The Broadview Anthology of

BRITISH LITERATURE

Volume 5
The Victorian Era
Third Edition

The Broadview Anthology of British Literature

The Medieval Period
The Renaissance and the Early Seventeenth Century
The Restoration and the Eighteenth Century
The Age of Romanticism
The Victorian Era
The Twentieth Century and Beyond

The Broadview Anthology of

BRITISH LITERATURE

Volume 5
The Victorian Era
Third Edition

GENERAL EDITORS

Joseph Black, University of Massachusetts
Kate Flint, University of Southern California
Isobel Grundy, University of Alberta
Don LePan, Broadview Press
Roy Liuzza, University of Tennessee
Jerome J. McGann, University of Virginia
Anne Lake Prescott, Barnard College
Jason R. Rudy, University of Maryland, College Park
Claire Waters, University of California, Davis

ASSOCIATE GENERAL EDITORS

Leonard Conolly, Trent University
Barry V. Qualls, Rutgers University

broadview press

BROADVIEW PRESS — www.broadviewpress.com
Peterborough, Ontario, Canada

Founded in 1985, Broadview Press remains a wholly independent publishing house. Broadview's focus is on academic publishing; our titles are accessible to university and college students as well as scholars and general readers. With 800 titles in print, Broadview has become a leading international publisher in the humanities, with world-wide distribution. Broadview is committed to environmentally responsible publishing and fair business practices.

© 2021 Broadview Press

LIBRARY AND ARCHIVES CANADA CATALOGUING IN PUBLICATION

Title: The Broadview anthology of British literature / general editors, Joseph Black (University of Massachusetts), Leonard Conolly (Trent University), Kate Flint (University of Southern California), Isobel Grundy (University of Alberta), Don LePan (Broadview Press), Roy Liuzza (University of Tennessee), Jerome J. McGann (University of Virginia), Anne Lake Prescott (Barnard College), Barry V. Qualls (Rutgers University), Claire Waters (University of California, Davis).
Other titles: British literature
Names: Black, Joseph, 1962- editor.
Description: Third edition. | Volume 5 has additional general editor, Jason R. Rudy, University of Maryland, College Park. | Includes bibliographical references and indexes. | Content: V. 5. The Victorian era.
Identifiers: Canadiana (print) 2014907235X | Canadiana (ebook) 20210158999 | ISBN 9781554814916 (paperback ; v. 5) | ISBN 9781770488076 (PDF ; v. 5) | ISBN 9781460407561 (EPUB ; v. 5)
Subjects: LCSH: English literature.
Classification: LCC PR1109 .B77 2015 | DDC 820.8—dc23

Broadview Press handles its own distribution in North America:
PO Box 1243, Peterborough, Ontario K9J 7H5, Canada
555 Riverwalk Parkway, Tonawanda, NY 14150, USA
Tel: (705) 743-8990; Fax: (705) 743-8353
email: customerservice@broadviewpress.com

For all territories outside of North America, distribution is handled by Eurospan Group.

Broadview Press acknowledges the financial support of the Government of Canada for our publishing activities.

Canada

Typeset by Kathryn Brownsey
Cover design by Lisa Brawn

PRINTED IN CANADA

CONTRIBUTING EDITORS AND WRITERS

MANAGING EDITOR	Laura Buzzard
DEVELOPMENTAL EDITOR	Jennifer McCue
GENERAL ACADEMIC AND TEXTUAL EDITORS	Laura Cardiff, Joe Davies, Colleen Franklin, Don LePan, Nora Ruddock, Helena Snopek Maxwell Uphaus
DESIGN COORDINATOR	Kathryn Brownsey

CONTRIBUTING EDITORS

Katherine O. Acheson
Suzy Anger
Melissa Bachynski
Robert Barrett
Gisele Baxter
Donald Beecher
Sandra Bell
Emily Bernhard Jackson
Joseph Black
Carol Blessing
Robert Boenig
Sarika Bose
Matthieu Boyd
Andrew Bretz
Benjamin Bruch
Laura Buzzard
Michael Calabrese
Laura Cardiff
Lisa Celovsky
Noel Chevalier
Mita Choudhury
Youngjin Chung
Massimo Ciavolella
Anna Clark
Elisha Cohn
Thomas J. Collins
Leonard Conolly
Matthew Davis
Darryl Domingo
Annmarie Drury
Dianne Dugaw
Siân Echard
Rose Eckert-Jantzie
Warren Edminster
Rachel Eisendrath
Garrett Epp
Michael Faletra

Emily Farrell
Christina Fawcett
Christina Fitzgerald
Adrienne Fitzpatrick
Andrew Fleck
Melissa Free
Maura Giles Watson
Stephen Glosecki
Amanda Goldrick-Jones
Katie Gramich
Erik Gray
John Greenwood
Melissa Gregory
Isobel Grundy
Stephen Guy-Bray
Douglas Hayes
Peter C. Herman
Heather Hill-Vasquez
John Holmes
Diane Jakacki
Eleanor Johnson
Ian Johnston
Essaka Joshua
Susan Kattwinkel
Michael Keefer
Amy King
Genevieve Kirk
David Klausner
Scott Kleinman
Chris Koenig-Woodyard
Gary Kuchar
Roger P. Kuin
Lydia K. Lake
Wendy Lee
Don LePan
Ruth Lexton
Roy Liuzza

Kirsten Lodge
Marie Loughlin
D.L. Macdonald
Hugh Magennis
Anne McWhir
Tobias Menely
Britt Mize
Alexander Mueller
Ian Munro
Sarah Neville
Meghan Nieman
David Oakleaf
Maureen Okun
Philip S. Palmer
Pam Perkins
Virginia Philipson
Jude Polsky
Kristen Pond
Anne Lake Prescott
Joyce Rappaport
Andrew Reszitnyk
Joseph Rezek
Shelby Richardson
Terry Robinson
Herbert Rosengarten
Nora Ruddock
Jason Rudy
Janice Schroeder
Chester Scoville
John T. Sebastian
Helena Snopek
Kelly Stage
Emily Steiner
Ashley Streeter
Martha Stoddard-Holmes
Julie Sutherland
David Swain

Carol Symes
Andrew Taylor
Peggy Thompson
Jane Tolmie
Rebecca Totaro
David Townsend
Yevgeniya Traps

Maxwell Uphaus
Melissa Valiska Gregory
Martine van Elk
Fred Waage
Andrea Walkden
Craig Walker
Claire Waters

David Watt
William Weaver
Vivienne Westbrook
Dan White
David Williams
Adrienne Williams Boyarin
James Winny

CONTRIBUTING WRITERS

Victoria Abboud
Jane Beal
Jennifer Beauvais
Rachel Bennett
Emily Bernhard Jackson
Rebecca Blasco
Matthieu Boyd
Julie Brennan
Andrew Bretz
Laura Buzzard
Laura Cardiff
Emily Cargan
Adrienne Eastwood
Wendy Eberle-Sinatra
Zachary Edwards
Peter Enman
Emily Farrell
Christina Fawcett
Joanne Findon
John Geddert
Jane Grove
Camille Isaacs

Erik Isford
Shoshannah Jones Square
Stephanie King
Chris Koenig-Woodyard
Gabrielle L'Archeveque
Don LePan
Anna Lepine
John McIntyre
Carrie Nartkler
Byron Nelson
Robin Norris
Kenna Olsen
Kendra O'Neal Smith
Lindsey E.R. O'Neil
Laura Pellerine
Virginia Philipson
Paige Pinto
Jude Polsky
Nora Ruddock
Jason Rudy
Anne Salo

Janice Schroeder
Carrie Shanafelt
Nicole Shukin
Helena Snopek
James Soderholm
Anne Sorbie
Jenna Stook
Ashley Streeter
Alexandria Stuart
Candace Taylor
Justin Thompson
Yevgeniya Traps
Maxwell Uphaus
David Van Belle
Sarah Vickers
Deirdra Wadden
Shari Watling
Matthew Williams
Bj Wray
Braedan Zimmer
Nicole Zylstra

LAYOUT AND TYPESETTING

Kathryn Brownsey

ILLUSTRATION FORMATTING AND ASSISTANCE

Cheryl Baldwin
Alexandria Stuart

Lisa Brawn

Eileen Eckert

PRODUCTION COORDINATORS

Tara Lowes

Tara Trueman

PERMISSIONS COORDINATORS

Merilee Atos
Chris Griffin

Emily Cargan
Jacqueline Kwan

Jennifer Elsayed
Amy Nimegeer

PROOFREADERS

Jennifer Bingham
Joe Davies
Lynn Fraser
Lynn Neufeld

Martin Boyne
Judith Earnshaw
Anne Hodgetts
Bethany Qualls

Lucy Conolly
Rose Eckert-Jantzie
Amy Neufeld

EDITORIAL ADVISORS

Rachel Ablow, University at Buffalo, SUNY
Phanuel Antwi, University of British Columbia
Dabney Bankert, James Madison University
Stephen C. Behrendt, University of Nebraska
Sumangala Bhattacharya, Pitzer College
Kim Blank, University of Victoria
Rita Bode, Trent University
Andrew Bretz, Wilfred Laurier University
David Brewer, Ohio State University
Susan Brown, University of Guelph
Daniel Burgoyne, Vancouver Island University
Catherine Burroughs, Wells College
Elizabeth Campbell, Oregon State University
William Christmas, San Francisco State University
Nancy Cirillo, University of Illinois, Chicago
Joanne Cordón, University of Connecticut
David Cowart, University of South Carolina
Alex Dick, University of British Columbia
Len Diepeveen, Dalhousie University
Daniel Fischlin, University of Guelph
Robert Forman, St. John's University
Peter Francev, Victor Valley College
Mark Fulk, Buffalo State College, SUNY
Julia Garrett, University of Wisconsin
Barbara Gates, University of Delaware
Dawn Goode, James Madison University
Chris Gordon-Craig, University of Alberta
Bruce Graver, Providence College
Natalie Grinnell, Wofford College
Jennifer Gustar, University of British Columbia, Okanagan
Stephen Guy-Bray, University of British Columbia
Tassie Gwilliam, University of Miami
Nathan Hensley, Georgetown University
Elizabeth Hodgson, University of British Columbia
John Holmes, University of Reading

Romana Huk, University of Notre Dame
Heidi Kaufman, University of Oregon
Michael Keefer, University of Guelph
Gordon Kipling, University of California, Los Angeles
Emily Kugler, University of California, San Diego
Sara Landreth, University of Ottawa
William Liston, Ball State University
Paula Loscocco, Lehman College
Kathleen Lundeen, Western Washington University
Peter Mallios, University of Maryland
Carl G. Martin, Norwich University
Martin McKinsey, University of New Hampshire
Rod Michell, Thompson Rivers University
Peter Murphy, Thompson Rivers University
Julie Nash, University of Massachusetts, Lowell
Byron Nelson, West Virginia University
Robin Norris, Carleton College
Michael North, University of California, Los Angeles
Nick Pawliuk, Thompson Rivers University
Lesley Peterson, University of North Alabama
John Pollock, San Jose State University
Joseph Rezek, Boston University
Andrew Scheil, University of Minnesota
Carol Senf, Georgia Tech
Ken Simpson, Thompson Rivers University
Sharon Smulders, Mount Royal University
Goran Stanivukovic, St. Mary's University
Marni Stanley, Vancouver Island University
Tim Stretton, St. Mary's University
Nanora Sweet, University of Missouri-St. Louis
Nicholas Watson, Harvard University
Kevin Whetter, Acadia University
Julian Yates, University of Delaware

CONTENTS

PREFACE

bound and expanded selection of eighteenth-century texts ... the Aesthetic Movement. Throughout the volume, introductions have been revised to reflect recent developments in scholarship and to bring greater balance to the anthology's treatment of gender, sexual orientation,

A FRESH APPROACH

The publication of the first edition of this anthology in 2006 was widely hailed as an exciting achievement, with many academics concluding that its comprehensiveness, its consistency, its visual appeal, and its fresh approach made the Broadview the "new standard" in anthologies of British literature. We have also taken a fresh approach in issuing new editions of the anthology's volumes. Rather than publishing new editions of each of the six volumes simultaneously, we are publishing new editions of the individual volumes at the rate of approximately one every year or two. Each volume thus appears in a new edition roughly every six to eight years. We recognize that our main competitors have in recent years made it a practice to issue new editions much more frequently than that, but our feeling is that it is better to allow several years to elapse between editions—not least of all, as a new edition may represent a considerable inconvenience to academics teaching from the anthology. (The approach also has real practical advantages for a smaller publisher such as Broadview; rather than gearing up for a massive process of revision every few years and then gearing down again in the wake of publication, we can proceed at a steady pace with the work of updating and revising.)

Among the numerous changes and additions made to this volume for the third edition, many are geared toward featuring a larger number of writers of color, not only from the British Isles but also from elsewhere in the British Empire. The volume now begins with Mary Prince; also new to the bound book are Mary Seacole, Mary Ann Shadd, T.N. Mukharji, Toru Dutt, Rabindranath Tagore, Tekahionwake (E. Pauline Johnson), Sarojini Naidu, and Rokeya Sakhawat Hossain. We are grateful to the volume's General Editors and to the numerous other scholars who identified the need for greater diversity in the volume's selections, and especially to Nathan Hensley, whose forceful commentary on whiteness in Victorian literature anthologies prompted us to make more significant changes and additions in this area than we might have otherwise.

With the anthology's third edition we are also striving to offer improved representation of Irish, Welsh, and Scottish literature, especially as its traditions differ from the English traditions that too often dominate literary studies of the British Isles. To that end, we have included a substantial new section titled "Ireland, Scotland, and Wales: Literary Currents in the Long Nineteenth Century." Other authors new to this edition include Harriet Martineau, Sheridan Le Fanu, Charlotte Brontë, Mary Elizabeth Braddon, and Arthur Morrison. The bound book features two new longer works—Le Fanu's *Carmilla* and Robert Louis Stevenson's *Strange Case of Dr. Jekyll and Mr. Hyde*—as well as new poetry by Elizabeth Barrett Browning, Robert Browning, Augusta Webster, Emily Brontë, Algernon Charles Swinburne, Thomas Hardy, Amy Levy, and Alfred, Lord Tennyson; new short fiction by Olive Schreiner; and new critical writing by Charles Dickens, George Eliot, Oscar Wilde, and Vernon Lee.

Significant changes have also been made to the anthology's contextual materials and apparatus. New "Contexts" sections addressing "Sexuality and Sexual Transgression" and "Nature and the Environment" have been added, as has a section on "The New Woman." (Note that we have streamlined the section on "Women in Society," and some selections previously appearing there can now be found among the "Sexuality" and "New Woman" materials.) The contextual materials addressing "Britain, Empire, and a Wider World" have been significantly revised and expanded to feature a larger proportion of writers of color in the bound book. We have also strengthened our coverage of important generic developments, with a revised "Contexts" section on "The Pre-Raphaelites" (now appearing in the bound book) and an expanded selection of materials relating to "The Aesthetic Movement." Throughout the volume, introductions have been revised to reflect recent developments in scholarship and to bring greater balance to the anthology's treatment of gender, sexual orientation, and race, as well as to more accurately represent the relationship between England and the rest of the British Empire. In response to feedback we received from academics teaching with the anthology, we have also revised the annotations throughout the volume to improve its accessibility for present-day students.

All this new material has resulted in a third edition that is substantially longer than the second. While we consider this increased length to be a necessary reflection of the increased diversity of the Victorian canon, we have, so as to keep the anthology at a manageable size, cut materials we have found to be taught infrequently. Thomas Babington Macaulay and Anthony Trollope, for example, are no longer represented by individual sections in the bound book. Any materials no longer included in the print volume remain available, however, as part of the anthology's online component. The website also features material new to the anthology that could not be accommodated in the bound book; highlights include Margaret Oliphant's novellas *The Library Window* and *Queen Eleanor and Fair Rosamond*; excerpts from Benjamin Disraeli's *Sybil* and George Eliot's *Middlemarch*; and short fiction by Henry James, Elizabeth Gaskell, and Harriet Martineau. A new "Contexts" section addressing Irish history, with particular emphasis on the Great Irish Famine, can also be found on the website, and new selections have been added to the online contextual materials addressing "Childhood and Children's Literature" and "Religion and Society."

As we have from the start with *The Broadview Anthology of British Literature*, we have enlisted the help of a substantial number of people in the preparation of this book's contents. Rather than dividing up the vast amount of work entailed in preparing such a large anthology among a relatively small number of academics, and asking each of them to handle on their own the work of choosing, annotating, and preparing introduc-

tions to texts in their own areas of specialization, we chose to involve a large number of contributors in the process (as the pages following the title page to this volume attest), and to encourage a high degree of collaboration at every level. First and foremost are the distinguished academics who serve as our General Editors for the project, but in all there have literally been hundreds of people involved at various stages in researching, drafting headnotes or annotations, reviewing material, editing material, and carrying out the work of designing and typesetting the texts and other materials. That approach allowed us to draw on a diverse range of talent, and to prepare the first edition of a large anthology with extraordinary efficiency. It has also facilitated the maintenance of a high degree of consistency. Material has been reviewed and revised in-house at Broadview, by outside editors, by a variety of academics with an extraordinarily diverse range of backgrounds and academic specialities, and by our team of General Editors for the project as a whole. The aim has been not only to ensure accuracy but also to make sure that the same standards are applied throughout the anthology to matters such as coverage provided in introductions, level of annotation, tone of writing, and student accessibility.

As with the first and second editions, several core principles have guided the selection of texts for this volume. We have endeavored to provide a selection that is broadly representative, while also being mindful of the importance of choosing texts that have the capacity to engage readers' interest today. We have for the most part made it a policy to include long works in their entirety or not at all; readers will find complete in *The Broadview Anthology* works such as *The History of Mary Prince* and *In Memoriam* that are often excerpted in (or omitted from) other anthologies. Where editions of works are available separately in our acclaimed Broadview Editions series, we have often decided to omit them from the anthology, on the grounds that those wishing to teach one or more such works may easily do so in a combination package with the anthology.

Any discussion of what is distinctive about *The Broadview Anthology of British Literature* must focus above all on the contents. In every volume of the anthology there is material that is distinctive and fresh—including not only selections by lesser-known writers but also less familiar selections from canonical writers. The anthology takes a fresh approach too to a great many canonical texts. The first volume of the anthology includes not only Roy Liuzza's translation of *Beowulf* (widely acclaimed as the most engaging and reliable translation available), but also new translations by Liuzza of many other works of Old English poetry and prose. Unique to the first volume of this anthology are a new verse translation of *Judith* by Stephen Glosecki and new translations by Claire Waters of several of the *Lais* of Marie de France. And so on through all six volumes.

In a number of these cases the distinctive form of the anthology facilitates the presentation of content in an engaging and practical fashion. Notably, the adoption of a two-column format allows for some translations (the Marie de France *Lais*, the James Winny translation of *Sir Gawain and the Green Knight*, poetry in Old Irish and other Celtic languages) to be presented in parallel column format alongside the original texts, allowing readers to experience something of the flavor of the original, while providing convenient access to an accessible translation. Similarly, passages from four translations of the Bible are laid out parallel to each other for ready comparison.

The large trim-size, two-column format also allows for greater flexibility in the presentation of visual materials. Throughout our intent is to make this an anthology that is fully alive to the connections between literary and visual culture, from the discussion of the CHI-RHO page of the Lindisfarne Gospels in the first volume of the anthology (and the accompanying color illustration) to the inclusion in Volume 6 of a number of selections (including Graham Greene's "The Basement Room," Tom Stoppard's "Professional Foul," and several skits from "Monty Python's Flying Circus") that may be discussed in connection with film or television versions. Along the way appear several full-page illustrations from the Ellesmere manuscript of Chaucer's *Canterbury Tales* and illustrations to a wide variety of

other works, from *Robinson Crusoe* and *Gulliver's Travels* to *The Adventure of the Speckled Band* and *The Road to Wigan Pier*.

CONTEXTUAL MATERIALS

Visual materials are also included in the background materials that form an important part of the anthology. These materials are presented in two ways. Several "Contexts" sections on particular topics or themes appear in each volume of the anthology, presented independent of any particular text or author. These include broadly based groupings of material on such topics as "Religion and Spiritual Life," "Print Culture," "India and the Orient," "Slavery and Its Abolition," "The New Art of Photography," and "The End of Empire." The groups of "In Context" materials each relate to a particular text or author. They range from the genealogical tables provided as a supplement to *Beowulf*; to materials on "The Eighteenth-Century Sexual Imagination" (presented in conjunction with Haywood's *Fantomina*); to a selection of materials relating to the Peterloo massacre (presented in conjunction with Percy Shelley's "The Mask of Anarchy"); to materials on "'The Vilest Scramble for Loot' in Central Africa" (presented in conjunction with Conrad's "An Outpost of Progress"). For the most part these contextual materials are, as the word suggests, included with a view to setting texts in their broader literary, historical, and cultural contexts; in some cases, however, the materials included in "Contexts" sections are themselves literary works of a high order. The autobiographical account by Eliza M. of nineteenth-century life in Cape Town, for example (included in the section in this volume on "Britain, Empire, and a Wider World"), is as remarkable for its literary qualities as it is for the light it sheds on the realities of colonial life. In the inclusion of texts such as these, as well as in other ways, the anthology aims to encourage readers to explore the boundaries of the literary and the non-literary, and the issue of what constitutes a "literary text."

TEXTS BY WOMEN WRITERS

A central element of the broadening of the canon of British literature in recent generations has of course been a great increase in the attention paid to texts by women writers. As one might expect from a publisher that has played an important role in making neglected works by women writers widely available, this anthology reflects the broadening of the canon quantitatively, by including a substantially larger number of women writers than have earlier anthologies of British literature. But it also reflects this broadening in other ways. In many anthologies of literature (anthologies of British literature, to be sure, but also anthologies of literature of a variety of other sorts) women writers are still too often set somewhat apart, referenced in introductions and headnotes only in relation to issues of gender, and treated as important only for the fact of their being women writers. *The Broadview Anthology* strenuously resists such segregation; while women writers are of course discussed in relation to gender issues, their texts are also presented and discussed alongside those by men in a wide variety of other contexts, including seventeenth-century religious and political controversies, the abolitionist movement, and World War I pacifism. Texts by women writers are front and center in the discussion of the development of realism in nineteenth-century fiction. And when it comes to the twentieth century, both Virginia Woolf and Dorothy Richardson are included alongside James Joyce as practitioners of groundbreaking modernist narrative techniques.

BOUNDARIES OF BRITISH LITERATURE

The broadening of English Studies, in conjunction with the expansion and subsequent contraction of British power and influence around the world, has considerably complicated the issue of exactly how inclusive anthologies should be. In several respects this anthology (like its two main competitors) is significantly more inclusive than its title suggests, including a number of non-British writers whose works connect in important ways with the traditions of British literature. We endeavor to portray the fluid and multilingual reality of the medieval period through the inclusion not only of works in Old and Middle English but also of works in Latin, in French, in Irish, in Welsh, and in Scots. We have extended this approach throughout the anthology with the inclusion of Celtic-language works from the early modern era, the long nineteenth century, and the twentieth century.

In later periods the word "British" becomes deeply problematic in different respects, but on balance we have preferred it to the only obvious alternative, "English." There are several objections to the latter in this context. Perhaps most obviously, "English" excludes authors or texts not only from Ireland but also from Scotland and from Wales, both of which retain to this day cultures quite distinct from that of the English. "English literature," of course, may also be taken to mean "literature written in English," but since the anthology does not cover *all* literature written in English (most obviously in excluding American literature), the ambiguity would not in this case be helpful.

The inclusion of Irish writers presents a related but even more tangled set of issues. At the beginning of the period covered by the six volumes of this anthology we find works, such as the *Book of Kells*, that may have been created in what is now England, in what is now Scotland, in what is now Ireland—or in some combination of these. Through most of the seventeenth, eighteenth, and nineteenth centuries almost the whole of Ireland was under British control—but for the most part unwillingly. In the period covered in the last of the six volumes Ireland was partitioned, with Northern Ireland becoming a part of the United Kingdom and the Republic of Ireland declared independent of Britain on 6 December 1921. Less than two months earlier, James Joyce had completed *Ulysses*, which was first published as a complete work the following year (in Paris, not in Britain). It would be obviously absurd to regard Joyce as a British writer up to just before the publication of *Ulysses*, and an Irish writer thereafter. And arguably he and other Irish writers should never be regarded as British, whatever the politics of the day. If on no other grounds than their overwhelming influence on and connection to the body of literature written in the British Isles, however, we have included Irish writers—among them Swift, Sheridan, Edgeworth, Wilde, Shaw, Beckett, Bowen, Muldoon, and Heaney as well as Joyce—throughout this anthology. We have also endeavored to give a real sense in the introductions to the six volumes of the anthology, in the headnotes to individual authors, and in the annotations to the texts themselves, of the ways in which the histories and the cultures of England, Ireland, Scotland, and Wales, much as they interact with one another, are also distinct.

Also included in this anthology are texts by writers from areas that are far removed geographically from the British Isles but that are or have been British possessions. Writers such as Mary Rowlandson, Olaudah Equiano, and Phillis Wheatley are included, as they spent all or most of their lives living in what were then British colonial possessions. Writers who came of age in an independent United States, on the other hand, are not included, unless (like T.S. Eliot) they subsequently put down roots in Britain and became important British literary figures. Substantial gray areas, of course, surround such issues. One might well argue, for example, that Henry James merits inclusion in an anthology of British literature, or that W.H. Auden and Thom Gunn are more American poets than British ones. But the chosen subject matter of James's work has traditionally been considered to mark him as having remained an American writer, despite having spent almost two-thirds of his life in England; he is therefore excluded from the bound book, though he is represented in the anthology's online component for those wishing to include him in their courses. And both Auden and Gunn so clearly made a mark in Britain before crossing the Atlantic that it would seem odd to exclude them from these pages on the grounds of their having lived the greater part of their adult lives in America. One of our competitors includes Sylvia Plath in their anthology of British literature; Plath lived in England for only five of her thirty years, though, and her poetry is generally agreed to have more in common with the traditions of Lowell, Merwin, and Sexton than with the currents of British poetry in the 1950s and '60s.

As a broad principle, we have been open to the inclusion of twentieth and twenty-first century work in English not only by writers from the British Isles but also by writers from British possessions overseas, and by writers from countries that were once British possessions and have remained a part of the British Commonwealth. In such cases we have often chosen selections that relate in one way or another to the tradition of British literature and the British colonial legacy. The Margaret Atwood selections in the anthology include work imagining the experience of British emigrants to Canada in the nineteenth century, while the selection by Tomson Highway addresses ongoing colonization in the twentieth; the Chinua Achebe story in the anthology concerns the divide between British colonial culture and traditional Nigerian culture; and so on.

THE HISTORY OF LANGUAGE, AND OF PRINT CULTURE

Among the liveliest discussions we had at meetings of our General Editors were those concerning the issue of whether or not to bring spelling and punctuation into accord with present-day practice. We finally decided that, in the interests of making the anthology accessible to the introductory student, we should *in most cases* bring spelling and punctuation in line with present-day practice. An important exception has been made for works in which modernizing spelling and punctuation would alter the meaning or the aural and metrical qualities. In practice this means that works before the late sixteenth century tend to be presented either in their original form or in translation, whereas later texts tend to have spelling and punctuation modernized. But where spelling and punctuation choices in later texts are known (or believed on reliable authority) to represent conscious choice on the part of the author rather than simply the common practice of the time, we have in those cases, too, made an exception and retained the original spelling and punctuation. (Among these are texts by Edmund Spenser; by William Cowper; by William Blake, John Clare, and several other poets of the Romantic era; by George Bernard Shaw; and by contemporary figures such as Linton Kwesi Johnson.)

Beyond this, we all agreed that we should provide for readers a real sense of the development of the language and of print culture. To that end we have included in each volume examples of texts in their original form—in some cases through the use of pages shown in facsimile, in others by providing short passages in which spelling and punctuation have not been modernized. A list of these appears near the beginning of each volume of the anthology.

We have also included a section of the history of the language as part of the introduction to each volume. And throughout the anthology we include materials—visual as well as textual—relating to the history of print culture.

A DYNAMIC AND FLEXIBLE ANTHOLOGY

Almost all major book publishing projects nowadays are accompanied by an adjunct website, and most large-scale anthologies are accompanied by websites that provide additional materials in electronic form. Since this anthology's inception, we have viewed its website component as precisely that—a *component* of the anthology itself. The notion of a website of this sort grew organically out of the process of trying to winnow down the contents of the first edition of the anthology to a manageable level—the point at which all the material to be included would fit within the covers of bound books that would not be overwhelmingly heavy. And we simply could not do it. After we had made a very substantial round of cuts we were still faced with a table of contents in which each volume was at least 200 or 300 pages longer than our agreed-upon maximum. Our solution was not to try to cut anything more, but rather to select a range of material to be made available in a website component of the anthology. This material is in every way produced according to the same high standards of the material in the bound books; the editorial standards, the procedures for annotation, the author introductions, and the page design and layout—all are

the same. The texts on the web, in short, are not "extra" materials; they are an integral part of the full anthology. In accordance with that principle, we have been careful to include a wide range of texts by lesser-known writers within the bound books, and a number of texts by canonical writers within the web component of the anthology.

The latter may be used in a variety of ways. Most obviously, readings from the web component are available to any purchaser of the book. Instructors who adopt *The Broadview Anthology of British Literature* as a course text are also granted permission to reproduce any web material for which Broadview holds copyright in a supplementary coursepack. An alternative for instructors who want to "create their own" anthology is to visit the "Custom Texts" page on the Broadview website or contact the publisher directly; Broadview can make available to students through their university bookstore a custom-made coursepack with precisely the desired materials included. Other options are available too. Volumes of the anthology itself may of course be shrink-wrapped together at special prices in any desired combination. They may also be combined in a shrink-wrapped package with one of the over 400 volumes in the Broadview Editions series, at no additional cost to the student (or with more than one edition for a modest additional charge).

We anticipate that over the years the web-based component of the anthology will continue to grow—every year there will be a greater choice of web-based texts in the anthology. But we do not foresee a day when the web will be the only option; we expect physical books always to remain central to Broadview's approach to publishing.

THE BROADVIEW LIST

One of the reasons we were able to bring a project of this sort to fruition in such a relatively short time was that we were able to draw on the resources of the full Broadview list: the many titles in the Broadview Editions series, and also the considerable range of other

Broadview anthologies. As the contributors' pages and the permissions acknowledgments pages indicate, a number of Broadview authors have acted as contributing editors to this volume, providing material from other volumes that has been adapted to suit the needs of the present anthology; we gratefully acknowledge their contribution.

As it has turned out, the number of cases where we have been able to draw on the resources of the Broadview list in the full sense, using in these pages texts and annotations in very much the same form in which they appear elsewhere, has been relatively small; whether because of an issue such as the level of textual modernization or one of style of annotation, we have more often than not ended up deciding that the requirements of this anthology were such that we could not use material from another Broadview source as-is. But even in these cases we often owe a debt of gratitude to the many academics who have edited outstanding editions and anthologies for Broadview. For even where we have not drawn directly from them, we have often been inspired by them—inspired to think of a wider range of texts as possibilities than we might otherwise have done, inspired to think of contextual materials in places where we might otherwise not have looked, inspired by the freshness of approach that so many of these titles exemplify.

EDITORIAL PROCEDURES AND CONVENTIONS, APPARATUS

The in-house set of editorial guidelines for *The Broadview Anthology of British Literature* runs to over 40 pages, covering everything from conventions for the spacing of marginal notes, to the use of small caps for the abbreviations CE and BCE, to the approach we have adopted to references in author headnotes to name changes. Perhaps the most important core principle in the introductions to the various volumes, in the headnotes for each author, in the introductions in "Contexts" sections, and in annotations throughout the anthology, is to endeavor to provide a sufficient amount of information to enable students to read and interpret these texts, but without making evaluative judgments or imposing particular interpretations. In practice that is all a good deal more challenging than it sounds; it is often extremely difficult to describe why a particular author is considered to be important without using language that verges on the interpretive or the evaluative. But it is a fine line that we have all agreed is worth trying to walk; we hope that readers will find that the anthology achieves an appropriate balance.

ANNOTATION: It is also often difficult to make judgments as to where it is appropriate to provide an explanatory annotation for a word or phrase. Our policy has been to annotate where we feel that most first- or second-year students are likely to have difficulty understanding the denotative meaning. (We have made it a practice not to provide notes discussing connotative meanings.) But in practice the vocabularies and levels of verbal facility of first- and second-year students may vary enormously, both from institution to institution and within any given college or university class. On the whole, we provide somewhat more annotation than our competitors, and somewhat less interpretation. Again, we hope that readers will find that the anthology has struck an appropriate balance.

THE ETHICS AND POLITICS OF ANNOTATION: On one issue regarding annotation we have felt that principles are involved that go beyond the pedagogical. Most anthologies of British literature allow many words or phrases of a racist, sexist, anti-Semitic, or homophobic nature either to pass entirely without comment, or to be glossed with apologist comments that leave the impression that such comments were excusable in the past, and may even be unobjectionable in the present. Where derogatory comments about Jewish people and money-lending are concerned, for example, anthologies often leave the impression that money-lending was a pretty unsavory practice that Jewish people entered by choice; it has been all too rare to provide readers with any sense of the degree to which English society consistently discriminated against Jews, expelling them entirely for several centuries, requiring them to wear physical marks identifying their Jewish status, prohibiting them from entering most professions, and so on. *The Broadview Anthology* endeavors in such cases, first of all, not to allow such words and phrases to pass without comment; and second, to gloss without glossing over.

DATES: We make it a practice to include the date when a work was first made public, whether publication in print or, in the case of dramatic works, made public through the first performance of the play. Where that date is known to differ substantially from the date of composition, a note to this effect is included in parentheses. With medieval works, where there is no equivalent to the "publication" of later eras, where texts often vary greatly from one manuscript copy to another, and where knowledge as to date of original composition is usually imprecise, the date that appears at the end of each work is an estimate of the date of the work's origin in the written form included in the anthology. Earlier oral or written versions are of course in some cases real possibilities.

TEXTS: Where translations appear in this anthology, a note at the bottom of the first page indicates what translation is being used. Similar notes also address overall textual issues where choice of copy text is particularly significant. Reliable editions of most works are listed in the bibliography for the anthology, which is included as part of the website component rather than in the bound books, to facilitate ready revision. (In addition to information as to reliable editions, the bibliography provides for each author and for each of the six periods select lists of important or useful historical and critical works.) Copyright information for texts not in the public domain, however, is provided within the bound books in a section listing Permissions Acknowledgments.

INTRODUCTIONS: In addition to the introductory headnotes for each author included in the anthology, each "Contexts" section includes a substantial introduction, and each volume includes an introduction to the period as a whole. These introductions to the six volumes of the anthology endeavor to provide a sense not only of the broad picture of literary developments in the period, but also of the historical, social, and political background, and of the cultural climate. Readers should be cautioned that, while there is inevitably some overlap between information presented here and information presented in the author headnotes, an effort has been made to avoid such repetition as much as possible; the general introduction to each period should thus be read in conjunction with the author headnotes. The general introductions aim not only to provide an overview of ways in which texts and authors included in these pages may connect with one another, but also to give readers a sense of connection with a range of other writers and texts of the period.

READING POETRY: For much of the glossary and for the "Reading Poetry" section that appears on the website component for this volume we have drawn on the superb material prepared by Herbert Rosengarten and Amanda Goldrick-Jones for *The Broadview Anthology of Poetry*; this section provides a concise but comprehensive introduction to the study of poetry. It includes discussions of diction, imagery, poetic figures, and various poetic forms, as well as offering an introduction to prosody.

MAPS: Also appearing within each of the bound books are maps especially prepared for this anthology, including, for each volume, a map of Britain showing towns and features of relevance during the pertinent period; a map showing the counties of Britain and of Ireland; maps both of the London area and of the inner city; and world maps indicating the locations of some of the significant places referenced in the anthology, and for later volumes showing the extent of Britain's overseas territories.

GLOSSARY: Some other anthologies of British literature include both glossaries of terms and essays introducing students to various political and religious categories in British history. Similar information is included in *The Broadview Anthology of British Literature*, but we have adopted a more integrated approach, including political and religious terms along with literary ones in a convenient general glossary available in the anthology's website component. While we recognize that looking to resources such as Wikipedia for information of this sort is often the student's first resort (and we recognize too the value of searching the web for the wealth of background reference information available there), we also recognize that not all online sources are equally reliable; it is our intent, through this glossary, through our introductions and headnotes, and through the wealth of accessible annotation in the anthology, to provide as part of the anthology a reliable core of information in the most convenient and accessible form possible.

OTHER MATERIALS: A chart of Monarchs and Prime Ministers is also provided within these pages. A range of other adjunct materials may be accessed through *The Broadview Anthology of British Literature* website. "Texts and Contexts" charts for each volume provide a convenient parallel reference guide to the dates of literary texts and historical developments. "Money in Britain" provides a thumbnail sketch of the world of pounds, shillings, and pence, together with a handy guide to estimating the current equivalents of monetary values from earlier eras. And the website offers, too, a variety of further aids for the student and the instructor. An up-to-date list of these appears on the site.

ACKNOWLEDGMENTS

The names of those on the Editorial Board that shaped this anthology appear on the title page, and those of the many who contributed directly to the writing, editing, and production of the project on the following two pages. Special acknowledgment for this new edition should go to Developmental Editor Jennifer McCue, who has been instrumental in tying together all the vast threads of this project and in making it a reality; to General Academic and Textual Editors Nora Ruddock, Maxwell Uphaus, and Helena Snopek, each of whom has played a key role in drafting introductory materials and annotations for the new material, and done so with great skill and unfailing grace; to Kathryn Brownsey, who has been responsible for design and typesetting, and has continued to do an outstanding job and to maintain her good spirits even when faced with near-impossible demands; to Joe Davies for the range of his general knowledge as well as for his keen eyes as our primary proofreader for the entire project; and to Jacqueline Kwan, who has done superb work on the complex job of clearing permissions for the anthology.

The academic general editors and all of us in-house at Broadview owe an enormous debt of gratitude to the hundreds of academics who have offered assistance at various stages of this project. In particular we would like to express our appreciation and our thanks to the following:

Rachel Ablow, University of Rochester
Katherine Acheson, University of Waterloo
Kenet Adamson, Southwestern Community College
Bryan Alexander, Middlebury College
Sharon Alker, Whitman College
James Allard, Brock University
Ella Allen, St. Thomas University
Rosemary Allen, Georgetown College
Laurel Amtower, San Diego State University
Robert Anderson, Oakland University
Christopher Armitage, University of North Carolina, Chapel Hill
Clinton Atchley, Henderson State University
Gerry Baillargeon, University of Victoria
John Baird, University of Toronto
William Baker, Northern Illinois University
Karen Bamford, Mount Allison University
John Batchelor, University of Newcastle
Lynn Batten, University of California, Los Angeles
Stephen Behrendt, University of Nebraska
Alexandra Bennett, Northern Illinois University
John Beynon, California State University, Fresno

Daniel Bivona, Arizona State University
Robert E. Bjork, Arizona State University
John Black, Moravian College
Scott Black, Villanova University
Rita Bode, Trent University
Robert Boenig, Texas A&M University
Matthew Borushko, Stonehill College
Rick Bowers, University of Alberta
Patricia Brace, Columbus State University
David Brewer, Ohio State University
William Brewer, Appalachian State University
Glen Brewster, Westfield State University
Susan Brown, University of Guelph
Sylvia Brown, University of Alberta
Sheila Burgar, University of Victoria
Catherine Burroughs, Wells College
Rebecca Bushnell, University of Pennsylvania
Michael Calabrese, California State University
Elizabeth Campbell, Oregon State University
Katey Castellano, James Madison University
Gregory Castle, Arizona State University
Cynthia Caywood, University of San Diego

Jane Chance, Rice University

Ranita Chatterjee, California State University, Northridge

William Christmas, San Francisco State University

Nancy Cirillo, University of Illinois, Chicago

Eric Clarke, University of Pittsburgh

Jeanne Clegg, University of Aquila, Italy

Thomas J. Collins, University of Western Ontario

Thomas L. Cooksey, Armstrong Atlantic State University

Kevin Cope, Louisiana State University

David Cowart, University of South Carolina

Catherine Craft-Fairchild, University of St. Thomas

Jenny Crisp, Dalton State College

Laura Dabundo, Kennesaw State University

Roger Davis, Red Deer College

Carol Davison, University of Windsor

JoEllen DeLucia, Central Michigan University

Alexander Dick, University of British Columbia

Len Diepeveen, Dalhousie University

Mary Dockray-Miller, Lesley College

James Doelman, Brescia University College, University of Western Ontario

Frank Donoghue, Ohio State University

Chris Downs, Saint James School

Alfred Drake, Chapman University

Ian Duncan, University of California, Berkeley

Julie Early, University of Alabama, Huntsville

Roxanne Eberle, University of Georgia

Siân Echard, University of British Columbia

Garrett Epp, University of Alberta

Joshua Eyler, Columbus State University

Ruth Feingold, St. Mary's College, Maryland

Dino Franco Felluga, Perdue University

Joanne Findon, Trent University

Larry Fink, Hardin Simmons University

Daniel Fischlin, University of Guelph

Christina Fitzgerald, University of Toledo

Verlyn Flieger, University of Maryland

Robert Forman, St. John's University

Allyson Foster, Hunter College

Lorcan Fox, University of British Columbia

Peter Francev, Victor Valley College

Roberta Frank, Yale University

Jeff Franklin, University of Colorado, Denver

Maria Frawley, George Washington University

Mark Fulk, Buffalo State College

Christine Gallant, Georgia State University

Andrew Galloway, Cornell University

Michael Gamer, University of Pennsylvania

Barbara Gates, University of Delaware

Laura George, Eastern Michigan University

Denise Gigante, Stanford University

Jonathan C. Glance, Mercer University

Susan Patterson Glover, Laurentian University

Jennifer Golightly, University of Denver

Daniel Gonzalez, University of New Orleans

Jan Gorak, University of Denver

Chris Gordon-Craig, University of Alberta

Evan Gottlieb, Oregon State University

Ann-Barbara Graff, Georgia Tech University

Bruce Graver, Providence College

Mary Griffin, Kwantlen University College

Michael Griffin, formerly of Southern Illinois University

George C. Grinnell, University of British Columbia, Okanagan

Jonathan Gross, DePaul University

Elisabeth Gruner, University of Richmond

Bonnie Gunzenhauser, Roosevelt University

Kevin Gustafson, University of Texas at Arlington

Stephen Guy-Bray, University of British Columbia

Ruth Haber, Worcester State College

Dorothy Hadfield, University of Guelph

Margaret Hadley, University of Calgary

Robert Hampson, Royal Holloway University of London

Carol Hanes, Howard College

Michael Hanly, Washington State University

Lila Harper, Central Washington State University

Joseph Harris, Harvard University

Katherine Harris, San Jose State University

Anthony Harrison, North Carolina State University

John Hart, Motlow State Community College

Douglas Hayes, Lakehead University

Jennifer Hellwarth, Allegheny University

David Herman, Ohio State University

Peter Herman, San Diego State University

Jillian Hess, Bronx Community College, CUNY
Kathy Hickock, Iowa State University
John Hill, US Naval Academy
Thomas Hill, Cornell University
Elizabeth Hodgson, University of British Columbia
Jim Hood, Guilford College
Joseph Hornsby, University of Alabama
Scott Howard, University of Denver
Jennifer Hughes, Averett University
Sylvia Hunt, Georgian College
Tara Hyland-Russell, St. Mary's College
Catherine Innes-Parker, University of Prince Edward
    Island
Jacqueline Jenkins, University of Calgary
John Johansen, University of Alberta
Gordon Johnston, Trent University
Essaka Joshua, University of Notre Dame
Richard Juang, Susquehanna University
Michael Keefer, University of Guelph
Sarah Keefer, Trent University
Lloyd Kermode, California State University,
    Long Beach
Brandon Kershner, University of Florida
Jon Kertzer, University of Calgary
Waqas Khwaja, Agnes State College
Helen Killoran, Ohio University
Gordon Kipling, University of California, Los Angeles
Anne Klinck, University of New Brunswick
Elizabeth Kraft, University of Georgia
Mary Kramer, University of Massachusetts, Lowell
Scott Krawczyk, United States Military Academy
Wai-Leung Kwok, San Francisco State University
Marilyn Lantz, East Mississippi Community College
Kate Lawson, University of Waterloo
Nathanial Leach, Cape Breton University
Linda Leeds, Bellevue Community College
Mary Elizabeth Leighton, University of Victoria
Eric Lindstrom, University of Vermont
Harriet Linkin, New Mexico State University
William Liston, Ball State University
Sharon Locy, Loyola Marymount University
Ross MacKay, Malaspina University-College
Peter Mallios, University of Maryland

Arnold Markley, Penn State University
Louis Markos, Houston Baptist University
Nick Mason, Brigham Young University
Pamela McCallum, University of Calgary
Patricia McCormack, Itawamba Community College
Kristen McDermott, Central Michigan University
John McGowan, University of North Carolina
Brian McHale, Ohio State University
Jim McKeown, McLennan Community College
Thomas McLean, University of Otago, New Zealand
Susan McNeill-Bindon, University of Alberta
Jodie Medd, Carleton University
Rod Michell, Thompson Rivers University
David Miller, Mississippi College
Kitty Millett, San Francisco State University
Britt Mize, Texas A&M University
Richard Moll, University of Western Ontario
Amy L. Montz, Texas A&M University
Monique Morgan, McGill University
John Morillo, North Carolina State University
Lucy Morrison, Salisbury University
Lorri Nandrea, University of Wisconsin-Steven's Point
Mara Narain, Texas Christian University
Byron Nelson, West Virginia University
Carolyn Nelson, West Virginia University
Claudia Nelson, Southwest Texas State University
Holly Faith Nelson, Trinity Western University
John Niles, University of Wisconsin, Madison
Michael North, University of California, Los Angeles
Mary Anne Nunn, Central Connecticut State University
David Oakleaf, University of Calgary
Tamara O'Callaghan, Northern Kentucky University
Karen Odden, Assistant Editor for *Victorian Literature
    and Culture* (formerly of University of Wisconsin,
    Milwaukee)
Erika Olbricht, Pepperdine University
Patrick O'Malley, Georgetown University
Patricia O'Neill, Hamilton College
Delilah Orr, Fort Lewis College
John Pagano, Barnard College
Kirsten Parkinson, Hiram College
Diana Patterson, Mount Royal College
Cynthia Patton, Emporia State University

Russell Perkin, St. Mary's University

Marjorie G. Perloff, Stanford University

Jim Persoon, Grand Valley State University

John Peters, University of North Texas

Todd Pettigrew, Cape Breton University

Alexander Pettit, University of North Texas

Jennifer Phegley, The University of Missouri, Kansas City

John Pollock, San Jose State University

Mary Poovey, New York University

Gautam Premnath, University of Massachusetts, Boston

Regina Psaki, University of Oregon

Laura Quinney, Brandeis University

Katherine Quinsey, University of Windsor

Tilottama Rajan, University of Western Ontario

Geoff Rector, University of Ottawa

Walter Reed, Emory University

Margaret Reeves, Atkinson College, York University

Cedric Reverand, University of Wyoming

Gerry Richman, Suffolk University

John Rickard, Bucknell University

Michelle Risdon, Lake Tahoe Community College

David Robinson, University of Arizona

Solveig C. Robinson, Pacific Lutheran University

Laura Rotunno, Pennsylvania State University, Altoona

Brian Rourke, New Mexico State University

Christopher Rovee, Louisiana State University

Nicholas Ruddick, University of Regina

Shannon Russell, John Cabot University

Donelle Ruwe, Northern Arizona University

Jon Saklofske, Acadia University

Michelle Sauer, Minot State University

John Savarese, University of Waterloo

SueAnn Schatz, Lock Haven University of Pennsylvania

Dan Schierenbeck, Central Missouri State University

Norbert Schürer, California State University, Long Beach

Debora B. Schwartz, California Polytechnic University

Janelle A. Schwartz, Loyola University

John T. Sebastian, Loyola University

David Seed, University of Liverpool

Karen Selesky, University College of the Fraser Valley

Carol Senf, Georgia Tech University

Sharon Setzer, North Carolina State University

Lynn Shakinovsky, Wilfred Laurier University

John Sider, Westmont College

Judith Slagle, East Tennessee State University

Johanna Smith, University of Texas at Arlington

Sharon Smulders, Mount Royal College

Jason Snart, College of DuPage

Malinda Snow, Georgia State University

Yasmin Solomonescu, University of Georgia

Goran Stanivukovic, St. Mary's University

Thomas Steffler, Carleton University

Richard Stein, University of Oregon

Eric Sterling, Auburn University Montgomery

James Stokes, University of Wisconsin, Stevens Point

Mary-Ann Stouck, Simon Fraser University

Nathaniel Strout, Hamilton College

Brad Sullivan, Western New England College

Lisa Surridge, University of Victoria

Joyce A. Sutphen, Gustavus Adolphus College

Beth Sutton-Ramspeck, Ohio State University

Nanora Sweet, University of Missouri, St. Louis

Dana Symons, Simon Fraser University

Andrew Taylor, University of Ottawa

Elizabeth Teare, University of Dayton

Doug Thorpe, University of Saskatchewan

Jane Toswell, University of Western Ontario

Kim Trainor, University of British Columbia

Herbert Tucker, University of Virginia

John Tucker, University of Victoria

Mark Turner, King's College, University of London

Eleanor Ty, Wilfrid Laurier University

Deborah Tyler-Bennett, Loughborough University

Kirsten Uszkalo, University of Alberta

Lisa Vargo, University of Saskatchewan

Gina Luria Walker, The New School, New York City

Kim Walker, Victoria University of Wellington

Miriam Wallace, New College of Florida

Orrin Wang, University of Maryland

Hayden Ward, West Virginia State University

David Watt, University of Manitoba

Ruth Wehlau, Queen's University

Lynn Wells, University of Regina

Dan White, University of Toronto at Mississauga
Patricia Whiting, Carleton University
Thomas Willard, University of Arizona
Tara Williams, Oregon State University
Chris Willis, Birkbeck University of London
Lisa Wilson, SUNY College at Potsdam
Ed Wiltse, Nazareth College
Anne Windholz, Augustana College
Rosemary Winslow, The Catholic University of
    America

Susan Wolfson, Princeton University
Kenneth Womack, Pennsylvania State University
Gillen Wood, University of Illinois,
    Urbana-Champaign
Carolyn Woodward, University of New Mexico
Julia Wright, Wilfrid Laurier University
Julian Yates, University of Delaware
Arlene Young, University of Manitoba
Lisa Zeitz, University of Western Ontario

The Victorian Era

The Victorian Era

The word "Victorian" conjures up a series of images that both accurately describe and misrepresent the literature and culture of the last two thirds of the nineteenth century in Britain. Stiff collars and stiff upper lips, draped table legs, exceedingly long novels, and gritty urban squalor have become the iconic images of Victorian Britain. But these images reveal only one dimension of what is a much more complex picture. While it is certainly the case that many Victorians tended to place a high value on such qualities as honor, duty, moral seriousness, and sexual propriety—at least officially—it is a mistake to assume that most were humorless or repressed. And while many of the best-known Victorian novels run to many hundreds of pages, we need to remember that Victorian audiences tended to read these in weekly or monthly installments, or in shorter volumes. Although brutal factory conditions, pitiful wages, and crowded cities impoverished many millions of people, the Victorian period also saw the passage of progressive labor laws, unprecedented wealth creation for some, and the first public sewage systems in Britain. And though "Victorian" still suggests "repressed" to many readers, historians and literary scholars alike have increasingly shown that discourses about sexuality developed and proliferated throughout the period, not least in its literary output.

In fact, it may be fair to say that there was never a single "Victorian mindset" or "Victorian value system" but rather a range of them, and that these shifted throughout the century. Indeed, there is no real consensus about when the Victorian era began and ended. Some point to the passage of the Reform Bill of 1832 as the dawn of a new era, others to the formal abolition of slavery in the British Empire in 1833. Still others argue for the unity of a longer period,[1] beginning perhaps with the end of the Napoleonic Wars in 1815 and ending with the outbreak of World War I in 1914. Perhaps the obvious choice is to date the period as starting with Victoria's ascension to the throne in 1837 and concluding with her death in 1901, but the identification of the period so entirely with her reign is ultimately arbitrary and tells us little about the Victorian era.

Franz Xaver Winterhalter, *Queen Victoria*, 1842.

Although a great deal of overlap can be found between what we now call the Romantic and Victorian periods, most scholars agree that the 1830s was a pivotal decade, marked by the transition of the monarchy from William IV to Victoria and by the spread of a spirit of

---

[1] Some historians have suggested that the period's beginning should perhaps be dated even earlier, with the seeds of "Victorianism" being planted as early as the late eighteenth century, with the re-emergence of Evangelicalism and the Methodist revival. The religious movement countered the ideals of the Enlightenment and may thus be said to mark the conclusion of the primary movement of the eighteenth century.

political and social reform that would characterize the next several decades. During the 1850s and 1860s, Britain emerged from a depressed economy and experienced a level of political and social stability that made these decades the most prosperous of the century. The mid-Victorian period is now often regarded as the most quintessentially "Victorian," both culturally and economically; the 1870s and 1880s saw some decline in the strength of the economy and in Britain's imperial dominance abroad, despite its continued acquisition of colonial possessions. These later decades were also marked by the glimmerings of social change, a wave that culminated in the fin-de-siècle spirit of the 1890s, which saw many challenges to the values and conventions of the preceding decades in literature, politics, and everyday life.

Photographer unknown, *Queen Victoria*, c. 1897.
A picture of Albert is in the background.

Photographer unknown, *Her Majesty the Queen*,
21 June 1887.

A GROWING POWER

During Victoria's reign, Britain was the richest nation and the most powerful empire on the globe, with unchallenged military supremacy until the latter decades of the century and an imperial reach that covered one-quarter of the earth's surface by 1897.[1] The British Isles also experienced both the benefits and the horrors of enormous population growth throughout the nineteenth century. The census of 1801 put the combined population of England and Wales slightly under 10.5 million people; at century's end that number had more than tripled to 32.5 million. Just as striking was the movement of this population, from 75 per cent rural distribution in the early decades to nearly the same percentage residing in urban districts by the end of the century. Northern industrial cities grew particularly fast: Manchester, a town of no more than 15,000 people in 1750, had grown to 75,000 by 1800, and to 125,000 by 1820; by 1850 its population was over 300,000. Between 1815 and 1914, more than 20 million people emigrated from Britain to other

---

[1] The scope of Britain's imperial holdings was memorably expressed in a popular saying of the period: "The sun never sets on the British empire." (A popular rejoinder to the sentiment was the saying that God did not trust the English in the dark.)

parts of the world, over half of them to the United States, but millions, too, to Australia and to Canada.

Fleet Street, London, c. 1890.

As the first industrialized country, Britain experienced a shift from an agrarian to an industrial wage economy that meant an increase in income for many people, creating a sector of the population that was neither rich nor poor and was increasingly termed "middle class." A spirit of entrepreneurship and market thinking—dominated by upwardly mobile men— gradually replaced what had once seemed an entrenched, unchangeable system of aristocratic patronage and paternalism in the world of business and trade. The Reform Bill of 1832 granted political representation in Parliament to certain sectors of the middle-class male population for the first time, although even with its passage, only one in six adult men could vote, and the

Construction of the sewer beneath Fleet Street, London, early 1860s. By 1858 the stench of sewage from the Thames had become so overwhelming that the Houses of Parliament at Westminster found it impossible to meet; construction of a city-wide underground system of sewers, under the direction of Joseph Bazalgette, began the following year.

Building the Holborn Viaduct across the Fleet valley (*Illustrated Times*, 18 September 1869). The viaduct, carrying both road and rail traffic, was a vast project carried out by the Corporation of the City of London between 1863 and 1869.

Alfred Morgan, *An Omnibus Ride to Piccadilly Circus— Mr. Gladstone Travelling with Ordinary Passengers*, 1885. The previous year Prime Minister William Gladstone's government had extended the franchise to working class men, through the Reform Bill of 1884.

suffrage was still linked to property ownership. Rail travel, the advent of the telegraph, daily newspapers, and the manufacture and import of goods via steamship from all over the globe collapsed time and space, and flooded the homes of the affluent with new luxuries and conveniences. The Great Exhibition of 1851, the first World's Fair, showcased Britain's industrial dominance with exhibits of new consumer goods and remarkable technologies; the event symbolized Britain's reputation as the "workshop of the world." Thus, for many the overall mood was positive, and Thomas Macaulay's confident assertions of the nation's progress in his bestselling *History of England* rang true for much of his audience.

GRINDING MILLS, GRINDING POVERTY

The paradox of the economic life of the time was summed up by Thomas Carlyle in 1843: "England is full of wealth," he wrote, "of multifarious produce, supply for human want in every kind; yet England is dying of inanition." For millions of people, low wages, unemployment, and fluctuations in trade created widespread misery in crowded industrial cities such as Manchester and Birmingham. According to one estimate, 70 per cent of the population at mid-century was considered poor. The New Poor Law,[1] passed in 1834, divided and categorized the poor as either "deserving" (the elderly and the physically infirm) or "undeserving" (the able-bodied but unemployed). The poor were now eligible to receive public assistance only in the notorious workhouses, also known as the "Poor Law Bastilles,"[2]

[1] The "Old Poor Law" was passed during the reign of Queen Elizabeth I.

[2] The Paris fortress-prison named the Bastille was stormed on 14 July 1789, initiating the French Revolution.

which often served to punish and stigmatize rather than relieve. In addition, inadequate housing and slum conditions led to frequent outbreaks of illness and disease. Between 1831 and 1866, four cholera epidemics killed more than 140,000 people, inaugurating Britain's first wide-scale public health movement. Scores of "Blue Books"—statistical investigations, surveys, and government reports on the condition of inner-city neighborhoods—culminated in the Public Health Acts of 1848 and the 1870s. Similarly, between 1802 and 1847, factories and mines producing iron, cotton, and coal, which had been unregulated, employing men, women, and children in conditions that were often dirty and dangerous, were made subject to a series of Factory Acts designed to force employers to limit work hours—14-hour workdays had been not uncommon—and prohibit the employment of children under the age of nine in certain industries.

In her poem, "The Cry of the Children" (1843), Elizabeth Barrett Browning drew attention to the problem of child labor, helping to create humanitarian awareness on the part of middle-class readers by asking "How long, O cruel nation, / Will you stand to move the world, on a child's heart?"[1] Thomas Hood's "The Song of the Shirt" (1843) focused on the plight of the genteel but impoverished female needle-worker who toils alone in grim conditions for meager wages. Cast in the elevated and stylized "voices" appropriated from their victimized speakers, such poems were both wildly popular and highly sentimental, qualities that have until recently served to exclude them from serious study by scholars of English literature. Yet these poems did as much as or more than government reports and statistical surveys to draw the attention of wealthy and middle-class readers to major social issues. So too did Carlyle's *Past and Present* (1843), which called England to take responsibility for the many starving workers in the land of "plenty":

We have more riches than any Nation ever had before: we have less good of them than any Nation had before. ... We have forgotten everywhere that *Cash-payment* is not the sole relation of human beings; we think, nothing doubting, that it absolves and liquidates all other engagements.

Even as such voices spoke up in support of the destitute and the working classes, over the course of the century, the voices of working-class people themselves were also increasingly heard. The 1828 publication of Robert Blincoe's *Memoir* of his appalling early life in the mills had a lasting impact; in addition to a direct effect on its readers, Blincoe's memoir provided much of the raw material for Frances Trollope's novel *Michael Armstrong: Factory Boy* (1840), and may also have inspired Charles Dickens's *Oliver Twist* (1838). Blincoe's memoir was followed by a number of other autobiographical narratives of working-class hardship; a particularly notable example of the genre was *A Narrative of the Experience and Sufferings of William Dodd* (1841). Ellen Johnson published a more wide-ranging memoir, *Autobiography of a Factory Girl* (1867), together with her poems and songs. Another prominent working-class poetic voice was that of Ebenezer Elliott, the "Corn-Law Rhymer" from Yorkshire who became an active force first in the Chartist movement and then in the struggle to repeal the Corn Laws (both of which will be discussed in more detail below). In his *Corn-Law Rhymes* (1831) and in subsequent work Elliott attacked

The deadly will that takes
What labour ought to keep;
It is the deadly power that makes
Bread dear and labour cheap.

How to best respond to the force of this "deadly power" remained a matter of debate and speculation. If some emphasized the need to continually press for political reform, others appealed emotionally for hearts

---

[1] Many of the poem's details were drawn from the 1842–43 Parliamentary commission report investigating the conditions of child employment in mines and factories. The report's author, R.H. Horne, was a close friend of the poet.

Thomas Iron Works, London, 1867.

Hatting mill, Manchester, 1890s.

to change; still others formulated new philosophical approaches to the underlying moral and socio-economic questions. Perhaps the most important of these approaches was Utilitarianism, a broad-reaching philosophy that had first been developed in the late eighteenth century, primarily by Jeremy Bentham, and that was expounded in a more careful, subtle, and thoroughgoing fashion by John Stuart Mill in the nineteenth.[1] Utilitarian thought began to shape governmental policy,

including the New Poor Law, in the middle decades of the nineteenth century—and continues to be a shaping force in the social policy of many nations today. In its crude form, Utilitarianism holds—in the words of Bentham's 1776 "A Fragment on Government"—that "it is the greatest happiness of the greatest number that is the measure of right and wrong." In other words, the central guiding principle of social morality should be the pursuit of that which is good for all members of society, with no one person or group's interests given special weight. But how does one calculate "the greatest happiness of the greatest number"? Can social, legal, economic, and political problems be resolved by a "moral arithmetic" that evaluates human pain and pleasure according to

---

[1] Mill first published *Utilitarianism*, his defense of the utilitarian philosophy in 1861, as a series of three articles in *Fraser's Magazine*. The essays appeared as a one-volume work in 1863.

entirely rationalist principles? According to some crude versions of utilitarian philosophy—though certainly not that of Mill—the answer is yes; imagination, feeling, and individual desire are obsolete impediments to the operation of the "laws" of social improvement, which may be derived from empirical observation and calculation.

Writers such as Elizabeth Barrett Browning, Dickens, Carlyle, and John Ruskin were intensely critical of Utilitarianism, taking its crudest forms as representative and regarding it as a morally and spiritually bankrupt response to the human condition. Dickens, in particular, caricatured utilitarian thinking with telling directness in his portrayal of Thomas Gradgrind in *Hard Times* (1854), a novel aimed at exposing the working conditions in English factories and at initiating reform.[1] As Dickens's work, and the work of others such as Barrett Browning amply demonstrated, opposition to the cruelties of poverty could be expressed—as plausibly and as powerfully—by means of emotional and aesthetic appeals as it could by means of the philosophical arguments of the Utilitarians.[2]

However, it may be fitting to understand the intensity of these writers' opposition to Utilitarianism in a larger context. For Mill, "the greatest number" included not only the poor white people of England but also people of other races in poverty the world over. This is not to suggest that Mill opposed colonization; in his view, the greatest good for Black people, Indigenous people, and people of color might well lie in colonization by benevolent, supposedly more civilized powers such as England. "Despotism," he wrote, "is a legitimate mode of government in dealing with barbarians, provided the end be their improvement." But even this pro-imperialist view was too much for Dickens, Carlyle, and Ruskin, who, for all their sympathy for the white British poor, at best disregarded the humanity of other races, and at worst regarded them with outright loathing.

CORN LAWS, POTATO FAMINE

As the powerful and privileged attempted to confront the range of social crises facing a newly industrialized nation, economic depression, unemployment, political instability in Europe, and a series of crop failures in the 1840s—a decade often dubbed the "Hungry Forties"—caused a disproportionate level of suffering for the poor. Artificial shortages of grain in the country inflated the price of bread beyond the reach of the working class, causing periodic bread riots and a discontented work force. These shortages were in part the result of the Corn Laws, which imposed heavy tariffs on imports of grain, and were intended to protect British agricultural interests and limit dependence on foreign supplies of cereal grains. The Corn Laws were repealed in 1846 under pressure from the Anti-Corn-Law League, an alliance of free-trade advocates and liberal, laissez-faire[3] trade reformers.

While the Corn Laws were being debated in the English parliament, in Ireland an outbreak of potato blight in 1845 marked the onset of what would become one of the most devastating human catastrophes of the nineteenth century. The tenant-farming rural poor of Ireland—who constituted the vast majority of the population—had for generations been subsisting very largely on the potatoes that they grew themselves on their meager plots of land. They could afford little else; the immense inequities of the Irish tenant farming system, together with the heavy tariffs imposed on imports of grain under the Corn Laws, ensured the Irish peasantry's near total dependence on the potato crop. The tenant farming population was thus desperately poor even before the famine of the 1840s. But as the potato blight spread throughout Ireland and persisted—devastating the crops of 1846, 1847, and 1848—outright starvation spread across the island, even as

[1] In a letter to his friend Charles Knight, Dickens accused the utilitarians of seeing "figures and averages, and nothing else."

[2] Although the "social novel" had its origins in the eighteenth century, it was developed and popularized as a genre during the Victorian period.

[3] From the French for "let do," the phrase "laissez-faire" came to be used in the late eighteenth century as a shorthand for the belief that government should intervene as little as possible in the workings of the economy. The term first appeared in English usage in George Whatley's *Principles of Trade* (1774), but it did not become popularized until James Mill's reference in an 1824 entry in *The Encyclopedia Britannica*.

Ireland continued to export to England vast quantities of meat, butter, and other food that remained unaffordable to the starving poor. (Anglo-Irish poet Jane Elgee's "The Famine Year" [1847], published under the pseudonym "Speranza," offers a lament for the "Fainting forms, hunger-stricken" who watch "Stately ships … bear our food away.") At the same time, desperately poor, mostly Catholic tenants were forced to pay rents (often extraordinarily high) to wealthy English or Anglo-Irish landowners, most of whom lived abroad. If the tenants failed to pay, eviction was the likely result—which often left the tenant facing imminent starvation.

Prime Minister Robert Peel's Conservative government attempted to alleviate the situation with make-work projects for the destitute and with emergency shipments of grain imported from the United States. The Irish famine was also an important factor in Peel's decision to support repeal of the Corn Laws; like many, he believed that cheaper grain would help alleviate the situation in Ireland. Peel succeeded in repealing the Corn Laws, but the issue split the Conservative party; he was forced into the opposition and his government was replaced in 1846 by the Whig[1] administration of Lord John Russell, which by the end of 1847 had greatly reduced funding of emergency aid for Ireland. The laissez-faire economic beliefs of many Whigs informed their decision to transfer the responsibility for famine relief to local authorities (who were in most cases utterly unable to fulfill such responsibilities) under the provisions of a new Irish Poor Law.

By the end of the decade, between 850,000 and 1,500,000 people—perhaps as much as 15 per cent of the Irish population—had died of starvation, and at least a million more had emigrated. Many have blamed this enormous scale of death and suffering on poor decision-making on the part of Peel, Russell, and others in the English government, including Sir Charles Trevelyan, who was responsible both for advising the government on the Irish situation and for implementing the government's relief policies in Ireland. Others have suggested that the indebtedness of the British government made it virtually impossible for England to provide help on the scale that was required. Still others have blamed the laissez-faire economic doctrines preached (if not always practiced) by the Whigs.

No doubt there is some truth to all these arguments, but two underlying truths are also inescapable. The first is that the structure of Irish society (with its absentee landlords and its vast inequities between rich and poor, between landowner and tenant, and between Protestant and Catholic) meant that the island was perpetually teetering on the edge of catastrophe. The second is that anti-Irish attitudes in England were so widespread and ran so deep in the general populace that it would in all probability have been impossible politically for any English leader—no matter how well-intentioned—to have succeeded in putting in place measures sufficiently wide-reaching to have prevented disaster. There is little question that Sir Charles Trevelyan was echoing the anti-Irish sentiments of many in England when he infamously claimed that "the judgement of God sent the calamity to teach the Irish a lesson, [and] that calamity must not be too much mitigated."

Even before the famine, nationalism and anti-English sentiment had been on the rise among Irish intellectuals. At the center of this moment was *The Nation*, a Dublin periodical founded in 1842 with the explicit aim of

> celebrating Irish language and history and of securing for Ireland a nationality which will not only raise our people from their poverty, by securing to them the blessings of a domestic legislature, but inflame and purify them with a lofty and heroic love of country—a nationality of the spirit as well as the letter—a nationality which may come to be stamped upon our manners, our literature, and our deeds.

The British government's obvious disregard for its Irish subjects during the famine only intensified the commitment of Irish nationalists. Writers linked to *The*

---

[1] At the beginning of the nineteenth century, the major political parties were Whigs and Tories. Very generally speaking, Whigs tended to espouse more liberal views and Tories tended to espouse more conservative views; in the 1830s the Tories evolved into the Conservative Party, and the Whigs were subsumed by the newly formed Liberal Party a few decades later.

Nation included James Clarence Mangan, who metaphorically evokes the anguish of the famine in poems such as "Siberia" (1846); William Carleton, who depicted the experiences of Ireland's rural poor in his novel *The Black Prophet: A Tale of Irish Famine* (1847), and poet and folklorist Jane Elgee (Speranza), who in 1848 demanded to know, "Is there one man that thinks that Ireland has not been sufficiently insulted, has not been sufficiently degraded in her honour and her rights, to justify her now in fiercely turning on her oppressor?"

NOTICE
TO
THE EARL OF CHARLEMONT'S TENANTRY.

IN consideration of the extensive failure in the POTATO CROP this Season, willing to bear his share in the general calamity, and anxious to relieve, as far as in him lies, his Poorer Tenants from an undue share of suffering under the Divine Will, LORD CHARLEMONT has directed that the following Scale of Reduction, in Payment of Rent, shall be adopted for this Year, upon his Estates in the COUNTIES of ARMAGH and TYRONE, viz. :—

25 per Cent. on Rents under £5	10 per Cent. on Rents under £20.	
20 per Cent. on Rents under £10	5 per Cent. on Rents under £30.	
15 per Cent. on Rents under £15	No Discount on Rents exceeding £30.	

Notice of a rent abatement by an Irish landlord, 1846.

On 29 June 1848, a group called the Young Irelanders—incensed by the famine and in part inspired by democratic revolutions occurring elsewhere in Europe—staged a rebellion. The group's grievances can be traced to the 1800 Acts of Union, which had dissolved the Irish Parliament; responsibility for the governance of Ireland had been transferred to the Houses of Parliament in London. Although the representation of Ireland in this body had been strengthened in 1829 (when legal restrictions on the political position of Catholics were lifted), many in Ireland continued to feel that the repeal of the Union and the establishment of self-government was the only effective response to the needs of Ireland.

The rebellion of the Young Irelanders was subdued within a day. Nevertheless, the seeds of the Irish independence movement had been effectively sown—not only in Ireland but also in the United States, where hundreds of thousands of Irish now lived. As these emigrants prospered in America, they provided more and more support for groups agitating for Irish inde-

Evicted family, Glenbeigh, Ireland, 1888. In the 1880s an economic depression coincided with the election of a substantial number of Irish Home Rule Members of Parliament (under Charles Parnell's leadership), and with a campaign by the Land League to resist the practice of evicting impoverished tenant farmers unable to pay their rent.

pendence. Chief among these was the Fenian movement, formed in the 1850s. The Fenians launched numerous attacks in the 1860s and 1870s, not only in England but also against symbols of colonial authority in British possessions in New Brunswick, Upper Canada, and Manitoba. The most significant Fenian uprising occurred in 1867; though unsuccessful in its aim of establishing an independent Irish Republic, it again brought the demands of Ireland to the forefront of public debate.

On the Parliamentary front, the demand for the repeal of the Union took the form of the Home Rule Movement; Home Rule for Ireland was the subject of heated debate through much of the latter half of the century. Its leading spokesperson was Charles Stewart Parnell, Ireland's greatest Parliamentarian during this time. (Parnell survived dozens of scurrilous attempts to discredit him over several decades; he was finally

Jabez Hughes, *Benjamin Disraeli*, c. 1877. Disraeli, who led the Conservative Party from 1868 to 1880 (serving as Prime Minister briefly in 1868 and then again from 1874 to 1880), was seen as something of an exotic within the English establishment. His parents were Jewish, but he was baptized as an infant and remained a practicing Anglican throughout his life. Disraeli's prolific literary career, which began with the publication of his first novel, *Vivian Grey*, in 1826, made him a well-known intellectual. A fashionable figure, Disraeli was derided by his strait-laced rival, Liberal leader William Gladstone, as "Asiatic"—a word often used in Victorian times, with obviously racist connotations, to mean "indulgent and irresponsible." But Disraeli remained a popular figure with much of the general population as well as with much of the establishment—and with the Queen.

brought down when his affair with a divorced woman became a public scandal.) Proposals to enact Home Rule were twice passed by the House of Commons—in 1886, when William Gladstone introduced a Home Rule bill, and then again in 1893. Both times the measure was defeated in the House of Lords. Another bill to enact Home Rule was put aside with the outbreak of World War I in 1914. Ultimately, independence was only achieved after the violent struggles of the 1916 Easter Uprising and the War of Independence of 1919–22. Even then, the British retained possession of a substantial area in Northern Ireland.

"THE TWO NATIONS"

In the 1830s and 1840s, the human cost of the Industrial Revolution—what became known as the "Condition of England" question—was scrutinized by legislators, workers, and writers. Carlyle, Dickens, Elizabeth Gaskell, Harriet Martineau, Benjamin Disraeli, and Henry Mayhew documented the daily existence of poor and working people, and criticized the laws that were supposed to address their suffering. The "social problem novel" or "industrial novel," an important subgenre of Victorian fiction, drew attention to class conflict and the social ramifications of laissez-faire economic policies. Prominent examples include Charles Kingsley's *Alton Locke* (1850), Charles Dickens's *Hard Times*, and Elizabeth Gaskell's *Mary Barton* (1848) and *North and South* (1854–55).

In his 1845 novel *Sybil*, future Prime Minister Benjamin Disraeli coined the phrase "the Two Nations" to describe the disparity in Britain between rich and poor. Novelists felt that their work could provoke social reform by exposing their middle-class audiences to the plight of the working classes, who were often portrayed as either vulnerable and victimized by forces beyond their control, or as a violent, angry "mass"; intervention by those of goodwill from other social classes is often implicitly recommended in such fiction as a way of ameliorating the situation and bridging "the Two Nations." For example, the use of the third-person omniscient narrator in Gaskell's novel *Mary Barton* allows Gaskell to move between the classes and present their viewpoints.

Non-fiction writing may have been as important as that of any novelist in nurturing the seeds of social change. Henry Mayhew's interviews with working people and street folk for the *Morning Chronicle* newspaper opened a window for its readers onto the daily existence of an often voiceless underclass. It must be said, however, that Mayhew's reports contained no overt political commentary or reform agenda. Friedrich Engels, by contrast, in his chronicle of urban squalor *The Condition of the Working Class in England in 1844*, not only described the extraordinary scale of the human suffering he witnessed but also placed the blame squarely on the shoulders of a class system created by industrial capitalism: "Power lies in the hands of those who own, directly or indirectly, foodstuffs and the means of production. The poor, having no capital, inevitably bear the consequences of defeat in the struggle."[1]

It was not only middle-class writers and observers who were bringing attention to the great divide between Britain's rich and poor. Chartism, a movement that initiated a series of political campaigns in the 1830s and 1840s, was a concrete expression of the desire of working-class people to resist economic and social disparity and press for political reform. The People's Charter of 1838, from which the movement took its name, petitioned the government to adopt a range of key reforms, including annual elections, universal male suffrage, and the abolition of the secret ballot and property qualifications for Members of Parliament. The mouthpiece of the Chartist movement was the *Northern Star* newspaper, one of many working-class periodicals that flourished in the early decades of the nineteenth century. The Chartist petitions were signed by up to five million people and presented to Parliament by a coalition of workers in 1839, 1842, and 1848, but were rejected each time. A number of middle-class writers sympathetic to the claims of the working classes were nevertheless suspicious of the Chartist movement, particularly in light of the political revolutions taking place in continental Europe in the late 1840s. In his

longing for the imagined social order of a feudal past, Carlyle denounced the "mad Chartisms" of the "anarchic multitude," comparing them to the events of the French Revolution and the Reign of Terror. With the defeat of the third petition, Chartism collapsed, but it had helped instigate a new level of class consciousness among ordinary people and set the stage for later working-class movements in Britain.

Chartist poster, 1838.

In the 1880s and 1890s various socialist movements emerged, partly on the strength of Karl Marx's theories of capital, which he formulated under the dome of the British Library after moving to London in 1849. The Fabian Society was one of the most influential socialist organizations. Its membership was mainly drawn from the middle class and included such notables as George Bernard Shaw, Sidney Webb, Beatrice Potter Webb, Edith Nesbit, and Annie Besant. The Fabians' tactics were reformist rather than revolutionary; they advocated

---

[1] Engels's treatise, first published in Germany in 1845, was not translated into English until 1892.

public ownership of utilities, affordable housing, improved wages, and greater access to higher education for all.

The Matchgirl Strike Committee, 1888. A threatened strike by Bryant and May Match Company employees—most of them girls of no more than 15, earning starvation wages and exposed to hazardous phosphorous fumes—became a *cause célèbre* in 1888, and forced the company to change its practices. The action was led by Annie Besant (who had initially become famous during her 1877 trial for obscenity—the charge being based on the distribution of her pamphlet offering practical advice on contraception).

Trade unions and labor movements also grew gradually in scope and strength throughout the century, with the Trade Union Act of 1871 granting legal status to unions for the first time. Newly mobilized workers in the 1880s organized to mount a series of strikes with varying degrees of success. Two of the most highly publicized of these were the match-girls' strike in 1888 and the London dock workers' strike of 1889. Union membership doubled in these years, partly because of the success of these labor actions.

The match-girls' strike began after the dismissal of one of the workers at the Bryant and May Factory in Bow, London, in early July 1888, but its real causes lay in the terrible working conditions at the factory, including 14-hour workdays, poor pay and excessive fines, and severe health complications resulting from working with dangerous materials. The strike attracted significant publicity, and factory owners were forced to concede to the strikers' demands for a better working-environment.

The London Dock Strike began on 14 August 1889. At a Parliamentary hearing on the issue, the general manager at the Millwall Docks testified about the physical conditions of the workers, which led to the strike:

> The poor fellows are miserably clad, scarcely with a boot on their foot, in a most miserable state. ... These are men who come to work in our docks who come on without having a bit of food in their stomachs, perhaps since the previous day; they have worked for an hour and have earned 5d. [5 pence, less than the cost of a loaf of bread]; their hunger will not allow them to continue: they take the 5d. in order that they may get food, perhaps the first food they have had for twenty-four hours.

The strike, which had succeeded in garnering strong middle-class support, ended in victory for the workers, whose principal demand had been for increased pay, and the establishment of unions for dock workers. In broad terms, the often oppressive conditions of England's modernizing economy turned the nation into a laboratory for developing strategies of social analysis and political activism—trade unions, general strikes, and other organized campaigns for change—that would remain powerful long after the Victorian era.

THE POSITION OF WOMEN

Gender consciousness was central to Victorian England's political scene in a number of significant ways. At the beginning of the Victorian period, middle-class women were shut out of most remunerative employments and institutions of higher education, could not vote, and had few legal rights. By the end of the century, the situation did not, on the surface, look radically different—universal female suffrage, for example, was not achieved in Britain until 1928—but several key developments heralded the changes to come in the twentieth century.

The first major challenges by Victorian "strong-minded women" to patriarchal control were in the area of marriage law. The common-law doctrine of coverture ensured that a woman's legal identity was subsumed in that of her husband's upon marriage. In effect, the law of coverture regarded the husband and wife as "one person": the husband. This meant that upon marriage a husband had full control of his wife's personal property and any earnings she acquired during the marriage; he had absolute authority over their home and children; and he could legally use physical force to discipline the members of his family. If he deserted his wife, she could not sue for divorce and had no custody rights to their children. No viable legal mechanism was available to an average woman to contest her husband's decisions, since husband and wife were "one body" under the law.[1] The essayist Frances Power Cobbe was among the most effective in pointing out the illogic of such arrangements, as well as the terrible toll they exacted. In contemplating, for example, the situation of "the poor woman whose husband has robbed her earnings, who leaves her and her children to starve, and then goes unpunished because the law can only recognize the relation of husband and wife as ... one before the law," Cobbe observed in her provocative 1868 essay "Criminals, Idiots, Women, and Minors" that

It is one of the numerous anomalies connected with women's affairs, that when they are under debate the same argument which would be held to determine other questions in one way is felt to settle theirs in another. If for instance it be proved of any other class of the community, that it is particularly liable to be injured, imposed upon, and tyrannized over (e.g., the children who work in factories), it is considered to follow as a matter of course that the law must step in for its protection. But it is the alleged *helplessness* of married women which, it is said, makes it indispensable to give all the support of the law, *not* to them, but to the stronger persons with whom they are unequally yoked.

Under pressure from organized networks of reformers, several major pieces of legislation were enacted that altered the status and position of married women. Perhaps the most economically significant of these was the Married Women's Property Act of 1870,[2] which finally allowed married women to legally own the money they earned and the property they inherited. In addition, the Matrimonial Causes Act of 1878 accorded some legal protection to female victims of domestic violence, and the Infant Custody Acts of 1839 and 1886 granted a woman custodial rights to her children. Although full equality within marriage was not realized in law until the twentieth century, the passage of the aforementioned legislation began to chip away at male patriarchal privilege and challenged the legal and religious "justifications" for women's oppression within the family.

In her 1851 essay "The Enfranchisement of Women" Harriet Taylor Mill addresses those "justifications" one by one, then proceeds to the heart of the matter: "The real question is, whether it is right and expedient that one half of the human race should pass through life in a state of forced subordination to the other half." *The Subjection of Women* (1869),[3] John Stuart Mill's famous extended essay on the topic, grew out of Taylor Mill's essay—the two worked largely collaboratively. "The Enfranchisement of Women" had

---

[1]   The tremendous pressures placed on women as a result of coverture are significant to the plot of a number of prominent Victorian novels, perhaps most notably Emily Brontë's *Wuthering Heights* (1847). In the novel, Heathcliff exploits marital coverture to usurp property as part of his plan for vengeance, repeatedly resorting to abuse and exploitation of the authority he is granted as husband.

[2]   The Act's full title was "An Act to amend the law relating to the property of married women." Although the Act effectively overturned coverture by allowing women to legally claim their own earnings and property, serious loopholes made it possible to easily evade the law, particularly in regard to inheritance. An additional problem was posed by the fact that the Act was not retroactive, thereby limiting its usefulness for many women. The Act also made it a woman's legal duty to financially maintain her children from profits earned. That is, the Act effectively established both parents as responsible for the financial support of their children.

[3]   The essay was completed in 1861, but Mill waited to publish the work until he felt it would be more influential.

Cartoon from *Votes for Women III* (7 January 1910).

The movement to win the vote for women began in the 1850s, and articles and petitions on the issue appeared with increasing frequency thereafter. Many of the early arguments drew parallels with other efforts to extend the franchise; as Mary Margaret Dilke observed in an 1889 article, "it is really an interesting study to notice how every argument used to delay the enfranchisement of working men and farm labourers reappears to do duty against women. How often has the question been asked, 'What does Hodge know about finance and foreign policy, colonial affairs and commercial interests?'"

As the suffrage movement grew, differences of opinion developed over the appropriate level of militancy to adopt and over whether the movement should press for universal suffrage or only for certain categories of women to be allowed to vote. The granting of the vote eventually came in two stages, with certain classes of propertied women granted the right to vote in 1918 (the same year the vote was granted to all men of 21 years or more), and all women over the age of 21 finally being granted the franchise in 1928.

set out with utmost clarity the ideal that is still being striven for today: "the principle which regulates the existing social relations between the two sexes—the legal subordination of one sex to the other—is wrong in itself and now one of the chief hindrances to human improvement ... it ought to be replaced by a principle of perfect equality, admitting no power or privilege on the one side, nor disability on the other."

The principles advocated by Cobbe, Taylor Mill, and Mill were, of course, not only matters of law and government; they pervaded every aspect of British life, from employment, to educational access, to a variety of cultural matters. The principle of "perfect equality" was very far from being realized in any of these areas even at century's end. But, by 1900, some at least were beginning to feel the effects of a slow movement toward greater acceptance of the principles of gender equality.

EMPIRE

Victorian Britain's internal politics, enormous wealth, and its sense of national and global identity cannot be adequately understood in isolation from its imperial rule abroad. In an address at Oxford in 1870, the highly influential critic and social thinker John Ruskin urged England to "found colonies as fast and as far as she is able, … seizing every piece of fruitful waste ground she can set her foot on, and there teaching these her colonists that their first aim is to be to advance the power of England by land and sea." And under Victoria's reign such power did indeed grow steadily, with eighteen major territories added to the British Empire, which already included India, Canada, Australia, New Zealand, and much of southern Africa and the Caribbean.

If the Empire arose largely from the desire to increase trade and maximize commercial interests, it also increasingly took hold of the political and cultural imagination. The often brutal effects of colonial domination were rationalized by a pseudo-science purporting to demonstrate the inferiority of dark-skinned peoples and by a keenly felt, much-encouraged sense of racial and cultural superiority over other peoples. A paternalistic sense of responsibility for people of the "inferior races" became known as the "white man's burden" in Rudyard Kipling's famous phrasing. Or, as evolutionary theorist Alfred Russel Wallace put it, "the relation of a civilized to an uncivilized race, over which it rules, is exactly that of parent to child, or generally adults to infants." In missionary work, travel and exploration, scientific writing, advertising, visual art, and literature, the culture and logic of imperial rule were formulated as part of the everyday "common sense" of the age.

Not everyone was in complete agreement about

Robert Bulwer-Lytton, Viceroy of India, Calcutta, 1877.

Britain's imperial policies and practices. Impassioned public debates about the moral and economic injustice of slavery had culminated in the legal abolition of the slave trade in 1807 and of slavery in most British possessions in 1833. Britain continued to rely on cheap imports of raw materials from its Caribbean colonies, however, and conditions for free workers were sometimes little better than they had been for enslaved people. Attention to British rule in the West Indies was renewed in 1865, following an uprising in which Black Jamaicans had killed about twenty white colonists. Governor Edward Eyre's response was to send troops, who killed more than four hundred Black Jamaicans, many of whom had not been involved in the revolt. Hundreds more people were also captured, some of whom were later executed, and Eyre's forces burned down more than 1,000 homes. The opinions of two of the century's most respected public intellectuals— Thomas Carlyle and John Stuart Mill—represented the opposing poles of the public's response, with Carlyle supporting Eyre's imposition of a harsh law to restore order, and Mill calling for Eyre to be tried for murder.

The "Indian Mutiny" of 1857–58 presented a major challenge to British rule in India, which until that point was still largely under the control of the East India Company. Sepoys—Indian men employed as soldiers by the British—staged a rebellion at Meerut in early 1857, killing British officers. The rebellion spread throughout northern territories and to Delhi, with massacres of British soldiers and civilians taking place at Cawnpore and Lucknow. British reprisals were swift and bloody, leading to summary executions, looting, and massacres of Indian civilians. The Indian resistance was motivated by religious, cultural, and political opposition to British policies, and had a lasting impact on British rule in India. One especially significant change was the transfer of colonial governance from the East India Company to the Crown in 1858. In the meantime, the English press was filled with lurid reports of the violence, resulting in greater public fascination with India than ever before. Countless eyewitness accounts, sermons, plays, novels, and poems—some written decades after the events—expressed moral outrage about the insurgency. There were also those, including Marx and the soon-to-be Prime Minister Benjamin Disraeli, who tried to contextualize the violence by criticizing Britain's exploitative attitudes and practices in India, but such dissenting voices remained very much a minority.

Britain participated in few major wars during Victoria's reign; when it did, the results were often less than heroic. In the Crimean War of 1854–56, Britain joined Turkey and France in fighting Russian encroachment into the Middle East, but the war did little to change the balance of power in Europe; it nonetheless resulted in the deaths of 21,000 British troops, 16,000 of whom died of disease.[1] In the Anglo-Zulu War of 1878–79, the Zulus of southern Africa had considerable initial success against British forces before being subdued, and in the Anglo-Afghan War of 1878–80, the British suffered various reversals before achieving a tenuous hold over Afghanistan. The Boer War of 1899–1902, in

Famine Victims, Madras, c. 1877. Famine was a recurrent reality in India throughout the nineteenth century, but the famine of the 1870s was particularly harsh. It gave rise to considerable controversy in Britain, with some (such as Florence Nightingale, the founder of modern nursing) pressing for investment in health, sanitation, and irrigation as well as short-term relief measures; others (in sympathy with the harsh approach taken by the Viceroy, Robert Bulwer-Lytton) saw such measures as too expensive or too "lenient."

South Africa, was fought between the British and the Boers over gold and diamond fields. For the Boers—white settlers of Dutch descent, also known as Afrikaaners—the war was part of a larger struggle to prevent the influence of foreign powers on agricultural lands they had claimed. A guerilla war ensued, and Britain's image as the greatest military power in the world suffered when the army was unable to defeat the vastly outnumbered Boers.

In England, popular support for the Empire reached its zenith in the 1880s and 1890s, as Britain accelerated the pace of its drive to increase its imperial acquisitions to compete with other European powers and with the United States. Queen Victoria's Golden and Diamond

---

[1] When the deplorable conditions of the military's hospitals became public knowledge through reports in *The Times*, Florence Nightingale was dispatched to the Crimea to superintend Britain's female nurses.

Florence Nightingale in the Crimea, c. 1856.

Queen Victoria and her servant Abdul Karim, 1893.

Jubilees, during which she celebrated the fiftieth and sixtieth anniversaries of her sovereignty, provided grand occasions for the expression of national pride. As *The Times* crowed, Britain was extolled as "the mightiest and most beneficial Empire ever known in the annals of mankind." Much popular reading in these decades was devoted to a celebration of Empire, though warnings of its imminent demise were also increasingly sounded. Boys' adventure stories in such publications as *The Boy's Own Annual* featured tales of manly prowess in the service of Empire and promoted the values of honor, courage, and duty to Queen and country. Travel and exploration narratives were popular, too—particularly those that recounted the heroic journeys of such larger-than-life figures as Richard Burton and David Livingstone. Burton (1821–90) was renowned for his travels throughout Asia and Africa and much celebrated for his mastery of foreign languages, of which he knew 29, by some counts. Perhaps his most famous exploit was traveling to Mecca in disguise, but he was also recognized for translating the complete *One Thousand and One Nights* from Arabic and for bringing the *Kama Sutra* to publication in English. Although he served as a symbol of the Empire's might, Burton was a prominent critic of colonial policies. David Livingstone (1813–73) renamed the Mosi-oa-Tunya—perhaps the world's most impressive waterfall—Victoria Falls in honor of the Queen. He was a national hero of sorts during the Victorian era, famed as a missionary, a scientist and explorer, and an idealistic imperialist who fought against slavery but advocated commercial empire. Speaking to students at Cambridge University in 1857, Livingstone declared,

People talk of the sacrifice I have made in spending so much of my life in Africa. Can that be called a sacrifice which is simply paid back as a small part of a great debt owing to our God, which we can never repay? Is that a sacrifice which brings its own blest reward in healthful activity, the consciousness of doing good, peace of mind, and a bright hope of a glorious destiny hereafter? Away with the word in such a view and with such a thought! It is emphatically no sacrifice. Say rather it is a privilege.

Engraving by G. Durand, after a sketch by H.M. Stanley, "The Meeting of Livingstone and Stanley in Central Africa" (from *The Graphic*, 3 August 1872). By 1869, it had been three years since the renowned missionary and explorer David Livingstone had embarked on an expedition in search of the source of the Nile River. American journalist Henry Morgan Stanley was commissioned in that year by a New York newspaper to find Livingstone; the story of the two finally meeting on the shores of Lake Tanganyika in 1871 became legendary. As Stanley described it, "I ... would have embraced him, only, he being an Englishman, I did not know how he would receive me; so I did what cowardice and false pride suggested was the best thing—walked deliberately to him, took off my hat, and said, 'Dr. Livingstone, I presume?'

"'Yes,' said he, with a kind smile, lifting his cap slightly."

Almost as popular as the narratives of Burton and Livingstone were travel journals by intrepid "lady explorers" such as Mary Kingsley and Isabella Bird, who unsettled conventional notions of Victorian femininity as they satisfied the public taste for true stories with fictionalized elements. Kingsley (1862–1900) first traveled to Africa in order to complete research for a book left unfinished by her father at the time of his death. She lived with local tribes in Angola. Upon her return to England, she toured the country, giving lectures in which she criticized missionaries for their attempts to change the local people—earning her much censure from the Church of England. She also defended African customs, including polygamy. Her books about her experiences—*Travels in Africa* (1897) and *West African Studies* (1899)—were best-sellers. Bird (1831–1904) traveled extensively, visiting Australia, Hawaii, and Colorado—then the most recent state to join the United States—where she covered more than 800 miles in the Rocky Mountains. The letters she wrote to her sister during this time were published as the immensely popular *A Lady's Life in the Rocky Mountains* (1879).

Treatments of the Empire in literature changed as the century progressed and Britain's grip on its colonies grew increasingly tenuous. Whereas early and mid-century Victorian fiction tended to imagine the Empire as a fairly static, unknown space to which characters can be exiled in the interests of narrative closure, late-century fiction often represented the Empire in darker, Gothic terms. Incorporating supernatural and psychological elements in their work, writers such as H. Rider Haggard, Arthur Conan Doyle, Rudyard Kipling, and Robert Louis Stevenson used colonial settings to explore themes of racial degeneration and human "savagery." In his 1899 novella, *Heart of Darkness*, Joseph Conrad, a Polish émigré to England, drew on his experience as a member of the merchant marine in his portrayal of imperial greed, exploitation, and corruption among ivory traders in the Congo. Even Kipling, called the "Laureate of Empire" for his energetic—and often jingoistic—portrayals of the glories of British imperialism, was not always unequivocal in his attitudes toward the Empire. In his 1897 poem "Recessional," he sounded a famous warning against imperial hubris: "Far-called, our navies melt away; / On dune and headland sinks the fire: / Lo, all our pomp of yesterday / Is one with Nineveh and Tyre!"[1]

FAITH AND DOUBT

At the beginning of the Victorian era, religion dominated social, moral, and intellectual life to a much greater degree than it had in the eighteenth century or would in the twentieth. One of the most unsettling developments for average citizens during the Victorian period was the growing opposition to the authority of Christian faith and the established church. A rapidly changing social order, combined with the growing predominance of scientific rationalism and empiricist

method, destabilized Christian certainty, creating a rising tide of secularism and religious skepticism. As critic J.A. Froude put it in 1841, "the very truths which have come forth have produced doubts ... this dazzle has too often ended in darkness."

The poet Arthur Hugh Clough was a central figure in the expression of the religious doubt of the age; in "Easter Day: Naples, 1849"—a poem whose title deliberately invokes the most sacred of days for Christians only for the poem to subvert the day's holiness—his verse conveys a strong sense of the intense emotion that could accompany such feelings:

> My heart was hot within me; till at last
> My brain was lightened when my tongue had said—
> Christ is not risen!
> Christ is not risen, no—
> He lies and moulders low.

Biblical scholars in England and Europe in the early decades of the century had begun to question the Scriptures as a source of literal truth and to present the figure of Jesus Christ as a mortal rather than a divine being. The German "higher critics" of the Bible—especially D.F. Strauss in his *Das Leben Jesu* (translated by George Eliot, 1844–46)[2]—were influential in this "scientific" discussion of biblical texts. Leading Victorian thinkers such as Carlyle, Eliot, and Martineau wrote of personal religious crises, and wrestled publicly with doubts about the value and meaning of Christian belief. As Matthew Arnold wrote in 1880, "There is not a creed which is not shaken, nor an accredited dogma which is not shown to be questionable, not a received tradition which does not threaten to dissolve." In this climate of uncertainty as to whether the divine could be knowable, Carlyle's arrival, in *Sartor Resartus* (1833–34), at an

---

[1] Nineveh, called an "exceeding great city" in the Book of Jonah, was the center of worship of the goddess Ishtar in Assyria; it was captured and razed in 612 BCE, signaling the end of the Assyrian Empire. Tyre—the largest and most important Phoenician city—was sacked by Alexander the Great during his campaign against Persia in 332 BCE.

[2] David Friedrich Strauss (1808–74) shocked and outraged Christian Europe with his depiction of the "historical Jesus." *Das Leben Jesu*, or *The Life of Jesus, Critically Examined*, caused a scandal with its insistence on the need to understand the miraculous events depicted in the Gospels as "mythical" in character. Eventually, Strauss's views came to dominate the new epoch of scriptural study, focused on textual interpretation.

affirmation of "natural supernaturalism" offers a telling statement of the almost desperate determination to find the divine in both nature and other human beings.

Traditional religious belief received its greatest challenge in the Victorian period from the evidence of the fossil record, and from Charles Darwin's theories of evolution and natural selection, which he advanced in *On the Origin of Species* (1859) and *The Descent of Man* (1871). While Darwin made a concerted effort in *On the Origin of Species* to avoid implying that his conclusions contradicted Christian faith in God, and while some theologians saw no contradiction between Darwin's views and Christianity, his work did certainly reject the Christian idea that human beings had been directly created in God's image and were thus of a different order than the rest of the natural world. In *Descent*, Darwin provoked and challenged his audience by declaring, "He who is not content to look, like a savage, at the phenomena of nature as disconnected, cannot any longer believe that man is the work of a separate act of creation."[1]

And religious controversy and doubt extended further still. Not only were the divinity of Christ, the literal truth of the Bible, and the processes of creation at issue, so too was the very existence of a creator or divine being. One of Darwin's strongest supporters, the scientist Thomas Henry Huxley, coined the term "agnostic" in 1869 at a party held in connection with the forming of the Metaphysical Society, a learned society that met regularly for over a decade to discuss theological issues, and whose members also included Tennyson, Ruskin, and Gladstone. The term agnostic named a person of a sort rarely acknowledged in earlier ages—one who

neither believes nor disbelieves in the existence of God, holding instead that it is simply impossible for humans to possess knowledge of such matters.[2] It is to such beliefs—or the lack thereof—that Matthew Arnold refers when he writes in "Dover Beach" (1867) of the ebbing tide of the "Sea of Faith." Whereas in the twentieth century that ebbing tide was sometimes welcomed as representing a freeing of human potential, Victorians tended to hear it in the way that Arnold heard it, inextricably associated with an "eternal note of sadness."

The established church of England and Scotland—the Anglican denomination—remained a powerful entity throughout the Victorian era, with the reigning monarch heading the Church as the "Defender of the Faith," as had been the case since Henry VIII's break with Rome in the 1530s. By century's end, however, its power was more social than political. Though only Anglicans could be admitted to Parliament until the late 1820s, and non-Anglicans were barred from taking degrees at Oxford and Cambridge until 1871, the changes in both policies demonstrated that allegiance to Anglicanism was no longer a necessary criterion for admission to the bastions of power.

The Church was also profoundly influenced by the gradual severance of church-state relations, as well as the increasing popularity of Evangelicalism, a broad-based movement comprising numerous Protestant denominations including Methodism and Presbyterianism. These "Dissenting" or "nonconformist" faiths transformed religious practice in Britain, stressing the importance of an individual's personal relationship with God, of prudence and temperance, of conversion, of missionary work, and of humanitarian activism. In 1865, the Methodist minister William Booth founded what became known as the Salvation Army, which ministered to the poor in London's East End and became the center of social purity campaigns stressing chastity and public decency for men as well as women. In general, Evangelical congregations were less hierarchical in organization than the traditional Anglican Church, were anti-Catholic in orientation, and

---

[1] Much recent debate has focused on the question of Darwin's own Christian faith. His *Autobiography* (completed in 1876, but first published in 1887, five years after his death) and letters suggest a growing agnosticism. In the *Autobiography*, Darwin recalls, "In my Journal I wrote that whilst standing in the midst of the grandeur of a Brazilian forest, 'it is not possible to give an adequate idea of the higher feelings of wonder, admiration, and devotion, which fill and elevate the mind.' I well remember my conviction that there is more in man than the mere breath of his body." But, toward the end of his life, he wrote to a correspondent, "I am sorry to have to inform you that I do not believe in the Bible as a divine revelation, & therefore not in Jesus Christ as the Son of God."

[2] Among Victorian authors, George Eliot is perhaps the most prominent to have described herself as an agnostic.

attracted both middle- and working-class believers who felt that Anglicanism had lost its spiritual power and had become a mere appendage of the state.

Henry Taunt, *Bible Stall at the St. Giles Fair, Oxford*, 1880.

Evangelicalism—and the resistance to it—within the Church of England resulted in a split between Anglican Evangelicals (commonly referred to as Low Church), progressives (Broad Church, sometimes called Latitudinarians), and Anglo-Catholics (High Church). An important High Church reaction to Evangelicalism took place in the 1830s and 1840s through the Oxford Movement, also called Tractarianism, led by Oxford theologians and intellectuals John Henry Newman, John Keble, and Edward Pusey. Celebrating the mystical and aesthetic elements of worship, they advocated an increased emphasis on religious ritual and a strict observance of clerical hierarchy within the Anglican communion. Newman's conversion to Roman Catholicism in 1845 spelled the end of the Oxford Movement, heralding a significant Catholic revival that saw many intellectuals rejecting Protestantism to embrace the Catholic faith and tradition. This was a significant

religious as well as political development, since Catholics in England and especially in Ireland had for centuries been subject to persecution.

Since the seventeenth century, the practice of Catholicism had been heavily penalized by the government, which imposed numerous legal restrictions on the ability of members of the Catholic Church to hold public office, to attend university or even to receive instruction in primary and secondary schools, to own or inherit land, and much more. These laws were known collectively as the Penal Laws. As Ireland's population was overwhelmingly Catholic, the practical effect of the Penal Laws was the near-complete exclusion of the vast majority of Irish people from public and political life. By the turn of the nineteenth century many of these laws had been changed or repealed, but several still remained. Importantly, Catholics were still unable to become Members of Parliament, meaning that legislation for Ireland was left in the hands of representatives whose interests were Protestant, pro-English, and largely upper-class as well.

The fight for Catholic rights—for "Catholic Emancipation," as it was generally referred to—was largely led by the charismatic leader Daniel O'Connell. O'Connell accused the government of despotism, positioning the call for Emancipation within the larger context of the call for liberty and equality that had been sweeping Europe since the end of the previous century. The Emancipation movement ostensibly achieved victory in 1829, with the passing of the Roman Catholic Relief Act, which annulled all previous restrictions on the ability of Catholics—including O'Connell himself— to be elected to Parliament. As some barriers were removed, however, others were erected. Notably, the financial requirement for running for Parliament was raised considerably: one needed now to own land worth at least ten pounds, a fivefold increase from the previous two-pound requirement. While not explicitly discriminatory toward the Irish, the requirement effectively excluded most Catholics, who were on average far poorer than the Protestant minority.

English Jews were also denied full rights of citizenship until a series of measures granted them access to Parliament, the military, the legal establishment, and

Illustrations by George Cruikshank to Charles Dickens's *Oliver Twist* (1838). The captions identify the figures in the above illustrations as "Fagin and the boys" and as "Monks [another character in the novel] and the Jew." As presented by Dickens and Cruikshank, the character of Fagin is a caricature of evil—and of Jewishness. In passages such as the following, Dickens's descriptions of Fagin give expression to some of the most extreme anti-Semitic stereotypes: "It seemed just the night when it befitted such a being as the Jew to be abroad. As he glided stealthily along, creeping beneath the shelter of the walls and doorways, the hideous old man seemed like some loathsome reptile, engendered in the slime and darkness through which he moved: crawling forth by night, in search of some rich offal for a meal." By repeatedly naming him as "the Jew" Dickens crudely implied that the characteristics of Fagin were also those of Jews in general. Dickens received complaints from readers on this score, and over time he altered his views. Beginning with the edition of 1867 he made revisions to *Oliver Twist*, changing to "Fagin" the previous references to "the Jew." The last novel Dickens completed, *Our Mutual Friend* (1864–65), is notable not least of all for the inclusion of a Jewish character (Riah) who is portrayed by Dickens in a positive light.

institutions of higher learning. Anti-Semitic stereotypes were legion in Victorian novels such as *Oliver Twist*. In at least a few cases the writings of non-Jewish novelists challenged the stereotypes—sometimes tentatively, in ways that to some extent still participated in the culture of prejudice (as in Anthony Trollope's wide-ranging novel of capitalism, marriage, and religion, *The Way We Live Now* [1875]), sometimes more clearly and un-equivocally (as in George Eliot's *Daniel Deronda* [1876][1]). And a significant body of Anglo-Jewish litera-

[1] Eliot's novel has been cited by Emma Lazarus and a number of other early Zionist leaders as highly influential in their decision to embrace Zionism. The narrative's treatment of Jews—contrasting their spirituality and connection to their community to the materialism and corruption of English society—was met with some hostility, and many reviewers remarked that the parts of *Daniel Deronda* focusing on

ture by writers such as Israel Zangwill and Amy Levy expressed a range of Jewish responses to social prejudice on the part of England's Christian majority.

Though the religious establishment suffered many challenges to its power, it would be a mistake to assume that secularism, Utilitarianism, and Darwinian theory stamped out religious faith or traditional religious practice: far from it. The Victorian period can be fairly characterized as an age of religious doubt that was also marked by intense religious feeling. As novels such as Anthony Trollope's *Barsetshire Chronicles*—a series of six novels published from 1855 to 1867—vividly convey, religious affiliation (irrespective of the strength of one's actual faith) shaped most people's sense of personal identity. And the quest for spiritual meaning was itself the driving force behind some of the most moving literary works of the age. One such work, Tennyson's *In Memoriam* (1849), an elegy for his friend Arthur Henry Hallam, chronicles the spiritual crisis of one man in the aftermath of his friend's death. By the end of the poem, the speaker has reconciled his religious doubts and scientific skepticism to re-embrace a Christian vision of the afterlife. In the closing lines of the poem the speaker exalts "That God, which ever lives and loves, / One God, one law, one element, / And one far-off divine event, / To which the whole creation moves."[1]

VICTORIAN DOMESTICITY: LIFE AND DEATH

The center of British religious, cultural, and emotional life in the nineteenth century was the family. As industrialization transformed the household from a workspace into its "opposite," the home came to be regarded as an almost sacred space, to be shielded from the aggressive competitiveness of the public world of work. The family, especially among the rising middle

Illustration, *Wonders of a Toy-Shop*, c. 1852. Though it is sometimes claimed that children were treated as "little adults" in the nineteenth century, that was far less frequently the case than it had been a century or two earlier. In many respects, indeed, the nineteenth century marks the coming into prominence of "childhood" as a cultural entity. The changing attitude towards children working in factories was one manifestation of change. Another was the evolution of "toy"—a word used before the nineteenth century to refer to a wide variety of trifles, but increasingly in the nineteenth century applied to playthings for children; toyshops specializing in such items became more and more widespread over the course of the Victorian period.

class, was increasingly nuclear in structure; the extended networks of friends and relations that had formed strong household connections in pre-industrial society became more and more tenuous. Increasingly, the social arrangement perceived as ideal among the better-off social classes consisted of a male breadwinner, employed outside the home, and his female helpmeet, who nurtured the children, managed the servants, and served as a paragon of domestic virtue. One of the key signs of a man's professional success was his wife's "idleness" within the home. The separation of work and family life was reflected in city planning with the construction of the first modern suburbs, supported by public transportation systems. Middle-class domestic archi-

Jewish characters were its weakest. The critic Edward Said has suggested, in "Zionism from the Standpoint of Its Victims" (1979), that the novel was a propaganda tool, used to encourage patriation of British-controlled Palestine by Jews.

[1] The importance of Tennyson's poem during the period is well illustrated by Queen Victoria's comment after the death of her husband Prince Albert in 1861 that "Next to the Bible, *In Memoriam* is my comfort."

tecture encouraged the display of wealth and the division of sexual labor amongst family members by dividing houses into "public" and "private" spaces. The middle-class family model became the ideal for the working class as well, although economic necessity continued to force many working-class wives and children to contribute to household earnings through paid labor, both inside and outside the home.

The domestic ideal and the emphasis on the family circle was shaped and promoted within the most privileged sphere of society. Throughout her reign, Queen Victoria was a paragon of good manners, restraint, and moral uprightness. In this she stood in contrast both to the escapades and excess that had surrounded the monarchies of her predecessors, George IV and William IV, and to the moral hypocrisy that characterized the reign of her son, Edward VII. In 1840, three years after her coronation, she married her first cousin,[1] Prince Albert of Saxe-Coburg-Gotha. Together, they had nine children, and Victoria became the nation's most revered icon of domestic femininity and maternal fecundity. Despite her own public role, she was a firm believer in separate spheres of influence and authority for men and women, voicing a then-conventional feminine distaste for power: "I am every day more convinced," she at one point declared, "that we women, if we are to be good women, feminine and amiable and domestic, are not fitted to reign." The Queen, not her husband, held the power of the monarch, but the royal family nonetheless projected an ideal of Victorian domesticity, with Albert exercising much influence over his wife's decisions, and Victoria displaying unwavering devotion to the practical, manly Albert.

Yet for all her outwardly conventional feminine attitudes, Victoria privately expressed ambivalence toward childbirth and marriage; she once complained in a letter to her daughter that giving birth made her feel like "a dog or a cow." In 1853, she agreed to undergo anesthesia during the birth of her son Leopold. This was a controversial new medical procedure, not least of all because it challenged the curse laid upon Eve (and therefore all women) in Genesis 1: "In sorrow shalt thou bring forth children." The queen's personal writings also reflect an intense attraction to Albert and an enthusiastic sexual appetite that were far from the passive ideal imposed on women during the period.

When Albert died of typhoid in 1861, the entire nation went into a state of mourning. Victoria was overwhelmed with grief, and for 15 years after his death she was rarely seen in public, except at the unveilings of the many public monuments she arranged to have erected to his memory. Eventually many began to regard her seclusion as self-indulgent and excessive, and her popularity among her subjects suffered for several years. Yet Victoria's long widowhood was in many ways a sign of the times; it both reflected and influenced the Victorian vogue for elaborate mourning rituals and conventions governing the public observance of death.

Life expectancy during the Victorian period was almost certainly higher than it was in the late eighteenth century, and it did improve over the period, but for most of the century it was nevertheless extraordinarily low by the standards of the developed world today—probably no higher than 40 years in many areas of the country. The death of relatively young people was far more common than it is today—not only deaths of children but also of young adults, many of diseases such as "consumption" (tuberculosis) and cholera. It was also very common for mothers to die in childbirth.

It is no exaggeration to say that death became a commercial industry in the nineteenth century; funerals provided a public occasion to mourn the passing of a loved one as much as they offered an opportunity for rich and middle-income people to display wealth. Strict observance of funerary rituals in details of dress and deportment became a social necessity, and commemorative memorabilia, such as tea sets, photographs, and mourning jewelry—often made from the hair of the deceased—could be found in most homes. Many families were prepared to spend the bulk of their savings on the funerals of loved ones. For the poor, the story was of course much different. The indigent were buried

---

[1] Marriage to one's cousin was considered unremarkable at the time, and was especially common among elites as a means of keeping wealth and power in the family.

with little or no ceremony in unmarked paupers' graves. Many working-class families contributed to burial clubs, an early form of insurance that guaranteed that at least a modest amount of money would be set aside for a respectable funeral for family members.

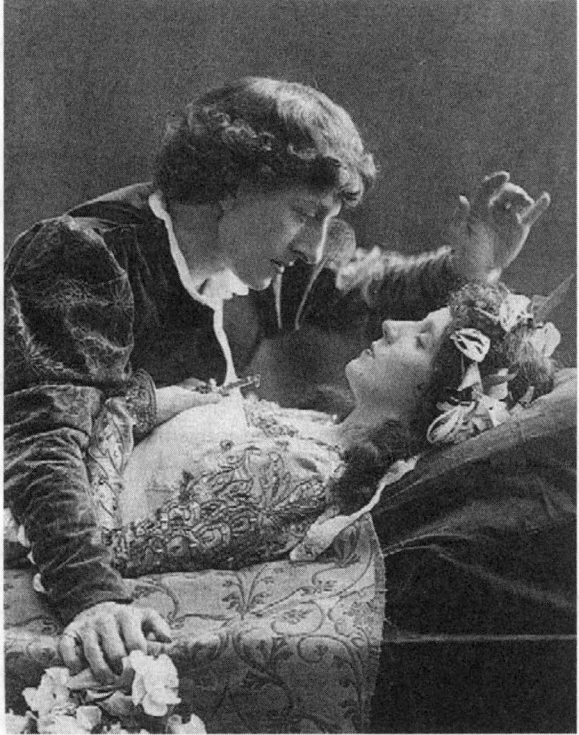

Romeo gazes at the dead Juliet: photograph of an 1895 production of Shakespeare's *Romeo and Juliet*, with Mrs. Patrick Campbell as Juliet.

The obsession with death in the Victorian period is reflected in much of the literature of the period; in Gaskell's novel *Mary Barton*, no fewer than 13 deaths either take place or are recounted within the first ten chapters. Tennyson's famed elegy *In Memoriam* is as much a meditation on death as it is a lament for the loss of a loved one. Countless Victorian novels feature prolonged death scenes, with grieving or greedy family members keeping vigil by the bedside of the dying. One of Dickens's most beloved characters, Little Nell in *The Old Curiosity Shop* (1840–41), was modeled on his

Advertisement from *The Lady*, 4 October 1900.

sister-in-law, Mary Hogarth, whose death had affected him deeply. Little Nell's death prompted an outpouring of grief from readers, many of whom wrote letters to Dickens in between installments of the novel imploring him to spare her.[1] The beautiful, often eroticized corpse—especially of a woman—was a favorite image in both visual art and poetry. In Christina Rossetti's "After Death" (1862), a female speaker observes her lover's attitude toward her corpse, and realizes, "He did not love me living; but once dead / He pitied me; and very sweet it is / To know he still is warm tho' I am cold."

---

[1] Not all were so moved. Of the death of Dickens's beloved character, Oscar Wilde famously opined, "One would have to have a heart of stone to read the death of little Nell without dissolving into tears … of laughter."

Though mortality rates, especially among infants, remained high throughout the century, there were significant medical advances in disease control and sanitation. Prominent among these was the verification of the bacterial theory of disease. Until late in the century, most medical practitioners and lay people believed that disease was spread through miasma, or the spread of harmful odors through the atmosphere. Susceptibility was routinely blamed on moral and social factors such as poverty, overcrowding, and sexual behaviors. During the cholera epidemics of the 1840s, researchers began to make links between incidents of the disease and water sources. Joseph Lister's work in the 1850s and 1860s confirmed the existence of micro-organisms, yet the miasma theory of disease was so entrenched that it was not until late in the century that the bacterial theory was fully accepted. By 1890, the pathogens for several diseases, including tuberculosis, cholera, typhoid, rabies, and diphtheria, had been identified. Surgical practice was also transformed by Lister's work on antiseptic treatments and the adoption of anesthetics, particularly ether and chloroform.

CULTURAL TRENDS

When the Duke of Wellington died in 1852, a million and a half people lined the streets of London to pay their last respects to the military hero who had defeated Napoleon at Waterloo. The deaths of the eminent were marked by elaborate, theatrical state funerals that fed an increasing appetite for public spectacles, epitomized by the Great Exhibition of 1851. The culture of Victorian Britain was very much a visual one, with public amusements, popular shows, traveling exhibitions, circuses, sporting events, holiday resorts, and public gardens to cater to every stratum of a society that had a growing amount of both disposable income and leisure time. London's theaters drew thousands of spectators every night to witness ingenious visual effects created by London's theater impresarios; live animals, underwater sequences, mob scenes, flying machines, sumptuous interiors, and innovations in lighting stoked the public mania for stage realism. Music halls aimed at lower middle- and working-class audiences featured a miscellany of comic songs, dance numbers, and magic shows by popular performers. Many public museums and galleries—which today draw thousands of visitors annually—were established in the Victorian period following the Great Exhibition, including the Victoria and Albert Museum, the National Portrait Gallery, and the Tate Gallery (founded by sugar magnate Henry Tate). Madame Tussaud's Wax Museum found a permanent home in London in 1835. From the 1870s and 1880s onwards, fashionable new shopping arcades and department stores filled with enticing consumer goods made shopping a respectable pastime for middle-class women.

Mass visual culture was inaugurated in the nineteenth century with the advent of a range of technologies, including the kaleidoscope, the daguerreotype, the photograph, and the cinema. As on the stage, visual technologies exploited light and movement in an effort to create the illusion of reality and transport viewers across time and space. Panoramas and dioramas[1] featured foreign cities, battlefields, landscapes, and natural disasters, and anticipated the "moving pictures" of the cinema. Innovations in print technology and the explosion of illustrated print material from the 1830s onwards signaled the public's increasing demand for the pictorial representation of daily events. The popular *Illustrated London News*, established in 1842, was the world's first illustrated weekly paper to hit newsstands; it used increasingly sophisticated technologies—from woodcuts to steel engravings to photographs—in its pictorial coverage of events at home and abroad. Serial novels published in periodicals were accompanied by wood-engraved illustrations intended to heighten the reader's appreciation of the narrative; popular engraver-illustrators such as George Cruikshank and Hablot K. Browne ("Phiz"), both of whom illustrated for Dickens, were initially as celebrated as the author himself.

---

[1] In a diorama, spectators view a partially translucent painting in a specially designed building, with variations of light cast upon the image to simulate the movement of light in a daytime scene. The diorama was first exhibited in London in 1823.

"View of the Grand Entrance to the Great Exhibition, 1851." The idea for what became the Great Exhibition grew out of a proliferation of smaller exhibitions of the products of craft and industry in the 1840s, and out of an awareness that Paris was contemplating its own large-scale international exhibition. Organized largely by Henry Cole, with the strong support of Prince Albert, the "Great Exhibition of the Works of Industry of All Nations" was held in Hyde Park in 1851. The Crystal Palace, centerpiece of the Exhibition, was later dismantled and re-assembled at Sydenham in south London as a home for permanent exhibitions, where it stood until it was destroyed by fire in 1936. (See Contexts: Britain, Empire, and a Wider World.)

Victorian painters benefited both from the emergence of a wealthy middle class able to purchase art for their homes and from the public's fascination with visual representation of contemporary life and historical drama. Scenes of everyday life with a narrative dimension and a moral message were especially popular with the viewing public. Like Victorian novelists and poets, many Victorian visual artists came to document the hardships of an industrial culture and landscape, depicting agricultural laborers, factory workers, and the unemployed in a highly realistic, yet often sentimental mode that has come to be known as social realism. Childhood innocence and scenes of domestic harmony were also common themes for many Victorian artists;

new and inexpensive methods of art reproduction meant that such pictures could be sold cheaply to a wide audience that was interested in seeing the values of home and family reflected on its walls. Panoramic views of Victorian life in all its colorful variety were also popular: William Powell Frith's *Derby Day* (1858) and *Railway Station* (1862) portrayed scenes of ordinary Victorians in such realistic detail that they caused a great sensation when they were first exhibited at the Royal Academy. Founded in the eighteenth century under George III, the Royal Academy of Arts was institutionalized as the most important mediator of public taste in art in the Victorian period. It offered a free training school to many of the century's most significant

William Powell Frith, *The Railway Station* (detail), 1862. The painting depicts a scene at Paddington Station in London.

artists, and its annual exhibitions of what it deemed the best works of the year drew thousands of spectators and buyers—as well as accusations of bias and preferential treatment on the part of those whose work had been excluded from the exhibitions or poorly hung.

The most influential movement in Victorian painting was the Pre-Raphaelite Brotherhood, composed of the artists John Everett Millais, William Holman Hunt, Thomas Woolner, James Collinson, Frederick George Stephens, and the brothers of Christina Rossetti, artist and poet Dante Gabriel Rossetti, and critic William Michael Rossetti. (Christina Rossetti herself, though she influenced and was influenced by the movement, was officially excluded from the Pre-Raphaelites on the grounds of gender.) At mid-century these artists began producing works that challenged the dominant taste for neoclassical style and subject matter by painting in a manner that shared commonalities with the work of medieval, pre-Renaissance artists and basing their aesthetic practice on styles common "before Raphael." Close attention to natural detail, flattened perspective, vivid colors, an interest in literary subject matter, and erotically charged images of spiritual and religious devotion were some of the hallmarks of the group. Their paintings of female figures as either ravishing "femmes fatales" or dreamy heroines in historical dress are today instantly recognizable (and are much reproduced). These paintings conveyed both women's power and vulnerability in nineteenth-century culture, and were sometimes twinned, in D.G. Rossetti's work especially, with a companion poem or with a quotation from a literary work. ("The Blessed Damozel" [1846] is one such example, in which the separation of two lovers by death in the poem is conveyed with two separate panels in the painting.) "Pre-Raphaelite," indeed, denotes a style of poetry as well as of painting; sensuous detail and a tendency to link earthly beauty to the divine are as characteristic of the poetry of D.G. Rossetti as they are of his paintings.

The Pre-Raphaelites should in part be considered alongside the Gothic Revival, a wave of interest in a medieval and Gothic aesthetic that had begun in the Romantic period and influenced Victorian painting,

Arthur Hughes, *The Long Engagement* (detail). Hughes (1832–1915) was one of the most prominent of the second wave of Pre-Raphaelite painters.

architecture, design, literature, and religious practice. The idealization of the Middle Ages is exemplified in the writing of Thomas Carlyle, John Ruskin, William Morris, and Alfred Tennyson. Ruskin, who in his art criticism also championed the work of the Pre-Raphaelites, argued in *The Stones of Venice* (1851–53) for the moral superiority of the Gothic style, in part because it was the product of artisan-workers who were free to use their creativity in their work, and so express their individual and spiritual nature. Ruskin urged his readers

The Palace of Westminster, home to both Houses of Parliament, was redesigned and rebuilt following the fire of 1834, in a vast project not completed until 1860. It is one of the most striking examples of the Gothic Revival style applied to a secular construction.

to re-examine the "ugly goblins" and "stern statues" of Gothic cathedrals, for "they are the signs of the life and liberty of every workman who struck the stone; a freedom of thought, and rank in scale of being, such as no laws, no charters, no charities can secure."

The Arts and Crafts movement of the last few decades of the century, led by William Morris and influenced by Ruskin's ideas, was dedicated to the production of hand-crafted furniture, glassware, books, and art objects. Design firms such as Morris and Co. and the Century Guild revived the medieval guild system of production, rejecting the mass-produced manufactures of the assembly line in favor of the freedom and spontaneity of craft and its makers. In their

critique of the ravages of industrial technology and the drudgery of mechanized labor, the practitioners of Gothic Revival imagined, and to some extent invented, the idea of the medieval past as a time of moral and religious stability, devotion to craft, and harmony with the rhythms of the natural world.

TECHNOLOGY

The technological invention that perhaps best exemplified the industrial age was the steam engine, a source and symbol of power both on land and at sea. Although the steam engine had been in use since the early eighteenth century, it was not until the nineteenth

Robert Howlett, "Isambard Kingdom Brunel and the Launching Chains of the *Great Eastern*," 1857. The ship (designed largely by Brunel) remained the largest in the world throughout its 31 years on the seas. Brunel, the leading engineer of the age, also played an important role in designing such Victorian landmarks as the Crystal Palace, the new Houses of Parliament, Paddington Station, and the Clifton Suspension Bridge at Bristol.

that steam technology—and the dependence on fossil fuels that it engendered—helped transform an entire economy and a way of life. Steam engines were adapted for use in the production of coal, textiles, heavy metals, and printing presses, thus becoming indispensable to Britain's industrial growth. Steamships powered the British Empire, with several major shipping lines established in the 1840s to serve routes to India, Africa, East Asia, and Australia. Railway steam locomotives epitomized the coming of the Victorian era, with the first local lines built in 1837 and 1838 as Victoria assumed the throne. In the "railway mania" of the 1840s, over 8,000 miles of new track were approved,

and, by 1900, over nine hundred million passengers were using Britain's rail system annually. London's underground rail system opened its first line in 1863, though horse-drawn transportation continued to dominate the streetscape until the end of the century. The convenience and speed of rail travel caught on quickly with everyone from the Queen to the ordinary worker. Rail companies established excursions to special events, such as horse races or the seaside, inaugurating local and national tourism on a mass scale. So important was the advent of railway travel to the development of English daily life, railway stations even became essential to the book trade and the spread of leisure reading; from the 1850s onward, book stalls catering to thousands of daily commuters began to stock their shelves with newspapers, magazines, and cheap, popular fiction, which became known as "railway literature."

Between transportation, industry, and the heating of homes, Britain used more coal per capita than any other nation. The burning of coal had a pronounced effect on urban landscapes, producing, especially toward the latter half of the century, what Londoners called a "gritty black" smog that coated everything from buildings to clothes and predisposed city-dwellers to deadly breathing ailments. In the last quarter of the century, bronchitis was the leading cause of death in industrial towns such as Manchester, where the medical officer Dr. John Leigh described the air quality thus:

> On the finest day, the vista is obscured by a column of haze, the accumulated density of which terminates the view by an apparent wall of fog. The smokey envelope of the town is very well seen from a distance of four or five miles in the country, particularly on the approach of evening, when the slanting rays of the sun give a remarkable definition to the black, cloudy covering, and indicate very distinctly the site and general boundaries of Manchester.

Despite its effects on their surroundings, many Victorians adored coal, viewing it as fundamental to the Empire's prosperity and global dominance. The prevailing fear regarding the long-term sustainability of coal was not that its environmental impact would be too much to bear but that the British Isles might eventually run out of it. As a writer in *The Times* declared in 1849, "if not the single element of our mercantile and political superiority, coal is at least absolutely essential; and could we suppose such an event as the exhaustion of the beds [coal deposits], it would be the final and utter catastrophe of our greatness."

CULTURAL IDENTITIES

The adoption of new technologies, the reorganization of employment, and the shift in power from the monarchy to the institutions of the modern liberal state revolutionized people's experience of work, family life, civic duty, and leisure time in the Victorian era. Such developments are almost always accompanied by shifts in the way people understand themselves as individuals in relation to their society. In the nineteenth century, the conditions and practices of one's class, gender, race, and sexuality began to acquire new meanings, to take on new importance, and to attract a new kind of attention. Changes in living conditions developed in connection with prescribed gender roles, which began to seem "natural" and "innate" because they supported the logic of industrial capital and bourgeois family life. Victorians tended to think about identity in terms of oppositions: male and female, rich and poor, Black and white, and, later in the century, homosexual and heterosexual. Such oppositions had the effect of establishing seemingly stable types and suggesting that the differences were natural and unchangeable. For example, the ideology of separate spheres for men and women proposed that gender and sexual identity were fixed categories and that "true womanhood" was the inherent opposite of normative manliness. Still, in the literary works of the period, the line between "opposites" was constantly crossed and revealed as problematic and variable.

The "Angel in the House"[1] became a common label for the Victorian ideal of respectable middle-class femininity. Quiet beauty, purity, devotion and selflessness were some of the essential features of the domestic wife and mother, who was described and exalted in advice literature and popular domestic novels aimed at female readers. "She must be enduringly, incorruptibly good," advised John Ruskin, "instinctively, infallibly wise—wise, not for self-development, but for self-renunciation; wise, not that she may set herself above her husband, but that she may never fall from his side." The absolute other to this paragon of virtue was the "fallen woman," a label that encompassed women with any form of sexual experience deemed improper or immoral. Prostitutes, rape survivors, unmarried mothers, adulteresses, homeless women, women deemed insane, and any woman who displayed rebellious passions could be labeled "fallen." Yet the boundary between the domestic angel and the fallen woman was extraordinarily narrow; one false step and innocence became wickedness, followed by ostracism from society, poverty, and almost certain death for the transgressor, at least according to dominant narratives of fallenness.[2] On the other hand, some fallen women were portrayed as penitent victims who embodied the feminine ideal even more fully than their uncorrupted female counterparts. Writers such as Elizabeth Gaskell, Christina Rossetti, George Eliot, Mary Elizabeth Braddon, Augusta Webster, and Thomas Hardy explored the tropes of purity and fallenness, bringing

[1] The phrase originated in the title of Coventry Patmore's long narrative poem. Patmore's "The Angel in the House"—first published in 1854, but revised several times for subsequent publication—was written about the author's wife, Emily, whom Patmore exalted as the perfect model of Victorian femininity and domesticity. The poem's opening lines—"Man must be pleased; but him to please / Is woman's pleasure"—rather neatly encapsulate the meaning and the message of the work. In "Professions for Women," a 1931 address given to the Women's Service League, Virginia Woolf argued that "part of the occupation ... of a woman writer" was to kill the "Angel in the House."

[2] In a famous moment in Dickens's *David Copperfield*, the narrator's recollection of a dangerous moment in the fallen Emily's early life leads him to wonder if it might not have been far better for her to have died rather than to have survived only to later "fall."

"pure" and "impure" women into each other's (and the reader's) proximity in order to probe the limits of the feminine ideal.

The male counterpart to the domestic angel was the Victorian gentleman, an heir of the chivalric ideal updated for the industrial age. In *The Idea of a University* (a series of lectures published as one volume in 1873), John Henry Newman characterized the gentleman as tender, merciful, prudent, patient, forbearing, resigned, and disciplined. Yet despite Newman's apparent confidence in this description, gentlemanliness was difficult to define: was it based on a man's mode of income or on his behavior? Was it a hereditary, professional, or moral category, or some combination? While eminent men were celebrated with great gusto in biography and prose works such as Carlyle's *On Heroes and Hero Worship* (1841), men were also often regarded as morally inferior to women because of their greater contact with the competition and corruption of the public world. (On the other hand, women could just as easily be pressed into the role of evil temptress in accounting for a man's fall from grace.) Tennyson's dramatic monologue "Ulysses" (1842) wrestles with two competing versions of masculinity: the thwarted Romantic hero, who longs for adventure and freedom from domestic encumbrance, and the reliable, managerial male who faithfully adheres to professional duty.

The concepts of the Victorian lady and gentleman were also class categories, serving to both reinforce and blur distinctions between various socio-economic groups. The boarding schools for the sons and daughters of the elite and the middle classes promulgated notions of proper female and male conduct in their curricula; increasingly, it was understood that one was not simply born a lady or a gentleman, but must learn to become one through rigorous training and constant self-scrutiny. As the terms "lady" and "gentleman" gradually lost their association with rank, socio-economic boundaries became increasingly difficult to distinguish, and novelists began to focus on the gendered and class behaviors of individuals for their narrative content. In Charlotte Brontë's *Jane Eyre* (1847), the moral awakening of the male hero, Edward Rochester, is achieved via the superior moral guidance of the "servant" governess, Jane Eyre, who avoids succumbing to pressure to become Rochester's mistress, and in doing so teaches him the true nature of domestic love and Christian sacrifice; Jane finally becomes Rochester's wife following his spiritual, moral rebirth. In Dickens's novels, including *David Copperfield* (1850) and *Great Expectations* (1860), the gentlemanly status of the male protagonists is achieved through diligence and perseverance rather than by birthright.

A best-selling advice book for men, *Self Help* (1859) by Samuel Smiles, stressed thrift, hard work, and optimism as essential qualities of the "self-made man," who, no matter what his social status, could achieve respectability and success, in part by following the example of heroic men whose accomplishments Smiles recounted. More generally, advice books, novels, and poems about the progress toward, or the fall from, "true" womanhood or manliness demonstrate that gendered and classed identities were cultural constructs that seemed "natural." The lady, the gentleman, the fallen woman, the hero—these gendered and class types, rationalized through the ideology of separate spheres—were cultural myths through which individuals made sense of their relationship to the social order.

As the century drew to a close, new styles of masculinity and femininity emerged to compete with the prevailing gender models of the previous decades. One of these emergent types was the "New Woman," a term that described a figure of greater sexual, economic, and social independence than the "Angel in the House." Although the term denoted a lifestyle and a literary category more than a political perspective, the figure of the New Woman was in part a product of the gains feminists had made by the 1880s and 1890s in the areas of higher education, employment, political and legal rights, and civic visibility. The New Woman quickly became a flashpoint for opinion makers on either side of the "Woman Question."[1] Smoking, swearing, riding a

---

[1] The question was largely one of the nature—and consequently, the proper role—of women. The "Woman Question" came to encompass the debates about the rights and responsibilities, as well as the place, of women in Victorian society.

Advertisement for Swift Cycles, c. 1895.

For Grand and other feminist writers, such as Mona Caird and Olive Schreiner, the portrayal of the New Woman hinged on a critique of the male sexual privilege that had already come under fire in the 1870s and 1880s during the social purity campaigns, including resistance to the Contagious Diseases Acts. This legislation, first enacted in the 1860s, allowed for the forcible confinement and internal examination of prostitutes by doctors in order to prevent the spread of venereal disease, first among the military, and then within civilian communities. Underwriting these Acts was the assumption that because male sexual urges were "uncontrollable," prostitution was a necessary evil that should be regulated because it could not be eradicated. The Act of 1864 decreed that infected women could be held in locked hospitals for three months; the Act of 1869 extended the period of confinement to a year. In 1867, there were proposals to extend the Acts to the north of England and the civilian population. Though the laws were ostensibly intended to combat the spread of disease by prostitutes, in practice, they essentially meant that any woman passing through a poor neighborhood was subject to compulsory medical examination and arrest. They also, as activists were quick to point out, hypocritically targeted prostitutes but not their clients. The campaign against the Acts, led by the charismatic Josephine Butler, condemned the sexual double standard and the humiliation of poor and vulnerable women by police and doctors, with Butler comparing the compulsory medical examinations to "instrumental rape." The Acts were struck down in 1886 after much public controversy; the movement to repeal them, led mostly by middle-class women, marked the first instance in which women publicly debated the subject of sex on a broad scale. It was also one of the most visible of the many social purity campaigns of the 1870s, 1880s, and 1890s, in which moral reformers engaged in the rescue and "reformation" of prostitutes and other "fallen women" and urged men to take a vow of chastity. The mandate of the National Vigilance Association, for example, was to "create a universal ethic of chastity, for all men and women alike." In calling for a single standard of behavior, many of the social purity

bicycle, debating in public, wearing men's clothes, and refusing marriage were some of the trademarks of the New Woman, who figured in novels, short stories, and popular journalism as someone either to emulate or to condemn. A number of male novelists, including George Gissing, George Moore, and Thomas Hardy, created memorable New Woman characters who grapple with the competing demands of personal autonomy and social expectation, while the works of many women writers, such as Sarah Grand's *The Heavenly Twins* (1893) and the semi-autobiographical *The Beth Book* (1897), presented New Woman characters who triumph over social convention and the sexual double standard.

groups espoused moral coerciveness and interventionist policies, which often ended up stigmatizing and further repressing the women and girls they were attempting to help.

The preoccupations of the purity campaigners were part of a renewed cultural and scientific interest in human sexuality among Victorians, dating from at least the early 1870s and the publication of Darwin's *The Descent of Man*. In that book, Darwin applied the theories from his *On the Origin of Species* to human evolution and behavior, positing that sexual selection among men and women accounted for their mental and physical differences. These "natural differences" were drawn straight from the catalogue of Victorian gender stereotypes, which held that men were inherently courageous, virile, and combative, and women intuitive, passive, and altruistic. The "complementarity" of these traits ensured the survival of the human "race," which evolutionists, anthropologists, and psychologists understood as a hierarchy: white European men at the top, followed by white women, white children, and the "primitive races." But, scientists wondered, how to explain the fact that some white men—seemingly nature's most civilized specimen—occasionally exhibited traits that resembled those of the women, children, primitives, and even the animals who were understood as biologically and mentally inferior? Such questions were compounded by fears that Britain's empire was crumbling because the purity of the "white race" was being diluted through racial mingling among English imperialists and the "savages" they ruled in the benighted labyrinths of the Empire. Closer to home, the poverty, crime, and vice of England's urban districts was often racialized: "As there is a darkest Africa is there not also a darkest England?" asked William Booth, founder of the Salvation Army. "Civilisation, which can breed its own barbarians, does it not also breed its own pygmies? May we not find a parallel at our own doors, and discover within a stone's throw of our cathedrals and palaces similar horrors to those which Stanley[1] has

found existing in the great Equatorial forest?" Social Darwinist theories of atavism (the reappearance of "primitive" characteristics in "advanced" populations) and degeneration (retrograde evolution) were formulated in the second half of the century to account for the "tendencies" of criminals, alcoholics, the poor, the mentally and physically disabled, and people with non-normative sexualities.

The first recorded English usage of the term "homosexual" did not occur until 1892; before that time "sodomy" was illegal (and punishable by death until 1861), but the concept of "the homosexual" as a distinct identity or way of being was not part of the Victorian worldview until the last decades of the century. With the emergence of a gay male subculture in London in the 1870s and 1880s, gay men—also called "sexual inverts"—became subject to increased scientific and legal scrutiny. Although "the lesbian" also emerged as a distinct identity in the 1890s, women were not subject to the same degree of persecution as gay men, in part because of the belief that women were unmotivated by sexual desire, and that their passionate female "friendships" were therefore innocent, merely temporary diversions from their true calling as wives and mothers. Bisexuality would not come to be widely considered a discrete sexuality until the twentieth century.

The Criminal Law Amendment Act of 1885, which raised the age of sexual consent from 13 to 16 under pressure from the social purity campaigners, contained a clause (known as the Labouchère Amendment, after Member of Parliament Henry Labouchère, who had introduced it) that mandated imprisonment for any man found guilty of "gross indecency"—effectively, any sexual act—with another man, even if the "indecency" was conducted entirely in private.[2] The Labouchère Amendment served to demonize gay men as "degenerates" whose "unnatural" desires threatened the stability of marriage, the future of the race, and the strength of the Empire. Feminized male types—the dandy, the aesthete, the fop—surfaced in visual art and

---

[1] Henry Morton Stanley (1841–1904) was a renowned journalist and explorer, best known for his travels in Africa.

[2] Many sexual acts were already illegal; in particular, "buggery"—a British term for anal sex—whether between two men or between a man and a woman, had been illegal since the Buggery Act of 1553.

literature alongside the masculinized New Woman figure to characterize a climate of sexual and gender experimentation at the fin-de-siècle that was celebrated by a few and denounced by many. As the popular satirical magazine *Punch* joked, "A new fear my bosom vexes; / Tomorrow there may be no sexes!"

In 1895, celebrity playwright Oscar Wilde[1] was brought to trial under the terms of the Labouchère Amendment and sentenced to two years in prison for "gross indecency." The highly publicized Wilde trials brought the moral panic of the preceding two decades to a crisis point. Yet Wilde's trial testimony, his writing, and that of his contemporaries such as John Addington Symonds, Algernon Charles Swinburne, "Michael Field," Sarah Grand, Mona Caird, Vernon Lee, and Edward Carpenter signaled a new level of consciousness regarding sexual and gender identity. With remarkable candor, the sexologist Havelock Ellis wrote that while "we may not know exactly what sex is … we do know that it is mutable, with the possibility of one sex being changed into the other sex, that its frontiers are often mutable, and that there are many stages between a complete male and a complete female." Ellis broke new ground with his multi-volume *The Psychology of Sex* (1897–1910), an early volume of which, *Sexual Inversion* (1897, coauthored with John Addington Symonds), was particularly noteworthy for treating same-sex sexuality in a purely descriptive fashion, rather than as a pathology. (In other volumes Ellis took a similar approach to many other topics, including "auto-erotism," or masturbation, and sado-masochism.) Sexuality and sexual practice had become topics of public conversation in a way that belies twentieth-century

"Two Seated Sicilian Youths," photograph from c. 1893 (Victoria and Albert Museum).

stereotypes of Victorian culture as sexually conservative or naïve. The apparent "repression" of sexual behaviors deemed improper or immoral only seemed to prohibit what was in fact an intense interest in the passions, proclivities, and practices of the "other" Victorians.[2]

REALISM

"Art is the nearest thing to life," wrote George Eliot in "The Natural History of German Life" (1856). "It is a mode of amplifying experience and extending our contact with our fellow-men beyond the bounds of our personal lot. All the more sacred is the task of the artist when he undertakes to paint the life of the People."

---

[1] Wilde was a married father of two young children, but rumors about his dalliances with men—many of working-class backgrounds, known as "rent-boys"—had abounded as his popularity increased. It was Wilde's involvement with Lord Alfred "Bosie" Douglas, the son of the 9th Marquess of Queensberry, that resulted in the rumors becoming a legal matter. The eccentric Queensberry, who believed his son had been corrupted by the older Wilde, left a note for Wilde at his club, accusing the playwright of "posing as a somdomite [*sic*]." Encouraged by Bosie, who hated his father, Wilde sued for libel; the resulting trial revealed a number of graphic details about Wilde's sexuality, and he was subsequently himself tried for acts of gross indecency.

[2] Steven Marcus's seminal exploration of Victorian expressions and repressions of sexuality, *The Other Victorians: A Study of Sexuality and Pornography in Mid-Nineteenth Century England* (1966) helped complicate the sometimes overly simplified early and mid-twentieth-century view of the Victorians as simply repressed and "anti-sexual."

Eliot's essay anticipated the masterpieces of realist fiction she would begin writing in just a few years—*Adam Bede* (1859), *The Mill on the Floss* (1860), and *Middlemarch* (1874) among them. For Eliot, as for many of her contemporaries, the true, even "sacred," purpose of art was to present an objective representation of real life that reflected the habits, desires, and aspirations of readers. For many novelists, realism seemed to be the form best suited to this purpose.

Victorian poetry too, especially at mid-century, was influenced by the predominance of realist fiction; long narrative poems, such as Tennyson's *Idylls of the King* (1856–85) and Robert Browning's *The Ring and the Book* (1868–69), appropriated novelistic forms of storytelling, combining trenchant social critique with formal experimentation. In Elizabeth Barrett Browning's "verse novel" and Bildungsroman[1] *Aurora Leigh* (1856), the speaker, Aurora Leigh herself, defines and defends her poetic practice of social engagement with the contemporary world, sounding very much like Eliot:

> Nay, if there's room for poets in this world
> A little overgrown (I think there is),
> Their sole work is to represent the age,
> Their age, not Charlemagne's …
> … this is living art,
> Which thus presents and thus records true life.

Much realist fiction of the Victorian period tended to center on the everyday experiences, moral progress, and inner struggles of an ordinary individual, while giving a sense of the connections between that individual and his or her broader social networks. Many realist novels, including those by Anthony Trollope, William Thackeray, Dickens, and Eliot contained multiple plot lines and a range of characters across socio-economic strata, representing both the cohesiveness and the disintegration of various social communities in an industrialized, commercializing society. Detailed descriptions of landscapes, city streets, and domestic interiors and close attention to the emotionally

complex motivations of characters—these too are characteristic of the realism of the Victorian novel. However, such broad vision is typically viewed from a single narrative perspective, whether that of the novel's protagonist or of an omniscient narrator.

Why did realism hold such appeal for Victorian novelists and their audiences? One explanation is that the revolutions of the nineteenth century created a climate in which people longed for a sense of verisimilitude in their literature in order to guide them through the changes and upheavals, both private and public, which they themselves faced. Many Victorian readers sought moral and ethical guidance from their authors, who assumed—or were thrust into—the role of "secular clerics" with varying degrees of confidence and authority. Realist fiction, along with other forms of writing such as biography, criticism, poetry, and history, was accepted as having a pedagogical function; such texts not only taught readers how to navigate the changes they were experiencing, but also how to imagine sympathetically and authentically the experiences of others. "We want to be taught to feel," wrote Eliot, "not for the heroic artisan or the sentimental peasant, but for the peasant in all his coarse apathy, and the artisan in all his suspicious selfishness."

In rejecting the heroic and the sentimental, Eliot positioned the realist novel in opposition to the heightened, "falsifying" sensibilities of the romantic mode, as did many others. In 1785, distinguishing between the romance and the newly emergent genre of the novel, Clara Reeve had observed that "the Novel is a picture of real life and manners, and of the times in which it was written. The Romance in lofty and elevated language, describes what never happened nor is likely to happen." Reeve's description of the novel could be applied to most Victorian fiction. Nonetheless, many of the best-known Victorian novels contain elements of the fantastic, the supernatural, or the mysterious: Dickens's *Oliver Twist* is like many of his others novels in that it sets out to realistically document the ravages of industrial poverty, but the novel's plot depends on outrageous coincidence, its story peopled with broadly

---

[1] "Novel of Education" (German).

Page of advertisements from the eighth number of the 1846 serial publication in ten numbers of Dickens's *Oliver Twist*. (Pages of advertisements appeared at the front and back of each number.)

drawn character types befitting the romance mode.[1] The novels of Charlotte and Emily Brontë memorably combine psychological realism with Gothic elements such as female imprisonment and suggestions of ghostly presences. The persistence of romantic elements in Victorian realist novels not only unsettles the confidence of our formal definitions, but also prompts us to consider just whose versions of "the real" were recognized as the most truthful.

Inevitably, realism's dominance in literature and in visual art came under attack. As early as the 1850s, but more widely in the 1880s and 1890s, visual artists, writers, and critics began to question the moral imperatives of realist art in a series of movements that have come to be referred to under the umbrella term "Aestheticism." In poetry, drama, criticism, and fiction, Aestheticism stressed experimentation in form and composition, independence of imagination and expression, and freedom of content, however perverse, morbid, or tawdry. In rebelling against the harsh brutalities of British industrial culture, the Aesthetes sought a "pure" art and formal beauty dissociated from the concerns and surroundings of the everyday. The Aesthetes were not interested in instructing or edifying a mass readership; rather, they advocated aesthetic withdrawal in order to pursue the essential forms of art. "Art for art's sake,"[2] translated from the French by art critic Walter Pater, became the rallying cry of the Aesthetes. "Art never expresses anything but itself," declares one of Oscar Wilde's speakers. "It has an independent life, just as Thought has, and develops purely on its own lines. It is not necessarily realistic in an age of realism, nor spiritual in an age of faith. So far from being a creation of its own time, it is usually in direct opposition to it." Similarly, Wilde concludes his preface to The Picture of Dorian Gray (1891) with the assertion that "All art is quite useless," having earlier stated that "There is no such thing as a moral or an immoral book."

By the 1890s, the aesthetic movement had been charged with elitism, hedonism, self-absorption, and same-sex sexuality.[3] Aestheticism by that time had shifted into Decadence, a term of either censure or praise, depending on who wielded it. The Decadents extended the precepts of Aestheticism in their affirmation of the perversity, artificiality, and overindulgence of a culture and a century that was nearing its end, and their works were often taken as evidence of social degeneration; in Degeneration (1892), the German critic Max Nordau attacked Decadent artists—including Wilde—as degenerates and argued that social decay is both reflected in and driven by art.

THE VICTORIAN NOVEL

The dominant Victorian literary form was the novel. Although the genre of the novel emerged well in advance of the Victorian period, the literary legitimacy and cultural authority the novel wields today were solidified in the nineteenth century. The novel was a dynamic form, shifting according to popular taste and critical assessments of its potential value to readers, who were offered an ever-expanding list of authors and subgenres from which to choose. While the early and mid-Victorian novels of men such as Dickens, Thackeray, and Trollope were wildly successful, both with the critical establishment and the reading public, many of the century's most influential and prolific novelists were women. These novelists—the Brontës, Eliot, Braddon, Gaskell, Charlotte Yonge, and Ellen Price Wood among them—paved the way for legions of other women to enter the field of fiction writing. Although the profession of "novelist" achieved new

[1] Oliver Twist is one of many orphans in Dickens's novels. Dickens's orphans inevitably confront the urban nightmares of Victorian life with well-nigh angelic purity—and, in Oliver's case, perfectly grammatical literary English.

[2] The French writer Théophile Gautier (1811–72) is generally credited with coining the phrase "l'art pour l'art" in the preface to his novel, Mademoiselle de Maupin (1836). A number of critics have contended that the idea—if not the precise phrase—dates back to ancient Rome.

[3] Wilde's The Picture of Dorian Gray, which first appeared in Lippincott's Monthly Magazine in 1890, was immediately accused of having homoerotic overtones and deemed "unclean," "effeminate," and "contaminating." Wilde made a number of changes to the novel before its publication as one volume in 1891, but these were not enough to keep the book from counting against him during his trial for acts of "gross indecency."

respectability in the period for both men and women alike, the novel continued in some circles to be maligned as lightweight and "pernicious," associated with frivolous lady scribblers and their female readers. As George Henry Lewes, George Eliot's partner, observed in "The Lady Novelists" (1852), "Of all departments of literature, Fiction is the one to which, by nature and by circumstance, women are best adapted. ... The very nature of fiction calls for that predominance of Sentiment which we have already attributed to the feminine mind."

The taste for particular subjects and approaches shifted regularly: the "silver fork" novels of the 1820s and 1830s centered on the extravagances and corruptions of the rich and fashionable, while the "social problem" novels of the 1840s depicted the minute details of life at the very opposite end of the social scale. Domestic novels by both the famous and the obscure focused on the quotidian; George Eliot's *Middlemarch*, rich in psychological complexity and moral analysis, is one of the most outstanding examples of domestic fiction of the Victorian period. A heightened form of this domestic-centered fiction was the "sensation" novel, which flourished in the 1860s and 1870s. Strong on dramatic incident and scandalous subject matter, such as bigamy, murder, madness, and crime, sensation novels exposed the hidden corruptions and dirty secrets of the outwardly respectable middle class; Wilkie Collins, Braddon, and Wood were some of the leading practitioners of this wildly popular and much maligned subgenre. The immense popular appeal of sensation novels was linked to the continued growth of a "mass readership," much to the chagrin of the critical elite, who bemoaned the "degradation" of literature as the century drew to a close. In the latter decades of the century, mystery novels, detective fiction, horror, and adventure stories soared in popularity, partly on the strength of an expanding audience of lower-income readers, rising literacy rates, and cheaper methods of book production. The counterpart to these often lurid and shocking tales were the naturalistic novels of Thomas Hardy, George Gissing, and George Moore, whose late-century fiction offers bleak, social Darwinist portraits of urban class struggle, slum life, rural poverty, and sexual frustration.

If the vogue for particular kinds of subject matter in novels shifted regularly, so too did their modes of publication, distribution, and consumption. One significant mode of publication was the three-volume edition, known as the "triple-decker." Readers who could not afford to buy the volumes themselves borrowed one volume at a time from lending libraries for a fee, generating huge profits for the most successful of these, Mudie's Select Library and W.H. Smith and Son. The triple-decker format was eventually supplanted by cheap single-volume editions that were sold in national book chains and at rail stations. Another mode of publication, one that made the novel a household word, was the monthly or weekly serial. Monthly installments of a few chapters, often accompanied by illustrations and advertisements, were initially published and purchased in separate parts with paper wrappers, generally appearing over a period of 19 months. By the 1860s, these serializations were more often appearing in monthly or weekly literary magazines. Dickens's enormously successful *Pickwick Papers* appeared in installments in 1836–37, launching the serial format as the most important publishing medium for Victorian fiction.[1] Serialization allowed readers with modest incomes to purchase new works when bound volumes were beyond their financial reach, and the regular continuation of a novel over a period of months or years meant that novels and novel reading became woven into the fabric of daily life, mingling with news, opinion, and readers' personal experience. The serialized format also had an influence on the novelistic genre, establishing a particular pace and necessitating "cliff-hangers," ensuring the return of the audience week after week.

---

[1] Long poems and works of non-fiction prose were also sometimes published serially; important examples include Robert Browning's *The Ring and the Book* and Matthew Arnold's *Culture and Anarchy* (serialized in *Cornhill Magazine* in 1867–68).

Cover, *Famous Crimes*, Police Budget Edition, c. 1890. Sensationalized stories of crime and horror, priced at one penny each and known as "penny dreadfuls," became hugely popular in the late nineteenth century.

POETRY

The novel's predominance and popularity have often meant that the significance of Victorian poetry is overlooked. Victorian poets throughout the century were greatly influenced by poets of the Romantic period, but key departures in form, content, and purpose set the Victorians apart from their predecessors. One of the most important of Victorian innovations was the development of the dramatic monologue, a lyric poem in the voice of a speaker who is not the poet and who occasionally addresses a silent auditor. Although the Victorians did not invent the dramatic monologue,

Robert Browning and Tennyson are typically credited with developing it into a form expressive of psychological complexity. Victorian psychologists were interested in exploring the boundary between sanity and madness, and the possibility of a lucid yet mentally unbalanced narrating persona appealed to Browning and Tennyson, who used the dramatic monologue to expose not only the unstable character of their speakers' passions, but also the social and cultural contexts that either produced or reflected their instability. Browning, in particular, chose a range of unstable, deluded, or even mentally deranged speakers whose self-perception is ironically distanced from the reader's, thus participating in pre-Freudian ideas about the divided self; perhaps the most famous of these is "My Last Duchess" (1842), which slowly reveals the fate of the speaker's wife. The dramatic monologue was also notably employed by other prominent poets including Elizabeth Barrett Browning, D.G. Rossetti, Christina Rossetti, Augusta Webster, Thomas Hardy, and Rudyard Kipling.

Many other poetic forms also flourished in the period. Perhaps surprisingly in an "age of realism," epic poems were a feature of the Victorian literary landscape, from Tennyson's *Idylls of the King* to George Eliot's *The Spanish Gypsy* (1868) and William Morris's *The Earthly Paradise* (1868–70). Sonnet sequences too were a popular form, particularly among women poets; notable examples include George Eliot's *Brother and Sister Sonnets* (1869), Christina Rossetti's *Monna Innominata* (1881), Augusta Webster's *Mother and Daughter Sonnets* (1895), and—most popular of all—Elizabeth Barrett Browning's *Sonnets from the Portuguese* (1850), a collection of 44 sonnets chronicling Barrett Browning's courtship with Robert Browning. Through the work of these writers and a host of others—from Felicia Hemans and Letitia Landon at the beginning of the period to Charlotte Mew and Mathilde Blind at its end—the "poetess" became an accepted part of the literary landscape.

The lyric introspection and self-exploration that is the hallmark of much Romantic verse was augmented in both form and content by a Victorian poetry of social engagement that strove to contextualize a speaker's moral and spiritual questions within the vicissitudes of contemporary life. In Tennyson's monologue *Maud* (1855), the tormented speaker's mental deterioration and reawakening are represented as continuous with the effects of industrialization and England's entry into the Crimean War. In Augusta Webster's dramatic monologue *A Castaway* (1870), a high-class prostitute's self-scrutiny illustrates the relationship between political economy and the commodification of female identity, with "coin" as a central metaphor for the connection between the two.

Not all poets accepted the view that poetry should speak to the issues and concerns of the present. In 1853, Matthew Arnold wrote that poets should respond to their world by mining "those elementary feelings which subsist permanently in the race, and are independent of time." In some of his later poetry, Arnold turned to classical rather than contemporary subjects as a way of rejecting what he saw as the crass materialism and spiritual futility of modern life. Yet for all his melancholia, Arnold did not advocate artistic isolation; whereas many poets of the second half of the century called for the independence of art from the imperative to offer moral instruction, Arnold continued to insist that the aesthetic endeavor necessarily involved ethical responsibility.

In contrast, Swinburne's poetry of sensual experience, his carnal subject matter and verbal pyrotechnics revel in the corporeality of poetry, so much so that he was accused in one famous review of "fleshliness" to the exclusion of "meditation" and "thought."[1] Swinburne's verse was important to the development of Aestheticism, influencing later poets such as Wilde and Symonds, whose poetry tended to emphasize formal beauty, sonic effects, and the momentary over the timeless. Like the Spasmodic poets of the 1840s and 1850s, like Arthur Hugh Clough in the late 1850s and early 1860s, and like Gerard Manley Hopkins at the

century's end, Swinburne also engaged in many challenging experiments with poetic form and meter, thereby anticipating some of the innovations and deliberate difficulties of modernist writing.

DRAMA

The Victorian period is not remembered for great stage dramas or for penetrating comedies, at least until the last decades of the century. Although Victorian audiences were avid theatergoers, they tended to prefer light-hearted entertainment to more serious fare. Comedies, pantomimes, farces, and musicals attracted audiences from across the social spectrum, but it was melodrama that became the most popular dramatic genre—albeit one that many critics during and since the Victorian era have dismissed as having little or no literary value. Disapprobation of the theater often invoked its tendency toward spectacle and its mass-market appeal in the same breath. The Victorian scholar Henry Morley, for example, lamented that "the great want of the stage in our day is an educated public" and that audiences

> clap their hands at pieces which are all leg and no brains; in which the male actor's highest ambition is to caper, slide, and stamp with the energy of a street-boy on a cellar flap, the actress shows plenty of thigh, and the dialogue, running entirely on the sound of words, hardly admits that they have any use at all as signs of thought[.]

While it did not conform to the aesthetic norms of the intellectual elite, melodrama did engage with the moral, social, and economic concerns of Victorians across classes, and it did so in a way that large numbers of people found compelling and entertaining. It thus opens a window onto the nature of power relations within modern market culture and the patriarchal family; sometimes it seems to support, and at other times to contest, these relations. With its sensational plots, stock characters, unadorned language, and a moral economy that unambiguously separates good from evil, melodrama exploited an audience's emotions, and in-

---

[1] The charge was made in Robert Buchanan's "The Fleshly School of Poetry," a review essay that first appeared in Volume 18 of *The Contemporary Review* in 1871. The review focused on D.G. Rossetti's *Poems*, citing Swinburne and Morris as other key figures in what Buchanan derisively termed "the Fleshly School," a mode he took to task for its "morbid deviation from the healthy forms of life."

variably ended on a happy note. (We need look no further than the mass appeal of the Hollywood films into which stage melodrama evolved to begin to understand why such performances were so popular.) Early in the century, melodramas often featured Gothic plots, settings, and characters, but the vogue for such subject matter gave way in the Victorian period to storylines centered on workaday conflicts in familiar settings, such as factories, cottages, and manor houses.

The most prolific and successful writer and adapter of melodramas was Dion Boucicault; his 1852 play *The Corsican Brothers* was such a hit with Queen Victoria that she saw it five times. Tom Taylor's popular *The Ticket-of-Leave Man* (1863) was set in recognizable London locations and featured a sleuth named Jack Hawksure who became a prototype for later stage detectives. Many popular novels, including works by Dickens, Collins, and Braddon, were adapted or pirated for the stage soon after they had been published. Ellen Price Wood's *East Lynne* (1861), a novel with a fallen woman theme, was adapted into several stage versions on the basis of its enormous success as one of the earliest sensation novels. Lines of influence between novels and stage melodrama ran in both directions: Dickens's employment of exaggerated characters, unlikely coincidences, and sentimental scenes reflects his love for the theater, and melodramatic elements can be seen in the work of many other novelists throughout the period, from Elizabeth Gaskell to Bram Stoker.

In 1881, theater impresario Richard D'Oyly Carte opened the Savoy Theatre in London for the express purpose of staging the comic operettas of W.S. Gilbert and Arthur Sullivan, whose collaboration had begun in 1875. Their most popular plays, such as *H.M.S. Pinafore* (1878), *The Mikado* (1885), and *Patience* (1881), are still regularly staged today. Gilbert's storylines and lyrics combined frivolous romance with witty and genial mockery of certain contemporary values,[1] as well as of

"A Gaiety Girl," music hall poster, 1893.

the formulaic nature of most London stage fare; Sullivan's alternately lilting and bouncy melodies proved irresistible, and "Gilbert and Sullivan" rapidly became a popular phenomenon. The Savoy Operas, as they came to be known, anticipated the new directions in British theater of the 1890s, epitomized in the comic plays of Oscar Wilde and the "problem plays" of George Bernard Shaw; both Wilde and Shaw offered serious critiques of their society while dazzling their audiences with their audacious wit, brilliant dialogue, and shocking candor.

[1] *Patience*, for example, satirized Aestheticism, prominently featuring a character known as Bunthorne, an aesthete poet. Though some critics have identified Oscar Wilde as the model for Bunthorne, Wilde's relative obscurity at the time of the operetta's composition suggests that the character is more likely a representation of then-

better-known poets such as Swinburne and D.G. Rossetti.

Prose Non-Fiction and Print Culture

Victorian writers of essays, criticism, history, and biography fully embraced the role of the public intellectual, whose particular mission was to instruct and edify readers about the day's key issues. Virtually no subject remained untouched: writers of non-fiction prose, also known as "sages," probed everything, from the latest scientific developments to religious controversies, from political and economic questions to gender issues, from aesthetic developments to social values and mores.

In an age of growing religious skepticism, readers looked to their "sages" as latter-day prophets and interpreters who were uniquely qualified to offer an almost divinely inspired wisdom. For men, this role of the secular cleric emerged along with the rise of the professional writer, or "man of letters," who could earn a comfortable living by the pen and maintain a level of gentlemanly respectability. For women writers, however, the decision to offer social and cultural critique often came at a price, since women were discouraged from involvement in—and even knowledge of—political issues. Arnold, Eliot, Ruskin, Pater, and Wilde produced some of the most influential literary and cultural criticism of the age, while Carlyle, Harriet Martineau, John Stuart Mill, Harriet Taylor Mill, and Frances Power Cobbe are among those better remembered for more overtly political commentary. What united most of these writers was their simultaneous position as societal outsiders and insiders: in a range of rhetorical styles, from prophetic to disinterested, prose writers typically argued from a marginal position under the assumption that their particular viewpoint had been abandoned or would be resisted by their readers. Yet it was precisely this outsider perspective that guaranteed the sage's unique authority within a society hungry for moral guidance by a voice not restrained by established cultural norms.

For every writer or sage celebrated by his or her reading public as a visionary, there were countless, often nameless "hack" writers who also contributed non-fiction prose, or, more properly, journalism, to newspapers and periodicals. Indeed, the periodical and

The opening of the Manchester Free Library, 1852. In 1845, local governments were given the authority to raise tax revenues to support the establishment of public libraries and museums. Free public libraries were distinguished from fee-charging circulating libraries such as Mudie's and W.H. Smith's.

newspaper press afforded both the sages and the hacks, as well as novelists and poets, a space to disseminate their work and reach ever-expanding audiences. In Wilkie Collins's words, it was "the age of periodicals." Early in the century, prominent literary journals such as the *Edinburgh Review*, *Blackwood's Magazine*, the *Quarterly Review*, *Fraser's Magazine*, and the *Athenaeum* attracted the most eminent writers. In the early Victorian era, writers in these journals generally published anonymously or under a pseudonym, no matter how distinguished they might be; not until the latter half of the century did signatures gradually begin to replace anonymity in many of the periodicals. Throughout the period, the number of periodicals steadily increased, until there was a magazine for every taste, every income level, every hobby group, every political and religious organization. Domestic magazines aimed at women readers, children's magazines, satirical or humor magazines, and monthly and quarterly miscellanies publishing fiction, poetry, criticism, and news all competed with each other for readers' interest, loyalty, and purchasing power in an increasingly diverse literary marketplace. Nearly all of the best-known literary writers across the genres saw their work published in magazines and newspapers: Barrett Browning's "The Cry of the Children" (1843) in *Blackwood's*, Dickens's *Oliver Twist* in *Bentley's Miscellany*, Arnold's *Culture and Anarchy* in the *Cornhill Magazine*, Yonge's *The Clever Woman of the Family* (1865) in the *Churchman's Family Magazine*.

The periodical press was also instrumental in the development of modern literary criticism. Book reviews in influential periodicals, such as the *Athenaeum*, could make or break a writer's reputation; prominent literary reviewers—some of whom, such as Henry James, were also celebrated authors in their own right—both forged a professional identity for themselves as literary critics and formulated principles of literary analysis that are today's tools of the trade.

Victorians were, in general, fascinated with characterizing their "age": Carlyle's "Signs of the Times," Mill's "Spirit of the Age," and Eliza Lynn Linton's "Girl of the Period" became popular catchphrases that signaled a self-conscious awareness of a society in transition. It was the "age of steam," the "age of doubt," and, perhaps most notably for students of literature, the "age of reading." Reading, like many other social institutions and cultural practices, gradually became democratized during Victoria's reign. The 1870 Education Act instituted compulsory elementary education in England and Wales for the first time; adult literacy was nearly universal by century's end. Readers were everywhere: in pubs, on trains, around the family hearth, at gentlemen's clubs, and in reading rooms.[1] The single reader—particularly the female reader—was a common subject for Victorian painters. Reading aloud was also a popular pastime; it was common for middle-class fathers to gather together their dependents, including the servants, at the end of

the day or week to read edifying family literature, such as sermons, tracts, and didactic fiction. Drawing on his background in the London theater, Dickens delivered public readings of his novels that attracted huge crowds and increased sales of his books. His performance of Little Nell's death scene famously left audiences weeping.

The explosion of reading and reading cultures in Victorian England went hand in hand with new mass-printing technologies, the rise of cheap wood-pulp paper in the last quarter of the century (facilitated by massive deforestation in Canada and elsewhere), the removal of prohibitive taxes on reading material, the ease of distribution made possible through the rail system, and political, economic, and social reforms that affected people at all levels of their existence. At the beginning of the century, mass literacy was regarded as a recipe for political revolution. From at least the middle of the century onwards, some worried that reading was becoming too popular, that it was a kind of "mania" or "disease" that "consumed" people. Critics such as Matthew Arnold argued that the newly literate but untutored masses lacked the necessary skills to distinguish between the timeless and the trashy, and that their rise therefore signaled the demise of English culture. Yet there were also those who argued that literacy was a human right, and it was ultimately this viewpoint that prevailed. In 1840, Carlyle wrote, "Books are written by martyr-men, not for rich men alone but for all men. If we consider it, every human being has, by the nature of the case, a *right* to hear what other wise human beings have spoken to him. It is one of the Rights of Men; a very cruel injustice if you deny it to a man."[2] The history of reading—the history of what and how different people read, the expectations that existed about what women and men should read, both in their leisure time and professionally—is ultimately inseparable from the history of the Victorian period.

---

[1] Private libraries where readers could pay an annual fee for access to current newspapers and the latest books and periodicals.

[2] It is unclear whether in this passage Carlyle meant "man" in the sense of "humanity" or in the narrower sense.

THE ENGLISH LANGUAGE IN THE VICTORIAN ERA

The English vocabulary continued to expand throughout the period. New words entered the language to name aspects of the changing world of work (*trade-union* is recorded as first having entered the language in 1831, for example; *margin*, used with reference to profit to mean "amount of money available once certain costs are covered," in the 1850s). New words were also needed to name aspects of human nature that were being seen in new ways or acknowledged for the first time (*personality*, used in the modern sense of "distinctive personal identity," in 1835; *sadism* in 1888; *homosexual* in 1892). New words were coined to name new religious movements (such as *evangelicanism*, *disestablishmentarianism*, and its famously long opposite *antidisestablishmentarianism*) and to name new developments in the culture of sports (*caddie* is first recorded in 1857). Less innocuously, new ways kept springing up to express old prejudices; *jew* is first recorded as being used derogatively as a transitive verb in 1845.

The coining of new words from Latin and Greek roots—especially new scientific terms—continued at a quickened pace, from *lithograph* and *locomotive*, to *photograph* and *phonograph*, to *telegraph*, *telephone*, and *dictaphone*. Far fewer new words were entering English from French, however; the flow of new words from French into English,[1] which had continued in the second half of the eighteenth century and the early years of the nineteenth at about the same pace as it had been a century earlier, slowed to a trickle in the Victorian era. It was far more characteristic of the eighteenth-century English to turn to the French for *etiquette* (1750) than it was for Victorians to turn to the French for *élan* (1880).

The expansion of English in the nineteenth century was not restricted to new noun coinages. A lively feature of the growth of the language during this period was an expansion in the use of verb-adverb combinations (e.g.,

bring up, *hold up*, *let up*, *pass up*, *shut up*—to name only a few of those involving *up*). With the spread of such coinages (as well as of an ever-growing number of slang expressions) into the written language came a gradual reduction in the level of formality of standard English.

The Western Electric multiple telephone switchboard, the Royal Exchange, Manchester, 1888. The spread of English as the leading language of communication world-wide was aided by the invention of the telegraph in 1837, and of the telephone later in the century.

A few centuries earlier, English as it was spoken in the British Isles had encompassed a vast range of dialects and variations in pronunciation. A reduction in these differences had begun with the imposition of English authority over Wales, Scotland, and Ireland; no doubt it was influenced, too, by the inherently stabilizing effects of print culture following the introduction of the printing press to England in the late fifteenth century. This trend toward greater standardization of vocabulary and of pronunciation continued through the nineteenth century. The spread of standardized pronunciation in particular was assisted by the growing influence of the elite boarding schools (known as "public schools") as the preferred sites of education for the privileged classes and for those who aspired to join them. Increasingly, in the late-Victorian period, girls as well as boys were sent to such schools; boarding schools such as St. Andrews (1877) and Roedean (1885) were the first institutions

---

[1] The importation of French words into English, often thought of as beginning with the Norman conquest in 1066, in fact did not occur with any great frequency until roughly a century later; the flow reached its peak in the late fourteenth century.

John Everett Millais, *Ophelia*, 1851–52. The drowning of Ophelia (from Shakespeare's *Hamlet*) was a frequent subject in Victorian painting; the best known representation is that of Millais. As the scene is described in Act 4, Scene 7 of the play, the mentally ill Ophelia comes to a stream "with fantastic garlands" of flowers. Distracted, she falls into the "weeping brook." For a while before she drowns, "her clothes spread wide" and hold her up.

Henry Wallis, *Chatterton*, 1856. The suicide of Thomas Chatterton (1752–70), of arsenic poisoning after a period of living close to starvation as a struggling poet, captured the Victorian imagination even more strongly than it had the Romantic one. Wallis's painting was widely praised when exhibited in 1856 at the Royal Academy; John Ruskin described it in his notes on the exhibit as "faultless and wonderful."

Thomas Jones Barker, *The Secret of England's Greatness* (detail), c. 1863. Barker's painting depicts the Queen presenting a Bible. The recipient and the specific occasion remain unidentified; in the background are Elizabeth, Duchess of Wellington (who served as Mistress of the Robes to the Queen); Prince Albert; Lord Palmerston (then serving as Prime Minister); and Lord John Russell (then serving as Foreign Secretary). An engraving of the painting was published under the fuller title, *The Bible: The Secret of England's Greatness*.

Franz Xaver Winterhalter, *The Royal Family in 1846* (detail), 1846.

Ford Madox Brown, *Work*, c. 1852–c. 1865. This famous painting (above), which took over twelve years to complete, brings together Victorians from an extraordinary range of backgrounds. The central group of excavators was the painting's starting point—the inspiration coming from the artist observing work on the construction of the London sewers. Less well-off members of society include the flower seller to the left and the orphaned children in the foreground, cared for by an older sibling. To the right are two "brain-workers" admired by the artist, Rev. F.D. Maurice (founder of the Working Man's College, where Brown was an art instructor) and Thomas Carlyle. In the background, members of the gentry on horseback observe the scene.

George Clausen,
The Stone Pickers, 1887.

William Holman Hunt, *The Awakening Conscience*, 1853–54. This canvas presents an elaborately coded story. In a letter to *The Times* of London, John Ruskin (signing himself as "The Author of Modern Painters") described the reaction of viewers—and elucidated the painting's intended significance: "… assuredly it is not understood. People gaze at it in a blank wonder, and leave it hopelessly; so that, although it is almost an insult to the painter to explain his thoughts in this instance, I cannot persuade myself to leave it thus misunderstood. The poor girl has been singing with her seducer; some chance words of the song "Oft in the stilly night" have struck upon the numbed places of her heart; she has started up in agony; he, not seeing her face, goes on singing, striking the keys carelessly with his gloved hand." As Ruskin discerned, the woman is evidently the mistress rather than the wife of the man; she wears a ring on every finger of her left hand except the fourth. The piece that has been played, "Oft in the stilly night," is a song in which a woman looks back to the innocence of her childhood. The doubling of the female figure through the use of the mirror suggests the possibility of a brighter future if she follows her awakened conscience and gives up the life of a "kept woman."

G.W. Joy, *General Gordon's Last Stand*, c. 1893. Gordon, who had held an administrative post in the Sudan in the 1870s (and played an important role during that period in ending the slave trade in the area), was sent again to the Sudan in 1884 on a mission to rescue garrisons of British troops that had been cut off after a remarkably successful rebellion led by Muhammad Ahmad. Ahmad, a Sudanese political leader and Islamic messianic figure known as the Madhi, had managed to unite many Sudanese people in the pursuit of independence from Ottoman-Egyptian powers (which were in turn largely dominated by British interests). Ahmad besieged Gordon's forces in Khartoum for ten months and finally overwhelmed them, and Gordon was killed during the battle (though almost certainly in the streets of the city, not as he is shown in Joy's iconic painting of the imagined scene). The incident became a *cause célèbre* in Britain, and there were many calls to avenge Gordon's death, but the Madhists managed to maintain independence for more than a decade; it was not until 1898 that the British under General Kitchener re-established British control of the Sudan.

Trade Emblem, Amalgamated Society of Engineers, Machinists, Millwrights, Smiths, and Pattern Makers, c. 1860.

Alfred Concanen, *Modern Advertising: A Railway Station in 1874*, 1874. This colored lithograph appeared as a fold-out frontispiece in the book *A History of Advertising from the Earliest Times.*

John O'Connor, *From Pentonville Road Looking West*, 1884. In the background is St. Pancras, one of the greatest of Victorian railway stations.

Advertisement, 1890s, "Cook's Tours in Scotland." Featured at lower left is the Firth of Forth Bridge (also known as the Forth Rail Bridge). The bridge, built in the wake of the collapse of the Firth of Tay Bridge, in which 75 lives had been lost, pioneered new techniques of cantilever construction; on its completion in 1890 it was by far the longest bridge in the world.

Benjamin Duterrau, *The Conciliation*, 1840. The painting shows a Methodist lay preacher instructing native Tasmanians.

Canadian election poster, 1891. The "Old Leader" was Sir John A. Macdonald, Canadian Prime Minister from 1867 to 1873 and again from 1878 to 1891. "The Old Policy" was Macdonald's National Policy, under the terms of which industries in the Dominion would be protected by a tariff on imports from the United States, but "imperial preference" exempted goods from Britain and its possessions from any tariff.

Emma Brownlow, *The Foundling Restored to Its Mother—An Incident in the Foundling Hospital*, 1858. Foundlings—deserted or abandoned children—were a frequent subject, both in Victorian literature and in the visual arts. The young girl portrayed here was indeed reclaimed soon after Brownlow had painted the picture. Most Victorian-era foundlings (like most orphans) were not so fortunate; they usually ended up not in the Foundling Hospital but in one of the workhouses established under the provisions of the 1834 Poor Law Amendment Act. Brownlow was herself raised in the Foundling Hospital—though not as a foundling; her father held a live-in position as administrator of the Thomas Coram Foundling Hospital.

(above) James Tissot, *Too Early*, 1873. The French painter Jacques-Joseph Tissot moved from Paris to London after being active in the 1871 Paris Commune; he took the Anglicized first name of James, and became both a popular and a highly regarded artist in his adopted home. Over the eleven years until his return to Paris in 1882 he painted many portraits, as well as many canvases depicting social interactions—often suggestive of a narrative. His narrative paintings include scenes of city streets, of harbor life, of garden parties, and of fashionable young women in a variety of sometimes surprising settings. Often dismissed in the twentieth century as a sentimentalist, Tissot is increasingly becoming recognized as an artist who provides a unique window into English social life in the 1870s and early 1880s.

(below) James Tissot, *An Interesting Story*, c. 1872. Of note: Tissot painted a very similar scene from a different angle, and gave it the title *A Tedious History*.

Joseph Nash, *The Great Industrial Exhibition of 1851: The Transept*, 1851. Nash's lithograph, from "his drawing in the possession of Her Majesty," was one of a series. The view was described as follows in the official catalogue: "the whole extent of the transept, interrupted only by the magnificent glass fountain of Messrs. Osler, and the groups of sculpture and tropical plants and trees, … flashes on the eye more like the fabled palace of Vathek than a structure reared in a few months by mortal hands." (For more on the Crystal Palace see the Contexts section on "Britain, Empire, and a Wider World.")

Franz Xaver Winterhalter, *The First of May, 1851*, 1851. The first of May, 1851 was the opening day of the Great Exhibition at the Crystal Palace; it was also the first birthday of the Queen's third son, Prince Arthur, and the eighty-second birthday of the Duke of Wellington; the "Iron Duke" is here shown presenting a gold casket decorated with jewels to mother and child (who is holding a sprig of lily of the valley). The scene in numerous respects follows traditional Christian iconography; Prince Albert stands behind the Queen, in the position occupied by Joseph in many depictions of Mary and her newborn son.

(For more on the Great Exhibition see the introduction to the Victorian Era and the Contexts section on "Britain, Empire, and a Wider World.")

for girls that paralleled centuries-old boys' schools such as Eton, Harrow, and Rugby.

Perhaps the greatest development relating to the history of the English language in the Victorian period was the initiation of a dictionary "on historical principles"—one that would record not only the various different meanings of words, but also how they had changed over time, and precisely when each meaning was first recorded in surviving written English. *The Oxford English Dictionary*, which was to be among the most ambitious of projects in an age of famously ambitious projects, had its origins in the work of the Philological Society, founded in 1842. In 1858, following the lead of a similar project initiated in Germany[1] and following years of discussion, the society issued a formal "Proposal for the Publication of a New Dictionary by the Philological Society." The society would invite volunteers to assist in sending in records they found of early or significant uses of words; eventually some six million slips with quotations written on them were submitted. By 1879, the Philological Society concluded that the project was so vast that it would not be able to complete it on its own, entering into an agreement with the Oxford University Press. Even with this assistance, it was not until 1884 that it proved possible to publish a volume covering one part of the letter *A*. By 1900, only four and one-half volumes had been published, and it was not until 1928 that a complete version of the full dictionary was available. (By then, of course, much of the early work was outdated; a second edition was published in 1989, and the *OED* is now continually being updated online.)

A less successful Victorian initiative was a multifaceted campaign to rationalize spelling—a campaign that extended in one form or another through almost the entire period as the prevalence of spellings that bear no relation to phonetic principles increasingly came to be criticized as antiquated and illogical.[2] In the early years of the Victorian era, interest in such matters was spurred by the introduction of Isaac Pitman's system of shorthand, with Pitman himself acting as a leading advocate for reform. By the 1850s, the Bible and a number of works were available in phonetic spelling versions, and by the end of the following decade, the Philological Society was taking an active role in airing all sides of the debate. Its American counterpart adopted a less impartial stance, calling in particular for the adoption of simplified phonetic spellings of words such as *tho*, *altho*, and *thruout*. Of their list only two—*program* and *catalog*—became generally adopted in the United States. In Britain resistance to such Americanisms carried the day—and in both countries, the campaign to rationalize spelling faltered by century's end in the face of a growing recognition of the degree to which English had become a written as well as a spoken language, with words comprehended very largely through the appearance on paper of the entire written word.

Resistance to Americanisms generally was felt not only in Britain itself, but also—indeed, perhaps even more strongly—in English Canada, in its unique position as staunchly British by history and by disposition but unavoidably "American" in the geographical sense. Complaints, such as those of a contributor to the *Canadian Journal* in 1857 against words and expressions "imported by travellers, daily circulated by American newspapers, and eagerly incorporated into the language of our Provincial press," were far from uncommon. Words such as *travellers* (in its British spelling; *travelers* according to common practice in the United States) themselves became points of contention. As the American spellings of such words—introduced by Noah Webster in his dictionary in 1825—became entrenched in the United States, Canadians began to develop a

---

[1] The *Deutsches Wörterbuch* was begun by the classicist Franz Passow and the philologists (and compilers of fairy tales) Jacob and Wilhelm Grimm.

---

[2] As a late-Victorian spelling reformer pointed out, the ways in which English words are spelled often bear so little connection to pronunciation that it would be possible to spell *fish* as *ghoti*, with the *gh* pronounced as we do the *gh* in *cough*; the *o* pronounced as we do the *o* in *women*; and the *ti* pronounced as we do the *ti* in *nation*. This now-famous example is thought to have been first given common currency by Bernard Shaw (who later became a crusader for spelling reform).

hybrid somewhere in between British and American spellings.

Conventions for marking direct speech and quoted material finally stabilized in the Victorian period in something close to their current form, though with what are now established differences between American and British conventions of punctuation still unsettled. Quotation marks themselves are a relatively recent invention; they became widely used only in the eighteenth century. Even in the late eighteenth century a number of different indicators for quoted material were still being used, the most common of which was to include quotation marks not only at the beginning of the quoted passage, but also at the beginning of each subsequent line for as long as the quotation extended. In the early Victorian period, it had become conventional to mark quotations with only an open quotation mark at the beginning of a passage and a closed quotation mark at the end—though it remained acceptable to use either single or double quotation marks.

The period also saw significant changes in the evolution of the paragraph as a primary means of signaling the shape of ideas in prose. The paragraph was originally simply a short horizontal marker added beneath a line in which a break in meaning occurred; in the sixteenth century, it became conventional to mark such shifts by setting off blocks of text through indentation at the beginning of each block. Until the late eighteenth century, however, paragraphs of English prose were often extremely long by modern standards, and one paragraph of expository or argumentative prose might hold a large number of only loosely related ideas. Even in the Romantic era, a paragraph might often run to a page or more. Through the nineteenth century, however, paragraphs gradually but steadily became shorter, and the principle of restricting each paragraph to a set of closely related ideas became much more widely followed.

History of the Language
and of Print Culture

In an effort to provide for readers a direct sense of the development of the language and of print culture, examples of texts in their original form (and of illustrations) have been provided in each volume. A list of materials related to Victorian period print culture and language within the present volume appears below. Overviews of "prose non-fiction and print culture" and of developments in the history of language during this period appear on pages xciv–xcviii.

MARY PRINCE
1788 – after 1833

"I will say the truth to the English people," declared the abolitionist Mary Prince, whose autobiography detailing her life in the West Indies is the earliest extant slave narrative by a woman. Published at a crucial moment in the campaign to end slavery in British possessions, *The History of Mary Prince* represents an important contribution to the abolitionist movement, as well as a work of historical and literary interest in its own right.

Mary Prince was born into bondage in the British colony of Bermuda, where for the first twelve years of her life she was, relatively speaking, spared the cruelty that dominated her adult years. Both her parents were also enslaved, the property of Charles Myners. After Myners died, Mary and her mother were sold to a Captain Williams, whose daughter Betsey treated Mary with racist condescension, but with relative compassion. Williams sold Prince to another family to raise money for his marriage, and in 1806 she was sent to work in the salt ponds of Turks Island: "This work was perfectly new to me. I was given a half barrel and shovel, and had to stand up to my knees in the water, from four o'clock in the morning till nine, when we were given some Indian corn boiled in water, which we were obliged to swallow as fast as we could for fear the rain should come on and melt the salt." In addition to these intolerable working conditions, Prince also endured physical and probably sexual abuse from her master.

In 1818, Prince was sold for three hundred dollars to John Wood, a plantation owner in Antigua, who beat, overworked, and otherwise abused her. By this time Prince had developed a serious skin problem, and while working for the Woods she became essentially crippled by severe rheumatism; her mistreatment would also eventually lead to damaged eyesight. Prince began attending meetings held at the Moravian Church, where various women taught her to read: "After we had done spelling, we tried to read in the Bible. After reading was over, the missionary gave out a hymn for us to sing." Prince was married in this church to Daniel Jones, a formerly enslaved man who had purchased his own freedom. Wood horsewhipped Prince when he discovered the marriage. In 1828 Wood took Prince to London as his servant. Abolitionist sympathizers helped her escape (which they were able to do because slavery was illegal in England), and she found employment as a domestic servant of Thomas Pringle, a Methodist and secretary of the Society for the Abolition of Slavery.

Pringle encouraged Prince to tell the story of her life and, in 1831, he arranged for the publication of her book, *The History of Mary Prince, a West-Indian Slave, Related by Herself.* In his "Preface" to the work, Pringle wrote: "The idea of writing Mary Prince's history was first suggested by herself. She wished it to be done, she said, that good people in England might hear from a slave what a slave had felt and suffered." Mary Prince told her story to Susanna Strickland (later Moodie), who recorded it in writing. It seems improbable that Strickland—who would later come to be regarded as one of Canada's most accomplished writers in the nineteenth century—would not at a minimum have edited the dictated narrative for grammar and syntax, and some have suggested that Pringle may have had some hand in shaping the manuscript so as to better serve abolitionist ends. (His insistence that the rhetorical flourish at the end of Prince's first paragraph is "given verbatim as uttered by Mary Prince" has struck more than one reader as rather forced.) But most scholars have stopped short of suggesting that material was fabricated by Pringle and Strickland, or that this is not in essence Prince's own narrative. Strickland herself attested that she had "been writing Mr. Pringle's black Mary's life from her own dictation and for her benefit adhering to her own simple story and language without deviating to the paths of flourish or romance."

The book was a great success, and gave rise to considerable controversy. *Blackwood's Magazine* and *The Glasgow Courier* claimed it was fraudulent and propagandistic. A number of libel suits resulted, with Wood suing Pringle and Pringle counter-suing. Wood claimed that the book had "endeavored to injure the character of my family by the most vile and infamous falsehoods." Wood lost the case, and the libel scandal served only to make Prince's work more widely known. It reached a third edition in the same year it was published, and it has since that time retained its place as one of the most moving, detailed, and comprehensive narratives of the life of an enslaved person.

Slavery was legally abolished in almost all British colonies in 1833. Little is known of Prince's life after the publication of her *History*, and we do not know when, where, or how she died.

⌘⌘⌘

The History of Mary Prince
A West Indian Slave
Related by Herself

PREFACE [BY THOMAS PRINGLE][1]

The idea of writing Mary Prince's history was first suggested by herself. She wished it to be done, she said, that good people in England might hear from a slave what a slave had felt and suffered; and a letter of her late master's, which will be found in the Supplement, induced me to accede to her wish without farther delay. The more immediate object of the publication will afterwards appear.

The narrative was taken down from Mary's own lips by a lady who happened to be at the time residing in my family as a visitor. It was written out fully, with all the narrator's repetitions and prolixities,[2] and afterwards pruned into its present shape; retaining, as far as was practicable, Mary's exact expressions and peculiar phraseology. No fact of importance has been omitted, and not a single circumstance or sentiment has been added. It is essentially her own, without any material alteration farther than was requisite to exclude redundances and gross grammatical errors, so as to render it clearly intelligible.

After it had been thus written out, I went over the whole, carefully examining her on every fact and circumstance detailed; and in all that relates to her residence in Antigua I had the advantage of being assisted in this scrutiny by Mr. Joseph Phillips, who was a resident in that colony during the same period, and had known her there.

The names of all the persons mentioned by the narrator have been printed in full, except those of Capt. I— and his wife, and that of Mr. D—, to whom conduct of peculiar atrocity is ascribed. These three individuals are now gone to answer at a far more awful tribunal than that of public opinion, for the deeds of which their former bondwoman accuses them; and to hold them up more openly to human reprobation could no longer affect themselves, while it might deeply lacerate the feelings of their surviving and perhaps innocent relatives, without any commensurate public advantage.

Without detaining the reader with remarks on other points which will be adverted to more conveniently in the Supplement, I shall here merely notice farther, that the Anti-Slavery Society have no concern whatever with this publication, nor are they in any degree responsible for the statements it contains. I have published the tract,

---

[1] *THOMAS PRINGLE*   Poet and abolitionist Thomas Pringle (1789–1834) was born in Scotland and lived in South Africa between 1820 and 1826, where he published a newspaper and a magazine. In 1826 he returned to England, where he devoted himself to the antislavery movement as secretary to the Society for the Abolition of Slavery.

[2] *prolixities*   Instances of wordiness.

not as their Secretary, but in my private capacity; and any profits that may arise from the sale will be exclusively appropriated to the benefit of Mary Prince herself.
THOMAS PRINGLE
7, Solly Terrace, Claremont Square,
January 25, 1831

P.S. Since writing the above, I have been furnished by my friend Mr. George Stephen, with the interesting narrative of Asa-Asa, a captured African, now under his protection; and have printed it as a suitable appendix to this little history.
T.P.

The History of Mary Prince

I was born at Brackish-Pond, in Bermuda, on a farm belonging to Mr. Charles Myners. My mother was a household slave; and my father, whose name was Prince, was a sawyer[1] belonging to Mr. Trimmingham, a shipbuilder at Crow-Lane. When I was an infant, old Mr. Myners died, and there was a division of the slaves and other property among the family. I was bought along with my mother by old Captain Darrel, and given to his grandchild, little Miss Betsey Williams. Captain Williams, Mr. Darrel's son-in-law, was master of a vessel which traded to several places in America and the West Indies, and he was seldom at home long together.

Mrs. Williams was a kind-hearted good woman, and she treated all her slaves well. She had only one daughter, Miss Betsey, for whom I was purchased, and who was about my own age. I was made quite a pet of by Miss Betsey, and loved her very much. She used to lead me about by the hand, and call me her little nigger.[2] This was the happiest period of my life; for I was too young to understand rightly my condition as a slave, and too thoughtless and full of spirits to look forward to the days of toil and sorrow.

My mother was a household slave in the same family. I was under her own care, and my little brothers and sisters were my play-fellows and companions. My mother had us several fine children after she came to Mrs. Williams, three girls and two boys. The tasks given out to us children were light, and we used to play together with Miss Betsey, with as much freedom almost as if she had been our sister.

My master, however, was a very harsh, selfish man; and we always dreaded his return from sea. His wife was herself much afraid of him; and, during his stay at home, seldom dared to show her usual kindness to the slaves. He often left her, in the most distressed circumstances, to reside in other female society, at some place in the West Indies of which I have forgot the name. My poor mistress bore his ill-treatment with great patience, and all her slaves loved and pitied her. I was truly attached to her, and, next to my own mother, loved her better than any creature in the world. My obedience to her commands was cheerfully given: it sprung solely from the affection I felt for her, and not from fear of the power which the white people's law had given her over me.

I had scarcely reached my twelfth year when my mistress became too poor to keep so many of us at home; and she hired me out to Mrs. Pruden, a lady who lived about five miles off, in the adjoining parish, in a large house near the sea. I cried bitterly at parting with my dear mistress and Miss Betsey, and when I kissed my mother and brothers and sisters, I thought my young heart would break, it pained me so. But there was no help; I was forced to go. Good Mrs. Williams comforted me by saying that I should still be near the home I was about to quit, and might come over and see her and my kindred whenever I could obtain leave of absence from Mrs. Pruden. A few hours after this I was taken to a strange house, and found myself among strange people. This separation seemed a sore trial to me then; but oh! 'twas light, light to the trials I have since endured!—'twas nothing—nothing to be mentioned with them; but I was a child then, and it was according to my strength.

I knew that Mrs. Williams could no longer maintain me; that she was fain to part with me for my food and clothing; and I tried to submit myself to the change. My

---

[1] *sawyer* Worker whose job it is to saw timber.

[2] *nigger* By the nineteenth century, this word had acquired the extremely derogatory connotations it carries today; it was, however, used freely by many white people.

new mistress was a passionate woman; but yet she did not treat me very unkindly. I do not remember her striking me but once, and that was for going to see Mrs. Williams when I heard she was sick, and staying longer than she had given me leave to do. All my employment at this time was nursing a sweet baby, little Master Daniel; and I grew so fond of my nursling that it was my greatest delight to walk out with him by the sea-shore, accompanied by his brother and sister, Miss Fanny and Master James.—Dear Miss Fanny! She was a sweet, kind young lady, and so fond of me that she wished me to learn all that she knew herself; and her method of teaching me was as follows:—Directly she had said her lessons to her grandmamma, she used to come running to me, and make me repeat them one by one after her; and in a few months I was able not only to say my letters but to spell many small words. But this happy state was not to last long. Those days were too pleasant to last. My heart always softens when I think of them.

At this time Mrs. Williams died. I was told suddenly of her death, and my grief was so great that, forgetting I had the baby in my arms, I ran away directly to my poor mistress's house; but reached it only in time to see the corpse carried out. Oh, that was a day of sorrow—a heavy day! All the slaves cried. My mother cried and lamented her sore; and I (foolish creature!) vainly entreated them to bring my dear mistress back to life. I knew nothing rightly about death then, and it seemed a hard thing to bear. When I thought about my mistress I felt as if the world was all gone wrong; and for many days and weeks I could think of nothing else. I returned to Mrs. Pruden's; but my sorrow was too great to be comforted, for my own dear mistress was always in my mind. Whether in the house or abroad, my thoughts were always talking to me about her.

I stayed at Mrs. Pruden's about three months after this; I was then sent back to Mr. Williams to be sold. Oh, that was a sad sad time! I recollect the day well. Mrs. Pruden came to me and said, "Mary, you will have to go home directly; your master is going to be married, and he means to sell you and two of your sisters to raise money for the wedding." Hearing this I burst out a crying,—though I was then far from being sensible of the full weight of my misfortune, or of the misery that waited for me. Besides, I did not like to leave Mrs. Pruden, and the dear baby, who had grown very fond of me. For some time I could scarcely believe that Mrs. Pruden was in earnest, till I received orders for my immediate return.—Dear Miss Fanny! how she cried at parting with me, whilst I kissed and hugged the baby, thinking I should never see him again. I left Mrs. Pruden's, and walked home with a heart full of sorrow. The idea of being sold away from my mother and Miss Betsey was so frightful, that I dared not trust myself to think about it. We had been bought of Mrs. Myners, as I have mentioned, by Miss Betsey's grandfather, and given to her, so that we were by right *her* property, and I never thought we should be separated or sold away from her.

When I reached the house, I went in directly to Miss Betsey. I found her in great distress; and she cried out as soon as she saw me, "Oh, Mary! my father is going to sell you all to raise money to marry that wicked woman. You are *my* slaves, and he has no right to sell you; but it is all to please her." She then told me that my mother was living with her father's sister at a house close by, and I went there to see her. It was a sorrowful meeting; and we lamented with a great and sore crying our unfortunate situation. "Here comes one of my poor piccaninnies!"[1] she said, the moment I came in, "one of the poor slave-brood who are to be sold tomorrow."

Oh dear! I cannot bear to think of that day,—it is too much.—It recalls the great grief that filled my heart, and the woeful thoughts that passed to and fro through my mind, whilst listening to the pitiful words of my poor mother, weeping for the loss of her children. I wish I could find words to tell you all I then felt and suffered. The great God above alone knows the thoughts of the poor slave's heart, and the bitter pains which follow such separations as these. All that we love taken away from us—oh, it is sad, sad! and sore to be borne!—I got no sleep that night for thinking of the morrow; and dear Miss Betsey was scarcely less distressed. She could not bear to part with her old playmates and she cried sore and would not be pacified.

---

[1] *piccaninnies* Children, usually applied derogatively to Black children.

The black morning at length came; it came too soon for my poor mother and us. Whilst she was putting on us the new osnaburgs[1] in which we were to be sold, she said, in a sorrowful voice, (I shall never forget it!) "See, I am *shrouding* my poor children; what a task for a mother!"—She then called Miss Betsey to take leave of us. "I am going to carry my little chickens to market," (these were her very words) "take your last look of them; may be you will see them no more." "Oh, my poor slaves! my own slaves!" said dear Miss Betsey, "you belong to me; and it grieves my heart to part with you."—Miss Betsey kissed us all, and, when she left us, my mother called the rest of the slaves to bid us good bye. One of them, a woman named Moll, came with her infant in her arms. "Ay!" said my mother, seeing her turn away and look at her child with the tears in her eyes, "your turn will come next." The slaves could say nothing to comfort us; they could only weep and lament with us. When I left my dear little brothers and the house in which I had been brought up, I thought my heart would burst.

Our mother, weeping as she went, called me away with the children Hannah and Dinah, and we took the road that led to Hamble Town, which we reached about four o'clock in the afternoon. We followed my mother to the market-place, where she placed us in a row against a large house, with our backs to the wall and our arms folded across our breasts. I, as the eldest, stood first, Hannah next to me, then Dinah; and our mother stood beside, crying over us. My heart throbbed with grief and terror so violently, that I pressed my hands quite tightly across my breast, but I could not keep it still, and it continued to leap as though it would burst out of my body. But who cared for that? Did one of the many bystanders, who were looking at us so carelessly, think of the pain that wrung the hearts of the negro woman and her young ones? No, no! They were not all bad, I dare say, but slavery hardens white people's hearts towards the blacks; and many of them were not slow to make their remarks upon us aloud, without regard to our grief—though their light words fell like cayenne on the fresh wounds of our hearts. Oh those white people have small hearts who can only feel for themselves.

At length the vendue[2] master, who was to offer us for sale like sheep or cattle, arrived, and asked my mother which was the eldest. She said nothing, but pointed to me. He took me by the hand, and led me out into the middle of the street, and, turning me slowly round, exposed me to the view of those who attended the vendue. I was soon surrounded by strange men, who examined and handled me in the same manner that a butcher would a calf or a lamb he was about to purchase, and who talked about my shape and size in like words—as if I could no more understand their meaning than the dumb beasts. I was then put up for sale. The bidding commenced at a few pounds, and gradually rose to fifty-seven, when I was knocked down to the highest bidder; and the people who stood by said that I had fetched a great sum for so young a slave.

I then saw my sisters led forth, and sold to different owners; so that we had not the sad satisfaction of being partners in bondage. When the sale was over, my mother hugged and kissed us, and mourned over us, begging of us to keep up a good heart, and do our duty to our new masters. It was a sad parting; one went one way, one another, and our poor mammy went home with nothing.

My new master was a Captain I—, who lived at Spanish Point. After parting with my mother and sisters, I followed him to his store, and he gave me into the charge of his son, a lad about my own age, Master Benjy, who took me to my new home. I did not know where I was going, or what my new master would do with me. My heart was quite broken with grief, and my thoughts went back continually to those from whom I had been so suddenly parted. "Oh, my mother! my mother!" I kept saying to myself, "Oh, my mammy and my sisters and my brothers, shall I never see you again!"

Oh, the trials! the trials! they make the salt water come into my eyes when I think of the days in which I was afflicted—the times that are gone; when I mourned and grieved with a young heart for those whom I

---

[1]   *osnaburgs*   Clothes made of osnaburg, a coarse linen.

[2]   *vendue*   Sale.

loved.—It was night when I reached my new home. The house was large, and built at the bottom of a very high hill; but I could not see much of it that night. I saw too much of it afterwards. The stones and the timber were the best things in it; they were not so hard as the hearts of the owners.

Before I entered the house, two slave women, hired from another owner, who were at work in the yard, spoke to me, and asked who I belonged to? I replied, "I am come to live here." "Poor child, poor child!" they both said; "you must keep a good heart, if you are to live here."—When I went in, I stood up crying in a corner. Mrs. I— came and took off my hat, a little black silk hat Miss Pruden made for me, and said in a rough voice, "You are not come here to stand up in corners and cry, you are come here to work." She then put a child into my arms, and, tired as I was, I was forced instantly to take up my old occupation of a nurse.—I could not bear to look at my mistress, her countenance was so stern. She was a stout tall woman with a very dark complexion, and her brows were always drawn together into a frown. I thought of the words of the two slave women when I saw Mrs. I—, and heard the harsh sound of her voice.

The person I took the most notice of that night was a French Black called Hetty, whom my master took in privateering from another vessel, and made his slave. She was the most active woman I ever saw, and she was tasked to her utmost. A few minutes after my arrival she came in from milking the cows, and put the sweet-potatoes on for supper. She then fetched home the sheep, and penned them in the fold; drove home the cattle, and staked them about the pond side; fed and rubbed down my master's horse, and gave the hog and the fed cow their suppers; prepared the beds, and un-dressed the children, and laid them to sleep. I liked to look at her and watch all her doings, for hers was the only friendly face I had as yet seen, and I felt glad that she was there. She gave me my supper of potatoes and milk, and a blanket to sleep upon, which she spread for me in the passage before the door of Mrs. I—'s chamber.

I got a sad fright, that night. I was just going to sleep, when I heard a noise in my mistress's room; and she presently called out to inquire if some work was finished that she had ordered Hetty to do. "No, Ma'am, not yet," was Hetty's answer from below. On hearing this, my master started up from his bed, and just as he was, in his shirt, ran down stairs with a long cow-skin in his hand. I heard immediately after, the cracking of the thong, and the house rang to the shrieks of poor Hetty, who kept crying out, "Oh, Massa! Massa! me dead. Massa! have mercy upon me—don't kill me out-right."—This was a sad beginning for me. I sat up upon my blanket, trembling with terror, like a frightened hound, and thinking that my turn would come next. At length the house became still, and I forgot for a little while all my sorrows by falling fast asleep.

The next morning my mistress set about instructing me in my tasks. She taught me to do all sorts of house-hold work; to wash and bake, pick cotton and wool, and wash floors, and cook. And she taught me (how can I ever forget it!) more things than these; she caused me to know the exact difference between the smart of the rope, the cart-whip, and the cow-skin, when applied to my naked body by her own cruel hand. And there was scarcely any punishment more dreadful than the blows I received on my face and head from her hard heavy fist. She was a fearful woman, and a savage mistress to her slaves.

There were two little slave boys in the house, on whom she vented her bad temper in a special manner. One of these children was a mulatto, called Cyrus, who had been bought while an infant in his mother's arms; the other, Jack, was an African from the coast of Guinea, whom a sailor had given or sold to my master. Seldom a day passed without these boys receiving the most severe treatment, and often for no fault at all. Both my master and mistress seemed to think that they had a right to ill-use them at their pleasure; and very often accompanied their commands with blows, whether the children were behaving well or ill. I have seen their flesh ragged and raw with licks.—Lick—lick—they were never secure one moment from a blow, and their lives were passed in continual fear. My mistress was not contented with using the whip, but often pinched their cheeks and arms in the most cruel manner. My pity for these poor boys was soon transferred to myself; for I was licked, and flogged, and pinched by her pitiless fingers in the neck and arms, exactly as they were. To strip me naked—to hang me up by the wrists and lay my flesh open with the cow-skin, was an ordinary punishment for even a slight offence. My mistress often robbed me too of the hours that belong to sleep. She used to sit up very late, frequently even until morning; and I had then to stand at a bench and wash during the greater part of the night, or pick wool and cotton and often I have dropped down overcome by sleep and fatigue, till roused from a state of stupor by the whip, and forced to start up to my tasks.

Poor Hetty, my fellow slave, was very kind to me, and I used to call her my Aunt; but she led a most miserable life, and her death was hastened (at least the slaves all believed and said so,) by the dreadful chastisement she received from my master during her pregnancy. It happened as follows. One of the cows had dragged the rope away from the stake to which Hetty had fastened it, and got loose. My master flew into a terrible passion, and ordered the poor creature to be stripped quite naked, notwithstanding her pregnancy, and to be tied up to a tree in the yard. He then flogged her as hard as he could lick, both with the whip and cow-skin, till she was all over streaming with blood. He rested, and then beat her again and again. Her shrieks were terrible. The consequence was that poor Hetty was brought to bed before her time, and was delivered after severe labour of a dead child. She appeared to recover after her confinement, so far that she was repeatedly flogged by both master and mistress afterwards; but her former strength never returned to her. Ere long her body and limbs swelled to a great size; and she lay on a mat in the kitchen, till the water burst out of her body and she died. All the slaves said that death was a good thing for poor Hetty; but I cried very much for her death. The manner of it filled me with horror. I could not bear to think about it; yet it was always present to my mind for many a day.

After Hetty died all her labours fell upon me, in addition to my own. I had now to milk eleven cows every morning before sunrise, sitting among the damp weeds; to take care of the cattle as well as the children; and to do the work of the house. There was no end to my toils—no end to my blows. I lay down at night and rose up in the morning in fear and sorrow; and often wished that like poor Hetty I could escape from this cruel bondage and be at rest in the grave. But the hand of that God whom then I knew not, was stretched over me; and I was mercifully preserved for better things. It was then, however, my heavy lot to weep, weep, weep, and that for years; to pass from one misery to another, and from one cruel master to a worse. But I must go on with the thread of my story. One day a heavy squall of wind and rain came on suddenly, and my mistress sent me round the corner of the house to empty a large earthen jar. The jar was already cracked with an old deep crack that divided it in the middle, and in turning it upside down to empty it, it parted in my hand. I could not help the accident, but I was dreadfully frightened, looking forward to a severe punishment. I ran crying to my mistress, "O mistress, the jar has come in two." "You have broken it, have you?" she replied; "come directly here to me." I came trembling: she stripped and flogged me long and severely with the cowskin; as long as she had strength to use the lash, for she did not give over till she was quite tired.—When my master came home at night, she told him of my fault; and oh, frightful! how he fell a swearing. After abusing me with every ill name he could think of, (too, too bad to speak in England,) and giving me several heavy blows with his hand, he said, "I shall come home tomorrow morning at twelve, on purpose to give you a round hundred." He kept his word—Oh sad for me! I cannot easily forget it. He tied me up upon a ladder, and gave me a hundred lashes with his own hand, and master Benjy stood by to count them for him. When he had licked me for some time he sat down to take breath; then after resting, he beat me again and again, until he was quite wearied, and so hot (for the weather was very sultry), that he sank back in his chair, almost like to faint. While my mistress went to bring him drink, there was a dreadful earthquake. Part of the roof fell down, and every thing in the house went—clatter, clatter, clatter. Oh I thought the end of all things near at hand;

and I was so sore with the flogging, that I scarcely cared whether I lived or died. The earth was groaning and shaking; every thing tumbling about; and my mistress and the slaves were shrieking and crying out, "The earthquake! the earthquake!" It was an awful day for us all.

During the confusion I crawled away on my hands and knees, and laid myself down under the steps of the piazza, in front of the house. I was in a dreadful state—my body all blood and bruises, and I could not help moaning piteously. The other slaves, when they saw me, shook their heads and said, "Poor child! poor child"—I lay there till the morning, careless of what might happen, for life was very weak in me, and I wished more than ever to die. But when we are very young, death always seems a great way off, and it would not come that night to me. The next morning I was forced by my master to rise and go about my usual work, though my body and limbs were so stiff and sore, that I could not move without the greatest pain.—Nevertheless, even after all this severe punishment, I never heard the last of that jar; my mistress was always throwing it in my face.

Some little time after this, one of the cows got loose from the stake, and eat one of the sweet-potato slips. I was milking when my master found it out. He came to me, and without any more ado, stooped down, and taking off his heavy boot, he struck me such a severe blow in the small of my back, that I shrieked with agony, and thought I was killed; and I feel a weakness in that part to this day. The cow was frightened by his violence, and kicked down the pail and spilt the milk all about. My master knew that this accident was his own fault, but he was so enraged that he seemed glad of an excuse to go on with his ill usage. I cannot remember how many licks he gave me then, but he beat me till I was unable to stand, and till he himself was weary.

After this I ran away and went to my mother, who was living with Mr. Richard Darrel. My poor mother was both grieved and glad to see me; grieved because I had been so ill used, and glad because she had not seen me for a long, long while. She dared not receive me into the house, but she hid me up in a hole in the rocks near,

and brought me food at night, after every body was asleep. My father, who lived at Crow-Lane, over the salt-water channel, at last heard of my being hid up in the cavern, and he came and took me back to my master. Oh I was loath, loath to go back; but as there was no remedy, I was obliged to submit.

When we got home, my poor father said to Capt. I—, "Sir, I am sorry that my child should be forced to run away from her owner; but the treatment she has received is enough to break her heart. The sight of her wounds has nearly broke mine.—I entreat you, for the love of God, to forgive her for running away, and that you will be a kind master to her in future." Capt. I— said I was used as well as I deserved, and that I ought to be punished for running away. I then took courage and said that I could stand the floggings no longer; that I was weary of my life, and therefore I had run away to my mother; but mothers could only weep and mourn over their children, they could not save them from cruel masters—from the whip, the rope, and the cow-skin. He told me to hold my tongue and go about my work, or he would find a way to settle me. He did not, however, flog me that day.

For five years after this I remained in his house, and almost daily received the same harsh treatment. At length he put me on board a sloop, and to my great joy sent me away to Turk's Island.[1] I was not permitted to see my mother or father, or poor sisters and brothers, to say good bye, though going away to a strange land, and might never see them again. Oh the Buckra[2] people who keep slaves think that black people are like cattle, without natural affection. But my heart tells me it is far otherwise.

We were nearly four weeks on the voyage, which was unusually long. Sometimes we had a light breeze, sometimes a great calm, and the ship made no way; so that our provisions and water ran very low, and we were put upon short allowance. I should almost have been starved had it not been for the kindness of a black man

---

[1] *sloop* Small ship; *Turk's Island* The southernmost and eastern-most island of the Bahamas.

[2] *Buckra* White.

called Anthony, and his wife, who had brought their own victuals, and shared them with me.

When we went ashore at the Grand Quay, the captain sent me to the house of my new master, Mr. D—, to whom Captain I— had sold me. Grand Quay is a small town upon a sandbank; the houses low and built of wood. Such was my new master's. The first person I saw, on my arrival, was Mr. D—, a stout sulky looking man, who carried me through the hall to show me to his wife and children. Next day I was put up by the vendue master to know how much I was worth, and I was valued at one hundred pounds currency.

My new master was one of the owners or holders of the salt ponds, and he received a certain sum for every slave that worked upon his premises, whether they were young or old. This sum was allowed him out of the profits arising from the salt works. I was immediately sent to work in the salt water with the rest of the slaves. This work was perfectly new to me. I was given a half barrel and a shovel, and had to stand up to my knees in the water, from four o'clock in the morning till nine, when we were given some Indian corn boiled in water, which we were obliged to swallow as fast as we could for fear the rain should come on and melt the salt. We were then called again to our tasks, and worked through the heat of the day; the sun flaming upon our heads like fire, and raising salt blisters in those parts which were not completely covered. Our feet and legs, from standing in the salt water for so many hours, soon became full of dreadful boils, which eat down in some cases to the very bone, afflicting the sufferers with great torment. We came home at twelve; ate our corn soup, called *blawly*, as fast as we could, and went back to our employment till dark at night. We then shovelled up the salt in large heaps, and went down to the sea, where we washed the pickle from our limbs, and cleaned the barrows and shovels from the salt. When we returned to the house, our master gave us each our allowance of raw Indian corn, which we pounded in a mortar and boiled in water for our suppers. We slept in a long shed, divided into narrow slips, like the stalls used for cattle. Boards fixed upon stakes driven into the ground, without mat or covering, were our only beds. On Sundays, after we had

washed the salt bags, and done other work required of us, we went into the bush and cut the long soft grass, of which we made trusses for our legs and feet to rest upon, for they were so full of the salt boils that we could get no rest lying upon the bare boards.

Though we worked from morning till night, there was no satisfying Mr. D—. I hoped, when I left Capt. I—, that I should have been better off, but I found it was but going from one butcher to another. There was this difference between them: my former master used to beat me while raging and foaming with passion; Mr. D— was usually quite calm. He would stand by and give orders for a slave to be cruelly whipped, and assist in the punishment, without moving a muscle of his face; walking about and taking snuff with the greatest composure. Nothing could touch his hard heart—neither sighs, nor tears, nor prayers, nor streaming blood; he was deaf to our cries, and careless of our sufferings.— Mr. D— has often stripped me naked, hung me up by the wrists, and beat me with the cow-skin, with his own hand, till my body was raw with gashes. Yet there was nothing very remarkable in this; for it might serve as a sample of the common usage of the slaves on that horrible island.

Owing to the boils in my feet, I was unable to wheel the barrow fast through the sand, which got into the sores, and made me stumble at every step; and my master, having no pity for my sufferings from this cause, rendered them far more intolerable, by chastising me for not being able to move so fast as he wished me. Another of our employments was to row a little way off from the shore in a boat, and dive for large stones to build a wall round our master's house. This was very hard work; and the great waves breaking over us continually, made us often so giddy that we lost our footing, and were in danger of being drowned.

Ah, poor me!—my tasks were never ended. Sick or well, it was work—work—work!—After the diving season was over, we were sent to the South Creek, with large bills, to cut up mangoes to burn lime with. Whilst one party of slaves were thus employed, another were sent to the other side of the island to break up coral out of the sea.

When we were ill, let our complaint be what it might, the only medicine given to us was a great bowl of hot salt water, with salt mixed with it, which made us very sick. If we could not keep up with the rest of the gang of slaves, we were put in the stocks,[1] and severely flogged the next morning. Yet, not the less, our master expected, after we had thus been kept from our rest, and our limbs rendered stiff and sore with ill usage, that we should still go through the ordinary tasks of the day all the same.—Sometimes we had to work all night, measuring salt to load a vessel; or turning a machine to draw water out of the sea for the salt-making. Then we had no sleep—no rest—but were forced to work as fast as we could, and go on again all next day the same as usual. Work—work—work—Oh that Turk's Island was a horrible place! The people in England, I am sure, have never found out what is carried on there. Cruel, horrible place!

Mr. D— had a slave called old Daniel, whom he used to treat in the most cruel manner. Poor Daniel was lame in the hip, and could not keep up with the rest of the slaves; and our master would order him to be stripped and laid down on the ground, and have him beaten with a rod of rough briar till his skin was quite red and raw. He would then call for a bucket of salt, and fling upon the raw flesh till the man writhed on the ground like a worm, and screamed aloud with agony. This poor man's wounds were never healed, and I have often seen them full of maggots, which increased his torments to an intolerable degree. He was an object of pity and terror to the whole gang of slaves, and in his wretched case we saw, each of us, our own lot, if we should live to be as old.

Oh the horrors of slavery!—How the thought of it pains my heart! But the truth ought to be told of it; and what my eyes have seen I think it is my duty to relate; for few people in England know what slavery is. I have been a slave—I have felt what a slave feels, and I know what a slave knows; and I would have all the good people in England to know it too, that they may break our chains, and set us free.

Mr. D— had another slave called Ben. He being very hungry, stole a little rice one night after he came in from work, and cooked it for his supper. But his master soon discovered the theft; locked him up all night; and kept him without food till one o'clock the next day. He then hung Ben up by his hands, and beat him from time to time till the slaves came in at night. We found the poor creature hung up when we came home; with a pool of blood beneath him, and our master still licking him, but this was not the worst. My master's son was in the habit of stealing the rice and rum. Ben had seen him do this, and thought he might do the same, and when master found out that Ben had stolen the rice and swore to punish him, he tried to excuse himself by saying that Master Dickey did the same thing every night. The lad denied it to his father, and was so angry with Ben for informing against him, that out of revenge he ran and got a bayonet, and whilst the poor wretch was suspended by his hands and writhing under his wounds, he run it quite through his foot. I was not by when he did it, but I saw the wound when I came home, and heard Ben tell the manner in which it was done.

I must say something more about this cruel son of a cruel father.—He had no heart—no fear of God; he had been brought up by a bad father in a bad path, and he delighted to follow in the same steps. There was a little old woman among the slaves called Sarah, who was nearly past work; and, Master Dickey being the overseer of the slaves just then, this poor creature, who was subject to several bodily infirmities, and was not quite right in her head, did not wheel the barrow fast enough to please him. He threw her down on the ground, and after beating her severely, he took her up in his arms and flung her among the prickly-pear[2] bushes, which are all covered over with sharp venomous prickles. By this her naked flesh was so grievously wounded, that her body swelled and festered all over, and she died in a few days after. In telling my own sorrows, I cannot pass by those of my fellow-slaves—for when I think of my own griefs, I remember theirs.

---

[1] *stocks*   Device for confining the ankles and sometimes the wrists.

[2] *prickly-pear*   Type of cactus.

I think it was about ten years I had worked in the salt ponds at Turk's Island, when my master left off business, and retired to a house he had in Bermuda, leaving his son to succeed him in the island. He took me with him to wait upon his daughters; and I was joyful, for I was sick, sick of Turk's Island, and my heart yearned to see my native place again, my mother, and my kindred.

I had seen my poor mother during the time I was a slave in Turk's Island. One Sunday morning I was on the beach with some of the slaves, and we saw a sloop come in loaded with slaves to work in the salt water. We got a boat and went aboard. When I came upon the deck I asked the black people, "Is there any one here for me?" "Yes," they said, "your mother." I thought they said this in jest—I could scarcely believe them for joy; but when I saw my poor mammy my joy was turned to sorrow, for she had gone from her senses. "Mammy," I said, "is this you!" She did not know me. "Mammy," I said, "what's the matter?" She began to talk foolishly and said that she had been under the vessel's bottom. They had been overtaken by a violent storm at sea. My poor mother had never been on the sea before, and she was so ill, that she lost her senses, and it was long before she came quite to herself again. She had a sweet child with her—a little sister I had never seen, about four years of age, called Rebecca. I took her on shore with me, for I felt I should love her directly; and I kept her with me a week. Poor little thing! her's has been a sad life, and continues so to this day. My mother worked for some years on the island, but was taken back to Bermuda some time before my master carried me again thither.

After I left Turk's Island, I was told by some negroes that came over from it, that the poor slaves had built up a place with boughs and leaves, where they might meet for prayers, but the white people pulled it down twice, and would not allow them even a shed for prayers. A flood came down soon after and washed away many houses, filled the place with sand, and overflowed the ponds: and I do think that this was for their wickedness; for the Buckra men there were very wicked. I saw and heard much that was very very bad at that place.

I was several years the slave of Mr. D— after I returned to my native place. Here I worked in the grounds. My work was planting and hoeing sweet-potatoes, Indian corn, plaintains, bananas, cabbages, pumpkins, onions, &c. I did all the household work, and attended upon a horse and cow besides,—going also upon all errands. I had to curry the horse—to clean and feed him—and sometimes to ride him a little. I had more than enough to do—but still it was not so very bad as Turk's Island.

My old master often got drunk, and then he would get in a fury with his daughter, and beat her till she was not fit to be seen. I remember on one occasion, I had gone to fetch water, and when I was coming up the hill I heard a great screaming; I ran as fast as I could to the house, put down the water, and went into the chamber, where I found my master beating Miss D— dreadfully. I strove with all my strength to get her away from him; for she was all black and blue with bruises. He had beat her with his fist, and almost killed her. The people gave me credit for getting her away. He turned round and began to lick me. Then I said, "Sir, this is not Turk's Island." I can't repeat his answer, the words were too wicked—too bad to say. He wanted to treat me the same in Bermuda as he had done in Turk's Island.

He had an ugly fashion of stripping himself quite naked and ordering me then to wash him in a tub of water. This was worse to me than all the licks. Sometimes when he called me to wash him I would not come, my eyes were so full of shame. He would then come to beat me. One time I had plates and knives in my hand, and I dropped both plates and knives, and some of the plates were broken. He struck me so severely for this, that at last I defended myself, for I thought it was high time to do so. I then told him I would not live longer with him, for he was a very indecent man—very spiteful, and too indecent; with no shame for his servants, no shame for his own flesh. So I went away to a neighbouring house and sat down and cried till the next morning, when I went home again, not knowing what else to do.

After that I was hired to work at Cedar Hills, and every Saturday night I paid the money to my master. I had plenty of work to do there—plenty of washing; but yet I made myself pretty comfortable. I earned two dollars and a quarter a week, which is twenty pence a day.

During the time I worked there, I heard that Mr. John Wood was going to Antigua. I felt a great wish to go there, and I went to Mr. D—, and asked him to let me go in Mr. Wood's service. Mr. Wood did not then want to purchase me; it was my own fault that I came under him, I was so anxious to go. It was ordained to be, I suppose; God led me there. The truth is, I did not wish to be any longer the slave of my indecent master.

Mr. Wood took me with him to Antigua, to the town of St. John's, where he lived. This was about fifteen years ago. He did not then know whether I was to be sold; but Mrs. Wood found that I could work, and she wanted to buy me. Her husband then wrote to my master to inquire whether I was to be sold? Mr. D— wrote in reply, "that I should not be sold to any one that would treat me ill." It was strange he should say this, when he had treated me so ill himself. So I was purchased by Mr. Wood for 300 dollars (or £100 Bermuda currency).

My work there was to attend the chambers and nurse the child, and to go down to the pond and wash clothes. But I soon fell ill of the rheumatism, and grew so very lame that I was forced to walk with a stick. I got the Saint Anthony's fire,[1] also, in my left leg, and became quite a cripple. No one cared much to come near me, and I was ill a long long time; for several months I could not lift the limb. I had to lie in a little old out-house, that was swarming with bugs and other vermin, which tormented me greatly; but I had no other place to lie in. I got the rheumatism by catching cold at the pond side, from washing in the fresh water; in the salt water I never got cold. The person who lived in next yard, (a Mrs. Greene,) could not bear to hear my cries and groans. She was kind, and used to send an old slave woman to help me, who sometimes brought me a little soup. When the doctor found I was so ill, he said I must be put into a bath of hot water. The old slave got the bark of some bush that was good for pains, which she boiled in the hot water, and every night she came and put me into the bath, and did what she could for me; I

don't know what I should have done, or what would have become of me, had it not been for her.—My mistress, it is true, did send me a little food; but no one from our family came near me but the cook, who used to shove my food in at the door, and say, "Molly, Molly, there's your dinner." My mistress did not care to take any trouble about me; and if the Lord had not put it into the hearts of the neighbours to be kind to me, I must, I really think, have lain and died.

It was a long time before I got well enough to work in the house. Mrs. Wood, in the meanwhile, hired a mulatto woman to nurse the child; but she was such a fine lady she wanted to be mistress over me. I thought it very hard for a coloured woman to have rule over me because I was a slave and she was free. Her name was Martha Wilcox; she was a saucy woman, very saucy; and she went and complained of me, without cause, to my mistress, and made her angry with me. Mrs. Wood told me that if I did not mind what I was about, she would get my master to strip me and give me fifty lashes: "You have been used to the whip," she said, "and you shall have it here." This was the first time she threatened to have me flogged; and she gave me the threatening so strong of what she would have done to me, that I thought I should have fallen down at her feet, I was so vexed and hurt by her words. The mulatto woman was rejoiced to have power to keep me down. She was constantly making mischief; there was no living for the slaves—no peace after she came.

I was also sent by Mrs. Wood to be put in the Cage one night, and was next morning flogged, by the magistrate's order, at her desire; and this all for a quarrel I had about a pig with another slave woman. I was flogged on my naked back on this occasion; although I was in no fault after all; for old Justice Dyett, when we came before him, said that I was in the right, and ordered the pig to be given to me. This was about two or three years after I came to Antigua.

When we moved from the middle of the town to the Point, I used to be in the house and do all the work and mind the children, though still very ill with the rheumatism. Every week I had to wash two large bundles of clothes, as much as a boy could help me to lift; but I

---

[1] *Saint Anthony's fire* Erysipelas or ergotism, diseases that cause intense redness, swelling of the skin, and severe pain.

could give no satisfaction. My mistress was always abusing and fretting after me. It is not possible to tell all her ill language.—One day she followed me foot after foot scolding and rating me. I bore in silence a great deal of ill words: at last my heart was quite full, and I told her that she ought not to use me so;—that when I was ill I might have lain and died for what she cared; and no one would then come near me to nurse me, because they were afraid of my mistress. This was a great affront. She called her husband and told him what I had said. He flew into a passion: but did not beat me then; he only abused and swore at me; and then gave me a note and bade me go and look for an owner. Not that he meant to sell me; but he did this to please his wife and to frighten me. I went to Adam White, a cooper,[1] a free black who had money, and asked him to buy me. He went directly to Mr. Wood, but was informed that I was not to be sold. The next day my master whipped me.

Another time (about five years ago) my mistress got vexed with me because I fell sick and I could not keep on with my work. She complained to her husband, and he sent me off again to look for an owner. I went to a Mr. Burchell, showed him the note, and asked him to buy me for my own benefit; for I had saved about 100 dollars, and hoped with a little help, to purchase my freedom. He accordingly went to my master: "Mr. Wood," he said, "Molly has brought me a note that she wants an owner. If you intend to sell her, I may as well buy her as another." My master put him off and said that he did not mean to sell me. I was very sorry at this, for I had no comfort with Mrs. Wood, and I wished greatly to get my freedom.

The way in which I made my money was this.— When my master and mistress went from home, as they sometimes did, and left me to take care of the house and premises, I had a good deal of time to myself and made the most of it. I took in washing, and sold coffee and yams and other provisions to the captains of ships. I did not sit still idling during the absence of my owners; for I wanted, by all honest means, to earn money to buy my freedom. Sometimes I bought a hog cheap on board

ship, and sold it for double the money on shore; and I also earned a good deal by selling coffee. By this means I by degrees acquired a little cash. A gentleman also lent me some to help to buy my freedom—but when I could not get free he got it back again. His name was Captain Abbot.

My master and mistress went on one occasion into the country, to Date Hill, for a change of air, and carried me with them to take charge of the children, and to do the work of the house. While I was in the country, I saw how the field negroes are worked in Antigua. They are worked very hard and fed but scantily. They are called out to work before daybreak, and come home after dark; and then each has to heave his bundle of grass for the cattle in the pen. Then, on Sunday morning, each slave has to go out and gather a large bundle of grass; and, when they bring it home, they have all to sit at the manager's door and wait till he comes out: often have they to wait there till past eleven o'clock without any breakfast. After that, those that have yams or potatoes, or fire-wood to sell, hasten to market to buy a dog's[2] worth of salt fish, or pork, which is a great treat for them. Some of them buy a little pickle out of the shad barrels, which they call sauce, to season their yams and Indian corn. It is very wrong, I know, to work on Sunday or go to market; but will not God call the Buckra men to answer for this on the great day of judgment—since they will give the slaves no other day?

While we were at Date Hill Christmas came; and the slave woman who had the care of the place (which then belonged to Mr. Roberts the marshal), asked me to go with her to her husband's house, to a Methodist meeting for prayer, at a plantation called Winthorps. I went; and they were the first prayers I ever understood. One woman prayed; and then they all sung a hymn; then there was another prayer and another hymn; and then they all spoke by turns of their own griefs as sinners. The husband of the woman I went with was a black driver. His name was Henry. He confessed that he had treated the slaves very cruelly; but said that he was compelled to obey the orders of his master. He prayed

---

[1] *cooper* Barrel- and tub-maker.

[2] *dog* Coin of low value.

them all to forgive him, and he prayed that God would forgive him. He said it was a horrid thing for a ranger to have sometimes to beat his own wife or sister; but he must do so if ordered by his master.

I felt sorry for my sins also. I cried the whole night, but I was too much ashamed to speak. I prayed God to forgive me. This meeting had a great impression on my mind, and led my spirit to the Moravian church; so that when I got back to town, I went and prayed to have my name put down in the Missionaries' book; and I followed the church earnestly every opportunity. I did not then tell my mistress about it; for I knew that she would not give me leave to go. But I felt I *must* go. Whenever I carried the children their lunch at school, I ran round and went to hear the teachers.

The Moravian ladies (Mrs. Richter, Mrs. Olufsen, and Mrs. Sauter) taught me to read in the class; and I got on very fast. In this class there were all sorts of people, old and young, grey headed folks and children; but most of them were free people. After we had done spelling, we tried to read in the Bible. After the reading was over, the missionary gave out a hymn for us to sing. I dearly loved to go to the church, it was so solemn. I never knew rightly that I had much sin till I went there. When I found out that I was a great sinner, I was very sorely grieved, and very much frightened. I used to pray God to pardon my sins for Christ's sake, and forgive me for every thing I had done amiss; and when I went home to my work, I always thought about what I had heard from the missionaries, and wished to be good that I might go to heaven. After a while I was admitted a candidate for the holy Communion.—I had been baptized long before this, in August 1817, by the Rev. Mr. Curtin, of the English Church, after I had been taught to repeat the Creed and the Lord's Prayer. I wished at that time to attend a Sunday School taught by Mr. Curtin, but he would not receive me without a written note from my master, granting his permission. I did not ask my owner's permission, from the belief that it would be refused; so that I got no farther instruction at that time from the English Church.

Some time after I began to attend the Moravian Church, I met with Daniel James, afterwards my dear husband. He was a carpenter and cooper to his trade; an honest, hard-working, decent black man, and a widower. He had purchased his freedom of his mistress, old Mrs. Baker, with money he had earned whilst a slave. When he asked me to marry him, I took time to consider the matter over with myself, and would not say yes till he went to church with me and joined the Moravians. He was very industrious after he bought his freedom; and he had hired a comfortable house, and had convenient things about him. We were joined in marriage, about Christmas 1826, in the Moravian Chapel at Spring Gardens, by the Rev. Mr. Olufsen. We could not be married in the English Church. English marriage is not allowed to slaves; and no free man can marry a slave woman.

When Mr. Wood heard of my marriage, he flew into a great rage, and sent for Daniel, who was helping to build a house for his old mistress. Mr. Wood asked him who gave him a right to marry a slave of his? My husband said, "Sir, I am a free man, and thought I had a right to choose a wife; but if I had known Molly was not allowed to have a husband, I should not have asked her to marry me." Mrs. Wood was more vexed about my marriage than her husband. She could not forgive me for getting married, but stirred up Mr. Wood to flog me dreadfully with his horsewhip. I thought it very hard to be whipped at my time of life for getting a husband—I told her so. She said that she would not have nigger men about the yards and premises, or allow a nigger man's clothes to be washed in the same tub where hers were washed. She was fearful, I think, that I should lose her time, in order to wash and do things for my husband: but I had then no time to wash for myself; I was obliged to put out my own clothes, though I was always at the wash-tub.

I had not much happiness in my marriage, owing to my being a slave. It made my husband sad to see me so ill-treated. Mrs. Wood was always abusing me about him. She did not lick me herself, but she got her husband to do it for her, whilst she fretted the flesh off my bones. Yet for all this she would not sell me. She sold five slaves whilst I was with her; but though she was always finding fault with me, she would not part with me. However, Mr. Wood afterwards allowed Daniel to have a place to live in our yard, which we were very thankful for.

After this, I fell ill again with the rheumatism, and was sick a long time; but whether sick or well, I had my work to do. About this time I asked my master and mistress to let me buy my own freedom. With the help of Mr. Burchell, I could have found the means to pay Mr. Wood; for it was agreed that I should afterwards serve Mr. Burchell a while, for the cash he was to advance for me. I was earnest in the request to my owners; but their hearts were hard—too hard to consent. Mrs. Wood was very angry—she grew quite outrageous—she called me a black devil, and asked me who had put freedom into my head. "To be free is very sweet," I said: but she took good care to keep me a slave. I saw her change colour, and I left the room.

About this time my master and mistress were going to England to put their son in school, and bring their daughters home; and they took me with them to take care of the child. I was willing to come to England: I thought that by going there I should probably get cured of my rheumatism, and should return with my master and mistress, quite well, to my husband. My husband was willing for me to come away, for he had heard that my master would free me,—and I also hoped this might prove true; but it was all a false report.

The steward of the ship was very kind to me. He and my husband were in the same class in the Moravian Church. I was thankful that he was so friendly, for my mistress was not kind to me on the passage; and she told me, when she was angry, that she did not intend to treat me any better in England than in the West Indies—that I need not expect it. And she was as good as her word.

When we drew near to England, the rheumatism seized all my limbs worse than ever, and my body was dreadfully swelled. When we landed at the Tower, I showed my flesh to my mistress, but she took no great notice of it. We were obliged to stop at the tavern till my master got a house; and a day or two after, my mistress sent me down into the wash-house to learn to wash in the English way. In the West Indies we wash with cold water—in England with hot. I told my

mistress I was afraid that putting my hands first into the hot water and then into the cold, would increase the pain in my limbs. The doctor had told my mistress long before I came from the West Indies, that I was a sickly body and the washing did not agree with me. But Mrs. Wood would not release me from the tub, so I was forced to do as I could. I grew worse, and could not stand to wash. I was then forced to sit down with the tub before me, and often through pain and weakness was reduced to kneel or to sit down on the floor, to finish my task. When I complained to my mistress of this, she only got into a passion as usual, and said washing in hot water could not hurt any one;—that I was lazy and insolent, and wanted to be free of my work; but that she would make me do it. I thought her very hard on me, and my heart rose up within me. However I kept still at that time, and went down again to wash the child's things; but the English washer-women who were at work there, when they saw that I was so ill, had pity upon me and washed them for me.

After that, when we came up to live in Leigh Street, Mrs. Wood sorted out five bags of clothes which we had used at sea, and also such as had been worn since we came on shore, for me and the cook to wash. Elizabeth the cook told her, that she did not think that I was able to stand to the tub, and that she had better hire a woman. I also said myself, that I had come over to nurse the child, and that I was sorry I had come from Antigua, since mistress would work me so hard, without compassion for my rheumatism. Mr. and Mrs. Wood, when they heard this, rose up in a passion against me. They opened the door and bade me get out. But I was a stranger, and did not know one door in the street from another, and was unwilling to go away. They made a dreadful uproar, and from that day they constantly kept cursing and abusing me. I was obliged to wash, though I was very ill. Mrs. Wood, indeed once hired a washer-woman, but she was not well treated, and would come no more.

My master quarrelled with me another time, about one of our great washings, his wife having stirred him up to do so. He said he would compel me to do the whole of the washing given out to me, or if I again refused, he would take a short course with me: he would either send me down to the brig in the river, to carry me back to Antigua, or he would turn me at once out of doors, and let me provide for myself. I said I would willingly go back, if he would let me purchase my own freedom. But this enraged him more than all the rest: he cursed and swore at me dreadfully, and said he would never sell my freedom—if I wished to be free, I was free in England, and I might go and try what freedom would do for me, and be d—d. My heart was very sore with this treatment, but I had to go on. I continued to do my work, and did all I could to give satisfaction, but all would not do.

Shortly after, the cook left them, and then matters went on ten times worse. I always washed the child's clothes without being commanded to do it, and any thing else that was wanted in the family; though still I was very sick—very sick indeed. When the great washing came round, which was every two months, my mistress got together again a great many heavy things, such as bed-ticks, bed-coverlets, &c. for me to wash. I told her I was too ill to wash such heavy things that day. She said, she supposed I thought myself a free woman, but I was not; and if I did not do it directly I should be instantly turned out of doors. I stood a long time before I could answer, for I did not know well what to do. I knew that I was free in England, but I did not know where to go, or how to get my living; and therefore, I did not like to leave the house. But Mr. Wood said he would send for a constable to thrust me out; and at last I took courage and resolved that I would not be longer thus treated, but would go and trust to Providence. This was the fourth time they had threatened to turn me out, and, go where I might, I was determined now to take them at their word; though I thought it very hard, after I had lived with them for thirteen years, and worked for them like a horse, to be driven out in this way, like a beggar. My only fault was being sick, and therefore unable to please my mistress, who thought she never could get work enough out of her slaves; and I told them so: but they only abused me and drove me out. This took place from two to three months, I think, after we came to England.

When I came away, I went to the man (one Mash) who used to black the shoes of the family, and asked his wife to get somebody to go with me to Hatton Garden to the Moravian Missionaries: these were the only persons I knew in England. The woman sent a young girl with me to the mission house, and I saw there a gentleman called Mr. Moore. I told him my whole story, and how my owners had treated me, and asked him to take in my trunk with what few clothes I had. The missionaries were very kind to me—they were sorry for my destitute situation, and gave me leave to bring my things to be placed under their care. They were very good people, and they told me to come to the church.

When I went back to Mr. Wood's to get my trunk, I saw a lady, Mrs. Pell, who was on a visit to my mistress. When Mr. and Mrs. Wood heard me come in, they set this lady to stop me, finding that they had gone too far with me. Mrs. Pell came out to me, and said, "Are you really going to leave, Molly? Don't leave, but come into the country with me." I believe she said this because she thought Mrs. Wood would easily get me back again. I replied to her, "Ma'am, this is the fourth time my master and mistress have driven me out, or threatened to drive me—and I will give them no more occasion to bid me go. I was not willing to leave them, for I am a stranger in this country, but now I must go—I can stay no longer to be used." Mrs. Pell then went up stairs to my mistress, and told that I would go, and that she could not stop me. Mrs. Wood was very much hurt and frightened when she found I was determined to go out that day. She said, "If she goes the people will rob her, and then turn her adrift." She did not say this to me, but she spoke it loud enough for me to hear; that it might induce me not to go, I suppose. Mr. Wood also asked me where I was going to. I told him where I had been, and that I should never have gone away had I not been driven out by my owners. He had given me a written paper some time before, which said that I had come with them to England by my own desire; and that was true. It said also that I left them of my own free will, because I was a free woman in England; and that I was idle and would not do my work—

which was not true. I gave this paper afterwards to a gentleman who inquired into my case.

I went into the kitchen and got my clothes out. The nurse and the servant girl were there, and I said to the man who was going to take out my trunk, "Stop, before you take up this trunk, and hear what I have to say before these people. I am going out of this house, as I was ordered; but I have done no wrong at all to my owners, neither here nor in the West Indies. I always worked very hard to please them, both by night and day; but there was no giving satisfaction, for my mistress could never be satisfied with reasonable service. I told my mistress I was sick, and yet she has ordered me out of doors. This is the fourth time; and now I am going out."

And so I came out, and went and carried my trunk to the Moravians. I then returned back to Mash the shoeblack's house, and begged his wife to take me in. I had a little West Indian money in my trunk; and they got it changed for me. This helped to support me for a little while. The man's wife was very kind to me. I was very sick, and she boiled nourishing things up for me. She also sent for a doctor to see me, and sent me medicine, which did me good, though I was ill for a long time with the rheumatic pains. I lived a good many months with these poor people, and they nursed me, and did all that lay in their power to serve me. The man was well acquainted with my situation, as he used to go to and fro to Mr. Wood's house to clean shoes and knives; and he and his wife were sorry for me.

About this time, a woman of the name of Hill told me of the Anti-Slavery Society, and went with me to their office, to inquire if they could do any thing to get me my freedom, and send me back to the West Indies. The gentlemen of the Society took me to a lawyer, who examined very strictly into my case; but told me that the laws of England could do nothing to make me free in Antigua. However they did all they could for me: they gave me a little money from time to time to keep me from want; and some of them went to Mr. Wood to try to persuade him to let me return a free woman to my husband; but though they offered him, as I have heard, a large sum for my freedom, he was sulky and obstinate, and would not consent to let me go free.

This was the first winter I spent in England, and I suffered much from the severe cold, and from the rheumatic pains, which still at times torment me. However, Providence was very good to me, and I got many friends—especially some Quaker ladies, who hearing of my case, came and sought me out, and gave me good warm clothing and money. Thus I had great cause to bless God in my affliction.

When I got better I was anxious to get some work to do, as I was unwilling to eat the bread of idleness. Mrs. Mash, who was a laundress, recommended me to a lady for a charwoman. She paid me very handsomely for what work I did, and I divided the money with Mrs. Mash; for though very poor, they gave me food when my own money was done, and never suffered me to want.

In the spring, I got into service with a lady, who saw me at the house where I sometimes worked as a charwoman. This lady's name was Mrs. Forsyth. She had been in the West Indies, and was accustomed to Blacks, and liked them. I was with her six months, and went with her to Margate. She treated me well, and gave me a good character when she left London.

After Mrs. Forsyth went away, I was again out of place, and went to lodgings, for which I paid two shillings a week, and found coals and candle. After eleven weeks, the money I had saved in service was all gone, and I was forced to go back to the Anti-Slavery office to ask a supply, till I could get another situation. I did not like to go back—I did not like to be idle. I would rather work for my living than get it for nothing. They were very good to give me a supply, but I felt shame at being obliged to apply for relief whilst I had strength to work.

At last I went into the service of Mr. and Mrs. Pringle, where I have been ever since, and am as comfortable as I can be while separated from my dear husband, and away from my own country and all old friends and connections. My dear mistress teaches me daily to read the word of God, and takes great pains to make me understand it. I enjoy the great privilege of being enabled to attend church three times on the Sunday; and I have met with many kind friends since I have been here, both clergymen and others. The Rev.

Mr. Young, who lives in the next house, has shown me much kindness, and taken much pains to instruct me, particularly while my master and mistress were absent in Scotland. Nor must I forget, among my friends, the Rev. Mr. Mortimer, the good clergyman of the parish, under whose ministry I have now sat for upwards of twelve months. I trust in God I have profited by what I have heard from him. He never keeps back the truth, and I think he has been the means of opening my eyes and ears much better to understand the word of God. Mr. Mortimer tells me that he cannot open the eyes of my heart, but that I must pray to God to change my heart, and make me to know the truth, and the truth will make me free.

I still live in the hope that God will find a way to give me my liberty, and give me back to my husband. I endeavour to keep down my fretting, and to leave all to Him, for he knows what is good for me better than I know myself. Yet, I must confess, I find it a hard and heavy task to do so.

I am often much vexed, and I feel great sorrow when I hear some people in this country say, that the slaves do not need better usage, and do not want to be free. They believe the foreign people, who deceive them, and say slaves are happy. I say, Not so. How can slaves be happy when they have the halter round their neck and the whip upon their back? and are disgraced and thought no more of than beasts?—and are separated from their mothers, and husbands, and children, and sisters, just as cattle are sold and separated? Is it happiness for a driver in the field to take down his wife or sister or child, and strip them, and whip them in such a disgraceful manner?—women that have had children exposed in the open field to shame! There is no modesty or decency shown by the owner to his slaves; men, women, and children are exposed alike. Since I have been here I have often wondered how English people can go out into the West Indies and act in such a beastly manner. But when they go to the West Indies, they forget God and all feeling of shame, I think, since they can see and do such

things. They tie up slaves like hogs—moor them up like cattle, and they lick them, so as hogs, or cattle, or horses never were flogged;—and yet they come home and say, and make some good people believe, that slaves don't want to get out of slavery. But they put a cloak about the truth. It is not so. All slaves want to be free—to be free is very sweet. I will say the truth to English people who may read this history that my good friend, Miss S—, is now writing down for me. I have been a slave myself—I know what slaves feel—I can tell by myself what other slaves feel, and by what they have told me. The man that says slaves be quite happy in slavery—that they don't want to be free—that man is either ignorant or a lying person. I never heard a slave say so. I never heard a Buckra man say so, till I heard tell of it in England. Such people ought to be ashamed of themselves. They can't do without slaves they say. What's the reason they can't do without slaves as well as in England? No slaves here—no whips—no stocks—no punishment, except for wicked people. They hire servants in England; and if they don't like them, they send them away: they can't lick them. Let them work ever so hard in England, they are far better off than slaves. If they get a bad master, they give warning and go hire to another. They have their liberty. That's just what *we* want. We don't mind hard work, if we had proper treatment, and proper wages like English servants, and proper time given in the week to keep us from breaking the Sabbath. But they won't give it; they will have work—work—work, night and day, sick or well, till we are quite done up; and we must not speak up nor look amiss, however much we be abused. And then when we are quite done up, who cares for us, more than for a lame horse? This is slavery. I tell it to let English people know the truth; and I hope they will never leave off to pray God, and call loud to the great King of England, till all the poor blacks be given free, and slavery done up for evermore.

—1831

IN CONTEXT

Mary Prince and Slavery

Mary Prince's Petition Presented to Parliament on 24 June 1829

A Petition of Mary Prince or James, commonly called Molly Wood, was presented, and read; setting forth, That the Petitioner was born a Slave in the colony of Bermuda, and is now about forty years of age; That the Petitioner was sold some years go for the sum of 300 dollars to Mr. John Wood, by whom the Petitioner was carried to Antigua, where she has since, until lately resided as a domestic slave on his establishment; that in December 1826, the Petitioner who is connected with the Moravian Congregation, was married in a Moravian Chapel at Spring Gardens, in the parish of Saint John's, by the Moravian minister, Mr. Ellesen, to a free Black of the name of Daniel James, who is a carpenter at Saint John's, in Antigua, and also a member of the same congregation; that the Petitioner and the said Daniel James have lived together ever since as man and wife; that about ten months ago the Petitioner arrived in London, with her master and mistress, in the capacity of nurse to their child; that the Petitioner's master has offered to send her back in his brig to the West Indies, to work in the yard; that the Petitioner expressed her desire to return to the West Indies, but not as a slave, and has entreated her master to sell her, her freedom on account of her services as a nurse to his child, but he has refused, and still does refuse; further stating the particulars of her case; and praying the House to take the same into their consideration, and to grant such relief as to them may, under the circumstances, appear right. Ordered, That the said Petition do lie upon the Table.

from Thomas Pringle, Supplement to *The History of Mary Prince* (1831)

It was through the auspices of Thomas Pringle that Mary Prince's narrative came to be published, and that Prince found employment in London. Pringle contributed a substantial *Supplement* to the *History* when it was first published; excerpts are reproduced below.

By the Original Editor, Thomas Pringle

L eaving Mary's narrative, for the present, without comment to the reader's reflections, I proceed to state some circumstances connected with her case which have fallen more particularly under my own notice, and which I consider it incumbent now to lay fully before the public.

About the latter end of November, 1828, this poor woman found her way to the office of the Anti-Slavery Society in Aldermanbury, by the aid of a person who had become acquainted with her situation, and had advised her to apply there for advice and assistance. After some preliminary examination into the accuracy of the circumstances related by her, I went along with her to Mr. George Stephen, solicitor, and requested him to investigate and draw up a statement of her case, and have it submitted to counsel, in order to ascertain whether or not, under the circumstances, her freedom could be legally established on her return to Antigua. On this occasion, in Mr. Stephen's presence and mine, she expressed, in very strong terms, her anxiety to return thither if she could go as a free person, and, at the same time, her extreme apprehensions of the fate that would probably await her if she returned as a slave. Her words were, "I would rather go into my grave than go back a slave to Antigua, though I wish to go back to my husband very much—very much—very much! I am much afraid my owners would separate me from my husband, and use me very hard, or perhaps sell me for a field negro;—and slavery is too too bad. I would rather go into my grave!"

The paper which Mr. Wood had given her before she left his house, was placed by her in Mr. Stephen's hands. It was expressed in the following terms:—

I have already told Molly, and now give it her in writing, in order that there may be no misunderstanding on her part, that as I brought her from Antigua at her own request and entreaty, and that she is consequently now free, she is of course at liberty to take her baggage and go where she pleases. And, in consequence of her late conduct, she must do one of two things—either quit the house, or return to Antigua by the earliest opportunity, as she does not evince a disposition to make herself useful. As she is a stranger in London, I do not wish to turn her out, or would do so, as two female servants are sufficient for my establishment. If after this she does remain, it will be only during her good behaviour; but on no consideration will I allow her wages or any other remuneration for her services.

JOHN A. WOOD
London, 18 August 1828

This paper, though not devoid of inconsistencies, which will be apparent to any attentive reader, is craftily expressed; and was well devised to serve the purpose which the writer had obviously in view, namely, to frustrate any appeal which the friendless black woman might make to the sympathy of strangers, and thus prevent her from obtaining an asylum, if she left his house, from any respectable family. As she had no one to refer to for a character in this country except himself, he doubtless calculated securely on her being speedily driven back, as soon as the slender fund she had in her possession was expended, to throw herself unconditionally upon his tender mercies; and his disappointment in this expectation appears to have exasperated his feelings of resentment towards the poor woman, to a degree which few persons alive to the claims of common justice, not to speak of Christianity or common humanity, could easily have anticipated. Such, at least, seems the only intelligible inference that can be drawn from his subsequent conduct.

The case having been submitted, by desire of the Anti-Slavery Committee, to the consideration of Dr. Lushington and Mr. Sergeant Stephen, it was found that there existed no legal means of compelling Mary's master to grant her manumission; and that if she returned to Antigua, she would inevitably fall again under his power, or that of his attorneys, as a slave. It was, however, resolved to try what could be effected for her by amicable negotiation; and with this view Mr. Ravenscroft, a solicitor, (Mr. Stephen's relative,) called upon Mr. Wood, in order to ascertain whether he would consent to Mary's manumission on any reasonable terms, and to refer, if required, the amount of compensation for her value to arbitration. Mr. Ravenscroft with some difficulty obtained one or two interviews, but found Mr. Wood so full of animosity against the woman, and so firmly bent against any arrangement having her freedom for its object, that the negotiation was soon broken off as hopeless. The angry slave-owner declared "that he would not move a finger about her in this country, or grant her manumission on any terms whatever; and that if she went back to the West Indies, she must take the consequences."

This unreasonable conduct of Mr. Wood, induced the Anti-Slavery Committee, after several other abortive attempts to effect a compromise, to think of bringing the case under the notice of

Parliament. The heads of Mary's statement were accordingly engrossed in a Petition, which Dr. Lushington offered to present, and to give notice at the same time of his intention to bring in a Bill to provide for the entire emancipation of all slaves brought to England with the owner's consent. But before this step was taken, Dr. Lushington again had recourse to negotiation with the master; and, partly through the friendly intervention of Mr. Manning, partly by personal conference, used every persuasion in his power to induce Mr. Wood to relent and let the bondwoman go free. Seeing the matter thus seriously taken up, Mr. Wood became at length alarmed,—not relishing, it appears, the idea of having the case publicly discussed in the House of Commons; and to avert this result he submitted to temporize—assumed a demeanour of unwonted civility, and even hinted to Mr. Manning (as I was given to understand) that if he was not driven to utter hostility by the threatened exposure, he would probably meet our wishes "in his own time and way." Having gained time by these manoeuvres, he adroitly endeavoured to cool the ardour of Mary's new friends, in her cause, by representing her as an abandoned and worthless woman, ungrateful towards him, and undeserving of sympathy from others; allegations which he supported by the ready affirmation of some of his West India friends, and by one or two plausible letters procured from Antigua. By these and like artifices he appears completely to have imposed on Mr. Manning, the respectable West India merchant whom Dr. Lushington had asked to negotiate with him; and he prevailed so far as to induce Dr. Lushington himself (actuated by the benevolent view of thereby best serving Mary's cause), to abstain from any remarks upon his conduct when the petition was at last presented in Parliament. In this way he dextrously contrived to neutralize all our efforts, until the close of the Session of 1829; soon after which he embarked with his family for the West Indies.

Every exertion for Mary's relief having thus failed; and being fully convinced from a twelve-month's observation of her conduct, that she was really a well-disposed and respectable woman; I engaged her, in December 1829, as a domestic servant in my own family. In this capacity she has remained ever since; and I am thus enabled to speak of her conduct and character with a degree of confidence I could not have otherwise done. …

I may here add a few words respecting the earlier portion of Mary Prince's narrative. The facts there stated must necessarily rest entirely,—since we have no collateral evidence,—upon their intrinsic claims to probability, and upon the reliance the reader may feel disposed, after perusing the foregoing pages, to place on her veracity. To my judgment, the internal evidence of the truth of her narrative appears remarkably strong. The circumstances are related in a tone of natural sincerity, and are accompanied in almost every case with characteristic and minute details, which must, I conceive, carry with them full conviction to every candid mind that this negro woman has actually seen, felt, and suffered all that she so impressively describes; and that the picture she has given of West Indian slavery is not less true than it is revolting.

But there may be some persons into whose hands this tract may fall, so imperfectly acquainted with the real character of Negro Slavery, as to be shocked into partial, if not absolute incredulity, by the acts of inhuman oppression and brutality related of Capt. I— and his wife, and of Mr. D—, the salt manufacturer of Turk's Island. Here, at least, such persons may be disposed to think, there surely must be *some* exaggeration; the facts are too shocking to be credible. The facts are indeed shocking, but unhappily not the less credible on that account. Slavery is a curse to the oppressor scarcely less than to the oppressed: its natural tendency is to brutalize both.

The Narrative of Ashton Warner

The History of Mary Prince was published in January of 1831. The following month Susanna Strickland recorded the narrative of the life of another enslaved person, Ashton Warner, which was published March 1st. No doubt inevitably, there is some similarity in the descriptions of horrific abuse in the two narratives, but there is also a good deal to suggest that Strickland was not being disingenuous in her assertion that she was quite faithful in recording these narratives as they were related to her; certainly there are noticeable differences between the narrative style of Warner and that of Prince. (Strickland's note inviting readers to "see and converse with themselves" if they doubt that someone of Warner's background would be able to express himself so well is particularly interesting in this connection.)

Advertisement

In consequence of the unexpected decease of Ashton Warner, while this little volume was in the press, the profits that may arise from its sale will no longer be required, as was originally designed, for his personal benefit. But, in compliance with a wish expressed by the poor negro on his death-bed, it is now proposed to appropriate the proceeds to the benefit of his aged mother, and the enfranchisement (should the amount prove so considerable) of his enslaved wife and child. And I have the satisfaction of being authorized to add, for the information of benevolent individuals disposed to contribute liberally towards the objects now intimated—whether by the purchase of copies of this volume, or by pecuniary donations—that the little charitable fund thus contemplated, will be placed under the immediate management of George Stephen, Esq., Solicitor, 17, King's Arms Yard, Coleman Street, and Thomas Pringle, Esq., Secretary of the Anti-Slavery Society, 18, Aldermanbury, who have kindly undertaken to superintend its proper application.

S. STRICKLAND.

from Introduction

In writing Ashton's narrative, I have adhered strictly to the simple facts, adopting, wherever it could conveniently be done, his own language, which, for a person in his condition, is remarkably expressive and appropriate. Had I been inclined to give a recital of revolting cruelty, I should have chosen another case; and for such, unhappily, I had not far to seek. But those who wish to read such mournful narratives of human depravity will find enough for their information (far too many for the honour of human nature!) recorded in the publications of the Anti-Slavery Society.

The profits arising from the sale of this tract will be appropriated to the benefit of Ashton, who has been for the last three months in England, endeavouring to establish his claims to freedom; and who is at present suffering under severe illness, without any adequate means of subsistence.

With a view to render this Sketch of Colonial Slavery more complete, and to enable the reader to compare the details given by Ashton with those recorded by intelligent and conscientious eye-witnesses from England, I have subjoined, as an Appendix, the very important testimonies on this subject of three highly respectable clergymen of the established Church, and of an excellent Wesleyan Missionary—testimonies as yet but partially known to the public, and which comprise a mass of information equally recent and interesting.

Should this little tract assist, however feebly, in the diffusion of correct information in regard to the general condition and the feelings of the slaves, and thus tend to promote the great and good cause of justice and mercy, the writer's object will be fully accomplished. Like the widow's mite cast into the sacred treasury,[1] those who love the truth will not deem it unworthy because its value is but humble.

London, 19 February 1831

S.S.

NEGRO SLAVERY

DESCRIBED

BY A NEGRO[1]

BEING

THE NARRATIVE OF ASHTON WARNER,

A NATIVE OF ST. VINCENT'S.

With an Appendix,

CONTAINING THE

TESTIMONY OF FOUR CHRISTIAN MINISTERS,

RECENTLY RETURNED FROM THE COLONIES,

ON THE SYSTEM OF SLAVERY AS IT NOW EXISTS.

BY

S. STRICKLAND.

"And tears and toil have been my lot
Since I the white man's thrall became;
And sorer griefs I wish forgot—
Harsh blows and burning shame!
Oh, Englishman! thou ne'er canst know
The injured bondman's bitter woe,
When round his heart, like scorpions, cling
Black thoughts that madden while they sting!"

LONDON:

SAMUEL MAUNDER, NEWGATE STREET.

1831.

from The Narrative of Ashton Warner (1831)

I was born in the Island of St. Vincent's, and baptized by the name of Ashton Warner, in the parish church, by the Rev. Mr. Gildon. My father and mother, at the time of my birth, were slaves on Cane Grove estate, in Bucumar Valley, then the property of Mr. Ottley. I was an infant at the breast when Mr. Ottley died; and shortly after the estate was put to sale, that the property might be divided among his family. Before Cane Grove was sold, my aunt, Daphne Crosbie, took the opportunity of buying my mother and me of Mr. Ottley's trustees. My aunt had been a slave, but a favoured one. She had money left her by a coloured gentleman of the name of Crosbie, with whom she lived, and whose name she took. After his death she went to reside at Kingston. Finding it a good thing to be free, aunt Daphne wished to make all her friends free also, particularly the slaves on the estate where she was born, and with whom she had shared, in her early days, all the sorrows of negro servitude. She had a large heart, and felt great kindness for her own people; but her means were not equal to her

---

[1] *widow's ... treasury* See Luke 21.1–4.

good wishes. She bought her old parents of Mr. Jackson, Mr. Ottley's executor; and, as it was her earnest desire to make us all happy, she would have bought my uncle John Baptiste (my mother's brother) too; but Mr. Wilson, the gentleman who purchased the estate, would not sell him. His reason for refusing my aunt never knew, for my uncle was an old man then, and nearly past work. Mr. Wilson sent him away to the Island of St. Lucia, and it was some years before aunt Daphne heard any tidings of him. At last some persons, coming from St. Lucia to St. Vincent's, told her that he lay very sick on Mr. Grant's estate. My aunt was glad to find that he was still living, and she went herself to make him free. She had never crossed the water, or been on the great sea, but she overcame her fears, and hired a small boat, and went directly to St. Lucia. She found my poor uncle in a very miserable state, and in this condition she bought him of his master, and brought him back to St. Vincent's. He was ill a long, long time; it was many long weary months before he could even take up a broom to sweep the house. He was very grateful to aunt Daphne for all that she had done for him; and so were we all. She was a very good, kind woman, and a Christian, though a black woman; and we (her relations) all loved her very, very much. We had no one else to love—she was all the world to us.

Whilst I lived with my aunt at Kingston I was very happy. I had no heavy tasks to do; and she was as careful over me as if she had been my own mother, and used to keep me with her in the house, that I might not be playing about in the streets with bad companions. My mother made sausages and *souse,*[1] and I used to help her to carry them to gentlemen's houses for sale. This was light labour to her, for she had been a field slave, kept at hard work, and driven to it by the whip. I am sure our best days were spent with my dear aunt; nor did she make us alone happy; all the money she could save went to purchase the freedom of slaves who had formerly been her companions in bondage at Cane Grove, or to make their condition better. There was not a person upon the island who did not speak well of Daphne Crosbie; black or white it was all the same. She bore a good character until the day she died.

I lived with my aunt till I was ten years old, when I was claimed as a slave belonging to the Cane Grove estate, by Mr. Wilson. This was a hard and unjust claim; but Mr. Wilson said, that though my mother was sold I was not—that the best slaves had been sold off the estate—that I was *his* property, and he would claim me wherever I was to be found. Now, he was wrong in all this, and I can prove to you, in two short minutes, that I did not belong to him. When my aunt manumitted my mother and me, Mr. Wilson had not-yet bought the estate; and in the Island of St. Vincent's it has always been a customary rule that the young child at the breast is sold as one with its mother, and does not become separate property till it is five or six years old; so that Mr. Wilson's claim was very unjust and oppressive.[2]

When my aunt found Mr. Wilson bent on taking me away by force, she went to Mr. Jackson, the gentleman from whom she had purchased my mother, and told him the state of the case, and he gave her a written paper to take to the Chief Justice of the island, to prove that I belonged to Daphne Crosbie, should Mr. Wilson continue to claim me. My aunt went to the Governor and showed him this paper, and also the manumission paper she had received from Mr. Jackson. The Governor, after looking at it, said that Mr. Wilson had no legal right to claim me upon the estate, and he promised my aunt that he would write to him to that effect. But we never knew whether he did or not, for we never got an answer from him. It is of no use trusting to what the white people in the West Indies say; they always forget their promises to slaves. Before this happened, my aunt had bound me apprentice

---

[1] [Strickland's note] Slices of pig's head, salted and prepared in a particular manner, and sold in the markets by the slaves.

[2] [Strickland's note] This is poor Ashton's own statement. Whether the Colonial *Slave Law* will support his claim for freedom on this ground, is a question which remains to be determined.—S.S.

to a cooper, to learn his trade. I was bound for seven years, and had signed the indenture myself, as a free black, by making a cross for my name.

My master's name was Pierre Wynn. He was a kind good master, and I never ceased to lament the cause which parted me from him. I had been with him between two and three months, and was busy one morning at work in the cooper's yard, helping the journeyman to truss a molasses-cask, when Mr. Wilson's manager, Mr. Donald, with two coloured men, and a white named Newman, came into the yard. This man, Newman, had informed Mr. Wilson where I was, and he sent his people to take me away by force. When the manager came into the yard, he said, "Which is Ashton?" I answered, quite innocently, not suspecting any mischief, "I am Ashton." Directly I said so the manager caught hold of me by the back of my neck. I did not know why he held me. I did not know what to think—I could not get my breath to speak—I was dreadfully frightened, and trembled all over. The other men got hold of me, and held me fast. They then led me away to Mr. Dalzell, Mr. Wilson's attorney, and shut me up in his office till Mr. Wilson came. Mr. Dalzell was afraid that I would try to make my escape, and to make sure of me one man kept watch at the window and another at the door. When Mr. Wilson came in he did not know me, and asked who I was. One of the men told him that I was Ashton. He said, "Very well; keep him here till I am ready to send him down to the estate." He then came up to the place where I was standing, and examined me from head to foot; then turned to Mr. Dalzell, and began talking to him about me. I was too young, and too much frightened at being stolen away, to remember much of their discourse; but I am very sure that I shall never forget that day.

Before Mr. Wilson left the office, my mother and Daphne Crosbie came to hear what was to be done with me, and why I had been taken away. But all they said was of no use; they could do no good where there was no justice to be had. Mr. Wilson insisted that I was a slave, and *his* slave, and he would have it so, in spite of my mother's tears and my aunt's entreaties. My poor mother was greatly distressed, and cried very bitterly. She entreated Mr. Wilson, if he thought he had a just claim for me, to put me in gaol till the question as to my freedom could be fairly settled; but he refused to do this, and when she continued her entreaties he grew angry, and ordered her not to stop in the yard, but to go away directly. And she and aunt Crosbie, on finding that nothing could be done for me there, were obliged to leave me in his hands.

The manager then put me into a boat, and took me down to the estate. It was rather late in the afternoon when we got there. I had nothing given me to do that day. It was Saturday, and I was not set to work till the Monday morning. I was very sad, and wished very much to run away. I could not bear the thought of being a slave, and I was very restless and unhappy.

On the Monday morning, John, the head cooper, took me down to the sugar works to help him; but I had no heart to work—I did nothing but think how I might run away. I was not knowing enough, however, to make my escape; and, after consulting with myself a long time, I found it would be the best plan to make myself as patient as I could. But still I was always thinking of my mother and aunt, and of Pierre Wynn, and the home I had been taken from. The estate of Cane Grove was in the middle of a deep valley, near the sea shore. Mr. Wilson's house stood upon the brow of the hill, and overlooked the whole sugar plantation. He had about three hundred slaves, and was considered one of the severest masters in the whole island.

As I have spoken of the condition of the field negroes as being so much worse than that of the mechanics among whom I was ranked on the estate, I shall here endeavour to describe the manner in which the field gang were worked on Cane Grove estate. They were obliged to be in the field before five o'clock in the morning; and, as the negro houses were at the distance of from three to four miles from the cane pieces, they were generally obliged to rise as early as four o'clock, to be at their work in time. The driver is first in the field, and calls the slaves together by cracking the whip or blowing the conch shell. Before five o'clock the overseer calls over the roll; and if any of the slaves are so unfortunate as to be too late, even by a few minutes, which, owing to the distance, is often the case, the driver flogs them as they come in, with the cart-whip, or with a scourge of tamarind rods. When flogged with the whip, they are stripped and held down upon the ground, and exposed in the most shameful manner.

In the cultivation of the canes the slaves work in a row. Each person has a hoe, and the women are expected to do as much as the men. This work is so hard that any slave, newly put to it, in the course of a month becomes so weak that often he is totally unfit for labour. If he falls back behind the rest, the driver keeps forcing him up with the whip.

They work from five o'clock to nine, when they are allowed to sit down for half an hour in the field, and take such food as they have been able to prepare over night. But many have no food ready, and so fast till mid-day.

They go to work again directly after half an hour's respite, and labour till twelve o'clock, when they leave off for dinner. They are allowed two hours of mid-day intermission, out of crop time, and an hour and a half in crop time.

During this interval every slave must pick a bundle of grass to bring home for the cattle at night. The grass grows in tufts, often scattered over a great space of ground, and, when the season is dry, it is very scarce and withered, so that the slaves collect it slowly and with difficulty, and are often employed most of the time allowed them for mid-day rest, in seeking for it. I have frequently known them occupied the whole two hours in collecting it.

They work again in gang from two till seven o'clock. It is then dark. When they return home the overseer calls over the roll, and demands of every man and woman their bundles of grass. He weighs with his hand each bundle as it is given in, and, if it be too light, the person who presents it is either instantly laid down and flogged severely with the cart-whip, or is put into the stocks for the whole night. If the slaves bring home no grass, they are not only put into the stocks all night, but are more severely flogged the next morning. This grass-picking is a very sore grievance to the field slaves.

When they are manuring the ground, the slaves are forced to carry the wet manure in open baskets upon their heads. This is most unpleasant as well as severe work. It is a usual occupation for wet weather, and the moisture from the manure drips constantly down upon the faces, and over the body and clothes of the slaves. They are forced to run with their loads as fast as they can; and, if they flag, the driver is instantly at their heels with the cart-whip.

The crop-time usually commences in January and lasts till June, and, if the season is wet, till July. During this season every slave must bring in a bundle of cane-tops for the cattle, instead of a bundle of grass. They then go immediately to the sugar works, where they have to take up the *mogass* which was spread out at nine o'clock in the morning to dry for fuel to boil the sugar. This mogass is the stalks of the cane after the juice has been squeezed out by the mill. The slaves are employed till ten at night in gathering in the mogass, that it may not be wetted with the dew and rendered unfit for immediate use. The overseer then calls over the roll, and issues orders for a certain spell of them to be up and at the works at one o'clock in the morning. After this the slaves have to prepare their suppers; for, if they have no very aged parents or friends belonging to them, they must do this themselves, which occupies them another hour. Every creature that is capable of work must take a part in the labours of the crop; and no person remains at home but those who are totally unfit for work. Slaves who are too old and weak to go to the field have to make up bundles of mogass, cut grass for the stock, &c.

During this season all the mechanics on the estate are employed to pot the sugar; carpenters, coopers, masons, and rum-distillers, even the pasture-boys who tend the cattle, are called in to assist. To the little people are given small tubs to carry the sugar into the curing house; and the grown-up slaves have shovels to fill the tubs for them. When employed in potting the sugar, we did not leave off to get our breakfast till ten or eleven o'clock, and I have known it mid-day before we have tasted food.

The whole gang of field slaves are divided into spells, and every man and woman able to work has not only to endure during crop-time the severe daily labour, but to work half the night also, or three whole nights in the week. The work is very severe, and great numbers of the slaves, during this period, sink under it, and become ill; but if they complain, their complaints are not readily believed, or are considered only a pretence to escape from labour. If they are so very ill that their inability to work can be no longer doubted, they are at length sent to the sick house.

The sick-house is just like a pen to keep pigs in; if you wish to keep yourself clean and decent, you cannot. It is one of the greatest punishments to the slaves to be sent there. When we were hard pressed, and had much sugar to pot, the manager would often send to the sick-house for the people who were sick, or lame with sores, to help us. If they refused to come, and said that they were unable to work, they were taken down and severely flogged, by the manager's order, with the cart-whip. There is nothing in slavery harder to bear than this. When you are ill and cannot work, your pains are made light of, and your complaints neither listened to, nor believed. I have seen people who were so sick that they could scarcely stand, dragged out of the sick-house, and tied up to a tree, and flogged in a shocking manner; then driven with the whip to the work. I have seen slaves in this state crawl away, and lie down among the wet trash to get a little ease, though they knew that it would most likely cause their death.

The quantity of food allowed the slaves is from two pounds and a half to three pounds of salt-fish per week, for each grown person. They could easily eat this in two days, but they must make it last till they receive a fresh allowance from the overseer. The rest of their food they raise upon their provision grounds. The owner gives to each slave from thirty to forty feet square of ground; not the best ground, but such as has been over-cropped, and is no longer productive for canes. This is taken from them the next year, when, by manuring and planting with yams and other things, it has been brought round, and recovered strength for the cultivation of sugar. The slaves are likewise permitted to cultivate waste pieces of ground, and the headlands of fields, that are unfit for planting. They work this ground every Sunday. It is generally given to them in March or April, and it is taken away in December or January. Besides the Sunday, they get part of twenty-six Saturdays, out of crop-time, to cultivate their grounds. What I mean by saying they get only *part* of these Saturdays is this—that they are employed in their master's work, such as carrying out trash, &c., from five to ten o'clock in the forenoon; and in the evening they must bring each his bundle of grass to deliver as usual at the calling of the lists; so that about seven hours, even of the day which is called their own, is occupied with their owner's work. They are obliged to work on these days at the provision grounds, if they wish ever so much for a holiday. If they are absent when the overseer inspects the grounds, they are flogged, or put in the stocks. The grounds produce plantains, yams, potatoes, pumpkins, calabashes, &c. On the Sunday, at every town, a market is held, in which the slaves are allowed to sell the produce of their grounds. Those that can save a little money, buy a pig and fatten it, that, in case of any death happening among their friends, they may sell the pig to provide a few necessaries for the funeral. They bury the dead during the night, being allowed no time during the day for their funerals.

In building their houses, they are allowed as much board as will form a window and a door. They go to the woods and cut wild canes, to form the walls and roof. The huts are thatched with cane-trash or tops.

For clothing, the owner gives to each slave in the year six yards of blue stuff, called bamboo, and six yards of brown. The young people and children are given a less allowance, in proportion to their size and age; the young children getting only a small stripe to tie round the waist. For bed-clothing, they give them only a blanket once in four or five years; and they are obliged to wear this till it falls in pieces. If the slaves require other clothes, they must buy them out of their own little savings. Many of the field negroes are very badly off for clothing. A good many are always to be seen with only a rag of cloth round their loins in all weathers.

People so hardly, so harshly, treated, and so destitute of every comfort, cannot be supposed to work with a willing mind. They have no home which they can well call their own. They are worked beyond their strength, and live in perpetual fear of the whip. They are insulted, tormented, and indecently exposed and degraded; yet English people wonder that they are not contented. Some have even said that they are happy! Let such people place themselves for a few minutes under the same yoke, and see if they could bear it. Such bondage is ruin both to the soul and body of the slave; and I hope every good Englishman will daily pray to God, that the yoke of slavery may soon be broken from off the necks of my unfortunate countrymen for ever.[1]

What made me feel more deeply for the sad condition of the field slaves was the circumstance of my having taken a wife from among them, after I had resided several years on Cane Grove estate. When I was about twenty-one years of age, finding my condition lonely, because I had no friends to manage for me, as the other slaves had, I wished to marry, and have a home of my own, and a kind partner to do for me. Among the field slaves there was a very respectable young woman, called Sally, for whom I had long felt a great deal of regard. At last I asked her to be my wife; and we stood up in her father's house, before her mother, and her uncle, and her sisters, and, holding each other by the hand, pledged our troth as husband and wife, and promised before God to be good and kind to each other, and to love and help each other, as long as we lived.

And so we married. And though it was not as white folks marry, before the parson, yet I considered her as much my wife, and I loved her as well, as though we had been married in the church; and she was as careful, and managed as well for me, as if she had been my mother. I could not bear to see her work in the field. It is, as I have already said, a very sad and hard condition of slavery; and the more my wife suffered, the more I wished to be free, and to make her so. When she was with child, she was flogged for not coming out early enough to work, and afterwards, when far advanced in pregnancy, she was put into the stocks by the manager, because she said she was unable to go to the field. My heart was almost broken to see her so treated, but I could do nothing to help her; and it would have made matters worse if I had attempted to speak up for her. She was twice punished in this cruel manner, though the overseer must have known that she was in no condition to work. After our child was born, she was again repeatedly flogged for not coming sooner to the field, though she had stopped merely to attend and suckle the baby. But they had no feeling for the mother or for her child, they cared only for the work. It is a dreadful thing to be a field negro; and it is scarcely less dreadful, if one's heart is not quite hardened, to have a wife, or a husband, or a child, in that condition. On this account I was often grieved that I had taken poor Sally to be my wife; for it caused her more suffering as a mother, while her cruel treatment wrung my heart, without my being able to move a finger, or utter a word, in her behalf.

---

[1] [Strickland's note] Such is the impressive language in which Ashton speaks of slavery. The above are his own expressions; for, though an uneducated, he is a very intelligent negro, and speaks remarkably good English. Any reader, who wishes it, may see and converse with himself, by making application through the publisher.—S.S.

Thomas Carlyle
1795 – 1881

Reviewing a book of selections from Thomas Carlyle's writings in 1855, George Eliot evaluated Carlyle's influence on his contemporaries: "There is hardly a superior or active mind of this generation that has not been modified by Carlyle's writings; there has hardly been an English book written for the last ten or twelve years that would not have been different if Carlyle had not lived. The character of his influence is best seen in the fact that many of the men who have the least agreement with his opinions are those to whom the reading of *Sartor Resartus* was an epoch in the history of their minds."

This evaluation stands as essentially correct. Whether it was Charles Dickens or John Ruskin, Robert Browning or Harriet Martineau, Matthew Arnold or George Eliot herself, Carlyle's thought and work affected the thinking and perspectives of those around him as that of few other writers did. This Victorian "sage" who was to become fluent in seven languages and count Johann Wolfgang von Goethe, J.S. Mill, Ralph Waldo Emerson, Alfred, Lord Tennyson, Charles Dickens, and Robert Browning among his friends, had very humble beginnings in the village of Ecclefechan, Scotland. Born in 1795, the eldest child of a poor, strict, Calvinist stonemason and a working class, uneducated mother, the young Carlyle showed early promise, and his parents were determined to give their son an education befitting his bright mind. At the age of 14, having attended local schools since he was five, Carlyle walked the nearly 100 miles from his home to enroll in a program at the University of Edinburgh, where he studied mathematics and prepared to enter the ministry. During his years at the University, however, his faith in God was challenged by his studies of skeptics such as David Hume, Voltaire, and Edward Gibbon. He left Edinburgh at age 19 without attaining a degree, and for some years he taught mathematics at Annan Academy.

He also continued what he began at Edinburgh: his life-long reading and study of German writers, whose work he was to introduce to English readers. In 1823 Carlyle completed a biography of the German poet Schiller, which was published serially in *The London Magazine*; his second publication was a translation of Goethe's *Wilhelm Meister* (1824). In 1827 he published an essay on Jean Paul Richter in the influential *Edinburgh Review*. This sign of recognition was repeated in 1829, when he published his "Signs of the Times" in the *Review*, the first of his essays that focused on the social problems of nineteenth-century England and its "Age of Machinery." With "Signs" and another essay, "Characteristics" (1831), the voice of a great social prophet of England emerged. Carlyle's importance increased with the publication of the semiautobiographical *Sartor Resartus* (1833–34), an unconventional work that, while its initial reception was lukewarm, would soon become widely influential.

It is in this period, as well, that Carlyle met and married Jane Baillie Welsh, the brilliant, articulate, talented daughter of a prosperous surgeon. She was well-placed to select from amongst many suitors; why she chose a coarse man from a working-class background was a mystery to her friends and a source of sorrow for her mother. Although their arguments were legendary, their union in 1826 was a true meeting of minds, Carlyle's creative genius and ambition matching Welsh's intellect and drive. In 1834, they moved to London, to a home in Cheyne Row in Chelsea, where Carlyle began the long career of writing that was to make him a prominent voice among his contemporaries, and where Jane Carlyle continued writing the letters that are amongst the most brilliant of all portraits of nineteenth-century London life.

Carlyle's work shows clearly and urgently the writer's confrontation with the age's dual heritage of religion and Romanticism, of tradition and the "march of mind." Carlyle discovered early on in his reading of Gibbon and the Germans that the "old theorem" of religion by which his own father had lived had "passed away," its "immaterialism, mysterious, divine though invisible character" banished by Locke and the mechanical world of the eighteenth century. For Carlyle, claiming that the Bible was factual truth "flatly contradicted all human science and experience." Yet he also believed that the Romantics' response to the passing of the "old beliefs"—the effort he saw in the early Goethe to form "his world out of himself"—led to despair and solipsism. Carlyle's celebration of Goethe's spiritual progress from narcissistic self-focus to a capacious view of humanity's role in a larger world became one of the main themes of his early work. This estimation was to become one of Carlyle's signature lines: "Close thy Byron, Open thy Goethe," commands Diogenes Teufelsdröckh, the questing protagonist of *Sartor Resartus*.

Carlyle began to achieve great fame with the publication of *The French Revolution* in 1836. His style resembled that of no other historian: highly metaphoric language, sentences that seemed "barbarous" because of their German-inflected structures and jarring syntax, the use of the present tense, representations of historical figures so vivid that they seemed like characters from a novel. Carlyle used this style to articulate the dangers that arise when the ruling classes lose sight of moral and social accountability: "French Revolution means here the open violent Rebellion, and Victory, of disimprisoned Anarchy against corrupt worn-out Authority" in which "Anarchy breaks prison; bursts up from the infinite Deep, and rages uncontrollable, immeasurable, enveloping a world."

In 1840 Carlyle gave a series of lectures, *On Heroes and Hero-Worship*, which he published in 1841. Here again he turns his attention to the sweep of historical transformation, now with a deeper focus on the role individual leaders play in history's unfolding. In these lectures, he argues that progress occurs only through the actions of "Great Men," whom the rest of humankind ought to worship: "No nobler feeling than this of admiration for one higher than himself dwells in the breast of man." The lectures take up as heroes such figures as the Norse god Odin, Muhammad, Shakespeare, Martin Luther, Robert Burns, Samuel Johnson, Oliver Cromwell, and Napoleon. Individuals such as these, Carlyle argues, apprehend the workings of the divine and can lead humankind out of darkness—if human beings will listen. In the nineteenth century, he laments, hero worship has fallen out of fashion, placing society in peril.

In Past and Present (1843), Carlyle further develops his views regarding the potential salvation of British politics and culture. By juxtaposing the medieval past of England, with its monks and serfs living in an organic community focused around a monastery, and the industrialism and *laissez-faire* economics of England's present that had produced poverty and starvation, Carlyle created a remarkable picture of the desperate social crises of the hungry forties. This latter-day England is populated by a group of vividly realized demons escaped out of Bunyan and the daily newspapers: Pandarus Dogdraught, Bobus of Houndsditch, Plugson of Undershot (a captain of industry), Sir Jabesh Windbag, the amphibious Pope, and the Dead Sea Apes (who believe that soul and stomach are synonymous). Through the biting depiction of such figures, Carlyle denounces the "Gospel of Enlightened Selfishness" that he and others saw as reducing the connections between human beings to those of a "cash nexus." The solution, Carlyle suggests, can be found in the redemptive powers of work—and especially in the efforts of heroes like Abbot Samson, a medieval figure whom Carlyle presents as a reformer who restored his degenerating society to its former glory. If the Victorian nation's "Captains of Industry" can develop the necessary nobility and heroism, then its people will transform from "a bewildered and bewildering mob" into "a firm regimented mass."

For many readers, Carlyle's exaltation of authority has represented a danger, and his conservative and authoritarian tendencies become more pronounced in his later work. *The Letters and Speeches of Oliver Cromwell* (1845) and *The History of Friedrich II of Prussia, Called Frederick the Great*, published between 1858 and 1865, furthered Carlyle's doctrine of hero-worship and his principles of order. He strongly opposed the enfranchisement of women and just as vehemently supported the enslavement of Black people in the West Indies. (Carlyle's 1849 essay on this topic ended his friendship with Mill, who wrote a spirited reply.) His 1850 publication of *Latter-Day Pamphlets*, with its corrosively satirical attacks on democracy and its representatives, is an extraordinarily splenetic outburst from a voice that had once challenged England to discover the godlike connections amongst all human beings.

Carlyle remained influential; Dickens, Browning, and John Ruskin all dedicated books to him. In 1874 he turned down a baronetcy offered by British Prime Minister Disraeli; he did, however, accept the Prussian Order of Merit in the same year. After his wife's death in 1866, he wrote little, though he did edit his wife's remarkable letters, *The Letters and Memorials of Jane Welsh Carlyle*, which were published after his own death. Carlyle, who had earlier stated his aversion to the idea of being buried in Westminster Abbey, was buried in 1881 beside his parents in Ecclefechan. George Eliot's estimation of Carlyle is an apt epitaph: "When he is saying the opposite of what we think, he says it so finely, with so hearty conviction—he makes the object about which we differ stand out in such grand relief under the clear light of his strong and honest intellect—he appeals so constantly to our sense of the manly and the truthful—that we are obliged to say 'Hear! Hear!' to the writer before we can give the decorous 'Oh! Oh!' to his opinions."

⌘ ⌘ ⌘

from *Sartor Resartus*

[In *Sartor Resartus* (Latin: "The Tailor Retailored"), Carlyle writes about the fictional German philosopher Diogenes Teufelsdröckh, the author of *Clothes: Their Origin and Influence*, whose name literally means "God-born devil's dung." Teufelsdröckh details his philosophy of clothes and clothing's relationship to Transcendentalist theories. Popular for a twenty-five year span within the Victorian period, Transcendentalism was a philosophical and literary movement that sought to integrate spirit and matter by integrating the natural and the supernatural worlds as "one great Unity." Teufelsdröckh also comments on clothing as an analogy for government and other institutions that "wear out" and need to

be replaced every so often. In this chapter and others, a fictional English editor comments on the professor's theories.]

from BOOK 3
CHAPTER 8—NATURAL SUPERNATURALISM

It is in his stupendous Section, headed *Natural Supernaturalism*, that the Professor first becomes a Seer; and, after long effort, such as we have witnessed, finally subdues under his feet this refractory[1] Clothes-Philosophy, and takes victorious possession thereof. Phantasms enough he has had to struggle with: "Cloth-

---

[1] *refractory* Stubborn; here, difficult to interpret or explain.

webs and Cobwebs," of Imperial Mantles,[1] Superannuated Symbols, and what not; yet still did he courageously pierce through. Nay, worst of all, two quite mysterious, world-embracing Phantasms, TIME and SPACE, have ever hovered round him, perplexing and bewildering; but with these also he now resolutely grapples, these also he victoriously rends asunder. In a word, he has looked fixedly on Existence, till, one after the other, its earthly hulls and garnitures[2] have all melted away; and now, to his rapt vision, the interior celestial Holy of Holies lies disclosed.

Here, therefore, properly it is that the Philosophy of Clothes attains to Transcendentalism;[3] this last leap, can we but clear it, takes us safe into the promised land, where *Palingenesis*,[4] in all senses, may be considered as beginning. "Courage, then!" may our Diogenes exclaim, with better right than Diogenes the First once did.[5] This stupendous Section we, after long painful meditation, have found not to be unintelligible, but, on the contrary, to grow clear, nay radiant, and all-illuminating. Let the reader, turning on it what utmost force of speculative intellect is in him, do his part, as we, by judicious selection and adjustment, shall study to do ours:

"Deep has been, and is, the significance of Miracles," thus quietly begins the Professor; "far deeper perhaps than we imagine. Meanwhile, the question of questions were: What specially is a Miracle? To that Dutch King of Siam, an icicle had been a miracle; whoso had carried with him an air-pump and vial of vitriolic ether,[6] might have worked a miracle. To my Horse, again, who unhappily is still more unscientific, do not I work a

miracle, and magical *Open sesame!*[7] every time I please to pay twopence and open for him an impassable *Schlagbaum*, or shut Turnpike?

"'But is not a real Miracle simply a violation of the Laws of Nature?' ask several. Whom I answer by this new question: What are the Laws of Nature? To me perhaps the rising of one from the dead were no violation of these Laws, but a confirmation, were some far deeper Law, now first penetrated into, and by Spiritual Force, even as the rest have all been, brought to bear on us with its Material Force.

"Here too may some inquire, not without astonishment: On what ground shall one, that can make Iron swim,[8] come and declare that therefore he can teach Religion? To us, truly, of the Nineteenth Century, such declaration were inept enough, which nevertheless to our fathers, of the First Century, was full of meaning.

"'But is it not the deepest Law of Nature that she be constant?' cries an illuminated class;[9] 'Is not the Machine of the Universe fixed to move by unalterable rules?' Probable enough, good friends; nay I, too, must believe that the God, whom ancient inspired men assert to be 'without variableness or shadow of turning,'[10] does indeed never change; that Nature, that the Universe, which no one whom it so pleases can be prevented from calling a Machine, does move by the most unalterable rules. And now of you, too, I make the old inquiry: What those same unalterable rules, forming the complete Statute-Book of Nature, may possibly be?

"They stand written in our Works of Science, say you, in the accumulated records of Man's Experience?—Was Man with his Experience present at the Creation, then, to see how it all went on? Have any deepest scientific individuals yet dived down to the foundations of the Universe and gauged everything there? Did the Maker take them into His counsel; that they read His groundplan of the incomprehensible All;

---

[1] *Mantles* Cloaks; also, responsibilities or roles.

[2] *garnitures* Ornaments.

[3] *Transcendentalism* In this case the professor refers to Transcendentalism's tendency to privilege the spiritual over the material. Nature, including human beings, has the powers, status, and authority traditionally attributed to an independent deity.

[4] *Palingenesis* Rebirth.

[5] *Courage, then! … once did* Third-century philosopher Diogenes Laërtius once told his listeners to have faith that his dull lecture would soon be over.

[6] *an air-pump … vitriolic ether* The evaporation of vitriolic ether (now called sulphuric ether) has a cooling effect that can be used to freeze water.

[7] *Open sesame!* Magical phrase used to open the cave in the story "Ali Baba and the Forty Thieves" in *The Arabian Nights*.

[8] *one … Iron swim* From 2 Kings 6.6, in which Elisha causes an iron axe head to swim.

[9] *illuminated class* Educated, knowledgeable.

[10] *without … turning* See James 1.17.

and can say, This stands marked therein, and no more than this? Alas, not in anywise! These scientific individuals have been nowhere but where we also are, have seen some handbreadths deeper than we see into the Deep that is infinite, without bottom as without shore.

"Laplace's Book on the Stars,[1] wherein he exhibits that certain Planets, with their Satellites, gyrate round our worthy Sun, at a rate and in a course, which, by greatest good fortune, he and the like of him have succeeded in detecting, is to me as precious as to another. But is this what thou namest 'Mechanism of the Heavens,' and 'System of the World'; this, wherein Sirius[2] and the Pleiades, and all Herschel's[3] Fifteen-thousand Suns per minute, being left out, some paltry handful of Moons, and inert Balls, had been—looked at, nicknamed, and marked in the Zodiacal Way-bill,[4] so that we can now prate of their Whereabout; their How, their Why, their What, being hid from us, as in the signless Inane?

"System of Nature! To the wisest man, wide as is his vision, Nature remains of quite *infinite* depth, of quite infinite expansion; and all Experience thereof limits itself to some few computed centuries and measured square miles. The course of Nature's phases, on this our little fraction of a Planet, is partially known to us; but who knows what deeper courses these depend on; what infinitely larger Cycle (of causes) our little Epicycle[5] revolves on? To the Minnow every cranny and pebble, and quality and accident,[6] of its little native Creek may have become familiar; but does the Minnow understand the Ocean Tides and periodic Currents, the Trade-winds, and Monsoons, and Moon's Eclipses, by all which the condition of its little Creek is regulated, and

may, from time to time (*un*miraculously enough), be quite overset and reversed? Such a minnow is Man; his Creek this Planet Earth; his Ocean the immeasurable All; his Monsoons and periodic Currents the mysterious Course of Providence through Aeons of Aeons.

"We speak of the Volume of Nature, and truly a Volume it is—whose Author and Writer is God. To read it! Dost thou, does man, so much as well know the Alphabet thereof? With its Words, Sentences, and grand descriptive Pages, poetical and philosophical, spread out through Solar Systems, and Thousands of Years, we shall not try thee. It is a Volume written in celestial hieroglyphs, in the true Sacred-writing, of which even Prophets are happy that they can read here a line and there a line. As for your Institutes, and Academies of Science, they strive bravely; and, from amid the thick-crowded, inextricably intertwisted hieroglyphic writing, pick out, by dexterous combination, some Letters in the vulgar Character, and therefrom put together this and the other economic[7] Recipe, of high avail in Practice. That Nature is more than some boundless Volume of such Recipes, or huge, well-nigh inexhaustible Domestic Cookery Book, of which the whole secret will in this manner one day evolve itself, the fewest dream.

"Custom," continues the Professor, "doth make dotards of us all.[8] Consider well, thou wilt find that Custom is the greatest of Weavers; and weaves air-raiment[9] for all the Spirits of the Universe; whereby indeed these dwell with us visibly, as ministering[10] servants, in our houses and workshops; but their spiritual nature becomes, to the most, forever hidden. Philosophy complains that Custom has hoodwinked us, from the first; that we do everything by Custom, even Believe by it; that our very Axioms, let us boast of Free-thinking as we may, are oftenest simply such Beliefs as we have never heard questioned. Nay, what is Philosophy throughout but a continual battle against Custom;

---

[1] *Laplace … Stars   Celestial Mechanics* (1799–1825), by French astronomer Pierre Simon, Marquis de Laplace.

[2] *Sirius*   The so-called "dog star," the brightest star in the constellation Canis Major (Latin: Big Dog).

[3] *Herschel*   English astronomer Sir William Herschel (1738–1822).

[4] *Way-bill*   Inventory of goods.

[5] *Epicycle*   The Ptolemaic description of the evolution of a planet in a small circle, the center of which is orbiting in the circumference of a larger circle.

[6] *accident*   Inessential or unimportant characteristic.

[7] *vulgar*   Vernacular; ordinary; *economic*   Practical, domestic.

[8] *Custom … us all*   Cf. Shakespeare's *Hamlet* 3.1.91: "Thus conscience does make cowards of us all."

[9] *raiment*   Clothing.

[10] *ministering*   Assisting.

an ever-renewed effort to *transcend* the sphere of blind Custom, and so become Transcendental?

"Innumerable are the illusions and legerdemain-tricks[1] of Custom; but of all these, perhaps the cleverest is her knack of persuading us that the Miraculous, by simple repetition, ceases to be Miraculous. True, it is by this means we live, for man must work as well as wonder; and herein is Custom so far a kind nurse,[2] guiding him to his true benefit. But she is a fond foolish nurse, or rather we are false foolish nurselings, when, in our resting and reflecting hours, we prolong the same deception. Am I to view the Stupendous with stupid indifference, because I have seen it twice, or two-hundred, or two-million times? There is no reason in Nature or in Art why I should; unless, indeed, I am a mere Work-Machine, for whom the divine gift of Thought were no other than the terrestrial gift of Steam is to the Steam-engine; a power whereby cotton might be spun, and money and money's worth realised.

"Notable enough too, here as elsewhere, wilt thou find the potency of Names, which indeed are but one kind of such custom-woven, wonder-hiding Garments. Witchcraft, and all manner of Spectre-work, and Demonology, we have now named Madness and Diseases of the Nerves. Seldom reflecting that still the new question comes upon us: What is Madness, what are Nerves? Ever, as before, does Madness remain a mysterious-terrific,[3] altogether *infernal* boiling-up of the Nether Chaotic Deep, through this fair-painted Vision of Creation, which swims thereon, which we name the Real. Was Luther's Picture of the Devil[4] less a Reality, whether it were formed within the bodily eye, or without it? In even the wisest Soul lies a whole world of internal Madness, an authentic Demon-Empire, out of which, indeed, his world of Wisdom has been creatively built together, and now rests there, as on its dark foundations does a habitable flowery Earth-rind.

"But deepest of all illusory Appearances, for hiding Wonder, as for many other ends, are your two grand fundamental world-enveloping Appearances, SPACE and TIME. These, as spun and woven for us from before Birth itself, to clothe our celestial ME for dwelling here, and yet to blind it—lie all-embracing, as the universal canvas, or warp and woof,[5] whereby all minor Illusions, in this Phantasm Existence, weave and paint themselves. In vain, while here on Earth, shall you endeavour to strip them off; you can, at best, but rend[6] them asunder for moments, and look through.

"Fortunatus had a wishing Hat, which when he put on, and wished himself Anywhere, behold he was There. By this means had Fortunatus triumphed over Space, he had annihilated Space; for him there was no Where, but all was Here. Were a Hatter to establish himself, in the Wahngasse of Weissnichtwo,[7] and make felts of this sort for all mankind, what a world we should have of it! Still stranger, should, on the opposite side of the street, another Hatter establish himself, and, as his fellow-craftsman made Space-annihilating Hats, make Time-annihilating! Of both would I purchase, were it with my last groschen,[8] but chiefly of this latter. To clap-on your felt, and, simply by wishing that you were Any*where*, straightway to be *There*! Next to clap-on your other felt, and, simply by wishing that you were Any*when*, straightway to be *Then*! This were indeed the grander; shooting at will from the Fire-Creation of the World to its Fire-Consummation; here historically present in the First Century, conversing face to face with Paul and Seneca;[9] there prophetically in the Thirty-first, conversing also face to face with other Pauls and Senecas, who as yet stand hidden in the depth of that late Time!

---

[1] *legerdemain-tricks* Sleights of hand.

[2] *nurse* Governess.

[3] *mysterious-terrific* Terrifying and mysterious.

[4] *Luther's Picture of the Devil* While he was translating the Psalms, German leader of the Protestant Reformation Martin Luther (1483–1546) threw his inkpot at an apparition of the devil.

[5] *warp and woof* Thread woven together to produce fabric; "warp" refers to the threads that run up and down, and "woof" refers to the threads that run across the fabric.

[6] *rend* Split; rip.

[7] *Wahngasse of Weissnichtwo* German: Delusion alley of I-know-not-where.

[8] *groschen* German coin.

[9] *Paul and Seneca* Roman philosopher Seneca (3 BCE to 65 CE) was said to have met and exchanged thoughts with his contemporary the apostle St. Paul.

"Or thinkest thou it were impossible, unimaginable? Is the Past annihilated, then, or only past; is the Future non-extant, or only future? Those mystic faculties of thine, Memory and Hope, already answer; already through those mystic avenues, thou the Earth-blinded summonest both Past and Future, and communest with them, though as yet darkly, and with mute beckonings. The curtains of Yesterday drop down, the curtains of Tomorrow roll up; but Yesterday and Tomorrow both *are*. Pierce through the Time-element, glance into the Eternal. Believe what thou findest written in the sanctuaries of Man's Soul, even as all Thinkers, in all ages, have devoutly read it there: that Time and Space are not God, but creations of God; that with God as it is a universal HERE, so is it an everlasting Now.

"And seest thou therein any glimpse of IMMORTALITY?—O Heaven! Is the white Tomb of our Loved One, who died from our arms, and had to be left behind us there, which rises in the distance, like a pale, mournfully receding Milestone, to tell how many toilsome un-cheered miles we have journeyed on alone,—but a pale spectral Illusion! Is the lost Friend still mysteriously Here, even as we are Here mysteriously, with God!—Know of a truth that only the Time-shadows have perished, or are perishable; that the real Being of what-ever was, and whatever is, and whatever will be, *is* even now and forever. This, should it unhappily seem new, thou mayest ponder at thy leisure, for the next twenty years, or the next twenty centuries; believe it thou must; understand it thou canst not.

"That the Thought-forms, Space and Time,[1] where-in, once for all, we are sent into this Earth to live, should condition and determine our whole Practical reasonings, conceptions, and imagings or imaginings, seems altogether fit, just, and unavoidable. But that they should, furthermore, usurp such sway over pure spiritual Meditation, and blind us to the wonder everywhere lying close on us, seems nowise so. Admit Space and Time to their due rank as Forms of Thought, nay even,

if thou wilt, to their quite undue rank of Realities; and consider, then, with thyself how their thin disguises hide from us the brightest God-effulgences! Thus, were it not miraculous, could I stretch forth my hand and clutch the Sun? Yet thou seest me daily stretch forth my hand and therewith clutch many a thing, and swing it hither and thither. Art thou a grown baby, then, to fancy that the Miracle lies in miles of distance, or in pounds avoirdupois[2] of weight; and not to see that the true inexplicable God-revealing Miracle lies in this, that I can stretch forth my hand at all; that I have free Force to clutch aught[3] therewith? Innumerable other of this sort are the deceptions, and wonder-hiding stupefactions, which Space practises, on us.

"Still worse is it with regard to Time. Your grand anti-magician, and universal wonder-hider, is this same lying Time. Had we but the Time-annihilating Hat, to put on for once only, we should see ourselves in a World of Miracles, wherein all fabled or authentic Thaumaturgy,[4] and feats of Magic, were outdone. But unhappily we have not such a Hat; and man, poor fool that he is, can seldom and scantily help himself without one.

"Were it not wonderful, for instance, had Orpheus, or Amphion,[5] built the walls of Thebes by the mere sound of his Lyre? Yet tell me, Who built these walls of Weissnichtwo; summoning out all the sandstone rocks, to dance along from the *Steinbruch* (now a huge Troglodyte[6] Chasm, with frightful green-mantled pools), and shape themselves into Doric and Ionic pillars,[7] squared ashlar[8] houses and noble streets? Was it not the still higher Orpheus, or Orpheuses, who, in past centuries, by the divine Music of Wisdom, succeeded in civilising

---

1 *Thought-forms, Space and Time* Pertaining to philosopher Immanuel Kant's (1724–1804) view that space and time are not external realities, but rather what he called "categories," or modes of perception.

2 *avoirdupois* System of measurement of weight; one stone is fourteen pounds avoirdupois.

3 *aught* Anything.

4 *Thaumaturgy* Working of miracles.

5 *Orpheus, or Amphion* Musicians of Greek myth whose music had marvelous powers.

6 *Troglodyte* Prehistoric cave-dweller, though here it seems to refer to the cave rather than the inhabitant.

7 *Doric and Ionic pillars* Two of the three styles of column used in ancient Greek architecture.

8 *ashlar* Stone block.

Man? Our highest Orpheus walked in Judea, eighteen-hundred years ago: his sphere-melody, flowing in wild native tones, took captive the ravished[1] souls of men; and, being of a truth sphere-melody, still flows and sounds, though now with thousandfold accompaniments, and rich symphonies, through all our hearts; and modulates, and divinely leads them. Is that a wonder, which happens in two hours; and does it cease to be wonderful if happening in two million? Not only was Thebes built by the music of an Orpheus, but without the music of some inspired Orpheus was no city ever built, no work that man glories in ever done.

"Sweep away the Illusion of Time; glance, if thou have eyes, from the near moving-cause to its far-distant Mover. The stroke that came transmitted through a whole galaxy of elastic balls, was it less a stroke than if the last ball only had been struck, and sent flying? O, could I (with the Time-annihilating Hat) transport thee direct from the Beginnings to the Endings, how were thy eyesight unsealed, and thy heart set flaming in the Light-sea of celestial wonder! Then sawest thou that this fair Universe, were it in the meanest province thereof, is in very deed the star-domed City of God; that through every star, through every grass-blade, and most through every Living Soul, the glory of a present God still beams. But Nature, which is the Time-vesture[2] of God, and reveals Him to the wise, hides Him from the foolish.

"Again, could anything be more miraculous than an actual authentic Ghost? The English Johnson longed, all his life, to see one, but could not, though he went to Cock Lane,[3] and thence to the church-vaults, and tapped on coffins. Foolish Doctor! Did he never, with the mind's eye as well as with the body's, look round him into that full tide of human Life he so loved; did he never so much as look into Himself? The good Doctor was a Ghost, as actual and authentic as heart could wish; well-nigh a million of Ghosts were travelling the streets by his side. Once more I say, sweep away the illusion of Time; compress the threescore[4] years into three minutes; what else was he, what else are we? Are we not Spirits, that are shaped into a body, into an Appearance, and that fade away again into air and Invisibility? This is no metaphor, it is a simple scientific *fact*: we start out of Nothingness, take figure, and are Apparitions; round us, as round the veriest spectre, is Eternity; and to Eternity minutes are as years and aeons. Come there not tones of Love and Faith, as from celestial harp-strings, like the Song of beatified Souls? And again, do not we squeak and jibber (in our discordant, screech-owlish debatings and recriminatings); and glide bodeful, and feeble, and fearful; or uproar (*poltern*), and revel in our mad Dance of the Dead—till the scent of the morning air[5] summons us to our still Home; and dreamy Night becomes awake and Day? Where now is Alexander of Macedon; does the steel Host, that yelled in fierce battle-shouts at Issus and Arbela,[6] remain behind him; or have they all vanished utterly, even as perturbed Goblins must? Napoleon too, and his Moscow Retreats and Austerlitz Campaigns![7] Was it all other than the veriest Spectre-hunt, which has now, with its howling tumult that made Night hideous, flitted away?—Ghosts! There are nigh a thousand-million walking the Earth openly at noontide; some half-hundred have vanished from it, some half-hundred have arisen in it, ere thy watch ticks once.

"O Heaven, it is mysterious, it is awful to consider that we not only carry each a future Ghost within him, but are, in very deed, Ghosts! These Limbs, whence had we them; this stormy Force; this life-blood with its burning Passion? They are dust and shadow; a Shadow-system gathered round our ME, wherein, through some moments or years, the Divine Essence is to be revealed in the Flesh. That warrior on his strong war-horse, fire flashes through his eyes; force dwells in his arm and

---

[1] *ravished* Entranced.

[2] *Time-vesture* Temporal clothing.

[3] *The English ... Cock Lane* Samuel Johnson investigated a ghost sighting, which turned out to be a hoax, on Cock Lane in London.

[4] *threescore* Sixty (a "score" is twenty).

[5] *scent of the morning air* See Shakespeare's *Hamlet* 1.5.66.

[6] *Alexander ... Arbela* Alexander the Great (356–323 BCE), King of Macedon, fought and won battles in Issus and Arbela in his quest to defeat the Persian Empire.

[7] *Napoleon ... Campaigns* French Emperor Napoleon Bonaparte was successful in his Austerlitz campaign but was defeated when he invaded Russia.

heart; but warrior and war-horse are a vision, a revealed Force, nothing more. Stately they tread the Earth, as if it were a firm substance; fool! the Earth is but a film; it cracks in twain, and warrior and war-horse sink beyond plummet's sounding.[1] Plummet's? Fantasy herself will not follow them. A little while ago, they were not; a little while, and they are not, their very ashes are not.

"So has it been from the beginning, so will it be to the end, Generation after generation takes to itself the Form of a Body; and forth-issuing from Cimmerian Night,[2] on Heaven's mission APPEARS. What Force and Fire is in each he expends; one grinding in the mill of Industry; one hunter-like climbing the giddy Alpine heights of Science; one madly dashed[3] in pieces on the rocks of Strife, in war with his fellow—and then the Heaven-sent is recalled; his earthly Vesture falls away, and soon even to Sense becomes a vanished Shadow. Thus, like some wild-flaming, wild-thundering train of Heaven's Artillery, does this mysterious MANKIND thunder and flame, in long-drawn, quick-succeeding grandeur, through the unknown Deep. Thus, like a God-created, fire-breathing Spirit-host, we emerge from the Inane; haste stormfully across the astonished Earth; then plunge again into the Inane.[4] Earth's mountains are levelled, and her seas filled up, in our passage; can the Earth, which is but dead and a vision, resist Spirits which have reality and are alive? On the hardest adamant[5] some footprint of us is stamped in; the last Rear of the host will read traces of the earliest Van.[6] But whence?—O Heaven, whither? Sense knows not; Faith knows not; only that it is through Mystery to Mystery, from God and to God.

We are such stuff
As dreams are made of, and our little Life
Is rounded with a sleep![7]

—1830–31

from *Past and Present*[8]

from BOOK 1
CHAPTER 6—HERO-WORSHIP

To the present Editor, not less than to Bobus,[9] a Government of the Wisest, what Bobus calls an Aristocracy of Talent, seems the one healing remedy; but he is not so sanguine as Bobus with respect to the means of realising it. He thinks that we have at once missed realising it, and come to need it so pressingly, by departing far from the inner eternal Laws, and taking-up with the temporary outer semblances of Laws. He thinks that "enlightened Egoism,"[10] never so luminous, is not the rule by which man's life can be led. That "Laissez-faire," "Supply-and-demand," "Cash-payment for the

---

[1] *plummet's sounding*   See Shakespeare's *The Tempest* 5.1.61; a plummet is a plumb-bob, a line with a weight on the end, used to determine a straight vertical line.

[2] *Cimmerian Night*   The Cimmerians of Homer's *Odyssey* (Book 11) lived in a land permanently enshrouded in darkness.

[3] *dashed*   Shattered.

[4] *Inane*   Here, void.

[5] *adamant*   Hard rock or mineral.

[6] *Van*   I.e., vanguard, the troops at the front of an army ("host").

[7] *We are … sleep!*   From Shakespeare's *The Tempest* 4.1.156–58; the original reads "dreams are made on."

[8] *Past and Present*   Carlyle wrote this treatise in seven weeks, in response to the lack of order and leadership that he felt was contributing to the widespread social and economic difficulties England was experiencing at that time. Carlyle blamed both the complacent aristocracy, which sought to maintain the status quo, and the spread of democracy, which he felt did little to provide heroic leaders. In 1837, industry in England entered into a depression that lasted several years. Many factories closed and others were forced to cut wages, which led to rioting in the manufacturing districts. By 1845, approximately one-twelfth of the population was unemployed, and many people ended up in overcrowded poorhouses. When the Chartists organized peaceful protests for social and economic reform, many British citizens began to fear a full-scale revolution.

[9] *Bobus*   Carlyle creates this fictional character, whom he earlier refers to as "Bobus Higgins, Sausage-maker on the great scale," as a caricature of members of the middle class who take a narrow-minded view of social reform.

[10] *enlightened Egoism*   I.e., rational egoism, according to which it is beneficial for society if individuals act in their own best interests.

sole nexus,"[1] and so forth, were not, are not and will never be, a practicable Law of Union for a Society of Men. The Poor and Rich, that Governed and Governing, cannot long live together on any such Law of Union. Alas, he thinks that man has a soul in him, *different* from the stomach in any sense of this word; that if said soul be asphyxied,[2] and lie quietly forgotten, the man and his affairs are in a bad way. He thinks that said soul will have to be resuscitated from its asphyxia; that if it prove irresuscitable, the man is not long for this world. In brief, that Midas-eared Mammonism, double-barrelled Dilettantism,[3] and their thousand adjuncts and corollaries, are *not* the Law by which God Almighty has appointed this his Universe to go; that, once for all, these are not the Law; and then, further, that we shall have to return to what *is* the Law—not by smooth flowery paths, it is like, and with "tremendous cheers" in our throat, but over steep untrodden places, through stormclad chasms, waste oceans, and the bosom of tornadoes; thank Heaven, if not through very Chaos and the Abyss! The resuscitating of a soul that has gone to asphyxia is no momentary or pleasant process, but a long and terrible one.

To the present Editor, Hero-worship, as he has elsewhere named it, means much more than an elected Parliament or stated Aristocracy of the Wisest; for in his dialect it is the summary, ultimate essence, and supreme practical perfection of all manner of worship, and true worthships and noblenesses whatsoever. Such blessed Parliament and, were it once in perfection, blessed Aristocracy of the Wisest, god-honoured and man-honoured, he does look for, more and more perfected—as the topmost blessed practical apex of a whole world reformed from sham-worship, informed anew with worship, with truth and blessedness! He thinks that Hero-worship, done differently in every different epoch of the world, is the soul of all social business among men; that the doing of it well, or the doing of it ill,[4] measures accurately what degree of well-being or of ill-being there is in the world's affairs. He thinks that we, on the whole, do our Hero-worship worse than any Nation in this world ever did it before; that the Burns an Exciseman, the Byron[5] a Literary Lion, are intrinsically, all things considered, a baser and falser phenomenon than the Odin[6] a God, the Mahomet a Prophet of God. It is this Editor's clear opinion, accordingly, that we must learn to do our Hero-worship better; that to do it better and better means the awakening of the Nation's soul from its asphyxia, and the return of blessed life to us—Heaven's blessed life, not Mammon's galvanic[7] accursed one. To resuscitate the Asphyxied, apparently now moribund and in the last agony if not resuscitated, such and no other seems the consummation.

"Hero-worship," if you will—yes, friends; but, first of all, by being ourselves of heroic mind. A whole world of Heroes; a world not of Flunkies, where no Hero-King *can* reign: that is what we aim at! We, for our share, will put away all Flunkyism, Baseness, Unveracity from us; we shall then hope to have Noblenesses and Veracities set over us; never till then. Let Bobus and Company sneer, "That is your Reform!" Yes, Bobus, that is our Reform; and except in that, and what will follow out of that, we have no hope at all. Reform, like Charity, O Bobus, must begin at home. Once well at home, how will it radiate outwards, irrepressible, into all that we touch and handle, speak and work; kindling ever new light, by incalculable contagion, spreading in geometric ratio, far and wide—doing good only, wheresoever it spreads, and not evil.

By Reform Bills, Anti-Corn-Law Bills, and thousand other bills and methods, we will demand of our Gover-

---

[1] *Laissez-faire*   Theory of economics, holding that the government should not interfere with business or trade, and that the market will regulate itself; *Cash … nexus*   I.e., cash is the only nexus (connection or bond) between people.

[2] *asphyxied*   Asphyxiated; suffocated.

[3] *Mammonism*   Worship of, or devotion to, Mammon, the personification of wealth. See Luke 16.13: "Ye cannot serve God and Mammon"; *Dilettantism*   Pursuit of knowledge in an art or science as an idle pastime, without any serious interest or goal.

[4] *ill*   Poorly; inadequately.

[5] *Exciseman*   Poet Robert Burns (1759–96), who worked as an excise officer. Burns came to be regarded as Scotland's national poet; *Byron*   Romantic poet George Gordon, Lord Byron (1788–1824).

[6] *Odin*   Norse god of war, art, and culture.

[7] *galvanic*   Applying electricity; having the effect of an electric shock.

nors, with emphasis, and for the first time not without effect, that they cease to be quacks, or else depart; that they set no quackeries and block-headisms anywhere to rule over us, that they utter or act no cant to us—it will be better if they do not. For we shall now know quacks when we see them; cant, when we hear it, shall be horrible to us! We will say, with the poor Frenchman at the Bar of the Convention, though in wiser style than he, and "for the space" not "of an hour" but of a life-time: "*Je demands l'arrestation des coquins et des laches.*" "Arrestment of the knaves and dastards." Ah, we know what a work that is; how long it will be before *they* are all or mostly got "arrested"—but here is one; arrest him, in God's name; it is one fewer! We will, in all practicable ways, by word and silence, by act and refusal to act, energetically demand that arrestment—"*je demande cette arrestation-la!*"—and by degrees infallibly attain it. Infallibly, for light spreads; all human souls, never so bedarkened, love light; light once kindled spreads, till all is luminous, till the cry, "*Arrest* your knaves and das-tards" rises imperative from millions of hearts, and rings and reigns from sea to sea. Nay, how many of them may we not "arrest" with our own hands, even now, we! Do not countenance[1] them, thou there: turn away from their lacquered sumptuosities, their belauded sophistries,[2] their serpent graciosities, their spoken and acted cant, with a sacred horror, with an *Apage Satanas.*[3] Bobus and Company, and all men, will gradually join us. We demand arrestment of the knaves and dastards, and begin by arresting our own poor selves out of that fraternity. There is no other reform conceivable. Thou and I, my friend, can, in the most flunky world, make, each of us, *one* non-flunky, one hero, if we like. That will be two heroes to begin with—Courage! even that is a whole world of heroes to end with, or what we poor Two can do in furtherance thereof!

Yes, friends: Hero-kings, and a whole world not unheroic—there lies the port and happy haven, towards which, through all these stormtost seas, French Revolu-

tions, Chartisms, Manchester Insurrections,[4] that make the heart sick in these bad days, the Supreme Powers are driving us. On the whole, blessed be the Supreme Powers, stern as they are! Towards that haven will we,[5] O friends; let all true men, with what of faculty is in them, bend valiantly, incessantly, with thousandfold endeavour, thither, thither! There, or else in the Ocean-abysses, it is very clear to me, we shall arrive.

Well, here truly is no answer to the Sphinx-question[6]—not the answer a disconsolate public, inquiring at the College of Health, was in hopes of! A total change of regimen, change of constitution and existence from the very centre of it; a new body to be got, with resuscitated soul—not without convulsive travail-throes, as all birth and new-birth presupposes travail! This is sad news to a disconsolate discerning Public, hoping to have got off by some Morrison's Pill,[7] some Saint-John's corrosive mixture and perhaps a little blistery friction on the back! We were prepared to part with our Corn-Law, with various Laws and Unlaws, but this, what is this?

Nor has the Editor forgotten how it fares with your ill-boding Cassandras in Sieges of Troy.[8] Imminent perdition is not usually driven away by words of warn-ing. Didactic Destiny has other methods in store, or these would fail always. Such words should, neverthe-less, be uttered, when they dwell truly in the soul of any man. Words are hard, are importunate; but how much harder the importunate events they foreshadow! Here

---

[1] *countenance* Approve of, tolerate.

[2] *sophistries* Intentionally misleading arguments.

[3] *Apage Satanas* Latin: Begone, Satan.

[4] *Chartisms* Movements by the Chartists, peaceful democratic reformers whose principles were set out in the "People's Charter," published in 1838; *Manchester Insurrections* Rioting in Manchester in 1842 resulted from the reduction of wages in both the coal mines and the factories. Manchester was also the site of the famous 1819 Peterloo Massacre, at which cavalry charged on an outdoor political meeting, killing at least eleven people and wounding several others.

[5] *Towards that haven will we* That haven shall be our aim.

[6] *Sphinx-question* Riddle, like those posed by the mythological sphinx, a winged half-woman, half-lion who would not allow travelers to pass unless they could correctly answer her riddle. If they answered incorrectly, they would be killed.

[7] *Morrison's Pill* I.e., a cure-all.

[8] *Cassandras ... Troy* Cassandra, daughter of the King of Troy, was given the gift of prophecy, but cursed so that nobody would believe her.

and there a human soul may listen to the words—who knows how many human souls?—whereby the importunate events, if not diverted and prevented, will be rendered *less* hard. The present Editor's purpose is to himself full of hope.

For though fierce travails, though wide seas and roaring gulfs lie before us, is it not something if a Loadstar,[1] in the eternal sky, do once more disclose itself; an everlasting light, shining through all cloud-tempests and roaring billows, ever as we emerge from the trough of the sea; the blessed beacon, far off on the edge of far horizons, towards which we are to steer incessantly for life? Is it not something, O Heavens, is it not all? There lies the Heroic Promised Land; under that Heaven's-light, my brethren, bloom the Happy Isles—there, O there! Thither will we;

"There dwells the great Achilles whom we knew."[2]

There dwell all Heroes, and will dwell: thither, all ye heroic-minded! The Heaven's Loadstar once clearly in our eye, how will each true man stand truly to *his* work in the ship; how, with undying hope, will all things be fronted, all be conquered. Nay, with the ship's prow once turned in that direction, is not all, as it were, already well? Sick wasting misery has become noble manful effort with a goal in our eye. The choking Nightmare chokes us no longer, for we *stir* under it; the Nightmare has already fled.

Certainly, could the present Editor instruct men how to know Wisdom, Heroism, when they see it, that they might do reverence to *it* only, and loyally make it ruler over them, yes, he were the living epitome of all Editors, Teachers, Prophets, that now teach and prophesy; he were an *Apollo*-Morrison, a Trismegistus[3] and

effective Cassandra! Let no Able Editor hope such things. It is to be expected the present laws of copyright, rate of reward per sheet, and other considerations will save him from that peril. Let no Editor hope such things; no—and yet let all Editors aim towards such things, and even towards such alone! One knows not what the meaning of editing and writing is, if even this be not it.

Enough, to the present Editor it has seemed possible some glimmering of light, for here and there a human soul might lie in these confused Paper-Masses now entrusted to him; wherefore he determines to edit the same. Out of old Books, new Writings, and much Meditation not of yesterday, he will endeavour to select a thing or two; and from the Past, in a circuitous way, illustrate the Present and the Future. The Past is a dim indubitable fact: the Future too is one, only dimmer; nay properly it is the *same* fact in new dress and development. For the Present holds it in both the whole Past and the whole Future—as the life-tree Igdrasil,[4] wide-waving, many-toned, has its roots down deep in the Death-kingdoms, among the oldest dead dust of men, and with its boughs reaches always beyond the stars, and in all times and places is one and the same Life-tree! …

from BOOK 3
CHAPTER 2—GOSPEL OF MAMMONISM

Reader, even Christian Reader as thy title goes, hast thou any notion of Heaven and Hell? I rather apprehend, not. Often as the words are on our tongue, they have got a fabulous or semi-fabulous character for most of us, and pass on like a kind of transient similitude, like a sound signifying little.

Yet it is well worth while for us to know, once and always, that they are not a similitude, nor a fable nor semi-fable; that they are an everlasting highest fact! "No Lake of Sicilian or other sulphur[5] burns now anywhere

---

[1] *Loadstar* Guiding star.

[2] *There dwells … knew* Cf. lines 63–64 of Alfred, Lord Tennyson's poem "Ulysses": "It may be we shall touch the Happy Isles, / And see the great Achilles, whom we knew." The Happy Isles were the Isles of the Blessed, supposedly (according to Greek myth) located in the Atlantic Ocean.

[3] *Apollo* Classical god of poetry, music, and prophecy; *Trismegistus* Greek: thrice great. This is an epithet of the classical god Hermes, the messenger and herald for the other gods.

[4] *Igdrasil* Great tree of Scandinavian mythology, the roots and branches of which stretched through the universe.

[5] *Lake … sulphur* Sulphur, often found near volcanic rocks, was formerly known as "brimstone" (i.e., "burning stone") and was thought to feed the fires of hell. At this time, Sicily was the world's primary source of sulphur.

in these ages," sayest thou? Well, and if there did not! Believe that there does not; believe it if thou wilt; nay, hold by it as a real increase, a rise to higher stages, to wider horizons and empires. All this has vanished, or has not vanished; believe as thou wilt as to all this. But that an Infinite of Practical Importance, speaking with strict arithmetical exactness, an *Infinite*, has vanished or can vanish from the Life of any Man, this thou shalt not believe! O brother, the Infinite of Terror, of Hope, of Pity, did it not at any moment disclose itself to thee, indubitable, unnameable? Came it never, like the gleam of eternal Oceans, like the voice of old Eternities, far-sounding through thy heart of hearts? Never? Alas, it was not thy Liberalism, then; it was thy Animalism! The Infinite is more sure than any other fact. But only men can discern it; mere building beavers, spinning arachnes, much more the predatory vulturous and vulpine species, do not discern it well!

"The word Hell," says Sauerteig,[1] "is still frequently in use among the English people, but I could not without difficulty ascertain what they meant by it. Hell generally signifies the Infinite Terror, the thing a man *is* infinitely afraid of, and shudders and shrinks from, struggling with his whole soul to escape from it. There is a Hell, therefore, if you will consider, which accompanies man in all stages of his history and religious or other development. But the Hells of men and Peoples differ notably. With Christians it is the infinite terror of being found guilty before the Just Judge. With old Romans, I conjecture, it was the terror not of Pluto,[2] for whom probably they cared little, but of doing unworthily, doing unvirtuously, which was their word for un*man*fully.[3] And now what is it, if you pierce through his Cants, his oft-repeated Hearsays, what he calls his Worships and so forth, what is it that the modern English soul does, in very truth, dread infinitely, and contemplate with entire despair? What *is* his Hell, after all these reputable, oft-repeated Hearsays, what is it?

With hesitation, with astonishment, I pronounce it to be the terror of 'Not succeeding'; of not making money, fame, or some other figure in the world—chiefly of not making money! Is not that a somewhat singular Hell?"

Yes, O Sauerteig, it is very singular.[4] If we do not "succeed," where is the use of us? We had better never have been born. "Tremble intensely," as our friend the Emperor of China says: *there* is the black Bottomless of Terror, what Sauerteig calls the "Hell of the English!" But indeed this Hell belongs naturally to the Gospel of Mammonism, which also has its corresponding Heaven. For there *is* one Reality among so many Phantasms; about one thing we are entirely in earnest: the making of money. Working Mammonism does divide the world with idle game-preserving Dilettantism—thank Heaven that there is even a Mammonism, *anything* we are in earnest about! Idleness is worst, Idleness alone is without hope: work earnestly at anything, you will by degrees learn to work at almost all things. There is endless hope in work, were it even work at making money.

True, it must be owned,[5] we for the present, with our Mammon-Gospel, have come to strange conclusions. We call it a Society; and go about professing openly the totalest separation, isolation. Our life is not a mutual helpfulness; but rather, cloaked under due laws-of-war, named "fair competition" and so forth, it is a mutual hostility. We have profoundly forgotten everywhere that *Cash payment* is not the sole relation of human beings; we think, nothing doubting, that *it* absolves and liquidates all engagements of man. "My starving workers?" answers the rich mill-owner: "Did not I hire them fairly in the market? Did I not pay them, to the last sixpence, the sum covenanted for? What have I to do with them more?" Verily Mammon-worship is a melancholy creed. When Cain, for his own behoof, had killed Abel, and was questioned, "Where is thy brother?" he too made answer, "Am I my brother's keeper?" Did I not pay my brother *his* wages, the thing he had merited from me?[6]

---

[1] *Sauerteig* Gottfried Sauerteig, the fictitious "Picturesque Tourist" who visits the St. Ives workhouse in Book 1, Chapter 1.

[2] *Pluto* Roman god of the underworld.

[3] *which was … unmanfully* The Latin word for man is *vir*.

[4] *singular* Remarkable; extraordinary.

[5] *owned* Admitted; confessed.

[6] *When Cain … me* See Genesis 4.9.

O sumptuous Merchant Prince, illustrious game-preserving Duke, is there no way of "killing" thy brother but Cain's rude way! "A good man by the very look of him, by his very presence with us as a fellow wayfarer in this Life-pilgrimage, *promises* so much." Woe to him if he forget all such promises, if he never know that they were given! To a deadened soul, seared with the brute Idolatry of Sense, to whom going to Hell is equivalent to not making money, all "promises" and moral duties, that cannot be pleaded for in Courts of Requests,[1] address themselves in vain. Money he can be ordered to pay, but nothing more. I have not heard in all Past History, and expect not to hear in all Future History, of any Society anywhere under God's Heaven, supporting itself on such Philosophy. The Universe is not made so; it is made otherwise than so. The man or nation of men that thinks it is made so, marches forward nothing doubting, step after step, but marches—whither we know! In these last two centuries of Atheistic Government (near two centuries now, since the blessed restoration of his Sacred Majesty, and Defender of the Faith, Charles Second[2]), I reckon that we have pretty well exhausted what of "firm earth" there was for us to march on—and are now, very ominously, shuddering, reeling, and let us hope trying to recoil, on the cliff's edge!

For out of this that we call Atheism come so many other *isms* and falsities, each falsity with its misery at its heels! A SOUL is not like wind (*spiritus*, or breath) contained within a capsule; the ALMIGHTY MAKER is not like a Clockmaker that once, in old immemorial ages, having *made* his Horologe[3] of a Universe, sits ever since and sees it go! Not at all. Hence comes Atheism; come, as we say, many other *isms*, and, as the sum of all, comes Valetism,[4] the *reverse* of Heroism—sad root of all

woes whatsoever. For indeed, as no man ever saw the above-said wind-element enclosed within its capsule, and finds it at bottom more deniable than conceivable; so too he finds, in spite of Bridgwater Bequests,[5] your Clockmaker Almighty an entirely questionable affair, a deniable affair—and accordingly denies it, and along with it so much else. Alas, one knows not what and how much else! For the faith in an Invisible, Unnameable, Godlike, present everywhere in all that we see and work and suffer, is the essence of all faith whatsoever; and that once denied, or still worse, asserted with lips only, and out of bound prayerbooks only, what other thing remains believable? That Cant well-ordered is marketable Cant; that Heroism means gas-lighted Histrionism;[6] that seen with "clear eyes" (as they call Valet-eyes) no man is a Hero, or ever was a Hero, but all men are Valets and Varlets. The accursed practical quintessence of all sorts of Unbelief! For if there be now no Hero, and the Histrio himself begin to be seen into, what hope is there for the seed of Adam here below? We are the doomed everlasting prey of the Quack; who, now in this guise, now in that, is to filch us, to pluck and eat us, by such modes as are convenient for him. For the modes and guises I care little. The Quack once inevitable, let him come swiftly, let him pluck and eat me—swiftly, that I may at least have done with him, for in his Quack-world I can have no wish to linger. Though he slay me, yet will I *not* trust in him. Though he conquer nations, and have all the Flunkies of the Universe shouting at his heels, yet will I know well that *he* is an Inanity; that for him and his there is no continuance appointed, save only in Gehenna and the Pool.[7] Alas, the Atheist world, from its utmost summits of Heaven and Westminster Hall,[8] downwards through poor seven-feet Hats and "Unveracities fallen hungry," down to the

[1] *Courts of Requests*   Court that examined the petitions of the poor.

[2] *the blessed ... Charles Second*   Restoration of the monarchy, which brought Charles II (r. 1660–85) to the throne of England after the country had been a republic for a little over a decade.

[3] *Horologe*   Clockwork.

[4] *Valetism*   I.e., the character of a valet. Carlyle defines valetism in Book 2 as "cloth-worship and quack-worship."

[5] *Bridgwater Bequests*   Francis Henry Egerton, 8th Earl of Bridgwater (1756–1829) left £8000 in his will to be awarded to the author of a treatise entitled "On the Power, Wisdom, and Goodness of God, as Manifested in the Creation."

[6] *gas-lighted*   I.e., lit with an early form of stage lighting; *Histrionism*   Acting.

[7] *Gehenna and the Pool*   I.e., Hell.

[8] *Westminster Hall*   Location of the British Houses of Parliament.

lowest cellars and neglected hunger-dens of it, is very wretched.

One of Dr. Alison's Scotch facts struck us much. A poor Irish Widow, her husband having died in one of the Lanes of Edinburgh, went forth with her three children, bare of all resource, to solicit help from the Charitable Establishments of that City. At this Charitable Establishment and then at that she was refused, referred from one to the other, helped by none, till she had exhausted them all, till her strength and heart failed her. She sank down in typhus-fever, died, and infected her Lane with fever, so that "seventeen other persons" died of fever there in consequence. The humane Physician asks thereupon, as with a heart too full for speaking, Would it not have been *economy* to help this poor Widow? She took typhus-fever, and killed seventeen of you! Very curious. The forlorn Irish Widow applies to her fellow-creatures, as if saying, "Behold I am sinking, bare of help. Ye must help me! I am your sister, bone of your bone; one God made us. Ye must help me!" They answer, "No, impossible; thou art no sister of ours." But she proves her sisterhood; her typhus-fever kills *them*. They actually were her brothers, though denying it! Had human creature ever to go lower for a proof?

For, as indeed was very natural in such case, all government of the Poor by the Rich has long ago been given over to Supply-and-demand, Laissez-faire and suchlike, and universally declared to be "impossible." "You are no sister of ours; what shadow of proof is there? Here are our parchments, our padlocks, proving indisputably our money-safes to be *ours*, and you to have no business with them. Depart! It is impossible!" Nay, what wouldst thou thyself have us do? cry indignant readers. Nothing, my friends—till you have got a soul for yourselves again. Till then all things are "impossible." Till then I cannot even bid you buy, as the old Spartans would have done, two-pence worth of powder and lead, and compendiously shoot to death this poor Irish Widow. Even that is "impossible" for you. Nothing is left but that she prove her sisterhood by dying, and infecting you with typhus. Seventeen of you lying dead will not deny such proof that she *was* flesh of your flesh; and perhaps some of the living may lay it to heart.

"Impossible": of a certain two-legged animal with feathers it is said, if you draw a distinct chalk-circle round him, he sits imprisoned, as if girt with the iron ring of Fate, and will die there, though within sight of victuals, or sit in sick misery there, and be fatted[1] to death. The name of this poor two-legged animal is—Goose; and they make of him, when well fattened, *Pâté de foie gras,* much prized by some! …

CHAPTER II—LABOUR

For there is a perennial nobleness, and even sacredness, in Work. Were he never so benighted, forgetful of his high calling, there is always hope in a man that actually and earnestly works: in Idleness alone is there perpetual despair. Work, never so Mammonish, mean, *is* in communication with Nature; the real desire to get Work done will itself lead one more and more to truth, to Nature's appointments and regulations, which are truth.

The latest Gospel in this world is, Know thy work and do it. "Know thyself": long enough has that poor "self" of thine tormented thee; thou wilt never get to "know" it, I believe! Think it not thy business, this of knowing thyself; thou art an unknowable individual. Know what thou canst work at, and work at it, like a Hercules![2] That will be thy better plan.

It has been written, "an endless significance lies in Work";[3] a man perfects himself by working. Foul jungles are cleared away, fair seedfields rise instead, and stately cities; and withal the man himself first ceases to be a jungle and foul unwholesome desert thereby. Consider how, even in the meanest sorts of Labour, the whole soul of a man is composed into a kind of real harmony the instant he sets himself to work! Doubt, Desire, Sorrow, Remorse, Indignation, Despair itself, all these like helldogs lie beleaguering the soul of the poor

---

[1] *fatted* Indulged; forced fed. *Pâté de foie gras* is made from goose or duck liver that has been made especially fatty through force-feeding.

[2] *Hercules* In Greek mythology, Hercules had to complete twelve labors.

[3] *an endless … Work* Probably a reference to German writer Johann Wolfgang von Goethe (1749–1832), who wrote on the value of work, and to whom Carlyle refers again later in this chapter.

dayworker, as of every man; but he bends himself with free valour against his task, and all these are stilled, all these shrink murmuring far off into their caves. The man is now a man. The blessed glow of Labour in him is it not as purifying fire, wherein all poison is burnt up, and of sour smoke itself there is made bright blessed flame!

Destiny, on the whole, has no other way of cultivating us. A formless Chaos, once set it *revolving*, grows round and ever rounder; ranges itself, by mere force of gravity, into strata, spherical courses; is no longer a Chaos, but a round compacted World. What would become of the Earth, did she cease[1] to revolve? In the poor old Earth, so long as she revolves, all inequalities, irregularities disperse themselves; all irregularities are incessantly becoming regular. Hast thou looked on the Potter's wheel, one of the venerablest objects, old as the Prophet Ezechiel[2] and far older? Rude lumps of clay, how they spin themselves up, by mere quick whirling, into beautiful circular dishes. And fancy the most assiduous Potter, but without his wheel, reduced to make dishes, or rather amorphous botches, by mere kneading and baking! Even such a Potter were Destiny, with a human soul that would rest and lie at ease, that would not work and spin! Of an idle unrevolving man the kindest Destiny, like the most assiduous Potter without wheel, can bake and knead nothing other than a botch; let her spend on him what expensive colouring, what gilding and enamelling she will, he is but a botch. Not a dish; no, a bulging, kneaded, crooked, shambling, squint-cornered, amorphous botch—a mere enamelled vessel of dishonour! Let the idle think of this.

Blessed is he who has found his work; let him ask no other blessedness. He has a work, a life-purpose; he has found it, and will follow it! How, as a free-flowing channel, dug and torn by noble force through the sour mud-swamp of one's existence, like an ever-deepening river there, it runs and flows, draining off the sour festering water, gradually from the root of the remotest grassblade, making, instead of pestilential swamp, a green fruitful meadow with its clear-flowing stream. How blessed for the meadow itself, let the stream and *its* value be great or small! Labour is Life: from the inmost heart of the Worker rises his god-given Force, the sacred celestial Life-essence breathed into him by Almighty God; from his inmost heart awakens him to all nobleness, to all knowledge, "self-knowledge" and much else, so soon as Work fitly begins. Knowledge? The knowledge that will hold good in working, cleave[3] thou to that; for Nature herself accredits that, says Yea to that. Properly thou hast no other knowledge but what thou hast got by working. The rest is yet all a hypothesis of knowledge, a thing to be argued of in schools, a thing floating in the clouds, in endless logic-vortices, till we try it and fix it. "Doubt, of whatever kind, can be ended by Action alone."

And again, hast thou valued Patience, Courage, Perseverance, Openness to light, readiness to own thyself mistaken, to do better next time? All these, all virtues, in wrestling with the dim brute Powers of Fact, in ordering of thy fellows in such wrestle, there and elsewhere not at all, thou wilt continually learn. Set down a brave Sir Christopher[4] in the middle of black ruined Stone-heaps, of foolish unarchitectural Bishops, redtape Officials, idle Nell-Gwyn Defenders[5] of the Faith, and see whether he will ever raise a Paul's Cathedral out of all that, yea or no! Rough, rude, contradictory are all things and persons, from the mutinous masons and Irish hodmen,[6] up to the idle Nell-Gwyn Defenders, to blustering redtape Officials, foolish unarchitectural Bishops. All these things and persons are there not for Christopher's sake and his Cathedral's; they are there for their own

---

[1] *did she cease* If she ceased.

[2] *Ezechiel* Hebrew prophet of the sixth century BCE.

[3] *cleave* Stick; adhere.

[4] *Sir Christopher* Christopher Wren (1632–1723), renowned English architect who was in charge of restoring London's public buildings and churches after the Great Fire of 1666. Wren constructed St. Paul's Cathedral, in which he is buried.

[5] *Nell-Gwyn Defenders* Actress Nell Gwyn was a mistress of Charles II. This epithet is a play on the title "Defender of the Faith," given to Henry VIII by the Pope in 1521 (and still a part of the English monarch's title).

[6] *hodmen* Those who prepare and carry the mortar and bricks to the builders.

sake mainly! Christopher will have to conquer and constrain all these, if he be able. All these are against him. Equitable Nature herself, who carries her mathematics and architectonics not on the face of her, but deep in the hidden heart of her, Nature herself is but partially for him—will be wholly against him, if he constrain her not! His very money, where is it to come from? The pious munificence of England lies far-scattered, distant, unable to speak and say, "I am here," must be spoken to before it can speak. Pious munificence, and all help, is so silent, invisible like the gods; impediment, contradictions manifold are so loud and near! O brave Sir Christopher, trust thou in those notwithstanding, and front all these; understand all these; by valiant patience, noble effort, insight, by man's-strength, vanquish and compel[1] all these, and, on the whole, strike down victoriously the last topstone of that Paul's Edifice, thy monument for certain centuries, the stamp "Great Man" impressed very legibly on Portland-stone[2] there!

Yes, all manner of help, and pious response from Men or Nature, is always what we call silent, cannot speak or come to light till it be seen, till it be spoken to. Every noble work is at first "impossible." In very truth, for every noble work the possibilities will lie diffused through Immensity, inarticulate, undiscoverable except to faith. Like Gideon thou shalt spread out thy fleece at the door of thy tent,[3] see whether under the wide arch of Heaven there be any bounteous moisture, or none. Thy heart and life-purpose shall be as a miraculous Gideon's fleece, spread out in silent appeal to Heaven; and from the kind Immensities, what from the poor unkind Localities and town and country Parishes there never could, blessed dew-moisture to suffice thee shall have fallen!

---

[1] *compel* I.e., drive away.

[2] *Portland-stone* Limestone mined on Portland Island, off the coast of Dorsetshire.

[3] *Gideon ... tent* See Judges 6.36–40, in which Gideon asks the Lord for proof that He will save Israel by Gideon's hand. First, Gideon puts a fleece of wool on the floor and asks that it be covered with dew in the morning, while the surrounding ground remains dry. When this occurs, Gideon asks that the following night the fleece be dry and the surrounding ground covered in dew. The Lord does this also.

Work is of a religious nature; work is of a *brave* nature, which it is the aim of all religion to be. All work of man is as the swimmer's: a waste ocean threatens to devour him; if he front it[4] not bravely, it will keep its word. By incessant wise defiance of it, lusty rebuke and buffet of it, behold how it loyally supports him, bears him as its conqueror along. "It is so," says Goethe, "with all things that man undertakes in this world."[5]

Brave Sea-captain, Norse Sea-king—Columbus, my hero, royalest Sea-king of all! It is no friendly environment this of thine, in the waste deep waters, around thee mutinous discouraged souls, behind thee disgrace and ruin, before thee the unpenetrated veil of Night. Brother, these wild water-mountains, bounding from their deep bases (ten miles deep, I am told), are not entirely there on thy behalf! Meseems *they* have other work than floating thee forward—and the huge Winds that sweep from Ursa Major to the Tropics and Equators, dancing their giant-waltz through the kingdoms of Chaos and Immensity, they care little about filling rightly or filling wrongly the small shoulder-of-mutton sails in this cockle-skiff of thine! Thou art not among articulate-speaking friends, my brother; thou art among immeasurable dumb monsters, tumbling, howling wide as the world here. Secret, far off, invisible to all hearts but thine, there lies a help in them: see how thou wilt get at that. Patiently thou wilt wait till the mad Southwester spend itself, saving thyself by dexterous science of defence, the while. Valiantly, with swift decision, wilt thou strike in, when the favouring East, the Possible, springs up. Mutiny of men thou wilt sternly repress; weakness, despondency, thou wilt cheerily encourage: thou wilt swallow down complaint, unreason, weariness, weakness of others and thyself—how much wilt thou swallow down! There shall be a depth of Silence in thee, deeper than this Sea, which is but ten miles deep, a Silence unsoundable, known to God only. Thou shalt be a Great Man. Yes, my World-Soldier, thou of the World Marine-service, thou wilt have to be *greater* than this tumultuous unmeasured World here round thee is.

---

[4] *front it* Confront it.

[5] *It is ... world* Cf. Goethe's *Wilhelm Meister's Apprenticeship* (1796).

Thou, in thy strong soul, as with wrestler's arms, shalt embrace it, harness it down, and make it bear thee on—to new Americas, or whither God wills! …

from BOOK 4
CHAPTER 4—CAPTAINS OF INDUSTRY

If I believed that Mammonism with its adjuncts was to continue henceforth the one serious principle of our existence, I should reckon it idle to solicit remedial measures from any Government, the disease being insusceptible of remedy. Government can do much, but it can in no wise[1] do all. Government, as the most conspicuous object in Society, is called upon to give signal of what shall be done; and, in many ways, to preside over, further, and command the doing of it. But the Government cannot do, by all its signaling and commanding, what the Society is radically indisposed to do. In the long-run every Government is the exact symbol of its People, with their wisdom and unwisdom; we have to say, Like People like Government. The main substance of this immense Problem of Organising Labour, and first of all of Managing the Working Classes, will, it is very clear, have to be solved by those who stand practically in the middle of it, by those who themselves work and preside over work. Of all that can be enacted by any Parliament in regard to it, the germs must already lie potentially extant in those two Classes, who are to obey such enactment. A Human Chaos *in* which there is no light, you vainly attempt to irradiate by light shed *on* it; order never can arise there.

But it is my firm conviction that the "Hell of England" will *cease* to be that of "not making money," that we shall get a nobler Hell and a nobler Heaven! I anticipate light *in* the Human Chaos, glimmering, shining more and more, under manifold[2] true signals from without That light shall shine. Our deity no longer being Mammon, O Heavens, each man will then say to himself, "Why such deadly haste to make money? I shall not go to Hell, even if I do not make money! There is another Hell, I am told!" Competition, at railway-speed, in all branches of commerce and work will then abate; good felt-hats for the head, in every sense, instead of seven-feet lath-and-plaster hats on wheels, will then be discoverable! Bubble-periods,[3] with their panics and commercial crises, will again become infrequent; steady modest industry will take the place of gambling speculation. To be a noble Master, among noble Workers, will again be the first ambition with some few; to be a rich Master only the second. How the Inventive Genius of England, with the whirr of its bobbins and billy-rollers[4] shoved somewhat into the backgrounds of the brain, will contrive and devise, not cheaper produce exclusively, but fairer distribution of the produce at its present cheapness! By degrees, we shall again have a Society with something of Heroism in it, something of Heaven's Blessing on it; we shall again have, as my German friend[5] asserts, "instead of Mammon-Feudalism with unsold cotton-shirts and Preservation of the Game, noble just Industrialism and Government by the Wisest!"

It is with the hope of awakening here and there a British man to know himself for a man and divine soul, that a few words of parting admonition, to all persons to whom the Heavenly Powers have lent power of any kind in this land, may now be addressed. And first to those same Master-Workers, Leaders of Industry, who stand nearest and in fact powerfulest, though not most prominent, being as yet in too many senses a Virtuality rather than an Actuality.

The Leaders of Industry, if Industry is ever to be led, are virtually the Captains of the World; if there be no nobleness in them, there will never be an Aristocracy more. But let the Captains of Industry consider: once again, are they born of other clay than the old Captains

---

[1]   *wise*   Way.

[2]   *manifold*   Many; various.

[3]   *Bubble-periods*   Violent fluctuations in the stock market.

[4]   *bobbins*   Wooden spools or cylinders on which cotton or thread is wound;   *billy-rollers*   Machines for preparing cotton or wool for spinning.

[5]   *German friend*   Reference to Teufelsdröckh, the protagonist of *Sartor Resartus* (1833–34).

of Slaughter, doomed forever to be no Chivalry, but a mere gold-plated *Doggery*—what the French well name *Canaille*, "Doggery" with more or less gold carrion at its disposal? Captains of Industry are the true Fighters, henceforth recognisable as the only true ones—Fighters against Chaos, Necessity, and the Devils and Jötuns[1]—and lead on Mankind in that great, and alone true and universal warfare; the stars in their courses fighting for them, and all Heaven and all Earth saying audibly, Well done! Let the Captains of Industry retire into their own hearts, and ask solemnly, If there is nothing but vulturous hunger for fine wines, valet reputation, and gilt carriages discoverable there? Of hearts made by the Almighty God I will not believe such a thing. Deep-hidden under wretchedest god-forgetting Cants, Epicurisms, Dead-Sea Apisms, forgotten as under foulest fat Lethe[2] mud and weeds, there is yet, in all hearts born into this God's-World, a spark of the Godlike slumbering. Awake, O nightmare sleepers; awake, arise, or be forever fallen![3] This is not playhouse poetry, it is sober fact. Our England, our world, cannot live as it is. It will connect itself with a God again, or go down with nameless throes and fire-consummation to the Devils. Thou who feelest aught of such a Godlike stirring in thee, any faintest intimation of it as through heavy-laden dreams, follow *it*, I conjure thee. Arise, save thyself, be one of those that save thy country.

Buccaneers, Chactaw Indians,[4] whose supreme aim in fighting is that they may get the scalps, the money, that they may amass scalps and money—out of such

came no Chivalry, and never will! Out of such came only gore and wreck, infernal rage and misery; desperation quenched in annihilation. Behold it, I bid thee; behold there, and consider! What is it that thou have a hundred thousand-pound bills laid-up in thy strong-room, a hundred scalps hung-up in thy wigwam?[5] I value not them or thee. Thy scalps and thy thousand-pound bills are as yet nothing, if no nobleness from within irradiate them; if no Chivalry, in action, or in embryo ever struggling towards birth and action, be there.

Love of men cannot be bought by cash-payment, and without love men cannot endure to be together. You cannot lead a Fighting World without having it regimented, chivalried; the thing, in a day, becomes impossible. All men in it, the highest at first, the very lowest at last, discern consciously, or by a noble instinct, this necessity. And can you any more continue to lead a Working World unregimented, anarchic? I answer, and the Heavens and Earth are now answering, No! The thing becomes not "in a day" impossible; but in some two generations it does. Yes, when fathers and mothers, in Stockport hunger-cellars, begin to eat their children; and Irish widows have to prove their relationship by dying of typhus-fever; and amid Governing "Corporations of the Best and Bravest," busy to preserve their game by "bushing,"[6] dark millions of God's human creatures start up in mad Chartisms, impracticable Sacred-Months,[7] and Manchester Insurrections; and there is a virtual Industrial Aristocracy as yet only half-alive, spell-bound amid money-bags and ledgers; and an actual Idle Aristocracy seemingly near dead in somnolent delusions, in trespasses and double-barrels, "sliding," as on inclined planes, which every new year they *soap* with new Hansard's-jargon under God's sky, and so

[1] *Jötuns* Members of a mythological Norse race of giants.

[2] *Epicurisms* Pursuits of sensual pleasures, luxury, and ease, so named after the philosophical system of third-century BCE Greek thinker Epicurus; *Dead-Sea Apisms* Reference to a Muslim fable in which a community living by the Dead Sea were transformed into apes on account of their failure to listen to Moses, God's prophet; *Lethe* River of forgetfulness in Hades, the classical underworld.

[3] *awake … fallen!* See Milton's *Paradise Lost*, 1.330.

[4] *Chactaw Indians* The Choctaw, who formerly inhabited central and southern Mississippi and southwest Alabama, were among many Native American tribes to practice scalping in warfare. Scalping became even more common, however, as the various colonial settlers offered rewards for the scalps of those who resisted them. In the nineteenth century, many Choctaw were forcibly removed from their lands in what is now Mississippi and made to relocate to Oklahoma.

[5] *wigwam* Traditional seasonal dwelling of some Indigenous North American cultures.

[6] *bushing* Placing bushes on the land in such a way as to prevent poachers from using nets to sweep for game.

[7] *Sacred-Months* Term used by Chartists at the 1839 National Convention to refer to general strikes.

are "sliding," ever faster, towards a "scale"[1] and balance-scale whereon is written *Thou art found Wanting*[2]—in such days, after a generation or two, I say, it does become, even to the low and simple, very palpably impossible! No Working World, any more than a Fighting World, can be led on without a noble Chivalry of Work, and laws and fixed rules which follow out of that, far nobler than any Chivalry of Fighting was. As an anarchic multitude on mere Supply-and-demand,[3] it is becoming inevitable that we dwindle in horrid suicidal convulsion and self-abrasion, frightful to the imagination, into *Chactaw* Workers. With wigwams and scalps, with palaces and thousand-pound bills, with savagery, depopulation, chaotic desolation! Good Heavens, will not one French Revolution and Reign of Terror[4] suffice us, but must there be two? There will be two if needed; there will be twenty if needed; there will be precisely as many as are needed. The Laws of Nature will have themselves fulfilled. That is a thing certain to me.

Your gallant battle-hosts and work-hosts,[5] as the others did, will need to be made loyally yours; they must and will be regulated, methodically secured in their just share of conquest under you—joined with you in veritable brotherhood, sonhood, by quite other and deeper ties than those of temporary day's wages! How would mere red-coated regiments, to say nothing of chivalries, fight for you, if you could discharge them on the evening of the battle, on payment of the stipulated shillings—and they discharge you on the morning of it!

Chelsea Hospitals,[6] pensions, promotions, rigorous lasting covenant on the one side and on the other, are indispensable even for a hired fighter. The Feudal Baron, much more—how could he subsist with mere temporary mercenaries round him at sixpence a day, ready to go over to the other side, if sevenpence were offered? He could not have subsisted, and his noble instinct saved him from the necessity of even trying! The Feudal Baron had a Man's Soul in him, to which anarchy, mutiny, and the other fruits of temporary mercenaries were intolerable; he had never been a Baron otherwise, but had continued a Chactaw and Buccaneer. He felt it precious, and at last it became habitual, and his fruitful enlarged existence included it as a necessity, to have men round him who in heart loved him; whose life he watched over with rigour yet with love; who were prepared to give their life for him, if need came. It was beautiful; it was human! Man lives not otherwise, nor can live contented, anywhere or anywhen. Isolation is the sum-total of wretchedness to man. To be cut off, to be left solitary; to have a world alien, not your world, all a hostile camp for you, not a home at all, of hearts and faces who are yours, whose you are! It is the frightfulest enchantment, too truly a work of the Evil One. To have neither superior, nor inferior, nor equal, united manlike to you. Without father, without child, without brother. Man knows no sadder destiny. "How is each of us," exclaims Jean Paul,[7] "so lonely in the wide bosom of the All!" Encased each as in his transparent "ice-palace," our brother visible in his, making signals and gesticulations to us—visible, but forever unattainable; on his bosom we shall never rest, nor he on ours. It was not a God that did this; no!

Awake, ye noble Workers, warriors in the one true war; all this must be remedied. It is you who are already half-alive, whom I will welcome into life, whom I will conjure, in God's name, to shake off your enchanted sleep, and live wholly! Cease to count scalps, gold-purses; not in these lies your or our salvation. Even

---

[1] *Idle Aristocracy ... scale* Deluded and idle Aristocrats obsess over game laws and possible trespassers on their game preserves, and over the "sliding scale" that sets the tariffs on grain (which were created to, among other things, enrich aristocratic landlords). To keep these benefits flowing they "soap" (with flattery) the scale in parliament ("Hansard's-jargon" refers to Parliamentary debate, the official report of which is known as "Hansard").

[2] *Thou ... Wanting* See Daniel 5.27.

[3] *Supply-and-demand* Forces that determine prices in an open, unregulated market.

[4] *Reign of Terror* Period of the French Revolution known for its violence, increased political instability, and numerous public executions, lasting from 1793 to 1794.

[5] *battle-hosts* Armies; *work-hosts* Assemblies of laborers.

[6] *Chelsea Hospitals* Homes such as the Chelsea Royal Hospital, for elderly or disabled veterans.

[7] *Jean Paul* German writer Jean Paul Richter (1763–1825).

these, if you count only these, will not long be left. Let buccaneering be put far from you; alter, speedily abrogate all laws of the buccaneers, if you would gain any victory that shall endure. Let God's justice, let pity, nobleness and manly valour, with more gold-purses or with fewer, testify themselves in this your brief Life-transit to all the Eternities, the Gods and Silences. It is to you I call; for ye are not dead, ye are already half-alive; there is in you a sleepless dauntless energy, the prime-matter of all nobleness in man. Honour to you in your kind. It is to you I call; ye know at least this, That the mandate of God to His creature man is Work! The future Epic of the World rests not with those that are near dead, but with those that are alive, and those that are coming into life.

Look around you. Your world-hosts are all in mutiny, in confusion, destitution; on the eve of fiery wreck and madness! They will not march farther for you, on the sixpence a day and supply-and-demand principle; they will not, nor ought they, nor can they. Ye shall reduce them to order, begin reducing them. To order, to just subordination; noble loyalty in return for noble guidance. Their souls are driven nigh[1] mad; let yours be sane and ever saner. Not as a bewildered bewildering mob, but as a firm regimented mass, with real captains over them, will these men march any more. All human interests, combined human endeavours, and social growths in this world, have, at a certain stage of their development, required organising; and Work, the grandest of human interests, does now require it.

God knows, the task will be hard; but no noble task was ever easy. This task will wear away your lives, and the lives of your sons and grandsons; but for what purpose, if not for tasks like this, were lives given to men? Ye shall cease to count your thousand-pound scalps; the noble of you shall cease! Nay, the very scalps, as I say, will not long be left if you count only these. Ye shall cease wholly to be barbarous vulturous Chactaws, and become noble European Nineteenth-Century Men. Ye shall know that Mammon, in never such gigs[2] and flunky "respectabilities," is not the alone God, that of himself he is but a Devil, and even a Brute-god.

Difficult? Yes, it will be difficult. The short-fibre cotton, that too was difficult. The waste cotton-shrub, long useless, disobedient, as the thistle by the wayside—have ye not conquered it, made it into beautiful bandana webs, white woven shirts for men, bright-tinted air-garments wherein flit goddesses? Ye have shivered mountains asunder, made the hard iron pliant to you as soft putty; the Forest-giants, Marsh-jötuns bear sheaves of golden-grain; Aegir[3] the Sea-demon himself stretches his back for a sleek highway to you, and on Firehorses and Windhorses ye career. Ye are most strong. Thor[4] red-bearded, with his blue sun-eyes, with his cheery heart and strong thunder-hammer, he and you have prevailed. Ye are most strong, ye Sons of the icy North, of the far East—far marching from your rugged Eastern Wildernesses, hitherward from the gray Dawn of Time! Ye are Sons of the *Jötun-land*, the land of Difficulties Conquered. Difficult? You must try this thing. Once try it with the understanding that it will and shall have to be done. Try it as ye try the paltrier thing, making of money! I will bet on you once more, against all Jötuns, Tailor-gods, Double-barrelled Law-wards, and Denizens of Chaos whatsoever!

—1843

---

[1] *nigh* Near.

[2] *gigs* Two-wheeled carriages. Ownership of a gig was a sign of social prestige.

[3] *Aegir* Norse god of the sea.

[4] *Thor* Norse god of thunder and rain.

URBAN WORK AND POVERTY

CONTEXTS

The Industrial Revolution brought rapid, pervasive, and frequently disorienting change to Britain. Manufacturing changed the face of the nation, from its physical appearance to the structure of family life. The Industrial Revolution had begun in the eighteenth century with the invention of new technology for spinning and weaving, and with the invention of the steam engine to power these machines, manufacturers established factories (originally called "mills") for centralized production. Mill towns such as Manchester boomed as workers crowded into cities seeking employment. There they lived in crowded, unsanitary conditions that bred disease—resulting in frequent epidemics of diseases such as cholera and typhoid. The second wave of the Industrial Revolution came with the spread of the railway in the 1840s, which allowed the iron and coal industries to flourish. Before legislation began to be passed in the 1840s, workers, including small children, worked long hours in dangerous, unhealthy conditions, without job security, insurance, or benefits. When occasional economic depressions caused factories and mines to close or cut down hours of operation, these workers often starved.

The lifelong damage resulting from the hardships faced by child workers is exemplified in the testimony of Elizabeth Bentley, one of the few women to speak before the 1832 Sadler Committee on the Labour of Children in Factories. Social reformer Michael Sadler had argued in Parliament for the passing of a Ten Hours Bill (limiting factory work to ten hours a day) and had detailed the suffering of child laborers in order to move his fellow members of Parliament to action. When the government asked for a committee of enquiry into the conditions of child laborers, Sadler chaired it, and the resulting testimony was published in Samuel Kydd's 1857 *History of the Factory Movement*. Bentley was one of thirty-eight workers (only three of whom were female) to be interviewed.

Andrew Ure's *The Philosophy of Manufactures* was one of the best-known works arguing in favor of the factory system. Ure viewed the factory system as a self-regulating organism that should be beyond government regulation, and into which workers should be introduced at a very young age, when they could be easily disciplined. While Ure speaks of the national wealth and prosperity that the factory system created, William Dodd, a child laborer, gives evidence in the excerpt following of the human costs of such "prosperity." Dodd's narrative of his life, which he published to expose the falsities of "eye-witness" accounts such as Ure's, details the lifetime of suffering and physical deformity that resulted from his early introduction to factory life. Prospects were not much better for adults employed in the mills; the reality for many working-class people was that they would work until they could work no more, at which point they would likely perish—a fate the woman in Thomas Hood's poem "Song of the Shirt" (reprinted below) seems eagerly to anticipate—or live the remainder of their days in a workhouse.

Friedrich Engels, author of *The Condition of the Working Class in England*, excerpted below, sought to expose not only the degrading conditions of the poor, but also the deliberate ways in which the middle classes shielded themselves from the realities of working-class people's suffering. Having come from Germany to study the cotton trade, Engels was struck by the conditions in England's urban centers. In this excerpt, he examines the living conditions of the working-class areas of Manchester (he also examines those of England's other "Great Towns," such as London) and the ways in which these areas are systematically hidden from the view of wealthier citizens. Engels went on to collaborate with Karl Marx on *The Communist Manifesto* (1848), and together the two thinkers laid the foundation of modern Communism.

The excerpt following, from Elizabeth Gaskell's novel *Mary Barton*, shows the opposing effects of industrialism on the rich and the poor, and the ways in which the factory system resulted in further alienation between classes. Gaskell contrasts the home lives of the rich and poor and details the private suffering of the latter during the economic depression known as the "hungry forties." *Mary Barton* was part of a developing genre known as the "social problem novel," which focused on the rampant poverty, unemployment, and disease that pervaded the Industrial Revolution. In his slightly later novel *Hard Times*, Charles Dickens details the dehumanizing effects of the factory system and factory managers' lack of recognition of the shared humanity of their employees. The fictional "Coketown" (so called because of the soot that blackens the city), in which his novel is set, is based on Dickens's observations of northern industrial towns such as Manchester and Preston.

One of the era's most influential depictions of working class and poor people was author and social reformer Henry Mayhew's *London Labour and the London Poor*, excerpted below. Asked by *The Morning Chronicle* to document, as metropolitan correspondent, the lives of the urban poor, Mayhew produced eighty-two articles that he later expanded into a four-volume collection of testimony of the lives of the lower class. He painted the underworld of Victorian society in unprecedented detail, shedding light on the specificities of economic exchange and the economic order that governed the poor. Perhaps more importantly, his work provided Victorians with a personal glimpse into the lives of the poor that helped to shape Victorian social theories. The serial newspaper publications were so popular that they resulted in the establishment of a fund to assist "Labour and the Poor." Mayhew had an ear for individual dialects, slang, and other oddities of speech, and composed each subject's narrative in language that, as closely as possible, imitated the speaker's own words. His characters were so compelling that Mayhew's narratives influenced the depiction of such characters in fiction, and writers such as Charles Dickens drew upon his representations of the poor to bring life to their own characters.

Overall, writings such as those reprinted here helped to make the middle and leisure classes more sympathetic to the hardships of poverty, and over the course of the nineteenth century some efforts were made to improve living and working conditions for the urban poor. Cities saw better sewer systems, cleaner water supplies, and in some cases the removal of slums—though the latter development had mixed effects on the slums' occupants, who, more often than not, were forced into even more crowded areas when their homes were demolished. Real wages for working people, however, increased, and a series of Factory Acts set requirements for ventilation, sanitation, and equipment safety, as well as limiting the working hours of women and children (a provision that effectively limited the working hours of many men as well). Many of these changes were achieved by the workers themselves; the century saw great strides in labor organization, with trade unions decriminalized in the 1860s. Yet labor for most working-class people remained dangerous, arduous, overlong, and underpaid well beyond the Victorian era.

⌘⌘⌘

from Elizabeth Bentley, *Testimony before the 1832 Committee on the Labour of Children in Factories* (1857)

"I am twenty-three years of age, and live at Leeds. I began to work at Mr. Busk's flax mill when I was six years old. I was then a little 'doffer.'[1] In that mill we worked from five in the morning till nine at night, when they were 'throng';[2] when they were not so 'throng,' the usual hours of labour were from six in the morning till seven at night. The time allowed for our meals was forty minutes at noon; not any time was allowed for breakfast or 'drinking': these we got as we could. When our work was bad, we had hardly any time to eat them at all: we were obliged to leave them or take them home. When we did not take our uneaten food home, the overlooker took it and gave it to his pigs. I consider 'doffing' to be a laborious employment. When the frames are full, the 'doffers' have to stop them, and take the 'flyers'[3] off, and take the full bobbins off, and carry them to the roller, and then put empty ones on, and set the frame going again. I was kept constantly on my feet; there were so many frames, and they run so quick, the labour was excessive, there was not time for anything. When the 'doffers' flagged[4] a little, or were too late, they were strapped. Those who were last in 'doffing' were constantly strapped—girls as well as boys. I have been strapped severely, and have been hurt by the strap excessively. The overlooker I was under was a very severe man. When I and others have been fatigued and worn out, and had not baskets enough to put the bobbins in, we used to put them in the window bottoms, and that broke the panes sometimes; and I broke one one time, and the overlooker strapped me on the arm, and it rose a blister, and I ran home to my mother. I worked at Mr. Busk's factory three or four years.

"When I left Mr. Busk's, I then went to Benyon's factory; I was about ten years of age, and was employed as a weigher in the card-room.[5] At Benyon's factory we worked from half-past five till eight at night; when they were 'throng,' until nine. The spinners at that mill were allowed forty minutes at noon for meals; no more time throughout the day was allowed. Those employed in the card-rooms had, in addition to the forty minutes at noon, a quarter of an hour allowed for their breakfast, and a quarter of an hour for their 'drinking.' The carding-room is more oppressive than the spinning department: those at work cannot see each other for dust. The 'cards' get so soon filled up with waste and dirt, they must be stopped or they would take fire: the stoppages are as much for the benefit of the employer as for the working people. The children at Benyon's factory were beat up to their labour with a strap. … The girls have many times had black marks upon their skins. Had the parents complained of this excessive ill-usage, the probable consequence would have been the loss of the employment of the child. Of this result the parents were afraid.

"I worked in the card-room; it was so dusty that the dust got upon my lungs, and the work was so hard. I was middling strong when I went there, but the work was so bad; I got so bad in health, that when I pulled the baskets down, I pulled my bones out of their places. The basket I pulled was a very large one; that was full of weights, upheaped, and pulling the basket, pulled my shoulder out of its place, and my ribs have grown over it. That hard work is generally done by women: it is not fit for children. There was no spinning for me, and I therefore did that work. …

"I am considerably deformed in person in consequence of this labour. I was about thirteen years old when my deformity began to come on, and it has got worse since. It is five years since my mother died, and she was never able to get me a pair of good stays[6] to hold me up; and when my mother died I had to do for myself,

---

[1] *doffer* Worker who assists the spinner by removing the full spindles, or bobbins, from the carding machine (which combs the cotton or wool) and replacing them with empty ones.

[2] *throng* Busy.

[3] *flyers* Part of the spinning machine that twists the thread and winds it upon the bobbin.

[4] *flagged* Slowed down.

[5] *card-room* Room that held the carding machines, which combed and cleaned the wool or cotton in preparation for spinning.

[6] *stays* Bodice stiffened with strips of whale-bone that gives support and shape to the figure; a corset.

and got me a pair. Before I worked at a mill I was as straight a little girl as ever went up and down town. I was straight until I was thirteen. I have been attended by a medical gentleman, Mr. Hare. He said it was owing to hard labour, and working in the factories. ...

"I have had the misfortune, from being a straight and healthful girl, to become very much otherwise in person. I do not know of any other girls that have become weak and deformed in like manner. I have known others who have been similarly injured in health. I am deformed in the shoulders; it is very common indeed to have weak ankles and crooked knees, that is brought on by stopping the spindle.

"I have had experience in wet spinning—it is very uncomfortable. I have stood before the frames till I have been wet through to my skin; and in winter-time, when myself and others have gone home, our clothes have been frozen, and we have nearly caught our death from cold. We have stopped at home one or two days, just as we were situated in our health; had we stopped away any length of time we should have found it difficult to keep our situation.

"I am now in the poor-house at Hunslet. Not any of my former employers come to see me. When I was at home, Mr. Walker made me a present of 1s. or 2s.,[1] but since I left my work and have gone to the poor-house, no one has come nigh[2] me. I was very willing to have worked as long as I was able, and to have supported my widowed mother. I am utterly incapable now of any exertion of that sort, and am supported by the parish."[3]

from Andrew Ure, *The Philosophy of Manufactures* (1835)

In its precise acceptation,[4] the factory system is of recent origin, and may claim England for its birth-place. The mills for throwing silk, or making organzine,[5] which were mounted centuries ago in several of the Italian states, and furtively transferred to this country by Sir Thomas Lombe in 1718, contained indeed certain elements of a factory, and probably suggested some hints of those grander and more complex combinations of self-acting machines, which were first embodied half a century later in our cotton manufacture by Richard Arkwright, assisted by gentlemen of Derby, well acquainted with its celebrated silk establishment. ...

When the first water-frames for spinning cotton were erected at Cromford, in the romantic valley of the Derwent, about sixty years ago, mankind were little aware of the mighty revolution which the new system of labour was destined by Providence to achieve, not only in the structure of British society, but in the fortunes of the world at large. Arkwright alone had the sagacity to discern, and the boldness to predict in glowing language, how vastly productive human industry would become, when no longer proportioned in its results to muscular effort, which is by its nature fitful and capricious, but when made to consist in the task of guiding the work of mechanical fingers and arms, regularly impelled with great velocity by some indefatigable physical power. What his judgment so clearly led him to perceive, his energy of will enabled him to realize with such rapidity and success, as would have done honour to the most influential individuals, but were truly wonderful in that obscure and indigent artisan. The main difficulty did not, to my apprehension, lie so much in the invention of a proper self-acting mechanism for drawing out and twisting cotton into a continuous thread, as in the distribution of the different members of the apparatus into one cooperative body, in impelling each organ with its appropriate delicacy and speed, and, above all, in training human beings to renounce their desultory[6] habits of work, and to identify themselves with the unvarying regularity of the complex automaton. To devise and administer a successful code of factory discipline, suited to the necessities of factory

---

[1]   *s.*   Shilling.

[2]   *nigh*   Near.

[3]   *supported by the parish*   I.e., with public funds.

[4]   *acceptation*   Customary explanation.

---

[5]   *organzine*   Silk yarn.

[6]   *desultory*   Half-hearted, lacking enthusiasm.

diligence, was the Herculean[1] enterprise, the noble achievement of Arkwright. Even at the present day, when the system is perfectly organized, and its labour lightened to the utmost, it is found nearly impossible to convert persons past the age of puberty, whether drawn from rural or from handicraft occupations, into useful factory hands. After struggling for a while to conquer their listless or restive habits, they either renounce the employment spontaneously, or are dismissed by the overlookers on account of inattention. ...

It required, in fact, a man of a Napoleon nerve and ambition to subdue the refractory tempers of work-people accustomed to irregular paroxysms of diligence,[2] and to urge on his multifarious and intricate constructions in the face of prejudice, passion, and envy. Such was Arkwright, who, suffering nothing to stay or turn aside his progress, arrived gloriously at the goal, and has for ever affixed his name to a great era in the annals of mankind, an era which has laid open unbounded prospects of wealth and comfort to the industrious, however much they may have been occasionally clouded by ignorance and folly.

... In my recent tour, continued during several months, through the manufacturing districts, I have seen tens of thousands of old, young, and middle-aged of both sexes, many of them too feeble to get their daily bread by any of the former modes of industry, earning abundant food, raiment,[3] and domestic accommodation, without perspiring at a single pore, screened meanwhile from the summer's sun and the winter's frost, in apartments more airy and salubrious[4] than those of the metropolis, in which our legislative and fashionable aristocracies assemble. In those spacious halls the benignant power of steam summons around

him his myriads of willing menials,[5] and assigns to each the regulated task, substituting for painful muscular effort on their part, the energies of his own gigantic arm, and demanding in return only attention and dexterity to correct such little aberrations as casually occur in his workmanship. The gentle docility of this moving force qualifies it for impelling the tiny bobbins of the lace-machine with a precision and speed inimitable by the most dexterous hands, directed by the sharpest eyes. Hence, under its auspices, and in obedience to Arkwright's polity,[6] magnificent edifices, surpassing far in number, value, usefulness, and ingenuity of construction, the boasted monuments of Asiatic, Egyptian, and Roman despotism, have, within the short period of fifty years, risen up in this kingdom, to show to what extent capital, industry, and science may augment the resources of a state, while they meliorate[7] the condition of its citizens. Such is the factory system, replete with prodigies in mechanics and political economy, which promises, in its future growth, to become the great minister of civilization to the terraqueous[8] globe, enabling this country, as its heart, to diffuse along with its commerce the life-blood of science and religion to myriads of people still lying "in the region and shadow of death."[9] ...

No master would wish to have any wayward children to work within the walls of his factory who do not mind their business without beating, and he therefore usually fines or turns away any spinners who are known to maltreat their assistants. Hence, ill-usage of any kind is a very rare occurrence. I have visited many factories, both in Manchester and in the surrounding districts, during a period of several months, entering the spinning rooms, unexpectedly, and often alone, at different times of the day, and I never saw a single instance of corporal chastisement inflicted on a child, nor indeed did I ever see children in ill-humour. They seemed to be always

[1] *Herculean* Monumental; laborious. The Roman hero and god Hercules is known for his strength and for the epic nature of the twelve labors he performed.

[2] *refractory tempers* Rebellious natures; *irregular paroxysms of diligence* Inconsistent spasms of industriousness.

[3] *raiment* Clothing.

[4] *salubrious* Favorable to health.

[5] *benignant* Benevolent; beneficial; *menials* Unskilled laborers; servants.

[6] *polity* Mode of administration.

[7] *meliorate* Improve.

[8] *terraqueous* Consisting of land and water.

[9] *in the ... death* From Matthew 4.16.

cheerful and alert, taking pleasure in the light play of their muscles—enjoying the mobility natural to their age. The scene of industry, so far from exciting sad emotions in my mind, was always exhilarating. It was delightful to observe the nimbleness with which they pieced the broken ends,[1] as the mule-carriage[1] began to recede from the fixed roller beam, and to see them at leisure, after a few seconds' exercise of their tiny fingers, to amuse themselves in any attitude they chose, till the stretch and winding-on were once more completed. The work of these lively elves seemed to resemble a sport, in which habit gave them a pleasing dexterity. Conscious of their skill, they were delighted to show it off to any stranger. As to exhaustion by the day's work, they evinced no trace of it on emerging from the mill in the evening; for they immediately began to skip about any neighbouring playground, and to commence their little amusements with the same alacrity as boys issuing from a school. It is moreover my firm conviction that if children are not ill-used by bad parents or guardians, but receive in food and raiment the full benefit of what they earn, they would thrive better when employed in our modern factories than if left at home in apartments too often ill-aired, damp, and cold.

from William Dodd, *A Narrative of the Experience and Sufferings of William Dodd, a Factory Cripple, Written by Himself* (1841)

Dear Reader,—I wish it to be distinctly and clearly understood, that, in laying before you the following sheets, I am not actuated[2] by any motive of ill-feeling to any party with whom I have formerly been connected; on the contrary, I have a personal respect for some of my former masters, and am convinced that, had they been in any other line of life, they would have shone forth as ornaments to the age in which they lived;

---

[1] *broken ends* I.e., of thread. This was the job of the "piecer," who ensured that the process of spinning could continue uninterrupted; *mule-carriage* The movable part of the mule, a kind of spinning machine, invented in 1779, that could spin yarn of varying thicknesses.

[2] *actuated* Driven; motivated.

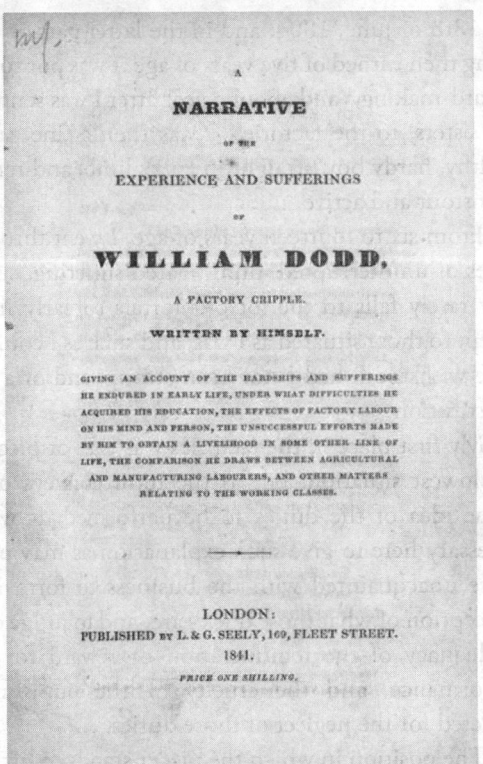

Title page from William Dodd, *A Narrative of the Experience and Sufferings of William Dodd, a Factory Cripple, Written by Himself* (1841).

but having witnessed the efforts of some writers (who can know nothing of the factories by experience) to mislead the minds of the public upon a subject of so much importance, I feel it to be my duty to give to the world a fair and impartial account of the working of the factory system, as I have found it in twenty-five years' experience.

… Of four children in our family, I was the only boy; and we were all, at different periods, as we could meet with employers, sent to work in the factories. My eldest sister was ten years of age before she went; consequently, she was, in a manner, out of harm's way, her bones having become firmer and stronger than ours, and capable of withstanding the hardships to which she was exposed much better than we could. … I was born on the 18th of June, 1804; and in the latter part of 1809, being then turned of five years of age, I was put to work at card-making,[1] and about a year after I was sent, with my sisters, to the factories. I was then a fine, strong, healthy, hardy boy, straight in every limb, and remarkably stout and active. ...

From six to fourteen years of age, I went through a series of uninterrupted, unmitigated suffering, such as very rarely falls to the lot of mortals so early in life, except to those situated as I was, and such as I could not have withstood, had I not been strong, and of a good constitution.

My first place in the factories was that of piecer, or the lowest situation: but as the term conveys only a vague idea of the duties to be performed, it will be necessary here to give such explanation as may enable those unacquainted with the business to form a just conception of what those duties are, and to judge of the inadequacy of the remuneration or reward for their performance, and the cruelty of the punishments inflicted for the neglect of those duties. ...

The position in which the piecer stands to his work is with his right foot forward, and his right side facing the frame: the motion he makes in going along in front of the frame, for the purpose of piecing, is neither forwards nor backwards, but in a sidling direction, constantly keeping his right side towards the frame. In this position he continues during the day, with his hands, feet, and eyes constantly in motion. It will be easily seen, that the chief weight of his body rests upon his right knee, which is almost always the first joint to give way. The number of cripples with the right knee in, greatly exceed those with the left knee in; a great many have both knees in such as my own from this cause.

Another evil resulting from the position in which the piecer stands, is what is termed "splay-foot," which may be explained thus: in a well-formed foot, there is a finely formed arch of bones immediately under the instep and ankle joint. The continual pressure of the body on this arch, before it is sufficiently strong to bear such pressure (as in the case of boys and girls in the factories) causes it to give way: the bones fall gradually down, the foot then becomes broad and flat, and the owner drags it after him with the broad side first. A great many factory cripples are in this state; this is very often attended with weak ankle and knee joints. I have a brother-in-law exactly thus, who has tried everything likely to do him good, but without success.

The spinner and the piecer are intimately connected together:[2] the spinner works by the piece, being paid by the stone[3] for the yarn spun; the piecer is hired by the week, and paid according to his abilities. The piecers are the servants of the spinners, and both are under an overlooker; and liable to be dismissed at a week's notice. Being thus circumstanced, it is clearly the advantage of the spinner to have good able piecers, who ought, in return, to be well paid. ...

In order to induce the piecer to do his work quick and well, the spinner has recourse to many expedients, such as offering rewards of a penny or two-pence for a good week's work inducing them to sing, which, like the music in the army, has a very powerful effect, and keeps them awake and active longer than any other thing; and, as a last resource, when nothing else will do, he takes the strap, or the billy-roller,[4] which are laid on[5] most unmercifully, accompanied by a round volley of oaths; and I pity the poor wretch who has to submit to the infliction of either.

On one occasion, I remember being thrashed with the billy-roller till my back, arms, and legs were covered with ridges as thick as my finger. This was more than I could bear, and, seeing a favourable opportunity, I slipped out and stole off home along some by-ways, so as not to be seen. Mother stripped me, and was shocked at my appearance. The spinner, not meeting with any

---

[1] *card-making* Cards combed and cleansed fibers in preparation for spinning.

[2] *The spinner ... together* The spinner, who ran the "billy" (or "slubbing," the machine that spins yarn) was dependent on the piecer for the preparation of the wool.

[3] *stone* Unit of measurement equal to 14 pounds.

[4] *billy-roller* Uppermost of a series of wooden rollers through which the wool is moved to the spindles. It was very long and easily removed from the billy; as a result, it was a notorious instrument of punishment to factory children.

[5] *laid on* Applied; here, used to hit with, for the purpose of punishment.

A wood engraving of a child mine-worker included in the *Report of the Commission of the Employment of Children and Young Persons in the Mines* (1842).

other to suit him, had the assurance[1] to come and beg that mother would let me go again, and promised not to strike me with the billy-roller any more. He kept his promise, but instead of using the roller, he used his fist.

... A piecer, it will be seen, is an important person in the factories, inasmuch as it is impossible to do without them. Formerly, boys and girls were sent to work in the factories as piecers at the early age of five or six years—as in my own case—but now, owing to the introduction of some wise laws for the regulation of factories,[2] they cannot employ any as piecers before they have attained the age of 9 years; at which age their bones are comparatively strong, generally speaking, and more able to endure the hardships to which they will be exposed.

They now enjoy many privileges that we had not, such as attending schools, limited hours of labour, &c.; but still it is far from being a desirable place for a child.

---

[1] *assurance* Audacity; boldness.

[2] *some wise ... factories* The 1833 Factory Act, which prevented children under nine from working in any factories except silk mills. It also decreed that children under 11 (and, eventually, under 13) could not work more than 9 hours a day or 48 hours a week, and that all working children had to be provided with education at the expense of the factory owners.

Formerly, it was nothing but work till we could work no longer. I have frequently worked at the frame till I could scarcely get home, and in this state have been stopped by people in the streets who noticed me shuffling along, and advised me to work no more in the factories: but I was not my own master. Thus year after year passed away, my afflictions and deformities increasing. I could not associate with anybody; on the contrary, I sought every opportunity to rest myself, and to shrink into any corner to screen myself from the prying eye of the curious and scornful! During the day, I frequently counted the clock, and calculated how many hours I had still to remain at work; my evenings were spent in preparing for the following day—in rubbing my knees, ankles, elbows, and wrists with oil, &c., and wrapping them in warm flannel! (for everything was tried to benefit me, except the right one—that of taking me from the work) after which, with a look at, rather than eating my supper (the bad smells of the factory having generally taken my appetite away) I went to bed, to cry myself to sleep, and pray that the Lord would take me to Himself before morning.

... A great many are made cripples by over-exertion. Among those who have been brought up from infancy

Thomas Annan, *Close No. 193, High Street, Glasgow*, 1868. Thomas Annan was hired by the Glasgow City Improvement Trust to photograph the city's slums before they were demolished. Many of his pictures show the open sewers and narrow passageways that were features of slum life. (See also Annan's photograph in the Contexts section on photography.)

with me in the factories, and whom death has spared, few have escaped without some injury. My brother-in-law and myself have been crippled by this cause, but in different ways; my sister partly by over-exertion and partly by machinery. On going home to breakfast one morning, I was much surprised at seeing several of the neighbours and two doctors in our house. On inquiring the cause, I found that my second sister had nearly lost her hand in the machinery. She had been working all night, and, fatigued and sleepy, had not been so watchful as she otherwise would have been; and consequently, her right hand became entangled in the machine which she was attending. Four iron teeth of a wheel, three-quarters of an inch broad, and one-quarter of an inch thick, had been forced through her hand, from the back

part, among the leaders, &c.; and the fifth iron tooth fell upon the thumb, and crushed it to atoms. It was thought, for some time, that she would lose her hand. But it was saved; and, as you may be sure, it is stiff and contracted, and is but a very feeble apology for a hand. This accident might have been prevented, if the wheels above referred to had been boxed off,[1] which they might have been for a couple of shillings; and the very next week after this accident, a man had two fingers taken off his hand, by the very same wheels—and still they are not boxed off!

Thomas Hood, "Song of the Shirt" (1843)

With fingers weary and worn,
    With eyelids heavy and red,
A woman sat, in unwomanly rags,
    Plying her needle and thread—
5 Stitch—stitch—stitch!
    In poverty, hunger, and dirt,
And still with a voice of dolorous pitch
    She sang the "Song of the Shirt."

"Work—work—work
10 Till the brain begins to swim;
Work—work—work
    Till the eyes are heavy and dim!
Seam, and gusset,[2] and band,
    Band, and gusset, and seam;
15 Till over the buttons I fall asleep,
    And sew them on in a dream!

"O! men, with sisters dear!
    O! men, with mothers and wives!
It is not linen you're wearing out,
20 But human creatures' lives!

---

[1] *the wheels … boxed off* The Factory Act of 1844 decreed that fly-wheels connected to mechanical parts, such as shafts, had to be boxed off or fenced. However, such a project would cost a few shillings per wheel, which would add up to a considerable expense, and would make it difficult for workers to clean the machinery. As a result, many factory owners ignored the law when it came into effect.

[2] *gusset* Triangular piece of material inserted into a piece of clothing to strengthen or enlarge some part.

Stitch—stitch—stitch,
In poverty, hunger, and dirt,
Sewing at once, with a double thread,
A shroud[1] as well as a shirt.

25   "But why do I talk of Death?
That phantom of grisly bone;
I hardly fear his terrible shape,
It seems so like my own—
It seems so like my own,
30   Because of the fasts I keep:
Oh! God! that bread should be so dear,
And flesh and blood so cheap!

"Work—work—work!
My labour never flags;
35   And what are its wages?
A bed of straw,
A crust of bread and rags,
That shatter'd roof, and this naked floor
A table—a broken chair—
40   A wall so blank, my shadow I thank
For sometimes falling there!

"Work—work—work!
From weary chime to chime,
Work—work—work
45   As prisoners work for crime!
Band, and gusset, and seam,
Seam, and gusset, and band,
Till the heart is sick, and the brain benumb'd,
As well as the weary hand.

50   "Work—work—work,
In the dull December light,
And work—work—work,
When the weather is warm and bright—
While underneath the eaves
55   The brooding swallows cling,
As if to show me their sunny backs
And twit me with the spring.

John Thomson's photograph of "The crawler," 1877. This photograph is taken from Thomson's famous project, *Street Life in London* (1877–78), one of the era's most influential pieces of social documentary. Thomson collaborated with Adolph Smith to create text to accompany the photographs. This picture, one of the best known, shows a destitute woman who told Thomson that she spent her nights on the steps of a workhouse and her days looking after a friend's baby, in exchange for a cup of tea and some bread.

"Oh! but to breathe the breath
Of the cowslip and primrose[2] sweet—
60   With the sky above my head,
And the grass beneath my feet,
For only one short hour
To feel as I used to feel,
Before I knew the woes of want
65   And the walk that costs a meal:

---

[1]   *shroud*   Sheet in which a corpse is wrapped for burial.

[2]   *cowslip … primrose*   Wildflowers.

"Oh, but for one short hour!
A respite, however brief!
No blessed leisure for Love or Hope,
But only time for grief!
70   A little weeping would ease my heart,
But in their briny head
My tears must stop, for every drop
Hinders needle and thread!"

With fingers weary and worn,
75   With eyelids heavy and red,
A woman sat, in unwomanly rags,
Plying her needle and thread—
Stitch—stitch—stitch!
In poverty, hunger, and dirt,
80   And still with a voice of dolorous pitch,
Would that its tone could reach the rich!
She sang this "Song of the Shirt!"

from Friedrich Engels, *The Condition of the Working Class in England in 1844*[1] (1845)

CHAPTER 3: THE GREAT TOWNS

Manchester lies at the foot of the southern slope of a range of hills, which stretch hither from Oldham, their last peak, Kersallmoor, being at once the racecourse and the Mons Sacer[2] of Manchester. Manchester proper lies on the left bank of the Irwell, between that stream and the two smaller ones, the Irk and the Medlock, which here empty into the Irwell. On the right bank of the Irwell, bounded by a sharp curve of the river, lies Salford, and farther westward Pendleton; northward from the Irwell lie Upper and Lower Broughton; northward of the Irk, Cheetham Hill; south of the Medlock lies Hulme; farther east Chorlton on Medlock; still farther, pretty well to the east of Manchester, Ardwick. The whole assemblage of buildings is commonly called Manchester, and contains about four hundred thousand inhabitants, rather more than less. The town itself is peculiarly built, so that a person may live in it for years, and go in and out daily without coming into contact with a working people's quarter or even with workers, that is, so long as he confines himself to his business or to pleasure walks. This arises chiefly from the fact that by unconscious tacit agreement, as well as with outspoken conscious determination, the working people's quarters are sharply separated from the sections of the city reserved for the middle class; or, if this does not succeed, they are concealed with the cloak of charity. Manchester contains, at its heart, a rather extended commercial district, perhaps half a mile long and about as broad, and consisting almost wholly of offices and warehouses. Nearly the whole district is abandoned by dwellers, and is lonely and deserted at night; only watchmen and policemen traverse its narrow lanes with their dark lanterns. This district is cut through by certain main thoroughfares upon which the vast traffic concentrates, and in which the ground level is lined with brilliant shops. In these streets the upper floors are occupied, here and there, and there is a good deal of life upon them until late at night. With the exception of this commercial district, all Manchester proper, all Salford and Hulme, a great part of Pendleton and Chorlton, two-thirds of Ardwick, and single stretches of Cheetham Hill and Broughton are all unmixed working people's quarters, stretching like a girdle, averaging a mile and a half in breadth, around the commercial district. Outside, beyond this girdle, lives the upper and middle bourgeoisie, the middle bourgeoisie in regularly laid out streets in the vicinity of the working quarters, especially in Chorlton and the lower lying portions of Cheetham Hill; the upper bourgeoisie in remoter villas with gardens in Chorlton and Ardwick, or on the breezy heights of Cheetham Hill, Broughton, and Pendleton, in free, wholesome country air, in fine, comfortable homes, passed once every half or quarter hour by omnibuses[3] going into the city. And the finest part of the arrangements is this, that the members of this money aristocracy can take the shortest road

---

[1] *The Condition ... 1844*   Translated by Florence Wischnewetzky, 1887.

[2] *Mons Sacer*   Latin: Sacred Mountain.

[3] *omnibuses*   Horse-drawn passenger vehicles used as urban transportation, ancestors of the modern transit bus.

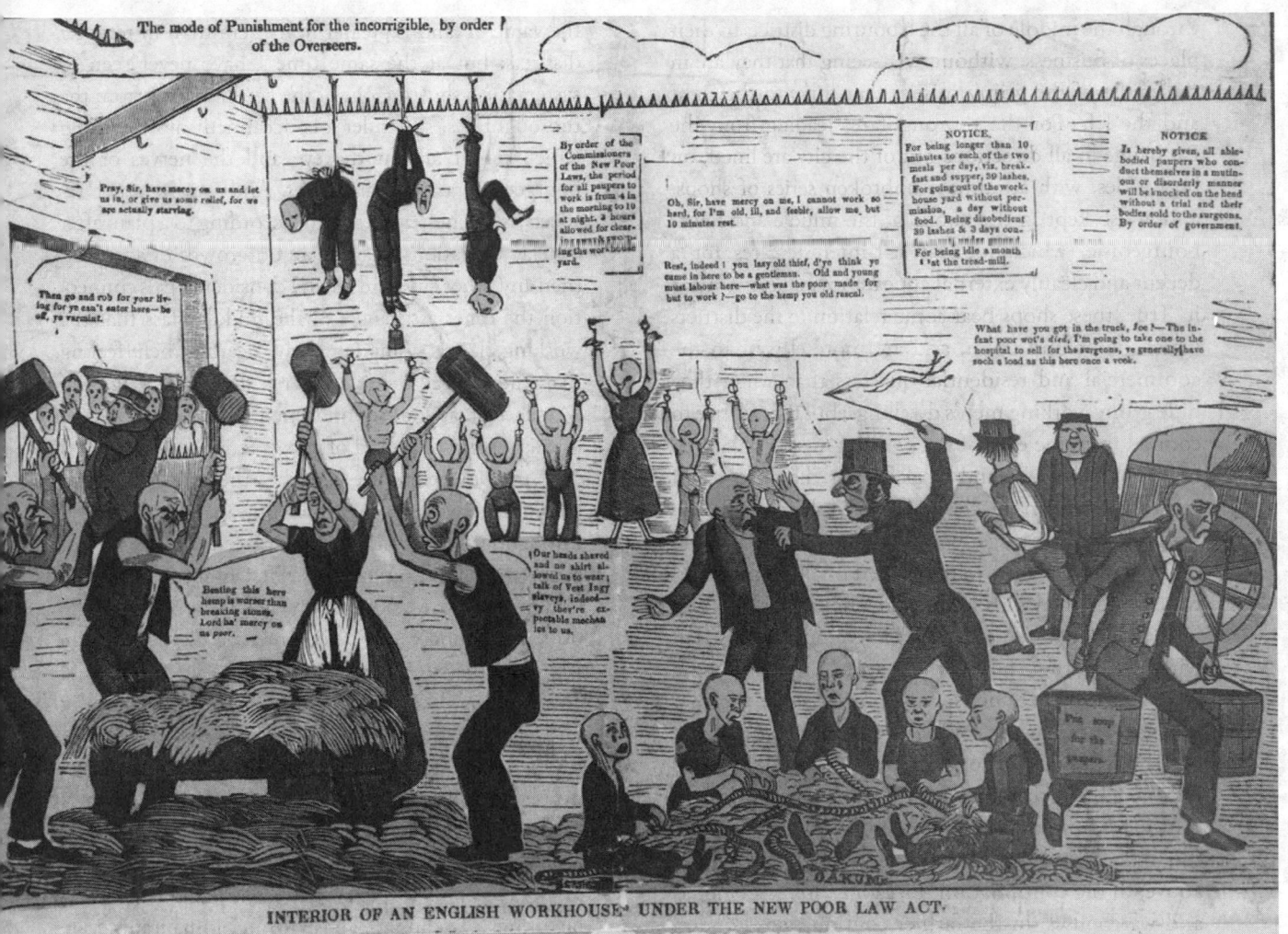

Anonymous, *The New Poor Law with a Description of the New Workhouses*, c. 1834. In the early nineteenth century, each parish administered its own relief for the poor. This might be provided in the form of a minimum allowance, or it might be provided via a workhouse, an institution in which the poor were given lodging and a minimal level of sustenance in exchange for work performed. This parish relief system was unpopular with a large proportion of the middle and leisure classes, who believed that many of the people the system supported were merely avoiding work out of laziness. Such concerns led to the passing of the 1834 Poor Law Amendment Act, which attempted to reduce the costs of poverty relief by discouraging people from claiming it. Allowances for the able-bodied were made illegal, and workhouses, the only remaining option, now consistently were designed to be as unpleasant as possible: families were separated by gender, strict discipline and uniforms were imposed, and food was unappealing. Residents of the workhouse were forbidden to leave without permission, and they were required to perform daily manual labor of a sort similar to the work assigned to prison inmates. Corporal punishment was sometimes used to keep workhouse inhabitants in line, but solitary confinement and denial of food were more usual disciplinary measures. The anonymous poster reproduced here reflects real workhouse practices—although many of them are represented in exaggerated form.

through the middle of all the labouring districts to their places of business, without ever seeing that they are in the midst of the grimy misery that lurks to the right and the left. For the thoroughfares leading from the Exchange in all directions out of the city are lined, on both sides, with an almost unbroken series of shops, and are so kept in the hands of the middle and lower bourgeoisie, which, out of self-interest, cares for a decent and cleanly external appearance and can *care* for it. True, these shops bear some relation to the districts which lie behind them, and are more elegant in the commercial and residential quarters than when they hide grimy working men's dwellings; but they suffice to conceal from the eyes of the wealthy men and women of strong stomachs and weak nerves the misery and grime which form the complement to their wealth. So, for instance, Deansgate, which leads from the Old Church directly southward, is lined first with mills and warehouses, then with second-rate shops and alehouses; farther south, when it leaves the commercial district, with less inviting shops, which grow dirtier and more interrupted by beer houses and gin palaces the farther one goes, until at the southern end the appearance of the shops leaves no doubt that workers and workers only are their customers. So Market Street running south-east from the Exchange; at first brilliant shops of the best sort, with counting-houses or warehouses above; in the continuation, Piccadilly, immense hotels and warehouses; in the farther continuation, London Road, in the neighbourhood of the Medlock, factories, beerhouses, shops for the humbler bourgeoisie and the working population; and from this point onward, large gardens and villas of the wealthier merchants and manufacturers. In this way anyone who knows Manchester can infer the adjoining districts, from the appearance of the thoroughfare, but one is seldom in a position to catch from the street a glimpse of the real labouring districts. I know very well that this hypocritical plan is more or less common to all great cities; I know, too, that the retail dealers are forced by the nature of their business to take possession of the great highways; I know that there are more good buildings than bad ones upon such streets everywhere, and that

the value of land is greater near them than in remoter districts; but at the same time I have never seen so systematic a shutting out of the working class from the thoroughfares, so tender a concealment of everything which might affront the eye and the nerves of the bourgeoisie, as in Manchester. And yet, in other respects, Manchester is less built according to a plan, after official regulations, is more an outgrowth of accident, than any other city; and when I consider in this connection the eager assurances of the middle class that the working class is doing famously, I cannot help feeling that the liberal manufacturers, the "Big Wigs" of Manchester, are not so innocent after all, in the matter of this sensitive method of construction.

I may mention just here that the mills almost all adjoin the rivers or the different canals that ramify[1] throughout the city, before I proceed at once to describe the labouring quarters. First of all, there is the Old Town of Manchester, which lies between the northern boundary of the commercial district and the Irk. Here the streets, even the better ones, are narrow and winding, like Todd Street, Long Millgate, Withy Grove, and Shude Hill, the houses dirty, old, and tumble-down, and the construction of the side streets utterly horrible. Going from the Old Church to Long Millgate, the stroller has at once a row of old-fashioned houses on the right, of which not one has kept its original level; these are remnants of the old pre-manufacturing Manchester, whose former inhabitants have removed with their descendants into better-built districts, and have left the houses, which were not good enough for them, to a working-class population strongly mixed with Irish blood. Here one is in an almost undisguised working men's quarter, for even the shops and beerhouses hardly take the trouble to exhibit a trifling degree of cleanliness. But all this is nothing in comparison with the courts and lanes which lie behind, to which access can be gained only through covered passages, in which no two human beings can pass at the same time. Of the irregular cramming together of dwellings in ways which defy all rational plan, of the

---

[1] *ramify* Branch.

tangle in which they are crowded literally one upon the other, it is impossible to convey an idea. And it is not the buildings surviving from the old times of Manchester which are to blame for this; the confusion has only recently reached its height when every scrap of space left by the old way of building has been filled up and patched over until not a foot of land is left to be further occupied. ...

The south bank of the Irk is here very steep and between fifteen and thirty feet high. On this abrupt slope there are planted three rows of houses, of which the lowest rise directly out of the river, while the front walls of the highest stand on the crest of the rise in Long Millgate. Among them are mills on the river; in short, the method of construction is as crowded and disorderly here as in the lower part of Long Millgate. Right and left a multitude of covered passages lead from the main street into numerous courts, and he who turns in thither gets into filth and disgusting grime, the equal of which is not to be found—especially in the courts which lead down to the Irk, and which contain unqualifiedly the most horrible dwellings which I have yet beheld. In one of these courts there stands directly at the entrance, at the end of the covered passage, a privy[1] without a door, so dirty that the inhabitants can pass into and out of the court only by passing through foul pools of stagnant urine and excrement. This is the first court on the Irk above Ducie Bridge—in case anyone should care to look into it. Below it on the river there are several tanneries which fill the whole neighbourhood with the stench of animal putrefaction. Below Ducie Bridge the only entrance to most of the houses is by means of narrow, dirty stairs and over heaps of refuse and filth. The first court below Ducie Bridge, known as Allen's Court, was in such a state at the time of the cholera[2] that the sanitary police ordered it evacuated, swept, and disinfected with chloride of lime. ... Since then, it seems to have been partially torn down and rebuilt; at least, looking down from Ducie Bridge, the passer-by sees several ruined walls and heaps of debris

with some newer houses. The view from this bridge, mercifully concealed from mortals of small stature by a parapet as high as a man, is characteristic for the whole district. At the bottom flows, or rather stagnates, the Irk, a narrow, coal-black, foul-smelling stream, full of debris and refuse, which it deposits on the lower right bank. In dry weather, a lone string of the most disgusting blackish-green slime pools are left standing on this bank, from the depths of which bubbles of miasmatic[3] gas constantly arise and give forth a stench unendurable even on the bridge forty or fifty feet above the surface of the stream. But besides this, the stream itself is checked every few paces by high weirs,[4] behind which slime and refuse accumulate and rot in thick masses. Above the bridge are tanneries, bone mills, and gasworks, from which all drains and refuse find their way into the Irk, which receives further the contents of all the neighbouring sewers and privies. It may be easily imagined, therefore, what sort of residue the stream deposits. Below the bridge you look upon the piles of debris, the refuse, filth, and offal[5] from the courts on the steep left bank; here each house is packed close behind its neighbour and a bit of each is visible, all black, smoky, crumbling, ancient, with broken panes and window-frames. The background is furnished by old barrack-like factory buildings. On the lower right bank stands a long row of houses and mills, the second row being a ruin without a roof, piled with debris; the third stands so low that the lowest floor is uninhabitable, and therefore without windows or doors. Here the background embraces the pauper burial-ground, the station of the Liverpool and Leeds railway, and, in the rear of this, the workhouse, the "Poor-Law Bastille"[6] of Manchester, which, like a citadel, looks threateningly down from behind its high walls and parapets on the

---

[1] *privy* Outhouse.

[2] *the time of the cholera* I.e., 1832.

[3] *miasmatic* Consisting of noxious vapor.

[4] *weirs* Human-made river barriers that control the flow of water.

[5] *offal* Garbage.

[6] *Poor-Law Bastille* Because of the terrible conditions in the workhouses (established by the Poor Laws in the 1830s), including poor food, monotonous make-work, and the separation of families, workhouses were often compared to prisons such as the famous Bastille in Paris.

A cross-section of working-class low-lodgings. The crowded rooms and open sewer running beneath the building provide examples of the sort of deplorable living conditions described by Engels in his examination of Manchester.

hilltop, upon the working people's quarter below. ...

Such is the Old Town of Manchester, and, on re-reading my description, I am forced to admit that instead of being exaggerated, it is far from black enough to convey a true impression of the filth, ruin, and uninhabitableness, the defiance of all considerations of cleanliness, ventilation, and health which characterize the construction of this single district, containing at least twenty to thirty thousand inhabitants. And such a district exists in the heart of the second city of England, the first manufacturing city of the world. If anyone

wishes to see in how little space a human being can move, how little air—and *such* air—he can breathe, how little of civilization he may share and yet live, it is only necessary to travel hither. True, this is the *Old* Town, and the people of Manchester emphasize the fact whenever anyone mentions to them the frightful condition of this Hell upon Earth; but what does that prove? Everything which here arouses horror and indignation is of recent origin, belongs to the *industrial epoch*. The couple of hundred houses which belong to Old Manchester have been long since abandoned by their original inhabitants; the industrial epoch alone has crammed into them the swarms of workers whom they now shelter; the industrial epoch alone has built up every spot between these old houses to make a covering for the masses whom it has conjured hither from the agricultural districts and from Ireland; the industrial epoch alone enables the owners of these cattle sheds to rent them for high prices to human beings, to plunder the poverty of the workers, to undermine the health of thousands, in order that they only, the owners, may grow rich. In the industrial epoch alone has it become possible that the worker scarcely freed from feudal servitude can be used as mere material, a mere chattel; that he must let himself be crowded into a dwelling too bad for every other, which he for his hard-earned wages buys the right to let go utterly to ruin. This is what manufacture has achieved, and, without these workers and their poverty, this slavery would have been impossible. True, the original construction of this quarter was bad, little good could have been made out of it; but, have the land-owners, has the municipality done anything to improve it when rebuilding? On the contrary, wherever a nook or corner was free, a house has been run up; where a superfluous passage remained, it has been built on; the value of land rose with the blossoming out of manufacture, and the more it rose, the more madly was the work of building carried on, without reference to the health or comfort of the inhabitants, with sole reference to the highest possible profit, on the principle that *no hole is so bad but that some poor creature must take it who can pay for nothing better*. However, it is the Old Town, and with this reflection the bourgeoisie is comforted.

from Elizabeth Gaskell, *Mary Barton* (1848)

CHAPTER 6

John Barton was not far wrong in his idea that the Messrs.[1] Carson would not be over-much grieved for the consequences of the fire in their mill. They were well insured; the machinery lacked the improvements of late years, and worked but poorly in comparison with that which might now be procured. Above all, trade was very slack; cottons could find no market, and goods lay packed and piled in many a warehouse. The mills were merely worked to keep the machinery, human and metal, in some kind of order and readiness for better times. So this was an excellent opportunity, Messrs. Carson thought, for refitting their factory with first-rate improvements, for which the insurance-money would amply pay. They were in no hurry about the business, however. The weekly drain of wages given for labour, useless in the present state of the market, was stopped. The partners had more leisure than they had known for years, and promised wives and daughters all manner of pleasant excursions, as soon as the weather should become more genial. It was a pleasant thing to be able to lounge over breakfast with a review or newspaper in hand; to have time for becoming acquainted with agreeable and accomplished daughters, on whose education no money had been spared, but whose fathers, shut up during a long day with calicoes[2] and accounts, had so seldom had leisure to enjoy their daughters' talents. There were happy family evenings, now that the men of business had time for domestic enjoyments. There is another side to the picture. There were homes over which Carsons' fire threw a deep, terrible gloom; the homes of those who would fain[3] work, and no man gave unto them—the homes of those to whom leisure was a curse. There, the family music was angry wails, when week after week passed by, and there was no work to be had, and consequently no wages to pay for the bread the children cried aloud for in their young impatience of suffering. There was no breakfast to lounge over; their lounge was taken in bed, to try and keep warmth in them that bitter March weather, and, by being quiet, to deaden the gnawing wolf within. Many a penny that would have gone little way enough in oatmeal or potatoes bought opium to still the hungry

---

[1] *Messrs.* Plural form of "Mr."

[2] *calicoes* Cotton cloths.

[3] *fain* Willingly.

little ones,[1] and make them forget their uneasiness in heavy troubled sleep. It was mother's mercy. The evil and the good of our nature came out strongly then. There were desperate fathers; there were bitter-tongued mothers (Oh God! what wonder!); there were reckless children; the very closest bonds of nature were snapped in that time of trial and distress. There was Faith such as the rich can never imagine on earth; there was "Love strong as death"; and, self-denial, among rude, coarse men, akin to that of Sir Philip Sidney's most glorious deed.[2] The vices of the poor sometimes astound us *here*; but when the secrets of all hearts shall be made known, their virtues will astound us in far greater degree. Of this I am certain.

As the cold, bleak spring came on (spring, in name alone), and consequently as trade continued dead, other mills shortened hours, turned off hands,[3] and finally stopped work altogether.

Barton worked short hours; Wilson, of course, being a hand in Carsons' factory, had no work at all. But his son, working at an engineer's, and a steady man, obtained wages enough to maintain all the family in a careful way. Still it preyed on Wilson's mind to be so long indebted to his son. He was out of spirits and depressed. Barton was morose, and soured towards mankind as a body, and the rich in particular. One evening, when the clear light at six o'clock contrasted strangely with the Christmas cold, and when the bitter wind piped down every entry, and through every cranny, Barton sat brooding over his stinted fire, and listening for Mary's step, in unacknowledged trust that her presence would cheer him. The door was opened, and Wilson came breathless in.

"You've not got a bit o' money by you, Barton?" asked he.

"Not I; who has now, I'd like to know. Whatten you want it for?"

"I donnot want it for mysel', tho' we've none to spare. But don[4] you know Ben Davenport as worked at Carsons'? He's down wi' the fever, and ne'er a stick o' fire nor a cowd[5] potato in the house."

"I han got no money, I tell ye," said Barton. Wilson looked disappointed. Barton tried not to be interested, but he could not help it in spite of his gruffness. He rose, and went to the cupboard (his wife's pride long ago). There lay the remains of his dinner, hastily put by ready for supper. Bread, and a slice of cold fat boiled bacon. He wrapped them in his handkerchief, put them in the crown of his hat and said—"Come, let's be going."

from Charles Dickens, *Hard Times* (1854)

CHAPTER 5: THE KEY-NOTE

Coketown, to which Messrs.[6] Bounderby and Grad-grind now walked, was a triumph of fact; it had no greater taint of fancy in it than Mrs. Gradgrind herself. Let us strike the key-note, Coketown, before pursuing our tune.

It was a town of red brick, or of brick that would have been red if the smoke and ashes had allowed it; but as matters stood it was a town of unnatural red and black like the painted face of a savage. It was a town of machinery and tall chimneys, out of which interminable serpents of smoke trailed themselves forever and ever, and never got uncoiled. It had a black canal in it, and a river that ran purple with ill-smelling dye, and vast piles of building full of windows where there was a rattling and trembling all day long, and where the piston of the steam-engine worked monotonously up and down, like the head of an elephant in a state of melancholy madness. It contained several large streets all very like one another, and many small streets still more like one

[1] *opium ... hungry little ones*   The apparently common practice among working-class families of giving sick or hungry infants opium or laudanum to help them sleep was frequently discussed at the time.

[2] *Sir Philip ... deed*   Poet and courtier Sir Philip Sidney (1554–86), who served in many diplomatic missions on the Continent, is said to have refused a glass of water offered to him when he lay dying on the battlefield at Zutphen, in the Netherlands. He instead gave the glass to a less seriously wounded soldier, saying "Thy necessity is greater than mine."

[3] *turned off hands*   I.e., laid off workers.

[4] *don*   Do.

[5] *cowd*   I.e., cold.

[6] *Messrs.*   Plural form of "Mr."

another, inhabited by people equally like one another, who all went in and out at the same hours, with the same sound upon the same pavements, to do the same work, and to whom every day was the same as yesterday and tomorrow, and every year the counterpart of the last and the next.

These attributes of Coketown were in the main inseparable from the work by which it was sustained; against them were to be set off, comforts of life which found their way all over the world, and elegancies of life which made, we will not ask how much of the fine lady, who could scarcely bear to hear the place mentioned. The rest of its features were voluntary, and they were these.

You saw nothing in Coketown but what was severely workful. If the members of a religious persuasion built a chapel there—as the members of eighteen religious persuasions had done—they made it a pious warehouse of red brick, with sometimes (but this is only in highly ornamental examples) a bell in a birdcage on the top of it. The solitary exception was the New Church; a stuccoed edifice with a square steeple over the door, terminating in four short pinnacles like florid wooden legs. All the public inscriptions in the town were painted alike, in severe characteristics of black and white. The jail might have been the infirmary, the infirmary might have been the jail, the town hall might have been either, or both, or anything else, for anything that appeared to the contrary in the graces of their construction. Fact, fact, fact, everywhere in the immaterial. The M'Choakumchild school was all fact, and the school of design was all fact, and the relations between master and man were all fact, and everything was fact between the lying-in hospital and the cemetery, and what you couldn't state in figures, or show to be purchaseable in the cheapest market and saleable in the dearest,[1] was not, and never should be, world without end, Amen.[2]

A town so sacred to fact, and so triumphant in its assertion, of course got on well? Why no, not quite well. No? Dear me!

No. Coketown did not come out of its own furnaces, in all respects like gold that had stood the fire. First, the perplexing mystery of the place was, Who belonged to the eighteen denominations? Because, whoever did, the labouring people did not. It was very strange to walk through the streets on a Sunday morning, and note how few of *them* the barbarous jangling of bells that was driving the sick and nervous mad, called away from their own quarter, from their own close rooms, from the corners of their own streets, where they lounged listlessly, gazing at all the church and chapel going, as at a thing with which they had no manner of concern. Nor was it merely the stranger who noticed this, because there was a native organization in Coketown itself, whose members were to be heard of in the House of Commons every session, indignantly petitioning for Acts of Parliament that should make these people religious by main force.[3] Then came the Teetotal Society, who complained that these same people *would* get drunk, and showed their tabular statements that they did get drunk, and proved at tea parties that no inducement, human or divine (except a medal), would induce them to forego their custom of getting drunk. Then came the chemist and druggist, with other tabular statements, showing that when they didn't get drunk, they took opium. Then came the experienced chaplain of the jail, with more tabular statements, outdoing all the previous tabular statements, and showing that the same people *would* resort to low haunts, hidden from the public eye, where they heard low singing and saw low dancing, and mayhap[4] joined in it; and where A.B., aged twenty-four next birthday, and committed for eighteen months' solitary,

---

[1] *dearest* Most expensive.

[2] *never should be … Amen* From the Anglican Book of Common Prayer: "Glory be to the Father, and to the Son, and to the Holy Ghost; as it was in the beginning, is now, and ever shall be, world without end. Amen."

[3] *members … main force* See Dickens's pamphlet *Sunday Under Three Heads* (written under the pseudonym "Timothy Sparks"), in which he vehemently opposes the "Sunday Observance Bill." Sir Andrew Agnew and his Evangelical group recommended to Parliament a series of moral reforms focusing on curtailing activities on Sunday, which Dickens contended would severely restrict the ability of the poor to enjoy their one day in the week that was free of labor.

[4] *mayhap* Perhaps.

London Nomads by John Thomson,
from *Street Life in London* (1877).

had himself said (not that he had ever shown himself particularly worthy of belief) his ruin began, as he was perfectly sure and confident that otherwise he would have been a tip-top moral specimen. Then came Mr. Gradgrind and Mr. Bounderby, the two gentlemen at this present moment walking through Coketown, and both eminently practical, who could, on occasion, furnish more tabular statements derived from their own personal experience, and illustrated by cases they had known and seen, from which it clearly appeared—in short, it was the only clear thing in the case—that these same people were a bad lot altogether, gentlemen; that do what you would for them they were never thankful for it, gentlemen; that they were restless, gentlemen; that they never knew what they wanted; that they lived upon the best, and bought fresh butter; and insisted on Mocha coffee, and rejected all but prime parts of meat, and yet were eternally dissatisfied and unmanageable. In short, it was the moral of the old nursery fable:

There was an old woman, and what do you think
She lived upon nothing but victuals and drink;
Victuals and drink were the whole of her diet,
And yet this old woman would NEVER be quiet.

from Henry Mayhew, *London Labour and the London Poor*, "Boy Crossing-Sweepers and Tumblers" (1851)

A remarkably intelligent lad, who, on being spoken to, at once consented to give all the information in his power, told me the following story of his life.

It will be seen from this boy's account, and the one or two following, that a kind of partnership exists among some of these young sweepers. They have associated themselves together, appropriated several crossings to their use, and appointed a captain over them. They have their forms of trial, and "jury-house" for the settlement of disputes; laws have been framed, which govern their commercial proceedings, and a kind of language adopted by the society for its better protection from the arch-enemy, the policeman.

I found the lad who first gave me an insight into the proceedings of the associated crossing-sweepers crouched on the stone steps of a door in Adelaide Street, Strand; and when I spoke to him he was preparing to settle down in a corner and go to sleep—his legs and body being curled round almost as closely as those of a cat on a hearth. The moment he heard my voice he was upon his feet, asking me to "give a halfpenny to poor little Jack."

He was a good-looking lad, with a pair of large mild eyes, which he took good care to turn up with an expression of supplication as he moaned for a halfpenny.

A cap, or more properly a stuff bag, covered a crop of hair which had matted itself into the form of so many paint-brushes, while his face, from its roundness of feature and the complexion of dirt, had an almost Indian look about it; the colour of his hands, too, was such that you could imagine he had been shelling walnuts.

He ran before me, treading cautiously with his naked feet, until I reached a convenient spot to take down his statement, which was as follows:

The boy crossing sweepers, from Henry Mayhew's *London Labour and the London Poor* (1861 edition).

"I've got no mother or father; mother has been dead for two years, and father's been gone for more than that—more nigh[1] five years—he died at Ipswich, in Suffolk. He was a perfumer by trade, and used to make hair-dye, and scent, and pomatum,[2] and all kinds of scents. He didn't keep a shop himself, but he used to serve them as did; he didn't hawk his goods about, neether, but had regular customers, what used to send him a letter, and then he'd take them what they wanted. Yes, he used to serve some good shops: there was H—'s, of London Bridge, what's a large chemist's. He used to make a good deal of money, but he lost it betting; and so his brother, my uncle, did all his. …

"After mother died, sister still kept on making nets,[3] and I lived with her for some time. But she was keeping company with a young man, and one day they went out, and came back and said they'd been and got married. It was him as got rid of me.

"He was kind to me for the first two or three months, while he was keeping her company; but before he was married he got a little cross, and after he was married he begun to get more cross, and used to send me to play in the streets, and tell me not to come home

A group of homeless boys just after being admitted to a shelter. (Photograph by John Thomson, c. 1880.)

again till night. One day he hit me, and I said I wouldn't be hit about by him, and then at tea that night sister gave me three shillings, and told me I must go and get my own living. So I bought a box and brushes (they cost me just the money) and went cleaning boots, and I done pretty well with them, till my box was stole from me by a boy where I was lodging. He's in prison now—got six calendar[4] for picking pockets. …

"I was fifteen the 24th of last May, sir, and I've been sweeping crossings now near upon two years. There's a party of six of us, and we have the crossings from St. Martin's Church as far as Pall Mall. I always go along with them as lodges in the same place as I do. In the daytime, if it's dry, we do anythink we can—open cabs, or anythink; but if it's wet, we separate, and I an' another gets a crossing—those who gets on it first, keeps it—and we stand on each side and take our chance.

---

[1] *more nigh* Closer to.

[2] *pomatum* Scented ointment for the hair.

[3] *nets* Meshwork or network, used for various purposes.

[4] *six calendar* I.e., six months.

Peter Henry Emerson and Thomas Frederick Goodall, "Coming Home from the Marshes," from *Life and Landscape on the Norfolk Broads*, 1887. While laborers in urban centers suffered deplorable living and working conditions, rural laborers also suffered from exploitative wages, long work hours, and poor housing. On the whole, rural families made do with dwellings, food, and clothing that were even worse than what their urban counterparts had—but poor people in the countryside nonetheless lived longer than those in the unsanitary, polluted cities and factory towns. This image, taken by the photographer Peter Henry Emerson in collaboration with Thomas Frederick Goodall, is part of their collection of photographs taken on the Norfolk Broads, where livelihoods were becoming increasingly precarious due to economic changes associated with England's industrialization. Influenced by the naturalist school of painting, Emerson and Goodall strove to capture what an observer would really see, but their photographs were nonetheless staged—a necessity given the long exposure time required by the camera they used.

"We do it this way: if I was to see two gentlemen coming, I should cry out, 'Two toffs!' and then they are mine; and whether they give me anythink or not they are mine, and my mate is bound not to follow them; for if he did he would get a hiding[1] from the whole lot of us. If we both cry out together, then we share. If it's a lady and a gentleman, then we cries, 'A toff and a doll!' Sometimes we are caught out in this way. Perhaps it is a lady and gentleman and a child; and if I was to see them, and only say, 'A toff and a doll,' and leave out the child, then my mate can add the child; and as he is right and I wrong, then it's his party.

"If there's a policeman coming we musn't ask for money; but we are always on the look-out for policemen, and if we see one, then we calls out 'Phillup!' for that's our signal. One of the policemen at St. Martin's Church—Bandy, we calls him—knows what Phillup means, for he's up to us; so we had to change the word. (At the request of the young crossing-sweeper the present signal is omitted.) ...

---

[1] *hiding* Walloping; beating.

"When we see the rain we say together, 'Oh! there's a jolly good rain! we'll have a good day tomorrow.' If a shower comes on, and we are at our room, which we general are about three o'clock, to get somethink to eat—besides, we general go there to see how much each other's taken in the day—why, out we run with our brooms.

"At night-time we tumbles[1]—that is, if the policeman ain't nigh. We goes general to Waterloo Place when the opera's on. We sends on one of us ahead, as a looker-out, to look for the policeman, and then we follows. It's no good tumbling to gentlemen *going* to the opera; it's when they're coming back they gives us money. When they've got a young lady on their arm they laugh at us tumbling; some will give us a penny, others threepence, sometimes a sixpence or a shilling, and sometimes a halfpenny. We either do the cat'un-wheel,[2] or else we keep before the gentleman and lady, turning head-over-heels, putting our broom on the ground and then turning over it. …

"When we are talking together we always talk in a kind of slang. Each policeman we gives a regular name—there's 'Bull's Head,' 'Bandy Shanks,' and 'Old Cherry Legs,' and 'Dot-and-carry-one'; they all knows their names as well as us. We never talks of crossings, but 'fakes.' We don't make no slang of our own, but uses the regular one."

---

[1] *tumbles* Perform leaps, somersaults, etc., like acrobats.   [2] *cat'unwheel* Cartwheel.

MARY SEACOLE
1805 – 1881

During the Crimean War in Russia (1854–56), two women particularly distinguished themselves for nursing wounded soldiers. One was the renowned "Lady with the Lamp," Florence Nightingale; the other was Mary Seacole, a native of Jamaica who had attempted to join Nightingale's nursing team but had been refused on the basis of her color. Seacole worked on the front lines in the Crimea, closer to the battlefields than any of Nightingale's nurses, and unlike Nightingale's, her journey, medicines, and supplies were self-funded. At the close of the war Seacole left the Crimea impoverished and ill. Fortunately, the famous war correspondent (later Sir) W.H. Russell recounted her story in *The Times*, and the same British public that had once ostracized her came to her aid. Seacole was also eventually recognized for her service by the French and Turkish governments, and in 1857 her autobiography, *Wonderful Adventures of Mrs. Seacole in Many Lands*, a lively narrative and telling commentary on Victorian attitudes toward race, became a bestseller.

Mary Grant was born a "free" Black in 1805 in the British colony of Jamaica. A self-described "Creole" with "good Scotch blood coursing" in her veins, Seacole later attributed her energy and work ethic to her father, a Scottish military officer, and her generous nature and vast knowledge of the medicinal arts to her Jamaican mother, a healer who ran a boardinghouse in Kingston for convalescing officers. Upon reaching adulthood, Seacole became an inveterate traveler, journeying to England, Haiti, the Bahamas, and Cuba. She married Edwin Horatio Seacole in 1836; together they continued to travel, but the marriage was cut short by his early death. Her mother died soon afterward, and Seacole took over her business and became known as a gifted healer herself, treating cholera and yellow fever victims in Jamaica and later in Panama. It was in the latter country that an American offered to bleach her "yeller" skin, which prompted the following reply: "As to the society which the process might gain me admission into, all I can say is, that, judging from the specimens I have met here and elsewhere, I don't think that I shall lose much by being excluded from it."

Back in Jamaica Seacole treated many British soldiers; when she heard that some were being sent to the war in the Crimea and that nurses were desperately needed for the cause, she undertook a voyage to England to offer her services. There, Seacole again felt the effects of discrimination. In her autobiography, Seacole describes her reaction after she had been denied support from the War Office and turned down by Florence Nightingale's recruitment staff: "Was it possible that American prejudices against colour had some root here? Did these ladies shrink from accepting my aid because my blood flowed beneath a somewhat duskier skin than theirs? Tears streamed down my foolish cheeks, as I stood in the fast thinning streets; tears of grief that any should doubt my motives." Determined to offer her services as a nurse, Seacole left for the Crimea at her own expense.

The Crimean War—a conflict in which Russian soldiers fought an alliance including British, French, and Turkish fighters—was bloody and deadly. Tens of thousands of soldiers on each side died of battle wounds, but far more were killed by disease. In Scutari, Turkey, she visited Nightingale's hospital and came away with this impression: "One thought never left my mind as I walked through the fearful miles of suffering in that great hospital. If it is so here, what must it not be at the scene of war—on the spot where the poor fellows are stricken down by pestilence or Russian bullets, and days and nights of agony must be passed before a woman's hand can dress their wounds. And I felt happy in the conviction that I must be useful three or four days nearer to their pressing wants than this." Thus it was that Seacole made the decision to tender her nursing services on the front lines in the Crimea.

Seacole set up the "British Hotel" near the front, accommodating, feeding, and treating British officers' ailments, and with the profits from this venture she purchased medicines and cared for wounded soldiers, both Allied and Russian, on the front. When the war ended, her services were redundant and her finances depleted. Taking up her cause, Russell publicized Seacole's charity and her devotion to the care of soldiers, and *Punch* magazine published a poem about the "kindly old soul" that prompted an outpouring of donations. By the time she died in London in 1881, Seacole had secured a comfortable income, partly acquired through proceeds from her autobiography.

⌘ ⌘ ⌘

from *Wonderful Adventures of Mrs. Seacole in Many Lands*

CHAPTER I
MY BIRTH AND PARENTAGE—EARLY TASTES AND TRAVELS—MARRIAGE AND WIDOWHOOD

I was born in the town of Kingston, in the island of Jamaica, some time in the present century. As a female, and a widow, I may well be excused giving the precise date of this important event. But I do not mind confessing that the century and myself were both young together, and that we have grown side by side into age and consequence. I am a Creole,[1] and have good Scotch blood coursing in my veins. My father was a soldier, of an old Scotch family; and to him I often trace my affection for a camp-life, and my sympathy with what I have heard my friends call "the pomp, pride, and circumstance of glorious war."[2] Many people have also traced to my Scotch blood that energy and activity which are not always found in the Creole race, and

which have carried me to so many varied scenes: and perhaps they are right. I have often heard the term "lazy Creole" applied to my country people; but I am sure I do not know what it is to be indolent. All my life long I have followed the impulse which led me to be up and doing; and so far from resting idle anywhere, I have never wanted[3] inclination to rove, nor will powerful enough to find a way to carry out my wishes. That these qualities have led me into many countries, and brought me into some strange and amusing adventures, the reader, if he or she has the patience to get through this book, will see. Some people, indeed, have called me quite a female Ulysses.[4] I believe that they intended it as a compliment; but from my experience of the Greeks, I do not consider it a very flattering one.

It is not my intention to dwell at any length upon the recollections of my childhood. My mother kept a boarding-house in Kingston, and was, like very many of the Creole women, an admirable doctress, in high repute with the officers of both services, and their wives, who were from time to time stationed at Kingston. It

---

[1] *Creole* In this case, a West Indian of mixed European and Black descent.

[2] *pomp ... war* From Shakespeare's *Othello*, 3.3.354. The line is slightly misquoted; it should read "pride, pomp and circumstance of glorious war."

[3] *wanted* Lacked.

[4] *Ulysses* Mythical hero of the Trojan War who roamed far and wide before returning to his home in Ithaca. "Ulysses" is the Roman name for the Greek Odysseus.

was very natural that I should inherit her tastes; and so I had from early youth a yearning for medical knowledge and practice which has never deserted me. When I was a very young child I was taken by an old lady, who brought me up in her household among her own grandchildren, and who could scarcely have shown me more kindness had I been one of them; indeed, I was so spoiled by my kind patroness that but for being frequently with my mother, I might very likely have grown up idle and useless. But I saw so much of her, and of her patients, that the ambition to become a doctress early took firm root in my mind; and I was very young when I began to make use of the little knowledge I had acquired from watching my mother, upon a great sufferer—my doll. I have noticed always what actors children are. If you leave one alone in a room, how soon it clears a little stage; and, making an audience out of a few chairs and stools, proceeds to act its childish griefs and blandishments upon its doll. So I also made good use of my dumb companion and confidante; and whatever disease was most prevalent in Kingston, be sure my poor doll soon contracted it. I have had many medical triumphs in later days, and saved some valuable lives; but I really think that few have given me more real gratification than the rewarding glow of health which my fancy used to picture stealing over my patient's waxen face after long and precarious illness.

Before long it was very natural that I should seek to extend my practice; and so I found other patients in the dogs and cats around me. Many luckless brutes were made to simulate diseases which were raging among their owners, and had forced down their reluctant throats the remedies which I deemed most likely to suit their supposed complaints. And after a time I rose still higher in my ambition; and despairing of finding another human patient, I proceeded to try my simples[1] and essences upon—myself.

When I was about twelve years old I was more frequently at my mother's house, and used to assist her in her duties; very often sharing with her the task of attending upon invalid officers or their wives, who came to her house from the adjacent camp at Up-Park,[2] or the military station at Newcastle.

As I grew into womanhood, I began to indulge that longing to travel which will never leave me while I have health and vigour. I was never weary of tracing upon an old map the route to England; and never followed with my gaze the stately ships homeward bound without longing to be in them, and see the blue hills of Jamaica fade into the distance. At that time it seemed most improbable that these girlish wishes should be gratified; but circumstances, which I need not explain, enabled me to accompany some relatives to England while I was yet a very young woman.

I shall never forget my first impressions of London. Of course, I am not going to bore the reader with them; but they are as vivid now as though the year 18— (I had very nearly let my age slip then) had not been long ago numbered in the past. Strangely enough, some of the most vivid of my recollections are the efforts of London street-boys to poke fun at my and my companion's complexion. I am only a little brown—a few shades duskier than the brunettes whom you all admire so much; but my companion was very dark, and a fair (if I can apply the term to her) subject for their rude wit. She was hot-tempered, poor thing! and as there were no policemen to awe the boys and turn our servants' heads in those days, our progress through the London streets was sometimes a rather chequered one.

I remained in England, upon the occasion of my first visit, about a year; and then returned to Kingston. Before long I again started for London, bringing with me this time a large stock of West Indian preserves and pickles for sale. After remaining two years here, I again started home and on the way my life and adventures were very nearly brought to a premature conclusion. Christmas day had been kept very merrily on board our ship the "Velusia"; and on the following day a fire broke out in the hold. I dare say it would have resisted all the crew's efforts to put it out, had not another ship appeared in sight; upon which the fire quietly allowed itself to be extinguished. Although considerably

---

[1] *simples* Medicines from plants.

[2] *Up-Park* Jamaican camp for British troops.

alarmed, I did not lose my senses; but during the time when the contest between fire and water was doubtful, I entered into an amicable arrangement with the ship's cook, whereby in consideration of two pounds—which I was not, however, to pay until the crisis arrived—he agreed to lash me on to a large hen-coop.

Before I had been long in Jamaica I started upon other trips, many of them undertaken with a view to gain. Thus I spent some time in New Providence,[1] bringing home with me a large collection of handsome shells and rare shell-work, which created quite a sensation in Kingston, and I had a rapid sale; I visited also Haiti and Cuba. But I hasten onward in my narrative.

Returned to Kingston, I nursed my old indulgent patroness in her long last illness. After she died, in my arms, I went to my mother's house, where I stayed, making myself useful in a variety of ways, and learning a great deal of Creole medicinal art, until I couldn't find courage to say "no" to a certain arrangement timidly proposed by Mr. Seacole, but married him, and took him down to Black River, where we established a store. Poor man! he was very delicate; and before I undertook the charge of him, several doctors had expressed most unfavourable opinions of his health. I kept him alive by kind nursing and attention as long as I could; but at last he grew so ill that we left Black River, and returned to my mother's house at Kingston. Within a month of our arrival there he died. This was my first great trouble, and I felt it bitterly. For days I never stirred—lost to all that passed around me in a dull stupor of despair. If you had told me that the time would soon come when I should remember this sorrow calmly, I should not have believed it possible: and yet it was so. I do not think that we hot-blooded Creoles sorrow less for showing it so impetuously; but I do think the sharp edge of our grief wears down sooner than theirs who preserve an outward demeanour of calmness, and nurse their woe secretly in their hearts.

CHAPTER 8
I Long to Join the British Army Before Sebastopol[2] —My Wanderings about London for That Purpose—How I Fail—Establishment of the Firm of "Day and Martin" —I Embark for Turkey

BEFORE I LEFT JAMAICA FOR NAVY BAY,[3] as narrated in the last chapter, war had been declared against Russia, and we were all anxiously expecting news of a descent upon the Crimea. Now, no sooner had I heard of war somewhere, than I longed to witness it; and when I was told that many of the regiments I had known so well in Jamaica had left England for the scene of action, the desire to join them became stronger than ever. I used to stand for hours in silent thought before an old map of the world, in a little corner of which some one had chalked a red cross, to enable me to distinguish where the Crimea was; and as I traced the route thither, all difficulties would vanish. But when I came to talk over the project with my friends, the best scheme I could devise seemed so wild and improbable, that I was fain to resign my hopes for a time, and so started for Navy Bay.

But all the way to England, from Navy Bay, I was turning my old wish over and over in my mind; and when I found myself in London, in the autumn of 1854, just after the battle of Alma[4] had been fought, and my old friends were fairly before the walls of Sebastopol, how to join them there took up far more of my thoughts than that visionary gold-mining speculation on the river Palmilla,[5] which seemed so feasible to us in New Granada, but was considered so wild and unprofitable a speculation in London. And, as time wore on, the inclination to join my old friends of the 97th, 48th and other regiments, battling with worse foes than yellow fever and cholera, took such exclusive possession of my mind, that I threw over the gold speculation altogether, and devoted all my energies to my new scheme.

---

[1] *New Providence* Island of the Bahamas.

[2] *SEBASTOPOL* Port city (now Sevastopol) in Crimea, a peninsula in the Black Sea. Sevastopol was the site of a major Russian naval base and was of strategic importance during the war.

[3] *NAVY BAY* In Panama (then under the rule of New Granada).

[4] *Alma* Site of the first battle of the Crimean War, won by the Allied forces.

[5] *river Palmilla* In Panama (then under the rule of New Granada).

Heaven knows it was visionary enough! I had no friends who could help me in such a project—nay, who would understand why I desired to go, and what I desired to do when I got there. My funds, although they might, carefully husbanded, carry me over the three thousand miles, and land me at Balaclava,[1] would not support me there long; while to persuade the public that an unknown Creole woman would be useful to their army before Sebastopol was too improbable to be thought of for an instant. Circumstances, however, assisted me.

As the winter wore on, came hints from various quarters of mismanagement, want, and suffering in the Crimea; and after the battles of Balaclava and Inkermann,[2] and the fearful storm of the 14th of November, the worst anticipations were realized. Then we knew that the hospitals were full to suffocation, that scarcity and exposure were the fate of all in the camp, and that the brave fellows for whom any of us at home would have split our last shilling, and shared our last meal, were dying thousands of miles away from the active sympathy of their fellow-countrymen. Fast and thick upon the news of Inkermann, fought by a handful of fasting and enfeebled men against eight times their number of picked Russians, brought fresh and animated to the contest, and while all England was reeling beneath the shock of that fearful victory, came the sad news that hundreds were dying whom the Russian shot and sword had spared, and that the hospitals of Scutari[3] were utterly unable to shelter, or their inadequate staff to attend to, the ship-loads of sick and wounded which were sent to them across the stormy Black Sea.

But directly England knew the worst, she set about repairing her past neglect. In every household busy fingers were working for the poor soldier—money flowed in golden streams wherever the need was—and Christian ladies, mindful of the sublime example, "I was sick, and ye visited me,"[4] hastened to volunteer their services by those sick-beds which only women know how to soothe and bless.

Need I be ashamed to confess that I shared in the general enthusiasm, and longed more than ever to carry my busy (and the reader will not hesitate to add experienced) fingers where the sword or bullet had been busiest, and pestilence most rife. I had seen much of sorrow and death elsewhere, but they had never daunted me; and if I could feel happy binding up the wounds of quarrelsome Americans and treacherous Spaniards,[5] what delight should I not experience if I could be useful to my own "sons," suffering for a cause it was so glorious to fight and bleed for! I never stayed to discuss probabilities, or enter into conjectures as to my chances of reaching the scene of action. I made up my mind that if the army wanted nurses, they would be glad of me, and with all the ardour of my nature, which ever carried me where inclination prompted, I decided that I would go to the Crimea; and go I did, as all the world knows.

Of course, had it not been for my old strong-mindedness (which has nothing to do with obstinacy, and is in no way related to it—the best term I can think of to express it being "judicious decisiveness"), I should have given up the scheme a score of times in as many days; so regularly did each successive day give birth to a fresh set of rebuffs and disappointments. I shall make no excuse to my readers for giving them a pretty full history of my struggles to become a Crimean heroine!

My first idea (and knowing that I was well fitted for the work, and would be the right woman in the right place, the reader can fancy my audacity) was to apply to the War Office for the post of hospital nurse. Among the diseases which I understood were most prevalent in the Crimea were cholera, diarrhoea, and dysentery, all of them more or less known in tropical climates; and with which, as the reader will remember, my Panama experi-

---

[1] *Balaclava*   Now Balaklava: site of the disastrous "Charge of the Light Brigade" in 1854, a battle immortalized by Alfred, Lord Tennyson in the same year.

[2] *Inkermann*   Site of the final of three battles fought before the siege of Sebastopol.

[3] *Scutari*   Allied jumping-off point in Turkey and location of the British Barrack Hospital where Florence Nightingale and her nurses worked.

[4] *I was sick, and ye visited me*   See Matthew 25.36.

[5] *binding … Spaniards*   Particularly in Panama, where Seacole nursed many foreigners with wounds or the symptoms of cholera.

ence had made me tolerably familiar. Now, no one will accuse me of presumption, if I say that I thought (and so it afterwards proved) that my knowledge of these human ills would not only render my services as a nurse more valuable, but would enable me to be of use to the overworked doctors. That others thought so too, I took with me ample testimony. I cannot resist the temptation of giving my readers one of the testimonials I had, it seems so eminently practical and to the point:—

"I became acquainted with Mrs. Seacole through the instrumentality of T.B. Cowan, Esq., H.B.M. Consul at Colon, on the Isthmus of Panama, and have had many opportunities of witnessing her professional zeal and ability in the treatment of aggravated forms of tropical diseases.

"I am personally much indebted for her indefatigable kindness and skill at a time when I am apt to believe the advice of a practitioner qualified in the North would have little availed.

"Her peculiar fitness, in a constitutional point of view, for the duties of a medical attendant, needs no comment.
(Signed) "A.G.M.,
"Late Medical Officer, West Granada
Gold-Mining Company."

So I made a long and unwearied application at the War Office, in blissful ignorance of the labour and time I was throwing away. I have reason to believe that I considerably interfered with the repose of sundry messengers, and disturbed, to an alarming degree, the official gravity of some nice gentlemanly young fellows, who were working out their salaries in an easy, off-hand way. But my ridiculous endeavours to gain an interview with the Secretary-at-War of course failed, and glad at last to oblige a distracted messenger, I transferred my attentions to the Quartermaster-General's department. Here I saw another gentleman, who listened to me with a great deal of polite enjoyment, and—his amusement ended—hinted, had I not better apply to the Medical Department; and accordingly I attached myself to their quarters with the same unwearying ardour. But, of course, I grew tired at last, and then changed my plans.

Now, I am not for a single instant going to blame the authorities who would not listen to the offer of a motherly yellow woman to go to the Crimea and nurse her "sons" there, suffering from the cholera, diarrhoea, and a host of lesser ills. In my country, where people know our use, it would have been different; but here it was natural enough—although I had references, and other voices spoke for me—that they should laugh, good-naturedly enough, at my offer. War, I know, is a serious game, but sometimes very humble actors are of great use in it, and if the reader, when he comes in time to peruse the evidence of those who had to do with the Sebastopol drama, of my share in it, will turn back to this chapter, he will confess perhaps that, after all, the impulse which led me to the War Department was not unnatural.

My new scheme was, I candidly confess, worse devised than the one which had failed. Miss Nightingale had left England for the Crimea, but other nurses were still to follow, and my new plan was simply to offer myself to Mrs. H—— as a recruit. Feeling that I was one of the very women most wanted, experienced and fond of the work, I jumped at once to the conclusion that they would gladly enrol me in their number. To go to Cox's, the army agents, who were most obliging to me, and obtain the Secretary-at-War's private address, did not take long; and that done, I laid the same pertinacious siege to his great house in —— —— Square, as I had previously done to his place of business.

Many a long hour did I wait in his great hall, while scores passed in and out; many of them looking curiously at me. The flunkeys,[1] noble creatures! marvelled exceedingly at the yellow woman whom no excuses could be got rid of, nor impertinence dismay, and showed me very clearly that they resented my persisting in remaining there in mute appeal from their sovereign will. At last I gave that up, after a message from Mrs. H. that the full complement of nurses had been secured, and that my offer could not be entertained. Once again I tried, and had an interview this time with one of Miss Nightingale's companions. She gave me the same reply,

---

[1] *flunkeys*   Male attendants or servants.

and I read in her face the fact, that had there been a vacancy, I should not have been chosen to fill it.

As a last resort, I applied to the manager of the Crimean Fund to know whether they would give me a passage to the camp—once there I would trust to something turning up. But this failed also, and one cold evening I stood in the twilight, which was fast deepening into wintry night, and looked back upon the ruins of my last castle in the air. The disappointment seemed a cruel one. I was so conscious of the unselfishness of the motives which induced me to leave England—so certain of the service I could render among the sick soldiery, and yet I found it so difficult to convince others of these facts. Doubts and suspicions arose in my heart for the first and last time, thank Heaven. Was it possible that American prejudices against colour had some root here? Did these ladies shrink from accepting my aid because my blood flowed beneath a somewhat duskier skin than theirs? Tears streamed down my foolish cheeks, as I stood in the fast thinning streets; tears of grief that any should doubt my motives—that Heaven should deny me the opportunity that I sought. Then I stood still, and looking upward through and through the dark clouds that shadowed London, prayed aloud for help. I dare say that I was a strange sight to the few passers-by, who hastened homeward through the gloom and mist of that wintry night. I dare say those who read these pages will wonder at me as much as they who saw me did; but you must all remember that I am one of an impulsive people, and find it hard to put that restraint upon my feelings which to you is so easy and natural.

The morrow, however, brought me fresh hope. A good night's rest had served to strengthen my determination. Let what might happen, to the Crimea I would go. If in no other way, then I would upon my own responsibility and at my own cost. There were those there who had known me in Jamaica, who had been under my care; doctors who would vouch for my skill and willingness to aid them, and a general who had more than once helped me, and would do so still. Why not trust to their welcome and kindness, and start at once? If the authorities had allowed me, I would willingly have given them my services as a nurse; but as they declined them, should I not open an hotel for invalids in the Crimea in my own way? I had no more idea of what the Crimea was than the home authorities themselves perhaps, but having once made up my mind, it was not long before cards were printed and speeding across the Mediterranean to my friends before Sebastopol. Here is one of them:—

"BRITISH HOTEL.
Mrs. Mary Seacole
(Late of Kingston, Jamaica),
Respectfully announces to her former kind friends,
and
to the Officers of the Army and Navy generally,
That she has taken her passage in the screw-steamer[1]
"Hollander," to start from London on the 25th of January, intending on her arrival at Balaclava to establish a mess table and comfortable quarters for sick and convalescent officers."

This bold programme would reach the Crimea in the end of January, at a time when any officer would have considered a stall in an English stable luxurious quarters compared to those he possessed, and had nearly forgotten the comforts of a mess-table. It must have read to them rather like a mockery, and yet, as the reader will see, I succeeded in redeeming my pledge.

While this new scheme was maturing, I again met Mr. Day in England. He was bound to Balaclava upon some shipping business, and we came to the understanding that (if it were found desirable) we should together open a store as well as an hotel in the neighbourhood of the camp. So was originated the well-known firm of Seacole and Day (I am sorry to say the camp wits dubbed it Day and Martin[2]), which, for so many months, did business upon the now deserted high-road from the then busy harbour of Balaclava to the front of the British army before Sebastopol.

---

[1] *screw-steamer* Steamboat driven by a propeller.

[2] *Day and Martin* Day & Martin, prosperous manufacturers of shoe blacking, or polish.

These new arrangements were not allowed to interfere in any way with the main object of my journey. A great portion of my limited capital was, with the kind aid of a medical friend, invested in medicines which I had reason to believe would be useful; with the remainder I purchased those home comforts which I thought would be most difficult to obtain away from England.

I had scarcely set my foot on board the "Hollander," before I met a friend. The supercargo[1] was the brother of the Mr. S——, whose death in Jamaica the reader will not have forgotten, and he gave me a hearty welcome. I thought the meeting augured well, and when I told him my plans he gave me the most cheering encouragement. I was glad, indeed, of any support, for, beyond all doubt, my project was a hazardous one.

So cheered at the outset, I watched without a pang the shores of England sink behind the smooth sea, and turned my gaze hopefully to the as yet landless horizon, beyond which lay that little peninsula to which the eyes and hearts of all England were so earnestly directed.

So, cheerily! the good ship ploughed its way eastward ho![2] for Turkey.

Chapter 9
Voyage to Constantinople—Malta—Gibraltar—Constantinople—And What I Thought of It—Visit to Scutari Hospital—Miss Nightingale

I am not going to risk the danger of wearying the reader with a long account of the voyage to Constantinople,[3] already worn threadbare by book-making tourists. It was not a very interesting one, and, as I am a good sailor, I had not even the temporary horrors of sea-sickness to mar it. The weather, although cold, was fine, and the sea good-humouredly calm, and I enjoyed the voyage amazingly. And as day by day we drew nearer to the scene of action, my doubts of success grew less and less, until I had a conviction of the rightness of the step I had

taken, which would have carried me buoyantly through any difficulties.

On the way, of course, I was called up from my berth at an unreasonable hour to gaze upon the Cape of St. Vincent, and expected to feel duly impressed when the long bay where Trafalgar's fight[4] was won came in view, with the white convent walls on the cliffs above bathed in the early sunlight. I never failed to take an almost childish interest in the signals which passed between the "Hollander" and the fleet of vessels whose sails whitened the track to and from the Crimea, trying to puzzle out the language these children of the ocean spoke in their hurried course, and wondering whether any, or what sufficiently important thing could happen which would warrant their stopping on their busy way.

We spent a short time at Gibraltar, and you may imagine that I was soon on shore making the best use of the few hours' reprieve granted to the "Hollander's" weary engines. I had an idea that I should do better alone, so I declined all offers of companionship, and selecting a brisk young fellow from the mob of cicerones[5] who offered their services, saw more of the art of fortification in an hour or so than I could understand in many years. The pleasure was rather fatiguing, and I was not sorry to return to the marketplace, where I stood curiously watching its strange and motley population. While so engaged, I heard for the first time an exclamation which became familiar enough to me afterwards.

"Why, bless my soul, old fellow, if this is not our good old Mother Seacole!" I turned round, and saw two officers, whose features, set in a broad frame of Crimean beard, I had some difficulty in recognising. But I soon remembered that they were two of the 48th, who had been often in my house at Kingston. Glad were the kind-hearted fellows, and not a little surprised withal, to meet their old hostess in the marketplace of Gibraltar, bound for the scene of action which they had left invalided; and it was not long before we were talking old

---

[1] *supercargo* Worker on a merchant ship who oversees the shipping and selling of cargo.

[2] *eastward ho!* Cf. Shakespeare's *Twelfth Night* 3.1.134: "Then westward-ho!"

[3] *Constantinople* Now Istanbul, Turkey.

[4] *Trafalgar's fight* A decisive naval battle at Trafalgar, in which Britain was victorious over the combined fleets of France and Spain (1805).

[5] *cicerones* Tourist guides.

times over some wine—Spanish, I suppose—but it was very nasty,

"And you are going to the front, old lady—you, of all people in the world?"

"Why not, my sons?—won't they be glad to have me there?"

"By Jove! yes, mother," answered one, an Irishman. "It isn't many women—God bless them!—we've had to spoil us out there. But it's not the place even for you, who know what hardship is? You'll never get a roof to cover you at Balaclava, or on the road either." So they rattled on, telling me of the difficulties that were in store for me. But they could not shake my resolution.

"Do you think I shall be of any use to you when I get there?"

"Surely."

"Then I'll go, were the place a hundred times worse than you describe it. Can't I rig up a hut with packing-cases, and sleep, if need be, on straw, like Margery Daw?"[1]

So they laughed, and drank success to me, and to our next meeting; for, although they were going home invalided, the brave fellows' hearts were with their companions, for all the hardships they had passed through.

We stopped at Malta also, where, of course, I landed, and stared about me, and submitted to be robbed by the lazy Maltese with all a traveller's resignation. Here, also, I met friends—some medical officers who had known me in Kingston; and one of them, Dr. F——, lately arrived from Scutari, gave me, when he heard my plans, a letter of introduction to Miss Nightingale, then hard at work, evoking order out of confusion, and bravely resisting the despotism of death, at the hospital of Scutari.

So on, past beautiful islands and shores, until we are steaming against a swift current, and an adverse wind, between two tower-crested promontories of rock, which they tell me stand in Europe and Asia, and are con-

nected with some pretty tale of love[2] in days long gone by. Ah! travel where a woman may, in the New World, or the Old, she meets this old, old tale everywhere. It is the one bond of sympathy which I have found existing in three quarters of the world alike. So on, until the cable rattles over the windlass,[3] as the good ship's anchor plunges down fathoms deep into the blue waters of the Bosphorus—her voyage ended.

I do not think that Constantinople impressed me so much as I had expected; and I thought its streets would match those of Navy Bay not unfairly. The caicques,[4] also, of which I had ample experience—for I spent six days here, wandering about Pera and Stamboul in the daytime, and returning to the "Hollander" at night-fall—might be made more safe and commodious for stout ladies, even if the process interfered a little with their ornament. Time and trouble combined have left me with a well-filled-out, portly form—the envy of many an angular Yankee female—and, more than once, it was in no slight danger of becoming too intimately acquainted with the temperature of the Bosphorus. But I will do the Turkish boatmen the justice to say that they were as politely careful of my safety as their astonishment and regard for the well-being of their caicques (which they appear to love as an Arab does his horse, or an Eskimo his dogs, and for the same reason perhaps) would admit. Somewhat surprised, also, seemed the cunning-eyed Greeks, who throng the streets of Pera, at the unprotected Creole woman who took Constantinople so coolly (it would require something more to surprise her); while the grave English raised their eyebrows wonderingly, and the more vivacious French shrugged their pliant shoulders into the strangest contortions. I accepted all this as a compliment to a stout female tourist, neatly dressed in a red or yellow dress, a plain shawl of some other colour, and a simple straw, wide-awake, with bright red streamers. I flatter myself that I woke up sundry sleepy-eyed Turks, who

---

[1] *Margery Daw* From a nursery rhyme: "See-saw, Margery Daw, / Sold her bed and lay on straw"; the name "Margery Daw" would have connoted a poor and untidy person.

[2] *some pretty tale of love* The story of Leander, who nightly swam the Hellespont (the Dardanelles) between Sestos and Abydos to visit his lover, Hero.

[3] *windlass* Cranking device used to raise an anchor.

[4] *caicques* Rowboats.

seemed to think that the great object of life was to avoid showing surprise at anything; while the Turkish women gathered around me, and jabbered about me, in the most flattering manner.

How I succeeded in getting Mr. Day's letters from the Post-office, Constantinople, puzzles me now; but I did—and I shall ever regard my success as one of the great triumphs of my life. Their contents were not very cheering. He gave a very dreary account of Balaclava and of camp life, and almost dissuaded me from continuing my journey; but his last letter ended by giving me instructions as to the purchases I had best make, if I still determined upon making the adventure; so I forgot all the rest, and busied myself in laying in the stores he recommended.

But I found time, before I left the "Hollander," to charter a crazy caicque, to carry me to Scutari, intending to present Dr. F——'s letter to Miss Nightingale.

It was afternoon when the boatmen set me down in safety at the landing-place of Scutari, and I walked up the slight ascent, to the great dull-looking hospital. Thinking of the many noble fellows who had been borne, or had painfully crept along this path, only to die within that dreary building, I felt rather dull; and directly I entered the hospital, and came upon the long wards of sufferers, lying there so quiet and still, a rush of tears came to my eyes, and blotted out the sight for a few minutes. But I felt at home, and looked about me with great interest. The men were, many of them, very quiet. Some of the convalescent formed themselves into little groups around one who read a newspaper; others had books in their hands, or by their side, where they had fallen when slumber overtook the readers, while hospital orderlies moved to and fro, and now and then the female nurses, in their quiet uniform, passed noise-lessly on some mission of kindness.

I was fortunate enough to find an old acquaintance, who accompanied me through the wards, and rendered it unnecessary for me to trouble the busy nurses. This was an old 97th man—a Sergeant T——, whom I had known in Kingston, and who was slowly recovering from an attack of dysentery, and making himself of use here until the doctors should let him go back and have

another "shy[1] at the Rooshians." He is very glad to meet me, and tells me his history very socially, and takes me to the bedsides of some comrades, who had also known me at Up-Park Camp. My poor fellows! how their eyes glisten when they light upon an old friend's face in these Turkish barracks—put to so sad a use, three thousand miles from home. Here is one of them—"hurt in the trenches," says the Sergeant, with shaven bandaged head, and bright, restless, Irish eyes, who hallooes out, "Mother Seacole! Mother Seacole!" in such an excited tone of voice; and when he has shaken hands a score of times, falls back upon his pillow very wearily. But I sit by his side, and try to cheer him with talk about the future, when he shall grow well, and see home, and hear them all thank him for what he has been helping to do, so that he grows all right in a few minutes; but, hearing that I am on the way to the front, gets excited again; for, you see, illness and weakness make these strong men as children, not least in the patient unmurmuring resigna-tion with which they suffer. I think my Irish friend had an indistinct idea of a "muddle" somewhere, which had kept him for weeks on salt meat and biscuit, until it gave him the "scurvy," for he is very anxious that I should take plenty of vegetables, of every sort. "And, oh! mother!"—and it is strange to hear his almost plaintive tone as he urges this—"take them plenty of eggs, mother; we never saw eggs over there."

At some slight risk of giving offence, I cannot resist the temptation of lending a helping hand here and there—replacing a slipped bandage, or easing a stiff one. But I do not think any one was offended; and one doctor, who had with some surprise and, at first, alarm on his face, watched me replace a bandage, which was giving pain, said, very kindly, when I had finished, "Thank you, ma'am."

One thought never left my mind as I walked through the fearful miles of suffering in that great hospital. If it is so here, what must it not be at the scene of war—on the spot where the poor fellows are stricken down by pestilence or Russian bullets, and days and nights of agony must be passed before a woman's hand

---

[1] *shy* Attempt.

can dress their wounds. And I felt happy in the conviction that I must be useful three or four days nearer to their pressing wants than this.

It was growing late before I felt tired, or thought of leaving Scutari, and Dr. S——, or some Jamaica friend, who had kindly borne me company for the last half-hour, agreed with me that the caicque was not the safest conveyance by night on the Bosphorus, and recommended me to present my letter to Miss Nightingale, and perhaps a lodging for the night could be found for me. So, still under the Sergeant's patient guidance, we thread our way through passages and corridors, all used as sick-wards, until we reach the corner tower of the building, in which are the nurses' quarters.

I think Mrs. B——, who saw me, felt more surprise than she could politely show (I never found women so quick to understand me as the men) when I handed her Dr. F——'s kind letter respecting me, and apologized for troubling Miss Nightingale. There is that in the Doctor's letter (he had been much at Scutari) which prevents my request being refused, and I am asked to wait until Miss Nightingale, whose every moment is valuable, can see me. Meanwhile Mrs. B. questions me very kindly, but with the same look of curiosity and surprise.

What object has Mrs. Seacole in coming out? This is the purport of her questions. And I say, frankly, to be of use somewhere; for other considerations I had not, until necessity forced them upon me. Willingly, had they accepted me, I would have worked for the wounded, in return for bread and water. I fancy Mrs. B—— thought that I sought for employment at Scutari, for she said, very kindly—

"Miss Nightingale has the entire management of our hospital staff, but I do not think that any vacancy—"

"Excuse me, ma'am," I interrupt her with, "but I am bound for the front in a few days"; and my questioner leaves me, more surprised than ever. The room I waited in was used as a kitchen. Upon the stoves were cans of soup, broth, and arrowroot, while nurses passed in and out with noiseless tread and subdued manner. I thought many of them had that strange expression of the eyes which those who have gazed long on scenes of woe or horror seldom lose.

In half an hour's time I am admitted to Miss Nightingale's presence. A slight figure, in the nurses' dress; with a pale, gentle, and withal firm face, resting lightly in the palm of one white hand, while the other supports the elbow—a position which gives to her countenance a keen inquiring expression, which is rather marked. Standing thus in repose, and yet keenly observant—the greatest sign of impatience at any time a slight, perhaps unwitting motion of the firmly planted right foot—was Florence Nightingale—that Englishwoman whose name shall never die, but sounds like music on the lips of British men until the hour of doom.

She has read Dr. F——'s letter, which lies on the table by her side, and asks, in her gentle but eminently practical and business-like way, "What do you want, Mrs. Seacole—anything we can do for you? If it lies in my power, I shall be very happy."

So I tell her of my dread of the night journey by caicque, and the improbability of my finding the "Hollander" in the dark; and, with some diffidence, threw myself upon the hospitality of Scutari, offering to nurse the sick for the night. Now unfortunately, for many reasons, room even for one in Scutari Hospital is at that time no easy matter to find; but at last a bed was discovered to be unoccupied at the hospital washerwoman's quarters.

My experience of washerwomen, all the world over, is the same—that they are kind soft-hearted folks. Possibly the soapsuds they almost live in find their way into their hearts and tempers, and soften them. This Scutari washerwoman is no exception to the rule, and welcomes me most heartily. With her, also, are some invalid nurses; and after they have gone to bed, we spend some hours of the night talking over our adventures, and giving one another scraps of our respective biographies. I hadn't long retired to my couch before I wished most heartily that we had continued our chat; for unbidden and most unwelcome companions took the washerwoman's place, and persisted not only in dividing my bed, but my plump person also. Upon my word, I believe the fleas are the only industrious creatures in all Turkey. Some of their relatives would seem to have migrated into Russia; for I found them in the

Crimea equally prosperous and ubiquitous.

In the morning, a breakfast is sent to my mangled remains, and a kind message from Mrs. B——, having reference to how I spent the night. And, after an interview with some other medical men, whose acquaintance I had made in Jamaica, I shake hands with the soft-hearted washerwoman, up to her shoulders in soap-suds already, and start for the "Hollander."

from CHAPTER 13
MY WORK IN THE CRIMEA

I hope the reader will give me credit for the assertion that I am about to make, viz., that I enter upon the particulars of this chapter with great reluctance; but I cannot omit them, for the simple reason that they strengthen my one and only claim to interest the public, viz., my services to the brave British army in the Crimea. But, fortunately, I can follow a course which will not only render it unnecessary for me to sound my own trumpet, but will be more satisfactory to the reader. I can put on record the written opinions of those who had ample means of judging and ascertaining how I fulfilled the great object which I had in view in leaving England for the Crimea; and before I do so, I must solicit my readers' attention to the position I held in the camp as doctress, nurse, and "mother."

I have never been long in any place before I have found my practical experience in the science of medicine useful. Even in London I have found it of service to others. And in the Crimea, where the doctors were so overworked, and sickness was so prevalent, I could not be long idle; for I never forgot that my intention in seeking the army was to help the kind-hearted doctors, to be useful to whom I have ever looked upon and still regard as so high a privilege.

But before very long I found myself surrounded with patients of my own, and this for two simple reasons. In the first place, the men (I am speaking of the "ranks" now) had a very serious objection to going into hospital for any but urgent reasons, and the regimental doctors were rather fond of sending them there; and, in the second place, they could and did get at my store sick-

comforts and nourishing food, which the heads of the medical staff would sometimes find it difficult to procure. These reasons, with the additional one that I was very familiar with the diseases which they suffered most from, and successful in their treatment (I say this in no spirit of vanity), were quite sufficient to account for the numbers who came daily to the British Hotel for medical treatment.

That the officers were glad of me as a doctress and nurse may be easily understood. When a poor fellow lay sickening in his cheerless hut and sent down to me, he knew very well that I should not ride up in answer to his message empty-handed. And although I did not hesitate to charge him with the value of the necessaries I took him, still he was thankful enough to be able to purchase them. When we lie ill at home surrounded with comfort, we never think of feeling any special gratitude for the sick-room delicacies which we accept as a consequence of our illness; but the poor officer lying ill and weary in his crazy hut, dependent for the merest necessaries of existence upon a clumsy, ignorant soldier-cook, who would almost prefer eating his meat raw to having the trouble of cooking it (our English soldiers are bad campaigners), often finds his greatest troubles in the want of those little delicacies with which a weak stomach must be humoured into retaining nourishment. How often have I felt sad at the sight of poor lads who in England thought attending early parade a hardship, and felt harassed if their neckcloths set awry, or the natty little boots would not retain their polish, bearing, and bearing so nobly and bravely, trials and hardships to which the veteran campaigner frequently succumbed. Don't you think, reader, if you were lying, with parched lips and fading appetite, thousands of miles from mother, wife, or sister, loathing the rough food by your side, and thinking regretfully of that English home where nothing that could minister to your great need would be left untried—don't you think that you would welcome the familiar figure of the stout lady whose bony horse has just pulled up at the door of your hut, and whose panniers[1] contain some cooling drink, a little

---

[1] *panniers* Baskets, in pairs, slung over the back of a horse or donkey.

broth, some homely[1] cake, or a dish of jelly or blanc-mange[2]—don't you think, under such circumstances, that you would heartily agree with my friend PUNCH'S remark:

> "That berry-brown face, with a kind heart's trace
>   Impressed on each wrinkle sly,
> Was a sight to behold, through the snow-clouds rolled
>   Across that iron sky."[3]

I tell you, reader, I have seen many a bold fellow's eyes moisten at such a season, when a woman's voice and a woman's care have brought to their minds recollections of those happy English homes which some of them never saw again; but many did, who will remember their woman-comrade upon the bleak and barren heights before Sebastopol.

Then their calling me "mother" was not, I think, altogether unmeaning. I used to fancy that there was something homely in the word; and, reader, you cannot think how dear to them was the smallest thing that reminded them of home.

—1857

---

[1] *homely*   In Britain, domestic (of the home).

[2] *blanc-mange*   Milk jelly.

[3] *That ... sky*   From "A Stir for Seacole," published in the satire and humor magazine *Punch* in December 1856.

HARRIET MARTINEAU
1802 – 1876

In her *Autobiography*, Harriet Martineau refers to her life as "somewhat remarkable"—something of an understatement, given the extraordinary interest that both her life and her work generated throughout much of the nineteenth century. While she is best known for her writings on controversial political issues—including political economy, women's rights, and slavery—she was also a prolific author of works on topics conventionally associated with women authors, such as domestic economy, education, and travel. Martineau often challenged traditional perspectives: she held an egalitarian view of marriage, she questioned the central tenets of the Christian faith, and she agitated for the rights of women, prisoners, and other oppressed groups. But she was also characteristically Victorian: she suffered periods of invalidism (a common malady among Victorian women), she wrestled with religious doubts for much of her life, and she wrote in a variety of popular Victorian genres. Martineau's celebrated status can be deduced both from the frequency with which her name appears in the letters and journals of her contemporaries, and from their comments about her; George Eliot, for example, described Martineau as "the only English woman" who "possesses thoroughly the art of writing." Though interest in Martineau waned in the twentieth century, scholars of recent generations have again begun to focus on this "literary lion" of the period.

Born in Norwich in 1802, Martineau was the sixth of eight children. Her father, Thomas Martineau, was a textile manufacturer; her mother, Elizabeth, was an austere woman who provided her children with every educational opportunity, but little affection. Martineau's education was superior to that given to most girls of her time; in her Unitarian home her intellectual curiosity was encouraged and she learned French, Latin, arithmetic, and writing. In addition, she had two experiences of formal schooling, first as one of fourteen girls at a Unitarian school for boys and later at her aunt's school for girls in Bristol.

Raised as a Unitarian, the young Martineau was encouraged to approach religious matters with a spirit of discussion and enquiry. Although Christianity was an important early influence in Martineau's life, when she was an adult her ties to the church loosened. A slow-growing disenchantment with religion caused her to eventually describe herself as a Christian only in the "free-thinking sense."

Around the age of twelve Martineau began to notice a loss of hearing, and by sixteen she was nearly deaf. Her condition heightened the isolation of what was already a difficult childhood, as the family either ignored her deafness or blamed her for not listening or responding appropriately. It was not until Martineau was twenty-eight that she began to use the ear trumpet that allowed her full engagement with the world around her.

Martineau was first encouraged to try writing by her brother James, who suggested it as a diversion. Her first two publications were articles in the Unitarian magazine *The Monthly Repository*: "Female Writers on Practical Divinity" (1822) and "On Female Education" (1823). Her early successes convinced her to try a career in writing as a way of helping the family out of straitened circumstances. Her father's finances had suffered from the effects of the economic crisis of 1825–26, and the family's situation was worsened by his failing health; he died in 1826.

The 1820s were a difficult time for Martineau. Her father's death was preceded by that of Thomas, her eldest brother, in 1824; both losses affected Martineau enormously. And in the same year that her father died, Martineau's fiancée, John Worthington, began to suffer from a serious mental illness; within a year, he too was dead. Martineau eventually came to doubt if she was in fact suited for marriage; she reflects in her *Autobiography* that she was "very thankful for not having married at all. … [M]y strong will, combined with anxiety of conscience, makes me fit only to live alone."

In February of 1832 Martineau published the first number of *Illustrations of Political Economy*, the work that would secure her lifelong fame. The work represented a new way of making basic economic principles intelligible to a general readership. Martineau's "illustrations" are fictional tales that aim to bring to life the reality of conditions such as poverty, overpopulation, and business-labor strife. The tales are explicitly didactic, with the principle that each tale is intended to illustrate set out at its conclusion. The *Illustrations* were published in 25 monthly numbers over the course of two years. Though some criticized Martineau's interpretation of economic principles as naïve, the tales proved to be extremely popular, achieving monthly sales in the range of 10,000 copies. (By comparison, novels sold in monthly numbers in the 1830s were considered successful if sales exceeded 2,000 copies per month.)

Martineau's two years of travel in America (1834–36) led to two books, *Society in America* (1837) and *Retrospect of Western Travel* (1838). In these writings, Martineau strove to judge American society on its own terms rather than by her foreign standards (an approach she advocated in *How to Observe Manners and Morals* [1838], often considered the first work of sociological methodology). Both her travel works were generally well-received by reviewers and readers in England, and they helped to make her reputation in America, where *Illustrations of Political Economy* had already made something of a mark. Martineau met with criticism in America, however—not surprisingly, since despite its sympathetic approach *Society in America* is both uncompromising in its antislavery principles and penetrating in its psychological assessment of the hypocrisy of Americans (Northerners as well as Southerners) who treat "people of colour" cruelly even as they "lay their hands on their hearts, and declare that all men are born free and equal."

Martineau's first novel, *Deerbrook* (1839), proved less successful, perhaps in part because it focused on a middle-class family at a time when audiences largely preferred stories involving the well-off or the desperately poor. Her only other novel, *The Hour and the Man* (1841), is a historical re-imagining of the experiences of Toussaint L'Ouverture, leader of the successful slave rebellion that resulted in the founding of Haiti as an independent nation.

After her return from America, Martineau suffered a period of illness and invalidism, which appears to have been the result of a uterine tumor. At the advice of friends, Martineau tried mesmerism—the results of which she lauded publically in "Letters on Mesmerism" (1844). Martineau also published *Life in the Sickroom* (1844), both a meditation on the psychological effects of invalidism and an advice book to others suffering from ill health.

After her recovery, Martineau chose to retire from her busy London life to the Lake District, by then a famous place of retirement for prominent literary figures. Thereafter she often spoke fondly of her property at Ambleside, where she named her house "The Knoll." Despite her more secluded life, Martineau continued to write prolifically. Her works from this period include *Eastern Life* (1848), about her travels to Egypt, and *Letters on the Laws and Nature of Man's Development* (1851). In the latter book, which Martineau co-wrote with Henry George Atkinson, an amateur scientist and philosopher, she discusses and questions many of the tenets of the Christian faith. Her beloved brother James was among those who reviewed the book negatively, and sister and brother neither saw nor wrote to each other again.

Martineau began to suffer from ill health again in 1854, and several physicians suspected heart trouble. Believing that she was likely soon to die, Martineau embarked on her *Autobiography*, which came to be acknowledged as among the great autobiographical writings of the period.

Defying her own expectations, Martineau went on to live another 22 years, during most of which time she continued to write prolifically. Her works from this period include two histories: *British Rule in India: A Historical Sketch* (1857), a response to what was at the time referred to as the Indian Mutiny of May 1857; and *History of England during the Thirty Years Peace: 1816–1846* (1849–50), a national history focused on political reforms. Martineau also collaborated with Florence Nightingale and Josephine Butler to write an *Appeal to the Women of England* (1869) denouncing the Contagious Diseases Acts that made any woman subject to forced medical examination upon suspicion that she was a prostitute.

Martineau died on 27 June, 1876 at the Knoll in Ambleside.

⌘ ⌘ ⌘

from *Letter to the Deaf*[1]

My Dear Companions,

The deafness under which I have now for some years past suffered, has become, from being an almost intolerable grievance, so much less of one to myself and my friends, than such a deprivation usually is, that I have often of late longed to communicate with my fellow-sufferers, in the hope of benefiting, by my experience, some to whom the discipline is newer than to myself.

I have for some time done what I could in private conversation; but it never occurred to me to print what I had to say, till it was lately not only suggested to me, but urged upon me as a duty. I adopt this method as the only means of reaching you all; and I am writing with the freedom which I should use in a private letter to each of you. It does not matter what may be thought of anything I now say, or of my saying it in this manner, by those who do not belong to our fraternity. I write merely for those who are deeply concerned in the

subject of my letter. The time may come when I shall tell the public some of our secrets, for other purposes than those which are now before me. At present I address only you; and as there is no need for us to tell our secrets to one another, there may be little here to interest any but ourselves. I am afraid I have nothing to offer to those of you who have been deaf from early childhood. Your case is very different from mine, as I have reason to know through my intimacy with a friend who became deaf at five years old. Before I was so myself, I had so prodigious a respect for this lady, (which she well deserves,) that if she could have heard the lightest whisper in which a timid girl ever spoke, I should not have dared to address her. Circumstances directed her attention towards me, and she began a correspondence, by letter, which flattered me, and gave me courage to converse with her when we met, and our acquaintance grew into an intimacy which enabled me at last to take a very bold step—to send her a sonnet, in allusion to our common infirmity; my deafness being then new, and the uppermost thing in my mind day and night. I was surprised and mortified at her not seeming to enter into what I had no doubt in the world must touch her very nearly; but I soon understood the reason. When we came to compare our experiences, we were

---

[1] *Letter to the Deaf*   The extract below is from an open letter to members of the public who have acquired deafness. It was first published in *Tait's Edinburgh Magazine*.

amused to find how differently we felt, and had always felt about our privation. Neither of us, I believe, much envies the other, though neither of us pretends to strike the balance of evil. She had suffered the most privation, and I the most pain. …

It is impossible for us to deny that if principles are ever needed, if methods are ever of use as supports and guides, it must be in a case where each of us must stand alone in the midst of temptations and irritations which beset us every hour, and against which no defence of habit has been set up, and no bond of companionship can strengthen us. What these temptations and irritations are, we all know: the almost impossibility of not seeming to hear when we do not, the persuasion that people are taking advantage of us in what they say—that they are discussing us, or laughing at us—that they do not care for us as long as they are merry—that the friend who takes the pains to talk to us might make us less conspicuous if he would—the vehement desire that we might be let alone, and the sense of neglect if too long let alone; all these, absurd and wicked fancies as they are seen to be when fairly set down, have beset us all in our time; have they not? For my own part, though I am never troubled with them now, I have so vivid a remembrance of them all, that I believe a thousand years would not weaken the impression. Surely that degree of suffering which lashes us into a temporary misanthropy when our neighbours are happiest, which makes us fly to our chambers, and lock ourselves in, to hide the burning tears which spring at the mirth of those we love best, which seduces us into falsehood or thanklessness to God and man, is enough to justify and require the most careful fixing of principles, and framing of methods. We might as well let our hearts and minds—our happiness—take their chance without discipline in all cases whatever, as neglect our own discipline in this. The first thing to be done is to fix upon our principle. This is easy enough. To give the least possible pain to others is the right principle. How to apply it requires more consideration. Let me just observe, that we are more inexcusable in forsaking our principle here than in any other case, and than the generality of people are in the generality of cases. Principles are usually forsaken from

being forgotten—from the occasion for them not being perceived. We have no such excuse while beginning to act upon our principle. We cannot forget—we cannot fail to perceive the occasion, for five minutes together, that we spend in society. By the time that we become sufficiently at ease to be careless, habit may, if we choose, have grown up to support our principle, and we may be safe.

Our principle requires that we should boldly review our case, and calmly determine for ourselves what we will give up, and what struggle to retain. It is a miserable thing to get on without a plan from day to day, nervously watching whether our infirmity lessens or increases, or choosing to take for granted that we shall be rid of it; or hopelessly and indolently giving up everything but a few selfish gratifications, or weakly refusing to resign what we can no longer enjoy. We must ascertain the probability for the future, if we can find physicians humane enough to tell us the truth: and where it cannot be ascertained, we must not delay making provision for the present. The greatest difficulty here arises from the mistaken kindness of friends. The physician had rather not say as mine said to me, "I consider yours a bad case." The parent entreats to be questioned about anything that passes; brothers and sisters wish that music should be kept up; and, what is remarkable, everybody has a vast deal of advice to give, if the subject be fairly mentioned; though everybody helps, by false tenderness, to make the subject too sacred an one to be touched upon. We sufferers are the persons to put an end to all this delusion and mismanagement. Advice must go for nothing with us in a case where nobody is qualified to advise. We must cross-question our physician, and hold him to it till he has told us all. We must destroy the sacredness of the subject, by speaking of it ourselves; not perpetually and sentimentally, but, when occasion arises, boldly, cheerfully, and as a plain matter of fact. When every body about us gets to treat it as a matter of fact, our daily difficulties are almost gone; and when we have to do with strangers, the simple, cheerful declaration, "I am very deaf," removes almost all trouble. Whether there was ever as much reluctance to acknowledge defective sight as there now is defective hearing—whether the mention of spectacles was ever as hateful as that of a trumpet is now, I do not know; but I was full as much grieved as amused lately at what was said to me in a shop where I went to try a new kind of trumpet: "I assure you, Ma'am," said the shopkeeper, "I dread to see a deaf person come into my shop. They all expect me to find them some little thing that they put into their ears, that will make them hear everything, without anybody finding out what is the matter with them."

Well, what must be given up, and what may be struggled for?

The first thing which we are disposed to give up is the very last which we ought to relinquish—society. How many good reasons we are apt to see—are we not?—why we should not dine out; why it is absurd to go into an evening party; why we ought to be allowed to remain quiet up stairs when visitors are below! This will not do. Social communication must be kept up through all its pains, for the sake of our friends as well as for our own. It can never be for the interest of our friends that we should grow selfish, or absorbed in what does not concern our day and generation, or nervous, dependent, and helpless in common affairs. The less able we become to pick up tidings of man and circumstance, the more diligently we must go in search of the information. The more our sympathies are in danger of contraction, the more must we put ourselves in the way of being interested by what is happening all about us. Society is the very last thing to be given up; but it must be sought, (and I say it with deep sympathy for those of you to whom the effort is new,) under a bondage of self-denial, which annihilates for a time almost all the pleasure. Whatever may be our fate—whether we may be set down at the end of a half circle, where nobody comes to address us, or whether we may be placed beside a lady who cannot speak above her breath, or a gentleman who shouts till everybody turns to see what is the matter; whether one well-meaning friend says across the room, in our behalf, "do tell that joke over again to ——," and all look to see how we laugh when they have done; or another kind of person says, "how I wish you could hear that song,"—or "that harp in the next room," or "those

sweet nightingales," if we happen to be out of doors—whether any or all these doings and sayings befall us, we must bravely go on taking our place in society.

Taking our place, I say. What is our place? It is difficult to decide. Certainly, not that of chief talker any more than that of chief listener. We must make up our minds for a time to hold the place that we may chance to be put into—to depend on the tact and kindness of those near us. This is not very pleasant; but if we cannot submit to it for a while, we cannot boast much of our humility, nor of our patience. We must submit to be usually insignificant, and sometimes ridiculous. Do not be dismayed, dear companions. This necessity will not last long, and it is well worthwhile undergoing it. Those who have strength of mind to seek society under this humiliation, and to keep their tempers through it, cannot long remain insignificant there. They must rise to their proper place, if they do but abstain from pressing beyond it. …

It is a matter of wonder that we are addressed so much as we are; and if, in addition to the difficulty of making us hear, we offer the disagreeableness of (not a constrained, that will be pitied, but) a frowning countenance, we may betake ourselves to the books of prints on the table, but may as well give up all hope of conversation. As a general rule, nothing can be worse than for people to think at all about their countenances; but in our case it is worthwhile, for a time, and to a certain extent. I was kindly told, a few years ago, that many people wished to converse with me, but that I looked as if I had rather not be spoken to. Well I might; for I then discovered that in trying to check one bad habit, I had fallen into another. I had a trick of sighing, to cover which I used to twist my fingers almost out of joint, (and so do you, I dare say,) and the pain of this process very naturally made me frown. My friend's hint put me on my guard. Instead of twisting my fingers, I recalled my vow of patience, and this made me smile; and the world has been a different place to me since. Some such little rule as turning every sigh into a smile will help you over a multitude of difficulties, and save you, at length, the trouble of thinking about either smiling or sighing.

It has always been my rule never to ask what is going

forward;[1] and the consequence has well compensated all I had to go through from the reproaches of kind friends, who were very anxious that I should trouble them in that way. Our principle plainly forbids the practice; and nothing can therefore justify it. There is at first no temptation; for we had then rather miss the sayings of the wise men of Greece, than obtain them by such means; but the practice once begun, there is no telling where it will stop. Have we not seen—it sickens me to think of it—restless, inquisitive, deaf people, who will have every insignificant thing repeated to them, to their own incessant disappointment, and the suffering of everybody about them, whom they make, but their appeals, almost as ridiculous as themselves. I never could tolerate the idea of any approach to the condition of one of these. I felt, besides, that it was impossible for me to judge of what might fairly be asked for, and what had better be let pass. I therefore obstinately adhered to my rule; and I believe that no one whom I have met in any society, (and I have seen a great deal,) has been enabled to carry away more that is valuable, or to enjoy it more thoroughly than myself. I was sure that I might trust to the kindness of my neighbours, if I was but careful not to vex and weary it; and my confidence has been fully justified. The duty extends to not looking as if you wanted to be amused. Your friends can have little satisfaction in your presence, if they believe that when you are not conversing you are no longer amused. "I wonder every day," said a young friend to me, when I was staying in a large well-filled country house, "what you do with yourself during our long dinners, when we none of us talk with you, because we have talked so much more comfortably on the lawn all the morning. I cannot think how you help going to sleep." "I watch how you help the soup," was my inconsiderate reply—I was not aware how inconsiderate, till I saw how she blushed every day after on taking up the ladle. I mentioned the soup only as a specimen of my occupations during dinner. There were also the sunset lights and shadows on the lawn to be watched, and the never-ceasing play of human countenances—our grand

resource when we have once gained ease enough to enjoy them at leisure. There were graceful and light-headed girls, and there was an originality of action in the whole family, which amused me from morning till night. The very apparatus of the table, and the various dexterities of the servants, are matters worth observing when we have nothing else to do. I never yet found a dinner too long, whether or not my next neighbour might be disposed for a tête-à-tête—never, I mean, since the time when every social occupation was to me full of weariness and constraint.

Another rule which I should recommend is always to wait to be addressed, except in our own houses, where the exception must be made with our guests. Some, I know, adopt a contrary rule, for this reason, that if we ask a question to which we can anticipate the answer, the awkwardness of a failure at the outset is prevented. But my own feeling is against obliging anyone to undertake the trouble of conversing with us. It is perfectly easy to show, at the moment of being addressed, that we are socially disposed, and grateful for being made companions; and I, at least, feel the pleasure to be greater for its having been offered me.

I think it best for us to give up also all undertakings and occupations in which we cannot mark and check our own failures; teaching anything which requires ear, preaching, and lecturing, and music. I gave up music, in opposition to much entreaty, some reproach, and strong secret inclination; because I knew that my friends would rather put up with a wrong bass in my playing, and false time in my singing, than deprive me of a resource. Our principle clearly forbids this kind of indulgence; therefore, however confident we may be of our musical ear, let us be quite sure that we shall never again be judges of our own music, or our own oratory, and avoid all wish of making others suffer needlessly by our privations. Listen to no persuasions, dear companions, if you are convinced that what I have said is right. ...

I do not know how sufficiently to enforce these sacrifices being made with frankness and simplicity; and nothing so much needs enforcing. If our friends were but aware how cruel an injury is the false delicacy which is so common, they would not encourage our false

---

[1] *what is going forward* I.e., what is going on or what is being said.

shame as they do. If they have known anything of the bondage of ordinary false shame, they may imagine something of our suffering in circumstances of irremediable singularity. Instead of putting the singularity out of sight, they should lead us to acknowledge it in words, prepare for it in habits, and act upon it in social intercourse. If they will not assist us here, we must do it for ourselves. Our principle, again, requires this. ...

And now, what may we struggle for? I dare say the words of the moralist lie as deep down in your hearts as in my own: "We must not repine, but we may lawfully struggle!"[1] I go further, and say that we are bound to struggle. Our principle requires it. We must struggle for whatever may be had, without encroaching on the comfort of others. With this limitation, we must hear all we can, for as long as we can. Yet how few of us will use the helps we might have! How seldom is a deaf person to be seen with a trumpet! I should have been diverted, if I had not been too much vexed, at the variety of excuses that I have heard on this head since I have been much in society. The trumpet makes the sound disagreeable; or is of no use; or is not wanted in a noise, because we hear better in a noise; nor in quiet, because we hear very fairly in quiet; or we think our friends do not like it; or we ourselves do not care for it, if it does not enable us to hear general conversation; or—a hundred other reasons just as good. Now, dear friends, believe me, these are but excuses. I have tried them all in turn, and I know them to be so. The sound soon becomes anything but disagreeable; and the relief to the nerves, arising from the use of such a help, is indescribable. None but the totally deaf can fail to find some kind of trumpet that will be of use to them, if they choose to look for it properly, and give it a fair trial. That it is not wanted in a noise is usually true; but we are seldom in a noise; and quiet is our greatest enemy,

(next to darkness, when the play of the countenance is lost to us). To reject a tête-à-tête in comfort because the same means will not afford us the pleasure of general conversation, is not very wise. Is it? As for the fancy, that our friends do not like it, it is a mistake, and a serious mistake. I can speak confidently of this. By means of galvanism[2] (which I do not, from my own experience, recommend) I once nearly recovered my hearing for a few weeks. It was well worthwhile being in a sort of nervous fever during those weeks, and more deaf than ever afterwards, for the enlightenment which I gained during the interval on various subjects, of which the one that concerns us now, is, the toil that our friends undergo on our account. This is the last topic on which I should speak to you, but for the prevalent unwillingness in our fraternity to use such helps as may ease the lungs of all around them as much as their own nerves. ...

Another struggle must be to seize or make opportunities for preserving or rectifying our associations, as far as they are connected with the sense which is imperfect. Hunger and thirst after all sounds that you can obtain, without trouble to others, and without disturbing your own temper; and do it more strenuously and cheerfully, the more reasons you have to apprehend the increase of your infirmity. ... We ought all to do so; losing no opportunity of associating sounds with other objects of sense, and of catching every breath of sound that passes us. We should note street cries; we should entice children to talk to us; we should linger in the neighbourhood of barrel organs, and go out of our way to walk by a dashing stream. We cannot tell how much wisdom we may at last find ourselves to have gained, by running out among the trees, when the quick coming and going of the sunshine tells us that the winds are abroad. Some day will show us from how much folly the chirp of an infant's voice may have saved us. I go so far as to recommend, certainly not any place of worship for purposes of experiment, but the theatre and the House of Commons, even when "the sough of words without the

---

[1] *We ... struggle!* Cf. Samuel Johnson, *The Rambler* 32, 7 July 1750. Here, Johnson urges that "In those evils which are allotted to us by Providence, such as deformity, privation of any of the senses, or old age, it is always to be remembered, that impatience can have no present effect, but to deprive us of the consolations which our condition admits. ... We are not to repine, but we may lawfully struggle; for the calamities of life, like the necessities of nature, are calls to labour and exercises of diligence" (2.43–44).

[2] *galvanism* According to Charles Henry Wilkinson's *The Effects of Electricity* (1799) and *Elements of Galvanism* (1804), electricity could be used as a treatment for many illnesses and conditions, including some types of deafness.

sense"[1] is all that can be had. The human voice is music, and carries sense, even then; and every tone is worth treasuring, when tones are likely to become scarce, or to cease. You will understand that it is only to those who can rule their own spirits that I recommend such an exercise as this last. If you cannot bear to enjoy less than the people about you, and in a different manner; or if you neglect what you came for, in mourning what you have lost, you are better at home. Nothing is worth the sacrifice of your repose of mind.

What else may we struggle for? For far more in the way of knowledge than I can now even intimate. I am not going to make out, as some would have me, that we lose nothing after all; that what we lose in one way we gain in another, and so on; pursuing a line of argument equally insulting to our own understandings, and the wisdom and benignity of Him who framed that curious instrument, the ear, and strung the chords of its nerves, and keeps up the perpetual harmonies of the atmosphere for its gratification. The ear was not made that men should be happier without it. To attempt to persuade *you* so, would above all be folly. But, in some sense there is a compensation to us, if we choose to accept it; and it is to improve this to the utmost that I would urge you and stimulate myself. We *have* some accomplishments which we may gratefully acknowledge, while the means by which we gain them must prevent our being proud of them. We are good physiognomists—good perceivers in every way, and have (if we are not idle) rather the advantage over others in the power of abstract reasoning. This union of two kinds of power, which in common cases are often cultivated at the expense of each other, puts a considerable amount of accurate knowledge within easier reach of us than of most other people. We must never forget what a vast quantity we must forego, but neither must we lose sight of whatever is peculiarly within our power. We have more time, too, than anybody else: more than the laziest lordling, who does nothing but let his ears be filled with nonsense from morning till night. The very busiest of our frater-

nity has, I should think, time every day for as much thought as is good for him, between the hours of rising and of rest.

These advantages make it incumbent upon us to struggle for such compensation as it is placed before us. We must set ourselves to gather knowledge from whatever we see and touch, and to digest it into wisdom during the extra time which is our privilege. What the sage goes out into the field at eventide[2] to seek, we can have at table, or in the thronged streets at noonday—opportunity for meditation, one of the chief means of wisdom. If to us the objects of sight are more vivid in their beauty, and more distinct in their suggestions than to others—if to us there is granted more leisure, and stronger inducement to study the movements of the mind within, from us may be expected a degree of certain kinds of attainment, in which it is as much of a sin as a misfortune for us to be deficient.

Finally, we, like all who are placed in uncommon circumstances, are so situated that our mental and moral constitution can scarcely fail of being either very weak or very strong. If we are dull and slow of observation, and indolent in thought, there is little chance of our being much wiser than infants; whereas, if we are acute and quick of observation, (and for us there is no medium), and disposed for thought, nothing is likely to prevent our going on to be wiser continually. ... I now suffer little or no pain from my privation, (except at moments when comparisons are forced upon me before I am ready for them); and I cannot help dreading a self-deception, to avoid which I would gladly endure over again all I have suffered. I had infinitely rather bear the perpetual sense of privation than become unaware of any thing that is true—of my intellectual deficiencies, of my disqualifications for society, of my errors in matters of fact, and of the burdens which I necessarily impose on those who surround me. My dependence for being reminded of these things is, not on those who incur trouble and sacrifice for my sake, but on the few occasional mortifications which I still meet with, and which are always welcomed for the sake of their office. We can

---

[1] *the ... sense* From an untitled poem by Elizabeth Hamilton (1758–1816) in which she reflects on her own deafness; *sough* Murmuring.

[2] *the ... eventide* Cf. Genesis 24.63: "And Isaac went out to meditate in the field in the evening."

never get beyond the necessity of keeping in full view the worst and the best that can be made of our lot. The worst is, either to sink under the trial, or to be made callous by it. The best is, to be as wise as is possible under a great disability, and as happy as is possible under a great privation. Believe me, with deep respect,

Your affectionate sister,
HARRIET MARTINEAU
March 16, 1834.

—1834

from *Retrospect of Western Travel*

from PREFACE

When I finished my late work on *Society in America*,[1] I had not the most remote idea of writing anything more on the subject of the New World. I have since been strongly solicited to communicate more of my personal narrative, and of the lighter characteristics of men, and incidents of travel, than it suited my purpose to give in the other work. It has also been represented to me that, as my published book concerns the Americans at least as much as the English, there is room for another which shall supply to the English what the Americans do not want—a picture of the aspect of the country, and of its men and manners. There seems no reason why such a picture should not be appended to an inquiry into the theory and practice of their society; especially as I believe that I have little to tell which will not strengthen the feelings of respect and kindness with which the people of Great Britain are more and more learning to regard the inhabitants of the Western Republic. I have, therefore, willingly acceded to

the desire of such of my readers as have requested to be presented with my *Retrospect of Western Travel*.

H. Martineau.

from FIRST IMPRESSIONS

… The moment of first landing in a foreign city is commonly spoken of as a perfect realization of forlornness. My entrance upon American life was anything but this. The spirits of my companions and myself were in a holy day dance while we were receiving our first impressions; and New York always afterward bore an air of gaiety to me from the association of the early pleasures of foreign travel. …

In the streets I was in danger of being run down by the fire-engines, so busy were my eyes with the novelties about me. These fire-engines run along the side-pavement, stopping for nobody; and I scarcely ever walked out in New York without seeing one or more out on business, or for an airing. The novelties which amused me were the spruce appearance of all the people; the pervading neatness and brightness, and the business-like air of the children. The car men were all well-dressed, and even two poor boys who were selling matches had clean shirt-collars and whole coats, though they were barefooted. The stocks of goods seemed large and handsome, and we were less struck with the indifference of manner commonly ascribed to American storekeepers than frequently afterward. The most unpleasant circumstance was the appearance and manner of the ladies whom we saw in the streets and stores. It was now the end of a very hot summer, and every lady we met looked as if she were emerging from the yellow fever;[2] and the languid and unsteady step betokened the reverse of health. …

One of the first impressions of a foreigner in New-York is of the extreme insolence and vulgarity of certain young Englishmen, who thus make themselves very conspicuous. Well-mannered Englishmen are scarcely

---

[1] *Society in America* Upon completion of her two-year tour of America, Martineau first wrote *Society in America* (1837), a description and assessment of American politics and culture which she calls her "more abstract American book." In her *Autobiography* she notes regarding *Retrospect of Western Travel* that readers "liked my second book best," perhaps because it offered a more concrete and personal narrative, as was traditional for travel books.

[2] *yellow fever* Viral disease spread by mosquitos; its symptoms can include yellowed skin. Although yellow fever is usually associated with tropical climates, America did see several outbreaks during the nineteenth century.

distinguishable from the natives, and thus escape observation; while every commercial traveller who sneers at republicanism all day long, and every impertinent boy, leaving home for the first time, with no understanding or sympathy for anything but what he has been accustomed to see at home, obtrudes himself upon the notice, and challenges the congeniality of such countrymen and countrywomen as he can contrive to put himself in the way of. I was annoyed this evening, on my return home, by a very complete specimen of the last-mentioned order of travellers.

Need I say, after thus detailing the little incidents which followed my landing in America, that my first impressions of the country were highly agreeable?

from NIAGARA

… It is not my intention to describe what we saw at Niagara so much as to relate what we did. To offer an idea of Niagara by writing of hues and dimensions is much like representing the kingdom of Heaven by images of jasper and topazes.

I visited the falls twice: first in October, 1834, in company with the party[1] with whom we traversed the state of New-York, when we stayed nearly a week; and again with Dr. and Mrs. F., and other friends,[2] in June, 1836, when we remained between two and three days. The first time we approached the falls from Buffalo, the next from Lewistown and Queenstown.

I expected to be disappointed in the first sight of the falls, and did not relish the idea of being questioned on the first day as to my "impressions." I therefore made a law, with the hearty agreement of the rest of the party,

that no one should ask an opinion of the spectacle for twenty-four hours. We stepped into the stage at Buffalo at half past eight in the morning on the 14th of October. At Black Rock we got out to cross the ferry. We looked at the green rushing waters we were crossing, and wondered whether they or we should be at the falls first. We had to wait some minutes for the stage on the Canada side, and a comely English woman invited us into her kitchen to warm ourselves. She was washing as well as cooking; and such a log was blazing under her boilers as no fireplace in England would hold. It looked like the entire trunk of a pine somewhat shortened. I could not help often wishing that some of the shivering poor of London could have supplies of the fuel which lies rotting in the American woods.

The road is extremely bad all the way from the ferry to the falls, and the bridges the rudest of the rude. The few farms looked decaying, and ill-clad children offered us autumn fruit for sale. We saw nothing to flatter our national complacency; for truly the contrast with the other side of the river was mournful enough. It was not till we had passed the inn with the sign of the "Chippeway Battle Ground" that we saw the spray from the falls. I believe we might have seen it sooner if we had known where to look. "Is that it?" we all exclaimed. It appeared on the left-hand side, whereas we had been looking to the right; and instead of its being suspended in the air like a white cloud, as we had imagined, it curled vigorously up, like smoke from a cannon or from a replenished fire. The winding of the road presently brought this round to our right hand. It seemed very near; the river, too, was as smooth as oil. The beginning of the Welland canal was next pointed out to me, but it was not a moment to care for canals. Then the little Round Island, covered with wood and surrounded by rapids, lay close at hand, in a recess of the Canada shore. Some of the rapids, of eight or ten feet descent, would be called falls elsewhere. They were glittering and foamy, with spaces of green water between. I caught a glimpse of a section of the cataract, but not any adequate view, before we were driven briskly up to the door of the hotel. We ran quickly from piazza to piazza till we reached the crown of the roof, where there is a space

---

[1] *the party* The Sedgwick family, including the novelist Catharine Maria Sedgwick (1789–1867). Martineau stayed with the Sedgwicks twice during her time in America: in September of 1834 and in the spring of 1836.

[2] *Dr. and Mrs. F.* Charles Follen (1796–1860), professor of German language and literature at Harvard University, and his wife Eliza Lee Follen (1787–1860), a poet and an author of children's books. Both were prominent abolitionists in Boston, and Dr. Follen was dismissed from Harvard for his abolitionism; *other friends* Ellis Gray Loring (1803–58), a lawyer and abolitionist, and Louisa Gilman Loring (1797–1868), his wife and a fellow abolitionist.

railed in for the advantage of the gazer who desires to reach the highest point. I think the emotion of this moment was never renewed or equalled. The morning had been cloudy, with a very few wandering gleams. It was now a little after noon; the sky was clearing, and at this moment the sun lighted up the Horseshoe Fall. I am not going to describe it. The most striking appearance was the slowness with which the shaded green waters rolled over the brink. This majestic oozing gives a true idea of the volume of the floods, but they no longer look like water.

We wandered through the wood, along Table Rock,[1] and to the ferry. We sat down opposite to the American Falls, finding them the first day or two more level to our comprehension than the Great Horseshoe Cataract;[2] yet through-out, the beauty was far more impressive to me than the grandeur. One's imagination may heap up almost any degree of grandeur; but the subtle colouring of this scene, tarrying with every breath of wind, refining upon the softness of driven snow, and dimming all the gems of the mine, is wholly inconceivable. The woods on Goat Island were in their gaudiest autumn dress; yet, on looking up to them from the fall, they seemed one dust colour. This will not be believed, but it is true.

The little detached fall on the American side piqued my interest at once. It looks solitary in the midst of the crowd of waters, coming out of its privacy in the wood to take its leap by itself. In the afternoon, as I was standing on Table Rock, a rainbow started out from the precipice a hundred feet below me, and curved upward as if about to alight on my head. Other such apparitions seemed to have a similar understanding with the sun. They went and came, blushed and faded, the floods rolling on, on, till the human heart, overcharged with beauty, could bear no more. …

from PRISONS[3]

… The first principle in the management of the guilty seems to me to be to treat them as men and women; which they were before they were guilty, and will be when they are no longer so; and which they are in the midst of it all. Their humanity is the principal thing about them; their guilt is a temporary state. The insane are first men, and secondarily diseased men; and in a due consideration of this order of things lies the main secret of the successful treatment of such. The drunkard is first a man, and secondarily a man with a peculiar weakness. The convict is, in like manner, first a man, and then a sinner. Now, there is something in the isolation of the convict which tends to keep this order of considerations right in the mind of his guardians. The warden and his prisoner converse like two men when they are face to face; but when the keeper watches a hundred men herded together in virtue of the one common characteristic of their being criminals, the guilt becomes the prominent circumstance, and there is an end of the brotherly faith in each, to which each must mainly owe his cure. This, in our human weakness, is the great evil attendant upon the good of collecting together sufferers under any particular physical or moral evil. Visitors are shy of the blind, the deaf and dumb, and insane, when they see them all together, while they would feel little or nothing of this shyness if they met each sufferer in the bosom of his own family. In the one case, the infirmity, defying sympathy, is the prominent circumstance; in the other, not. It follows from this, that such an association of prisoners as that at Auburn must be more difficult to reform, more difficult to do the state's duty by, than any number or kind of criminals

---

[1] *Table Rock* Rock shelf near Niagara Falls. Portions of the rock collapsed over the course of the eighteenth century, and the protruding part of the rock is no longer there.

[2] *We sat down … Great Horseshoe Cataract* Niagara Falls is made up of three falls named, from largest to smallest, the Horseshoe Falls, the American Falls, and the Bridal Veil Falls. Horseshoe Falls is located mostly on the Canadian side, separated from American Falls by Goat Island. Bridal Veil Falls is on the American side and separated from the other two falls by Luna Island; *Cataract* Waterfall.

[3] *PRISONS* It was a common practice of British travelers to visit institutions such as prisons and insane asylums, but Martineau was also more generally interested in prison reform, which was a pressing matter during this period. See her essay on "Prison Discipline" included in the website component of this anthology, as well as the footnote to that selection explaining some of the major reforms in the period.

who are classed by some other characteristic, or not classed at all.

The wonderfully successful friend of criminals, Captain Pillsbury, of the Weathersfield prison, has worked on this principle, and owes his success to it. His moral power over the guilty is so remarkable, that prison-breakers who can be confined nowhere else are sent to him to be charmed into staying their term out. It was told of his treatment of two such. One was a gigantic personage, the terror of the country, who had plunged deeper and deeper in crime for seventeen years. Captain Pillsbury told him when he came that he hoped he would not repeat the attempts to escape which he had made elsewhere. "It will be best," said he, "that you and I should treat each other as well as we can. I will make you as comfortable as I possibly can, and shall be anxious to be your friend; and I hope you will not get me into any difficulty on your account. There is a cell intended for solitary confinement, but we have never used it, and I should be sorry ever to have to turn the key upon anybody in it. You may range the place as freely as I do if you will trust me as I shall trust you." The man was sulky, and for weeks showed only very gradual symptoms of softening under the operation of Captain Pillsbury's cheerful confidence. At length information was given to the captain of this man's intention to break prison. The captain called him, and taxed him with it; the man preserved a gloomy silence. He was told that it was now necessary for him to be locked in the solitary cell, and desired to follow the captain, who went first, carrying a lamp in one hand and the key in the other. In the narrowest part of the passage the captain (who is a small, slight man) turned round and looked in the face of the stout criminal. "Now," said he, "I ask you whether you have treated me as I deserve? I have done everything I could think of to make you comfortable; I have trusted you, and you have never given me the least confidence in return, and have even planned to get me into difficulty. Is this kind? And yet I cannot bear to lock you up. If I had the least sign that you cared for me. ..." The man burst into tears. "Sir," said he, "I have been a very devil these seventeen years; but you treat me like a man." "Come, let us go

back," said the captain. The convict had the free range of the prison as before. From this hour he began to open his heart to the captain, and cheerfully fulfilled his whole term of imprisonment, confiding to his friend, as they arose, all impulses to violate his trust, and all facilities for doing so which he imagined he saw.

The other case was a criminal of the same character, who went so far as to make the actual attempt to escape. He fell, and hurt his ankle very much. The captain had him brought in and laid on his bed, and the ankle attended to, every one being forbidden to speak a word of reproach to the sufferer. The man was sullen, and would not say whether the bandaging of his ankle gave him pain or not. This was in the night, and every one returned to bed when this was done. But the captain could not sleep. He was distressed at the attempt, and thought he could not have fully done his duty by any man who would make it. He was afraid the man was in great pain. He rose, threw on his gown, and went with a lamp to the cell. The prisoner's face was turned to the wall, and his eyes were closed, but the traces of suffering were not to be mistaken. The captain loosened and replaced the bandage, and went for his own pillow to rest the limb upon, the man neither speaking nor moving all the time. Just when he was shutting the door the prisoner started up and called him back. "Stop, sir. Was it all to see after my ankle that you have got up?"

"Yes, it was. I could not sleep for thinking of you."

"And you have never said a word of the way I have used you!"

"I do feel hurt with you, but I don't want to call you unkind while you are suffering as you are now."

The man was in an agony of shame and grief. All he asked was to be trusted again when he should have recovered. He was freely trusted, and gave his generous friend no more anxiety on his behalf.

Captain Pillsbury is the gentleman who, on being told that a desperate prisoner had sworn to murder him speedily, sent for him to shave him, allowing no one to be present. He eyed the man, pointed to the razor, and desired him to shave him. The prisoner's hand trembled, but he went through it very well. When he had done the captain said, "I have been told you meant to murder me, but I thought I might trust you." "God bless you, sir! you may," replied the regenerated man. Such is the power of faith in man!

The greatest advantage of solitary confinement[1] is that it presents the best part of a prisoner's mind to be acted upon by his guardians; and the next is, that the prisoner is preserved from the evil influences of vicious companionship, of shame within the prison walls, and of degradation when he comes out. I am persuaded that no system of secondary punishment has yet been devised that can be compared with this. I need not, at this time of day, explain that I mean solitary imprisonment with labour, and with frequent visits from the guardians of the prisoner. Without labour, the punishment is too horrible and unjust to be thought of. The reflective man would go mad, and the clown would sleep away his term, and none of the purposes of human existence could be answered. Work is, in prison as out of it, the grand equaliser, stimulus, composer, and rectifier; the prime obligation and the prime privilege. It is delightful to see how soon its character is recognised there. In the Philadelphia penitentiary work is forbidden to the criminal for two days subsequent to his entrance; he petitions for it before the two days are out, however doggedly he may have declared that he will never work. Small incidents show what a resource it is. A convict shoemaker mentioned to a visitor a very early hour of the winter day as that at which he began to work. "But how can you see at that time of a winter's morning? It must be nearly dark." "I hammer my leather. That requires very little light. I get up and hammer my leather." ...

from FIRST SIGHT OF SLAVERY

... From the day of my entering the States till that of my leaving Philadelphia I had seen society basking in one bright sunshine of good-will. The sweet temper and kindly manners of the Americans are so striking to foreigners, that it is some time before the dazzled stranger perceives that, genuine as is all this good, evils as black as night exist along with it. I had been received with such hearty hospitality everywhere, and had lived among friends so conscientious in their regard for human rights, that, though I had heard of abolition riots, and had observed somewhat of the degradation of the blacks, my mind had not yet been really troubled about the enmity of the races. The time of awakening must come. It began just before I left Philadelphia.

I was calling on a lady[2] whom I had heard speak with strong horror of the abolitionists (with whom I had then no acquaintance); and she turned round upon me with the question whether I would not prevent, if I could, the marriage of a white person with a person of colour. I saw at once the beginning of endless troubles in this inquiry, and was very sorry it had been made; but my determination had been adopted long before, never to evade the great question of colour; never to provoke it; but always to meet it plainly in whatever form it should be presented. I replied that I would never, under any circumstances, try to separate persons who really loved, believing such to be truly those whom God had joined; but I observed that the case she put was one not likely to happen, as I believed the blacks were no more disposed to marry the whites than the whites to marry the blacks. "You are an amalgamationist!" cried she. I told her that the party term was new to me; but that she must give what name she pleased to the principle I had declared in answer to her question. This lady is an eminent religionist, and denunciations spread rapidly from her. The day before I left Philadelphia my old shipmate, the Prussian physician,[3] arrived there, and lost no time in calling to tell me, with much agitation, that I must not go a step farther south; that he had heard on

---

[1] *solitary confinement* One of the punishments believed to have the greatest effect on reforming prisoners. In connection with the idea of religious reformation, solitude was believed to prevent the spread of vice among the prisoners and to encourage reflection that would induce prisoners to convert.

[2] *a lady* Most likely Deborah Norris Logan (1761–1839), diarist, memoirist, and historian. Her diary includes accounts of Martineau's visits.

[3] *Prussian physician* Nicolaus Heinrich Julius (1783–1862). Martineau describes him in her *Autobiography* as "a philanthropist going to America ... to inquire into the state of prison discipline there" and notes that there was "something mysterious and doubtful about him."

all hands, within two hours of his arrival, that I was an amalgamationist, and that my having published a story against slavery would be fatal to me in the slave states. I did not give much credit to the latter part of this news, and saw plainly that all I had to do was to go straight on. I really desired to see the working of the slave system, and was glad that my having published against its principles[1] divested me altogether of the character of a spy, and gave me an unquestioned liberty to publish the results of what I might observe. In order to see things as they were, it was necessary that people's minds should not be prepossessed by my friends as to my opinions and conduct; and therefore forbade my Philadelphia friends to publish in the newspapers, as they wished, an antidote to the charges already current against me.

The next day I first set foot in a slave state, arriving in the evening at Baltimore. I dreaded inexpressibly the first sight of a slave, and could not help speculating on the lot of every person of colour I saw from the windows the first few days. The servants in the house where I was were free blacks.

Before a week was over I perceived that all that is said in England of the hatred of the whites to the blacks in America is short of the truth. The slanders that I heard of the free blacks were too gross to injure my estimation of any but those who spoke them. In Baltimore the bodies of coloured people exclusively are taken for dissection, "because the whites do not like it, and the coloured people cannot resist." It is wonderful that the bodily structure can be (with the exception of the colouring of the skin) thus assumed to be the pattern of that of the whites; that the exquisite nervous system, the instrument of moral as well as physical pleasures and pains, can be nicely investigated, on the ground of its being analogous with that of the whites; that not only the mechanism, but the sensibilities of the degraded race should be argued from to those of the exalted order, and

that men come from such a study with contempt for these brethren in their countenances, hatred in their hearts, and insult on their tongues. These students are the men who cannot say that the coloured people have not nerves that quiver under moral injury, nor a brain that is on fire with insult, nor pulses that throb under oppression. These are the men who should stay the hand of the rash and ignorant possessors of power, who crush the being of creatures, like themselves, "fearfully and wonderfully made."[2] But to speak the right word, to hold out the helping hand, these searchers into man have not light nor strength.

It was in Baltimore that I heard Miss Edgeworth[3] denounced as a woman of no intelligence or delicacy, whose works could never be cared for again, because, in *Belinda*, poor Juba was married, at length, to an English farmer's daughter! The incident is so subordinate that I had entirely forgotten it; but a clergyman's lady threw the volume to the opposite corner of the floor when she came to the page. As I have said elsewhere, Miss Edgeworth is worshipped throughout the United States; but it is in spite of this terrible passage, this clause of a sentence in *Belinda*, which nobody in America can tolerate, while no one elsewhere ever, I should think, dreamed of finding fault with it.

A lady from New-England, staying in Baltimore, was one day talking over slavery with me, her detestation of it being great, when I told her I dreaded seeing a slave. "You have seen one," said she. "You were waited on by a slave yesterday evening." She told me of a gentleman who let out and lent out his slaves to wait at gentlemen's houses, and that the tall handsome mulatto who handed the tea at a party the evening before was one of these. I was glad it was over for once; but I never lost the painful feeling caused to a stranger by intercourse with slaves. No familiarity with them, no mirth and contentment on their part, ever soothed the miserable restlessness caused by the presence of a deeply-injured fellow-being. No wonder or ridicule on the spot avails anything to the

---

[1] *my having ... its principles*   In "Demerara" (1832), one of the tales in her *Illustrations of Political Economy*, Martineau critiques slavery, primarily on economic principles. Martineau also wrote two antislavery articles that appeared in the *Monthly Repository* in 1830 and 1831.

[2] *fearfully and wonderfully made*   Cf. Psalm 139.14.

[3] *Miss Edgeworth*   Maria Edgeworth (1768–1849), one of the most popular and prolific early nineteenth-century British writers. Her second novel, *Belinda*, includes an interracial marriage.

stranger. He suffers, and must suffer from this, deeply and long, as surely as he is human and hates oppression. The next slave that I saw, knowing that it was a slave, was at Washington, where a little negro child took hold of my gown in the passage of our boarding-house, and entered our drawing-room with me. She shut the door softly, as asking leave to stay. I took up a newspaper. She sat at my feet, and began amusing herself with my shoestrings. Finding herself not discouraged, she presently begged play by peeping at me above and on each side the newspaper. She was a brighteyed, merry-hearted child; confiding, like other children, and dreading no evil, but doomed, hopelessly doomed, to ignorance, privation, and moral degradation. When I looked at her, and thought of the fearful disobedience to the first of moral laws, the cowardly treachery, the cruel abuse of power involved in thus dooming to blight a being so helpless, so confiding, and so full of promise, a horror came over me which sickened my very soul. To see slaves is not to be reconciled to slavery. ...

from LIFE AT WASHINGTON

... Washington is no place for persons of domestic tastes. Persons who love dissipation, persons who love to watch the game of politics, and those who make a study of strong minds under strong excitements, like a season at Washington; but it is dreary to those whose pursuits and affections are domestic. I spent five weeks there, and was heartily glad when they were over. I felt the satisfaction all the time of doing something that was highly useful; of getting knowledge that was necessary to me, and could not be otherwise obtained; but the quiet delights of my Philadelphia home[1] (though there half our time was spent in visiting) had spoiled me for such a life as every one leads at the metropolis. I have always looked back upon the five weeks at Washington as one of the most profitable, but by far the least agreeable, of my residences in the United States. ...

At the president's[2] I met a very large party, among whom there was more stiffness than I saw in any other society in America. It was not the fault of the president or his family, but of the way in which the company was unavoidably brought together. With the exception of my party, the name of everybody present began with J, K, or L; that is to say, it consisted of members of Congress, who are invited alphabetically, to ensure none being left out. This principle of selection is not, perhaps, the best for the promotion of ease and sociability; and well as I liked the day, I doubt whether many others could say they enjoyed it. When we went in the president was standing in the middle of the room to receive his guests. After speaking a few words with me, he gave me into the charge of Major Donelson, his secretary, who seated me, and brought up for introduction each guest as he passed from before the president. A congressional friend of mine (whose name began with a J) stationed himself behind my chair, and gave me an account of each gentleman who was introduced to me; where he came from, what his politics were, and how, if at all, he had distinguished himself. All this was highly amusing. At dinner the president was quite disposed for conversation. Indeed, he did nothing but talk. His health is poor, and his diet of the sparest. We both talked freely of the governments of England and France; I, novice in American politics as I was, entirely forgetting that the great French question[3] was pending, and that the president and the King of the French were then bandying very hard words. I was most struck and surprised with the president's complaints of the American Senate, in which there was at that time a small majority against the administration. He told me that I must not judge of the body by what I saw it then, and that after the 4th of March I should behold a Senate

[1] *Philadelphia home* Martineau stayed in the home of William Henry Furness (1802–96), a Unitarian pastor.

[2] *the president* Andrew Jackson, who served as president from 1829 to 1837.

[3] *French question* In 1831 the French government signed a treaty with the United States dictating the payment of 25 million francs to the United States in return for reduced duties on French wines. France failed to pay this money; by 1834 relations between the two countries were tense, and President Jackson made several public addresses against the French. The matter was settled in the spring of 1836 when France finally paid the money in installments.

more worthy of the country. After the 4th of March there was, if I remember rightly, a majority of two in favour of the government. The ground of his complaint was, that the senators had sacrificed their dignity by disregarding the wishes of their constituents. The other side of the question is, that the dignity of the Senate is best consulted by its members following their own convictions, declining instructions for the term for which they are elected. It is a serious difficulty, originating in the very construction of the body, and not to be settled by dispute.

The president offered me bonbons for a child belonging to our part at home, and told me how many children (of his nephew's and his adopted son's) he had about him, with a mildness and kindliness which contrasted well with his tone upon some public occasions. He did the honours of his house with gentleness and politeness to myself, and, as far as I saw, to every one else. About an hour after dinner he rose, and we led the way into the drawing-room, where the whole company, gentlemen as well as ladies, followed to take coffee; after which every one departed, some homeward, some to make evening calls, and others, among whom were ourselves, to a splendid ball at the other extremity of the city. …

from THE CAPITOL

… Those whose taste is the contemplation of great and original men may always have it gratified by going to Washington. Whatever may be thought of the form and administration of government there; however certain it may be that the greatest of men are not, in this age of the world, to be found in political life, it cannot be but that, among the real representatives of a composite and self-governing nation, there must be many men of power; power of intellect, of goodness, or, at least, of will.

from CITY LIFE IN THE SOUTH

… I made it a rule to allow others to introduce the subject of slavery, knowing that they would not fail to do so, and that I might learn as much from their method of approaching the topic as from anything they could say upon it. Before half an hour had passed, every man, woman, or child I might be conversing with had entered upon the question. As it was likewise a rule with me never to conceal or soften my own opinions, and never to allow myself to be irritated by what I heard (for it is too serious a subject to indulge frailties with), the best understanding existed between slaveholders and myself. We never quarrelled, while, I believe, we never failed to perceive the extent of the difference of opinion and feeling between us. I met with much more cause for admiration in their frankness than reason to complain of illiberality. …

Charleston is the place in which to see those contrasting scenes of human life brought under the eye which moralists gather together for the purpose of impressing the imagination. The stranger has but to pass from street to street, to live from hour to hour in this city, to see in conjunction the extremes between which there is everywhere else a wide interval. The sights of one morning I should remember if every other particular of my travels were forgotten. I was driven round the city by a friend[1] whose conversation was delightful all the way. Though I did not agree in all his views of society, the thoughtfulness of his mind and the benevolence of his exertions betokened a healthy state of feeling, and gave value to all he said. He had been a friend of the lamented Grimké;[2] and he showed me the house where Grimké lived and died, and told me much of him; of the nobleness of his character, the extent of his attainments, and how, dying at fifty-four, he had lived by industry a long life. My mind was full of the contemplation of the heights which human beings are destined to reach, when I was plunged into a new scene; one which it was my own conscientious choice to visit,

---

[1] *a friend* Samuel Gilman (1791–1858), a Unitarian minister who hosted Martineau during her stay in the city.

[2] *Grimké* Thomas Smith Grimké (1786–1834), a lawyer, politician, and native of Charleston. His political and social beliefs are reflected in his service on the board of the American Institute of Education and the new American Peace Society against war, as well as his involvement in the temperance movement in South Carolina.

but for which the preceding conversation had ill-prepared me. I went into the slave market, a place which the traveller ought not to avoid to spare his feelings. There was a table on which stood two auctioneers, one with a hammer, the other to exhibit "the article" and count the bids. The slaves for sale were some of them in groups below, and some in a long row behind the auctioneers. The sale of a man was just concluding when we entered the market. A woman, with two children, one at the breast, and another holding by her apron, composed the next lot. The restless, jocose zeal of the auctioneer who counted the bids was the most infernal sight I ever beheld. The woman was a mulatto; she was neatly dressed, with a clean apron and a yellow head-handkerchief. The elder child clung to her. She hung her head low, lower, and still lower on her breast, yet turning her eyes incessantly from side to side, with an intensity of expectation which showed that she had not reached the last stage of despair. I should have thought that her agony of shame and dread would have silenced the tongue of every spectator; but it was not so. A lady[1] chose this moment to turn to me and say, with a cheerful air of complacency, "You know my theory, that one race must be subservient to the other. I do not care which; and if the blacks should ever have the upper hand, I should not mind standing on that table, and being sold with two of my children." Who could help saying within himself, "Would you were! so that that mother were released!" Who could help seeing in vision the blacks driving the whites into the field, and preaching from the pulpits of Christian churches the doctrines now given out there, that God has respect of persons; that men are to hold each other as property, instead of regarding each other as brethren; and that the right interpretation of the golden rule by the slaveholder is, "Do unto your slaves as you would wish your master to do unto you if you were a slave!" A little boy of eight or nine years old apparently, was next put up alone. There was no bearing the child's look of helplessness and shame. It seemed like an outrage to be among the starers

from whom he shrunk, and we went away before he was disposed of. ...

from Signs of the Times in Massachusetts

... I was at this time slightly acquainted with three or four abolitionists, and I was distrusted by most or all of the body who took any interest in me at all. My feelings were very different from theirs about the slaveholders of the South; naturally enough, as these Southern slaveholders were nothing else in the eyes of abolitionists, while to me they were, in some cases, personal friends, and, in more, hospitable entertainers. It was known, however, that I had declared my intention of attending an abolition meeting. This was no new resolution. From the outset of my inquiry into the question, I had declared that, having attended colonization meetings, and heard all that the slaveholders had to say for themselves and against abolitionists, I felt myself bound to listen to the other side of the question. I always professed my intention of seeking acquaintance with the abolitionists, though I then fully and involuntarily believed two or three charges against them which I found to be wholly groundless. The time was now come for discharging this duty.

On the Monday, two friends, then only new acquaintances, called on me at the house of a clergyman where I was staying, three miles from Boston. A late riot at Salem was talked over, a riot in which the family of Mr. Thompson[2] had been driven from one house to another three times in one night, the children being snatched from their beds, carried abroad in the cold, and injuriously terrified. It was mentioned that the ladies of the Anti-slavery Society were going to attempt a meeting on the next Wednesday, and I was asked whether I was in earnest in saying that I would attend one of their meetings. Would I go to this one if I should be invited? I replied that it depended entirely on the nature of the meeting. If it was merely a meeting for the settlement of accounts and the despatch of business, where I should not learn what I wanted, I should wait

---

[1] *A lady* In her *Autobiography*, Martineau ascribes this comment to Caroline Howard Gilman (1794–1888), an author of poetry, children's books, housekeeping manuals, and a memoir.

[2] *Mr. Thompson* George Thompson (1804–78), a prominent abolitionist.

for a less perilous time; if it was a bona fide public meeting, a true reflection of the spirit and circumstances of the time and the cause, I would go. The matter was presently decided by the arrival of a regular official invitation to me to attend the meeting, and to carry with me the friend who was my travelling companion,[1] and any one else who might be disposed to accompany me.

Trifling as these circumstances may now appear, they were no trifles at the time; and many considerations were involved in the smallest movement a stranger made on the question. The two first things I had to take care of were to avoid involving my host[2] in any trouble I might get into, and to afford opportunity to my companion to judge for herself what she would do. My host had been reviled in the newspapers already for having read a notice (among several others) of an anti-slavery meeting from Dr. Channing's pulpit, where he was accidentally[3] preaching. My object was to prevent his giving an opinion on anything that I should do, that he might not be made more or less responsible for my proceedings. I handed the invitation to my companion, with a hint not to speak of it. We separately made up our minds to go, and announced our determination to our host and hostess. Between joke and earnest, they told us we should be mobbed; and the same thing was repeated by many who were not in joke at all.

At two o'clock on the Wednesday we arrived at the house of a gentleman where we were to meet a few of the leading abolitionists, and dine, previous to the meeting. Our host was miserably ill that day, unfit to be out of his chamber; but he exerted himself to the utmost, being resolved to escort his wife to the meeting. During dinner, the conversation was all about the Southern gentry, in whose favour I said all I could, and

much more than the party could readily receive; which was natural enough, considering that they and I looked at the people of the South from different points of view. Before we issued forth on our expedition I was warned once more that exertions had been made to get up a mob, and that it was possible we might be dispersed by violence. When we turned into the street where the house of meeting stood, there were about a dozen boys hooting before the door, as they saw ladies of colour entering. We were admitted without having to wait an instant on the steps, and the door was secured behind us. The ladies assembled in two drawing-rooms, thrown into one by the folding-doors being opened. The total number was a hundred and thirty. The president sat at a small table by the folding doors, and before her was a large Bible, paper, pens, and ink, and the secretary's papers. There were only three gentlemen in the house, its inhabitant, the gentleman who escorted us, and a clergyman who had dined with us. They remained in the hall, keeping the front door fastened, and the back way clear for our retreat, if retreat should be necessary. But the number of hooters in the streets at no time exceeded thirty, and they treated us to nothing worse than a few yells.

A lady who sat next me amused me by inquiring, with kindness, whether it revolted my feelings to meet thus in assembly with people of colour. She was as much surprised as pleased with my English deficiency of all feeling on the subject. My next neighbour on the other hand was Mrs. Thompson,[4] the wife of the anti-slavery lecturer, who had just effected his escape, and was then on the sea. The proceedings began with the reading of a few texts of Scripture by the president. My first impression was that the selection of these texts gave out a little vainglory about the endurance of persecution; but when I remembered that this was the reunion of persons who had been dispersed by a mob, and when I afterward became aware how cruelly many of the members had been wounded in their moral sense, their domestic affections, and their prospects in life, I was

---

[1] *travelling companion* Louisa Jeffrey accompanied Martineau in return for her expenses paid.

[2] *my host* Martineau was staying with the abolitionists Ellis Gray Loring and Louisa Gilman Loring.

[3] *Dr. Channing* William Ellery Channing (1780–1842), transcendentalist and minister of Federal Street Church in Boston; *accidentally* By chance.

[4] *Mrs. Thompson* Wife of George Thompson, who in November 1835 was pursued by a Boston mob and forced to escape in a rowboat; he then sailed back to England.

quite ready to yield my too nice[1] criticism. A prayer then followed, the spirit of which appeared to me perfect in hopefulness, meekness, and gentleness. While the secretary was afterward reading her report, a note was handed to me, the contents of which sunk my spirits fathom deep for the hour. It was a short pencil note from one of the gentlemen[2] in the hall; and it asked me whether I had any objection to give a word of sympathy to the meeting, fellow-labourers as we had long been in behalf of the principles in whose defence they were met. The case was clear as daylight to my conscience. If I had been a mere stranger, attending with a mere stranger's interest to the proceedings of a party of natives, I might and ought to have declined mixing myself up with their proceedings. But I had long before published against slavery, and always declared my conviction that this was a question of humanity, not of country or race; a moral, not a merely political question; a general affair, and not one of city, state, party, or nation. Having thus declared on the safe side of the Atlantic, I was bound to act up to my declaration on the unsafe side, if called upon. I thought it a pity that the call had been made, though I am now very glad that it was, as it was the means of teaching me more of the temper and affairs of the times than I could have known by any other means, and as it ripened the regard which subsisted between myself and the writer of the note into a substantial, profitable, and delightful friendship; but, at the moment, I foresaw none of these good consequences, but a formidable array of very unpleasant ones. I foresaw that almost every house in Boston, except those of the abolitionists, would be shut against me; that my relation to the country would be completely changed, as I should be suddenly transformed from being a guest and an observer to being considered a missionary or a spy; and results even more serious than this might reasonably be anticipated. During the few minutes I had for consideration, the wife of the writer of the note came to me, and asked what I thought of it, begging me to feel quite at liberty to attend to it or not, as I liked. I felt that I had no such liberty. I was presently introduced to the meeting, when I offered the note as my reason for breaking the silence of a stranger, and made the same declarations of my abhorrence of slavery and my agreement in the principles of the abolitionists which I had expressed throughout the whole of my travels through the South.

Of the consequences of this simple affair it is not my intention to give any account, chiefly because it would be impossible to convey to my English readers my conviction of the smallness of the portion of American society which was concerned in the treatment inflicted upon me. The hubbub was so great, and the modes of insult were so various, as to justify distant observers in concluding that the whole nation had risen against me. I soon found how few can make a great noise, while the many are careless or ignorant of what is going on about a person or a party with whom they have nothing to do; and while not a few are rendered more hearty in their regard and more generous in their hospitality by the disgraces of the individual who is under the oppression of public censure. All that I anticipated at the moment of reading the note came to pass, but only for a time. Eventually, nothing remained which in the slightest degree modified my opinions or impaired my hopes of the society I was investigating. ...

—1838

---

[1] *nice* Exacting.

[2] *one of the gentlemen* In her *Autobiography* Martineau identifies this man as her host, Ellis Gray Loring.

JOHN STUART MILL
1806 – 1873

Philosopher, social reformer, economist, and politician, John Stuart Mill was one of the most influential of Victorian thinkers. His breadth of knowledge and interests was staggering, as was the range of subject matter that he chose to examine in his writing, including women's rights, civil liberties, economic theories, logic, and poetics. Mill's *Utilitarianism* and *On Liberty* are both still regarded as central works in the fields of moral and social philosophy and political science.

Mill seemed destined from an early age to become a polymath—his childhood was practically a monument to over-achievement. He was born in London in 1806, the first child of Harriet Burrow and James Mill, a distinguished psychologist, philosopher, and historian. James was a disciple of Jeremy Bentham, who had founded the philosophical school of utilitarianism, an ethical doctrine whose main premise is that an action ought to be taken only if it produces happiness for all involved (later refined by J.S. Mill into the "greatest happiness principle," which suggests that people ought to act in ways that produce the greatest happiness for all involved). Participating in an experiment devised in part by Bentham, James decided that his eldest son would be a guinea pig for his educational theories, and at a very young age John began a rigorous education aimed at preparing him to become a future leader of the Benthamites.

In his autobiography, Mill described his formal instruction as beginning with Greek at age three; by the age of eight he could translate the works of Plato. He then learned Latin well enough to translate such masters as Horace and Ovid, and also studied mathematics, the sciences, and English literature. Not being content to allow his son to learn simply by rote, James heavily emphasized rhetoric and debate, insisting that John make moral decisions about the principles he was learning. By the time he was 14, his father considered him to be ready for university study but felt that an institution would hold him back, and thus Mill began his career a full "quarter of a century before his contemporaries," as he would say in his autobiography.

James's experiment succeeded—John was a brilliant and erudite child, able to converse and debate with adults and to tutor all of his siblings from an early age. The daily ten-hour study regime, however, took a toll on him, and in his early twenties Mill experienced a period of deep depression that was relieved only when he discovered the poetry of William Wordsworth. During this time he pondered the virtues of Bentham's utilitarianism, which seemed to favor the good of the majority at the expense of the individual, who, Mill felt, is the best judge of his or her own happiness. Although he himself was an empiricist, he felt that Bentham's philosophy promoted the "science" of ethics at the expense of real life. Mill said of Bentham's utilitarianism: "It is wholly empirical and the empiricism of one who has had little experience." After reading the Romantic poets—Wordsworth in particular—Mill began to appreciate the therapeutic effects of poetry and the arts and the importance of an emotional life. The essay "What Is Poetry?" (1833) speaks to his concerns about the necessity of individual pleasure.

After studying law for two years, Mill worked for decades in the East India Office, first as a clerk and then as head of his department, but he continued to be an outspoken advocate for individual rights and freedoms (he had been arrested as a teenager for disseminating literature in support of birth control). He published a modification of Bentham's philosophy, later reworked as *Utilitarianism* (1863); his most ambitious early work was *System of Logic*, published in 1843 and still highly regarded in philosophical circles today. The book that followed, *Principles of Political Economy* (1848), commands a similar level of respect in the field of economics. In 1859 Mill wrote another key work: *On Liberty*, a treatise that continued his theme of support for individual rights, deriding democratic majorities that conform to tradition and smother individuality.

In the planning and to some extent the writing of both these and subsequent works, Mill was assisted by Harriet Taylor, an aspiring author whom Mill had first met in 1831 and with whom he began to work closely. (The precise extent of Taylor's involvement remains the subject of debate among scholars). The two were married in 1851 after her husband's death. Mill and Taylor never moved freely in society together, however; many of his friends, Carlyle and Tennyson included, viewed their relationship as inappropriate.

After serving as Member of Parliament from 1865 to 1868, Mill published *The Subjection of Women* (1869). He had worked on this book for years, and it had become a passionate subject for both Mill and Taylor. *The Subjection of Women* spoke to the rights of women, both legally and practically, arguing for government reforms of property and divorce laws, women's enfranchisement, and advocating the end of "slavery" in the home. Mill even argued in Parliament—well ahead of his time—for non-sexist language and the rewording of parliamentary bills to remove gender-specific terms.

Mill died in 1873 in Avignon, France, and was buried beside his wife, who had died prematurely in 1858. In his eloquent and insightful *Autobiography*, published shortly after his death, Mill wrote candidly about his childhood experiences with a demanding father and a thoroughly rational education; about his mental breakdown and his discovery of the value of works of the imagination; about his relationship with Harriet Taylor; and about his writing. The *Autobiography* is valued both as a work of literature in its own right and as a record of the remarkable life of a profoundly influential thinker.

⌘ ⌘ ⌘

What Is Poetry?

It has often been asked, what is poetry? And many and various are the answers which have been returned. The vulgarest of all—one with which no person possessed of the faculties to which poetry addresses itself can ever have been satisfied—is that which confounds poetry with metrical composition: yet to this wretched mockery of a definition, many have been led back, by the failure of all their attempts to find any other that would distinguish what they have been accustomed to call poetry, from much which they have known only under other names.

That, however, the word *poetry* does import[1] something quite peculiar in its nature, something which may exist in what is called prose as well as in verse, something which does not even require the instrument of words, but can speak, through those other audible symbols called musical sounds, and even through the

_____
[1] *import* Signify.

visible ones, which are the language of sculpture, painting, and architecture; all this, as we believe, is and must be felt, though perhaps indistinctly, by all upon whom poetry in any of its shapes produces any impression beyond that of tickling the ear. To the mind, poetry is either nothing, or it is the better part of all art whatever, and of real life too; and the distinction between poetry and what is not poetry, whether explained or not, is felt to be fundamental.

Where everyone feels a difference, a difference there must be. All other appearance may be fallacious, but the appearance of a difference is itself a real difference. Appearances too, like other things, must have a cause, and that which can cause anything, even an illusion, must be a reality. And hence, while a half-philosophy disdains the classifications and distinctions indicated by popular language, philosophy carried to its highest point may frame new ones, but never sets aside the old, content with correcting and regularizing them. It cuts fresh channels for thought, but it does not fill up such as it finds ready-made, but traces, on the contrary, more deeply, broadly, and distinctly, those into which the current has spontaneously flowed.

Let us then attempt, in the way of modest inquiry, not to coerce and confine nature within the bounds of an arbitrary definition, but rather to find the boundaries which she herself has set, and erect a barrier round them; not calling mankind to account for having misapplied the word *poetry*, but attempting to clear up to them the conception[1] which they already attach to it, and to bring before their minds as a distinct principle that which, as a vague feeling, has really guided them in their actual employment of the term.

The object of poetry is confessedly to act upon the emotions; and therein is poetry sufficiently distinguished from what Wordsworth affirms to be its logical opposite, namely, not prose, but matter of fact or science.[2] The one addresses itself to the belief, the other to the feelings. The one does its work by convincing or persuading, the other by moving. The one acts by presenting a proposition to the understanding, the other by offering interesting objects of contemplation to the sensibilities.

This, however, leaves us very far from a definition of poetry. We have distinguished it from one thing, but we are bound to distinguish it from everything. To present thoughts or images to the mind for the purpose of acting upon the emotions, does not belong to poetry alone. It is equally the province (for example) of the novelist: and yet the faculty of the poet and the faculty of the novelist are as distinct as any other two faculties; as the faculty of the novelist and of the orator, or of the poet and the metaphysician. The two characters may be united, as characters the most disparate may; but they have no natural connection.

Many of the finest poems are in the form of novels, and in almost all good novels there is true poetry. But there is a radical distinction between the interest felt in a novel as such, and the interest excited by poetry; for the one is derived from incident, the other from the representation of feeling. In one, the source of the emotion excited is the exhibition of a state or states of human sensibility;[3] in the other, of a series of states of mere outward circumstances. Now, all minds are capable of being affected more or less by representations of the latter kind, and all, or almost all, by those of the former; yet the two sources of interest correspond to two distinct and (as respects their greatest development) mutually exclusive characters of mind. So much is the nature of poetry dissimilar to the nature of fictitious narrative, that to have a really strong passion for either of the two, seems to presuppose or to superinduce[4] a comparative indifference to the other.

At what age is the passion for a story, for almost any kind of story, merely as a story, the most intense? In childhood. But that also is the age at which poetry, even of the simplest description, is least relished and least understood; because the feelings with which it is especially conversant are yet undeveloped, and not having been even in the slightest degree experienced, cannot be sympathized with. In what stage of the progress of

---

[1] *conception* Idea.

[2] *Wordsworth … science* See William Wordsworth's "Note" in "Preface" to *Lyrical Ballads* (1800).

[3] *sensibility* Emotional and aesthetic sensitivity.

[4] *superinduce* Introduce additionally.

society, again, is storytelling most valued, and the storyteller in greatest request and honor? In a rude state; like that of the Tartars[1] and Arabs at this day, and of almost all nations in the earliest ages. But in this state of society there is little poetry except ballads, which are mostly narrative, that is, essentially stories, and derive their principal interest from the incidents. Considered as poetry, they are of the lowest and most elementary kind: the feelings depicted, or rather indicated, are the simplest our nature has; such joys and griefs as the immediate pressure of some outward event excites in rude minds, which live wholly immersed in outward things, and have never, either from choice or a force they could not resist, turned themselves to the contemplation of the world within. Passing now from childhood, and from the childhood of society, to the grown-up men and women of this most grown-up and unchildlike age—the minds and hearts of greatest depth and elevation are commonly those which take greatest delight in poetry; the shallowest and emptiest, on the contrary, are, by universal remark, the most addicted to novel reading. This accords, too, with all analogous experience of human nature. The sort of persons whom not merely in books but in their lives, we find perpetually engaged in hunting for excitement from without,[2] are invariably those who do not possess, either in the vigor of their intellectual powers or in the depth of their sensibilities, that which would enable them to find ample excitement nearer at home. The same persons whose time is divided between sightseeing, gossip, and fashionable dissipation,[3] take a natural delight in fictitious narrative; the excitement it affords is of the kind which comes from without. Such persons are rarely lovers of poetry, though they may fancy themselves so, because they relish novels in verse. But poetry, which is the delineation of the deeper and more secret workings of the human heart, is interesting only to those to whom it recalls what they have felt, or

whose imagination it stirs up to conceive what they could feel, or what they might have been able to feel, had their outward circumstances been different.

Poetry, when it is really such, is truth; and fiction also, if it is good for anything, is truth: but they are different truths. The truth of poetry is to paint the human soul truly: the truth of fiction is to give a true picture of life. The two kinds of knowledge are different, and come by different ways, come mostly to different persons. Great poets are often proverbially ignorant of life. What they know has come by observation of themselves; they have found there one highly delicate, and sensitive, and refined specimen of human nature, on which the laws of human emotion are written in large characters, such as can be read off without much study: and other knowledge of mankind, such as comes to men of the world by outward experience, is not indispensable to them as poets: but to the novelist such knowledge is all in all; he has to describe outward things, not the inward man; actions and events, not feelings; and it will not do for him to be numbered among those who, as Madame Roland said of Brissot,[4] know man but not men.

All this is no bar to the possibility of combining both elements, poetry and narrative or incident, in the same work, and calling it either a novel or a poem; but so may red and white combine on the same human features, or on the same canvas; and so may oil and vinegar, though opposite natures, blend together in the same composite taste. There is one order of composition which requires the union of poetry and incident, each in its highest kind—the dramatic. Even there the two elements are perfectly distinguishable, and may exist of unequal quality, and in the most various proportion. The incidents of a dramatic poem may be scant and ineffective, though the delineation of passion and character may be of the highest order; as in Goethe's

---

[1] *rude* Unrefined; *Tartars* Term once used to describe most peoples of north and central Asia, and associated with the Turco-Mongol tradition. The majority of Tatars today live in Ukraine, Russia, and Uzbekistan, and are predominantly Muslim.

[2] *from without* From external sources.

[3] *dissipation* Indulgence.

[4] *Madame Roland* See Marie Jeanne Philipon Roland de la Platière's *Appeal to Impartial Posterity* (1796); *Brissot* Jacques-Pierre Brissot (1754–93), a French journalist and leader of the Girondists during the French Revolution, was executed by the Jacobins in 1793.

glorious *Torquato Tasso*;[1] or again, the story as a mere story may be well got up for effect, as is the case with some of the most trashy productions of the Minerva press:[2] it may even be, what those are not, a coherent and probable series of events, though there be scarcely a feeling exhibited which is not exhibited falsely, or in a manner absolutely commonplace. The combination of the two excellencies is what renders Shakespeare so generally acceptable, each sort of readers finding in him what is suitable to their faculties. To the many he is great as a storyteller, to the few as a poet.

In limiting poetry to the delineation of states of feeling, and denying the name where nothing is delineated but outward objects, we may be thought to have done what we promised to avoid—to have not found, but made a definition, in opposition to the usage of the English language, since it is established by common consent that there is a poetry called descriptive. We deny the charge. Description is not poetry because there is descriptive poetry, no more than science is poetry because there is such a thing as a didactic poem; no more, we might almost say, than Greek or Latin is poetry because there are Greek and Latin poems. But an object which admits of being described, or a truth which may fill a place in a scientific treatise, may also furnish an occasion for the generation of poetry, which we thereupon choose to call descriptive or didactic. The poetry is not in the object itself, nor in the scientific truth itself, but in the state of mind in which the one and the other may be contemplated. The mere delineation of the dimensions and colors of external objects is not poetry, no more than a geometrical ground plan of St. Peter's or Westminster Abbey[3] is painting. Descriptive poetry consists, no doubt, in description, but in description of things as they appear, not as they are; and

it paints them not in their bare and natural lineaments, but arranged in the colors and seen through the medium of the imagination set in action by the feelings. If a poet is to describe a lion, he will not set about describing him as a naturalist would, nor even as a traveler would, who was intent upon stating the truth, the whole truth, and nothing but the truth. He will describe him by imagery, that is, by suggesting the most striking likenesses and contrasts which might occur to a mind contemplating the lion, in the state of awe, wonder, or terror, which the spectacle naturally excites, or is, on the occasion, supposed to excite. Now this is describing the lion professedly, but the state of excitement of the spectator really. The lion may be described falsely or in exaggerated colors, and the poetry be all the better; but if the human emotion be not painted with the most scrupulous truth, the poetry is bad poetry, i.e., is not poetry at all, but a failure.

Thus far our progress towards a clear view of the essentials of poetry has brought us very close to the last two attempts at a definition of poetry which we happen to have seen in print, both of them by poets and men of genius. The one is by Ebenezer Elliott, the author of *Corn-Law Rhymes*, and other poems of still greater merit. "Poetry," says he, "is impassioned truth."[4] The other is by a writer in *Blackwood's Magazine*, and comes, we think, still nearer the mark. We forget his exact words, but in substance he defined poetry as "man's thoughts tinged by his feelings." There is in either definition a near approximation to what we are in search of. Every truth which man can announce, every thought, even every outward impression, which can enter into his consciousness, may become poetry when shown through any impassioned medium, when invested with the coloring of joy, or grief, or pity, or affection, or admiration, or reverence, or awe, or even hatred or terror: and, unless so colored, nothing, be it as interesting as it may, is poetry. But both these definitions fail to discriminate between poetry and eloquence. Eloquence, as well as poetry, is impassioned truth; eloquence, as well as poetry, is thoughts colored by the feelings. Yet common apprehension and philosophic

---

[1] *Goethe's glorious Torquato Tasso*   Reference to the late eighteenth-century play by Johann Wolfgang von Goethe, about sixteenth-century Italian poet Torquato Tasso.

[2] *Minerva press*   Publishing company (1790–1820) that specialized in cheap, and many would say tasteless, novels.

[3] *St. Peter's*   St. Peter's Basilica, a large, lavish church in Vatican City where the pope often delivers sermons and liturgies; *Westminster Abbey*   Gothic-style church in central London that is the traditional coronation and burial site of the British monarchy.

[4] *Poetry ... truth*   See "Preface" to Elliot's *Corn-Law Rhymes* (1828).

criticism alike recognize a distinction between the two: there is much that everyone would call eloquence, which no one would think of classing as poetry. A question will sometimes arise, whether some particular author is a poet; and those who maintain the negative commonly allow, that though not a poet, he is a highly eloquent writer.

The distinction between poetry and eloquence appears to us to be equally fundamental with the distinction between poetry and narrative, or between poetry and description. It is still farther from having been satisfactorily cleared up than either of the others, unless, which is highly probable, the German artists and critics[1] have thrown some light upon it which has not yet reached us. Without a perfect knowledge of what they have written, it is something like presumption to write upon such subjects at all, and we shall be the foremost to urge that, whatever we may be about to submit, may be received, subject to correction from them.

Poetry and eloquence are both alike the expression or uttering forth of feeling. But if we may be excused the seeming affectation of the antithesis, we should say that eloquence is *heard*, poetry is *over*heard. Eloquence supposes an audience; the peculiarity of poetry appears to us to lie in the poet's utter unconsciousness of a listener. Poetry is feeling confessing itself to itself, in moments of solitude, and bodying itself forth in symbols which are the nearest possible representations of the feeling in the exact shape in which it exists in the poet's mind. Eloquence is feeling pouring itself forth to other minds, courting their sympathy, or endeavoring to influence their belief, or move them to passion or to action.

All poetry is of the nature of soliloquy. It may be said that poetry, which is printed on hot-pressed paper, and sold at a bookseller's shop, is a soliloquy in full dress, and upon the stage. But there is nothing absurd in the idea of such a mode of soliloquizing. What we have said to ourselves, we may tell to others afterwards; what

we have said or done in solitude, we may voluntarily reproduce when we know that other eyes are upon us. But no trace of consciousness that any eyes are upon us must be visible in the work itself. The actor knows that there is an audience present; but if he act as though he knew it, he acts ill. A poet may write poetry with the intention of publishing it; he may write it even for the express purpose of being paid for it; that it should be poetry, being written under any such influences, is far less probable; not, however, impossible; but not otherwise possible than if he can succeed in excluding from his work every vestige of such lookings-forth into the outward and everyday world, and can express his feelings exactly as he has felt them in solitude, or as he feels that he should feel them, though they were to remain forever unuttered. But when he turns round and addresses himself to another person; when the act of utterance is not itself the end, but a means to an end—viz.,[2] by the feelings he himself expresses to work upon the feelings, or upon the belief, or the will of another—when the expression of his emotions, or of his thoughts, tinged by his emotions, is tinged also by that purpose, by that desire of making an impression upon another mind, then it ceases to be poetry, and becomes eloquence.

Poetry, accordingly, is the natural fruit of solitude and meditation; eloquence, of intercourse[3] with the world. The persons who have most feeling of their own, if intellectual culture have given them a language in which to express it, have the highest faculty of poetry; those who best understand the feelings of others, are the most eloquent. The persons, and the nations, who commonly excel in poetry, are those whose character and tastes render them least dependent for their happiness upon the applause, or sympathy, or concurrence of the world in general. Those to whom that applause, that sympathy, that concurrence are most necessary, generally excel most in eloquence. And hence, perhaps, the French, who are the least poetical of all great and refined nations, are among the most eloquent: the French, also,

---

[1] *the German artists and critics* Throughout the mid-nineteenth century, the works of Goethe and other figures of German Romanticism were seen as ground-breaking by the British intellectual elite.

[2] *viz.* Abbreviation of the Latin *videlicet*, meaning "namely" or "that is to say."

[3] *intercourse* Communication.

being the most sociable, the vainest, and the least self-dependent.

If the above be, as we believe, the true theory of the distinction commonly admitted between eloquence and poetry; or though it be not that, yet if, as we cannot doubt, the distinction above stated be a real bona fide distinction, it will be found to hold, not merely in the language of words, but in all other language, and to intersect the whole domain of art.

Take, for example, music: we shall find in that art, so peculiarly the expression of passion, two perfectly distinct styles; one of which may be called the poetry, the other the oratory of music. This difference being seized[1] would put an end to much musical sectarianism. There has been much contention whether the character of Rossini's[2] music—the music, we mean, which is characteristic of that composer—is compatible with the expression of passion. Without doubt, the passion it expresses is not the musing, meditative tenderness, or pathos, or grief of Mozart,[3] the great poet of his art. Yet it is passion, but garrulous passion—the passion which pours itself into other ears; and therein the better calculated for dramatic effect, having a natural adaptation for dialogue. Mozart also is great in musical oratory; but his most touching compositions are in the opposite style—that of soliloquy. Who can imagine "*Dove sono*"[4] *heard?* We imagine it *over*-heard. The same is the case with many of the finest national airs. Who can hear those words, which speak so touchingly the sorrows of a mountaineer in exile:

My heart's in the Highlands[5]—my heart is not here;
My heart's in the Highlands, a-chasing the deer,
A-chasing the wild-deer, and following the roe—
My heart's in the Highlands, wherever I go.

Who can hear those affecting words, married to as affecting an air, and fancy that he sees the singer? That song has always seemed to us like the lament of a prisoner in a solitary cell, ourselves listening, unseen, in the next. As the direct opposite of this, take "Scots wha hae wi' Wallace bled,"[6] where the music is as oratorical as the poetry.

Purely pathetic[7] music commonly partakes of soliloquy. The soul is absorbed in its distress, and though there may be bystanders, it is not thinking of them. When the mind is looking within and not without, its state does not often or rapidly vary; and hence the even, uninterrupted flow, approaching almost to monotony, which a good reader, or a good singer, will give to words or music of a pensive or melancholy cast. But grief, taking the form of a prayer, or of a complaint becomes oratorical; no longer low, and even, and subdued, it assumes a more emphatic rhythm, a more rapidly returning accent; instead of a few slow, equal notes, following one after another at regular intervals, it crowds note upon note, and oft-times assumes a hurry and bustle like joy. Those who are familiar with some of the best of Rossini's serious compositions, such as the air "*Tu che i miseri conforti,*" in the opera of *Tancredi*, or the duet "*Ebben per mia memoria,*" in *La Gazza Ladra*, will at once understand and feel our meaning. Both are highly tragic and passionate; the passion of both is that of oratory, not poetry. The like may be said of that most moving prayer in Beethoven's *Fidelio*, "*Komm, Hoffnung, lass das letzte Stern / Der Müde nicht erbleichen*";[8] in which Madame Devrient,[9] last summer, exhibited such consummate powers of pathetic expression. How different from Winter's beautiful "*Paga pii*,"[10] the very soul of melancholy exhaling itself in solitude; fuller of meaning, and, therefore, more profoundly poetical than the words

---

[1] *seized*   Understood; accepted.

[2] *Rossini*   Gioachino Antonio Rossini (1792–1868), a composer best known for operatic works such as *The Barber of Seville.*

[3] *Mozart*   Wolfgang Amadeus Mozart (1756–91), recognized as one of the most influential composers in the Western classical tradition.

[4] *Dove sono*   From Mozart's *The Marriage of Figaro*, 1786.

[5] *My heart's ... Highlands*   From a poem of the same name by Robert Burns (1798).

[6] *Scots ... bled*   By Robert Burns (1793).

[7] *pathetic*   Evoking strong emotion.

[8] *Komm ... erbleichen*   Beethoven's exact lines are "*Komm, Hoffnung, lass den letzten Stern / Der Müden nicht erbleichen,*" which translate to "Come, Hope, do not let the last star of the weary fade away."

[9] *Madame Devrient*   Famous opera singer Madame Wilhelmine Schröder-Devrient (1804–60).

[10] *Paga pii*   Aria from Peter Winter's *Il ratto di Proserpina* (1804).

for which it was composed—for it seems to express not simply melancholy, but the melancholy of remorse.

If, from vocal music, we now pass to instrumental, we may have a specimen of musical oratory in any fine military symphony or march: while the poetry of music seems to have attained its consummation in Beethoven's Overture to *Egmont*.[1] We question whether so deep an expression of mixed grandeur and melancholy was ever in any other instance produced by mere sounds.

In the arts which speak to the eye, the same distinctions will be found to hold, not only between poetry and oratory, but between poetry, oratory, narrative, and simple imitation or description.

Pure description is exemplified in a mere portrait or a mere landscape—productions of art, it is true, but of the mechanical rather than of the fine arts, being works of simple imitation, not creation. We say, a mere portrait, or a mere landscape, because it is possible for a portrait or a landscape, without ceasing to be such, to be also a picture. A portrait by Lawrence, or one of Turner's[2] views, is not a mere copy from nature: the one combines with the given features that particular expression (among all good and pleasing ones) which those features are most capable of wearing, and which, therefore, in combination with them, is capable of producing the greatest positive beauty. Turner, again, unites the objects of the given landscape with whatever sky, and whatever light and shade, enable those particular objects to impress the imagination most strongly. In both, there is creative art—not working after an actual model, but realizing an idea.

Whatever in painting or sculpture expresses human feeling, or character, which is only a certain state of feeling grown habitual, may be called, according to circumstances, the poetry or the eloquence of the painter's or the sculptor's art; the poetry, if the feeling declares itself by such signs as escape from us when we are unconscious of being seen; the oratory, if the signs are those we use for the purpose of voluntary communication.

The poetry of painting seems to be carried to its highest perfection in the *Peasant Girl* of Rembrandt,[3] or in any Madonna or Magdalen of Guido;[4] that of sculpture, in almost any of the Greek statues of the gods; not considering these in respect to the mere physical beauty, of which they are such perfect models, not undertaking either to vindicate or to contest the opinion of philosophers, that even physical beauty is ultimately resolvable into expression; we may safely affirm, that in no other of man's works did so much of soul ever shine through mere inanimate matter.

The narrative style answers to what is called historical painting, which it is the fashion among connoisseurs to treat as the climax of the pictorial art. That it is the most difficult branch of the art, we do not doubt, because, in its perfection, it includes, in a manner, the perfection of all the other branches. As an epic poem, though, insofar as it is epic (i.e., narrative), it is not poetry at all, is yet esteemed the greatest effort of poetic genius, because there is no kind whatever of poetry which may not appropriately find a place in it. But a historical picture, as such, that is, as the representation of an incident, must necessarily, as it seems to us, be poor and ineffective. The narrative powers of painting are extremely limited. Scarcely any picture, scarcely any series even of pictures, which we know of, tells its own story without the aid of an interpreter; you must know the story beforehand; then, indeed, you may see great beauty and appropriateness in the painting. But it is the single figures which, to us, are the great charm even of a historical picture. It is in these that the power of the art is really seen: in the attempt to narrate, visible and permanent signs are far behind the fugitive audible ones which follow so fast one after another, while the faces and figures in a narrative picture, even though they be Titian's,[5] stand still. Who would not prefer one *Virgin and Child* of Raphael,[6] to all the pictures which

---

[1] *Egmont* Ludwig van Beethoven, Opus 84 (1809).

[2] *Lawrence* Sir Thomas Lawrence (1769–1830); *Turner* J.M.W. Turner (1775–1851).

[3] *Rembrandt* Rembrandt Harmenzoon Van Rijn (1606–69).

[4] *Guido* Guido Reni (1575–1642).

[5] *Titian's* Referring to the work of the Venetian painter Tiziano Vecellio (c. 1485–1576).

[6] *Raphael* Raffaelo Sanzio (1483–1520).

Rubens,[1] with his fat, frowzy Dutch Venuses, ever painted? Though Rubens, besides excelling almost everyone in his mastery over all the mechanical parts of his art, often shows real genius in grouping his figures, the peculiar problem of historical painting. But, then, who, except a mere student of drawing and coloring, ever cared to look twice at any of the figures themselves? The power of painting lies in poetry, of which Rubens had not the slightest tincture—not in narrative, where he might have excelled.

The single figures, however, in an historical picture, are rather the eloquence of painting than the poetry: they mostly (unless they are quite out of place in the picture) express the feelings of one person as modified by the presence of others. Accordingly the minds whose bent leads them rather to eloquence than to poetry, rush to historical painting. The French painters, for instance, seldom attempt, because they could make nothing of, single heads, like those glorious ones of the Italian masters, with which they might glut themselves day after day in their own Louvre.[2] They must all be historical; and they are, almost to a man, attitudinizers. If we wished to give to any young artist the most impressive warning our imaginations could devise, against that kind of vice in the pictorial, which corresponds to rant in the histrionic art, we would advise him to walk once up and once down the gallery of the Luxembourg;[3] even now when David,[4] the great corrupter of taste, has been translated from this world to the next, and from the Luxembourg, consequently, into the more elevated sphere of the Louvre. Every figure in French painting or statuary seems to be showing itself off before spectators: they are in the worst style of corrupted eloquence, but in no style of poetry at all. The best are stiff and unnatural; the worst resemble figures of cataleptic patients. The French artists fancy themselves imitators of the classics, yet they seem to have no understanding and no feeling of that repose which was the peculiar and pervading character of Grecian art, until it began to decline: a repose tenfold more indicative of strength than all their stretching and straining; for strength, as Thomas Carlyle says, does not manifest itself in spasms.[5]

There are some productions of art which it seems at first difficult to arrange in any of the classes above illustrated. The direct aim of art as such, is the production of the beautiful; and as there are other things beautiful besides states of mind, there is much of art which may seem to have nothing to do with either poetry or eloquence as we have defined them. Take for instance a composition of Claude, or Salvator Rosa.[6] There is here creation of new beauty: by the grouping of natural scenery, conformably indeed to the laws of outward nature, but not after any actual model; the result being a beauty more perfect and faultless than is perhaps to be found in any actual landscape. Yet there is a character of poetry even in these, without which they could not be so beautiful. The unity, and wholeness, and aesthetic congruity of the picture still lies in singleness of expression; but it is expression in a different sense from that in which we have hitherto employed the term. The objects in an imaginary landscape cannot be said, like the words of a poem or the notes of a melody, to be the actual utterance of a feeling; but there must be some feeling with which they harmonize, and which they have a tendency to raise up in the spectator's mind. They must inspire a feeling of grandeur, a loveliness, a cheerfulness, a wildness, a melancholy, a terror. The painter must surround his principal objects with such imagery as would spontaneously arise in a highly imaginative mind, when contemplating those objects under the impression of the feelings which they are intended to inspire. This, if it be not poetry, is so nearly allied to it, as scarcely to require being distinguished.

In this sense we may speak of the poetry of architecture. All architecture, to be impressive, must be the expression or symbol of some interesting idea; some thought, which has power over the emotions. The

---

1 *Rubens* Peter Paul Rubens (1577–1640).

2 *Louvre* Large, prestigious art museum in Paris.

3 *the gallery of the Luxembourg* Paris art museum that was, for most of the nineteenth century, dedicated to contemporary art.

4 *David* Jacques-Louis David (1748–1825).

5 *for strength … in spasms* See Thomas Carlyle's review of Ebenezer Elliott's "Corn-Law Rhymes" in the *Edinburgh Review*, July 1832.

6 *Claude* Claude Lorrain (c. 1600–82); *Salvator Rosa* (1615–73).

reason why modern architecture is so paltry, is simply that it is not the expression of any idea; it is a mere parroting of the architectural tongue of the Greeks, or of our Teutonic ancestors, without any conception of a meaning.

To confine ourselves, for the present, to religious edifices: these partake of poetry, in proportion as they express, or harmonize with, the feelings of devotion. But those feelings are different according to the conception entertained of the beings, by whose supposed nature they are called forth. To the Greek, these beings were incarnations of the greatest conceivable physical beauty, combined with supernatural power: and the Greek temples express this, their predominant character being graceful strength; in other words, solidity, which is power, and lightness which is also power, accomplishing with small means what seemed to require great; to combine all in one word, *majesty*. To the Catholic, again, the Deity was something far less clear and definite; a being of still more resistless power than the heathen divinities; greatly to be loved; still more greatly to be feared; and wrapped up in vagueness, mystery, and incomprehensibility. A certain solemnity, a feeling of doubting and trembling hope, like that of one lost in a boundless forest who thinks he knows his way but is not sure, mixes in all the genuine expressions of Catholic devotion. This is eminently the expression of the pure Gothic cathedral; conspicuous equally in the mingled majesty and gloom of its vaulted roofs and stately aisles, and in the "dim religious light"[1] which steals through its painted windows.

There is no generic[2] distinction between the imagery which is the expression of feeling and the imagery which is felt to harmonize with feeling. They are identical. The imagery in which feeling utters itself forth from within, is also that in which it delights when presented to it from without. All art, therefore, in proportion as it produces its effects by an appeal to the emotions partakes of poetry, unless it partakes of oratory, or of

narrative. And the distinction which these three words indicate, runs through the whole field of the fine arts.

The above hints have no pretension to the character of a theory. They are merely thrown out for the consideration of thinkers, in the hope that if they do not contain the truth, they may do somewhat to suggest it. Nor would they, crude as they are, have been deemed worthy of publication, in any country but one in which the philosophy of art is so completely neglected, that whatever may serve to put any inquiring mind upon this kind of investigation, cannot well, however imperfect in itself, fail altogether to be of use.

—1833

from *The Subjection of Women*

CHAPTER 1

If people are mostly so little aware how completely, during the greater part of the duration of our species, the law of force was the avowed rule of general conduct, any other being only a special and exceptional consequence of peculiar[3] ties—and from how very recent a date it is that the affairs of society in general have been even pretended to be regulated according to any moral law; as little do people remember or consider, how institutions and customs which never had any ground but the law of force, last on into ages and states of general opinion which never would have permitted their first establishment. Less than forty years ago, Englishmen might still by law hold human beings in bondage as saleable property: within the present century they might kidnap them and carry them off, and work them literally to death.[4] This absolutely extreme case of the law of force, condemned by those who can tolerate almost every other form of arbitrary power, and which, of all others, presents features the most revolting to the feelings of all who look at it from an impartial position, was the law of civilized and Christian England within

---

[1] *dim religious light*   See John Milton's *Il Penseroso* (1632), line 160.

[2] *generic*   Categorical.

[3] *peculiar*   Particular.

[4] *Less than forty ... literally to death*   The *Slavery Abolition Act* (1833) prohibited slavery in almost all British-held territory.

the memory of persons now living: and in one half of Anglo-Saxon America three or four years ago, not only did slavery exist, but the slave trade, and the breeding of slaves expressly for it, was a general practice between slave states.[1] Yet not only was there a greater strength of sentiment against it, but, in England at least, a less amount either of feeling or of interest in favour of it, than of any other of the customary abuses of force: for its motive was the love of gain, unmixed and undisguised; and those who profited by it were a very small numerical fraction of the country, while the natural feeling of all who were not personally interested in it, was unmitigated abhorrence. So extreme an instance makes it almost superfluous to refer to any other: but consider the long duration of absolute monarchy.[2] In England at present it is the almost universal conviction that military despotism is a case of the law of force, having no other origin or justification. Yet in all the great nations of Europe except England it either still exists, or has only just ceased to exist, and has even now a strong party favourable to it in all ranks of the people, especially among persons of station and consequence. Such is the power of an established system, even when far from universal; when not only in almost every period of history there have been great and well-known examples of the contrary system, but these have almost invariably been afforded by the most illustrious and most prosperous communities. In this case, too, the possessor of the undue power, the person directly interested in it, is only one person, while those who are subject to it and suffer from it are literally all the rest. The yoke is naturally and necessarily humiliating to all persons, except the one who is on the throne, together with, at most, the one who expects to succeed to it. How different are these cases from that of the power of men over women! I am not now prejudging the question of its justifiableness. I am showing how vastly more

permanent it could not but be, even if not justifiable, than these other dominations which have nevertheless lasted down to our own time. Whatever gratification of pride there is in the possession of power, and whatever personal interest in its exercise, is in this case not confined to a limited class, but common to the whole male sex. Instead of being, to most of its supporters, a thing desirable chiefly in the abstract, or, like the political ends usually contended for by factions, of little private importance to any but the leaders; it comes home to the person and hearth of every male head of a family, and of everyone who looks forward to being so. The clodhopper[3] exercises, or is to exercise, his share of the power equally with the highest nobleman. And the case is that in which the desire of power is the strongest: for everyone who desires power, desires it most over those who are nearest to him, with whom his life is passed, with whom he has most concerns in common, and in whom any independence of his authority is oftenest likely to interfere with his individual preferences. If, in the other cases specified, powers manifestly grounded only on force, and having so much less to support them, are so slowly and with so much difficulty got rid of, much more must it be so with this, even if it rests on no better foundation than those. We must consider, too, that the possessors of the power have facilities[4] in this case, greater than in any other, to prevent any uprising against it. Every one of the subjects lives under the very eye, and almost, it may be said, in the hands, of one of the masters—in closer intimacy with him than with any of her fellow-subjects; with no means of combining against him, no power of even locally overmastering him, and, on the other hand, with the strongest motives for seeking his favour and avoiding to give him offence. In struggles for political emancipation, everybody knows how often its champions are bought off by bribes, or daunted by terrors. In the case of women, each individual of the subject-class is in a chronic state of bribery and intimidation combined. In setting up the standard of resistance, a large number of the leaders, and still

---

[1] *in one half ... between slave states*   Before the end of the American Civil War (1861–65), the nation was largely divided into "slave states," where slavery was entirely legal, and "free states," where it was not.

[2] *absolute monarchy*   Form of government in which the monarch's authority is not limited by, for example, a constitution or a legislative body.

[3] *clodhopper*   Here, an unrefined or working-class man.

[4] *facilities*   Capabilities.

more of the followers, must make an almost complete sacrifice of the pleasures or the alleviations of their own individual lot. If ever any system of privilege and enforced subjection had its yoke tightly riveted on the necks of those who are kept down by it, this has. I have not yet shown that it is a wrong system: but everyone who is capable of thinking on the subject must see that even if it is, it was certain to outlast all other forms of unjust authority. And when some of the grossest of the other forms still exist in many civilized countries, and have only recently been got rid of in others, it would be strange if that which is so much the deepest rooted had yet been perceptibly shaken anywhere. There is more reason to wonder that the protests and testimonies against it should have been so numerous and so weighty as they are.

Some will object, that a comparison cannot fairly be made between the government of the male sex and the forms of unjust power which I have adduced[1] in illustration of it, since these are arbitrary, and the effect of mere usurpation, while it on the contrary is natural. But was there ever any domination which did not appear natural to those who possessed it? There was a time when the division of mankind into two classes, a small one of masters and a numerous one of slaves, appeared, even to the most cultivated minds, to be a natural, and the only natural, condition of the human race. No less an intellect, and one which contributed no less to the progress of human thought, than Aristotle,[2] held this opinion without doubt or misgiving; and rested it on the same premises on which the same assertion in regard to the dominion of men over women is usually based, namely that there are different natures among mankind, free natures, and slave natures; that the Greeks were of a free nature, the barbarian races of Thracians[3] and Asiatics of a slave nature. But why need I go back to Aristotle? Did not the slaveowners of the Southern United States maintain the same doctrine, with all the fanaticism with which men cling to the theories that justify their pas-

sions and legitimate their personal interests? Did they not call heaven and earth to witness that the dominion of the white man over the black is natural, that the black race is by nature incapable of freedom, and marked out for slavery? some even going so far as to say that the freedom of manual labourers is an unnatural order of things anywhere. Again, the theorists of absolute monarchy have always affirmed it to be the only natural form of government; issuing from the patriarchal, which was the primitive and spontaneous form of society, framed on the model of the paternal, which is anterior to[4] society itself, and, as they contend, the most natural authority of all. Nay, for that matter, the law of force itself, to those who could not plead any other, has always seemed the most natural of all grounds for the exercise of authority. Conquering races hold it to be Nature's own dictate that the conquered should obey the conquerors, or, as they euphoniously paraphrase it, that the feebler and more unwarlike races should submit to the braver and manlier. The smallest acquaintance with human life in the middle ages, shows how supremely natural the dominion of the feudal nobility over men of low condition appeared to the nobility themselves, and how unnatural the conception seemed, of a person of the inferior class claiming equality with them, or exercising authority over them. It hardly seemed less so to the class held in subjection. The emancipated serfs and burgesses,[5] even in their most vigorous struggles, never made any pretension to a share of authority; they only demanded more or less of limitation to the power of tyrannizing over them. So true is it that unnatural generally means only uncustomary, and that everything which is usual appears natural. The subjection of women to men being a universal custom, any departure from it quite naturally appears unnatural. But how entirely, even in this case, the feeling is dependent on custom, appears by ample experience. Nothing so much astonishes the people of distant parts of the world, when they first learn anything about England, as to be told that it is under a queen: the

---

[1] *adduced* Presented as evidence.

[2] *Aristotle* See Aristotle's *Politics*.

[3] *Thracians* A warring group of tribes, the Thracians occupied the area north of Greece from 700 BCE to 4 CE.

---

[4] *anterior to* Here, a precondition of.

[5] *burgesses* Townsfolk, especially those who are not vassals to a lord.

thing seems to them so unnatural as to be almost incredible. To Englishmen this does not seem in the least degree unnatural, because they are used to it; but they do feel it unnatural that women should be soldiers or members of parliament. In the feudal ages, on the contrary, war and politics were not thought unnatural to women, because not unusual; it seemed natural that women of the privileged classes should be of manly character, inferior in nothing but bodily strength to their husbands and fathers. The independence of women seemed rather less unnatural to the Greeks than to other ancients, on account of the fabulous Amazons[1] (whom they believed to be historical), and the partial example afforded by the Spartan[2] women; who, though no less subordinate by law than in other Greek states, were more free in fact, and being trained to bodily exercises in the same manner with men, gave ample proof that they were not naturally disqualified for them. There can be little doubt that Spartan experience suggested to Plato,[3] among many other of his doctrines, that of the social and political equality of the two sexes.

But, it will be said, the rule of men over women differs from all these others in not being a rule of force: it is accepted voluntarily; women make no complaint, and are consenting parties to it. In the first place, a great number of women do not accept it. Ever since there have been women able to make their sentiments known by their writings (the only mode of publicity which society permits to them), an increasing number of them have recorded protests against their present social condition: and recently many thousands of them, headed by the most eminent women known to the public, have petitioned parliament for their admission to the Parliamentary Suffrage.[4] The claim of women to be educated as solidly, and in the same branches of knowledge, as men, is urged with growing intensity, and

with a great prospect of success; while the demand for their admission into professions and occupations hitherto closed against them, becomes every year more urgent. Though there are not in this country, as there are in the United States, periodical Conventions and an organized party to agitate for the Rights of Women, there is a numerous and active Society organized and managed by women, for the more limited object of obtaining the political franchise. Nor is it only in our own country and in America that women are beginning to protest, more or less collectively, against the disabilities under which they labour. France, and Italy, and Switzerland, and Russia now afford examples of the same thing. How many more women there are who silently cherish similar aspirations, no one can possibly know; but there are abundant tokens how many *would* cherish them, were they not so strenuously taught to repress them as contrary to the proprieties of their sex. It must be remembered, also, that no enslaved class ever asked for complete liberty at once. When Simon de Montfort[5] called the deputies of the commons to sit for the first time in parliament, did any of them dream of demanding that an assembly, elected by their constituents, should make and destroy ministries, and dictate to the king in affairs of state? No such thought entered into the imagination of the most ambitious of them. The nobility had already these pretensions;[6] the commons pretended to nothing but to be exempt from arbitrary taxation, and from the gross individual oppression of the king's officers. It is a political law of nature that those who are under any power of ancient origin, never begin by complaining of the power itself, but only of its oppressive exercise. There is never any want[7] of women who complain of ill usage by their husbands. There would be infinitely more, if complaint were not the greatest of all provocatives to a repetition and increase of the ill usage. It is this which frustrates all attempts to maintain the power but protect the woman

---

[1] *Amazons* A mythical race of women warriors.

[2] *Spartan* In Classical Greece, the Spartans were known for their austerity, their militarism, and relative equality between men and women.

[3] *Plato* See Plato's *Republic*, 5.

[4] *petitioned ... Parliamentary Suffrage* Mill himself also introduced such a petition to the House of Commons in 1866.

---

[5] *Simon de Montfort* The Earl of Leicester (c. 1205–65) led a baronial revolt against Henry III and subsequently established a newly representative parliament.

[6] *pretensions* Aspirations; demands.

[7] *want* Lack.

against its abuses. In no other case (except that of a child) is the person who has been proved judicially to have suffered an injury, replaced under the physical power of the culprit who inflicted it. Accordingly wives, even in the most extreme and protracted cases of bodily ill usage, hardly ever dare avail themselves of the laws made for their protection: and if, in a moment of irrepressible indignation, or by the interference of neighbours, they are induced to do so, their whole effort afterwards is to disclose as little as they can, and to beg off[1] their tyrant from his merited chastisement.

All causes, social and natural, combine to make it unlikely that women should be collectively rebellious to the power of men. They are so far in a position different from all other subject classes, that their masters require something more from them than actual service. Men do not want solely the obedience of women, they want their sentiments. All men, except the most brutish, desire to have, in the woman most nearly connected with them, not a forced slave but a willing one, not a slave merely, but a favourite.[2] They have therefore put everything in practice to enslave their minds. The masters of all other slaves rely, for maintaining obedience, on fear; either fear of themselves, or religious fears. The masters of women wanted more than simple obedience, and they turned the whole force of education to effect their purpose. All women are brought up from the very earliest years in the belief that their ideal of character is the very opposite to that of men; not self-will, and government by self-control, but submission, and yielding to the control of others. All the moralities tell them that it is the duty of women, and all the current sentimentalities that it is their nature, to live for others; to make complete abnegation of themselves, and to have no life but in their affections. And by their affections are meant the only ones they are allowed to have—those to the men with whom they are connected, or to the children who constitute an additional and indefeasible tie between them and a man. When we put together three things—first, the natural attraction between opposite sexes; secondly, the wife's entire dependence on the husband, every privilege or pleasure she has being either his gift, or depending entirely on his will; and lastly, that the principal object of human pursuit, consideration, and all objects of social ambition, can in general be sought or obtained by her only through him, it would be a miracle if the object of being attractive to men had not become the polar star of feminine education and formation of character. And, this great means of influence over the minds of women having been acquired, an instinct of selfishness made men avail themselves of it to the utmost as a means of holding women in subjection, by representing to them meekness, submissiveness, and resignation of all individual will into the hands of a man, as an essential part of sexual attractiveness. Can it be doubted that any of the other yokes which mankind have succeeded in breaking, would have subsisted till now if the same means had existed, and had been so sedulously[3] used, to bow down their minds to it? If it had been made the object of the life of every young plebeian to find personal favour in the eyes of some patrician, of every young serf with some seigneur;[4] if domestication with him, and a share of his personal affections, had been held out as the prize which they all should look out for, the most gifted and aspiring being able to reckon on the most desirable prizes; and if, when this prize had been obtained, they had been shut out by a wall of brass from all interests not centering in him, all feelings and desires but those which he shared or inculcated; would not serfs and seigneurs, plebeians and patricians, have been as broadly distinguished at this day as men and women are? and would not all but a thinker here and there, have believed the distinction to be a fundamental and unalterable fact in human nature?

The preceding considerations are amply sufficient to show that custom, however universal it may be, affords in this case no presumption, and ought not to create any prejudice, in favour of the arrangements which place women in social and political subjection to men. But I

---

[1] *beg off* Excuse.

[2] *favourite* Chosen companion of a person with superior status.

[3] *sedulously* Diligently.

[4] *plebeian* Commoner; *patrician* Aristocrat; *serf* Laborer in a condition of servitude; *seigneur* Feudal lord.

may go farther, and maintain that the course of history, and the tendencies of progressive human society, afford not only no presumption in favour of this system of inequality of rights, but a strong one against it; and that, so far as the whole course of human improvement up to this time, the whole stream of modern tendencies, warrants any inference on the subject, it is, that this relic of the past is discordant with the future, and must necessarily disappear.

For, what is the peculiar character of the modern world—the difference which chiefly distinguishes modern institutions, modern social ideas, modern life itself, from those of times long past? It is, that human beings are no longer born to their place in life, and chained down by an inexorable bond to the place they are born to, but are free to employ their faculties, and such favourable chances as offer, to achieve the lot which may appear to them most desirable. Human society of old was constituted on a very different principle. All were born to a fixed social position, and were mostly kept in it by law, or interdicted[1] from any means by which they could emerge from it. As some men are born white and others black, so some were born slaves and others freemen and citizens; some were born patricians, others plebeians; some were born feudal nobles, others commoners and *roturiers*.[2] A slave or serf could never make himself free, nor, except by the will of his master, become so. In most European countries it was not till towards the close of the middle ages, and as a consequence of the growth of regal power, that commoners could be ennobled. Even among nobles, the eldest son was born the exclusive heir to the paternal possessions, and a long time elapsed before it was fully established that the father could disinherit him. Among the industrious classes, only those who were born members of a guild, or were admitted into it by its members, could lawfully practise their calling within its local limits; and nobody could practise any calling deemed important, in any but the legal manner—by processes authoritatively prescribed. Manufacturers have

stood in the pillory[3] for presuming to carry on their business by new and improved methods. In modern Europe, and most in those parts of it which have participated most largely in all other modern improvements, diametrically opposite doctrines now prevail. Law and government do not undertake to prescribe by whom any social or industrial operation shall or shall not be conducted, or what modes of conducting them shall be lawful. These things are left to the unfettered choice of individuals. Even the laws which required that workmen should serve an apprenticeship, have in this country been repealed: there being ample assurance that in all cases in which an apprenticeship is necessary, its necessity will suffice to enforce it. The old theory was, that the least possible should be left to the choice of the individual agent; that all he had to do should, as far as practicable, be laid down for him by superior wisdom. Left to himself he was sure to go wrong. The modern conviction, the fruit of a thousand years of experience, is, that things in which the individual is the person directly interested, never go right but as they are left to his own discretion; and that any regulation of them by authority, except to protect the rights of others, is sure to be mischievous. This conclusion, slowly arrived at, and not adopted until almost every possible application of the contrary theory had been made with disastrous result, now (in the industrial department) prevails universally in the most advanced countries, almost universally in all that have pretensions to any sort of advancement. It is not that all processes are supposed to be equally good, or all persons to be equally qualified for everything; but that freedom of individual choice is now known to be the only thing which procures the adoption of the best processes, and throws each operation into the hands of those who are best qualified for it. Nobody thinks it necessary to make a law that only a strong-armed man shall be a blacksmith. Freedom and competition suffice to make blacksmiths strong-armed men, because the weak-armed can earn more by engaging in occupations for which they are more fit. In

---

[1]   *interdicted* Prohibited.

[2]   *roturiers* Commoners who owned land in feudal times.

[3]   *pillory* Wooden framework in which wrongdoers were locked and exposed to public derision.

consonance[1] with this doctrine, it is felt to be an over-stepping of the proper bounds of authority to fix beforehand, on some general presumption, that certain persons are not fit to do certain things. It is now thoroughly known and admitted that if some such presumptions exist, no such presumption is infallible. Even if it be well grounded in a majority of cases, which it is very likely not to be, there will be a minority of exceptional cases in which it does not hold: and in those it is both an injustice to the individuals, and a detriment to society, to place barriers in the way of their using their faculties for their own benefit and for that of others. In the cases, on the other hand, in which the unfitness is real, the ordinary motives of human conduct will on the whole suffice to prevent the incompetent person from making, or from persisting in, the attempt.

If this general principle of social and economical science is not true; if individuals, with such help as they can derive from the opinion of those who know them, are not better judges than the law and the government, of their own capacities and vocation; the world cannot too soon abandon this principle, and return to the old system of regulations and disabilities. But if the principle is true, we ought to act as if we believed it, and not to ordain that to be born a girl instead of a boy, any more than to be born black instead of white, or a commoner instead of a nobleman, shall decide the person's position through all life—shall interdict people from all the more elevated social positions, and from all, except a few, respectable occupations. Even were we to admit the utmost that is ever pretended as to the superior fitness of men for all the functions now reserved to them, the same argument applies which forbids a legal qualification for members of parliament. If only once in a dozen years the conditions of eligibility exclude a fit person, there is a real loss, while the exclusion of thousands of unfit persons is no gain; for if the constitution of the electoral body disposes them to choose unfit persons, there are always plenty of such persons to choose from. In all things of any difficulty and importance, those who can do them well are fewer than the need, even with the most unrestricted latitude of choice:

and any limitation of the field of selection deprives society of some chances of being served by the competent, without ever saving it from the incompetent.

At present, in the more improved countries, the disabilities of women are the only case, save one, in which laws and institutions take persons at their birth, and ordain that they shall never in all their lives be allowed to compete for certain things. The one exception is that of royalty. Persons still are born to the throne; no one, not of the reigning family, can ever occupy it, and no one even of that family can, by any means but the course of hereditary succession, attain it. All other dignities and social advantages are open to the whole male sex: many indeed are only attainable by wealth, but wealth may be striven for by anyone, and is actually obtained by many men of the very humblest origin. The difficulties, to the majority, are indeed insuperable[2] without the aid of fortunate accidents; but no male human being is under any legal ban: neither law nor opinion superadd[3] artificial obstacles to the natural ones. Royalty, as I have said, is excepted: but in this case everyone feels it to be an exception—an anomaly in the modern world, in marked opposition to its customs and principles, and to be justified only by extraordinary special expediencies, which, though individuals and nations differ in estimating their weight, unquestionably do in fact exist. But in this exceptional case, in which a high social function is, for important reasons, bestowed on birth instead of being put up to competition, all free nations contrive to adhere in substance to the principle from which they nominally derogate; for they circumscribe this high function by conditions avowedly intended to prevent the person to whom it ostensibly belongs from really performing it; while the person by whom it is performed, the responsible minister, does obtain the post by a competition from which no full-grown citizen of the male sex is legally excluded. The disabilities, therefore, to which women are subject from the mere fact of their birth, are the solitary examples of the kind in modern legislation. In no instance except

---

[1] *consonance* Agreement.

[2] *insuperable* Insurmountable.

[3] *superadd* Add additionally.

this, which comprehends[1] half the human race, are the higher social functions closed against anyone by a fatality of birth which no exertions, and no change of circumstances, can overcome; for even religious disabilities (besides that in England and in Europe they have practically almost ceased to exist) do not close any career to the disqualified person in case of conversion.[2]

The social subordination of women thus stands out an isolated fact in modern social institutions; a solitary breach of what has become their fundamental law; a single relic of an old world of thought and practice exploded in everything else, but retained in the one thing of most universal interest; as if a gigantic dolmen, or a vast temple of Jupiter Olympus, occupied the site of St. Paul's[3] and received daily worship, while the surrounding Christian churches were only resorted to on fasts and festivals. This entire discrepancy between one social fact and all those which accompany it, and the radical opposition between its nature and the progressive movement which is the boast of the modern world, and which has successively swept away everything else of an analogous character, surely affords, to a conscientious observer of human tendencies, serious matter for reflection. It raises a *prima facie*[4] presumption on the unfavourable side, far outweighing any which custom and usage could in such circumstances create on the favourable; and should at least suffice to make this, like the choice between republicanism[5] and royalty, a balanced question.

---

[1]   *comprehends*   Encompasses.

[2]   *for even religious ... in case of conversion*   In Britain, laws preventing Catholics and Nonconformist Protestants from attending university, holding public office, and entering several professions were largely removed during the late eighteenth and early nineteenth centuries. Prior to that, these restrictions could be evaded only by those willing to declare their allegiance to the Church of England;   *disabilities*   Here, legal limitations.

[3]   *exploded*   Rejected, condemned; *dolmen*   Celtic monument associated with pagan rituals; *temple of Jupiter Olympus*   Temple honoring Jupiter, king of the gods in Roman mythology; *St. Paul's*   Anglican cathedral in central London, where it is a significant landmark.

[4]   *prima facie*   Latin: arising at first sight.

[5]   *republicanism*   I.e., democratic rule, as opposed to rule by a monarch.

The least that can be demanded is, that the question should not be considered as prejudged by existing fact and existing opinion, but open to discussion on its merits, as a question of justice and expediency: the decision on this, as on any of the other social arrangements of mankind, depending on what an enlightened estimate of tendencies and consequences may show to be most advantageous to humanity in general, without distinction of sex. And the discussion must be a real discussion, descending to foundations, and not resting satisfied with vague and general assertions. It will not do, for instance, to assert in general terms, that the experience of mankind has pronounced in favour of the existing system. Experience cannot possibly have decided between two courses, so long as there has only been experience of one. If it be said that the doctrine of the equality of the sexes rests only on theory, it must be remembered that the contrary doctrine also has only theory to rest upon. All that is proved in its favour by direct experience, is that mankind have been able to exist under it, and to attain the degree of improvement and prosperity which we now see; but whether that prosperity has been attained sooner, or is now greater, than it would have been under the other system, experience does not say. On the other hand, experience does say, that every step in improvement has been so invariably accompanied by a step made in raising the social position of women, that historians and philosophers have been led to adopt their elevation or debasement as on the whole the surest test and most correct measure of the civilization of a people or an age. Through all the progressive period of human history, the condition of women has been approaching nearer to equality with men. This does not of itself prove that the assimilation[6] must go on to complete equality; but it assuredly affords some presumption that such is the case.

Neither does it avail anything to say that the *nature* of the two sexes adapts them to their present functions and position, and renders these appropriate to them. Standing on the ground of common sense and the constitution of the human mind, I deny that anyone knows, or can know, the nature of the two sexes, as long

---

[6]   *assimilation*   Process of becoming similar.

as they have only been seen in their present relation to one another. If men had ever been found in society without women, or women without men, or if there had been a society of men and women in which the women were not under the control of the men, something might have been positively known about the mental and moral differences which may be inherent in the nature of each. What is now called the nature of women is an eminently artificial thing—the result of forced repression in some directions, unnatural stimulation in others. It may be asserted without scruple, that no other class of dependents have had their character so entirely distorted from its natural proportions by their relation with their masters; for, if conquered and slave races have been, in some respects, more forcibly repressed, whatever in them has not been crushed down by an iron heel has generally been let alone, and if left with any liberty of development, it has developed itself according to its own laws; but in the case of women, a hot-house and stove cultivation[1] has always been carried on of some of the capabilities of their nature, for the benefit and pleasure of their masters. Then, because certain products of the general vital force sprout luxuriantly and reach a great development in this heated atmosphere and under this active nurture and watering, while other shoots from the same root, which are left outside in the wintry air, with ice purposely heaped all round them, have a stunted growth, and some are burnt off with fire and disappear; men, with that inability to recognise their own work which distinguishes the unanalytic mind, indolently believe that the tree grows of itself in the way they have made it grow, and that it would die if one half of it were not kept in a vapour bath and the other half in the snow.

Of all difficulties which impede the progress of thought, and the formation of well-grounded opinions on life and social arrangements, the greatest is now the unspeakable ignorance and inattention of mankind in respect to the influences which form human character. Whatever any portion of the human species now are, or seem to be, such, it is supposed, they have a natural tendency to be: even when the most elementary knowl-edge of the circumstances in which they have been placed, clearly points out the causes that made them what they are. Because a cottier[2] deeply in arrears to his landlord is not industrious, there are people who think that the Irish are naturally idle. Because constitutions can be overthrown when the authorities appointed to execute them turn their arms against them, there are people who think the French incapable of free government.[3] Because the Greeks cheated the Turks, and the Turks only plundered the Greeks, there are persons who think that the Turks are naturally more sincere:[4] and because women, as is often said, care nothing about politics except their personalities, it is supposed that the general good is naturally less interesting to women than to men. History, which is now so much better understood than formerly, teaches another lesson: if only by showing the extraordinary susceptibility of human nature to external influences, and the extreme variableness of those of its manifestations which are supposed to be most universal and uniform. But in history, as in travelling, men usually see only what they already had in their own minds; and few learn much from history, who do not bring much with them to its study.

Hence, in regard to that most difficult question, what are the natural differences between the two sexes—a subject on which it is impossible in the present state of society to obtain complete and correct knowl-edge—while almost everybody dogmatizes upon it, almost all neglect and make light of the only means by which any partial insight can be obtained into it. This is, an analytic study of the most important department of psychology, the laws of the influence of circumstances on character. For, however great and apparently ineradi-

---

1 *hot-house and stove cultivation* Literally, artificial methods used to enhance the growth of plants.

2 *cottier* Tenant who rents a cottage and often works for a landlord in return. Exploitative landlords were a significant problem in nineteenth-century Ireland.

3 *Because constitutions ... free government* In the wake of the French Revolution of 1789, regime stability was often short-lived, and throughout the nineteenth century there were several failed and often violent attempts to establish political order.

4 *Because the Greeks ... more sincere* Greece was occupied by the Ottoman Empire from the mid-fifteenth century until the Greek War of Independence (1821–30). The suggestion that the "Greeks cheated the Turks" may allude to the guerilla tactics used in the uprising.

cable the moral and intellectual differences between men and women might be, the evidence of there being natural differences could only be negative. Those only could be inferred to be natural which could not possibly be artificial—the residuum,[1] after deducting every characteristic of either sex which can admit of being explained from education or external circumstances. The profoundest knowledge of the laws of the formation of character is indispensable to entitle anyone to affirm even that there is any difference, much more what the difference is, between the two sexes considered as moral and rational beings; and since no one, as yet, has that knowledge (for there is hardly any subject which, in proportion to its importance, has been so little studied), no one is thus far entitled to any positive opinion on the subject. Conjectures are all that can at present be made; conjectures more or less probable, according as more or less authorized by such knowledge as we yet have of the laws of psychology, as applied to the formation of character.

Even the preliminary knowledge, what the differences between the sexes now are, apart from all question as to how they are made what they are, is still in the crudest and most incomplete state. Medical practitioners and physiologists have ascertained, to some extent, the differences in bodily constitution; and this is an important element to the psychologist: but hardly any medical practitioner is a psychologist. Respecting the mental characteristics of women; their observations are of no more worth than those of common men. It is a subject on which nothing final can be known, so long as those who alone can really know it, women themselves, have given but little testimony, and that little, mostly suborned.[2] It is easy to know stupid women. Stupidity is much the same all the world over. A stupid person's notions and feelings may confidently be inferred from those which prevail in the circle by which the person is surrounded. Not so with those whose opinions and feelings are an emanation from their own nature and faculties. It is only a man here and there who has any

tolerable knowledge of the character even of the women of his own family. I do not mean, of their capabilities; these nobody knows, not even themselves, because most of them have never been called out. I mean their actually existing thoughts and feelings. Many a man thinks he perfectly understands women, because he has had amatory relations with several, perhaps with many of them. If he is a good observer, and his experience extends to quality as well as quantity, he may have learnt something of one narrow department of their nature—an important department, no doubt. But of all the rest of it, few persons are generally more ignorant, because there are few from whom it is so carefully hidden. The most favourable case which a man can generally have for studying the character of a woman, is that of his own wife: for the opportunities are greater, and the cases of complete sympathy not so unspeakably rare. And in fact, this is the source from which any knowledge worth having on the subject has, I believe, generally come. But most men have not had the opportunity of studying in this way more than a single case: accordingly one can, to an almost laughable degree, infer what a man's wife is like, from his opinions about women in general. To make even this one case yield any result, the woman must be worth knowing, and the man not only a competent judge, but of a character so sympathetic in itself, and so well adapted to hers, that he can either read her mind by sympathetic intuition, or has nothing in himself which makes her shy of disclosing it. Hardly anything, I believe, can be more rare than this conjunction. It often happens that there is the most complete unity of feeling and community of interests as to all external things, yet the one has as little admission into the internal life of the other as if they were common acquaintance. Even with true affection, authority on the one side and subordination on the other prevent perfect confidence. Though nothing may be intentionally withheld, much is not shown. In the analogous relation of parent and child, the corresponding phenomenon must have been in the observation of everyone. As between father and son, how many are the cases in which the father, in spite of real affection on both sides, obviously to all the world does not know, nor suspect,

---

[1] *the residuum* What is left over.

[2] *suborned* Obtained through bribery or coercion, especially in the case of false testimony.

parts of the son's character familiar to his companions and equals. The truth is, that the position of looking up to another is extremely unpropitious[1] to complete sincerity and openness with him. The fear of losing ground in his opinion or in his feelings is so strong, that even in an upright character, there is an unconscious tendency to show only the best side, or the side which, though not the best, is that which he most likes to see: and it may be confidently said that thorough knowledge of one another hardly ever exists, but between persons who, besides being intimates, are equals. How much more true, then, must all this be, when the one is not only under the authority of the other, but has it inculcated on her as a duty to reckon everything else subordinate to his comfort and pleasure, and to let him neither see nor feel anything coming from her, except what is agreeable to him. All these difficulties stand in the way of a man's obtaining any thorough knowledge even of the one woman whom alone, in general, he has sufficient opportunity of studying. When we further consider that to understand one woman is not necessarily to understand any other woman; that even if he could study many women of one rank, or of one country, he would not thereby understand women of other ranks or countries; and even if he did, they are still only the women of a single period of history; we may safely assert that the knowledge which men can acquire of women, even as they have been and are, without reference to what they might be, is wretchedly imperfect and superficial, and always will be so, until women themselves have told all that they have to tell.

And this time has not come; nor will it come otherwise than gradually. It is but of yesterday that women have either been qualified by literary accomplishments or permitted by society, to tell anything to the general public. As yet very few of them dare tell anything, which men, on whom their literary success depends, are unwilling to hear. Let us remember in what manner, up to a very recent time, the expression, even by a male author, of uncustomary opinions, or what are deemed eccentric feelings, usually was, and in some degree still is, received; and we may form some faint conception

under what impediments a woman, who is brought up to think custom and opinion her sovereign rule, attempts to express in books anything drawn from the depths of her own nature. The greatest woman who has left writings behind her sufficient to give her an eminent rank in the literature of her country, thought it necessary to prefix as a motto to her boldest work, "Un homme peut braver l'opinion; une femme doit s'y soumettre."[2] The greater part of what women write about women is mere sycophancy to men. In the case of unmarried women, much of it seems only intended to increase their chance of a husband. Many, both married and unmarried, overstep the mark, and inculcate a servility beyond what is desired or relished by any man, except the very vulgarest. But this is not so often the case as, even at a quite late period, it still was. Literary women are becoming more freespoken, and more willing to express their real sentiments. Unfortunately, in this country especially, they are themselves such artificial products, that their sentiments are compounded of a small element of individual observation and consciousness, and a very large one of acquired associations. This will be less and less the case, but it will remain true to a great extent, as long as social institutions do not admit the same free development of originality in women which is possible to men. When that time comes, and not before, we shall see, and not merely hear, as much as it is necessary to know of the nature of women, and the adaptation of other things to it.

I have dwelt so much on the difficulties which at present obstruct any real knowledge by men of the true nature of women, because in this as in so many other things "opinio copiæ inter maximas causas inopiæ est;"[3] and there is little chance of reasonable thinking on the matter, while people flatter themselves that they perfectly understand a subject of which most men know absolutely nothing, and of which it is at present impos-

---

[1] *unpropitious* Unfavorable.

[2] [Mill's note] Title-page of Mme. de Staël's *Delphine*. [The French novelist's (1766–1817) words translate as: "A man can brave (public) opinion; a woman must submit to it."]

[3] *opinio copiæ … inopiæ est* Latin: the belief in sufficiency is one of the greatest causes of insufficiency.

sible that any man, or all men taken together, should have knowledge which can qualify them to lay down the law to women as to what is, or is not, their vocation. Happily, no such knowledge is necessary for any practical purpose connected with the position of women in relation to society and life. For, according to all the principles involved in modern society, the question rests with women themselves—to be decided by their own experience, and by the use of their own faculties. There are no means of finding what either one person or many can do, but by trying—and no means by which anyone else can discover for them what it is for their happiness to do or leave undone.

One thing we may be certain of—that what is contrary to women's nature to do, they never will be made to do by simply giving their nature free play. The anxiety of mankind to interfere in behalf of nature, for fear lest nature should not succeed in effecting its purpose, is an altogether unnecessary solicitude. What women by nature cannot do, it is quite superfluous to forbid them from doing. What they can do, but not so well as the men who are their competitors, competition suffices to exclude them from; since nobody asks for protective duties and bounties in favour of women; it is only asked that the present bounties and protective duties in favour of men should be recalled. If women have a greater natural inclination for some things than for others, there is no need of laws or social inculcation to make the majority of them do the former in preference to the latter. Whatever women's services are most wanted for, the free play of competition will hold out the strongest inducements to them to undertake. And, as the words imply, they are most wanted for the things for which they are most fit; by the apportionment of which to them, the collective faculties of the two sexes can be applied on the whole with the greatest sum of valuable result.

The general opinion of men is supposed to be, that the natural vocation of a woman is that of a wife and mother. I say, is supposed to be, because, judging from acts—from the whole of the present constitution of society—one might infer that their opinion was the direct contrary. They might be supposed to think that the alleged natural vocation of women was of all things the most repugnant to their nature; insomuch that if they are free to do anything else—if any other means of living, or occupation of their time and faculties, is open, which has any chance of appearing desirable to them—there will not be enough of them who will be willing to accept the condition said to be natural to them. If this is the real opinion of men in general, it would be well that it should be spoken out. I should like to hear somebody openly enunciating the doctrine (it is already implied in much that is written on the subject)—"It is necessary to society that women should marry and produce children. They will not do so unless they are compelled. Therefore it is necessary to compel them." The merits of the case would then be clearly defined. It would be exactly that of the slaveholders of South Carolina and Louisiana. "It is necessary that cotton and sugar should be grown. White men cannot produce them. Negroes will not, for any wages which we choose to give. *Ergo* they must be compelled." An illustration still closer to the point is that of impressment.[1] Sailors must absolutely be had to defend the country. It often happens that they will not voluntarily enlist. Therefore there must be the power of forcing them. How often has this logic been used! and, but for one flaw in it, without doubt it would have been successful up to this day. But it is open to the retort—First pay the sailors the honest value of their labour. When you have made it as well worth their while to serve you, as to work for other employers, you will have no more difficulty than others have in obtaining their services. To this there is no logical answer except "I will not": and as people are now not only ashamed, but are not desirous, to rob the labourer of his hire, impressment is no longer advocated. Those who attempt to force women into marriage by closing all other doors against them, lay themselves open to a similar retort. If they mean what they say, their opinion must evidently be, that men do not render the married condition so desirable to women, as to induce them to accept it for its own recommendations. It is not a sign of one's thinking the boon one offers very

---

[1] *impressment* Policy that pressed men into public service, even against their will; this practice was discontinued after 1835.

attractive, when one allows only Hobson's choice,[1] "that or none." And here, I believe, is the clue to the feelings of those men, who have a real antipathy to the equal freedom of women. I believe they are afraid, not lest women should be unwilling to marry, for I do not think that anyone in reality has that apprehension; but lest they should insist that marriage should be on equal conditions; lest all women of spirit and capacity should prefer doing almost anything else, not in their own eyes degrading, rather than marry, when marrying is giving themselves a master, and a master too of all their earthly possessions. And truly, if this consequence were necessarily incident to marriage, I think that the apprehension would be very well founded. I agree in thinking it probable that few women, capable of anything else, would, unless under an irresistible *entrainement*,[2] rendering them for the time insensible to anything but itself, choose such a lot, when any other means were open to them of filling a conventionally honourable place in life: and if men are determined that the law of marriage shall be a law of despotism, they are quite right, in point of mere policy, in leaving to women only Hobson's choice. But, in that case, all that has been done in the modern world to relax the chain on the minds of women, has been a mistake. They never should have been allowed to receive a literary education. Women who read, much more women who write, are, in the existing constitution of things, a contradiction and a disturbing element: and it was wrong to bring women up with any acquirements but those of an odalisque,[3] or of a domestic servant.

—1869

---

[1] *boon* Favor, beneficial gift; *Hobson's choice* Expression originating from a Cambridge-London carrier, Thomas Hobson (1544–1630), who refused, when hiring out his horses, to allow any to leave the stable out of turn.

[2] *entrainement* Enchantment or charm.

[3] *odalisque* Concubine.

WOMEN IN SOCIETY

CONTEXTS

There was much debate concerning the proper place of women and the ideal characteristics of femininity throughout the nineteenth century. In a nation ruled by a female queen who supported education for women but not female suffrage, the lines between conventional masculine and feminine realms were often blurred. The traditional roles of wives, mothers, and daughters; the structure of the family; the nature of marriage; and how society ought to treat those unwilling or unable to conform to its standards of womanhood—all these subjects were open for examination by both men and women, and many writers and thinkers voiced opinions on them.

Sarah Stickney Ellis, the author of *The Women of England*, ran a school for girls but did not support intellectual advancement for women. Instead, she educated her pupils to become capable managers of their homes, from which they could best facilitate the advancement of their husbands and sons. Her numerous guides to female conduct, including *The Daughters of England* (1842), *The Wives of England* (1843), and *The Mothers of England* (1845), were extremely popular.

As the selection from *Fraser's Magazine* shows, the role of the governess in Victorian society posed issues of both gender and class. The growing prosperity of the middle classes enabled more and more families to afford governesses—and the increased emphasis on education (for females as well as for males) led to a widespread acknowledgment of the importance of the role governesses played as educators. In Victorian social hierarchy, the governess was a "lady"; this was *socially* a desirable occupation for many women, especially those daughters of tradespeople who sought to "better themselves." But as a paid employee (albeit often a poorly paid one) the governess was part of the work force—a status that would normally disqualify a woman from being considered a "lady." Consequently, the situation of the governess was rife with tensions, and the daily reality of her life was often very difficult; Charlotte Brontë complained of the "wretched bondage" of being a governess.

The women's suffrage campaign, which began in the 1850s, heightened the debate over women's proper role in society. Suffragists' frustration over the lack of female vote was exacerbated by a series of Reform Acts, which extended the vote to a much greater proportion of men than had previously been entitled, but explicitly excluded all women. There were a variety of arguments used in the effort to justify the political subordination of women to men; these included the scientific argument, which presented evidence for women's supposed intellectual and physical inferiority, and the "divine will" argument, which portrayed female inferiority as part of the natural order established by God in Genesis. In her argument for female suffrage in *The Enfranchisement of Women*, Harriet Taylor presents—and attacks—some additional arguments used to protest women's entrance into politics.

Coventry Patmore's long poem *The Angel in the House*, which became extraordinarily popular in both Britain and the United States, is a sentimental depiction of the ideal female as conceived by many Victorian men of the upper and middle classes. The poem, which celebrated Patmore's first wife (he remarried twice after her death) details their courtship and marriage and epitomizes the view of women held by many men at the time. In the twentieth century the poem became the object of attacks by many feminist critics, notably Virginia Woolf, and the phrase "angel in the house" was commonly used as a sort of shorthand to refer to an oppressive Victorian attitude towards gender roles.

During this era, when the "angel in the house" was seen by many as the ideal to which every woman should aspire, growing numbers of women were actually unmarried—an uncomfortable fact that had long been true but began to generate considerable commentary in the latter half of the century. It was generally believed that the "problem" was demographic: there were too many women relative to men, and so some women—commonly referred to as "odd" or "redundant" women—were left without a partner. While emigration and military service occupied many men who might otherwise have started families, the low marriage rate was also a result of individual choice; initially, it was a choice made by men who did not want or could not afford to marry, leaving an abundance of single women (especially those of the middle class) competing for the narrow range of jobs that were considered appropriate for them. But as many in the first generation of "odd women" found single life a viable option, more and more women began to feel free either to postpone marriage or to reject it altogether. To conventional writers such as William Rathbone Greg, who tackles the question in his essay "Why Are Women Redundant?," the "odd women" were to be pitied for their inability—or derided for their refusal—to fulfill their natural destinies as wives and mothers. For feminists such as Frances Power Cobbe, as she argues in a response to Greg's article, the "odd women" were a clear illustration of the problems with a societal model that forced women to choose between marriage and financial desperation. The debate surrounding the "odd women" thus became part of a larger debate raging in the late nineteenth century: the argument over "the woman question."

Conversation about "the woman question" was heated, and the proponents of women's rights were often viciously attacked in print. As the satirical cartoon reproduced below demonstrates, suffragists were often viewed as the antithesis of the ideal woman, epitomizing instead traditionally "masculine" characteristics. In the excerpt following, Eliza Lynn Linton, perhaps the most vocal anti-feminist of the period, criticizes what she sees as the unnatural, masculine boldness of the "modern girl," whose unwillingness to serve and support her husband and nurture her children, Linton argues, makes her not only unsuitable for marriage, but a disgrace to England's national character.

The idea that a woman ought to be subordinate to her husband was not only a matter of social expectation; it was also incorporated into English law. For much of the nineteenth century, in most respects the law treated a husband and wife as a single person, with many of the wife's rights—including her right to the possession of her own property—subsumed by her husband's. In her article "Criminals, Idiots, Women, and Minors," Frances Power Cobbe describes and criticizes the common arguments used to justify depriving married women of the legal rights that even convicted felons were afforded. Women began campaigning against these laws in the 1850s, and the Married Women's Property Acts were passed in 1870 and 1882, allowing married women the same property rights as unmarried women.

Within Victorian society's complex network of gender and class distinctions, many citizens relied upon printed material for guidance in matters of conduct and etiquette, as well as for practical advice on household management and professional opportunities. *The Girl's Own Paper*, a weekly paper founded in 1880 as a companion to the very successful *Boy's Own Paper*, provided such information to many female readers. According to its editor, the paper, which was published by the Religious Tract Society, aimed to instruct its readers "in the moral and domestic virtues, preparing them for the responsibility of womanhood and for a heavenly home."

Despite the efforts of such organs as *The Girl's Own Paper*, the traditional paradigm of wifehood and motherhood that it espoused had, by the end of the nineteenth century, begun to lose its primacy in the minds of many women. This rejection of conventional gender ideologies shifted into high gear near the end of the century, when "the marriage question" came to occupy a central position in debates concerning women's political rights, their education, and their need for social and economic independence. These debates, which coalesced during the 1890s around the controversial figure of the so-called "New Woman," are addressed in another Contexts section later in this anthology.

⌘ ⌘ ⌘

from Sarah Stickney Ellis, *The Daughters of England: Their Position in Society, Character and Responsibilities* (1842)

… The sphere upon which a young woman enters on first leaving school, or, to use a popular phrase, on "completing her education," is so entirely new to her, her mind is so often the subject of new impressions, and her attention so frequently absorbed by new motives for exertion, that, if at all accustomed to reflect, we cannot doubt but she will make these, or similar questions, the subject of serious inquiry—"What is my position in society? What do I aim at? And what means do I intend to employ for the accomplishment of my purpose?" …

As women, then, the first thing of importance is to be content to be inferior to men—inferior in mental power, in the same proportion that you are inferior in bodily strength. Facility of movement, aptitude, and grace, the bodily frame of woman may possess in a higher degree than that of man; just as in the softer touches of mental and spiritual beauty her character may present a lovelier page than his. Yet, as the great attribute of power must still be wanting there, it becomes more immediately her business to inquire how this want may be supplied.

An able and eloquent writer on "Woman's Mission"[1] has justly observed that woman's strength is in her influence. And, in order to render this influence more complete, you will find on examination that you are by nature endowed with peculiar[2] faculties—with a quickness of perception, facility of adaptation, and acuteness of feeling, which fit you especially for the part you have to act in life; and which, at the same time, render you, in a higher degree than men, susceptible both of pain and pleasure. …

* * *

I have already stated that women, in their position in life, must be content to be inferior to men; but as their inferiority consists chiefly in their want of power, this deficiency is abundantly made up to them by their capability of exercising influence; it is made up to them also in other ways, incalculable in their number and extent; but in none so effectually as by that order of Divine Providence which places them, in a moral and religious point of view, on the same level with man; nor can it be a subject of regret to any right-minded woman that they are not only exempt from the most laborious occupations both of mind and body, but also from the necessity of engaging in those eager pecuniary speculations, and in that fierce conflict of worldly interests by which men are so deeply occupied as to be in a manner compelled to stifle their best feelings, until they become in reality the characters they at first only assumed. Can it be a subject of regret to any kind and feeling woman that her sphere of action is one adapted to the exercise

[1] *An able … Mission* Sarah Lewis, whose *Woman's Mission*, a popular book on female conduct, was published in 1839.

[2] *peculiar* Particular.

of the affections, where she may love, and trust, and hope, and serve, to the utmost of her wishes? Can it be a subject of regret that she is not called upon, so much as man, to calculate, to compete, to struggle, but rather to occupy a sphere in which the elements of discord cannot with propriety be admitted—in which beauty and order are expected to denote her presence, and where the exercise of benevolence is the duty she is most frequently called upon to perform.

Women almost universally consider themselves, and wish to be considered by others, as extremely affectionate; scarcely can a more severe libel be pronounced upon a woman than to say that she is not so. Now the whole law of woman's life is a law of love. I propose, therefore, to treat the subject in this light—to try whether the neglect of their peculiar duties does not imply an absence of love, and whether the principle of love, thoroughly carried out, would not so influence their conduct and feelings as to render them all which their best friends could desire.

Let us, however, clearly understand each other at the outset. To love, is a very different thing from a desire to be beloved. To love, is woman's nature—to be beloved is the consequence of her having properly exercised and controlled that nature. To love, is a woman's duty—to be beloved, is her reward.

* * *

… There is yet another flight of female ambition, another course which the love of distinction is apt to make, more product of folly, and of disappointment, perhaps, than all the rest. It is the ambition of the female author who writes for fame. Could those young aspirants know how little real dignity there is connected with the *trade* of authorship, their harps would be exchanged for distaffs,[1] their rose-tinted paper would be converted into ashes, and their Parnassus[2] would dwin-

dle to a molehill. … The same want of sympathy which so often inspires the first effort of female authorship, might often find a sweet and abundant interchange of kindness in many a faithful heart beside the homely hearth. And after all, there is more true poetry in the fire-side affections of early life than in all those sympathetic associations with unknown and untried developments of mind which ever have existed either amongst the sons or the daughters of men.

Taking a more sober view of the case, there are, unquestionably, subjects of deep interest with which women have opportunities peculiar to themselves of becoming acquainted, and thus of benefiting their fellow creatures through the medium of their writings. But, after all, literature is not the natural channel for a woman's feelings; and pity, not envy, ought to be the meed[3] of her who writes for the public. How much of what with other women is reserved for the select and chosen intercourse of affection, with her must be laid bare to the coarse cavillings,[4] and coarser commendations, of amateur or professional critics. How much of what no woman loves to say, except to the listening ear of domestic affection, by her must be told—nay, blazoned—to the world. And then, in her season of depression, or of wounded feeling, when her spirit yearns to sit in solitude, or even in darkness, so that it may be still; to know and feel that the very essence of that spirit, now embodied in a palpable form, has become an article of sale and bargain, tossed over from the hands of one workman to another, free alike to the touch of the prince and the peasant, and no longer to be reclaimed at will by the original possessor, let the world receive it as it may.

Is such, I ask, an enviable distinction?

---

[1] *distaff* Staff on which wool or flax was wound when spinning.

[2] *Parnassus* Mountain in Greece sacred to the Muses, the nine daughters of Zeus and Mnemosyne, each of whom presided over, and provided inspiration for, a different aspect of the arts and sciences.

---

[3] *meed* Recompense; reward.

[4] *intercourse* Conversation; *cavillings* Unfair or petty fault-finding.

from Anonymous, "Hints on the Modern Governess System," *Fraser's Magazine* (November 1844)

.... To trace the growth of woman's desire after knowledge would be the task of a philosopher; for us, it suffices to see that it is, that it has been from all ages. The barter of Paradise for the means of knowledge is the first recorded act of woman's life; she tempted man to forego all tried blessings, for the untried boon of "knowing good and evil."[1] Thenceforth, man wreaked his vengeance upon woman, for the loss of ease and plenty, by keeping her ignorant, and, consequently, helpless. But since the day that Christianity dawned on the world, an emancipation of the weak out of the power of the strong has been silently progressing. The faint cry, uplifted at intervals, swelled into a chorus; there was a sudden rush; all the world clamoured for a better education for women; no wonder, in such a struggle, that the greater number mistook chaff and husks[2] for bread. The movement was all too sudden. Education, in as far as it implies intellectual and moral growth, is the work of life; its operations are as secret and as self-derived as the gradual shooting of the green blade into the wheat-ear.

Now, when that cry of women after knowledge pierced the air, a thousand sprang up, mushroomwise, in a night, to answer it. Mothers who had only read their Bibles and receipt-books[3] found themselves unprepared for the emergency—we have so little patience, so little foresight. Then, teaching, that holy vocation of a woman, became a trade. An universal demand creates its own supply. Here was a tempting opening to all aspiring women, who were free to try a new field; the unmarried daughters of the gentry left with scanty portions had, till now, been content to eke out their small incomes in trade; many were the gentlewomen, in our great-grandmothers' days, who lived in honoured independence, though they kept small shops, to which their old friends resorted. They did not lose caste[4] because they sat for part of the day behind the counter. However, this refuge grew insecure from the outward pressure of public opinion in favour of refinement. ... Many left their quiet homes for the schoolrooms of halls and castles. As they mounted the stair, others came from a lower rank, and filled the vacant steps. The restless rage to push on had stirred all classes. Those who, disappointed in their new stand, looked wistfully back to the old, found that when they would[5] return they could not. There was no place left for them but that which they had chosen. Like much else, it looked best from a distance. Here, then, was a whole class of women driven into a new line, for which they had received no fitting preparation. ... The new generation, thirsting to be taught, found teachers at their mercy, hanging between two ranks. Do the weak desire to learn what they may expect from the strong? Let them ponder deeply the governess system of the present day. This was the watch-word, "Teach us on our own terms, or work, and cease to be gentlewomen." To the newly risen race of governesses, even such equivocal gentility was preferable to a second change, though it was to be gained at the price of isolation. ...

The policy of the world is to take advantage of want. It became apparent that a whole family of daughters might be taught by one of these single women, struggling for bread, for less than it formerly cost to send one girl to school. Where competition was so great, there

---

[1] *The barter of Paradise ... good and evil*   In Genesis 3, Eve, the first woman, eats the fruit of the tree that grants knowledge of good and evil, which has been forbidden by God; Adam, the first man, also eats it at her urging. As punishment, Adam and Eve are banished from the Garden of Eden.

[2] *chaff and husks*   Material separated out from grains when threshing cereal crops.

[3] *receipt-books*   I.e., recipe books.

[4] *lose caste*   I.e., lose their position in society.

[5] *would*   Wished to.

was no difficulty in driving a bargain. The means of instruction might be had so cheaply that the grocer's daughters could be taught to read *Paul and Virginia* in the original tongue, and to strum *The Fall of Paris*.[1] In process of time, therefore, a governess became a necessary appanage[2] in every family.

Whether it be right or wrong, as a general rule, for mothers to delegate their most sacred trust to hired strangers, we are not here to discuss. The fact exists. Is the system carried out fairly for all parties? Is there any question astir as to its abuse? Philanthropic eyes are scanning many social evils. Is it yet considered how far a whole race of women are dragging out weary lives under a mass of trials, the detail of which would fill a "blue book"[3] by themselves? True, if the case were known, "a thousand voices" would be "uplifted."[4] The miseries of the governess may even swell that sickening clamour about the "rights of women," which would never have been raised had women been true to themselves. But that trite saying in this case has its point. The modern governess system is a case between woman and woman. Before one sex demands its due from the other, let it be just to itself.

Punch has ably pleaded in the cause of salaries and qualifications.[5] The statistics touching lunatic asylums give a frightful proportion of governesses in the list of the insane.[6] But has the whole life in home schoolrooms ever been investigated? We ask this with a real wish to be informed, with a hope of directing eyes to this unknown page of human life. Have kind, ladylike, cultivated women ever reflected on the relation which subsists between themselves and others of like minds, and, perhaps, formerly in similar circumstances? Have they ever tried to put themselves in the position of the young women devoting themselves to the education of their children, who yet live as strangers in the midst of their homes? …

… When the lesson-books are closed, and the little ones have capered out of the school-room, what becomes of the teacher, who has not exchanged a thought or a word with any one of congenial mind all day? Hour after hour she has *bent down* her mind, and *raised* the children's to given points, which, however interesting, are exhausting. A young thing, perhaps, still herself, ready to spring up again at one kindly touch. Do not even fond mothers, who teach their own children, feel that after the labours of the day they need some interchange of *mind*? They have often felt refreshed when husband or friend has given them a new thought, or understood an articulated feeling, after the repression of the day, necessary in fulfilling the duty of teaching. Who is there that has not known the dryness of spending time with people of more limited capacities and interests than one's own? … Let mothers ask if they would not expect their own daughters to languish in spirits and energy, if they had no intercourse[7] with older companions. Whilst the children are with their parents

---

[1] *Paul and Virginia*   The sentimental French novel *Paul et Virginie* (1787), by Jacques-Henri Bernadin de St. Pierre; *strum*   Play poorly on the piano; *The Fall of Paris*   Popular song of the period.

[2] *appanage*   Possession, perquisite.

[3] *blue book*   Parliamentary report.

[4] *a thousand … uplifted*   A reference to the epigraph of this article, from French novelist George Sand's collection of fictional letters, *Lettres à Marcie* (1837): "Society is full of abuses. Women complain of being brutally enslaved, badly brought up, badly educated, badly treated, and badly defended. All this is, unfortunately, true. These complaints are just, and do not doubt but that before long a thousand voices will be uplifted to remedy the evil."

[5] *Punch has … qualifications*   The satirical weekly magazine *Punch* had recently printed numerous articles advocating the improvement of conditions for governesses.

---

[6] *The statistics … insane*   During the early and mid nineteenth century it was a commonplace that governesses tended toward mental instability as a result of the stressful nature of their employment. While some statistics did show that there was a high percentage of governesses in asylums, this may have been due in part to the fact that private asylums sometimes provided the cheapest respectable accommodation for women without family or employment.

[7] *intercourse*   Communication.

and their guests, the governess, quite as often as not, is expected to remain in the school-room, unless specially invited to join the circle. This is peculiarly[1] the case in large establishments, where the school-room arrangements are distinct from the rest of the family. We believe that most young women of delicate perceptions would prefer their desolate apartment to feeling themselves clogs[2] upon the family party. But do people know what they are about when they leave young creatures alone, long evening after evening, following days of seclusion and exhaustion? Factory-girls, shop-women, teachers of accomplishments, return to their homes at night. The servants gather round the work-table or the hall-fire. Prisoners in gaol[3] may collect together in knots in their yards, look in each other's faces, hear the sound of human voices, tell their troubles and joys, and listen to their neighbours. Solitary confinement, even for felons, is reserved to punish some special offence. It is only the governess, and a certain class of private tutors, who must hear the echoes from the drawing-room and the offices, feeling that, in a house full of people, they dwell alone. Nervous irritability, dejection, loss of energy, are the inevitable results which follow a too solitary life in youth. Yet, without elasticity in her own frame, how can the governess be a fitting companion and teacher of such gay, volatile creatures as children—so easily cowed and spirit-broken by harshness or settled sadness in those who live with them? Would not querulous temper of depression of spirits in the governess be complained of by the parents? Do they consider, when they expect cheerfulness and an even composure of spirits from one fretted with children's restless waywardness, and chilled by the frosty indifference and neglect of the grown-up members of the family, that they ask an impossible thing?

---

[1] *peculiarly* Particularly.

[2] *clogs* Encumbrances. Literally, blocks of wood attached to the leg or neck of a person or animal to prevent escape.

[3] *gaol* I.e., jail.

from Harriet Taylor, *The Enfranchisement of Women* (1851)

When a prejudice, which has any hold on the feeling, finds itself reduced to the unpleasant necessity of assigning reasons, it thinks it has done enough when it has re-asserted the very point in the dispute, in phrases which appeal to the pre-existing feelings. Thus, many persons think they have sufficiently justified the restrictions on women's field of action when they have said that the pursuits from which women are excluded are *unfeminine*, and that the *proper sphere* of women is not politics or publicity, but private and domestic life.

We deny the right of any portion of the species to decide for another portion, or any individual for another individual, what is and what is not their "proper sphere." The proper sphere for all human beings is the largest and highest which they are able to attain to. …

We shall follow the very proper convention, in not entering into the question of the alleged differences in physical or mental qualities between the sexes; not because we have nothing to say, but because we have too much. … But if those who assert that the "proper sphere" for women is the domestic, mean by this that they have not shown themselves qualified for any other, the assertion evinces great ignorance of life and of history. Women have shown fitness for the highest social functions, exactly in proportion as they have been admitted to them. By a curious anomaly, though ineligible to even the lowest offices of state, they are in some countries admitted to the highest of all, the regal; and if there is any one function for which they have shown a decided vocation, it is that of reigning. …

Concerning the fitness, then, of women for politics, there can be no question: but the dispute is more likely to turn upon the fitness of politics for women. When the reasons alleged for excluding women from active life in all its higher departments are stripped of their garb of declamatory phrases, and reduced to the simple expression of a meaning, they seem to be mainly three: the incompatibility of active life with maternity and with the cares of a household; secondly, its alleged hardening effect on the character; and thirdly, the inexpediency of making an addition to the already excessive pressure of competition in every kind of professional or lucrative employment.

The first, the maternity argument, is usually laid most stress upon: although (it needs hardly be said) this reason, if it be one, can apply only to mothers. It is neither necessary nor just to make imperative on women that they shall be either mothers or nothing; or that if they have been mothers once, they shall be nothing else during the whole remainder of their lives. Neither women nor men need any law to exclude them from an occupation if they have undertaken another which is incompatible with it. No one proposes to exclude the male sex from Parliament because a man may be a soldier or sailor in active service, or a merchant whose business requires all his time and energies. Nine-tenths of the occupations of men exclude them *de facto*[1] from public life, as effectually as if they were excluded by law; but that is no reason for making laws to exclude even the nine-tenths, much less the remaining tenth. The reason of the case is the same for women as for men. There is no need to make provision by law that a woman shall not carry on the active details of a household, or of the education of children, and at the same time practise a profession or be elected to Parliament. Where incompatibility is real, it will take care of itself: but there is gross injustice in making the incompatibility a pretence for the exclusion of those in whose case it does not exist. And these, if they were free to choose, would be a very large proportion. The maternity argument deserts its supporters in the case of single women, a large and increasing class of the population; a fact which, it is not irrelevant to remark, by tending to diminish the excessive competition of numbers, is calculated to assist greatly the prosperity of all. There is no inherent reason or necessity that all women should voluntarily choose to devote their lives to one animal function and its consequences. Numbers of women are wives and mothers only because there is no other career open to them, no other occupation for their feelings or

their activities. Every improvement in their education, and enlargement of their faculties—everything which renders them more qualified for any other mode of life, increases the number of those to whom it is an injury and an oppression to be denied the choice. To say that women must be excluded from active life because maternity disqualifies them for it, is in fact to say that every other career should be forbidden them in order that maternity may be their only resource.

But secondly, it is urged that to give the same freedom of occupation to women as to men would be an injurious addition to the crowd of competitors, by whom the avenues to almost all kinds of employment are choked up, and its remuneration depressed. This argument, it is to be observed, does not reach the political question. It gives no excuse for withholding from women the rights of citizenship. The suffrage, the jury-box, admission to the legislature and to office, it does not touch. It bears only on the industrial branch of the subject. Allowing it, then, in an economical point of view, its full force; assuming that to lay open to women the employments now monopolized by men, would tend, like the breaking down of other monopolies, to lower the rate of remuneration in those employments; let us consider what is the amount of this evil consequence, and what the compensation for it. The worst ever asserted, much worse than is at all likely to be realized, is that if women competed with men, a man and a woman could not together earn more than is now earned by the man alone. Let us make this supposition, the most favourable supposition possible: the joint income of the two would be the same as before, while the woman would be raised from the position of a servant to that of a partner. Even if every woman, as matters now stand, had a claim on some man for support, how infinitely preferable is it that part of the income should be of the woman's earning, even if the aggregate sum were but little increased by it, rather than that she should be compelled to stand aside in order that men may be the sole earners, and the sole dispensers of what is earned. Even under the present laws respecting the property of women, a woman who contributes materially to the support of the family cannot be treated

---

[1] *de facto* Latin: in reality; as a matter of fact.

in the same contemptuously tyrannical manner as one who, however she may toil as a domestic drudge, is a dependent on the man for subsistence. As for the depression of wages by increase of competition, remedies will be found for it in time. Palliatives might be applied immediately; for instance, a more rigid exclusion of children from industrial employment, during the years in which they ought to be working only to strengthen their bodies and minds for after life. Children are necessarily dependent, and under the power of others; and their labour, being not for themselves but for the gain of their parents, is a proper subject for legislative regulation. With respect to the future, we neither believe that improvident multiplication, and the consequent excessive difficulty of gaining a subsistence, will always continue, nor that the division of mankind into capitalists and hired labourers, and the regulation of the reward of labourers mainly by demand and supply, will be for ever, or even much longer, the rule of the world. But so long as competition is the general law of human life, it is tyranny to shut out one half of the competitors. All who have attained the age of self-government have an equal claim to be permitted to sell whatever kind of useful labour they are capable of, for the price which it will bring.

The third objection to the admission of women to political or professional life, its alleged hardening tendency, belongs to an age now past, and is scarcely to be comprehended by people of the present time. There are still, however, persons who say that the world and its avocations render men selfish and unfeeling; that the struggles, rivalries, and collisions of business and of politics make them harsh and unamiable; that if half the species must unavoidably be given up to these things, it is the more necessary that the other half should be kept free from them; that to preserve women from the bad influences of the world is the only chance of preventing men from being wholly given up to them.

There would have been plausibility in this argument when the world was still in the age of violence; when life was full of physical conflict, and every man had to redress his injuries or those of others, by the sword or by the strength of his arm. Women, like priests, by being exempted from such responsibilities, and from some part of the accompanying dangers, may have been enabled to exercise a beneficial influence. But in the present condition of human life, we do not know where those hardening influences are to be found, to which men are subject and from which women are at present exempt. Individuals now-a-days are seldom called upon to fight hand to hand, even with peaceful weapons; personal enmities and rivalries count for little in worldly transactions; the general pressure of circumstances, not the adverse will of individuals, is the obstacle men now have to make head against. That pressure, when excessive, breaks the spirit, and cramps and sours the feelings, but not less of women than of men, since they suffer certainly not less from its evils. There are still quarrels and dislikes, but the sources of them are changed. The feudal chief once found his bitterest enemy in his powerful neighbour, the minister or courtier in his rival for place: but opposition of interest in active life, as a cause of personal animosity, is out of date; the enmities of the present day arise not from great things but small, from what people say of one another, more than from what they do; and if there are hatred, malice, and all uncharitableness, they are to be found among women fully as much as among men. In the present state of civilization, the notion of guarding women from the hardening influences of the world could only be realized by secluding them from society altogether. The common duties of common life, as at present constituted, are incompatible with any other softness in women than weakness. Surely weak minds in weak bodies must ere long[1] cease to be even supposed to be either attractive or amiable.

But, in truth, none of these arguments and considerations touch the foundations of the subject. The real question is, whether it is right and expedient that one half of the human race should pass through life in a state of forced subordination to the other half. If the best state of human society is that of being divided into two parts, one consisting of persons with a will and a substantive existence, the other of humble companions to these persons, attached, each of them to one, for the

---

[1] *ere long* Before long.

purpose of bringing up *his* children, and making *his* home pleasant to him; if this is the place assigned to women, it is but kindness to educate them for this; to make them believe that the greatest good fortune which can befall them is to be chosen by some man for this purpose; and that every other career which the world deems happy or honourable is closed to them by the law, not of social institutions, but of nature and destiny.

When, however, we ask why the existence of one-half the species should be merely ancillary to that of the other—why each woman should be a mere appendage to a man, allowed to have no interests of her own, that there may be nothing to compete in her mind with his interests and his pleasure; the only reason which can be given is, that men like it. It is agreeable to them that men should live for their own sake, women for the sake of men: and the qualities and conduct in subjects which are agreeable to rulers, they succeed for a long time in making the subjects themselves consider as their appropriate virtues.

from Coventry Patmore, *The Angel in the House* (1854–56)

THE WIFE'S TRAGEDY

Man must be pleased; but him to please
 Is woman's pleasure; down the gulf
Of his condoled[1] necessities
 She casts her best, she flings herself.
5 How often flings for nought!° and yokes *nothing*
 Her heart to an icicle or whim,
Whose each impatient word provokes
 Another, not from her, but him;
While she, too gentle even to force
10 His penitence by kind replies,
Waits by, expecting his remorse,
 With pardon in her pitying eyes;
And if he once, by shame oppressed,
 A comfortable word confers,
15 She leans and weeps against his breast,

---

[1] *condoled* Sympathized with.

And seems to think the sin was hers;
And whilst his love has any life,
 Or any eye to see her charms,
At any time, she's still his wife,
20 Dearly devoted to his arms;
She loves with love that cannot tire;
 And when, ah woe, she loves alone,
Through passionate duty love flames higher,
 As grass grows taller round a stone. ...

THE FOREIGN LAND

A woman is a foreign land,
 Of which, though there he settle young
A man will ne'er quite understand
 The customs, politics, and tongue.
5 The foolish hie° them post-haste through, *hasten*
 See fashions odd, and prospects fair,
Learn of the language, "How-d'ye do,"
 And go and brag that they've been there.
The most for leave to trade apply,
10 For once, at Empire's seat her heart,
Then get what knowledge ear and eye
 Glean chancewise in the life-long mart.° *market*
And certain others few and fit,
 Attach them to the Court, and see
15 The country's best, its accent hit,
 And partly sound its polity.

from William Rathbone Greg, "Why Are Women Redundant?" (1862)

... [T]here is an enormous and increasing number of single women in the nation, a number quite disproportionate and quite abnormal; a number which, positively and relatively, is indicative of an unwholesome social state, and is both productive and prognostic[2] of much wretchedness and wrong. There are hundreds of thousands of women—not to speak more largely still— scattered through all ranks, but proportionally most

---

[2] *prognostic* Predictive.

numerous in the middle and upper classes—who have to earn their own living instead of spending and husbanding[1] the earnings of men; who, not having the natural duties and labours of wives and mothers, have to carve out artificial and painfully-sought occupations for themselves; who, in place of completing, sweetening, and embellishing the existence of others, are compelled to lead an independent and incomplete existence of their own. In the manufacturing districts thousands of girls are working in mills and earning ample wages, instead of performing, or preparing and learning to perform, the functions and labours of domestic life. In great cities, thousands, again, are toiling in the ill-paid *métier*[2] of seamstresses and needlewomen, wasting life and soul, gathering the scantiest subsistence, and surrounded by the most overpowering and insidious temptations. As we go a few steps higher in the social scale, we find two classes of similar abnormal existences; women, more or less well educated, spending youth and middle life as governesses, living laboriously, yet perhaps not uncomfortably, but laying by[3] nothing, and retiring to a lonely and destitute old age: and old maids, with just enough income to live upon, but wretched and deteriorating, their minds narrowing, and their hearts withering, because they have nothing to do, and none to love, cherish, and obey. A little further upwards, how many do we daily see, how many have we all known, who are raised by fortune above the necessity of caring for their own subsistence, but to whom employment is a necessity as imperious as to the milliner or the husbandman,[4] because only employment can fill the dreary void of an unshared existence—beautiful lay nuns, involuntary takers of the veil, who pine for work, who beg for occupation, who pant for interest in life, as the hart panteth after the water-brooks, and dig for it more earnestly than for hid treasures.[5] With most women, probably, this phase comes at some epoch in their course; with numbers, alas,

it never passes into any other. Some rush to charity, and do partial good or much mischief; some find solace in literary interests and work, and these, though the fewest, are perhaps the most fortunate of all; some seek in the excessive development of the religious affections a pale ideal substitute for the denied human ones—a substitute of which God forbid that we should speak slightingly, but which is seldom wholly satisfactory or wholly safe. Lastly, as we ascend into the highest ranks of all, we come upon crowds of the same unfulfilled destinies—the same *existences manquées*[6]—women who have gay society,[7] but no sacred or suffering home, whose dreary round of pleasure is yet sadder, less remunerative, and less satisfying, than the dreary round of toil trodden by their humble sisters. The very being of all these various classes is a standing proof of, and protest against, that "something wrong," on which we have a few words to say—that besetting problem which, like the sphinx's,[8] society must solve or die. …

… Therefore it is that all those efforts, on which chivalric or compassionate benevolence is now so intent, to render single life as easy, as attractive, and as lucrative to women, as unhappily other influences to which we have alluded have already made it to men, *are efforts in a wrong direction*—spontaneous and natural, no doubt, to the tender heart of humanity, which always seeks first to relieve suffering, and only at a later date begins to think of curing disorder—but not to be smiled upon or aided by wise prescribers for the maladies of states. … To endeavour to make women independent of men; to multiply and facilitate their employments; to enable them to earn a separate and ample subsistence by competing with the hardier sex in those careers and occupations hitherto set apart for that sex alone; to induct them generally into avocations, not only as interesting and beneficent, and therefore *appropriate*, but specially and definitely as *lucrative*; to surround single life for them with so smooth an entrance, and such a pleasant, ornamented,

---

[1] *husbanding*   Using economically.

[2] *métier*   French: employment.

[3] *laying by*   Saving.

[4] *husbandman*   Farmer.

[5] *as the hart … water-brooks*   Expression of longing for God in Psalm 42.1; *dig for … hid treasures*   Description of longing for death in Job 3.21.

---

[6] *existences manquées*   French: lost lives.

[7] *gay society*   Pleasant, carefree social circle.

[8] *sphinx*   Mythical creature said to guard the entrance to the Greek city of Thebes. She posed a riddle to all travelers attempting to enter the city and killed those unable to solve it.

comfortable path, that marriage shall almost come to be regarded, not as their most honourable function and especial calling, but merely as one of many ways open to them, competing on equal terms with other ways for their cold and philosophic choice: this would appear to be the aim and theory of many female reformers. …

from Frances Power Cobbe, "What Shall We Do with Our Old Maids?" (1862)

… It appears that there is a natural excess of four or five per cent of females over the males in our population. This, then, might be assumed to be the limits within which female celibacy was normal and inevitable.

There is, however, an actual ratio of thirty per cent of women now in England who never marry, leaving one-fourth of both sexes in a state of celibacy. This proportion further appears to be constantly on the increase. It is obvious enough that these facts call for a revision of many of our social arrangements. The old assumption that marriage was the sole destiny of woman, and that it was the business of her husband to afford her support, is brought up short by the statement that one woman in four is certain not to marry, and that three millions of women earn their own living at this moment in England. We may view the case two ways: either—

1st, We must frankly accept this new state of things, and educate women and modify trade in accordance therewith, so as to make the condition of celibacy as little injurious as possible; or—

2nd, We must set ourselves vigorously to stop the current which is leading men and women away from the natural order of Providence. We must do nothing whatever to render celibacy easy or attractive; and we must make the utmost efforts to promote marriage by emigration of women to the colonies,[1] and all other means in our power.

The second of these views we shall in the first place consider. It may be found to colour the ideas of a vast number of writers, and to influence essentially the decisions made on many points—as the admission of women to university degrees, to the medical profession, and generally to free competition in employment. Lately it has met a powerful and not unkindly exposition in an article in a contemporary quarterly, entitled, "Why Are Women Redundant?" Therein it is plainly set forth that all efforts to make celibacy easy for women are labours in a wrong direction, and are to be likened to the noxious exertions of quacks to mitigate the symptoms of disease, and allow the patient to persist in his evil courses. …

A little deeper reflection, however, discloses a very important point which has been dropped out of the argument. Marriage is, indeed, the happiest and best condition for mankind. But does anyone think that all marriages are so? When we make the assertion that marriage is good and virtuous, do we mean a marriage of interest,[2] a marriage for wealth, for position, for rank, for support? Surely nothing of the kind. Such marriages as these are the sources of misery and sin, not of happiness and virtue, nay, their moral character, to be fitly designated, would require stronger words than we care to use. There is only one kind of marriage which makes good the assertion that it is the right and happy condition for mankind, and that is a marriage founded on free choice, esteem, and affection—in one word, on love. If, then, we seek to promote the happiness and virtue of the community, our efforts must be directed to encouraging *only* marriages which are of the sort to produce them—namely, marriages founded on love. All marriages founded on interest, on the desire for position, support, or the like, we must discourage to the utmost of our power, as the sources of nothing but wretchedness. Where, now, have we reached? Is it not to the conclusion that to make it a woman's *interest* to marry, to force her, by barring out every means of self-support and all fairly remunerative labour, to look to

1 *emigration of … the colonies* One course of action recommended in "Why Are Women Redundant?" by William Rathbone Greg, the article to which Cobbe is responding. A selection from Greg's article is reproduced above.

2 *interest* I.e., self-interest.

marriage as her sole chance of competency,[1] is precisely to drive her into one of those sinful and unhappy marriages? It is quite clear we can never drive her into *love*. That is a sentiment which poverty, friendlessness, and helplessness can by no means call out. Nor, on the contrary, can competence and freedom in any way check it. It will arise under its natural conditions, if we will but leave the matter alone. A loving marriage can never become a matter of "cold philosophic choice."[2] And if *not* a loving one, then, for Heaven's sake, let us give no motive for choice at all.

Let the employments of women be raised and multiplied as much as possible, let their labour be as fairly remunerated, let their education be pushed as high, let their whole position be made as healthy and happy as possible, and there will come out once more, here as in every other department of life, the triumph of the Divine laws of our nature. Loving marriages are (we cannot doubt) what God has designed, not marriages of interest. When we have made it *less* women's interest to marry, we shall indeed have less and fewer interested marriages, with all their train of miseries and evils. But we shall also have more *loving* ones, more marriages founded on free choice and free affection. Thus we arrive at the conclusion that for the very end[3] of promoting marriage—that is, such marriage as it is alone desirable to promote—we should pursue a precisely opposite course to that suggested by the Reviewer or his party. Instead of leaving single women as helpless as possible, and their labour as ill-rewarded—instead of dinning into their ears from childhood that marriage is their one vocation and concern in life, and securing afterwards if they miss it that they shall find no other vocation or concern—instead of all this, we shall act exactly on the reverse principle. We shall make single life so free and happy that they shall have not one temptation to change it save the only temptation which *ought* to determine them—namely, love. Instead of making marriage a case

of "Hobson's choice"[4] for a woman, we shall endeavour to give her such independence of all interested considerations that she may make it a choice, not indeed "cold and philosophic," but warm from the heart, and guided by heart and conscience only.

from Eliza Lynn Linton, "The Girl of the Period," *Saturday Review* (March 1868)

Time was when the stereotyped phrase "a fair young English girl" meant the ideal of womanhood, to us, at least, of home birth[5] and breeding. It meant a creature generous, capable, and modest; something franker than a Frenchwoman, more to be trusted than an Italian, as brave as an American but more refined, as domestic as a German and more graceful. It meant a girl who could be trusted alone if need be, because of the innate purity and dignity of her nature, but who was neither bold in bearing nor masculine in mind; a girl who, when she married, would be her husband's friend and companion, but never his rival; one who would consider their interests identical, and not hold him as just so much fair game for spoil; who would make his house his true home and place of rest, not a mere passage-place for vanity and ostentation to go through; a tender mother, an industrious housekeeper, a judicious mistress. We prided ourselves as a nation on our women. We thought we had the pick of creation in this fair young English girl of ours, and envied no other men their own. ... This was in the old time, and when English girls were content to be what God and nature had made them. Of late years we have changed the pattern, and have given to the world a race of women as utterly unlike the old insular ideal as if we had created another nation altogether. The girl of the period and the fair young English girl of the past have nothing in common save[6] ancestry and their mother-tongue; and

---

[1] *competency*   Here, financial sufficiency.

[2] *cold philosophic choice*   Phrase used by Greg in "Why Are Women Redundant?"

[3] *end*   Purpose.

[4] *Hobson's choice*   Choice in which only one thing is offered, and one must accept it or make do with nothing.

[5] *home birth*   Here, birth in the home country.

[6] *save*   Except.

"THE ANGEL IN 'THE HOUSE;'" OR, THE RESULT OF FEMALE SUFFRAGE.
(*A Troubled Dream of the Future.*)

This cartoon appeared in the 14 June 1884 edition of *Punch*. A satirical representation of the suffragist, here having gained the vote and a position of political power, speaking in the House of Commons. She is knitting a "blue stocking," an allusion to the term "bluestocking," a derogatory term that began to be applied to free-thinking women in the eighteenth century.

even of this last the modern version makes almost a new language, through the copious additions it has received from the current slang of the day.

The girl of the period is a creature who dyes her hair and paints her face, as the first articles of her personal religion; whose sole idea of life is plenty of fun and luxury; and whose dress is the object of such thought and intellect as she possesses. Her main endeavour in this is to outvie her neighbours in the extravagance of fashion. No matter whether, as in the time of crinolines,[1] she sacrificed decency, or, as now, in the time of trains, she sacrifices cleanliness; no matter either, whether she makes herself a nuisance and an inconvenience to every one she meets. The girl of the period has

---

[1] *crinolines* Stiff undergarments designed to hold out and give shape to skirts.

done away with such moral muffishness[1] as consideration for others, or regard for counsel and rebuke. It was all very well in old-fashioned times, when fathers and mothers had some authority and were treated with respect, to be tutored and made to obey, but she is far too fast and flourishing to be stopped in mid-career[2] by these slow old morals; and as she dresses to please herself, she does not care if she displeases everyone else. Nothing is too extraordinary and nothing too exaggerated for her vitiated[3] taste; and things which in themselves would be useful reforms if let alone become monstrosities worse than those which they have displaced so soon as she begins to manipulate and improve. If a sensible fashion lifts the gown out of the mud, she raises hers midway to her knee. If the absurd structure of wire and buckram,[4] once called a bonnet, is modified to something that shall protect the wearer's face without putting out the eyes of her companion, she cuts hers down to four straws and a rosebud, or a tag of lace and a bunch of glass beads! … She has blunted the fine edges of feeling so much that she cannot understand why she should be condemned for an imitation of form which does not include imitation of fact; she cannot be made to see that modesty of appearance and virtue ought to be inseparable, and that no good girl can afford to appear bad, under penalty of receiving the contempt awarded to the bad.

This imitation of the *demi-monde*[5] in dress leads to something in manner and feeling, not quite so pronounced perhaps, but far too like to be honourable to herself or satisfactory to her friends. It leads to slang, bold talk, and fastness; to the love of pleasure and indifference to duty; to the desire of money before either love or happiness; to uselessness at home, dissatisfaction with the monotony of ordinary life, and horror of all useful work; in a word, to the worst forms of luxury and selfishness, to the most fatal effects arising from want of high principle and absence of tender feeling. … No one can say of the modern English girl that she is tender, loving, retiring, or domestic. The old fault so often found by keen-sighted Frenchwomen, that she was so fatally *romanesque*,[6] so prone to sacrifice appearances and social advantages for love, will never be set down to the girl of the period. Love indeed is the last thing she thinks of, and the least of the dangers besetting her. Love in a cottage, that seductive dream which used to vex the heart and disturb the calculations of prudent mothers, is now a myth of past ages. The legal barter of herself for so much money, representing so much dash,[7] so much luxury and pleasure—that is her idea of marriage; the only idea worth entertaining. For all seriousness of thought respecting the duties or the consequences of marriage, she has not a trace. If children come, they find but a stepmother's cold welcome from her; and if her husband thinks that he has married anything that is to belong to him—a *tacens et placens uxor*[8] pledged to make him happy—the sooner he wakes from his hallucination and understands that he has simply married someone who will condescend to spend his money on herself, and who will shelter her indiscretions behind the shield of his name, the less severe will be his disappointment. She has married his house, his carriage, his balance at the bankers, his title; and he himself is just the inevitable condition clogging the wheel of her fortune; at best an adjunct, to be tolerated with more or less patience as may chance. For it is only the old-fashioned sort, not girls of the period *pur sang*,[9] that marry for love, or put the husband before the banker. But she does not marry easily. Men are afraid of her; and with reason. They may amuse themselves with her of an evening, but they do not take her readily for life. …

The marvel, in the present fashion of life among women, is how it holds its ground in spite of the disap-

---

[1] *muffishness* Foolishness, often describing someone or something seen as old-fashioned.

[2] *mid-career* Mid-motion.

[3] *vitiated* Corrupted.

[4] *buckram* Stiff cotton cloth.

[5] *demi-monde* French: literally, "half world"; figuratively, the world existing below the level of respectable society. The term was often used to denote the world of the courtesan.

[6] *romanesque* French: romantic.

[7] *dash* Fancy display.

[8] *tacens … uxor* Latin: silent and pleasing wife.

[9] *pur sang* French: pure-blooded.

probation of men. It used to be an old-time notion that the sexes were made for each other, and that it was only natural for them to please each other, and to set themselves out for that end. But the girl of the period does not please men. She pleases them as little as she elevates them; and how little she does that, the class of women she has taken as her models of itself testifies. All men whose opinion is worth having prefer the simple and genuine girl of the past, with her tender little ways and pretty bashful modesties, to this loud and rampant modernization, with her false red hair and painted skin, talking slang as glibly as a man, and by preference leading the conversation to doubtful subjects. She thinks she is piquante[1] and exciting when she thus makes herself the bad copy of a worse original; and she will not see that though men laugh with her they do not respect her, though they flirt with her they do not marry her; she will not believe that she is not the kind of thing they want, and that she is acting against nature and her own interests when she disregards their advice and offends their taste. We do not see how she makes out her account, viewing her life from any side; but all we can do is to wait patiently until the national madness has passed, and our women have come back again to the old English ideal, once the most beautiful, the most modest, the most essentially womanly in the world.

from Frances Power Cobbe, "Criminals, Idiots, Women, and Minors," *Fraser's Magazine* (December 1868)

There was an allegory rather popular about thirty years ago, whose manifest purpose was to impress on the juvenile mind that tendency which Mr. Matthew Arnold has ingeniously designated "Hebraism."[2] The hero of the tale descends upon earth from some distant planet, and is conducted by a mundane cicerone[3] through one of our great cities, where he beholds the docks and arsenals, the streets and marts, the galleries of art, and the palaces of royalty. The visitor admires everything till he happens to pass a graveyard. "What is that gloomy spot?" he asks of his companion. "It is a cemetery," replies the guide.

"A—what did you say?" inquires the son of the star.

"A graveyard; a place of public interment; where we bury our dead," reiterates the cicerone.

The visitor, pale with awe and terror, learns at last that there is in this world such a thing as *Death*, and (as he is forbidden to return to his own planet) he resolves to dedicate every moment left to him to prepare himself for that fearful event and all that may follow it.

Had that visitor heard for the first time upon his arrival on earth of another incident of human existence—namely, *Marriage*, it may be surmised that his astonishment and awe would also have been considerable. To his eager inquiry whether men and women earnestly strove to prepare themselves for so momentous an occurrence, he would have received the puzzling reply that women frequently devoted themselves with perfectly Hebraistic singleness of aim to that special purpose; but that men, on the contrary, very rarely included any preparation for the married state among the items of their widest Hellenistic culture. But this anomaly would be trifling compared to others which would be revealed to him. "Ah," we can hear him say to his guide as they pass into a village church. "What a pretty sight is this! What is happening to that sweet young woman in white who is giving her hand to the good-looking fellow beside her, all the company decked in holiday attire, and the joy-bells shaking the old tower overhead? She is receiving some great honour, is she not? The Prize of Virtue, perhaps?"

"Oh, yes," would reply the friend; "an honour certainly. She is being Married." After a little further explanation the visitor would pursue his inquiry:

"Of course, having entered this honourable state of matrimony, she has some privilege above the women

---

[1] *piquante* Stimulating.

[2] *Hebraism* Originally denoting an attribute of the Hebrew people, the term was used by Arnold to describe a moral (rather than intellectual) theory of life. Arnold used the term "Hellenistic," in contrast, to denote the intellectual culture or way of life typified by the ancient Greeks.

[3] *cicerone* Guide.

who are not chosen by anybody? I notice her husband has just said, 'With all my worldly goods I thee endow.' Does that mean that she will henceforth have the control of his money altogether, or only that he takes her into partnership?"

"*Pas précisément*,[1] my dear sir. By our law it is *her* goods and earnings, present and future, which belong to him from this moment."

"You don't say so? But then, of course, his goods are hers also?"

"Oh dear, no! not at all. He is only bound to find her food; and truth to tell, not very strictly or efficaciously bound to do that."

"How! do I understand you? Is it possible that here in the most solemn religious act, which I perceive your prayer book calls 'The Solemnisation of Holy Matrimony,' every husband makes a generous promise, which promise is not only a mockery, but the actual reverse and parody of the real state of the case: the man who promises giving nothing, and the woman who is silent giving all?"

"Well, yes; I suppose that is something like it, as to the letter of the law. But then, of course, practically—"

"Practically, I suppose few men can really be so unmanly and selfish as the law warrants them in being. Yet some, I fear, may avail themselves of such authority. May I ask another question? As you subject women who enter the marriage state to such very severe penalties as this, what worse have you in store for women who lead a dissolute life, to the moral injury of the community?"

"Oh, the law takes nothing from them. Whatever they earn or inherit is their own. They are able, also, to sue the fathers of their children for their maintenance, which a wife, of course, is not allowed to do on behalf of *her* little ones, because she and her husband are one in the eye of the law."

"One question still further—your criminals? Do they always forfeit their entire property on conviction?"

"Only for the most heinous crimes; felony and murder, for example."

"Pardon me; I must seem to you so stupid! Why is the property of the woman who commits Murder, and the property of the woman who commits Matrimony, dealt with alike by your law?"

Leaving our little allegory and in sober seriousness, we must all admit that the just and expedient treatment of women by men is one of the most obscure problems, alike of equity and of policy. Nor of women only, but of all classes and races of human beings whose condition is temporarily or permanently one of comparative weakness and dependence. ...

By the common law of England a married woman has no legal existence, so far as property is concerned, independently of her husband. The husband and wife are assumed to be one person, and that person is the husband. The wife can make no contract, and can neither sue nor be sued. Whatever she possess of personal property at the time of her marriage, or whatever she may afterwards earn or inherit, belongs to her husband, without control on her part. ... If she possess real estate, so long as her husband lives he receives and spends the income derived from it, being only forbidden to sell it without her consent. From none of her property is he bound to reserve anything, or make any provision for her maintenance or that of her children. This is the law for all, but practically it affects only two classes of women, *viz.*[2] those who marry hurriedly or without proper advisers, and those whose property at the time of marriage is too small to permit of the expense of a settlement; in other words, the whole middle and lower ranks of women, and a certain portion of the upper ranks. Women of the richer class, with proper advisers, never come under the provisions of the Common Law, being carefully protected therefrom by an intricate system elaborated for the purpose by the courts of Equity,[3] to which the victims of the Common Law have for years applied for redress. That system always involves considerable legal expenses, and an arrangement

---

[1] *Pas précisément* French: Not exactly.

[2] *viz.* Latin: namely; that is to say (an abbreviation of *videlicet*).

[3] *the courts of Equity* In particular the Court of Chancery, which based decisions on principles of equity (i.e., fairness) and was not bound by precedents set by common law courts.

with trustees which is often extremely inconvenient and injurious to the interests of the married couple; nevertheless it is understood to be so great a boon[1] that none who can afford to avail themselves of it fail to do so.

What then is the principle on which the Common Law mulcts[2] the poorer class of women of their property and earnings, and entails on the rich, if they wish to evade it, the costs and embarrassment of a marriage settlement? There is, of course, a principle in it, and one capable of clear statement. There are grounds for the law; first of Justice, then of Expediency, lastly (and as we believe) most influential of all, of Sentiment.

First, the grounds of Justice.

Man is the natural bread-winner. Woman lives by the bread which man has earned. Ergo, it is fit and right that the man who wins should have absolute disposal, not only of his winnings, but of every other small morsel or fraction of earning or property she may possess. It is a fair return to him for his labour in the joint interests of both. ... The woman's case is that of a pauper who enters a workhouse.[3] The ratepayers are bound to support him; but if he have any savings they must be given up to the board. HE cannot claim support and keep independent property.

Then for Expediency. "How can two walk together except they be agreed?" says the Bible.[4] "How can they walk together except one of them have it all his own way?" says the voice of rough and ready practicality. Somebody must rule in a household, or everything will go to rack and ruin; and disputes will be endless. If somebody is to rule it can only be the husband, who is wiser, stronger, knows more of the world, and in any case has not the slightest intention of yielding his predominance. But to give a man such rule he must be allowed to keep the purse. Nothing but the power of the purse—in default of the stick—can permanently and thoroughly secure authority. ...

Lastly, for the sentimental view. How painful is the notion of a wife holding back her money from him who is every day toiling for her support! How fair is the ideal picture of absolute concession on her part of all she possesses of this world's dross[5] to the man to whom she gives her heart and life! ... The young man and maiden, after years of affection, and carefully laying by of provision for the event, take each other at last, to be henceforth no more twain, but one flesh. Both have saved a little money, but it now belongs to the husband alone. He lays it out in the purchase of a cottage where they are henceforth to dwell. Day by day he goes forth to his labour, and weekly he brings home his earnings and places them in his wife's lap, bidding her spend them as she knows best for the supply of their homely board,[6] their clothing which her deft fingers will make and many a time repair, and last for their common treasures, the little children who gather around them. Thus they grow old in unbroken peace and love, the man's will having never once been disputed, the wide yielding alike from choice and from necessity to his superior sense and his legal authority.

Surely this idea of life, for which the Common Law of England has done its utmost to provide, is well worth the pondering before we attempt to meddle with any of its safeguards? Who will suggest anything better in its room?[7]

Alas, there are other scenes besides idylls of domestic peace and obedience promoted by the laws we are considering. ...

The existing Common Law is not *Just*, because it neither can secure nor actually even attempts to secure for the woman the equivalent support for whose sake she is forced to relinquish her property.

It is not *Expedient*, because while in happy marriages it is superfluous and useless, in unhappy ones it becomes highly injurious; often causing the final ruin of a family

---

[1] *boon* Advantage.

[2] *mulcts* Swindles.

[3] *workhouse* Institution in which the poor were given lodging and a minimal level of sustenance in exchange for work performed. They were designed to be as unpleasant as possible so as to discourage people from entering them.

[4] *How can ... says the Bible* See Amos 3.3.

[5] *dross* Impure matter of little value.

[6] *homely board* Table; i.e., meals.

[7] *in its room* Instead.

which the mother (if upheld by law) might have supported single-handed. It is also shown not to be considered expedient by the conduct of the entire upper class of the country, and even of the legislature itself in the system of the Court of Chancery. Where no one who can afford to evade the law fails to evade it, the pretence that it is believed to be generally expedient is absurd. Further, the classes which actually evade it, and the countries where it is non-existing, show in no degree less connubial harmony than those wherein it is enforced.

Lastly, it does not tend to fulfil, but to counteract, the *Sentiment* regarding the marriage union, to which it aims to add the pressure of force. Real unanimity is not produced between two parties by forbidding one of them to have any voice at all. The hard mechanical contrivance of the law for making husband and wife of one heart and mind is calculated to produce a precisely opposite result.

from "Between School and Marriage," *The Girl's Own Paper* (4 September 1886)

This time in a girl's life corresponds to that in a man's which is passed in a university, or in learning the work of his profession. Too many girls look on it as a *mauvais quart d'heure*,[1] which may be dawdled through in an irresponsible way until they have a house of their own. Marriage represents a home, a position; sometimes even less than that—a trousseau,[2] or a wedding tour. So they hasten through the years of adolescence as well as may be in order to reach the end of a wearisome task.

And yet if the girl is mother to the woman—that is to say, if the woman will be what the girl now is, this time, which is essentially one for settling habits, cannot be anything less than the most important in life. If the girl spend it in thoughtless idleness and discontented trifling, the result will be seen in the character of the woman. It is well for any of us when our work is cut out for us, so to speak, and we have not to look about for a profitable way of passing the time; but this last is the miserable condition of many girls belonging to daughter-full houses in easy circumstances. What can they do between school and marriage?

When the financial resources of her father are slender, a girl is quite right to seek for some employment by which she may earn her own living, and perhaps help her brothers and sisters; but when this is not the case, let no feeling of quixotic[3] restlessness induce her to rashly leave home. It may be her plain duty to remain at home, and she may be independent and pay her way quite as much as one who earns and pays current coin. She can pay her way by filling in the little spaces in home life as only a dear daughter can, by lifting the weight of care from her mother, and by slipping in a soft word or a smile where it is like oil on the troubled waters of a father's spirit. What better remuneration can a father have for his expenditure upon his daughters than their laughter, good humour, and sympathy?…

from Emma Brewer, "Our Friends the Servants," *The Girl's Own Paper* (25 March 1893)

Among mistresses[4] who earnestly desire the welfare of their servants there is no question which causes more trouble and anxiety than that of allowing visitors in the kitchen, men visitors especially. It is indeed a difficult question, and cannot be solved for every one alike.

I know several ladies who have thought it right that such of their maids as were engaged should be permitted to receive their sweethearts from time to time in the kitchen; but in every case where this has been granted that has come under my notice, the results have been so disastrous as to necessitate the withdrawal of the privilege. It was found utterly destructive of harmony in the kitchen, and gave no real pleasure to anyone. In some

---

[1] *mauvais quart d'heure* French: an unpleasant time (literally, an unpleasant quarter of an hour), from the French expression "*passer un mauvais quart d'heure*," meaning "to have a bad time of it."

[2] *trousseau* A bride's collection of clothing and linens.

[3] *quixotic* Foolishly idealistic.

[4] *mistresses* Married women with the responsibility of maintaining a household.

The Girl's Own Paper, sold weekly for a penny, was mainly marketed to working- and middle-class women, but it was read by women from all classes and age groups and soon after its founding reached a circulation of over 250,000.

cases the fickle men forsook their old love in favour of some younger and more attractive of the fellow-servants, and it is not difficult to imagine the bitterness, anger, and sharp words which became the fashion after such faithlessness.

In others the sweethearts borrowed money of all the foolish girls in order to lay it upon horses[1] in which they were interested; in others, where more stimulant had been taken than was good for them, they have boasted among other men of the beautiful silver,[2] etc., in the houses where their young women lived, with what results may be guessed.

In simple fairness the privilege cannot be granted to one without extending it to all; this, in many houses, would fill the kitchens of an evening; for no maid would acknowledge that she had no young man, and would get one on the spot without considering his character, and such a one would scarcely add to the safety or morality of the kitchen. …

There are a few things in the relationship between mistress and maid which distress me greatly, because I know they are utterly destructive of home-peace and comfort; one is a mistress reproving her servant in public, another is a maid answering her mistress rudely, and a third is a mistress finding fault with servants out of the room to one who is waiting in the room.

No good servant would endure the first nor be guilty of the second, but one and all are evil in their result, and it is easy to see that, let the fault be what it may, it cannot be remedied in this fashion.

Servants have feelings to be wounded and rights to be respected, and when these are ignored they feel that their occupation is compromising to their respectability and freedom.

We lose many good servants in this way, and get in their place large importations of very inferior ones from the Continent.[3] It gives one a feeling of sadness that while the mother country stands in increased need of good and trustworthy servants, she cannot retain them or make friends of them, but has to look on while her colonies attract those she herself would so gladly keep.

I do not know if all are aware that every month ships leave England with a number of servants on board; indeed, as many as fourteen vessels go over to Queensland alone, carrying, on an average, two hundred

---

[1] *lay it upon horses* Bet on horse races.

[2] *the beautiful silver* Cutlery and other items plated with silver.

[3] *the Continent* The European mainland.

servants on each ship. Any young woman with good health and good character can get a free passage to Queensland if she is under thirty-five years of age. This colony, even above others, values highly our friends the servants, whose success is undoubted. They try to live up to the high opinion formed of them, but it is grievous to see them leaving the old country which wants them even more than the colonies.

ELIZABETH BARRETT BROWNING
1806 – 1861

Now widely considered one of the foremost poets of the Victorian era, Elizabeth Barrett Browning was equally highly regarded in her day, admired by contemporaries such as Wordsworth and Dickinson, critics, and the general public alike. Strongly associated in popular consciousness with the romantic vision of her *Sonnets from the Portuguese*—"How do I love thee? Let me count the ways," the first line of "Sonnet 43," remains one of the most famous lines in English literature—she was also a boldly political poet with a range of emotion and subject matter extending far beyond the romantic. Many critics consider her greatest achievement to be *Aurora Leigh*, a semi-autobiographical long poem in which Barrett Browning articulates her "highest convictions upon Life and Art."

Elizabeth Barrett was the eldest of twelve children born to a wealthy plantation-owning family in Durham, England. Just prior to her birth her parents, Edward Barrett Moulton-Barrett and Mary Graham Clarke Moulton-Barrett, moved from their slave plantation in Jamaica to raise a family in England. The young Barrett grew up in the sheltered environment of a country manor called Hope End, learning languages and studying the classics, at a time when a young woman's education was typically restricted to the domestic sphere. An exceptional and intellectually voracious student, Barrett learned Latin, Greek, and French from her brothers' tutors and studied philosophical, historical, and religious works on her own. She had read Milton's *Paradise Lost* by the time she was 10 years old and, encouraged by her parents, anonymously published her first poem, an epic entitled *The Battle of Marathon*, a few years later. In 1826, she published *An Essay on Mind and Other Poems*. In 1833 she published her translation from the Greek of Aeschylus' *Prometheus Bound*; she also included some of her own poems in the volume.

Due to the abolition of slavery, the Barretts' fortune began to wane, and in 1832 they were required to sell Hope End, eventually moving to Wimpole Street in London. Her father was overly protective of his children, however, and Barrett fell into semi-seclusion within the family home; her seclusion was compounded by illnesses that had begun to plague her when she was about 12 years old. Critics speculate as to the exact nature of those illnesses, but there is evidence to suggest that Barrett may have suffered from tuberculosis and possibly from a spinal injury. Her maladies were no doubt exacerbated by the opiates prescribed by doctors and the depression that followed the accidental death of her beloved brother Edward, who had accompanied her while she recuperated in the south of England. This tragedy, and Barrett's subsequent feelings of anguish and guilt, inspired some of her best-known poems, including the elegiac sonnet "Grief."

Much has been written about Barrett's middle years, but the image of the bed-ridden recluse remains somewhat at odds with the prolific reader and writer who wrote poetry, essays, reviews, and criticism for magazines and journals and published *The Seraphim and Other Poems* in 1838. The two-volume collection of her *Poems* published in 1844 contains some of her most politically charged poetry, including "The Cry of the Children," which condemned the employment of children in factories. During these years, Barrett kept up an active correspondence with many writers, critics, and artists and accepted occasional visitors in the confines of her family home. It was in this way that she met Robert Browning, who called upon her after the 1844 collection appeared. He visited her after first writing to express his admiration for work that had already made Barrett famous in England and was rapidly gaining recognition in the United States.

The subsequent exchange of 574 letters between Barrett and Browning, and their eventual elopement, have received much attention, with some suggesting that Barrett Browning's best work was inspired by this passionate relationship. It is worth noting here that she had already begun to write love poetry, having translated Petrarch's sonnets and written her own before she met Browning. There is no doubt, however, that the force of their relationship inspired some of her most enduring work, notably her famous *Sonnets from the Portuguese*, written during her courtship with Browning and published in 1850. "My little Portuguese," an allusion to her dark skin, was Browning's pet name for his wife.

Her 1846 marriage to Browning and their ensuing life together in Italy were a boon to Barrett Browning's health and her work. Her beloved father, however, who had forbidden his children to marry, refused to speak to or see his daughter again, going so far as to return her letters unopened. In 1849 the Brownings' only child, Robert Wiedemann Barrett Browning (nicknamed "Pen"), was born in Casa Guidi, just outside Florence.

Not long after the publication of *Sonnets*, Barrett Browning published *Casa Guidi Windows*, which promoted the cause of *Risorgimento*, the Italian struggle for unification and independence from foreign domination (the subject also of many of the later *Poems before Congress*). In 1850, she published the abolition poem "The Runaway Slave at Pilgrim's Point," one of the great dramatic monologues and political-protest poems written in English in the nineteenth century. Barrett Browning's comment on Harriet Beecher Stowe's *Uncle Tom's Cabin* summarizes her consistent response to critics who questioned her choice of subjects: "… is it possible you think a woman has no business with questions like the question of slavery? Then she had better use a pen no more. She had better subside into slavery and concubinage herself, I think, as in the times of old, shut herself up with the Penelopes in the 'women's apartment,' and take no rank among thinkers and speakers."

The 1856 work *Aurora Leigh* further cemented Barrett Browning's immense popularity, even though its candid sexual content and direct treatment of gender inequality were deemed scandalous by many at the time. An ambitious "novel in verse" (as Barrett Browning styled it), *Aurora Leigh* is narrated in nine books of blank verse and is the zenith of Barrett Browning's life work, encompassing her convictions on desire, power, art, love, romance, race, class structures, and the subjugation of women. The independent and progressive heroine of the books is named in part after Barrett Browning's idol, French writer George Sand (née Aurore Dupin), known for her liberal, feminist views and her penchant for wearing men's clothing. Like Sand, and also like Barrett Browning herself, Aurora Leigh is a writer, one who questions her identity as both artist and woman, and who struggles to achieve independence from staid societal mores and yet still preserve the ability to attain love and companionship. As Barrett Browning herself would observe, "never did a book so divide opinions in London. Some persons can't bear it—& others [are] crying it up as what I am too modest to write"; John Ruskin, for example, pronounced it the greatest poem of the century. It would later be praised by Virginia Woolf for capturing essential qualities of the Victorian intellectual landscape: "Aurora Leigh, with her passionate interest in social questions, her conflict as artist and woman, her longing for knowledge and freedom, is the true daughter of her age."

Elizabeth Barrett Browning predeceased her husband by 28 years when she passed away in his arms in 1861; she is buried in the Protestant cemetery in Florence. By the early twentieth century, *Sonnets from the Portuguese* was still widely read, but the rest of her work had fallen out of fashion. It remained so, despite praise from Woolf and a few other individual critics, until the growth of feminist criticism in the 1970s, which restored attention to her broader oeuvre; now, her work is as highly valued as it was during her lifetime.

⌘⌘⌘

The Young Queen[1]

"This awful[2] responsibility is imposed upon me so suddenly, and at so early a period of my life, that I should feel myself utterly oppressed by the burden, were I not sustained by the hope that Divine Providence, which has called me to this work, will give me strength for the performance of it."

The Queen's Declaration in Council[3]

The shroud is yet unspread
  To wrap our crownèd dead;
His soul hath scarcely hearkened for the thrilling[4]
  word of doom;
And Death that makes serene
5 Ev'n brows where crowns have been,
Hath scarcely time to meeten° his, for   *prepare*
  silence of the tomb.

St. Paul's king-dirging[5] note
The city's heart hath smote—
The city's heart is struck with thought more solemn
  than the tone!
10 A shadow sweeps apace°   *swiftly*
Before the nation's face,
Confusing in a shapeless blot the sepulchre and throne.

The palace sounds with wail—
The courtly dames are pale—
15 A widow o'er the purple[6] bows, and weeps its
  splendour dim:
And we who hold the boon,
A king for freedom won,
Do feel eternity rise up between our thanks and him.

And while all things express
20 All glory's nothingness,
A royal maiden treadeth firm where that departed
  trod!
The deathly scented crown
Weighs her shining ringlets down;
But calm she lifts her trusting face, and calleth
  upon God.

---

1 *The Young Queen* Written in July 1837, this poem responds to the ascension of Victoria to the throne upon the death of her uncle, King William IV. Victoria was only eighteen years old.

2 *awful* Awe-inspiring; intimidating.

3 *The Queen's Declaration in Council* From Victoria's first official address as Queen of the United Kingdom, given on 21 June 1837.

4 *thrilling* Shudder-inducing; frightening.

5 *St. Paul's* Anglican cathedral in London, whose bells would have rung to announce the king's death; *king-dirging* A dirge is a funeral song.

6 *widow* William IV's wife, queen consort Adelaide of Saxe-Meiningen; *purple* Color associated with royalty, and sometimes the color of the cloth used to cover a royal coffin.

25   Her thoughts are deep within her:
No outward pageants[1] win her
From memories that in her soul are rolling wave
     on wave—
Her palace walls enring
The dust that was a king—
30   And very cold beneath her feet, she feels her father's
     grave[2]

And One, as fair as she,[3]
Can scarce forgotten be—
Who clasped a little infant dead, for all a kingdom's
     worth!
The mournèd, blessèd One,
35   Who views Jehovah's throne,
Aye smiling to the angels, that she lost a throne on
     earth.

Perhaps our youthful Queen
Remembers what has been—
Her childhood's rest by loving heart, and sport on
     grassy sod—
40   Alas! can others wear
A mother's heart for her?
But calm she lifts her trusting face, and calleth
     upon God

Yea! Call on God, thou maiden
Of spirit nobly laden,
45   And leave such happy days behind, for
     happy-making years!
A nation looks to thee
For steadfast sympathy:
Make room within thy bright clear eyes, for all its
     gathered tears.

And so the grateful isles
50   Shall give thee back their smiles,

---

[1]   *pageants*   Performances; false displays.

[2]   *father's grave*   Victoria's father, Edward, Duke of Kent and Strathearn, had died in 1820.

[3]   *One, as fair as she*   Allusion to Princess Charlotte, daughter of George IV, who had died after giving birth to a stillborn child in 1817.

And as thy mother joys in thee, in them shalt thou
     rejoice;
Rejoice to meekly bow
A somewhat paler brow,
While the King of kings[4] shall bless thee by the
     British people's voice!
—1837

The Cry of the Children[5]

"Φεῦ, φεῦ, τί προσδέρκεσθέ μ' ὄμμασιν, τέκνα;"[6] —Medea.

1

Do ye hear the children weeping, O my brothers,
     Ere the sorrow comes with years?
They are leaning their young heads against their
     mothers,
       And *that* cannot stop their tears.
5   The young lambs are bleating in the meadows,
     The young birds are chirping in the nest,
The young fawns are playing with the shadows,
     The young flowers are blowing toward the west—
But the young, young children, O my brothers,
10   They are weeping bitterly!
They are weeping in the playtime of the others,
     In the country of the free.

2

Do you question the young children in the sorrow
     Why their tears are falling so?
The old man may weep for his tomorrow
15   Which is lost in Long Ago;
The old tree is leafless in the forest,

---

[4]   *King of kings*   I.e., Jesus Christ.

[5]   *The Cry of the Children*   This poem was written in response to Richard Hengist Horne's 1843 "Report of the Children's Employment Commission" regarding child labor in the mining and manufacturing industries (see "In Context: Children in the Mines," on the companion website). Horne was the author of the epic poem *Orion* and the play *Cosmo de' Medici*, as well as *A New Spirit of the Age*, co-written with Elizabeth Barrett.

[6]   *Φεῦ … τέκνα*   From Euripides's *Medea* (431 BCE) 1.1040, in which Medea says, upon killing her children: "Alas, why do you gaze at me thus, my children?"

The old year is ending in the frost,
The old wound, if stricken, is the sorest,
20   The old hope is hardest to be lost.
But the young, young children, O my brothers,
        Do you ask them why they stand
Weeping sore before the bosoms of their mothers,
        In our happy Fatherland?

3

25 They look up with their pale and sunken faces,
        And their looks are sad to see,
For the man's hoary[1] anguish draws and presses
        Down the cheeks of infancy.
"Your old earth," they say, "is very dreary;
30   Our young feet," they say, "are very weak!
Few paces have we taken, yet are weary—
        Our grave rest is very far to seek.
Ask the aged why they weep, and not the children;
        For the outside earth is cold;
35 And we young ones stand without, in our
                bewildering,
        And the graves are for the old."

4

"True," say the children, "it may happen
        That we die before our time;
Little Alice died last year—her grave is shapen
40   Like a snowball, in the rime.°   frost
We looked into the pit prepared to take her:
        Was no room for any work in the close clay![2]
From the sleep wherein she lieth none will wake her,
        Crying, 'Get up, little Alice! it is day.'
45 If you listen by that grave, in sun and shower,
        With your ear down, little Alice never cries;
Could we see her face, be sure we should not know her,
        For the smile has time for growing in her eyes:
And merry go her moments, lulled and stilled in
50   The shroud[3] by the kirk° chime.   church
It is good when it happens," say the children,
        "That we die before our time."

---

[1] *hoary* Old and gray.

[2] *clay* Grave dirt.

[3] *shroud* Sheet used to wrap the dead for burial.

5

Alas, alas, the children! they are seeking
        Death in life, as best to have;
55 They are binding up their hearts away from breaking,
        With a cerement° from the grave.   *shroud*
Go out, children, from the mine and from the city,
        Sing out, children, as the little thrushes do;
Pluck you handfuls of the meadow cowslips[4] pretty,
60   Laugh aloud, to feel your fingers let them through!
But they answer, "Are your cowslips of the meadows
        Like our weeds anear° the mine?   *near*
Leave us quiet in the dark of the coal shadows,
        From your pleasures fair and fine!

6

65 "For oh," say the children, "we are weary,
        And we cannot run or leap;
If we cared for any meadows, it were merely
        To drop down in them and sleep.
Our knees tremble sorely in the stooping,
70   We fall upon our faces, trying to go;
And, underneath our heavy eyelids drooping,
        The reddest flower would look as pale as snow;
For, all day, we drag our burden tiring
        Through the coal dark, under ground;
75 Or, all day, we drive the wheels of iron
        In the factories, round and round.

7

"For all day, the wheels are droning, turning;
        Their wind comes in our faces,
Till our hearts turn, our heads with pulses burning,
80   And the walls turn in their places:
Turns the sky in the high window blank and reeling,
        Turns the long light that drops adown the wall,
Turn the black flies that crawl along the ceiling,
        All are turning, all the day, and we with all.
85 And all day, the iron wheels are droning,
        And sometimes we could pray,
'O ye wheels,' (breaking out in a mad moaning)
        'Stop! be silent for today!'"

---

[4] *cowslips* Fragrant yellow flowers commonly found in pastures.

8

Aye, be silent! Let them hear each other breathing
90   For a moment, mouth to mouth!
Let them touch each other's hands, in a fresh wreathing
        Of their tender human youth!
Let them feel that this cold metallic motion
        Is not all the life God fashions or reveals:
95 Let them prove[1] their living souls against the notion
        That they live in you, or under you, O wheels!
Still, all day, the iron wheels go onward,
        Grinding life down from its mark;
And the children's souls, which God is calling sunward,
100   Spin on blindly in the dark.

9

Now tell the poor young children, O my brothers,
        To look up to Him and pray;
So the blessed One who blesseth all the others,
        Will bless them another day.
105 They answer, "Who is God that He should hear us,
        While the rushing of the iron wheels is stirred?
When we sob aloud, the human creatures near us
        Pass by, hearing not, or answer not a word.
And *we* hear not (for the wheels in their resounding)
110   Strangers speaking at the door:
Is it likely God, with angels singing round him,
        Hears our weeping any more?

10

"Two words, indeed, of praying we remember,
        And at midnight's hour of harm,
115 'Our Father,' looking upward in the chamber,
        We say softly for a charm.[2]
We know no other words except 'Our Father,'
        And we think that, in some pause of angels' song,
God may pluck them with the silence sweet to gather,
120   And hold both within His right hand which is strong.

---

[1] *prove* Test.

[2] [Barrett Browning's note] A fact rendered pathetically historical by Mr. Horne's report of his commission. The name of the poet of *Orion* and *Cosmo de' Medici* has, however, a change of associations, and comes in time to remind me that we have some noble poetic heat of literature still, however open to the reproach of being somewhat gelid in our humanity. [*gelid* Cold.]

'Our Father!' If He heard us, He would surely
        (For they call Him good and mild)
Answer, smiling down the steep world very purely,
        'Come and rest with me, my child.'"

11

125 "But no!" say the children, weeping faster,
        "He is speechless as a stone:
And they tell us, of His image is the master
        Who commands us to work on.
Go to!" say the children,—"up in heaven,
130   Dark, wheel-like, turning clouds are all we find.
Do not mock us; grief has made us unbelieving:
        We look up for God, but tears have made us blind."
Do you hear the children weeping and disproving,
        O my brothers, what ye preach?
135 For God's possible is taught by His world's loving,
        And the children doubt of each.

12

And well may the children weep before you!
        They are weary ere they run;
They have never seen the sunshine, nor the glory
140   Which is brighter than the sun.
They know the grief of man, without its wisdom;
        They sink in man's despair, without its calm;
Are slaves, without the liberty in Christdom,
        Are martyrs, by the pang without the palm;[3]
145 Are worn as if with age, yet unretrievingly
        The harvest of its memories cannot reap,—
Are orphans of the earthly love and heavenly.
        Let them weep! let them weep!

13

They look up with their pale and sunken faces,
150   And their look is dread to see,
For they mind you of their angels in high places,
        With eyes turned on Deity!
"How long," they say, "how long, O cruel nation,
        Will you stand, to move the world, on a child's heart,—

---

[3] *palm* In Christianity, a symbol of spiritual victory especially associated with martyrs.

55 Stifle down with a mailed° heel its palpitation,   *armored*
    And tread onward to your throne amid the mart?[1]
Our blood splashes upward, O gold-heaper,
    And your purple shows your path!
But the child's sob in the silence curses deeper
60   Than the strong man in his wrath."
—1844

To George Sand[2]
A Desire

Thou large-brained woman and large-hearted man,
    Self-called George Sand! whose soul, amid the lions
Of thy tumultuous senses, moans defiance
And answers roar for roar, as spirits can:
5 I would some mild miraculous thunder ran
Above the applauded circus, in appliance°   *application*
Of thine own nobler nature's strength and science,
Drawing two pinions,° white as wings of swan,   *wings*
From thy strong shoulders, to amaze the place
10 With holier light! that thou to woman's claim
And man's, mightst join beside the angel's grace
Of a pure genius sanctified from blame,
Till child and maiden pressed to thine embrace
To kiss upon thy lips a stainless fame.
—1844

To George Sand
A Recognition

True genius, but true woman! dost deny
    The woman's nature with a manly scorn,
And break away the gauds° and armlets worn   *ornaments*
By weaker women in captivity?
5 Ah, vain denial! that revolted cry

Is sobbed in by a woman's voice forlorn,—
Thy woman's hair, my sister, all unshorn
Floats back dishevelled strength in agony,
Disproving thy man's name: and while before
10 The world thou burnest in a poet fire,
We see thy woman heart beat evermore
Through the large flame. Beat purer, heart, and higher,
Till God unsex[3] thee on the heavenly shore
Where unincarnate spirits purely aspire!
—1844

A Year's Spinning[4]

1

He listened at the porch that day,
    To hear the wheel go on, and on;
And then it stopped, ran back away,
    While through the door he brought the sun:
    5 But now my spinning is all done.

2

He sat beside me, with an oath
    That love ne'er ended, once begun;
I smiled—believing for us both,
    What was the truth for only one:
10   And now my spinning is all done.

3

My mother cursed me that[5] I heard
    A young man's wooing as I spun:
Thanks, cruel mother, for that word—
    For I have, since, a harder known!
15   And now my spinning is all done.

4

I thought—O God!—my firstborn's cry
    Both voices to mine ear would drown:

---

1   *mart* Marketplace, especially a crowded one.

2   *George Sand* Pseudonym of French author Amandine Aurore Lucie Dupin (1804–76), who was often condemned for her free-spirited ways, which included wearing men's clothing. For images of Sand see "In Context: Images of George Sand," on the companion website.

3   *unsex* Here, remove the qualities traditionally associated with femininity.

4   *Spinning* The act of producing yarn or thread with the use of the spinning wheel.

5   *cursed me that* Berated me because.

I listened in mine agony—
    It was the *silence* made me groan!
20   And now my spinning is all done.

5

Bury me 'twixt my mother's grave,
    (Who cursed me on her deathbed lone)
And my dead baby's (God it save!)
    Who, not to bless me, would not moan.
25   And now my spinning is all done.

6

A stone upon my heart and head,
    But no name written on the stone!
Sweet neighbours, whisper low instead,
    "This sinner was a loving one—
30   And now her spinning is all done."

7

And let the door ajar remain,
    In case he should pass by anon;°   *at some time*
And leave the wheel out very plain,—
    That HE, when passing in the sun,
35   May see the spinning is all done.
—1850

The Runaway Slave at Pilgrim's Point

1

I stand on the mark beside the shore
    Of the first white pilgrim's bended knee,
Where exile turned to ancestor,[1]
    And God was thanked for liberty.
5 I have run through the night, my skin is as dark,
I bend my knee down on this mark:
    I look on the sky and the sea.

2

O pilgrim-souls, I speak to you!
    I see you come proud and slow
10 From the land of the spirits pale as dew
    And round me and round me ye go.
O pilgrims, I have gasped and run
All night long from the whips of one
    Who in your names works sin and woe!

3

15 And thus I thought that I would come
    And kneel here where you knelt before,
And feel your souls around me hum
    In undertone to the ocean's roar;
And lift my black face, my black hand,
20 Here, in your names, to curse this land
    Ye blessed in freedom's, evermore.

4

I am black, I am black,
    And yet God made me, they say:
But if He did so, smiling back
25   He must have cast His work away
Under the feet of His white creatures,
With a look of scorn, that the dusky features
    Might be trodden again to clay.

5

And yet He has made dark things
30   To be glad and merry as light:
There's a little dark bird sits and sings,
    There's a dark stream ripples out of sight,
And the dark frogs chant in the safe morass,°   *swamp*
And the sweetest stars are made to pass
35   O'er the face of the darkest night.

6

But *we* who are dark, we are dark!
    Ah God, we have no stars!
About our souls in care and cark°   *troubles*
    Our blackness shuts like prison bars:
40 The poor souls crouch so far behind

---

[1] *Where exile turned to ancestor* The place where colonists, now ancestors, once stood. Though not exiles in the strictest sense, many early colonists left Britain to escape religious persecution.

That never a comfort can they find
　　By reaching through the prison bars.

7

Indeed we live beneath the sky,
　　That great smooth Hand of God stretched out
45 On all his children fatherly,
　　To save them from the dread and doubt
Which would be if, from this low place,
All opened straight up to His face
　　Into the grand eternity.

8

50 And still God's sunshine and His frost,
　　They make us hot, they make us cold,
As if we were not black and lost;
　　And the beasts and birds, in wood and fold,
Do fear and take us for very men:
55 Could the whippoorwill or the cat of the glen
　　Look into my eyes and be bold?

9

I am black, I am black!
　　But, once, I laughed in girlish glee,
For one of my colour stood in the track
60 　Where the drivers drove, and looked at me,
And tender and full was the look he gave—
Could a slave look *so* at another slave?—
　　I look at the sky and sea.

10

And from that hour our spirits grew
65 　As free as if unsold, unbought:
Oh, strong enough, since we were two,
　　To conquer the world, we thought.
The drivers drove us day by day;
We did not mind, we went one way,
70 　And no better a freedom sought.

11

In the sunny ground between the canes,°   *sugar canes*
　　He said "I love you" as he passed;

When the shingle roof rang sharp with the rains,
　　I heard how he vowed it fast:
75 While others shook he smiled in the hut,
　　As he carved me a bowl of the coconut
　　Through the roar of the hurricanes.

12

I sang his name instead of a song,
　　Over and over I sang his name,
80 Upward and downward I drew it along
　　My various notes,—the same, the same!
I sang it low, that the slave girls near
Might never guess, from aught they could hear,
　　It was only a name—a name.

13

85 I look on the sky and the sea.
　　We were two to love, and two to pray:
Yes, two, O God, who cried to Thee,
　　Though nothing didst Thou say!
Coldly Thou sat'st behind the sun:
90 And now I cry who am but one,
　　Thou wilt not speak today.

14

We were black, we were black,
　　We had no claim to love and bliss,
What marvel if each went to wrack?°   *ruin*
95 　They wrung my cold hands out of his
They dragged him—where? I crawled to touch
His blood's mark in the dust ... not much,
　　Ye pilgrim-souls, though plain as this!

15

Wrong, followed by a deeper wrong!
100 　Mere grief's too good for such as I:
So the white men brought the shame ere long
　　To strangle the sob of my agony.
They would not leave me for my dull
Wet eyes!—it was too merciful
105 　To let me weep pure tears and die.

16

I am black, I am black!
   I wore a child upon my breast,
An amulet that hung too slack,
   And, in my unrest, could not rest:
110 Thus we went moaning, child and mother,
One to another, one to another,
   Until all ended for the best.

17

For hark! I will tell you low, low,
   I am black, you see,—
115 And the babe who lay on my bosom so,
   Was far too white, too white for me;
As white as the ladies who scorned to pray
Beside me at church but yesterday,
   Though my tears had washed a place for my knee.

18

120 My own, own child! I could not bear
   To look in his face, it was so white;
I covered him up with a kerchief there,
   I covered his face in close and tight:
And he moaned and struggled, as well might be,
125 For the white child wanted his liberty—
   Ha, ha! he wanted the master right.

19

He moaned and beat with his head and feet,
   His little feet that never grew;
He struck them out, as it was meet,°   *proper*
130   Against my heart to break it through:
I might have sung and made him mild,
But I dared not sing to the white-faced child
   The only song I knew.

20

I pulled the kerchief very close:
135   He could not see the sun, I swear,
More, then, alive, than now he does
   From between the roots of the mango … where?
I know where. Close! A child and mother

Do wrong to look at one another
140   When one is black and one is fair.

21

Why, in that single glance I had
   Of my child's face, … I tell you all,
I saw a look that made me mad!
   The master's look, that used to fall
145 On my soul like his lash … or worse!
And so, to save it from my curse,
   I twisted it round in my shawl.

22

And he moaned and trembled from foot to head,
   He shivered from head to foot;
150 Till after a time, he lay instead
   Too suddenly still and mute.
I felt, beside, a stiffening cold:
I dared to lift up just a fold,
   As in lifting a leaf of the mango fruit.

23

155 But *my* fruit … ha, ha!—there, had been
   (I laugh to think on't at this hour!)
Your fine white angels (who have seen
   Nearest the secret of God's power)
And plucked my fruit to make them wine,
160 And sucked the soul of that child of mine
   As the hummingbird sucks the soul of the flower.

24

Ha, ha, the trick of the angels white!
   They freed the white child's spirit so.
I said not a word, but day and night
165   I carried the body to and fro,
And it lay on my heart like a stone, as chill.
—The sun may shine out as much as he will:
   I am cold, though it happened a month ago.

25

From the white man's house, and the black man's hut,
170   I carried the little body on;

The forest's arms did round us shut,
    And silence through the trees did run:
They asked no question as I went,
They stood too high for astonishment,
175   They could see God sit on His throne.

26

My little body, kerchiefed fast,
    I bore it on through the forest, on;
And when I felt it was tired at last,
    I scooped a hole beneath the moon:
180 Through the forest tops the angels far,
With a white sharp finger from every star,
    Did point and mock at what was done.

27

Yet when it was all done aright,—
    Earth, 'twixt me and my baby, strewed,—
185 All, changed to black earth,—nothing white,—
    A dark child in the dark!—ensued
Some comfort, and my heart grew young;
I sat down smiling there and sung
    The song I learnt in my maidenhood.

28

190 And thus we two were reconciled,
    The white child and black mother, thus;
For as I sang it soft and wild,
    The same song, more melodious,
Rose from the grave whereon I sat:
195 It was the dead child singing that,
    To join the souls of both of us.

29

I look on the sea and the sky.
    Where the pilgrims' ships first anchored lay
The free sun rideth gloriously,
200   But the pilgrim-ghosts have slid away
Through the earliest streaks of the morn:
My face is black, but it glares with a scorn
    Which they dare not meet by day.

30

Ha!—in their stead, their hunter sons!
205   Ha, ha! they are on me—they hunt in a ring!
Keep off! I brave you all at once,
    I throw off your eyes like snakes that sting!
You have killed the black eagle at nest, I think:
Did you ever stand still in your triumph, and shrink
210   From the stroke of her wounded wing?

31

(Man, drop that stone you dared to lift!—)
    I wish you who stand there five abreast,
Each, for his own wife's joy and gift,
    A little corpse as safely at rest
215 As mine in the mangoes! Yes, but she
May keep live babies on her knee,
    And sing the song she likes the best.

32

I am not mad: I am black.
    I see you staring in my face—
220 I know you staring, shrinking back,
    Ye are born of the Washington race,
And this land is the free America,
And this mark on my wrist—(I prove what I say)
    Ropes tied me up here to the flogging place.

33

225 You think I shrieked then? Not a sound!
    I hung, as a gourd hangs in the sun;
I only cursed them all around
    As softly as I might have done
My very own child: from these sands
230 Up to the mountains, lift your hands,
    O slaves, and end what I begun!

34

Whips, curses; these must answer those!
    For in this UNION you have set
Two kinds of men in adverse rows,
235   Each loathing each; and all forget
The seven wounds in Christ's body fair,
While HE sees gaping everywhere
    Our countless wounds that pay no debt.

35

Our wounds are different. Your white men
240   Are, after all, not gods indeed,
Nor able to make Christs again
         Do good with bleeding. We who bleed
(Stand off!) we help not in our loss!
We are too heavy for our cross,
245   And fall and crush you and your seed.

36

I fall, I swoon! I look at the sky.
         The clouds are breaking on my brain;
I am floated along, as if I should die
         Of liberty's exquisite pain.
250   In the name of the white child waiting for me
In the death dark where we may kiss and agree,
White men, I leave you all curse-free
         In my broken heart's disdain!
—1850

from *Sonnets from the Portuguese*

1

I thought once how Theocritus[1] had sung
Of the sweet years, the dear and wished-for years,
Who each one in a gracious hand appears
To bear a gift for mortals, old or young:
5   And, as I mused it in his antique tongue,[2]
I saw, in gradual vision through my tears,
The sweet, sad years, the melancholy years,
Those of my own life, who by turns had flung
A shadow across me. Straightway I was 'ware,
10   So weeping, how a mystic Shape did move
Behind me, and drew me backward by the hair;
And a voice said in mastery, while I strove—
"Guess now who holds thee?"—"Death," I said. But,
         there,
The silver answer rang—"Not Death, but Love."

---

[1] *Theocritus*   Greek poet of the third century BCE who created the genre of the pastoral (characterized by idyllic country life and love between shepherds and shepherdesses).

[2] *antique tongue*   Ancient Greek language.

7

The face of all the world is changed, I think,
Since first I heard the footsteps of thy soul
Move still, oh, still, beside me, as they stole
Betwixt me and the dreadful outer brink
5   Of obvious death, where I, who thought to sink,
Was caught up into love, and taught the whole
Of life in a new rhythm. The cup of dole[3]
God gave for baptism, I am fain° to drink,   *glad*
And praise its sweetness, Sweet, with thee anear.
10   The names of country, heaven, are changed away
For where thou art or shalt be, there or here;
And this … this lute and song … loved yesterday,
(The singing angels know) are only dear
Because thy name moves right in what they say.

13

And wilt thou have me fasten into speech
The love I bear thee, finding words enough,
And hold the torch out, while the winds are rough,
Between our faces, to cast light on each?—
5   I drop it at thy feet. I cannot teach
My hand to hold my spirit so far off
From myself—me—that I should bring thee proof
In words, of love hid in me out of reach.
Nay, let the silence of my womanhood
10   Commend my woman-love to thy belief—
Seeing that I stand unwon, however wooed,
And rend the garment of my life, in brief,
By a most dauntless, voiceless fortitude,
Lest one touch of this heart convey its grief.

21

Say over again, and yet once over again,
That thou dost love me. Though the word repeated
Should seem "a cuckoo-song," as thou dost treat it,
Remember, never to the hill or plain,
5   Valley and wood, without her cuckoo-strain
Comes the fresh Spring in all her green completed.
Belovèd, I, amid the darkness greeted

---

[3] *dole*   Misery. See Mark 10.38: "Ye know not what ye ask: can ye drink of the cup that I drink of? and be baptized with the baptism that I am baptized with?"

By a doubtful spirit-voice, in that doubt's pain
Cry, "Speak once more—thou lovest!" Who can fear
10 Too many stars, though each in heaven shall roll,
Too many flowers, though each shall crown the year?
Say thou dost love me, love me, love me—toll
The silver iterance![1]—only minding, Dear,
To love me also in silence with thy soul.

22

When our two souls stand up erect and strong,
  Face to face, silent, drawing nigh°   *near*
  and nigher,
Until the lengthening wings break into fire
At either curvèd point—what bitter wrong
5 Can the earth do to us, that we should not long
Be here contented? Think. In mounting higher,
The angels would press on us and aspire
To drop some golden orb of perfect song
Into our deep, dear silence. Let us stay
10 Rather on earth, Belovèd—where the unfit
Contrarious moods of men recoil away
And isolate pure spirits, and permit
A place to stand and love in for a day,
With darkness and the death hour rounding it.

24

Let the world's sharpness, like a clasping knife,
  Shut in upon itself and do no harm
In this close hand of Love, now soft and warm,
And let us hear no sound of human strife
5 After the click of the shutting. Life to life—
I lean upon thee, Dear, without alarm,
And feel as safe as guarded by a charm
Against the stab of worldlings, who if rife[2]
Are weak to injure. Very whitely still
10 The lilies of our lives may reassure
Their blossoms from their roots, accessible
Alone to heavenly dews that drop not fewer,
Growing straight, out of man's reach, on the hill.
God only, who made us rich, can make us poor.

26

I lived with visions for my company
  Instead of men and women, years ago,
And found them gentle mates, nor thought to know
A sweeter music than they played to me.
5 But soon their trailing purple[3] was not free
Of this world's dust, their lutes did silent grow,
And I myself grew faint and blind below
Their vanishing eyes. Then *thou* didst come—to be,
Belovèd, what they seemed. Their shining fronts,
10 Their songs, their splendours (better, yet the same,
As river water hallowed into fonts[4]),
Met in thee, and from out thee overcame
My soul with satisfaction of all wants:
Because God's gifts put man's best dreams to shame.

28

My letters! all dead paper, mute and white!
  And yet they seem alive and quivering
Against my tremulous hands which loose the string
And let them drop down on my knee tonight.
5 This said—he wished to have me in his sight
Once, as a friend: this fixed a day in spring
To come and touch my hand … a simple thing,
Yet I wept for it!—this, … the paper's light …
Said, *Dear, I love thee*; and I sank and quailed
10 As if God's future thundered on my past.
This said, *I am thine*—and so its ink has paled
With lying at my heart that beat too fast.
And this … O Love, thy words have ill availed
If, what this said, I dared repeat at last!

43

How do I love thee? Let me count the ways.
  I love thee to the depth and breadth and height
My soul can reach, when feeling out of sight
For the ends of Being and ideal Grace.
5 I love thee to the level of every day's
Most quiet need, by sun and candle-light.
I love thee freely, as men strive for Right;
I love thee purely, as they turn from Praise.

---

1 *iterance* Repetition.

2 *if rife* Even if widespread.

3 *their trailing purple* Purple robes are closely associated with royalty.

4 *hallowed* Made holy; *fonts* Vessels used for holy water.

I love thee with the passion put to use
10 In my old griefs, and with my childhood's faith.
I love thee with a love I seemed to lose
With my lost saints[1]—I love thee with the breath,
Smiles, tears, of all my life!—and, if God choose,
I shall but love thee better after death.
—1845–47

Aurora Leigh

Published in 1856, *Aurora Lee* dazzled and baffled its first readers because of its size (close to 11,000 lines) and its focus on a fictional female poet. This mixed reception changed by the end of the century, when it was embraced for its poetics and treatment of gender politics. In 1857, George Eliot remarked that the poem gave her "a deeper sense of communion with a large as well as beautiful mind." Her religious language is telling. Indeed, when in 1896, Fanny Zampini-Salazer described the poem as "the gospel of woman," she captured Browning's engagement with the issues of sexual, political, artistic, and economic liberty that one observes in Rossetti's "Goblin Market," Mill's *The Subjection of Women*, and Sarah Grand's writing—the issues that inform the "New Woman" debate.

The poem is a *Künstlerroman*, the story of a poet's artistic development as she loses her parents and travels from her childhood home in Italy to England. There she discovers books and a desire to write, and struggles to find her voice as she contends with the patriarchal world: the marital advances of her cousin Romney; the story of the "fallen woman" Marian Erle; and her growth as a poet who finds critical but little popular or financial success.

In such a world, Aurora's struggles as a woman and as a poet are intertwined as she attempts to throw "off the old conventions"—literary and cultural (1.177). Although Browning commented that the poem is "an autobiography of a poetess— (not me)," her life and Aurora's overlap. Both poets work to craft a female voice in a patriarchal literary tradition. Dubbing *Aurora Leigh* "a novel-poem," Browning established a feminist, hybridic genre that shares narrative elements with the Victorian novel.

There is also an epic quality to the poem that places it alongside Milton's *Paradise Lost*, Tennyson's *In Memoriam*, and Wordsworth's *Prelude*. All are epics that expand and reinvent the conventions and history of the genre, and in this context Browning faces the challenge of all poets: writing in the present, in the "throbbing age," with a "double vision" that requires keeping the past in sight (5. 184–203). In doing so, she explores gendered aesthetics in political and cultural contexts of Victorian England but with an eye to the future. She offers a forward-looking epic in many ways resembling that which Thomas Carlyle has in mind in *Past and Present*: "The future Epic of the World rests not with those that are near dead, but with those that are alive, and those that are coming into life" (38).

from *Aurora Leigh*

BOOK 1

Of writing many books there is no end;[2]
And I who have written much in prose and verse
For others' uses, will write now for mine—
Will write my story for my better self,
5 As when you paint your portrait for a friend,
Who keeps it in a drawer and looks at it
Long after he has ceased to love you, just
To hold together what he was and is.

I, writing thus, am still what men call young;
10 I have not so far left the coasts of life
To travel inward, that I cannot hear
That murmur of the outer Infinite[3]
Which unweaned babies smile at in their sleep
When wondered at for smiling; not so far,

---

[1] *lost saints* Saints for whom the speaker no longer feels youthful religious fervor.

[2] *Of writing … end* See Ecclesiastes 12.12: "[O]f making many books there is no end; and much study is a weariness of the flesh."

[3] *I have not so far … outer Infinite* Cf. William Wordsworth's "Ode: Intimations of Immortality from Recollections of Early Childhood," 9.

15 But still I catch my mother at her post
Beside the nursery door, with finger up,
"Hush, hush—here's too much noise!" while her
    sweet eyes
Leap forward, taking part against her word
In the child's riot. Still I sit and feel
20 My father's slow hand, when she had left us both,
Stroke out my childish curls across his knee,
And hear Assunta's daily jest (she knew
He liked it better than a better jest)
Inquire how many golden scudi[1] went
25 To make such ringlets. O my father's hand,
Stroke heavily, heavily the poor hair down,
Draw, press the child's head closer to thy knee!
I'm still too young, too young, to sit alone.

I write. My mother was a Florentine,
30 Whose rare blue eyes were shut from seeing me
When scarcely I was four years old, my life
A poor spark snatched up from a failing lamp
Which went out therefore. She was weak and frail;
She could not bear the joy of giving life,
35 The mother's rapture slew her. If her kiss
Had left a longer weight upon my lips
It might have steadied the uneasy breath,
And reconciled and fraternised° my soul   *befriended*
With the new order. As it was, indeed,
40 I felt a mother-want about the world,
And still went seeking, like a bleating lamb
Left out at night in shutting up the fold—
As restless as a nest-deserted bird
Grown chill through something being away, though
    what
45 It knows not. I, Aurora Leigh, was born
To make my father sadder, and myself
Not overjoyous, truly. Women know
The way to rear up children (to be just),
They know a simple, merry, tender knack
50 Of tying sashes, fitting baby shoes,
And stringing pretty words that make no sense,
And kissing full sense into empty words,

Which things are corals[2] to cut life upon,
Although such trifles: children learn by such,
55 Love's holy earnest in a pretty play
And get not over-early solemnised,
But seeing, as in a rose-bush, Love's Divine
Which burns and hurts not,[3]—not a single bloom—
Become aware and unafraid of Love.
60 Such good do mothers. Fathers love as well
—Mine did, I know—but still with heavier brains,
And wills more consciously responsible,
And not as wisely, since less foolishly;
So mothers have God's license to be missed.

65 My father was an austere Englishman,
Who, after a dry lifetime spent at home
In college learning, law, and parish talk,
Was flooded with a passion unaware,
His whole provisioned and complacent past
70 Drowned out from him that moment. As he stood
In Florence, where he had come to spend a month
And note the secret of da Vinci's drains,[4]
He musing somewhat absently perhaps
Some English question … whether men should pay
75 The unpopular but necessary tax
With left or right hand—in the alien sun
In that great square of the Santissima[5]
There drifted past him (scarcely marked°   *noticed*
    enough
To move his comfortable island scorn)
80 A train of priestly banners, cross and psalm,
The white-veiled rose-crowned maidens holding up
Tall tapers, weighty for such wrists, aslant
To the blue luminous tremor of the air,
And letting drop the white wax as they went
85 To eat the bishop's wafer[6] at the church;

---

[1] *scudi* Italian coins no longer in use.

[2] *corals* Babies' teething toys made of polished coral.

[3] *rose-bush … hurts not* See Exodus 3.2, in which God appears in a burning bush.

[4] *da Vinci's drains* Leonardo da Vinci (1452–1519), Renaissance painter, sculptor, architect, and engineer, invented a system of drainage canals.

[5] *Santissima* Florence's baroque church of Santissima Annunziata.

[6] *eat the bishop's wafer* Receive Holy Communion.

From which long trail of chanting priests and girls,
A face flashed like a cymbal on his face
And shook with silent clangour brain and heart,
Transfiguring him to music. Thus, even thus,
90 He too received his sacramental gift
With eucharistic[1] meanings; for he loved.

And thus beloved, she died. I've heard it said
That but to see him in the first surprise
Of widower and father, nursing me,
95 Unmothered little child of four years old,
His large man's hands afraid to touch my curls,
As if the gold would tarnish—his grave lips
Contriving such a miserable smile
As if he knew needs must, or I should die,
100 And yet 'twas hard—would almost make the stones
Cry out for pity.[2] There's a verse he set
In Santa Croce[3] to her memory—
"Weep for an infant too young to weep much
When death removed this mother"—stops the mirth
105 Today on women's faces when they walk
With rosy children hanging on their gowns,
Under the cloister[4] to escape the sun
That scorches in the piazza.[5] After which
He left our Florence and made haste to hide
110 Himself, his prattling child, and silent grief,
Among the mountains above Pelago;[6]
Because unmothered babes, he thought, had need
Of mother nature more than others use,
And Pan's[7] white goats, with udders warm and full
115 Of mystic contemplations, come to feed
Poor milkless lips of orphans like his own—
Such scholar-scraps he talked, I've heard from friends,

For even prosaic men who wear grief long
Will get to wear it as a hat aside
120 With a flower stuck in't. Father, then, and child,
We lived among the mountains many years,
God's silence on the outside of the house,
And we who did not speak too loud within,
And old Assunta to make up the fire,
125 Crossing herself whene'er a sudden flame
Which lightened from the firewood, made alive
That picture of my mother on the wall.

The painter drew it after she was dead,
And when the face was finished, throat and hands,
130 Her cameriera[8] carried him, in hate
Of the English-fashioned shroud, the last brocade
She dressed in at the Pitti;[9] "he should paint
No sadder thing than that," she swore, "to wrong
Her poor signora." Therefore very strange
135 The effect was. I, a little child, would crouch
For hours upon the floor with knees drawn up,
And gaze across them, half in terror, half
In adoration, at the picture there—
That swan-like supernatural white life
140 Just sailing upward from the red stiff silk
Which seemed to have no part in it nor power
To keep it from quite breaking out of bounds.
For hours I sat and stared. Assunta's awe
And my poor father's melancholy eyes
145 Still pointed that way. That way went my thoughts
When wandering beyond sight. And as I grew
In years, I mixed, confused, unconsciously,
Whatever I last read or heard or dreamed,
Abhorrent, admirable, beautiful,
150 Pathetical, or ghastly, or grotesque,
With still that face … which did not therefore change,
But kept the mystic level of all forms,
Hates, fears, and admirations, was by turns
Ghost, fiend, and angel, fairy, witch, and sprite,

---

[1] *eucharistic* Having to do with the Christian rite of Communion.

[2] *make the stones / Cry out for pity* Cf. Jesus' speech to the Pharisees in Luke 19.40: "If these should hold their peace, the stones would immediately cry out."

[3] *Santa Croce* Gothic church in Florence.

[4] *cloister* Covered walkway, usually between a wall and an open area.

[5] *piazza* City square.

[6] *Pelago* Village near Florence.

[7] *Pan* Greek god of Nature who was half goat and half man, and to whom white goats were sacred.

---

[8] *cameriera* Maid.

[9] *Pitti* Renaissance palace in Florence, former home of the Medicis and other royal families.

155 A dauntless Muse who eyes a dreadful Fate,[1]
A loving Psyche[2] who loses sight of Love,
A still Medusa[3] with mild milky brows
All curdled and all clothed upon with snakes
Whose slime falls fast as sweat will; or anon
160 Our Lady of the Passion, stabbed with swords
Where the Babe sucked; or Lamia[4] in her first
Moonlighted pallor, ere she shrunk and blinked
And shuddering wriggled down to the unclean;
Or my own mother, leaving her last smile
165 In her last kiss upon the baby-mouth
My father pushed down on the bed for that—
Or my dead mother, without smile or kiss,
Buried at Florence. All which images,
Concentred[5] on the picture, glassed themselves
170 Before my meditative childhood, as
The incoherencies of change and death
Are represented fully, mixed and merged,
In the smooth fair mystery of perpetual Life.

And while I stared away my childish wits
175 Upon my mother's picture (ah, poor child!),
My father, who through love had suddenly
Thrown off the old conventions, broken loose
From chin-bands of the soul, like Lazarus,[6]

Yet had no time to learn to talk and walk
180 Or grow anew familiar with the sun—
Who had reached to freedom, not to action, lived,
But lived as one entranced, with thoughts, not aims—
Whom love had unmade from a common man
But not completed to an uncommon man—
185 My father taught me what he had learnt the best
Before he died and left me—grief and love.
And, seeing we had books among the hills,
Strong words of counselling souls confederate°   allied
With vocal pines and waters—out of books
190 He taught me all the ignorance of men,
And how God laughs in heaven when any man
Says "Here I'm learned; this, I understand;
In that, I am never caught at fault or doubt."
He sent the schools to school, demonstrating
195 A fool will pass for such through one mistake,
While a philosopher will pass for such,
Through said mistakes being ventured in the gross
And heaped up to a system.
                                              I am like,
They tell me, my dear father. Broader brows
200 Howbeit, upon a slenderer undergrowth
Of delicate features—paler, near as grave;
But then my mother's smile breaks up the whole,
And makes it better sometimes than itself.

So, nine full years, our days were hid with God
205 Among his mountains: I was just thirteen,
Still growing like the plants from unseen roots
In tongue-tied Springs—and suddenly awoke
To full life and life's needs and agonies
With an intense, strong, struggling heart beside
210 A stone-dead father. Life, struck sharp on death,
Makes awful lightning. His last word was "Love—"
"Love, my child, love, love!"—(then he had done with
    grief)
"Love, my child." Ere I answered he was gone,
And none was left to love in all the world.

215 There, ended childhood. What succeeded next
I recollect as, after fevers, men
Thread back the passage of delirium,

---

[1] *Muse* One of the nine goddesses of the arts and sciences in Greek and Roman mythology; *Fate* One of three goddesses of fate and destiny in Greek and Roman mythology.

[2] *Psyche* Mortal daughter of royalty in Greek mythology. Eros, the god of love, visited Psyche in the dark of night as her lover, but he abandoned her after she disobeyed his command not to look at him.

[3] *Medusa* One of the three Gorgons, who was made mortal after claiming she was more beautiful than Athena. Medusa was transformed into a monster with hair made of snakes, whose gaze would turn men to stone.

[4] *Lady … Babe sucked* Catholic iconology portrays the Virgin Mary stabbed through the heart with the seven swords of grief (the seven sorrows) upon the events leading up to and the crucifixion of Christ, her son; *Lamia* After the goddess Hera killed her children, the mortal Lamia turned to killing others' children out of revenge.

[5] *Concentred* Converged.

[6] *chin-bands … Lazarus* Cloth used to hold a corpse's mouth closed. John 11.44 speaks of Lazarus rising from the dead, "bound hand and foot with graveclothes: and his face was bound about with a napkin. Jesus saith unto them, Loose him, and let him go."

Missing the turn still, baffled by the door;
Smooth endless days, notched here and there with knives,
220   A weary, wormy darkness, spurred i' the flank
With flame, that it should eat and end itself
Like some tormented scorpion.[1] Then at last
I do remember clearly how there came
A stranger with authority, not right
225   (I thought not), who commanded, caught me up
From old Assunta's neck; how, with a shriek,
She let me go—while I, with ears too full
Of my father's silence to shriek back a word,
In all a child's astonishment at grief
230   Stared at the wharf edge where she stood and moaned,
My poor Assunta, where she stood and moaned!
The white walls, the blue hills, my Italy,
Drawn backward[2] from the shuddering steamer deck,
Like one in anger drawing back her skirts
235   Which suppliants catch at. Then the bitter sea
Inexorably pushed between us both
And, sweeping up the ship with my despair,
Threw us out as a pasture to the stars.

Ten nights and days we voyaged on the deep;
240   Ten nights and days without the common face
Of any day or night; the moon and sun
Cut off from the green reconciling earth,
To starve into a blind ferocity
And glare unnatural; the very sky
245   (Dropping its bell-net down upon the sea,
As if no human heart should 'scape alive)
Bedraggled with the desolating salt,
Until it seemed no more that holy heaven
To which my father went. All new and strange;
250   The universe turned stranger, for a child.

Then, land!—then, England! oh, the frosty cliffs
Looked cold upon me. Could I find a home
Among those mean red houses through the fog?
And when I heard my father's language first
255   From alien lips which had no kiss for mine

I wept aloud, then laughed, then wept, then wept,
And someone near me said the child was mad
Through much seasickness. The train swept us on:
Was this my father's England? the great isle?
260   The ground seemed cut up from the fellowship
Of verdure,° field from field, as man from man;   greenery
The skies themselves looked low and positive,
As almost you could touch them with a hand,
And dared to do it they were so far off
265   From God's celestial crystals;[3] all things blurred
And dull and vague. Did Shakespeare and his mates
Absorb the light here?—not a hill or stone
With heart to strike a radiant colour up
Or active outline on the indifferent air.

270   I think I see my father's sister stand
Upon the hall step of her country house
To give me welcome. She stood straight and calm,
Her somewhat narrow forehead braided tight
As if for taming accidental thoughts
275   From possible pulses; brown hair pricked with gray
By frigid use of life (she was not old,
Although my father's elder by a year),
A nose drawn sharply, yet in delicate lines;
A close mild mouth, a little soured about
280   The ends, through speaking unrequited loves
Or peradventure niggardly° half-truths;   stingy
Eyes of no colour—once they might have smiled,
But never, never have forgot themselves
In smiling; cheeks, in which was yet a rose
285   Of perished summers, like a rose in a book,
Kept more for ruth° than pleasure—if past bloom,   pity
Past fading also.
                    She had lived, we'll say,
A harmless life, she called a virtuous life,
A quiet life, which was not life at all
290   (But that, she had not lived enough to know),
Between the vicar and the county squires,
The lord-lieutenant looking down sometimes
From the empyrean° to assure their souls   heaven

---

[1] *flame … scorpion* When surrounded by fire a scorpion will arch its back in protection; this habit is the source of the myth that it is stinging itself and dying by suicide.

[2] *Drawn backward* Receding.

[3] *God's celestial crystals* Reference to the notion from classical astronomy that the moon, stars, and other celestial or heavenly bodies were embedded in spheres made of crystal that rotated around the Earth.

Against chance vulgarisms, and, in the abyss,
295 The apothecary,[1] looked on once a year
To prove their soundness of humility.
The poor-club[2] exercised her Christian gifts
Of knitting stockings, stitching petticoats,
Because we are of one flesh, after all,
300 And need one flannel[3] (with a proper sense
Of difference in the quality)—and still
The book-club, guarded from your modern trick
Of shaking dangerous questions from the crease,
Preserved her intellectual. She had lived
305 A sort of cage-bird life, born in a cage,
Accounting that to leap from perch to perch
Was act and joy enough for any bird.
Dear heaven, how silly are the things that live
In thickets, and eat berries!
                               I, alas,
310 A wild bird scarcely fledged,[4] was brought to her cage,
And she was there to meet me. Very kind.
Bring the clean water, give out the fresh seed.

She stood upon the steps to welcome me,
Calm, in black garb. I clung about her neck—
315 Young babes, who catch at every shred of wool
To draw the new light closer, catch and cling
Less blindly. In my ears my father's word
Hummed ignorantly, as the sea in shells,
"Love, love, my child." She, black there with my grief,
320 Might feel my love—she was his sister once—
I clung to her. A moment she seemed moved,
Kissed me with cold lips, suffered me to cling,
And drew me feebly through the hall into
The room she sat in.
                        There, with some strange spasm
325 Of pain and passion, she wrung loose my hands
Imperiously, and held me at arm's length,
And with two grey-steel naked-bladed eyes
Searched through my face—ay, stabbed it through
   and through,

Through brows and cheeks and chin, as if to find
330 A wicked murderer in my innocent face,
If not here, there perhaps. Then, drawing breath,
She struggled for her ordinary calm—
And missed it rather—told me not to shrink,
As if she had told me not to lie or swear—
335 "She loved my father and would love me too
As long as I deserved it." Very kind.

I understood her meaning afterward;
She thought to find my mother in my face,
And questioned it for that. For she, my aunt,
340 Had loved my father truly, as she could,
And hated, with the gall of gentle souls,
My Tuscan mother who had fooled away
A wise man from wise courses, a good man
From obvious duties, and, depriving her,
345 His sister, of the household precedence,°   superiority
Had wronged his tenants, robbed his native land,
And made him mad, alike by life and death,
In love and sorrow. She had pored° for years   pondered
What sort of woman could be suitable
350 To her sort of hate, to entertain it with,
And so, her very curiosity
Became hate too, and all the idealism
She ever used in life was used for hate,
Till hate, so nourished, did exceed at last
355 The love from which it grew, in strength and heat,
And wrinkled her smooth conscience with a sense
Of disputable virtue (say not, sin)
When Christian doctrine was enforced at church.

And thus my father's sister was to me
360 My mother's hater. From that day she did
Her duty to me (I appreciate it
In her own word as spoken to herself),
Her duty, in large measure, well pressed out
But measured always. She was generous, bland,
365 More courteous than was tender, gave me still
The first place—as if fearful that God's saints
Would look down suddenly and say "Herein
You missed a point, I think, through lack of love."
Alas, a mother never is afraid

---

1 *apothecary* One who dispenses medicines (a low status profession).
2 *poor-club* Society for gathering and distributing material assistance to the poor.
3 *flannel* Soft, woven fabric made from wool or cotton.
4 *fledged* Mature enough to fly.

370 Of speaking angerly to any child,
Since love, she knows, is justified of love.

And I, I was a good child on the whole,
A meek and manageable child. Why not?
I did not live, to have the faults of life:
375 There seemed more true life in my father's grave
Than in all England. Since *that* threw me off
Who fain would cleave[1] (his latest will, they say,
Consigned me to his land), I only thought
Of lying quiet there where I was thrown
380 Like seaweed on the rocks, and suffering her
To prick me to a pattern with her pin,
Fibre from fibre, delicate leaf from leaf,
And dry out from my drowned anatomy
The last sea-salt left in me.
                               So it was.
385 I broke the copious curls upon my head
In braids, because she liked smooth-ordered hair.
I left off saying my sweet Tuscan words
Which still at any stirring of the heart
Came up to float across the English phrase
390 As lilies (*Bene* or *Che che*[2]), because
She liked my father's child to speak his tongue.
I learnt the collects and the catechism,[3]
The creeds, from Athanasius back to Nice,[4]
The Articles, the Tracts *against* the times[5]
395 (By no means Buonaventure's "Prick of Love"[6]),
And various popular synopses° of   *summaries*

Inhuman doctrines never taught by John,[7]
Because she liked instructed piety.
I learnt my complement of classic French
400 (Kept pure of Balzac and neologism[8])
And German also, since she liked a range
Of liberal education—tongues, not books.
I learnt a little algebra, a little
Of the mathematics—brushed with extreme flounce[9]
405 The circle of the sciences, because
She misliked women who are frivolous.
I learnt the royal genealogies
Of Oviedo,[10] the internal laws
Of the Burmese empire—by how many feet
410 Mount Chimborazo outsoars Teneriffe.[11]
What navigable river joins itself
To Lara,[12] and what census of the year five
Was taken at Klagenfurt,[13]—because she liked
A general insight into useful facts.
415 I learnt much music—such as would have been
As quite impossible in Johnson's day[14]
As still it might be wished—fine sleights of hand
And unimagined fingering, shuffling off
The hearer's soul through hurricanes of notes
420 To a noisy Tophet;° and I drew ... costumes   *Hell*
From French engravings, nereids° neatly   *sea nymphs*
         draped
(With smirks of simmering godship): I washed in
Landscapes from nature (rather say, washed out).

---

[1] *Who fain would cleave*   Who would gladly stay attached.

[2] *Bene or Che che*   Common Italian sayings.

[3] *collects*   Short prayers; *catechism*   Questions and answers in the Anglican *Book of Common Prayer*.

[4] *Athanasius ... Nice*   Doctrines of Athanasia and the Nicene Council, creeds of the Church of England.

[5] *Articles*   Thirty-nine articles in the Anglican doctrine; *the Tracts against the times*   Referring to the *Tracts for the Times*. The first tract was composed by John Henry Newman in 1833 and called for a return to the Catholic roots of the Anglican Church.

[6] *Buonaventure's "Prick of Love"*   Once incorrectly attributed to the thirteenth-century Franciscan theologian St. Bonaventure, *Stimulus Divini Amoris* ("God of Love") was actually written by Jacobus Mediolanensis in the fourteenth century. The devotional text concentrates on the emotional aspect of spirituality.

[7] *John*   One of Christ's twelve apostles and purported author of five books belonging to the New Testament.

[8] *Balzac*   French novelist Honoré de Balzac (1799–1850); *neologism* Newly invented language.

[9] *flounce*   Impatient speed.

[10] *Oviedo*   Gonzalo Fernandez de Oviedo y Valdez (1478–1557), Spanish historian, wrote a posthumously published book on the natural history of the Americas.

[11] *Mount Chimborazo outsoars Teneriffe*   One of Spain's Canary Islands, Tenerife has a peak just over half the height of Chimborazo, the highest mountain in the Andes of Ecuador.

[12] *Lara*   Town in Spain.

[13] *Klagenfurt*   Capital city of Carinthia (Kärnten) in Austria.

[14] *music ... Johnson's day*   The Classical and Baroque music popular during "Johnson's day" was extraordinarily difficult to play. Samuel Johnson (1709–84) once famously said of a renowned violinist's musical choice: "Difficult do you call it, Sir? I would it had been impossible."

I danced the polka and Cellarius,[1]
25 Spun glass, stuffed birds, and modelled flowers in wax,
Because she liked accomplishments in girls.
I read a score of books on womanhood
To prove, if women do not think at all,
They may teach thinking (to a maiden aunt
30 Or else the author)—books that boldly assert
Their right of comprehending husband's talk
When not too deep, and even of answering
With pretty "may it please you," or "so it is"—
Their rapid insight and fine aptitude,
35 Particular worth and general missionariness,
As long as they keep quiet by the fire
And never say "no" when the world says "ay,"
For that is fatal—their angelic reach
Of virtue, chiefly used to sit and darn,
40 And fatten household sinners—their, in brief,
Potential faculty in everything
Of abdicating power in it: she owned°   *declared*
She liked a woman to be womanly,
And English women, she thanked God and sighed
45 (Some people always sigh in thanking God)
Were models to the universe. And last
I learnt cross-stitch, because she did not like
To see me wear the night with empty hands
A-doing nothing. So, my shepherdess
50 Was something after all (the pastoral saints
Be praised for't), leaning lovelorn with pink eyes
To match her shoes, when I mistook the silks;
Her head uncrushed by that round weight of hat
So strangely similar to the tortoise-shell
55 Which slew the tragic poet.[2]
                                By the way,
The works of women are symbolical.
We sew, sew, prick our fingers, dull our sight,
Producing what? A pair of slippers, sir,
To put on when you're weary—or a stool
60 To stumble over and vex you … "curse that stool!"
Or else at best, a cushion, where you lean

And sleep, and dream of something we are not
But would be for your sake. Alas, alas!
This hurts most, this—that, after all, we are paid
465 The worth of our work, perhaps.
                                In looking down
Those years of education (to return)
I wonder if Brinvilliers suffered more
In the water torture[3] … flood succeeding flood
To drench the incapable throat and split the veins …
470 Than I did. Certain of your feebler souls
Go out in such a process; many pine°   *waste away*
To a sick, inodorous light; my own endured:
I had relations in the Unseen, and drew
The elemental nutriment and heat
475 From nature, as earth feels the sun at nights,
Or as a babe sucks surely in the dark.
I kept the life thrust on me, on the outside
Of the inner life with all its ample room
For heart and lungs, for will and intellect,
480 Inviolable by conventions. God,
I thank thee for that grace of thine!
                                At first
I felt no life which was not patience—did
The thing she bade me, without heed to a thing
Beyond it, sat in just the chair she placed,
485 With back against the window, to exclude
The sight of the great lime-tree on the lawn,
Which seemed to have come on purpose from the woods
To bring the house a message—ay, and walked
Demurely in her carpeted low rooms,
490 As if I should not, hearkening my own steps,
Misdoubt[4] I was alive. I read her books,
Was civil to her cousin, Romney Leigh,
Gave ear to her vicar, tea to her visitors,
And heard them whisper, when I changed a cup
495 (I blushed for joy at that)—"The Italian child,
For all her blue eyes and her quiet ways,
Thrives ill in England: she is paler yet
Than when we came the last time; she will die."

---

[1] *Cellarius* Waltz-Mazurka named after dance master Henri Cellarius in 1842.

[2] *tortoise-shell … poet* Greek tragedian Aeschylus (c. 525–456 BCE) was said to have been killed when an eagle dropped a tortoise on his bald head in order to crack the tortoise's shell.

---

[3] *Brinvilliers … water torture* The Parisian Marquise de Brinvilliers (1630–76) was tortured and eventually beheaded after being convicted of poisoning various members of her family.

[4] *Misdoubt* Question whether.

"Will die." My cousin, Romney Leigh, blushed too,
500 With sudden anger, and approaching me
Said low between his teeth, "You're wicked now?
You wish to die and leave the world a-dusk
For others, with your naughty light blown out?"
I looked into his face defyingly;
505 He might have know that, being what I was,
'Twas natural to like to get away
As far as dead folk can: and then indeed
Some people make no trouble when they die.
He turned and went abruptly, slammed the door,
510 And shut his dog out.
                              Romney, Romney Leigh.
I have not named my cousin hitherto,
And yet I used him as a sort of friend;
My elder by few years, but cold and shy
And absent … tender, when he thought of it,
515 Which scarcely was imperative, grave betimes,[1]
As well as early master of Leigh Hall,
Whereof the nightmare sat upon his youth,
Repressing all its seasonable delights,
And agonising with a ghastly sense
520 Of universal hideous want° and wrong   lack
To incriminate possession. When he came
From college to the country, very oft
He crossed the hill on visits to my aunt,
With gifts of blue grapes from the hothouses,
525 A book in one hand—mere statistics (if
I chanced to lift the cover), count of all
The goats whose beards grow sprouting down toward
      hell
Against God's separative judgment hour.[2]
And she, she almost loved him—even allowed
530 That sometimes he should seem to sigh my way;
It made him easier to be pitiful,
And sighing was his gift. So, undisturbed,
At whiles° she let him shut my music up   times
And push my needles down, and lead me out
535 To see in that south angle of the house
The figs grow black as if by a Tuscan rock,
On some light pretext. She would turn her head

At other moments, go to fetch a thing,
And leave me breath enough to speak with him,
540 For his sake; it was simple.
                              Sometimes too
He would have saved me utterly, it seemed,
He stood and looked so.
                              Once, he stood so near,
He dropped a sudden hand upon my hand
Bent down on woman's work, as soft as rain—
545 But then I rose and shook it off as fire,
The stranger's touch that took my father's place
Yet dared seem soft.
                              I used him for a friend
Before I ever knew him for a friend.
'Twas better, 'twas worse also, afterward:
550 We came so close, we saw our differences
Too intimately. Always Romney Leigh
Was looking for the worms, I for the gods.
A godlike nature his; the gods look down,
Incurious of themselves; and certainly
555 'Tis well I should remember, how, those days,
I was a worm too, and he looked on me.

A little by his act perhaps, yet more
By something in me, surely not my will,
I did not die. But slowly, as one in swoon,
560 To whom life creeps back in the form of death,
With a sense of separation, a blind pain
Of blank obstruction, and a roar i' the ears
Of visionary chariots which retreat
As earth grows clearer … slowly, by degrees;
565 I woke, rose up … where was I? in the world;
For uses therefore I must count worthwhile.

I had a little chamber in the house,
As green as any privet hedge a bird
Might choose to build in, though the nest itself
570 Could show but dead-brown sticks and straws; the walls
Were green, the carpet was pure green, the straight
Small bed was curtained greenly, and the folds
Hung green about the window which let in
The outdoor world with all its greenery.
575 You could not push your head out and escape
A dash of dawn-dew from the honeysuckle,

---

[1] *betimes*   Here, at an early age.
[2] *The goats … judgment hour*   See Matthew 25.32–33, 41.

But so you were baptized into the grace
And privilege of seeing ...
            First, the lime
(I had enough there, of the lime, be sure—
580 My morning-dream was often hummed away
By the bees in it); past the lime, the lawn,
Which, after sweeping broadly round the house,
Went trickling through the shrubberies in a stream
Of tender turf, and wore and lost itself
585 Among the acacias, over which you saw
The irregular line of elms by the deep lane
Which stopped the grounds and dammed the overflow
Of arbutus and laurel. Out of sight
The lane was; sunk so deep, no foreign tramp
590 Nor drover[1] of wild ponies out of Wales
Could guess if lady's hall or tenant's lodge
Dispensed such odours—though his stick well crooked
Might reach the lowest trail of blossoming briar
Which dipped upon the wall. Behind the elms,
595 And through their tops, you saw the folded hills
Striped up and down with hedges (burly oaks
Projecting from the line to show themselves),
Through which my cousin Romney's chimneys smoked
As still as when a silent mouth in frost
600 Breathes, showing where the woodlands hid Leigh Hall;
While, far above, a jut of tableland,
A promontory without water, stretched—
You could not catch it if the days were thick,
Or took it for a cloud; but, otherwise,
605 The vigorous sun would catch it up at eve
And use it for an anvil till he had filled
The shelves of heaven with burning thunderbolts,
Protesting against night and darkness:—then,
When all his setting trouble was resolved
610 To a trance of passive glory, you might see
In apparition on the golden sky
(Alas, my Giotto's background!)[2] the sheep run
Along the fine clear outline, small as mice
That run along a witch's scarlet thread.[3]

615 Not a grand nature. Not my chestnut woods
Of Vallombrosa,[4] cleaving° by the spurs   *clinging*
To the precipices. Not my headlong leaps
Of waters, that cry out for joy or fear
In leaping through the palpitating pines,
620 Like a white soul tossed out to eternity
With thrills of time upon it. Not indeed
My multitudinous mountains, sitting in
The magic circle, with the mutual touch
Electric, panting from their full deep hearts
625 Beneath the influent[5] heavens, and waiting for
Communion and commission. Italy
Is one thing, England one.
              On English ground
You understand the letter—ere the fall
How Adam lived in a garden. All the fields
630 Are tied up fast with hedges, nosegay-like;
The hills are crumpled plains, the plains parterres,[6]
The trees, round, woolly, ready to be clipped,
And if you seek for any wilderness
You find, at best, a park. A nature tamed
635 And grown domestic like a barn-door fowl,
Which does not awe you with its claws and beak,
Nor tempt you to an eyrie too high up,
But which, in cackling, sets you thinking of
Your eggs tomorrow at breakfast, in the pause
640 Of finer meditation.
              Rather say,
A sweet familiar nature, stealing in
As a dog might, or child, to touch your hand
Or pluck° your gown, and humbly mind you so   *tug*
Of presence and affection, excellent
645 For inner uses, from the things without.

I could not be unthankful, I who was
Entreated thus and holpen.° In the room   *helped*
I speak of, ere the house was well awake,
And also after it was well asleep,
650 I sat alone, and drew the blessing in
Of all that nature. With a gradual step,

---

[1] *drover* Herder of animals.

[2] *golden sky ... background* Renaissance Florentine painter Giotto (1267–1337) often used gold as a background color.

[3] *small as mice ... scarlet thread* Meaning obscure.

[4] *Vallombrosa* Summer resort in the mountains near Florence.

[5] *influent* Exerting celestial, astral, or occult power.

[6] *parterres* Patterned ornamental gardens.

A stir among the leaves, a breath, a ray,
It came in softly, while the angels made
A place for it beside me. The moon came,
655 And swept my chamber clean of foolish thoughts.
The sun came, saying, "Shall I lift this light
Against the lime-tree, and you will not look?
I make the birds sing—listen! but, for you,
God never hears your voice, excepting when
660 You lie upon the bed at nights and weep."

Then, something moved me. Then, I wakened up
More slowly than I verily write now,
But wholly, at last, I wakened, opened wide
The window and my soul, and let the airs
665 And outdoor sights sweep gradual gospels in,
Regenerating what I was. O, Life,
How oft we throw it off and think—"Enough,
Enough of life in so much!—here's a cause
For rupture;—herein we must break with Life,
670 Or be ourselves unworthy; here we are wronged,
Maimed, spoiled for aspiration: farewell, Life!"
And so, as froward° babes, we hide our eyes   obstinate
And think all ended.—Then, Life calls to us
In some transformed, apocalyptic voice,
675 Above us, or below us, or around:
Perhaps we name it Nature's voice, or Love's,
Tricking ourselves, because we are more ashamed
To own our compensations than our griefs:
Still, Life's voice!—still, we make our peace with Life.

680 And I, so young then, was not sullen. Soon
I used to get up early, just to sit
And watch the morning quicken[1] in the gray,
And hear the silence open like a flower
Leaf after leaf—and stroke with listless hand
685 The woodbine through the window, till at last
I came to do it with a sort of love,
At foolish unaware: whereat I smiled—
A melancholy smile, to catch myself
Smiling for joy.
                    Capacity for joy
690 Admits temptation. It seemed, next, worthwhile

To dodge the sharp sword set against my life;
To slip downstairs through all the sleepy house,
As mute as any dream there, and escape
As a soul from the body, out of doors,
695 Glide through the shrubberies, drop into the lane,
And wander on the hills an hour or two,
Then back again before the house should stir.

Or else I sat on in my chamber green,
And lived my life, and thought my thoughts, and prayed
700 My prayers without the vicar; read my books
Without considering whether they were fit
To do me good. Mark, there. We get no good
By being ungenerous, even to a book,
And calculating profits—so much help
705 By so much reading. It is rather when
We gloriously forget ourselves and plunge
Soul-forward, headlong, into a book's profound,
Impassioned for its beauty and salt of truth—
'Tis then we get the right good from a book.

710 I read much. What my father taught before
From many a volume, Love re-emphasised
Upon the self-same pages: Theophrast[2]
Grew tender with the memory of his eyes,
And Ælian[3] made mine wet. The trick of Greek
715 And Latin he had taught me, as he would
Have taught me wrestling or the game of fives[4]
If such he had known—most like a shipwrecked man
Who heaps his single platter with goats' cheese
And scarlet berries; or like any man
720 Who loves but one, and so gives all at once,
Because he has it, rather than because
He counts it worthy. Thus, my father gave;
And thus, as did the women formerly

---

1 *quicken* Come alive.

2 *Theophrast* Greek philosopher (c. 370–287 BCE), student and successor of Aristotle at the Lyceum, the Athenian philosophical school founded by Aristotle.

3 *Ælian* Greek rhetorician (c. 170–c. 230) and author of Greek books on natural history.

4 *game of fives* Handball game similar to the game of squash.

By young Achilles,[1] when they pinned a veil
725 Across the boy's audacious front, and swept
With tuneful laughs the silver-fretted rocks,
He wrapt his little daughter in his large
Man's doublet,° careless did it fit or no.   *jacket*

But, after I had read for memory,
730 I read for hope. The path my father's foot
Had trod me out (which suddenly broke off
What time he dropped the wallet of the flesh[2]
And passed), alone I carried on, and set
My child-heart 'gainst the thorny underwood,
735 To reach the grassy shelter of the trees.
Ah babe i' the wood, without a brother-babe!
My own self-pity, like the red-breast bird,
Flies back to cover all that past with leaves.[3]

Sublimest danger, over which none weeps,
740 When any young wayfaring soul goes forth
Alone, unconscious of the perilous road,
The day-sun dazzling in his limpid eyes,
To thrust his own way, he an alien, through
The world of books! Ah, you!—you think it fine,
745 You clap hands—"A fair day!"—you cheer him on,
As if the worst, could happen, were to rest
Too long beside a fountain. Yet, behold,
Behold!—the world of books is still the world,
And worldlings° in it are less merciful   *worldly people*
750 And more puissant.° For the wicked there   *powerful*
Are winged like angels; every knife that strikes
Is edged from elemental fire to assail
A spiritual life; the beautiful seems right
By force of beauty, and the feeble wrong
755 Because of weakness; power is justified
Though armed against Saint Michael;[4] many a crown

Covers bald foreheads. In the book world, true,
There's no lack, neither, of God's saints and kings,
That shake the ashes of the grave aside
760 From their calm locks and undiscomfited
Look steadfast truths against Time's changing mask.
True, many a prophet teaches in the roads;
True, many a seer pulls down the flaming heavens
Upon his own head in strong martyrdom
765 In order to light men a moment's space.
But stay!—who judges?—who distinguishes
'Twixt Saul and Nahash[5] justly, at first sight,
And leaves king Saul precisely at the sin,
To serve king David?[6] who discerns at once
770 The sound of the trumpets, when the trumpets blow
For Alaric as well as Charlemagne?[7]
Who judges wizards, and can tell true seers
From conjurers? the child, there? Would you leave
That child to wander in a battlefield
775 And push his innocent smile against the guns;
Or even in a catacomb—his torch
Grown ragged in the fluttering air, and all
The dark a-mutter round him? not a child.

I read books bad and good—some bad and good
780 At once (good aims not always make good books:
Well-tempered spades turn up ill-smelling soils
In digging vineyards even); books that prove
God's being so definitely, that man's doubt
Grows self-defined the other side the line,
785 Made atheist by suggestion; moral books,
Exasperating to license; genial books,
Discounting from the human dignity;
And merry books, which set you weeping when
The sun shines—ay, and melancholy books,
790 Which make you laugh that anyone should weep
In this disjointed life for one wrong more.

---

[1] *as did the women ... Achilles* The Greek god Thetis disguised her son Achilles as a girl and hid him among the women of the court in order to prevent him from perishing in the Trojan War.

[2] *the wallet of the flesh* I.e., his body.

[3] *babe i' the wood ... leaves* Cf. the British children's ballad "The Babes in the Woods," in which two children are abandoned in the wood. After they die, robins come to cover them with leaves.

[4] *Saint Michael* One of the principal archangels, known as a protector and figured with a sword.

---

[5] *Saul and Nahash* See 1 Samuel 11: Saul was named king of Israel over his rival Nahash.

[6] *king David* David succeeded Saul as king of Israel.

[7] *Alaric* Visigoth king (c. 370–410 CE) and conqueror of much of the Eastern and Roman empires; *Charlemagne* Charles the Great (742?–814), emperor of the West and king of the Franks.

The world of books is still the world, I write,
And both worlds have God's providence, thank God,
To keep and hearten: with some struggle, indeed,
795   Among the breakers,[1] some hard swimming through
The deeps—I lost breath in my soul sometimes
And cried "God save me if there's any God,"
But, even so, God saved me; and, being dashed
From error on to error, every turn
800   Still brought me nearer to the central truth.

I thought so. All this anguish in the thick
Of men's opinions … press and counter-press,
Now up, now down, now underfoot, and now
Emergent … all the best of it, perhaps,
805   But throws you back upon a noble trust
And use of your own instinct—merely proves
Pure reason stronger than bare inference
At strongest. Try it—fix against heaven's wall
The scaling-ladders of school logic—mount
810   Step by step!—sight goes faster; that still ray
Which strikes out from you, how, you cannot tell,
And why, you know not (did you eliminate,
That such as you indeed should analyse?)
Goes straight and fast as light, and high as God.

815   The cygnet° finds the water, but the man   *young swan*
Is born in ignorance of his element
And feels out blind at first, disorganised
By sin i' the blood—his spirit-insight dulled
And crossed°by his sensations. Presently   *betrayed*
820   He feels it quicken in the dark sometimes,
When, mark, be reverent, be obedient,
For such dumb motions of imperfect life
Are oracles of vital Deity
Attesting the Hereafter. Let who says
825   "The soul's a clean white paper," rather say,
A palimpsest,[2] a prophet's holograph[3]
Defiled, erased and covered by a monk's—

The apocalypse, by a Longus![4] poring on
Which obscene text, we may discern perhaps
830   Some fair, fine trace of what was written once,
Some upstroke of an alpha and omega[5]
Expressing the old scripture.

                    Books, books, books!
I had found the secret of a garret room
Piled high with cases in my father's name,
835   Piled high, packed large—where, creeping in and out
Against the giant fossils of my past,
Like some small nimble mouse between the ribs
Of a mastodon, I nibbled here and there
At this or that box, pulling through the gap,
840   In heats of terror, haste, victorious joy,
The first book first. And how I felt it beat
Under my pillow, in the morning's dark,
An hour before the sun would let me read!
My books! At last because the time was ripe,
845   I chanced upon the poets.

                    As the earth
Plunges in fury, when the internal fires
Have reached and pricked her heart, and, throwing flat
The marts°and temples, the triumphal gates   *marketplaces*
And towers of observation, clears herself
850   To elemental freedom—thus, my soul,
At poetry's divine first finger-touch,
Let go conventions and sprang up surprised,
Convicted of the great eternities
Before two worlds.

                    What's this, Aurora Leigh,
855   You write so of the poets, and not laugh?
Those virtuous liars, dreamers after dark,
Exaggerators of the sun and moon,
And soothsayers in a teacup?

                    I write so
Of the only truth-tellers now left to God,
860   The only speakers of essential truth,

---

[1]   *breakers* Breaking waves.

[2]   *palimpsest* Paper or manuscript that has been written upon, rubbed out and written upon again, either partially or wholly obliterating the original.

[3]   *holograph* Document handwritten by its author.

[4]   *Longus* Greek poet of the third or fourth century, author of *Daphnis and Chloë* and originator of the pastoral romance, which often articulates intense physical desire.

[5]   *alpha and omega* First and last letters of the Greek alphabet; metaphorically, the be all and end all. See Revelation 1.11, in which God says: "I am Alpha and Omega, the first and the last: and, What thou seest, write in a book."

Opposed to relative, comparative,
And temporal truths; the only holders by
His sun-skirts, through conventional gray glooms;
The only teachers who instruct mankind
865 From just a shadow on a charnel° wall   mortuary
To find man's veritable stature out
Erect, sublime—the measure of a man,
And that's the measure of an angel, says
The apostle.[1] Ay, and while your common men
870 Lay telegraphs, gauge railroads, reign, reap, dine,
And dust the flaunty°carpets of the world   showy
For kings to walk on, or our president,
The poet suddenly will catch them up
With his voice like a thunder—"This is soul,
875 This is life, this word is being said in heaven,
Here's God down on us! what are you about?"
How all those workers start amid their work,
Look round, look up, and feel, a moment's space,
That carpet dusting, though a pretty trade,
880 Is not the imperative labour after all.

My own best poets, am I one with you,
That thus I love you—or but one through love?
Does all this smell of thyme about my feet
Conclude my visit to your holy hill
885 In personal presence, or but testify
The rustling of your vesture° through my dreams   clothing
With influent odours? When my joy and pain,
My thought and aspiration like the stops
Of pipe or flute, are absolutely dumb°   silent
890 Unless melodious, do you play on me
My pipers—and if, sooth,° you did not blow,   truly
Would no sound come? or is the music mine,
As a man's voice or breath is called his own,
Inbreathed by the Life-breather? There's a doubt
895 For cloudy seasons!
                    But the sun was high
When first I felt my pulses set themselves
For concord;°when the rhythmic turbulence   harmony
Of blood and brain swept outward upon words,
As wind upon the alders, blanching them
900 By turning up their under-natures till

They trembled in dilation. O delight
And triumphs of the poet, who would say
A man's mere "yes," a woman's common "no,"
A little human hope of that or this,
905 And says the word so that it burns you through
With a special revelation, shakes the heart
Of all the men and women in the world,
As if one came back from the dead and spoke,
With eyes too happy, a familiar thing
910 Become divine i' the utterance! while for him
The poet, speaker, he expands with joy;
The palpitating angel in his flesh
Thrills inly with consenting fellowship
To those innumerous spirits who sun themselves
915 Outside of time.
                    O life, O poetry,
—Which means life in life! cognisant of life
Beyond this blood-beat, passionate for truth
Beyond these senses!—poetry, my life,
My eagle, with both grappling feet still hot
920 From Zeus's thunder, who hast ravished me
Away from all the shepherds, sheep, and dogs,
And set me in the Olympian roar and round
Of luminous faces for a cupbearer,[2]
To keep the mouths of all the godheads moist
925 For everlasting laughters—I myself
Half drunk across the beaker° with their eyes!   cup
How those gods look!
                    Enough so, Ganymede,
We shall not bear above° a round or two.   more than
We drop the golden cup at Heré's[3] foot
930 And swoon back to the earth—and find ourselves
Face down among the pinecones, cold with dew,
While the dogs bark, and many a shepherd scoffs,
"What's come now to the youth?" Such ups and downs
Have poets.
                    Am I such indeed? The name
935 Is royal, and to sign it like a queen

---

[1] *measure of a man ... apostle* See Revelation 21.17.

[2] *Zeus's thunder ... cupbearer* Zeus, king of the Greek gods, un-
leashed a thunderstorm on earth to confuse mortals and steal away the
beautiful shepherd boy Ganymede. Zeus made the boy immortal and
brought him to Olympus to serve as cupbearer to the gods; *ravished*
Abducted, especially for sexual purposes.

[3] *Heré* Hera, wife of Zeus.

Is what I dare not—though some royal blood
Would seem to tingle in me now and then,
With sense of power and ache—with
    imposthumes°   *abscesses*
And manias usual to the race. Howbeit
940 I dare not: 'tis too easy to go mad
And ape a Bourbon in a crown of straws;[1]
The thing's too common.

                      Many fervent souls
Strike rhyme on rhyme, who would strike steel on steel
If steel had offered, in a restless heat
945 Of doing something. Many tender souls
Have strung their losses on a rhyming thread,
As children cowslips:[2] the more pains they take,
The work more withers. Young men, ay, and maids,
Too often sow their wild oats in tame verse,
950 Before they sit down under their own vine[3]
And live for use. Alas, near all the birds
Will sing at dawn—and yet we do not take
The chaffering° swallow for the holy lark.   *chattering*

In those days, though, I never analysed,
955 Not even myself. Analysis comes late.
You catch a sight of Nature, earliest,
In full front sun-face, and your eyelids wink
And drop before the wonder of 't; you miss
The form, through seeing the light. I lived, those days,
960 And wrote because I lived—unlicensed else;
My heart beat in my brain. Life's violent flood
Abolished bounds—and, which my neighbour's field,
Which mine, what mattered? it is thus in youth!
We play at leapfrog over the god Term;[4]
965 The love within us and the love without
Are mixed, confounded; if we are loved or love,
We scarce distinguish: thus, with other power;
Being acted on and acting seem the same:
In that first onrush of life's chariot-wheels,
970 We know not if the forests move or we.

And so, like most young poets, in a flush
Of individual life I poured myself
Along the veins of others, and achieved
Mere lifeless imitations of live verse,
975 And made the living answer for the dead,
Profaning nature. "Touch not, do not taste,
Nor handle,"[5]—we're too legal,[6] who write young:
We beat the phorminx° till we hurt our thumbs,   *lyre*
As if still ignorant of counterpoint;°   *interwoven melodies*
980 We call the Muse—"O Muse, benignant[7] Muse,"—
As if we had seen her purple-braided head,
With the eyes in it, start between the boughs
As often as a stag's. What make-believe,
With so much earnest! what effete° results   *overrefined*
985 From virile efforts! what cold wire-drawn° odes   *detailed*
From such white heats!—bucolics,[8] where the cows
Would scare the writer if they splashed the mud
In lashing off the flies—didactics,[9] driven
Against the heels of what the master said;
990 And counterfeiting epics, shrill with trumps[10]
A babe might blow between two straining cheeks
Of bubbled rose, to make his mother laugh;
And elegiac griefs, and songs of love,
Like cast-off nosegays° picked up on the road,   *bouquets*
995 The worse for being warm: all these things, writ
On happy mornings, with a morning heart,
That leaps for love, is active for resolve,
Weak for art only. Oft, the ancient forms
Will thrill, indeed, in carrying the young blood.
1000 The wine-skins, now and then, a little warped,
Will crack even, as the new wine gurgles in.
Spare the old bottles!—spill not the new wine.[11]

---

[1] *Bourbon in a crown of straws* The Bourbon dynasty was founded by Napoleon, who of course had no real title to the Crown of France.

[2] *cowslips* Fragrant pasture flowers, sometimes made into garlands.

[3] *sit down under their own vine* See 1 Kings 4.25.

[4] *Term* Terminus, Roman god of boundaries.

[5] *Touch not … handle* From Colossians 2.21–22: "Touch not; taste not; handle not; Which all are to perish with the using."

[6] *legal* Dedicated to the law.

[7] *benignant* Benevolent.

[8] *bucolics* Pastoral poems.

[9] *didactics* Writings that contain a lesson or moral.

[10] *trumps* Trumpeting sounds.

[11] *Spare … wine* See Matthew 9.17: "Neither do men put new wine into old bottles: else the bottles break, and the wine runneth out, and the bottles perish: but they put new wine into new bottles, and both are preserved."

By Keats's[1] soul, the man who never stepped
In gradual progress like another man,
1005 But, turning grandly on his central self,
Ensphered himself in twenty perfect years
And died, not young (the life of a long life
Distilled to a mere drop, falling like a tear
Upon the world's cold cheek to make it burn
1010 Forever); by that strong excepted° soul,   *exceptional*
I count it strange and hard to understand
That nearly all young poets should write old,
That Pope was sexagenary at sixteen,
And beardless Byron[2] academical,
1015 And so with others. It may be perhaps
Such have not settled long and deep enough
In trance, to attain to clairvoyance—and still
The memory mixes with the vision, spoils,
And works it turbid.
                              Or perhaps, again,
1020 In order to discover the Muse-Sphinx,[3]
The melancholy desert must sweep round,
Behind you as before.—
                              For me, I wrote
False poems, like the rest, and thought them true
Because myself was true in writing them.
1025 I peradventure° have writ true ones since   *perhaps*
With less complacence.
                              But I could not hide
My quickening inner life from those at watch.
They saw a light at a window, now and then,
They had not set there: who had set it there?
1030 My father's sister started when she caught
My soul agaze in my eyes. She could not say
I had no business with a sort of soul,
But plainly she objected—and demurred
That souls were dangerous things to carry straight
1035 Through all the spilt saltpetre[4] of the world.

She said sometimes "Aurora, have you done
Your task this morning? have you read that book?
And are you ready for the crochet here?"—
As if she said "I know there's something wrong;
1040 I know I have not ground you down enough
To flatten and bake you to a wholesome crust
For household uses and proprieties,
Before the rain has got into my barn
And set the grains a-sprouting. What, you're green
1045 With outdoor impudence? you almost grow?"
To which I answered, "Would she hear my task,[5]
And verify my abstract of the book?
Or should I sit down to the crochet work?
Was such her pleasure?" Then I sat and teased
1050 The patient needle till it split the thread,
Which oozed off from it in meandering lace
From hour to hour. I was not, therefore, sad;
My soul was singing at a work apart
Behind the wall of sense, as safe from harm
1055 As sings the lark when sucked up out of sight
In vortices of glory and blue air.

And so, through forced work and spontaneous work,
The inner life informed the outer life,
Reduced the irregular blood to a settled rhythm,
1060 Made cool the forehead with fresh-sprinkling dreams,
And, rounding to the spheric soul the thin,
Pined body, struck a colour up the cheeks
Though somewhat faint. I clenched my brows across
My blue eyes greatening in the looking-glass,
1065 And said "We'll live, Aurora! we'll be strong.
The dogs are on us—but we will not die."

Whoever lives true life will love true love.
I learnt to love that England. Very oft,
Before the day was born, or otherwise
1070 Through secret windings of the afternoons,
I threw my hunters off and plunged myself
Among the deep hills, as a hunted stag
Will take the waters, shivering with the fear
And passion of the course. And when at last
1075 Escaped, so many a green slope built on slope

---

[1] *Keats* Romantic poet John Keats (1795–1821).

[2] *Pope … Byron* Both Alexander Pope (1688–1744) and Lord Byron (1788–1824) were precocious poets who published while still in their teens.

[3] *Sphinx* In Greek mythology the Sphinx is represented with the body of a lion and the head of a woman. The Sphinx would pose a riddle to passersby and destroy them if they could not solve it.

[4] *saltpetre* Potassium nitrate, a component in explosives.

[5] *task* Here, completed assignment.

Betwixt me and the enemy's house behind,
I dared to rest, or wander, in a rest
Made sweeter for the step upon the grass,
And view the ground's most gentle dimplement[1]
1080 (As if God's finger touched but did not press
In making England), such an up and down
Of verdure—nothing too much up or down,
A ripple of land; such little hills, the sky
Can stoop to tenderly and the wheatfields climb;
1085 Such nooks of valleys lined with orchises,°   orchids
Fed full of noises by invisible streams;
And open pastures where you scarcely tell
White daisies from white dew—at intervals
The mythic oaks and elm trees standing out
1090 Self-poised upon their prodigy of shade—
I thought my father's land was worthy too
Of being my Shakespeare's.
                                    Very oft alone,
Unlicensed; not unfrequently with leave
To walk the third with Romney and his friend
1095 The rising painter, Vincent Carrington,
Whom men judge hardly as bee-bonneted,[2]
Because he holds that, paint a body well,
You paint a soul by implication,[3] like
The grand first Master. Pleasant walks! for if
1100 He said "When I was last in Italy,"
It sounded as an instrument that's played
Too far off for the tune—and yet it's fine
To listen.
                    Often we walked only two
If cousin Romney pleased to walk with me.
1105 We read, or talked, or quarrelled, as it chanced.
We were not lovers, nor even friends well-matched:
Say rather, scholars upon different tracks,
And thinkers disagreed: he, overfull
Of what is, and I, haply,° overbold   by chance

1110 For what might be.
                                    But then the thrushes sang,
And shook my pulses and the elms' new leaves:
At which I turned, and held my finger up,
And bade him mark that, howsoe'er the world
Went ill, as he related, certainly
1115 The thrushes still sang in it. At the word
His brow would soften—and he bore with me
In melancholy patience, not unkind,
While breaking into voluble° ecstasy   talkative
I flattered all the beauteous country round,
1120 As poets use, the skies, the clouds, the fields,
The happy violets hiding from the roads
The primroses run down to, carrying gold;
The tangled hedgerows, where the cows push out
Impatient horns and tolerant churning mouths
1125 'Twixt dripping ash boughs—hedgerows all alive
With birds and gnats and large white butterflies
While look as if the mayflower had caught life
And palpitated forth upon the wind;
Hills, vales, woods, netted in a silver mist,
1130 Farms, granges, doubled up among the hills;
And cattle grazing in the watered vales,
And cottage chimneys smoking from the woods,
And cottage gardens smelling everywhere,
Confused with smell of orchards. "See," I said,
1135 "And see! is God not with us on the earth?
And shall we put Him down by aught we do?
Who says there's nothing for the poor and vile
Save poverty and wickedness? behold!"
And ankle-deep in English grass I leaped
1140 And clapped my hands, and called all very fair.

In the beginning when God called all good,
Even then was evil near us,[4] it is writ;
But we indeed who call things good and fair,
The evil is upon us while we speak;
1145 Deliver us from evil,[5] let us pray.

---

[1] *dimplement*   Dimple (Barrett Browning coined this word).

[2] *bee-bonneted*   Slang: obsessed with something odd.

[3] *paint a body ... soul by implication*   Cf. Robert Browning's "Fra Lippo Lippi" 179–83, in which the painter/narrator says, "Your business is not to catch men with show, / With homage to the perishable clay, / But lift them over it, ignore it all, / Make them forget there's such a thing as flesh. / Your business is to paint the souls of men."

---

[4] *In the beginning ... near us*   See Genesis 1.1, 1.31, and 2.9.

[5] *Deliver us from evil*   From Matthew 6.13.

from BOOK 2

Times followed one another. Came a morn
I stood upon the brink of twenty years,
And looked before and after, as I stood
Woman and artist—either incomplete,
5 Both credulous of completion. There I held
The whole creation in my little cup,
And smiled with thirsty lips before I drank
"Good health to you and me, sweet neighbour mine,
And all these peoples."
            I was glad, that day;
10 The June was in me, with its multitudes
Of nightingales all singing in the dark,
And rosebuds reddening where the calyx[1] split.
I felt so young, so strong, so sure of God!
So glad, I could not choose be very wise!
15 And, old at twenty, was inclined to pull
My childhood backward in a childish jest
To see the face of 't once more, and farewell!
In which fantastic mood I bounded forth
At early morning—would not wait so long
20 As even to snatch my bonnet by the strings,
But, brushing a green trail across the lawn
With my gown in the dew, took will and away
Among the acacias of the shrubberies,
To fly my fancies in the open air
25 And keep my birthday, till my aunt awoke
To stop good dreams. Meanwhile I murmured on
As honeyed bees keep humming to themselves,
"The worthiest poets have remained uncrowned
Till death has bleached their foreheads to the bone;
30 And so with me it must be unless I prove
Unworthy of the grand adversity,
And certainly I would not fail so much.
What, therefore, if I crown myself today
In sport, not pride, to learn the feel of it,
35 Before my brows be numbed as Dante's[2] own
To all the tender pricking of such leaves?
Such leaves! what leaves?"
            I pulled the branches down

To choose from.
            "Not the bay![3] I choose no bay
(The fates deny us if we are overbold),
40 Nor myrtle[4]—which means chiefly love; and love
Is something awful which one dares not touch
So early o' mornings. This verbena[5] strains
The point of passionate fragrance; and hard by,
This guelder rose, at far too slight a beck
45 Of the wind, will toss about her flower-apples.
Ah—there's my choice—that ivy on the wall,
That headlong ivy! not a leaf will grow
But thinking of a wreath. Large leaves, smooth leaves,
Serrated like my vines, and half as green.
50 I like such ivy, bold to leap a height
'Twas strong to climb; as good to grow on graves
As twist about a thyrsus;[6] pretty too
(And that's not ill) when twisted round a comb."

Thus speaking to myself, half singing it,
55 Because some thoughts are fashioned like a bell
To ring with once being touched, I drew a wreath
Drenched, blinding me with dew, across my brow,
And fastening it behind so, turning faced
… My public!—cousin Romney—with a mouth
60 Twice graver than his eyes.
            I stood there fixed—
My arms up, like the caryatid,[7] sole
Of some abolished temple, helplessly
Persistent in a gesture which derides
A former purpose. Yet my blush was flame,
65 As if from flax, not stone.
            "Aurora Leigh,
The earliest of Auroras!"[8]
            Hand stretched out
I clasped, as shipwrecked men will clasp a hand,

---

[1] *calyx* Outer leaves of a bud.

[2] *Dante* Italian poet Dante Alighieri (1265–1321), author of *The Divine Comedy*.

[3] *bay* Sacred tree of the Greek god Apollo; famous poets in Greece were given laurel wreaths as a symbol of honor.

[4] *myrtle* Plant sacred to Venus, Roman goddess of love.

[5] *verbena* Type of flowering plant.

[6] *thyrsus* Spear or staff of the Greek god Dionysus, tipped with a pinecone and entwined with vines.

[7] *caryatid* Building column sculpted in the figure of a woman.

[8] *Auroras* Dawns; personification of Aurora, Roman goddess of the dawn.

Indifferent to the sort of palm. The tide
Had caught me at my pastime, writing down
70   My foolish name too near upon the sea
Which drowned me with a blush as foolish. "You,
My cousin!"
                    The smile died out in his eyes
And dropped upon his lips, a cold dead weight,
For just a moment, "Here's a book I found!
75   No name writ on it—poems, by the form;
Some Greek upon the margin—lady's Greek
Without the accents. Read it? Not a word.
I saw at once the thing had witchcraft in't,
Whereof the reading calls up dangerous spirits:
80   I rather bring it to the witch."
                                            "My book.
You found it"…
                    "In the hollow by the stream
That beech leans down into—of which you said
The Oread in it has a Naiad's[1] heart
And pines for waters."
                            "Thank you."
                                                "Thanks to *you*
85   My cousin! that I have seen you not too much
Witch, scholar, poet, dreamer, and the rest,
To be a woman also."
                            With a glance
The smile rose in his eyes again and touched
The ivy on my forehead, light as air.
90   I answered gravely "Poets needs must be
Or° men or women—more's the pity."   *either*
                                    "Ah,
But men, and still less women, happily,
Scarce need be poets. Keep to the green wreath,
Since even dreaming of the stone and bronze
95   Brings headaches, pretty cousin, and defiles
The clean white morning dresses."
                                    "So you judge!
Because I love the beautiful I must
Love pleasure chiefly, and be overcharged
For ease and whiteness! well, you know the world,
100 And only miss your cousin, 'tis not much.
But learn this; I would rather take my part

With God's Dead, who afford to walk in white
Yet spread His glory, than keep quiet here
And gather up my feet from even a step
105 For fear to soil my gown in so much dust.
I choose to walk at all risks.—Here, if heads
That hold a rhythmic thought, much ache perforce,[2]
For my part I choose headaches—and today's
My birthday."
                    "Dear Aurora, choose instead
110 To cure them. You have balsams."°   *salves*
                            "I perceive.
The headache is too noble for my sex.
You think the heartache would sound decenter,[3]
Since that's the woman's special, proper ache,
And altogether tolerable, except
115 To a woman."
                    Saying which, I loosed my wreath,
And swinging it beside me as I walked,
Half-petulant, half-playful, as we walked,
I sent a sidelong look to find his thought—
As falcon set on falconer's finger may,
120 With sidelong head, and startled, braving eye,
Which means, "You'll see—you'll see! I'll soon take flight,
You shall not hinder." He, as shaking out
His hand and answering "Fly then," did not speak,
Except by such a gesture. Silently
125 We paced, until, just coming into sight
Of the house windows, he abruptly caught
At one end of the swinging wreath, and said
"Aurora!" There I stopped short, breath and all.

"Aurora, let's be serious, and throw by
130 This game of head and heart. Life means, be sure,
Both heart and head—both active, both complete,
And both in earnest. Men and women make
The world, as head and heart make human life.
Work man, work woman, since there's work to do
135 In this beleaguered earth, for head and heart,
And thought can never do the work of love:
But work for ends, I mean for uses, not
For such sleek fringes (do you call them ends,

---

[1] *Oread* Mountain nymph; *Naiad* River nymph.

[2] *perforce* Unavoidably.

[3] *decenter* More decent.

Still less God's glory?) as we sew ourselves
40 Upon the velvet of those baldaquins°   *canopies*
Held 'twixt us and the sun. That book of yours,
I have not read a page of; but I toss
A rose up—it falls calyx down, you see!
The chances are that, being a woman, young
45 And pure, with such a pair of large, calm eyes,
You write as well … and ill … upon the whole,
As other women. If as well, what then?
If even a little better, … still, what then?
We want the Best in art now, or no art.
50 The time is done for facile° settings up   *superficial*
Of minnow gods, nymphs here and tritons[1] there;
The polytheists have gone out in God,
That unity of Bests. No best, no God!
And so with art, we say. Give art's divine,
55 Direct, indubitable, real as grief,
Or leave us to the grief we grow ourselves
Divine by overcoming with mere hope
And most prosaic patience. You, you are young
As Eve with nature's daybreak on her face,
60 But this same world you are come to, dearest coz,[2]
Has done with keeping birthdays, saves her wreaths
To hang upon her ruins—and forgets
To rhyme the cry with which she still beats back
Those savage, hungry dogs that hunt her down
65 To the empty grave of Christ. The world's hard
        pressed;
The sweat of labour in the early curse
Has (turning acrid in six thousand years[3])
Become the sweat of torture. Who has time,
An hour's time … think!—to sit upon a bank
70 And hear the cymbals tinkle[4] in white hands?
When Egypt's slain, I say, let Miriam sing!—

Before—where's Moses?"[5]
                        "Ah, exactly that.
Where's Moses?—is a Moses to be found?
You'll seek him vainly in the bulrushes,[6]
175 While I in vain touch cymbals. Yet concede,
Such sounding brass[7] has done some actual good
(The application in a woman's hand,
If that were credible, being scarcely spoilt,)
In colonising beehives."
                        "There it is!—
180 You play beside a deathbed like a child,
Yet measure to yourself a prophet's place
To teach the living. None of all these things
Can women understand. You generalise
Oh, nothing—not even grief! Your quick-breathed
        hearts,
185 So sympathetic to the personal pang,
Close on each separate knife stroke, yielding up
A whole life at each wound, incapable
Of deepening, widening a large lap of life
To hold the world-full woe. The human race
190 To you means, such a child, or such a man,
You saw one morning waiting in the cold,
Beside that gate, perhaps. You gather up
A few such cases, and when strong sometimes
Will write of factories and of slaves, as if
195 Your father were a negro, and your son
A spinner[8] in the mills. All's yours and you,
All, coloured with your blood, or otherwise
Just nothing to you. Why, I call you hard
To general suffering. Here's the world half-blind
200 With intellectual light, half-brutalised
With civilisation, having caught the plague
In silks from Tarsus,[9] shrieking east and west

---

1 *minnow* Tiny, insignificant; *nymphs* Classical nature spirits; *tritons* Reference to Triton, Greek god of the sea. See Shakespeare's *Coriolanus* 3.1.92: "Hear you this Triton of the minnows?"

2 *coz* Term of familiarity; shortened form of cousin.

3 *six thousand years* Approximate age of the earth, according to a literal interpretation of the Bible.

4 *cymbals tinkle* See 1 Corinthians 13.1.

5 *Egypt's slain … Moses* According to Exodus 15.19–22, Miriam sang and danced after the Pharaoh and his men drowned and Moses led the Jewish people through the Red Sea.

6 *bulrushes* In Exodus 2.3 Moses' mother hides her son in an ark made from bulrushes.

7 *sounding brass* From 1 Corinthians 13.1: "Though I speak with the tongues of men and of angels, and have not charity, I am become as sounding brass, or a tinkling cymbal."

8 *spinner* Here, a wage-laborer involved in the industrial manufacture of yarn or thread for textile production.

9 *Tarsus* City in Turkey.

Along a thousand railroads, mad with pain
And sin too! ... does one woman of you all
205 (You who weep easily) grow pale to see
This tiger shake his cage?—does one of you
Stand still from dancing, stop from stringing pearls,
And pine and die because of the great sum
Of universal anguish?—Show me a tear
210 Wet as Cordelia's,[1] in eyes bright as yours,
Because the world is mad. You cannot count,
That you should weep for this account, not you!
You weep for what you know. A red-haired child
Sick in a fever, if you touch him once,
215 Though but so little as with a fingertip,
Will set you weeping; but a million sick ...
You could as soon weep for the rule of three[2]
Or compound fractions. Therefore, this same world,
Uncomprehended by you, must remain
220 Uninfluenced by you.—Women as you are,
Mere women, personal and passionate,
You give us doting mothers, and perfect wives,
Sublime Madonnas, and enduring saints!
We get no Christ from you—and verily
225 We shall not get a poet, in my mind."

"With which conclusion you conclude!"...
                                           "But this,
That you, Aurora, with the large live brow
And steady eyelids, cannot condescend
To play at art, as children play at swords,
230 To show a pretty spirit, chiefly admired
Because true action is impossible.
You never can be satisfied with praise
Which men give women when they judge a book
Not as mere work but as mere woman's work,
235 Expressing the comparative respect
Which means the absolute scorn. 'Oh, excellent,
What grace, what facile turns, what fluent sweeps,
What delicate discernment ... almost thought!
The book does honour to the sex, we hold.
240 Among our female authors we make room
For this fair writer, and congratulate

The country that produces in these times
Such women, competent to ... spell.'"
                                           "Stop there,"
I answered, burning through his thread of talk
245 With a quick flame of emotion—"You have read
My soul, if not my book, and argue well
I would not condescend ... we will not say
To such a kind of praise (a worthless end
Is praise of all kinds), but to such a use
250 Of holy art and golden life. I am young,
And peradventure° weak—you tell me so—   perhaps
Through being a woman. And, for all the rest,
Take thanks for justice. I would rather dance
At fairs on tightrope, till the babies dropped
255 Their gingerbread for joy—than shift the types[3]
For tolerable verse, intolerable
To men who act and suffer. Better far
Pursue a frivolous trade by serious means,
Than a sublime art frivolously."
                                           "You,
260 Choose nobler work than either, O moist eyes
And hurrying lips and heaving heart! We are young,
Aurora, you and I. The world—look round—
The world, we're come to late, is swollen hard
With perished generations and their sins:
265 The civiliser's spade grinds horribly
On dead men's bones, and cannot turn up soil
That's otherwise than fetid. All success
Proves partial failure; all advance implies
What's left behind; all triumph, something crushed
270 At the chariot wheels; all government, some wrong
And rich men make the poor, who curse the rich,
Who agonise together, rich and poor,
Under and over, in the social spasm
And crisis of the ages. Here's an age
275 That makes its own vocation! here we have stepped
Across the bounds of time! here's nought to see,
But just the rich man and just Lazarus,
And both in torments, with a mediate° gulf,   dividing
Though not a hint of Abraham's bosom.[4] Who

---

[1] *tear ... Cordelia's* See Shakespeare's *King Lear* 4.7.80.

[2] *rule of three* Mathematical method of cross-multiplication.

[3] *types* Moveable type, or letters, used in the printing process.

[4] *rich man ... Abraham's bosom* From Luke 16.19–22: the rich man who denied food to the beggar Lazarus was sent to hell, while Lazarus was sent to join Abraham in heaven.

280　Being man, Aurora, can stand calmly by
　　And view these things, and never tease his soul
　　For some great cure? No physic° for this grief,　*medicine*
　　In all the earth and heavens too?"
　　　　　　　　　　　　　　　　　　"You believe
　　In God, for your part?—ay? that He who makes
285　Can make good things from ill things, best from worst,
　　As men plant tulips upon dunghills when
　　They wish them finest?"
　　　　　　　　　　　　　　　　"True. A death-heat is
　　The same as life-heat, to be accurate,
　　And in all nature is no death at all,
290　As men account of death, so long as God
　　Stands witnessing for life perpetually,
　　By being just God. That's abstract truth, I know,
　　Philosophy, or sympathy with God:
　　But I, I sympathise with man, not God
295　(I think I was a man for chiefly this),
　　And when I stand beside a dying bed,
　　'Tis death to me. Observe—it had not much
　　Consoled the race of mastodons to know,
　　Before they went to fossil, that anon°　　*soon*
300　Their place would quicken with the elephant.
　　They were not elephants but mastodons;
　　And I, a man, as men are now and not
　　As men may be hereafter, feel with men
　　In the agonising present."
　　　　　　　　　　　　　　　　"Is it so,"
305　I said, "my cousin? is the world so bad,
　　While I hear nothing of it through the trees?
　　The world was always evil—but so bad?"

　　"So bad, Aurora. Dear, my soul is gray
　　With poring over the long sum of ill;
310　So much for vice, so much for discontent,
　　So much for the necessities of power,
　　So much for the connivances of fear,
　　Coherent in statistical despairs
　　With such a total of distracted life, …
315　To see it down in figures on a page,
　　Plain, silent, clear, as God sees through the earth
　　The sense of all the graves—that's terrible
　　For one who is not God, and cannot right
　　The wrong he looks on. May I choose indeed,

320　But vow away my years, my means, my aims,
　　Among the helpers, if there's any help
　　In such a social strait?[1] The common blood
　　That swings along my veins is strong enough
　　To draw me to this duty."
　　　　　　　　　　　　　　　Then I spoke.
325　"I have not stood long on the strand° of life,　*shore*
　　And these salt waters have had scarcely time
　　To creep so high up as to wet my feet:
　　I cannot judge these tides—I shall, perhaps.
　　A woman's always younger than a man
330　At equal years, because she is disallowed
　　Maturing by the outdoor sun and air,
　　And kept in long-clothes past the age to walk.
　　Ah well, I know you men judge otherwise!
　　You think a woman ripens, as a peach,
335　In the cheeks chiefly. Pass it to me now;
　　I'm young in age, and younger still, I think,
　　As a woman. But a child may say amen
　　To a bishop's prayer and feel the way it goes,
　　And I, incapable to loose the knot
340　Of social questions, can approve, applaud
　　August compassion, Christian thoughts that shoot
　　Beyond the vulgar white° of personal aims.　*archery target*
　　Accept my reverence."
　　　　　　　　　　　　　　There he glowed on me
　　With all his face and eyes. "No other help?"
345　Said he—"no more than so?"
　　　　　　　　　　　　　　　　"What help?" I asked.
　　"You'd scorn my help—as Nature's self, you say,
　　Has scorned to put her music in my mouth
　　Because a woman's. Do you now turn round
　　And ask for what a woman cannot give?"

350　"For what she only can, I turn and ask,"
　　He answered, catching up my hands in his,
　　And dropping on me from his high-eaved brow
　　The full weight of his soul—"I ask for love,
　　And that, she can; for life in fellowship
355　Through bitter duties—that, I know she can;
　　For wifehood—will she?"
　　　　　　　　　　　　　　　　"Now," I said, "may God

---

[1] *strait* Difficult situation.

Be witness 'twixt us two!" and with the word,
Meseemed[1] I floated into a sudden light
Above his stature—"am I proved too weak
360 To stand alone, yet strong enough to bear
Such leaners on my shoulder? poor to think,
Yet rich enough to sympathise with thought?
Incompetent to sing, as blackbirds can,
Yet competent to love, like HIM?"
                                                I paused;
365 Perhaps I darkened, as the lighthouse will
That turns upon the sea. "It's always so.
Anything does for a wife."
                                "Aurora, dear,
And dearly honoured,"—he pressed in at once
With eager utterance—"you translate me ill.
370 I do not contradict my thought of you
Which is most reverent, with another thought
Found less so. If your sex is weak for art
(And I, who said so, did but honour you
By using truth in courtship), it is strong
375 For life and duty. Place your fecund heart
In mine, and let us blossom for the world
That wants love's colour in the grey of time.
My talk, meanwhile, is arid to you, ay,
Since all my talk can only set you where
380 You look down coldly on the arena-heaps
Of headless bodies, shapeless, indistinct!
The Judgment-Angel scarce would find his way
Through such a heap of generalised distress
To the individual man with lips and eyes,
385 Much less Aurora. Ah, my sweet, come down,
And hand in hand we'll go where yours shall touch
These victims, one by one! till, one by one,
The formless, nameless trunk of every man
Shall seem to wear a head with hair you know,
390 And every woman catch your mother's face
To melt you into passion."
                                "I am a girl,"
I answered slowly; "you do well to name
My mother's face. Though far too early, alas,
God's hand did interpose 'twixt it and me,
395 I know so much of love as used to shine

In that face and another. Just so much;
No more indeed at all. I have not seen
So much love since, I pray you pardon me,
As answers even to make a marriage with
400 In this cold land of England. What you love
Is not a woman, Romney, but a cause:
You want a helpmate, not a mistress, sir,
A wife to help your ends[2]—in her no end.
Your cause is noble, your ends excellent,
405 But I, being most unworthy of these and that,
Do otherwise conceive of love. Farewell."

"Farewell, Aurora? you reject me thus?"
He said.
            "Sir, you were married long ago.
You have a wife already whom you love,
410 Your social theory. Bless you both, I say.
For my part, I am scarcely meek enough
To be the handmaid of a lawful spouse.
Do I look a Hagar,[3] think you?"
                                "So you jest."

"Nay, so, I speak in earnest," I replied.
415 "You treat of marriage too much like, at least,
A chief apostle: you would bear with you
A wife … a sister[4] … shall we speak it out?
A sister of charity."
                        "Then, must it be
Indeed farewell? And was I so far wrong
420 In hope and in illusion, when I took
The woman to be nobler than the man,
Yourself the noblest woman, in the use
And comprehension of what love is—love,
That generates the likeness of itself
425 Through all heroic duties? so far wrong,
In saying bluntly, venturing truth on love,
'Come, human creature, love and work with me,'—
Instead of 'Lady, thou art wondrous fair,
And, where the Graces[5] walk before, the Muse

---

1 *Meseemed*   It seemed to me.

2 *ends*   Goals, purposes.

3 *Hagar*   See Genesis 16.1–4: Hagar was handmaid to Sarah, Abraham's wife, and she also bore Abraham's child, as Sarah was unable to conceive.

4 *chief apostle … sister*   See 1 Corinthians 9.5.

5 *Graces*   In Greek mythology, three goddesses of beauty and charm.

30 Will follow at the lightning of their eyes,
And where the Muse walks, lovers need to creep:
Turn round and love me, or I die of love.'"
With quiet indignation I broke in.
"You misconceive the question like a man,
35 Who sees a woman as the complement
Of his sex merely. You forget too much
That every creature, female as the male,
Stands single in responsible act and thought
As also in birth and death. Whoever says
40 To a loyal woman, 'Love and work with me,'
Will get fair answers if the work and love,
Being good themselves, are good for her—the best
She was born for. Women of a softer mood,
Surprised by men when scarcely awake to life,
45 Will sometimes only hear the first word, love,
And catch up with it any kind of work,
Indifferent, so that dear love go with it.
I do not blame such women, though, for love,
They pick much oakum;[1] earth's fanatics make
50 Too frequently heaven's saints. But *me* your work
Is not the best for—nor your love the best,
Nor able to commend the kind of work
For love's sake merely. Ah, you force me, sir,
To be overbold in speaking of myself:
55 I too have my vocation—work to do,
The heavens and earth have set me since I changed[2]
My father's face for theirs, and, though your world
Were twice as wretched as you represent,
Most serious work, most necessary work
60 As any of the economists'. Reform,
Make trade a Christian possibility,
And individual right no general wrong;
Wipe out earth's furrows of the Thine and Mine,
And leave one green[3] for men to play at bowls,
65 With innings for them all! … What then, indeed,
If mortals are not greater by the head
Than any of their prosperities? what then,
Unless the artist keep up open roads
Betwixt the seen and unseen—bursting through

---

[1] *oakum* Rope fibers acquired by untwisting and picking at old rope, a chore commonly assigned to prisoners or the workhouse poor.

[2] *changed* Exchanged.

[3] *green* Public field.

470 The best of your conventions with his best,
The speakable, imaginable best
God bids him speak, to prove what lies beyond
Both speech and imagination? A starved man
Exceeds a fat beast: we'll not barter, sir,
475 The beautiful for barley.—And, even so,
I hold you will not compass your poor ends
Of barley-feeding and material ease,
Without a poet's individualism
To work your universal. It takes a soul,
480 To move a body: it takes a high-souled man,
To move the masses, even to a cleaner sty:
It takes the ideal, to blow a hair's-breadth off
The dust of the actual.—Ah, your Fouriers[4] failed,
Because not poets enough to understand
485 That life develops from within.—For me,
Perhaps I am not worthy, as you say,
Of work like this: perhaps a woman's soul
Aspires, and not creates: yet we aspire,
And yet I'll try out your perhapses, sir,
490 And if I fail … why, burn me up my straw
Like other false works—I'll not ask for grace;
Your scorn is better, cousin Romney. I
Who love my art, would never wish it lower
To suit my stature. I may love my art.
495 You'll grant that even a woman may love art,
Seeing that to waste true love on anything
Is womanly, past question."
                                        I retain
The very last word which I said that day,
As you the creaking of the door, years past,
500 Which let upon you such disabling news
You ever after have been graver. He,
His eyes, the motions in his silent mouth,
Were fiery points on which my words were caught,
Transfixed for ever in my memory
505 For his sake, not their own. And yet I know
I did not love him … nor he me … that's sure …
And what I said is unrepented of,
As truth is always. Yet … a princely man!—
If hard to me, heroic for himself!
510 He bears down on me through the slanting years,

---

[4] *Fourier* Charles Fourier (1772–1837), French socialist philosopher and utopian theorist.

Arthur Hughes, *Aurora Leigh's Dismissal of Romney*, 1860.

The stronger for the distance. If he had loved,
Ay, loved me, with that retributive face, ...
I might have been a common woman now
And happier, less known and less left alone,
515 Perhaps a better woman after all,
With chubby children hanging on my neck
To keep me low and wise. Ah me, the vines
That bear such fruit are proud to stoop with it.
The palm stands upright in a realm of sand.

520

And I, who spoke the truth then, stand upright,
Still worthy of having spoken out the truth,
By being content I spoke it though it set
Him there, me here.—O woman's vile remorse,
525 To hanker after a mere name, a show,
A supposition, a potential love!
Does every man who names love in our lives
Become a power for that? is love's true thing
So much best to us, that what personates loveIs next
530 best? A potential love, forsooth!
I'm not so vile. No, no—he cleaves, I think,
This man, this image—chiefly for the wrong

And shock he gave my life, in finding me
Precisely where the devil of my youth
535 Had set me, on those mountain-peaks of hope[1]
All glittering with the dawn-dew, all erect
And famished for the noon—exclaiming, while
I looked for empire and much tribute, "Come,
I have some worthy work for thee below.
540 Come, sweep my barns and keep my hospitals,
And I will pay thee with a current coin
Which men give women."
...

from BOOK 5

Aurora Leigh, be humble. Shall I hope
To speak my poems in mysterious tune
With man and nature?—with the lava-lymph
That trickles from successive galaxies
5 Still drop by drop adown the finger of God
In still new worlds?—with summer days in this
That scarce dare breathe they are so beautiful?
With spring's delicious trouble in the ground,
Tormented by the quickened blood of roots,
10 And softly pricked by golden crocus sheaves
In token of the harvest-time of flowers?
With winters and with autumns—and beyond
With the human heart's large seasons, when it hopes
And fears, joys, grieves, and loves?—with all that strain
15 Of sexual passion, which devours the flesh
In a sacrament of souls? with mother's breasts
Which, round the new-made creatures hanging there,
Throb luminous and harmonious like pure spheres?—
With multitudinous life, and finally
20 With the great escapings of ecstatic souls,
Who, in a rush of too long prisoned flame,
Their radiant faces upward, burn away
This dark of the body, issuing on a world
Beyond our mortal?—can I speak my verse
25 So plainly in tune to these things and the rest
That men shall feel it catch them on the quick
As having the same warrant over them

---

[1] *devil ... hope* See Luke 4.5: "And the devil, taking him [Jesus] up into an high mountain, showed unto him all the kingdoms of the world in a moment of time."

To hold and move them if they will or no,
Alike imperious as the primal rhythm
30 Of that theurgic[1] nature?—I must fail,
Who fail at the beginning to hold and move
One man—and he my cousin, and he my friend,
And he born tender, made intelligent,
Inclined to ponder the precipitous sides
35 Of difficult questions; yet, obtuse to *me*,
Of *me*, incurious! likes me very well,
And wishes me a paradise of good,
Good looks, good means, and good digestion—ay,
But otherwise evades me, puts me off
40 With kindness, with a tolerant gentleness—Too light a
book for a grave man's reading! Go,
Aurora Leigh: be humble.
                                    There it is,
We women are too apt to look to one,
Which proves a certain impotence in art.
45 We strain our natures at doing something great,
Far less because it's something great to do,
Than haply that we, so, commend ourselves
As being not small, and more appreciable
To some one friend. We must have mediators
50 Betwixt our highest conscience and the judge;
Some sweet saint's blood must quicken in our palms,
Or all the like in heaven seems slow and cold:
Good only being perceived as the end of good,
And God alone pleased—that's too poor, we think,
55 And not enough for us by any means.
Ay—Romney, I remember, told me once
We miss the abstract when we comprehend.
We miss it most when we aspire—and fail.

Yet, so, I will not.—This vile woman's way
60 Of trailing garments shall not trip me up:
I'll have no traffic with the personal thought
In Art's pure temple. Must I work in vain,
Without the approbation of a man?
It cannot be; it shall not. Fame itself,
65 That approbation of the general race,
Presents a poor end (though the arrow speed
Shot straight with vigorous finger to the white),

And the highest fame was never reached except
By what was aimed above it. Art for art,
70 And good for God Himself, the essential Good!
We'll keep our aims sublime, our eyes erect,
Although our woman-hands should shake and fail;
And if we fail ... But must we?—
                                    Shall I fail?
The Greeks said grandly in their tragic phrase,
75 "Let no one be called happy till his death."[2]
To which I add—Let no one till his death
Be called unhappy. Measure not the workUntil the day's
out and the labour done,
Then bring your gauges. If the day's work's scant,
80 Why, call it scant; affect no compromise;
And, in that we have nobly striven at least,
Deal with us nobly, women though we be,
And honour us with truth if not with praise.
…
The critics say that epics have died out
140 With Agamemnon[3] and the goat-nursed gods;[4]
I'll not believe it. I could never deem,° *think*
As Payne Knight[5] did (the mythic mountaineer
Who travelled higher than he was born to live,
And showed sometimes the goitre[6] in his throat
145 Discoursing of an image seen through fog),
That Homer's heroes measured twelve feet high.[7]
They were but men:—his Helen's hair turned grey
Like any plain Miss Smith's who wears a front;[8]

---

[1] *theurgic* Pertaining to the operation of the gods or the supernatural in human affairs.

[2] *Let no one ... death* The final lines of Sophocles's *Oedipus Rex*: "From hence the lesson draw, / To reckon no man happy till ye see / The closing day; until he pass the bourn / Which severs life from death, unscathed by woe."

[3] *Agamemnon* King of Mycenae and head of the Greek forces in the Trojan War; Agamemnon was murdered by his wife and her lover.

[4] *goat-nursed gods* Zeus, the supreme god of Greek mythology, was nursed by a goat as a baby.

[5] *Payne Knight* Radical historian and author of much commentary on Greek mythology; Richard Payne Knight (1750–1824) released an edition of the *Iliad* and the *Odyssey* that deleted many of Homer's passages.

[6] *goitre* Thyroid swelling in the neck, occurring disproportionately in people who dwell in mountainous areas.

[7] *Homer's ... high* Payne Knight felt that Greek art and literature idealized humans.

[8] *front* False hair that covers the forehead.

And Hector's infant whimpered at a plume[1]
150   As yours last Friday at a turkey-cock.
All actual heroes are essential[2] men,
And all men possible heroes: every age,
Heroic in proportions, double-faced,
Looks backward and before, expects a morn
155   And claims an epos.°   *epic poem*
                    Ay, but every age
Appears to souls who live in't (ask Carlyle) Most
unheroic.[3] Ours, for instance, ours:
The thinkers scout° it, and the poets abound   *mock*
Who scorn to touch it with a fingertip:
160   A pewter age—mixed metal, silver-washed;
An age of scum, spooned off the richer past,
An age of patches for old gaberdines,°   *woolen cloths*
An age of mere transition,[4] meaning nought
Except that what succeeds must shame it quite
165   If God please. That's wrong thinking, to my mind,
And wrong thoughts make poor poems.
                                        Every age,
Through being beheld too close, is ill-discerned
By those who have not lived past it. We'll suppose
Mount Athos carved, as Alexander schemed,
170   To some colossal statue of a man.[5]
The peasants, gathering brushwood in his ear,
Had guessed as little as the browsing goats
Of form or feature of humanity
Up there—in fact, had travelled five miles off
175   Or ere the giant image broke on them,
Full human profile, nose and chin distinct,

Mouth, muttering rhythms of silence up the sky
And fed at evening with the blood of suns;
Grand torso—hand, that flung perpetually
180   The largesse of a silver river down
To all the country pastures. 'Tis even thus
With times we live in—evermore too great
To be apprehended near.
                            But poets should
Exert a double vision; should have eyes
185   To see near things as comprehensively
As if afar they took their point of sight,
And distant things as intimately deepAs if they touched
them. Let us strive for this.
I do distrust the poet who discerns
190   No character or glory in his times,
And trundles back his soul five hundred years,
Past moat and drawbridge, into a castle court,
To sing—oh, not of lizard or of toad
Alive i' the ditch there—'twere excusable,
195   But of some black chief, half knight, half sheep-lifter,[6]
Some beauteous dame, half chattel[7] and half queen,
As dead as must be, for the greater part,
The poems made on their chivalric bones;
And that's no wonder: death inherits death.
200   Nay, if there's room for poets in this world
A little overgrown (I think there is),
Their sole work is to represent the age,
Their age, not Charlemagne's,[8]—this live, throbbing
       age,
That brawls, cheats, maddens, calculates, aspires,
205   And spends more passion, more heroic heat,
Betwixt the mirrors of its drawing-rooms,
Than Roland with his knights at Roncesvalles.[9]
To flinch from modern varnish, coat or flounce,[10]
Cry out for togas and the picturesque,

---

[1]   *Hector's ... plume*   In Homer's *Iliad* 6.575–78, Hector's son recoils in fear upon seeing his warrior father's plumed helmet.

[2]   *essential*   In their essence, their fundamental qualities.

[3]   *every age ... unheroic*   Thomas Carlyle wrote in *On Heroes, Hero-Worship, and the Heroic in History* (1840) that the heroism of any given age is never recognized in its time.

[4]   *An age of mere transition*   In *The Spirit of the Age* (1831) John Stuart Mill wrote: "In the present age of transition, everything must be subordinate to freedom of inquiry."

[5]   *Mount Athos ... man*   In Plutarch's *The Life of Alexander*, the sculptor Stasicrates proposed to Alexander that he carve out of Mount Athos "a most enduring and most conspicuous statue of the king, which in its left hand should hold a city of ten thousand inhabitants, and with its right should pour forth a river running with generous current into the sea."

[6]   *sheep-lifter*   Sheep-thief.

[7]   *chattel*   Here, enslaved person.

[8]   *Charlemagne*   Charles the Great (742–814), ruler of much of Europe in the early years of the ninth century.

[9]   *Roland ... Roncesvalles*   Roland, Charlemagne's commander, was immortalized in *Chanson de Roland*, which relates his death in a battle at Roncesvalles.

[10]   *flounce*   Decorative material added to embellish clothing or curtains.

Is fatal—foolish too. King Arthur's self
Was commonplace to Lady Guenever;
And Camelot to minstrels seemed as flat
As Fleet Street[1] to our poets.
                                    Never flinch,
But still, unscrupulously epic, catch
Upon the burning lava of a song
The full-veined, heaving, double-breasted Age:
That, when the next shall come, the men of thatMay
touch the impress[2] with reverent hand, and say
"Behold—behold the paps° we have all sucked!   nipples
This bosom seems to beat still, or at least
It sets ours beating: this is living art,
Which thus presents and thus records true life."
—1857

210
215
220

A Curse for a Nation

PROLOGUE

I heard an angel speak last night,
        And he said "Write!
Write a nation's curse for me,
And send it over the Western Sea."

I faltered, taking up the word:
        "Not so, my lord!
If curses must be, choose another
To send thy curse against my brother.

"For I am bound by gratitude,
        By love and blood,
To brothers of mine across the sea,
Who stretch out kindly hands to me."

"Therefore," the voice said, "shalt thou write
        My curse tonight.
From the summits of love a curse is driven,
As lightning is from the tops of heaven."

5

10

15

"Not so," I answered. "Evermore
        My heart is sore
For my own land's sins: for little feet
Of children bleeding along the street:

"For parked-up[3] honors that gainsay
        The right of way:
For almsgiving through a door that is
Not open enough for two friends to kiss:

"For love of freedom which abates
        Beyond the straits:
For patriot virtue starved to vice on
Self-praise, self-interest, and suspicion:

"For an oligarchic[4] parliament,
        And bribes well-meant.
What curse to another land assign,
When heavy-souled for the sins of mine?"

"Therefore," the voice said, "shalt thou write
        My curse tonight.
Because thou hast strength to see and hate
A foul thing done within thy gate."

"Not so," I answered once again.
        "To curse, choose men.
For I, a woman, have only known
How the heart melts and the tears run down."

"Therefore," the voice said, "shalt thou write
        My curse tonight.
Some women weep and curse, I say
(And no one marvels), night and day.

"And thou shalt take their part tonight,
        Weep and write.
A curse from the depths of womanhood
Is very salt, and bitter, and good."

20

25

30

35

40

45

---

[1] *Fleet Street* In London, then the hub of the news and publishing industries.

[2] *impress* Mark or stamp.

[3] *parked-up* Here, fenced in, as one might enclose a park.

[4] *oligarchic* Governed by a small, elite group.

So thus I wrote, and mourned indeed,
50　　　What all may read.
And thus, as was enjoined on me,
I send it over the Western Sea.

THE CURSE

1

Because ye have broken your own chain
　　With the strain
55 Of brave men climbing a nation's height,
Yet thence bear down with brand and thong[1]
On souls of others—for this wrong
　　This is the curse. Write.

Because yourselves are standing straight
60　　In the state
Of Freedom's foremost acolyte,
Yet keep calm footing all the time
On writhing bond-slaves—for this crime
　　This is the curse. Write.

65 Because ye prosper in God's name,
　　With a claim
To honor in the old world's sight,
Yet do the fiend's° work perfectly　　　　　　*Devil's*
In strangling martyrs—for this lie
70　　This is the curse. Write.

2

Ye shall watch while kings conspire
Round the people's smouldering fire,
　　And, warm for your part,
Shall never dare—O shame!
75 To utter the thought into flame
　　Which burns at your heart.
　　This is the curse. Write.

Ye shall watch while nations strive
With the bloodhounds, die or survive,
80　　Drop faint from their jaws,
Or throttle them backward to death;
And only under your breath

Shall favor the cause.
　　This is the curse. Write.

85 Ye shall watch while strong men draw
The nets of feudal law
　　To strangle the weak;
And, counting the sin for a sin,
Your soul shall be sadder within
90　　Than the word ye shall speak.
　　This is the curse. Write.

When good men are praying erect
That Christ may avenge His elect
　　And deliver the earth,
95 The prayer in your ears, said low,
Shall sound like the tramp of a foe
　　That's driving you forth.
　　This is the curse. Write.

When wise men give you their praise,
100 They shall praise in the heat of the phrase,
　　As if carried too far.
When ye boast your own charters kept true,
Ye shall blush; for the thing which ye do
　　Derides what ye are.
105　　This is the curse. Write.

When fools cast taunts at your gate,
Your scorn ye shall somewhat abate
　　As ye look o'er the wall;
For your conscience, tradition, and name
110 Explode with a deadlier blame
　　Than the worst of them all.
　　This is the curse. Write.

Go, wherever ill deeds shall be done,
Go, plant your flag in the sun
115　　Beside the ill-doers!
And recoil from clenching the curse
Of God's witnessing universe
　　With a curse of yours.
　　This is the curse. Write.
—1860

---

[1] *brand* Branding iron; *thong* Whip.

Mother and Poet

Browning wrote the following poem in 1861, after learning that the Italian writer Olimpia Savio (1815–89) had recently lost her second son, Emilio, in the Siege of Gaeta. The siege was an important victory for the Italian Unification movement or *Risorgimento*, a political, social, and military effort to free the various Italian states from foreign control and to unify the country. The movement was a success, resulting in the formation of the Kingdom of Italy and ending with the kingdom's expansion to include the Papal States, with Rome as its capital.

Savio—who lived in Turin, where she wrote poetry and articles in support of Italian Unifi-cation—had also lost her first son, Alfredo, in the Siege of Ancona in 1860. The loss of two of her sons made Savio a symbol of the sacrifices made by the Italian people during the *Risorgimento*.

Turin, after news from Gaeta, 1861

1

Dead! One of them shot by the sea in the east,
     And one of them shot in the west by the sea.[1]
Dead! both my boys! When you sit at the feast
     And are wanting a great song for Italy free,
5   Let none look at *me*!

2

Yet I was a poetess only last year,
     And good at my art, for a woman, men said;
But *this* woman, *this*, who is agonized here,
     —The east sea and west sea rhyme on in her head
10   For ever instead.

3

What art can a woman be good at? Oh, vain!
     What art *is* she good at, but hurting her breast
With the milk-teeth° of babes, and a smile   *baby teeth*
          at the pain?

Ah boys, how you hurt! you were strong as you
          pressed,
15   And I proud, by that test.

4

What art's for a woman? To hold on her knees
     Both darlings! to feel all their arms round her throat,
Cling, strangle a little! to sew by degrees
     And 'broider° the long-clothes[2] and neat   *embroider*
          little coat;
20   To dream and to dote.

5

To teach them ... It stings there! *I* made them indeed
     Speak plain° the word *country*. I taught   *clearly*
          them, no doubt,
That a country's a thing men should die for at need.
     I prated[3] of liberty, rights, and about
25   The tyrant cast out.

6

And when their eyes flashed ... O my beautiful eyes! ...
     I exulted; nay, let them go forth at the wheels
Of the guns, and denied not. But then the surprise
     When one sits quite alone! Then one weeps, then
          one kneels!
30   God, how the house feels!

7

At first, happy news came, in gay letters moiled°   *soiled*
     With my kisses—of camp-life and glory, and how
They both loved me; and, soon coming home to be
          spoiled
     In return would fan off every fly from my brow
35   With their green laurel-bough.[4]

---

[1] *One of them shot ... west by the sea* Ancona and Gaeta, the places where Savio's sons were killed, are on opposite coasts of Italy.

[2] *long-clothes* Clothing worn by babies before they learn to walk.

[3] *prated* Talked at length, talked foolishly.

[4] *laurel-bough* The laurel is symbolic of military victory and poetic distinction.

8

Then was triumph at Turin: "Ancona was free!"[1]
    And some one came out of the cheers in the street,
With a face pale as stone, to say something to me.
    My Guido[2] was dead! I fell down at his feet,
40   While they cheered in the street.

9

I bore it; friends soothed me; my grief looked sublime
    As the ransom of Italy. One boy remained
To be leant on and walked with, recalling the time
    When the first grew immortal, while both of us
    strained
45   To the height he had gained.

10

And letters still came, shorter, sadder, more strong,
    Writ now but in one hand, "I was not to faint—
One loved me for two—would be with me ere long:
    And *Viva l'Italia!*—he died for, our saint,
50   Who forbids our complaint."

11

My Nanni[3] would add, "he was safe, and aware
    Of a presence that turned off the balls—was imprest[4]
It was Guido himself, who knew what I could bear,
    And how 'twas impossible, quite dispossessed,
55   To live on for the rest."

12

On which, without pause, up the telegraph line
    Swept smoothly the next news from Gaeta: *Shot.*
Tell his mother. Ah, ah, "his," "their" mother—not
    "mine,"
No voice says "My mother" again to me. What!
60   You think Guido forgot?

13

Are souls straight[5] so happy that, dizzy with Heaven,
    They drop earth's affections, conceive not of woe?
I think not. Themselves were too lately forgiven
    Through THAT Love and Sorrow which
    reconciled so
65   The Above and Below.

14

O Christ of the seven wounds,[6] who look'dst
    through the dark
To the face of Thy mother! consider, I pray,
How we common mothers stand desolate, mark,
    Whose sons, not being Christs, die with eyes
    turned away,
70   And no last word to say!

15

Both boys dead? but that's out of nature. We all
    Have been patriots, yet each house must always
    keep one.
'Twere imbecile, hewing out roads to a wall;
    And, when Italy's made, for what end is it done
75   If we have not a son?

16

Ah, ah, ah! when Gaeta's taken, what then?
    When the fair wicked queen sits no more at her
    sport[7]
Of the fire-balls of death crashing souls out of men?
    When the guns of Cavalli[8] with final retort
80   Have cut the game short?

---

1 *triumph ... free* I.e., news of the victory at Ancona was heard in Turin.

2 *Guido* Nickname for Savio's son Alfredo.

3 *Nanni* Nickname for Savio's son Emilio.

4 *balls* Cannonballs or musket balls; *imprest* Convinced.

---

5 *straight* Straightaway, immediately.

6 *seven wounds* In some traditions, Christ is said to have received seven wounds in the course of his execution.

7 *fair ... sport* Queen Maria Sophie of the Two Sicilies (1841–1925) and her husband Ferdinand II took up residence in the fortress at Gaeta, where they were besieged by the Garibaldine forces who wished to overthrow them in the effort to unify Italy. Maria Sophie became known as a kind of warrior queen for her strenuous efforts to rally the defenders of Gaeta.

8 *guns of Cavalli* Giovanni Cavalli (1808–79) invented a new cannon that could be loaded from the back and fire shot at a faster rate.

17

When Venice and Rome keep their new jubilee,
    When your flag takes all heaven for its white,
        green, and red,
When you have your country from mountain to sea,
    When King Victor[1] has Italy's crown on his head,
85   (And I have my Dead)—

18

What then? Do not mock me. Ah, ring your bells low,
    And burn your lights faintly! *My* country is *there*,
Above the star pricked by the last peak of snow:
    My Italy's THERE, with my brave civic Pair,
90   To disfranchise despair![2]

19

Forgive me. Some women bear children in strength,
    And bite back the cry of their pain in self-scorn;
But the birth-pangs of nations will wring us at length
    Into wail such as this—and we sit on forlorn
95   When the man-child is born.

20

Dead! One of them shot by the sea in the east,
    And one of them shot in the west by the sea.
Both! both my boys! If in keeping the feast
    You want a great song for your Italy free,
100   Let none look at *me*![3]
  —1862 (WRITTEN 1861)

A Musical Instrument

1

What was he doing, the great god Pan,[4]
    Down in the reeds by the river?
Spreading ruin and scattering ban,°   *curses*
Splashing and paddling with hoofs of a goat,
5 And breaking the golden lilies afloat
    With the dragonfly on the river.

2

He tore out a reed, the great god Pan,
    From the deep cool bed of the river:
The limpid water turbidly ran,
10 And the broken lilies a-dying lay,
And the dragonfly had fled away,
    Ere he brought it out of the river.

3

High on the shore sat the great god Pan
    While turbidly flowed the river;
15 And hacked and hewed as a great god can,
With his hard bleak steel at the patient reed,
Till there was not a sign of the leaf indeed
    To prove it fresh from the river.

4

He cut it short, did the great god Pan,
20   (How tall it stood in the river!)
Then drew the pith, like the heart of a man,
Steadily from the outside ring,
And notched the poor dry empty thing
    In holes, as he sat by the river.

1 *King Victor* King Victor Emmanuel II (1820–78) was King of Sardinia until 1861, when he became King of Italy, having succeeded in his efforts to unify large parts of the region.

2 *disfranchise despair* Deprive despair of its due rights.

3 [Browning's note] This was Laura Savio, of Turin, a poetess and patriot, whose sons were killed at Ancona and Gaeta.

4 *Pan* Greek god of nature who was half goat and half man. After the nymph Syrinx turned herself into a bed of reeds in order to escape him, Pan created an instrument (the panpipe) out of the reeds.

5

25 "This is the way," laughed the great god Pan
    (Laughed while he sat by the river),
"The only way, since gods began
To make sweet music, they could succeed."
Then, dropping his mouth to a hole in the reed,
30   He blew in power by the river.

6

Sweet, sweet, sweet, O Pan!
    Piercing sweet by the river!
Blinding sweet, O great god Pan!
The sun on the hill forgot to die,
35 And the lilies revived, and the dragonfly
    Came back to dream on the river.

7

Yet half a beast is the great god Pan,
    To laugh as he sits by the river,
Making a poet out of a man:
40 The true gods sigh for the cost and pain—
For the reed which grows nevermore again
    As a reed with the reeds in the river.
—1862

ALFRED, LORD TENNYSON
1809 – 1892

I n 1850, the novelist and critic Charles Kingsley praised Tennyson's dramatic monologue "Locksley Hall" as the poem that "has had most influence on the minds of the young men of our day." Throughout his long career, Tennyson's poems continued to resonate with Victorian audiences. The self-reflective grief of *In Memoriam* (1850) touched a chord of genuine sympathy in nineteenth-century readers, including Queen Victoria herself, much as Tennyson's re-telling of Arthurian legend in *Idylls of the King* (1859–85) echoed—while also questioning—the nationalistic zeal of the later Victorian period. Britain's poet laureate from 1850 to his death in 1892, Tennyson was the quintessential poet of his age.

He was born in 1809 in Somersby, Lincolnshire, to a privileged family, and his poetic gifts became apparent early on. At age eight, Tennyson was composing pages of blank verse in the style of James Thomson; by ten or eleven he had graduated to studying the work of Alexander Pope, imitating hundreds of lines of Pope's translation of Homer's *Iliad*. At twelve, Tennyson set to work on his first epic, a six-thousand-line experiment that mimicked Walter Scott's octo-syllabic extravaganzas of war and romance. "I wrote as much as seventy lines at one time," he later recalled, "and used to go shouting them about the fields in the dark." By age fourteen, with an Elizabethan-style drama entitled *The Devil and the Lady*, Tennyson's work was approaching the sonorous agility and understated pathos for which it would be known. His first publication, *Poems by Two Brothers* (1827), a collaborative effort by Tennyson and his two older brothers, Frederick and Charles, was completed just prior to Tennyson's entrance to Trinity College, Cambridge.

Tennyson distinguished himself at Cambridge, establishing his reputation as both a deep thinker and a poet. In June of 1829, he won the chancellor's Gold Medal with a blank-verse poem, *Timbuctoo*. Some time in that year, Tennyson met Arthur Henry Hallam, who was to become the poet's closest friend and companion. It was also in 1829 that Tennyson joined the Cambridge Apostles, an undergraduate debating society of which Hallam and many of Tennyson's other Cambridge friends were a part. The year 1830 saw the publication of Tennyson's first important volume, *Poems, Chiefly Lyrical,* which Hallam reviewed for the *Englishman's Magazine* in an essay entitled "On Some of the Characteristics of Modern Poetry and on the Lyrical Poems of Alfred Tennyson." Hallam describes Tennyson as a poet of "sensation," one of a school of poets, including Shelley and Keats, whose "fine organs tremble into emotion at colors, and sounds, and movements" and who translate this physiological sensitivity into their verses. It was precisely such sensitivity that Christopher North (the pseudonym of John Wilson) later attacked in his 1832 *Blackwood's* review of the volume. Subsequently many critics have charted Tennyson's gradual movement away from a poetics of sensation and toward a more restrained poetic style.

The early 1830s were a difficult time for the young poet. Following the death of his father in 1831, Tennyson left Cambridge without taking his degree. Soon afterward, his brother Edward lost his sanity, succumbing to what was known as the "black blood" of the Tennyson family. Finally, and perhaps most devastatingly, Arthur Hallam died suddenly in 1833, apparently of a stroke or a brain hemorrhage. Having published one volume, *Poems*, in 1832, Tennyson would remain silent as a poet for the next ten years, refusing to publish his many works in progress until the *Poems* of 1842, the work that brought him his reputation as both a remarkable poet and a great voice of his age. During the "ten years' silence," however, Tennyson composed much of what many consider his masterwork, *In Memoriam* (1850), in addition to the innovative dramatic monologues of the 1842 *Poems*, including "Ulysses," "Locksley Hall," and "St Simeon Stylites."

In 1847, Tennyson published *The Princess*, a poetic medley that explored, through a wildly improbable narrative, the relations between the sexes and the viability of education for women. Interspersed throughout the work are many of Tennyson's best-known lyrics: "Sweet and Low," "The Splendour Falls," and "Tears, Idle Tears," among others. In 1850, Tennyson ascended to the laureateship and married Emily Sellwood, to whom he had been engaged for thirteen years. That same year, Tennyson also published *In Memoriam*, the elegy on which he had been at work since Arthur Hallam's death. The first of many of Tennyson's books to sell in large numbers, *In Memoriam* went into three editions in its first year alone. Amid a rising swell of scientific discovery and industrial transformation, the poem captured the mood of the era, alternating between faith in science and faith in religion, and reflecting the hopes, doubts, and beliefs of the Victorians.

Tennyson's life changed notably as a result of both his marriage and his suddenly public role as poet laureate. The Tennysons had two sons within the next four years, the elder of whom was named Hallam after Tennyson's deceased friend. (After his father's death, Hallam Tennyson wrote a biography entitled *Alfred Lord Tennyson: A Memoir*, and he penned a second volume in 1911, *Tennyson and His Friends*. Alfred Tennyson's grandson Charles also wrote a biography in 1949.)

Many critics have argued that Tennyson's style changed after his appointment as Poet Laureate. Certainly it is true that he assumed a different voice in the occasional poems composed in his role as poet laureate, most notably the "Ode on the Death of the Duke of Wellington" (1852); likewise "The Charge of the Light Brigade" (1854) projects an explicit political stance largely absent in his earlier works. But Tennyson continued to evolve as a poet, publishing an experimental "monodrama," *Maud*, in 1855 and the first four segments of his epic, *Idylls of the King*, in 1859. *Maud* was in many ways Tennyson's most controversial publication. Critics complained of the poem's irregular rhythms and of the "screed of bombast" that seemed to some like "the rasping of a blacksmith's file." *Idylls of the King*, on the other hand, was largely—though not universally—hailed as a *magnum opus*. Tennyson had contemplated writing an epic from his childhood; the finished *Idylls* reflects the poet's mature thoughts about Victorian life, politics, and culture through the world of Camelot and King Arthur.

Tennyson's later publications include the plays *Queen Mary* (1875), *The Falcon* (1879), and *The Promise of May* (1882), all of which were produced on the Victorian stage, and numerous volumes of poetry, including *Enoch Arden* (1864), *Tiresias, and Other Poems* (1885), *Locksley Hall Sixty Years After* (1886), and *Demeter and Other Poems* (1889). In 1883, Tennyson accepted a barony and took a seat in the House of Lords. When he died in 1892, over 11,000 people applied for tickets to his funeral at Westminster Abbey, though only 1,000 were permitted to attend. He is buried beside Robert Browning in the Poets' Corner of the Abbey.

⌘ ⌘ ⌘

She only said, "My life is dreary,
    He cometh not," she said;
10 She said, "I am aweary, aweary,
    I would that I were dead!"

Her tears fell with the dews at even;°   *evening*
    Her tears fell ere° the dews were dried;   *before*
15 She could not look on the sweet heaven,
    Either at morn or eventide.
After the flitting of the bats,
    When thickest dark did trance° the sky,   *entrance*
    She drew her casement-curtain by,
20 And glanced athwart° the glooming flats.[3]   *across*
    She only said, "The night is dreary,
        He cometh not," she said;
    She said, "I am aweary, aweary,
        I would that I were dead!"

25 Upon the middle of the night,
    Waking she heard the night-fowl crow:
The cock sung out an hour ere light:
    From the dark fen° the oxen's low   *lowlands*
Came to her: without hope of change,
30   In sleep she seemed to walk forlorn,
    Till cold winds woke the gray-eyed morn
About the lonely moated grange.
    She only said, "The day is dreary,
        He cometh not," she said;
35   She said, "I am aweary, aweary,
        I would that I were dead!"

About a stone-cast from the wall
    A sluice with blackened waters slept,
And o'er it many, round and small,
40   The clustered marish-mosses[4] crept.
Hard by° a poplar shook alway,°   *nearby / always*
    All silver-green with gnarlèd bark:
    For leagues no other tree did mark
The level waste, the rounding gray.
45   She only said, "My life is dreary,

Julia Margaret Cameron, *Mariana*, 1875.

Mariana

Mariana in the moated grange
           (*Measure for Measure*)[1]

With blackest moss the flower-plots
    Were thickly crusted, one and all:
The rusted nails fell from the knots
    That held the pear to the gable-wall.[2]
5 The broken sheds looked sad and strange:
    Unlifted was the clinking latch;
    Weeded and worn the ancient thatch
Upon the lonely moated grange.

---

[1] *Mariana ... Measure* Tennyson's epigraph is adapted from the words of the Duke in Shakespeare's *Measure for Measure*, 3.1.277: "There, at the moated grange, lies this dejected Mariana." Earlier in the scene, the Duke has recounted how Mariana, having lost her dowry (and her brother) in a shipwreck, has been deserted by her betrothed; *moated grange* Cottage or small farmhouse surrounded by a moat, or water-filled ditch.

[2] *The rusted ... gable-wall* The pear has been espaliered, or trained to grow against a wall on a lattice or framework of stakes.

---

[3] *flats* Flatlands or lowlands.

[4] [Tennyson's note] *Marish-mosses*, the little marsh-moss lumps that float on the surface of the water.

He cometh not," she said;
    She said, "I am aweary, aweary,
      I would that I were dead!"

And ever when the moon was low,
50   And the shrill winds were up and away,
In the white curtain, to and fro,
    She saw the gusty shadow sway.
But when the moon was very low,
    And wild winds bound within their cell,[1]
55   The shadow of the poplar fell
Upon her bed, across her brow.
    She only said, "The night is dreary,
      He cometh not," she said;
    She said, "I am aweary, aweary,
60   I would that I were dead!"

All day within the dreamy house,
    The doors upon their hinges creaked;
The blue fly sung in the pane; the mouse
    Behind the mouldering wainscot[2] shrieked,
65 Or from the crevice peered about.
    Old faces glimmered through the doors,
    Old footsteps trod the upper floors,
Old voices called her from without.
    She only said, "My life is dreary,
70   He cometh not," she said;
    She said, "I am aweary, aweary,
      I would that I were dead!"

The sparrow's chirrup on the roof,
    The slow clock ticking, and the sound
75 Which to the wooing wind aloof
    The poplar made, did all confound
Her sense; but most she loathed the hour
    When the thick-moted[3] sunbeam lay
    Athwart the chambers, and the day
80 Was sloping toward his western bower.
    Then, said she, "I am very dreary,

---

[1] *wild winds … their cell*   Reference to Virgil's *Aeneid*, 1.52, in which Aeolus, god of winds, keeps the winds imprisoned in a cavern.

[2] *wainscot*   Wood paneling on the lower part of a wall.

[3] *thick-moted*   I.e., thick with motes of dust.

    He will not come," she said;
    She wept, "I am aweary, aweary,
      Oh God, that I were dead!"
—1830

The Palace of Art

I built my soul a lordly pleasure-house,
    Wherein at ease for aye° to dwell.   *ever*
I said, "O Soul, make merry and carouse,
    Dear soul, for all is well."

5 A huge crag-platform, smooth as burnished brass
    I chose. The rangèd ramparts bright
From level meadow-bases of deep grass
    Suddenly scaled the light.

Thereon I built it firm. Of ledge or shelf
10   The rock rose clear, or winding stair.
My soul would live alone unto herself
    In her high palace there.

And "while the world runs round and round," I said,
    "Reign thou apart, a quiet king,
15 Still as, while Saturn whirls, his steadfast shade
    Sleeps on his luminous ring."

To which my soul made answer readily:
    "Trust me, in bliss I shall abide
In this great mansion, that is built for me,
20   So royal-rich and wide."

*

Four courts I made, East, West and South and North,
    In each a squared lawn, wherefrom
The golden gorge of dragons spouted forth
    A flood of fountain-foam.

25 And round the cool green courts there ran a row
    Of cloisters, branched like mighty woods,

Echoing all night to that sonorous flow
    Of spouted fountain-floods.

And round the roofs a gilded gallery
30   That lent broad verge° to distant lands,   *view*
Far as the wild swan wings, to where the sky
    Dipped down to sea and sands.

From those four jets four currents in one swell
    Across the mountain streamed below
35 In misty folds, that floating as they fell
    Lit up a torrent-bow.[1]

And high on every peak a statue seemed
    To hang on tiptoe, tossing up
A cloud of incense of all odour steamed
40   From out a golden cup.

So that she thought, "And who shall gaze upon
    My palace with unblinded eyes,
While this great bow will waver in the sun,
    And that sweet incense rise?"

45 For that sweet incense rose and never failed,
    And, while day sank or mounted higher,
The light aerial gallery, golden-railed,
    Burnt like a fringe of fire.

Likewise the deep-set windows, stained and traced,[2]
50   Would seem slow-flaming crimson fires
From shadowed grots° of arches interlaced,   *grottoes*
    And tipped with frost-like spires.

*

Full of long-sounding corridors it was,
    That over-vaulted grateful° gloom,   *pleasing*
55 Through which the livelong day my soul did pass,
    Well-pleased, from room to room.

Full of great rooms and small the palace stood,
    All various, each a perfect whole
From living Nature, fit for every mood
60   And change of my still soul.

For some were hung with arras° green and blue,   *tapestries*
    Showing a gaudy summer-morn,
Where with puffed cheek the belted hunter blew
    His wreathèd bugle-horn.

65 One seemed all dark and red—a tract of sand,
    And someone pacing there alone,
Who paced forever in a glimmering land,
    Lit with a low large moon.

One showed an iron coast and angry waves.
70   You seemed to hear them climb and fall
And roar rock-thwarted under bellowing caves,
    Beneath the windy wall.

And one, a full-fed river winding slow
    By herds upon an endless plain,
75 The ragged rims of thunder brooding low,
    With shadow-streaks of rain.

And one, the reapers at their sultry toil.
    In front they bound the sheaves. Behind
Were realms of upland, prodigal in oil,
80   And hoary to the wind.[3]

And one a foreground black with stones and slags,[4]
    Beyond, a line of heights, and higher
All barred with long white cloud the scornful crags,
    And highest, snow and fire.

85 And one, an English home—gray twilight poured
    On dewy pastures, dewy trees,
Softer than sleep—all things in order stored,
    A haunt of ancient Peace.

---

[1] *torrent-bow* Rainbow formed in the spray of a torrent.

[2] *traced* Outlined with tracery, delicately carved strips of stone used to separate segments of stained glass.

[3] *hoary to the wind* White underside of the olive leaves are exposed by the wind.

[4] *slags* Chunks of volcanic rock.

Nor these alone, but every landscape fair,
90   As fit for every mood of mind,
Or gay, or grave, or sweet, or stern, was there
       Not less than truth designed.

*

Or the maid-mother by a crucifix,
       In tracts of pasture sunny-warm,
95 Beneath branch-work of costly sardonyx[1]
       Sat smiling, babe in arm.

Or in a clear-walled city on the sea,
       Near gilded organ-pipes, her hair
Wound with white roses, slept St. Cecily;[2]
100   An angel looked at her.

Or thronging all one porch of Paradise
       A group of Houris[3] bowed to see
The dying Islamite, with hands and eyes
       That said, We wait for thee.

105 Or mythic Uther's deeply-wounded son[4]
       In some fair space of sloping greens
Lay, dozing in the vale of Avalon,
       And watched by weeping queens.

Or hollowing one hand against his ear,
110   To list° a foot-fall, ere he saw   *hear*
The wood-nymph, stayed the Ausonian king[5] to hear
       Of wisdom and of law.

Or over hills with peaky tops engrailed,°   *serrated*
       And many a tract of palm and rice.

115 The throne of Indian Cama[6] slowly sailed
       A summer fanned with spice.

Or sweet Europa's[7] mantle° blew unclasped,   *loose cloak*
       From off her shoulder backward borne:
From one hand drooped a crocus: one hand grasped
120   The mild bull's golden horn.

Or else flushed Ganymede,[8] his rosy thigh
       Half-buried in the Eagle's down,
Sole as a flying star shot through the sky
       Above the pillared town.

125 Nor these alone: but every legend fair
       Which the supreme Caucasian[9] mind
Carved out of Nature for itself, was there,
       Not less than life, designed.

*

Then in the towers I placed great bells that swung,
130   Moved of themselves, with silver sound;
And with choice paintings of wise men I hung
       The royal dais round.

For there was Milton like a seraph° strong,   *angel*
       Beside him Shakespeare bland° and mild; *gentle*
135 And there the world-worn Dante grasped his song,
       And somewhat grimly smiled.

And there the Ionian father[10] of the rest;
       A million wrinkles carved his skin;

---

[1] *sardonyx*   Onyx striped with sard, a yellow or orange quartz.

[2] *St. Cecily*   St. Cecilia, patron saint of music.

[3] *Houris*   Nymphs of Muslim paradise.

[4] *Uther's deeply-wounded son*   King Arthur, son of Uther Pendragon, badly wounded in his last battle and carried to the mystic island of Avalon to heal.

[5] *Ausonian king*   Numa, the legendary second king of Rome, who was said to have received the laws of the kingdom from the nymph Egeria; "Ausonia" was an ancient name for Italy often used by poets.

[6] [Tennyson's note]   The Hindu God of young love, son of Brahma.

[7] *Europa*   In Greek legend, the beautiful daughter of the king of Phoenicia. Zeus fell in love with her and assumed the shape of a bull in order to carry her off.

[8] *Ganymede*   In Greek legend, a beautiful youth who was carried up to heaven at the command of Zeus, who made him cupbearer to the gods.

[9] *Caucasian*   Here, Indo-European; the term is used here not in the sense of "white race," but in a sense encompassing peoples of Europe and parts of Asia including the Indian subcontinent.

[10] *Ionian father*   Homer.

A hundred winters snowed upon his breast,
140   From cheek and throat and chin.

Above, the fair hall-ceiling stately-set
    Many an arch high up did lift,
And angels rising and descending met
    With interchange of gift.

145 Below was all mosaic choicely planned
    With cycles of the human tale
Of this wide world, the times of every land
    So wrought, they will not fail.

The people here, a beast of burden slow,
150   Toiled onward, pricked with goads and stings;[1]
Here played, a tiger, rolling to and fro
    The heads and crowns of kings;

Here rose, an athlete, strong to break or bind
    All force in bonds that might endure,
155 And here once more like some sick man declined,
    And trusted any cure.

But over these she trod: and those great bells
    Began to chime. She took her throne:
She sat betwixt the shining Oriels,°   *windows*
160   To sing her songs alone.

And through the topmost Oriels' coloured flame
    Two godlike faces gazed below;
Plato the wise, and large-browed Verulam,[2]
    The first of those who know.

165 And all those names, that in their motion were
    Full-welling fountainheads of change,
Betwixt the slender shafts were blazoned[3] fair
    In diverse raiment° strange: *clothing*

Through which the lights, rose, amber, emerald, blue,
170   Flushed in her temples and her eyes,
And from her lips, as morn from Memnon, drew
    Rivers of melodies.[4]

No nightingale delighteth to prolong
    Her low preamble all alone,
175 More than my soul to hear her echoed song
    Throb through the ribbèd stone;

Singing and murmuring in her feastful mirth,
    Joying to feel herself alive,
Lord over Nature, Lord of the visible earth,
180   Lord of the senses five;

Communing with herself: "All these are mine,
    And let the world have peace or wars,
'Tis one to me." She—when young night divine
    Crowned dying day with stars,

185 Making sweet close of his delicious toils—
    Lit light in wreaths and anadems,°   *garlands*
And pure quintessences of precious oils
    In hollowed moons of gems,

To mimic heaven; and clapped her hands and cried,
190   "I marvel if my still° delight   *constant*
In this great house so royal-rich, and wide,
    Be flattered to the height.

"O all things fair to sate my various eyes!
    O shapes and hues that please me well!
195 O silent faces of the Great and Wise,
    My Gods, with whom I dwell!

"O God-like isolation which art mine,
    I can but count thee perfect gain,
What time I watch the darkening droves of swine
200   That range on yonder plain.

---

[1] *goads and stings*   I.e., sharp-pointed rods.

[2] *Oriels' coloured ... Verulam*   Recessed stained-glass windows with images of Plato and Francis Bacon, one of whose titles was Baron Verulam.

[3] *blazoned*   Brightly painted, as one would a coat of arms.

[4] *morn from ... melodies*   The statue of the legendary Ethiopian king Memnon at Thebes was said by the ancient Greeks to produce beautiful music when touched by the rays of the dawning sun.

"In filthy sloughs they roll a prurient° skin,   *itching*
    They graze and wallow, breed and sleep;
And oft some brainless devil enters in,
    And drives them to the deep."[1]

205 Then of the moral instinct would she prate
    And of the rising from the dead,
As hers by right of full-accomplished Fate;
    And at the last she said:

"I take possession of man's mind and deed.
210   I care not what the sects may brawl.
I sit as God holding no form of creed,
    But contemplating all."

                   *

Full oft the riddle of the painful earth
    Flashed through her as she sat alone,
215 Yet not the less held she her solemn mirth,
    And intellectual throne.

And so she throve and prospered: so three years
    She prospered: on the fourth she fell,
Like Herod, when the shout was in his ears,
220   Struck through with pangs of hell.[2]

Lest she should fail and perish utterly,
    God, before whom ever lie bare
The abysmal deeps of Personality,
    Plagued her with sore despair.

225 When she would think, where'er she turned her sight
    The airy hand confusion wrought,

Wrote, "Mene, mene,"[3] and divided quite
    The kingdom of her thought.

Deep dread and loathing of her solitude
230   Fell on her, from which mood was born
Scorn of herself; again, from out that mood
    Laughter at her self-scorn.

"What! is not this my place of strength," she said,
    "My spacious mansion built for me,
235 Whereof the strong foundation-stones were laid
    Since my first memory?"

But in dark corners of her palace stood
    Uncertain shapes; and unawares
On white-eyed phantasms weeping tears of blood,
240   And horrible nightmares,

And hollow shades enclosing hearts of flame,
    And, with dim fretted foreheads all,
On corpses three-months-old at noon she came,
    That stood against the wall.

245 A spot of dull stagnation, without light
    Or power of movement, seemed my soul,
'Mid onward-sloping motions infinite
    Making for one sure goal.

A still salt pool, locked in with bars of sand,
250   Left on the shore; that hears all night
The plunging seas draw backward from the land
    Their moon-led waters white.

A star that with the choral starry dance
    Joined not, but stood, and standing saw

---

1 *oft some ... the deep*   See Matthew 8.28–32, in which Jesus casts devils out of two men and into a herd of swine, whereupon the herd stampedes off a cliff into the sea.

2 *Herod, when ... of hell*   See Acts 12.21–23, where King Herod is struck dead as a crowd of his subjects shout that he is a god and not a man.

---

3 *Mene, mene*   The first of the words, seen by the Babylonian king Belshazzar, that are mysteriously written on the wall by a disembodied hand in Daniel 5.25–26. Daniel's interpretation of the words for the frightened king concludes with the phrase "Thy kingdom is divided."

55 The hollow orb of moving Circumstance
        Rolled round by one fixed law.[1]

    Back on herself her serpent pride had curled.
        "No voice," she shrieked in that lone hall,
    "No voice breaks through the stillness of this world:
60   One deep, deep silence all!"

    She, mouldering with the dull earth's mouldering sod,
        Inwrapt tenfold in slothful shame,
    Lay there exilèd from eternal God,
        Lost to her place and name;

65 And death and life she hated equally,
        And nothing saw, for her despair,
    But dreadful time, dreadful eternity,
        No comfort anywhere;

    Remaining utterly confused with fears,
70   And ever worse with growing time,
    And ever unrelieved by dismal tears,
        And all alone in crime:

    Shut up as in a crumbling tomb, girt round
        With blackness as a solid wall,
75 Far off she seemed to hear the dully° sound   faint
        Of human footsteps fall.

    As in strange lands a traveller walking slow,
        In doubt and great perplexity,
    A little before moon-rise hears the low
80   Moan of an unknown sea;

    And knows not if it be thunder, or a sound
        Of rocks thrown down, or one deep cry
    Of great wild beasts; then thinketh, "I have found
        A new land, but I die."

85 She howled aloud, "I am on fire within.
        There comes no murmur of reply.

What is it that will take away my sin,
    And save me lest I die?"

So when four years were wholly finished,
290   She threw her royal robes away.
"Make me a cottage in the vale," she said,
    "Where I may mourn and pray.

"Yet pull not down my palace towers, that are
    So lightly, beautifully built:
295 Perchance I may return with others there
    When I have purged my guilt."
—1832 (REVISED 1842)

The Lady of Shalott [2]

PART I

O n either side the river lie
    Long fields of barley and of rye,
That clothe the wold° and meet the sky;   plain
And through the field the road runs by
5   To many-towered Camelot;[3]
And up and down the people go,
Gazing where the lilies blow°   bloom
Round an island there below,
    The island of Shalott.

10 Willows whiten,[4] aspens quiver,
Little breezes dusk° and shiver   darken
Through the wave that runs for ever
By the island in the river
    Flowing down to Camelot.
15 Four gray walls, and four gray towers,

---

1 *A star ... one fixed law* Reference to the North Star, which is aligned with Earth's axis of rotation, and so appears fixed in the night sky.

2 *The Lady of Shalott* The title character is based on the figure of Elaine in the Arthurian romances, who dies for love of Lancelot; she is called "the lily maid of Astolat" in Malory's *Morte d'Arthur*. Tennyson first encountered the story, however, in a medieval Italian romance called "La Donna di Scalotta" and changed the name to Shalott for a softer sound.

3 *Camelot* Legendary location of King Arthur's court.

4 *Willows whiten* I.e., the wind exposes the white undersides of the leaves.

Overlook a space of flowers,
And the silent isle imbowers°   *encloses*
    The Lady of Shalott.

By the margin,° willow-veiled,   *shore*
20 Slide the heavy barges trailed
By slow horses; and unhailed
The shallop¹ flitteth silken-sailed
    Skimming down to Camelot:
But who hath seen her wave her hand?
25 Or at the casement seen her stand?
Or is she known in all the land,
    The Lady of Shalott?

Only reapers, reaping early
In among the bearded barley,
30 Hear a song that echoes cheerly
From the river winding clearly,
    Down to towered Camelot:
And by the moon the reaper weary,
Piling sheaves in uplands airy,
35 Listening, whispers "'Tis the fairy
    Lady of Shalott."

PART 2

There she weaves by night and day
A magic web with colours gay.
She has heard a whisper say,
40 A curse is on her if she stay
    To look down to Camelot.
She knows not what the curse may be,
And so she weaveth steadily,
And little other care hath she,
45   The Lady of Shalott.

And moving through a mirror clear
That hangs before her all the year,
Shadows of the world appear.
There she sees the highway near
50   Winding down to Camelot:
There the river eddy whirls,

And there the surly village-churls,°   *peasants*
And the red cloaks of market girls,
    Pass onward from Shalott.

55 Sometimes a troop of damsels glad,
An abbot on an ambling pad,°   *horse*
Sometimes a curly shepherd-lad,
Or long-haired page² in crimson clad,
    Goes by to towered Camelot;
60 And sometimes through the mirror blue
The knights come riding two and two:
She hath no loyal knight and true,
    The Lady of Shalott.

But in her web she still delights
65 To weave the mirror's magic sights,
For often through the silent nights
A funeral, with plumes and lights
    And music, went to Camelot:
Or when the moon was overhead,
70 Came two young lovers lately wed;
"I am half sick of shadows," said
    The Lady of Shalott.

PART 3

A bow-shot from her bower-eaves,
He rode between the barley-sheaves,
75 The sun came dazzling through the leaves,
And flamed upon the brazen greaves³
    Of bold Sir Lancelot.
A red-cross knight⁴ for ever kneeled
To a lady in his shield,
80 That sparkled on the yellow field,
    Beside remote Shalott.

The gemmy° bridle glittered free,   *brilliant*
Like to some branch of stars we see
Hung in the golden Galaxy.

---

¹ *shallop* Light open boat for use in shallow water.

² *page* Boy who waits on a knight or other person of high rank.

³ *greaves* Armor worn below the knee.

⁴ *red-cross knight* Knight wearing the cross of St. George, patron saint of England.

85 The bridle bells rang merrily
      As he rode down to Camelot:
  And from his blazoned baldric° slung   *shoulder-strap*
  A mighty silver bugle hung,
  And as he rode his armour rung,
90   Beside remote Shalott.

  All in the blue unclouded weather
  Thick-jewelled shone the saddle-leather,
  The helmet and the helmet-feather
  Burned like one burning flame together,
95   As he rode down to Camelot.
  As often through the purple night,
  Below the starry clusters bright,
  Some bearded meteor, trailing light,
      Moves over still Shalott.

100 His broad clear brow in sunlight glowed;
  On burnished hooves his war-horse trode;
  From underneath his helmet flowed
  His coal-black curls as on he rode,
      As he rode down to Camelot.
105 From the bank and from the river
  He flashed into the crystal mirror,
  "Tirra lirra," by the river
      Sang Sir Lancelot.

  She left the web, she left the loom,
110 She made three paces through the room,
  She saw the water-lily bloom,
  She saw the helmet and the plume,
      She looked down to Camelot.
  Out flew the web and floated wide;
115 The mirror cracked from side to side;
  "The curse is come upon me," cried
      The Lady of Shalott.

PART 4

  In the stormy east-wind straining,
  The pale yellow woods were waning,
120 The broad stream in his banks complaining,
  Heavily the low sky raining

      Over towered Camelot;
  Down she came and found a boat
  Beneath a willow left afloat,
125 And round about the prow she wrote
      The Lady of Shalott.

  And down the river's dim expanse
  Like some bold seer in a trance,
  Seeing all his own mischance—
130 With a glassy countenance[1]
      Did she look to Camelot.
  And at the closing of the day
  She loosed the chain, and down she lay;
  The broad stream bore her far away,
135   The Lady of Shalott.

  Lying, robed in snowy white
  That loosely flew to left and right—
  The leaves upon her falling light—
  Through the noises of the night
140   She floated down to Camelot:
  And as the boat-head wound along
  The willowy hills and fields among,
  They heard her singing her last song,
      The Lady of Shalott.

145 Heard a carol, mournful, holy,
  Chanted loudly, chanted lowly,
  Till her blood was frozen slowly,
  And her eyes were darkened wholly,
      Turned to towered Camelot.
150 For ere she reached upon the tide
  The first house by the water-side,
  Singing in her song she died,
      The Lady of Shalott.

  Under tower and balcony,
155 By garden-wall and gallery,
  A gleaming shape she floated by,
  Dead-pale between the houses high,
      Silent into Camelot.

---

[1] *countenance* Facial expression.

Out upon the wharfs they came,
160 Knight and burgher,[1] lord and dame,
And round the prow they read her name,
    The Lady of Shalott.

Who is this? and what is here?
And in the lighted palace near
165 Died the sound of royal cheer;
And they crossed themselves for fear,
    All the knights at Camelot:
But Lancelot mused a little space;[2]
He said, "She has a lovely face;
170 God in his mercy lend her grace,
    The Lady of Shalott."
—1832 (REVISED 1842)

The Lotos-Eaters[3]

"Courage!" he said, and pointed toward the
    land,
    "This mounting wave will roll us shoreward
        soon."
In the afternoon they came unto a land
In which it seemed always afternoon.
5 All round the coast the languid air did swoon,
Breathing like one that hath a weary dream.
Full-faced above the valley stood the moon;
And like a downward smoke, the slender stream
Along the cliff to fall and pause and fall did seem.

10 A land of streams! some, like a downward smoke,
Slow-dropping veils of thinnest lawn,[4] did go;

---

[1] *burgher* Wealthy citizen of a town.

[2] *a little space* For a short while.

[3] *Lotos-Eaters* In Homer's *Odyssey* (9.82–104), the Lotus Eaters were a race of people who inhabited a remote island; they existed in peaceful apathy because of the narcotic effects of the lotus plants they ate. When Odysseus landed on the island, some of his men ate the lotus plants and wanted to stay on the island, rather than return home to their families. The speaker in line 1 is Odysseus; his men sing the "Choric Song" beginning at line 46.

[4] *lawn* Fine fabric.

And some through wavering lights and shadows broke,
Rolling a slumbrous sheet of foam below.
They saw the gleaming river seaward flow
15 From the inner land: far off, three mountain-tops,
Three silent pinnacles of agèd snow,
Stood sunset-flushed: and, dewed with showery drops,
Up-clomb the shadowy pine above the woven
    copse.°   *thicket*

The charmèd sunset lingered low adown
20 In the red West: through mountain clefts the dale
Was seen far inland, and the yellow down
Bordered with palm, and many a winding vale
And meadow, set with slender galingale;[5]
A land where all things always seemed the same!
25 And round about the keel with faces pale,
Dark faces pale against that rosy flame,
The mild-eyed melancholy Lotos-eaters came.

Branches they bore of that enchanted stem,
Laden with flower and fruit, whereof they gave
30 To each, but whoso did receive of them,
And taste, to him the gushing of the wave
Far far away did seem to mourn and rave
On alien shores; and if his fellow spake,
His voice was thin, as voices from the grave;
35 And deep-asleep he seemed, yet all awake,
And music in his ears his beating heart did make.

They sat them down upon the yellow sand,
Between the sun and moon upon the shore;
And sweet it was to dream of Fatherland,
40 Of child, and wife, and slave; but evermore
Most weary seemed the sea, weary the oar,
Weary the wandering fields of barren foam.
Then some one said, "We will return no more";
And all at once they sang, "Our island home
45 Is far beyond the wave; we will no longer roam."

---

[5] *galingale* Species of sedge.

Choric Song[1]

1

There is sweet music here that softer falls
Than petals from blown[2] roses on the grass,
Or night-dews on still waters between walls
Of shadowy granite, in a gleaming pass;
50 Music that gentlier on the spirit lies,
Than tired eyelids upon tired eyes;
Music that brings sweet sleep down from the blissful skies.
Here are cool mosses deep,
And through the moss the ivies creep,
55 And in the stream the long-leaved flowers weep,
And from the craggy ledge the poppy hangs in sleep.

2

Why are we weighed upon with heaviness,
And utterly consumed with sharp distress,
While all things else have rest from weariness?
60 All things have rest: why should we toil alone,
We only toil, who are the first of things,
And make perpetual moan,
Still from one sorrow to another thrown:
Nor ever fold our wings,
65 And cease from wanderings,
Nor steep our brows in slumber's holy balm;
Nor harken what the inner spirit sings,
"There is no joy but calm!"
Why should we only toil, the roof and crown of things?

3

70 Lo! in the middle of the wood,
The folded leaf is wooed from out the bud
With winds upon the branch, and there
Grows green and broad, and takes no care,
Sun-steeped at noon, and in the moon
75 Nightly dew-fed; and turning yellow
Falls, and floats adown the air.
Lo! sweetened with the summer light,
The full-juiced apple, waxing over-mellow,
Drops in a silent autumn night.

80 All its allotted length of days,
The flower ripens in its place,
Ripens and fades, and falls, and hath no toil,
Fast-rooted in the fruitful soil.

4

Hateful is the dark-blue sky,
85 Vaulted o'er the dark-blue sea.
Death is the end of life; ah, why
Should life all labour be?
Let us alone. Time driveth onward fast,
And in a little while our lips are dumb.
90 Let us alone. What is it that will last?
All things are taken from us, and become
Portions and parcels of the dreadful Past.
Let us alone. What pleasure can we have
To war with evil? Is there any peace
95 In ever climbing up the climbing wave?
All things have rest, and ripen toward the grave
In silence; ripen, fall and cease:
Give us long rest or death, dark death, or dreamful ease.

5

How sweet it were, hearing the downward stream,
100 With half-shut eyes ever to seem
Falling asleep in a half-dream!
To dream and dream, like yonder amber light,
Which will not leave the myrrh-bush[3] on the height;
To hear each other's whispered speech;
105 Eating the Lotos day by day,
To watch the crisping ripples on the beach,
And tender curving lines of creamy spray;
To lend our hearts and spirits wholly
To the influence of mild-minded melancholy;
110 To muse and brood and live again in memory,
With those old faces of our infancy
Heaped over with a mound of grass,
Two handfuls of white dust,[4] shut in an urn of brass!

---

[1] CHORIC SONG Song sung in unison (like that performed by the Chorus in an ancient Greek play).

[2] blown Having blossomed.

[3] myrrh-bush Thorny bush that produces a resin used to make incense and medicine.

[4] white dust I.e., cremated remains.

6

Dear is the memory of our wedded lives,
115 And dear the last embraces of our wives
And their warm tears: but all hath suffered change:
For surely now our household hearths are cold:
Our sons inherit us: our looks are strange:
And we should come like ghosts to trouble joy.
120 Or else the island princes over-bold
Have eat our substance,[1] and the minstrel sings
Before them of the ten years' war in Troy,
And our great deeds, as half-forgotten things.
Is there confusion in the little isle?
125 Let what is broken so remain.
The Gods are hard to reconcile:
'Tis hard to settle order once again.
There *is* confusion worse than death,
Trouble on trouble, pain on pain,
130 Long labour unto agèd breath,
Sore task to hearts worn out by many wars
And eyes grown dim with gazing on the pilot-stars.

7

But, propped on beds of amaranth and moly,[2]
How sweet (while warm airs lull us, blowing lowly)
135 With half-dropped eyelid still,
Beneath a heaven dark and holy,
To watch the long bright river drawing slowly
His waters from the purple hill—
To hear the dewy echoes calling
140 From cave to cave through the thick-twinèd vine—
To watch the emerald-coloured water falling
Through many a woven acanthus[3]-wreath divine!
Only to hear and see the far-off sparkling brine,
Only to hear were sweet, stretched out beneath the pine.

8

145 The Lotos blooms below the barren peak:
The Lotos blows by every winding creek:
All day the wind breathes low with mellower tone:
Through every hollow cave and alley lone
Round and round the spicy downs the yellow
    Lotos-dust is blown.
150 We have had enough of action, and of motion we,
Rolled to starboard, rolled to larboard,° when   port
    the surge was seething free,
Where the wallowing monster spouted his foam-
    fountains in the sea.
Let us swear an oath, and keep it with an equal mind,
In the hollow Lotos-land to live and lie reclined
155 On the hills like Gods together, careless of mankind.
For they lie beside their nectar, and the bolts[4] are hurled
Far below them in the valleys, and the clouds are
    lightly curled
Round their golden houses, girdled with the gleaming
    world:
Where they smile in secret, looking over wasted lands,
160 Blight and famine, plague and earthquake, roaring
    deeps and fiery sands,
Clanging fights, and flaming towns, and sinking
    ships, and praying hands.
But they smile, they find a music centred in a doleful
    song
Steaming up, a lamentation and an ancient tale of
    wrong,
Like a tale of little meaning though the words are strong;
165 Chanted from an ill-used race of men that cleave the
    soil,
Sow the seed, and reap the harvest with enduring toil,
Storing yearly little dues of wheat, and wine and oil;
Till they perish and they suffer—some, 'tis whispered
    —down in hell
Suffer endless anguish, others in Elysian[5] valleys dwell,
170 Resting weary limbs at last on beds of asphodel.[6]
Surely, surely, slumber is more sweet than toil, the shore

---

[1] *Have eat our substance* I.e., have consumed our goods and property. As the sailors rightly surmise, in the years that they have been away from their home island of Ithaca (the "little isle" of line 124) following Odysseus to fight the Trojan War, the other princes of Ithaca and the neighboring islands have encroached upon their homes.

[2] *amaranth* Mythical flower that never wilted; *moly* Herb with magical protective powers.

[3] *acanthus* Plant native to Mediterranean shores. The Greeks and Romans esteemed the plant for the elegance of its leaves.

[4] *bolts* Lightning bolts.

[5] *Elysian* Heavenly. According to the ancient Greeks, Elysium was the dwelling place of the blessed after death.

[6] *asphodel* Plant said to cover the Elysian fields.

Than labour in the deep mid-ocean, wind and wave
    and oar;
Oh rest ye, brother mariners, we will not wander more.
—1832 (REVISED 1842)

Ulysses[1]

It little profits that an idle king,
  By this still hearth, among these barren crags,
Matched with an agèd wife, I mete[2] and dole
Unequal laws unto a savage race,
5 That hoard, and sleep, and feed, and know not me.

I cannot rest from travel: I will drink
Life to the lees:° all times I have enjoyed   *dregs*
Greatly, have suffered greatly, both with those
That loved me, and alone; on shore, and when
10 Thro' scudding° drifts the rainy Hyades[3]   *wind-driven*
Vexed the dim sea: I am become a name;
For always roaming with a hungry heart
Much have I seen and known; cities of men
And manners, climates, councils, governments,
15 Myself not least, but honoured of them all;
And drunk delight of battle with my peers,
Far on the ringing plains of windy Troy.[4]
I am a part of all that I have met;
Yet all experience is an arch wherethrough
20 Gleams that untravelled world, whose margin°   *horizon*
    fades
For ever and for ever when I move.
How dull it is to pause, to make an end,

To rust unburnished, not to shine in use!
As though to breathe were life. Life piled on life
25 Were all too little, and of one to me
Little remains: but every hour is saved
From that eternal silence, something more,
A bringer of new things; and vile it were
For some three suns to store and hoard myself,
30 And this gray spirit yearning in desire
To follow knowledge like a sinking star,
Beyond the utmost bound of human thought.

    This is my son, mine own Telemachus,
To whom I leave the sceptre and the isle—
35 Well-loved of me, discerning to fulfil
This labour, by slow prudence to make mild
A rugged people, and through soft degrees
Subdue them to the useful and the good.
Most blameless is he, centred in the sphere
40 Of common duties, decent not to fail
In offices of tenderness, and pay
Meet° adoration to my household gods,   *fitting*
When I am gone. He works his work, I mine.

    There lies the port; the vessel puffs her sail:
45 There gloom the dark broad seas. My mariners,
Souls that have toiled, and wrought, and thought
    with me—
That ever with a frolic welcome took
The thunder and the sunshine, and opposed
Free hearts, free foreheads—you and I are old;
50 Old age hath yet his honour and his toil;
Death closes all: but something ere the end,
Some work of noble note, may yet be done,
Not unbecoming men that strove with Gods.

The lights begin to twinkle from the rocks:
55 The long day wanes: the slow moon climbs: the deep
Moans round with many voices. Come, my friends,
'Tis not too late to seek a newer world.
Push off, and sitting well in order smite
The sounding furrows; for my purpose holds
60 To sail beyond the sunset, and the baths
Of all the western stars, until I die.
It may be that the gulfs will wash us down:

---

[1] *Ulysses* Latin name for Odysseus, the hero of Homer's *Odyssey*, which culminates in his reunion (after nearly twenty years) with his wife Penelope and his only son Telemachus (see line 33) and his regaining the throne of Ithaca. Here, some time after the adventures recounted by Homer, the aged yet restless Ulysses prepares to embark on one last voyage of discovery. Tennyson was inspired by a passage in Dante's *Inferno* (Canto 26), in which the shade of Ulysses recounts the story of that final voyage.

[2] *mete* Portion out.

[3] *Hyades* Group of stars near the constellation Taurus and associated with rainstorms.

[4] *Troy* Ancient city in what is now modern Turkey, and site of the Trojan War, in which Ulysses was a participant.

It may be we shall touch the Happy Isles,[1]
And see the great Achilles,[2] whom we knew.
65   Though much is taken, much abides; and though
We are not now that strength which in old days
Moved earth and heaven; that which we are, we are;
One equal temper of heroic hearts,
Made weak by time and fate, but strong in will
70   To strive, to seek, to find, and not to yield.
    —1842 (WRITTEN 1833)

The Epic[3]

At Francis Allen's on the Christmas-eve,—
    The game of forfeits[4] done—the girls all kissed
Beneath the sacred bush[5] and past away—
The parson Holmes, the poet Everard Hall,
5   The host, and I sat round the wassail-bowl,[6]
Then half-way ebbed: and there we held a talk,
How all the old honour had from Christmas gone,
Or gone, or dwindled down to some odd games
In some odd nooks like this; till I, tired out
10   With cutting eights[7] that day upon the pond,
Where, three times slipping from the outer edge,
I bumped the ice into three several stars,
Fell in a doze; and half-awake I heard
The parson taking wide and wider sweeps,
15   Now harping on the church-commissioners,
Now hawking at Geology and schism;[8]

Until I woke, and found him settled down
Upon the general decay of faith
Right through the world, "at home was little left,
20   And none abroad: there was no anchor, none,
To hold by." Francis, laughing, clapped his hand
On Everard's shoulder, with "I hold by him."
"And I," quoth Everard, "by the wassail-bowl."
"Why yes," I said, "we knew your gift that way
25   At college: but another which you had,
I mean of verse (for so we held it then),
What came of that?" "You know," said Frank, "he burnt
His epic, his King Arthur, some twelve books"—
And then to me demanding why? "Oh, sir,
30   He thought that nothing new was said, or else
Something so said 'twas nothing—that a truth
Looks freshest in the fashion of the day:
God knows: he has a mint of reasons: ask.
It pleased me well enough." "Nay, nay," said Hall,
35   "Why take the style of those heroic times?
For nature brings not back the Mastodon,[9]
Nor we those times; and why should any man
Remodel models? these twelve books of mine
Were faint Homeric echoes, nothing-worth,
40   Mere chaff and draff,[10] much better burnt." "But I,"
Said Francis, "picked the eleventh from this hearth
And have it: keep a thing, its use will come.
I hoard it as a sugar-plum for Holmes."
He laughed, and I, though sleepy, like a horse
45   That hears the corn-bin open, pricked my ears;
For I remembered Everard's college fame
When we were freshmen: then at my request
He brought it; and the poet little urged,
But with some prelude of disparagement,
50   Read, mouthing out his hollow oes and aes,
Deep-chested music, and to this result.

---

[1] *Happy Isles*   Elysium, or Isles of the Blessed, where heroes enjoyed the afterlife.

[2] *Achilles*   Greek hero of the Trojan War, the central character of Homer's *Iliad*.

[3] *The Epic*   Tennyson wrote this poem as a poetic "frame" for "Morte d'Arthur," which follows; together the two poems make up a single work. "The Epic" itself consists of the fifty-one lines that precede the "Morte d'Arthur," plus the thirty-one lines that follow.

[4] *forfeits*   Parlor game popular in the nineteenth century.

[5] *sacred bush*   Mistletoe.

[6] *wassail-bowl*   Punch bowl containing spiced ale.

[7] *cutting eights*   Skating figure-eights.

[8] *church-commissioners ... Geology ... schism*   References to contemporary religious and scientific controversies.

[9] *Mastodon*   Extinct elephant-like mammal; evidence of its existence was first discovered in the eighteenth century, and the name first applied in the early nineteenth.

[10] *chaff and draff*   Here, refuse, material of little worth.

Morte d'Arthur[1]

So all day long the noise of battle rolled
   Among the mountains by the winter sea;
Until King Arthur's table, man by man,
Had fallen in Lyonnesse[2] about their Lord,
5 King Arthur: then, because his wound was deep,
The bold Sir Bedivere uplifted him,
Sir Bedivere, the last of all his knights,
And bore him to a chapel nigh° the field,   *near*
A broken chancel[3] with a broken cross,
10 That stood on a dark strait of barren land.
On one side lay the ocean, and on one
Lay a great water, and the moon was full.

   Then spake King Arthur to Sir Bedivere:
"The sequel of today unsolders all
15 The goodliest fellowship of famous knights
Whereof this world holds record. Such a sleep
They sleep—the men I loved. I think that we
Shall never more, at any future time,
Delight our souls with talk of knightly deeds,
20 Walking about the gardens and the halls
Of Camelot,[4] as in the days that were.
I perish by this people which I made,—
Though Merlin[5] sware° that I should   *promised*
    come again
To rule once more—but let what will be, be,
25 I am so deeply smitten through the helm[6]
That without help I cannot last till morn.
Thou therefore take my brand° Excalibur,   *sword*

Which was my pride: for thou rememberest how
In those old days, one summer noon, an arm
30 Rose up from out the bosom of the lake,
Clothed in white samite,° mystic, wonderful,   *silk*
Holding the sword—and how I rowed across
And took it, and have worn it, like a king:
And, wheresoever I am sung or told
35 In aftertime, this also shall be known:
But now delay not: take Excalibur,
And fling him far into the middle mere:[7]
Watch what thou seest, and lightly bring me word."

   To him replied the bold Sir Bedivere:
40 "It is not meet,° Sir King, to leave thee thus,   *appropriate*
Aidless, alone, and smitten through the helm.
A little thing may harm a wounded man.
Yet I thy hest° will all perform at full,   *command*
Watch what I see, and lightly bring thee word."

45   So saying, from the ruined shrine he stepped
And in the moon athwart the place of tombs,
Where lay the mighty bones of ancient men,
Old knights, and over them the sea-wind sang
Shrill, chill, with flakes of foam. He, stepping down
50 By zig-zag paths, and juts of pointed rock,
Came on the shining levels of the lake.

   There drew he forth the brand Excalibur,
And o'er him, drawing it, the winter moon,
Brightening the skirts of a long cloud, ran forth
55 And sparkled keen with frost against the hilt:
For all the haft° twinkled with diamond sparks, *handle*
Myriads of topaz-lights, and jacinth[8]-work
Of subtlest jewellery. He gazed so long
That both his eyes were dazzled, as he stood,
60 This way and that dividing the swift mind,
In act to throw: but at the last it seemed
Better to leave Excalibur concealed
There in the many-knotted waterflags,°   *reeds*
That whistled stiff and dry about the marge.°   *shore*
65 So strode he back slow to the wounded King.

---

[1] *Morte d'Arthur* French: The Death of [King] Arthur. This poem was later incorporated into the final book of Tennyson's epic *Idylls of the King.* As his kingdom and the knightly Order of the Round Table fall into disorder, Arthur faces a rebellion led by his nephew Modred; in one final battle Arthur defeats Modred, but his knights are almost all killed and Arthur himself gravely wounded by a blow to the head.

[2] [Tennyson's note] The country of legend that lay between Cornwall and the Scilly Islands.

[3] *chancel* Area around the altar.

[4] *Camelot* Legendary location of King Arthur's court.

[5] *Merlin* Wizard, advisor, and manipulator of events in Arthurian legend.

[6] *smitten through the helm* Pierced through the helmet.

[7] *middle mere* Middle of the lake.

[8] *jacinth* Reddish-orange gem.

Then spake King Arthur to Sir Bedivere:
"Hast thou performed my mission which I gave?
What is it thou hast seen? or what hast heard?"

And answer made the bold Sir Bedivere:
70 "I heard the ripple washing in the reeds,
And the wild water lapping on the crag."

To whom replied King Arthur, faint and pale:
"Thou hast betrayed thy nature and thy name,
Not rendering true answer, as beseemed
75 Thy fealty,° nor like a noble knight: sworn allegiance
For surer sign had followed, either hand,
Or voice, or else a motion of the mere.
This is a shameful thing for men to lie.
Yet now, I charge thee,[1] quickly go again
80 As thou art lief° and dear, and do the thing   beloved
I bad[2] thee, watch, and lightly bring me word."

Then went Sir Bedivere the second time
Across the ridge, and paced beside the mere,
Counting the dewy pebbles, fix'd in thought;
85 But when he saw the wonder of the hilt,
How curiously and strangely chased,° he smote   engraved
His palms together, and he cried aloud,

"And if indeed I cast the brand away,
Surely a precious thing, one worthy note,
90 Should thus be lost for ever from the earth,
Which might have pleased the eyes of many men.
What good should follow this, if this were done?
What harm, undone? deep harm to disobey,
Seeing obedience is the bond of rule.
95 Were it well to obey then, if a king demand
An act unprofitable, against himself?
The King is sick, and knows not what he does.
What record, or what relic of my lord
Should be to aftertime, but empty breath
100 And rumours of a doubt? but were this kept,
Stored in some treasure-house of mighty kings,
Some one might show it at a joust of arms,

Saying, 'King Arthur's sword, Excalibur,
Wrought by the lonely maiden of the Lake.
105 Nine years she wrought it, sitting in the deeps
Upon the hidden bases of the hills.'
So might some old man speak in the aftertime
To all the people, winning reverence.
But now much honour and much fame were lost."

110 So spake he, clouded with his own conceit,
And hid Excalibur the second time,
And so strode back slow to the wounded King.

Then spoke King Arthur, breathing heavily:
"What is it thou hast seen? or what hast heard?"

115 And answer made the bold Sir Bedivere:
"I heard the water lapping on the crag,
And the long ripple washing in the reeds."

To whom replied King Arthur, much in wrath:
"Ah, miserable and unkind, untrue,
120 Unknightly, traitor-hearted! Woe is me!
Authority forgets a dying king,
Laid widowed of the power in his eye
That bowed the will. I see thee what thou art,
For thou, the latest-left° of all my knights,   last
125 In whom should meet the offices of all,
Thou wouldst betray me for the precious hilt;
Either from lust of gold, or like a girl
Valuing the giddy pleasure of the eyes.
Yet, for a man may fail in duty twice,
130 And the third time may prosper, get thee hence:
But, if thou spare to fling Excalibur,
I will arise and slay thee with my hands."

Then quickly rose Sir Bedivere, and ran,
And, leaping down the ridges lightly, plunged
135 Among the bulrush-beds, and clutched the sword,
And strongly wheeled and threw it. The great brand
Made lightnings in the splendour of the moon,
And flashing round and round, and whirled in an arch,
Shot like a streamer of the northern morn,[3]

---

[1] *I charge thee* I command you.

[2] *bad* I.e., bade, commanded.

---

[3] *northern morn* Aurora borealis.

140 Seen where the moving isles of winter[1] shock
By night, with noises of the northern sea.
So flashed and fell the brand Excalibur:
But ere he dipped the surface, rose an arm
Clothed in white samite, mystic, wonderful,
145 And caught him by the hilt, and brandished him
Three times, and drew him under in the mere.
And lightly went the other to the King.

Then spoke King Arthur, drawing thicker breath:
"Now see I by thine eyes that this is done.
150 Speak out: what is it thou hast heard, or seen?"

And answer made the bold Sir Bedivere:
"Sir King, I closed mine eyelids, lest the gems
Should blind my purpose, for I never saw,
Nor shall see, here or elsewhere, till I die,
155 Not though I live three lives of mortal men,
So great a miracle as yonder hilt.
Then with both hands I flung him, wheeling him;
But when I looked again, behold an arm,
Clothed in white samite, mystic, wonderful,
160 That caught him by the hilt, and brandished him
Three times, and drew him under in the mere."

And answer made King Arthur, breathing hard:
"My end draws nigh; 'tis time that I were gone.
Make broad thy shoulders to receive my weight,
165 And bear me to the margin;° yet I fear   shore
My wound hath taken cold, and I shall die."

So saying, from the pavement he half rose,
Slowly, with pain, reclining on his arm,
And looking wistfully with wide blue eyes
170 As in a picture. Him Sir Bedivere
Remorsefully regarded through his tears,
And would have spoken, but he found not words,
Then took with care, and kneeling on one knee,
O'er both his shoulders drew the languid hands,
175 And rising bore him through the place of tombs.

But, as he walked, King Arthur panted hard,
Like one that feels a nightmare on his bed
When all the house is mute. So sighed the King,
Muttering and murmuring at his ear, "Quick, quick!
180 I fear it is too late, and I shall die."
But the other swiftly strode from ridge to ridge,
Clothed with his breath, and looking, as he walked,
Larger than human on the frozen hills.
He heard the deep behind him, and a cry
185 Before. His own thought drove him, like a goad.
Dry clashed his harness in the icy caves
And barren chasms, and all to left and right
The bare black cliff clanged round him, as he based
His feet on juts of slippery crag that rang
190 Sharp-smitten with the dint of armèd heels—
And on a sudden, lo! the level lake,
And the long glories of the winter moon.
Then saw they how there hove° a dusky barge,   floated
Dark as a funeral scarf from stem to stern,
195 Beneath them; and descending they were ware°   aware
That all the decks were dense with stately forms
Black-stoled,[2] black-hooded, like a dream—by these
Three Queens with crowns of gold—and from them rose
A cry that shivered to the tingling stars,
200 And, as it were one voice, an agony
Of lamentation, like a wind, that shrills
All night in a waste land, where no one comes,
Or hath come, since the making of the world.

Then murmured Arthur, "Place me in the barge,"
205 And to the barge they came. There those three Queens
Put forth their hands, and took the King, and wept.
But she, that rose the tallest of them all
And fairest, laid his head upon her lap,
And loosed the shattered casque,° and chafed   helmet
    his hands,
210 And called him by his name, complaining loud,
And dropping bitter tears against his brow
Striped with dark blood: for all his face was white
And colourless, and like the withered moon
Smote by the fresh beam of the springing east;
215 And all his greaves and cuisses[3] dashed with drops

---

[1] *isles of winter* Icebergs.

[2] *Black-stoled* Wearing black cloaks.

[3] *greaves and cuisses* Armor for shins and thighs.

Of onset;[1] and the light and lustrous curls—
That made his forehead like a rising sun
High from the dais-throne—were parched with dust;
Or, clotted into points and hanging loose,
220 Mix'd with the knightly growth that fringed his lips.
So like a shattered column lay the King;
Not like that Arthur who, with lance in rest,
From spur to plume a star of tournament,
Shot through the lists[2] at Camelot, and charged
225 Before the eyes of ladies and of kings.

    Then loudly cried the bold Sir Bedivere,
"Ah! my Lord Arthur, whither shall I go?
Where shall I hide my forehead and my eyes?
For now I see the true old times are dead,
230 When every morning brought a noble chance,
And every chance brought out a noble knight.
Such times have been not since the light that led
The holy Elders[3] with the gift of myrrh.
But now the whole Round Table is dissolved
235 Which was an image of the mighty world;
And I, the last, go forth companionless,
And the days darken round me, and the years,
Among new men, strange faces, other minds."

    And slowly answered Arthur from the barge:
240 "The old order changeth, yielding place to new,
And God fulfils Himself in many ways,
Lest one good custom should corrupt the world.
Comfort thyself: what comfort is in me?
I have lived my life, and that which I have done
245 May He within Himself make pure! but thou,
If thou shouldst never see my face again,
Pray for my soul. More things are wrought by prayer
Than this world dreams of. Wherefore, let thy voice
Rise like a fountain for me night and day.
250 For what are men better than sheep or goats
That nourish a blind life within the brain,
If, knowing God, they lift not hands of prayer

Both for themselves and those who call them friend?
For so the whole round earth is every way
255 Bound by gold chains about the feet of God.
But now farewell. I am going a long way
With these thou seest—if indeed I go—
(For all my mind is clouded with a doubt)
To the island-valley of Avilion;[4]
260 Where falls not hail, or rain, or any snow,
Nor ever wind blows loudly; but it lies
Deep-meadowed, happy, fair with orchard-lawns
And bowery hollows crown'd with summer sea,
Where I will heal me of my grievous wound."

265 So said he, and the barge with oar and sail
Moved from the brink, like some full-breasted swan
That, fluting a wild carol ere her death,[5]
Ruffles her pure cold plume, and takes the flood
With swarthy webs.[6] Long stood Sir Bedivere
270 Revolving many memories, till the hull
Looked one black dot against the verge of dawn,
And on the mere the wailing died away.

———————

Here ended Hall,[7] and our last light, that long
Had winked and threatened darkness, flared and fell:
At which the Parson, sent to sleep with sound,
[55] And waked with silence, grunted "Good!" but we
Sat rapt: it was the tone with which he read—
Perhaps some modern touches here and there
Redeemed it from the charge of nothingness—
Or else we loved the man, and prized his work;
[60] I know not: but we sitting, as I said,
The cock crew loud; as at that time of year
The lusty bird takes every hour for dawn:[8]
Then Francis, muttering, like a man ill-used,

———————

[1] *onset* Rush of battle (which has splattered his armor).

[2] *lists* Arenas in which jousting and tilting tournaments were held.

[3] *holy Elders* Three kings who brought gifts, including myrrh, at the birth of Jesus (Matthew 2.11).

[4] *Avilion* Avalon, a magical island frequently featured in Arthurian legend.

[5] *swan … death* Swans were said to sing only once, at their deaths.

[6] *webs* I.e., webbed feet.

[7] *Here ended Hall* "The Epic" here resumes, as Everard Hall has finished reading out his poem.

[8] *The cock … for dawn* For the belief that the rooster crows all night long on Christmas Eve, see Shakespeare, *Hamlet*, 1.1.158–60.

"There now—that's nothing!" drew a little back,
[65] And drove his heel into the smouldered log,
That sent a blast of sparkles up the flue:
And so to bed; where yet in sleep I seemed
To sail with Arthur under looming shores,
Point after point; till on to dawn, when dreams
[70] Begin to feel the truth and stir of day,
To me, methought, who waited with a crowd,
There came a bark° that, blowing forward, bore   *ship*
King Arthur, like a modern gentleman
Of stateliest port;° and all the people cried,   *bearing*
[75] "Arthur is come again: he cannot die."
Then those that stood upon the hills behind
Repeated—"Come again, and thrice as fair";
And, further inland, voices echoed—"Come
With all good things, and war shall be no more."
[80] At this a hundred bells began to peal,
That with the sound I woke, and heard indeed
The clear church-bells ring in the Christmas-morn.
—1842 (WRITTEN 1833–34)

[Break, break, break]

Break, break, break,
On thy cold gray stones, O Sea!
And I would that my tongue could utter
The thoughts that arise in me.

5   O well for the fisherman's boy,
That he shouts with his sister at play!
O well for the sailor lad,
That he sings in his boat on the bay!

And the stately ships go on
10   To their haven under the hill;
But O for the touch of a vanished hand,
And the sound of a voice that is still![1]

Break, break, break,
At the foot of thy crags, O Sea!

---

[1] *But ... still* Probably a reference to Tennyson's closest friend, Arthur Hallam, who had died in 1833.

15 But the tender grace of a day that is dead
Will never come back to me.
—1842 (WRITTEN 1834?)

St Simeon Stylites[2]

Although I be the basest of mankind,
From scalp to sole one slough and crust of sin,
Unfit for earth, unfit for heaven, scarce meet
For troops of devils, mad with blasphemy,
5   I will not cease to grasp the hope I hold
Of saintdom, and to clamour, mourn and sob,
Battering the gates of heaven with storms of prayer,
Have mercy, Lord, and take away my sin.

Let this avail, just, dreadful, mighty God,
10 This not be all in vain, that thrice ten years,
Thrice multiplied by superhuman pangs,
In hungers and in thirsts, fevers and cold,
In coughs, aches, stitches, ulcerous throes and cramps,
A sign betwixt the meadow and the cloud,
15 Patient on this tall pillar I have borne
Rain, wind, frost, heat, hail, damp, and sleet, and snow;
And I had hoped that ere this period closed
Thou wouldst have caught me up into thy rest,
Denying not these weather-beaten limbs
20 The meed° of saints, the white robe and the   *reward*
palm.

O take the meaning, Lord: I do not breathe,
Not whisper, any murmur of complaint.
Pain heaped ten-hundred-fold to this, were still
Less burthen, by ten-hundred-fold, to bear,
25 Than were those lead-like tons of sin, that crushed
My spirit flat before thee.
O Lord, Lord,

---

[2] *St Simeon Stylites* Simeon was an early fifth-century Christian ascetic who gained fame for the extreme form of self-denial he practiced: he lived for nearly forty years atop a pillar in the Syrian desert. (*Stylites* is Greek for "of the pillar.") Pilgrims flocked to see him and other pillar-saints imitated his example.

Thou knowest I bore this better at the first,
For I was strong and hale of body then;
And though my teeth, which now are dropt away,
30 Would chatter with the cold, and all my beard
Was tagged with icy fringes in the moon,
I drowned the whoopings of the owl with sound
Of pious hymns and psalms, and sometimes saw
An angel stand and watch me, as I sang.
35 Now am I feeble grown; my end draws nigh;
I hope my end draws nigh: half deaf I am,
So that I scarce can hear the people hum
About the column's base, and almost blind,
And scarce can recognise the fields I know;
40 And both my thighs are rotted with the dew;
Yet cease I not to clamour and to cry,
While my stiff spine can hold my weary head,
Till all my limbs drop piecemeal from the stone,
Have mercy, mercy: take away my sin.

45 O Jesus, if thou wilt not save my soul,
Who may be saved? who is it may be saved?
Who may be made a saint, if I fail here?
Show me the man hath suffered more than I.
For did not all thy martyrs die one death?
50 For either they were stoned, or crucified,
Or burned in fire, or boiled in oil, or sawn
In twain beneath the ribs; but I die here
Today, and whole years long, a life of death.
Bear witness, if I could have found a way
55 (And heedfully I sifted all my thought)
More slowly-painful to subdue this home
Of sin, my flesh, which I despise and hate,
I had not stinted° practice, O my God.   spared

For not alone this pillar-punishment,
60 Not this alone I bore: but while I lived
In the white convent down the valley there,
For many weeks about my loins I wore
The rope that haled the buckets from the well,
Twisted as tight as I could knot the noose;
65 And spake not of it to a single soul,
Until the ulcer, eating through my skin,
Betrayed my secret penance, so that all

My brethren marvelled greatly. More than this
I bore, whereof, O God, thou knowest all.

70 Three winters, that my soul might grow to thee,
I lived up there on yonder mountain side.
My right leg chained into the crag, I lay
Pent in a roofless close of ragged stones;
Inswathed sometimes in wandering mist, and twice
75 Blacked with thy branding thunder, and sometimes
Sucking the damps for drink, and eating not,
Except the spare chance-gift of those that came
To touch my body and be healed, and live:
And they say then that I worked miracles,
80 Whereof my fame is loud amongst mankind,
Cured lameness, palsies, cancers. Thou, O God,
Knowest alone whether this was or no.
Have mercy, mercy! cover all my sin.

Then, that I might be more alone with thee,
85 Three years I lived upon a pillar, high
Six cubits,[1] and three years on one of twelve;
And twice three years I crouched on one that rose
Twenty by measure; last of all, I grew
Twice ten long weary weary years to this,
90 That numbers forty cubits from the soil.

I think that I have borne as much as this—
Or else I dream—and for so long a time,
If I may measure time by yon slow light,
And this high dial, which my sorrow crowns—
95 So much—even so.
                      And yet I know not well,
For that the evil ones come here, and say,
"Fall down, O Simeon: thou hast suffered long
For ages and for ages!" then they prate°   chatter
Of penances I cannot have gone through,
100 Perplexing me with lies; and oft I fall,
Maybe for months, in such blind lethargies
That Heaven, and Earth, and Time are choked.
                                          But yet

---

[1] *cubits* Unit of measure equal to the length of a forearm, or about half a meter.

Bethink thee, Lord, while thou and all the saints
Enjoy themselves in heaven, and men on earth
105 House in the shade of comfortable roofs,
Sit with their wives by fires, eat wholesome food,
And wear warm clothes, and even beasts have stalls,
I, 'tween the spring and downfall of the light,
Bow down one thousand and two hundred times,
110 To Christ, the Virgin Mother, and the saints;
Or in the night, after a little sleep,
I wake: the chill stars sparkle; I am wet
With drenching dews, or stiff with crackling frost.
I wear an undressed goatskin on my back;
115 A grazing iron collar grinds my neck;
And in my weak, lean arms I lift the cross,
And strive and wrestle with thee till I die:
O mercy, mercy! wash away my sin.

O Lord, thou knowest what a man I am;
120 A sinful man, conceived and born in sin:[1]
'Tis their own doing; this is none of mine;
Lay it not to me. Am I to blame for this,
That here come those that worship me? Ha! ha!
They think that I am somewhat. What am I?
125 The silly people take me for a saint,
And bring me offerings of fruit and flowers:
And I, in truth (thou wilt bear witness here)
Have all in all endured as much, and more
Than many just and holy men, whose names
130 Are registered and calendared for saints.

Good people, you do ill to kneel to me.
What is it I can have done to merit this?
I am a sinner viler than you all.
It may be I have wrought some miracles,
135 And cured some halt° and maimed; but what   *lame*
    of that?
It may be, no one, even among the saints,
May match his pains with mine; but what of that?
Yet do not rise; for you may look on me,
And in your looking you may kneel to God.
140 Speak! is there any of you halt or maimed?

I think you know I have some power with Heaven
From my long penance: let him speak his wish.

Yes, I can heal him. Power goes forth from me.[2]
They say that they are healed. Ah, hark! they shout
145 "St Simeon Stylites." Why, if so,
God reaps a harvest in me. O my soul,
God reaps a harvest in thee. If this be,
Can I work miracles and not be saved?
This is not told of any. They were saints.
150 It cannot be but that I shall be saved;
Yea, crowned a saint. They shout, "Behold a saint!"
And lower voices saint me from above.
Courage, St Simeon! This dull chrysalis°   *cocoon*
Cracks into shining wings, and hope ere death
155 Spreads more and more and more, that God hath now
Sponged and made blank of crimeful record all
My mortal archives.
          O my sons, my sons,
I, Simeon of the pillar, by surname
Stylites, among men; I, Simeon,
160 The watcher on the column till the end;
I, Simeon, whose brain the sunshine bakes;
I, whose bald brows in silent hours become
Unnaturally hoar with rime,[3] do now
From my high nest of penance here proclaim
165 That Pontius and Iscariot[4] by my side
Showed like fair seraphs.° On the coals I lay,   *angels*
A vessel full of sin: all hell beneath
Made me boil over. Devils plucked my sleeve,
Abaddon and Asmodeus[5] caught at me.
170 I smote them with the cross; they swarmed again.
In bed like monstrous apes they crushed my chest:
They flapped my light out as I read: I saw
Their faces grow between me and my book;
With colt-like whinny and with hoggish whine
175 They burst my prayer. Yet this way was left,

---

[1] *O Lord ... in sin* Cf. Psalm 51.5: "Behold, I was shapen in iniquity; and in sin did my mother conceive me."

[2] *Power goes ... me* Cf. Luke 8.46, where it is Jesus who says, when healing the sick, "power [has] gone out from me."

[3] *hoar with rime* White with frost.

[4] *Pontius and Iscariot* Pontius Pilate, who condemned Jesus to death; Judas Iscariot, the disciple of Jesus who betrayed him.

[5] *Abaddon and Asmodeus* Evil spirits mentioned in the Bible.

And by this way I 'scaped them. Mortify
Your flesh, like me, with scourges and with thorns;
Smite, shrink not, spare not. If it may be, fast
Whole Lents, and pray. I hardly, with slow steps,
180   With slow, faint steps, and much exceeding pain,
Have scrambled past those pits of fire, that still
Sing in mine ears. But yield not me the praise:
God only through his bounty hath thought fit,
Among the powers and princes of this world,
185   To make me an example to mankind,
Which few can reach to. Yet I do not say
But that a time may come—yea, even now,
Now, now, his footsteps smite the threshold stairs
Of life—I say, that time is at the doors
190   When you may worship me without reproach;
For I will leave my relics in your land,
And you may carve a shrine about my dust,
And burn a fragrant lamp before my bones,
When I am gathered to the glorious saints.

195   While I spake then, a sting of shrewdest°   *sharpest*
            pain
Ran shrivelling through me, and a cloudlike change,
In passing, with a grosser film made thick
These heavy, horny eyes. The end! the end!
Surely the end! What's here? a shape, a shade,
200   A flash of light. Is that the angel there
That holds a crown? Come, blessed brother, come.
I know thy glittering face. I waited long;
My brows are ready. What! deny it now?
Nay, draw, draw, draw nigh. So I clutch it. Christ!
205   'Tis gone: 'tis here again; the crown! the crown!
So now 'tis fitted on and grows to me,
And from it melt the dews of Paradise,
Sweet! sweet! spikenard, and balm, and frankincense.[1]
Ah! let me not be fooled, sweet saints: I trust
210   That I am whole, and clean, and meet for Heaven.

        Speak, if there be a priest, a man of God,
Among you there, and let him presently
Approach, and lean a ladder on the shaft,

And climbing up into my airy home,
215   Deliver me the blessed sacrament;
For by the warning of the Holy Ghost,
I prophesy that I shall die tonight,
A quarter before twelve.
                                    But thou, O lord,
Aid all this foolish people; let them take
220   Example, pattern: lead them to thy light.
—1842 (WRITTEN 1833)

Locksley Hall

Comrades, leave me here a little, while as yet 'tis
    early morn:
Leave me here, and when you want me, sound upon
    the bugle-horn.

'Tis the place, and all around it, as of old, the
    curlews[2] call,
Dreary gleams about the moorland flying over
    Locksley Hall;

5   Locksley Hall, that in the distance overlooks the
    sandy tracts,
And the hollow ocean-ridges roaring into cataracts.

Many a night from yonder ivied casement, ere I went
    to rest,
Did I look on great Orion[3] sloping slowly to the West.

Many a night I saw the Pleiads,[4] rising through the
    mellow shade,
10   Glitter like a swarm of fire-flies tangled in a silver braid.

Here about the beach I wandered, nourishing a
    youth sublime
With the fairy tales of science, and the long result of
    Time;

---

[1] *spikenard, and balm, and frankincense*   Aromatic oils mentioned in
the Bible.

[2] *curlews* Species of shore-dwelling birds.

[3] *Orion* The constellation named after the hunter of Greek legend.
It sets in November and so was associated with rains and storms.

[4] *Pleiads* The constellation commonly known as the Pleiades (named
after the seven daughters of Atlas), which rises in May and sets in
November.

When the centuries behind me like a fruitful land reposed;
When I clung to all the present for the promise that it
    closed:

15   When I dipped into the future far as human eye
    could see;
Saw the Vision of the world, and all the wonder that
    would be.—

In the Spring a fuller crimson comes upon the robin's
    breast;
In the Spring the wanton lapwing[1] gets himself
    another crest;

In the Spring a livelier iris changes on the burnished
    dove;
20   In the Spring a young man's fancy lightly turns to
    thoughts of love.

Then her cheek was pale and thinner than should be
    for one so young,
And her eyes on all my motions with a mute
    observance hung.

And I said, "My cousin Amy, speak, and speak the
    truth to me,
Trust me, cousin, all the current of my being sets to
    thee."

25   On her pallid cheek and forehead came a colour and a
    light,
As I have seen the rosy red flushing in the northern
    night.

And she turned—her bosom shaken with a sudden
    storm of sighs—
All the spirit deeply dawning in the dark of hazel eyes—

Saying, "I have hid my feelings, fearing they should
    do me wrong";
30   Saying, "Dost thou love me, cousin?" weeping, "I
    have loved thee long."

Love took up the glass of Time,[2] and turned it in
    his glowing hands;
Every moment, lightly shaken, ran itself in golden sands.

Love took up the harp of Life, and smote on all the
    chords with might;
Smote the chord of Self, that, trembling, passed in
    music out of sight.

35   Many a morning on the moorland did we hear the
    copses° ring,   *thickets*
And her whisper thronged my pulses with the fullness
    of the Spring.

Many an evening by the waters did we watch the
    stately ships,
And our spirits rushed together at the touching of
    the lips.

O my cousin, shallow-hearted! O my Amy, mine no
    more!
40   O the dreary, dreary moorland! O the barren, barren
    shore!

Falser than all fancy fathoms,° falser than all   *apprehends*
    songs have sung,
Puppet to a father's threat, and servile to a shrewish
    tongue!

Is it well to wish thee happy?—having known me—to
    decline
On a range of lower feelings and a narrower heart
    than mine!

45   Yet it shall be: thou shalt lower to his level day by day,
What is fine within thee growing coarse to sympathise
    with clay.

As the husband is, the wife is: thou art mated with a
    clown,[3]

---

[1] *lapwing* A plover, a type of wading bird.

[2] *glass of Time* Hourglass.

[3] *clown* Rustic, boorish fellow.

And the grossness of his nature will have weight to
    drag thee down.

He will hold thee, when his passion shall have spent
    its novel force,
50 Something better than his dog, a little dearer than his
    horse.

What is this? his eyes are heavy: think not they are
    glazed with wine.
Go to him: it is thy duty: kiss him: take his hand in
    thine.

It may be my lord is weary, that his brain is overwrought:
Soothe him with thy finer fancies, touch him with
    thy lighter thought.

55 He will answer to the purpose, easy things to
    understand—
Better thou wert dead before me, though I slew thee
    with my hand!

Better thou and I were lying, hidden from the heart's
    disgrace,
Rolled in one another's arms, and silent in a last embrace.

Cursèd be the social wants that sin against the
    strength of youth!
60 Cursèd be the social lies that warp us from the
    living truth!

Cursèd be the sickly forms that err from honest
    Nature's rule!
Cursèd be the gold that gilds the straitened forehead
    of the fool![1]

Well—'tis well that I should bluster!—Hadst thou
    less unworthy proved—
Would to God—for I had loved thee more than ever
    wife was loved.

65 Am I mad, that I should cherish that which bears but
    bitter fruit?
I will pluck it from my bosom, though my heart be at
    the root.

Never, though my mortal summers to such length
    of years should come
As the many-wintered crow that leads the clanging
    rookery[2] home.

Where is comfort? in division of the records of the mind?
70 Can I part her from herself, and love her, as I knew
    her, kind?

I remember one that perished: sweetly did she speak
    and move:
Such a one do I remember, whom to look at was to love.

Can I think of her as dead, and love her for the love
    she bore?
No—she never loved me truly: love is love for evermore.

75 Comfort? comfort scorned of devils! this is truth the
    poet sings,
That a sorrow's crown of sorrow is remembering
    happier things.[3]

Drug thy memories, lest thou learn it, lest thy heart be
    put to proof,
In the dead unhappy night, and when the rain is on
    the roof.

Like a dog, he hunts in dreams, and thou art staring at
    the wall,
80 Where the dying night-lamp flickers, and the
    shadows rise and fall.

Then a hand shall pass before thee, pointing to his
    drunken sleep,

---

[1] *straitened ... fool* Narrow or low foreheads were thought to indicate stupidity; *straitened* Narrowed.

[2] *rookery* Here, gathering of crows.

[3] *this is truth ... happier things* Cf. Dante, *Inferno* 5.121–23: "No greater grief than to remember joy, when misery is at hand."

To thy widowed[1] marriage-pillows, to the tears that
    thou wilt weep.

Thou shalt hear the "Never, never," whispered by the
    phantom years,
And a song from out the distance in the ringing of
    thine ears;

85 And an eye shall vex thee, looking ancient kindness on
    thy pain.
Turn thee, turn thee on thy pillow: get thee to thy
    rest again.

Nay, but Nature brings thee solace; for a tender
    voice will cry.
'Tis a purer life than thine; a lip to drain thy trouble dry.

Baby lips will laugh me down: my latest rival brings
    thee rest.
90 Baby fingers, waxen touches, press me from the
    mother's breast.

O, the child too clothes the father with a dearness not
    his due.
Half is thine and half is his: it will be worthy of the two.

O, I see thee old and formal, fitted to thy petty part,
With a little hoard of maxims preaching down a
    daughter's heart.

95 "They were dangerous guides the feelings—she[2]
    herself was not exempt—
Truly, she herself had suffered"—Perish in thy self-
    contempt!

Overlive it—lower yet—be happy! wherefore should I
    care?
I myself must mix with action, lest I wither by despair.

What is that which I should turn to, lighting upon
    days like these?
100 Every door is barred with gold, and opens but to
    golden keys.

Every gate is thronged with suitors, all the markets
    overflow.
I have but an angry fancy: what is that which I should
    do?

I had been content to perish, falling on the foeman's
    ground,
When the ranks are rolled in vapour, and the winds
    are laid with sound.

105 But the jingling of the guinea° helps the hurt   *coin*
    that Honour feels,
And the nations do but murmur, snarling at each
    other's heels.

Can I but relive in sadness? I will turn that earlier page.
Hide me from my deep emotion, O thou wondrous
    Mother-Age!

Make me feel the wild pulsation that I felt before the
    strife,
110 When I heard my days before me, and the tumult of
    my life;

Yearning for the large excitement that the coming
    years would yield,
Eager-hearted as a boy when first he leaves his father's
    field,

And at night along the dusky highway near and
    nearer drawn,
Sees in heaven the light of London flaring like a
    dreary dawn;

115 And his spirit leaps within him to be gone before him
    then,
Underneath the light he looks at, in among the
    throngs of men:

---

1 *widowed* In that she and her husband are emotionally estranged.

2 *she* The woman, Amy, is pictured in the future, speaking of herself
in the third person to her daughter.

Men, my brothers, men the workers, ever reaping
    something new:
That which they have done but earnest of the things
    that they shall do:

For I dipped into the future, far as human eye could
    see,
120   Saw the Vision of the world, and all the wonder that
    would be;

Saw the heavens fill with commerce, argosies[1] of
    magic sails,
Pilots of the purple twilight, dropping down with
    costly bales;

Heard the heavens fill with shouting, and there rained
    a ghastly dew
From the nations' airy navies grappling in the central blue;

125   Far along the world-wide whisper of the south-wind
    rushing warm,
With the standards° of the peoples plunging   *flags*
    through the thunder-storm;

Till the war-drum throbbed no longer, and the
    battle-flags were furled
In the Parliament of man, the Federation of the world.

There the common sense of most shall hold a fretful
    realm in awe,
130   And the kindly earth shall slumber, lapped in
    universal law.

So I triumphed ere my passion sweeping through me
    left me dry,
Left me with the palsied heart, and left me with the
    jaundiced eye;

Eye, to which all order festers, all things here are out
    of joint:

Science moves, but slowly slowly, creeping on from
    point to point:
135   Slowly comes a hungry people, as a lion creeping
    nigher,°   *closer*
Glares at one that nods and winks behind a slowly-
    dying fire.

Yet I doubt not through the ages one increasing
    purpose runs,
And the thoughts of men are widened with the
    process of the suns.

What is that to him that reaps not harvest of his
    youthful joys,
140   Though the deep heart of existence beat forever like a boy's?

Knowledge comes, but wisdom lingers, and I linger
    on the shore,
And the individual withers, and the world is more
    and more.

Knowledge comes, but wisdom lingers, and he bears a
    laden breast,
Full of sad experience, moving toward the stillness of
    his rest.

145   Hark, my merry comrades call me, sounding on the
    bugle-horn,
They to whom my foolish passion were a target for
    their scorn:

Shall it not be scorn to me to harp on such a
    mouldered string?
I am shamed through all my nature to have loved so
    slight a thing.

Weakness to be wroth° with weakness!   *angry*
    woman's pleasure, woman's pain—
150   Nature made them blinder motions bounded in a
    shallower brain:

---

1 *argosies* Fleets of merchants ships. In this couplet and the next the
speaker predicts that commerce and warfare will someday be carried
out by aircraft.

Woman is the lesser man, and all thy passions,
    matched with mine,
Are as moonlight unto sunlight, and as water unto
    wine[1]—

Here at least, where nature sickens, nothing. Ah, for
    some retreat
Deep in yonder shining Orient, where my life began
    to beat;

5 Where in wild Mahratta-battle[2] fell my father evil-
    starred;[3]—
I was left a trampled orphan, and a selfish uncle's
    ward.[4]

Or to burst all links of habit—there to wander far away,
On from island unto island at the gateways of the day.

Larger constellations burning, mellow moons and
    happy skies,
160 Breadths of tropic shade and palms in cluster, knots of
    Paradise.

Never comes the trader, never floats an European flag,
Slides the bird o'er lustrous woodland, swings the
    trailer[5] from the crag;

Droops the heavy-blossomed bower, hangs the heavy-
    fruited tree—
Summer isles of Eden lying in dark-purple spheres of sea.

165 There methinks would be enjoyment more than in
    this march of mind,
In the steamship, in the railway, in the thoughts
    that shake mankind.

There the passions cramped no longer shall have
    scope and breathing space;
I will take some savage woman, she shall rear my
    dusky race.

Iron jointed, supple-sinewed, they shall dive, and they
    shall run,
170 Catch the wild goat by the hair, and hurl their lances
    in the sun;

Whistle back the parrot's call, and leap the rainbows
    of the brooks,
Not with blinded eyesight poring over miserable books—

Fool, again the dream, the fancy! but I *know* my
    words are wild,
But I count the gray barbarian lower than the
    Christian child.

175 I, to herd with narrow foreheads, vacant of our
    glorious gains,
Like a beast with lower pleasures, like a beast with
    lower pains!

Mated with a squalid savage—what to me were sun or
    clime?
I the heir of all the ages, in the foremost files[6] of time—

I that rather held it better men should perish one
    by one,
180 Than that earth should stand at gaze like Joshua's
    moon in Ajalon![7]

Not in vain the distance beacons. Forward,
    forward let us range,
Let the great world spin forever down the ringing
    grooves of change.

Through the shadow of the globe we sweep into
    the younger day:

---

1 *as water unto wine* See John 2.1–11, in which Jesus is said to have miraculously transformed water into wine at a wedding feast.

2 *Mahratta-battle* Conflict between the British and the Mahratta soldiers from Bombay in 1818.

3 *evil-starred* Cursed with bad luck.

4 *ward* Minor placed in the care of a guardian.

5 *trailer* Vine or hanging branch.

---

6 *files* The ages of time pictured as men marching in file.

7 *Joshua's moon in Ajalon* In Joshua 10.12–13, Joshua makes the moon and sun stand still during a battle in the valley of Ajalon.

Better fifty years of Europe than a cycle of
    Cathay.°   *China*

185   Mother-Age (for mine I knew not) help me as
    when life begun:
Rift° the hills, and roll the waters, flash the   *split open*
    lightnings, weigh[1] the Sun.

O, I see the crescent promise of my spirit hath not set.
Ancient founts of inspiration well through all my
    fancy yet.

Howsoever these things be, a long farewell to Locksley
    Hall!
190   Now for me the woods may wither, now for me the
    roof-tree fall.

Comes a vapour from the margin, blackening over
    heath and holt,°   *wood*
Cramming all the blast before it, in its breast a
    thunderbolt.

Let it fall on Locksley Hall, with rain or hail, or fire or
    snow;
For the mighty wind arises, roaring seaward, and I go.
  —1842

from *The Princess*

[*Sweet and Low*]

Sweet and low, sweet and low,
    Wind of the western sea,
Low, low, breathe and blow,
    Wind of the western sea!
5 Over the rolling waters go,
Come from the dying moon, and blow,
    Blow him again to me;
While my little one, while my pretty one, sleeps.

Sleep and rest, sleep and rest,
10   Father will come to thee soon;
Rest, rest, on mother's breast,
    Father will come to thee soon;
Father will come to his babe in the nest,
Silver sails all out of the west
15   Under the silver moon:
Sleep, my little one, sleep, my pretty one, sleep.

[*The Splendour Falls*]

The splendour falls on castle walls
    And snowy summits old in story:
The long light shakes across the lakes,
    And the wild cataract° leaps in glory.   *waterfall*
5 Blow, bugle, blow, set the wild echoes flying,
Blow, bugle; answer, echoes, dying, dying, dying.

O hark, O hear! how thin and clear,
    And thinner, clearer, farther going!
O sweet and far from cliff and scar[2]
10   The horns of Elfland faintly blowing!
Blow, let us hear the purple glens replying:
Blow, bugle; answer, echoes, dying, dying, dying.

O love, they die in yon rich sky,
    They faint on hill or field or river:
15 Our echoes roll from soul to soul,
    And grow for ever and for ever.
Blow, bugle, blow, set the wild echoes flying,
And answer, echoes, answer, dying, dying, dying.

[*Tears, Idle Tears*]

Tears, idle tears, I know not what they mean,
    Tears from the depth of some divine despair
Rise in the heart, and gather to the eyes,
In looking on the happy Autumn-fields,
5 And thinking of the days that are no more.

---

1 *weigh* Raise or bring up, as in "weigh anchor."

2 *scar* Steep, craggy portion of mountainside.

Fresh as the first beam glittering on a sail,
That brings our friends up from the underworld,
Sad as the last which reddens over one
That sinks with all we love below the verge;°   *horizon*
10 So sad, so fresh, the days that are no more.

Ah, sad and strange as in dark summer dawns
The earliest pipe of half-awakened birds
To dying ears, when unto dying eyes
The casement° slowly grows a glimmering   *window*
    square;
15 So sad, so strange, the days that are no more.

Dear as remembered kisses after death,
And sweet as those by hopeless fancy feigned
On lips that are for others; deep as love,
Deep as first love, and wild with all regret;
20 O Death in Life, the days that are no more.

[Now Sleeps the Crimson Petal]

Now sleeps the crimson petal, now the white;
    Nor waves the cypress[1] in the palace walk;
Nor winks the gold fin in the porphyry[2] font:
The fire-fly wakens: waken thou with me.

5 Now droops the milkwhite peacock like a ghost,
And like a ghost she glimmers on to me.

Now lies the Earth all Danaë[3] to the stars,
And all thy heart lies open unto me.

Now slides the silent meteor on, and leaves
10 A shining furrow, as thy thoughts in me.

Now folds the lily all her sweetness up,
And slips into the bosom of the lake:

So fold thyself, my dearest, thou, and slip
Into my bosom and be lost in me.

[Come Down, O Maid]

Come down, O maid, from yonder
    mountain height:
What pleasure lives in height (the shepherd sang)
In height and cold, the splendour of the hills?
But cease to move so near the Heavens, and cease
5 To glide a sunbeam by the blasted Pine,
To sit a star upon the sparkling spire;
And come, for Love is of the valley, come,
For Love is of the valley, come thou down
And find him; by the happy threshold, he,
10 Or hand in hand with Plenty in the maize,°   *corn*
Or red with spurted purple of the vats,
Or foxlike in the vine;[4] nor cares to walk
With Death and Morning on the silver horns,
Nor wilt thou snare him in the white ravine,
15 Nor find him dropped upon the firths° of ice,   *juttings*
That huddling slant in furrow-cloven falls
To roll the torrent out of dusky doors:
But follow; let the torrent dance thee down
To find him in the valley; let the wild
20 Lean-headed Eagles yelp alone, and leave
The monstrous ledges there to slope, and spill
Their thousand wreaths of dangling water-smoke,
That like a broken purpose waste in air:
So waste not thou; but come; for all the vales
25 Await thee; azure pillars of the hearth[5]
Arise to thee; the children call, and I
Thy shepherd pipe, and sweet is every sound,
Sweeter thy voice, but every sound is sweet;
Myriads of rivulets hurrying through the lawn,
30 The moan of doves in immemorial elms,
And murmuring of innumerable bees.

---

[1] *cypress* Type of evergreen tree, classically associated with mourning and death.

[2] *porphyry* Beautiful, polished purple stone.

[3] *Danaë* In Greek mythology, a princess visited by Zeus in the form of a shower of gold.

---

[4] *foxlike in the vine* See Song of Solomon 2.15: "Take us the foxes, the little foxes, that spoil the vines. …"

[5] *azure pillars of the hearth* Columns of bluish smoke rising from household fires.

[*The Woman's Cause Is Man's*][1]

"Blame not thyself too much," I said, "nor
    blame
Too much the sons of men and barbarous laws;
These were the rough ways of the world till now.
Henceforth thou hast a helper, me, that know
5 The woman's cause is man's: they rise or sink
Together, dwarfed or godlike, bond or free:
For she that out of Lethe[2] scales with man
The shining steps of Nature, shares with man
His nights, his days, moves with him to one goal,
10 Stays° all the fair young planet in her hands—   *sustains*
If she be small, slight-natured, miserable,
How shall men grow? but work no more alone!
Our place is much: as far as in us lies
We two will serve them both in aiding her—
15 Will clear away the parasitic forms
That seem to keep her up but drag her down—
Will leave her space to burgeon out of all
Within her—let her make herself her own
To give or keep, to live and learn and be
20 All that not harms distinctive womanhood.
For woman is not undeveloped man,
But diverse:° could we make her as the man,   *different*
Sweet Love were slain: his dearest bond is this,
Not like to like, but like in difference.
25 Yet in the long years liker must they grow;
The man be more of woman, she of man;
He gain in sweetness and in moral height,
Nor lose the wrestling thews° that throw   *muscles*
    the world;
She mental breadth, nor fail in childward care,
30 Nor lose the childlike in the larger mind;
Till at the last she set herself to man,
Like perfect music unto noble words;
And so these twain, upon the skirts° of Time,   *borders*

35 Sit side by side, full-summed in all their powers,
Dispensing harvest, sowing the To-be,
Self-reverent each and reverencing each,
Distinct in individualities,
But like each other even as those who love.
Then comes the statelier Eden back to men:
40 Then reign the world's great bridals, chaste and calm:
Then springs the crowning race of humankind.
May these things be!"
                    Sighing she spoke "I fear
They will not."
                  "Dear, but let us type[3] them now
In our own lives, and this proud watchword rest
45 Of equal; seeing either sex alone
Is half itself, and in true marriage lies
Nor equal, nor unequal: each fulfils
Defect in each, and always thought in thought,
Purpose in purpose, will in will, they grow,
50 The single pure and perfect animal,
The two-celled heart beating, with one full stroke,
Life."
  And again sighing she spoke: "A dream
That once was mine! what woman taught you this?"
—1847 (REVISED AND SUPPLEMENTED 1850)

―――――

In Memoriam A.H.H.

Arthur Henry Hallam, who attended Cambridge's
Trinity College at the same time as Tennyson, was
regarded by many who knew him as among the
most promising poetic talents of his generation.
Eighteen months younger than Tennyson, Hallam
was also far more outgoing. The two became friends
and fierce supporters of each other's work. Both also
became members of the famous Cambridge intellectual society, the Apostles, and after meeting Tennyson's family, Hallam became engaged to Tennyson's
sister Emily. Hallam and Tennyson remained in
close contact even after the death of Tennyson's
father forced him to leave Cambridge; they traveled
together to the Pyrenees in 1830, and to the Rhine-

---

[1] *The Woman's Cause Is Man's* This passage from late in *The Princess*
(7.239–91) shows the reconciliation between the princess, who hoped
to live in an environment from which all men were excluded, and the
narrator, a prince who wishes to marry her.

[2] *Lethe* In Greek myth, one of the rivers of Hades. Drinking its
waters caused the souls of the dead to forget their past lives.

[3] *type* Serve as a model for.

land in 1832. In 1833, however, while on a trip to Vienna with his family, Hallam suffered a stroke and died; he was 22 years old.

Hallam's unexpected death had a profound and lasting effect on many of his friends; for Tennyson it marked the beginning of a long period of self-reflection and questioning. He began writing the lyric poems that would eventually form the basis of *In Memoriam* within a few weeks of Hallam's death— some seventeen years before the full poem was eventually published. According to the poet's own account, "the sections were written at many different places" and over the course of many years. He did not at first think of "weaving them into a whole"; only later did the longer work begin to take shape in his mind. The ultimate arrangement is loosely chronological, with the elegy as a whole tracing a three-year journey through the grieving process, punctuated by three Christmas scenes (sections 30, 78, and 105).

As Tennyson continued to reflect on Hallam's death, his subject matter broadened and deepened. The many moods of grief provide occasions for the poem to interrogate matters as wide-ranging as the character of scientific inquiry, the origin of human life, and the nature of religious faith. The Victorian "crisis of faith" that is often associated with the publication of Darwin's *On the Origin of Species* in 1859 is sometimes said to have begun before the Victorian age itself—with the publication just before Hallam's death of Charles Lyell's *Principles of Geology*, a book that made it far more difficult to accept the Christian account of Creation as being true in any literal sense. Perhaps more than any other work of the age, *In Memoriam* gave voice to the resulting uncertainty of a society trying to make room for both God and science. But for Tennyson, as for many Victorians, the scientific challenge made religious faith more vitally important than ever before. "The different moods of sorrow as in a drama are dramatically given," Tennyson said of the full poem, as was his "conviction that fear, doubts, and suffering will find answer and relief only through Faith in a God of Love."

The 133 sections that make up *In Memoriam* vary widely in length and style as well as mood. Yet they are all written in the form that has come to be known as the "In Memoriam stanza": a stanza of four lines in iambic tetrameter, with an ABBA rhyme scheme.

In Memoriam appeared in 1850 to near-universal acclaim. Initially it was published anonymously, but the identity of the author quickly became well-known; Charles Kingsley was not alone in believing (as Kingsley wrote in a September 1850 review of the poem) that there was only "one man in England possessed at once of poetic talent and artistic experience sufficient for so noble a creation." The poem cemented Tennyson's reputation, and he was appointed to the position of Poet Laureate before the year was out.

In Memoriam A.H.H.[1]

[PROLOGUE[2]]

Strong Son of God, immortal Love,
  Whom we, that have not seen Thy face,
  By faith, and faith alone, embrace,
Believing where we cannot prove;

5 Thine are these orbs of light and shade;
  Thou madest Life in man and brute;
  Thou madest Death; and lo, Thy foot
Is on the skull which Thou hast made.

Thou wilt not leave us in the dust:
10 Thou madest man, he knows not why,
  He thinks he was not made to die;
And Thou hast made him: Thou art just.

---

[1] *In Memoriam A.H.H.*   Latin: In memory of A.H.H.; the title was apparently suggested by the poet's fiancée. The published poem did not bear either Tennyson's name or Arthur Henry Hallam's, only the dedication "In Memoriam A.H.H. obiit MDCCCXXXIII" (In memory of A.H.H., died 1833).

[2] *PROLOGUE*   The Prologue was composed in 1849 after the rest of the poem was completed.

Thou seemest human and divine,
    The highest, holiest manhood, Thou:
15   Our wills are ours, we know not how;
Our wills are ours, to make them Thine.

Our little systems[1] have their day;
    They have their day and cease to be:
    They are but broken lights of Thee,
20 And Thou, O Lord, art more than they.

We have but faith: we cannot know;
    For knowledge is of things we see;
    And yet we trust it comes from Thee,
A beam in darkness: let it grow.

25 Let knowledge grow from more to more,
    But more of reverence in us dwell;
    That mind and soul, according well,
May make one music as before,[2]

But vaster. We are fools and slight;
30   We mock Thee when we do not fear:
    But help Thy foolish ones to bear;
Help Thy vain worlds to bear Thy light.

Forgive what seemed my sin in me;
    What seemed my worth since I began;
35   For merit lives from man to man,
And not from man, O Lord, to Thee.

Forgive my grief for one removed,
    Thy creature, whom I found so fair.
    I trust he lives in Thee, and there
40 I find him worthier to be loved.

Forgive these wild and wandering cries,
    Confusions of a wasted youth;
    Forgive them where they fail in truth,
And in Thy wisdom make me wise.
—1849

1

I held it truth, with him who sings
    To one clear harp in diverse tones,
    That men may rise on stepping-stones
Of their dead selves to higher things.[3]

5 But who shall so forecast the years
    And find in loss a gain to match?
    Or reach a hand through time to catch
The far-off interest of tears?

Let Love clasp Grief lest both be drowned,
10   Let darkness keep her raven gloss:
    Ah, sweeter to be drunk with loss,
To dance with death, to beat the ground,

Than that the victor Hours[4] should scorn
    The long result of love, and boast,
15   "Behold the man that loved and lost,
But all he was is overworn."

2

Old Yew,[5] which graspest at the stones
    That name the under-lying dead,
    Thy fibres net the dreamless head,
Thy roots are wrapped about the bones.

5 The seasons bring the flower again,
    And bring the firstling[6] to the flock;
    And in the dusk of thee, the clock
Beats out the little lives of men.

O not for thee the glow, the bloom,
10   Who changest not in any gale,

---

[1] *Our little systems* Philosophical, scientific, and theological ways of thinking that Tennyson here indicates as belonging to humankind.

[2] [Tennyson's note] As in the ages of faith.

[3] *him … things* The reference here is unclear. Tennyson said that he was alluding to a work by the German poet Goethe; however, the passage does not appear to correspond to any of Goethe's works.

[4] *Hours* Horai, Greek goddesses of time and of the changing of seasons.

[5] *Yew* Species of tree, often planted in graveyards and thus associated poetically with mourning. The English Yew, an extraordinarily long-lived tree, is evergreen as opposed to deciduous; its leaves do not change color and fall off in the autumn.

[6] *firstling* Offspring born first in the season.

Nor branding summer suns avail
    To touch thy thousand years of gloom:

And gazing on thee, sullen tree,
    Sick[1] for thy stubborn hardihood,
5   I seem to fail from out my blood
And grow incorporate into thee.

3

O Sorrow, cruel fellowship,
    O Priestess in the vaults of Death,
    O sweet and bitter in a breath,
What whispers from thy lying lip?

5 "The stars," she whispers, "blindly run;
    A web is woven across the sky;
    From out waste places comes a cry,
And murmurs from the dying sun:[2]

  "And all the phantom, Nature, stands—
10   With all the music in her tone,
    A hollow echo of my own,—
A hollow form with empty hands."

And shall I take a thing so blind,
    Embrace her as my natural good;
15   Or crush her, like a vice of blood,
Upon the threshold of the mind?

4

To Sleep I give my powers away;
    My will is bondsman° to the dark;   *slave*
    I sit within a helmless bark,°   *ship*
And with my heart I muse and say:

5 O heart, how fares it with thee now,
    That thou should'st fail from thy desire,
    Who scarcely darest to inquire,
"What is it makes me beat so low?"

---

1 *Sick* I.e., with envy.

2 *dying sun* Tennyson was writing at a time when the hypothesis that the sun was a dying star had been recently advanced by astronomers.

Something it is which thou hast lost,
10   Some pleasure from thine early years.
    Break, thou deep vase of chilling tears,
That grief hath shaken into frost!

Such clouds of nameless trouble cross
    All night below the darkened eyes;
15   With morning wakes the will, and cries,
"Thou shalt not be the fool of loss."

5

I sometimes hold it half a sin
    To put in words the grief I feel;
    For words, like Nature, half reveal
And half conceal the Soul within.

5 But, for the unquiet heart and brain,
    A use in measured language lies;
    The sad mechanic exercise,
Like dull narcotics, numbing pain.

In words, like weeds,[3] I'll wrap me o'er,
10   Like coarsest clothes against the cold:
    But that large grief which these enfold
Is given in outline and no more.

6

One writes, that "Other friends remain,"
    That "Loss is common to the race"—
    And common is the commonplace,
And vacant chaff well meant for grain.

5 That loss is common would not make
    My own less bitter, rather more:
    Too common! Never morning wore
To evening, but some heart did break.

O father, wheresoe'er thou be,
10   Who pledgest° now thy gallant son;   *drink a toast to*
    A shot, ere half thy draught be done,
Hath stilled the life that beat from thee.

---

3 *weeds* In Victorian times, this word was also used to refer to mourning clothes.

O mother, praying God will save
   Thy sailor,—while thy head is bowed,
15   His heavy-shotted° hammock-shroud[1]   *weighted*
Drops in his vast and wandering grave.

Ye know no more than I who wrought
   At that last hour to please him well;
   Who mused on all I had to tell,
20 And something written, something thought;

Expecting still his advent[2] home;
   And ever met him on his way
   With wishes, thinking, "here today,"
Or "here tomorrow will he come."

25 O somewhere, meek, unconscious dove,[3]
   That sittest ranging° golden hair;   *arranging*
   And glad to find thyself so fair,
Poor child, that waitest for thy love!

For now her father's chimney glows
30   In expectation of a guest;
   And thinking "this will please him best,"
She takes a riband° or a rose;   *ribbon*

For he will see them on tonight;
   And with the thought her colour burns;
35   And, having left the glass, she turns
Once more to set a ringlet right;

And, even when she turned, the curse
   Had fallen, and her future Lord°   *husband*
   Was drowned in passing through the ford,[4]
40 Or killed in falling from his horse.

O what to her shall be the end?
   And what to me remains of good?

---

[1] *hammock-shroud* Hammock, commonly used for sleeping on sailing ships, used here to wrap a corpse for burial at sea.

[2] *advent* Arrival of something or someone important.

[3] *dove* I.e., young maiden.

[4] *ford* Shallow place where one crosses a river.

To her, perpetual maidenhood,
And unto me no second friend.

7

Dark house,[5] by which once more I stand
   Here in the long unlovely street,
   Doors, where my heart was used to beat
So quickly, waiting for a hand,

5 A hand that can be clasped no more—
   Behold me, for I cannot sleep,
   And like a guilty thing I creep
At earliest morning to the door.

He is not here; but far away
10   The noise of life begins again,
   And ghastly through the drizzling rain
On the bald street breaks the blank day.

8

A happy lover who has come
   To look on her that loves him well,
   Who 'lights[6] and rings the gateway bell,
And learns her gone and far from home;

5 He saddens, all the magic light
   Dies off at once from bower[7] and hall,
   And all the place is dark, and all
The chambers emptied of delight:

So find I every pleasant spot
10   In which we two were wont to meet,
   The field, the chamber and the street,
For all is dark where thou art not.

Yet as that other, wandering there
   In those deserted walks, may find
15   A flower beat with rain and wind,
Which once she fostered up with care;

---

[5] *Dark house* I.e., Hallam's house in London.

[6] *'lights* Alights from a horse.

[7] *bower* Inner room, bedchamber.

So seems it in my deep regret,
   O my forsaken heart, with thee
   And this poor flower of poesy
Which little cared for fades not yet.

But since it pleased a vanished eye,
   I go to plant it on his tomb,
   That if it can it there may bloom,
Or dying, there at least may die.

9

Fair ship, that from the Italian shore[1]
   Sailest the placid ocean-plains
   With my lost Arthur's loved remains,
Spread thy full wings, and waft him o'er.

So draw him home to those that mourn
   In vain; a favourable speed
   Ruffle thy mirrored mast, and lead
Through prosperous floods his holy urn.

All night no ruder° air perplex   *turbulent*
   Thy sliding keel, till Phosphor,[2] bright
   As our pure love, through early light
Shall glimmer on the dewy decks.

Sphere all your lights around, above;
   Sleep, gentle heavens, before the prow;
   Sleep, gentle winds, as he sleeps now,
My friend, the brother of my love;

My Arthur, whom I shall not see
   Till all my widowed race be run;
   Dear as the mother to the son,
More than my brothers are to me.

10

I hear the noise about thy keel;
   I hear the bell struck in the night:

I see the cabin-window bright;
   I see the sailor at the wheel.

Thou bring'st the sailor to his wife,
   And travelled men from foreign lands;
   And letters unto trembling hands;
And, thy dark freight, a vanished life.

So bring him: we have idle dreams:
   This look of quiet flatters thus
   Our home-bred fancies: O to us,
The fools of habit, sweeter seems

To rest beneath the clover sod,
   That takes the sunshine and the rains,
   Or where the kneeling hamlet[3] drains
The chalice of the grapes of God;[4]

Than if with thee the roaring wells
   Should gulf him fathom-deep in brine;
   And hands so often clasped in mine,
Should toss with tangle° and with shells.   *seaweed*

11

Calm is the morn without a sound,
   Calm as to suit a calmer grief,
   And only through the faded leaf
The chestnut pattering to the ground:

Calm and deep peace on this high wold,°   *plain*
   And on these dews that drench the furze,[5]
   And all the silvery gossamers°   *cobwebs*
That twinkle into green and gold:

Calm and still light on yon great plain
   That sweeps with all its autumn bowers,
   And crowded farms and lessening towers,
To mingle with the bounding main:°   *sea*

---

[1] *Fair ... shore* Sections 9–19 imaginatively reconstruct the journey of the ship that bore Hallam's body back to England; he died in Vienna and his body was shipped from Italy.

[2] *Phosphor* The planet Venus, also called the morning star.

[3] *hamlet* I.e., the citizens of a hamlet.

[4] *drains ... God* I.e., partakes in communion.

[5] *furze* Evergreen shrubs.

Calm and deep peace in this wide air,
  These leaves that redden to the fall;
15   And in my heart, if calm at all,
If any calm, a calm despair:

Calm on the seas, and silver sleep,
  And waves that sway themselves in rest,
  And dead calm in that noble breast
20 Which heaves but with the heaving deep.

12

Lo, as a dove when up she springs
  To bear through Heaven a tale of woe,
  Some dolorous message knit below
The wild pulsation of her wings;

5 Like her I go; I cannot stay;
  I leave this mortal ark behind,[1]
  A weight of nerves without a mind,
And leave the cliffs, and haste away

O'er ocean-mirrors rounded large,
10 And reach the glow of southern skies,
  And see the sails at distance rise,
And linger weeping on the marge,[2]

And saying; "Comes he thus, my friend?
  Is this the end of all my care?"
15 And circle moaning in the air:
"Is this the end? Is this the end?"

And forward dart again, and play
  About the prow, and back return
  To where the body sits, and learn
20 That I have been an hour away.

13

Tears of the widower, when he sees
  A late-lost form that sleep reveals,
And moves his doubtful arms, and feels
Her place is empty, fall like these;

5 Which weep a loss forever new,
  A void where heart on heart reposed;
  And, where warm hands have pressed and closed,
Silence, till I be silent too.

Which weep the comrade of my choice,
10 An awful thought, a life removed,
  The human-hearted man I loved,
A Spirit, not a breathing voice.

Come Time, and teach me, many years,
  I do not suffer in a dream;
15 For now so strange do these things seem,
Mine eyes have leisure for their tears;

My fancies time to rise on wing,
  And glance about the approaching sails,
  As though they brought but merchants' bales,[3]
20 And not the burden that they bring.

14

If one should bring me this report,
  That thou° hadst touched the land today,   *i.e., the ship*
  And I went down unto the quay,
And found thee lying in the port;

5 And standing, muffled round with woe,
  Should see thy passengers in rank
  Come stepping lightly down the plank,
And beckoning unto those they know;

And if along with these should come
10 The man I held as half-divine;
  Should strike a sudden hand in mine,
And ask a thousand things of home;

And I should tell him all my pain,
  And how my life had drooped of late,

---

[1] *I leave … behind* The poet's spirit, like the dove sent forth by Noah (Genesis 8) leaves the "ark" (his body) behind.

[2] *marge* Water's edge; shore.

[3] *bales* I.e., of cotton or other trade goods.

5   And he should sorrow o'er my state
    And marvel what possessed my brain;

    And I perceived no touch of change,
        No hint of death in all his frame,
        But found him all in all the same,
20 I should not feel it to be strange.

15

    Tonight the winds begin to rise
        And roar from yonder dropping day:
        The last red leaf is whirled away,
        The rooks° are blown about the skies;   *crows*

5   The forest cracked, the waters curled,
        The cattle huddled on the lea;°   *pasture*
        And wildly dashed on tower and tree
    The sunbeam strikes along the world:

    And but for fancies, which aver°   *declare*
10   That all thy motions gently pass
        Athwart a plane of molten glass,
    I scarce could brook the strain and stir

    That makes the barren branches loud;
        And but for fear it is not so,
15   The wild unrest that lives in woe
    Would dote and pore on yonder cloud

    That rises upward always higher,
        And onward drags a labouring breast,
        And topples round the dreary west,
20 A looming bastion° fringed with fire.   *fortress*

16

    What words are these have fallen from me?
        Can calm despair and wild unrest
        Be tenants of a single breast,
    Or sorrow such a changeling be?

5   Or doth she only seem to take
        The touch of change in calm or storm;

    But knows no more of transient form
    In her deep self, than some dead lake

    That holds the shadow of a lark
10   Hung in the shadow of a heaven?
        Or has the shock, so harshly given,
    Confused me like the unhappy bark°   *boat*

    That strikes by night a craggy shelf,[1]
        And staggers blindly ere she sink?
15   And stunned me from my power to think
    And all my knowledge of myself;

    And made me that delirious man
        Whose fancy fuses old and new,
        And flashes into false and true,
20 And mingles all without a plan?

17

    Thou comest, much wept for: such a breeze
        Compelled thy canvas, and my prayer
        Was as the whisper of an air
    To breathe thee over lonely seas.

5   For I in spirit saw thee move
        Through circles of the bounding sky,
        Week after week: the days go by:
    Come quick, thou bringest all I love.

    Henceforth, wherever thou mayst roam,
10   My blessing, like a line of light,
        Is on the waters day and night,
    And like a beacon guards thee home.

    So may whatever tempest mars
        Mid-ocean, spare thee, sacred bark;
15   And balmy drops in summer dark
    Slide from the bosom of the stars.

    So kind an office hath been done,
        Such precious relics brought by thee;

---

[1] *craggy shelf* Reef.

The dust of him I shall not see
20   Till all my widowed race be run.

18

'Tis well; 'Tis something; we may stand
    Where he in English earth is laid,
    And from his ashes may be made
The violet of his native land.

5   'Tis little; but it looks in truth
    As if the quiet bones were blest
    Among familiar names to rest
And in the places of his youth.

Come then, pure hands, and bear the head
10   That sleeps or wears the mask of sleep,
    And come, whatever loves to weep,
And hear the ritual of the dead.

Ah yet, even yet, if this might be,
    I, falling on his faithful heart,
15   Would breathing through his lips impart
The life that almost dies in me;

That dies not, but endures with pain,
    And slowly forms the firmer mind,
    Treasuring the look it cannot find,
20   The words that are not heard again.

19

The Danube[1] to the Severn[2] gave
    The darkened heart that beat no more;
    They laid him by the pleasant shore,
And in the hearing of the wave.

5   There twice a day the Severn fills;
    The salt sea-water passes by,

And hushes half the babbling Wye,[3]
And makes a silence in the hills.

The Wye is hushed nor moved along,
10   And hushed my deepest grief of all,
    When filled with tears that cannot fall,
I brim with sorrow drowning song.

The tide flows down, the wave again
    Is vocal in its wooded walls;
15   My deeper anguish also falls,
And I can speak a little then.

20

The lesser griefs that may be said,
    That breathe a thousand tender vows,
    Are but as servants in a house
Where lies the master newly dead;

5   Who speak their feeling as it is,
    And weep the fullness from the mind:
    "It will be hard," they say, "to find
Another service such as this."[4]

My lighter moods are like to these,
10   That out of words a comfort win;
    But there are other griefs within,
And tears that at their fountain freeze;

For by the hearth the children sit
    Cold in that atmosphere of Death,
15   And scarce endure to draw the breath,
Or like to noiseless phantoms flit:

But open converse is there none,
    So much the vital spirits sink
    To see the vacant chair, and think,
20   "How good! how kind! and he is gone."

---

[1] *Danube* River that flows through Vienna.

[2] *Severn* River in England. Hallam is buried at Clevedon, in Somerset, overlooking the Severn estuary.

[3] *Wye* The River Wye empties into the Severn; twice a day its flow is stopped by the incoming tide.

[4] *It will … this* I.e., it will be difficult to find employment with a master as good as this one.

21

I sing to him that rests below,
    And, since the grasses round me wave,
    I take the grasses of the grave,
And make them pipes whereon to blow.[1]

The traveller hears me now and then,
    And sometimes harshly will he speak:
    "This fellow would make weakness weak,
And melt the waxen hearts of men."

Another answers, "Let him be,
    He loves to make parade of pain,
    That with his piping he may gain
The praise that comes to constancy."

A third is wroth:° "Is this an hour   indignant
    For private sorrow's barren song,
    When more and more the people throng°   crowd
The chairs and thrones of civil power?

"A time to sicken and to swoon,
    When Science reaches forth her arms
    To feel from world to world, and charms
Her secret from the latest moon?"

Behold, ye speak an idle thing:
    Ye never knew the sacred dust:
    I do but sing because I must,
And pipe but as the linnets[2] sing:

And one is glad; her note is gay,
    For now her little ones have ranged;
    And one is sad: her note is changed,
Because her brood is stolen away.

22

The path by which we twain did go,
    Which led by tracts that pleased us well,

Through four sweet years arose and fell,
    From flower to flower, from snow to snow:

And we with singing cheered the way,
    And, crowned with all the season lent,
    From April on to April went,
And glad at heart from May to May:

But where the path we walked began
    To slant the fifth autumnal slope,[3]
    As we descended following Hope,
There sat the Shadow feared of man;

Who broke our fair companionship,
    And spread his mantle° dark and cold,   cloak
    And wrapped thee formless in the fold,
And dulled the murmur on thy lip,

And bore thee where I could not see
    Nor follow, though I walk in haste,
    And think, that somewhere in the waste
The Shadow sits and waits for me.

23

Now, sometimes in my sorrow shut,
    Or breaking into song by fits,
    Alone, alone, to where he sits,
The Shadow cloaked from head to foot,

Who keeps the keys of all the creeds,
    I wander, often falling lame,
    And looking back to whence I came,
Or on to where the pathway leads;

And crying, How changed from where it ran
    Through lands where not a leaf was dumb;°   silent
    But all the lavish hills would hum
The murmur of a happy Pan:[4]

---

[1] *And make ... to blow* Tennyson is here employing the conventions of the pastoral elegy; the speaker here is a shepherd singing or playing a flute.

[2] *linnets* Species of songbirds.

[3] *fifth ... slope* I.e., in the autumn of their fifth year of friendship.

[4] *Pan* Greek god of flocks and sheep, a common presence in English pastoral poetry. To the Romans, he was a universal god, the god of Nature.

When each by turns was guide to each,
    And Fancy light from Fancy caught,
15   And Thought leapt out to wed with Thought
Ere Thought could wed itself with Speech;

And all we met was fair and good,
    And all was good that Time could bring,
    And all the secret of the Spring
20   Moved in the chambers of the blood;

And many an old philosophy
    On Argive° heights divinely sang,   *Greek*
    And round us all the thicket rang
To many a flute of Arcady.[1]

24

And was the day of my delight
    As pure and perfect as I say?
    The very source and fount of Day
Is dashed with wandering isles of night.[2]

5 If all was good and fair we met,
    This earth had been the Paradise
    It never looked to human eyes
Since our first Sun arose and set.

And is it that the haze of grief
10   Makes former gladness loom so great?
    The lowness of the present state,
That sets the past in this relief?

Or that the past will always win
    A glory from its being far;
15   And orb into the perfect star
We saw not, when we moved therein?

25

I know that this was Life,—the track
    Whereon with equal feet we fared;

And then, as now, the day prepared
The daily burden for the back.

5 But this it was that made me move
    As light as carrier-birds[3] in air;
    I loved the weight I had to bear,
Because it needed help of Love:

Nor could I weary, heart or limb,
10   When mighty Love would cleave in twain
    The lading° of a single pain,   *burden*
And part it, giving half to him.

26

Still onward winds the dreary way;
    I with it; for I long to prove
    No lapse of moons[4] can canker° Love,   *tarnish*
Whatever fickle tongues may say.

5 And if that eye which watches guilt
    And goodness, and hath power to see
    Within the green the mouldered tree,
And towers fallen as soon as built—

Oh, if indeed that eye foresee
10   Or see (in Him is no before)
    In more of life true life no more
And Love the indifference to be,

Then might I find, ere yet the morn
    Breaks hither over Indian seas,
15   That Shadow waiting with the keys,
To shroud me from my proper° scorn.   *own*

27

I envy not in any moods
    The captive void of noble rage,
    The linnet[5] born within the cage,
That never knew the summer woods:

---

[1] *Arcady* Arcadia, a hilly area of central Greece, said to be the home of Pan.

[2] *source ... night* The Sun, dotted with sunspots.

[3] *carrier-birds* Here, carrier pigeons.

[4] *lapse ... moons* Span of time.

[5] *linnet* Small bird of the finch family, a popular pet in the nineteenth and early twentieth centuries.

5 I envy not the beast that takes
     His license in the field of time,
     Unfettered by the sense of crime,
   To whom a conscience never wakes;

   Nor, what may count itself as blest,
10   The heart that never plighted troth[1]
     But stagnates in the weeds of sloth;
   Nor any want-begotten rest.

   I hold it true, whate'er befall;
     I feel it, when I sorrow most;
15   'Tis better to have loved and lost
   Than never to have loved at all.[2]

28
   The time draws near the birth of Christ:[3]
     The moon is hid; the night is still;
     The Christmas bells from hill to hill
   Answer each other in the mist.

5 Four voices of four hamlets round,
     From far and near, on mead° and moor,   *meadow*
     Swell out and fail, as if a door
   Were shut between me and the sound:

   Each voice four changes[4] on the wind,
10   That now dilate, and now decrease,
     Peace and goodwill, goodwill and peace,
   Peace and goodwill, to all mankind.

   This year I slept and woke with pain,
     I almost wished no more to wake,
15   And that my hold on life would break
   Before I heard those bells again:

   But they my troubled spirit rule,
     For they controlled me when a boy;
     They bring me sorrow touched with joy,
20   The merry merry bells of Yule.

29
   With such compelling cause to grieve
     As daily vexes household peace,
     And chains regret to his decease,
   How dare we keep our Christmas-eve;

5 Which brings no more a welcome guest
     To enrich the threshold of the night
     With showered largess of delight
   In dance and song and game and jest?

   Yet go, and while the holly boughs
10   Entwine the cold baptismal font,[5]
     Make one wreath more for Use and Wont,[6]
   That guard the portals of the house;

   Old sisters of a day gone by,
     Gray nurses, loving nothing new;
15   Why should they miss their yearly due
   Before their time? They too will die.

30
   With trembling fingers did we weave
     The holly round the Christmas hearth;
     A rainy cloud possessed the earth,
   And sadly fell our Christmas-eve.

5 At our old pastimes in the hall
     We gambolled,° making vain pretence   *danced*
     Of gladness, with an awful[7] sense
   Of one mute Shadow watching all.

   We paused: the winds were in the beech:
10   We heard them sweep the winter land;

---

[1] *plighted troth* Vowed faithfulness.

[2] *'Tis better ... loved at all* These lines are repeated in section 85.

[3] *The time ... Christ* The poem returns three times to the poet's experience of Christmas in the wake of Hallam's death. Sections 28–30 focus on the first Christmas after the death. See also sections 78 and 105.

[4] *changes* Sequences of notes played by church bells.

[5] *baptismal font* Basin used to hold water for Christian baptism.

[6] *Use and Wont* I.e., habit and custom.

[7] *awful* Full of awe.

And in a circle hand-in-hand
Sat silent, looking each at each.

Then echo-like our voices rang;
   We sung, though every eye was dim,
15   A merry song we sang with him
Last year: impetuously we sang:

We ceased: a gentler feeling crept
   Upon us: surely rest is meet:°   *appropriate*
   "They rest," we said, "their sleep is sweet,"
20 And silence followed, and we wept.

Our voices took a higher range;
   Once more we sang: "They do not die
   Nor lose their mortal sympathy,
Nor change to us, although they change;

25 "'Rapt from the fickle and the frail
   With gathered power, yet the same,
   Pierces the keen seraphic flame[1]
From orb to orb, from veil to veil."

Rise, happy morn, rise, holy morn,
30   Draw forth the cheerful day from night:
   O Father, touch the east, and light
The light that shone when Hope was born.

31

When Lazarus left his charnel-cave,
   And home to Mary's house returned,[2]
   Was this demanded—if he yearned
To hear her weeping by his grave?

5 "Where wert thou, brother, those four days?"
   There lives no record of reply,
   Which telling what it is to die
Had surely added praise to praise.

From every house the neighbours met,
10   The streets were filled with joyful sound,
   A solemn gladness even crowned
The purple brows of Olivet.[3]

Behold a man raised up by Christ!
   The rest remaineth unrevealed;
15   He told it not; or something sealed
The lips of that Evangelist.[4]

32

Her eyes are homes of silent prayer,
   Nor other thought her mind admits
   But, he was dead, and there he sits,
And He that brought him back is there.

5 Then one deep love doth supersede
   All other, when her ardent gaze
   Roves from the living brother's face,
And rests upon the Life[5] indeed.

All subtle thought, all curious fears,
10   Borne down by gladness so complete,
   She bows, she bathes the Saviour's feet
With costly spikenard[6] and with tears.[7]

Thrice blest whose lives are faithful prayers,
   Whose loves in higher love endure;
15   What souls possess themselves so pure,
Or is there blessedness like theirs?

33

O thou[8] that after toil and storm
   Mayst seem to have reached a purer air,
   Whose faith has centre everywhere,
Nor cares to fix itself to form,

---

1 *seraphic flame* Intense, purifying fire, associated with the angel-like Seraphim.

2 *Lazarus … returned* See John 11.1–44, in which Jesus raises Lazarus from the dead. The biblical account does not include any mention of Lazarus returning home to his sister Mary.

3 *Olivet* Mount of Olives, in Jerusalem.

4 *Evangelist* John, who recorded the event in his Gospel.

5 *Life* I.e., Christ. See John 11.25: "I am the Resurrection and the Life."

6 *spikenard* Expensive aromatic oil.

7 *bathes … tears* See John 12.3.

8 *thou* Addressed to an unspecified (implicitly male) listener.

5 Leave thou thy sister when she prays,
       Her early Heaven, her happy views;
       Nor thou with shadowed hint confuse
   A life that leads melodious days.

   Her faith through form is pure as thine,
10   Her hands are quicker unto good:
       Oh, sacred be the flesh and blood
   To which she links a truth divine!

   See thou, that countest reason ripe
       In holding by the law within,
15   Thou fail not in a world of sin,
   And even for want of such a type.

34

   My own dim life should teach me this,
       That life shall live for evermore,
       Else earth is darkness at the core,
   And dust and ashes all that is;

5 This round of green, this orb of flame,[1]
       Fantastic beauty; such as lurks
       In some wild Poet, when he works
   Without a conscience or an aim.

   What then were God to such as I?
10   'Twere hardly worth my while to choose
       Of things all mortal, or to use
   A little patience ere I die;

   'Twere best at once to sink to peace,
       Like birds the charming serpent draws,
15   To drop head-foremost in the jaws
   Of vacant darkness and to cease.

35

   Yet if some voice that man could trust
       Should murmur from the narrow house,[2]
       "The cheeks drop in; the body bows;
   Man dies: nor is there hope in dust":

---

[1] *round ... flame* I.e., the earth and the sun.

[2] *narrow house* Implies the grave.

5 Might I not say? "Yet even here,
       But for one hour, O Love, I strive
       To keep so sweet a thing alive":
   But I should turn mine ears and hear

   The moanings of the homeless sea,
10   The sound of streams that swift or slow
       Draw down Æonian° hills,[3] and sow   *eternal*
   The dust of continents to be;

   And Love would answer with a sigh,
       "The sound of that forgetful shore
15   Will change my sweetness more and more,
   Half-dead to know that I shall die."

   O me, what profits it to put
       An idle case? If Death were seen
       At first as Death, Love had not been,
20 Or been in narrowest working shut,

   Mere fellowship of sluggish moods,
       Or in his coarsest Satyr-shape[4]
       Had bruised the herb and crushed the grape,
   And basked and battened° in the woods.   *thrived*

36

   Though truths in manhood darkly join,
       Deep-seated in our mystic frame,
       We yield all blessing to the name
   Of Him that made them current coin;

5 For Wisdom dealt with mortal powers,
       Where truth in closest[5] words shall fail,
       When truth embodied in a tale
   Shall enter in at lowly doors.

---

[3] *Draw ... hills* Tennyson turns again to the subject of hills in section 123.

[4] *Satyr-shape* In the shape of satyrs; half-human, half-beast. I.e., if we believed that death ended all, love would never have progressed beyond mere animalistic impulse.

[5] *closest* Most tightly reasoned.

And so the Word had breath,[1] and wrought
10   With human hands the creed of creeds
      In loveliness of perfect deeds,
More strong than all poetic thought;

Which he may read that binds the sheaf,
      Or builds the house, or digs the grave,
15   And those wild eyes that watch the wave
In roarings round the coral reef.

37

Urania[2] speaks with darkened brow:
      "Thou pratest° here where thou art least;   chatter
      This faith has many a purer priest,
And many an abler voice than thou.

5   "Go down beside thy native rill,°   stream
      On thy Parnassus[3] set thy feet,
      And hear thy laurel whisper sweet
About the ledges of the hill."

And my Melpomene[4] replies,
10   A touch of shame upon her cheek:
      "I am not worthy even to speak
Of thy prevailing mysteries;

"For I am but an earthly Muse,
      And owning but a little art
15   To lull with song an aching heart,
And render human love his dues;

"But brooding on the dear one dead,
      And all he said of things divine,[5]

(And dear to me as sacred wine
20   To dying lips is all he said),

"I murmured, as I came along,
      Of comfort clasped in truth revealed;
      And loitered in the master's field,
And darkened sanctities with song."

38

With weary steps I loiter on,
      Though always under altered skies
      The purple from the distance dies,
My prospect and horizon gone.

5   No joy the blowing° season gives,   blooming
      The herald melodies of spring,
      But in the songs I love to sing
A doubtful gleam of solace lives.

If any care for what is here
10   Survive in spirits rendered free,
      Then are these songs I sing of thee
Not all ungrateful to thine ear.

39

Old warder of these buried bones,
      And answering now my random stroke
      With fruitful cloud and living smoke,
Dark yew, that graspest at the stones

5   And dippest toward the dreamless head,
      To thee too comes the golden hour
      When flower is feeling after flower;
But Sorrow—fixed upon the dead,

And darkening the dark graves of men,—
10   What whispered from her lying lips?
      Thy gloom is kindled at the tips,
And passes into gloom again.

40

Could we forget the widowed hour
      And look on Spirits breathed away,

---

1 *Word had breath* See John 1.14: "The Word became flesh and
dwelt among us."

2 *Urania* Greek Muse of astronomy; invoked by the poet Milton as
a source of divine wisdom.

3 *thy Parnassus* I.e., your home. Mount Parnassus was the home of
the Muses.

4 *Melpomene* Greek Muse of tragedy.

5 *And all … divine* Tennyson admired Hallam's ideas and writings
on theological subjects.

As on a maiden in the day
    When first she wears her orange-flower!¹

5 When crowned with blessing she doth rise
    To take her latest leave of home,
    And hopes and light regrets that come
Make April of her tender eyes,

And doubtful joys the father move,
10   And tears are on the mother's face,
    As parting with a long embrace
She enters other realms of love;

Her office there to rear, to teach,
    Becoming as is meet° and fit   *proper*
15   A link among the days, to knit
The generations each with each;

And, doubtless, unto thee is given
    A life that bears immortal fruit
    In those great offices that suit
20 The full-grown energies of heaven.

Ay me, the difference I discern!
    How often shall her old fireside
    Be cheered with tidings of the bride,
How often she herself return,

25 And tell them all they would have told,
    And bring her babe, and make her boast,
    Till even those that missed her most
Shall count new things as dear as old:

But thou and I have shaken hands,
30   Till growing winters lay me low;
    My paths are in the fields I know,
And thine in undiscovered lands.²

---

¹ *orange-flower* Brides often wore wreaths of orange-flowers in this period.

² *undiscovered lands* See *Hamlet* 3.1.79–80, in which death is "the undiscovered country, from whose bourne / No traveller returns."

41

Thy spirit ere our fatal loss
    Did ever rise from high to higher;
    As mounts the heavenward altar-fire,
As flies the lighter through the gross.°   *heavier*

5 But thou art turned to something strange,
    And I have lost the links that bound
    Thy changes; here upon the ground,
No more partaker of thy change.

Deep folly! yet that this could be—
10   That I could wing° my will with might   *hurl*
    To leap the grades of life and light,
And flash at once, my friend, to thee.

For though my nature rarely yields
    To that vague fear implied in death;
15   Nor shudders at the gulfs beneath,
The howlings from forgotten fields;

Yet oft when sundown skirts the moor
    An inner trouble I behold,
    A spectral° doubt which makes me cold,   *ghostly*
20 That I shall be thy mate no more,

Though following with an upward mind
    The wonders that have come to thee,
    Through all the secular to-be,
But evermore a life behind.

42

I vex my heart with fancies dim:
    He still outstripped me in the race;
    It was but unity of place
That made me dream I ranked with him.

5 And so may Place retain us still,
    And he the much-beloved again,
    A lord of large experience, train
To riper growth the mind and will:

And what delights can equal those
10   That stir the spirit's inner deeps,
    When one that loves but knows not, reaps
A truth from one that loves and knows?

43

If Sleep and Death be truly one,
    And every spirit's folded bloom
    Through all its intervital[1] gloom
In some long trance should slumber on;

5 Unconscious of the sliding hour,
    Bare of the body, might it last,
    And silent traces of the past
Be all the colour of the flower:

So then were nothing lost to man;
10   So that still garden of the souls
    In many a figured leaf enrolls
The total world since life began;

And love will last as pure and whole
    As when he loved me here in Time,
15   And at the spiritual prime°   *rebirth*
Rewaken with the dawning soul.

44

How fares it with the happy dead?
    For here the man is more and more;
    But he forgets the days before
God shut the doorways of his head.[2]

5 The days have vanished, tone and tint,
    And yet perhaps the hoarding sense
    Gives out at times (he knows not whence)
A little flash, a mystic hint;

And in the long harmonious years
10   (If Death so taste Lethean springs[3]),
    May some dim touch of earthly things
Surprise thee° ranging with thy peers.   *Hallam*

If such a dreamy touch should fall,
    O turn thee round, resolve the doubt;
15   My guardian angel will speak out
In that high place, and tell thee all.

45

The baby new to earth and sky,
    What time his tender palm is pressed
    Against the circle of the breast,
Has never thought that "this is I":

5 But as he grows he gathers much,
    And learns the use of "I," and "me,"
    And finds "I am not what I see,
And other than the things I touch."

So rounds he to a separate mind
10   From whence clear memory may begin,
    As through the frame that binds him in
His isolation grows defined.

This use may lie in blood and breath,
    Which else were fruitless of their due,
15   Had man to learn himself anew
Beyond the second birth of Death.

46

We ranging down this lower track,
    The path we came by, thorn and flower,
    Is shadowed by the growing hour,
Lest life should fail in looking back.

5 So be it: there no shade can last
    In that deep dawn behind the tomb,

---

[1] *intervital* Between two stages of existence.

[2] *the doorways of his head* The baby's soft-spot, or fontanel: the anatomical opening in the skull at birth. The speaker notes that we cannot remember the days of infancy before the fontanel closes, and asks whether the dead likewise forget their previous life.

[3] *Lethean springs* According to Greek mythology, drinking from the River Lethe in Hades caused the dead to forget their previous existences.

But clear from marge° to marge shall bloom   *shore*
The eternal landscape of the past;

A lifelong tract of time revealed;
10   The fruitful hours of still increase;
    Days ordered in a wealthy peace,
And those five years its richest field.

O Love, thy province were not large,
    A bounded field, nor stretching far;
15   Look also, Love, a brooding star,
A rosy warmth from marge to marge.

47

That each, who seems a separate whole,
    Should move his rounds, and fusing all
    The skirts of self again, should fall
Remerging in the general Soul,[1]

5 Is faith as vague as all unsweet:
    Eternal form shall still divide
    The eternal soul from all beside;
And I shall know him when we meet:

And we shall sit at endless feast,
10   Enjoying each the other's good:
    What vaster dream can hit the mood
Of Love on earth? He seeks at least

Upon the last and sharpest height,
    Before the spirits fade away,
15   Some landing-place, to clasp and say,
"Farewell! We lose ourselves in light."

48

If these brief lays,° of Sorrow born,   *songs*
    Were taken to be such as closed
    Grave doubts and answers here proposed,
Then these were such as men might scorn:

5 Her care is not to part and prove;
    She takes, when harsher moods remit,

---

[1] *Remerging ... Soul* Losing individual personality in the afterlife.

What slender shade of doubt may flit,
And makes it vassal unto love:

And hence, indeed, she sports with words,
10   But better serves a wholesome law,
    And holds it sin and shame to draw
The deepest measure from the chords;

Nor dare she trust a larger lay,
    But rather loosens from the lip
15   Short swallow-flights of song, that dip
Their wings in tears, and skim away.

49

From art, from nature, from the schools,
    Let random influences glance,
    Like light in many a shivered° lance   *splintered*
That breaks about the dappled pools:

5 The lightest wave of thought shall lisp,
    The fancy's tenderest eddy wreathe,
    The slightest air of song shall breathe
To make the sullen surface crisp.°   *ripple*

And look thy look, and go thy way,
10   But blame not thou the winds that make
    The seeming-wanton ripple break,
The tender-pencilled shadow play.

Beneath all fancied hopes and fears
    Ay me, the sorrow deepens down,
15   Whose muffled motions blindly drown
The bases of my life in tears.

50

Be near me[2] when my light is low,
    When the blood creeps, and the nerves prick
    And tingle; and the heart is sick,
And all the wheels of Being slow.

5 Be near me when the sensuous frame
    Is racked with pangs that conquer trust;

---

[2] *Be near me* Section 50 is directly addressed to Hallam.

And Time, a maniac scattering dust,
And Life, a Fury[1] slinging flame.

Be near me when my faith is dry,
10   And men the flies of latter spring,
That lay their eggs, and sting and sing
And weave their petty cells and die.

Be near me when I fade away,
To point the term of human strife,
15   And on the low dark verge of life
The twilight of eternal day.

51

Do we indeed desire the dead
Should still be near us at our side?
Is there no baseness we would hide?
No inner vileness that we dread?

5   Shall he for whose applause I strove,
I had such reverence for his blame,
See with clear eye some hidden shame
And I be lessened in his love?

I wrong the grave with fears untrue:
10   Shall love be blamed for want of faith?
There must be wisdom with great Death:
The dead shall look me through and through.

Be near us when we climb or fall:
Ye watch, like God, the rolling hours
15   With larger other eyes than ours,
To make allowance for us all.

52

I cannot love thee as I ought,
For love reflects the thing beloved;
My words are only words, and moved
Upon the topmost froth of thought.

"Yet blame not thou thy plaintive song,"   5
The Spirit of true love replied;
"Thou canst not move me from thy side,
Nor human frailty do me wrong.

"What keeps a spirit wholly true
To that ideal which he bears?   10
What record? not the sinless years
That breathed beneath the Syrian blue:[2]

"So fret not, like an idle girl,
That life is dashed with flecks of sin.
Abide: thy wealth is gathered in,   15
When Time hath sundered shell from pearl."

53

How many a father have I seen,
A sober man, among his boys,
Whose youth was full of foolish noise,
Who wears his manhood hale° and green: robust

And dare we to this fancy give,   5
That had the wild oat not been sown,
The soil, left barren, scarce had grown
The grain by which a man may live?

Or, if we held the doctrine sound
For life outliving heats of youth,   10
Yet who would preach it as a truth
To those that eddy round and round?

Hold thou the good: define it well:
For fear divine Philosophy
Should push beyond her mark, and be   15
Procuress to the Lords of Hell.

54

Oh yet we trust that somehow good
Will be the final goal of ill,[3]

---

[1] *Fury* Reference to the Furies, a trio of avenging goddesses of Greek mythology.

[2] *Syrian blue* Blue skies of Syria, commonly used as a term for the land in which Christ lived.

[3] *Oh yet ... of ill* Section 54–56 together address this topic.

To pangs of nature, sins of will,
Defects of doubt, and taints of blood;

5 That nothing walks with aimless feet;
  That not one life shall be destroyed,
  Or cast as rubbish to the void,
When God hath made the pile complete,

That not a worm is cloven¹ in vain;
10 That not a moth with vain desire
  Is shrivelled in a fruitless fire,
Or but subserves another's gain.

Behold, we know not anything;
  I can but trust that good shall fall
15 At last—far off—at last, to all,
And every winter change to spring.

So runs my dream: but what am I?
  An infant crying in the night:
  An infant crying for the light:
20 And with no language but a cry.

                    55
The wish, that of the living whole
  No life may fail beyond the grave,
  Derives it not from what we have
The likest God within the soul?

5 Are God and Nature then at strife,
  That Nature lends such evil dreams?
  So careful of the type° she seems,   species
So careless of the single life;

That I, considering everywhere
10 Her secret meaning in her deeds,
  And finding that of fifty seeds
She often brings but one to bear,

I falter where I firmly trod,
  And falling with my weight of cares

15 Upon the great world's altar-stairs
That slope through darkness up to God,

I stretch lame hands of faith, and grope,
  And gather dust and chaff, and call
  To what I feel is Lord of all,
20 And faintly trust the larger hope.

                    56
"So careful of the type?" but no.
  From scarpèd² cliff and quarried stone
  She cries, "A thousand types are gone:
I care for nothing, all shall go.³

5 "Thou makest thine appeal to me:
  I bring to life, I bring to death:
  The spirit does but mean the breath:
I know no more." And he, shall he,

Man, her last work, who seemed so fair,
10 Such splendid purpose in his eyes,
  Who rolled the psalm to wintry skies,
Who built him fanes° of fruitless prayer,   temples

Who trusted God was love indeed
  And love Creation's final law—
15 Though Nature, red in tooth and claw
With ravine,° shrieked against his creed—   violence

Who loved, who suffered countless ills,
  Who battled for the True, the Just,
  Be blown about the desert dust,
20 Or sealed within the iron hills?

No more? A monster then, a dream,
  A discord. Dragons° of the prime,   dinosaurs

---

¹ cloven Cut in two.

² scarpèd Steeply cut.

³ A thousand ... shall go A reference to the geological discoveries of Charles Lyell, whose Principles of Geology (1830–33) Tennyson had read. The fossil record evident in exposed rocks and cliffs reveals that entire species have become extinct.

That tare° each other in their slime,   *tore*
Were mellow music matched with him.[1]

25   O life as futile, then, as frail!
    O for thy voice to soothe and bless!
    What hope of answer, or redress?
Behind the veil, behind the veil.

57

Peace; come away: the song of woe
    Is after all an earthly song:
    Peace; come away: we do him wrong
To sing so wildly: let us go.

5   Come; let us go: your cheeks are pale;
    But half my life I leave behind:
    Methinks my friend is richly shrined;
But I shall pass; my work will fail.

Yet in these ears, till hearing dies,
10   One set slow bell will seem to toll
    The passing of the sweetest soul
That ever looked with human eyes.

I hear it now, and o'er and o'er,
    Eternal greetings to the dead;
15   And "Ave,° Ave, Ave," said,   *hail*
"Adieu,° adieu" for evermore.   *farewell*

58

In those sad words I took farewell:
    Like echoes in sepulchral° halls,   *tomb-like*
    As drop by drop the water falls
In vaults and catacombs, they fell;

5   And, falling, idly broke the peace
    Of hearts that beat from day to day,
    Half-conscious of their dying clay,
And those cold crypts where they shall cease.

---

[1] *Dragons ... with him* I.e., if the natural world reflects a universe based in destruction rather than love, then the dinosaurs are more in accord with nature than humankind, which is deluded in its pursuit of religion (see lines 11–12).

The high Muse answered: "Wherefore grieve
10   Thy brethren with a fruitless tear?
    Abide a little longer here,
And thou shalt take a nobler leave."

59

O Sorrow, wilt thou live with me
    No casual mistress, but a wife,
    My bosom-friend and half of life;
As I confess it needs must be;

5   O Sorrow, wilt thou rule my blood,
    Be sometimes lovely like a bride,
    And put thy harsher moods aside,
If thou wilt have me wise and good.

My centred passion cannot move,
10   Nor will it lessen from today;
    But I'll have leave at times to play
As with the creature of my love;

And set thee forth, for thou art mine,
    With so much hope for years to come,
15   That, howsoe'er I know thee, some
Could hardly tell what name were thine.

60

He passed; a soul of nobler tone:
    My spirit loved and loves him yet,
    Like some poor girl whose heart is set
On one whose rank exceeds her own.

5   He mixing with his proper sphere,
    She finds the baseness of her lot,
    Half jealous of she knows not what,
And envying all that meet him there.

The little village looks forlorn;
10   She sighs amid her narrow days,
    Moving about the household ways,
In that dark house where she was born.

The foolish neighbours come and go,
    And tease her till the day draws by:
15   At night she weeps, "How vain am I!
How should he love a thing so low?"

61

If, in thy second state sublime,[1]
    Thy ransomed reason change replies[2]
    With all the circle of the wise,
The perfect flower of human time;

5 And if thou cast thine eyes below,
    How dimly charactered and slight,
    How dwarfed a growth of cold and night,
How blanched with darkness must I grow!

Yet turn thee to the doubtful shore,[3]
10   Where thy first form was made a man;
    I loved thee, Spirit, and love, nor can
The soul of Shakespeare love thee more.[4]

62

Though if an eye that's downward cast
    Could make thee somewhat blench° or fail,   *flinch*
    Then be my love an idle tale,
And fading legend of the past;

5 And thou, as one that once declined°   *stooped*
    When he was little more than boy,
    On some unworthy heart with joy,
But lives to wed an equal mind;

And breathes a novel world, the while
10   His other passion wholly dies,
    Or in the light of deeper eyes
Is matter for a flying smile.

---

1 *in thy ... sublime* I.e., in heaven.

2 *Thy ransomed ... replies* Your redeemed mind exchanged words.

3 *to the doubtful shore* I.e., to life on earth, now not easily remembered or seen.

4 *nor can ... more* The poet expresses love for his beloved friend here directly but also in the entire series of poems, as Shakespeare did in his Sonnets.

63

Yet pity for a horse o'er-driven,
    And love in which my hound has part,
    Can hang no weight upon my heart
In its assumptions° up to heaven;   *aspirations*

5 And I am so much more than these,
    As thou, perchance, art more than I,
    And yet I spare them sympathy,
And I would set their pains at ease.

So mayst thou watch me where I weep,
10   As, unto vaster motions bound,
    The circuits of thine orbit round
A higher height, a deeper deep.

64

Dost thou look back on what hath been,
    As some divinely gifted man,
    Whose life in low estate began
And on a simple village green;

5 Who breaks his birth's invidious° bar,   *discriminatory*
    And grasps the skirts of happy chance,
    And breasts° the blows of circumstance,   *meets*
And grapples with his evil star;

Who makes by force his merit known
10   And lives to clutch the golden keys,[5]
    To mould a mighty state's decrees,
And shape the whisper of the throne;

And moving up from high to higher,
    Becomes on Fortune's crowning slope
15   The pillar of a people's hope,
The centre of a world's desire;

Yet feels, as in a pensive dream,
    When all his active powers are still,
    A distant dearness in the hill,
20 A secret sweetness in the stream,

---

5 *the golden keys* Symbolically, the keys to public office.

The limit of his narrower fate,
    While yet beside its vocal springs
    He played at counsellors and kings,
With one that was his earliest mate;

25   Who ploughs with pain his native lea°   land
    And reaps the labour of his hands,
    Or in the furrow musing stands;
"Does my old friend remember me?"

65

Sweet soul, do with me as thou wilt;
    I lull a fancy trouble-tossed
    With "Love's too precious to be lost,
A little grain shall not be spilt."

5   And in that solace can I sing,
    Till out of painful phases wrought
    There flutters up a happy thought,
Self-balanced on a lightsome wing:

Since we deserved the name of friends,
10   And thine effect so lives in me,
    A part of mine may live in thee
And move thee on to noble ends.

66

You thought my heart too far diseased;
    You wonder when my fancies play
    To find me gay among the gay,
Like one with any trifle pleased.

5   The shade by which my life was crossed,
    Which makes a desert in the mind,
    Has made me kindly with my kind,
And like to him whose sight is lost;

Whose feet are guided through the land,
10   Whose jest among his friends is free,
    Who takes the children on his knee,
And winds their curls about his hand:

He plays with threads,[1] he beats his chair
    For pastime, dreaming of the sky;
15   His inner day can never die,
His night of loss is always there.

67

When on my bed the moonlight falls,
    I know that in thy place of rest
    By that broad water of the west,[2]
There comes a glory° on the walls;   halo

5   Thy marble bright in dark appears,
    As slowly steals a silver flame
    Along the letters of thy name,
And o'er the number of thy years.

The mystic glory swims away;
10   From off my bed the moonlight dies;
    And closing eaves of wearied eyes
I sleep till dusk is dipped in gray:

And then I know the mist is drawn
    A lucid veil from coast to coast,
15   And in the dark church like a ghost
Thy tablet glimmers to the dawn.

68

When in the down I sink my head,
    Sleep, Death's twin-brother, times my breath;
    Sleep, Death's twin-brother, knows not Death,
Nor can I dream of thee as dead:

5   I walk as ere I walked forlorn,
    When all our path was fresh with dew,
    And all the bugle breezes blew
Reveillée[3] to the breaking morn.

But what is this? I turn about,
10   I find a trouble in thine eye,

---

1   *plays with threads*   Suggests a kind person who plays the game of
cat's cradle to amuse children.

2   *broad … west*   I.e., the Severn Estuary.

3   *Reveillée*   Music played to awaken soldiers in the morning.

Which makes me sad I know not why,
Nor can my dream resolve the doubt:

But ere the lark hath left the lea
   I wake, and I discern the truth;
15   It is the trouble of my youth
That foolish sleep transfers to thee.

69

I dreamed there would be Spring no more,
   That Nature's ancient power was lost:
   The streets were black with smoke and frost,
They chattered trifles at the door:

5   I wandered from the noisy town,
   I found a wood with thorny boughs:
   I took the thorns to bind my brows,
I wore them like a civic crown:[1]

I met with scoffs, I met with scorns
10   From youth and babe and hoary° hairs: *gray*
   They called me in the public squares
The fool that wears a crown of thorns:

They called me fool, they called me child:
   I found an angel of the night;
15   The voice was low, the look was bright;
He looked upon my crown and smiled:

He reached the glory of a hand,
   That seemed to touch it into leaf:
   The voice was not the voice of grief,
20 The words were hard to understand.

70

I cannot see the features right,
   When on the gloom I strive to paint
   The face I know; the hues are faint
And mix with hollow masks of night;

5   Cloud-towers by ghostly masons wrought,
   A gulf that ever shuts and gapes,
   A hand that points, and pallèd° shapes   *veiled*
In shadowy thoroughfares of thought;

And crowds that stream from yawning doors,
10   And shoals of puckered faces drive;
   Dark bulks that tumble half alive,
And lazy lengths on boundless shores;

Till all at once beyond the will
   I hear a wizard music roll,
15   And through a lattice on the soul
Looks thy fair face and makes it still.

71

Sleep, kinsman thou to death and trance
   And madness, thou hast forged at last
   A night-long Present of the Past
In which we went through summer France.[2]

5   Hadst thou such credit with the soul?
   Then bring an opiate trebly° strong,   *triply*
   Drug down the blindfold sense of wrong
That so my pleasure may be whole;

While now we talk as once we talked
10   Of men and minds, the dust of change,
   The days that grow to something strange,
In walking as of old we walked

Beside the river's wooded reach,
   The fortress, and the mountain ridge,
15   The cataract° flashing from the bridge,   *waterfall*
The breaker breaking on the beach.

---

[1] *civic crown* Highly prized garland of oak leaves and acorns, bestowed upon one who has saved the life of another in war.

[2] *France* Tennyson and Hallam vacationed together in France in 1830.

72

Risest thou thus, dim dawn, again,[1]
   And howlest, issuing out of night,
   With blasts that blow the poplar white,[2]
And lash with storm the streaming pane?

5   Day, when my crowned estate begun
     To pine in that reverse of doom,
     Which sickened every living bloom,
   And blurred the splendour of the sun;

Who usherest in the dolorous hour
10   With thy quick tears that make the rose
     Pull sideways, and the daisy close
   Her crimson fringes to the shower;

Who might'st have heaved a windless flame
     Up the deep East, or, whispering, played
15   A chequer-work of beam and shade
   Along the hills, yet looked the same,

As wan,° as chill, as wild as now;   *pale*
     Day, marked as with some hideous crime,
     When the dark hand struck down through time,
20   And cancelled nature's best: but thou,

Lift as thou mayst thy burdened brows
     Through clouds that drench the morning star,[3]
     And whirl the ungarnered sheaf[4] afar,
   And sow the sky with flying boughs,

25   And up thy vault with roaring sound
     Climb thy thick noon, disastrous day;
     Touch thy dull goal of joyless gray,
   And hide thy shame beneath the ground.

73

So many worlds, so much to do,
   So little done, such things to be,
   How know I what had need of thee,
For thou wert strong as thou wert true?

5   The fame is quenched that I foresaw,
     The head hath missed an earthly wreath:
     I curse not nature, no, nor death;
   For nothing is that errs from law.

We pass; the path that each man trod
10   Is dim, or will be dim, with weeds:
     What fame is left for human deeds
In endless age? It rests with God.

O hollow wraith of dying fame,
     Fade wholly, while the soul exults,
15   And self-infolds the large results
Of force that would have forged a name.

74

As sometimes in a dead man's face,
   To those that watch it more and more,
   A likeness, hardly seen before,
Comes out—to some one of his race:°   *family*

5   So, dearest, now thy brows are cold,
     I see thee what thou art, and know
     Thy likeness to the wise below,[5]
Thy kindred with the great of old.

But there is more than I can see,
10   And what I see I leave unsaid,
     Nor speak it, knowing Death has made
His darkness beautiful with thee.

75

I leave thy praises unexpressed
   In verse that brings myself relief,
   And by the measure of my grief
I leave thy greatness to be guessed;

---

[1] *Risest ... again* Refers to the anniversary of the day Hallam died (15 September). The second anniversary of Hallam's death is commemorated in section 99, where the same first line is used.

[2] *blow ... white* I.e., reveal the white underside of poplar leaves.

[3] *morning star* The planet Venus.

[4] *ungarnered sheaf* Bundle of grain stalks that has not been put in storage.

[5] *likeness ... below* Similarity to wise people in the past.

What practice howsoe'er expert
   In fitting aptest words to things,
   Or voice the richest-toned that sings,
Hath power to give thee as thou wert?

I care not in these fading days
   To raise a cry that lasts not long,
   And round thee with the breeze of song
To stir a little dust of praise.

Thy leaf has perished in the green,
   And, while we breathe beneath the sun,
   The world which credits what is done
Is cold to all that might have been.

So here shall silence guard thy fame;
   But somewhere, out of human view,
   Whate'er thy hands are set to do
Is wrought with tumult of acclaim.

76

Take wings of fancy, and ascend,
   And in a moment set thy face
   Where all the starry heavens of space
Are sharpened to a needle's end;

Take wings of foresight; lighten through
   The secular abyss[1] to come,
   And lo, thy deepest lays° are dumb   *songs*
Before the mouldering of a yew;[2]

And if the matin songs,[3] that woke
   The darkness of our planet, last,
   Thine own shall wither in the vast,
Ere half the lifetime of an oak.

Ere these have clothed their branchy bowers
   With fifty Mays, thy songs are vain;

---

1. *secular abyss* Depth of ages.
2. *yew* A tree that lives a very long time.
3. *matin songs* Morning songs (matins is the service that precedes the first mass of the day); here, referring to the earliest recorded works of poetry.

And what are they when these remain
The ruined shells of hollow towers?

77

What hope is here for modern rhyme
   To him, who turns a musing eye
   On songs, and deeds, and lives, that lie
Foreshortened in the tract of time?

These mortal lullabies of pain
   May bind a book, may line a box,
   May serve to curl a maiden's locks;[4]
Or when a thousand moons shall wane

A man upon a stall may find,
   And, passing, turn the page that tells
   A grief, then changed to something else,
Sung by a long-forgotten mind.

But what of that? My darkened ways
   Shall ring with music all the same;
   To breathe my loss is more than fame,
To utter love more sweet than praise.

78

Again at Christmas did we weave
   The holly round the Christmas hearth;
   The silent snow possessed the earth,
And calmly fell our Christmas-eve:

The yule-clog[5] sparkled keen with frost,
   No wing of wind the region swept,
   But over all things brooding slept
The quiet sense of something lost.

As in the winters left behind,
   Again our ancient games had place,
   The mimic picture's breathing grace,
And dance and song and hoodman-blind.[6]

---

4. *May ... locks* Rolls of paper may be worn in the hair to help it to curl.
5. *yule-clog* Large log of wood burnt at Christmas.
6. *hoodman-blind* Blind-man's-bluff.

Who showed a token of distress?
 No single tear, no mark of pain:
15   O sorrow, then can sorrow wane?
 O grief, can grief be changed to less?

 O last regret, regret can die!
  No—mixed with all this mystic frame,
  Her deep relations are the same,
20 But with long use her tears are dry.

79

"More than my brothers are to me,"—
 Let this not vex thee, noble heart![1]
 I know thee of what force thou art
To hold the costliest love in fee.[2]

5 But thou and I are one in kind,
 As moulded like in Nature's mint;
 And hill and wood and field did print
The same sweet forms in either mind.

For us the same cold streamlet curled
10 Through all his eddying coves; the same
 All winds that roam the twilight came
In whispers of the beauteous world.

At one dear knee we proffered vows,
 One lesson from one book we learned,
15 Ere childhood's flaxen ringlet turned
To black and brown on kindred brows.

And so my wealth resembles thine,
 But he was rich where I was poor,
 And he supplied my want the more
20 As his unlikeness fitted mine.

80

If any vague desire should rise,
 That holy Death ere Arthur died

---

[1] *More ... heart!* Tennyson quotes section 9, line 20, and asks his brother (probably Charles, the one to whom he was closest) not to be offended.

[2] *in fee* In possession.

Had moved me kindly from his side,
And dropped the dust on tearless eyes;

5 Then fancy shapes, as fancy can,
 The grief my loss in him had wrought,
 A grief as deep as life or thought,
But stayed in peace with God and man.

I make a picture in the brain;
10 I hear the sentence that he speaks;
 He bears the burden of the weeks
But turns his burden into gain.

His credit thus shall set me free;
 And, influence-rich to soothe and save,
15 Unused example from the grave
Reach out dead hands to comfort me.

81

Could I have said while he was here,
 "My love shall now no further range;
 There cannot come a mellower change,
For now is love mature in ear."[3]

5 Love, then, had hope of richer store:
 What end is here to my complaint?
 This haunting whisper makes me faint,
"More years had made me love thee more."

But Death returns an answer sweet:
10 "My sudden frost was sudden gain,
 And gave all ripeness to the grain,
It might have drawn from after-heat."

82

I wage not any feud with Death
 For changes wrought on form and face;
 No lower life that earth's embrace
May breed with him, can fright my faith.

5 Eternal process moving on,
 From state to state the spirit walks;

---

[3] *ear* I.e., of grain.

And these are but the shattered stalks,
Or ruined chrysalis[1] of one.

Nor blame I Death, because he bare°   bore
10   The use of virtue out of earth:
   I know transplanted human worth
Will bloom to profit, otherwhere.

For this alone on Death I wreak
   The wrath that garners in my heart;
15   He put our lives so far apart
We cannot hear each other speak.

83

Dip down upon the northern shore,
   O sweet new-year delaying long;
   Thou doest expectant nature wrong;
Delaying long, delay no more.

5   What stays thee from the clouded noons,
   Thy sweetness from its proper place?
   Can trouble live with April days,
Or sadness in the summer moons?

Bring orchis,° bring the foxglove spire,   orchid
10   The little speedwell's[2] darling blue,
   Deep tulips dashed with fiery dew,
Laburnums,[3] dropping-wells of fire.

O thou, new-year, delaying long,
   Delayest the sorrow in my blood,
15   That longs to burst a frozen bud
And flood a fresher throat with song.

84

When I contemplate all alone
   The life that had° been thine below,   would have

And fix my thoughts on all the glow
   To which thy crescent would have grown;

5   I see thee sitting crowned with good,
   A central warmth diffusing bliss
   In glance and smile, and clasp and kiss,
On all the branches of thy blood;

Thy blood, my friend, and partly mine;
10   For now the day was drawing on,
   When thou shouldst link thy life with one
Of mine own house,[4] and boys of thine

Had babbled "Uncle" on my knee;
   But that remorseless iron hour
15   Made cypress[5] of her orange flower,
Despair of Hope, and earth of thee.

I seem to meet their least desire,
   To clap their cheeks, to call them mine.
   I see their unborn faces shine
20 Beside the never-lighted fire.

I see myself an honoured guest,
   Thy partner in the flowery walk
   Of letters, genial table-talk,
Or deep dispute, and graceful jest;

25 While now thy prosperous labour fills
   The lips of men with honest praise,
   And sun by sun the happy days
Descend below the golden hills

With promise of a morn as fair;
30   And all the train of bounteous hours
   Conduct by paths of growing powers,
To reverence and the silver hair;

Till slowly worn her earthly robe,
   Her lavish mission richly wrought,

---

[1] *chrysalis* Cocoon that a caterpillar occupies during its transformation and sheds to reveal itself as having evolved into a butterfly.

[2] *speedwell* Plant with small, usually violet-blue flowers.

[3] *Laburnums* Trees with hanging bunches of bright yellow flowers.

---

[4] *thou shouldst ... house* Hallam had been engaged to Tennyson's sister Emily.

[5] *cypress* Tree symbolic of mourning.

35   Leaving great legacies of thought,
        Thy spirit should fail from off the globe;

        What time mine own might also flee,
            As linked with thine in love and fate,
            And, hovering o'er the dolorous strait
40   To the other shore, involved in thee,

        Arrive at last the blessèd goal,
            And He that died in Holy Land[1]
            Would reach us out the shining hand,
        And take us as a single soul.

45   What reed was that on which I leant?
            Ah, backward fancy, wherefore wake
            The old bitterness again, and break
        The low beginnings of content.

                        85

        This truth came borne with bier[2] and pall,[3]
            I felt it, when I sorrowed most,
            'Tis better to have loved and lost,
        Than never to have loved at all[4]—

5   O true in word, and tried in deed,[5]
            Demanding, so to bring relief
            To this which is our common grief,
        What kind of life is that I lead;

        And whether trust in things above
10   Be dimmed of sorrow, or sustained;
            And whether love for him have drained
        My capabilities of love;

        Your words have virtue such as draws
            A faithful answer from the breast,

15   Through light reproaches, half expressed,
        And loyal unto kindly laws.

        My blood an even tenor kept,
            Till on mine ear this message falls,
            That in Vienna's fatal walls
20   God's finger touched him, and he slept.

        The great Intelligences° fair   *angels*
            That range above our mortal state,
            In circle round the blessèd gate,
        Received and gave him welcome there;

25   And led him through the blissful climes,
            And showed him in the fountain fresh
            All knowledge that the sons of flesh
        Shall gather in the cycled times.

        But I remained, whose hopes were dim,
30   Whose life, whose thoughts were little worth,
            To wander on a darkened earth,
        Where all things round me breathed of him.

        O friendship, equal-poised control,
            O heart, with kindliest motion warm,
35   O sacred essence, other form,
        O solemn ghost, O crownèd soul!

        Yet none could better know than I,
            How much of act at human hands
            The sense of human will demands
40   By which we dare to live or die.

        Whatever way my days decline,
            I felt and feel, though left alone,
            His being working in mine own,
        The footsteps of his life in mine;

45   A life that all the Muses decked
            With gifts of grace, that might express
            All-comprehensive tenderness,
        All-subtilising° intellect: *elevating*

---

[1] *He ... Land*   I.e., Christ.

[2] *bier*   Moveable stand on which a corpse is carried to the grave.

[3] *pall*   Cloth that covers a corpse or a coffin.

[4] *'Tis better ... loved at all*   These lines are repeated in section 27.

[5] *O ... deed*   This section is addressed to a friend of both Tennyson and Hallam, Edmund Lushington (1811–93); see also note to Epilogue.

And so my passion hath not swerved
50   To works of weakness, but I find
      An image comforting the mind,
And in my grief a strength reserved.

Likewise the imaginative woe,
    That loved to handle spiritual strife,
55   Diffused the shock through all my life,
But in the present broke the blow.

My pulses therefore beat again
    For other friends that once I met;
      Nor can it suit me to forget
60 The mighty hopes that make us men.

I woo your love: I count it crime
    To mourn for any overmuch;
      I, the divided half of such
A friendship as had mastered Time;

65 Which masters Time indeed, and is
    Eternal, separate from fears:
      The all-assuming months and years
Can take no part away from this:

But Summer on the steaming floods,
70   And Spring that swells the narrow brooks,
      And Autumn, with a noise of rooks,
That gather in the waning woods,

And every pulse of wind and wave
    Recalls, in change of light or gloom,
75   My old affection of the tomb,
And my prime° passion in the grave: *first*

My old affection of the tomb,
    A part of stillness, yearns to speak:
      "Arise, and get thee forth and seek
80 A friendship for the years to come.

"I watch thee from the quiet shore;
    Thy spirit up to mine can reach;

But in dear words of human speech
We two communicate no more."

85 And I, "Can clouds of nature stain
    The starry clearness of the free?
      How is it? Canst thou feel for me
Some painless sympathy with pain?"

And lightly does the whisper fall;
90   "'Tis hard for thee to fathom this;
      I triumph in conclusive bliss,
And that serene result of all."

So hold I commerce° with the dead;   *conversation*
    Or so methinks the dead would say;
95   Or so shall grief with symbols play
And pining life be fancy-fed.

Now looking to some settled end,
    That these things pass, and I shall prove
      A meeting somewhere, love with love,
100 I crave your pardon, O my friend;

If not so fresh, with love as true,
    I, clasping brother-hands, aver
      I could not, if I would, transfer
The whole I felt for him to you.

105 For which be they that hold apart
    The promise of the golden hours?
      First love, first friendship, equal powers,
That marry with the virgin heart.

Still mine, that cannot but deplore,°   *weep*
110   That beats within a lonely place,
      That yet remembers his embrace,
But at his footstep leaps no more,

My heart, though widowed, may not rest
    Quite in the love of what is gone,
115   But seeks to beat in time with one
That warms another living breast.

Ah, take the imperfect gift I bring,
   Knowing the primrose[1] yet is dear,
   The primrose of the later year,
120 As not unlike to that of Spring.

86

Sweet after showers, ambrosial air,
   That rollest from the gorgeous gloom
   Of evening over brake° and bloom   *fern*
And meadow, slowly breathing bare

5 The round of space, and rapt below
   Through all the dewy-tasselled wood,
   And shadowing down the hornèd flood[2]
In ripples, fan my brows and blow

The fever from my cheek, and sigh
10   The full new life that feeds thy breath
   Throughout my frame, till Doubt and Death,
Ill brethren, let the fancy fly

From belt to belt of crimson seas
   On leagues of odour streaming far,
15   To where in yonder orient star
A hundred spirits whisper "Peace."

87

I passed beside the reverend walls[3]
   In which of old I wore the gown;
   I roved at random through the town,
And saw the tumult of the halls;

5 And heard once more in college fanes°   *chapels*
   The storm their high-built organs make,
   And thunder-music, rolling, shake
The prophet blazoned on the panes;

And caught once more the distant shout,
10   The measured pulse of racing oars
   Among the willows; paced the shores
And many a bridge, and all about

The same gray flats again, and felt
   The same, but not the same; and last
15   Up that long walk of limes I passed
To see the rooms in which he dwelt.

Another name was on the door:
   I lingered; all within was noise
   Of songs, and clapping hands, and boys
20 That crashed the glass and beat the floor;

Where once we held debate, a band
   Of youthful friends, on mind and art,
   And labour, and the changing mart,°   *market*
And all the framework of the land;

25 When one would aim an arrow fair,
   But send it slackly from the string;
   And one would pierce an outer ring,
And one an inner, here and there;

And last the master-bowman, he,
30   Would cleave the mark. A willing ear
   We lent him. Who but hung to hear
The rapt oration flowing free

From point to point, with power and grace
   And music in the bounds of law,
35   To those conclusions when we saw
The God within him light his face,

And seem to lift the form, and glow
   In azure orbits heavenly-wise;
   And over those ethereal eyes
40 The bar[4] of Michael Angelo.

---

[1] *primrose* Flowering plant, often with pale yellow flowers.

[2] *hornèd flood* Body of water that splits into two prongs to flow around an object. See Milton, *Paradise Lost* 11.831; see also Ben Jonson, *Volpone* 3.7.153.

[3] *reverend walls* Trinity College, Cambridge, where Tennyson and Hallam had been students, and where they first met.

[4] *bar* Forehead ridge. According to Tennyson's *Memoir* (1.38), Hallam once told Tennyson "Alfred, look over my eyes; surely I have the bar of Michael Angelo."

88

Wild bird, whose warble, liquid sweet,
    Rings Eden through the budded quicks,°   hedgerows
        O tell me where the senses mix,
O tell me where the passions meet,

5   Whence radiate: fierce extremes employ
        Thy spirits in the darkening leaf,
        And in the midmost heart of grief
Thy passion clasps a secret joy:

And I—my harp would prelude woe—
10   I cannot all command the strings;
        The glory of the sum of things
Will flash along the chords and go.

89

Witch-elms that counterchange° the floor   checker
    Of this flat lawn with dusk and bright;
        And thou, with all thy breadth and height
Of foliage, towering sycamore;

5   How often, hither wandering down,
        My Arthur found your shadows fair,
        And shook to all the liberal air
The dust and din and steam of town:

He brought an eye for all he saw;
10   He mixed in all our simple sports;
        They pleased him, fresh from brawling courts
And dusty purlieus[1] of the law.

O joy to him in this retreat,
    Immantled° in ambrosial dark,   cloaked
15   To drink the cooler air, and mark
The landscape winking through the heat:

O sound to rout the brood of cares,
    The sweep of scythe in morning dew,
        The gust that round the garden flew,
20 And tumbled half the mellowing pears!

O bliss, when all in circle drawn
    About him, heart and ear were fed
        To hear him, as he lay and read
The Tuscan poets[2] on the lawn:

25 Or in the all-golden afternoon
        A guest, or happy sister, sung,
        Or here she brought the harp and flung
A ballad to the brightening moon:

Nor less it pleased in livelier moods,
30   Beyond the bounding hill to stray,
        And break the livelong summer day
With banquet in the distant woods;

Whereat we glanced from theme to theme,
    Discussed the books to love or hate,
35   Or touched the changes of the state,
Or threaded some Socratic[3] dream;

But if I praised the busy town,
    He loved to rail against it still,
        For "ground in yonder social mill
40 We rub each other's angles down,

"And merge," he said, "in form and gloss
    The picturesque of man and man."
        We talked: the stream beneath us ran,
The wine-flask lying couched in moss,

45 Or cooled within the glooming wave;
        And last, returning from afar,
        Before the crimson-circled star[4]
Had fallen into her father's grave,

---

[1] *purlieus* Physical bounds, limits.

[2] *Tuscan poets* Dante and Petrarch.

[3] *Socratic* Relating to the Greek philosopher Socrates and/or his mode of philosophical inquiry through dialogue. Originally Tennyson wrote "Platonic"; he may have changed the word because "Platonic" was sometimes employed as a euphemism for "gay."

[4] *crimson-circled star* Venus, often referred to as the "evening star." Her "father," mentioned in the next line, may be the classical sky god Caelus; in some accounts of Venus's birth, she emerged from the sea after Caelus's genitals were thrown into it.

And brushing ankle-deep in flowers,
50   We heard behind the woodbine[1] veil
    The milk that bubbled in the pail,
And buzzings of the honeyed hours.

90

He tasted love with half his mind,
    Nor ever drank the inviolate spring
    Where nighest° heaven, who first could fling   *nearest*
This bitter seed among mankind;

5   That could the dead, whose dying eyes
    Were closed with wail, resume their life,
    They would but find in child and wife
An iron welcome when they rise:

    'Twas well, indeed, when warm with wine,
10   To pledge them with a kindly tear,
    To talk them o'er, to wish them here,
    To count their memories half divine;

But if they came who passed away,
    Behold their brides in other hands;
15   The hard heir strides about their lands,
And will not yield them for a day.

Yea, though their sons were none of these,
    Not less the yet-loved sire would make
    Confusion worse than death, and shake
20   The pillars of domestic peace.

Ah dear, but come thou back to me:
    Whatever change the years have wrought,
    I find not yet one lonely thought
That cries against my wish for thee.

91

When rosy plumelets tuft the larch,
    And rarely pipes the mounted thrush;
    Or underneath the barren bush
Flits by the sea-blue bird[2] of March;

5   Come, wear the form by which I know
    Thy spirit in time among thy peers;
    The hope of unaccomplished years
Be large and lucid round thy brow.

When summer's hourly-mellowing change
10   May breathe, with many roses sweet,
    Upon the thousand waves of wheat,
That ripple round the lonely grange;°   *farmhouse*

Come: not in watches of the night,
    But where the sunbeam broodeth warm,
15   Come, beauteous in thine after form,
And like a finer light in light.

92

If any vision should reveal
    Thy likeness, I might count it vain
    As but the canker of the brain;
Yea, though it spake and made appeal

5   To chances where our lots were cast
    Together in the days behind,
    I might but say, I hear a wind
Of memory murmuring the past.

Yea, though it spake and bared to view
10   A fact within the coming year;
    And though the months, revolving near,
Should prove the phantom-warning true,

They might not seem thy prophecies,
    But spiritual presentiments,
15   And such refraction of events
As often rises ere they rise.

93

I shall not see thee. Dare I say
    No spirit ever brake the band
    That stays him from the native land
Where first he walked when clasped in clay?

---

[1]   *woodbine*   Plant also known as honeysuckle.

[2]   *sea-blue bird*   Kingfisher.

5   No visual shade of some one lost,
      But he, the Spirit himself, may come
      Where all the nerve of sense is numb;
   Spirit to Spirit, Ghost to Ghost.

   O, therefore from thy sightless range
10   With gods in unconjectured bliss,
      O, from the distance of the abyss
   Of tenfold-complicated change,

   Descend, and touch, and enter; hear
      The wish too strong for words to name;
15   That in this blindness of the frame[1]
   My Ghost may feel that thine is near.

94

How pure at heart and sound in head,
    With what divine affections bold
    Should be the man whose thought would hold
An hour's communion with the dead.

5   In vain shalt thou, or any, call
      The spirits from their golden day,
      Except, like them, thou too canst say,
   My spirit is at peace with all.

   They haunt the silence of the breast,
10   Imaginations calm and fair,
      The memory like a cloudless air,
   The conscience as a sea at rest:

   But when the heart is full of din,
      And doubt beside the portal waits,
15   They can but listen at the gates,
   And hear the household jar° within.   *sound*

95

By night we lingered on the lawn,
    For underfoot the herb was dry;
    And genial warmth; and o'er the sky
The silvery haze of summer drawn;

5   And calm that let the tapers burn
      Unwavering: not a cricket chirred:
      The brook alone far-off was heard,
   And on the board the fluttering urn:[2]

   And bats went round in fragrant skies,
10   And wheeled or lit the filmy shapes[3]
      That haunt the dusk, with ermine[4] capes
   And woolly breasts and beaded eyes;

   While now we sang old songs that pealed
      From knoll to knoll, where, couched at ease,
15   The white kine° glimmered, and the trees   *cattle*
   Laid their dark arms about the field.

   But when those others, one by one,
      Withdrew themselves from me and night,
      And in the house light after light
20   Went out, and I was all alone,

   A hunger seized my heart; I read
      Of that glad year which once had been,[5]
      In those fallen leaves which kept their green,
   The noble letters of the dead:

25   And strangely on the silence broke
      The silent-speaking words, and strange
      Was love's dumb cry defying change
   To test his worth; and strangely spoke

   The faith, the vigour, bold to dwell
30   On doubts that drive the coward back,
      And keen through wordy snares to track
   Suggestion to her inmost cell.

   So word by word, and line by line,
      The dead man touched me from the past,

---

1   *the frame*   The human body.

2   *board*   Table set with food; *urn*   Vessel used to heat water for tea.

3   *filmy shapes*   I.e., moths.

4   *ermine*   White fur of a weasel-like animal of the same name.

5   *that glad ... been*   The time of the friendship.

35   And all at once it seemed at last
        The living soul was flashed on mine,

        And mine in this was wound, and whirled
            About empyreal° heights of thought,   *heavenly*
            And came on that which is, and caught
40   The deep pulsations of the world,

        Æonian° music measuring out   *eternal*
            The steps of Time—the shocks of Chance—
            The blows of Death. At length my trance
        Was cancelled, stricken through with doubt.

45   Vague words! but ah, how hard to frame
            In matter-moulded forms of speech,
            Or even for intellect to reach
        Through memory that which I became:

        Till now the doubtful dusk revealed
50   The knolls once more where, couched at ease,
            The white kine glimmered, and the trees
        Laid their dark arms about the field:

        And sucked from out the distant gloom
            A breeze began to tremble o'er
55   The large leaves of the sycamore,
        And fluctuate all the still perfume,

        And gathering freshlier overhead,
            Rocked the full-foliaged elms, and swung
            The heavy-folded rose, and flung
60   The lilies to and fro, and said

        "The dawn, the dawn," and died away;
            And East and West, without a breath,
            Mixed their dim lights, like life and death,
        To broaden into boundless day.

96

        You say, but with no touch of scorn,
            Sweet-hearted, you, whose light-blue eyes

        Are tender over drowning flies,
        You tell me, doubt is Devil-born.[1]

5   I know not: one[2] indeed I knew
            In many a subtle question versed,
            Who touched a jarring lyre at first,
        But ever strove to make it true:

        Perplexed in faith, but pure in deeds,
10   At last he beat his music out.
            There lives more faith in honest doubt,
        Believe me, than in half the creeds.

        He fought his doubts and gathered strength,
            He would not make his judgment blind,
15   He faced the spectres of the mind
        And laid them: thus he came at length

        To find a stronger faith his own;
            And Power was with him in the night,
            Which makes the darkness and the light,
20   And dwells not in the light alone,

        But in the darkness and the cloud,
            As over Sinai's peaks of old,
            While Israel made their gods of gold,
        Although the trumpet blew so loud.[3]

97

        My love has talked with rocks and trees;
            He finds on misty mountain-ground
            His own vast shadow glory-crowned;
        He sees himself in all he sees.

5   Two partners of a married life—
            I looked on these and thought of thee
            In vastness and in mystery,
        And of my spirit as of a wife.

---

[1] *You say ... Devil-born* These lines may be addressed to Emily Sellwood, the woman Tennyson eventually married; the long delay was due partly to her concern that he lacked sufficient religious faith.

[2] [Tennyson's note] A.H.H.

[3] *Sinai's ... loud* See Exodus 19.16–19, Exodus 32.1–5.

These two—they dwelt with eye on eye,
10   Their hearts of old have beat in tune,
        Their meetings made December June,
Their every parting was to die.

Their love has never passed away;
        The days she never can forget
15   Are earnest° that he loves her yet,   *a token*
Whate'er the faithless people say.

Her life is lone, he sits apart,
        He loves her yet, she will not weep,
        Though rapt in matters dark and deep
20 He seems to slight her simple heart.

He thrids° the labyrinth of the mind,   *threads*
        He reads the secret of the star,
        He seems so near and yet so far,
He looks so cold: she thinks him kind.

25 She keeps the gift of years before,
        A withered violet is her bliss:
        She knows not what his greatness is,
For that, for all, she loves him more.

For him she plays, to him she sings
30   Of early faith and plighted vows;
        She knows but matters of the house,
And he, he knows a thousand things.

Her faith is fixed and cannot move,
        She darkly feels him great and wise,
35   She dwells on him with faithful eyes,
"I cannot understand: I love."

98

You leave us:[1] you will see the Rhine,
        And those fair hills I sailed below,
        When I was there with him; and go
By summer belts of wheat and vine

5 To where he breathed his latest breath,
        That City.[2] All her splendour seems
        No livelier than the wisp that gleams
On Lethe[3] in the eyes of Death.

Let her great Danube[4] rolling fair
10   Enwind her isles, unmarked of me:
        I have not seen, I will not see
Vienna; rather dream that there,

A treble darkness, Evil haunts
        The birth, the bridal; friend from friend
15   Is oftener parted, fathers bend
Above more graves, a thousand wants

Gnarr° at the heels of men, and prey   *snarl*
        By each cold hearth, and sadness flings
        Her shadow on the blaze of kings:
20 And yet myself have heard him say,

That not in any mother town
        With statelier progress to and fro
        The double tides of chariots flow
By park and suburb under brown

25 Of lustier° leaves; nor more content,   *more robust*
        He told me, lives in any crowd,
        When all is gay with lamps, and loud
With sport and song, in booth and tent,

Imperial halls, or open plain;
30   And wheels the circled dance, and breaks
        The rocket molten into flakes
Of crimson or in emerald rain.

---

[1] *You leave us* Addressed to Tennyson's brother Charles, who traveled down the Rhine on his honeymoon. Tennyson and Hallam also visited the Rhine together, in 1832.

[2] *That City* Vienna, where Hallam died.

[3] *Lethe* In Greek mythology, one of the five rivers of the underworld; it is known as the river of forgetfulness or oblivion.

[4] *Danube* Europe's second longest river, flowing through Vienna and Budapest and emptying in to the Black Sea.

99

Risest thou thus, dim dawn, again,[1]
  So loud with voices of the birds,
  So thick with lowings of the herds,
Day, when I lost the flower of men;

5 Who tremblest through thy darkling° red   *darkening*
  On yon swollen brook that bubbles fast
  By meadows breathing of the past,
And woodlands holy to the dead;

Who murmurest in the foliaged eaves
10   A song that slights the coming care,
  And Autumn laying here and there
A fiery finger on the leaves;

Who wakenest with thy balmy breath
  To myriads on the genial earth,
15   Memories of bridal, or of birth,
And unto myriads more, of death.

O wheresoever those may be,
  Betwixt the slumber of the poles,
  Today they count as kindred souls;
20 They know me not, but mourn with me.

100[2]

I climb the hill: from end to end
  Of all the landscape underneath,
  I find no place that does not breathe
Some gracious memory of my friend;

5 No gray old grange, or lonely fold,
  Or low morass° and whispering reed,   *swamp*
  Or simple stile from mead° to mead,   *meadow*
Or sheepwalk up the windy wold;°   *moor*

Nor hoary° knoll of ash and haw°   *old / hawthorn*
10   That hears the latest linnet trill,

Nor quarry trenched along the hill
And haunted by the wrangling daw;°   *jackdaw*

Nor runlet tinkling from the rock;
  Nor pastoral rivulet that swerves
15   To left and right through meadowy curves,
That feed the mothers of the flock;

But each has pleased a kindred eye,
  And each reflects a kindlier day;
  And, leaving these, to pass away,
20 I think once more he seems to die.

101

Unwatched, the garden bough shall sway,
  The tender blossom flutter down,
  Unloved, that beech will gather brown,
This maple burn itself away;

5 Unloved, the sun-flower, shining fair,
  Ray round with flames her disk of seed,
  And many a rose-carnation feed
With summer spice the humming air;

Unloved, by many a sandy bar,
10   The brook shall babble down the plain,
  At noon or when the lesser wain[3]
Is twisting round the polar star;

Uncared for, gird° the windy grove,   *surround*
  And flood the haunts of hern° and crake;°   *heron / crow*
15   Or into silver arrows break
The sailing moon in creek and cove;

Till from the garden and the wild
  A fresh association blow,
  And year by year the landscape grow
20 Familiar to the stranger's child;

---

[1] *Risest ... again* This section begins with the same line as section 72 and marks the second anniversary of Hallam's death.

[2] *100* Sections 100–03 record Tennyson's feelings at having to move, together with his family, from the house in Lincolnshire where they had grown up, and where Hallam had often visited, to a new home outside of London.

[3] *lesser wain* Constellation of Ursa Minor. Ursa Major and Ursa Minor (Latin: Great Bear and Little Bear) each contain seven stars. These are known as Charles's Wain and Lesser Wain. A wain is a wagon, with poles used for hitching a horse; the word "pole," or "plow," gives rise to the common names for the stars, "Great Plough" and "Little Plough."

As year by year the labourer tills
    His wonted glebe,[1] or lops the glades;
    And year by year our memory fades
From all the circle of the hills.

102

We leave the well-belovèd place
    Where first we gazed upon the sky;
    The roofs, that heard our earliest cry,
Will shelter one of stranger race.

5   We go, but ere we go from home,
    As down the garden-walks I move,
    Two spirits of a diverse love
Contend for loving masterdom.

One whispers, "Here thy boyhood sung
10   Long since its matin° song, and heard   *morning*
    The low love-language of the bird
In native hazels tassel-hung."

The other answers, "Yea, but here
    Thy feet have strayed in after hours
15   With thy lost friend among the bowers,
And this hath made them trebly° dear."   *triply*

These two have striven half the day,
    And each prefers his separate claim,
    Poor rivals in a losing game,
20 That will not yield each other way.

I turn to go: my feet are set
    To leave the pleasant fields and farms;
    They mix in one another's arms
To one pure image of regret.

103

On that last night before we went
    From out the doors where I was bred,
    I dreamed a vision of the dead,
Which left my after-morn content.

5   Methought I dwelt within a hall,
    And maidens[2] with me: distant hills
    From hidden summits fed with rills°   *creeks*
A river sliding by the wall.

The hall with harp and carol rang.
10   They sang of what is wise and good
    And graceful. In the centre stood
A statue veiled, to which they sang;

And which, though veiled, was known to me,
    The shape of him I loved, and love
15   Forever: then flew in a dove
And brought a summons from the sea:

And when they learnt that I must go
    They wept and wailed, but led the way
    To where a little shallop° lay   *dinghy*
20 At anchor in the flood below;

And on by many a level mead,
    And shadowing bluff that made the banks,
    We glided winding under ranks
Of iris, and the golden reed;

25 And still as vaster grew the shore
    And rolled the floods in grander space,
    The maidens gathered strength and grace
And presence, lordlier than before;

And I myself, who sat apart
30 And watched them, waxed[3] in every limb;
    I felt the thews of Anakim,[4]
The pulses of a Titan's[5] heart;

As one would sing the death of war,
    And one would chant the history

---

2 [Tennyson's note] They are the Muses, poetry, arts—all that made life beautiful here, which we hope will pass with us beyond the grave.

3 *waxed* Grew stronger.

4 *thews* Muscles and tendons; *Anakim* Race of giants mentioned in the biblical books of Deuteronomy and Joshua.

5 *Titan* Giant in Greek mythology.

---

1 *wonted glebe* Customary field.

35   Of that great race, which is to be,
        And one the shaping of a star;

        Until the forward-creeping tides
            Began to foam, and we to draw
            From deep to deep, to where we saw
40   A great ship lift her shining sides.

        The man we loved was there on deck,
            But thrice as large as man he bent
            To greet us. Up the side I went,
        And fell in silence on his neck:

45   Whereat those maidens with one mind
            Bewailed their lot; I did them wrong:
            "We served thee here," they said, "so long,
        And wilt thou leave us now behind?"

        So rapt I was, they could not win
50   An answer from my lips, but he
            Replying, "Enter likewise ye
        And go with us": they entered in.

        And while the wind began to sweep
            A music out of sheet and shroud,[1]
55   We steered her toward a crimson cloud
        That landlike slept along the deep.

104

        The time draws near the birth of Christ;
            The moon is hid, the night is still;
            A single church below the hill
        Is pealing, folded in the mist.

5   A single peal of bells below,
            That wakens at this hour of rest
            A single murmur in the breast,
        That these are not the bells I know.[2]

Like strangers' voices here they sound,
10   In lands where not a memory strays,
        Nor landmark breathes of other days,
    But all is new unhallowed ground.

105

Tonight ungathered let us leave
    This laurel, let this holly stand:
    We live within the stranger's land,
And strangely falls our Christmas-eve.

5   Our father's dust is left alone
        And silent under other snows:
        There in due time the woodbine blows,
    The violet comes, but we are gone.

No more shall wayward grief abuse
10   The genial hour with mask and mime;
        For change of place, like growth of time,
    Has broke the bond of dying use.

Let cares that petty shadows cast,
    By which our lives are chiefly proved,
15   A little spare the night I loved,
    And hold it solemn to the past.

But let no footstep beat the floor,
    Nor bowl of wassail mantle[3] warm;
    For who would keep an ancient form
20 Through which the spirit breathes no more?

Be neither song, nor game, nor feast;
    Nor harp be touched, nor flute be blown;
    No dance, no motion, save alone
What lightens in the lucid east

25 Of rising worlds by yonder wood.
        Long sleeps the summer in the seed;
        Run out your measured arcs, and lead
    The closing cycle rich in good.

---

[1] *sheet and shroud* Ropes on a ship.

[2] *these ... know* Because he is now in his new, unfamiliar home.

[3] *wassail* Mulled punch associated with Yuletide; *mantle* Covering of foam on an alcoholic drink.

106

Ring out, wild bells, to the wild sky,
   The flying cloud, the frosty light:
   The year is dying in the night;
Ring out, wild bells, and let him die.

5   Ring out the old, ring in the new,
   Ring, happy bells, across the snow:
   The year is going, let him go;
Ring out the false, ring in the true.

Ring out the grief that saps the mind,
10   For those that here we see no more;
   Ring out the feud of rich and poor,
Ring in redress to all mankind.

Ring out a slowly dying cause,
   And ancient forms of party strife;
15   Ring in the nobler modes of life,
With sweeter manners, purer laws.

Ring out the want, the care, the sin,
   The faithless coldness of the times;
   Ring out, ring out my mournful rhymes,
20   But ring the fuller minstrel in.

Ring out false pride in place and blood,
   The civic slander and the spite;
   Ring in the love of truth and right,
Ring in the common love of good.

25   Ring out old shapes of foul disease;
   Ring out the narrowing lust of gold;
   Ring out the thousand wars of old,
Ring in the thousand years of peace.

Ring in the valiant man and free,
30   The larger heart, the kindlier hand;
   Ring out the darkness of the land,
Ring in the Christ that is to be.

107

It is the day when he was born,[1]
   A bitter day that early sank
   Behind a purple-frosty bank
Of vapour, leaving night forlorn.

5   The time admits not flowers or leaves
   To deck the banquet. Fiercely flies
   The blast of North and East, and ice
Makes daggers at the sharpened eaves,

And bristles all the brakes° and thorns   *thickets*
10   To yon hard crescent, as she hangs
   Above the wood which grides° and clangs   *scrapes*
Its leafless ribs and iron horns

Together, in the drifts that pass
   To darken on the rolling brine
15   That breaks the coast. But fetch the wine,
Arrange the board and brim the glass;

Bring in great logs and let them lie,
   To make a solid core of heat;
   Be cheerful-minded, talk and treat
20   Of all things even as he were by;

We keep the day. With festal cheer,
   With books and music, surely we
   Will drink to him, whate'er he be,
And sing the songs he loved to hear.

108

I will not shut me from my kind,
   And, lest I stiffen into stone,
   I will not eat my heart alone,
Nor feed with sighs a passing wind:

5   What profit lies in barren faith,
   And vacant yearning, though with might
   To scale the heaven's highest height,
Or dive below the wells of Death?

---

[1] *day ... born* Hallam's birthday.

What find I in the highest place,
10   But mine own phantom chanting hymns?
        And on the depths of death there swims
The reflex° of a human face.   *reflection*

I'll rather take what fruit may be
        Of sorrow under human skies:
15   'Tis held that sorrow makes us wise,
Whatever wisdom sleep with thee.

109

Heart-affluence in discursive talk
        From household fountains never dry;
        The critic clearness of an eye,
That saw through all the Muses' walk;[1]

5   Seraphic intellect and force
        To seize and throw the doubts of man;
        Impassioned logic, which outran
The hearer in its fiery course;

High nature amorous of the good,
10   But touched with no ascetic gloom;
        And passion pure in snowy bloom
Through all the years of April blood;

A love of freedom rarely felt,
        Of freedom in her regal seat
15   Of England; not the schoolboy heat,
The blind hysterics of the Celt;

And manhood fused with female grace
        In such a sort, the child would twine
        A trustful hand, unasked, in thine,
20 And find his comfort in thy face;

All these have been, and thee mine eyes
        Have looked on: if they looked in vain,
        My shame is greater who remain,
Nor let thy wisdom make me wise.

110

Thy converse drew us with delight,
        The men of rathe° and riper years: *younger*
        The feeble soul, a haunt of fears,
Forgot his weakness in thy sight.

5   On thee the loyal-hearted hung,
        The proud was half disarmed of pride,
        Nor cared the serpent at thy side
To flicker with his double tongue.

The stern were mild when thou wert by,
10   The flippant put himself to school
        And heard thee, and the brazen fool
Was softened, and he knew not why;

While I, thy nearest, sat apart,
        And felt thy triumph was as mine;
15   And loved them more, that they were thine,
The graceful tact, the Christian art;

Nor mine the sweetness or the skill,
        But mine the love that will not tire,
        And, born of love, the vague desire
20 That spurs an imitative will.

111

The churl in spirit, up or down
        Along the scale of ranks, through all,
        To him who grasps a golden ball,[2]
By blood a king, at heart a clown;°   *peasant*

5   The churl in spirit, howe'er he veil
        His want in forms for fashion's sake,
        Will let his coltish nature break
At seasons through the gilded pale:°   *fence*

For who can always act? but he,
10   To whom a thousand memories call,
        Not being less but more than all
The gentleness he seemed to be,

---

1 *saw ... walk*   The speaker here is praising Hallam's genius, which suggested great potential in the areas of philosophy and literature.

---

2 *golden ball*   I.e., the orb of the monarch.

Best seemed the thing he was, and joined
    Each office of the social hour
    To noble manners, as the flower
And native growth of noble mind;

Nor ever narrowness or spite,
    Or villain fancy fleeting by,
    Drew in the expression of an eye,
Where God and Nature met in light;

And thus he bore without abuse
    The grand old name of gentleman,
    Defamed by every charlatan,
And soiled with all ignoble use.

112

High wisdom holds my wisdom less,
    That I, who gaze with temperate eyes
    On glorious insufficiencies,
Set light by narrower perfectness.

But thou, that fillest all the room
    Of all my love, art reason why
    I seem to cast a careless eye
On souls, the lesser lords of doom.

For what wert thou? some novel power
    Sprang up forever at a touch,
    And hope could never hope too much,
In watching thee from hour to hour,

Large elements in order brought,
    And tracts of calm from tempest made,
    And world-wide fluctuation swayed
In vassal tides that followed thought.

113

'Tis held that sorrow makes us wise;
    Yet how much wisdom sleeps with thee
    Which not alone had guided me,
But served the seasons that may rise;

For can I doubt, who knew thee keen
    In intellect, with force and skill
    To strive, to fashion, to fulfil—
I doubt not what thou wouldst have been:

A life in civic action warm,
    A soul on highest mission sent,
    A potent voice of Parliament,
A pillar steadfast in the storm,

Should licensed boldness gather force,
    Becoming, when the time has birth,
    A lever to uplift the earth
And roll it in another course,

With thousand shocks that come and go,
    With agonies, with energies,
    With overthrowings, and with cries,
And undulations to and fro.

114

Who loves not Knowledge? Who shall rail
    Against her beauty? May she mix
    With men and prosper! Who shall fix
Her pillars?[1] Let her work prevail.

But on her forehead sits a fire:
    She sets her forward countenance
    And leaps into the future chance,
Submitting all things to desire.

Half-grown as yet, a child, and vain—
    She cannot fight the fear of death.
    What is she, cut from love and faith,
But some wild Pallas[2] from the brain

Of Demons? fiery-hot to burst
    All barriers in her onward race

---

[1] *pillars* Outer limits. In classical mythology this refers to the Pillars of Hercules, which marked the outer limits of the known world.

[2] *Pallas* Pallas Athena, Greek goddess of wisdom, who was said to have leapt out from the forehead of Zeus, rather than having been born in the usual manner.

15   For power. Let her know her place;
    She is the second, not the first.

    A higher hand must make her mild,
        If all be not in vain; and guide
        Her footsteps, moving side by side
20 With wisdom, like the younger child:

    For she is earthly of the mind,
        But Wisdom heavenly of the soul.
        O, friend, who camest to thy goal
    So early, leaving me behind,

25 I would the great world grew like thee,
        Who grewest not alone in power
        And knowledge, but by year and hour
    In reverence and in charity.

115

    Now fades the last long streak of snow,
        Now burgeons every maze of quick°   *vegetation*
        About the flowering squares, and thick
    By ashen roots the violets blow.

5   Now rings the woodland loud and long,
        The distance takes a lovelier hue,
        And drowned in yonder living blue
    The lark becomes a sightless song.

    Now dance the lights on lawn and lea,
10   The flocks are whiter down the vale,
        And milkier every milky sail
    On winding stream or distant sea;

    Where now the seamew° pipes, or dives   *seagull*
        In yonder greening gleam, and fly
15   The happy birds, that change their sky
    To build and brood; that live their lives

    From land to land; and in my breast
        Spring wakens too; and my regret
    Becomes an April violet,
20 And buds and blossoms like the rest.

116

    Is it, then, regret for buried time
        That keenlier in sweet April wakes,
        And meets the year, and gives and takes
    The colours of the crescent prime?°   *new moon*

5   Not all: the songs, the stirring air,
        The life re-orient out of dust,
        Cry through the sense to hearten trust
    In that which made the world so fair.

    Not all regret: the face will shine
10   Upon me, while I muse alone;
        And that dear voice, I once have known,
    Still speak to me of me and mine:

    Yet less of sorrow lives in me
        For days of happy commune dead;
15   Less yearning for the friendship fled,
    Than some strong bond which is to be.

117

    O days and hours, your work is this
        To hold me from my proper place,
        A little while from his embrace,
    For fuller gain of after bliss:

5   That out of distance might ensue
        Desire of nearness doubly sweet;
        And unto meeting when we meet,
    Delight a hundredfold accrue,

    For every grain of sand that runs,
10   And every span of shade¹ that steals,
        And every kiss of toothèd wheels,²
    And all the courses of the suns.

---

¹ [Tennyson's note] The sun-dial.

² *toothèd wheels* Gears of a clock.

118

Contemplate all this work of Time,[1]
  The giant labouring in his youth;
  Nor dream of human love and truth,
As dying Nature's earth and lime;[2]

5 But trust that those we call the dead
  Are breathers of an ampler day
  For ever nobler ends. They[3] say,
The solid earth whereon we tread

In tracts of fluent heat began,
10 And grew to seeming-random forms,
  The seeming prey of cyclic storms,
Till at the last arose the man;

Who throve and branched from clime to clime,
  The herald of a higher race,
15 And of himself in higher place,
If so he type this work of time

Within himself, from more to more;
  Or, crowned with attributes of woe
  Like glories, move his course, and show
20 That life is not as idle ore,

But iron dug from central gloom,
  And heated hot with burning fears,
  And dipped in baths of hissing tears,
And battered with the shocks of doom

25 To shape and use. Arise and fly
  The reeling Faun,[4] the sensual feast;
  Move upward, working out the beast,
And let the ape and tiger die.

119

Doors, where my heart was used to beat[5]
  So quickly, not as one that weeps
  I come once more; the city sleeps;
I smell the meadow in the street;

5 I hear a chirp of birds; I see
  Betwixt the black fronts long-withdrawn
  A light-blue lane of early dawn,
And think of early days and thee,

And bless thee, for thy lips are bland,°   *gentle*
10 And bright the friendship of thine eye;
  And in my thoughts with scarce a sigh
I take the pressure of thine hand.

120

I trust I have not wasted breath:
  I think we are not wholly brain,
  Magnetic mockeries;[6] not in vain,
Like Paul with beasts,[7] I fought with Death;

5 Not only cunning casts in clay:
  Let Science prove we are, and then
  What matters Science unto men,
At least to me? I would not stay.

Let him, the wiser man who springs
10 Hereafter, up from childhood shape
  His action like the greater ape,
But I was *born* to other things.

121

Sad Hesper[8] o'er the buried sun
  And ready, thou, to die with him,

---

1 *Contemplate ... Time* Section 118 marks a return to the ideas expressed in sections 55 and 56 about recent scientific discoveries and their impact on religious faith and morality.

2 *lime* Quicklime, sometimes scattered on corpses during burial.

3 *They* Probably refers to scientists such as Lyell, Chambers, and Cuvier.

4 *Faun* In classical mythology, a creature who is half goat and half human.

5 *Doors ... beat* Hallam's house; see section 7, to which this section responds.

6 *Magnetic mockeries* The brain's electrical impulses, another contemporary scientific discovery.

7 *Paul ... beasts* See 1 Corinthians 15.32: "If I fought wild beasts in Ephesus for merely human reasons, what have I gained? If the dead are not raised, 'Let us eat and drink, for tomorrow we die.'"

8 *Hesper* Hesperus, the so-called evening star; actually, the planet Venus, which doubles as the morning star, or "Phosphor" (line 9).

Thou watchest all things ever dim
And dimmer, and a glory done:

5   The team[1] is loosened from the wain,°   *cart*
    The boat is drawn upon the shore;
    Thou listenest to the closing door,
And life is darkened in the brain.

Bright Phosphor, fresher for the night,
10   By thee the world's great work is heard
    Beginning, and the wakeful bird;
Behind thee comes the greater light:

The market boat is on the stream,
    And voices hail it from the brink;
15   Thou hear'st the village hammer clink,
And see'st the moving of the team.

Sweet Hesper-Phosphor, double name
    For what is one, the first, the last,
    Thou, like my present and my past,
20 Thy place is changed; thou art the same.

122

Oh, wast thou with me, dearest, then,
    While I rose up against my doom,
    And yearned to burst the folded gloom,
To bare the eternal Heavens again,

5   To feel once more, in placid awe,
    The strong imagination roll
    A sphere of stars about my soul,
In all her motion one with law;

If thou wert with me, and the grave
10   Divide us not, be with me now,[2]
    And enter in at breast and brow,
Till all my blood, a fuller wave,

Be quickened with a livelier breath,
    And like an inconsiderate boy,

---

[1] *team* I.e., of horses or oxen.

[2] *be … now* Cf. section 50.

15 As in the former flash of joy,
I slip the thoughts of life and death;

And all the breeze of Fancy blows,
    And every dew-drop paints a bow,°   *rainbow*
    The wizard lightnings[3] deeply glow,
20 And every thought breaks out a rose.

123

There rolls the deep where grew the tree.
    O earth, what changes hast thou seen!
    There where the long street roars, hath been
The stillness of the central sea.

5   The hills are shadows, and they flow
    From form to form, and nothing stands;
    They melt like mist, the solid lands,
Like clouds they shape themselves and go.[4]

But in my spirit will I dwell,
10   And dream my dream, and hold it true;
    For though my lips may breathe adieu,
I cannot think the thing farewell.

124

That which we dare invoke to bless;
    Our dearest faith; our ghastliest doubt;
    He, They, One, All; within, without;
The Power in darkness whom we guess;

5   I found Him not in world or sun,
    Or eagle's wing, or insect's eye;
    Nor through the questions men may try,
The petty cobwebs[5] we have spun:

If e'er when faith had fallen asleep,
10   I heard a voice "believe no more"

---

[3] *wizard lightnings* Northern lights, or aurora borealis.

[4] *O earth … and go* The images that Tennyson uses here are inspired by Charles Lyell's geological discoveries as described in his work *The Principles of Geology* (1830–33). See also section 35.

[5] *petty cobwebs* Here, the arguments of natural theology, which suggested that God could be inferred from evidence in nature.

And heard an ever-breaking shore
That tumbled in the Godless deep;

A warmth within the breast would melt
   The freezing reason's colder part,
5   And like a man in wrath the heart
Stood up and answered "I have felt."

No, like a child in doubt and fear:
   But that blind clamour made me wise;
   Then was I as a child that cries,
10 But, crying, knows his father near;[1]

And what I am beheld again
   What is, and no man understands;
   And out of darkness came the hands
That reach through nature, moulding men.

125

Whatever I have said or sung,
   Some bitter notes my harp would give,
   Yea, though there often seemed to live
A contradiction on the tongue,

5 Yet Hope had never lost her youth;
   She did but look through dimmer eyes;
   Or Love but played with gracious lies,
Because he felt so fixed in truth:

And if the song were full of care,
10 He breathed the spirit of the song;
   And if the words were sweet and strong
He set his royal signet° there;   *seal*

Abiding with me till I sail
   To seek thee on the mystic deeps,
15 And this electric force, that keeps
A thousand pulses dancing,[2] fail.

126

Love is and was my Lord and King,
   And in his presence I attend°   *wait*
   To hear the tidings of my friend,
Which every hour his couriers bring.

5 Love is and was my King and Lord,
   And will be, though as yet I keep
   Within his court on earth, and sleep
Encompassed by his faithful guard,

And hear at times a sentinel
10 Who moves about from place to place,
   And whispers to the worlds of space,
In the deep night, that all is well.

127

And all is well, though faith and form[3]
   Be sundered in the night of fear;
   Well roars the storm to those that hear
A deeper voice across the storm,

5 Proclaiming social truth shall spread,
   And justice, even though thrice again
   The red fool-fury of the Seine[4]
Should pile her barricades with dead.

But ill for him that wears a crown,
10 And him, the lazar,° in his rags: *leper*
   They tremble, the sustaining crags;
The spires of ice are toppled down,

And molten up, and roar in flood;
   The fortress crashes from on high,
15 The brute earth lightens to the sky,
And the great Æon° sinks in blood,   *eon*

And compassed by the fires of Hell;
   While thou, dear spirit, happy star,

---

[1] *But … near* Cf. section 54.

[2] *this electric … dancing* Electrical impulses in the nervous system as understood by contemporary science.

---

[3] *form* I.e., religious doctrine.

[4] *red … Seine* I.e., the slaughter during the French Revolution. The Seine is the river that runs through Paris.

O'erlook'st the tumult from afar,
20   And smilest, knowing all is well.

128

The love that rose on stronger wings,
    Unpalsied when he met with Death,
    Is comrade of the lesser faith
That sees the course of human things.

5   No doubt vast eddies in the flood
    Of onward time shall yet be made,
    And thronèd races may degrade;
Yet O ye mysteries of good,

Wild Hours that fly with Hope and Fear,
10   If all your office had to do
    With old results that look like new;
If this were all your mission here,

To draw, to sheathe a useless sword,
    To fool the crowd with glorious lies,
15   To cleave a creed in sects and cries,
To change the bearing of a word,

To shift an arbitrary power,
    To cramp the student at his desk,
    To make old bareness picturesque
20   And tuft with grass a feudal tower;

Why then my scorn might well descend
    On you and yours. I see in part
    That all, as in some piece of art,
Is toil cöoperant to an end.

129

Dear friend, far off, my lost desire,
    So far, so near in woe and weal;
    O loved the most, when most I feel
There is a lower and a higher;

5   Known and unknown; human, divine;
    Sweet human hand and lips and eye;

Dear heavenly friend that canst not die,
Mine, mine, for ever, ever mine;

Strange friend, past, present, and to be;
10   Loved deeplier, darklier understood;
    Behold, I dream a dream of good,
And mingle all the world with thee.

130

Thy voice is on the rolling air;
    I hear thee where the waters run;
    Thou standest in the rising sun,
And in the setting thou art fair.

5   What art thou then? I cannot guess;
    But though I seem in star and flower
    To feel thee some diffusive power,
I do not therefore love thee less:

My love involves the love before;
10   My love is vaster passion now;
    Though mixed with God and Nature thou,
I seem to love thee more and more.

Far off thou art, but ever nigh;
    I have thee still, and I rejoice;
15   I prosper, circled with thy voice;
I shall not lose thee though I die.

131

O living will that shalt endure
    When all that seems shall suffer shock,
    Rise in the spiritual rock,[1]
Flow through our deeds and make them pure,

5   That we may lift from out of dust
    A voice as unto him that hears,
    A cry above the conquered years
To one that with us works, and trust,

---

[1] *spiritual rock*   See 1 Corinthians 10.4: "They drink of that spiritual
Rock that followed them: and that Rock was Christ."

With faith that comes of self-control,
    The truths that never can be proved
    Until we close with all we loved,
And all we flow from, soul in soul.

[EPILOGUE]

O true and tried, so well and long,
    Demand not thou a marriage lay;
    In that it is thy marriage day
Is music more than any song.[1]

5 Nor have I felt so much of bliss
    Since first he[2] told me that he loved
    A daughter of our house; nor proved
Since that dark day a day like this;

Though I since then have numbered o'er
10   Some thrice three years: they went and came,
    Remade the blood and changed the frame,
And yet is love not less, but more;

No longer caring to embalm
    In dying songs a dead regret,
15   But like a statue solid-set,
And moulded in colossal calm.

Regret is dead, but love is more
    Than in the summers that are flown,
    For I myself with these have grown
20 To something greater than before;

Which makes appear the songs I made
    As echoes out of weaker times,
    As half but idle brawling rhymes,
The sport of random sun and shade.

25 But where is she, the bridal flower,
    That must be made a wife ere noon?

---

[1] *O true … song* The Epilogue is a wedding song for Edmund Lushington (see note to 85.5), who married Tennyson's sister Cecilia in 1842.

[2] *he* I.e., Hallam, who fell in love with Tennyson's sister Emily.

She enters, glowing like the moon
Of Eden on its bridal bower:

On me she bends her blissful eyes
30   And then on thee; they meet thy look
    And brighten like the star that shook
Betwixt the palms of paradise.

O when her life was yet in bud,
    He too foretold the perfect rose.
35   For thee she grew, for thee she grows
Forever, and as fair as good.

And thou art worthy; full of power;
    As gentle; liberal-minded, great,
    Consistent; wearing all that weight
40 Of learning lightly like a flower.

But now set out: the noon is near,
    And I must give away the bride;
    She fears not, or with thee beside
And me behind her, will not fear.

45 For I that danced her on my knee,
    That watched her on her nurse's° arm,   *nanny*
    That shielded all her life from harm
At last must part with her to thee;

Now waiting to be made a wife,
50   Her feet, my darling, on the dead;
    Their pensive tablets° round her head,   *monuments*
And the most living words of life

Breathed in her ear. The ring is on,
    The "wilt thou" answered, and again
55   The "wilt thou" asked, till out of twain
Her sweet "I will" has made you one.

Now sign your names, which shall be read,
    Mute symbols of a joyful morn,
    By village eyes as yet unborn;
60 The names are signed, and overhead

Begins the clash and clang that tells
    The joy to every wandering breeze;
    The blind wall rocks, and on the trees
The dead leaf trembles to the bells.

65   O happy hour, and happier hours
      Await them. Many a merry face
      Salutes them—maidens of the place,
    That pelt us in the porch with flowers.

O happy hour, behold the bride
70   With him to whom her hand I gave.
      They leave the porch, they pass the grave
That has today its sunny side.

Today the grave is bright for me,
    For them the light of life increased,
75   Who stay to share the morning feast,
Who rest tonight beside the sea.

Let all my genial spirits advance
    To meet and greet a whiter sun;
    My drooping memory will not shun
80   The foaming grape of eastern France.

It circles round, and fancy plays,
    And hearts are warmed and faces bloom,
    As drinking health to bride and groom
We wish them store of happy days.

85   Nor count me all to blame if I
      Conjecture of a stiller guest,
      Perchance, perchance, among the rest,
And, though in silence, wishing joy.

But they must go, the time draws on,
90   And those white-favoured horses wait;
      They rise, but linger; it is late;
Farewell, we kiss, and they are gone.

A shade falls on us like the dark
    From little cloudlets on the grass,

95   But sweeps away as out we pass
To range the woods, to roam the park,

Discussing how their courtship grew,
    And talk of others that are wed,
    And how she looked, and what he said,
100 And back we come at fall of dew.

Again the feast, the speech, the glee,
    The shade of passing thought, the wealth
    Of words and wit, the double health,
The crowning cup, the three-times-three,[1]

105 And last the dance;—till I retire:
    Dumb is that tower which spake so loud,
    And high in heaven the streaming cloud,
And on the downs a rising fire:

And rise, O moon, from yonder down,
110   Till over down[2] and over dale
    All night the shining vapour sail
And pass the silent-lighted town,

The white-faced halls, the glancing rills,
    And catch at every mountain head,
115 And o'er the friths[3] that branch and spread
Their sleeping silver through the hills;

And touch with shade the bridal doors,
    With tender gloom the roof, the wall;
    And breaking let the splendour fall
120 To spangle all the happy shores

By which they rest, and ocean sounds,
    And, star and system rolling past,
    A soul shall draw from out the vast
And strike his being into bounds,[4]

---

1 *three-times-three* A toast: "Three-times-three cheers for the bride and groom!"

2 *down* Open, rolling land.

3 *friths* Inlets, or estuaries.

4 *A soul ... bounds* I.e., a child shall be conceived on this wedding night.

And, moved through life of lower phase
   Result in man, be born and think,
   And act and love, a closer link
Betwixt us and the crowning race

Of those that, eye to eye, shall look
   On knowledge; under whose command
   Is Earth and Earth's, and in their hand
Is Nature like an open book;

No longer half-akin to brute,
   For all we thought and loved and did,
   And hoped, and suffered, is but seed
Of what in them is flower and fruit;

Whereof the man, that with me trod
   This planet, was a noble type
   Appearing ere the times were ripe,
That friend of mine who lives in God,

That God, which ever lives and loves,
   One God, one law, one element,
   And one far-off divine event,
To which the whole creation moves.
—1850

The Eagle
[Fragment]

He clasps the crag with crooked hands;
Close to the sun in lonely lands,
Ringed with the azure world, he stands.

The wrinkled sea beneath him crawls;
He watches from his mountain walls,
And like a thunderbolt he falls.
—1851 (WRITTEN 1833?)

The Charge of the Light Brigade

In one of the most notorious events of the Crimean War (1853–56), a miscommunication within the British chain of military command on 24 October 1854 caused a cavalry of lightly armed troops to be sent into a frontal assault upon far more heavily armed Russian troops; despite being obviously unmatched to the task, the cavalry obeyed their orders and entered into a short and extremely unequal battle by the end of which over 100 of the Light Brigade's 670 troops had been killed, with many more wounded or taken prisoner. The episode has often been held up as an example of the bravery of the British troops; it has often been taken too as emblematic of the general mismanagement and futility of the Crimean War. Debates over who was to blame for the blunder raged for years.

The three senior officers involved in the misunderstanding were all members of the aristocracy. Lord Raglan commanded the entire British military force; Lord Lucan commanded the two cavalry brigades (Heavy and Light); Lord Cardigan had been given command of the Light Brigade by Lord Lucan. A junior officer, Captain Louis Nolan, carried over to Lord Lucan an order that Lord Raglan had shouted out. The order as Lucan had understood it was then relayed to Lord Cardigan, who led the charge.

Tennyson wrote the first draft of this famous poem on 2 December 1854 after having read accounts in *The Times* of the disastrous charge. A fragmentary report of the incident had appeared in the 11 November issue of *The Times*, and a much fuller report by *Times* correspondent William Howard Russell had been published in the 14 November issue. Tennyson appears to have also drawn on the long editorial on the subject that appeared in the 13 November issue; in that editorial the phrase "some hideous blunder" is used. Excerpts from some of these *Times* pieces appear below. Tennyson evidently drew on other texts as well; as Herman Melville was among the first to point out, the poem follows very closely the rhythm of certain stanzas of "Agincourt," a seventeenth-century battle poem by Michael Drayton ("They now to fight are gone, / Armour on armour shone …").

The poem was first published in a weekly newspaper, *The Examiner*, on 9 December 1854. A facsimile of the galley proofs of the *Examiner* text, with Tennyson's corrections, is the first version of the poem provided below. A significantly altered version appeared in *Maud and Other Poems* (published in July, 1855); Tennyson substantially shortened the poem, and removed any reference to a "blunder." By this time, however, the original *Examiner* version had become well known and had been fairly widely circulated; it was said to have been recited by some of the soldiers serving in Crimea. A chaplain working in Crimea for The Society for the Propagation of the Gospel suggested that the poem be reprinted for wider circulation among the troops. Tennyson was happy to approve the request—but which of the two versions should be used? On reflection Tennyson concluded that the heavily revised 1855 *Maud and Other Poems* version had been a mistake—that "the criticism of one or two London friends" had induced him to spoil the original poem. Given that it had been the *Examiner* version that had already been known and recited in the Crimea, Tennyson now referred to that version as "the soldiers' version." In a letter to publisher John Forster he gave the following instructions: "The soldiers are the best critics in what pleases them. I send you a copy which retains the 'Light Brigade' and the 'blunder'd'; and I declare that it is the best of the two [versions]." A postscript reiterated the point: "P.S. I am convinced now after writing it out that this *is* the best version."

As can be seen below, the text he then sent off (which became the standard text, printed in the 1856 edition of *Maud and Other Poems* and in subsequent editions of Tennyson's poetry), does not in fact represent a complete return to the 1854 *Examiner* "soldier's version." Though the two are substantially the same, the opening of the 1856 version is altered (with one "blundered" rather than two), and the fourth stanza is significantly altered as well. These and other smaller changes are itemized in the footnotes to the 1856 version.

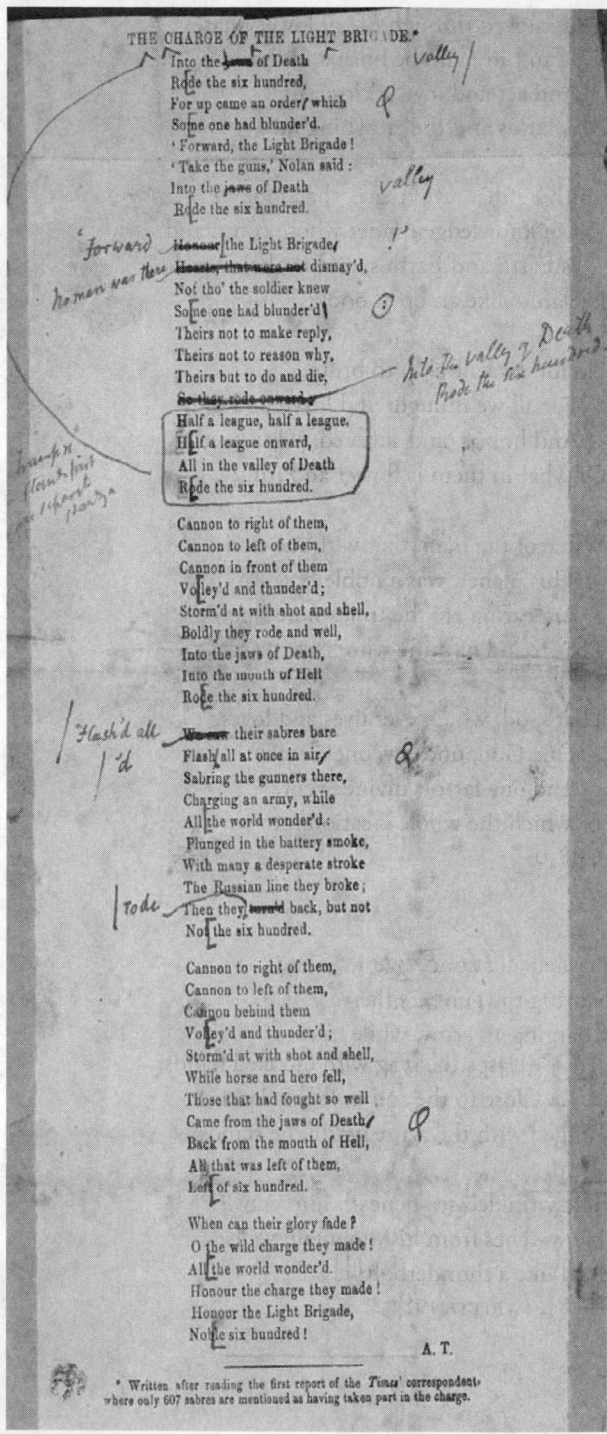

The galley proofs of the initial *Examiner* text, with Tennyson's hand-written corrections.

The Charge of the Light Brigade
[1855 version]

1

Half a league,[1] half a league,
Half a league onward,
All in the valley of Death[2]
    Rode the six hundred.
5 "Charge," was the captain's cry;
Theirs not to reason why,
Theirs not to make reply,
Theirs but to do and die,
Into the valley of Death
10   Rode the six hundred.

2

Cannon to right of them,
Cannon to left of them,
Cannon in front of them
    Volleyed and thundered;
15 Stormed at with shot and shell,
Boldly they rode and well;
Into the jaws of Death,
Into the mouth of Hell,
    Rode the six hundred.

3

20 Flashed all their sabres[3] bare,
Flashed all at once in air,
Sabring the gunners there,
Charging an army, while
    All the world wondered:
25 Plunged in the battery-smoke
Fiercely the line they broke;
Strong was the sabre-stroke;
Making an army reel
    Shaken and sundered.
30 Then they rode back, but not,
Not the six hundred.

---

1 *league* About three miles.

2 *valley of Death* See Psalm 23.4: "Yea, though I walk through the valley of the shadow of death." The phrase "valley of death" also appears in the 14 November *Times* account.

3 *sabres* Long, curved swords.

The Charge of the Light Brigade
[1856 version]

1

Half a league,[4] half a league,
Half a league onward,
All in the valley of Death
    Rode the six hundred.[5]
5 "Forward, the Light Brigade!
Charge for the guns!" he said:[6]
Into the valley of Death
    Rode the six hundred.

2

"Forward, the Light Brigade!"
10 Was there a man dismayed?[7]
Not though the soldier knew
    Some one had blundered:
Theirs not to make reply,
Theirs not to reason why,
15 Theirs but to do and die:
Into the valley of Death
    Rode the six hundred.

3

Cannon to right of them,
Cannon to left of them,
20 Cannon in front of them
    Volleyed and thundered;
Stormed at with shot and shell,
Boldly they rode and well,
Into the jaws of Death,
25 Into the mouth of Hell
    Rode the six hundred.

---

4 *league* About three miles.

5 *Rode the six hundred* In the *Examiner* version the following two lines are added here: "For up came an order which / Some one had blundered."

6 *Charge for the guns! he said* In the *Examiner* version, "'Take the guns,' Nolan said."

7 *Was there a man dismayed?* In the *Examiner* version, "No man was there dismayed."

4

Cannon to right of them,
Cannon to left of them,
Cannon behind them
35   Volleyed and thundered;
Stormed at with shot and shell,
They that had struck so well
Rode thro' the jaws of Death,
Half a league back again,
40 Up from the mouth of Hell,
All that was left of them,
      Left of six hundred.

5

Honour the brave and bold!
Long shall the tale be told,
45 Yea, when our babes are old—
      How they rode onward.
—1854 (REVISED 1855)

4

Flashed all their sabres bare,
Flashed as they turned[1] in air
Sabring the gunners there,
30 Charging an army, while
      All the world wondered:
Plunged in the battery-smoke
Right through the line they broke;
Cossack[2] and Russian
35 Reeled from the sabre-stroke
      Shattered and sundered.[3]
Then they rode back, but not
      Not the six hundred.

5

Cannon to right of them,
40 Cannon to left of them,
Cannon behind them
      Volleyed and thundered;
Stormed at with shot and shell,
While horse and hero fell,
45 They[4] that had fought so well
Came through[5] the jaws of Death,
Back from the mouth of Hell,
All that was left of them,[6]
      Left of six hundred.

6

50 When can their glory fade?
O the wild charge they made!
      All the world wondered.
Honour the charge they made!
Honour the Light Brigade,
55   Noble six hundred!
—1854 (REVISED 1856)

---

[1] *as they turned* In the *Examiner* version, "all at once."

[2] *Cossack* Cossacks, members of an ethnic and cultural group from a region north of the Black and Caspian Seas, played an important role in the Imperial Russian Army.

[3] *Right through ... sundered* In the *Examiner* version, two lines take the place of these four: "With many a desperate stroke / The Russian line they broke."

[4] *They* In the *Examiner* version, "Those."

[5] *through* In the *Examiner* version, "from."

[6] *All ... them* Hundreds of soldiers died or were wounded.

In Context

The Charge of the Light Brigade as Reported in *The Times*

from "The Attack on Balaklava," *The Times* (13 November 1854)

The long 13 November report in *The Times* of the action in the Crimea included two letters from the principals—one from Lord Raglan and one from Lord Lucan.

[from Letter to the Duke of Newcastle from FitzRoy James Henry Somerset, Lord Raglan]

... The charge of this brigade was one of the most successful I ever witnessed, was never for a moment doubtful, and is in the highest degree creditable to Brigadier-General Scarlett[1] and the officers and men engaged in it.

As the enemy withdrew from the ground which they had momentarily occupied, I directed the cavalry, supported by the Fourth Division, under Lieutenant-General Sir George Cathcart, to move forward, and take advantage of any opportunity to regain the heights; and, not having been able to accomplish this immediately, and it appearing that an attempt was making to remove the captured guns, the Earl of Lucan was desired to advance rapidly, follow the enemy in their retreat, and try to prevent them from effecting their objects.

In the meanwhile the Russians had time to reform on their own ground, with artillery in front and upon their flanks.

From some misconception of the instruction to advance, the Lieutenant-General considered that he was bound to attack at all hazards, and he accordingly ordered Major-General the Earl of Cardigan[2] to move forward with the Light Brigade.

This order was obeyed in the most spirited and gallant manner. Lord Cardigan charged with the utmost vigour, attacked a battery which was firing upon the advancing squadrons, and, having passed beyond it, engaged the Russian cavalry in its rear; but there his troops were assailed by artillery and infantry as well as cavalry, and necessarily retired, after having committed much havoc upon the enemy.

They effected this movement without haste or confusion; but the loss they have sustained has, I deeply lament, been very severe in officers, men, and horses, only counterbalanced by the brilliancy of the attack and the gallantry, order, and discipline which distinguished it, forming a striking contrast to the conduct of the enemy's cavalry which had previously been engaged with the heavy brigade. ...

---

[1] *Brigadier-General Scarlett* James Yorke Scarlett (1799–1871), General in command of the Heavy Brigade that was also present during the battle.

[2] *Major-General the Earl of Cardigan* James Thomas Brudenell (1797–1868), commander of the Light Brigade.

[from LETTER FROM GEORGE BINGHAM, LORD LUCAN]

… The Heavy Brigade having now joined the Light Brigade, the division took up a position with a view of supporting an attack upon the heights, when, being instructed to make a rapid advance to our front, to prevent the enemy carrying the guns lost by the Turkish troops in the morning, I ordered the Light Brigade to advance in two lines, and supported them with the Heavy Brigade. This attack of the Light Cavalry was very brilliant and daring; exposed to a fire from heavy batteries on their front and two flanks, they advanced unchecked until they reached the batteries of the enemy, and cleared them of their gunners, and only retired when they found themselves engaged with a very superior force of cavalry in the rear. Major-General the Earl of Cardigan led this attack in the most gallant and intrepid manner; and his Lordship has expressed himself to me as admiring in the highest degree the courage and zeal of every officer, non-commissioned officer, and man who assisted.

The Heavy Brigade advanced to the support of the attack under a very galling fire from the batteries and infantry in a redoubt,[1] and acted with most perfect steadiness, and in a manner to deserve all praise.

The losses, my Lord, it grieves me to state, have been very great indeed, and, I fear, will be much felt by your Lordship.

I cannot too strongly recommend to your Lordship the two General officers commanding the brigades, all the officers in command of regiments, as also the divisional and brigade staffs; indeed, the conduct of every individual, of every rank, I feel to be deserving of my entire praise, and, I hope, of your Lordship's approbation. …

from Editorial, *The Times* (13 November 1854)

The phrase "some hideous blunder" in the conclusion to this piece appears to have prompted Tennyson's use of the verb "blundered" in his poem.

We now know the details of the attack on Balaklava on the 25th, and with them much that is glorious and much that is reassuring. The worst is comprehended in a melancholy loss of men, chiefly in that arm of the service which could least bear it[.] … We have, then, in the despatches before us nearly the whole of the loss, which it would be vain to conceal is most lamentable[.] … The disaster, then, of which the mere shadow has darkened so many a household among us for the last ten days is not more, but it is not much less, than the annihilation of the Light Cavalry Brigade. It entered into action about 700 strong, and mustered only 191 on its return, though, of course, some afterwards rejoined their comrades. Of the missing, it is to be feared that the majority are killed, as the Russians, who would make the most of their prisoners, do not account for half as many. Had there been the smallest use in the movement that has cost us so much—had it been the necessity of a retreat or part of any plan whatever, we should endeavour to bear this sad loss as we do the heaps of human life lavished in an assault. Even accident would have made it more tolerable. But it was a mere mistake—evidently a mistake, and perceived to be such when it was too late to correct it. The affair then assumed the terrible form of a splendid self-sacrifice. Two great armies, composed of four nations, saw from the slopes of a vast amphitheatre seven hundred British cavalry proceed at a rapid pace, and in perfect order, to certain destruction. Such a spectacle was never seen before, and we trust will never be repeated. There are two consolations—the first that, owing to the very incomplete state

---

[1] *redoubt* Stronghold.

of our regiments, there were not more to exhibit in this fearful death-parade; and, secondly, that even in that awful progress, when officer and soldier felt themselves hurried to their doom by some inextricable error, they still kept their ranks, went fiercely on, rode up hills, stormed batteries, and sold their lives as dearly as the manifest odds against them would allow.

The error was one of unusual simplicity, and requires no science to understand it. There was no surprise, not even too short a notice. There was no misconception of the enemy's strength. There was no inevitable train of consequences, in which disaster was the slow result of successive operations. … It was about noon … that the fatal movement took place. The cavalry then received an order to advance rapidly to the front, to follow the enemy, and attempt to prevent them carrying off the guns; and, as the circumstances under which the order was received were not a little formidable, they were told that the French cavalry were on their left. How far the order was itself the result of a misconception, or was intended to be executed at discretion, does not appear, and will probably afford the subject of painful but vain recrimination. It was interpreted as leaving no discretion at all, and the whole brigade advanced at a trot for more than a mile, down a valley, with a murderous flank fire of Minié muskets[1] and shells from hills on both sides. It charged batteries, took guns, sabred[2] the gunners, and charged the Russian cavalry beyond; but, not being supported—and, under the circumstances, perhaps it is fortunate it was not—and being attacked by cavalry in front and rear, it had to cut its way through them, and return through the same cavalry and the same fire. The brigade was simply pounded by the shot, shell, and Minié bullets from the hills. Not more than a dozen were killed by the Russian cavalry, who, if they had been good for anything, would have taken care that not a single British soldier should return to tell the tale. Causeless as the sacrifice was, it was most glorious. A French General who saw the advance, and apprehended at once its fatal issue, exclaimed, "*C'est très magnifique, mais ce n'est pas la guerre.*"[3] The enthusiasm of the moment, and the fellow-feeling of the two armies, almost led the Chasseurs d'Afrique[4] to follow the British brigade to its doom, but they were wisely restrained, and did much better service by charging a Russian battery on the flank, and for a time checking its fire.

It is difficult not to regard such a disaster in a light of its own, and to separate it from the general sequence of affairs. Causeless and fruitless, it stands by itself, as a grand heroic deed, surpassing even that spectacle of a shipwrecked regiment, settling down into the waves, each man still in his rank. The British soldier will do his duty, even to certain death, and is not paralyzed by feeling that he is the victim of some hideous blunder. Whatever the case of the common soldier, and however little he might know the full horrors of his position till death had done its work all around him, the officers who led him on, with a conspicuous gallantry that extorted the admiration of the foe, knew well what they were about. Nor were those officers mere soldiers of fortune, with nothing to lose but themselves, and no inducements out of their profession. They were men who risked on that day all the enjoyments that rank, wealth, good social position, and many fortunate circumstances can offer to those who are content to stay at home. Splendid as the event was on the Alma,[5] yet that rugged ascent in the face of heights blazing with destruction was scarcely so glorious as the progress of the

[1] *Minié muskets* Rifles that came into use during the mid-nineteenth century. They had a longer range and greater accuracy than most similar guns of the period, and fired Minié bullets, which were easier to load than their predecessors.

[2] *sabred* I.e., attacked with sabres, curved swords.

[3] *C'est très … la guerre* French: This is very magnificent, but this is not war.

[4] *Chasseurs d'Afrique* Light cavalry branch of the French Armé d'Afrique, who were normally stationed in France's colonial possessions in North Africa, but also participated in the Crimean War.

[5] *Alma* Crimean river, the site of the Battle of the Alma on 20 September 1854.

cavalry through and through that valley of death,[1] with a murderous fire, not only in front, but on both sides, above, and even in the rear. ...

from "The Cavalry Action at Balaclava," *The Times* (14 November 1854)

> Though the report from which the following excerpt is taken appeared in the 14 November issue of *The Times*, the dispatch from *The Times*' correspondent (William Howard Russell) is dated 25 October.

... **A**s they passed towards the front, the Russians opened on them from the guns in the redoubt on the right, with volleys of musketry and rifles. They swept proudly past, glittering in the morning sun in all the pride and splendour of war. We could scarcely believe the evidence of our senses! Surely that handful of men are not going to charge an army in position? Alas! it was but too true—their desperate valour knew no bounds, and far indeed was it removed from its so-called better part—discretion. They advanced in two lines, quickening their pace as they closed towards the enemy. A more fearful spectacle was never witnessed than by those who, without the power to aid, beheld their heroic countrymen rushing to the arms of death. At the distance of 1,200 yards the whole line of the enemy belched forth, from 30 iron mouths, a flood of smoke and flame, through which hissed the deadly balls. Their flight was marked by instant gaps in our ranks by dead men and horses, by steeds flying wounded or riderless across the plain. The first line is broken, it is joined by the second, they never halt or check their speed an instant; with diminished ranks, thinned by those 30 guns, which the Russians had laid with the most deadly accuracy, with a halo of flashing steel above their heads, and with a cheer which was many a noble fellow's death-cry, they flew into the smoke of the batteries, but ere they were lost from view the plain was strewed with their bodies and with the carcasses of horses. They were exposed to an oblique fire from the batteries on the hills on both sides, as well as to a direct fire of musketry. Through the clouds of smoke we could see their sabres flashing as they rode up to the guns and dashed between them, cutting down the gunners as they stood. We saw them riding through the guns, as I have said; to our delight we saw them returning, after breaking through a column of Russian infantry, and scattering them like chaff, when the flank fire of the battery on the hill swept them down, scattered and broken as they were. Wounded men and dismounted troopers flying towards us told the sad tale—demi-gods could not have done what we had failed to do. ...

---

[1] *valley of death*   See Psalm 23.4: "Yea, though I walk through the valley of the shadow of death."

[*Flower in the Crannied Wall*]

Flower in the crannied wall,
I pluck you out of the crannies,
I hold you here, root and all, in my hand,
Little flower—but *if* I could understand
5 What you are, root and all, and all in all,
I should know what God and man is.
—1869

Vastness

1

Many a hearth upon our dark globe sighs after many
    a vanished face,
Many a planet by many a sun may roll with the dust
    of a vanished race.

2

Raving politics, never at rest—as this poor earth's
    pale history runs,—
What is it all but a trouble° of ants in the gleam   *agitation*
    of a million million of suns?

3

5 Lies upon this side, lies upon that side, truthless violence
    mourned by the Wise,
Thousands of voices drowning his own in a popular
    torrent of lies upon lies;

4

Stately purposes, valour in battle, glorious annals of
    army and fleet,
Death for the right cause, death for the wrong cause,
    trumpets of victory, groans of defeat;

5

Innocence seethed° in her mother's milk,[1] and   *boiled*
    Charity setting the martyr aflame;

10 Thraldom° who walks with the banner of   *bondage*
    Freedom, and recks not[2] to ruin a realm in her name.

6

Faith at her zenith, or all but lost in the gloom of doubts
    that darken the schools;
Craft with a bunch of all-heal[3] in her hand,
    followed up by her vassal° legion of fools;   *servile*

7

Trade flying over a thousand seas with her spice
    and her vintage, her silk and her corn;°   *grain*
Desolate offing,[4] sailorless harbours, famishing
    populace, wharves forlorn;

8

15 Star of the morning, Hope in the sunrise;
    gloom of the evening, Life at a close;
Pleasure who flaunts on her wide down-way
    with her flying robe and her poisoned rose;

9

Pain, that has crawled from the corpse of Pleasure,
    a worm which writhes all day, and at night
Stirs up again in the heart of the sleeper, and stings
    him back to the curse of the light;

10

Wealth with his wines and his wedded harlots;
    honest Poverty, bare to the bone;
20 Opulent Avarice, lean as Poverty; Flattery gilding
    the rift in a throne;

11

Fame blowing out from her golden trumpet
    a jubilant challenge to Time and to Fate;
Slander, her shadow, sowing the nettle on all the
    laurelled[5] graves of the Great;

---

1 *Innocence ... milk* See Exodus 34.26: "Thou shalt not seethe a kid in his mother's milk."

2 *recks not* Is not reluctant.

3 *all-heal* Name given to various plants believed to possess healing properties.

4 *offing* Most distant part of the sea visible from shore.

5 *laurelled* Decorated with laurel, signifying military victory or poetic achievement.

12

Love for the maiden, crowned with marriage,
  no regrets for aught° that has been,   *anything*
Household happinesss, gracious children,
  debtless competence,° golden mean;   *sufficiency*

13

25 National hatreds of whole generations, and
    pigmy° spites of the village spire;   *trivial*
  Vows that will last to the last death-ruckle,°   *death-rattle*
    and vows that are snapped in a moment of fire;

14

He that has lived for the lust of the minute,
  and died in the doing it, flesh without mind;
He that has nailed all flesh to the Cross,
  till Self died out in the love of his kind;

15

Spring and Summer and Autumn and Winter,
  and all these old revolutions of earth;
30 All new-old revolutions of Empire—change of the
    tide—what is all of it worth?

16

What the philosophies, all the sciences, poesy,
  varying voices of prayer?
All that is noblest, all that is basest, all that is filthy
  with all that is fair?

17

What is it all, if we all of us end but in being our own
  corpse-coffins at last,
Swallowed in Vastness, lost in Silence, drowned
  in the deeps of a meaningless Past?

18

35 What but a murmur of gnats in the gloom,
    or a moment's anger of bees in their hive?—

*   *   *

Peace, let it be! for I loved him, and love him for ever:
  the dead are not dead but alive.
—1885; 1889

Crossing the Bar [1]

Sunset and evening star,
  And one clear call for me!
And may there be no moaning of the bar,
  When I put out to sea,

5 But such a tide as moving seems asleep,
    Too full for sound and foam,
When that which drew from out the boundless deep
    Turns again home.

Twilight and evening bell,
10   And after that the dark!
And may there be no sadness of farewell,
    When I embark;

For though from out our bourne° of Time and   *limit*
    Place
    The flood may bear me far,
15 I hope to see my Pilot face to face
    When I have crossed the bar.
—1889

---

1 *Bar* Sandbank across the mouth of a harbor or estuary.

IN CONTEXT

Images of Tennyson

Particularly in his later years, Tennyson became an iconic figure in Victorian Britain. The best known photographic images of him are those taken by Julia Margaret Cameron, two of which are reproduced below. (Another appears in the introduction to Tennyson, above.) Tennyson as a younger man is described below by Thomas Carlyle.

Julia Margaret Cameron, *Alfred Tennyson*, 1865. Tennyson nicknamed this photograph "the dirty monk" and claimed that it was his favorite photograph of himself.

Julia Margaret Cameron, *Alfred, Lord Tennyson*, 1866.

from Thomas Carlyle, Letter to Ralph Waldo Emerson, 5 August 1844

Alfred is one of the few British or Foreign Figures (a not increasing number I think!) who are and remain beautiful to me;—a true human soul, or some authentic approximation thereto, to whom your own soul can say, Brother!—However, I doubt[1] he will not come; he often skips me, in these brief visits to Town; skips everybody indeed; being a man solitary and sad, as certain men are, dwelling in an element of gloom,—carrying a bit of Chaos about him, in short, which he is manufacturing into Cosmos!

Alfred is the son of a Lincolnshire Gentleman Farmer, I think; indeed, you see in his verses that he is a native of "moated granges,"[2] and green, fat pastures, not of mountains and their torrents and

---

[1] *doubt* Suspect.

[2] *moated granges* See Tennyson's poem, "Mariana" (above).

storms. He had his breeding at Cambridge, as if for the Law or Church; being master of a small annuity on his Father's decease, he preferred clubbing[1] with his Mother and some Sisters, to live unpromoted and write Poems. In this way he lives still, now here, now there; the family always within reach of London, never in it; he himself making rare and brief visits, lodging in some old comrade's rooms. I think he must be under forty, not much under it.[2] One of the finest-looking men in the world. A great shock of rough dusty-dark hair; bright-laughing hazel eyes; massive aquiline face, most massive yet most delicate; of sallow-brown complexion, almost Indian-looking; clothes cynically loose, free-and-easy;—smokes infinite tobacco. His voice is musical metallic,—fit for loud laughter and piercing wail, and all that may lie between; speech and speculation free and plenteous: I do not meet, in these late decades, such company over a pipe!—We shall see what he will grow to. He is often unwell; very chaotic,—his way is through Chaos and the Bottomless and Pathless; not handy for making out many miles upon.

IN CONTEXT

Victorian Images of Arthurian Legend

Arthurian romance was a frequent subject of Victorian painting and photography as well as Victorian literature; a sampling is reproduced below.

Julia Margaret Cameron, *The Parting of Lancelot and Guinevere*, 1874.

Julia Margaret Cameron, *Vivien and Merlin*, 1874.

---

[1] *clubbing* Being in the company of.

[2] *not much under it* In fact, Tennyson was just about to turn thirty-five when this was written.

John William Waterhouse, *The Lady of Shalott*, 1888.

William Holman Hunt, *The Lady of Shalott*, 1857.

Henry Peach Robinson, *The Lady of Shalott*, c. 1860.

In Context

Crimea and the Camera

The Crimean War was the first to be photographed extensively—most notably by Roger Fenton, who spent three months in Crimea in 1855. Both the technology of the time and the demands of Victorian taste militated against shooting scenes of battle directly; unlike Matthew Brady and other photographers of the American Civil War a few years later, Fenton took no pictures of bloody and mangled corpses.

Fenton's most famous photograph of the war, *Valley of the Shadow of Death*, came to be closely associated with Tennyson's famous 1854 poem, "The Charge of the Light Brigade." The connection is not entirely a direct one, however. It was not the valley where the charge occurred that Fenton photographed but another valley in the vicinity—one that had begun to be referred to by soldiers as "the valley of the shadow of death" (in an echo both of Tennyson's poem and of the Bible) because of the frequency with which the Russians shelled it.

Roger Fenton, *Group of Croat Chiefs*, 1855.

Roger Fenton, *Cookhouse of the 8th Hussars*, 1855.

Roger Fenton, *Valley of the Shadow of Death*, 1855.

CHARLES DARWIN
1809 – 1882

The name Charles Darwin has become synonymous in many minds with the theory of evolution, but theories of evolution did not begin with Darwin. Long before the Victorian era the ancient Greek thinkers Anaximander (611–547 BCE), Empedocles (492–432 BCE), and Aristotle (384–322 BCE) all speculated that life as we know it evolved from sea creatures. In the year Darwin was born, the French biologist Lamarck suggested that species respond and adapt to their environments and then transmit these adaptive traits to their offspring. And in 1850, drawing on the theories of Charles Lyell and Robert Chambers, Tennyson speculated on the idea of evolution in his poetic elegy *In Memoriam*. But when the unassuming British naturalist Charles Darwin articulated his acceptance of the concept of evolution and published his theory of natural selection in 1859 in *On the Origin of Species*, his views provoked comment and controversy internationally. He had offered a detailed, cogent, and plausible theory that to many appeared to call into question the idea of divine creation, as well as assumptions about human beings' innate superiority to, and difference from, other creatures.

Charles Robert Darwin was born in 1809 in Shrewsbury, England, to Robert Waring Darwin, a successful doctor (and son of the famous physician, botanist, philosopher, and poet Erasmus Darwin), and Susannah Wedgwood Darwin, daughter of the pottery manufacturer Josiah Wedgwood. Charles distinguished himself neither at school nor at the University of Edinburgh, where his father sent him to study medicine. He often complained throughout his school years of being bored, although he always showed an active interest in and enthusiasm for the natural sciences and for specimen collection. When he left medical school without taking his degree, his father pushed him into a second career track; ironically, the man who would be reviled by religious fundamentalists next studied theology at Cambridge with a view to joining the clergy. Darwin again became bored with his studies, preferring to spend his time collecting and studying beetles. He did make an important friend at Cambridge; his botany professor, John Henslow, recognized Darwin's potential as a natural scientist and recommended him for a position on the H.M.S. Beagle, the ship that would take him around the world to collect biological specimens and data. On this pivotal five-year voyage, Darwin compiled meticulous records of his findings along with an engaging account of his travels and the cultures he encountered, which he subsequently published as *The Voyage of the Beagle* in 1839.

Influenced by James Hutton's geological theories and Charles Lyell's *Principles of Geology*, Darwin also collected fossils and noted the relationship between creatures and their environments, particularly among the unique fauna of the Galapagos Islands. These isolated islands contained species of birds completely unlike those on the mainland, as well as others that closely resembled species of South America. After completing the voyage, Darwin devoted the rest of his career to researching and attempting to explain the differences between such species and their ancestors. After reading Thomas Malthus's *An Essay on the Principle of Population*, he came up with his answer: individuals that are strong enough to survive environmental pressures pass their favorable traits on to successive generations, and thus species adapt and gradually form new species, a process Darwin called "natural selection." Moreover, according to Darwinian theory this process has persisted for millions of years, with all species having evolved from a single life form.

Although he wrote essays on his evolutionary ideas, Darwin did not publish his findings for 20 years, until another naturalist, Alfred Russel Wallace, sent him a paper that included similar conclusions about natural selection. The two agreed to present a joint paper in 1858 to the Linnaean Society in London, and the next year Darwin published *On the Origin of Species*. *Origin* sold out its entire print run amidst a storm of protest and indignation. In the decade following its publication, responses to the book abounded in the literary world, with authors such as Charles Kingsley and Samuel Butler opposing Darwin, while George Eliot, Thomas Hardy, and Joseph Conrad drew on his theories and modes of explanation.

For the rest of his life, Darwin lived in his country house with his wife, his cousin Emma Wedgwood, whom he had married in 1839, and his many children, studying flora and fauna and publishing his findings. Although the world around him struggled to absorb the impact of his evolutionary theory, Darwin refused to engage in debates about the questions that haunted so many: are humans really evolved from lower life forms, and where does this theory leave the Bible's teachings? In *The Descent of Man, and Selection in Relation to Sex* (1871) Darwin explicitly extended his evolutionary theory to human beings and put forward the notion of sexual selection.

In 1882, after suffering from ill health for many years, quite possibly from a disease acquired during his voyage on the H.M.S. Beagle, Darwin died. He was buried next to Sir Isaac Newton in Westminster Abbey.

⌘ ⌘ ⌘

from *The Voyage of the Beagle*

from CHAPTER 10: TIERRA DEL FUEGO

December 17th, 1832.—Having now finished with Patagonia[1] and the Falkland Islands, I will describe our first arrival in Tierra del Fuego.[2] A little after noon we doubled Cape St. Diego, and entered the famous strait of Le Maire. We kept close to the Fuegian shore, but the outline of the rugged, inhospitable Staten-land was visible amidst the clouds. In the afternoon we anchored in the Bay of Good Success. While entering we were saluted in a manner becoming[3] the inhabitants of this savage land. A group of Fuegians partly concealed by the entangled forest, were perched on a wild point overhanging the sea; and as we passed by, they sprang up and waving their tattered cloaks sent forth a loud and sonorous shout. The savages followed the ship, and just before dark we saw their fire, and again heard their wild cry. The harbour consists of a fine piece of water half surrounded by low rounded mountains of clay-slate, which are covered to the water's edge by one dense gloomy forest. A single glance at the landscape was sufficient to show me how widely different it was from any thing I had ever beheld. At night it blew a gale of wind, and heavy squalls from the mountains swept past us. It would have been a bad time out at sea, and we, as well as others, may call this Good Success Bay.

---

[1] *Patagonia*   Southern portion of South America.

[2] *Tierra del Fuego*   Southernmost tip of South America.

[3] *becoming*   Appropriate to.

In the morning the Captain sent a party to communicate with the Fuegians. When we came within hail, one of the four natives who were present advanced to receive us, and began to shout most vehemently, wishing to direct us where to land. When we were on shore the party looked rather alarmed, but continued talking and making gestures with great rapidity. It was without exception the most curious and interesting spectacle I ever beheld. I could not have believed how wide was the difference between savage and civilized man: it is greater than between a wild and domesticated animal, inasmuch as in man there is a greater power of improvement. The chief spokesman was old, and appeared to be the head of the family; the three others were powerful young men, about six feet high. The women and children had been sent away. These Fuegians are a very different race from the stunted, miserable wretches farther westward; and they seem closely allied to the famous Patagonians of the Strait of Magellan. Their only garment consists of a mantle made of guanaco[1] skin, with the wool outside; this they wear just thrown over their shoulders, leaving their persons as often exposed as covered. Their skin is of a dirty coppery red colour.

The old man had a fillet[2] of white feathers tied round his head, which partly confined his black, coarse, and entangled hair. His face was crossed by two broad transverse bars; one, painted bright red, reached from ear to ear and included the upper lip; the other, white like chalk, extended above and parallel to the first, so that even his eyelids were thus coloured. The other two men were ornamented by streaks of black powder, made of charcoal. The party altogether closely resembled the devils which come on the stage in plays like *Der Freischutz*.[3]

Their very attitudes were abject, and the expression of their countenances[4] distrustful, surprised, and startled. After we had presented them with some scarlet cloth, which they immediately tied round their necks, they became good friends. This was shown by the old man patting our breasts, and making a chuckling kind of noise, as people do when feeding chickens. I walked with the old man, and this demonstration of friendship was repeated several times; it was concluded by three hard slaps, which were given me on the breast and back at the same time. He then bared his bosom for me to return the compliment, which being done, he seemed highly pleased. The language of these people, according to our notions, scarcely deserves to be called articulate. Captain Cook[5] has compared it to a man clearing his throat, but certainly no European ever cleared his throat with so many hoarse, guttural, and clicking sounds.

They are excellent mimics: as often as we coughed or yawned, or made any odd motion, they immediately imitated us. Some of our party began to squint and look awry; but one of the young Fuegians (whose whole face was painted black, excepting a white band across his eyes) succeeded in making far more hideous grimaces. They could repeat with perfect correctness each word in any sentence we addressed them, and they remembered such words for some time. Yet we Europeans all know how difficult it is to distinguish apart the sounds in a foreign language. Which of us, for instance, could follow an American Indian through a sentence of more than three words? All savages appear to possess, to an uncommon degree, this power of mimicry. I was told, almost in the same words, of the same ludicrous habit among the Caffres:[6] the Australians, likewise, have long been notorious for being able to imitate and describe the gait of any man, so that he may be recognized. How can this faculty be explained? Is it a consequence of the more practised habits of perception and keener senses, common to all men in a savage state, as compared with those long civilized?

When a song was struck up by our party, I thought the Fuegians would have fallen down with astonishment. With equal surprise they viewed our dancing; but one of the young men, when asked, had no objection to a little

---

[1] *guanaco* Wild llama, the coat of which is a red-brown wool.

[2] *fillet* Headband.

[3] *Der Freischutz* 1820 opera by Carl Maria von Weber.

[4] *countenances* Faces.

[5] *Captain Cook* James Cook (1728–79), English explorer.

[6] *Caffres* Kaffirs, a common term for native Africans (now considered to be derogatory).

waltzing. Little accustomed to Europeans as they appeared to be, yet they knew and dreaded our fire-arms; nothing would tempt them to take a gun in their hands. They begged for knives, calling them by the Spanish word "cuchilla." They explained also what they wanted, by acting as if they had a piece of blubber in their mouth, and then pretending to cut instead of tear it.

I have not as yet noticed[1] the Fuegians whom we had on board. During the former voyage of the *Adventure* and *Beagle* in 1826 to 1830, Captain Fitz Roy[2] seized on a party of natives, as hostages for the loss of a boat, which had been stolen, to the great jeopardy of a party employed on the survey; and some of these natives, as well as a child whom he bought for a pearl-button, he took with him to England, determining to educate them and instruct them in religion at his own expense. To settle these natives in their own country, was one chief inducement to Captain Fitz Roy to undertake our present voyage; and before the Admiralty had resolved to send out this expedition, Captain Fitz Roy had generously chartered a vessel, and would himself have taken them back. The natives were accompanied by a missionary, R. Matthews; of whom and of the natives, Captain Fitz Roy has published a full and excellent account. Two men, one of whom died in England of the smallpox, a boy and a little girl, were originally taken; and we had now on board, York Minster, Jemmy Button (whose name expresses his purchase-money), and Fuegia Basket. York Minster was a full-grown, short, thick, powerful man: his disposition was reserved, taciturn, morose, and when excited violently passionate; his affections were very strong towards a few friends on board; his intellect good. Jemmy Button was a universal favourite, but likewise passionate; the expression of his face at once showed his nice disposition. He was merry and often laughed, and was remarkably sympathetic with any one in pain: when the water was rough, I was often a little seasick, and he used to come to me and say in a plaintive voice, "Poor, poor fellow!" but the notion, after his aquatic life, of a

man being sea-sick, was too ludicrous, and he was generally obliged to turn on one side to hide a smile or laugh, and then he would repeat his "Poor, poor fellow!" He was of a patriotic disposition; and he liked to praise his own tribe and country, in which he truly said there were "plenty of trees," and he abused all the other tribes: he stoutly declared that there was no Devil in his land. Jemmy was short, thick, and fat, but vain of his personal appearance; he used to wear gloves, his hair was neatly cut, and he was distressed if his well-polished shoes were dirtied. He was fond of admiring himself in a looking-glass; and a merry-faced little Indian boy from the Rio Negro, whom we had for some months on board, soon perceived this, and used to mock him: Jemmy, who was always rather jealous of the attention paid to this little boy, did not at all like this, and used to say, with rather a contemptuous twist of his head, "Too much skylark." It seems yet wonderful to me, when I think over all his many good qualities, that he should have been of the same race, and doubtless partaken of the same character, with the miserable, degraded savages whom we first met here. Lastly, Fuegia Basket was a nice, modest, reserved young girl, with a rather pleasing but sometimes sullen expression, and very quick in learning anything, especially languages. This she showed in picking up some Portuguese and Spanish, when left on shore for only a short time at Rio de Janeiro and Monte Video, and in her knowledge of English. York Minster was very jealous of any attention paid to her; for it was clear he determined to marry her as soon as they were settled on shore.

Although all three could both speak and understand a good deal of English, it was singularly difficult to obtain much information from them, concerning the habits of their countrymen: this was partly owing to their apparent difficulty in understanding the simplest alternative. Every one accustomed to very young children, knows how seldom one can get an answer even to so simple a question as whether a thing is black *or* white; the idea of black or white seems alternately to fill their minds. So it was with these Fuegians, and hence it was generally impossible to find out, by cross-questioning, whether one had rightly understood anything which

[1] *noticed* Mentioned.

[2] *Captain Fitz Roy* Robert Fitz Roy (1805–65).

they had asserted. Their sight was remarkably acute: it is well known that sailors, from long practice, can make out a distant object much better than a landsman; but both York and Jemmy were much superior to any sailor on board: several times they have declared what some distant object has been, and though doubted by every one, they have proved right, when it has been examined through a telescope. They were quite conscious of this power; and Jemmy, when he had any little quarrel with the officer on watch, would say, "Me see ship, me no tell."

It was interesting to watch the conduct of the savages, when we landed, towards Jemmy Button: they immediately perceived the difference between him and ourselves, and held much conversation one with another on the subject. The old man addressed a long harangue to Jemmy, which it seems was to invite him to stay with them. But Jemmy understood very little of their language, and was, moreover, thoroughly ashamed of his countrymen. When York Minster afterwards came on shore, they noticed him in the same way, and told him he ought to shave; yet he had not twenty dwarf hairs on his face, whilst we all wore our untrimmed beards. They examined the colour of his skin, and compared it with ours. One of our arms being bared, they expressed the liveliest surprise and admiration at its whiteness, just in the same way in which I have seen the ourang-outang do at the Zoological Gardens. We thought that they mistook two or three of the officers, who were rather shorter and fairer, though adorned with large beards, for the ladies of our party. The tallest among the Fuegians was evidently much pleased at his height being noticed. When placed back to back with the tallest of the boat's crew, he tried his best to edge on higher ground, and to stand on tiptoe. He opened his mouth to show his teeth, and turned his face for a side view; and all this was done with such alacrity, that I dare say he thought himself the handsomest man in Tierra del Fuego. After our first feeling of grave astonishment was over, nothing could be more ludicrous than the odd mixture of surprise and imitation which these savages every moment exhibited. ...

December 25th.—Close by the cove, a pointed hill, called Rater's Peak, rises to the height of 1700 feet. The surrounding islands all consist of conical masses of greenstone, associated sometimes with less regular hills of baked and altered clay-slate. This part of Tierra del Fuego may be considered as the extremity of the submerged chain of mountains already alluded to. The cove takes its name of "Wigwam" from some of the Fuegian habitations; but every bay in the neighbourhood might be so called with equal propriety. The inhabitants, living chiefly upon shell-fish, are obliged constantly to change their place of residence; but they return at intervals to the same spots, as is evident from the piles of old shells, which must often amount to many tons in weight. These heaps can be distinguished at a long distance by the bright green colour of certain plants, which invariably grow on them. Among these may be enumerated the wild celery and scurvy grass, two very serviceable plants, the use of which has not been discovered by the natives.

The Fuegian wigwam resembles, in size and dimensions, a haycock.[1] It merely consists of a few broken branches stuck in the ground, and very imperfectly thatched on one side with a few tufts of grass and rushes. The whole cannot be the work of an hour, and it is only used for a few days. At Goeree Roads I saw a place where one of these naked men had slept, which absolutely offered no more cover than the form of a hare. The man was evidently living by himself, and York Minster said he was "very bad man," and that probably he had stolen something. On the west coast, however, the wigwams are rather better, for they are covered with seal-skins. We were detained here several days by the bad weather. The climate is certainly wretched: the summer solstice was now passed, yet every day snow fell on the hills, and in the valleys there was rain, accompanied by sleet. The thermometer generally stood about 45°, but in the night fell to 38° or 40°. From the damp and boisterous state of the atmosphere, not cheered by a gleam of sunshine, one fancied the climate even worse than it really was.

While going one day on shore near Wollaston Island, we pulled alongside a canoe with six Fuegians. These were the most abject and miserable creatures I

---

[1] *haycock* Haystack.

anywhere beheld. On the east coast the natives, as we have seen, have guanaco cloaks, and on the west, they possess seal-skins. Amongst these central tribes the men generally have an otter-skin, or some small scrap about as large as a pocket-handkerchief, which is barely sufficient to cover their backs as low down as their loins. It is laced across the breast by strings, and according as the wind blows, it is shifted from side to side. But these Fuegians in the canoe were quite naked, and even one full-grown woman was absolutely so. It was raining heavily, and the fresh water, together with the spray, trickled down her body. In another harbour not far distant, a woman, who was suckling a recently-born child, came one day alongside the vessel, and remained there out of mere curiosity, whilst the sleet fell and thawed on her naked bosom, and on the skin of her naked baby! These poor wretches were stunted in their growth, their hideous faces bedaubed with white paint, their skins filthy and greasy, their hair entangled, their voices discordant, and their gestures violent. Viewing such men, one can hardly make oneself believe that they are fellow-creatures, and inhabitants of the same world. It is a common subject of conjecture what pleasure in life some of the lower animals can enjoy: how much more reasonably the same question may be asked with respect to these barbarians! At night, five or six human beings, naked and scarcely protected from the wind and rain of this tempestuous climate, sleep on the wet ground coiled up like animals. Whenever it is low water, winter or summer, night or day, they must rise to pick shellfish from the rocks; and the women either dive to collect sea-eggs, or sit patiently in their canoes, and with a baited hairline without any hook, jerk out little fish. If a seal is killed, or the floating carcass of a putrid whale discovered, it is a feast; and such miserable food is assisted by a few tasteless berries and fungi.

They often suffer from famine: I heard Mr. Low, a sealingmaster intimately acquainted with the natives of this country, give a curious account of the state of a party of one hundred and fifty natives on the west coast, who were very thin and in great distress. A succession of gales prevented the women from getting shell-fish on the rocks, and they could not go out in their canoes to

catch seal. A small party of these men one morning set out, and the other Indians explained to him, that they were going a four days' journey for food: on their return, Low went to meet them, and he found them excessively tired, each man carrying a great square piece of putrid whales-blubber with a hole in the middle, through which they put their heads, like the Gauchos[1] do through their ponchos or cloaks. As soon as the blubber was brought into a wigwam, an old man cut off thin slices, and muttering over them, broiled them for a minute, and distributed them to the famished party, who during this time preserved a profound silence. Mr. Low believes that whenever a whale is cast on shore, the natives bury large pieces of it in the sand, as a resource in time of famine; and a native boy, whom he had on board, once found a stock thus buried. ...

The different tribes have no government or chief; yet each is surrounded by other hostile tribes, speaking different dialects, and separated from each other only by a deserted border or neutral territory: the cause of their warfare appears to be the means of subsistence. Their country is a broken mass of wild rocks, lofty hills, and useless forests: and these are viewed through mists and endless storms. The habitable land is reduced to the stones on the beach; in search of food they are compelled unceasingly to wander from spot to spot, and so steep is the coast, that they can only move about in their wretched canoes. They cannot know the feeling of having a home, and still less that of domestic affection; for the husband is to the wife as a brutal master to a laborious slave. Was a more horrid deed ever perpetrated, than that witnessed on the west coast by Byron,[2] who saw a wretched mother pick up her bleeding dying infant-boy, whom her husband had mercilessly dashed on the stones for dropping a basket of sea-eggs! How little can the higher powers of the mind be brought into play: what is there for imagination to picture, for reason to compare, for judgment to decide upon? To knock a

[1] *Gauchos* South American horsemen of mixed Native American and European descent.

[2] *Byron* John Byron (1723–86), British vice-admiral and explorer, and grandfather of the poet George Gordon, Lord Byron. See his *Narrative of Great Distresses on the Shores of Patagonia* (1768).

limpet[1] from the rock does not require even cunning, that lowest power of the mind. Their skill in some respects may be compared to the instinct of animals; for it is not improved by experience: the canoe, their most ingenious work, poor as it is, has remained the same, as we know from Drake,[2] for the last two hundred and fifty years. Whilst beholding these savages, one asks, whence have they come? What could have tempted, or what change compelled a tribe of men, to leave the fine regions of the north, to travel down the Cordillera or backbone of America, to invent and build canoes, which are not used by the tribes of Chile, Peru, and Brazil, and then to enter on one of the most inhospitable countries within the limits of the globe? Although such reflections must at first seize on the mind, yet we may feel sure that they are partly erroneous. There is no reason to believe that the Fuegians decrease in number; therefore we must suppose that they enjoy a sufficient share of happiness, of whatever kind it may be, to render life worth having. Nature by making habit omnipotent, and its effects hereditary, has fitted the Fuegian to the climate and the productions of his miserable country. ...

January 19th, 1833—Three whale-boats and the yawl,[3] with a party of twenty-eight, started under the command of Captain Fitz Roy. In the afternoon we entered the eastern mouth of the channel, and shortly afterwards found a snug little cove concealed by some surrounding islets. Here we pitched our tents and lighted our fires. Nothing could look more comfortable than this scene. The glassy water of the little harbour, with the branches of the trees hanging over the rocky beach, the boats at anchor, the tents supported by the crossed oars, and the smoke curling up the wooded valley, formed a picture of quiet retirement.[4] The next day (20th) we smoothly glided onwards in our little fleet, and came to a more inhabited district. Few if any of these natives could ever have seen a white man;

certainly nothing could exceed their astonishment at the apparition of the four boats. Fires were lighted on every point (hence the name of Tierra del Fuego, or the land of fire), both to attract our attention and to spread far and wide the news. Some of the men ran for miles along the shore. I shall never forget how wild and savage one group appeared: suddenly four or five men came to the edge of an overhanging cliff; they were absolutely naked, and their long hair streamed about their faces; they held rugged staffs in their hands, and, springing from the ground, they waved their arms round their heads, and sent forth the most hideous yells.

At dinner-time we landed among a party of Fuegians. At first they were not inclined to be friendly; for until the Captain pulled in ahead of the other boats, they kept their slings in their hands. We soon, however, delighted them by trifling presents, such as tying red tape round their heads. They liked our biscuit: but one of the savages touched with his finger some of the meat preserved in tin cases which I was eating, and feeling it soft and cold, showed as much disgust at it, as I should have done at putrid blubber. ...

On the last day of February in the succeeding year (1834), the *Beagle* anchored in a beautiful little cove at the eastern entrance of the Beagle Channel. Captain Fitz Roy determined on the bold, and as it proved successful, attempt to beat against the westerly winds by the same route, which we had followed in the boats to the settlement at Woollya. We did not see many natives until we were near Ponsonby Sound, where we were followed by ten or twelve canoes. The natives did not at all understand the reason of our tacking,[5] and, instead of meeting us at each tack, vainly strove to follow us in our zig-zag course. I was amused at finding what a difference the circumstance of being quite superior in force made, in the interest of beholding these savages. While in the boats I got to hate the very sound of their voices, so much trouble did they give us. The first and last word was "yammerschooner." When, entering some quiet

---

[1] *limpet* Marine snail with a low conical shell.

[2] *Drake* Sir Francis Drake (c. 1540–96), English explorer. In 1577 his travels took him past Tierra del Fuego.

[3] *yawl* Small boat.

[4] *retirement* Seclusion.

[5] *tacking* Sailing maneuver in which a ship zig-zags between two courses, enabling it to make progress against a wind blowing from the direction of intended travel.

little cove, we have looked round and thought to pass a quiet night, the odious word "yammerschooner" has shrilly sounded from some gloomy nook, and then the little signal-smoke has curled up to spread the news far and wide. On leaving some place we have said to each other, "Thank Heaven, we have at last fairly left these wretches!" when one more faint halloo from an all-powerful voice, heard at a prodigious distance, would reach our ears, and clearly could we distinguish— "yammerschooner." But now, the more Fuegians the merrier; and very merry work it was. Both parties laughing, wondering, gaping at each other; we pitying them, for giving us good fish and crabs for rags, *et cetera*; they grasping at the chance of finding people so foolish as to exchange such splendid ornaments for a good supper. It was most amusing to see the undisguised smile of satisfaction with which one young woman with her face painted black, tied several bits of scarlet cloth round her head with rushes. Her husband, who enjoyed the very universal privilege in this country of possessing two wives, evidently became jealous of all the attention paid to his young wife; and, after a consultation with his naked beauties, was paddled away by them.

Some of the Fuegians plainly showed that they had a fair notion of barter. I gave one man a large nail (a most valuable present) without making any signs for a return; but he immediately picked out two fish, and handed them up on the point of his spear. If any present was designed for one canoe, and it fell near another, it was invariably given to the right owner. The Fuegian boy, whom Mr. Low had on board, showed, by going into the most violent passion, that he quite understood the reproach of being called a liar, which in truth he was. We were this time, as on all former occasions, much surprised at the little notice, or rather none whatever, which was taken of many things, the use of which must have been evident to the natives. Simple circumstances—such as the beauty of scarlet cloth or blue beads, the absence of women, our care in washing ourselves—excited their admiration far more than any grand or complicated object, such as our ship. Bougain-

ville[1] has well remarked concerning these people, that they treat the "chefs d'oeuvres de l'industrie humaine, comme ils traitent les loix de la nature et ses phenomenes."[2]

On the 5th of March, we anchored in the cove at Woollya, but we saw not a soul there. We were alarmed at this, for the natives in Ponsonby Sound showed by gestures, that there had been fighting; and we afterwards heard that the dreaded Oens men had made a descent. Soon a canoe, with a little flag flying, was seen approaching, with one of the men in it washing the paint off his face. This man was poor Jemmy—now a thin haggard savage, with long disordered hair, and naked, except a bit of a blanket round his waist. We did not recognize him till he was close to us; for he was ashamed of himself, and turned his back to the ship. We had left him plump, fat, clean, and well dressed—I never saw so complete and grievous a change. As soon however as he was clothed, and the first flurry was over, things wore a good appearance. He dined with Captain Fitz Roy, and ate his dinner as tidily as formerly. He told us he had "too much" (meaning enough) to eat, that he was not cold, that his relations were very good people, and that he did not wish to go back to England: in the evening we found out the cause of this great change in Jemmy's feelings, in the arrival of his young and nice-looking wife. With his usual good feeling, he brought two beautiful otter-skins for two of his best friends, and some spear-heads and arrows made with his own hands for the Captain. He said he had built a canoe for himself, and he boasted that he could talk a little of his own language! But it is a most singular fact, that he appears to have taught all his tribe some English: an old man spontaneously announced "Jemmy Button's wife." Jemmy had lost all his property. He told us that York Minster had built a large canoe, and with his wife Fuegia, had several months since gone to his own country, and had taken farewell by an act of consummate villainy; he persuaded Jemmy and his mother to come with him, and then on the way deserted them by night, stealing every article of their property.

---

[1] *Bougainville* Louis de Bougainville (1729–1811), French navigator.

[2] *chefs d'oeuvres … phenomenes* French: masterworks of human industry as they treat the laws of nature and its phenomena.

Jemmy went to sleep on shore, and in the morning returned, and remained on board till the ship got under weigh, which frightened his wife, who continued crying violently till he got into his canoe. He returned loaded with valuable property. Every soul on board was heartily sorry to shake hands with him for the last time. I do not now doubt that he will be as happy as, perhaps happier than, if he had never left his own country. Every one must sincerely hope that Captain Fitz Roy's noble hope may be fulfilled, of being rewarded for the many generous sacrifices which he made for these Fuegians, by some shipwrecked sailor being protected by the descendants of Jemmy Button and his tribe! When Jemmy reached the shore, he lighted a signal fire, and the smoke curled up, bidding us a last and long farewell, as the ship stood on her course into the open sea.

The perfect equality among the individuals composing the Fuegian tribes, must for a long time retard their civilization. As we see those animals, whose instinct compels them to live in society and obey a chief, are most capable of improvement, so is it with the races of mankind. Whether we look at it as a cause or a consequence, the more civilized always have the most artificial governments. For instance, the inhabitants of Otaheite,[1] who, when first discovered, were governed by hereditary kings, had arrived at a far higher grade than another branch of the same people, the New Zealanders—who, although benefited by being compelled to turn their attention to agriculture, were republicans in the most absolute sense. In Tierra del Fuego, until some chief shall arise with power sufficient to secure any acquired advantage, such as the domesticated animals, it seems scarcely possible that the political state of the country can be improved. At present, even a piece of cloth given to one is torn into shreds and distributed; and no one individual becomes richer than another. On the other hand, it is difficult to understand how a chief can arise till there is property of some sort by which he might manifest his superiority and increase his power.

I believe, in this extreme part of South America, man exists in a lower state of improvement than in any other part of the world. The South Sea islanders of the two races inhabiting the Pacific, are comparatively civilized. The Esquimaux,[2] in his subterranean hut, enjoys some of the comforts of life, and in his canoe, when fully equipped, manifests much skill. Some of the tribes of southern Africa, prowling about in search of roots, and living concealed on the wild and arid plains, are sufficiently wretched. The Australian, in the simplicity of the arts of life, comes nearest the Fuegian: he can, however, boast of his boomerang, his spear and throwing-stick, his method of climbing trees, of tracking animals, and of hunting. Although the Australian may be superior in acquirements, it by no means follows that he is likewise superior in mental capacity: indeed, from what I saw of the Fuegians when on board, and from what I have read of the Australians, I should think the case was exactly the reverse.

from CHAPTER 17: GALAPAGOS ARCHIPELAGO[3]

… The natural history of these islands is eminently curious, and well deserves attention. Most of the organic productions are aboriginal[4] creations, found nowhere else; there is even a difference between the inhabitants of the different islands; yet all show a marked relationship with those of America, though separated from that continent by an open space of ocean, between 500 and 600 miles in width. The archipelago is a little world within itself, or rather a satellite attached to America, whence it has derived a few stray colonists, and has received the general character of its indigenous productions. Considering the small size of these islands, we feel the more astonished at the number of their aboriginal beings, and at their confined range. Seeing every height crowned with its crater, and the boundaries of most of the lava-streams still distinct, we are led to believe that within a period, geologically recent, the unbroken ocean

[1] *Otaheite* Tahiti.

[2] *Esquimaux* Inuk, or Inuit person.

[3] *GALAPAGOS ARCHIPELAGO* Series of islands off the coast of Ecuador, named after the Spanish word for tortoise.

[4] *aboriginal* Local.

was here spread out. Hence, both in space and time, we seem to be brought somewhat near to that great fact—that mystery of mysteries—the first appearance of new beings on this earth. …

The tortoises, when purposely moving towards any point, travel by night and day, and arrive at their journey's end much sooner than would be expected. The inhabitants, from observing marked individuals, consider that they travel a distance of about eight miles in two or three days. One large tortoise, which I watched, walked at the rate of sixty yards in ten minutes, that is 360 yards in the hour, or four miles a day—allowing a little time for it to eat on the road. During the breeding season, when the male and female are together, the male utters a hoarse roar or bellowing, which, it is said, can be heard at the distance of more than a hundred yards. The female never uses her voice, and the male only at these times; so that when the people hear this noise, they know that the two are together. They were at this time (October) laying their eggs. The female, where the soil is sandy, deposits them together, and covers them up with sand; but where the ground is rocky she drops them indiscriminately in any hole: Mr. Bynoe found seven placed in a fissure. The egg is white and spherical; one which I measured was seven inches and three-eighths in circumference, and therefore larger than a hen's egg. The young tortoises, as soon as they are hatched, fall a prey in great numbers to the carrion-feeding buzzard. The old ones seem generally to die from accidents, as from falling down precipices: at least, several of the inhabitants told me, that they had never found one dead without some evident cause. The inhabitants believe that these animals are absolutely deaf; certainly they do not overhear a person walking close behind them. I was always amused when overtaking one of these great monsters, as it was quietly pacing along, to see how suddenly, the instant I passed, it would draw in its head and legs, and uttering a deep hiss fall to the ground with a heavy sound, as if struck dead. I frequently got on their backs, and then giving a few

raps on the hinder part of their shells, they would rise up and walk away—but I found it very difficult to keep my balance. The flesh of this animal is largely employed, both fresh and salted; and a beautifully clear oil is prepared from the fat. When a tortoise is caught, the man makes a slit in the skin near its tail, so as to see inside its body, whether the fat under the dorsal plate is thick. If it is not, the animal is liberated; and it is said to recover soon from this strange operation. In order to secure the tortoises, it is not sufficient to turn them like turtle,[1] for they are often able to get on their legs again.

There can be little doubt that this tortoise is an aboriginal inhabitant of the Galapagos; for it is found on all, or nearly all, the islands, even on some of the smaller ones where there is no water; had it been an imported species, this would hardly have been the case in a group which has been so little frequented. …

… [T]his archipelago, though standing in the Pacific Ocean, is zoologically part of America.

If this character were owing merely to immigrants from America, there would be little remarkable in it; but we see that a vast majority of all the land animals, and that more than half of the flowering plants, are aboriginal productions. It was most striking to be surrounded by new birds, new reptiles, new shells, new insects, new plants, and yet by innumerable trifling details of structure, and even by the tones of voice and plumage of the birds, to have the temperate plains of Patagonia, or the hot dry deserts of northern Chile, vividly brought before my eyes. Why, on these small points of land, which within a late geological period must have been covered by the ocean, which are formed of basaltic lava, and therefore differ in geological character from the American continent, and which are placed under a peculiar climate—why were their aboriginal inhabitants, associated, I may add, in different proportions both in kind and number from those on the continent, and therefore acting on each other in a different manner—why were

---

[1] *turn them like turtle* Here, turn them onto their backs.

they created on American types of organization? It is probable that the islands of the Cape de Verd[1] group resemble, in all their physical conditions, far more closely the Galapagos Islands than these latter physically resemble the coast of America; yet the aboriginal inhabitants of the two groups are totally unlike; those of the Cape de Verd Islands bearing the impress of Africa, as the inhabitants of the Galapagos Archipelago are stamped with that of America.

I have not as yet noticed by far the most remarkable feature in the natural history of this archipelago; it is, that the different islands to a considerable extent are inhabited by a different set of beings. My attention was first called to this fact by the Vice-Governor, Mr. Lawson, declaring that the tortoises differed from the different islands, and that he could with certainty tell from which island any one was brought. I did not for some time pay sufficient attention to this statement, and I had already partially mingled together the collections from two of the islands. I never dreamed that islands, about fifty or sixty miles apart, and most of them in sight of each other, formed of precisely the same rocks, placed under a quite similar climate, rising to a nearly equal height, would have been differently tenanted; but we shall soon see that this is the case. It is the fate of most voyagers, no sooner to discover what is most interesting in any locality, than they are hurried from it; but I ought, perhaps, to be thankful that I obtained sufficient material to establish this most remarkable fact in the distribution of organic beings.

The inhabitants, as I have said, state that they can distinguish the tortoises from the different islands; and that they differ not only in size, but in other characters. Captain Porter[2] has described those from Charles and from the nearest island to it, namely, Hood Island, as having their shells in front thick and turned up like a Spanish saddle, whilst the tortoises from James Island are rounder, blacker, and have a better taste when cooked. M. Bibron,[3] moreover, informs me that he has seen what he considers two distinct species of tortoise from the Galapagos, but he does not know from which islands. The specimens that I brought from three islands were young ones; and probably owing to this cause, neither Mr. Gray[4] nor myself could find in them any specific differences. I have remarked that the marine Amblyrhynchus[5] was larger at Albemarle Island than elsewhere; and M. Bibron informs me that he has seen two distinct aquatic species of this genus; so that the different islands probably have their representative species or races of the Amblyrhynchus, as well as of the tortoise.

—1839

[1] *Cape de Verd* Cape Verde, a group of islands off the northwest coast of Africa, due west of Senegal.

[2] *Captain Porter* David Porter (1780–1843), captain of the *Essex*, who recorded his travels in *Journal of a Cruise* (1812).

[3] *M. Bibron* (Monsieur) Gabriel Bibron (1806–48), French zoologist.

[4] *Mr. Gray* Asa Gray (1810–88), a Harvard botanist and one of Darwin's strongest supporters.

[5] *marine Amblyrhynchus* Galapagos marine iguana (*Amblyrhynchus cristatus*).

IN CONTEXT

Images from *The Beagle*

There are extensive visual records of Darwin's voyages—perhaps most notably, the watercolor drawings of Conrad Martens, who was for nine months official artist on the *Beagle*. Several of these drawings were widely circulated in Victorian times in the form of engravings by Thomas Landseer that were based on original sketches by Martens and others sailing with Darwin.

George Richmond, *Charles Darwin*, 1840.

Conrad Martens, *Fuegian of the Yapoo Tekeenica Tribe*, 1832.

Conrad Martens, *H.M.S. Beagle*, Tierra del Fuego, c. 1832.

Conrad Martens, *Charles Island, Galapagos*, 1835.

from *On the Origin of Species*

INTRODUCTION

When on board H.M.S. "Beagle," as naturalist,[1] I was much struck with certain facts in the distribution of the inhabitants of South America, and in the geological relations of the present to the past inhabitants of that continent. These facts seemed to me to throw some light on the origin of species—that mystery of mysteries, as it has been called by one of our greatest philosophers. On my return home, it occurred to me, in 1837, that something might perhaps be made out on this question by patiently accumulating and reflecting on all sorts of facts which could possibly have any bearing on it. After five years' work I allowed myself to speculate on the subject, and drew up some short notes; these I enlarged in 1844 into a sketch of the conclusions, which then seemed to me probable: from that period to the present day I have steadily pursued the same object. I hope that I may be excused for entering on these personal details, as I give them to show that I have not been hasty in coming to a decision.

My work is now nearly finished; but as it will take me two or three more years to complete it, and as my health is far from strong, I have been urged to publish this abstract. I have more especially been induced to do this, as Mr. Wallace,[2] who is now studying the natural history of the Malay archipelago, has arrived at almost exactly the same general conclusions that I have on the origin of species. Last year he sent to me a memoir on this subject, with a request that I would forward it to Sir Charles Lyell,[3] who sent it to the Linnean Society,[4] and it is published in the third volume of the Journal of that Society. Sir C. Lyell and Dr. Hooker,[5] who both knew of my work—the latter having read my sketch of 1844—honoured me by thinking it advisable to publish, with Mr. Wallace's excellent memoir, some brief extracts from my manuscripts.

This abstract, which I now publish, must necessarily be imperfect. I cannot here give references and authorities for my several statements; and I must trust to the reader reposing some confidence in my accuracy. No doubt errors will have crept in, though I hope I have always been cautious in trusting to good authorities alone. I can here give only the general conclusions at which I have arrived, with a few facts in illustration, but which, I hope, in most cases will suffice. No one can feel more sensible than I do of the necessity of hereafter publishing in detail all the facts, with references, on which my conclusions have been grounded; and I hope in a future work to do this. For I am well aware that scarcely a single point is discussed in this volume on which facts cannot be adduced,[6] often apparently leading to conclusions directly opposite to those at which I have arrived. A fair result can be obtained only by fully stating and balancing the facts and arguments on both sides of each question; and this cannot possibly be here done.

I much regret that want of space prevents my having the satisfaction of acknowledging the generous assistance which I have received from very many naturalists, some of them personally unknown to me. I cannot, however, let this opportunity pass without expressing my deep obligations to Dr. Hooker, who for the last fifteen years has aided me in every possible way by his large stores of knowledge and his excellent judgment.

In considering the origin of species, it is quite conceivable that a naturalist, reflecting on the mutual affinities of organic beings, on their embryological relations, their geographical distribution, geological succession, and other such facts, might come to the conclusion that each species had not been independently created, but had descended, like varieties, from other species. Nevertheless, such a conclusion, even if well founded, would be unsatisfactory, until it could be

---

[1] *When on board ... naturalist* Darwin traveled on the *Beagle* between 1831 and 1836.

[2] *Mr. Wallace* Alfred Russel Wallace (1823–1913), English naturalist and social critic.

[3] *Sir Charles Lyell* British geologist (1797–1875).

[4] *Linnean Society* Prominent London scientific society.

[5] *Dr. Hooker* Joseph Dalton Hooker (1817–1911), botanist and friend of Darwin.

[6] *adduced* Brought forth.

shown how the innumerable species inhabiting this world have been modified, so as to acquire that perfection of structure and coadaptation which most justly excites our admiration. Naturalists continually refer to external conditions, such as climate, food, *et cetera*, as the only possible cause of variation. In one very limited sense, as we shall hereafter see, this may be true; but it is preposterous to attribute to mere external conditions, the structure, for instance, of the woodpecker, with its feet, tail, beak, and tongue, so admirably adapted to catch insects under the bark of trees. In the case of the mistletoe, which draws its nourishment from certain trees, which has seeds that must be transported by certain birds, and which has flowers with separate sexes absolutely requiring the agency of certain insects to bring pollen from one flower to the other, it is equally preposterous to account for the structure of this parasite, with its relations to several distinct organic beings, by the effects of external conditions, or of habit, or of the volition of the plant itself.

The author of the "Vestiges of Creation"[1] would, I presume, say that, after a certain unknown number of generations, some bird had given birth to a woodpecker, and some plant to the mistletoe, and that these had been produced perfect as we now see them; but this assumption seems to me to be no explanation, for it leaves the case of the coadaptations of organic beings to each other and to their physical conditions of life, untouched and unexplained.

It is, therefore, of the highest importance to gain a clear insight into the means of modification and coadaptation. At the commencement of my observations it seemed to me probable that a careful study of domesticated animals and of cultivated plants would offer the best chance of making out this obscure problem. Nor have I been disappointed; in this and in all other perplexing cases I have invariably found that our knowledge, imperfect though it be, of variation under domestication, afforded the best and safest clue. I may venture to express my conviction of the high value of such

studies, although they have been very commonly neglected by naturalists.

From these considerations, I shall devote the first chapter of this abstract to variation under domestication. We shall thus see that a large amount of hereditary modification is at least possible, and, what is equally or more important, we shall see how great is the power of man in accumulating by his selection successive slight variations. I will then pass on to the variability of species in a state of nature; but I shall, unfortunately, be compelled to treat this subject far too briefly, as it can be treated properly only by giving long catalogues of facts. We shall, however, be enabled to discuss what circumstances are most favourable to variation. In the next chapter the struggle for existence amongst all organic beings throughout the world, which inevitably follows from their high geometrical ratio of increase, will be treated of. This is the doctrine of Malthus,[2] applied to the whole animal and vegetable kingdoms. As many more individuals of each species are born than can possibly survive; and as, consequently, there is a frequently recurring struggle for existence, it follows that any being, if it vary however slightly in any manner profitable to itself, under the complex and sometimes varying conditions of life, will have a better chance of surviving, and thus be *naturally selected*. From the strong principle of inheritance, any selected variety will tend to propagate its new and modified form.

This fundamental subject of natural selection will be treated at some length in the fourth chapter; and we shall then see how natural selection almost inevitably causes much extinction of the less improved forms of life and induces what I have called divergence of character. In the next chapter I shall discuss the complex and little known laws of variation and of correlation of growth. In the four succeeding chapters, the most apparent and gravest difficulties on the theory will be given: namely, first, the difficulties of transitions, or in understanding how a simple being or a simple organ can be changed and perfected into a highly developed being or elabo-

---

[1] *Vestiges of Creation* 1844 book, published anonymously but written by Robert Chambers, which suggests that progressive evolution is God's act of creation through geological time.

[2] *Malthus* Thomas Robert Malthus (1766–1834), who theorized in his 1798 work *An Essay on the Principle of Population* that the human population would eventually outstrip its food resources.

rately constructed organ; secondly the subject of instinct, or the mental powers of animals, thirdly, hybridism, or the infertility of species and the fertility of varieties when intercrossed; and fourthly, the imperfection of the geological record. In the next chapter I shall consider the geological succession of organic beings throughout time; in the eleventh and twelfth, their geographical distribution throughout space; in the thirteenth, their classification or mutual affinities, both when mature and in an embryonic condition. In the last chapter I shall give a brief recapitulation of the whole work, and a few concluding remarks.

No one ought to feel surprise at much remaining as yet unexplained in regard to the origin of species and varieties, if he makes due allowance for our profound ignorance in regard to the mutual relations of all the beings which live around us. Who can explain why one species ranges widely and is very numerous, and why another allied species has a narrow range and is rare? Yet these relations are of the highest importance, for they determine the present welfare, and, as I believe, the future success and modification of every inhabitant of this world. Still less do we know of the mutual relations of the innumerable inhabitants of the world during the many past geological epochs in its history. Although much remains obscure, and will long remain obscure, I can entertain no doubt, after the most deliberate study and dispassionate judgment of which I am capable, that the view which most naturalists entertain, and which I formerly entertained—namely, that each species has been independently created—is erroneous. I am fully convinced that species are not immutable; but that those belonging to what are called the same genera[1] are lineal descendants of some other and generally extinct species, in the same manner as the acknowledged varieties of any one species are the descendants of that species. Furthermore, I am convinced that natural selection has been the main but not exclusive means of modification.

---

[1] *genera*   Latin: groupings of species. Plural of "genus."

from Chapter 3: Struggle for Existence

Before entering on the subject of this chapter, I must make a few preliminary remarks, to show how the struggle for existence bears on natural selection. It has been seen in the last chapter that amongst organic beings in a state of nature there is some individual variability; indeed I am not aware that this has ever been disputed. It is immaterial for us whether a multitude of doubtful forms be called species or sub-species or varieties; what rank, for instance, the two or three hundred doubtful forms of British plants are entitled to hold, if the existence of any well-marked varieties be admitted. But the mere existence of individual variability and of some few well-marked varieties, though necessary as the foundation for the work, helps us but little in understanding how species arise in nature. How have all those exquisite adaptations of one part of the organisation to another part, and to the conditions of life, and of one distinct organic being to another being, been perfected? We see these beautiful co-adaptations most plainly in the woodpecker and mistletoe; and only a little less plainly in the humblest parasite which clings to the hairs of a quadruped or feathers of a bird; in the structure of the beetle which dives through the water; in the plumed seed which is wafted by the gentlest breeze; in short, we see beautiful adaptations everywhere and in every part of the organic world.

Again, it may be asked, how is it that varieties, which I have called incipient species, become ultimately converted into good and distinct species, which in most cases obviously differ from each other far more than do the varieties of the same species? How do those groups of species, which constitute what are called distinct genera, and which differ from each other more than do the species of the same genus, arise? All these results, as we shall more fully see in the next chapter, follow inevitably from the struggle for life. Owing to this struggle for life, any variation, however slight and from whatever cause proceeding, if it be in any degree profitable to an individual of any species, in its infinitely complex relations to other organic beings and to external nature, will tend to the preservation of that individual, and will generally be inherited by its offspring. The offspring, also, will thus have a better chance of surviving, for, of the many individuals of any species which are periodically born, but a small number can survive. I have called this principle, by which each slight variation, if useful, is preserved, by the term of natural selection, in order to mark its relation to man's power of selection. We have seen that man by selection can certainly produce great results, and can adapt organic beings to his own uses, through the accumulation of slight but useful variations, given to him by the hand of nature. But natural selection, as we shall hereafter see, is a power incessantly ready for action, and is as immeasurably superior to man's feeble efforts, as the works of nature are to those of art.

We will now discuss in a little more detail the struggle for existence. In my future work this subject shall be treated, as it well deserves, at much greater length. The elder De Candolle[1] and Lyell have largely and philosophically shown that all organic beings are exposed to severe competition. In regard to plants, no one has treated this subject with more spirit and ability than W. Herbert,[2] Dean of Manchester, evidently the result of his great horticultural knowledge. Nothing is easier than to admit in words the truth of the universal struggle for life, or more difficult—at least I have found it so—than constantly to bear this conclusion in mind. Yet unless it be thoroughly engrained in the mind, I am convinced that the whole economy of nature, with every fact on distribution, rarity, abundance, extinction, and variation, will be dimly seen or quite misunderstood. We behold the face of nature bright with gladness, we often see superabundance of food; we do not see, or we forget, that the birds which are idly singing round us mostly live on insects or seeds, and are thus constantly destroying life; or we forget how largely these songsters, or their eggs, or their nestlings, are destroyed by birds and beasts of prey; we do not always bear in mind, that though food may be now superabundant, it is not so at all seasons of each recurring year.

[1] *The elder De Candolle* Augustin-Pyramus de Candolle (1778–1841), Swiss botanist.

[2] *W. Herbert* William Herbert (1778–1847).

I should premise that I use the term struggle for existence in a large and metaphorical sense, including dependence of one being on another, and including (which is more important) not only the life of the individual, but success in leaving progeny. Two canine animals in a time of dearth, may be truly said to struggle with each other which shall get food and live. But a plant on the edge of a desert is said to struggle for life against the drought, though more properly it should be said to be dependent on the moisture. A plant which annually produces a thousand seeds, of which on an average only one comes to maturity, may be more truly said to struggle with the plants of the same and other kinds which already clothe the ground. The mistletoe is dependent on the apple and a few other trees, but can only in a far-fetched sense be said to struggle with these trees, for if too many of these parasites grow on the same tree, it will languish and die. But several seedling mistletoes, growing close together on the same branch, may more truly be said to struggle with each other. As the mistletoe is disseminated by birds, its existence depends on birds; and it may metaphorically be said to struggle with other fruit-bearing plants, in order to tempt birds to devour and thus disseminate its seeds rather than those of other plants. In these several senses, which pass into each other, I use for convenience' sake the general term of struggle for existence.

A struggle for existence inevitably follows from the high rate at which all organic beings tend to increase. Every being, which during its natural lifetime produces several eggs or seeds, must suffer destruction during some period of its life, and during some season or occasional year, otherwise, on the principle of geometrical increase, its numbers would quickly become so inordinately great that no country could support the product. Hence, as more individuals are produced than can possibly survive, there must in every case be a struggle for existence, either one individual with another of the same species, or with the individuals of distinct species, or with the physical conditions of life. It is the doctrine of Malthus applied with manifold force to the whole animal and vegetable kingdoms; for in this case there can be no artificial increase of food, and no prudential restraint from marriage. Although some species may be now increasing, more or less rapidly, in numbers, all cannot do so, for the world would not hold them.

There is no exception to the rule that every organic being naturally increases at so high a rate, that if not destroyed, the earth would soon be covered by the progeny of a single pair. Even slow-breeding man has doubled in twenty-five years, and at this rate, in a few thousand years, there would literally not be standing room for his progeny. Linnaeus[1] has calculated that if an annual plant produced only two seeds—and there is no plant so unproductive as this—and their seedlings next year produced two, and so on, then in twenty years there would be a million plants. The elephant is reckoned to be the slowest breeder of all known animals, and I have taken some pains to estimate its probable minimum rate of natural increase: it will be under the mark to assume that it breeds when thirty years old, and goes on breeding till ninety years old, bringing forth three pair of young in this interval; if this be so, at the end of the fifth century there would be alive fifteen million elephants, descended from the first pair.

But we have better evidence on this subject than mere theoretical calculations, namely, the numerous recorded cases of the astonishingly rapid increase of various animals in a state of nature, when circumstances have been favourable to them during two or three following seasons. Still more striking is the evidence from our domestic animals of many kinds which have run wild in several parts of the world: if the statements of the rate of increase of slow-breeding cattle and horses in South America, and latterly in Australia, had not been well authenticated, they would have been quite incredible. So it is with plants: cases could be given of introduced plants which have become common throughout whole islands in a period of less than ten years. Several of the plants now most numerous over the wide plains of La Plata,[2] clothing square leagues of surface almost to the exclusion of all other plants, have been introduced from Europe;

and there are plants which now range in India, as I hear from Dr. Falconer,[3] from Cape Comorin[4] to the Himalaya, which have been imported from America since its discovery. In such cases, and endless instances could be given, no one supposes that the fertility of these animals or plants has been suddenly and temporarily increased in any sensible degree. The obvious explanation is that the conditions of life have been very favourable, and that there has consequently been less destruction of the old and young, and that nearly all the young have been enabled to breed. In such cases the geometrical ratio of increase, the result of which never fails to be surprising, simply explains the extraordinarily rapid increase and wide diffusion of naturalised[5] productions in their new homes. ...

Many cases are on record showing how complex and unexpected are the checks and relations between organic beings, which have to struggle together in the same country. I will give only a single instance, which, though a simple one, has interested me. In Staffordshire, on the estate of a relation where I had ample means of investigation, there was a large and extremely barren heath, which had never been touched by the hand of man; but several hundred acres of exactly the same nature had been enclosed twenty-five years previously and planted with Scotch fir. The change in the native vegetation of the planted part of the heath was most remarkable, more than is generally seen in passing from one quite different soil to another: not only the proportional numbers of the heath-plants were wholly changed, but twelve species of plants (not counting grasses and carices[6]) flourished in the plantations, which could not be found on the heath. The effect on the insects must have been still greater, for six insectivorous birds were very common in the plantations, which were not to be seen on the heath; and the heath was frequented by two or three distinct insectivorous birds. Here we see how potent has been the effect of the introduction of a single tree,

[1] *Linnaeus* Carolus Linnaeus (1707–78), Swedish scientist who laid the foundations of modern taxonomy.

[2] *La Plata* Region of Argentina.

[3] *Dr. Falconer* Hugh Falconer (1808–65), one of the pre-eminent British palaeontologists of the time.

[4] *Cape Comorin* Southernmost point of the Indian subcontinent.

[5] *naturalised* Recently introduced and acclimatized.

[6] *carices* Sedges.

nothing whatever else having been done, with the exception that the land had been enclosed, so that cattle could not enter. But how important an element enclosure is, I plainly saw near Farnham, in Surrey. Here there are extensive heaths, with a few clumps of old Scotch firs on the distant hill-tops: within the last ten years large spaces have been enclosed, and self-sown firs are now springing up in multitudes, so close together that all cannot live. When I ascertained that these young trees had not been sown or planted, I was so much surprised at their numbers that I went to several points of view, whence I could examine hundreds of acres of the unenclosed heath, and literally I could not see a single Scotch fir, except the old planted clumps. But on looking closely between the stems of the heath, I found a multitude of seedlings and little trees, which had been perpetually browsed down by the cattle. In one square yard, at a point some hundreds yards distant from one of the old clumps, I counted thirty-two little trees; and one of them, judging from the rings of growth, had during twenty-six years tried to raise its head above the stems of the heath, and had failed. No wonder that, as soon as the land was enclosed, it became thickly clothed with vigorously growing young firs. Yet the heath was so extremely barren and so extensive that no one would ever have imagined that cattle would have so closely and effectually searched it for food.

Here we see that cattle absolutely determine the existence of the Scotch fir; but in several parts of the world insects determine the existence of cattle. Perhaps Paraguay offers the most curious instance of this; for here neither cattle nor horses nor dogs have ever run wild, though they swarm southward and northward in a feral state; and Azara and Rengger[1] have shown that this is caused by the greater number in Paraguay of a certain fly, which lays its eggs in the navels of these animals when first born. The increase of these flies, numerous as they are, must be habitually checked by some means, probably by birds. Hence, if certain insectivorous birds (whose numbers are probably regulated by hawks or beasts of prey) were to increase in Paraguay, the flies would decrease—then cattle and horses would become feral, and this would certainly greatly alter (as indeed I have observed in parts of South America) the vegetation: this again would largely affect the insects; and this, as we just have seen in Staffordshire, the insectivorous birds, and so onwards in ever-increasing circles of complexity. We began this series by insectivorous birds, and we have ended with them. Not that in nature the relations can ever be as simple as this. Battle within battle must ever be recurring with varying success; and yet in the long-run the forces are so nicely balanced, that the face of nature remains uniform for long periods of time, though assuredly the merest trifle would often give the victory to one organic being over another. Nevertheless so profound is our ignorance, and so high our presumption, that we marvel when we hear of the extinction of an organic being; and as we do not see the cause, we invoke cataclysms to desolate the world, or invent laws on the duration of the forms of life!

I am tempted to give one more instance showing how plants and animals, most remote in the scale of nature, are bound together by a web of complex relations. I shall hereafter have occasion to show that the exotic *Lobelia fulgens*,[2] in this part of England, is never visited by insects, and consequently, from its peculiar structure, never can set a seed. Many of our orchidaceous plants absolutely require the visits of moths to remove their pollen-masses and thus to fertilise them. I have, also, reason to believe that humble-bees[3] are indispensable to the fertilisation of the heartsease (*Viola tricolor*), for other bees do not visit this flower. From experiments which I have tried, I have found that the visits of bees, if not indispensable, are at least highly beneficial to the fertilisation of our clovers; but humble-bees alone visit the common red clover (*Trifolium pratense*), as other bees cannot reach the nectar. Hence I have very little doubt, that if the whole genus of humble-bees became extinct or very rare in England, the

---

[1] *Azara and Rengger*   Félix de Azara (1746–1821), Spanish explorer and naturalist, and Johann Rudolph Rengger (1795–1832), German naturalist. In the early part of the nineteenth century, both published influential studies on Paraguayan fauna.

[2] *Lobelia fulgens*   Queen Victoria Cardinal flower.

[3] *humble-bees*   Bumblebees.

heartsease and red clover would become very rare, or wholly disappear. The number of humble-bees in any district depends in a great degree on the number of field-mice, which destroy their combs and nests; and Mr. H. Newman,[1] who has long attended to the habits of humble-bees, believes that "more than two thirds of them are thus destroyed all over England." Now the number of mice is largely dependent, as every one knows, on the number of cats; and Mr. Newman says, "Near villages and small towns I have found the nests of humble-bees more numerous than elsewhere, which I attribute to the number of cats that destroy the mice." Hence it is quite credible that the presence of a feline animal in large numbers in a district might determine, through the intervention first of mice and then of bees, the frequency of certain flowers in that district!

from CHAPTER 14: RECAPITULATION AND CONCLUSION

… I have now recapitulated the chief facts and considerations which have thoroughly convinced me that species have changed, and are still slowly changing by the preservation and accumulation of successive slight favourable variations. Why, it may be asked, have all the most eminent living naturalists and geologists rejected this view of the mutability of species? It cannot be asserted that organic beings in a state of nature are subject to no variation; it cannot be proved that the amount of variation in the course of long ages is a limited quantity; no clear distinction has been, or can be, drawn between species and well-marked varieties. It cannot be maintained that species when intercrossed are invariably sterile, and varieties invariably fertile; or that sterility is a special endowment and sign of creation. The belief that species were immutable productions was almost unavoidable as long as the history of the world was thought to be of short duration; and now that we have acquired some idea of the lapse of time, we are too apt to assume, without proof, that the geological record is so perfect that it would have afforded us plain evidence of the mutation of species, if they had undergone mutation.

But the chief cause of our natural unwillingness to admit that one species has given birth to other and distinct species, is that we are always slow in admitting any great change of which we do not see the intermediate steps. The difficulty is the same as that felt by so many geologists, when Lyell first insisted that long lines of inland cliffs had been formed, and great valleys excavated, by the slow action of the coast-waves. The mind cannot possibly grasp the full meaning of the term of a hundred million years; it cannot add up and perceive the full effects of many slight variations, accumulated during an almost infinite number of generations.

Although I am fully convinced of the truth of the views given in this volume under the form of an abstract, I by no means expect to convince experienced naturalists whose minds are stocked with a multitude of facts all viewed, during a long course of years, from a point of view directly opposite to mine. It is so easy to hide our ignorance under such expressions as the "plan of creation," "unity of design,"[2] et cetera, and to think that we give an explanation when we only restate a fact. Any one whose disposition leads him to attach more weight to unexplained difficulties than to the explanation of a certain number of facts will certainly reject my theory. A few naturalists, endowed with much flexibility of mind, and who have already begun to doubt on the immutability of species, may be influenced by this volume; but I look with confidence to the future, to young and rising naturalists, who will be able to view both sides of the question with impartiality. Whoever is led to believe that species are mutable will do good service by conscientiously expressing his conviction; for only thus can the load of prejudice by which this subject is overwhelmed be removed. …

When the views entertained in this volume on the origin of species, or when analogous views are generally admitted, we can dimly foresee that there will be a considerable revolution in natural history. Systematists will be able to pursue their labours as at present; but

----

[1] *Mr. H. Newman*   Unidentified.

[2] *plan of creation*   Phrase implying that God created the universe and has a plan for its unfolding; *unity of design*   Phrase suggesting that it is possible to deduce from evidence found in nature that it is the product of a single creator's purpose or design.

they will not be incessantly haunted by the shadowy doubt whether this or that form be in essence a species. This I feel sure, and I speak after experience, will be no slight relief. The endless disputes whether or not some fifty species of British brambles are true species will cease. Systematists will have only to decide (not that this will be easy) whether any form be sufficiently constant and distinct from other forms, to be capable of definition; and if definable, whether the differences be sufficiently important to deserve a specific name. This latter point will become a far more essential consideration than it is at present; for differences, however slight, between any two forms, if not blended by intermediate gradations, are looked at by most naturalists as sufficient to raise both forms to the rank of species. Hereafter we shall be compelled to acknowledge that the only distinction between species and well-marked varieties is, that the latter are known, or believed, to be connected at the present day by intermediate gradations, whereas species were formerly thus connected. Hence, without quite rejecting the consideration of the present existence of intermediate gradations between any two forms, we shall be led to weigh more carefully and to value higher the actual amount of difference between them. It is quite possible that forms now generally acknowledged to be merely varieties may hereafter be thought worthy of specific names, as with the primrose and cowslip;[1] and in this case scientific and common language will come into accordance. In short, we shall have to treat species in the same manner as those naturalists treat genera, who admit that genera are merely artificial combinations made for convenience. This may not be a cheering prospect; but we shall at least be freed from the vain search for the undiscovered and undiscoverable essence of the term species.

The other and more general departments of natural history will rise greatly in interest. The terms used by naturalists of affinity, relationship, community of type, paternity, morphology, adaptive characters, rudimentary and aborted organs, *et cetera*, will cease to be metaphorical, and will have a plain signification. When we no longer look at an organic being as a savage looks at a ship, as at something wholly beyond his comprehension; when we regard every production of nature as one which has had a history; when we contemplate every complex structure and instinct as the summing up of many contrivances, each useful to the possessor, nearly in the same way as when we look at any great mechanical invention as the summing up of the labour, the experience, the reason, and even the blunders of numerous workmen; when we thus view each organic being, how far more interesting, I speak from experience, will the study of natural history become!

A grand and almost untrodden field of inquiry will be opened, on the causes and laws of variation, on correlation of growth, on the effects of use and disuse, on the direct action of external conditions, and so forth. The study of domestic productions will rise immensely in value. A new variety raised by man will be a far more important and interesting subject for study than one more species added to the infinitude of already recorded species. Our classifications will come to be, as far as they can be so made, genealogies; and will then truly give what may be called the plan of creation. The rules for classifying will no doubt become simpler when we have a definite object in view. We possess no pedigrees or armorial bearings;[2] and we have to discover and trace the many diverging lines of descent in our natural genealogies, by characters of any kind which have long been inherited. Rudimentary organs will speak infallibly with respect to the nature of long-lost structures. Species and groups of species, which are called aberrant, and which may fancifully be called living fossils, will aid us in forming a picture of the ancient forms of life. Embryology will reveal to us the structure, in some degree obscured, of the prototypes of each great class.

When we can feel assured that all the individuals of the same species, and all the closely allied species of most genera, have within a not very remote period descended from one parent, and have migrated from some one birthplace; and when we better know the many means of migration, then, by the light which geology now throws,

---

[1] *primrose and cowslip* Flowers common in England.

[2] *armorial bearings* Coats of arms.

and will continue to throw, on former changes of climate and of the level of the land, we shall surely be enabled to trace in an admirable manner the former migrations of the inhabitants of the whole world. Even at present, by comparing the differences of the inhabitants of the sea on the opposite sides of a continent, and the nature of the various inhabitants of that continent in relation to their apparent means of immigration, some light can be thrown on ancient geography.

The noble science of geology loses glory from the extreme imperfection of the record. The crust of the earth with its embedded remains must not be looked at as a well-filled museum, but as a poor collection made at hazard and at rare intervals. The accumulation of each great fossiliferous formation will be recognised as having depended on an unusual concurrence of circumstances, and the blank intervals between the successive stages as having been of vast duration. But we shall be able to gauge with some security the duration of these intervals by a comparison of the preceding and succeeding organic forms. We must be cautious in attempting to correlate as strictly contemporaneous two formations, which include few identical species, by the general succession of their forms of life. As species are produced and exterminated by slowly acting and still existing causes, and not by miraculous acts of creation and by catastrophes; and as the most important of all causes of organic change is one which is almost independent of altered and perhaps suddenly altered physical conditions, namely, the mutual relation of organism to organism—the improvement of one being entailing the improvement or the extermination of others; it follows, that the amount of organic change in the fossils of consecutive formations probably serves as a fair measure of the lapse of actual time. A number of species, however, keeping in a body might remain for a long period unchanged, whilst within this same period, several of these species, by migrating into new countries and coming into competition with foreign associates, might become modified; so that we must not overrate the accuracy of organic change as a measure of time. During early periods of the earth's history, when the forms of life were probably fewer and simpler, the rate of change

was probably slower; and at the first dawn of life, when very few forms of the simplest structure existed, the rate of change may have been slow in an extreme degree. The whole history of the world, as at present known, although of a length quite incomprehensible by us, will hereafter be recognised as a mere fragment of time, compared with the ages which have elapsed since the first creature, the progenitor of innumerable extinct and living descendants, was created.

In the distant future I see open fields for far more important researches. Psychology will be based on a new foundation, that of the necessary acquirement of each mental power and capacity by gradation. Light will be thrown on the origin of man and his history.

Authors of the highest eminence seem to be fully satisfied with the view that each species has been independently created. To my mind it accords better with what we know of the laws impressed on matter by the Creator, that the production and extinction of the past and present inhabitants of the world should have been due to secondary causes, like those determining the birth and death of the individual. When I view all beings not as special creations, but as the lineal descendants of some few beings which lived long before the first bed of the Silurian[1] system was deposited, they seem to me to become ennobled. Judging from the past, we may safely infer that not one living species will transmit its unaltered likeness to a distant futurity. And of the species now living very few will transmit progeny of any kind to a far distant futurity; for the manner in which all organic beings are grouped, shows that the greater number of species of each genus, and all the species of many genera, have left no descendants, but have become utterly extinct. We can so far take a prophetic glance into futurity as to foretell that it will be the common and widely-spread species, belonging to the larger and dominant groups, which will ultimately prevail and procreate new and dominant species. As all the living forms of life are the lineal descendants of those which lived long before the Silurian epoch, we may feel certain that the ordinary succession by genera-

---

[1] *Silurian* Geological time period approximately 440 million to 410 million years ago.

tion has never once been broken, and that no cataclysm has desolated the whole world. Hence we may look with some confidence to a secure future of equally inappreciable length. And as natural selection works solely by and for the good of each being, all corporeal and mental endowments will tend to progress towards perfection.

It is interesting to contemplate an entangled bank, clothed with many plants of many kinds, with birds singing on the bushes, with various insects flitting about, and with worms crawling through the damp earth, and to reflect that these elaborately constructed forms, so different from each other, and dependent on each other in so complex a manner, have all been produced by laws acting around us. These laws, taken in the largest sense, being growth with reproduction; inheritance which is almost implied by reproduction; variability from the indirect and direct action of the external conditions of life, and from use and disuse; a ratio of increase so high as to lead to a struggle for life, and as a consequence to natural selection, entailing divergence of character and the extinction of less-improved forms. Thus, from the war of nature, from famine and death, the most exalted object which we are capable of conceiving, namely, the production of the higher animals, directly follows. There is grandeur in this view of life, with its several powers, having been originally breathed into a few forms or into one; and that, whilst this planet has gone cycling on according to the fixed law of gravity, from so simple a beginning endless forms most beautiful and most wonderful have been, and are being, evolved.
—1859

from *The Descent of Man*

from CHAPTER 19
SECONDARY SEXUAL CHARACTERS OF MAN

With mankind the differences between the sexes are greater than in most species of Quadrumana, but not so great as in some, for instance, the mandrill.[1] Man on an average is considerably taller, heavier, and stronger than woman, with squarer shoulders and more plainly-pronounced muscles. Owing to the relation which exists between muscular development and the projection of the brows, the superciliary ridge[2] is generally more strongly marked in man than in woman. His body, and especially his face, is more hairy, and his voice has a different and more powerful tone. In certain tribes the women are said, whether truly I know not, to differ slightly in tint from the men; and with Europeans, the women are perhaps the more brightly coloured of the two, as may be seen when both sexes have been equally exposed to the weather.

Man is more courageous, pugnacious and energetic than woman, and has a more inventive genius. His brain is absolutely[3] larger, but whether relatively to the larger size of his body, in comparison with woman, has not, I believe, been fully ascertained. In woman the face is rounder; the jaws and the base of the skull smaller; the outlines of the body rounder, in parts more prominent; and her pelvis is broader than in man; but this latter character may perhaps be considered rather as a primary than a secondary sexual character. She comes to maturity at an earlier age than man.

As with animals of all classes, so with man, the distinctive characters of the male sex are not fully developed until he is nearly mature; and if emasculated[4] they never appear. The beard, for instance, is a secondary sexual character, and male children are beardless, though at an early age they have abundant hair on the head. It is probably due to the rather late appearance in life of the successive variations, by which man acquired his masculine characters, that they are transmitted to the

---

[1] *Quadrumana* Primates with, literally, "four hands," in that both the hind and forefeet have opposable thumbs. This category, now obsolete, included all primates other than human beings; *mandrill* Earlier, Darwin describes the adult male mandrill (close relative of the baboon) as possessing "extraordinary" bright coloration and facial protuberances that are "scarcely perceptible" in the female.

[2] *superciliary ridge* Ridge of bone above the eye sockets.

[3] *absolutely* In absolute, as opposed to relative, terms.

[4] *emasculated* Castrated.

male sex alone. Male and female children resemble each other closely, like the young of so many other animals in which the adult sexes differ; they likewise resemble the mature female much more closely than the mature male. The female, however, ultimately assumes certain distinctive characters, and in the formation of her skull is said to be intermediate between the child and the man. ...

The half-human progenitors of man, and men in a savage state, have struggled together during many generations for the possession of the females. But mere bodily strength and size would do little for victory, unless associated with courage, perseverance, and determined energy. With social animals, the young males have to pass through many a contest before they win a female, and the older males have to retain their females by renewed battles. They have, also, in the case of mankind, to defend their females, as well as their young, from enemies of all kinds, and to hunt for their joint subsistence. But to avoid enemies or to attack them with success, to capture wild animals, and to invent and fashion weapons, requires the aid of the higher mental faculties, namely, observation, reason, invention, or imagination. These various faculties will thus have been continually put to the test and selected during manhood; they will, moreover, have been strengthened by use during this same period of life. Consequently, in accordance with the principle often alluded to,[1] we might expect that they would at least tend to be transmitted chiefly to the male offspring at the corresponding period of manhood.

Now, when two men are put into competition, or a man with a woman, who possess every mental quality with the same perfection, with the exception that the one has the higher energy, perseverance, and courage, this one will generally become more eminent, whatever the object may be, and will gain victory. He may be said to possess genius—for genius has been declared by a great authority to be patience;[2] and patience, in this sense, mean unflinching, undaunted perseverance. But this view of genius is perhaps deficient; for without the higher powers of the imagination and reason, no eminent success in many subjects can be gained. But these latter as well as the former faculties will have developed in man, partly through sexual selection—that is, through the contest of rival males, and partly through natural selection—that is, from success in the general struggle for life; and as in both cases the struggle will have been during maturity, the characters thus gained will have been transmitted more fully to the male than to the female offspring. Thus man has ultimately become superior to woman. It is, indeed, fortunate that the law of the equal transmission of characters to both sexes has commonly prevailed throughout the whole class of mammals; otherwise, it is probable that man would have become as superior in mental endowment to woman, as the peacock is in ornamental plumage to the peahen. ...

from CHAPTER 21
GENERAL SUMMARY AND CONCLUSION

A brief summary will be sufficient to recall to the reader's mind the more salient points in this work. Many of the views which have been advanced are highly speculative, and some no doubt will prove erroneous; but I have in every case given the reasons which have led me to one view rather than to another. It seemed worthwhile to try how far the principle of evolution would throw light on some of the more complex problems in the natural history of man. False facts are highly injurious to the progress of science, for they often endure long; but false views, if supported by some evidence, do little harm, for every one takes a salutary pleasure in proving their falseness: and when this is done, one path towards error is closed and the road to truth is often at the same time opened.

[1] *the principle often alluded to* I.e., the principle that characteristics appearing in one sex after maturity will more likely be transmitted to that sex alone.

[2] *genius has ... patience* The proverbial statement "genius is eternal patience" is often attributed to the Italian sculptor Michelangelo (1475–1564).

The main conclusion here arrived at, and now held by many naturalists who are well competent to form a sound judgment is that man is descended from some less highly organised form. The grounds upon which this conclusion rests will never be shaken, for the close similarity between man and the lower animals in embryonic development, as well as in innumerable points of structure and constitution both of high and of the most trifling importance—the rudiments which he retains, and the abnormal reversions to which he is occasionally liable—are facts which cannot be disputed. They have long been known, but until recently they told us nothing with respect to the origin of man. Now when viewed by the light of our knowledge of the whole organic world, their meaning is unmistakable. The great principle of evolution stands up clear and firm, when these groups or facts are considered in connection with others, such as the mutual affinities of the members of the same group, their geographical distribution in past and present times, and their geological succession. It is incredible that all these facts should speak falsely. He who is not content to look, like a savage, at the phenomena of nature as disconnected, cannot any longer believe that man is the work of a separate act of creation. He will be forced to admit that the close resemblance of the embryo of man to that, for instance, of a dog—the construction of his skull, limbs and whole frame on the same plan with that of other mammals, independently of the uses to which the parts may be put—the occasional re-appearance of various structures, for instance of several muscles, which man does not normally possess, but which are common to the Quadrumana—and a crowd of analogous facts—all point in the plainest manner to the conclusion that man is the co-descendant with other mammals of a common progenitor.

We have seen that man incessantly presents individual differences in all parts of his body and in his mental faculties. These differences or variations seem to be induced by the same general causes, and to obey the same laws as with the lower animals. In both cases similar laws of inheritance prevail. Man tends to increase at a greater rate than his means of subsistence; consequently he is occasionally subjected to a severe struggle for existence, and natural selection will have effected whatever lies within its scope. A succession of strongly-marked variations of a similar nature is by no means requisite; slight fluctuating differences in the individual suffice for the work of natural selection; not that we have any reason to suppose that in the same species, all parts of the organization tend to vary to the same degree. We may feel assured that the inherited effects of the long-continued use or disuse of parts will have done much in the same direction with natural selection. Modifications formerly of importance, though no longer of any special use, are long-inherited. When one part is modified, other parts change through the principle of correlation, of which we have instances in many curious cases of correlated monstrosities.[1] Something may be attributed to the direct and definite action of the surrounding conditions of life, such as abundant food, heat or moisture; and lastly, many characters of slight physiological importance, some indeed of considerable importance, have been gained through sexual selection.

No doubt man, as well as every other animal, presents structures, which seem to our limited knowledge, not to be now of any service to him, nor to have been so formerly, either for the general conditions of life, or in the relations of one sex to the other. Such structures cannot be accounted for by any form of selection, or by the inherited effects of the use and disuse of parts. We know, however, that many strange and strongly-marked peculiarities of structure occasionally appear in our domesticated productions, and if their unknown causes were to act more uniformly, they would probably become common to all the individuals of the species. We may hope hereafter to understand something about the causes of such occasional modifications, especially through the study of monstrosities: hence the labours of experimentalists such as those of M. Camille Dareste,[2] are full of promise for the future. In general we can only say that the cause of each slight

---

[1] *monstrosities* Physical anomalies.

[2] *M. Camille Dareste* (Monsieur) Camille Dareste, French zoologist (1822–99), founder of experimental teratology, the study of abnormalities in plants and animals.

variation and of each monstrosity lies much more in the constitution of the organism, than in the nature of the surrounding conditions; though new and changed conditions certainly play an important part in exciting organic changes of many kinds. Through the means just specified, aided perhaps by others as yet undiscovered, man has been raised to his present state. But since he attained to the rank of manhood, he has diverged into distinct races, or as they may be more fitly called sub-species. Some of these, such as the Negro and European, are so distinct that, if specimens had been brought to a naturalist without any further information, they would undoubtedly have been considered by him as good and true species. Nevertheless all the races agree in so many unimportant details of structure and in so many mental peculiarities that these can be accounted for only by inheritance from a common progenitor; and a progenitor thus characterised would probably deserve to rank as man.

It must not be supposed that the divergence of each race from the other races, and of all from a common stock, can be traced back to any one pair of progenitors. On the contrary, at every stage in the process of modification, all the individuals which were in any way better fitted for their conditions of life, though in different degrees, would have survived in greater numbers than the less well-fitted. The process would have been like that followed by man, when he does not intentionally select particular individuals, but breeds from all the superior individuals, and neglects the inferior. He thus slowly but surely modifies his stock, and unconsciously forms a new strain. So with respect to modifications acquired independently of selection, and due to variations arising from the nature of the organism and the action of the surrounding conditions, or from changed habits of life, no single pair will have been modified much more than the other pairs inhabiting the same country, for all will have been continually blended through free intercrossing.

By considering the embryological structure of man—the homologies[1] which he presents with the lower animals—the rudiments which he retains—and the reversions to which he is liable, we can partly recall in imagination the former condition of our early progenitors; and can approximately place them in their proper place in the zoological series. We thus learn that man is descended from a hairy, tailed quadruped, probably arboreal in its habits, and an inhabitant of the Old World. This creature, if its whole structure had been examined by a naturalist, would have been classed amongst the Quadrumana, as surely as the still more ancient progenitor of the Old and New World monkeys. The Quadrumana and all the higher mammals are probably derived from an ancient marsupial animal, and this through a long series of diversified forms, from some amphibian-like creature, and this again from some fish-like animal. In the dim obscurity of the past we can see that the early progenitor of all the Vertebrata must have been an aquatic animal provided with branchiae,[2] with the two sexes united in the same individual, and with the most important organs of the body (such as the brain and heart) imperfectly or not at all developed. This animal seems to have been more like the larvae of the existing marine Ascidians[3] than any other known form. …

The belief in God has often been advanced as not only the greatest, but the most complete of all the distinctions between man and the lower animals. It is however impossible, as we have seen, to maintain that this belief is innate or instinctive in man. On the other hand a belief in all-pervading spiritual agencies seems to be universal; and apparently follows from a considerable advance in man's reason, and from a still greater advance in his faculties of imagination, curiosity and wonder. I am aware that the assumed instinctive belief in God has been used by many persons as an argument for His existence. But this is a rash argument, as we should thus be compelled to believe in the existence of many cruel and malignant spirits, only a little more powerful than man; for the belief in them is far more general than in a beneficent Deity. The idea of a univer-

---

[1] *homologies* Similarities of structure due to common descent.

[2] *Vertebrata* Vertebrates, animals having a spinal column; *branchiae* Breathing apparatus, gills.

[3] *Ascidians* Molluscs.

sal and beneficent Creator does not seem to arise in the mind of man, until he has been elevated by long-continued culture.

He who believes in the advancement of man from some low organised form, will naturally ask how does this bear on the belief in the immortality of the soul. The barbarous races of man, as Sir J. Lubbock[1] has shown, possess no clear belief of this kind; but arguments derived from the primeval beliefs of savages are, as we have just seen, of little or no avail. Few persons feel any anxiety from the impossibility of determining at what precise period in the development of the individual, from the first trace of a minute germinal vesicle,[2] man becomes an immortal being; and there is no greater cause for anxiety because the period cannot possibly be determined in the gradually ascending organic scale.

I am aware that the conclusions arrived at in this work will be denounced by some as highly irreligious; but he who denounces them is bound to show why it is more irreligious to explain the origin of man as a distinct species by descent from some lower form, through the laws of variation and natural selection, than to explain the birth of the individual through the laws of ordinary reproduction. The birth both of the species and of the individual are equally parts of that grand sequence of events, which our minds refuse to accept as the result of blind chance. The understanding revolts at such a conclusion, whether or not we are able to believe that every slight variation of structure—the union of each pair in marriage—the dissemination of each seed— and other such events, have all been ordained for some special purpose.

Sexual selection has been treated at great length in this work; for, as I have attempted to show, it has played an important part in the history of the organic world. I am aware that much remains doubtful, but I have endeavoured to give a fair view of the whole case. In the lower divisions of the animal kingdom, sexual selection seems to have done nothing: such animals are often affixed for life to the same spot, or have the sexes combined in the same individual, or what is still more important, their perceptive and intellectual faculties are not sufficiently advanced to allow of the feelings of love and jealousy, or of the exertion of choice. When, however, we come to the Arthropoda[3] and Vertebrata, even to the lowest classes in these two great sub-kingdoms, sexual selection has effected much.

In the several great classes of the animal kingdom— in mammals, birds, reptiles, fishes, insects, and even crustaceans—the differences between the sexes follow nearly the same rules. The males are almost always the wooers; and they alone are armed with special weapons for fighting with their rivals. They are generally stronger and larger than the females, and are endowed with the requisite qualities of courage and pugnacity. They are provided, either exclusively or in a much higher degree than the females, with organs for vocal or instrumental music, and with odoriferous glands. They are ornamental with infinitely diversified appendages, and with the most brilliant or conspicuous colours, often arranged in elegant patterns, whilst the females are unadorned. When the sexes differ in more important structures, it is the male which is provided with special sense-organs for discovering the female, with locomotive organs for reaching her, and often with prehensile organs for holding her. These various structures for charming or securing the female are often developed in the male during only part of the year, namely the breeding-season. They have in many cases been more or less transferred to the females; and in the latter case they often appear in her as mere rudiments. They are lost or never gained by the males after emasculation. Generally they are not developed in the male during early youth, but appear a short time before the age for reproduction. Hence in most cases the young of both sexes resemble each other; and the female somewhat resembles her young offspring throughout life. In almost every great class a few anomalous cases occur, where there has been an almost complete transposition of the characters proper to the two sexes; the females assuming characters which properly belong to the males. This surprising

---

[1] *Sir J. Lubbock* John Lubbock, Lord Avebury (1834–1913), in his book *Prehistoric Times* (1865).

[2] *germinal vesicle* Nucleus of animals' permanent ovum.

---

[3] *Arthropoda* Sub-kingdom which includes insects, spiders, crustaceans, etc.

uniformity in the laws regulating the differences between the sexes in so many and such widely separated classes, is intelligible if we admit the action of one common cause, namely sexual selection.

Sexual selection depends on the success of certain individuals over others of the same sex, in relation to the propagation of the species; whilst natural selection depends on the success of both sexes, at all ages, in relation to the general conditions of life. The sexual struggle is of two kinds; in the one it is between individuals of the same sex, generally the males, in order to drive away or kill their rivals, the females remaining passive; whilst in the other, the struggle is likewise between the individuals of the same sex, in order to excite or charm those of the opposite sex, generally the females, which no longer remain passive, but select the more agreeable partners. This latter kind of selection is closely analogous to that which man unintentionally, yet effectually, brings to bear on his domesticated productions, when he preserves during a long period the most pleasing or useful individuals, without any wish to modify the breed.

The laws of inheritance determine whether characters gained through sexual selection by either sex shall be transmitted to the same sex, or to both; as well as the age at which they shall be developed. It appears that variations arising late in life are commonly transmitted to one and the same sex. Variability is the necessary basis for the action of selection, and is wholly independent of it. It follows from this, that variations of the same general nature have often been taken advantage of and accumulated through sexual selection in relation to the propagation of the species, as well as through natural selection in relation to the general purposes of life. Hence secondary sexual characters, when equally transmitted to both sexes can be distinguished from ordinary specific characters only by the light of analogy. The modifications acquired through sexual selection are often so strongly pronounced that the two sexes have frequently been ranked as distinct species, or even as distinct genera.[1] Such strongly-marked differences must be in some manner

highly important; and we know that they have been acquired in some instances at the cost not only of inconvenience, but of exposure to actual danger.

The belief in the power of sexual selection rests chiefly on the following considerations. Certain characters are confined to one sex; and this alone renders it probable that in most cases they are connected with the act of reproduction. In innumerable instances these characters are fully developed only at maturity, and often during only a part of the year, which is always the breeding-season. The males (passing over a few exceptional cases) are the more active in courtship; they are the better armed, and are rendered the more attractive in various ways. It is to be especially observed that the males display their attractions with elaborate care in the presence of the females; and that they rarely or never display them excepting during the season of love. It is incredible that all this should be purposeless. Lastly we have distinct evidence with some quadrupeds and birds, that the individuals of one sex are capable of feeling a strong antipathy or preference for certain individuals of the other sex.

Bearing in mind these facts, and the marked results of man's unconscious selection, when applied to domesticated animals and cultivated plants, it seems to me almost certain that if the individuals of one sex were during a long series of generations to prefer pairing with certain individuals of the other sex, characterised in some peculiar manner, the offspring would slowly but surely become modified in this same manner. I have not attempted to conceal that, excepting when the males are more numerous than the females, or when polygamy prevails, it is doubtful how the more attractive males succeed in leaving a large number of offspring to inherit their superiority in ornaments or other charms than the less attractive males; but I have shown that this would probably follow from the females—especially the more vigorous ones, which would be the first to breed—preferring not only the more attractive but at the same time the more vigorous and victorious males.

Although we have some positive evidence that birds appreciate bright and beautiful objects, as with the bower-birds of Australia, and although they certainly

---

[1] *genera* Latin: groups of species. Plural of "genus."

appreciate the power of song, yet I fully admit that it is astonishing that the females of many birds and some mammals should be endowed with sufficient taste to appreciate ornaments, which we have reason to attribute to sexual selection; and this is even more astonishing in the case of reptiles, fish, and insects. But we really know little about the minds of the lower animals. It cannot be supposed, for instance, that male birds of paradise or peacocks should take such pains in erecting, spreading, and vibrating their beautiful plumes before the females for no purpose. We should remember the fact given on excellent authority in a former chapter, that several peahens, when debarred from an admired male, remained widows during a whole season rather than pair with another bird.

Nevertheless I know of no fact in natural history more wonderful than that of the female Argus pheasant should appreciate the exquisite shading of the ball-and-socket ornaments and the elegant patterns on the wing-feathers of the male. He who thinks that the male was created as he now exists must admit that the great plumes, which prevent the wings from being used for flight, and which are displayed during courtship and at no other time in a manner quite peculiar to this one species, were given to him as an ornament. If so, he must likewise admit that the female was created and endowed with the capacity of appreciating such ornaments. I differ only in the conviction that the male Argus pheasant acquired his beauty gradually, through the preference of the females during many generations for the more highly ornamented males; the aesthetic capacity of the females having been advanced through exercise or habit, just as our own taste is gradually improved. In the male through the fortunate chance of a few feathers, being left, unchanged, we can distinctly trace how simple spots with a little fulvous[1] shading on one side may have been developed by small steps into the wonderful ball-and-socket ornaments; and it is probable that they were actually thus developed.

Everyone who admits the principle of evolution, and yet feels great difficulty in admitting that female mammals, birds, reptiles, and fish, could have acquired the high taste implied by the beauty of the males, and which generally coincides with our own standard, should reflect that the nerve-cells of the brain in the highest as well as in the lowest members of the Vertebrate series, are derived from those of the common progenitor of this great kingdom. For we can thus see how it has come to pass that certain mental faculties, in various and widely distinct groups of animals, have been developed in nearly the same manner and to nearly the same degree.

The reader who has taken the trouble to go through the several chapters devoted to sexual selection, will be able to judge how far the conclusions at which I have arrived are supported by sufficient evidence. If he accepts these conclusions he may, I think, safely extend them to mankind; but it would be superfluous here to repeat what I have so lately said on the manner in which sexual selection apparently has acted on man, both on the male and female side, causing the two sexes to differ in body and mind, and the several races to differ from each other in various characters, as well as from their ancient and lowly-organised progenitors. He who admits the principle of sexual selection will be led to the remarkable conclusion that the nervous system not only regulates most of the existing functions of the body, but has indirectly influenced the progressive development of various bodily structures and of certain mental qualities. Courage, pugnacity, perseverance, strength and size of body, weapons of all kinds, musical organs, both vocal and instrumental, bright colours and ornamental appendages, have all been indirectly gained by the one sex or the other, through the exertion of choice, the influence of love and jealousy, and the appreciation of the beautiful in sound, colour or form; and these powers of the mind manifestly depend on the development of the brain.

Man scans with scrupulous care the character and pedigree of his horses, cattle, and dogs before he matches them; but when he comes to his own marriage he rarely, or never, takes any such care. He is impelled by nearly the same motives as the lower animals, when they are left to their own free choice, though he is in so far superior to them that he highly values mental charms

---

[1] *fulvous* Brownish- or reddish-yellow.

and virtues. On the other hand he is strongly attracted by mere wealth or rank. Yet he might by selection do something not only for the bodily constitution and frame of his offspring, but for their intellectual and moral qualities. Both sexes ought to refrain from marriage if they are in any marked degree inferior in body or mind; but such hopes are Utopian and will never be even partially realised until the laws of inheritance are thoroughly known. Everyone does good service who aids towards this end. When the principles of breeding and inheritance are better understood, we shall not hear ignorant members of our legislature rejecting with scorn a plan for ascertaining whether or not consanguineous marriages[1] are injurious to man.

The advancement of the welfare of mankind is a most intricate problem: all ought to refrain from marriage who cannot avoid abject poverty for their children; for poverty is not only a great evil, but tends to its own increase by leading to recklessness in marriage. On the other hand as Mr. Galton[2] has remarked, if the prudent avoid marriage, whilst the reckless marry, the inferior members tend to supplant the better members of society. Man, like every other animal, has no doubt advanced to his present high condition through a struggle for existence consequent on his rapid multiplication; and if he is to advance still higher, it is to be feared that he must remain subject to a severe struggle. Otherwise he would sink into indolence, and the more gifted men would not be more successful in the battle of life than the less gifted. Hence our natural rate of increase, though leading to many and obvious evils, must not be greatly diminished by any means. There should be open competition for all men; and the most able should not be prevented by laws or customs from succeeding best and rearing the largest number of offspring. Important as the struggle for existence has been and even still is, yet as far as the highest part of man's nature is concerned there are other agencies more important. For the moral qualities are advanced, either

directly or indirectly, much more through the effects of habit, the reasoning powers, instruction, religion, *et cetera*, than through natural selection; though to this latter agency may be safely attributed the social instincts, which afforded the basis for the development of the moral sense.

The main conclusion arrived at in this work, namely, that man is descended from some lowly organised form, will, I regret to think, be highly distasteful to many. But there can hardly be a doubt that we are descended from barbarians. The astonishment which I felt on first seeing a party of Fuegians on a wild and broken shore will never be forgotten by me, for the reflection at once rushed into my mind—such were our ancestors. These men were absolutely naked and bedaubed with paint, their long hair was tangled, their mouths frothed with excitement, and their expression was wild, startled, and distrustful. They possessed hardly any arts, and like wild animals lived on what they could catch; they had no government, and were merciless to every one not of their own small tribe. He who has seen a savage in his native land will not feel much shame, if forced to acknowledge that the blood of some more humble creature flows in his veins. For my own part I would as soon be descended from that heroic little monkey, who braved his dreaded enemy in order to save the life of his keeper, or from that old baboon, who descending from the mountains, carried away in triumph his young comrade from a crowd of astonished dogs—as from a savage who delights to torture his enemies, offers up bloody sacrifices, practises infanticide without remorse, treats his wives like slaves, knows no decency, and is haunted by the grossest superstitions.

Man may be excused for feeling some pride at having risen, though not through his own exertions, to the very summit of the organic scale; and the fact of his having thus risen, instead of having been aboriginally placed there, may give him hope for a still higher destiny in the distant future. But we are not here concerned with hopes or fears, only with the truth as far as our reason permits us to discover it; and I have given the evidence to the best of my ability. We must, however, acknowledge, as it seems to me, that man with all

---

[1] *consanguineous marriages* Marriages between blood relatives.

[2] *Mr. Galton* Sir Francis Galton (1822–94), Darwin's half cousin, one of the founders of eugenics, the "science" that aimed to improve the human species through selective breeding.

his noble qualities, with sympathy which feels for the most debased, with benevolence which extends not only to other men but to the humblest living creature, with his god-like intellect which has penetrated into the movements and constitution of the solar system—with all these exalted powers—Man still bears in his bodily frame the indelible stamp of his lowly origin. —1871

IN CONTEXT

Defending and Attacking Darwin

One of Darwin's most important defenders was Thomas Henry Huxley (1825–95), a naturalist and essayist who in the 1870s developed the concept of agnosticism. In 1860 he became known as "Darwin's Bulldog" for his aggressive and persuasive efforts to popularize the theory of natural selection—and counter the backlash against it. He continued to write about evolutionary theory throughout the rest of his life.

from Thomas Huxley, "Criticisms on *The Origin of Species*" (1864)

It is singular how differently one and the same book will impress different minds. That which struck the present writer most forcibly on his first perusal of the "Origin of Species" was the conviction that teleology,[1] as commonly understood, had received its deathblow at Mr. Darwin's hands. For the teleological argument runs thus: an organ or organism (A) is precisely fitted to perform a function or purpose (B); therefore it was specially constructed to perform that function. In Paley's[2] famous illustration, the adaptation of all the parts of the watch to the function, or purpose, of showing the time, is held to be evidence that the watch was specially contrived to that end; on the ground, that the only cause we know of, competent to produce such an effect as a watch which shall keep time, is a contriving intelligence adapting the means directly to that end.

Suppose, however, that any one had been able to show that the watch had not been made directly by any person, but that it was the result of the modification of another watch which kept time but poorly; and that this again had proceeded from a structure which could hardly be called a watch at all—seeing that it had no figures on the dial and the hands were rudimentary; and that going back and back in time we came at last to a revolving barrel as the earliest traceable rudiment of the whole fabric. And imagine that it had been possible to show that all these changes had resulted, first, from a tendency of the structure to vary indefinitely; and secondly, from something in the surrounding world which helped all variations in the direction of an accurate time-keeper, and checked[3] all those in other directions; then it is obvious that the force of Paley's argument would be gone. For it would be demonstrated that an apparatus thoroughly well adapted to a particular purpose might be the result of a method of trial and error worked by unintelligent agents, as well as of the direct application of the means appropriate to that end, by an intelligent agent.

---

[1]   *teleology*   Study of intelligent design or purpose in nature.

[2]   *Paley*   William Paley (1743–1805), English philosopher. Huxley refers to Paley's 1802 book, *Natural Theology, or Evidences of the Existence and Attributes of the Deity Collected from the Appearances of Nature.*

[3]   *checked*   Stopped.

Now it appears to us that what we have here, for illustration's sake, supposed to be done with the watch, is exactly what the establishment of Darwin's theory will do for the organic world. For the notion that every organism has been created as it is and launched straight at a purpose, Mr. Darwin substitutes the conception of something which may fairly be termed a method of trial and error. Organisms vary incessantly; of these variations the few meet with surrounding conditions which suit them and thrive; the many are unsuited and become extinguished.

from Thomas Huxley, "Mr. Darwin's Critics" (1871)

The gradual lapse of time has now separated us by more than a decade from the date of the publication of the "Origin of Species"—and whatever may be thought or said about Mr. Darwin's doctrines, or the manner in which he has propounded them, this much is certain, that, in a dozen years, the "Origin of Species" has worked as complete a revolution in biological science as the "Principia"[1] did in astronomy—and it has done so, because, in the words of Helmholtz,[2] it contains "an essentially new creative thought."

And as time has slipped by, a happy change has come over Mr. Darwin's critics. The mixture of ignorance and insolence which, at first, characterised a large proportion of the attacks with which he was assailed, is no longer the sad distinction of anti-Darwinian criticism. Instead of abusive nonsense, which merely discredited its writers, we read essays, which are, at worst, more or less intelligent and appreciative; while, sometimes, like that which appeared in the "North British Review" for 1867, they have a real and permanent value.

The several publications of Mr. Wallace and Mr. Mivart[3] contain discussions of some of Mr. Darwin's views, which are worthy of particular attention, not only on account of the acknowledged scientific competence of these writers, but because they exhibit an attention to those philosophical questions which underlie all physical science, which is as rare as it is needful.

from *Punch*

The humor magazine *Punch* continued to lampoon Darwin's theories in its cartoons even after they had become widely accepted in the community at large. The first of the cartoons below (depicting a gorilla as a social "lion"), was published in 1861, the second (a response to Darwin's 1881 *The Formation of Vegetable Mould Through the Action of Worms*) in 1882.

---

[1] *Principia* Sir Isaac Newton's *Philosophiae Naturalis Principia Mathematica* (1687).

[2] *Helmholtz* Hermann Ludwig Ferdinand von Helmholtz (1821–94), German professor of physiology and physics.

[3] *Mr. Wallace* Alfred Russel Wallace (1823–1913), English naturalist and social critic; *Mr. Mivart* St. George Jackson Mivart (1827–1900), British biologist. His *Genesis of Species* (1871) established him as a leading opponent of Darwin's theory.

THE LION OF THE SEASON.

MAN·IS·BVT·A·WORM.

IN CONTEXT

Social Darwinism

The term "Social Darwinism" is used to refer to ideas that attempt to apply certain evolutionary notions to social issues. Chief among the Victorian "Social Darwinists" was Herbert Spencer, a wide-ranging thinker who coined the term "survival of the fittest" in an 1852 essay, "A Theory of Population." Like that work, his 1851 book *Social Statics* (from which excerpts are reprinted below) pre-dates Darwin's *On the Origin Species* by several years. In fact the tenets of Social Darwinism were quite independent of Darwin's biological theories, and were in no way necessarily embraced by the same people.

from Herbert Spencer, *Social Statics: or, the Conditions Essential to Human Happiness Specified, and the First of Them Developed* (1851)

Pervading all nature we may see at work a stern discipline, which is a little cruel that it may be very kind. That state of universal warfare maintained throughout the lower creation, to the great perplexity of many worthy people, is at bottom the most merciful provision which the circumstances admit of. It is much better that the ruminant animal, when deprived by age of the vigour which made its existence a pleasure, should be killed by some beast of prey, than that it should linger out a life made painful by infirmities, and eventually die of starvation. By the destruction of all such, not only is existence ended before it becomes burdensome, but room is made for a younger generation capable of the fullest enjoyment; and, moreover, out of the very act of substitution happiness is derived for a tribe of predatory creatures. Note further, that their carnivorous enemies not only remove from herbivorous herds individuals past their prime, but also weed out the sickly, the malformed, and the least fleet or powerful. By the aid of which purifying process, as well as by the fighting, so universal in the pairing season, all vitiation[1] of the race through the multiplication of its inferior samples is prevented; and the maintenance of a constitution completely adapted to surrounding conditions, and therefore most productive of happiness, is ensured.

The development of the higher creation is a progress towards a form of being capable of a happiness undiminished by these drawbacks. It is in the human race that the consummation[2] is to be accomplished. Civilization is the last stage of its accomplishment. And the ideal man is the man in whom all the conditions of that accomplishment are fulfilled. Meanwhile the well-being of existing humanity, and the unfolding of it into this ultimate perfection, are both secured by that same beneficent, though severe discipline, to which the animate creation at large is subject: a discipline which is pitiless in the working out of good: a felicity-pursuing law which never swerves for the avoidance of partial and temporary suffering. The poverty of the incapable, the distresses that come upon the imprudent, the starvation of the idle, and those shoulderings aside of the weak by the strong, which leave so many "in shallows and in miseries,"[3] are the decrees of a large, far-seeing benevolence. It seems hard that an unskilfulness which with all his efforts he cannot overcome, should entail hunger upon the artisan. It seems hard that a labourer incapacitated by sickness from competing with his stronger fellows, should have to bear the resulting privations. It seems hard that widows and orphans should be left to struggle for life or death. Nevertheless, when regarded not separately, but in connection with the interests of universal humanity, these harsh fatalities are seen to be full of the highest beneficence—the same beneficence which brings to early graves the children of diseased parents, and singles out the low-spirited,[4] the intemperate,[5] and the debilitated as the victims of an epidemic.

There are many very amiable people—people over whom in so far as their feelings are concerned we may fitly rejoice—who have not the nerve to look this matter fairly in the face. Disabled as they are by their sympathies with present suffering, from duly regarding ultimate consequences, they pursue a course which is very injudicious, and in the end even cruel. We do not consider it true kindness in a mother to gratify her child with sweetmeats[6] that are certain to make it ill. We should think it a very foolish sort of benevolence which led a surgeon to let his patient's disease progress to a fatal issue, rather than inflict pain by an operation. Similarly, we must call those spurious philanthropists, who, to prevent present misery, would entail greater misery upon future generations. All defenders of a poor-law[7] must, however, be classed amongst such. That rigorous necessity which, when allowed to act on them, becomes so sharp a spur to the lazy, and so strong a bridle to the random, these paupers' friends would repeal, because of the wailings it here and there produces. Blind to the fact, that under the natural order of things society is constantly excreting its unhealthy, imbecile, slow, vacillating, faithless members, these unthinking, though well-meaning, men advocate

---

[1] *vitiation* Impairment.

[2] *consummation* Culmination.

[3] *in ... miseries* From Shakespeare's *Julius Caesar* 4.2.70–73: "There is a tide in the affairs of men, / Which taken at the flood leads on to fortune; / Omitted, all the voyage of that life / Is bound in shallows and in miseries."

[4] *low-spirited* Depressed.

[5] *intemperate* Heavy drinkers.

[6] *sweetmeats* Confections, such as candied fruits and nuts.

[7] *poor-law* Law providing for the support of the poor at public expense.

an interference which not only stops the purifying process, but even increases the vitiation[1]—absolutely encourages the multiplication of the reckless and incompetent by offering them an unfailing provision, and discourages the multiplication of the competent and provident by heightening the prospective difficulty of maintaining a family. And thus, in their eagerness to prevent the really salutary[2] sufferings that surround us, these sigh-wise and groan-foolish people bequeath to posterity a continually increasing curse.

At first sight these considerations seem conclusive against *all* relief to the poor—voluntary as well as compulsory; and it is no doubt true that they imply a condemnation of whatever private charity enables the recipients to elude the necessities of our social existence. With this condemnation, however, no rational man will quarrel. That careless squandering of pence which has fostered into perfection a system of organized begging—which has made skilful mendicancy[3] more profitable than ordinary manual labour—which induces the simulation of palsy, epilepsy, cholera, and no end of diseases and deformities—which has called into existence warehouses for the sale and hire of impostor's dresses[4]—which has given to pity-inspiring babes a market value of *9d.* per day—the unthinking benevolence which has generated all this, cannot but be disapproved by every one. Now it is only against this injudicious charity that the foregoing argument tells. To that charity which may be described as helping men to help themselves, it makes no objection—countenances[5] it rather. And in helping men to help themselves, there remains abundant scope for the exercise of a people's sympathies. Accidents will still supply victims on whom generosity may be legitimately expended. Men thrown upon their backs by unforeseen events, men who have failed for want of knowledge inaccessible to them, men ruined by the dishonesty of others, and men in whom hope long delayed has made the heart sick, may, with advantage to all parties, be assisted. Even the prodigal,[6] after severe hardship has branded his memory with the unbending conditions of social life to which he must submit, may properly have another trial afforded him. And, although by these ameliorations the process of adaptation must be remotely interfered with, yet in the majority of cases, it will not be so much retarded in one direction as it will be advanced in another. ...

Progress ... is not accident, but a necessity. Instead of civilisation being artificial, it is part of nature; all of a piece with the development of the embryo or the unfolding of a flower. The modifications mankind have undergone, and are still undergoing, result from a law underlying the whole organic creation; and provided the human race continues, and the constitution of things remains the same, those modifications must end in completeness. As surely as the tree becomes bulky when it stands alone, and slender if one of a group ... so surely must things be called evil and immoral disappear; so surely must man become perfect.

[1] *vitiation*   Deterioration.

[2] *salutary*   Beneficial, healthy.

[3] *mendicancy*   Begging.

[4] *impostor's dresses*   Here, misleadingly tattered clothing.

[5] *countenances*   Approves of.

[6] *prodigal*   Excessively wasteful.

NATURE AND THE ENVIRONMENT
CONTEXTS

The views of nature put forward in the Romantic period—in particular, those put forward by the English Romantic poets—have continued ever since to exert a strong influence on the ways in which we view non-human environments and humans' relationship to them. Many Victorians agreed with the Wordsworth of 1799 that the experience of wild nature is of vital importance to the human psyche; that nature may inspire within us "the joy of elevated thoughts"; that Nature herself may take on an almost godlike status. They felt themselves at one with the Wordsworth who had described himself as a "worshipper of Nature"—and not a few adopted a worshipful attitude towards Wordsworth himself. Unlike the other great Romantic poets, Wordsworth himself lived on, honored as Poet Laureate for the last seven years of his life, and becoming a figure almost as important to the Victorian era as he had been to the Romantic one. Letitia Landon's "Rydal Water and Grasmere Lake, The Residence of Wordsworth" illustrates both the reverence that many Victorians felt for the man himself and the degree to which Wordsworthian views of nature exerted a powerful hold on the Victorian poetic imagination. The approach to life and to learning that Eliza Cook describes herself as having adopted—"the woods and forests became my tutors"—evokes the central theme of Wordsworth's "Tables Turned": "Let Nature be your teacher." Even at the end of the century, Wordsworth remained a frequent reference point; the degree to which Henry Salt quotes Wordsworth in the selections included here was not at all unusual. But for a significant portion of the Victorian era Wordsworth was also an active participant in Victorian debates about environmental issues—most notably, the vexed issue of the degree to which railways should be allowed to encroach upon the beauty of Britain's natural scenery. The selection included here is part of a debate over the preservation of natural beauty and of wilderness that continued throughout the century—and indeed, has continued through to our day. (The National Trust, a body charged with the task of preserving places of natural beauty and structures of historic importance, was founded in 1895 by Octavia Hill and others; Britain's first three national parks—in the Lake District, the Peaks District, and Snowdonia (Cenedlaethol Eryri)—were created in 1951.)

If the idea of a godlike Nature remained a touchstone throughout the Victorian period, so too did the notion that God—for most Britons a Christian, specifically Protestant, God—expresses Himself in large part *through* the beauties of nature. Adelaide Proctor's "Two Worlds" is a striking poetic expression of this sort of notion.

The word "environment" in the sense of "the conditions in general affecting the life, existence, or properties of an organism or object" is first recorded by the *OED* as having been used in 1866[1]—the same year in which the word "ecology" was first coined. Though the concepts of *nature* and of *environment* and *ecology* all overlap, the latter two suggest webs of connectivity rather different from those that the word *nature* suggests—webs in which God plays a less central part, and science and technology a greater one. During the Victorian era the extent of the environmental harms that

---

[1] The word is not, however, recorded by the *OED* as having been used prior to the 1940s in one of the ways that we often employ it today—prefaced by "the" to denote "the natural world or physical surroundings in general, either as a whole or within a particular geographical area, esp. as affected by human activity."

humankind in the capitalist era can cause became steadily more visible—in the thick smoke from the factories that blanketed Britain's cities, in the depletion of her forests, in the polluting of her waterways, and in countless other forms. Much as scientific and technological developments had made possible the smoke, pollution, and so on, it also became plain to Victorians that addressing these problems would entail bringing science and technology to bear in the search for solutions—as the documents included here in the "State of the Thames" section make clear.

John Ruskin was oriented neither towards scientific and technological fixes for environmental degradation nor towards the grubby work of trying to effect political solutions to such problems. Yet he played a vitally important role in making Britons aware of the damage that was being done. In his lecture "Traffic" and in many other writings, Ruskin linked such damage not only to the economic mechanisms of capitalism but also to associated social attitudes—to Britons' obeisance towards "the god of getting on." In considering what was happening to the farms and fields, to the wild landscapes, and to the architecture of Britain, he brought to bear considerations of aesthetics, ethics, history, political economy, social class, and religion. Ruskin's ideas in these areas influenced generations of painters, architects, urban planners, and literary figures.

It has often been suggested that Ruskin, in his *Storm-Cloud of the Nineteenth Century*, was also among the first to recognize the phenomenon of climate change. Ruskin's ruminations on what he described as a "plague cloud" are wide ranging, and embrace moral, aesthetic, and spiritual commentary at least as much as they do scientific observation. How best to interpret them remains the subject of rich debate. Several key passages from *Storm-Cloud* are included in these pages; much more substantial excerpts are included in the anthology's website component.

In the later Victorian period, the degradation of the environment gave rise to another strain of thought—environmental utopianism and dystopianism. Richard Jeffries' *After London*, which is arguably the best-known example of this genre, is excerpted in these pages, while two other such works—W.H. Hudson's *A Crystal Age* (1887), and William Morris's *News from Nowhere* (1890)—are excerpted in the anthology's website component.

In Victorian times non-human animals were part of the human environment—including the urban environment—to a far greater degree than is the case in developed societies today. For the Victorians, then, it is not surprising that concern for the world around them should have embraced animate as well as inanimate nature. The movement to curb human cruelty towards non-human animals has roots in the eighteenth century and achieved its first great successes in the 1820s with the passage in 1822 of the Act to Prevent the Cruel and Improper Treatment of Cattle, and the founding in 1824 of the Society for the Prevention of Cruelty to Animals. But it gathered considerable steam in the 1830s and 1840s with the passage of several more pieces of animal cruelty legislation and through the writings of Lewis Gompertz (see the online component of volume 4 of this anthology). Later in the century it was given further momentum by the anti-vivisection movement; by Anna Sewell's *Black Beauty* (1877) and the crusade against cruelty to horses; and, towards the end of the century, by the writings of environmental activists such as Henry Salt. Salt and others—among them Thomas Hardy—took issue with those crude versions of Charles Darwin's thought that took "survival of the fittest" to be a moral code that gave license to humans to behave cruelly; instead, they took Darwin's theory as supporting the view that we should acknowledge humans to be more closely related to the "lower animals" than had previously been recognized, and on that account that we should accord them a higher moral status than we had previously assigned to them—and treat them with greater respect.[1]

The ways in which environmentalism interacts with considerations of social class is a subject to which Victorians paid a good deal of attention. An ongoing theme (reflected in several of the documents provided here, from Wordsworth's reflections on railway excursions through to those of Henry Salt and Octavia Hill) was how best to balance the interests of the masses with those of the environment; how could every Briton—including members of the working classes—be provided with access to the beauties of nature without unleashing the full environmental impact of mass tourism? Another perspective on such questions is provided by Eliza Cook in her 1870 poem "Song of the City Artisan"—a moving reflection on the effect on urban workers of being unable to experience "Nature, fresh and free," to enjoy "the sunlight and the mountain air."

If environmentalism—and, indeed, nature writing—tend to be associated with the middle and upper classes, they tend too to be associated with white people. The writings of Tekahionwake are a reminder that Indigenous people throughout the British Empire were at least as capable of feeling close connections to nature as any white person in England. (Tekahionwake's "The Happy Hunting Grounds" is included in these pages; the selection of her work that appears elsewhere in this volume also includes several poems that are of interest in part for the way in which they treat environmental topics.) And the descriptions provided in 1874 by !kweitan ta //ken of how her people employ the substance known as *rooi klip* is a reminder of the tremendous variety of ways in which, at different locations within the British Empire during the Victorian period, humans interacted with nature. Even as the /Xam people in the mountains north of Cape Town were adorning themselves with *rooi klip* in the hope of affecting the weather locally, the factories that Ruskin described as the "Manchester devil" were beginning, in ways still unknown to science, to affect the climate world-wide.

⌘ ⌘ ⌘

from Letitia Landon, "Rydal Water and Grasmere Lake, The Residence of Wordsworth" (1838)

Landon (1802–38), who was among the most popular and prolific poets of the Romantic era, eventually became as famous for her allegedly scandalous life and for her mysterious death by poison as for her verse. Her poem in praise of Wordsworth evidences the degree to which Wordsworthian reverence for Nature (both for itself and for the "associate thought" it gave rise to) had become ingrained in the English psyche at the dawn of the Victorian era.

Included here are the first three stanzas of Landon's poem, together with the final stanza.

[N.B. Landon is accorded a full author entry in the Romantic Period volume of this anthology.]

Not for the glory on their heads
  Those stately hill-tops wear,
Although the summer sunset sheds
  Its constant crimson there.
5 Not for the gleaming lights that break
  The purple of the twilight lake,
Half dusky and half fair,
  Does that sweet valley seem to be
A sacred place on earth to me.

10 The influence of a moral spell
  Is found around the scene,

---

[1] See also, elsewhere in this volume, the "In Context" materials accompanying the selections from Darwin's work (pages 318–22).

Giving new shadows to the dell,
    New verdure to the green.
With every mountain-top is wrought
15   The presence of associate thought,
A music that has been;
    Calling that loveliness to life
With which the inward world is rife.

His home—our English poet's home—
20   Amid these hills is made;
Here, with the morning, hath he come,
    There, with the night delayed.
On all things is his memory cast,
    For every place wherein he past
25 Is with his mind arrayed
    That, wandering in a summer hour,
Asked wisdom of the leaf and flower. ...

Eternal as the hills thy name,
    Eternal as thy strain;
30 So long as ministers of Fame
    Shall Love and Hope remain.
The crowded city in its streets,
    The valley, in its green retreats,
Alike thy words retain.
35   What need hast thou of sculptured stone?
Thy temple, is thy name alone.

from Anna Atkins, *Photographs of British Algae: Cyanotype Impressions* (1843)

Anna Atkins (1799–1871) was a photographer and
botanist; her 1843 volume *Photographs of British
Algae: Cyanotype Impressions* is the first book known
to have been illustrated with photographic images.
Atkins was acquainted both with photographic pioneer William Henry Fox Talbot and with Sir John
Herschel (1792–1871), the famous astronomer, who
in 1839 had coined the term "photography" and
invented the "sun-printing" process for creating the
photographic images that he termed cyanotypes—a
process later employed in creating blueprints for use
in architecture and engineering.

Atkins also created (together with Anne Dixon)
two other collections of cyanotypes: *Cyanotypes of
British and Foreign Ferns* (1853) and *Cyanotypes of
British and Foreign Flowering Plants and Ferns* (1854).

from the INTRODUCTION

The difficulty of making accurate drawings of objects
so minute as many of the algae and confervae has
induced me to avail myself of Sir John Herschel's
beautiful process of cyanotype to obtain impressions of
the plants themselves, which I have much pleasure in
offering to my botanist friends.

I hope that in general the impressions will be found
sharp and well defined, but in some instances ... the
thickness of the specimens makes it impossible to press
the glass used in taking photographs sufficiently close to
them to ensure a perfect representation of every part. ...

Cystoseira granulata.

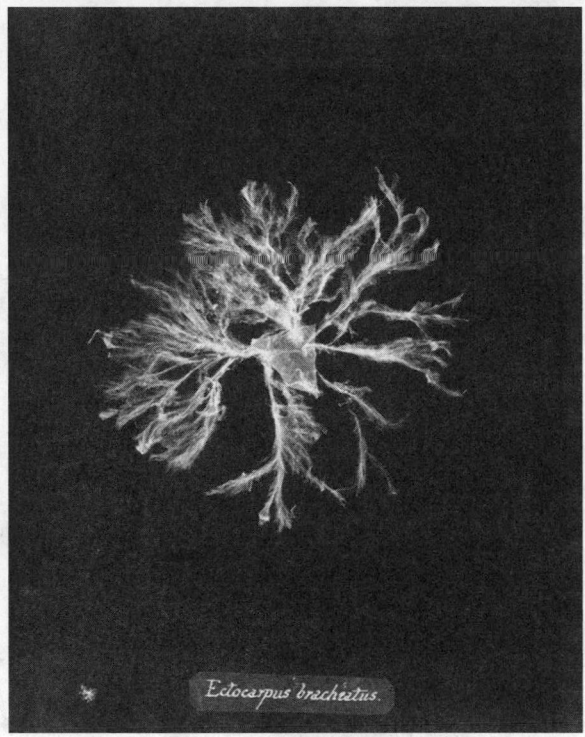

Ectocarpus brachiatus.

William Wordsworth, On the Projected Kendal and Windermere Railway

Wordsworth loomed as large in the Victorian period as he had done in the Romantic. He was accorded extraordinary respect throughout the period—widely regarded as something of a spokesperson for nature. (In 1906 Ernest de Selincourt wrote of his connection to the Lake District that "nowadays, alike by tourist and by student, Wordsworth is regarded not merely as the prophet of the Lakeland, but almost as its first discoverer.") But Wordsworth himself was also very much alive through the first thirteen years of Victoria's reign—still active as a poet, and still engaged in the issues of the day.

One of the most interesting subjects of that engagement was the issue of how railways would affect the environment—and affect the human experience of natural beauty. The 16 October 1844 issue of *The Morning Post*, a leading conservative

daily newspaper in London, included a new sonnet by Wordsworth on the subject of a proposed new railway into the Lake District. The sonnet was followed by a brief commentary by the poet—and preceded on the previous page by a brief commentary by the paper's editors. Wordsworth's views excited some controversy; in *The Morning Chronicle* of 23 October "Mr. Wordsworth and his clique" were accused of seeking to prevent the common people from gaining access to the beauties of the Lake District; a long letter in support of Wordsworth's position appeared in the 24 October *Morning Post*.

Wordsworth himself then wrote at greater length on the subject in two letters to the *Morning Post*, the first published on 9 December and the second on 20 December. The "Able Talk" columnist in the same paper also weighed in, on 18 December, in support of Wordsworth's arguments.

Wordsworth published revised versions of these letters in a pamphlet, and he also included revised versions as an appendix to subsequent editions of his *Guide through the District of the Lakes in the North of England*. (Confusingly, the fifth edition "with considerable additions," among them this material from 1844, retains the date "1835" on the title page.) The excerpts included here are from the original letters themselves, except where otherwise indicated.

from *The Morning Post* (16 October 1844)

[BY THE EDITORS]

Delighted, as we always are, to be the means of giving to the public anything from the pen of Mr. Wordsworth, we have an especial satisfaction in publishing the sonnet that appears in our paper of this day.

Perhaps no living man except the venerable Poet-Laureate could have infused the spirit of poetry into so unromantic a subject as a railroad; that he has done so, our readers will acknowledge. They will also admit, when they know the circumstances, that he had ample reason for selecting such a theme. The proposed railway that is to disturb the beauty of a region of which beauty is the "staple commodity"—for no case of traffic can honestly be made out[1]—has alarmed most of the old[2] residents in the country, and we hope the speculators in railroad shares will yet be prevented from forcing this ugly and useless infliction on the most beautiful and least commercial district in England. The railroad at Kendal will be near enough to the Lakes—within seven miles of Windermere. And the line from Kendal over Shap Falls, and via Penrith (for Carlisle and Scotland), will bring tourists within five miles of Ullswater,[3] without cutting and blasting through the very heart of the scenery and destroying its character.

Can we wonder that one, with such singular susceptibility of the beauties of nature as Mr. Wordsworth, should express himself strongly at this needless destruction of them?

SONNET ON THE PROJECTED KENDAL AND WINDERMERE RAILWAY

Is then no nook of English ground secure
From rash assault? Schemes of
    retirement° sown   *restful seclusion*
In youth, and mid the busy world kept pure
As when their earliest flowers of hope were
    blown,°   *bloomed*
5   Must perish; how can they this blight endure?
And must he too his old delights disown[4]
Who scorns a false utilitarian lure
Mid his paternal fields at random thrown?

10 Baffle the threat, bright Scene, from Orrest-head[5]
Given to the pausing traveller's rapturous glance!
Plead for thy peace, thou beautiful romance
Of nature; and, if human hearts be dead,
Speak, passing winds; ye torrents, with your strong
And constant voice, protest against the wrong!

> William Wordsworth.
> Rydal Mount, October 12th, 1844

Let not the above be considered as merely a poetical effusion. The degree and kind of attachment which many of the yeomanry feel to their small inheritances can scarcely be overrated. Near the house of one of them stands a magnificent tree, which a neighbour of the owner advised him to fell for profit's sake. "Fell it," exclaimed the yeoman, "I had rather fall on my knees and worship it." It happens, I believe, that the intended railway would pass through this little property, and I hope that an apology for the answer will not be thought necessary by one who enters into the strength of the feeling.

> W.W.

from *The Morning Post* (9 December 1844)

[TO THE EDITOR]

Sir,

Some little time ago you did me the favour of inserting a sonnet expressive of the regret and indignation which, in common with others all over these Islands, I felt at the proposal of a railway to extend from Kendal to Low Woods, near the head of Windermere. The project was so offensive to a large majority of the proprietors through whose lands the line, after it came in view of the lake, was to pass, that, for this reason, and the avowed one of the heavy expense without which the difficulties in the way could not be overcome, it has been partially abandoned, and the terminus is now

---

[1] *no case of traffic can honestly be made out* I.e., no argument for allowing commercial traffic in the region can reasonably be put forward.

[2] *old* Long-established.

[3] *Windermere … Ullswater* Two of the most prominent bodies of water in the Lakes district.

[4] *his old delights disown* In later versions Wordsworth revised this line, substituting "the ruthless change bemoan" for "his old delights disown."

[5] *Orrest-head* Hill in the Lake District that affords a panoramic view of Windermere and its environs.

announced to be at a spot within a mile of Bowness. But as no guarantee can be given that the project will not hereafter be revived, and an attempt made to carry the line forward through the vales of Ambleside and Grasmere, and as in one main particular the case remains essentially the same, allow me to address you upon certain points which merit more consideration than the favourers of the scheme have yet given them. ...

In this district the manufactures are trifling; mines it has none, and its quarries are either wrought out or superseded; the soil is light, and the cultivatable parts of the country are very limited; so that it has little to send out, and little has it also to receive. Summer tourists (and the very word precludes the notion of a railway) it has in abundance; but the inhabitants are so few and their intercourse with other places so infrequent, that one daily coach, which could not be kept going but through its connection with the Post-office, suffices for three-fourths of the year along the line of country as far as Keswick. The staple of the district is, in fact, its beauty and its character of seclusion and retirement; and to these topics and to others connected with them my remarks shall be confined.

The projectors have induced many to favour their schemes by declaring that one of their main objects is to place the beauties of the Lake District within easier reach of those who cannot afford to pay for ordinary conveyances. Look at the facts. Railways are completed, which, joined with others in rapid progress, will bring travellers who prefer approaching by Ullswater to within four miles of that lake. The Lancaster and Carlisle Railway will approach the town of Kendal, about eight or nine miles from eminences that command the whole vale of Windermere. The lakes are therefore at present of very easy access for *all* persons; but if they be not made still more so, the poor, it is said, will be wronged. Before this be admitted let the question be fairly looked into, and its different bearings examined. ...

[Before the poet Thomas Gray's] time, with the exception of the passage from Thomas Burnet[1] just

alluded to, there is not, I believe, a single English traveler whose published writings would disprove the assertion, that, where precipitous rocks and mountains are mentioned at all, they are spoken of as objects of dislike and fear, and not of admiration. Even Gray himself, describing, in his Journal, the steeps at the entrance of Borrowdale, expresses his terror in the language of Dante: "Let us not speak of them, but look and pass on." In my youth, I lived some time in the vale of Keswick, under the roof of a shrewd and sensible women, who more than once exclaimed in my hearing, "Bless me! folk are always talking about prospects: when I was young there was never sic a thing neamed."[2] In fact, our ancestors, as everywhere appears, in choosing the site of their houses, looked only at shelter and convenience, especially of water, and often would place a barn or any other out-house directly in front of their habitations, however beautiful the landscape which their windows might otherwise have commanded. The first house that was built in the Lake District for the sake of the beauty of the country was the work of Mr. English, who had often travelled in Italy, and chose for its site, some eighty years ago, the great island of Windermere; but it was sold before his building was finished, and he showed how little he was capable of appreciating the character of the situation by setting up a length of high garden-wall, as exclusive as it was ugly, almost close to the house. The nuisance was swept away when the late Mr. Curwen became the owner of this favoured spot. Mr. English was followed by Mr. Pocklington, a native of Nottinghamshire, who played strange pranks by his buildings and plantations upon Vicar's Island, in Derwentwater, which his admiration, such as it was, of the country, and probably a wish to be a leader in a new fashion, had tempted him to purchase. But what has all this to do with the subject? Why, to show that a vivid perception of romantic scenery is neither inherent in mankind, nor a necessary consequence of even a comprehensive education. It is benignly ordained that green fields, clear blue skies, running streams of pure water,

---

[1] *Thomas Burnet* English theologian (c. 1635–1715) who wrote about Earth's origins.

[2] *sic a thing neamed* Such a thing named.

rich groves and woods, orchards, and all the ordinary varieties of rural nature, should find an easy way to the affections of all men, and more or less so from early childhood till the senses are impaired by old age and the sources of mere earthly enjoyment have in a great measure failed. But a taste beyond this, however desirable it may be that every one should possess it, is not to be implanted at once; it must be gradually developed both in nations and individuals. Rocks and mountains, torrents and wide-spread waters, and all those features of nature which go to the composition of such scenes as this part of England is distinguished for, cannot, in their finer relations to the human mind, be comprehended, or even very imperfectly conceived, without processes of culture or opportunities of observation in some degree habitual. In the eye of thousands and tens of thousands, a rich meadow, with fat cattle grazing upon it, or the sight of what they would call a heavy crop of corn, is worth all that the Alps and Pyrenees in their utmost grandeur and beauty could show to them; and, notwithstanding the grateful influence, as we have observed, of ordinary nature and the productions of the fields, it is noticeable what trifling conventional prepossessions will, in common minds, not only preclude pleasure from the sight of natural beauty, but will even turn it into an object of disgust. "If I had to do with this garden," said a respectable person, one of my neighbours, "I would sweep away all the black and dirty stuff from that wall." The wall was backed by a bank of earth, and was exquisitely decorated with ivy, flowers, moss, and ferns, such as grow of themselves in like places; but the mere notion of fitness associated with a trim garden-wall prevented, in this instance, all sense of the spontaneous bounty and delicate care of nature. In the midst of small pleasure-ground, immediately below my house, rises a detached rock, equally remarkable for the beauty of its form, the ancient oaks that grow out of it, and the flowers and shrubs which adorn it. "What a nice place would this be," said a Manchester tradesman, pointing to the rock, "if that ugly lump were but out of the way." Men as little advanced in the pleasure which such objects give to others are so far from being rare, that they may be said to represent a large majority of mankind. This is a fact, and none but the deceiver and the willingly deceived can be offended by its being stated. But as a more susceptible taste is undoubtedly a great acquisition, and has been spreading among us for some years, the question is, what means are most likely to be beneficial in extending its operation? Surely that good is not to be obtained by transferring at once uneducated persons in large bodies to particular spots, where the combinations of natural objects are such as would afford the greatest pleasure to those who have been in the habit of observing and studying the peculiar character of such scenes, and how they differ one from another. Instead of tempting artisans and labourers, and the humbler classes of shopkeepers, to ramble to a distance, let us rather look with lively sympathy upon persons in that condition, when, upon a holiday, or on the Sunday, after having attended divine worship, they make little excursions with their wives and children among neighbouring fields, whither the whole of each family might stroll, or be conveyed, at much less cost than would be required to take a single individual of their number to the shores of Windermere by the cheapest conveyance. It is in some such way as this one, that persons who must labour daily with their hands for bread in large towns, or are subject to confinement through the week, can be trained to a profitable intercourse with nature where she is the most distinguished by the majesty and sublimity of her forms. …

The widespread waters of these regions are in their nature peaceful; so are the steep mountains and the rocky glens; nor can they be profitably enjoyed but by a mind disposed to peace. Go to a pantomime, a farce, or a puppet-show, if you want noisy pleasure—the crowd of spectators who partake your enjoyment will, by their presence and acclamations, enhance it. But may those who have given proof that they prefer other gratifications continue to be safe from the molestation of cheap trains pouring out their hundreds at a time along the margin of Windermere; nor let any one be liable to the charge of being selfishly disregardful of the poor, and their innocent and salutary enjoyments, if he does not congratulate himself upon the especial benefit which would thus be conferred on such a concourse.

O, Nature, a' thy shows an' forms,
  To feeling pensive hearts hae charms![1]

So exclaimed the Ayrshire ploughman, speaking of ordinary rural nature under the varying influences of the seasons, and the sentiment has found an echo in the bosoms of thousands in as humble a condition as he himself was when he gave vent to it. But then they were feeling, pensive hearts; men who would be among the first to lament the facility with which they had approached this region, by a sacrifice of so much of its quiet and beauty, as, from the intrusion of a railway would be inseparable. What can, in truth, be more absurd than that either rich or poor should be spared the trouble of travelling by the high roads over so short a space, according to their respective means, if the unavoidable consequence must be a great disturbance of the retirement, and in many places a destruction of the beauty of the country, which the parties are come in search of? …

Having, I trust, given sufficient reason for the belief that the imperfectly educated classes are not likely to draw much good from rare visits to the lakes performed in this way, and surely on their own account it is not desirable that the visits should be frequent, let us glance at the mischief which such facilities would certainly produce. The directors of railway companies are always ready to devise or encourage entertainments for tempting the humbler classes to leave their homes. Accordingly, for the profit of the shareholders and that of the lower class of inn-keepers, we should have wrestling matches, horse and boat races without number, and pot-houses[2] and beer-shops would keep pace with these excitements and recreations, most of which might too easily be had elsewhere. The injuring which would thus be done to morals, both among this influx of strangers and the lower class of inhabitants, is obvious. …

… [B]e it remembered that this case is, as has been said before, a peculiar one, and that the staple of the country is its beauty and its character of retirement. Let then the beauty be undisfigured and the retirement unviolated, unless there be reason for believing that rights and interests of a higher kind and more apparent than those which have been urged in behalf of the projected intrusion will compensate the sacrifice.

Thanking you for the judicious observations that have appeared in your paper upon the subject of railways,

I remain, Sir,

Your obliged,

Wm. Wordsworth

from *The Morning Post* (20 December 1844)

[TO THE EDITOR]

Sir,

As you obligingly found space in your journal for observations of mine upon the intended Kendal and Windermere Railway, I venture to send you some further remarks upon the same subject. … The scope of the main argument, it will be recollected, was to prove that the perception of what has acquired the name of picturesque and romantic scenery is far from being intuitive, that it can be produced only by a slow and gradual process of culture; and to show, as a consequence, that the humbler ranks of society are not, and cannot be, in a state to gain material benefit from a more speedy access than they now have to this beautiful region. …

[I have learned by experience] how many men of the same rank, living from birth in this very region, are indifferent to those objects around them in which a cultivated taste takes so much pleasure. I should not have detained the reader so long upon this point of the subject, had I not heard that among the affluent and benevolent manufacturers of Yorkshire and Lancashire are some who already entertain the thought of sending, at their own expense, large bodies of their workmen, by railway, to the

---

[1] *O, Nature … charms* From "To William Simpson of Ochiltree" (1785) by the Scottish poet Robert Burns, who came from a humble farming background in the Scottish region of Ayrshire.

[2] *pot-houses* Taverns.

banks of Windermere. Surely those gentlemen will think a little more before they put such a scheme into practice. The rich man cannot benefit the poor, nor the superior the inferior, by anything that degrades him. Packing off men after this fashion for holiday entertainment is, in fact, treating them like children. They go at the will of their masters, and must return at the same, or they will be dealt with as transgressors. …

It will be felt by those who think with me upon this occasion that I have been writing on behalf of a social condition which no one who is competent to judge of it will be willing to subvert, and that I have been endeavouring to support moral sentiments and intellectual pleasures of a high order against an enmity which seems growing more and more formidable every day; I mean "Utilitarianism," serving as a mask for cupidity and gambling speculations. My business with this evil lies in its reckless mode of action by railways, now its favourite instruments. Upon good authority I have been told that there was lately an intention of driving one of these pests, as they are likely too often to prove, through a part of the magnificent ruins of Furness Abbey[1]—an outrage which was prevented by some one pointing out how easily a devastation might be made; and the hint produced its due effect upon the engineer. …

Even a broad highway may in some places greatly impair the characteristic beauty of the country, as will be readily acknowledged by those who remember what the Lake of Grasmere was before the new road that runs along its eastern margin had been constructed.… As it once was, and fringed with wood, instead of the breastwork of bare wall that now confines it. In the same manner has the beauty, and still more the sublimity of many Passes in the Alps been injuriously affected. …

Similar remarks might be applied to the mountainous country of Wales; but there too, the plea of utility, especially as expediting the communication between England and Ireland, more than justifies the labours of the Engineer. Not so would it be with the Lake District.

A railroad is already planned along the sea coast, and another from Lancaster to Carlisle is in great forwardness: an intermediate one is therefore, to say the least of it, superfluous. Once for all let me declare that it is not against Railways but against the abuse of them that I am contending.[2] …

I have now done with the subject. The time of life at which I have arrived may, I trust, if nothing else will, guard me from the imputation of having written from any selfish interest, or from fear of disturbance which a railway might cause to myself. If gratitude for what repose and quiet in a district hitherto, for the most part, not disfigured but beautified by human hands, have done for me through the course of a long life, and hope that others might hereafter be benefited in the same manner and in the same country, be selfishness, then, indeed, but not otherwise, I plead guilty of the charge. We have too much hurrying about in these islands; much for idle pleasure, and more from over activity in the pursuit of wealth. It might be added that this habit is too apt to degenerate into the love of gain, pursued without regard to the real good or happiness of others.

Proud were ye, Mountains, when, in times of old,
Your patriot sons, to stem invasive war,
Intrenched your brows; ye gloried in each scar:
Now, for your shame, a Power, the Thirst of Gold,
5   That rules o'er Britain like a baneful star,
Wills that your peace, your beauty, shall be sold,
And clear way made for her triumphal car
Through the beloved retreats your arms enfold!
Here YE that Whistle? As her long-linked Train
10   Swept onwards, did the vision cross your view?
Yes, ye were startled; and, in balance true,
Weighing the mischief with the promised gain,
Mountains, and Vales, and Floods, I call on you
To share the passion of a just disdain.
          William Wordsworth

---

[1] *Furness Abbey* Former monastery located in the same area of northern England as the Lake District.

[2] *It will be felt … I am contending* These paragraphs are among those added by Wordsworth in later versions of the text; they do not appear in his original letter to *The Morning Post*.

Note: If any one, from the perusal of these letters, should suppose that I am blind to the power by which railways have been produced and the good that may be expected from their *legitimate* application, let him take the trouble, if he think it worthwhile, to read a sonnet of mine, published some years ago, entitled "Steam-boats, Viaducts, and Railways."

W.W.
Rydal Mount, Dec. 17, 1844

(The sonnet above adverted to will be found in the fifth volume of Mr. Wordsworth's Collected poems, edition of 1837.—Ed. Morning Post)

[Here follows the text of the sonnet referred to]

STEAMBOATS AND RAILWAYS[1]

Motions and Means, on sea on land at war
With old poetic feeling, not for this
Shall ye, by poets even, be judged amiss!
Nor shall your presence, howsoe'er it mar
5 The loveliness of nature, prove a bar
To the mind's gaining that prophetic sense
Of future good, that point of vision, whence
May be discovered what in soul ye are;
In spite of all that Beauty must disown
10 In your harsh features, Nature doth embrace
Her lawful offspring in man's Art; and Time,
Pleased with your triumphs o'er her brother Space,
Accepts from your bold hand the proffered crown
Of Hope, and welcomes you with cheer sublime.

Eliza Cook, Poems

Eliza Cook (1818–89) was the child of a London brass-worker and his wife; the family moved to a small farm outside the city when she was still a child. Cook published her first volume of poems at the age of 17; a year later she published "The Thames" in the *Weekly Dispatch*. Cook remained for many decades a popular author, writing essays on a variety of public issues as well as publishing several volumes of poetry. She was a strong advocate for women's and for workers' rights; her body of work includes a variety of domestic poems, patriotic poems, and poems of "reflective morality," as well as many nature poems.

"The Thames" (1836)

Let the Rhine be blue and bright
In its path of liquid light,
Where the red grapes fling a beam
Of glory on the stream;
5 Let the gorgeous beauty there
Mingle all that's rich and fair;
Yet to me it ne'er could be
Like that river great and free,
    The Thames! the mighty Thames!

10 Though it bear no azure wave,
Though no pearly foam may lave,
Or leaping cascades pour
Their rainbows on its shore;
Yet I ever loved to dwell
15 Where I heard its gushing swell,
And never skimmed its breast
But I warmly praised and blest
    The Thames! the mighty Thames!

Can ye find in all the world
20 A braver flag unfurled
Than that which floats above
The stream I sing and love?
O, what a burning glow
Has thrilled my breast and brow,
25 To see that proud flag come
With glory to its home,
    The Thames! the mighty Thames!

---

[1] *STEAMBOATS AND RAILWAYS* The sonnet as printed in *The Morning Post* varies in several small respects from the version first published in 1835 as "Steamboats, Viaducts, and Railways."

Did ribs more firm and fast
Ere meet the shot or blast
30   Than the gallant barks° that glide   *ships*
On its full and steady tide?
Would ye seek a dauntless crew
With hearts to dare and hands to do?
You 'll find the foe proclaims
35   They are cradled on the Thames;
    The Thames! the mighty Thames!

They say the mountain child
Oft loves its torrent wild
So well, that should he part
40   He breaks his pining heart;
He grieves with smothered sighs
Till his wearying spirit dies;
And so I yearn to thee,
Thou river of the free,
45   My own, my native Thames!

from Preface to *Poems, Second Series* (1845)

... I remember seeing a review of my earliest writings where the critic attempted to sneer me down as being "a poet of and for the lower classes." Short sighted man of letters! ... Surely it is no mean end to lay fast hold on sentiments unwarped by classic learning, and excite sympathy with feelings that live in simple bosoms, deep, strong, and unbiased. ...

I have been told that I write too boldly—that a feminine pen should never have traced such songs as "The Englishman" and "Old Time." ... Is there a line offensive to national pride, or reflective morality? To such narrow-minded grumblers I can only say that I fear the fault lies in their weak powers of digestion than in my plain, substantial food. ...

I can only write from my heart, and that heart has been left from infancy to the mercy of its own intense impulses. My rhyming tendency developed itself at a very early age, but the tones of judicious praise or improving censure never met my ear. The advantage of an enlightened—nay, even a common—education was denied me. ... I was left like a wild colt on the fresh and boundless common of Nature to pick up a mouthful of truth where I could. The woods and forests became my tutors; the rippling stream and bulrush sighing in the wind whispered to me in sweet and gentle breathings; the silver stars in the measureless night sky and the bright flowers in my morning path awoke my wonder, and opened the portals that led to the high and mysterious temple of Thought. God and Creation were before my eyes in all their glory, and as an untaught child I worshipped the Being who had endowed me with power to contemplate his works. ...

"God Hath a Voice" (1845)

God hath a voice that ever is heard
In the peal of the thunder, the chirp of the bird;
It comes in the torrent, all rapid and strong,
In the streamlet's soft gush as it ripples along;
5   It breathes in the zephyr,[1] just kissing the bloom;
It lives in the rush of the seeping simoom;°   *desert wind*
Let the hurricane whistle, or warblers rejoice,
What do they tell thee, but God hath a voice!

God hath a presence, and that ye may see
10   In the fold of the flower, the leaf of the tree;
In the sun of the noonday, the star of the night;
In the storm-wind of darkness, the rainbow of light;
In the waves of the ocean, the furrows of land;
In the mountain of granite, the atom of sand;
15   Turn where ye may, from the sky to the sod,
Where can ye gaze that ye see not a God!

---

[1]   *zephyr*   West wind, synonymous with a gentle and pleasant breeze.

"Lines Written for the Sheffield Mechanics' Exhibition" (1846)

The ice-bound tide, with currents pent beneath,
　Is stagnant, dreary, dull, and sad as Death:
Black, frowning clouds hang like a pall unfurled
Above the source whose Commerce aids a world.
5　The river's frozen—and the "outward bound"
Lies like a coffin in the ice-grave round.

The stripling boy with dust-polluted skin,
Hears no soft bubble-plash to tempt him in;
The famished wild dove, fluttering far to seek
10　For water, falls with stiff, unmoistened beak;
And vernal° bloom that fain would   *springtime*
　　deck the bank,
Crushed by the chill breath, leaves a cheerless blank.

But see; the summer sun with glowing beam
Flings radiant warmth upon the torpid stream;
15　The dense and blackened mass is seen no more;
Life stirs the waters—Joy is on the shore;
And fast and fresh the tide goes rolling by
Beneath the glory of a cloudless sky.

The laden bark° hastes onward with her freight;   *ship*
20　Destined to cheer some lone and distant state:
The growing children loiter by the side,
Watching the waves that sparkle as they glide;
Wading knee-deep, to touch the lily's brim,
Till bold in Hope—they plunge—strike out—
　　and swim.

25　The bird, whose soft notes hail Affection's nest,
Comes nigh to drink and lave its downy breast;
The flowers that spring burst forth with deeper hue,
With sweeter perfume, and a richer dew;
And the pure river, spreading as it goes;
30　Bears Health and Loveliness where'er it flows.

Knowledge, bright Knowledge, so *thy* sun must shine,
And leave unchained the spirit-stream divine.
Knowledge, fair Knowledge, 'tis alone thy ray

Can melt the bars of mortal ice away:
35　Thy honest sunshine only can unbind
The hard cold fetters freezing up the *Mind*;
Letting the tide of Intellect run free
With clear, warm gush to the Eternal Sea.

Fair Knowledge pleads the Universal Cause;
40　Truth in her language—Justice in her laws:
Leading rude° Ignorance with gentle hand   *unsophisticated*
To join Creation's highest, noblest band,
Loudly proclaiming that her humblest halls
Aid Peace and Virtue more than prison walls.
45　There do we list the teachings that impart
Strength to the brain, and Beauty to the heart—
There do we gain the wisdom that bestows
Balm for our own and care for others' woes;
There do we learn to prize the mercies sent,
50　And hail the giver with a glad content;
And *all* must bless the Temple that is raised
Where Man grows happier, while GOD is praised.

"Song of the City Artisan" (1870)

I never murmur at the lot
　That dooms me as the rich man's slave;
His wealthy ease I covet not—
　　No power I seek, no wealth I crave.

5　Labor is good, my strong right hand
　　Is ever ready to endure;
Though meanly° born, I bless my land,   *humbly*
　　Content to be among its poor.

But look upon this forehead pale,
10　　This tintless cheek, this rayless eye;
What do they ask?—the mountain gale,
　　The dewy turf, and open sky.

I read of high and grassy hills,
　　Of balmy dells and tangled woods;
15　Of lily-cups where dew distils,
　　Of hawthorns where the ringdove broods.

I hear of bright and perfumed flowers,
  That spring to kiss the wanderer's feet;
Of forests where the young fawn cowers,
20   Of streamlets rippling, cool and sweet.

They tell of waving fields of grain,
  Of purple fruit and shining leaves;
Of scattered seed and laden wain,°   *wagon*
  Of furrowed glebe° and rustling sheaves.   *field*

25 They speak of Nature, fresh and free,
  Lighting the dullest eyes that look;
Bards sing its glory—but to me
  It is a sealed and hidden book.

The radiant summer beams may fall,
30   But fail to break my cheerless gloom:
They cannot pierce the dusty wall
  Where pallid fingers ply the loom.

No warbler sings his grateful joys,
  No laden bee goes humming by;
35 Nought breaks the shifting shuttle's noise
  But angry oath or suffering sigh.

Pent with the crowd, oppressed and faint,
  My brow is damp, my breath is thick
And though my spirit yield no plaint,
40   My pining heart is deadly sick.

Give me a spade to delve the soil
  From early dawn to closing night;
The plough, the flail, or any toil
  That will not shut me from the light.

45 I often dream of an old tree,
  With violets round it, growing wild;
I know that happy dream must be
  Of where I played, a tiny child:

A dog-rose hedge, a cottage door,
50   Still linger in my wearied brain;
I feel my soul yearn more and more
  To see that hedgerow once again.

Double the labor of my task,
  Lessen my poor and scanty fare!
55 But give, oh! give me what I ask—
  The sunlight and the mountain air.

Roger Fenton, Early Photographs

Landscape photography was one of several branches of the new art in which Roger Fenton (1819–69) was a leading figure. In 1858 the *Journal of the Photographic Society* was unstinting in its praise:

> No one can touch Fenton in landscape: he seems to be to photography what Turner was to painting—our greatest landscape photographer; not that there is any similarity between the aerial perspectives of Turner, and the substantial and real we get transferred by Fenton. … There is such an artistic feeling about the whole of these pictures, the gradations of tint are so admirably given, that they cannot fail to strike the beholder as being something more than mere photographs.

Roger Fenton, *Wharfe and Pool, Below the Strid*, 1854. This area is described in *Black's Picturesque Guide to Yorkshire* (1862):

The Strid ..., receives its name from the ledges of rock by which the torrent is hemmed in, being here so near to each other that it is easy to stride across. ... Either side of the Wharfe [River] ... is overhung with solemn woods, from which huge, perpendicular masses of grey rock jut out at intervals. ... Here a tributary stream rushes from a waterfall and bursts through a woody glen to mingle its waters with the Wharfe; there the Wharfe itself is nearly lost in a deep cleft in the rock. ...

Roger Fenton, *Kirkstone Pass, Westmoreland*, 1857. By the 1850s this viewpoint had come to be regarded by many sightseers as among the most scenic in the Lake District. Lake Windermere is visible in the distance.

Roger Fenton, *Falls of the Llugwy, at Pont-y-Pair*, 1857. The location is in North Wales, near the village of Bettws-y-Coed.

Roger Fenton, *The Thames and the Houses of Parliament*, c. 1858.

The State of the Thames

In the mid-nineteenth century raw sewage was still being dumped directly into the Thames at London—resulting not only in an appalling odor but also in frequent outbreaks of cholera and other water-borne illnesses (though until the 1850s their cause was more often the subject of speculation than of science). The outbreak of cholera in London that John Snow famously linked to polluted water supply at a Broad Street pump occurred in 1854; a year later it had become widely accepted that cholera was a water-borne disease, and that human waste was frequently its carrier. Snow had advanced these ideas years earlier, however; he presented the paper excerpted below to a meeting of the Westminster Medical Society in September of 1849.

The famous scientist Michael Faraday (1791–1867) was among those who made "the state of the Thames" a public issue in the 1850s; his letter to *The Times* is reprinted below, together with cartoons from Punch and excerpts from the Parliamentary debates of 1858. Construction of sewers to address the problem was finally begun in 1859, though it was not completed until 1875; carried out under the

direction of chief engineer Joseph Bazalgette, it was one of the most ambitious of Victorian engineering projects.

The process of addressing sewage pollution in Britain's waterways continued well into the twentieth century. A Royal Commission on Sewage Disposal was established by the British government in 1898, and continued its work until 1912; its recommendations were not all acted on for many decades more.

from John Snow, "On the Mode of Communication of Cholera" (1849)

... Although there are a great number of pumps, supplied by wells, in this metropolis, yet by far the greater part of the water used for drinking and for culinary purposes is furnished by the various Water Companies. On the south side of the Thames the water works all obtain their supply from that river, at parts where it is much polluted by the sewers; none of them obtaining their water higher up the stream than Vauxhall Bridge—the position of the South London Water Works. Now as soon as the cholera began to prevail in

London, part of the water which had been contained in the evacuations of the patients would begin to enter the mains of the Water Works: whether the *materies morbi*[1] of cholera—which, it has been shewn, there is good reason for believing is contained in the evacuations—would be sent round to the inhabitants, would depend on whether the water were kept in the reservoirs till this *materies morbi* settled down or was destroyed; or whether it could be separated by the filtration through gravel and sand, which the water is stated to undergo. Notwithstanding this filtration, the water in this part of town is not always quite clear, and sometimes it has an offensive smell when clear. The deaths from cholera in this district, which contains a very little more than a quarter of the population, have been more numerous than in all the other districts put together; as will be seen ... [in] the reports of the Registrar-General. Out of the 7,466 deaths in the metropolis, 4,001 have occurred on the south side of the Thames, being nearly eight to each thousand of the inhabitants. ...

The whole of the Central Districts are likewise supplied from the New River,[2] and this part of the town has suffered much less from cholera, hitherto, than the south and east divisions; although many portions of it are quite on a par with the worst parts on the south of the Thames as regards overcrowding and bad smells. ... The West Districts, together with Marylebone, are supplied with Thames water by the West Middlesex, Grand Junction, and Chelsea Water Works. The West Middlesex Company obtain their water above Hammersmith, and the Grand Junction at Brentford; both these places, and especially the latter, are, by the meandering course of the river, several miles above London; and unless, perhaps, at certain parts of the tide, are free from sewage water, except that of certain towns—as Richmond, Barnes, etc.—in which the cholera has not yet been prevalent. The Chelsea Company, which supply Chelsea, Pimlico, Westminster, and part of Brompton, get their water at Chelsea, only one or two miles above Vauxhall; but they take great pains to filter it carefully. It will perhaps be remarked that the dilution of the cholera poison in the Thames would most likely render it innocuous; but as far as can be judged from analogy, the poison consists probably of organized particles, extremely small no doubt, but not capable of indefinite division, so long as they retain their properties. ...

It will probably be objected to the views advanced in this paper, that animal poisons, when swallowed, are generally destroyed in the stomach by the process of digestion; and, indeed, it is not improbable that the material which gives rise to cholera is often thus destroyed, and its effects resisted, since the complaint is very often observed to come on when the digestive powers have been weakened by a fit of drunkenness. ...

It should be observed, that the mode of contracting the malady here indicated does not altogether preclude the possibility of its being transmitted a short distance through the air; for the organic part of the fæces, when dry, might be wafted as a fine dust, in the same way as the spores of cryptogamic plants, or the germs of animalcules,[3] and entering the mouth, might be swallowed. In this manner, open sewers, as their contents are continually becoming dry on the sides, might be means of conveying cholera, independently of their mixing with water used for drinking. Mr. Russell, of Horsley-down, who attended the two first cases of the disease occurring in London last autumn—that of John Harnold, a seaman just arrived from Hamburg, where the disease was prevailing, and that of a man named Blenkinsopp, who came, after the death of the former, to lodge and sleep in the same room, and had the cholera eight days after him—states that the next cases in Horsleydown, which commenced three or four days afterwards, were in a situation a little way removed from

---

[1] *materies morbi* Latin: diseased matter; by extension, the material cause of the disease.

[2] *New River* Artificial waterway, opened in 1613, that supplied London with drinking water from the River Lea, a tributary of the Thames.

[3] *animalcules* Microscopic organisms.

that of the two preceding, and having no apparent connection with it, except that an open sewer, up which the tide flows, runs past both places, and the sewage from the houses in the first neighbourhood is, when the tide rises, carried past those in the second. ...

Michael Faraday, Letter to *The Times*, 7 July 1855

Sir,

I traversed this day by steam-boat the space between London and Hangerford Bridges between half-past one and two o'clock; it was low water, and I think the tide must have been near the turn. The appearance and the smell of the water forced themselves at once on my attention. The whole of the river was an opaque pale brown fluid. In order to test the degree of opacity, I tore up some white cards into pieces, moistened them so as to make them sink easily below the surface, and then dropped some of these pieces into the water at every pier the boat came to; before they had sunk an inch below the surface they were indistinguishable, though the sun shone brightly at the time; and when the pieces fell edgeways the lower part was hidden from sight before the upper part was under water. This happened at St. Paul's Wharf, Blackfriars Bridge, Temple Wharf, Southwark Bridge, and Hungerford; and I have no doubt would have occurred further up and down the river. Near the bridges the feculence[1] rolled up in clouds so dense that they were visible at the surface, even in water of this kind.

The smell was very bad, and common to the whole of the water; it was the same as that which now comes up from the gully-holes in the streets; the whole river was for the time a real sewer. Having just returned from out of the country air, I was, perhaps, more affected by

it than others; but I do not think I could have gone on to Lambeth or Chelsea, and I was glad to enter the streets for an atmosphere which, except near the sink-holes, I found much sweeter than that on the river.

I have thought it a duty to record these facts, that they may be brought to the attention of those who exercise power or have responsibility in relation to the condition of our river; there is nothing figurative in the words I have employed, or any approach to exaggeration; they are the simple truth. If there be sufficient authority to remove a putrescent pond from the neighbourhood of a few simple dwellings, surely the river which flows for so many miles through London ought not to be allowed to become a fermenting sewer. The condition in which I saw the Thames may perhaps be considered as exceptional, but it ought to be an impossible state, instead of which I fear it is rapidly becoming the general condition. If we neglect this subject, we cannot expect to do so with impunity; nor ought we to be surprised if, ere many years are over, a hot season give us sad proof of the folly of our carelessness.

I am, Sir,
Your obedient servant,

M. Faraday
Royal Institution

from *Punch* (21 July 1855)

Faraday's letter was widely noted; among the reactions was the cartoon below, which appeared in the magazine *Punch* later that same month with the caption "Faraday Giving His Card to Father Thames," and with an additional comment by the magazine's editors below the caption: "And we hope the Dirty Fellow will consult the learned Professor."

---

[1] *feculence* Filth.

from *Hansard's Parliamentary Debates* (1858)

HOUSE OF COMMONS: FROM 28 MAY 1858 DEBATES

State of the Thames—

Question: Mr. Brady said he wished to put a question to the noble Lord the Chief Commissioner of Works with regard to the state of the River Thames. It was a notorious fact that hon. Gentlemen sitting in the Committee Rooms and in the Library were utterly unable to remain there in consequence of the stench which arose from the river; and he wished to know if the noble Lord has taken any measures for mitigating the effluvium[1] and discontinuing the nuisance.

Lord John Manners said he was very sorry to tell the hon. Gentleman that the River Thames was not in his jurisdiction, and therefore not under his control.

_____

[1] *effluvium* Disgusting odor.

HOUSE OF COMMONS: FROM 15 JUNE 1858 DEBATES

State of the Thames—

Question—Mr. Mangles: I wish to ask the noble Lord the Chief Commissioner of Works whether he intends to take any steps with regard to the present state of the River Thames. [*Laughter and Cheers.*] My question, I perceive, excited the laughter of some hon. Gentlemen, but I can assure them that if they lived in the vicinity of the Thames they would not think my question one of little importance. By a perverse ingenuity, one of the noblest of rivers has been changed into a cesspool, and I wish to ask whether Her Majesty's Government intend to take any steps to remedy the evil?

Lord John Manners: Sir, in answer to the question which has been somewhat unexpectedly put to me by the hon. Gentleman, I can only say, and he must be as well aware of the facts as myself, that Her Majesty's Government have nothing whatever to do with the state of the Thames; that by a recent Act of Parliament the whole jurisdiction over it has been committed to the Metropolitan Board of Works, and that Her Majesty's Government can only exercise a sort of veto upon any plan which they may propose for its purification. No scheme which they may propose for its purification can be carried into effect unless it has received the approbation of the Chief Commissioner of Works. All I can say is, that up to the present moment I have not received any scheme from the Metropolitan Board of Works to which I can give my assent, or from which I can withhold it. It may be satisfactory to know that in my individual capacity I am at this moment serving on a Committee which has been appointed for the purpose of investigating some scheme for the purification of the Thames. When the researches of that Committee terminate, it will be open to the hon. Gentleman to ask me any questions with reference to the subject, and I shall be glad to afford him all the information in my power.

from *Punch* (10 July 1858)

This cartoon, depicting the figure of Death taking lives as he rows along the Thames, appeared in the 10 July 1858 issue of the magazine *Punch*, with the caption "The Silent Highwayman."

Pre-Raphaelite Nature Painting

In their approach to nature, the Pre-Raphaelites were inspired in large part by John Ruskin's directive to young painters in his conclusion to the first volume of *Modern Painters* (1847): "They should go to nature in all singleness of heart, and walk with her laboriously and trustingly, having no other thought but how best to penetrate her meaning; rejecting nothing, selecting nothing, and scorning nothing; believing all things to be right and good, and rejoicing always in the truth."

Pre-Raphaelite nature paintings are notable not least of all for the attention they pay to detail. William Holman Hunt (1827–1910) spent several months in 1852 at the site near Hastings that is the subject of the painting he titled *Our English Coasts* when he showed it at the Royal Academy Exhibition in 1853. (When he exhibited it again in 1855 in Paris he re-titled it *Strayed Sheep*.)

Rosa Brett (1829–82) and John Brett (1831–1902) were siblings, children of an army veterinarian and his wife who paid for both to have art lessons in the 1840s. Both became important Pre-Raphaelite artists—though John enjoyed greater success. (Rosa exhibited for many years under the pseudonym Rosarius.) Like that of Holman Hunt, the work of both Bretts is notable for its detail. John seems to have taken on subjects suggestive of the sublime more often than did Rosa, but the seeming differences in preferred subject matter may be more apparent than real; as Rosa revealed in the diary she kept during the period when the two shared a studio, she sometimes painted works (she mentions specifically a painting entitled *Fungus*) that passed for her brother's.

John's *The Glacier of Rosenlaui* was painted during a trip to Switzerland he took in 1856, after having been inspired by his reading of volume 4 of Ruskin's *Modern Painters* ("Of Mountain Beauty"). When Brett returned, he showed the painting to Dante Gabriel Rossetti, who in turn showed it to Ruskin; both praised it highly.

When Rosa's painting *Thistles* was shown at the 1861 Royal Academy exhibition the Art-Journal reviewer gave it a mixed review: "It might be difficult to get more interesting thistles than those … painted by Rosarius, whoever he may be; but they are only thistles after all, and no means within the domain of Art will magnify the down into importance, even though every fibre were as fully represented as in nature."

Anna Blunden (1829–1915), who was for many years close to Ruskin, is best known for a portrait entitled *The Seamstress* (alternatively known as *Song of the Shirt*, after the Thomas Hood poem that inspired it). She was also for many years an accomplished landscape painter; *Kynance Cove* was well received when it was exhibited at the Royal Academy show in 1863.

[N.B. A separate section on The Pre-Raphaelites appears elsewhere in this anthology; see also the author entries for Dante Gabriel Rossetti and John Ruskin.]

William Holman Hunt, *Our English Coasts / Strayed Sheep*, 1852.

John Brett, *The Glacier of Rosenlaui*, 1856.

Rosa Brett, *Thistles*, 1861.

Anna Blunden, *Kynance Cove, Cornwall*, undated (c. 1860?).

Adelaide Proctor, "Two Worlds" (1861)

Adelaide Proctor (1825–64) was among the most popular poets of the Victorian period—almost as popular as Tennyson, by some accounts. Though a Catholic, she is said to have been Queen Victoria's favorite poet. Her nature poetry, like much of her other poetry, is strongly colored by her religious beliefs.

God's world is bathed in beauty,
    God's world is steeped in light;
It is the self-same glory
    That makes the day so bright,
5 Which thrills the earth with music,
    Or hangs the stars in night.

Hid in earth's mines of silver,
    Floating on clouds above—
Ringing in Autumn's tempest,
10   Murmured by every dove—
One thought fills God's creation,
    His own great name of Love!

In God's world Strength is lovely,
    And so is Beauty strong,
15 And Light—God's glorious shadow—
    To both great gifts belong;
And they all melt into sweetness,
    And fill the earth with Song.

Above God's world bends Heaven,
20   With day's kiss pure and bright,
Or folds her still more fondly
    In tender shade of night;
And she casts back Heaven's sweetness,
    In fragrant love and light.

25 God's world has one great echo;
    Whether calm blue mists are curled,
Or lingering dew-drops quiver,
    Or red storms are unfurled;

The same deep love is throbbing
30   Through the great heart of God's world.

Man's world is black and blighted,
    Steeped through with self and sin;
And should his feeble purpose
    Some feeble good begin,
35 The work is marred and tainted
    By leprosy within.

Man's world is bleak and bitter;
    Wherever he has trod,
He spoils the tender beauty
40   That blossoms on the sod,
And blasts the loving Heaven
    Of the great, good world of God.

There strength on coward weakness
    In cruel might will roll;
45 Beauty and Joy are cankers
    That eat away the soul;
And Love—O God, avenge it—
    The plague-spot of the whole.

Man's world is pain and terror;
50   He found it pure and fair,
And wove in nets of sorrow
    The golden summer air.
Black, hideous, cold, and dreary,
    Man's curse, not God's, is there.

55 And yet God's world is speaking:
    Man will not hear it call;
But listens where the echoes
    Of his own discords fall,
Then clamors back to Heaven
60   That God has done it all.

O God, man's heart is darkened,
    He will not understand!
Show him Thy cloud and fire;
    And, with Thine own right hand,

65   Then lead him through his desert,
        Back to Thy Holy Land!

John Ruskin, "Traffic" (1864)

In 1864 Ruskin accepted an invitation to speak in the town hall at Bradford on the subject of that city's projected new Exchange building;[1] the lecture he delivered, entitled "Traffic,"[2] ranged far beyond the topic of architecture. In its 28 April 1864 issue, the *Bradford Observer* informed its readers that "about seven hundred people" had assembled to hear "eloquence—not of the mere word-painting type—but of the higher kind that emanates from a mind deeply imbued with a grand philosophy." Such eloquence, the writer continued—"eloquence unsullied by the hot breath of politics, or the spitting venom of sectarianism, is so rare a thing that we can mark but few days in our diary that have been so brightened." The writer then provides something by way of a summary of Ruskin's remarks, but in doing so treads noticeably lightly when it comes to reporting on the degree to which Ruskin took issue in his lecture with the materialistic philosophy that Ruskin presumed many of his listeners to be adhering to. (There is only one reference in the article to "the goddess of getting on.")

The *Bradford Observer* reporter remarks that the room "was filled to its utmost corner, and the lot of most of the audience was that of having expected much and having got more." The final paragraph notes that Mr. H.W. Ripley, who chaired the event, took pains to make it clear in his closing remarks that the directors of the Bradford Exchange had not as yet "fixed upon or discussed any style of architecture" for the new Exchange building; and to make it clear as well that the Committee which had "formed

itself for the express purpose of inviting" Ruskin to deliver the lecture was a body entirely separate from the Board of Directors of the Exchange.

Ruskin's lecture was published later in 1864 in *The Crown of Wild Olive: Three Lectures on Work, Traffic, and War*. The new Bradford Exchange was completed three years later; a sketch of the building (and a report on its opening) appear following the excerpts from Ruskin's lecture.

My good Yorkshire friends, you asked me down here among your hills that I might talk to you about this Exchange you are going to build: but earnestly and seriously asking you to pardon me, I am going to do nothing of the kind. I cannot talk, or at least can say very little, about this same Exchange. I must talk of quite other things, though not willingly; I could not deserve your pardon, if when you invited me to speak on one subject, I wilfully spoke on another. But I cannot speak, to purpose, of anything about which I do not care; and most simply and sorrowfully I have to tell you, in the outset, that I do *not* care about this Exchange of yours.

If, however, when you sent me your invitation, I had answered, "I won't come, I don't care about the Exchange of Bradford," you would have been justly offended with me, not knowing the reasons of so blunt a carelessness. So I have come down, hoping that you will patiently let me tell you why. …

Look at the essential circumstances of the case, which you, as business men, know perfectly well, though perhaps you think I forget them. You are going to spend 30,000*l.*, which to you, collectively, is nothing; the buying a new coat is, as to the cost of it, a much more important matter of consideration to me than building a new Exchange is to you. But you think you may as well have the right thing for your money. You know there are a great many odd styles of architecture about; you don't want to do anything ridiculous; you hear of me, among others, as a respectable architectural … [authority] and you send for me, that I may tell you the leading fashion. …

Now, pardon me for telling you frankly, you cannot have good architecture merely by asking people's advice

---

[1]   *Exchange building*   Building designed to provide a space to facilitate the buying and selling of goods or services. Exchanges may be devoted to the sale and purchase of a particular type of good or service (e.g., a grain exchange, a stock exchange) or to a wider range (e.g., a commodities exchange—or, as in this case, simply an exchange).

[2]   *Traffic*   Buying and selling of goods. (Nowadays this meaning is maintained only in the context of "drug trafficking.")

on occasion. All good architecture is the expression of national life and character; and it is produced by a prevalent and eager national taste, or desire for beauty. And I want you to think a little of the deep significance of this word "taste"; for no statement of mine has been more earnestly or oftener controverted than that good taste is essentially a moral quality. "No," say many of my antagonists, "taste is one thing, morality is another. Tell us what is pretty; we shall be glad to know that; but preach no sermons to us."

Permit me, therefore, to fortify this old dogma of mine somewhat. Taste is not only a part and an index of morality—it is the only morality. ...

But you may answer or think, "Is the liking for outside ornaments—for pictures, or statues, or furniture, or architecture—a moral quality?" Yes, most surely, if a rightly set liking. Taste for *any* pictures or statues is not a moral quality, but taste for good ones is. Only here again we have to define the word "good." I don't mean by "good," clever—or learned—or difficult in the doing. ...

[A]ll delight in art, and all love of it, resolve themselves into simple love of that which deserves love. That deserving is the quality which we call "loveliness" (we ought to have an opposite word, hateliness, to be said of the things which deserve to be hated); and it is not an indifferent nor optional thing whether we love this or that; but it is just the vital function of all our being. What we *like* determines what we *are*, and is the sign of what we are; and to teach taste is inevitably to form character. ...

I notice that among all the new buildings that cover your once wild hills, churches and schools are mixed in due, that is to say, in large proportion, with your mills and mansions, and I notice also that the churches and schools are almost always Gothic, and the mansions and mills are never Gothic. Will you allow me to ask precisely the meaning of this? For, remember, it is peculiarly a modern phenomenon. ...

[C]onsider what a wide significance this fact has; and remember that it is not you only, but all the people of England, who are behaving thus just now.

You have all got into the habit of calling the church "the house of God." I have seen, over the doors of many churches, the legend actually carved, "*This* is the house of God, and this is the gate of heaven."[1] ...

But the perpetual and insolent warping of that strong verse to serve a merely ecclesiastical purpose, is only one of the thousand instances in which we sink back into gross Judaism.[2] ...

Now, you feel, as I say this to you—I know you feel—as if I were trying to take away the honour of your churches. Not so; I am trying to prove to you the honour of your houses and your hills; I am trying to show you—not that the Church is not sacred—but that the whole Earth is. ...

"But what has all this to do with our Exchange?" you ask me, impatiently. My dear friends, it has just everything to do with it; on these inner and great questions depend all the outer and little ones; and if you have asked me down here to speak to you, because you had before been interested in anything I have written, you must know that all I have yet said about architecture was to show this. The book I called *The Seven Lamps* was to show that certain right states of temper and moral feeling were the magic powers by which all good architecture, without exception, had been produced. *The Stones of Venice*, had, from beginning to end, no other aim than to show that the Gothic architecture of Venice had arisen out of, and indicated in all its features, a state of pure national faith, and of domestic virtue; and that its Renaissance architecture had arisen out of, and in all its features indicated, a state of concealed national infidelity, and of domestic corruption. And now, you ask me what style is best to build in; and how can I answer, knowing the meaning of the two styles, but by another question—do you mean to build as Christians or as Infidels? And still more—do you mean to build as honest Christians or as honest Infidels? ... You don't like to be asked such rude questions. I cannot help it; they are of much more importance than

---

[1] *This ... heaven* See Genesis 28.17.

[2] *Judaism* In this context, overly legalistic and literal-minded religion.

this Exchange business; and if they can be at once answered, the Exchange business settles itself in a moment. But, before I press them farther, I must ask leave to explain one point clearly. In all my past work, my endeavour has been to show that good architecture is essentially religious—the production of a faithful and virtuous, not of an infidel and corrupted people. ...

You know we are speaking always of the real, active, continual, national worship; that by which men act while they live; not that which they talk of when they die. Now, we have, indeed, a nominal religion, to which we pay tithes of property, and sevenths of time;[1] but we have also a practical and earnest religion, to which we devote nine-tenths of our property and six-sevenths of our time. And we dispute a great deal about the nominal religion; but we are all unanimous about this practical one, of which I think you will admit that the ruling goddess may be best generally described as the "Goddess of Getting-on,"[2] or "Britannia of the Market." ... And all your great architectural works, are, of course, built to her. It is long since you built a great cathedral; and how you would laugh at me, if I proposed building a cathedral on the top of one of these hills of yours, taking it for an Acropolis! But your railroad mounds, prolonged masses of Acropolis; your railroad stations, vaster than the Parthenon, and innumerable; your chimneys, how much more mighty and costly than cathedral spires! your harbour-piers; your warehouses; your exchanges!—all these are built to your great Goddess of "Getting-on"; and she has formed, and will continue to form, your architecture, as long as you worship her; and it is quite vain to ask me to tell you how to build to *her*; you know far better than I.

There might indeed, on some theories, be a conceivably good architecture for Exchanges—that is to say if there were any heroism in the fact or deed of exchange,

which might be typically carved on the outside of your building. For, you know, all beautiful architecture must be adorned with sculpture or painting; and for sculpture or painting, you must have a subject. And hitherto it has been a received opinion among the nations of the world that the only right subjects for either, were *heroisms* of some sort. ...

The wonder has always been great to me, that heroism has never been supposed to be in anywise consistent with the practice of supplying people with food, or clothes; but rather with that of quartering oneself upon them for food, and stripping them of their clothes. ...

Are not all forms of heroism, conceivable in doing these serviceable deeds? You doubt who is strongest? It might be ascertained by push of spade, as well as push of sword. Who is wisest? There are witty things to be thought of in planning other business than campaigns. Who is bravest? There are always the elements to fight with, stronger than men; and nearly as merciless. The only absolutely and unapproachably heroic element in the soldier's work seems to be—that he is paid little for it—and regularly: while you traffickers, and exchangers, and others occupied in presumably benevolent business, like to be paid much for it[.] ...

Your ideal of human life ... is, I think, that it should be passed in a pleasant undulating world, with iron and coal everywhere underneath it. On each pleasant bank of this world is to be a beautiful mansion, with two wings; and stables, and coach-houses; a moderately sized park; a large garden and hot houses; and pleasant carriage drives through the shrubberies. In this mansion are to live the favoured votaries of the Goddess; the English gentleman, with his gracious wife, and his beautiful family; always able to have the boudoir and the jewels for the wife, and the beautiful ball dresses for the daughters, and hunters for the sons, and a shooting in the Highlands for himself. At the bottom of the bank, is to be the mill; not less than a quarter of a mile long, with a steam engine at each end, and two in the middle, and a chimney three hundred feet high. In this mill are to be in constant employment from eight hundred to a thousand workers, who never drink, never strike, always

---

[1] *sevenths of time* I.e., every seventh day (Sunday) is devoted to religious practice. Ruskin is punning on the original meaning of "tithe" as the tenth of one's possessions one was supposed to donate to the Church.

[2] *Getting-on* Making your way in the world—especially, making your way by becoming wealthier.

go to church on Sunday, and always express themselves in respectful language.

Is not that, broadly, and in the main features, the kind of thing you propose to yourselves? It is very pretty indeed seen from above; not at all so pretty, seen from below. For, observe, while to one family this deity is indeed the Goddess of Getting-on, to a thousand families she is the Goddess of *not* Getting-on. "Nay," you say, "they have all their chance." Yes, so has every one in a lottery, but there must always be the same number of blanks. "Ah! but in a lottery it is not skill and intelligence which take the lead, but blind chance." What then! do you think the old practice, that "they should take who have the power, and they should keep who can,"[1] is less iniquitous, when the power has become power of brains instead of fist? and that, though we may not take advantage of a child's or a woman's weakness, we may of a man's foolishness? "Nay, but finally, work must be done, and some one must be at the top, some one at the bottom." Granted, my friends. Work must always be, and captains of work must always be; and if you in the least remember the tone of any of my writings, you must know that they are thought unfit for this age, because they are always insisting on need of government, and speaking with scorn of liberty. But I beg you to observe that there is a wide difference between being captains or governors of work, and taking the profits of it. It does not follow, because you are general of an army, that you are to take all the treasure, or land, it wins (if it fight for treasure or land); neither, because you are king of a nation, that you are to consume all the profits of the nation's work. Real kings, on the contrary, are known invariably by their doing quite the reverse of this—by their taking the least possible quantity of the nation's work for themselves. There is no test of real kinghood so infallible as that. Does the crowned creature live simply, bravely, unostentatiously? probably he *is* a King. Does he cover his body with jewels, and his table with delicates? in all probability he is *not* a King. It is possible he may be, as Solomon was;

but that is when the nation shares his splendour with him. Solomon made gold, not only to be in his own palace as stones, but to be in Jerusalem as stones. But even so, for the most part, these splendid kinghoods expire in ruin, and only the true kinghoods live, which are of royal labourers governing loyal labourers; who, both leading rough lives, establish the true dynasties. Conclusively you will find that because you are king of a nation, it does not follow that you are to gather for yourself all the wealth of that nation; neither, because you are king of a small part of the nation, and lord over the means of its maintenance—over field, or mill, or mine, are you to take all the produce of that piece of the foundation of national existence for yourself.

You will tell me I need not preach against these things, for I cannot mend them. No, good friends, I cannot; but you can, and you will; or something else can and will. Do you think these phenomena are to stay always in their present power or aspect? All history shows, on the contrary, that to be the exact thing they never can do. Change *must* come; but it is ours to determine whether change of growth, or change of death. Shall the Parthenon be in ruins on its rock, and Bolton priory in its meadow, but these mills of yours be the consummation of the buildings of the earth, and their wheels be as the wheels of eternity? Think you that "men may come, and men may go," but—mills—go on forever? Not so; out of these, better or worse shall come; and it is for you to choose which.

I know that none of this wrong is done with deliberate purpose. I know, on the contrary, that you wish your workmen well; that you do much for them, and that you desire to do more for them, if you saw your way to it safely. I know that many of you have done, and are every day doing, whatever you feel to be in your power; and that even all this wrong and misery are brought about by a warped sense of duty, each of you striving to do his best, without noticing that this best is essentially and centrally the best for himself, not for others. And all this has come of the spreading of that thrice accursed, thrice impious doctrine of the modern economist, that "To do the best for yourself, is finally to do the best for others." Friends, our great Master said not so; and most

---

[1] *they … can* From "Rob Roy's Grave" (1803), by William Wordsworth (lines 39–40).

absolutely we shall find this world is not made so. Indeed, to do the best for others, is finally to do the best for ourselves; but it will not do to have our eyes fixed on that issue. [I]n our own Scriptural tradition … [it is said that, within human hearts God's nature was full so long as] they were submissive to the sacred laws, and carried themselves lovingly to all that had kindred with them in divineness; for their uttermost spirit was faithful and true, and in every wise great; so that, in all meekness of wisdom, they dealt with each other, and took all the chances of life; and despising all things except virtue, they cared little what happened day by day, and *bore lightly the burden* of gold and of possessions; for they saw that, if only their common love and virtue increased, all these things would be increased together with them; but to set their esteem and ardent pursuit upon material possession would be to lose that first, and their virtue and affection together with it.

from "The New Exchange Building, Bradford," *The Illustrated London News* (16 March 1867)

The opening of the new Exchange at Bradford took place on Wednesday last. … The building is designed in the Gothic style, adapted to modern wants and requirements. It was desirable that no projections or recesses should occur in Market Street, and the Market Street front was therefore kept unbroken. At the east end, and forming the entrance, is placed the clock tower, which rises to the height of 150 ft. The windows to the principal front have coupled shafts, in serpentine marble; and the building is crowned by an open and pierced parapet, terminated at each angle by corbelled turrets. … Between each of the large windows on the ground floor are circular medallions containing heads of men who have contributed to the commercial enterprise of the country and the prosperity of this town.

The principal contractors are Messrs. J. and W. Beauland, of Bradford. The building has cost about £30,000, and has been erected from the designs of Messrs. Lockwood and Mawson, architects, of Bradford and London.

from William Stanley Jevons, *The Coal Question* (1866)

Jevons (1835–82) was among the leading economists of the Victorian era; he is credited with having made a significant contribution to the development of political economy as a discipline that drew substantially upon mathematics and statistics in formulating conclusions. In *The Coal Question: An Inquiry Concerning the Progress of the Nation, and the Probable Exhaustion of the Coal Mines*, a foundational work in linking political economy to concerns regarding what we now call sustainability, Jevons posed for Britons what he called a "truly solemn question—Are we wise in allowing the commerce of this country to rise beyond the point at which we can long maintain it?"

Jevons's work first appeared in 1865; in the second edition, which appeared the following year, Jevons added a preface in which he declared that "renewed reflection" had further convinced him of his "main position"—that "we cannot long progress as we are now doing."

(Please note that a more substantial selection of excerpts from Jevons's work is included in this anthology's website component.)

from CHAPTER 1: INTRODUCTION AND OUTLINE

Day by day it becomes more evident that the coal we happily[1] possess in excellent quality and abundance is the mainspring of modern material civilization. As the source of fire, it is the source at once of mechanical motion and of chemical change. Accordingly it is the chief agent in almost every improvement or discovery in the arts which the present age brings forth. It is to us indispensable for domestic purposes, and it has of late years been found to yield a series of organic substances, which puzzle us by their complexity, please us by their beautiful colours, and serve us by their various utility.

And as the source especially of steam and iron, coal is all powerful. This age has been called the Iron Age, and it is true that iron is the material of most great novelties. By its strength, endurance, and wide range of qualities, this metal is fitted to be the fulcrum and lever of great works, while steam is the motive power. But coal alone can command in sufficient abundance either the iron or the steam; and coal, therefore, commands this age—the Age of Coal.

Coal in truth stands not beside but entirely above all other commodities. It is the material energy of the country—the universal aid—the factor in everything we do. With coal almost any feat is possible or easy; without it we are thrown back into the laborious poverty of early times.

With such facts familiarly before us, it can be no matter of surprise that year by year we make larger

draughts upon[2] a material of such myriad qualities—of such miraculous powers. But it is at the same time impossible that men of foresight should not turn to compare with some anxiety the masses yearly drawn with the quantities known or supposed to lie within these islands. ...

This question concerning the duration of our present cheap supplies of coal cannot but excite deep interest and anxiety wherever or whenever it is mentioned: for a little reflection will show that coal is almost the sole necessary basis of our material power, and is that, consequently, which gives efficiency to our moral and intellectual capabilities. England's manufacturing and commercial greatness, at least, is at stake in this question, nor can we be sure that material decay may not involve us in moral and intellectual retrogression. [I]t is in a subsequent chapter on the Export and Import of Coal conclusively shown that we cannot make up for a future want of coal by importation from other countries, it will appear that there is no reasonable prospect of any relief from a future want of the main agent of industry.[3] We must lose that which constitutes our peculiar energy. And considering how greatly our manufactures and navigation depend upon coal, and how vast is our consumption of it compared with that of other nations, it cannot be supposed we shall do without coal more than a fraction of what we do with it. ...

from CHAPTER 18: CONCLUDING REFLECTIONS

... [I]t is impossible to close without a few further remarks upon the truly solemn question—are we wise in allowing the commerce of this country to rise beyond the point at which we can long maintain it? To say the simple truth, will it not appear evident, soon after the final adoption of Free Trade principles, that our own

---

[1] *happily* Fortunately.

[2] *make larger draughts upon* Use larger and larger quantities of, thus drawing down the supply.

[3] *no reasonable prospect ... of industry* I.e., no reasonable chance that we can escape shortages of the material [coal] on which our industry primarily relies.

resources are just those to which such principles ought to be applied last and most cautiously? To part in trade with the surplus yearly interest of the soil may be unalloyed gain, but to disperse so lavishly the cream of our mineral wealth is to be spendthrifts of our capital—to part with that which will never come back.

And after all commerce is but a means to an end, the diffusion of civilization and wealth. To allow commerce to proceed until the source of civilization is weakened and overturned is like killing the goose to get the golden egg. Is the immediate creation of material wealth to be our only object? Have we not hereditary possessions in our just laws, our free and nobly developed constitution, our rich literature and philosophy, incomparably above material wealth, and which we are beyond all things bound to maintain, improve, and hand down in safety? And do we accomplish this duty in encouraging a growth of industry which must prove unstable, and perhaps involve all things in its fall? …

!kweiten ta //ken, "What the Maidens Do with *Rooi Klip*" (1874)

In 1874 !kweiten ta //ken, together with her husband and two of her young children, came to Cape Town (then the capital of Cape Colony, a semi-autonomous jurisdiction within the British Empire) from her home in the Katrop Mountains to the north; she stayed in the city until January of the following year. While there, she was interviewed numerous times by Lucy Lloyd, who was working with linguist William Bleek to record the (now extinct) /Xam language and to record the *kukummi* (aggregated information, stories, and myths) of the /Xam people. It is not clear exactly what the substance referred to as *rooi klip* consists of, but in a note to the original text Lloyd provides this

additional gloss: "The bushgirls put it round the springs, and adorn the springs with it, so that the water shall not dry up—R. [another /Xam informant] tells me. The women paint their cheeks with it, and also their *karosses*, R. says. The maidens put it on the men's backs." M.J. Daymond and her fellow editors, who include this selection in their *Women Writing Africa: The Southern Region* volume, provide further information on !kweiten ta //ken and Lloyd; the text itself is part of the University of Cape Town Libraries Bleek Collection.

The maiden, she ornaments the spring with [*rooi klip*] when she becomes a maiden; she wishes that the spring may not dry up [literally, "go out"]; because she wishes that the water might remain quietly in the spring. Because she wishes that the water may not dry up; that the water may remain in the spring. Therefore, they adorn the spring, when they become maidens. Therefore, they adorn the spring on account of it; because they wish that the spring may not dry up, that it [the water] might remain quietly on account of it. Therefore, the old women tell them about it; therefore, they [the maidens] adorn the water's springs, on account of it. They wish that the spring may not become dry.

Thence it is that the girls adorn the young men, because they wish that the rain may not lightning kill them [the young men]. Therefore, they adorn them, on account of it.

The Water's Story.

Therefore, they [the maidens] adorn the young men, on account of it; for the rain comes out [in] the young men. Therefore, they [the maidens] adorn them on account of it, with [*rooi klip*], [so] that the rain may not come out [upon them]. Therefore, they adorn them, on account of it.

Thomas Talbot Bury, *View of the Liverpool and Manchester Railway across Chat Moss*, 1831. Chat Moss is a deep peat bog (now located within the city boundaries of Salford); in the nineteenth century, building a stable trackbed in such locations was a significant engineering challenge.

from Samuel Smiles, *Lives of the Engineers* (1874–77)

Scottish writer and political reformer Samuel Smiles (1812–1904) is most famous for his groundbreaking 1859 book *Self-Help; with Illustrations of Character and Conduct*, but he also authored numerous biographies, most notably the multi-volume *Lives of the Engineers* (1862). Here, Smiles celebrates the innovation and industriousness of a variety of British engineers whose work in remaking the British environment with railways, canals, and steamships he saw as essential to nineteenth-century social and economic development; the sections included in this anthology's online component focus primarily on the early railway developers George Stephenson (1781–1848) and his son Robert Stephenson (1803–59).

Smiles continued to revise the text throughout the late nineteenth century and the work was reissued several times, most notably in the five volumes published from 1874 to 1877. A brief excerpt from the introduction is included here; substantial excerpts appear as part of the anthology's website component.

from VOLUME 1

from INTRODUCTION

Our engineers may be regarded in some measure as the makers of modern civilisation. The problems of political history cannot properly be interpreted without reference to the people themselves—how they lived and how they worked, and what they did to promote the civilisation of the nation to which they belonged. Hence English engineers are not unworthy to be considered in the history of their country. For what were England without its roads, its bridges, its canals, its docks, and its harbours? What were it without its tools, its machinery, its steam-engine, its steam-ships, and its locomotive? Are not the men who have made the motive power of the country, and immensely increased its productive strength, the men above all others who have tended to make the country what it is? ...

The object of this work is to give an account of some of the principal men by whom this nation has been made so great and prosperous as it is—the men by whose skill and industry large tracts of fertile land have been won from the sea, the bog, and the fen,[1] and made available for human habitation and sustenance; who, by their industry, skill, and genius, have made England the busiest of workshops; who have rendered the country accessible in all directions by roads, bridges, canals, and railways; and who have built lighthouses, breakwaters, docks, and harbours, for the protection and accommodation of our vast home and foreign commerce.

---

[1] *fen* Marshland.

Mathilde Blind, Poems

Born in Germany, Blind led a lively childhood, as her mother and stepfather engaged in revolutionary activities in several European countries before moving to London in 1852 (where their household remained a gathering spot for political activists). Blind herself was also a republican and a socialist, as well as being active in the movement for women's rights. Many of her poems concern the natural world, and the interaction between human and non-human nature. She is known for exploring Darwinian themes in her writing—notably in her long poem *The Ascent of Man* (1889)—which is followed in the same volume by a group of poems entitled "Poems of the Open Air"; "On a Forsaken Lark's Nest" and "Reapers" appear together in that group.

"Entangled," 1867

I stood as one enchanted,
  All in the forest deep:
As one that wond'ring wanders,
  Dream-bound within his sleep.

5 A thousand rustling footsteps
  Pattered upon the ground;
A thousand whisp'ring voices
  Made the wide silence, sound.

Some murmured deep and deeper,
10 Like waves in solemn seas;
Some breathèd sweet and sweeter,
  Like elves on moon-lit leas.°   *meadows*

Tall ferns, washed down in sunlight,
  Beckoned with fingers green;
15 Tall flowers nodded strangely,
  With white and glimm'ring sheen;

They sighed, they sang so softly,
  They stretched their arms to me;

My heart, it throbbed so wildly,
20 In weird tumultuous glee.

I staggered in the mosses,
  It seemed to drag me down
Into the gleaming bushes;
  To fall, to sink, to drown.

25 When lo! thro' scared foliage,
  A lovely bird did fly;
And looked at me so knowing,
  With bright and curious eye;

It broke out into warbles,
30 And singing sped away;
But I, like one awakened,
  Fled down the mossy way.

"On a Forsaken Lark's Nest," 1889

Lo, where left 'mid the sheaves, cut down by the iron-fanged reaper,
Eating its way as it clangs fast through the wavering wheat,
Lies the nest of a lark, whose little brown eggs could not keep her
As she, affrighted and scared, fled from the harvester's feet.

5 Ah, what a heartful of song that now will never awaken,
Closely packed in the shell, awaited love's fostering,
That should have quickened to life what, now a-cold and forsaken,
Never, enamoured of light, will meet the dawn on the wing.

Ah, what paeans of joy, what raptures no mortal can measure,
10 Sweet as honey that's sealed in the cells of the honeycomb,

Would have ascended on high in jets of mellifluous
　　pleasure,
Would have dropped from the clouds to nest in its
　　gold-curtained home.

Poor, pathetic brown eggs! Oh, pulses that never will
　　quicken
Music mute in the shell that hath been turned to a
　　tomb!
15　Many a sweet human singer, chilled and adversity-
　　stricken,
Withers benumbed in a world his joy might have
　　helped to illume.

"Reapers," 1889

Sun-tanned men and women, toiling there together;
　Seven I count in all, in yon field of wheat,
Where the rich ripe ears in the harvest weather
Glow an orange gold through the sweltering heat.

5　Busy life is still, sunk in brooding leisure:
Birds have hushed their singing in the hushed tree-tops;
Not a single cloud mars the flawless azure;
Not a shadow moves o'er the moveless crops;

In the glassy shallows, that no breath is creasing,
10　Chestnut-coloured cows in the rushes dank
Stand like cows of bronze, save when they flick the
　　teasing
Flies with switch of tail from each quivering flank.

Nature takes a rest—even her bees are sleeping,
And the silent wood seems a church that's shut;
15　But these human creatures cease not from their reaping
While the corn stands high, waiting to be cut.

Thomas Hardy,
On Human and Non-Human Animals

The ways in which the natural world is depicted and characterized in the work of Thomas Hardy have been much discussed, with considerable attention often paid to the treatment he accords relationships between human and non-human animals. *Far from the Madding Crowd*, Hardy's first novel to reach a wide readership, focuses a good deal on the natural world: on its great cycles; on the awe that Nature is capable of inspiring in humans; on the role that chance plays in natural events that affect humans; and on the relationship between humans and non-human animals. Its protagonist, Gabriel Oak, is a shepherd of uncommon ability; in one pivotal scene late in the novel he performs a difficult procedure on dozens of sheep suffering from bloat, thereby saving the lives of many of them (and saving the flock of Bathsheba Everdene, the novel's other main character). A brief descriptive and reflective passage from the novel's second chapter is included here; the excerpts included as part of the anthology's website component include an early scene in which sheep and cows have given birth; a description of sheep shearing; and a scene in which Gabriel and his flock suffer an extraordinary piece of bad luck.

If Hardy is warmly sympathetic towards humans engaged in animal agriculture, he is also acutely aware of the ways in which almost any form of animal agriculture requires cruelty by humans towards non-humans—requires, for example, that "every shepherd [be] an arrant traitor to his defenseless sheep." "The Puzzled Game-Birds" conveys similar ideas—but here Hardy adopts the viewpoint of the non-human animals.

Hardy's 1910 letter to *The Times* voices his views as to the ethical implications of Darwinian science so far as human interaction with non-human animals is concerned. (For more on this topic see the "In Context" materials following Darwin's author entry.)

from *Far from the Madding Crowd* (1874)

from CHAPTER 2

It was nearly midnight on the eve of St. Thomas's, the shortest day in the year. A desolating wind wandered from the north over the hill whereon Oak had watched the yellow wagon and its occupant[1] in the sunshine of a few days earlier.

Norcombe Hill—not far from lonely Toller-Down—was one of the spots which suggest to a passer-by that he is in the presence of a shape approaching the indestructible as nearly as any to be found on earth. It was a featureless convexity of chalk and soil—an ordinary specimen of those smoothly-outlined protuberances of the globe which may remain undisturbed on some great day of confusion, when far grander heights and dizzy granite precipices topple down.

The hill was covered on its northern side by an ancient and decaying plantation of beeches, whose upper verge formed a line over the crest, fringing its arched curve against the sky, like a mane. Tonight these trees sheltered the southern slope from the keenest blasts, which smote the wood and floundered through it with a sound as of grumbling, or gushed over its crowning boughs in a weakened moan. The dry leaves in the ditch simmered and boiled in the same breezes, a tongue of air occasionally ferreting out a few, and sending them spinning across the grass. A group or two of the latest in date amongst the dead multitude had remained till this very mid-winter time on the twigs which bore them and in falling rattled against the trunks with smart taps.

Between this half-wooded half-naked hill, and the vague still horizon that its summit indistinctly commanded, was a mysterious sheet of fathomless shade—the sounds from which suggested that what it concealed bore some reduced resemblance to features here. The thin grasses, more or less coating the hill, were touched by the wind in breezes of differing powers, and almost of differing natures—one rubbing the blades heavily, another raking them piercingly, another brushing them like a soft broom. The instinctive act of humankind was to stand and listen, and learn how the trees on the right and the trees on the left wailed or chaunted to each other in the regular antiphonies of a cathedral choir; how hedges and other shapes to leeward[2] then caught the note, lowering it to the tenderest sob; and how the hurrying gust then plunged into the south, to be heard no more.

The sky was clear—remarkably clear—and the twinkling of all the stars seemed to be but throbs of one body, timed by a common pulse. The North Star was directly in the wind's eye, and since evening the Bear had swung round it outwardly to the east, till he was now at a right angle with the meridian. A difference of colour in the stars—oftener read of than seen in England—was really perceptible here. The sovereign brilliancy of Sirius pierced the eye with a steely glitter, the star called Capella was yellow, Aldebaran and Betelgueux shone with a fiery red.

To persons standing alone on a hill during a clear midnight such as this, the roll of the world eastward is almost a palpable movement. The sensation may be caused by the panoramic glide of the stars past earthly objects, which is perceptible in a few minutes of stillness, or by the better outlook upon space that a hill affords, or by the wind, or by the solitude; but whatever be its origin, the impression of riding along is vivid and abiding. The poetry of motion is a phrase much in use, and to enjoy the epic form of that gratification it is necessary to stand on a hill at a small hour of the night, and, having first expanded with a sense of difference from the mass of civilised mankind, who are dream-wrapt and disregardful of all such proceedings at this time, long and quietly watch your stately progress through the stars. After such a nocturnal reconnoitre it is hard to get back to earth, and to believe that the consciousness of such majestic speeding is derived from a tiny human frame.

[1] *its occupant* Bathsheba Everdene.

[2] *to leeward* Located on the side of the hill sheltered from the wind.

"The Puzzled Game-Birds" (1902)

(*Triolet*)[1]

They are not those who used to feed us
    When we were young—they cannot be—
These shapes that now bereave and bleed us?
They are not those who used to feed us,
5   For did we then cry, they would heed us.
—If hearts can house such treachery
They are not those who used to feed us
When we were young—they cannot be!

"On Animals' Rights," *The Times* (3 May 1910)

The following letter has been addressed by Mr. Thomas Hardy to the Editor of *The Humanitarian* on the occasion of the Humanitarian League attaining its twentieth year:

    The Athenaeum, Pall Mall, SW, April 10, 1910
Sir,

I am glad to think that the Humanitarian League has attained the handsome age of twenty years—the Animals' Defence League particularly.

Few people seem to perceive fully as yet that the most far-reaching consequence of the establishment of the common origin of all species is ethical; that it logically involved a readjustment of altruistic morals, by enlarging, as a necessity of rightness, the application of what has been called "the Golden Rule" from the area of mere mankind to that of the whole animal kingdom. Possibly Darwin himself did not quite perceive it.

While man was deemed to be a creation apart from all other creations, a secondary or tertiary morality was considered good enough to practice towards the "inferior" races; but no person who reasons nowadays can escape the trying conclusion that this is not maintain-

able. And though we may not at present see how the principle of equal justice all round is to be carried out in its entirety, I recognize that the league is grappling with the question. Your obedient servant,

                                    Thomas Hardy

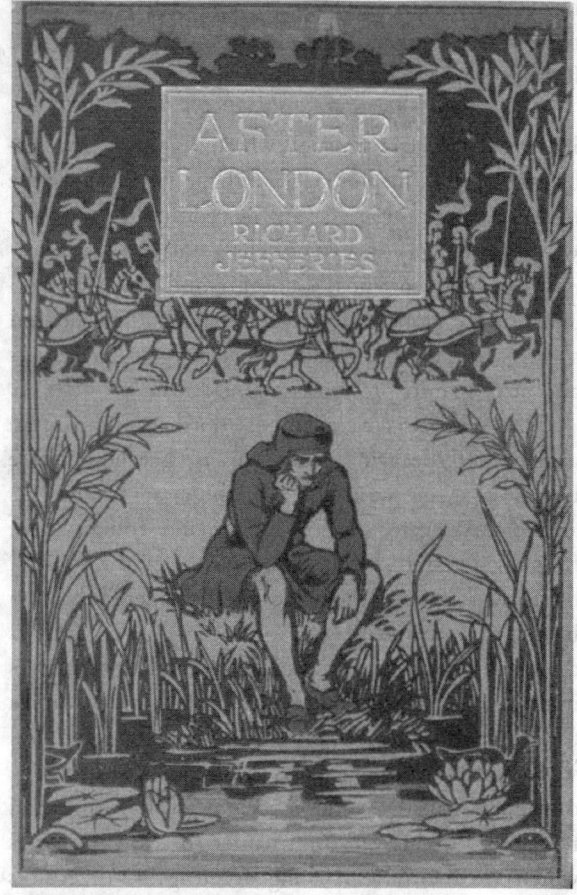

Cover image, *After London* (1885).

from Richard Jefferies, *After London* (1885)

Richard Jeffries (1848–87) was among the best-known nature writers of the late Victorian period. Excerpts from two of his essays, "Nature Near London (1883) and "Hours of Spring" (1899) are included as part of the website component of this anthology. Jeffries is best-known today for *After London* (1885), which is often described as the

---

[1] *Triolet* Verse form consisting of a single eight-line stanza in which the fourth line repeats the first line, and the last two lines repeat the first two lines.

progenitor of the modern genre of the post-apocalyptic novel. Its first section, "The Relapse into Barbarism," describes how, in the wake of a catastrophe that has severely depopulated England, nature reclaims the formerly "civilized" landscape. The novel's second part, "Wild England," includes a description of the former city of London, now reverted to swampland.

from PART I: THE RELAPSE INTO BARBARISM
from CHAPTER 1: THE GREAT FOREST

The old men say their fathers told them that soon after the fields were left to themselves a change began to be visible. It became green everywhere in the first spring, after London ended, so that all the country looked alike.

The meadows were green, and so was the rising wheat which had been sown, but which neither had nor would receive any further care. Such arable fields as had not been sown, but where the last stubble had been ploughed up, were overrun with couch-grass, and where the short stubble had not been ploughed, the weeds hid it. So that there was no place which was not more or less green; the footpaths were the greenest of all, for such is the nature of grass where it has once been trodden on, and by-and-by, as the summer came on, the former roads were thinly covered with the grass that had spread out from the margin.

In the autumn, as the meadows were not mown, the grass withered as it stood, falling this way and that, as the wind had blown it; the seeds dropped, and the bennets[1] became a greyish-white, or, where the docks and sorrel were thick, a brownish-red. The wheat, after it had ripened, there being no one to reap it, also remained standing, and was eaten by clouds of sparrows, rooks, and pigeons, which flocked to it and were undisturbed, feasting at their pleasure. As the winter came on, the crops were beaten down by the storms, soaked with rain, and trodden upon by herds of animals.

Next summer the prostrate straw of the preceding year was concealed by the young green wheat and barley that sprang up from the grain sown by dropping from the ears, and by quantities of docks, thistles, oxeye daisies, and similar plants. This matted mass grew up through the bleached straw. Charlock,[2] too, hid the rotting roots in the fields under a blaze of yellow flower. The young spring meadow-grass could scarcely push its way up through the long dead grass and bennets of the year previous, but docks and thistles, sorrel, wild carrots, and nettles, found no such difficulty.

Footpaths were concealed by the second year, but roads could be traced, though as green as the sward, and were still the best for walking, because the tangled wheat and weeds, and, in the meadows, the long grass, caught the feet of those who tried to pass through. Year by year the original crops of wheat, barley, oats, and beans asserted their presence by shooting up, but in gradually diminished force, as nettles and coarser plants, such as the wild parsnips, spread out into the fields from the ditches and choked them.

Aquatic grasses from the furrows and water-carriers extended in the meadows, and, with the rushes, helped to destroy or take the place of the former sweet herbage. Meanwhile, the brambles, which grew very fast, had pushed forward their prickly runners farther and farther from the hedges till they had now reached ten or fifteen yards. The briars had followed, and the hedges had widened to three or four times their first breadth, the fields being equally contracted. Starting from all sides at once, these brambles and briars in the course of about twenty years met in the centre of the largest fields.

Hawthorn bushes sprang up among them, and, protected by the briars and thorns from grazing animals, the suckers of elm-trees rose and flourished. Sapling ashes, oaks, sycamores, and horse-chestnuts, lifted their heads. Of old time the cattle would have eaten off the seed leaves with the grass so soon as they were out of the ground, but now most of the acorns that were dropped

---

[1] *bennets* Grass-stalks.

[2] *Charlock* Field-mustard.

by birds, and the keys[1] that were wafted by the wind, twirling as they floated, took root and grew into trees. By this time the brambles and briars had choked up and blocked the former roads, which were as impassable as the fields.

No fields, indeed, remained, for where the ground was dry, the thorns, briars, brambles, and saplings already mentioned filled the space, and these thickets and the young trees had converted most part of the country into an immense forest. Where the ground was naturally moist, and the drains had become choked with willow roots, which, when confined in tubes, grow into a mass like the brush of a fox, sedges and flags and rushes covered it. Thorn bushes were there, too, but not so tall; they were hung with lichen. Besides the flags and reeds, vast quantities of the tallest cow-parsnips or "gicks" rose five or six feet high, and the willow herb with its stout stem, almost as woody as a shrub, filled every approach.

By the thirtieth year there was not one single open place, the hills only excepted, where a man could walk, unless he followed the tracks of wild creatures or cut himself a path. The ditches, of course, had long since become full of leaves and dead branches, so that the water which should have run off down them stagnated, and presently spread out into the hollow places and by the corner of what had once been fields, forming marshes where the horsetails, flags, and sedges hid the water.

As no care was taken with the brooks, the hatches upon them gradually rotted, and the force of the winter rains carried away the weak timbers, flooding the lower grounds, which became swamps of larger size. The dams, too, were drilled by water-rats, and the streams percolating through, slowly increased the size of these tunnels till the structure burst, and the current swept on and added to the floods below. Mill-dams stood longer, but, as the ponds silted up, the current flowed round and even through the mill-houses, which, going by degrees to ruin, were in some cases undermined till they fell.

Everywhere the lower lands adjacent to the streams had become marshes, some of them extending for miles in a winding line, and occasionally spreading out to a mile in breadth. This was particularly the case where brooks and streams of some volume joined the rivers, which were also blocked and obstructed in their turn, and the two, overflowing, covered the country around; for the rivers brought down trees and branches, timbers floated from the shore, and all kinds of similar materials, which grounded in the shallows or caught against snags, and formed huge piles where there had been weirs.

Sometimes, after great rains, these piles swept away the timbers of the weir, driven by the irresistible power of the water, and then in its course the flood, carrying the balks[2] before it like battering rams, cracked and split the bridges of solid stone which the ancients had built. These and the iron bridges likewise were overthrown, and presently quite disappeared, for the very foundations were covered with the sand and gravel silted up.

Thus, too, the sites of many villages and towns that anciently existed along the rivers, or on the lower lands adjoining, were concealed by the water and the mud it brought with it. The sedges and reeds that arose completed the work and left nothing visible, so that the mighty buildings of olden days were by these means utterly buried. And, as has been proved by those who have dug for treasures, in our time the very foundations are deep beneath the earth, and not to be got at for the water that oozes into the shafts that they have tried to sink through the sand and mud banks.

From an elevation, therefore, there was nothing visible but endless forest and marsh. On the level ground and plains the view was limited to a short distance, because of the thickets and the saplings which had now become young trees. The downs only were still partially open, yet it was not convenient to walk upon them except in the tracks of animals, because of the long grass which, being no more regularly grazed upon by sheep, as was once the case, grew thick and tangled. Furze, too, and heath covered the slopes, and in places

---

[1] *keys* Dry tree-fruits.

[2] *balks* Wooden beams.

vast quantities of fern. There had always been copses of fir and beech and nut-tree covers, and these increased and spread, while bramble, briar, and hawthorn extended around them.

By degrees the trees of the vale seemed as it were to invade and march up the hills, and, as we see in our time, in many places the downs are hidden altogether with a stunted kind of forest. But all the above happened in the time of the first generation. Besides these things a great physical change took place; but before I speak of that, it will be best to relate what effects were produced upon animals and men.

In the first years after the fields were left to themselves, the fallen and over-ripe corn crops became the resort of innumerable mice. They swarmed to an incredible degree, not only devouring the grain upon the straw that had never been cut, but clearing out every single ear in the wheat-ricks that were standing about the country. Nothing remained in these ricks but straw, pierced with tunnels and runs, the home and breeding-place of mice, which thence poured forth into the fields. Such grain as had been left in barns and granaries, in mills, and in warehouses of the deserted towns, disappeared in the same manner.

When men tried to raise crops in small gardens and enclosures for their sustenance, these legions of mice rushed in and destroyed the produce of their labour. Nothing could keep them out, and if a score were killed, a hundred more supplied their place. These mice were preyed upon by kestrel hawks, owls, and weasels; but at first they made little or no appreciable difference. In a few years, however, the weasels, having such a super-abundance of food, trebled in numbers, and in the same way the hawks, owls, and foxes increased. There was then some relief, but even now at intervals districts are invaded, and the granaries and the standing corn suffer from these depredations.

This does not happen every year, but only at intervals, for it is noticed that mice abound very much more in some seasons than others. The extraordinary multiplication of these creatures was the means of providing food for the cats that had been abandoned in the towns, and came forth into the country in droves. Feeding on

the mice, they became, in a very short time, quite wild, and their descendants now roam the forest. ...

from PART 2: WILD ENGLAND
from CHAPTER 5: THE LAKE

There now only remains the geography of our country to be treated of before the history is commenced. Now the most striking difference between the country as we know it and as it was known to the ancients is the existence of the great Lake in the centre of the island. ...

The Lake is also divided into two unequal portions by the straits of White Horse, where vessels are often weather-bound, and cannot make way against the wind, which sets a current through the narrow channel. There is no tide; the sweet waters do not ebb and flow; but while I thus discourse, I have forgotten to state how they came to fill the middle of the country. Now, the philosopher Silvester, and those who seek after marvels, say that the passage of the dark body through space caused an immense volume of fresh water to fall in the shape of rain, and also that the growth of the forests distilled rain from the clouds. Let us leave these speculations to dreamers, and recount what is known to be.

For there is no tradition among the common people, who are extremely tenacious of such things, of any great rainfall, nor is there any mention of floods in the ancient manuscripts, nor is there any larger fall of rain now than was formerly the case. But the Lake itself tells us how it was formed, or as nearly as we shall ever know, and these facts were established by the expeditions lately sent out.

At the eastern extremity the Lake narrows, and finally is lost in the vast marshes which cover the site of the ancient London. Through these, no doubt, in the days of the old world there flowed the river Thames. By changes of the sea level and the sand that was brought up there must have grown great banks, which obstructed the stream. I have formerly mentioned the vast quantities of timber, the wreckage of towns and bridges which was carried down by the various rivers, and by none more so than by the Thames. These added to the accumulation, which increased the faster because the foundations of the ancient bridges held it like piles driven in for the purpose. And before this the river had become partially choked from the cloacæ[1] of the ancient city which poured into it through enormous subterranean aqueducts and drains.

After a time all these shallows and banks became well matted together by the growth of weeds, of willows, and flags, while the tide, ebbing lower at each drawing back, left still more mud and sand. Now it is believed that when this had gone on for a time, the waters of the river, unable to find a channel, began to overflow up into the deserted streets, and especially to fill the underground passages and drains, of which the number and extent was beyond all the power of words to describe. These, by the force of the water, were burst up, and the houses fell in.

For this marvellous city, of which such legends are related, was after all only of brick, and when the ivy grew over and trees and shrubs sprang up, and, lastly, the waters underneath burst in, this huge metropolis was soon overthrown. At this day all those parts which were built upon low ground are marshes and swamps. Those houses that were upon high ground were, of course, like the other towns, ransacked of all they contained by the remnant that was left; the iron, too, was extracted. Trees growing up by them in time cracked the walls, and they fell in. Trees and bushes covered them; ivy and nettles concealed the crumbling masses of brick.

The same was the case with the lesser cities and towns whose sites are known in the woods. For though many of our present towns bear the ancient names, they do not stand upon the ancient sites, but are two or three, and sometimes ten miles distant. The founders carried with them the name of their original residence. Thus the low-lying parts of the mighty city of London became swamps, and the higher grounds were clad with bushes. The very largest of the buildings fell in, and there was nothing visible but trees and hawthorns on the upper lands, and willows, flags, reeds, and rushes on the lower. These crumbling ruins still more choked the stream, and almost, if not quite, turned it back. If any

water ooze past, it is not perceptible, and there is no channel through to the salt ocean. It is a vast stagnant swamp, which no man dare enter, since death would be his inevitable fate.

There exhales from this oozy mass so fatal a vapour that no animal can endure it. The black water bears a greenish-brown floating scum, which for ever bubbles up from the putrid mud of the bottom. When the wind collects the miasma, and, as it were, presses it together, it becomes visible as a low cloud which hangs over the place. The cloud does not advance beyond the limit of the marsh, seeming to stay there by some constant attraction; and well it is for us that it does not, since at such times when the vapour is thickest, the very wild-fowl leave the reeds, and fly from the poison. There are no fishes, neither can eels exist in the mud, nor even newts. It is dead. ...

Air Pollution in the Victorian City

The *Oxford English Dictionary* records the terms "air pollution" and "water pollution" as first having been used in 1874 (in an American journal, the *Medical and Surgical Reporter*); in a discussion of how best to keep hospital air pure, one participant emphasized the importance of preventing the air and the water from being polluted by "the products of decomposing filth." The labeling of the effects of factory smoke as "pollution" lagged some distance behind, but the reality of significant air pollution predates the Victorian period; even in the early nineteenth century industrialization had created considerable air pollution in urban areas. By mid-century the problem had grown considerably worse; at the opening of *Bleak House* (1853), Dickens describes the contribution smoke was making to the fog that so often enveloped British cities: "smoke lowering down from chimney-pots, making a soft black drizzle, with flakes of soot in it as big as full-grown snowflakes—gone into mourning, one might imagine, for the death of the sun." But for much of the Victorian period factory smoke tended more often than not to be seen as a sign of progress, even

---

[1] *cloacæ* Latin: sewers.

among progressives; the first legislation against air pollution was the 1875 Public Health Act, which prescribed various smoke abatement measures intended to improve urban air quality.

Wentworth Works, Sheffield, England, c. 1850.

Lever Brothers soap factory, Port Sunlight, Liverpool, 1890.

View from Newport Bridge, Middlesborough, c. 1900.

from John Ruskin, *The Storm-Cloud of the Nineteenth Century* (1884)

The pair of lectures Ruskin delivered on 4 and 11 February 1884 in London (later published under the title *The Storm-Cloud of the Nineteenth Century*) together form one of his most extraordinary works. Over the years Ruskin had grown increasingly strident in some of his views, launching diatribes against the scientific approach and against modernity. (At one point in the 1880s he described railroads as "the loathsomest form of devilry now extant, animated and deliberate earthquakes, destructive of all wise social habit or possible natural beauty, carriages of damned souls on the ridges of their own graves.") In the view of many, he had also by the 1880s become increasingly erratic; he had begun in 1878 to suffer from periodic breakdowns in his mental health. But he remained a lucid and powerful writer and speaker, and an influential thinker.

Is *The Storm-Cloud of the Nineteenth Century* evidence of Ruskin himself being "in the clouds," as one newspaper suggested at the time? (Several newspaper reports are included below.) Does the lecture constitute, as some in the second half of the twentieth century suggested, a "crusade against pollution"? Is it, at least in part, a prescient commentary on the phenomenon of global warming, as some in the twenty-first century have suggested? Such suggestions must necessarily be to some degree qualified; far from appealing to science, as do modern-day appeals for action against climate change, Ruskin disparages the contributions of scientists. And in the final analysis he appears to regard the "plague cloud" less as a physical phenomenon than as a reflection of humans' moral and spiritual failings—our failings not specifically in mistreating the environment but more generally (in our warlike behavior, in our selfishness, and so on). Are such suggestions the crackpot musings of an intellectual who has become lost in the clouds? Or is Ruskin grasping, in some inchoate form, a larger web of connections that even now is not entirely clear to us?

PREFACE

The following lectures, drawn up under the pressure of more imperative and quite otherwise directed work, contain many passages which stand in need of support, and some, I do not doubt, more or less of correction, which I always prefer to receive openly from the better knowledge of friends, after setting down my own impressions of the matter in clearness as far as they reach, than to guard myself against by submitting my manuscript, before publication, to annotators whose stricture or suggestion I might often feel pain in refusing, yet hesitation in admitting.

But though thus hastily, and to some extent incautiously, thrown into form, the statements in the text are founded on patient and, in all essential particulars, accurately recorded observations of the sky, during fifty years of a life of solitude and leisure; and in all they contain of what may seem to the reader questionable, or astonishing, are guardedly and absolutely true.

In many of the reports given by the daily press, my assertion of radical change, during recent years, in weather aspect was scouted[1] as imaginary, or insane. I am indeed, every day of my yet spared life, more and more grateful that my mind is capable of imaginative vision, and liable to the noble dangers of delusion which separate the speculative intellect of humanity from the dreamless instinct of brutes: but I have been able, during all active work, to use or refuse my power of contemplative imagination, with as easy command of it as a physicist's of his telescope: the times of morbid are just as easily distinguished by me from those of healthy vision, as by men of ordinary faculty, dream from waking; nor is there a single fact stated in the following pages which I have not verified with a chemist's analysis, and a geometer's precision.

The first lecture is printed, with only addition here and there of an elucidatory word or phrase, precisely as it was given on the 4th February. In repeating it on the 11th, I amplified several passages, and substituted for the concluding one, which had been printed with accuracy in most of the leading journals, some observations which I thought calculated to be of more general interest. To these, with the additions in the first text, I have now prefixed a few explanatory notes, to which numeral references are given in the pages they explain, and have arranged the fragments in connection clear enough to allow of their being read with ease as a second Lecture.

Herne Hill, 12th March, 1884.

from LECTURE 1

… Tonight … [I] propose to bring to your notice a series of cloud phenomena, which, so far as I can weigh existing evidence, are peculiar to our own times; yet which have not hitherto received any special notice or description from meteorologists.

So far as the existing evidence, I say, of former literature can be interpreted, the storm-cloud—or more accurately plague-cloud, for it is not always stormy—which I am about to describe to you, never was seen but by now living, or *lately* living eyes. It is not yet twenty years that this—I may well call it, wonderful,[2] cloud has been, in its essence, recognizable. There is no description of it, so far as I have read, by any ancient observer. Neither Homer nor Virgil, neither Aristophanes nor Horace,[3] acknowledge any such clouds among those compelled by Jove. Chaucer[4] has no word of them, nor Dante;[5] Milton none, nor Thomson.[6] In modern times,

---

[1] *scouted* Dismissed as absurd; scorned.

[2] *wonderful* Astonishing, unusual, portentous.

[3] *Homer* Legendary Greek poet (c. 8th century BCE); *Virgil* Latin poet of the first century BCE, author of *The Aeneid*; *Aristophanes* Greek comedy writer (c. 448–380 BCE); *Horace* Latin lyric poet of the first century BCE.

[4] *Jove* Jupiter; *Chaucer* English poet (c. 1342–1400).

[5] [Ruskin's note] The vapor over the pool of Anger in the "Inferno," the clogging stench which rises from Caina, and the fog of the circle of Anger in the "Purgatorio" resemble, indeed, the cloud of the Plague-wind very closely—but are conceived only as supernatural. The reader will no doubt observe, throughout the following lecture, my own habit of speaking of beautiful things as "natural," and of ugly ones as "unnatural." … [*Dante* Dante Alighieri (1265–1321), Italian poet and author of the long narrative poem *The Divine Comedy* (1320).]

[6] *Milton* English poet (1608–74); *Thomson* Poet James Thomson (1700–48).

Scott, Wordsworth and Byron[1] are alike unconscious of them; and the most observant and descriptive of scientific men, De Saussure,[2] is utterly silent concerning them. Taking up the traditions of air from the year before Scott's death, I am able, by my own constant and close observation, to certify you that in the forty following years (1831 to 1871 approximately—for the phenomena in question came on gradually)—no such clouds as these are, and are now often for months without intermission, were ever seen in the skies of England, France, or Italy.

In those old days, when weather was fine, it was luxuriously fine; when it was bad—it was often abominably bad, but it had its fit of temper and was done with it—it didn't sulk for three months without letting you see the sun—nor send you one cyclone inside out, every Saturday afternoon, and another outside in, every Monday morning.

In fine weather the sky was either blue or clear in its light; the clouds, either white or golden, adding to, not abating, the luster of the sky. In wet weather, there were two different species of clouds—those of beneficent rain, which for distinction's sake I will call the non-electric rain-cloud, and those of storm, usually charged highly with electricity. The beneficent rain-cloud was indeed often extremely dull and gray for days together, but gracious nevertheless, felt to be doing good, and often to be delightful after drought; capable also of the most exquisite coloring, under certain conditions;[3] and continually traversed in clearing by the rainbow—and, secondly, the storm-cloud, always majestic, often dazzlingly beautiful, and felt also to be beneficent in its own way, affecting the mass of the air with vital agitation, and purging it from the impurity of all morbific[4] elements.

In the entire system of the Firmament,[5] thus seen and understood, there appeared to be, to all the thinkers of those ages, the incontrovertible and unmistakable evidence of a Divine Power in creation, which had fitted, as the air for human breath, so the clouds for human sight and nourishment[.] …

… If you watch the steam coming strongly out of an engine-funnel, at the top of the funnel it is transparent—you can't see it, though it is more densely and intensely there than anywhere else. Six inches out of the funnel it becomes snow-white—you see it, and you see it, observe, exactly where it is—it is then a real and proper cloud. Twenty yards off the funnel it scatters and melts away; a little of it sprinkles you with rain if you are underneath it, but the rest disappears; yet it is still there—the surrounding air does not absorb it all into space in a moment; there is a gradual diffusing current of invisible moisture at the end of the visible stream—an invisible, yet quite substantial, vapour; but not, according to our definition, a cloud, for a cloud is vapour *visible*.

Then the next bit of the question, of course, is, What makes the vapour visible, when it is so? Why is the compressed steam transparent, the loose steam white, the dissolved steam transparent again?

The scientific people tell you that the vapour becomes visible, and chilled, as it expands. Many thanks to them; but can they show us any reason why particles of water should be more opaque when they are separated than when they are close together, or give us any idea of the difference of the state of a particle of water, which won't *sink* in the air, from that of one that won't *rise* in it?[6]

---

[1] *Scott* Sir Walter Scott, Scots author noted for his ballads and for developing the historical novel (1771–1832); *Wordsworth* English poet William Wordsworth (1770–1850); *Byron* George Gordon, Lord Byron, English poet (1788–1824).

[2] *De Saussure* Horace Bénédict de Saussure (1740–99), geologist and physicist who laid the foundations of modern meteorology.

[3] [Ruskin's note] These conditions are mainly in the arrangement of the lower rain-clouds in flakes thin and detached enough to be illuminated by early or late sunbeams: their textures are then more softly blended than those of the upper cirri, and have the qualities of painted, instead of burnished or inflamed, color.

[4] *morbific* Disastrous.

[5] *Firmament* Arch or vault of heaven.

[6] [Ruskin's note] The opposed conditions of the higher and lower orders of cloud, with the balanced intermediate one, are beautifully seen on mountain summits of rock or earth. On snowy ones they are far more complex: but on rock summits there are three [continued …]

And here I must parenthetically give you a little word of, I will venture to say, extremely useful, advice about scientific people in general. Their first business is, of course, to tell you things that are so, and do happen—as that, if you warm water, it will boil; if you cool it, it will freeze; and if you put a candle to a cask of gunpowder, it will blow you up. Their second, and far more important business, is to tell you what you had best do under the circumstances—put the kettle on in time for tea; powder your ice and salt, if you have a mind for ices; and obviate the chance of explosion by not making the gunpowder. But if, beyond this safe and beneficial business, they ever try to *explain* anything to you, you may be confident of one of two things—either that they know nothing (to speak of) about it, or that they have only seen one side of it—and not only haven't seen, but usually have no mind to see, the other. When, for instance, Professor Tyndall explains the twisted beds of the Jungfrau to you by intimating that the Matterhorn is growing flat; or the clouds on the lee side of the Matterhorn by the wind's rubbing against the windward side of it,[1] you may be pretty sure the scientific people don't know much (to speak of) yet, either about rock-beds, or cloud-beds. And even if the explanation, so to

call it, be sound on one side, windward or lee, you may, as I said, be nearly certain it won't do on the other. Take the very top and centre of scientific interpretation by the greatest of its masters: Newton explained to you—or at least was once supposed to have explained—why an apple fell; but he never thought of explaining the exactly correlative, but infinitely more difficult question, how the apple got up there! …

In Diagram 4, Mr. Severn has beautifully enlarged my sketch of a July thunder-cloud of the year 1858, on the Alps of the Val d'Aosta,[2] seen from Turin, that is to say, some twenty-five or thirty miles distant. You see that no mistake is possible here about what is good weather and what bad, or which is cloud and which is sky; but I show you this sketch especially to give you the scale of heights for such clouds in the atmosphere. These thunder cumuli entirely *hide* the higher Alps. It does not, however, follow that they have buried them, for most of their own aspect of height is owing to the approach of their nearer masses; but at all events, you have cumulus there rising from its base, at about three thousand feet above the plain, to a good ten thousand in the air.

White cirri,[3] in reality parallel, but by perspective radiating, catch the sunshine above, at a height of from fifteen to twenty thousand feet; but the storm on the mountains gathers itself into a full mile's depth of massy cloud—every fold of it involved with thunder, but every form of it, every action, every color, magnificent: doing its mighty work in its own hour and its own dominion, nor snatching from you for an instant, nor defiling with a stain, the abiding blue of the transcendent sky, or the fretted silver of its passionless clouds. …

distinct forms of attached cloud in serene weather; the first that of cloud veil laid over them, and *falling* in folds through their ravines (the obliquely descending clouds of the entering chorus in Aristophanes); secondly, the ascending cloud, which develops itself loosely and independently as it rises, and does not attach itself to the hill-side, while the falling veil cloud clings to it close all the way down; and lastly the throned cloud, which rests indeed on the mountain summit, with its base, but rises high above into the sky, continually changing its outlines, but holding its seat perhaps all day long. …

[1] [Ruskin's note] "Glaciers of the Alps," page 146—"The sun was near the western horizon, and I remained alone upon the Grat to see his last beams illuminate the mountains, which, with one exception, were without a trace of cloud. …" [The Irish scientist John Tyndall was, from 1853 to 1887, professor of physics at the Royal Institution of Great Britain in London; the Jungfrau and the Matterhorn are both mountains in the Alps, which Tyndall, a pioneering mountaineer and glaciologist, visited frequently.]

[2] *Severn … Val d'Aosta* The English artist Joseph Severn (1793–1879), best known as a friend of John Keats early in the century, became a friend of Ruskin's in later years. It is Ruskin's original rather than Severn's enlarged version that is reproduced here.

[3] *cirri* Cirrus clouds, a type of cloud characterized by thin, wispy strands.

John Ruskin, *A July Thunder Cloud, Val d'Aosta*, 1858. Joseph Severn's enlarged version of this watercolor sketch by John Ruskin was shown to the audience when Ruskin delivered the lecture. Ruskin himself also painted during the same year a version of the scene in oil.

Thus far then of clouds that were once familiar; now at last, entering on my immediate subject, I shall best introduce it to you by reading an entry in my diary which gives progressive description of the most gentle aspect of the modern plague-cloud.

Bolton Abbey, 4th July, 1875.

Half-past eight, morning; the first bright morning for the last fortnight.

At half-past five it was entirely clear, and entirely calm; the moorlands glowing, and the Wharfe glittering in sacred light, and even the thin-stemmed field-flowers quiet as stars, in the peace in which—

All trees and simples, great and small,
That balmy leaf do bear,
Than they were painted on a wall,
No more do move, nor steir.[1]

But, an hour ago, the leaves at my window first shook slightly. They are now trembling *continuously*, as those of all the trees, under a gradually rising wind, of which the tremulous action scarcely per-

mits the direction to be defined, but which falls and returns in fits of varying force, like those which precede a thunderstorm—never wholly ceasing: the direction of its upper current is shown by a few ragged white clouds, moving fast from the north, which rose, at the time of the first leaf-shaking, behind the edge of the moors in the east.

This wind is the plague-wind of the eighth decade of years in the nineteenth century; a period which will assuredly be recognized in future meteorological history as one of phenomena hitherto unrecorded in the courses of nature, and characterized pre-eminently by the almost ceaseless action of this calamitous wind. While I have been writing these sentences, the white clouds above specified have increased to twice the size they had when I began to write; and in about two hours from this time—say by eleven o'clock, if the wind continue—the whole sky will be dark with them, as it was yesterday, and has been through prolonged periods during the last five years. I first noticed the definite character of this wind, and of the clouds it brings with it, in the year 1871, … I am able now to state positively that its range of power extends from the North of England to Sicily; and that it blows more or less during the whole of the year, except the early autumn. This autumnal abdication is, I hope, beginning; it blew but feebly yesterday, though without intermission, from the north, making every shady place cold, while the sun was burning; its effect on the sky being only to dim the blue of it between masses of ragged cumulus. Today it has entirely fallen; and there seems hope of bright weather, the first for me since the end of May, when I had two fine days at Aylesbury; the third, May 28th, being black again from morning to evening. There seems to be some reference to the blackness caused by the prevalence of this wind in the old French name of Bise, '*gray* wind'; and, indeed, one of the darkest and bitterest days of it I ever saw was at Vevay in 1872.

The first time I recognized the clouds brought by the plague-wind as distinct in character was in walking back from Oxford, after a hard day's work, to Abingdon, in the early spring of 1871: it would take too long to give you any

---

[1] *All trees … steir* From "Of the Day Estivall" (1599), by the Scottish poet Alexander Hume; *simples* Plants; *steir* Stir.

account this evening of the particulars which drew my attention to them; but during the following months I had too frequent opportunities of verifying my first thoughts of them, and on the first of July in that year wrote the description of them which begins the "Fors Clavigera"[1] of August, thus:

> It is the first of July, and I sit down to write by the dismalest light that ever yet I wrote by; namely, the light of this midsummer morning, in mid-England, (Matlock, Derbyshire), in the year 1871.
>
> For the sky is covered with gray cloud—not rain-cloud, but a dry black veil, which no ray of sunshine can pierce; partly diffused in mist, feeble mist, enough to make distant objects unintelligible, yet without any substance, or wreathing, or color of its own. And everywhere the leaves of the trees are shaking fitfully, as they do before a thunder-storm; only not violently, but enough to show the passing to and fro of a strange, bitter, blighting wind. Dismal enough, had it been the first morning of its kind that summer had sent. But during all this spring, in London, and at Oxford, through meager March, through changelessly sullen April, through despondent May, and darkened June, morning after morning has come gray-shrouded thus.
>
> And it is a new thing to me, and a very dreadful one. I am fifty years old, and more; and since I was five, have gleaned the best hours of my life in the sun of spring and summer mornings; and I never saw such as these, till now.
>
> And the scientific men are busy as ants, examining the sun, and the moon, and the seven stars,[2] and can tell me all about *them*, I believe, by this time; and how they move, and what they are made of.
>
> And I do not care, for my part, two copper spangles how they move, nor what they are made of. I can't move them any other way than they go, nor make them of anything else, better than they are made. But I would care much and give much, if I

> could be told where this bitter wind comes from, and what *it* is made of.
>
> For, perhaps, with forethought, and fine laboratory science, one might make it of something else.
>
> It looks partly as if it were made of poisonous smoke; very possibly it may be: there are at least two hundred furnace chimneys in a square of two miles on every side of me. But mere smoke would not blow to and fro in that wild way. It looks more to me as if it were made of dead men's souls—such of them as are not gone yet where they have to go, and may be flitting hither and thither, doubting, themselves, of the fittest place for them.
>
> You know, if there *are* such things as souls, and if ever any of them haunt places where they have been hurt, there must be many about us, just now, displeased enough!

The last sentence refers of course to the battles of the Franco-German campaign,[3] which was especially horrible to me, in its digging, as the Germans should have known, a moat flooded with waters of death between the two nations for a century to come.

Since that Midsummer day, my attention, however otherwise occupied, has never relaxed in its record of the phenomena characteristic of the plague-wind[.] …

Now … —take the following sequences of accurate description of thunderstorm, *with* plague-wind.

> 22d June, 1876.
>
> Thunderstorm; pitch dark, with no *blackness*, but deep, high, *filthiness* of lurid, yet not sublimely lurid, smoke-cloud; dense manufacturing mist; fearful squalls of shivery wind, making Mr. Severn's sail quiver like a man in a fever fit—all about four, afternoon—but only two or three claps of thunder, and feeble, though near, flashes. I never saw such a dirty, weak, foul storm. It cleared suddenly, after raining all afternoon, at half-past eight to nine, into pure, natural weather—low rain-clouds on quite clear, green, wet hills.

---

[1] *Fors Clavigera* Title of a series of open letters, published as pamphlets, that Ruskin wrote in the 1870s, addressed to British workmen.

[2] *seven stars* I.e., planets, seven of which had been identified by the time Ruskin wrote.

[3] *Franco-German campaign* I.e., the Franco-Prussian War (1870–71).

Brantwood, 13th August, 1879.

The most terrific and horrible thunderstorm, this morning, I ever remember. It waked me at six, or a little before—then rolling incessantly, like railway luggage trains, quite ghastly in its mockery of them—the air one loathsome mass of sultry and foul fog, like smoke; scarcely raining at all, but increasing to heavier rollings, with flashes quivering vaguely through all the air, and at last terrific double streams of reddish-violet fire, not forked or zigzag, but rippled rivulets—two at the same instant some twenty to thirty degrees apart, and lasting on the eye at least half a second, with grand artillery-peals following; not rattling crashes, or irregular crack-lings, but delivered volleys. It lasted an hour, then passed off, clearing a little, without rain to speak of—not a glimpse of blue—and now, half-past seven, seems settling down again into Manchester devil's darkness.

Quarter to eight, morning. Thunder returned, all the air collapsed into one black fog, the hills invisible, and scarcely visible the opposite shore; heavy rain in short fits, and frequent, though less formidable, flashes, and shorter thunder. While I have written this sentence the cloud has again dissolved itself, like a nasty solution in a bottle, with miraculous and unnatural rapidity, and the hills are in sight again; a double-forked flash—rippled, I mean, like the others—starts into its frightful ladder of light between me and Wetherlam, as I raise my eyes. All black above, a rugged spray cloud on the Eaglet. (The "Eaglet" is my own name for the bold and elevated crag to the west of the little lake above Coniston mines. It had no name among the country people, and is one of the most conspicuous features of the mountain chain, as seen from Brantwood.)

Half-past eight. Three times light and three times dark since last I wrote, and the darkness seeming each time as it settles more loathsome, at last stopping my reading in mere blindness. One lurid gleam of white cumulus in upper lead-blue sky, seen for half a minute through the sulphurous chimney-pot vomit of blackguardly cloud beneath, where its rags were thinnest. ...

John Ruskin, *Cloud Study*, 1880.

And now I come to the most important sign of the plague-wind and the plague-cloud: that in bringing on their peculiar darkness, they *blanch* the sun instead of reddening it. And here I must note briefly to you the uselessness of observation by instruments, or machines, instead of eyes. In the first year when I had begun to notice the specialty of the plague-wind, I went of course to the Oxford observatory to consult its registrars. They have their anemometer always on the twirl, and can tell you the force, or at least the pace, of a gale, by day or night. But the anemometer can only record for you how often it has been driven round, not at all whether it went round *steadily*, or went round *trembling*. And on that point depends the entire question whether it is a plague breeze or a healthy one: and what's the use of telling you whether the wind's strong or not, when it can't tell you whether it's a strong medicine, or a strong poison? ...

Blanched Sun—blighted grass—blinded man. If, in conclusion, you ask me for any conceivable cause or meaning of these things—I can tell you none, according to your modern beliefs; but I can tell you what meaning it would have borne to the men of old time. Remember, for the last twenty years, England, and all foreign nations, either tempting her, or following her, have blasphemed the name of God deliberately and openly; and have done iniquity by proclamation, every man doing as much injustice to his brother as it is in his power to do. ...

What is best to be done, do you ask me? The answer is plain. Whether you can affect the signs of the sky or

not, you *can* the signs of the times. Whether you can bring the *sun* back or not, you can assuredly bring back your own cheerfulness, and your own honesty. You may not be able to say to the winds, "Peace; be still,"[1] but you can cease from the insolence of your own lips, and the troubling of your own passions. And all *that* it would be extremely well to do, even though the day *were* coming when the sun should be as darkness, and the moon as blood.[2] But, the paths of rectitude and piety once regained, who shall say that the promise of old time would not be found to hold for us also?— "Bring ye all the tithes into my storehouse, and prove me now herewith, saith the Lord God, if I will not open you the windows of heaven, and pour you out a blessing, that there shall not be room enough to receive it."[3]
—1884

Newspaper Reports of Ruskin's "Storm-Cloud" Lecture

Ruskin's lecture was widely reported on in the press, with the majority of newspapers and magazines that carried accounts of the lecture praising it respectfully and emphasizing Ruskin's closing remarks—his calling upon his listeners to address the "moral gloom" of the nation by addressing that within their own souls. The *Morning Post*, *The Standard*, and the *Pall Mall Gazette* all devoted half or more of their reports to quoting or paraphrasing Ruskin's final few paragraphs. The report in *The Graphic*, with its passages of gentle mockery, was an outlier.

The excerpt from an article published in the *Liverpool Mercury* more than three months after Ruskin's address illustrates the degree to which his notions concerning new meteorological phenomena

had become widely known—and applied in a variety of contexts. (For more on "the earthquake in Java" see "The Remarkable Sunsets" in the website component of this "Contexts" section.)

from "Mr. Ruskin at the London Institution," *The Morning Post* (5 February 1884)

Yesterday afternoon Mr. Ruskin lectured to an audience which completely crowded the theatre of the London institution on "The Storm Clouds of the Nineteenth Century." The address, which was illustrated by some drawings of cloud phenomena enlarged from sketches by Professor Ruskin himself, was listened to with profound attention, some of the more eloquent passages being loudly applauded. The lecture was a description of "black clouds and plague winds," which Mr. Ruskin has observed since 1871; but as to which he only began to make regular entries in his diary since 1875. Formerly, he says, we had storm clouds and rain clouds, fogs and mists, but these had some settled characteristics, and we knew what to expect of them. ... With the plague wind, however, ... clouds instantly darkened the sky. This malignant wind was unconnected with any particular corner of the compass, but blew indifferently from them all, polluting the character as well as enhancing the violence of all natural and necessary storms. ...

"If," said Mr. Ruskin, "you ask me in conclusion, what is the meaning of all this—of blanched sun, of blighted grass, of blinded man; if you ask me for any conceivable cause or meaning of these things, I can give you none according to your modern beliefs and knowledge. I can tell you what meaning it would have borne to the men of olden times. But remember, for the last 20 years England and all foreign nations ... [The article then quotes almost verbatim the final two paragraphs of Ruskin's address] ... shall not be room enough to receive it."

---

[1] *Peace; be still* In Mark 4.39, Jesus calms a storm on the Sea of Galilee with these words.

[2] *the sun ... blood* See Acts 2.20: "The sun shall be turned into darkness, and the moon into blood, before the great and notable day of the Lord come."

[3] *Bring ye ... receive it* See Malachi 3.10.

"Mr. Ruskin in the Clouds," *The Graphic* (9 February 1884)

Few probably of those who went to hear Mr. Ruskin lecture at the London Institution expected to gain any solid meteorological information. Nevertheless, the address was fairly interesting and decidedly original. He could not open his lips without charming his hearers by some passages glowing with poetry, nor, on the other hand, with such a subject before him, could he fail to gird at[1] the men of science—"falsely so called," Mr. Ruskin evidently believes. They know very little that they ought to know. Professor Tyndall is but a shallow geologist, and though scientists can tell us why an apple falls from a tree, they cannot disclose the greater secret how it climbed up there. Were it not that Mr. Ruskin is Mr. Ruskin, and that most of us are aware that this is "only pretty Fanny's way,"[2] we should be inclined to call these satirical passages both puerile and untrue. As for the apple, unless Mr. Ruskin means that scientific men have failed to penetrate the mystery of life, in other respects they, or any intelligent school-girl, can tell him how the apple, by successive stages, climbed out of the earth to its place on the branch. And we wonder that such a keen observer of Nature as Mr. Ruskin should attempt to draw a hard-and-fast distinction between mists that brood on the earth and clouds that hang above it. Any one who has been to the top of a mountain knows that cloud and mist are practically interchangeable terms. But the most wonderful of Mr. Ruskin's discoveries is his "plague-cloud." It only began to appear, he says, in 1871. We admit that, owing perhaps to the machinations of the American forecasters, the weather has not been all it should be for some years past, but we cannot swallow the "plague-cloud." It no doubt has a real existence—in Mr. Ruskin's own bodily sensations. A time comes to all of us as we grow old, when the nipping eager air which we laughingly breasted in youth chills us to the marrow. In that sense we are content to accept the "plague cloud."

from *The Liverpool Mercury* (26 August 1884)

One of Mr. Ruskin's storm clouds seems to have come up on London today. While holiday-makers have been enjoying the sunshine on the Kentish coast, we have been half-disposed to shiver at the sudden change of temperature. The morning broke with heavy rain, and in a few moments the dawn lit up the heavens with fiery lights which resembled those summer sunsets of which so much was said by wise philosophers who traced them to the earthquake in Java. From dawn to dusk the thermometer has been steadily falling; and we are disposed tonight to close our windows against a chilling wind. The suddenness of the change is favorable to rheumatism; but it is hardly a relief, for though the breeze is cool it is not bracing. The sky seems to have fallen on our heads, and a sense of oppression greater than that caused by yesterday's heat seems to be universal.

Private Land, Common Land

From the late medieval period through to the early nineteenth century, the enclosure movement was a constant in English life; land that had been held in common (typically as communal grazing land) gradually became "enclosed" under private ownership and devoted to the farming of cash crops. The late nineteenth century saw at least a partial reversal of that trend. Activists began to press for national landmarks to be held in public hands, and for the maintenance of public access to be preserved throughout the country. Bodies such as the Commons Preservation Society (formed in 1865), the National Footpath Preservation Society (founded in 1884), and the National Trust (founded in 1895) worked with some success to influence both public

---

[1] *gird at* Swipe or scoff at.
[2] *only pretty Fanny's way* From "An Elegy, To an Old Beauty," by the Anglo-Irish poet Thomas Parnell (1679–1718). According to the poem, "all that's madly wild, or oddly gay, / We call it only pretty Fanny's way."

opinion and the legislative and regulatory climate.

Octavia Hill, a Christian socialist who became one of the founders of the National Trust, was for decades among the leaders of this movement. Hill's career as a social reformer began in the 1860s and early 1870s as she endeavored to improve housing conditions for the poor. In 1876–77 she first became engaged with the issue of preserving the commons, pressing for improvements to the 1876 Act for Facilitating the Regulation and Improvement of Commons. A number of her essays and speeches from this period were published in 1877 under the title *Our Common Land and Other Short Essays*. As the excerpts below suggest, she was a particularly eloquent advocate for improving access to nature for the general public.

So too was Samuel Plimsoll (1824–98), a member of the radical faction within the Liberal Party who had become famous for his efforts to improve the lot of sailors. With the Lake District becoming a more and more popular tourist destination, many of the region's ancient footpaths had been closed to the public, as landowners reacted against the increase in foot traffic. The closure of footpaths on Latrigg, a Lake District hill that had long been a popular climb, sparked special outrage—as the account in the *Pall Mall Gazette* makes clear. Eventually two of three footpaths on Latrigg were reopened, their status as ancient rights of way confirmed.

Environmentalists continued to press both for preservation (of open spaces and of scenic landscapes) and for public access to the landscape—including via footpaths crossing private land. In the mid-1890s a considerable measure of success was achieved on two fronts. In 1894 a new Local Government Act set out national guidelines on the basis of which local authorities could more readily protect existing rights of way—and create new ones. And in 1895 the National Trust was created, with a mandate "to promote the permanent preservation for the benefit of the Nation of lands and ... buildings of beauty or historic interest."

from Octavia Hill, "Our Common Land" (1877)

Probably few persons who have a choice of holidays select a bank holiday,[1] which falls in the spring or summer, as one on which they will travel or stroll in the country, unless, indeed, they live in neighbourhoods very far removed from large towns. Every railway station is crowded; every booking-office thronged; every seat—nay, all standing room—is occupied in every kind of public conveyance; the roads leading out of London for miles are crowded with every description of vehicle—van, cart, chaise, gig—drawn by every size and sort of donkey, pony, or horse; if it be a dusty day, a great, dull unbroken choking cloud of dust hangs over every line of road.

Yet in spite of all this, and in spite of the really bad sights to be seen at every public house along the road, in spite of the wild songs and boisterous behaviour, and reckless driving home at night, which shows how sadly intoxication is still bound up with the idea and practical use of a holiday to hundreds of our people, how much intense enjoyment the day gives! how large a part of this enjoyment is unmixed good! And the evil is kept in check very much. We may see the quiet figure of a policeman as we drive home, dark in the twilight, dark amidst the dust, keeping order among the vehicles, making the drunken drivers mind what they are doing. He keeps very tolerable order. And then these days in the country ought to lessen the number of drunkards every year; and more and more we shall be able to trust to the public opinion of the quiet many to preserve order.

And watch, when at last the open spaces are reached towards which all these lines of vehicles are tending—be it Epping, or Richmond, or Greenwich, or Hampstead[2]—every place seems swarming with an undisciplined, but heartily happy crowd. The swings, the roundabouts, the donkeys, the stalls, are beset by dozens

---

[1] *bank holiday* Public holiday; statutory holiday on which banks are closed.

[2] *Epping ... Hampstead* In the 1870s, all areas with a considerable amount of green space, located not far from London. (All except Epping are now within Greater London.)

or even hundreds of pleasure-seekers, gay and happy, though they are not always the gentlest or most refined. Look at the happy family groups—father, and mother, and children, with their picnic dinners neatly tied up in handkerchiefs; watch the joy of eager children leaping out of vans to purchase for a halfpenny the wonderful pink streamers which they will stick proudly in their caps; see the merry little things running untiringly up and down the bank of sand or grass; notice the affectionate father bringing out the pot of ale to the wife as she sits comfortably tucked up in shawls in the little cart, or treating the children to sweetmeats; sympathize in the hearty energy of the great rough lads who have walked miles, as their dusty boots well show; their round, honest faces have beamed with rough mirth at every joke that has come in their way all day. ... To all these the day brings unmixed good.

Now, have you ever paused to think what Londoners would do without this holiday, or what it would be without open spaces? Cooped up for many weeks in close rooms, compelled on their holiday to travel for miles in a crowded stream, first between houses, and then between dusty high hedges, suddenly they expand into free uncrowded space under spreading trees, or onto the wide Common from which blue distance is visible; the eye, long unrefreshed with sight of growing grass, or star-like flowers, is rejoiced by them again. To us the Commons or forest looks indeed crowded with people, but to them the feeling is one of sufficient space, free air, green grass, and colour, with a life without which they might think the place dull. Every atom of open space you have left to these people is needed; take care you lose none of it; it is becoming yearly of more vital importance to save or increase it. ...

from Octavia Hill, "The Future of Our Commons" (1877)

Is all the land, from sea to sea, to be used for corn-growing or building-over only? Are those who own estates to have their gardens, and the people to have none? ...

Surely we want some beauty in our lives; they cannot be all labour, they cannot be all feeding. When the work is done, when the eating is finished, the soul and spirit of men ask for rest; they want air, they want the sense of peace, they want the sense of space, they want the influence of beauty. Men seek it on the rocky sea-shore, on the peaks of the mountains, by the streams in the valleys, or on the heather-covered moorlands. Over-excited in the cities, overstrained by toil, they need, if it were but once in their lives, that wonderful sense of pause and peace which the near-presence of the great creations of God gives. The silence brings them marvellous messages, the clouds seem their companions, the lights which pass over the heather-covered hills fill them with an immeasurable joy. Old cares seem so far away as hardly to be real; and in the great space which surrounds them the whole spirit is brought into harmony with grander music, tuned to nobler imaginings, and nerved for mightier struggles. ... [All] this, as individuals, we know. There are signs that, as a nation, we are beginning to see it.

from "Rights of Way in Lakeland: The Capture of Latrigg, by one who assisted," *Pall Mall Gazette* (3 October 1887)

On Saturday afternoon, in beautiful sunshine, a solid phalanx of ... about two thousand in number, asserted the public right of access to the top of Latrigg, in Keswick Vale. There have been demonstrations on a similar kind on the shores of Windermere, but never, within the frontiers of Lakeland and within the memory of the oldest inhabitant, was such an extraordinary and significant event known as that under consideration. The hero of the day was Mr. Samuel Plimsoll, who "came to the rescue." ...

Mr. Plimsoll then, amidst tremendous cheering ..., said he did not think it necessary to vindicate his presence there, neither was it necessary to justify it to the great bulk of the country; but still, there were some who might ask, "what business that fellow had there." His answer was a denial that the rights which they had come that day, in such large numbers and in such orderly array, to vindicate, are the rights of Keswick alone. He maintained that they are the rights of the people of England, and as one of that people he was there. He said further that these rights, valuable as they are, are not merely the possession of the people of today. We must see to it that this grand old country of ours may be handed down to our children as good as we found it. Now, certain landlords don't understand this. ...

It is said that [Mr. Anthony Spedding, owner of the Greta Bank estate] claims this beautiful hill in virtue of the Commons Enclosure Act of 1810. But ... what Parliament has given Parliament can take away. ... The pretexts put forward by the landlords in the early part of this century to enclose the common lands which belong to the people have been a "desire to increase the food supply," which they have made scarce. Well, the sheep can graze on Latrigg when it is open as well as when it is closed. ... The property in land has never been, is not, and never can be as absolute as personal property. If all the landlords said, "We will grow no food on the land," they would be shown that the land was only theirs as trustees for the nation. This has been illustrated in the case of railways. Parliament gave the railways power to take the land, whether the owners desired it or no, thus affirming the public interest to be paramount. There are some landlords who imagine the earth belongs to them. ...

I say one word to these pretty tyrants who have obtained 97 percent of everything that is going, and want to take the other three from the hard-working people. I want to say, be wise in time: if you won't be guided by the easy snaffle of public opinion, you will be restrained by the bit and curb of parliamentary restraint. (Great cheering.)

... Presently the whole body of vindicators, following the picturesque zigzag path, and many singing "Rule Britannia" and other iconoclastic songs, had assembled on the summit of Latrigg, where cheers were given for everybody. Derwentwater lay like a mirror beneath, broken here and there by the sheen in the wake of lazily-moving pleasure-boats.

Keswick and Derwentwater, from Latrigg (illustration printed in the *Monthly Chronicle*, April 1890).

Henry Salt, On Humans, Nature, and Non-Human Animals

Henry Salt (1851–1939), a naturalist, literary scholar, and classicist, was also an activist on many fronts—among them the preservation of the British landscape, prison reform, and the promotion of socialist ideals. He remains best known for his writings on human and non-human animals, and in particular for having been the first to put forward an extended argument for animal rights. Salt's writings have been influential not only in the Western world, but worldwide; Mohandas Gandhi's advocacy of vegetarianism was influenced by Salt.

The poem with which Salt opens *On Cambrian and Cumbrian Hills* is dated 1879; the full book was published in 1908. A brief excerpt from the book is included here; longer excerpts are included as part of the anthology's website component.

A brief selection from Salt's *Animals' Rights: Considered in Relation to Social Progress* (1894) may be found below; again, longer excerpts are included as part of the anthology's website component.

from *On Cambrian and Cumbrian Hills* (1879, 1908)

I send thee, love, this upland flower I found,
   While wandering lonely with o'erclouded heart,
Hid in a grey recess of rocky ground
   Among the misty mountains far apart;
5 And there I heard the wild wind's luring sound,
   Which whoso trusts, is healed of earthborn care,
And watched the lofty ridges loom around,
   Yet yearned in vain their secret faith to share.
When lo! the sudden sunlight, sparkling keen,
10 Poured full upon the vales the glorious day,
And bared the abiding mountain-tops serene,
   And swept the shifting vapour-wreaths away—
Then with the hills' true heart my heart beat true,
Heavens opened, cloud-thoughts vanished,
     and I knew.

from CHAPTER 7: SLAG HEAP OR SANCTUARY?

[I]t must not be supposed that Lakeland has not suffered even as Wales has done, though in a less degree, from the ravages of commercialism. Coniston is a sad proof of the contrary, where that once beautiful mountain, the Old Man, has been so ruined by the copper-mines that, as has been said of the gold-fields of Colorado, "the hills have been flayed of all their grass and scalped of all their timber; they are scarred and gashed and ulcerated all over from past mining operations. ..." I was told by Ruskin, whose windows at Brantwood looked westward across Coniston Water to the Old Man, that he thought the very sky above the mountain-top was poisoned and clouded by the mines.

Take the case of Thirlmere, too, that once wild and winding tarn,[1] so narrow at the middle that it was spanned by a rustic bridge, but now enlarged into a Manchester water-tank. ...

The desecration of our mountains is but part of the widespread contempt for natural scenery which may be seen from end to end of the land; but it is among mountains, where Nature is at her wildest, that it strikes us the most. From what filthy-mindedness comes the strange conviction that a clear, swift stream is the right and proper receptacle for the rubbish of human homes? I know a Welsh village, the type, alas! Of many villages in Wales, and elsewhere, in which from the houses built on the steep bank of a pure mountain torrent there dribbles down into the river a tributary river of filth—dust, broken bottles, paper, old boots, decaying vegetables, and all kinds of refuse. ...

There is only one thorough solution of the problem, and that is to nationalize such districts as Snowdonia, Lakeland, the Peak of Derbyshire, and other public holiday-haunts, and so to preserve them for the use and enjoyment of the people for all time. If parks, open spaces, railways, tramways, water, and other public needs can be municipalized, why not mountains? It is impossible to over-estimate the value of mountains as a recreation-ground for soul and body, yet, while we are awaking to the need of maintaining public rights in other directions, we are allowing our mountains—in North Wales and elsewhere—to be sacrificed to commercial selfishness. If Snowdon, for instance, had been purchased by the public twenty years ago, the investment would have been a great deal more profitable than those in which we usually engage; but while we are willing to spend vast sums on grabbing other people's territory, we have not, of course, a penny to spare for the preservation of our own.[2]

What we need, in short, is the appointment of mountain sanctuaries—highland parks, where the hills themselves, with the wild animals and plants whose life is of the hills, shall be preserved in their wildness as the cherished property of the people—consecrated places, where everyone shall be entitled to walk, to climb, to rest, to meditate, to study Nature, to disport himself as he will, but *not* to injure or destroy. When we truly care for these hills of ours, we shall remove them from the

---

[1] *tarn* Mountain lake.

[2] *If Snowdon ... preservation of our own* In 1951 Britain finally did create three such national parks—in the Lake District, the Peaks District, and Snowdonia (Cenedlaethol Eryri).

tender mercies of the mine-owners and railway lords, who now seek profit in their disfigurement, and shall place them under a council of mountaineers and naturalists and nature lovers who understand and reverence them, with the instruction that they shall so administer their charge as to add to the present happiness and the permanent wealth of the nation. How long will it take us, hag-ridden as we are by the nightmare of private ownership, to awake to the necessity of such a change?

from Animals' Rights: Considered in Relation to Social Progress (1894)

from CHAPTER 5:
THE SLAUGHTER OF ANIMALS FOR FOOD

... [E]xperience has shown that flesh-food is wholly unnecessary for the support of healthy life. The importance of this more general recognition of a truth which has in all ages been familiar to a few enlightened thinkers, can hardly be over-estimated in its bearing on the question of animals' rights. ...

The most mischievous effect of the practice of flesh-eating, in its influence on the study of animals' rights at the present time, is that it so stultifies and debases the very *raison d'etre* of countless myriads of beings—it brings them into life for no better purpose than to deny their right to live. It is idle to appeal to the internecine warfare that we see in some aspects of wild nature, where the weaker animal is often the prey of the stronger, for there (apart from the fact that co-operation largely modifies competition) the weaker races at least live their own lives and take their chance in the game, whereas the victims of the human carnivora are bred, and fed, and from the first predestined to untimely slaughter, so that their whole mode of living is warped from its natural standard, and they are scarcely more than animated beef or mutton or pork. This, I contend, is a flagrant violation of the rights of the lower animals, as those rights are now beginning to be apprehended by the humaner conscience of mankind. It has been well said that "to keep a man (slave or servant) for your own

advantage merely, to keep an animal that you may *eat* it, is a lie. You cannot look that man or animal in the face."[1] ...

from CHAPTER 8: LINES OF REFORM

... [T]his brings us back to the moral of the whole matter. The idea of Humanity is no longer confined to man; it is beginning to extend itself to the lower animals, as in the past it has been gradually extended to savages and slaves. ... [W]hat has long been felt by the poet is now being scientifically corroborated by the anthropologist and philosopher. ... "The standpoint of modern thought," says Büchner, "no longer recognises in animals a difference of kind, but only a difference of degree, and sees the principle of intelligence developing through an endless and unbroken series."[2]

It is noteworthy that, on this point, evolutionary science finds itself in agreement with oriental tradition. ...

It is not human life only that is lovable and sacred, but *all* innocent and beautiful life: the great republic of the future will not confine its beneficence to man. The isolation of man from Nature, by our persistent culture of the ratiocinative faculty, and our persistent neglect of the instinctive, has hitherto been the penalty we have had to pay for our incomplete and partial "civilization"; there are many signs that the tendency will now be towards that "Return to Nature" of which Rousseau was the prophet. But let it not for a moment be supposed that an acceptance of the gospel of Nature implies an abandonment or depreciation of intellect—on the contrary, it is the assertion that reason itself can never be at its best, can never be truly rational, except when it is in perfect harmony with the deep-seated emotional instincts and sympathies which underlie all thought.

---

[1] *to keep a man ... the face*   In a footnote, Salt identifies the quotation as being from Edward Carpenter's "England's Ideal." That article by the influential socialist and gay rights activist appeared in the May 1884 issue of the magazine *To-day*.

[2] [Salt's note] "Mind in Animals," translated by Annie Besant. [Ludwig Büchner (1824–99), a German philosopher, was a noted exponent of scientific materialism.]

The true scientist and humanist is he who will reconcile brain to heart, and show us how, without any sacrifice of what we have gained in knowledge, we may resume what we have temporarily lost during the process of acquiring that knowledge—the sureness of intuitive faculty which is originally implanted in men and animals alike. Only by this return to the common fount of feeling will it be possible for man to place himself in right relationship towards the lower animals, and to break down the fatal barrier of antipathy that he has himself erected. …

Tekahionwake/E. Pauline Johnson, "The Happy Hunting Grounds" (1889)

Tekahionwake/E. Pauline Johnson (1861–1913), the child of an Englishwoman and a Mohawk father, became something of a literary celebrity in the late nineteenth and early twentieth centuries, performing in the garb of "an Indian Princess." In 1895 Hector Charlesworth, a leading arbiter of colonial taste in Canada, declared that "for the past five years Miss Pauline Johnson has been the most popular figure in Canadian literature, and in many respects the most prominent one." Her poetry as well as her performances were taken seriously by mainstream critics such as Charlesworth, who expressed admiration for its "charm and power and music."

Many of Tekahionwake's most popular poems—"The Happy Hunting Grounds" among them—evoked the natural world in treating Indigenous themes. In her more popular poems she was careful not to offend mainstream white sensibilities; in poems such as "The Corn Husker," however, she wrote directly and starkly of the oppression her people had suffered. (See the author entry elsewhere in this anthology for that and other poems.)

Into the rose gold westland, its yellow prairies roll,
World of the bison's freedom, home of the
      Indian's soul.
Roll out, O seas! in sunlight bathed,
Your plains wind-tossed, and grass enswathed.

5 Farther than vision ranges, farther than eagles fly,
Stretches the land of beauty, arches the perfect sky,
Hemmed through the purple mists afar
By peaks that gleam like star on star.

Fringing the prairie billows, fretting horizon's line,
10 Darkly green are slumb'ring wildernesses of pine,
Sleeping until the zephyrs[1] throng
To kiss their silence into song.

Whispers freighted with odour swinging into the air,
Russet needles as censers swing to an altar, where
15 The angels' songs are less divine
Than duo sung twixt breeze and pine.

Laughing into the forest, dimples a mountain stream,
Pure as the airs above it, soft as a summer dream,
O! Lethean[2] spring thou'rt only found
20 In this ideal hunting ground.

Surely the great Hereafter cannot be more than this,
Surely we'll see that country after Time's farewell kiss.
Who would his lovely faith condole?
Who envies not the Red-skin's soul,

25 Sailing into the cloud land, sailing into the sun,
Into the crimson portals ajar when life is done?
O! dear dead race, my spirit too
Would fain sail westward unto you.

---

[1] *zephyrs* West winds, synonymous with gentle and pleasant breezes.

[2] *Lethean* In Greek mythology, the water of the River Lethe, one of the rivers of the underworld, caused forgetfulness of the past.

Mary Coleridge, Poems

Mary Coleridge (1861–1907), the great-grandniece of Samuel Taylor Coleridge, had two slim volumes of poetry printed privately in 1896 and 1897, under the pen-name Anodos; a few of her poems were also published in 1898 in a collection entitled *The Garland*. Most of her poetry was published after her death, and the dates of composition are thus in many cases uncertain.

"The Lady of Trees," 1898

By a lake below the mountain
   Hangs the birch, as if, in glee,
The lake had flung the moon a fountain,
   She had turned it to a tree.

5 Therefore do her dull leaves glimmer
   Like the waves that mothered them.
Therefore flits a moony shimmer
   Always round her curvèd stem.

"In London Town," 1908

It was a bird of Paradise,
   Over the roofs he flew.
All the children, in a trice,
Clapped their hands and cried, "How nice!"
5   "Look—his wings are blue!"

His body was of ruby red,
   His eyes were burning gold.
All the grown-up people said,
"What a pity the creature is not dead,
10   For then it could be sold!"

One was braver than the rest.
   He took a loaded gun;
Aiming at the emerald crest,
He shot the creature through the breast.
15   Down it fell in the sun.

It was not heavy, it was not fat,
   And folk began to stare.
"We cannot eat it, that is flat!
And such outlandish feathers as that
20   Why, who could ever wear?"[1]

They flung it into the river brown.
   "A pity the creature died!"
With a smile and with a frown,
Thus they did in London town;
25   But all the children cried.

---

[1] *who could ever wear?* The feathers of the bird of paradise evidently were frequently worn; see elsewhere in this section Henry Salt's discussion of millinery (Chapter 6 of *Animals' Rights*).

ELIZABETH GASKELL
1810 – 1865

Mrs. Gaskell, as she was known to nineteenth-century readers, became famous both for her gentle portrayals in fiction of genteel village life and as one of the first authors of the Victorian era to write "social protest" novels dealing with contemporary issues of poverty, industrialization, and social life in both rural and urban England. Gaskell presents brutally honest portrayals of very different sorts of Victorian reality—conditions of poor factory workers in *Mary Barton* and *North and South*, for example, and of the plight of an unwed mother in *Ruth*.

Elizabeth Cleghorn Stevenson was born in 1810 near London to William Stevenson, a Unitarian preacher and civil servant, and Elizabeth Holland, who died soon after childbirth. From the age of one, Elizabeth was raised by a beloved aunt in the village of Knutsford (the model for Gaskell's novel *Cranford*), near Manchester in northern England. She received a liberal, modern education at a boarding school in Warwick, in central England, and when she came of age went to visit a distant relative in Manchester, where she met her future husband, William Gaskell, a Unitarian minister.

According to Unitarian practices, the two pursued a degree of gender equality far greater than was typical for a Victorian marriage, with Gaskell free to pursue her own interests. For the first twelve years of their marriage, however, she devoted herself to the upbringing and education of her five children and performed many of the duties of her role as a minister's wife, which entailed teaching at a charity school and visiting poor parishioners. By listening to these people's tales of hardship and observing the conditions in factories and homes, Gaskell acquired much of the inspiration for her books. She wrote a small number of short stories and co-authored a poem with her husband while raising her children, but it was not until her infant son died of scarlet fever in 1845 that she began to write novels and stories in earnest, an activity her husband recommended as a partial remedy for the depression brought on by loss.

Mary Barton, Gaskell's first novel, was published in 1848. In it, she exposed the desperation and hopelessness of poverty-stricken millworkers who toiled in miserable, unhealthy conditions in the industrial city of Manchester. Although the book was originally published under the pseudonym "Cotton Mather Mills, Esq.," it was not long before the public's and critics' curiosity unmasked Gaskell. Even though many society people found her portrayal of factory owners to be harsh and unfair, she became an esteemed guest at literary gatherings and social events. Charles Dickens was so impressed with her writing that he asked her to contribute "a short tale or any number of tales" to his magazine, *Household Words*. Gaskell agreed and contributed numerous stories over the next several years; the first, "Our Society at Cranford," appeared in the 13 December 1851 issue. Eight other humorous tales followed, all concerning the same group of upper- and middle-class women and their milieu in a peaceful country village. The tales were extremely well received, and were soon published together as the novel *Cranford* (1853).

Gaskell's next novel was not received as enthusiastically as *Cranford* had been. *Ruth*, also published in 1853, tells the story of a woman who has a child out of wedlock. The subject would have been criticized in any event, but Gaskell's sympathetic portrayal of the woman and her exposure of the hypocrisy of Victorian society deeply angered many people. The book was so controversial that some parishioners burned their copies, and it was banned in many homes, including, ironically, Gaskell's own—even she felt that the subject matter was unsuitable for children. On the other hand, notable women writers such as Elizabeth Barrett Browning, George Eliot, and Charlotte Brontë spoke out in praise of the book. In her next novel, *North and South* (1855), also published in *Household Words* (1854–55), Gaskell returned to issues of factory workers, comparing life in both the rural and urban south with the harsh lives of the working poor in the north. Like *Mary Barton*, *North and South* addressed the need for factory owners to reform workplace conditions and for workers to fight for their rights.

After Charlotte Brontë's death in 1855, Gaskell wrote her biography at the behest of Charlotte's father, Patrick Brontë. Influenced by her close friendship with Charlotte, Gaskell created a very sympathetic portrait of the Brontës, and she included their outspoken opinions about various friends and acquaintances. Unfortunately, Gaskell's loyalty to her subject landed her in trouble when one of those maligned by the Brontës threatened legal action. Under pressure from her publisher, Gaskell was forced to apologize publicly, and the questionable material was removed from the book's subsequent editions. *The Life of Charlotte Brontë* (1857) remains, however, a highly readable biography and a masterpiece of characterization—and it did a great deal to defend Brontë's reputation, ensuring that her work would continue to be read.

Gaskell had almost completed her final novel, *Wives and Daughters*, when she collapsed and died suddenly in 1865. Often compared with the novels of Jane Austen and George Eliot, *Wives and Daughters* exposes the social workings of various classes in a small country town, expressing social critique with the delicate wit and sly humor for which the author was known. Gaskell was buried beside the Unitarian chapel in Knutsford, the town of her childhood that she had so loved and had immortalized in her stories.

Our Society at Cranford [1]

In the first place, Cranford is in possession of the Amazons;[2] all the holders of houses, above a certain rent, are women. If a married couple come to settle in the town, somehow the gentleman disappears; he is either fairly frightened to death by being the only man in the Cranford evening parties, or he is accounted for by being with his regiment, his ship, or closely engaged in business all the week in the great neighbouring commercial town of Drumble, distant only twenty miles on a railroad.[3] In short, whatever does become of the gentlemen, they are not at Cranford. What could they do if they were there? The surgeon has his round of thirty miles, and sleeps at Cranford; but every man cannot be a surgeon. For keeping the trim gardens full of choice flowers without a weed to speck them; for frightening away little boys who look wistfully at the said flowers through the railings; for rushing out at the geese that occasionally venture into the gardens if the gates are left open; for deciding all questions of literature and politics without troubling themselves with unnecessary reasons or arguments; for obtaining clear and correct knowledge of everybody's affairs in the parish; for keeping their neat maid-servants in admirable order; for kindness (somewhat dictatorial) to the poor, and real tender good offices to each other whenever any are in distress, the ladies of Cranford are quite sufficient. "A man," as one of them observed to me once, "is *so* in the way in the house!" Although the ladies of Cranford know all each other's proceedings, they are exceedingly indifferent to each other's opinions. Indeed as each has her own individuality, not to say eccentricity, pretty strongly developed, nothing is so easy as verbal retaliation; but somehow good-will reigns among them to a considerable degree.

The Cranford ladies have only an occasional little quarrel, spirited out in a few peppery words and angry jerks of the head; just enough to prevent the even tenor[4] of their lives from becoming too flat. Their dress is very independent of fashion; as they observe, "What does it signify how we dress here at Cranford, where everybody knows us?" And if they go from home, their reason is equally cogent: "What does it signify how we dress here, where nobody know us?" The materials of their clothes are, in general, good and plain, and most of them are nearly as scrupulous as Miss Tyler, of cleanly[5] memory; but I will answer for it, the last gigot,[6] the last tight and scanty petticoat in war in England, was seen in Cranford—and seen without a smile.

I can testify to a magnificent family red silk umbrella, under which a gentle little spinster, left alone of many brothers and sisters, used to patter to church on rainy days. Have you any red silk umbrellas in London? We had a tradition of the first that had ever been seen in Cranford; and the little boys mobbed it, and called it "a stick in petticoats." It might have been the very red silk one I have described, held by a strong father over a troop of little ones; the poor little lady—the survivor of all—could scarcely carry it.

Then there were rules and regulations for visiting and calls; and they were announced to any young people, who might be staying in the town, with all the solemnity with which the old Manx laws were read once a year on the Tyne-wold.[7]

---

[1] *Our Society at Cranford* Published in *Household Words*, a weekly magazine edited by Charles Dickens. Starting in March 1850, *Household Words* was published every Wednesday for nine years. The magazine combined fiction—often serialized novels—and nonfiction; most of the writing was concerned with prominent social issues of the mid-Victorian period. "Our Society at Cranford" was first published in *Household Words* as a stand-alone piece; at Dickens's urging, Gaskell wrote eight more parts, with the concluding section appearing in 1853. The same year, the episodes were collected into the novel *Cranford* and published as a complete volume. Gaskell was apparently working on her novel *Ruth* (1853) concurrently with the publication of *Cranford* in *Household Words*.

[2] *Amazons* In classical Greek mythology, a legendary tribe of self-sufficient female warriors, often at war with the Greeks. The name has since come to signify "woman warriors" more generally.

[3] *the great neighbouring commercial town ... a railroad* Gaskell's Cranford is modeled on Knutsford, a town in Cheshire that is approximately 20 miles southwest of the city of Manchester.

[4] *tenor* Tone.

[5] *cleanly* Pure or innocent.

[6] *gigot* Style of sleeve that is very puffy at the shoulder and narrow at the wrist. It was out of fashion by the end of the 1830s, but became popular again toward the end of the century.

[7] *Manx laws* Common law system on the Isle of Man; *Tyne-wold* Tynwald is the name of the Isle of Man parliament.

"Our friends have sent to inquire how you are after your journey tonight, my dear" (fifteen miles, in a gentleman's carriage); "they will give you some rest tomorrow, but the next day, I have no doubt, they will call; so be at liberty after twelve—from twelve to three are our calling-hours."

Then, after they had called, "It is the third day; I dare say your Mamma has told you, my dear, never to let more than three days elapse between receiving a call[1] and returning it; and also, that you are never to stay longer than a quarter of an hour."

"But am I to look at my watch? How am I to find out when a quarter of an hour has passed?"

"You must keep thinking about the time, my dear, and not allow yourself to forget it in conversation."

As everybody had this rule in their minds, whether they received or paid a call, of course no absorbing subject was ever spoken about. We kept ourselves to short sentences of small talk, and were punctual to our time.

I imagine that a few of the gentlefolks of Cranford were poor, and had some difficulty in making both ends meet; but they were like Spartans,[2] and concealed their smart under a smiling face. We none of us spoke of money, because that subject savoured of commerce and trade, and though some might be poor, we were all aristocratic. The Cranfordians had that kindly *esprit de corps*[3] which made them overlook all deficiencies in success when some among them tried to conceal their poverty. When Mrs. Forrester gave a party in her baby-house of a dwelling, and the little maiden disturbed the ladies on the sofa by a request that she might get the tea-tray out from underneath, every one took this novel proceeding as the most natural thing in the world; and talked on about household forms and ceremonies, as if we all believed that our hostess had a regular servants' hall, second table, with housekeeper and steward;[4]

instead of the one little charity-school maiden, whose short ruddy arms could never have been strong enough to carry the tray upstairs, if she had not been assisted in private by her mistress, who now sat in state, pretending not to know what cakes were sent up; though she knew, and we knew, and she knew that we knew, and we knew that she knew, she had been busy all the morning making tea-bread and sponge-cakes.

There were one or two consequences arising from this general but unacknowledged poverty, and this very much acknowledged gentility, which were not amiss, and which might be introduced into many circles of society to their great improvement. For instance, the inhabitants of Cranford kept early hours, and clattered home in their pattens,[5] under the guidance of a lantern-bearer, about nine o'clock at night; and the whole town was abed and asleep by half-past ten. Moreover, it was considered "vulgar" (a tremendous word in Cranford) to give anything expensive, in the way of eatable or drinkable, at the evening entertainments. Wafer bread-and-butter and sponge-biscuits were all that the Honourable Mrs. Jamieson gave; and she was sister-in-law to the late Earl of Cranford, although she did practise such "elegant economy."

"Elegant economy!" How naturally one falls back into the phraseology of Cranford! There, economy was always "elegant," and money-spending always "vulgar and ostentatious"; a sort of sour-grapeism, which made us very peaceful and satisfied. I never shall forget the dismay felt when a certain Captain Brown came to live at Cranford, and openly spoke about his being poor. Not in a whisper to an intimate friend, the doors, and windows being previously closed; but, in the public street! in a loud military voice! alleging his poverty as a reason for not taking a particular house. The ladies of Cranford were already rather moaning over the invasion of their territories by a man and a gentleman. He was a half-pay Captain, and had obtained some situation[6] on

---

[1] *call* Formal visit.

[2] *Spartans* The ancient inhabitants of Sparta were known for their stoical spirit (as well as for their plainness, scrupulousness, fortitude, and prowess in battle).

[3] *esprit de corps* French: group spirit, comradeship.

[4] *steward* Servant who manages a household or estate.

[5] *pattens* Thick-soled shoes, or overshoes, meant to be worn on wet or muddy ground.

[6] *half-pay Captain* Retired officers, as well as those waiting for a new assignment, were given "half-pay." (The term is misleading, as the officers received a great deal more than half of the pay for working officers, whose pay levels were lower on the grounds that they also

a neighbouring railroad, which had been vehemently petitioned against by the little town; and if, in addition to his masculine gender, and his connexion with the obnoxious railroad, he was so brazen as to talk of being poor—why! then, indeed, he must be sent to Coventry.[1] Death was as true and as common as poverty; yet people never spoke about that, loud out in the streets. It was a word not to be mentioned to ears polite. We had tacitly agreed to ignore that any with whom we associated on terms of visiting equality could ever be prevented by poverty from doing anything that they wished. If we walked home to or from a party, it was because the night was *so* fine, or the air *so* refreshing; not because sedan-chairs[2] were expensive. If we wore prints,[3] instead of summer silks, it was because we preferred a washing material; and so on, till we blinded ourselves to the vulgar fact that we were, all of us, people of very moderate means. Of course, then, we did not know what to make of a man who could not speak of poverty as if it was not a disgrace. Yet, somehow Captain Brown made himself respected in Cranford, and was called upon, in spite of all resolutions to the contrary. I was surprised to hear his opinions quoted as authority, at a visit which I paid to Cranford about a year after he had settled in the town. My own friends had been among the bitterest opponents of any proposal to visit Captain Brown and his daughters only twelve months before; and now he was even admitted in the tabooed hours before twelve. True, it was to discover the cause of a smoking chimney, before the fire was lighted; but still Captain Brown walked upstairs, nothing daunted, spoke in a voice too large for the room, and joked quite in the way of a tame man, about the house. He had been blind to all the small slights and omissions of trivial ceremonies with

which he had been received. He had been friendly, though the Cranford ladies had been cool: he had answered small sarcastic compliments in good faith; and, with his manly frankness, had overpowered all the shrinking which met him as a man who was not ashamed to be poor. And, at last, his excellent masculine common sense and his facility in devising expedients to overcome domestic dilemmas, had gained him an extraordinary place as authority among the Cranford ladies. He, himself, went on in his course, as unaware of his popularity as he had been of the reverse; and I am sure he was startled one day, when he found his advice so highly esteemed as to make some counsel which he had given in jest, be taken in sober, serious earnest.

It was on this subject—an old lady had an Alderney cow,[4] which she looked upon as a daughter. You could not pay the short quarter-of-an-hour call without being told of the wonderful milk or wonderful intelligence of this animal. The whole town knew and kindly regarded Miss Betsy Barker's Alderney; therefore great was the sympathy and regret when, in an unguarded moment, the poor cow tumbled into a lime-pit.[5] She moaned so loudly that she was soon heard, and rescued; but meanwhile the poor beast had lost most of her hair, and came out looking naked, cold, and miserable, in a bare skin. Everybody pitied the animal, though a few could not restrain their smiles at her droll appearance. Miss Betsy Barker absolutely cried with sorrow and dismay; and it was said she thought of trying a bath of oil. This remedy, perhaps, was recommended by some one of the number whose advice she asked; but the proposal, if ever it was made, was knocked on the head by Captain Brown's decided, "Get her a flannel waistcoat and flannel drawers, Ma'am, if you wish to keep her alive. But my advice is, kill the poor creature at once."

Miss Betsy Barker dried her eyes, and thanked the Captain heartily; she set to work, and by-and-by all the town turned out to see the Alderney meekly going to her pasture, clad in dark grey flannel. I have watched her myself many a time. Do you ever see cows dressed in grey flannel in London?

---

received room and board; in many cases, the "half-pay" of retired officers was higher than the salary paid those currently in service); *situation* Position of employment.

[1] *sent to Coventry* The expression suggests the refusal to interact with an undesirable member of a group, or the desire to exclude someone from society.

[2] *sedan-chairs* Fashionable vehicles, seating one passenger, carried by two bearers holding on to two poles.

[3] *prints* Printed fabric, likely calico, a relatively inexpensive cotton textile.

[4] *Alderney cow* Breed of dairy cow.

[5] *lime-pit* Pit used to remove hair from animal hides.

Captain Brown had taken a small house on the outskirts of the town, where he lived with his two daughters. He must have been upwards of sixty at the time of the first visit I paid to Cranford, after I had left it as a residence. But he had a wiry, well-trained, elastic figure; a stiff military throw-back of his head, and a springing step, which made him appear much younger than he was. His eldest daughter looked almost as old as himself, and betrayed the fact that his real was more than his apparent age. Miss Brown must have been forty; she had a sickly, pained, careworn expression on her face, and looked as if the gaiety of youth had long faded out of sight. Even when young she must have been plain and hard-featured. Miss Jessie Brown was ten years younger than her sister, and twenty shades prettier. Her face was round and dimpled. Miss Jenkyns once said, in a passion against Captain Brown (the cause of which I will tell you presently), "that she thought it was time for Miss Jessie to leave off her dimples, and not always be trying to look like a child." It was true there was something child-like in her face; and there will be, I think, till she dies, though she should live to a hundred. Her eyes were large blue wandering eyes, looking straight at you; her nose was unformed and snub, and her lips were red and dewy; she wore her hair, too, in little rows of curls, which heightened this appearance. I do not know if she was pretty or not; but I liked her face, and so did everybody, and I do not think she could help her dimples. She had something of her father's jauntiness of gait and manner; and any female observer might detect a slight difference in the attire of the two sisters—that of Miss Jessie being about two pounds per annum more expensive than Miss Brown's. Two pounds was a large sum in Captain Brown's annual disbursements.[1]

Such was the impression made upon me by the Brown family, when I first saw them altogether in Cranford church. The Captain I had met before—on the occasion of the smoky chimney, which he had cured by some simple alteration in the flue. In church, he held his double eye-glass to his eyes during the morning hymn, and then lifted up his head erect, and sang out loud joyfully. He made the responses louder than the

clerk—an old man with a piping feeble voice, who, I think, felt aggrieved at the Captain's sonorous bass, and quavered higher and higher in consequence.

On coming out of church, the brisk Captain paid the most gallant attention to his two daughters. He nodded and smiled to his acquaintances; but he shook hands with none until he had helped Miss Brown to unfurl her umbrella, had relieved her of her prayer-book, and had waited patiently till she, with trembling nervous hands, had taken up her gown to walk through the wet roads.

I wondered what the Cranford ladies did with Captain Brown at their parties. We had often rejoiced, in former days, that there was no gentleman to be attended to, and to find conversation for, at the card-parties. We had congratulated ourselves upon the snugness of the evenings; and, in our love for gentility and distaste of mankind, we had almost persuaded ourselves that to be a man was to be "vulgar"; so that when I found my friend and hostess, Miss Jenkyns, was going to have a party in my honour, and that Captain and the Miss Browns were invited, I wondered much what would be the course of the evening. Card-tables, with green baize[2] tops, were set out by daylight, just as usual; it was the third week in November, so the evenings closed in about four. Candles, and clean packs of cards, were arranged on each table. The fire was made up, the neat maid-servant had received her last directions; and, there we stood dressed in our best, each with a candle-lighter in our hands, ready to dart at the candles as soon as the first knock came. Parties in Cranford were solemn festivities, making the ladies feel gravely elated, as they sat together in their best dresses. As soon as three had arrived, we sat down to "Preference,"[3] I being the unlucky fourth. The next four comers were put down immediately to another table; and, presently, the tea-trays, which I had seen set out in the store-room as I passed in the morning, were placed

---

[1] *disbursements* Spending.

[2] *baize* Coarse woolen material, typically used for coverings or linings.

[3] *Preference* Card game, typically involving three players using a thirty-two card deck, in which the trump card is established through bidding.

each on the middle of a card-table. The china was delicate egg-shell; the old-fashioned silver glittered with polishing; but the eatables were of the slightest description. While the trays were yet on the tables, Captain and the Miss Browns came in; and I could see, that somehow or other, the Captain was a favourite with all the ladies present. Ruffled brows were smoothed, sharp voices lowered at his approach. Miss Brown looked ill, and depressed almost to gloom. Miss Jessie smiled as usual, and seemed nearly as popular as her father. He immediately and quietly assumed the man's place in the room; attended to every one's wants, lessened the pretty maid-servant's labour by waiting on empty cups, and bread-and-butterless ladies; and yet did it all in so easy and dignified a manner, and so much as if it were a matter of course for the strong to attend to the weak, that he was a true man throughout. He played for three-penny points with as grave an interest as if they had been pounds; and yet, in all his attention to strangers, he had an eye on his suffering daughter; for suffering I was sure she was, though to many eyes she might only appear to be irritable. Miss Jessie could not play cards; but she talked to the sitters-out, who, before her coming, had been rather inclined to be cross. She sang, too, to an old cracked piano, which I think had been a spinnet[1] in its youth. Miss Jessie sang "Jock of Hazeldean"[2] a little out of tune; but we were none of us musical, though Miss Jenkyns beat time, out of time, by way of appearing to be so.

It was very good of Miss Jenkyns to do this; for I had seen that, a little while before, she had been a good deal annoyed by Miss Jessie Brown's unguarded admission (à-propos of Shetland wool) that she had an uncle, her mother's brother, who was a shopkeeper in Edinburgh. Miss Jenkyns tried to drown this confession by a terrible cough—for the Honourable Mrs. Jamieson was sitting at the card-table nearest Miss Jessie, and what would she say or think if she found out she was in the same room with a shopkeeper's niece! But Miss Jessie Brown (who had no tact, as we all agreed, the next

morning) *would* repeat the information, and assure Miss Pole she could easily get her the identical Shetland wool required, "through my uncle, who has the best assortment of Shetland goods of any one in Edinbro'." It was to take the taste of this out of our mouths, and the sound of this out of our ears, that Miss Jenkyns proposed music; so I say again, it was very good of her to beat time to the song.

When the trays reappeared with biscuits and wine, punctually at a quarter to nine, there was conversation; comparing of cards, and talking over tricks; but, by-and-by, Captain Brown sported[3] a bit of literature.

"Have you seen any numbers of 'Hood's Own?'"[4] said he. (It was then publishing in parts.) "Capital thing!"

Now, Miss Jenkyns was daughter of a deceased rector of Cranford; and, on the strength of a number of manuscript sermons, and a pretty good library of divinity, considered herself literary, and looked upon any conversation about books as a challenge to her. So she answered and said, "Yes, she had seen it; indeed, she might say she had read it."

"And what do you think of it?" exclaimed Captain Brown. "Isn't it famously good?" So urged, Miss Jenkyns could not but speak.

"I must say I don't think it is by any means equal to Dr. Johnson.[5] Still, perhaps, the author is young. Let him persevere, and who knows what he may become if he will take the great Doctor for his model." This was evidently too much for Captain Brown to take placidly; and I saw the words on the tip of his tongue before Miss

---

[1] *spinnet* Musical instrument, resembling a small harpsichord, with each of its strings designed for a single note.

[2] *Jock of Hazeldean* Scottish ballad, with words by Sir Walter Scott.

[3] *tricks* Cards won during play; *sported* Casually brought up.

[4] *Hood's Own* Thomas Hood (1799–1845), a poet and humorist and publisher of *Comic Annual*, was the author of political satires and caricatures, as well as comic sketches, that appeared monthly and were eventually collected as *Hood's Own, or, Laughter from Year to Year* (1838–39). This reference is one of the alterations made by Charles Dickens; Gaskell's original wording (reinstated in *Cranford*) was "'...any numbers of The Pickwick Papers,' said he"—a reference to Dickens's early work of fiction (published in parts from April 1836 to November 1837). See "In Context" below for further information.

[5] *Dr. Johnson* Samuel Johnson (1709–84), influential poet, essayist, lexicographer (he was responsible for the *Dictionary of the English Language*, published in 1755), and critic. He was frequently held up as a model man of letters during the Victorian period.

Jenkyns had finished her sentence.

"It is quite a different sort of thing, my dear madam," he began.

"I am quite aware of that," returned she. "And I make allowances, Captain Brown."

"Just allow me to read you a scene out of this month's number," pleaded he. "I had it only this morning, and I don't think the company can have read it yet."

"As you please," said she, settling herself with an air of resignation. He read the account of the gentleman who was terrified out of his wits by political events, who "could no more collect himself than the Irish tithes."[1] Some of us laughed heartily. *I* did not dare, because I was staying in the house. Miss Jenkyns sat in patient gravity. When it was ended, she turned to me, and said with mild dignity, "Fetch me 'Rasselas,'[2] my dear, out of the book-room."

When I brought it to her, she turned to Captain Brown: "Now allow *me* to read you a scene, and then the present company can judge between your favourite, Mr. Hood, or Dr. Johnson."

She read one of the conversations between Rasselas and Imlac,[3] in a high-pitched majestic voice; and when she had ended, she said, "I imagine I am now justified in my preference of Dr. Johnson, as a writer of fiction." The Captain screwed his lips up, and drummed on the table, but he did not speak. She thought she would give a finishing blow or two.

"I consider it vulgar, and below the dignity of literature, to publish in numbers."[4]

"How was the 'Rambler'[5] published, Ma'am?" asked Captain Brown, in a low voice; which I think Miss Jenkyns could not have heard.

"Dr. Johnson's style is a model for young beginners. My father recommended it to me when I began to write letters. I have formed my own style upon it; I recommend it to your favourite."

"I should be very sorry for him to exchange his style for any such pompous writing," said Captain Brown.

Miss Jenkyns felt this as a personal affront, in a way of which the Captain had not dreamed. Epistolary writing,[6] she and her friends considered her *forte*. Many a copy of many a letter have I seen written and corrected on the slate, before she "seized the half-hour just previous to post-time to assure" her friends of this or of that; and Dr. Johnson was, as she said, her model in these compositions. She drew herself up with dignity, and only replied to Captain Brown's last remark by saying, with marked emphasis on every syllable, "I prefer Dr. Johnson to Mr. Hood."

It is said—I won't vouch for the fact—that Captain Brown was heard to say, *sotto voce*,[7] "D—n Dr. Johnson!" If he did, he was penitent afterwards, as he showed by going to stand near Miss Jenkyns's armchair, and endeavouring to beguile her into conversation on some more pleasing subject. But she was inexorable. The next day, she made the remark I have mentioned, about Miss Jessie's dimples.

It was impossible to live a month at Cranford and not know the daily habits of each resident; and long before my visit was ended, I knew much concerning the whole Brown trio. There was nothing new to be discovered respecting their poverty; for they had spoken simply and openly about that from the very first. They

[1] *the account ... Irish tithes* The Tithe War (1830–36) was a largely nonviolent reaction to the enforcement of a tithe, or tax-like payment, on Irish farmers by the Church of Ireland. The already financially pressed farmers increasingly began to resist making the payments. Although the farmers typically employed civil disobedience, the conflict produced casualties, most notably in 1835, when seventeen people were killed and thirty wounded as part of an enforcement attempt.

This reference was one of the alterations made by Charles Dickens. In Gaskell's original (and in *Cranford*), the text reads as follows: "... the account of the 'swarry' which Sam Weller gave at Bath,"—a reference to Chapter 37 of Dickens's *The Pickwick Papers*.

[2] *Rasselas* Samuel Johnson's *The History of Rasselas, Prince of Abissinia* (1759), an allegorical work on the subject of happiness.

[3] *Rasselas and Imlac* Rasselas is the titular Abissinian prince, confined to a beautiful valley as he awaits ascension to the throne. Eventually, Rasselas flees, accompanied by his faithful friend, the poet Imlac (as well as his sister and her attendant).

[4] *publish in numbers* Publish in parts; serialize.

[5] *Rambler* Samuel Johnson published *The Rambler*, a series of short papers on various topics, every Tuesday and Saturday from 1750 to 1752. Altogether, Johnson produced over two hundred articles, written in an elevated style, on subjects ranging from literature to politics.

[6] *Epistolary writing* The writing of letters.

[7] *sotto voce* Italian: in a soft voice; under his breath.

made no mystery of the necessity for their being economical. All that remained to be discovered was the Captain's infinite kindness of heart, and the various modes in which, unconsciously to himself, he manifested it. Some little anecdotes were talked about for some time after they occurred. As we did not read much, and as all the ladies were pretty well suited with servants, there was a dearth of subjects for conversation. We, therefore, discussed the circumstance of the Captain taking a poor old woman's dinner out of her hands, one very slippery Sunday. He had met her returning from the bakehouse[1] as he came from church, and noticed her precarious footing; and with the grave dignity with which he did everything, he relieved her of her burden, and steered along the street by her side, carrying her baked mutton and potatoes safely home. This was thought very eccentric; and it was rather expected that he would pay a round of calls, on the Monday morning, to explain and apologise to the Cranford sense of propriety: but he did no such thing; and then it was decided that he was ashamed, and was keeping out of sight. In a kindly pity for him, we began to say—"After all, the Sunday morning's occurrence showed great goodness of heart"; and it was resolved that he should be comforted on his next appearance amongst us; but, lo! he came down upon us, untouched by any sense of shame, speaking loud and bass as ever, his head thrown back, his wig as jaunty and well-curled as usual, and we were obliged to conclude he had forgotten all about Sunday.

Miss Pole and Miss Jessie Brown had set up a kind of intimacy, on the strength of the Shetland wool and the new knitting stitches; so it happened that when I went to visit Miss Pole, I saw more of the Browns than I had done while staying with Miss Jenkyns; who had never got over what she called Captain Brown's disparaging remarks upon Dr. Johnson, as a writer of light and agreeable fiction. I found that Miss Brown was seriously ill of some lingering, incurable complaint, the pain occasioned by which gave the uneasy expression to her face that I had taken for unmitigated crossness. Cross, too, she was at times, when the nervous irritability occasioned by her disease became past endurance. Miss Jessie bore with her at these times even more patiently than she did with the bitter self-upbraidings by which they were invariably succeeded. Miss Brown used to accuse herself, not merely of hasty and irritable temper; but also of being the cause why her father and sister were obliged to pinch, in order to allow her the small luxuries which were necessaries in her condition. She would so fain[2] have made sacrifices for them and have lightened their cares, that the original generosity of her disposition added acerbity to her temper. All this was borne by Miss Jessie and her father with more than placidity—with absolute tenderness. I forgave Miss Jessie her singing out of time, and her juvenility of dress, when I saw her at home. I came to perceive that Captain Brown's dark Brutus wig[3] and padded coat (alas! too often threadbare) were remnants of the military smartness of his youth, which he now wore unconsciously. He was a man of infinite resources, gained in his barrack experience. As he confessed, no one could black his boots to please him except himself; but, indeed, he was not above saving the little maid-servant's labours in every way, feeling probably that his daughter's illness made the place[4] a hard one.

He endeavoured to make peace with Miss Jenkyns soon after the memorable dispute I have named, by a present of a wooden fire-shovel (his own making), having heard her say how much the grating of an iron one annoyed her. She received the present with cool gratitude, and thanked him formally. When he was gone, she bade me put it away in the lumber-room; feeling, probably, that no present from a man who preferred Mr. Hood to Dr. Johnson could be less jarring than an iron fire-shovel.

Such was the state of things when I left Cranford and went to Drumble. I had, however, several corre-

---

[1] *bakehouse* House where bread is baked. The poor could in many cases take their meals to be heated at the local bakehouse (which would charge a modest fee for the service).

[2] *fain* Gladly.

[3] *Brutus wig* Wig styled in an uneven crop and named after Lucius Junius Brutus, the Roman Republic's founder.

[4] *place* Job.

spondents who kept me *au fait*[1] to the proceedings of the dear little town. There was Miss Pole, who was becoming as much absorbed in crochet as she had been once in knitting; and the burden[2] of whose letter was something like, "But don't you forget the white worsted at Flint's," of the old song;[3] for, at the end of every sentence of news came a fresh direction as to some crochet commission which I was to execute for her. Miss Matilda Jenkyns (who did not mind being called Miss Matey, when Miss Jenkyns was not by); wrote nice, kind, rambling letters; now and then venturing into an opinion of her own; but suddenly pulling herself up, and either begging me not to name what she had said, as Deborah thought differently, and *she* knew; or else, putting in a postscript to the effect that, since writing the above, she had been talking over the subject with Deborah, and was quite convinced that, &c.—(here, probably, followed a recantation of every opinion she had given in the letter). Then came Miss Jenkyns— Deborah, as she liked Miss Matey to call her; her father having once said that the Hebrew name ought to be so pronounced. I secretly think she took the Hebrew prophetess[4] for a model in character; and, indeed, she was not unlike the stern prophetess in some ways; making allowance, of course, for modern customs and difference in dress. Miss Jenkyns wore a cravat, and a little bonnet like a jockey-cap, and altogether had the appearance of a strong-minded woman; therefore, she would have despised the modern idea of women being equal to men. Equal, indeed! She knew they were superior.—But to return to her letters. Everything in them was stately and grand, like herself. I have been looking them over (dear Miss Jenkyns, how I loved her!) and I will give an extract, more especially because it relates to our friend Captain Brown:

"The Honourable Mrs. Jamieson has only just quitted me;[5] and, in the course of conversation she communicated to me the intelligence, that she had yesterday received a call from her revered husband's quondam[6] friend, Lord Mauleverer. You will not easily conjecture what brought his lordship within the precincts of our little town. It was to see Captain Brown, with whom, it appears, his lordship was acquainted in the 'plumed wars,'[7] and who had the privilege of averting destruction from his lordship's head, when some great peril was impending over it, off the misnomered Cape of Good Hope.[8] You know our friend the Honourable Mrs. Jamieson's deficiency in the spirit of innocent curiosity; and you will, therefore, not be so much surprised when I tell you she was quite unable to disclose to me the exact nature of the peril in question. I was anxious, I confess, to ascertain in what manner Captain Brown, with his limited establishment, could receive so distinguished a guest; and I discovered that his lordship retired to rest; and, let us hope to refreshing slumbers, at the Angel Hotel; but shared the Brunonian[9] meals during the two days that he honoured Cranford with this august presence. Mrs. Johnson, our civil butcher's wife, informs me that Miss Jessie purchased a leg of lamb; but, besides this, I can hear of no preparation whatever to give a suitable reception to so distinguished a visitor. Perhaps they entertained him with 'the feast of reason and the flow of soul';[10] and to us, who are acquainted with Captain Brown's sad want of relish, for

[1] *au fait* French: up-to-date; fully informed.

[2] *burden* Here, primary meaning carried by a communication; also, the chorus of a song.

[3] *But don't ... old song* The "old song" in question is "Country Commissions," which takes the form of a letter, each verse ending with a reminder to procure a "skein of white worsted at Flint's."

[4] *Deborah ... Hebrew prophetess* Prophet and Judge, or legal and military leader, of the ancient Israelites, Deborah successfully mounted a counterattack against the king of Canaan, a military triumph recounted in the biblical Book of Judges.

[5] *quitted me* Left me.

[6] *quondam* Latin: former; retired.

[7] *plumed wars* Napoleonic Wars, fought between England and France (1803–15), so-called because of the plumed helmets worn by the soldiers.

[8] *Cape of Good Hope* Part of the Atlantic coast on the Cape Peninsula of South Africa; the rocky terrain was first dubbed "Cape of Tempests" by the Portuguese explorer Bartolemeu Dias, who first rounded it in 1488.

[9] *Brunonian* Related to Brown.

[10] *the feast ... soul* Cf. Alexander Pope, *Imitations of Horace*, "The First Satire of the Second Book of Horace, Imitated," 130.

'the pure wells of English undefiled,'[1] it may be matter for congratulation, that he has had the opportunity of improving his taste by holding converse with an elegant and refined member of the British aristocracy. But from some mundane feelings who is free?"

Miss Pole and Miss Matey wrote to me by the same post. Such a piece of news as Lord Mauleverer's visit was not to be lost on the Cranford letter-writers: they made the most of it. Miss Matey humbly apologised for writing at the same time as her sister, who was so much more capable than she to describe the honour done to Cranford; but, in spite of a little bad spelling, Miss Matey's account gave me the best idea of the commotion occasioned by his lordship's visit, after it had occurred; for, except the people at the Angel, the Browns, Mrs. Jamieson, and a little lad his lordship had sworn at for driving a dirty hoop against the aristocratic legs, I could not hear of any one with whom his lordship had held conversation.

My next visit to Cranford was in the summer. There had been neither births, deaths, nor marriages since I was there last. Everybody lived in the same house, and wore pretty nearly the same well-preserved, old-fashioned clothes. The greatest event was that Miss Jenkyns had purchased a new carpet for the drawing-room. O, the busy work Miss Matey and I had in chasing the sunbeams, as they fell in an afternoon right down on this carpet through the blindless window! We spread newspapers over the places, and sat down to our book or work; and, lo! in a quarter of an hour the sun had moved, and was blazing away on a fresh spot; and down again we went on our knees to alter the position of the newspapers. We were very busy, too, one whole morning before Miss Jenkyns gave her party, in following her directions, and in cutting out and stitching together pieces of newspaper, so as to form little paths to every chair, set for the expected visitors, lest their shoes might dirty or defile the purity of the carpet. Do you make paper paths for every guest to walk upon in London?

Captain Brown and Miss Jenkyns were not very cordial to each other. The literary dispute, of which I had seen the beginning, was a "raw," the slightest touch on which made them wince. It was the only difference of opinion they had ever had; but that difference was enough. Miss Jenkyns could not refrain from talking *at* Captain Brown; and though he did not reply, he drummed with his fingers; which action she felt and resented as very disparaging to Dr. Johnson. He was rather ostentatious in his preference of the writings of Mr. Hood; would walk through the street so absorbed in them, that he all but ran against Miss Jenkyns; and though his apologies were earnest and sincere, and though he did not, in fact, do more than startle her and himself, she owned to me she had rather he had knocked her down, if he had only been reading a higher style of literature. The poor, brave Captain! he looked older, and more worn, and his clothes were very threadbare. But he seemed as bright and cheerful as ever, unless he was asked about his daughter's health.

"She suffers a great deal, and she must suffer more; we do what we can to alleviate her pain—God's will be done!" He took off his hat at these last words. I found, from Miss Pole, that everything had been done, in fact. A medical man, of high repute in that country neighbourhood, had been sent for, and every injunction he had given was attended to, regardless of expense. Miss Pole was sure they denied themselves many things in order to make the invalid comfortable; but they never spoke about it; and as for Miss Jessie! "I really think she's an angel," said poor Miss Pole, quite overcome. "To see her way of bearing with Miss Brown's crossness, and the bright face she puts on after she's been sitting up a whole night and scolded above half of it, is quite beautiful. Yet she looks as neat and as ready to welcome the Captain at breakfast-time, as if she had been asleep in the Queen's bed all night. My dear! you could never laugh at her prim little curls or her pink bows again, if you saw her as I have done." I could only feel very penitent, and greet Miss Jessie with double respect when I met her next. She looked faded and pinched; and her lips began to quiver, as if she was very weak, when she

---

[1] *the pure wells … undefiled* The poet Edmund Spenser (c. 1552–99) deemed the works of Geoffrey Chaucer (c. 1343–1400) a "well of English pure and undefiled."

spoke of her sister. But she brightened, and sent back the tears that were glittering in her pretty eyes, as she said:

"But, to be sure, what a town Cranford is for kindness! I don't suppose any one has a better dinner than usual cooked, but the best part of all comes in a little covered basin for my sister. The poor people will leave their earliest vegetables at our door for her. They speak short and gruff, as if they were ashamed of it; but I am sure it often goes to my heart to see their thoughtfulness." The tears now came back and overflowed; but after a minute or two, she began to scold herself, and ended by going away, the same cheerful Miss Jessie as ever.

"But why does not this Lord Mauleverer do something for the man who saved his life?" said I.

"Why, you see, unless Captain Brown has some reason for it, he never speaks about being poor; and he walked along by his lordship, looking as happy and cheerful as a prince; and as they never call attention to their dinner by apologies, and as Miss Brown was better that day, and all seemed bright, I dare say his lordship never knew how much care there was in the background. He did send game in the winter pretty often, but now he is gone abroad."

I had often occasion to notice the use that was made of fragments and small opportunities in Cranford; the rose-leaves that were gathered ere they fell, to make into a potpourri for some one who had no garden; the little bundles of lavender-flowers sent to strew the drawers of some town-dweller, or to burn in the chamber of some invalid. Things that many would despise, and actions which it seemed scarcely worthwhile to perform, were all attended to in Cranford. Miss Jenkyns stuck an apple full of cloves to be heated and smell pleasantly in Miss Brown's room; and as she put in each clove, she uttered a Johnsonian sentence. Indeed, she never could think of the Browns without talking Johnson; and, as they were seldom absent from her thoughts just then, I heard many a rolling three-piled[1] sentence.

Captain Brown called one day to thank Miss Jenkyns for many little kindnesses, which I did not know until then that she had rendered. He had sud-

denly become like an old man; his deep bass voice had a quavering in it; his eyes looked dim, and the lines on his face were deep. He did not—could not—speak cheerfully of his daughter's state, but he talked with manly pious resignation, and not much. Twice over he said, "What Jessie has been to us, God only knows!" and after the second time, he got up hastily, shook hands all round without speaking, and left the room.

That afternoon we perceived little groups in the street, all listening with faces aghast to some tale or other. Miss Jenkyns wondered what could be the matter for some time before she took the undignified step of sending Jenny out to inquire.

Jenny came back with a white face of terror. "Oh, Ma'am! oh, Miss Jenkyns, Ma'am! Captain Brown is killed by them nasty cruel railroads!" and she burst into tears. She, along with many others, had experienced the poor Captain's kindness.

"How?—where—where? Good God! Jenny, don't waste time in crying, but tell us something." Miss Matey rushed out into the street at once, and collared the man who was telling the tale.

"Come in—come to my sister at once,—Miss Jenkyns, the rector's daughter. Oh, man, man! say it is not true,"—she cried, as she brought the affrighted carter,[2] sleeking down his hair, into the drawing-room, where he stood with his wet boots on the new carpet, and no one regarded it.

"Please, mum, it is true. I seed it myself," and he shuddered at the recollection. "The Captain was a-reading some new book as he was deep in, a-waiting for the down train;[3] and there was a little lass as wanted to come to its mammy, and gave its sister the slip, and came toddling across the line. And he looked up sudden at the sound of the train coming, and seed the child, and he darted on the line and cotched it up, and his foot slipped, and the train came over him in no time. Oh Lord, Lord! Mum, it's quite true—and they've come over to tell his daughters. The child's safe, though, with

---

[1] *three-piled* Sophisticated, polished, elegant.

[2] *carter* Cart driver.

[3] *down train* Train headed away from a main terminus (such as London or Manchester); the train headed in the opposite direction may similarly be referred to as the up train.

only a bang on its shoulder, as he threw it to its mammy. Poor Captain would be glad of that, mum, would not he, God bless him!" The great rough carter puckered up his manly face, and turned away to hide his tears. I turned to Miss Jenkyns. She looked very ill, as if she were going to faint, and signed to me to open the window.

"Matilda, bring me my bonnet. I must go to those girls. God pardon me if ever I have spoken contemptuously to the Captain!"

Miss Jenkyns arrayed herself to go out, telling Miss Matilda to give the man a glass of wine. While she was away, Miss Matey and I huddled over the fire, talking in a low and awestruck voice. I know we cried quietly all the time.

Miss Jenkyns came home in a silent mood, and we durst not ask her many questions. She told us that Miss Jessie had fainted, and that she and Miss Pole had had some difficulty to bring her round; but that, as soon as she recovered, she begged one of them to go and sit with her sister.

"Dr. Colburn says she cannot live many days, and she shall be spared this shock," said Miss Jessie, shivering with feelings to which she dared not give way.

"But how can you manage, my dear?" asked Miss Jenkyns; "you cannot bear up—she must see your tears."

"God will help me—I will not give way—she was asleep when the news came; she may be asleep yet. She would be so utterly miserable, not merely at my father's death, but to think of what would become of me; she is so good to me." She looked up earnestly in their faces with her soft true eyes, and Miss Pole told Miss Jenkyns afterwards she could hardly bear it, knowing, as she did, how Miss Brown treated her sister.

However, it was settled according to Miss Jessie's wish. Miss Brown was to be told her father had been summoned to take a short journey on railway business. They had managed it in some way—Miss Jenkyns could not exactly say how. Miss Pole was to stop with Miss Jessie. Mrs. Jamieson had sent to inquire: And this was all we heard that night; and a sorrowful night it was. The next day a full account of the fatal accident was in the country paper, which Miss Jenkyns took in. Her

eyes were very weak, she said, and she asked me to read it. When I came to "the gallant gentleman was deeply engaged in the perusal of Hood's Poems,[1] which he had just received," Miss Jenkyns shook her head long and solemnly, and then sighed out, "Poor, dear, infatuated man!"

The corpse was to be taken from the station to the parish church, there to be interred. Miss Jessie had set her heart on following it to the grave; and no dissuasives could alter her resolve. Her restraint upon herself made her almost obstinate; she resisted all Miss Pole's entreaties, and Miss Jenkyns's advice. At last Miss Jenkyns gave up the point; and after a silence, which I feared portended some deep displeasure against Miss Jessie, Miss Jenkyns said she should accompany the latter to the funeral.

"It is not fit for you to go alone. It would be against both propriety and humanity were I to allow it."

Miss Jessie seemed as if she did not half like this arrangement; but her obstinacy, if she had any, had been exhausted in her determination to go to the interment. She longed, poor thing! I have no doubt, to cry alone over the grave of the dear father, to whom she had been all in all; and to give way, for one little half-hour, uninterrupted by sympathy, and unobserved by friendship. But it was not to be. That afternoon Miss Jenkyns sent out for a yard of black crape,[2] and employed herself busily in trimming the little black silk bonnet I have spoken about. When it was finished she put it on, and looked at us for approbation—admiration she despised. I was full of sorrow, but, by one of those whimsical thoughts which come unbidden into our heads, in times of deepest grief, I no sooner saw the bonnet than I was reminded of a helmet; and in that hybrid bonnet, half-helmet, half-jockey cap, did Miss Jenkyns attend Captain Brown's funeral; and I believe supported Miss Jessie with a tender indulgent firmness which was invaluable, allowing her to weep her passionate fill before they left.

---

[1] *Hood's Poems*   One of Dickens's alterations; Gaskell's original reads "a number of Pickwick."

[2] *black crape*   Fabric traditionally used for clothing worn during periods of mourning.

Miss Pole, Miss Matey, and I, meanwhile, attended to Miss Brown: and hard work we found it to relieve her querulous and never-ending complaints. But if we were so weary and dispirited, what must Miss Jessie have been! Yet she came back almost calm, as if she had gained a new strength. She put off her mourning dress, and came in, looking pale and gentle; thanking us each with a soft long pressure of the hand. She could even smile—a faint, sweet, wintry smile, as if to reassure us of her power to endure; but her look made our eyes fill suddenly with tears, more than if she had cried outright.

It was settled that Miss Pole was to remain with her all the watching live-long night; and that Miss Matey and I were to return in the morning to relieve them, and give Miss Jessie the opportunity for a few hours of sleep. But when the morning came, Miss Jenkyns appeared at the breakfast table, equipped in her helmet bonnet, and ordered Miss Matey to stay at home, as she meant to go and help to nurse. She was evidently in state of great friendly excitement, which she showed by eating her breakfast standing, and scolding the household all round.

No nursing—no energetic strong-minded woman could help Miss Brown now. There was that in the room as we entered, which was stronger than us all, and made us shrink into solemn awestruck helplessness. Miss Brown was dying. We hardly knew her voice, it was so devoid of the complaining tone we had always associated with it. Miss Jessie told me afterwards that it, and her face too, were just what they had been formerly, when her mother's death left her the young anxious head of the family, of whom only Miss Jessie survived.

She was conscious of her sister's presence, though not, I think, of ours. We stood a little behind the curtain; Miss Jessie knelt with her face near her sister's, in order to catch the last soft awful whispers.

"Oh, Jessie! Jessie! How selfish I have been! God forgive me for letting you sacrifice yourself for me as you did. I have so loved you—and yet I have thought only of myself. God forgive me!"

"Hush, love! hush!" said Miss Jessie, sobbing.

"And my father! my dear, dear father! I will not complain now, if God will give me strength to be patient. But, oh, Jessie! tell my father how I longed and yearned to see him at last, and to ask his forgiveness. He can never know now how I loved him—oh! if I might but tell him, before I die, what a life of sorrow his has been, and I have done so little to cheer him!"

A light came into Miss Jessie's face. "Would it comfort you, dearest, to think that he does know—would it comfort you, love, to know that his cares, his sorrows—" Her voice quivered, but she steadied it into calmness,—"Mary! he has gone before you to the place where the weary are at rest. He knows now how you loved him."

A strange look, which was not distress, came over Miss Brown's face. She did not speak for some time, but then we saw her lips form the words, rather than heard the sound—"Father, mother, Harry, Archy!"—then, as if it was a new idea throwing a filmy shadow over her darkening mind—"But you will be alone—Jessie!"

Miss Jessie had been feeling this all during the silence, I think; for the tears rolled down her cheeks like rain at these words; and she could not answer at first. Then she put her hands together tight, and lifted them up, and said—but not to us—

"Though He slay me, yet will I trust in Him."[1]

In a few moments more, Miss Brown lay calm and still; never to sorrow or murmur more.

After this second funeral, Miss Jenkyns insisted that Miss Jessie should come to stay with her, rather than go back to the desolate house; which, in fact, we learned from Miss Jessie, must now be given up, as she had not wherewithal to maintain it. She had something about twenty pounds per annum, besides the interest of the money for which the furniture would sell; but she could not live upon that; and so we talked over her qualifications for earning money.

"I can sew neatly," said she, "and I like nursing. I think, too, I could manage a house, if anyone would try me as housekeeper; or I would go into a shop, as saleswoman, if they would have patience with me at first."

Miss Jenkyns declared, in an angry voice, that she should do no such thing; and talked to herself about "some people having no idea of their rank as a Captain's daughter," nearly an hour afterwards, when she brought

---

[1] *Though He ... trust in Him* Cf. Job 13.15.

Miss Jessie up a basin of delicately-made arrow-root,[1] and stood over her like a dragoon[1] until the last spoonful was finished: then she disappeared. Miss Jessie began to tell me some more of the plans which had suggested themselves to her, and insensibly fell into talking of the days that were past and gone, and interested me so much, I neither knew nor heeded how time passed. We were both startled when Miss Jenkyns reappeared, and caught us crying. I was afraid lest she would be displeased, as she often said that crying hindered digestion, and I knew she wanted Miss Jessie to get strong; but, instead, she looked queer and excited, and fidgeted round us without saying anything. At last she spoke. "I have been so much startled—no, I've not been at all startled—don't mind me, my dear Miss Jessie—I've been very much surprised—in fact, I've had a caller, whom you knew once, my dear Miss Jessie—"

Miss Jessie went very white, then flushed scarlet, and looked eagerly at Miss Jenkyns—

"A gentleman, my dear, who wants to know if you would see him."

"Is it?—it is not—" stammered out Miss Jessie—and got no farther.

"This is his card," said Miss Jenkyns, giving it to Miss Jessie; and while her head was bent over it, Miss Jenkyns went through a series of winks and odd faces to me, and formed her lips into a long sentence, of which, of course, I could not understand a word.

"May he come up?" asked Miss Jenkyns, at last.

"Oh, yes! certainly!" said Miss Jessie, as much as to say, this is your house, you may show any visitor where you like. She took up some knitting of Miss Matey's, and began to be very busy, though I could see how she trembled all over.

Miss Jenkyns rang the bell, and told the servant who answered it to show Major Campbell upstairs; and, presently, in walked a tall, fine, frank-looking man of forty, or upwards. He shook hands with Miss Jessie; but he could not see her eyes, she kept them so fixed on the ground. Miss Jenkyns asked me if I would come and help her to tie up the preserves in the store-room; and, though Miss Jessie plucked at my gown and even looked up at me with begging eye, I durst not refuse to go where Miss Jenkyns asked. Instead of tying up preserves in the store-room, however, we went to talk in the dinning-room; and there Miss Jenkyns told me what Major Campbell had told her—how he had served in the same regiment with Captain Brown, and had become acquainted with Miss Jessie, then a sweet-looking, blooming girl of eighteen; how the acquaintance had grown into love, on his part, though it had been some years before he had spoken; how, on becoming possessed, through the will of an uncle, of a good estate in Scotland, he had offered, and been refused, though with so much agitation, and evident distress, that he was sure she was not indifferent to him; and how he had discovered that the obstacle was the fell[2] disease which was, even then, too surely threatening her sister. She had mentioned that the surgeons foretold intense suffering; and there was no one but herself to nurse her poor Mary, or cheer and comfort her father during the time of illness. They had had long discussions; and, on her refusal to pledge herself to him as his wife, when all should be over, he had grown angry, and broken off entirely, and gone abroad, believing that she was a cold-hearted person, whom he would do well to forget. He had been travelling in the East, and was on his return home when, at Rome, he saw the account of Captain Brown's death in "Galignani."[3]

Just then Miss Matey, who had been out all the morning, and had only lately returned to the house, burst in with a face of dismay and outraged propriety—

"Oh, goodness me!" she said. "Caroline, there's a gentleman sitting in the drawing-room, with his arm round Miss Jessie's waist!" Miss Matey's eyes looked large with terror.

Miss Jenkyns snubbed her down in an instant:

---

[1] *arrow-root* Food prepared from the starchy tuberous plant *Maranta*, indigenous to the West Indies; *dragoon* Cavalry soldier, particularly one armed with a musket (which, because it "breathes fire," is sometimes called a "dragoon").

[2] *fell* Cruel, deadly.

[3] *Galignani Galignani's Messenger* was a daily English-language newspaper published in Paris by Giovanni Antonio Galignani (1757–1821), an Italian-born newspaper publisher.

"The most proper place in the world for his arm to be in. Go away, Matilda, and mind your own business." This from her sister, who had hitherto been a model of feminine decorum, was a blow for poor Miss Matey, and with a double shock she left the room.

The last time I ever saw poor Miss Jenkyns was many years after this. Mrs. Campbell had kept up a warm and affectionate intercourse[1] with all at Cranford. Miss Jenkyns, Miss Matey, and Miss Pole had all been to visit her, and returned with wonderful accounts of her house, her husband, her dress, and her looks. For, with happiness, something of her early bloom returned; she had been a year or two younger than we had taken her for. Her eyes were always lovely and, as Mrs. Campbell, her dimples were not out of place. At the time to which I have referred, when I last saw Miss Jenkyns, that lady was old and feeble, and had lost something of her strong mind. Little Flora Campbell was staying with the Misses Jenkyns, and when I came in she was reading aloud to Miss Jenkyns, who lay feeble and changed on the sofa. Flora put down the Rambler when I came in. "Ah!" said Miss Jenkyns, "you find me changed, my dear. I can't see as I used to do. If Flora were not here to read to me, I hardly know how I should get through the day. Did you ever read the Rambler? It's a wonderful book—wonderful! and the most improving reading for Flora"—(which I dare say it would have been if she could have read half the words without spelling, and could have understood the meaning of a third)—"better than that strange old book, with the queer name, poor Captain Brown was killed for reading—that book by Mr. Hood, you know—Hood—Admiral Hood; when I was a girl; but that's a long time ago—I wore a cloak with a red Hood"—she babbled on long enough for Flora to get a good long spell at "Miss Kilmansegg and her Golden Leg,"[2] which Miss Matey had left on the table.

Poor, dear Miss Jenkyns! Cranford is Man-less now.[3]
—1851

---

[1] *intercourse* Communication.

[2] *Miss Kilmansegg and her Golden Leg* Poem by the popular eighteenth-century writer Thomas Hood. The decision to include this reference was made by Charles Dickens in his capacity as the editor of *Household Words*; Gaskell's original had Flora turn her attention to Dickens's own *Christmas Carol* (1843). (See the "In Context" material below.)

[3] *Poor, dear … Man-less now* This sentence does not appear in *Cranford*. (See the "In Context" materials below.)

IN CONTEXT

Charles Dickens and the Publication History of "Our Society at Cranford"

Dickens's editorial interventions in the publication of Gaskell's "Our Society at Cranford" were the subject of some dispute between the two. Dickens evidently felt uncomfortable at the reference to his own works *The Pickwick Papers* and *A Christmas Carol* in the text of Gaskell's story; without consulting her, he edited the piece so as to remove the references. Precisely what other changes may have been in dispute is not clear—Gaskell's letters to Dickens concerning the matter have not survived—but the *Household Words* story includes a final sentence that Gaskell did not include in *Cranford*, in which the second chapter concludes as follows:

"Ah!" said Miss Jenkyns, "you find me changed, my dear. I can't see as I used to do. If Flora were not here to read to me, I hardly know how I should get through the day. Did you ever read the Rambler? It's a wonderful book—wonderful! and the most improving reading for Flora" (which I daresay it would have been, if she could have read half the words without spelling, and could have understood the meaning of a third), "better than that strange old book, with the queer name, poor Captain Brown was killed for reading—that book by Mr Boz, you know—'Old Poz'; when I was a girl—but that's a long time ago—I acted Lucy in 'Old Poz.'" She babbled on long enough for Flora to get a good long spell at the Christmas Carol, which Miss Matty had left on the table.

In Gaskell's text Miss Jenkyns confusedly runs together the name under which much of Dickens's early work appeared—"Boz"—with the name of Maria Edgeworth's 1795 children's play "Old Poz," in which one of the characters is named Lucy. Dickens made a stab at conveying the same sort of confusion as that which Miss Jenkyns makes between a work written for adults and one written for children with his reference to a poem by Thomas Hood and to Little Red Riding Hood, but—not surprisingly—Gaskell was displeased at such changes having been made without her consent. Though Dickens did manage to placate her (and to persuade her to publish in *Household Words* the subsequent pieces that together became *Cranford*), their relationship thereafter was far from entirely smooth.

Included below is Dickens's January 1850 letter inviting Gaskell to contribute to the magazine, together with two letters to her from December 1851.

LETTER FROM CHARLES DICKENS TO ELIZABETH GASKELL

31 January 1850
Devonshire Terrace

My Dear Mrs. Gaskell,

You may perhaps have seen an announcement in the papers of my intention to start a new cheap weekly journal of general literature.

I do not know what your literary vows of temperance or abstinence may be, but as I do honestly know that there is no living English writer whose aid I would desire to enlist in preference to the authoress of "Mary Barton" (a book that most profoundly affected and impressed me), I venture to ask you whether you can give me any hope that you will write a short tale, or any number of tales, for the projected pages.

No writer's name will be used, neither my own nor any other; every paper will be published without any signature, and all will seem to express the general mind and purpose of the journal, which is the raising up of those that are down, and the general improvement of our social condition. I should set a value on your help which your modesty can hardly imagine; and I am perfectly sure that the least result of your reflection or observation in respect of the life around you, would attract attention and do good.

Of course I regard your time as valuable, and consider it so when I ask you if you could devote any of it to this purpose.

If you could and would prefer to speak to me on the subject, I should be very glad indeed to come to Manchester for a few hours and explain anything you might wish to know. My unaffected[1] and great admiration of your book makes me very earnest in all relating to you. Forgive my troubling you for this reason, and believe me ever,

Faithfully yours.

P.S.—Mrs. Dickens and her sister send their love.

LETTER FROM CHARLES DICKENS TO ELIZABETH GASKELL

Thursday Afternoon, 5 December 1851
Tavistock House

My Dear Mrs. Gaskell,

I write in great haste to tell you that Mr. Wills, in the utmost consternation, has brought me your letter, just received (four o'clock), and that it is <u>too late</u> to recall your tale. I was so delighted with it that I put it first in the number (not hearing of any objection to my proposed alteration by return of post), and the number is now made up and in the printer's hands. I cannot possibly take the tale out—it has departed from me.

I am truly concerned for this, but I hope you will not blame me for what I have done in perfect good faith. Any recollection of me from your pen cannot (as I think you know) be otherwise than truly gratifying to me; but with my name on every page of "Household Words," there would be—or at least I should feel—an impropriety in so mentioning myself. I was particular, in changing the

---

[1] *unaffected* Genuine.

author, to make it "Hood's Poems" in the most important place—I mean where the captain is killed—and I hope and trust that the substitution will not be any serious drawback to the paper in any eyes but yours. I would do anything rather than cause you a minute's vexation arising out of what has given me so much pleasure, and I sincerely beseech you to think better of it, and not to fancy that any shade has been thrown on your charming writing, by

The unfortunate but innocent.

P.S.—I write at a gallop, not to lose another post.

Letter from Charles Dickens to Elizabeth Gaskell

Sunday, 21 December 1851
Tavistock House

My Dear Mrs. Gaskell,

If you were not the most suspicious of women, always looking for soft sawder[1] in the purest metal of praise, I should call your paper delightful, and touched in the tenderest and most delicate manner. Being what you are, I confine myself to the observation that I have called it "A Love Affair at Cranford,"[2] and sent it off to the printer.

Faithfully yours ever.

---

[1] *soft sawder*   Flattery, insincere or disingenuous praise.

[2] *A Love Affair at Cranford*   Title given to the second installment in the series of stories that eventually grew into the novel *Cranford*.

ROBERT BROWNING
1812 — 1889

"The spirit of passionate and imaginative poetry is not dead among us," wrote an exultant R.H. Horne in 1844, while reviewing the poems of the young Robert Browning. But Browning, for all his passion and imagination, was not a popular poet for much of his lifetime. Indeed, until the 1860s, Browning was better known as the husband of Elizabeth Barrett. His own poetry, in the eyes of many of his contemporaries, was far too obscure, littered as it was with recondite historical and literary references and with dubious subject matter—husbands murdering their wives, artists frolicking with prostitutes. Fame did come, however, and scholars now credit Browning for having realized new possibilities in the dramatic monologue, a form of poetry that, like a monologue in a dramatic production, showcases the speech of a character to an implied or imaginary audience. The poems are, in Browning's own words, "so many utterances of so many imaginary persons, not mine." As Browning's dramatic monologues unfold, their speakers reveal levels of psychological complexity that have inspired generations of poets, from the Pre-Raphaelites who were coming of age in the 1840s to Modernists such as Ezra Pound and T.S. Eliot.

Browning was the eldest of two children born in an upper middle-class suburb of London to a scholarly father and a devout, Protestant mother, Sarah Anna Wiedemann. An opponent of slavery, Robert Browning, Sr. rejected employment on his family's plantation in St. Kitts in favor of less lucrative but more morally acceptable work as a clerk for the Bank of England. Both parents helped to shape Browning's religious, social, and intellectual tastes and values, with Browning, Sr. in particular feeding his son's voracious appetite for knowledge. The young Browning composed his first poem at the age of six. He attended Peckham School between the ages of ten and twelve and later some classes at University College in London. But the great majority of his schooling took place at home with tutors, and he spent many hours studying the books in his family's voluminous library.

Browning first arrived on the literary scene with the publication in 1833 of *Pauline: A Fragment of a Confession*, a long poem in the style of Shelley's *Alastor* (1816). John Stuart Mill credited *Pauline* with "considerable poetic powers" that yet revealed "a more intense and morbid self-consciousness than I ever knew in any sane human being." The volume, published with family funds, apparently sold not even a single copy. It was followed in 1835 by *Paracelsus*, which, though similarly obscure, at least made Browning known to a few important critics and ultimately brought him into contact with Carlyle, Dickens, and Wordsworth, among others. With *Sordello* (1840), Browning secured his reputation for writing poetry of bewildering difficulty. Browning claimed that his "stress [in *Sordello*] lay on the incidents in the development of a soul: little else is worth study," and yet few could make sense of such incidents as Browning had chosen to portray them.

In 1842 Browning published a volume of shorter poems, *Dramatic Lyrics*, which marked an important break from his earlier productions. Included were many of the poems on which his reputation came to be based: "My Last Duchess," "Soliloquy of the Spanish Cloister," "Johannes Agricola in Meditation," and "Porphyria's Lover," the last two of which had been published in the

Monthly Repository of 1836 under the heading "Madhouse Cells." With *Dramatic Romances and Lyrics* (1845) and *Men and Women* (1855), Browning confirmed his literary reputation as the foremost innovator of the dramatic monologue; he remained, however, little known among contemporary Victorians. *Men and Women* contained now-canonical poems such as "Fra Lippo Lippi" and "Andrea del Sarto." In Browning's volume, wrote George Eliot in the *Westminster Review*, the reader will find "no conventionality, no melodious commonplace, but freshness, originality, sometimes eccentricity of expression; no didactic laying-out of a subject, but dramatic indication, which requires the reader to trace by his own mental activity the underground stream of thought that jets out in elliptical and pithy verse." Eliot's commentary draws attention not only to Browning's unconventional subject matter and dramatic presentation, but also to the range of his accomplishment in poetic form, his lack of "melodious commonplace." Victorian critics noted with varying degrees of wonder and consternation the degree to which Browning experimented with rhythm and meter, an experimentation that in the early twentieth century earned him the nickname "Old Hippety-Hop o' the accents" from Ezra Pound.

In January of 1845 Browning began what became a celebrated correspondence with the already-famous poet Elizabeth Barrett. Even before meeting her personally (an event that took place after four months of writing), Browning praised Barrett's 1844 volume *Poems* with the words, "I do, as I say, love these books with all my heart—and I love you too." Barrett fell in love with Browning after meeting him, and in 1846, despite her chronic illness and her father's command never to marry, the two eloped in London and moved to Italy, where they remained for the rest of her life. Their only child, Robert Wiedemann Barrett Browning (nicknamed "Pen"), was born in 1849 in their Florence home, Casa Guidi.

Browning returned to London and society life after his wife's death in 1861. 1864 brought the publication of *Dramatis Personae*, the first of his volumes to be popular among British readers. This was followed in 1868–69 by his twelve-part epic "murder-poem" (as Browning called it), *The Ring and the Book*. Browning conceived the idea of writing this epic in 1860, when in a Florence market he chanced upon a book of documents concerning a 1698 murder trial. He organized the story so that each book in the epic gives voice to a different participant in the event: the murderer, various onlookers, the victim, and even the Pope. In juxtaposing these varying testimonies, Browning suggests the impossibility of ever finding a coherent or truthful narrative and the importance of recognizing the relativity of points of view—something enacted in his dramatic monologues. These "filthy rags of speech," says the Pope, are "tatters all too contaminate for use."

The 1879–80 volumes of *Dramatic Idyls* brought the poet even greater fame, both in England and internationally; the public in the United States flocked to buy his books, and wearing brown articles of clothing in his honor became fashionable. In 1889, on the day his final volume of poems, *Asolando*, was published, Robert Browning died at his son's home in Venice. He is buried next to Alfred, Lord Tennyson, in the Poets' Corner of Westminster Abbey.

⌘ ⌘ ⌘

Porphyria's Lover

The rain set early in tonight,
    The sullen wind was soon awake,
It tore the elm tops down for spite,
    And did its worst to vex the lake:
5   I listened with heart fit to break.
When glided in Porphyria; straight
    She shut the cold out and the storm,
And kneeled and made the cheerless grate
    Blaze up, and all the cottage warm;
10   Which done, she rose, and from her form
Withdrew the dripping cloak and shawl,
    And laid her soiled gloves by, untied
Her hat and let the damp hair fall,
    And, last, she sat down by my side
15   And called me. When no voice replied,
She put my arm about her waist,
    And made her smooth white shoulder bare,
And all her yellow hair displaced,
    And, stooping, made my cheek lie there,
20   And spread, o'er all, her yellow hair,
Murmuring how she loved me—she
    Too weak, for all her heart's endeavour,
To set its struggling passion free
    From pride, and vainer ties dissever,°   sever
25   And give herself to me forever.
But passion sometimes would prevail,
    Nor could tonight's gay feast restrain
A sudden thought of one so pale
    For love of her, and all in vain:
30   So, she was come through wind and rain.
Be sure I looked up at her eyes
    Happy and proud; at last I knew
Porphyria worshipped me; surprise
    Made my heart swell, and still it grew
35   While I debated what to do.
That moment she was mine, mine, fair,
    Perfectly pure and good: I found
A thing to do, and all her hair
    In one long yellow string I wound
40   Three times her little throat around,
And strangled her. No pain felt she;

I am quite sure she felt no pain.
As a shut bud that holds a bee,
    I warily oped her lids: again
45   Laughed the blue eyes without a stain.
And I untightened next the tress
    About her neck; her cheek once more
Blushed bright beneath my burning kiss:
    I propped her head up as before,
50   Only, this time my shoulder bore
Her head, which droops upon it still:
    The smiling rosy little head,
So glad it has its utmost will,
    That all it scorned at once is fled,
55   And I, its love, am gained instead!
Porphyria's love: she guessed not how
    Her darling one wish would be heard.
And thus we sit together now,
    And all night long we have not stirred,
60   And yet God has not said a word!
—1836

Soliloquy of the Spanish Cloister

1

Gr-r-r—there go, my heart's abhorrence!
    Water your damned flowerpots, do!
If hate killed men, Brother Lawrence,
    God's blood, would not mine kill you!
5   What? your myrtle bush[1] wants trimming?
    Oh, that rose has prior claims—
Needs its leaden vase filled brimming?
    Hell dry you up with its flames!

2

At the meal we sit together:
10   *Salve tibi!*[2] I must hear
Wise talk of the kind of weather,
    Sort of season, time of year:
Not a plenteous cork crop: scarcely

---

[1]   *myrtle bush* Aromatic evergreen shrub with white flowers.
[2]   *Salve tibi* Hail to thee.

Dare we hope oak galls,[1] I doubt:
15 What's the Latin name for "parsley"?
    What's the Greek name for Swine's Snout?[2]

3

Whew! We'll have our platter burnished,
    Laid with care on our own shelf!
With a fire-new spoon we're furnished,
20   And a goblet for ourself,
Rinsed like something sacrificial
    Ere 'tis fit to touch our chaps°—   *jaws*
Marked with L. for our initial!
    (He-he! There his lily snaps!)

4

25 *Saint*, forsooth! While brown Dolores
    Squats outside the Convent bank
With Sanchicha, telling stories,
    Steeping tresses in the tank,
Blue-black, lustrous, thick like horsehairs,
30   —Can't I see his dead eye glow,
Bright as 'twere a Barbary corsair's?[3]
    (That is, if he'd let it show!)

5

When he finishes refection,°   *a meal*
    Knife and fork he never lays
35 Crosswise, to my recollection,
    As do I, in Jesu's praise.
I the Trinity illustrate,
    Drinking watered orange pulp—
In three sips the Arian[4] frustrate;
40   While he drains his at one gulp.

6

Oh, those melons? If he's able
    We're to have a feast! so nice!
One goes to the Abbot's table,
    All of us get each a slice.
45 How go on your flowers? None double?
    Not one fruit-sort can you spy?
Strange!—And I, too, at such trouble,
    Keep them close-nipped on the sly!

7

There's a great text in Galatians,
50   Once you trip on it, entails
Twenty-nine distinct damnations,[5]
    One sure, if another fails:
If I trip him just a-dying,
    Sure of heaven as sure can be,
55 Spin him round and send him flying
    Off to hell, a Manichee?[6]

8

Or, my scrofulous° French novel   *morally corrupt*
    On grey paper with blunt type!
Simply glance at it, you grovel
60   Hand and foot in Belial's° gripe: *the devil's*
If I double down its pages
    At the woeful sixteenth print,
When he gathers his greengages,°   *plums*
    Ope a sieve and slip it in't?

9

65 Or, there's Satan!—one might venture
    Pledge one's soul to him, yet leave
Such a flaw in the indenture[7]
    As he'd miss till, past retrieve,
Blasted lay that rose acacia

---

[1] *oak galls* Growths on oak trees that are used to produce certain inks and tannins.

[2] *Swine's Snout* Dandelion.

[3] *Barbary corsair* Pirate of the Barbary Coast (former name of the Mediterranean coastal region of North Africa).

[4] *Arian* Follower of Arius (256–336), considered a heretic in his day for his disavowal of the notion (inherent in the concept of the Trinity) that Jesus Christ was of the same essence or substance as God.

---

[5] *Galatians ... damnations* See Galatians 5.19–21 for a list of 17, not 29, sins.

[6] *Manichee* Heretic; follower of the Persian theologian Mani's third-century beliefs in dualism.

[7] *indenture* Binding contract of servitude.

70   We're so proud of! *Hy, Zy, Hine*[1] ...
        'St, there's Vespers! *Plena gratiâ*
            Ave, Virgo![2] Gr-r-r—you swine!
        —1842

My Last Duchess[3]

Ferrara

That's my last Duchess painted on the wall,
Looking as if she were alive. I call
That piece a wonder, now: Frà° Pandolf's hands   brother
Worked busily a day, and there she stands.
5   Will't please you sit and look at her? I said
"Frà Pandolf" by design, for never read
Strangers like you that pictured countenance,°   face
The depth and passion of its earnest glance,
But to myself they turned (since none puts by
10 The curtain I have drawn for you, but I)
And seemed as they would ask me, if they durst,
How such a glance came there; so, not the first
Are you to turn and ask thus. Sir, 'twas not
Her husband's presence only, called that spot
15 Of joy into the Duchess' cheek: perhaps
Frà Pandolf chanced to say "Her mantle° laps   cloak
Over my lady's wrist too much," or "Paint
Must never hope to reproduce the faint
Half-flush that dies along her throat": such stuff
20 Was courtesy, she thought, and cause enough
For calling up that spot of joy. She had
A heart—how shall I say?—too soon made glad,
Too easily impressed; she liked whate'er
She looked on, and her looks went everywhere.
25 Sir, 'twas all one! My favour° at her breast,   gift
The dropping of the daylight in the West,
The bough of cherries some officious fool
Broke in the orchard for her, the white mule
She rode with round the terrace—all and each
30 Would draw from her alike the approving speech,
Or blush, at least. She thanked men—good! but
            thanked
Somehow—I know not how—as if she ranked
My gift of a nine-hundred-years-old name
With anybody's gift. Who'd stoop to blame
35 This sort of trifling? Even had you skill
In speech—(which I have not)—to make your will
Quite clear to such an one, and say, "Just this
Or that in you disgusts me; here you miss,
Or there exceed the mark"—and if she let
40 Herself be lessoned so, nor plainly set
Her wits to yours, forsooth,° and made excuse,   truly
—E'en then would be some stooping; and I choose
Never to stoop. Oh sir, she smiled, no doubt,
Whene'er I passed her; but who passed without
45 Much the same smile? This grew; I gave commands;
Then all smiles stopped together. There she stands
As if alive. Will't please you rise? We'll meet
The company below, then. I repeat,
The Count your master's known munificence
50 Is ample warrant that no just pretence
Of mine for dowry will be disallowed;
Though his fair daughter's self, as I avowed
At starting, is my object. Nay, we'll go
Together down, sir. Notice Neptune,[4] though,
55 Taming a seahorse, thought a rarity,
Which Claus of Innsbruck cast in bronze for me!
—1842

---

[1] *Hy, Zy, Hine* The meaning of these words is uncertain; some critics
have suggested that they are the opening words of a spell, or that they
mimic the sound of the bell that rings for Vespers (evening prayers).

[2] *Plena ... Virgo* Version of the Latin prayer "Ave Maria": "Full of
grace / Hail, Virgin."

[3] *My Last Duchess* According to Louis S. Friedland, Browning likely
modeled the speaker of this poem on Alfonso II (1533–98), Duke of
Ferrara. His first wife, a member of the wealthy Medici family, was
only fourteen years old when they married. Only three days after the
wedding, Alfonso left his wife for two years, and she died of suspicious
causes a year after he returned.

---

[4] *Neptune* Roman god of the sea, who rides in a chariot pulled by
seahorses.

Home-Thoughts, from Abroad

1

Oh, to be in England
      Now that April's there,
And whoever wakes in England
Sees, some morning, unaware,
5   That the lowest boughs and the brushwood sheaf
Round the elm-tree bole° are in tiny leaf,   trunk
While the chaffinch[1] sings on the orchard bough
In England—now!

2

And after April, when May follows,
10   And the whitethroat[2] builds, and all the swallows!
Hark, where my blossomed pear tree in the hedge
Leans to the field and scatters on the clover
Blossoms and dewdrops—at the bent spray's[3] edge—
That's the wise thrush; he sings each song twice over,
15   Lest you should think he never could recapture
The first fine careless rapture!
And though the fields look rough with hoary[4] dew
All will be gay when noontide wakes anew
The buttercups, the little children's dower—
20   Far brighter than this gaudy melon flower!
—1845

The Bishop Orders His Tomb at Saint Praxed's Church

Rome, 15—

Vanity, saith the preacher, vanity![5]
      Draw round my bed: is Anselm keeping back?
Nephews—sons mine ... ah God, I know not! Well—
She, men would have to be your mother once,
5   Old Gandolf envied me, so fair she was!
What's done is done, and she is dead beside,
Dead long ago, and I am Bishop since,
And as she died so must we die ourselves,
And thence ye may perceive the world's a dream.
10   Life, how and what is it? As here I lie
In this state chamber, dying by degrees,
Hours and long hours in the dead night, I ask
"Do I live, am I dead?" Peace, peace seems all.
Saint Praxed's ever was the church for peace;
15   And so, about this tomb of mine. I fought
With tooth and nail to save my niche, ye know:
—Old Gandolf cozened° me, despite my care;   cheated
Shrewd was that snatch from out the corner south
He graced his carrion with, God curse the same!
20   Yet still my niche is not so cramped but thence
One sees the pulpit o' the epistle side,[6]
And somewhat of the choir, those silent seats,
And up into the aery dome where live
The angels, and a sunbeam's sure to lurk:
25   And I shall fill my slab of basalt there,
And 'neath my tabernacle take my rest,
With those nine columns round me, two and two,
The odd one at my feet where Anselm stands:
Peach-blossom marble all, the rare, the ripe
30   As fresh-poured red wine of a mighty pulse.
—Old Gandolf with his paltry onion-stone,[7]
Put me where I may look at him! True peach,
Rosy and flawless: how I earned the prize!
Draw close: that conflagration of my church
35   —What then? So much was saved if aught[8] were missed!
My sons, ye would not be my death? Go dig
The white-grape vineyard where the oil-press stood,
Drop water gently till the surface sink,
And if ye find ... Ah God, I know not, I! ...
40   Bedded in store of rotten fig leaves soft,
And corded up in a tight olive-frail,°   basket

---

[1]   *chaffinch*   Small songbird of the finch family.

[2]   *whitethroat*   Small migrating songbird of the warbler family.

[3]   *spray*   Tree branch appealingly covered with blossoms.

[4]   *hoary*   Silvery-gray.

[5]   *Vanity, saith the preacher, vanity*   From Ecclesiastes 1.2: "Vanity of vanities, saith the Preacher, vanity of vanities; all is vanity."

[6]   *epistle side*   Right-hand side, where the pulpit is and from which the epistles are read.

[7]   *onion-stone*   Variety of less expensive marble that is named for its tendency to peel into layers.

[8]   *aught*   Anything.

Some lump, ah God, of *lapis lazuli*,[1]
Big as a Jew's head cut off at the nape,
Blue as a vein o'er the Madonna's[2] breast …
45 Sons, all have I bequeathed you, villas, all,
That brave Frascati[3] villa with its bath,
So, let the blue lump poise between my knees,
Like God the Father's globe on both his hands
Ye worship in the Jesu Church[4] so gay,
50 For Gandolf shall not choose but see and burst!
Swift as a weaver's shuttle fleet our years:[5]
Man goeth to the grave, and where is he?[6]
Did I say basalt for my slab, sons? Black—
'Twas ever antique-black° I meant! How else   *black marble*
55 Shall ye contrast my frieze[7] to come beneath?
The bas-relief in bronze ye promised me,
Those Pans and Nymphs[8] ye wot° of, and   *know*
    perchance
Some tripod, thyrsus,[9] with a vase or so,
The Saviour at his sermon on the mount,[10]
60 Saint Praxed[11] in a glory,° and one Pan[12]   *halo, lightbeam*

Ready to twitch the Nymph's last garment off,
And Moses with the tables[13] … but I know
Ye mark me not! What do they whisper thee,
Child of my bowels, Anselm? Ah, ye hope
65 To revel down my villas while I gasp
Bricked o'er with beggar's mouldy travertine°   *limestone*
Which Gandolf from his tomb top chuckles at!
Nay, boys, ye love me—all of jasper,° then!   *precious stone*
'Tis jasper ye stand pledged to, lest I grieve
70 My bath must needs be left behind, alas!
One block, pure green as a pistachio nut,
There's plenty jasper somewhere in the world—
And have I not Saint Praxed's ear to pray
Horses for ye, and brown Greek manuscripts,
75 And mistresses with great smooth marbly limbs?
—That's if ye carve my epitaph aright,
Choice Latin, picked phrase, Tully's[14] every word,
No gaudy ware like Gandolf's second line—
Tully, my masters? Ulpian[15] serves his need!
80 And then how I shall lie through centuries,
And hear the blessed mutter of the mass,
And see God made and eaten all day long,
And feel the steady candle flame, and taste
Good strong thick stupefying incense smoke!
85 For as I lie here, hours of the dead night,
Dying in state and by such slow degrees,
I fold my arms as if they clasped a crook,°   *bishop's staff*
And stretch my feet forth straight as stone can point,
And let the bedclothes, for a mortcloth,[16] drop
90 Into great laps and folds of sculptor's work:
And as yon tapers[17] dwindle, and strange thoughts
Grow, with a certain humming in my ears,
About the life before I lived this life,
And this life too, popes, cardinals and priests,
95 Saint Praxed at his sermon on the mount,
Your tall pale mother with her talking eyes,

---

[1] *lapis lazuli*   Semi-precious blue stone; the altar-tomb of St. Ignatius at Il Gesù (Church of the Holy Name of Jesus) in Rome is decorated with huge columns made from lapis lazuli.

[2] *Madonna*   Mary, the mother of Jesus.

[3] *Frascati*   Summer resort near Rome.

[4] *Jesu Church*   Il Gesù.

[5] *Swift … years*   From Job 7.6: "My days are swifter than a weaver's shuttle, and are spent without hope"; *shuttle*   Weaver's instrument used to pass the yarn across the loom.

[6] *Man goeth … where is he?*   From Job 7.9: "As the cloud is consumed and vanisheth away: so he that goeth down to the grave shall come up no more."

[7] *frieze*   Painted or sculpted band on a wall or column.

[8] *bas-relief … Pans and Nymphs*   Shallow carvings that depict Greek mythological figures alongside biblical figures.

[9] *tripod*   Vessel on which sat the Oracle at Delphi, where she delivered her prophecies; *thyrsus*   Staff adorned with a pine cone and ivy, carried by Dionysus, the Greek god of wine, and his followers.

[10] *sermon on the mount*   Series of teachings by Jesus Christ, recorded in the Gospel of Matthew. Jesus is often depicted delivering them to a crowd of listeners.

[11] *Saint Praxed*   Roman virgin of the second century who gave away all of her wealth to the poor.

[12] *Pan*   Greek shepherd god of nature, who chased the nymph Syrinx until she turned herself into a bed of reeds.

[13] *tables*   Tablets with the Ten Commandments inscribed upon them.

[14] *Tully*   Commonly known as Cicero, Roman orator, philosopher, and political figure of the first century BCE.

[15] *Ulpian*   Roman jurist (?–228 CE), whose writings were acknowledged to be of a lower standard than Cicero's.

[16] *mortcloth*   Funeral cloth draped over the dead.

[17] *tapers*   Candles.

And newfound agate urns as fresh as day,
And marble's language, Latin pure, discreet,
—Aha, ELUCESCEBAT[1] quoth our friend?
100 No Tully, said I, Ulpian at the best!
Evil and brief hath been my pilgrimage.[2]
All *lapis*, all, sons! Else I give the Pope
My villas! Will ye ever eat my heart?
Ever your eyes were as a lizard's quick,
105 They glitter like your mother's for my soul,
Or ye would heighten my impoverished frieze,
Piece out its starved design, and fill my vase
With grapes, and add a vizor and a Term,[3]
And to the tripod ye would tie a lynx
110 That in his struggle throws the thyrsus down,
To comfort me on my entablature°   column
Whereon I am to lie till I must ask
"Do I live, am I dead?" There, leave me, there!
For ye have stabbed me with ingratitude
115 To death—ye wish it—God, ye wish it! Stone—
Gritstone, a-crumble! Clammy squares which sweat
As if the corpse they keep were oozing through—
And no more lapis to delight the world!
Well go! I bless ye. Fewer tapers there,
120 But in a row: and, going, turn your backs
—Ay, like departing altar ministrants,
And leave me in my church, the church for peace,
That I may watch at leisure if he leers—
Old Gandolf, at me, from his onion-stone,
125 As still he envied me, so fair she was!
—1845

---

[1] *ELUCESCEBAT* Latin: He was illustrious. *Elucescebat* is a later Latin verb form; Cicero would have written *elucebat*.

[2] *Evil … pilgrimage* Cf. Genesis 47.9: "Jacob said unto Pharaoh … few and evil have the days of the years of my life been, and have not attained unto the days of the years of the life of my fathers in the days of their pilgrimage."

[3] *vizor* Helmet piece represented in Roman sculpture; *Term* Statue of Terminus, Roman god of boundaries.

Meeting at Night

1

The grey sea and the long black land;
And the yellow half moon large and low;
And the startled little waves that leap
In fiery ringlets from their sleep,
5 As I gain the cove with pushing prow,
And quench its speed i' the slushy sand.

2

Then a mile of warm sea-scented beach;
Three fields to cross till a farm appears;
A tap at the pane, the quick sharp scratch
10 And blue spurt of a lighted match,
And a voice less loud, thro' its joys and fears,
Than the two hearts beating each to each!
—1845

Parting at Morning

Round the cape of a sudden came the sea,
And the sun looked over the mountain's rim:
And straight was a path of gold for him,
And the need of a world of men for me.
—1845

How It Strikes a Contemporary

I only knew one poet in my life:
And this, or something like it, was his way.

You saw go up and down Valladolid,[4]
A man of mark, to know next time you saw.
5 His very serviceable suit of black
Was courtly once and conscientious still,
And many might have worn it, though none did:
The cloak, that somewhat shone and showed the
    threads,
Had purpose, and the ruff, significance.

---

[4] *Valladolid* City in Spain north of Madrid.

10 He walked and tapped the pavement with his cane,
Scenting the world, looking it full in face,
An old dog, bald and blindish, at his heels.
They turned up, now, the alley by the church,
That leads nowhither; now, they breathed themselves
15 On the main promenade just at the wrong time:
You'd come upon his scrutinizing hat,
Making a peaked shade blacker than itself
Against the single window spared some house
Intact yet with its mouldered Moorish work—
20 Or else surprise the ferrel° of his stick   *metal cap*
Trying the mortar's temper 'tween the chinks
Of some new shop a-building, French and fine.
He stood and watched the cobbler at his trade,
The man who slices lemons into drink,
25 The coffee roaster's brazier, and the boys
That volunteer to help him turn its winch.
He glanced o'er books on stalls with half an eye,
And fly-leaf ballads on the vendor's string,
And broad-edge bold-print posters by the wall.
30 He took such cognizance of men and things,
If any beat a horse, you felt he saw;
If any cursed a woman, he took note;
Yet stared at nobody—you stared at him,
And found, less to your pleasure than surprise,
35 He seemed to know you and expect as much.
So, next time that a neighbour's tongue was loosed,
It marked the shameful and notorious fact,
We had among us, not so much a spy,
As a recording chief inquisitor,
40 The town's true master if the town but knew!
We merely kept a governor for form,[1]
While this man walked about and took account
Of all thought, said and acted, then went home,
And wrote it fully to our Lord the King
45 Who has an itch to know things, he knows why,
And reads them in his bedroom of a night.
Oh, you might smile! there wanted not a touch,
A tang of … well, it was not wholly ease
As back into your mind the man's look came.
50 Stricken in years a little—such a brow
His eyes had to live under!—clear as flint

On either side the formidable nose
Curved, cut and coloured like an eagle's claw.
Had he to do with A.'s surprising fate?
55 When altogether old B. disappeared
And young C. got his mistress—was't our friend,
His letter to the King, that did it all?
What paid the bloodless man for so much pains?
Our Lord the King has favourites manifold,
60 And shifts his ministry some once a month;
Our city gets new governors at whiles—
But never word or sign, that I could hear,
Notified to this man about the streets
The King's approval of those letters conned°   *studied*
65 The last thing duly at the dead of night.
Did the man love his office? Frowned our Lord,
Exhorting when none heard—"Beseech me not!
Too far above my people—beneath me!
I set the watch—how should the people know?
70 Forget them, keep me all the more in mind!"
Was some such understanding 'twixt the two?

     I found no truth in one report at least—
That if you tracked him to his home, down lanes
Beyond the Jewry,[2] and as clean to pace,
75 You found he ate his supper in a room
Blazing with lights, four Titians[3] on the wall,
And twenty naked girls to change his plate!
Poor man, he lived another kind of life
In that new stuccoed third house by the bridge,
80 Fresh-painted, rather smart than otherwise!
The whole street might o'erlook him as he sat,
Leg crossing leg, one foot on the dog's back,
Playing a decent cribbage with his maid
(Jacynth, you're sure her name was) o'er the cheese
85 And fruit, three red halves of starved winter pears,
Or treat of radishes in April. Nine,
Ten, struck the church clock, straight to bed went he.

---

[1] *for form*   For the sake of formality or appearances.

[2] *Jewry*   Area of the city in which Jews were required to live.
[3] *Titians*   Paintings by the Venetian artist Titian (c. 1490–1576).

My father, like the man of sense he was,
Would point him out to me a dozen times;
90 "'St—'St," he'd whisper, "the Corregidor!"°   *magistrate*
I had been used to think that personage
Was one with lacquered breeches, lustrous belt,
And feathers like a forest in his hat,
Who blew a trumpet and proclaimed the news,
95 Announced the bullfights, gave each church its turn,
And memorized the miracle in vogue!
He had a great observance from us boys;
We were in error; that was not the man.

    I'd like now, yet had haply° been afraid,   *perhaps*
100 To have just looked, when this man came to die,
And seen who lined the clean gay garret sides
And stood about the neat low truckle-bed,[1]
With the heavenly manner of relieving guard.[2]
Here had been, mark, the general-in-chief,
105 Thro' a whole campaign of the world's life and death,
Doing the King's work all the dim day long,
In his old coat and up to knees in mud,
Smoked like a herring, dining on a crust—
And, now the day was won, relieved at once!
110 No further show or need for that old coat,
You are sure, for one thing! Bless us, all the while
How sprucely we are dressed out, you and I!
A second, and the angels alter that.
Well, I could never write a verse—could you?
115 Let's to the Prado[3] and make the most of time.
    —1855

---

[1] *truckle-bed*   Trundle bed (one that can be pushed under a bed of regular height).

[2] *relieving guard*   Guards replacing those on duty.

[3] *Prado*   Museum in Madrid.

Memorabilia[4]

1

Ah, did you once see Shelley plain,
    And did he stop and speak to you
And did you speak to him again?
    How strange it seems and new!

2

5 But you were living before that,
    And also you are living after;
And the memory I started at—
    My starting moves your laughter.

3

I crossed a moor, with a name of its own
10   And a certain use in the world no doubt,
Yet a hand's-breath of it shines alone
    'Mid the blank miles round about:

4

For there I picked up on the heather
    And there I put inside my breast
15 A moulted feather, an eagle feather!
    Well, I forget the rest.
—1855

Love Among the Ruins

1

Where the quiet-coloured end of evening smiles,
    Miles and miles
On the solitary pastures where our sheep
    Half-asleep
5 Tinkle homeward thro' the twilight, stray or stop
    As they crop°—   *graze*

---

[4] [Browning's note] I was one day in the bookshop of Hodgson, the well-known London bookseller, when a stranger came in, who, in the course of conversation with the bookseller, spoke of something that Shelley had once said to him. Suddenly, the stranger paused, and burst into laughter as he observed me staring at him with blanched face; and … I still vividly remember how strangely the presence of a man who had seen and spoken with Shelley affected me. [Percy Bysshe Shelley (1792–1822) was an influential Romantic poet.]

Was the site once of a city great and gay,
    (So they say)
Of our country's very capital, its prince
10   Ages since
Held his court in, gathered councils, wielding far
    Peace or war.

2

Now—the country does not even boast a tree,
    As you see,
15 To distinguish slopes of verdure,[1] certain rills°   *brooks*
    From the hills
Intersect and give a name to, (else they run
    Into one)
Where the domed and daring palace shot its spires
20   Up like fires
O'er the hundred-gated circuit of a wall
    Bounding all
Made of marble, men might march on nor be pressed,[2]
    Twelve abreast.

3

25 And such plenty and perfection, see, of grass
    Never was!
Such a carpet as, this summer-time, o'erspreads
    And embeds
Every vestige of the city, guessed alone,
30   Stock° or stone—   *stump*
Where a multitude of men breathed joy and woe
    Long ago;
Lust of glory pricked their hearts up, dread of shame
    Struck them tame;
35 And that glory and that shame alike, the gold
    Bought and sold.

4

Now—the single little turret that remains
    On the plains,

By the caper overrooted, by the gourd[3]
40   Overscored,
While the patching houseleek's[4] head of blossom winks
    Through the chinks—
Marks the basement whence a tower in ancient time
    Sprang sublime,
45 And a burning ring, all round, the chariots traced
    As they raced,
And the monarch and his minions and his dames
    Viewed the games.

5

And I know, while thus the quiet-coloured eve
50   Smiles to leave
To their folding,[5] all our many-tinkling fleece°   *sheep*
    In such peace,
And the slopes and rills in undistinguished grey
    Melt away—
55 That a girl with eager eyes and yellow hair
    Waits me there
In the turret whence the charioteers caught soul
    For the goal,
When the king looked, where she looks now,
    breathless, dumb°   *silent*
60   Till I come.

6

But he looked upon the city, every side,
    Far and wide,
All the mountains topped with temples, all the glades'
    Colonnades,[6]
65 All the causeys,° bridges, aqueducts—and then, *raised roads*
    All the men!

---

[3] *caper* Flowering Mediterranean plant that grows on walls and in other rocky, inhospitable locations; *gourd* Family of climbing or trailing plants that includes pumpkins and squashes.

[4] *houseleek* Hardy flowering succulent suited to dry and rocky climates. Common houseleeks were traditionally planted on roofs, where they were thought to exert protective properties against lightning, decay, and evil magic.

[5] *their folding* I.e., their return to the sheepfold.

[6] *Colonnades* Rows of columns, especially as part of a covered structure.

---

[1] *verdure* Vegetation.

[2] *nor be pressed* Without being pressed close together.

When I do come, she will speak not, she will stand,
    Either hand
On my shoulder, give her eyes the first embrace
70   Of my face,
Ere we rush, ere we extinguish sight and speech
    Each on each.

7

In one year they sent a million fighters forth
    South and North,
75 And they built their gods a brazen pillar[1] high
    As the sky
Yet reserved a thousand chariots in full force—
    Gold, of course.
O heart! oh blood that freezes, blood that burns!
80   Earth's returns
For whole centuries of folly, noise and sin!
    Shut them in,
With their triumphs and their glories and the rest!
    Love is best.
    —1855, REVISED 1863

"Childe Roland to the Dark Tower Came"
(*See Edgar's song in* Lear[2])

1

My first thought was, he lied in every word,
    That hoary° cripple, with malicious eye   *wizened*
    Askance to watch the working of his lie
On mine, and mouth scarce able to afford°   *provide*

---

1 *brazen pillar* Brass pillar. See 1 Kings 7.15, in which Solomon, who is overseeing the construction of a magnificent temple, has "two pillars of brass" cast for the building. Browning's line may also reference the Tower of Babel: in Genesis 11.1–9, the people of the earth share one language, and they attempt to build a tower to reach to heaven. When God sees the tower, he scatters the people and diversifies their languages so that they cannot work together to accomplish such ambitious projects.

2 *Edgar … Lear* From Shakespeare's *King Lear* 3.4.130–32, in which the character Edgar, disguised as the beggar Poor Tom, sings about the French hero Rowland, nephew of Charlemagne: "Child Rowland to the dark tower came, / His word was still, Fie, foh, and fum, / I smell the blood of a British man." "Childe" refers to a youth born of noble stock, who would usually become a candidate for knighthood.

5 Suppression of the glee, that pursed and scored
    Its edge, at one more victim gained thereby.

2

What else should he be set for, with his staff?
    What, save to waylay with his lies, ensnare
    All travellers who might find him posted there,
10 And ask the road? I guessed what skull-like laugh
Would break, what crutch 'gin° write my epitaph   *begin*
    For pastime in the dusty thoroughfare,

3

If at his counsel I should turn aside
    Into that ominous tract which, all agree,
15   Hides the Dark Tower. Yet acquiescingly
I did turn as he pointed: neither pride
Nor hope rekindling at the end descried,°   *glimpsed*
    So much as gladness that some end might be.

4

For, what with my whole world-wide wandering,
20   What with my search drawn out thro' years, my
        hope
    Dwindled into a ghost not fit to cope
With that obstreperous joy success would bring—
I hardly tried now to rebuke the spring
    My heart made, finding failure in its scope.

5

25 As when a sick man very near to death
    Seems dead indeed, and feels begin and end
    The tears and takes the farewell of each friend,
And hears one bid the other go, draw breath
Freelier outside ("since all is o'er," he saith,
30   "And the blow fallen no grieving can amend");

6

While some discuss if near the other graves
    Be room enough for this, and when a day
    Suits best for carrying the corpse away,
With care about the banners, scarves and staves:
35 And still the man hears all, and only craves
    He may not shame such tender love and stay.

7

Thus, I had so long suffered in this quest,
    Heard failure prophesied so oft, been writ
    So many times among "The Band"—to wit,
40 The knights who to the Dark Tower's search addressed
Their steps—that just to fail as they, seemed best,
    And all the doubt was now—should I be fit?

8

So, quiet as despair, I turned from him,
    That hateful cripple, out of his highway
45   Into the path he pointed. All the day
Had been a dreary one at best, and dim
Was settling to its close, yet shot one grim
    Red leer to see the plain catch its estray.°   *stray animal*

9

For mark! no sooner was I fairly found
50   Pledged to the plain, after a pace or two,
    Than, pausing to throw backward a last view
O'er the safe road, 'twas gone; grey plain all round:
Nothing but plain to the horizon's bound.
    I might go on; nought else remained to do.

10

55 So, on I went. I think I never saw
    Such starved ignoble nature; nothing throve:
    For flowers—as well expect a cedar grove!
But cockle, spurge,[1] according to their law
Might propagate their kind, with none to awe,
60   You'd think; a burr had been a treasure trove.

11

No! penury, inertness and grimace,
    In some strange sort, were the land's portion. "See
    Or shut your eyes," said Nature peevishly,
"It nothing skills:[2] I cannot help my case:
65 'Tis the Last Judgment's fire must cure this place,
    Calcine° its clods and set   *burn completely*
        my prisoners free."

---

[1] *cockle, spurge* Types of weeds.

[2] *It nothing skills* It doesn't matter.

12

If there pushed any ragged thistle-stalk
    Above its mates, the head was chopped; the
        bents°   *reed-like grasses*
    Were jealous else. What made those holes and rents
70 In the dock's° harsh swarth° leaves,   *weed's / dark*
        bruised as to baulk
All hope of greenness? 'tis a brute must walk
    Pashing° their life out, with a brute's intents.   *smashing*

13

As for the grass, it grew as scant as hair
    In leprosy; thin dry blades pricked the mud
75   Which underneath looked kneaded up with blood.
One stiff blind horse, his every bone a-stare,
Stood stupefied, however he came there:
    Thrust out past service from the devil's stud!

14

Alive? he might be dead for aught° I know,   *all*
80   With that red gaunt and colloped[3] neck a-strain,
    And shut eyes underneath the rusty mane;
Seldom went such grotesqueness with such woe;
I never saw a brute I hated so;
    He must be wicked to deserve such pain.

15

85 I shut my eyes and turned them on my heart.
    As a man calls for wine before he fights,
    I asked one draught of earlier, happier sights,
Ere fitly I could hope to play my part.
Think first, fight afterwards—the soldier's art:
90   One taste of the old time sets all to rights.

16

Not it! I fancied Cuthbert's reddening face
    Beneath its garniture of curly gold,
    Dear fellow, till I almost felt him fold
An arm in mine to fix me to the place,
95 That way he used. Alas, one night's disgrace!
    Out went my heart's new fire and left it cold.

---

[3] *colloped* Having folds of fat.

17

Giles then, the soul of honour—there he stands
    Frank as ten years ago when knighted first.
    What honest man should dare (he said) he durst.
00 Good—but the scene shifts—faugh! what hangman
        hands
Pin to his breast a parchment? His own bands
    Read it. Poor traitor, spit upon and curst!

18

Better this present than a past like that;
    Back therefore to my darkening path again!
    No sound, no sight as far as eye could strain.
05 Will the night send a howlet° or a bat?   *owl*
I asked: when something on the dismal flat
    Came to arrest my thoughts and change their train.

19

A sudden little river crossed my path
110   As unexpected as a serpent comes.
    No sluggish tide congenial to the glooms;
This, as it frothed by, might have been a bath
For the fiend's glowing hoof—to see the wrath
    Of its black eddy bespate° with flakes and   *flooded*
        spumes.°   *foam*

20

115 So petty yet so spiteful! All along,
    Low scrubby alders kneeled down over it;
    Drenched willows flung them headlong in a fit
Of mute despair, a suicidal throng:
The river which had done them all the wrong,
120   Whate'er that was, rolled by, deterred no whit.

21

Which, while I forded—good saints, how I feared
    To set my foot upon a dead man's cheek,
    Each step, or feel the spear I thrust to seek
For hollows, tangled in his hair or beard!
125 —It may have been a water-rat I speared,
    But, ugh! it sounded like a baby's shriek.

22

Glad was I when I reached the other bank.
    Now for a better country. Vain presage!°   *omen*
    Who were the strugglers, what war did they wage,
130 Whose savage trample thus could pad the dank
Soil to a plash?° Toads in a poisoned tank,   *pool*
    Or wild cats in a red-hot iron cage—

23

The fight must so have seemed in that fell cirque.[1]
    What penned them there, with all the plain to
        choose?
135   No footprint leading to that horrid mews,
None out of it. Mad brewage set to work
Their brains, no doubt, like galley slaves the Turk
    Pits for his pastime, Christians against Jews.

24

And more than that—a furlong[2] on—why, there!
140   What bad use was that engine for, that wheel,
    Or brake, not wheel—that harrow[3] fit to reel
Men's bodies out like silk? with all the air
Of Tophet's° tool, on earth left unaware,   *hell's*
    Or brought to sharpen its rusty teeth of steel.

25

145 Then came a bit of stubbed ground, once a wood,
    Next a marsh, it would seem, and now mere earth
    Desperate and done with; (so a fool finds mirth,
Makes a thing and then mars it, till his mood
Changes and off he goes!) within a rood°—   *quarter acre*
150   Bog, clay and rubble, sand and stark black dearth.

26

Now blotches rankling, coloured gay and grim,
    Now patches where some leanness of the soil's
    Broke into moss or substances like boils;
Then came some palsied[4] oak, a cleft in him

---

[1] *fell cirque* Dreadful arena.

[2] *furlong* 220 yards.

[3] *harrow* Iron-toothed implement dragged over ploughed fields to break up clods of earth.

[4] *palsied* Here, weathered and bent with age.

155 Like a distorted mouth that splits its rim
    Gaping at death, and dies while it recoils.

27

And just as far as ever from the end!
    Nought in the distance but the evening, nought
    To point my footstep further! At the thought,
160 A great black bird, Apollyon's[1] bosom-friend,
Sailed past, nor beat his wide wing dragon-
      penned°   *winged*
    That brushed my cap—perchance the guide I sought.

28

For, looking up, aware I somehow grew,
    'Spite of the dusk, the plain had given place
165   All round to mountains—with such name to grace
Mere ugly heights and heaps now stolen in view.
How thus they had surprised me,—solve it, you!
    How to get from them was no clearer case.

29

Yet half I seemed to recognize some trick
170   Of mischief happened to me, God knows when—
    In a bad dream perhaps. Here ended, then,
Progress this way. When, in the very nick
Of giving up, one time more, came a click
    As when a trap shuts—you're inside the den!

30

175 Burningly it came on me all at once,
    This was the place! those two hills on the right,
    Crouched like two bulls locked horn in horn in
      fight;
While to the left, a tall scalped mountain … Dunce,
Dotard, a-dozing at the very nonce,°   *moment*
180   After a life spent training for the sight!

31

What in the midst lay but the Tower itself?
    The round squat turret, blind as the fool's heart,
    Built of brown stone, without a counterpart
In the whole world. The tempest's mocking elf

185 Points to the shipman° thus the unseen shelf   *sailor*
    He strikes on, only when the timbers start.

32

Not see? because of night perhaps?—why, day
    Came back again for that! before it left,
    The dying sunset kindled through a cleft:
190 The hills, like giants at a hunting, lay,
Chin upon hand, to see the game at bay,—
    "Now stab and end the creature—to the
      heft!"°   *sword handle*

33

Not hear? when noise was everywhere! it tolled
    Increasing like a bell. Names in my ears
195   Of all the lost adventurers my peers—
How such a one was strong, and such was bold,
And such was fortunate, yet each of old
    Lost, lost! one moment knelled the woe of years.

34

There they stood, ranged along the hillsides, met
200   To view the last of me, a living frame
    For one more picture! in a sheet of flame
I saw them and I knew them all. And yet
Dauntless the slug-horn° to my lips I set,   *trumpet*
    And blew. *"Childe Roland to the Dark Tower came."*
—1855

Fra Lippo Lippi[2]

I am poor brother Lippo, by your leave![3]
  You need not clap your torches to my face.
Zooks,[4] what's to blame? you think you see a monk!
What, 'tis past midnight, and you go the rounds,
5 And here you catch me at an alley's end

[1] *Apollyon* Devil, or winged "angel of the bottomless pit," in Revelations 9.11.

[2] *Fra Lippo Lippi* Browning extracted details of the life of Florentine painter and Carmelite monk Fra (Brother) Filippo Lippi (1406–69) from Giorgio Vasari's *The Lives of the Painters* (1550); the art theory Lippi propounds, however, is envisioned by Browning.

[3] *by your leave* Conventional expression of respect or politeness.

[4] *Zooks* Exclamation of surprise.

Where sportive[1] ladies leave their doors ajar?
The Carmine's[2] my cloister: hunt it up,
Do—harry out,[3] if you must show your zeal,
Whatever rat, there, haps° on his wrong hole,   *happens*
10 And nip each softling of a wee white mouse,
Weke, weke, that's crept to keep him company!
Aha, you know your betters! Then, you'll take
Your hand away that's fiddling on my throat,
And please to know me likewise. Who am I?
15 Why, one, sir, who is lodging with a friend
Three streets off—he's a certain … how d'ye call?
Master—a … Cosimo of the Medici,[4]
I' the house that caps the corner. Boh! you were best!
Remember and tell me, the day you're hanged,
20 How you affected such a gullet's-gripe!°   *stranglehold*
But you, sir, it concerns you that your knaves
Pick up a manner nor discredit you:
Zooks, are we pilchards,[5] that they sweep the streets
And count fair prize what comes into their net?
25 He's Judas to a tittle,[6] that man is!
Just such a face! Why, sir, you make amends.
Lord, I'm not angry! Bid your hangdogs[7] go
Drink out this quarter-florin[8] to the health
Of the munificent House that harbours me
30 (And many more beside, lads! more beside!)
And all's come square again. I'd like his face—
His, elbowing on his comrade in the door
With the pike and lantern—for the slave that holds
John Baptist's head a-dangle by the hair[9]
35 With one hand ("Look you, now," as who should say)

And his weapon in the other, yet unwiped!
It's not your chance to have a bit of chalk,
A wood-coal or the like? or you should see!
Yes, I'm the painter, since you style me so.
40 What, brother Lippo's doings, up and down,
You know them and they take you?[10] like enough!
I saw the proper twinkle in your eye—
'Tell you, I liked your looks at very first.
Let's sit and set things straight now, hip to haunch.
45 Here's spring come, and the nights one makes up bands
To roam the town and sing out carnival,[11]
And I've been three weeks shut within my
       mew,°   *confined space*
A-painting for the great man, saints and saints
And saints again. I could not paint all night—
50 Ouf! I leaned out of window for fresh air.
There came a hurry of feet and little feet,
A sweep of lute strings, laughs, and whifts of song—
Flower o' the broom,
Take away love, and our earth is a tomb![12]
55 *Flower o' the quince,*
I let Lisa go, and what good in life since?
Flower o' the thyme—and so on. Round they went.
Scarce had they turned the corner when a titter
Like the skipping of rabbits by moonlight—three slim
       shapes,
60 And a face that looked up … zooks, sir, flesh and blood,
That's all I'm made of! Into shreds it went,
Curtain and counterpane° and coverlet,   *bedspread*
All the bed furniture—a dozen knots,
There was a ladder! Down I let myself,
65 Hands and feet, scrambling somehow, and so dropped,
And after them. I came up with the fun
Hard by Saint Laurence,[13] hail fellow, well met—
Flower o' the rose,
If I've been merry, what matter who knows?
70 And so as I was stealing back again
To get to bed and have a bit of sleep

---

1 *sportive* Here, promiscuous or engaging in prostitution.

2 *Carmine* Lippi was raised an orphan and eventually took his vows in Santa Maria del Carmine, a Carmelite monastery.

3 *harry out* Flush out; chase into the open.

4 *Cosimo of the Medici* The wealthy Medici family, headed up by Lippi's patron, Cosimo dé Medici (1389–1464), ruled Florence for many years.

5 *pilchards* Herring-like fish.

6 *to a tittle* Exactly (a "tittle" is a letter stroke or punctuation mark).

7 *hangdogs* Wretched, low people.

8 *florin* Florentine currency.

9 *the slave that … the hair* John Baptist's martyrdom by beheading has often been depicted in this manner in religious paintings.

---

10 *they take you?* You like them?

11 *carnival* Celebrations before Lent.

12 *Flower … tomb* This song takes the form of a *stornelli*, a three-line Italian folk song about a flower.

13 *Saint Laurence* Church of San Lorenzo in Florence.

Ere I rise up tomorrow and go work
On Jerome[1] knocking at his poor old breast
With his great round stone to subdue the flesh,
75 You snap me of the sudden. Ah, I see!
Though your eye twinkles still, you shake your head—
Mine's shaved—a monk, you say—the sting's in that!
If Master Cosimo announced himself,
Mum's the word naturally; but a monk!
80 Come, what am I a beast for? tell us, now!
I was a baby when my mother died
And father died and left me in the street.
I starved there, God knows how, a year or two
On fig skins, melon parings, rinds and shucks,
85 Refuse and rubbish. One fine frosty day,
My stomach being empty as your hat,
The wind doubled me up and down I went.
Old Aunt Lapaccia trussed me with one hand,
(Its fellow was a stinger as I knew)
90 And so along the wall, over the bridge,
By the straight cut to the convent. Six words there,
While I stood munching my first bread that month:
"So, boy, you're minded," quoth the good fat father
Wiping his own mouth, 'twas refection°-time—   meal
"To quit this very miserable world?
Will you renounce"… "the mouthful of bread?"
    thought I;
By no means! Brief, they made a monk of me;
I did renounce the world, its pride and greed,
Palace, farm, villa, shop and banking-house,
100 Trash, such as these poor devils of Medici
Have given their hearts to—all at eight years old.
Well, sir, I found in time, you may be sure,
'Twas not for nothing—the good bellyful,
The warm serge and the rope that goes all round,[2]
105 And day-long blessed idleness beside!
"Let's see what the urchin's fit for"—that came next.
Not overmuch their way, I must confess.
Such a to-do! They tried me with their books:
Lord, they'd have taught me Latin in pure waste!

110 Flower o' the clove,
    All the Latin I construe is, "amo," I love!
But, mind you, when a boy starves in the streets
Eight years together, as my fortune was,
Watching folk's faces to know who will fling
115 The bit of half-stripped grape bunch he desires,
And who will curse or kick him for his pains—
Which gentleman processional and fine,
Holding a candle to the Sacrament,
Will wink and let him lift a plate and catch
120 The droppings of the wax to sell again,
Or holla for the Eight[3] and have him whipped—
How say I?—nay, which dog bites, which lets drop
His bone from the heap of offal in the street—
Why, soul and sense of him grow sharp alike,
125 He learns the look of things, and none the less
For admonition from the hunger pinch.
I had a store of such remarks, be sure,
Which, after I found leisure, turned to use.
I drew men's faces on my copy books,
130 Scrawled them within the antiphonary's marge,[4]
Joined legs and arms to the long music notes,
Found eyes and nose and chin for A's and B's,
And made a string of pictures of the world
Betwixt the ins and outs of verb and noun,
135 On the wall, the bench, the door. The monks looked
    black.
"Nay," quoth the Prior, "turn him out, d'ye say?
In no wise. Lose a crow and catch a lark.
What if at last we get our man of parts,[5]
We Carmelites, like those Camaldolese
140 And Preaching Friars,[6] to do our church up fine
And put the front on it that ought to be!"
And hereupon he bade me daub away.
Thank you! my head being crammed, the walls a blank,
Never was such prompt disemburdening.
145 First, every sort of monk, the black and white,
I drew them, fat and lean: then, folk at church,

---

1 *Jerome* The ascetic St. Jerome, who lived many years as a hermit in the Syrian desert.

2 *serge* Cotton fabric commonly used to make monks' robes; *rope …
round* I.e., rope belt.

---

3 *Eight* The eight magistrates who governed Florence.

4 *antiphonary's marge* Margin of a book of choral—or antiphonal—music, normally sung in harmony by two choirs.

5 *man of parts* Man of intellect, ability.

6 *Preaching Friars* Dominican monks.

From good old gossips waiting to confess
Their cribs° of barrel droppings, candle ends— *pilferings*
To the breathless fellow at the altar foot,
50 Fresh from his murder, safe[1] and sitting there
With the little children round him in a row
Of admiration, half for his beard and half
For that white anger of his victim's son
Shaking a fist at him with one fierce arm,
55 Signing himself[2] with the other because of Christ
(Whose sad face on the cross sees only this
After the passion of a thousand years)
Till some poor girl, her apron o'er her head,
(Which the intense eyes looked through) came at eve
60 On tiptoe, said a word, dropped in a loaf,
Her pair of earrings and a bunch of flowers
(The brute took growling), prayed, and so was gone.
I painted all, then cried "'Tis ask and have;
Choose, for more's ready!"—laid the ladder flat,
65 And showed my covered bit of cloister wall.
The monks closed in a circle and praised loud
Till checked, taught what to see and not to see,
Being simple bodies—"That's the very man!
Look at the boy who stoops to pat the dog!
70 That woman's like the Prior's niece who comes
To care about his asthma: it's the life!"
But there my triumph's straw-fire flared and
     funked;°   *smoked*
Their betters took their turn to see and say:
The Prior and the learned pulled a face
75 And stopped all that in no time. "How? what's here?
Quite from the mark of painting, bless us all!
Faces, arms, legs and bodies like the true
As much as pea and pea! it's devil's game!
Your business is not to catch men with show,
180 With homage to the perishable clay,[3]
But lift them over it, ignore it all,
Make them forget there's such a thing as flesh.
Your business is to paint the souls of men—
Man's soul, and it's a fire, smoke … no, it's not …

185 It's vapour done up like a newborn babe—
(In that shape when you die it leaves your mouth)
It's … well, what matters talking, it's the soul!
Give us no more of body than shows soul!
Here's Giotto,[4] with his Saint a-praising God,
190 That sets us praising—why not stop with him?
Why put all thoughts of praise out of our head
With wonder at lines, colours, and what not?
Paint the soul, never mind the legs and arms!
Rub all out, try at it a second time.
195 Oh, that white smallish female with the breasts,
She's just my niece … Herodias, I would say—
Who went and danced and got men's heads cut off![5]
Have it all out!" Now, is this sense, I ask?
A fine way to paint soul, by painting body
200 So ill, the eye can't stop there, must go further
And can't fare worse! Thus, yellow does for white
When what you put for yellow's simply black,
And any sort of meaning looks intense
When all beside itself means and looks nought.
205 Why can't a painter lift each foot in turn,
Left foot and right foot, go a double step,
Make his flesh liker and his soul more like,
Both in their order? Take the prettiest face,
The Prior's niece … patron saint—is it so pretty
210 You can't discover if it means hope, fear,
Sorrow or joy? won't beauty go with these?
Suppose I've made her eyes all right and blue,
Can't I take breath and try to add life's flash,
And then add soul and heighten them threefold?
215 Or say there's beauty with no soul at all—
(I never saw it—put the case the same—)
If you get simple beauty and nought else,
You get about the best thing God invents:
That's somewhat: and you'll find the soul you have
     missed,
220 Within yourself, when you return him thanks.

---

[1] *fellow … safe* Safe from prosecution within the church.

[2] *Signing himself* Making the sign of the cross.

[3] *clay* Here, physical body; a reference to Genesis 2.7, where God makes human beings out of earth.

[4] *Giotto* Renowned Florentine artist (1267–1337), whose works consist mainly of religious paintings and frescoes.

[5] *Herodias … heads cut off* According to Matthew 14.6–10, King Herod's niece Salomé (the daughter of his sister Herodias) danced for the king and then requested that he bring her the head of John the Baptist, now the patron saint of Florence.

"Rub all out!" Well, well, there's my life, in short,
And so the thing has gone on ever since.
I'm grown a man no doubt, I've broken bounds:
You should not take a fellow eight years old
225 And make him swear to never kiss the girls.
I'm my own master, paint now as I please—
Having a friend, you see, in the Corner-house!
Lord, it's fast holding by the rings in front—
Those great rings serve more purposes than just
230 To plant a flag in, or tie up a horse!
And yet the old schooling sticks, the old grave eyes
Are peeping o'er my shoulder as I work,
The heads shake still—"It's art's decline, my son!
You're not of the true painters, great and old;
235 Brother Angelico's the man, you'll find;
Brother Lorenzo[1] stands his single peer:
Fag° on at flesh, you'll never make the third!"   drudge
Flower o' the pine,
You keep your mistr ... manners, and I'll stick to mine!
240 I'm not the third, then: bless us, they must know!
Don't you think they're the likeliest to know,
They with their Latin? So, I swallow my rage,
Clench my teeth, suck my lips in tight, and paint
To please them—sometimes do and sometimes don't;
245 For, doing most, there's pretty sure to come
A turn, some warm eve finds me at my saints—
A laugh, a cry, the business of the world—
(*Flower o' the peach,*
Death for us all, and his own life for each!)
250 And my whole soul revolves, the cup runs over,[2]
The world and life's too big to pass for a dream,
And I do these wild things in sheer despite,
And play the fooleries you catch me at,
In pure rage! The old mill-horse, out at grass
255 After hard years, throws up his stiff heels so,
Although the miller does not preach to him
The only good of grass is to make chaff.°   hay
What would men have? Do they like grass or no—
May they or mayn't they? all I want's the thing

260 Settled forever one way. As it is,
You tell too many lies and hurt yourself:
You don't like what you only like too much,
You do like what, if given you at your word,
You find abundantly detestable.
265 For me, I think I speak as I was taught;
I always see the garden and God there
A-making man's wife;[3] and, my lesson learned,
The value and significance of flesh,
I can't unlearn ten minutes afterwards.

270   You understand me: I'm a beast, I know.
But see, now—why, I see as certainly
As that the morning star's about to shine,
What will hap some day. We've a youngster here
Comes to our convent, studies what I do,
275 Slouches and stares and lets no atom drop:
His name is Guidi[4]—he'll not mind the monks—
They call him Hulking Tom, he lets them talk—
He picks my practice up—he'll paint apace,
I hope so—though I never live so long,
280 I know what's sure to follow. You be judge!
You speak no Latin more than I, belike;°   likely
However, you're my man, you've seen the world
—The beauty and the wonder and the power,
The shapes of things, their colours, lights and shades,
285 Changes, surprises—and God made it all!
—For what? Do you feel thankful, ay or no,
For this fair town's face, yonder river's line,
The mountain round it and the sky above,
Much more the figures of man, woman, child,
290 These are the frame to? What's it all about?
To be passed over, despised? or dwelt upon,
Wondered at? oh, this last of course!—you say.
But why not do as well as say—paint these
Just as they are, careless what comes of it?
295 God's works—paint anyone, and count it crime
To let a truth slip. Don't object, "His works

---

1 *Brother Angelico ... Brother Lorenzo* Italian Renaissance artists who painted in the early 1400s in the conventional style, as opposed to Lippi's naturalist style.

2 *the cup runs over* See Psalm 23.5.

3 *I always see ... man's wife* Reference to Genesis 2, in which God creates the first woman to be a companion for the first man.

4 *Guidi* Tommaso Guidi (1401–28), who became known as Masaccio, was highly skilled at creating naturalistic portrayals of human figures; he was likely Lippi's teacher, not his student.

Are here already; nature is complete:
Suppose you reproduce her—(which you can't)
There's no advantage! you must beat her, then."
300 For, don't you mark? we're made so that we love
First when we see them painted, things we have passed
Perhaps a hundred times nor cared to see;
And so they are better, painted—better to us,
Which is the same thing. Art was given for that;
305 God uses us to help each other so,
Lending our minds out. Have you noticed, now,
Your cullion's° hanging face? A bit of chalk,   *scoundrel's*
And trust me but you should, though! How much
    more,
If I drew higher things with the same truth!
310 That were to take the Prior's pulpit place,
Interpret God to all of you! Oh, oh,
It makes me mad to see what men shall do
And we in our graves! This world's no blot for us,
Nor blank; it means intensely, and means good:
315 To find its meaning is my meat and drink.
"Ay, but you don't so instigate to prayer!"
Strikes in the Prior: "when your meaning's plain
It does not say to folk—remember matins,[1]
Or, mind you fast next Friday!" Why, for this
320 What need of art at all? A skull and bones,
Two bits of stick nailed crosswise, or, what's best,
A bell to chime the hour with, does as well.
I painted a Saint Laurence[2] six months since
At Prato,[3] splashed the fresco in fine style:
325 "How looks my painting, now the scaffold's down?"
I ask a brother: "Hugely," he returns—
"Already not one phiz° of your three slaves   *face*
Who turn the Deacon off his toasted side,
But's scratched and prodded to our heart's content,
330 The pious people have so eased their own
With coming to say prayers there in a rage:
We get on fast to see the bricks beneath.
Expect another job this time next year,

For pity and religion grow i' the crowd—
335 Your painting serves its purpose!" Hang the fools!

   —That is—you'll not mistake an idle word
Spoke in a huff by a poor monk, God wot,°   *knows*
Tasting the air this spicy night which turns
The unaccustomed head like Chianti wine!
340 Oh, the church knows! don't misreport me, now!
It's natural a poor monk out of bounds
Should have his apt word to excuse himself:
And hearken how I plot to make amends.
I have bethought me: I shall paint a piece
345 … There's for you! Give me six months, then go, see
Something in Sant'Ambrogio's![4] Bless the nuns!
They want a cast o' my office. I shall paint
God in the midst, Madonna and her babe,[5]
Ringed by a bowery flowery angel brood,
350 Lilies and vestments and white faces, sweet
As puff on puff of grated orris-root[6]
When ladies crowd to Church at midsummer.
And then i' the front, of course a saint or two—
Saint John,[7] because he saves the Florentines,
355 Saint Ambrose,[8] who puts down in black and white
The convent's friends and gives them a long day,
And Job, I must have him there past mistake,
The man of Uz[9] (and Us without the z,
Painters who need his patience). Well, all these
360 Secured at their devotion, up shall come
Out of a corner when you least expect,
As one by a dark stair into a great light,
Music and talking, who but Lippo! I!—

[1] *matins* Morning prayer services.

[2] *Saint Laurence* Roman deacon (?–258 CE) who was martyred by being burnt on a gridiron, an instrument of torture.

[3] *Prato* Town west of Florence.

[4] *Sant' Ambrogio's* Lippi painted *Coronation of the Virgin* for the main altar of Florence's Sant' Ambrogio convent.

[5] *Madonna and her babe* Mary, mother of Jesus, depicted holding him as an infant, the subject of a mid-fifteenth-century painting by Fra Filippo Lippi.

[6] *orris-root* Roots of the iris flower, used as a fragrant cosmetic powder.

[7] *Saint John* St. John the Baptist, patron saint of Florence.

[8] *Saint Ambrose* Aurelius Ambrosius (c. 340–97), Archbishop of Milan, influential Christian theologian.

[9] *man of Uz* See Job 1.1: Job was a righteous man who lost everything when God allowed Satan to challenge his faith.

Mazed,[1] motionless and moonstruck—I'm the man!
365 Back I shrink—what is this I see and hear?
I, caught up with my monk's things by mistake,
My old serge gown and rope that goes all round,
I, in this presence, this pure company!
Where's a hole, where's a corner for escape?
370 Then steps a sweet angelic slip of a thing
Forward, puts out a soft palm—"Not so fast!"
—Addresses the celestial presence, "nay—
He made you and devised you, after all,
Though he's none of you! Could Saint John there draw—
375 His camel hair[2] make up a painting brush?
We come to brother Lippo for all that,
Iste perfecit opus![3] So, all smile—
I shuffle sideways with my blushing face
Under the cover of a hundred wings
380 Thrown like a spread of kirtles° when you're gay   *skirts*
And play hot cockles,[4] all the doors being shut,
Till, wholly unexpected, in there pops
The hothead husband! Thus I scuttle off
To some safe bench behind, not letting go
385 The palm of her, the little lily thing
That spoke the good word for me in the nick,
Like the Prior's niece … Saint Lucy,[5] I would say.
And so all's saved for me, and for the church
A pretty picture gained. Go, six months hence!
390 Your hand, sir, and goodbye: no lights, no lights!
The street's hushed, and I know my own way back,
Don't fear me! There's the grey beginning. Zooks!
—1855

---

[1] *Mazed* Stunned, bewildered.

[2] *Saint John … camel hair* St. John the Baptist "was clothed in camel hair," according to Mark 1.6.

[3] *Iste perfecit opus* Latin: He caused the work to be created; inscription on the *Coronation*, placed beside a portrait that Browning (following Vasari) mistakenly took to be Lippi's.

[4] *hot cockles* Christmas game played blindfolded.

[5] *Saint Lucy* Virgin martyr of Sicily (? –304? CE).

The Last Ride Together

1

I said—Then, dearest, since 'tis so,
Since now at length my fate I know,
Since nothing all my love avails,
Since all, my life seemed meant for, fails,
5   Since this was written and needs must be—
My whole heart rises up to bless
Your name in pride and thankfulness!
Take back the hope you gave—I claim
Only a memory of the same,
10 —And this beside, if you will not blame,
Your leave for one more last ride with me.

2

My mistress bent that brow of hers;
Those deep dark eyes where pride demurs
When pity would be softening through,
15 Fixed me a breathing-while or two
With life or death in the balance: right!
The blood replenished me again;
My last thought was at least not vain:
I and my mistress, side by side
20 Shall be together, breathe and ride,
So, one day more am I deified.
Who knows but the world may end tonight?

3

Hush! if you saw some western cloud
All billowy-bosomed, over-bowed
25 By many benedictions—sun's
And moon's and evening-star's at once—
And so, you, looking and loving best,
Conscious grew, your passion drew
Cloud, sunset, moonrise, star-shine too,
30 Down on you, near and yet more near,
Till flesh must fade for heaven was here!—
Thus leant she and lingered—joy and fear!
Thus lay she a moment on my breast.

4

Then we began to ride. My soul
5 Smoothed itself out, a long-cramped scroll
Freshening and fluttering in the wind.
Past hopes already lay behind.
    What need to strive with a life awry?
Had I said that, had I done this,
10 So might I gain, so might I miss.
Might she have loved me? just as well
She might have hated, who can tell!
Where had I been now if the worst befell?
    And here we are riding, she and I.

5

45 Fail I alone, in words and deeds?
Why, all men strive and who succeeds?
We rode; it seemed my spirit flew,
Saw other regions, cities new,
    As the world rushed by on either side.
50 I thought—All labour, yet no less
Bear up beneath their unsuccess.
Look at the end of work, contrast
The petty done, the undone vast,
    This present of theirs with the hopeful past!
55   I hoped she would love me; here we ride.

6

What hand and brain went ever paired?
What heart alike conceived and dared?
What act proved all its thought had been?
What will but felt the fleshly screen?
60   We ride and I see her bosom heave.
There's many a crown for who can reach.
Ten lines, a statesman's life in each!
The flag stuck on a heap of bones,
A soldier's doing! what atones?
65 They scratch his name on the Abbey[1] stones.
    My riding is better, by their leave.

7

What does it all mean, poet? Well,
Your brains beat into rhythm, you tell
What we felt only; you expressed

(continued)

70 You hold things beautiful the best,
    And pace them in rhyme so, side by side.
'Tis something, nay 'tis much: but then,
Have you yourself what's best for men?
Are you—poor, sick, old ere your time—
75 Nearer one whit your own sublime
Than we who never have turned a rhyme?
    Sing, riding's a joy! For me, I ride.

8

And you, great sculptor—so, you gave
A score of years to Art, her slave,
80 And that's your Venus,[2] whence we turn
To yonder girl that fords the burn!°   *stream*
    You acquiesce, and shall I repine?°   *complain*
What, man of music, you grown grey
With notes and nothing else to say,
85 Is this your sole praise from a friend,
"Greatly his opera's strains intend,
But in music we know how fashions end!"
    I gave my youth; but we ride, *in fine*.[3]

9

Who knows what's fit for us? Had fate
90 Proposed bliss here should sublimate
My being—had I signed the bond—
Still one must lead some life beyond,
    Have a bliss to die with, dim-descried.
This foot once planted on the goal,
95 This glory-garland round my soul,
Could I descry such? Try and test!
I sink back shuddering from the quest.
Earth being so good, would heaven seem best?
    Now, heaven and she are beyond this ride.

10

100 And yet—she has not spoke so long!
What if heaven be that, fair and strong
At life's best, with our eyes upturned
Whither life's flower is first discerned,
    We, fixed so, ever should so abide?

---

1 *Abbey* Westminster Abbey.

2 *Venus* Roman goddess of love.

3 *in fine* In the end.

105 What if we still ride on, we two
With life forever old yet new,
Changed not in kind but in degree,
The instant made eternity—
And heaven just prove that I and she
110   Ride, ride together, forever ride?
—1855

Andrea del Sarto[1]

(Called "The Faultless Painter")

But do not let us quarrel any more,
No, my Lucrezia;[2] bear with me for once:
Sit down and all shall happen as you wish.
You turn your face, but does it bring your heart?
5 I'll work then for your friend's friend, never fear,
Treat his own subject after his own way,
Fix his own time, accept too his own price,
And shut the money into this small hand
When next it takes mine. Will it? tenderly?
10 Oh, I'll content him—but tomorrow, Love!
I often am much wearier than you think,
This evening more than usual, and it seems
As if—forgive now—should you let me sit
Here by the window with your hand in mine
15 And look a half-hour forth on Fiesole,[3]
Both of one mind, as married people use,
Quietly, quietly the evening through,
I might get up tomorrow to my work
Cheerful and fresh as ever. Let us try.
20 Tomorrow, how you shall be glad for this!
Your soft hand is a woman of itself,
And mine the man's bared breast she curls inside.
Don't count the time lost, neither; you must serve
For each of the five pictures we require:

25 It saves a model. So! keep looking so—
My serpentining beauty, rounds on rounds!
—How could you ever prick those perfect ears,
Even to put the pearl there! oh, so sweet—
My face, my moon, my everybody's moon,
30 Which everybody looks on and calls his,
And, I suppose, is looked on by in turn,
While she looks—no one's: very dear, no less.
You smile? why, there's my picture ready made,
There's what we painters call our harmony!
35 A common greyness silvers everything—
All in a twilight, you and I alike
—You, at the point of your first pride in me
(That's gone you know)—but I, at every point;
My youth, my hope, my art, being all toned down
40 To yonder sober pleasant Fiesole.
There's the bell clinking from the chapel top;
That length of convent wall across the way
Holds the trees safer, huddled more inside;
The last monk leaves the garden; days decrease,
45 And autumn grows, autumn in everything.
Eh? the whole seems to fall into a shape
As if I saw alike my work and self
And all that I was born to be and do,
A twilight piece. Love, we are in God's hand.
50 How strange now, looks the life he makes us lead;
So free we seem, so fettered° fast we are!   shackled
I feel he laid the fetter: let it lie!
This chamber for example—turn your head—
All that's behind us! You don't understand
55 Nor care to understand about my art,
But you can hear at least when people speak:
And that cartoon,° the second from the door   sketch
—It is the thing, Love! so such things should be—
Behold Madonna![4]—I am bold to say.
60 I can do with my pencil what I know,
What I see, what at bottom of my heart
I wish for, if I ever wish so deep—
Do easily, too—when I say, perfectly,
I do not boast, perhaps: yourself are judge,
65 Who listened to the Legate's[5] talk last week,

---

[1] *Andrea del Sarto* Browning's poem explores the life of the painter Andrea del Sarto (1486–1531), as narrated by Giorgio Vasari (once del Sarto's pupil) in *The Lives of the Painters*. In this biography, Vasari speculates as to why del Sarto (translated, this name means "son of a tailor") failed to fulfill the promise of his early paintings.

[2] *Lucrezia* Lucrezia del Fede, del Sarto's wife and model.

[3] *Fiesole* Hill town near Florence.

[4] *Madonna* Mary, the mother of Jesus.

[5] *Legate* Representative of the Pope.

And just as much they used to say in France.
At any rate 'tis easy, all of it!
No sketches first, no studies, that's long past:
I do what many dream of, all their lives,
70 —Dream? strive to do, and agonize to do,
And fail in doing. I could count twenty such
On twice your fingers, and not leave this town,
Who strive—you don't know how the others strive
To paint a little thing like that you smeared
75 Carelessly passing with your robes afloat—
Yet do much less, so much less, Someone says,
(I know his name, no matter)—so much less!
Well, less is more, Lucrezia: I am judged.
There burns a truer light of God in them,
80 In their vexed beating stuffed and stopped-up brain,
Heart, or whate'er else, than goes on to prompt
This low-pulsed forthright craftsman's hand of mine.
Their works drop groundward, but themselves, I know,
Reach many a time a heaven that's shut to me,
85 Enter and take their place there sure enough,
Though they come back and cannot tell the world.
My works are nearer heaven, but I sit here.
The sudden blood of these men! at a word—
Praise them, it boils, or blame them, it boils too.
90 I, painting from myself and to myself,
Know what I do, am unmoved by men's blame
Or their praise either. Somebody remarks
Morello's[1] outline there is wrongly traced,
His hue mistaken; what of that? or else,
95 Rightly traced and well ordered; what of that?
Speak as they please, what does the mountain care?
Ah, but a man's reach should exceed his grasp,
Or what's a heaven for? All is silver-grey
Placid and perfect with my art: the worse!
100 I know both what I want and what might gain,
And yet how profitless to know, to sigh
"Had I been two, another and myself,
Our head would have o'erlooked the world!" No doubt.
Yonder's a work now, of that famous youth
105 The Urbinate[2] who died five years ago.

('Tis copied, George Vasari sent it me.)
Well, I can fancy how he did it all,
Pouring his soul, with kings and popes to see,
Reaching, that heaven might so replenish him,
110 Above and through his art—for it gives way;
That arm is wrongly put—and there again—
A fault to pardon in the drawing's lines,
Its body, so to speak: its soul is right,
He means right—that, a child may understand.
115 Still, what an arm! and I could alter it:
But all the play, the insight and the stretch—
Out of me, out of me! And wherefore out?
Had you enjoined them on me, given me soul,
We might have risen to Rafael, I and you!
120 Nay, Love, you did give all I asked, I think—
More than I merit, yes, by many times.
But had you—oh, with the same perfect brow,
And perfect eyes, and more than perfect mouth,
And the low voice my soul hears, as a bird
125 The fowler's pipe,[3] and follows to the snare—
Had you, with these the same, but brought a mind!
Some women do so. Had the mouth there urged
"God and the glory! never care for gain.
The present by the future, what is that?
130 Live for fame, side by side with Agnolo![4]
Rafael is waiting: up to God, all three!"
I might have done it for you. So it seems:
Perhaps not. All is as God over-rules.
Beside, incentives come from the soul's self;
135 The rest avail not. Why do I need you?
What wife had Rafael, or has Agnolo?
In this world, who can do a thing, will not;
And who would do it, cannot, I perceive:
Yet the will's somewhat—somewhat, too, the power—
140 And thus we half-men struggle. At the end,
God, I conclude, compensates, punishes.
'Tis safer for me, if the award be strict,
That I am something underrated here,
Poor this long while, despised, to speak the truth.
145 I dared not, do you know, leave home all day,

---

[1] *Morello*   Monte Morello, a mountain near Florence.

[2] *Urbinate*   The painter Raphael (1483–1520), who was born in Urbino.

[3] *fowler's pipe*   Call used by hunters to lure fowl.

[4] *Agnolo*   I.e., Michelangelo Buonarroti (1475–1564), sculptor and painter.

For fear of chancing on the Paris lords.[1]
The best is when they pass and look aside;
But they speak sometimes; I must bear it all.
Well may they speak! That Francis, that first time,
150 And that long festal year at Fontainebleau!
I surely then could sometimes leave the ground,
Put on the glory, Rafael's daily wear,
In that humane great monarch's golden look—
One finger in his beard or twisted curl
155 Over his mouth's good mark that made the smile,
One arm about my shoulder, round my neck,
The jingle of his gold chain in my ear,
I painting proudly with his breath on me,
All his court round him, seeing with his eyes,
160 Such frank French eyes, and such a fire of souls
Profuse, my hand kept plying by those hearts—
And, best of all, this, this, this face beyond,
This in the background, waiting on my work,
To crown the issue with a last reward!
165 A good time, was it not, my kingly days?
And had you not grown restless ... but I know—
'Tis done and past; 'twas right, my instinct said;
Too live the life grew, golden and not grey,
And I'm the weak-eyed bat no sun should tempt
170 Out of the grange whose four walls make his world.
How could it end in any other way?
You called me, and I came home to your heart.
The triumph was—to reach and stay there; since
I reached it ere the triumph, what is lost?
175 Let my hands frame your face in your hair's gold,
You beautiful Lucrezia that are mine!
"Rafael did this, Andrea painted that;
The Roman's is the better when you pray,
But still the other's Virgin was his wife—"
180 Men will excuse me. I am glad to judge
Both pictures in your presence; clearer grows
My better fortune, I resolve to think.
For, do you know, Lucrezia, as God lives,
Said one day Agnolo, his very self,
185 To Rafael ... I have known it all these years ...

(When the young man was flaming out his thoughts
Upon a palace wall for Rome to see,[2]
Too lifted up in heart because of it)
"Friend, there's a certain sorry little scrub
190 Goes up and down our Florence, none cares how,
Who, were he set to plan and execute
As you are, pricked on[3] by your popes and kings,
Would bring the sweat into that brow of yours!"
To Rafael's!—And indeed the arm is wrong.
195 I hardly dare ... yet, only you to see,
Give the chalk here—quick, thus the line should go!
Ay, but the soul! he's Rafael! rub it out!
Still, all I care for, if he spoke the truth,
(What he? why, who but Michel Agnolo?
200 Do you forget already words like those?)
If really there was such a chance, so lost—
Is, whether you're—not grateful—but more pleased.
Well, let me think so. And you smile indeed!
This hour has been an hour! Another smile?
205 If you would sit thus by me every night
I should work better, do you comprehend?
I mean that I should earn more, give you more.
See, it is settled dusk now; there's a star;
Morello's gone, the watch-lights show the wall,
210 The cue-owls[4] speak the name we call them by.
Come from the window, love—come in, at last,
Inside the melancholy little house
We built to be so gay with. God is just.
King Francis may forgive me: oft at nights
215 When I look up from painting, eyes tired out,
The walls become illumined, brick from brick
Distinct, instead of mortar, fierce bright gold,
That gold of his I did cement them with!
Let us but love each other. Must you go?
220 That cousin here again? he waits outside?
Must see you—you, and not with me? Those loans?
More gaming debts to pay? you smiled for that?
Well, let smiles buy me! have you more to spend?
While hand and eye and something of a heart

---

[1] *For fear ... lords* According to Vasari, del Sarto absconded with funds given to him at Fontainebleau by his patron, King Francis I of France.

[2] *When the young ... to see* Many of Raphael's most famous works are frescoes on the walls of the Apostolic Palace in the Vatican.

[3] *pricked on* Goaded.

[4] *cue-owls* Also known as scops-owls, whose cry sounds like "cue."

25 Are left me, work's my ware, and what's it worth?
I'll pay my fancy. Only let me sit
The grey remainder of the evening out,
Idle, you call it, and muse perfectly
How I could paint, were I but back in France,
30 One picture, just one more—the Virgin's face,
Not yours this time! I want you at my side
To hear them—that is, Michel Agnolo—
Judge all I do and tell you of its worth.
Will you? Tomorrow, satisfy your friend.
235 I take the subjects for his corridor,
Finish the portrait out of hand—there, there,
And throw him in another thing or two
If he demurs; the whole should prove enough
To pay for this same cousin's freak.° Beside,   whim
240 What's better and what's all I care about,
Get you the thirteen scudi° for the ruff!   Italian currency
Love, does that please you? Ah, but what does he,
The cousin! what does he to please you more?

    I am grown peaceful as old age tonight.
245 I regret little, I would change still less.
Since there my past life lies, why alter it?
The very wrong to Francis!—it is true
I took his coin, was tempted and complied,
And built this house and sinned, and all is said.
250 My father and my mother died of want.
Well, had I riches of my own? you see
How one gets rich! Let each one bear his lot.
They were born poor, lived poor, and poor they died:
And I have laboured somewhat in my time
255 And not been paid profusely. Some good son
Paint my two hundred pictures—let him try!
No doubt, there's something strikes a balance. Yes,
You loved me quite enough, it seems tonight.
This must suffice me here. What would one have?
260 In heaven, perhaps, new chances, one more chance—
Four great walls in the New Jerusalem,[1]
Meted on each side by the angel's reed,
For Leonard,[2] Rafael, Agnolo and me

To cover—the three first without a wife,
265 While I have mine! So—still they overcome
Because there's still Lucrezia—as I choose.

Again the cousin's whistle! Go, my Love.
—1855

A Woman's Last Word

1
Let's contend no more, Love,
    Strive nor weep:
All be as before, Love,
    —Only sleep!

2
5 What so wild as words are?
    I and thou
In debate, as birds are,
    Hawk on bough!

3
See the creature stalking
10   While we speak!
Hush and hide the talking,
    Cheek on cheek!

4
What so false as truth is,
    False to thee?
15 Where the serpent's tooth is
    Shun the tree—

5
Where the apple reddens
    Never pry—
Lest we lose our Edens,
20   Eve and I.[3]

1 *Four … Jerusalem* See Revelations 21.10.
2 *Leonard* Artist Leonardo da Vinci (1452–1519).
3 *Where the serpent's tooth … Eve and I* See Genesis 3.

6

Be a god and hold me
      With a charm!
Be a man and fold me
      With thine arm!

7

25 Teach me, only teach, Love!
      As I ought
I will speak thy speech, Love,
      Think thy thought—

8

Meet, if thou require it,
30   Both demands,
Laying flesh and spirit
      In thy hands.

9

That shall be tomorrow
      Not tonight:
35 I must bury sorrow
      Out of sight:

10

—Must a little weep, Love,
      (Foolish me!)
And so fall asleep, Love,
40   Loved by thee.
—1855

Caliban[1] *upon Setebos*
Or, Natural Theology[2] *in the Island*

"Thou thoughtest that I was altogether such a one as thyself."[3]

['W ill sprawl, now that the heat of day is best,
      Flat on his belly in the pit's much mire,
With elbows wide, fists clenched to prop his chin.
And, while he kicks both feet in the cool slush,
5 And feels about his spine small eft-things° course,   *lizards*
Run in and out each arm, and make him laugh:
And while above his head a pompion-plant,°   *pumpkin*
Coating the cave-top as a brow its eye,
Creeps down to touch and tickle hair and beard,
10 And now a flower drops with a bee inside,
And now a fruit to snap at, catch and crunch—
He looks out o'er yon sea which sunbeams cross
And recross till they weave a spider-web
(Meshes of fire, some great fish breaks at times)
15 And talks to his own self, howe'er he please,
Touching that other, whom his dam[4] called God.
Because to talk about Him, vexes—ha,
Could He but know! and time to vex is now,
When talk is safer than in winter-time.
20 Moreover Prosper and Miranda[5] sleep
In confidence he drudges at their task,
And it is good to cheat the pair, and gibe,
Letting the rank tongue blossom into speech.][6]

---

[1] *Caliban* Wild, deformed, and unruly half-human half-monster character in Shakespeare's *The Tempest*; Caliban ascribes to his god, Setebos, characteristics that he sees in himself.

[2] *Natural Theology* Theology based upon observable facts, rather than Scripture.

[3] *Thou ... thyself* From Psalms 50.21, in which God speaks to his people.

[4] *his dam* Sycorax, Caliban's mother. Caliban speaks of himself in third person, indicated by lowercase "he," "him," or "his."

[5] *Prosper and Miranda* Prospero, magician and father of Miranda, fled his home in Milan and landed on the island where Caliban dwelled; he made Caliban his servant.

[6] *['Will sprawl ... speech]* The first and also the final stanzas of the poem, both set off by square brackets, represent those lines that Caliban thinks to himself and does not speak aloud. An apostrophe before a word generally signals that the missing word is "Caliban"; i.e.,

Setebos, Setebos, and Setebos!
5 'Thinketh, He dwelleth i' the cold o' the moon.

'Thinketh He made it, with the sun to match,
But not the stars; the stars came otherwise;
Only made clouds, winds, meteors, such as that:
Also this isle, what lives and grows thereon,
10 And snaky sea which rounds and ends the same.

'Thinketh, it came of being ill at ease:
He hated that He cannot change His cold,
Nor cure its ache. 'Hath spied an icy fish
That longed to 'scape the rock-stream where she lived,
35 And thaw herself within the lukewarm brine
O' the lazy sea her stream thrusts far amid,
A crystal spike 'twixt two warm walls of wave;
Only, she ever sickened, found repulse
At the other kind of water, not her life,
40 (Green-dense and dim-delicious, bred o' the sun)
Flounced back from bliss she was not born to breathe,
And in her old bounds buried her despair,
Hating and loving warmth alike: so He.

'Thinketh, He made thereat the sun, this isle,
45 Trees and the fowls here, beast and creeping thing.
Yon otter, sleek-wet, black, lithe as a leech;
Yon auk,° one fire-eye in a ball of foam,   *diving bird*
That floats and feeds; a certain badger brown
He hath watched hunt with that slant white-wedge eye
50 By moonlight; and the pie° with the long tongue   *magpie*
That pricks deep into oakwarts for a worm,
And says a plain word when she finds her prize,
But will not eat the ants; the ants themselves
That build a wall of seeds and settled stalks
55 About their hole—He made all these and more,
Made all we see, and us, in spite: how else?
He could not, Himself, make a second self
To be His mate; as well have made Himself:
He would not make what he mislikes or slights,
60 An eyesore to Him, or not worth His pains:
But did, in envy, listlessness or sport,
Make what Himself would fain, in a manner, be—

Weaker in most points, stronger in a few,
Worthy, and yet mere playthings all the while,
65 Things He admires and mocks too—that is it.
Because, so brave, so better though they be,
It nothing skills if He begin to plague.
Look now, I melt a gourd-fruit into mash,
Add honeycomb and pods, I have perceived,
70 Which bite like finches when they bill and kiss—
Then, when froth rises bladdery, drink up all,
Quick, quick, till maggots scamper through my brain;
Last, throw me on my back i' the seeded thyme,
And wanton, wishing I were born a bird.
75 Put case, unable to be what I wish,
I yet could make a live bird out of clay:
Would not I take clay, pinch my Caliban
Able to fly?—for, there, see, he hath wings,
And great comb like the hoopoe's° to admire,   *colorful bird's*
80 And there, a sting to do his foes offence,
There, and I will that he begin to live,
Fly to yon rock-top, nip me off the horns
Of grigs° high up that make the merry din,   *crickets*
Saucy through their veined wings, and mind me not.
85 In which feat, if his leg snapped, brittle clay,
And he lay stupid-like—why, I should laugh;
And if he, spying me, should fall to weep,
Beseech me to be good, repair his wrong,
Bid his poor leg smart less or grow again—
90 Well, as the chance were, this might take or else
Not take my fancy: I might hear his cry,
And give the mankin[1] three sound legs for one,
Or pluck the other off, leave him like an egg,
And lessoned he was mine and merely clay.
95 Were this no pleasure, lying in the thyme,
Drinking the mash, with brain become alive,
Making and marring clay at will? So He.

'Thinketh, such shows nor right nor wrong in Him,
Nor kind, nor cruel: He is strong and Lord.
100 'Am strong myself compared to yonder crabs
That march now from the mountain to the sea,
'Let twenty pass, and stone the twenty-first,
Loving not, hating not, just choosing so.

Caliban speaks of himself in third person.

[1] *mankin* Little man, i.e., human.

'Say, the first straggler that boasts purple spots
105 Shall join the file, one pincer twisted off;
'Say, this bruised fellow shall receive a worm,
And two worms he whose nippers end in red;
As it likes me each time, I do: so He.

Well then, 'supposeth He is good i' the main,
110 Placable if His mind and ways were guessed,
But rougher than His handiwork, be sure!
Oh, He hath made things worthier than Himself,
And envieth that, so helped, such things do more
Than He who made them! What consoles but this?
115 That they, unless through Him, do nought at all,
And must submit: what other use in things?
'Hath cut a pipe of pithless elder joint[1]
That, blown through, gives exact the scream o' the jay
When from her wing you twitch the feathers blue:
120 Sound this, and little birds that hate the jay
Flock within stone's throw, glad their foe is hurt:
Put case such pipe could prattle and boast forsooth
"I catch the birds, I am the crafty thing,
I make the cry my maker cannot make
125 With his great round mouth; he must blow through
    mine!"
Would not I smash it with my foot? So He.

But wherefore rough, why cold and ill at ease?
Aha, that is a question! Ask, for that,
What knows—the something over Setebos
130 That made Him, or He, may be, found and fought,
Worsted, drove off and did to nothing, perchance.
There may be something quiet o'er His head,
Out of His reach, that feels nor joy nor grief,
Since both derive from weakness in some way.
135 I joy because the quails come; would not joy
Could I bring quails here when I have a mind:
This Quiet,° all it hath a mind to, doth.   *another deity*
'Esteemeth stars the outposts of its couch,
But never spends much thought nor care that way.
140 It may look up, work up—the worse for those
It works on! 'Careth but for Setebos
The many-handed as a cuttle-fish,°   *octopus*

Who, making Himself feared through what He does,
Looks up, first, and perceives he cannot soar
145 To what is quiet and hath happy life;
Next looks down here, and out of very spite
Makes this a bauble-world to ape yon real,
These good things to match those as hips°   *rosehips*
    do grapes.
'Tis solace making baubles, ay, and sport.
150 Himself peeped late, eyed Prosper at his books
Careless and lofty, lord now of the isle:
Vexed, 'stitched a book of broad leaves, arrow-shaped,
Wrote thereon, he knows what, prodigious words;
Has peeled a wand and called it by a name;
155 Weareth at whiles for an enchanter's robe
The eyed skin of a supple oncelot;°   *ocelot*
And hath an ounce[2] sleeker than youngling mole,
A four-legged serpent he makes cower and couch,
Now snarl, now hold its breath and mind his eye,
160 And saith she is Miranda and my wife:
'Keeps for his Ariel[3] a tall pouch-bill crane
He bids go wade for fish and straight disgorge;
Also a sea-beast, lumpish, which he snared,
Blinded the eyes of, and brought somewhat tame,
165 And split its toe-webs, and now pens the drudge
In a hole o' the rock and calls him Caliban;
A bitter heart that bides its time and bites.
'Plays thus at being Prosper in a way,
Taketh his mirth with make-believes: so He.

170 His dam held that the Quiet made all things
Which Setebos vexed only: 'holds not so.
Who made them weak, meant weakness He might vex.
Had He meant other, while His hand was in,
Why not make horny eyes no thorn could prick,
175 Or plate my scalp with bone against the snow,
Or overscale my flesh 'neath joint and joint,
Like an orc's° armour? Ay—so spoil His sport! *sea monster's*
He is the One now: only He doth all.
'Saith, He may like, perchance, what profits Him.
180 Ay, himself loves what does him good; but why?

---

[1] *elder joint* Branch of an elder tree.

[2] *ounce* Cheetah-like cat.

[3] *Ariel* Air spirit of *The Tempest*, who once served and then was freed
by the evil witch Sycorax; thereafter Ariel was bound to serve Prospero.

'Gets good no otherwise. This blinded beast
Loves whoso places flesh meat on his nose,
But, had he eyes, would want no help, but hate
Or love, just as it liked him: He hath eyes.
185 Also it pleaseth Setebos to work,
Use all His hands, and exercise much craft,
By no means for the love of what is worked.
'Tasteth, himself, no finer good i' the world
When all goes right, in this safe summertime,
190 And he wants little, hungers, aches not much,
Than trying what to do with wit and strength.
'Falls to make something: 'piled yon pile of turfs,
And squared and stuck there squares of soft white
    chalk,
And, with a fish tooth, scratched a moon on each,
195 And set up endwise certain spikes of tree,
And crowned the whole with a sloth's skull a-top,
Found dead i' the woods, too hard for one to kill.
No use at all i' the work, for work's sole sake;
'Shall some day knock it down again: so He.

200 'Saith He is terrible: watch His feats in proof!
One hurricane will spoil six good months' hope.
He hath a spite against me, that I know,
Just as He favours Prosper, who knows why?
So it is, all the same, as well I find.
205 'Wove wattles° half the winter, fenced   *twigs, branches*
    them firm
With stone and stake to stop she-tortoises
Crawling to lay their eggs here: well, one wave,
Feeling the foot of Him upon its neck,
Gaped as a snake does, lolled out its large tongue,
210 And licked the whole labour flat: so much for spite.
'Saw a ball flame down late (yonder it lies)
Where, half an hour before, I slept i' the shade:
Often they scatter sparkles: there is force!
'Dug up a newt He may have envied once
215 And turned to stone, shut up inside a stone.
Please Him and hinder this?—What Prosper does?
Aha, if He would tell me how! Not He!
There is the sport: discover how or die!
All need not die, for of the things o' the isle

220 Some flee afar, some dive, some run up trees;
Those at His mercy—why, they please Him most
When … when … well, never try the same way twice!
Repeat what act has pleased, He may grow wroth.°   *angry*
You must not know His ways, and play Him off,
225 Sure of the issue. 'Doth the like himself:
'Spareth a squirrel that it nothing fears
But steals the nut from underneath my thumb,
And when I threat, bites stoutly in defence:
'Spareth an urchin° that contrariwise,   *hedgehog*
230 Curls up into a ball, pretending death
For fright at my approach: the two ways please.
But what would move my choler° more than this,   *anger*
That either creature counted on its life
Tomorrow and next day and all days to come,
235 Saying, forsooth, in the inmost of its heart,
"Because he did so yesterday with me,
And otherwise with such another brute,
So must he do henceforth and always."—Ay?
Would teach the reasoning couple what "must" means!
240 'Doth as he likes, or wherefore Lord? So He.

'Conceiveth all things will continue thus,
And we shall have to live in fear of Him
So long as He lives, keeps His strength: no change,
If He have done His best, make no new world
245 To please Him more, so leave off watching this—
If He surprise not even the Quiet's self
Some strange day—or, suppose, grow into it
As grubs grow butterflies: else, here are we,
And there is He, and nowhere help at all.

250 'Believeth with the life, the pain shall stop.
His dam held different, that after death
He both plagued enemies and feasted friends:
Idly! He doth His worst in this our life,
Giving just respite lest we die through pain,
255 Saving last pain for worst—with which, an end.
Meanwhile, the best way to escape His ire
Is, not to seem too happy. 'Sees, himself,
Yonder two flies, with purple films and pink,
Bask on the pompion-bell above: kills both.

260 'Sees two black painful beetles roll their ball
On head and tail as if to save their lives:
Moves them the stick away they strive to clear.

Even so, 'would have Him misconceive, suppose
This Caliban strives hard and ails no less,
265 And always, above all else, envies Him;
Wherefore he mainly dances on dark nights,
Moans in the sun, gets under holes to laugh,
And never speaks his mind save housed as now:
Outside, 'groans, curses. If He caught me here,
270 O'erheard this speech, and asked "What chucklest at?"
'Would, to appease Him, cut a finger off,
Or of my three kid yearlings burn the best,
Or let the toothsome apples rot on tree,
Or push my tame beast for the orc to taste:
275 While myself lit a fire, and made a song
And sung it, "*What I hate, be consecrate
To celebrate Thee and Thy state, no mate
For Thee; what see for envy in poor me?*"

Hoping the while, since evils sometimes mend,
280 Warts rub away and sores are cured with slime,
That some strange day, will either the Quiet catch
And conquer Setebos, or likelier He
Decrepit may doze, doze, as good as die.

[What, what? A curtain o'er the world at once!
285 Crickets stop hissing; not a bird—or, yes,
There scuds His raven that has told Him all!
It was fool's play, this prattling! Ha! The wind
Shoulders the pillared dust, death's house o' the move,
And fast invading fires begin! White blaze—
290 A tree's head snaps—and there, there, there, there, there,
His thunder follows! Fool to gibe at Him!
Lo! 'Lieth flat and loveth Setebos!
'Maketh his teeth meet through his upper lip,
Will let those quails fly, will not eat this month
295 One little mess of whelks,° so he may 'scape!]   *shellfish*
—1864

CHARLES DICKENS
1812 – 1870

Few English novelists have attracted the vast audiences and lasting fame of Charles Dickens. People the world over are familiar with the moral transformation of *A Christmas Carol*'s Ebenezer Scrooge and the life of the orphan Oliver Twist, immortalized in his piteous request for a second bowl of watery gruel: "Please, sir, I want some more." From Pickwick and Sam Weller in *The Pickwick Papers* to Mr. Micawber in *David Copperfield* to Pip in *Great Expectations*, from Mr. Guppy and Mrs. Jellyby in *Bleak House* to Mr. Gradgrind in *Hard Times* and Flora Finching in *Little Dorrit*, Dickens created a panoply of memorable characters. Combining comic genius with astute criticisms of the laws, institutions, and the social order of Victorian society, he created novels that continue to command the attention of critics and the general public alike. His novels still stand as a testament to his stature both as a popular writer and as a social critic.

Dickens's early childhood was signally important as source material for the concerns and themes of his novels. His father worked as a naval office clerk in Portsmouth when Charles was born in 1812, the second of 10 children (two died in infancy). John and Elizabeth Dickens aspired to a middle-class life, but had unending difficulties controlling their spending and were always on the brink of penury. At one time, they served a four-month stint in the Marshalsea debtors' prison. Charles was able to attend school in Chatham, near London, after the family was transferred to the dockyards there, but in 1823 his education was halted, and he joined his parents in Camden Town, London. The young Dickens worked at odd jobs for his parents and was eventually sent off to work at Warren's Boot Blacking Factory at the age of 12. The psychological impact of this environment on Dickens was permanent; he never forgot the humiliation he had suffered or the dismay he had felt at the relatively harsh working conditions under which he and other children were forced to toil.

After the family came into a modest inheritance, Dickens returned to school, but in 1827, at just 15 years of age, he left school again because his father was unable to pay the fees. Working as a clerk in a law firm, he studied shorthand in his spare time, eventually becoming a parliamentary reporter. In 1833, *Monthly Magazine* published Dickens's first story, "A Dinner at Poplar Walk." While working as a newspaper reporter the next year, he launched a highly popular series of articles that were eventually collected and published as *Sketches by Boz* (his journalistic pseudonym) in 1836. The success of this book allowed Dickens to marry Catherine Hogarth and to begin another series that cemented his fame and secured his financial stability. A monthly illustrated serial about the Pickwick Club was commissioned by publishers Chapman and Hall, and the absurd characters of Mr. Pickwick, Mr. Winkle, Mr. Tupman, Mr. Snodgrass, and Sam Weller soon had people all over England clamoring for the latest installment of *The Pickwick Papers*. Dickens consolidated this success by beginning *Oliver Twist* (1837–38) in *Bentley's Miscellany*, which he had begun editing, and then launching *Nicholas Nickleby* (1838–39) as a monthly serial.

In 1837, Dickens and his wife began to raise a family (they eventually had 10 children). In this same year, he lost his beloved sister-in-law, Mary Hogarth, who would become the inspiration for Little Nell in *The Old Curiosity Shop* (1840–41) and for many of the childlike women that constitute the "good angels" of his novels. By the time this book was published, Dickens's fame had spread throughout North America; eager fans would line the piers in New York waiting for the latest installment of a Dickens story to arrive from England.

In 1842, Dickens journeyed to the United States to take advantage of his fame, but the trip turned out to be a disappointment. The hordes that crowded around him relentlessly, trying to speak to, touch, or even just glimpse the famous author were only part of the problem. He scorned, publicly and at any opportunity, the lack of international copyright laws, which meant that Americans could pirate editions of his books without any of the proceeds going to him. Dickens set out his disdain for American habits (such as chewing and spitting tobacco) and for American institutions, such as slavery and what he thought was a ruthless prison system in a book about his travels, *American Notes* (1842), and made Americans the object of derision in his novel *Martin Chuzzlewit* (1843–44). Americans were incensed and reacted with an outpouring of vindictive editorials in the press. As it happened, *Martin Chuzzlewit* did not sell well on either side of the Atlantic. Americans began to forgive Dickens after the appearance of the overwhelmingly successful *A Christmas Carol* (1843), the first in his Christmas book series and a novel that is all about forgiveness and redemption.

Dickens was an astonishingly energetic and prolific writer, becoming the editor of *Household Words* in 1850, while writing and acting in theatrical works, traveling widely, and working in various social causes. Throughout the 1840s and 1850s, he published at an unprecedented rate: *Dombey and Son* (1846–48), *David Copperfield* (his most autobiographical work, 1849–50), *Bleak House* (1852–53), *Hard Times* (1854), *Little Dorrit* (1855–57), *A Tale of Two Cities* (1859), *Great Expectations* (1861), and *Our Mutual Friend* (1865). All of these novels were first published in serial form. This approach necessitated an episodic structure, prompting him to develop methods of characterization that allowed immediate identification of characters by readers waiting for weekly or monthly installments. He also developed an extraordinary talent for weaving together numerous strands of story material and coincidental events that, however implausible they might appear, somehow strike the reader as persuasive.

Dickens not only edited *Household Words*; he also wrote many of the pieces himself, both fiction and non-fiction. In fact, he referred to himself as the "conductor" of the magazine, not its editor. Had he never written any of his novels or short stories, he would still be remembered for the extraordinary body of non-fiction he produced. His essays for the magazine deal with a wide variety of topics, but again and again he returns in one way or another to the condition of the poor—the great issue of his time. The condition of poor children was a particular concern for Dickens—as his 1850 essay "A Walk in the Workhouse" suggests. But, as the 1854 essay "The Quiet Poor" demonstrates, his sympathetic understanding for poor people both *en masse* and as individuals could operate just as keenly for those "who are never to be seen in workhouses and prisons." That essay also illustrates Dickens's abiding interest in public policy; he believed in the power of the human heart to bring change (and he strove in his writing to tug at the heartstrings of his readers), but he was also an advocate for changes to social and economic legislation.

In 1858 Dickens separated from Catherine; the break was complicated by his relationship with the actress Ellen Ternan and by the degree of publicity that (partly at Dickens's instigation) attended his change in marital status. In that same year, Dickens began an extensive series of public readings, a lucrative but exhausting enterprise that severely compromised his health. He continued touring throughout the 1860s while editing his new journal, *All the Year Round* (begun in 1859). Dickens was at work on *The Mystery of Edwin Drood* when he died in 1870 during a grueling schedule of readings. In his will Dickens requested that he be buried at Rochester, Kent, near his home. Under public pressure the family agreed to allow him to be buried instead in Poet's Corner in Westminster Abbey. Dickens's instructions that the funeral be "unostentatious, and strictly private" were followed, however; there were only a dozen present for the ceremony in the cathedral.

⌘ ⌘ ⌘

A Walk in the Workhouse[1]

On a certain Sunday I formed one of the congregation assembled in the chapel of a large metropolitan Workhouse. With the exception of the clergyman and clerk, and a very few officials, there were none but paupers present. The children sat in the galleries; the women in the body of the chapel, and in one of the side aisles; the men in the remaining aisle. The service was decorously performed, though the sermon might have been much better adapted to the comprehension and to the circumstances of the hearers. The usual supplications were offered, with more than the usual significancy in such a place, for the fatherless children and widows, for all sick persons and young children, for all that were desolate and oppressed, for the comforting and helping of the weak-hearted, for the raising up of them that had fallen; for all that were in danger, necessity, and tribulation. The prayers of the congregation were desired "for several persons in the various wards dangerously ill"; and others who were recovering returned their thanks to Heaven.

Among this congregation were some evil-looking young women, and beetle-browed young men; but not many—perhaps that kind of characters kept away. Generally, the faces (those of the children excepted) were depressed and subdued, and wanted colour. Aged people were there in every variety. Mumbling, bleareyed, spectacled, stupid, deaf, lame; vacantly winking in the gleams of sun that now and then crept in through the open doors, from the paved yard; shading their listening ears, or blinking eyes, with their withered hands; poring over their books, leering at nothing, going to sleep, crouching and drooping in corners. There were weird old women, all skeleton within, all bonnet and cloak without, continually wiping their eyes with dirty dusters of pocket handkerchiefs; and there were ugly old crones, both male and female, with a ghastly kind of contentment upon them which was not at all comforting to see. Upon the whole, it was the dragon, Pauperism, in a very weak and impotent condition: toothless, fangless, drawing his breath heavily enough, and hardly worth chaining up.

When the service was over, I walked with the humane and conscientious gentleman whose duty it was to take that walk, that Sunday morning, through the little world of poverty enclosed within the workhouse walls. It was inhabited by a population of some fifteen hundred or two thousand paupers, ranging from the infant newly born or not yet come into the pauper world, to the old man dying on his bed.

In a room opening from a squalid yard, where a number of listless women were lounging to and fro, trying to get warm in the ineffectual sunshine of the tardy May morning—in the "Itch Ward," not to compromise the truth—a woman such as HOGARTH[2] has often drawn, was hurriedly getting on her gown before a dusty fire. She was the nurse, or wardswoman, of that insalubrious department—herself a pauper—flabby, raw-boned, untidy—unpromising and coarse of aspect as need be. But, on being spoken to about the patients whom she had in charge, she turned round, with her shabby gown half on, half off, and fell a crying with all

---

[1] *A Walk in the Workhouse* This essay appeared in 1850 in Dickens's magazine *Household Words*.

[2] *HOGARTH* Artist and printmaker William Hogarth (1687–1764) was greatly admired by Dickens for his satirical paintings and prints of eighteenth-century London life.

her might. Not for show, not querulously, not in any mawkish sentiment, but in the deep grief and affliction of her heart; turning away her dishevelled head: sobbing most bitterly, wringing her hands, and letting fall abundance of great tears, that choked her utterance. What was the matter with the nurse of the itch ward? Oh, "the dropped child" was dead! Oh, the child that was found in the street, and she had brought up ever since, had died an hour ago, and see where the little creature lay, beneath this cloth! The dear, the pretty dear!

The dropped child seemed too small and poor a thing for Death to be in earnest with, but Death had taken it; and already its diminutive form was neatly washed, composed, and stretched as if in sleep upon a box. I thought I heard a voice from Heaven saying, It shall be well for thee, O nurse of the itch ward, when some less gentle pauper does those offices to thy cold form, that such as the dropped child are the angels who behold my Father's face!

In another room were several ugly old women crouching, witch-like, round a hearth, and chattering and nodding, after the manner of the monkeys. "All well here? And enough to eat?" A general chattering and chuckling; at last an answer from a volunteer. "Oh yes, gentleman! Bless you, gentleman! Lord bless the Parish of St. So-and-So! It feed the hungry, sir, and give drink to the thusty, and it warm them which is cold, so it do, and good luck to the parish of St. So-and-So, and thankee, gentleman!" Elsewhere, a party of pauper nurses were at dinner. "How do YOU get on?" "Oh pretty well, sir! We works hard, and we lives hard—like the sodgers!"[1]

In another room, a kind of purgatory or place of transition, six or eight noisy madwomen were gathered together, under the superintendence of one sane attendant. Among them was a girl of two or three and twenty, very prettily dressed, of most respectable appearance and good manners, who had been brought in from the house where she had lived as domestic servant (having, I suppose, no friends), on account of being subject to epileptic fits, and requiring to be removed

under the influence of a very bad one. She was by no means of the same stuff, or the same breeding, or the same experience, or in the same state of mind, as those by whom she was surrounded; and she pathetically complained that the daily association and the nightly noise made her worse, and was driving her mad—which was perfectly evident. The case was noted for inquiry and redress, but she said she had already been there for some weeks.

If this girl had stolen her mistress's watch, I do not hesitate to say she would have been infinitely better off. We have come to this absurd, this dangerous, this monstrous pass, that the dishonest felon is, in respect of cleanliness, order, diet, and accommodation, better provided for, and taken care of, than the honest pauper.

And this conveys no special imputation on the workhouse of the parish of St. So-and-So, where, on the contrary, I saw many things to commend. It was very agreeable, recollecting that most infamous and atrocious enormity committed at Tooting[2]—an enormity which, a hundred years hence, will still be vividly remembered in the byways of English life, and which has done more to engender a gloomy discontent and suspicion among many thousands of the people than all the Chartist leaders[3] could have done in all their lives—to find the pauper children in this workhouse looking robust and well, and apparently the objects of very great care. In the Infant School—a large, light, airy room at the top of the building—the little creatures, being at dinner, and eating their potatoes heartily, were not cowed by the presence of strange visitors, but stretched out their small hands to be shaken, with a very pleasant confidence. And it was comfortable to see two mangy pauper rocking-horses rampant in a corner. In the girls' school, where the dinner was also in progress, everything bore a cheerful and healthy aspect. The meal was over in the boys' school by the time of our arrival there, and the room was not yet quite rearranged; but the boys were

---

[1] *sodgers* I.e., soldiers.

[2] *Tooting* In 1849, after four half-starved children had died of cholera in a Tooting workhouse, the proprietor was found guilty of manslaughter.

[3] *Chartist leaders* The Chartist movement pressed for political (and by implication, social and economic) reform from 1836 onwards.

roaming unrestrained about a large and airy yard, as any other schoolboys might have done. Some of them had been drawing large ships upon the schoolroom wall; and if they had a mast with shrouds and stays set up for practice (as they have in the Middlesex House of Correction), it would be so much the better. At present, if a boy should feel a strong impulse upon him to learn the art of going aloft, he could only gratify it, I presume, as the men and women paupers gratify their aspirations after better board and lodging, by smashing as many workhouse windows as possible, and being promoted to prison.

In one place, the Newgate[1] of the workhouse, a company of boys and youths were locked up in a yard alone; their dayroom being a kind of kennel where the casual poor used formerly to be littered down at night. Diverse of them had been there some long time. "Are they never going away?" was the natural inquiry. "Most of them are crippled, in some form or other," said the wardsman, "and not fit for anything." They slunk about, like dispirited wolves or hyenas; and made a pounce at their food when it was served out, much as those animals do. The big-headed idiot shuffling his feet along the pavement, in the sunlight outside, was a more agreeable object everyway.

Groves of babies in arms; groves of mothers and other sick women in bed; groves of lunatics; jungles of men in stone-paved downstairs dayrooms, waiting for their dinners; longer and longer groves of old people, in upstairs infirmary wards, wearing out life, God knows how—this was the scenery through which the walk lay, for two hours. In some of these latter chambers, there were pictures stuck against the wall, and a neat display of crockery and pewter on a kind of sideboard; now and then it was a treat to see a plant or two; in almost every ward there was a cat.

In all of these long walks of aged and infirm, some old people were bedridden, and had been for a long time; some were sitting on their beds half naked; some dying in their beds; some out of bed, and sitting at a table near the fire. A sullen or lethargic indifference to what was asked, a blunted sensibility to everything but

warmth and food, a moody absence of complaint as being of no use, a dogged silence and resentful desire to be left alone again, I thought were generally apparent. On our walking into the midst of one of these dreary perspectives of old men, nearly the following little dialogue took place, the nurse not being immediately at hand:

"All well here?"

No answer. An old man in a Scotch cap[2] sitting among others on a form at the table, eating out of a tin porringer,[3] pushes back his cap a little to look at us, claps it down on his forehead again with the palm of his hand, and goes on eating.

"All well here?" (repeated).

No answer. Another old man sitting on his bed, paralytically peeling a boiled potato, lifts his head and stares.

"Enough to eat?"

No answer. Another old man, in bed, turns himself and coughs.

"How are YOU today?" To the last old man.

That old man says nothing; but another old man, a tall old man of very good address, speaking with perfect correctness, comes forward from somewhere, and volunteers an answer. The reply almost always proceeds from a volunteer, and not from the person looked at or spoken to.

"We are very old, sir," in a mild, distinct voice. "We can't expect to be well, most of us."

"Are you comfortable?"

"I have no complaint to make, sir." With a half shake of his head, a half shrug of his shoulders, and a kind of apologetic smile.

"Enough to eat?"

"Why, sir, I have but a poor appetite," with the same air as before; "and yet I get through my allowance very easily."

"But," showing a porringer with a Sunday dinner in it; "here is a portion of mutton, and three potatoes. You can't starve on that?"

---

[1] *Newgate* Newgate was London's main prison.

[2] *Scotch cap* Woolen hat worn in the Highlands.

[3] *porringer* Bowl for porridge, soups, and other runny foods.

"Oh dear no, sir," with the same apologetic air. "Not starve."

"What do you want?"

"We have very little bread, sir. It's an exceedingly small quantity of bread."

The nurse, who is now rubbing her hands at the questioner's elbow, interferes with, "It ain't much raly, sir. You see they've only six ounces a day, and when they've took their breakfast, there CAN only be a little left for night, sir." Another old man, hitherto invisible, rises out of his bedclothes, as out of a grave, and looks on.

"You have tea at night?" The questioner is still addressing the well-spoken old man.

"Yes, sir, we have tea at night."

"And you save what bread you can from the morning, to eat with it?"

"Yes, sir—if we can save any."

"And you want more to eat with it?"

"Yes, sir." With a very anxious face.

The questioner, in the kindness of his heart, appears a little discomposed, and changes the subject.

"What has become of the old man who used to lie in that bed in the corner?"

The nurse don't remember what old man is referred to. There has been such a many old men. The well-spoken old man is doubtful. The spectral old man who has come to life in bed says "Billy Stevens." Another old man who has previously had his head in the fireplace, pipes out, "Charley Walters."

Something like a feeble interest is awakened. I suppose Charley Walters had conversation in him.

"He's dead," says the piping old man.

Another old man, with one eye screwed up, hastily displaces the piping old man, and says.

"Yes! Charley Walters died in that bed, and—and—"

"Billy Stevens," persists the spectral old man.

"No, no! and Johnny Rogers died in that bed, and—and—they're both on 'em dead—and Sam'l Bowyer"; this seems very extraordinary to him; "he went out!"

With this he subsides, and all the old men (having had quite enough of it) subside, and the spectral old man goes into his grave again, and takes the shade of Billy Stevens with him.

As we turn to go out at the door, another previously invisible old man, a hoarse old man in a flannel gown, is standing there, as if he had just come up through the floor.

"I beg your pardon, sir, could I take the liberty of saying a word?"

"Yes, what is it?"

"I am greatly better in my health, sir; but what I want, to get me quite round," with his hand on his throat, "is a little fresh air, sir. It has always done my complaint so much good, sir. The regular leave for going out, comes round so seldom, that if the gentlemen, next Friday, would give me leave to go out walking, now and then—for only an hour or so, sir!—"

Who could wonder, looking through those weary vistas of bed and infirmity, that it should do him good to meet with some other scenes, and assure himself that there was something else on earth? Who could help wondering why the old men lived on as they did; what grasp they had on life; what crumbs of interest or occupation they could pick up from its bare board; whether Charley Walters had ever described to them the days when he kept company with some old pauper woman in the bud, or Billy Stevens ever told them of the time when he was a dweller in the far off foreign land called Home!

The morsel of burnt child, lying in another room, so patiently, in bed, wrapped in lint, and looking steadfastly at us with his bright quiet eyes when we spoke to him kindly, looked as if the knowledge of these things, and of all the tender things there are to think about, might have been in his mind as if he thought, with us, that there was a fellow-feeling in the pauper nurses which appeared to make them more kind to their charges than the race of common nurses in the hospitals—as if he mused upon the future of some older children lying around him in the same place, and thought it best, perhaps, all things considered, that he should die—as if he knew, without fear, of those many coffins, made and unmade, piled up in the store below—and of his unknown friend, "the dropped child," calm upon the box lid covered with a cloth. But there was something wistful and appealing, too, in his tiny face, as if, in the midst of all the hard necessities and incongruities he pondered on, he pleaded, in behalf of the helpless and the aged poor, for a little more liberty—and a little more bread.

—1850

Preface to *Oliver Twist* (1850)

Dickens's second novel, *Oliver Twist* (1837–38), includes a grim description of Jacob's Island, one of London's most appalling slums. The slum, Dickens wrote, featured

> rooms so small, so filthy, so confined, that the air would seem too tainted even for the dirt and squalor which they shelter; wooden chambers thrusting themselves out above the mud, and threatening to fall into it—as some have done; dirt-besmeared walls and decaying foundations; every repulsive lineament of poverty, every loathsome indication of filth, rot, and garbage[.] …
>
> In Jacob's Island, the warehouses are roofless and empty; the walls are crumbling down; the windows are windows no more; the doors are falling into the streets; the chimneys are blackened, but they yield no smoke. … The houses have no owners; they are broken open, and entered upon by those who have the courage; and there they live, and there they die. They must have powerful motives for a secret residence, or be reduced to a destitute condition indeed, who seek a refuge in Jacob's Island.

The following preface to *Oliver Twist* appeared as part of Dickens's first collected novels, a series titled the "Cheap Edition" and marketed toward readers of lower income. Writing thirteen years after the novel's initial publication, Dickens used the preface to contradict those who questioned the accuracy of *Oliver Twist*'s depiction of urban squalor—and even denied the existence of Jacob's Island itself.

from *Oliver Twist*

PREFACE TO THE PRESENT EDITION

At page 267 of this present edition of Oliver Twist, there is a description of "the filthiest, the strangest, the most extraordinary, of the many localities that are hidden in London." And the name of this place is Jacob's Island.

Eleven or twelve years have elapsed since the description was first published. I was as well convinced then, as I am now, that nothing effectual can be done for the elevation of the poor in England, until their dwelling-places are made decent and wholesome. I have always been convinced that this reform must precede all other Social Reforms; that it must prepare the way for Education, even for Religion; and that, without it, those classes of the people which increase the fastest, must become so desperate, and be made so miserable, as to bear within themselves the certain seeds of ruin to the whole community.

The metropolis (of all places under heaven) being excluded from the provisions of the Public Health Act, passed last year, a society has been formed called the Metropolitan Sanitary Association, with the view of remedying this grievous mistake. The association held its first public meeting at Freemason's Hall, on Wednesday the sixth of February last; the Bishop of London presiding. It happened that this very place, Jacob's Island, had lately attracted the attention of the Board of Health, in consequence of its having been ravaged by cholera; and that the Bishop of London had in his hands the result of an inquiry under the Metropolitan Sewers Commission, shewing, by way of proof of the cheapness of sanitary improvements, an estimate of the probable cost at which the houses in Jacob's Island could be rendered fit for human habitation—which cost was stated at about a penny three farthings per week per house. The Bishop referred to this paper, with the moderation and forbearance which pervaded all his observations, and did me the honour to mention that I had described Jacob's Island. When I subsequently made a few observations myself, I confessed that soft impeachment.[1]

Now, the vestry[2] of Marylebone parish, meeting on the following Saturday, had the honour to be addressed by Sir Peter Laurie;[3] a gentleman of infallible authority, of great innate modesty, and of a most sweet humanity. This remarkable alderman, as I am informed by *The Observer* newspaper, then and there delivered himself (I quote the passage without any correction) as follows:

> Having touched upon the point of saving to the poor, he begged to illustrate it by reading for them the particulars of a survey that had been made in a locality called—"Jacob's Island"—(a laugh)—where, according to the surveyor, 1300 houses were erected on forty acres of ground. The surveyor asserted and laid down that each house could be supplied with a constant supply of pure water—secondly, that each house could be supplied with a sink—thirdly, a water-closet—fourthly, a drain—fifthly, a, foundation drain—and, sixthly, the accommodation of a dust bin (laughter), and all at the average rate of 13s. 4d.[4] per week (oh, oh, and laughter).
>
> Mr. G. Bird: Can Sir Peter Laurie tell the vestry where "Jacob's Island" is? (laughter).
>
> Sir P. Laurie: That was just what he was about to tell them. The Bishop of London, poor soul, in his simplicity, thought there really was such a place, which he had been describing so minutely, *whereas it turned out that it ONLY existed in a work of fiction, written by Mr. Charles Dickens ten years ago* (roars of laughter). *The fact was admitted by Mr. Charles Dickens himself at the meeting*, and he (Sir P. Laurie) had extracted his words from the same paper, the

Morning Herald. Mr. Dickens said "Now the first of these classes proceeded generally on the supposition that the compulsory improvement of these dwellings, when exceedingly defective, would be very expensive. But that was a great mistake, for nothing was cheaper than good sanitary improvements, as they knew in this case of 'Jacob's Island' (laughter), which he had described in a work of fiction some ten or eleven years ago."

When I came to read this, I was so much struck by the honesty, by the truth, and by the wisdom of this logic, as well as by the fact of the sagacious vestry, including members of parliament, magistrates, officers, chemists, and I know not who else listening to it meekly (as became them), that I resolved to record the fact here, as a certain means of making it known to, and causing it to be reverenced by, many thousands of people. Reflecting upon this logic, and its universal application; remembering that when Fielding described Newgate,[5] the prison immediately ceased to exist; that when Smollett took Roderick Random to Bath,[6] that city instantly sank into the earth; that when Scott exercised his genius on Whitefriars,[7] it incontinently glided into the Thames; that an ancient place called Windsor was entirely destroyed in the reign of Queen Elizabeth by two Merry Wives of that town, acting under the direction of a person of the name of Shakespeare;[8] and that Mr. Pope, after having at a great expense completed his grotto at Twickenham, incautiously reduced it to ashes by writing a poem upon it[9]—I say, when I came to consider these things, I was inclined to make this preface the vehicle of my humble tribute of admiration to Sir

---

[1] *confessed that ... impeachment* I.e., confessed to the "crime" of having written about Jacob's Island.

[2] *vestry* Members of a parish who meet to conduct church and community business.

[3] *Sir Peter Laurie* British politician (1778–1861) and former Lord Mayor of London who had also served as an alderman (a position similar to that of city councilor).

[4] *13s. 4d.* 13 shillings and 4 pence.

[5] *Fielding ... Newgate* See Henry Fielding's novel *Amelia* (1751), in which Fielding, who had visited London's notorious Newgate Prison in the course of his work as a magistrate, describes the appalling conditions there.

[6] *Smollett ... Bath* See Tobias Smollett, *The Adventures of Roderick Random* (1748).

[7] *Whitefriars* London neighborhood described in Sir Walter Scott's novel *The Fortunes of Nigel* (1822).

[8] *an ancient place ... Shakespeare* See Shakespeare's *The Merry Wives of Windsor* (1602). Windsor is a town near London.

[9] *Mr. Pope ... upon it* See Alexander Pope, "On His Grotto at Twickenham" (written 1740).

Peter Laurie. But, I am restrained by a very painful consideration—by no less a consideration than the impossibility of *his* existence. For Sir Peter Laurie having been himself described in a book (as I understand he was, one Christmas time, for his conduct on the seat of Justice[1]), it is but too clear that there CAN be no such man!

Otherwise, I should have been quite sure of his concurrence in the following passage, written thirty years ago by my late lamented friend the Reverend Sydney Smith, that great master of wit, and terror of noodles;[2] but singularly applicable to the present occasion.

We have been thus particular in stating the case, that we may make an answer to those profligate persons who are always ready to fling an air of ridicule upon the labours of humanity, because they

are desirous that what they have not the virtue to do themselves, should appear to be foolish and romantic when done by others. A still higher degree of depravity than this, is to want[3] every sort of compassion for human misery, when it is accompanied by filth, poverty, and ignorance. To regulate humanity by the income tax, and to deem the bodily wretchedness and the dirty tears of the poor, a fit subject for pleasantry and contempt. We should have been loth to believe that such deep-seated and disgusting immorality existed in these days; but the notice of it is forced upon us.[4]

Devonshire Terrace, March, 1850.

—1850

---

[1] *as I ... of Justice* In the Christmas novella *The Chimes* (1844), Dickens satirized Laurie's oppressive policies toward the poor via the character of Alderman Cute.

[2] *noodles* Fools.

[3] *want* Lack.

[4] *We have ... upon us* See Reverend Sydney Smith, "Chimney Sweepers," *Edinburgh Review* (1819).

SHERIDAN LE FANU
1814 – 1873

As Henry James wrote in 1884, a novel by Sheridan Le Fanu was "customary ... for the bedside; the ideal reading in a country house for the hours after midnight." A formative influence on the British ghost story, Le Fanu was a best-selling author for most of the second half of the nineteenth century. He was also an accomplished periodical editor and a writer in many genres including poetry, historical romance, criticism, and journalism. It is his Gothic and sensation fiction, however, for which he is now mainly remembered. Some critics have derided his writing as uneven, churned out rapidly to profit from the popular press, but many have lauded his best work for its mastery of atmosphere and for its deep exploration of characters' psychological torment.

Joseph Thomas Sheridan Le Fanu was born in 1814 in Dublin and spent much of his childhood on the grounds of the nearby military school where his father was chaplain. His family had long belonged to the Protestant elite class that held the majority of political power in Ireland: descended from Huguenot (French Calvinist) nobility, Le Fanu was also related to the eighteenth-century playwright Richard Brinsley Sheridan. During Le Fanu's teenage years, the family moved to Abingdon, where his father was to serve as a Church of Ireland minister. The family began to experience financial troubles when the area's Catholic inhabitants, as part of a resistance campaign against Anglican dominance, refused to pay the legally mandated tithes. Le Fanu nonetheless received an aristocratic education: he was privately tutored as a child, and in 1833 went on to Trinity College, Dublin, where he was the president of the College Historical Society and received an Honors degree in Classics. He then studied law at the King's Inns, Dublin, though he would never fully commit to the law as an occupation. By 1838, a year before he would be called to the Irish bar, his writing career was already underway with the publication of his first short story, "The Ghost and the Bone-Setter," in the *Dublin University Magazine*.

Le Fanu published prolifically in the late 1830s through the 40s, with much of his short fiction linked via the character of Father Purcell, an eighteenth-century Catholic priest embroiled in various Gothic horrors in the ancient castles of Ireland. Collected after Le Fanu's death as *The Purcell Papers* (1880), these stories reflect the influence of earlier Gothic writers such as Ann Radcliffe as well as that of Irish folk tales. During this period, he also purchased full or partial ownership of several conservative newspapers, including *The Warder* and the *Statesman*. He also published his first novels, works of historical fiction in the tradition established by Walter Scott: *The Cock and Anchor* (1845) and *The Fortunes of Colonel Torlogh O'Brien* (1847), both set against the backdrop of past centuries of conflict between Ireland's Catholic and Protestant inhabitants. Though his supernatural short stories were popular, these novels were not as well received.

In 1843, Le Fanu married Susanna Bennett, a barrister's daughter; the couple would have four children. Prompted at least in part by the financial needs of his growing family, he turned away from fiction to focus on his journalistic career. The shape of his family changed again when, after several illnesses and periods of ill psychological health, Susanna died in 1858. Le Fanu was plagued by guilt and grief following her death, and his diaries reflect a period of intense religious and spiritual exploration. These events did not, however, bring an end to his writing career; on the contrary, in 1861 he purchased the *Dublin University Magazine* and began to act as its editor. In the same year, he recommended publishing fiction, beginning a prolific period that would produce his most critically acclaimed work, much of which possessed a darker tone that many scholars have attributed to his personal misfortune.

The *Dublin University Magazine* served as a vehicle for much of this fiction, including the serial publication of his next novel, *The House by the Churchyard* (1861–63), arguably the best-known of his novels set in Ireland and his only popularly successful historical romance. While he retained the interest in Irish history that informed the settings of his earlier work, after *The House by the Churchyard* Le Fanu would largely adapt his novels to the demands of the larger, more commercially viable English publishing market. English readers wanted, as one of his publishers phrased it, "the story of an English subject and in modern times," and Le Fanu attempted to make his work conform to this description. In many respects, however, his writing retained an Irish flavor, and some of his novels—including his most famous, *Uncle Silas* (1864)—adapted earlier fiction he had set in Ireland to English locations.

A sensational tale of murder, family intrigue, and inheritance, *Uncle Silas* (1864) also reflects Le Fanu's intense interest in the spiritualist writings of Emanuel Swedenborg (1688–1772). Swedenborg, a scientist-turned-theologian, believed himself to have received a divine revelation that constituted the "second coming" prophesied in the Bible, and he claimed to have been given the task of reforming Christianity according to this revelation. Among his tenets were the beliefs that the material plane of existence is a lesser reflection of the spiritual plane, and that it is possible for living people to perceive the spirits of the dead. *Uncle Silas* concludes with a direct statement of Swedenborgian philosophy: "This world is a parable—the habitation of symbols—the phantoms of spiritual things immortal shown in material shape. May the blessed second-sight be mine—to recognize under these beautiful forms of earth the ANGELS who wear them; for I am sure we may walk with them if we will, and hear them speak!" Other important works by Le Fanu, including the short story "Green Tea," also display Swedenborg's influence.

In addition to *Uncle Silas* and *The House by the Churchyard*, Le Fanu published more than ten novels in the last decade of his life, generally in the Gothic and sensation fiction genres. As a novelist, he became so strongly associated with sensation fiction that critics called him "the Irish Wilkie Collins" after the most popular writer in the genre, despite Le Fanu's own protests that he considered "sensation fiction" a "degrading term" he did not wish to see applied to his own work. His novels continued, however, to display the hallmarks of the genre: complex plots incorporating scandalous crime and intrigue, stock characters such as beautiful heiresses and evil uncles, and domestic settings with an often sinister aspect. Alongside these novels, he continued to publish short fiction—some in his own *Dublin University Magazine* and, increasingly, in more successful English periodicals; several of his stories, as well as two of his serialized novels, appeared in Charles Dickens's magazine *All the Year Round*.

Many of Le Fanu's best shorter periodical works were collected under the title *In a Glass Darkly* (1872), where they are united by their association with the character Martin Hesselius, a German doctor specializing in the occult. The volume's fictional editor claims to have found the stories in Hesselius's papers, and some of them include him as a narrator or character. While the doctor frequently posits a cause for the supernatural events in each story, the treatment of the supernatural is inconsistent. For example, in stories such as "Green Tea," in which the protagonist is haunted by a monkey who drives him to suicide, Hesselius's diagnosis is "hereditary suicidal mania," but it remains unclear whether the monkey should be considered a demon or a hallucination. "The Room in the Dragon Volant," while gruesome, involves no supernatural elements at all, but features a group of thieves who bury their victims alive. At the other extreme, the events of "Carmilla," an account of a young woman's complex relationship to a beautiful vampire, Hesselius endorses the reality of vampires in his afterword. *In a Glass Darkly* was met with a mixed critical reception: the *Saturday Review* dismissed its contents as "foolish and vulgar ghost stories," while the *Athenaeum* praised their Gothic effects: "Our author's pride is to make his reader's 'flesh creep,' and in this achievement we do not doubt his success."

When Le Fanu died in 1873, he was remembered for his commercial more than his literary achievements; one obituary placed him "in the foremost ranks of popular-novelists," observing that "[h]ardly a magazine exists to which he has not contributed the leading serial." Yet his work made an impression on avant-garde as well as popular literature: *The House by the Churchyard* is a recurring reference point in James Joyce's *Finnegans Wake* (1939). It is in the genre of horror and Gothic fiction, however, that Le Fanu has had the most lasting influence: his depiction of sexualized women vampires in "Carmilla," in particular, has set the tone for many later works of horror, from Bram Stoker's *Dracula* (1897) to films such as Danish director Carl Theodor Dreyer's classic *Vampyr* (1932) and the 1970 cult hit *The Vampire Lovers*. More generally, Le Fanu's body of work influenced later supernatural authors such as M.R. James, who in the 1930s championed Le Fanu's Gothic stories, writing that he "succeeds in inspiring a mysterious terror better than any other writer."

⌘ ⌘ ⌘

Carmilla

PROLOGUE

Upon a paper attached to the Narrative which follows, Doctor Hesselius has written a rather elaborate note, which he accompanies with a reference to his Essay on the strange subject which the MS.[1] illuminates.

This mysterious subject he treats in that Essay, with his usual learning and acumen, and with remarkable directness and condensation. It will form but one volume of the series of that extraordinary man's collected papers.

As I publish the case, in these volumes, simply to interest the "laity," I shall forestall the intelligent lady,

who relates it, in nothing;[2] and, after due consideration, I have determined, therefore, to abstain from presenting any précis[3] of the learned Doctor's reasoning, or extract from his statement on a subject which he describes as "involving, not improbably, some of the profoundest arcana of our dual existence, and its intermediates."

I was anxious, on discovering this paper, to re-open the correspondence commenced by Doctor Hesselius, so many years before, with a person so clever and careful as his informant seems to have been. Much to my regret, however, I found that she had died in the interval.

She, probably, could have added little to the Narrative which she communicates in the following pages, with, so far as I can pronounce, such a conscientious particularity.

---

[1] *MS.* Manuscript.

[2] *As I publish ... in nothing* Because I am publishing this woman's story for a general audience, I will add nothing to delay the beginning of her narrative.

[3] *précis* Summary.

Chapter I
An Early Fright

In Styria,[1] we, though by no means magnificent people, inhabit a castle, or schloss.[2] A small income, in that part of the world, goes a great way. Eight or nine hundred a year does wonders. Scantily enough ours would have answered among wealthy people at home. My father is English, and I bear an English name, although I never saw England. But here, in this lonely and primitive place, where everything is so marvellously cheap, I really don't see how ever so much more money would at all materially add to our comforts, or even luxuries.

My father was in the Austrian service, and retired upon a pension and his patrimony, and purchased this feudal residence, and the small estate on which it stands, a bargain.

Nothing can be more picturesque or solitary. It stands on a slight eminence in a forest. The road, very old and narrow, passes in front of its drawbridge, never raised in my time, and its moat, stocked with perch, and sailed over by many swans, and floating on its surface white fleets of water-lilies.

Over all this the schloss shows its many-windowed front; its towers, and its Gothic chapel.

The forest opens in an irregular and very picturesque glade before its gate, and at the right a steep Gothic bridge carries the road over a stream that winds in deep shadow through the wood.

I have said that this is a very lonely place. Judge whether I say truth. Looking from the hall door towards the road, the forest in which our castle stands extends fifteen miles to the right, and twelve to the left. The nearest inhabited village, is about seven of your English miles to the left. The nearest inhabited schloss of any historic associations, is that of old General Spielsdorf, nearly twenty miles away to the right.

I have said "the nearest inhabited village," because there is, only three miles westward, that is to say in the direction of General Spielsdorf's schloss, a ruined village, with its quaint little church, now roofless, in the aisle of which are the mouldering tombs of the proud family of Karnstein, now extinct, who once owned the equally desolate château which, in the thick of the forest, overlooks the silent ruins of the town.

Respecting the cause of the desertion of this striking and melancholy spot, there is a legend which I shall relate to you another time.

I must tell you now, how very small is the party who constitute the inhabitants of our castle. I don't include servants, or those dependents who occupy rooms in the buildings attached to the schloss. Listen, and wonder! My father, who is the kindest man on earth, but growing old; and I, at the date of my story, only nineteen. Eight years have passed since then. I and my father constituted the family at the schloss. My mother, a Styrian lady, died in my infancy, but I had a good-natured governess, who had been with me from, I might almost say, my infancy. I could not remember the time when her fat, benignant[3] face was not a familiar picture in my memory. This was Madame Perrodon, a native of Berne,[4] whose care and good nature in part supplied to me the loss of my mother, whom I do not even remember, so early I lost her. She made a third at our little dinner party. There was a fourth, Mademoiselle De Lafontaine, a lady such as you term, I believe, a "finishing governess." She spoke French and German, Madame Perrodon French and broken English, to which my father and I added English, which, partly to prevent its becoming a lost language among us, and partly from patriotic motives, we spoke every day. The consequence was a Babel,[5] at which strangers used to laugh, and which I shall make no attempt to reproduce in this narrative. And there were two or three young lady friends besides, pretty nearly of my own age, who were occasional visitors, for longer or shorter terms; and these visits I sometimes returned.

---

1 *Styria* Southern Austrian region known for its castles.

2 *schloss* German term for a castle or manor.

3 *benignant* Kind.

4 *Berne* Major city in Switzerland.

5 *Babel* Here, a mix of different languages. In Genesis 11.1–9, humans attempt to build the Tower of Babel, a tower that would reach heaven; God thwarts them by giving them different languages and scattering them around the earth.

These were our regular social resources; but of course there were chance visits from "neighbours" of only five or six leagues[1] distance. My life was, notwithstanding, rather a solitary one, I can assure you.

My gouvernantes[2] had just so much control over me as you might conjecture such sage persons would have in the case of a rather spoiled girl, whose only parent allowed her pretty nearly her own way in everything.

The first occurrence in my existence, which produced a terrible impression upon my mind, which, in fact, never has been effaced, was one of the very earliest incidents of my life which I can recollect. Some people will think it so trifling that it should not be recorded here. You will see, however, by-and-bye, why I mention it. The nursery, as it was called, though I had it all to myself, was a large room in the upper story of the castle, with a steep oak roof. I can't have been more than six years old, when one night I awoke, and looking round the room from my bed, failed to see the nursery-maid. Neither was my nurse there; and I thought myself alone. I was not frightened, for I was one of those happy children who are studiously kept in ignorance of ghost stories, of fairy tales, and of all such lore as makes us cover up our heads when the door creaks suddenly, or the flicker of an expiring candle makes the shadow of a bed-post dance upon the wall, nearer to our faces. I was vexed and insulted at finding myself, as I conceived, neglected, and I began to whimper, preparatory to a hearty bout of roaring; when to my surprise, I saw a solemn, but very pretty face looking at me from the side of the bed. It was that of a young lady who was kneeling, with her hands under the coverlet. I looked at her with a kind of pleased wonder, and ceased whimpering. She caressed me with her hands, and lay down beside me on the bed, and drew me towards her, smiling; I felt immediately delightfully soothed, and fell asleep again. I was wakened by a sensation as if two needles ran into my breast very deep at the same moment, and I cried loudly. The lady started back, with her eyes fixed on me,

and then slipped down upon the floor, and, as I thought, hid herself under the bed.

I was now for the first time frightened, and I yelled with all my might and main. Nurse, nursery-maid, housekeeper, all came running in, and hearing my story, they made light of it, soothing me all they could meanwhile. But, child as I was, I could perceive that their faces were pale with an unwonted look of anxiety, and I saw them look under the bed, and about the room, and peep under tables and pluck open cupboards; and the housekeeper whispered to the nurse: "Lay your hand along that hollow in the bed; some one did lie there, so sure as you did not; the place is still warm."

I remember the nursery-maid petting me, and all three examining my chest, where I told them I felt the puncture, and pronouncing that there was no sign visible that any such thing had happened to me.

The housekeeper and the two other servants who were in charge of the nursery, remained sitting up all night; and from that time a servant always sat up in the nursery until I was about fourteen.

I was very nervous for a long time after this. A doctor was called in, he was pallid[3] and elderly. How well I remember his long saturnine[4] face, slightly pitted with small-pox, and his chesnut wig. For a good while, every second day, he came and gave me medicine, which of course I hated.

The morning after I saw this apparition I was in a state of terror, and could not bear to be left alone, daylight though it was, for a moment.

I remember my father coming up and standing at the bedside, and talking cheerfully, and asking the nurse a number of questions, and laughing very heartily at one of the answers; and patting me on the shoulder, and kissing me, and telling me not to be frightened, that it was nothing but a dream and could not hurt me.

But I was not comforted, for I knew the visit of the strange woman was not a dream; and I was awfully frightened.

I was a little consoled by the nursery-maid's assuring me that it was she who had come and looked at me, and

---

[1] *five or six leagues*   About fifteen to eighteen miles; one league is about three miles.

[2] *gouvernantes*   Governesses.

[3] *pallid*   Pale or sickly.

[4] *saturnine*   Somber or gloomy.

lain down beside me in the bed, and that I must have been half-dreaming not to have known her face. But this, though supported by the nurse, did not quite satisfy me.

I remember, in the course of that day, a venerable old man, in a black cassock,[1] coming into the room with the nurse and housekeeper, and talking a little to them, and very kindly to me; his face was very sweet and gentle, and he told me they were going to pray, and joined my hands together, and desired me to say, softly, while they were praying, "Lord hear all good prayers for us, for Jesus' sake." I think these were the very words, for I often repeated them to myself, and my nurse used for years to make me say them in my prayers.

I remember so well the thoughtful sweet face of that white-haired old man, in his black cassock, as he stood in that rude,[2] lofty, brown room, with the clumsy furniture of a fashion three hundred years old, about him, and the scanty light entering its shadowy atmosphere through the small lattice. He kneeled, and the three women with him, and he prayed aloud with an earnest quavering voice for, what appeared to me, a long time. I forget all my life preceding that event, and for some time after it is all obscure also, but the scenes I have just described stand out vivid as the isolated pictures of the phantasmagoria[3] surrounded by darkness.

CHAPTER 2
A GUEST

I am now going to tell you something so strange that it will require all your faith in my veracity to believe my story. It is not only true, nevertheless, but truth of which I have been an eye-witness.

It was a sweet summer evening, and my father asked me, as he sometimes did, to take a little ramble with him along that beautiful forest vista which I have mentioned as lying in front of the schloss.

"General Spielsdorf cannot come to us so soon as I had hoped," said my father, as we pursued our walk.

He was to have paid us a visit of some weeks, and we had expected his arrival next day. He was to have brought with him a young lady, his niece and ward, Mademoiselle Rheinfeldt, whom I had never seen, but whom I had heard described as a very charming girl, and in whose society I had promised myself many happy days. I was more disappointed than a young lady living in a town, or a bustling neighbourhood can possibly imagine. This visit, and the new acquaintance it promised, had furnished my day dream for many weeks.

"And how soon does he come?" I asked.

"Not till autumn. Not for two months, I dare say," he answered. "And I am very glad now, dear, that you never knew Mademoiselle Rheinfeldt."

"And why?" I asked, both mortified and curious.

"Because the poor young lady is dead," he replied. "I quite forgot I had not told you, but you were not in the room when I received the General's letter this evening."

I was very much shocked. General Spielsdorf had mentioned in his first letter, six or seven weeks before, that she was not so well as he would wish her, but there was nothing to suggest the remotest suspicion of danger.

"Here is the General's letter," he said, handing it to me. "I am afraid he is in great affliction; the letter appears to me to have been written very nearly in distraction."

We sat down on a rude bench, under a group of magnificent lime-trees. The sun was setting with all its melancholy splendour behind the sylvan[4] horizon, and the stream that flows beside our home, and passes under the steep old bridge I have mentioned, wound through many a group of noble trees, almost at our feet, reflecting in its current the fading crimson of the sky. General Spielsdorf's letter was so extraordinary, so vehement, and in some places so self-contradictory, that I read it twice over—the second time aloud to my father—and was still unable to account for it, except by supposing that grief had unsettled his mind.

It said "I have lost my darling daughter, for as such I loved her. During the last days of dear Bertha's illness I was not able to write to you. Before then I had no idea

---

[1] *cassock*   Long garment worn by a priest.

[2] *rude*   Rough and simple.

[3] *phantasmagoria*   Dream-like succession of images, usually odd or unsettling.

[4] *sylvan*   Wooded.

of her danger. I have lost her, and now learn all, too late. She died in the peace of innocence, and in the glorious hope of a blessed futurity.[1] The fiend who betrayed our infatuated[2] hospitality has done it all. I thought I was receiving into my house innocence, gaiety, a charming companion for my lost Bertha. Heavens! what a fool have I been! I thank God my child died without a suspicion of the cause of her sufferings. She is gone without so much as conjecturing the nature of her illness, and the accursed passion of the agent of all this misery. I devote my remaining days to tracking and extinguishing a monster. I am told I may hope to accomplish my righteous and merciful purpose. At present there is scarcely a gleam of light to guide me. I curse my conceited incredulity,[3] my despicable affectation of superiority, my blindness, my obstinacy—all—too late. I cannot write or talk collectedly now. I am distracted. So soon as I shall have a little recovered, I mean to devote myself for a time to enquiry, which may possibly lead me as far as Vienna. Some time in the autumn, two months hence, or earlier if I live, I will see you—that is, if you permit me; I will then tell you all that I scarce dare put upon paper now. Farewell. Pray for me, dear friend."

In these terms ended this strange letter. Though I had never seen Bertha Rheinfeldt my eyes filled with tears at the sudden intelligence; I was startled, as well as profoundly disappointed.

The sun had now set, and it was twilight by the time I had returned the General's letter to my father.

It was a soft clear evening, and we loitered, speculating upon the possible meanings of the violent and incoherent sentences which I had just been reading. We had nearly a mile to walk before reaching the road that passes the schloss in front, and by that time the moon was shining brilliantly. At the drawbridge we met Madame Perrodon and Mademoiselle De Lafontaine, who had come out, without their bonnets, to enjoy the exquisite moonlight.

We heard their voices gabbling in animated dialogue as we approached. We joined them at the drawbridge, and turned about to admire with them the beautiful scene.

The glade through which we had just walked lay before us. At our left the narrow road wound away under clumps of lordly trees, and was lost to sight amid the thickening forest. At the right the same road crosses the steep and picturesque bridge, near which stands a ruined tower which once guarded that pass; and beyond the bridge an abrupt eminence rises, covered with trees, and showing in the shadows some grey ivy-clustered rocks.

Over the sward[4] and low grounds a thin film of mist was stealing, like smoke, marking the distances with a transparent veil; and here and there we could see the river faintly flashing in the moonlight.

No softer, sweeter scene could be imagined. The news I had just heard made it melancholy; but nothing could disturb its character of profound serenity, and the enchanted glory and vagueness of the prospect.

My father, who enjoyed the picturesque, and I, stood looking in silence over the expanse beneath us. The two good governesses, standing a little way behind us, discoursed upon the scene, and were eloquent upon the moon.

Madame Perrodon was fat, middle-aged, and romantic, and talked and sighed poetically. Mademoiselle De Lafontaine—in right of her father, who was a German, assumed to be psychological, metaphysical, and something of a mystic—now declared that when the moon shone with a light so intense it was well known that it indicated a special spiritual activity. The effect of the full moon in such a state of brilliancy was manifold. It acted on dreams, it acted on lunacy, it acted on nervous people; it had marvellous physical influences connected with life. Mademoiselle related that her cousin, who was mate of a merchant ship, having taken a nap on deck on such a night, lying on his back, with his face full in the light of the moon, had wakened, after a dream of an old woman clawing him by the cheek, with his features horribly drawn to one side; and his

---

[1] *in the … blessed futurity* I.e., in hope of heaven.

[2] *infatuated* Foolish, excessive.

[3] *incredulity* Unwillingness to believe.

[4] *sward* Grassy area.

countenance[1] had never quite recovered its equilibrium.

"The moon, this night," she said, "is full of odylic and magnetic influence[2]—and see, when you look behind you at the front of the schloss, how all its windows flash and twinkle with that silvery splendour, as if unseen hands had lighted up the rooms to receive fairy guests."

There are indolent states of the spirits in which, indisposed to talk ourselves, the talk of others is pleasant to our listless ears; and I gazed on, pleased with the tinkle of the ladies' conversation.

"I have got into one of my moping moods to-night," said my father, after a silence, and quoting Shakespeare, whom, by way of keeping up our English, he used to read aloud, he said:

"In truth I know not why I am so sad:
It wearies me; you say it wearies you;
But how I got it—came by it."[3]

"I forget the rest. But I feel as if some great misfortune were hanging over us. I suppose the poor General's afflicted letter has had something to do with it."

At this moment the unwonted[4] sound of carriage wheels and many hoofs upon the road, arrested our attention.

They seemed to be approaching from the high ground overlooking the bridge, and very soon the equipage[5] emerged from that point. Two horsemen first crossed the bridge, then came a carriage drawn by four horses, and two men rode behind.

It seemed to be the travelling carriage of a person of rank; and we were all immediately absorbed in watching that very unusual spectacle. It became, in a few moments, greatly more interesting, for just as the carriage had passed the summit of the steep bridge, one of the leaders, taking fright, communicated his panic to the rest, and after a plunge or two, the whole team broke into a wild gallop together, and dashing between the horsemen who rode in front, came thundering along the road towards us with the speed of a hurricane.

The excitement of the scene was made more painful by the clear, long-drawn screams of a female voice from the carriage window.

We all advanced in curiosity and horror; my father in silence, the rest with various ejaculations[6] of terror.

Our suspense did not last long. Just before you reach the castle drawbridge, on the route they were coming, there stands by the roadside a magnificent lime-tree, on the other stands an ancient stone cross, at sight of which the horses, now going at a pace that was perfectly frightful, swerved so as to bring the wheel over the projecting roots of the tree.

I knew what was coming. I covered my eyes, unable to see it out, and turned my head away; at the same moment I heard a cry from my lady-friends, who had gone on a little.

Curiosity opened my eyes, and I saw a scene of utter confusion. Two of the horses were on the ground, the carriage lay upon its side with two wheels in the air; the men were busy removing the traces,[7] and a lady, with a commanding air and figure had got out, and stood with clasped hands, raising the handkerchief that was in them every now and then to her eyes. Through the carriage door was now lifted a young lady, who appeared to be lifeless. My dear old father was already beside the elder lady, with his hat in his hand, evidently tendering his aid and the resources of his schloss. The lady did not appear to hear him, or to have eyes for anything but the slender girl who was being placed against the slope of the bank.

I approached; the young lady was apparently stunned, but she was certainly not dead. My father, who piqued[8] himself on being something of a physician, had just had his fingers to her wrist and assured the lady,

---

[1] *countenance* Facial appearance.

[2] *odylic and magnetic influence* Reference to the ideas of German pseudoscientist Baron Carl von Reichenbach (1788–1869), who argued for the existence of an "odic force" related to electromagnetism. Some people, he thought, could see the auras produced by the force, which was supposed to have a range of properties including hypnotic effects.

[3] *In truth ... came by it* Opening lines of Shakespeare's *The Merchant of Venice* (1605).

[4] *unwonted* Unusual or unexpected.

[5] *equipage* Carriage, horses, and attendants.

---

[6] *ejaculations* Spontaneous expressions of emotion.

[7] *traces* Straps attaching the horses to the carriage.

[8] *piqued* Prided.

who declared herself her mother, that her pulse, though faint and irregular, was undoubtedly still distinguishable. The lady clasped her hands and looked upward, as if in a momentary transport[1] of gratitude; but immediately she broke out again in that theatrical way which is, I believe, natural to some people.

She was what is called a fine looking woman for her time of life, and must have been handsome; she was tall, but not thin, and dressed in black velvet, and looked rather pale, but with a proud and commanding countenance, though now agitated strangely.

"Was ever being so born to calamity?" I heard her say, with clasped hands, as I came up. "Here am I, on a journey of life and death, in prosecuting[2] which to lose an hour is possibly to lose all. My child will not have recovered sufficiently to resume her route for who can say how long. I must leave her; I cannot, dare not, delay. How far on, sir, can you tell, is the nearest village? I must leave her there; and shall not see my darling, or even hear of her till my return, three months hence."

I plucked my father by the coat, and whispered earnestly in his ear: "Oh! papa, pray[3] ask her to let her stay with us—it would be so delightful. Do, pray."

"If Madame will entrust her child to the care of my daughter, and of her good gouvernante, Madame Perrodon, and permit her to remain as our guest, under my charge, until her return, it will confer a distinction[4] and an obligation upon us, and we shall treat her with all the care and devotion which so sacred a trust deserves."

"I cannot do that, sir, it would be to task your kindness and chivalry too cruelly," said the lady, distractedly.

"It would, on the contrary, be to confer on us a very great kindness at the moment when we most need it. My daughter has just been disappointed by a cruel misfortune, in a visit from which she had long anticipated a great deal of happiness. If you confide this young lady to our care it will be her best consolation. The nearest village on your route is distant, and affords no such inn as you could think of placing your daughter at; you cannot allow her to continue her journey for any considerable distance without danger. If, as you say, you cannot suspend your journey, you must part with her to-night, and nowhere could you do so with more honest assurances of care and tenderness than here."

There was something in this lady's air and appearance so distinguished, and even imposing, and in her manner so engaging, as to impress one, quite apart from the dignity of her equipage, with a conviction that she was a person of consequence.

By this time the carriage was replaced in its upright position, and the horses, quite tractable, in the traces again.

The lady threw on her daughter a glance which I fancied was not quite so affectionate as one might have anticipated from the beginning of the scene; then she beckoned slightly to my father, and withdrew two or three steps with him out of hearing; and talked to him with a fixed and stern countenance, not at all like that with which she had hitherto spoken.

I was filled with wonder that my father did not seem to perceive the change, and also unspeakably curious to learn what it could be that she was speaking, almost in his ear, with so much earnestness and rapidity.

Two or three minutes at most I think she remained thus employed, then she turned, and a few steps brought her to where her daughter lay, supported by Madame Perrodon. She kneeled beside her for a moment and whispered, as Madame supposed, a little benediction[5] in her ear; then hastily kissing her she stepped into her carriage, the door was closed, the footmen in stately liveries jumped up behind, the outriders spurred on, the postillions[6] cracked their whips, the horses plunged and broke suddenly into a furious canter that threatened soon again to become a gallop, and the carriage whirled away, followed at the same rapid pace by the two horsemen in the rear.

---

[1] *transport*   State of overwhelming emotion.

[2] *prosecuting*   Completing.

[3] *pray*   Please.

[4] *distinction*   Honor.

[5] *benediction*   Blessing or prayer for divine help.

[6] *liveries*   Uniforms worn by servants; *outriders*   Servants who ride beside the carriage; *postillions*   Servants who ride on the horses that pull a carriage.

CHAPTER 3
WE COMPARE NOTES

We followed the cortège[1] with our eyes until it was swiftly lost to sight in the misty wood; and the very sound of the hoofs and the wheels died away in the silent night air.

Nothing remained to assure us that the adventure had not been an illusion of a moment but the young lady, who just at that moment opened her eyes. I could not see, for her face was turned from me, but she raised her head, evidently looking about her, and I heard a very sweet voice ask complainingly, "Where is mamma?"

Our good Madame Perrodon answered tenderly, and added some comfortable assurances.

I then heard her ask:

"Where am I? What is this place?" and after that she said, "I don't see the carriage; and Matska, where is she?"

Madame answered all her questions in so far as she understood them; and gradually the young lady remembered how the misadventure came about, and was glad to hear that no one in, or in attendance on, the carriage was hurt; and on learning that her mamma had left her here, till her return in about three months, she wept.

I was going to add my consolations to those of Madame Perrodon when Mademoiselle De Lafontaine placed her hand upon my arm, saying:

"Don't approach, one at a time is as much as she can at present converse with; a very little excitement would possibly overpower her now."

As soon as she is comfortably in bed, I thought, I will run up to her room and see her.

My father in the meantime had sent a servant on horseback for the physician, who lived about two leagues away; and a bedroom was being prepared for the young lady's reception.

The stranger now rose, and leaning on Madame's arm, walked slowly over the drawbridge and into the castle gate.

In the hall, servants waited to receive her, and she was conducted forthwith to her room.

The room we usually sat in as our drawing-room is long, having four windows, that looked over the moat and drawbridge, upon the forest scene I have just described.

It is furnished in old carved oak, with large carved cabinets, and the chairs are cushioned with crimson Utrecht velvet.[2] The walls are covered with tapestry, and surrounded with great gold frames, the figures being as large as life, in ancient and very curious costume, and the subjects represented are hunting, hawking, and generally festive. It is not too stately to be extremely comfortable; and here we had our tea, for with his usual patriotic leanings he insisted that the national beverage should make its appearance regularly with our coffee and chocolate.

We sat here this night, and with candles lighted, were talking over the adventure of the evening.

Madame Perrodon and Mademoiselle De Lafontaine were both of our party. The young stranger had hardly lain down in her bed when she sank into a deep sleep; and those ladies had left her in the care of a servant.

"How do you like our guest?" I asked, as soon as Madame entered. "Tell me all about her?"

"I like her extremely," answered Madame, "she is, I almost think, the prettiest creature I ever saw; about your age, and so gentle and nice."

"She is absolutely beautiful," threw in Mademoiselle, who had peeped for a moment into the stranger's room.

"And such a sweet voice!" added Madame Perrodon.

"Did you remark a woman in the carriage, after it was set up again, who did not get out," inquired Mademoiselle, "but only looked from the window?"

"No, we had not seen her."

Then she described a hideous black woman, with a sort of coloured turban on her head, who was gazing all the time from the carriage window, nodding and grinning derisively towards the ladies, with gleaming eyes and large white eye-balls, and her teeth set as if in fury.

"Did you remark what an ill-looking pack of men the servants were?" asked Madame.

"Yes," said my father, who had just come in, "ugly,

---

[1] *cortège*   Procession, especially one that is grand or dignified.

[2] *Utrecht velvet*   Expensive, thick velvet stamped with patterns.

hang-dog[1] looking fellows, as ever I beheld in my life. I hope they mayn't rob the poor lady in the forest. They are clever rogues, however; they got everything to rights in a minute."

"I dare say they are worn out with too long travelling," said Madame. "Besides looking wicked, their faces were so strangely lean, and dark, and sullen. I am very curious, I own; but I dare say the young lady will tell us all about it to-morrow, if she is sufficiently recovered."

"I don't think she will," said my father, with a mysterious smile, and a little nod of his head, as if he knew more about it than he cared to tell us.

This made me all the more inquisitive as to what had passed between him and the lady in the black velvet, in the brief but earnest interview that had immediately preceded her departure.

We were scarcely alone, when I entreated him to tell me. He did not need much pressing.

"There is no particular reason why I should not tell you. She expressed a reluctance to trouble us with the care of her daughter, saying she was in delicate health and nervous, but not subject to any kind of seizure—she volunteered that—nor to any illusion; being, in fact, perfectly sane."

"How very odd to say all that!" I interpolated. "It was so unnecessary."

"At all events it was said," he laughed, "and as you wish to know all that passed, which was indeed very little, I tell you. She then said, 'I am making a long journey of vital importance—she emphasized the word—rapid and secret; I shall return for my child in three months; in the meantime, she will be silent as to who we are, whence we come, and whither we are travelling.' That is all she said. She spoke very pure French. When she said the word 'secret,' she paused for a few seconds, looking sternly, her eyes fixed on mine. I fancy she makes a great point of that. You saw how quickly she was gone. I hope I have not done a very foolish thing, in taking charge of the young lady."

For my part, I was delighted. I was longing to see and talk to her; and only waiting till the doctor should give me leave. You, who live in towns, can have no idea

how great an event the introduction of a new friend is, in such a solitude as surrounded us.

The doctor did not arrive till nearly one o'clock; but I could no more have gone to my bed and slept, than I could have overtaken, on foot, the carriage in which the princess in black velvet had driven away.

When the physician came down to the drawing-room, it was to report very favourably upon his patient. She was now sitting up, her pulse quite regular, apparently perfectly well. She had sustained no injury, and the little shock to her nerves had passed away quite harmlessly. There could be no harm certainly in my seeing her, if we both wished it; and, with this permission, I sent, forthwith, to know whether she would allow me to visit her for a few minutes in her room.

The servant returned immediately to say that she desired nothing more.

You may be sure I was not long in availing myself of this permission.

Our visitor lay in one of the handsomest rooms in the schloss. It was, perhaps, a little stately. There was a sombre piece of tapestry opposite the foot of the bed, representing Cleopatra with the asps to her bosom;[2] and other solemn classic scenes were displayed, a little faded, upon the other walls. But there was gold carving, and rich and varied colour enough in the other decorations of the room, to more than redeem the gloom of the old tapestry.

There were candles at the bed side. She was sitting up; her slender pretty figure enveloped in the soft silk dressing gown, embroidered with flowers, and lined with thick quilted silk, which her mother had thrown over her feet as she lay upon the ground.

What was it that, as I reached the bed-side and had just begun my little greeting, struck me dumb[3] in a moment, and made me recoil a step or two from before her? I will tell you.

I saw the very face which had visited me in my childhood at night, which remained so fixed in my

---

[1] *hang-dog* Disreputable.

[2] *Cleopatra ... bosom* According to legend, Egyptian Pharaoh Cleopatra VII (69–30 BCE) died by suicide, using poisonous snakes whom she provoked to bite her.

[3] *dumb* Unable to speak.

memory, and on which I had for so many years so often ruminated with horror, when no one suspected of what I was thinking.

It was pretty, even beautiful; and when I first beheld it, wore the same melancholy expression.

But this almost instantly lighted into a strange fixed smile of recognition.

There was a silence of fully a minute, and then at length she spoke; I could not.

"How wonderful!" she exclaimed, "Twelve years ago, I saw your face in a dream, and it has haunted me ever since."

"Wonderful indeed!" I repeated, overcoming with an effort the horror that had for a time suspended my utterances. "Twelve years ago, in vision or reality, I certainly saw you. I could not forget your face. It has remained before my eyes ever since."

Her smile had softened. Whatever I had fancied strange in it, was gone, and it and her dimpling cheeks were now delightfully pretty and intelligent.

I felt reassured, and continued more in the vein which hospitality indicated, to bid her welcome, and to tell her how much pleasure her accidental arrival had given us all, and especially what a happiness it was to me.

I took her hand as I spoke. I was a little shy, as lonely people are, but the situation made me eloquent, and even bold. She pressed my hand, she laid hers upon it, and her eyes glowed, as, looking hastily into mine, she smiled again, and blushed.

She answered my welcome very prettily. I sat down beside her, still wondering; and she said:

"I must tell you my vision about you; it is so very strange that you and I should have had, each of the other so vivid a dream, that each should have seen, I you and you me, looking as we do now, when of course we both were mere children. I was a child, about six years old, and I awoke from a confused and troubled dream, and found myself in a room, unlike my nursery, wainscoted clumsily in some dark wood, and with cupboards and bedsteads, and chairs, and benches placed about it. The beds were, I thought, all empty, and the room itself without anyone but myself in it; and I, after looking about me for some time, and admiring especially an iron candlestick, with two branches, which I should certainly know again, crept under one of the beds to reach the window; but as I got from under the bed, I heard some one crying; and looking up, while I was still upon my knees, I saw you—most assuredly you—as I see you now; a beautiful young lady, with golden hair and large blue eyes, and lips—your lips—you, as you are here. Your looks won me; I climbed on the bed and put my arms about you, and I think we both fell asleep. I was aroused by a scream; you were sitting up screaming. I was frightened, and slipped down upon the ground, and, it seemed to me, lost consciousness for a moment; and when I came to myself, I was again in my nursery at home. Your face I have never forgotten since. I could not be misled by mere resemblance. You are the lady whom I then saw."

It was now my turn to relate my corresponding vision, which I did, to the undisguised wonder of my new acquaintance.

"I don't know which should be most afraid of the other," she said, again smiling—"If you were less pretty I think I should be very much afraid of you, but being as you are, and you and I both so young, I feel only that I have made your acquaintance twelve years ago, and have already a right to your intimacy; at all events it does seem as if we were destined, from our earliest childhood, to be friends. I wonder whether you feel as strangely drawn towards me as I do to you; I have never had a friend—shall I find one now?" She sighed, and her fine dark eyes gazed passionately on me.

Now the truth is, I felt rather unaccountably towards the beautiful stranger. I did feel, as she said, "drawn towards her," but there was also something of repulsion. In this ambiguous feeling, however, the sense of attraction immensely prevailed. She interested and won me; she was so beautiful and so indescribably engaging.

I perceived now something of langour and exhaustion stealing over her, and hastened to bid her good night.

"The doctor thinks," I added, "that you ought to have a maid to sit up with you to-night; one of ours is waiting, and you will find her a very useful and quiet creature."

"How kind of you, but I could not sleep, I never could with an attendant in the room. I shan't require any assistance—and, shall I confess my weakness, I am haunted with a terror of robbers. Our house was robbed once, and two servants murdered, so I always lock my door. It has become a habit—and you look so kind I know you will forgive me. I see there is a key in the lock."

She held me close in her pretty arms for a moment and whispered in my ear, "Good night, darling, it is very hard to part with you, but good-night; to-morrow, but not early, I shall see you again."

She sank back on the pillow with a sigh, and her fine eyes followed me with a fond and melancholy gaze, and she murmured again "Good night, dear friend."

Young people like, and even love, on impulse. I was flattered by the evident, though as yet undeserved, fondness she showed me. I liked the confidence with which she at once received me. She was determined that we should be very near friends.

Next day came and we met again. I was delighted with my companion; that is to say, in many respects.

Her looks lost nothing in daylight—she was certainly the most beautiful creature I had ever seen, and the unpleasant remembrance of the face presented in my early dream, had lost the effect of the first unexpected recognition.

She confessed that she had experienced a similar shock on seeing me, and precisely the same faint antipathy that had mingled with my admiration of her. We now laughed together over our momentary horrors.

CHAPTER 4
HER HABITS—A SAUNTER

I told you that I was charmed with her in most particulars.

There were some that did not please me so well.

She was above the middle height of women. I shall begin by describing her. She was slender, and wonderfully graceful. Except that her movements were languid—very languid—indeed, there was nothing in her appearance to indicate an invalid. Her complexion was rich and brilliant; her features were small and beautifully formed; her eyes large, dark, and lustrous; her hair was quite wonderful, I never saw hair so magnificently thick and long when it was down about her shoulders; I have often placed my hands under it, and laughed with wonder at its weight. It was exquisitely fine and soft, and in colour a rich very dark brown, with something of gold. I loved to let it down, tumbling with its own weight, as, in her room, she lay back in her chair talking, in her sweet low voice, I used to fold and braid it, and spread it out and play with it. Heavens! If I had but known all!

I said there were particulars which did not please me. I have told you that her confidence won me the first night I saw her; but I found that she exercised with respect to herself, her mother, her history, everything in fact connected with her life, plans, and people, an ever wakeful reserve. I dare say I was unreasonable, perhaps I was wrong; I dare say I ought to have respected the solemn injunction laid upon my father by the stately lady in black velvet. But curiosity is a restless and unscrupulous passion, and no one girl can endure, with patience, that hers should be baffled by another. What harm could it do anyone to tell me what I so ardently desired to know? Had she no trust in my good sense or honour? Why would she not believe me when I assured her, so solemnly, that I would not divulge one syllable of what she told me to any mortal breathing.

There was a coldness, it seemed to me, beyond her years, in her smiling melancholy persistent refusal to afford me the least ray of light.

I cannot say we quarrelled upon this point, for she would not quarrel upon any. It was, of course, very unfair of me to press her, very ill-bred, but I really could not help it; and I might just as well have let it alone.

What she did tell me amounted, in my unconscionable[1] estimation—to nothing.

It was all summed up in three very vague disclosures:

First.—Her name was Carmilla.

Second.—Her family was very ancient and noble.

Third.—Her home lay in the direction of the west.

---

[1] *unconscionable* Unreasonable.

She would not tell me the name of her family, nor their armorial bearings,[1] nor the name of their estate, nor even that of the country they lived in.

You are not to suppose that I worried her incessantly on these subjects. I watched opportunity, and rather insinuated than urged my inquiries. Once or twice, indeed, I did attack her more directly. But no matter what my tactics, utter failure was invariably the result. Reproaches and caresses were all lost upon her. But I must add this, that her evasion was conducted with so pretty a melancholy and deprecation,[2] with so many, and even passionate declarations of her liking for me, and trust in my honour, and with so many promises that I should at last know all, that I could not find it in my heart long to be offended with her.

She used to place her pretty arms about my neck, draw me to her, and laying her cheek to mine, murmur with her lips near my ear, "Dearest, your little heart is wounded; think me not cruel because I obey the irresistible law of my strength and weakness; if your dear heart is wounded, my wild heart bleeds with yours. In the rapture of my enormous humiliation I live in your warm life, and you shall die—die, sweetly die—into mine. I cannot help it; as I draw near to you, you, in your turn, will draw near to others, and learn the rapture of that cruelty, which yet is love; so, for a while, seek to know no more of me and mine, but trust me with all your loving spirit."

And when she had spoken such a rhapsody,[3] she would press me more closely in her trembling embrace, and her lips in soft kisses gently glow upon my cheek.

Her agitations and her language were unintelligible to me.

From these foolish embraces, which were not of very frequent occurrence, I must allow, I used to wish to extricate myself; but my energies seemed to fail me. Her murmured words sounded like a lullaby in my ear, and soothed my resistance into a trance, from which I only seemed to recover myself when she withdrew her arms.

In these mysterious moods I did not like her. I experienced a strange tumultuous excitement that was pleasurable, ever and anon,[4] mingled with a vague sense of fear and disgust. I had no distinct thoughts about her while such scenes lasted, but I was conscious of a love growing into adoration, and also of abhorrence. This I know is paradox, but I can make no other attempt to explain the feeling.

I now write, after an interval of more than ten years, with a trembling hand, with a confused and horrible recollection of certain occurrences and situations, in the ordeal through which I was unconsciously passing; though with a vivid and very sharp remembrance of the main current of my story. But, I suspect, in all lives there are certain emotional scenes, those in which our passions have been most wildly and terribly roused, that are of all others the most vaguely and dimly remembered.

Sometimes after an hour of apathy, my strange and beautiful companion would take my hand and hold it with a fond pressure, renewed again and again; blushing softly, gazing in my face with languid and burning eyes, and breathing so fast that her dress rose and fell with the tumultuous respiration. It was like the ardour of a lover; it embarrassed me; it was hateful and yet over-powering; and with gloating eyes she drew me to her, and her hot lips travelled along my cheek in kisses; and she would whisper, almost in sobs, "You are mine, you shall be mine, you and I are one for ever." Then she has thrown herself back in her chair, with her small hands over her eyes, leaving me trembling.

"Are we related," I used to ask; "what can you mean by all this? I remind you perhaps of some one whom you love; but you must not, I hate it; I don't know you—I don't know myself when you look so and talk so."

She used to sigh at my vehemence, then turn away and drop my hand.

Respecting these very extraordinary manifestations I strove in vain to form any satisfactory theory—I could not refer them to affectation or trick. It was unmistakably the momentary breaking out of suppressed instinct

---

[1] *armorial bearings*   Heraldry or coat of arms.

[2] *deprecation*   Heartfelt expressions of opposition.

[3] *rhapsody*   Intense display of emotion.

[4] *ever and anon*   Periodically.

and emotion. Was she, notwithstanding her mother's volunteered denial, subject to brief visitations of insanity; or was there here a disguise and a romance? I had read in old story books of such things. What if a boyish lover had found his way into the house, and sought to prosecute his suit in masquerade, with the assistance of a clever old adventuress? But there were many things against this hypothesis, highly interesting as it was to my vanity.

I could boast of no little attentions such as masculine gallantry delights to offer. Between these passionate moments there were long intervals of common-place, of gaiety, of brooding melancholy, during which, except that I detected her eyes so full of melancholy fire, following me, at times I might have been as nothing to her. Except in these brief periods of mysterious excitement her ways were girlish; and there was always a languor about her, quite incompatible with a masculine system in a state of health.

In some respects her habits were odd. Perhaps not so singular in the opinion of a town lady like you, as they appeared to us rustic people. She used to come down very late, generally not till one o'clock, she would then take a cup of chocolate, but eat nothing; we then went out for a walk, which was a mere saunter, and she seemed, almost immediately, exhausted, and either returned to the schloss or sat on one of the benches that were placed, here and there, among the trees. This was a bodily languor in which her mind did not sympathise. She was always an animated talker, and very intelligent.

She sometimes alluded for a moment to her own home, or mentioned an adventure or situation, or an early recollection, which indicated a people of strange manners, and described customs of which we knew nothing. I gathered from these chance hints that her native country was much more remote than I had at first fancied.

As we sat thus one afternoon under the trees a funeral passed us by. It was that of a pretty young girl, whom I had often seen, the daughter of one of the rangers of the forest. The poor man was walking behind the coffin of his darling; she was his only child, and he looked quite heartbroken. Peasants walking two-and-two came behind, they were singing a funeral hymn.

I rose to mark my respect as they passed, and joined in the hymn they were very sweetly singing.

My companion shook me a little roughly, and I turned surprised.

She said brusquely, "Don't you perceive how discordant that is?"

"I think it very sweet, on the contrary," I answered, vexed at the interruption, and very uncomfortable, lest the people who composed the little procession should observe and resent what was passing.

I resumed, therefore, instantly, and was again interrupted. "You pierce my ears," said Carmilla, almost angrily, and stopping her ears with her tiny fingers. "Besides, how can you tell that your religion and mine are the same; your forms wound me, and I hate funerals. What a fuss! Why you must die—everyone must die; and all are happier when they do. Come home."

"My father has gone on with the clergyman to the churchyard. I thought you knew she was to be buried to-day."

"She? I don't trouble my head about peasants. I don't know who she is," answered Carmilla, with a flash from her fine eyes.

"She is the poor girl who fancied she saw a ghost a fortnight[1] ago, and has been dying ever since, till yesterday, when she expired."

"Tell me nothing about ghosts. I shan't sleep to-night, if you do."

"I hope there is no plague or fever coming; all this looks very like it," I continued. "The swineherd's young wife died only a week ago, and she thought something seized her by the throat as she lay in her bed, and nearly strangled her. Papa says such horrible fancies do accompany some forms of fever. She was quite well the day before. She sank afterwards, and died before a week."

"Well, her funeral is over, I hope, and her hymn sung; and our ears shan't be tortured with that discord and jargon. It has made me nervous. Sit down here, beside me; sit close; hold my hand; press it hard—hard—harder."

---

[1] *a fortnight* Two weeks.

We had moved a little back, and had come to another seat.

She sat down. Her face underwent a change that alarmed and even terrified me for a moment. It darkened, and became horribly livid;[1] her teeth and hands were clenched, and she frowned and compressed her lips, while she stared down upon the ground at her feet, and trembled all over with a continued shudder as irrepressible as ague.[2] All her energies seemed strained to suppress a fit, with which she was then breathlessly tugging; and at length a low convulsive cry of suffering broke from her, and gradually the hysteria subsided. "There! That comes of strangling people with hymns!" she said at last. "Hold me, hold me still. It is passing away."

And so gradually it did; and perhaps to dissipate the sombre impression which the spectacle had left upon me, she became unusually animated and chatty; and so we got home.

This was the first time I had seen her exhibit any definable symptoms of that delicacy of health which her mother had spoken of. It was the first time, also, I had seen her exhibit anything like temper.

Both passed away like a summer cloud; and never but once afterwards did I witness on her part a momentary sign of anger. I will tell you how it happened.

She and I were looking out of one of the long drawing-room windows, when there entered the court-yard, over the drawbridge, a figure of a wanderer whom I knew very well. He used to visit the schloss generally twice a year.

It was the figure of a hunchback, with the sharp lean features that generally accompany deformity. He wore a pointed black beard, and he was smiling from ear to ear, showing his white fangs. He was dressed in buff, black, and scarlet, and crossed with more straps and belts than I could count, from which hung all manner of things. Behind, he carried a magic-lantern, and two boxes, which I well knew, in one of which was a sala-mander, and in the other a mandrake.[3] These monsters used to make my father laugh. They were compounded of parts of monkeys, parrots, squirrels, fish, and hedge-hogs, dried and stitched together with great neatness and startling effect. He had a fiddle, a box of conjuring apparatus, a pair of foils and masks attached to his belt, several other mysterious cases dangling about him, and a black staff with copper ferrules[4] in his hand. His companion was a rough spare dog, that followed at his heels, but stopped short, suspiciously at the drawbridge, and in a little while began to howl dismally.

In the meantime, the mountebank,[5] standing in the midst of the court-yard, raised his grotesque hat, and made us a very ceremonious bow, paying his compliments very volubly[6] in execrable French, and German not much better. Then, disengaging his fiddle, he began to scrape a lively air, to which he sang with a merry discord, dancing with ludicrous airs and activity, that made me laugh, in spite of the dog's howling.

Then he advanced to the window with many smiles and salutations, and his hat in his left hand, his fiddle under his arm, and with a fluency that never took breath, he gabbled a long advertisement of all his accomplishments, and the resources of the various arts which he placed at our service, and the curiosities and entertainments which it was in his power, at our bidding, to display.

"Will your ladyships be pleased to buy an amulet against the oupire,[7] which is going like the wolf, I hear, through these woods," he said, dropping his hat on the pavement. "They are dying of it right and left, and here is a charm that never fails; only pinned to the pillow, and you may laugh in his face."

---

[1] *livid* Gray-toned, especially as a result of extreme anger.

[2] *ague* Fever with shivering.

[3] *magic-lantern* Small projector used to display images for entertainment; *salamander* Small lizard, associated in folklore with fire and poison; *mandrake* Plant with roots shaped like a human figure, thought in folklore to have magical properties.

[4] *foils* Long, thin swords used in fencing; *ferrules* End caps, here protecting the staff from splitting.

[5] *mountebank* Traveling performer who sells useless medicines and supposed magical items.

[6] *volubly* With rapid speech.

[7] *oupire* Vampire; the term is borrowed from Slavic languages.

SHERIDAN LE FANU

These charms consisted of oblong slips of vellum, with cabalistic ciphers[1] and diagrams upon them.

Carmilla instantly purchased one, and so did I.

He was looking up, and we were smiling down upon him, amused; at least, I can answer for myself. His piercing black eye, as he looked up in our faces, seemed to detect something that fixed for a moment his curiosity.

In an instant he unrolled a leather case, full of all manner of odd little steel instruments.

"See here, my lady," he said, displaying it, and addressing me, "I profess, among other things less useful, the art of dentistry. Plague take the dog!" he interpolated. "Silence, beast! He howls so that your ladyships can scarcely hear a word. Your noble friend, the young lady at your right, has the sharpest tooth—long, thin, pointed, like an awl,[2] like a needle; ha, ha! With my sharp and long sight, as I look up, I have seen it distinctly; now if it happens to hurt the young lady, and I think it must, here am I, here are my file, my punch, my nippers; I will make it round and blunt, if her ladyship pleases; no longer the tooth of a fish, but of a beautiful young lady as she is. Hey? Is the young lady displeased? Have I been too bold? Have I offended her?"

The young lady, indeed, looked very angry as she drew back from the window.

"How dares that mountebank insult us so? Where is your father? I shall demand redress from him. My father would have had the wretch tied up to the pump, and flogged with a cart-whip, and burnt to the bones with the castle brand!"

She retired from the window a step or two, and sat down, and had hardly lost sight of the offender, when her wrath subsided as suddenly as it had risen, and she gradually recovered her usual tone, and seemed to forget the little hunchback and his follies.

My father was out of spirits that evening. On coming in he told us that there had been another case very similar to the two fatal ones which had lately occurred. The sister of a young peasant on his estate, only a mile away, was very ill, had been, as she described

it, attacked very nearly in the same way, and was now slowly but steadily sinking.

"All this," said my father, "is strictly referable to natural causes. These poor people infect one another with their superstitions, and so repeat in imagination the images of terror that have infested their neighbours."

"But that very circumstance frightens one horribly," said Carmilla.

"How so?" inquired my father.

"I am so afraid of fancying I see such things; I think it would be as bad as reality."

"We are in God's hands; nothing can happen without his permission, and all will end well for those who love him. He is our faithful creator; He has made us all, and will take care of us."

"Creator! Nature!" said the young lady in answer to my gentle father. "And this disease that invades the country is natural. Nature. All things proceed from Nature—don't they? All things in the heaven, in the earth, and under the earth, act and live as Nature ordains? I think so."

"The doctor said he would come here to-day," said my father, after a silence. "I want to know what he thinks about it, and what he thinks we had better do."

"Doctors never did me any good," said Carmilla.

"Then you have been ill?" I asked.

"More ill than ever you were," she answered.

"Long ago?"

"Yes, a long time. I suffered from this very illness; but I forget all but my pain and weakness, and they were not so bad as are suffered in other diseases."

"You were very young then?"

"I dare say; let us talk no more of it. You would not wound a friend?" She looked languidly in my eyes, and passed her arm round my waist lovingly, and led me out of the room. My father was busy over some papers near the window.

"Why does your papa like to frighten us?" said the pretty girl, with a sigh and a little shudder.

"He doesn't, dear Carmilla, it is the very furthest thing from his mind."

"Are you afraid, dearest?"

---

[1] *vellum* Fine parchment made from calfskin; *cabalistic ciphers* Mystical symbols.

[2] *awl* Tool used to puncture holes, usually in leather.

"I should be very much if I fancied there was any real danger of my being attacked as those poor people were."

"You are afraid to die?"

"Yes, every one is."

"But to die as lovers may—to die together, so that they may live together. Girls are caterpillars while they live in the world, to be finally butterflies when the summer comes; but in the meantime there are grubs and larvæ, don't you see—each with their peculiar propensities, necessities and structure. So says Monsieur Buffon, in his big book, in the next room."

Later in the day the doctor came, and was closeted with papa for some time. He was a skilful man, of sixty and upwards, he wore powder, and shaved[1] his pale face as smooth as a pumpkin. He and papa emerged from the room together, and I heard papa laugh, and say as they came out:

"Well, I do wonder at a wise man like you. What do you say to hippogriffs and dragons?"

The doctor was smiling, and made answer, shaking his head—

"Nevertheless life and death are mysterious states, and we know little of the resources of either."

And so they walked on, and I heard no more. I did not then know what the doctor had been broaching, but I think I guess it now.

CHAPTER 5
A WONDERFUL LIKENESS

This evening there arrived from Gratz[2] the grave, dark-faced son of the picture cleaner, with a horse and cart laden with two large packing cases, having many pictures in each. It was a journey of ten leagues, and whenever a messenger arrived at the schloss from our little capital of Gratz, we used to crowd about him in the hall, to hear the news.

This arrival created in our secluded quarters quite a sensation. The cases remained in the hall, and the messenger was taken charge of by the servants till he had eaten his supper. Then with assistants, and armed with hammer, ripping-chisel, and turnscrew, he met us in the hall, where we had assembled to witness the unpacking of the cases.

Carmilla sat looking listlessly on, while one after the other the old pictures, nearly all portraits, which had undergone the process of renovation, were brought to light. My mother was of an old Hungarian family, and most of these pictures, which were about to be restored to their places, had come to us through her.

My father had a list in his hand, from which he read, as the artist rummaged out the corresponding numbers. I don't know that the pictures were very good, but they were, undoubtedly, very old, and some of them very curious also. They had, for the most part, the merit of being now seen by me, I may say, for the first time; for the smoke and dust of time had all but obliterated them.

"There is a picture that I have not seen yet," said my father. "In one corner, at the top of it, is the name, as well as I could read, 'Marcia Karnstein,' and the date '1698' and I am curious to see how it has turned out."

I remembered it; it was a small picture, about a foot and a half high, and nearly square, without a frame; but it was so blackened by age that I could not make it out.

The artist now produced it, with evident pride. It was quite beautiful; it was startling; it seemed to live. It was the effigy of Carmilla!

"Carmilla, dear, here is an absolute miracle. Here you are, living, smiling, ready to speak, in this picture. Isn't it beautiful, papa? And see, even the little mole on her throat."

My father laughed, and said "Certainly it is a wonderful likeness," but he looked away, and to my surprise seemed but little struck by it, and went on talking to the picture cleaner, who was also something of an artist, and discoursed with intelligence about the portraits or other works, which his art had just brought into light and colour, while I was more and more lost in wonder the more I looked at the picture.

"Will you let me hang this picture in my room, papa?" I asked.

---

1 *wore powder ... shaved* Wearing powder and fully shaving the face were outdated fashions.

2 *Gratz* Capital of Styria.

"Certainly, dear," said he, smiling, "I'm very glad you think it so like. It must be prettier even than I thought it, if it is."

The young lady did not acknowledge this pretty speech, did not seem to hear it. She was leaning back in her seat, her fine eyes under their long lashes gazing on me in contemplation, and she smiled in a kind of rapture.

"And now you can read quite plainly the name that is written in the corner. It is not Marcia; it looks as if it was done in gold. The name is Mircalla, Countess Karnstein, and this is a little coronet[1] over it, and underneath A.D. 1698. I am descended from the Karnsteins; that is, mamma was."

"Ah!" said the lady, languidly, "so am I, I think, a very long descent, very ancient. Are there any Karnsteins living now?"

"None who bear the name, I believe. The family were ruined, I believe, in some civil wars, long ago, but the ruins of the castle are only about three miles away."

"How interesting!" she said, languidly. "But see what beautiful moonlight!" She glanced through the hall-door, which stood a little open. "Suppose you take a little ramble round the court, and look down at the road and river."

"It is so like the night you came to us," I said.

She sighed, smiling.

She rose, and each with her arm about the other's waist, we walked out upon the pavement.

In silence, slowly we walked down to the draw-bridge, where the beautiful landscape opened before us.

"And so you were thinking of the night I came here?" she almost whispered. "Are you glad I came?"

"Delighted, dear Carmilla," I answered.

"And you asked for the picture you think like me, to hang in your room," she murmured with a sigh, as she drew her arm closer about my waist, and let her pretty head sink upon my shoulder.

"How romantic you are, Carmilla," I said. "Whenever you tell me your story, it will be made up chiefly of some one great romance."

She kissed me silently.

"I am sure, Carmilla, you have been in love; that there is, at this moment, an affair of the heart going on."

"I have been in love with no one, and never shall," she whispered, "unless it should be with you."

How beautiful she looked in the moonlight!

Shy and strange was the look with which she quickly hid her face in my neck and hair, with tumultuous sighs, that seemed almost to sob, and pressed in mine a hand that trembled.

Her soft cheek was glowing against mine. "Darling, darling," she murmured, "I live in you; and you would die for me, I love you so."

I started from her.

She was gazing on me with eyes from which all fire, all meaning had flown, and a face colourless and apathetic.

"Is there a chill in the air, dear?" she said drowsily. "I almost shiver; have I been dreaming? Let us come in. Come; come; come in."

"You look ill, Carmilla; a little faint. You certainly must take some wine," I said.

"Yes, I will. I'm better now. I shall be quite well in a few minutes. Yes, do give me a little wine," answered Carmilla, as we approached the door. "Let us look again for a moment; it is the last time, perhaps, I shall see the moonlight with you."

"How do you feel now, dear Carmilla? Are you really better?" I asked.

I was beginning to take alarm, lest she should have been stricken with the strange epidemic that they said had invaded the country about us.

"Papa would be grieved beyond measure," I added, "if he thought you were ever so little ill, without immediately letting us know. We have a very skilful doctor near this, the physician who was with papa to-day."

"I'm sure he is. I know how kind you all are; but, dear child, I am quite well again. There is nothing ever wrong with me, but a little weakness. People say I am languid; I am incapable of exertion; I can scarcely walk as far as a child of three years old; and every now and then the little strength I have falters, and I become as you have just seen me. But after all I am very easily set up again; in a moment I am perfectly myself. See how I have recovered."

---

[1] *coronet* Small crown symbolic of nobility.

So, indeed, she had; and she and I talked a great deal, and very animated she was; and the remainder of that evening passed without any recurrence of what I called her infatuations. I mean her crazy talk and looks, which embarrassed, and even frightened me.

But there occurred that night an event which gave my thoughts quite a new turn, and seemed to startle even Carmilla's languid nature into momentary energy.

CHAPTER 6
A VERY STRANGE AGONY

When we got into the drawing-room, and had sat down to our coffee and chocolate, although Carmilla did not take any, she seemed quite herself again, and Madame, and Mademoiselle De Lafontaine, joined us, and made a little card party, in the course of which papa came in for what he called his "dish of tea."

When the game was over he sat down beside Carmilla on the sofa, and asked her, a little anxiously, whether she had heard from her mother since her arrival.

She answered "No."

He then asked whether she knew where a letter would reach her at present.

"I cannot tell," she answered ambiguously, "but I have been thinking of leaving you; you have been already too hospitable and too kind to me. I have given you an infinity of trouble, and I should wish to take a carriage to-morrow, and post[1] in pursuit of her; I know where I shall ultimately find her, although I dare not yet tell you."

"But you must not dream of any such thing," exclaimed my father, to my great relief. "We can't afford to lose you so, and I won't consent to your leaving us, except under the care of your mother, who was so good as to consent to your remaining with us till she should herself return. I should be quite happy if I knew that you heard from her; but this evening the accounts of the progress of the mysterious disease that has invaded our neighbourhood, grow even more alarming; and my beautiful guest, I do feel the responsibility, unaided by advice from your mother, very much. But I shall do my best; and one thing is certain, that you must not think of leaving us without her distinct direction to that effect. We should suffer too much in parting from you to consent to it easily."

"Thank you, sir, a thousand times for your hospitality," she answered, smiling bashfully. "You have all been too kind to me; I have seldom been so happy in all my life before, as in your beautiful château, under your care, and in the society of your dear daughter."

So he gallantly, in his old-fashioned way, kissed her hand, smiling and pleased at her little speech.

I accompanied Carmilla as usual to her room, and sat and chatted with her while she was preparing for bed.

"Do you think," I said at length, "that you will ever confide fully in me?"

She turned round smiling, but made no answer, only continued to smile on me.

"You won't answer that?" I said. "You can't answer pleasantly; I ought not to have asked you."

"You were quite right to ask me that, or anything. You do not know how dear you are to me, or you could not think any confidence too great to look for. But I am under vows, no nun half so awfully, and I dare not tell my story yet, even to you. The time is very near when you shall know everything. You will think me cruel, very selfish, but love is always selfish; the more ardent the more selfish. How jealous I am you cannot know. You must come with me, loving me—to death; or else hate me and still come with me, and hating me through death and after. There is no such word as indifference in my apathetic nature."

"Now, Carmilla, you are going to talk your wild nonsense again," I said hastily.

"Not I, silly little fool as I am, and full of whims and fancies; for your sake I'll talk like a sage. Were you ever at a ball?"

"No; how you do run on. What is it like? How charming it must be."

"I almost forget, it is years ago."

---

[1] *post* Travel using post-horses, horses available for hire who could be exchanged as they were exhausted so that a traveler would not have to wait for them to rest.

I laughed.

"You are not so old. Your first ball can hardly be forgotten yet."

"I remember everything about it—with an effort. I see it all, as divers see what is going on above them, through a medium, dense, rippling, but transparent. There occurred that night what has confused the picture, and made its colours faint. I was all but assassinated in my bed, wounded here," she touched her breast, "and never was the same since."

"Were you near dying?"

"Yes, very—a cruel love—strange love, that would have taken my life. Love will have its sacrifices. No sacrifice without blood. Let us go to sleep now; I feel so lazy. How can I get up just now and lock my door?"

She was lying with her tiny hands buried in her rich wavy hair, under her cheek, her little head upon the pillow, and her glittering eyes followed me wherever I moved, with a kind of shy smile that I could not decipher.

I bid her good-night, and crept from the room with an uncomfortable sensation.

I often wondered whether our pretty guest ever said her prayers. I certainly had never seen her upon her knees. In the morning she never came down until long after our family prayers were over, and at night she never left the drawing-room to attend our brief evening prayers in the hall.

If it had not been that it had casually come out in one of our careless talks that she had been baptised, I should have doubted her being a Christian. Religion was a subject on which I had never heard her speak a word. If I had known the world better, this particular neglect or antipathy would not have so much surprised me.

The precautions of nervous people are infectious, and persons of a like temperament are pretty sure, after a time, to imitate them. I had adopted Carmilla's habit of locking her bedroom door, having taken into my head all her whimsical alarms about midnight invaders and prowling assassins. I had also adopted her precaution of making a brief search through her room, to satisfy herself that no lurking assassin or robber was "ensconced."[1]

These wise measures taken, I got into my bed and fell asleep. A light was burning in my room. This was an old habit, of very early date, and which nothing could have tempted me to dispense with.

Thus fortified I might take my rest in peace. But dreams come through stone walls, light up dark rooms, or darken light ones, and their persons make their exits and their entrances as they please, and laugh at locksmiths.

I had a dream that night that was the beginning of a very strange agony.

I cannot call it a nightmare, for I was quite conscious of being asleep. But I was equally conscious of being in my room, and lying in bed, precisely as I actually was. I saw, or fancied I saw, the room and its furniture just as I had seen it last, except that it was very dark, and I saw something moving round the foot of the bed, which at first I could not accurately distinguish. But I soon saw that it was a sooty-black animal that resembled a monstrous cat. It appeared to me about four or five feet long, for it measured fully the length of the hearth-rug as it passed over it; and it continued to-ing and fro-ing with the lithe sinister restlessness of a beast in a cage. I could not cry out, although as you may suppose, I was terrified. Its pace was growing faster, and the room rapidly darker and darker, and at length so dark that I could no longer see anything of it but its eyes. I felt it spring lightly on the bed. The two broad eyes approached my face, and suddenly I felt a stinging pain as if two large needles darted, an inch or two apart, deep into my breast. I waked with a scream. The room was lighted by the candle that burnt there all through the night, and I saw a female figure standing at the foot of the bed, a little at the right side. It was in a dark loose dress, and its hair was down and covered its shoulders. A block of stone could not have been more still. There was not the slightest stir of respiration. As I stared at it, the figure appeared to have changed its place, and was now nearer the door; then, close to it, the door opened, and it passed out.

I was now relieved, and able to breathe and move. My first thought was that Carmilla had been playing me a trick, and that I had forgotten to secure my door. I

---

[1] *ensconced* Concealed.

hastened to it, and found it locked as usual on the inside. I was afraid to open it—I was horrified. I sprang into my bed and covered my head up in the bed-clothes, and lay there more dead than alive till morning.

CHAPTER 7
DESCENDING

It would be vain my attempting to tell you the horror with which, even now, I recall the occurrence of that night. It was no such transitory terror as a dream leaves behind it. It seemed to deepen by time, and communicated itself to the room and the very furniture that had encompassed the apparition.

I could not bear next day to be alone for a moment. I should have told papa, but for two opposite reasons. At one time I thought he would laugh at my story, and I could not bear its being treated as a jest; and at another, I thought he might fancy that I had been attacked by the mysterious complaint which had invaded our neighbourhood. I had myself no misgivings of the kind, and as he had been rather an invalid for some time, I was afraid of alarming him.

I was comfortable enough with my good-natured companions, Madame Perrodon, and the vivacious Mademoiselle De Lafontaine. They both perceived that I was out of spirits and nervous, and at length I told them what lay so heavy at my heart.

Mademoiselle laughed, but I fancied that Madame Perrodon looked anxious.

"By-the-by," said Mademoiselle, laughing, "the long lime-tree walk, behind Carmilla's bedroom-window, is haunted!"

"Nonsense!" exclaimed Madame, who probably thought the theme rather inopportune, "and who tells that story, my dear?"

"Martin says that he came up twice, when the old yard-gate was being repaired, before sunrise, and twice saw the same female figure walking down the lime-tree avenue."

"So he well might, as long as there are cows to milk in the river fields," said Madame.

"I daresay; but Martin chooses to be frightened, and never did I see fool more frightened."

"You must not say a word about it to Carmilla, because she can see down that walk from her room window," I interposed, "and she is, if possible, a greater coward than I."

Carmilla came down rather later than usual that day.

"I was so frightened last night," she said, so soon as were together, "and I am sure I should have seen something dreadful if it had not been for that charm I bought from the poor little hunchback whom I called such hard names. I had a dream of something black coming round my bed, and I awoke in a perfect horror, and I really thought, for some seconds, I saw a dark figure near the chimney-piece, but I felt under my pillow for my charm, and the moment my fingers touched it, the figure disappeared, and I felt quite certain, only that I had it by me, that something frightful would have made its appearance, and, perhaps, throttled me, as it did those poor people we heard of."

"Well, listen to me," I began, and recounted my adventure, at the recital of which she appeared horrified.

"And had you the charm near you?" she asked, earnestly.

"No, I had dropped it into a china vase in the drawing-room, but I shall certainly take it with me to-night, as you have so much faith in it."

At this distance of time I cannot tell you, or even understand, how I overcame my horror so effectually as to lie alone in my room that night. I remember distinctly that I pinned the charm to my pillow. I fell asleep almost immediately, and slept even more soundly than usual all night.

Next night I passed as well. My sleep was delightfully deep and dreamless. But I wakened with a sense of lassitude[1] and melancholy, which, however, did not exceed a degree that was almost luxurious.

"Well, I told you so," said Carmilla, when I described my quiet sleep, "I had such delightful sleep myself last night; I pinned the charm to the breast of my night-dress. It was too far away the night before. I am quite sure it was all fancy, except the dreams. I used to think that evil spirits made dreams, but our doctor told me it is no such thing. Only a fever passing by, or some

---

[1] *lassitude* Mental or physical weariness.

other malady, as they often do, he said, knocks at the door, and not being able to get in, passes on, with that alarm."

"And what do you think the charm is?" said I.

"It has been fumigated or immersed in some drug, and is an antidote against the malaria," she answered.

"Then it acts only on the body?"

"Certainly; you don't suppose that evil spirits are frightened by bits of ribbon, or the perfumes of a druggist's shop? No, these complaints, wandering in the air, begin by trying the nerves, and so infect the brain, but before they can seize upon you, the antidote repels them. That I am sure is what the charm has done for us. It is nothing magical, it is simply natural."

I should have been happier if I could have quite agreed with Carmilla, but I did my best, and the impression was a little losing its force.

For some nights I slept profoundly; but still every morning I felt the same lassitude, and a languor weighed upon me all day. I felt myself a changed girl. A strange melancholy was stealing over me, a melancholy that I would not have interrupted. Dim thoughts of death began to open, and an idea that I was slowly sinking took gentle, and, somehow, not unwelcome, possession of me. If it was sad, the tone of mind which this induced was also sweet. Whatever it might be, my soul acquiesced in it.

I would not admit that I was ill, I would not consent to tell my papa, or to have the doctor sent for.

Carmilla became more devoted to me than ever, and her strange paroxysms of languid adoration more frequent. She used to gloat[1] on me with increasing ardour the more my strength and spirits waned. This always shocked me like a momentary glare of insanity.

Without knowing it, I was now in a pretty advanced stage of the strangest illness under which mortal ever suffered. There was an unaccountable fascination in its earlier symptoms that more than reconciled me to the incapacitating effect of that stage of the malady. This fascination increased for a time, until it reached a certain point, when gradually a sense of the horrible mingled itself with it, deepening, as you shall hear, until it

discoloured and perverted the whole state of my life.

The first change I experienced was rather agreeable. It was very near the turning point from which began the descent of Avernus.[2]

Certain vague and strange sensations visited me in my sleep. The prevailing one was of that pleasant, peculiar cold thrill which we feel in bathing, when we move against the current of a river. This was soon accompanied by dreams that seemed interminable, and were so vague that I could never recollect their scenery and persons, or any one connected portion of their action. But they left an awful impression, and a sense of exhaustion, as if I had passed through a long period of great mental exertion and danger. After all these dreams there remained on waking a remembrance of having been in a place very nearly dark, and of having spoken to people whom I could not see; and especially of one clear voice, of a female's, very deep, that spoke as if at a distance, slowly, and producing always the same sensation of indescribable solemnity and fear. Sometimes there came a sensation as if a hand was drawn softly along my cheek and neck. Sometimes it was as if warm lips kissed me, and longer and more lovingly as they reached my throat, but there the caress fixed itself. My heart beat faster, my breathing rose and fell rapidly and full drawn; a sobbing, that rose into a sense of strangulation, supervened,[3] and turned into a dreadful convulsion, in which my senses left me and I became unconscious.

It was now three weeks since the commencement of this unaccountable state. My sufferings had, during the last week, told upon my appearance. I had grown pale, my eyes were dilated and darkened underneath, and the languor which I had long felt began to display itself in my countenance.

My father asked me often whether I was ill; but, with an obstinacy which now seems to me unaccountable, I persisted in assuring him that I was quite well.

In a sense this was true. I had no pain, I could complain of no bodily derangement.[4] My complaint

---

[1] *gloat* Look passionately.

[2] *descent of Avernus* Here, descent into the underworld.

[3] *supervened* Interrupted.

[4] *derangement* Disorder.

seemed to be one of the imagination, or the nerves, and, horrible as my sufferings were, I kept them, with a morbid reserve, very nearly to myself.

It could not be that terrible complaint which the peasants called the oupire, for I had now been suffering for three weeks, and they were seldom ill for much more than three days, when death put an end to their miseries.

Carmilla complained of dreams and feverish sensations, but by no means of so alarming a kind as mine. I say that mine were extremely alarming. Had I been capable of comprehending my condition, I would have invoked aid and advice on my knees. The narcotic of an unsuspected influence was acting upon me, and my perceptions were benumbed.

I am going to tell you now of a dream that led immediately to an odd discovery.

One night, instead of the voice I was accustomed to hear in the dark, I heard one, sweet and tender, and at the same time terrible, which said, "Your mother warns you to beware of the assassin." At the same time a light unexpectedly sprang up, and I saw Carmilla, standing, near the foot of my bed, in her white night-dress, bathed, from her chin to her feet, in one great stain of blood.

I wakened with a shriek, possessed with the one idea that Carmilla was being murdered. I remember springing from my bed, and my next recollection is that of standing on the lobby, crying for help.

Madame and Mademoiselle came scurrying out of their rooms in alarm; a lamp burned always on the lobby, and seeing me, they soon learned the cause of my terror.

I insisted on our knocking at Carmilla's door. Our knocking was unanswered. It soon became a pounding and an uproar. We shrieked her name, but all was vain.

We all grew frightened, for the door was locked. We hurried back, in panic, to my room. There we rang the bell long and furiously. If my father's room had been at that side of the house, we would have called him up at once to our aid. But, alas! he was quite out of hearing, and to reach him involved an excursion for which we none of us had courage.

Servants, however, soon came running up the stairs; I had got on my dressing-gown and slippers meanwhile, and my companions were already similarly furnished. Recognising the voices of the servants on the lobby, we sallied out[1] together; and having renewed, as fruitlessly, our summons at Carmilla's door, I ordered the men to force the lock. They did so, and we stood, holding our lights aloft, in the doorway, and so stared into the room.

We called her by name; but there was still no reply. We looked round the room. Everything was undisturbed. It was exactly in the state in which I had left it on bidding her good night. But Carmilla was gone.

CHAPTER 8
SEARCH

At sight of the room, perfectly undisturbed except for our violent entrance, we began to cool a little, and soon recovered our senses sufficiently to dismiss the men. It had struck Mademoiselle that possibly Carmilla had been wakened by the uproar at her door, and in her first panic had jumped from her bed, and hid herself in a press,[2] or behind a curtain, from which she could not, of course, emerge until the majordomo and his myrmidons[3] had withdrawn. We now recommenced our search, and began to call her by name again.

It was all to no purpose. Our perplexity and agitation increased. We examined the windows, but they were secured. I implored of Carmilla, if she had concealed herself, to play this cruel trick no longer—to come out, and to end our anxieties. It was all useless. I was by this time convinced that she was not in the room, nor in the dressing room, the door of which was still locked on this side. She could not have passed it. I was utterly puzzled. Had Carmilla discovered one of those secret passages which the old house-keeper said were known to exist in the schloss, although the tradition of their exact situation had been lost? A little time

1 *sallied out* Went forth (the term especially refers to a military force attacking after a retreat).

2 *press* Cupboard for storing linens.

3 *majordomo* Head servant; *myrmidons* Followers (here, the other servants).

would, no doubt, explain all—utterly perplexed as, for the present, we were.

It was past four o'clock, and I preferred passing the remaining hours of darkness in Madame's room. Daylight brought no solution of the difficulty.

The whole household, with my father at its head, was in a state of agitation next morning. Every part of the château was searched. The grounds were explored. Not a trace of the missing lady could be discovered. The stream was about to be dragged; my father was in distraction; what a tale to have to tell the poor girl's mother on her return. I, too, was almost beside myself, though my grief was quite of a different kind.

The morning was passed in alarm and excitement. It was now one o'clock, and still no tidings. I ran up to Carmilla's room, and found her standing at her dressing-table. I was astounded. I could not believe my eyes. She beckoned me to her with her pretty finger, in silence. Her face expressed extreme fear.

I ran to her in an ecstasy of joy; I kissed and embraced her again and again. I ran to the bell and rang it vehemently, to bring others to the spot, who might at once relieve my father's anxiety.

"Dear Carmilla, what has become of you all this time? We have been in agonies of anxiety about you," I exclaimed. "Where have you been? How did you come back?"

"Last night has been a night of wonders," she said.

"For mercy's sake, explain all you can."

"It was past two last night," she said, "when I went to sleep as usual in my bed, with my doors locked, that of the dressing-room, and that opening upon the gallery. My sleep was uninterrupted, and, so far as I know, dreamless; but I awoke just now on the sofa in the dressing-room there, and I found the door between the rooms open, and the other door forced. How could all this have happened without my being wakened? It must have been accompanied with a great deal of noise, and I am particularly easily wakened; and how could I have been carried out of my bed without my sleep having been interrupted, I whom the slightest stir startles?"

By this time, Madame, Mademoiselle, my father, and a number of the servants were in the room. Carmilla was, of course, overwhelmed with inquiries, congratulations, and welcomes. She had but one story to tell, and seemed the least able of all the party to suggest any way of accounting for what had happened.

My father took a turn up and down the room, thinking. I saw Carmilla's eye follow him for a moment with a sly, dark glance.

When my father had sent the servants away, Mademoiselle having gone in search of a little bottle of valerian and sal-volatile,[1] and there being no one now in the room with Carmilla, except my father, Madame, and myself, he came to her thoughtfully, took her hand very kindly, led her to the sofa, and sat down beside her.

"Will you forgive me, my dear, if I risk a conjecture, and ask a question?"

"Who can have a better right?" she said. "Ask what you please, and I will tell you everything. But my story is simply one of bewilderment and darkness. I know absolutely nothing. Put any question you please. But you know, of course, the limitations mamma has placed me under."

"Perfectly, my dear child. I need not approach the topics on which she desires our silence. Now, the marvel of last night consists in your having been removed from your bed and your room, without being wakened, and this removal having occurred apparently while the windows were still secured, and the two doors locked upon the inside. I will tell you my theory, and first ask you a question."

Carmilla was leaning on her hand dejectedly; Madame and I were listening breathlessly.

"Now, my question is this. Have you ever been suspected of walking in your sleep?"

"Never, since I was very young indeed."

"But you did walk in your sleep when you were young?"

"Yes; I know I did. I have been told so often by my old nurse."

My father smiled and nodded.

---

[1]   *valerian*   Herb used to induce calm; *sal-volatile*   Smelling salts.

"Well, what has happened is this. You got up in your sleep, unlocked the door, not leaving the key, as usual, in the lock, but taking it out and locking it on the outside; you again took the key out, and carried it away with you to some one of the five-and-twenty rooms on this floor, or perhaps up-stairs or down-stairs. There are so many rooms and closets, so much heavy furniture, and such accumulations of lumber,[1] that it would require a week to search this old house thoroughly. Do you see, now, what I mean?"

"I do, but not all," she answered.

"And how, papa, do you account for her finding herself on the sofa in the dressing-room, which we had searched so carefully?"

"She came there after you had searched it, still in her sleep, and at last awoke spontaneously, and was as much surprised to find herself where she was as any one else. I wish all mysteries were as easily and innocently explained as yours, Carmilla," he said, laughing. "And so we may congratulate ourselves on the certainty that the most natural explanation of the occurrence is one that involves no drugging, no tampering with locks, no burglars, or poisoners, or witches—nothing that need alarm Carmilla, or any one else, for our safety."

Carmilla was looking charmingly. Nothing could be more beautiful than her tints. Her beauty was, I think, enhanced by that graceful languor that was peculiar to her. I think my father was silently contrasting her looks with mine, for he said:

"I wish my poor Laura was looking more like herself," and he sighed.

So our alarms were happily ended, and Carmilla restored to her friends.

CHAPTER 9
THE DOCTOR

As Carmilla would not hear of an attendant sleeping in her room, my father arranged that a servant should sleep outside her door, so that she could not attempt to make another such excursion without being arrested at her own door.

---

[1] *lumber* Miscellaneous stored items.

That night passed quietly; and next morning early, the doctor, whom my father had sent for without telling me a word about it, arrived to see me.

Madame accompanied me to the library; and there the grave little doctor, with white hair and spectacles, whom I mentioned before, was waiting to receive me.

I told him my story, and as I proceeded he grew graver and graver.

We were standing, he and I, in the recess of one of the windows, facing one another. When my statement was over, he leaned with his shoulders against the wall, and with his eyes fixed on me earnestly, with an interest in which was a dash of horror.

After a minute's reflection, he asked Madame if he could see my father.

He was sent for accordingly, and as he entered, smiling, he said:

"I dare say, doctor, you are going to tell me that I am an old fool for having brought you here; I hope I am."

But his smile faded into shadow as the doctor, with a very grave face, beckoned him to him.

He and the doctor talked for some time in the same recess where I had just conferred with the physician. It seemed an earnest and argumentative conversation. The room is very large, and I and Madame stood together, burning with curiosity, at the further end. Not a word could we hear, however, for they spoke in a very low tone, and the deep recess of the window quite concealed the doctor from view, and very nearly my father, whose foot, arm, and shoulder only could we see; and the voices were, I suppose, all the less audible for the sort of closet which the thick wall and window formed.

After a time my father's face looked into the room; it was pale, thoughtful, and, I fancied, agitated.

"Laura, dear, come here for a moment. Madame, we shan't trouble you, the doctor says, at present."

Accordingly I approached, for the first time a little alarmed; for, although I felt very weak, I did not feel ill; and strength, one always fancies, is a thing that may be picked up when we please.

My father held out his hand to me, as I drew near, but he was looking at the doctor, and he said:

"It certainly is very odd; I don't understand it quite. Laura, come here, dear; now attend to Doctor Spielsberg, and recollect yourself."

"You mentioned a sensation like that of two needles piercing the skin, somewhere about your neck, on the night when you experienced your first horrible dream. Is there still any soreness?"

"None at all," I answered.

"Can you indicate with your finger about the point at which you think this occurred?"

"Very little below my throat—here," I answered.

I wore a morning dress, which covered the place I pointed to.

"Now you can satisfy yourself," said the doctor. "You won't mind your papa's lowering your dress a very little. It is necessary, to detect a symptom of the complaint under which you have been suffering."

I acquiesced. It was only an inch or two below the edge of my collar.

"God bless me!—so it is," exclaimed my father, growing pale.

"You see it now with your own eyes," said the doctor, with a gloomy triumph.

"What is it?" I exclaimed, beginning to be frightened.

"Nothing, my dear young lady, but a small blue spot, about the size of the tip of your little finger; and now," he continued, turning to papa, "the question is what is best to be done?"

"Is there any danger?" I urged, in great trepidation.

"I trust not, my dear," answered the doctor. "I don't see why you should not recover. I don't see why you should not begin immediately to get better. That is the point at which the sense of strangulation begins?"

"Yes," I answered.

"And—recollect as well as you can—the same point was a kind of centre of that thrill which you described just now, like the current of a cold stream running against you?"

"It may have been; I think it was."

"Ay, you see?" he added, turning to my father. "Shall I say a word to Madame?"

"Certainly," said my father.

He called Madame to him, and said:

"I find my young friend here far from well. It won't be of any great consequence, I hope; but it will be necessary that some steps be taken, which I will explain by-and-bye; but in the meantime, Madame, you will be so good as not to let Miss Laura be alone for one moment. That is the only direction I need give for the present. It is indispensable."

"We may rely upon your kindness, Madame, I know," added my father.

Madame satisfied him eagerly.

"And you, dear Laura, I know you will observe the doctor's direction."

"I shall have to ask your opinion upon another patient, whose symptoms slightly resemble those of my daughter, that have just been detailed to you—very much milder in degree, but I believe quite of the same sort. She is a young lady—our guest; but as you say you will be passing this way again this evening, you can't do better than take your supper here, and you can then see her. She does not come down till the afternoon."

"I thank you," said the doctor. "I shall be with you, then, at about seven this evening."

And then they repeated their directions to me and to Madame, and with this parting charge my father left us, and walked out with the doctor; and I saw them pacing together up and down between the road and the moat, on the grassy platform in front of the castle, evidently absorbed in earnest conversation.

The doctor did not return. I saw him mount his horse there, take his leave, and ride away eastward through the forest.

Nearly at the same time I saw the man arrive from Dranfeld with the letters, and dismount and hand the bag to my father.

In the meantime, Madame and I were both busy, lost in conjecture as to the reasons of the singular and earnest direction which the doctor and my father had concurred in imposing. Madame, as she afterwards told me, was afraid the doctor apprehended a sudden seizure, and that, without prompt assistance, I might either lose my life in a fit, or at least be seriously hurt.

This interpretation did not strike me; and I fancied,

perhaps luckily for my nerves, that the arrangement was prescribed simply to secure a companion, who would prevent my taking too much exercise, or eating unripe fruit, or doing any of the fifty foolish things to which young people are supposed to be prone.

About half-an-hour after my father came in—he had a letter in his hand—and said:

"This letter had been delayed; it is from General Spielsdorf. He might have been here yesterday, he may not come till to-morrow, or he may be here to-day."

He put the open letter into my hand; but he did not look pleased, as he used when a guest, especially one so much loved as the General, was coming. On the contrary, he looked as if he wished him at the bottom of the Red Sea. There was plainly something on his mind which he did not choose to divulge.

"Papa, darling, will you tell me this?" said I, suddenly laying my hand on his arm, and looking, I am sure, imploringly in his face.

"Perhaps," he answered, smoothing my hair caressingly over my eyes.

"Does the doctor think me very ill?"

"No, dear; he thinks, if right steps are taken, you will be quite well again, at least, on the high road to a complete recovery, in a day or two," he answered, a little drily. "I wish our good friend, the General, had chosen any other time; that is, I wish you had been perfectly well to receive him."

"But do tell me, papa," I insisted, "what does he think is the matter with me?"

"Nothing; you must not plague me with questions," he answered, with more irritation than I ever remember him to have displayed before; and seeing that I looked wounded, I suppose, he kissed me, and added, "You shall know all about it in a day or two; that is, all that I know. In the meantime you are not to trouble your head about it."

He turned and left the room, but came back before I had done wondering and puzzling over the oddity of all this; it was merely to say that he was going to Karnstein, and had ordered the carriage to be ready at twelve, and that I and Madame should accompany him; he was going to see the priest who lived near those picturesque grounds, upon business, and as Carmilla had never seen them, she could follow, when she came down, with Mademoiselle, who would bring materials for what you call a pic-nic, which might be laid for us in the ruined castle.

At twelve o'clock, accordingly, I was ready, and not long after, my father, Madame and I set out upon our projected drive.

Passing the drawbridge we turn to the right, and follow the road over the steep gothic bridge, westward, to reach the deserted village and ruined castle of Karnstein.

No sylvan drive can be fancied prettier. The ground breaks into gentle hills and hollows, all clothed with beautiful wood, totally destitute of the comparative formality which artificial planting and early culture and pruning impart.

The irregularities of the ground often lead the road out of its course, and cause it to wind beautifully round the sides of broken hollows and the steeper sides of the hills, among varieties of ground almost inexhaustible.

Turning one of these points, we suddenly encountered our old friend, the General, riding towards us, attended by a mounted servant. His portmanteaus[1] were following in a hired waggon, such as we term a cart.

The General dismounted as we pulled up, and, after the usual greetings, was easily persuaded to accept the vacant seat in the carriage, and send his horse on with his servant to the schloss.

---

[1] *portmanteaus* Large trunks.

CHAPTER 10
BEREAVED

It was about ten months since we had last seen him; but that time had sufficed to make an alteration of years in his appearance. He had grown thinner; something of gloom and anxiety had taken the place of that cordial serenity which used to characterise his features. His dark blue eyes, always penetrating, now gleamed with a sterner light from under his shaggy grey eyebrows. It was not such a change as grief alone usually induces, and angrier passions seemed to have had their share in bringing it about.

We had not long resumed our drive, when the General began to talk, with his usual soldierly directness, of the bereavement, as he termed it, which he had sustained in the death of his beloved niece and ward; and he then broke out in a tone of intense bitterness and fury, inveighing against the "hellish arts" to which she had fallen a victim, and expressing, with more exasperation than piety, his wonder that Heaven should tolerate so monstrous an indulgence of the lusts and malignity[1] of hell.

My father, who saw at once that something very extraordinary had befallen, asked him, if not too painful to him, to detail the circumstances which he thought justified the strong terms in which he expressed himself.

"I should tell you all with pleasure," said the General, "but you would not believe me."

"Why should I not?" he asked.

"Because," he answered testily, "you believe in nothing but what consists with your own prejudices and illusions. I remember when I was like you, but I have learned better."

"Try me," said my father; "I am not such a dogmatist as you suppose. Besides which, I very well know that you generally require proof for what you believe, and am, therefore, very strongly pre-disposed to respect your conclusions."

"You are right in supposing that I have not been led lightly into a belief in the marvellous—for what I have experienced is marvellous—and I have been forced by

extraordinary evidence to credit that which ran counter, diametrically, to all my theories. I have been made the dupe of a preternatural conspiracy."

Notwithstanding his professions of confidence in the General's penetration, I saw my father, at this point, glance at the General, with, as I thought, a marked suspicion of his sanity.

The General did not see it, luckily. He was looking gloomily and curiously into the glades and vistas of the woods that were opening before us.

"You are going to the Ruins of Karnstein?" he said. "Yes, it is a lucky coincidence; do you know I was going to ask you to bring me there to inspect them. I have a special object in exploring. There is a ruined chapel, ain't there, with a great many tombs of that extinct family?"

"So there are—highly interesting," said my father. "I hope you are thinking of claiming the title and estates?"

My father said this gaily, but the General did not recollect the laugh, or even the smile, which courtesy exacts for a friend's joke; on the contrary, he looked grave and even fierce, ruminating on a matter that stirred his anger and horror.

"Something very different," he said, gruffly. "I mean to unearth some of those fine people. I hope, by God's blessing, to accomplish a pious sacrilege here, which will relieve our earth of certain monsters, and enable honest people to sleep in their beds without being assailed by murderers. I have strange things to tell you, my dear friend, such as I myself would have scouted as incredible a few months since."

My father looked at him again, but this time not with a glance of suspicion—with an eye, rather, of keen intelligence and alarm.

"The house of Karnstein," he said, "has been long extinct: a hundred years at least. My dear wife was maternally descended from the Karnsteins. But the name and title have long ceased to exist. The castle is a ruin; the very village is deserted; it is fifty years since the smoke of a chimney was seen there; not a roof left."

"Quite true. I have heard a great deal about that since I last saw you; a great deal that will astonish you. But I had better relate everything in the order in which

---

[1] *malignity* Evil, malice.

it occurred," said the General. "You saw my dear ward—my child, I may call her. No creature could have been more beautiful, and only three months ago none more blooming."

"Yes, poor thing! when I saw her last she certainly was quite lovely," said my father. "I was grieved and shocked more than I can tell you, my dear friend; I knew what a blow it was to you."

He took the General's hand, and they exchanged a kind pressure. Tears gathered in the old soldier's eyes. He did not seek to conceal them. He said:

"We have been very old friends; I knew you would feel for me, childless as I am. She had become an object of very near interest to me, and repaid my care by an affection that cheered my home and made my life happy. That is all gone. The years that remain to me on earth may not be very long; but by God's mercy I hope to accomplish a service to mankind before I die, and to subserve[1] the vengeance of Heaven upon the fiends who have murdered my poor child in the spring of her hopes and beauty!"

"You said, just now, that you intended relating everything as it occurred," said my father. "Pray do; I assure you that it is not mere curiosity that prompts me."

By this time we had reached the point at which the Drunstall road, by which the General had come, diverges from the road which we were travelling to Karnstein.

"How far is it to the ruins?" inquired the General, looking anxiously forward.

"About half a league," answered my father. "Pray let us hear the story you were so good as to promise."

CHAPTER II
THE STORY

"With all my heart," said the General, with an effort; and after a short pause in which to arrange his subject, he commenced one of the strangest narratives I ever heard.

"My dear child was looking forward with great pleasure to the visit you had been so good as to arrange

for her to your charming daughter." Here he made me a gallant but melancholy bow. "In the meantime we had an invitation to my old friend the Count Carlsfeld, whose schloss is about six leagues to the other side of Karnstein. It was to attend the series of fêtes which, you remember, were given by him in honour of his illustrious visitor, the Grand Duke Charles."[2]

"Yes; and very splendid, I believe, they were," said my father.

"Princely! But then his hospitalities are quite regal. He has Aladdin's lamp. The night from which my sorrow dates was devoted to a magnificent masquerade. The grounds were thrown open, the trees hung with coloured lamps. There was such a display of fireworks as Paris itself had never witnessed. And such music— music, you know, is my weakness—such ravishing music! The finest instrumental band, perhaps, in the world, and the finest singers who could be collected from all the great operas in Europe. As you wandered through these fantastically illuminated grounds, the moon-lighted château throwing a rosy light from its long rows of windows, you would suddenly hear these ravishing voices stealing from the silence of some grove, or rising from boats upon the lake. I felt myself, as I looked and listened, carried back into the romance and poetry of my early youth.

"When the fireworks were ended, and the ball beginning, we returned to the noble suite of rooms that were thrown open to the dancers. A masked ball, you know, is a beautiful sight; but so brilliant a spectacle of the kind I never saw before.

"It was a very aristocratic assembly. I was myself almost the only 'nobody' present.

"My dear child was looking quite beautiful. She wore no mask. Her excitement and delight added an unspeakable charm to her features, always lovely. I remarked[3] a young lady, dressed magnificently, but wearing a mask, who appeared to me to be observing my ward with extraordinary interest. I had seen her, earlier in the evening, in the great hall, and again, for a few

---

[1] *subserve* Assist.

[2] *fêtes* French: parties; *Grand Duke Charles* Charles, Grand Duke of Baden (1786–1818).

[3] *remarked* Noticed.

minutes, walking near us, on the terrace under the castle windows, similarly employed. A lady, also masked, richly and gravely dressed, and with a stately air, like a person of rank, accompanied her as a chaperon. Had the young lady not worn a mask, I could, of course, have been much more certain upon the question whether she was really watching my poor darling. I am now well assured that she was.

"We were now in one of the salons. My poor dear child had been dancing, and was resting a little in one of the chairs near the door; I was standing near. The two ladies I have mentioned had approached, and the younger took the chair next my ward; while her companion stood beside me, and for a little time addressed herself, in a low tone, to her charge.

"Availing herself of the privilege of her mask, she turned to me, and in the tone of an old friend, and calling me by my name, opened a conversation with me, which piqued my curiosity a good deal. She referred to many scenes where she had met me—at Court, and at distinguished houses. She alluded to little incidents which I had long ceased to think of, but which, I found, had only lain in abeyance in my memory, for they instantly started into life at her touch.

"I became more and more curious to ascertain who she was, every moment. She parried my attempts to discover very adroitly and pleasantly. The knowledge she showed of many passages in my life seemed to me all but unaccountable; and she appeared to take a not unnatural pleasure in foiling my curiosity, and in seeing me flounder, in my eager perplexity, from one conjecture to another.

"In the meantime the young lady, whom her mother called by the odd name of Millarca, when she once or twice addressed her, had, with the same ease and grace, got into conversation with my ward.

"She introduced herself by saying that her mother was a very old acquaintance of mine. She spoke of the agreeable audacity which a mask rendered practicable; she talked like a friend; she admired her dress, and insinuated very prettily her admiration of her beauty. She amused her with laughing criticisms upon the people who crowded the ball-room, and laughed at my

poor child's fun. She was very witty and lively when she pleased, and after a time they had grown very good friends, and the young stranger lowered her mask, displaying a remarkably beautiful face. I had never seen it before, neither had my dear child. But though it was new to us, the features were so engaging, as well as lovely, that it was impossible not to feel the attraction powerfully. My poor girl did so. I never saw anyone more taken with another at first sight, unless, indeed, it was the stranger herself, who seemed quite to have lost her heart to her.

"In the meantime, availing myself of the licence of a masquerade, I put not a few questions to the elder lady.

"'You have puzzled me utterly,' I said, laughing. 'Is that not enough? won't you, now, consent to stand on equal terms, and do me the kindness to remove your mask?'

"'Can any request be more unreasonable?' she replied. 'Ask a lady to yield an advantage! Beside, how do you know you should recognise me? Years make changes.'

"'As you see,' I said, with a bow, and, I suppose, a rather melancholy little laugh.

"'As philosophers tell us,' she said; 'and how do you know that a sight of my face would help you?'

"'I should take chance for that,' I answered. 'It is vain trying to make yourself out an old woman; your figure betrays you.'

"'Years, nevertheless, have passed since I saw you, rather since you saw me, for that is what I am considering. Millarca, there, is my daughter; I cannot then be young, even in the opinion of people whom time has taught to be indulgent, and I may not like to be compared with what you remember me. You have no mask to remove. You can offer me nothing in exchange.'

"'My petition is to your pity, to remove it.'

"'And mine to yours, to let it stay where it is,' she replied.

"'Well, then, at least you will tell me whether you are French or German; you speak both languages so perfectly.'

"'I don't think I shall tell you that, General; you intend a surprise, and are meditating the particular point of attack.'

"'At all events, you won't deny this,' I said, 'that being honoured by your permission to converse, I ought to know how to address you. Shall I say Madame la Comtesse?'

"She laughed, and she would, no doubt, have met me with another evasion—if, indeed, I can treat any occurrence in an interview every circumstance of which was pre-arranged, as I now believe, with the profoundest cunning, as liable to be modified by accident.[1]

"'As to that,' she began; but she was interrupted, almost as she opened her lips, by a gentleman, dressed in black, who looked particularly elegant and distinguished, with this drawback, that his face was the most deadly pale I ever saw, except in death. He was in no masquerade—in the plain evening dress of a gentleman; and he said, without a smile, but with a courtly and unusually low bow—

"'Will Madame la Comtesse permit me to say a very few words which may interest her?'

"The lady turned quickly to him, and touched her lip in token of silence; she then said to me, 'Keep my place for me, General; I shall return when I have said a few words.'

"And with this injunction, playfully given, she walked a little aside with the gentleman in black, and talked for some minutes, apparently very earnestly. They then walked away slowly together in the crowd, and I lost them for some minutes.

"I spent the interval in cudgelling my brains for a conjecture as to the identity of the lady who seemed to remember me so kindly, and I was thinking of turning about and joining in the conversation between my pretty ward and the Countess's daughter, and trying whether, by the time she returned, I might not have a surprise in store for her, by having her name, title, château, and estates at my fingers' ends. But at this moment she returned, accompanied by the pale man in black, who said:

"'I shall return and inform Madame la Comtesse when her carriage is at the door.'

"He withdrew with a bow."

---

[1] *accident* Chance.

CHAPTER 12
A PETITION

"'Then we are to lose Madame la Comtesse, but I hope only for a few hours,' I said, with a low bow.

"'It may be that only, or it may be a few weeks. It was very unlucky his speaking to me just now as he did. Do you now know me?'

"I assured her I did not.

"'You shall know me,' she said, 'but not at present. We are older and better friends than, perhaps, you suspect. I cannot yet declare myself. I shall in three weeks pass your beautiful schloss, about which I have been making enquiries. I shall then look in upon you for an hour or two, and renew a friendship which I never think of without a thousand pleasant recollections. This moment a piece of news has reached me like a thunderbolt. I must set out now, and travel by a devious route, nearly a hundred miles, with all the dispatch I can possibly make. My perplexities multiply. I am only deterred by the compulsory reserve I practise as to my name from making a very singular request of you. My poor child has not quite recovered her strength. Her horse fell with her, at a hunt which she had ridden out to witness, her nerves have not yet recovered the shock, and our physician says that she must on no account exert herself for some time to come. We came here, in consequence, by very easy stages—hardly six leagues a day. I must now travel day and night, on a mission of life and death—a mission the critical and momentous nature of which I shall be able to explain to you when we meet, as I hope we shall, in a few weeks, without the necessity of any concealment.'

"She went on to make her petition, and it was in the tone of a person from whom such a request amounted to conferring, rather than seeking a favour. This was only in manner, and, as it seemed, quite unconsciously. Than the terms in which it was expressed, nothing could be more deprecatory.[2] It was simply that I would consent to take charge of her daughter during her absence.

---

[2] *deprecatory* Apologetic or appeasing.

"This was, all things considered, a strange, not to say, an audacious request. She in some sort disarmed me, by stating and admitting everything that could be urged against it, and throwing herself entirely upon my chivalry. At the same moment, by a fatality that seems to have predetermined all that happened, my poor child came to my side, and, in an undertone, besought me to invite her new friend, Millarca, to pay us a visit. She had just been sounding her,[1] and thought, if her mamma would allow her, she would like it extremely.

"At another time I should have told her to wait a little, until, at least, we knew who they were. But I had not a moment to think in. The two ladies assailed me together, and I must confess the refined and beautiful face of the young lady, about which there was something extremely engaging, as well as the elegance and fire of high birth, determined me; and, quite overpowered, I submitted, and undertook, too easily, the care of the young lady, whom her mother called Millarca.

"The Countess beckoned to her daughter, who listened with grave attention while she told her, in general terms, how suddenly and peremptorily she had been summoned, and also of the arrangement she had made for her under my care, adding that I was one of her earliest and most valued friends.

"I made, of course, such speeches as the case seemed to call for, and found myself, on reflection, in a position which I did not half like.

"The gentleman in black returned, and very ceremoniously conducted the lady from the room.

"The demeanour of this gentleman was such as to impress me with the conviction that the Countess was a lady of very much more importance than her modest title alone might have led me to assume.

"Her last charge to me was that no attempt was to be made to learn more about her than I might have already guessed, until her return. Our distinguished host, whose guest she was, knew her reasons.

"'But here,' she said, 'neither I nor my daughter could safely remain for more than a day. I removed my mask imprudently for a moment, about an hour ago, and, too late, I fancied you saw me. So I resolved to seek an opportunity of talking a little to you. Had I found that you had seen me, I should have thrown myself on your high sense of honour to keep my secret for some weeks. As it is, I am satisfied that you did not see me; but if you now suspect, or, on reflection, should suspect, who I am, I commit myself, in like manner, entirely to your honour. My daughter will observe the same secrecy, and I well know that you will, from time to time, remind her, lest she should thoughtlessly disclose it.'

"She whispered a few words to her daughter, kissed her hurriedly twice, and went away, accompanied by the pale gentleman in black, and disappeared in the crowd.

"'In the next room,' said Millarca, 'there is a window that looks upon the hall door. I should like to see the last of mamma, and to kiss my hand to her.'

"We assented, of course, and accompanied her to the window. We looked out, and saw a handsome old-fashioned carriage, with a troop of couriers and footmen. We saw the slim figure of the pale gentleman in black, as he held a thick velvet cloak, and placed it about her shoulders and threw the hood over her head. She nodded to him, and just touched his hand with hers. He bowed low repeatedly as the door closed, and the carriage began to move.

"'She is gone,' said Millarca, with a sigh.

"'She is gone,' I repeated to myself, for the first time—in the hurried moments that had elapsed since my consent—reflecting upon the folly of my act.

"'She did not look up,' said the young lady, plaintively.

"'The Countess had taken off her mask, perhaps, and did not care to show her face,' I said; 'and she could not know that you were in the window.'

"She sighed, and looked in my face. She was so beautiful that I relented. I was sorry I had for a moment repented of my hospitality, and I determined to make her amends for the unavowed churlishness[2] of my reception.

"The young lady, replacing her mask, joined my ward in persuading me to return to the grounds, where the concert was soon to be renewed. We did so, and

[1] *sounding her* Getting to know her.

[2] *unavowed churlishness* Unspoken discourteousness.

walked up and down the terrace that lies under the castle windows. Millarca became very intimate with us, and amused us with lively descriptions and stories of most of the great people whom we saw upon the terrace. I liked her more and more every minute. Her gossip, without being ill-natured, was extremely diverting to me, who had been so long out of the great world. I thought what life she would give to our sometimes lonely evenings at home.

"This ball was not over until the morning sun had almost reached the horizon. It pleased the Grand Duke to dance till then, so loyal people could not go away, or think of bed.

"We had just got through a crowded saloon,[1] when my ward asked me what had become of Millarca. I thought she had been by her side, and she fancied she was by mine. The fact was, we had lost her.

"All my efforts to find her were vain. I feared that she had mistaken, in the confusion of a momentary separation from us, other people for her new friends, and had, possibly, pursued and lost them in the extensive grounds which were thrown open to us.

"Now, in its full force, I recognised a new folly in my having undertaken the charge of a young lady without so much as knowing her name; and fettered as I was by promises, of the reasons for imposing which I knew nothing, I could not even point my inquiries by saying that the missing young lady was the daughter of the Countess who had taken her departure a few hours before.

"Morning broke. It was clear daylight before I gave up my search. It was not till near two o'clock next day that we heard anything of my missing charge.

"At about that time a servant knocked at my niece's door, to say that he had been earnestly requested by a young lady, who appeared to be in great distress, to make out where she could find the General Baron Spielsdorf and the young lady his daughter, in whose charge she had been left by her mother.

"There could be no doubt, notwithstanding the slight inaccuracy,[2] that our young friend had turned up; and so she had. Would to heaven we had lost her!

"She told my poor child a story to account for her having failed to recover us for so long. Very late, she said, she had got to the housekeeper's bedroom in despair of finding us, and had then fallen into a deep sleep which, long as it was, had hardly sufficed to recruit her strength after the fatigues of the ball.

"That day Millarca came home with us. I was only too happy, after all, to have secured so charming a companion for my dear girl."

CHAPTER 13
THE WOOD-MAN

"There soon, however, appeared some drawbacks. In the first place, Millarca complained of extreme languor—the weakness that remained after her late illness—and she never emerged from her room till the afternoon was pretty far advanced. In the next place, it was accidentally discovered, although she always locked her door on the inside, and never disturbed the key from its place till she admitted the maid to assist at her toilet,[3] that she was undoubtedly sometimes absent from her room in the very early morning, and at various times later in the day, before she wished it to be understood that she was stirring. She was repeatedly seen from the windows of the schloss, in the first faint grey of the morning, walking through the trees, in an easterly direction, and looking like a person in a trance. This convinced me that, she walked in her sleep. But this hypothesis did not solve the puzzle. How did she pass out from her room, leaving the door locked on the inside? How did she escape from the house without unbarring door or window?

"In the midst of my perplexities, an anxiety of a far more urgent kind presented itself.

---

[1] *saloon* Salon, a large room used to entertain guests.

[2] *slight inaccuracy* Millarca incorrectly confers the title of Baron upon the General.

[3] *toilet* Routine care for one's appearance, including styling one's hair, applying cosmetics, and dressing.

"My dear child began to lose her looks and health, and that in a manner so mysterious, and even horrible, that I became thoroughly frightened.

"She was at first visited by appalling dreams; then, as she fancied, by a spectre, sometimes resembling Millarca, sometimes in the shape of a beast, indistinctly seen, walking round the foot of her bed, from side to side. Lastly came sensations. One, not unpleasant, but very peculiar, she said, resembled the flow of an icy stream against her breast. At a later time, she felt something like a pair of large needles pierce her, a little below the throat, with a very sharp pain. A few nights after, followed a gradual and convulsive sense of strangulation; then came unconsciousness."

I could hear distinctly every word the kind old General was saying, because by this time we were driving upon the short grass that spreads on either side of the road as you approach the roofless village which had not shown the smoke of a chimney for more than half a century.

You may guess how strangely I felt as I heard my own symptoms so exactly described in those which had been experienced by the poor girl who, but for the catastrophe which followed, would have been at that moment a visitor at my father's château. You may suppose, also, how I felt as I heard him detail habits and mysterious peculiarities which were, in fact, those of our beautiful guest, Carmilla!

A vista opened in the forest; we were on a sudden under the chimneys and gables of the ruined village, and the towers and battlements of the dismantled castle, round which gigantic trees are grouped, overhung us from a slight eminence.

In a frightened dream I got down from the carriage, and in silence, for we had each abundant matter for thinking; we soon mounted the ascent, and were among the spacious chambers, winding stairs, and dark corridors of the castle.

"And this was once the palatial residence of the Karnsteins!" said the old General at length, as from a great window he looked out across the village, and saw the wide, undulating expanse of forest. "It was a bad family, and here its blood-stained annals were written,"

he continued. "It is hard that they should, after death, continue to plague the human race with their atrocious lusts. That is the chapel of the Karnsteins, down there."

He pointed down to the grey walls of the gothic building, partly visible through the foliage, a little way down the steep.[1] "And I hear the axe of a woodman," he added, "busy among the trees that surround it; he possibly may give us the information of which I am in search, and point out the grave of Mircalla, Countess of Karnstein. These rustics preserve the local traditions of great families, whose stories die out among the rich and titled so soon as the families themselves become extinct."

"We have a portrait, at home, of Mircalla, the Countess Karnstein; should you like to see it?" asked my father.

"Time enough, dear friend," replied the General. "I believe that I have seen the original; and one motive which has led me to you earlier than I at first intended, was to explore the chapel which we are now approaching."

"What! see the Countess Mircalla," exclaimed my father; "why, she has been dead more than a century!"

"Not so dead as you fancy, I am told," answered the General.

"I confess, General, you puzzle me utterly," replied my father, looking at him, I fancied, for a moment with a return of the suspicion I detected before. But although there was anger and detestation, at times, in the old General's manner, there was nothing flighty.

"There remains to me," he said, as we passed under the heavy arch of the gothic church—for its dimensions would have justified its being so styled—"but one object which can interest me during the few years that remain to me on earth, and that is to wreak on her the vengeance which, I thank God, may still be accomplished by a mortal arm."

"What vengeance can you mean?" asked my father, in increasing amazement.

"I mean, to decapitate the monster," he answered, with a fierce flush, and a stamp that echoed mournfully through the hollow ruin, and his clenched hand was at the same moment raised, as if it grasped the handle of

---

[1] *steep*   Slope.

an axe, while he shook it ferociously in the air.

"What?" exclaimed my father, more than ever bewildered.

"To strike her head off."

"Cut her head off!"

"Aye, with a hatchet, with a spade, or with anything that can cleave through her murderous throat. You shall hear," he answered, trembling with rage. And hurrying forward he said:

"That beam will answer for a seat; your dear child is fatigued; let her be seated, and I will, in a few sentences, close my dreadful story."

The squared block of wood, which lay on the grass-grown pavement of the chapel, formed a bench on which I was very glad to seat myself, and in the mean-time the General called to the woodman, who had been removing some boughs which leaned upon the old walls; and, axe in hand, the hardy old fellow stood before us.

He could not tell us anything of these monuments; but there was an old man, he said, a ranger of this forest, at present sojourning in the house of the priest, about two miles away, who could point out every monument of the old Karnstein family; and, for a trifle,[1] he under-took to bring him back with him, if we would lend him one of our horses, in little more than half-an-hour.

"Have you been long employed about this forest?" asked my father of the old man.

"I have been a woodman here," he answered in his patois,[2] "under the forester, all my days; so has my father before me, and so on, as many generations as I can count up. I could show you the very house in the village here, in which my ancestors lived."

"How came the village to be deserted?" asked the General.

"It was troubled by revenants,[3] sir; several were tracked to their graves, there detected by the usual tests, and extinguished in the usual way, by decapitation, by the stake, and by burning; but not until many of the villagers were killed.

"But after all these proceedings according to law," he continued—"so many graves opened, and so many vampires deprived of their horrible animation—the village was not relieved. But a Moravian[4] nobleman, who happened to be travelling this way, heard how matters were, and being skilled—as many people are in his country—in such affairs, he offered to deliver the village from its tormentor. He did so thus: There being a bright moon that night, he ascended, shortly after sunset, the towers of the chapel here, from whence he could distinctly see the churchyard beneath him; you can see it from that window. From this point he watched until he saw the vampire come out of his grave, and place near it the linen clothes in which he had been folded, and then glide away towards the village to plague its inhabitants.

"The stranger, having seen all this, came down from the steeple, took the linen wrappings of the vampire, and carried them up to the top of the tower, which he again mounted. When the vampire returned from his prowlings and missed his clothes, he cried furiously to the Moravian, whom he saw at the summit of the tower, and who, in reply, beckoned him to ascend and take them. Whereupon the vampire, accepting his invitation, began to climb the steeple, and so soon as he had reached the battlements, the Moravian, with a stroke of his sword, clove his skull in twain, hurling him down to the churchyard, whither, descending by the winding stairs, the stranger followed and cut his head off, and next day delivered it and the body to the villagers, who duly impaled and burnt them.

"This Moravian nobleman had authority from the then head of the family to remove the tomb of Mircalla, Countess Karnstein, which he did effectually, so that in a little while its site was quite forgotten."

"Can you point out where it stood?" asked the General, eagerly.

The forester shook his head and smiled.

"Not a soul living could tell you that now," he said; "besides, they say her body was removed; but no one is sure of that either."

---

[1] *trifle* Small amount of money; a tip.

[2] *patois* Regional dialect.

[3] *revenants* Undead people.

[4] *Moravian* From the region of Moravia, now part of the Czech Republic.

Having thus spoken, as time pressed, he dropped his axe and departed, leaving us to hear the remainder of the General's strange story.

CHAPTER 14
THE MEETING

"My beloved child," he resumed, "was now growing rapidly worse. The physician who attended her had failed to produce the slightest impression upon her disease, for such I then supposed it to be. He saw my alarm, and suggested a consultation. I called in an abler physician, from Gratz. Several days elapsed before he arrived. He was a good and pious, as well as a learned man. Having seen my poor ward together, they withdrew to my library to confer and discuss. I, from the adjoining room, where I awaited their summons, heard these two gentlemen's voices raised in something sharper than a strictly philosophical discussion. I knocked at the door and entered. I found the old physician from Gratz maintaining his theory. His rival was combatting it with undisguised ridicule, accompanied with bursts of laughter. This unseemly manifestation subsided and the altercation ended on my entrance.

"'Sir,' said my first physician, 'my learned brother seems to think that you want a conjuror, and not a doctor.'

"'Pardon me,' said the old physician from Gratz, looking displeased, 'I shall state my own view of the case in my own way another time. I grieve, Monsieur le Général, that by my skill and science I can be of no use. Before I go I shall do myself the honour to suggest something to you.'

"He seemed thoughtful, and sat down at a table and began to write. Profoundly disappointed, I made my bow, and as I turned to go, the other doctor pointed over his shoulder to his companion who was writing, and then, with a shrug, significantly touched his forehead.

"This consultation, then, left me precisely where I was. I walked out into the grounds, all but distracted. The doctor from Gratz, in ten or fifteen minutes, overtook me. He apologised for having followed me, but said that he could not conscientiously take his leave without a few words more. He told me that he could not be mistaken; no natural disease exhibited the same symptoms; and that death was already very near. There remained, however, a day, or possibly two, of life. If the fatal seizure were at once arrested, with great care and skill her strength might possibly return. But all hung now upon the confines of the irrevocable. One more assault might extinguish the last spark of vitality which is, every moment, ready to die.

"'And what is the nature of the seizure you speak of?' I entreated.

"'I have stated all fully in this note, which I place in your hands upon the distinct condition that you send for the nearest clergyman, and open my letter in his presence, and on no account read it till he is with you; you would despise it else, and it is a matter of life and death. Should the priest fail you, then, indeed, you may read it.'

"He asked me, before taking his leave finally, whether I would wish to see a man curiously learned upon the very subject, which, after I had read his letter, would probably interest me above all others, and he urged me earnestly to invite him to visit him there; and so took his leave.

"The ecclesiastic[1] was absent, and I read the letter by myself. At another time, or in another case, it might have excited my ridicule. But into what quackeries will not people rush for a last chance, where all accustomed means have failed, and the life of a beloved object is at stake?

"Nothing, you will say, could be more absurd than the learned man's letter. It was monstrous enough to have consigned him to a madhouse. He said that the patient was suffering from the visits of a vampire! The punctures which she described as having occurred near the throat, were, he insisted, the insertion of those two long, thin, and sharp teeth which, it is well known, are peculiar to vampires; and there could be no doubt, he added, as to the well-defined presence of the small livid[2] mark which all concurred in describing as that induced

---

[1] *ecclesiastic* Clergy member.

[2] *livid* Greyish blue or purple.

by the demon's lips, and every symptom described by the sufferer was in exact conformity with those recorded in every case of a similar visitation.

"Being myself wholly sceptical as to the existence of any such portent as the vampire, the supernatural theory of the good doctor furnished, in my opinion, but another instance of learning and intelligence oddly associated with some one hallucination. I was so miserable, however, that, rather than try nothing, I acted upon the instructions of the letter.

"I concealed myself in the dark dressing-room, that opened upon the poor patient's room, in which a candle was burning, and watched there till she was fast asleep. I stood at the door, peeping through the small crevice, my sword laid on the table beside me, as my directions prescribed, until, a little after one, I saw a large black object, very ill-defined, crawl, as it seemed to me, over the foot of the bed, and swiftly spread itself up to the poor girl's throat, where it swelled, in a moment, into a great, palpitating mass.

"For a few moments I had stood petrified. I now sprang forward, with my sword in my hand. The black creature suddenly contracted toward the foot of the bed, glided over it, and, standing on the floor about a yard below the foot of the bed, with a glare of skulking ferocity and horror fixed on me, I saw Millarca. Speculating I know not what, I struck at her instantly with my sword; but I saw her standing near the door, unscathed. Horrified, I pursued, and struck again. She was gone; and my sword flew to shivers against the door.

"I can't describe to you all that passed on that horrible night. The whole house was up and stirring. The spectre Millarca was gone. But her victim was sinking fast, and before the morning dawned, she died."

The old General was agitated. We did not speak to him. My father walked to some little distance, and began reading the inscriptions on the tombstones; and thus occupied, he strolled into the door of a side-chapel to prosecute his researches. The General leaned against the wall, dried his eyes, and sighed heavily. I was relieved on hearing the voices of Carmilla and Madame, who were at that moment approaching. The voices died away.

In this solitude, having just listened to so strange a story, connected, as it was, with the great and titled dead, whose monuments were mouldering among the dust and ivy round us, and every incident of which bore so awfully upon my own mysterious case—in this haunted spot, darkened by the towering foliage that rose on every side, dense and high above its noiseless walls—a horror began to steal over me, and my heart sank as I thought that my friends were, after all, not about to enter and disturb this triste[1] and ominous scene.

The old General's eyes were fixed on the ground, as he leaned with his hand upon the basement[2] of a shattered monument.

Under a narrow, arched doorway, surmounted by one of those demoniacal grotesques[3] in which the cynical and ghastly fancy of old Gothic carving delights, I saw very gladly the beautiful face and figure of Carmilla enter the shadowy chapel.

I was just about to rise and speak, and nodded smiling, in answer to her peculiarly engaging smile; when with a cry, the old man by my side caught up the woodman's hatchet, and started forward. On seeing him a brutalised change came over her features. It was an instantaneous and horrible transformation, as she made a crouching step backwards. Before I could utter a scream, he struck at her with all his force, but she dived under his blow, and unscathed, caught him in her tiny grasp by the wrist. He struggled for a moment to release his arm, but his hand opened, the axe fell to the ground, and the girl was gone.

He staggered against the wall. His grey hair stood upon his head, and a moisture shone over his face, as if he were at the point of death.

The frightful scene had passed in a moment. The first thing I recollect after, is Madame standing before me, and impatiently repeating again and again, the question, "Where is Mademoiselle Carmilla?"

I answered at length, "I don't know—I can't tell—she went there," and I pointed to the door through

---

[1] *triste* Sad.

[2] *basement* Foundation or foot.

[3] *grotesques* Bizarre or deformed carved figures.

which Madame had just entered; "only a minute or two since."

"But I have been standing there, in the passage, ever since Mademoiselle Carmilla entered; and she did not return."

She then began to call "Carmilla," through every door and passage and from the windows, but no answer came.

"She called herself Carmilla?" asked the General, still agitated.

"Carmilla, yes," I answered.

"Aye," he said; "that is Millarca. That is the same person who long ago was called Mircalla, Countess Karnstein. Depart from this accursed ground, my poor child, as quickly as you can. Drive to the clergyman's house, and stay there till we come. Begone! May you never behold Carmilla more; you will not find her here."

CHAPTER 15
ORDEAL AND EXECUTION

As he spoke one of the strangest looking men I ever beheld, entered the chapel at the door through which Carmilla had made her entrance and her exit. He was tall, narrow-chested, stooping, with high shoulders, and dressed in black. His face was brown and dried in with deep furrows; he wore an oddly-shaped hat with a broad leaf.[1] His hair, long and grizzled, hung on his shoulders. He wore a pair of gold spectacles, and walked slowly, with an odd shambling gait, with his face sometimes turned up to the sky, and sometimes bowed down toward the ground, seemed to wear a perpetual smile; his long thin arms were swinging, and his lank hands, in old black gloves ever so much too wide for them, waving and gesticulating in utter abstraction.

"The very man!" exclaimed the General, advancing with manifest delight. "My dear Baron, how happy I am to see you, I had no hope of meeting you so soon." He signed to my father, who had by this time returned, and leading the fantastic old gentleman, whom he called the Baron, to meet him. He introduced him formally, and they at once entered into earnest conversation. The stranger took a roll of paper from his pocket, and spread it on the worn surface of a tomb that stood by. He had a pencil case in his fingers, with which he traced imaginary lines from point to point on the paper, which from their often glancing from it, together, at certain points of the building, I concluded to be a plan of the chapel. He accompanied what I may term his lecture, with occasional readings from a dirty little book, whose yellow leaves were closely written over.

They sauntered together down the side aisle, opposite to the spot where I was standing, conversing as they went; then they began measuring distances by paces, and finally they all stood together, facing a piece of the side-wall, which they began to examine with great minuteness; pulling off the ivy that clung over it, and rapping the plaster with the ends of their sticks, scraping here, and knocking there. At length they ascertained the existence of a broad marble tablet, with letters carved in relief upon it.

With the assistance of the woodman, who soon returned, a monumental inscription and carved escutcheon[2] were disclosed. They proved to be those of the long lost monument of Mircalla, Countess Karnstein.

The old General, though not I fear given to the praying mood, raised his hands and eyes to heaven, in mute thanksgiving for some moments.

"To-morrow," I heard him say; "the commissioner will be here, and the Inquisition[3] will be held according to law."

Then turning to the old man with the gold spectacles, whom I have described, he shook him warmly by both hands and said:

"Baron, how can I thank you? How can we all thank you? You will have delivered this region from a plague that has scourged its inhabitants for more than a century. The horrible enemy, thank God, is at last tracked."

My father led the stranger aside, and the General followed. I knew that he had led them out of hearing, that he might relate my case, and I saw them glance often quickly at me, as the discussion proceeded.

[1] *leaf* Brim.

[2] *escutcheon* Shield with a coat of arms.

[3] *Inquisition* Official investigation.

My father came to me, kissed me again and again, and leading me from the chapel, said:

"It is time to return, but before we go home, we must add to our party the good priest, who lives but a little way from this; and persuade him to accompany us to the schloss."

In this quest we were successful: and I was glad, being unspeakably fatigued when we reached home. But my satisfaction was changed to dismay, on discovering that there were no tidings of Carmilla. Of the scene that had occurred in the ruined chapel, no explanation was offered to me, and it was clear that it was a secret which my father for the present determined to keep from me.

The sinister absence of Carmilla made the remembrance of the scene more horrible to me. The arrangements for that night were singular. Two servants, and Madame were to sit up in my room that night; and the ecclesiastic with my father kept watch in the adjoining dressing-room.

The priest had performed certain solemn rites that night, the purport of which I did not understand any more than I comprehended the reason of this extraordinary precaution taken for my safety during sleep.

I saw all clearly a few days later.

The disappearance of Carmilla was followed by the discontinuance of my nightly sufferings.

You have heard, no doubt, of the appalling superstition that prevails in Upper and Lower Styria, in Moravia, Silisia, in Turkish Servia,[1] in Poland, even in Russia; the superstition, so we must call it, of the Vampire.

If human testimony, taken with every care and solemnity, judicially, before commissions innumerable, each consisting of many members, all chosen for integrity and intelligence, and constituting reports more voluminous perhaps than exist upon any one other class of cases, is worth anything, it is difficult to deny, or even to doubt the existence of such a phenomenon as the Vampire.

For my part I have heard no theory by which to explain what I myself have witnessed and experienced, other than that supplied by the ancient and well-attested belief of the country.

The next day the formal proceedings took place in the Chapel of Karnstein. The grave of the Countess Mircalla was opened; and the General and my father recognised each his perfidious and beautiful guest, in the face now disclosed to view. The features, though a hundred and fifty years had passed since her funeral, were tinted with the warmth of life. Her eyes were open; no cadaverous smell exhaled from the coffin. The two medical men, one officially present, the other on the part of the promoter of the inquiry, attested the marvellous fact, that there was a faint but appreciable respiration, and a corresponding action of the heart. The limbs were perfectly flexible, the flesh elastic; and the leaden coffin floated with blood, in which to a depth of seven inches, the body lay immersed. Here then, were all the admitted signs and proofs of vampirism. The body, therefore, in accordance with the ancient practice, was raised, and a sharp stake driven through the heart of the vampire, who uttered a piercing shriek at the moment, in all respects such as might escape from a living person in the last agony. Then the head was struck off, and a torrent of blood flowed from the severed neck. The body and head were next placed on a pile of wood, and reduced to ashes, which were thrown upon the river and borne away, and that territory has never since been plagued by the visits of a vampire.

My father has a copy of the report of the Imperial Commission, with the signatures of all who were present at these proceedings, attached in verification of the statement. It is from this official paper that I have summarized my account of this last shocking scene.

CHAPTER 16
CONCLUSION

I write all this you suppose with composure. But far from it; I cannot think of it without agitation. Nothing but your earnest desire so repeatedly expressed, could have induced me to sit down to a task that has unstrung

---

[1] *Silisia* Region in what is now modern Poland; *Turkish Servia* Serbia, which was part of the Ottoman Empire from the late Middle Ages until the late nineteenth century.

my nerves for months to come, and reinduced a shadow of the unspeakable horror which years after my deliverance continued to make my days and nights dreadful, and solitude insupportably terrific.

Let me add a word or two about that quaint Baron Vordenburg, to whose curious lore we were indebted for the discovery of the Countess Mircalla's grave.

He had taken up his abode in Gratz, where, living upon a mere pittance, which was all that remained to him of the once princely estates of his family, in Upper Styria, he devoted himself to the minute and laborious investigation of the marvellously authenticated tradition of Vampirism. He had at his fingers' ends all the great and little works upon the subject. "Magia Posthuma," "Phlegon de Mirabilibus," "Augustinus de curâ pro Mortuis," "Philosophicæ et Christiæ Cogitationes de Vampiris," by John Christofer Herenberg;[1] and a thousand others, among which I remember only a few of those which he lent to my father. He had a voluminous digest of all the judicial cases, from which he had extracted a system of principles that appear to govern—some always, and others occasionally only—the condition of the vampire. I may mention, in passing, that the deadly pallor attributed to that sort of revenants, is a mere melodramatic fiction. They present, in the grave, and when they show themselves in human society, the appearance of healthy life. When disclosed to light in their coffins, they exhibit all the symptoms that are enumerated as those which proved the vampire-life of the long-dead Countess Karnstein.

How they escape from their graves and return to them for certain hours every day, without displacing the clay or leaving any trace of disturbance in the state of the coffin or the cerements,[2] has always been admitted to be utterly inexplicable. The amphibious[3] existence of the vampire is sustained by daily renewed slumber in the grave. Its horrible lust for living blood supplies the vigour of its waking existence. The vampire is prone to be fascinated with an engrossing vehemence, resembling the passion of love, by particular persons. In pursuit of these it will exercise inexhaustible patience and stratagem, for access to a particular object may be obstructed in a hundred ways. It will never desist until it has satiated its passion, and drained the very life of its coveted victim. But it will, in these cases, husband and protract its murderous enjoyment with the refinement of an epicure,[4] and heighten it by the gradual approaches of an artful courtship. In these cases it seems to yearn for something like sympathy and consent. In ordinary ones it goes direct to its object, overpowers with violence, and strangles and exhausts often at a single feast.

The vampire is, apparently, subject, in certain situations, to special conditions. In the particular instance of which I have given you a relation, Mircalla seemed to be limited to a name which, if not her real one, should at least reproduce, without the omission or addition of a single letter, those, as we say, anagrammatically, which compose it. Carmilla did this; so did Millarca.

My father related to the Baron Vordenburg, who remained with us for two or three weeks after the expulsion of Carmilla, the story about the Moravian nobleman and the vampire at Karnstein churchyard, and then he asked the Baron how he had discovered the exact position of the long-concealed tomb of the Countess Millarca? The Baron's grotesque features puckered up into a mysterious smile; he looked down, still smiling on his worn spectacle-case and fumbled with it. Then looking up, he said:

"I have many journals, and other papers, written by that remarkable man; the most curious among them is one treating of the visit of which you speak, to Karnstein. The tradition, of course, discolours and distorts a little. He might have been termed a Moravian nobleman, for he had changed his abode to that territory, and was, beside, a noble. But he was, in truth, a native of Upper Styria. It is enough to say that in very early youth he had been a passionate and favoured lover

---

[1] *Magia Posthuma ... Herenberg* Classical and eighteenth-century works on vampirism and on death in general.

[2] *cerements* Waxed linens used to wrap bodies for burial.

[3] *amphibious* Possessing a dual character (here, that of being dead and alive).

[4] *husband* Manage and care for judiciously, as one manages a household economy or cultivates a farm; *epicure* Person who is devoted to physical pleasures.

of the beautiful Mircalla, Countess Karnstein. Her early death plunged him into inconsolable grief. It is the nature of vampires to increase and multiply, but according to an ascertained and ghostly law.

"Assume, at starting, a territory perfectly free from that pest. How does it begin, and how does it multiply itself? I will tell you. A person, more or less wicked, puts an end to himself. A suicide, under certain circumstances, becomes a vampire. That spectre visits living people in their slumbers; they die, and almost invariably, in the grave, develop into vampires. This happened in the case of the beautiful Mircalla, who was haunted by one of those demons. My ancestor, Vordenburg, whose title I still bear, soon discovered this, and in the course of the studies to which he devoted himself, learned a great deal more.

"Among other things, he concluded that suspicion of vampirism would probably fall, sooner or later, upon the dead Countess, who in life had been his idol. He conceived a horror, be she what she might, of her remains being profaned by the outrage of a posthumous execution. He has left a curious paper to prove that the vampire, on its expulsion from its amphibious existence, is projected into a far more horrible life; and he resolved to save his once beloved Mircalla from this.

"He adopted the stratagem of a journey here, a pretended removal of her remains, and a real obliteration of her monument. When age had stolen upon him, and from the vale of years[1] he looked back on the scenes he was leaving, he considered, in a different spirit, what he had done, and a horror took possession of him. He made the tracings and notes which have guided me to the very spot, and drew up a confession of the deception that he had practised. If he had intended any further action in this matter, death prevented him; and the hand of a remote descendant has, too late for many, directed the pursuit to the lair of the beast."

We talked a little more, and among other things he said was this:

"One sign of the vampire is the power of the hand. The slender hand of Mircalla closed like a vice of steel on the General's wrist when he raised the hatchet to strike. But its power is not confined to its grasp; it leaves a numbness in the limb it seizes, which is slowly, if ever, recovered from."

The following Spring my father took me on a tour through Italy. We remained away for more than a year. It was long before the terror of recent events subsided; and to this hour the image of Carmilla returns to memory with ambiguous alternations—sometimes the playful, languid, beautiful girl; sometimes the writhing fiend I saw in the ruined church; and often from a reverie I have started, fancying I heard the light step of Carmilla at the drawing-room door.

THE END
—1871–72 (REVISED 1872)

---

[1] *vale of years* Perspective of old age.

IN CONTEXT

Carmilla Illustrated

Carmilla was first published as a serial fiction in *Dark Blue*, an eclectic English literary magazine whose contributors included prominent Victorians such as Dante Gabriel Rossetti, Algernon Charles Swinburne, and Mathilde Blind. The illustrations reproduced below appeared with *Carmilla* in its serial form, each accompanying one of the novella's monthly installments; they are followed by the first page of the story as it appeared in the first edition of Le Fanu's collection *In a Glass Darkly* (1872).

Michael Fitzgerald, illustration for *Carmilla*, 1872. This image appears to illustrate the following passage from Chapter 4:

> She sat down. Her face underwent a change that alarmed and even terrified me for a moment. It darkened, and became horribly livid; her teeth and hands were clenched, and she frowned and compressed her lips[.] ... All her energies seemed strained to suppress a fit, with which she was breathlessly tugging; and at length a low convulsive cry of suffering broke from her.

David Henry Friston, illustration for *Carmilla*, 1872. In this image, General Spielsdorf witnesses Millarca's attack on his niece Bertha (Chapter 14).

PROLOGUE.

～～～

UPON a paper attached to the Narrative which follows, Doctor Hesselius
has written a rather elaborate note, which
he accompanies with a reference to his
Essay on the strange subject which the MS.
illuminates.

This mysterious subject, he treats, in that
Essay, with his usual learning and acumen,
and with remarkable directness and condensation. It will form but one volume of the

VOL. III.   E

Facsimile page from Sheridan Le Fanu, *In a Glass Darkly*, 1872.

CHARLOTTE BRONTË
1816 – 1855

Charlotte Brontë's first published novel, *Jane Eyre* (1847), is among the most enduringly beloved novels in the English language. Simultaneously a rousing tale of mystery and romantic passion and a powerful, incisive depiction of Victorian class boundaries and gender roles, its language and subject matter led many reviewers of the time to speculate about the identity and gender of its author, who chose to publish all her works under the pseudonym "Currer Bell." To those critics, Brontë boldly declared in 1849: "To you I am neither Man nor Woman—I come before you as an Author only—it is the sole standard by which you have a right to judge me—the sole ground on which I accept your judgment." Though her work would never entirely escape the gendered criticism of more conservative readers, over the course of her brief career Brontë nevertheless became one of the most renowned novelists of her era.

Brontë was born in April 1816 in the village of Thornton, West Yorkshire, the third child of Irish emigrant and Anglican priest Patrick Brontë and his wife Maria Branwell Brontë. Three more children were born to the Brontës in quick succession: Patrick Branwell in 1817, Emily Jane in 1818, and Anne in 1820. Shortly after Anne's birth, the Brontës moved to the village of Haworth, where Patrick took up the curacy of St. Michael and All Angels' Church. Haworth was a small and isolated working village, later described by Brontë as a "strange uncivilized place." With no family connections nearby and little inclination to make friends amongst the villagers, the children grew intensely dependent upon one another for companionship.

The first of many tragedies struck the family in 1821, with Maria Branwell Brontë's death. Three years later, the four eldest girls, Maria, Elizabeth, Charlotte, and Emily, were enrolled in the Clergy Daughters' School in Cowan Bridge, a boarding school for the daughters of poor members of the clergy. The girls' time at the institution proved disastrous. Living conditions were crowded, cold, and unsanitary, the food often extremely poorly cooked; many of the teachers were harsh disciplinarians with little regard for the Brontës' imaginative personalities, and Charlotte experienced bullying on account of her small physique and short-sightedness. Early in 1825, the school was swept by a typhoid epidemic. The Brontës were withdrawn from the school in the spring, but Maria and Elizabeth, who had already been sickly upon their arrival, were weakened by the experience; both died of what was probably tuberculosis not long after their return home. Charlotte was now left the eldest Brontë child.

For the next few years, the remaining children were educated informally at home, and were otherwise left mostly to their own devices. They read extensively (Patrick Brontë had remarkably liberal literary tastes for a curate of his time), with Charlotte developing a particular fondness for the popular but controversial Romantic poet Lord Byron. The children spent a great deal of their free time wandering the Haworth moors and playing highly imaginative games together, inventing the elaborate fantasy worlds of Angria and Gondal; these worlds, inspired by real-world political events, by adventure narratives, and by Romantic literature, would provide the settings for the sisters' earliest writings.

Brontë's formal education resumed in 1831, when she attended the small boarding school of Roe Head. After completing her education, she returned to Roe Head in 1835 as a teacher, the first in a series of teaching jobs she took on with the aim of supporting her financially struggling family; she hated the work, finding it psychologically and creatively stifling, but teaching was among the few money-making options available to single women of her class. Over the course of the next few years she also worked twice as a governess in wealthy households—a demeaning experience that would profoundly inform *Jane Eyre*. In 1842, Charlotte and Emily traveled to Brussels to improve their French, where they attended a boarding school run by Zoë and Constantin Héger. To help pay for their tuition and board, Charlotte taught English at the school, and Emily taught music. Charlotte became passionately attached to Constantin, who taught her French literature; the connection was at once intellectually fulfilling and emotionally painful, as the intensity of Charlotte's feelings for the married Héger appears to have been largely unrequited. Brontë's experiences in Brussels provided the setting and central themes for two of her novels, *The Professor* (published posthumously in 1857) and *Villette* (1853).

In 1845, Brontë stumbled across a notebook of Emily's poetry. Deeply moved by her sister's depth of poetic talent, Brontë persuaded her sisters to collaborate on a volume of poetry, which was published under ambiguously gendered pseudonyms in 1846. *The Poems of Currer, Ellis, and Acton Bell* barely sold, but the few reviews that were published over the next few months were modestly encouraging, and gave the sisters some hope. Before long, all three had completed novels: *The Professor* (Charlotte), *Wuthering Heights* (Emily), and *Agnes Grey* (Anne). Brontë struggled to find a publisher for this first effort—*The Professor* would ultimately not be published until after her death—but she persevered with a second novel. This latter effort was accepted with enthusiasm by the influential publishers Smith, Elder & Co.; *Jane Eyre* was published under Brontë's pseudonym in October 1847.

Influenced by eighteenth-century Gothic literature, by the burgeoning genre of the *bildungsroman* (coming-of-age story), and by Victorian social novels, *Jane Eyre* proved an almost overnight success. Its eponymous heroine is a poor, unconnected orphan whose "plain" looks, quiet demeanor, and passionate, rebellious spirit have often led her to be interpreted as a psychological self-portrait of Brontë. The boarding school Jane attends as a child is clearly a fictionalized version of the Clergy Daughters' School, and the portrayal of Jane's time as a governess expresses many of Brontë's own experiences in that role. Reviews of the novel were overwhelmingly positive, but a vocal minority found the novel's passionate language, Jane's yearning for emotional freedom, and her romance with her mysterious, Byronic employer Mr. Rochester to be "coarse" and vulgar—especially, some said, if Currer Bell were in fact a woman, a topic of popular speculation. Nevertheless, enthusiasm for the novel's psychological power prevailed; it had gone into a third edition by the spring of 1848.

Brontë's next work, *Shirley*—a historical novel set against the backdrop of the 1811 Luddite uprisings in Yorkshire—was published in 1849, around the tail end of a series of tragedies that had begun to beset the Brontë family during the previous autumn. Branwell Brontë, who had been struggling with substance addiction for years, died of tuberculosis in September 1848; Emily died of the same disease three months later, and in May 1849, Anne, too, died of what was probably tuberculosis. From that point the grieving Charlotte remained at Haworth to care for her father, now his only surviving child. She began working on revised editions of her sisters' earlier novels, *Wuthering Heights* and *Agnes Grey*; both editions, published in 1850, included a biographical preface in which Brontë revealed the true identities of Currer, Ellis, and Acton Bell, putting to rest the public debate that had been growing ever since *Jane Eyre*'s publication. Two years later, Brontë published her third novel, *Villette*; though not nearly as much of a popular success as *Jane Eyre*, it was praised by some readers as a more sophisticated work.

Brontë married her father's curate, Arthur Bell Nicholls, in 1854. Their marriage appears to have formed a very happy period in Brontë's life, though she also found her increased household duties to be a frustrating impingement upon her writing time. Brontë began showing signs of what was probably *hyperemesis gravidarum*, a particularly severe form of morning sickness, early in the new year; she died on 31 March 1855, nine months into her marriage, leaving unfinished a final novel, *Emma*. After her death, Patrick Brontë approached the writer Elizabeth Gaskell, who had befriended Brontë in the 1850s, to write a biography of his daughter. Gaskell's resultant *The Life of Charlotte Brontë* (1857), which was immensely popular and is still considered a masterpiece of life writing, minimized Brontë's unconventionality and presented her to the Victorian public as a woman whose first care was her domestic life. The biography bolstered Brontë's reputation and helped cement her importance to the canon of nineteenth-century women writers, a position she has continued to hold to this day. Modern audiences have, however, embraced Brontë's transgressive strength and intensity of feeling—the very elements of her writing that had alienated some of her contemporaries.

⌘ ⌘ ⌘

from *Jane Eyre*[1]

At this point in the novel, the protagonist and speaker, Jane Eyre, has been living at a charity boarding school called the Lowood Institution. She was sent there by her aunt Reed, who had brought her up—grudgingly and at times cruelly—after the death of her parents. The school follows harsh educational methods and is guided by narrow-minded religious ideas; it also provides poor-quality food and clothing. One kind teacher, Miss Temple, acts as the school's superintendent, and she tries to shield the students from the cruelties of the school supervisor, Mr. Brocklehurst.

CHAPTER 9

But the privations,[2] or, rather, the hardships of Lowood, lessened. Spring drew on; she was, indeed, already come; the frosts of winter had ceased; its snows were melted; its cutting winds ameliorated. My wretch-ed feet, flayed and swelled to lameness by the sharp air of January, began to heal and subside under the gentler breathings of April. The nights and mornings no longer, by their Canadian temperature, froze the very blood in our veins; we could now endure the play-hour passed in the garden. Sometimes, on a sunny day, it began even to be pleasant and genial; and a greenness grew over those brown beds which, freshening daily, suggested the thought that Hope traversed them at night, and left each morning brighter traces of her steps. Flowers peeped out among the leaves—snowdrops, crocuses, purple auriculas, and golden-eyed pansies. On Thursday afternoons (half holidays) we now took walks, and found still sweeter flowers opening by the wayside, under the hedges.

I discovered, too, that a great pleasure—an enjoyment which the horizon only bounded—lay all outside the high and spike-guarded walls of our garden. This pleasure consisted in a prospect of noble summits girdling a great hill-hollow, rich in verdure and shadow; in a bright beck,[3] full of dark stones and sparkling

---

[1] *Jane Eyre* The text presented here is based on the 1848 third edition of *Jane Eyre*.

[2] *privations* Instances of being deprived of food and other necessaries.

[3] *beck* Stream.

eddies. How different had this scene looked when I viewed it laid out beneath the iron sky of winter, stiffened in frost, shrouded with snow—when mists as chill as death wandered to the impulse of east winds along those purple peaks, and rolled down "ing" and holm[1] till they blended with the frozen fog of the beck! That beck itself was then a torrent, turbid and curbless;[2] it tore asunder the wood, and sent a raving sound through the air, often thickened with wild rain or whirling sleet; and for the forest on its banks, *that* showed only ranks of skeletons.

April advanced to May. A bright, serene May it was; days of blue sky, placid sunshine, and soft western or southern gales filled up its duration. And now vegetation matured with vigor; Lowood shook loose its tresses; it became all green, all flowery; its great elm, ash, and oak skeletons were restored to majestic life; woodland plants sprung up profusely in its recesses; unnumbered varieties of moss filled its hollows; and it made a strange ground-sunshine out of the wealth of its wild primrose plants; I have seen their pale, gold gleam, in overshadowed spots, like scatterings of the sweetest luster. All this I enjoyed often and fully, free, unwatched, and almost alone; for this unwonted liberty and pleasure there was a cause, to which it now becomes my task to advert.

Have I not described a pleasant site for a dwelling, when I speak of it as bosomed in hill and wood, and rising from the verge of a stream? Assuredly, pleasant enough; but whether healthy or not is another question.

That forest dell, where Lowood lay, was the cradle of fog and fog-bred pestilence;[3] which, quickening[4] with the quickening spring, crept into the Orphan Asylum, breathed typhus through its crowded school-room and dormitory, and, ere May arrived, transformed the seminary[5] into an hospital.

Semi-starvation and neglected colds had pre-disposed most of the pupils to receive infection. Forty-five out of the eighty girls lay ill at one time. Classes were broken up, rules relaxed. The few who continued well were allowed almost unlimited license, because the medical attendant insisted on the necessity of frequent exercise to keep them in health; and had it been otherwise, no one had leisure to watch or restrain them. Miss Temple's whole attention was absorbed by the patients; she lived in the sick room, never quitting it except to snatch a few hours' rest at night. The teachers were fully occupied with packing up and making other necessary preparations for the departure of those girls who were fortunate enough to have friends and relations able and willing to remove them from the seat of contagion. Many, already smitten, went home only to die; some died at the school, and were buried quietly and quickly, the nature of the malady forbidding delay.

While disease had thus become an inhabitant of Lowood, and death its frequent visitor; while there was gloom and fear within its walls; while its rooms and passages steamed with hospital smells—the drug and the pastile striving vainly to overcome the effluvia[6] of mortality—that bright May shone unclouded over the bold hills and beautiful woodland out-of-doors. Its garden, too, glowed with flowers; hollyhocks had sprung up tall as trees, lilies had opened, dahlias and roses were in bloom; the borders of the little beds were gay with pink thrift and crimson double-daisies; the sweet-briers gave out, morning and evening, their scent of spice and apples; and these fragrant treasures were all useless for most of the inmates of Lowood, except to furnish now and then a handful of herbs and blossoms to put in a coffin.

But I, and the rest who continued well, enjoyed fully the beauties of the scene and season. They let us ramble in the wood, like gypsies, from morning till night; we

---

[1] *ing* A north-of-England name for a meadow bordering a river; *holm* Low-lying grassy land by a river; can also mean an island in a river.

[2] *turbid* Opaque, muddy; *curbless* Unrestrained.

[3] *fog-bred pestilence* In the nineteenth century, the "miasma" theory of illness was still prevalent—the idea that illness was primarily caused by inhaling corrupted air. Fog was seen as particularly dangerous and almost certain to contain miasma.

[4] *quickening* Coming to life.

---

[5] *typhus* Reference either to typhus or typhoid fever—both cause high fever and rash, and both thrive in unhealthy, crowded environments; *seminary* School.

[6] *pastile* Lozenge; *effluvia* Smells.

did what we liked—went where we liked; we lived better, too. Mr. Brocklehurst and his family never came near Lowood now; household matters were not scrutinized into; the cross housekeeper was gone, driven away by the fear of infection; her successor, who had been matron at the Lowton Dispensary,[1] unused to the ways of her new abode, provided with comparative liberality. Besides, there were fewer to feed; the sick could eat little; our breakfast-basins were better filled; when there was no time to prepare a regular dinner, which often happened, she would give us a large piece of cold pie, or a thick slice of bread and cheese, and this we carried away with us to the wood, where we each chose the spot we liked best, and dined sumptuously.

My favorite seat was a smooth and broad stone, rising white and dry from the very middle of the beck, and only to be got at by wading through the water—a feat I accomplished barefoot. The stone was just broad enough to accommodate comfortably me and another girl—at that time my chosen comrade—one Mary Ann Wilson, a shrewd, observant personage, whose society I took pleasure in, partly because she was witty and original, and partly because she had a manner which set me at my ease. Some years older than I, she knew more of the world, and could tell me many things I liked to hear. With her, my curiosity found gratification. To my faults, also, she gave ample indulgence, never imposing curb or rein on anything I said. She had a turn for narrative—I for analysis; she liked to inform—I to question; so we got on swimmingly together, deriving much entertainment, if not much improvement, from our mutual intercourse.

And where, meantime, was Helen Burns?[2] Why did I not spend these sweet days of liberty with her? Had I forgotten her? Or was I so worthless as to have grown tired of her pure society? Surely the Mary Ann Wilson I have mentioned was inferior to my first acquaintance; she could only tell me amusing stories, and reciprocate any racy and pungent gossip I chose to indulge in; while, if I have spoken truth of Helen, she was qualified to give those who enjoyed the privilege of her converse a taste of far higher things.

True, reader, and I knew and felt this; and though I am a defective being, with many faults and few redeeming points, yet I never tired of Helen Burns, nor ever ceased to cherish for her a sentiment of attachment as strong, tender, and respectful as any that ever animated my heart. How could it be otherwise, when Helen, at all times and under all circumstances, evinced for me a quiet and faithful friendship, which ill-humor never soured nor irritation ever troubled! But Helen was ill at present; for some weeks she had been removed from my sight to I knew not what room, upstairs. She was not, I was told, in the hospital portion of the house with the fever patients; for her complaint was consumption,[3] not typhus; and by consumption I, in my ignorance, understood something mild, which time and care would be sure to alleviate.

I was confirmed in this idea by the fact of her once or twice coming downstairs on very warm, sunny afternoons, and being taken by Miss Temple into the garden; but, on these occasions, I was not allowed to go and speak to her; I only saw her from the school-room window, and then not distinctly, for she was much wrapped up, and sat at a distance under the verandah.

One evening, in the beginning of June, I had stayed out very late with Mary Ann in the wood; we had, as usual, separated ourselves from the others, and had wandered far—so far that we lost our way, and had to ask it at a lonely cottage, where a man and woman lived, who looked after a herd of half-wild swine that fed on the mast[4] in the wood. When we got back, it was after moonrise; a pony, which we knew to be the surgeon's, was standing at the garden-door. Mary Ann remarked, that she supposed someone must be very ill, as Mr. Bates had been sent for at that time of the evening. She went into the house. I stayed behind a few minutes to

---

[1] *Dispensary* Apothecary's shop, where medicines were prepared and sold.

[2] *Helen Burns* Dear friend of Jane's at Lowood: a well-read, gentle, religious, and at times visionary person.

[3] *consumption* Tuberculosis.

[4] *mast* Nuts from the trees of the forest, especially beech, chestnut, and oak.

plant in my garden[1] a handful of roots I had dug up in the forest, and which I feared would wither if I left them till morning. This done, I lingered yet a little longer; the flowers smelled so sweet as the dew fell; it was such a pleasant evening, so serene, so warm; the still glowing west promised so fairly another fine day on the morrow; the moon rose with such majesty in the grave east. I was noting these things, and enjoying them as a child might, when it entered my mind, as it had never done before:

"How sad to be lying now on a sick bed, and to be in danger of dying! This world is pleasant; it would be dreary to be called from it, and to have to go—who knows where?"

And then my mind made its first earnest effort to comprehend what had been infused into it concerning heaven and hell, and for the first time it recoiled, baffled; and, for the first time, glancing behind, on each side, and before it, it saw all round an unfathomed gulf; it felt the one point where it stood—the present; all the rest was formless cloud and vacant depth, and it shuddered at the thought of tottering, and plunging amid that chaos. While pondering this new idea, I heard the front door open; Mr. Bates came out, and with him was a nurse. After she had seen him mount his horse and depart, she was about to close the door, but I ran up to her.

"How is Helen Burns?"

"Very poorly," was the answer.

"Is it her Mr. Bates has been to see?"

"Yes."

"And what does he say about her?"

"He says she'll not be here long."

This phrase, uttered in my hearing yesterday, would have only conveyed the notion that she was about to be removed to Northumberland, to her own home. I should not have suspected that meant she was dying; but I knew instantly now; it opened clear on my comprehension that Helen Burns was numbering her last days in this world, and that she was going to be taken to the region of spirits, if such region there were. I experi-

enced a shock of horror, then a strong thrill of grief, then a desire—a necessity—to see her; and I asked in what room she lay.

"She is in Miss Temple's room," said the nurse.

"May I go up and speak to her?"

"Oh, no, child! It is not likely: and now it is time for you to come in; you'll catch the fever if you stop out when the dew is falling."

The nurse closed the front door; I went in by the side entrance which led to the school-room; I was just in time; it was nine o'clock, and Miss Miller was calling the pupils to go to bed.

It might be two hours later, probably near eleven, when I—not having been able to fall asleep, and deeming, from the perfect silence of the dormitory, that my companions were all wrapped in profound repose—rose softly, put on my frock over my night-dress, and, without shoes, crept from the apartment, and set off in quest of Miss Temple's room. It was quite at the other end of the house; but I knew my way; and the light of the unclouded summer moon, entering here and there at passage windows, enabled me to find it without difficulty. An odor of camphor and burned vinegar warned me when I came near the fever room; and I passed its door quickly, fearful lest the nurse who sat up all night should hear me. I dreaded being discovered and sent back; for I *must* see Helen—I must embrace her before she died—I must give her one last kiss, exchange with her one last word.

Having descended a staircase, traversed a portion of the house below, and succeeded in opening and shutting, without noise, two doors, I reached another flight of steps; these I mounted, and then just opposite to me was Miss Temple's room. A light shone through the keyhole, and from under the door: a profound stillness pervaded the vicinity. Coming near, I found the door slightly ajar; probably to admit some fresh air into the close abode of sickness. Indisposed to hesitate, and full of impatient impulses—soul and senses quivering with keen throes[2]—I put it back and looked in. My eye sought Helen, and feared to find death.

[1] *my garden* The students at Lowood each have their own garden plot to tend.

[2] *throes* Pains.

Close by Miss Temple's bed, and half covered with its white curtains, there stood a little crib. I saw the outline of a form under the clothes, but the face was hid by the hangings: the nurse I had spoken to in the garden sat in an easy chair, asleep; an unsnuffed candle burned dimly on the table. Miss Temple was not to be seen: I knew afterward that she had been called to a delirious patient in the fever-room. I advanced; then paused by the crib side: my hand was on the curtain, but I preferred speaking before I withdrew it. I still recoiled at the dread of seeing a corpse.

"Helen!" I whispered softly; "are you awake?"

She stirred, herself put back the curtain, and I saw her face, pale, wasted, but quite composed; she looked so little changed that my fear was instantly dissipated.

"Can it be you, Jane?" she asked in her own gentle voice.

"Oh!" I thought, "she is not going to die; they are mistaken: she could not speak and look so calmly if she were."

I got on to her crib and kissed her: her forehead was cold, and her cheek both cold and thin, and so were her hand and wrist; but she smiled as of old.

"Why are you come here, Jane? It is past eleven o'clock; I heard it strike some minutes since."

"I came to see you, Helen; I heard you were very ill, and I could not sleep till I had spoken to you."

"You came to bid me goodbye, then; you are just in time, probably."

"Are you going somewhere, Helen? Are you going home?"

"Yes; to my long home—my last home."

"No, no, Helen." I stopped, distressed. While I tried to devour my tears, a fit of coughing seized Helen; it did not, however, wake the nurse; when it was over, she lay some minutes exhausted; then she whispered—

"Jane, your little feet are bare; lie down and cover yourself with my quilt."

I did so; she put her arm over me, and I nestled close to her. After a long silence, she resumed; still whispering—

"I am very happy, Jane; and when you hear that I am dead you must be sure and not grieve; there is nothing to grieve about. We all must die one day, and the illness which is removing me is not painful; it is gentle and gradual; my mind is at rest. I leave no one to regret me much; I have only a father; and he is lately married, and will not miss me. By dying young I shall escape great sufferings. I had not qualities or talents to make my way very well in the world; I should have been continually at fault."

"But where are you going to, Helen? Can you see? Do you know?"

"I believe; I have faith; I am going to God."

"Where is God? What is God?"

"My maker and yours; who will never destroy what he created. I rely implicitly on his power, and confide wholly in his goodness; I count the hours till that eventful one arrives which shall restore me to him, reveal him to me."

"You are sure, then, Helen, that there is such a place as heaven; and that our souls can get to it when we die?"

"I am sure there is a future state; I believe God is good; I can resign my immortal part to him without any misgiving. God is my father; God is my friend; I love him; I believe he loves me."

"And shall I see you again, Helen, when I die?"

"You will come to the same region of happiness; be received by the same mighty, universal Parent, no doubt, dear Jane."

Again I questioned; but this time only in thought. "Where is that region? Does it exist?" And I clasped my arms closer round Helen; she seemed dearer to me than ever; I felt as if I could not let her go; I lay with my face hidden on her neck. Presently she said, in the sweetest tone—

"How comfortable I am! That last fit of coughing has tired me a little; I feel as if I could sleep; but don't leave me, Jane; I like to have you near me."

"I'll stay with you, *dear* Helen; no one shall take me away."

"Are you warm, darling?"

"Yes."

"Goodnight, Jane."

"Goodnight, Helen."

She kissed me, and I her; and we both soon slumbered.

When I awoke it was day: an unusual movement roused me; I looked up; I was in somebody's arms; the nurse held me; she was carrying me through the passage back to the dormitory. I was not reprimanded for leaving my bed; people had something else to think about: no explanation was afforded then to my many questions; but a day or two afterward I learned that Miss Temple, on returning to her own room at dawn, had found me laid in the little crib; my face against Helen Burns's shoulder, my arms round her neck. I was asleep, and Helen was—dead.

Her grave is in Brocklebridge churchyard; for fifteen years after her death it was only covered by a grassy mound; but now a gray marble tablet marks the spot, inscribed with her name, and the word "Resurgam."[1]
—1847

In Context

Brontë's Development as a Writer

Correspondence with Robert Southey (1837)

By 1836, Brontë had begun to take seriously the notion of writing professionally. That December, she wrote to Robert Southey, English Poet Laureate, seeking his feedback on a sample of her poetry. Her initial missive has not survived, but we know that along with the sample, she sent Southey an earnest letter describing her emotional plight and her struggle to reconcile herself to the drudgery of daily life. His response was mixed; though it has since become infamous for its urging that "Literature cannot be the business of a woman's life"—and that Brontë's literary yearnings might subside once she married and had children—Southey also acknowledged that she had considerable poetic talent, and encouraged her to "write poetry for its own sake ... and not with a view to celebrity; the less you aim at that, the more likely you will be to deserve and finally to obtain it." A follow-up letter included an invitation for Brontë to visit Southey in the Lakes District. Though this apparent offer of friendship did not come to fruition—and though Southey's obvious prejudice against the idea of women writers was undoubtedly discouraging—Brontë would prize the brief correspondence for the rest of her life.

[1] *Resurgam* Latin: I shall rise again.

Keswick, 12 March 1837

Madam,

... It is not my advice that you have asked as to the direction of your talents, but my opinion of them; and yet the opinion may be worth little, and the advice much. You evidently possess, and in no inconsiderable degree, what Wordsworth[1] calls "the faculty of verse." I am not depreciating it when I say that in these times it is not rare. Many volumes of poems are now published every year without attracting public attention, any one of which, if it had appeared half a century ago, would have obtained a high reputation for its author. Whoever, therefore, is ambitious of distinction in this way, ought to be prepared for disappointment.

But it is not with a view to distinction that you should cultivate this talent, if you consult your own happiness. I, who have made literature my profession, and devoted my life to it, and have never for a moment repented of the deliberate choice, think myself nevertheless bound in duty to caution every young man who applies as an aspirant to me for encouragement and advice against taking so perilous a course. You will say, that a woman has no need of such a caution: there can be no peril in it for her. In a certain sense this is true; but there is a danger of which I would, with all kindness and all earnestness, warn you. The daydreams in which you habitually indulge are likely to induce a distempered state of mind; and in proportion as all the ordinary uses of the world seem to you flat and unprofitable, you will be unfitted for them without becoming fitted for anything else. Literature cannot be the business of a woman's life, and it ought not to be. The more she is engaged in her proper duties, the less leisure will she have for it even as an accomplishment and a recreation. To those duties you have not yet been called, and, when you are, you will be less eager for celebrity. You will not seek in imagination for excitement, of which the vicissitudes of this life, and the anxieties from which you must not hope to be exempted, be your state what it may, will bring with them but too much.

But do not suppose that I disparage the gift which you possess; nor that I would discourage you from exercising it. I only exhort you so to think of it, and so to use it, as to render it conducive to your own permanent good. Write poetry for its own sake; not in a spirit of emulation, and not with a view to celebrity: the less you aim at that, the more likely you will be to deserve, and finally to obtain it. So written, it is wholesome both for the heart and soul; it may be made the surest means, next to religion, of soothing the mind, and elevating it. You may embody in it your best thoughts and your wisest feelings, and in so doing discipline and strengthen them.

Farewell, Madam. It is not because I have forgotten that I was once young myself, that I write to you in this strain; but because I remember it. You will neither doubt my sincerity, nor my goodwill; and, however ill what has here been said may accord with your present views and temper, the longer you live the more reasonable it will appear to you. Though I may be but an ungracious adviser, you will allow me, therefore, to subscribe myself, with the best wishes for your happiness here and hereafter,

Your true friend,

Robert Southey

---

[1] *Wordsworth* Romantic poet William Wordsworth (1770–1850), a friend of Southey's who would become Poet Laureate after Southey's death.

March 16 [1837]

Sir,

I cannot rest till I have answered your letter, even though by addressing you a second time I should appear a little intrusive; but I must thank you for the kind and wise advice you have condescended to give me. I had not ventured to hope for such a reply; so considerate in its tone, so noble in its spirit. I must suppress what I feel, or you will think me foolishly enthusiastic.

At the first perusal of your letter I felt only shame and regret that I had ever ventured to trouble you with my crude rhapsody; I felt a painful heat rise to my face when I thought of the quires[1] of paper I had covered with what once gave me so much delight, but which now was only a source of confusion; but after I had thought a little, and read it again and again, the prospect seemed to clear. You do not forbid me to write; you do not say that what I write is utterly destitute of merit. You only warn me against the folly of neglecting real duties for the sake of imaginative pleasures; of writing for the love of fame; for the selfish excitement of emulation. You kindly allow me to write poetry for its own sake, provided I leave undone nothing which I ought to do, in order to pursue that single, absorbing, exquisite gratification. I am afraid, sir, you think me very foolish. I know the first letter I wrote to you was all senseless trash from beginning to end; but I am not altogether the idle dreaming being it would seem to denote. My father is a clergyman of limited though competent income, and I am the eldest of his children. He expended quite as much in my education as he could afford in justice to the rest. I thought it therefore my duty, when I left school, to become a governess. In that capacity I find enough to occupy my thoughts all day long, and my head and hands too, without having a moment's time for one dream of the imagination. In the evenings, I confess, I do think, but I never trouble anyone else with my thoughts. I carefully avoid any appearance of preoccupation and eccentricity, which might lead those I live amongst to suspect the nature of my pursuits. Following my father's advice—who from my childhood has counselled me, just in the wise and friendly tone of your letter—I have endeavoured not only attentively to observe all the duties a woman ought to fulfil, but to feel deeply interested in them. I don't always succeed, for sometimes when I'm teaching or sewing I would rather be reading or writing; but I try to deny myself; and my father's approbation amply rewarded me for the privation. Once more allow me to thank you with sincere gratitude. I trust I shall never more feel ambitious to see my name in print; if the wish should rise, I'll look at Southey's letter, and suppress it. It is honour enough for me that I have written to him, and received an answer. That letter is consecrated; no one shall ever see it but papa and my brother and sisters. Again I thank you. This incident, I suppose, will be renewed no more; if I live to be an old woman, I shall remember it thirty years hence as a bright dream. The signature which you suspected of being fictitious is my real name. Again, therefore, I must sign myself

C. Brontë

---

[1] *quires* Sheets.

Keswick, March 22, 1837

Dear Madam,

Your letter has given me great pleasure, and I should not forgive myself if I did not tell you so. You have received admonition as considerately and as kindly as it was given. Let me now request that, if you ever should come to these lakes[1] while I am living here, you will let me see you. You would then think of me afterwards with the more goodwill, because you would perceive that there is neither severity nor moroseness in the state of mind to which years and observation have brought me.

It is, by God's mercy, in our power to attain a degree of self-government, which is essential to our own happiness, and contributes greatly to that of those around us. Take care of over-excitement, and endeavour to keep a quiet mind (even for your health it is the best advice that can be given you): your moral and spiritual improvement will then keep pace with the culture of your intellectual powers.

And now, Madam, God bless you! Farewell, and believe me to be your sincere friend,

Robert Southey

from Elizabeth Gaskell's *Life of Charlotte Brontë*, Volume 2, Chapter 1 (1857)

The following excerpts from Gaskell's biography focus on Brontë's process of composition, and on her work process for *Jane Eyre* in particular.

… I remember, however, many little particulars which Miss Brontë gave me, in answer to my inquiries respecting her mode of composition, etc. She said, that it was not every day that she could write. Sometimes weeks or even months elapsed before she felt that she had anything to add to that portion of her story which was already written. Then, some morning, she would waken up, and the progress of her tale lay clear and bright before her, in distinct vision. When this was the case, all her care was to discharge her household and filial duties, so as to obtain leisure to sit down and write out the incidents and consequent thoughts, which were, in fact, more present to her mind at such times than her actual life itself. Yet notwithstanding this "possession" (as it were), those who survive, of her daily and household companions, are clear in their testimony, that never was the claim of any duty, never was the call of another for help, neglected for an instant. …

Anyone who has studied her writings—whether in print or in her letters; anyone who has enjoyed the rare privilege of listening to her talk, must have noticed her singular felicity in the choice of words. She herself, in writing her books, was solicitous on this point. One set of words was the truthful mirror of her thoughts; no others, however apparently identical in meaning, would do. She had that strong practical regard for the simple holy truth of expression, which Mr. Trench[2] has enforced, as a duty too often neglected. She would wait patiently searching for the right term, until it presented itself to her. It might be provincial, it might be derived from the Latin; so that it accurately represented her idea, she did not mind whence it came; but this care makes her style present the finish of a piece of mosaic. Each component part, however small, has been dropped into the right place. She never wrote down a sentence until she clearly understood what she wanted to say, had deliberately chosen the words, and arranged them in their right order. Hence it comes that, in the scraps of paper

---

[1] *these lakes*   I.e., the Lake District, the picturesque region of northwestern England where many Romantic poets, including Southey and Wordsworth, resided.

[2] *Mr. Trench*   Richard Chenevix Trench (1807–86) was an Anglo-Irish archbishop and philologist who wrote extensively about language, particularly his views that truth, historical and moral, can be found in the study of words.

covered with her pencil writing which I have seen, there will occasionally be a sentence scored out, but seldom, if ever, a word or an expression. She wrote on these bits of paper in a minute hand, holding each against a piece of board, such as is used in binding books, for a desk. This plan was necessary for one so short-sighted as she was; and, besides, it enabled her to use pencil and paper, as she sat near the fire in the twilight hours, or if (as was too often the case) she was wakeful for hours in the night. Her finished manuscripts were copied from these pencil scraps, in clear, legible, delicate traced writing, almost as easy to read as print.

The sisters retained the old habit, which was begun in their aunt's lifetime, of putting away their work at nine o'clock, and beginning their study, pacing up and down the sitting room. At this time, they talked over the stories they were engaged upon, and described their plots. Once or twice a week, each read to the others what she had written, and heard what they had to say about it. Charlotte told me, that the remarks made had seldom any effect in inducing her to alter her work, so possessed was she with the feeling that she had described reality; but the readings were of great and stirring interest to all, taking them out of the gnawing pressure of daily-recurring cares, and setting them in a free place. It was on one of these occasions, that Charlotte determined to make her heroine [of *Jane Eyre*] plain, small, and unattractive, in defiance of the accepted canon.

The writer of the beautiful obituary article on "the death of Currer Bell"[1] most likely learnt from herself what is there stated, and which I will take the liberty of quoting, about *Jane Eyre*.

> She once told her sisters that they were wrong—even morally wrong—in making their heroines beautiful as a matter of course. They replied that it was impossible to make a heroine interesting on any other terms. Her answer was, "I will prove to you that you are wrong; I will show you a heroine as plain and as small as myself, who shall be as interesting as any of yours." Hence "Jane Eyre," said she in telling the anecdote: "but she is not myself, any further than that." As the work went on, the interest deepened to the writer. When she came to "Thornfield" she could not stop. Being short-sighted to excess, she wrote in little square paper-books, held close to her eyes, and (the first copy) in pencil. On she went, writing incessantly for three weeks; by which time she had carried her heroine away from Thornfield, and was herself in a fever which compelled her to pause.

This is all, I believe, which can now be told respecting the conception and composition of this wonderful book. …

---

[1] *obituary … Bell*   Anonymous obituary that was published in the *Leeds Mercury* newspaper on 7 April 1855.

GRACE AGUILAR
1816 – 1847

During her all-too-short literary career, Grace Aguilar managed to be many things. She was an advocate for Jewish emancipation and an empowering voice for Jewish women; a pioneering female-centered theologian; an early Zionist; a mediator between late Romantic and early Victorian poetry; and an innovator in domestic and historical fiction, to name a few. Aguilar's writing includes history, theology, religious apologetics, scriptural interpretation, prayers, and sermons, as well as poems, historical romances, and domestic novels. Her work was recognized in her lifetime, and still more after her death, for the way that it sought to raise the status of both the Jewish community within predominantly Christian Britain and of women within Judaism: in one tribute, a group

of Jewish women wrote that until Aguilar began writing, it had "in modern times never been the case that a woman … should stand forth the public advocate of the faith of Israel." In addition, Aguilar's writing explores themes at the very center of Victorian literature and thought, including the status and nature of religious belief; the relationship between private and public spheres; the extent and limits of English identity; and the interaction of the various national and religious communities comprising Britain.

Aguilar was born in London to Sarah Dias Fernandes and Emanuel Aguilar, both of Portuguese-Jewish descent; they had come to England in order to avoid the Spanish Inquisition. As a child, Aguilar suffered from illness and was regularly sent from London to the south coast of England, which was thought to be better for her health but which separated her from the bulk of England's Jewish community. Mainly educated by her parents, she spent much time in isolation, reading books from a precocious age and writing in her journals, which she continued to keep throughout her life. Before she reached her teens, she had begun writing poems and had completed a play. Some of Aguilar's early poetry was eventually published in her first collection, *The Magic Wreath* (1835). These early writings already display Aguilar's abiding interest in Jewish people and traditions.

When Aguilar began writing, British Jews were trying to obtain full civil rights while also fending off increasing pressure to assimilate or convert to Christianity. This pressure especially targeted Jewish women, who were widely perceived by non-Jews to be uneducated and oppressed, and who were, in fact, frequently marginalized within their community. Much of Aguilar's writing addresses these intertwined issues of religion and gender. Her popular poem "The Wanderers" (1845), for example, uses its sympathetic re-imagining of the biblical story of Hagar—who was sent into exile by Abraham's wife, Sarah, for conceiving Abraham's child—to dramatize the contemporary Jewish experience of alienation within Britain. Aguilar also defended both Jewish rights and women's rights in her copious nonfictional prose, which includes *The Spirit of Judaism* (1842), a theological treatise; *The Jewish Faith* (1846), an imaginary dialogue between two women on faith and conversion; and *The Women of Israel* (1845), a series of biographical studies of biblical, historical, and modern Jewish women. These works argued for both external recognition of Jewish rights and internal Jewish religious reform, including the wider liturgical use of English rather than Hebrew and the expansion of educational and other opportunities for women. They also engaged with the questions—pressing for many Victorians—of who and what religion was for, how it should be practiced, and what its relationship with the rest of society and of life should be.

Aguilar similarly spoke to both her community's immediate concerns and broader Victorian preoccupations in her fiction. She wrote historical fiction as well as novels centered on contemporary, mainly female, domestic experience; in both cases, she wrote about Jews and non-Jews alike. Aguilar's domestic fiction includes the novel *Home Influence* (1847)—which became her most popular work—and its follow-ups, *Woman's Friendship* (1850) and *A Mother's Recompense* (1851), as well as the short-story collection *Home Scenes and Heart Studies* (1852). Her writing in this vein reflects not only on the vexed Victorian issue of "separate spheres" but also on her own status as a female professional writer. Aguilar's short story "The Authoress," for example, concerns a woman writer, Clara Stanley, whose suitor Granville Dudley rejects her when a friend advises him that "A literary woman is the very antipodes of domestic happiness." The two ultimately marry when Dudley discovers that Clara's writing is motivated not by money or ambition but by a sense of feminine duty to her readers, which leads him to conclude that she "unite[s] … perfectly the literary and domestic characters."

Aguilar's historical fiction includes *The Vale of Cedars* (1850), a depiction of a Jewish family trying to evade the Spanish Inquisition, and *Days of Bruce* (1852), a romance about Scotland in the Middle Ages. In these novels, too, Aguilar deepened and complicated the exploration of a topic at the core of nineteenth-century British culture: the nature of national identity, especially in a multinational state such as Britain, and the tension between ethnic particularity and affiliation with "Britishness." Aguilar's literary depictions of Jewish history, together with her historical study "The History of the Jews in England" (1847), portray Jews as both at home in their host countries and set apart from them—both "Englishmen" and "Hebrews"—in a way that reflects and augments nineteenth-century British attempts to reckon with Britain's complex status as a nation of nations.

During her lifetime, Aguilar reached a considerable audience of both Jewish and non-Jewish readers on both sides of the Atlantic. She published much of her work in major Jewish periodicals such as *The Occident*, becoming one of this American magazine's highest-paid writers, but she also published in Christian women's magazines, and she earned a good living by her pen. However, she had been in poor health since her earliest childhood and was further weakened in 1838 by a bout of measles. She became increasingly frail, to the point that, in 1847, her brother Emanuel persuaded her to visit him in Frankfurt to consult a German physician. It was there that Aguilar died, at the age of thirty-one. Her mother later edited and published several volumes of her work, and her readership increased after her death.

⌘ ⌘ ⌘

Past, Present, and Future: A Sketch

It was a place of graves, and still and lone,
As all of life's strange history were flown,
And nothing left but the cold stones, that lay
Thick-crested o'er with emblems of decay—
5   High wavy grass, where never flowers had rest,
And the dull clinging moss, that lay caressed
E'en by the pale cold marble. There was one,
A mother's last low resting; and her child
Stood gazing round bewildered. There was none
10 Like that her soul trail pictured, undefiled
By Time's too with'ring hand. She sought a stone,
Pure in its spotless marble—standing lone,
With its brief record of a loved one gone,
And all untouched by shadow of decay;
15 For, oh! that full heart, but yesterday
It felt, since they had laid her there, alas!
Through bloomless weeds, and melancholy grass.
They led her where a lowly grave reposed,
Whose marble shrine thick clustering weeds enclosed,
20 There! lay she there! her tomb by Time's cold hand
Touched as all others, in that grave-girt sand,
When scarcely seemed it that a week had passed
Since those fond eyes had looked and smiled their last;
Since that loved voice its last low whisper said,
25 And breathed its blessing on that mourner's head.
Were these but memories now? and could it be
Long months had passed into eternity?
That time had flung his mantle o'er the grave,
And when the long grass in dark masses wave,
30 Low wailing accents filled the breezy blast;
"The loved, the mourned, the cherished, all are past."
Shrine of the past! that solitude—around,
Beneath, that word of woe hath impress[1] found—
Impress and echo; but on that lone heart
35 The past was present, sweeter joys t'impart
In shadow than in being. From the cup
Of mem'ry, life in such sweet hues gleamed up,
And brought forth bliss which had been with such
        power,

How might she deem them phantoms of the hour,
40 To shine a while and pass? Too soon she felt
They were but shadows, in her heart that dwelt
And mingled with her being. Oh! the woe
Of such awak'ning! Fled the sunny glow,
The cherished dream—the past once more was past,
45 And the dim present all its misery cast
One little moment; then, by Mercy sent,
The future to the present radiance lent,
And o'er that mourning spirit softly stole
Sweet visions of the freed, the heaven-born soul,
50 Awaiting hers in those fair realms of love,
Which smiled in beauty, life's last home, above.
The past, the present, merged in Faith's fond thought,
Which such bright glimpses of the future brought,
And softened that deep woe—and she hath bowed,
55 Believing and adoring, while the cloud
Folding that spirit, melted into tears,
Which grief assuaging, e'en its pang endears—
She knew her heart must wear a while its chain,
But earth in Faith's effulgence smiled again.
—1842

The Hebrew's Appeal

On Occasion of the Late Fearful Ukase Promoted by the Emperor of Russia[2]

Awake! arise! ye friends of Israel's race,
The wail of thousands lingers on the air,

---

[1] *impress* Impression upon the psyche.

[2] [Aguilar's note] The above poem was written nearly six months ago, when the Russian ukase [decree] was first made public, and sent to the only paper in England devoted to Jewish interests—the Voice of Jacob—the writer wishing to prove that at least one female Jewish heart and voice were raised in an appeal for her afflicted brethren. The editor of the V. of J. did not insert it, on the plea of having so much press of matter as to prevent giving it the required space. The Christian Lady's Magazine not only accepted and inserted it, but in bold and spirited prose appealed to her countrymen on the same subject. Still a Jewish paper is the natural channel for the public appearance of the poem, and therefore the writer sends it to the Occident, believing that though somewhat late, it will not there be disregarded. [Aguilar's poem responds to an 1844 proclamation by Emperor Nicolas I restricting Russian Jews' activities and ordering them to resettle on the Russian/Polish border.]

By heavy pinions° borne, through realms of space,   *wings*
'Til Israel shudd'ring, Israel's woe must bear;
5   The voice of suff'ring echoes to the skies,
And oh, not yet! one pitying heart replies.

List to the groan from manly bosoms rent,°   *torn*
The wilder sob from weaker spirits wrung,
The deep woe that hath in voice no vent,
10   Yet round the heart her deathly robe has flung,
And childish tears flow thick and fast like rain,
From eyes that never wept, and ne'er shall weep again.

Vain, vain, the mother's piteous shriek of woe,
Her dying infants clinging to her breast;
15   And age infirm, and youth, whose high hearts glow;
Vain, vain their cry for mercy on the oppressed.
The Ukase has gone forth—a word, a breath,
And thousands are cast out, to exile and to death.

Ay, death! for such is exile—fearful doom,
20   From homes expelled—yet still to Poland chained;
'Til want and famine mind and life consume,
And sorrow's poisoned chalice, all is drained.
Oh God, that this should be! that one frail man
Hath power to crush a nation 'neath his ban.°   *edict*

25   Will none arise! with outstretched hand to save!
No prayer for pity, and for aid awake?
Will She° who gave to Liberty the slave,   *England*
For God's own people not one effort make?
Will She not rise once more, in mercy clad,
30   And heal the bleeding heart, and Sorrow's sons make
    glad?

Will England sleep, when Justice bids her wake,
And send her voice all thrillingly afar?
Will England sleep, when her rebuke might shake
With shame and terror, e'en the tyrant Czar,

35   And 'neath the magic of her mild appeal,
Move Russia's frozen soul for Israel to feel?

Oh England! thou hast called us to thy breast,
And done to orphans all a mother's part,
And given them peace, and liberty, and rest,
40   And healing poured into the homeless heart;
Then, oh once more, let Israel mercy claim,
And suff'ring thousands bless our England's honoured
    name.

And let one prayer from Hebrew hearths ascend
To Israel's God, that He may deign reply,
45   And yet again His chosen race defend,
And "have respect"[1] once more "unto their cry,"[2]
And e'en from depths of darkness and despair,
Give freedom to His own, and "all their burden bear."[3]

For shall we sink, though dark our way and drear,
50   And Hope hath found in misery a tomb?
Though man be silent, Mercy hath no tear,
And Love and Joy are withered 'neath the gloom?
No! God is near to hear us while we crave,
And He will "bare His holy arm, to shield us and to
    save."[4]
—1844

---

[1] *have respect*   From Leviticus 26.9, in which God says to the Jewish people, "I will have respect unto you, and make you fruitful, and multiply you, and establish my covenant with you."

[2] *unto their cry*   From Psalms 34.15: "The eyes of the Lord are upon the righteous, and his ears are open unto their cry."

[3] *all their burden bear*   See Psalms 55.22: "Cast thy burden upon the Lord, and he shall sustain thee: he shall never suffer the righteous to be moved."

[4] *bare ... save*   See Isaiah 52.10: "The Lord hath made bare His holy arm in the eyes of all the nations; and all the ends of the earth shall see the salvation of our God."

The Wanderers
Genesis 21, 14–20[1]

With saddened heart and tearful eye the mother
    went her way,
The Patriarch's[2] mandate had gone forth, and Hagar
    must not stay.
Oh! who can tell the emotions deep that pressed on
    Abra'am's heart—
As thus, obedient to his God, from Ismael called to
    part!

5   But God had spoken, and he knew His word was
    changeless truth,
He could not doubt His blessing would protect the
    friendless youth;
He bade him go, nor would he heed the anguish of
    his soul;
He turned aside—a father's woe in silence to control.

Now hand in hand they wend their way, o'er hills and
    vale and wild;
10 The mother's heart was full of grief, but smiled in glee
    her child:
Fearless and free, he felt restraint would never gall
    him now—
And hailed with joy the fresh'ning breeze that fanned
    his fair young brow.

His mother's heart was desolate, and tears swelled in
    her eye;
Scarce to his artless words of love her quiv'ring lips
    reply.
15 *She* only saw the *future* as a lone and dreary wild:
The *present* stood before the lad in joyance undefiled.

She knew, alas! his boyish strength too soon would
    droop and fade;
And who was, in that lonely scene, to give them food
    and aid?
With trembling gaze she oft would mark° the   *observe*
    flushing of his cheek,
20 And list in terror, lest he should 'gin falteringly to
    speak!

Fatigue she felt not for herself, not heeded care nor
    pain—
But nearer, nearer to her breast her boy at times she'd
    strain;
Beersheba's[3] wilderness they see before them dark and
    wide;
Oh, who across its scorching sand their wandering
    steps will guide?

25 The flush departed from the cheek which she so oft
    has kissed;
To his glad tones of childish glee no longer may
    she list;°   *listen*
A pallor as of death is spread o'er those sweet features
    now—
She sees him droop before the blast that fanned his
    aching brow.

"Oh, mother lay me down," he cried, "I know not
    what I feel,
30 But something cold and rushing seems thro' all my
    limbs to steal—
Oh kiss me, mother dear, and then ah, lay me down
    to sleep—
Nay, do not look upon me thus—kiss me and do not
    weep!"

Scarce could her feeble arms support her child, and lay
    him where
Some clustering shrubs might shield him from the
    heavy scorching air;

---

[1] *Genesis 21, 14–20* In which God orders Abraham to cast out his mistress, Hagar, and their illegitimate son, Ishmael, upon the birth of a son by his wife, Sarah. Hagar wanders the parched desert and has just given up hope for Ishmael's life, when God sees her sorrow, leads her to water, and promises her that Ishmael will begin "a great nation."

[2] *Patriarch* I.e., Abraham.

---

[3] *Beersheba* City in the Negev desert region of what is now modern Israel.

35   His drooping eyelids closed; his breath came painfully
      and slow—
She bent her head on his a while in wild yet speechless
      woe.

Then from his side she hurried, as impelled she knew
      not why,
Save that she could not linger there—she could not
      see him die—
She lifted up her voice and wept—and o'er the lonely
      wild
40   "Let me not see his death!" was borne, "my Ismael,
      my child!"

And silence came upon her then, her stricken soul to
      calm;
And suddenly and strange there fell a soft and
      soothing balm—
And then a voice came stealing, on the still and
      fragrant air—
A still small voice[1] that would be heard, tho' solitude
      was there.

45   "What aileth thee, oh Hagar?" thus it spoke: "fear not,
      for God hath heard
The lad's voice where he is—and thou, trust in thy
      Maker's word!
Awake! arise! lift up the lad and hold him in thine
      hand—
I will of him a nation make, before Me, he shall
      stand."[2]

It ceased, that voice; and silence now, as strangely soft
      and still,
50   The boundless desert once again with eloquence
      would fill—
And strength returned to Hagar's frame, for God hath
      oped her eyes—
And lo! amid the arid sands a well of water lies!

Quick to her boy, with beating heart, the anxious
      mother flies,
And to his lips, and hands, and brow, the cooling
      draught applies—
55   He wakes! he breathes! the flush of life is mantling[3]
      on his cheek—
He smiles! he speaks! oh those quick tears his mother's
      joy shall speak!

She held him to her throbbing breast, she gazed upon
      his face—
The beaming features, one by one, in silent love to
      trace.
She bade him kneel to bless the Hand that saved him
      in the wild—
60   But oh! few words her lips could speak, save these
      —"My child, my child!"

—1845

---

[1] *A still small voice*   See 1 Kings 19.12.

[2] *What aileth ... stand*   From Genesis 21.17.

[3] *mantling*   Here, blushing.

EMILY BRONTË
1818 – 1848

It would seem that there were two Emily Brontës: one a shy, introverted, and unremarkable young woman, and the other the strong-willed, brilliant, and legendary woman who became almost a mythic figure after her death at the age of thirty. Both versions develop from the impressions her sister Charlotte gave of her in the preface to the second edition of *Wuthering Heights*, published shortly after her death. It is for this novel that she is now best known, although she is also widely lauded for the emotional intensity, enigmatic mysticism, and linguistic ingenuity of her poetry—much of which was not published until the twentieth century. She was at work on a second, lost novel at the time of her death. While many Victorians were suspicious of *Wuthering Heights* on account of its expressions of passion and of violence, it became a classic text in the twentieth century. Its reputation has been enhanced by film adaptations, particularly by the 1939 version starring Laurence Olivier, which helped make it into a by-word for romantic tragedy.

Emily Brontë's literary talent flourished in a house of creative writers that included her sisters Charlotte (best known for *Jane Eyre*) and Anne (*The Tenant of Wildfell Hall*). Emily was the fifth child of Patrick Brontë and Maria Branwell, born in 1818 into poor circumstances in Thornton, Yorkshire. Maria died just two years later, not long after Patrick, an Anglican clergy member, had taken a post in nearby Haworth, where he and the children remained for practically all their lives. The six children were cared for by Maria's sister, Elizabeth Branwell, and educated primarily by Patrick (who had graduated from Cambridge). For the most part the children had the run of the stone parsonage that sat next to a graveyard in the desolate West Yorkshire moors. At the same time, industrial Yorkshire was close at hand.

When she was just five years old, Emily followed her three elder sisters to a charity school for the daughters of poor clergy, a harsh institution that Charlotte would later depict in *Jane Eyre*. The conditions there were wretched, and all the sisters returned home when the two eldest, Maria and Elizabeth, contracted tuberculosis; they died soon afterward. The remaining children were left mainly to their own devices, performing household chores, reading literary classics and current affairs periodicals, walking on the moors, and writing elaborate plays and stories together. The two oldest children, Charlotte and Branwell, created an imaginary kingdom called "Angria"; the two younger children, Emily and Anne, fashioned the island of "Gondal," inspired by their father's colorful descriptions of political and historical events. Although the children's transcripts of Gondal no longer exist, Brontë continued its themes in her later, published poems.

Brontë again went off to school when she was seventeen, to a small institution at which Charlotte was now working as a teacher; Brontë, who had been reluctant to leave Haworth to begin with, grew intensely homesick, and returned home after only six months. Two years later she left home for another brief sojourn—this time to teach—but her homesickness and what she called her life of slavery brought her back again soon afterward. Her last stint away from home was in 1842, when she joined Charlotte at a teaching institution in Brussels. The two had planned to open their own school in Yorkshire, hoping they could turn around the family's desperate financial circumstances.

Charlotte eventually persuaded her sisters to publish a volume of their poems using pseudonyms. Unfortunately, *The Poems of Currer, Ellis, and Acton Bell* (1846), which was published with their own funds, sold only two copies and was ignored by most reviewers, although one did say that Ellis (Emily) showed the most promise. Within a year, however, all three Brontë sisters had completed novels: Charlotte, *The Professor*; Emily, *Wuthering Heights*; and Anne, *Agnes Grey*. When Charlotte's subsequently published novel, *Jane Eyre*, became a bestseller, Emily's and Anne's books were also published together in three volumes (*Agnes Grey* being the third). All three sisters used their pseudonyms.

Wuthering Heights is a book so full of passion and violence that the Victorian public assumed it had been written by a man (some even speculated that Branwell Brontë penned it), and some conjectured that the author of *Jane Eyre* had written it. Its dark and brooding story is set against the wild and bleak landscape of the Yorkshire moors. Highly charged with sexuality and with powerful moral ambiguities, the novel broke many conventions of the time. The marriage plot is at once respected (the "good characters," Cathy Linton and Hareton Earnshaw, inherit their rightful property and a happy ending) and damned (the "lovers" Catherine and Heathcliff both meet with an unhappy end, even if they are rumored to still roam the moors). The idea of love, so central to Victorian realism, is in *Wuthering Heights* as much frightening as comforting. It is no wonder that some reviewers found the novel gloomy, too unrelenting in its violence, and morally suspect. Even Charlotte Brontë, who always championed the novel as a work of genius, questioned its meaning.

Much of Brontë's poetry shares the bleakness of *Wuthering Heights* and its preoccupation with passion, loss, and death. Many of the poems display a desire for transcendence reminiscent of Catherine and Heathcliff's yearnings and yet a tenderness that is not evident in them or in the narrators of the novel. There is often in the poems a view of an existence free of the restraints of everyday life, even though this existence is often realized only through the realm of the imagination—perspectives that connect Brontë to her Romantic predecessors much more than to her Victorian contemporaries.

In 1848 the only Brontë son, Branwell, died of tuberculosis hastened by the effects of long-term alcohol and drug addiction. Emily Brontë soon began to show symptoms of tuberculosis herself, dying of the disease in December of 1848—only one year after the publication of *Wuthering Heights*. She left behind more than 150 poems in manuscript form; after her death Charlotte arranged for the publication of a few of these, but the majority did not appear in print until the early 1900s.

⌘ ⌘ ⌘

Remembrance

C old in the earth—and the deep snow piled above
    thee,
    Far, far removed, cold in the dreary grave!
Have I forgot, my only Love, to love thee,
    Severed at last by Time's all-severing wave?

5   Now, when alone, do my thoughts no longer hover
    Over the mountains, on that northern shore,

Resting their wings where heath and fern-leaves cover
    Thy noble heart for ever, ever more?

Cold in the earth—and fifteen wild Decembers,
10   From those brown hills, have melted into spring:
Faithful, indeed, is the spirit that remembers
    After such years of change and suffering!

Sweet Love of youth, forgive, if I forget thee,
    While the world's tide is bearing me along;

15 Other desires and other hopes beset me,
    Hopes which obscure, but cannot do thee wrong!

No later light has lightened up my heaven,
    No second morn has ever shone for me;
All my life's bliss from thy dear life was given,
20   All my life's bliss is in the grave with thee.

But when the days of golden dreams had perished,
    And even Despair was powerless to destroy;
Then did I learn how existence could be cherished,
    Strengthened, and fed without the aid of joy.

25 Then did I check° the tears of useless passion,   *restrain*
    Weaned my young soul from yearning after thine;
Sternly denied its burning wish to hasten
    Down to that tomb already more than mine.

And, even yet, I dare not let it languish,
30   Dare not indulge in memory's rapturous pain;
Once drinking deep of that divinest anguish,
    How could I seek the empty world again?
    —1846

Plead for Me

Oh, thy bright eyes must answer now,
    When Reason, with a scornful brow,
Is mocking at my overthrow!
Oh, thy sweet tongue must plead for me
5 And tell, why I have chosen thee!

Stern Reason is to judgment come,
Arrayed in all her forms of gloom:
Wilt thou, my advocate, be dumb?°   *silent*
No, radiant angel, speak and say,
10 Why I did cast the world away.

Why I have persevered to shun
The common paths that others run,
And on a strange road journeyed on,

Heedless, alike, of wealth and power—
15 Of glory's wreath and pleasure's flower.

These, once, indeed, seemed Beings Divine;
And they, perchance, heard vows of mine,
And saw my offerings on their shrine;
But, careless gifts are seldom prized,
20 And mine were worthily despised.

So, with a ready heart I swore
To seek their altar-stone no more;
And gave my spirit to adore
Thee, ever-present, phantom thing;
25 My slave, my comrade, and my king,

A slave, because I rule thee still;
Incline thee to my changeful will,
And make thy influence good or ill:
A comrade, for by day and night
30 Thou art my intimate delight,—

My darling pain that wounds and sears
And wrings a blessing out from tears
By deadening me to earthly cares;
And yet, a king, though prudence well
35 Have taught thy subject to rebel.

And am I wrong to worship, where
Faith cannot doubt, nor hope despair,
Since my own soul can grant my prayer?
Speak, God of visions, plead for me,
40 And tell why I have chosen thee!
    —1846

The Old Stoic

Riches I hold in light esteem;
    And love I laugh to scorn;
And lust of fame was but a dream
    That vanished with the morn:

5   And if I pray, the only prayer
        That moves my lips for me
    Is, "Leave the heart that now I bear,
        And give me liberty!"[1]

    Yes, as my swift days near their goal,
10   'Tis all that I implore;
    In life and death, a chainless soul,
        With courage to endure.
        —1846 (WRITTEN 1841)

My Comforter

Well hast thou spoken, and yet, not taught
    A feeling strange or new;
Thou hast but roused a latent thought,
A cloud-closed beam of sunshine, brought
5   To gleam in open view.

Deep down, concealed within my soul,
    That light lies hid from men;
Yet, glows unquenched—though shadows roll,
Its gentle ray cannot control,
10   About the sullen den.

Was I not vexed, in these gloomy ways
    To walk alone so long?
Around me, wretches uttering praise,
Or howling o'er their hopeless days,
15   And each with Frenzy's tongue;—

A brotherhood of misery,
    Their smiles as sad as sighs;
Whose madness daily maddened me,
Distorting into agony
20   The bliss before my eyes!

So stood I, in Heaven's glorious sun,
    And in the glare of Hell;
My spirit drank a mingled tone,
Of seraph's° song, and demon's moan;   *angel's*
25 What my soul bore, my soul alone
        Within itself may tell!

Like a soft air, above a sea,
    Tossed by the tempest's stir;
A thaw-wind, melting quietly
30 The snow-drift, on some wintry lea;°   *meadow*
No: what sweet thing resembles thee,
        My thoughtful Comforter?

And yet a little longer speak,
    Calm this resentful mood;
35 And while the savage heart grows meek,
For other token do not seek,
But let the tear upon my cheek
        Evince my gratitude!
        —1846

[Loud without the wind was roaring]

Loud without the wind was roaring
    Through the waned autumnal sky,
Drenching wet, the cold rain pouring
    Spoke of stormy winters nigh.

5   All too like that dreary eve
    Sighed within repining grief—
    Sighed at first—but sighed not long
    Sweet—How softly sweet it came!
    Wild words of an ancient song—
10   Undefined, without a name—

"It was spring, for the skylark was singing."
Those words they awakened a spell—
They unlocked a deep fountain whose springing
Nor absence nor distance can quell.

---

[1] *give me liberty!* Cf. Patrick Henry's 1775 speech, in which he recommended that his fellow Virginians rise in arms against British rule: "I know not what course others may take; but as for me, give me liberty or give me death!"

15 In the gloom of a cloudy November
They uttered the music of May—
They kindled the perishing ember
Into fervour that could not decay

Awaken on all my dear moorlands
20 The wind in its glory and pride!
O call me from valleys and highlands
To walk by the hill-river's side!

It is swelled with the first snowy weather;
The rocks they are icy and hoar[1]
25 And darker waves round the long heather
And the fern-leaves are sunny no more

There are no yellow-stars on the mountain,
The bluebells have long died away
From the brink of the moss-bedded fountain,
30 From the side of the wintery brae°—   *hillside*

But lovelier than cornfields[2] all waving
In emerald and scarlet and gold
Are the slopes where the north wind is raving
And the glens where I wandered of old—

35 "It was morning; the bright sun was beaming."
How sweetly that brought back to me
The time when nor labour nor dreaming
Broke the sleep of the happy and free

But blithely we rose as the dusk heaven
40 Was melting to amber and blue—
And swift were the wings to our feet given
While we traversed the meadows of dew.

For the moors, for the moors where the short grass
Like velvet beneath us should lie!
45 For the moors, for the moors where each high pass
Rose sunny against the clear sky!

For the moors, where the linnet° was trilling   *songbird*
Its song on the old granite stone—
Where the lark—the wild skylark was filling
50 Every breast with delight like its own.

What language can utter the feeling
That rose when, in exile afar,
On the brow of a lonely hill kneeling
I saw the brown heath growing there.

55 It was scattered and stunted, and told me
That soon even that would be gone:
It whispered, "The grim walls enfold me
I have bloomed in my last summer's sun."

But not the loved music whose waking
60 Makes the soul of the Swiss die away
Has a spell more adored and heartbreaking
Than in its half-blighted bells lay—

The spirit that bent 'neath its power
How it longed, how it burned to be free!
65 If I could have wept in that hour
Those tears had been heaven to me—

Well, well the sad minutes are moving
Though loaded with trouble and pain—
And sometime the loved and the loving
70 Shall meet on the mountains again—
—1850 (WRITTEN 1835)

[A little while, a little while]

A little while, a little while
The noisy crowd are barred away;
And I can sing and I can smile—
A little while I've holiday!

5 Where wilt thou go my harassed heart?
Full many a land invites thee now;
And places near, and far apart
Have rest for thee, my weary brow—

---

[1] *hoar*   White with frost.

[2] *cornfields*   Fields of grain.

There is a spot 'mid barren hills
10   Where winter howls and driving rain
But if the dreary tempest chills
There is a light that warms again

The house is old, the trees are bare
And moonless bends the misty dome
15   But what on earth is half so dear—
So longed for as the hearth of home?

The mute bird sitting on the stone,
The dank moss dripping from the wall,
The garden-walk with weeds o'ergrown
20   I love them—how I love them all!

Shall I go there? Or shall I seek
Another clime, another sky.
Where tongues familiar music speak
In accents dear to memory?

25   Yes, as I mused, the naked room,
The flickering firelight died away
And from the midst of cheerless gloom
I passed to bright, unclouded day—

A little and a lone green lane
30   That opened on a common[1] wide
A distant, dreamy, dim blue chain
Of mountains circling every side—

A heaven so clear, an earth so calm,
So sweet, so soft, so hushed an air
35   And, deepening still the dreamlike charm,
Wild moor-sheep feeding everywhere—

That was the scene—I knew it well
I knew the pathways far and near
That winding o'er each billowy swell
40   Marked out the tracks of wandering deer

Could I have lingered but an hour
It well had paid a week of toil

---

[1]   *common*   Open piece of land intended for public use.

But truth has banished fancy's power
I hear my dungeon bars recoil—

45   Even as I stood with raptured eye
Absorbed in bliss so deep and dear
My hour of rest had fleeted by
And given me back to weary care—
—1850 (WRITTEN 1838)

[Shall Earth no more inspire thee]

Shall Earth no more inspire thee,
Thou lonely dreamer now?
Since passion may not fire thee
Shall nature cease to bow?

5   Thy mind is ever moving
In regions dark to thee;
Recall its useless roving—
Come back and dwell with me.

I know my mountain breezes
10   Enchant and soothe thee still—
I know my sunshine pleases
Despite thy wayward will.

When day with evening blending
Sinks from the summer sky,
15   I've seen thy spirit bending
In fond idolatry.

I've watched thee every hour;
I know my mighty sway,
I know my magic power
20   To drive thy griefs away.

Few hearts to mortals given
On earth so wildly pine;
Yet none would ask a heaven
More like this earth than thine.

25   Then let my winds caress thee;
Thy comrade let me be—

original spelling

Since nought beside can bless thee,
Return and dwell with me.
—1850 (WRITTEN 1841)

[*No coward soul is mine*][1]

No coward soul is mine
No trembler in the world's storm-troubled sphere
I see Heaven's glories shine
And Faith shines equal arming me from Fear

5   O God within my breast
Almighty ever-present Deity
Life, that in me hast rest
As I Undying Life, have power in Thee

Vain are the thousand creeds
10 That move men's hearts, unutterably vain,
Worthless as withered weeds
Or idlest froth amid the boundless main°   *sea*

To waken doubt in one
Holding so fast by thy infinity
15 So surely anchored on
The steadfast rock of Immortality.

With wide-embracing love
Thy spirit animates eternal years
Pervades and broods above,
20 Changes, sustains, dissolves, creates and rears

Though Earth and moon were gone
And suns and universes ceased to be
And thou wert left alone
Every Existence would exist in thee

25 There is not room for Death
Nor atom that his might could render void
Since thou art Being and Breath
And what thou art may never be destroyed.
—1850 (WRITTEN 1846)

[*Often rebuked, yet always back returning*][2]

Often rebuked, yet always back returning
To those first feelings that were born with me,
And leaving busy chase of wealth and learning
For idle dreams of things which cannot be:

5   Today, I will seek not the shadowy region;
Its unsustaining vastness waxes drear;
And visions rising, legion after legion,
Bring the unreal world too strangely near.

I'll walk, but not in old heroic traces,°   *tracks*
10 And not in paths of high morality,
And not among the half-distinguished faces,
The clouded forms of long-past history.

I'll walk where my own nature would be leading:
It vexes me to choose another guide:
15 Where the gray flocks in ferny glens are feeding;
Where the wild wind blows on the mountain side.

What have those lonely mountains worth revealing?
More glory and more grief than I can tell:
The earth that wakes *one* human heart to feeling
20 Can centre both the worlds of heaven and hell.
—1850[3]

---

1   *No coward soul is mine*   Like much of Brontë's poetry, this poem
was not published until after her death. In preparing the poems for
publication in 1850, Charlotte Brontë made some alterations in
punctuation and syntax. The copy printed here is from the original
1846 manuscript, which is largely unpunctuated.

2   *Often rebuked … returning*   The authorship of "Often rebuked" has
been variously credited to Emily, Charlotte, and Anne Brontë; when
the poem was first printed it was recorded as having been written by
Emily.

3   *1850*   Brontë did not record the date on which she composed this
poem.

[*The night is darkening round me*]¹

The night is darkening round me
    The wild winds coldly blow
But a tyrant spell has bound me
And I cannot cannot go

5   The giant trees are bending
    Their bare boughs weighed with snow
    And the storm is fast descending
    And yet I cannot go

    Clouds beyond clouds above me
10 Wastes beyond wastes below
    But nothing drear can move me
    I will not cannot go

original spelling

    I'll come when thou art saddest
    Laid alone in the darkened room
    When the mad day's mirth has vanished
    And the smile of joy is banished
5   From evening's chilly gloom

    I'll come when the heart's real feeling
    Has entire unbiased sway
    And my influence o'er thee stealing
    Grief deepening joy congealing
10 Shall bear thy soul away

    Listen 'tis just the hour
    The awful time for thee
    Dost thou not feel upon thy soul
    A flood of strange sensations roll
15 Forerunners of a sterner power
    Heralds of me

---

¹ *The night … me* Sometimes considered three separate poems, "The Night" is unfinished. Brontë tended even in her published work to punctuate less heavily than most Victorian poets. As this poem demonstrates, the tendency was far more pronounced in her written drafts.

I would have touched the heavenly key
That spoke alike of bliss and thee
I would have woke the entrancing song
But its words died upon my tongue
5   And then I knew that entheal° strain   *divine*
Could never speak of joy again
And then I felt
—1902 (WRITTEN 1837)

original spelling

[*I'll come when thou art saddest*]

I'll come when thou art saddest,
Laid alone in the darkened room;
When the mad day's mirth has vanished
And the smile of joy is banished
5   From evening's chilly gloom.

I'll come when the heart's real feeling
Has entire, unbiased sway,
And my influence o'er thee stealing,
Grief deepening, joy congealing,
10 Shall bear thy soul away.

Listen! 'tis just the hour,
The awful time for thee:
Dost thou not feel upon thy soul
A flood of strange sensations roll,
15 Forerunners of a sterner power,
Heralds of me?
—1902 (WRITTEN 1837)

[*I'm happiest when most away*]

I'm happiest when most away
I can bear my soul from its home of clay
On a windy night when the moon is bright
And the eye can wander through worlds of light—

5 When I am not and none beside—
Nor earth nor sea nor cloudless sky—
But only spirit wandering wide
Through infinite immensity.
    —1910 (WRITTEN 1838)

[*If grief for grief can touch thee*]

If grief for grief can touch thee,
If answering woe for woe,
If any ruth° can melt thee   compassion
Come to me now!

5 I cannot be more lonely,
More drear I cannot be!

My worn heart throbs so wildly
'Twill break for thee—

10 And when the world despises—
When heaven repels my prayer—
Will not mine angel comfort?
Mine idol hear?

Yes by the tears I've poured,
By all my hours of pain
15 O I shall surely win thee
Beloved, again!
    —1902 (WRITTEN 1840)

THE NEW ART OF PHOTOGRAPHY

CONTEXTS

If the Victorian era was in many ways an "age of realism" in literature, it was also an age in which the "real" was given new definition through the medium of photography. Photography was developed virtually simultaneously by Louis Daguerre and Henry Fox Talbot, with the Frenchman and the Englishman making announcements of their discoveries within three weeks of each other in 1839. As Charles Dickens describes in his essay on "Photography" (excerpted in this section), the technologies developed by the two were quite distinct; the "daguerreotype" resulted in a single image, while the calotype technology developed by Talbot involved paper negatives from which multiple images could be created. Later in the century a variety of other techniques were developed, including glass plate technology, which provided levels of photographic detail that remain virtually unrivaled, even in the twenty-first century. By the 1890s, the advent of the portable "Kodak" camera had put photography into the reach of the middle classes. Not only was it possible for one to obtain a few images of one's loved ones from a professional; one could also take up the activity of photography as an amateur. But even in the 1840s, the new science and art of photography was helping to transform a number of aspects of Victorian culture.

Photography had a particularly strong impact on print culture. Engraving had for centuries made possible the reproduction of illustrations, and wood engraving, one of the first methods used to produce illustrations in books, enjoyed a renaissance in the period, as did all things medieval. Metal engravings, a slightly later invention, enjoyed a short revival in popularity during the nineteenth century—particularly steel engravings, which could be used to produce a large number of proofs. This practice was soon superceded, however, by photo-engraving, a photomechanical process by which a photographic image was recorded on a sensitized metal plate, which was then etched in an acid bath and used to reproduce the photograph. The widespread reproduction of actual photographs in newspapers and magazines did not come until the early twentieth century, but these engraving techniques, pioneered in such publications as the satirical magazine *Punch* (founded in 1841), and, especially, in *The Illustrated London News* (founded 14 May 1842), allowed engravings based on photographic images to be reproduced—and to give readers a sense of the world being shown to them as it really was.

The connections between photography and print were not restricted to newspapers and magazines, of course; new technologies such as the engraving machine (created in the 1830s) enabled an unprecedented expansion of book illustration in the Victorian period. And sometimes the connections between literature and photography were entirely direct; Tennyson, for example, commissioned the photographer Julia Margaret Cameron to illustrate his *Idylls of the King*.

Photography interacted just as powerfully with other arts. The connection between photography and painting was an obvious one, and certainly many artists began to use photographs in their work, sometimes merely as an *aide memoire*, sometimes as a "copy text," sometimes as something in-between. For his famous panorama of *Derby Day* (1856–58), for example, the painter William Powell Frith commissioned the photographer Robert Howlett to take photographs not of the entire scene in which Frith was interested (for which Frith relied on his own sketches from life) but of a range of different individuals within it, so that he could fill in human details with greater accuracy and completeness.

Some expressed an outright preference for the newer art over the arts of painting and drawing. In an essay that appeared in the 21 January 1857 issue of the *Journal of the Photographic Society*, for example, "Theta" argued that "what in painting is a tiresome pedantry of observation, becomes in photography an inexhaustible delight, a study, and a piece of instruction. What we cared not for in nature, becomes a joy and wonder in the photographic picture." But when practitioners of the new art began to stake claims for an artistic status that went beyond fidelity to nature and aspired to the condition of "High Art," they met with considerable resistance. A landmark was the exhibition in 1857 at the Art Treasures Exhibition in Manchester (the first major exhibition to showcase photography alongside painting and other traditional visual arts). The most controversial work exhibited was Oscar Rejlander's vast photographic tableau, *The Two Ways of Life*, in which a montage of photographic images of allegorical figures are brought together against an artificial backdrop. To many, the artistic presumption of the work crossed a line; reviewing the exhibition in *The Art-Journal*, Robert Hunt allowed that "the pose of each figure is good and the grouping of the whole as nearly perfect as possible," but nevertheless concluded that "we do not … desire to see many advances in this direction. Works of High Art are not to be executed by a mechanical contrivance. The hand of man, guided by the heaven-born mind, can alone achieve greatness in this direction."

Rejlander was not alone in his desire to create photographs that would be recognized as "High Art," that is, in the same sorts of ways as oil paintings were received. Henry Peach Robinson argued unabashedly in "Pictorial Effect in Photography" (1867) for the use of the photographer's artifice to contrive a pleasing result: "any dodge, trick, and conjuration of any kind is open to the photographer's use. His imperative duty is to avoid the mean, the base, and the ugly, and to aim to elevate his subject, … to correct the unpicturesque. … A great deal can be done and very beautiful pictures made, by a mixture of the real and the artificial in a picture." Robinson's most controversial work of precisely this sort was *Fading Away* (1858), a composition combining images from five negatives, with the full image depicting a girl dying of consumption. Some saw the result of Robinson's artistry as a tasteless exploitation of grief, but the image was extremely popular (Prince Albert was prompted by his admiration of *Fading Away* to place a standing order for a copy of any composite photograph Robinson produced).

A very different approach to the art of photography was taken by Henry Emerson, who strongly criticized the approaches of photographers such as Rejlander, Robinson, and Julia Margaret Cameron. "Photograph people as they really are," he advised in *Naturalistic Photography* (1886). "Do not dress them up. … The photographic technique is perfect." Emerson's recommended photographic techniques, however, were themselves highly original—and in their own way as consciously artistic as those of Robinson or Cameron. In Emerson's view, one should emulate the natural, and "nothing in nature has a hard outline, but everything is seen against something else, and its outlines fade gently into something else, often so subtly that you cannot distinguish clearly where one ends and the other begins." To represent nature as the eye perceives it, then, Emerson recommended shooting photographs slightly out of focus. Emerson's impressionistic approach was popular for a time (and continued to influence some important photographers well into the twentieth century), but by the 1890s it was in painting rather than in photography that impressionism was putting down deep roots. Emerson himself came to recant his earlier views; in "The Death of Naturalistic Photography" (1890), he wrote that he had given up hope of photography being able to compete with painting; and regretting that he had compared "photographs to great works of art, and photographers to great artists … I throw in my lot with those who say Photography is a very limited Art."

But "limited" was by then precisely what photography had proven it was *not*. Within Britain and its colonies alone, the medium had produced the war photographs, nature photographs, and still-lifes of Roger Fenton; the social realism of John Thomson and Thomas Annan; the memorably idealized expressions of female beauty of Julia Margaret Cameron and Lady Clementina Hawarden; suggestive representations of the exotic by Fenton, Thomson, Cameron, Francis Frith, and others; powerful representations by Howlett and others of the vitality of industrial Britain, and Annan's and Thomson's equally powerful images of its brutality; Frank Sutcliffe's and Henry Taunt's evocative images of village and rural life; and the compelling portraiture of Cameron, Lewis Carroll, William Notman, and many others.

The practice of photography was diverse, too. Early on it had become established as a professional pursuit—in the 1851 census there were already 51 British citizens who listed "photographer" as their occupation. But aristocratic amateurs such as Cameron, Hawarden, and Talbot continued to make their marks. With the notable exception of Lady Elizabeth Butler, women remained excluded from the ranks of accepted artists in the medium of painting; in photography, however, Cameron, Hawarden—and, later in the century, Anna Atkins and others—were leading figures.

More generally, it was also true that the sorts of individuals who were attracted to photography formed a diverse group. The barriers that today divide photography as an artistic pursuit from its commercial and scientific applications had for the most part not yet been erected in the Victorian era. Even those who saw photography as an art simultaneously appreciated it as science; Roger Fenton, for example, in his 1852 "Proposal for the Formation of a Photographic Society" (reprinted in this section), refers to photography both as an art and as a "branch of natural science," and proposes to open the society to opticians and chemists as well as artists and "practical photographers, both professional and amateur." One influential photographer whose work straddled the line between art and science was Eadweard Muybridge, who created a famous serious of photographs to answer the question—until then unresolved—of whether a horse becomes momentarily airborne while trotting or galloping. After nearly six years spent at work on a process involving multiple cameras with a brief exposure time, he captured *The Horse in Motion* (1878). He continued to use photography to study different forms of movement, eventually developing faster shutter speeds and faster film; his work ultimately paved the way for the creation of motion pictures.

As Muybridge's achievements demonstrate, the nineteenth century was a period of rapid advancement in the technology of photography—a medium that in the mid-century was not only extremely new but also severely limited. No means existed, for example, to enlarge photographic images, and the very long exposure times required in photography's early years meant that it remained impossible for a photograph to "capture a moment"; figures passing quickly in front of the camera would remain entirely unrecorded. (That Fenton's most famous photograph of the Crimean War showed cannon balls in an empty valley was a reflection of Victorian sensibilities, but also a reflection of the limits of technology: he could have depicted dead bodies, but to photograph the action of battle was still impossible.) The diversity and the depth of the achievement of practitioners of the photographic arts in the Victorian era are all the more impressive for the technical obstacles that they faced.

⌘ ⌘ ⌘

Roger Fenton, "Proposal for the Formation of a Photographic Society" (1852)

Roger Fenton, a 32-year-old painter and sometime law student, was among the many in whom the displays at the Great Exhibition of 1851 sparked an interest in the new art of photography. Much of the finest work displayed at the Exhibition was by French photographers (prominent among them Hippolyte Bayard and Gustave Le Gray), and in October of 1851, Fenton traveled to Paris to meet members of the Societé Héliographique, the world's first photographic society. By the summer of 1852, Fenton was becoming prominent in English photographic circles, and later that year he put forward the proposal reprinted here, for the formation of a new society. The Photographic Society came into existence in 1853, with the Queen and Prince Albert as patrons; in 1894 the name was changed to The Royal Photographic Society.

The science of Photography gradually progressing for several years, seems to have advanced at a more rapid pace during and since the Exhibition of 1851. Its lovers and students in all parts of Europe were brought into more immediate and frequent communication.

Ideas of theory and methods of practice were interchanged, the pleasure and the instruction were mutual. In order that this temporary may become the normal condition of the art and of its professors, it is proposed to unite in a common society, with a fixed place of meeting, and a regular official organization, all those gentlemen whose tastes have led them to the cultivation of this branch of natural science.

As the object proposed is not only to form a pleasant and convenient Photographic Club, but a society that shall be as advantageous for the art as is the Geographic Society[1] to the advancement of knowledge in its department, it follows necessarily that it shall include among its members men of all ranks of life; that while men of eminence, from their fortune, social position, or scientific reputation, are welcomed, no photographer of respectability in his particular sphere of life be rejected.

The society then will consist of those eminent in the study of natural philosophy,[2] of opticians, chemists, artists, and practical photographers, professional and amateur. It will admit both town and country members. It is proposed:—

That, after the society has been once organized, persons who may in future wish to become members will have to be proposed and seconded, a majority of votes deciding their election.

That the entrance fee and subscription shall be as small as possible, in order that none may be excluded by the narrowness of their means.

That there shall be an entrance fee of £2.2s.—a subscription of £1.1s.

That the society should have appropriate premises fitted up with laboratory, glass operating room, and salon,[3] in which to hold its meetings.

That such meetings should be periodically held, for the purpose of hearing and discussing written or verbal communications on the subject of Photography, receiving and verifying claims as to priority of invention, exhibiting and comparing pictures produced by different applications of photographic principles; making known improvements in construction of cameras and lenses; and, in fine, promoting by emulation and comparison the progress of the art.

That the proceedings of the society shall be published regularly in some acknowledged organ, which shall be sent to all subscribing members.

That a library of works bearing upon the history or tending to the elucidation of the principles of the science be formed upon the premises, and at the expense of the society, to be used by the members, subject to such rules as may hereafter be agreed upon.

That the society should publish an annual album, of which each member should receive a copy, who had contributed a good negative photograph to its formation, other members having to pay (and the public being charged at the rate of   )?[4]

---

[1] *Geographic Society* Founded in 1830, the Geographic Society was a supporter of many exploratory expeditions, including those of Charles Darwin and David Livingston.

[2] *natural philosophy* I.e., science.

[3] *salon* Gathering room, especially one used for intellectual discussion.

[4] *rate of   )?* The space left here, together with the question mark, suggest that the specific amount was an issue left for later discussion.

The heaviest expense attendant upon this plan would be leasing or construction of convenient premises, and this expense might be lessened by the letting off[1] the lower part as a shop for the sale of photographic chemicals, and the upper part to some person who would form a commercial establishment for the printing of positives.[2]

Before any progress can be made in the organization of such a society as the foregoing, it is necessary first to ascertain the amount of support which it would be likely to obtain. If those gentlemen, therefore, who feel inclined to become members of such a society will send in their names and addresses to R. FENTON, Esq., 2, Albert Terrace, and 50, King William Street, City,[3] together with any suggestion which may occur to them individually on the perusal of this outline of a plan, arrangements will be made as soon as a sufficient number of persons have sent in their names, to hold a meeting in some central situation, to which they will be invited to discuss the matter and to elect a committee for the organization of a society.

from Charles Dickens, "Photography," *Household Words* (1853)

Among Dickens's many contributions to *Household Words* (a widely-circulated miscellany of articles and literary pieces) were installments of his fiction, essays on political issues, and articles on various cultural topics—such as the selection excerpted below.

... Light from the sky is, in fact, the chief part of the stock-in-trade of a photographer. Other light than the sun's can be employed; but, while the sun continues to pour down to us a daily flow of light of the best quality, as cheap as health (we will not say as cheap as dirt, for dirt is a dear article), sunlight will be consumed by the photographers in preference to any other. A diffused, mellow light from the sky, which moderates the dark-ness of all shadows, is much better suited to the purpose of photography than a direct sunbeam; which creates hard contrasts of light and shade. For in the picture formed by light, whether on metal, glass, or paper, such hard contrasts will be made still harder. Lumpy shadows haunt the chambers of all bad photographers.

He who would not be vexed by them and would produce a portrait in which the features shall be represented with the necessary softness, finds it generally advantageous not only to let the shades be cast upon the face in a room full of diffused rays—that is to say, under a skylight—but also by the waving of large black velvet screens over the head to moderate and stint the quantity of light that falls on features not thrown into shadow. For this reason few very good photographic pictures can be taken from objects illuminated only by a side light, as in a room with ordinary windows. The diffused light of cloudy weather, if the air be free from fog, hinders the process of photography only by lengthening the time occupied in taking impressions. Light, when it is jaundiced by a fog, is quite as liable as jaundiced men to give erroneous views of mankind.

Photography, out of England, has made its most rapid advances, and produced its best results in the United States and in France; but, although both the French and the Americans have the advantage of a much purer and more certain supply of sunlight, it is satisfactory to know that the English photographers have thrown as much light of their own on the new science as any of their neighbours. ...

The den of the photographer, in which he goes through those mysterious operations which are not submitted to the observation of the sitter, is a small room lighted by a window, and communicating into a dark closet, veiled with heavy curtains. Our sense of the supernatural, always associated with dark closets, was excited strongly in this chamber, by the sound of a loud rumbling in the bowels of the house, and the visible departure of a portion of the wall to lower regions. "We thought instinctively of bandits who wind victims up and down in moveable rooms or turn them up in treacherous screw bedsteads. But, of course, there was no danger to be apprehended. What we saw was, of

[1] *letting off* Renting out a portion of a property.

[2] *positives* Photographs, as opposed to "negatives" from which photographic prints are made.

[3] *City* I.e., the City of London.

course, only a contrivance to save labour in conveying pictures up or down for colouring or framing. Our consciences having been satisfied on this point, the expert magician took a plate of the prescribed size, made ready to his hand. Such plates consist of a thin layer of silver fixed upon copper, and are provided to the artist highly polished; but a final and superlative polish is given to each plate, with a "buff" or pad like a double handled razor strop, tinged with a fine mineral powder. Simple as it appears, the final polishing of the plate is an operation that can only succeed well under a practised pair of hands, that regulate their pressure by a refined sense of touch. The plate thus polished was brushed over finally and very lightly, as with the touch of a cat's paw, with a warm pad of black velvet freshly taken from an oven.

To witness the next process we went into the dark closet itself, the very head quarters of spectredom. There, having carefully excluded daylight, the operator lifted up the lid of a small bin, rapidly fixed the plate, silver side downwards, in a place made underneath for its reception, shut down the lid, and began to measure seconds by counting, talking between whiles, thus:— "One—that box—two contains—three—chloride of iodine—four—strewn—five—six—at the bottom. Now!" (Presto, out came the plate in a twinkling, and was held against a sheet of white paper, upon which it reflected a ghastly straw colour by the light of a small jet of gas.) "Ah, tint not deep enough!" The plate was popped into its vapour bath again with magic quickness. "Seven—the action of the iodine" (continued the operator, counting seconds, and teaching us our lesson in the same breath) "rising in vapour upon the surface— eleven—of the plate—twelve—causes it to take in succession—thirteen—fourteen—fifteen—all the colours of the spectrum—sixteen—seventeen; and deposits upon it a film." As he went on solemnly counting, we asked how long he exposed the plate to the visitation of that potent vapour. "A very short time," he replied; "but it varies—thirty—thirty-one—according to the light in the next room—thirty-five—thirty-six—thirty-seven. Adjusting the plate to the weather, thirty-eight—is the result of an acquired instinct—thirty-nine—forty. Now it is ready." The plate was out, and its change to a

deeper straw colour was shown. The lid of an adjoining bin was lifted, and the iodized plate was hung in the same way over another vapour; that of the chloride of bromine, that the wraiths of the two vapours might mingle, mingle, mingle as black spirits with white, blue spirits with gray. In this position it remained but a very short time, while we stood watching by in the dark cupboard. The plate having had its temper worked upon by these mysterious agencies was rendered so extremely sensitive, that it was requisite to confine it at once, in a dark hole or solitary cell, made ready for it in a wooden frame; a wooden slide was let down over it, and it was ready to be carried to the camera.

Before quitting this part of the subject, we must add to the preceding description two or three external facts. We have been discussing hitherto the kernel without touching the nutshell in which these, like all other reasonable matters in this country, may be (and usually are) said to lie. The nutshell is in fact as important to a discussion in this country as the small end of the wedge or the British Lion:[1]—In the action of light upon surfaces prepared in a certain manner lies the whole idea of photography. The camera-obscura is an old friend; how to fix chemically the illuminated images formed in the camera by light, was a problem at which Sir Humphrey Davy,[2] half a century ago, was one of the first men who worked. Sir Humphrey succeeded no farther than in the imprinting of a faint image, but as he could not discover how to fix it, the whole subject was laid aside. Between the years 1814 and 1828, two Frenchmen, M. Daguerre and M. Nièpce,[3] were at work upon the problem. In 1827 M. Nièpce produced before the Royal

---

[1] *small end … British Lion* Commonplace expressions referring, respectively, to an apparently small thing with significant consequences, and to the lion as a symbol of England.

[2] *camera-obscura* Box or darkened room in which an optical effect is produced by light passing through a pinhole or lens, projecting an image of external objects onto a surface; *Sir Humphrey Davy* English scientist (1778–1829) best known as the discoverer of several chemical elements.

[3] *two Frenchmen … Nièpce* Louis-Jacques-Mandé Daguerre (1787–1851), now more commonly referred to as "Louis Daguerre," inventor of the daguerreotype process of photography, and Nicéphore Niépce, said by many to have produced the world's first photograph.

Society what he then called heliographs, sun-pictures, formed and fixed upon glass, copper plated with silver, and well-polished tin. But, as he kept the secret of his processes, no scientific use was made of his discovery. M. Daguerre, working at the same problem, succeeded about the same time in fixing sun-pictures on paper impregnated with nitrate of silver. M. Daguerre and M. Nièpce having combined their knowledge to increase the value of their art, the French government—in the year 1839—acting nobly, as it has often acted in the interests of science, bought for the free use of the world the details of the new discovery. For the full disclosure of their secrets there was granted to M. Daguerre a life pension of two hundred and forty pounds (he died not many months ago), and a pension of one hundred and sixty pounds to the son of M. Nièpce, with the reversion of one half to their widows.

Six months before the disclosure of the processes in France, Mr. Fox Talbot[1] in England had discovered a process leading to a like result—the fixing of sun-pictures upon paper. As the English parliament buys little for science, nothing unfortunately hindered the patenting of Mr. Talbot's method. That patent in certain respects very much obstructed the advance of photography in this country, and great credit is due to Mr. Talbot for having recently and voluntarily abandoned his exclusive rights, and given his process to the public for all purposes and uses, except that of the portrait-taker. By so doing he acted in the spirit of a liberal art born in our own days, and peculiarly marked with the character of our own time. It does one good to think how photographers, even while exercising the new art for money, have pursued it with a generous ardour for its own sake, and emulate each other in the magnanimity with which they throw their own discoveries into the common heap, and scorn to check the progress of their art for any selfish motive. After the completion of the French discovery two daguerreotype establishments were formed in London armed with patent rights, and their proprietors, Messrs. Claudet and Beard, do in fact still hold those rights, of which they have long cheerfully

permitted the infringement. Mr. Beard tried to enforce them only once, we believe; and M. Claudet, with distinguished liberality, never. …

And we may observe here that another illustration of our vanities was furnished to us on a different occasion. Daguerreotype plates commonly present faces as they would be seen in a looking-glass, that is to say, reversed: the left side of the face, in nature, appearing upon the right side of the miniature. That is the ordinary aspect in which every one sees his own face, for it is only possible for him to behold it reflected in a mirror. This reversing, of course, alters in the slightest degree the similitude … and it is a curious fact that few of us are content to have even our faces shown to us as others see them. The non-inverted daguerreotypes differ too much from the dear images of self that we are used to learn by heart out of our looking-glasses. They invariably please the friend to whom they are to be given, but they frequently displease the sitter. … A daguerreotype, formed in the usual way and inverted, if held before a looking-glass, becomes again inverted, and shows therefore a non-inverted picture of the person whom it represents.

… There are many processes by which photographic impressions may be taken upon paper and glass; a book full of them lies at this moment before us: we have ourselves seen two, and shall confine ourselves to the telling of a part of our experience. We rang the artist's bell of Mr. Henneman in Regent-street, who takes very good portraits upon paper by a process cousin to the Talbotype. By that gentleman we were introduced into a neat little chamber lighted by gas, with a few pans and chemicals upon a counter. His process was excessively simple: he would show it to us. He took a square of glass, cleaned it very perfectly, then holding it up by one corner with the left hand, he poured over the centre of the glass some collodion, which is, as most people know, gun-cotton dissolved in ether. By a few movements of the left hand, which appear easy, but are acquired with trouble, the collodion was caused to flow into an even coat over the surface of the glass, and the excess was poured off at another corner. To do this by a few left-handed movements without causing any ripple upon the collodion adhering to the glass is really very difficult.

---

[1] *Mr. Fox Talbot* Henry Fox Talbot (1800–77), English scientist and mathematician, inventor of the calotype photographic process.

This done, the plate was left till the ether had almost evaporated, and deposited a film of gun-cotton—which is in fact a delicate paper—spread evenly over the surface of the glass. The glass covered with this delicate paper, before it was yet quite dry, was plunged carefully into a pan or bath, containing a solution of nitrate of silver, about eight grains of it to every hundred of distilled water. In about two minutes it was taken out, and ready for the camera. It was a sheet of glass covered with a fine film of cotton-paper impregnated with nitrate of silver, a colourless salt blackened by light.

It was removed in a dark frame to the camera. Then an assistant, opening a book, assumed an attitude and sat for his picture. In a few seconds it was taken in the usual way, and the glass carried again into the operator's room. There it was dipped into another bath—a bath of pyrogallic acid—and the impression soon became apparent. To bring it out with greater force it was then dipped into a second and much weaker bath of nitrate of silver. The image was then made perfect; but, as the light parts were all depicted by the blackest shades, and the black parts were left white, the courteous assistant was there represented as a negro.

That negro stage was not of course the finished portrait, it was "the negative"—or stereotype plate, as it were—from which, after it had been fixed with a solution of the sulphate of the peroxyde of iron, any number of impressions could be taken. For it is obvious that if a plate like this be placed on sensitive paper, and exposed to daylight, the whole process will be reversed. The black face will obstruct the passage of the light and leave a white face underneath, the white hair will allow the light to pass, making black hair below, and so on. Impressions thus taken on paper, and afterwards fixed, may either serve for portraits, as they are, or, like the silver plates, they may be coloured.

… Photography already has been found available by the astronomer; the moon has sat for a full-face picture,[1]

and there is hope that in a short time photographic paper will become a common auxiliary to the telescope. History will be indebted to photography for facsimiles of documents and volumes that have perished; travellers may bring home incontestible transcripts of inscriptions upon monuments, or foreign scenery. The artist will no longer be delayed in travelling to execute his sketches on the spot. He can now wander at his ease, and bring home photographic views, from which to work, as sculptors from the model. Photography is a young art, but from its present aspect we can judge what power it will have in its maturity. The mind may readily become bewildered among expectations, but one thing will suggest many. We understand that a catalogue of the national library of Paris has been commenced, in which each work is designated by a photographic miniature of its title-page.

Photography and Immortality

The following brief extracts are from a letter of poet Elizabeth Barrett (later Elizabeth Barrett Browning) to a friend, and from a speech by one of the first presidents of the photographic society. Pollock's belief was that photography was first and foremost "a *practical science*," but his enthusiasm for it was no less than that of those who valued it more as an art.

from Elizabeth Barrett, Letter to Mary Russell Mitford, 1843

Do you know anything about that wonderful invention of the day, called the Daguerrotype? Think of a man sitting down in the sun and leaving his facsimile in all its full completion of outline and shadow, steadfast on a plate, at the end of a minute and a half! The Mesmeric[2] disembodiment of spirits strikes one as a degree less marvelous. … It is not merely the likeness which is

---

[1] *moon has sat for a full-face picture* Amateur photographer John Dillwyn Llewelyn (1810–82) and his daughter Thereza Llewelyn were pioneers in astronomical photography, taking pictures of the moon through the telescope Llewelyn had constructed in 1851 at his estate in Wales.

[2] *Mesmeric* Franz Mesmer (1734–1835) claimed to have discovered a mysterious force he termed "animal magnetism"; it was termed *mesmerism* by others.

precious in such cases—but the association and the sense of nearness involved in the thing ... the fact of the very shadow of the person lying there fixed for ever! It is the very sanctification of portraits.

from Sir Frederick Pollock, "Presidential Address," Photographic Society (1855)

The varied objects to which Photography can address itself, its power of rendering permanent that which appears to be as fleeting as the shadows that go across the dial,[1] the power that it possesses of giving fixedness to instantaneous objects, are for the purposes of history ... a matter of the greatest importance. It is not too much to say that no individual—not merely individual man, but no individual substance, no individual matter, nothing that is extraordinary in art, that is celebrated in architecture, that is calculated to excite the imagination of those who behold it, need now perish; but may be rendered immortal by the assistance of Photography.

Henry Fox Talbot, *The Haystack*, 1844. Talbot wrote of this photo, "[o]ne advantage of the discovery of the Photographic Art will be, that it will enable us to introduce into our pictures a multitude of minute details which add to the truth and reality of the representation, but which no artist would take the trouble to copy faithfully from nature."

---

[1] *dial* Sundial.

Henry Fox Talbot, *Nelson's Column under Construction, Trafalgar Square*, 1844.

Roger Fenton, *The British Museum*, 1857.

Roger Fenton, *Fruit and Flowers*, 1860.

Roger Fenton, *The Long Walk, Windsor*, 1860.

Oscar Gustav Rejlander, *The Two Ways of Life* (detail), 1857.

Robert Howlett, *The Great Eastern: Isambard Kingdom Brunel Inspecting Construction Work* (detail), 1857.

Oscar Gustav Rejlander, *Homeless*, c. 1860. (This well-known and widely praised photograph was also sometimes referred to as *A Night in Town* or *Poor Joe*.)

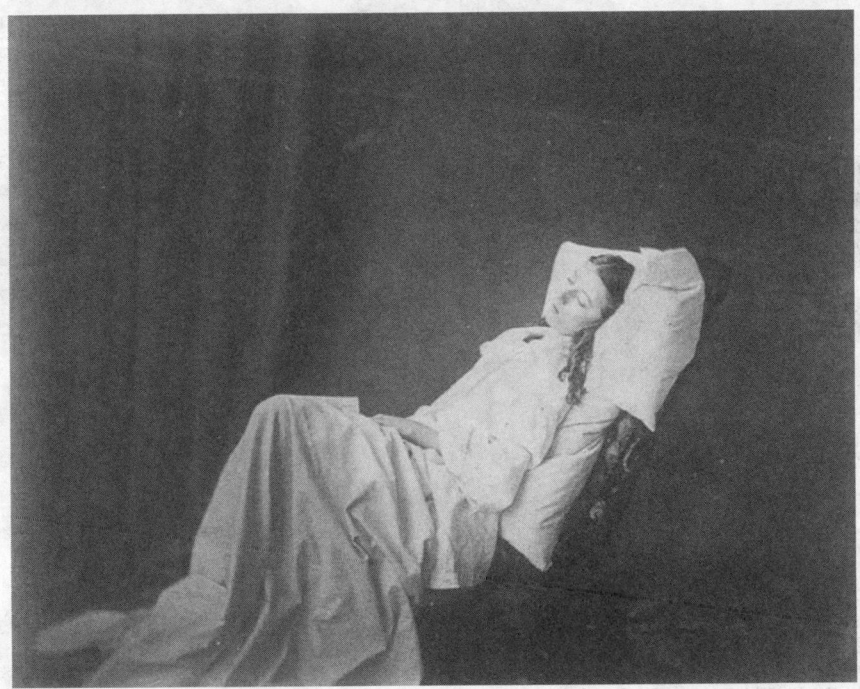

A preliminary study for *Fading Away*, this photograph was exhibited with the following verse:

> She never told her Love
> But let concealment, like a
>   worm i' the bud,
> Feed on her damask cheek.
>   Shakespeare

Henry Peach Robinson, *She Never Told Her Love*, 1857.

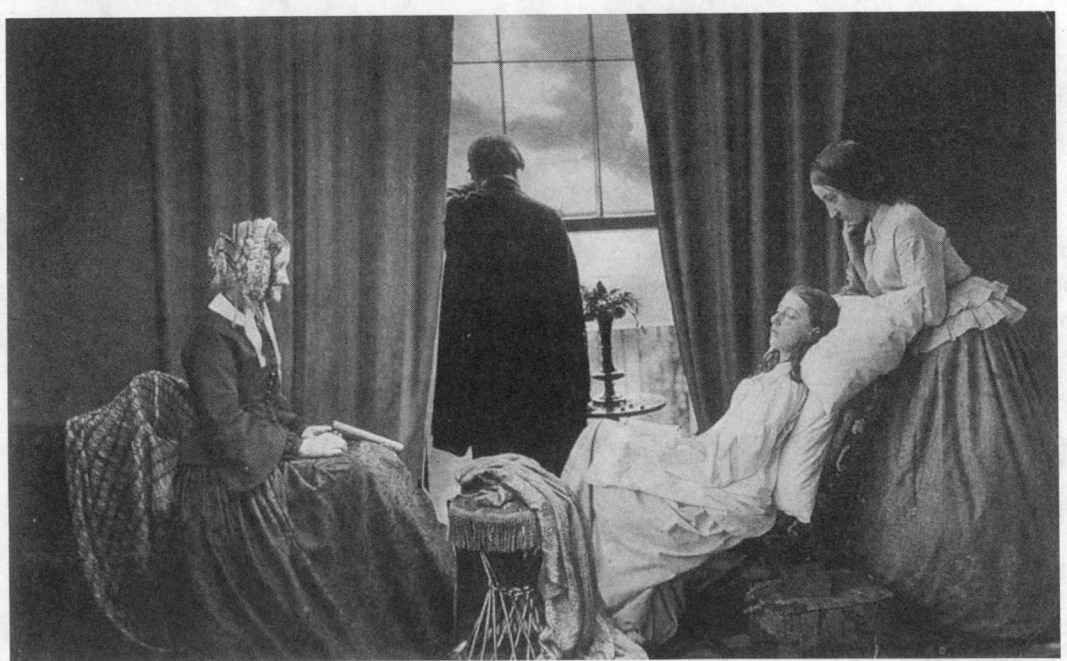

Henry Peach Robinson, *Fading Away*, 1858. Robinson inscribed "First Impression" on the printed mat along with the following verse: "Must then that peerless form, / Which love and admiration cannot view / Without a beating heart, those azure veins / Which steal like streams along a field of snow, / As breathing marble, perish! Shelley"

Francis Frith, *The Pyramids of Dahshoor, From the East*, c. 1857.

Francis Frith, *Crocodile on a Sand-Bank* (detail), 1057.

Camille Silvy, Sarah Forbes Bonetta (Sarah Davies), 1862. The daughter of a Yoruba chief, Sarah Forbes Bonetta was born Oboma Aina in 1843. Captured in an attack by the Kingdom of Dahomey as a child, she was enslaved and eventually given as a gift to diplomat Frederick Forbes, who renamed her and brought her to England. There, she became a protégée of Queen Victoria, who supported her education and later became godmother to her daughter.

Camille Silvy, James Pinson Labulo Davies and Sarah Forbes Bonetta (Sarah Davies), 1862. Bonetta married the Sierra Leonian entrepreneur Davies in 1862, just a few weeks before this photograph was taken. They eventually settled in Lagos.

Lady Clementina Hawarden, *The Toilette*, c. 1864.

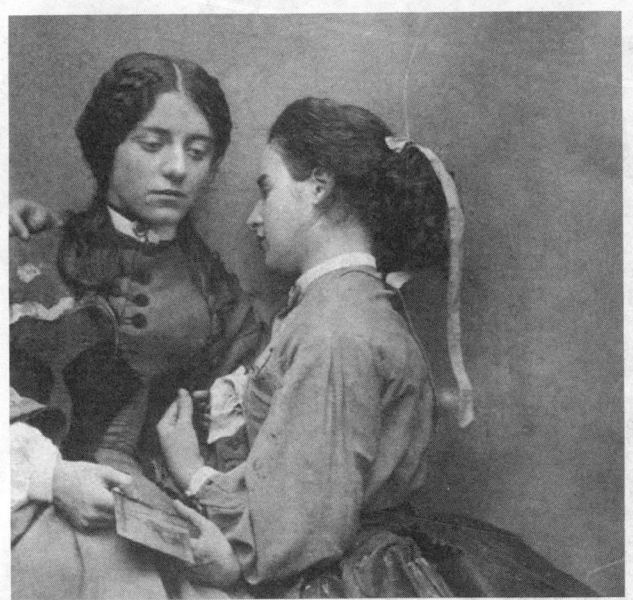

Lady Clementina Hawarden, *Lady Isabella Grace and Clementina Maude, 5 Princes Gardens*, c. 1862–63.

Lewis Carroll, *Ellen Watts (Ellen Terry)*, 1865.

Lewis Carroll, *Tuning*, 1876.

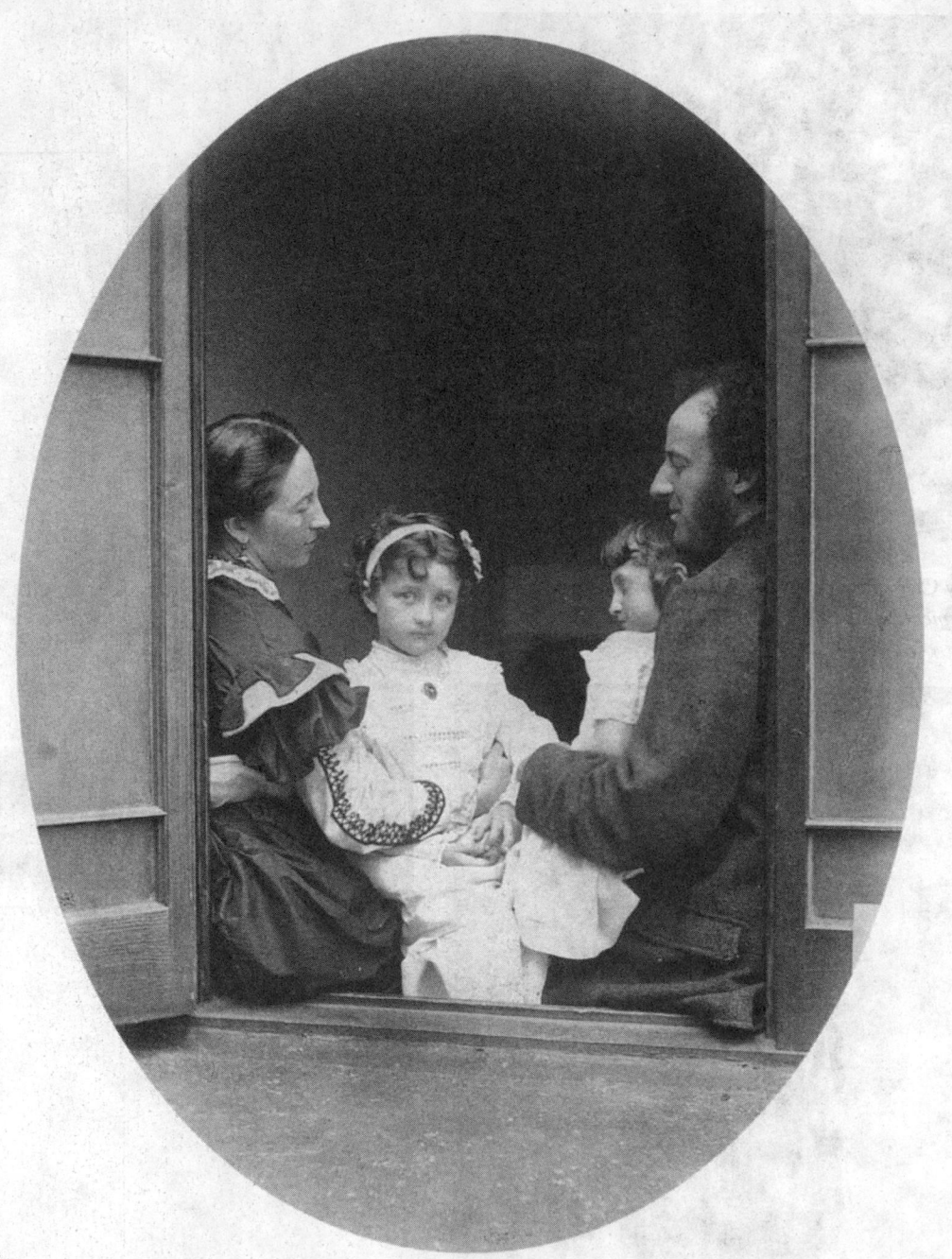

Lewis Carroll, *John Everett Millais, His Wife, and Two of Their Daughters*, 1865.

Francis Bedford, *A Peaceful Village*, 1859.

Julia Margaret Cameron, *Annie—My First Success*, 1864. Cameron maintained that this image was her first successful photograph.

Julia Margaret Cameron, *Thomas Carlyle*, 1867. Carlyle wrote of the photo, "it is as if it suddenly began to speak, terrifically ugly and woebegone!"

Julia Margaret Cameron, *Ophelia*, 1867.

Julia Margaret Cameron, *The Angel at the Sepulchre*, 1869.

Julia Margaret Cameron, *Cingalese Girl*, 1875.

Julia Margaret Cameron, *The Passing of Arthur*, 1875.

Bourne & Shepherd, *Man Singh, Rajah of Dhrangadhra*, c. 1870.

Thomas Annan, *Close No. 46, Saltmarket, Glasgow*, 1868.

William Notman, *Miss Thomas, Montreal, QC*, c. 1868.

Eadweard Muybridge, *The Horse in Motion*, 1878.

John Thomson, *Physic Street, Canton*, c. 1869.

William Notman, *Blackfoot Brave, near Calgary, Alberta*, 1889.

Peter Henry Emerson, *Gathering Water-Lilies*, 1886.

Frederick Evans, *A Sea of Steps, Wells Cathedral*, c. 1903.

Frederick Evans, *Lincoln Cathedral: From the Castle*, 1896.

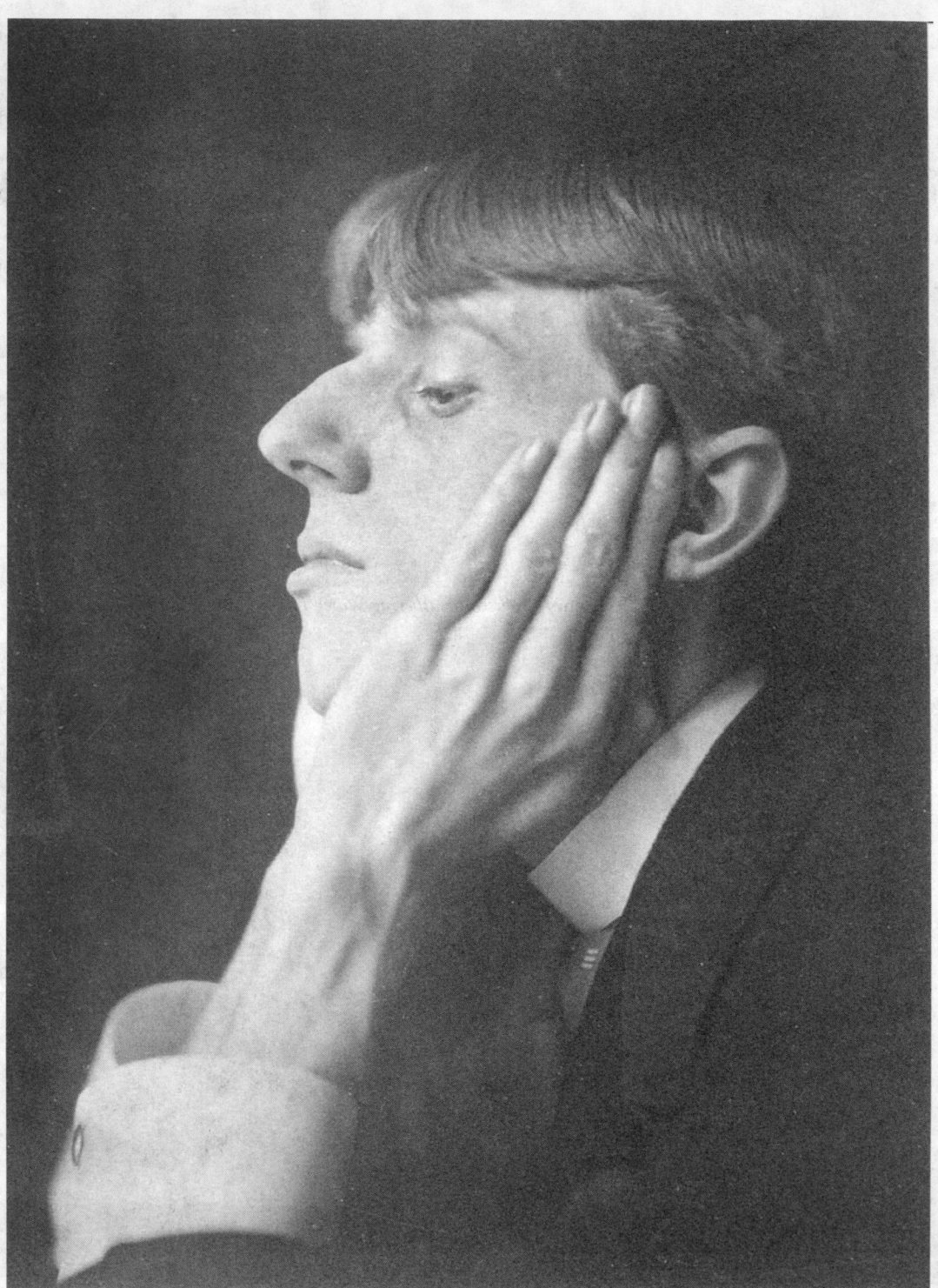

Frederick Evans, *Portrait of Aubrey Beardsley*, c. 1894.

London Stereoscopic Company, *Johanna Jonkers, The African Choir*, 1891. This is one of a series of photographic portraits taken of the sixteen members of the African Choir, a group of Christian South African singers, during their acclaimed British tour in the early 1890s.

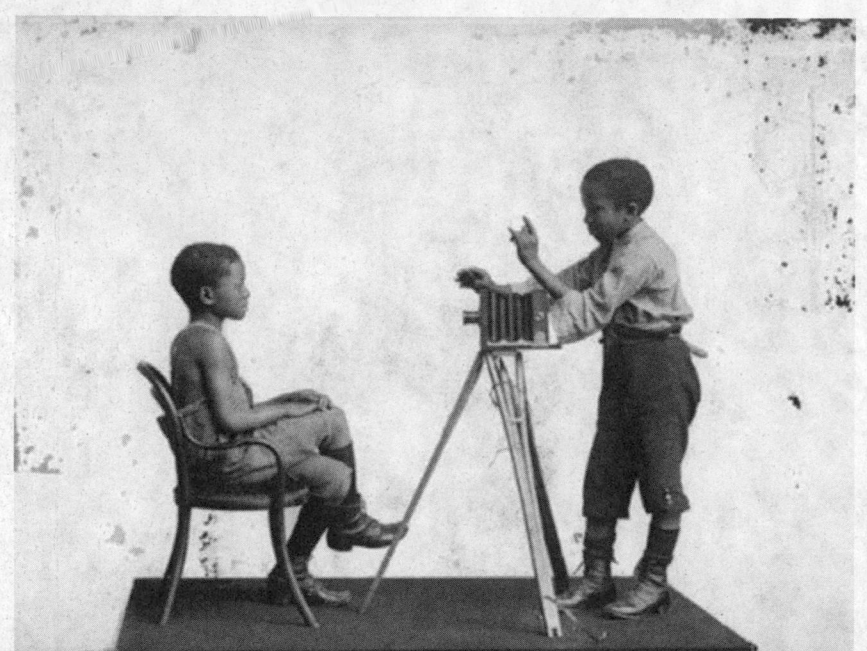

London Stereoscopic Company, *Albert Jonas and John Xiniwe,*
The African Choir, 1891.

London Stereoscopic Company, *Unknown*
Member of the African Choir, 1891.

London Stereoscopic Company, *Eleanor*
Xiniwe, The African Choir, 1891.

GEORGE ELIOT
1819 – 1880

George Eliot chose her masculine pen name with good reason: she did not wish to be received by the public as a woman writer and judged by terms thought to be appropriate to women's work. At a time when women were often prevented from engaging in such work, Eliot was a scholar and editor, publishing groundbreaking essays, literary criticism, and translations. When she turned to fiction, Eliot was a writer who valued sympathy above all other qualities; hers was a notable intellectual voice that produced some of the most remarkable novels of the Victorian period, including *Adam Bede*, *The Mill on the Floss*, *Middlemarch*, and *Daniel Deronda*. She was hailed for her intimate portrayal of the social and spiritual lives of her characters, particularly for the psychological acuity with which she brought them to life. Her novels garnered her fame in her lifetime, and it has been widely acknowledged since that her work holds a central place in the tradition of novel-writing in English.

Mary Anne Evans (she also used Mary Ann and later Marian) was born in rural Warwickshire, England, in 1819, the third child of Christiana Pearson and Robert Evans. This landscape was to figure in almost all her fiction. She was educated at various boarding schools where she distinguished herself as a studious, shy, and introspective child. At one school, a compassionate teacher named Maria Lewis took her under her wing and molded her spiritual development, instilling evangelical beliefs that would persist into early adulthood. When Eliot's mother died in 1836, her formal education came to an end, but she continued to study theology, languages, philosophy, Romantic poetry, and German literature while caring for her father.

Her close relationship with her father was tested in 1842 when she announced her loss of faith in Christianity and organized religion, after falling under the influence of the freethinking, radical intellectuals Charles and Caroline Bray and Caroline's brother, Charles Hennell. Hennell urged her to translate *The Life of Jesus*, by the German "higher critic" David Friedrich Strauss; the translation appeared in 1846. This study considered the Bible's texts not as factual histories ordained by God, but rather as myths, the products of people living in a specific historical period trying to find language to articulate their sense of the powers that ruled the universe. In 1854, Eliot published her translation of Ludwig Feuerbach's *Essence of Christianity* (1854), her only publication to bear the name of Marian Evans on its title page. Here again she continued her radical work of introducing ideas that challenged traditional religious beliefs. Before this work, in 1851, she had become assistant editor of the radical *Westminster Review*, a position she held for two years, helping to restore the magazine to the high intellectual standards it had attained while under the editorship of the philosopher John Stuart Mill. Even after leaving her position at the *Review*, George Eliot continued to contribute many important essays to the magazine, among them "Silly Novels by Lady Novelists" and "The Natural History of German Life" (1856).

In 1851 she met George Henry Lewes, biographer, novelist, botanist, and literary and theatrical critic. In 1854, they began to live together (though he was married). The decision to live in a common-law "marriage," as they called it (indeed, George Eliot called herself and became known to many as "Mrs. Lewes"), came at great personal expense; the brother to whom she had once been very close persuaded the entire family to shun her, which they did for the duration of her quarter-century relationship with Lewes. The relationship also constricted her involvement in the literary and intellectual world of London, especially in the early years of her writing career.

George Eliot's novels and shorter fiction (three novellas were published in *Blackwood's Magazine* under her pseudonym and collected in *Scenes of Clerical Life* in 1858) mostly harken back to the early part of the century in pre-industrial England and concentrate on the lives of ordinary people at a time when great changes were on the horizon; she draws readers' attention to how tragedy, as well as sublime comedy, may form part of the lives of common people. In a passage in *The Mill on the Floss*, George Eliot explains the appeal of the Midland landscape and its Wordsworthian influence upon her imagination: "These familiar flowers, these well-remembered bird-notes, this sky, with its fitful brightness, these furrowed and grassy fields ... such things as these are the mother tongue of our imagination, the language that is laden with all the subtle inextricable associations the fleeting hours of our childhood left behind them. Our delight in the sunshine on the deep-bladed grass to-day, might be no more than the faint perception of wearied souls, if it were not for the sunshine and the grass in the far-off years which still live in us, and transform our perception into love." These scenes become the sources of the moral imagination, "with its deep immoveable roots in memory." They are also the sources of George Eliot's moral realism. As she wrote in Chapter 17 of *Adam Bede*, her focus was not heroes or sublimely beautiful women, but people who do "the rough work of the world" because human beings need to reverence "that other beauty ... which lies in no secret of proportion, but in the secret of deep human sympathy."

Even though George Eliot was almost forty when she began writing fiction, once she began she was prolific. *Adam Bede* appeared in 1859 to great critical acclaim (Queen Victoria was among its admirers); *The Mill on the Floss* was published in 1860 and *Silas Marner* in 1861; her Renaissance historical novel, *Romola*, in 1863; *Felix Holt, the Radical*, a book about the First Reform Bill, in 1866; a collection of poetry, *The Spanish Gypsy*, in 1868; and *Middlemarch* in 1871–72. This novel, widely thought to be among the greatest written in English, is set in the time leading up to the 1832 Reform Bill, which significantly expanded the male electorate and accomplished a more equal distribution of Parliamentary seats, particularly benefiting manufacturing towns and cities. At this historical moment, when the forces of progress were struggling with countervailing conservative reaction, Eliot traces the interwoven lives of the inhabitants of the fictive town of Middlemarch and the lands surrounding it, particularly the lives of Dorothea Brooke, an idealistic, ardent, and intelligent young woman, and of Tertius Lydgate, an ambitious young doctor who longs to make important medical discoveries. The omniscient narrator's sympathy and intellectual generosity continually guide the reader's impressions; while capable of incisive satire, the narrator nevertheless finds redemptive qualities even in the most flawed characters. The profound degree of social and psychological insight displayed in the novel reflects Eliot's professed aim for her writings, "that those who read them should be better able to *imagine* and to *feel* the pains and the joys of those who differ from themselves in everything but the broad fact of being struggling, erring, human creatures."[1]

Daniel Deronda (1876) was George Eliot's final novel. Her interest in Judaism and in the Hebrew language informed this epic story, set in contemporary England, of a woman who is forced into an

---

[1] From a letter to Charles Bray, 5 July 1859.

oppressive marriage with an aristocrat and of an idealistic young man, the eponymous Daniel, who discovers his Jewish roots and works toward a renewal of the Jewish nation. For the agnostic George Eliot, the appeal of Judaism lay in its role as the foundation of the images and texts that inform a morality divinely human; Judaism was the source of western culture's moral imagination. She may not have been a believer, but her fiction finds much of its life in the tropes and images of the religious imagination as she found them in the King James Bible, Milton, Bunyan, and the English hymns. This most intellectually sophisticated of all Victorian novelists was also one of its most deeply traditional.

In 1878, George Eliot's beloved partner Lewes died. In May of 1880, she married John Walter Cross, a man 20 years her junior. She died in December 1880, and was buried beside Lewes in Highgate Cemetery. Before her death she reconciled with her brother Isaac, who welcomed the "legitimacy" of her marriage to Cross. Five years after her death, Cross published a reverent biography of Mary Anne Evans, entitled *George Eliot's Life as Related in Her Letters and Journals*.

⌘ ⌘ ⌘

O, May I Join the Choir Invisible

Longum illud tempus, quum non ero, magis me movet, quam hoc exiguum.[1]
—CICERO, ad Att., 12.18.

O, may I join the choir invisible
Of those immortal dead who live again
In minds made better by their presence: live
In pulses stirred to generosity,
5   In deeds of daring rectitude, in scorn
For miserable aims that end with self,
In thoughts sublime that pierce the night like stars,
And with their mild persistence urge man's search
To vaster issues.
          So to live is heaven:
10   To make undying music in the world,
Breathing as beauteous order that controls
With growing sway the growing life of man.
So we inherit that sweet purity
For which we struggled, failed, and agonised
15   With widening retrospect that bred despair.
Rebellious flesh that would not be subdued,

A vicious parent shaming still its child,
Poor anxious penitence, is quick dissolved;
Its discords, quenched by meeting harmonies,
20   Die in the large and charitable air.
And all our rarer, better, truer self,
That sobbed religiously in yearning song,
That watched to ease the burthen° of the world,   burden
Laboriously tracing what must be,
25   And what may yet be better—saw within
A worthier image for the sanctuary,
And shaped it forth before the multitude
Divinely human, raising worship so
To higher reverence more mixed with love—
30   That better self shall live till human Time
Shall fold its eyelids, and the human sky
Be gathered like a scroll within the tomb
Unread forever.
          This is life to come,
Which martyred men have made more glorious
35   For us who strive to follow. May I reach
That purest heaven, be to other souls
The cup of strength in some great agony,
Enkindle generous ardour, feed pure love,
Beget the smiles that have no cruelty—
40   Be the sweet presence of a good diffused,
And in diffusion ever more intense.

---

[1] *Longum … exiguum* Latin: And the great length of time after I shall cease to be matters more to me than the short time I have here.

So shall I join the choir invisible,
Whose music is the gladness of the world.
—1867

from *Brother and Sister Sonnets*

SONNET 11

School parted us; we never found again
That childish world where our two spirits mingled
Like scents from varying roses that remain
One sweetness, nor can evermore be singled.

5   Yet the twin habit of that early time
Lingered for long about the heart and tongue:
We had been natives of one happy clime,°   *environment*
And its dear accent to our utterance clung.

Till the dire years whose awful° name is   *awe-inspiring*
    Change
10 Had grasped our souls still yearning in divorce,
And pitiless shaped them in two forms that range
Two elements which sever their life's course.

But were another childhood world my share,
I would be born a little sister there.
—1874

from *Adam Bede*

CHAPTER 17: IN WHICH THE STORY PAUSES A LITTLE

"This Rector of Broxton is little better than a pagan!" I hear one of my readers exclaim. "How much more edifying it would have been if you had made him give Arthur some truly spiritual advice. You might have put into his mouth the most beautiful things—quite as good as reading a sermon."

Certainly I could, if I held it the highest vocation of the novelist to represent things as they never have been and never will be. Then, of course, I might refashion life and character entirely after my own liking; I might select the most unexceptionable type of clergyman, and put my own admirable opinions into his mouth on all occasions. But it happens, on the contrary, that my strongest effort is to avoid any such arbitrary picture, and to give a faithful account of men and things as they have mirrored themselves in my mind. The mirror is doubtless defective; the outlines will sometimes be disturbed, the reflection faint or confused; but I feel as much bound to tell you as precisely as I can what that reflection is, as if I were in the witness-box narrating my experience on oath.

Sixty years ago—it is a long time, so no wonder things have changed—all clergymen were not zealous; indeed there is reason to believe that the number of zealous clergymen was small, and it is probable that if one among the small minority had owned the livings of Broxton and Hayslope in the year 1799, you would have liked him no better than you like Mr. Irwine. Ten to one, you would have thought him a tasteless, indiscreet, methodistical[1] man. It is so very rarely that facts hit that nice[2] medium required by our own enlightened opinions and refined taste! Perhaps you will say, "Do improve the facts a little, then; make them more accordant with those correct views which it is our privilege to possess. The world is just what we like; do touch it up with a tasteful pencil, and make believe it is not quite such a mixed entangled affair. Let all people who hold unexceptionable opinions act unexceptionably. Let your most faulty characters always be on the wrong side, and your virtuous ones on the right. Then we shall see at a glance whom we are to condemn, and whom we are to approve. Then we shall be able to admire, without the slightest disturbance of our prepossessions: we shall hate and despise with that true ruminant relish which belongs to undoubting confidence."

But, my good friend, what will you do then with your fellow parishioner who opposes your husband in

---

[1]   *methodistical* Rigidly adhering to systems and methods.

[2]   *nice* Precise.

the vestry?[1]—with your newly-appointed vicar, whose style of preaching you find painfully below that of his regretted predecessor?—with the honest servant who worries your soul with her one failing?—with your neighbour, Mrs. Green, who was really kind to you in your last illness, but has said several ill-natured things about you since your convalescence?—nay, with your excellent husband himself, who has other irritating habits besides that of not wiping his shoes? These fellow mortals, every one, must be accepted as they are: you can neither straighten their noses, nor brighten their wit, nor rectify their dispositions; and it is these people—amongst whom your life is passed—that it is needful you should tolerate, pity, and love: it is these more or less ugly, stupid, inconsistent people, whose movements of goodness you should be able to admire—for whom you should cherish all possible hopes, all possible patience. And I would not, even if I had the choice, be the clever novelist who could create a world so much better than this, in which we get up in the morning to do our daily work, that you would be likely to turn a harder, colder eye on the dusty streets and the common green fields—on the real breathing men and women, who can be chilled by your indifference or injured by your prejudice, who can be cheered and helped onward by your fellow feeling, your forbearance, your outspoken, brave justice.

So I am content to tell my simple story, without trying to make things seem better than they were; dreading nothing, indeed, but falsity, which, in spite of one's best efforts, there is reason to dread. Falsehood is so easy, truth so difficult. The pencil is conscious of a delightful facility in drawing a griffin[2]—the longer the claws, and the larger the wings, the better; but that marvellous facility which we mistook for genius is apt to forsake us when we want to draw a real unexaggerated lion. Examine your words well, and you will find that even when you have no motive to be false, it is a very

hard thing to say the exact truth, even about your own immediate feelings—much harder than to say something fine about them which is *not* the exact truth.

It is for this rare, precious quality of truthfulness that I delight in many Dutch paintings, which lofty-minded people despise. I find a source of delicious sympathy in these faithful pictures of a monotonous homely existence, which has been the fate of so many more among my fellow mortals than a life of pomp or of absolute indigence, of tragic suffering or of world-stirring actions. I turn, without shrinking, from cloud-borne angels, from prophets, sibyls, and heroic warriors, to an old woman bending over her flowerpot, or eating her solitary dinner, while the noonday light, softened perhaps by a screen of leaves, falls on her mob cap,[3] and just touches the rim of her spinning-wheel, and her stone jug, and all those cheap common things which are the precious necessaries of life to her—or I turn to that village wedding, kept between four brown walls, where an awkward bridegroom opens the dance with a high-shouldered, broad-faced bride, while elderly and middle-aged friends look on, with very irregular noses and lips, and probably with quart-pots in their hands, but with an expression of unmistakeable contentment and goodwill. "Foh!" says my idealistic friend, "what vulgar details! What good is there in taking all these pains to give an exact likeness of old women and clowns?[4] What a low phase of life!—what clumsy, ugly people!"

But bless us, things may be lovable that are not altogether handsome, I hope? I am not at all sure that the majority of the human race have not been ugly, and even among those "lords of their kind," the British, squat figures, ill-shapen nostrils, and dingy complexions are not startling exceptions. Yet there is a great deal of family love amongst us. I have a friend or two whose class of features is such that the Apollo curl[5] on the summit of their brows would be decidedly trying; yet to

---

[1] *vestry* Here, meeting of members of a parish to conduct church business.

[2] *griffin* Mythological creature with features of both an eagle and a lion.

[3] *mob cap* Women's cotton bonnet with a ruffled edge that ties under the chin.

[4] *clowns* Rural people.

[5] *Apollo curl* I.e., curl like that of the Greek god Apollo.

my certain knowledge tender hearts have beaten for them, and their miniatures[1]—flattering, but still not lovely—are kissed in secret by motherly lips. I have seen many an excellent matron, who could never in her best days have been handsome, and yet she had a packet of yellow love-letters in a private drawer, and sweet children showered kisses on her sallow cheeks. And I believe there have been plenty of young heroes, of middle stature and feeble beards, who have felt quite sure they could never love anything more insignificant than a Diana,[2] and yet have found themselves in middle life happily settled with a wife who waddles. Yes! thank God; human feeling is like the mighty rivers that bless the earth: it does not wait for beauty—it flows with resistless force and brings beauty with it.

All honour and reverence to the divine beauty of form! Let us cultivate it to the utmost in men, women, and children—in our gardens and in our houses. But let us love that other beauty too, which lies in no secret of proportion, but in the secret of deep human sympathy. Paint us an angel, if you can, with a floating violet robe, and a face paled by the celestial light; paint us yet oftener a Madonna,[3] turning her mild face upward and opening her arms to welcome the divine glory; but do not impose on us any aesthetic rules which shall banish from the region of Art those old women scraping carrots with their work-worn hands, those heavy clowns taking holiday in a dingy pot-house,[4] those rounded backs and stupid[5] weather-beaten faces that have bent over the spade and done the rough work of the world—those homes with their tin pans, their brown pitchers, their rough curs, and their clusters of onions. In this world there are so many of these common coarse people, who have no picturesque sentimental wretchedness! It is so needful we should remember their existence, else we may happen to leave them quite out of our religion and philosophy, and frame lofty theories which only fit a world of extremes. Therefore let Art always remind us of them; therefore let us always have men ready to give the loving pains of a life to the faithful representing of commonplace things—men who see beauty in these commonplace things, and delight in showing how kindly the light of heaven falls on them. There are few prophets in the world; few sublimely beautiful women; few heroes. I can't afford to give all my love and reverence to such rarities; I want a great deal of those feelings for my everyday fellow men, especially for the few in the foreground of the great multitude, whose faces I know, whose hands I touch, for whom I have to make way with kindly courtesy. Neither are picturesque lazzaroni[6] or romantic criminals half so frequent as your common labourer, who gets his own bread, and eats it vulgarly but creditably with his own pocketknife. It is more needful that I should have a fibre of sympathy connecting me with that vulgar citizen who weighs out my sugar in a vilely assorted cravat[7] and waistcoat, than with the handsomest rascal in red scarf and green feathers—more needful that my heart should swell with loving admiration at some trait of gentle goodness in the faulty people who sit at the same hearth with me, or in the clergyman of my own parish, who is perhaps rather too corpulent, and in other respects is not an Oberlin or a Tillotson,[8] than at the deeds of heroes whom I shall never know except by hearsay, or at the sublimest abstract of all clerical graces that was ever conceived by an able novelist.

And so I come back to Mr. Irwine, with whom I desire you to be in perfect charity, far as he may be from satisfying your demands on the clerical character. Perhaps you think he was not—as he ought to have been—a living demonstration of the benefits attached to a national church? But I am not sure of that; at least I know that the people in Broxton and Hayslope would

---

[1] *miniatures* Small painted portraits, often held as keepsakes.

[2] *Diana* Roman goddess of the hunt.

[3] *Madonna* Mary, mother of Jesus.

[4] *pot-house* Tavern.

[5] *stupid* In a stupor.

[6] *lazzaroni* Vagabonds or beggars.

[7] *cravat* Neck scarf.

[8] *Oberlin* German pastor J.F. Oberlin (1740–1826), who cared for Livonian author J.M.R. Lenz, and about whom Eliot might have read in Georg Büchner's novella *Lenz* (1850); *Tillotson* John Tillotson (1630–94), Archbishop of Canterbury.

have been very sorry to part with their clergyman, and that most faces brightened at his approach; and until it can be proved that hatred is a better thing for the soul than love, I must believe that Mr. Irwine's influence in his parish was a more wholesome one than that of the zealous Mr. Ryde, who came there twenty years afterwards, when Mr. Irwine had been gathered to his fathers. It is true, Mr. Ryde insisted strongly on the doctrines of the Reformation,[1] visited his flock a great deal in their own homes, and was severe in rebuking the aberrations of the flesh—put a stop, indeed, to the Christmas rounds of the church singers, as promoting drunkenness, and too light a handling of sacred things. But I gathered from Adam Bede, to whom I talked of these matters in his old age, that few clergymen could be less successful in winning the hearts of their parishioners than Mr. Ryde. They learned a great many notions about doctrine from him, so that almost every churchgoer under fifty began to distinguish as well between the genuine gospel and what did not come precisely up to that standard, as if he had been born and bred a Dissenter;[2] and for some time after his arrival there seemed to be quite a religious movement in that quiet rural district. "But," said Adam, "I've seen pretty clear, ever since I was a young un, as religion's something else besides notions. It isn't notions sets people doing the right thing—it's feelings. It's the same with the notions in religion as it is with mathematics—a man may be able to work problems straight off in's head as he sits by the fire and smokes his pipe; but if he has to make a machine or a building, he must have a will and a resolution, and love something else better than his own ease. Somehow, the congregation began to fall off, and people began to speak light o' Mr. Ryde. I believe he meant right at bottom; but, you see, he was sourish-tempered, and was for beating down prices with the people as worked for him; and his preaching wouldn't go down well with that sauce. And he wanted to be like my lord judge i' the parish, punishing folks for doing wrong; and he scolded 'em from the pulpit as if he'd been a Ranter,[3] and yet he couldn't abide the Dissenters, and was a deal more set against 'em than Mr. Irwine was. And then he didn't keep within his income, for he seemed to think at first go-off that six hundred a year was to make him as big a man as Mr. Donnithorne; that's a sore mischief I've often seen with the poor curates jumping into a bit of a living all of a sudden. Mr. Ryde was a deal thought on at a distance, I believe, and he wrote books, but as for mathematics and the natur o' things, he was as ignorant as a woman. He was very knowing about doctrines, and used to call 'em the bulwarks[4] of the Reformation, but I've always mistrusted that sort o' learning as leaves folks foolish and unreasonable about business. Now Mester Irwine was as different as could be, as quick!—he understood what you meant in a minute; and he knew all about building, and could see when you'd made a good job. And he behaved as much like a gentleman to the farmers, and th' old women and the labourers, as he did to the gentry. You never saw *him* interfering and scolding, and trying to play th' emperor. Ah! he was a fine man as ever you set eyes on, and so kind to's mother and sisters. That poor sickly Miss Anne—he seemed to think more of her than of anybody else in the world. There wasn't a soul in the parish had a word to say against him; and his servants stayed with him till they were so old and pottering, he had to hire other folks to do their work."

"Well," I said, "that was an excellent way of preaching in the weekdays; but I daresay, if your old friend Mr. Irwine were to come to life again, and get into the pulpit next Sunday, you would be rather ashamed that he didn't preach better after all your praise of him."

"Nay, nay," said Adam, broadening his chest and throwing himself back in his chair, as if he were ready to meet all inferences, "nobody has ever heard me say Mr. Irwine was much of a preacher. He didn't go into deep

[1] *Reformation* Sixteenth-century religious movement that sought to reform the Catholic Church and eventually established the Protestant religion.

[2] *Dissenter* Member of a Protestant sect that rebelled against and eventually broke with the Church of England.

[3] *Ranter* Member of a religious sect called "Primitive Methodist," whose name arose from a tradition of singing in the streets.

[4] *bulwarks* Potent defenses.

speritial experience; and I know there's a deal in a man's inward life as you can't measure by the square, and say, 'Do this and that'll follow,' and, 'Do that and this'll follow.' There's things go on in the soul, and times when feelings come into you like a rushing mighty wind, as the Scripture says, and part your life in two a'most, so as you look back on yourself as if you was somebody else. Those are things as you can't bottle up in a 'do this' and 'do that'; and I'll go so far with the strongest Methodist ever you'll find. That shows me there's deep speritial things in religion. You can't make much out wi' talking about it, but you feel it. Mr. Irwine didn't go into those things; he preached short moral sermons, and that was all. But then he acted pretty much up to what he said; he didn't set up for being so different from other folks one day, and then be as like 'em as two peas the next. And he made folks love him and respect him, and that was better nor stirring up their gall wi' being over busy. Mrs. Poyser used to say—you know she would have her word about everything—she said, Mr. Irwine was like a good meal o' victual, you were the better for him without thinking on it, and Mr. Ryde was like a dose o' physic,[1] he gripped you and worreted[2] you, and after all he left you much the same."

"But didn't Mr. Ryde preach a great deal more about that spiritual part of religion that you talk of, Adam? Couldn't you get more out of his sermons than out of Mr. Irwine's?"

"Eh, I knowna. He preached a deal about doctrines. But I've seen pretty clear ever since I was a young un, as religion's something else besides doctrines and notions. I look at it as if the doctrines was like finding names for your feelings, so as you can talk of 'em when you've never known 'em, just as a man may talk o' tools when he knows their names, though he's never so much as seen 'em, still less handled 'em. I've heard a deal o' doctrine i' my time, for I used to go after the dissenting preachers along wi' Seth, when I was a lad o' seventeen, and got puzzling myself a deal about th' Arminians and the Calvinists. The Wesleyans,[3] you know, are strong Arminians; and Seth, who could never abide anything harsh, and was always for hoping the best, held fast by the Wesleyans from the very first; but I thought I could pick a hole or two in their notions, and I got disputing wi' one o' the class leaders down at Treddles'on, and harassed him so, first o' this side and then o' that, till at last he said, 'Young man, it's the devil making use o' your pride and conceit as a weapon to war against the simplicity o' the truth.' I couldn't help laughing then, but as I was going home, I thought the man wasn't far wrong. I began to see as all this weighing and sifting what this text means and that text means, and whether folks are saved all by God's grace, or whether there goes an ounce o' their own will to 't, was no part o' real religion at all. You may talk o' these things for hours on end, and you'll only be all the more coxy[4] and conceited for 't. So I took to going nowhere but to church, and hearing nobody but Mr. Irwine, for he said nothing but what was good, and what you'd be the wiser for remembering. And I found it better for my soul to be humble before the mysteries o' God's dealings, and not be making a clatter about what I could never understand. And they're poor foolish questions after all; for what have we got either inside or outside of us but what comes from God? If we've got a resolution to do right, He gave it us, I reckon, first or last; but I see plain enough we shall never do it without a resolution, and that's enough for me."

Adam, you perceive, was a warm admirer, perhaps a partial judge, of Mr. Irwine, as, happily, some of us still are of the people we have known familiarly. Doubtless it will be despised as a weakness by that lofty order of minds who pant after the ideal, and are oppressed by a general sense that their emotions are of too exquisite a

---

1 *physic* Medicine.

2 *worreted* Annoyed.

3 *Arminians* Followers of Dutch Protestant theologian James Arminius (1560–1609), who opposed certain Calvinist doctrines, such as predestination, original sin, and the notion that God is the creator of both good and evil; *Calvinists* Also called "Reformed Protestants"; Christian followers of John Calvin (1509–64); *Wesleyans* Methodists; followers of John Wesley (1703–91), who embraced Arminian theology and founded Methodism.

4 *coxy* Cocky.

character to find fit objects among their everyday fellow men. I have often been favoured with the confidence of these select natures, and find them concur in the experience that great men are over-estimated and small men are insupportable; that if you would love a woman without ever looking back on your love as a folly, she must die while you are courting her; and if you would maintain the slightest belief in human heroism, you must never make a pilgrimage to see the hero. I confess I have often meanly shrunk from confessing to these accomplished and acute gentlemen what my own experience has been. I am afraid I have often smiled with hypocritical assent, and gratified them with an epigram on the fleeting nature of our illusions, which anyone moderately acquainted with French literature can command at a moment's notice. Human converse,[1] I think some wise man has remarked, is not rigidly sincere. But I herewith discharge my conscience, and declare that I have had quite enthusiastic movements of admiration towards old gentlemen who spoke the worst English, who were occasionally fretful in their temper, and who had never moved in a higher sphere of influence than that of parish overseer; and that the way in which I have come to the conclusion that human nature is lovable—the way I have learnt something of its deep pathos, its sublime mysteries—has been by living a great deal among people more or less commonplace and vulgar, of whom you would perhaps hear nothing very surprising if you were to inquire about them in the neighbourhoods where they dwelt. Ten to one most of the small shopkeepers in their vicinity saw nothing at all in them. For I have observed this remarkable coincidence, that the select natures who pant after the ideal, and find nothing in pantaloons or petticoats great enough to command their reverence and love, are curiously in unison with the narrowest and pettiest. For example, I have often heard Mr. Gedge, the landlord of the Royal Oak, who used to turn a bloodshot eye on his neighbours in the village of Shepperton, sum up his opinion of the people in his own parish—and they were

all the people he knew—in these emphatic words: "Ay, sir, I've said it often, and I'll say it again, they're a poor lot i' this parish—a poor lot, sir, big and little." I think he had a dim idea that if he could migrate to a distant parish, he might find neighbours worthy of him; and indeed he did subsequently transfer himself to the Saracen's Head, which was doing a thriving business in the back street of a neighbouring market-town. But, oddly enough, he has found the people up that back street of precisely the same stamp as the inhabitants of Shepperton—"a poor lot, sir, big and little, and them as comes for a go o' gin are no better than them as comes for a pint o' twopenny[2]—a poor lot."
—1859

Silly Novels by Lady Novelists

Silly novels by Lady Novelists are a genus with many species, determined by the particular quality of silliness that predominates in them—the frothy, the prosy, the pious, or the pedantic. But it is a mixture of all these—a composite order of feminine fatuity, that produces the largest class of such novels, which we shall distinguish as the *mind-and-millinery*[3] species. The heroine is usually an heiress, probably a peeress[4] in her own right, with perhaps a vicious baronet, an amiable duke, and an irresistible younger son of a marquis as lovers in the foreground, a clergyman and a poet sighing for her in the middle distance, and a crowd of undefined adorers dimly indicated beyond. Her eyes and her wit are both dazzling; her nose and her morals are alike free from any tendency to irregularity; she has a superb *contralto* and a superb intellect; she is perfectly well-dressed and perfectly religious; she dances like a sylph,[5] and reads the Bible in the original tongues. Or it may be that the heroine is not an heiress—that rank and wealth

---

[1] *converse* Conversation.

[2] *twopenny* Ale.

[3] *millinery* Women's hats.

[4] *peeress* Member of the nobility.

[5] *sylph* Mythical being whose element is air.

are the only things in which she is deficient; but she infallibly gets into high society, she has the triumph of refusing many matches and securing the best, and she wears some family jewels or other as a sort of crown of righteousness at the end. Rakish[1] men either bite their lips in impotent confusion at her repartees, or are touched to penitence by her reproofs, which, on appropriate occasions, rise to a lofty strain of rhetoric; indeed, there is a general propensity in her to make speeches, and to rhapsodize at some length when she retires to her bedroom. In her recorded conversations she is amazingly eloquent, and in her unrecorded conversations, amazingly witty. She is understood to have a depth of insight that looks through and through the shallow theories of philosophers, and her superior instincts are a sort of dial by which men have only to set their clocks and watches, and all will go well. The men play a very subordinate part by her side. You are consoled now and then by a hint that they have affairs,[2] which keeps you in mind that the working-day business of the world is somehow being carried on, but ostensibly the final cause of their existence is that they may accompany the heroine on her "starring" expedition through life. They see her at a ball, and are dazzled; at a flower show, and they are fascinated; on a riding excursion, and they are witched by her noble horsemanship; at church, and they are awed by the sweet solemnity of her demeanour. She is the ideal woman in feelings, faculties, and flounces. For all this, she as often as not marries the wrong person to begin with, and she suffers terribly from the plots and intrigues of the vicious baronet; but even death has a soft place in his heart for such a paragon, and remedies all mistakes for her just at the right moment. The vicious baronet is sure to be killed in a duel, and the tedious husband dies in his bed requesting his wife, as a particular favour to him, to marry the man she loves best, and having already dispatched a note to the lover informing him of the comfortable arrangement. Before matters arrive at this desirable issue our feelings are tried

by seeing the noble, lovely, and gifted heroine pass through many *mauvais*[3] moments, but we have the satisfaction of knowing that her sorrows are wept into embroidered pocket handkerchiefs, that her fainting form reclines on the very best upholstery, and that whatever vicissitudes she may undergo, from being dashed out of her carriage to having her head shaved in a fever, she comes out of them all with a complexion more blooming and locks more redundant than ever.

We may remark, by the way, that we have been relieved from a serious scruple by discovering that silly novels by lady novelists rarely introduce us into any other than very lofty and fashionable society. We had imagined that destitute women turned novelists, as they turned governesses, because they had no other "ladylike" means of getting their bread. On this supposition, vacillating syntax and improbable incident had a certain pathos for us, like the extremely supererogatory[4] pincushions and ill-devised nightcaps that are offered for sale by a blind man. We felt the commodity to be a nuisance, but we were glad to think that the money went to relieve the necessitous, and we pictured to ourselves lonely women struggling for a maintenance, or wives and daughters devoting themselves to the production of "copy"[5] out of pure heroism—perhaps to pay their husband's debts, or to purchase luxuries for a sick father. Under these impressions we shrank from criticising a lady's novel; her English might be faulty, but, we said to ourselves, her motives are irreproachable; her imagination may be uninventive, but her patience is untiring. Empty writing was excused by an empty stomach, and twaddle was consecrated by tears. But no! This theory of ours, like many other pretty theories, has had to give way before observation. Women's silly novels, we are now convinced, are written under totally different circumstances. The fair writers have evidently never talked to a tradesman except from a carriage window; they have no notion of the working classes

---

[1] *Rakish* Fashionable; slightly suggestive of immorality.

[2] *affairs* Matters to attend to, usually of a business nature.

[3] *mauvais* French: bad.

[4] *supererogatory* Unnecessary.

[5] *copy* Text to be printed.

except as "dependents"; they think five hundred a year a miserable pittance; Belgravia[1] and "baronial halls" are their primary truths; and they have no idea of feeling interest in any man who is not at least a great landed proprietor, if not a prime minister. It is clear that they write in elegant boudoirs, with violet-coloured ink and a ruby pen; that they must be entirely indifferent to publishers' accounts, and inexperienced in every form of poverty except poverty of brains. It is true that we are constantly struck with the want of verisimilitude in their representations of the high society in which they seem to live; but then they betray no closer acquaintance with any other form of life. If their peers and peeresses are improbable, their literary men, tradespeople, and cottagers are impossible; and their intellect seems to have the peculiar impartiality of reproducing both what they *have* seen and heard, and what they have *not* seen and heard, with equal unfaithfulness.

There are few women, we suppose, who have not seen something of children under five years of age, yet in "Compensation,"[2] a recent novel of the mind-and-millinery species, which calls itself a "story of real life," we have a child of four and a half years old talking in this Ossianic[3] fashion—

> "Oh, I am so happy, dear gran'mamma—I have seen—I have seen such a delightful person; he is like everything beautiful—like the smell of sweet flowers, and the view from Ben Lomond—or no, *better than that*—he is like what I think of and see when I am very, very happy; and he is really like mamma, too, when she sings; and his forehead is like *that distant sea*," she continued, pointing to the blue Mediterranean; "there seems no end—no end; or like the clusters of stars I like best to look at on a warm night ... Don't look so ... your forehead is like Loch Lomond, when the wind is blowing and

the sun is gone in; I like the sunshine best when the lake is smooth. ... So now—I like it better than ever ... it is more beautiful still from the dark cloud that has gone over it, *when the sun suddenly lights up all the colours of the forests and shining purple rocks, and it is all reflected in the waters below.*"

We are not surprised to learn that the mother of this infant phenomenon, who exhibits symptoms so alarmingly like those of adolescence repressed by gin, is herself a phoenix.[4] We are assured, again and again, that she had a remarkably original mind, that she was a genius, and "conscious of her originality," and she was fortunate enough to have a lover who was also a genius, and a man of "most original mind."

This lover, we read, though "wonderfully similar" to her "in powers and capacity," was "infinitely superior to her in faith and development," and she saw in him the "'Agape'[5]—so rare to find—of which she had read and admired the meaning in her Greek Testament; having, *from her great facility in learning languages,* read the Scriptures in their original *tongues.*" Of course! Greek and Hebrew are mere play to a heroine; Sanskrit is no more than *a b c* to her; and she can talk with perfect correctness in any language except English. She is a polking polyglot,[6] a Creuzer[7] in crinoline. Poor men! There are so few of you who know even Hebrew; you think it something to boast of if, like Bolingbroke,[8] you only "understand that sort of learning, and what is writ about it"; and you are perhaps adoring women who can think slightingly of you in all the Semitic languages successively. But, then, as we are almost invariably told, that a heroine has a "beautifully small head," and as her intellect has probably been early invigorated by an

---

[1] *Belgravia* Fashionable district in London.

[2] *Compensation* Subtitled "A Story of Real Life Thirty Years Ago," by Georgiana, Lady Chatterton; published in the *Athenaeum* in 1856.

[3] *Ossianic* Resembling the poetry of the supposed ancient Gaelic poet Ossian, which was later discovered to have been written by the eighteenth-century Scottish poet James Macpherson.

[4] *phoenix* Figuratively, from the mythical bird of which there was said to be only one, a unique person.

[5] *Agape* Greek: Spiritual (as opposed to sexual) love.

[6] *polking polyglot* Dancing master of languages.

[7] *Creuzer* German philologist Georg Friedrich Creuzer (1771–1858).

[8] *Bolingbroke* English politician and humanist Henry St. John, Viscount Bolingbroke (1678–1751).

attention to costume and deportment, we may conclude that she can pick up the Oriental tongues, to say nothing of their dialects, with the same aerial facility that the butterfly sips nectar. Besides, there can be no difficulty in conceiving the depth of the heroine's erudition, when that of the authoress is so evident.

In "Laura Gay,"[1] another novel of the same school, the heroine seems less at home in Greek and Hebrew, but she makes up for the deficiency by a quite playful familiarity with the Latin classics—with the "dear old Virgil," "the graceful Horace, the humane Cicero, and the pleasant Livy";[2] indeed, it is such a matter of course with her to quote Latin, that she does it at a picnic in a very mixed company of ladies and gentlemen, having, we are told, "no conception that the nobler sex were capable of jealousy on this subject. And if, indeed," continues the biographer of Laura Gay, "the wisest and noblest portion of that sex were in the majority, no such sentiment would exist; but while Miss Wyndhams and Mr. Redfords abound, great sacrifices must be made to their existence." Such sacrifices, we presume, as abstaining from Latin quotations, of extremely moderate interest and applicability, which the wise and noble minority of the other sex would be quite as willing to dispense with as the foolish and ignoble majority. It is as little the custom of well-bred men as of well-bred women to quote Latin in mixed parties; they can contain their familiarity with "the humane Cicero" without allowing it to boil over in ordinary conversation, and even references to "the pleasant Livy" are not absolutely irrepressible. But Ciceronian Latin is the mildest form of Miss Gay's conversational power. Being on the Palatine[3] with a party of sightseers, she falls into the following vein of well-rounded remark: "Truth can only be pure objectively, for even in the creeds where it predominates, being subjective, and parcelled out into

portions, each of these necessarily receives a hue of idiosyncrasy, that is, a taint of superstition more or less strong; while in such creeds as the Roman Catholic, ignorance, interest, the bias of ancient idolatries, and the force of authority, have gradually accumulated on the pure truth, and transformed it, at last, into a mass of superstition for the majority of its votaries; and how few are there, alas! whose zeal, courage, and intellectual energy are equal to the analysis of this accumulation, and to the discovery of the pearl of great price which lies hidden beneath this heap of rubbish." We have often met with women much more novel and profound in their observations than Laura Gay, but rarely with any so inopportunely long winded. A clerical lord, who is half in love with her, is alarmed by the daring remarks just quoted, and begins to suspect that she is inclined to free thinking. But he is mistaken; when in a moment of sorrow he delicately begs leave to "recall to her memory, a *depot* of strength and consolation under affliction, which, until we are hard pressed by the trials of life, we are too apt to forget," we learn that she really has "recurrence to that sacred depot," together with the teapot. There is a certain flavour of orthodoxy mixed with the parade of fortunes and fine carriages in "Laura Gay," but it is an orthodoxy mitigated by study of the humane Cicero, and by an "intellectual disposition to analyse."

"Compensation" is much more heavily dosed with doctrine, but then it has a treble amount of snobbish worldliness and absurd incident to tickle the palate of pious frivolity. Linda, the heroine, is still more speculative and spiritual than Laura Gay, but she has been "presented," and has more, and far grander, lovers; very wicked and fascinating women are introduced—even a French *lionne*;[4] and no expense is spared to get up as exciting a story as you will find in the most immoral novels. In fact, it is a wonderful *potpourri* of Almack's,[5] Scotch second sight, Mr. Rogers's breakfasts,[6] Italian

---

[1] *Laura Gay*   Author anonymous; published 1856 in the *Athenaeum*.

[2] *Virgil*   Latin poet of the first century BCE, author of *The Aeneid*; *Horace*   Latin lyric poet of the first century BCE; *Cicero*   Roman orator, philosopher, and politician of the first century BCE; *Livy*   First century BCE historian and author of *The History of Rome*.

[3] *Palatine*   One of the seven hills of the ancient city of Rome.

[4] *lionne*   Literary celebrity.

[5] *Almack's*   Almack's Assembly Rooms, where fashionable subscription dances were held.

[6] *Mr. Rogers's breakfasts*   English poet Samuel Rogers (1763–1855) was known for holding breakfasts for the literary elite.

brigands, deathbed conversions, superior authoresses, Italian mistresses, and attempts at poisoning old ladies, the whole served up with a garnish of talk about "faith and development," and "most original minds." Even Miss Susan Barton, the superior authoress, whose pen moves in a "quick decided manner when she is composing," declines the finest opportunities of marriage, and though old enough to be Linda's mother (since we are told that she refused Linda's father), has her hand sought by a young earl, the heroine's rejected lover. Of course, genius and morality must be backed by eligible offers, or they would seem rather a dull affair; and piety, like other things, in order to be *comme il faut*,[1] must be in "society," and have admittance to the best circles.

"Rank and Beauty"[2] is a more frothy and less religious variety of the mind-and-millinery species. The heroine, we are told, "if she inherited her father's pride of birth and her mother's beauty of person, had in herself a tone of enthusiastic feeling that perhaps belongs to her age even in the lowly born, but which is refined into the high spirit of wild romance only in the far descended, who feel that it is their best inheritance." This enthusiastic young lady, by dint of reading the newspaper to her father, falls in love with the *prime minister*, who, through the medium of leading articles and "the *resumé* of the debates," shines upon her imagination as a bright particular star, which has no parallax[3] for her, living in the country as simple Miss Wyndham. But she forthwith becomes Baroness Umfraville in her own right, astonishes the world with her beauty and accomplishments when she bursts upon it from her mansion in Spring Gardens, and, as you foresee, will presently come into contact with the unseen *objet aimé*.[4]

Perhaps the words "prime minister" suggest to you a wrinkled or obese sexagenarian;[5] but pray dismiss the image. Lord Rupert Conway has been "called while still almost a youth to the first situation[6] which a subject can hold in the universe," and even leading articles and a *resumé* of the debates have not conjured up a dream that surpasses the fact.

The door opened again, and Lord Rupert Conway entered. Evelyn gave one glance. It was enough; she was not disappointed. It seemed as if a picture on which she had long gazed was suddenly instinct[7] with life, and had stepped from its frame before her. His tall figure, the distinguished simplicity of his air—it was a living Vandyke,[8] a cavalier, one of his noble cavalier ancestors, or one to whom her fancy had always likened him, who long of yore had, with an Umfraville, fought the Paynim[9] far beyond sea. Was this reality?

Very little like it, certainly.

By and by, it becomes evident that the ministerial heart is touched. Lady Umfraville is on a visit to the Queen at Windsor, and,

The last evening of her stay, when they returned from riding, Mr. Wyndham took her and a large party to the top of the Keep,[10] to see the view. She was leaning on the battlements, gazing from that "stately height" at the prospect beneath her, when Lord Rupert was by her side. "What an unrivalled view!" exclaimed she.

"Yes, it would have been wrong to go without having been up here. You are pleased with your visit?"

[1] *comme il faut* Proper; correct (from the French: "as it must be").
[2] *Rank and Beauty* Subtitled "The Young Baroness," published 1856; author anonymous.
[3] *resumé* Summary; *parallax* Reference to stellar parallax, the apparent movement of some stars relative to others. This effect, which is caused by changes in the position of the earth, becomes more difficult to detect the farther away a given star is.
[4] *objet aimé* French: object of affection.
[5] *sexagenerian* Person in their sixties.
[6] *situation* Position of employment.
[7] *instinct* Filled.
[8] *Vandyke* I.e., like a portrait by seventeenth-century Flemish artist Anthony Van Dyke, elegant, noble, and aristocratic.
[9] *Paynim* Non-Christians, generally Muslims.
[10] *Keep* Castle tower.

"Enchanted! A Queen to live and die under, to live and die for!"

"Ha!" cried he, with sudden emotion, and with a *eureka* expression of countenance, as if he had *indeed found a heart in unison with his own.*

The "*eureka* expression of countenance," you see at once to be prophetic of marriage at the end of the third volume; but before that desirable consummation, there are very complicated misunderstandings, arising chiefly from the vindictive plotting of Sir Luttrell Wycherley, who is a genius, a poet, and in every way a most remarkable character indeed. He is not only a romantic poet, but a hardened rake[1] and a cynical wit; yet his deep passion for Lady Umfraville has so impoverished his epigrammatic[2] talent, that he cuts an extremely poor figure in conversation. When she rejects him, he rushes into the shrubbery, and rolls himself in the dirt, and on recovering, devotes himself to the most diabolical and laborious schemes of vengeance, in the course of which he disguises himself as a quack physician, and enters into general practice, foreseeing that Evelyn will fall ill, and that he shall be called in to attend her. At last, when all his schemes are frustrated, he takes leave of her in a long letter, written, as you will perceive from the following passage, entirely in the style of an eminent literary man:

"Oh, lady, nursed in pomp and pleasure, will you ever cast one thought upon the miserable being who addresses you? Will you ever, as your gilded galley is floating down the unruffled stream of prosperity, will you ever, while lulled by the sweetest music—thine own praises,—hear the far off sigh from that world to which I am going?"

On the whole, however, frothy as it is, we rather prefer "Rank and Beauty" to the other two novels we have mentioned. The dialogue is more natural and spirited; there is some frank ignorance, and no pedantry; and you are allowed to take the heroine's astounding intellect upon trust, without being called on to read her conversational refutations of sceptics and philosophers, or her rhetorical solutions of the mysteries of the universe.

Writers of the mind-and-millinery school are remarkably unanimous in their choice of diction. In their novels, there is usually a lady or gentleman who is more or less of a upas tree:[3] the lover has a manly breast; minds are redolent of various things; hearts are hollow; events are utilized; friends are consigned to the tomb; infancy is an engaging period; the sun is a luminary that goes to his western couch, or gathers the raindrops into his refulgent[4] bosom; life is a melancholy boon; Albion and Scotia[5] are conversational epithets. There is a striking resemblance, too, in the character of their moral comments, such, for instance, as that "It is a fact, no less true than melancholy, that all people, more or less, richer or poorer, are swayed by bad example"; that "Books, however trivial, contain some subjects from which useful information may be drawn"; that "Vice can too often borrow the language of virtue"; that "Merit and nobility of nature must exist, to be accepted, for clamour and pretension cannot impose upon those too well read in human nature to be easily deceived"; and that, "In order to forgive, we must have been injured." There is, doubtless, a class of readers to whom these remarks appear peculiarly pointed and pungent, for we often find them doubly and trebly scored with the pencil, and delicate hands giving in their determined adhesion to these hardy novelties by a distinct *très vrai*,[6] emphasized by many notes of exclamation. The colloquial style of these novels is often marked by much ingenious inversion, and a careful avoidance of such cheap phraseology as can be heard every day. Angry young gentlemen exclaim—"'Tis ever thus, methinks"; and in the half hour before dinner a young lady informs her next neighbour that the first day she read Shakespeare she "stole away into the park, and beneath the

---

[1] *rake* Fashionable man of loose character.

[2] *epigrammatic* Witty.

[3] *upas tree* Notoriously poisonous tree.

[4] *refulgent* Radiant.

[5] *Albion and Scotia* Archaic names for England and Scotland, their use here signifying pretension.

[6] *très vrai* French: very true.

shadow of the greenwood tree, devoured with rapture the inspired page of the great magician." But the most remarkable efforts of the mind-and-millinery writers lie in their philosophic reflections. The authoress of "Laura Gay," for example, having married her hero and heroine, improves the event by observing that "if those sceptics, whose eyes have so long gazed on matter that they can no longer see aught else in man, could once enter with heart and soul into such bliss as this, they would come to say that the soul of man and the polypus[1] are not of common origin, or of the same texture." Lady novelists, it appears, can see something else besides matter; they are not limited to phenomena, but can relieve their eyesight by occasional glimpses of the *noumenon*,[2] and are, therefore, naturally better able than anyone else to confound sceptics, even of that remarkable, but to us unknown school, which maintains that the soul of man is of the same texture as the polypus.

The most pitiable of all silly novels by lady novelists are what we may call the *oracular* species—novels intended to expound the writer's religious, philosophical, or moral theories. There seems to be a notion abroad among women, rather akin to the superstition that the speech and actions of idiots are inspired, and that the human being most entirely exhausted of common sense is the fittest vehicle of revelation. To judge from their writings, there are certain ladies who think that an amazing ignorance, both of science and of life, is the best possible qualification for forming an opinion on the knottiest moral and speculative questions. Apparently, their recipe for solving all such difficulties is something like this: Take a woman's head, stuff it with a smattering of philosophy and literature chopped small, and with false notions of society baked hard, let it hang over a desk a few hours every day, and serve up hot in feeble English, when not required. You will rarely meet with a lady novelist of the oracular class who is diffident of her ability to decide on theological ques-

tions—who has any suspicion that she is not capable of discriminating with the nicest[3] accuracy between the good and evil in all church parties—who does not see precisely how it is that men have gone wrong hitherto—and pity philosophers in general that they have not had the opportunity of consulting her. Great writers, who have modestly contented themselves with putting their experience into fiction, and have thought it quite a sufficient task to exhibit men and things as they are, she sighs over as deplorably deficient in the application of their powers. "They have solved no great questions"—and she is ready to remedy their omission by setting before you a complete theory of life and manual of divinity, in a love story, where ladies and gentlemen of good family go through genteel vicissitudes, to the utter confusion of Deists, Puseyites,[4] and ultra-Protestants, and to the perfect establishment of that particular view of Christianity which either condenses itself into a sentence of small caps,[5] or explodes into a cluster of stars on the three hundred and thirtieth page. It is true, the ladies and gentlemen will probably seem to you remarkably little like any you have had the fortune or misfortune to meet with, for, as a general rule, the ability of a lady novelist to describe actual life and her fellow men, is in inverse proportion to her confident eloquence about God and the other world, and the means by which she usually chooses to conduct you to true ideas of the invisible is a totally false picture of the visible.

As typical a novel of the oracular kind as we can hope to meet with, is "The Enigma: a Leaf from the Chronicles of the Wolchorley House."[6] The "enigma" which this novel is to solve, is certainly one that demands powers no less gigantic than those of a lady

---

[1] *polypus* Octopus.

[2] *noumenon* Greek: intangible article that is known only through the intellect.

[3] *nicest* Most precise.

[4] *Puseyites* Followers of Edward Bouverie Pusey (1800–82), English clergy member, leader of the Oxford Movement, and supporter of the Anglican church.

[5] *small caps* Short capital letters, often used in texts of the period to add emphasis or to indicate significance.

[6] *The Enigma ... House* Published 1856 in the *Athenaeum*; author anonymous.

novelist, being neither more nor less than the existence of evil. The problem is stated, and the answer dimly foreshadowed on the very first page. The spirited young lady, with raven hair, says, "All life is an inextricable confusion"; and the meek young lady, with auburn hair, looks at the picture of the Madonna[1] which she is copying, and—"*There* seemed the solution of that mighty enigma." The style of this novel is quite as lofty as its purpose; indeed, some passages on which we have spent much patient study are quite beyond our reach, in spite of the illustrative aid of italics and small caps; and we must await further "development" in order to understand them. Of Ernest, the model young clergyman, who sets everyone right on all occasions, we read, that "he held not of marriage in the marketable kind, after a social desecration"; that, on one eventful night, "sleep had not visited his divided heart, where tumultuated, in varied type and combination, the aggregate feelings of grief and joy"; and that, "for the *marketable* human article he had no toleration, be it of what sort, or set for what value it might, whether for worship or class, his upright soul abhorred it, whose ultimatum, the self-deceiver, was to him THE *great spiritual lie*, 'living in a vain show, deceiving and being deceived'; since he did not suppose the phylactery[2] and enlarged border on the garment to be *merely* a social trick." (The italics and small caps are the author's, and we hope they assist the reader's comprehension.) Of Sir Lionel, the model old gentleman, we are told that "the simple ideal of the middle age, apart from its anarchy and decadence, in him most truly seemed to live again, when the ties which knit men together were of heroic cast. The first-born colours of pristine faith and truth engraven on the common soul of man, and blent into the wide arch of brotherhood, where the primeval law of *order* grew and multiplied, each perfect after his kind, and mutually interdependent." You see clearly, of course, how colours are first engraven on a soul, and then blent into a wide arch, on which arch of colours—apparently a rainbow—the law of order grew and multiplied, each—apparently the arch and the law—perfect after his kind? If, after this, you can possibly want any further aid towards knowing what Sir Lionel was, we can tell you, that in his soul "the scientific combinations of thought could educe[3] no fuller harmonies of the good and the true, than lay in the primeval pulses which floated as an atmosphere around it!" and that, when he was sealing a letter, "Lo! the responsive throb in that good man's bosom echoed back in simple truth the honest witness of a heart that condemned him not, as his eye, bedewed with love, rested, too, with something of ancestral pride, on the undimmed motto of the family—'LOIAUTÉ.'"[4]

The slightest matters have their vulgarity fumigated out of them by the same elevated style. Commonplace people would say that a copy of Shakespeare lay on a drawing-room table; but the authoress of "The Enigma," bent on edifying periphrasis,[5] tells you that there lay on the table, "that fund of human thought and feeling, which teaches the heart through the little name, 'Shakespeare.'" A watchman sees a light burning in an upper window rather longer than usual, and thinks that people are foolish to sit up late when they have an opportunity of going to bed; but, lest this fact should seem too low and common, it is presented to us in the following striking and metaphysical manner: "He marvelled—as man *will* think for others in a necessarily separate personality, consequently (though disallowing it) in false mental premise—how differently *he* should act, how gladly *he* should prize the rest so lightly held of within." A footman—an ordinary Jeames, with large calves and aspirated vowels—answers the doorbell, and the opportunity is seized to tell you that he was a "type of the large class of pampered menials, who follow the

[1] *the Madonna* Mary, mother of Jesus.

[2] *phylactery* Small boxes containing religious verses, traditionally worn on the head and arm by Jewish men. See Matthew 23.5: "But all their works they do for to be seen of men: they make broad their phylacteries, and enlarge the borders of their garments."

[3] *educe* Draw out.

[4] *LOIAUTÉ* Old French: Loyalty.

[5] *periphrasis* Figure of speech by which a meaning is expressed by many words rather than few or one.

curse of Cain[1]—'vagabonds' on the face of the earth, and whose estimate of the human class varies in the graduated scale of money and expenditure. ... These, and such as these, O England, be the false lights of thy morbid civilization!" We have heard of various "false lights," from Dr. Cumming to Robert Owen,[2] from Dr. Pusey to the Spirit-rappers,[3] but we never before heard of the false light that emanates from plush and powder.

In the same way very ordinary events of civilized life are exalted into the most awful crises, and ladies in full skirts and *manches à la Chinoise*,[4] conduct themselves not unlike the heroines of sanguinary[5] melodramas. Mrs. Percy, a shallow woman of the world, wishes her son Horace to marry the auburn-haired Grace, she being an heiress; but he, after the manner of sons, falls in love with the raven-haired Kate, the heiress's portionless cousin; and, moreover, Grace herself shows every symptom of perfect indifference to Horace. In such cases, sons are often sulky or fiery, mothers are alternately manoeuvering and waspish, and the portionless young lady often lies awake at night and cries a good deal. We are getting used to these things now, just as we are used to eclipses of the moon, which no longer set us howling and beating tin kettles. We never heard of a lady in a fashionable "front"[6] behaving like Mrs. Percy under these circumstances. Happening one day to see Horace talking to Grace at a window, without in the least knowing what they are talking about, or having the least reason to believe that Grace, who is mistress of the house and a person of dignity, would accept her son if he were to offer himself, she suddenly rushes up to them

and clasps them both, saying, "with a flushed countenance[7] and in an excited manner"—"This is indeed happiness; for, may I not call you so, Grace?—my Grace—my Horace's Grace!—my dear children!" Her son tells her she is mistaken, and that he is engaged to Kate, whereupon we have the following scene and tableau:

Gathering herself up to an unprecedented height, (!) her eyes lightning forth the fire of her anger—

"Wretched boy!" she said, hoarsely and scornfully, and clenching her hand, "Take then the doom of your own choice! Bow down your miserable head and let a mother's—"

"Curse not!" spake a deep low voice from behind, and Mrs. Percy started, scared, as though she had seen a heavenly visitant appear, to break upon her in the midst of her sin.

Meantime, Horace had fallen on his knees at her feet, and hid his face in his hands.

Who, then, is she—who! Truly his "guardian spirit" hath stepped between him and the fearful words, which, however unmerited, must have hung as a pall over his future existence—a spell which could not be unbound—which could not be unsaid.

Of an earthly paleness, but calm with the still, iron-bound calmness of death—the only calm one there—Katherine stood; and her words smote on the ear in tones whose appallingly slow and separate intonation rung on the heart like the chill, isolated tolling of some fatal knell.

"He would have plighted me his faith, but I did not accept it; you cannot, therefore—you *dare* not curse him. And here," she continued, raising her hand to heaven, whither her large dark eyes also rose with a chastened glow, which, for the first time, *suffering* had lighted in those passionate orbs,— "here I promise, come weal, come woe, that Horace Wolchorley and I do never interchange vows without his mother's sanction—without his mother's blessing!"

---

[1] *Cain* First son of Adam and Eve, who killed his brother Abel, and was cursed by God, condemned to be a restless wanderer (see Genesis 4).

[2] *Dr. Cumming* The Reverend John Cumming (1807–81), Calvinist preacher; *Robert Owen* Social reformer (1771–1858).

[3] *Spirit-rappers* Mediums who performed séances and claimed to communicate with the dead, interpreting the knocking sounds allegedly made by their spirits.

[4] *manches à la Chinoise* French: Chinese sleeves.

[5] *sanguinary* Featuring bloodshed.

[6] *front* False curls worn on the forehead.

[7] *countenance* Facial appearance.

Here, and throughout the story, we see that confusion of purpose which is so characteristic of silly novels written by women. It is a story of quite modern drawing-room society—a society in which polkas are played and Puseyism discussed; yet we have characters, and incidents, and traits of manner introduced, which are mere shreds from the most heterogeneous romances. We have a blind Irish harper, "relic of the picturesque bards of yore," startling us at a Sunday-school festival of tea and cake in an English village; we have a crazy gipsy, in a scarlet cloak, singing snatches of romantic song, and revealing a secret on her deathbed which, with the testimony of a dwarfish miserly merchant, who salutes strangers with a curse and a devilish laugh, goes to prove that Ernest, the model young clergyman, is Kate's brother; and we have an ultra-virtuous Irish Barney, discovering that a document is forged, by comparing the date of the paper with the date of the alleged signature, although the same document has passed through a court of law, and occasioned a fatal decision. The "Hall" in which Sir Lionel lives is the venerable country seat of an old family, and this, we suppose, sets the imagination of the authoress flying to donjons[1] and battlements, where "lo! the warder blows his horn"; for, as the inhabitants are in their bedrooms on a night certainly within the recollection of Pleaceman X., and a breeze springs up, which we are at first told was faint, and then that it made the old cedars bow their branches to the greensward,[2] she falls into this mediaeval vein of description (the italics are ours): "The banner *unfurled it* at the sound, and shook its guardian wing above, while the startled owl *flapped her* in the ivy; the firmament looking down through her 'argus eyes,'[3]—

Ministers of heaven's mute melodies.

And lo! two strokes tolled from out the warder tower, and 'Two o'clock' re-echoed its interpreter below."

---

1 *donjon* The main tower within a walled castle or fortress.

2 *greensward* Grassy ground.

3 *argus eyes* Intensely watching eyes. Argus, a giant from Greek mythology, described as having as many as a hundred eyes.

Such stories as this of "The Enigma" remind us of the pictures clever children sometimes draw "out of their own head," where you will see a modern villa on the right, two knights in helmets fighting in the foreground, and a tiger grinning in a jungle on the left, the several objects being brought together because the artist thinks each pretty, and perhaps still more because he remembers seeing them in other pictures.

But we like the authoress much better on her mediaeval stilts than on her oracular ones—when she talks of the *Ich*[4] and of "subjective" and "objective," and lays down the exact line of Christian verity, between "right-hand excesses and left-hand declensions."[5] Persons who deviate from this line are introduced with a patronizing air of charity. Of a certain Miss Inshquine she informs us, with all the lucidity of italics and small caps, that "*function, not form,* AS *the inevitable outer expression of the spirit in this tabernacled age,*[6] weakly engrossed her." And *à propos* of Miss Mayjar, an evangelical lady who is a little too apt to talk of her visits to sick women and the state of their souls, we are told that the model clergyman is "not one to disallow, through the *super* crust, the undercurrent towards good in the *subject,* or the positive benefits, nevertheless, to the *object.*" We imagine the double-refined accent and protrusion of chin which are feebly represented by the italics in this lady's sentences! We abstain from quoting any of her oracular doctrinal passages, because they refer to matters too serious for our pages just now.

The epithet "silly" may seem impertinent, applied to a novel which indicates so much reading and intellectual activity as "The Enigma"; but we use this epithet advisedly. If, as the world has long agreed, a very great amount of instruction will not make a wise man, still less will a very mediocre amount of instruction make a wise woman. And the most mischievous form of femi-

---

4 *Ich* German: I.

5 *right-hand ... declensions* See Michael Shields, *Faithful Contendings Displayed* (1780), in which the author identifies "the extremes of left-hand declensions and right-hand extravagancies" as threats to the Church; *declensions* Declines, especially in faith or loyalty.

6 *tabernacled age* Here, age of churches.

nine silliness is the literary form, because it tends to confirm the popular prejudice against the more solid education of women. When men see girls wasting their time in consultations about bonnets and ball dresses, and in giggling or sentimental love confidences, or middle-aged women mismanaging their children, and solacing themselves with acrid gossip, they can hardly help saying, "For Heaven's sake, let girls be better educated; let them have some better objects of thought —some more solid occupations." But after a few hours' conversation with an oracular literary woman, or a few hours' reading of her books, they are likely enough to say, "After all, when a woman gets some knowledge, see what use she makes of it! Her knowledge remains acquisition, instead of passing into culture; instead of being subdued into modesty and simplicity by a larger acquaintance with thought and fact, she has a feverish consciousness of her attainments; she keeps a sort of mental pocket mirror, and is continually looking in it at her own 'intellectuality'; she spoils the taste of one's muffin by questions of metaphysics; 'puts down' men at a dinner table with her superior information; and seizes the opportunity of a *soirée* to catechise us on the vital question of the relation between mind and matter. And then, look at her writings! She mistakes vagueness for depth, bombast for eloquence, and affectation for originality; she struts on one page, rolls her eyes on another, grimaces in a third, and is hysterical in a fourth. She may have read many writings of great men, and a few writings of great women; but she is as unable to discern the difference between her own style and theirs as a Yorkshireman is to discern the difference between his own English and a Londoner's: rhodomontade[1] is the native accent of her intellect. No—the average nature of women is too shallow and feeble a soil to bear much tillage; it is only fit for the very lightest crops."

It is true that the men who come to such a decision on such very superficial and imperfect observation may not be among the wisest in the world; but we have not now to contest their opinion—we are only pointing out how it is unconsciously encouraged by many women who have volunteered themselves as representatives of the feminine intellect. We do not believe that a man was ever strengthened in such an opinion by associating with a woman of true culture, whose mind had absorbed her knowledge instead of being absorbed by it. A really cultured woman, like a really cultured man, is all the simpler and the less obtrusive for her knowledge; it has made her see herself and her opinions in something like just proportions; she does not make it a pedestal from which she flatters herself that she commands a complete view of men and things, but makes it a point of observation from which to form a right estimate of herself. She neither spouts poetry nor quotes Cicero on slight provocation; not because she thinks that a sacrifice must be made to the prejudices of men, but because that mode of exhibiting her memory and Latinity does not present itself to her as edifying or graceful. She does not write books to confound philosophers, perhaps because she is able to write books that delight them. In conversation she is the least formidable of women, because she understands you, without wanting to make you aware that you *can't* understand her. She does not give you information, which is the raw material of culture—she gives you sympathy, which is its subtlest essence.

A more numerous class of silly novels than the oracular, (which are generally inspired by some form of High Church, or transcendental Christianity) is what we may call the *white neck-cloth* species, which represent the tone of thought and feeling in the Evangelical party.[2] This species is a kind of genteel tract on a large scale, intended as a sort of medicinal sweetmeat[3] for Low Church young ladies; an Evangelical substitute for the fashionable novel, as the May Meetings[4] are a substitute

---

[1] *rhodomontade* Pretentious, inflated style of speaking.

[2] *High Church ... Evangelical party* The Anglican Church (the Church of England) split into factions, with the High Church practicing the more formal rituals and ceremonies of Catholicism and the Low Church, or Evangelical branch, rejecting them.

[3] *sweetmeat* Confection, such as candied fruit or nuts.

[4] *May Meetings* Yearly Missionary Society meetings for the Church of England were held in May.

for the Opera. Even Quaker[1] children, one would think, can hardly have been denied the indulgence of a doll; but it must be a doll dressed in a drab gown and a coal-scuttle bonnet[2]—not a wordly doll, in gauze and spangles. And there are no young ladies, we imagine —unless they belong to the Church of the United Brethren, in which people are married without any love-making[3]—who can dispense with love stories. Thus, for Evangelical young ladies there are Evangelical love stories, in which the vicissitudes of the tender passion are sanctified by saving views of Regeneration and the Atonement. These novels differ from the oracular ones, as a Low Churchwoman often differs from a High Churchwoman: they are a little less supercilious, and a great deal more ignorant, a little less correct in their syntax, and a great deal more vulgar.

The Orlando[4] of Evangelical literature is the young curate, looked at from the point of view of the middle class, where cambric bands are understood to have as thrilling an effect on the hearts of young ladies as epaulettes[5] have in the classes above and below it. In the ordinary type of these novels, the hero is almost sure to be a young curate,[6] frowned upon, perhaps, by worldly mammas, but carrying captive the hearts of their daughters, who can "never forget *that* sermon"; tender glances are seized from the pulpit stairs instead of the opera box; tête-à-têtes[7] are seasoned with quotations from Scripture, instead of quotations from the poets; and questions as to the state of the heroine's affections are mingled with anxieties as to the state of her soul. The young curate

always has a background of well-dressed and wealthy, if not fashionable society—for Evangelical silliness is as snobbish as any other kind of silliness; and the Evangelical lady novelist, while she explains to you the type of the scapegoat on one page, is ambitious on another to represent the manners and conversation of aristocratic people. Her pictures of fashionable society are often curious studies considered as efforts of the Evangelical imagination; but in one particular the novels of the White Neck-cloth School are meritoriously realistic—their favourite hero, the Evangelical young curate, is always rather an insipid personage.

The most recent novel of this species that we happen to have before us, is "The Old Grey Church."[8] It is utterly tame and feeble; there is no one set of objects on which the writer seems to have a stronger grasp than on any other; and we should be entirely at a loss to conjecture among what phases of life her experience has been gained, but for certain vulgarisms of style which sufficiently indicate that she has had the advantage, though she has been unable to use it, of mingling chiefly with men and women whose manners and characters have not had all their bosses[9] and angles rubbed down by refined conventionalism. It is less excusable in an Evangelical novelist, than in any other, gratuitously to seek her subjects among titles and carriages. The real drama of Evangelicalism—and it has abundance of fine drama for anyone who has genius enough to discern and reproduce it—lies among the middle and lower classes; and are not Evangelical opinions understood to give an especial interest in the weak things of the earth, rather than in the mighty? Why then, cannot our Evangelical lady novelists show us the operation of their religious views among people (there really are many such in the world) who keep no carriage, "not so much as a brass-bound gig,"[10] who even manage to eat their dinner without a silver fork, and in whose mouths the authoress's questionable English would be strictly consistent?

---

[1] *Quaker* Also known as the Society of Friends, a dissenting group of Protestants associated with a simple and austere mode of living.

[2] *coal-scuttle bonnet* Scoop-shaped bonnet commonly worn by Quaker women in the nineteenth century.

[3] *Church of the United Brethren* Protestant denomination formed in Pennsylvania, drawing on the practices of several Christian religious communities; *love-making* Courtship.

[4] *Orlando* Hero of medieval romance.

[5] *cambric bands* Strips of fine linen that hang from the neck of clerics' dress; *epaulettes* Worn on the shoulders of officers' uniforms.

[6] *curate* Pastor.

[7] *tête-à-têtes* French: literally, "head to heads," private conversations between two people.

[8] *The Old Grey Church* By Lady Caroline Scott, published 1856 in the *Athenaeum*.

[9] *bosses* Protuberances; bumps.

[10] *gig* Light, two-wheeled carriage pulled by one horse.

Why can we not have pictures of religious life among the industrial classes in England, as interesting as Mrs. Stowe's pictures of religious life among the negroes?[1] Instead of this, pious ladies nauseate us with novels which remind us of what we sometimes see in a worldly woman recently "converted"—she is as fond of a fine dinner table as before, but she invites clergymen instead of beaux;[2] she thinks as much of her dress as before, but she adopts a more sober choice of colours and patterns; her conversation is as trivial as before, but the triviality is flavoured with gospel instead of gossip. In "The Old Grey Church," we have the same sort of Evangelical travesty of the fashionable novel, and of course the vicious, intriguing baronet is not wanting. It is worthwhile to give a sample of the style of conversation attributed to this high-born rake—a style that in its profuse italics and palpable innuendoes, is worthy of Miss Squeers.[3] In an evening visit to the ruins of the Colosseum, Eustace, the young clergyman, has been withdrawing the heroine, Miss Lushington, from the rest of the party, for the sake of a *tête-à-tête*. The baronet is jealous, and vents his pique in this way:

There they are, and Miss Lushington, no doubt, quite safe; for she is under the holy guidance of Pope Eustace the First, who has, of course, been delivering to her an edifying homily on the wickedness of the heathens of yore, who, as tradition tells us, in this very place let loose the wild *beastises* on poor St. Paul![4]—Oh, no! by the bye, I believe I am wrong, and betraying my want of clergy, and that it was not at all St. Paul, nor was it here. But no matter, it would equally serve as a text to preach

from, and from which to diverge to the degenerate *heathen* Christians of the present day, and all their naughty practices, and so end with an exhortation to "come out from among them, and be separate"[5]—and I am sure, Miss Lushington, you have most scrupulously conformed to that injunction this evening, for we have seen nothing of you since our arrival. But everyone seems agreed it has been a *charming party of pleasure,* and I am sure we all feel *much indebted* to Mr. Grey for having *suggested* it; and as he seems so capital a cicerone,[6] I hope he will think of something else equally agreeable to *all.*

This drivelling kind of dialogue, and equally drivelling narrative, which, like a bad drawing, represents nothing, and barely indicates what is meant to be represented, runs through the book; and we have no doubt is considered by the amiable authoress to constitute an improving novel, which Christian mothers will do well to put into the hands of their daughters. But everything is relative; we have met with American vegetarians whose normal diet was dry meal, and who, when their appetite wanted stimulating, tickled it with *wet* meal; and so, we can imagine that there are Evangelical circles in which "The Old Grey Church" is devoured as a powerful and interesting fiction.

But, perhaps, the least readable of silly women's novels, are the *modern-antique* species, which unfold to us the domestic life of Jannes and Jambres, the private love affairs of Sennacherib, or the mental struggles and ultimate conversion of Demetrius the silversmith.[7] From most silly novels we can at least extract a laugh; but those of the modern antique school have a ponderous, a leaden kind of fatuity, under which we groan. What can be more demonstrative of the inability of literary women to measure their own powers, than their frequent assumption of a task which can only be justified

---

[1] *Mrs. Stowe's ... negroes* In Harriet Beecher Stowe's novels *Uncle Tom's Cabin* (1852), and *Dred* (1856).

[2] *beaux* Male suitors.

[3] *Miss Squeers* Pathetic character in Charles Dickens's *Nicholas Nickleby* (1838).

[4] *St. Paul* St. Paul (c. 5–65 CE) was an important figure in the early spread of Christianity. He is believed to have spent the last years of his life in Rome. According to tradition, he was beheaded as part of a wave of religious persecution—not killed by animals, as some other victims were.

[5] *come out ... be separate* See 2 Corinthians 6.17, of which St. Paul is believed to be the author.

[6] *cicerone* Guide to antiquities.

[7] *Jannes and Jambres* Egyptian magicians in 2 Timothy 3.8; *Sennacherib* Biblical king of Assyria; see 2 Kings 18.13; *Demetrius the silversmith* See Acts 19.24.

by the rarest concurrence of acquirement with genius? The finest effort to reanimate the past is of course only approximative—is always more or less an infusion of the modern spirit into the ancient form—

> Was ihr den Geist der Zeiten heisst,
> Das ist im Grund der Herren eigner Geist,
> In dem die Zeiten sich bespiegeln.[1]

Admitting that genius which has familiarized itself with all the relics of an ancient period can sometimes, by the force of its sympathetic divination, restore the missing notes in the "music of humanity,"[2] and reconstruct the fragments into a whole which will really bring the remote past nearer to us, and interpret it to our duller apprehension—this form of imaginative power must always be among the very rarest, because it demands as much accurate and minute knowledge as creative vigour. Yet we find ladies constantly choosing to make their mental mediocrity more conspicuous, by clothing it in a masquerade of ancient names; by putting their feeble sentimentality into the mouths of Roman vestals[3] or Egyptian princesses, and attributing their rhetorical arguments to Jewish high priests and Greek philosophers. A recent example of this heavy imbecility is "Adonijah, a Tale of the Jewish Dispersion,"[4] which forms part of a series, "uniting," we are told, "taste, humour, and sound principles." "Adonijah," we presume, exemplifies the tale of "sound principles"; the taste and humour are to be found in other members of the series. We are told on the cover, that the incidents of this tale are "fraught with unusual interest," and the preface winds up thus: "To those who feel interested in the dispersed of Israel and Judea, these pages may afford, perhaps, information on an important subject, as well as amusement." Since the "important subject" on which this book is to afford information is not specified, it may possibly lie in some esoteric meaning to which we have no key; but if it has relation to the dispersed of Israel and Judea at any period of their history, we believe a tolerably well-informed schoolgirl already knows much more of it than she will find in this "Tale of the Jewish Dispersion." "Adonijah" is simply the feeblest kind of love story, supposed to be instructive, we presume, because the hero is a Jewish captive, and the heroine a Roman vestal; because they and their friends are converted to Christianity after the shortest and easiest method approved by the "Society for Promoting the Conversion of the Jews"; and because, instead of being written in plain language, it is adorned with that peculiar style of grandiloquence which is held by some lady novelists to give an antique colouring, and which we recognise at once in such phrases as these: "the splendid regnal talents undoubtedly possessed by the Emperor Nero"—"the expiring scion of a lofty stem"—"the virtuous partner of his couch"—"ah, by Vesta!"—and "I tell thee, Roman." Among the quotations which serve at once for instruction and ornament on the cover of this volume, there is one from Miss Sinclair,[5] which informs us that "Works of imagination are *avowedly* read by men of science, wisdom, and piety"; from which we suppose the reader is to gather the cheering inference that Dr. Daubeny, Mr. Mill, or Mr. Maurice,[6] may openly indulge himself with the perusal of "Adonijah," without being obliged to secrete it among the sofa cushions, or read it by snatches under the dinner table.

"Be not a baker if your head be made of butter," says a homely proverb, which, being interpreted, may mean, let no woman rush into print who is not prepared for the consequences. We are aware that our remarks are in a very different tone from that of the reviewers who, with a perennial recurrence of precisely similar emotions, only paralleled, we imagine, in the experience of

---

[1] *Was ihr ... bespiegeln* German, from Johann Wolfgang von Goethe's *Faust*: "That which people call the spirit of the times is actually their own spirit reflecting the past."

[2] *music of humanity* From William Wordsworth's "Tintern Abbey," line 91.

[3] *vestals* Priestesses of Vesta, Roman goddess of the hearth.

[4] *Adonijah ... Dispersion* 1856, by Jane Margaret Strickland.

[5] *Miss Sinclair* Scottish novelist Catherine Sinclair (1800–64).

[6] *Dr. Daubeny* English chemist and botanist Charles Giles Bridle Daubeny (1795–1867); *Mr. Mill* English philosopher John Stuart Mill (1806–73); *Mr. Maurice* English theologian Rev. Frederick D. Maurice (1805–72).

monthly nurses,[1] tell one lady novelist after another that they "hail" her productions "with delight." We are aware that the ladies at whom our criticism is pointed are accustomed to be told, in the choicest phraseology of puffery, that their pictures of life are brilliant, their characters well drawn, their style fascinating, and their sentiments lofty. But if they are inclined to resent our plainness of speech, we ask them to reflect for a moment on the chary praise, and often captious blame, which their panegyrists[2] give to writers whose works are on the way to become classics. No sooner does a woman show that she has genius or effective talent, than she receives the tribute of being moderately praised and severely criticised. By a peculiar thermometric adjustment, when a woman's talent is at zero, journalistic approbation is at the boiling pitch; when she attains mediocrity, it is already at no more than summer heat; and if ever she reaches excellence, critical enthusiasm drops to the freezing point. Harriet Martineau, Currer Bell, and Mrs. Gaskell[3] have been treated as cavalierly as if they had been men. And every critic who forms a high estimate of the share women may ultimately take in literature, will, on principle, abstain from any exceptional indulgence towards the productions of literary women. For it must be plain to everyone who looks impartially and extensively into feminine literature, that its greatest deficiencies are due hardly more to the want of intellectual power than to the want of those moral qualities that contribute to literary excellence—patient diligence, a sense of the responsibility involved in publication, and an appreciation of the sacredness of the writer's art. In the majority of women's books you see that kind of facility which springs from the absence of any high standard; that fertility in imbecile combination or feeble imitation which a little self-criticism would check and

reduce to barrenness, just as with a total want[4] of musical ear people will sing out of tune, while a degree more melodic sensibility would suffice to render them silent. The foolish vanity of wishing to appear in print, instead of being counter-balanced by any consciousness of the intellectual or moral derogation[5] implied in futile authorship, seems to be encouraged by the extremely false impression that to write *at all* is a proof of superiority in a woman. On this ground, we believe that the average intellect of women is unfairly represented by the mass of feminine literature, and that while the few women who write well are very far above the ordinary intellectual level of their sex, the many women who write ill are very far below it. So that, after all, the severer critics are fulfilling a chivalrous duty in depriving the mere fact of feminine authorship of any false prestige which may give it a delusive attraction, and in recommending women of mediocre faculties—as at least a negative service they can render their sex—to abstain from writing.

The standing apology for women who become writers without any special qualification is that society shuts them out from other spheres of occupation. Society is a very culpable entity, and has to answer for the manufacture of many unwholesome commodities, from bad pickles to bad poetry. But society, like "matter," and Her Majesty's Government, and other lofty abstractions, has its share of excessive blame as well as excessive praise. Where there is one woman who writes from necessity, we believe there are three women who write from vanity; and, besides, there is something so antiseptic in the mere healthy fact of working for one's bread, that the most trashy and rotten kind of feminine literature is not likely to have been produced under such circumstances. "In all labour there is profit";[6] but ladies' silly novels, we imagine, are less the result of labour than of busy idleness.

---

[1] *monthly nurses* Women hired to assist a mother during and after the delivery of a child.

[2] *chary* Careful; *captious* Crafty; *panegyrists* Those who deliver praise.

[3] *Harriet Martineau* British journalist (1802–76); *Currer Bell* Pseudonym of British novelist Charlotte Brontë (1816–55); *Mrs. Gaskell* British novelist Elizabeth Gaskell (1810–65).

---

[4] *check* Restrain; *want* Lack.

[5] *derogation* Decline in reputation.

[6] *In all labour there is profit* From Proverbs 14.23.

Happily, we are not dependent on argument to prove that Fiction is a department of literature in which women can, after their kind, fully equal men. A cluster of great names, both living and dead, rush to our memories in evidence that women can produce novels not only fine, but among the very finest—novels, too, that have a precious speciality, lying quite apart from masculine aptitudes and experience. No educational restrictions can shut women out from the materials of fiction, and there is no species of art which is so free from rigid requirements. Like crystalline masses, it may take any form, and yet be beautiful; we have only to pour in the right elements—genuine observation, humour, and passion. But it is precisely this absence of rigid requirement which constitutes the fatal seduction of novel writing to incompetent women. Ladies are not wont to be very grossly deceived as to their power of playing on the piano; here certain positive difficulties of execution have to be conquered, and incompetence inevitably breaks down. Every art which has its absolute *technique* is, to a certain extent, guarded from the intrusions of mere left-handed[1] imbecility. But in novel writing there are no barriers for incapacity to stumble against, no external criteria to prevent a writer from mistaking foolish facility for mastery. And so we have again and again the old story of La Fontaine's ass,[2] who puts his nose to the flute, and, finding that he elicits some sound, exclaims, "Moi, aussi, je joue de la flute"[3]—a fable which we commend, at parting, to the consideration of any feminine reader who is in danger of adding to the number of "silly novels by lady novelists."
—1856

---

[1] *left-handed* Inept.

[2] *La Fontaine's ass* French poet Jean de la Fontaine (1621–95) wrote many fables, but "The Ass and the Flute" was written by Tomás de Iriarte (1750–91).

[3] *Moi, aussi … flute* French: I too play the flute.

from *The Natural History of German Life*

It is an interesting branch of psychological observation to note the images that are habitually associated with abstract or collective terms—what may be called the picture-writing of the mind, which it carries on concurrently with the more subtle symbolism of language. Perhaps the fixity or variety of these associated images would furnish a tolerably fair test of the amount of concrete knowledge and experience which a given word represents, in the minds of two persons who use it with equal familiarity. The word *railways*, for example, will probably call up, in the mind of a man who is not highly locomotive, the image either of a "Bradshaw,"[4] or of the station with which he is most familiar, or of an indefinite length of tram-road; he will alternate between these three images, which represent his stock of concrete acquaintance with railways. But suppose a man to have had successively the experience of a "navvy,"[5] an engineer, a traveller, a railway director and shareholder, and a landed proprietor in treaty with a railway company, and it is probable that the range of images which would by turns present themselves to his mind at the mention of the *word* "railways," would include all the essential facts in the existence and relations of the *thing*. Now it is possible for the first-mentioned personage to entertain very expanded views as to the multiplication of railways in the abstract, and their ultimate function in civilization. He may talk of a vast network of railways stretching over the globe, of future "lines" in Madagascar, and elegant refreshment rooms in the Sandwich Islands, with none the less glibness because his distinct conceptions on the subject do not extend beyond his one station and his indefinite length of tram-road. But it is evident that if we want a railway to be made, or its affairs to be managed, this man of wide views and narrow observation will not serve our purpose.

Probably, if we could ascertain the images called up by the terms "the people," "the masses," "the proletar-

---

[4] *Bradshaw* British train schedule.

[5] *navvy* Worker at an unskilled job; laborer.

iat," "the peasantry," by many who theorize on those bodies with eloquence, or who legislate for them without eloquence, we should find that they indicate almost as small an amount of concrete knowledge—that they are as far from completely representing the complex facts summed up in the collective term, as the railway images of our non-locomotive gentleman. How little the real characteristics of the working classes are known to those who are outside them, how little their natural history has been studied, is sufficiently disclosed by our art as well as by our political and social theories. Where, in our picture exhibitions, shall we find a group of true peasantry? What English artist even attempts to rival in truthfulness such studies of popular life as the pictures of Teniers or the ragged boys of Murillo?[1] Even one of the greatest painters of the pre-eminently realistic school,[2] while, in his picture of *The Hireling Shepherd*, he gave us a landscape of marvellous truthfulness, placed a pair of peasants in the foreground who were not much more real than the idyllic swains and damsels of our chimney ornaments. Only a total absence of acquaintance and sympathy with our peasantry, could give a moment's popularity to such a picture as *Cross Purposes*, where we have a peasant girl who looks as if she knew L.E.L.'s[3] poems by heart, and English rustics, whose costume seems to indicate that they are meant for ploughmen, with exotic features that remind us of a handsome *primo tenore*.[4] Rather than such cockney sentimentality as this, as an education for the taste and sympathies, we prefer the most crapulous[5] group of boors that Teniers ever painted. But even those among our painters who aim at giving the rustic type of features, who are far above the effeminate feebleness of the "Keepsake" style,[6] treat their subjects under the influ-

ence of traditions and prepossessions rather than of direct observation. The notion that peasants are joyous, that the typical moment to represent a man in a smock-frock is when he is cracking a joke and showing a row of sound teeth, that cottage matrons are usually buxom, and village children necessarily rosy and merry, are prejudices difficult to dislodge from the artistic mind, which looks for its subjects into literature instead of life. The painter is still under the influence of idyllic literature, which has always expressed the imagination of the cultivated and town-bred, rather than the truth of rustic life. Idyllic ploughmen are jocund when they drive their team afield; idyllic shepherds make bashful love under hawthorn bushes; idyllic villagers dance in the chequered shade and refresh themselves, not immoderately, with spicy nut-brown ale. But no one who has seen much of actual ploughmen thinks them jocund; no one who is well acquainted with the English peasantry can pronounce them merry. The slow gaze, in which no sense of beauty beams, no humour twinkles—the slow utterance, and the heavy slouching walk, remind one rather of that melancholy animal the camel, than of the sturdy countryman, with striped stockings, red waistcoat, and hat aside, who represents the traditional English peasant. Observe a company of haymakers. When you see them at a distance, tossing up the forkfuls of hay in the golden light, while the wagon creeps slowly with its increasing burthen over the meadow, and the bright green space which tells of work done gets larger and larger, you pronounce the scene "smiling," and you think these companions in labour must be as bright and cheerful as the picture to which they give animation. Approach nearer, and you will certainly find that haymaking time is a time for joking, especially if there are women among the labourers; but the coarse laugh that bursts out every now and then, and expresses the triumphant taunt, is as far as possible from your conception of idyllic merriment. That delicious effervescence of the mind which we call fun, has no equivalent for the northern peasant, except tipsy revelry; the only realm of fancy and imagination for the English clown exists at

---

[1]   *Teniers*   Flemish painter David Teniers the Elder (1582–1649);
Murillo   Spanish painter Bartolomé Estéban Murillo (1617–82).

[2]   *one of the greatest ... school*   William Holman Hunt (1827–1910).

[3]   *L.E.L.*   Letitia Elizabeth Landon (1802–38).

[4]   *primo tenore*   Operatic first tenor.

[5]   *crapulous*   Excessive drinking and eating.

[6]   *"Keepsake" style*   I.e., in the style of the popular gift books which were given as "keepsakes" in the period.

the bottom of the third quart pot.[1]

The conventional countryman of the stage, who picks up pocketbooks and never looks into them, and who is too simple even to know that honesty has its opposite, represents the still lingering mistake, that an unintelligible dialect is a guarantee for ingenuousness, and that slouching shoulders indicate an upright disposition. It is quite true that a thresher is likely to be innocent of any adroit arithmetical cheating, but he is not the less likely to carry home his master's corn in his shoes and pocket; a reaper is not given to writing begging letters, but he is quite capable of cajoling the dairymaid into filling his small beer bottle with ale. The selfish instincts are not subdued by the sight of buttercups, nor is integrity in the least established by that classic rural occupation, sheep washing. To make men moral, something more is requisite than to turn them out to grass.

Opera peasants, whose unreality excites Mr. Ruskin's[2] indignation, are surely too frank an idealization to be misleading; and since popular chorus is one of the most effective elements of the opera, we can hardly object to lyric rustics in elegant laced bodices and picturesque motley, unless we are prepared to advocate a chorus of colliers[3] in their pit costume, or a ballet of charwomen[4] and stocking weavers. But our social novels profess to represent the people as they are, and the unreality of their representations is a grave evil. The greatest benefit we owe to the artist, whether painter, poet, or novelist, is the extension of our sympathies. Appeals founded on generalizations and statistics require a sympathy ready made, a moral sentiment already in activity; but a picture of human life such as a great artist can give, surprises even the trivial and the selfish into that attention to what is apart from themselves, which may be called the raw material of moral sentiment. When Scott takes us into Luckie Mucklebackit's cottage,[5] or tells the story of "The Two Drovers"—when Wordsworth sings to us the reverie of "Poor Susan"[6] —when Kingsley shows us Alton Locke gazing yearningly over the gate which leads from the highway into the first wood he ever saw[7]—when Hornung[8] paints a group of chimney sweepers—more is done towards linking the higher classes with the lower, towards obliterating the vulgarity of exclusiveness, than by hundreds of sermons and philosophical dissertations. Art is the nearest thing to life; it is a mode of amplifying experience and extending our contact with our fellow men beyond the bounds of our personal lot. All the more sacred is the task of the artist when he undertakes to paint the life of the people. Falsification here is far more pernicious than in the more artificial aspects of life. It is not so very serious that we should have false ideas about evanescent fashions—about the manners and conversation of beaux and duchesses; but it *is* serious that our sympathy with the perennial joys and struggles, the toil, the tragedy, and the humour in the life of our more heavily laden fellow men, should be perverted, and turned towards a false object instead of the true one.

This perversion is not the less fatal because the misrepresentation which gives rise to it has what the artist considers a moral end. The thing for mankind to know is, not what are the motives and influences which the moralist thinks *ought* to act on the labourer or the artisan, but what are the motives and influences which *do* act on him. We want to be taught to feel, not for the heroic artisan or the sentimental peasant, but for the peasant in all his coarse apathy, and the artisan in all his suspicious selfishness.

---

[1] *quart pot* I.e., of beer.

[2] *Mr. Ruskin* Literary, art, and social critic John Ruskin (1819–1900); see Ruskin's *Modern Painters*, 3.5.

[3] *colliers* Coal miners.

[4] *charwomen* Cleaning women, usually day laborers.

[5] *Luckie Mucklebackit's cottage* In Sir Walter Scott's *The Antiquary* (1816).

[6] *Poor Susan* "The Reverie of Poor Susan" by William Wordsworth (1798).

[7] *Kingsley … saw* In Charles Kingsley's novel *Alton Locke, Tailor and Poet: An Autobiography* (1850).

[8] *Hornung* Swiss painter Joseph Hornung (1792–1870).

We have one great novelist[1] who is gifted with the utmost power of rendering the external traits of our town population; and if he could give us their psychological character—their conceptions of life, and their emotions—with the same truth as their idiom and manners, his books would be the greatest contribution art has ever made to the awakening of social sympathies. But while he can copy Mrs. Plornish's[2] colloquial style with the delicate accuracy of a sun picture, while there is the same startling inspiration in his description of the gestures and phrases of "Boots,"[3] as in the speeches of Shakespeare's mobs or numbskulls, he scarcely ever passes from the humorous and external to the emotional and tragic, without becoming as transcendent in his unreality as he was a moment before in his artistic truthfulness. But for the precious salt of his humour, which compels him to reproduce external traits that serve, in some degree, as a corrective to his frequently false psychology, his preternaturally virtuous poor children and artisans, his melodramatic boatmen and courtesans, would be as noxious as Eugène Sue's[4] idealized proletaires in encouraging the miserable fallacy that high morality and refined sentiment can grow out of harsh social relations, ignorance, and want; or that the working classes are in a condition to enter at once into a millennial state of *altruism*, wherein everyone is caring for everyone else, and no one for himself.

If we need a true conception of the popular character to guide our sympathies rightly, we need it equally to check our theories, and direct us in their application. The tendency created by the splendid conquests of modern generalization, to believe that all social questions are merged in economical science, and that the relations of men to their neighbours may be settled by algebraic equations—the dream that the uncultured classes are prepared for a condition which appeals principally to their moral sensibilities—the aristocratic

dilettantism which attempts to restore the "good old times" by a sort of idyllic masquerading, and to grow feudal fidelity and veneration as we grow prize turnips, by an artificial system of culture—none of these diverging mistakes can co-exist with a real knowledge of the people, with a thorough study of their habits, their ideas, their motives. The landholder, the clergyman, the mill owner, the mining agent, have each an opportunity for making precious observations on different sections of the working classes, but unfortunately their experience is too often not registered at all, or its results are too scattered to be available as a source of information and stimulus to the public mind generally. If any man of sufficient moral and intellectual breadth, whose observations would not be vitiated by a foregone conclusion, or by a professional point of view, would devote himself to studying the natural history of our social classes, especially of the small shopkeepers, artisans, and peasantry—the degree in which they are influenced by local conditions, their maxims and habits, the points of view from which they regard their religious teachers, and the degree in which they are influenced by religious doctrines, the interaction of the various classes on each other, and what are the tendencies in their position towards disintegration or towards development—and if, after all this study, he would give us the result of his observations in a book well nourished with specific facts, his work would be a valuable aid to the social and political reformer. ...

—1856

Margaret Fuller and Mary Wollstonecraft[5]

The dearth of new books just now gives us time to recur to less recent ones which we have hitherto noticed but slightly, and among these we choose the late

---

[1] *one great novelist* English novelist Charles Dickens (1812–70).

[2] *Mrs. Plornish* Character in *Little Dorrit* (1855–57).

[3] *Boots* Character in Dickens's *The Holly-Tree* (1855).

[4] *Eugène Sue* French author Joseph Marie Eugène Sue (1804–57).

[5] *Margaret Fuller* American feminist and essayist (1810–50), co-editor of *The Dial*, an art and literary journal, and author of *Woman in the Nineteenth Century* (1855); *Mary Wollstonecraft* British feminist and author (1759–97), whose work includes *A Vindication of the Rights of Woman* (1792).

edition of Margaret Fuller's *Woman in the Nineteenth Century*, because we think it has been unduly thrust into the background by less comprehensive and candid productions on the same subject. Notwithstanding certain defects of taste and a sort of vague spiritualism and grandiloquence which belong to all but the very best American writers, the book is a valuable one; it has the enthusiasm of a noble and sympathetic nature, with the moderation and breadth and large allowance of a vigorous and cultivated understanding. There is no exaggeration of woman's moral excellence or intellectual capabilities; no injudicious insistence on her fitness for this or that function hitherto engrossed by men; but a calm plea for the removal of unjust laws and artificial restrictions, so that the possibilities of her nature may have room for full development, a wisely stated demand to disencumber her of the

> Parasitic forms
> That seem to keep her up, but drag her down—
> And leave her field to burgeon and to bloom
> From all within her, make herself her own
> To give or keep, to live and learn and be
> All that not harms distinctive womanhood.[1]

It is interesting to compare this essay of Margaret Fuller's published in its earliest form in 1843, with a work on the position of woman, written between sixty and seventy years ago—we mean Mary Wollstonecraft's *Rights of Woman*. The latter work was not continued beyond the first volume, but so far as this carries the subject, the comparison, at least in relation to strong sense and loftiness of moral tone, is not at all disadvantageous to the woman of the last century. There is in some quarters a vague prejudice against the *Rights of Woman* as in some way or other a reprehensible book, but readers who go to it with this impression will be surprised to find it eminently serious, severely moral, and withal rather heavy—the true reason, perhaps, that no edition has been published since 1796, and that it is

now rather scarce. There are several points of resemblance, as well as of striking difference, between the two books. A strong understanding is present in both, but Margaret Fuller's mind was like some regions of her own American continent, where you are constantly stepping from the sunny "clearings" into the mysterious twilight of the tangled forest—she often passes in one breath from forcible reasoning to dreamy vagueness; moreover, her unusually varied culture gives her great command of illustration. Mary Wollstonecraft, on the other hand, is nothing if not rational; she has no erudition, and her grave pages are lit up by no ray of fancy. In both writers we discern, under the brave bearing of a strong and truthful nature, the beating of a loving woman's heart, which teaches them not to undervalue the smallest offices of domestic care or kindliness. But Margaret Fuller, with all her passionate sensibility, is more of the literary woman, who would not have been satisfied without intellectual production; Mary Wollstonecraft, we imagine, wrote not at all for writing's sake, but from the pressure of other motives. So far as the difference of date allows, there is a striking coincidence in their trains of thought; indeed, every important idea in the *Rights of Woman*, except the combination of home education with a common day-school for boys and girls, reappears in Margaret Fuller's essay.

One point on which they both write forcibly is the fact that, while men have a horror of such faculty or culture in the other sex as tends to place it on a level with their own, they are really in a state of subjection to ignorant and feeble-minded women. Margaret Fuller says:

> Wherever man is sufficiently raised above extreme poverty or brutal stupidity, to care for the comforts of the fireside, or the bloom and ornament of life, woman has always power enough, if she choose to exert it, and is usually disposed to do so, in proportion to her ignorance and childish vanity. Unacquainted with the importance of life and its purposes, trained to a selfish coquetry and love of petty power, she does not look beyond the pleasure of making herself felt at the moment, and governments are shaken and commerce broken up to gratify the

---

[1] *Parasitic forms … womanhood* From Alfred, Lord Tennyson's *The Princess* (1850) 7.253–58.

MARGARET FULLER AND MARY WOLLSTONECRAFT

pique of a female favourite. The English shop-keeper's wife does not vote, but it is for her interest that the politician canvasses by the coarsest flattery.

Again:

All wives, bad or good, loved or unloved, inevitably influence their husbands from the power their position not merely gives, but necessitates of colour-ing evidence and infusing feelings in hours when the—patient, shall I call him?—is off his guard.

Hear now what Mary Wollstonecraft says on the same subject:

Women have been allowed to remain in ignorance and slavish dependence many, very many years, and still we hear of nothing but their fondness of plea-sure and sway, their preference of rakes and soldiers, their childish attachment to toys, and the vanity that makes them value accomplishments more than virtues. History brings forward a fearful catalogue of the crimes which their cunning has produced, when the weak slaves have had sufficient address to over-reach their masters. ... When, therefore, I call women slaves, I mean in a political and civil sense; for indirectly they obtain too much power, and are debased by their exertions to obtain illicit sway. ... The libertinism, and even the virtues of superior men, will always give women of some description great power over them; and these weak women, under the influence of childish passions and selfish vanity, *will throw a false light over the objects which the very men view with their eyes who ought to en-lighten their judgment.* Men of fancy, and those sanguine characters who mostly hold the helm of human affairs in general, relax in the society of women; and surely I need not cite to the most superficial reader of history the numerous examples of vice and oppression which the private intrigues of female favourites have produced; not to dwell on the mischief that naturally arises from the blundering interposition of well-meaning folly. *For in the transactions of business it is much better to have to deal with a knave than a fool, because a knave adheres to some plan, and any plan of reason may be seen through*

sooner than a sudden flight of folly. The power which vile and foolish women have had over wise men who possessed sensibility is notorious.

There is a notion commonly entertained among men that an instructed woman, capable of having opinions, is likely to prove an impracticable yoke-fellow, always pulling one way when her husband wants to go the other, oracular in tone, and prone to give curtain lectures on metaphysics. But surely, so far as obstinacy is concerned, your unreasoning animal is the most unmanageable of creatures, where you are not allowed to settle the question by a cudgel, a whip and bridle, or even a string to the leg. For our own parts, we see no consistent or commodious medium between the old plan of corporal discipline and that thorough education of women which will make them rational beings in the highest sense of the word. Wherever weakness is not harshly controlled it must *govern,* as you may see when a strong man holds a little child by the hand, how he is pulled hither and thither, and wearied in his walk by his submission to the whims and feeble movements of his companion. A really cultured woman, like a really cultured man, will be ready to yield in trifles. So far as we see, there is no indissoluble connection between infirmity of logic and infirmity of will, and a woman quite innocent of an opinion in philosophy, is as likely as not to have an indomitable opinion about the kitchen. As to airs of superiority, no woman ever had them in consequence of true culture, but only because her culture was shallow or unreal, only as a result of what Mrs. Malaprop well calls "the ineffectual qualities in a woman"[1]—mere acquisitions carried about, and not knowledge thoroughly assimilated so as to enter into the growth of the character.

To return to Margaret Fuller, some of the best things she says are on the folly of absolute definitions of woman's nature and absolute demarcations of woman's

---

[1] *Mrs. Malaprop* Character in Richard Sheridan's play *The Rivals* (1775), after whom the term "malapropism" was coined, for her humorous misuse of words; *"the ineffectual ... woman"* From *The Rivals* 3.3.12–13.

mission. "Nature," she says, seems to delight in varying the arrangements, as if to show that she will be fettered by no rule; and we must admit the same varieties that she admits." Again: "If nature is never bound down, nor the voice of inspiration stifled, that is enough. We are pleased that women should write and speak, if they feel need of it, from having something to tell; but silence for ages would be no misfortune, if that silence be from divine command, and not from man's tradition." And here is a passage, the beginning of which has been often quoted:

> If you ask me what offices they [women] may fill, I reply—any. I do not care what case you put; let them be sea captains if you will. I do not doubt there are women well fitted for such an office, and, if so, I should be as glad as to welcome the Maid of Saragossa, or the Maid of Missolonghi, or the Suliote heroine, or Emily Plater.[1] I think women need, especially at this juncture, a much greater range of occupation than they have, to rouse their latent powers. ... In families that I know, some little girls like to saw wood, others to use carpenters' tools. Where these tastes are indulged, cheerfulness and good-humour are promoted. Where they are forbidden, because "such things are not proper for girls," they grow sullen and mischievous. Fourier[2] had observed these wants of women, as no one can fail to do who watches the desires of little girls, or knows the *ennui* that haunts grown women, except where they make to themselves a serene little world by art of some kind. He, therefore, in proposing a great variety of employments, in manufactures or the care of plants and animals, allows for one-third of women as likely to have a taste for masculine pursuits, one-third of men for feminine. ... I have no doubt, however, that a large proportion of women would give themselves to the same employments as now, because there are circumstances that must lead them. Mothers will delight to make the nest soft and warm. Nature would take care of that;

no need to clip the wings of any bird that wants to soar and sing, or finds in itself the strength of pinion[3] for a migratory flight unusual to its kind. The difference would be that *all* need not be constrained to employments for which *some* are unfit.

A propos of the same subject, we find Mary Wollstonecraft offering a suggestion which the women of the United States have already begun to carry out. She says:

> Women, in particular, all want to be ladies, Which is simply to have nothing to do, but listlessly to go they scarcely care where, for they cannot tell what. But what have women to do in society? I may be asked, but to loiter with easy grace; surely you would not condemn them all to suckle fools and chronicle small beer.[4] No. *Women might certainly study the art of healing, and be physicians as well as nurses.* ... Business of various kinds they might likewise pursue, if they were educated in a more orderly manner. ... Women would not then marry for a support, as men accept of places under government, and neglect the implied duties.

Men pay a heavy price for their reluctance to encourage self-help and independent resources in women. The precious meridian years of many a man of genius have to be spent in the toil of routine, that an "establishment" may be kept up for a woman who can understand none of his secret yearnings, who is fit for nothing but to sit in her drawing-room like a doll-Madonna in her shrine. No matter. Anything is more endurable than to change our established formulæ about women, or to run the risk of looking up to our wives instead of looking down on them. *Sit divus, dummodo non sit vivus* (let him be a god, provided he be not living), said the Roman magnates of Romulus;[5] and so men say of women, let them be idols, useless absorbents of precious

---

[1] *Maid of Saragossa ... Emily Plater* Heroines who distinguished themselves in battle.

[2] *Fourier* Charles Fourier (1772–1837), French social philosopher.

[3] *pinion* Wing.

[4] *suckle fools ... small beer* Shakespeare, *Othello* 2.1.159.

[5] *Romulus* Founder of Rome, who according to legend eventually became a god.

things, provided we are not obliged to admit them to be strictly fellow-beings, to be treated, one and all, with justice and sober reverence.

On one side we hear that woman's position can never be improved until women themselves are better; and, on the other, that women can never become better until their position is improved—until the laws are made more just, and a wider field opened to feminine activity. But we constantly hear the same difficulty stated about the human race in general. There is a perpetual action and reaction between individuals and institutions; we must try and mend both by little and little—the only way in which human things can be mended. Unfortunately, many over-zealous champions of women assert their actual equality with men—nay, even their moral superiority to men—as a ground for their release from oppressive laws and restrictions. They lose strength immensely by this false position. If it were true, then there would be a case in which slavery and ignorance nourished virtue, and so far we should have an argument for the continuance of bondage. But we want freedom and culture for woman, because subjection and ignorance have debased her, and with her, Man; for—

> If she be small, slight-natured, miserable,
> How shall men grow?[1]

Both Margaret Fuller and Mary Wollstonecraft have too much sagacity to fall into this sentimental exaggeration. Their ardent hopes of what women may become do not prevent them from seeing and painting women as they are. On the relative moral excellence of men and women Mary Wollstonecraft speaks with the most decision:

Women are supposed to possess more sensibility, and even humanity, than men, and their strong attachments and instantaneous emotions of compassion are given as proofs; but the clinging affection of ignorance has seldom anything noble in it, and may mostly be resolved into selfishness, as well as the affection of children and brutes. I have known many weak women whose sensibility was entirely engrossed by their husbands; and as for their humanity, it was very faint indeed, or rather it was only a transient emotion of compassion. Humanity does not consist "in a squeamish ear," says an eminent orator.[2] "It belongs to the mind as well as to the nerves." But this kind of exclusive affection, though it degrades the individual, should not be brought forward as a proof of the inferiority of the sex, because it is the natural consequence of confined views; for even women of superior sense, having their attention turned to little employments and private plans, rarely rise to heroism, unless when spurred on by love! and love, as an heroic passion, like genius, appears but once in an age. I therefore agree with the moralist who asserts "that women have seldom so much generosity as men"; and that their narrow affections, to which justice and humanity are often sacrificed, render the sex apparently inferior, especially as they are commonly inspired by men; but I contend that the heart would expand as the understanding gained strength, if women were not depressed from their cradles.

We had marked several other passages of Margaret Fuller's for extract, but as we do not aim at an exhaustive treatment of our subject, and are only touching a few of its points, we have, perhaps, already claimed as much of the reader's attention as he will be willing to give to such desultory material.

—1855

---

[1] *If she ... grow?* From Tennyson's *The Princess* 7.249–50.

[2] *eminent orator* Charles James Fox (1749–1806), British politician.

SEXUALITY AND SEXUAL TRANSGRESSION

CONTEXTS

When it comes to sexual morality, the Victorian age has long been associated with prudishness. It is true that the century's repressive laws led to the imprisonment of such men as Oscar Wilde; that anxiety surrounded sexuality and especially masturbation as a perceived threat to mental and physical health; and that many forms of sexual expression could carry extreme social consequences, especially for women. It is also true, however, that Victorian attitudes toward and experiences of sexuality were far more varied than these facts suggest. The era also saw, for example, the growth of gay and lesbian subcultures, especially in literary and artistic communities; the development of a scientific discourse that addressed human sexuality and sexual variation head-on; and a movement led by women to challenge the unfair burdens placed on their gender by the sexual double standard. Toward the end of the century, the relaxation of sexual mores and the expansion of conversation surrounding sexuality had progressed to an extent that one conservative editorial, printed in 1895, demanded, "What does all this perpetual discussion of sex mean? Wherefore this constant analysis of the passions? How does it come that the people today are filled with nothing but sex, sex, sex?"

The stereotype of Victorian repression was to a certain extent accurate with regard to the law surrounding sexuality between men. At the beginning of the century, execution was the sentence for "buggery," a category that encompassed sodomy (anal sex) and bestiality, treating them as equivalent evils. The last execution for same-sex relations was in 1836; for the next several decades men continued to be sentenced to death as indicated by law, but in actuality the sentences were commuted to anything ranging from a year's imprisonment to a life sentence of penal servitude. The death penalty for sodomy was, finally, officially removed in 1861, when it was replaced with the sentence of penal servitude for a minimum of ten years. Throughout the century's middle decades, the extent of punishment endured by men arrested for sodomy varied dramatically from case to case, often according to the class status of the individual; while wealthy men saw their reputations ruined and were sometimes forced to leave Britain, it was generally the less wealthy who received long, grueling prison sentences.

The legal landscape changed, however, in 1885 with a brief addition to the Criminal Law Amendment Act known as the "Labouchère Amendment," named for its virulently homophobic champion Henry Labouchère. While on the surface the Labouchère Amendment softened the law—the maximum sentence was reduced to two years' hard labor—in both intention and reality its effect was to crack down on sexuality between men. The shorter sentences made juries less hesitant to convict on the type of evidence usually available in sodomy cases. More importantly, the law made convictions much easier to obtain by replacing "sodomy" or "buggery" with the crime of "gross indecency," a term that was never defined but came in practice to refer to *any* type of sex act between men. The amendment became known as "The Blackmailer's Charter," since this dramatic decrease in the burden of proof made all men who took part in any form of same-sex sexuality tremendously vulnerable to the courts. The trial of Oscar Wilde—sentenced to two years' hard labor—was undoubtedly one of the most sensational outcomes of Labouchère's law, but hundreds of men would be imprisoned under the amendment before the end of the century, and thousands more before its repeal in 1967.

Despite the potential legal and social consequences, desire between men flourished in various subcultural enclaves. Many boys wealthy enough to attend boys' schools such as Harrow and Eton had same-sex experiences there; for those of the middle- and upper-classes who continued to act on same-sex desire in their adulthood, London offered brothels, private gatherings, and the streets of certain neighborhoods, where paid liaisons could be obtained with working-class men and boys. A culture of drag (a word first recorded in the mid-nineteenth century) offered modes of gender as well as sexual expression beyond the mainstream norms.[1] Romantic and sexual relations brought together men whose backgrounds would otherwise have precluded social connection: as the poet and critic John Addington Symonds mused regarding his romance with a Venetian gondolier, "Had it not been for my abnormal desire, I could never have learned to know and appreciate a human being so far removed from me in position, education, national quality and physique." But these relationships were infused with power imbalance; upper-class men tended to objectify those of the working classes, whom they perceived as rugged and authentic, and to seek a stereotypically sensual, often racialized exoticism in the men and boys they encountered outside the British Isles. From the teenage student to the telegraph boy or the Sicilian youth, the ideal object of desire was, for many wealthier men, much younger as well as socially subordinate.

This was especially the case for a loosely connected circle of intellectuals known as the "Uranian poets," who found inspiration in ancient Greek culture's embrace of male-male sexuality, especially between older men and youths. Symonds describes his first encounter with descriptions of same-sex love in Plato as follows:

> I had obtained the sanction of the love which had been ruling me from childhood. Here was the poetry, the philosophy of my own enthusiasm for male beauty, expressed with all the magic of unrivalled style. And, what was more, I now became aware that the Greek race—the actual historical Greeks of antiquity—treated this love seriously, invested it with moral charm, endowed it with sublimity.

For some associated with the Uranian movement, such as Symonds in *A Problem in Greek Ethics* (1883) and Edward Carpenter in *Homogenic Love and Its Place in a Free Society* (1894), Greek philosophy formed a starting place for the explicit discussion of sexual morality between men. For other Uranians, allusions to Greek culture could be used to express same-sex desire covertly; a poem such as William Cory's "Heraclitus" (1858), for example, was widely popular as an evocation of passionate friendship between men—but its Greek background conveyed obvious homoeroticism for readers prepared to acknowledge it. In general, Victorians accepted writing in which men expressed deep affection for other men so long as it was possible to interpret them as friends rather than lovers. Tennyson's extravagant and poignant expressions of love for his friend Arthur Henry Hallam in *In Memoriam A.H.H.*, for example, made it one of the most popular poems of the century—and one that continues to be interpreted as homoerotic by some readers but not others.

---

[1] The complex relationship between sexuality and gender during this period makes it sometimes difficult to distinguish people who cross-dressed and had same-sex relationships from people who, in anachronistic terms, might be considered transgender. Certainly, the use of women's names and clothes was common in what were ostensibly communities of men who loved men; the use of men's names and clothes was similarly common among people in ostensibly lesbian relationships.

While Victorian culture allowed some space for love between men so long as it took the form of friendship (or could be disguised as such), it allowed even more space for such love between women. Many Victorians felt that sexuality between women was an impossibility—at least among civilized Englishwomen—and intensely passionate, physically affectionate friendships between women were not just tolerated but actively condoned. This expansive view of friendship provided effective cover for some women to pursue sexual and romantic relationships, including unofficial marriages, while raising minimal suspicion; it can also make it difficult to determine from surviving writings whether or not the individuals involved in a given passionate connection perceived it as a sexual one. Overt sexuality between women could, if discovered, have disastrous material and social consequences—as demonstrated by the case excerpted below of Marianne Woods and Jane Pirie, teachers forced out of work by rumors that they had a sexual relationship—but it was not criminalized. Apocryphally, a law against it was considered and then rejected, because Queen Victoria refused to believe such a thing existed.

Much as sexual attraction between women may not have been acknowledged as a possibility in respectable mid-Victorian society, "Sapphism" (or "tribadism") was certainly a presence in many pornographic publications of the Victorian era. Most such works were entirely the products of the authors' fantasies, but with notable exceptions; many scholars have concluded that the anonymous (but almost certainly male-authored) erotic book *My Secret Life* (1888), for example, is unusual in that it is likely as much memoir as it is fantasy. Mentions of "tribadism" in works such as *My Secret Life* and same-sex encounters recorded in the diary of Anne Lister (1791–1840) suggest that women who loved other women were at least sometimes able to find and connect with each other; Lister, a wealthy entrepreneur, recorded in often explicit terms her sexual relationships with a number of women. There is, however, little evidence to suggest that, without leaving the British Isles, women had access to anything resembling the public spaces of the sort where men sought other men during the era.

Toward the end of the century, lesbian existence began to become more visible, and an intellectual community of lesbian women writers took shape. The New Woman movement, with its challenge to the male-dominated norms of conventional marriage,[1] and the Aesthetic movement, with its avant-garde repudiation of gender and sexual norms, encompassed women of all sexualities and encouraged greater freedom of sexual expression in art. Many significant writers with passionate feelings for women (and, in some cases, for men as well), such as Charlotte Mew, Vernon Lee, Amy Levy, Mathilde Blind, and Michael Field (a pseudonym shared by Katharine Harris Bradley and Edith Emma Cooper), had at least social connections with one or both of these movements.

It was also in the 1880s and 1890s that doctors and scientists began to devote attention to the study of sexualities deemed deviant—including those involving attraction to people ostensibly of the same sex. A distinction between sexual orientation and gender identity had not yet been drawn, and some theorists proposed multiple categories of gender as well as of sexual attraction; some argued, further, that genital and other physical differences marked those whose desires they considered pathological. Arguably the most influential of these early sexual studies was Richard von Krafft-Ebing's *Psychopathia Sexualis* (first published in Germany in 1886). Krafft-Ebing's work—which appeared in English translation in 1892 despite concerns that, as the translator wrote, "a pornographic interest on the part of the public" might motivate its wide readership—coined or popularized a number of terms now commonplace in English, including "homosexuality," "heterosexuality," "sadism," and "masochism." A few years later saw the publication of the first volume of pioneering

---

[1] See "Contexts: The New Woman," elsewhere in this volume, for further discussion of sexuality and New Women.

English scholar Havelock Ellis's *The Psychology of Sex* (1897–1928). Ellis would eventually publish seven volumes of his study; the first, titled *Sexual Inversion*, was a collaboration with John Addington Symonds and addressed what we would now term gay, lesbian, and bisexual sexuality. While such studies tended to cast same-sex sexuality as a medical abnormality, many of the people they described saw them as liberating in their suggestion that sexual orientation might be a congenital attribute rather than simply an immoral personal choice.

In relationships between women and men, medical, legal, and social pressures converged to place the social and physical burdens associated with sexuality on women. Safe, effective methods of abortion and contraception (apart from abstinence) were unavailable, and childbirth and pregnancy posed a significant risk to the health of a mother—as well as, for unmarried women, an immense social and financial cost that drove some mothers to commit infanticide or give up their newborns. While only some Victorians believed that, as the doctor William Acton infamously claimed at mid-century, "a modest woman seldom desires any sexual gratification for herself," a sexual double standard allowed men a considerable degree of leniency in their sexual activity with women, while granting almost no such freedom to women themselves. An 1857 law, for example, permitted husbands to divorce their wives on the grounds of the woman's adultery alone—but decreed that for a wife to divorce her husband, she must prove him guilty not just of adultery but of adultery combined with another offence, such as incest, rape, or sodomy.

Victorian women were haunted by the specter of the "fallen woman" whose sexual transgression—a relationship out of wedlock, an adulterous affair, or an act of prostitution, regardless of its motivation— caused her to be cast out of her family and society, able to support herself only through a miserable and short life of prostitution from which there was no escape. Prostitution, known as "the great social evil," was seen variously as the last resort of victims of desperate poverty, as evidence of the moral degradation of the lower classes, and even as the inevitable consequence of individual women's failures to control their unnatural lust. The fallen woman archetype appeared often in literature, but the reality for prostitutes was not so clear-cut; while they were often mistreated as social outcasts and certainly faced the serious risks of disease, abuse, and unwanted pregnancy, many worked as prostitutes only occasionally, and others eventually married or transitioned to more "respectable" careers—or enjoyed relative security as madams or the "kept women" of upper-class men.[1] To many lower-class women, the relative freedom and financial security that prostitution offered represented the best of a narrow range of options—but however the lives of real prostitutes varied, public perception regarding prostitution tended overwhelmingly towards either pity or condemnation.

In the last half of the nineteenth century, the treatment of prostitutes became a subject of heated debate when campaigners drew public attention to the provisions of the Contagious Diseases Acts. The Acts, passed in 1864, 1867, and 1869, gave police and medical professionals greater legal power over suspected prostitutes, with the stated purpose of protecting the British military from venereal disease. According to the Acts, police could arrest any woman they believed to be a prostitute, subject her to a forced physical examination by a doctor, and require her to appear at regular intervals for further examinations. If she was found to have a venereal disease, the doctor could detain her in a designated "lock hospital" until the disease was cured. These measures were only applied to women;

---

[1] Augusta Webster's dramatic monologue "A Castaway" (included elsewhere in this volume) is written from the point of view of one who has "a home / All velvet" but sees herself as the kindred soul of "any drab" prostitute selling herself on the street. Thomas Hardy challenges sentimental, moralizing literary perspectives on prostitution in his poem "The Ruined Maid" (also included elsewhere in this volume), in which a young woman from the country is saved from a life of drudgery by a lucrative career as a city prostitute.

men who solicited prostitutes were subject to no such compulsory examination or treatment. The first Contagious Disease Act was limited to a few towns with military bases, but with each Act the area of application expanded, and supporters of the Acts tried to have them extended to the whole country.

The Acts were met with serious opposition, however, from many who saw them as an attack on civil liberties and as an appalling illustration of Victorian society's double standard regarding the sexes. People of all classes and both sexes were involved in the campaign against the Acts, but the strongest voices were those of the middle- and upper-class women who organized the resistance—the members of the Ladies' National Association for the Repeal of the Contagious Diseases Acts. Social purity values were a prominent element of this early feminist campaign: a key argument against the Contagious Diseases Acts was that they enshrined a sexual double standard in law, placing the burden of disease control on women who had turned to prostitution for their livelihoods while imposing no consequences on the men who exploited them. A better solution, many argued, was that men should stop seeking prostitutes for sex.

As women who defied convention by speaking in public on political matters—especially matters of sexual morality—the association's members often faced violence and verbal abuse, but they succeeded in their aim. As a result of pressure from the protest movement, the Contagious Diseases Acts were suspended in 1883 and repealed in 1886. The campaign had a lasting influence on the growth of feminist activism—as a successful political movement led and organized by women, it inspired thousands of women to enter the political sphere for the first time. While the social purity values underlying the movement were by no means embraced by feminists across the board, they would remain a current in feminist politics well into the twentieth century; one 1913 campaign, for example, would endorse "Votes for Women and Chastity for Men."

⌘ ⌘ ⌘

Sexuality and the Law

from *The Trying and Pillorying of the Vere-Street Club* (1810)

In 1810, the Bow Street Runners (London's first official police force) raided the White Swan on Vere Street and arrested about two dozen people. The White Swan was a molly house—a meeting place for men seeking paid or casual sex with other men—and six of those arrested were convicted of attempted sodomy. Their sentences ranged from one to three years in prison and, for all but one of those convicted, an hour spent in the pillory, a device in which people are restrained in a public place where anyone is free to abuse them. Two other patrons of the White Swan, not present on the night of the raid, were later convicted of sodomy and hanged. 1810 marked a peak in early nineteenth-century

hatred of sexuality between men, and the pillorying of the "Vere Street Coterie" was exceptionally brutal; it was, however, only one of many legal persecutions of men in same-sex relationships during the period.

The disgust felt by all ranks of Society at the detestable conduct of these wretches occasioned many thousands to become spectators of their punishment. At an early hour the Old Bailey was completely blockaded, and the increase of the mob about 1 o'clock, put a stop to the business of the Sessions.[1] The shops from Ludgate-Hill to the Haymarket[2] were shut up, and the

---

[1] *Old Bailey* London's central criminal court; *Sessions* I.e., court sessions.

[2] *Ludgate-Hill* Hill where the Old Bailey is located; *Haymarket* London street a little over two kilometers from Ludgate Hill.

streets lined with people, waiting to see the offenders pass. …

Shortly after twelve, the ammunition wagons from the neighbouring markets appeared in motion. These consisted of a number of carts which were driven by butchers' boys, who had previously taken care to fill them with the offal, dung &c. appertaining to their several slaughter-houses. A number of hucksters were also put in requisition,[1] who carried on their heads baskets of apples, potatoes, turnips, cabbage-stalks and other vegetables, together with the remains of diverse[2] dogs and cats. The whole of these were sold to the populace at a high price, who spared no expense to provide themselves with the necessary articles of assault.

A number of fishwomen attended with stinking flounders and the entrails of other fish which had been in preparation for several days. These articles, however, were not to be sold, as their proprietors, hearty in the cause, declared they wanted them "for their own use." …

Before they reached half way to the scene of their exposure, they were not discernible as human beings. If they had had much further to go, the cart would have been absolutely filled over them. The one who sat rather aloof from the rest, was the landlord of the house, a fellow of a stout bulky figure, who could not stow himself away as easily as the others, who were slighter; he was therefore, as well on account of his being known, attacked with double fury. Dead cats and dogs, offal, potatoes, turnips &c. rebounded from him on every side; while his apparently manly appearance drew down peculiar execrations on him, and nothing but the motion of the cart prevented his being killed on the spot. At one o'clock four of them were exalted on a new pillory, made purposely for their accommodation. The remaining two, Cooke and Amos, were honoured by being allowed to enjoy a triumph in the pillory alone. … Cook, (who had been the landlord) and Amos, alias Fox, were desired to mount. Cook held his hand to his head, and complained of the blows he had already received; and Amos made the same complaint, and shewed a large brick-bat,[3] which had struck him in the face. The Under Sheriff told them that the sentence must be executed, and they reluctantly mounted. Cook said nothing; but Amos seeing the preparations that were [being made], declared in the most solemn manner that he was innocent; but it was vociferated from all quarters that he had been convicted before, and in one minute they appeared a complete heap of mud, and their faces were much more battered than those of the former four. Cook received several hits in his face, and he had a lump raised upon his eyebrow as large as an egg. Amos's two eyes were completely closed up; and when they were untied, Cook appeared almost insensible, and it was necessary to help them both down and into the cart, when they were conveyed to Newgate[4] by the same road they had come, and in their passage they continued to receive the same salutations the spectators had given them in going out. Cook continued to lie upon the seat in the cart, but Amos lay down among the filth, till their entrance into Newgate sheltered the wretches from the further indignation of the most enraged populace we ever saw. As they passed the end of Catherine-street, Strand, on their return, a coachman stood upon his box, and gave Cook five or six cuts with his whip.

It is impossible for language to convey an adequate idea of the universal expressions of execration which accompanied these monsters on their journey; it was fortunate for them that the weather was dry, had it been otherwise they would have been smothered. From the moment the cart was in motion, the fury of the mob began to display itself in showers of mud and filth of every kind. Before the cart reached Temple-bar, the wretches were so thickly covered with filth, that a vestige of the human figure was scarcely discernible. They were chained, and placed in such a manner that they could not lie down in the cart, and could only hide and shelter their heads from the storm by stooping. This, however,

---

[1] *hucksters* Street vendors; *put in requisition* Called into service.

[2] *diverse* Various.

[3] *brick-bat* Piece of brick used as a projectile.

[4] *Newgate* Prison near the Old Bailey.

could afford but little protection. Some of them were cut in the head with the brickbats, and bled profusely. The streets, as they passed, resounded with the universal shouts and execrations of the populace.

from Lord Meadowbank's statements, *Miss Marianne Woods and Miss Jane Pirie against Dame Helen Cumming Gordon* (1811)

In 1810, Marianne Woods (1781–1870) and Jane Pirie (1779–1833), the operators of an Edinburgh boarding school, were accused of licentious behavior by one of their pupils, sixteen-year old Jane Cumming. As she would report in the trial that followed, Cumming, who slept in the same bed as one of the teachers, claimed to have been frequently awakened by hearing them "kissing and shaking the bed" as she lay on the other side. Cumming's grandmother, Dame Helen Cumming Gordon, shared these accusations with the families of other students, and soon all the students had withdrawn from the school. Their livelihoods destroyed, Woods and Pirie sued Dame Gordon for libel in 1811. The teachers lost the first trial (the panel of seven judges split 4–3); an 1812 review of the case again resulted in a 4–3 split, but this time the judgment was in favor of Woods and Pirie. It is unclear how much, if anything, Dame Gordon eventually paid in damages, or what became of Woods, Pirie, or Cumming after the scandal.

The judges voting in favor of Woods and Pirie gave a number of sometimes contradictory reasons for their decisions, including disbelief in the possibility that seemingly decent British women could be capable of such acts. The judgment was to a considerable degree racialized; it was considered by some to be more plausible that Cumming—a half-Indian young woman who had spent her early years in a hot climate—could invent a tale of unspeakable debauchery than that two respectable Scottish women could engage in the debauchery she described.

No cause was ever more extraordinary, or required a more grave and mature consideration. The pursuers[1] are two women of fair and irreproachable character, whose ruin has been accomplished by communications relative to their conduct, which, however confidentially conceived, could not fail to produce that effect. The defender is an honourable and very respectable Scottish Matron, who thought herself called upon, by the strongest moral duties, to save from contamination her own grandchildren, that she had placed at the pursuers' school; and to apprise the friends and relatives of others, that had been placed there, as she might suppose, in consequence of her recommendation or example[.] … There are also the young persons, or at least one young person, from whom the fatal imputation proceeded—one, unfortunately, wanting in the advantages of legitimacy,[2] and of a European complexion—and of consequence the more dependent on the favour of her connections and protectors. … And in my mind, there is a fourth party whose interest is deeply at stake, I mean the public; for the virtues, the comforts and the freedom of domestic intercourse,[3] mainly depend on the purity of female manners, and that, again, on their habits of intercourse remaining as they have hitherto been—free from suspicion. …

I must acknowledge that with respect to the nature of the crime charged, I labour under a very high degree of incredulity. … There is no sort of doubt that women of a peculiar conformation,[4] from an elongation of the clitoris, are capable both of giving and receiving venereal pleasure, in intercourse with women, by imitating the functions of a male in copulation; and that in some countries this conformation is so common that circumcision of the clitoris is practised as a religious rite. … Nor is it to be disputed that, by means of tools, women may artificially accomplish the venereal gratification. But, in this case, the use of tools is excluded by the defender's evidence, … [Jane Pirie] is represented as always performing the male functions, which surely

---

[1] *pursuers* Plaintiffs; i.e., Woods and Pirie.

[2] *legitimacy* I.e., married parents.

[3] *intercourse* Relationships (here, not necessarily sexual).

[4] *conformation* Configuration of physical parts.

could afford no gratification to herself if performed only by means of tools. ...

But if tools and tribadism[1] are out of the question, then I state as the ground of my incredulity ... the important fact that the imputed vice has been hitherto unknown in Britain. Neither the pruriency of corrupt imaginations has brought it forward in works of professed obscenity, nor has the wantonness of satire ever ventured to suggest it as a ground of obloquy.[2] ... Your Lordships, then, will judge as to the probabilities of two Scotch women, of admitted intelligence, educated, as it is established the pursuers were educated, and undertaking such a profession as they did undertake, discovering a venereal gratification which Lucian was not able to describe,[3] and rushing into a vice which, hitherto, even the most corrupt imaginations in this country had not so much as fancied; and what is perhaps equally extraordinary, that they should have dared to disclose to each other the secret of such depraved inclinations, and that, too, while it is still problematical, whether a venereal gratification can in this manner be accomplished or not. ...

... [N]othing short of the clearest and most decisive evidence can authorise a Judge to find the pursuers guilty of a crime, while, if I may so express myself, the *corpus delicti*[4] of a crime is still a question, and even if there were such a crime in possibility, while it has hitherto remained unknown, and even unthought of, in this part of the world.

---

[1] *tribadism* Usually a now-archaic term for "lesbianism," here used specifically to refer to the "peculiar conformation" Meadowbank describes above.

[2] *obloquy* Slander, insult.

[3] *Lucian was ... describe* In Assyrian satirist Lucian's *Dialogues of the Courtesans* (second century CE), one courtesan tries to convince another to describe how she has had sex with women; the experienced courtesan refuses to explain the mechanics involved.

[4] *corpus delicti* Latin: body of the crime. This legal term refers to the principle that, in order for a person to be convicted of a crime, it must first be proved that the crime was committed.

from Edward E. Deacon, *Digest of the Criminal Law of England* (1831)

Barrister Edward E. Deacon's *Digest of the Criminal Law of England* is an alphabetical reference work discussing how English law applies to various crimes, from abduction to treason. Notably, Deacon declares in his introduction to the book that capital punishment should be administered "as seldom as possible," but in the passage excerpted below, which addresses sodomy, he advocates venomously for the death penalty as an appropriate sentence.

1. Sodomy is that horrible sin against nature, and the ordinance of the Almighty,[5] which the English law (in the language of the indictment for the offence) most fitly describes as one not even to be named amongst Christians. The least notice, that could be taken of this detestable crime, would certainly be the best; but those who profess to expound the criminal law, as well as those whose duty is to administer it, must not shrink from the task, disgusting though it be, of explaining with clearness and precision that dreadful crime, of which the inevitable consequence is death to those convicted of it, besides indelible and lasting infamy to their names—which the slightest suspicion of the least propensity to, drives them as pestilential outcasts from society—and which, even to mention by its odious appellation, is pollution to the lips that utter it, or the pen transcribing it. But the offence, revolting as it is, must be defined: it is a carnal knowledge committed against the order of nature by man with man, or in the same unnatural means with woman, or by man or woman in any manner with beast[.] ...

2. To the credit of the law of England, this abominable crime, ever since it was introduced into this country

---

[5] [Deacon's note] Leviticus, xx, 13, 15, 16. [Leviticus 20.13: "If a man also lie with mankind, as he lieth with a woman, both of them have committed an abomination: they shall surely be put to death; their blood shall be upon them."]

by the Lombards,[1] has been visited with the *penalty of death*—a punishment, which is sanctioned by the voice of nature and of reason, as well as the express law of God. ...

Fanny (right) and Stella (left), 1869. Fanny and Stella—also known as Thomas Boulton and Frederick Park—were actors who performed women's roles onstage, a practice that was socially acceptable. They also spent a significant proportion of their offstage time dressed as women, and they conducted their romantic relationships with men as Fanny and Stella. The friends became the subject of a London media frenzy in 1870, when they were arrested leaving a theater dressed as women; papers followed in detail the subsequent court case in which Boulton and Park's clothing, bodies, sleeping arrangements, and romantic relationships were intensely scrutinized, with particular attention to a period Stella spent living as the wife of the politician Lord Arthur Clinton. Boulton and Park were tried for sodomy, and the trial—which included the first mention of the word "drag" in official English records—ended in their acquittal, as the prosecution failed to provide sufficient evidence to support the accusation.

from An Act to Amend the Law Relating to Divorce and Matrimonial Causes in England (1857)

27. It shall be lawful for any husband to present a petition to the said Court, praying that his marriage may be dissolved, on the ground that his wife has since the celebration thereof been guilty of adultery; and it shall be lawful for any wife to present a petition to the said Court, praying that her marriage may be dissolved, on the ground that since the celebration thereof her husband has been guilty of incestuous adultery, or of bigamy with adultery, or of rape, or of sodomy or bestiality, or of adultery coupled with such cruelty as without adultery would have entitled her to a divorce a mensa et thoro,[2] or of adultery coupled with desertion, without reasonable excuse, for two years or upwards. ...

---

[1] *Lombards* Deacon likely means "Lollards," members of a reformist religious sect active in the late Middle Ages; some writers associated Lollards and other heretical groups with sodomy, and some believed it had not been practiced in England until the Lollards' arrival.

[2] *a mensa et thoro* Latin: from bed and table. This term is applied to legally approved separation, in which spouses live apart but are not fully divorced.

Cover of the *Illustrated Police News*, 9 October 1880. One of the illustrations on this cover depicts a police raid on a private ball held in Hulme, Manchester. The event was widely reported; the *Dundee Advertiser*, for example, described it as follows:

... About nine o'clock cabs began to arrive containing young men, most of whom had portmanteaus or boxes or bags with them. A considerable number were in female attire, the costumes being of the most gorgeous description, with bracelets, &c. ... The officers [hidden in preparation for the raid] saw 47 persons enter the building, 22 being dressed as women, and at first were supposed to be women. Dancing commenced about ten o'clock to the strains of a harmonium

played by a blind man. [Detective] Caminada saw through a window from the roof of an adjoining building what transpired, and having seen certain improprieties ordered the raid. A signal was given, and the police followed Caminada to the door. In answer to his knock some one called, "Who's there?" and on giving the password "Sister" he was admitted. The police were at once set upon, and Caminada was thrown back; but after a short scuffle, during which some of the men threw off their female attire and one tried to jump through a window, they were all secured, handcuffed, and removed to the cells at the Town Hall. ...

The ball's attendees were required to pay two £25 sureties to be "of good behaviour" for twelve months; many were severely impacted socially, as their names were printed in the *Manchester Evening News*.

from Section 2, Criminal Law Amendment Act (1885)

This portion of the Criminal Law Amendment Act is more commonly known as the Labouchère Amendment for Henry Labouchère, the homophobic MP who proposed it. Apart from this brief addition, the act was otherwise focused on preventing the sexual exploitation of teenage girls. The Labouchère Amendment remained in force until 1967.

11. Any male person who, in public or private, commits, or is a party to the commission of, or procures or attempts to procure the commission by any male person of, any act of gross indecency with another male person, shall be guilty of a misdemeanor, and being convicted thereof shall be liable at the discretion of the Court to be imprisoned for any term not exceeding two years, with or without hard labour.

Love, Sex, and Friendship between Men

from William Johnson Cory, *Ionica* (1858)

William Johnson, later William Johnson Cory (1823–92), was for decades a successful teacher at the prestigious preparatory school Eton, but was eventually forced into retirement amid rumors that his relationships with students were inappropriately intimate. He is now best known for his anonymously published volume *Ionica*, a collection addressed to a young man whom he taught at Eton. The book's homoeroticism—entwined with its allusions to ancient Greek culture's accommodation of love between men—were sufficiently subtle that the book was well-received; Cory's translation from the Greek of "Heraclitus," an elegy for the poet Heraclitus of Halicarnassus by the ancient Lybian poet Callimachus, became a widely read Victorian standard.

HERACLITUS

They told me, Heraclitus, they told me you were
  dead,
They brought me bitter news to hear and bitter tears
  to shed.
I wept, as I remembered, how often you and I
Had tired the sun with talking and sent him down
  the sky.

5   And now that thou art lying, my dear old Carian[1] guest,
A handful of grey ashes, long, long ago at rest,
Still are thy pleasant voices, thy nightingales, awake;
For Death, he taketh all away, but them he cannot take.

DETERIORA[2]

One year I lived in high romance,
10   A soul ennobled by the grace
Of one whose very frowns enhance
    The regal lustre of the face,

And in the magic of a smile
I dwelt as in Calypso's[3] isle.

15   One year, a narrow line of blue,
    With clouds both ways awhile held back:
And dull the vault that line goes through,
    And frequent now the crossing rack;[4]
And who shall pierce the upper sky,
20   And count the spheres? Not I, not I!

Sweet year, it was not hope you brought,
    Nor after toil and storm repose,
But a fresh growth of tender thought,
    And all of love my spirit knows.
25   You let my lifetime pause, and bade
The noontide dial cast no shade.

If fate and nature screen from me
    The sovran° front I bowed before,   *sovereign*
And set the glorious creature free,
30   Whom I would clasp, detain, adore;
If I forego that strange delight,
Must all be lost? Not quite, not quite.

Die, little Love, without complaint,
    Whom Honour standeth by to shrive:[5]
35   Assoilèd° from all selfish taint,   *absolved*
    Die, Love, whom Friendship will survive.
Nor heat nor folly gave thee birth;
And briefness does but raise thy worth.

Let the grey hermit Friendship hoard
40   Whatever sainted Love bequeathed,
And in some hidden scroll record
    The vows in pious moments breathed.
Vex not the lost with idle suit,
Oh lonely heart, be mute, be mute.

---

[1] *Carian* From Caria, a region of what is now Turkey.

[2] *DETERIORA* Latin: Worse.

---

[3] *Calypso* In Homer's *Odyssey*, Calypso is a sea-nymph who falls in love with Odysseus and keeps him, by means of enchantment, on her island for seven years.

[4] *rack* Fast-moving mass of clouds.

[5] *shrive* Hear confession and absolve of sins.

John Addington Symonds, "From Friend to Friend" (1880)

The following poem was included in the 1880 collection *New and Old: A Volume of Verse* by John Addington Symonds (1840–93); it appears below in an earlier, privately published form. The subject of the poem is likely Willie Dyer, a fellow student Symonds fell in love with while attending Harrow, a prestigious boys' school. Symonds ended the relationship at his father's urging, but would later write in his memoirs that "I have never felt the same unreason and unreasoning emotion for another human being."

Dear Friend, I know not if such aching nights
    Of sweet strange comradeship as we have spent,
Or if twin minds with equal ardour spent,
To search the world's unspeakable delights
5   Or if long days passed on Parnassian[1] heights
Together in rapt interminglement
    Of heart with heart on hope sublime intent,
Or if the tide of turbulent appetites
    That sway both breasts in harmony, have wrought
10 Our spirits to communion:[2] but I swear
    That neither chance or change nor time nor aught
That makes the future of our lives less fair,
    Shall sunder us who once have breathed this air
Of soul-commingling friendship passion-wrought.

---

[1] *Parnassian* Of Parnassus, a mountain in Greece that, according to myth, was sacred to Apollo and the Muses, and was therefore seen as the home of artistic inspiration.

[2] *Or if the tide … communion* In the published version of the poem, these lines were altered as follows: "Or if the spark of heaven-born fire that lights / Love in both breasts from boyhood, thus have wrought / Our spirits to communion."

John Gambril Nicholson, "In Working Dress" (1892)

John Gambril Nicholson (1866–1931) is considered one of the Uranian poets; this poem from his first collection, *Love in Earnest: Sonnets, Ballades, and Lyrics* (1892), evokes an attraction to working-class men common among Uranian writers.

'Twas on a hot midsummer day,
    When I had looked for you in vain
    In garden, stable, barn and lane,
I found you mowing in the hay.

5 I came upon you unaware.
    Suffused with sweat you swung the scythe;
    A stooping figure, strong and lithe,
With arms above the elbow bare.

In trousers of stiff corduroy,
10   A cotton shirt, a leather belt,
    A drooping hat of dingy felt—
I scarcely recognised my boy!

Behind you all unmarked I came,
    Watching how well your work you did;
15   Your back was bent, your face was hid,
And dubiously I spoke your name.

You turned; and, hotter than before,
    With the broad hat your brow you fanned,
    And giving me a moist brown hand,
20 Glanced at the clumsy boots you wore.

For, as I gazed, you did not guess
    How fair you seemed in such disguise;
    Your deprecating down-cast eyes
Said, Please excuse my working-dress!

25 Not in your Sunday fineries,
    Nor clad in flannels for your play,
    But as you were that working-day
Of you my sweetest memory is!

Lord Alfred Douglas, "Two Loves" (1894)

Writer and editor Lord Alfred Douglas (1870–
1945) is best remembered for his relationship with
Oscar Wilde; Douglas's father, the Marquess of
Queensbury's public attacks on the relationship led
Wilde to charge him with libel, and the evidence
uncovered in the course of that trial led to Wilde's
own conviction and incarceration for "gross indecency." The following poem, written by Douglas,
was published in *The Chameleon: A Bazaar of Dangerous and Smiling Chances*, an Oxford undergraduate periodical that only ran for one issue. Wilde also
contributed an essay to the issue, and Douglas's
poem and other contents of the volume were submitted as evidence against Wilde in court.

I dreamed I stood upon a little hill,
  And at my feet there lay a ground, that seemed
Like a waste° garden, flowering at its will   *wild*
With buds and blossoms. There were pools that dreamed
5 Black and unruffled; there were white lilies
A few, and crocuses, and violets
Purple or pale, snake-like fritillaries[1]
Scarce seen for the rank grass, and through green nets
Blue eyes of shy pervenche° winked in the sun. *periwinkle*
10 And there were curious flowers, before unknown,
Flowers that were stained with moonlight, or with shades
Of Nature's wilful moods; and here a one
That had drunk in the transitory tone
Of one brief moment in a sunset; blades
15 Of grass that in an hundred springs had been
Slowly but exquisitely nurtured by the stars,
And watered with the scented dew long cupped
In lilies, that for rays of sun had seen
Only God's glory, for never a sunrise mars
20 The luminous air of Heaven. Beyond, abrupt,
A grey stone wall, o'ergrown with velvet moss
Uprose; and gazing I stood long, all mazed°   *amazed*
To see a place so strange, so sweet, so fair.
And as I stood and marvelled, lo! across

25 The garden came a youth; one hand he raised
To shield him from the sun, his wind-tossed hair
Was twined with flowers, and in his hand he bore
A purple bunch of bursting grapes, his eyes
Were clear as crystal, naked all was he,
30 White as the snow on pathless mountains frore,° *frozen*
Red were his lips as red wine-spilth[2] that dyes
A marble floor, his brow chalcedony.[3]
And he came near me, with his lips uncurled
And kind, and caught my hand and kissed my mouth,
35 And gave me grapes to eat, and said, "Sweet friend,
Come I will show thee shadows of the world
And images of life. See from the South
Comes the pale pageant that hath never an end."
And lo! within the garden of my dream
40 I saw two walking on a shining plain
Of golden light. The one did joyous seem
And fair and blooming, and a sweet refrain
Came from his lips; he sang of pretty maids
And joyous love of comely girl and boy,
45 His eyes were bright, and 'mid the dancing blades
Of golden grass his feet did trip for joy;
And in his hands he held an ivory lute
With strings of gold that were as maidens' hair,
And sang with voice as tuneful as a flute,
50 And round his neck three chains of roses were.
But he that was his comrade walked aside;
He was full sad and sweet, and his large eyes
Were strange with wondrous brightness, staring wide
With gazing; and he sighed with many sighs
55 That moved me, and his cheeks were wan and white
Like pallid lilies, and his lips were red
Like poppies, and his hands he clenchèd tight,
And yet again unclenchèd, and his head
Was wreathed with moon-flowers pale as lips of death.
60 A purple robe he wore, o'erwrought in gold
With the device° of a great snake, whose breath *emblem*
Was like curved flame: which when I did behold
I fell a-weeping, and I cried, "Sweet youth,

---

[1] *fritillaries* Type of bell-shaped flowers.

[2] *wine-spilth* Spilled wine.

[3] *chalcedony* Type of quartz that is often translucent.

Tell me why, sad and sighing, thou dost rove
65 These pleasant realms? I pray thee speak me
        sooth°   *truth*
What is thy name?" He said, "My name is Love."
Then straight the first did turn himself to me
And cried, "He lieth, for his name is Shame,
70 But I am Love, and I was wont to be
Alone in this fair garden, till he came
Unasked by night; I am true Love, I fill
The hearts of boy and girl with mutual flame."
Then sighing, said the other, "Have thy will,
I am the Love that dare not speak its name."

Love, Sex, and Friendship between Women

from Anne Lister, Diaries (1806–40)

For most of her life, Anne Lister (1791–1840), a well-to-do and well-educated West Yorkshire woman of conservative political views, kept a most extraordinary diary. Most of the entries are hand-written in the usual way; frequently, however, there are also entries that are written in a code that Lister herself devised using Greek letters and other symbols. In the 1890s, Lister's descendant John Lister and his friend Arthur Burrell cracked the code. In a 1936 letter to the Halifax Borough librarian, Burrell described the discovery:

> [We realized that] the word "hope" was in cipher. With these four letters almost certain we began very late at night to find the remaining clues. We finished at 2 am. … The part written in cipher—turned out after examination to be entirely unpublishable. Mr. Lister was distressed but he refused to take my advice, which was that he should burn all 26 volumes. He was as you know an antiquarian and my suggestion seemed sacrilege, which perhaps it was.

Burrell made plain why he considered the "contents of this cipher" to be unpublishable: they comprised "an intimate account of homosexual practices among Miss Lister and her many 'friends'; hardly any one of them escaped her."

Thursday 26 August [1819, Halifax]

Miss Browne and I walked leisurely along and got to Shibden by 5. Sat ten minutes alone in the drawing-room. Then my aunt came and afterwards, Isabella. Stayed with them (excused ten minutes for my dinner) till Miss Inman and the Miss Knights rapped at the door. Then dressed in half an hour and went in to tea. Walked a turn or two in the garden, showed Isabella's prints, etc. and the evening went off pleasantly, I taking care to pay rather more attention to Miss Browne than the other young ladies. Her brother and Mr. William Knight came for their sisters at eight. John Oates brought a small instrument to procure a light by the compression of air enclosed in a tube. All pleased with it[.] … They all went about 8:30 …

[in code] Just before we came in from the garden, contrived to be a few minutes alone with only Tib and Miss Browne. The former gave me a kiss and I made it an excuse to kiss Miss Browne on her lips, a very little, moistly. She looked shamefacedly. Were, a few minutes afterwards, us three in the hall. Miss Browne said kissing was an odd thing and people made queer remarks about it. "These," said I, "none of us understand." But I think she did not very much dislike it after all. [end of coded passage]

Miss Browne looked very neat, pretty and like a gentle-woman. They all thought so and could not do otherwise.

Sunday 29 August [1819, Halifax]

All went to morning church. …

[in code] In passing Miss Browne, smiled very graciously. I fancied she looked rather sheepish. What has she thought of my kissing her when she was here on Thursday? Tib said she pulled her bonnet over her face the moment after I had done it.

Thursday 18 November [1819, Manchester]

[in code] … Not much conversation before getting into

bed. … C— made no objection to her coming to Manchester when he heard she was to meet me. … [He] would give her till eight o'clock to be at home tomorrow. … Asked how often they were connected and, guessing, found might be at the rate of about twenty times a year. Got into bed. She seemed to want a kiss. It was more than I did. The tears gushed to my eyes. I felt I know not what and she perceived that I was much agitated. She bade me not or she should begin too and I knew not how she would suffer. She guessed not what passed within me. They were not tears of adoration. I felt that she was another man's wife. I shuddered at the thought and at the conviction that no sophistry[1] could gloss over the criminality of our connection. It seemed not that the like had occurred to her[.] …

Saturday 16 September [1820, Halifax] [in code] Talking about Isabella, my aunt said a good deal about her being no companion for them, being stupid when I was not downstairs, about her pulling my face, etc. and being so unmindful of these things before my uncle and herself and my father, and indeed, James—such a lad as James—a servant! Indeed, she never felt so little in her life. Wondered Miss Norcliffe should let herself down so. I said what I could. Laid it on the manners of the world. My aunt said I did not understand her. In fact, it would not seem to understand. Tib was too fond, I know, though I cannot well choose to appear to know. She observed how different Mary was. Said I, "They are such different characters they cannot be compared, but Mary says she has just as much regard for me as Tib." My aunt seemed to doubt I believed she had just as much or more, however diffident her manner of shewing it. My aunt seemed still incredulous. I wonder if she smokes[2] Tib? Surely she has not nous[3] enough, though Tib is, indeed, shockingly barefaced. I must manage things better in the future.

Friday 17 November [1820, Langton] [in code] Not long with Miss Vallance but long enough to say, in brief, that Tib and I … had had a row … about drinking so much wine. Tib was very violent after she came into bed at night. We renewed the conversation and she was a good deal more violent than before … I stood by the fire, talking very calmly, I daresay an hour, while she was in bed, repeating what I had said before. She still swore by all that is sacred she never took more than five glasses a day; one at luncheon, one at supper, one at dinner, and two at tea. I repeated that I could, if I chose, mention a time (alluding to when she was last at Shibden) when, for several days she not only took more than five but more than six or seven glasses. She called God and all the angels of heaven to witness it was a lie and wished herself at the devil if it was not false. I still quietly persisted that I knew that thing to be fact. She declared it an infamous lie, that I would not mention the time and place where, because I could not… I told her a great many home truths. When the converse ceased, I began to curl and get into bed. She was soon snoring, and we never spoke after my getting into bed.

Wednesday 20 December [1820, Langton] [in code] One and a half hours, just after tea, with Anne in her room. In low spirits. Mentioned, as frequent causes of this sort of thing, my father's having so lost the manners of a gentleman, the bad luck of his estate at Weighton, and, above all, Mary's marriage, etc. Anne must and does think me very much attached to Mary and must guess our hopes of eventually coming together. One and a half an hour with Anne after she was in bed. Talking, at first, much in the same style as in the evening, just before, but then got more loving. Kissed her, told her I had a pain in my knees—my expression to her for desire—and saw plainly she likes me and would yield again, without much difficulty, to opportunity and importunity.

---

[1] *sophistry*   Clever but fallacious reasoning.

[2] *smokes*   Suspects.

[3] *nous*   Greek: intellect, mind, intuition.

Friday 22 December [1820, Langton]
From 3 to 4, walked with Anne Belcombe in the East Balk field.

[in code] In the evening, Mrs. Milne played. Hung over her at the instrument. Afterwards, sat next to her and paid her marked attention … Came upstairs at 10:40. Near half an hour in Mrs. Milne's room. Near an hour with Anne Belcombe. She told me of my attention to Mrs. Milne and that I had taken no notice of her or Miss Vallance and that she was sure Miss Vallance had observed it and felt as she did. Said I could not help it. Miss Milne was fascinating. Then went half an hour to Miss Vallance. Got out of her that she had observed me to Mrs. Milne and was a little jealous. Anne then came to my room, having expected me again in hers, and stayed almost until I got into bed. Her love for me gets quite as evident as I could wish.

Monday 29 January [1821, Halifax]
Cutting curl-papers half an hour … Arranging and putting away my last year's letters. Looked over and burnt several very old ones from indifferent people. … [in code] Burnt … Mr. Montagu's farewell verse [so] that no trace of any man's admiration may remain. It is not meet[1] for me. I love, and only love, the fairer sex and, thus beloved by them in turn, my heart revolts from any other love than theirs.

Thursday 8 February [1821, Halifax]
Came upstairs at 11 a.m.

[in code] Spent my time from then until 3 writing to Mary very affectionately, more so than I remember to have done for long. … Wrote the following crypt; "I can live upon hope, forget that we grow older, and love you as warmly as ever. Yes, Mary, you cannot doubt the love of one who has waited for you so long and patiently. You can give me all of happiness I care for and, pressed to the heart which I believe my own, caressed and treasured there, I will indeed be constant and never, from that moment, feel a wish of thought for any other than my wife. You shall have every smile and every

Charlotte Cushman and Matilda Hays, c. 1855. Charlotte Cushman (1816–76), an American actor, and Matilda Hays (1820–97), an English writer and translator, had a decade-long relationship, much of which they spent living in Rome as part of an expatriate community of lesbian artists and intellectuals. Elizabeth Barrett Browning, who knew the couple, described their relationship in an 1848 letter to her sister as "a female marriage," writing that Cushman and Hays "have made vows of celibacy & of eternal attachment to each other—they live together, dress alike."

breath of tenderness. 'One shall our union and our interests be' and every wish that love inspires, and every kiss and every dear feeling of delight shall only make me more securely and entirely yours." Then, after hoping to see her in York next winter and at Steph's before the end of the summer, I further wrote in crypt as follows, "I do not like to be too long estranged from you sometimes, for, Mary, there is a nameless tie in that soft intercourse which blends us into one and makes me feel that you are mine. There is no feeling like it. There is no pledge which gives such sweet possession."

---

[1] meet Appropriate, well suited.

Simeon Solomon, *Sappho and Erinna in a Garden at Mytilene*, 1864. Born into a middle-class Jewish family, Pre-Raphaelite painter Simeon Solomon (1840–1905) enjoyed a successful career until 1873, when he was arrested for attempted sodomy. His reputation plummeted after the incident, and he became reliant on workhouses and the support of his friends for sustenance. He remained, however, a part of Pre-Raphaelite and Aesthetic circles and continued to produce influential work until the end of his life. Some of Solomon's best-known paintings have homoerotic themes; this painting depicts the ancient Greek poet Sappho, who wrote numerous love poems about women, embracing another Greek poet, Erinna.

Monday 12 February [1821, Halifax]
Letter from Anne Belcombe (Petergate, York) ...
[in code] nothing but news and concluded, "from your ever sincere, affectionate, Anne Belcome." The seal, Cupid in a boat guided by a star. "*Si je te perds, je suis*

perdu."[1] Such letters as these will keep up much love on my part. I shall not think much about her but get out of the scrape as well as I can, sorry and remorseful to have been in it at all. Heaven forgive me, and may Mary never know it.

---

[1] *Si je te perds, je suis perdu*   French: If I lose you, I am lost.

from Edith Simcox, *Autobiography of a Shirtmaker* (written 1876–1900)

Edith Simcox (1844–1901) was a woman of wide-ranging interests and talents. From 1875 until 1884 she managed a shirt-making cooperative that she had with a friend; the enterprise aimed to provide employment at fair wages and under good working conditions for women (who, then as now, were often exploited in the textile industry). She was for three years an elected member of the London School Board, representing the Radical Party. As an author, she was active for several decades, contributing numerous articles and reviews to publications such as *Fraser's Magazine*, *Longman's Magazine*, and *Nineteenth Century*; she also wrote a two-volume study of property ownership in early civilizations (in which she made the case that the more advanced civilizations were those in which women were allowed to own property).

Simcox gave the title *Autobiography of a Shirtmaker* to the personal journal that she kept from 1876 to 1900; until 1880 the journal's focus is very largely on Simcox's passionate attachment to the novelist George Eliot. Though Eliot appears to have felt no answering passion, she and George Henry Lewes maintained a cordial and friendly relationship with Simcox, and often welcomed her into their home.

Simcox's journal became known to scholars in the 1950s, but a full transcription was not published until 1998. Included here are excerpts representative of Simcox's expressed feelings for Eliot, together with the only surviving letter from Simcox to Eliot.

November 7, 1877

My whole soul is a longing question. I am going to see her. It rained this morning; now the sun is coming out. I feel as if that were a bad omen. She will be pre-engaged.

November 9, 1877

I was ushered in without hesitation. They[1] were together sitting reading; he was at the second day of headache. I tried to say something easy—that it was fate not to get rid of me. She—that it seemed rather hard on me on Sunday—and—was she afraid of my poisoning Johnny's shirts? [Mr. Lewes had invited me to come early on Sunday, before other people; but I only contrived to get a few minutes short of J.C.] which she seemed inclined to parry by saying many other people came. They had tried battledore and shuttlecock[2] as a substitute for the exercise of lawn tennis which had done her so much good. He had a letter from a young Cambridge man, who had dreamt so vividly and repeatedly that she was ill that he couldn't help writing to ask—enclosing a directed card for reply "only a dream" or something of the sort to prove that he was not in quest of an autograph. She said, perhaps that would make me more charitable to men-folk. I protested I wasn't otherwise, and she said she had always owed me a grudge for not being grateful enough to the Italian officer who was kind to me when the train was snowed up beyond Foggia. She said, unlike most people, she believed I should have thought more of the adventure if a woman had been kind to me. I said I might have if I had the opportunity of being kind to a woman, but that I had no prejudice whatever against men. He and she said as they have before, that among chance acquittances men are more appreciative and courteous to her than women. I said that I found women kinder than men, which she was "glad to hear," as showing they could be kind to each other—and I didn't explain either that I had always taken their kindness as a sign that I was half a man— and they knew it; or that I thought it rather hard she should visit, as a fault, my constitutional want of charm for men. I did not stay long and she only said—Are you going soon. ....

---

[1] *They* Novelist George Eliot and author and editor George Henry Lewes, with whom Eliot lived for the last twenty-four years of Lewes's life.

[2] *battledore and shuttlecock* Game similar to badminton.

January 27, 1878

Today I have written to her, in lightly loving strain—after burning two sheets of more earnest matter. ...

February 6, 1878

Yesterday I went to see her, and have been in a calm glow of happiness since—for no special reason, only that to have been near her happens to have that effect on me. She had had headaches and was in a somewhat despondent mood, so I did nothing but make reckless love to her.[1] ... I brought her two of the least spoilt of my Valentines, which she humanely forbore to read in my presence. She said it was a pity my letters could not be kept some five centuries to show a more sober posterity what hyperbole had once been possible. I asked if she took so gloomy a view of the future as to think five centuries hence there would be no one as adorable as herself—of that, said Lewis, you may be sure. I agreed and she professed to be silenced in confusion. I had told her of my ambition to be allowed to lie silently at her feet as she pursued her occupations, and that made her refer to my last letter. She also—as she once wrote—that I "knew all the craft of fine loving," as she also tells her husband; he and I pelted her with a little loving chaff about her own unamiableness, and when he affected to agree with her I said it was a mean attempt to curry favour with divinity—I would be no party to such hypocrisy—unless I had as much as he to gain! I tore myself away with difficulty, choked with tears in the passages—and so came away. ...

December 23, 1880

She was alone when I arrived. I was too shy to ask for any special greeting—only kissed her again and again as she sat. Mr. Cross came in soon and noticed his countenance was transfigured—a calm look of pure *beatitude* had succeeded the ordinary good nature—poor fellow! She was complaining of a slight sore throat, when he came in and touched her hand, said she felt the reverse of better. I only stayed half an hour therefore; she said

do not go, but I gave as a reason that she should not tire her throat and then she asked me and I only asked after his health—she had spoken before of being quite well and I thought it was only a passing cold—she thought it was caught at the Agamemnon. I meant to call again tomorrow and take her some snowdrops. This morning I heard from Johnny—she died at 10 last night! On Tuesday, I was stuck by something ominous, a sentence in a novel: "There is only one remedy for a chronic misunderstanding—Death." One slender comfort is left me—that I saw and kissed her so near the end. I thought—though I did not say—God grant I may die after such a meeting as this—and it is dead. Now all is over. I have nothing more to wait and long for—alone forevermore!

Edith Simcox, Letter to George Eliot, 28 March 1880

Sunday, 1 Douro Place
Victoria Road, W

My own Darling,

There are no posts in particular at Sark and as I am going there especially to be out of temptation to torment you, I want as a reward, leave for one more last caress. For my own, you have "done your duty" to us, and as I can't forget how hard that is, I can't help loving you even more and more dearly for the sake of the sweet patience that bears and does what is so hard. And, therefore darling, I do want you to leave us before you are quite outworn, and I ought to be able to let you go without moaning; it is like dying once a year and each year is harder than the last.

It seems horrible that I should be better off than you, and yet, while you are here, I cannot help being happy for every moment in your presence. A word you let fall on Thursday makes me want to say one thing: You said some people wrote to you more freely from thinking you were alone. Darling, just because my love for you is the one great joy and blessing of my life, I should like you to know that if you had been alone seven years ago, I should not have ventured to let the

---

[1]   *make reckless love to her*   Make reckless romantic overtures to her.

love I felt have its way. I dared to love you like this and to tell you so because he likes for you to be told, and all one's love could not be more than he thought due, than he liked to have poured at your feet. He delighted in sharing the blessedness of loving you and but for the sweet memory of his generous welcome, I could not bear to be glad in feeling your dearness now. All my little bits of good fortune seemed to come through him, and the thought of him is never more vividly present than when I am happiest in your love. If it were not so, it would seem a disloyalty—as it is—I often half-hate myself because your happiness is dead and mine because of yours—I must live while you do.

One more little confession: It does not hurt me in the least to say it, but "Sweet Mother" has come a hundred times to the tip of my pen since it was told not. Do you see darling, that I can only love you three lawful ways: idolatrously as Frater the Virgin Mary, in romance wise as Petrarch,[1] Laura, or with a child's fondness for the mother one leans on notwithstanding the irreverence of one's longing to pet and take care of her? Sober friendship seems to make the ugliest claim to a kind equality; friendship is a precious thing indeed, but between friends I think if there is love at all it must be equal, and whichever way we take it, our relation is between unequals. It is a quite unpractical trifle, but I am impelled to say this because any change in one's speech seems to imply a change in feeling and there has been none in my feeling for you except a growing desire not to make any burdensome claim, not even to weary you with the boundless, grateful love that must still always be yours—as I am.

Edith

7 kisses are launched upon the foggy air. Goodbye, darling.

---

[1] *Frater* Friar, member of a religious order; *Petrarch* Italian poet (1304–74) best known for his sonnets dedicated to a woman named Laura, the object of his unrequited love.

Amy Levy, "At a Dinner Party" (1889)

Anglo-Jewish poet and novelist Amy Levy (1861–89) was part of an intellectual and social circle of feminist "New Women"; she also had, in addition to other romantic connections, a strong and apparently unrequited attachment to the Aesthetic writer Vernon Lee. The following poem is one of several in Levy's posthumously published final collection, *A London Plane-Tree and Other Verse* (1889), that touch on same-sex desire.

With fruit and flowers that board is deckt
    The wine and laughter flow;
I'll not complain—could one expect
    So dull a world to know?

5 You look across the fruit and flowers,
    My glance your glances find.—
It is our secret, only ours,
    Since all the world is blind.

from Frances Power Cobbe, *Life of Frances Power Cobbe, as Told by Herself* (1904)

Crusading journalist Frances Power Cobbe (1822–1904) and sculptor Mary Lloyd (1819–96) met in Rome in 1861; by 1863 they were living together in London. They later moved to an estate in Wales. The two remained together until Lloyd's death in 1896, and Cobbe frequently referred to Lloyd as either her "husband" or her "wife."

The first edition of Cobbe's autobiography was published in 1894. The passage below, which was added after Lloyd's death, appears in the final pages of later editions.

from CHAPTER 21

September 1898

The grey granite stone is standing already in Llanelltyd burying ground, though my place beneath it still waits for me. The friend who made my life so happy when I wrote the last pages of this book, and who had then done so for thirty-four blessed years, lies there, under the rose trees and the mignonette; alone, until I may be laid beside her.

It would be some poor comfort to me in my loneliness to write here some little account of Mary Charlotte Lloyd, and to describe her keen, highly-cultivated intellect, her quick sense of humour, her gifts as sculptor and painter (the pupil and friend of John Gibson and of Rosa Bonheur[1]), her practical ability and strict justice in the administration of her estate, above all to speak of her character. "Cast"—as one who knew her from childhood said—"in an heroic mould" of fortitude and loftiness, her absolute unselfishness in all things large and small. But the reticence which belonged to the greatness of her nature made her always refuse to allow me to lead her into the more public life whereto my work necessarily brought me, and in her last sacred directions she forbids me to commemorate her by any written record. Only then, in the hearts of the few who really knew her, must her noble memory live.

I wrote the following lines to her some twenty-five years ago when spending a few days away from her and our home in London. I found them again after her death among her papers. They have a doubled meaning for me now, when the time has come for me to need her most of all.

To Mary C. Lloyd
Written in Hartley Combe, Liss, about 1873

Friend of my life! When'er my eyes
Rest with sudden, glad surprise
On Nature's scenes of earth and air
Sublimely grand, or sweetly fair,
5   I want you—Mary.

When men and women gifted, free,
Speak their fresh thoughts ungrudgingly,

And spring forth, each kindling mind
Streams like a meteor in the wind,
10   I want you—Mary.

When soft the summer evenings close,
And crimson in the sunset rose,
Our Cader[2] glows, majestic, grand,
The crown of all your lovely land,
15   I want you—Mary.

When the dark winter nights come round
To our "ain fireside,"[3] cheerly bound,
With our dear Rembrandt[4] girl, so brown,
Smiling serenely on us down,
20   I want you—Mary.

Now, while the vigorous pulses leap
Still strong within my spirit's deep;
Now, while my yet unwearied brain
Weaves its thick web of throughs amain,
25   I want you—Mary.

Hereafter, when slow ebbs the tide,
And age drains out my strength and pride,
And dim-grown eyes and trembling hand
No longer list[5] my soul's command,
30   I want you—Mary.

In joy and grief, in good and ill,
Friend of my heart! I need you still;
My Playmate, Friend, Companion, Love
To dwell with here, to clasp above,
35   I want you—Mary.

For O! If past the gates of Death
To me the Unseen openeth

---

[1] *John Gibson* Welsh sculptor (1790–1886); *Rosa Bonheur* French painter and sculptor (1822–99). Both Gibson and Bonheur had same-sex relationships.

[2] *Cader* Cader Idris, an imposing mountain in Wales, located near the home of Power Cobbe and Lloyd.

[3] *ain fireside* Reference to "My Ain Fireside," a popular ballad written by Elizabeth Hamilton in the early nineteenth century.

[4] *Rembrandt* Dutch painter (1606–69).

[5] *list* Listen to.

Immortal joys to angels given,
Upon the holy heights of Heaven,
                    I'll want you—Mary!

God has given me two priceless benedictions in life: in my youth a perfect mother, and in my later years, a perfect friend. No other gifts, had I possessed them, genius, or beauty, or fame, or the wealth of the Indies, would have been worthy to compare with the joy of those affections. To live in companionship, almost unbroken by separation and never marred by doubt or a rough word, with a mind in whose workings my own found inexhaustible interest, and my hearts its rest; a friend who knew me better than anyone beside could ever know me, and yet—strange to think!—could love me better than any other. This was happiness for which, even now that it is over, I thank God from the depths of my soul. I thank Him that I have had such a Friend. And I thank Him that she died without prolonged suffering or distress, with her head resting on my breast and her hand pressing mine; calm and courageous to the last. Her old physician said, when all was over, "I have seen many, a *great* many, men and women die; but I never saw one die so bravely."

Sexuality and Medical Discourse

from William Acton, *The Functions and Disorders of the Reproductive Organs* (1858, revised 1875)

English doctor William Acton (1813–75), a specialist in venereal disease, focuses on the sexual health of men in *The Functions and Disorders of the Reproductive Organs* (1858), his best-known work. The views on masturbation and women's sexuality expressed in the passages below are often quoted as examples of typical Victorian opinion; they were certainly held by some medical professionals but were by no means universal.

from CHAPTER 2
MASTURBATION

from SECTION 2
MASTURBATION IN THE YOUTH AND ADULT

... I now proceed to point out what the results of masturbation are, when the vicious habit is practised after the age at which semen begins to be secreted.

THE SYMPTOMS.—It is often difficult to obtain much certain information on the subject during the early practice of the vice. Its unfortunate victims, so long as they can practise it with impunity, or are ignorant of its consequences, can hardly be induced to make the confession. And few authors who could avoid the task, have ventured even to speculate on the frequency of a vice at once so wide-spread and so deplorable. ...

If the struggle is severe for a youth to extricate himself from these vicious propensities, experience teaches me that it is very doubtful if, when the practice has been much indulged in, the physical frame will ever be wholly built up again; the haggard expression,[1] the sunken eye, the long, cadaverous-looking countenance, the downcast expression, which seems to arise from the dread of looking a fellow-creature in the face, may be carried to the grave. Undoubtedly care and attention

---

[1] [Acton's note] Since writing the above a very favorable case of recovery has come under my notice. About six years ago a youth consulted me, suffering from some of the worst effects of masturbation. He has lately come to ask my opinion on the advisability of marriage. I find that, intellectually and physically, my patient has to a great extent recovered, but he still retains the peculiar physiognomy which, to me, is very characteristic. There is the hollow, sunken eye still left, although nature has filled up all other interstices. The expression has nearly become natural, but still the practiced eye sees that there remains an unsettled look, very different from the calm, steady gaze of other men. In this case I was able to give my sanction to an early marriage, strict continence having always been maintained, only occasional emissions occurring, and I have little doubt that a few years of married life will still further improve the expression of the face.

This opinion was borne out by the results. I have lately (1874) met my former patient, an altered man, much improved in appearance, and we had much earnest conversation as to how he should protect his growing-up boys from falling into a condition similar to that of their father.

may do much in remedying the intellectual wreck which we notice in such youths.

It will be remembered that I am describing the results of only the worst and longest continued cases. The probability is that in many who read these pages and who have at some time or other practised this vice, but have early abandoned it, the symptoms will be of the slightest kind, and a speedy cure may be promised. ...

I could speak, from my own experience, of the many wrecks of high intellectual attainments, and the foul blot which has been made on the virgin page of youth—of shocks from which the youth's nervous system will never, in my opinion, be able to rally—of maladies engendered which no after course of treatment can altogether cure, although surgery may do much to alleviate symptoms as they arise.

One of the chief causes which impede recovery, and interfere with the action of any remedies, is the mental anguish arising from the horror and remorse which the patient experiences. ...

If, however, a patient will not attempt self-control, mental as well as physical, and if—instead of consulting a qualified medical man, hearing from him a statement of the consequences of the practice, strictly following out the treatment recommended, and giving up the vile habit—he should abandon himself to humiliation and despair, the downward course may be very rapid and fatal. When this frame of mind has completely got possession of a man, the step to insanity in its worst and most hopeless forms is alarmingly short. ...

from CHAPTER 5
MARITAL EXCESSES

It is a common notion among the public, and even among professional men, that the word *excess* chiefly applies to *illicit* sexual connection. Of course, whether extravagant in degree or not, all such connection is, from one point of view, an *excess*. But any warning against sexual dangers would be very incomplete if it did not extend to the excesses too often committed by married persons in ignorance of their ill-effects. Too frequent emission of the life-giving fluid, and too frequent sexual excitement of the nervous system, are, as we have seen, in themselves most destructive. The result is the same within the marriage bond as without it. The married man who thinks that, because he is a married man, he can commit no excess, however often the act of sexual congress is repeated, will suffer as certainly and as seriously as the unmarried debauchee who acts on the same principle in his indulgences—perhaps more certainly, from his very ignorance, and from his not taking those precautions and following those rules which a career of vice is apt to teach the sensualist. Many a man has, until his marriage, lived a most continent life;—so has his wife. As soon as they are wedded, intercourse is indulged in night after night; neither party having any idea that these repeated sexual acts are excesses, which the system of neither can with impunity bear, and which to the delicate man, at least, is occasionally absolute ruin. The practice is continued till health is impaired, sometimes permanently; and when a patient is at last obliged to seek medical advice, his usual surgeon may have no idea or suspicion of the excess, and treat the symptom without recommending the removal of the cause, namely the sexual excess; hence it is that the patient experiences no relief for the indigestion, lowness of spirits, or general debility from which he may be suffering. If, however, the patient comes under the care of a medical man in the habit of treating such cases, the invalid is thunderstruck at learning that his sufferings arise from excesses unwittingly committed. Married people often appear to think that connection may be repeated just as regularly and almost as often as their meals. Till they are told of the danger, the idea never enters their heads that they have been guilty of great and almost criminal excess; nor is this to be wondered at, since the possibility of such a cause of disease is seldom hinted at. ...

I have taken pains to obtain and compare abundant evidence on this subject, and the result of my inquiries I may briefly epitomise as follows: I should say that the majority of women (happily for society) are not very much troubled with sexual feeling of any kind. What men are habitually, women are only exceptionally. It is too true, I admit, as the Divorce Court shows, that there are some few women who have sexual desires so strong that they surpass those of men, and shock public feeling by their consequences. I admit, of course, the existence of sexual excitement terminating even in nymphomania,[1] a form of insanity that those accustomed to visit lunatic asylums must be fully conversant with; but, with these sad exceptions, there can be no doubt that sexual feeling in the female is in the majority of cases in abeyance, and that it requires positive and considerable excitement to be roused to all; and ever if roused (which in many instances it never can be) it is very moderate compared with that of the male. ...

I am ready to maintain that there are many females who never feel any sexual excitement whatever. Others, again, immediately after each period, do become, to a limited degree, capable of experiencing it; but this capacity is often temporary, and may entirely cease till the next menstrual period. Many of the best mothers, wives, and managers of households, know little of or are careless about sexual indulgences. Love of home, of children, and of domestic duties are the only passions they feel.

As a general rule, a modest woman seldom desires any sexual gratification for herself. She submits to her husband's embraces, but principally to gratify him; and, were it not for the desire of maternity, would far rather be relieved from his attentions. No nervous or feeble young man need, therefore, be deterred from marriage by an exaggerated notion of the arduous duties required from

him. Let him be well assured, on my authority backed by the opinion of many, that the married woman has no wish to be placed on the footing of a mistress. ...

Representing the debilitated state of the body from the effects of onanism or Self-pollution.

"Representing the debilitated state of the body from the effects of Onanism or Self-Pollution," illustration from R.J. Brodie & Co., *The Secret Companion, a Medical Work on Onanism or Self-Pollution,* 1848. Concerns that frequent orgasms were bad for one's health prompted some people to resist masturbation and even to limit intercourse with their spouses. This engraving from a work on the subject by "R.J. Brodie & Co., Consulting Surgeons" depicts the negative health effects masturbation ("onanism") was supposed to cause.

---

[1] [Acton's note] I shall probably have no other opportunity of noticing that, as excision of the clitoris has been recommended for the cure of this complaint, Köbelt thinks that it would not be necessary to remove the whole of the clitoris in nymphomania, the same results (that is destruction of venereal desire) would follow if the glans clitoridis had been alone removed, as it is now considered that it is the glans alone in which the sensitive nerves expand. This view I do not agree with, as I have already stated with regard to the analogous structure of the penis, p. 180. I am fully convinced that in many women there is no special sexual sensation in the clitoris, and I am as positive that the special sensibility dependent on the erectile tissue exists in several portions of the vaginal canal.

from James Paget, "Sexual Hypochondriasis" (1870)

Prominent surgeon and pathologist James Paget (1814–99) made several medical discoveries, published numerous books and articles, and served as president of the Royal College of Surgeons, in addition to practicing at St. Bartholomew's Hospital in London. In the following excerpt from a clinical lecture, he discusses patients' anxieties regarding sexual health and especially masturbation.

... Ignorance about sexual affairs seems to be a notable characteristic of the more civilised part of the human race. Brutes, even those most changed by our domestication, copulate as naturally as they eat or defaecate. As the instinct for food leads them to eat, and carries with it all the knowledge necessary for the choice and taking of their food, so the sexual instinct has with it the knowledge how to copulate. It is the same, I believe, with the least civilised of our race; but it is not so with the most civilised. It seems as if, in the course of generations, the transmission of intellectual powers gained by education had the effect of subduing or superseding those of instinct. How far up the grades of civilisation this change begins, I do not know; but among ourselves it is certain that the method of copulating needs to be taught, and that they to whom it is not taught remain quite ignorant about it; as ignorant as, I suppose, we should be of what to eat and drink if we were not taught. Of course very few, I mean very few of our sex, grow-up without being taught, either by the talk of schoolfellows or by books or other means; but a few grow-up and even marry in complete ignorance; and this ignorance, which is rare among men, is very common among well-educated women.

The fact is of much interest in relation both to the natural history of our race, and to the frequency of sexual disorders dependent on the mind or on the nervous system. For sexual desire arises and grows without the knowledge how to satisfy it; and in the learning how to satisfy it errors and fancies and things half understood get into the mind, and become to some men sources of misery and fright, and to some the subjects of hypochondriac gloom and watchfulness.

Among the merely ignorant you will find that, if they be otherwise sensible people, they need only to be told the truth concerning the disorders, real or imaginary, for which they consult you. Knowledge will cure them. But if they be or have become hypochondriac they will not receive, or will not retain, knowledge; their erroneous beliefs will be to their minds stronger than your truths. ...

But on some subjects of your teaching you will have to be very clear as to matters of fact; especially, for instance, as to the practice of masturbation, to which many of your patients will ascribe their chief distresses.

Now, I believe you may teach positively that masturbation does neither more nor less harm than sexual intercourse practised with the same frequency in the same conditions of general health and age and circumstance. Practised frequently by the very young, that is, at any time before or at the beginning of puberty, masturbation is very likely to produce exhaustion, effeminacy, over-sensitiveness and nervousness; just as equally frequent copulation at the same age would probably produce them. Or, practised every day, or many times in one day, at any age, either masturbation or copulation is likely to produce similar mischiefs or greater. And the mischiefs are especially likely or nearly sure to happen, and to be greatest, if the excesses are practised by those who, by inheritance or circumstances, are liable to any nervous disease—to "spinal irritation," epilepsy, insanity, or any other. But the mischiefs are due to the quantity, not to the method, of the excesses; and the quantity is to be estimated in relation to age and the power of the nervous system. I have seen as numerous and as great evils consequent on excessive sexual intercourse as on excessive masturbation: but I have not seen or heard anything to make me believe that occasional masturbation has any other effects on one who practises it than has occasional sexual intercourse, nor anything justifying the dread with which sexual hypochondriacs regard the having occasionally practised it. I wish that I could say something worse of so nasty a practice; an uncleanliness, a filthiness forbidden by GOD, an unmanliness despised by men. ...

from Richard von Krafft-Ebing, *Psychopathia Sexualis*[1] (first edition 1886, English translation 1892)

"Very few ever fully appreciate the powerful influence which sexuality exercises over feeling, thought, and conduct, both in the individual and in society," wrote psychologist Richard von Krafft-Ebing (1840–1902) in the preface to his groundbreaking book *Psychopathia Sexualis* (1886), a study of what he considered the "pathological manifestations of the sexual life." The text, which consisted of case studies interspersed with Krafft-Ebing's own theories and commentary, went through numerous editions, each larger than the last, as Krafft-Ebing added new categories of deviance as well as new case studies, many of them autobiographical writings submitted voluntarily by individuals who saw their experiences reflected in his work.

from CHAPTER 3
GENERAL PATHOLOGY

ACQUIRED HOMOSEXUALITY

Case 99. Autobiography

… I feel like a woman in a man's form, and even though I often am sensible of the man's form, yet it is always in a feminine sense. Thus, for example, I feel the penis as clitoris; the urethra as urethra and vaginal orifice, which always feels a little wet, even when it is actually dry; the scrotum as labia majora; in short, I always feel the vulva. And all that that means one alone can know who feels or has felt so. But the skin all over my body feels feminine; it receives all impressions, whether of touch, of warmth, or whether unfriendly, as feminine, and I have the sensations of a woman. I cannot go with bare hands, as both heat and cold trouble me. When

the time is past when we men are permitted to carry sun-umbrellas, I have to endure great sensitiveness of the skin of my face, until sun-umbrellas can again be used. On awaking in the morning, I am confused for a few moments, as if I were seeking for myself; then the imperative feeling of being a woman awakens. …

… How the feeling for dress and ornament lowers a man! Even in his changed form, even when he can no longer recall the masculine sexual feeling, he would not wish to be forced to feel like a woman. … At last he longs for a moment in which he might raise his mask; but that moment does not come. He can only find amelioration of his misery when he can put on some bit of female attire or finery, an undergarment, etc.; for he dare not go about as a woman. To be compelled to fulfill all the duties of a calling with the feeling of being a woman costumed as a man, and to see no end of it, is no trifle. Religion alone saves from a great lapse; but it does not prevent the pain when temptation affects the man who feels as a woman; and so it must be felt and endured! …

The foregoing autobiography, scientifically so important, was accompanied by the following no less interesting letter:

SIR: I must next beg your indulgence for troubling you with my communication. I lost all control, and thought of myself only as a monster before which I myself shuddered. Then your work gave me courage again; and I determined to go to the bottom of the matter, and examine my past life, let the result be what it might. It seemed a duty of gratitude to you to tell you the result of my recollection and observation, since I had not seen any description by you of an analogous case; and, finally, I also thought it might perhaps interest you to learn, from the pen of a physician, how such a worthless human, or masculine, being thinks and feels under the

---

[1] *Psychopathia Sexualis*   Translation of the seventh German edition by Charles Gilbert Chaddock.

weight of the imperative idea of being a woman.

It is not perfect; but I no longer have the strength to reflect more upon it, and have no desire to go into the matter more deeply. Much is repeated; but I beg you to remember that any mask may be allowed to fall off, particularly when it is not voluntarily worn, but enforced.

After reading your work, I hope that, if I fulfill my duties as physician, citizen, father, and husband, I may still count myself among human beings who do not deserve merely to be despised. ...

Case 109. *Psychical Hermaphroditism. Autobiography.*—"I was born in 1868. The families of both my parents are healthy; at any rate, mental disease has never occurred in them. My father was a merchant; he is now sixty-five years old, and for years has been nervous and especially inclined to be melancholic. Before his marriage, my father is said to have lived fast. My mother is healthy, though not very strong. There are two other healthy children.

"I was very early developed sexually, and in my fourteenth year was so much troubled by pollutions[1] that I was frightened. Under what circumstances they occurred, particularly the nature of the dreams that were connected with them, I am no longer able to state. The fact is, that for years I have only felt myself drawn toward men sexually; and, with every effort and a terrible struggle, I am still unable to overcome this unnatural impulse that is so repugnant to me. It is said that I had many severe illnesses in my childhood, and that my life was often despaired of. To this was probably due the fact that I was spoiled and made very delicate. I was always much in the house, preferred to play with dolls rather than with soldiers, and I liked to play quietly in the house better than to play noisily in the streets. I entered the Gymnasium[2] at the age of ten. Though I was lazy, I was among the best scholars; for I learned very easily, and was the favorite of my teacher. From my earliest childhood (seventh year), I took pleasure in little girls. I remember that, even until my thirteenth year, I had formal love-affairs with them, and was jealous of those who associated with them; that I took pleasure in looking under the petticoats of my sister's friends and the servants; and that I had erections when touching the persons of my female playmates. I can, however, recall with certainty that boys attracted and excited me sexually just as early and powerfully. I always took great delight in reading and in the theatre. I had a doll-theatre, with which I played by preference. I knew whole pieces by heart, and copied the actors I saw, taking especially the female parts, in which I was delighted to put on female attire.

"As my sexual life became more pronounced, my inclination for boys won the upper hand. I fell completely in love with my companions, and had lustful feeling if one of them who pleased me touched my body. I became very shy, and refused to take gymnastic and swimming lessons. I thought I was different from my comrades, and did not like to undress before them. I liked to look at the penes of my companions and easily had erections. I masturbated but once, and that in my youth. When a friend told me that one could have pleasure without women, I likewise tried it; but I found no pleasure in it. At that time, also, a book fell in my hands which warned against the effects of onanism.[3] After that one trial I never did it again. In my fourteenth or fifteenth year, I made the acquaintance of two younger boys who excited me sexually to the highest degree. I was especially in love with one of them. ...

"At the age of nineteen I went to the University. My first semester was spent at the University of B., and it is still terrible to recall it. My sexual appetite powerfully excited me, and at night, for hours at a time, I ran about looking for men, especially when I was intoxicated. The next morning I would be crazy about myself. Fortunately, I found no one. In the second semester, I went to M. This was my happiest time. I had pleasant friends,

---

[1] *pollutions* Ejaculations, especially during sleep.

[2] *Gymnasium* School intended to prepare students for university.

[3] *onanism* Masturbation.

and, for a wonder, took pleasure in women, and was very happy about it. I had a love-affair with a young girl of spoiled character, with whom I spent wild nights. I was extraordinarily virile. I, who had formerly been chaste, also associated with other women, as never before. I felt fresh and well after coitus. I was not charmed so much by the female figure, which was never beautiful to me, as by—I know not what. In short, I knew women whose touch immediately induced erection. This joy and state of delight did not last long. I was so foolish as to take rooms with a friend. We had one sleeping-room. My friend was very talented and amiable, and a favorite with women; and it was by these characteristics that he at first so strongly attracted me. In fact, I love only highly-educated men; uneducated, powerful persons are able excite me intensely only for the moment, and cannot retain my affections. I soon fell in love with my friend. Then came the terrible time that destroyed my health. I slept in the same room with my friend, and had to see him undress daily; so that it required all my strength to keep from betraying myself. I became nervous, cried easily, and was jealous of those who associated with my friend. I still associated with women; but it was only with difficulty that I could perform coitus, which, like woman, was repugnant to me. The same women who had excited me intensely, no longer had any effect on me. I followed my friend to W., where he met an earlier friend with whom he associated. I became jealous and sick with love and longing. At the same time, I associated with women again, but seldom and only with difficulty, indulged in coitus. I became terribly depressed and almost insane. Work was out of the question. I led a foolish, wild life, and spent a great amount of money, almost throwing it away. Then, after six weeks of it, I broke down, and had to visit a water-cure,[1] where I spent many months. There I came to myself again, and soon became much liked; for I can be very gay, and I take great pleasure in the society of educated ladies. In conversation, I prefer married women to younger girls; I am also very gay in

the society of gentlemen at the beer-table and bowling-alley.

"At the sanitarium I met a man of twenty-nine, who was apparently constituted like myself. The fellow forced himself upon me, and wanted to embrace and kiss me; but he was very repugnant to me, though he excited me, and his touch caused erection, and even ejaculation. One evening he got me to perform mutual onanism. After it I spent a most frightful, sleepless night; I was terribly disgusted with the whole affair, and thought I should never do such a thing with a man again. …

"… As long as I have control of myself, I use all my strength to combat my nature. It is terrible when one can have no pleasure in associating with friends, and every erect soldier or butcher-boy makes one tremble and throb. It is frightful when night comes, and I watch at the window for some one to urinate against a wall across the way, and give me an opportunity to see his genitals. These thoughts are terrible; and besides, there is the consciousness of the immorality and criminality of my state of mind and my longing. I have a repugnance for myself that I cannot describe. I consider my condition abnormal; I cannot think that it is congenital, but I believe that the impulse was bred in me by faulty education. My suffering makes me reckless and egotistical; it takes away all kindness of disposition, and makes me careless about my family. I am moody, and often almost insane; often I am so depressed that I know not what to do, and then am easily moved to tears. And yet I have a horror of sexual intercourse with men. One evening when I came from a drinking-party, drunk and excited and in a half-conscious state, and, full of desire, was wandering about, I met a young man, who got me to perform mutual masturbation. Though he excited me, after the act I was beside myself. Today, when I go by the place, I am overcome with horror; and lately, when riding by it, without any cause, I fell from my gentle horse, that I know so well—I was so overcome by the memory of my unworthy deed.

"I love my family life and children, and social intercourse; and, with my position in society, I am suited to have a family. But I must give up all that; and

---

[1] *water-cure* Place where one's ailments are treated by a variety of means including drinking and bathing in water.

yet, I cannot abandon hope of cure. And so I vacillate between hopeful gaiety and frightful hopelessness, and neglect business and family. Indeed, I do not ask that I may marry and found a family; I wish only to overcome the terrible inclination for the male sex; only to associate quietly with my friends, and to learn to respect myself again. ..."

Last fall I made the patient's acquaintance. He is destitute of degenerative signs, and of perfectly masculine appearance, even though he is delicately formed and slender. Genitals perfectly normal. Appearance distinguished, with nothing striking. He is much troubled about his sexual perversion, and wishes to be freed from it at any price. In spite of the greatest effort on the part of both physician and patient, only a slight degree of hypnosis, insufficient for suggestive treatment, could be induced.

B. *Homo-Sexual Feeling as an Abnormal Congenital Manifestation*. ... The essential feature of this strange manifestation of the sexual life is the want[1] of sexual sensibility for the opposite sex, even to the extent of horror, while sexual inclination and impulse toward the same sex are present. At the same time, the genitals are normally developed, the sexual glands perform their functions properly, and the sexual type is completely differentiated. ...

From the cases published up to 1877, I have designated this peculiar sexual feeling as a functional sign of degeneration, and as a partial manifestation of a neuro-psychopathic state,[2] in most cases hereditary—a supposition which has found renewed confirmation in a consideration of additional cases. The following peculiarities may be given as the signs of this neuro-psychopathic taint:

1. The sexual life of individuals thus organized manifests itself, as a rule, abnormally early, and thereafter with abnormal power. Not infrequently still other perverse manifestations are presented besides the abnormal method of sexual satisfaction, which in itself is conditioned by the peculiar sexual feeling.

2. The psychical love manifest in these men is, for the most part, exaggerated and exalted in the same way as their sexual instinct is manifested in consciousness, with a strange and even compelling force.

3. By the side of the functional signs of degeneration attending contrary sexual feeling are found other functional, and in many cases anatomical, evidences of degeneration.

4. Neuroses (hysteria, neurasthenia,[3] epileptoid states, etc.) co-exist. Almost always the existence of temporary or lasting neurasthenia may be proved. As a rule, this is constitutional, having its root in congenital conditions. It is awakened and maintained by masturbation or enforced abstinence. ...

5. In the majority of cases, psychical anomalies (brilliant endowment in art, especially music, poetry, etc., by the side of bad intellectual powers or original eccentricity) are present, which may even go so far as pronounced conditions of mental degeneration (dementia, moral insanity).

In many urnings,[4] either temporarily or permanently, insanity of a degenerative character (pathological emotional states, periodical insanity, paranoia, etc.) makes its appearance.

6. In almost all cases where an examination of the physical and mental peculiarities of the ancestors and blood-relations has been possible, neuroses, psychoses, degenerative signs, etc., have been found in the families. ...

The depth of congenital contrary feeling is shown by the fact that the lustful dream of the male-loving urning has for its content only male individuals; that of the

---

[1] *want* Lack.

[2] *neuro-psychopathic state* State of mental illness involving the physical brain.

[3] *neurasthenia* Psychological disorder involving fatigue and physical discomfort.

[4] *urnings* Now-archaic term for gay men. In his discussion of male homosexuality, Krafft-Ebing draws a distinction between homosexuals of other sorts and urnings, whose "love for their own sex" is not merely physical, but "emotional and passionate."

female-loving woman, only female individuals, with corresponding situations. … [I]n many instances, the consciousness of the abnormality of the condition is wanting. The majority of urnings are happy in their perverse sexual feeling and impulse, and unhappy only in so far as social and legal barriers stand in the way of the satisfaction of the instinct toward their own sex. …

1. *Psychical Hermaphroditism.*[1]—The characteristic mark of this degree of inversion of the sexual instinct is that, by the side of the pronounced sexual instance and desire for the same sex, a desire toward the opposite sex is present; but the latter is much weaker and is manifested episodically only, while the homo-sexuality is primary, and, in time and intensity, forms the most striking feature of the vita sexualis.[2] …

from CHAPTER 5
PATHOLOGICAL SEXUALITY IN ITS LEGAL ASPECTS

LESBIAN LOVE

… Lesbian Love does not seem to approach urningism in frequency. The majority of female urnings do not act in obedience to an innate impulse, but they are developed under conditions analogous to those which produce the urning by cultivation.

These "forbidden friendships" flourish especially in penal institutions for females.

Kraussold[3] … reports: "The female prisoners have such friendships, which, when possible, extend to mutual manustupration.[4] But temporary manual gratification is not the only purpose of such friendships. They are made to be enduring—entered into systematically, so to speak—and intense jealousy and passion for love are developed, which can scarcely be surpassed between persons of opposite sex. When the friend of one prisoner is merely smiled at by another, there are often the most violent scenes of jealousy, and even beatings. …

Coffignon[5] reports (… p. 301) that this vice is, of late, quite the fashion—partly owing to novels on the subject, and partly as a result of … the sleeping of female servants in the same bed, seduction in schools by depraved pupils, or seduction of daughters by perverse servants.

The author declares that this vice ("sapphism") is met with more frequently among ladies of the aristocracy and prostitutes. …

John Addington Symonds, letter to Richard von Krafft-Ebing (1889, 1899)

The following letter, in which Symonds anonymously critiques Krafft-Ebing's theories regarding homosexuality, first appeared in an expanded 1889 edition of *Psychopathia Sexualis*, where Krafft-Ebing printed it as a case study. Symonds then reprinted the letter himself as part of his own book *A Problem in Modern Ethics: Being an Enquiry into the Phenomenon of Sexual Inversion, Addressed Especially to Medical Psychologists and Jurists* (privately published in 1891). He retained his anonymity by introducing the letter as follows:

At the close of this enquiry into medical theories of sexual inversion, all of which assume that the phenomenon is morbid, it may not be superfluous to append the protest of an Urning against that solution of the problem. I translate it from the original document published by Krafft-Ebing (pp. 216–219). He says that the writer is "a man of high position in London"; but whether the communication was made in German or in English, does not appear.

---

[1] [Krafft-Ebing's note] Comp. author's work, "Ueber psychosexuales Zwitterthum," in the internationalen Centralblatt f. d. Physiologie u. Pathologie der Harn und Sexualorgane, Bd. i, Heft 2.

[2] *vita sexualis* Sexual life.

[3] *Kraussold* See Carl Kraussold, *Melancholie und Schuld*, 1884.

[4] *manustupration* Now-archaic term for masturbation.

---

[5] *Coffignon* Paris journalist Ali Coffignon. The material Krafft-Ebing refers to appears in his *La Corruption à Paris* (1888).

You have no conception what sustained and difficult struggles we all of us (the thoughtful and refined among us most of all) have to carry on, and how terribly we are forced to suffer under the false opinions which still prevail regarding us and our so-called immorality.

Your view that, in most cases, the phenomenon in question has to be ascribed to congenital morbidity, offers perhaps the easiest way of overcoming popular prejudices, and awakening sympathy instead of horror and contempt for us poor "afflicted" creatures. Still, while I believe that this view is the most favourable for us in the present state of things, I am unable in the interest of science to accept the term morbid without qualification, and venture to suggest some further distinctions bearing on the central difficulties of the problem.

The phenomenon is certainly anomalous; but the term morbid carries a meaning which seems to me inapplicable to the subject, or at all events to very many cases which have come under my cognisance. I will concede à priori that a far larger proportion of mental disturbance, nervous hyper-sensibility, &c., can be proved in Urnings[1] than in normal men. But ought this excess of nervous erethism[2] to be referred necessarily to the peculiar nature of the Urning? Is not this the true explanation, in a vast majority of cases, that the Urning, owing to present laws and social prejudices, cannot like other men obtain a simple and easy satisfaction of his inborn sexual desires?

To begin with the years of boyhood: an Urning, when he first becomes aware of sexual stirrings in his nature, and innocently speaks about them to his comrades, soon finds that he is unintelligible. So he wraps himself within his own thoughts. Or should he attempt to tell a teacher or his parents about these feelings, the inclination, which for him is as natural as swimming to a fish, will be treated by them as corrupt and sinful; he is exhorted at any cost to overcome and trample on it. Then there begins in him a hidden conflict, a forcible suppression of the sexual impulse; and in proportion as the natural satisfaction of his craving is denied, fancy works with still more lively efforts, conjuring up those seductive pictures which he would fain expel from his imagination. The more energetic is the youth who has to fight this inner battle, the more seriously must his whole nervous system suffer from it. It is this forcible suppression of an instinct so deeply rooted in our nature, it is this, in my humble opinion, which first originates the morbid symptoms, that may often be observed in Urnings. But such consequences have nothing in themselves to do with the sexual inversion proper to the Urning.

Well then; some persons prolong this never-ending inner conflict, and ruin their constitutions in course of time; others arrive eventually at the conviction that an inborn impulse, which exists in them so powerfully, cannot possibly be sinful—so they abandon the impossible task of suppressing it. But just at this point begins in real earnest the Iliad[3] of their sufferings and constant nervous excitations. The normal man, if he looks for means to satisfy his sexual inclinations, knows always where to find that without trouble. Not so the Urning. He sees the men who attract him; he dares not utter, nay, dares not even let it be perceived, what stirs him. He imagines that he alone of all the people in the world is the subject of emotions so eccentric. Naturally, he cultivates the society of young men, but does not venture to confide in them. So at last he is driven to seek some relief in himself, some makeshift for the satisfaction he cannot obtain. This results in masturbation, probably excessive, with its usual pernicious consequences to health. When, after the lapse of a certain time, his nervous system is gravely compromised, this morbid phenomenon ought not to be ascribed to sexual inversion in itself; far rather we have to regard it as the logical issue[4] of the Urning's position, driven as he is by dominant opinion to forego the gratification which for him is natural and normal, and to betake himself to onanism.

[1] *Urnings* Now-archaic term for gay men.
[2] *erethism* Here, psychological over-activity.
[3] *Iliad* I.e., long story of successive catastrophes.
[4] *issue* Outcome.

But let us now suppose that the Urning has enjoyed the exceptional good-fortune of finding upon his path in life a soul who feels the same as he does, or else that he has been early introduced by some initiated friend into the circles of the Urning-world. In this case, it is possible that he will have escaped many painful conflicts; yet a long series of exciting cares and anxieties attend on every step he takes. He knows indeed now that he is by no means the only individual in the world who harbours these abnormal emotions; he opens his eyes, and marvels to discover how numerous are his comrades in all social spheres and every class of industry; he also soon perceives that Urnings, no less than normal men and women, have developed prostitution, and that male strumpets can be bought for money just as easily as females. Accordingly, there is no longer any difficulty for him in gratifying his sexual impulse. But how differently do things develop themselves in his case! How far less fortunate is he than normal man!

Let us assume the luckiest case that can befall him. The sympathetic friend, for whom he has been sighing all his life, is found. Yet he cannot openly give himself up to this connection, as a young fellow does with the girl he loves. Both of the comrades are continually forced to hide their liaison; their anxiety on this point is incessant; anything like an excessive intimacy, which could arouse suspicion (especially when they are not of the same age, or do not belong to the same class in society), has to be concealed from the external world. In this way, the very commencement of the relation sets a whole chain of exciting incidents in motion: and the dread lest the secret should be betrayed or divined, prevents the unfortunate lover from ever arriving at a simple happiness. Trifling circumstances, which would have no importance for another sort of man, make him tremble: lest suspicion should awake, his secret be discovered, and he become a social outcast, lose his official appointment, be excluded from his profession. Is it conceivable that this incessant anxiety and care should pass over him without a trace, and not react upon his nervous system?

Another individual, less lucky, has not found a sympathetic comrade, but has fallen into the hands of some pretty fellow, who at the outset readily respond to his wishes, till he drew the very deepest secret of h nature forth. At that point the subtlest methods of blackmailing begin to be employed. The miserable persecuted wretch, placed between the alternative of paying money down or of becoming socially impossible, losing a valued position, seeing dishonour bursting upon himself and family, pays, and still the more he pays, the greedier becomes the vampire who sucks his life-blood, until at last there lies nothing else before him except total financial ruin or disgrace. Who will be astonished if the nerves of an individual in this position are not equal to the horrid strain?

In some cases the nerves give way altogether: mental alienation sets in; at last the wretch finds in a madhouse that repose which life would not afford him. Others terminate their unendurable situation by the desperate act of suicide. How many unexplained cases of suicide in young men ought to be ascribed to this cause!

I do not think I am far wrong when I maintain that at least half of the suicides of young men are due to this one circumstance. Even in cases where no merciless blackmailer persecutes the Urning, but a connection has existed which lasted satisfactorily on both sides, still in these cases discovery, or the dread of discovery, leads only too often to suicide. How many officers, who have had connection with their subordinates, how many soldiers, who have lived in such relation with a comrade, where they thought they were about to be discovered, have put a bullet through their brains to avoid the coming disgrace! And the same might be said about all the other callings in life.

In consequence of all this, it seems clear that if, as a matter of fact, mental abnormalities and real disturbances of the intellect are commoner with Urnings than in the case of other men, this does not establish an inevitable connection between the mental eccentricity and the Urning's specific temperament, or prove that the latter causes the former. According to my firm conviction, mental disturbances and morbid symptoms which may be observed in Urnings ought in the large majority of instances not be so referred to their sexual anomaly; the real fact is that they are induced in them the prevalent false theory of sexual inversion, together with the legislation in force against Urnings and the reigning tone of public opinion. It is only one who has some approximate notion of the mental and moral sufferings, of the anxieties and perturbations, to which an Urning is exposed, who knows the never ending hypocrisies and concealments he must practise in order to cloak his indwelling inclination, who comprehends the infinite difficulties which oppose the natural satisfaction of his sexual desire—it is only such a one, I say, who is able properly to wonder at the comparative rarity of mental aberrations and nervous ailments in the class of Urnings. The larger proportion of these morbid circumstances would certainly not be developed if the Urning, like the normal man, could obtain a simple and facile gratification of his sexual appetite, and if he were not everlastingly exposed to the continuing anxieties I have attempted to describe.

from Havelock Ellis and John Addington Symonds, *Sexual Inversion* (1897)

The first English-language book dedicated to the medical study of same-sex sexuality, *Sexual Inversion* was a collaboration between John Addington Symonds (1840–93) and Havelock Ellis (1859–1939), a pioneering writer and researcher for whom the book was a starting point for his seven-volume *Studies in the Psychology of Sex* (1897–1928). Published in German in 1896 and in English a year later, *Sexual Inversion* was subject to controversy and repression; Symonds had died before the work's publication, and his literary executor bought most of the first English print run to protect the family's reputation. Another edition was published with Symonds uncredited, but the book was soon declared obscene and banned in Britain. Ellis would publish future volumes of *Studies in the Psychology of Sex* in the United States, and *Sexual Inversion* remained banned in Britain until the mid-1930s.

from GENERAL PREFACE

... It is a mistake, *they* [many of my friends] say, to try to uncover these *things*; leave the sexual instincts alone, to grow up and develop in the shy solitude they love, and they will be sure to grow up and develop wholesomely. But, as a matter of fact, that is precisely what we cannot and will not ever allow them to do. There are very few middle-aged men and women who can clearly recall the facts of their lives and tell you in all honesty that their sexual instincts have developed easily and wholesomely throughout. And it should not be difficult to see why this is so. Let my friends try to transfer their feelings and theories from the reproductive region to, let us say, the nutritive region, the only other which can be compared to it for importance. Suppose that eating and drinking were never spoken of openly, save in veiled or poetic language, and that no one ever ate food publicly, because it was considered immoral and immodest to reveal the mysteries of this natural function. We know what would occur. A considerable proportion of the community, more especially the more youthful members, possessed by an instinctive and legitimate curiosity, would concentrate their thoughts on the subject. They would have so many problems to puzzle over: How often ought I to eat? What ought I to eat? Is it wrong to eat fruit, which I like? Ought I to eat grass, which I don't like? Instinct notwithstanding, we may be quite sure that only a small minority would succeed in eating reasonably and wholesomely. The sexual secrecy of life is even more disastrous than such a nutritive secrecy would be[.] ...

from PREFACE TO *SEXUAL INVERSION*

... There can be no doubt that a peculiar amount of ignorance exists regarding the subject of sexual inversion. I know medical men of many years' general experience who have never, to their knowledge, come across a single case. We may remember, indeed, that some fifteen years ago the total number of cases recorded in scientific literature scarcely equalled those of British race which I have obtained, and that before my first cases were published not a single British case, unconnected with the asylum or the prison, had ever been recorded. Probably not a very large number of people are even aware that the turning in of the sexual instinct towards persons of the same sex can ever be regarded as in-born, so far as any sexual instinct is in-born. And very few indeed would not be surprised if it were possible to publish a list of the names of sexually inverted persons. Shortly before Mr. Symonds' death he drew up a list of men of British race whom of his own knowledge or from trustworthy information he knew to be inverted. The list contained fifty-two names, many of them honourably known in Church, State, Society, Art, and Letters. I could supplement this list by another of sexually inverted women, of whom a considerable proportion are widely and honourably known in litera-ture or otherwise, while many of the others are individu-als of more than average ability or character.

It cannot be positively affirmed of all these persons that they were born inverted, but in most the inverted tendency seems to be instinctive, and appears at a somewhat early age. In any case, however, it must be realised that in this volume we are not dealing with subjects belonging to the lunatic asylum or the prison. We are concerned with individuals who live in freedom, some of them suffering intensely from their abnormal organisation, but otherwise ordinary members of society. In a few cases, we are concerned with individu-als whose moral or artistic ideals have widely influenced their fellows who know nothing of the peculiar organi-sation which has largely moulded those ideals. ...

from SEXUAL INVERSION IN MEN

... I do not propose to adopt any more complex classifi-cation than the clinical distinction between simple inversion and psycho-sexual hermaphroditism, as it is usually called; the first class including all those individu-als who are sexually attracted only to their own sex, the second class those who are attracted to both sexes. ...

Case V.—Physician, unmarried, English, aged 60. Feels sure that in his own case heredity must be the

cause. His father suffered from severe attacks of melan-cholia; he himself from the age of 13–14, without any incitement of an external kind, and with every good influence around him and a severe, heartfelt striving on his own part after all that was good, nevertheless felt this instinct form and get strength within him. Prayers, struggles, all means used were of no avail. The thoughts, the imagination remained bent in one fixed direction.

His has been a miserable life. Death, even if it meant nothing but a passage into nothingness, he says, would be a thousand times preferable. As to investigating the subject scientifically, nothing could come of it. There are so many deviations from the normal mental and moral (who, indeed, is without them?), and yet they do not constitute insanity. This he regards as one of them. In another communication he says, "If all the miserable hours of wretchedness and despair could be counted up which I have suffered in my life, they would form a hell. Even now I cannot decide for myself how far one is exactly accountable for morbid instincts and feeling from which no prayers, no struggle, can deliver one. My own opinion is that in one way or another no one is blameless, but that there is great difference in the moral nature, and that in the case of a great many persons stains are not felt as stains." ...

The next ... cases are told in the subject's own words.

Case VI.—"My parentage is very sound and healthy. Both my parents (who belong to the professional middle class) have good general health; nor can I trace any marked abnormal or diseased tendency, of mind or body, in any records of the family.

"Though of a strongly nervous temperament myself, and sensitive, my health is good. I am not aware of any tendency to physical disease. In early manhood, how-ever, owing, I believe, to the great emotional tension under which I lived, my nervous system was a good deal shattered and exhausted. Mentally and morally my nature is pretty well balanced, and I have never had any serious perturbations in these departments. ...

"As a boy, I was attracted in general by boys rather older than myself; after leaving school I still fell in love, in a romantic vein, with comrades of my own standing. Now—at the age of 37—my ideal of love is a powerful, strongly built man, of my own age or rather younger—preferably of the working class. Though having solid sense and character, he need not be too glib or refined. Anything effeminate in a man, or anything of the cheap intellectual style, repels me very decisively.

"I have never had to do with actual paederasty, so-called. My chief desire in love is bodily nearness or contact, as to sleep naked with a naked friend; the specially sexual, though urgent enough, seems a secondary matter. Paederasty, either active or passive, might seem in place to me with one I loved very devotedly and who also loved me to that degree—but I think not otherwise. I am an artist by temperament and choice, fond of all beautiful things especially the male human form; of active, slight, muscular build; and sympathetic, but somewhat indecisive, character, though possessing self-control.

"I cannot regard my sexual feelings as unnatural or abnormal, since they have disclosed themselves so perfectly naturally and spontaneously within me. All that I have read in books or heard spoken about the ordinary sexual love, its intensity and passion, life-long devotion, love at first sight, etc., seems to me to be easily matched by my own experiences in the homosexual form; and with regard to the morality of this complex subject, my feeling is that it is the same as should prevail in love between man and woman—namely, that no bodily satisfaction should be sought at the cost of another person's distress or degradation. I am sure that this kind of love is, notwithstanding the physical difficulties that attend it, as deeply stirring and ennobling as the other kind, if not more so; and I think that for a perfect relationship the actual sex gratifications (whatever they may be) probably hold a less important place in this love than in the other."

PSYCHOSEXUAL HERMAPHRODITISM

This is the somewhat awkward name given to that form of inversion in which there exists a sexual attraction to both sexes. It is decidedly less common than simple inversion. We are only justified in including within this group those persons who find sexual pleasure and satisfaction both with men and with women, but in more than one of the following cases the homosexual is more powerful than the heterosexual instinct, and it is possible that these should really be regarded as cases of simple inversion. We have to remember that there is every inducement for the sexual invert to cultivate a spurious attraction to the opposite sex. ...

Case XXV.—Englishman, 40 years of age, retired from business. So far as he knows, belongs to a family that is quite normal.

Homosexual desires began at the age of 11 at a small private school, and were afterwards developed at a large public school. He did not practise masturbation. His erotic dreams were connected with individuals of both sexes, but more usually, he thinks, with women. He likes women in a general way and enjoys their society, but has always had a greater feeling of attraction towards a beautiful youth of 18 or 20 than towards a girl of the same age. He has often had connection with women, but, though he liked it, he has always preferred that with men. He has never been able to make up his mind to marry.

When a young boy he liked boys of his own age, but as he grew older preferred those aged between 20 and 28, as also he does at present. Those belonging to his own social position, and clerks in business, he likes best, but is not averse at times to servants, sailors and soldiers, provided they are clean, manly, and attractive in voice and manner. His usual method of gratification is intercrural connection, but at times he has been willing to practice *paedicatio.*[1]

He was fond of riding, boating and sports as a boy; he is also fond of music and painting. His chief regret in connection with his homosexual instincts is that he is obliged to lead a double life.

---

[1] *intercrural connection* Sex in which one partner's penis is placed between the other's thighs; *paedicatio* Anal sex.

from SEXUAL INVERSION IN WOMEN

… [W]e know comparatively little of sexual inversion in woman; of the total number of recorded cases of this abnormality, now very considerable, but a small proportion are in women, and the chief monographs on the subject devote but little space to women.

I think there are several reasons for this. Notwithstanding the severity with which homosexuality in women has been visited in a few cases, for the most part men seem to have been indifferent towards it; when it has been made a crime or a cause for divorce in men, it has usually been considered as no offence at all in women.[1] Another reason is that it is less easy to detect in women; we are accustomed to a much greater familiarity and intimacy between women than between men, and we are less apt to suspect the existence of any abnormal passion. And allied with this cause we have also to bear in mind the extreme ignorance and the extreme reticence of women regarding any abnormal or even normal manifestation of their sexual life. A woman may feel a high degree of sexual attraction for another woman without realising that her affection is sexual, and when she does realise it she is nearly always very unwilling to reveal the nature of her intimate experience, even with the adoption of precautions, and although the fact may be present to her that by helping to reveal the nature of her abnormality she may be helping to lighten the burden of it on other women. Among the numerous confessions voluntarily sent to Krafft-Ebing there is not one by a woman. There is, I think, one other reason why sexual inversion is less obvious in a woman. We have some reason to believe that, while a slight degree of homosexuality is commoner in women than in men, and is favoured by the conditions under which women

live, well marked and fully developed cases of inversion are rarer in women than in men. This result would be in harmony with what we know as to the greater affectibility of the feminine organism to slight stimuli, and its less liability to serious variation.[2] …

Case XXVIII.—Miss S, age 38, living in a city of the United States of America, a business woman of fine intelligence, prominent in professional and literary circles. Her general health is good, but she belongs to a family in which there is a marked neuropathic element. She is of rather phlegmatic temperament, well poised, always perfectly calm and self-possessed, rather retiring in disposition, with gentle, dignified bearing.

She says she cannot care of men, but that all her life has been "glorified and made beautiful by friendship with women," whom she loves as a man loves women. Her character is, however, well disciplined, and her friends are not aware of the nature of her affections. She tries not to give all her love to one person, and endeavours (as she herself expresses it) to use this "gift of loving" as a stepping-stone to high mental and spiritual attainments. She is described by one who has known her for several years as "having a high nature, and instincts unerringly toward high things."

from CHAPTER 6
THE THEORY OF SEXUAL INVERSION

The analysis of these cases leads directly up to a question of the first importance: What is sexual inversion? Is it, as many would have us believe, an abominable acquired vice, to be stamped out by the prison? or is it, as a few assert, a beneficial variety of human emotion which should be tolerated or even fostered? Is it a diseased condition which qualifies its subject for the lunatic asylum? or is it a natural monstrosity, a human "sport," the manifestations of which must be regulated when they become anti-social? There is probably an element of truth in more than one of these views. I am prepared

---

[1] [Ellis and Symonds's note] This apparently widespread opinion is represented by the remark of a young man in the last century (concerning the Lesbian friend of the woman he wishes to marry), quoted in the Comte de Tilly's *Souvenirs*: "J'avoue que c'est un genre de rivalité qui ne me donne aucune humeur; au contraire, cela m'amuse et j'ai l'immoralité d'en rire." [French: "I confess that this sort of rivalry gives me no ill humour; on the contrary, it amuses me, and I have the immorality to laugh about it."]

[2] [Ellis and Symonds's note] See H. Ellis, *Man and Woman*, chs. xiii and xv.

to admit that very widely divergent views of sexual inversion are largely justified by the position and attitude of the investigator. It is natural that the police official should find that his cases are largely mere examples of disgusting vice and crime. It is natural that the asylum superintendent should find that we are chiefly dealing with a form of insanity. It is equally natural that the sexual invert himself should find that he and his inverted friends are not so very unlike ordinary persons. We have to recognise the influence of professional and personal bias and the influence of environment, one investigator basing his conclusions on one class of cases, another on a quite different class of cases. Naturally, I have largely founded my own conclusions on my own cases. I believe, however, that my cases and my attitude towards them justify me in doing this with some confidence. I am not in the position of one who is pleading *pro domo*, nor of the police official, nor even of the physician, for these persons have not come to me for treatment. I approach the matter as a psychologist who has ascertained certain definite facts, and who is founding his conclusions on those facts.

The first point which impresses me is that we must regard sexual inversion as largely a congenital phenomenon, or, to speak more accurately, as a phenomenon which is based on congenital conditions. ... It must also be pointed out that the argument for acquired or suggested inversion logically involves the assertion that normal sexuality is also acquired or suggested. If a man becomes attracted to his own sex simply because the fact or the image of such attraction is brought before him, then we are bound to believe that a man becomes attracted to the opposite sex only because the fact or the image of such attraction is brought before him. This theory is wholly unworkable. In nearly every country of the world men associate with men, and women with women; if association and suggestion were the only influential causes, then inversion, instead of being the exception, ought to be the rule throughout the human species, if not, indeed, throughout the whole zoological series. ...

If, then, we must postulate a congenital abnormality in order to account satisfactorily for at least a large

proportion of sexual inverts, wherein does that abnormality consist? ...

We can probably grasp the nature of the abnormality better if we reflect on the development of the sexes and on the latent organic bi-sexuality in each sex. ... Putting the matter in a purely speculative shape, it may be said that at conception the organism is provided with about 50 per cent. of male germs and about 50 per cent. of female germs, and that as development proceeds either the male or the female germs assume the upper hand, killing out those of the other sex, until in a maturely developed individual only a few aborted germs of the opposite sex are left. In the homosexual person, however, and in the psychosexual hermaphrodite, we may imagine that the process has not proceeded normally, on account of some peculiarity in the number or character of either the original male germs or female germs, or both; the result being that we have a person who is organically twisted into a shape that is more fitted for the exercise of the inverted than of the normal sexual impulse, or else equally fitted to both.[1]

Thus in sexual inversion we have what may fairly be called a "sport" or variation, one of those organic aberrations which we see throughout living nature, in plants and in animals.[2] ...

---

[1] [Ellis and Symonds's note] I do not present this view as more than a picture which helps us to realise the actual phenomena which we witness in homosexuality[.] ...

[2] [Ellis and Symonds's note] The idea that sexual inversion is a variation, perhaps due to imperfect sexual differentiation, or reversion of type, was suggested in America by Kiernan (*Am. Lancet*, 1884, and *Med. Standard*, Nov.–Dec., 1888), and Lydston (*Phil. Med. and Surg. Reporter*, Sept., 1889, and *Addresses and Essays*, 1892). In this work (p. 246) he remarks: "Just as we may have variations of physical form and of mental attributes, in general, so we may have variations and perversions of that intangible entity, sexual affinity"; and (p. 46) he refers to failure of development and imperfect differentiation of generative centres, comparable to conditions like hypospadias and epispadias. In Germany a patient of Krafft-Ebing has worked out the same idea, connecting inversion with foetal bisexuality (8th ed. *Psych Sex.*, p. 227). Krafft-Ebing himself simply asserts that, whether congenital or acquired, there must be *Belastung*; inversion is a "degenerative phenomenon," a functional sign of degeneration (Krafft-Ebing, "Zur Erklärung der conträren Sexualempfindung," *Jahrbuch für Psychiatrie*, 1894).

from "Sex-Mania," *Reynolds's Newspaper* (21 April 1895)

> *Reynolds's Newspaper* frequently ran vehement editorials advocating social purity values; the week before this article appeared, the paper had condemned "The Notorious Mr. Wilde" in a front-page headline.

... What does all this perpetual discussion of sex mean? Wherefore this constant analysis of the passions? How does it come that the people today are filled with nothing but sex, sex, sex? Influenza is not the only new plague which has come to reside among us. Rather a more terrible plague has taken hold of the nation—sex mania.

Now what is this prevailing lunacy of sex, but a violent reaction from the Puritanical constraints and artificial up-bringing of both. ... To repress every manifestation of passion is the cardinal doctrine of English home training. The result is that the schools of both sexes have become hot-beds of vice, and the Universities—public women being excluded from the University towns—are the homes of unnatural offences. All this is reflected in our literature and in the social movements of the day. The "New Woman" is, to a certain extent, a development of sex-mania: the male decadent is the victim, and the rising population are being affected physically and mentally by symptoms of the same disease.

For, after all, this perpetual brooding on sex is as much a disease or form of madness, or hundreds of other tendencies for the manifestation of which we lock people in asylums. Any doctor will say as much. Pederasty, Sadism, Masochism, Fetischism, Androgyny, Gynandry,[1] are forms of pure madness, which drive the

sufferers to lunatic asylums, or to suicide[.] ... Already, indeed, and more specifically on the Continent, these abnormal tendencies are being treated by hypnotic suggestion. Dr. R. von Krafft-Ebing, the Professor of Psychiatry and Neurology in the University of Vienna, indeed, goes so far as to treat excessive devotion to religion as a form of sex-mania. He says: "For the most part, [such devotions] rest upon sexuality which manifests itself in a sexual impulse that is abnormally early and intense. The *libido* finds satisfaction in ... exaggerated religious enthusiasm[.] ..." And no one who knows anything of the practice of our criminal courts can be unaware that the defense of uncontrollable sex tendency, amounting to partial lunacy, is being more frequently put forward as a plea in answer to offenses of this character. If the truth were known Jack the Ripper was nothing but a sex maniac in the sense of the term which we have been using.

These alarming symptoms of national life are likely to spread with the increasing lunacy of the age and the ever-growing population who live on the labours of others. And to all there can be but one end. History teaches us that moral corruption has always been the forerunner of the downfall of nations. It was so in Greece, Rome, the Italian Republics, and France before the Revolution. There is no example to the contrary. So we may take it that the shocking depravity of the English idle classes at this moment is a symptom of our approaching dissolution. ...

The English classes have been justly accused of being the most hypocritical the world has known. Our society is honeycombed with corruption as a decaying cheese is with maggots[.] ... The Magistrates and the judges of criminal courts spend a large portion of public funds in hearing charges of sexual offences against state Church clergymen and old men. Scarcely indeed is the child out of arms, but we hear of some criminal assault attempted. Our streets are strewn with the bodies of new-born babies illicitly begotten. Luxury, more cruel than war, is descending from the patrician caste: its example is demoralizing all grades of Society. And in the face of this foul dream of lust, this Walpurg's Night of Corruption, the State's clergy, themselves connected by blood

---

[1] *Pederasty ... Gynandry* Terms used in Richard von Krafft-Ebing's *Psychopathia Sexualis* (1886, English translation 1892) to describe what he considers various sexual pathologies. He uses "pederasty" to refer to anal sex, and "androgyny" and "gynandry" to refer to people whose appearance and behavior are the opposite of that usually associated with their genitals.

with the criminals, are dumb![1]

We have already referred to the morals of the aristocracy. For a body so limited in numbers, the amount and the gravity of their offences against public and private morals are astounding. By what is revealed we may guess what is concealed. Every effort is made to hush up aristocratic scandals. Numerous offences of this character are the subject of private conversation, although they never find their way into the public courts or the newspapers. …

Yet what shall we say to a woman like Lady Henry Somerset, screaming in an American magazine, the *Arena*, against what she calls "compulsory motherhood"?[2] Where does the compulsion come in? Women are not forced to marry in these days nor are they bound, except in the way of business, to speak to men. … We are not overburdened with admiration for former times, but certainly the Englishwoman of the last and preceding centuries seem to have been a brighter influence, and to have induced a more healthy feeling in the community among whom they moved. It is not necessary that woman should confine herself to making jam; but if there was a little more of that kind of domestic industry, not only would it add immeasurably to the comfort and convenience of our homes, but it would provide a useful occupation for persons like Lady Somerset[.] …

———

[1] *Walpurg's Night* Night on which, according to German folklore, witches hold a debauched celebration; *dumb* Silent.

[2] *Lady Henry … motherhood* Reference to "The Welcome Child," an essay by women's rights activist Lady Isabella Somerset. This essay does not include the phrase "compulsory motherhood," but a piece on her article in *The Review of Reviews* attributes to her the view that "'if voluntary motherhood is the crown of the race, involuntary compulsory motherhood is the very opposite.'" Somerset's name was associated with a public scandal surrounding her separation from her husband, who was gay.

Prostitution, Social Purity, and the Contagious Diseases Acts

Thomas Hood, "The Bridge of Sighs" (1844)

One of the most popular pieces by the widely read poet Thomas Hood (1799–1845), "The Bridge of Sighs" sensationally mourns the death of a prostitute whose only means of escape from a life of sin—and the abject suffering it engenders—is suicide. The poem proved to be inspirational subject matter for artists, and the image of a fallen woman contemplating or having carried out suicide by drowning appeared in a variety of paintings and illustrations in the following decades.

"DROWNED! DROWNED!"[3]—HAMLET

O   ne more Unfortunate,
      Weary of breath,
Rashly importunate,[4]
Gone to her death!

5   Take her up tenderly,
     Lift her with care;
     Fashioned so slenderly,
     Young, and so fair!

     Look at her garments
10   Clinging like cerements;[5]
     Whilst the wave constantly
     Drips from her clothing;
     Take her up instantly,
     Loving, not loathing.

15   Touch her not scornfully;
     Think of her mournfully,
     Gently and humanly;

———

[3] *DROWNED! DROWNED!* From Shakespeare's *Hamlet* 4.7.183; the Queen's line upon learning that Ophelia, mad with grief, has drowned.

[4] *importunate* Here, acting at the wrong time.

[5] *cerements* Cloths used to wrap a body for burial.

Not of the stains of her,
All that remains of her
20   Now is pure womanly.

Make no deep scrutiny
Into her mutiny
Rash and undutiful:
Past all dishonour,
25   Death has left on her
Only the beautiful.

Still, for all slips of hers,
One of Eve's family—
Wipe those poor lips of hers
30   Oozing so clammily.

Loop up her tresses
Escaped from the comb,
Her fair auburn tresses;
Whilst wonderment guesses
35   Where was her home?

Who was her father?
Who was her mother?
Had she a sister?
Had she a brother?
40   Or was there a dearer one
Still, and a nearer one
Yet, than all other?

Alas! for the rarity
Of Christian charity
45   Under the sun!
Oh! it was pitiful!
Near a whole city full,
Home she had none.

Sisterly, brotherly,
50   Fatherly, motherly
Feelings had changed:
Love, by harsh evidence,
Thrown from its eminence;
Even God's providence
55   Seeming estranged.

Where the lamps quiver
So far in the river,
With many a light
From window and casement,
60   From garret to basement,
She stood, with amazement,
Houseless by night.

The bleak wind of March
Made her tremble and shiver;
65   But not the dark arch,
Or the black flowing river:
Mad from life's history,
Glad to death's mystery,
Swift to be hurled—
70   Anywhere, anywhere
Out of the world!

In she plunged boldly
No matter how coldly
The rough river ran—
75   Over the brink of it,
Picture it—think of it,
Dissolute Man!
Lave° in it, drink of it,   *wash*
Then, if you can!

80   Take her up tenderly,
Lift her with care;
Fashioned so slenderly,
Young, and so fair!

Ere her limbs frigidly
85   Stiffen too rigidly,
Decently—kindly—
Smooth and compose them;
And her eyes, close them,
Staring so blindly!

90   Dreadfully staring
Through muddy impurity,
As when with the daring
Last look of despairing
Fixed on futurity.

95   Perishing gloomily,
      Spurred by contumely,°   *scornful abuse*
      Cold inhumanity,
      Burning insanity,
      Into her rest.
100   Cross her hands humbly
      As if praying dumbly,
      Over her breast!

      Owning her weakness,
      Her evil behaviour,
105   And leaving, with meekness,
      Her sins to her Saviour!

from Henry Mayhew, "Labour and the Poor: The Metropolitan Districts," *The Morning Chronicle* (1849)

In the 1840s, the reporter Henry Mayhew (1812–87) undertook an extensive project interviewing impoverished Londoners and recounting his findings in the newspaper *The Morning Chronicle*; the resulting articles later appeared in Mayhew's collection *London Labour and the London Poor* (1851). The following selection is from the stories Mayhew recorded of London needlewomen; women in this profession often chose or were forced into prostitution as an escape from the meager payment, long work hours, and cruel treatment from employers they received in the clothing industry.

… "I make moleskin[1] trousers. I get 7*d*. and 8*d*.[2] per pair. I can do two pairs in a day, and twelve, when there is full employment, in a week. But some weeks I have no work at all. I work from six in the morning to ten at night; that is what I call my day's work. When I am fully employed I get from 7*s*. to 8*s*.[3] a week. My ex-penses out of that for twist,[4] thread, and candles are about 1*s*. 6*d*. a week, leaving me about 6*s*. a week clear. But there's coals to pay for out of this, and that's at the least 6*d*. or more; so 5*s*. 6*d*. is the very outside of what I earn when I'm in full work. Lately I have been dreadfully slack; so we are every winter, all of us "sloppers,"[5] and that's the time when we wants the most money. The week before last I had but two pair to make all the week, so that I only earnt 1*s*. clear. For this last month I'm sure I haven't done any more than that each week. Taking one week with another, all the year round, I don't make above 3*s*. clear money each week. I don't work at any other kind of slop work. The trousers work is held to be the best paid of all. I give 1*s*. a week rent.

"My father died when I was five years of age. My mother is a widow, upwards of 66 years of age, and seldom has a day's work. Generally once in the week she is employed pot-scouring—that is, cleaning publicans' pots.[6] She is paid 4*d*. a dozen for that, and does about four dozen and a half, so that she gets about 1*s*. 6*d*. in the day by it. For the rest she is dependent upon me. I am 20 years of age the 25th of this month. We earn together, to keep the two of us, from 4*s*. 6*d*. to 5*s*. each week. Out of this we have to pay 1*s*. rent, and there remains 3*s*. 6*d*. to 4*s*. to find us both in food and clothing. It is of course impossible for us to live upon it, and the consequence is I am obligated to go in a bad way.

"I have been three years working at slop work. I was virtuous when I first went to work, and I remained so till this last twelvemonth. I struggled very hard to keep myself chaste, but I found that I couldn't get food and clothing for myself and mother, so I took to live with a young man. He is turned 20. He is a tinman. He did promise to marry me, but his sister made mischief between me and him, so that parted us. I have not seen him now for about six months, and I can't say whether

---

[1] *moleskin*   Heavy cotton fabric, once commonly used to make trousers.

[2] *7d. and 8d.*   Seven and eight pence. There are twelve pence in a shilling, and twenty shillings in a pound.

[3] *7s. to 8s.*   Seven to eight shillings.

[4] *twist*   Strong thread made of multiple strands twisted together.

[5] *sloppers*   Slop workers, producers of cheap, low-quality clothing.

[6] *publicans' pots*   Pewter drinking vessels used by the working-class customers of pubs.

he will keep his promise or not. I am now pregnant by him, and expect to be confined[1] in two months' time. He knows of my situation, and so does my mother. My mother believed me to be married to him. She knows otherwise now. I was very fond of him, and had known him for two years before he seduced me. He could make 14s. a week. He told me if I came to live with him he'd take care I shouldn't want, and both mother and me had been very bad off before. He said, too, he'd make me his lawful wife, but I hardly cared so long as I could get food for myself and mother.

"Many young girls at the shop advised me to go wrong. They told me how comfortable they was off; they said they could get plenty to eat and drink, and good clothes. There isn't one young girl as can get her living by slop work. The masters all know this, but they wouldn't own to it, of course. It stands to reason that no one can live and pay rent, and find clothes, upon 3s. a week, which is the most they make clear, even the best hands, at the moleskin and cord trousers[2] work. There's poor people moved out of our house that was making ¾d. shirts. I am satisfied there is not one young girl that works at slop work that is virtuous, and there are some thousands in the trade. They may do very well if they have got mothers and fathers to find them a home and food, and to let them have what they earn for clothes; then they may be virtuous, but not without. I've heard of numbers who have gone from slop work to the streets altogether for a living, and I shall be obliged to do the same thing myself unless something better turns up for me.

"If I was never allowed to speak no more, it was the little money I got by my labour that led me to go wrong. Could I have honestly earnt enough to have subsisted upon, to find me in proper food and clothing, such as is necessary, I should not have gone astray; no, never—As it was I fought against it as long as I could—that I did—to the last. I hope to be able to get a ticket for a midwife;[3] a party has promised me as much, and, he says, if possible, he'll get me an order for a box of linen. My child will only increase my burdens, and if my young man won't support my child I must go on the streets altogether. I know how horrible all this is. It would have been much better for me to have subsisted upon a dry crust and water rather than be as I am now. But no one knows the temptations of us poor girls in want. Gentlefolks can never understand it. If I had been born a lady it wouldn't have been very hard to have acted like one. To be poor and to be honest, especially with young girls, is the hardest struggle of all. There isn't one in a thousand that can get the better of it. I am ready to say again, that it was want, and nothing more, that made me transgress. If I had been better paid I should have done better. Young as I am, my life is a curse to me. If the Almighty would please to take me before my child is born, I should die happy."

from W.R. Greg, "Prostitution," *Westminster Review* (January 1850)

This review of mid-nineteenth-century research on prostitution, by essayist William Rathbone Greg (1809–81), expresses views that were commonly held on the subject during the period.

… [W]e feel called upon to protest against the manner in which prostitutes are almost universally regarded, spoken of, and treated in this country, as dishonouring alike to our religion and our manhood. This iniquity pervades all classes, and both sexes. No language is too savage for these wretched women. They are outcasts, Pariahs, lepers. Their touch, even in the extremity of suffering, is shaken off as if it were pollution and disease. It is discreditable to a woman even to be supposed to know of their existence. They are kicked, cuffed, trampled on with impunity by everyone. Their oaths are seldom regarded in a court of justice, scarcely

---

[1] *confined*   Engaged in childbirth, or in a period of rest undertaken before or after the birth.

[2] *cord trousers*   Trousers made of corduroy.

[3] *ticket for a midwife*   I.e., document issued by a charity that has paid for the recipient to receive a midwife's services.

ever in a police court. They seem to be considered far more out of the pale[1] of the humanity than negroes on a slave plantation. …

The world—the unknowing world—is apt to fancy[2] [a prostitute] revelling in the *enjoyment* of licentious pleasures; lost and dead to all sense of remorse and shame; wallowing in mire because she loves it. Alas! there is no truth in *this* conception, or only in the most exceptional cases. Passing over all the agonies of grief and terror she must have endured before she reached her present degradation; the vain struggles to retrieve the first false, fatal step; the feeling of her inevitable future pressing her down with all the hopeless weight of destiny; the dreams of a happy past that haunt her in the night-watches, and keep her ever trembling on the verge of madness—passing over all this, what is her position when she has reached the last step of her downward progress, and has become a common prostitute? Every calamity that can afflict human nature seems to have gathered round her—cold, hunger, disease, often absolute starvation. Insufficiently fed, insufficiently clad, she is driven out alike by necessity and by the dread of solitude, to wander through the streets by night, for the chance of earning a meal by the most loathsome labour that imagination can picture, or a penal justice could inflict. For, be it remembered, desire has, by this time, long ceased; the mere momentary excitement of sexual indulgence is no longer attainable; repetition has changed pleasure into absolute repugnance; and these miserable women ply their wretched trade with a loathing and abhorrence which only perpetual semi-intoxication can deaden or endure. The curses, the blows, the nameless brutalities they have to submit to from their ruffianly associates of the brothel and saloon, are as nothing to the hideous punishment inherent in the daily practice of their sin. Their evidence, and the evidence of all who have come in contact with them is unanimous on this point—that gin alone enables them to live or act; that

without its constant stimulus and stupefaction, they would long since have died from mere physical exhaustion, or gone mad from mental horrors. …

The career of these women is a brief one; their downward path a marked and inevitable one; and they know this well. They are almost never rescued; escape themselves they cannot. *Vestigia nulla retrorsum*.[3] The swindler may repent, the drunkard may reform; society aids and encourages them in their thorny path of repentance and atonement, and welcomes back with joy and generous forgetfulness the lost sheep and the prodigal son.[4] But the prostitute may *not* pause—*may* NOT *recover*: at the very first halting, timid step she may make to the right or to the left, with a view to flight from her appalling doom, the whole resistless influences of the surrounding world, the good as well as bad, close around her to hunt her back into perdition.

Then comes the last sad scene of all, when drink, disease, and starvation have laid her on her death-bed. On a wretched pallet in a filthy garret, with no companions but the ruffians, drunkards, and harlots with whom she had cast in her lot; amid brutal curses, ribald language, and drunken laughter; with a past—which, even were there no future, would be dreadful to contemplate—laying its weight of despair upon her soul; with a prospective[5] beyond the grave which the little she retains of her early religion lights up for her with the lurid light of hell—this poor daughter of humanity terminates a life, of which, if the sin has been grievous and the weakness lamentable, the expiation[6] has been fearfully tremendous.

---

[1] *pale* Boundary.

[2] *fancy* Imagine.

[3] *Vestigia nulla retrorsum* Latin: No steps backward.

[4] *the lost … prodigal son* Refers to two biblical parables. In the former, a shepherd leaves his flock to recover a single lost sheep; in the latter, a father celebrates the return home of a son who has repented after squandering his inheritance.

[5] *prospective* Expectation of the future.

[6] *expiation* Penalty.

THE GREAT SOCIAL EVIL.

TIME :—Midnight. A Sketch not a Hundred Miles from the Haymarket.

Bella. "AH ! FANNY ! HOW LONG HAVE YOU BEEN *GAY* ?"

This cartoon by John Leech appeared in the 10 January 1857 edition of *Punch.* "The Great Social Evil" was a term frequently used to refer to prostitution. The phrase "not a hundred miles from the Haymarket" is here used ironically; the Haymarket area in London was itself notorious for vice of all sorts: in *Household Words* in September 1857, Albert Smith described the area at night as "absolutely hideous, with its sparring snobs, and flashing satins, and sporting gents, and painted cheeks, and brandy-sparkling eyes, and bad tobacco, and hoarse horse-laughs, and loud indecency." The word "gay" was, in the nineteenth century, a euphemism for "engaged in prostitution."

from The Contagious Diseases Act (1866)

PERIODICAL MEDICAL EXAMINATIONS

15. Where an information on oath is laid before a justice by a superintendent of police, charging to the effect that the informant has good cause to believe that a woman therein named is a common prostitute, and either is resident within the limits of any place to which this Act applies,[1] or, being resident within five miles of those limits, has, within fourteen days before the laying of the information, been within those limits for the purpose of prostitution, the justice may, if he thinks fit, issue a notice thereof addressed to such a woman, which notice the superintendent of police shall cause to be served on her. ...

16. ... The justice present, on oath being made before him substantiating the matter of the information to his satisfaction, may, if he thinks fit, order that the woman be subject to a periodical medical examination by the visiting surgeon for any period not exceeding one year, for the purpose of ascertaining at the time of each such examination whether she is affected with a contagious disease; and thereupon she shall be subject to such a periodical medical examination, and the order shall be a sufficient warrant for the visiting surgeon to conduct such examination accordingly. ...

DETENTION IN HOSPITAL

20. If on any such examination the woman examined is found to be affected with a contagious disease, she shall thereupon be liable to be detained in a certified hospital, subject and according to the provisions of this Act. ...

21. Any woman to whom any such certificate of the visiting surgeon relates may, if she thinks fit, proceed to the certified hospital named in that certificate, and place herself there for medical treatment, but if after the certificate is delivered to her she neglects or refuses to do so, the superintendent of police or a constable acting under his orders, shall apprehend her, and convey her with all practicable speed to that hospital, and place her there for medical treatment, and the certificate of the visiting surgeon shall be a sufficient authority to him for so doing. ...

22. Where a woman certified by the visiting surgeon to be affected with a contagious disease, places herself, or is placed as aforesaid, in a certified hospital for medical treatment, she shall be detained there for that purpose by the chief medical officer of the hospital until discharged by him by writing under his hand. ...

24. Provided always, that any woman shall not be detained under any one certificate for a longer time than three months, unless the chief medical officer of the hospital in which she is detained, and the inspector of certified hospitals, or the visiting surgeon for the place whence she came, or was brought, conjointly certify that her further detention for medical treatment is requisite (which certificate shall be in duplicate, and one of the originals thereof shall be delivered to the woman); and in that case she may be further detained in the hospital in which she is, at the expiration of the said period of three months, by the chief medical officer, until discharged by him by writing under his hand; but so that any woman be not detained under any one certificate for a longer time in the whole than six months.[2] ...

26. Every woman conveyed or transferred under this Act to a certified hospital shall, while being so conveyed or transferred thither, and also while detained there, be deemed to be legally in the custody of the person conveying, transferring, or detaining her. ...

REFUSAL TO BE EXAMINED, &C.

28. In the following cases, namely—

If any woman subjected by order of a justice under this Act to periodical medical examination at any time

---

[1] *any place ... Act applies* The stated purpose of the Act was to protect the health of soldiers and sailors; the Act was therefore limited to specific port towns and towns with army bases. The 1869 Act extended this coverage to several more towns, including Southampton, which did not have a military base.

[2] *six months* This maximum was increased to nine months by the Contagious Diseases Act of 1869.

peremptorily[1] absents herself in order to avoid submitting herself to such examination on any occasion on which she ought so to submit herself, or refuses or wilfully neglects to submit herself to such examination on any such occasion;

If any woman authorized by this Act to be detained in a certified hospital for medical treatment quits the hospital without being discharged therefrom by the chief medical officer thereof by writing under his hand (the proof whereof shall lie on the accused);

If any woman authorized by this Act to be detained in a certified hospital for medical treatment, or any woman being in a certified hospital under medical treatment for a contagious disease, refuses or wilfully neglects while in the hospital to conform to the regulations thereof approved under this Act;

Then and in every such case such woman shall be guilty of an offence against this Act, and on summary conviction[2] shall be liable to imprisonment, with or without hard labour, in the case of a first offence for any term not exceeding one month, and in the case of a second or any subsequent offence for any term not exceeding three months; and in the case of the offence of quitting the hospital without being discharged as aforesaid the woman may be taken into custody without warrant by any constable.

from Harriet Martineau, "The Contagious Diseases Acts—II," *Daily News* (29 December 1869)

Journalist and social theorist Harriet Martineau (1802–76) was one of many influential members of the Ladies' National Association for the Repeal of the Contagious Diseases Acts. The following is part of a series of letters she published in the *Daily News* as part of the repeal campaign.

TO THE EDITORS OF THE DAILY NEWS

SIR, It is natural that the first shock given by these Acts to the women of England, and indeed to every good citizen, should be in the fact that legal safeguards of vital importance to their security and freedom have been set aside, and liabilities[3] of the most fearful kind have been introduced, without any adequate warrant, without due warning, and actually without the knowledge of the people, or of any class among them; and even without any consciousness on the part of Parliament itself. Up to the date of the passage of these Bills every woman in the country had the same rights as men over her own person; and the law extended its protection over all alike—of both sexes, and altogether without regard to any question of character, manners, and calling. Prostitutes were as other women, and as men, in their claims upon the law. Now it is so no longer. Any woman of whom a policeman swears that he has reason to believe that she is a prostitute is helpless in the hands of the administrators of the new law. She is subject to the extremity of outrage under the eyes, hands, and instruments of surgeons, for the protection of the sex which is the cause of the sin, which is to be protected in further indulgence in it, and which is passed over by the law, while the victim is punished. If a tithe[4] of the stories were told which might be truly told of innocent women who have confessed, under the torture of the new peril, sin which they never dreamed of, or of real sinners so unable to endure what is now imposed upon them as to faint or to go mad, the people of the country would be heartbroken. Meanwhile, the men who have contrived this curse for their country and nation are always ready with their assurances that that sort of women get used to the new treatment. It is sad work at first, but they get used to it, and in time they leave off caring for anything. No doubt it will be new to many readers that the chance of retrieval[5] has lately been cut

---

[1] *peremptorily* I.e., without providing valid reasons for refusing examination.

[2] *summary conviction* Conviction given by a judge of a lower court without trial by jury. Minor offenses were typically tried in this way.

[3] *liabilities* Here, legal punishments.

[4] *tithe* Tenth.

[5] *of retrieval* I.e., of reforming prostitutes.

off in this way from that class of women wherever the new Acts operate; it will be new to them that the legal position of women has been deprived of its most essential security. But the incredible part of the case will be that this has been effected in the dark and in silence. The press has not fulfilled its function and its trust in regard to the more recent Act.[1] In Parliament no warning voice was raised. The most sacred liberties of half the people of England are gone, without being missed; and now it is the women, for the most part, who have to insist on their restoration. No one can wonder that when my countrywomen become conscious of their loss, and find on every hand that most men know nothing about it, that many care nothing about it, and that there are professional men who say that honest women ought to be thankful for the institution of a test of their innocence, under the chance of false accusation—no one can wonder if, in such a posture of affairs, the first protest of honourable women should be against privation of sacred rights, wrought under cover of that ignorance of the country, and that negligence of the press and of Parliament, which have imposed upon women the painful task of agitation for the recovery of what they have lost, and the vindication of what remains.

Again, it is a new and menacing fact that, in a country where civil liberty is professed, and for the most part enjoyed, penal consequences are imposed on an assumed offence which is not defined.[2] A woman, chaste or unchaste, is charged by a policeman, rightly or wrongly, with being a prostitute. The law makes no distinctions of degrees or kinds, provides the accused with no means of trial or defence, but subjects her to legal violation. If she refuses submission, she is liable to imprisonment with hard labour for terms according to her persistence in refusal. If she had sense and courage to ask for a precise legal definition of her imputed offence, she would not get it. The loose description which stands in the Act, and is the substance of the policeman's charge, is the ground on which she, and she alone, is subject to judgment and punishment—to moral torture if unresisting, to imprisonment with hard labour—for life if she holds by her personal rights. This is contrary to all precedent, and to the whole spirit and method of British penal law.

And why is this innovation ventured upon? For whose sake are such encroachments on personal liberties perpetrated? Here, again, we see why it is that the Matronage[3] of England is moved to avowal and action which it would have supposed impossible till these new perils became manifest.

The mothers of sons do not desire that the ways of vice should be made easy and safe to men; and further, they do not desire that the victims of the vice of men should bear the whole penalty of their common license.[4] The extension of the recent Act to the whole civil population[5] would cover with the protection of the law the brothel, *as* brothel, as expressly as the school or the church. Prostitutes, observing the provisions of the Act, are pursuing their trade under the sanction of Parliament. Young men, entering the world, find this kind of vice recognized as necessary by Parliament, the police, the magistracy, and the law; and with this discovery a host of scruples and shames and difficulties vanish. What is felt by mothers who find law and Government enlisted on the side of animal passion, and against the old institutions of Marriage and the Home, may be conceived. To such mothers it is almost worse that the sex most guilty in regard to the sin should be protected from the natural retribution by the sacrifice of the victimized sex. The law lays hold of the woman for the

---

[1] *the more recent Act*   The Contagious Diseases Act of 1869, the third and final Act, which expanded the areas of the program's operation and extended the length of time for which women could be held.

[2] *not defined*   The Acts applied to anyone police had "good cause" to believe was "a common prostitute"; the Acts themselves did not provide explicit definitions of "common prostitute" or of what constituted "good cause" to believe a woman was one.

[3] *Matronage*   Married women.

[4] *common license*   Shared immorality.

[5] *The extension … civil population*   The Acts were for the most part limited to towns with nearby military bases; the Association for the Extension of the Contagious Diseases Acts was campaigning for the Acts to be applied to the whole country.

purpose of preventing her injuring the man. It nowhere proposes to protect the woman from precisely the same injury by the man. Many thousands of girls, as innocent as any of their countrymen, have been courted down in the rural districts by a soldier, idling away his days, or a commercial traveller, appearing periodically, or a lawyer going the circuit,[1] or some other heartless vagabond. Each of those many thousands has probably believed herself the favourite of Fortune—destined to marry a great man in the great town—London or other. After an agonizing decline and a heartbreaking struggle, she finds herself an outcast in the streets of the great town— doomed to a fearful fate, from the earliest days of the existence of her calling: but now—What is it now under this new legislation? The mothers of sons, sinning sons as well as pure, shrink from any sort of countenance[2] of a law which, on the one hand, proposes to render vice safe from its worst penalty, and, on the other, compels the wronged and deluded victim of man's guile and selfishness and grossness to bear the penal consequences, while all is arranged for the escape of the stronger and grosser sinner. The Matronage of England protest, as some of them are showing at this moment, against the selfishness and cowardness of men—whether sons or strangers—being made a shield against the retribution they have risked, and against the powerful influence of men—in army or navy, parliament, hospital, or Council board—being brought to bear upon ruined women in their weakness, to place them where they may intercept the visitations of disease, and be made to endure sufferings inconceivable or incredible[3] by men, in order to enable men to indulge in license with the least risk of incurring any suffering at all. This is a part which the mothers of England do not desire that their sons should enact, and therefore they rouse their courage to denounce the law which so arranges the role of both sexes in regard to their common sin. ...

---

[1] *going the circuit* Working in a circuit court, which toured an assigned district to hold trials in communities outside London.

[2] *countenance* Acceptance.

[3] *incredible* Not believable.

from Josephine Butler, *Personal Reminiscences of a Great Crusade* (1896)

A prolific writer and speaker and a passionate Christian feminist reformer, Josephine Butler (1828–1906) was the public face of the Ladies' National Association for the Repeal of the Contagious Diseases Acts. In the following passage from her autobiography, she describes public response to the association's activism.

In the autumn of 1872 an opportunity ... arose, through an election at Pontefract,[4] of reminding the government once more that the claims of the Abolitionists[5] could not safely be ignored. The Right Hon. H. Childers[6] was obliged, by certain changes in the Ministry, to seek re-election. He had been first Lord of the Admiralty,[7] and in that office it had fallen to his lot to administer the obnoxious regulations in connection with our Naval Stations.[8] Several orders had been issued from the Admiralty during his term of office concerning the administration of the system at Plymouth and Portsmouth—orders which had shocked the moral sense of many persons who had not previously been able to see clearly through the conventional wording of the Law itself the iniquity of the principles on which it was based. ...

On the first day of his canvass,[9] Mr. Childers having engaged the Town Hall at Knottingley[10] to address the electors there at nine o'clock on the evening of the 13th August, the Abolitionists, wishing to have the first word, secured the same Hall for seven o'clock, agreeing to

---

[4] *Pontefract* Constituency in Yorkshire, in northern England.

[5] *Abolitionists* I.e., opponents of the Contagious Diseases Acts.

[6] *Right Hon. H. Childers* Hugh Childers (1827–96). He was a Member of Parliament for Pontefract from 1860 to 1885 and occupied several influential government positions.

[7] *first Lord of the Admiralty* Civilian president of the Board of Admiralty, which commanded the British Navy.

[8] *obnoxious regulations ... Naval Stations* The Contagious Diseases Acts applied almost exclusively to towns near army and navy bases.

[9] *canvass* Effort to gain political support.

[10] *Knottingley* Town in the Pontefract constituency.

move out in time to leave the building clear for their opponents. The Mr. Childers' party attempted to checkmate them by announcing that he would address the electors at a much earlier hour, and from the windows of the Buck Inn instead of the Town Hall. This enabled us to be present, and to hear what Mr. Childers had to say. He made the customary excuses concerning the delicacy of the subject, and asked those who desired it to be dropped to hold up their hands. Mr. H.J. Wilson[1] here enquired whether he, as a non-elector (for Pontefract), might ask a question, and the reply from the window was, "No! you are not an elector, you are not wanted." Groans followed this answer, and a hubbub ensued. Mr. Wilson would have been roughly handled had not a body of working men placed themselves on each side of him, saying "Stand still; don't move an inch; you shall be heard; ask your questions; we want to hear the answers." During this time Mr. Childers' chairman, carried away with passion, was trying to reach Mr. Wilson's head in order to castigate him with his umbrella. The crowd swayed backwards and forwards, and Mr. Wilson stood firm, with a smile upon his face. Some questions were asked from the crowd, and not at all satisfactorily answered by Mr. Childers.

Suddenly a voice shouted, "To the Town Hall!" (for our meeting). The cry was taken up, and the crowd started in that direction. With some other ladies I had been watching the scene from a window, when several gentlemen came up to us, and proposed to escort us to the Town Hall by way of a quiet back street. Thereupon some of the working men cried out, "No; never go down a back way. Come along through the middle of the crowd, and before their windows; we will protect you." Our progress to the Town Hall was thus converted in to a sort of triumphal procession, Mr. Wilson walking first, with the Blue Book of the Royal Commis-

sion[2] under his arm, attended by Mr. Edmondson[3] and others, and loudly cheered by the crowd of men and women in whose midst they moved; while Mr. Childers and his friends looked with perplexed faces from the windows of the Buck Inn upon their retreating audience, which had gone wholly over to the opposition. It was not an encouraging scene for a Parliamentary candidate.

One of Mr. Childers' friends had, however, hurried to the Town Hall, and, reaching the platform before we arrived, offered himself as chairman. Mr. Wilson proposed another chairman, and a new disturbance arose, which lasted for about half an hour. Eventually, however, Mr. Wilson and others were heard with much attention and applause.

Mr. Childers' party retorted by attacking and dispersing a meeting of women the following day. We had arranged to hold this meeting of women in the afternoon, when Mr. Childers was again to address a large concourse from the window of a house. We had decided to hold our meeting at the same hour, thinking we should be unmolested.[4] We had been obliged to go all over the town before we found anyone bold enough to grant us a place to meet in. At last we found a large hay-loft over an empty room on the outskirts of the town. We could only ascend to it by means of a kind of ladder, leading through a trap-door in the floor. However, the place was large enough to hold a good meeting, and was soon filled. Mr. Stuart[5] had run on in advance and paid for the room in his own name, and had again looked in to see that all was right. He found the floor strewn with cayenne pepper in order to make it impossible for us to speak, and there were some bundles of

---

[1] *Mr. H.J. Wilson* Henry Joseph Wilson (1833–1914), a radical Liberal politician who played a major organizational role in the movement against the Contagious Diseases Acts.

[2] *Blue Book … Commission* I.e., the Royal Commission's report on the Contagious Diseases Acts. Royal Commission "Blue Books" were in-depth government studies of social issues.

[3] *Mr. Edmondson* Joseph Edmondson (1831–1908), a Quaker minister heavily involved in the campaign against the Contagious Diseases Acts.

[4] *unmolested* Not bothered.

[5] *Mr. Stuart* James Stuart (1843–1913), a politician who supported women's causes.

straw in the empty room below. He got a poor woman to help him, and with buckets of water they managed to drench the floor and sweep together the cayenne pepper. Still, when we arrived, it was very unpleasant for eyes and throat. We began our meeting with prayer, and the women were listening to our words with increasing determination never to forsake the good cause, when a smell of burning was perceived, smoke began to curl up through the floor, and a threatening noise was heard below at the door. The bundles of straw beneath had been set on fire, and the smoke much annoyed us. Then, to our horror, looking down the room to the trap-door entrance, we saw appearing head after head of men with countenances[1] full of fury; man after man came in, until they crowded the place. There was no possible exit for us, the windows being too high above the ground, and we women were gathered into one end of the room like a flock of sheep surrounded by wolves. Few of these men, we learned, were Yorkshire people; they were led on by two persons whose *dress* was that of gentlemen.

It is difficult to describe in words what followed. It was a time which required strong faith and calm courage. Mrs. Wilson[2] and I stood in front of the company of women, side by side. She whispered in my ear, "Now is the time to trust in God; do not let us fear"; and a comforting sense of the Divine presence came to us both. It was not personal violence that we feared so much as the mental pain inflicted by the rage, profanity, and obscenity of the men, of their words and their threats. Their language was hideous. They shook their fists in our faces, with volleys of oaths. This continued for some time, and we had no defence or means of escape. Their chief rage was directed against Mrs. Wilson and me. We understood by their language that certain among them had a personal and vested interest in the evil thing we were opposing.[3] It was clear that

they understood that "their craft was in danger."[4] The new teaching and revolt of women had stirred up the very depths of hell. We said nothing, for our voices could not have been heard. We simply stood shoulder to shoulder—Mrs. Wilson and I—and waited and endured; and it seemed all the time as if some strong angel were present; for when these men's hands were literally upon us, they were held back by an unseen power. There was among our audience a young Yorkshire woman, strong and stalwart, with bare muscular arms, and a shawl over her head. She dashed forward, fought her way through the crowd of men, and, running as fast as she could, she found Mr. Stuart on the outskirts of Mr. Childers' meeting, and cried to him, "Come! Run! They are killing the ladies." He did run, and came up the ladder stairs into the midst of the crowd. As soon, however, as they perceived he was our defender, they turned upon him. A strong man seized him in his arms; another opened the window; and they were apparently about to throw him headlong out. Some of us ran forward between him and the window, thus just giving him time to slip from between the man's arms to the floor, and glide away to the side where we were. He then asked to be allowed to say a few words to them, and, with good temper and coolness, he argued that he had taken[5] the room, that it was his, and if they would kindly let the ladies go he would hear what they had to say. A fierce argument ensued. Meanwhile stones were thrown into the window, and broken glass flew across the room. While all this was going on (it seemed to us like hours of horrible endurance), hope came at last, in the shape of two or three helmeted policemen, whose heads appeared one by one through the trap-door. "Now," we thought, "we are safe!" *But no!* These were Metropolitans[6] who had come from London for the

---

[1] *countenances* Facial expressions.

[2] *Mrs. Wilson* Charlotte Wilson (1833–1921), who participated in reform movements, including the campaign against the Contagious Diseases Acts. She was married to Henry J. Wilson.

[3] *certain among ... were opposing* I.e., they were pimps.

---

[4] *their craft was in danger* Reference to Acts 19, in which the manufacturers of idols are afraid of losing their profits due to the spread of belief in Christ. They form an angry mob and trap a group of Jews in a theater.

[5] *taken* Here, rented.

[6] *Metropolitans* Members of the Metropolitan Police Service, Greater London's police force.

occasion of the election; they simply looked at the scene with a cynical smile, and left the place without an attempt to defend us. My heart grew sick as I saw them disappear. Our case seemed now to become desperate. Mrs. Wilson and I whispered to each other in the midst of the din, "Let us ask God to help us, and then make a rush for the entrance." Two or three working women placed themselves in front of us, and we pushed our way, I scarcely know how, to the stairs. It was only myself and one or two other ladies that the men really cared to insult and terrify, so if we could get away we felt sure the rest would be safe. I made a dash forward, and took one leap from the trap-door to the ground-floor below. Being light, I came down safely. I found Mrs. Wilson with me very soon in the street. Once in the open street, these cowards did not dare to offer us violence. We went straight to our own hotel, and there we had a magnificent women's meeting. Such a revulsion of feeling came over the inhabitants of Pontefract when they heard of this disgraceful scene that they flocked to hear us, many of the women weeping. We were advised to turn the lights low, and close the windows, on account of the mob; but the hotel was literally crowded with women, and we scarcely needed to speak; events had spoken for us, and all honest hearts were won.

from Josephine Butler, *Some Thoughts on the Present Aspect of the Crusade Against the State Regulation of Vice* (1874)

In the following excerpt from one of her pamphlets opposing the Contagious Diseases Acts, Josephine Butler connects the campaign with Christianity, with opposition to the sexual double standard, and with feminist social justice in general.

... [T]he pure and refined among women, it is asserted, ought never even to know of, much less to come in contact with, the social evils in our midst, even with a view to oppose and overcome them, or to leave their own "sphere" in order to save women who are "not worth saving." The practical heathenism of this judgment can only be seen in its true colours by setting it side by side with the example and character of Christ. Did he refuse the grace and purity of his presence to the darkest abodes of earth? Were any beings in human shape not worth saving in his estimation?

It is clear that no perceptible impression can be made on the institution of harlotry, as represented by the female slave population of our cities who are devoted to a life of shame, until the stronghold—the accepted base standard in regard to male purity—is assailed and overthrown. Men have imposed on women a stricter rule in morality than they have imposed on themselves, or are willing themselves to obey. This may be to some extent the secret of the unwillingness of many men to see women laying siege in earnest to the great instituted iniquity; they fear lest a discovery of practice as well as theory, too lax to be defended by the least thoughtful, should come to the light, and disturb the social order, or rather disorder, which men have hitherto ordained. There are, however, many who ... sincerely believe that the influence of good women is impaired by any courageous opposition to known and scandalous evils. Those who thus judge have missed the Christian ideal in the picture they have presented to their own imaginations of the perfection either of true womanhood or true manhood. They prate of Christ; but what do they know of him? Have they ever looked full at that image of him given by the evangelists? Can they imagine any gulf which it would be possible for a pure human being to bridge over, in order to save a fellow creature, to be compared with the gulf which he bridged over in order to identify himself with human nature in its lowest estate, and to restore the lost and guilty? The way in which even good men, professing to be believers in Jesus of Nazareth, judge this matter, the way in which they cling to their unequal judgments of unchaste men and unchaste women, and continue to separate, by an impassable barrier, the lapsed[1] among women from the pure or the so called pure; the way in

---

[1] *lapsed* Fallen into sin.

which they dread any probing of the subject, and deprecate the direct action, and the searching and purifying influence of enlightened women in the matter, is so un-Christlike, so unholy, that it calls for the most stern and constantly repeated rebuke. It is an infamy which flouts the heavens. Remembering how the Holiest could say to one such erring woman, "neither do I condemn thee, go and sin no more," I would, if I were a man, (with my hand on my heart, I say it) take off my hat and stand bareheaded[1] before the most degraded of these women, before I would dare to speak of them as greater sinners than myself, even if I were myself blameless; for, as a man, I should feel ashamed and penitent on behalf of other men, for whom and by whom these helpless ones have been cast forth and branded.

How is it that we may search the Gospels through and through, and not find one word of reproof to the poor, the down trodden, and the suffering? Not because Christ did not see *their* sins as well as the sins of the Scribes and Pharisees;[2] but he knew, he felt, with that divine insight of his, that they were not in the same degree responsible while bound hand and foot with the chains society had riveted upon their weak limbs. I fail to understand how any man or woman can initiate the restoration of such by preaching to them concerning their sins, and threatening them with the judgment of God. Rather would I begin by making them women first; by restoring their womanhood. I would seat them by my side, side by side with me, or higher if need be, and then, after that, if they fall, say to them—"O my sisters, ye have sinned; kneel down, and pray for strength to sin no more, by the side of your fellow sinner—*me*." It is *we*, not they, who ought to cover our faces and blush as they pass us by; for the sin of society

is *ours*. Are there not many of us who must confess that we have sinned up to the measure of our opportunities and enlightenment? What more have they done who had neither opportunities nor enlightenment? Therefore I would call upon the purest men and women among us to repent; to weep with me for the destruction of the daughter of my people, and to oppose, by every means and at every turn, the falsehoods prevalent in society, by which the present state of things is maintained.

De Tocqueville says, "Nothing is more customary in man than to recognize superior wisdom in the person of his oppressor."[3] Slaves have done so; women have done so. In reply to letters addressed to women of the upper classes (who are naturally much more enslaved to conventional ideas than ourselves) I have frequently been told that I ought to leave this whole subject of the degradation and enslavement of women to the superior wisdom of men; and only a few weeks ago a lady writing in an Oxford newspaper against the opposition to Mr. Lewis's[4] candidature, asserted that it was impossible for women to understand such a subject. To those who regard freedom as a holy thing, this slavery of the intellect and judgment appears the most dangerous and deadening of all forms of slavery. We must cease to "recognize superior wisdom" in those who oppress us, and learn to abhor the despotism of a public opinion formed by men, which has so long, and with such calamitous results, aimed at holding in bondage even the inmost thoughts of women. Not for spiritual bondage and moral freedom alone do we pray; we supplicate God to grant us also the emancipation of the intellect and the judgment from every theoretic falsehood and injustice. "For myself, when I feel the hand of power lie heavy on my brow, I care but little to know who oppresses me; and I am not the more disposed to pass under the yoke, because it is held out to me by the

---

[1] *neither do ... no more* Jesus' words to an adulterous woman in John 8.11. When the woman is about to be stoned for her crime, Jesus invites anyone who is without sin to throw the first stone. The crowd disperses, leaving the woman unharmed; *take off ... bareheaded* Display of respect or humility.

[2] *the Scribes and Pharisees* Scribes were keepers of Jewish law and tradition; the Pharisees were a sect of strict Jews. Jesus condemns the Scribes and the Pharisees as hypocrites for valuing status and appearances at the expense of genuine spirituality (Matthew 23).

[3] *Nothing is ... his oppressor* From Alexis de Tocqueville's *Democracy in America* (1835–40) 2.1.2.

[4] *Mr. Lewis* John Delaware Lewis (1828–84) lost the 1874 election for Member of Parliament for Oxford. During the campaign, pamphlets circulated deriding his support of the Contagious Diseases Acts.

arms of a million of men."[1] The public opinion which rules us in this vital matter of the relations of the sexes, upheld by millions of men, and backed by the whole weight of the authority of many centuries, is a despotism against which we proclaim ourselves rebels. Between the rebels and the despot there can be no longer any truce.

Mr. Herbert Spencer[2] has lately endorsed the opinion which male writers have been so long accustomed to express, that men possess strongly the sense of justice, and that women are weak in this sense. I am grieved that so excellent a man should have ventured on such an assertion at such a time as this. It would, I think, have been more modest if Mr. Spencer had postponed the utterance of that sentiment until the Contagious Diseases Acts were repealed. Men framed those Acts—Acts whose cowardliness, tyrannous injustice, flagrant inequality and cruelty have probably never been equalled in the history of the world; and men now refuse to repeal those Acts, in the face of the bitter cry of outraged womanhood, and the persistent demands of men whose sense of justice has been roused by that cry. It is true that the sense of justice in women is weak. Like many other qualities and powers possessed by women, it has been deadened through the want of exercise. The depressed[3] condition of woman has prevented the free exercise of her judgment; her natural sense of justice has been, in secret, outraged almost to extinction; she has not been permitted to exercise or express it in any open or legitimate manner, nor encouraged to bring it to bear on any large or public questions. No wonder that it has become enfeebled. But the sense of justice in man has been impaired, well nigh[4] to extinction, by a different process. It has been warped and corrupted by the almost exclusive possession of power in one direction, and by

the privilege he has assumed to himself of forming a judgment on all that concerns one half of the human race, irrespective of any judgment which that half of the human race may have formed concerning their own interests. Privilege, even more than subjection, corrupts, deadens, and kills the sense of justice within the human soul. …

Surely if any time of the world's history ever called for courageous and independent speech, and for typical and Christ like acts on the part of women towards their fallen sisters and fallen brothers, this age of ours, this very year of 1874, calls for such! …

from W.T. Stead, "The Maiden Tribute of Modern Babylon 1," *Pall Mall Gazette* (6 July 1885)

"The Maiden Tribute of Modern Bablyon" (1885), a series of articles written for the *Pall Mall Gazette* by investigative journalist W.T. Stead (1849–1912), shocked readers with its sensational portrayal of child abduction and forced prostitution in London. Among other appalling details, Stead reported that, as part of his investigation, he had been able to purchase a girl from her mother for £5; despite his benevolent intentions, he spent three months in jail for the crime. The mass outrage Stead's series provoked was a significant factor in the passage, the same year, of the Criminal Law Amendment Act raising the age of consent for girls from 13 to 16.

INTRODUCTION

In ancient times, if we may believe the myths of Hellas,[5] Athens, after a disastrous campaign, was compelled by her conqueror to send once every nine years a tribute to Crete of seven youths and seven maidens. The doomed fourteen, who were selected by lot amid the lamentations of the citizens, returned no more. The vessel that bore them to Crete unfurled black sails as the symbol of despair, and on arrival her passen-

---

[1] *For myself … of men* From de Tocqueville's *Democracy in America* 2.1.2.

[2] *Herbert Spencer* Philosopher and political theorist (1820–1903). Initially an advocate of women's suffrage, he later decided that women lacked the necessary rational abilities.

[3] *depressed* Held down.

[4] *nigh* Near.

[5] *Hellas* I.e., Greece.

gers were flung into the famous Labyrinth of Daedalus, there to wander about blindly until such time as they were devoured by the Minotaur, a frightful monster, half man, half bull, the foul product of an unnatural lust. …

The fact that the Athenians should have taken so bitterly to heart the paltry maiden tribute that once in nine years they had to pay to the Minotaur seems incredible, almost inconceivable. This very night in London, and every night, year in and year out, not seven maidens only, but many times seven, selected almost as much by chance as those who in the Athenian market-place drew lots as to which should be flung into the Cretan labyrinth, will be offered up as the Maiden Tribute of Modern Babylon.[1] Maidens they were when this morning dawned, but tonight their ruin will be accomplished, and tomorrow they will find themselves within the portals of the maze of London brotheldom. Within that labyrinth wander, like lost souls, the vast host of London prostitutes, whose numbers no man can compute, but who are probably not much below 50,000 strong. Many, no doubt, who venture but a little way within the maze make their escape. But multitudes are swept irresistibly on and on to be destroyed in due season, to give place to others, who also will share their doom.

The maw of the London Minotaur is insatiable, and none that go into the secret recesses of his lair return again. After some years' dolorous wandering in this palace of despair—for "hope of rest to solace there is none, nor e'en of milder pang," save the poisonous anodyne of drink—most of those ensnared tonight will perish, some of them in horrible torture. Yet, so far from this great city being convulsed with woe, London cares for none of these things, and the cultured man of the world, the heir of all the ages, the ultimate product of a long series of civilizations and religions, will shrug his shoulders in scorn at the folly of any one who ventures in public print to raise even the mildest protest against a horror a thousand times more horrible than that which, in the youth of the world, haunted like a night-

mare the imagination of mankind. Nevertheless, I have not yet lost faith in the heart and conscience of the English folk, the sturdy innate chivalry and right thinking of our common people; and although I am no vain dreamer of Utopias peopled solely by Sir Galahads and vestal virgins,[2] I am not without hope that there may be some check placed upon this vast tribute of maidens, unwitting or unwilling, which is nightly levied in London by the vices of the rich upon the necessities of the poor.

London's lust annually uses up many thousands of women, who are literally killed and made away with—living sacrifices slain in the service of vice. That may be inevitable, and with that I have nothing to do. But I do ask that those doomed to the house of evil fame shall not be trapped into it unwillingly, and that none shall be beguiled into the chamber of death before they are of an age to read the inscription above the portal—"All hope abandon ye who enter here."[3] If the daughters of the people must be served up as dainty morsels to minister to the passions of the rich, let them at least attain an age when they can understand the nature of the sacrifice which they are asked to make. And if we must cast maidens—not seven, but seven times seven—nightly into the jaws of vice, let us at least see to it that they assent to their own immolation, and are not unwilling sacrifices procured by force and fraud.

That is surely not too much to ask from the dissolute rich. Even considerations of self-interest might lead our rulers to assent to so modest a demand. For the hour of Democracy has struck, and there is no wrong which a man resents like this. If it has not been resented hitherto, it is not because it was not felt. … [U]nless the levying of the maiden-tribute in London is shorn of its worst abuses—at present, as I shall show, flourishing

---

[1] *Babylon* Proverbially decadent or sinful large city.

[2] *Sir Galahads* In many versions of Arthurian legend, Sir Galahad, one of King Arthur's knights, is depicted as a deeply religious virgin; *vestal virgins* Ancient Roman priestesses devoted to Vesta, goddess of the hearth. They took vows of chastity during the period of their service.

[3] *All hope … enter here* Phrase said to be inscribed at the gates of hell in Dante's *Inferno* 3.9.

unchecked—resentment, which might be appeased by reform, may hereafter be the virus of a social revolution. It is the one explosive which is strong enough to wreck the Throne.

LIBERTY FOR VICE, REPRESSION FOR CRIME

To avoid all misapprehension as to the object with which I propose to set forth the ghastly and criminal features of this infernal traffic, I wish to say emphatically at the outset that, however strongly I may feel as to the imperative importance of morality and chastity, I do not ask for any police interference with the liberty of vice. I ask only for the repression of crime.

… To extirpate vice by Act of Parliament is impossible; but because we must leave vice free that is no reason why we should acquiesce helplessly in the perpetration of crime. And that crime of the most ruthless and abominable description is constantly and systematically practised in London without let or hindrance, I am in a position to prove from my own personal knowledge—a knowledge purchased at a cost of which I prefer not to speak. Those crimes may be roughly classified as follows:

I. The sale and purchase and violation of children.
II. The procuration of virgins.
III. The entrapping and ruin of women.
IV. The international slave trade in girls.
V. Atrocities, brutalities, and unnatural crimes.

That is what I call sexual criminality, as opposed to sexual immorality. It flourishes in all its branches on every side to an extent of which even those specially engaged in rescue work have but little idea. Those who are constantly engaged in its practice naturally deny its existence. But I speak of that which I do know, not from hearsay or rumour, but of my own personal knowledge. …

THE VIOLATION OF VIRGINS

This branch of the subject is one upon which even the coolest and most scientific observer may well find it difficult to speak dispassionately in a spirit of calm and philosophic investigation. The facts, however, as they have been elucidated in the course of a careful and painstaking inquiry are so startling, and the horror which they excite so overwhelming, that it is doubly necessary to approach the subject with a scepticism proof against all but the most overwhelming demonstration. It is, however, a fact that there is in full operation among us a system of which the violation of virgins is one of the ordinary incidents; that these virgins are mostly of tender age, being too young in fact to understand the nature of the crime of which they are the unwilling victims; that these outrages are constantly perpetrated with almost absolute impunity; and that the arrangements for procuring, certifying, violating, repairing, and disposing of these ruined victims of the lust of London are made with a simplicity and efficiency incredible to all who have not made actual demonstration of the facility with which the crime can be accomplished.

To avoid misapprehension, I admit that the vast majority of those who are on the streets in London have not come there by the road of organized rape. Most women fall either by the seduction of individuals or by the temptation which well-dressed vice can offer to the poor. But there is a minority which has been as much the victim of violence as were the Bulgarian maidens with whose wrongs Mr. Gladstone made the world ring some eight years ago. Some are simply snared, trapped and outraged either when under the influence of drugs or after a prolonged struggle in a locked room, in which the weaker succumbs to sheer downright force. Others are regularly procured; bought at so much per head in some cases, or enticed under various promises into the fatal chamber from which they are never allowed to emerge until they have lost what woman ought to value more than life. It is to this department of the subject that I now address myself.

Before beginning this inquiry I had a confidential interview with one of the most experienced officers who for many years was in a position to possess an intimate acquaintance with all phases of London crime. I asked him, "Is it or is it not a fact that, at this moment, if I were to go to the proper houses, well introduced, the keeper would, in return for money down, supply me in due time with a maid—a genuine article, I mean, not a mere prostitute tricked out as a virgin, but a girl who had never been seduced?" "Certainly," he replied without a moment's hesitation. "At what price?" I continued. "That is a difficult question," he said. "I remember one case which came under my official cognizance in Scotland yard in which the price agreed upon was stated to be £20. Some parties in Lambeth undertook to deliver a maid for that sum to a house of ill fame, and I have no doubt it is frequently done all over London."

"But," I continued, "are these maids willing or unwilling parties to the transaction—that is, are they really maiden, not merely in being each a virgo intacta in the physical sense, but as being chaste girls who are not consenting parties to their seduction?" He looked surprised at my question, and then replied emphatically: "Of course they are rarely willing, and as a rule they do not know what they are coming for." "But," I said in amazement, "then do you mean to tell me that in very truth actual rapes, in the legal sense of the word, are constantly being perpetrated in London on unwilling virgins, purveyed and procured to rich men at so much a head by keepers of brothels?" "Certainly," said he, "there is not a doubt of it." "Why," I exclaimed, "the very thought is enough to raise hell." "It is true," he said; "and although it ought to raise hell, it does not even raise the neighbours."

"But do the girls cry out?" "Of course they do. But what avails screaming in a quiet bedroom? Remember, the utmost limit of howling or excessively violent screaming, such as a man or woman would make if actual murder was being attempted, is only two minutes, and the limit of screaming of any kind is only five. Suppose a girl is being outraged in a room next to your house. You hear her screaming, just as you are dozing to sleep. Do you get up, dress, rush downstairs, and insist on admittance? Hardly. But suppose the screams continue and you get uneasy, you begin to think whether you should not do something? Before you have made up your mind and got dressed the screams cease, and you think you were a fool for your pains." "But the policeman on the beat?" "He has no right to interfere, even if he heard anything. Suppose that a constable had a right to force his way into any house where a woman screamed fearfully, policemen would be almost as regular attendants at childbed as doctors. Once a girl gets into such a house she is almost helpless, and may be ravished with comparative safety."

"But surely rape is a felony punishable with penal servitude. Can she not prosecute?" "Whom is she to prosecute? She does not know her assailant's name. She might not even be able to recognize him if she met him outside. Even if she did, who would believe her? A woman who has lost her chastity is always a discredited witness. The fact of her being in a house of ill fame would possibly be held to be evidence of her consent. The keeper of the house and all the servants would swear she was a consenting party; they would swear that she had never screamed, and the woman would be condemned as an adventuress who wished to levy black mail." "And this is going on today?" "Certainly it is, and it will go on, and you cannot help it, as long as men have money, procuresses are skilful, and women are weak and inexperienced." …

from Sarah Grand, *The Beth Book* (1897)

The writer and politician who coined the phrase "New Woman," Sarah Grand (1854–1943) is best known for novels and nonfiction that advocate greater educational opportunities and independence for women—and that condemn licentiousness in married men for the distress and disease it imposes on their wives. In the episode excerpted below from her novel *The Beth Book*, Grand's protagonist, trapped in a miserable unequal marriage, discovers that her husband is a doctor complicit in the injustices of the Contagious Diseases Acts.

"I am afraid I have taken you by surprise," Mrs. Kilroy began rather nervously.

"Will you sit down?" Beth said coldly. "You cannot wonder if I am surprised to see you. This is the first visit you have paid me, although we met directly after I came to Slane—some years ago. You were kind and cordial on that occasion, but the next time I saw you—at that ball—you slighted[1] me; and after that you shunned me until I met you the other day at Mrs. Carne's, and then you seemed inclined to take me up again. I do not understand such caprices,[2] and I do not like them."

"It was not caprice," Mrs. Kilroy assured her. "I liked you very much the first time we met, and I should have called immediately; but when I asked for your address I was told that your husband was in charge of the Lock Hospital[3]—"

"Yes, the hospital for the diseases of women," Beth said. "But what difference does that make?"

"It made me jump to the hasty conclusion that you approved of the degradation of your own sex," said Angelica.

"The degradation of my own sex!" said Beth bewildered. "What is a Lock Hospital?"

Angelica explained the whole horrible apparatus for the special degradation of women.[4]

"Now, perhaps, you will understand what we felt about you," Angelica concluded, "we who are loyal to our own sex and have a sense of justice, when we thought you were content to live on the means your husband makes in such a shameful way."

An extraordinary look of relief came into Beth's face. "Then it was not my fault—not because I was horrid?" she exclaimed. All the slights were as nothing the moment she gathered that she had not deserved them. Angelica stared at her; but it was not in Beth's nature to think long about herself, only the full force of what she had just heard as it concerned others did not come to her for some seconds. When it did she was overcome. "How could you suppose that I knew?" she gasped at last. "This is the first hint I have had of the loathsome business. My husband talks to me about—many things that he had better not have mentioned, but about this

he has never said a word."

"Then he must have suspected that you would disapprove," said Mrs. Kilroy.

"Disapprove!" Beth ejaculated.[5] "The whole thing makes me sick; I ought to have been told before I married him. I never would have spoken to a man in such a position had I known; you did well to avoid me."

"No," said Angelica. "I did ill and I feel humiliated for my own want of penetration,[6] for my hasty conclusion. It was Sir George Galbraith who first made me suspect that you knew nothing about it, and I would have come at once to make sure; but we were just leaving the neighbourhood, and we only returned yesterday. Ideala did not believe that you knew it either, and she rated[7] us all for the way we had treated you. She has been in America ever since she met you at Mrs. Carne's, but she is coming home next week, and has written to entreat me to ask you to meet her. Will you? Will you come and stay with me? Do, and talk this over with us. I can see that it has been a great shock to you."

"I cannot answer you now," said Beth, "I must think—I must think what I had better do."

"Yes, think it over," said Angelica, "then write and tell me when you will come. Only do come. You will find yourself among friends—congenial friends, I venture to prophesy."

When Mrs. Kilroy had gone, Beth went to her bedroom and waited there for Dan. It was the only place where she could be sure of seeing him alone. He dressed for dinner now that Miss Petterick was with them.

Dan came in whistling hilariously. He stopped short when he saw Beth's face.

"What's up?" he asked.

"Mrs. Kilroy has been here."

"I hope you thanked her for nothing!"

"I'm afraid I forgot to thank her at all," Beth said, "although she has put me under an obligation to her."

"May I ask what the obligation is?"

---

[1] *slighted* Disrespected, ignored.

[2] *caprices* Games.

[3] *Lock Hospital* Hospital for the treatment of venereal diseases, where women were held under the Contagious Diseases Acts.

[4] *Angelica explained ... of women* This line does not appear in some early editions.

[5] *ejaculated* Exclaimed.

[6] *did ill* Acted badly; *want of penetration* Lack of insight.

[7] *rated* Rebuked.

"She told me frankly why no decent woman will associate with us. It is not my fault after all, it seems, but yours—you and your Lock Hospital. It is against the Anglo-Saxon spirit to admit panders[1] into society."

"So she told you about that, did she, the meddling busybody!" he answered coolly. "I was afraid they would, some of them, damn them! and I knew you would go into hysterics. She didn't tell you the necessity for it, I suppose, nor the good it is doing; but I will, so just listen to me, then you'll see, perhaps, that I know more about it than these canting[2] sentimentalists."

Beth, sitting in judgment on him, set her mouth and listened in silence until he stopped. In his own defence he gave her many revolting details couched in the coarsest language.

"But, then, in the name of justice," she exclaimed, "what means do you take to protect those poor unfortunate women from disease? What do you do to the men who spread it? What becomes of diseased men?"

"Oh, they marry, I suppose. Anyhow, that is not my business. Doctors cannot be expected to preach morals. Sanitation is our business."

"But aren't morals closely connected with sanitation?" Beth said. "And why, if sanitation is your business, do you take no radical measures with regard to this horrible disease? Why do you not have it reported, never mind who gets it, as scarlet fever, smallpox, and other diseases—all less disastrous to the general health of the community—are reported?"

Dan shrugged his shoulders. "It's a deuced[3] awkward thing for a man to be suspected of disease. It's a stigma, and might spoil his prospects. Women are so cursedly prying nowadays. They've got wind of its being incurable, and many a one won't marry a man if a suspicion of it attaches to him."

"I see," said Beth. "The principles of the medical profession with regard to sanitation when women are in question seem to be peculiar. I wish to Heaven I had known them sooner." She hid her face in her hands and suddenly burst into tears.

Dan scowled. "Well, this is nice!" he exclaimed. "I have had a devilish hard day's work and come in cheery, as usual, to do my best to make things pleasant for you, and this is the reception I get! You're a nice pill, indeed!" He went off muttering into his dressing-room and slammed the door.

When he appeared in the drawing-room he found Beth and Bertha chatting together as usual, and as during the rest of the evening he could detect no difference in Beth's manner, he congratulated himself that she was going to accept the position as inevitable and say no more about it. It was not Beth's way to return to a disagreeable subject once it had been discussed unless she meant to do something in the matter, and Dan conceived that there was nothing to be done in this instance. He considered that he was not the sort of man it was safe for women to interfere with, and he guessed she knew it!

He was mistaken, however, when he supposed that she had let the subject drop, and was going to resign herself to an invidious[4] position. She was merely letting it lapse until she understood it. It was all as new to her as it was horrifying, and she required time to study both sides of the question. Her own sense of justice was too acute to let her accept at once the accusation—that so-called civilised men, who boast of their chivalrous protection of the "weaker sex," had imposed upon women a special public degradation while the most abandoned and culpable of their own sex were not only allowed to go unpunished, but to spread vice and disease where they listed.[5]

---

[1] *panders* Pimps; facilitators of prostitution.

[2] *canting* Hypocritically preaching.

[3] *deuced* Slang word similar to "darned."

[4] *invidious* Unjust, provoking hatred or anger.

[5] *listed* Wished.

JOHN RUSKIN
1819 – 1900

John Ruskin was a painter and a poet, author of dozens of books on the arts and sciences, and a dedicated believer in fundamental links between all disciplines. Famous as a critic of art, culture, and society, Ruskin synthesized subjects in fluid and poetic ways, and he exerted an enormous influence on the aesthetic, philosophical, and political sensibilities of his day. This influence bore heavily on the work of the Pre-Raphaelite painters, notably Dante Gabriel Rossetti, John Everett Millais, and William Holman Hunt. In addition, Ruskin's opposition to industrialization and his ideas about the sacredness of human work inspired William Morris and the Arts and Crafts Movement. Mahatma Gandhi, who translated Ruskin's *Unto the Last* into Gujarati, said about the work's effect on him, "I believe that I discovered some of my deepest convictions reflecting on this great book of Ruskin's, [… which] captured me and made me transform my life."

Ruskin was born in London in 1819 to Margaret Cox and John James Ruskin, a successful wine merchant. Possibly because the couple bore John in midlife and had no other children, the Evangelical Ruskins raised their child in an overprotective and cloistered manner, allowing him neither friends nor toys. The young John's schooling, administered by his mother, was strict and included hours of Bible study every day (the two would read the entire Bible and then resume from the beginning), while his father, also a stern Evangelical, procured tutors for the arts and languages. When Ruskin came of age, he attended Oxford (where he won the Newdigate Prize for poetry), but even then his mother accompanied him, living in rooms nearby, and his father joined the two every weekend.

Even though he had a talent for both poetry and painting, Ruskin realized after graduation that he did not wish to pursue either as a career. His admiration for the British painter J.M.W. Turner, however, led to his first work of art criticism, which evolved into the five-volume *Modern Painters*, published over a period of more than a decade. The first volume of *Modern Painters* was a defense of Turner's "fidelity" to his landscapes and his ability to see and express "truth" in nature. It was not only Ruskin's aesthetic analyses that attracted attention, however, but also his elegant and engaging prose style.

In 1848, Ruskin entered into a disastrous marriage with Euphemia ("Effie") Chalmers, which ended six years later in an annulment on the grounds that the marriage had never been consummated. The following year Effie married the painter John Everett Millais. Throughout his life, Ruskin's relationships with women were fraught, most notably his relationship with Rose La Touche, whom he met in 1858 when she was only nine years old. Ruskin proposed marriage to Rose in 1866, but she ultimately rejected his offer, both because of his earlier annulment and because she was a strict Evangelical, while he had lost his religious faith (he said he had been "unconverted" while attending church in Turin). Not long after her death in 1875, Ruskin suffered an attack of madness, the first of many such episodes he experienced throughout his life.

Although there were times when Ruskin could not function due to mental illness, he was astonishingly prolific: his *Collected Works* fill thirty-nine volumes, and he wrote thousands of letters. His books on architecture, *The Seven Lamps of Architecture* (1849) and the three-volume *Stones of Venice* (1851–53), were so influential that they provoked a revival of Gothic architecture that in some ways ran counter to his philosophies. Ruskin felt that the hand of God was present in those who labored on the stone buildings of the Middle Ages, and that the magnificent Gothic architecture of Venice was a manifestation of a virtuous and honorable people. His writing inspired many to support the preservation and restoration of architectural treasures. Ruskin himself, however, promoted a social, rather than simply an architectural, restoration.

Ruskin's attacks on society became increasingly focused on the effects of modern production, and he became an outspoken challenger of the Industrial Age. His views on economic and social reform, radical at the time, have affected social thinking to this day. Ruskin was strongly opposed to *laissez faire* economics and advocated the organization of labor (the founders of the Labour Party in Britain attributed their ideas to Ruskin), cooperative business ventures, an old-age pension, a minimum wage, public libraries and art galleries, a national health service, equal education opportunities, and pollution control, among many other initiatives. In 1878, Ruskin founded the Guild of St. George, an organization that still exists today, in order to educate the public and to preserve and support small businesses and the production of local crafts. This is not to say that Ruskin's political views could in any way be considered wholly progressive; for example, his 1865 two-part essay *Sesame and Lilies*, in which he defines the qualities and ideal roles of men and women, was popular in his own era but roundly condemned by feminist critics in the late twentieth century. He was also a supporter of British imperialism. He considered Britain to be superior in civilization to nations such as India, and, in 1865 he was an outspoken defender of the infamous Jamaican Governor Edward John Eyre, who had committed a shocking series of atrocities to repress a rebellion.

After writing and lecturing throughout the 1860s, Ruskin was offered the first Slade Professorship of Fine Arts at Oxford, where he delivered (and subsequently published) many famous lectures and speeches to awestruck students, including the young Oscar Wilde. During this decade he also began a series of letters addressed to English laborers, published as *Fors Clavigera*. Ruskin was forced to resign his position at Oxford in 1880 due to mental illness, and although he resumed his professorship for a brief period and published two final books of lectures, *The Pleasures of England* and *The Art of England*, these years were not good to him. He managed to write many installments of his brilliant autobiography, *Praeterita*, but it remained unfinished. After a long illness he died in 1900. Although Westminster Abbey offered a resting place, Ruskin's last wishes were honored, and he was buried near his home in the Coniston graveyard. For the great Russian writer Leo Tolstoy, and for many others, Ruskin's legacy remained alive: "Ruskin was one of the most remarkable of men, not only of England and our time but of all countries and all times. He was one of those rare men who think with their hearts, and so he thought and said not only what he himself had seen and felt, but what everyone will think and say in the future."

N.B. Additional Ruskin selections are included in the "Nature and the Environment" Contexts section.

⌘⌘⌘

from *Modern Painters*

A DEFINITION OF GREATNESS IN ART

Painting, or art generally, as such, with all its technicalities, difficulties, and particular ends, is nothing but a noble and expressive language, invaluable as the vehicle of thought, but by itself nothing. He who has learned what is commonly considered the whole art of painting, that is, the art of representing any natural object faithfully, has as yet only learned the language by which his thoughts are to be expressed. He has done just as much towards being that which we ought to respect as a great painter, as a man who has learned how to express himself grammatically and melodiously has towards being a great poet. The language is, indeed, more difficult of acquirement in the one case than in the other, and possesses more power of delighting the sense, while it speaks to the intellect; but it is, nevertheless, nothing more than language, and all those excellences which are peculiar[1] to the painter as such, are merely what rhythm, melody, precision, and force are in the words of the orator and the poet, necessary to their greatness, but not the tests of their greatness. It is not by the mode of representing and saying, but by what is represented and said, that the respective greatness either of the painter or the writer is to be finally determined. ...

So that, if I say that the greatest picture is that which conveys to the mind of the spectator the greatest number of the greatest ideas, I have a definition which will include as subjects of comparison every pleasure which art is capable of conveying. If I were to say, on the contrary, that the best picture was that which most closely imitated nature, I should assume that art could only please by imitating nature; and I should cast out of the pale[2] of criticism those parts of works of art which are not imitative, that is to say, intrinsic beauties of colour and form, and those works of art wholly, which, like the Arabesques of Raffaelle[3] in the Loggias,[4] are not imitative at all. Now, I want a definition of art wide enough to include all its varieties of aim. I do not say, therefore, that the art is greatest which gives most pleasure, because perhaps there is some art whose end is to teach, and not to please. I do not say that the art is greatest which teaches us most, because perhaps there is some art whose end is to please, and not to teach. I do not say that the art is greatest which imitates best, because perhaps there is some art whose end is to create and not to imitate. But I say that the art is greatest which conveys to the mind of the spectator, by any means whatsoever, the greatest number of the greatest ideas; and I call an idea great in proportion as it is received by a higher faculty of the mind, and as it more fully occupies, and in occupying, exercises and exalts, the faculty by which it is received.

If this, then, be the definition of great art, that of a great artist naturally follows. He is the greatest artist who has embodied, in the sum of his works, the greatest number of the greatest ideas. ...

OF TRUTH OF WATER

I believe it is a result of the experience of all artists, that it is the easiest thing in the world to give a certain degree of depth and transparency to water; but that it is next to impossible, to give a full impression of surface. If no reflection be given, a ripple being supposed, the water looks like lead: if reflection be given, it, in nine cases out of ten, looks *morbidly* clear and deep, so that we always go down *into* it, even when the artist most wishes us to glide *over* it. Now, this difficulty arises from the very same circumstance which occasions the frequent failure in effect of the best-drawn foregrounds ... the change, namely, of focus necessary in the eye in order to receive rays of light coming from different distances. Go to the edge of a pond in a perfectly calm day, at some place where there is duckweed floating on the surface, not thick, but a leaf here and there. Now, you may either see in the water the reflection of the sky, or you may see the duckweed; but you cannot, by any effort, see both together. If you look for the reflection, you will be sensible of a sudden change or effort in the eye, by

---

[1] *peculiar* Specific.

[2] *pale* Territory with defined boundaries.

[3] *Raffaelle* I.e., Raphael (1483–1520), Italian Renaissance painter.

[4] *Loggias* Open-air galleries.

which it adapts itself to the reception of the rays which have come all the way from the clouds, have struck on the water, and so been sent up again to the eye. The focus you adopt is one fit for great distance; and, accordingly, you will feel that you are looking down a great way under the water, while the leaves of the duckweed, though they lie upon the water at the very spot on which you are gazing so intently, are felt only as a vague uncertain interruption, causing a little confusion in the image below, but entirely undistinguishable as leaves, and even their colour unknown and unperceived. Unless you think of them, you will not even feel that anything interrupts your sight, so excessively slight is their effect. If, on the other hand, you make up your mind to look for the leaves of the duckweed, you will perceive an instantaneous change in the effort of the eye, by which it becomes adapted to receive near rays, those which have only come from the surface of the pond. You will then see the delicate leaves of the duckweed with perfect clearness, and in vivid green; but, while you do so, you will be able to perceive nothing of the reflections in the very water on which they float, nothing but a vague flashing and melting of light and dark hues, without form or meaning, which to investigate, or find out what they mean or are, you must quit your hold of the duckweed, and plunge down.

Hence it appears, that whenever we see plain reflections of comparatively distant objects, in near water, we cannot possibly see the surface, and *vice versa;* so that when in a painting we give the reflections with the same clearness with which they are visible in nature, we presuppose the effort of the eye to look under the surface, and, of course, destroy the surface, and induce an effect of clearness which, perhaps, the artist has not particularly wished to attain, but which he has found himself forced into, by his reflections, in spite of himself. And the reason of this effect of clearness appearing preternatural is, that people are not in the habit of looking at water with the distant focus adapted to the reflections, unless by particular effort. We invariably, under ordinary circumstances, use the surface focus; and, in consequence, receive nothing more than a vague

and confused impression of the reflected colours and lines, however clearly, calmly, and vigorously all may be defined underneath, if we choose to look for them. We do not look for them, but glide along over the surface, catching only playing light and capricious colour for evidence of reflection, except where we come to images of objects close to the surface, which the surface focus is of course adapted to receive; and these we see clearly, as of the weeds on the shore, or of sticks rising out of the water, etc. Hence, the ordinary effect of water is only to be rendered by giving the reflections of the *margin* clear and distinct (so clear they usually are in nature, that it is impossible to tell where the water begins); but the moment we touch the reflection of distant objects, as of high trees or clouds, that instant we must become vague and uncertain in drawing, and, though vivid in colour and light as the object itself, quite indistinct in form and feature. If we take such a piece of water as that in the foreground of Turner's[1] Château of Prince Albert, the first impression from it is, "What a wide *surface*!" We glide over it a quarter of a mile into the picture before we know where we are, and yet the water is as calm and crystalline as a mirror; but we are not allowed to tumble into it, and gasp for breath as we go down, we are kept upon the surface, though that surface is flashing and radiant with every hue of cloud, and sun, and sky, and foliage. But the secret is in the drawing of these reflections. We cannot tell, when we look *at* them and *for* them, what they mean. They have all character, and are evidently reflections of something definite and determined; but yet they are all uncertain and inexplicable; playing colour and palpitating shade, which, though we recognize them in an instant for images of something, and feel that the water is bright, and lovely, and calm, we cannot penetrate nor interpret; we are not allowed to go down to them, and we repose, as we should in nature, upon the lustre of the level surface. It is in this power of saying everything, and yet saying nothing too plainly, that the perfection of art here, as in all other cases, consists.

—1843

---

[1] *Turner*   J.M.W. Turner (1775–1851), English landscape artist.

from *The Stones of Venice*

THE NATURE OF GOTHIC

... In the definition proposed, I shall only endeavour to analyze the idea which I suppose already to exist in the reader's mind. We all have some notion, most of us a very determined one, of the meaning of the term Gothic, but I know that many persons have this idea in their minds without being able to define it: that is to say, understanding generally that Westminster Abbey is Gothic, and St. Paul's is not, that Strasburg Cathedral is Gothic, and St. Peter's[1] is not, they have, nevertheless, no clear notion of what it is that they recognize in the one or miss in the other, such as would enable them to say how far the work at Westminster or Strasburg is good and pure of its kind; still less to say of any nondescript building, like St. James's Palace or Windsor Castle,[2] how much right Gothic element there is in it, and how much wanting. And I believe this inquiry to be a pleasant and profitable one; and that there will be found something more than usually interesting in tracing out this grey, shadowy, many-pinnacled image of the Gothic spirit within us; and discerning what fellowship there is between it and our Northern hearts. And if, at any point of the inquiry, I should interfere with any of the reader's previously formed conceptions, and use the term Gothic in any sense which he would not willingly attach to it, I do not ask him to accept, but only to examine and understand, my interpretation, as necessary to the intelligibility of what follows in the rest of the work. ...

I believe, then, that the characteristic or moral elements of Gothic are the following, placed in the order of their importance:

1. Savageness.
2. Changefulness.
3. Naturalism.
4. Grotesqueness.
5. Rigidity.
6. Redundance.

These characters are here expressed as belonging to the building; as belonging to the builder, they would be expressed thus:—1. Savageness or Rudeness.[3] 2. Love of Change. 3. Love of Nature. 4. Disturbed Imagination. 5. Obstinacy. 6. Generosity. And I repeat, that the withdrawal of any one, or any two, will not at once destroy the Gothic character of a building, but the removal of a majority of them will. I shall proceed to examine them in their order.

(1.) Savageness. I am not sure when the word "Gothic" was first generically applied to the architecture of the North; but I presume that, whatever the date of its original usage, it was intended to imply reproach, and express the barbaric character of the nations among whom that architecture arose. It never implied that they were literally of Gothic lineage, far less that their architecture had been originally invented by the Goths[4] themselves; but it did imply that they and their buildings together exhibited a degree of sternness and rudeness, which, in contradistinction to the character of Southern and Eastern nations, appeared like a perpetual reflection of the contrast between the Goth and the Roman in their first encounter. And when that fallen Roman, in the utmost impotence of his luxury, and insolence of his guilt, became the model for the imitation of civilized Europe, at the close of the so-called Dark ages,[5] the word Gothic became a term of unmitigated contempt, not unmixed with aversion. From that contempt, by the exertion of the antiquaries and architects of this century, Gothic architecture has been

---

[1] *Westminster Abbey* Medieval church in London where coronations and burials of British monarchs are held; *St. Paul's* English baroque-style cathedral in central London; *Strasburg Cathedral* Late medieval cathedral in Strasbourg, France; *St. Peter's* Renaissance-style church in Vatican City, completed in 1626.

[2] *St. James's Palace* Tudor-style palace in London, built in the sixteenth century and used as a residence by several monarchs; *Windsor Castle* Residence of the British royal family, located in Windsor.

[3] *Rudeness* Roughness.

[4] *Goths* Eastern-European Germanic-speaking peoples, in part responsible for the collapse of the Roman Empire.

[5] *Dark ages* Term used to refer to the Middle Ages or the early centuries of the Middle Ages, usually suggesting that they were a period of ignorance and intellectual stagnation.

sufficiently vindicated; and perhaps some among us, in our admiration of the magnificent science of its structure, and sacredness of its expression, might desire that the term of ancient reproach should be withdrawn, and some other, of more apparent honourableness, adopted in its place. There is no chance, as there is no need, of such a substitution. As far as the epithet was used scornfully, it was used falsely; but there is no reproach in the word, rightly understood; on the contrary, there is a profound truth, which the instinct of mankind almost unconsciously recognizes. It is true, greatly and deeply true, that the architecture of the North is rude and wild; but it is not true, that, for this reason, we are to condemn it, or despise. Far otherwise: I believe it is in this very character that it deserves our profoundest reverence.

The charts of the world which have been drawn up by modern science have thrown into a narrow space the expression of a vast amount of knowledge, but I have never yet seen any one pictorial enough to enable the spectator to imagine the kind of contrast in physical character which exists between Northern and Southern countries. We know the differences in detail, but we have not that broad glance and grasp which would enable us to feel them in their fulness. We know that gentians grow on the Alps, and olives on the Apennines;[1] but we do not enough conceive for ourselves that variegated mosaic of the world's surface which a bird sees in its migration, that difference between the district of the gentian and of the olive which the stork and the swallow see far off, as they lean upon the sirocco wind.[2] Let us, for a moment, try to raise ourselves even above the level of their flight, and imagine the Mediterranean lying beneath us like an irregular lake, and all its ancient promontories sleeping in the sun: here and there an angry spot of thunder, a grey stain of storm, moving upon the burning field; and here and there a fixed wreath of white volcano smoke, surrounded by its circle of ashes; but for the most part a great peacefulness of light, Syria and Greece, Italy and Spain, laid like pieces

of a golden pavement into the sea-blue, chased,[3] as we stoop nearer to them, with bossy beaten work of mountain chains, and glowing softly with terraced gardens, and flowers heavy with frankincense, mixed among masses of laurel, and orange, and plumy palm, that abate with their grey-green shadows the burning of the marble rocks, and of the ledges of porphyry[4] sloping under lucent sand. Then let us pass farther towards the north, until we see the orient colours change gradually into a vast belt of rainy green, where the pastures of Switzerland, and poplar valleys of France, and dark forests of the Danube and Carpathians stretch from the mouths of the Loire to those of the Volga,[5] seen through clefts in grey swirls of rain-cloud and flaky veils of the mist of the brooks, spreading low along the pasture lands: and then, farther north still, to see the earth heave into mighty masses of leaden rock and heathy moor, bordering with a broad waste of gloomy purple that belt of field and wood, and splintering into irregular and grisly islands amidst the northern seas, beaten by storm, and chilled by ice-drift, and tormented by furious pulses of contending tide, until the roots of the last forests fail from among the hill ravines, and the hunger of the north wind bites their peaks into barrenness; and, at last, the wall of ice, durable like iron, sets, deathlike, its white teeth against us out of the polar twilight. And, having once traversed in thought this gradation of the zoned iris of the earth in all its material vastness, let us go down nearer to it, and watch the parallel change in the belt of animal life; the multitudes of swift and brilliant creatures that glance in the air and sea, or tread the sands of the southern zone; striped zebras and spotted leopards, glistening serpents, and birds arrayed in purple and scarlet. Let us contrast their delicacy and brilliancy of colour, and swiftness of motion, with the frost-cramped strength, and shaggy covering, and dusky plumage of the northern tribes; contrast the Arabian horse with the Shetland, the tiger and leopard with the

---

[1] *gentians* Flowering herbs; *Apennines* Chain of mountain ranges running through most of the Italian peninsula.

[2] *sirocco wind* Hot, moist wind from North Africa.

[3] *chased* Engraved.

[4] *porphyry* Red crystalline rock.

[5] *Danube* River flowing across Central and Eastern Europe; *Carpathians* Mountain range in Central and Eastern Europe; *Loire* River in France; *Volga* River in Russia.

wolf and bear, the antelope with the elk, the bird of paradise with the osprey;[1] and then, submissively acknowledging the great laws by which the earth and all that it bears are ruled throughout their being, let us not condemn, but rejoice in the expression by man of his own rest in the statutes of the lands that gave him birth. Let us watch him with reverence as he sets side by side the burning gems, and smoothes with soft sculpture the jasper pillars, that are to reflect a ceaseless sunshine, and rise into a cloudless sky: but not with less reverence let us stand by him, when, with rough strength and hurried stroke, he smites an uncouth animation out of the rocks which he has torn from among the moss of the moorland, and heaves into the darkened air the pile of iron buttress and rugged wall, instinct with work of an imagination as wild and wayward as the northern sea; creatures of ungainly shape and rigid limb, but full of wolfish life; fierce as the winds that beat, and changeful as the clouds that shade them. …

In … the first volume of this work, it was noticed that the systems of architectural ornament, properly so called, might be divided into three:—1. Servile ornament, in which the execution or power of the inferior workman is entirely subjected to the intellect of the higher;—2. Constitutional ornament, in which the executive inferior power is, to a certain point, emancipated and independent, having a will of its own, yet confessing its inferiority and rendering obedience to higher powers;—and . 3. Revolutionary ornament, in which no executive inferiority is admitted at all. I must here explain the nature of these divisions at somewhat greater length.

Of Servile ornament, the principal schools are the Greek, Ninevite,[2] and Egyptian; but their servility is of different kinds. The Greek master-workman was far advanced in knowledge and power above the Assyrian or Egyptian. Neither he nor those for whom he worked could endure the appearance of imperfection in anything; and, therefore, what ornament he appointed to be done by those beneath him was composed of mere geometrical forms—balls, ridges, and perfectly symmetrical foliage—which could be executed with absolute precision by line and rule, and were as perfect in their way, when completed, as his own figure sculpture. The Assyrian and Egyptian, on the contrary, less cognizant of accurate form in anything, were content to allow their figure sculpture to be executed by inferior workmen, but lowered the method of its treatment to a standard which every workman could reach, and then trained him by discipline so rigid, that there was no chance of his falling beneath the standard appointed. The Greek gave to the lower workman no subject which he could not perfectly execute. The Assyrian gave him subjects which he could only execute imperfectly, but fixed a legal standard for his imperfection. The workman was, in both systems, a slave.

But in the mediaeval, or especially Christian, system of ornament, this slavery is done away with altogether; Christianity having recognized, in small things as well as great, the individual value of every soul. But it not only recognizes its value; it confesses its imperfection, in only bestowing dignity upon the acknowledgment of unworthiness. That admission of lost power and fallen nature, which the Greek or Ninevite felt to be intensely painful, and, as far as might be, altogether refused, the Christian makes daily and hourly, contemplating the fact of it without fear, as tending, in the end, to God's greater glory. Therefore, to every spirit which Christianity summons to her service, her exhortation is: Do what you can, and confess frankly what you are unable to do; neither let your effort be shortened for fear of failure, nor your confession silenced for fear of shame. And it is, perhaps, the principal admirableness of the Gothic schools of architecture, that they thus receive the results of the labour of inferior minds; and out of fragments full of imperfection, and betraying that imperfection in every touch, indulgently raise up a stately and unaccusable whole. …

---

[1] *Shetland* Shetland pony, a Scottish breed of short-legged pony, originating in the Shetland Islands; *bird of paradise* Fruit-eating bird known for its brightly colored and elaborate feathers, and found predominantly in New Guinea and eastern Australia; *osprey* Grey and brown bird of prey, found on all continents except the Antarctic.

[2] *Ninevite* Referring to the ancient Assyrian city of Nineveh (c. 3000–612 BCE), a site of archaeological interest in Ruskin's time, where several large bas-reliefs had recently been unearthed, along with thousands of cuneiform tablets. At its height, the Assyrian empire (c. 2500–609 BCE) covered large portions of the Middle East, including much of modern Iraq and Egypt.

And now, reader, look round this English room of yours, about which you have been proud so often, because the work of it was so good and strong, and the ornaments of it so finished. Examine again all those accurate mouldings, and perfect polishings, and un-erring adjustments of the seasoned wood and tempered steel. Many a time you have exulted over them, and thought how great England was, because her slightest work was done so thoroughly. Alas! if read rightly, these perfectnesses are signs of a slavery in our England a thousand times more bitter and more degrading than that of the scourged African, or helot[1] Greek. Men may be beaten, chained, tormented, yoked like cattle, slaugh-tered like summer flies, and yet remain in one sense, and the best sense, free. But to smother their souls with them, to blight and hew into rotting pollards[2] the suckling branches of their human intelligence, to make the flesh and skin which, after the worm's work on it, is to see God, into leathern thongs to yoke machinery with—this is to be slave-masters indeed; and there might be more freedom in England, though her feudal lords' lightest words were worth men's lives, and though the blood of the vexed husbandman[3] dropped in the furrows of her fields, than there is while the animation of her multitudes is sent like fuel to feed the factory smoke, and the strength of them is given daily to be wasted into the fineness of a web, or racked into the exactness of a line.

And, on the other hand, go forth again to gaze upon the old cathedral front, where you have smiled so often at the fantastic ignorance of the old sculptors: examine once more those ugly goblins, and formless monsters, and stern statues, anatomiless and rigid; but do not mock at them, for they are signs of the life and liberty of every workman who struck the stone; a freedom of thought, and rank in scale of being, such as no laws, no charters, no charities can secure; but which it must be the first aim of all Europe at this day to regain for her children. …

We have much studied and much perfected, of late, the great civilized invention of the division of labour; only we give it a false name. It is not, truly speaking, the labour that is divided; but the men: divided into mere segments of men—broken into small fragments and crumbs of life; so that all the little piece of intelligence that is left in a man is not enough to make a pin, or a nail, but exhausts itself in making the point of a pin or the head of a nail. Now it is a good and desirable thing, truly, to make many pins in a day; but if we could only see with what crystal sand their points were polished—sand of human soul, much to be magnified before it can be discerned for what it is—we should think there might be some loss in it also. And the great cry that rises from all our manufacturing cities, louder than their furnace blast, is all in very deed for this—that we manufacture everything there except men; we blanch cotton, and strengthen steel, and refine sugar, and shape pottery; but to brighten, to strengthen, to refine, or to form a single living spirit, never enters into our estimate of advantages. And all the evil to which that cry is urging our myriads can be met only in one way: not by teaching nor preaching, for to teach them is but to show them their misery, and to preach to them, if we do nothing more than preach, is to mock at it. It can be met only by a right understanding, on the part of all classes, of what kinds of labour are good for men, raising them, and making them happy; by a determined sacri-fice of such convenience, or beauty, or cheapness as is to be got only by the degradation of the workman; and by equally determined demand for the products and results of healthy and ennobling labour.

And how, it will be asked, are these products to be recognized, and this demand to be regulated? Easily: by the observance of three broad and simple rules:

1. Never encourage the manufacture of any article not absolutely necessary, in the production of which *Invention* has no share.

2. Never demand an exact finish for its own sake, but only for some practical or noble end.

3. Never encourage imitation or copying of any kind, except for the sake of preserving records of great works.

---

[1] *helot* Of a class of serfs, falling between slave and citizen in the Spartan social hierarchy.

[2] *pollards* Trees whose branches have been lopped off to shape them.

[3] *husbandman* Farmer.

The second of these principles is the only one which directly rises out of the consideration of our immediate subject; but I shall briefly explain the meaning and extent of the first also, reserving the enforcement of the third for another place.

1. Never encourage the manufacture of anything not necessary, in the production of which invention has no share.

For instance. Glass beads are utterly unnecessary, and there is no design or thought employed in their manufacture. They are formed by first drawing out the glass into rods; these rods are chopped up into fragments of the size of beads by the human hand, and the fragments are then rounded in the furnace. The men who chop up the rods sit at their work all day, their hands vibrating with a perpetual and exquisitely timed palsy,[1] and the beads dropping beneath their vibration like hail. Neither they, nor the men who draw out the rods or fuse the fragments, have the smallest occasion for the use of any single human faculty; and every young lady, therefore, who buys glass beads is engaged in the slave-trade, and in a much more cruel one than that which we have so long been endeavouring to put down. …

[One example to] show the reader what I mean [comes] from the manufacture already alluded to, that of glass. Our modern glass is exquisitely clear in its substance, true in its form, accurate in its cutting. We are proud of this. We ought to be ashamed of it. The old Venice glass[2] was muddy, inaccurate in all its forms, and clumsily cut, if at all. And the old Venetian was justly proud of it. For there is this difference between the English and Venetian workman, that the former thinks only of accurately matching his patterns, and getting his curves perfectly true and his edges perfectly sharp, and becomes a mere machine for rounding curves and sharpening edges; while the old Venetian cared not a whit whether his edges were sharp or not, but he invented a new design for every glass that he made, and never moulded a handle or a lip without a new fancy in

it. And therefore, though some Venetian glass is ugly and clumsy enough when made by clumsy and uninventive workmen, other Venetian glass is so lovely in its forms that no price is too great for it; and we never see the same form in it twice. Now you cannot have the finish and the varied form too. If the workman is thinking about his edges, he cannot be thinking of his design; if of his design, he cannot think of his edges. Choose whether you will pay for the lovely form or the perfect finish, and choose at the same moment whether you will make the worker a man or a grindstone.

Nay, but the reader interrupts me—"If the workman can design beautifully, I would not have him kept at the furnace. Let him be taken away and made a gentleman, and have a studio, and design his glass there, and I will have it blown and cut for him by common workmen, and so I will have my design and my finish too."

All ideas of this kind are founded upon two mistaken suppositions: the first, that one man's thoughts can be, or ought to be, executed by another man's hands; the second, that manual labour is a degradation, when it is governed by intellect.

On a large scale, and in work determinable by line and rule, it is indeed both possible and necessary that the thoughts of one man should be carried out by the labour of others; in this sense I have already defined the best architecture to be the expression of the mind of manhood by the hands of childhood. But on a smaller scale, and in a design which cannot be mathematically defined, one man's thoughts can never be expressed by another: and the difference between the spirit of touch of the man who is inventing, and of the man who is obeying directions, is often all the difference between a great and a common work of art. How wide the separation is between original and second-hand execution, I shall endeavour to show elsewhere; it is not so much to our purpose here as to mark the other and more fatal error of despising manual labour when governed by intellect; for it is no less fatal an error to despise it when thus regulated by intellect, than to value it for its own sake. We are always in these days endeavouring to separate the two; we want one man to be always thinking, and another to be always working, and we call one

---

[1] *palsy* Shaking.

[2] *Venice glass* Long famous for its ornamental and colorful glassware, Venice has been the site of glass production since approximately 450 CE.

a gentleman, and the other an operative; whereas the workman ought often to be thinking, and the thinker often to be working, and both should be gentlemen, in the best sense. As it is, we make both ungentle, the one envying, the other despising, his brother; and the mass of society is made up of morbid thinkers, and miserable workers. Now it is only by labour that thought can be made healthy, and only by thought that labour can be made happy, and the two cannot be separated with impunity. It would be well if all of us were good handi-craftsmen in some kind, and the dishonour of manual labour done away with altogether; so that though there should still be a trenchant distinction of race between nobles and commoners, there should not, among the latter, be a trenchant distinction of employment, as between idle and working men, or between men of liberal and illiberal professions. All professions should be liberal, and there should be less pride felt in peculiarity of employment, and more in excellence of achievement. And yet more, in each several[1] profession, no master should be too proud to do its hardest work. The painter should grind his own colours; the architect work in the mason's yard with his men. … Hitherto I have used the words imperfect and perfect merely to distinguish between work grossly unskilful, and work executed with average precision and science; and I have been pleading that any degree of unskilfulness should be admitted, so only that the labourer's mind had room for expression. But, accurately speaking, no good work whatever can be perfect, and *the demand for perfection is always a sign of a misunderstanding of the ends of art.*

This for two reasons, both based on everlasting laws. The first, that no great man ever stops working till he has reached his point of failure: that is to say, his mind is always far in advance of his powers of execution, and the latter will now and then give way in trying to follow it; … And therefore, if we are to have great men work-ing at all, or less men doing their best, the work will be imperfect, however beautiful. Of human work none but what is bad can be perfect, in its own bad way.

The second reason is, that imperfection is in some sort essential to all that we know of life. It is the sign of life in a mortal body, that is to say, of a state of progress and change. Nothing that lives is, or can be, rigidly perfect; part of it is decaying, part nascent. The foxglove blossom—a third part bud, a third part past, a third part in full bloom—is a type of the life of this world. And in all things that live there are certain irregularities and deficiencies which are not only signs of life, but sources of beauty. No human face is exactly the same in its lines on each side, no leaf perfect in its lobes, no branch in its symmetry. All admit irregularity as they imply change; and to banish imperfection is to destroy expression, to check[2] exertion, to paralyze vitality. All things are literally better, lovelier, and more beloved for the imperfections which have been divinely appointed, that the law of human life may be Effort, and the law of human judgment, Mercy.

Accept this then for a universal law, that neither architecture nor any other noble work of man can be good unless it be imperfect; and let us be prepared for the otherwise strange fact, which we shall discern clearly as we approach the period of the Renaissance, that the first cause of the fall of the arts of Europe was a relent-less requirement of perfection, incapable alike either of being silenced by veneration for greatness, or softened into forgiveness of simplicity.

Thus far then of the Rudeness or Savageness, which is the first mental element of Gothic architecture. It is an element in many other healthy architectures also, as the Byzantine and Romanesque;[3] but true Gothic cannot exist without it.

The second mental element above named was Changefulness, or Variety.

I have already enforced the allowing independent operation to the inferior workman, simply as a duty *to him,* and as ennobling the architecture by rendering it more Christian. We have now to consider what reward

---

[1] *several* Different.

[2] *check* Restrict.

[3] *Byzantine* The architecture of Byzantium (fourth–fifteenth centuries CE), once the eastern portion of the Roman Empire, was a strong influence on medieval European architecture; *Romanesque* Style of medieval European architecture that borrowed aspects of Roman and Byzantine architecture, most notably the rounded arch.

we obtain for the performance of this duty, namely, the perpetual variety of every feature of the building.

Wherever the workman is utterly enslaved, the parts of the building must of course be absolutely like each other; for the perfection of his execution can only be reached by exercising him in doing one thing, and giving him nothing else to do. The degree in which the workman is degraded may be thus known at a glance, by observing whether the several parts of the building are similar or not; and if, as in Greek work, all the capitals are alike, and all the mouldings unvaried, then the degradation is complete; if, as in Egyptian or Ninevite work, though the manner of executing certain figures is always the same, the order of design is perpetually varied, the degradation is less total; if, as in Gothic work, there is perpetual change both in design and execution, the workman must have been altogether set free.

How much the beholder gains from the liberty of the labourer may perhaps be questioned in England, where one of the strongest instincts in nearly every mind is that love of order which makes us desire that our house windows should pair like our carriage horses, and allows us to yield our faith unhesitatingly to architectural theories which fix a form for everything, and forbid variation from it. I would not impeach love of order: it is one of the most useful elements of the English mind; it helps us in our commerce and in all purely practical matters; and it is in many cases one of the foundation stones of morality. Only do not let us suppose that love of order is love of art. It is true that order, in its highest sense, is one of the necessities of art, just as time is a necessity of music; but love of order has no more to do with our right enjoyment of architecture or painting, than love of punctuality with the appreciation of an opera. ...

From these general uses of variety in the economy of the world, we may at once understand its use and abuse in architecture. The variety of the Gothic schools is the more healthy and beautiful, because in many cases it is entirely unstudied, and results, not from mere love of change, but from practical necessities. For in one point of view Gothic is not only the best, but the *only rational* architecture, as being that which can fit itself most easily to all services, vulgar or noble. Undefined in its slope of roof, height of shaft, breadth of arch, or disposition of ground plan, it can shrink into a turret, expand into a hall, coil into a staircase, or spring into a spire, with undegraded grace and unexhausted energy; and whenever it finds occasion for change in its form or purpose, it submits to it without the slightest sense of loss either to its unity or majesty,—subtle and flexible like a fiery serpent, but ever attentive to the voice of the charmer. And it is one of the chief virtues of the Gothic builders, that they never suffered ideas of outside symmetries and consistencies to interfere with the real use and value of what they did. If they wanted a window, they opened one; a room, they added one; a buttress, they built one; utterly regardless of any established conventionalities of external appearance, knowing (as indeed it always happened) that such daring interruptions of the formal plan would rather give additional interest to its symmetry than injure it. ...

The third constituent element of the Gothic mind was stated to be Naturalism; that is to say, the love of natural objects for their own sake, and the effort to represent them frankly, unconstrained by artistical laws.

This characteristic of the style partly follows in necessary connection with those named above. For, so soon as the workman is left free to represent what subjects he chooses, he must look to the nature that is round him for material, and will endeavour to represent it as he sees it, with more or less accuracy according to the skill he possesses, and with much play of fancy, but with small respect for law. There is, however, a marked distinction between the imaginations of the Western and Eastern races, even when both are left free; the Western, or Gothic, delighting most in the representation of facts, and the Eastern (Arabian, Persian, and Chinese) in the harmony of colours and forms. ...

Now the noblest art is an exact unison of the abstract value, with the imitative power, of forms and colours. It is the noblest composition, used to express the noblest facts. But the human mind cannot in general unite the two perfections: it either pursues the fact to the neglect of the composition, or pursues the composition to the neglect of the fact.

And it is intended by the Deity that it *should* do this: the best art is not always wanted. Facts are often wanted without art, as in a geological diagram; and art often without facts, as in a Turkey carpet. And most men have been made capable of giving either one or the other, but not both; only one or two, the very highest, can give both. ...

We have now, I believe, obtained a sufficiently accurate knowledge both of the spirit and form of Gothic architecture; but it may, perhaps, be useful to the general reader, if, in conclusion, I set down a few plain and practical rules for determining, in every instance, whether a given building be good Gothic or not, and, if not Gothic, whether its architecture is of a kind which will probably reward the pains of careful examination.

First, look if the roof rises in a steep gable, high above the walls. If it does not do this, there is something wrong: the building is not quite pure Gothic, or has been altered.

Secondly, look if the principal windows and doors have pointed arches with gables over them. If not pointed arches, the building is not Gothic; if they have not any gables over them, it is either not pure, or not first-rate.

If, however, it has the steep roof, the pointed arch, and gable all united, it is nearly certain to be a Gothic building of a very fine time. ...

... See if it looks as if it had been built by strong men; if it has the sort of roughness, and largeness, and nonchalance, mixed in places with the exquisite tenderness which seems always to be the sign-manual of the broad vision, and massy[1] power of men, who can see

past the work they are doing, and betray here and there something like disdain for it. ...

Secondly, observe if it be irregular, its different parts fitting themselves to different purposes, no one caring what becomes of them, so that they do their work. If one part always answers accurately to another part, it is sure to be a bad building; and the greater and more conspicuous the irregularities, the greater the chances are

The Ducal Palace—Bird's Eye View.

that it is a good one. For instance, in the Ducal Palace,[2] of which a rough woodcut [appears here], the general idea is sternly symmetrical; but two windows are lower than the rest of the six; and if the reader will count the arches of the small arcade as far as to the great balcony, he will find it is not in the centre, but set to the right-hand side by the whole width of one of those arches. We may be pretty sure that the building is a good one; none but a master of his craft would have ventured to do this. —1853

---

[1] *sign-manual* Authenticating signature; *massy* Heavy.

[2] *Ducal Palace* Gothic palace in Venice.

MATTHEW ARNOLD
1822 – 1888

Nicknamed "the Emperor" by his friends and family, Matthew Arnold was an ardent and, in the view of some Victorians, arrogant critic of modernity. Arnold embodied both the idealist expectations and the apocalyptic anxieties of the approaching *fin-de-siécle* in his poetry and prose. In the face of an increasingly materialistic mass culture, dominated by what he considered the vacuity of "the average man" or "Philistine" of the democratized middle classes, Arnold sought to revive

culture in the image of liberal humanism. Only an education in the ostensibly timeless and universal works of masters like Marcus Aurelius, Tolstoy, Homer, and Wordsworth, Arnold believed, could cure the *malaise* of modern life.

"For the creation of a masterwork of literature, two powers must concur," Arnold wrote in 1865, "The power of the man and the power of the moment, and the man is not enough without the moment." Arnold believed that modern industrial life and the materialism it had made possible were radically indisposed towards artistic genius and indeed had created a climate of psychological and moral enervation that poetry was powerless to heal. The *Zeitgeist* (one of his terms for the powerful work of modern popular culture) was profoundly "unpoetical," and was best anatomized through prose. His own career shows symptoms of the fragmentation he analyzed. Arnold incisively broke with the often melancholic poetry of his early years in order to pursue prose criticism, for him the best possible literary work, he

believed, in an era that he saw as spiritually bankrupt. Modern society was in no condition to produce great poets; the best that modern life could muster, according to Arnold, were powerful critics—*if* they stayed away from the politics of the passing moment.

The River Thames ran past the village of Laleham where Matthew Arnold was born in 1822. Arnold was the eldest son of Mary Penrose Arnold and Dr. Thomas Arnold. His father, a clergy member and headmaster of Rugby School, was celebrated for reforming the school's curriculum to foreground Christian values, classical languages, and competitive games. Ironically, Arnold, who in later life would come to resemble his father by valuing above all else great humanist texts and a classical education, was lazy, laconic, and flippant as a student. Upon meeting the young dilettante, Charlotte Brontë wrote that "his manner displeases, from its seeming foppery." Yet, in spite of a flamboyant indifference to academia and a studied attempt to dissociate himself from all that his father represented, he amazed family and friends by winning a scholarship to Oxford's Balliol College in 1840, the prodigious Newdigate Prize for poetry in 1843, and a Fellowship at Oriel College in 1845.

Wordsworth, a friend of the family, was one of the most tangible influences on Arnold's poetry. When Wordsworth died, Arnold wondered sadly, "Who will teach us how to feel?" He frequently fled from classes to wander the countryside around the Lake District or to hike in the Alps, landscapes memorialized by Wordsworth and Coleridge. Many critics claim that Arnold was most accomplished as a poet of nature. The "simple joy the country yields," rendered in poems like "Thyrsis," reveals a surprising affinity with the quiet style of Thomas Gray; his "Resignation" speaks to Wordsworth's "Tintern Abbey." Arnold's personal manner, reminiscent of his idols Lord Byron and Goethe, did not cancel out a heartfelt relation to nature, whose unadorned expression modeled the "high seriousness" he admired in Sophocles and Aeschylus.

In 1847, Arnold obtained employment in London as a private secretary to the liberal politician Lord Lansdowne, beginning a period during which he produced most of his poetry. The 1849 publication of *The Strayed Reveller, and Other Poems*, by "A," was followed by *Empedocles on Etna, and Other Poems* (1852). The controversial preface to *Poems* (1853) provoked heated debate. Here Arnold focused on the ponderous force of the "unpoetical" nineteenth century writ large over his earlier work and damned the "dialogue of the mind with itself" that his *Empedocles on Etna* exhibited. Great poetry, Arnold claimed, must be distinguished from verse produced by a restless intellect fragmented by attempts to address the problems of contemporary life. Poetry should create works of beauty and unity that rise above the historical moment to "inspirit and rejoice" readers.

Letters to his best friend and fellow poet Arthur Hugh Clough, who did address the intellectual issues of the current moment, provide valuable insight into the demanding standards Arnold set for poetry. "I am glad you like the *Gypsy Scholar*," he wrote, "—but what does it *do* for you? Homer *animates*—Shakespeare *animates*—in its poor way I think *Sohrab and Rustum animates*—the *Gypsy Scholar* at best awakens a pleasing melancholy." Considered an often biting critic of the work of his contemporaries, including Clough, Arnold's harshest criticisms were first addressed to his own work. His poem "Dover Beach," probably written in 1851, but published in 1867, is considered one of English literature's profound expressions of modernity's disaffection with itself. Yet perceiving that his own poetry seemed passively ensnared in the "continual state of mental distress" that he took to task in the preface to *Poems*, he largely ceased writing poetry from the mid-1850s onward. After *New Poems* (1867), Arnold would refashion himself as a prose writer. According to Lionel Trilling, Arnold "perceived in himself the poetic power, but knew that his genius was not of the greatest, that the poetic force was not irresistible in him," not enough, at any rate, to act as a transformative agent in an age of disillusionment.

Arnold married Frances Lucy Wightman in 1851, and to support his family he accepted a position as a public school inspector. Initially thinking the job would suffice "for the next three or four years," Arnold continued to be employed in the public service for three and a half decades, writing only in his spare time. He believed that his inspections of schools in Britain and across Europe gave him first-hand experience to support his conviction that educating the public in a classical humanist tradition was key to "civilizing the next generation of the lower classes."

In 1857, Arnold was elected Professor of Poetry at Oxford University, where he delivered public lectures for the following ten years. Though a proponent of an exacting standard of classical scholarship, Arnold was the first to lecture in English rather than Latin, altering an elitist institutional practice that acted as a barrier to the kind of education that, in his opinion, the nineteenth century urgently needed. Arnold turned many of his lectures into essays and books, including *On Translating Homer* (1861) and *Friendship's Garland* (1871).

Though by his own standards of greatness Arnold could not transform society as a poet, as a critic he was determined to reform it. In his famous essay "The Function of Criticism at the Present Time," published in *Essays in Criticism* (1865), Arnold helped raise the value of criticism from its status as a "baneful and injurious employment" to a creative activity in its own right. Deftly juxtaposing snatches from tabloids alongside texts of high culture, Arnold's critical methodology foreshadowed the kind of work pursued in cultural studies today. While few have unanimously agreed with Arnold's pronouncements on literature and society, his critical work has had a profound impact on the work of the twentieth-century critics that followed him, such as T.S. Eliot, Virginia Woolf, F.R. Leavis, Lionel Trilling, and Raymond Williams.

In *Culture and Anarchy* (1869), arguably his most important work of social criticism, Arnold proposed that antagonistic factions of British society could learn to overcome their differences through an education in "disinterested" and universal human values. The differences allowed expression in democratic societies would disintegrate into anarchic disorder, thought Arnold, unless tethered to the "higher" ideals of the humanist tradition. His witty veneer and Apollonian appeal to transcendent virtues of "sweetness and light" sometimes enamored, and sometimes exasperated, a public whose prominent figures he often singled out by name for critical interrogation. Leslie Stephen, Virginia Woolf's father, remarked drily, "I often wished ... that I too had a little sweetness and light that I might be able to say such nasty things of my enemies."

During the 1870s, Arnold published a series of attacks on orthodox religion: *St. Paul and Protestantism* (1870), *Literature and Dogma* (1873), and *God and the Bible* (1875). Even in a period that witnessed the challenges to traditional religious belief posed by Darwin's theories, the work of geologists, and the "higher criticism" of the Bible that came from Germany and elsewhere, Arnold's religious critiques scandalized many Victorians. He recommended that Victorians exchange their faith in a religion founded on the assumption of the truth of the Bible for faith in a transcendent, secular humanism. When he returned to literary criticism in "The Study of Poetry" (1880), he claimed, as Thomas Carlyle had before him in the 1830s, that "most of what now passes for religion and philosophy will be replaced by poetry."

Arnold embarked on a lecture tour of the United States in 1883. Tired and burdened by debts, Arnold saw the trip as a money-making venture that would also allow him to visit a daughter who had married an American. He was loved in Washington but received with mixed success in other cities. He compiled his lectures in *Discourses in America* (1885), which contains his discussion of Emerson as well as the essay "Literature and Science." Here Arnold responds to Thomas Huxley's claim in "Science and Culture" (1881) that "for the purpose of attaining real culture, an exclusively scientific education is at least as effectual as an exclusively literary education." Especially in America, Arnold argued, where the democratic impulse to glorify "the average man" was particularly enthusiastic, education must safeguard the guiding ideals of the Western tradition, "the best that is known and thought."

Arnold died suddenly of a heart attack in 1888, leaving behind him a remarkable body of cultural criticism and a few poems familiar to all readers of English poetry. His statement about Oxford and modernity in *Culture and Anarchy* may well be taken as fitting epitaph: "We in Oxford ... have not failed to seize one truth,—the truth that beauty and sweetness are essential characters of a complete human perfection.... We have not won our political battles, we have not carried our main points, we have not stopped our adversaries' advance, we have not marched victoriously with the modern world; but we have told silently upon the mind of the century, we have prepared currents of feeling which sap our adversaries' position when it seems gained, we have kept up our communications with the future."

⌘ ⌘ ⌘

The Forsaken Merman

Come, dear children, let us away;
Down and away below!
Now my brothers call from the bay,
Now the great winds shoreward blow,
5 Now the salt tides seaward flow;
Now the wild white horses play,
Champ and chafe and toss in the spray.
Children dear, let us away!
This way, this way!

10 Call her once before you go—
Call once yet!
In a voice that she will know:
"Margaret! Margaret!"
Children's voices should be dear
15 (Call once more) to a mother's ear;
Children's voices, wild with pain—
Surely she will come again!
Call her once and come away;
This way, this way!
20 "Mother dear, we cannot stay!
The wild white horses foam and fret."
Margaret! Margaret!

Come, dear children, come away down;
Call no more!
25 One last look at the white-walled town,
And the little grey church on the windy shore,
Then come down!
She will not come though you call all day;
Come away, come away!

30 Children dear, was it yesterday
We heard the sweet bells over the bay?
In the caverns where we lay,
Through the surf and through the swell,
The far-off sound of a silver bell?
35 Sand-strewn caverns, cool and deep,
Where the winds are all asleep;

Where the spent lights quiver and gleam,
Where the salt weed sways in the stream,
Where the sea-beasts, ranged all round,
40 Feed in the ooze of their pasture-ground;
Where the sea-snakes coil and twine,
Dry their mail and bask in the brine;
Where great whales come sailing by,
Sail and sail, with unshut eye,
45 Round the world for ever and aye?
When did music come this way?
Children dear, was it yesterday?

Children dear, was it yesterday
(Call yet once) that she went away?
50 Once she sat with you and me,
On a red gold throne in the heart of the sea,
And the youngest sat on her knee.
She combed its bright hair, and she tended it well,
When down swung the sound of a far-off bell.
55 She sighed, she looked up through the clear green
     sea;
She said: "I must go, for my kinsfolk pray
In the little grey church on the shore today.
'Twill be Easter-time in the world—ah me!
And I lose my poor soul, Merman! here with
     thee."[1]
60 I said: "Go up, dear heart, through the waves;
Say thy prayer, and come back to the kind
     sea-caves!"
She smiled, she went up through the surf in the
     bay.
Children dear, was it yesterday?

Children dear, were we long alone?
65 The sea grows stormy, the little ones moan;
"Long prayers," I said, "in the world they say;
Come!" I said; and we rose through the surf in the
     bay.

---

[1] *I lose ... thee* According to popular folk belief, mermaids and mermen had no souls, and humans who went to live with them would lose theirs as well.

We went up the beach, by the sandy down°   *dune*
Where the sea-stocks bloom, to the white-walled
    town;
70 Through the narrow paved streets, where all was
    still,
To the little grey church on the windy hill.
From the church came a murmur of folk at their
    prayers,
But we stood without in the cold blowing airs.
We climbed on the graves, on the stones worn with
    rains,
75 And we gazed up the aisle through the small leaded
    panes.
She sat by the pillar; we saw her clear:
"Margaret, hist!¹ come quick, we are here!
Dear heart," I said, "we are long alone;
The sea grows stormy, the little ones moan."
80 But, ah, she gave me never a look,
For her eyes were seal'd to the holy book!
Loud prays the priest; shut stands the door.
Come away, children, call no more!
Come away, come down, call no more!

85   Down, down, down!
Down to the depths of the sea!
She sits at her wheel in the humming town,
Singing most joyfully.
Hark what she sings: "O joy, O joy,
90 For the humming street, and the child with its toy!
For the priest, and the bell, and the holy well;
For the wheel where I spun,
And the blessed light of the sun!"
And so she sings her fill,
95 Singing most joyfully,
Till the spindle drops from her hand,
And the whizzing wheel stands still.
She steals to the window, and looks at the sand,
And over the sand at the sea;
100 And her eyes are set in a stare;
And anon° there breaks a sigh,   *soon*
And anon there drops a tear,

From a sorrow-clouded eye,
And a heart sorrow-laden,
105 A long, long sigh;
For the cold strange eyes of a little Mermaiden
And the gleam of her golden hair.

    Come away, away children;
Come children, come down!
110 The hoarse wind blows coldly;
Lights shine in the town.
She will start from her slumber
When gusts shake the door;
She will hear the winds howling,
115 Will hear the waves roar.
We shall see, while above us
The waves roar and whirl,
A ceiling of amber,
A pavement of pearl.
120 Singing: "Here came a mortal,
But faithless was she!
And alone dwell for ever
The kings of the sea."

But, children, at midnight,
125 When soft the winds blow,
When clear falls the moonlight,
When spring-tides are low;
When sweet airs come seaward
From heaths starred with broom,²
130 And high rocks throw mildly
On the blanched sands a gloom;
Up the still, glistening beaches,
Up the creeks we will hie,°   *hasten*
Over banks of bright seaweed
135 The ebb-tide leaves dry.
We will gaze, from the sand-hills,
At the white, sleeping town;
At the church on the hill-side—
And then come back down.
140 Singing: "There dwells a loved one,
But cruel is she!

---

1 *hist* Exclamation made as a request for silence or attention.

2 *broom* Type of shrub bearing yellow flowers, common in England.

She left lonely for ever
The kings of the sea."
—1849

Isolation. To Marguerite [1]

We were apart; yet, day by day,
   I bade my heart more constant be.
I bade it keep the world away,
And grow a home for only thee;
5   Nor feared but thy love likewise grew,
Like mine, each day, more tried, more true.

The fault was grave! I might have known,
What far too soon, alas! I learned—
The heart can bind itself alone,
10   And faith may oft be unreturned.
Self-swayed our feelings ebb and swell—
Thou lov'st no more—Farewell! Farewell!

Farewell!—and thou, thou lonely heart,
Which never yet without remorse
15   Even for a moment didst depart
From thy remote and sphered course
To haunt the place where passions reign—
Back to thy solitude again!

Back! with the conscious thrill of shame
20   Which Luna felt, that summer-night,
Flash through her pure immortal frame,
When she forsook the starry height
To hang over Endymion's sleep
Upon the pine-grown Latmian steep. [2]

25   Yet she, chaste queen, had never proved
How vain a thing is mortal love,

Wandering in Heaven, far removed.
But thou hast long had place to prove
This truth—to prove, and make thine own:
30   "Thou hast been, shalt be, art, alone."

Or, if not quite alone, yet they
Which touch thee are unmating things—
Ocean and clouds and night and day;
Lorn autumns and triumphant springs;
35   And life, and others' joy and pain,
And love, if love, of happier men.

Of happier men—for they, at least,
Have *dream'd* two human hearts might blend
In one, and were through faith released
40   From isolation without end
Prolong'd; nor knew, although not less
Alone than thou, their loneliness.
—1857 (1849)

To Marguerite—Continued

Yes! in the sea of life enisled,
   With echoing straits between us thrown,
Dotting the shoreless watery wild,
We mortal millions live *alone*.
5   The islands feel the enclasping flow,
And then their endless bounds they know.

But when the moon their hollows lights,
And they are swept by balms of spring,
And in their glens, on starry nights,
10   The nightingales divinely sing;
And lovely notes, from shore to shore,
Across the sounds and channels pour—

Oh! then a longing like despair
Is to their farthest caverns sent;
15   For surely once, they feel, we were
Parts of a single continent!
Now round us spreads the watery plain—
Oh might our marges° meet again!   borders

---

[1] *Marguerite*   An unidentified woman, perhaps someone Arnold met in Switzerland in the 1840s, or Mary Claude, an Englishwoman Arnold knew during that same time.

[2] *Which Luna ... steep*   Luna (or Diana), goddess of chastity and the moon, fell in love with the shepherd boy Endymion when she found him sleeping on Mount Latmos.

Who ordered, that their longing's fire
20 Should be, as soon as kindled, cooled?
Who renders vain their deep desire?—
A God, a God their severance ruled!
And bade betwixt their shores to be
The unplumbed, salt, estranging sea.
—1852 (1849)

The Buried Life

Light flows our war of mocking words, and yet,
     Behold, with tears mine eyes are wet!
I feel a nameless sadness o'er me roll.
Yes, yes, we know that we can jest,
5   We know, we know that we can smile!
But there's a something in this breast,
To which thy light words bring no rest,
And thy gay smiles no anodyne.°   remedy
Give me thy hand, and hush awhile,
10 And turn those limpid° eyes on mine,   clear
And let me read there, love! thy inmost soul.

Alas! is even love too weak
To unlock the heart, and let it speak?
Are even lovers powerless to reveal
15 To one another what indeed they feel?
I knew the mass of men concealed
Their thoughts, for fear that if revealed
They would by other men be met
With blank indifference, or with blame reproved;
20 I knew they lived and moved
Tricked° in disguises, alien to the rest   dressed up
Of men, and alien to themselves—and yet
The same heart beats in every human breast!

But we, my love!—doth a like spell benumb
25 Our hearts, our voices?—must we too be dumb?

Ah! well for us, if even we,
Even for a moment, can get free
Our heart, and have our lips unchained;
For that which seals them hath been deep-ordained!

30 Fate, which foresaw
How frivolous a baby man would be—
By what distractions he would be possessed,
How he would pour himself in every strife,
And well-nigh° change his own identity—   nearly
35 That it might keep from his capricious play
His genuine self, and force him to obey
Even in his own despite his being's law,
Bade through the deep recesses of our breast
The unregarded river of our life
40 Pursue with indiscernible flow its way;
And that we should not see
The buried stream, and seem to be
Eddying at large in blind uncertainty,
Though driving on with it eternally.

45 But often, in the world's most crowded streets,
But often, in the din of strife,
There rises an unspeakable desire
After the knowledge of our buried life;
A thirst to spend our fire and restless force
50 In tracking out our true, original course;
A longing to inquire
Into the mystery of this heart which beats
So wild, so deep in us—to know
Whence our lives come and where they go.
55 And many a man in his own breast then delves,
But deep enough, alas! none ever mines.
And we have been on many thousand lines,
And we have shown, on each, spirit and power;
But hardly have we, for one little hour,
60 Been on our own line, have we been ourselves—
Hardly had skill to utter one of all
The nameless feelings that course through our breast,
But they course on for ever unexpressed.
And long we try in vain to speak and act
65 Our hidden self, and what we say and do
Is eloquent, is well—but 'tis not true!
And then we will no more be racked
With inward striving, and demand
Of all the thousand nothings of the hour
70 Their stupefying power;
Ah yes, and they benumb us at our call!

Yet still, from time to time, vague and forlorn,
From the soul's subterranean depth upborne
As from an infinitely distant land,
75 Come airs, and floating echoes, and convey
A melancholy into all our day.

Only—but this is rare—
When a beloved hand is laid in ours,
When, jaded with the rush and glare
80 Of the interminable hours,
Our eyes can in another's eyes read clear,
When our world-deafened ear
Is by the tones of a loved voice caressed—
A bolt is shot back somewhere in our breast,
85 And a lost pulse of feeling stirs again.
The eye sinks inward, and the heart lies plain,
And what we mean, we say, and what we would, we
        know.
A man becomes aware of his life's flow,
And hears its winding murmur; and he sees
90 The meadows where it glides, the sun, the breeze.

And there arrives a lull in the hot race
Wherein he doth for ever chase
That flying and elusive shadow, rest.
An air of coolness plays upon his face,
95 And an unwonted calm pervades his breast.
And then he thinks he knows
The hills where his life rose,
And the sea where it goes.
—1852

The Scholar-Gipsy[1]

Go, for they call you, shepherd, from the hill;
Go, shepherd, and untie the wattled cotes![2]
    No longer leave thy wistful flock unfed,
    Nor let thy bawling fellows rack their throats,
5   Nor the cropped herbage shoot another head.
            But when the fields are still,
        And the tired men and dogs all gone to rest,
        And only the white sheep are sometimes seen
        Cross and recross the strips of moon-blanched
            green,
10 Come, shepherd, and again begin the quest!

Here, where the reaper was at work of late—
    In this high field's dark corner, where he leaves
        His coat, his basket, and his earthen cruse,° jug
    And in the sun all morning binds the sheaves,
15   Then here, at noon, comes back his stores to
            use—
            Here will I sit and wait,
        While to my ear from uplands far away
        The bleating of the folded° flocks is borne, enclosed

1 The Scholar-Gipsy Arnold said this poem was inspired by the
following passage in Joseph Glanville's Vanity of Dogmatizing (1661):

There was very lately a lad in the University of Oxford, who was
by his poverty forced to leave his studies there; and at last to join
himself to a company of vagabond gypsies. Among these extravagant people, by the insinuating subtilty of his carriage, he quickly
got so much of their love and esteem as that they discovered to
him their mystery. After he had been a pretty while exercised in
the trade, there chanced to ride by a couple of scholars, who had
formerly been of his acquaintance. They quickly spied out their
old friend among the gypsies; and he gave them an account of the
necessity which drove him to that kind of life, and told them that
the people he went with were not such imposters as they were
taken for, but that they had a traditional kind of learning among
them, and could do wonders by the power of imagination, their
fancy binding that of others; that he himself had learned much of
their art, and when he had compassed the whole secret, he
intended, he said, to leave their company, and give the world an
account of what he had learned.

Arnold imagines this student still roaming the area surrounding
Oxford, where Arnold spent "the freest and most delightful part,
perhaps, of my life."

2 wattled cotes Sheepfolds made of woven sticks.

With distant cries of reapers in the corn°— *grain*
20   All the live murmur of a summer's day.

Screened is this nook o'er the high, half-reaped field,
    And here till sun-down, shepherd! will I be.
        Through the thick corn the scarlet poppies peep,
    And round green roots and yellowing stalks I see
25   Pale pink convolvulus[1] in tendrils creep;
            And air-swept lindens[2] yield
    Their scent, and rustle down their perfumed
            showers
        Of bloom on the bent grass where I am laid,
        And bower me from the August sun with shade;
30   And the eye travels down to Oxford's towers.

And near me on the grass lies Glanvil's book—
    Come, let me read the oft-read tale again!
        The story of the Oxford scholar poor,
    Of pregnant[3] parts and quick inventive brain,
35   Who, tired of knocking at preferment's door,
            One summer-morn forsook
    His friends, and went to learn the gipsy-lore,
        And roamed the world with that wild
            brotherhood,
        And came, as most men deemed, to little good,
40   But came to Oxford and his friends no more.

But once, years after, in the country-lanes,
    Two scholars, whom at college erst° he knew, *once*
        Met him, and of his way of life enquired;
    Whereat he answered, that the gipsy-crew,
45   His mates, had arts to rule as they desired
            The workings of men's brains,
    And they can bind them to what thoughts they
            will.
        "And I," he said, "the secret of their art,
        When fully learned, will to the world impart;
50   But it needs heaven-sent moments for this skill."

___

[1] *convolvulus* Morning-glory.

[2] *lindens* Type of deciduous trees known for their pleasant-smelling flowers.

[3] *pregnant* Full of ideas.

This said, he left them, and returned no more.
    But rumours hung about the country-side,
        That the lost Scholar long was seen to stray,
    Seen by rare glimpses, pensive and tongue-tied,
55   In hat of antique shape, and cloak of grey,
            The same the gypsies wore.
    Shepherds had met him on the Hurst[4] in spring;
        At some lone alehouse in the Berkshire moors,
        On the warm ingle-bench,[5] the smock-frocked
            boors° *rustics*
60   Had found him seated at their entering,

But, 'mid their drink and clatter, he would fly.
    And I myself seem half to know thy looks,
        And put the shepherds, wanderer! on thy trace;[6]
    And boys who in lone wheatfields scare the rooks[7]
65   I ask if thou hast passed their quiet place;
            Or in my boat I lie
    Moored to the cool bank in the summer-heats,
        'Mid wide grass meadows which the sunshine
            fills,
        And watch the warm, green-muffled Cumner
            hills,
70   And wonder if thou haunt'st their shy retreats.

For most, I know, thou lov'st retired ground!
    Thee at the ferry Oxford riders blithe,
        Returning home on summer-nights, have met
    Crossing the stripling Thames at Bab-lock-hithe,
75   Trailing in the cool stream thy fingers wet,
            As the punt's[8] rope chops round;
    And leaning backward in a pensive dream,
        And fostering in thy lap a heap of flowers
        Plucked in shy fields and distant Wychwood
            bowers,
80   And thine eyes resting on the moonlit stream.

___

[4] *the Hurst* Hill outside Oxford. All the places mentioned in the stanzas following are located in the area surrounding Oxford.

[5] *ingle-bench* Fireside bench.

[6] *trace* Trail.

[7] *rooks* Crows.

[8] *punt* Small, shallow boat propelled with a long pole pushed against the river bottom.

And then they land, and thou art seen no more!
   Maidens, who from the distant hamlets come
      To dance around the Fyfield elm in May,
   Oft through the darkening fields have seen thee
      roam,
5   Or cross a stile into the public way.
      Oft thou hast given them store
   Of flowers—the frail-leafed, white anemone,
      Dark bluebells drenched with dews of summer
      eves,
      And purple orchises with spotted leaves—
00 But none hath words she can report of thee.

And, above Godstow Bridge, when hay-time's here
   In June, and many a scythe in sunshine flames,
      Men who through those wide fields of breezy
      grass
   Where black-winged swallows haunt the glittering
      Thames,
95   To bathe in the abandoned lasher pass,[1]
      Have often passed thee near
   Sitting upon the river bank o'ergrown;
      Marked thine outlandish garb, thy figure
      spare,
      Thy dark vague eyes, and soft abstracted air—
00 But, when they came from bathing, thou wast gone!

At some lone homestead in the Cumner hills,
   Where at her open door the housewife darns,
      Thou hast been seen, or hanging on a gate
   To watch the threshers in the mossy barns.
05   Children, who early range these slopes and late
      For cresses[2] from the rills,°   *creeks*
   Have known thee eyeing, all an April-day,
      The springing pastures and the feeding kine;° *cows*
      And marked thee, when the stars come out
      and shine,
110 Through the long dewy grass move slow away.

In autumn, on the skirts of Bagley Wood—
   Where most the gypsies by the turf-edged way
      Pitch their smoked tents, and every bush you
      see
   With scarlet patches tagged and shreds of grey,[3]
115   Above the forest-ground called Thessaly—
      The blackbird, picking food,
   Sees thee, nor stops his meal, nor fears at all;
      So often has he known thee past him stray,
      Rapt, twirling in thy hand a withered spray,
120 And waiting for the spark from heaven to fall.

And once, in winter, on the causeway chill
   Where home through flooded fields foot-travellers
      go,
      Have I not passed thee on the wooden bridge,
   Wrapt in thy cloak and battling with the snow,
125   Thy face toward Hinksey and its wintry ridge?
      And thou hast climbed the hill,
   And gained the white brow of the Cumner range;
      Turned once to watch, while thick the
      snowflakes fall,
      The line of festal light in Christ-Church hall[4]—
130 Then sought thy straw in some sequestered grange.

But what—I dream! Two hundred years are flown
   Since first thy story ran through Oxford halls,
      And the grave Glanvil did the tale inscribe
   That thou wert wandered from the studious walls
135   To learn strange arts, and join a gipsy-tribe;
      And thou from earth art gone
   Long since, and in some quiet churchyard laid—
      Some country-nook, where o'er thy unknown
      grave
      Tall grasses and white flowering nettles wave,
140 Under a dark, red-fruited yew-tree's shade.

—No, no, thou hast not felt the lapse of hours!
   For what wears out the life of mortal men?

---

[1] *lasher pass* Place where water collects after spilling over a dam.

[2] *cresses* Strongly flavored leaf vegetables, especially watercress, which grows naturally in small bodies of fresh water.

[3] *With scarlet ... grey* Reference to the clothes of the gypsies, which they hang on the bushes to dry.

[4] *Christ-Church hall* Dining hall of Christ Church, an Oxford College.

'Tis that from change to change their being
  rolls;
'Tis that repeated shocks, again, again,
145   Exhaust the energy of strongest souls
    And numb the elastic powers.
Till having used our nerves with bliss and
  teen,°   *vexation*
  And tired upon a thousand schemes our wit,
  To the just-pausing Genius[1] we remit
150 Our worn-out life, and are—what we have been.

Thou hast not lived, why should'st thou perish, so?
  Thou hadst *one* aim, *one* business, *one* desire;
   Else wert thou long since numbered with the
    dead!
  Else hadst thou spent, like other men, thy fire!
155   The generations of thy peers are fled,
    And we ourselves shall go;
  But thou possessest an immortal lot,
   And we imagine thee exempt from age
   And living as thou liv'st on Glanvil's page,
160 Because thou hadst—what we, alas! have not.

For early didst thou leave the world, with powers
Fresh, undiverted to the world without,
  Firm to their mark, not spent on other things;
·Free from the sick fatigue, the languid doubt,
165   Which much to have tried, in much been
    baffled, brings.
   O life unlike to ours!
Who fluctuate idly without term or scope,
  Of whom each strives, nor knows for what he
   strives,
  And each half lives a hundred different lives;
170 Who wait like thee, but not, like thee, in hope.

Thou waitest for the spark from heaven! and we,
  Light half-believers of our casual creeds,
   Who never deeply felt, nor clearly willed,
  Whose insight never has borne fruit in deeds,
175   Whose vague resolves never have been fulfilled;

For whom each year we see
Breeds new beginnings, disappointments new;
  Who hesitate and falter life away,
  And lose tomorrow the ground won today—
180 Ah! do not we, wanderer! await it too?

Yes, we await it!—but it still delays,
  And then we suffer! and amongst us one,
   Who most has suffered,[2] takes dejectedly
  His seat upon the intellectual throne;
185   And all his store of sad experience he
    Lays bare of wretched days;
Tells us his misery's birth and growth and signs,
  And how the dying spark of hope was fed,
  And how the breast was soothed, and how the
   head,
190 And all his hourly varied anodynes.° *pain relievers*

This for our wisest! and we others pine,
  And wish the long unhappy dream would end,
   And waive all claim to bliss, and try to bear;
With close-lipped patience for our only friend,
195   Sad patience, too near neighbour to despair—
    But none has hope like thine!
Thou through the fields and through the woods
  dost stray,
  Roaming the country-side, a truant boy,
  Nursing thy project in unclouded joy,
200 And every doubt long blown by time away.

O born in days when wits were fresh and clear,
  And life ran gaily as the sparkling Thames;
   Before this strange disease of modern life,
  With its sick hurry, its divided aims,
205   Its heads o'ertaxed, its palsied hearts, was rife—
    Fly hence, our contact fear!
Still fly, plunge deeper in the bowering wood!
  Averse, as Dido did with gesture stern

[1] *Genius* Attendant spirit that accompanies a soul from birth to death and shapes his or her character.

[2] *one … suffered* Reference probably either to Tennyson—whose *In Memoriam* appeared in 1850, the year he succeeded Wordsworth as Poet Laureate—or to German philosopher Johann Wolfgang von Goethe (1749–1832).

From her false friend's approach in Hades turn,[1]
10   Wave us away, and keep thy solitude!

Still nursing the unconquerable hope,
   Still clutching the inviolable shade,
     With a free, onward impulse brushing through,
   By night, the silvered branches of the glade—
15   Far on the forest-skirts, where none pursue.
        On some mild pastoral slope
     Emerge, and resting on the moonlit pales
     Freshen thy flowers as in former years
   With dew, or listen with enchanted ears,
20   From the dark dingles,[2] to the nightingales!

But fly our paths, our feverish contact fly!
   For strong the infection of our mental strife,
     Which, though it gives no bliss, yet spoils for rest;
   And we should win thee from thy own fair life,
25   Like us distracted, and like us unblest.
        Soon, soon thy cheer would die,
   Thy hopes grow timorous, and unfixed thy powers,
     And thy clear aims be cross and shifting made;
     And then thy glad perennial youth would fade,
30   Fade, and grow old at last, and die like ours.

Then fly our greetings, fly our speech and smiles!
   —As some grave Tyrian[3] trader, from the sea,
     Descried at sunrise an emerging prow
   Lifting the cool-haired creepers° stealthily,   *vines*
35   The fringes of a southward-facing brow
        Among the Aegean isles;
   And saw the merry Grecian coaster[4] come,
     Freighted with amber grapes, and Chian[5] wine,

Green, bursting figs, and tunnies°   *tuna fish*
     steeped in brine—
240   And knew the intruders on his ancient home,

The young light-hearted masters of the waves—
   And snatched his rudder, and shook out more sail;
     And day and night held on indignantly
   O'er the blue Midland waters with the gale,
245   Betwixt the Syrtes[6] and soft Sicily,
        To where the Atlantic raves
   Outside the western straits; and unbent sails
     There, where down cloudy cliffs, through
        sheets of foam,
     Shy traffickers, the dark Iberians[7] come;
250   And on the beach undid his corded bales.
—1853

Stanzas from *The Grande Chartreuse*[8]

Through Alpine meadows soft-suffused
   With rain, where thick the crocus blows,°   *blooms*
Past the dark forges long disused,
The mule-track from Saint Laurent goes.
5   The bridge is crossed, and slow we ride,
Through forest, up the mountain-side.

The autumnal evening darkens round,
The wind is up, and drives the rain;

---

[1] *as Dido … turn*   In Virgil's *Aeneid*, Dido, Queen of Carthage, dies by suicide when her lover, Aeneas, deserts her. When he encounters her in Hades, she turns away from him.

[2] *dingles*   Wooded dales.

[3] *Tyrian*   From Tyre, ancient capital of Phoenicia.

[4] *coaster*   Ship that trades along a coast.

[5] *Chian*   From the Greek island of Chios.

[6] *Syrtes*   Two treacherous gulfs off the coast of northern Africa.

[7] *dark Iberians*   Inhabitants of Spain or Portugal. The story of these "shy traffickers" comes from fifth-century BCE Greek historian Herodotus's *History*, in which he explains that the Carthaginians would sail through the Strait of Gibraltar to trade with the West Africans. In a unique trading process, these Carthaginians would leave their goods on the beach, withdrawing to their ships. The Africans would come out of their hiding places and leave gold beside the goods they wished to purchase. After they had retreated, the Carthaginians would return and decide if this was adequate payment. The process would be repeated until the two sides reached an agreement.

[8] *Grande Chartreuse*   Carthusian monastery in a nearly inaccessible valley in the French Alps, established by Saint Bruno in 1804. Arnold visited the monastery on his honeymoon in 1851. The Carthusians are known for their austerity, and devote their time to fasting, solitary contemplation, and prayer.

While, hark! far down, with strangled sound
10 Doth the Dead Guier's[1] stream complain,
Where that wet smoke, among the woods,
Over his boiling cauldron broods.

Swift rush the spectral vapours white
Past limestone scars with ragged pines,
15 Showing—then blotting from our sight!—
Halt—through the cloud-drift something shines!
High in the valley, wet and drear,
The huts of Courrerie appear.

Strike leftward! cries our guide; and higher
20 Mounts up the stony forest-way.
At last the encircling trees retire;
Look! through the showery twilight grey
What pointed roofs are these advance?
A palace of the Kings of France?

25 Approach, for what we seek is here!
Alight, and sparely sup, and wait
For rest in this outbuilding near;
Then cross the sward[2] and reach that gate.
Knock; pass the wicket! Thou art come
30 To the Carthusians' world-famed home.

The silent courts, where night and day
Into their stone-carved basins cold
The splashing icy fountains play—
The humid corridors behold!
35 Where, ghostlike in the deepening night,
Cowled[3] forms brush by in gleaming white.

The chapel, where no organ's peal
Invests the stern and naked prayer—
With penitential cries they kneel
40 And wrestle; rising then, with bare
And white uplifted faces stand,
Passing the Host from hand to hand;

Each takes, and then his visage wan
Is buried in his cowl once more.
45 The cells!—the suffering Son of Man
Upon the wall—the knee-worn floor—
And where they sleep, that wooden bed,
Which shall their coffin be, when dead![4]

The library, where tract and tome
50 Not to feed priestly pride are there,
To hymn the conquering march of Rome,
Nor yet to amuse, as ours are!
They paint of souls the inner strife,
Their drops of blood, their death in life.

55 The garden, overgrown—yet mild,
See, fragrant herbs[5] are flowering there!
Strong children of the Alpine wild
Whose culture is the brethren's care;
Of human tasks their only one,
60 And cheerful works beneath the sun.

Those halls, too, destined to contain
Each its own pilgrim-host of old,
From England, Germany, or Spain—
All are before me! I behold
65 The House, the Brotherhood austere!
—And what am I, that I am here?

For rigorous teachers seized my youth,
And purged its faith, and trimmed° its fire,   *tended*
Showed me the high, white star of Truth,
70 There bade me gaze, and there aspire.
Even now their whispers pierce the gloom:
What dost thou in this living tomb?

Forgive me, masters of the mind!
At whose behest I long ago
75 So much unlearnt, so much resigned—
I come not here to be your foe!

---

[1] *Dead Guier* Guiers Mort, a river that flows down past the monastery and into the Guiers Vif (French: Living Guiers).

[2] *sward* Stretch of grass.

[3] *Cowled* Dressed in a cowl, a monk's hooded garment.

---

[4] *that wooden … dead* Carthusians are buried on wooden planks. They are sometimes (incorrectly) thought to sleep in their coffins.

[5] *fragrant herbs* From which the Carthusians make the liqueur Chartreuse, the sales of which provide their primary source of income.

I seek these anchorites,[1] not in ruth,°   *remorse*
To curse and to deny your truth;

Not as their friend, or child, I speak!
80 But as, on some far northern strand,
Thinking of his own Gods, a Greek
In pity and mournful awe might stand
Before some fallen Runic[2] stone—
For both were faiths, and both are gone.

85 Wandering between two worlds, one dead,
The other powerless to be born,
With nowhere yet to rest my head,
Like these, on earth I wait forlorn.
Their faith, my tears, the world deride—
90 I come to shed them at their side.

Oh, hide me in your gloom profound,
Ye solemn seats of holy pain!
Take me, cowled forms, and fence me round,
Till I possess my soul again;
95 Till free my thoughts before me roll,
Not chafed by hourly false control!

For the world cries your faith is now
But a dead time's exploded dream;
My melancholy, sciolists[3] say,
100 Is a passed mode, an outworn theme—
As if the world had ever had
A faith, or sciolists been sad!

Ah, if it *be* passed, take away,
At least, the restlessness, the pain;
105 Be man henceforth no more a prey
To these out-dated stings again!
The nobleness of grief is gone—
Ah, leave us not the fret alone!

But—if you cannot give us ease—
110 Last of the race of them who grieve

Here leave us to die out with these
Last of the people who believe!
Silent, while years engrave the brow;
Silent—the best are silent now.

115 Achilles[4] ponders in his tent,
The kings of modern thought are dumb;°   *silent*
Silent they are, though not content,
And wait to see the future come.
They have the grief men had of yore,
120 But they contend and cry no more.

Our fathers[5] watered with their tears
This sea of time whereon we sail,
Their voices were in all men's ears
Who passed within their puissant° hail.   *powerful*
125 Still the same ocean round us raves,
But we stand mute, and watch the waves.

For what availed it, all the noise
And outcry of the former men?
Say, have their sons achieved more joys,
130 Say, is life lighter now than then?
The sufferers died, they left their pain—
The pangs which tortured them remain.

What helps it now, that Byron bore,
With haughty scorn which mocked the smart,
135 Through Europe to the Aetolian shore[6]
The pageant of his bleeding heart?
That thousands counted every groan,
And Europe made his woe her own?

What boots it, Shelley! that the breeze
140 Carried thy lovely wail away,
Musical through Italian trees

---

[1] *anchorites* Religious hermits.

[2] *Runic* Carved with runes (early Norse letters).

[3] *sciolists* Pretenders to knowledge.

[4] *Achilles* Greek warrior who, during the Trojan War, stayed in his tent, refusing to participate, until the death of his best friend, Patrocles, in battle, moved him to action.

[5] *Our fathers* I.e., the previous generation of writers.

[6] *Aetolian shore* In Greece, where the English poet George Gordon, Lord Byron, died.

Which fringe thy soft blue Spezzian bay?[1]
Inheritors of thy distress
Have restless hearts one throb the less?

145   Or are we easier, to have read,
O Obermann![2] the sad, stern page,
Which tells us how thou hidd'st thy head
From the fierce tempest of thine age
In the lone brakes° of Fontainebleau,   thickets
150   Or chalets near the Alpine snow?

Ye slumber in your silent grave!
The world, which for an idle day
Grace to your mood of sadness gave,
Long since hath flung her weeds[3] away.
155   The eternal trifler breaks your spell;
But we—we learnt your lore too well!

Years hence, perhaps, may dawn an age,
More fortunate, alas! than we,
Which without hardness will be sage,
160   And gay without frivolity.
Sons of the world, oh, speed those years;
But, while we wait, allow our tears!

Allow them! We admire with awe
The exulting thunder of your race;
165   You give the universe your law,
You triumph over time and space!
Your pride of life, your tireless powers,
We laud them, but they are not ours.

We are like children reared in shade
170   Beneath some old-world abbey wall,
Forgotten in a forest-glade,
And secret from the eyes of all.
Deep, deep the greenwood round them waves,
Their abbey, and its close° of graves!   enclosure

175   But, where the road runs near the stream,
Oft through the trees they catch a glance
Of passing troops in the sun's beam—
Pennon,[4] and plume, and flashing lance!
Forth to the world those soldiers fare,
180   To life, to cities, and to war!

And through the wood, another way,
Faint bugle-notes from far are borne,
Where hunters gather, staghounds bay,°   bark
Round some fair forest-lodge at morn.
185   Gay dames are there, in sylvan° green;   forest
Laughter and cries—those notes between!

The banners flashing through the trees
Make their blood dance and chain their eyes;
That bugle-music on the breeze
190   Arrests them with a charmed surprise.
Banner by turns and bugle woo:
Ye shy recluses, follow too!

O children, what do ye reply?
"Action and pleasure, will ye roam
195   Through these secluded dells to cry
And call us?—but too late ye come!
Too late for us your call ye blow,
Whose bent was taken long ago.

"Long since we pace this shadowed nave;
200   We watch those yellow tapers shine,
Emblems of hope over the grave,
In the high altar's depth divine;
The organ carries to our ear
Its accents of another sphere.

205   "Fenced early in this cloistral round
Of reverie, of shade, of prayer,
How should we grow in other ground?
How should we flower in foreign air?
—Pass, banners, pass, and bugles, cease;
210   And leave our desert to its peace!"
                                                          —1855

---

1   *Spezzian bay*   Where English poet Percy Bysshe Shelley drowned,
in Italy.

2   *Obermann*   Protagonist of the 1804 novel of that name by Étienne
Pivert de Senancour (1770–1846).

3   *weeds*   Mourning garments.

---

4   *Pennon*   Narrow triangular flag, usually borne on the head of a
lance.

Dover Beach

The sea is calm tonight.
　　The tide is full, the moon lies fair
Upon the straits—on the French coast the light
Gleams and is gone; the cliffs of England stand,
5　Glimmering and vast, out in the tranquil bay.
Come to the window, sweet is the night-air!
Only, from the long line of spray
Where the sea meets the moon-blanched land,
Listen! you hear the grating roar
10　Of pebbles which the waves draw back, and fling,
At their return, up the high strand,°   *shore*
Begin, and cease, and then again begin,
With tremulous cadence slow, and bring
The eternal note of sadness in.

15　Sophocles long ago
Heard it on the Aegean, and it brought
Into his mind the turbid ebb and flow
Of human misery;[1] we
Find also in the sound a thought,
20　Hearing it by this distant northern sea.

The Sea of Faith
Was once, too, at the full, and round earth's shore
Lay like the folds of a bright girdle° furled.   *belt*
But now I only hear
25　Its melancholy, long, withdrawing roar.
Retreating, to the breath
Of the night-wind, down the vast edges drear
And naked shingles[2] of the world.

30　Ah, love, let us be true
To one another! for the world, which seems
To lie before us like a land of dreams,
So various, so beautiful, so new,
Hath really neither joy, nor love, nor light,
Nor certitude, nor peace, nor help for pain;
35　And we are here as on a darkling[3] plain
Swept with confused alarms of struggle and flight,
Where ignorant armies clash by night.[4]
—1867

East London[5]

'Twas August, and the fierce sun overhead
　　Smote on the squalid streets of Bethnal Green,
And the pale weaver, through his windows seen
In Spitalfields, looked thrice dispirited.

5　I met a preacher there I knew, and said:
"Ill and o'erworked, how fare you in this scene?"
"Bravely!" said he; "for I of late have been
Much cheered with thoughts of Christ, *the living bread*."[6]

O human soul! as long as thou canst so
10　Set up a mark of everlasting light,
Above the howling senses' ebb and flow,

To cheer thee, and to right thee if thou roam—
Not with lost toil thou labourest through the night!
Thou mak'st the heaven thou hop'st indeed thy
　　home.
—1867

---

[1] *Sophocles … misery* Cf. Sophocles's *Antigone* 583–91: "Blest are those whose days have not tasted of evil. For when a house has once been shaken by the gods, no form of ruin is lacking, but it spreads over the bulk of the race, just as, when the surge is driven over the darkness of the deep by the fierce breath of Thracian sea-winds, it rolls up the black sand from the depths, and the wind-beaten headlands that front the blows of the storm give out a mournful roar."

[2] *shingles* Rocky beaches.

[3] *darkling* Dark, or darkening.

[4] *as on … night* Reference to Thucydides's *History of the Peloponnesian War*, in which the invading Athenians became confused as night fell on the battle at Epipolae. Combatants could not tell friend from foe in the moonlight.

[5] *East London* Working-class area of the city. Bethnal Green and Spitalfields are districts in East London.

[6] *the living bread* See John 6.51: "I am the living bread which came down from heaven: if any man eat of this bread, he shall live for ever."

West London[1]

Crouched on the pavement, close by Belgrave
        Square,
A tramp I saw, ill, moody, and tongue-tied.
A babe was in her arms, and at her side
A girl; their clothes were rags, their feet were bare.

5   Some labouring men, whose work lay somewhere
            there,
    Passed opposite; she touched her girl, who hied°   *hastened*
    Across, and begged, and came back satisfied.
    The rich she had let pass with frozen stare.

    Thought I: "Above her state this spirit towers;
10   She will not ask of aliens, but of friends,
    Of sharers in a common human fate.

    "She turns from that cold succour, which attends
    The unknown little from the unknowing great,
    And points us to a better time than ours."
    —1867

Preface to the First Edition of Poems

In two small volumes of poems, published anonymously, one in 1849, the other in 1852, many of the
poems which compose the present volume have already
appeared. The rest are now published for the first time.

I have, in the present collection, omitted the poem
from which the volume published in 1852 took its title.[2]
I have done so, not because the subject of it was a
Sicilian Greek born between two and three thousand
years ago, although many persons would think this a
sufficient reason. Neither have I done so because I had,
in my own opinion, failed in the delineation which I
intended to effect. I intended to delineate the feelings of
one of the last of the Greek religious philosophers, one of

the family of Orpheus and Musaeus, having survived his
fellows, living on into a time when the habits of Greek
thought and feeling had begun fast to change, character
to dwindle, the influence of the Sophists[3] to prevail. Into
the feelings of a man so situated there entered much that
we are accustomed to consider as exclusively modern;
how much, the fragments of Empedocles[4] himself which
remain to us are sufficient at least to indicate. What
those who are familiar only with the great monuments of
early Greek genius suppose to be its exclusive characteristics, have disappeared; the calm, the cheerfulness, the
disinterested[5] objectivity have disappeared; the dialogue
of the mind with itself has commenced; modern problems have presented themselves; we hear already the
doubts, we witness the discouragement, of Hamlet and
of Faust.[6]

The representations of such a man's feelings must be
interesting, if consistently drawn. We all naturally take
pleasure, says Aristotle, in any imitation or representation whatever: this is the basis of our love of Poetry: and
we take pleasure in them, he adds, because all knowledge is naturally agreeable to us; not to the philosopher
only, but to mankind at large. Every representation
therefore which is consistently drawn may be supposed
to be interesting, inasmuch as it gratifies this natural
interest in knowledge of all kinds. What is not interesting, is that which does not add to our knowledge of any
kind; that which is vaguely conceived and loosely
drawn; a representation which is general, indeterminate,
and faint, instead of being particular, precise, and firm.

---

[1]   *West London*   Wealthy end of the city. Belgrave Square was (and is)
a particularly affluent district.

[2]   *the poem … title*   Arnold's *Empedocles on Etna*.

[3]   *Orpheus*   Legendary Thracian poet and musician; *Musaeus*   Pupil
of Orpheus; *Sophists*   Itinerant teachers and intellectuals of ancient
Greece whose name became negatively associated with the use of clever
but misleading argument.

[4]   *fragments of Empedocles*   Fragments of Empedocles's scientific
treatises survive.

[5]   *disinterested*   Impartial.

[6]   *Hamlet*   Indecisive, self-questioning protagonist of Shakespeare's
1609 tragedy of the same name; *Faust*   Legendary German doctor
who makes a bargain with Satan to gain exceptional knowledge and
pleasure. The Faust story has inspired numerous literary works,
including Christopher Marlowe's play *Doctor Faustus* (c. 1588), and
Goethe's tragedy *Faust* (1808).

Any accurate representation may therefore be expected to be interesting; but, if the representation be a poetical one, more than this is demanded. It is demanded, not only that it shall interest, but also that it shall inspirit and rejoice the reader: that it shall convey a charm, and infuse delight. For the Muses, as Hesiod says, were born that they might be "a forgetfulness of evils, and a truce from cares":[1] and it is not enough that the Poet should add to the knowledge of men, it is required of him also that he should add to their happiness. "All art," says Schiller, "is dedicated to Joy, and there is no higher and no more serious problem, than how to make men happy. The right art is that alone, which creates the highest enjoyment."[2]

A poetical work, therefore, is not yet justified when it has been shown to be an accurate, and therefore interesting representation; it has to be shown also that it is a representation from which men can derive enjoyment. In presence of the most tragic circumstances, represented in a work of Art, the feeling of enjoyment, as is well known, may still subsist: the representation of the most utter calamity, of the liveliest anguish, is not sufficient to destroy it: the more tragic the situation, the deeper becomes the enjoyment; and the situation is more tragic in proportion as it becomes more terrible.

What then are the situations, from the representation of which, though accurate, no poetical enjoyment can be derived? They are those in which the suffering finds no vent in action; in which a continuous state of mental distress is prolonged, unrelieved by incident, hope, or resistance; in which there is everything to be endured, nothing to be done. In such situations there is inevitably something morbid, in the description of them something monotonous. When they occur in actual life, they are painful, not tragic; the representation of them in poetry is painful also.

To this class of situations, poetically faulty as it appears to me, that of Empedocles, as I have endeavoured to represent him, belongs; and I have therefore excluded the poem from the present collection.

And why, it may be asked, have I entered into this explanation respecting a matter so unimportant as the admission or exclusion of the poem in question? I have done so, because I was anxious to avow that the sole reason for its exclusion was that which has been stated above; and that it has not been excluded in deference to the opinion which many critics of the present day appear to entertain against subjects chosen from distant times and countries: against the choice, in short, of any subjects but modern ones.

"The poet," it is said, and by an intelligent critic, "the poet who would really fix the public attention must leave the exhausted past, and draw his subjects from matters of present import, and therefore both of interest and novelty."[3]

Now this view I believe to be completely false. It is worth examining, inasmuch as it is a fair sample of a class of critical dicta[4] everywhere current at the present day, having a philosophical form and air, but no real basis in fact; and which are calculated to vitiate the judgement of readers of poetry, while they exert, so far as they are adopted, a misleading influence on the practice of those who make it.

What are the eternal objects of poetry, among all nations and at all times? They are actions; human actions; possessing an inherent interest in themselves, and which are to be communicated in an interesting manner by the art of the poet. Vainly will the latter imagine that he has everything in his own power; that he can make an intrinsically inferior action equally delightful with a more excellent one by his treatment of it; he may indeed compel us to admire his skill, but his work will possess, within itself, an incurable defect.

The poet, then, has in the first place to select an excellent action; and what actions are the most excellent? Those, certainly, which most powerfully appeal to

---

[1] *Muses* In Greek mythology, the nine daughters of Zeus and Mnemosyne, each of whom presided over and provided inspiration for an aspect of the arts and sciences; *a forgetfulness ... cares* From early Greek poet Hesiod's *Theogony*.

[2] *All art ... enjoyment* From celebrated German dramatist and poet Friedrich von Schiller's *On the Use of the Chorus in Tragedy* (1803).

[3] [Arnold's note] In the *Spectator* of April 2nd, 1853. The words quoted were not used with reference to poems of mine.

[4] *dicta* Authoritative or generally accepted pronouncements.

the great primary human affections: to those elementary feelings which subsist permanently in the race, and which are independent of time. These feelings are permanent and the same; that which interests them is permanent and the same also. The modernness or antiquity of an action, therefore, has nothing to do with its fitness for poetical representation; this depends upon its inherent qualities. To the elementary part of our nature, to our passions, that which is great and passionate is eternally interesting; and interesting solely in proportion to its greatness and to its passion. A great human action of a thousand years ago is more interesting to it than a smaller human action of today, even though upon the representation of this last the most consummate skill may have been expended, and though it has the advantage of appealing by its modern language, familiar manners, and contemporary allusions, to all our transient feelings and interests. These, however, have no right to demand of a poetical work that it shall satisfy them; their claims are to be directed elsewhere. Poetical works belong to the domain of our permanent passions: let them interest these, and the voice of all subordinate claims upon them is at once silenced.

Achilles, Prometheus, Clytemnestra, Dido[1]—what modern poem presents personages as interesting, even to us moderns, as these personages of an "exhausted past"? We have the domestic epic dealing with the details of modern life which pass daily under our eyes; we have poems representing modern personages in contact with the problems of modern life, moral, intellectual, and social; these works have been produced by poets the most distinguished of their nation and time; yet I fearlessly assert that *Hermann and Dorothea, Childe Harold, Jocelyn, The Excursion*,[2] leave the reader cold in comparison with the effect produced upon him by the later books of the *Iliad*, by the *Oresteia*, or by the episode of Dido. And why is this? Simply because in the three last-named cases the action is greater, the personages nobler, the situations more intense: and this is the true basis of the interest in a poetical work, and this alone.

It may be urged, however, that past actions may be interesting in themselves, but that they are not to be adopted by the modern poet, because it is impossible for him to have them clearly present to his own mind, and he cannot therefore feel them deeply, nor represent them forcibly. But this is not necessarily the case. The externals of a past action, indeed, he cannot know with the precision of a contemporary; but his business is with its essentials. The outward man of Oedipus or of Macbeth,[3] the houses in which they lived, the ceremonies of their courts, he cannot accurately figure to himself; but neither do they essentially concern him. His business is with their inward man; with their feelings and behaviour in certain tragic situations, which engage their passions as men; these have in them nothing local and casual; they are as accessible to the modern poet as to a contemporary.

The date of an action, then, signifies nothing: the action itself, its selection and construction, this is what is all-important. This the Greeks understood far more clearly than we do. The radical difference between their poetical theory and ours consists, as it appears to me, in this: that, with them, the poetical character of the action in itself, and the conduct of it, was the first consideration; with us, attention is fixed mainly on the value of the separate thoughts and images which occur in the treatment of an action. They regarded the whole; we regard the parts. With them, the action predominated over the expression of it; with us, the expression predominates over the action. Not that they failed in expression or were inattentive to it; on the contrary, they are the highest models of expression, the unapproached masters of the grand style: but their expression is so excellent because it is so admirably kept in its right degree of prominence; because it is so simple and so well subordinated; because it draws its force directly from the

1 *Achilles … Dido* Major characters in ancient Greek and Roman classic works—Homer's *Iliad* (c. eighth century BCE), Hesiod's *Theogony* (c. 700 BCE), the *Oresteia* trilogy by Aeschylus (fifth century BCE), and Virgil's *Aeneid* (19 BCE) respectively.

2 *Hermann … Excursion* Poems by Johann Wolfgang von Goethe (1797), Lord Byron (1818), Alphonse de Lamartine (1836), and William Wordsworth (1814).

3 *Oedipus* Central character of the tragedy *Oedipus the King* (429 BCE) by Greek playwright Sophocles; *Macbeth* Titular character of Shakespeare's 1606 tragedy.

pregnancy of the matter which it conveys. For what reason was the Greek tragic poet confined to so limited a range of subjects? Because there are so few actions which unite in themselves, in the highest degree, the conditions of excellence: and it was not thought that on any but an excellent subject could an excellent poem be constructed. A few actions, therefore, eminently adapted for tragedy, maintained almost exclusive possession of the Greek tragic stage; their significance appeared inexhaustible; they were as permanent problems, perpetually offered to the genius of every fresh poet. This too is the reason of what appears to us moderns a certain baldness of expression in Greek tragedy; of the triviality with which we often reproach the remarks of the chorus, where it takes part in the dialogue: that the action itself, the situation of Orestes, or Merope, or Alcmaeon,[1] was to stand the central point of interest, unforgotten, absorbing, principal; that no accessories were for a moment to distract the spectator's attention from this; that the tone of the parts was to be perpetually kept down, in order not to impair the grandiose effect of the whole. The terrible old mythic story on which the drama was founded stood, before he entered the theatre, traced in its bare outlines upon the spectator's mind; it stood in his memory, as a group of statuary, faintly seen, at the end of a long and dark vista: then came the poet, embodying outlines, developing situations, not a word wasted, not a sentiment capriciously thrown in: stroke upon stroke, the drama proceeded: the light deepened upon the group; more and more it revealed itself to the rivetted gaze of the spectator: until at last, when the final words were spoken, it stood before him in broad sunlight, a model of immortal beauty.

This was what a Greek critic demanded; this was what a Greek poet endeavoured to effect. It signified nothing to what time an action belonged; we do not find that the *Persae*[2] occupied a particularly high rank among the dramas of Aeschylus because it represented a matter of contemporary interest: this was not what a cultivated Athenian required; he required that the permanent elements of his nature should be moved; and dramas of which the action, though taken from a long-distant mythic time, yet was calculated to accomplish this in a higher degree than that of the *Persae*, stood higher in his estimation accordingly. The Greeks felt, no doubt, with their exquisite sagacity of taste, that an action of present times was too near them, too much mixed up with what was accidental and passing, to form a sufficiently grand, detached, and self-subsistent object for a tragic poem: such objects belonged to the domain of the comic poet, and of the lighter kinds of poetry. For the more serious kinds, for pragmatic poetry, to use an excellent expression of Polybius,[3] they were more difficult and severe in the range of subjects which they permitted. Their theory and practice alike, the admirable treatise of Aristotle, and the unrivalled works of their poets, exclaim with a thousand tongues—"All depends upon the subject; choose a fitting action, penetrate yourself with the feeling of its situations; this done, everything else will follow."

But for all kinds of poetry alike there was one point on which they were rigidly exacting; the adaptability of the subject to the kind of poetry selected, and the careful construction of the poem.

How different a way of thinking from this is ours! We can hardly at the present day understand what Menander[4] meant, when he told a man who inquired as to the progress of his comedy that he had finished it, not having yet written a single line, because he had constructed the action of it in his mind. A modern critic would have assured him that the merit of his piece depended on the brilliant things which arose under his pen as he went along. We have poems which seem to exist merely for the sake of single lines and passages; not for the sake of producing any total-impression. We have critics who seem to direct their attention merely to detached expressions, to the language about the action, not to the action itself. I verily think that the majority of them do not in their hearts believe that there is such a thing as a total-impression to be derived from a poem at

---

[1] *Orestes ... Alcmaeon* Central characters in ancient Greek tragedies.

[2] *Persae* Play by Aeschylus, set during a Greek victory over the invading Persians, one that had occurred a few years before.

[3] *Polybius* Second-century BCE Greek historian; author of a forty-volume history of Rome, of which only five volumes survive.

[4] *Menander* Fourth-century BCE comic dramatist.

all, or to be demanded from a poet; they think the term a common-place of metaphysical criticism. They will permit the poet to select any action he pleases, and to suffer that action to go as it will, provided he gratifies them with occasional bursts of fine writing, and with a shower of isolated thoughts and images. That is, they permit him to leave their poetical sense ungratified, provided that he gratifies their rhetorical sense and their curiosity. Of his neglecting to gratify these, there is little danger; he needs rather to be warned against the danger of attempting to gratify these alone; he needs rather to be perpetually reminded to prefer his action to everything else; so to treat this, as to permit its inherent excellences to develop themselves, without interruption from the intrusion of his personal peculiarities: most fortunate, when he most entirely succeeds in effacing himself, and in enabling a noble action to subsist as it did in nature.

But the modern critic not only permits a false practice; he absolutely prescribes false aims.—"A true allegory of the state of one's own mind in a representative history," the poet is told, "is perhaps the highest thing that one can attempt in the way of poetry."[1]—And accordingly he attempts it. An allegory of the state of one's own mind, the highest problem of an art which imitates actions! No assuredly, it is not, it never can be so: no great poetical work has ever been produced with such an aim. *Faust* itself, in which something of the kind is attempted, wonderful passages as it contains, and in spite of the unsurpassed beauty of the scenes which relate to Margaret,[2] *Faust* itself, judged as a whole, and judged strictly as a poetical work, is defective: its illustrious author, the greatest poet of modern times, the greatest critic of all times, would have been the first to acknowledge it; he only defended his work, indeed, by asserting it to be "something incommensurable."

The confusion of the present times is great, the multitude of voices counselling different things bewildering, the number of existing works capable of attracting a young writer's attention and of becoming his models, immense: what he wants is a hand to guide him through the confusion, a voice to prescribe to him the aim which he should keep in view, and to explain to him that the value of the literary works which offer themselves to his attention is relative to their power of helping him forward on his road towards this aim. Such a guide the English writer at the present day will nowhere find. Failing this, all that can be looked for, all indeed that can be desired, is, that his attention should be fixed on excellent models; that he may reproduce, at any rate, something of their excellence, by penetrating himself with their works and by catching their spirit, if he cannot be taught to produce what is excellent independently.

Foremost among these models for the English writer stands Shakespeare: a name the greatest perhaps of all poetical names; a name never to be mentioned without reverence. I will venture, however, to express a doubt whether the influence of his works, excellent and fruitful for the readers of poetry, for the great majority, has been of unmixed advantage to the writers of it. Shakespeare indeed chose excellent subjects—the world could afford no better than Macbeth, or Romeo and Juliet, or Othello:[3] he had no theory respecting the necessity of choosing subjects of present import, or the paramount interest attaching to allegories of the state of one's own mind; like all great poets, he knew well what constituted a poetical action; like them, wherever he found such an action, he took it; like them, too, he found his best in past times. But to these general characteristics of all great poets he added a special one of his own; a gift, namely, of happy, abundant, and ingenious expression, eminent and unrivalled: so eminent as irresistibly to strike the attention first in him, and even to throw into comparative shade his other excellences as a poet. Here has been the mischief. These other excellences were his fundamental excellences as a poet; what distinguishes the artist from the mere amateur, says Goethe, is *Architectonicè* in the highest sense; that power of execution, which creates, forms, and constitutes: not the profoundness of single thoughts, not the richness of imagery, not the abundance of illustration. But these attractive accessories of a poetical work being more easily seized than the spirit of the whole, and these

---

[1] *A true ... poetry* From *North British Review* 19 (August 1853).

[2] *Margaret* Faust's lover in Goethe's tragedy.

[3] *Othello* Titular character of Shakespeare's 1603 tragedy.

accessories being possessed by Shakespeare in an un-equalled degree, a young writer having recourse to Shakespeare as his model runs great risk of being vanquished and absorbed by them, and, in consequence, of reproducing, according to the measure of his power, these, and these alone. Of this preponderating quality of Shakespeare's genius, accordingly, almost the whole of modern English poetry has, it appears to me, felt the influence. To the exclusive attention on the part of his imitators to this it is in a great degree owing, that of the majority of modern poetical works the details alone are valuable, the composition worthless. In reading them one is perpetually reminded of that terrible sentence on a modern French poet—*Il dit tout ce qu'il veut, mais malheureusement il n'a rien à dire.*[1]

Let me give an instance of what I mean. I will take it from the works of the very chief among those who seem to have been formed in the school of Shakespeare: of one whose exquisite genius and pathetic[2] death render him for ever interesting. I will take the poem of *Isabella, or the Pot of Basil*, by Keats. I choose this rather than the *Endymion*,[3] because the latter work (which a modern critic has classed with the *Fairy Queen*![4]), although undoubtedly there blows through it the breath of genius, is yet as a whole so utterly incoherent, as not strictly to merit the name of a poem at all. The poem of *Isabella*, then, is a perfect treasure-house of graceful and felicitous words and images: almost in every stanza there occurs one of those vivid and picturesque turns of expression, by which the object is made to flash upon the eye of the mind, and which thrill the reader with a sudden delight. This one short poem contains, perhaps, a greater number of happy single expressions which one could quote than all the extant tragedies of Sophocles.[5] But the action, the story? The action in itself is an excellent one; but so feebly is it conceived by the poet, so loosely constructed, that the effect produced by it, in

and for itself, is absolutely null. Let the reader, after he has finished the poem of Keats, turn to the same story in the Decameron:[6] he will then feel how pregnant and interesting the same action has become in the hands of a great artist, who above all things delineates his object; who subordinates expression to that which it is designed to express.

I have said that the imitators of Shakespeare, fixing their attention on his wonderful gift of expression, have directed their imitation to this, neglecting his other excellences. These excellences, the fundamental excellences of poetical art, Shakespeare no doubt possessed them—possessed many of them in a splendid degree; but it may perhaps be doubted whether even he himself did not sometimes give scope to his faculty of expression to the prejudice of a higher poetical duty. For we must never forget that Shakespeare is the great poet he is from his skill in discerning and firmly conceiving an excellent action, from his power of intensely feeling a situation, of intimately associating himself with a character; not from his gift of expression, which rather even leads him astray, degenerating sometimes into a fondness for curiosity of expression, into an irritability of fancy, which seems to make it impossible for him to say a thing plainly, even when the press of the action demands the very directest language, or its level character the very simplest. Mr. Hallam,[7] than whom it is impossible to find a saner and more judicious critic, has had the courage (for at the present day it needs courage) to remark, how extremely and faultily difficult Shakespeare's language often is. It is so: you may find main scenes in some of his greatest tragedies, *King Lear* for instance, where the language is so artificial, so curiously tortured, and so difficult, that every speech has to be read two or three times before its meaning can be comprehended. This over-curiousness of expression is indeed but the excessive employment of a wonderful gift—of the power of saying a thing in a happier way

---

[1] *Il dit ... dire* French: He says everything he wishes to, but unfortunately he has nothing to say.

[2] *pathetic* Evoking strong emotion.

[3] *Endymion* 1818 epic poem by John Keats.

[4] *Fairy Queen* I.e., Edmund Spenser's *The Faerie Queene*.

[5] *Sophocles* Greek playwright (c. 497–405 BCE).

[6] *the Decameron* Book of connected tales written in the fourteenth century by the Italian author Boccaccio; Keats's poem *Isabella* is based on one of the stories in the collection.

[7] *Mr. Hallam* Henry Hallam, author of *Introduction to the Literature of Europe* (1838–39).

than any other man; nevertheless, it is carried so far that one understands what M. Guizot[1] meant, when he said that Shakespeare appears in his language to have tried all styles except that of simplicity. He has not the severe and scrupulous self-restraint of the ancients, partly no doubt, because he had a far less cultivated and exacting audience: he has indeed a far wider range than they had, a far richer fertility of thought; in this respect he rises above them: in his strong conception of his subject, in the genuine way in which he is penetrated with it, he resembles them, and is unlike the moderns: but in the accurate limitation of it, the conscientious rejection of superfluities, the simple and rigorous development of it from the first line of his work to the last, he falls below them, and comes nearer to the moderns. In his chief works, besides what he has of his own, he has the elementary soundness of the ancients; he has their important action and their large and broad manner: but he has not their purity of method. He is therefore a less safe model; for what he has of his own is personal, and inseparable from his own rich nature; it may be imitated and exaggerated, it cannot be learned or applied as an art; he is above all suggestive; more valuable, therefore, to young writers as men than as artists. But clearness of arrangement, rigour of development, simplicity of style—these may to a certain extent be learned: and these may, I am convinced, be learned best from the ancients, who although infinitely less suggestive than Shakespeare, are thus, to the artist, more instructive.

What then, it will be asked, are the ancients to be our sole models? the ancients with their comparatively narrow range of experience, and their widely different circumstances? Not, certainly, that which is narrow in the ancients, nor that in which we can no longer sympathize. An action like the action of the *Antigone* of Sophocles, which turns upon the conflict between the heroine's duty to her brother's corpse and that to the laws of her country, is no longer one in which it is possible that we should feel a deep interest. I am speaking too, it will be remembered, not of the best sources of intellectual stimulus for the general reader, but of the best models of instruction for the individual writer. This last may certainly learn of the ancients, better than anywhere else, three things which it is vitally important for him to know: the all-importance of the choice of a subject; the necessity of accurate construction; and the subordinate character of expression. He will learn from them how unspeakably superior is the effect of the one moral impression left by a great action treated as a whole, to the effect produced by the most striking single thought or by the happiest image. As he penetrates into the spirit of the great classical works, as he becomes gradually aware of their intense significance, their noble simplicity, and their calm pathos, he will be convinced that it is this effect, unity and profoundness of moral impression, at which the ancient poets aimed; that it is this which constitutes the grandeur of their works, and which makes them immortal. He will desire to direct his own efforts towards producing the same effect. Above all, he will deliver himself from the jargon of modern criticism, and escape the danger of producing poetical works conceived in the spirit of the passing time, and which partake of its transitoriness.

The present age makes great claims upon us: we owe it service, it will not be satisfied without our admiration. I know not how it is, but their commerce with the ancients appears to me to produce, in those who constantly practise it, a steadying and composing effect upon their judgement, not of literary works only, but of men and events in general. They are like persons who have had a very weighty and impressive experience; they are more truly than others under the empire of facts, and more independent of the language current among those with whom they live. They wish neither to applaud nor to revile their age: they wish to know what it is, what it can give them, and whether this is what they want. What they want, they know very well; they want to educe and cultivate what is best and noblest in themselves: they know, too, that this is no easy task— χαλεπὸν as Pittacus said, χαλεπὸν ἐσθλὸν ἔμμεναι[2]—and they ask themselves sincerely whether their age and its literature can assist them in the at-

---

[1] *M. Guizot* French historian (1787–1874). His discussion of Shakespeare is found in his *Shakespeare et son temps* (1852).

[2] χαλεπὸν ἐσθλὸν ἔμμεναι Greek: It is hard to be good. Pittacus was a seventh-century BCE Greek political and military figure.

tempt. If they are endeavouring to practise any art, they remember the plain and simple proceedings of the old artists, who attained their grand results by penetrating themselves with some noble and significant action, not by inflating themselves with a belief in the pre-eminent importance and greatness of their own times. They do not talk of their mission, nor of interpreting their age, nor of the coming poet; all this, they know, is the mere delirium of vanity; their business is not to praise their age, but to afford to the men who live in it the highest pleasure which they are capable of feeling. If asked to afford this by means of subjects drawn from the age itself, they ask what special fitness the present age has for supplying them: they are told that it is an era of progress, an age commissioned to carry out the great ideas of industrial development and social amelioration. They reply that with all this they can do nothing; that the elements they need for the exercise of their art are great actions, calculated powerfully and delightfully to affect what is permanent in the human soul; that so far as the present age can supply such actions, they will gladly make use of them; but that an age wanting in moral grandeur can with difficulty supply such, and an age of spiritual discomfort with difficulty be powerfully and delightfully affected by them.

A host of voices will indignantly rejoin that the present age is inferior to the past neither in moral grandeur nor in spiritual health. He who possesses the discipline I speak of will content himself with remembering the judgements passed upon the present age, in this respect, by the two men, the one of strongest head, the other of widest culture, whom it has produced; by Goethe and by Niebuhr.[1] It will be sufficient for him that he knows the opinions held by these two great men respecting the present age and its literature; and that he feels assured in his own mind that their aims and demands upon life were such as he would wish, at any rate, his own to be; and their judgement as to what is impeding and disabling such as he may safely follow. He will not, however, maintain a hostile attitude towards the false pretensions of his age; he will content himself with not being overwhelmed by them. He will esteem

himself fortunate if he can succeed in banishing from his mind all feelings of contradiction, and irritation, and impatience; in order to delight himself with the contemplation of some noble action of a heroic time, and to enable others, through his representation of it, to delight in it also.

I am far indeed from making any claim, for myself, that I possess this discipline; or for the following poems, that they breathe its spirit. But I say, that in the sincere endeavour to learn and practise, amid the bewildering confusion of our times, what is sound and true in poetical art, I seemed to myself to find the only sure guidance, the only solid footing, among the ancients. They, at any rate, knew what they wanted in art, and we do not. It is this uncertainty which is disheartening, and not hostile criticism. How often have I felt this when reading words of disparagement or of cavil:[2] that it is the uncertainty as to what is really to be aimed at which makes our difficulty, not the dissatisfaction of the critic, who himself suffers from the same uncertainty. *Non me tua fervida terrent Dicta: Dii me terrent, et Jupiter hostis.*[3]

Two kinds of *dilettanti*, says Goethe, there are in poetry: he who neglects the indispensable mechanical part, and thinks he has done enough if he shows spirituality and feeling; and he who seeks to arrive at poetry merely by mechanism, in which he can acquire an artisan's readiness, and is without soul and matter. And he adds, that the first does most harm to art, and the last to himself. If we must be *dilettanti*: if it is impossible for us, under the circumstances amidst which we live, to think clearly, to feel nobly, and to delineate firmly: if we cannot attain to the mastery of the great artists—let us, at least, have so much respect for our art as to prefer it to ourselves: let us not bewilder our successors: let us transmit to them the practice of poetry, with its boundaries and wholesome regulative laws, under which excellent works may again, perhaps, at some future time, be produced, not yet fallen into oblivion through our

---

[1] *Niebuhr* German historian Barthold Georg Niebuhr (1776–1831).

[2] *cavil* Petty complaint.

[3] *Non me ... hostis* Latin: Your fiery words do not frighten me; the gods frighten me, as does the enmity of Jupiter. (From *Aeneid* 12.894–95, in which Turnus, a warrior forsaken by the gods, responds to Aeneas, who has mocked his fear.)

neglect, not yet condemned and cancelled by the influence of their eternal enemy, Caprice.

—1853

from *The Function of Criticism at the Present Time*

Many objections have been made to a proposition which, in some remarks of mine on translating Homer,[1] I ventured to put forth; a proposition about criticism, and its importance at the present day. I said: "Of the literature of France and Germany, as of the intellect of Europe in general, the main effort, for now many years, has been a critical effort; the endeavour, in all branches of knowledge, theology, philosophy, history, art, science, to see the object as in itself it really is." I added, that owing to the operation in English literature of certain causes, "almost the last thing for which one would come to English literature is just that very thing which now Europe most desires—criticism"; and that the power and value of English literature was thereby impaired. More than one rejoinder declared that the importance I here assigned to criticism was excessive, and asserted the inherent superiority of the creative effort of the human spirit over its critical effort. And the other day, having been led by a Mr. Shairp's excellent notice of Wordsworth[2] to turn again to his biography, I found, in the words of this great man, whom I, for one, must always listen to with the profoundest respect, a sentence passed on the critic's business, which seems

to justify every possible disparagement of it. Wordsworth says in one of his letters:

> The writers in these publications [the reviews], while they prosecute their inglorious employment, can not be supposed to be in a state of mind very favourable for being affected by the finer influences of a thing so pure as genuine poetry.

And a trustworthy reporter of his conversation quotes a more elaborate judgement to the same effect:

> Wordsworth holds the critical power very low, infinitely lower than the inventive; and he said today that if the quantity of time consumed in writing critiques on the works of others were given to original composition, of whatever kind it might be, it would be much better employed; it would make a man find out sooner his own level, and it would do infinitely less mischief. A false or malicious criticism may do much injury to the minds of others, a stupid invention, either in prose or verse, is quite harmless.

It is almost too much to expect of poor human nature, that a man capable of producing some effect in one line of literature, should, for the greater good of society, voluntarily doom himself to impotence and obscurity in another. Still less is this to be expected from men addicted to the composition of the "false or malicious criticism" of which Wordsworth speaks. However, everybody would admit that a false or malicious criticism had better never been written. Everybody, too, would be willing to admit, as a general proposition, that the critical faculty is lower than the inventive. But is it true that criticism is really, in itself, a baneful and injurious employment; is it true that all time given to writing critiques on the works of others would be much better employed if it were given to original composition of whatever kind this may be? Is it true Johnson had better have gone on producing more *Irenes* instead of

---

[1] *in some ... Homer* In Arnold's *On Translating Homer* (1861).

[2] [Arnold's note] I cannot help thinking that a practice, common in England during the last century, and still followed in France, of printing a notice of this kind—a notice by competent critics—to serve as an introduction to an eminent author's works, might be revived among us with advantage. To introduce all succeeding editions of Wordsworth, Mr. Shairp's notice might, it seems it me, excellently serve; it is written from the point of view of an admirer, nay, or a disciple, and that is right; but then the disciple must also be, as in this case he is, a critic, a man of letters, not, as too often happens, some relation or friend with no qualification for his task except affection for his author. [Arnold refers to J.C. Shairp's essay *Wordsworth: The Man and the Poet* (1864).]

writing his *Lives of the Poets*;[1] nay, is it certain that Wordsworth himself was better employed in making his Ecclesiastical Sonnets than when he made his celebrated Preface,[2] so full of criticism, and criticism of the works of others? Wordsworth was himself a great critic, and it is to be sincerely regretted that he has not left us more criticism; Goethe[3] was one of the greatest of critics, and we may sincerely congratulate ourselves that he has left us so much criticism. Without wasting time over the exaggeration which Wordsworth's judgement on criticism clearly contains, or over an attempt to trace the causes—not difficult, I think, to be traced—which may have led Wordsworth to this exaggeration, a critic may with advantage seize an occasion for trying[4] his own conscience, and for asking himself of what real service at any given moment the practice of criticism either is or may be made to his own mind and spirit, and to the minds and spirits of others.

The critical power is of lower rank than the creative. True; but in assenting to this proposition, one or two things are to be kept in mind. It is undeniable that the exercise of a creative power, that a free creative activity, is the highest function of man; it is proved to be so by man's finding in it his true happiness. But it is undeniable, also, that men may have the sense of exercising this free creative activity in other ways than in producing great words of literature or art; if it were not so, all but a very few men would be shut out from the true happiness of all men. They may have it in well-doing, they may have it in learning, they may have it even in criticising. This is one thing to be kept in mind. Another is, that the exercise of the creative power in the production of great works of literature or art, however high this exercise of it may rank, is not at all epochs and under all conditions possible; and that therefore labour may be vainly spent in attempting it, which might with more fruit be used in preparing for it, in rendering it possible. This creative power works with elements, with materials; what if it has not those materials, those elements, ready for its use? In that case it must surely wait till they are ready. Now in literature—I will limit myself to literature, for it is about literature that the question arises—the elements with which the creative power works are ideas; the best ideas, on every matter which literature touches, current at the time. At any rate we may lay it down as certain that in modern literature no manifestation of the creative power not working with these can be very important or fruitful. And I say current at the time, not merely accessible at the time; for creative literary genius does not principally show itself in discovering new ideas; that is rather the business of the philosopher. The grand work of literary genius is a work of synthesis and exposition, not of analysis and discovery; its gift lies in the faculty of being happily inspired by a certain intellectual and spiritual atmosphere, by a certain order of ideas, when it finds itself in them; of dealing divinely with these ideas, presenting them in the most effective and attractive combinations—making beautiful works with them, in short. But it must have the atmosphere, it must find itself amidst the order of ideas, in order to work freely; and these it is not so easy to command. This is why great creative epochs in literature are so rare, this is why there is so much that is unsatisfactory in the productions of many men of real genius; because, for the creation of a masterwork of literature two powers must concur, the power of the man and the power of the moment, and the man is not enough without the moment; the creative power has, for its happy exercise, appointed elements, and those elements are not in its own control.

Nay, they are more within the control of the critical power. It is the business of the critical power, as I said in the words already quoted, "in all branches of knowledge, theology, philosophy, history, art, science, to see the object as in itself it really is." Thus it tends, at last, to make an intellectual situation of which the creative power can profitably avail itself. It tends to establish an order of ideas, if not absolutely true, yet true by compar-

---

[1] *Johnson ... Poets* In the nineteenth century Samuel Johnson was perhaps most celebrated for his biographical and critical work *Lives of the English Poets* (1779–81), while his play *Irene* (1736) has never been highly regarded.

[2] *Preface* To Wordsworth and Coleridge's *Lyrical Ballads* (1800). His *Ecclesiastical Sonnets* is not his best-known work.

[3] *Goethe* German poet and dramatist Johann Wolfgang von Goethe (1749–1832).

[4] *trying* Testing.

ison with that which it displaces; to make the best ideas prevail. Presently these new ideas reach society, the touch of truth is the touch of life, and there is a stir and growth everywhere; out of this stir and growth come the creative epochs of literature.

Or, to narrow our range, and quit these considerations of the general march of genius and of society—considerations which are apt to become too abstract and impalpable—every one can see that a poet, for instance, ought to know life and the world before dealing with them in poetry; and life and the world being in modern times very complex things, the creation of a modern poet, to be worth much, implies a great critical effort behind it; else it must be a comparatively poor, barren, and short-lived affair. This is why Byron's[1] poetry had so little endurance in it, and Goethe's so much; both Byron and Goethe had a great productive power, but Goethe's was nourished by a great critical effort providing the true materials for it, and Byron's was not; Goethe knew life and the world, the poet's necessary subjects, much more comprehensively and thoroughly than Byron. He knew a great deal more of them, and he knew them much more as they really are.

It has long seemed to me that the burst of creative activity in our literature, through the first quarter of this century, had about it in fact something premature; and that from this cause its productions are doomed, most of them, in spite of the sanguine[2] hopes which accompanied and do still accompany them, to prove hardly more lasting than the productions of far less splendid epochs. And this prematureness comes from its having proceeded without having its proper data, without sufficient materials to work with. In other words, the English poetry of the first quarter of this century, with plenty of energy, plenty of creative force, did not know enough. This makes Byron so empty of matter, Shelley[3] so incoherent, Wordsworth even, profound as he is, yet so wanting in completeness and variety. Wordsworth cared little for books, and disparaged Goethe. I admire

Wordsworth, as he is, so much that I cannot wish him different; and it is vain, no doubt, to imagine such a man different from what he is, to suppose that he could have been different. But surely the one thing wanting to make Wordsworth an even greater poet than he is—his thought richer, and his influence of wider application—was that he should have read more books, among them, no doubt, those of that Goethe whom he disparaged without reading him.

But to speak of books and reading may easily lead to a misunderstanding here. It was not really books and reading that lacked to our poetry at this epoch; Shelley had plenty of reading, Coleridge[4] had immense reading. Pindar and Sophocles[5]—as we all say so glibly, and often with so little discernment of the real import of what we are saying—had not many books; Shakespeare was no deep reader. True; but in the Greece of Pindar and Sophocles, in the England of Shakespeare, the poet lived in a current of ideas in the highest degree animating and nourishing to the creative power; society was, in the fullest measure, permeated by fresh thought, intelligent and alive. And this state of things is the true basis for the creative power's exercise, in this it finds its data, its materials, truly ready for its hand; all the books and reading in the world are only valuable as they are helps to this. Even when this does not actually exist, books and reading may enable a man to construct a kind of semblance of it in his own mind, a world of knowledge and intelligence in which he may live and work. This is by no means an equivalent to the artist for the nationally diffused life and thought of the epochs of Sophocles or Shakespeare; but, besides that it may be a means of preparation for such epochs, it does really constitute, if many share in it, a quickening and sustaining atmosphere of great value. Such an atmosphere the many-sided learning and the long and widely combined critical effort of Germany formed for Goethe, when he lived and worked. There was no national glow of life and thought there, as in the Athens of Pericles or the

---

[1] *Byron* George Gordon, Lord Byron (1788–1824), English Romantic poet.

[2] *sanguine* Optimistic.

[3] *Shelley* Percy Bysshe Shelley (1792–1822), English Romantic poet.

[4] *Coleridge* Samuel Taylor Coleridge (1772–1834), English Romantic poet.

[5] *Pindar* Greek lyric poet of the fifth century BCE; *Sophocles* Greek tragedian (c. 497–405 BCE).

England of Elizabeth.[1] That was the poet's weakness. But there was a sort of equivalent for it in the complete culture and unfettered thinking of a large body of Germans. That was his strength. In the England of the first quarter of this century there was neither a national glow of life and thought, such as we had in the age of Elizabeth, nor yet a culture and a force of learning and criticism such as were to be found in Germany. Therefore the creative power of poetry wanted, for success in the highest sense, materials and a basis; a thorough interpretation of the world was necessarily denied to it.

... The Englishman has been called a political animal, and he values what is political and practical so much that ideas easily become objects of dislike in his eyes, and thinkers "miscreants," because ideas and thinkers have rashly meddled with politics and practice. This would be all very well if the dislike and neglect confined themselves to ideas transported out of their own sphere, and meddling rashly with practice; but they are inevitably extended to ideas as such, and to the whole life of intelligence; practice is everything, a free play of the mind is nothing. The notion of the free play of the mind upon all subjects being a pleasure in itself, being an object of desire, being an essential provider of elements without which a nation's spirit, whatever compensations it may have for them, must, in the long run, die of inanition, hardly enters into an Englishman's thoughts. It is noticeable that the word *curiosity*, which in other languages is used in a good sense, to mean, as a high and fine quality of man's nature, just this disinterested love of a free play of the mind on all subjects, for its own sake—it is noticeable, I say, that this word has in our language no sense of the kind, no sense but a rather bad and disparaging one. But criticism, real criticism, is essentially the exercise of this very quality; it obeys an instinct prompting it to try to know the best that is known and thought in the world, irrespectively of practice, politics, and everything of the kind; and to value knowledge and thought as they approach this best,

without the intrusion of any other considerations whatever. This is an instinct for which there is, I think, little original sympathy in the practical English nature, and what there was of it has undergone a long benumbing period of blight and suppression in the epoch of concentration which followed the French Revolution.

But epochs of concentration cannot well endure for ever; epochs of expansion, in the due course of things, follow them. Such an epoch of expansion seems to be opening in this country. In the first place all danger of a hostile forcible pressure of foreign ideas upon our practice has long disappeared; like the traveller in the fable, therefore, we begin to wear our cloak a little more loosely.[2] Then, with a long peace, the ideas of Europe steal gradually and amicably in, and mingle, though in infinitesimally small quantities at a time, with our own notions. Then, too, in spite of all that is said about the absorbing and brutalising influence of our passionate material progress, it seems to me indisputable that this progress is likely, though not certain, to lead in the end to an apparition of intellectual life; and that man, after he has made himself perfectly comfortable and has now to determine what to do with himself next, may begin to remember that he has a mind, and that the mind may be made the source of great pleasure. I grant it is mainly the privilege of faith, at present, to discern this end to our railways, our business, and our fortune-making; but we shall see if, here as elsewhere, faith is not in the end the true prophet. Our ease, our travelling, and our unbounded liberty to hold just as hard and securely as we please to the practice to which our notions have given birth, all tend to beget an inclination to deal a little more freely with these notions themselves, to canvass them a little, to penetrate a little into their real nature. Flutterings of curiosity, in the foreign sense of the word, appear amongst us, and it is in these that criticism must look to find its account. Criticism first; a time of true creative activity, perhaps—which, as I

---

[1] *Athens of Pericles* Pericles was a prominent Athenian political leader of the early fifth century BCE and was responsible for the construction of the Parthenon; *Elizabeth* Elizabeth I reigned as Queen of England and Ireland from 1558 to 1603.

[2] *like the ... loosely* In one of Aesop's fables, the wind and the sun compete to see who is more powerful, betting on which of them can cause a traveler to take his cloak off first. The wind attempts to use force, but the fierce gusts only cause the traveler to clutch his cloak more tightly. When the sun shines on him, however, the traveler is persuaded to take off his cloak.

have said, must inevitably be preceded amongst us by a time of criticism—hereafter, when criticism has done its work.

It is of the last importance that English criticism should clearly discern what rule for its course, in order to avail itself of the field now opening to it, and to produce fruit for the future, it ought to take. The rule may be summed up in one word—*disinterestedness*.[1] And how is criticism to show disinterestedness? By keeping aloof from what is called "the practical view of things"; by resolutely following the law of its own nature, which is to be a free play of the mind on all subjects which it touches. By steadily refusing to lend itself to any of those ulterior, political, practical considerations about ideas, which plenty of people will be sure to attach to them, which perhaps ought often to be attached to them, which in this country at any rate are certain to be attached to them quite sufficiently, but which criticism has really nothing to do with. Its business is, as I have said, simply to know the best that is known and thought in the world, and by in its turn making this known, to create a current of true and fresh ideas. Its business is to do this with inflexible honesty, with due ability; but its business is to do no more, and to leave alone all questions of practical consequences and applications, questions which will never fail to have due prominence given to them. Else criticism, besides being really false to its own nature, merely continues in the old rut which it has hitherto followed in this country, and will certainly miss the chance now given to it. For what is at present the bane of criticism in this country? It is that practical considerations cling to it and stifle it. It subserves interests not its own. Our organs of criticism are organs of men and parties having practical ends to serve, and with them those practical ends are the first thing and the play of the mind the second; so much play of mind as is compatible with the prosecution of those practical ends is all that is wanted. An organ like the *Revue des Deux Mondes*,[2] having for its main function to understand and utter the best that is known and thought in the world, existing, it may be said, as just an organ for a free play of the mind, we have not. But we have the *Edinburgh Review*, existing as an organ of the old Whigs, and for as much play of the mind as may suit its being that; we have the *Quarterly Review*, existing as an organ of the Tories, and for as much play of mind as may suit its being that; we have the *British Quarterly Review*, existing as an organ of the political Dissenters,[3] and for as much play of mind as may suit its being that; we have *The Times*, existing as an organ of the common, satisfied, well-to-do Englishman, and for as much play of mind as may suit its being that. And so on through all the various fractions, political and religious, of our society; every fraction has, as such, its organ of criticism, but the notion of combining all fractions in the common pleasure of a free disinterested play of mind meets with no favour. Directly this play of mind wants to have more scope, and to forget the pressure of practical considerations a little, it is checked, it is made to feel the chain. We saw this the other day in the extinction, so much to be regretted, of the *Home and Foreign Review*.[4] Perhaps in no organ of criticism in this country was there so much knowledge, so much play of mind; but these could not save it. The *Dublin Review* subordinates play of mind to the practical business of English and Irish Catholicism, and lives. It must needs be that men should act in sects and parties, that each of these sects and parties should have its organ, and should make this organ subserve the interests of its action; but it would be well, too, that there should be a criticism, not the minister of these interests, not their enemy, but absolutely and entirely independent of them. No other criticism will ever attain any real authority or make any real way towards its end—the creating a current of true and fresh ideas.

It is because criticism has so little kept in the pure intellectual sphere, has so little detached itself from practice, has been so directly polemical and controversial, that it has so ill accomplished, in this country, its best spiritual work; which is to keep man from a self-

---

[1]   *disinterestedness*   I.e., objectivity.

[2]   *Revue ... Mondes*   International magazine founded in Paris in 1829.

[3]   *Dissenters*   Nonconformist Protestants, opposed to the beliefs and practices of the Church of England.

[4]   *Home ... Review*   Liberal, predominantly Catholic periodical (1862–64).

satisfaction which is retarding and vulgarizing, to lead him towards perfection, by making his mind dwell upon what is excellent in itself, and the absolute beauty and fitness of things. A polemical practical criticism makes men blind even to the ideal imperfection of their practice, makes them willingly assert its ideal perfection, in order the better to secure it against attack; and clearly this is narrowing and baneful for them. If they were reassured on the practical side, speculative considerations of ideal perfection they might be brought to entertain, and their spiritual horizon would thus gradually widen. Sir Charles Adderley[1] says to the Warwickshire farmers—

> Talk of the improvement of breed! Why, the race we ourselves represent, the men and women, the old Anglo-Saxon race, are the best breed in the whole world ... The absence of a too enervating climate, too unclouded skies, and a too luxurious nature, has produced so vigorous a race of people, and has rendered us so superior to all the world.

Mr. Roebuck says to the Sheffield cutlers[2]—

> I look around me and ask what is the state of England? Is not property safe? Is not every man able to say what he likes? Can you not walk from one end of England to the other in perfect security? I ask you whether, the world over or in past history, there is anything like it? Nothing. I pray that our unrivaled happiness may last.

Now obviously there is a peril for poor human nature in words and thoughts of such exuberant self-satisfaction, until we find ourselves safe in the streets of the Celestial City.

> *Das wenige verschwindet leicht dem Blicke*
> *Der vorwärts sieht, wie viel noch übrig bleibt*[3]—

says Goethe; "the little that is done seems nothing when we look forward and see how much we have yet to do." Clearly this is a better line of reflection for weak humanity, so long as it remains on this earthly field of labour and trial.

But neither Sir Charles Adderley nor Mr. Roebuck is by nature inaccessible to considerations of this sort. They only lose sight of them owing to the controversial life we all lead, and the practical from which all speculation takes with us. They have in view opponents whose aim is not ideal, but practical; and in their zeal to uphold their own practice against these innovators, they go so far as even to attribute to this practice an ideal perfection. Somebody has been wanting to introduce a six-pound franchise, or to abolish church-rates,[4] or to collect agricultural statistics by force, or to diminish local self-government. How natural, in reply to such proposals, very likely improper or ill-timed, to go a little beyond the mark and to say stoutly, "such a race of people as we stand, so superior to all the world! The Old Anglo-Saxon race, the best breed in the whole world! I pray that our unrivaled happiness may last! I ask you whether, the world over or in past history, there is anything like it?" And so long as criticism answers this dithyramb[5] by insisting that the old Anglo-Saxon race would be still more superior to all others if it had no church-rates, or that our unrivalled happiness would last yet longer with a six-pound franchise, so long will the strain, "The best breed in the whole world!" swell louder and louder, everything ideal and refining will be lost out of sight, and both the assailed and their critics will remain in a sphere, to say the truth, perfectly unvital, a sphere in which spiritual progression is impossible. But let criticism leave church-rates and the franchise alone, and in the most candid spirit, without a single lurking thought of practical innovation, confront with our dithyramb this paragraph on which I stumbled in a newspaper immediately after reading Mr. Roebuck:

---

[1] *Sir Charles Adderley* Conservative member of Parliament and landowner (1814–1905).

[2] *Sheffield cutlers* Sheffield, in South Yorkshire, was a long-standing center of cutlery manufacture.

[3] *Das wenige ... bleibt* Goethe's *Iphigenie auf Tauris* 1.291–92.

[4] *six-pound franchise* Proposal to extend voting rights to anyone whose property was worth six pounds or more annual rent—a radical idea at the time; *church-rates* Taxes paid to support the Church of England.

[5] *dithyramb* Emotionally inflated speech, poem, or song.

A shocking child murder has just been committed at Nottingham. A girl named Wragg left the workhouse[1] there on Saturday morning with her young illegitimate child. The child was soon afterwards found dead on Mapperly Hills, having been strangled. Wragg is in custody.

Nothing but that; but, in juxtaposition with the absolute eulogies of Sir Charles Adderley and Mr. Roebuck, how eloquent, how suggestive are those few lines! "Our old Anglo-Saxon breed, the best in the whole world!"—how much that is harsh and ill-favoured there is in this best! *Wragg*! If we are to talk of ideal perfection of "the best in the whole world," has any one reflected what a touch of grossness in our race, what an original shortcoming in the more delicate spiritual perceptions, is shown by the natural growth amongst us of such hideous names—Higginbottom, Stiggins, Bugg! In Ionia and Attica[2] they were luckier in this respect than "the best race in the world"; by the Ilissus[3] there was no Wragg, poor thing! And "our unrivaled happiness"—what an element of grimness, bareness, and hideousness mixes with it and blurs it; the workhouse, the dismal Mapperly Hills[4]—how dismal those who have seen them will remember—the gloom, the smoke, the cold, the strangled illegitimate child! "I ask you whether, the world over or in past history, there is anything like it?" Perhaps not, one is inclined to answer; but at any rate, in that case, the world is very much to be pitied. And the final touch—short, bleak, and inhuman: *Wragg is in custody*. The sex lost in the confusion of our unrivalled happiness; or (shall I say?) the superfluous Christian name lopped off by the straightforward vigour of our old Anglo-Saxon breed! There is profit for the spirit in such contrasts as this; criticism serves the cause of perfection by establish-

ing them. By eluding sterile conflict, by refusing to remain in the sphere where alone narrow and relative conceptions have any worth and validity, criticism may diminish its momentary importance, but only in this way has it a chance of gaining admittance for those wider and more perfect conceptions to which all its duty is really owed. Mr. Roebuck will have a poor opinion of an adversary who replies to his defiant songs of triumph only by murmuring under his breath, *Wragg is in custody*; but in no other way will these songs of triumph be induced gradually to moderate themselves, to get rid of what in them is excessive and offensive, and to fall into a softer and truer key.

It will be said that it is a very subtle and indirect action which I am thus prescribing for criticism, and that, by embracing in this manner the Indian virtue of detachment and abandoning the sphere of practical life, it condemns itself to a slow and obscure work. Slow and obscure it may be, but it is the only proper work of criticism. The mass of mankind will never have any ardent zeal for seeing things as they are; very inadequate ideas will always satisfy them. On these inadequate ideas reposes, and must repose, the general practice of the world. That is as much as saying that whoever sets himself to see things as they are will find himself one of a very small circle; but it is only by this small circle resolutely doing its own work that adequate ideas will ever get current at all. The rush and roar of practical life will always have a dizzying and attracting effect upon the most collected spectator, and tend to draw him into its vortex; most of all will this be the case where that life is so powerful as it is in England. But it is only by remaining collected, and refusing to lend himself to the point of view of the practical man, that the critic can do the practical man any service; and it is only by the greatest sincerity in pursuing his own course, and by at last convincing even the practical man of his sincerity, that he can escape misunderstandings which perpetually threaten him.

For the practical man is not apt for fine distinctions, and yet in these distinctions truth and the highest culture greatly find their account. But it is not easy to lead a practical man—unless you reassure him as to your practical intentions, you have no chance of leading

---

[1] *workhouse* Institution in which the poor were given lodging and a minimal level of sustenance in exchange for work performed. They were designed to be as unpleasant as possible so as to discourage people from entering them.

[2] *Ionia* Ancient region of Greek settlements in what is now western Turkey; *Attica* Greek peninsula containing Athens, strongly associated with the classical period.

[3] *Ilissus* River in Attica.

[4] *Mapperly Hills* Located near the coal-mining, industrial area of Nottingham.

him—to see a thing which he has always been used to look at from one side only, which he greatly values, and which, looked at from that side, quite deserves, perhaps, all the prizing and admiring which he bestows upon it—that this thing, looked at from another side, may appear much less beneficent and beautiful, and yet retain all its claims to our practical allegiance. Where shall we find language innocent enough, how shall we make the spotless purity of our intentions evident enough, to enable us to say to the political Englishman that the British Constitution itself, which, seen from the practical side, looks such a magnificent organ of progress and virtue, seen from the speculative side—with its compromises, its love of facts, its horror of theory, its studied avoidance of clear thoughts—that, seen from this side, our august Constitution sometimes looks—forgive me, shade of Lord Somers![1]—a colossal machine for the manufacture of Philistines?[2] How is Cobbett[3] to say this and not be misunderstood, blackened as he is with the smoke of a lifelong conflict in the field of political practice? How is Mr. Carlyle to say it and not be misunderstood, after his furious raid into this field with his Latter-day Pamphlets?[4] How is Mr. Ruskin, after his pugnacious political economy?[5] I say, the critic must keep out of the region of immediate practice in the political, social, humanitarian sphere, if he wants to make a beginning for that more free speculative treatment of things, which may perhaps one day make its benefits felt even in this sphere, but in a natural and thence irresistible manner. ...

If I have insisted so much on the course which criticism must take where politics and religion are concerned, it is because, where these burning matters are in question, it is most likely to go astray. I have wished, above all, to insist on the attitude which criticism should adopt towards things in general; on its right tone and temper of mind. But then comes another question as to the subject-matter which literary criticism should most seek. Here, in general, its course is determined for it by the idea which is the law of its being; the idea of a disinterested endeavour to learn and propagate the best that is known and thought in the world, and thus to establish a current of fresh and true ideas. By the very nature of things, as England is not all the world, much of the best that is known and thought in the world cannot be of English growth, must be foreign; by the nature of things, again, it is just this that we are least likely to know, while English thought is streaming in upon us from all sides, and takes excellent care that we shall not be ignorant of its existence. The English critic of literature, therefore, must dwell much on foreign thought, and with particular heed on any part of it, which, while significant and fruitful in itself, is for any reason specially likely to escape him. Again, judging is often spoken of as the critic's one business, and so in some sense it is; but the judgement which almost insensibly forms itself in a fair and clear mind, along with fresh knowledge, is the valuable one; and thus knowledge, and ever fresh knowledge, must be the critic's great concern for himself. And it is by communicating fresh knowledge, and letting his own judgement pass along with it—but insensibly, and in the second place, not the first, as a sort of companion and clue, not as an abstract lawgiver—that the critic will generally do most good to his readers. Sometimes, no doubt, for the sake of establishing an author's place in literature, and his relation to a central standard (and if this is not done, how are we to get at our best in the world?) criticism may have to deal with a subject-matter so familiar that fresh knowledge is out of the question, and then it must be all judgement; an enunciation and detailed application of principles. Here the great safeguard is never to let oneself become abstract, always to retain an intimate and lively consciousness of the truth of what one is saying, and, the moment this fails us, to be sure that something is wrong. Still, under all circum-

---

[1] *Lord Somers* Political leader who presided over the creation of the Declaration of Rights (1689).

[2] *Philistines* Members of the Biblical tribe that fought against the Israelites. Here Arnold uses the term humorously to denote the unenlightened middle classes; "the enemy."

[3] *Cobbett* William Cobbett (1762–1835), farmer and radical political writer.

[4] *Latter-day Pamphlets* Satirical pamphlets, published in 1850, in which Thomas Carlyle expressed vehement anti-democratic views.

[5] *Mr. Ruskin ... economy* In his *Unto the Last* (1862), John Ruskin moved away from art criticism and attacked laissez-faire economics.

stances, this mere judgement and application of principles is, in itself, not the most satisfactory work to the critic; like mathematics, it is tautological, and cannot well give us, like fresh learning, the sense of creative activity.

But stop, someone will say; all this talk is of no practical use to us whatever; this criticism of yours is not what we have in our minds when we speak of criticism; when we speak of critics and criticism, we mean critics and criticism of the current English literature of the day; when you offer to tell criticism of its function, it is to this criticism that we expect you to address yourself. I am sorry for it, for I am afraid I must disappoint these expectations. I am bound by my own definition of criticism: a disinterested endeavour to learn and propagate the best that is known and thought in the world. How much of current English literature comes into this "best that is known and thought in the world"? Not very much, I fear; certainly less, at this moment, than of the current literature of France or Germany. Well, then, am I to alter my definition of criticism, in order to meet the requirements of a number of practising English critics, who, after all, are free in their choice of a business? That would be making criticism lend itself just to one of those alien practical considerations, which, I have said, are so fatal to it. One may say, indeed, to those who have to deal with the mass—so much better disregarded—of current English literature, that they may at all events endeavour, in dealing with this, to try it, so far as they can, by the standard of the best that is known and thought in the world; one may say, that to get anywhere near this standard, every critic should try and possess one great literature, at least, besides his own; and the more unlike his own, the better. But, after all, the criticism I am really concerned with—the criticism which alone can much help us for the future, the criticism which, throughout Europe, is at the present day meant, when so much stress is laid on the importance of criticism and the critical spirit—is a criticism which regards Europe as being, for intellectual and spiritual purposes, one great confederation, bound to a joint action and working to a common result; and whose members have, for their proper outfit, a knowledge of Greek, Roman, and

Eastern antiquity, and of one another. Special, local, and temporary advantages being put out of account, that modern nation will in the intellectual and spiritual sphere make most progress, which most thoroughly carries out this programme. And what is that but saying that we too, all of us, as individuals, the more thoroughly we carry it out, shall make the more progress?

There is so much inviting us!—what are we to take? what will nourish us in growth towards perfection? That is the question which, with the immense field of life and of literature lying before him, the critic has to answer; for himself first, and afterwards for others. In this idea of the critic's business the essays brought together in the following pages have had their origin; in this idea, widely different as are their subjects, they have, perhaps, their unity.

I conclude with what I said at the beginning: to have the sense of creative activity is the great happiness and the great proof of being alive, and it is not denied to criticism to have it; but then criticism must be sincere, simple, flexible, ardent, ever widening its knowledge. Then it may have, in no contemptible measure, a joyful sense of creative activity; a sense which a man of insight and conscience will prefer to what he might derive from a poor, starved, fragmentary, inadequate creation. And at some epochs no other creation is possible.

Still, in full measure, the sense of creative activity belongs only to genuine creation; in literature we must never forget that. But what true man of letters ever can forget it? It is no such common matter for a gifted nature to come into possession of a current of true and living ideas, and to produce amidst the inspiration of them, that we are likely to underrate it. The epochs of Aeschylus and Shakespeare make us feel their preeminence. In an epoch like those is, no doubt, the true life of literature; there is the promised land, towards which criticism can only beckon. That promised land it will not be ours to enter, and we shall die in the wilderness: but to have desired to enter it, to have saluted it from afar, is already, perhaps, the best distinction among contemporaries; it will certainly be the best title to esteem with posterity.

—1864

from *Culture and Anarchy*[1]

from CHAPTER I: SWEETNESS AND LIGHT

The disparagers of culture make its motive curiosity; sometimes, indeed, they make its motive mere exclusiveness and vanity. The culture which is supposed to plume itself on a smattering of Greek and Latin is a culture which is begotten by nothing so intellectual as curiosity; it is valued either out of sheer vanity and ignorance or else as an engine of social and class distinction, separating its holder, like a badge or title, from other people who have not got it. No serious man would call this *culture*, or attach any value to it, as culture, at all. To find the real ground for the very different estimate which serious people will set upon culture, we must find some motive for culture in the terms of which may lie a real ambiguity; and such a motive the word *curiosity* gives us.

I have before now pointed out that we English do not, like the foreigners, use this word in a good sense as well as in a bad sense. With us the word is always used in a somewhat disapproving sense. A liberal and intelligent eagerness about the things of the mind may be meant by a foreigner when he speaks of curiosity, but with us the word always conveys a certain notion of frivolous and unedifying activity. In the *Quarterly Review*, some little time ago, was an estimate of the celebrated French critic, M. Sainte-Beuve,[2] and a very inadequate estimate it in my judgement was. And its inadequacy consisted chiefly in this: that in our English

way it left out of sight the double sense really involved in the word *curiosity*, thinking enough was said to stamp M. Sainte-Beuve with blame if it was said that he was impelled in his operations as a critic by curiosity, and omitting either to perceive that M. Sainte-Beuve himself, and many other people with him, would consider that this was praiseworthy and not blameworthy, or to point out why it ought really to be accounted worthy of blame and not of praise. For as there is a curiosity about intellectual matters which is futile, and merely a disease, so there is certainly a curiosity—a desire after the things of the mind simply for their own sakes and for the pleasure of seeing them as they are—which is, in an intelligent being, natural and laudable. Nay, and the very desire to see things as they are implies a balance and regulation of mind which is not often attained without fruitful effort, and which is the very opposite of the blind and diseased impulse of mind which is what we mean to blame when we blame curiosity. Montesquieu says: "The first motive which ought to impel us to study is the desire to augment the excellence of our nature, and to render an intelligent being yet more intelligent."[3] This is the true ground to assign for the genuine scientific passion, however manifested, and for culture, viewed simply as a fruit of this passion; and it is a worthy ground, even though we let the term *curiosity* stand to describe it.

But there is of culture another view, in which not solely the scientific passion, the sheer desire to see things as they are, natural and proper in an intelligent being, appears as the ground of it. There is a view in which all the love of our neighbour, the impulses towards action, help, and beneficence, the desire for removing human error, clearing human confusion, and diminishing human misery, the noble aspiration to leave the world better and happier than we found it—motives eminently such as are called social—come in as part of the grounds of culture, and the main and pre-eminent part. Culture is then properly described not as having its origin in curiosity, but as having its origin in the love of

---

[1] *Culture and Anarchy* This work grew out of Arnold's last Oxford lecture, in 1869, and responds to the political climate surrounding the passage of the Second Reform Bill in 1867. Arnold feared that the individualism, or self-serving attitude, that seemed to fuel much of laissez-faire capitalism would lead to a state of anarchy—a state in which no culture could flourish. "Sweetness and light" is taken from a fable in Jonathan Swift's *The Battle of the Books* (1704). In this fable, the bee (who represents ancient culture) travels far to fill its hive with honey and wax (which is used to make candles). The bee thus provides "the two noblest things, which are sweetness and light," while the spider (representing modern culture) stays at home and forms its own web, producing "nothing at all but flybane and cobweb."

[2] *M. Sainte-Beuve* French critic Charles Augustin Sainte-Beuve (1804–69).

[3] *The first ... intelligent* See the French political philosopher Montesquieu's *Discours sur les motifs qui doivent nous encourager aux science* (1725).

perfection; it is *a study of perfection*. It moves by the force, not merely or primarily of the scientific passion for pure knowledge, but also of the moral and social passion for doing good. As, in the first view of it, we took for its worthy motto Montesquieu's words: "To render an intelligent being yet more intelligent!" so, in the second view of it, there is no better motto which it can have than these words of Bishop Wilson:[1] "To make reason and the will of God prevail!"[2] ...

Nothing is more common than for people to confound the inward peace and satisfaction which follows the subduing of the obvious faults of our animality with what I may call absolute inward peace and satisfaction—the peace and satisfaction which are reached as we draw near to complete spiritual perfection, and not merely to moral perfection, or rather to relative moral perfection. No people in the world have done more and struggled more to attain this relative moral perfection than our English race has. For no people in the world has the command to *resist the devil, to overcome the wicked one*, in the nearest and most obvious sense of those words, had such a pressing force and reality. And we have had our reward, not only in the great worldly prosperity which our obedience to this command has brought us, but also, and far more, in great inward peace and satisfaction. But to me few things are more pathetic than to see people, on the strength of the inward peace and satisfaction which their rudimentary efforts towards perfection have brought them, employ, concerning their incomplete perfection and the religious organisations within which they have found it, language which properly applies only to complete perfection, and is a far-off echo of the human soul's prophecy of it. Religion itself, I need hardly say, supplies them in abundance with this grand language. And very freely do they use it; yet it is really the severest possible criticism of such an incomplete perfection as alone we have yet reached through our religious organisations.

The impulse of the English race towards moral development and self-conquest has nowhere so powerfully manifested itself as in Puritanism.[3] Nowhere has Puritanism found so adequate an expression as in the religious organisation of the Independents.[4] The modern Independents have a newspaper, the *Nonconformist*, written with great sincerity and ability. The motto, the standard, the profession of faith which this organ of theirs carries aloft, is: "The Dissidence of Dissent and the Protestantism of the Protestant religion." There is sweetness and light, and an ideal of complete harmonious human perfection! One need not go to culture and poetry to find language to judge it. Religion, with its instinct for perfection, supplies language to judge it, language, too, which is in our mouths every day. "Finally, be of one mind, united in feeling," says St. Peter.[5] There is an ideal which judges the Puritan ideal: "The Dissidence of Dissent and the Protestantism of the Protestant religion!" And religious organisations like this are what people believe in, rest in, would give their lives for! Such, I say, is the wonderful virtue of even the beginnings of perfection, of having conquered even the plain faults of our animality, that the religious organisation which has helped us to do it can seem to us something precious, salutary, and to be propagated, even when it wears such a brand of imperfection on its forehead as this. And men have got such a habit of giving to the language of religion a special application, of making it a mere jargon, that for the condemnation which religion itself passes on the shortcomings of their religious organisations they have no ear; they are sure to cheat themselves and to explain this condemnation away. They can only be reached by the criticism which culture, like poetry, speaking a language not to be sophisticated, and resolutely testing these organisations by the ideal of a human perfection complete on all sides, applies to them.

---

[1] *Bishop Wilson* Church of England clergy member (1663–1755) whose *Maxims* Arnold admired.

[2] *To make ... prevail!* Bishop Thomas Wilson, *Sacra Privata* (1781). [This is from the same source as noted above.]

[3] *Puritanism* Form of strict English Protestant religious observance dating from the sixteenth century. In general, Puritans embraced an austere mode of living and distanced themselves from the practices of the Church of England.

[4] *Independents* Members of a seventeenth-century Puritan sect.

[5] *Finally ... Peter* From 1 Peter 3.8.

But men of culture and poetry, it will be said, are again and again failing, and failing conspicuously, in the necessary first stage to a harmonious perfection, in the subduing of the great obvious faults of our animality, which it is the glory of these religious organisations to have helped us to subdue. True, they do often so fail. They have often been without the virtues as well as the faults of the Puritan; it has been one of their dangers that they so felt the Puritan's faults that they too much neglected the practice of his virtues. I will not, however, exculpate them at the Puritan's expense. They have often failed in morality, and morality is indispensable. And they have been punished for their failure, as the Puritan has been rewarded for his performance. They have been punished wherein they erred; but their ideal of beauty, of sweetness and light, and a human nature complete on all its sides, remains the true ideal of perfection still; just as the Puritan's ideal of perfection remains narrow and inadequate, although for what he did well he has been richly rewarded. Notwithstanding the mighty results of the Pilgrim Fathers' voyage, they and their standard of perfection are rightly judged when we figure to ourselves Shakespeare or Virgil[1]—souls in whom sweetness and light, and all that in human nature is most humane, were eminent—accompanying them on their voyage, and think what intolerable company Shakespeare and Virgil would have found them! In the same way let us judge the religious organisations which we see all around us. Do not let us deny the good and the happiness which they have accomplished; but do not let us fail to see clearly that their idea of human perfection is narrow and inadequate, and that the Dissidence of Dissent and the Protestantism of the Protestant religion will never bring humanity to its true goal. As I said with regard to wealth: Let us look at the life of those who live in and for it—so I say with regard to the religious organisations. Look at the life imaged in such a newspaper as the *Nonconformist*—a life of jealousy of the Establishment,[2] disputes, tea-meetings, openings of chapels, sermons; and then think of it as an ideal of a human life completing itself on all sides, and aspiring with all its organs after sweetness, light, and perfection!

Another newspaper, representing, like the *Nonconformist*, one of the religious organisations of this country, was a short time ago giving an account of the crowd at Epsom on the Derby day,[3] and of all the vice and hideousness which was to be seen in that crowd; and then the writer turned suddenly round upon Professor Huxley,[4] and asked him how he proposed to cure all this vice and hideousness without religion. I confess I felt disposed to ask the asker this question: and how do you propose to cure it with such a religion as yours? How is the ideal of a life so unlovely, so unattractive, so incomplete, so narrow, so far removed from a true and satisfying ideal of human perfection, as is the life of your religious organisation as you yourself reflect it, to conquer and transform all this vice and hideousness? Indeed, the strongest plea for the study of perfection as pursued by culture, the clearest proof of the actual inadequacy of the idea of perfection held by the religious organisations—expressing, as I have said, the most widespread effort which the human race has yet made after perfection—is to be found in the state of our life and society with these in possession of it, and having been in possession of it I know not how many hundred years. We are all of us included in some religious organisation or other; we all call ourselves, in the sublime and aspiring language of religion which I have before noticed, children of God. Children of God—it is an immense pretension!—and how are we to justify it? By the works which we do, and the words which we speak. And the work which we collective children of God do, our grand centre of life, our city which we have builded for us to dwell in, is London! London, with its unutterable external hideousness, and with its internal canker of *publice egestas, privatim opulentia*—to use the

---

[1] *the Pilgrim Fathers' voyage* Reference to the voyage of the *Mayflower*, which brought the first group of Puritan settlers to New England in 1620; *Virgil* Roman poet (70–19 BCE) best known for his epic the *Aeneid*.

[2] *Establishment* I.e., the established Church, the Church of England.

[3] *Epsom … day* The Derby Stakes, a thoroughbred horse race, is held every June in Epsom, Surrey.

[4] *Professor Huxley* Thomas Huxley (1825–95), biologist, educator, and vocal supporter of the theory of evolution.

words which Sallust puts into Cato's[1] mouth about Rome—unequalled in the world! The word, again, which we children of God speak, the voice which most hits our collective thought, the newspaper with the largest circulation in England, nay, with the largest circulation in the whole world, is the *Daily Telegraph*! I say that when our religious organisations—which I admit to express the most considerable effort after perfection that our race has yet made—land us in no better result than this, it is high time to examine carefully their idea of perfection, to see whether it does not leave out of account sides and forces of human nature which we might turn to great use; whether it would not be more operative if it were more complete. And I say that English reliance on our religious organisations and on their ideas of human perfection just as they stand, is like our reliance on freedom, on muscular Christianity,[2] on population, on coal, on wealth—mere belief in machinery, and unfruitful; and that it is wholesomely counteracted by culture, bent on seeing things as they are, and on drawing the human race onwards to a more complete, a harmonious perfection.

Culture, however, shows its single-minded love of perfection, its desire simply to make reason and the will of God prevail, its freedom from fanaticism, by its attitude towards all this machinery, even while it insists that it is machinery. Fanatics, seeing the mischief men do themselves by their blind belief in some machinery or other—whether it is wealth and industrialism, or whether it is the cultivation of bodily strength and activity, or whether it is a political organisation—or whether it is a religious organisation—oppose with might and main the tendency to this or that political and religious organisation, or to games and athletic exercises, or to wealth and industrialism, and try violently to stop it. But the flexibility which sweetness and light give, and which is one of the rewards of culture pursued in good faith, enables a man to see that a tendency may be necessary, and even, as a preparation for something in the future, salutary, and yet that the generations or individuals who obey this tendency are sacrificed to it, that they fall short of the hope of perfection by following it; and that its mischiefs are to be criticised, lest it should take too firm a hold and last after it has served its purpose. ...
—1868

---

[1] *publice ... opulentia* Latin: public poverty; private opulence; *Sallust* First-century BCE Roman historian; *Cato* Roman political figure Cato the Younger (95–46 BCE).

[2] *muscular Christianity* Victorian-era movement promoting moral development through sport and exercise.

MARY ANN SHADD
1823 – 1893

Though she is relatively unknown, Mary Ann Shadd was a figure of real importance to mid nineteenth-century American and Canadian history. As founder and editor of *The Provincial Freeman and Daily Advertiser*, she has the distinction of being the first woman to start a newspaper in Canada, as well as the first Black woman newspaper editor in North America. Later in life she attended Howard University School of Law—and became as influential a figure in the women's rights movement as she had been earlier in her life as a leader in Canadian and American Black communities. As an educator, Shadd worked tirelessly to improve conditions for Black children, and founded several schools; she also worked to educate people who had been freed from slavery or had escaped slavery. As an abolitionist, Shadd was particularly active in both Canada and the United States during the decade prior to the American Civil War, and she played an important role in encouraging the emigration of Black people into Canada.

Shadd grew up in a family of free Blacks in the slave state of Delaware. "Freedom," however, for Black citizens of Delaware was a relative term; even free Blacks were subject to widespread persecution during this era, throughout the United States and (arguably to a somewhat lesser extent) in Canada. Her father, Abraham Shadd, a shoemaker with shops in both Wilmington, Delaware, and West Chester, Pennsylvania, used the family home as a refuge for fugitives from slavery, and was a representative for the state of Delaware at conventions for the Improvement of Free People of Color; later, he became the first Black to hold elected office in British North America when, in 1859, he won a seat on the Raleigh Town Council. A similar determination to improve the situation of her people became a powerful force in Mary Shadd's own life. At the age of 16, after completing her education at a Quaker school for free Blacks in West Chester, Shadd went on to form her own school in Wilmington. She soon became active more widely in the issues of the day; in the late 1840s her letters were published and her work discussed in the pages of Frederick Douglass's newspaper, the *North Star*.

With the passage of the Fugitive Slave Act of 1850, life became increasingly hazardous for free Blacks (see below). Largely in order to avoid the risk of enslavement, Shadd's family joined the exodus into what was then Canada West.[1] Shadd saw the need for the education of people in Canada who had escaped from slavery, and soon opened up a school in Windsor with the financial support of the American Mission Association. She was also an advocate for emigration to Canada as a strategy of opposition to the oppression of Blacks in the United States—an issue on which the Black community was divided. Shadd put forward her case in an 1852 pamphlet "for the information of colored immigrants" entitled *A Plea for Emigration; or Notes of Canada West*.

Shadd's founding of *The Provincial Freeman* in 1853 (initially under the name of journalist Samuel Ringgold Ward to conceal its female authorship) provided her with another platform for putting forward her views—not only in favor of abolition, but also on education, on the role of

---

[1] *Canada West* What is now Southern Ontario was the British Colony of Upper Canada from 1791 until 1841. (What is now the southern half of Quebec was during that period the British colony of Lower Canada—"lower" because it was downstream on the St. Lawrence River from the upper reaches of that river and from the other rivers and lakes that flow into it.) In 1841 Upper and Lower Canada together became the United Province of Canada, and from that time until 1867 what is now southern Ontario was known as Canada West. Only with Confederation in 1867 did the provinces of Ontario and Quebec come into existence.

women in society, on temperance (which she strongly supported), and against "exclusivity" (segregation, as it is termed today). As a staunch integrationist, Shadd was at odds with the segregationist leanings of some other abolitionists and activists of the era. In particular, she clashed with the well-known activist Henry Bibb (1815–54), editor of the newspaper *Voice of the Fugitive* and director of the Refugee Home Society, a settlement intended exclusively for people freed from slavery. Their disagreements—over the issue of exclusivity, various concerns relating to education, and what Shadd considered to be Bibb's unethical financial practices—ultimately led to the American Mission Association pulling funding from her school. Shadd gave lectures around the U.S. in order to raise funds for the school; she eventually relocated to Toronto, from where she continued for some years to edit *The Provincial Freeman*.

In 1856 Shadd married Toronto barber Thomas Cary, with whom she would have two children before his death in 1860. The *Freeman*, which had always struggled financially, folded in 1857, after being turned over to Mary's brother Isaac. (As had been the case when she founded it, there was resistance to the notion of a woman running a newspaper; her brother, however, turned out to be no better able to make a financial success of the paper.)

Like many who came to Canada through the "Underground Railroad," Shadd returned to the United States with the Emancipation Proclamation and the end of slavery. She assisted in the recruitment of Black soldiers, and later worked in the education and settlement of emancipated enslaved people. After teaching in Detroit and Washington, D.C., Shadd entered Howard Law School in 1868; in 1883 she completed her degree, becoming the second Black woman to earn a law degree in the United States.

In the 1870s and 1880s Shadd became increasingly active in the suffrage movement (and in the movement regarding women's rights more generally); her work was recognized by, among others, Elizabeth Cady Stanton (arguably the leading figure in the suffrage movement in America). Shadd remained active as a writer for various newspapers, and continued to work to improve the lives of African Americans (including, in the 1870s, as an agent for Frederick Douglass's newspaper, the *New National Era*).

Shadd died in Washington in 1893. Until her death she continued to teach and to promote the causes of women's rights and Black education.

⌘ ⌘ ⌘

A Plea for Emigration[1]
INTRODUCTORY REMARKS

The increasing desire on the part of the colored people to become thoroughly informed respecting the Canadas, and particularly that part of the province called Canada West[2]—to learn of the climate, soil, and production, and of the inducements offered generally to emigrants, and to them particularly, since that the passage of the odious Fugitive Slave Law[3] has made a

---

[1] *A Plea for Emigration* Phanuel Antwi (of the University of British Columbia) has provided invaluable editorial assistance in the preparation of this text. Punctuation and paragraph breaks have been modernized, but the American spelling of the original has been retained.

[2] *Canadas … Canada West* Prior to 1841 the provinces of Upper and Lower Canada were independent political entities. After British Parliament passed the Act of Union in 1840 they became one single province, divided into the administrative districts of Canada West and Canada East, which correspond with present-day Ontario and Quebec.

[3] *Fugitive Slave Law* Enacted by U.S. Congress in 1850, this law mandated the hiring of officials and issuing of warrants for hunting down and arresting fugitive slaves. $10 rewards were given for the return of slaves, and $5 for the capture of freed Blacks. Penalties for hindering this process were substantially increased.

residence in the United States to many of them dangerous in the extreme—this consideration, and the absence of condensed information accessible to all, is my excuse for offering this tract to the notice of the public.

The people are in a strait.[1] On the one hand, a proslavery administration, with its entire controllable force, is bearing upon them with fatal effect: on the other, the Colonization Society,[2] in the Garb of *Christianity* and *Philanthropy*, is seconding the efforts of the first named power, by bringing into the lists a vast social and immoral influence, thus making more effective the agencies employed. Information is needed. Tropical Africa, the land of promise of the colonizationists, teeming as she is with breath of pestilence, a burning sun, and fearful maladies, bids them welcome; she feelingly invites [them] to moral and physical death, under a voluntary escort of their most bitter enemies at home. Again, many look with dreadful forebodings to the probability of worse than inquisitorial inhumanity in the Southern States from the operation of the Fugitive Law. Certain that neither a home in Africa, nor in the Southern States, is desireable under present circumstances, inquiry is made respecting Canada. I have endeavored to furnish information to a certain extent, to that end, and believing that more reliance would be placed upon a statement of facts obtained in that country, from reliable sources and from observation, than upon a repetition of current statements made elsewhere, however honestly made, I determined to visit Canada, and to there collect such information as most

persons desire. These pages contain the result of much inquiry—matter obtained both from individuals and from documents and papers of unquestionable character in the province.

—1852

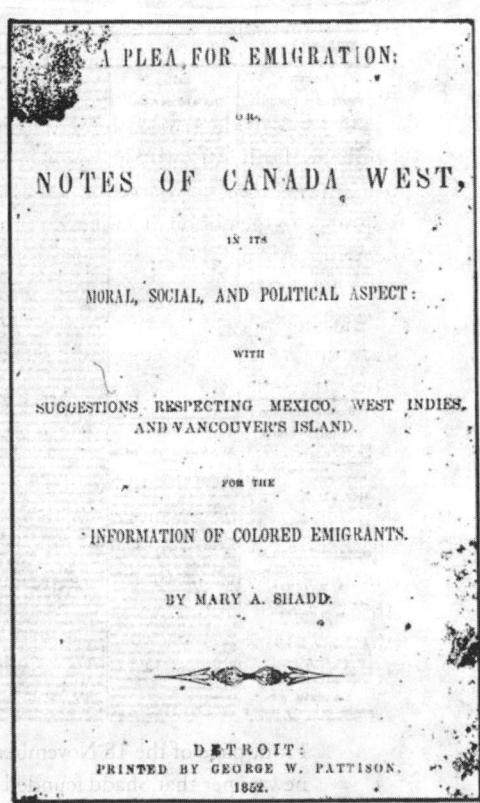

Title page of *A Plea for Emigration* in its original 1852 pamphlet form.

---

[1] *strait* Dilemma.

[2] *Colonization Society* The American Society for Colonizing the Free People of Color of the United States, an organization of white Americans that encouraged the emigration of Blacks from America to Africa; it was under the auspices of the Society that a settlement for formerly enslaved Americans was established in Liberia, in West Africa.

Front page of the 18 November 1854 issue of the *Provincial Freeman*, the newspaper that Shadd founded and edited for several years in the 1850s.

from *The Provincial Freeman*
(24 March 1854)

The three pieces included here all appeared in the 24 March 1854 issue of the paper. The first two are unsigned editorials, in all likelihood written by Shadd herself. The third was reprinted in *The Provincial Freeman* from the Toronto *Globe* and includes the editorial preface to the address that had appeared in that paper.

RELATIONS OF CANADA TO AMERICAN SLAVERY

The fact that this is a British Province, and that slavery has no existence on British soil, the fact that this soil never was polluted by slaver, and the fact that (since the ever memorable Somerset decision[1]) the slave of another country became a freeman by touching our soil, place us in relations of antagonism to slavery. This

---

[1] *Somerset decision* Landmark 1772 legal ruling that was popularly interpreted to mean that slavery was illegal in Britain, though not in its colonies—and that an enslaved person automatically became free upon entering Britain.

was early seen and felt by the slave, and as early seen and felt by the slaveholder. Accordingly, so early as 1825, the attention of the U.S. Government was directed to this point. In the month of May, of that year, the House of Representatives passed a resolution calling upon the President to enter into correspondence with the British Government, for the recovery of slaves who had escaped into Canada. … From that time to 1842, the number of slaves escaping to Canada constantly and rapidly increased. Then, when a treaty was made between the two Governments, called the Ashburton Treaty, it was most earnestly sought, on the part of the United States Government … to have an article inserted which should authorize slave catching in Canada; … but the Court of St. James[1] promptly refused … to allow the American slaveholder to use Canada as a park to chase human game in. … Canada, therefore, from her connection with the British Crown, is legally and constitutionally in an attitude of antagonism to American slavery. She offers and secures to the American slave, the moment he arrives here, Freedom—British Freedom—impartial Freedom. And when he has stood his seven years' probation, and taken the oath of allegiance, Canada secures to him, at home and abroad, in law and in equity, all the rights and immunities of a British subject.

But there is another view of our relations to this subject. It is painful to admit it … but disgraceful as it is, it is useless to conceal it. Friendliness to slavery is to be found in this Province in more forms than one.

1. There are some parties here who practised slave-driving in the South. They love slavery as they love the gain they derived from wielding the whip over its victims. A sprinkling of such customers is to be found here and there, the Province over.

2. There are others, too, who have married heiresses to slave estates. Having received their wives and slaves by the same act of matrimony, they are strongly tempted to regard slavery to be as sacred as marriage itself.

3. Then there are persons resident in Canada who were once slaveholders in the West Indies. The glorious people of Great Britain, determined to have the great

principle of British freedom applied practically to the enslaved, as well as to all others, like Job, they, through the Government, "broke the jaws of the wicked, and delivered the spoiled out of their teeth."[2] But these ex-slaveholders were never convinced of the sin of slave-holding—or, if convinced of it, they then were con-verted from it. Hence they are in spirit now, what they were in practice before the act of '32.[3] The influence of these parties is as deeply and wickedly pro-slavery as that of the vilest slaveocrats of New York, Boston, Philadel-phia or Baltimore.

4. As a born Yankee, we are ashamed of it, but it is true that too many of the natives of the United States have brought their pro-slaveryism with them, from the other side. Like the refugee slaves, they come here to enjoy an improvement of their condition, and like them, too, they enjoy the protecting care of this good British realm; but they turn scornfully upon the black man, and do what [they can] to rob him of his rights—to which the latter is as fully entitled as themselves. From sympathy with their native country, and from their own negro-hate, they maintain a constant and growing pro-slavery influence wherever they are settled. There are but very few exceptions to this rule, for it is a rule; and most safely may it be said, that while the Yankees are far from being the only negro-haters, or pro-slavery parties, whose principles disgrace our country, it is nevertheless true that the mass of them are the most decided slaveocrats in the land; and what is more, they most industriously spread and promulgate their sentiments, and seek to make them prevalent and controlling, even to the violation of Her Majesty's laws. We could give abundant illustrations of this.

5. It remains to be said, that the prejudice against negroes, so prevalent in various parts of the Province, as maintained by many persons of all nations, including, of course, native Canadians, is one of the strongest pro-slavery influences that disgraces and degrades our fair county; it does more to place us side by side with

---

[1] *Court of St. James* Court of the British sovereign, concerned primarily with foreign affairs.

[2] *broke the … their teeth* Cf. Job 29.17.

[3] *act of '32* The *Act for the Abolition of Slavery throughout the British Colonies* was in fact passed by Parliament in August 1833, and began to take effect in August 1834.

American oppressors than any other thing. Everybody knows that it is the North and not the South that supplies the power of public opinion, of the pulpit, the press, commerce, manufactures, literature, religion, politics, everything that keeps slavery alive. Now the sentiment—the controlling sentiment of the people of the North, that renders them the volunteer bodyguard of slavery—is their negro-hate. The maintenance of a like negro-hate here, of course, encourages the same feeling there, and aids it in doing its very worst work. Every Canadian negro-hater is a volunteer British slaveocrat. Every such one is a strengthener of the slave system, and we repeat, that there should be such, is one of the worst facts—the foulest disgrace, the deepest degradation—in all our history.

So long as these facts exist, we shall want anti-slavery labors, organizations, agitation, and newspapers in Canada. Our humble life shall be devoted to the counteracting of the pro-slaveryism of our adopted country. It is for this reason that we leave our own hearthstone, and expose ourselves to so many disagreeables, as a lecturing agent of the Canadian Anti-Slavery Society. Hence it is we consent, without pay, to scribble for the *Provincial Freeman*. And we do believe that the education and improvement of our own people will lay this enmity to liberty and humanity—this friendship for despotism—low, in a death and burial that shall know no resurrection, and that at no very distant day. At any rate we shall labor on in hope.

Let the pro-slaveryism of Canada be overcome, and let the anti-slavery influence of our laws, constitution, and position be fully and freely exerted, and there is no portion of the British Empire whose influence against slavery would be so healthful and so potent as that of Canada.

Union

We have frequently heard it said that no people are so much given to party divisions, dissensions and disunions as the colored people. But we question the correctness of this very prevalent opinion. The Irish are divided into

Orangemen[1] and Catholics; the Scotch into Highlanders and Lowlanders; the English into as many divisors as there are counties in England almost. Then each of these dislikes, and is divided against all the rest. Come to religious denominations, and any town in the British Empire will furnish abundant proof that the black people are very far from either enjoying or suffering a monopoly of disunionism. The truth is, that in this respect, the colored people are precisely like any other people, especially are they like any other ignorant people;[2] and the more we see of other people, the more deeply are we impressed, not only with the oneness, but with the likeness of the human family, in this, as in all other respects.

Some fear that the differences of opinion existing among our people, in respect to certain public matters, will prove disastrous. We have no such fears. It would be no mark of manliness in us, to think, according to the dictum of every man assuming to be a leader among us, or who should please to lord it over us. We freely confess that we desire no union at the expense of free independent thinking and action. We ask no one blindly to follow, or agree with us, upon the pain of being denounced as a disunionist; and He who made us knows, that we will follow no demagogue, black or white, in doctrine or practice, into that which our judgment and conscience disapprove, for fear of incurring the blame of any who esteem union as of all things most valuable. Union is desirable—very desirable—and worthy of forbearance, forgiveness, self-denial, and charity for its obtainment; but union purchased at the expense of moral principle, is purchased at too dear a rate.[3] It is better to stand alone, upon principle, than to go with any multitude, compromising principle.

American Slavery

[The following address to the Women of the Union States has been prepared by the Toronto Ladies Associa-

[1] *Orangemen* I.e., Protestants.

[2] *ignorant people* I.e., people who are denied the benefits of education.

[3] *at too dear a rate* Too expensively.

tion for the relief of Destitute Colored Fugitives. It is written in a good spirit, and contains suggestions which it is the legitimate province of women to carry out into practical action. Much may be effected by female influence, especially in family arrangements, and in the education of those who are to be the future legislators and the wives of legislators. There is about this address also what will commend it the more to the people of the United States—a plainness of speech which they like. It expresses the truth in courteous terms, and seeks not to sweeten the unpalatable fact that slavery is a sin which ought to be abolished at once by every Christian nation—*Globe*]

The affectionate address of thousands of the women of Canada to their sisters, the women of the United States of America.

"While the women of England, with whom we in this Colony are identified, propose to address you on the subject of Negro Slavery, it may not seem an unfitting occasion for us to add, in the name of Christian spirit, our suggestions and entreaties. Living so near to the scene of slavery, and coming daily into contest with its bitter fruits, in the persons of those unhappy fugitives who have been compelled by law to seek an asylum in our country, we cannot but deeply deplore its continuance in the world, and especially in your mighty nation—a nation whose influence for good might be co-extensive with the civilized world, were it not for this foul blot, which mars its glory and paralyzes its power.

"We would then ask you, in the spirit of Christian love, to use that influence which, as sisters, as daughters, and as mothers, you possess, for the abolition of a system, which deprives its victims of the fruits of their labor; which substitutes concubinage for the sacred institution of marriage; which abrogates the relation of parent and child, tearing children from the arms of their parents, and parents from each other; which shrouds the intellect of rational beings in the dark gloom of ignorance and forbids the souls of immortal beings from holding communion with their maker; and which degrades man, created in the Divine image, to the level of a beast. We repeat not this dark catalogue of crimes,

needlessly to wound your feelings, or in a spirit of self complacency, as if we and our fathers were free from all guilt, but with the view of sufferers. We ask you to ponder seriously and dispassionately the fact that the system which generates such evils is becoming daily more deeply rooted in your soil, and hence more difficult to be cured or eradicated. We presume not to dictate to you the mode of action to which your sympathies should lead, but would affectionately suggest the following as peculiarly suited to your sex: to soften the harsh and cruel, to remonstrate with the unfeeling and unjust, to confirm the wavering and to encourage the timid. We do not forget that there are many masters of slaves, who like Patrick Henry, confess their guilt, and so far pay 'their devoirs to virtue as to own the excellence and rectitude of her precepts, and lament their want of conformity to them.'[1] In the case of such, use your influence to win them into the path of virtue. We believe that there are many who, like your celebrated Pinckney, declare 'that by the eternal principles of natural justice, no master in the State has a right to hold his slave in bondage a single hour' but who are yet timid

---

[1] *like Patrick Henry … conformity to them* One of the American Founders, Patrick Henry (1736–99) twice served as Governor of Virginia. Famous for his rousing oratory against the British in the period leading up to the American Revolution ("Give me liberty or give me death," he famously declared), Henry never did grant liberty to the people he enslaved. The passage here quoted is from a 13 January 1773 letter to John Alsop, a Quaker who had written to Henry to plead the case against slavery. Henry declared that he would "honor the Quakers for their noble efforts to abolish Slavery," and acknowledged that he remained an enslaver merely from "the general inconvenience of living without them." Nevertheless, he remained an enslaver and defender of slavery in the circumstances of his own time. The furthest he would go in that context was to urge that enslaved people be treated leniently:

I will not—I cannot justify [slavery], however culpable my conduct. I will so far pay my devoir to Virtue, as to own the excellence and rectitude of her precepts, and to lament my want of conformity to them. I believe a time will come when an opportunity will be afforded to abolish this lamentable evil. Everything we can do, is to improve it, if it happens in our day; if not, let us transmit to our descendants, together with our slaves, a pity for their unhappy lot, and an abhorrence of Slavery. If we cannot reduce this wished-for reformation to practice, let us treat the unhappy victims with lenity. It is the furthest advancement we can make toward justice.

in their action.[1] Encourage and determine such by your counsel and approbation. In the quiet seclusion of domestic privacy, warn those who desire to extend the area of slavery, of the difficulties that surround its present limits, and beseech them to think of the final results. Above all, let mothers prayerfully imbue the youthful hearts of their children with those important scripture truths which declare 'That God hath made out of one blood all nations of men to dwell on all the face of the earth.'[2] 'There is no respect of persons with God.'[3] 'Forbear threatening, for both your and their master is in heaven.'[4] 'Give unto your servants (slaves) that which is just and equal.'[5] 'Do unto others as you would that they should do unto you;'[6] and we venture to predict that ere another generation pass away 'every bond shall be broken,'[7] and the oppressed will go free; and your great Republic, free from its heavy incubus, will then truly be a land in which 'all men are equal, and have a right to life, liberty, and the pursuit of happiness.' Women of America, your power for good is great, and great are your responsibilities. Many of you by your talents, your advocacy of the rights and liberties of mankind, and your self-denying labors on behalf of the injured African race, command the admiration of mankind. To encourage such in their works of love, and to arouse others to use more energetically the means with which Nature hath endowed them for similar purposes, we now venture to address you, and earnestly pray that to you, the women of the United States, may belong the imperishable honor of removing from your soil the iniquitous system of slavery, which that noble spirit—the ornament of your country—Judge Jay,[8] has described as 'a sin of crimson dye,' and the 'abolition of which in your land was amongst the first wishes of the immortal Washington.'"

—1854

[1] *Pinckney ... action*   Charles Cotesworth Pinckney (1746–1825), a South Carolina politician who ran twice for the Presidency. Though he was an enslaver and defended the institution of slavery, he had supported the abolition of the slave trade in 1808.

[2] *That God ... the earth*   Cf. Acts 17.26.

[3] *There is ... with God*   Cf. Romans 2.11.

[4] *Forbear ... heaven*   Cf. Ephesians 6.9.

[5] *Give unto ... and equal*   Cf. Colossians 4.1.

[6] *Do unto ... unto you*   Cf. Matthew 7.12.

[7] *every bond shall be broken*   Phrase commonly used in antislavery rhetoric. Also cf. Isaiah 58.6.

[8] *Judge Jay*   John Jay (1745–1829). One of the Founders of the United States, Jay was a leading opponent of slavery. In 1789 he became the first Chief Justice of the United States.

GEORGE MEREDITH
1828 – 1909

George Meredith was well-known as both a novelist and a poet. Although he struggled to establish his reputation and his works had never achieved great commercial success, by the end of his life he was celebrated, especially by other writers, as the author of intellectually challenging and artistically complex work. Today, his novels remain well regarded but they are also little read and rarely taught. Meredith is now best known for his sonnet sequence, *Modern Love*, published in 1862. This innovative narrative poem turned an unflinching eye on the problems of contemporary marriage. The poem was considered by many critics at the time to be shocking in its explicit consideration of sexual desire and striking in the frankness with which it depicted modern, middle-class life.

Meredith was born on 12 February 1828, in Portsmouth, England, to a tailor and an innkeeper's daughter. Taught to be ambitious despite his lower-middle-class status, he was reticent about the details of his youth, preferring not even to reveal the location of his birth. His family traced their ancestry to Welsh princes and were able to send George to be educated in Germany at a school suited to a gentleman's son. After completing his schooling, Meredith was articled to a London solicitor, Richard Stephen Charnock, with whom he began to produce a handwritten magazine, "The Monthly Observer." Through the small circle of friends involved with the magazine, he met Mary Ellen Peacock Nicolls, the charismatic daughter of the English satirical writer Thomas Love Peacock and also a writer herself. They married in 1849. Mary Ellen, a widowed young mother almost seven years older than Meredith, was connected with artists and other writers and she encouraged Meredith's literary aspirations. His first poem, "Chillianwallah," was published in *Chambers' Edinburgh Journal* in 1849; his first collection, *Poems*, appeared in 1851. Their son Arthur Gryffydh Meredith was born in 1853. By 1856, however, the couple was living separately and in 1858, Mary Ellen left Meredith for the Pre-Raphaelite painter Henry Wallis. Although she was pregnant with her lover's child—which at the time constituted grounds for divorce—Meredith did not take legal action, though he did seek to prevent her from visiting their son.

Meredith drew on autobiographical materials in his writing after the separation. His first novel, *The Ordeal of Richard Feverel* (1859), concerns a single father raising his only son, and his second, *Evan Harrington* (1860–61), is about a tailor attempting to raise himself in the world. Meredith's personal life also informed *Modern Love*, which he wrote following Mary Ellen's death in 1861. While the poem certainly reflects some of Meredith's experiences, it is much more than a record of his own marital discord. It was published alongside several other kinds of poems in a volume entitled *Modern Love and Poems of the English Roadside, with Poems and Ballads* in 1862, the same year that he briefly shared Queen's House in Chelsea with fellow poets Dante Gabriel Rossetti, William Michael Rossetti, and Algernon Charles Swinburne. Meredith remarried in 1864.

Meredith's subsequent career focused mainly on writing novels. He also published in magazines and worked as a manuscript reader for the publisher Chapman and Hall, where he encouraged the early efforts of younger writers such as Thomas Hardy and George Gissing. His most successful later novels both concerned women's subjugation in marriage: *The Egoist* (1879), a comedy about a woman's efforts to escape from a stifling engagement; and *Diana of the Crossways* (1885), based on the ordeal of Caroline Norton, a woman whose powerful husband had sued for adultery in the late 1830s, prompting her to agitate for women's legal rights. He also published another volume of poetry in 1883.

Meredith was accorded great respect in later life; he was elected President of the Society of Authors in 1892, his works were reissued in Editions de Luxe from 1896 to 1911, and he was awarded the Order of Merit in 1905. Yet younger writers remembered him best for the intellectual challenges posed by his style. Oscar Wilde commented in "The Decay of Lying" (1891): "Ah, Meredith! Who can define him? His style is chaos illumined by flashes of lightning. As a writer he has mastered everything except language: as a novelist he can do everything, except tell a story." Virginia Woolf likewise distinguished between Meredith's style and his social vision, writing, "His mind was too self-conscious, and too sophisticated to stay lyrical for long. He does not sing only; he dissects."

Modern Love

Modern Love dissects a marriage. The sonnets recount a husband's suspicion of his wife's infidelity, his efforts to forgive, his inner turmoil when they hide their misery in front of others, his inability to cease caring for her, his taking a lover, a final grasp at marital reconciliation, and eventually, the wife's suicide. Following this story line can be difficult, as a reviewer writing in the *Athenaeum* in 1862 pointed out: "The story of 'Modern Love' is rather hinted at than told." Some sonnets directly address the wife, called "Madam" throughout, or the mistress, called "Lady." Most are written in the first person from the husband's point of view, which is often itself untrustworthy, confused, or contradictory. Others, especially at the beginning and end of the sequence, are either written in the third person or mix the two perspectives. Although patterns of imagery appear across sonnets, the tone and style of the whole text varies considerably, ranging from domestic vignette to pastoral satire to elegy. Finally, many of the developments depicted in the narrative are internal shifts in the husband's own feelings (and his feelings *about* his feelings) rather than outward actions. By turns histrionic, self-pitying, self-condemning, and detached, the speaker's turbulent psyche showcases the difficulty of bringing to consciousness a sustained, coherent account of unconscious motivations and desires. This variability and inscrutability was linked by some critics, unfavorably, to the recent "Spasmodic" movement in poetry, which solicited readers' visceral responses by emphasizing vivid first-person sensations in long, first-person poems. However, the long narrative poem was a powerful vehicle in the nineteenth century for meditations on both personal and political matters; many poets experimented with longer poems to diverse effects.

Although the long poem was an open-ended form, Meredith gave it shape by using the highly structured sonnet form to tell a story. Linking a series of sonnets to create a narrative, Meredith took a traditional form of love poetry in a new direction. And although Meredith employed many classical, biblical, and English references, he used this established form to address problems of modernity, particularly what was known as the Woman Question.

His adaptation of the sonnet to this new context is evident even at a formal level. The sonnet is conventionally a fourteen-line poem in iambic pentameter that follows one of two fixed rhyme schemes (although there are numerous variants). The first originated in Italy with the work of Francesco Petrarch and was circulated in English by Sir Thomas Wyatt. The second was developed in England and popularized by William Shakespeare. Both the Petrarchan and the Shakespearean sonnet develop a key idea, usually from a first-person point of view, in several stages. The Petrarchan sonnet divides into two units: the eight-line octave proposing a problem, and the six-line sestet, which begins with a *volta*, or turn, in thought and offers resolution. The octave uses an *abbaabba* rhyme scheme, while the sestet uses a *cdecde* or *cdcdcd* scheme. The Shakespearean sonnet follows a four-part pattern resolving in a rhyming couplet: *abab cdcd efef gg*. Meredith mixes and alters these forms. He adds two lines, creating a sixteen-line sonnet with four stanzas each using the same rhyme scheme: *abba cddc effe ghhg*. In essence, he extends the pattern of the Italian octave across the Shakespearean four-part structure. A key effect of this change is that it eliminates the parts of the sonnet usually associated with resolution.

The sequence innovates upon the sonnet tradition not only formally but also in its exploration of gender roles and marital customs. The mid-nineteenth century was a time of significant debate about the role of women. Conduct books, lectures, and poems such as Coventry Patmore's *The Angel in the House* (1854–62) commonly advocated women's subservience to men and dedication to the household, but mores were changing. By the 1850s, English women were beginning to seek access to higher education, employment outside the home, property rights, and the ability to pursue divorce. Marriage in the nineteenth century was structured by the legal idea of coverture, which subsumed (or "covered") a wife's legal existence in her husband's. Coverture transferred all legal power as well as control of all property to the husband; it began to be dismantled in 1870 with the first Married Women's Property Act. Divorce law began to change in 1857, when the Matrimonial Causes Act made divorce considerably more accessible than it had been; whereas divorce had previously required a ruinously expensive private Bill of Parliament, the 1857 Act classified it as a civil proceeding. It also allowed wives as well as husbands to pursue legal separation. However, the Act preserved a marked imbalance of power. While it permitted a husband to pursue divorce if he could prove his wife had committed adultery, a wife had to prove not only adultery but also another offense (such as cruelty, desertion, or bigamy). Although Meredith himself could have sought a divorce under this new law, he chose not to do so. The protagonist of *Modern Love*, in contrast, has a murkier legal outlook since it is not certain that his wife has consummated a sexual relationship outside of the marriage.

Meredith was not the only writer to treat contemporary marriage critically—Elizabeth Barrett Browning's long poem *Aurora Leigh* (1853) had also done so influentially. But the sexual frankness and lack of moral clarity in *Modern Love* offended many of its early readers. As the *Athenaeum* critic put it, "We are not sure that, after great labor, we have arrived at Mr. Meredith's drift; but we are quite sure that, if we have, we do not care for it." R.H. Hutton, writing in *The Spectator*, argued that Meredith treats "a deep and painful subject on which he has no conviction to express," concluding that the sequence was "simply bad and [in] prurient taste." In contrast, the young poet Swinburne—Meredith's housemate for a brief time—was a comparatively rare champion of the poem, defending it in a subsequent issue of the same journal: "Mr. Meredith is one of the three or four poets now alive whose work, perfect or imperfect, is always as noble in design as it is often faultless in result."

Meredith would go on to write other sonnets after those of *Modern Love*, notably "Lucifer in Starlight." But most of his other published poetry was lyric rather than narrative. *Modern Love* appears in the middle of Meredith's second volume of poems between two sections that were both better received. It was preceded by two poems, "Grandfather Bridgman" and "The Meeting," and followed by a section entitled "Roadside Philosophers"; these poems all addressed modernity from the point of view of socially alienated first-person speakers. The volume's final section, "Poems and Ballads," included numerous meditations on nature, particularly the complex lyric "Ode to the Spirit of the Earth in Autumn." Contemporary critics preferred these sections, even while recognizing that *Modern*

Love was the most ambitious portion of the volume; some implied that Meredith would reveal the true depths of his talents if he would only find more suitable topics. For critics today, however, *Modern Love* occupies a secure position among Meredith's most important work—formally experimental and socially radical for its time.

⌘ ⌘ ⌘

Modern Love

1

By this he knew she wept with waking eyes:
That, at his hand's light quiver by her head,
The strange low sobs that shook their common bed,
Were called into her with a sharp surprise,
5   And strangled mute, like little gaping snakes,
Dreadfully venomous to him. She lay
Stone-still, and the long darkness flowed away
With muffled pulses. Then, as midnight makes
Her giant heart of Memory and Tears
10   Drink the pale drug of silence, and so beat
Sleep's heavy measure, they from head to feet
Were moveless, looking through their dead black years,
By vain regret scrawled over the blank wall.
Like sculptured effigies they might be seen
15   Upon their marriage-tomb, the sword between;
Each wishing for the sword that severs all.

2

It ended, and the morrow brought the task.
Her eyes were guilty gates, that let him in
By shutting all too zealous for their sin:
Each sucked a secret, and each wore a mask.
5   But, oh, the bitter taste her beauty had!
He sickened as at breath of poison-flowers:
A languid humour stole among the hours,
And if their smiles encountered, he went mad,
And raged deep inward, till the light was brown
10   Before his vision, and the world forgot,
Looked wicked as some old dull murder-spot.
A star with lurid beams, she seemed to crown
The pit of infamy: and then again

He fainted on his vengefulness, and strove
15   To ape° the magnanimity of love,   *imitate*
And smote himself, a shuddering heap of pain.

3

This was the woman; what now of the man?
But pass him. If he comes beneath a heel,
He shall be crushed until he cannot feel,
Or, being callous, haply till he can.
5   But he is nothing—nothing? Only mark
The rich light striking out from her on him!
Ha! what a sense it is when her eyes swim
Across the man she singles, leaving dark
All else! Lord God, who mad'st the thing so fair,
10   See that I am drawn to her even now!
It cannot be such harm on her cool brow
To put a kiss? Yet if I meet him there!
But she is mine! Ah, no! I know too well
I claim a star whose light is overcast:
15   I claim a phantom-woman in the Past.
The hour has struck, though I heard not the bell!

4

All other joys of life he strove to warm,
And magnify, and catch them to his lip:
But they had suffered shipwreck with the ship,
And gazed upon him sallow from the storm.
5   Or if Delusion came, 'twas but to show
The coming minute mock the one that went.
Cold as a mountain in its star-pitched tent,
Stood high Philosophy, less friend than foe:
Whom self-caged Passion, from its prison-bars,
10   Is always watching with a wondering hate.
Not till the fire is dying in the grate,
Look we for any kinship with the stars.

Oh, wisdom never comes when it is gold,
And the great price we pay for it full worth:

15   We have it only when we are half earth.
Little avails that coinage to the old!

5

A message from her set his brain aflame.
A world of household matters filled her mind,
Wherein he saw hypocrisy designed:
She treated him as something that is tame,

5   And but at other provocation bites.
Familiar was her shoulder in the glass,
Through that dark rain: yet it may come to pass
That a changed eye finds such familiar sights
More keenly tempting than new loveliness.

10   The "What has been" a moment seemed his own:
The splendours, mysteries, dearer because known,
Nor less divine: Love's inmost sacredness,
Called to him, "Come!"—In his restraining start,
Eyes nurtured to be looked at, scarce could see

15   A wave of the great waves of Destiny
Convulsed at a checked impulse of the heart.

6

It chanced his lips did meet her forehead cool.
She had no blush, but slanted down her eye.
Shamed nature, then, confesses love can die:
And most she punishes the tender fool

5   Who will believe what honours her the most!
Dead! is it dead? She has a pulse, and flow
Of tears, the price of blood-drops, as I know,
For whom the midnight sobs around Love's ghost,
Since then I heard her, and so will sob on.

10   The love is here; it has but changed its aim.
O bitter barren woman! what's the name?
The name, the name, the new name thou hast won?
Behold me striking the world's coward stroke!
That will I not do, though the sting is dire.

15   —Beneath the surface this, while by the fire
They sat, she laughing at a quiet joke.

7

She issues radiant from her dressing-room,
Like one prepared to scale an upper sphere:
—By stirring up a lower, much I fear!
How deftly that oiled barber lays his bloom!

5   That long-shanked dapper Cupid[1] with frisked curls,
Can make known women torturingly fair;
The gold-eyed serpent dwelling in rich hair,
Awakes beneath his magic whisks and twirls.
His art can take the eyes from out my head,

10   Until I see with eyes of other men;
While deeper knowledge crouches in its den,
And sends a spark up—is it true we are wed?
Yea! filthiness of body is most vile,
But faithlessness of heart I do hold worse.

15   The former, it were not so great a curse
To read on the steel-mirror of her smile.

8

Yet it was plain she struggled, and that salt
Of righteous feeling made her pitiful.
Poor twisting worm, so queenly beautiful!
Where came the cleft between us? whose the fault?

5   My tears are on thee, that have rarely dropped
As balm for any bitter wound of mine:
My breast will open for thee at a sign!
But, no: we are two reed-pipes, coarsely stopped:
The God once filled them with his mellow breath;

10   And they were music till he flung them down,
Used! used! Hear now the discord-loving clown° *peasant*
Puff his gross spirit in them, worse than death!
I do not know myself without thee more:
In this unholy battle I grow base:

15   If the same soul be under the same face,
Speak, and a taste of that old time restore!

9

He felt the wild beast in him between whiles
So masterfully rude, that he would grieve
To see the helpless delicate thing receive
His guardianship through certain dark defiles.

---

1 *Cupid* Roman god of love.

5   Had he not teeth to rend, and hunger too?
    But still he spared her. Once: "Have you no fear?"
    He said: 'twas dusk; she in his grasp; none near.
    She laughed: "No, surely; am I not with you?"
    And uttering that soft starry "you," she leaned
10 Her gentle body near him, looking up;
    And from her eyes, as from a poison-cup,
    He drank until the flittering eyelids screened.
    Devilish malignant witch! and oh, young beam
    Of heaven's circle-glory! Here thy shape
15 To squeeze like an intoxicating grape—
    I might, and yet thou goest safe, supreme.

10

    But where began the change; and what's my crime?
    The wretch condemned, who has not been arraigned,
    Chafes at his sentence. Shall I, unsustained,
    Drag on Love's nerveless body through all time?
5   I must have slept, since now I wake. Prepare,
    You lovers, to know Love a thing of moods:
    Not like hard life, of laws. In Love's deep woods,
    I dreamt of loyal Life—the offence is there!
    Love's jealous woods about the sun are curled;
10 At least, the sun far brighter there did beam.—
    My crime is that, the puppet of a dream,
    I plotted to be worthy of the world.
    Oh, had I with my darling helped to mince
    The facts of life, you still had seen me go
15 With hindward feather and with forward toe,
    Her much-adored delightful Fairy Prince!

11

    Out in the yellow meadows, where the bee
    Hums by us with the honey of the Spring,
    And showers of sweet notes from the larks on wing,
    Are dropping like a noon-dew, wander we.
5   Or is it now? or was it then? for now,
    As then, the larks from running rings send showers:
    The golden foot of May is on the flowers,
    And friendly shadows dance upon her brow.
    What's this, when Nature swears there is no change
10 To challenge eyesight? Now, as then, the grace
    Of heaven seems holding earth in its embrace.

    Nor eyes, nor heart, has she to feel it strange?
    Look, woman, in the West. There wilt thou see
    An amber cradle near the sun's decline:
15 Within it, featured even in death divine,
    Is lying a dead infant, slain by thee.

12

    Not solely that the Future she destroys,
    And the fair life which in the distance lies
    For all men, beckoning out from dim rich skies:
    Nor that the passing hour's supporting joys
5   Have lost the keen-edged flavour, which begat
    Distinction in old times, and still should breed
    Sweet Memory, and Hope—earth's modest seed,
    And heaven's high-prompting: not that the world is flat
    Since that soft-luring creature I embraced,
10 Among the children of Illusion went:
    Methinks with all this loss I were content,
    If the mad Past, on which my foot is based,
    Were firm, or might be blotted: but the whole
    Of life is mixed: the mocking Past will stay:
15 And if I drink oblivion of a day,
    So shorten I the stature of my soul.

13

    "I play for Seasons; not Eternities!"
    Says Nature, laughing on her way. "So must
    All those whose stake is nothing more than dust!"
    And lo, she wins, and of her harmonies
5   She is full sure! Upon her dying rose,
    She drops a look of fondness, and goes by,
    Scarce any retrospection in her eye;
    For she the laws of growth most deeply knows,
    Whose hands bear, here, a seed-bag—there, an urn.
10 Pledged she herself to aught, 'twould mark her end!
    This lesson of our only visible friend,
    Can we not teach our foolish hearts to learn?
    Yes! yes!—but, oh, our human rose is fair
    Surpassingly! Lose calmly Love's great bliss,
15 When the renewed for ever of a kiss
    Whirls life within the shower of loosened hair!

14

What soul would bargain for a cure that brings
Contempt the nobler agony to kill?
Rather let me bear on the bitter ill,
And strike this rusty bosom with new stings!
5 It seems there is another veering fit,
Since on a gold-haired lady's eyeballs pure,
I looked with little prospect of a cure,
The while her mouth's red bow loosed shafts of wit.
Just heaven! can it be true that jealousy
10 Has decked the woman thus? and does her head
Swim somewhat for possessions forfeited?
Madam, you teach me many things that be.
I open an old book, and there I find,
That "Women still may love whom they deceive."
15 Such love I prize not, madam: by your leave,
The game you play at is not to my mind.

15

I think she sleeps: it must be sleep, when low
Hangs that abandoned arm toward the floor;
The face turned with it. Now make fast the door.
Sleep on: it is your husband, not your foe!
5 The Poet's black stage-lion of wronged love,
Frights not our modern dames:—well if he did!
Now will I pour new light upon that lid,
Full-sloping like the breasts beneath. "Sweet dove,
Your sleep is pure. Nay, pardon: I disturb.
10 I do not? good!" Her waking infant-stare
Grows woman to the burden my hands bear:
Her own handwriting to me when no curb
Was left on Passion's tongue. She trembles through;
A woman's tremble—the whole instrument—
15 I show another letter lately sent.
The words are very like: the name is new.

16

In our old shipwrecked days there was an hour,
When in the firelight steadily aglow,
Joined slackly, we beheld the red chasm grow
Among the clicking coals. Our library-bower
5 That eve was left to us: and hushed we sat
As lovers to whom Time is whispering.

From sudden-opened doors we heard them sing:
The nodding elders mixed good wine with chat.
Well knew we that Life's greatest treasure lay
10 With us, and of it was our talk. "Ah, yes!
Love dies!" I said: I never thought it less.
She yearned to me that sentence to unsay.
Then when the fire domed blackening, I found
Her cheek was salt against my kiss, and swift
15 Up the sharp scale of sobs her breast did lift:—
Now am I haunted by that taste! that sound!

17

At dinner, she is hostess, I am host.
Went the feast ever cheerfuller? She keeps
The Topic over intellectual deeps
In buoyancy afloat. They see no ghost.
5 With sparkling surface-eyes we play the ball:
It is in truth a most contagious game:
HIDING THE SKELETON, shall be its name.
Such play as this, the devils might appal!
But here's the greater wonder; in that we
10 Enamoured of an acting nought can tire,
Each other, like true hypocrites, admire;
Warm-lighted looks, Love's ephemerioe,[1]
Shoot gaily o'er the dishes and the wine.
We waken envy of our happy lot.
15 Fast, sweet, and golden, shows the marriage-knot.
Dear guests, you now have seen Love's corpse-light
    shine.

18

Here Jack and Tom are paired with Moll and Meg.
Curved open to the river-reach is seen
A country merry-making on the green.
Fair space for signal shakings of the leg.
5 That little screwy° fiddler from his booth,   *tipsy*
Whence flows one nut-brown stream, commands the joints
Of all who caper here at various points.
I have known rustic revels in my youth:
The May-fly[2] pleasures of a mind at ease.

---

1 *ephemerioe* Short-lived or fleeting aspects; ephemera.

2 *May-fly* Insect that lives only for one day.

10 An early goddess was a county lass:
A charmed Amphion-oak[1] she tripped the grass.
What life was that I lived? The life of these?
Heaven keep them happy! Nature they seem near.
They must, I think, be wiser than I am;
15 They have the secret of the bull and lamb.
'Tis true that when we trace its source, 'tis beer.

19

No state is enviable. To the luck alone
Of some few favoured men I would put claim.
I bleed, but her who wounds I will not blame.
Have I not felt her heart as 'twere my own
5 Beat thro' me? could I hurt her? heaven and hell!
But I could hurt her cruelly! Can I let
My Love's old time-piece to another set,
Swear it can't stop, and must for ever swell?
Sure, that's one way Love drifts into the mart°   market
10 Where goat-legged[2] buyers throng. I see not plain—
My meaning is, it must not be again.
Great God! the maddest gambler throws his heart.
If any state be enviable on earth,
'Tis yon born idiot's, who, as days go by,
15 Still rubs his hands before him, like a fly,
In a queer sort of meditative mirth.

20

I am not of those miserable males
Who sniff at vice and, daring not to snap,
Do therefore hope for heaven. I take the hap°   result
Of all my deeds. The wind that fills my sails,
5 Propels; but I am helmsman. Am I wrecked,
I know the devil has sufficient weight
To bear: I lay it not on him, or fate.
Besides, he's damned. That man I do suspect
A coward, who would burden the poor deuce
10 With what ensues from his own slipperiness.
I have just found a wanton-scented tress

---

[1] *Amphion-oak*   In Roman myth, Amphion was the son of Zeus and
Antiope. Given a lyre by the goddess Hermes, he played it with such
magical beauty that the stones and trees danced.

[2] *goat-legged*   Lustful.

In an old desk, dusty for lack of use.
Of days and nights it is demonstrative,
That, like some aged star, gleam luridly
15 If for those times I must ask charity,
Have I not any charity to give?

21

We three are on the cedar-shadowed lawn;
My friend being third. He who at love once laughed
Is in the weak rib by a fatal shaft
Struck through, and tells his passion's bashful dawn
5 And radiant culmination, glorious crown,
When "this" she said: went "thus": most wondrous she!
Our eyes grow white, encountering: that we are three,
Forgetful; then together we look down.
But he demands our blessing; is convinced
10 That words of wedded lovers must bring good.
We question; if we dare! or if we should!
And pat him, with light laugh. We have not winced.
Next, she has fallen. Fainting points the sign
To happy things in wedlock. When she wakes,
15 She looks the star that through the cedar shakes:
Her lost moist hand clings mortally to mine.

22

What may the woman labour to confess?
There is about her mouth a nervous twitch.
'Tis something to be told, or hidden—which?
I get a glimpse of hell in this mild guess.
5 She has desires of touch, as if to feel
That all the household things are things she knew.
She stops before the glass. What sight in view?
A face that seems the latest to reveal!
For she turns from it hastily, and tossed
10 Irresolute, steals shadow-like to where
I stand; and wavering pale before me there,
Her tears fall still as oak-leaves after frost.
She will not speak. I will not ask. We are
League-sundered by the silent gulf between.
15 You burly lovers on the village green,
Yours is a lower, and a happier star!

23

'Tis Christmas weather, and a country house
Receives us: rooms are full: we can but get
An attic-crib.[1] Such lovers will not fret
At that, it is half-said. The great carouse
5 Knocks hard upon the midnight's hollow door,
But when I knock at hers, I see the pit.
Why did I come here in that dullard° fit?   *stupid*
I enter, and lie couched upon the floor.
Passing, I caught the coverlet's quick beat:—
10 Come, Shame, burn to my soul! and Pride, and Pain—
Foul demons that have tortured me, enchain!
Out in the freezing darkness the lambs bleat.
The small bird stiffens in the low starlight.
I know not how, but shuddering as I slept,
15 I dreamed a banished angel to me crept:
My feet were nourished on her breasts all night.

24

The misery is greater, as I live!
To know her flesh so pure, so keen her sense,
That she does penance now for no offence,
Save against Love. The less can I forgive!
5 The less can I forgive, though I adore
That cruel lovely pallor which surrounds
Her footsteps; and the low vibrating sounds
That come on me, as from a magic shore.
Low are they, but most subtle to find out
10 The shrinking soul. Madam, 'tis understood
When women play upon their womanhood,
It means, a Season gone. And yet I doubt
But I am duped. That nun-like look waylays
My fancy. Oh! I do but wait a sign!
15 Pluck out the eyes of pride! thy mouth to mine!
Never! though I die thirsting. Go thy ways!

25

You like not that French novel? Tell me why.
You think it quite unnatural. Let us see.
The actors are, it seems, the usual three:
Husband, and wife, and lover. She—but fie!
5 In England we'll not hear of it. Edmond,
The lover, her devout chagrin doth share;
Blanc-mange[2] and absinthe are his penitent fare,
Till his pale aspect makes her over-fond:
So, to preclude fresh sin, he tries rosbif.[3]
10 Meantime the husband is no more abused:
Auguste forgives her ere the tear is used.
Then hangeth all on one tremendous IF—
If she will choose between them! She does choose;
And takes her husband, like a proper wife.
15 Unnatural? My dear, these things are life:
And life, some think, is worthy of the Muse.

26

Love ere he bleeds, an eagle in high skies,
Has earth beneath his wings: from reddened eve
He views the rosy dawn. In vain they weave
The fatal web below while far he flies.
5 But when the arrow strikes him, there's a change.
He moves but in the track of his spent pain,
Whose red drops are the links of a harsh chain,
Binding him to the ground, with narrow range.
A subtle serpent then has Love become.
10 I had the eagle in my bosom[4] erst:°   *at first*
Henceforward with the serpent I am cursed.[5]
I can interpret where the mouth is dumb.°   *silent*
Speak, and I see the side-lie of a truth.
Perchance my heart may pardon you this deed:
15 But be no coward—you that made Love bleed,
You must bear all the venom of his tooth!

---

1 *crib* Small living space.

2 *Blanc-mange* Milk jelly.

3 *rosbif* French: roast beef.

4 *I had ... bosom* Reference to the Greek myth of Prometheus, a Titan who stole fire from the gods and gave it to humankind. As punishment he was chained to a rock, where an eagle (in some versions, a vulture) fed on his liver, which grew back daily.

5 *Henceforward ... cursed* See Genesis 3.15, where God curses the serpent who tempted Eve to eat the forbidden fruit, leading to Adam and Eve's expulsion from the paradise of Eden: "And I will put enmity between thee and the woman, and between thy seed and her seed; it shall bruise thy head, and thou shalt bruise his heel."

27

Distraction is the panacea, Sir!
I hear my oracle of Medicine say.
Doctor! that same specific yesterday
I tried, and the result will not deter
5 A second trial. Is the devil's line
Of golden hair, or raven black, composed?
And does a cheek, like any seashell rosed,
Or clear as widowed sky, seem most divine?
No matter, so I taste forgetfulness.
10 And if the devil snare me, body and mind,
Here gratefully I score—he seemëd kind,
When not a soul would comfort my distress!
O sweet new world, in which I rise new made!
O Lady, once I gave love: now I take!
15 Lady, I must be flattered. Shouldst thou wake
The passion of a demon, be not afraid.

28

I must be flattered. The imperious
Desire speaks out. Lady, I am content
To play with you the game of Sentiment,
And with you enter on paths perilous;
5 But if across your beauty I throw light,
To make it threefold, it must be all mine.
First secret; then avowed. For I must shine
Envied—I, lessened in my proper sight!
Be watchful of your beauty, Lady dear!
10 How much hangs on that lamp you cannot tell.
Most earnestly I pray you, tend it well:
And men shall see me as a burning sphere;
And men shall mark you eyeing me, and groan
To be the God of such a grand sunflower!
15 I feel the promptings of Satanic power,
While you do homage unto me alone.

29

Am I failing? For no longer can I cast
A glory° round about this head of gold.   halo
Glory she wears, but springing from the mould
Not like the consecration of the Past!
5 Is my soul beggared? Something more than earth

I cry for still: I cannot be at peace
In having Love upon a mortal lease.
I cannot take the woman at her worth!
Where is the ancient wealth wherewith I clothed
10 Our human nakedness, and could endow
With spiritual splendour a white brow
That else had grinned at me the fact I loathed?
A kiss is but a kiss now! and no wave
Of a great flood that whirls me to the sea.
15 But, as you will! we'll sit contentedly,
And eat our pot of honey on the grave.

30

What are we first? First, animals; and next
Intelligences at a leap; on whom
Pale lies the distant shadow of the tomb,
And all that draweth on the tomb for text,
5 Into which state comes Love, the crowning sun:
Beneath whose light the shadow loses form.
We are the lords of life, and life is warm.
Intelligence and instinct now are one.
But nature says: "My children most they seem
10 When they least know me: therefore I decree
That they shall suffer." Swift doth young Love flee,
And we stand wakened, shivering from our dream.
Then if we study Nature we are wise.
Thus do the few who live but with the day:
15 The scientific animals are they.—
Lady, this is my sonnet to your eyes.

31

This golden head has wit in it. I live
Again, and a far higher life, near her.
Some women like a young philosopher;
Perchance because he is diminutive.
5 For woman's manly god must not exceed
Proportions of the natural nursing size.
Great poets and great sages draw no prize
With women: but the little lap-dog breed,
Who can be hugged, or on a mantel-piece
10 Perched up for adoration, these obtain
Her homage. And of this we men are vain?
Of this! 'Tis ordered for the world's increase!°   procreation

Small flattery! Yet she has that rare gift
To beauty, Common Sense. I am approved.
15 It is not half so nice as being loved,
And yet I do prefer it. What's my drift?

32

Full faith I have she holds that rarest gift
To beauty, Common Sense. To see her lie
With her fair visage an inverted sky
Bloom-covered, while the underlids uplift,
5 Would almost wreck the faith; but when her mouth
(Can it kiss sweetly? sweetly!) would address
The inner me that thirsts for her no less,
And has so long been languishing in drought,
I feel that I am matched; that I am man!
10 One restless corner of my heart or head,
That holds a dying something never dead,
Still frets, though Nature giveth all she can.
It means, that woman is not, I opine,[1]
Her sex's antidote. Who seeks the asp
15 For serpent's bites? 'Twould calm me could I clasp
Shrieking Bacchantes[2] with their souls of wine!

33

"In Paris, at the Louvre, there have I seen
The sumptuously-feathered angel pierce
Prone Lucifer, descending.[3] Looked he fierce,
Showing the fight a fair one? Too serene!
5 The young Pharsalians[4] did not disarray
Less willingly their locks of floating silk:
That suckling mouth of his, upon the milk
Of heaven might still be feasting through the fray.
Oh, Raphael! when men the Fiend do fight,
10 They conquer not upon such easy terms.
Half serpent in the struggle grow these worms.

---

[1] *I opine* I hold the opinion.

[2] *Bacchantes* Female followers of Bacchus, Roman god of wine, whose revelries included wild, orgiastic dancing.

[3] *sumptuously-feathered… descending* *St. Michael Vanquishing Satan*, painting by Raphael (1483–1520) depicting St. Michael forcing Satan into Hell.

[4] *Pharsalians* Followers of Julius Caesar who won a decisive victory over Pompey in the Battle of Pharsalia in 48 BCE.

And does he grow half human, all is right."
This to my Lady in a distant spot,
Upon the theme: *While mind is mastering clay,*
15 *Gross clay invades it.* If the spy you play,
My wife, read this! Strange love talk, is it not?

34

Madam would speak with me. So, now it comes:
The Deluge or else Fire! She's well; she thanks
My husbandship. Our chain on silence clanks.
Time leers between, above his twiddling thumbs.
5 Am I quite well? Most excellent in health!
The journals, too, I diligently peruse.
Vesuvius[5] is expected to give news:
Niagara[6] is no noisier. By stealth
Our eyes dart scrutinizing snakes.
10 She's glad I'm happy, says her quivering under-lip.
"And are not you?" "How can I be?" "Take ship!
For happiness is somewhere to be had."
"Nowhere for me!" Her voice is barely heard.
I am not melted, and make no pretence.
15 With commonplace I freeze her, tongue and sense.
Niagara, or Vesuvius, is deferred.

35

It is no vulgar nature I have wived,
Secretive, sensitive, she takes a wound
Deep to her soul, as if the sense had swooned,
And not a thought of vengeance had survived.
5 No confidences has she: but relief
Must come to one whose suffering is acute.
O have a care of natures that are mute!
They punish you in acts: their steps are brief.
What is she doing? What does she demand
10 From Providence, or me? She is not one
Long to endure this torpidly, and shun
The drugs that crowd about a woman's hand.

---

[5] *Vesuvius* Mount Vesuvius, an active volcano on the Bay of Naples.

[6] *Niagara* Niagara Falls, waterfalls on the Niagara River.

At Forfeits[1] during snow we played, and I
Must kiss her. "Well performed!" I said: then she:
15 "'Tis hardly worth the money, you agree?"
Save her? What for? To act this wedded lie!

36

My Lady unto Madam makes her bow.
The charm of women is, that even while
You're probed by them for tears, you yet may smile,
Nay, laugh outright, as I have done just now.
5 The interview was gracious: they anoint
(To me aside) each other with fine praise:
Discriminating compliments they raise,
That hit with wondrous aim on the weak point:
My Lady's nose of Nature might complain.
10 It is not fashioned aptly to express
Her character of large-browed steadfastness.
But Madam says: Thereof she may be vain!
Now, Madam's faulty feature is a glazed
And inaccessible eye, that has soft fires,
15 Wide gates, at love-time only. This admires
My Lady. At the two I stand amazed.

37

Along the garden terrace, under which
A purple valley (lighted at its edge
By smoky torch-flame on the long cloud-ledge
Whereunder dropped the chariot[2]), glimmers rich,
5 A quiet company we pace, and wait
The dinner-bell in pre-digestive calm.
So sweet up violet banks the Southern balm
Breathes round, we care not if the bell be late:
Though here and there grey seniors question Time
10 In irritable coughings. With slow foot
The low rosed moon, the face of Music mute,
Begins among her silent bars to climb.
As in and out, in silvery dusk, we thread,

I hear the laugh of Madam, and discern
15 My Lady's heel before me at each turn.
Our tragedy, is it alive or dead?

38

Give to imagination some pure light
In human form to fix it, or you shame
The devils with that hideous human game:—
Imagination urging appetite!
5 Thus fallen have earth's greatest Gogmagogs,[3]
Who dazzle us, whom we can not revere:
Imagination is the charioteer
That, in default of better, drives the hogs.
So, therefore, my dear Lady, let me love!
10 My soul is arrowy to the light in you.
You know me that I never can renew
The bond that woman broke: what would you have?
'Tis Love, or Vileness! not a choice between,
Save petrifaction! What does Pity here?
15 She killed a thing, and now it's dead, 'tis dear.
Oh, when you counsel me, think what you mean!

39

She yields: my Lady in her noblest mood
Has yielded: she, my golden-crownèd rose!
The bride of every sense! more sweet than those
Who breathe the violet breath of maidenhood.
5 O visage of still music in the sky!
Soft moon! I feel thy song, my fairest friend!
True harmony within can apprehend
Dumb harmony without. And hark! 'tis nigh!
Belief has struck the note of sound: a gleam
10 Of living silver shows me where she shook
Her long white fingers down the shadowy brook,
That sings her song, half waking, half in dream.
What two come here to mar this heavenly tune?
A man is one: the woman bears my name,

---

1 *Forfeits* Game in which players give up articles as penalties for mistakes made and then redeem those articles by performing small tasks.

2 *the chariot* Here, the sun, often represented in classical mythology as a chariot driven across the sky by a god.

3 *Gogmagogs* Giants. Gogmagog was the greatest of British giants, according to the history of Britain by Geoffrey of Monmouth (c. 1100–54). In British legend, Gog and Magog were two giants who were taken prisoner and forced to serve as porters at the royal palace. In Revelation 20.8, Gog and Magog represent the superhuman adversaries of the Kingdom of God at the end of time.

15 And honour. Their hands touch! Am I still tame?
   God, what a dancing spectre seems the moon!

40

I bade my Lady think what she might mean.
Know I my meaning, I? Can I love one,
And yet be jealous of another? None
Commits such folly. Terrible Love, I ween,°   think
5 Has might, even dead, half sighing to upheave
The lightless seas of selfishness amain:[1]
Seas that in a man's heart have no rain
To fall and still them. Peace can I achieve,
By turning to this fountain-source of woe,
10 This woman, who's to Love as fire to wood?
She breathed the violet breath of maidenhood
Against my kisses once! but I say, No!
The thing is mocked at! Helplessly afloat,
I know not what I do, whereto I strive,
15 The dread that my old love may be alive,
Has seized my nursling new love by the throat.

41

How many a thing which we cast to the ground,
When others pick it up becomes a gem!
We grasp at all the wealth it is to them;
And by reflected light its worth is found.
5 Yet for us still 'tis nothing! and that zeal
Of false appreciation quickly fades.
This truth is little known to human shades,
How rare from their own instinct 'tis to feel!
They waste the soul with spurious desire,
10 That is not the ripe flame upon the bough:
We two have taken up a lifeless vow
To rob a living passion: dust for fire!
Madam is grave, and eyes the clock that tells
Approaching midnight. We have struck despair
15 Into two hearts. O, look we like a pair
Who for fresh nuptials joyfully yield all else?

42

I am to follow her. There is much grace
In woman when thus bent on martyrdom.
They think that dignity of soul may come,
Perchance, with dignity of body. Base!
5 But I was taken by that air of cold
And statuesque sedateness, when she said
"I'm going"; lit a taper,° bowed her head,   candle
And went, as with the stride of Pallas[2] bold.
Fleshly indifference horrible! The hands
10 Of Time now signal: O, she's safe from me!
Within those secret walls what do I see?
Where first she set the taper down she stands:
Not Pallas: Hebe[3] shamed! Thoughts black as death,
Like a stirred pool in sunshine break. Her wrists
15 I catch: she faltering, as she half resists,
"You love …? love …? love …?" all in an indrawn breath.

43

Mark where the pressing wind shoots javelin-like,
Its skeleton shadow on the broad-backed wave!
Here is a fitting spot to dig Love's grave;
Here where the ponderous breakers plunge and strike,
5 And dart their hissing tongues high up the sand:
In hearing of the ocean, and in sight
Of those ribbed wind-streaks running into white.
If I the death of Love had deeply planned,
I never could have made it half so sure,
10 As by the unblest kisses which upbraid
The full-waked sense; or failing that, degrade!
'Tis morning: but no morning can restore
What we have forfeited. I see no sin:
The wrong is mixed. In tragic life, God wot,°   knows
15 No villain need be! Passions spin the plot:
We are betrayed by what is false within.

[1] *amain* At full speed, in full force.

[2] *Pallas* Epithet of Athena, Greek goddess of wisdom, protectress of towns, and patroness of the arts.

[3] *Hebe* Goddess of youth and spring, the cup-bearer of Olympus until accused of immodesty by Jupiter and dismissed.

44

They say, that Pity in Love's service dwells,
A porter at the rosy temple's gate.
I missed him going: but it is my fate
To come upon him now beside his wells;
5 Whereby I know that I Love's temple leave,
And that the purple doors have closed behind.
Poor soul! if in those early days unkind,
Thy power to sting had been but power to grieve,
We now might with an equal spirit meet,
10 And not be matched like innocence and vice.
She for the Temple's worship has paid price,
And takes the coin of Pity as a cheat.
She sees through simulation to the bone:
What's best in her impels her to the worst:
15 Never, she cries, shall Pity soothe Love's thirst,
Or foul hypocrisy for truth atone!

45

It is the season of the sweet wild rose,
My Lady's emblem in the heart of me!
So golden-crownèd shines she gloriously,
And with that softest dream of blood she glows:
5 Mild as an evening heaven round Hesper[1] bright!
I pluck the flower, and smell it, and revive
The time when in her eyes I stood alive.
I seem to look upon it out of Night.
Here's Madam, stepping hastily. Her whims
10 Bid her demand the flower, which I let drop.
As I proceed, I feel her sharply stop,
And crush it under heel with trembling limbs.
She joins me in a cat-like way, and talks
Of company, and even condescends
15 To utter laughing scandal of old friends.
These are the summer days, and these our walks.

46

At last we parley: we so strangely dumb
In such a close communion! It befell

About the sounding of the Matin-bell,[2]
And lo! her place was vacant, and the hum
5 Of loneliness was round me. Then I rose,
And my disordered brain did guide my foot
To that old wood where our first love-salute
Was interchanged: the source of many throes![3]
There did I see her, not alone. I moved
10 Toward her, and made proffer of my arm.
She took it simply, with no rude alarm;
And that disturbing shadow passed reproved.
I felt the pained speech coming, and declared
My firm belief in her, ere she could speak.
15 A ghastly morning came into her cheek,
While with a widening soul on me she stared.

47

We saw the swallows gathering in the sky,
And in the osier-isle[4] we heard their noise.
We had not to look back on summer joys,
Or forward to a summer of bright dye:
5 But in the largeness of the evening earth
Our spirits grew as we went side by side.
The hour became her husband and my bride.
Love that had robbed us so, thus blessed our dearth!
The pilgrims of the year waxed very loud
10 In multitudinous chatterings, as the flood
Full brown came from the West, and like pale blood
Expanded to the upper crimson cloud.
Love that had robbed us of immortal things,
This little moment mercifully gave
15 Where I have seen across the twilight wave,
The swan sail with her young beneath her wings.

48

Their sense is with their senses all mixed in,
Destroyed by subtleties these women are!
More brain, O Lord, more brain! or we shall mar
Utterly this fair garden we might win.

---

1 *Hesper* I.e., Hesperus, the evening star.

---

2 *Matin-bell* Bell announcing the start of the service of matins, which precedes the first mass of the day.

3 *throes* Severe pangs or spasms, here of pain or longing.

4 *osier-isle* Island of willow trees.

5 Behold! I looked for peace, and thought it near.
   Our inmost hearts had opened, each to each.
   We drank the pure daylight of honest speech.
   Alas! that was the fatal draught, I fear.
   For when of my lost Lady came the word,
10 This woman, O this agony of flesh!
   Jealous devotion bade her break the mesh,
   That I might seek that other like a bird.
   I do adore the nobleness! despise
   The act! She has gone forth, I know not where.
15 Will the hard world my sentience of her share?
   I feel the truth; so let the world surmise.

49

   He found her by the ocean's moaning verge,°   edge
   Nor any wicked change in her discerned;
   And she believed his old love had returned,
   Which was her exultation, and her scourge.
5 She took his hand, and walked with him, and seemed
   The wife he sought, though shadow-like and dry.
   She had one terror, lest her heart should sigh,
   And tell her loudly she no longer dreamed.
   She dared not say, "This is my breast: look in."
10 But there's a strength to help the desperate weak.
   That night he learned how silence best can speak
   The awful things when Pity pleads for Sin.
   About the middle of the night her call
   Was heard, and he came wondering to the bed.
15 "Now kiss me, dear! it may be, now!" she said.
   Lethe[1] had passed those lips, and he knew all.

50

   Thus piteously Love closed what he begat:
   The union of this ever-diverse pair!
   These two were rapid falcons in a snare,
   Condemned to do the flitting of the bat.
5 Lovers beneath the singing sky of May,
   They wandered once; clear as the dew on flowers:
   But they fed not on the advancing hours:

----

[1] *Lethe* A river in Hades (the underworld in Greek mythology) the waters of which produced forgetfulness of the past in those who drank it.

   Their hearts held cravings for the buried day.
   Then each applied to each that fatal knife,
10 Deep questioning, which probes to endless dole.°   sorrow
   Ah, what a dusty answer gets the soul
   When hot for certainties in this our life!—
   In tragic hints here see what evermore
   Moves dark as yonder midnight ocean's force,
15 Thundering like ramping° hosts of warrior horse,   rearing
   To throw that faint thin line upon the shore!
   —1862

Ode to the Spirit of Earth in Autumn

Fair Mother Earth lay on her back last night,
   To gaze her fill on autumn's sunset skies,
When at a waving of the fallen light
Sprang realms of rosy fruitage[2] o'er her eyes.
5 A lustrous heavenly orchard hung the West,
Wherein the blood of Eden bloomed again:
Red were the myriad cherub°-mouths that pressed,   angel
Among the clusters, rich with song, full°   completely
   fain,°   glad
But dumb,° because that overmastering spell   silent
10 Of rapture held them dumb: then, here and there,
A golden harp lost strings; a crimson shell
Burnt grey; and sheaves of lustre fell to air.
The illimitable° eagerness of hue   boundless
Bronzed, and the beamy winged bloom that flew
15 'Mid those bunched fruits and thronging figures failed.
A green-edged lake of saffron touched the blue,
With isles of fireless purple lying through:
And Fancy on that lake to seek lost treasures sailed.

   Not long the silence followed:
      The voice that issues from thy breast,
         O glorious South-west,
20   Along the gloom-horizon holloa'd;°   called out
   Warning the valleys with a mellow roar
   Through flapping wings; then sharp the woodland bore
25   A shudder and a noise of hands:

----

[2] *fruitage* Process of bearing fruit.

A thousand horns from some far vale
In ambush sounding on the gale.
Forth from the cloven° sky came bands   split
Of revel-gathering spirits; trooping down,
30   Some rode the tree-tops; some on torn cloud-strips
Burst screaming thro' the lighted town:
And scudding[1] seaward, some fell on big ships:
Or mounting the sea-horses blew
Bright foam-flakes on the black review
35   Of heaving hulls and burying beaks.[2]

Still on the farthest line, with outpuffed cheeks,
'Twixt dark and utter dark, the great wind drew
From heaven that disenchanted harmony
To join earth's laughter in the midnight blind:
40   Booming a distant chorus to the shrieks
Preluding° him: then he,   preceding, introducing
His mantle streaming thunderingly behind,
Across the yellow realm of stiffened Day,
Shot thro' the woodland alleys signals three;
45   And with the pressure of a sea,
Plunged broad upon the vale that under lay.

Night on the rolling foliage fell:
But I, who love old hymning night,
And know the Dryad° voices well,   wood-nymph
50   Discerned them as their leaves took flight,
Like souls to wander after death:
Great armies in imperial dyes,°   colors
And mad to tread the air and rise,
The savage freedom of the skies
55   To taste before they rot. And here,
Like frail white-bodied girls in fear,
The birches swung from shrieks to sighs;
The aspens, laughers at a breath,
In showering spray-falls mixed their cries,
60   Or raked a savage ocean-strand
With one incessant drowning screech.

Here stood a solitary beech,
That gave its gold with open hand,
And all its branches, toning chill,[3]
65   Did seem to shut their teeth right fast,
To shriek more mercilessly shrill,
And match the fierceness of the blast.

But heard I a low swell that noised
Of far-off ocean, I was 'ware°   aware
70   Of pines upon their wide roots poised,
Whom never madness in the air
Can draw to more than loftier stress
Of mournfulness, not mournfulness
For melancholy, but Joy's excess,
75   That singing, on the lap of sorrow faints:
And Peace, as in the hearts of saints
Who chant unto the Lord their God;
Deep Peace below upon the muffled sod,
The stillness of the sea's unswaying floor.
80   Could I be sole there not to see
The life within the life awake;
The spirit bursting from the tree,
And rising from the troubled lake?
Pour, let the wines of Heaven pour!
85   The Golden Harp is struck once more,
And all its music is for me!
Pour, let the wines of Heaven pour!
And, ho, for a night of Pagan glee!

There is a curtain o'er us.
90   For once, good souls, we'll not pretend
To be aught° better than her who bore us,   any
And is our only visible friend.
Hark to her laughter! who laughs like this,
Can she be dead, or rooted in pain?
95   She has been slain by the narrow brain,
But for us who love her she lives again.
Can she die? O, take her kiss!

---

[1]   *scudding* Moving swiftly, pushed by wind; also a nautical term describing a method of sailing in a gale.

[2]   *beaks* Pointed projections attached to the prows of ancient war vessels.

[3]   *toning chill* Assuming a chill tone.

The crimson-footed nymph is panting up the glade,
With the wine-jar at her arm-pit, and the drunken
    ivy-braid[1]
100 Round her forehead, breasts, and thighs: starts° *out leaps*
    a Satyr,[2] and they speed:
Hear the crushing of the leaves: hear the cracking of
    the bough!
And the whistling of the bramble, the piping of the
    weed!

    But the bull-voiced oak is battling now:
    The storm has seized him half-asleep,
105 And round him the wild woodland throngs
    To hear the fury of his songs,
    The uproar of an outraged deep.
    He wakes to find a wrestling giant
    Trunk to trunk and limb to limb,
110 And on his rooted force reliant
    He laughs and grasps the broadened giant,
    And twist and roll the Anakim;[3]
And multitudes, acclaiming to the cloud,
    Cry which is breaking, which is bowed.

115   Away, for the cymbals clash aloft
    In the circles of pine, on the moss-floor soft.
    The nymphs of the woodland are gathering there.
They huddle° the leaves, and trample, and toss;   *heap*
They swing in the branches, they roll in the moss,
120   They blow the seed on the air.
Back to back they stand and blow
The winged seed on the cradling air,
A fountain of leaves over bosom and back.
The pipe of the Faun[4] comes on their track

125 And the weltering[5] alleys overflow
With musical shrieks and wind-wedded hair.
The riotous companies melt to a pair.
    Bless them, mother of kindness!

    A star has nodded through
130   The depths of the flying blue.
    Time only to plant the light
    Of a memory in the blindness.
    But time to show me the sight
    Of my life thro' the curtain of night;
135   Shining a moment, and mixed
    With the onward-hurrying stream,
    Whose pressure is darkness to me;
    Behind the curtain, fixed,
    Beams with endless beam
140   That star on the changing sea.

Great Mother Nature! teach me, like thee,
To kiss the season and shun regrets.
And am I more than the mother who bore,
Mock me not with thy harmony!
145   Teach me to blot regrets,
    Great Mother! me inspire
    With faith that forward sets
    But feeds the living fire,
    Faith that never frets
150   For vagueness in the form.
    In life, O keep me warm!
    For, what is human grief?
    And what do men desire?
Teach me to feel myself the tree,
155   And not the withered leaf.
Fixed am I and await the dark to-be!

    And O, green bounteous Earth!
Bacchante[6] Mother! stern to those
Who live not in thy heart of mirth;
160 Death shall I shrink from, loving thee?

---

[1] *nymph is ... ivy-braid* The nymph is identified as a follower of Bacchus (god of wine and bringer of ecstasy, associated with the fertility of nature) by her wine-jug and the ivy decorating her body.

[2] *Satyr* Half man, half beast (usually goat or horse) of classical mythology; a woodland companion of Bacchus. Depictions of Bacchus's arrival often include a procession of reveling nymphs and satyrs.

[3] *Anakim* Member of a biblical race of giants. (See Joshua 15.14; Judges 1.20; Numbers 13.33.)

[4] *Faun* Woodland deity that is part man, part goat.

[5] *weltering* In a state of agitation or turmoil.

[6] *Bacchante* Priestess of Bacchus, Roman god of agriculture, fertility, and wine.

Into the breast that gives the rose,
    Shall I with shuddering fall?

    Earth, the mother of all,
    Moves on her steadfast way,
165   Gathering, flinging, sowing.
    Mortals, we live in her day,
    She in her children is growing.

She can lead us, only she,
Unto God's footstool, whither she reaches:
170 Loved, enjoyed, her gifts must be,
Reverenced the truths she teaches,
Ere a man may hope that he
Ever can attain the glee
Of things without a destiny!

175   She knows not loss:
    She feels but her need,
    Who the winged seed
    With the leaf doth toss.

And may not men to this attain?
180 That the joy of motion, the rapture of being,
Shall throw strong light when our season is fleeing,
Nor quicken aged blood in vain,
At the gates of the vault, on the verge° of the plain?   *edge*
Life thoroughly lived is a fact in the brain,
185   While eyes are left for seeing.

Behold, in yon stripped autumn, shivering grey,
    Earth knows no desolation.
    She smells regeneration
    In the moist breath of decay.

190 Prophetic of the coming joy and strife,
    Like the wild western war-chief sinking
    Calm to the end he eyes unblinking,
Her voice is jubilant in ebbing life.

    He for his happy hunting-fields
195   Forgets the droning chant, and yields
    His numbered breaths to exultation

In the proud anticipation:
Shouting the glories of his nation,
Shouting the grandeur of his race,
200 Shouting his own great deeds of daring:
And when at last death grasps his face,
And stiffened on the ground in peace
He lies with all his painted terrors glaring;
Hushed are the tribe to hear a threading cry:
205   Not from the dead man;
    Not from the standers-by:
    The spirit of the red man[1]
Is welcomed by his fathers up on high.
—1862

The Lark Ascending

He rises and begins to round,
  He drops the silver chain of sound
Of many links without a break,
In chirrup, whistle, slur and shake,
5 All intervolved° and spreading wide,   *intertwined*
Like water-dimples down a tide
Where ripple ripple overcurls
And eddy into eddy whirls;
A press of hurried notes that run
10 So fleet° they scarce are more than one,   *swift*
Yet changeingly the trills repeat
And linger ringing while they fleet,°   *pass*
Sweet to the quick[2] o' the ear, and dear
To her beyond and handmaid° ear,   *attendant*
15 Who sits beside our inner springs,
Too often dry for this he brings,
Which seems the very jet of earth
At sight of sun, her music's mirth,
As up he wings° the spiral stair,   *flies*
20 A song of light, and pierces air
With fountain ardour, fountain play
To reach the shining tops of day,

---

1 *the red man* Offensive term for Indigenous person of North America.

2 *the quick* The vital part; the core.

And drink in everything discerned.
An ecstasy to music turned,
25 Impelled by what his happy bill
Disperses; drinking, showering still,
Unthinking save that he may give
His voice the outlet, there to live
Renewed in endless notes of glee,
30 So thirsty of his voice is he,
For all to hear and all to know
That he is joy, awake, aglow,
The tumult of the heart to hear
Through pureness filtered crystal-clear,
35 And know the pleasure sprinkled bright
By simply singing of delight,
Shrill, irreflective,° unrestrained,   *unthinking*
Rapt, ringing, on the jet sustained
Without a break, without a fall,
40 Sweet-silvery, sheer lyrical,
Perennial, quavering up the chord
Like myriad dews of sunny sward°   *turf*
That trembling into fullness shine,
And sparkle dropping argentine;°   *silver*
45 Such wooing as the ear receives
From zephyr° caught in choric leaves[1]   *soft wind*
Of aspens when their chattering net
Is flushed to white with shivers wet;[2]
And such the water-spirit's chime
50 On mountain heights in morning's prime,
Too freshly sweet to seem excess,
Too animate to need a stress;
But wider over many heads
The starry voice ascending spreads,
55 Awakening, as it waxes° thin,   *grows*
The best in us to him akin;
And every face to watch him raised,
Puts on the light of children praised,
So rich our human pleasure ripes°   *ripens*
60 When sweetness on sincereness pipes,
Though nought be promised from the seas,

But only a soft-ruffling breeze
Sweep glittering on a still content,
Serenity in ravishment.

65 For singing till his heaven fills,
'Tis love of earth that he instils,
And ever winging up and up,
Our valley is his golden cup,
And he the wine which overflows
70 To lift us with him as he goes:
The woods and brooks, the sheep and kine.°   *cattle*
He is, the hills, the human line,
The meadows green, the fallows brown,
The dreams of labour in the town;
75 He sings the sap, the quickened veins;
The wedding song of sun and rains
He is, the dance of children, thanks
Of sowers,[3] shout of primrose-banks,
And eye of violets while they breathe;
80 All these the circling song will wreathe,
And you shall hear the herb and tree,
The better heart of men shall see,
Shall feel celestially, as long
As you crave nothing save the song.

85 Was never voice of ours could say
Our inmost in the sweetest way,
Like yonder voice aloft, and link
All hearers in the song they drink:
Our wisdom speaks from failing blood,
90 Our passion is too full in flood,
We want° the key of his wild note   *lack*
Of truthful in a tuneful throat,
The song seraphically° free   *angelically*
Of taint of personality,
95 So pure that it salutes the suns
The voice of one for millions,
In whom the millions rejoice
For giving their one spirit voice.

---

[1] *choric leaves* Leaves in a chorus.

[2] *Of aspens … shivers wet* The leaves of aspen trees flutter with a distinctive sound and motion, often described as "quaking."

---

[3] *sowers* Those who sow seeds.

Yet men have we, whom we revere,
100   Now names, and men still housing here,
Whose lives by many a battle-dint[1]
Defaced, and grinding wheels on flint,
Yield substance, though they sing not, sweet
For song our highest heaven to greet:
105   Whom heavenly singing gives us new,
Enspheres them brilliant in our blue,
From firmest base to farthest leap,
Because their love of Earth is deep,
And they are warriors in accord
110   With life to serve and pass reward,

So touching purest and so heard
In the brain's reflex of yon bird;
Wherefore their soul in me, or mine,
Through self-forgetfulness divine,
115   In them, that song aloft maintains,
To fill the sky and thrill the plains
With showerings drawn from human stores,
As he to silence nearer soars,
Extends the world at wings and dome,
120   More spacious making more our home,
Till lost on his aërial rings
In light, and then the fancy sings.
—1881

---

[1]   *battle-dint*   Blow received in battle.

Dante Gabriel Rossetti
1828 – 1882

"Youth and Death, Destiny and Fortune, Fame, Poetic Fame, Memory, Oblivion"—these, according to Walter Pater, are among the "mysterious powers" at the center of Dante Gabriel Rossetti's work. But "enthroned" among these, Pater wrote, is "the ideal intensity of love." The ethereal yet sensuous aesthetic Rossetti developed to evoke these mysteries in painting as well as poetry exerted a strong influence on poets and artists of the late nineteenth and early twentieth centuries.

Stylized and radiant scenes of knights, maidens, and lovers—soon synonymous with Rossetti's name—found their original inspiration in works of early Italian, Christian, and medieval iconography. The subject of "The Blessed Damozel," one of Rossetti's finest poems, glows with the spiritually luminous effects associated with the religious poetry of Dante (Rossetti's namesake). Yet Rossetti also endowed his damsel with an earthly voluptuousness. Borrowing from Dantesque and Arthurian mythology, Rossetti created fantasies whose "stained glass" quality reflects both the literary outlines of religious allegory and the sensual strokes of an artist enraptured by the female figure. It was an artistic approach that ran the risk of causing offense at a time when soul and body, love and sex, were separate compartments of Victorian life, and Rossetti's work was frequently attacked in the later half of his career for trying to solder spiritual to "fleshly" desires.

Born in 1828 into an erudite family, Rossetti was the second child and eldest son of four children. He was a competitive yet fiercely fond older brother to his sister, the future poet Christina. His mother, Frances Polidori Rossetti, was Anglo-Italian; his father, Gabriele Rossetti, an exiled Italian patriot, was a Professor at King's College, London. The Rossettis' childhood home, with its assortment of orthodox and unorthodox books, was a meeting place where politicized ex-patriots spent many an evening debating the past and future of Italy. From the stream of sketches and literary compositions issuing from the temperamental imaginations of Dante Gabriel and Christina, it was apparent early on that the two Rossettis were extraordinarily gifted. Their parents held high hopes that Dante Gabriel would become a great painter, even though his schooling in painting and his knowledge of European painting were not extensive.

Rossetti was a moody student at the Royal Academy of Arts in 1848 when he co-founded the Pre-Raphaelite Brotherhood with fellow painters William Holman Hunt, John Everett Millais, James Collinson, Frederic George Stephens, Thomas Woolner, and Dante Gabriel's brother, critic William Michael Rossetti. In a letter to his sister Christina, Rossetti spoke of the group as a "Round Table" whose knights shared a mutual love of Keats. They also adored Malory's *Morte Darthur*, the novels of Walter Scott, and the work of Blake, Dante, Tennyson, and Browning. By referencing early Florentine and Sienese schools (dubbed "the Italian Primitives" because they predated the High Renaissance), the Pre-Raphaelites sought to reform what they saw as the florid emptiness of Victorian art and its lack of truth to nature. "Sincerity" as a quality of near-devotional feeling communicated through purity of line and color was more important to the Pre-Raphaelites than mere technical virtuosity. As one critic put it, the Pre-Raphaelites favored "primitive but vital imperfection, as opposed to lifeless perfection." A movement in both literature and painting, Pre-Raphaelitism was identified with a vivid palette, formal patterning, and symbolic details woven into exotic scenes of religious or romantic love whose settings evoked a sumptuous "elsewhere." In Pre-Raphaelite poetry and painting, there was always a "definiteness of sensible imagery," as Pater said of "The Blessed Damozel."

When sixteen-year old Christina published *Verses* in 1847, Rossetti was compelled to try with meter what he was doing with color. "Colour and metre," Rossetti claimed, "are the true parents of nobility in painting and poetry." In 1850, the Pre-Raphaelite Brotherhood published a journal of poems and illustrations entitled *The Germ*, in which Rossetti's "The Blessed Damozel" first appeared. The publication gained Rossetti a small group of admirers that would steadily increase. John Ruskin, who helped turn the tide in his favor by praising the art of the Pre-Raphaelites in *The Times* in 1851, became one of Rossetti's prominent patrons and closest friends. Rossetti cherished intellectual friendships with Robert Browning and William Morris, and socialized with the flamboyant Algernon Swinburne. He obtained stable employment teaching art at the Working Men's College. Stumbling across a book of William Blake's poems and paintings, Rossetti discovered another kindred spirit, albeit one who had died a year before he was born. Having secured his own reputation, Rossetti was able to rescue Blake from near oblivion, rediscovering him for a Victorian audience. In 1861, he also published *The Early Italian Poets*, which introduced, through his translations of the *Vita Nuova* and other poems by Dante and his predecessors and contemporaries, many poets whose work had been unknown in England.

Rossetti was also prone to what one biographer calls "rescue missions" of unknown beauties. Elizabeth Gaskell wrote that Rossetti was "hair-mad," with a penchant for the wavy tresses of women he and his friends called "stunners." On the one hand, Rossetti supported the equality and independence of working-class women like Elizabeth Siddal, whom he eventually married. On the other hand, his rescue of beautiful women from their class obscurity dramatized a sexual imbalance of power that was titillating; like many Victorian men, Rossetti enjoyed the license to "fall in love" with working-class women without seriously compromising his reputation, a license prohibited to women under the double standards of Victorian society.

Siddal, a model for the Pre-Raphaelites and an artist and poet in her own right, died by suicide in 1862, two years after her marriage to Rossetti. Invoking Dante's dead beloved, Beatrice, Rossetti memorialized Siddal in a painting entitled *Beata Beatrix* (c. 1863). Seized with remorse at her funeral, he tucked a manuscript of poems into her coffin. He had them exhumed years later in order to publish his first collection of verse, *Poems* (1870). Though Rossetti afterwards lived with Fanny Cornforth, he fell in love with Jane Burden, the wife of William Morris. Both Fanny and "Janey" came from working-class backgrounds and modeled for Rossetti, becoming sensuously stylized objects of desire in paintings such as *Proserpine* (1874).

Soon after the appearance of Rossetti's *The House of Life*, a sequence of sonnets that appeared in his first volume of poetry, the poet Robert Buchanan denounced its "animalism" in a scalding critique entitled *The Fleshly School of Poetry* (1871). According to Buchanan, Rossetti's "house of life" was suggestive of a brothel and his sonnets bore the stamp of "the same sense of weary, wasting, yet exquisite sensuality." Rossetti counterattacked with "The Stealthy School of Criticism" (1872), and he would make significant additions and revisions to *The House of Life* over the next decade.

Rossetti's mental health had long been unstable, and Buchanan's attack provoked a serious breakdown. Though Yeats's youthful claim that he was "in all things Pre-Raphaelite" was proof of Rossetti's influence on the next generation of poets, Rossetti himself never fully recovered from being "stigmatized as a sensualist," in the words of one critic. He continued to paint and write, however, and in 1881 he published *Ballads and Sonnets*, a collection featuring several long ballads as well as an expanded version of *The House of Life*. Bouts of nervous depression, made worse by the consumption of whiskey and narcotics, led to a decline in Rossetti's health; he died in 1882.

⌘ ⌘ ⌘

The Blessed Damozel [1]

The blessed damozel leaned out
    From the gold bar of Heaven;
Her eyes were deeper than the depth
    Of waters stilled at even;
5 She had three lilies in her hand,
    And the stars in her hair were seven.

Her robe, ungirt from clasp to hem,
    No wrought flowers did adorn,
But a white rose of Mary's [2] gift,
10   For service meetly° worn;   *properly*
Her hair that lay along her back
    Was yellow like ripe corn.°   *grain*

Herseemed she scarce had been a day
    One of God's choristers;
15 The wonder was not yet quite gone
    From that still look of hers;
Albeit, to them she left, her day
    Had counted as ten years.

(To one, it is ten years of years.
20   … Yet now, and in this place,
Surely she leaned o'er me—her hair
    Fell all about my face. …
Nothing: the autumn-fall of leaves.
    The whole year sets apace.)

25 It was the rampart of God's house
    That she was standing on;
By God built over the sheer depth
    The which is Space begun;
So high, that looking downward thence
30   She scarce could see the sun.

It lies in Heaven, across the flood
    Of ether, [3] as a bridge.
Beneath, the tides of day and night
    With flame and darkness ridge
35 The void, as low as where this earth
    Spins like a fretful midge. [4]

Around her, lovers, newly met
    'Mid deathless love's acclaims,
Spoke evermore among themselves
40   Their heart-remembered names;
And the souls mounting up to God
    Went by her like thin flames.

And still she bowed herself and stooped
    Out of the circling charm;
45 Until her bosom must have made
    The bar she leaned on warm,
And the lilies lay as if asleep
    Along her bended arm.

From the fixed place of Heaven she saw
50   Time like a pulse shake fierce
Through all the worlds. Her gaze still strove
    Within the gulf to pierce

---

[1] *The Blessed Damozel* After the poem's publication, Rossetti told novelist Hall Caine that he had written it as something of a sequel to Edgar Allen Poe's poem "The Raven" (1845): "I saw that Poe had done the utmost it was possible to do with the grief of the lover on earth, and so determined to reverse the conditions, and give utterance to the yearning of the loved one in heaven." A "damozel" is a damsel, a young, unmarried woman.

[2] *Mary* Mother of Jesus.

[3] *ether* Substance once speculated to fill the space between the stars and planets in the sky.

[4] *midge* Small fly.

Dante Gabriel Rossetti, *The Blessed Damozel*, 1875–78.

Its path; and now she spoke as when
    The stars sang in their spheres.[1]

55 The sun was gone now; the curled moon
    Was like a little feather
Fluttering far down the gulf; and now
    She spoke through the still weather.

60 Her voice was like the voice the stars
    Had when they sang together.

(Ah sweet! Even now, in that bird's song,
    Strove not her accents there,
Fain° to be hearkened? When those bells   *gladly*
    Possessed the mid-day air,
65 Strove not her steps to reach my side
    Down all the echoing stair?)

---

[1] *as when ... spheres*   See Job 38.7, in which the morning stars sing on
creation day. Rossetti probably also refers to the Pythagorean concept
of the music of the spheres, inaudible to those on earth.

"I wish that he were come to me,
    For he will come," she said.
"Have I not prayed in Heaven?—on earth,
    Lord, Lord, has he not prayed?
Are not two prayers a perfect strength?
    And shall I feel afraid?

"When round his head the aureole° clings,   halo
    And he is clothed in white,
I'll take his hand and go with him
    To the deep wells of light;
As unto a stream we will step down,
    And bathe there in God's sight.

"We two will stand beside that shrine,
    Occult,° withheld, untrod,   secret
Whose lamps are stirred continually
    With prayer sent up to God;
And see our old prayers, granted, melt
    Each like a little cloud.

"We two will lie i'the shadow of
    That living mystic tree[1]
Within whose secret growth the Dove[2]
    Is sometimes felt to be,
While every leaf that His plumes touch
    Saith His Name audibly.

"And I myself will teach to him,
    I myself, lying so,
The songs I sing here; which his voice
    Shall pause in, hushed and slow,
And find some knowledge at each pause,
    Or some new thing to know."

(Alas! We two, we two, thou say'st!
    Yea, one wast thou with me
That once of old. But shall God lift
    To endless unity
The soul whose likeness with thy soul
    Was but its love for thee?)

"We two," she said, "will seek the groves
    Where the lady Mary is,
With her five handmaidens, whose names
    Are five sweet symphonies,
Cecily, Gertrude, Magdalen,
    Margaret and Rosalys.[3]

"Circlewise sit they, with bound locks
    And foreheads garlanded;
Into the fine cloth white like flame
    Weaving the golden thread,
To fashion the birth-robes for them
    Who are just born, being dead.

"He shall fear, haply,° and be dumb: perchance
    Then will I lay my cheek
To his, and tell about our love,
    Not once abashed or weak:
And the dear Mother will approve
    My pride, and let me speak.

"Herself shall bring us, hand in hand,
    To him round whom all souls
Kneel, the clear-ranged unnumbered heads
    Bowed with their aureoles:°   haloes
And angels meeting us shall sing
    To their citherns and citoles.[4]

"There will I ask of Christ the Lord
    Thus much for him and me:
Only to live as once on earth
    With Love—only to be,
As then awhile, for ever now
    Together, I and he."

She gazed and listened and then said,
    Less sad of speech than mild—

---

[1] *living mystic tree* Tree of life (See Revelation 22.2).

[2] *Dove* Holy Spirit.

[3] *Cecily ... Rosalys* Cecilia, Gertrude, Margaret, and Rosalia are all saints; Mary Magdalene appears in the Bible as a follower of Jesus who witnessed his death and resurrection.

[4] *citherns* Guitar-like instruments strung with wire and played with a quill, popular in the sixteenth and seventeenth centuries; *citoles* Stringed instruments common in the thirteenth to fifteenth centuries.

135 "All this is when he comes." She ceased.
  The light thrilled towards her, filled
With angels in strong level flight.
  Her eyes prayed, and she smiled.

(I saw her smile.) But soon their path
140   Was vague in distant spheres:
And then she cast her arms along
  The golden barriers,
And laid her face between her hands,
  And wept. (I heard her tears.)
 —1850

Jenny

"Vengeance of Jenny's case! Fie on her!
Never name her, child"

     (Mrs. Quickly.)[1]

Lazy laughing languid Jenny,
 Fond of a kiss and fond of a guinea,[2]
Whose head upon my knee to-night
Rests for a while, as if grown light
5 With all our dances and the sound
To which the wild tunes spun you round:
Fair Jenny mine, the thoughtless queen
Of kisses which the blush between
Could hardly make much daintier;
10 Whose eyes are as blue skies, whose hair
Is countless gold incomparable;
Fresh flower, scarce touched with signs that tell
Of Love's exuberant hotbed—Nay,
Poor flower left torn since yesterday
15 Until to-morrow leave you bare;
Poor handful of bright spring-water
Flung in the whirlpool's shrieking face;
Poor shameful Jenny, full of grace
Thus with your head upon my knee—

20 Whose person or whose purse may be
The lodestar[3] of your reverie?

 This room of yours, my Jenny, looks
A change from mine so full of books,
Whose serried[4] ranks hold fast, forsooth,
25 So many captive hours of youth—
The hours they thieve from day and night
To make one's cherished work come right,
And leave it wrong for all their theft,
Even as to-night my work was left:
30 Until I vowed that since my brain
And eyes of dancing seemed so fain,°   *willing*
My feet should have some dancing too—
And thus it was I met with you.
Well, I suppose 'twas hard to part,
35 For here I am. And now, sweetheart,
You seem too tired to get to bed.

 It was a careless life I led
When rooms like this were scarce so strange
Not long ago. What breeds the change—
40 The many aims or the few years?
Because to-night it all appears
Something I do not know again.

 The cloud's not danced out of my brain—
The cloud that made it turn and swim
45 While hour by hour the books grew dim.
Why, Jenny, as I watch you there,
For all your wealth of loosened hair,
Your silk ungirdled and unlaced
And warm sweets open to the waist,
50 All golden in the lamplight's gleam,
You know not what a book you seem,
Half-read by lightning in a dream!
How should you know, my Jenny? Nay,
And I should be ashamed to say—
55 Poor beauty, so well worth a kiss!
But while my thought runs on like this

---

[1] *Vengeance … Quickly* From Shakespeare's *The Merry Wives of Windsor* 1.1. The rest of Mistress Quickly's speech reads, "if she be a whore."

[2] *guinea* English gold coin.

[3] *lodestar* Pole star; i.e., guiding star.

[4] *serried* Pressed close together.

With wasteful whims more than enough,
I wonder what you're thinking of.

    If of myself you think at all,
60 What is the thought?—conjectural
On sorry matters best unsolved?—
Or inly° is each grace revolved   *inwardly*
To fit me with a lure?—or (sad
To think!) perhaps you're merely glad
65 That I'm not drunk or ruffianly
And let you rest upon my knee.

    For sometimes, were the truth confessed,
You're thankful for a little rest—
Glad from the crush to rest within,
70 From the heart-sickness and the din
Where envy's voice at virtue's pitch
Mocks you because your gown is rich;
And from the pale girl's dumb° rebuke,   *silent*
Whose ill-clad grace and toil-worn look
75 Proclaim the strength that keeps her weak
And other nights than yours bespeak;
And from the wise unchildish elf,
To schoolmate lesser than himself
Pointing you out, what thing you are—
80 Yes, from the daily jeer and jar,
From shame and shame's outbraving too,
Is rest not sometimes sweet to you?
But most from the hatefulness of man
Who spares not to end what he began,
85 Whose acts are ill and his speech ill,
Who, having used you at his will,
Thrusts you aside, as when I dine
I serve the dishes and the wine.

    Well, handsome Jenny mine, sit up,
90 I've filled our glasses, let us sup,
And do not let me think of you,
Lest shame of yours suffice for two.
What, still so tired? Well, well then, keep
Your head there, so you do not sleep;
95 But that the weariness may pass
And leave you merry, take this glass.

Ah! lazy lily hand, more blessed
If ne'er in rings it had been dressed
Nor ever by a glove concealed!

100 Behold the lilies of the field,
They toil not neither do they spin;[1]
(So doth the ancient text begin—
Not of such rest as one of these
Can share.) Another rest and ease
105 Along each summer-sated path
From its new lord the garden hath,
Than that whose spring in blessings ran
Which praised the bounteous husbandman,
Ere yet, in days of hankering breath,
110 The lilies sickened unto death.

    What, Jenny, are your lilies dead?
Aye, and the snow-white leaves are spread
Like winter on the garden-bed.
But you had roses left in May—
115 They were not gone too. Jenny, nay,
But must your roses die, and those
Their purfled[2] buds that should unclose?
Even so; the leaves are curled apart,
Still red as from the broken heart,
120 And here's the naked stem of thorns.

    Nay, nay, mere words. Here nothing warns
As yet of winter. Sickness here
Or want alone could waken fear—
Nothing but passion wrings a tear.
125 Except when there may rise unsought
Haply° at times a passing thought   *perchance*
Of the old days which seem to be
Much older than any history
That is written in any book;
130 When she would lie in fields and look
Along the ground through the blown grass,
And wonder where the city was,

---

[1] *Behold ... spin* Reference to Matthew 6.28: "And why take ye thought for raiment? Consider the lilies of the field, how they grow; they toil not, neither do they spin."

[2] *purfled* Edged with another color.

Far out of sight, whose broil° and bale°   *tumult / woe*
They told her then for a child's tale.

135   Jenny, you know the city now.
A child can tell the tale there, how
Some things which are not yet enrolled
In market-lists are bought and sold
Even till the early Sunday light,
140 When Saturday night is market-night
Everywhere, be it dry or wet,
And market-night in the Haymarket.[1]
Our learned London children know,
Poor Jenny, all your pride and woe;
145 Have seen your lifted silken skirt
Advertise dainties through the dirt;
Have seen your coach-wheels splash rebuke
On virtue; and have learned your look
When, wealth and health slipped past, you stare
150 Along the streets alone, and there,
Round the long park, across the bridge,
The cold lamps at the pavement's edge
Wind on together and apart,
A fiery serpent for your heart.

155   Let the thoughts pass, an empty cloud!
Suppose I were to think aloud—
What if to her all this were said?
Why, as a volume seldom read
Being opened halfway shuts again,
160 So might the pages of her brain
Be parted at such words, and thence
Close back upon the dusty sense.
For is there hue or shape defined
In Jenny's desecrated mind,
165 Where all contagious currents meet,
A Lethe[2] of the middle street?
Nay, it reflects not any face,
Nor sound is in its sluggish pace,

But as they coil those eddies clot,
170 And night and day remember not.

Why, Jenny, you're asleep at last!
Asleep, poor Jenny, hard and fast—
So young and soft and tired; so fair,
With chin thus nestled in your hair,
175 Mouth quiet, eyelids almost blue
As if some sky of dreams shone through!

Just as another woman sleeps!
Enough to throw one's thoughts in heaps
Of doubt and horror—what to say
180 Or think—this awful secret sway,
The potter's power over the clay!
Of the same lump (it has been said)
For honour and dishonour made,
Two sister vessels.[3] Here is one.

185   My cousin Nell is fond of fun,
And fond of dress, and change, and praise,
So mere a woman in her ways:
And if her sweet eyes rich in youth
Are like her lips that tell the truth,
190 My cousin Nell is fond of love.
And she's the girl I'm proudest of.
Who does not prize her, guard her well?
The love of change, in cousin Nell,
Shall find the best and hold it dear:
195 The unconquered mirth turn quieter
Not through her own, through others' woe:
The conscious pride of beauty glow
Beside another's pride in her,
One little part of all they share.
200 For Love himself shall ripen these
In a kind soil to just increase
Through years of fertilizing peace.

---

1 *Haymarket* Street in London's theater district, at the time a center of prostitution.

2 *Lethe* River in Hades (the underworld of classical mythology) whose waters bring forgetfulness to those who drink from them.

---

3 *The potter's … vessels* Reference to Romans 9.21: "Hath not the potter power over the clay, of the same lump to make one vessel unto honor, and another unto dishonor?"

Of the same lump (as it is said)
For honour and dishonour made,
Two sister vessels. Here is one.

It makes a goblin of the sun.

So pure—so fallen! How dare to think
Of the first common kindred link?
Yet, Jenny, till the world shall burn
It seems that all things take their turn;
And who shall say but this fair tree
May need, in changes that may be,
Your children's children's charity?
Scorned then, no doubt, as you are scorned!
Shall no man hold his pride forewarned
Till in the end, the Day of Days,
At Judgment, one of his own race,
As frail and lost as you, shall rise—
His daughter, with his mother's eyes?

How Jenny's clock ticks on the shelf!
Might not the dial scorn itself
That has such hours to register?
Yet as to me, even so to her
Are golden sun and silver moon,
In daily largesse of earth's boon,
Counted for life-coins to one tune.
And if, as blindfold fates are tossed,
Through some one man this life be lost,
Shall soul not somehow pay for soul?

Fair shines the gilded aureole°   halo
In which our highest painters place
Some living woman's simple face.
And the stilled features thus descried
As Jenny's long throat droops aside—
The shadows where the cheeks are thin,
And pure wide curve from ear to chin—
With Raffael's, Leonardo's[1] hand
To show them to men's souls, might stand,
Whole ages long, the whole world through,

For preachings of what God can do.
What has man done here? How atone,
Great God, for this which man has done?
And for the body and soul which by
Man's pitiless doom must now comply
With lifelong hell, what lullaby
Of sweet forgetful second birth
Remains? All dark. No sign on earth
What measure of God's rest endows
The many mansions of his house.[2]

If but a woman's heart might see
Such erring heart unerringly
For once! But that can never be.

Like a rose shut in a book
In which pure women may not look,
For its base pages claim control
To crush the flower within the soul;
Where through each dead rose-leaf that clings,
Pale as transparent psyche-wings,[3]
To the vile text, are traced such things
As might make lady's cheek indeed
More than a living rose to read;
So nought save foolish foulness may
Watch with hard eyes the sure decay;
And so the life-blood of this rose,
Puddled with shameful knowledge, flows
Through leaves no chaste hand may unclose:
Yet still it keeps such faded show
Of when 'twas gathered long ago,
That the crushed petals' lovely grain,
The sweetness of the sanguine[4] stain,
Seen of a woman's eyes, must make
Her pitiful heart, so prone to ache,
Love roses better for its sake—
Only that this can never be:
Even so unto her sex is she.

---

[1] *Raffael, Leonardo*   I.e., Italian painters Raphael (1483–1520) and Leonardo da Vinci (1452–1519).

[2] *The many mansions of his house*   See John 14.2.

[3] *psyche-wings*   Psyche, Greek goddess of the soul, is often depicted with butterfly wings.

[4] *sanguine*   Here, blood-red or blushing.

Yet, Jenny, looking long at you,
The woman almost fades from view.
A cipher of man's changeless sum
Of lust, past, present, and to come,
280 Is left. A riddle that one shrinks
To challenge from the scornful sphinx.[1]

Like a toad within a stone
Seated while Time crumbles on;[2]
Which sits there since the earth was cursed
285 For Man's transgression at the first;[3]
Which, living through all centuries,
Not once has seen the sun arise;
Whose life, to its cold circle charmed,
The earth's whole summers have not warmed;
290 Which always—whitherso the stone
Be flung—sits there, deaf, blind, alone;
Aye, and shall not be driven out
Till that which shuts him round about
Break at the very Master's stroke,
295 And the dust thereof vanish as smoke,
And the seed of Man vanish as dust—
Even so within this world is Lust.

Come, come, what use in thoughts like this?
Poor little Jenny, good to kiss—
300 You'd not believe by what strange roads
Thought travels, when your beauty goads
A man to-night to think of toads!
Jenny, wake up ... Why, there's the dawn!

And there's an early wagon drawn
305 To market, and some sheep that jog
Bleating before a barking dog;
And the old streets come peering through
Another night that London knew;
And all as ghostlike as the lamps.

310 So on the wings of day decamps
My last night's frolic. Glooms begin
To shiver off as lights creep in
Past the gauze curtains half drawn-to,
And the lamp's doubled shade grows blue—
315 Your lamp, my Jenny, kept alight,
Like a wise virgin's, all one night!
And in the alcove coolly spread
Glimmers with dawn your empty bed;
And yonder your fair face I see
320 Reflected lying on my knee,
Where teems with first foreshadowings
Your pier-glass[4] scrawled with diamond rings:
And on your bosom all night worn
Yesterday's rose now droops forlorn
325 But dies not yet this summer morn.

And now without, as if some word
Had called upon them that they heard,
The London sparrows far and nigh
Clamour together suddenly;
330 And Jenny's cage-bird grown awake
Here in their song his part must take,
Because here too the day doth break.

And somehow in myself the dawn
Among stirred clouds and veils withdrawn
335 Strikes greyly on her. Let her sleep.
But will it wake her if I heap
These cushions thus beneath her head
Where my knee was? No—there's your bed,
My Jenny, while you dream. And there
340 I lay among your golden hair
Perhaps the subject of your dreams,
These golden coins.

---

[1] *sphinx* Winged creature of Greek mythology who killed those who could not answer its riddles.

[2] *Like a ... on* Phenomenon of living toads, frogs, or other creatures trapped in stone or wood is one that has been occasionally reported. One such instance occurred in 1865, when workers excavating in Hartlepool, England, split open a magnesium limestone rock found 25 feet underground to discover a living toad. The *Hartlepool Free Press* reported, "The cavity was no larger than its body, and presented the appearance of being cast for it." There was no evidence as to how the toad could have gotten into the stone or survived in it for any length of time. But, from its appearance and the age of the rock in which it was found, the toad was estimated to be over 6,000 years old.

[3] *Man's ... the first* Reference to the fall of Adam and Eve; see Genesis 3.

[4] *pier-glass* Large, tall mirror.

For still one deems
That Jenny's flattering sleep confers
345   New magic on the magic purse—
Grim web, how clogged with shrivelled flies!
Between the threads fine fumes arise
And shape their pictures in the brain.
There roll no streets in glare and rain,
350   Nor flagrant man-swine whets his tusk;
But delicately sighs in musk
The homage of the dim boudoir;
Or like a palpitating star
Thrilled into song, the opera-night
355   Breathes faint in the quick pulse of light;
Or at the carriage-window shine
Rich wares for choice; or, free to dine,
Whirls through its hour of health (divine
For her) the concourse of the Park.
360   And though in the discounted dark
Her functions there and here are one,
Beneath the lamps and in the sun
There reigns at least the acknowledged belle
Apparelled beyond parallel.
365   Ah Jenny, yes, we know your dreams.

For even the Paphian Venus[1] seems
A goddess o'er the realms of love,
When silver-shrined in shadowy grove:
Aye, or let offerings nicely placed
370   But hide Priapus[2] to the waist,
And whoso looks on him shall see
An eligible deity.

Why, Jenny, waking here alone
May help you to remember one,
375   Though all the memory's long outworn
Of many a double-pillowed morn.
I think I see you when you wake,
And rub your eyes for me, and shake

My gold, in rising, from your hair,
380   A Danaë[3] for a moment there.

Jenny, my love rang true! for still
Love at first sight is vague, until
That tinkling makes him audible.

And must I mock you to the last,
385   Ashamed of my own shame—aghast
Because some thoughts not born amiss
Rose at a poor fair face like this?
Well, of such thoughts so much I know:
In my life, as in hers, they show,
390   By a far gleam which I may near,
A dark path I can strive to clear.

Only one kiss. Goodbye, my dear.
—1848

My Sister's Sleep

She fell asleep on Christmas Eve:
    At length the long-ungranted shade
    Of weary eyelids overweighed
The pain nought else might yet relieve.

5   Our mother, who had leaned all day
    Over the bed from chime to chime,
    Then raised herself for the first time,
And as she sat her down, did pray.

Her little work-table was spread
10   With work to finish. For the glare
    Made by her candle, she had care
To work some distance from the bed.

Without, there was a cold moon up,
    Of winter radiance sheer and thin;

---

[1] *Paphian Venus* Venus, goddess of love, was said to have been born of sea-foam, but emerged on the island of Paphos, Cyprus.

[2] *Priapus* God of procreation, and a personification of an erect phallus.

[3] *Danaë* According to Greek mythology, Acrisius imprisoned his daughter Danaë in a room of bronze to ensure she would never conceive a son. Zeus, however, fell in love with Danaë and came to her through the ceiling as a shower of gold that fell in her lap.

15   The hollow halo it was in
Was like an icy crystal cup.

Through the small room, with subtle sound
    Of flame, by vents the fireshine drove
    And reddened. In its dim alcove
20 The mirror shed a clearness round.

I had been sitting up some nights,
    And my tired mind felt weak and blank;
    Like a sharp strengthening wine it drank
The stillness and the broken lights.

25 Twelve struck. That sound, by dwindling years
    Heard in each hour, crept off; and then
    The ruffled silence spread again,
Like water that a pebble stirs.

Our mother rose from where she sat:
30   Her needles, as she laid them down,
    Met lightly, and her silken gown
Settled: no other noise than that.

"Glory unto the Newly Born!"
    So, as said angels, she did say;
35   Because we were in Christmas Day,
Though it would still be long till morn.

Just then in the room over us
    There was a pushing back of chairs,
    As some who had sat unawares
40 So late, now heard the hour, and rose.

With anxious softly-stepping haste
    Our mother went where Margaret lay,
    Fearing the sounds o'erhead—should they
Have broken her long watched-for rest!

45 She stopped an instant, calm, and turned;
    But suddenly turned back again;
    And all her features seemed in pain
With woe, and her eyes gazed and yearned.

For my part, I but hid my face,
50   And held my breath, and spoke no word:
    There was none spoken; but I heard
The silence for a little space.

Our mother bowed herself and wept:
    And both my arms fell, and I said,
55   "God knows I knew that she was dead."
And there, all white, my sister slept.

Then kneeling, upon Christmas morn
    A little after twelve o'clock
    We said, ere the first quarter struck,
60 "Christ's blessing on the newly born!"
    —1850

Sibylla Palmifera[1]

Under the arch of Life, where love and death,
    Terror and mystery, guard her shrine, I saw
    Beauty enthroned; and though her gaze struck awe,
I drew it in as simply as my breath.
5   Hers are the eyes which, over and beneath,
    The sky and sea bend on thee—which can draw,
    By sea or sky or woman, to one law,
The allotted bondman of her palm and wreath.

This is that Lady Beauty, in whose praise
10   Thy voice and hand shake still—long known to thee
        By flying hair and fluttering hem—the beat
        Following her daily of thy heart and feet,
    How passionately and irretrievably,
In what fond flight, how many ways and days!
    —1868

---

[1] *Sibylla Palmifera* This sonnet was composed to accompany the painting of the same title, also reproduced here; the poem later appeared under the title "Soul's Beauty" in the 1881 version of Rossetti's sonnet sequence *The House of Life*. The Sibyl (prophet) of Cumae wrote her prophesies on palm leaves.

Dante Gabriel Rossetti, *Sybilla Palmifera*, 1868.

Lady Lilith[1]

Of Adam's first wife, Lilith, it is told
(The witch he loved before the gift of Eve)
That, ere the snake's, her sweet tongue could deceive,
And her enchanted hair was the first gold.
5   And still she sits, young while the earth is old,
And, subtly of herself contemplative,
Draws men to watch the bright web she can weave,
Till heart and body and life are in its hold.

Rose, foxglove, poppy are her flowers: for where
10   Is he not found, O Lilith, whom shed scent
And soft-shed fingers and soft sleep shall snare?
Lo! as that youth's eyes burned at thine, so went
Thy spell through him, and left his straight neck
    bent
And round his heart one strangling golden hair.
—1868

Mary Magdalene at the Door of Simon the Pharisee[2]

(For a Drawing)[3]

"Why wilt thou cast the roses from thine hair?
Nay, be thou all a rose—wreath, lips, and
    cheek.

Dante Gabriel Rossetti, *Mary Magdalene at the Door of Simon the Pharisee*, 1858.

Nay, not this house—that banquet-house we seek;
See how they kiss and enter; come thou there.
5   This delicate day of love we two will share
Till at our ear love's whispering night shall speak.
What, sweet one—hold'st thou still the foolish
    freak?°   whim
Nay, when I kiss thy feet they'll leave the stair."

"Oh loose me! See'st thou not my Bridegroom's face
10   That draws me to Him? For His feet my kiss,
My hair, my tears He craves to-day—and oh!
What words can tell what other day and place
Shall see me clasp those blood-stained feet of His?
He needs me, calls me, loves me: let me go!"
—1870

[1] *Lady Lilith* This sonnet was composed to accompany a painting of the same title, reproduced here. In the extended version of Rossetti's sonnet sequence *The House of Life* (1881), it appeared with the title "Body's Beauty." Lilith was the first wife of Adam; according to Talmudic legend, she rejected Adam when she refused to accept a subservient position in sexual intercourse. She left the Garden of Eden and mated with various demons.

[2] *Mary ... Pharisee* See Luke 7.36–50, which tells how an anonymous penitent, often assumed to be Mary Magdalene, burst into the house of Simon, a Pharisee, where Jesus was dining. She prostrated herself at his feet, which she then washed with her tears and dried with her hair.

[3] [Rossetti's note] In the drawing Mary has left a procession of revellers, and is ascending by a sudden impulse the steps of the house where she sees Christ. Her lover has followed her and is trying to turn her back.

Sonnets and Songs,
Towards a Work to Be Called

"The House of Life"[1]

1. BRIDAL BIRTH

As when desire, long darkling,[2] dawns, and first
The mother looks upon the newborn child,
Even so my Lady stood at gaze and smiled
When her soul knew at length the Love it nursed.
5 Born with her life, creature of poignant thirst
    And exquisite hunger, at her heart Love lay
    Quickening in darkness, till a voice that day
Cried on him, and the bonds of birth were burst.

Now, shielded in his wings, our faces yearn
10 Together, as his fullgrown feet now range
    The grove, and his warm hands our couch prepare:
Till to his song our bodiless souls in turn
    Be born his children, when Death's nuptial change
    Leaves us for light the halo of his hair.

2. LOVE'S REDEMPTION

O Thou who at Love's hour ecstatically
    Unto my lips dost evermore present
    The body and blood of Love in sacrament;

Whom I have neared and felt thy breath to be
5 The inmost incense of his sanctuary;
    Who without speech hast owned him, and intent
    Upon his will, thy life with mine hast blent,°   *mingled*
And murmured o'er the cup, Remember me!

O what from thee the grace, for me the prize,
10 And what to Love the glory—when the whole
    Of the deep stair thou tread'st to the dim shoal°   *bank*
And weary water of the place of sighs,
And there dost work deliverance, as thine eyes
    Draw up my prisoned spirit to thy soul!

3. LOVESIGHT

When do I see thee most, beloved one?
    When in the light the spirits of mine eyes
    Before thy face, their altar, solemnize
The worship of that Love through thee made known?
5 Or when in the dusk hours, (we two alone)
    Close-kissed and eloquent of still replies
    Thy twilight-hidden glimmering visage° lies,   *face*
And my soul only sees thy soul its own?

O love, my love! if I no more should see
10 Thyself, nor on the earth the shadow of thee,
    Nor image of thine eyes in any spring—
How then should sound upon life's darkening slope
The ground-whirl of the perished leaves of Hope,
    The wind of Death's imperishable wing?

4. THE KISS

What smouldering senses in death's sick delay
    Or seizure of malign vicissitude
    Can rob this body of honour, or denude
This soul of wedding-raiment worn today?
5 For lo! even now my lady's lips did play
    With these my lips such consonant interlude
    As laurelled Orpheus[3] longed for when he wooed

---

[1] *Sonnets and … of Life*   The text of *The House of Life* reprinted here is that of the first published version, which was included in Rossetti's *Poems* (1870) and is composed of 50 sonnets and 11 songs. Rossetti introduced this preliminary version with the following description: "The first twenty-eight sonnets and the seven first songs treat of love. These and the others would belong to separate sections of the projected work."
   Rossetti continued revising and adding to the work until 1881, when he published the expanded *House of Life*—a sequence of 101 sonnets, plus one introductory one—as part of his collection *Ballads and Sonnets*. Removed from this final edition were all 11 songs as well as one sonnet—"Nuptial Sleep," which had been the subject of fierce attack by Robert Buchanan in his review of the 1870 *House of Life*, titled "The Fleshly School of Poetry" (see the excerpts elsewhere in this anthology). With their first publication, the *House of Life* sonnets were extremely influential, sparking a trend among contemporary poets of writing sonnet sequences.

[2] *darkling*   Dark or darkening.

[3] *laurelled Orpheus*   Orpheus was a legendary ancient Greek poet who almost succeeded in winning his wife back from the underworld with his song. Celebrated poets were crowned with wreaths of laurel in ancient Greece.

The half-drawn hungering face with that last lay.°   *song*
I was a child beneath her touch—a man
10   When breast to breast we clung, even I and she—
     A spirit when her spirit looked through me—
A god when all our life-breath met to fan
Our life-blood, till love's emulous[1] ardours ran,
     Fire within fire, desire in deity.

5. NUPTIAL SLEEP

At length their long kiss severed, with sweet
     smart;°   *pain*
     And as the last slow sudden drops are shed
     From sparkling eaves when all the storm has fled,
So singly flagged the pulses of each heart.
5 Their bosoms sundered, with the opening start
     Of married flowers to either side outspread
     From the knit stem; yet still their mouths, burnt red,
Fawned on each other where they lay apart.

Sleep sank them lower than the tide of dreams,
10   And their dreams watched them sink, and slid away.
Slowly their souls swam up again, through gleams
     Of watered light and dull drowned waifs[2] of day;
Till from some wonder of new woods and streams
     He woke, and wondered more: for there she lay.

6. SUPREME SURRENDER

To all the spirits of love that wander by
     Along the love-sown fallowfield[3] of sleep
     My lady lies apparent; and the deep
Calls to the deep; and no man sees but I.
5 The bliss so long afar, at length so nigh,
     Rests there attained. Methinks proud Love must weep
     When Fate's control doth from his harvest reap
The sacred hour for which the years did sigh.

First touched, the hand now warm around my neck
10   Taught memory long to mock desire: and lo!
     Across my breast the abandoned hair doth flow,
Where one shorn tress long stirred the longing ache:
And next the heart that trembled for its sake
     Lies the queen-heart in sovereign overthrow.°   *defeat*

7. LOVE'S LOVERS

Some ladies love the jewels in Love's zone°   *belt*
     And gold-tipped darts he hath for painless play
     In idle scornful hours he flings away;
And some that listen to his lute's soft tone
Do love to vaunt° the silver praise their own;   *boast*
     Some prize his blindfold[4] sight; and there be they
     Who kissed his wings which brought him yesterday
And thank his wings today that he is flown.

My lady only loves the heart of Love:
10   Therefore Love's heart, my lady, hath for thee
     His bower° of unimagined flower and tree: *arbor*
There kneels he now, and all-anhungered[5] of
Thine eyes grey-lit in shadowing hair above,
     Seals with thy mouth his immortality.

8. PASSION AND WORSHIP

One flame-winged brought a white-winged
     harp-player
     Even where my lady and I lay all alone;
     Saying: "Behold, this minstrel is unknown;
Bid him depart, for I am minstrel here:
5 Only my strains are to Love's dear ones dear."
     Then said I: "Through thine hautboy's°   *oboe's*
     rapturous tone
     Unto my lady still this harp makes moan,
And still she deems the cadence deep and clear."

Then said my lady: "Thou art Passion of Love,
10   And this Love's Worship: both he plights°   *pledges*
     to me.

---

[1] *emulous* Desiring, jealous.

[2] *waifs* Figuratively, objects floating in the water; outcasts.

[3] *fallowfield* Field that is not being used to produce crops; fields are
left fallow to allow the soil to regain its fertility.

---

[4] *blindfold* Cupid was often depicted blindfolded.

[5] *anhungered* Overcome with hunger.

Thy mastering music walks the sunlit sea:
But where wan water trembles in the grove
And the wan moon is all the light thereof,
    This harp still makes my name its voluntary."[1]

9. THE PORTRAIT

O Lord of all compassionate control,
  O Love! let this my lady's picture glow
Under my hand to praise her name, and show
Even of her inner self the perfect whole:
5 That he who seeks her beauty's furthest goal,
  Beyond the light that the sweet glances throw
  And refluent° wave of the sweet   *flowing back*
     smile, may know
The very sky and sea-line of her soul.

Lo! it is done. Above the long lithe throat
10   The mouth's mould testifies of voice and kiss,
    The shadowed eyes remember and foresee.
Her face is made her shrine. Let all men note
  That in all years (O Love, thy gift is this!)
    They that would look on her must come to me.

10. THE LOVE-LETTER

Warmed by her hand and shadowed by her hair
  As close she leaned and poured her heart
    through thee,
  Whereof the articulate throbs accompany
The smooth black stream that makes thy whiteness
    fair—
5 Sweet fluttering sheet, even of her breath aware—
  Oh let thy silent song disclose to me
    That soul wherewith her lips and eyes agree
Like married music in Love's answering air.

Fain° had I watched her when, at some fond   *gladly*
    thought,
10   Her bosom to the writing closelier° pressed, *more closely*
    And her breast's secrets peered into her breast;

When, through eyes raised an instant, her soul sought
My soul, and from the sudden confluence caught
    The words that made her love the loveliest.

11. THE BIRTH-BOND

Have you not noted, in some family
  Where two were born of a first marriage-bed,[2]
  How still they own their gracious bond, though fed
And nursed on the forgotten breast and knee?—
5 How to their father's children they shall be
  In act and thought of one goodwill; but each
  Shall for the other have, in silence speech,
And in a word complete community?

Even so, when first I saw you, seemed it, love,
10   That among souls allied to mine was yet
One nearer kindred than life hinted of.
  O born with me somewhere that men forget,
  And though in years of sight and sound unmet,
Known for my soul's birth-partner well enough!

12. A DAY OF LOVE

Those envied places which do know her well,
  And are so scornful of this lonely place,
  Even now for once are emptied of her grace:
Nowhere but here she is: and while Love's spell
5 From his predominant presence doth compel
  All alien hours, an outworn° populace,   *worn out*
  The hours of Love fill full the echoing space
With sweet confederate° music favourable.   *united*

Now many memories make solicitous
10   The delicate love-lines of her mouth, till, lit
  With quivering fire, the words take wing from it;
As here between our kisses we sit thus
  Speaking of things remembered, and so sit
Speechless while things forgotten call to us.

---

1 *voluntary* Musical solo in a church service.

2 *born of … marriage-bed* Born of a first marriage (i.e., born to a mother who is now dead and a father who is now remarried).

13. LOVE-SWEETNESS

Sweet dimness of her loosened hair's downfall
   About thy face; her sweet hands round thy head
   In gracious fostering union garlanded;
Her tremulous smiles; her glances' sweet recall
5 Of love; her murmuring sighs memorial;
     Her mouth's culled[1] sweetness by thy kisses shed
     On cheeks and neck and eyelids, and so led
Back to her mouth which answers there for all:

What sweeter than these things, except the thing
10   In lacking which all these would lose their sweet:
     The confident heart's still fervour; the swift beat
And soft subsidence° of the spirit's wing,   *fall*
Then when it feels, in cloud-girt° wayfaring,   *surrounded*
     The breath of kindred plumes against its feet?

14. LOVE'S BAUBLES

I stood where Love in brimming armfuls bore
   Slight wanton flowers and foolish toys of fruit,
   And round him ladies thronged in warm pursuit,
Fingered and lipped and proffered the strange store:
5 And from one hand the petal and the core
     Savoured of sleep; and cluster and curled shoot
     Seemed from another hand like shame's salute—
Gifts that I felt my cheek was blushing for.

At last Love bade my Lady give the same:
10   And as I looked, the dew was light thereon;
     And as I took them, at her touch they shone
With inmost heaven-hue of the heart of flame.
     And then Love said: "Lo! when the hand is hers,
     Follies of love are love's true ministers."

15. WINGED HOURS

Each hour until we meet is as a bird
   That wings from far his gradual way along
   The rustling covert° of my soul—his song   *covering*
Still loudlier trilled through leaves more deeply stirred:

5 But at the hour of meeting, a clear word
   Is every note he sings, in Love's own tongue;
   Yet, Love, thou know'st the sweet strain suffers wrong,
Through our contending kisses oft unheard.

What of that hour at last, when for her sake
10   No wing may fly to me nor song may flow;
   When, wandering round my life unleaved,[2] I know
The bloodied feathers scattered in the brake,°   *thicket*
     And think how she, far from me, with like eyes
     Sees through the untuneful bough the wingless skies?

16. LIFE-IN-LOVE

Not in thy body is thy life at all
   But in this lady's lips and hands and eyes;
   Through these she yields thee life that vivifies
What else were sorrow's servant and death's thrall.°   *slave*
5 Look on thyself without her, and recall
     The waste remembrance and forlorn surmise
     That lived but in a dead-drawn breath of sighs
O'er vanished hours and hours eventual.

Even so much life hath the poor tress of hair
10   Which, stored apart, is all love hath to show
   For heart-beats and for fire-heats long ago;
Even so much life endures unknown, even where,
   'Mid change the changeless night
     environeth,°   *encompasses*
Lies all that golden hair undimmed in death.

17. THE LOVE-MOON

"When that dead face, bowered° in the   *shaded*
   furthest years,
   Which once was all the life years held for thee,
   Can now scarce bid the tides of memory
Cast on thy soul a little spray of tears—
5 How canst thou gaze into these eyes of hers
     Whom now thy heart delights in, and not see

---

[1] *culled* Picked (like fruit or flowers).

[2] *unleaved* Bare of leaves.

Within each orb Love's philtred euphrasy[1]
Make them of buried troth°   *faithfulness*
    remembrancers?"°   *reminders*

"Nay, pitiful Love, nay, loving Pity!, Well
10   Thou knowest that in these twain° I have   *two*
            confessed
Two very voices of thy summoning bell.
    Nay, Master, shall not Death make manifest
In these the culminant changes which approve
The love-moon that must light my soul to Love?"

18. The Morrow's Message

"Thou Ghost," I said, "and is thy name Today?—
    Yesterday's son, with such an abject brow!
    And can Tomorrow be more pale than thou?"
While yet I spoke, the silence answered: "Yea,
5   Henceforth our issue° is all grieved and grey,   *offspring*
        And each beforehand makes such poor avow°   *offering*
        As of old leaves beneath the budding bough
Or night-drift° that the sundawn shreds away."   *mist*

Then cried I: "Mother of many malisons,°   *curses*
10   O Earth, receive me to thy dusty bed!"
        But therewithal the tremulous silence said:
"Lo! Love yet bids thy lady greet thee once—
Yea, twice—whereby thy life is still the sun's;
        And thrice—whereby the shadow of death is dead."

19. Sleepless Dreams

Girt° in dark growths, yet glimmering   *surrounded*
    with one star,
    O night desirous as the nights of youth!
    Why should my heart within thy spell, forsooth,
Now beat, as the bride's finger-pulses are
5   Quickened within the girdling° golden bar?   *encircling*
        What wings are these that fan my pillow, smooth?

And why does Sleep, waved back by Joy and
    Ruth,°   *sorrow*
Tread softly round and gaze at me from far?

Nay, night deep-leaved! And would Love feign in thee
    Some shadowy palpitating grove that bears
    Rest for man's eyes and music for his ears?
O lonely night! art thou not known to me,
A thicket hung with masks of mockery
    And watered with the wasteful warmth of tears?

20. Secret Parting

Because our talk was of the cloud-control
    And moon-track of the journeying face of Fate,
    Her tremulous kisses faltered at love's gate
And her eyes dreamed against a distant goal:
5   But soon, remembering her how brief the whole
        Of joy, which its own hours annihilate,
        Her set gaze gathered, thirstier than of late,
And as she kissed, her mouth became her soul.

Thence in what ways we wandered, and how strove
10   To build with fire-tried vows the piteous home
        Which memory haunts and whither sleep may
            roam—
They only know for whom the roof of Love
Is the still-seated secret of the grove,
    Nor spire may rise nor bell be heard therefrom.

21. Parted Love

What shall be said of this embattled day
    And armed occupation of this night
    By all thy foes beleaguered—now when sight
Nor sound denotes the loved one far away?
5   Of these thy vanquished hours what shalt thou say—
        As every sense to which she dealt delight
        Now labours lonely o'er the stark noon-height
To reach the sunset's desolate disarray?

Stand still, fond fettered wretch! while Memory's art
10   Parades the Past before thy face, and lures
        Thy spirit to her passionate portraitures:

---

[1] *philtred* Enchanted (a philtre is a love potion); *euphrasy* Plant used to treat weak eyes. Its name comes from the Greek word for gladness.

Till the tempestuous tide-gates flung apart
Flood with wild will the hollows of thy heart,
   And thy heart rends thee, and thy body endures.

22. BROKEN MUSIC

The mother will not turn, who thinks she hears
   Her nursling's speech first grow articulate;
   But breathless with averted eyes elate
She sits, with open lips and open ears,
5 That it may call her twice. 'Mid doubts and fears
   Thus oft my soul has hearkened; till the song,
   A central moan for days, at length found tongue.
And the sweet music welled and the sweet tears.

But now, whatever while[1] the soul is fain°   *glad*
10   To list° that wonted° murmur,   *listen to / accustomed*
      as it were
The speech-bound sea-shell's low importunate strain—
   No breath of song, thy voice alone is there,
O bitterly beloved! and all her gain
   Is but the pang of unpermitted prayer.[2]

23. DEATH-IN-LOVE

There came an image in Life's retinue
   That had Love's wings and bore his gonfalon:° *banner*
   Fair was the web,° and nobly wrought *woven fabric*
     thereon,
O soul-sequestered face, thy form and hue!
5 Bewildering sounds, such as Spring wakens to,
   Shook in its folds; and through my heart its power
   Sped trackless as the immemorable hour
When birth's dark portal groaned and all was new.

But a veiled woman followed, and she caught
10   The banner round its staff, to furl and cling—
   Then plucked a feather from the bearer's wing,
And held it to his lips that stirred it not,
   And said to me, "Behold, there is no breath:
   I and this Love are one, and I am Death."

---

[1] *whatever while* Whenever.

[2] *unpermitted prayer* Prayer for something that will not be granted.

24, 25, 26, 27. WILLOWWOOD

1

I sat with Love upon a woodside well,
   Leaning across the water, I and he;
   Nor ever did he speak nor looked at me,
But touched his lute wherein was audible:
5 The certain secret thing he had to tell:
   Only our mirrored eyes met silently
   In the low wave; and that sound came to be
The passionate voice I knew; and my tears fell.

And at their fall, his eyes beneath grew hers;
10 And with his foot and with his wing-feathers
   He swept the spring that watered my heart's
     drouth.°   *drought*
Then the dark ripples spread to waving hair,
   And as I stooped, her own lips rising there
   Bubbled with brimming kisses at my mouth.

2

And now Love sang: but his was such a song,
   So meshed with half-remembrance hard to free,
   As souls disused in death's sterility
May sing when the new birthday tarries long.
5 And I was made aware of a dumb° throng   *silent*
   That stood aloof, one form by every tree,
   All mournful forms, for each was I or she,
The shades of those our days that had no tongue.

They looked on us, and knew us and were known;
10 While fast together, alive from the abyss,
   Clung the soul-wrung implacable close kiss;
And pity of self through all made broken moan
   Which said, "For once, for once, for once alone!"
   And still Love sang, and what he sang was this:

3

"O Ye, all ye that walk in Willowwood,
   That walk with hollow faces burning white;
What fathom-depth[3] of soul-struck widowhood,
   What long, what longer hours, one lifelong night,

---

[3] *fathom-depth* Six feet.

5   Ere ye again, who so in vain have wooed
        Your last hope lost, who so in vain invite
    Your lips to that their unforgotten food,
        Ere ye, ere ye again shall see the light!

    Alas! the bitter banks in Willowwood,
10   With tear-spurge wan, with bloodwort[1] burning red:
    Alas! if ever such a pillow could
        Steep deep the soul in sleep till she were dead—
    Better all life forget her than this thing,
    That Willowwood should hold her wandering!"

                         4

    So sang he: and as meeting rose and rose
        Together cling through the wind's wellaway,°   *lament*
        Nor change at once, yet near the end of day
    The leaves drop loosened where the heart-stain glows—
5   So when the song died did the kiss unclose;
        And her face fell back drowned, and was as grey
        As its grey eyes; and if it ever may
    Meet mine again I know not if Love knows.

    Only I know that I leaned low and drank
10 A long draught from the water where she sank,
        Her breath and all her tears and all her soul:
    And as I leaned, I know I felt Love's face
    Pressed on my neck with moan of pity and grace,
        Till both our heads were in his aureole.[2]

              28. STILLBORN LOVE

    The hour which might have been yet might not be,
        Which man's and woman's heart conceived and
            bore
        Yet whereof life was barren—on what shore
    Bides it the breaking of Time's weary sea?
5   Bondchild of all consummate joys set free,
        It somewhere sighs and serves, and mute before

    ---

    [1] *tear-spurge* Spurge is a type of plant with milky juice; *blood-wort* Name applied to various plants with red roots or red leaves.

    [2] *aureole* Circle of radiance, usually surrounding the body of a holy being.

    The house of Love, hears through the echoing door
    His hours elect in choral consonancy.°   *harmony*

    But lo! what wedded souls now hand in hand
10 Together tread at last the immortal strand°   *shore*
        With eyes where burning memory lights love home?
    Lo! how the little outcast hour has turned
    And leaped to them and in their faces yearned—
        "I am your child: O parents, ye have come!"

              29. INCLUSIVENESS

    The changing guests, each in a different mood,
        Sit at the roadside table and arise:
        And every life among them in likewise
    Is a soul's board set daily with new food.
5   What man has bent o'er his son's sleep, to brood
        How that face shall watch his when cold it lies?—
        Or thought, as his own mother kissed his eyes,
    Of what her kiss was when his father wooed?

    May not this ancient room thou sit'st in dwell
10   In separate living souls for joy or pain?
        Nay, all its corners may be painted plain
    Where Heaven shows pictures of some life spent well;
        And may be stamped, a memory all in vain,
    Upon the sight of lidless eyes in Hell.

              30. KNOWN IN VAIN

    As two whose love, first foolish, widening scope,
        Knows suddenly, with music high and soft,
        The Holy of holies; who because they scoffed
    Are now amazed with shame, nor dare to cope
5   With the whole truth aloud, lest heaven should
            ope;°   *open*
        Yet, at their meetings, laugh not as they laughed
        In speech; nor speak, at length; but sitting oft
    Together, within hopeless sight of hope

    For hours are silent: So it happeneth
10   When Work and Will awake too late, to gaze
    After their life sailed by, and hold their breath.
        Ah! who shall dare to search through what sad maze

Thenceforth their incommunicable ways
Follow the desultory° feet of Death?   *random, purposeless*

31. THE LANDMARK

Was *that* the landmark? What, the foolish well
Whose wave, low down, I did not stoop to drink,
But sat and flung the pebbles from its brink
In sport to send its imaged skies pell-mell,
5 (And mine own image, had I noted well!)—
Was that my point of turning?—I had thought
The stations of my course should rise unsought,
As altar-stone or ensigned[1] citadel.

But lo! the path is missed, I must go back,
10 And thirst to drink when next I reach the spring
Which once I stained, which since may have grown
    black.
Yet though no light be left nor bird now sing
As here I turn, I'll thank God, hastening,
That the same goal is still on the same track.

32. A DARK DAY

The gloom that breathes upon me with these airs
Is like the drops which strike the traveller's brow
Who knows not, darkling, if they bring him now
Fresh storm, or be old rain the covert° bears.   *thicket*
5 Ah! bodes this hour some harvest of new tares,°   *seeds*
Or hath but memory of the day whose plough
Sowed hunger once—the night at length when thou,
O prayer found vain, didst fall from out my prayers?

How prickly were the growths which yet how smooth,
10 Along the hedgerows of this journey shed,
Lie by Time's grace till night and sleep may soothe!
Even as the thistledown from pathsides dead
Gleaned° by a girl in autumns of her youth,   *gathered*
Which one new year makes soft her marriage-bed.

33. THE HILL SUMMIT

This feast-day of the sun, his altar there
In the broad west has blazed for vesper-song;[2]
And I have loitered in the vale too long
And gaze now a belated worshipper.
5 Yet may I not forget that I was 'ware,°   *aware*
So journeying, of his face at intervals
Transfigured where the fringed horizon fails—
A fiery bush with coruscating° hair.   *sparkling*

And now that I have climbed and won this height,
10 I must tread downward through the sloping shade
And travel the bewildered tracks till night.
Yet for this hour I still may here be stayed
And see the gold air and the silver fade
And the last bird fly into the last light.

34. BARREN SPRING

Once more the changed year's turning wheel returns:
And as a girl sails balanced in the wind,
And now before and now again behind
Stoops as it swoops, with cheek that laughs and burns—
5 So Spring comes merry towards me now, but earns
No answering smile from me, whose life is twined
With the dead boughs that winter still must bind,
And whom today the Spring no more concerns.

Behold, this crocus is a withering flame;
10 This snowdrop, snow; this apple-blossom's part
To breed the fruit that breeds the serpent's art.
Nay, for these Spring-flowers, turn thy face from them,
Nor gaze till on the year's last lily-stem
The white cup shrivels round the golden heart.

35, 36, 37. THE CHOICE

I

Eat thou and drink; tomorrow thou shalt die.
Surely the earth, that's wise being very old,
Needs not our help. Then loose me, love, and hold

---

[1] *ensigned* I.e., decorated with a sign or banner.

[2] *vesper-song* Evening prayer in the Christian Church.

Thy sultry hair up from my face; that I
5   May pour for thee this golden wine, brim-high,
      Till round the glass thy fingers glow like gold.
      We'll drown all hours: thy song, while hours are
         tolled,
Shall leap, as fountains veil the changing sky.

Now kiss, and think that there are really those,
10   My own high-bosomed beauty, who increase
      Vain gold, vain lore,° and yet might   *knowledge*
        choose our way
      Through many days they toil; then comes a day
They die not—never having lived—but cease;
And round their narrow lips the mould falls close.

2

Watch thou and fear: tomorrow thou shalt die.
   Or art thou sure thou shalt have time for death?
Is not the day which God's word promiseth
To come man knows not when? In yonder sky,
5   Now while we speak, the sun speeds forth: can I
      Or thou assure him of his goal? God's breath
      Even at the moment haply° quickeneth   *perhaps*
The air to a flame; till spirits, always nigh,
Though screened and hid, shall walk the daylight here.
10   And dost thou prate° of all that   *chatter trivially*
        man shall do?
      Canst thou, who hast but plagues, presume to be
      Glad in his gladness that comes after thee?
Will *his* strength slay *thy* worm in Hell? Go to:
Cover thy countenance,° and watch, and fear.   *face*

3

Think thou and act; tomorrow thou shalt die.
   Outstretched in the sun's warmth upon the shore,
   Thou say'st: "Man's measured path is all gone o'er:
Up all his years, steeply, with strain and sigh,
5   Man clomb° until he touched the truth; and I,   *climbed*
      Even I, am he whom it was destined for."
      How should this be? Art thou then so much more
Than they who sowed, that thou shouldst reap thereby?

Nay, come up hither. From this wave-washed mound
10   Unto the furthest flood-brim look with me;

Then reach on with thy thought till it be drowned.
   Miles and miles distant though the grey line be,
And though thy soul sail leagues and leagues beyond—
   Still, leagues beyond those leagues, there is more sea.

38. HOARDED JOY

I said: "Nay, pluck not—let the first fruit be:
  Even as thou sayest, it is sweet and red,
  But let it ripen still. The tree's bent head
Sees in the stream its own fecundity°   *fertility*
5   And bides the day of fulness. Shall not we
      At the sun's hour that day possess the shade,
      And claim our fruit before its ripeness fade,
And eat it from the branch and praise the tree?"

I say: "Alas! our fruit hath wooed the sun
10   Too long—'tis fallen and floats adown the stream.
Lo, the last clusters! Pluck them every one,
   And let us sup with summer; ere the gleam
Of autumn set the year's pent sorrow free,
And the woods wail like echoes from the sea."

39. VAIN VIRTUES

What is the sorriest thing that enters Hell?
   None of the sins—but this and that fair deed
   Which a soul's sin at length could supersede.
These yet are virgins, whom death's timely knell[1]
5   Might once have sainted; whom the fiends compel
      Together now, in snake-bound shuddering
      sheaves°   *bundles*
      Of anguish, while the scorching bridegroom leaves
Their refuse maidenhood abominable.

Night sucks them down, the garbage of the pit,
10   Whose names, half entered in the book of Life,
      Were God's desire at noon. And as their hair
And eyes sink last, the Torturer deigns°   *condescends*
      no whit[2]
      To gaze, but, yearning, waits his worthier wife,

---

[1] *knell* Sound of the bell rung to mark a person's death.

[2] *no whit* Not at all.

The Sin still blithe° on earth that   *careless, joyful*
   sent them there.

40. LOST DAYS

The lost days of my life until today,
   What were they, could I see them on the street
   Lie as they fell? Would they be ears of wheat
Sown once for food but trodden into clay?
5   Or golden coins squandered and still to pay?
      Or drops of blood dabbling the guilty feet?
      Or such spilt water as in dreams must cheat
The throats of men in Hell, who thirst alway?

I do not see them here; but after death
10   God knows I know the faces I shall see,
Each one a murdered self, with low last breath.
      "I am thyself—what hast thou done to me?"
   "And I—and I—thyself" (lo! each one saith),
      "And thou thyself to all eternity!"

41. DEATH'S SONGSTERS

When first that horse, within whose populous womb
   The birth was death, o'ershadowed Troy with
      fate,
   Her elders, dubious of its Grecian freight,
Brought Helen there to sing the songs of home:[1]
5   She whispered, "Friends, I am alone; come, come!"
      Then, crouched within, Ulysses waxed° afraid,   *grew*
      And on his comrades' quivering mouths he laid
His hands, and held them till the voice was dumb.

The same was he who, lashed to his own mast,
10   There where the sea-flowers screen the charnel-caves,[2]

Beside the sirens' singing island passed,
   Till sweetness failed along the
      inveterate° waves.[3] …   *lasting, persistent*
Say, soul—are songs of Death no heaven to thee,
Nor shames her lip the cheek of Victory?

42. "RETRO ME, SATHANA!"[4]

Get thee behind me. Even as, heavy-curled,
   Stooping against the wind, a charioteer
   Is snatched from out his chariot by the hair,
So shall Time be; and as the void° car,°   *empty | chariot*
   hurled
5   Abroad by reinless steeds, even so the world:
      Yea, even as chariot-dust upon the air,
      It shall be sought and not found anywhere.
Get thee behind me, Satan. Oft unfurled,

Thy perilous wings can beat and break like lath[5]
10   Much mightiness of men to win thee praise.
      Leave these weak feet to tread in narrow ways.
Thou still, upon the broad vine-sheltered path,
Mayst wait the turning of the phials of wrath[6]
   For certain years, for certain months and days.

43. LOST ON BOTH SIDES

As when two men have loved a woman well,
   Each hating each, through Love's and Death's
      deceit;
   Since not for either this stark marriage-sheet
And the long pauses of this wedding-bell;
5   Yet o'er her grave the night and day dispel
      At last their feud forlorn, with cold and heat;

---

[1] *When first … home* Reference to a legend of the Trojan War with the Ancient Greeks. The Greeks, unable to get inside the walls of Troy, hide themselves within a large, hollow wooden horse, which is then presented as a gift of peace to the Trojans. Suspicious, the Trojans have Helen of Troy (whose abduction had started the war) pretend to be alone and attempt to lure any hidden cargo out of the horse. Ulysses suspects a trick and keeps his men quiet. Once the Trojans are asleep, the Greeks climb out and conquer the city.

[2] *charnel-caves* I.e., caves of death, or caves full of corpses.

[3] *The same … inveterate waves* Another story of Ulysses. Sirens are mythological women who dwell on rocky islands and lure sailors to shipwreck; Ulysses resists their enchanting song by having himself tied to the mast of his ship.

[4] *RETRO ME, SATHANA* "Get behind me, Satan," Jesus' words in Mark 8.33. The words are traditionally spoken as a charm to resist temptation or drive away evil.

[5] *lath* Thin strip of wood.

[6] *phials of wrath* At the apocalypse, God instructs angels to "pour out the vials of the wrath of God upon the earth" (Revelation 17.1).

Nor other than dear friends to death may
    fleet°   *quickly pass*
The two lives left that most of her can tell—

So separate hopes, which in a soul had wooed
    The one same Peace, strove with each other long,
        And Peace before their faces perished since:
So through that soul, in restless brotherhood,
    They roam together now, and wind among
        Its by-streets, knocking at the dusty inns.

10 *(left margin)*

44. The Sun's Shame

Beholding youth and hope in mockery caught
    From life; and mocking pulses that remain
    When the soul's death of bodily death is
        fain;°   *necessitated*
Honour unknown, and honour known unsought;
And penury's° sedulous°   *poverty's / persistent*
    self-torturing thought
        On gold, whose master therewith buys his bane;
        And longed-for woman longing all in vain
For lonely man with love's desire distraught;

And wealth, and strength, and power, and pleasantness,
    Given unto bodies of whose souls men say,
    None poor and weak, slavish and foul, as they:
Beholding these things, I behold no less
The blushing morn and blushing eve confess
    The shame that loads the intolerable day.

45. The Vase of Life

Around the vase of Life at your slow pace
    He has not crept, but turned it with his hands,
    And all its sides already understands.
There, girt,° one breathes alert for some   *surrounded*
    great race;
Whose road runs far by sands and fruitful space;
    Who laughs, yet through the jolly throng has passed;
    Who weeps, nor stays for weeping; who at last,
A youth, stands somewhere crowned, with silent face.

And he has filled this vase with wine for blood,
    With blood for tears, with spice for burning vow,
        With watered flowers for buried love most fit;
And would have cast it shattered to the flood,
    Yet in Fate's name has kept it whole; which now
    Stands empty till his ashes fall in it.

46. A Superscription[1]

Look in my face; my name is Might-have-been
    I am also called No-more, Too-late, Farewell;
    Unto thine ear I hold the dead-sea shell
Cast up thy Life's foam-fretted feet between;
Unto thine eyes the glass where that is seen
    Which had Life's form and Love's, but by my spell
    Is now a shaken shadow intolerable,
Of ultimate things unuttered the frail screen.

Mark me, how still I am! But should there dart
    One moment through thy soul the soft surprise
    Of that winged Peace which lulls the breath of sighs—
Then shalt thou see me smile, and turn apart
Thy visage° to mine ambush at thy heart   *face*
    Sleepless with cold commemorative eyes.

47. He and I

Whence came his feet into my field, and why?
    How is it that he sees it all so drear?°   *dreary*
    How do I see his seeing, and how hear
The name his bitter silence knows it by?
This was the little fold of separate sky
    Whose pasturing clouds in the soul's atmosphere
    Drew living light from one continual year:
How should he find it lifeless? He, or I?

Lo! this new Self now wanders round my field,
    With plaints° for every flower, and for   *complaints*
        each tree
        A moan, the sighing wind's auxiliary:
And o'er sweet waters of my life, that yield

---

[1] *Superscription* Something written above (a text or a picture).

Unto his lips no draught° but tears unsealed,   *medicine*
    Even in my place he weeps. Even I, not he.

48, 49. NEWBORN DEATH

1

Today Death seems to me an infant child
    Which her worn mother Life upon my knee
    Has set to grow my friend and play with me;
If haply° so my heart might be beguiled   *by chance*
5 To find no terrors in a face so mild—
    If haply so my weary heart might be
    Unto the newborn milky eyes of thee,
O Death, before resentment reconciled.

How long, O Death? And shall thy feet depart
10   Still a young child's with mine, or wilt thou stand
Fullgrown the helpful daughter of my heart,
    What time with thee indeed I reach the strand°   *shore*
Of the pale wave which knows thee what thou art,
    And drink it in the hollow of thy hand?

2

And thou, O Life, the lady of all bliss,
    With whom, when our first heart beat full and fast,
    I wandered till the haunts of men were passed,
And in fair places found all bowers° amiss   *shelters*
5 Till only woods and waves might hear our kiss,
    While to the winds all thought of Death we cast—
    Ah, Life! and must I have from thee at last
No smile to greet me and no babe but this?

Lo! Love, the child once ours; and Song, whose hair
10   Blew like a flame and blossomed like a wreath;
And Art, whose eyes were worlds by God found fair;
    These o'er the book of Nature mixed their breath
With neck-twined arms, as oft we watched them there:
    And did these die that thou mightst bear me Death?

50. THE ONE HOPE

When vain desire at last and vain regret
    Go hand in hand to death, and all is vain,
What shall assuage the unforgotten pain

And teach the unforgetful to forget?
5 Shall Peace be still a sunk stream long unmet—
    Or may the soul at once in a green plain
    Stoop through the spray of some sweet life-fountain
And cull° the dew-drenched flowering   *pick*
    amulet?°   *protective charm*

Ah! when the wan soul in that golden air
10   Between the scriptured[1] petals softly blown
    Peers breathless for the gift of grace unknown—
Ah! let none other written spell soe'er
But only the one Hope's one name be there—
    Not less nor more, but even that word alone.

SONG 1. LOVE-LILY

Between the hands, between the brows,
    Between the lips of Love-Lily,
A spirit is born whose birth endows
    My blood with fire to burn through me;
5 Who breathes upon my gazing eyes,
    Who laughs and murmurs in mine ear,
At whose least touch my colour flies,
    And whom my life grows faint to hear.

Within the voice, within the heart,
10   Within the mind of Love-Lily,
A spirit is born who lifts apart
    His tremulous wings and looks at me;
Who on my mouth his finger lays,
    And shows, while whispering lutes confer,
15 That Eden of Love's watered ways
    Whose winds and spirits worship her.

Brows, hands, and lips, heart, mind, and voice,
    Kisses and words of Love-Lily—
Oh! bid me with your joy rejoice
20   Till riotous longing rest in me!
Ah! let not hope be still distraught,
    But find in her its gracious goal,
Whose speech Truth knows not from her thought
    Nor Love her body from her soul.

---

1 *scriptured* Inscribed with letters.

SONG 2. FIRST LOVE REMEMBERED

Peace in her chamber, wheresoe'er
   It be, a holy place:
The thought still brings my soul such grace
   As morning meadows wear.

5 Whether it still be small and light,
      A maid's who dreams alone,
   As from her orchard-gate the moon
      Its ceiling showed at night:

   Or whether, in a shadow dense
10   As nuptial° hymns invoke,   *wedding*
   Innocent maidenhood awoke
      To married innocence:

   There still the thanks unheard await
      The unconscious gift bequeathed;
15 For there my soul this hour has breathed
      An air inviolate.

SONG 3. PLIGHTED[1] PROMISE

In a soft-complexioned sky,
   Fleeting rose and kindling grey,
Have you seen Aurora[2] fly
   At the break of day?
5 So my maiden, so my plighted may
      Blushing cheek and gleaming eye
         Lifts to look my way.

   Where the inmost leaf is stirred
      With the heart-beat of the grove,
10 Have you heard a hidden bird
      Cast her note above?
   So my lady, so my lovely love,
      Echoing Cupid's[3] prompted word,
         Makes a tune thereof.

---

1 *PLIGHTED*   Solemnly vowed, especially in reference to promises of love and marriage.

2 *Aurora*   Classical goddess of the dawn.

3 *Cupid*   Classical god of desire and erotic love.

15 Have you seen, at heaven's mid-height,
      In the moon-rack's[4] ebb and tide,
   Venus[5] leap forth burning white,
      Dian[6] pale and hide?
20 So my bright breast-jewel, so my bride,
      One sweet night, when fear takes flight,
         Shall leap against my side.

SONG 4. SUDDEN LIGHT

I have been here before,
   But when or how I cannot tell:
I know the grass beyond the door,
   The sweet keen smell,
5 The sighing sound, the lights around the shore.

   You have been mine before—
      How long ago I may not know:
   But just when at that swallow's soar
      Your neck turned so,
10 Some veil did fall—I knew it all of yore.

   Then, now—perchance again! ...
      O round mine eyes your tresses shake!
   Shall we not lie as we have lain
      Thus for Love's sake,
15 And sleep, and wake, yet never break the chain?

SONG 5. A LITTLE WHILE

A little while a little love
   The hour yet bears for thee and me
   Who have not drawn the veil to see
If still our heaven be lit above.
5 Thou merely, at the day's last sigh,
   Hast felt thy soul prolong the tone;
And I have heard the night-wind cry
   And deemed its speech mine own.

---

4 *rack*   Mass of clouds.

5 *Venus*   Classical goddess of beauty and love.

6 *Dian*   Classical goddess of the moon, virginity, and the hunt.

A little while a little love
10   The scattering autumn hoards for us
        Whose bower[1] is not yet ruinous°   *in ruins*
Nor quite unleaved[2] our songless grove
Only across the shaken boughs
        We hear the flood-tides seek the sea,
15 And deep in both our hearts they rouse
        One wail for thee and me.

A little while a little love
        May yet be ours who have not said
        The word it makes our eyes afraid
20 To know that each is thinking of.
Not yet the end: be our lips dumb
        In smiles a little season yet:
I'll tell thee, when the end is come,
        How we may best forget.

SONG 6. THE SONG OF THE BOWER[3]

Say, is it day, is it dusk in thy bower,
        Thou whom I long for, who longest for me?
Oh! be it light, be it night, 'tis Love's hour,
        Love's that is fettered as Love's that is free.
5 Free Love has leaped to that innermost chamber,
        Oh! the last time, and the hundred before:
Fettered Love, motionless, can but remember,
        Yet something that sighs from him passes the door.

Nay, but my heart when it flies to thy bower,
10   What does it find there that knows it again?
There it must droop like a shower-beaten flower,
        Red at the rent° core and dark with the rain.   *torn*
Ah! yet what shelter is still shed above it—
        What waters still image° its leaves torn apart?   *show*
15 Thy soul is the shade that clings round it to love it,
        And tears are its mirror deep down in thy heart.

---

[1] *bower* Shelter or shady place in a forest.

[2] *unleaved* Bare of leaves.

[3] BOWER Sheltered place in a forest; can also refer to a lover's bedroom.

What were my prize, could I enter thy bower,
        This day, tomorrow, at eve or at morn?
Large lovely arms and a neck like a tower,
20   Bosom then heaving that now lies forlorn.
Kindled with love-breath, (the sun's kiss is colder!)
        Thy sweetness all near me, so distant today;
My hand round thy neck and thy hand on my shoulder,
        My mouth to thy mouth as the world melts away.

25 What is it keeps me afar from thy bower,
        My spirit, my body, so fain° to be there?   *desirous*
Waters engulfing or fires that devour?
        Earth heaped against me or death in the air?
Nay, but in day-dreams, for terror, for pity,
30   The trees wave their heads with an omen to tell;
Nay, but in night-dreams, throughout the dark city,
        The hours, clashed together, lose count in the bell.

Shall I not one day remember thy bower,
        One day when all days are one day to me?
35 Thinking, "I stirred not, and yet had the power"—
        Yearning, "Ah God, if again it might be!"
Peace, peace! such a small lamp illumes, on this highway,
        So dimly so few steps in front of my feet—,
Yet shows me that her way is parted from my way. . . .
40   Out of sight, beyond light, at what goal may we meet?

SONG 7. PENUMBRA[4]

I did not look upon her eyes
    (Though scarcely seen, with no surprise,
'Mid many eyes a single look),
Because they should not gaze rebuke,
5 At night, from stars in sky and brook.

I did not take her by the hand
(Though little was to understand
From touch of hand all friends might take),
Because it should not prove a flake
10 Burnt in my palm to boil and ache.

---

[4] PENUMBRA Shadow of a partial eclipse.

I did not listen to her voice
(Though none had noted, where at choice
All might rejoice in listening),
Because no such a thing should cling
15 In the wood's moan at evening.

I did not cross her shadow once
(Though from the hollow west the sun's
Last shadow runs along so far),
Because in June it should not bar
20 My ways, at noon when fevers are.

They told me she was sad that day
(Though wherefore tell what love's soothsay,° *prediction*
Sooner than they, did register?),
And my heart leapt and wept to her,
25 And yet I did not speak nor stir.

So shall the tongues of the sea's foam
(Though many voices therewith come
From drowned hope's home to cry to me),
Bewail one hour the more, when sea
30 And wind are one with memory.

SONG 8. THE WOODSPURGE[1]

The wind flapped loose, the wind was still,
    Shaken out dead from tree and hill:
I had walked on at the wind's will—
I sat now, for the wind was still.

5   Between my knees my forehead was—
My lips, drawn in, said not Alas!
My hair was over in the grass,
My naked ears heard the day pass.

My eyes, wide open, had the run
10 Of some ten weeds to fix upon;
Among those few, out of the sun,
The woodspurge flowered, three cups in one.

---

[1] *WOODSPURGE* Plant with green, cup-shaped flowers, usually in groups of three.

From perfect grief there need not be
Wisdom or even memory:
15 One thing then learnt remains to me—
The woodspurge has a cup of three.

SONG 9. THE HONEYSUCKLE

I plucked a honeysuckle where
    The hedge on high is quick° with thorn,   *alive*
    And climbing for the prize, was torn,
And fouled my feet in quag°-water;   *marsh*
5   And by the thorns and by the wind
    The blossom that I took was thinned
And yet I found it sweet and fair.

Thence to a richer growth I came,
    Where, nursed in mellow intercourse,
10   The honeysuckles sprang by scores,°   *twenties*
Not harried like my single stem,
    All virgin lamps of scent and dew.
    So from my hand that first I threw,
Yet plucked not any more of them.

SONG 10. A YOUNG FIR-WOOD

These little firs today are things
    To clasp into a giant's cap,
    Or fans to suit his lady's lap.
From many winters many springs
5   Shall cherish them in strength and sap,
    Till they be marked upon the map,
A wood for the wind's wanderings.

All seed is in the sower's hands:
    And what at first was trained to spread
10   Its shelter for some single head—
Yea, even such fellowship of wands—
    May hide the sunset, and the shade
    Of its great multitude be laid
Upon the earth and elder sands.

SONG II. THE SEA-LIMITS

Consider the sea's listless chime:
  Time's self it is, made audible—
    The murmur of the earth's own shell.
Secret continuance sublime
5   Is the sea's end: our sight may pass
    No furlong[1] further. Since time was,
This sound hath told the lapse of time.

No quiet, which is death's—it hath
  The mournfulness of ancient life,
10   Enduring always at dull strife.
As the world's heart of rest and wrath,
  Its painful pulse is in the sands.
  Last utterly, the whole sky stands,
Grey and not known, along its path.

15 Listen alone beside the sea,
  Listen alone among the woods;
  Those voices of twin solitudes
Shall have one sound alike to thee:
  Hark where the murmurs of thronged men
20   Surge and sink back and surge again—
Still the one voice of wave and tree.

Gather a shell from the strown[2] beach
  And listen at its lips: they sigh
  The same desire and mystery,
25 The echo of the whole sea's speech.
  And all mankind is thus at heart
  Not anything but what thou art:
And Earth, Sea, Man, are all in each.
—1870 (WRITTEN 1847–70)

Silent Noon[3]

Your hands lie open in the long fresh grass—
  The finger-points look through like rosy blooms:
    Your eyes smile peace. The pasture gleams and
      glooms
'Neath billowing skies that scatter and amass.
5 All round our nest, far as the eye can pass,
    Are golden kingcup-fields with silver edge
    Where the cow-parsley skirts the hawthorn-hedge.
'Tis visible silence, still as the hour-glass.

Deep in the sun-searched growths the dragon-fly
10 Hangs like a blue thread loosened from the sky—
    So this winged hour is dropped to us from above.
Oh! clasp we to our hearts, for deathless dower,
This close-companioned inarticulate hour
    When twofold silence was the song of love.
—1870

[A Sonnet is a moment's monument][4]

A Sonnet is a moment's monument—
  Memorial from the Soul's eternity
    To one dead deathless hour. Look that it be,
Whether for lustral° rite or dire portent,   *purification*
5 Of its own arduous fulness reverent:
    Carve it in ivory or in ebony,
    As Day or Night may rule; and let Time see
Its flowering crest impearled and orient.°   *lustrous*

---

1 *furlong* Measure indicating the length of a field—220 yards or 200 meters.

2 *strown* Strewn (with shells).

3 *Silent Noon* Originally published as an individual sonnet in *Poems* (1870), this poem was incorporated as Sonnet 19 into the expanded version of *The House of Life* sonnet sequence that was published in 1881.

4 *A Sonnet … monument* This poem was first published as an introduction to the 1881 version of Rossetti's sonnet sequence *The House of Life*.

A Sonnet is a coin: its face reveals
10   The soul—its converse, to what Power 'tis due—
Whether for tribute to the august appeals
    Of Life, or dower in Love's high retinue,

It serve; or, 'mid the dark wharf's cavernous breath,
In Charon's[1] palm it pay the toll to Death.
—1881

In Context

The "Fleshly School" Controversy

The attack by poet and critic Robert Buchanan on D.G. Rossetti (whom Buchanan grouped with William Morris, Algernon Charles Swinburne, and others) is an oft-quoted reference point in discussions of Victorian poetry. Buchanan's long review article appeared in the October 1871 issue of the *Contemporary Review*; it was published under the pseudonym "Thomas Maitland." Rossetti managed to discover Buchanan's true identity, and published his response—"The Stealthy School of Criticism"—in *The Athenaeum*. Swinburne responded to Buchanan at greater length with *Under the Microscope* (1872), a 98-page pamphlet. The Buchanan and Rossetti pieces, which are excerpted below, are both included in their entirety as part of the website component of this anthology.

from Thomas Maitland [Robert Buchanan], "The Fleshly School of Poetry: Mr. D.G. Rossetti"[2] (1871)

If, on the occasion of any public performance of Shakespeare's great tragedy, the actors who perform the parts of Rosencrantz and Guildenstern[3] were, by a preconcerted arrangement and by means of what is technically known as "gagging," to make themselves fully as prominent as the leading character, and to indulge in soliloquies and business strictly belonging to Hamlet himself, the result would be, to say the least of it, astonishing; yet a very similar effect is produced on the unprejudiced mind when the "walking gentlemen" of the fleshly[4] school of poetry, who bear precisely the same relation to Mr. Tennyson[5] as Rosencrantz and Guildenstern do to the Prince of Denmark in the play, obtrude their lesser identities and parade their smaller idiosyncrasies in the front rank of leading performers. In their own place, the gentlemen are interesting and useful. ...

This may seem a frivolous and inadequate way of opening our remarks on a school of verse-writers which some people regard as possessing great merits; but in good truth, it is scarcely possible to discuss with any seriousness the pretensions with which foolish friends and small critics have surrounded the fleshly school, which, in spite of its spasmodic ramifications in the erotic direction, is merely one of the many sub-Tennysonian schools expanded to supernatural dimensions, and

---

[1] *Charon* Classical figure responsible for ferrying dead souls across the river separating the world of the living from the underworld. It was customary to bury people with a coin to pay for this service.

[2] *The Fleshly ... Rossetti* Buchanan wrote this review of the fifth edition of Rossetti's *Poems* for the *Contemporary Review*, using the pseudonym "Thomas Maitland."

[3] *Rosencrantz and Guildenstern* Minor characters in Shakespeare's *Hamlet*.

[4] *fleshly* Carnal.

[5] *Mr. Tennyson* Alfred, Lord Tennyson (1809–92), English poet and Poet Laureate of the United Kingdom.

endeavouring by affectations all its own to overshadow its connection with the great original. ... [Fleshliness] is a quality which becomes unwholesome when there is no moral or intellectual quality to temper and control it. Fully conscious of this themselves, the fleshly gentlemen have bound themselves by solemn league and covenant[1] to extol fleshliness as the distinct and supreme end of poetic and pictorial art; to aver that poetic expression is greater than poetic thought, and by inference that the body is greater than the soul, and sound superior to sense; and that the poet, properly to develop his poetic faculty, must be an intellectual hermaphrodite, to whom the very facts of day and night are lost in a whirl of aesthetic terminology. ... It would be scarcely worthwhile, however, to inquire into the pretensions of the writers on merely literary grounds, because sooner or later all literature finds its own level, whatever criticism may say or do in the matter; but it unfortunately happens in the present case that the fleshly school of verse-writers are, so to speak, public offenders, because they are diligently spreading the seeds of disease broadcast wherever they are read and understood. Their complaint too is catching, and carries off many young persons. What the complaint is, and how it works, may be seen on a very slight examination of the works of Mr. Dante Gabriel Rossetti, to whom we shall confine our attention in the present article.

Mr. Rossetti has been known for many years as a painter of exceptional powers, who, for reasons best known to himself, has shrunk from publicly exhibiting his pictures, and from allowing anything like a popular estimate to be formed of their qualities. He belongs, or is said to belong, to the so-called Pre-Raphaelite school, a school which is generally considered to exhibit much genius for colour, and great indifference to perspective. ... [O]f his capabilities in colour we cannot speak, though we should guess that they are great; for if there is any good quality by which his poems are specially marked, it is a great sensitiveness to hues and tints as conveyed in poetic epithet. These qualities, which impress the casual spectator of the photographs from his pictures, are to be found abundantly among his verses. There is the same thinness and transparence of design, the same combination of the simple and the grotesque, the same morbid deviation from healthy forms of life, the same sense of weary, wasting, yet exquisite sensuality; nothing virile, nothing tender, nothing completely sane; a superfluity of extreme sensibility, of delight in beautiful forms, hues, and tints, and a deep-seated indifference to all agitating forces and agencies, all tumultuous griefs and sorrows, all the thunderous stress of life, and all the straining storm of speculation. Mr. Morris is often pure, fresh, and wholesome as his own great model; Mr. Swinburne startles us more than once by some fine flash of insight; but the mind of Mr. Rossetti is like a glassy mere,[2] broken only by the dive of some water-bird or the hum of winged insects, and brooded over by an atmosphere of insufferable closeness, with a light blue sky above it, sultry depths mirrored within it, and a surface so thickly sown with waterlilies that it retains its glassy smoothness even in the strongest wind. Judged relatively to his poetic associates, Mr. Rossetti must be pronounced inferior to either. He cannot tell a pleasant story like Mr. Morris, nor forge alliterative thunderbolts like Mr. Swinburne. It must be conceded, nevertheless, that he is neither so glibly imitative as the one, nor so transcendently superficial as the other.

Although he has been known for many years as a poet as well as a painter—as a painter and poet idolized by his own family and personal associates—and although he has once or twice appeared in print as a contributor to magazines, Mr. Rossetti did not formally appeal to the public until rather more than a year ago, when he published a copious volume of poems, with the announcement that the book, although it contained pieces composed at intervals during a period of many years, "included

---

[1] *solemn league and covenant* Here, oath; *The Solemn League and Covenant* (1643) was a document forming an alliance between Scottish and English opponents of the king during the First English Civil War.

[2] *mere* Pond.

nothing which the author believes to be immature." … No sooner had the work appeared than the chorus of eulogy began. "The book is satisfactory from end to end," wrote Mr. Morris in the *Academy*; "I think these lyrics, with all their other merits, the most complete of their time; nor do I know what lyrics of any time are to be called *great*, if we are to deny the title to these." On the same subject Mr. Swinburne went into a hysteria of admiration: "golden affluence," "jewel-coloured words," "chastity of form," "harmonious nakedness," "consummate fleshly sculpture," and so on in Mr. Swinburne's well-known manner when reviewing his friends. Other critics, with a singular similarity of phrase, followed suit. Strange to say, moreover, no one accused Mr. Rossetti of naughtiness. What had been heinous in Mr. Swinburne was majestic exquisiteness in Mr. Rossetti. Yet we question if there is anything in the unfortunate *Poems and Ballads*[1] quite so questionable on the score of thorough naughtiness as many pieces in Mr. Rossetti's collection. Mr. Swinburne was wilder, more outrageous, more blasphemous, and his subjects were more atrocious in themselves; yet the hysterical tone slew the animalism, the furiousness of epithet lowered the sensation; and the first feeling of disgust at such themes as "Laus Veneris" and "Anactoria,"[2] faded away into comic amazement. It was only a little mad boy letting off squibs,[3] not a great strong man, who might be really dangerous to society. "I *will* be naughty!" screamed the little boy; but, after all, what did it matter? It is quite different, however, when a grown man, with the self-control and easy audacity of actual experience, comes forward to chronicle his amorous sensations, and, first proclaiming in a loud voice his literary maturity, and consequent responsibility, shamelessly prints and publishes such a piece of writing as this sonnet on "Nuptial Sleep":

[Here Buchanan quotes "Nuptial Sleep" in its entirety.]

This, then, is "the golden affluence of words, the firm outline, the justice and chastity of form." Here is a full-grown man, presumably intelligent and cultivated, putting on record for other full-grown men to read, the most secret mysteries of sexual connection, and that with so sickening a desire to reproduce the sensual mood, so careful a choice of epithet to convey mere animal sensations, that we merely shudder at the shameless nakedness. We are no purists in such matters. We hold the sensual part of our nature to be as holy as the spiritual or intellectual part, and we believe that such things must find their equivalent in all; but it is neither poetic, nor manly, nor even human, to obtrude such things as the themes of whole poems. It is simply nasty. Nasty as it is, we are very mistaken if many readers do not think it nice. … In poems like "Nuptial Sleep," the man who is too sensitive to exhibit his pictures, and so modest that it takes him years to make up his mind to publish his poems, parades his private sensations before a coarse public, and is gratified by their applause.

It must not be supposed that all Mr. Rossetti's poems are made up of trash like this. Some of them are as noteworthy for delicacy of touch as others are for shamelessness of exposition. They contain some exquisite pictures of nature, occasional passages of real meaning, much beautiful phraseology, lines of peculiar sweetness, and epithets chosen with true literary cunning. But the fleshly feeling is everywhere. Sometimes, as in "The Stream's Secret," it is deliciously modulated, and adds greatly to our emotion of pleasure at perusing a finely-wrought poem; at other times, as in the "Last Confession," it is fiercely held in check by the exigencies of a powerful situation and the strength of

[1] *Poems and Ballads* Algernon Charles Swinburne's *Poems and Ballads* (1866) shocked Victorian readers with its radical politics, its rejection of Christianity, and its celebration of sexuality.

[2] *Laus Veneris* Latin: In Praise of Venus (classical goddess of love); *Anactoria* Lover of the ancient Greek poet Sappho. "Laus Veneris" and "Anactoria" are poems appearing in *Poems and Ballads*.

[3] *squibs* Fireworks.

a dramatic speaker; but it is generally in the foreground, flushing the whole poem with unhealthy rose-colour, stifling the senses with overpowering sickliness, as of too much civet.[1] Mr. Rossetti is never dramatic, never impersonal—always attitudinizing, posturing, and describing his own exquisite emotions. He is the "Blessed Damozel,"[2] leaning over the "gold bar of heaven," and seeing

> Time like a pulse shake fierce
>   Through all the worlds;

he is "heaven-born Helen, Sparta's queen," whose "each twin breast is an apple sweet"; he is Lilith the first wife of Adam; he is the rosy Virgin of the poem called "Ave," and the Queen in the "Staff and Scrip"; he is "Sister Helen" melting her waxen man; he is all these, just as surely as he is Mr. Rossetti soliloquizing over Jenny in her London lodging,[3] or the very nuptial person writing erotic sonnets to his wife. In petticoats or pantaloons, in modern times or in the middle ages, he is just Mr. Rossetti, a fleshly person, with nothing particular to tell us or teach us, with extreme self-control, a strong sense of colour, and a careful choice of diction. Amid all his "affluence of jewel-coloured words," he has not given us one rounded and noteworthy piece of art; though his verses are all art, not one poem which is memorable for its own sake, and quite separable from the displeasing identity of the composer. The nearest approach to a perfect whole is the "Blessed Damozel," a peculiar poem, placed first in the book, perhaps by accident, perhaps because it is a key to the poems which follow. This poem appeared in a rough shape many years ago in the *Germ*, an unwholesome periodical started by the Pre-Raphaelites, and suffered, after gasping through a few feeble numbers, to die the death of all such publications. In spite of its affected title, and of numberless affectations throughout the text, the "Blessed Damozel" has great merits of its own, and a few lines of real genius. We have heard it described as the record of actual grief and love, or, in simple words, the apotheosis of one actually lost by the writer; but, without having any private knowledge of the circumstance of its composition, we feel that such an account of the poem is inadmissible. It does not contain one single note of sorrow. It is a "composition," and a clever one. ...

We cannot forbear expressing our wonder, by the way, at the kind of women whom it seems the unhappy lot of these gentlemen to encounter. We have lived as long in the world as they have, but never yet came across persons of the other sex who conduct themselves in the manner described. Females who bite, scratch, scream, bubble, munch, sweat, writhe, twist, wriggle, foam, and in a general way slaver over their lovers, must surely possess some extraordinary qualities to counteract their otherwise most offensive mode of conducting themselves. It appears, however, on examination, that their poet-lovers conduct themselves in a similar manner. They, too, bite, scratch, scream, bubble, munch, sweat, writhe, twist, wriggle, foam, and slaver, in a style frightful to hear of. Let us hope that it is only their fun, and that they don't mean half they say. At times, in reading such books as this, one cannot help wishing that things had remained forever in the asexual state described in Mr. Darwin's great chapter on Palingenesis.[4] We get very weary of this protracted hankering after a person of the other sex; it seems meat, drink, thought, sinew, religion for the fleshly school. ... Whether he is writing of the holy Damozel, or of the Virgin herself, or of Lilith, or Helen, or of Dante, or of

---

[1] *civet* Strong-smelling glandular secretion of the civet cat, used in perfume.

[2] *Blessed Damozel* One of the poems in Rossetti's collection reviewed here.

[3] *Jenny ... lodging* "Jenny" is the title of one of Rossetti's poems in *Poems*. The subject of the poem, Jenny, is a prostitute.

[4] *Palingenesis* According to the now discredited theory of palingenesis, a developing organism passes through the forms of its evolutionary ancestors.

Jenny the street-walker, he is fleshly all over, from the roots of his hair to the tip of his toes; never a true lover merging his identity into that of the beloved one; never spiritual, never tender; always self-conscious and aesthetic. "Nothing," says a modern writer, "in human life is so utterly remorseless—not love, not hate, not ambition, not vanity—as the artistic or aesthetic instinct morbidly developed to the suppression of conscience and feeling"; and at no time do we feel more fully impressed with this truth than after the perusal of "Jenny," in some respects the finest poem in the volume, and in all respects the poem best indicative of the true quality of the writer's humanity. ...

What we object to in this poem is not the subject, which any writer may be fairly left to choose for himself; nor anything particularly vicious in the poetic treatment of it; nor any bad blood bursting through in special passages. But the whole tone, without being more than usually coarse, seems heartless. There is not a drop of piteousness in Mr. Rossetti. He is just to the outcast, even generous; severe to the seducer; sad even at the spectacle of lust in dimity[1] and fine ribbons. Notwithstanding all this, and a certain delicacy and refinement of treatment unusual with this poet, the poem repels and revolts us, and we like Mr. Rossetti least after its perusal. We are angry with the fleshly person at last. The "Blessed Damozel" puzzled us, the "Song of the Bower" amused us, the love-sonnet depressed and sickened us, but "Jenny," though distinguished by less special viciousness of thought and style than any of these, fairly makes us lose patience. We detect its fleshliness at a glance; we perceive that the scene was fascinating less through its human tenderness than because it, like all the others, possessed an inherent quality of animalism. ...

Without pausing to criticise a thing so trifling—as well might we dissect a cobweb or anatomize a medusa[2]—let us ask the reader's attention to a peculiarity to which all the students of the fleshly school must sooner or later give their attention—we mean the habit of accenting the last syllable in words which in ordinary speech are accentuated on the penultimate:

> Between the hands, between the brows,
> Between the lips of Love-Lil*ee*!

which may be said to give to the speaker's voice a sort of cooing tenderness just bordering on a loving whistle. Still better as an illustration are the lines:

> Saturday night is market night
> Everywhere, be it dry or wet,
> And market night in the Haymar-*ket*!

It is unnecessary to multiply examples of an affectation which disfigures all these writers ... distinguish their attempt at leading business by affecting the construction of their grandfathers and great-grandfathers, and the accentuation of the poets of the court of James I.[3] It is in all respects a sign of remarkable genius, from this point of view, to rhyme "was" with "grass," "death" with "lièth," "love" with "of," "once" with "suns," and so on *ad nauseam*. We are far from disputing the value of bad rhymes used occasionally to break up the monotony of verse, but the case is hard when such blunders become the rule and not the exception, when writers deliberately lay themselves out to be as archaic and affected as possible. Poetry is perfect human speech, and these archaisms are the mere fiddlededeeing of empty heads and hollow hearts. Bad as they are, they are the true indication of falser

---

[1] *dimity* Sheer cotton fabric.

[2] *medusa* Jellyfish.

[3] *James I* King of England and Ireland from 1603 to 1625, and, as James VI, King of Scotland.

tricks and affectations which lie far deeper. They are trifles, light as air, showing how the wind blows. The soul's speech and the heart's speech are clear, simple, natural, and beautiful, and reject the meretricious[1] tricks to which we have drawn attention. …

The great strong current of English poetry rolls on, ever mirroring in its bosom new prospects of fair and wholesome thought. Morbid deviations are endless and inevitable; there must be marsh and stagnant mere as well as mountain and wood. Glancing backward into the shady places of the obscure, we see the once prosperous nonsense-writers each now consigned to his own little limbo—Skelton and Gower still playing fantastic tricks with the mother-tongue; Gascoigne outlasting the applause of all, and living to see his own works buried before him; Sylvester doomed to oblivion by his own fame as a translator; Carew the idol of the courts, and Donne[2] the beloved of the schoolmen, both buried in the same oblivion … and so on, through league after league of a flat and desolate country which once was prosperous, till we come again to these fantastic figures of the fleshly school, with their droll medieval garments, their funny archaic speech, and the fatal marks of literary consumption in every pale and delicate visage. Our judgment on Mr. Rossetti, to whom we in the meantime confine our judgment, is substantially that of the *North American Reviewer*, who believes that "we have in him another poetical man, and a man markedly poetical, and of a kind apparently, though not radically, different from any of our secondary writers of poetry, but that we have not in him a new poet of any weight," and that he is "so affected, sentimental, and painfully self-conscious, that the best to be done in his case is to hope that this book of his, having unpacked his bosom of so much that is unhealthy, may have done him more good than it has given others pleasure." Such, we say, is our opinion, which might very well be wrong, and have to undergo modification, if Mr. Rossetti was younger and less self-possessed. His "maturity" is fatal.

from Dante Gabriel Rossetti, *The Stealthy School of Criticism*[3] (1872)

Your paragraph, a fortnight ago, relating to the pseudonymous authorship of an article, violently assailing myself and other writers of poetry, in the *Contemporary Review* for October last, reveals a species of critical masquerade which I have expressed in the heading given to this letter. Since then, Mr. Sidney Colvin's[4] note, qualifying the report that he intends to "answer" that article, has appeared in your pages; and my own view as to the absolute forfeit, under such conditions, of all claim to honourable reply, is precisely the same as Mr. Colvin's. For here a critical organ, professedly adopting the principle of open signature, would seem, in reality, to assert (by silent practice, however, not by enunciation), that if the anonymous in criticism was—as itself originally inculcated—but an early caterpillar stage, the nominate too is found to be no better than a homely transitional chrysalis, and

---

[1] *meretricious* Superficially appealing; or, related to prostitution.

[2] *Skelton … Donne* English poets of the late medieval to early modern period.

[3] *The Stealthy School of Criticism* Rossetti addressed this letter to the *Contemporary Review*, after the journal published Thomas Maitland's "The Fleshly School of Poetry: Mr. D.G. Rossetti." Before publishing his rejoinder in *The Athenaeum*, Rossetti uncovered the identity of Robert Buchanan, the author of the brutally critical piece. Rossetti included this poem as a preface to his letter:

> As a critic, the poet Buchanan
> Thinks the Pseudo worth two of the Anon—
> Into Maitland he's slunk;
> Yet what gift of the skunk
> Guides the shuddering nose to Buchanan?

[4] *Mr. Sidney Colvin* Professor and author of books on literature and arts (1847–1927).

that the ultimate butterfly form for a critic who likes to sport in sunlight and yet to elude the grasp, is after all the pseudonymous. But, indeed, what I may call the "Siamese" aspect of the entertainment provided by the *Review* will elicit but one verdict. Yet I may, perhaps, as the individual chiefly attacked, be excused for asking your assistance now in giving a specific denial to specific charges which, if unrefuted, may still continue, in spite of their author's strategic fiasco, to serve his purpose against me to some extent.

The primary accusation, on which this writer grounds all the rest, seems to be that others and myself "extol fleshliness as the distinct and supreme end of poetic and pictorial art; aver that poetic expression is greater than poetic thought; and, by inference, that the body is greater than the soul, and sound superior to sense." ...

A Sonnet entitled "Nuptial Sleep" is quoted and abused at page 338 of the *Review*, and is there dwelt upon as a "whole poem," describing "merely animal sensations." It is no more a whole poem in reality, than is any single stanza of any poem throughout the book. The poem, written chiefly in sonnets, and of which this is one sonnet-stanza, is entitled "The House of Life," and even in my first published instalment of the whole work (as contained in the volume under notice) ample evidence is included that no such passing phase of description as the one headed "Nuptial Sleep" could possibly be put forward by the author of "The House of Life" as his own representative view of the subject of love. In proof of this, I will direct attention (among the love-sonnets of this poem) to Nos. 2, 8, 11, 17, 28, and more especially 13, which, indeed, I had better print here.

[Here Rossetti quotes sonnet 13, "Love-Sweetness," in full.]

Any reader may bring any artistic charge he pleases against the above sonnet; but one charge it would be impossible to maintain against the writer of the series in which it occurs, and that is, the wish on his part to assert that the body is greater than the soul. For here all the passionate and just delights of the body are declared—somewhat figuratively, it is true, but unmistakably—to be as naught if not ennobled by the concurrence of the soul at all times. Moreover, nearly one half of this series of sonnets has nothing to do with love, but treats of quite other life influences. I would defy anyone to couple with fair quotation of Sonnets 29, 30, 31, 39, 40, 41, 43, or others, the slander that their author was not impressed, like all other thinking men, with the responsibilities and higher mysteries of life, while Sonnets 35, 36, and 37, entitled "The Choice," sum up the general view taken in a manner only to be evaded by conscious insincerity. Thus much for "The House of Life," of which the sonnet "Nuptial Sleep" is one stanza, embodying, for its small constituent share, a beauty of natural universal function, only to be reprobated in art if dwelt on (as I have shown that it is not here) to the exclusion of those other highest things of which it is the harmonious concomitant.

At page 342, an attempt is made to stigmatize four short quotations as being specially "my own property," that is, (for the context shows the meaning), as being grossly sensual, though all guiding reference to any precise page or poem in my book is avoided here. The first of these unspecified quotations is from the "Last Confession," and is the description referring to the harlot's laugh, the hideous character of which, together with its real or imagined resemblance to the laugh heard soon afterwards from the lips of one long cherished as an ideal, is the immediate cause which makes the maddened hero of the poem a murderer. Assailants may say what they please, but no poet or poetic reader will blame me for making the incident recorded in these seven lines as repulsive to the reader as it was to the hearer and beholder. Without this, the chain of motive and result would remain obviously incomplete. Observe also that these are but seven lines in a poem of some five hundred, not one other of which could be classed with them.

A second quotation gives the last two lines *only* of the following sonnet, which is the first of four sonnets in "The House of Life" jointly entitled "Willowwood":

[Here Rossetti quotes "Willowwood" in its entirety.]

The critic has quoted (as I said) only the last two lines, and he has italicized the second as something unbearable and ridiculous. Of course the inference would be that this was really my own absurd bubble-and-squeak[1] notion of an actual kiss. The reader will perceive at once, from the whole sonnet transcribed above, how untrue such an inference would be. The sonnet describes a dream or trance of divided love momentarily reunited by the longing fancy; and in the imagery of the dream, the face of the beloved rises through deep dark waters to kiss the lover. Thus the phrase, "Bubbled with brimming kisses," &c., bears purely on the special symbolism employed, and from that point of view will be found, I believe, perfectly simple and just. ...

I have selected, amid much railing on my critic's part, what seemed the most representative indictment against me, and have, so far, answered it. Its remaining clauses set forth how others and myself "aver that poetic expression is greater than poetic thought ... and sound superior to sense"—an accusation elsewhere, I observe, expressed by saying that we "wish to create form for its own sake." ... [Notice that this accusation] is not against the poetic value of certain work, but against its primary and (by assumption) its admitted aim. And to this I must reply that so far, assuredly, not even Shakespeare himself could desire more arduous human tragedy for development in art than belongs to the themes I venture to embody, however incalculably higher might be his power of dealing with them. What more inspiring for poetic effort than the terrible love turned to hate—perhaps the deadliest of all passion-woven complexities—which is the theme of "Sister Helen." ... What, again, more so than the ... baffling problems which the face of Jenny conjures up—or than the analysis of passion and feeling attempted in "The House of Life" and others among the more purely lyrical poems? I speak here, as does my critic in the clause adduced, of *aim* not of *achievement*, and so far, the mere summary is instantly subversive of the preposterous imputation. To assert that the poet whose matter is such as this aims chiefly at "creating form for its own sake," is, in fact, almost an ingenuous kind of dishonesty. ... Yet this may fairly be taken as an example of the spirit in which a constant effort is here made against me to appeal to those who either are ignorant of what I write, or else belong to the large class too easily influenced by an assumption of authority in addressing them. The false name appended to the article must, as is evident, aid this position vastly; for who, after all, would not be apt to laugh at seeing one poet confessedly come forward as aggressor against another in the field of criticism? ...

Thus far, then, let me thank you for the opportunity afforded me to join issue with the Stealthy School of Criticism. As for any literary justice to be done on this particular Mr. Robert-Thomas,[2] I will merely ask the reader whether, once identified, he does not become manifestly his own best "sworn tormentor"? For who will then fail to discern all the palpitations which preceded his final resolve in the great question whether to be or not to be his acknowledged self when he became an assailant? And yet this is he who, from behind his mask, ventures to charge another with "bad blood," with "insincerity," and the rest of it (and that where poetic fancies are alone in question), while every word on his own tongue is covert rancour, and every stroke from his pen perversion of truth. Yet, after all, there is nothing wonderful in the lengths to which a fretful poet-critic will carry such grudges

---

[1] *bubble-and-squeak*   English breakfast hash traditionally made from leftover cabbage, potatoes, and meat.

[2] *Mr. Robert-Thomas*   Rossetti combines Buchanan's real first name (Robert) and that of his pseudonymous character, "Thomas Maitland."

as he may bear, while publisher and editor can both be found who are willing to consider such means admissible, even to the clear subversion of first professed tenets in the *Review* which they conduct.

In many phases of outward nature, the principle of chaff[1] and grain holds good—the base enveloping the precious continually, but an untruth was never yet the husk of a truth. Thresh and riddle and winnow it as you may—let it fly in shreds to the four winds—falsehood only will be that which flies and that which stays. And thus the sheath of deceit which this pseudonymous undertaking presents at the outset insures in fact what will be found to be its real character to the core.

---

[1] *chaff* Outer covering found on seeds and grains.

THE PRE-RAPHAELITES

CONTEXTS

The Pre-Raphaelites were a group of passionate young artists and intellectuals who wanted to break away from the cultural establishment of their day and work toward a new aesthetic ideal. They took inspiration from the critic John Ruskin, following his advice to artists: "go to nature in all singleness of heart." In their painting, the group sought a sharp and detailed realism, both physical and psychological, while also emulating late medieval Italian art, which the Pre-Raphaelites admired for its grace and simplicity, as well as for its depth of color, emotion, and detail. Using a rich, jewel-like palette of sensual colors, the Pre-Raphaelites rejected everyday, domestic scenes and chose serious subjects for their pictures, often based on scenes from the Bible, literary works, and classical mythology. In 1848, William Holman Hunt, John Everett Millais, and Dante Gabriel Rossetti formed what they called the Pre-Raphaelite Brotherhood, and within its first year others joined, including James Collinson, Frederic George Stephens, Thomas Woolner, and William Michael Rossetti, who acted as the group's secretary. While some members were poets or critics who developed Pre-Raphaelitism as a literary movement, most members were painters, and visual arts dominated the Brotherhood.

The group members asserted their artistic vision against what they saw to be a limited and unnatural ideal promoted by the Royal Academy, which considered the Italian High Renaissance to be the epitome of achievement in art. The Academy taught students to emulate the work of Raphael, whose careful perspective and balanced compositions created idealized and highly finished paintings. Students were taught to paint the figures first, and then the background, blending color gradually to bring the significant parts of the painting into sharper focus. The Pre-Raphaelites found this system of instruction to be stifling, mechanistic, and artificial. Instead, they sought to bring *every* part of the canvas into equal focus by flattening perspective in the manner of medieval Italian artists. They painted the background first, then the figures, painting from life to create naturalistic representations of both their human models and the architecture, fauna, and flora that surrounded them. While the group did not have an official manifesto, they did believe in the potential for art to change society, offering beauty and simplicity as counteracting forces against the rapidly industrializing world in which they lived. The movement was in some ways paradoxical: seeking to revolutionize the present by reviving elements of a distant past.

When members of the Pre-Raphaelites showed paintings in the 1850 Royal Academy Exhibition, including Millais's *Christ in the House of His Parents* and Hunt's *A Converted British Family*, their work was received with outrage. Critics, including Charles Dickens, reacted against the paintings' lack of symmetry and linear perspective, as well as against their hyper-realism, especially in Millais's depiction of Christ at home with his working-class family. John Ruskin—one of few critics not hostile to the new movement—wrote letters to the *Times* in defense of the new style of painting, as well as an essay in support of the movement, entitled *Pre-Raphaelitism* (1851). The Pre-Raphaelites also began publishing a magazine, *The Germ* (1850), where they could explore and promote their ideas. Only four issues of the magazine were published, but they documented the Pre-Raphaelites' breadth of interests; the magazine contained images, poems, reviews, essays, and designs, showing that the aesthetic vision behind the movement applied not only to paintings, but also to illustration, textiles, and literature.

Although the Pre-Raphaelites were, officially, a "brotherhood," there were many women artists and writers associated with the movement, and their influence was formative; many curators and critics have now begun to group the contributions of these women under the umbrella of the "Pre-Raphaelite Sisters" or "Sisterhood." Indeed, some of the women saw themselves in this way: painter Anna Mary Howitt, in her book *An Art-Student in Munich* (1854), envisioned "a beautiful sisterhood in Art, of which we have all dreamed long, and by which association we might be enabled to do noble things." Some of the women painters associated with the Pre-Raphaelites include Elizabeth Siddal, Joanna Mary Boyce Wells, Emma Sandys, Barbara Leigh Smith Bodichon, and Evelyn De Morgan. Some were also activists for feminist causes; Bodichon, for example, founded the group "The Ladies of Langham Place" to campaign for women's rights.

Some women connected to the Pre-Raphaelites became famous as models and muses for the male painters, including Siddal, Fanny Eaton, Jane Morris, Fanny Cornforth, and Marie Zambaco. Christina Rossetti, one of the century's most accomplished poets, published seven poems in *The Germ* (under the pseudonym "Ellen Alleyn") and was painted and drawn repeatedly by the members. Her sonnet "In an Artist's Studio" reveals the uncomfortable position women, particularly the models, held in relation to Pre-Raphaelite men, who idealized each model's beauty but used it in service of their own imaginative vision; the model, Rossetti wrote, appears in the painting "Not as she is, but as she fills his dream."

The Pre-Raphaelite Brotherhood dissolved after about five years, as the members traveled abroad and developed in their own directions, though they all continued to work within the aesthetic they had promoted as Pre-Raphaelites. A "second wave" of Pre-Raphaelitism emerged in 1857, with Edward Burne-Jones and William Morris joining Dante Gabriel Rossetti to create a set of murals based on Arthurian legends. In 1861, Morris, Burne-Jones, Rossetti, Ford Madox Brown, and others created a decorative arts company that would eventually become known as Morris & Company. Dedicated to handcrafting beautiful objects made of natural materials, the company was also a socialist response to the inhumanity and ugliness of mass-production. Later in the century, through the work of Morris, the critic Walter Pater, and others, many of the values of Pre-Raphaelitism would be taken in new directions by the Aesthetic and Symbolist movements.

The materials presented below include substantial excerpts from an account by Millais's son, John G. Millais, of how his father painted what became perhaps the most controversial of all Pre-Raphaelite works, "Christ in the House of His Parents"; from Charles Dickens's scathing response to that painting and, more generally, to the Pre-Raphaelite work exhibited at the 1850 Royal Academy show; from one highly critical review of the Pre-Raphaelite paintings exhibited at the 1851 Royal Academy show; from Ruskin's letter in response to such scathing reviews; and from a 50-page pamphlet Ruskin published later that year entitled *Pre-Raphaelitism*. We have also included excerpts from essays discussing Pre-Raphaelite aesthetics: one by William Michael Rossetti on the evolution and aims of the Pre-Raphaelites; one by John Seward on Pre-Raphaelite admiration of early Italian art; and one by Oscar Wilde reflecting, at the close of the century, on the importance of the Pre-Raphaelite movement.

In addition to the images included below and in the Dante Gabriel Rossetti and Christina Rossetti sections of this anthology, reproductions of Pre-Raphaelite works (notably Millais's *Ophelia* and Hunt's *The Awakening Conscience*) are included in the color insert of this anthology.

⌘⌘⌘

from William Michael Rossetti, *Dante Gabriel Rossetti; His Family Letters, with a Memoir by William Michael Rossetti* (1895)

[The incident that sparked the establishment of the Pre-Raphaelite Brotherhood occurred] the month of August or of September 1848, when Hunt was twenty-one years of age, Rossetti twenty, and Millais nineteen. They had thus barely ceased to be big boys; but Hunt and Millais were already very capable and recognized painters, and all three were enthusiasts—enthusiasts with a difference. Millais perceived within himself powers which far exceeded those of most of the acknowledged heads of his profession, … Hunt was not only stubbornly persistent, but eagerly desirous of developing something at once solid and uncommon; Rossetti, a beginner in the art, was fired with inventive imaginings, and a love of beauty, and was just as anxious as his colleagues to distinguish himself, if as yet not equally certain to do so. All three condemned the commonplace anecdotal subjects of most British painters of the day, and their flimsy pretences at cleverness of execution, unsupported by either clear intuition into the facts of Nature, or by lofty or masculine style; or by an effort at sturdy realization. …

[The three young men] hated the cant about Raphael[1] and the Great Masters, and utter cant it was in the mouths of such underlings of the brush as they saw all around them. They determined to make a new start on a firm basis. What was the basis to be? It was to be serious and elevated invention of subject, along with earnest scrutiny of visible facts, and an earnest endeavour to represent them voraciously and exactly.

This does not fully account for them calling themselves Pre-Raphaelites. Mr. Hunt says—and he must be correct—that the word Pre-Raphaelites "had first been used as a term of contempt by our enemies"; founded, it would seem, more upon the talk of the young men than upon anything … which they had actually done. Hunt's pictures as yet had no distinctive Pre-Raphaelite

quality, Millais's were quite in the contrary line, and Rossetti was not known to have painted at all. But they saw, in the Italian painters from Giotto to Leonardo,[2] and in certain early Flemish and German painters, so far as they knew about them (which was little), a manifest emotional sincerity, expressed sometimes in a lofty and solemn way, and sometimes with a candid *naiveté*; they saw strong evidences of grace, decorative charm, observation and definition of certain appearances of Nature, and patient and loving but not mechanical labour. …

It was with this feeling, and obviously not with any idea of actually imitating any painters who had preceded Raphael, that the youths adopted as a designation … the word Pre-Raphaelite. The word "Brotherhood" was, it seems, Rossetti's term, put forward as being preferable—which it most certainly was—to any such term as Clique or Association. And thus was the Pre-Raphaelite Brotherhood constituted as the autumn of 1848 began. …

As it was, Pre-Raphaelitism proved to be very uphill work. It was more abused, as being a principle of a few men in unison, than it would have been if exemplified by one of them only; but the very abuse was the beginning of its triumph. Any one of them, if acting by himself, might have been recognized as a man of genius; he would hardly have become a power in art. If the invention of "the Pre-Raphaelite Brotherhood" was a craze, it was a craze spiced with a deal of long-headedness. Some method in that sort of madness. …

Had the Pre-Raphaelite Brotherhood any ulterior aim beyond that of producing good works of art? Yes, and No. Assuredly they had the aim of developing such *ideas* as are suited to the medium of fine art, as a bridging the arts of form into general unison with what is highest in other arts, especially poetry. … In the person of at least two of its members, Hunt and Collins, it had also a definite relation to a Christian, and not a pagan or

---

[1]   *Raphael*   Raffaello Sanzio da Urbino (1483–1520), Italian painter and sculptor, regarded in the mid-nineteenth century as the greatest artist of the Italian Renaissance.

[2]   *Giotto to Leonardo*   Giotto di Bondone (c. 1266–1337), leading Italian artist of the late medieval/early Renaissance period; Leonardo da Vinci (1452–1519) leading artist of the Italian Renaissance, from the generation immediately preceding that of Raphael.

latitudinarian,[1] line of thought. On the other hand, the notion that the Brotherhood, as such, had anything whatever to do with particular movements in the religious world … is totally … erroneous. To say that Pre-Raphaelitism was part of "the ever rising protest of our century against artificial authority," as in the cases of "The French Revolution" and Wordsworth and Darwin, etc.,[2] is indeed not untrue, but is far too vague to account for anything. … Neither was Ruskin their inciter, though it is true that Hunt had read and laid to heart in 1847 the first volume of *Modern Painters*, the only thing then current as Ruskin's work. …

That the Pre-Raphaelites valued moral and spiritual ideas as an important section of the ideas germane to fine art is most true, and not one of them was in the least any inclined to do any work of a gross, lascivious, or sensual description; but neither did they limit the province of art to the spiritual or the moral. I will therefore take it upon me to say that the bond of union among the members of the Brotherhood was really and simply this: 1) to have genuine ideas to express; 2) to study Nature attentively, so as to know how to express them; 3) to sympathize with what is direct and serious and heartfelt in previous art, to the exclusion of what is conventional and self-parading and learned by rote; and 4) and most indispensable of all, to produce thoroughly good pictures and statues.

from John Seward, "The Purpose and Tendency of Early Italian Art," The Germ: Thoughts Toward Nature in Poetry, Literature, and Art (31 January 1850)

In this essay, the Pre-Raphaelite art critic Frederic George Stephens (1827–1907), under the pseudonym "John Seward," articulates Pre-Raphaelite ideals in art by considering the virtues of the medieval Italian painters the group admired. The essay was published in *The Germ*, the Pre-Raphaelite magazine that was launched to promote the group's ideas.

… The modern artist does not retire to monasteries, or practise discipline;[3] but he may show his participation in the same high feeling by a firm attachment to truth in every point of representation, which is the most just method. For how can good be sought by evil means, or by falsehood, or by slight in any degree? By a determination to represent the thing and the whole of the thing, by training himself to the deepest observation of its fact and detail, enabling himself to reproduce, as far as possible, nature herself, the painter will best evince his share of faith.

It is by this attachment to truth in its most severe form that the followers of the Arts have to show that they share in the peculiar character of the present age—a humility of knowledge, a diffidence of attainment. …

It has been said that there is presumption in this movement of the modern school, a want[4] of deference to established authorities, a removing of ancient landmarks. This is best answered by the profession that nothing can be more humble than the pretension to the observation of facts alone, and the truthful rendering of them. If we are not to depart from established principles, how are we to advance at all? Are we to remain still? Remember, nothing remains still; that which does not advance falls backward. That this movement is an advance, and that it is of nature herself, is shown by its going nearer to truth in every object produced, and by its being guided by the very principles the ancient painters followed, as soon as they attained the mere power of representing an object faithfully. These principles are now revived, not from them, though through their example, but from nature herself. …

Let us have the mind and the mind's-workings, not the remains of earnest thought which has been frittered

[1] *latitudinarian* Latitudinarians believed that the Church should try to accommodate a diverse range of views when it came to issues of liturgy and of theological doctrine.

[2] *the ever rising … Darwin., etc.* [Author's note] See Mrs. Wood's *Dante Rossetti and the Pre-Raphaelite Movement*, page 9. [A history of the Pre-Raphaelite movement, written by Ester Wood and published in 1894.]

[3] *practise discipline* Impose self-punishment—such as fasting or flagellation—as an expression of religious penance.

[4] *want* Lack.

away by a long dreary course of preparatory study, by which all life has been evaporated. Never forget that there is in the wide river of nature something which everybody who has a rod and line may catch, precious things which everyone may dive for. ...

The sciences have become almost exact within the present century. Geology and chemistry are almost re-instituted. The first has been nearly created; the second expanded so widely that it now searches and measures the creation. And how has this been done but by bringing greater knowledge to bear upon a wider range of experiment; by being precise in the search after truth? If this adherence to fact, to experiment and not theory—to begin at the beginning and not fly to the end—has added so much to the knowledge of man in science; why may it not greatly assist the moral purposes of the Arts? It cannot be well to degrade a lesson by falsehood. Truth in every particular ought to be the aim of the artist. Admit no untruth: let the priest's garment be clean. ...

That the real power of the Arts, in conjunction with Poetry, upon the actions of any age is, or might be, predominant above all others will be readily allowed by all that have given any thought to the subject: and that there is no assignable limit to the good that may be wrought by their influence is another point on which there can be small doubt. Let us then endeavour to call up and exert this power in the worthiest manner, not forgetting that we chose a difficult path, in which there are many snares, and holding in mind the motto, "No Cross, no Crown."[1]

Believe that there is that in the fact of truth, though it be only in the character of a single leaf earnestly studied, which may do its share in the great labor of the world: remember that it is by truth alone that the Arts can ever hold the position for which they were intended, as the most powerful instruments, the most gentle guides; that, of all classes, there is none to whom the celebrated words of Lessing, "That the destinies of a nation depend upon its young men between nineteen and twenty-five years of age,"[2] can apply so well as to yourselves. Recollect, that your portion in this is most important: that your share is with the poet's share; that, in every careless thought or neglected doubt, you shelve your duty, and forsake your trust; fulfil and maintain these, whether in the hope of personal fame and fortune, or from a sense of power used to its intentions; and you may hold out both hands to the world. Trust it, and it will have faith in you; will hearken to the precepts you may have permission to impart.

from John Guille Millais, *The Life and Letters of Sir John Everett Millais* (1899)

... In the following year [1850] was exhibited the picture commonly known as *Christ in the Home of His Parents*, but with no other title than the following quotation from Zechariah 13.6: "and one shall say unto Him, 'what are these wounds in thine hands?' Then He shall answer, 'those with which I was wounded in the house of my friends.'" It was painted on precisely the same principle as was that which had called forth the derision of the multitude, and [given that] both Rossetti and Mr. Hunt exhibited at the same time important pictures of the same school, there could no longer be any doubt as to the serious meaning of the movement. Then, with one accord, there opponents fell upon Millais as the prime mover in the rebellion against established precedent. ...

The picture itself, devotional and symbolic in intent, is too well known to need any description. The child Christ is seen in His Father's workshop with blood flowing from his hand, the result of a recent wound, while His Mother waits upon Him with loving sympathy. This is the main subject. And now let us see how it was treated by the Press.

Blackwood's Magazine dealt with it in this wise: "We can hardly imagine anything more ugly, graceless, and unpleasant than Mr. Millais' picture of 'Christ in the

---

1   *No Cross, no Crown*   I.e., no triumph without suffering; the phrase references Christ's crucifixion and subsequent enthronement in heaven.

2   *Lessing ... age*   Stephens attributes this quotation to the German philosopher G.E. Lessing (1729–81).

Carpenter's Shop.' Such a collection of splay feet, puffed joints, and misshapen limbs was assuredly never before made in so small a compass. We have great difficulty in believing a report that his unpleasing and atrociously effected picture has found a purchaser at a high price. Another specimen from the same brush inspires rather laughter than disgust." …

Another critic, bent on displaying his wit at the expense of the artist, said: "Mr. Millais' picture looks as if it had passed through a mangle." And even Charles Dickens, who in later years was a firm friend of Millais and a great admirer of his works, denounced the picture in a leading article in *Household Words* as "mean, odious, revolting, and repulsive."

But perhaps the most unreasonable notice of all was the following, which appeared in *The Times*: "Mr. Millais' principal picture is, to speak plainly, revolting. The attempts to associate the Holy Family with the meanest details of a carpenter's shop, with no conceivable omission of misery, of dirt, of even disease, all finished with the same loathsome minuteness is disgusting; and with a surprising power of imitation, this picture serves to show how far mere imitation may fall short … of all dignity and truth."

In an interesting note on this picture Mr. Edward Benest (Millais' cousin) says:

During the three years I was working in London I was a frequent visitor to the Gower Street House.[1] … From the intellectual point of view this picture may be said to be the outcome of the combined brains of the Millais family. Every little portion of the whole canvas was discussed, considered, and settled upon by the father, mother, and Johnnie (the artist) before a touch was placed on the canvas, although sketches had been made. Of course, coming frequently, I used to criticize too; and if I suggested any alteration, Johnnie used to say in his determined way, "no, Ned: that has all been settled by us, and I shan't alter it."

Everything in that house was characteristic of the great devotion of all to the young artist; and yet he was in no way spoilt. Whilst he was at work his father and mother sat beside him most of the time, the mother constantly reading to him on every imaginable subject that interested the boy, or stopping to discuss matters with him. The boy himself, whilst working, joined freely and cleverly in any conversation that was going on; and once when I asked him how he could possibly paint and talk at the same time, and throw such energy into both, he said, tapping his forehead, "Oh, that's all right. I have painted every touch in my head, as it were, long ago, and have now only to transfer it to canvas." …

The principal point of discussion with regards to The "Carpenter's Shop" related to the head of the Virgin Mary. At first, as the sketches show, she was represented as being kissed by the child Christ; but this idea was [soon] altered to the present position of the figures, and the mother is now shown embracing her Son. These two figures were constantly painted and repainted in various attitudes, and finished only a short time before the picture was exhibited. The figure, too, of St. John carrying a bowl of water was inserted at the last moment.

The picture, when finished (not before), was sold for £150 to a dealer named Farrer, whose confidence in the young artist was amusingly displayed by pasting on the back of it all the adverse criticisms that appeared.

… In painting [the picture], Millais was so determined to be accurate in every detail that he used to take the canvas down to a carpenter's shop and paint the interior direct from what he saw there. The figure of Joseph he took from the carpenter himself, saying that it was "the only way to get the development of the muscles right"; but the head was painted from Millais' father. His great difficulty was with the sheep, for there were no flocks within miles of Gower Street. At last, only a few days before the picture had to be sent to the Royal Academy, he went to a neighbouring butcher's, where he bought two sheeps' heads with the wool on, and from these he painted the flock. …

[1] *the Gower Street House* Millais was living with his parents on Gower Street in London.

John Everett Millais, *Christ in the House of His Parents* (also known as "The Carpenter's Shop"), 1849–50. When first exhibited at the Royal Academy's show in 1850, the picture appeared without a title; the following words from the Bible were displayed beside it: "And one shall say unto him, 'What are these wounds in thine hands?' Then he shall answer. 'Those with which I was wounded in the house of my friends.'" (The passage, from Zechariah 13.6, is often read as foreshadowing the crucifixion of Christ.)

from Charles Dickens, "Old Lamps for New Ones," *Household Words* (15 June 1850)

... In the fifteenth century, a certain feeble lamp of art arose in the Italian town of Urbino. This poor light, Raphael Sanzio by name, better known to a few miserably mistaken wretches in these later days, as Raphael (another burned at the same time, called Titian[1]), was fed with a preposterous idea of Beauty with a ridiculous power of etherealising, and exalting to the Very Heaven of Heavens, what was most sublime and lovely in the

expression of the human face divine on Earth with the truly contemptible conceit of finding in poor humanity the fallen likeness of the angels of GOD, and raising it up again to their pure spiritual condition. This very fantastic whim effected a low revolution in Art, in this wise, that Beauty came to be regarded as one of its indispensable elements. In this very poor delusion, Artists have continued until the present nineteenth century, when it was reserved for some bold aspirants to "put it down."

The Pre-Raphael Brotherhood, Ladies and Gentlemen, is the dread Tribunal which is to set this matter right. Walk up, walk up and here, conspicuous on the wall of the Royal Academy of Art in England, in the eighty-second year of their annual exhibition, you shall

---

[1] *another burned ... Titian* I.e., another "lamp of art" burned— that of the great Renaissance artist Tiziano Vecelli or Tiziano Vecellio (c. 1489–1576), known as Titian.

see what this new Holy Brotherhood, this terrible Police that is to disperse all Post-Raphael offenders, has "been and done!"

You come in this Royal Academy Exhibition, which is familiar with the works of Wilkie, Collins, Etty, Eastlake, Mulready, Leslie, Maclise, Turner, Stanfield, Landseer, Roberts, Danby, Creswisk, Lee, Webster, Herbert, Dyce, Cope, and others who would have been renowned as great masters in any age or country you come, in this place, to the contemplation of a Holy Family. You will have the goodness to discharge from your minds all Post-Raphael ideas, all religious aspirations, all elevating thoughts, all tender, awful, sorrowful, ennobling, sacred, graceful, or beautiful associations, and to prepare yourselves, as befits such a subject Pre-Raphaelly considered for the lowest depths of what is mean,[1] odious, repulsive, and revolting.

You behold the interior of a carpenter's shop. In the foreground of that carpenter's shop is a hideous, wry-necked, blubbering, red-headed boy, in a bed-gown, who appears to have received a poke in the hand, from the stick of another boy with whom he has been playing in an adjacent gutter, and to be holding it up for the contemplation of a kneeling woman, so horrible in her ugliness, that (supposing it were possible for any human creature to exist for a moment with that dislocated throat) she would stand out from the rest of the company as a Monster, in the vilest cabaret[2] in France, or the lowest ginshop in England. Two almost naked carpenters, master and journeyman, worthy companions of this agreeable female, are working at their trade; a boy, with some small flavor of humanity in him, is entering with a vessel of water; and nobody is paying any attention to a snuffy old woman who seems to have mistaken that shop for the tobacconist's next door, and to be hopelessly waiting at the counter to be served with half an ounce of her favourite mixture. Wherever it is possible to express ugliness of feature, limb, or attitude, you have it expressed. Such men as the carpenters might be undressed in any hospital where dirty drunkards, in a high state of varicose veins, are received. ...

This, in the nineteenth century, and in the eighty-second year of the annual exhibition of the National Academy of Art, is the Pre-Raphael representation to us, Ladies and Gentlemen, of the most solemn passage which our minds can ever approach. This, in the nineteenth century, and in the eighty-second year of the annual exhibition of the National Academy of Art, is what Pre-Raphael Art can do to render reverence and homage to the faith in which we live and die! ...

from *The Times*, "Review of the Annual Exhibition at the Royal Academy" (May 1851)

... These young artists have unfortunately become notorious by addicting themselves to an antiquated style, and an affected simplicity in painting, which is to genuine art what the medieval ballads and designs in *Punch* are to Chaucer and Giotto. With the utmost readiness to humour even the caprices of art, when they bear the stamp of originality and genius, we can extend no toleration to a mere servile imitation of the cramped style, false perspective, and crude colour of remote antiquity. We do not want to see ... drapery "snapped instead of folded," faces bloated into apoplexy or extenuated to skeletons, colour borrowed from the jars in a druggist's shop, and expression forced into caricature. It is said that the gentlemen have the power to do better things. ... But we must doubt a capacity of which we have seen so little proof, and if any such capacity did exist in them, we fear it has already been overlaid by mannerism and conceit. To become great in art, it has been said that a painter must become as a little child, though not childish; but the authors of these offensive and absurd productions have contrived to combine the puerility or infancy of their art with the upishness and self sufficiency of a different period of life. That morbid infatuation which sacrifices truth, beauty, and genuine feeling to mere eccentricity deserves no quarter at the hands of the public. ...

---

[1] *mean* Lowly, undignified.

[2] *cabaret* Drinking house.

from John Ruskin, Letter to *The Times* (May 1851)

Sir:

Your usual liberty will, I trust, give a place in your columns to this expression of my regret that the tone of the critique which appeared in *The Times* of Wednesday last of the works of Mr. Millais and Mr. Hunt, now of the Royal Academy, should have been scornful as well as severe.

I regret it, first, because the mere labour bestowed upon these works, and their fidelity to a certain order of truth … ought at once to have placed them above the level of mere contempt; and, secondly, because I believe these young artists to be at a most critical period of their career—at a turning point, from which they may either sink into nothingness or rise to a very real greatness; and I believe also, that whether they choose the upward or downward path may in no small degree depend upon the character of the criticism which their works have to sustain. … [W]hen I first saw the chief picture by Millais in the exhibition last year I had nearly come to the same conclusions myself. But I ask for your permission, in justice to artists who have at least given much time and toil to their pictures, to institute some more serious inquiry into their merits and faults than your general notice of the Academy could have possibly admitted.

Let me state, in the first place, that I have no acquaintance with these artists and very imperfect sympathy with them. No one who has met with any of my writings will suspect me of desiring to encourage them in their Romanist and Tractarian tendencies.[1] I am glad to see that Mr. Millais's lady in blue is heartily tired of her painted window and idolatrous toilet table, and I have no particular respect for Mr. Collinson's *Lady in White*, because her sympathies are limited by a dead wall

James Collinson, *Convent Thoughts*, 1850. In the letter excerpted here, Ruskin refers to this picture as *Lady in White*.

or divided between some goldfish and a tadpole. …! But I happen to have a special acquaintance with the water plant, *Alisma Plantago*, among which the said goldfish are swimming; and as I never saw it so thoroughly or so well drawn, I must take leave to remonstrate with you, when you say sweepingly that these men "sacrifice truth as well as feeling to eccentricity." For as a mere botanical study … this picture would be invaluable to me, and I heartily wish it were mine.

But, before entering into such particulars, let me correct an impression which your article is likely to induce in most minds, and which is all together false.

---

[1] *Romanist and Tractarian tendencies*   John Henry Newman, Edward Pusey, John Keble, and other so-called "tractarians" (they were also referred to as the Oxford Movement) were known for writing tracts in defense of the heritage of the Church of England—including its Roman Catholic heritage. (Newman later converted to Catholicism.) William Holman Hunt's paintings were frequently criticized for their perceived Catholic leanings; Ruskin defended Hunt's *The Light of the World* against such charges in 1853.

John Everett Millais, *Mariana*, 1851. The painting depicts a character from Shakespeare's *Measure for Measure*. After Mariana loses her dowry in a shipwreck, her fiancé, Angelo, abandons her, but she remains in love with him. When the painting was first shown, it was accompanied by lines from an 1830 poem by Alfred Tennyson, also entitled "Mariana":

> She only said, "My life is dreary—
> He cometh not!" she said;
> She said, "I am aweary, aweary—
> I would that I were dead!"

These Pre-Raphaelites (I cannot compliment them on common sense in choice of a *nom de guerre*[1]) do *not* desire nor pretend in any way to imitate antique painting, as such. They know very little of ancient paintings who suppose the works of these young artists to resemble them. As far as I can judge their aim—for, as I've said, I do not know the men themselves—the Pre-Raphaelites intend to surrender no advantage which the knowledge

Marie Spartali Stillman, *Mariana*, c. 1867–69. Stillman worked as a model for the Pre-Raphaelites and also had a long and prolific career as a painter.

of inventions of the present time can afford to their art. They intend to return to early days in this one point only—that ... they will draw either what they see, or what they suppose might have been the actual facts of the scene they desire to represent, irrespective of any conventional rules of picture making; and they have chosen their unfortunate though not inaccurate name because all artists did this before Raphael's time, and after Raphael's time did *not* do this, but sought to paint fair pictures, rather than represent stern facts, of which the consequence has been that from Raphael's time to this day historical art has been in acknowledged decadence. ...

[T]here was not one single error in perspective in four out of the five pictures in question; and ... in Millais' *Mariana* there is but this one—the top of the green

---

[1] *nom de guerre* French: name adopted for battle. In English the phrase usually means "pseudonym"; here it refers to the movement's self-chosen title, "Pre-Raphaelite."

curtain in the distant window has too low a vanishing point. … I will undertake, if need be, to point out and prove a dozen worse errors in perspective in any twelve pictures, containing architecture, taken at random from among the works of the popular painters of the day. …

[F]urther: … as studies both of drapery and of every minor detail, there is nothing in art so earnest or so complete as these pictures since the days of Albert Durer.[1] This I assert generally and fearlessly. On the other hand, I am perfectly ready to admit that Mr. Hunt's *Sylvia* is not a person whom Proteus or anyone else would have been likely to fall in love with at first sight; and that one cannot feel very sincere that Mr. Millais's *Wives of the Sons of Noah* should have escaped the Deluge; and many other faults besides on which I will not enlarge at present, because I have already occupied too much of your valuable space, and I hope to enter into more special criticism in a future letter. I have the honour to be, Sir,

Your obedient servant,

The author of *Modern Painters*

from John Ruskin, *Pre-Raphaelitism* (1851)

… The infinite absurdity and failure of our present training consists mainly of this, that we do not rank imagination and invention high enough, and suppose that they *can* be taught. Throughout every sentence that I have written, the reader will find the same rank attributed to these powers,—the rank of a purely divine gift, not to be attained, increased, or in any wise modified by teaching[.] … [I]f we had sense, should we not rather restrain and bridle the first flame of invention in early youth, heaping material on it as one would on the first sparks and tongues of a fire which we desired to feed into greatness? Should we not educate the whole intellect in general strength, and all the affections into warmth and honesty, and look to heaven for the rest? This, I say, we should have sense enough to do …: but, … to produce a poet on canvas, what is our way of setting to work? We

begin, in all probability, by telling the youth of 15 or 16 that Nature is full of faults, and that he is to improve her; but then Raphael is perfection, and the more he copies Raphael the better; that after much copying of Raphael, he is to try what he can do himself in a Raphaelesque, but yet original, manner: that is to say, he is to try to do something very clever, all out of his own head, but yet this clever something is to be properly subjected to Raphaelesque rules, is to have a principle light occupying 1/7 of its space, and a principle shadow occupying 1/3 of the same; that no two people's heads in the picture are to be turned the same way, and that all the personages represented are to possess ideal beauty of the highest order, which ideal beauty consists partly in Greek outlines of nose, partly in proportions expressible in decimal fractions between the lips and chin, but partly also in that degree of improvement which the youth of 16 is to bestow upon God's work in general. This I say is the kind of teaching which through various channels, Royal Academy lecturing, press criticisms, public enthusiasm, and not least by solid weight of gold, we give to our young men. And we wonder we have no painters!

[Ruskin here discusses a number of Victorian painters as cases in point—particularly J.M.W. Turner, whose paintings from about 1800 onwards Ruskin regarded as displaying the highest genius. It is only towards the end of the pamphlet that he turns his attention to the painters who styled themselves as Pre-Raphaelites.]

It is not, however, only in invention that men overwork themselves, but in execution also; and here I have a word to say to the Pre-Raphaelites specially. They are working too hard. There is evidence in failing portions of their pictures, showing that they have wrought so long upon them that their very sight has failed for weariness, and that the hand refused anymore to obey the heart; and besides this, there are certain qualities of drawing which they miss from over-carefulness. For, let them be assured, there is a great truth working in that common desire of men to see things

---

[1] *Durer* Albrecht Dürer (1471–1528), German painter.

done in what they call a "masterly," or "bold," or "broad," manner: a truth oppressed and abused, like almost every other in this world, but an eternal true one nevertheless; and whatever mischief may have followed from men's looking for nothing else but this facility of execution, and supposing that a picture was assuredly all right if only it were done with broad dashes of the brush, still the truth remains the same: … the noblest results [should only be] attainable by a certain ease and decision of manipulation. … The freedom of the lines of Nature can only be represented by a similar freedom in the hand that follows them; there are curves in the flow of the hair, and in the form of the features, and in the muscular or outline of the body, which can in no wise be caught but by a sympathetic freedom in the stroke of the pencil. I do not care what example is taken, be it the most subtle and careful work of Leonardo himself, there will be found a play and power and ease in the outlines which no *slow* effort could ever imitate.

from Oscar Wilde, *The English Renaissance of Art* (1882, 1907)

Wilde delivered this lecture during his 1882 North American tour. In it, he argues that the nineteenth century in Britain had seen "a sort of new birth of the spirit of man … in its desire for a more gracious and comely way of life, its passion for physical beauty, its exclusive attention to form, its seeking for new subjects for poetry, new forms of art, new intellectual and imaginative enjoyments." Wilde traces the beginnings of this movement in the works of the English Romantic poets, particularly in the poems of John Keats, and traces it onward to the Pre-Raphaelite movement.

… As regards the pre-Raphaelites the story is simple enough. In the year 1847 a number of young men in London, poets and painters, passionate admirers of Keats all of them, formed the habit of meeting together for discussions on art, the result of such discussions being that the English Philistine[1] public was roused

___
[1] *Philistine* Uneducated, hostile to the arts.

suddenly from its ordinary apathy by hearing that there was in its midst a body of young men who had determined to revolutionise English painting and poetry. They called themselves the pre-Raphaelite Brotherhood.

In England, then as now, it was enough for a man to try and produce any serious beautiful work to lose all his rights as a citizen; and besides this, the pre-Raphaelite Brotherhood—among whom the names of Dante Rossetti, Holman Hunt and Millais will be familiar to you—had on their side three things that the English public never forgives: youth, power and enthusiasm.

Satire, always as sterile as it is shameful and as impotent as it is insolent, paid them that usual homage which mediocrity pays to genius—doing, here as always, infinite harm to the public, blinding them to what is beautiful, teaching them that irreverence which is the source of all vileness and narrowness of life, but harming the artist not at all, rather confirming him in the perfect rightness of his work and ambition. For to disagree with three-fourths of the British public on all points is one of the first elements of sanity, one of the deepest consolations in all moments of spiritual doubt.

As regards the ideas these young men brought to the regeneration of English art, we may see at the base of their artistic creations a desire for a deeper spiritual value to be given to art as well as a more decorative value.

Pre-Raphaelites they called themselves; not that they imitated the early Italian masters at all, but that in their work, as opposed to the facile abstractions of Raphael, they found a stronger realism of imagination, a more careful realism of technique, a vision at once more fervent and more vivid, an individuality more intimate and more intense.

For it is not enough that a work of art should conform to the aesthetic demands of its age: there must be also about it, if it is to affect us with any permanent delight, the impress of a distinct individuality, an individuality remote from that of ordinary men, and coming near to us only by virtue of a certain newness and wonder in the work, and through channels whose very strangeness makes us more ready to give them welcome.

Evelyn de Morgan, *Night and Sleep*, 1878.

La personalité, said one of the greatest of modern French critics, *voilà ce qui nous sauvera*.[1]

But above all things was it a return to Nature—that formula which seems to suit so many and such diverse movements: they would draw and paint nothing but what they saw, they would try and imagine things as they really happened. Later there came to the old house by Blackfriars Bridge,[2] where this young brotherhood used to meet and work, two young men from Oxford, Edward Burne-Jones and William Morris—the latter substituting for the simpler realism of the early days a more exquisite spirit of choice, a more faultless devotion to beauty, a more intense seeking for perfection: a master of all exquisite design and of all spiritual vision. It is of the school of Florence rather than of that of Venice that he is kinsman, feeling that the close imitation of Nature is a disturbing element in imaginative art. The visible aspect of modern life disturbs him not; rather is it for him to render eternal all that is beautiful in Greek, Italian, and Celtic legend. To Morris we owe poetry whose perfect precision and clearness of word and vision has not been excelled in the literature of our country, and by the revival of the decorative arts he has given to our individualised romantic movement the social idea and the social factor also.

But the revolution accomplished by this clique of young men, with Ruskin's faultless and fervent eloquence to help them, was not one of ideas merely but of execution, not one of conceptions but of creations. ...

Pre-Raphaelite Models: Fanny Eaton

The women who modeled for the Pre-Raphaelite painters portrayed a wide range of literary figures, Biblical heroines, and goddesses from Greek mythology. Many of them were artists themselves, and most were discovered in their places of work—Elizabeth Siddal, for example, worked at a dressmaker's; Fanny Cornforth as a servant; and Annie Miller in a pub. The models were creative participants in the work of painting: Siddal famously remained in a tub so long for Millais's *Drowning Ophelia* (1852) that she came down with a severe illness. The models most often posed for several painters in the movement, each of whom would portray the women with their own distinctive imaginative visions. The following set of images are all depictions of the Jamaica-born model Fanny Eaton (1835–1924) by a variety of Pre-Raphaelite artists. Eaton worked as an artist's model for the Pre-Raphaelites between 1859 and 1867, to supplement her income as a household servant and to help support her ten children.

---

[1] *La personalité ... sauvera* French: It is personality that will save us. The quotation is adapted from Émile Zola's seventh essay in his series *Les Romanciers Naturalistes* (1881).

[2] *old house ... Blackfriars Bridge* In 1852, Dante Gabriel Rossetti moved to a studio near Blackfriars Bridge, London.

Simeon Solomon, *The Mother of Moses*, 1860.

Joanna Boyce Wells, *Fanny Eaton*, 1861.

Rebecca Solomon, *The Young Teacher*, 1861.

Frederick Sandys, *Study for the Head of Morgan le Fay*, c. 1862.

Frederick Sandys, *Morgan le Fay*, 1863–64.

CHRISTINA ROSSETTI
1830 – 1894

To the late-Victorian critic Edmund Gosse, Christina Rossetti was "one of the most perfect poets of the age." Her melding of sensuous imagery and precise form earned her the admiration and devotion of many nineteenth-century readers, an admiration that has only increased in the generations that followed. Praised for being, as one critic wrote in 1862, "remarkably fresh and free," Rossetti's lyric voice is marked by its concision and symbolic richness, and by a pervasive spiritual dimension, even when the subject matter is secular. The quality of her faith, and of her doubt, lends an intensity to her poems that places her writing in kinship with the work of Emily Brontë, Emily Dickinson, and Gerard Manley Hopkins.

She was born in London in 1830, the youngest of four children. Her father, Gabriele Rossetti, was a scholar and an Italian exile, and her mother, Frances Polidori, also a scholar, was the daughter of an Italian exile. Italian revolutionaries-in-exile frequented the Rossetti home, creating a provocative and unconventional environment for the Rossetti children. Frances and Gabriele educated all their four children themselves, including Christina, who dedicated all her work to her mother. Other influences included their mother's devotion to Christianity and visits to their maternal grandfather's rural home. "If any one thing schooled me in the direction of poetry," Rossetti was later to write, "it was perhaps the delightful idle liberty to prowl all alone about my grandfather's cottage-grounds some thirty miles from London." Rossetti's grandfather Polidori printed her first volume of poems, *Verses*, in 1847. These poems of the sixteen-year-old Rossetti already exhibited many of the qualities for which her work would later be known: directness of expression, and narratives colored with vivid and often sensuous detail. The poems in this collection reflected her literary influences: Gothic fiction and the poetry of George Herbert, William Blake, John Keats, and the Italian poets Dante and Tasso.

In 1850 her two brothers, Dante Gabriel and William Michael, helped found the Pre-Raphaelite Brotherhood, a group of writers and painters that shared certain aesthetic goals. Rossetti was both part of, and not part of, this "Brotherhood": she published several poems in *The Germ*, the journal of the Brotherhood, and she also served as a model for several paintings in the early years of the movement. Her aesthetic sense—and especially her attention to color and detail—link her to the movement, as do her devotion to the faithful representation of nature and her interest in symbolic representation. As a woman, however, she was not invited to their meetings, and in later years she became more and more critical of the Brotherhood's increasingly secular orientation and its objectification of women (such criticism is apparent in poems such as "In an Artist's Studio").

The 1850s were a difficult time for Rossetti. Early in the decade she rejected, most likely on religious grounds, a suitor to whom she had been engaged for two years, the Pre-Raphaelite painter James Collinson. Collinson had converted to Anglicanism to please Rossetti, but he ultimately returned to his original faith, Catholicism. (In 1866 Rossetti appears to have rejected a second suitor,

Charles Bagot Cayley, perhaps because he was an agnostic.) In 1854 Rossetti volunteered to join Florence Nightingale's nursing efforts in the Crimean War, but she was rejected for being too young. She volunteered instead at the Highgate Penitentiary for "fallen women," where she was known as "sister Christina." When on duty at the penitentiary, she would live there for two-week intervals, and her experiences with the inmates influenced her literary work (particularly her development of the themes of betrayal and illicit love in her poetry), as well as spurring her activism against child prostitution. Her social activism extended to protesting vivisection and other animal experimentation; she was also openly critical of slavery and imperialism. Throughout this period, she lived with her mother, sister, and brother William in the family home.

Rossetti first gained attention in the literary world with her 1862 publication of *Goblin Market and Other Poems*. Before publication of the volume, the eminent critic John Ruskin had declared the poems irregular in their rhyme schemes and meters. Ruskin advised Rossetti to "exercise herself in the severest commonplace of metre until she [could] write as the public like." Rossetti nevertheless went ahead with publication, and the vast majority of her Victorian critics praised the volume for what one reviewer called its "very decided character and originality, both in theme and treatment." *Goblin Market* remains among her most discussed works. Few readers have believed William Michael Rossetti's insistence that his sister "did not mean anything profound" by *Goblin Market*, and the poem has been interpreted in countless ways, including as an examination of female relationship, as a Christian allegory, and as a story of the redemption of a fallen woman.

More volumes followed, among the most important of which were *The Prince's Progress and Other Poems* (1866), *Sing-Song* (1872), and *A Pageant and Other Poems* (1881). *Sing-Song* is a collection of children's verses and nursery rhymes that have proved enduringly popular. With "Monna Innominata," the "sonnet of sonnets" published in *A Pageant and Other Poems,* Rossetti offered her own bold contribution to the sonnet-sequence tradition. In the prose preface to "Monna Innominata," Rossetti notes that women such as Dante's Beatrice and Petrarch's Laura were denied the opportunity to speak for themselves. If either had spoken in her own voice, Rossetti writes, "the portrait left us might have appeared more tender, if less dignified, than any drawn even by a devoted friend." Rossetti's sonnets speak of unfulfilled yearning and painful loss, bringing to the sonnet form the voice of a woman's suffering such as Rossetti argued had never before been written.

The role of faith in Rossetti's life was central: it guided her decisions and actions, as well as her literary output. More than half of her poems are devotional, and as she grew older her writing became almost exclusively religious. The Rossettis were High Anglicans, and Christina was influenced by the Oxford Movement, an intellectual movement within the Anglican church that led to Anglo-Catholicism. Some of her key devotional works include *Annus Domini: A Prayer for Each Day of the Year* (1874), *Time Flies: A Reading Diary* (1885), and *The Face of the Deep* (1892). *Verses* (1893), her last book of poetry, collects poems from her devotional works, and is a passionate record of her desire for union with Christ. In her essay "I Am Christina Rossetti," Virginia Woolf writes that "the pressure of a tremendous faith circles and clamps together these little songs," and, addressing Rossetti directly, observes, "No sooner have you feasted on beauty with your eyes than your mind tells you that beauty is vain and beauty passes. Death, oblivion, and rest lap round your songs with their dark wave."

In 1871, Rossetti was stricken with Graves's disease, which led her to retreat even further into an already quiet life as she continued to live with and care for her mother and two aunts. She lived to see editions of her collected poems published in 1875 and then again in 1890. Rossetti underwent surgery for breast cancer in 1892, and died of the disease in 1894.

⌘ ⌘ ⌘

Goblin Market

In 1859, Rossetti became a voluntary lay sister at St. Mary Magdalene Penitentiary in Highgate, an institution founded to reform prostitutes and other so-called "fallen women" and help them regain what Victorian society defined as respectability. Highgate was not the only such establishment at the time—an indication of a growing belief that the harms of sexual transgression were not indelible—but the prevailing view was nevertheless that women could not be redeemed once they had "fallen." Rossetti's involvement at Highgate puts her on the side of the reformers, who believed that God's power was enough not only to save the souls of the worst of sinners (as such women were perceived to be), but also to transform infamy into decency in this life; the fallen could be raised and welcomed in good society once again.

It was during her tenure at Highgate that Rossetti wrote *Goblin Market*. The timing cannot have been a coincidence; the poem's themes of sisterhood, temptation, and redemption are clearly linked to her reform work. But while it may have found its catalyst there, *Goblin Market* goes well beyond a concern with the rehabilitation of prostitutes. The poem offers much more than a single view, opening windows onto a breadth of topics as diverse as gender violence, women's sexuality, Christian salvation, female friendship, substance abuse, and mercantile capitalism. It is at once a poem for children and for adults—pairing bright, memorable fairytale imagery and a singing tone with an unexpected sensuality and a wealth of insight into some of the most serious difficulties and joys of adult life. As such, it resonates with a wide range of readers.

As the anchor piece of the volume *Goblin Market and Other Poems*, the poem found a publisher, Alexander MacMillan, in 1862. Before the book went to press, MacMillan read *Goblin Market* to a society for working-class men in Cambridge. In a letter to Rossetti's brother Gabriel, he described their reaction: "They seemed at first to wonder whether I was making fun of them; by degrees they got as still as death, and when I finished there was a tremendous burst of applause." These men were not the sort of audience that one might first think of as

naturally receptive to such a work, but their response is indicative of the poem's potency, and it is unsurprising that, of Rossetti's corpus, *Goblin Market* remains the most widely read and commented on, even as interest in the rest of Rossetti's output has intensified over the past three decades. The striking depth of *Goblin Market*, despite a steadily increasing enthusiasm for its exploration, has not yet been plumbed.

Goblin Market

Morning and evening
Maids heard the goblins cry:
"Come buy our orchard fruits,
Come buy, come buy:
5 Apples and quinces,
Lemons and oranges,
Plump unpecked cherries,
Melons and raspberries,
Bloom-down-cheeked peaches,
10 Swart°-headed mulberries,   *dark*
Wild free-born cranberries,
Crabapples, dewberries,
Pine-apples, blackberries,
Apricots, strawberries;—
15 All ripe together
In summer weather,—
Morns that pass by,
Fair eves that fly;
Come buy, come buy:
20 Our grapes fresh from the vine,
Pomegranates full and fine,
Dates and sharp bullaces,
Rare pears and greengages,
Damsons[1] and bilberries
25 Taste them and try:
Currants and gooseberries,
Bright-fire-like barberries,[2]

---

[1] *bullaces ... Damsons* Bullaces, greengages, and damsons are all varieties of plums.

[2] *barberries* Red, acidic berries, used in cooking for their sour flavor.

Figs to fill your mouth,
Citrons from the South,
30 Sweet to tongue and sound to eye;
Come buy, come buy."

Evening by evening
Among the brookside rushes,
Laura bowed her head to hear,
35 Lizzie veiled her blushes:
Crouching close together
In the cooling weather,
With clasping arms and cautioning lips,
With tingling cheeks and finger tips.
40 "Lie close," Laura said,
Pricking up her golden head:
"We must not look at goblin men,
We must not buy their fruits:
Who knows upon what soil they fed
45 Their hungry thirsty roots?"
"Come buy," call the goblins
Hobbling down the glen.
"Oh," cried Lizzie, "Laura, Laura,
You should not peep at goblin men."
50 Lizzie covered up her eyes,
Covered close lest they should look;
Laura reared her glossy head,
And whispered like the restless brook:
"Look, Lizzie, look, Lizzie,
55 Down the glen tramp little men.
One hauls a basket,
One bears a plate,
One lugs a golden dish
Of many pounds weight.
60 How fair the vine must grow
Whose grapes are so luscious;
How warm the wind must blow
Through those fruit bushes."
"No," said Lizzie: "No, no, no;
65 Their offers should not charm us,
Their evil gifts would harm us."
She thrust a dimpled finger
In each ear, shut eyes and ran:
Curious Laura chose to linger

70 Wondering at each merchant man.
One had a cat's face,
One whisked a tail,
One tramped at a rat's pace,
One crawled like a snail,
75 One like a wombat prowled obtuse and furry,
One like a ratel° tumbled hurry skurry.   *badger*
She heard a voice like voice of doves
Cooing all together:
They sounded kind and full of loves
80 In the pleasant weather.

Laura stretched her gleaming neck
Like a rush-imbedded swan,
Like a lily from the beck,°   *stream*
Like a moonlit poplar branch,
85 Like a vessel at the launch
When its last restraint is gone.

Backwards up the mossy glen
Turned and trooped the goblin men,
With their shrill repeated cry,
90 "Come buy, come buy."
When they reached where Laura was
They stood stock still upon the moss,
Leering at each other,
Brother with queer brother;
95 Signalling each other,
Brother with sly brother.
One set his basket down,
One reared his plate;
One began to weave a crown
100 Of tendrils, leaves, and rough nuts brown
(Men sell not such in any town);
One heaved the golden weight
Of dish and fruit to offer her:
"Come buy, come buy," was still their cry.
105 Laura stared but did not stir,
Longed but had no money:
The whisk-tailed merchant bade her taste
In tones as smooth as honey,
The cat-faced purr'd,
110 The rat-paced spoke a word

Of welcome, and the snail-paced even was heard;
One parrot-voiced and jolly
Cried "Pretty Goblin" still for "Pretty Polly";—
One whistled like a bird.

115 But sweet-tooth Laura spoke in haste:
"Good Folk, I have no coin;
To take were to purloin:
I have no copper in my purse,
I have no silver either,
120 And all my gold is on the furze°   *evergreen shrub*
That shakes in windy weather
Above the rusty heather."
"You have much gold upon your head,"
They answered all together:
125 "Buy from us with a golden curl."
She clipped a precious golden lock,
She dropped a tear more rare than pearl,
Then sucked their fruit globes fair or red.
Sweeter than honey from the rock,[1]
130 Stronger than man-rejoicing wine,
Clearer than water flowed that juice;
She never tasted such before,
How should it cloy with length of use?
She sucked and sucked and sucked the more
135 Fruits which that unknown orchard bore;
She sucked until her lips were sore;
Then flung the emptied rinds away
But gathered up one kernel-stone,
And knew not was it night or day
140 As she turned home alone.

Lizzie met her at the gate
Full of wise upbraidings:
"Dear, you should not stay so late,
Twilight is not good for maidens;
145 Should not loiter in the glen
In the haunts of goblin men.
Do you not remember Jeanie,
How she met them in the moonlight,
Took their gifts both choice and many,
150 Ate their fruits and wore their flowers

Plucked from bowers
Where summer ripens at all hours?
But ever in the noonlight
She pined and pined away;
155 Sought them by night and day,
Found them no more but dwindled and grew grey;
Then fell with the first snow,
While to this day no grass will grow
Where she lies low:
160 I planted daisies there a year ago
That never blow.°   *bloom*
You should not loiter so."
"Nay, hush," said Laura:
"Nay, hush, my sister:
165 I ate and ate my fill,
Yet my mouth waters still;
Tomorrow night I will
Buy more": and kissed her:
"Have done with sorrow;
170 I'll bring you plums tomorrow
Fresh on their mother twigs,
Cherries worth getting;
You cannot think what figs
My teeth have met in,
175 What melons icy cold
Piled on a dish of gold
Too huge for me to hold,
What peaches with a velvet nap,
Pellucid° grapes without one seed: *translucent*
180 Odorous indeed must be the mead
Whereon they grow, and pure the wave they drink
With lilies at the brink,
And sugar-sweet their sap."

Golden head by golden head,
185 Like two pigeons in one nest
Folded in each other's wings,
They lay down in their curtained bed:
Like two blossoms on one stem,
Like two flakes of new-fall'n snow,
190 Like two wands of ivory
Tipped with gold for awful° kings.   *awe-inspiring*
Moon and stars gazed in at them,

---

[1] *honey from the rock*   See Deuteronomy 32.13.

Wind sang to them lullaby,
Lumbering owls forbore to fly,
195 Not a bat flapped to and fro
Round their rest:
Cheek to cheek and breast to breast
Locked together in one nest.

Early in the morning
200 When the first cock crowed his warning,
Neat like bees, as sweet and busy,
Laura rose with Lizzie:
Fetched in honey, milked the cows,
Aired and set to rights the house,
205 Kneaded cakes of whitest wheat,
Cakes for dainty mouths to eat,
Next churned butter, whipped up cream,
Fed their poultry, sat and sewed;
Talked as modest maidens should:
210 Lizzie with an open heart,
Laura in an absent dream,
One content, one sick in part;
One warbling for the mere bright day's delight,
One longing for the night.

215 At length slow evening came:
They went with pitchers to the reedy brooks;
Lizzie most placid in her look,
Laura most like a leaping flame.
They drew the gurgling water from its deep.
220 Lizzie plucked purple and rich golden flags,°   irises
Then turning homeward said: "The sunset flushes
Those furthest loftiest crags;
Come Laura, not another maiden lags.
No wilful squirrel wags,
225 The beasts and birds are fast asleep."
But Laura loitered still among the rushes,
And said the bank was steep.

And said the hour was early still,
The dew not fall'n, the wind not chill;
230 Listening ever, but not catching
The customary cry,
"Come buy, come buy,"

With its iterated jingle
Of sugar-baited words:
235 Not for all her watching
Once discerning even one goblin
Racing, whisking, tumbling, hobbling—
Let alone the herds
That used to tramp along the glen,
240 In groups or single,
Of brisk fruit-merchant men.
Till Lizzie urged, "O Laura, come;
I hear the fruit-call, but I dare not look:
You should not loiter longer at this brook:
245 Come with me home.
The stars rise, the moon bends her arc,
Each glowworm winks her spark,
Let us get home before the night grows dark:
For clouds may gather
250 Though this is summer weather,
Put out the lights and drench us thro';
Then if we lost our way what should we do?"

Laura turned cold as stone
To find her sister heard that cry alone,
255 That goblin cry,
"Come buy our fruits, come buy."
Must she then buy no more such dainty fruit?
Must she no more such succous° pasture find,   juicy
Gone deaf and blind?
260 Her tree of life drooped from the root:
She said not one word in her heart's sore ache;
But peering through the dimness, nought discerning,
Trudged home, her pitcher dripping all the way;
So crept to bed, and lay
265 Silent till Lizzie slept;
Then sat up in a passionate yearning,
And gnashed her teeth for baulked desire, and wept
As if her heart would break.

Day after day, night after night,
270 Laura kept watch in vain
In sullen silence of exceeding pain.
She never caught again the goblin cry,
"Come buy, come buy"—

She never spied the goblin men
75 Hawking their fruits along the glen:
But when the noon waxed bright
Her hair grew thin and grey;
She dwindled, as the fair full moon doth turn
To swift decay and burn
80 Her fire away.

One day remembering her kernel-stone
She set it by a wall that faced the south;
Dewed it with tears, hoped for a root,
Watched for a waxing shoot,
85 But there came none.
It never saw the sun,
It never felt the trickling moisture run:
While with sunk eyes and faded mouth
She dreamed of melons, as a traveller sees
90 False waves in desert drouth°   drought
With shade of leaf-crowned trees,
And burns the thirstier in the sandful breeze.

She no more swept the house,
Tended the fowl or cows,
295 Fetched honey, kneaded cakes of wheat,
Brought water from the brook:
But sat down listless in the chimney-nook
And would not eat.

Tender Lizzie could not bear
300 To watch her sister's cankerous care,
Yet not to share.
She night and morning
Caught the goblins' cry:
"Come buy our orchard fruits,
305 Come buy, come buy:"—
Beside the brook, along the glen,
She heard the tramp of goblin men,
The voice and stir
Poor Laura could not hear;
310 Longed to buy fruit to comfort her,
But feared to pay too dear.
She thought of Jeanie in her grave,
Who should have been a bride;

But who for joys brides hope to have
315 Fell sick and died
In her gay prime,
In earliest winter time,
With the first glazing rime,°   frost
With the first snow-fall of crisp Winter time.

320 Till Laura dwindling
Seemed knocking at Death's door.
Then Lizzie weighed no more
Better and worse;
But put a silver penny in her purse,
325 Kissed Laura, crossed the heath with clumps of furze
At twilight, halted by the brook:
And for the first time in her life
Began to listen and look.

Laughed every goblin
330 When they spied her peeping:
Came towards her hobbling,
Flying, running, leaping,
Puffing and blowing,
Chuckling, clapping, crowing.
335 Clucking and gobbling,
Mopping and mowing,
Full of airs and graces,
Pulling wry faces,
Demure grimaces,
340 Cat-like and rat-like,
Ratel- and wombat-like,
Snail-paced in a hurry,
Parrot-voiced and whistler,
Helter skelter, hurry skurry,
345 Chattering like magpies,
Fluttering like pigeons,
Gliding like fishes,—
Hugged her and kissed her:
Squeezed and caressed her:
350 Stretched up their dishes,
Panniers,[1] and plates:
"Look at our apples
Russet and dun,

---

[1] *Panniers* Baskets, especially ones used in the transport of goods.

Bob at our cherries,
355   Bite at our peaches,
Citrons and dates,
Grapes for the asking,
Pears red with basking
Out in the sun,
360   Plums on their twigs;
Pluck them and suck them,—
Pomegranates, figs."

"Good folk," said Lizzie,
Mindful of Jeanie:
365   "Give me much and many"—
Held out her apron,
Tossed them her penny.
"Nay, take a seat with us,
Honour and eat with us,"
370   They answered grinning:
"Our feast is but beginning.
Night yet is early,
Warm and dew-pearly,
Wakeful and starry:
375   Such fruits as these
No man can carry;
Half their bloom would fly,
Half their dew would dry,
Half their flavour would pass by.
380   Sit down and feast with us,
Be welcome guest with us,
Cheer you and rest with us."—
"Thank you," said Lizzie: "But one waits
At home alone for me:
385   So without further parleying,°   *discussion*
If you will not sell me any
Of your fruits though much and many,
Give me back my silver penny
I tossed you for a fee."—
390   They began to scratch their pates,°   *heads*
No longer wagging, purring,
But visibly demurring,
Grunting and snarling.
One called her proud,
395   Cross-grained, uncivil;

Their tones waxed loud,
Their looks were evil.
Lashing their tails
They trod and hustled her,
400   Elbowed and jostled her,
Clawed with their nails,
Barking, mewing, hissing, mocking,
Tore her gown and soiled her stocking,
Twitched her hair out by the roots,
405   Stamped upon her tender feet,
Held her hands and squeezed their fruits
Against her mouth to make her eat.

White and golden Lizzie stood,
Like a lily in a flood,—
410   Like a rock of blue-veined stone
Lashed by tides obstreperously,—
Like a beacon left alone
In a hoary° roaring sea,   *silvery*
Sending up a golden fire,—
415   Like a fruit-crowned orange tree
White with blossoms honey-sweet
Sore beset by wasp and bee,—
Like a royal virgin town
Topped with gilded dome and spire
420   Close beleaguered by a fleet
Mad to tug her standard° down.   *flag*

One may lead a horse to water,
Twenty cannot make him drink.
Though the goblins cuffed and caught her,
425   Coaxed and fought her,
Bullied and besought her,
Scratched her, pinched her black as ink,
Kicked and knocked her,
Mauled and mocked her,
430   Lizzie uttered not a word;
Would not open lip from lip
Lest they should cram a mouthful in:
But laughed in heart to feel the drip
Of juice that syruped all her face,
435   And lodged in dimples of her chin,
And streaked her neck which quaked like curd.

At last the evil people,
Worn out by her resistance,
Flung back her penny, kicked their fruit
140 Along whichever road they took,
Not leaving root or stone or shoot;
Some writhed into the ground,
Some dived into the brook
With ring and ripple,
145 Some scudded on the gale without a sound,
Some vanished in the distance.

In a smart, ache, tingle,
Lizzie went her way;
Knew not was it night or day;
450 Sprang up the bank, tore through the furze,
Threaded copse° and dingle,°   *thicket / dell*
And heard her penny jingle
Bouncing in her purse,
Its bounce was music to her ear.
455 She ran and ran
As if she feared some goblin man
Dogged her with gibe or curse
Or something worse:
But not one goblin skurried after,
460 Nor was she pricked by fear;
The kind heart made her windy-paced
That urged her home quite out of breath with haste
And inward laughter.

She cried, "Laura," up the garden,
465 "Did you miss me?
Come and kiss me.
Never mind my bruises,
Hug me, kiss me, suck my juices
Squeezed from goblin fruits for you,
470 Goblin pulp and goblin dew.
Eat me, drink me, love me;
Laura, make much of me;
For your sake I have braved the glen
And had to do with goblin merchant men."

475 Laura started from her chair,
Flung her arms up in the air,

Clutched her hair:
"Lizzie, Lizzie, have you tasted
For my sake the fruit forbidden?
480 Must your light like mine be hidden,
Your young life like mine be wasted,
Undone in mine undoing,
And ruined in my ruin,
Thirsty, cankered, goblin-ridden?"—
485 She clung about her sister,
Kissed and kissed and kissed her:
Tears once again
Refreshed her shrunken eyes,
Dropping like rain
490 After long sultry drouth;
Shaking with aguish[1] fear, and pain,
She kissed and kissed her with a hungry mouth.

Her lips began to scorch,
That juice was wormwood[2] to her tongue,
495 She loathed the feast:
Writhing as one possessed she leaped and sung,
Rent all her robe, and wrung
Her hands in lamentable haste,
And beat her breast.
500 Her locks streamed like the torch
Borne by a racer at full speed,
Or like the mane of horses in their flight,
Or like an eagle when she stems the light
Straight toward the sun,
505 Or like a caged thing freed,
Or like a flying flag when armies run.

Swift fire spread through her veins, knocked at her
      heart,
Met the fire smouldering there
And overbore its lesser flame;
510 She gorged on bitterness without a name:
Ah! fool, to choose such part
Of soul-consuming care!
Sense failed in the mortal strife:
Like the watchtower of a town

---

1   *aguish* Feverish.

2   *wormwood* Type of bitter herb.

515   Which an earthquake shatters down,
       Like a lightning-stricken mast,
       Like a wind-uprooted tree
       Spun about,
       Like a foam-topped waterspout
520   Cast down headlong in the sea,
       She fell at last;
       Pleasure past and anguish past,
       Is it death or is it life?

       Life out of death.
525   That night long Lizzie watched by her,
       Counted her pulse's flagging stir,
       Felt for her breath,
       Held water to her lips, and cooled her face
       With tears and fanning leaves.
530   But when the first birds chirped about their eaves,
       And early reapers plodded to the place
       Of golden sheaves,
       And dew-wet grass
       Bowed in the morning winds so brisk to pass,
535   And new buds with new day
       Opened of cup-like lilies on the stream,
       Laura awoke as from a dream,
       Laughed in the innocent old way,
       Hugged Lizzie but not twice or thrice;
540   Her gleaming locks showed not one thread of grey,
       Her breath was sweet as May,
       And light danced in her eyes.

       Days, weeks, months, years
       Afterwards, when both were wives
545   With children of their own;
       Their mother-hearts beset with fears,
       Their lives bound up in tender lives;
       Laura would call the little ones
       And tell them of her early prime,
550   Those pleasant days long gone
       Of not-returning time:
       Would talk about the haunted glen,
       The wicked quaint fruit-merchant men,
       Their fruits like honey to the throat
555   But poison in the blood;
       (Men sell not such in any town):
       Would tell them how her sister stood
       In deadly peril to do her good,
       And win the fiery antidote:
560   Then joining hands to little hands
       Would bid them cling together,—
       "For there is no friend like a sister
       In calm or stormy weather;
       To cheer one on the tedious way,
565   To fetch one if one goes astray,
       To lift one if one totters down,
       To strengthen whilst one stands."
       —1862

IN CONTEXT

Illustrating *Goblin Market*

1862 Macmillan edition—illustration by D.G. Rossetti.

The first edition of *Goblin Market* appeared in 1862 with a frontispiece by the author's brother, the Pre-Raphaelite painter and poet Dante Gabriel Rossetti. The round inset above the drawing of sisters Laura and Lizzie depicts the goblins carrying their fruits to market. Another notable edition was that of 1893, with art nouveau illustrations by artist and writer Laurence Housman (brother of poet A.E. Housman).

Illustration by Laurence Housman from the 1893
Macmillan edition.

And one was blue with famine after love,
     Who like a harpstring snapped rang harsh and low
The burden of what those were singing of.
One shamed herself in love; one temperately
10   Grew gross in soulless love, a sluggish wife;
One famished died for love. Thus two of three
     Took death for love and won him after strife;
One droned in sweetness like a fattened bee:
     All on the threshold, yet all short of life.
—1862

Remember

Remember me when I am gone away,
     Gone far away into the silent land;
     When you can no more hold me by the hand,
Nor I half turn to go yet turning stay.
5   Remember me when no more day by day
     You tell me of our future that you planned:
     Only remember me; you understand
It will be late then to counsel or to pray.
Yet if you should forget me for a while
10   And afterwards remember, do not grieve:
     For if the darkness and corruption leave
     A vestige of the thoughts that once I had,
Better by far you should forget and smile
     Than that you should remember and be sad.
—1862

A Triad

Three sang of love together: one with lips
     Crimson, with cheeks and bosom in a glow,
Flushed to the yellow hair and finger tips;
     And one there sang who soft and smooth as snow
5   Bloomed like a tinted hyacinth at a show;

A Birthday

My heart is like a singing bird
     Whose nest is in a watered shoot;
My heart is like an apple tree
     Whose boughs are bent with thickset fruit;
5   My heart is like a rainbow shell
     That paddles in a halcyon° sea;   *calm*
My heart is gladder than all these
     Because my love is come to me.

Raise me a dais of silk and down;
10   Hang it with vair° and purple dyes;   *squirrel fur*
Carve it in doves and pomegranates,
       And peacocks with a hundred eyes;
Work it in gold and silver grapes,
       In leaves, and silver fleurs-de-lys;
15   Because the birthday of my life
       Is come, my love is come to me.
—1861

After Death

The curtains were half drawn, the floor was swept
       And strewn with rushes, rosemary and may
Lay thick upon the bed on which I lay,
Where thro' the lattice ivy-shadows crept.
5   He leaned above me, thinking that I slept
       And could not hear him; but I heard him say:
"Poor child, poor child": and as he turned away
Came a deep silence, and I knew he wept.
He did not touch the shroud, or raise the fold
10   That hid my face, or take my hand in his,
       Or ruffle the smooth pillows for my head:
       He did not love me living; but once dead
He pitied me; and very sweet it is
To know he still is warm tho' I am cold.
—1862

An Apple-Gathering

I plucked pink blossoms from mine apple tree
       And wore them all that evening in my hair:
Then in due season when I went to see
       I found no apples there.

5   With dangling basket all along the grass
       As I had come I went the selfsame track:
My neighbours mocked me while they saw me pass
       So empty-handed back.

Lilian and Lilias smiled in trudging by,
10   Their heaped-up basket teazed me like a jeer;
Sweet-voiced they sang beneath the sunset sky,
       Their mother's home was near.

Plump Gertrude passed me with her basket full,
       A stronger hand than hers helped it along;
15   A voice talked with her thro' the shadows cool
       More sweet to me than song.

Ah Willie, Willie, was my love less worth
       Than apples with their green leaves piled above?
I counted rosiest apples on the earth
20   Of far less worth than love.

So once it was with me you stooped to talk
       Laughing and listening in this very lane;
To think that by this way we used to walk
       We shall not walk again!

25   I let my neighbours pass me, ones and twos
       And groups; the latest said the night grew chill,
And hastened: but I loitered, while the dews
       Fell fast I loitered still.
—1862

Echo

Come to me in the silence of the night;
       Come in the speaking silence of a dream;
Come with soft rounded cheeks and eyes as bright
       As sunlight on a stream;
       Come back in tears,
5   O memory, hope, love of finished years.

O dream how sweet, too sweet, too bitter sweet,
       Whose wakening should have been in Paradise,
Where souls brimfull of love abide and meet;
10   Where thirsting longing eyes
       Watch the slow door
That opening, letting in, lets out no more.

Yet come to me in dreams, that I may live
　　My very life again tho' cold in death:
15　Come back to me in dreams, that I may give
　　　Pulse for pulse, breath for breath:
　　　　Speak low, lean low,
As long ago, my love, how long ago.
—1862

Winter: My Secret

I tell my secret? No indeed, not I:
　Perhaps some day, who knows?
But not today; it froze, and blows, and snows,
　And you're too curious: fie!
5　You want to hear it? well:
Only, my secret's mine, and I won't tell.

Or, after all, perhaps there's none:
Suppose there is no secret after all,
　But only just my fun.
10　Today's a nipping day, a biting day;
　In which one wants a shawl,
A veil, a cloak, and other wraps:
I cannot ope to every one who taps,
And let the draughts come whistling thro' my hall;
15　Come bounding and surrounding me,
Come buffeting, astounding me,
Nipping and clipping thro' my wraps and all.
I wear my mask for warmth: who ever shows
　His nose to Russian snows
20　To be pecked at by every wind that blows?
You would not peck? I thank you for good will,
Believe, but leave that truth untested still.

Spring's an expansive time: yet I don't trust
March with its peck of dust,
25　Nor April with its rainbow-crowned brief showers,
　Nor even May, whose flowers
One frost may wither thro' the sunless hours.

Perhaps some languid summer day,
When drowsy birds sing less and less,
30　And golden fruit is ripening to excess,
If there's not too much sun nor too much cloud,
And the warm wind is neither still nor loud,
Perhaps my secret I may say,
Or you may guess.
—1862

"No, Thank You, John"

I never said I loved you, John:
　Why will you teaze me day by day,
And wax a weariness to think upon
　With always "do" and "pray"?°   *please*

5　You know I never loved you, John;
　No fault of mine made me your toast:[1]
Why will you haunt me with a face as wan
　As shows an hour-old ghost?

I dare say Meg or Moll would take
10　Pity upon you, if you'd ask:
And pray don't remain single for my sake
　Who can't perform that task.

I have no heart?—Perhaps I have not;
　But then you're mad to take offence
15　That I don't give you what I have not got:
　Use your own common sense.

Let bygones be bygones:
　Don't call me false, who owed not to be true:
I'd rather answer "No" to fifty Johns
20　Than answer "Yes" to you.

Let's mar our pleasant days no more,
　Songbirds of passage, days of youth:
Catch at today, forget the days before:
　I'll wink at your untruth.

1　*your toast* I.e., the woman to whom John would raise a glass when toasting his lady.

25　Let us strike hands as hearty friends;
　　　　No more, no less; and friendship's good:
　　Only don't keep in view ulterior ends,
　　　　And points not understood

　　In open treaty. Rise above
30　　　Quibbles and shuffling off and on:
　　Here's friendship for you if you like; but love,—
　　　　No, thank you, John.
　　　　　—1862

A Pause of Thought

I looked for that which is not, nor can be,
　　And hope deferred made my heart sick in truth:
　　　But years must pass before a hope of youth
　　　　Is resigned utterly.

5　I watched and waited with a steadfast will:
　　　And though the object seemed to flee away
　　　That I so longed for, ever day by day
　　　　I watched and waited still.

　　Sometimes I said, "This thing shall be no more;
10　　My expectation wearies and shall cease;
　　　I will resign it now and be at peace:"
　　　　Yet never gave it o'er.

　　Sometimes I said, "It is an empty name
　　　I long for; to a name why should I give
15　　The peace of all the days I have to live?"—
　　　　Yet gave it all the same.

　　Alas, thou foolish one! alike unfit
　　　For healthy joy and salutary pain:
　　　Thou knowest the chase useless, and again
20　　　Turnest to follow it.
　　　　　—1848

Song

She sat and sang alway
　　By the green margin of a stream,
Watching the fishes leap and play
　　　Beneath the glad sunbeam.
5　I sat and wept alway
　　　Beneath the moon's most shadowy beam,
Watching the blossoms of the May
　　　Weep leaves into the stream.

　　I wept for memory;
10　　She sang for hope that is so fair:
My tears were swallowed by the sea;
　　　Her songs died on the air.
　　　　—1862

Song

When I am dead, my dearest,
　　　Sing no sad songs for me;
Plant thou no roses at my head,
　　　Nor shady cypress[1] tree.
5　Be the green grass above me
　　　With showers and dewdrops wet;
And if thou wilt, remember,
　　　And if thou wilt, forget.

　　I shall not see the shadows,
10　　I shall not feel the rain;
I shall not hear the nightingale
　　　Sing on as if in pain.
And dreaming through the twilight
　　　That doth not rise nor set,
15　Haply° I may remember,   *by chance*
　　　And haply may forget.
　　　　—1862

---

[1] *cypress* Type of coniferous tree long associated with mourning and death.

Dead before Death

Ah! changed and cold, how changed and very cold!
   With stiffened smiling lips and cold calm eyes:
      Changed, yet the same; much knowing, little wise;
This was the promise of the days of old!
5 Grown hard and stubborn in the ancient mould,
      Grown rigid in the sham of lifelong lies:
      We hoped for better things as years would rise,
But it is over as a tale once told.
All fallen the blossom that no fruitage bore,
10   All lost the present and the future time,
All lost, all lost, the lapse that went before:
So lost till death shut-to the opened door,
      So lost from chime to everlasting chime,
So cold and lost for ever evermore.
      —1862

Monna Innominata [1]
A Sonnet of Sonnets

Beatrice, immortalized by "*altissimo poeta … cotanto amante*";[2] Laura, celebrated by a great though an inferior bard[3]—have alike paid the exceptional penalty of exceptional honour, and have come down to us resplendent with charms, but (at least, to my apprehension) scant of attractiveness.

   These heroines of worldwide fame were preceded by a bevy of unnamed ladies "*donne innominate*" sung by a school of less conspicuous poets; and in that land and that period which gave simultaneous birth to Catholics, to Albigenses, and to Troubadours,[4] one can imagine many a lady as sharing her lover's poetic aptitude, while the barrier between them might be one held sacred by

both, yet not such as to render mutual love incompatible with mutual honour.

   Had such a lady spoken for herself, the portrait left us might have appeared more tender, if less dignified, than any drawn even by a devoted friend. Or had the Great Poetess[5] of our own day and nation only been unhappy instead of happy, her circumstances would have invited her to bequeath to us, in lieu of the "Portuguese Sonnets," an inimitable "*donna innominata*" drawn not from fancy but from feeling, and worthy to occupy a niche beside Beatrice and Laura.

1

"Lo dì che han detto a' dolci amici addio."—DANTE
"Amor, con quanto sforzo oggi mi vinci!"—PETRARCA [6]

Come back to me, who wait and watch for you:—
   Or come not yet, for it is over then,
      And long it is before you come again,
So far between my pleasures are and few.
5 While, when you come not, what I do I do
      Thinking "Now when he comes," my sweetest "when":
      For one man is my world of all the men
This wide world holds; O love, my world is you.
Howbeit, to meet you grows almost a pang
10   Because the pang of parting comes so soon;
      My hope hangs waning, waxing, like a moon
         Between the heavenly days on which we meet:
Ah me, but where are now the songs I sang
      When life was sweet because you called them sweet?

2

"Era già l'ora che volge il desio."—DANTE
"Ricorro al tempo ch' io vi vidi prima."—PETRARCA[7]

I wish I could remember that first day,
   First hour, first moment of your meeting me,

---

[1]   *Monna Innominata*   Italian: Unnamed Lady.

[2]   *altissimo poeta … cotanto amante*   Italian: loftiest poet … equally great lover. Rossetti refers to Italian poet Dante Alighieri (1265–1321), whose muse was Beatrice.

[3]   *great … bard*   Italian poet Francesco Petrarca (1304–74) wrote sonnets dedicated to Laura.

[4]   *Albigenses*   Albigensians were members of a religious sect of the twelfth and thirteenth centuries; *Troubadours*   Wandering lyric poets of the eleventh to thirteenth centuries.

---

[5]   *Great Poetess*   Elizabeth Barrett Browning.

[6]   *DANTE*   From *Purgatorio* 8.3: "Who in the morn have bid sweet friends farewell"; *PETRARCA*   From *Canzone* 85.12: "Love, with what forces you conquer me now!"

[7]   *DANTE*   From *Purgatorio* 8.1: "Now was the hour that wakens fond desire"; *PETRARCA*   From Sonnet 20.3: "I remember when I saw you for the first time."

If bright or dim the season, it might be
  Summer or winter for aught I can say;
5 So unrecorded did it slip away,
  So blind was I to see and to foresee,
  So dull to mark the budding of my tree
That would not blossom yet for many a May.
If only I could recollect it, such
10 A day of days! I let it come and go
  As traceless as a thaw of bygone snow;
It seemed to mean so little, meant so much;
If only now I could recall that touch,
  First touch of hand in hand—Did one but know!

3

"O ombre vane, fuor che ne l'aspetto!"—DANTE
"Immaginata guida la conduce."—PETRARCA[1]

I dream of you to wake: would that I might
  Dream of you and not wake but slumber on;
  Nor find with dreams the dear companion gone,
As summer ended summer birds take flight.
5 In happy dreams I hold you full in sight,
  I blush again who waking look so wan;
  Brighter than sunniest day that ever shone,
In happy dreams your smile makes day of night.
Thus only in a dream we are at one,
10 Thus only in a dream we give and take
    The faith that maketh rich who take or give;
  If thus to sleep is sweeter than to wake,
    To die were surely sweeter than to live,
Tho' there be nothing new beneath the sun.

4

"Poca favilla gran fiamma seconda."—DANTE
"Ogni altra cosa, ogni pensier va fore,
  E sol ivi con voi rimansi amore."—PETRARCA[2]

I loved you first: but afterwards your love,
  Outsoaring mine, sang such a loftier song
As drowned the friendly cooings of my dove.
  Which owes the other most? My love was long,
5 And yours one moment seemed to wax° *grow*
    more strong;
I loved and guessed at you, you construed me
And loved me for what might or might not be—
  Nay, weights and measures do us both a wrong.
For verily love knows not "mine" or "thine";
10 With separate "I" and "thou" free love has done,
    For one is both and both are one in love:
Rich love knows nought of "thine that is not mine";
    Both have the strength and both the length
      thereof,
  Both of us, of the love which makes us one.

5

"Amor che a nullo amato amar perdona."—DANTE
"Amor m'addusse in sì gioiosa spene."—PETRARCA[3]

O my heart's heart, and you who are to me
  More than myself myself, God be with you,
  Keep you in strong obedience leal° and true *loyal*
To Him whose noble service setteth free;
5 Give you all good we see or can foresee,
  Make your joys many and your sorrows few,
  Bless you in what you bear and what you do,
Yea, perfect you as He would have you be.
So much for you; but what for me, dear friend?
10 To love you without stint and all I can
Today, tomorrow, world without an end;
    To love you much and yet to love you more,
  As Jordan[4] at his flood sweeps either shore;
Since woman is the helpmeet made for man.[5]

---

[1] DANTE From *Purgatorio* 2.79: "Oh vain shadows, except in outward aspect"; PETRARCA From *Canzone* 277.9: "An imagined guide leads her."

[2] DANTE From *Paradiso* 1.34: "From a small spark a great flame rises"; PETRARCA From *Canzone* 72.44–45: "All other hopes, all other thoughts are gone, and love with you remains there alone."

[3] DANTE From *Inferno* 5.103: "Love, that denial takes from none beloved"; PETRARCA From Sonnet 56.11: "Love urged me in this gladness to believe."

[4] *Jordan* The River Jordan, in the Middle East, is significant to Christianity and Judaism.

[5] *woman … for man* See Genesis 2.18: "And the Lord God said, It is not good that the man should be alone; I will make him an help meet for him."

6

> "Or puoi la quantitate
> Comprender de l'amor che a te mi scalda."—DANTE
> "Non vo'che da tal nodo amor mi sciolglia."—PETRARCA[1]

Trust me, I have not earned your dear rebuke,
  I love, as you would have me, God the most;
  Would lose not Him, but you, must one be lost,
Nor with Lot's wife cast back a faithless look,[2]
5 Unready to forego what I forsook;
  This say I, having counted up the cost,
  This, tho' I be the feeblest of God's host,
The sorriest sheep Christ shepherds with His crook.
Yet while I love my God the most, I deem
10   That I can never love you overmuch;
    I love Him more, so let me love you too;
  Yea, as I apprehend it, love is such
I cannot love you if I love not Him,
    I cannot love Him if I love not you.

7

> "Qui primavera sempre ed ogni frutto."—DANTE
> "Ragionando con meco ed io con lui."—PETRARCA[3]

"Love me, for I love you"—and answer me,
  "Love me, for I love you": so shall we stand
  As happy equals in the flowering land
Of love, that knows not a dividing sea.
5 Love builds the house on rock and not on sand,
  Love laughs what while the winds rave desperately;
  And who hath found love's citadel unmanned?
    And who hath held in bonds love's liberty?—
My heart's a coward tho' my words are brave—
10   We meet so seldom, yet we surely part
    So often; there's a problem for your art!
  Still I find comfort in his Book, who saith,

Tho' jealousy be cruel as the grave,
  And death be strong, yet love is strong as death.[4]

8

> "Come dicesse a Dio, D'altro non calme."—DANTE
> "Spero trovar pietà non che perdono."—PETRARCA[5]

"I, if I perish, perish"—Esther spake:[6]
  And bride of life or death she made her fair
  In all the lustre of her perfumed hair
And smiles that kindle longing but to slake.
5 She put on pomp of loveliness, to take
  Her husband through his eyes at unaware;
  She spread abroad her beauty for a snare,
Harmless as doves and subtle as a snake.
She trapped him with one mesh of silken hair,
10   She vanquished him by wisdom of her wit,
    And built her people's house that it should
      stand:—
    If I might take my life so in my hand,
And for my love to Love put up my prayer,
  And for love's sake by Love be granted it!

9

> "O dignitosa coscienza e netta!"—DANTE
> "Spirto più acceso di virtuti ardenti."—PETRARCA[7]

Thinking of you, and all that was, and all
  That might have been and now can never be,
  I feel your honoured excellence, and see
Myself unworthy of the happier call:

---

[1] *DANTE* From *Purgatorio* 21.133–34: "Now has thou proved the force and ardor of the love I bear thee"; *PETRARCA* From *Canzone* 59.17: "I do not wish love to release me from this knot."

[2] *Lot's wife … look* See Genesis 19.26: "[Lot's] wife looked back from behind him, and she became a pillar of salt."

[3] *DANTE* From *Purgatorio* 28.143: "Perpetual spring and every fruit"; *PETRARCA* From *Canzone* 35.14: "Speaking with me and I with him."

[4] *his Book … death* See The Song of Solomon 6: "Set me as a seal upon your heart, as a seal upon your arm; for love is strong as death, passion fierce as the grave."

[5] *DANTE* From *Purgatorio* 8.12: "As if telling God, 'I care for nothing else'"; *PETRARCA* From *Canzone* 1.8: "I hope to find pity, not just forgiveness."

[6] *I … spake* From Esther 4.16, in which Queen Esther says to Mordecai, before donning beautiful robes and appealing to her husband to cease his mission to kill her people, the Jews: "Go, gather together all the Jews … and neither eat nor drink three days, night or day: I also and my maidens will fast likewise; and so will I go in unto the king, which is not according to the law: and if I perish, I perish."

[7] *DANTE* From *Purgatorio* 3.8: "Oh conscience clear and upright!"; *PETRARCA* From *Canzone* 283.3: "Spirit dazzling with blazing virtues."

5 For woe is me who walk so apt to fall,
     So apt to shrink afraid, so apt to flee,
     Apt to lie down and die (ah woe is me!)
  Faithless and hopeless turning to the wall.
  And yet not hopeless quite nor faithless quite,
10 Because not loveless; love may toil all night,
     But take at morning; wrestle till the break
       Of day, but then wield power with God and
         man:—
     So take I heart of grace as best I can,
  Ready to spend and be spent for your sake.

10

"Con miglior corso e con migliore stella."—DANTE
"La vita fugge e non s'arresta un' ora."—PETRARCA[1]

Time flies, hope flags, life plies a wearied wing;
     Death following hard on life gains ground apace;
     Faith runs with each and rears an eager face,
  Outruns the rest, makes light of everything,
5 Spurns earth, and still finds breath to pray and sing;
     While love ahead of all uplifts his praise,
     Still asks for grace and still gives thanks for grace,
  Content with all day brings and night will bring.
  Life wanes; and when love folds his wings above
10   Tired hope, and less we feel his conscious pulse,
       Let us go fall asleep, dear friend, in peace:
       A little while, and age and sorrow cease;
     A little while, and life reborn annuls
  Loss and decay and death, and all is love.

11

"Vien dietro a me e lascia dir le genti."—DANTE
"Contando i casi della vita nostra."—PETRARCA[2]

Many in aftertimes will say of you
     "He loved her"—while of me what will they say?
     Not that I loved you more than just in play,

For fashion's sake as idle women do.
5 Even let them prate; who know not what we knew
     Of love and parting in exceeding pain,
     Of parting hopeless here to meet again,
  Hopeless on earth, and heaven is out of view.
  But by my heart of love laid bare to you,
10   My love that you can make not void nor vain,
  Love that foregoes you but to claim anew
       Beyond this passage of the gate of death,
     I charge you at the Judgment make it plain
       My love of you was life and not a breath.

12

"Amor, che ne la mente mi ragiona."—DANTE
"Amor vien nel bel viso di costei."—PETRARCA[3]

If there be any one can take my place
     And make you happy whom I grieve to grieve,
     Think not that I can grudge it, but believe
  I do commend you to that nobler grace,
5 That readier wit than mine, that sweeter face;
     Yea, since your riches make me rich, conceive
     I too am crowned, while bridal crowns I weave,
  And thread the bridal dance with jocund° pace.   *merry*
  For if I did not love you, it might be
10   That I should grudge you some one dear delight;
       But since the heart is yours that was mine own,
     Your pleasure is my pleasure, right my right,
  Your honourable freedom makes me free,
       And you companioned I am not alone.

13

"E drizzeremo glí occhi al Primo Amore."—DANTE
"Ma trovo peso non de le mie braccia."—PETRARCA[4]

If I could trust mine own self with your fate,
     Shall I not rather trust it in God's hand?
     Without Whose Will one lily doth not stand,

---

[1] *DANTE* From *Paradiso* 1.40: "In best course and in happiest constellation"; *PETRARCA* From *Canzone* 272.1: "Life flies and doesn't stay for an hour."

[2] *DANTE* From *Purgatorio* 5.13: "Come after me, and leave behind the people's babblings"; *PETRARCA* From *Canzone* 285.12: "Telling of the changes in our lives."

[3] *DANTE* From *Purgatorio* 2.112: "Love that discourses in my thoughts"; *PETRARCA* From *Canzone* 13.2: "Love appears in the beautiful face of this lady."

[4] *DANTE* From *Paradiso* 32.142: "And our eyes will turn unto the First Love"; *PETRARCA* From Sonnet 20.5: "The burden I find too great a weight for my arms."

Nor sparrow fall at His appointed date;
5   Who numbereth the innumerable sand,
Who weighs the wind and water with a weight,
To Whom the world is neither small nor great,
      Whose knowledge foreknew every plan we planned.
Searching my heart for all that touches you,
10   I find there only love and love's goodwill
Helpless to help and impotent to do,
            Of understanding dull, of sight most dim;
            And therefore I commend you back to Him
      Whose love your love's capacity can fill.

14
"E la Sua Volontade è nostra pace."—DANTE
"Sol con questi pensier, con altre chiome."—PETRARCA[1]

Youth gone, and beauty gone if ever there
      Dwelt beauty in so poor a face as this;
      Youth gone and beauty, what remains of bliss?
I will not bind fresh roses in my hair,
5 To shame a cheek at best but little fair,—
      Leave youth his roses, who can bear a thorn,—
I will not seek for blossoms anywhere,
      Except such common flowers as blow with corn.[2]
Youth gone and beauty gone, what doth remain?
10   The longing of a heart pent up forlorn,
            A silent heart whose silence loves and longs;
            The silence of a heart which sang its songs
      While youth and beauty made a summer morn,
Silence of love that cannot sing again.
—1881

Cobwebs

It is a land with neither night nor day,
Nor heat nor cold, nor any wind, nor rain,
      Nor hills nor valleys; but one even plain
Stretches thro' long unbroken miles away:

While thro' the sluggish air a twilight grey
5
      Broodeth; no moons or seasons wax and wane,
      No ebb and flow are there along the main,°   sea
No bud-time no leaf-falling there for aye,°   any
No ripple on the sea, no shifting sand,
10   No beat of wings to stir the stagnant space,
No pulse of life thro' all the loveless land:
And loveless sea; no trace of days before,
      No guarded home, no toil-won resting place
No future hope no fear for evermore.
—1896 (WRITTEN 1855)

Dante Gabriel Rossetti's *Beata Beatrix*, 1864–70.

In an Artist's Studio

One face[3] looks out from all his canvasses,
      One selfsame figure sits or walks or leans:
      We found her hidden just behind those screens,
That mirror gave back all her loveliness.

---

[1] *DANTE* From *Paradiso* 3.85: "And in his will is our tranquility";
PETRARCA From *Canzone* 30.32: "Alone with these thoughts, with
time-altered locks of hair."

[2] *blow* Blossom; *corn* Grain.

[3] *One face* I.e., Elizabeth (Lizzie) Siddal's. Siddal (1829–62) was
D.G. Rossetti's model for *Beata Beatrix* and many other paintings; the
two eventually married. She was a poet and artist in her own right.

5   A queen in opal or in ruby dress,
           A nameless girl in freshest summer-greens,
           A saint, an angel;—every canvass means
       The same one meaning, neither more nor less.
       He feeds upon her face by day and night,
10   And she with true kind eyes looks back on him,
       Fair as the moon and joyful as the light:
           Not wan with waiting, nor with sorrow dim;
       Not as she is, but was when hope shone bright;
           Not as she is, but as she fills his dream.
       —1896

Promises like Pie-Crust[1]

Promise me no promises,
    So will I not promise you;
Keep we both our liberties,
    Never false and never true:
5 Let us hold the die uncast,
    Free to come as free to go;
For I cannot know your past,
    And of mine what can you know?

You, so warm, may once have been
10   Warmer towards another one;
I, so cold, may once have seen
    Sunlight, once have felt the sun:
Who shall show us if it was
    Thus indeed in time of old?
15 Fades the image from the glass
    And the fortune is not told.

If you promised, you might grieve
    For lost liberty again;
If I promised, I believe
20   I should fret to break the chain:
Let us be the friends we were,
    Nothing more but nothing less;
Many thrive on frugal fare
    Who would perish of excess.
—1896 (WRITTEN 1861)

---

[1] *Promises like Pie-Crust*   See Jonathan Swift's comment: "Promises and pie-crust are made to be broken."

In Progress

Ten years ago it seemed impossible
    That she should ever grow so calm as this,
    With self-remembrance in her warmest kiss
And dim dried eyes like an exhausted well.
5 Slow-speaking when she has some fact to tell,
    Silent with long-unbroken silences,
    Centred in self yet not unpleased to please,
Gravely monotonous like a passing bell.
Mindful of drudging daily common things,
10   Patient at pastime, patient at her work,
Wearied perhaps but strenuous certainly.
Sometimes I fancy we may one day see
    Her head shoot forth seven stars from where they
        lurk
And her eyes lightnings and her shoulders wings.
—1896

Sleeping at Last

Sleeping at last, the trouble & tumult over,
    Sleeping at last, the struggle & horror past,
Cold & white out of sight of friend & of lover
Sleeping at last.

5 No more a tired heart downcast or overcast,
No more pangs that wring or shifting fears that hover,
Sleeping at last in a dreamless sleep locked fast.

Fast asleep. Singing birds in their leafy cover
Cannot wake her, nor shake her gusty blast.
10 Under the purple thyme & the purple clover
Sleeping at last.
—1896

LEWIS CARROLL
1832 – 1898

Charles Dodgson (better known by his pseudonym, "Lewis Carroll") created some of his era's most beloved and enduring literature for children. *Alice's Adventures in Wonderland* and *Through the Looking-Glass* have remained perennially popular since their first publication. His famously frustrated protagonist, who engages in bewildering exchanges with such memorable characters as the Mad Hatter, the Cheshire Cat, the March Hare, and the Mock Turtle, is as familiar a figure as any character in nineteenth-century fiction.

Charles Lutwidge Dodgson was the third of eleven children born to Frances Jane Lutwidge and the Reverend Charles Dodgson, who was a mathematician and later a curate in Daresbury, Cheshire. Because they lived in a remote village, the Dodgson children were largely schooled at home and relied on one another for amusement; Charles contributed many stories and drawings to their various family magazines. He became a fine student when he later entered boarding school, winning many awards and scholarships.

Dodgson continued to excel at Oxford University, where he followed in his father's footsteps and took first place honors in mathematics. He thereafter spent almost his entire life as a lecturer in mathematics at Oxford, where he was given a lifetime fellowship, with the stipulation that he enter the ministry and refrain from marrying. During his early years there, he took up the then-new art of photography as a hobby and devoted himself to taking exquisite photographs—primarily of children, although he later also became known for his portraits of famous literary figures, Alfred, Lord Tennyson and Dante Gabriel Rossetti among them.

Dodgson eventually became acquainted with the family of Henry Liddell, who was then Dean of Christ Church College. As he had done with many other children, Dodgson endeared himself to the three Liddell daughters by weaving elaborate tales for their amusement. On one occasion, Dodgson and a friend took advantage of a beautiful summer's day to go boating down the Thames with the Liddell girls. During the outing Dodgson began making up the story of Alice's adventures underground, wherein Alice goes down a rabbit hole and meets various characters that both fascinate and confound her. He later often looked back upon this day wistfully, as when he wrote of the "birth" of the Alice of his tales: "I can call it up almost as clearly as if it were yesterday—the cloudless blue above, the watery mirror below, the boat drifting idly on its way, the tinkle of the drops that fell from the oars … the three eager faces, hungry for news of fairy-land, and who would not be said 'nay' to: from whose lips 'Tell us a story, please,' had all the stern immutability of Fate!"

After Dodgson had complied with Alice Liddell's request to write up the story for her, Henry Kingsley (brother of novelist Charles Kingsley) saw the manuscript and persuaded him to publish it. Having already published several books on mathematics under his own name, he took the name Lewis, which he anglicized from "Ludovicus," the Latin word for "Lutwidge," and Carroll from "Carolus," Latin for "Charles." *Alice's Adventures in Wonderland* appeared in 1865 with illustrations by *Punch* cartoonist John Tenniel. From that point on, Lewis Carroll's fame far surpassed that of Charles Dodgson. In 1872 he published the sequel *Through the Looking-Glass and What Alice Found There*, which continued the tale of Alice as she passes through a mirror and finds herself engaged as a pawn in a topsy-turvy game of chess.

By the time *Through the Looking-Glass* was published, Dodgson was entirely estranged from the Liddells. The reason for this remains unclear, as the relevant pages were removed from Dodgson's diary; some scholars have since suggested that Carroll was sexually attracted to children and the break occurred as a result of his romantic interest in Alice. Other scholars argue that he had no such interest and offer different explanations for the estrangement, including the possibility that he had been caught in romantic pursuit of the Liddells' governess. The former critics tend to see undertones of sexual desire in Carroll's photographs and literary portrayals of girl children, while the latter tend to interpret the same elements as reflective of typical Victorian aesthetics and attitudes regarding childhood.

Carroll later wrote three books of nonsense poems, including *The Hunting of the Snark* (1876). He also published *Sylvie and Bruno* and *Sylvie and Bruno Concluded* (1889 and 1893), but the novel and its sequel never achieved the fame of the Alice series. The author died of bronchitis in 1898; he is buried in a cemetery near the home he bought for his family in Surrey.

⌘⌘⌘

Verses Recited by Humpty Dumpty[1]

In winter when the fields are white,
I sing this song for your delight.

In spring, when woods are getting green,
I'll try and tell you what I mean.

5   In summer, when the days are long,
Perhaps you'll understand the song.

In autumn, when the leaves are brown,
Take pen and ink and write it down.

I sent a message to the fish:
10 I told them "This is what I wish."

The little fishes of the sea,
They sent an answer back to me.

The little fishes' answer was
"We cannot do it, sir, because."

15 I sent to them again to say
"It will be better to obey."

The fishes answered with a grin,
"Why, what a temper you are in!"

I told them once, I told them twice;
20 They would not listen to advice.

I took a kettle large and new,
Fit for the deed I had to do.

My heart went hop, my heart went thump;
I filled the kettle at the pump.

25 Then someone came to me and said,
"The little fishes are in bed."

I said to him, I said it plain,
"Then you must wake them up again."

I said it very loud and clear;
30 I went and shouted in his ear.

---

[1] *Verses ... Dumpty* From *Through the Looking-Glass and What Alice Found There*, Ch. 6: "Humpty Dumpty."

But he was very stiff and proud;
He said, "You needn't shout so loud!"

And he was very proud and stiff;
He said, "I'd go and wake them, if ——"

35   I took a corkscrew from the shelf;
I went to wake them up myself.

And when I found the door was locked,
I pulled and pushed and kicked and knocked.

And when I found the door was shut,
40   I tried to turn the handle, but ——
("That's all," said Humpty Dumpty.)
    —1872

Jabberwocky[1]

'Twas brillig and the slithy toves
    Did gyre and gimble in the wabe;
All mimsy were the borogroves,
    And the mome raths outgrabe.

5   "Beware the Jabberwock, my son!
    The jaws that bite, the claws that catch!
Beware the Jubjub bird, and shun
    The frumious Bandersnatch!"

He took his vorpal sword in hand:
10   Long time the manxome foe he sought—
So rested he by the Tumtum tree.
    And stood awhile in thought.

And as in uffish thought he stood,
    The Jabberwock, with eyes of flame,
15   Came whiffling through the tulgey wood,
    And burbled as it came!

John Tenniel, *Slaying the Jabberwock*, from
Lewis Carroll, *Through the Looking-Glass*, 1872.

One, two! One, two! And through and through
    The vorpal blade went snicker-snack!
He left it dead, and with its head
20   He went galumphing back.

"And hast thou slain the Jabberwock?
    Come to my arms, my beamish boy!
O frabjous day! Callooh! Callay!"
    He chortled in his joy.

25   'Twas brillig and the slithy toves
    Did gyre and gimble in the wabe;
All mimsy were the borogroves,
    And the mome raths outgrabe.
    —1872

---

[1] *Jabberwocky* From *Through the Looking-Glass and What Alice
Found There*, Ch. 1: "Looking-Glass House."

IN CONTEXT

"Jabberwocky"

The poem "Jabberwocky" appears in the first chapter of *Through the Looking-Glass and What Alice Found There*. The first of the following excerpts provides the surrounding context in that chapter; the second is an excerpt from later in the book, when the poem is again discussed.

from Lewis Carroll, *Through the Looking-Glass and What Alice Found There* (1872)

from CHAPTER 1: LOOKING-GLASS HOUSE

There was a book lying near Alice on the table, and while she sat watching the White King (for she was still a little anxious about him, and had the ink all ready to throw over him, in case he fainted again), she turned over the leaves, to find some part that she could read, "—for it's all in some language I don't know," she said to herself.

It was like this.

> YKCOWREBBAJ
>
> sevot yhtils eht dna ,gillirb sawT'
> ebaw eht ni elbmig dna eryg diD
> ,sevorgorob eht erew ysmim llA
> .ebargtuo shtar emom eht dnA

She puzzled over this for some time, but at last a bright thought struck her. "Why, it's a looking-glass book, of course! And if I hold it up to a glass, the words will all go the right way again."

This was the poem that Alice read.

[Here the poem appears.]

"It seems very pretty," she said when she had finished it, "but it's rather hard to understand." (You see she didn't like to confess, even to herself, that she couldn't make it out at all.) "Somehow it seems to fill my head with ideas—only I don't exactly know what they are! However, somebody killed something: that's clear, at any rate—."

from CHAPTER 6: HUMPTY DUMPTY

"You seem very clever at explaining words, sir," said Alice. "Would you kindly tell me the meaning of the poem called 'Jabberwocky'?"

"Let's hear it," said Humpty Dumpty. "I can explain all the poems that ever were invented—and a good many that haven't been invented just yet."

This sounded very hopeful, so Alice repeated the first verse:

> "'Twas brillig, and the slithy toves
> Did gyre and gimble in the wabe;
> All mimsy were the borogroves,
> And the mome raths outgrabe."

"That's enough to begin with," Humpty Dumpty interrupted: "there are plenty of hard words there. '*Brillig*' means four o'clock in the afternoon—the time when you begin *broiling* things for dinner."

"That'll do very well," said Alice: "and '*slithy*'?"

"Well, '*slithy*' means 'lithe and slimy.' 'Lithe' is the same as 'active.' You see it's like a portmanteau[1]—there are two meanings packed up into one word."

"I see it now," Alice remarked thoughtfully: "and what about '*toves*'?"

"Well, '*toves*' are something like badgers—they're something like lizards—and they're something like corkscrews."

"They must be very curious-looking creatures."

"They are that," said Humpty Dumpty: "also they made their nests under sundials—also they live on cheese."

"And what's to '*gyre*' and to '*gimble*'?"

"To '*gyre*' is to go round and round like a gyroscope. To '*gimble*' is to make holes like a gimlet."[2]

"And 'the *wabe*' is the grass plot round a sundial, I suppose?" said Alice, surprised at her own ingenuity.

"Of course it is. It's called '*wabe*,' you know, because it goes a long way before it, and a long way behind it——"

"And a long way beyond it on each side," Alice added.

"Exactly so. Well, then, '*mimsy*' is 'flimsy and miserable' (there's another portmanteau for you). And a '*borogrove*' is a thin, shabby-looking bird with its feathers sticking out all round—something like a live mop."

"And then '*mome raths*'?" said Alice. "If I'm not giving you too much trouble."

"Well, a '*rath*' is a sort of green pig; but '*mome*' I'm not certain about. I think it's short for '*from home*'—meaning that they'd lost their way, you know."

"And what does '*outgrabe*' mean?"

"Well, '*outgribing*' is something between bellowing and whistling, with a kind of sneeze in the middle: however, you'll hear it done, maybe—down in the wood yonder—and when you've once heard it you'll be *quite* content. Who's been repeating all that hard stuff to you?"

"I read it in a book," said Alice.

═══════

IN CONTEXT

The Photographs of Lewis Carroll

Though as a photographer Carroll is best known for his images of children—and of Alice Liddell in particular—he was among the most accomplished of Victorian portrait photographers. Like many photographers of the time, he often portrayed his subjects in dramatic roles.

---

[1] *portmanteau* Leather carrying case; "portmanteau" has since entered the English language in the sense to which Humpty Dumpty refers, i.e., a blended word.

[2] *gimlet* Small tool used for boring holes.

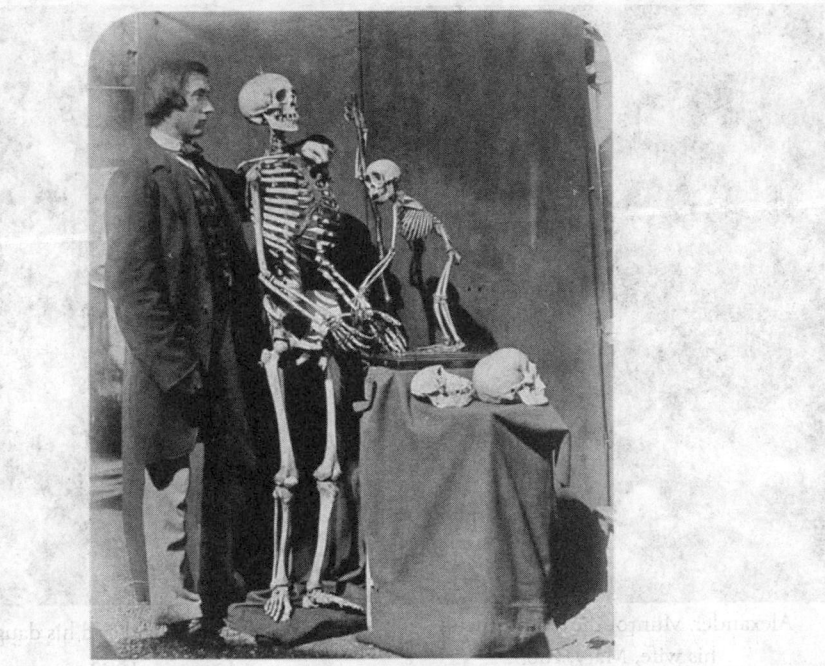

Reginald Southey and Skeletons, 1857.

Alice, Lorina, Harry, and Edith Liddell, 1860.

Alice Liddell as "The Beggar Maid,"
1858.

Alexander Munro, the sculptor with
his wife, Mary, 1863.

George MacDonald and his daughter Lily,
1863.

Ella Chlora Monier-Williams, 1866.

Andromeda, 1865.

Captive Princess, 1875.

IRELAND, SCOTLAND, AND WALES: LITERARY CURRENTS IN THE LONG NINETEENTH CENTURY

For those studying English history and literary history, there is some logic to seeing the 1830s as a turning point. In English history, the tumultuous events of the early and mid 1830s—chief among them the Reform Bill of 1832 and the abolition of slavery in 1833–34—give plausibility to the notion that Victoria's accession to the throne in 1837 was part of the dawn of a new era. And in literary history—to grossly oversimplify—the 1830s mark a divide on one side of which is Romanticism and revolution (with poetry the dominant genre), and on the other side of which is realism (with prose fiction the dominant genre). The Reform Bill was of some importance for Scotland and Wales too, but it is far from obvious that the 1830s mark a natural divide in the history or the literary history of Ireland, Scotland, or Wales.

For Ireland in particular, it seems more natural to think in terms of what historians of Europe often refer to as the long nineteenth century—the period from the beginning of the French Revolution in 1789 to the beginning of the First World War in 1914. For Ireland the revolt that was in part inspired by the French, as well as aided by them—the United Irishmen Rebellion of 1798 ("the year of the French")—marks a much more natural start to a historical era than do the 1830s, just as the outbreak of World War I (and the Easter Rising of 1916) mark a more natural end to it than does the end of the nineteenth century or the end of Victoria's reign. (The tumultuous history of Ireland over this period—the rebellion of '98, the Acts of Union, Catholic Emancipation, the Great Irish Famine, and the long struggle over Home Rule—is accorded a substantial Contexts section in the website component of this anthology.)

One thread above all—aside from a shared linguistic background—ties together the literatures of Ireland, Scotland, and Wales in the medieval era and into the early modern period: the presence of a bardic tradition. A *bard* (Gaelic spelling) or *bardd* (Welsh spelling) was a poet and storyteller by profession; bards underwent long training in their art, and became adept at writing in a variety of genres, each with its own conventions as to meter and rhyme as well as appropriate subject matter and tone. Bards wrote elegies, eulogies and other praise poems, satires, and love poetry. They were well versed in history and legend, and were expected to be able to compose new work in these areas too (as well as to know and to be able to recite traditional works). Typically they worked for hire, under the patronage of a chief or nobleman—though during some eras they might move from place to place or compose work for more than one patron. Though it had died out as a living tradition by the eighteenth century, the idea of the bard carried on as a cultural reference point—and to some extent as a rallying cry.

Nowhere had the bardic tradition been stronger than in Ireland—and in no other area did it survive so long: the last great work in Irish in the bardic tradition is a 1,026 line narrative poem by Brian Merriman (1747–1805), *Cúirt an Mheon-Oíche*, composed in or around 1780. Usually given the title *The Midnight Court* in English translations (of which there at least eleven), the poem is by turns satirical, erotic, and broadly comical; the "court" in question is run by fairies trying to reach a judgment concerning the complaints of Irish women who say they have been suffering from sexual neglect (as their husbands think only of war and politics).

Many have judged *The Midnight Court* to be among the finest of all works of Irish poetry, but it marks the end of a line. By the early nineteenth century the old "hedge schools" were dying out and formal education was becoming available to Catholics; as in Protestant schools, formal schooling was conducted entirely in English; not surprisingly, therefore, nineteenth-century Irish poetry—and Irish literature generally—is almost entirely dominated by English-language writing. A widespread opinion has long been (as Thomas Kinsella put it in a widely quoted 1971 essay) that this change represents a virtually unmitigated disaster; the "dullness of the nineteenth century" in Irish literature in general, and Irish poetry in particular, seems to Kinsella so extreme that he characterizes the period between the age of Merriman and the age of Yeats as, in literary terms, "one of total silence." When it comes to individual writers, though, even critics such as Kinsella acknowledge some merit in the established canon of mid-nineteenth-century writers—a group that includes James Clarence Mangan, Samuel Ferguson, and William Allingham. They acknowledge too the social and political significance of the century's literature. In this regard, a pivotal development was the 1842 founding of *The Nation*, a weekly newspaper that had extraordinary ambitions. Founded by two Catholics (Charles Gavan Duffy, its first editor, and John Blake Dillon) and a Protestant (Thomas Davis), it aimed, in the words of the prospectus for the publication, to foster

> a nationality which will not only raise our people from their poverty, by securing to them the blessings of a domestic legislature, but inflame and purify them with a lofty and heroic love of country … a nationality which may come to be stamped upon our manners, our literature, and our deeds—a nationality which may embrace Protestant, Catholic … a nationality which would be recognized by the world, and sanctified by wisdom, virtue, and time.

The magnitude of the struggles that the Irish faced over the course of the long nineteenth century is truly extraordinary: the struggle for better living conditions for tenant farmers and for the poor generally; the struggle for better education; the fight over tithes and, more broadly, the struggle for Catholic emancipation; the struggle for Home Rule; the wrenching effects of mass emigration; and, most dramatic and heart-wrenching of all, the struggle for survival during the famine of 1845–47, when over a million people are estimated to have died of starvation or famine-related disease, and perhaps twice that number were forced to emigrate. Given the degree to which these struggles were all a part of a larger struggle against the centuries-long history of English oppression, it should not surprise us that so much of Irish literature during the long nineteenth century is infused with political content. From the late nineteenth century through to the late twentieth, it was the habit of many critics and literary historians to regard such content in a negative light—to disparage the literary qualities of works that broadcast a clear political agenda. So it was, for example, that the novels of Sydney Owenson (included in the website component of Volume 4 of this anthology), whose lively "national tales" had an overtly political purpose, were frequently dismissed as "escapist" and the novels of William Carleton as "polemical." To some extent such views have persisted into the twenty-first century. Lucy Collins, for example, reaches the following conclusion in the introduction to her fine anthology of the work of nineteenth- and twentieth-century women poets: "while engagement with the Gaelic past had a largely revivifying effect on Irish writing in the nineteenth century, an exclusive focus on nationalist feeling generally detracted from the aesthetic value of the poetry, privileging political conviction over artistic complexity." On the whole, however, critics and literary historians have come increasingly to the view that political conviction and artistic merit are far from mutually exclusive—and that a good deal of both is to be found in Irish literature of the nineteenth century. To be sure, they acknowledge the dearth of famous names over the period between the great Irish writers of the late eighteenth and early nineteenth centuries (Merriman, and also the Anglo-Irish writers Richard Brinsley Sheridan and Maria Edgeworth) and the extraordinary cluster of major writers in the very late nineteenth century and the first half of the twentieth (Bernard Shaw and Oscar Wilde as well as W.B. Yeats, James Joyce, John Millington Synge, Sean O'Casey, and Samuel Beckett). But there is an increasing interest in exploring the writings of the nineteenth-century Irish writers who inhabit the space between those two clusters—and an increasing willingness to acknowledge that much of their work is extraordinarily interesting as well as remarkably varied.

For most of the twentieth century, Irish literature in the nineteenth and early twentieth centuries was often taken to be an almost entirely male preserve (Kinsella's 1986 *Oxford Book of Irish Verse*, for example, includes no nineteenth- or twentieth-century women writers). Over the past generation or two, however—as prominent modern writers such as Eavan Boland and Nuala Ní Dhomhnaill have spoken up powerfully against "the traditional exclusion" of women from Irish literary history—it has come to be increasingly appreciated in recent decades that the work of writers such as Emily Lawless, Katherine Tynan, Eve Gore-Booth, and Winnifred Mary Letts was in fact just as accomplished—and just as informed politically—as the work of Mangan, Ferguson, or Davis had been, while, arguably, being broader in scope. It should perhaps not surprise us that open-minded inquiry brings to light as many accomplished women writers as their male counterparts during this period, for—unlike in Scotland—education was not a male preserve. By the 1870s, indeed, there were as many female as male students in Irish schools.

That there are fewer Scottish authors represented in this section than there are Irish or Welsh authors is a reflection not of any ebb in the importance of Scottish writers to British literature over the course of the long nineteenth century—quite the reverse. From the late eighteenth to the early twentieth centuries no fewer than ten Scottish writers (Robert Burns, Joanna Baillie, James Hogg, Sir Walter Scott, James Macpherson, Thomas Carlyle, Margaret Oliphant, James Thomson, Robert Louis Stevenson, and Sir Arthur Conan Doyle) are accorded author entries in this anthology—a remarkable number, given that the Scots made up no more than 10 per cent of the British population during this period. And that list does not include several outstanding writers whose work is not easy to anthologize—such as the novelist Susan Ferrier, the fantasy writer George Macdonald, and J.M. Barrie, creator of *Peter Pan*.

Literature is in no way an extraordinary case here; from the great figures of the Scottish Enlightenment in the mid eighteenth century—Adam Smith and David Hume chief among them—through to the early years of the twentieth century, Scottish notables make up an outsized proportion of the leading figures in any number of fields. In science and technology James Watt, George Stevenson, and John McAdam revolutionized industry and transportation with the steam engine, the modern railway, and the gravel roadbed; in engineering Thomas Telford broke new ground in his designs for bridges and canals (and it was Scottish engineer and railway builder Sandford Fleming who invented standard time); Joseph Lister revolutionized medicine by introducing the concept of sterilization; and the list goes on.

The Scottish influence was strong not just within Britain, but around the world. Scots such as Lachlan Macquarie in Australia and John A. Macdonald in Canada became colonial leaders; Scotsman David Livingstone redefined the role of the missionary in his explorations of southern Africa; Scotsman James Mill set colonial policy on a new path with his *History of British India*; and Scots were disproportionately represented in business enterprises in all corners of the globe (in the early nineteenth century, 80 per cent of those on the payroll of the Hudson's Bay Company, for example, were Scottish).

There is no single cultural or socio-economic explanation for Scotland's extraordinary prominence through this period, but it has often been surmised that Scottish accomplishments in this era are not unconnected to the state of religion in Scotland. Unlike in Ireland and Wales, the established Church in Scotland was not a branch of the Anglican Church; the Church of Scotland had long been Presbyterian and Calvinist.[1] There was thus little or no parallel in Scotland to the sense that prevailed among the majority in Ireland of the established Church as an oppressive force. That it not to say that religious affairs were without controversy—far from it. There were numerous and ongoing tensions both between secular and religious influences in society and between different strains of Protestantism. Moderate Presbyterians had defeated Evangelicals in their 1757 bid to control the Church of Scotland, but Evangelicals continued to agitate through the early decades of the nineteenth century against Church of Scotland policies such as the practice of allowing influential landowners to influence the choosing of local ministers in the Church. Finally, the Disruption of 1843 resulted in the formation of the breakaway Free Church of Scotland—which in turn would merge in 1900 with the United Presbyterian Church to form the United Free Church of Scotland. In whatever its forms, Scottish Presbyterianism continued throughout the period to promote what Max Weber famously termed the "Protestant work ethic" perhaps more effectively than did any other branch of Protestantism. But the workings of any society's psyche resist easy generalizations; as the excerpt below from the oft-mocked *Self-Help* suggests, even such an exemplar of the principles of the work ethic as Samuel Smiles is not easy to pigeonhole.

If religious currents may help to explain Scottish exceptionalism, so too may education. The Scots were, on average, better educated than the English—from the sixteenth century onwards Scottish Presbyterians had been world leaders in this regard. By the 1830s, however, the old system of parish schools and "dame schools" (which taught girls to read and to sew—but not to write) was becoming inadequate to the needs of a modern nation. George Lewis's *Scotland: A Half Educated Nation* (1834) provided a wake-up call, and in the second half of the century the burden of educating the people began to shift from church to secular authorities; the 1872 Education Act made schooling compulsory for all children between the ages of five and thirteen, and transferred responsibility to State authorities.

Education was almost always in English rather than in Gaelic, however, and by 1911 only 4.2 per cent of Scotland's 4,500,000 people spoke Gaelic. More broadly, the culture of the Gaelic-speaking Highlands had long been in decline—along with the Highland population. Not until 1885 did the Highlands and Island Crofting Act end the centuries-old practice of landlords evicting tenant farmers *en masse* and destroying entire communities in order to clear the land for more profitable activities (such as sheep farming).

By the end of the century, then, some of the greatest contrasts in the industrialized world were in Scotland. One could find one of the world's great urban economies—powered by engineering, ship-building, steel-making, and textiles. But one could also find abject urban poverty—and abject

---

[1] The Anglican Church (or "Scottish Episcopal Church") did retain a presence in Scotland, but its numbers were small and its influence minimal. As J.M. Barrie observed, in the eyes of many Presbyterians there was little difference between being a member of the "English Kirk" (as the Anglican Church was often referred to) and being a Roman Catholic.

rural poverty among the people who still remained in the Highland counties. One could find a deep-rooted literary culture—but one could also find a culture in which women were only beginning to be taught how to write.

The nineteenth century is a century of paradox in the history of Welsh culture. The best-known of all Welsh writers of the century—Felicia Hemans—is famous most of all for poems expressing sentimental patriotic feeling not towards Wales, but towards England. Wales enjoyed considerable economic growth over the course of the century, but key sectors of the economy—most notably, coal mining—continued to be notorious for low wages and horrendous working conditions until well into the twentieth century.

Religion played a central role in nineteenth-century Wales—and here too there were numerous paradoxes. The most important religious event of the century occurred in 1811, when the Welsh Methodists broke free from the control of the Anglican Church. Culturally, however, religion was far from a liberating force. With the great growth during the century of Nonconformist or "Dissenting" forms of religion (i.e., those dissenting from and not conforming with the Anglican Church, which remained throughout the century the established church), strictures against alcoholic drink and sexual licentiousness became more and more widespread—and so too did strictures against the "sins" of dancing, secular music, and works of fiction. Censorious attitudes took hold not only in Methodism but in most other Nonconformist denominations as well. To be sure, such strictures were not universal—and Dissenters were not uniformly censorious or puritanical. One of the century's most notable cultural developments was the founding in 1845 by Lewis Edwards, a Welsh Calvinist minister, of *Y Traethodydd* (The Essayist), a Welsh-language organ of culture that has survived into the twenty-first century. And the old medieval tradition of *eisteddfodau* (festivals of literature, dance, and music), which had been revived in the eighteenth century, was carried on through the nineteenth; despite considerable opposition, a national *Eisteddfod* was established in the second half of the century.

Given the degree to which strict Nonconformist strains of Christianity dominated Welsh life in this period, it is ironic that Anglican authorities continued to characterize the bulk of the Welsh people as being sexually irresponsible and of doubtful moral character generally. Notoriously, the 1847 Report of the Commission of Enquiry into the State of Education in Wales (known as the "Blue Books") veered from educational into cultural commentary of the most dubious sort, suggesting that the natural state of the majority of the population was an "utter vacuity of thought" and maligning the Welsh language as "a vast drawback to Wales, and a manifold barrier to the moral progress of the people."

The Welsh language certainly came under pressure during this century, but by its end there had been only a modest decline in its use. By 1911 there were still approximately 1,000,000 speakers of the language, out of a total population of just over 2,400,000. As the selections here—perhaps most memorably, Evan James's "Land of my Fathers"—suggest, pride in the language remained a powerful rallying cry throughout the century. In the end, the greatest legacy left by the "Blue Books" was the degree to which they united the Welsh in support of Welsh language and culture.

The century saw a considerable growth in formal education—passage of the Intermediate Schools Act in 1889 was a notable milestone—but at century's end a substantial gulf remained between the well-educated and almost entirely English-speaking privileged classes and the much less educated mass of the Welsh people. There was nevertheless a significant growth in Welsh literary culture. A significant milestone was the publication between 1838 and 1849 of Charlotte Guest's translation of *The Four Branches of the Mabinogi* and related poems (which together she termed *The Mabinogion*).

Much as her translation is now faulted, the works themselves, which were little-known before Guest's work, are now universally acknowledged as foundational classics of Welsh culture.

A striking number of the outstanding Welsh writers of the long nineteenth century are women. The list of prominent Anglo-Welsh writers includes not only Jane Cave, Mary Robinson, and Hemans (all of whom are accorded full author entries in this anthology) and the writers included below, but also Ann Griffiths (1776–1805), a noted author of hymns; Maria James (1795–1868), a woman of working class background whose family emigrated to America when she was ten, and whose poetry returns frequently to themes of cultural and linguistic loss; and Emily Jane Pfeiffer (1827–90), an Anglo-Welsh poet whose writing often took issue with the domination of Britain by England over Wales, Scotland, and Ireland, and with the domination of men over women.

Religious conservatism does not always imply political conservatism, and certainly it did not always do so in nineteenth-century Wales. In the first half of the century there were numerous uprisings against oppressively high taxes and a lack of adequate support for farmers (notably, the Rebecca riots of 1839–43 in south and mid-Wales), and against low wages and high unemployment (notably, the Merthyr Rising of 1831 in south Wales). In the second half of the century there came to be considerable support for socialist causes—again, especially in the more heavily populated and more heavily industrialized south. There were protests too against British military action—as the selection below by Samuel Roberts illustrates. Anti-war sentiment was not confined to Radicals such as Roberts; many mainstream nonconformists were also opposed to British militarism. (During WWI in the early twentieth century, acrimonious divisions among religious nonconformists in Wales opened up over the pacifist cause.)

As in Ireland there was a strong push in Wales for Home Rule—though in Wales the agitation for Home Rule, which gathered steam only in the second half of the nineteenth century, was less vehement. Few in Wales called for outright independence from Britain, but the *Cymru Fydd* (Young Wales) movement, which was outspoken in its demands for a separate Welsh parliament, was for a time in the 1880s and 1890s a force to be reckoned with. One of the leading lights of *Cymru Fydd* was David Lloyd George (see below), later to play a key role in British politics as the force behind the "People's Budget" of 1909–10 and as Prime Minister during WWI.

⌘ ⌘ ⌘

IRELAND

SONGS OF '98

The Rebellion of 1798 became the subject of many poems and songs; two of the best known are included here. (For background on the rebellion see the Contexts section "Ireland in the Long Nineteenth Century" in the website component of this anthology.)

Slievenamon [1]

Slievenamon, a low mountain in Tipperary, figures prominently in Irish history and myth. The battle referenced in this song took place 23 July 1798.

It is my sorrow that this day's troubles
Poor Irishmen so sore did strike,
Because our tyrants are laughing at us,
And say they fear neither fork nor pike;

---

[1] *Slievenamon* Translated from the Irish by Frank O'Connor. Not to be confused with this song is the well-known nineteenth-century poem of the same name by Charles Kickham.

5 Our Major never came to lead us,
       We had no orders and drifted on
   As you'd send a drover[1] with a cow to the fair
       On the sunny side of Slievenamon.

   Ross[2] was the place we were defeated,
10   There we left many a pikeman dead,
   Little children burned to ashes,
       Women in holes and ditches hid.
   But I promise you the men that slew them
       We'll meet them yet with pike and gun,
15 And we'll drive the yeomen[3] in flight before us
       When we pay them back on Slievenamon.

   The sturdy Frenchman with ships in order
       Beneath sharp masts is long at sea;
   They're always saying they will come to Ireland,
20   And they will set the Irish free.
   Light as a blackbird on a green bough swinging
       Would be my heart if the French would come—
   O the broken ranks and the trumpets ringing
       On the sunny side of Slievenamon!
   —DATE UNKNOWN

CARROLL MALONE, *The Croppy[4] Boy*

There is more than one version of this nineteenth
century song. That which Patrick Crotty includes in
The Penguin Book of Irish Poetry includes only nine
stanzas; in that anonymously authored version the
young man is betrayed not by a soldier pretending
to be a priest (as in the Malone version below), but
by a relative:

> My own first cousin did me betray
> And for one bare guinea stole my life away.

The lyrics below were published in the 4 January
1845 issue of *The Nation*, and credited to Carroll
Malone (the pen name of poet William B. McBurney
[d. 1892]). It is the Malone version that now has
particularly deep roots in Irish culture. James Joyce
refers to it in *Ulysses*, and wrote of it as well in a letter
to his son:

> It is a pure and noble musical poem, pro-
> foundly sincere and dramatic … This is not a
> patriotic song like "Wearing of the Green."
> You could sing it just as well at Sheffield as at
> Cork.[5] Study every word of it and you will
> make it into a masterpiece.

"The Croppy Boy" is usually sung to the tune *Cailín
Óg a Stór*—an air that is many centuries old.

"Good men and true in this house who dwell,
   To a stranger bouchal[6] I pray you tell:
Is the priest at home, or may he be seen?
I would speak a word with Father Green."

5 "The Priest's at home, boy, and may be seen;
'Tis easy speaking with Father Green.
But you must wait till I go and see
If the Holy Father alone may be."

The youth has entered an empty hall—
10 What a lonely sound has his light footfall!
And the gloomy chamber's chill and bare,
With a vested priest in a lonely chair.

The youth has knelt to tell his sins:
"Nomine Dei," the youth begins;
15 At "mea culpa"[7] he beats his breast,
And in broken murmurs he speaks the rest.

---

[1] *drover* Person who drives livestock to market.

[2] *Ross* New Ross, a site of one of the 1798 Rebellion's significant battles; after their victory, the British Army massacred uninvolved civilians as well as rebel fighters.

[3] *yeomen* Government soldiers in the British army.

[4] *Croppy* Slang designation for a young man fighting in the Irish Rebellion of 1798; these men were known for having short cropped hair.

[5] *as well at Sheffield as at Cork* Sheffield is in England, Cork in Ireland.

[6] *bouchal* Irish: young man. (The more common spelling today is *buachaill*.)

[7] *Nomine Dei … mea culpa* Latin phrases used in the Catholic ritual of confessing one's sins; *Nomine Dei* In the name of our Lord; *mea culpa* I have sinned.

"At the siege of Ross did my father fall,
And at Gorey my loving brothers all.
I alone am left of my name and race;
20   I will go to Wexford[1] and take their place.

"I cursed three times since last Easter day;
At mass-time once I went to play;
I passed the churchyard one day in haste,
And forgot to pray for my mother's rest.

25   "I bear no grudge against living thing,
But I love my country above the king.
Now, Father! bless me, and let me go
To die, if God has ordained it so."

The priest said nought, but a rustling noise
30   Made the youth look about in wild surprise;
The robes were off, and in scarlet there
Sat a yeoman[2] captain with fiery glare.

With fiery glare and with fury hoarse,
Instead of a blessing, he breathed a curse:
35   "'Twas a good thought, boy, to come here and shrive,[3]
For one short hour is your time to live.

"Upon yon river three tenders[4] float;
The priest's in one—if he isn't shot!
We hold his house for our Lord the King,
40   And, amen say I, may all traitors swing!"

At Geneva Barrack that young man died,
And at Passage[5] they have his body laid.
Good people who live in peace and joy,
Breathe a prayer and a tear for the Croppy Boy.
—1845

WILLIAM CARLETON (1794–1869)

Novelist William Carleton—"the great novelist of Ireland," in W.B. Yeats's view—is known for his lively and influential—if sometimes stereotypical—depictions of the rural Irish character in the nineteenth century; a review of his *Traits and Stories* in *Blackwood's Edinburgh Magazine* called his tales "Admirable, truly! Intensely Irish," and claimed that "never were that wild, imaginative people better described."

Carleton was born in County Tyrone in 1798 to a farming family; his Irish-speaking parents instilled in him a love of literature and song at an early age. He lived a rather peripatetic life for several years, working at various jobs before publishing *Traits and Stories* in 1830. An immediate success, this collection of sketches and stories was followed some years later by a second series of stories. In 1847 Carleton published *The Black Prophet: A Tale of Irish Famine*, in which he vividly describes the bleak realities of rural communities during the Famine.

Though born a Catholic, Carleton converted to Protestantism in early adulthood, and became the target of criticism for the sometimes-satirical perspective towards Catholicism adopted in certain of his later writings. Despite the success of his work, Carleton's last years were spent in relative poverty; he died in 1869.

---

[1] *Ross … Wexford*   Two significant clashes during the 1798 Rebellion took place at the towns of New Ross and Gorey; both are located in County Wexford, which was the center of the rebellion. (Another name for the rebels was "Wexford boys.")

[2] *yeoman*   Government soldier in the British Army.

[3] *shrive*   Present oneself to a priest for the purposes of confessing one's sins and receiving absolution.

[4] *tenders*   Boats used for transporting people, especially between shore and a larger vessel.

[5] *Geneva Barrack … Passage*   Geneva Barracks (now a ruin) is located in the town of Waterford in southeast Ireland; the community of Passage (or Passage East) is located on the narrow passage into Waterford Harbor.

from *The Black Prophet; A Tale of Irish Famine*

from CHAPTER 6: A RUSTIC MISER AND HIS ESTABLISHMENT

There is to be found in Ireland, and, we presume, in all other countries, a class of hardened wretches, who look forward to a period of dearth as to one of great gain and advantage, and who contrive, by exercising the most heartless and diabolical principles, to make the sickness, famine, and general desolation which scourge their fellow-creatures, so many sources of successful extortion and rapacity, and consequently of gain to themselves. These are country misers or money-lenders, who are remarkable for keeping meal until the arrival of what is termed a hard year, or a dear summer, when they sell it out at an enormous or usurious prices, and who, at all times, and under all circumstances, dispose of it only at terms dictated by their own griping spirit and the crying necessity of the unhappy purchasers.

The houses and places of such persons are always remarkable for a character in their owners of hard and severe saving, which at a first glance has the appearance of that rare virtue in our country, called frugality—a virtue which, upon a closer inspection, is found to be nothing with them but selfishness, sharpened up into the most unscrupulous avarice and penury.

About half a mile from the Sullivans', lived a remarkable man of this class, named Darby Skinadre. In appearance he was lank and sallow, with a long, thin, parched-looking face, and a miserable crop of yellow beard, which no one could pronounce as anything else than "a dead failure"; added to this were two piercing ferret eyes, always sore and with a tear standing in each, or trickling down his fleshless cheeks; so that, to persons disposed to judge only by appearances, he looked very like a man in a state of perpetual repentance for his transgressions, or, what was still farther from the truth, who felt a most Christian sympathy with the distresses of the poor. In his house, and about it, there was much, no doubt, to be commended, for there was much to mark the habits of the saving man. Everything was neat and clean, not so much from any innate love of neatness and cleanliness, as because these qualities were economical in themselves. His ploughs and farming implements were all snugly laid up, and covered, lest they might be injured by exposure to the weather; and his house was filled with large chests and wooden hogsheads, trampled hard with oatmeal, which, as they were never opened unless during a time of famine, had their joints and crevices festooned by innumerable mealy-looking cobwebs, which description of ornament extended to the dresser itself, where they might be seen upon most of the cold-looking shelves, and those neglected utensils, that in other families are mostly used for food. His haggard[1] was also remarkable for having in it, throughout all the year, a remaining stack or two of oats or wheat, or perhaps one or two large ricks of hay, tanned by the sun of two or three summers into tawny hue—each or all kept in the hope of a failure and a famine.

In a room from the kitchen, he had a beam, a pair of scales, and a set of weights, all of which would have been vastly improved by a visit from the lord mayor, had our mealmonger lived under the jurisdiction of that civic gentleman. He was seldom known to use metal weights when disposing of his property; in lieu of these he always used round stones, which, upon the principle of the Scottish proverb, that "many a little makes a muckle,"[2] he must have found a very beneficial mode of transacting business.

If anything could add to the iniquity of his principles, as a plausible but most unscrupulous cheat, it was the hypocritical prostitution of the sacred name and character of religion to his own fraudulent impositions upon the poor and the distressed. Outwardly, and to the eye of men, he was proverbially strict and scrupulous in the observation of its sanctions, but outrageously severe and unsparing upon all who appeared to be influenced either by a negligent or worldly spirit, or who omitted the least title of its forms. Religion and its duties, therefore, were perpetually in his

---

[1] *haggard* Storeroom for hay and grains.

[2] *muckle* Scots: a large amount.

mouth but never with such apparent zeal and sincerity as when enforcing his most heartless and hypocritical exactions upon the honest and struggling creatures whom necessity or neglect had driven into his meshes.

Such was Darby Skinadre; and certain we are that the truth of the likeness we have given of him will be at once recognized by our readers as that of the roguish hypocrite, whose rapacity is the standing curse of half the villages of the country, especially during the seasons of distress, or failure of crops.

Skinadre, on the day we write of, was reaping a rich harvest from the miseries of the unhappy people. In a lower room of his house, to the right of the kitchen as you entered it, he stood over the scales, weighing out with a dishonest and parsimonious hand, the scanty pittance which poverty enabled the wretched creatures to purchase from him; and in order to give them a favourable impression of his piety, and consequently of his justice, he had placed against the wall a delf[1] crucifix, with a semi-circular receptacle at the bottom of it for holding holy water. This was as much as to say "how could I cheat you, with the image of our Blessed Redeemer before my eyes to remind me of my duty, and to teach me, as He did, to love my fellow-creatures?" And with many of the simple people, he actually succeeded in making the impression he wished; for they could not conceive it possible that any principle, however rapacious, could drive a man to the practice of such sacrilegious imposture.

There stood Skinadre, like the very Genius of Famine, surrounded by distress, raggedness, feeble hunger, and tottering disease, in all the various aspects of pitiable suffering, hopeless desolation, and that agony of the heart which impresses wildness upon the pale cheek, makes the eye at once dull and eager, parches the mouth and gives to the voice of misery tones that are hoarse and hollow. There he stood, striving to blend consolation with deceit, and in the name of religion and charity subjecting the helpless wretches to fraud and extortion. Around him was misery, multiplied into all her most appalling shapes. Fathers of families were

---

[1] *delf* Delft (type of earthenware originating in the Dutch town of Delft).

there, who could read in each other's faces too truly the gloom and anguish that darkened the brow and wrung the heart. The strong man, who had been not long before a comfortable farmer, now stood dejected and apparently broken down, shorn of his strength, without a trace of either hope or spirit; so woefully shrunk away too, from his superfluous apparel, that the spectators actually wondered to think that this was the large man, of such powerful frame, whose feats of strength had so often heretofore filled them with amazement. But, alas! what will not sickness and hunger do? …

And there was the widower, on behalf of his mother-less children, coming with his worn and desolate look of sorrow, almost thankful to God that his Kathleen was not permitted to witness the many-shaped miseries of this woeful year; and yet experiencing the sharp and bitter reflection that now, in all their trials—in his poor children's want and sickness—in their moanings by day and their cries for her by night, they have not the soft affection of her voice nor the tender touch of her hand to soothe their pain—nor has he that smile, which was ever his, to solace him now, nor that faithful heart to soothe him with its affection, or to cast its sweetness into the bitter cup of affliction. …

It is impossible, however, to describe the various aspects and claims of misery which presented themselves at Skinadre's house. The poor people flitted to and fro silently and dejectedly, wasted, feeble, and sickly—sometimes in small groups of twos and threes, and sometimes a solitary individual might be seen hastening with earnest but languid speed, as if the life of some dear child or beloved parent, of a husband or wife, or perhaps, the lives of a whole family, depended upon his or her arrival with food.

CHAPTER 7: A PANORAMA OF MISERY

Skinadre, thin and mealy, with his coat off, but wearing a waistcoat to which were attached flannel sleeves, was busily engaged in his agreeable task of administering to their necessities. Such was his smoothness of manner, and the singular control which a long life of hypocrisy had given him over his feelings, that it was impossible to draw any correct distinction between that which he only assumed, and that which he really felt. This consequently gave him an immense advantage over everyone with whom he came in contact, especially the artless and candid, and all who were in the habit of expressing what they thought. We shall, however, take the liberty of introducing him to the reader, and allow honest Skinadre to speak for himself.

"They're beggars—thim three—that woman and her two childre; still my heart bleeds for them, bekase[1] we should love our neighbours as ourselves; but I have given away as much meal in charity, an' me can so badly afford it, as would—I can't now, indeed, my poor woman! Sick—troth they look sick, an' you look sick yourself. Here, Paddy Lenahan, help that woman an' her two poor childre out of that half bushel of meal you've got; you won't miss a handful for God's sake."

This he said to a poor man who had just purchased some oatmeal from him; for Skinadre was one of those persons who, however he might have neglected works of mercy himself, took great delight in encouraging others to perform them.

"Troth it's not at your desire I do it, Darby," replied the man; "but bekase she an' they wants it, God help them. Here, poor creature, take this for the honour of God: an' I'm only sorry, for both our sakes, that I can't do more."

"Well, Jemmy Duggan," proceeded the miser, addressing a new-comer, "what's the news wid you? They're hard times, Jemmy; we all know that an' feel it too, and yet we live, most of us, as if there wasn't a God ta punish us."

"At all events," replied the man, "we feel what sufferin' is now, God help us! Between hunger and sickness, the counthry was never in sich a state widin[2] the memory of man. What, in the name o' God, will become of the poor people, I know not. The Lord pity them an' relieve them!"

"Amen, amen, Jemmy! Well, Jemmy, can I do anything for you? But Jemmy, in regard to that, the thruth is, we have brought all these scourges on us by our sins and our transgressions; thim that sins, Jemmy, must suffer."

"There's no one denyin' it, Darby; but you're axin' me can you do anything for me, an' my answer to that is, that you can, if you like."

"Ah! Jemmy, you wor ever an' always a wild, heedless, heerum-skeerum rake,[3] that never was likely to do much good; little religion ever rested on you, an' now I'm afeard no signs on it."

"Well, well, who's widout sin? I'm sure I'm not. What I want is, to know if you'll credit me for a hundred of meal till the times mends a trifle. I have the six o' them at home widout their dinner this day, an' must go widout if you refuse me. When the harvest comes round, I'll pay you."

"Jemmy, you owe three half-year's, rent; an' as for the harvest an' what it'll bring, only jist look at the day that's in it. It goes to my heart to refuse you, poor man; but Jemmy, you see you have brought this on yourself. If you had been an attentive, industrious man, an' minded your religion, you wouldn't be as you are now. Six you have at home, you say?"

"Ay, not to speak of the woman an' myself. I know you won't refuse them, Darby, bekase if we're hard pushed now, it's a'most everybody's case as well as mine. Be what I may, you know I'm honest."

"I don't doubt your honesty, Jemmy; but Jemmy, if I sell my meal to a man that can pay and won't, or if I sell my meal to a man that would pay and can't, by which do I lose most? There it is, Jemmy—think o' that now. Six in family, you say?"

"Six in family, wid the woman an' myself." ...

"It goes to my heart, Jemmy, to refuse you—six in family, an' the two of yourselves. Troth it does, to my very heart itself; but stay, maybe we may manage it. You have no money, you say?"

"No money now, but won't be so long, plaise God."

"Well, but havn't you value of any kind? sure, God help them, they can't starve, poor creatures—the Lord pity them!" Here he wiped away a drop of villainous

---

[1] *bekase* Because.

[2] *widin* Within.

[3] *rake* Scots slang: someone who is always trying to get more money.

rheum which ran down his cheek, and he did it with such an appearance of sympathy, that almost anyone would have imagined it was a tear of compassion for the distresses of the poor man's family.

"Oh! no, they can't starve. Have you no valuables of any kind, Jemmy?—ne'er a baste[1] now, or anything that way?"

"Why, there's a young heifer; but I'm strugglin' to keep it to help me in the rent. I was obliged to sell my pig long ago, for I had no way of feedin' it."

"Well, bring me the heifer, Jemmy, an' I won't let the crathurs[2] starve. We'll see what can be done when it comes here. An' now, Jemmy, let me ax if you wint to hear mass on last Sunday?"

"Troth I didn't like to go in this trim. Peggy has a web of frieze[3] half made this good while; it'll be finished some time, I hope."

"Ah! Jemmy, Jemmy, it's no wondher the world's

the way it is, for indeed there's little thought of God or religion in it. You passed last Sunday like a haythen, an' now you see how you stand today for the same."

"You'll let me bring some o' the meal home wid me now," said the man; "the poor cratures tasted hardly anything today yet, an' they wor cryin' whin I left home. I'll come back wid the heifer fullfut. Troth they're in outher misery, Darby."

"Poor things! an' no wondher, wid such a haythen of a father; but, Jemmy, bring the heifer here first till I look at it, an' the sooner you bring it here the sooner they'll have relief, the crathurs."

It is not our intention to follow up this iniquitous bargain any further; it is enough to say that the heifer passed from Jemmy's possession into his, at about the fourth part of its value. ...

—1847

IN CONTEXT

W.B. Yeats, from Introduction to *Stories from Carleton* (1889)

In 1889, when the Walter Scott publishing company issued *Stories from Carleton* in their Camelot Series of reprints—"monthly shilling volumes," as they were advertised, ranging from Plutarch's *Lives* to Thoreau's *Walden*—Carleton himself had been dead for twenty years. Nobel-Prize winning poet William Butler Yeats (1865–1939), for his part, was at this time just 23; *The Wind among the Reeds*, his first volume of poetry, was still ten years away.

At the end of the last century, there lived in the townland of Prillisk, in the parish of Clogher, in the county of Tyrone,[4] a farmer named Carleton. Among his neighbours, he was noted for his great memory. A pious Catholic, he could repeat almost the whole of the Old and New Testament, and no man ever heard tell of Gaelic charm, rann,[5] poem, prophesy, miracle, tale of blessed priest or friar, revelation of ghost or fairy, that did not already lie on this man's tongue.

His wife, Mary, was even better known. Hers was the sweetest voice within the range of many Baronies. When she went to sing at wake or wedding the neighbours for miles round would flock in to hear, as city folk do for some famous prima donna. She had a great store of old Gaelic songs and

---

1   *baste*   Beast; animal.

2   *crathurs*   Creatures.

3   *web of frieze*   Knitted woolen garment in a frieze pattern.

4   *Tyrone*   Located in what is now Northern Ireland.

5   *rann*   Style of Irish verse.

tunes, many an air, sung once under all Irish roof-trees, has gone into the grave with her. The words she sang were Gaelic. Once they asked her to sing the air,[1] "The Red-Haired Man's Wife," to English words. "I will sing for you," she answered, "but the English words and the air are like a quarrelling man and wife. The Irish melts into the tune: the English does not." She could repeat many poems, some handed down for numberless years, others written by her own grandfather and uncle, who were noted peasant poets in their day. She was a famous keener,[2] likewise. No one could load the wild funeral song with so deep sorrow. Often and often when she caught up the cry, the other keeners would become silent in admiration.

On Shrove-Tuesday, in the year 1798, when pitch-caps[3] were well in fashion, was born to these two a son, whom they called William Carleton. He was the youngest of fourteen children.

Before long his mind was brimful of his father's stories and his mother's songs. In after days he recorded how many times, when his mother sat by her spinning wheel, singing "Shule agra" or the "Trougha," or some other "song of sorrow," he would go over with tears in his eyes, and whisper, "Mother dear, don't sing that song; it makes me sorrowful." Fifty years later his mind was still full of old songs that had died on all other lips than his.

At this time Ireland was plentifully stored with hedge schoolmasters. Government had done its best to crush out education, and only succeeded in doing what like policy had done for the priestcraft—surrounding it with a halo. Ditchers and plough-boys developed the strangest enthusiasm for Greek and Latin. The worst of it was, the men who set up schools behind the hedges were often sheer imposters. Among them, however, were a few worthy of fame, like Andrew Magrath, the Munster poet, who sang his allegiance to the fairy, "Dawn of the Ocean Vats."

The boy Carleton sat under three hedge schoolmasters in succession—Pat Fryne, called Mat Kavanagh in the stories; O'Beirne of Findramore; and another, the master in "The Poor Scholar," whose name Carleton never recorded, as he had nothing but evil to say of him. ...

William Carleton was a great Irish historian. The history of a nation is not in parliaments and battlefields, but in what the people say to each other on fair days and high days, and how they farm, and quarrel, and go on pilgrimage. These things has Carleton recorded.

He is the great novelist of Ireland, by right of the most Celtic eyes that ever gazed from under the brows of storyteller. His equals in gloomy and tragic power, Michael and John Banim,[4] had nothing of his Celtic humour. One man alone stands near him there—Charles Kickham,[5] of Tipperary. ... But, then, he had not Carleton's intensity. ...

There is no wistfulness in the works of Carleton. I find there, especially in his longer novels, a kind of clay-cold melancholy. One is not surprised to hear, great humourist though he was, that his conversation was more mournful than humorous. He seems, like the animals in Milton,[6] half emerged only from the earth and its brooding. When I read any portion of the "Black Prophet," ... I seem to

---

[1] *air* Song.

[2] *keener* One who performs keens, or lamentations for the dead, at Irish funerals and wakes.

[3] *pitch-caps* The pitch-cap was a method of torture, famously used by the British military upon participants in the United Irishmen Rebellion of 1798; it involved placing a "cap" of boiling tar onto the victim's head.

[4] *Michael and John Banim* Irish writers of the early 1800s.

[5] *Charles Kickham* Irish writer and revolutionary (1828–82).

[6] *Milton* John Milton (1608–74), English poet and dramatist. His account of the sixth day of Creation (*Paradise Lost*, 7.449ff.) includes descriptions of the creation of various animals—among them the lion who, when half created, paws the ground as he struggles to be free of the "grassy clods" of the "fertile womb" of Earth that is giving birth to him.

be looking out at the wild, torn storm-clouds that lie in heaps at sundown along the western seas of Ireland; all nature, and not merely man's nature, seems to pour out for me its inbred fatalism.

JAMES CLARENCE MANGAN (1803–1849)

Dublin-born poet James Clarence Mangan was a self-taught translator of languages as diverse as German, Irish, and Persian, and was during his lifetime known at least as much for his translations as for his original poetry. His writings became increasingly patriotic and political during the Great Famine, and many of his best-known poems—including "Dark Rosaleen"—were published in *The Nation*. Though Mangan lived his latter years in poverty and died of cholera (likely brought on by malnutrition and alcoholism) at the age of 46, he is now recognized as one of most important Irish poets of the nineteenth century.

The Woman of Three Cows[1]

from the Irish[2]

O Woman of Three Cows, *agragh*![3] don't let
   your tongue thus rattle!
O, don't be saucy, don't be stiff, because you may
   have cattle.
I have seen—and, here's my hand to you, I only
   say what's true—
A many a one with twice your stock not half so proud
   as you.

5   Good luck to you, don't scorn the poor, and don't
   be their despiser,
For worldly wealth soon melts away, and cheats the
   very miser,

And Death soon strips the proudest wreath
   from haughty human brows;
Then don't be stiff, and don't be proud, good
   Woman of Three Cows!

See where Momonia's[4] heroes lie, proud Owen
   More's descendants,
10   'Tis they that won the glorious name, and had the
   grand attendants!
If *they* were forced to bow to Fate, as every mortal bows,
Can *you* be proud, can *you* be stiff, my Woman of
   Three Cows!

The brave sons of the Lord of Clare,[5] they left the
   land to mourning;
Movrone![6] for they were banished, with no hope of
   their returning—
15   Who knows in what abodes of want those youths
   were driven to house?
Yet *you* can give yourself these airs, O Woman of
   Three Cows!

O, think of Donnell of the Ships,[7] the Chief
   whom nothing daunted—
See how he fell in distant Spain, unchronicled,
   unchanted!

---

[1] *The Woman of Three Cows*   Based on an anonymous Irish poem.

[2] *from the Irish*   Mangan used this phrase to identify poems whose subject matter originated in an Irish language poem. Such poems are not properly speaking translations; Mangan often drew on literal translations of the Irish originals, but his own poems are poetic re-workings rather than translations.

[3] *agragh*   Irish: my love.

[4] *Momonia*   Munster, one of the four provinces of Ireland and formerly the Kingdom of Munster; its kings were said to be descended from the mythological Éogan Mór, or Owen More.

[5] *brave sons ... of Clare*   Daniel and Charles O'Brien, both of whom fought for the Jacobites in the Irish army and died in battle abroad; along with the many Irish soldiers who fought for foreign armies between the sixteenth and eighteenth centuries, they were part of the group known as the "Wild Geese."

[6] *Movrone*   From the Irish *mo bhrón*: my sorrow.

[7] *Donnell of the Ships*   Donal Cam O'Sullivan Beare (1561–1618), among the last Gaelic lords of Ireland; after losing a battle at his stronghold at Dunboy Castle, he was exiled to Spain and eventually murdered there by an Englishman from Dublin.

He sleeps, the great O'Sullivan, where thunder
    cannot rouse—
20 Then ask yourself, should *you* be proud, good
    Woman of Three Cows!

O'Ruark, Maguire,[1] those souls of fire, whose names
    are shrined in story—
Think how their high achievements once made
    Erin's[2] highest glory—
Yet now their bones lie mouldering under weeds
    and cypress boughs,
And so, for all your pride, will yours, O Woman
    of Three Cows!

25 The O'Carrolls,[3] also, famed when Fame was only
    for the boldest,
Rest in forgotten sepulchres with Erin's best and oldest;
Yet who so great as they of yore in battle or carouse?
Just think of that, and hide your head, good
    Woman of Three Cows!

Your neighbour's poor, and you, it seems, are big
    with vain ideas,
30 Because, *inagh*![4] you've got three cows—one more,
    I see, than *she* has.
That tongue of yours wags more at times than
    Charity allows,
But if you're strong, be merciful, great Woman of
    Three Cows!
    —1840

Kathaleen Ny-Houlahan[5]

Long they pine in weary woe, the nobles of our land,
Long they wander to and fro, proscribed, alas!
    and banned;
Feastless, houseless, altarless, they bear the exile's brand;
But their hope is in the coming-to of Kathaleen
    Ny-Houlahan.

5 Think her not a ghostly hag, too hideous to be seen,
Call her not unseemly names, our matchless Kathaleen!
Young she is, and fair she is, and would be crowned
    a queen,
Were the king's son at home here with Kathaleen
    Ny-Houlahan!

Sweet and mild would look her face, O, none so
    sweet and mild,
10 Could she crush the foes by whom her beauty is reviled;
Woolen plaids[6] would grace herself, and robes of silk
    her child,
If the king's son were living here with Kathaleen
    Ny-Houlahan!

Sore disgrace it is to see the Arbitress° of thrones,   *ruler*
Vassal° to a Saxoneen[7] of cold and   *servant*
    sapless bones!
15 Bitter anguish wrings our souls—with heavy sighs
    and groans
We wait the Young Deliverer of Kathaleen
    Ny-Houlahan!

---

[1] *O'Ruark, Maguire* Brian O'Rourke (c. 1540–91) and Hugh Maguire (d. 1600), both supporters of O'Sullivan Beare in the Nine Years' War.

[2] *Erin* From the Irish *Éire* or *Éireann*, common poetic name for Ireland.

[3] *The O'Carrolls* Significant Gaelic noble family, who once ruled the Kingdom of Éile.

[4] *inagh!* An exclamation in Irish.

---

[5] *Kathaleen Ny-Houlahan* Figure of Irish nationalist mythology (more commonly spelled Kathleen Ni Houlihan), generally depicted as a woman who calls for the help and sacrifice of young men to help her take back her rightful land; she is most famously depicted in the play of the same name (1902) written by W.B. Yeats and Lady Augusta Gregory.

[6] *plaids* Garments in tartan patterns, generally associated with the Scottish Highlands but also sometimes with Ireland (especially during the rise of Irish nationalism).

[7] *Saxoneen* Mocking diminutive for Saxon, i.e., English person.

Let us pray to Him who holds life's issues in His
    hands—
Him who formed the mighty globe, with all its
    thousand lands;
Girding them with seas and mountains, rivers deep,
    and strands,
20 To cast a look of pity upon Kathaleen Ny-Houlahan!

He, who over sands and waves led Israèl along—
He, who fed with heavenly bread, that chosen tribe
    and throng—
He who stood by Moses when his foes were fierce
    and strong—
May He show forth His might in saving Kathaleen
    Ny-Houlahan.
—1841

Dark Rosaleen[1]

from the Irish

O my Dark Rosaleen,
    Do not sigh, do not weep!
The priests are on the ocean green,
    They march along the deep.
5 There's wine from the royal Pope,
    Upon the ocean green;
And Spanish ale shall give you hope,[2]
    My Dark Rosaleen!
    My own Rosaleen!
10 Shall glad your heart, shall give you hope,
Shall give you health, and help, and hope,
    My Dark Rosaleen.

Over hills and through dales,
    Have I roamed for your sake;
15 All yesterday I sailed with sails

On river and on lake.
The Erne,[3] at its highest flood,
    I dashed across unseen,
For there was lightning in my blood,
20   My Dark Rosaleen!
    My own Rosaleen!
Oh! there was lightning in my blood,
Red lightning lightened through my blood,
    My Dark Rosaleen!

25 All day long in unrest
    To and fro do I move,
The very soul within my breast
    Is wasted for you, love!
The heart in my bosom faints
30   To think of you, my Queen,
My life of life, my saint of saints,
    My Dark Rosaleen!
    My own Rosaleen!
To hear your sweet and sad complaints,
35 My life, my love, my saint of saints,
    My Dark Rosaleen!

Woe and pain, pain and woe,
    Are my lot night and noon,
To see your bright face clouded so,
40   Like to the mournful moon.
But yet will I rear your throne
    Again in golden sheen;
'Tis you shall reign, shall reign alone,
    My Dark Rosaleen!
45   My own Rosaleen!
'Tis you shall have the golden throne,
'Tis you shall reign, and reign alone,
    My Dark Rosaleen!

Over dews, over sands
50   Will I fly for your weal;
Your holy delicate white hands
    Shall girdle me with steel.
At home in your emerald bowers,

---

[1] *Dark Rosaleen* The poem is an adaptation of the Irish song *Róisín Dubh*, meaning "Dark Róisín," said to be named after the daughter of the Earl of Tyrone; the name Róisín has come to be taken as a poetic name for Ireland.

[2] *Spanish ale ... you hope* Referring to Spanish sympathies with Ireland, as a fellow Catholic country.

[3] *The Erne* River in Ulster, the northern province of Ireland.

From morning's dawn till e'en,°   *evening*
55 You'll pray for me, my flower of flowers,
      My Dark Rosaleen!
      My fond Rosaleen!
You'll think of me through daylight hours,
My virgin flower, my flower of flowers,
60   My Dark Rosaleen!

I could scale the blue air,
      I could plough the high hills,
Oh, I could kneel all night in prayer,
      To heal your many ills!
65 And one beamy smile from you
      Would float like light between
My toils and me, my own, my true,
      My Dark Rosaleen!
      My fond Rosaleen!
70 Would give me life and soul anew,
      A second life, a soul anew,
      My Dark Rosaleen!

O! the Erne shall run red
      With redundance of blood,
75 The earth shall rock beneath our tread,
      And flames wrap hill and wood,
And gun-peal, and slogan cry,
      Wake many a glen serene,
Ere you shall fade, ere you shall die,
80   My Dark Rosaleen!
      My own Rosaleen!
The Judgement Hour must first be nigh,
Ere you can fade, ere you can die,
      My Dark Rosaleen!
—1846

The Nameless One

Roll forth, my song, like the rushing river,
      That sweeps along to the mighty sea;
God will inspire me while I deliver
      My soul of thee!

5 Tell thou the world, when my bones lie whitening
      Amid the last homes of youth and eld,°   *old age*
That once there was one whose veins ran lightning
      No eye beheld.

Tell how his boyhood was one drear night-hour,
10   How shone for him, through his griefs and gloom,
No star of all heaven sends to light our
      Path to the tomb.

Roll on, my song, and to after ages
      Tell how, disdaining all earth can give,
15 He would have taught men, from wisdom's pages,
      The way to live.

And tell how trampled, derided, hated,
      And worn by weakness, disease, and wrong,
He fled for shelter to God, who mated
20   His soul with song.

With song which alway, sublime or vapid,
      Flowed like a rill° in the morning beam,   *small river*
Perchance not deep, but intense and rapid—
      A mountain stream.

25 Tell how this Nameless, condemned for years long
      To herd with demons from hell beneath,
Saw things that made him, with groans and tears, long
      For even death.

Go on to tell how, with genius wasted,
30   Betrayed in friendship, befooled in love,
With spirit shipwrecked, and young hopes blasted,
      He still, still strove;

Till, spent with toil, dreeing° death for others   *suffering*
      (And some whose hands should have wrought
           for him,
35 If children live not for sires° and mothers,)   *fathers*
      His mind grew dim;

And he fell far through that pit abysmal,
    The gulf and grave of Maginn and Burns,[1]
And pawned his soul for the devil's dismal
40   Stock of returns.

But yet redeemed it in days of darkness,
    And shapes and signs of the final wrath,
When death, in hideous and ghastly starkness,
    Stood on his path.

45 And tell how now, amid wreck and sorrow,
    And want, and sickness, and houseless nights,
He bides in calmness the silent morrow
    That no ray lights.

And lives he still, then? Yes! Old and hoary
50   At thirty-nine, from despair and woe,
He lives, enduring what future story
    Will never know.

Him grant a grave to, ye pitying noble,
    Deep in your bosoms: there let him dwell!
55 He, too, had tears for all souls in trouble,
    Here, and in hell.
   —1849(?)

SAMUEL FERGUSON (1810–1886)

A lawyer by profession, Samuel Ferguson was also a poet, antiquarian, and general enthusiast of Irish history. Born in Belfast, he lived in numerous regions throughout Ireland, and became a regular contributor to publications such as *Blackwood's Edinburgh Magazine* and the *Dublin University Magazine*. His travels throughout Great Britain and Ireland provided the material for an archaeological text on Celtic Ogham inscriptions, and he also published several volumes of poetry. Ferguson was a supporter of the nationalist Young Ireland movement, and through this association met writer and activist Thomas Davis, who became a beloved friend; Ferguson's "Lament for the Death of Thomas Davis" was written in grief at the young man's early death. Ferguson was knighted in 1878.

Lament for the Death of Thomas Davis

I walked through Ballinderry[2] in the spring-time,
    When the bud was on the tree;
And I said, in every fresh-ploughed field beholding
    The sowers striding free,
5 Scattering broadside° forth the corn in   *widely*
    golden plenty
    On the quick seed-clasping soil,
"Even such this day, among the fresh-stirred hearts
    of Erin.[3]
    Thomas Davis, is thy toil!"

I sat by Ballyshannon[4] in the summer,
10   And saw the salmon leap;
And I said, as I beheld the gallant creatures
    Spring glittering from the deep,
Through the spray, and through the prone heaps
    striving onward
    To the calm, clear streams above,
15 "So seekest thou thy native founts of freedom,
    Thomas Davis,
    In thy brightness of strength and love!"

I stood on Derrybawn[5] in the autumn,
    I heard the eagle call,
With a clangorous cry of wrath and lamentation,
20   That filled the wide mountain hall,
O'er the bare deserted place of his plundered eyrie;
    And I said, as he screamed and soared,
"So callest thou, thou wrathful-soaring Thomas Davis,
    For a nation's rights restored!"

---

[1] *Maginn and Burns* William Maginn (1794–1842) and Robert Burns (1759–96), writers known for the unhappy circumstances of their deaths, both rumored to have been alcoholics.

[2] *Ballinderry* Small parish in Northern Ireland.

[3] *Erin* Name for Ireland, stemming from the Irish endonym *Éire*.

[4] *Ballyshannon* Town in County Donegal.

[5] *Derrybawn* Mountain in County Wicklow.

5 And, alas! to think but now, and thou art lying
      Dear Davis, dead at thy mother's knee;
  And I, no mother near, on my own sick bed,
      That face on earth shall never see;
  I may lie and try to feel that I am dreaming,
10   I may lie and try to say, "Thy will be done"—
  But a hundred such as I will never comfort Erin
      For the loss of the noble son!

  Young husbandman of Erin's fruitful seed-time,
      In the fresh track of danger's plough!
35 Who will walk the heavy, toilsome, perilous furrow,
      Girt with freedom's seed-sheets now?
  Who will banish with the wholesome crop of knowledge
      The flaunting weed and the bitter thorn,
  Now that thou thyself art but a seed for hopeful
          planting
40   Against the resurrection[1] morn?

  Young salmon of the flood-tide of freedom
      That swells round Erin's shore!
  Thou wilt leap against their loud oppressive torrent
      Of bigotry and hate no more:
45 Drawn downward by their prone material instinct
      Let them thunder on their rocks, and foam—
  Thou hast leapt, aspiring soul, to founts beyond
          their raging,
      Where troubled waters never come!

  But I grieve not, eagle of the empty eyrie,
50   That thy wrathful cry is still;
  And that the songs alone of peaceful mourners
      Are heard today on Erin's hill:
  Better far, if brothers' war be destined for us
      (God avert that horrid day I pray!)
55 That ere our hands be stained with slaughter fratricidal,
      Thy warm hand should be cold in clay.

  But my trust is strong in God, who made us brothers,
      That he will not suffer their right hands
  Which thou hast joined in holier rites than wedlock,
60   To draw opposing brands.
  Oh, many a tuneful tongue that thou mad'st vocal
      Would lie cold and silent then—
  And songless long once more, should often-widowed
          Erin
      Mourn the loss of her brave young men.

65 Oh, brave young men, my love, my pride, my promise,
      'Tis on you my hopes are set,
  In manliness, in kindliness, in justice
      To make Erin a nation yet:
  Self-respecting, self-relying, self-advancing,
70   In union or in severance, free and strong—
  And if God grant this, then, under God, to Thomas
          Davis
      Let the greater praise belong!
  —1847

Dear Dark Head

  Put your head, darling, darling, darling,
      Your darling black head my heart above;
  Oh, mouth of honey, with the thyme for fragrance,
      Who, with heart in breast, could deny you love?

5 Oh, many and many a young girl for me is pining,
      Letting her locks of gold to the cold wind free,
  For me, the foremost of our gay young fellows;
      But I'd leave a hundred, pure love, for thee!

  Then put your head, darling, darling, darling,
10   Your darling black head my heart above;
  Oh, mouth of honey, with the thyme for fragrance,
      Who, with heart in breast, could deny you love?
  —1867

---

[1] *resurrection* I.e., the raising of the dead at the Day of Judgment.

THOMAS DAVIS (1814–1845)

Born in County Cork, Thomas Davis studied law at Trinity College in Dublin before becoming a leader of the nationalist Young Ireland movement. Hoping for unity between Protestants and Catholics in support of the Irish cause, he helped to establish the influential weekly newspaper *The Nation*, and wrote numerous nationalist ballads. Though he died of scarlet fever at the age of 30, his accomplishments during his brief years were such that he provided significant inspiration to later nationalists such as Patrick (or Pádraig) Pearse.

A Nation Once Again

When boyhood's fire was in my blood,
    I read of ancient freemen,
For Greece and Rome who bravely stood,
    Three Hundred men and Three men.[1]
5 And then I prayed I yet might see
    Our fetters rent° in twain,°   torn / two
And Ireland, long a province, be
    A Nation once again

And, from that time, through wildest woe,
10   That hope has shone, a far light;
Nor could love's brightest summer glow
    Outshine that solemn starlight:
It seemed to watch above my head
    In forum, field, and fane;°   church
15 Its angel voice sang round my bed,
    "A Nation once again."

It whispered, too, that "freedom's ark
    And service high and holy,
Would be profaned by feelings dark,
20   And passions vane or lowly;
For freedom comes from God's right hand,
    And needs a godly train;
And righteous men must make our land
    A Nation once again."

25 So, as I grew from boy to man,
    I bent me to that bidding—
My spirit of each selfish plan
    And cruel passion ridding;
For, thus I hoped one day to aid—
30   Oh! can such hope be vain?
When my dear country shall be made
    A Nation once again.
—1845

AODH MAC DOMHNAILL (1802–1867)

Mac Domhnaill wrote poetry in Irish during a period when the use of that language was declining dramatically. For many years he was employed by the Irish Society, a Protestant-run organization which aimed to give Irish speakers throughout Ireland access to the Scriptures in their native language; he also worked collecting Irish-language songs, stories, and manuscripts. Among Mac Domhnaill's own writings—many of which were elegies to figures such as the Catholic leader Daniel O'Connell—are three poems written during various stages of the Great Famine. The details of the last few years of Mac Domhnaill's life are unclear; he died in a poorhouse in County Cavan in 1867.

---

[1] [Davis's note] The Three Hundred Greeks who died at Thermopylæ, and the Three Romans who kept the Sublician Bridge.

Milleadh na bPrátaí

Níl file ná fáidh dár ghnáthaigh cumann na Naoi,
Níl ollamh ná bard le fáil a bhlas an sruth sí,
Níl duine den dáil gan cháin gan donas gan díth,
Faoi chogadh lucht Beárla a sháraigh orainn le dlí.

5   Ach dá mairfeadh i stát san áit seo curaidh mar bhí,
Mac Cumhaill is mac Dáire is ní áirím Conchúr an rí,
Cú Chulainn, Conall Cearnach is ar sáraíodh uilig sa
        maidhm,
Ba ghairid an spás go gcarnfaí Bhullaí sa ngríb.

Ach ó d'imigh gan dáil na táinte a chleacht inár dtír,
10 Is gan againn 'na n-áit ach bearnadh, gorta is íot',
Ní chluintear in álraibh cárlach is ceiliúr ar chraobh,
Is níl bric san áill mar ghnách in Oileán na Naomh.

Níl fear i gcrích Fáil ná mná is leinbh na cích',
Níl scafaire breá ná stáidbhean mhascalach mhín,
15 Níl bacach ar shráid ach cráite is torrach a chaoi,
Ó tháinig an phláigh ar phrátaí, is díomhaoin dubh
        díth'.

The Spoiling of the Potatoes[1]

There's neither poet nor prophet with the Muses
        acquainted,
Nor ollave,[2] nor bard, the enchanted stream that has
        tasted,
Not one of them is free of censure, misery, and want,
After the war of the English speakers who with laws
        have oppressed us.

5   But if the heroes of old held sway in this place,
Mac Cumhaill, mac Dáire or, even, Conchúr the king,[3]
Cú Chulainn, Conall Cearnach[4] and all who were
        bested in the attack,
They wouldn't be long driving Billy[5] into the mud.

But since the wealth we knew in this land was divested,
10 And in its place only destruction, famine and thirst,
The song of the birds in glen or on branch is heard not,
There's no longer trout in the streams of the Island of
        Saints.[6]

There's no man in Ireland, nor woman, nor suckling
        babe,
There's no strapping fellow nor stately woman,
        strong and fine,
15 There's no beggar on the street that is not tormented
        and care-laden;
Since the potatoes were blighted, they are destitute
        and sorely wanting.

---

[1] *The Spoiling of the Potatoes*   The translation is by Fionntán DeBrun (translation copyright © Fionntán DeBrun 2018).

[2] *ollave*   Highest class of poets. (The Irish spelling *ollamh* is often used in English as well.)

[3] *Mac Cumhaill*   Fionn mac Cumhaill, also known in English as Finn MacCool, a celebrated hunter-warrior of Irish mythology, featured in the Fenian Cycle; *mac Dáire* Legendary warrior-king of Munster; *Conchúr the king* Conchobar mac Nessa, legendary king of Ulster.

[4] *Cú Chulainn*   Legendary warrior of Ulster, known for his ability to go into a terrifying battle frenzy; *Conall Cearnach* Legendary warrior.

[5] *Billy*   Anglicization of an Irish word for the English.

[6] *Island of Saints*   Common epithet for Ireland.

Is an measann sibh a chairde an rá seo uile bheith fíor,
Gurbh é siocair na mbráithre a sháraigh aithne na
    naomh,
Nó cionnfáth na banríona a d'áirigh muintir na crích',
20 Nó an dtáinig an phláigh mar thámhaibh eile ón
    ngaoth?

Ní chreidim go bráth is a shárfhios anois ag mo chroí
Gurbh é mallacht an Phápa ar Mháirtín fá bhriseadh
    an dlí
A thug milleadh ar bharr na bprátaí uilig san oích'—
Is feicfidh tú bearnadh is bánú eile ar Sheán Bhuí.

25 Guímse an tAthair is Banríon Fhlaitheas na Naomh,
Peadar 's a' Papa, Pádraig is easpaig an tsaoil,
Sagairt is bráithre cráifeach is manaigh le brí
Go dtige na Spáinnigh le prátaí chugainn arís.
    —1846

And friends, do you think that all that is said is true,
That this was the fault of the friars who broke the
    commandments of saints,
Or the reason the queen counted the people of the land?[1]
20 Or did the blight come like other plagues from the wind?

I will never believe it for I now know it right well in
    my heart,
That it was the Pope's curse on Martin[2] for breaking
    the law
That brought destruction on all the potato crop in the
    night—
And you'll yet see John Bull[3] breached and laid to
    waste.

25 I pray in earnest to the Father and the Queen of
    Heaven,
Peter and the Pope, Patrick[4] and all the world's bishops,
Priests and pious friars and monks
That the Spanish may come to us with potatoes again.[5]
    —TRANSLATION 2018

---

[1] *the queen … the land* Reference to the census taken in 1841 (the
monarch at the time was Queen Victoria).

[2] *Martin* Martin Luther (1483–1546), German religious leader
whose attacks on ecclesiastical corruption began the Protestant Reformation in Europe; he was excommunicated by the Pope for his anti-
Church writings.

[3] *John Bull* Common personification of England.

[4] *Peter* Saint Peter, one of Jesus' apostles, traditionally considered
the first pope by Roman Catholics; *Patrick* Patron saint of Ireland,
traditionally considered the first bishop of Armagh and the founder of
Christianity on the island.

[5] *the Spanish … potatoes again* The earliest-known cultivation of the
potato was by the Incas in South America; following the conquest of
Peru by Spain in 1536, the Spanish introduced the potato to Europe.

BOY AND GIRL AT CAHERA.

A temporary roadside home of a landless family, late nineteenth century. No photographs of the suffering endured by the Irish peasantry during the Great Famine are known to exist. Photographs such as this one from later in the century, however, provide evidence of how little improvement there was in housing conditions for the very poor, even many decades after the famine. (For more on this subject, see the section "Contexts: Ireland in the Long Nineteenth Century" in the online component of this anthology.)

James Mahoney, *Boy and Girl at Cahera*. This sketch was one of several published in the 13 February 1847 and 20 February 1847 issues of *The Illustrated London News*. The accompanying story provided the background: "The sketch is taken on the road, at Cahera, of a famished boy and girl turning up the ground to seek for a potato to appease their hunger. 'Not far from the spot where I made this sketch,' says Mr. Mahoney, 'is another of the many sepulchres above ground, where six dead bodies had lain for twelve days, without the least chance of interment, owing to their being so far from the town.'" Substantial excerpts from these illustrated articles, together with other background documents pertaining to the Great Famine, are available in the online component of this anthology, in the section "Contexts: Ireland in the Long Nineteenth Century."

LADY JANE WILDE (SPERANZA) (1821–1896)

Poet, nationalist, and women's rights campaigner Lady Jane Wilde, née Elgee, was born in Wexford in 1821. Though today less well-known than her son Oscar, in her own time Wilde was a popular and respected member of literary circles in Dublin and London, and hosted a salon in the home in which her son grew up. Wilde wrote poetry for the influential and controversial nationalist newspaper *The Nation* in the 1840s, alternately using the pen names John Fenshaw Ellis and "Speranza"—meaning "hope" in Italian; she became an editor of the newspaper in 1848. Wilde also published two volumes of poetry and a collection of Irish folktales. Upon the bankruptcy and death of her husband, Lady Wilde moved to London to join Oscar and his brother Willie, where she lived in relative poverty until her death in 1896.

The Famine Year

1

Weary men, what reap ye?—Golden corn for the stranger.[1]
What sow ye?—Human corses° that wait   *corpses*
    for the avenger.
Fainting forms, hunger-stricken, what see you
    in the offing?°   *distance*
Stately ships to bear our food away, amid the
    stranger's scoffing.
5   There's a proud array of soldiers—what do they
    round your door?
They guard our masters' granaries from the thin
    hands of the poor.
Pale mothers, wherefore weeping?—Would to God
    that we were dead—
Our children swoon° before us, and we   *faint*
    cannot give them bread.

2

Little children, tears are strange upon your infant
    faces,
10   God meant you but to smile within your mother's
    soft embraces.
Oh! we know not what is smiling, and we know
    not what is dying;
But we're hungry, very hungry, and we cannot stop
    our crying.
And some of us grow cold and white—we know not
    what it means;
But, as they lie beside us, we tremble in our dreams.
15   There's a gaunt crowd on the highway—are ye come
    to pray to man,
With hollow eyes that cannot weep, and for words
    your faces wan?°   *pale, sickly*

3

No; the blood is dead within our veins—we care
    not now for life;
Let us die hid in the ditches, far from children and
    from wife;
We cannot stay and listen to their raving, famished
    cries—
20   Bread! Bread! Bread! and none to still their agonies.
We left our infants playing with their dead mother's
    hand:
We left our maidens maddened by the fever's
    scorching brand:
Better, maiden, thou were strangled in thy own
    dark-twisted tresses—
Better, infant, thou wert smothered in thy mother's
    first caresses.

4

25   We are fainting in our misery, but God will hear
    our groan;
Yet, if fellow-men desert us, will He hearken°   *listen*
    from His Throne?
Accursed are we in our own land, yet toil we still
    and toil;
But the stranger reaps our harvest—the alien owns
    our soil.

---

[1] *Golden corn ... the stranger* Aside from the blight upon potatoes, during the famine actual shortage of food in Ireland was never as extreme as might be expected; rather, the issue at hand was the continued export of Irish crops to England and abroad, even throughout the height of starvation; *corn* Any edible grain, such as wheat.

O Christ! how have we sinned, that on our native
    plains
30 We perish houseless, naked, starved, with branded
    brow, like Cain's?[1]
Dying, dying wearily, with a torture sure and slow—
Dying, as a dog would die, by the wayside as we go.

5

One by one they're falling round us, their pale faces
    to the sky;
We've no strength left to dig them graves—there let
    them lie.
35 The wild bird, if he's stricken, is mourned by the
    others,
But we—we die in Christian land—we die amid our
    brothers,
In the land which God has given, like a wild beast in
    his cave,
Without a tear, a prayer, a shroud, a coffin, or a grave.
Ha! but think ye the contortions on each livid face ye see,
40 Will not be read on judgment-day by eyes of Deity?

6

We are wretches, famished, scorned, human tools to
    build your pride,
But God will yet take vengeance for the souls for
    whom Christ died.
Now is your hour of pleasure—bask ye in the world's
    caress;
But our whitening bones against ye will arise as
    witnesses,
45 From the cabins and the ditches, in their charred,
    uncoffined masses,
For the Angel of the Trumpet[2] will know them as he
    passes.
A ghastly, spectral army, before the great God we'll stand,
And arraign ye as our murderers, the spoilers of our
    land.
—1864

---

[1] *Cain* In Genesis 4, Cain murders his brother Abel, and is thenceforth marked and cursed by God.

[2] *Angel of the Trumpet* I.e., the angel or angels who will sound the
trumpets to announce the coming of the Last Judgment.

WILLIAM ALLINGHAM (1824–1889)

Though today remembered mostly for "The Fairies"
and a small number of similar poems, William
Allingham was a relatively influential writer during
his own day, and was a contemporary and friend of
poets such as Alfred Tennyson and Dante Gabriel
Rossetti. Besides being a writer of original poetry,
Allingham was also a collector of ballads, and
published a popular volume of British ballads in
1864. His own poetry was significant in the
development of the Celtic revival movement, and in
this capacity inspired later Irish poets such as W.B.
Yeats.

The Fairies
(A Child's Song)

Up the airy mountain,
    Down the rushy glen,
We daren't go a-hunting
    For fear of little men;
5 Wee folk, good folk,[3]
    Trooping all together;
Green jacket, red cap,
    And white owl's feather!

Down along the rocky shore
10   Some make their home,
They live on crispy pancakes
    Of yellow tide-foam;
Some in the reeds
    Of the black mountain lake,
15 With frogs for their watch-dogs,
    All night awake.

High on the hill-top
    The old King sits;
He is now so old and grey
20   He's nigh lost his wits.
With a bridge of white mist

---

[3] *good folk* Common epithet in Ireland for the fairies.

Columbkill[1] he crosses,
  On his stately journeys
    From Slieveleague to Rosses;[2]
25 Or going up with music
    On cold starry nights,
To sup with the Queen
    Of the gay Northern Lights.

They stole little Bridget
30   For seven years long;
When she came down again
    Her friends were all gone.
They took her lightly back,
    Between the night and morrow;
35 They thought that she was fast asleep,
    But she was dead with sorrow.
They have kept her ever since
    Deep within the lakes,
On a bed of flag-leaves,
40   Watching till she wakes.

By the craggy hill-side,
  Through the mosses bare,
They have planted thorn-trees
  For pleasure here and there.
45 Is any man so daring
    As dig one up in spite,
He shall find their sharpest thorns
    In his bed at night.

Up the airy mountain,
50   Down the rushy glen,
We daren't go a-hunting
    For fear of little men;
Wee folk, good folk,
    Trooping all together;
55 Green jacket, red cap,
    And white owl's feather!
—1849

---

[1] *Columbkill* Coloumbkille Lough in County Donegal, named after
Saint Columba or Colm Cille, a significant early missionary said to
have been born in Donegal.

[2] *Slieveleague to Rosses* Set of sea cliffs and geographical area,
respectively, in County Donegal.

THOMAS D'ARCY MCGEE (1825–1868)

Although he is more widely known as the Irish-Canadian politician who successfully pushed for Confederation in the 1860s, Thomas D'Arcy McGee (1825–68) was also a prolific writer, and was indeed regarded by some as among the finest Irish poets of the nineteenth century. Born in Louth and raised largely in Wexford, McGee received little formal education, instead attending informal hedge schools. At the age of seventeen he emigrated to the United States, where he wrote for Irish-American journals such as *The Boston Pilot* and spoke in favor of repealing the Irish Acts of Union. Three years later he returned to Ireland and became involved with the radical nationalist paper *The Nation* and the Young Irelander Rebellion of 1848; when the rebellion failed, he fled back to the United States. After this period his political views grew increasingly conservative. He moved to Canada in 1857 and denounced the radicalism of the growing Fenian Movement. After a decade of success as a Canadian politician, McGee was assassinated in 1868; his funeral was attended by thousands.

Throughout the changing periods of his political career, McGee remained known and respected for his poetry, much of which takes inspiration from the history and mythology of his native Ireland. The text of the following poems is taken from the posthumous collection of his poetry, *The Poems of Thomas D'Arcy McGee*, edited by Irish author Mary Anne Sadlier in 1869. In her preface to the volume, Sadlier notes that some poems have been changed very slightly "to correct errors, which the author himself would have done in a general revision."

The Celts

Long, long ago, beyond the misty space
  Of twice a thousand years,
In Erin[3] old there dwelt a mighty race,
  Taller than Roman spears;
5 Like oaks and towers, they had a giant grace,
  Were fleet as deers,

---

[3] *Erin* From the Irish name for Ireland, Éire.

With winds and wave they made their
    'biding°-place,   *abiding*
  These Western shepherd-seers.

Their ocean-god was Mân-â-nân M'Lir,[1]
10   Whose angry lips,
In their white foam, full often would inter
  Whole fleets of ships;
Cromah,[2] their day-god and their thunderer,
  Made morning and eclipse;
15 Bride[3] was their queen of song, and unto her
  They prayed with fire-touched lips.

Great were their deeds, their passions, and their sports;
  With clay and stone
They piled on strath[4] and shore those mystic forts
20   Not yet o'erthrown;
On cairn-crowned hills they held their council-courts;
  While youths alone,
With giant dogs, explored the elk resorts,
  And brought them down.

25 Of these was Finn,[5] the father of the bard
  Whose ancient song
Over the clamor of all change is heard,
  Sweet-voiced and strong.
Finn once o'ertook Granu,[6] the golden-haired,
30   The fleet and young;

From her the lovely, and from him the feared,
  The primal poet sprung.

Ossian! two thousand years of mist and change
  Surround thy name—
35 Thy Finian[7] heroes now no longer range
  The hills of fame.
The very name of Finn and Gaul[8] sound strange—
  Yet thine the same—
By miscalled lake and desecrated grange—
40   Remains, and shall remain!

The Druid's[9] altar and the Druid's creed
  We scarce can trace,
There is not left an undisputed deed
  Of all your race,
45 Save your majestic song, which hath their speed,
  And strength and grace;
In that sole song they live, and love, and bleed—
  It bears them on through space.

Oh, inspired giant! shall we e'er behold
50   In our own time
One fit to speak your spirit on the wold,°   *open moor*
  Or seize your rhyme?
One pupil of the past, as mighty souled
  As in the prime,
55 Were the fond, fair, and beautiful, and bold—
  They, of your song sublime!
—1869

---

[1] *Mân-â-nân M'Lir*   Celtic sea god.

[2] *Cromah*   Likely Crom Cruach, Celtic god with unclear associations and origins, who has been described variously as a sun god, a god of fertility, or a violent god propitiated by human sacrifice.

[3] *Bride*   Also known as Brigid, Celtic goddess of spring, fertility, and poetry, whose mythology may have merged with that of the popular Catholic Saint Brigid; traditions in the veneration of both the goddess and the saint involve tending a sacred fire.

[4] *strath*   Broad river valley.

[5] *Finn*   Fionn mac Cumhaill or Finn MacCool, famed hunter-warrior of Irish mythology and father of the mythological poet Oisín, or Ossian.

[6] *Granu*   Probably Gráinne, mythological wife of Fionn; however, according to the dominant mythology, Gráinne vehemently disliked her husband and eventually separated from him; the poet Oisín is thus said to have been the son of Fionn and another woman, Sadhbh.

Home Thoughts

If will had wings, how fast I'd flee
To the home of my heart o'er the seething sea!

---

[7] *Finian*   Referring to the Fenian Cycle, the body of mythological accounts describing the life of Fionn mac Cumhaill and his relations.

[8] *Gaul*   Probably Goll mac Morna, Fionn's sometime-enemy and sometime-ally.

[9] *Druid*   Member of an ancient, semi-mythological Celtic order of magicians, sorcerers, and soothsayers.

If wishes were power, if words were spells,
I'd be this hour where my own love dwells.

5   My own love dwells in the storied land,
Where the holy wells sleep in yellow sand;
And the emerald lustre of Paradise beams
Over homes that cluster round singing streams.

I, sighing, alas! exist alone—
10 My youth is as grass on an unsunned stone,
Bright to the eye, but unfelt below—
As sunbeams that lie over Arctic snow.

My heart is a lamp that love must relight,
Or the world's fire-damp will quench it quite;
15 In the breast of my dear, my life-tide springs—
Oh! I'd tarry none here, if will had wings.
—1869

The Irish Wife

Earl Desmond's Apology[1]

I would not give my Irish wife
For all the dames of the Saxon land—
I would not give my Irish wife
For the Queen of France's hand;
5   For she to me is dearer
Than castles strong, or lands, or life—
An outlaw—so I'm near her
To love till death my Irish wife.

Oh, what would be this home of mine—
10 A ruined, hermit-haunted place,
But for the light that nightly shines
Upon its walls from Kathleen's face?

What comfort in a mine of gold—
What pleasure in a royal life,
15 If the heart within lay dead and cold,
If I could not wed my Irish wife?

I knew the law forbade the banns[2]—
I knew my king abhorred her race—
Who never bent before their clans,
20 Must bow before their ladies' grace.
Take all my forfeited domain,
I cannot wage with kinsmen strife—
Take knightly gear and noble name,
And I will keep my Irish wife.

25 My Irish wife has clear blue eyes,
My heaven by day, my stars by night—
And, twin-like, truth and fondness lie
Within her swelling bosom white.
My Irish wife has golden hair—
30 Apollo's[3] harp had once such strings—
Apollo's self might pause to hear
Her bird-like carol when she sings.

I would not give my Irish wife
For all the dames of the Saxon land—
35 I would not give my Irish wife
For the Queen of France's hand;
For she to me is dearer
Than castles strong, or lands, or life—
In death I would lie near her,
40 And rise beside my Irish wife.
—1869

Memories

I left two loves on a distant strand,
One young, and fond, and fair, and bland;[4]

---

[1] *Earl Desmond's Apology*   The poem is apparently inspired by the marriage in 1418 of Thomas Fitzgerald, 5th Earl of Desmond—an Anglo-Norman peer—and the Gaelic woman Catherine MacCormac. The marriage violated the Statutes of Kilkenny, which forbade English settlers from marrying into old Irish families; Fitzgerald was thereby dispossessed of his lands. The marriage also inspired a poem by Irish poet Thomas Moore (1779–1852), "Desmond's Song"; *Apology* Defense.

[2] *banns*   Public declaration of an intention to marry.

[3] *Apollo*   Greek god of music.

[4] *bland*   Gentle; mild-mannered.

One fair, and old, and sadly grand—
My wedded wife and my native land.

5   One tarrieth sad and seriously
Beneath the roof that mine should be;
One sitteth sibyl-like[1] by the sea,
Chanting a grave song mournfully.

A little life I have not seen
10 Lies by the heart that mine hath been;
A cypress wreath darkles now, I ween,°   *think*
Upon the brow of my love in green.

The mother and wife shall pass away,
Her hands be dust, her lips be clay;
15 But my other love on earth shall stay,
And live in the life of a better day.

Ere we were born my first love was,
My sires° were heirs to her holy cause;   *fathers*
And she yet shall sit in the world's applause,
20 A mother of men and blessèd laws.

I hope and strive the while I sigh,
For I know my first love cannot die;
From the chain of woes that loom so high
Her reign shall reach to eternity.
—1869

EMILY LAWLESS (1845–1913)

Born into an aristocratic Anglo-Irish family (her father became a baron while she was a child), Lawless spent much of her childhood at the estate of her mother's family in Country Galway, and became much affected by the rugged scenery of western Ireland. She began to write while in her thirties; her first novel, the three-volume *A Chelsea Householder*, was published in 1882. Her third novel, *Hurrish*, set a remote area of County Clare, established Lawless as a popular novelist.

[1] *sibyl-like* Resembling the sibyls, women of classical mythology with powers of divination, often characterized as frenzied or witch-like.

Lawless wrote history as well as fiction and poetry, and her novels and poems are often set in earlier eras. She seems to have had more sympathy with the cause of rebellion against English oppression in earlier eras than she did in her own. She supported the Land League's efforts to improve the lot of Irish tenant farmers (a cause bitterly opposed by her landowner brother), but she was no revolutionary; rather than Home Rule for Ireland, she advocated a continuance of the union between Ireland and the rest of Britain.

Her best-known poems appear in the volume *With the Wild Geese* (1902), which had originally appeared in a privately printed edition in 1898. It came to the attention of Stopford Brooke, who encouraged her to seek a wider audience for the poems; she agreed on the condition that he write an introduction that would fill in for English readers the historical context for the poems. Here is the explanation given for the meaning of "wild geese" in this context:

> The "Wild Geese" was the name given by the romantic and sorrowful imaginings of the Irish to the exiles who, like the wild birds and with their wailing cry, migrated to the Continent before and after the Battle of Aughrim, and the Surrender of Limerick in 1691. The Irish officers and soldiers were permitted by the Treaty of Limerick to go where they pleased in ships provided by the English government. Twenty thousand sorrowing men … sailed to Brest. … They were only the forerunners of a great exodus of Irishmen flying from the iniquities of the penal laws to give their swords to France, an exodus which lasted fully a hundred years.

Lawless never married; towards the end of the century she moved to Surrey, south of London, where she appears to have shared a household with Lady Sarah Spencer. In *A Garden Diary* (1902), which she dedicates "To the Garden's Chief owner, and the Gardener's Friend," Lawless published selections from a diary in which she writes of their garden, of their household, of world affairs (especially of the Boer War that was then raging), and—with passionate intensity in the 25 August 1900 entry reproduced below—of their friendship.

After Aughrim[1]

She said, "They gave me of their best,
They lived, they gave their lives for me;[2]
I tossed them to the howling waste,
And flung them to the foaming sea."

5 She said, "I never gave them aught,
Not mine the power, if mine the will;
I let them starve, I let them bleed—
They bled and starved, and loved me still."

She said, "Ten times they fought for me,
10 Ten times they strove with might and main,
Ten times I saw them beaten down,
Ten times they rose and fought again."

She said, "I stayed alone at home,
A dreary woman, grey and cold;
15 I never asked them how they fared,
Yet still they loved me as of old."

She said, "I never called them sons,
I almost ceased to breathe their name,
Then caught it echoing down the wind,
20 Blown backwards from the lips of Fame."

She said, "Not mine, not mine the fame;
Far over sea, far over land,
Cast forth like rubbish from my shores,
They won it yonder, sword in hand."

25 She said, "God knows they owe me nought,
I tossed them to the foaming sea,
I tossed them to the howling waste,
Yet still their love comes home to me."
—1902

---

[1] *Aughrim*   At the battle of Aughrim (1691), fought near Galway in western Ireland, between 5,000 and 10,000 lives were lost as the English army defeated the Jacobite army; the Jacobites were never again a significant force.

[2] *me*   The voice here is that of Ireland personified as a woman—a literary device long common in Irish literature.

Clare Coast[3]

Circa 1720

See, cold island, we stand
Here tonight on your shore,
Tonight, but never again;
Lingering a moment more.
5 See, beneath us our boat
Tugs at its tightening chain,
Holds out its sail to the breeze,
Pants to be gone again.
Off then with shouts and mirth,
10 Off with laughter and jests,
Mirth and song on our lips,
Hearts like lead in our breasts.

Death and the grave behind,
Death and a traitor's bier;
15 Honour and fame before,
Why do we linger here?
Why do we stand and gaze,
Fools, whom fools despise,
Fools untaught by the years,
20 Fools renounced by the wise?

Heartsick, a moment more,
Heartsick, sorry, fierce,
Lingering, lingering on,
Dreaming the dreams of yore;
25 Dreaming the dreams of our youth,
Dreaming the days when we stood
Joyous, expectant, serene,
Glad, exultant of mood,
Singing with hearts afire,
30 Singing with joyous strain,
Singing aloud in our pride,
"We shall redeem her again!"

---

[3] *Clare Coast*   The poem, part of Lawless's collection *With the Wild Geese* (1902), takes as its subject the "Wild Geese," exiled soldiers who left Ireland to fight in continental armies between the sixteenth and eighteenth centuries; many of those soldiers were Irish Catholics, who were barred by the Penal Laws from entering the armed forces in their own country; *Clare* County on the west coast of Ireland.

Ah, not tonight that strain—
Silent tonight we stand,
35 A scanty, a toil-worn crew,
Strangers, foes in the land!
Gone the light of our youth,
Gone forever, and gone,
Hope with the beautiful eyes,
40 Who laughed as she lured us on;
Lured us to danger and death,
To honour, perchance to fame—
Empty fame at the best,
Glory half dimmed with shame.
45 War-battered dogs are we,
Fighters in every clime,
Fillers of trench and of grave,
Mockers, bemocked by time.
War-dogs, hungry and grey,
50 Gnawing a naked bone,
Fighters in every clime,
Every cause but our own.

See us, cold isle of our love!
Coldest, saddest of isles—
55 Cold as the hopes of our youth,
Cold as your own wan smiles.
Coldly your streams outpour,
Each apart on the height,
Trickling, indifferent, slow,
60 Lost in the hush of the night.
Colder, sadder the clouds,
Comfortless bringers of rain;
Desolate daughters of air,
Sweep o'er your sad grey plain
65 Hiding the form of your hills,
Hiding your low sand duns;°   *dunes*
But coldest, saddest, oh isle!
Are the homeless hearts of your sons.

Coldest, and saddest there,
70 In yon sun-lit land of the south,
Where we sicken, and sorrow, and pine,
And the jest flies from mouth to mouth,
And the church bells crash overhead,

And the idle hours flit by,
75 And the beaded wine-cups clink.
And the sun burns fierce in the sky;
And your exiles, the merry of heart,
Laugh and boast with the best,
Boast, and extol their part,
80 Boast, till some lifted brow,
Crossed with a line severe,
Seems with displeasure to ask,
"Are these loud braggarts we hear,
Are they the sons of the West,
85 The wept-for, the theme of songs,
The exiled, the injured, the banned,
The men of a thousand wrongs?"

Fool, did you never hear
Of sunshine which broke through rain?
90 Sunshine which came with storm?
Laughter that rang of pain?
Boastings begotten of grief,
Vauntings to hide a smart,
Braggings with trembling lip,
95 Tricks of a broken heart?

Sudden some wayward gleam,
Sudden some passing sound—
The careless splash of an oar,
The idle bark of a hound,
100 A shadow crossing the sun,
An unknown step in the hall,
A nothing, a folly, a straw!
Back it returns—all—all!
Back with the rush of a storm,
105 Back the old anguish and ill,
The sad, green landscape of home,
The small grey house by the hill,
The wide grey shores of the lake,
The low sky, seeming to weave
110 Its tender pitiful arms
Round the sick lone landscape at eve.
Back with its pains and its wrongs,
Back with its toils and its strife,
Back with its struggle and woe,

115 Back flows the stream of our life.
Darkened with treason and wrong,
Darkened with anguish and ruth,°   *sorrow*
Bitter, tumultuous, fierce,
Yet glad in the light of our youth.

120 So, cold island, we stand
Here tonight on your shore—
Tonight, but never again,
Lingering a moment more.
See, beneath us our boat,
125 Tugs at its tightening chain,
Holds out its sail to the breeze,
Pants to be gone again.
Off then with shouts and mirth,
Off with laughter and jests,
130 Jests and song on our lips,
Hearts like lead in our breasts.
—1902

To _____, Aged Twenty-Two

You will recall perchance some summer day,
Not this year, or e'en the next, but some far year,
What time we two have stood together here,
Under this friendly cloudflecked sky of May.

5 The late-come swallows in their devious way,
The urgent questings of bewildered bees,
The chirp of some proud mother from the trees,
And the warm promise of the procreant clay,

All these will perhaps return, and if with these,
10 With sun and cloud and bird and budding trees
There mingle some old memories of me,
Keep them, but do not grieve. For naught abides,
The untiring river rolls, and down its tides
Wave follows wave into the same old sea.
—1909

Emigrants

Like sea-pools on some restless, rock-strewn shore
These bog-pools flutter ere they sink to rest,
And o'er this surface, level as a floor,
Yon blue reek° trails its idle way to west   *chimney-smoke*
5 It comes from thee, brown shieling,[1] late bereft
Of thy last fledgelings; tenement outworn,
Long marked for desolation, and now left
To two old hearts, submissive, but forlorn.

How like some wintry nest it shows tonight;
10 While over its bent thatch a young curved moon
Peers through thin clouds scarce greyer than her light
Peers wistfully, as if arrived too soon,
Or doubtful of her welcome. While I stand
A string of wild duck speeds across her horn,
15 Six, seven, eleven—Oh adventurous band!
Westward you stream, due west, and now are gone.

Gone! Gone! They leave us! Yet the brown pools there
Still dance and flutter in this crisping wind,
And still the blue reek gaily mounts to where
20 That new-born moon, so timid, yet so kind,
Peers earthward, as if curious to mark
A scene less often honoured of the sun.
Slowly the shadows lengthen, while the dark
Grows deeper; and another day is done.
—1906

from *A Garden Diary*

September 4, 1899

It has been wet, and is now fine again, consequently
our view of the downs exhibits those tones of vinous[2]
purple, shading into indigo, that in moments of patriotic expansion I am apt to call Irish. I do not think it is
quite friendly of our neighbours, especially those who

---

1 *shieling*   Rustic house on a pasture.

2 *vinous*   Wine-like.

live upon the ridge above our heads, to smile so significantly whenever that word "view" happens to slip out, as it did just now, in alluding to our new possession, and its prospects. For what, after all, is a view? The question seems to suggest a reference to the dictionary, and here is Webster, ponderous in brown calf.[1] "View. 1st. Act of seeing, or beholding; sight; survey; examination by the eye. That which is looked towards, or kept in sight; an appearance; a show." Well, have we not something to look towards, to keep in sight, some appearance, some show? For that matter, so, it may be urged, has the habitant of the "two pair back,"[2] or the rustic whose prospect is limited to a survey of his or her neighbours' under garments—those "short and simple flannels of the poor" hung to dry in silhouette against a back fence. The truth is it is not at all desirable to be so haughty. I will not go so far as to say that it is unchristian, but it is certainly unbecoming, for are we not all fellow-creatures? What if you *can* command seven counties from your windows? What if on one particular morning—to me incredible—you did see three ships cross Shoreham gap?[3] What if from your garden chair you can be regaled by a fantasia of changing lights and shadows? be lapped into peace upon summer afternoons, or stirred by the drama of battle clouds, flung into blackness by a storm? Well, if you can, be glad of it, but for pity's sake abstain from bragging! "Gi' God thanks, and say no more o' it." Believe me it is not even commonly lucky to be so proud, and I speak with some little authority upon that subject.

For as regards this matter of views, I too have been haughty to the point of insupportableness. I too have believed that the possession of wide prospects argued some peculiar, some ineffable superiority in myself. There was a time when nothing short of an entire ocean, none of your petty babbling channels, but the whole thundering Atlantic, sufficed for my ambition. In those days only upon the largest combination of sea, sky, mountain; seascape, landscape, cloudscape, did it seem

possible adequately to exist. As for a mere rustic landscape, as for a confined one, as for a humdrum English one, above all as for a landscape within fifty miles of London, why the mention of such things merely moved my commiseration! Those were the days when to be called upon to leave what is sometimes uncivilly called the ruder[4] island, and to repair, even temporarily, to the more prosperous one, seemed a fall and a degradation hardly to be measured by words. When the contraction of the horizon seemed like a contraction of all life, and of all that made life worth having. When the remembrance that one would have to wake in the morning with no dim blue line to greet one, appeared, to a patriotic, a self-respecting being, to be a wrong and an indignity hardly to be endured without revolt.

Such an attitude is, I now hold, unbecoming in mere mortals, and, like other vaulting ambitions, is apt to precede a fall. The man who starts in life determined to be either Cæsar, or nothing, frequently fails to become Cæsar, whereas with regard to the other alternative, the gods are quite capable of taking him at his word. Happily, life is for most of us a liberal education, and the narrowing of the horizon comes to be endured with a philosophy born of other, and more serious deprivations. It may even be open to question whether any man or woman ever yet was made the better by the possession of a noble view? That he or she ought to have been made so is quite true, but as a matter of fact, have they? We are moulded out of exceedingly stubborn stuff, and are not often ennobled, I suspect, by the landscapes that surround us, any more than we are by the pursuits we follow, or the names that we carry about with us. Furthermore the essentials of all landscape show a considerable similarity. Much the same sort of clouds and sunshine, much the same sort of nights and days, much the same sort of summers and winters, visit alike the tamest and the wildest of them. Even the more dramatic and exciting fluctuations—snow, and hail, storm, and lightning—exhibit a greater impartiality than might have been expected. The gale that has just unroofed your lordly tower, had equally swept the tiles

---

[1] *calf* Calfskin; i.e., bound in leather.

[2] *two pair back* Room at the back of a house's second floor.

[3] *Shoreham gap* The opening to the harbor at Shoreham-on-Sea (in West Sussex).

[4] *ruder* Humbler; less civilized (as Ireland was often thought of by the English).

off our humble porch; in the same way that moralists are fond of assuring us that sickness and sorrow, loss and pain, old age and death, fall equally upon the homes of beggars and of kings.

Never having belonged to the last of these classes, I cannot take it upon me to answer for the discomforts that pertain to it. With regard to the other, though I have often seen myself figuring, or upon the point of figuring, amongst its sad and tattered ranks, the impression has never been a particularly agreeable one, and I prefer, therefore, not to dwell upon it. It was moreover the subject of landscapes, I think, not of either kings or beggars, that was under discussion? But that is the sort of thing that is always happening! Of all the unsatisfactory stock to keep, ideas are in my experience the most unsatisfactory; equally whether they are winged, or entirely wingless ones. As for a diary—which, to be of the slightest use, ought to act as a kind of cow-boy, or goose-girl, to them, and keep them in order—on the contrary it seems merely to follow their waddling and gyrations with the most foolish, and unnecessary submissiveness. The result is that one starts intending to fill a page with one subject, and before one has got very far one discovers that in reality one is filling it up with quite another! ...

August 25, 1900

From gropings along unlit ways, and towards an undiscoverable goal, what a pleasant experience it is to turn suddenly back to the well-trodden paths of a near and a tried companionship! It is almost an exact parallel to the sensations of the child who, having rushed out of its home into the wild winter night, full of hollow reverberations, and perturbing gleams, suddenly retreats, and finds itself once more beside the hearth, with an absolutely new sense of its security, and wide-armed delightfulness.

Upon few topics has more ink been expended than upon this one of friendship. As regards one point all the pens have I think been agreed, and that is that diversity constitutes its soundest basis. If a truism, this is at least one of those truisms that every day's experience throws into new relief. Friendship demands absolutely no conformity, but lives, thrives, and has its being upon the most absolutely radical differences. Friend and friend may differ by nearly everything that can differentiate one human being from another. By the tenor of their thoughts; by the circumstances of their lives; by the very texture of their brains, their souls, their hearts, their entire natures. Friendship makes light of such little discrepancies as these. Its roots push down to a stratum where even the largest of them become mere accidents, and at that serene depth they meet and lock securely under them all.

To say that such a tie is the great ameliorator of life, the soother of its sorrows, the encourager of its brighter moments, is to say ridiculously little. To say that it is one that we could hardly endure to think of existing without, is to say almost less. The very notion of such a deprivation produces a sort of vertigo; a species of mental confusion, akin to the thought of losing identity itself. Worse, indeed, for it is not merely the everyday, the vulgar self, that such a loss—supposing it to be complete—would deprive one of. It is that other, better, and more shining self, which only really exists inside the enchanted walls of a loving, sympathetic friendship. Within those fostering walls it grows, expands, and flourishes, but outside of them it sickens, pines away, and dies.

It is a very singular tie, when one reflects a little upon it; so close often that no nearness of blood, no identity of name, could, so far as one can see, make it any closer. It seems to be antecedent, not alone to itself, but to the whole social warp and woof,[1] of which it is an outcome. Just as the trees in one wood seem, to anyone who wanders often in it, to have acquired a sort of identity, so two who have walked for some time very closely together, though they may differ as widely as an ash does from a pine, as an oak does from a hornbeam, acquire a sort of similarity, due to the same sunshine having warmed, the same storms having shaken and darkened both. It is well to speak a good word now and then of a personage whom one habitually abuses, so let

---

[1] *warp and woof* In weaving, the *warp* and *woof* are threads which cross each other at right angles to form the finished piece; thus, the social "fabric."

it be recorded in favour of that odd compound of good and ill which we call our existence that, if it has thwarted our desires, dwarfed our ambitions, nipped in our joys, chilled back our aspirations, cut down our hopes, and not infrequently wrung our hearts, at least—it has given us our friends!

—1901

JOHN KEEGAN CASEY (1846–1870)

Born during the Great Famine, Irish revolutionary John Keegan Casey wrote numerous articles for the later incarnation of the nationalist *Nation* newspaper, and was imprisoned for his participation in the Fenian Rising of 1867. He is best known for "The Rising of the Moon," a popular and much-performed ballad that exists in several variants.

The Rising of the Moon[1]

"Tell me, tell me, Shawn O'Farrell,
    Why it is you hurry so?"
"Hush *ma bouchal*,[2] hush and listen,"
    And his cheeks were in a glow.
5 "I bear orders from the captain,
    Get you ready quick and soon,
For our pikes[3] must be together
    By the rising of the moon."

"Tell me, tell me, Shawn O'Farrell,
10   Where the gathering is to be."
"At the old spot by the river
    That's well known to you and me.
One word more, our signal token,
    Whistle up the marching tune,

---

[1] *The Rising of the Moon*   The poem memorializes aspects of the Irish Rebellion of 1798, an uprising against British rule led by the United Irishmen; the rebellion was ultimately a failure, and many suspected rebels were brutally executed.

[2] *ma bouchal*   From the Irish *mo bhuachaill*, meaning "my boy."

[3] *pikes*   Long spears, the weapon most commonly used by the rebels in the Rebellion.

15 Hurrah, my boys, for Ireland's freedom,
        By the rising of the moon."

Down by the lonely river,
    A dark mass of men were seen,
Far above the starry banner
20   Hung our own immortal green.
"Death to every foe and traitor,
    Forward on the marching tune,"
And a million pikes were shining
    By the rising of the moon.

25 Out of every mud wall cabin
        Eyes were watching all the night,
Many a manly breast was throbbing
    For the blessed morning light.
Murmurs passed along the valley
30   Like the banshee's lonely croon,
And a million pikes were shining
    By the rising of the moon.

Well they fought for poor old Ireland,
    And bitter was their fate,
35 What a feeling of pride and sorrow
        Fills the name of Ninety-Eight.
But yet we have in poor old Ireland
    Hearts that beat as firm and true,
We will follow in their footsteps
40   By the rising of the moon.
—1866

WINIFRED M. LETTS (1882–1972)

Though Winifred M. Letts was born in England, she spent most of her life in her maternal home country of Ireland. She began her literary career writing plays for the Abbey Theatre in Dublin, but turned to poetry with the publication of her first collection in 1913. Her poem "The Deserter" is an oft-anthologized poem of the First World War.

Deirdre[1] in the Street

Deirdre is dead, and all her beauty blown
Like wind-swept petals underneath the thorn.
If beauty dies, then beauty is new-born,
And Deirdre met me in the street today,
5 Her hair like blackbirds' breasts, her shadowed eyes
Two hazel-circled pools beneath grey skies.
Proudly she walked as women from the hills,
Her basket full of early daffodils.

Deirdre is dead, and beauty, like a smoke,
10 Passes its phantom way into the air.
But other women are as young and fair.
Here at my elbow with soft hurried speech
She urged her wares. And in this dreary place
I looked upon a princess face to face.
15 Backed by a hoarding fierce with garish bills,
Deirdre stood crying—"Buy the daffodils."
—1913

The Old Wexford Woman

What do I think of the women that's in it?
'Tis little enough;
If you offered them flax would they trouble to spin it?
Faith! I've a notion before they'd begin it
5   You'd wait for your stuff.

Would they pick wool from the hedges and ditches?
We did in my day.
But it's easier plans they have now to make riches:
Why would you sew when machines makes your
stitches?
10   Sure, that's what they say.

'Tis truth I'd no hand for making a letter,
But where was the lack?[2]
An' I couldn't read books any more than that setter.[3]
But for baking or stitching there wasn't a better,
15   Or making a brack.[4]

The black fasts[5] were kept without hesitation,
I tell you no lie.
Arrah![6] now there's no manner of strength in the nation,
It's sorra a one but needs dispensation[7]
20   For fear they would die.

The way they are now they're seeking their pleasure,
The days are too slow.
They'd look twice at a spade were they hunting for
treasure,
It's towns that they want, and evenings of leisure
25   To streel[8] to and fro.

What is it they're after there in the city
That takes them away?
It's new clothes they'll be buying to make themselves
pretty;
No value at all—an' that is the pity.
30   They'll know it some day.

What do I think of the race that we're rarin'?
They're not worth my shawl.
For it's sooner they're threadbare an' nobody carin'.
Mine was the days—but there's no good comparin'.
35   God help us all!
—1913

---

1 *Deirdre*   Deirdre is a popular figure of Irish mythology, a beautiful and tragic heroine who is betrothed from birth to King Conchubar. She falls in love with Naoise and runs off with him, but she is later recaptured, and forced to marry Conchubar after her lover is slain. When Conchubar is dissatisfied with Deirdre's coldness towards him, he tries to marry her off to Naoise's murderer as a punishment; she kills herself in anguish and protest.

2 *lack*   Shame.

3 *setter*   Type of dog.

4 *brack*   Fruitcake or loaf.

5 *black fasts*   Severe forms of fasting, often practiced by Catholics during the observation of Lent.

6 *Arrah!*   Exclamation used in Irish English.

7 *dispensation*   Official permission from the Church to be exempt from the full terms of a fast, sometimes claimed for one's health or for other reasons.

8 *streel*   Stroll aimlessly.

The Deserter

There was a man—don't mind his name,
  Whom Fear had dogged by night and day.
He could not face the German guns
And so he turned and ran away,

5 Just that—he turned and ran away,
But who can judge him, you or I?
God makes a man of flesh and blood
Who yearns to live and not to die.
And this man when he feared to die

10 Was scared as any frightened child,
His knees were shaking under him,
His breath came fast, his eyes were wild.
I've seen a hare with eyes as wild,
With throbbing heart and sobbing breath.

15 But oh! it shames one's soul to see
A man in abject fear of death,
But fear had gripped him, so had death;
His number had gone up that day,
They might not heed his frightened eyes,

20 They shot him when the dawn was grey.
Blindfolded, when the dawn was grey,
He stood there in a place apart,
The shots rang out and down he fell.
An English bullet in his heart.

25 An English bullet in his heart!
But here's the irony of life—
His mother thinks he fought and fell,
A hero, foremost in the strife.
So she goes proudly; to the strife

30 Her best, her hero son she gave.
O well for her she does not know
He lies in a deserter's grave.
    —1916

SCOTLAND

JOHN GALT (1779–1839)

Perhaps a precursor to the historical novel popularized by later writers such as Sir Walter Scott, John Galt's *Annals of the Parish* was one of what the author called his "theoretical histories." Not quite a novel, this relatively plot-less work purports to chronicle the life of a small parish town in Scotland as witnessed by the Reverend Micah Balwhidder. The novel was an immediate success, Balwhidder becoming one of Galt's most beloved characters. Balwhidder, whose tenure as minister of Dalmailing coincides with the first fifty years of King George III's reign, provides a reliable lens through which the reader witnesses changes such as the Industrial Revolution and the rise of international trade, and the effects these events had on ordinary citizens in Scotland. Written in a fluid mixture of English and Scots, and with a sense of humor not unlike that of Galt's contemporary Jane Austen, *Annals* paints a lively portrait of village life in eighteenth- and early-nineteenth-century Scotland.

from *Annals of the Parish: or, The Chronicle of Dalmailing; during the ministry of the Rev. Micah Balwhidder, written by himself*

CHAPTER 4: YEAR 1763

Charles Malcolm's return from sea—Kate Malcolm is taken to live with Lady Macadam—Death of the first Mrs. Balwhidder.

The An. Dom.[1] 1763, was, in many a respect, a memorable year, both in public and in private. The King granted peace to the French,[2] and Charlie Malcolm, that went to sea in the Tobacco trader, came home to see his mother. The ship, after being at America, had gone down to Jamaica, an island in the West Indies, with a cargo of live lumber, as Charlie told me himself, and had come home with more than a hundred and fifty hoggits of sugar, and sixty-three puncheons[3] full of rum; for she was, by all accounts, a stately galley, and almost two hundred tons in the burthen,[4] being the largest vessel then sailing from the creditable town of Port-Glasgow. Charlie was not expected; and his coming was a great thing to us all, so I will mention the whole particulars.

One evening, towards the gloaming,[5] as I was taking my walk of meditation, I saw a brisk sailor laddie coming towards me. He had a pretty green parrot sitting on a bundle, tied in a Barcelona silk handkerchief, which he carried with a stick over his shoulder, and in this bundle was a wonderful big nut, such as no one in our parish had ever seen. It was called a cocker-nut.[6]

This blithe callant[7] was Charlie Malcolm, who had come all the way that day his leaful lane,[8] on his own legs from Greenock, where the Tobacco trader was then 'livering her cargo. I told him how his mother, and his brothers, and his sisters were all in good health, and went to convoy him home; and as we were going along he told me many curious things, and he gave me six beautiful yellow limes, that he had brought in his pouch all the way across the seas, for me to make a bowl of punch with, and I thought more of them than if they had been golden guineas, it was so mindful of the laddie.

When we got to the door of his mother's house, she was sitting at the fireside, with her three other bairns[9] at their bread and milk, Kate being then with Lady Skimmilk at the Breadland[10] sewing. It was between the day and dark, when the shuttle stands still till the lamp is lighted. But such a shout of joy and thankfulness as rose from that hearth, when Charlie went in! The very parrot, ye would have thought, was a participator, for the beast gied a skraik that made my whole head dirl;[11] and the neighbours came flying and flocking to see what was the matter, for it was the first parrot ever seen within the bounds of the parish, and some thought it was but a foreign hawk, with a yellow head and green feathers.

In the midst of all this, Effie Malcolm had run off to the Breadland for her sister Kate, and the two lassies came flying breathless, with Miss Girzie Gilchrist, the Lady Skimmilk pursuing them like desperation, or a griffin, down the avenue; for Kate, in her hurry, had flung down her seam, a new printed gown, that she was helping to make, and it had fallen into a boyne[12] of milk that was ready for the creaming, by which ensued a double misfortune to Miss Girzie, the gown being not

---

[1] *An. Dom* Anno Domini; Latin: Year of our Lord.

[2] *The King ... the French* Referring to the 1763 Treaty of Paris, which ended the Seven Years' War with a British victory over France; the end of the war has been commonly viewed as marking the beginning of the era of British imperial dominance.

[3] *hoggits* Hogsheads; large casks; *puncheons* Casks for alcoholic beverages.

[4] *burthen* Carrying capacity.

[5] *gloaming* Twilight.

[6] *cocker-nut* Coconut.

[7] *callant* Young man.

[8] *leaful lane* All alone.

[9] *bairns* Children.

[10] *Breadland* Estate of Balwhidder's late patron, the Laird of Breadland.

[11] *gied a skraik* Gave a screech; *dirl* Shake; ring.

[12] *boyne* Milk dish.

only ruined, but licking up the cream. For this, poor Kate was not allowed ever to set her face in the Breadland again.

When Charlie Malcolm had staid about a week with his mother, he returned to his berth in the Tobacco trader, and shortly after his brother Robert was likewise sent to serve his time to the sea, with an owner that was master of his own bark, in the coal trade at Irville. Kate, who was really a surprising lassie for her years, was taken off her mother's hands by the old Lady Macadam, that lived in her jointure house,[1] which is now the Cross Keys Inn. Her ladyship was a woman of high breeding, her husband having been a great general, and knighted by the King for his exploits; but she was lame, and could not move about in her dining-room without help, so hearing from the first Mrs. Balwhidder how Kate had done such an unatonable deed to Miss Girzie Gilchrist, she sent for Kate, and finding her sharp and apt, she took her to live with her as a companion. This was a vast advantage, for the lady was versed in all manner of accomplishments, and could read and speak French with more ease than any professor at that time would do in the College of Glasgow; and she had learnt to sew flowers on satin, either in a nunnery abroad, or in a boarding-school in England, and took pleasure in teaching Kate all she knew, and how to behave herself like a lady.

In the summer of this year, old Mr. Patrick Dilworth, that had so long been doited with the paralytics,[2] died, and it was a great relief to my people, for the heritors[3] could no longer refuse to get a proper schoolmaster; so we took on trial Mr. Lorimore, who has ever since the year after, with so much credit to himself, and usefulness to the parish, been schoolmaster, session-clerk, and precentor[4]—a man of great mildness, and

extraordinary particularity. He was then a very young man, and some objection was made on account of his youth, to his being session-clerk, especially as the smuggling immorality still gave us much trouble in the making up of irregular marriages; but his discretion was greater than could have been hoped for from his years; and after a twelvemonth's probation in the capacity of schoolmaster, he was installed in all the offices that had belonged to his predecessor, old Mr. Patrick Dilworth that was.

But the most memorable thing that befell among my people this year, was the burning of the lint-mill on the Lugton Water,[5] which happened, of all the days of the year, on the very self-same day that Miss Girzie Gilchrist, better known as Lady Skim-milk, hired the chaise[6] from Mrs. Watts of the New Inns of Irville, to go with her brother the Major, to consult the faculty in Edinburgh,[7] concerning his complaints. For, as the chaise was coming by the mill, William Huckle, the miller that was, came flying out of the mill like a demented man, crying fire!—and it was the driver that brought the melancholy tidings to the clachan[8]—and melancholy they were; for the mill was utterly destroyed, and in it not a little of all that year's crop of lint in our parish. The first Mrs. Balwhidder lost upwards of twelve stone, which we had raised on the glebe with no small pains, watering it in the drouth, as it was intended for sarking to ourselves, and sheets and napery.[9] A great loss indeed it was, and the vexation thereof had a visible effect on Mrs. Balwhidder's health, which from the spring had been in a dwining[10] way. But for it, I think she might have wrestled through the winter: however, it was ordered otherwise, and she was removed from mine to Abraham's bosom on Christmas Day, and buried on

---

[1] *jointure house* Property inherited by a woman in the event of her husband's death (jointures were arranged primarily among the wealthy).

[2] *doited* Mentally impaired; *paralytics* Paralysis; Dilworth may have been affected by a stroke.

[3] *heritors* Privileged parish landowners responsible for the financial upkeep of the church, schools, etc.

[4] *precentor* Leader of the church choir.

[5] *lint-mill* Flax mill, for the making of linen; *Lugton Water* River in western Scotland.

[6] *chaise* Light open carriage.

[7] *the faculty in Edinburgh* I.e., the medical faculty.

[8] *clachan* Village.

[9] *glebe* Parish minister's land; *drouth* Drought; *sarking* Linen undergarments; *napery* Table linen.

[10] *dwining* Dwindling; sickly.

Hogmanay,[1] for it was thought uncanny to have a dead corpse in the house on the new-year's day. She was a worthy woman, studying with all her capacity to win the hearts of my people towards me—in the which good work she prospered greatly; so that, when she died, there was not a single soul in the parish that was not contented with both my walk[2] and conversation. Nothing could be more peaceable than the way we lived together. Her brother Andrew, a fine lad, I had sent to the College at Glasgow, at my own cost, and when he came out to the burial, he stayed with me a month, for the Manse after her decease was very dull, and it was during this visit that he gave me an inkling of his wish to go out to India as a cadet, but the transactions anent[3] that fall within the scope of another year—as well as what relates to her headstone, and the epitaph in metre, which I indicated myself thereon; John Truel the mason carving the same, as may be seen in the kirkyard,[4] where it wants a little reparation and setting upright, having settled the wrong way when the second Mrs. Balwhidder was laid by her side. But I must not here enter upon an anticipation.

CHAPTER 5: YEAR 1764

He gets a marble headstone for Mrs. Balwhidder, and writes an Epitaph for it—He is afflicted with melancholy, and thinks of writing a book—Nichol Snipe the gamekeeper's device when reproved in church.

This year well deserved the name of the monumental year in our parish; for the young Laird[5] of the Breadland, that had been my pupil, being learning to be an advocate among the faculty in Edinburgh, with his lady mother, who had removed thither with the young ladies her daughters, for the benefit of education, sent out to be put up in the kirk, under the loft over the family vault, an elegant marble headstone, with an epitaph engraven thereon, in fair Latin, setting forth many excellent qualities which the old laird, my patron that was, the inditer[6] thereof, said he possessed. I say the inditer, because it could no have been the young laird himself, although he got the credit o't on the stone, for he was nae daub in my aught at the Latin or any other language. However, he might improve himself at Edinburgh, where a' manner of genteel things were then to be got at an easy rate, and doubtless, the young laird got a probationer at the College to write the epitaph; but I have often wondered sin' syne,[7] how he came to make it in Latin, for assuredly his dead parent, if he could have seen it, could not have read a single word o't, notwithstanding it was so vaunty[8] about his virtues, and other civil and hospitable qualifications.

The coming of the laird's monumental stone had a great effect on me, then in a state of deep despondency, for the loss of the first Mrs. Balwhidder; and I thought I could not do a better thing, just by way of diversion in my heavy sorrow, than to get a well-shapen headstone made for her—which, as I have hinted at in the record of the last year, was done and set up. But a headstone without an epitaph, is no better than a body without the breath of life in't; and so it behoved me to make a posey[9] for the monument, the which I conned[10] and pondered upon for many days. I thought as Mrs. Balwhidder, worthy woman as she was, did not understand the Latin tongue, it would not do to put on what I had to say in that language, as the laird had done—nor indeed would it have been easy, as I found upon the experimenting, to tell what I had to tell in Latin, which is naturally a crabbed[11] language, and very difficult to write properly. I therefore, after mentioning her age and the dates of her birth and departure, composed in sedate poetry, the following epitaph, which may yet be seen on the tombstone.

---

1 *Hogmanay* New Year's Eve.

2 *walk* I.e., of life; manner of living.

3 *anent* Regarding.

4 *kirkyard* Churchyard.

5 *Laird* Estate owner.

6 *inditer* Writer.

7 *sin' syne* Since then.

8 *vaunty* Boastful.

9 *posey* Poesy; poem.

10 *conned* Pored over.

11 *crabbed* Difficult.

EPITAPH

A lovely Christian, spouse, and friend,
Pleasant in life, and at her end.
A pale consumption dealt the blow
That laid her here, with dust below.
Sore was the cough that shook her frame;
That cough her patience did proclaim—
And as she drew her latest breath,
She said, "The Lord is sweet in death."
O pious reader, standing by,
Learn like this gentle one to die.
The grass doth grow and fade away,
And time runs out by night and day;
The King of Terrors has command
To strike us with his dart in hand.
Go where we will by flood or field,
He will pursue and make us yield.
But though to him we must resign
The vesture of our part divine,
There is a jewel in our trust,
That will not perish in the dust,
A pearl of price, a precious gem,
Ordained for Jesus' diadem;
Therefore, be holy while you can,
And think upon the doom of man.
Repent in time and sin no more,
That when the strife of life is o'er,
On wings of love your soul may rise,
To dwell with angels in the skies,
Where psalms are sung eternally,
And martyrs ne'er again shall die;
But with the saints still bask in bliss,
And drink the cup of blessedness.

This was greatly thought of at the time, and Mr. Loremore, who had a nerve for poesy himself in his younger years, was of opinion, that it was so much to the purpose and suitable withal, that he made his scholars write it out for their examination copies, at the reading whereof before the heritors, when the examination of the school came round, the tear came into my eye, and everyone present sympathized with me in my great affliction for the loss of the first Mrs. Balwhidder.

Andrew Lanshaw, as I have recorded, having come from the Glasgow College to the burial of his sister, my wife that was, stayed with me a month to keep me company; and staying with me, he was a great cordial, for the weather was wet and sleety, and the nights were stormy, so that I could go little out, and few of the elders came in, they being at that time old men in a feckless condition, not at all qualified to warsle[1] with the blasts of winter. But when Andrew left me to go back to his classes, I was eerie[2] and lonesome, and but for the getting of the monument ready, which was a blessed entertainment to me in those dreary nights, with consulting anent the shape of it with John Truel, and meditating on the verse for the epitaph, I might have gone altogether demented. However, it pleased HIM, who is the surety of the sinner, to help me through the Slough of Despond,[3] and to set my feet on fair land, establishing my way thereon.

But the work of the monument, and the epitaph, could not endure for a constancy, and after it was done, I was again in great danger of sinking into the hypochonderies[4] a second time. However, I was enabled to fight with my affliction, and by and by, as the spring began to open her green lattice, and to set out her flower-pots to the sunshine, and the time of the singing of birds was come, I became more composed, and like myself, so I often walked in the fields, and held communion with nature, and wondered at the mysteries thereof.

On one of these occasions, as I was sauntering along the edge of Eaglesham-wood, looking at the industrious bee going from flower to flower, and the idle butterfly, that layeth up no store, but perisheth ere it is winter, I felt as it were a spirit from on high descending upon me, a throb at my heart, and a thrill in my brain, and I was transported out of myself, and seized with the notion of

---

[1] *warsle* Wrestle.

[2] *eerie* Gloomy.

[3] *Slough of Despond* Name of a bog in John Bunyan's *The Pilgrim's Progress* (1678) that represents a state of moral degradation and sinfulness.

[4] *hypochonderies* Melancholia; depression.

writing a book—but what it should be about, I could not settle to my satisfaction. Sometimes I thought of an orthodox poem, like Paradise Lost,[1] by John Milton, wherein I proposed to treat more at large of Original Sin, and the great mystery of Redemption; at others, I fancied that a connect treatise on the efficacy of Free Grace[2] would be more taking; but although I made diverse beginnings in both subjects, some new thought ever came into my head, and the whole summer passed away, and nothing was done. I therefore postponed my design of writing a book till the winter, when I would have the benefit of the long nights. Before that, however, I had other things of more importance to think about. My servant lasses, having no eye of a mistress over them, wastered everything at such a rate, and made such a galravitching[3] in the house, that, long before the end of the year, the year's stipend was all spent, and I did not know what to do. At lang and length I mustered courage to send for Mr. Auld, who was then living, and an elder. He was a douce[4] and discreet man, fair and well-doing in the world, and had a better handful of strong common sense than many even of the heritors. So I told him how I was situate, and conferred with him, and he advised me, for my own sake, to look out for another wife, as soon as decency would allow, which, he thought, might very properly be after the turn of the year, by which time the first Mrs. Balwhidder would be dead more than twelve months; and when I mentioned my design to write a book, he said (and he was a man of good discretion), that the doing of the book was a thing that would keep, but wasterful servants were a growing evil; so, upon his counselling, I resolved not to meddle with the book till I was married again, but employ the interim, between then and the turn of the year, in looking out for a prudent woman to be my second wife,

strictly intending, as I did perform, not to mint[5] a word about my choice, if I made one, till the whole twelve months and a day, from the date of the first Mrs. Balwhidder's interment, had run out.

In this the hand of Providence was very visible, and lucky for me it was that I had sent for Mr. Auld when I did send, as the very week following, a sound began to spread in the parish, that one of my lassies had got herself with bairn, which was an awful thing to think had happened in the house of her master, and that master a minister of the gospel. Some there were, for backbiting appertaineth to all conditions, that jealoused[6] and wondered if I had not a finger in the pie; which, when Mr. Auld heard, he bestirred himself in such a manful and godly way in my defence, as silenced the clash, telling that I was utterly incapable of any such thing, being a man of a guileless heart, and a spiritual simplicity, that would be ornamental in a child. We then had the latheron[7] summoned before the Session, and was not long of making her confess, that the father was Nichol Snipe, Lord Glencairn's gamekeeper; and both her and Nichol were obligated to stand in the kirk, but Nichol was a graceless reprobate, for he came with two coats, one buttoned behind him, and another buttoned before him, and two wigs of my lord's, lent him by the valet-de-chamer;[8] the one over his face, and the other in the right way; and he stood with his face to the church-wall. When I saw him from the pu'-pit,[9] I said to him—"Nichol, you must turn your face towards me!" At the which, he turned round to be sure, but there he presented the same show as his back. I was confounded, and did not know what to say, but cried out, with a voice of anger—"Nichol, Nichol! if ye had been a' back, ye would nae hae[10] been there this day"; which had such an effect on the whole congregation,

---

[1] *Paradise Lost* Epic poem (1667) recounting the fall of the angel Satan and the loss of the Garden of Eden by Adam and Eve.

[2] *connect* Orderly; *Free Grace* The idea that one can be saved by God's grace through one's own faith alone, regardless of prior sins; a central tenet of Protestant theology.

[3] *wastered* Wasted; *galravitching* Extravagance.

[4] *douce* Sober, judicious.

[5] *mint* Speak; hint at.

[6] *jealoused* Suspected.

[7] *latheron* Laidron or ladrone; slattern; derogatory word for a "loose" woman.

[8] *valet-de-chamer* Valet-de-chambre; personal servant of a gentleman.

[9] *pu'-pit* Pulpit.

[10] *nae hae* Not have.

that the poor fellow suffered afterwards more derision, than if I had rebuked him in the manner prescribed by the Session.

This affair, with the previous advice of Mr. Auld, was, however, a warning to me, that no pastor of his parish should be long without a helpmate. Accordingly, as soon as the year was out, I set myself earnestly about the search for one, but as the particulars fall properly within the scope and chronicle of the next year, I must reserve them for it; and I do not recollect that anything more particular befell in this, excepting that William Mutchkins, the father of Mr. Mutchkins, the great spirit-dealer in Glasgow, set up a change house[1] in the clachan, which was the first in the parish, and which, if I could have helped, it would have been the last; for it was opening a howf[2] to all manner of wickedness, and was an immediate get and offspring of the smuggling trade, against which I had so set my countenance. But William Mutchkins himself was a respectable man, and no house could be better ordered than his change. At a stated hour he made family worship, for he brought up his children in the fear of God and the Christian religion; and although the house was full, he would go in to the customers, and ask them if they would want anything for half an hour, for that he was going to make exercise with his family; and many a wayfaring traveller has joined in the prayer. There is no such thing, I fear, now-a-days, of publicans entertaining travellers in this manner.

CHAPTER 6: YEAR 1765

Establishment of a whisky distillery—He is again married to Miss Lizy Kibbock—Her industry in the dairy—Her example diffuses a spirit of industry through the parish.

As there was little in the last year that concerned the parish, but only myself, so in this the like fortune continued; and saving a rise in the price of barley, occasioned, as was thought, by the establishment of a house for brewing whisky in a neighbouring parish, it could not be said that my people were exposed to the mutations and influences of the stars, which ruled in the seasons of Ann. Dom. 1765. In the winter there was a dearth[3] of fuel, such as has not been since; for when the spring loosened the bonds of the ice, three new coal-heughs were shanked[4] in the Douray moor, and ever since there has been a great plenty of that necessary article. Truly, it is very wonderful to see how things come round; when the talk was about the shanking of their heughs, and a paper to get folk to take shares in them, was carried through the circumjacent parishes, it was thought a gowk's[5] errand; but no sooner was the coal reached, but up sprung such a traffic, that it was a God-send to the parish, and the opening of a trade and commerce, that has, to use an old byword, brought gold in gowpins amang[6] us. From that time my stipend has been on the regular increase, and therefore I think that the incoming of the heritors must have been in like manner augmented.

Soon after this, the time was drawing near for my second marriage. I had placed my affections, with due consideration, on Miss Lizy Kibbock, the well-brought-up daughter of Mr. Joseph Kibbock, of the Gorbyholm, who was the first that made a speculation in the farming way in Ayrshire, and whose cheese were of such an excellent quality, that they have, under the name of Delap-cheese, spread far and wide over the civilized world. Miss Lizy and me were married on the 29th day of April, with some inconvenience to both sides, on account of the dread that we had of being married in May, for it is said,

> "Of the marriages in May,
> The bairns die of a decay."

However, married we were, and we hired the Irville chaise, and with Miss Jenny her sister, and Becky Cairns

---

[1] *change house* Inn; pub.

[2] *howf* Abode; housing place (often with the implication of housing something disreputable).

[3] *dearth* Shortage.

[4] *coal-heughs* Coal quarries; *shanked* Sunk; mined.

[5] *gowk* Fool.

[6] *gowpins* Handfuls; *amang* Among.

her niece, who sat on a portmanty[1] at our feet, we went on a pleasure jaunt to Glasgow, where we bought a miracle[2] of useful things for the Manse, that neither the first Mrs. Balwhidder nor me ever thought of; but the second Mrs. Balwhidder that was, had a geni[3] for management, and it was extraordinary what she could go through. Well may I speak of her with commendations; for she was the bee that made my honey, although at first things did not go so clear with us. For she found the Manse rookit and herrit, and there was such a supply of plenishing of all sort wanted,[4] that I thought myself ruined and undone by her care and industry. There was such a buying of wool to make blankets, with a booming of the meikle wheel to spin the same, and such birring of the little wheel for sheets and napery, that the Manse was for many a day like an organ kist.[5] Then we had milk cows, and the calves to bring up, and a kirning[6] of butter, and a making of cheese; in short, I was almost by myself[7] with the jangle and din, which prevented me from writing a book as I had proposed, and I for a time thought of the peaceful and kindly nature of the first Mrs. Balwhidder with a sigh; but the outcoming was soon manifest. The second Mrs. Balwhidder sent her butter on the market-days to Irville, and her cheese from time to time to Glasgow, to Mrs. Firlot, that kept the huxtry[8] in the Saltmarket, and they were both so well made, that our dairy was just a coining of money, insomuch, that after the first year, we had the whole tot[9] of my stipend to put untouched into the bank.

But I must say, that although we were thus making siller like sclate[10] stones, I was not satisfied in my own mind, that I had got the Manse merely to be a factory of butter and cheese, and to breed up veal calves for the slaughter; so I spoke to the second Mrs. Balwhidder, and pointed out to her what I thought the error of our way; but she had been so ingrained with the profitable management of cows and grumphies[11] in her father's house, that she could not desist, at the which I was greatly grieved. By and by, however, I began to discern that there was something as good in her example, as the giving of alms to the poor folk. For all the wives of the parish were stirred up by it into a wonderful thrift, and nothing was heard of in every house, but of quiltings and wabs[12] to weave; insomuch, that before many years came round, there was not a better stocked parish, with blankets and napery, than mine was, within the bounds of Scotland. ...

—1821

JANET HAMILTON (1795–1873)

James Thomson and Mary Brownlee Thomson, Janet Hamilton's parents, were field laborers for much of her childhood; her father also worked at different times as a shoemaker. Married when she was thirteen to another shoemaker, Hamilton bore ten children in the years 1810–25. She received no formal education but was taught by her mother to read; she did not learn how to write until she was in her fifties. Hamilton's first book, *Poems and Essays of a Miscellaneous Character*, was published by subscription in 1863. By the time her third volume, *Poems and Ballads* (1868) was published, her work was widely and very positively reviewed. As *The Glasgow Herald* put it, "the name of Janet Hamilton is one of the most remarkable in the history of Scottish poetry. That a woman in humble life, who did not enjoy the advantages of a school education, should, at the age of 73, and while now blind, be

---

[1] *portmanty* Portmanteau, traveling case.

[2] *miracle* Impressively large amount.

[3] *geni* Genius.

[4] *rookit* Dirty; *herrit* Plundered, stripped of goods; *wanted* Lacking.

[5] *meikle* Large; *birring* Whirring; *kist* Chest or trunk in which clothes or valuables are kept.

[6] *kirning* Churning.

[7] *by myself* Beside myself; out of my wits.

[8] *huxtry* Small shop.

[9] *tot* Lot.

[10] *siller* Silver; money; *sclate* Slate, i.e., for roofing.

[11] *grumphies* Pigs.

[12] *wabs* Webs, i.e., of woven fabric.

capable of composing verse at all, is singular enough; but that these verses should possess the verve, pathos, and genuine truthfulness of ... a Burns (in all but his best pieces) can only be accounted for by the inheritance of genius."

Hamilton has been known largely for her poems in Scottish dialect, but she was also a highly accomplished writer in standard English of poems, prose essays, and sketches.

Lines on the Long and Beautiful Summer of 1865, in Connection with the Cattle Plague Then Raging [1]

The first recorded case in the cattle plague (also known as *rinderpest*) of 1865 was 24 June; the disease quickly spread throughout much of England, Wales, and Scotland. On 29 September a Royal Commission was appointed to investigate the plague's causes and make recommendations as to how best to deal with it. By February 1866 the government had placed increased restrictions on cattle movement and made the mass slaughter of diseased animals obligatory; by the following summer the plague had been brought under control. The plague is estimated to have killed 75–80 per cent of the animals affected, and approximately 8 per cent of the total British cattle population.

At the height of the plague there were widespread calls for days of public fasting and humiliation—the idea being that the plague had been sent by God as punishment for human sin. Though such notions would become far less widely held in Britain in the twentieth century, they have a long history, and in the mid nineteenth century they were certainly not relics of a distant past; nevertheless, such calls were not always made without controversy or resistance. In 1865 the Queen sided with the Archbishop of Canterbury in approving a special prayer for protection against the plague, but did not declare a day of fasting and humiliation.

Lines on the Summer of the Cattle Plague, 1865

Summer long, and bright, and glowing,
Flowers in triple plenty blowing,
Flushed the garden, field and glade,
Tints of every hue and shade.
5 Woods and fields more richly green,
Waters placid, pure and sheen,
Singing, sparkling, danced along,
Musical as merles'° song.   *blackbirds'*
Ne'er did "incense breathing morn"[2]
10 O'er green fields of springing corn,
Flowery lea, and moorland heath,
Shed more balmy odorous breath.
Such pearl-drops ne'er, I ween,°   *think*
Gathered were on village green,
15 On sweet May, by sportive girls,
They the purest, fairest pearls,
'Sixty-five as thou hast given
From the dewy morning heaven.
With the first faint streak of morn,
20 When the cock first winds his horn,
Wakes the music of the woods,
Rising, swelling into floods
Of melody! Sweet warbling throats!
How ye poured your jubilant notes
25 Of love and joy, devoid of fear:
No tuneless Winter chilled your cheer.
In that Summer, long and glowing,
Nature from her lap o'erflowing
Spread around an ample feast
30 With full hand for bird and beast.
Ah! what pleasure 'twas to see
Straying o'er the daisied lea,°   *grass*

---

[1] This is the retrospective title given the poem when it appears in the 1868 *Poems and Ballads* volume and also the 1880 posthumous volume *Poems, Essays and Sketches: Comprising the Principal Pieces from Her Complete Works*. Where the poem itself appears in the tables of contents of those volumes, however, it is given the shorter title "Lines on the Summer of the Cattle Plague, 1865." The wording of the poem itself ("Now alas!," "not now the milkmaid's song," etc.) seems to suggest that the poem dates at the latest from early in 1866.

[2] *incense breathing morn*   The phrase is from the line that opens the fifth stanza of Thomas Gray's "Elegy Written in a Country Churchyard": "The breezy call of incense-breathing Morn."

Or, recumbent on the sward,°   *grassy field*
"The milky mothers of the herd,"
35   Udder rich in lacteal wealth,
Full of lusty life and health—
Richest clover, greenest grass,
Cropping quietly.
                    Now, alas!
Sore, plague-smitten, dying, dead,
40   On the pastures where they fed!
Thousands upon thousands gone—
Deep the loss, and sad the moan
In the dairies and the farms,
Where each day brings fresh alarms:
45   And the wonder ever grows
Whence the dire distemper flows.
Ah! not now the milkmaid's song,
As she drives the herd along,
Comes on woodland echoes borne,
50   At gloamin'° grey or dewy morn.   *twilight*
Now she walks with mournful tread
Through each empty stall and shed;
Meets her ear no welcome low:
All is deathly silence now.
55   For your suff'rings, sinless things,
Weeps the muse even while she sings:
Guilt not yours brought down the rod
Of a just and righteous God.
To that God we now appeal:
60   He has wounded, He can heal;
He alone can grant release
From this dark and fell° disease.   *cruel*
From our sinful, suff'ring land,
Lord, remove Thy chast'ning hand!
—1866

Rhymes for the Times IV—1865

Juist noo° there are mony wha°   *now / many who*
  rin° to an' fro,   *run*
An' knowledge increases, abune° an' below;   *above*
The yird's° like a riddle,[1] pits, tunnels, an' bores,   *earth*
Whaur° bodies, like mowdies,° by   *where / moles*
  hunners° an' scores,[2]   *hundreds*
5   Are houkin',° an' holin', an' blastin' the rocks;   *digging*
An' droonin's° an' burnin's, explosions   *drownings*
  an' shocks,
An' a' ither meagries,° amang us are rife;   *misfortunes*
Oh, mony's the slain in the battle o' life!
It's Mammon[3] we worship, wi' graspin' an' greed,
10   Wi' sailin' an' railin' at telegraph speed,
Get gowd oot° the ironstone,   *gold out of*
  an' siller frae° coal,   *silver from*
An' thoosan's on thoosan's draw oot o' ae° hole.   *one*
Wi' oil shale aneath° us, an' fire-warks abune,   *beneath*
I think we'll tak' lowe,° an' bleeze°   *fire / blaze*
  up to the mune.°   *moon*
15   The kintra's° contentit an' hale°   *country's / healthy*
  at the heart;
That gleg birkie, Gladstone,[4] has weel
  dune° his part;   *well done*
Exchequer's big pouches o' siller are fu',°   *full*
An' mony's the taxes that's dune awa' noo;
An' labour's weel paid, an' the flour an' the meal
20   At a wanworth[5]—an' sae we micht fen
  unco weel.°   *fare very well*
Oor Premier has promised to stan' for reform;[6]

---

[1] *riddle*   Sieve; piece of coarse mesh.

[2] *scores*   Groups of twenty.

[3] *Mammon*   Wealth or material things, personified as a devil-figure.

[4] *gleg* Sharp-witted; *birkie* Spirited or assertive man; *Gladstone* William Gladstone (1809–98), later Prime Minister, served as Chancellor of the Exchequer from 1859 to 1866.

[5] *wanworth*   Cost below actual value.

[6] *Oor Premier ... for reform*   Perhaps alluding to the struggle for electoral reform, which came to fruition in Scotland with the Representation of the People Act 1868.

The Fins an' the Yankees are brewin' a storm,[1]
They're swallin'° an' frothin' wi' bunkum   *swelling*
    an' bosh,°   *nonsense*
But they daurna° come near oor bit   *dare not*
    islan' sae cosh.°   *comfortable*
25 There's a bee in the bannet o' some o' the cloth,[2]
The Sabbath's the subject, an' wow but I'm wroth
To see the blin'° leaders lead blin' men awa',   *blind*
Till into the ditch they baith stumble an' fa'.
"The soul is immortal," tak' that for a text,
30 "The body is perishin'," tak' for the next;
To whilk o' the twa° shou'd the   *which of the two*
    Sabbath be given?
To the body?—then what for the soul an' for heaven?
—1868

Auld Mither Scotlan'[3]
A Lay of the Doric[4]

Na, na, I wunna pairt° wi' that   *would not part*
    I downa° gi'e it up;   *do not*
O' Scotlan's hamely° mither tongue   *homely*
    I canna quat the grup.[5]
5 It's 'bedded° in my very heart,   *embedded*
    Ye needna rive an' rug;[6]
It's in my e'en° an' on my tongue,   *eye*
    An' singin' in my lug.°   *ear*

Oh, leeze me on[7] the Scottish lass,
10   Fresh frae her muirlan'° hame,   *moorland*
Wi' gowden° or wi' coal-black hair,   *golden*

Row'd° up wi' bucklin came;[8]   *twisted*
Or wavin' roun her snawy broo,°   *snowy brow*
    Sae bonnie, braid,° an' brent,°   *broad / smooth*
15 Gaun barefit wi' her kiltit[9] coat,
    Blythe singin' ower the bent!

I heard her sing "Auld Robin Gray,"[10]
    An' "Yarrow's Dowie Den"[11]—
O' Flodden,[12] an' oor° forest   *our*
    flouris°   *flourishing*
20   Cut doon by Englishmen;
My saul was fir'd, my heart was fu',
    The tear was in my e'e:°   *eye*
Let ither lan's ha ither sangs,
    Auld Scotlan's sangs for me.

25 What words mair tender, kin' an' true,
    Can wooer ha'e to say,
Whan doun the burn at gloamin' fa',°   *nightfall*
    He meets his bonnie May?
Or words mair sweet, mair saft an' dear,
30   Can lassie ha'e to speak,
Whan love is dancin' in her e'e
    An' glowin' on her cheek!

For, oh, the meltin' Doric lay,
    In cot or clachan° sung,   *village*
35 The words that drap like hinny dew
    Frae mither Scotlan's tongue,
Ha'e power to thrill the youthfu' heart
    An' fire the patriot's min';
To saften grief in ilka° form   *every*
40   It comes to human kin'.

I saw a waefu' mither kneel
    On weary, tremblin' knee,

---

[1] *The Fins ... a storm* Allusion to the American Civil War (1861–65).

[2] *o' the cloth* Of the Church; i.e., the clergy.

[3] *Auld Mither Scotlan'* Hamilton in fact wrote two poems by this title; the following text is taken from the memorial volume *Poems, Essays, and Sketches* published posthumously in 1880; *Mither* Mother.

[4] *Lay* Song; *Doric* Scottish dialect.

[5] *quat the grup* Relinquish the grip; let go.

[6] *rive an' rug* Struggle.

[7] *leeze me on* Dear to me is.

[8] *bucklin came* Comb for pinning up the hair.

[9] *kiltit* Tucked in or held up for freedom of movement.

[10] *Auld Robin Gray* Popular Scots ballad written by Lady Anne Lindsay (1750–1825).

[11] *Yarrow's Dowie Den* Scottish folk ballad.

[12] *Flodden* At the Battle of Flodden (1513), English troops killed thousands of Scottish soldiers, including King James IV.

Beside the cradle, where she laid
   Her bairnie° doon to dee.°   *child / die*
45 An' aye she kissed the cauld white cheek,
   An' aye she made her mane,°   *lament*
"My ain wee lamb, my ain sweet doo,
   Frae me forever gane!"

The faither straikit° back her hair,   *stroked*
50   An' dichtit saft her e'en,[1]
"Wee Willie's gane, thy marrow's° here,   *husband*
   Thy life-lang, lovin' frien'."
She leant her on his faithfu' breast,
   An' sabbed "Wilt thou forgi'e
55 My sinfu' grief for bairnie lost,
   Whan I ha'e God an' thee.

"My mither, tho' the snaws o' eld
   Are on my pow° an' thine,   *head*
My heart is leal to thee as in
60   The days o' auld langsyne.[2]
Thy hamely worth, thy couthie° speech,   *kindly*
   Are dear—hoo dear to me!
An' neist° to God, my John, an' bairns,   *next*
   Thy place sall ever be."
—1868

Effie—A Ballad

She was wearin' awa'! she was wearin' awa'!
   Wi' the leaves in October, we thocht she
      wad fa',°   *fall*
For her cheek was owre red, an' her e'e° was   *eye*
   owre bricht,°   *bright*
Whaur the saul leukit oot[3] like an angel o' licht.

5 She dwalt in the muirlans° amang the   *moorlands*
   red bells
O' the sweet hinny heather that blooms on the fells,

Whaur the peesweep an' plover[4] are aye on the wing,
An' the lilt o' the lav'rock's° first heard   *skylark*
   in the Spring.

As black as a craw, an' as saft as the silk,
10 Were the lang locks that fell on a neck like the milk;
She was lithesome an' lo'esome° as lassie   *lonesome*
   micht be,
An' saft was the love-licht that danc'd in her e'e.

Puir Effie had lov'd; a' the hopes an' the fears,
The plagues an' the pleasures, the smiles an' the tears
15 O' love she had kenn'd°—she had gone thro'   *known*
   them a'
For fause° Jamie Crichton—oh, black be   *false*
   his fa'!°   *fate*

The auldest o' five, whan a lassie o' ten,
She had baith the hoose an' the bairnies°   *children*
   to fen';°   *care for*
The mither° had gane when she was but a bairn,   *mother*
20 Sae Effie had mony° sad lessons to learn.   *many*

At hame, had ye seen her amang the young chips,
The sweet law o' kindness was aye on her lips;
She kamed oot their hair, wash'd their wee
   hackit° feet,   *white*
Wi' sae tentie a haun° that a bairn   *gentle a hand*
   wadna greet.°   *complain*

25 She was to her faither the licht o' his een,°   *eye*
He said she was be what her mither had been—
A fair an' sweet sample o' true womanhood,
Sae carefu' an' clever, sae bonnie an' guid.

The cot-house it stood on the lip o' the burn,°   *river*
30 That wimpled an' jinkit[5] wi' mony a turn
Roun' the fit o' the heather-fring'd
   gowany brae,°   *flower-covered hill*
Whaur the ae cow was tether'd, an' bairnies at play.

---

[1] *dichtit saft her e'en* Softly wiped [the tears from] her eye.

[2] *auld langsyne* Times gone by.

[3] *saul leukit oot* Soul looks out.

[4] *peesweep an' plover* Birds common to the Scottish Highlands;
peesweep Lapwing or peewit.

[5] *wimpled an' jinkit* Twisted and turned; meandered.

Sweet Effie was juist in the midst o' her teens
Whan she gat the first inkling o' what wooing means
35 Frae a chiel° in the clachan, wha aften   *young man*
    was seen
Stealin' up the burnside to the cot-hoose° at e'en.   *cottage*

On a saft simmer° gloamin' I saw them mysel'   *summer*
On the bank o' the burnie, an' well I cou'd tell,
By the hue on her cheek, an' the blink o' her e'e,
40 That her young love was his, an' wad evermair be.

Belyve° to fair Effie cam' wooers galore,   *soon*
An' mony saft tirlin's° at e'en on the door;   *knocks*
She smiled on them a', but gied° welcome to   *gave*
    nane—
Her first love an' last was young Jamie's alane.

45 An' Jamie, wha ne'er was a week frae her side,
Had vowed e'er a towmond[1] to mak' her his bride;
Her troth° she had gi'en him wi'   *promise, betrothal*
    blushes an' tears—
It was sweet—oh, how sweet! tho' whiles she had fears;

For a wee burdie sang, as roun' her it flew,
50 Sweet lassie, tak' tent—he's owre sweet to be true;
He's oot in the e'enin's whan ye dinna ken,°   *do not know*
An' they say he's been seen wi' Kate o' the Glen.

But Effie wad lauch,° an' wad sae to hersel',   *laugh*
What lees° an' what clashes° thae   *lies / gossip*
    bodies maun° tell,   *must*
55 For my Jamie has sworn to be true to the death,
An' nocht noo° can pairt us as lang's we   *nothing now*
    ha'e breath.

Ae° short winter Sabbath, juist as it grew mirk,° *one / dark*
The faither cam' hame—he had been at the kirk;°   *church*
His cheek was sae white, an' his leuk was sae queer,
60 That Effie glower'd at him in dredour an' fear.

Then he said, "My ain Effie, puir mitherless°   *motherless*
    lass!
Oh, wha wad ha'e thocht this wad e'er come to pass?
Thy Jamie, this day, in the kirk was proclaim'd,
An' Katie MacLean for his bride they ha'e named.

65 "I was tauld on the road by ane that maun ken,
Her grannie was ance the gudewife o' the Glen,
An' she left to young Katie a hantle o' gear[2]—
It's gear Jamie wants, an' there's naething o't here."

An' what said puir Effie? She stood like a stane,
70 But faintin', or greetin', or cryin' was nane;
Her sweet lips they quiver'd, the bluid frae her cheek
Flew back to her heart, but nae word cou'd she speak.

The faither sat doun, laid her head on his breast:
"On God an' her faither my Effie maun rest,
75 They ne'er will deceive thee—thy wrangs are richt sair;
Gin Jamie had wed thee they micht ha'e been mair."

Sune Effie gat up, gied her faither some meat,
Put the bairnies to bed, yet ne'er could she greet—
Her young heart was stricken—the fountains were dry
80 That gush frae the een wi' a tearfu' supply.

That nicht at the reading she joined in the psalm,
Her cheek it was pale, but her brow it was calm;
An' faither he pray'd, as she knelt by his side,
That God his dear lassie wad comfort an' guide.

85 The winter gaed by, an' the hale° simmer thro'   *whole*
She tosh'd° up the hoose, fed an' milkit the cow;   *tidied*
The cauld warl' had nocht that she cared for ava,°   *at all*
Her life it was silently meltin' awa'.

Oh! whaur noo the love-licht that sparkled ere while
90 In her bonny black e'e? Oh! whaur noo the smile
That dimpled her cheek? They were gane! they were
    gane!
Yet she ne'er shed a tear, an' ne'er made a mane.°   *moan*

---

[1] *e'er a towmond* Within a year.

[2] *hantle o' gear* Large amount of wealth.

An sae she was wearin', fast wearin awa'!
Wi' the leaves in October sweet Effie did fa'!
95 Her mournin' was ended, an' blissfu' an' bricht
The dear lassie dwells wi' the angels o' licht.
—1868

SAMUEL SMILES (1812–1904)

Smiles's most famous book, *Self-Help; with Illustrations of Character and Conduct* (1859), is renowned as a ground-breaking work of popular non-fiction—the forerunner that gave its name to an entire genre. By the end of the nineteenth century *Self-Help* had sold a quarter of a million copies.

The degree to which doctrines of individual enterprise are today associated with political conservativism has led many to assume that Smiles himself must have been to the right of center politically. In fact he was a strong advocate of causes such as parliamentary reform and women's suffrage, and a strong critic of *rentier* capitalists who obtain wealth merely through deploying their capital and through the labor of others rather that through their own hard work. He was not against government measures to help the poor or government measures to further the progress of the nation; he was simply of the view that the actions of individuals would, collectively, have greater impact than the actions of governments.

Raised near Edinburgh, Smiles attended the University of Edinburgh. He began to attract attention during the 1840s when he was editor of the *Leeds Times*; it was during his time in Leeds that he began to give lectures to groups of working men on the subject of self-help. Though self-reliance is said by many to be a characteristically Scottish trait, Smiles himself was so far from being a Scottish nationalist that he writes of England as "our nation."

from *Self-Help*[1]

from CHAPTER I: SELF-HELP—NATIONAL AND INDIVIDUAL

"The worth of a State, in the long run, is the worth of the individuals composing it."—J.S. Mill[2]

"We put too much faith in systems, and look too little to men."—B. Disraeli[3]

... National progress is the sum of individual industry, energy, and uprightness, as national decay is of individual idleness, selfishness, and vice. What we are accustomed to decry as great social evils, will, for the most part, be found to be but the outgrowth of man's own perverted life; and though we may endeavour to cut them down and extirpate them by means of Law, they will only spring up again with fresh luxuriance in some other form, unless the conditions of personal life and character are radically improved. If this view be correct, then it follows that the highest patriotism and philanthropy consist, not so much in altering laws and modifying institutions, as in helping and stimulating men to elevate and improve themselves by their own free and independent individual action.

It may be of comparatively little consequence how a man is governed from without, whilst everything depends upon how he governs himself from within. The greatest slave is not he who is ruled by a despot, great though that evil be, but he who is the thrall of his own moral ignorance, selfishness, and vice. Nations who are thus enslaved at heart cannot be freed by any mere changes of masters or of institutions; and so long as the fatal delusion prevails, that liberty solely depends upon and consists in government, so long will such changes, no matter at what cost they may be effected, have as little

---

[1] *Self-Help*   The text used here is that of the "new edition" of 1896, for which Smiles made a number of revisions.

[2] *J.S. Mill*   John Stuart Mill, English philosopher and proponent of the doctrine of utilitarianism; the quotation is from the last paragraph of *On Liberty* (1859).

[3] *B. Disraeli*   Benjamin Disraeli (1804–81), writer and Prime Minister of the United Kingdom.

practical and lasting result as the shifting of the figures in a phantasmagoria.[1] The solid foundations of liberty must rest upon individual character; which is also the only sure guarantee for social security and national progress. John Stuart Mill truly observes that "even despotism does not produce its worst effects so long as individuality exists under it; and whatever crushes individuality is despotism, by whatever name it be called."[2]

Old fallacies as to human progress are constantly turning up. Some call for Caesars,[3] others for Nationalities,[4] and others for Acts of Parliament. We are to wait for Caesars, and when they are found, "happy the people who recognise and follow them."[5] This doctrine shortly means, everything *for* the people, nothing *by* them—a doctrine which, if taken as a guide, must, by destroying the free conscience of a community, speedily prepare the way for any form of despotism. Caesarism is human idolatry in its worst form—a worship of mere power, as degrading in its effects as the worship of mere wealth would be. A far healthier doctrine to inculcate among[6] the nations would be that of Self-Help; and so soon as it is thoroughly understood and carried into action, Caesarism will be no more. The two principles are directly antagonistic; and what Victor Hugo said of the Pen and the Sword alike applies to them, "Ceci tuera cela."[7]

The power of Nationalities and Acts of Parliament is also a prevalent superstition. What William Dargan,[8]

---

[1] *phantasmagoria* Exhibition of optical illusions using artificial light.

[2] *even despotism ... be called* See *On Liberty* (1859).

[3] *Caesars* I.e., strong political leaders.

[4] *Nationalities* I.e., nationalism; movements for national autonomy.

[5] *happy the ... follow them* From Napoleon III's *History of Julius Caesar* (1865–66).

[6] *inculcate among* Impress upon.

[7] *Ceci tuera cela* French: This will kill that. Smiles may have confused the classic proverb regarding the pen being mightier than the sword with this phrase by Victor Hugo (1802–85) regarding the pen (or the book) and religion. In Hugo's novel *Notre-Dame de Paris* (English translations of which have often been published under the title *The Hunchback of Notre Dame*) the character Claude Frollo, a priest attached to Notre-Dame cathedral in Paris, points to a book as he looks at the cathedral tower and says "This [the book] will kill that [religion, as symbolized by the cathedral]."

[8] *William Dargan* Irish rail engineer (1799–1867).

one of Ireland's truest patriots, said at the closing of the first Dublin Industrial Exhibition, may well be quoted now: "To tell the truth," he said, "I never heard the word independence mentioned that my own country and my own fellow townsmen did not occur to my mind. I have heard a great deal about the independence that we were to get from this, that, and the other place, and of the great expectations we were to have from persons from other countries coming amongst us. Whilst I value as much as any man the great advantages that must result to us from that intercourse, I have always been deeply impressed with the feeling that our industrial independence is dependent upon ourselves. I believe that with simple industry and careful exactness in the utilization of our energies, we never had a fairer chance nor a brighter prospect than the present. We have made a step, but perseverance is the great agent of success; and if we but go on zealously, I believe in my conscience that in a short period we shall arrive at a position of equal comfort, of equal happiness, and of equal independence, with that of any other people."

All nations have been made what they are by the thinking and the working of many generations of men. Patient and persevering labourers in all ranks and conditions of life, cultivators of the soil and explorers of the mine, inventors and discoverers, manufacturers, mechanics and artisans, poets, philosophers, and politicians, all have contributed towards the grand result, one generation building upon another's labours, and carrying them forward to still higher stages. This constant succession of noble workers—the artisans of civilisation—has served to create order out of chaos in industry, science, and art; and the living race has thus, in the course of nature, become the inheritor of the rich estate provided by the skill and industry of our forefathers, which is placed in our hands to cultivate, and to hand down, not only unimpaired but improved, to our successors.

The spirit of self-help, as exhibited in the energetic action of individuals, has in all times been a marked feature in the English character, and furnishes the true measure of our power as a nation. Rising above the heads of the mass, there were always to be found a series of individuals distinguished beyond others, who commanded the public homage. But our progress has also been owing to multitudes of smaller and less known men. Though only the generals' names may be remembered in the history of any great campaign, it has been in a great measure through the individual valour and heroism of the privates that victories have been won. And life, too, is "a soldiers' battle,"—men in the ranks having in all times been amongst the greatest of workers. Many are the lives of men unwritten, which have nevertheless as powerfully influenced civilisation and progress as the more fortunate Great whose names are recorded in biography. Even the humblest person, who sets before his fellows an example of industry, sobriety, and upright honesty of purpose in life, has a present as well as a future influence upon the well-being of his country; for his life and character pass unconsciously into the lives of others, and propagate good example for all time to come.

Daily experience shows that it is energetic individualism which produces the most powerful effects upon the life and action of others, and really constitutes the best practical education. ...

—1859, 1896

JOHN A. MACDONALD (1815–1891)

Though Macdonald's family emigrated from Scotland in 1820, when he was still a child, he remained proudly attached to his Scottish heritage throughout his life. He was a leading force behind the drive to unite the British colonies in the northern part of North America into one entity, and became Canada's first Prime Minister following Confederation in 1867. (He was, it must be noted, also a forceful proponent of the worst harms associated with the foundation of Canada, including the policy of cultural genocide the Canadian government implemented against the Indigenous peoples whose land the British Empire had colonized.) Macdonald delivered the speech excerpted below at a conference held in Quebec to consider the possibility of uniting Upper and Lower Canada with the Atlantic colonies of Nova Scotia, New Brunswick, and Prince Edward Island; in the excerpts presented here he compares

the nature of the proposed Canadian union to the union between Scotland and England and the union of United States to the south.

from *Speech on the Quebec Resolution*,[1] 6 February 1865

... The relations between England and Scotland are very similar to that which obtains[2] between the Canadas. The union between them, in matters of legislation, is of a federal character, because the Act of Union[3] between the two countries provides that the Scottish law cannot be altered, except for the manifest advantage of the people of Scotland. This stipulation has been held to be so obligatory on the Legislature of Great Britain, that no measure affecting the law of Scotland is passed unless it receives the sanction of a majority of the Scottish members in Parliament. No matter how important it may be for the interests of the empire as a whole to alter the laws of Scotland—no matter how much it may interfere with the symmetry of the general law of the United Kingdom, that law is not altered, except with the consent of the Scottish people, as expressed by their representatives in Parliament. (Hear, hear.) Thus, we have, in Great Britain, to a limited extent, an example of the working and effects of a Federal Union, as we might expect to witness them in our own Confederation.

The whole scheme of Confederation, as propounded by the Conference, as agreed to and sanctioned by the Canadian Government, and as now presented for the consideration of the people, and the Legislature, bears upon its face the marks of compromise. Of necessity there must have been a great deal of mutual concession.

---

[1] *Quebec Resolution* Collection of resolutions drafted at the October 1864 Quebec Conference laying down the foundation for the eventual Canadian Confederation; a fundamental aspect of the resolution was the establishment of a strong central government.

[2] *obtains* Exists.

[3] *Act of Union* The Acts of Union between England and Scotland were passed in 1707, joining the two kingdoms (previously separate though ruled by the same monarch) into the United Kingdom of Great Britain; one of the Acts' provisions stipulated that Scots law would remain unchanged.

When we think of the representatives of five colonies, all supposed to have different interests, meeting together, charged with the duty of protecting those interests and of pressing the views of their own localities and sections, it must be admitted that had we not met in a spirit of conciliation, and with an anxious desire to promote this union; if we had not been impressed with the idea contained in the words of the resolution—"That the best interests and present and future prosperity of British North America would be promoted by a Federal Union under the Crown of Great Britain,"—all our efforts might have proved to be of no avail. If we had not felt that, after coming to this conclusion, we were bound to set aside our private opinions on matters of detail, if we had not felt ourselves bound to look at what was practicable, not obstinately rejecting the opinions of others nor adhering to our own; if we had not met, I say, in a spirit of conciliation, and with an anxious, overruling desire to form one people under one government, we never would have succeeded. ...

Prior to the formation of the American Union, as we all know, the different states which entered into it were separate colonies. They had no connection with each other further than that of having a common sovereign, just as with us at present. Their constitutions and their laws were different. They might and did legislate against each other, and when they revolted against the Mother Country they acted as separate sovereignties, and carried on the war by a kind of treaty of alliance against the common enemy. Ever since the union was formed the difficulty of what is called "State Rights" has existed, and this had much to do in bringing on the present unhappy war in the United States.[1] They commenced, in fact, at the wrong end. They declared by their Constitution that each state was a sovereignty in itself, and that all the powers incident to a sovereignty belonged to each state, except those powers which, by the Constitution, were conferred upon the General Government and Congress.

Here we have adopted a different system. We have strengthened the General Government.[2] We have given the General Legislature all the great subjects of legislation. We have conferred on them, not only specifically and in detail, all the powers which are incident to sovereignty, but we have expressly declared that all subjects of general interest not distinctly and exclusively conferred upon the local governments and local legislatures, shall be conferred upon the General Government and Legislature. We have thus avoided that great source of weakness which has been the cause of the disruption of the United States. We have avoided all conflict of jurisdiction and authority, and if this Constitution is carried out, as it will be in full detail in the Imperial Act to be passed if the colonies adopt the scheme, we will have in fact, as I said before, all the advantages of a legislative union under one administration, with, at the same time the guarantees for local institutions and for local laws, which are insisted upon by so many in the provinces now, I hope, to be united. ...
—1865

ELIZA OGILVY (1822–1912)

Born in 1822, Scottish writer Eliza Ogilvy is best known for her poems on motherhood, as well as for her poems and stories that illustrate Scottish history and myth. She married in 1843 and wrote "A Natal Address" on the occasion of the birth of her first child, Rose. The death of Rose less than two years later inspired Ogilvy's first full volume, the solemn *Rose Leaves* (1845). The following year she published *A Book of Highland Minstrelsy*, in which each poem is prefaced by a background piece in prose. Ogilvy put out several more volumes of verse over the years, one of which was written while living in Florence, Italy, where she and her family befriended the English poets Robert and Elizabeth Barrett

---

[1] *Ever since ... United States* The first constitution of the United States, formed during the Revolutionary War, had guaranteed individual states almost complete sovereignty; while the authority of the central government was strengthened with the creation of the new Constitution in 1789, questions surrounding the sovereignty of individual states continued to figure prominently in American political discourse. The American Civil War (1861–65) was fought in large part over the claims of Southern states that they had a constitutional right to maintain the institution of slavery.

[2] *General Government* I.e., the central government.

Browning. Upon their return to Britain Ogilvy concentrated on her prose writing, publishing stories and articles in periodicals, and also wrote a memoir of E.B. Browning.

A Natal Address to My Child, March 19th 1844

Hail to thy puggy nose, my Darling,
Fair womankind's last added scrap,
That, callow° as an unfledged starling,   bald
Liest screaming in the Nurse's lap.

5   No locks thy tender cranium boasteth,
No lashes veil thy gummy eye
And, like some steak gridiron° toasteth,   griddle
Thy skin is red and crisp and dry.

Thy mouth is swollen past describing
10   Its corners twisted as in scorn
Of all the leech° is now prescribing   doctor, physician
To doctor° thee, the newly born.   treat

Sweet little lump of flannel binding,
Thou perfect cataract° of clothes,   waterfall
15   Thy many folds there's no unwinding
Small mummy without arms or toes!

And am I really then thy Mother?
My very child I cannot doubt thee,
Remembering all the fuss and bother
20   And moans and groans I made about thee!

'Tis now thy turn to groan and grumble,
As if afraid to enter life,
To dare each whipping scar and tumble
And task and toil with which 'tis rife.

25   O Baby of the wise round forehead,
Be not too thoughtful ere thy time;
Life is not truly quite so horrid—
Oh! how she squalls!—she can't bear rhyme!
—1844

The Imprecation[1] by the Cradle

A young lady of rank, belonging to an ancient family in the north of Scotland, was betrothed, with the consent of her relations, to a gentleman of equal birth. Their union being delayed by unforeseen obstacles, the lover found means to ruin the unhappy girl, whose affection for her plighted husband left her more exposed to his unprincipled passion. Then, notwithstanding the wealth to which she was heiress, he deserted her, and completed his perfidy[2] by carrying his addresses to the daughter of a neighbouring earl, by whom they were accepted.

The distracted[3] lady heard of his new betrothal when on the point of becoming a mother. With a strength almost supernatural in one so delicately reared, she rose from her bed the very day her child was born, and attiring herself in costly garments, went to a public assembly,[4] where her fickle lover and his engaged wife were to be present. There she danced so gaily and so lightly as completely to belie the rumours scandal had circulated regarding her.

But shortlived was her assumed gaiety. Returned to her dishonoured home, heartbroken and a prey to her emotions, she knelt down by the cradle of her son and prayed that on the father's head sorrow and retribution might descend, and that he might never know happiness in his home or child in his wedlock.

Her adjuration seemed a prophecy, for she who had filled her place in his affections, learning the story of her hapless rival, conceived a violent hatred for her husband. So far did this dislike proceed that her mind became unsettled. She repeatedly attempted both her own and her husband's life; and at last, confined to prevent fatal consequences, she died a raving and a childless maniac.

The boy, whose birth had brought misfortune on both his parents and caused so much sorrow on all sides, grew to manhood, when he distinguished himself

---

[1]   *Imprecation*   Invocation of vengeance; curse.

[2]   *perfidy*   Deceit.

[3]   *distracted*   Distressed.

[4]   *assembly*   Ball; party.

greatly in the profession of arms, gaining both honour and wealth in his country's service.

Such are the romantic incidents of a story which is literally true.

PART 1

Slumber sweet, my babie,
  Slumber peacefullie,
Mickle° grief and mickle wrang°   *much / wrong*
  I have borne for thee!

5 Hush thee, heir of sorrow!
  Sleep and sleep away,
All of thy fause° father's heart   *false*
  Mingled with thy clay.°   *body*

Dinna° wear his likeness,   *do not*
10 Dinna smile his smile;
I should hate thee, innocent,
  For that look of guile!

Dinna speak his accents,
  Lest my heart of fire
15 Spurn the child for blandishments
  Borrowed from the sire.°   *father*

Faint with mother-anguish
  From my bed I rose,
Kamed° the locks he praised so weel,° *combed / well, highly*
20 Donned my richest clothes,

Danced amang the blythest,
  Gay as ony° bride,   *any*
All the weakness of my limbs
  Iron-braced by pride.

25 Fair is Lady Ellen,
  He her hand did hold,
Breathed to her the flatteries
  Breathed to me of old.

Dancing down the measure,
30 Ne'er his thoughts could be
How to him a child was born
  That dark day by me.

Oh! ye dreams of vengeance,
  Which the injured haunt,
35 If ye come like evil powers
  Evil prayers to grant,

Cursèd be his union!
  Cursèd be his name!
Trodden in forgetfulness,
40 Blotted out in shame!

Barren be his wedlock,
  Desolate his hearth,
Never may his ancient halls
  Echo children's mirth.

45 Childless Lady Ellen!
  Never may her hand
Rock the cradled little one,
  Heir of all her land.

Land and lordly glories
50 Passing to another,
Never may a lawful heir
  Mock his elder brother!

Slumber sweet, my babie,
  Slumber peacefullie,
55 Mickle grief and mickle wrang
  Life has yet for thee!

PART 2

Slumber sweet, my mother,
  Slumber peacefullie,
Dinna heed the grief and wrang
  Life has brought to me!

5   Dinna heed the scorning
         Of thy haughty kin,
     Dinna weep sae° bitterlie   *so*
         Lang° repented sin!   *long*

     Dinna heed the portion
10   Lawful heirs enjoy,
     Forfeit lands and forfeit name
         Wrested from thy boy.

     Dinna weep the traitor
         Who thy youth betrayed,
15   Wooed thee in the sunny time,
         Left thee in the shade.

     For the curse is working,
         At my birth conjured,
     Sharper griefs are piercing him
20   Than thyself endured!

     Lonely are his castles,
         Desolate his halls,
     Never child hath propped the house
         Which to ruin falls.

25   Hate is in her bosom,
         Who the long night lies
     Gazing in his haggard face
         With unquiet eyes.

     Crazed is Lady Ellen,
30   She whose beauty won
     Lover from his plighted bride,
         Father from his son.

     Crazed is Lady Ellen,
         Yet her madness knows
35   Horror for his perjury,
         Pity for thy woes.

     Softly sleep, my mother,
         He can sleep no more,

     Fearfulness and gaunt remorse
40   Knocking at his door.

     Outcast from my lineage,
         He to me denied
     Father's love and father's name,
         Wealth and rank and pride;

45   Yet my blood is burning
         With ancestral fires,
     And the glory of the child
         Shall outshine the sire's.

     And the landless soldier,
50   From the gory field,
     From the ramparts won shall carve
         His unspotted shield.

     Softly sleep, my mother,
         Slumber peacefullie,
55   Justice for its cruel wrong
         Life shall yield to me!
                                    —1846

The Portents of the Night

Night to the devout Highlander was a time to rest within doors, and renew the strength by sleep. Evil spirits were abroad, the Prince of Darkness[1] roamed over the hills: it was presumption to dare his presence, and drew upon itself the neglect of all angelic guardians. It is rather difficult to reconcile this timorous avoidance of danger with the thousand recorded facts of nightly creaghs,[2] nightly robberies, nightly assassinations; but we must remember, that even in the most superstitious the overwhelming passion of the moment has silenced the voice of fear. The constantly recurring disasters of these evil undertakings was, of course, attributed by the neighbours to the contemptuous presumption which

---

1 *Prince of Darkness* I.e., the devil; Satan.
2 *creaghs* Cattle raids.

overlooked the peril. It was then held an established axiom, that evil spirits were to be shunned, not braved. Those whose necessary tasks detained them out of doors beyond nightfall were not so liable to harm as the daring loiterer, who was sure to suffer for his boldness by an encounter with the wicked demons let loose upon the earth during the dark hours.

The vision of armed horsemen riding along the face of an impassable precipice is taken from a narration of a similar appearance in the daytime on the mountains of Cumberland.[1] It is given in detail by Sir David Brewster,[2] in his work on "Natural Magic." Scott[3] likewise speaks, in his "Lady of the Lake," of a presage of coming death of a similar character:

> Sounds, too, had come in midnight blast
> Of charging steeds careering fast
> Along Benharrow's shingly side,
> Where mortal horseman ne'er might ride.

The birk scarred by the witch's ban[4] recalls an idea entertained in many parts of the Highlands, that these ill-omened crones could wither a tree by their curses, so that the sap should dry up in the trunk, and the whole become blighted and unfruitful, as if scathed by lightning.

It was sometimes the custom to baptize an infant over a drawn sword, in the emergency of illness and distance from a priest. The rite of baptism was highly prized among the Highlanders; they regarded it as an unfailing passport to heaven for the child who died in earliest infancy. On the other hand, those unhappy ones whose parents, through accident or neglect, had omitted ensuring for them the entrance into happiness, were lost forever and ever, as much as the most hardened sinner. Their voices were heard in the woods bewailing their wretched fate, and upbraiding their forgetful parents.

To "win west" was a proverbial expression for reaching heaven. The Highlanders to this day suppose the realms of everlasting glory to be situate to the westward. This fancy has probably remained to them from an extinct Druidical[5] superstition, which fixed the locality of the eternal mansions in the island of Hath Innis, among the more remote of the Hebridean archipelago.[6]

The water of three streams at their confluence possessed, it was said, singular properties. Hither bereaved parents came with the elfin changeling, whom the fairies had substituted for their own fair mortal child. The infant being left all night at this gathering of the waters, was found in the morning the very one whom the "gude people"[7] had stolen, the magic of the spot forcing the dishonest elves to restore their prize. The ford crossed on occasion of a burial by a funeral party, was called the Ford of the Dead and the Living. Its waters were of potent efficacy to counteract evil spells, witchcraft, and all delusions of the devil, but the ford itself was generally haunted, especially on the approach of a death among the neighbouring inhabitants. The spectre seen by the traveller had its face hidden—a circumstance usually held to portend evil to the spectator himself, who saw in the muffled form his shadowy likeness. The gazer, when such an appearance came before him, could, by reversing his plaid[8] or any other part of his vestments, ascertain this fact to his satisfaction, as the spectre, if his own, would undergo a similar change. The "Legend of Montrose"[9] illustrates this most dramatically in the dialogue between Ranald of the Mist and Allan Macaulay.

The compatibility of such a superstitious disposition with a religious and sincere faith has been before commented on; the effect of those visions would be to sink

---

[1] *Cumberland* Mountainous region in northwestern England, on the Scottish border.

[2] *Sir David Brewster* Scottish academic and scientist (1781–1868), who wrote a series of letters addressed to Sir Walter Scott on various topics including "spectral apparitions."

[3] *Scott* Scottish poet and novelist Sir Walter Scott (1771–1832).

[4] *birk* Birch tree; *ban* Curse.

[5] *Druidical* Originating with the Druids, ancient figures of Celtic history and myth who often figure in legend as magicians, sorcerers, and soothsayers.

[6] *Hebridean archipelago* Group of remote islands off the northwest coast of Scotland.

[7] *gude people* Good people; common epithet for the fairies.

[8] *plaid* Woolen cloak in a tartan pattern, worn as part of traditional Highland dress.

[9] *Legend of Montrose* 1819 novel by Sir Walter Scott.

every serious Highlander on his knees. In his habitual reference of every occurrence, natural or extraordinary, to the watchful superintendence of an all-wise Deity, the Gael has left his posterity a lesson of true wisdom.

THE PORTENTS OF THE NIGHT

"What saw ye outbye in the gloamin',°   *twilight*
gudeman?°   *husband*
Your teeth chatter sairly, your colour is wan!
Did ye venture the pass o' the mountain by night?
Ye surely have witnessed some terrible sight;
5 Was it aught° o' this warld, or a kelpie, or   *anything*
   sprite?"

"I cam' by the pass o' the mountain, gudewife,
But I'll never return a' the days of my life;
The calm caller° moonlight was stirred on   *cool*
   the crags
By the glinting of harness, the fluttering of flags;
10 A troop of armed horsemen rode gallantly by
Where a goat couldna° creep on the   *could not*
   precipice high,
In a long single file, horse by horse, round the cliff;
The flash o' their weapons gaed° past in   *went*
   a gliff.°   *instant*
Sure never was seen at sic° hour, in sic place,   *such*
15 Or rider or steed of this earth's mortal race;
And I knelt there in fear wi' my plaid on my face."

"That troop boded naething but evil, gudeman;
The voice o' dissension is loud in the lan';
The horse o' the Saxon° shall trample   *i.e., the English*
   he vale,
20 And faggot[1] and sword be the meed° o'   *reward*
   the Gael.
But saw ye nae sicht° in the forest, gudeman,   *sight*
Where the birks are all scaured by the dour witch's ban?
Your teeth chatter sairly, your colour is wan!"

"Nae sight have I seen in the forest, gudewife,
25 But I heard what I ne'er shall forget in my life,—
A moanin' and sobbin' of infant in pain,
A dreary cry over and over again.
It was na the wind, for the wind it was still;
It was na the burn, for there's frost on the hill;
30 'Twas the voice of a child, girning° sadly   *crying*
   and sair,
Sounding close at my footsteps and filling the air;
And I searched the dark wood, but no baby was there."

"'Twas the voice o' your baby unchristened, gudeman;
Unblessed by the priest was her life's little span;
35 No waters of mercy were poured on her head,
And therefore she waileth so sair from the dead,
And haunteth the forest, and canna find rest;
Unsealed by redemption, she canna win west.
Oh! would I had crossed thee with naked claymore[2]
40 Than barred thee from heaven, my babe that I bore!
Or would I had ta'en° thee though   *taken*
   corri° and spate,°   *valley / flood*
Through the drifts of the snow to the priest's very gate,
Or ever thou cam'st to such terrible fate!
But saw ye nae sicht by the water, gudeman?
45 Your teeth chatter sairly, your colour is wan!
Did ye come by the ford where the three rivers meet,
Where the widowed and childless gae aften to greet
By the graves that lie close at the kirk's°   *church's*
   holy feet?"

"I cam' by the kirk o' the rivers, gudewife,
50 'Tis the last time I ever shall pass it in life.
As the ford o' the Dead and the Living I crossed,
I saw a drooned man° in the wild billows   *drowned*
   tossed;
The features were downward, no face could I see,
But closely he drifted, he brushed by my knee;
55 And still when the plaid or the hair I would grasp,
The wet spray alone did I find in my clasp,
Till the corse° floated seaward with shrieks   *corpse*
   on the breeze,

---

[1] *faggot* Bundle of sticks used for fuel; here, for burning out the Scots.

[2] *claymore* Two-handed sword with a double-edged blade, formerly used by Scottish Highlanders.

With the roar of the river, the sigh of the trees,
And my heart 'gan to swim, and my pulses to freeze."

60 "Ohone[1] for my Donald! ohone, my gudeman!
Was ever sic sorrow since life first began?
Not many may look on their ain ghastly wraith,
Not many like thee hae sic warnin' o' death;
For lo! as I sat here at evening's dark close,
65 And toasted your bannocks and thickened your brose,[2]
The river seemed suddenly rushing beside,
And I saw a drooned man swept away by the tide—
I saw 'twas your face as it hurled o'er the
    linn,°   waterfall
There was shrieking without and that vision within.
70 As swift as it came so it vanished away,
And nocht at my feet but the black poussie° lay;   cat
He shivered wi' terror, I greeted full sore,
Till your hand at the latch and your foot on the floor
Gar'd me rise up to meet you and clasp you once more."

75 "Your words are a warning of evil, gudewife!
Short, short is the thread o' my fast-dwindled life;
And mickle° my sinnin' and hardened my soul,   great
And far is my heart frae the heavenly goal.
The path o' the just is a steep whinny[3] brae,°   hill
80 And aft did I stumble, and aft did I stray:
Kneel down by the ingle, gudewife, and we'll pray!"
—1846

JOHN DAVIDSON (1857–1909)

Much of the work of Scottish-born writer John Davidson is notable for its blending of lyric poetry and philosophy, and for the scientific influence that is evident in his ideas. In the decade leading up to his death Davidson wrote four "Testaments," long poems which express his Materialist philosophical vision; he claimed in 1904 that the purpose of the series was "to aid in the overthrow of the rotten financial investment called Christendom." Plagued by financial difficulties and depression, Davidson died by suicide at the age of 50.

[N.B. One poem of Davidson's ("A Northern Suburb") is also included in "The Aesthetic Movement" section of this volume.]

Waiting

Within unfriendly walls
    We starve—or starve by stealth.
Oxen fatten in their stalls;
    You guard the harrier's° health: hunting hound
5 They never can be criminals,
    And can't compete for wealth.
        From the mansion and the palace
            Is there any help or hail°   protection
        For the tenants of the alleys,
10   Of the workhouse[4] and the jail?

Though lands await our toil,[5]
    And earth half-empty rolls,
Cumberers° of English soil,   burdens
    We cringe for orts° and doles°—   scraps / charity
15 Prosperity's accustomed foil,
    Millions of useless souls.
        In the gutters and the ditches
            Human vermin festering lurk—
        We, the rust upon your riches;
20   We, the flaw in all your work.

Come down from where you sit;
    We look to you for aid.
Take us from the miry pit,
    And lead us out undismayed:

---

[1] *Ohone* Exclamation of grief.

[2] *brose* Type of porridge.

[3] *whinny* Covered in furze-bushes; thorny.

[4] *workhouse* Especially after the Poor Law Amendment Act of 1834, most other forms of financial relief for the impoverished and unemployed were replaced by the workhouse, an institution to which people could go to perform labor in exchange for food and shelter; conditions at these workhouses were often made intentionally severe in order to discourage the poor from seeking even this degree of aid.

[5] *Though lands ... our toil* Many believed that a solution to poverty and unemployment would be found in encouraging emigration to the "half-empty" colonies.

25   Say, "Even you, outcast, unfit,
     Forward with sword and spade!"
       And myriads of us idle
         Would thank you through our tears,
     Though you drove us with a bridle,
30   And a whip about our ears!

   From cloudy cape to cape
     The teeming waters seethe;
   Golden grain and purple grape
     The regions overwreathe.
35   Will no one help up to escape?
     We scarce have room to breathe.
       You might try to understand us:
         We are waiting night and day
     For a captain to command us,
40   And the word we must obey.
—1897

from *The Testament of an Empire Builder*

…

Do I believe in Heaven and Hell? I do;
   We have them here; the world is nothing else.
Beauty and power and splendor and delight
Of chosen ones, elect ere Time began,
5   In loathsomeness, debility, disgrace,
Humiliation, travail, terror, woe,
Of multitudes, of myrmidons,[1] of all
The labourers, soldiers, servants, rooted deep:
He is a slave: a prisoner: damned: in Hell,
10   Whose daily bread depends on toil approved.
For me, I clambered into Heaven at once
And stayed there; joined the warfare of the times
In corner, trust, and syndicate: upheaved
A furrow, hissing through the angry world,
15   A redhot ploughshare in a frozen glebe,°   *field*
And reaped my millions long before my prime.

Then, being English, one of the elect
Above all folks, within me fate grew strong.
The authentic mandate of imperial doom
20   Silenced the drowsy lullaby of love,
(Though now my turbid[2] blood and nerves disused
Complain of mystery unrevealed, and haunt
Imagination day and night with looks—
With beckoning looks, soft arms and fragrant breath;
25   For even in Heaven each ransomed soul frequents
A private, an inevitable Hell!)
Undid my simple, immature design,
And made me—What! tenfold a criminal?
No other name for Hastings, Clive,[3] and me!
30   I broke your slothful dream of folded wings,
Of work achieved and empire circumscribed,
Dispelled the treacherous flatteries of peace,
And thrust upon you in your dull despite
The one thing needful, half a continent
35   Of habitable land! The English Hell
Forever crowds upon the English Heaven.
Secure your birthright; set the world at naught;
Confront your fate; regard the naked deed;
Enlarge your Hell; preserve it in repair;
40   Only a splendid Hell keeps Heaven fair.
—1902

WALES

FELICIA HEMANS (1793–1835)

A separate author entry for Hemans appears elsewhere in this anthology; included here are two poems from her largely forgotten 1822 collection *Welsh Melodies*, together with one of her more popular poems ("The Better Land") that has interesting parallels to "The Cambrian in America."

---

[1] *myrmidons* Subservient followers. In Greek mythology, the Myrmidons were loyal warriors who followed Achilles into battle against Troy.

[2] *turbid* Thick, muddled.

[3] *Hastings, Clive* Warren Hastings (1732–1818) and Robert Clive (1725–74) were both controversial Governors-General of India who contributed to consolidating British rule in the subcontinent; Clive in particular has been harshly criticized for his policies, which led to famine and hardship for many while enabling Clive to amass a great deal of personal wealth.

The Cambrian[1] in America

When the last flush of eve is dying
  On boundless lakes afar that shine:
When winds amidst the palms are sighing,
  And fragrance breathes from every pine:[2]
5 When stars through cypress boughs are gleaming,
  And fire-flies wander bright and free,
Still of thy harps, thy mountains dreaming,
  My thoughts, wild Cambria! dwell with thee!
Alone o'er green savannas roving,
10 Where some broad stream in silence flows,
Or through the eternal forests moving,
  One only home my spirit knows!
Sweet land, whence memory ne'er hath parted!
  To thee on sleep's light wing I fly;
15 But happier could the weary-hearted
  Look on his own blue hills and die!
—1822

Taliesin's[3] Prophecy

[A prophecy of Taliesin relating to the Ancient Britons
is still extant, and has been strikingly verified. It is to the
following effect:
     Their God they shall worship,
     Their language they shall retain,
     Their land they shall lose,
     Except wild Wales.]

A voice from time departed yet floats thy hills among,
  O Cambria! thus thy prophet bard, thy Taliesin
    sung:
"The path of unborn ages is traced upon my soul,
The clouds which mantle things unseen away before
  me roll,

5 A light the depths revealing hath o'er my spirit passed,
A rushing sound from days to be swells fitful in the
    blast,
And tells me that forever shall live the lofty tongue
To which the harp of Mona's[4] woods by freedom's
    hand was strung.

"Green island of the mighty![5] I see thine ancient race
10 Driven from their father's realm to make the rocks
    their dwelling-place!
I see from Uthyr's[6] kingdom the sceptre pass away,
And many a line of bards and chiefs and princely
    men decay.
But long as Arvon's mountains[7] shall lift their
    sovereign forms,
And wear the crown to which is given dominion
    o'er the storms,
15 So long, their empire sharing, shall live the lofty tongue
To which the harp of Mona's woods by freedom's
    hand was strung!"
—1822

The Better Land

"I hear thee speak of the better land,
  Thou call'st its children a happy band;
Mother! oh, where is that radiant shore?
Shall we not seek it, and weep no more?
5 Is it where the flower of the orange blows,
And the fire-flies glance through the myrtle boughs?"
  —"Not there, not there, my child!"

"Is it where the feathery palm-trees rise,
And the date grows ripe under sunny skies?

---

[1] *Cambrian* Welsh person; "Cambria" is the Anglicized version of
the Welsh name for Wales, *Cymru*.

[2] [Hemans's note] The aromatic odor of the pine has frequently
been mentioned by travellers.

[3] *Taliesin* Sixth-century Celtic bard, the reputed author of many
texts including a Welsh manuscript known as *The Book of Taliesin*.

[4] *harp* National instrument of Wales; *Mona* The island of
Anglesey in northern Wales, also known in Welsh as *Ynys Môn*.

[5] [Hemans's note] *Ynys y Cedeirn*, or Isle of the Mighty—an ancient
name given to Britain.

[6] [Hemans's note] Uthyr Pendragon, king of Britain, supposed to
have been the father of Arthur.

[7] *Arvon's mountains* Wales's highest mountains are located in Arfon,
in the northern part of the country.

10   Or midst the green islands of glittering seas,
     Where fragrant forests perfume the breeze,
     And strange, bright birds on their starry wings,
     Bear the rich hues of all glorious things?"
        —"Not there, not there, my child!"

15   "Is it far away, in some region old,
     Where the rivers wander o'er sands of gold?—
     Where the burning rays of the ruby shine,
     And the diamond lights up the secret mine,
     And the pearl gleams forth from the coral strand?—
20   Is it there, sweet mother, that better land?"
        —"Not there, not there, my child!

     "Eye hath not seen it, my gentle boy!
     Ear hath not heard its deep songs of joy;
     Dreams cannot picture a world so fair—
25   Sorrow and death may not enter there;

Time doth not breathe on its fadeless bloom,
For beyond the clouds, and beyond the tomb,
    It is there, it is there, my child!"
—1828

JOHN BLACKWELL (ALUN) (1797–1840)

Born in the town of Mold in Wales, John Blackwell—who adopted the bardic name Alun—received little to no formal education, but learned to read and write while apprenticing to a shoemaker who had an interest in poetry. An enthusiastic student of both English and Welsh poetic traditions, he attended local *eisteddfodau*—Welsh competitive literary festivals—and became editor of a Welsh-language magazine. He is best remembered for lyric poems such as *"Cathl i'r Eos."*

Cathl i'r Eos

Pan guddio nos in daear gu
    O dan ei du adenydd
Y clywir dy delori mwyn,
    A chôr llwyn yn llonydd;
5   Ac os bydd pigyn dan dy fron
     Yn peri i'th galon guro,
Ni wnei, nes torro'r wawrddydd hael,
    Ond canu, a gadael iddo.

A thebyg it yw'r feinir wâr
10   Sydd gymar gwell na gemau:
Er cilio haul a hulio bro
    Â miloedd o gymylau,
Pan dawo holl gysurwyr dydd,
    Hi lyna yn ffyddlonaf;
15   Yn nyfnder nos o boen a thrais
    Y dyry lais felysaf.

Song to the Nightingale[1]

When our dear earth is hid by night
    Under its black wing,
The woodland choir is mute, but you
    Then gently sing,
5   And if against your heart a thorn
    Throbs beneath your breast,
You, till generous day should break,
    Will but sing, and leave the rest.

And like you is this gentle girl,
10   Partner more than rubies dear,
At sunset, though across the land
    A thousand clouds appear,
When all day's comforters are dumb°   *silent*
    Her fidelity's complete;
15   In the night's anguish and dismay
    Never sounded voice so sweet.

---

[1] *Song to the Nightingale*   Translated by Anthony Conran, 1967.

Er dichon fod ei chalon wan
    Yn delwi dan y dulid,
Ni chwyna, i flino'i hannwyl rai,
    Ei gwên a guddia'i gofid;
Na pheidia'i chân trwy ddunos faith,
    Nes gweled gobaith golau
Yn t'wynnu, megis llygad aur,
    Trwy bur amrantau'r borau.
—c. 1830?

Though the worry almost numbs her heart
    She'll not complain
Nor tire her dear ones with distress—
    Her smile hides her pain;
Nor ends her song the long night through
    Until bright hope shall dawn,
Shining like an eye of gold
    Through the clear lids of morn.
—1967

SAMUEL ROBERTS (1800–1885)

Welsh minister Samuel Roberts became known for his radical political writings in the 1840s, many of which were published in his Welsh-language periodical, *Y Cronicl*. Among the causes he adopted were the abolition of slavery, women's suffrage, and the recognition of the rights of tenant farmers. He frequently gave voice to his disdain for British imperialism and militarism; in the following piece on the Crimean War,[1] Roberts condemns Britain and its allies for their roles in the conflict.

A Pacifist's Credo

In times of difficulty governments like individuals tend to be very stubborn and selfish. Many a country, at such times, has been terribly selfish, and madly boastful: but we acknowledge despite our shame that we do not believe any country (either civilized or barbarian) has ever deigned to boast more and so outrageously than England has done these last two years; and its proud boasting will remain a stain on its name for as long as the Thames flows through the centre of its capital city. And it weighs heavily on us to confess our belief that the war [in Crimea] will continue, and get worse, and spread, multiplying the losses and dangers of the king-

doms of Europe if the voice of England were to carry the day in the conferences which have recently been considering the matter. One of the blackest pages in the historiography of the world is the one dealing with "the wars of England." It is to be hoped to God she will change her tune and her spirit with a view to the usefulness and "glory" of her military institutions. If she will not, her name will be accursed all over the world and will remain so until the last afternoon of the earth.

The chief and foremost announcement made by England up to now has been that it wishes to replenish its armies, and build up its navy, and reinforce its defences and strengthen and increase the number of all its military institutions. In this it is setting the worst example to other kingdoms. It is in fact making them increase their armies according to the English pattern, to the detriment of the world. Instead of devoting its talent and influence to excelling in love and good works, it is leading the way in barbarism of the worst kind.

It is claimed boldly that the war is "for civilization and Christendom." We have wondered a great deal about the barbarism of such a claim. Furthering civilization by war! Perfecting European civilization by spreading the barbarism of war throughout Europe! Pleading virtue by means of vice! Kindness by rashness! Love by cruelty! Patience and order through riot and anarchy! Restraint and wealth through waste and damage! Courtesy and civilization through the most atrocious plans and slaughter! We can only say that people who hold to such a philosophy are uncivilized barbarians. Though

---

[1] *Crimean War*   Fought on the Crimean Peninsula (then part of the Russian Empire) between 1853 and 1856, the Crimean War pitted Russia against an alliance of France, Britain, the Ottoman Empire, and Sardinia in a battle over control of certain parts of the Middle East, including the Holy Land. The war was notorious for its high number of casualties and increasingly perceived ineffectualness.

they wear scarlet and silks, they are barbarians. Though they have golden chains about their necks, they are barbarians. Though they live in marble palaces, they are barbarians. Though the finest food and wine is on their tables, they are barbarians. Though they are fluent in parliamentary debates, they are barbarians. And barbarians they will remain until there is a change. Yes, they are fond of talking about "war to further Christianity!" "To further Christianity by war!" That is the blackest calumny[1] that has ever passed the lips of the superstitious, the blackest ever uttered in the name of atheism. Yes, they say, war is necessary for the furtherance of Christianity. No, no, I say, the history of the late war is everlasting evidence against Turkey, France, and England, that Christianity's influence, the influence of the gospels of peace, has been completely gagged in the spheres of their authority. …

Who does not pray—and pray more earnestly—for the dawning of a day, yes, for the imminent dawning of a fair and peaceful day when kind-hearted, courteous, and peace-loving men will administer the courts of Europe! Then their peace shall flow out like a river, and justice be guided like waves of the sea.

—1855

EVAN JAMES (1809–1878)

Evan James was a weaver by trade; he also wrote poetry and essays and was an active member of Welsh-language communities. His "*Hen Wlad fy Nhadau*" or "Land of my Fathers" has been the unofficial but widely used national anthem of Wales since the early twentieth century. It is said that James's son, James James, composed the melody one day while walking along the banks of the River Rhonda, though it is uncertain whether this preceded or followed the writing of the lyrics.

Hen Wlad fy Nhadau

Mae hen wlad fy nhadau yn annwyl i mi,
Gwlad beirdd a chantorion, enwogion o fri,
Ei gwrol ryfelwyr, gwladgarwyr tra mad,
Dros ryddid gollasant eu gwa'd.

5   Gwlad, Gwlad, pleidiol wyf i'm gwlad.
Tra môr yn fur i'r bur hoff bau,
O bydded i'r heniaih barhau.

Hen Gymru fynyddig, paradwys y bardd,
Pob dyffryn, pob clogwyn, i'm golwg sydd hardd,
10   Trwy deimlad gwladgarol, mor swynol yw si
Ei nentydd, afonydd, i fi.

Os treisiodd y gelyn fy ngwlad dan ei droed,
Mae hen iaith y Cymry mor fyw ag erioed,
Ni luddiwyd yr awen dan erchyll law brad,
15   Na thelyn berseiniol fy ngwlad.
—1856

Old Land of My Fathers[2]

Old land of my fathers, land of my choice,
The land in which bards and minstrels rejoice;
Land whose stern warriors were true as could be;
They gave their blood to be free.

5   Wales! Wales! I'll be faithful to Wales!
The sea is her wall; may nought 'ere befall
The pure, loved land, and th' old language of Wales.

Old mountains of Cambria,[3] bards' paradise,
Each hill and each valley the eye delights;
10   To the ears of her patriots how charming still seems
The music that forever flows in her streams.

If my land be by enemies harshly oppressed
The old Welsh tongue never dies, never rests;
The muse has slipped the traitor's noose—she's gone,
15   And the harp of my country plays on.
—2019

---

[1] *calumny* Lie.

[2] *Old Land of My Fathers* The present translation has been prepared by the editors of this anthology, in consultation with several of the extant translations.

[3] *Cambria* Latinized form of the Welsh name for Wales, *Cymru*.

SARAH JANE REES (CRANOGWEN) (1839–1916)

The daughter of a master mariner, Sarah Jane Rees had a fascinatingly varied career, during which she taught at a school of marine navigation, campaigned on behalf of the women's temperance movement, and wrote numerous works of prose and poetry. Like many Welsh poets of her era, she gained much of her literary skill and fame through participation in local *eisteddfodau*, competitive literary festivals. She was also editor of the Welsh-language women's periodical *Y Frythones*, and spoke on behalf of many progressive causes throughout her life.

The End of the Year[1]

Almost, almost done, another year,
And I go forward, forward, drawing near;
Many a year is now left high and dry,
And my life, my only life, is passing by:
5   I feel now that my journey's a descent
A rapid one—Oh strange how downward bent!
The day—the month—the year, all onward brings,
Hastening past, as if on speedy, tiny wings;
While I am contemplating them with joy,
10 They fly past, making of my mind a toy,
If one must sing happily at their birth,
One must do the same now, or the knell of death
Will sound with sorrow from the brink of their grave,
And thus does all in this sad world its ending have.

15 What?—Does the speed of time increase,
As it draws near the end of its lease?
Is there some great Power which pulls at it?
Perhaps a new name is given to it?
Is it true that the whole of the present,
20 While toward eternity it follows the current,
With its great powers sucking ardently,
Speeds on time's wheels, which turn more quickly?
It's as if we're in reach of the tide of Eternity,
And everything goes speeding on at a gallop,

25 But oh how I long to be able to say "stop"!
But no, too quickly the twilight falls for me!

There's work to be done, but time pays me no heed,
I think of doing, but time goes on with speed,
I decide to do, I plan, and I make haste,
30 While the day, the month, the year, speed past;
Each morning the day begins to die,
And the week just disappears, goes powering by,
The year, as if it were running a race,
Eager to reach its end, it speeds apace!

35 What is going on?—Where is everything going
Like this, powering onward, unstoppable, turning?
Is there no rest sometimes, no respite?
Day follows day, a new year comes to light;
But to my eyes everything seems restrained,
40 Everything's smaller, quicker, contained:
As it drives forward like this, before long it's sure
The end will be reached, the eternal cure,
And then—what, my Lord, will be thy behest?
A great stillness, and everything at rest?
45 The eager wheels of changeful time will
Beyond this boundary, be completely still?
Do the years there live and die?
Does the tide there have a neap[2] and high?
Are there boundaries to that Continent,
50 Does its moon change from waning to crescent?
Oh my Lord God, how boundless is Eternity!
How incomprehensible is that place to me!
How impossible to plumb that Ocean's deeps,
Whose tide is high and brooks no neaps!
55 I feel myself being pulled towards it!
What, oh what will be my fate within it?
You plumb its very depths, entirely!
Oh grant that I may know you fully,
And shelter always in your shadow!
60 I'll release myself into the eternal now
Quietly, trusting always in you!
—1870(?)

---

[1] *The End of the Year* Translated by Katie Gramich for *Welsh Women's Poetry 1460–2001: An Anthology*. Copyright © Katie Gramich 2003.

[2] *neap* Period in which the high tide is at its lowest, and there is little difference between high and low tide.

DAVID LLOYD GEORGE (1863–1945)

Of all British Prime Ministers, David Lloyd George is said to number among the handful of greatest English orators. He is also the only British Prime Minister for whom English was a second language; born in northern England to Welsh parents, he grew up with Welsh as his first language.

In the early 1890s (when a Liberal member of Parliament) Lloyd George devoted a considerable amount of time to setting up new branches of the *Cymru Fydd* League; the speech excerpted here was delivered at such an occasion in Cardiff.

from *Speech delivered at the inaugural meeting of the Cardiff branch of the Cymru Fydd League*, October 1894

... No one can fairly lay cowardice to the charge of any Celtic race.[1] Their bravery has stood the severest test to which courage can be put. They have been beaten, baffled, discomfited, disappointed, times innumerable. They know more of the "hope deferred that maketh the heart sick"[2] than almost any branch of the human race. They have been trodden on and despised for centuries in their own land, but their indomitable spirit is still unbroken. There is one thing, however, that their fortitude does not seem to be equal to. You cannot get the Celt to face a disagreeable fact. His fiery nature always shies at an unpleasant truth. There is but one way of curing him of his fault, and that is by adopting a method used by trainers when a spirited horse starts at an object on the roadway turn his head towards it and compel him, whether he will or not, to stare at it. ... Let us pursue the same strategy with the Welsh spirit. Get it to look steadily at the disturbing facts along the path of its national progress. It will get on its journey very much more surely and speedily for the experience. ...

... During the last twenty-six years Wales has returned a preponderating majority of Liberal members to Parliament. ... Liberal Ministries have ... been dependent for their very existence upon the loyalty of their Welsh supporters. But, in spite of all this, Wales has not during the whole of that time had a single measure of reform from any Liberal Government dealing with any of the special topics in which she is more immediately interested. I would say more than that she has not had in the aggregate one week out of the whole of those fourteen years for the discussion of her special concerns. The result is surely not a promising one. ... Of course we may be told that this sterility of results is attributable entirely to Tory obstruction. ... [But] in spite of Tory obstruction England has always had her wants attended to without delay. ... If any one suffers from the obstruction of the reactionary forces represented in the House of Commons, it is the Celtic nationalities of this kingdom. ...

—1894

---

[1] *Celtic race* Twenty-first-century Welsh, Scottish, and Irish people have grown to be highly suspicious of generalizations about "the Celts" or "the Celtic races," which (quite aside from the issue of oversimplification) have a long history of being advanced in disparaging or patronizing ways. Lloyd George's speech is evidence that such terms were sometimes also employed by those of Welsh, Scottish, or Irish background in support of the cause of "Celtic peoples."

[2] *hope deferred ... sick* The quotation is from Proverbs 13.12.

William Morris
1834 – 1896

William Morris applied his prodigious, pragmatic creativity to a staggering array of artistic and social pursuits: poetry, translation, painting, woodcuts, furniture, wallpaper and textile design, illuminated manuscripts, stained glass windows, and commerce. His work was also informed by an acute political consciousness of his good fortune in "being born prosperous and rich." Fiercely committed to breaking down class distinctions between "intellectual" and "workman," Morris was an artist-activist who insisted on manually producing his own designs. At a time when crafts such as embroidery were regarded as lesser, feminine arts, Morris researched long-forgotten techniques to authenticate the organic integrity of his designs, and promptly took up the needle himself. In giving serious regard to textile arts and in sharing unusual techniques with the women who helped to produce his designs, Morris was what one critic calls "the prophet of the subversive stitch."

Born in 1834 to prosperous Evangelical parents, Morris was brought up in the Essex countryside. At four years old he was reading novels. By the time he was seven, he had devoured the works of Walter Scott, an author whose imaginative vision, especially in the Waverley novels, would never wear thin for Morris. Scott's work, Malory's *Morte Darthur*, and John Ruskin's *Modern Painters* and *Stones of Venice* provided the formulative influences for his life's work, whether in poetry or crafts or his socialist politics. Although Morris enjoyed a golden childhood and cherished his Welsh roots, he eventually rebelled against a stolid family dynasty which seemed to personify capitalism's more boorish traits. Morris saw little of a father who had secured the family fortune by investing in copper mines, an industry whose exploitation of workers and of the environment was diametrically opposed to the principles of socialist utopia Morris would depict in the novel *News from Nowhere* (1890). Morris's mother, though in some ways a fond presence during his childhood, embodied to him an intellectual vacancy that he would increasingly associate with the bourgeoisie.

In 1848, Morris was sent to Marlborough College. At Marlborough, lessons were a daily grind of learning by rote; the crushing monotony surely contributed to Morris's later stand as an educational anarchist in the tradition of writers such as William Godwin. Acquaintances recall Morris sitting at his desk compulsively weaving nets for catching fish and birds, an image of manual dexterity and absorption in the making of objects simultaneously decorative and useful that would repeat itself throughout his days: Morris at embroidery, Morris knotting rugs and tapestries, Morris stirring dyes mixed from original recipes in his quest for purity of color, Morris arranging exquisite type for his Kelmscott Press.

Morris met Edward Burne-Jones, an aspiring painter, as a student at Oxford. He was to prove a lifelong friend. They read Tennyson and Ruskin, and admired Ruskin's critique of Victorian industrialization and its de-valuation of the worker. Morris pursued a radical yet thorough study of Oxford's historic architecture; to his mind, Oxford was a precious remnant of medieval life threatened by the rising tide of mechanization and industrialization. In 1877, he would found the Society for the Protection of Ancient Buildings, fighting off a species of commercial restoration that he saw as destructive of the original beauty of England's architecture.

Through Burne-Jones, Morris was introduced to poet and painter Dante Gabriel Rossetti and the Pre-Raphaelite Brotherhood. Morris's artistic gifts were immediately recognized by the fraternity, though he lacked charm with women, which made him the target of some of the members of the group. For years both Burne-Jones and Rossetti sketched caricatures of Morris, Rossetti cruelly exaggerating Morris as a skulking or hulking sexual buffoon. The antagonism that marked Rossetti's and Morris's friendship intensified when Morris proposed to Jane Burden, the beautiful laboring-class daughter of a stablehand, whom Rossetti had "discovered" and used as a model. An offer of marriage from a man of wealth was too good to be refused. Yet their marriage in 1859 initiated an unhappy life together, one aggravated by a long love affair between Jane Morris and Rossetti.

Morris, who had planned to become an architect, was inspired by his connections with the Pre-Raphaelites to turn to painting and poetry. In his first volume of poetry, *The Defence of Guenevere and Other Poems* (1858), Morris recreates a medieval world, and in the title poem gives a powerful, sensuous voice to King Arthur's Queen. In his recreation, he adheres to what he would later describe (in 1891) as the primary characteristics of the Pre-Raphaelite school: "Naturalism," "the conscientious presentment of incident," and "a definite, harmonious, conscious beauty." His popular poem *The Life and Death of Jason* (1867), about the search for the Golden Fleece, was followed by a masterful homage to Chaucer, *The Earthly Paradise* (1868–70). As a series of twenty-four stories related by different narrators, the multi-volume narrative poem echoed the structure of Chaucer's *The Canterbury Tales*. In place of English characters, however, Morris wrote of a band of fourteenth-century Norsemen fleeing the Black Death and searching for a rumored Earthly Paradise "where none grow old." Paradise never found, the band returns home, and on feast-days each of them take turns telling tales of their voyage. With *The Earthly Paradise*, Morris enjoyed tremendous popularity as a poet, nearly becoming Tennyson's successor as Poet Laureate.

In 1861 he opened Morris & Co., a design-manufacturing firm that would become the best-known decorating business in Victorian Britain, producing stained-glass windows, wallpapers, furniture, carpets, and tapestries. The vision of Morris & Co. was best expressed by Morris himself when he said, "Have nothing in your houses which you do not know to be useful or believe to be beautiful." Around this time, the bard in Morris began to gravitate northward, drawn to the bluntness and stoicism of Icelandic sagas. In 1871 he set sail on the first of two voyages to Iceland. His voyages inspired him to write *The Story of Sigurd the Volsung* (1876), described by one critic as "a Nordic cathedral, a strong and simple edifice of anapestic couplets in four colossal books." Upon co-translating the *Volsunga Saga*, Morris emerged as an authority on Icelandic lore.

Morris underwent what he called a "conversion" to socialism in 1883. If his life and work had been a steady accumulation of evidence against industrial capitalism, it finally found its full articulation in the socialist cause. Morris organized, lectured, and contributed regular articles to socialist journals. In 1884 he founded the Socialist League and its official journal, *The Commonweal*. In "How I Became a Socialist," published in *Justice* magazine in 1894, Morris declared: "Apart from the desire to produce beautiful things, the leading passion of my life has been and is hatred of modern civilization."

Politically disillusioned by growing rifts in the Socialist League, Morris eventually retreated to his favorite house, Kelmscott Manor, and set up a small press. Its finest work was the Kelmscott Chaucer, an edition of *The Canterbury Tales* complete with Edward Burne-Jones's illustrations and Morris's own designs. But age came upon Morris suddenly; his tremendous energies were finally spent and he died in 1896, aged sixty-two. His pastoral idealization of earlier times, and the futurist paradise envisioned in *News from Nowhere*, had challenged Victorian culture with the radical possibility of social equality and happiness valued for its own sake. As C.S. Lewis argued, "Morris may build a world in some ways happier than the real one, but happiness puts as stern a question as misery."

⌘ ⌘ ⌘

The Defence of Guenevere[1]

But, knowing now that they would have her speak,
She threw her wet hair backward from her brow,
Her hand close to her mouth touching her cheek,

As though she had had there a shameful blow,
5   And feeling it shameful to feel aught° but shame   *anything*
All through her heart, yet felt her cheek burned so,

She must a little touch it; like one lame
She walked away from Gauwaine,[2] with her head
Still lifted up; and on her cheek of flame

10   The tears dried quick; she stopped at last and said:
"O knights and lords, it seems but little skill°   *use*
To talk of well-known things past now and dead.

"God wot° I ought to say, I have done ill,   *knows*
And pray you all forgiveness heartily!
15   Because you must be right, such great lords—still

"Listen, suppose your time were come to die,
And you were quite alone and very weak;
Yea, laid a dying while very mightily

"The wind was ruffling up the narrow streak
20   Of river through your broad lands running well:
Suppose a hush should come, then some one speak:

"'One of these cloths is heaven, and one is hell,
Now choose one cloth for ever; which they be,
I will not tell you, you must somehow tell

25   "'Of your own strength and mightiness; here, see!'
Yea, yea, my lord, and you to ope° your eyes,   *open*
At foot of your familiar bed to see

"A great God's angel standing, with such dyes,°   *colors*
Not known on earth, on his great wings, and hands
30   Held out two ways, light from the inner skies

"Showing him well, and making his commands
Seem to be God's commands, moreover, too,
Holding within his hands the cloths on wands;

"And one of these strange choosing cloths was blue,
35   Wavy and long, and one cut short and red;
No man could tell the better of the two.

"After a shivering half-hour you said:
'God help! heaven's colour, the blue'; and he said, 'hell.'
Perhaps you then would roll upon your bed,

40   "And cry to all good men that loved you well,
'Ah Christ! if only I had known, known, known';
Launcelot went away, then I could tell,

"Like wisest man how all things would be, moan,
And roll and hurt myself, and long to die,
45   And yet fear much to die for what was sown.

"Nevertheless you, O Sir Gauwaine, lie,
Whatever may have happened through these years,
God knows I speak truth, saying that you lie."

---

[1] *Guenevere* Wife of King Arthur, Guenevere has a love affair with Lancelot, one of Arthur's Knights of the Round Table. Here, Morris envisions Guenevere defending herself against Gawain's accusation of adultery.

[2] *Gauwaine* Arthur's nephew and one of the chief knights of the Round Table.

Her voice was low at first, being full of tears,
50   But as it cleared, it grew full loud and shrill,
Growing a windy shriek in all men's ears,

A ringing in their startled brains, until
She said that Gauwaine lied, then her voice sunk,
And her great eyes began again to fill,

55   Though still she stood right up, and never shrunk,
But spoke on bravely, glorious lady fair!
Whatever tears her full lips may have drunk,

She stood, and seemed to think, and wrung her hair,
Spoke out at last with no more trace of shame,
60   With passionate twisting of her body there:

"It chanced upon a day that Launcelot came
To dwell at Arthur's court: at Christmas-time
This happened; when the heralds sung his name,

"'Son of King Ban of Benwick,'[1] seemed to chime
65   Along with all the bells that rang that day,
O'er the white roofs, with little change of rhyme.

"Christmas and whitened winter passed away,
And over me the April sunshine came,
Made very awful with black hail-clouds, yea

70   "And in the Summer I grew white with flame,
And bowed my head down—Autumn, and the sick
Sure knowledge things would never be the same,

"However often Spring might be most thick
Of blossoms and buds, smote° on me, and I grew   shone
75   Careless of most things, let the clock tick, tick,

"To my unhappy pulse, that beat right through
My eager body; while I laughed out loud,
And let my lips curl up at false or true,

"Seemed cold and shallow without any cloud.
80   Behold my judges, then the cloths were brought:
While I was dizzied thus, old thoughts would crowd,

"Belonging to the time ere° I was bought   before
By Arthur's great name and his little love;
Must I give up for ever then, I thought,

85   "That which I deemed would ever round me move
Glorifying all things; for a little word,
Scarce ever meant at all, must I now prove

"Stone-cold for ever? Pray you, does the Lord
Will that all folks should be quite happy and good?
90   I love God now a little, if this cord

"Were broken, once for all what striving could
Make me love anything in earth or heaven?
So day by day it grew, as if one should

"Slip slowly down some path worn smooth and even,
95   Down to a cool sea on a summer day;
Yet still in slipping there was some small leaven[2]

"Of stretched hands catching small stones by the way,
Until one surely reached the sea at last,
And felt strange new joy as the worn head lay

100 "Back, with the hair like sea-weed; yea all past
Sweat of the forehead, dryness of the lips,
Washed utterly out by the dear waves o'ercast

"In the lone sea, far off from any ships!
Do I not know now of a day in Spring?
105 No minute of that wild day ever slips

"From out my memory; I hear thrushes sing,
And wheresoever I may be, straightway°   immediately
Thoughts of it all come up with the most fresh sting;

---

[1] *King … Benwick* Lancelot's father, King of Brittany in France.

[2] *leaven* Tempering element.

"I was half mad with beauty on that day,
10 And went without my ladies all alone,
In a quiet garden walled round every way;

"I was right joyful of that wall of stone,
That shut the flowers and trees up with the sky,
And trebled all the beauty: to the bone,

15 "Yea right through to my heart, grown very shy
With weary thoughts, it pierced, and made me glad;
Exceedingly glad, and I knew verily,°   *truly*

"A little thing just then had made me mad;
I dared not think, as I was wont° to do,   *accustomed*
20 Sometimes, upon my beauty; if I had

"Held out my long hand up against the blue,
And, looking on the tenderly darken'd fingers,
Thought that by rights one ought to see quite through,

"There, see you, where the soft still light yet lingers,
25 Round by the edges; what should I have done,
If this had joined with yellow spotted singers,

"And startling green drawn upward by the sun?
But shouting, loosed out, see now! all my hair,
And trancedly stood watching the west wind run

130 "With faintest half-heard breathing sound—why there
I lose my head e'en now in doing this;
But shortly listen—In that garden fair

"Came Launcelot walking; this is true, the kiss
Wherewith we kissed in meeting that spring day,
135 I scarce dare talk of the remember'd bliss,

"When both our mouths went wandering in one way,
And aching sorely, met among the leaves;
Our hands being left behind strained far away.

"Never within a yard of my bright sleeves
140 Had Launcelot come before—and now, so nigh!
After that day why is it Guenevere grieves?

"Nevertheless you, O Sir Gauwaine, lie,
Whatever happened on through all those years,
God knows I speak truth, saying that you lie.

145 "Being such a lady could I weep these tears
If this were true? A great queen such as I
Having sinn'd this way, straight her conscience sears;

"And afterwards she liveth hatefully,
Slaying and poisoning, certes° never weeps,— *certainly*
150 Gauwaine be friends now, speak° me lovingly. *address*

"Do I not see how God's dear pity creeps
All through your frame, and trembles in your mouth?
Remember in what grave your mother sleeps,

"Buried in some place far down in the south,
155 Men are forgetting as I speak to you;
By her head sever'd in that awful drouth° *drought*

"Of pity that drew Agravaine's fell blow,[1]
I pray your pity! let me not scream out
For ever after, when the shrill winds blow

160 "Through half your castle-locks![2] let me not shout
For ever after in the winter night
When you ride out alone! in battle-rout° *battle formation*

"Let not my rusting tears make your sword light!
Ah! God of mercy, how he turns away!
165 So, ever must I dress me° to the fight; *prepare myself*

"So—let God's justice work! Gauwaine, I say,
See me hew down your proofs:[3] yea, all men know
Even as you said how Mellyagraunce[4] one day,

---

[1] *By ... blow* Morgause (Arthur's half-sister) was murdered by her sons Gawain, Gaheris, Mordred, and Agravaine after they discovered her having a love affair with a young knight, Sir Lamorak.

[2] *castle-locks* Castle casements, hatches, wickets.

[3] *hew* Cut; *proofs* Evidence.

[4] *Mellyagraunce* Outlaw knight who captures Guenevere.

"One bitter day in *la Fausse Garde*,[1] for so
170   All good knights held it after, saw—
Yea, sirs, by cursed unknightly outrage; though

"You, Gauwaine, held his word without a flaw,
This Mellyagraunce saw blood upon my bed[2]—
Whose blood then pray you? is there any law

175   "To make a queen say why some spots of red
Lie on her coverlet? or will you say,
'Your hands are white, lady, as when you wed,

"'Where did you bleed?' and must I stammer out—'Nay,
I blush indeed, fair lord, only to rend
180   My sleeve up to my shoulder, where there lay

"'A knife-point last night': so must I defend
The honour of the lady Guenevere?
Not so, fair lords, even if the world should end

"This very day, and you were judges here
185   Instead of God. Did you see Mellyagraunce
When Launcelot stood by him? what white fear

"Curdled his blood, and how his teeth did dance,
His side sink in? as my knight cried and said,
'Slayer of unarm'd men,[3] here is a chance!

190   "'Setter of traps, I pray you guard your head,
By God I am so glad to fight with you,
Stripper of ladies, that my hand feels lead

"'For driving weight; hurrah now! draw and do,
For all my wounds are moving in my breast,
195   And I am getting mad with waiting so.'

"He struck his hands together o'er the beast,
Who fell down flat, and grovell'd at his feet,
And groan'd at being slain so young—'at least.'

"My knight said: 'Rise you, sir, who are so fleet
200   At catching ladies, half-arm'd will I fight,
My left side all uncovered!' then I weet,[4]

"Up sprang Sir Mellyagraunce with great delight
Upon his knave's face; not until just then
Did I quite hate him, as I saw my knight

205   "Along the lists[5] look to my stake and pen
With such a joyous smile, it made me sigh
From agony beneath my waist-chain, when

"The fight began, and to me they drew nigh;°   near
Ever Sir Launcelot kept him on the right,
210   And traversed warily, and ever high

"And fast leapt caitiff's° sword, until my knight   villain's
Sudden threw up his sword to his left hand,
Caught it, and swung it; that was all the fight.

"Except a spout of blood on the hot land;
215   For it was hottest summer; and I know
I wonder'd how the fire, while I should stand,

"And burn, against the heat, would quiver so,
Yards above my head; thus these matters went;
Which things were only warnings of the woe

220   "That fell on me. Yet Mellyagraunce was shent,°   ruined
For Mellyagraunce had fought against the Lord;
Therefore, my lords, take heed lest you be blent[6]

"With all this wickedness; say no rash word
Against me, being so beautiful; my eyes,
225   Wept all away to grey, may bring some sword

"To drown you in your blood; see my breast rise,
Like waves of purple sea, as here I stand;
And how my arms are moved in wonderful wise,

---

1 *la Fausse Garde*   The False Keep, Mellyagraunce's castle.

2 *blood … bed*   Taken as evidence for Guenevere's infidelity.

3 *Slayer … men*   Just after abducting Guenevere, Mellyagraunce had
his soldiers attack Lancelot, who was unarmed.

4 *uncovered* Unarmored; *weet* Know.

5 *lists* Place for combat.

6 *blent* Mingled.

"Yea also at my full heart's strong command,
230 See through my long throat how the words go up
In ripples to my mouth; how in my hand

"The shadow lies like wine within a cup
Of marvellously colour'd gold; yea now
This little wind is rising, look you up,

235 "And wonder how the light is falling so
Within my moving tresses: will you dare,
When you have looked a little on my brow,

"To say this thing is vile? or will you care
For any plausible lies of cunning woof,°   *weave*
240 When you can see my face with no lie there

"For ever? am I not a gracious proof—
'But in your chamber Launcelot was found'—
Is there a good knight then would stand aloof,

"When a queen says with gentle queenly sound:
245 'O true as steel, come now and talk with me,
I love to see your step upon the ground

"'Unwavering, also well I love to see
That gracious smile light up your face, and hear
Your wonderful words, that all mean verily

250 "'The thing they seem to mean: good friend, so dear
To me in everything, come here to-night,
Or else the hours will pass most dull and drear;

"'If you come not, I fear this time I might
Get thinking over much of times gone by,
255 When I was young, and green hope was in sight:

"'For no man cares now to know why I sigh;
And no man comes to sing me pleasant songs,
Nor any brings me the sweet flowers that lie

"'So thick in the gardens; therefore one so longs
260 To see you, Launcelot; that we may be
Like children once again, free from all wrongs

"'Just for one night.' Did he not come to me?
What thing could keep true Launcelot away
If I said 'Come'? there was one less than three

265 "In my quiet room that night, and we were gay;
Till sudden I rose up, weak, pale, and sick,
Because a bawling broke our dream up, yea

"I looked at Launcelot's face and could not speak,
For he looked helpless too, for a little while;
270 Then I remember how I tried to shriek,

"And could not, but fell down; from tile to tile
The stones they threw up rattled o'er my head
And made me dizzier; till within a while

"My maids were all about me, and my head
275 On Launcelot's breast was being soothed away
From its white chattering, until Launcelot said—

"By God! I will not tell you more to-day,
Judge any way you will—what matters it?
You know quite well the story of that fray,°   *noisy quarrel*

280 "How Launcelot still'd their bawling, the mad fit
That caught up Gauwaine—all, all, verily,
But just that which would save me; these things flit.[1]

"Nevertheless you, O Sir Gauwaine, lie,
Whatever may have happen'd these long years,
285 God knows I speak truth, saying that you lie!

"All I have said is truth, by Christ's dear tears."
She would not speak another word, but stood
Turn'd sideways; listening, like a man who hears

His brother's trumpet sounding through the wood
290 Of his foes' lances. She lean'd eagerly,
And gave a slight spring sometimes, as she could

---

[1] *flit* Have passed.

At last hear something really; joyfully
Her cheek grew crimson, as the headlong speed
Of the roan charger[1] drew all men to see,
295   The knight who came was Launcelot at good need.[2]
    —1858

William Morris, *Queen Guenevere*, 1858.

The Haystack in the Floods

Had she come all the way for this,
    To part at last without a kiss?
Yea, had she borne the dirt and rain
That her own eyes might see him slain
5   Beside the haystack in the floods?

Along the dripping leafless woods,
The stirrup touching either shoe,
She rode astride as troopers° do;   horse soldiers
With kirtle kilted[3] to her knee,
10   To which the mud splash'd wretchedly;
And the wet dripp'd from every tree
Upon her head and heavy hair,
And on her eyelids broad and fair;
The tears and rain ran down her face.
15   By fits and starts they rode apace,[4]
And very often was his place
Far off from her; he had to ride
Ahead, to see what might betide°   happen
When the roads cross'd; and sometimes, when
20   There rose a murmuring from his men,
Had to turn back with promises;
Ah me! she had but little ease;
And often for pure doubt and dread
She sobb'd, made giddy in the head
25   By the swift riding; while, for cold,
Her slender fingers scarce could hold
The wet reins; yea, and scarcely, too,
She felt the foot within her shoe
Against the stirrup: all for this,
30   To part at last without a kiss
Beside the haystack in the floods.

For when they near'd that old soak'd hay,
They saw across the only way
That Judas, Godmar, and the three
35   Red running lions dismally
Grinn'd from his pennon,° under which,   flag

---

[1] *roan charger* Horse with coat of mixed color.

[2] *at … need* Just in time.

---

[3] *kirtle* Long gown; *kilted* Fastened or tied up.

[4] *apace* At a good pace.

In one straight line along the ditch,
They counted thirty heads.
               So then,
While Robert turn'd round to his men,
40 She saw at once the wretched end,
And, stooping down, tried hard to rend
Her coif° the wrong way from her head,   *cap*
And hid her eyes; while Robert said:
"Nay, love, 'tis scarcely two to one,
45 At Poictiers[1] where we made them run
So fast—why, sweet my love, good cheer.
The Gascon frontier[2] is so near,
Nought° after this."   *nothing*

          But, "O," she said,
"My God! my God! I have to tread
50 The long way back without you; then
The court at Paris; those six men;
The gratings of the Chatelet;[3]
The swift Seine[4] on some rainy day
Like this, and people standing by,
55 And laughing, while my weak hands try
To recollect how strong men swim.
All this, or else a life with him,
For which I should be damned at last,
Would God[5] that this next hour were past!"

60 He answer'd not, but cried his cry,
"St. George for Marny!"[6] cheerily;
And laid his hand upon her rein.
Alas! no man of all his train°   *retinue*
Gave back that cheery cry again;

65 And, while for rage his thumb beat fast
Upon his sword-hilt, some one cast
About his neck a kerchief long,
And bound him.

          Then they went along
To Godmar; who said: "Now, Jehane,
70 Your lover's life is on the wane
So fast, that, if this very hour
You yield not as my paramour,°   *mistress*
He will not see the rain leave off—
Nay, keep your tongue from gibe° and scoff, *taunts*
75 Sir Robert, or I slay you now."

She laid her hand upon her brow,
Then gazed upon the palm, as though
She thought her forehead bled, and—"No!"
She said, and turn'd her head away,
80 As there were nothing else to say,
And everything were settled: red
Grew Godmar's face from chin to head:
"Jehane, on yonder hill there stands
My castle, guarding well my lands:
85 What hinders me from taking you,
And doing that I list° to do   *like*
To your fair wilful body, while
Your knight lies dead?"

          A wicked smile
Wrinkled her face, her lips grew thin,
90 A long way out she thrust her chin:
"You know that I should strangle you
While you were sleeping; or bite through
Your throat, by God's help—ah!" she said,
"Lord Jesus, pity your poor maid!
95 For in such wise they hem me in,
I cannot choose but sin and sin,
Whatever happens: yet I think
They could not make me eat or drink,
And so should I just reach my rest."
100 "Nay, if you do not my behest,°   *bidding*
O Jehane! though I love you well,"
Said Godmar, "would I fail to tell
All that I know?" "Foul lies," she said.

[1] *Poictiers* I.e., Poitiers, a city in west-central France where England won a decisive victory over French forces in 1356.

[2] *Gascon* Gascony, province of southern France that served as a major battlefield in the Hundred Years' War (1337–1453); *frontier* Border.

[3] *Chatelet* The Châtelet prison at Paris.

[4] *Seine* River flowing through Paris.

[5] *Would God* I wish to God.

[6] *St. George* Patron saint of England; *St. ... Marny* Battle-cry asking St. George to help Sir Robert de Morny, the "Robert" of the poem.

"Eh? lies, my Jehane? by God's head,
105 At Paris folks would deem° them true!   *judge*
Do you know, Jehane, they cry for you,
'Jehane the brown! Jehane the brown!
Give us Jehane to burn or drown!'—
Eh—gag me Robert!—sweet my friend,
110 This were indeed a piteous end
For those long fingers, and long feet,
And long neck, and smooth shoulders sweet;
An end that few men would forget
That saw it—So, an hour yet:
115 Consider, Jehane, which to take
Of life or death!"
                              So, scarce awake,
Dismounting, did she leave that place,
And totter some yards: with her face
Turn'd upward to the sky she lay,
120 Her head on a wet heap of hay,
And fell asleep: and while she slept,
And did not dream, the minutes crept
Round to the twelve again; but she,
Being waked at last, sigh'd quietly,
125 And strangely childlike came, and said:
"I will not." Straightway Godmar's head,
As though it hung on strong wires, turn'd
Most sharply round, and his face burn'd.

For Robert—both his eyes were dry,
130 He could not weep, but gloomily
He seem'd to watch the rain; yea, too,
His lips were firm; he tried once more
To touch her lips, she reach'd out, sore
And vain desire so tortured them,
135 The poor grey lips, and now the hem
Of his sleeve brush'd them.
                                        With a start
Up Godmar rose, thrust them apart;
From Robert's throat he loosed the bands
Of silk and mail; with empty hands
140 Held out, she stood and gazed, and saw,
The long bright blade without a flaw
Glide out from Godmar's sheath, his hand
In Robert's hair; she saw him bend

Back Robert's head; she saw him send
145 The thin steel down; the blow told well,[1]
Right backward the knight Robert fell,
And moan'd as dogs do, being half dead,
Unwitting,° as I deem: so then   *senseless*
Godmar turn'd grinning to his men,
150 Who ran, some five or six, and beat
His head to pieces at their feet.

Then Godmar turn'd again and said
"So, Jehane, the first fitte[2] is read!
Take note, my lady, that your way
155 Lies backward to the Chatelet!"
She shook her head and gazed awhile
At her cold hands with a rueful smile,
As though this thing had made her mad.

This was the parting that they had
160 Beside the haystack in the floods.
—1858

How I Became a Socialist

I am asked by the Editor to give some sort of a history of the above conversion, and I feel that it may be of some use to do so, if my readers will look upon me as a type of a certain group of people, but not so easy to do clearly, briefly, and truly. Let me, however, try. But first, I will say what I mean by being a Socialist, since I am told that the word no longer expresses definitely and with certainty what it did ten years ago. Well, what I mean by Socialism is a condition of society in which there should be neither rich nor poor, neither master nor master's man, neither idle nor overworked, neither brain-sick brain workers, nor heart-sick hand workers, in a word, in which all men would be living in equality of condition, and would manage their affairs unwastefully, and with the full consciousness that harm to one would mean harm to all—the realization at last of the meaning of the word COMMONWEALTH.

---

[1] *told well* Landed accurately.

[2] *fitte* Section of a poem or song.

Now this view of Socialism which I hold today, and hope to die holding, is what I began with; I had no transitional period, unless you may call such a brief period of political radicalism during which I saw my ideal clear enough, but had no hope of any realization of it. That came to an end some months before I joined the (then) Democratic Federation,[1] and the meaning of my joining that body was that I had conceived a hope of the realization of my ideal. If you ask me how much of a hope, or what I thought we Socialists then living and working would accomplish towards it, or when there would be effected any change in the face of society, I must say, I do not know. I can only say that I did not measure my hope, nor the joy that it brought me at the time. For the rest, when I took that step I was blankly ignorant of economics; I had never so much as opened Adam Smith, or heard of Ricardo, or of Karl Marx.[2] Oddly enough, I *had* read some of Mill, to wit, those posthumous papers of his (published, was it, in the *Westminster Review* or the *Fortnightly*?) in which he attacks Socialism in its Fourierist[3] guise. In those papers he put the arguments, as far as they go, clearly and honestly, and the result, so far as I was concerned, was to convince me that Socialism was a necessary change, and that it was possible to bring it about in our own days. Those papers put the finishing touch to my conversion to Socialism. Well, having joined a Socialist body (for the Federation soon became definitely Socialist), I put some conscience[4] into trying to learn the economical side of Socialism, and even tackled Marx, though I must confess that, whereas I thoroughly enjoyed the historical part of *Capital*,[5] I suffered agonies of confusion of the brain over reading the pure economics of that great work. Anyhow, I read what I could, and will hope that some information stuck to me from my reading; but more, I must think, from continuous conversation with such friends as Bax and Hyndman and Scheu,[6] and the brisk course of propaganda meetings which were going on at the time, and in which I took my share. Such finish to what of education in practical Socialism as I am capable of I received afterwards from some of my Anarchist friends, from whom I learned, quite against their intention, that Anarchism was impossible, much as I learned from Mill against *his* intention that Socialism was necessary.

But in this telling how I fell into *practical* Socialism I have begun, as I perceive, in the middle, for in my position of a well-to-do man, not suffering from the disabilities which oppress a working man at every step, I feel that I might never have been drawn into the practical side of the question if an ideal had not forced me to seek towards it. For politics as politics, i.e., not regarded as a necessary if cumbersome and disgustful means to an end, would never have attracted me, nor when I had become conscious of the wrongs of society as it now is, and the oppression of poor people, could I have ever believed in the possibility of a *partial* setting right of those wrongs. In other words, I could never have been such a fool as to believe in the happy and "respectable" poor.

If, therefore, my ideal forced me to look for practical Socialism, what was it that forced me to conceive of an

---

[1] *Democratic Federation* The Social Democratic Federation, Britain's first official socialist political party, was founded in 1881.

[2] *Adam Smith* Scottish political economist (1723–90) credited with outlining the foundation of free-market economic theory in his *Wealth of Nations* (1776); *Ricardo* David Ricardo (1772–1823), British free-market economist; *Karl Marx* German economist, philosopher, and social revolutionary (1818–83) whose *Das Kapital* (1867) and *The Communist Manifesto* (1848) heavily influenced modern conceptions of socialism.

[3] *Mill* John Stuart Mill (1806–73), highly influential British philosopher and political economist who advocated utilitarianism, a theory holding that the highest ethical goal is to promote the greatest good for the greatest number of people; *Westminster Review* Periodical established in 1824 showcasing the work of progressive intellectuals; *Fortnightly* Periodical established in 1865; like the *Westminster Review*, it was associated with liberalism; *Fourierist* Characteristic of the social reforms advocated by Charles Fourier (1772–1837), who proposed that society be organized into small, self-sufficient groups of no more than 1,500 people, who would be interdependent in terms of labor, wealth, and housing.

[4] *conscience* Here, conscientiousness, mindful effort.

[5] *Capital* Marx's *Das Kapital* (1867).

[6] *Bax* Ernest Belfort Bax (1854–1926), British socialist philosopher; *Hyndman* H.H. Hyndman (1842–1921), founder of the Social Democratic Federation; *Scheu* Andreas Scheu (1844–1927), pioneer in the social democratic movement in Austria and co-founder of the Social Democratic Federation.

ideal? Now, here comes in what I said of my being (in this paper) a type of a certain group of mind.

Before the uprising of *modern* Socialism almost all intelligent people either were, or professed themselves to be, quite contented with the civilization of this century. Again, almost all of these really were thus contented, and saw nothing to do but to perfect the said civilization by getting rid of a few ridiculous survivals of the barbarous ages. To be short, this was the *Whig*[1] frame of mind, natural to the modern prosperous middle-class men, who, in fact, as far as mechanical progress is concerned, have nothing to ask for, if only Socialism would leave them alone to enjoy their plentiful style.

But besides these contented ones there were others who were not really contented, but had a vague sentiment of repulsion to the triumph of civilization, but were coerced into silence by the measureless power of Whiggery.[2] Lastly, there were a few who were in open rebellion against the said Whiggery—a few, say two, Carlyle and Ruskin.[3] The latter, before my days of practical Socialism, was my master towards the ideal aforesaid, and, looking backward, I cannot help saying, by the way, how deadly dull the world would have been twenty years ago but for Ruskin! It was through him that I learned to give form to my discontent, which I must say was not by any means vague. Apart from the desire to produce beautiful things, the leading passion of my life has been and is hatred of modern civilization. What shall I say of it now, when the words are put into my mouth, my hope of its destruction—what shall I say of its supplanting by Socialism?

What shall I say concerning its mastery of and its waste of mechanical power, its commonwealth so poor, its enemies of the commonwealth so rich, its stupendous organization—for the misery of life! Its contempt of simple pleasures which everyone could enjoy but for its folly? Its eyeless[4] vulgarity which has destroyed art, the one certain solace of labour? All this I felt then as now, but I did not know why it was so. The hope of the past times was gone, the struggles of mankind for many ages had produced nothing but this sordid, aimless, ugly confusion; the immediate future seemed to me likely to intensify all the present evils by sweeping away the last survivals of the days before the dull squalor of civilization had settled down on the world. This was a bad look-out[5] indeed, and, if I may mention myself as a personality and not as a mere type, especially so to a man of my disposition, careless of metaphysics and religion, as well as of scientific analysis, but with a deep love of the earth and the life on it, and a passion for the history of the past of mankind. Think of it! Was it all to end in a counting-house[6] on the top of a cinder-heap,[7] with Podsnap's[8] drawing-room in the offing,[9] and a Whig committee dealing out champagne to the rich and margarine to the poor in such convenient proportions as would make all men contented together, though the pleasure of the eyes was gone from the world, and the place of Homer[10] was to be taken by Huxley?[11] Yet, believe me, in my heart, when I really forced myself to look towards the future, that is what I saw in it, and, as far as I could tell, scarce anyone seemed to think it worth while to struggle against such a consummation of civilization. So there I was in for a fine pessimistic end of life, if it had not somehow dawned on me that amidst all this filth of civilization the seeds of a great change, what we others call Social-Revolution, were beginning to germinate. The whole face of things was changed to me by that discovery, and all I had to do then in order to become a Socialist was to hook myself on to the

---

[1]   *Whig*   Liberal.

[2]   *Whiggery*   Whig principles.

[3]   *Carlyle*   Thomas Carlyle (1795–1881), British historian, essayist and political critic; *Ruskin*   John Ruskin (1819–1900), British author and art critic.

[4]   *eyeless*   Undiscriminating.

[5]   *look-out*   Outlook, prospective condition.

[6]   *counting-house*   Office.

[7]   *cinder-heap*   Area of refuse from iron production.

[8]   *Podsnap's*   Belonging to Mr. Podsnap, a wealthy character from Charles Dickens's last novel, *Our Mutual Friend* (1865).

[9]   *in the offing*   Likely to happen in the near future.

[10]   *Homer*   Greek epic poet (c. 850 BCE?) to whom two of the most influential Western literary works are attributed—the *Iliad* and the *Odyssey*.

[11]   *Huxley*   Thomas Huxley (1825–95), Victorian essayist and educator.

practical movement, which, as before said, I have tried to do as well as I could.

To sum up, then, the study of history and the love and practice of art forced me into a hatred of the civilization which, if tilings were to stop as they are, would turn history into inconsequent nonsense, and make art a collection of the curiosities of the past, which would have no serious relation to the life of the present.

But the consciousness of revolution stirring amidst our hateful modern society prevented me, luckier than many others of artistic perceptions, from crystallizing into a mere railer against "progress" on the one hand, and on the other from wasting time and energy in any of the numerous schemes by which the quasi-artistic of the middle classes hope to make art grow when it has no longer any root, and thus I became a practical Socialist.

A last word or two. Perhaps some of our friends will say, what have we to do with these matters of history and art? We want by means of Social-Democracy to win a decent livelihood, we want in some sort to live, and that at once. Surely anyone who professes to think that the question of art and cultivation must go before that of the knife and fork (and there are some who do propose that) does not understand what art means, or how that its root must have a soil of a thriving and unanxious life. Yet it must be remembered that civilization has reduced the workman to such a skinny and pitiful existence, that he scarcely knows how to frame a desire for any life much better than that which he now endures perforce.[1] It is the province of art to set the true ideal of a full and reasonable life before him, a life to which the perception and creation of beauty, the enjoyment of real pleasure that is, shall be felt to be as necessary to man as his daily bread, and that no man, and no set of men, can be deprived of this except by mere opposition, which should be resisted to the utmost.

—1894

---

[1] *perforce* Inevitably, unavoidably.

IN CONTEXT

William Morris and Edward Burne-Jones

Frederick Mollyer, *William Morris and Edward Burne-Jones with their families*, c. 1880. Burne-Jones (1833–98) was, with Morris, a key figure in the Arts and Crafts movement and the most significant of the second generation of Pre-Raphaelite artists.

Morris is standing in the back at the right of the photograph, and Burne-Jones is seated in the center. Morris's wife Jane (née Burden), the inspiration for and subject of many Pre-Raphaelite works, is in front of Morris and Burne-Jones; Burne-Jones's father stands at the rear left.

MARY ELIZABETH BRADDON
1835 – 1915

Together with contemporaries Ellen Wood and Wilkie Collins, Mary Elizabeth Braddon created the popular and controversial genre of sensation fiction. Sometimes referred to as the "Queen of the Circulating Library" (referring to the public libraries then associated with middle-class readers), Braddon is best known for the sensation novels *Lady Audley's Secret* and *Aurora Floyd*, but she was a prolific writer and editor: in addition to writing over eighty novels, she also published short fiction, essays, poetry, and plays, and served as editor of the literary magazines *Temple Bar* and *Belgravia*.

Braddon was born on 4 October 1835, the youngest child of Fanny White and Henry Braddon. The family began encountering financial difficulties in the late 1830s, and by 1839 Braddon's parents had separated, with Fanny continuing to raise the children as a single parent. For a number of years, Fanny and her children lived a somewhat nomadic life, at times supported through their recurrent monetary struggles by various family members. Braddon's education began with lessons from her mother, whom she describes in her unpublished memoirs as a thorough teacher: "I had no dry-as-dust lessons to learn by rote, but I had to write a good deal—little bits of history, geography, a good deal of French … [filling] a goodly pile of exercise books in the course of my studies." At the age of nine, she began attending boarding school at Dartmouth Lodge.

Braddon and her mother (Braddon's siblings had both left England upon reaching adulthood) moved to Bath in 1852, where the seventeen-year-old hoped to launch a career in acting—a highly controversial choice for a respectable young woman. She took the stage name Mary Seyton, and found modest success touring the provincial circuit, acting mostly in comedies and farces, but also occasionally in burlesques, pantomimes, and Shakespearean productions. Her work eventually took her to London for a season in 1856, but reviews were mixed, and she soon returned to the provincial circuit.

Braddon began writing poetry in the late 1850s, publishing under her stage name in provincial publications such as the *Beverley Recorder*, the *General Advertiser*, and the *Brighton Herald*. Finding some success in this medium, she moved to London and began writing short fiction under the name M.E. Braddon. Her first novel, *Three Times Dead*, was published in 1860, while she was simultaneously working on an epic poem about the Italian revolutions for a wealthy patron named John Gilby; the collection *Garibaldi and Other Poems* was published in 1861. Neither work sold particularly well, but Braddon's career took off when she met prominent London publisher John Maxwell. In 1861 Maxwell reissued *Three Times Dead* as *The Trail of the Serpent* in the more marketable three-volume format; under this title the novel sold a thousand copies in its first week.

Braddon began writing for Maxwell's various literary publications, which ranged from lowbrow to middlebrow in their style and target audiences. *Lady Audley's Secret* first appeared as a serial in *Robin Goodfellow*, and then in *The Sixpenny Magazine* after the first magazine went bankrupt and readers demanded the story's continuation. By the time *Lady Audley's Secret* was published as a three-volume hardcover in 1862, Braddon was practically a household name; readers were both aghast at and enraptured by her sensational portrayal of the murderous and bigamous Lady Audley. By this time Braddon had also become romantically involved with Maxwell—who himself had a wife still living, incarcerated at a mental asylum in Ireland. Braddon moved in with Maxwell in 1861, and had her first child by him the following year. When the details of this relationship became publicly known, many critics were quick to suggest connections between Braddon's private life and the lives of her characters.

Despite the continuing controversy surrounding both Braddon's private life and the perceived immorality of her writing, her popularity continued to soar over the course of the coming years. She wrote numerous three-volume novels—which were broadly distributed in the subscription libraries of the day—and also continued to publish short stories and serialized "penny dreadfuls" in lowbrow magazines, usually anonymously or under a pseudonym. With her work now the primary source of income for her family with Maxwell, she was almost always working on numerous stories at once, a state she frequently lamented as distracting from her higher literary aspirations. Nevertheless, some of her work did engage with more obviously "literary" themes; *The Doctor's Wife* (1864), for example, was an adaptation of Gustave Flaubert's 1856 realist novel *Madame Bovary*. Braddon thus challenged the conventionally accepted genre and class boundaries of earlier nineteenth-century literature, and in doing so provoked the ire of many reviewers. Critic W.F. Rae attacked Braddon—and the sensation fiction genre as a whole—in an 1865 review, writing sarcastically that Braddon "may boast without fear of contradiction, of having temporarily succeeded in making the literature of the Kitchen the favourite reading of the Drawing-room." As a financially successful woman writer whose female characters often challenged Victorian ideals of femininity, Braddon was particularly vulnerable to such criticism. But she was also vocally defended from many quarters; Henry James, who judged that her work was "from a literary point of view, ... contemptible," nevertheless praised her mastery of this new kind of literature, asserting that she did this work "like an artist."

Braddon became more deeply immersed in the world of periodical publishing as her career progressed, founding and taking on an editorial role for the somewhat "racy" magazine *Belgravia* in 1866, and also for a period working as an editor for the more conventional literary publication *Temple Bar*. In 1868, Braddon suffered a mental breakdown—likely prompted in part by her feverish writing pace as well as by the deaths of her mother and sister—and ceased writing for two years. She took up the pen again in 1871, and would produce on average one book a year for most of the rest of her life. Braddon and Maxwell had had six children together by 1870; they married in 1874, after the death of Maxwell's first wife, and thereby put to rest most of the gossip surrounding their relationship. Braddon's work gained increasing respect after this period; Margaret Oliphant, previously a critic of sensation fiction, wrote in 1892 that Braddon had invented "that gentle and amiable heroine, fair-haired, blue-eyed, and capable of every crime, who has been so often repeated since," and that she had the "power of interesting and occupying the public, which is one of the first qualities of the novelist." Braddon died of a brain aneurysm on 4 February 1915; her last novel, *Mary*, was published the following year.

In 1901, Arnold Bennett wrote that "you would travel far before you reached the zone where the name of Braddon failed of recognition." Indeed, her work remained popular well into the twentieth century; *Lady Audley's Secret* was adapted for silent film twice before Braddon's death. But her work fell into relative obscurity after her death, and for decades she was dismissed as a minor novelist. As the canon has expended in the twenty-first century to include more popular literature and women writers, Braddon has re-emerged as a central figure in Victorian literature and culture.

⌘ ⌘ ⌘

The Mystery at Fernwood [1]

I

"No, Isabel, I do *not* consider that Lady Adela seconded her son's invitation at all warmly."

This was the third time within the last hour that my aunt had made this above remark. We were seated opposite each other in a first-class carriage of the York express, and the flat fields of ripening wheat were flitting by us like yellow shadows under the afternoon sunshine. We were going on a visit to Fernwood, a country mansion twenty miles from York, in order that I might become acquainted with the family of Mr. Lewis Wendale, to whose only son Laurence I was engaged to be married.

Laurence Wendale and I had only been acquainted during the brief May and June of my first London season,[2] which I—the orphan heiress of a wealthy Calcutta merchant—had passed under the roof of my aunt, Mrs. Maddison Trevor, the dashing widow of a major in the Life Guards,[3] and the only sister of my dead father. Mrs. Trevor had made many objections to this brief six weeks' engagement between Laurence and I; but the impetuous young Yorkshireman had overruled everything. What objection could there be? he asked.

He was to have two thousand a year and Fernwood at his father's death; forty thousand pounds from a maiden aunt the day he came of age—for he was not yet one-and-twenty, my impetuous young lover. As for his family, let Mrs. Trevor look into Burke's "Country Families"[4] for the Wendales of Fernwood. His mother was Lady Adela, youngest daughter of Lord Kingwood, of Castle Kingwood, county Kildare. What objections could my aunt have, then? His family did not know me, and might not approve of the match, urged my aunt. Laurence laughed aloud; a long ringing peal of that merry, musical laughter I loved so well to hear.

"Not approve!" he cried, "not love my little Bella! That is too good a joke!" On which immediately followed an invitation to Fernwood, seconded by a note from Lady Adela Wendale.

It was to this very note my aunt was never tired of taking objection. It was cold, it was stiff, constrained; it had been only written to please Laurence. How little I thought of the letter! And yet it was the first faint and shadowy indication of that terrible rock ahead upon which my life was to be wrecked; the first feeble link to the chain of the one great mystery in which the fate of so many was involved.

The letter was cold, certainly. Lady Adela started by declaring she should be most happy to see us; she was all anxiety to be introduced to her charming daughter-in-law. And then my lady ran off to tell us how dull Fernwood was, and how she feared we should regret our long journey into the heart of Yorkshire to a lonely country-house, where we should find no one but a

---

[1] *The Mystery at Fernwood* First published in two installments, appearing in volume 3 (November 1861) and volume 4 (March 1862) of *Temple Bar: A London Magazine for Town and Country Readers*, "The Mystery at Fernwood" was also published in 1862 in Braddon's collection *Ralph the Bailiff and Other Stories*. In the latter it appears without any numbering of parts; a line space is all that marks the division between the two.

[2] *season* The London social season took place roughly while Parliament was in session, from late autumn to early summer. Many wealthy families spent the rest of the year at their country homes.

[3] *Life Guards* Cavalry regiment of the British Army, formed in 1788.

[4] *Burke's "Country Families"* Volume from Burke's Peerage, a genealogical publisher that records the ancestry and heraldry of the peerage, baronetage, knightage, and landed gentry of the United Kingdom.

captious invalid, a couple of nervous women, and a young man devoted to farming and field-sports.

But I was not afraid of being dull where my light-hearted Laurence was; and I overruled all my aunt's objections, ordered half a dozen new dresses, and carried Mrs. Maddison Trevor off to the Great Northern Station before she had time to remonstrate.

Laurence had gone on before to see that all was prepared for us; and had promised to meet us at York, and drive us over to Fernwood in his mail-phaeton.[1] He was standing on the platform as the train entered the station, with the sunshine glittering about his chestnut curls, and his clear blue eyes radiant with life and happiness.

Laurence Wendale was very handsome; but perhaps his greatest charm consisted in that wonderful vitality, that untiring energy and indomitable spirit, which made him so different from all other young men whom I had met. So great was this vitality that, by some magnetic influence, it seemed to communicate itself to others. I was never tired when Laurence was with me. I could waltz longer with him for my partner; ride longer in the Row[2] with him for my cavalier; sit out an opera or examine an exhibition of pictures with less fatigue when he was near. His presence pervaded a whole house; his joyous laugh ran through every room. It seemed as if where he was sorrow could not come.

I felt this more than ever as we drew nearer Fernwood. The country was bleak and bare; wide wastes of moorland stretched away on either side of the by-road down which we drove. The afternoon sunshine had faded out, leaving a cold gray sky, with low masses of leaden cloud brooding close over the landscape, and shutting in the dim horizon. But no influence of scenery or atmosphere could affect Laurence. His spirits were even higher than usual this afternoon.

"They have fitted up the oak-rooms for you, ladies," he said. "Such solemn and stately chambers, with high-canopied beds crowned with funeral plumes; black-oak paneling; portraits of dead-and-gone Wendales: Mistress Aurora, with pannier-hoops[3] and a shepherdess's crook; Mistress Lydia, with ringlets *à la Sévigné*[4] and a pearl necklace; Mortimer Wendale, in a Ramillies wig;[5] Theodore, with love-locks, velvet doublet, and Spanish-leather boots.[6] Such a collection of them! You may expect to see them all descend from their frames in the witching time of night to warm their icy fingers at your sea-coal fires. Your expected arrival has made quite a sensation in our dull old abode. My mother has looked up from the last new novel she had from Mudie[7] half a dozen times this day, I verily believe, to ask if all due preparations were being made; while my dear, active, patient, indefatigable sister Lucy has been running about superintending the arrangements ever since breakfast."

"Your sister Lucy!" I said, catching at his last words; "I shall so love her, Laurence."

"I hope you will, darling," he answered, almost gravely, "for she has been the best and dearest sister to me. And yet I'm half afraid; Lucy is ten years older than you—grave, reserved, sometimes almost melancholy; but if ever there was a banished angel treading this earth in human form, my sister Lucy surely is that guardian spirit."

"Is she like you, Laurence?"

"Like me! Oh, no, not in the least. She is only my half-sister, you know. She resembles her mother, who died young."

---

[1] *mail-phaeton* Open horse-drawn carriage.

[2] *the Row* Rotten Row, fashionable horse-riding track in Hyde Park, London.

[3] *pannier-hoops* Stiff, framed undergarments designed to hold wide skirts out at the hips, creating the fashionable silhouette of the eighteenth century.

[4] *ringlets à la Sévigné* Marie de Rabutin-Chantal, Marquise de Sévigné (1626–96) was famous both for her writing and for her hairstyle, which featured a series of ringlets on each side, extending below her chin.

[5] *Ramillies wig* Men's wig with a long queue hanging down at the back, often tied with a velvet bow, fashionable in the eighteenth century.

[6] *love-locks ... boots* Men's fashions of approximately the sixteenth century; a "love-lock" was a single lock of hair worn longer than the rest, often draped romantically over the front of the shoulder.

[7] *Mudie* Mudie's Lending Library was a popular circulating library in London, established by Charles Edward Mudie in 1842.

We were at the gates of Fernwood when he said this—high wooden gates, with stone pillars moss-grown and dilapidated; a tumble-down-looking lodge, kept by a slatternly woman, whose children were at play in a square patch of ground planted with cabbages and currant-bushes, fenced in with a rotten paling, and ambitiously called a garden. From this lodge-entrance a long avenue stretched away for about half a mile, at the end of which a great red-brick mansion, built in the Tudor style, frowned at us, rather as if in defiance than in welcome. The park was entirely uncultivated: the trunks of the trees were choked with the tangled under-wood; the fern grew deep in the long vistas, broken here and there by solitary pools of black water, on whose quiet borders we heard the flap of the heron's wing, and the dull croaking of an army of frogs.

Lady Adela was right. Fernwood *was* a dull place. I could scarcely repress a shudder as we drove along the dark avenue, while my poor aunt's teeth chattered audibly. Accustomed to spend three parts of the year in Onslow Square, and the autumn months at Brighton or Ryde,[1] this dreary Yorkshire mansion was a terrible trial to her rather over-sensitive nerves.

Laurence seemed to divine the reason of our silence. "The place is frightfully neglected, Mrs. Trevor," he said apologetically; "but I do not mean this sort of thing to last, I assure you. Before ever I bring my delicate little Bella to Fernwood, I shall have landscape-gardeners and upholsterers down by the score, and do my best to convert this dreary wilderness into a terrestrial paradise. I cannot tell you why the place has been suffered to fall into decay; certainly not for want of money, still less for want of opportunity, for my father is an idle man, to whom one would imagine restoring and rebuilding would afford a delightful hobby. No, there is no reason why the place should have been so neglected."

He said this more to himself than to us, as if the words were spoken in answer to some long train of thought of his own. I watched his face earnestly, for I

had seldom seen him look so thoughtful. Presently he said, with more of his usual manner,

"As you are close upon the threshold of Fernwood now, ladies, I ought perhaps to tell you that you will find ours a most low-spirited family. With everything in life to make us happy, we seem forever under a cloud. Ever since I can remember my poor father, he has been sinking slowly into decay, almost in the same way as this neglected place, till now he is a confirmed invalid, without any positive illness. My mother reads novels all day, and half lives upon sal volatile[2] and spirits of lavender. My sister, the only active person in the house, is always thoughtful, and very often melancholy. Mind, I merely tell you this to prepare you for anything you may see; not to depress you, for you may depend upon my exertions towards reforming this dreary household, which has sunk into habitual despondency from sheer easy fortune and want of vexation."

The phaeton drew up before a broad flight of stone steps as Laurence ceased speaking, and in five minutes more he had assisted my aunt and myself to alight, and had ushered us into the presence of Lady Adela and Miss Lucy Wendale.

We found Lady Adela, as her son's description had given us reason to expect, absorbed in a novel. She threw down her book as we entered, and advanced to meet us with considerable cordiality; rather, indeed, as if she really were grateful to us for breaking in upon her solitary life.

"It is so good of you to come," she said, folding me in her slender arms with an almost motherly embrace, "and so kind of you, too, my dear Mrs. Trevor, to abandon all your town pleasures for the sake of bringing this dear girl to me. Believe me, we will do all in our power to make you comfortable, if you can put up with very limited society; for we have received no company whatever since my son's childhood, and I do not think my visiting-list could muster half a dozen names."

Lady Adela was an elegant-looking woman, in the very prime of life; but her handsome face was thin and careworn, and premature wrinkles gathered about her melancholy blue eyes and thoughtful mouth. While she was talking to my aunt, Lucy Wendale and I drew nearer to each other.

Laurence's half-sister was by no means handsome; pale and sallow, with dark hair and rather dull gray eyes, she looked as if some hidden sorrow had quenched out the light of her life long ago, in her earliest youth; some sorrow that had neither been forgotten nor decreased by time, but that had rather grown with her growth, and strengthened with her strength, until it had become a part of her very self—some disappointed attachment, I thought, some cruel blow that had shattered a girl's first dream, and left a broken-hearted woman to mourn the fatal delusion. In my utter ignorance of life, I thought these were the only griefs which ever left a woman's life desolate.

"You will try and be happy at Fernwood, Isabel," Lucy Wendale said gently, as she drew me into a seat by her side, while Laurence bent fondly over us both. I do not believe, dear as we were to each other, that my Laurence ever loved me as he loved this pale-faced half-sister. "You will try and be happy, will you not, dear Isabel? Laurence has been breaking-in the prettiest chestnut mare in all Yorkshire, I think, that you may explore the country with us. I have heard what a daring horsewoman you are. The pianos have been put in tune for you, and the billiard-table re-covered, that you may have exercise on rainy days; and if we cannot give you much society, we will do all else to prevent your feeling dull."

"I shall be very happy here with you, dear Lucy," I said; "but you tell me so much of the dullness of Fernwood, while, I daresay, you yourself have a hundred associations that make the old place very dear to you."

She looked down as I spoke, and a very faint flush broke through the sallow paleness of her complexion.

"I am not very fond of Fernwood," she said gravely.

It was at Fernwood, then, that the great sorrow of her life came upon her, I thought.

"No, Lucy," said Laurence, almost impatiently, "everybody knows this dull place is killing you by inches, and yet nothing on earth can induce you to quit

it. When we all go to Scarborough or Burlington, when mamma goes to Harrogate, when I run up to town[1] to rub off my provincial rust, and see what the world is made of outside these dreary gates—you obstinately persist in staying at home; and the only reason you can urge for doing so is, that you must remain here to take care of that unfortunate invalid of yours, Mr. Thomas."

I was holding Lucy's hand in mine, and I felt the poor wasted little fingers tremble as her brother spoke. My curiosity wag strongly aroused.

"Mr. Thomas!" I exclaimed, half involuntarily.

"Ah, to be sure, Bella, I forgot to tell you of that member of our household, but as I have never seen him, I may be forgiven the omission. This Mr. Thomas is a poor relative of my father's: a hopeless invalid, bedridden, I believe—is he not, Lucy?—who requires a strong man and an experienced nurse to look after him, and who occupies the entire upper story of one wing of the house. Poor Mr. Thomas, invalid as he is, must certainly be a most fascinating person. My mother goes to see him every day, but as stealthily as if she were paying a secret visit to some condemned criminal. I have often met my father coming away from his rooms, pale and melancholy; and, as for my sister Lucy, she is so attached to this sick dependent of ours, that, as I have just said, nothing will induce her to leave the house for fear his nurse or his valet should fail in their care of him."

I still held Lucy's hand, but it was perfectly steady now. Could this poor relative, this invalid dependent, have any part in the sorrowful mystery that had overshadowed her life? And yet, no; I thought that could scarcely be, for she looked up with such perfect self-possession as she answered her brother,

"My whole life has gradually fallen into the duty of attendance upon this poor young man, Laurence; and I will never leave Fernwood while he lives."

A young man! Mr. Thomas was a young man, then.

Lucy herself led us to the handsome suite of apartments prepared for us. Mrs. Trevor's room was separated from mine by a corridor, out of which opened two

---

[1]   *town*   I.e., London.

dressing-rooms and a pretty little boudoir, all looking on to the park. My room was at the extreme angle of the building; it had two doors, one leading to the corridor communicating with my aunt's apartments, the other opening into a gallery running the entire length of the house. Looking out into this gallery, I saw that the opposite wing was shut in by a baize door.[1] I looked with some curiosity at this heavy baize door. It was most likely the barrier which closed the outer world upon Laurence Wendale's invalid relation.

Lucy left us as soon as she had installed my aunt and I in our apartments. While I was dressing for dinner, the housekeeper, a stout, elderly woman, came to ask me if I found everything I required.

"As you haven't brought your own servant with you, miss," she said, "Miss Lucy told me to place her maid Sarah entirely at your service. Miss gives very little work to a maid herself, so Sarah has plenty of leisure time on her hands, and you'll find her a very respectable young woman."

I told her that I could do all I wanted for myself; but before she left me I could not resist asking her one question about the mysterious invalid.

"Are Mr. Thomas's rooms at this end of the house?" I asked.

The woman looked at me with an almost scared expression, and was silent for a moment.

"Has Mr. Laurence been saying anything to you about Mr. Thomas?" she said, rather anxiously as I thought.

"Mr. Laurence and his sister Miss Lucy were both talking of him just now."

"Oh, indeed, miss," answered the woman with an air of relief; "the poor gentleman's rooms are at the other end of the gallery, miss."

"Has he lived here long?" I asked.

"Nigh upon twenty years, miss—above twenty years, I'm thinking."

---

[1] *baize door* Baize is a durable woolen fabric, most often used on billiards tables, but also used to insulate or sound proof doors. In the Victorian era, a baize door was often found at the entrance to the living quarters of domestic servants.

"I suppose he is distantly related to the family."

"Yes, miss."

"And quite dependent on Mr. Wendale?"

"Yes, miss."

"It is very good of your master to have supported him for so many years, and to keep him in such comfort."

"My master is a very good man, miss."

The woman seemed determined to give me as little information as possible; but I could not resist one more question.

"How is it that in all these years Mr. Laurence has never seen this invalid relation?" I asked.

It seemed that this question, of all others, was the most embarrassing to the housekeeper. She turned first red and then pale, and said, in a very confused manner, "The poor gentleman never leaves his room, miss; and Mr. Laurence has such high spirits, bless his dear heart, and has such a noisy, rackety way with him, that he is no fit company for an invalid."

It was evidently useless trying for further information, so I abandoned the attempt, and bidding the housekeeper good afternoon, began to dress my hair before the massive oak-framed looking-glass.

"The truth of the matter is," I said to myself, "that after all there is nothing more to be said about it. I have tried to create a mystery out of the simplest possible family arrangement. Mr. Wendale has a bedridden relative, too poor and too helpless to support himself. What more natural than that he should give him house-room in this dreary old mansion, where there seems space enough to lodge a regiment?"

I found the family assembled in the drawing-room. Mr. Wendale was the wreck of a very handsome man. He must in early life have resembled Laurence; but, as my lover had said, it seemed indeed as if he and the house and grounds of Fernwood had fallen into decay together. But notwithstanding his weak state of health, he gave us a warm welcome, and did the honours of his hospitable dinner-table with the easy grace of a finished gentleman.

After dinner, my aunt and Lady Adela sat at one of the windows talking; while Laurence, Lucy, and I gathered together upon a long stone terrace outside the drawing-room, watching the last low crimson streak of the August sunset fade behind the black trunks of the trees, and melt away into faint red splashes upon the water-pools amongst the brushwood. We were very happy together; Laurence and I talking of a hundred different subjects, telling Lucy our London adventures, describing our fashionable friends, our drives and rides, *fêtes*, balls, and dinners; she, with a grave smile upon her lips, listening to us with almost maternal patience.

"I must take you over the old house tomorrow, Isabel," Laurence said in the course of the evening. "I suppose Lucy did not tell you that she had put you into the haunted room?"

"No, indeed!"

"You must not listen to this silly boy, my dear Isabel," said Miss Wendale. "Of course, like all other old houses, Fernwood can boast its ghost-story; but since no one in my father's lifetime has ever seen the phantom, you may imagine that it is not a very formidable one."

"But you own there *is* a ghost!" I exclaimed eagerly, "Pray tell me the story."

"I'll tell you, Bella," answered Laurence, "and then you'll know what sort of a visitor to expect when the bells of Fernwood church, hidden away behind the elms yonder, tremble on the stroke of midnight. A certain Sir Humphrey Wendale, who lived in the time of Henry the Eighth,[1] was wronged by his wife, a very beautiful woman. Had he acted according to the ordinary fashion of the time, he would have murdered the lady and his rival; but our ancestor was of a more original turn of mind, and he hit upon an original plan of vengeance. He turned every servant out of Fernwood House; and one morning, when the unhappy lady was sleeping, he locked every door of the mansion, secured every outlet and inlet, and rode away merrily in the summer sunshine, leaving his wife to die the slow and hideous death of starvation. Fernwood is lonely enough even now, Heaven knows! But it was lonelier in those distant days. A passing traveller may now and then have glanced

upward at the smokeless chimneys, dimly visible across the trees, as he rode under the park-palings; but none ever dreamed that the deserted mansion had one luckless tenant. Fifteen months afterwards, when Sir Humphrey rode home from foreign travel, he had some difficulty in forcing the door of the chamber in which you are to sleep: the withered and skeleton form of his dead wife had fallen across the threshold."

"What a horrible story!" I exclaimed, with a shiver.

"It is only a legend, dear Isabel," said Lucy; "like all tradition, exaggerated and distorted into due proportions of poetic horror. Pray, do not suffer your mind to dwell upon such a fable."

"Indeed I hope it is not true," I answered. "How fond people are of linking mysteries and horrors such as this with the history of an old family! And yet we never fall across any such family mystery in our own days."

I slept soundly that night at Fernwood, undisturbed by the attenuated shadow of Sibyl Wendale, Sir Humphrey's unhappy wife. The bright sunshine was reflected in the oak panels of my room, and the larks were singing high up in a cloudless blue sky, when I awoke. I found my aunt quite reconciled to her visit.

"Lady Adela is a very agreeable woman," she said; "quiet, perhaps, to a fault, but with that high tone of matter which is always charming. Lucy Wendale seems a dear good girl, though evidently a confirmed old maid. You will find her of inestimable use when you are married—that is to say, if you ever have to manage this great rambling place, which will of course fall to your lot in the event of poor Mr. Wendale's death."

As for myself, I was as happy at Fernwood as the August days were long. Lucy Wendale rode remarkably well. It was the only amusement for which she cared; and she and her horses were on terms of the most devoted attachment. Laurence, his sister, and I were therefore constantly out together, riding amongst the hills about Fernwood, and exploring the country for twenty miles round.

Indoors, Lucy left us very much to ourselves. She was the ruling spirit of the house, and but for her everything must have fallen utterly to decay. Lady Adela read novels, or made a feeble attempt at amusing my

---

[1] *the time of Henry the Eighth* Henry VIII was King of England from 1509 to 1547.

aunt with her conversation. Mr. Wendale kept his room during the fore part of the day; while Laurence and I played, sang, sketched, and rattled the billiard-balls over the green cloth whenever bad weather drove us to indoor amusements.

It was one day that I was sketching the castellated facade of the old mansion, I noticed a peculiar circumstance connected with the suite of rooms occupied by the invalid, Mr. Thomas. These rooms were at the extreme left angle of the building, and were lighted by a range of six windows. I was surprised by observing that every one of these windows was of ground glass.[1] I asked Laurence the reason of this.

"Why, I believe the glare of light was too much for Mr. Thomas," he answered; "so my father, who is the kindest creature in Christendom, had the windows made opaque, as you see them now."

"Has the alteration been long made?"

"It was made when I was about six years old; I have rather a vague recollection of the event, and I should not perhaps remember it but for one circumstance. I was riding about down here one morning on my Shetland pony, when my attention was attracted by a child who was looking through one of those windows. I was not near enough to see his face, but I fancy he must have been about my own age. He beckoned to me, and I was riding across the grass to respond to his invitation, when my sister Lucy appeared at the window and snatched the child away. I suppose he was some one belonging to the female attendant upon Mr. Thomas, and had strayed unnoticed into the invalid's rooms. I never saw him again; and the next day a glazier came over from York, and made the alteration in the windows."

"But Mr. Thomas must have air; I suppose the windows are sometimes opened," I said.

"Never; they are each ventilated by a single pane, which, if you observe, is open now."

"I cannot help pitying this poor man," I said, after a pause, "shut out almost from the light of heaven by his infirmities, deprived of all society."

"Not entirely so," answered Laurence. "No one knows how many stolen hours my sister Lucy devotes to her poor invalid."

"Perhaps he is a very studious man, and finds his consolation in literary or scientific pursuits," I said; "does he read very much?"

"I think not. I never heard of his having any books got for him."

"But one thing has puzzled me, Laurence," I continued. "Lucy spoke of him the other day as a young man, and yet Mrs. Porson, your housekeeper, told me he had lived at Fernwood for upwards of twenty years."

"As for that," answered Laurence carelessly, "Lucy no doubt remembers him as a young man upon his first arrival here, and continues to call him so from mere force of habit. But, pray, my little inquisitive Bella, do not rack your brains about this poor relation of ours. To tell the truth, I have become so used to his unseen presence in the house, that I have ceased to think of him at all. I meet a grim woman, dressed in black merino, coming out of the green-baize door, and I know that she is Mr. Thomas's nurse; or I see a solemn-faced man, and I am equally assured that he is Mr. Thomas's servant, James Beck, who has grown grey in his office; I encounter the doctor riding away from Fernwood on his brown cob, and I feel convinced that he has just looked in to see how Mr. Thomas is going on; if I miss my sister for an hour in the twilight, I know that she is in the west wing talking to Mr. Thomas; but as nobody ever calls upon me to do anything for the poor man, I think no more of the matter."

I felt these words almost a reproof to what might have appeared idle, or even impertinent, curiosity on my part. And yet the careless indifference of Laurence's manner seemed to jar upon my senses. Could it be that this glad and high-hearted being, whom I so tenderly loved, was selfish—heedless of the sufferings of others? No, it was surely not this that prompted his thoughtless words. It is a positive impossibility for one whose whole nature is life and motion, animation and vigour, to comprehend for one brief moment the horror of the invalid's darkened rooms and solitary days.

[1] *ground glass* Glass that has been ground to give it a matte, opaque appearance.

I had been nearly a month at Fernwood, when, for the first time during our visit, Laurence left us. One of his old schoolfellows, a lieutenant in the army, was quartered with his regiment at York, and Laurence had promised to dine with the mess. Though I had been most earnest in requesting him to accept this invitation, I could not help feeling dull and dispirited as I watched him drive away down the avenue, and felt that for the first time we were to spend the long autumn evening without him. Do what I would, the time hung heavily on my hands. The September sunset was beautiful, and Lucy and I walked up and down the terrace after dinner, while Mr. Wendale slept in his easy-chair, and my Aunt and Lady Adela exchanged drowsy monosyllabic sentences on a couch near the fire, which was always lighted in the evening.

It was in vain that I tried to listen to Lucy's conversation. My thoughts wandered in spite of myself—sometimes to Laurence in the brilliantly-lighted mess-room, enlivening a circle of *blasé* officers with his boisterous gaiety; sometimes, as if in contrast to this, to the dark west rooms in which the invalid counted the long hours; sometimes to that dim future in whose shadowy years death was to claim our weary host, and Laurence and I were to be master and mistress at Fernwood. I had often tried to picture the place as it would be when it fell into Laurence's hands, and architects and landscape-gardeners came to work their wondrous transformations; but, do what I would, I could never imagine it otherwise than as it was—with straggling ivy hanging forlornly about the moss-stained walls, and solitary pools of stagnant water hiding amongst the tangled brushwood.

Laurence and I were to be married in the following spring. He would come of age in February, and I should be twenty in March—scarcely a year between our ages, and both a great deal too young to marry, my aunt said. After tea Lucy and I sang and played. Dreary music it seemed to me that night. I thought my voice and the piano were both out of tune, and I left Lucy very rudely in the middle of our favourite duet. I took up twenty books from the crowded drawing-room table, only to throw them wearily down again. Never had Lady Adela's novels seemed so stupid as when I looked into them that night; never had my aunt's conversation sounded so tiresome. I looked from my watch to the old-fashioned timepiece upon the chimney half a dozen times, to find at last that it was scarcely ten o'clock. Laurence had promised to be home by eleven, and had begged Lucy and me to sit up for him.

Eleven struck at last; but Laurence had not kept his promise. My aunt and Lady Adela rose to light their candles. Mr. Wendale always retired a little after nine. I pleaded for half an hour longer, and Lucy was too kind not to comply readily.

"Isabel is right," she said; "Laurence is a spoilt boy, you know, mamma, and will feel himself very much ill-used if he finds no one up to hear his description of the mess-dinner."

"Only half an hour, then, mind, young ladies," said my aunt. "I cannot allow you to spoil your complexions on account of dissipated people who drive twenty miles to a military dinner. One half-hour; not a moment more, or I shall come down again to scold you both."

We promised obedience, and my aunt left us. Lucy and I seated ourselves on each side of the low fire, which had burned dull and hollow. I was too much dispirited to talk, and I sat listening to the ticking of the clock, and the occasional falling of a cinder in the bright steel fender. Then that thought came to me which comes to all watchers. What if anything had happened to Laurence? I went to one of the windows and pulled back the heavy shutters. It was a lovely night; clear, though not moonlight, and myriads of stars gleamed in the cloudless sky. I stood at the window for some time, listening for the wheels and watching for the lamps of the phaeton.

I too was a spoilt child; life had for me been bright and smooth, and the least thought of grief or danger to those I loved filled me with a wild panic. I turned suddenly round to Lucy, and cried out, "Lucy! Lucy, I am getting frightened! Suppose anything should have happened to Laurence. Those horses are wild and unmanageable sometimes. If he had taken a few glasses of wine—if he trusted the groom to drive—if—"

She came over to me, and took me in her arms as if I had been indeed a little child.

"My darling," she said, "my darling Isabel, you must not distress yourself by such fancies as these. He is only half an hour later than he said, and as for danger, dearest, he is beneath the shelter of Providence, without whose safeguard those we love are never secure even for a moment."

Her quiet manner calmed my agitation. I left the window, and returned shivering to the expiring fire.

"It is nearly three-quarters of an hour now, Bella, dear," she said presently; "we must keep our promise, and as for Laurence, you will hear the phaeton drive in before you go to sleep, I dare say."

"I shall not go to sleep until I do hear it," I answered, as I bade her good night.

I could not help listening for the welcome sound of the carriage-wheels as I crossed the hall and went upstairs. I stopped in the corridor to look into my aunt's room; but she was fast asleep, and I closed the door as softly as I had opened it. It was as I left this room that, glancing down the corridor, I was surprised to see that there was a light in my own bed-chamber. I was prepared to find a fire there, but the light shining through the half-open door was something brighter than the red glow of a fire. I had joined Laurence in laughing at the ghost-story, but my first thought on seeing this light was of the shadow of the wretched Lady Sybil. What if I found her crouching over my hearth?

I had half a mind to go back to my aunt's room, awake her, and tell her my fears; but one moment's reflection made me ashamed of my cowardice. I went on, and pushed open the door of my room. There was no pale phantom shivering over the open hearth. There was an old-fashioned silver candlestick upon the table, and Laurence, my lover, was seated by the blazing fire; not dressed in the evening costume he had wore for the dinner-party, but wrapped in a loose gray woollen dressing-gown, and wearing a black-velvet smoking-cap upon his chestnut hair.

Without stopping to think of the strangeness of his appearance in my room; without wondering at the fact of his having entered the house unknown either to Lucy or myself; without one thought but joy and relief of mind in seeing him once more, I ran forward to him,

crying out, "Laurence, Laurence, I am so glad you have come back!"

He—Laurence, my lover, as I thought, the man, the horrible shadow, the dreadful being—rose from his chair, and snatching up some papers that lay loosely on the table by his side, crumpled them into a ball with one fierce gesture of his strong hand, and flung them at my feet; then, with a harsh dissonant laugh that seemed a mocking echo of the joyous music I loved so well, he stalked out of the door opening on the gallery. I tried to scream, but my dry lips and throat could form no sound. The oak-panelling of the room spun round, the walls and ceiling contracted, as if they had been crushing in upon me to destroy me. I fell heavily to the floor; but as I fell I heard the phaeton-wheels upon the carriage-drive below, and Laurence Wendale's voice calling to the servants.[1]

2

I can remember little more that happened upon that horrible night. I have a vague recollection of opening my eyes upon a million dazzling lights, which slowly resolved themselves into the one candle held in Lucy Wendale's hand, as she stood beside the bed upon which I was lying. My aunt, wrapped in her dressing-gown, sat by my pillow. My face and hair were dripping with the vinegar-and-water they had thrown over me, and I could hear Laurence, in the corridor outside my bedroom door, asking again and again, "Is she better? Has she quite come to?"

But of all this I was only dimly conscious; a load of iron seemed pressing upon my forehead, and icy hands seemed riveted upon the back of my head, holding it tightly to the pillow on which it lay. I could no more have lifted it than I could have lifted a ton-weight. I could only lie staring with stupid dull eyes at Lucy's pale face, silently wishing that she and my aunt would go, and leave me to myself.

---

[1] The first instalment in *Temple Bar* (published in the November 1861 issue) ends here; the second installment was published in the March 1862 issue.

I suppose I was feverish and a little light-headed all that night—acting over and over again the brief scene of my meeting with the weird shadow of my lover. All the stories I had laughed at might be true, then. I had seen the phantom of the man I loved! The horrible double, shaped perhaps out of impalpable air, but as terribly distinct to the eye as if it had been a form of flesh and blood.

Lucy was sitting by my bedside when I awoke from a short sleep which had succeeded the long night of fever. How intensely refreshing that brief but deep slumber was to me! How delicious the gradual fading-out of the sense of horror and bewilderment, with all the hideous confusions of delirium, into the blank tranquillity of dreamless sleep! When I awoke my head was still painful, and my frame as feeble as if I had lain for a week on a sickbed; but my brain was cleared, and I was able to think quietly of what had happened.

"Lucy," I said, "you do not know what frightened me or why I fainted."

"No, dearest, not exactly."

"But you can know nothing of it, Lucy. You were not with me when I came into this room last night. You did not see—"

I paused, unable to finish my sentence.

"Did not see whom—or what, dear Isabel?"

"The shadow of your brother Laurence."

My whole frame trembled with the recollection of my terror of the night before, as I said this; yet I was able to observe Lucy's face, and I saw that its natural hue had faded to an ashen pallor.

"The shadow, Isabel!" she faltered; not as if in any surprise at my words, but rather as if she merely spoke because she felt obliged to make some reply to me.

"Yes, Lucy," I said, raising myself upon the pillow, and grasping her wrist, "the shadow of your brother Laurence. The living, breathing, moving image of your brother, with every lineament and every shade of colouring reflected in the phantom face as they would be reflected in a mirror. Not shadowy, transparent, or vanishing, but as distinct as you are to me at this very moment. Good heavens! Lucy, I give you my solemn word that I heard the phantom footsteps along that gallery as distinctly as I have ever heard the steps of Laurence himself; the firm heavy tread of a strong man."

Lucy Wendale sat for some time perfectly silent, looking straight before her—not at me, but out at the half-open window, round which the ivy-leaves were fluttering, to the dim moorland melting into purple distance above the tree-tops in the park. Her profile was turned towards me; but I could see by her firmly-compressed lips and fixed eyes that she was thinking deeply.

Presently she said, slowly and deliberately, without once looking at me as she spoke, "You must be fully aware, my dearest Isabel, that these delusions are of common occurrence with people of an extremely sensitive temperament. You may be one of these delicately organised persons; you had thrown yourself last night into a very nervous and hysterical state in your morbid anxiety about Laurence. With your whole mind full of his image, with all kinds of shadowy terrors about danger to him, what more likely than that you should conjure up an object such as that which you fancy you saw last night?"

"But so palpable, Lucy, so distinct!"

"It would be as easy for the brain to shape a distinct as an indistinct form. Grant the possibility of optical delusion—a fact established by a host of witnesses—and you cannot limit the character of the delusion. But I must get our doctor, Mr. Arden, to talk to you about this. He is something of a metaphysician as well as a medical man, and will be able to cure your mental ills, and regulate this feverish pulse of yours at the same time. Laurence has ridden over to York to fetch him, and I daresay they will both be here directly."

"Lucy, remember you must never tell Laurence the cause of my last night's fainting fit."

"Never, Isobel. I was about to make the very same request to you. It is much better that he should not know it."

"Much better; for, oh, Lucy, do you remember that in all ghost-stories the appearance of the shadow, or double, of a living person is a presage of death to that person? The thought of this brings back all my terror. My Laurence, my darling, if anything should happen to him!"

"Come, Bella, Mr. Arden must talk to you. In the meantime, here comes Mrs. Porson with your breakfast. While you are taking it, I will go to the library, and look for Sir Walter Scott's *Demonology*.[1] You will find several instances in that book of the optical delusions I have spoken of."

The housekeeper came bustling into the room with a breakfast-tray, which she placed on a table by the bed. When she had arranged everything for my comfort, and propped me up with a luxurious pile of pillows, she turned round to speak to Lucy.

"Oh, Miss Lucy," she said, "poor Beck is so awfully cut up. If you'd only just see him, and tell him—"

Lucy silenced her with one look; a brief but all-expressive glance of warning and reproval. I could not help wondering what possible reason there could be for making a mystery of some little trouble of James Beck's.

Mr. Arden, the York surgeon, was the most delightful of men. He came with Lucy into my room, and laughed and chatted me out of my low spirits before he had been with me a quarter of an hour. He talked so much of hysteria, optical delusions, false impressions of outward objects, abnormal conditions of the organ of sight, and other semi-mental, semi-physical infirmities, that he fairly bewildered me into agreeing with and believing all he said.

"I hear you are a most accomplished horsewoman, Miss Morley," he said, as he rose to leave us; "and as the day promises to be fine, I most strongly recommend a canter across the moors, with Mr. Wendale as your cavalier. Go to sleep between this and luncheon; rise in time to eat a mutton-chop and drink a glass of bitter ale; ride for two hours in the sunniest part of the afternoon, take a light dinner, and go to bed early; and I will answer for your seeing no more of the ghost. You have no idea how much indigestion has to do with these things. I daresay if I were to see your bill of fare for yesterday I should discover that Lady Adela's cook is responsible for the phantom, and that he made his first appearance among the *entrées*. Who can wonder that the Germans are a ghost-seeing people, when it is remembered that they eat raspberry-jam with roast veal?"[2]

I followed the doctor's advice to the letter; and at three o'clock in the afternoon Laurence and I were galloping across the moorland, tinged with a yellow hazy light in the September sunshine. Like most impressionable people, I soon recovered from my nervous shock; and by the time I sprang from the saddle before the wide stone portico at Fernwood I had almost forgotten my terrors of the night before.

A fortnight after this my aunt and I left Yorkshire for Brighton, whither Laurence speedily followed us. Before leaving I did all in my power to induce Lucy to accompany us, but in vain. She thanked my aunt for her cordial invitation, but declared that she could not leave Fernwood. We departed, therefore, without having won her, as I had hoped to have done, from the monotony of her solitary life, and without having seen Mr. Wendale's invalid dependent, the mysterious occupant of the west wing.

Early in November Laurence was summoned from Brighton by the arrival of a black-bordered letter, written by Lucy, and telling him of his father's death. Mr. Wendale had been found by his servant, seated in an easy-chair in his study, with his head lying back upon the cushions, and an open book on the carpet at his feet, dead. He had long suffered from disease of the heart.

My lover wrote me long letters from Yorkshire, telling me how his mother and sister bore the blow which had fallen upon them so suddenly. It was a quiet and subdued sorrow, rather than any tempestuous grief, which reigned in the narrow circle at Fernwood. Mr. Wendale had been an invalid for many years, giving very little of his society to his wife and daughter. His death, therefore, though sudden, had not been unexpected, nor did his loss leave any great blank in that quiet home.

---

[1] *Sir Walter Scott's Demonology* Scott's *Letters on Witchcraft and Demonology* (1830) examines alleged supernatural phenomena from the Old Testament to the nineteenth century, taking a rational and often skeptical approach.

[2] *Who can wonder ... with roast veal* I.e., it should not surprise us that the Germans are so strange as to believe they see ghosts, given that they do things as strange as eating raspberry jam as a condiment accompanying roast veal.

Laurence spent Christmas at Fernwood, but returned to us for the new year; and it was then settled that we should go down to Yorkshire early in February, in order to superintend the restoration and alteration of the old place.

All was arranged for our journey, when, on the very day on which we were to start, Laurence came to Onslow Square with a letter from his mother, which he had only just received. Lady Adela wrote a few hurried lines to beg us to delay our visit for some days, as they had decided on removing Mr. Thomas, before the alterations were commenced, to a cottage which was being prepared for him near York. The invalid had not been left a pauper by the death of his patron, as by Mr. Wendale's will an annuity of two hundred a year was left to Thomas Wendale.[1]

"I will not hear of this visit being delayed an hour," Laurence said impatiently, as he thrust Lady Adela's crumpled letter into his pocket. "My poor foolish mother and sister are really too absurd about this first or fifth cousin of ours, Thomas Wendale. Let him leave Fernwood, or let him stay at Fernwood, just as he, or his nurse, or his medical man, may please; but I certainly shall not allow his arrangements to interfere with ours. So, ladies, I shall be perfectly ready to escort you by the eleven o'clock express."

Mrs. Trevor remonstrated, declaring that she would rather delay our visit according to Lady Adela's wish; but my impetuous Laurence would not hear a word, and under a black and moonless February sky we drove up the avenue at Fernwood.

---

[1] In the *Ralph the Bailiff and Other Stories* version this sentence is replaced by a somewhat longer passage, as follows:

His patron's death did not leave the invalid dependent on the bounty of Laurence or Lady Adela. Mr. Wendale had bequeathed a small estate, worth three hundred a year, in trust for the sole use and benefit of this Mr. William Wendale.

Neither Laurence nor I understood why the money should have been left in trust rather than unconditionally to the man himself. But neither he nor I felt deeply interested in the subject; and Laurence was far too careless of business matters to pry into the details of his succession. He knew himself to be the owner of Fernwood and of a handsome income, and that was all he cared to know.

We met Mr. Arden in the hall as we entered. There seemed something ominous in receiving our first greeting from the family doctor; and Laurence was for a moment alarmed by his presence.

"My mother—Lucy!" he said anxiously; "they are well, I hope?"

"Perfectly well. I have not been attending them; I have just come from Mr. Thomas."

"Is he worse?"

"I fear he is rather worse than usual."

Our welcome was scarcely a cordial one, for both Lucy and Lady Adela were evidently embarrassed by our unexpected arrival. Their black dresses, half-covered with crape,[2] the mourning liveries of the servants, the vacant seat of the master, the dismal winter weather and ceaseless beating of the rain upon the window-panes without, gave a more than usually dreary aspect to the place, and seemed to chill us to the very soul.

Those who at any period of their lives have suffered some terrible and crushing affliction, some never-to-be-forgotten trouble, for which even the hand of Time has no lessening influence, which increases rather than diminishes as the slow course of a hopeless life carries us further from it, so that as we look back we do not ask ourselves why the trial seemed so bitter, but wonder rather how we endured even as we did—those only who have sunk under such a grief as this can know how difficult it is to dissociate the period preceding the anguish from the hour in which it came. I say this lest I should be influenced by after-feelings when I describe the dismal shadows that seemed to brood over the hearth round which Lady Adela, my aunt, Laurence, and myself gathered upon the night of our return to Fernwood.

Lucy had left us, and when her brother inquired about her, Lady Adela said she was with Mr. Thomas.

As usual, Laurence chafed at the answer. It was hard, he said, that his sister should have to act as sick-nurse to this man.

---

[2] *crape* Thin woven fabric, often dyed black and used for mourning garments.

"James Beck has gone to York to prepare for Thomas," answered Lady Adela, "and the poor boy has no one with him but his nurse."

The poor boy! I wondered why it was that Lady Adela and her stepdaughter always alluded to Mr. Thomas as a young man.

Early the next morning, Laurence insisted upon our accompanying him on a circuit of the house, to discuss the intended alterations. I have already described the gallery, running the whole length of the building, at one end of which was situated the suite of rooms occupied by Mr. Thomas, and at the other extremity those devoted to Mrs. Trevor and myself. Lady Adela's apartments were nearest to those of the invalid, Lucy's next, then the billiard-room, and opening out of that the bed and dressing-room occupied by Laurence. On the other side of the gallery were servants' and visitors' rooms, and a pretty boudoir sacred to Lady Adela.

Laurence was in very high spirits, planning alterations here and renovations there—bay-windows to be thrown out in one direction, and folding-doors knocked through in another—till we laughed heartily at him on finding that the pencil-memorandum he was preparing for the architect resolved itself into an order for knocking down the old house and building a new one. We had explored every nook and corner in the place, with the one exception of those mysterious apartments in the left wing. Laurence Wendale paused before the green-baize door, but after a moment's hesitation tapped for admittance.

"I have never seen Mr. Thomas, and it is rather awkward to have to ask to look at his rooms while he is in them; but the necessity of the case will be my excuse for intruding on him. The architect will be here tomorrow, and I want to have all my plans ready to submit to him."

The baize door was opened by Lucy Wendale; she started at seeing us.

"What do you want, Laurence?" she said.

"To see Mr. Thomas's rooms. I shall not disturb him, if he will kindly allow me to glance round the apartments."

I could see that there was an inner half-glass door behind that at which Lucy was standing.

"You cannot possibly see the rooms today, Laurence," she said, hurriedly. "Mr. Thomas leaves early tomorrow morning."

She came out into the gallery, closing the baize door behind her; but as the shutting of the door reverberated through the gallery, I heard another sound that turned my blood to ice, and made me cling convulsively to Laurence's arm.

The laugh, the same dissonant laugh, that I had heard from the spectral lips of my lover's shadow!

"Lucy," I said, "did you hear that?"

"What?"

"The laugh, the laugh I heard the night that—"

Laurence had thrown his arm round me, alarmed by my terror. His sister was standing a little way behind him; she put her finger to her lips, looking at me significantly.

"You must be mistaken, Isabel," she said quietly.

There was some mystery, then, connected with this Mr. Thomas—a mystery which for some especial reason was to be concealed from Laurence.

Half an hour after this, Lucy Wendale came to me as I was searching for a book in the library.

"Isabel," she said, "I wish to say a few words to you."

"Yes, dear Lucy."

"You are to be my sister, and I have perhaps done wrong in concealing from you the one unhappy secret which has clouded the lives of my poor father, my stepmother, and myself. But long ago, when Laurence was a child, it was deemed expedient that the grief which was so heavy a load for us should, if possible, be spared to him. My father was so passionately devoted to his handsome light-hearted boy, that he shrank day by day from the thought of revealing to him the afflicting secret which was such a source of grief to himself. We found that, by constant care and watchfulness, it was possible to conceal all from Laurence, and up to this hour we have done so. But it is perhaps better that you should know all; for you will be able to aid us in keeping the knowledge from Laurence, or, if absolutely necessary, you may by and by break it to him gently, and reconcile him to an irremediable affliction."

"But this secret—this affliction—it concerns your invalid relation, Mr. Thomas?"

"It does, Isabel,"

I know that the words which were to reveal all were trembling upon her lips, that in one brief moment she would have spoken, and I should have known all. I should have known in time—but before she could utter a syllable the door was opened by one of the women-servants.

"O, miss, if you please," she said, "Mrs. Peters says would you step upstairs this minute?"

Mrs. Peters was the nurse who attended on Mr. Thomas.

Lucy pressed my hand. "Tomorrow, dearest, tomorrow I will tell you all."

She hurried from the room, and I sank into a chair by the fire, with my book lying open in my lap, unable to read a line, unable to think, except upon one subject—the secret which I was so soon to learn. If she had but spoken then! A few words more, and what unutterable misery might have been averted!

I was aroused from my reverie by Laurence, who came to challenge me to a game at billiards. On my pleading fatigue as an excuse for refusing, he seated himself on a low stool at my feet, offering to read aloud to me.

"What shall it be, Bella? *Paradise Lost*, *Martin Chuzzlewit*, Byron, Shelley, Tennyson[1]—?"

"Tennyson by all means! The dreary rain-blotted sky outside those windows, and the bleak moorland in the distance, are perfectly Tennysonian. Read *Locksley Hall*."[2]

His deep melodious voice rolled out the swelling verses; but I heard the sound without its meaning. I could only think of the mystery which had been kept so long a secret from my lover. When he had finished the poem he threw aside his book, and sat looking earnestly at me.

"My solemn Bella," he said, "what on earth are you thinking about?"

The broad glare of the blaze from an enormous sea-coal fire was full upon his handsome face. I tried to rouse myself, and, laying my hands upon his forehead, pushed back his curling chestnut hair. As I did so I for the first time perceived a cicatrice[3] across his left temple. A deep gash, as if from the cut of a knife; but a wound of far-distant date.

"Why, Laurence," I said, "you tell me you were never thrown, and yet you have a scar here that looks like the evidence of some desperate fall. Did you get it in hunting?"

"No, my inquisitive Bella! No horse is to blame for that personal embellishment. I believe it was done when I was a child of two or three years old; but I have no positive recollection of the event, though I have a vague remembrance of wearing a sticking-plaster bandage across my forehead, and being unconscionably petted by Lucy and my mother."

"But it looks like a scar from a cut—from the cut of a knife."

"I must have fallen upon some sharp instrument—the edge of one of the stone steps, perhaps, or a metal scraper."

"My poor Laurence, the blow might have killed you!"

He looked grave.

"Do you know, Bella," he said, "how difficult it is to dissociate the vague recollections of the actual events of our childhood from childish dreams that are scarcely more vague? Sometimes I have a strange fancy that I can remember getting this cut, and that it was caused by a knife thrown at me by another child."

"Another child! What child?"

"A boy of my own age and size."

---

[1] *Paradise Lost* Epic poem by John Milton (1667–74); *Martin Chuzzlewit* Picaresque novel by Charles Dickens published serially from 1842 to 1844; *Byron* Romantic poet George Gordon, Lord Byron (1788–1824); *Shelley* Romantic poet Percy Bysshe Shelley (1792–1822); *Tennyson* Alfred, Lord Tennyson, who was Poet Laureate of the U.K. from 1850 to 1892.

[2] *Locksley Hall* Tennyson's 1842 poem narrated by a lovelorn man returning to his childhood home of Locksley Hall, reminiscing about the woman who has rejected him.

[3] *cicatrice* Scar.

"Was he your playfellow?"

"I can't tell; I can remember nothing but the circumstance of his throwing the knife at me, and the sensation of the hot blood streaming into my eyes and blinding me."

"Can you remember where it occurred?"

"Yes, in the gallery upstairs."

We lunched at two. After luncheon, Laurence went to his own room to write some letters; Lady Adela and my aunt read and worked in the drawing-room, while I sat at the piano, rambling through some sonatas of Beethoven.

We were occupied in this manner when Lucy came into the room, dressed for walking. "I have ordered the carriage, mamma," she said. "I am going over to York to see that Beck has everything prepared. I shall be back to dinner."

Lady Adela seemed to grow more helpless every day; every day to rely more and more on her stepdaughter.

"You are sure to do all for the best, Lucy," she said. "Take plenty of wraps, for it is bitterly cold."

"Shall I go with you, Lucy?" I asked.

"You! Oh, on no account, dear Isabel. What would Laurence say to me if I carried you off for a whole afternoon?"

She hurried from the room, and in two minutes the lumbering close carriage drove away from the portico. My motive in asking to accompany her was a selfish one. I thought it possible she might resume the morning's interrupted conversation during our drive.

If I had but gone with her!

It is so difficult to reconcile one's self to the irrevocable decrees of Providence; it is so difficult to bow the head in meek submission to the awful fiat; so difficult not to look back to the careless hours which preceded the falling of the blow, and calculate how it might have been averted.

The February twilight was closing in. My aunt and Lady Adela had fallen asleep by the fire. I stole softly out of the room to fetch a book which I had left upstairs. There was more light in the hall and on the staircase than in the drawing-room; but the long gallery was growing dark, the dusky shadows gathering about the faded portraits of my lover's ancestry. I stopped at the top of the staircase, and looked for a moment towards the billiard-room. The door was open, and I could see a light streaming from Laurence's little study. I went to my own room, contrived to find the book I wanted, and returned to the gallery. As I left my room I saw that the green-baize door at the extreme end of the gallery was wide open.

An irresistible curiosity attracted me towards those mysterious apartments. As I drew nearer to the staircase, I could plainly perceive the figure of a man standing at the half-glass door within. The light of a fire shining in the room behind him threw the outline of his head and figure into sharp relief. There was no possibility of mistaking that well-known form—the broad shoulders, the massive head, and clusters of curling hair. It was Laurence Wendale looking through the glass door of the invalid's apartments. He had penetrated those forbidden chambers, then. I thought immediately of the mystery connected with the invalid, and of Lucy's anxiety that it should be kept from her brother, and I hurried forward towards the baize door. As I advanced he saw me, and rattled impatiently at the lock of the inner door. It was locked, but the key was on the outside. He did not speak, but rattled the lock incessantly, signifying by a gesture of his head that I was to open the door. I turned the key, the door opened outwards, and I was nearly knocked down by the force with which he flung it back and dashed past me.

"Laurence!" I said, "Laurence! what have you been doing here, and who locked you in?"

He did not answer me, but strode along the gallery, looking at each of the doors till he came to the only open one, that of the billiard-room, which he entered.

I was wounded by this rude manner; but I scarcely thought of that, for I was on the threshold of the apartments occupied by the mysterious invalid, and I could not resist one hurried peep into the room behind the half-glass door.

It was a roomy apartment, very plainly furnished; a large fire burned in the grate, which was closely guarded by a very high brass fender, the highest I had ever seen. There was an easy-chair close to this fender, and on the floor beside it a heap of old childish books, with glaring coloured prints, some of them torn to shreds. On the mantelpiece there was a painted wooden figure, held together by strings, such as children play with. Exactly opposite to where I stood there was another door, which was half-open, and through which I saw a bedroom, furnished with two iron bedsteads, placed side by side. There were no hangings either to these bedsteads or to the windows in the sitting-room, and the latter were protected by iron bars. A horrible fear came over me. Mr. Thomas was perhaps a madman. The seclusion, the locked doors, the guarded fireplace and windows, the dreary curtainless beds, the watchfulness of Lucy, James Beck, and the nurse—all pointed to this conclusion.

Tenantless as the rooms looked, the maniac might be lurking in the shadow. I turned to hurry back to the gallery, and found myself face to face with Mrs. Peters, the nurse, with a small tea-tray in her hands.

"My word, miss," she said, "how you did startle me, to be sure! What are you doing here? and why have you unlocked this door?"

"To let out Mr. Laurence."

"Mr. Laurence!" she exclaimed, in a terrified voice.

"Yes; he was inside this door. Some one had locked him in, I suppose, and he told me to open it for him."

"Oh miss, what have you done! what have you done! Today, above all things, when we've had such an awful time with him! What have you done!"

What had I done? I thought the woman must herself be half distraught, so unaccountable was the agitation of her manner.

Oh merciful Heaven, the laugh! the harsh, mocking, exulting, idiotic laugh! This time it rang in loud and discordant peals to the very rafters of the old house.

"O, for pity's sake," I cried, clinging to the nurse, "what is it, what is it?"

She threw me off, and, rushing to the balustrades at the head of the staircase, called loudly, "Andrew, Henry! Bring lights!"

They came, the two men-servants—old men, who had served in that house for thirty or forty years—they came with candles, and followed the nurse to the billiard-room.

The door of communication between that and Laurence Wendale's study was wide open, and on the threshold, with the light shining upon him from within the room, stood the double of my lover; the living, breathing image of my Laurence, the creature I had seen at the half-glass door, and had mistaken for Laurence himself. His face was distorted by a ghastly grin, and he was uttering some strange unintelligible sounds as we approached him—guttural and unearthly murmurs horrible to hear. Even in that moment of bewilderment and terror I could see that the cambric about his right wrist was splashed with blood.

The nurse looked at him severely; he slunk away like a frightened child, and crept into a corner of the billiard-room, where he stood grinning and mouthing at the blood-stains upon his wrist.

We rushed into the little study. Oh horror of horrors! The writing-table was overturned; ink, papers, pens, all scattered and trampled on the floor; and in the midst of the confusion lay Laurence Wendale, the blood slowly ebbing away, with dull gurgling sound, from a hideous gash in his throat.

A penknife, with which he had been, it is imagined, mending pens when disturbed by his horrible visitor, lay amongst the trampled papers, crimsoned to the hilt.

Laurence Wendale had been murdered by his idiot[1] twin-brother.

*   *   *

There was an inquest. I can recall at any hour, or at any moment, the whole agony of the scene. The dreary room, adjoining that in which the body lay; the dull February sky; the monotonous voice of the coroner, and the medical men; and myself, or some wretched, shuddering, white-lipped creature that I could scarcely believe to be myself, giving evidence. Lady Adela was reproved for having kept her idiot son at Fernwood without the knowledge of the murdered man; but every effort was made to hush up the terrible story. Thomas

---

[1] *idiot* Archaic term for a person with a severe mental disability, now considered offensive.

Wendale was tried at York, and transferred to the county lunatic asylum, there to be detained during her Majesty's pleasure. His unhappy brother was quietly buried in the Wendale vault, the chief mausoleum in a damp moss-grown church close to the gates of Fernwood.

It is upwards of ten years since all this happened, but the horror of that February twilight is as fresh in my mind today as it was when I lay stricken—not senseless, but stupefied with anguish—on a sofa in the drawing-room at Fernwood, listening to the wailing of the wretched mother and sister.

The misery of that time changed me at once from a young woman to an old one; not by any sudden blanching of my dark hair, but by the blotting-out of every girlish feeling in the dull monotony of resignation. This change in my own nature has drawn Lucy Wendale and I together with a link far stronger than any common sisterhood. Lady Adela died two years after the murder of her son. The Fernwood property (forfeited by the idiot's crime, but afterwards restored by the clemency of the crown) has passed into the hands of the heir-at-law.

Lucy lives with me at the Isle of Wight. She is my protectress, my elder sister, without whom I should be lost, for I am but a poor helpless creature.

It was months after the quiet funeral in Fernwood church before Lucy spoke to me of the wretched being who had been the author of so much misery.

"The idiocy of my unhappy brother," she said, "was caused by a fall from his nurse's arms, which resulted in a fatal injury to the brain. The two children were infants at the time of the accident, and so much alike that we could only distinguish Laurence from Thomas by the different colour of the ribbons with which the nurse tied the sleeves of the children's little white frocks. My poor father suffered bitterly from his son's affliction, sometimes cherishing hope even in the face of the verdict which medical science pronounced upon the poor child's case, sometimes succumbing to utter despair. It was the intense misery which he himself endured that made him resolve on the course which ultimately led to so fatal a catastrophe. He determined on concealing Thomas's affliction from his twin-brother. At a very early age the idiot child was removed to the apartments in which he lived until the day of his brother's murder. James Beck and the nurse, both experienced in the treatment of mental affliction, were engaged to attend him; and, indeed, the strictest precaution seemed necessary, as, on the only occasion of the two children meeting, Thomas evinced a determined animosity to his brother, and inflicted a blow with a knife, the traces of which Laurence carried to his grave. The doctors attributed this violent hatred to some morbid feeling respecting the likeness between the two boys. Thomas flew at his brother as some wild animal springs upon its reflection in a glass. With me, in his most violent moments, he was comparatively tractable; but the strictest surveillance was always necessary, and the fatal deed which the wretched, but irresponsible, creature at last committed might never have been done but for the imprudent absence of James Beck and myself."

—1861–62

AUGUSTA WEBSTER
1837 – 1894

Among nineteenth-century women poets, Augusta Webster was, according to Christina Rossetti, "by far the most formidable." Frequently praised during her lifetime for the "power" and "strength" of her work, Webster is best known for bold poetic portraits that give dramatic voice to social issues in Victorian culture. Webster's dramatic monologues—written from the perspectives of characters both modern, such as prostitutes and preachers, and mythical, such as the legendary ancient Greek figures Circe and Medea—address some of the central concerns of her era, including the status of women; courtship, marriage, and sexuality; problems of religious faith; and the tension between pursuing an artistic vocation and meeting the demands of the marketplace. Webster's treatment of such subjects stands out for its social and psychological realism as well as for its eschewal of the conventional pieties that characterized much Victorian thinking about these issues. Webster also made a mark on Victorian culture not only through her dramatic monologues but through a larger body of work that includes essays, a novel, verse dramas, and a posthumously published sonnet sequence exploring her relationship with her daughter; through her status as a respected translator of Ancient Greek; and through her work as a campaigner for women's rights.

Born in 1837 to Julia Hume Davies and Vice-Admiral George Davies of the British Navy in Poole, Dorset, Julia Augusta Davies spent her earliest years on board her father's ship, the *Griper*. It is said that Webster learned Greek at a young age to help her brother with his lessons; her mastery of a classical language traditionally reserved for male education may also have been motivated by literary ambitions, anticipating a career which included two translations of Greek plays. Webster attended the Cambridge School of Art and was admitted to the South Kensington Art School where, according to Ray Strachey, she "nearly dashed the prospects of women art students for ever by being expelled for whistling." In 1863 she married Thomas Webster, a fellow and law lecturer at Trinity College in Cambridge. Their only child, Margaret, is memorialized in one of Webster's finest works, the posthumously published sonnet sequence *Mother and Daughter*.

While no personal documents exist to shed light on the Websters' marriage, the couple's decision to move to London suggests that it was not conventionally patriarchal; giving up a prestigious position in Cambridge, Webster's husband supported a move which would enable his wife to develop professionally in proximity to some of her literary models, such as Robert Browning and Alfred, Lord Tennyson. In London, Webster was poetry reviewer for the *Athenaeum* for a decade, and wrote regular columns for the *Examiner*. She also campaigned on behalf of women's suffrage and education, becoming one of the first women to be elected to the London School Board.

Webster's writing is rich with social commentary. Her poem "A Castaway," praised by Robert Browning and called "her masterpiece" by the critic Theodore Watts-Dunton, presents through the persona of a prostitute a powerful critique of the Victorian "economy of love" (to borrow the phrase of Webster scholar Christine Sutphin). "A Castaway," like "The Happiest Girl in the World" and "Jeanne D'Arc," is written in the poetic genre in which Webster excelled, the dramatic monologue. Two collections of monologues, *Dramatic Studies* (1866) and *Portraits* (1870), mark Webster's most lasting contribution to English poetry. In contrast to the psychological interiors dramatized by Robert Browning in monologues such as "Fra Lippo Lippi," Webster skillfully crafted the monologue to speak to external social circumstances. Webster was able to give voice to a sensual and political potency prohibited Victorian women by speaking through mythological surrogates in "Medea in Athens" and "Circe." While the implied, silent listener addressed within conventional dramatic monologues is often absent from Webster's treatments (leading the *London Review* to describe *Dramatic Studies* as "a set of soliloquies"), her monologues stage a voice whose message is a moving social performance.

The essays on love and marriage that Webster regularly contributed to the *Examiner* were, like most submissions to Victorian periodicals, anonymous. The editor of the *Examiner* held Webster's essay "A Translation and a Transcription" in high esteem, ranking it "the best article which ever appeared in its pages." Webster's first two books, *Blanche Lisle and Other Poems* (1860) and a narrative poem in blank verse entitled *Lilian Gray* (1864), were published under the pseudonym Cecil Home. All subsequent work, ranging from lyrics to verse dramas, appeared under Webster's own name. She even daringly attached her own name to her translations of *The Medea of Euripides* and *The Prometheus Bound of Aeschylus* at a time when scholarship in classical languages was considered to be strictly the province of "gentlemen."

By the time Webster died in 1894, her work had already ceased to receive substantial critical or popular attention, and this pattern would continue for nearly a century. A few notable figures protested against this neglect: Rossetti criticized Webster's exclusion from a "list of poetesses" assembled in 1890 by William Gladstone, and Watts-Dunton proclaimed it "a monstrous thing that such poetry as Augusta Webster's should be unknown." However, Webster lacked sufficient powerful connections to secure her reputation, and the politics of twentieth-century canon formation did not favor writers like her—especially those whose most significant works were longer dramatic monologues and verse dramas. It was not until the 1980s and 90s that feminist scholarship rediscovered Webster. Today, she is increasingly regarded as a major voice in Victorian literature and one of the most innovative writers of her time.

⌘ ⌘ ⌘

A Castaway

Poor little diary, with its simple thoughts,
　Its good resolves, its "Studied French an hour,"
"Read Modern History," "Trimmed up my grey hat,"
"Darned stockings," "Tatted,"[1] "Practiced my new song,"
5　"Went to the daily service," "Took Bess soup,"
"Went out to tea." Poor simple diary!
And did *I* write it? Was I this good girl,

This budding colourless young rose of home?
Did I so live content in such a life,
10　Seeing no larger scope, nor asking it,
Than this small constant round—old clothes to mend,
New clothes to make, then go and say my prayers,
Or carry soup, or take a little walk
And pick the ragged-robins[2] in the hedge?
15　Then, for ambition, (was there ever life
That could forego that?) to improve my mind

1　*Tatted* Made lace.

2　*ragged-robin* Common English flower.

And know French better and sing harder songs;
For gaiety, to go, in my best white
Well washed and starched and freshened with new bows,
20 And take tea out to meet the clergyman.
No wishes and no cares, almost no hopes,
Only the young girl's hazed and golden dreams
That veil the future from her.

            So long since:
And now it seems a jest to talk of me
25 As if I could be one with her, of me
Who am … me.

         And what is that? My looking-glass
Answers it passably; a woman sure,
No fiend, no slimy thing out of the pools,
A woman with a ripe and smiling lip
30 That has no venom in its touch I think,
With a white brow on which there is no brand;[1]
A woman none dare call not beautiful,
Not womanly in every woman's grace.

      Aye, let me feed upon my beauty thus,
35 Be glad in it like painters when they see
At last the face they dreamed but could not find
Look from their canvas on them, triumph in it,
The dearest thing I have. Why, 'tis my all,
Let me make much of it: is it not this,
40 This beauty, my own curse at once and tool
To snare men's souls (I know what the good say
Of beauty in such creatures), is it not this
That makes me feel myself a woman still,
With still some little pride, some little—

                 Stop!
45 "Some little pride, some little"—Here's a jest!
What word will fit the sense but modesty?
A wanton° I, but modest!   *prostitute*

        Modest, true;
I'm not drunk in the streets, ply not for hire

At infamous corners with my likenesses
50 Of the humbler kind; yes, modesty's my word—
'Twould shape my mouth well too, I think I'll try:
"Sir, Mr. What-you-will, Lord Who-knows-what,
My present lover or my next to come,
Value me at my worth, fill your purse full,
55 For I am modest; yes, and honour me
As though your schoolgirl sister or your wife
Could let her skirts brush mine or talk of me;
For I am modest."

        Well, I flout myself:
But yet, but yet—

           Fie, poor fantastic fool,
60 Why do I play the hypocrite alone,
Who am no hypocrite with others by?
Where should be my "But yet"? I am that thing
Called half a dozen dainty names, and none
Dainty enough to serve the turn and hide
65 The one coarse English worst that lurks beneath:
Just that, no worse, no better.

             And, for me,
I say let no one be above her trade;
I own my kindredship with any drab[2]
Who sells herself as I, although she crouch
70 In fetid garrets and I have a home
All velvet and marqueterie and pastilles,[3]
Although she hide her skeleton in rags
And I set fashions and wear cobweb lace:
The difference lies but in my choicer ware,
75 That I sell beauty and she ugliness;
Our traffic's one—I'm no sweet slaver-tongue
To gloze[4] upon it and explain myself
A sort of fractious angel misconceived—
Our traffic's one: I own it. And what then?
80 I know of worse that are called honourable.
Our lawyers, who with noble eloquence

---

[1] *brand* Revealing mark or sign.

[2] *drab* Common prostitute.

[3] *marqueterie* Inlaid mosaic work decorating furniture; *pastilles* Aromatic pastes burnt as perfumes.

[4] *gloze* Interpret deceitfully or flatteringly.

And virtuous outbursts lie to hang a man,
Or lie to save him, which way goes the fee:
Our preachers, gloating on your future hell
5   For not believing what they doubt themselves:
Our doctors, who sort poisons out by chance
And wonder how they'll answer, and grow rich:
Our journalists, whose business is to fib
And juggle truths and falsehoods to and fro:
10 Our tradesmen, who must keep unspotted names
And cheat the least like stealing that they can:
Our —— all of them, the virtuous worthy men
Who feed on the world's follies, vices, wants,
And do their businesses of lies and shams
95 Honestly, reputably, while the world
Claps hands and cries "good luck," which of their
        trades,
Their honourable trades, barefaced like mine,
All secrets brazened out, would show more white?

And whom do I hurt more than they? as much?
00 The wives? Poor fools, what do I take from them
Worth crying for or keeping? If they knew
What their fine husbands look like seen by eyes
That may perceive there are more men than one!
But, if they can, let them just take the pains
05 To keep them: 'tis not such a mighty task
To pin an idiot to your apron-string;
And wives have an advantage over us,
(The good and blind ones have) the smile or pout
Leaves them no secret nausea at odd times.
10 Oh, they could keep their husbands if they cared,
But 'tis an easier life to let them go,
And whimper at it for morality.

Oh! those shrill carping virtues, safely housed
From reach of even a smile that should put red
115 On a decorous cheek, who rail at us
With such a spiteful scorn and rancorousness,
(Which maybe is half envy at the heart)

And boast themselves so measurelessly good
And us so measurelessly unlike them,
120 What is their wondrous merit that they stay
In comfortable homes whence not a soul
Has ever thought of tempting them, and wear
No kisses but a husband's upon lips
There is no other man desires to kiss—
125 Refrain in fact from sin impossible?
How dare they hate us so? what have they done,
What borne, to prove them other than we are?
What right have they to scorn us—glass-case saints,
Dianas[1] under lock and key—what right
130 More than the well-fed helpless barn-door fowl
To scorn the larcenous wild-birds?

                            Pshaw, let be!
Scorn or no scorn, what matter for their scorn?
I have outfaced my own—that's harder work.
Aye, let their virtuous malice dribble on—
135 Mock snowstorms on the stage—I'm proof long since:
I have looked coolly on my what and why,
And I accept myself.

                            Oh I'll endorse
The shamefullest revilings mouthed at me,
Cry "True! Oh perfect picture! Yes, that's I!"
140 And add a telling blackness here and there,
And then dare swear you, every nine of ten,
My judges and accusers, I'd not change
My conscience against yours, you who tread out
Your devil's pilgrimage along the roads
145 That take in church and chapel, and arrange
A roundabout and decent way to hell.

Well, mine's a short way and a merry one:
So says my pious hash of ohs and ahs,
Choice texts and choicer threats, appropriate names,

----

[1] *Diana* Roman goddess of virginity.

150   (Rahabs and Jezebels[1]) some fierce Tartuffe[2]
       Hurled at me through the post. We had rare fun
       Over that tract[3] digested with champagne.
       Where is it? where's my rich repertory
       Of insults Biblical?[4] "*I prey on souls*"—
155   Only my men have oftenest none I think:
       "*I snare the simple ones*"—but in these days
       There seem to be none simple and none snared
       And most men have their favourite sinnings planned
       To do them civilly and sensibly:
160   "*I braid my hair*"—but braids are out of date:
       "*I paint my cheeks*"—I always wear them pale:
       "*I—*"

           Pshaw! the trash is savourless today:
       One cannot laugh alone. There, let it burn.
       What, does the windy dullard think one needs
165   His wisdom dove-tailed on to Solomon's,[5]
       His threats out-threatening God's, to teach the news
       That those who need not sin have safer souls?
       We know it, but we've bodies to save too;
       And so we earn our living.

                       Well lit, tract!
170   At least you've made me a good leaping blaze.
       Up, up, how the flame shoots! and now 'tis dead.

       Oh proper finish, preaching to the last—
       No such bad omen either; sudden end,
       And no sad withering horrible old age.
175   How one would clutch at youth to hold it tight!
       And then to know it gone, to see it gone,
       Be taught its absence by harsh careless looks,
       To live forgotten, solitary, old—
       The cruellest word that ever woman learns.
180   Old—that's to be nothing, or to be at best
       A blurred memorial that in better days
       There was a woman once with such a name.
       No, no, I could not bear it: death itself
       Shows kinder promise ... even death itself,
185   Since it must come one day—

                       Oh this grey gloom!
       This rain, rain, rain, what wretched thoughts it brings!
       Death: I'll not think of it.

                       Will no one come?
       'Tis dreary work alone.

                       Why did I read
       That silly diary? Now, sing-song, ding-dong,
190   Come the old vexing echoes back again,
       Church bells and nursery good-books, back again
       Upon my shrinking ears that had forgotten—
       I hate the useless memories: 'tis fools' work
       Singing the hackneyed° dirge of "better days":   stale
195   Best take Now kindly, give the past good-bye,
       Whether it were a better or a worse.

           Yes, yes, I listened to the echoes once,
       The echoes and the thoughts from the old days.
       The worse for me: I lost my richest friend,
200   And that was all the difference. For the world,
       I would not have that flight known. How they'd roar:
       "What! Eulalie, when she refused us all,
       'Ill' and 'away,' was doing Magdalene,[6]

---

1   *Rahabs and Jezebels*   I.e., harlots. Rahab was a biblical harlot whose family was saved from the destruction of Jericho because she hid messengers that had been sent by Joshua to spy on the city. (See Joshua 6.17–25.) Jezebel was a Phoenician princess who married Ahab, King of Israel. She refused to worship Yahweh, continuing to practice her country's traditional worship instead, and murdered Yahweh's prophets. Her name is often used to denote a cruel, sexually predatory woman. (See 1 Judges 16 and 18.)

2   *Tartuffe*   Hypocritical character who feigned virtue in Molière's 1664 play of that name.

3   *tract*   Religious pamphlet.

4   *insults Biblical*   See Ecclesiastes 7.26: "And I find more bitter than death the woman, whose heart is snares and nets, and her hands as bands: whoso pleaseth God shall escape from her; but the sinner shall be taken by her," and 1 Timothy 2.9–10, which advises women to "adorn themselves in modest apparel, with shamefacedness and sobriety; not with braided hair, or gold, or pearls, or costly array; / But (which becometh women professing godliness) with good works."

5   *Solomon*   Biblical king of Israel who was known for his wisdom.

6   *doing Magdalene*   Becoming a reformed prostitute, so called after Mary Magdalene of the New Testament, one of Jesus' disciples. The houses in Victorian England to which prostitutes could come to reform were known as "Magdalene houses."

Tears, ashes, and her Bible, and then off
05   To hide her in a Refuge[1] … for a week!"

    A wild whim that, to fancy I could change
My new self for my old because I wished!
Since then, when in my languid days there comes
That craving, like homesickness, to go back
10   To the good days, the dear old stupid days,
To the quiet and the innocence, I know
'Tis a sick fancy and try palliatives.

    What is it? You go back to the old home,
And 'tis not *your* home, has no place for you,
15   And, if it had, you could not fit you in it.
And could I fit me to my former self?
If I had had the wit, like some of us,
To sow my wild-oats into three per cents,[2]
Could I not find me shelter in the peace
220   Of some far nook where none of them would come,
Nor whisper travel from this scurrilous world
(That gloats, and moralizes through its leers)
To blast me with my fashionable shame?
There I might—oh my castle in the clouds!
225   And where's its rent?—but there, were there a there,
I might again live the grave blameless life
Among such simple pleasures, simple cares:
But could they be my pleasures, be my cares?
The blameless life, but never the content—
230   Never. How could I henceforth be content
With any life but one that sets the brain
In a hot merry fever with its stir?
What would there be in quiet rustic days,
Each like the other, full of time to think,
235   To keep one bold enough to live at all?
Quiet is hell, I say—as if a woman
Could bear to sit alone, quiet all day,
And loathe herself and sicken on her thoughts.

    They tried it at the Refuge, and I failed:
240   I could not bear it. Dreary hideous room,

Coarse pittance, prison rules, one might bear these
And keep one's purpose; but so much alone,
And then made faint and weak and fanciful
By change from pampering to half-famishing—
245   Good God, what thoughts come! Only one week more
And 'twould have ended: but in one day more
I must have killed myself. And I loathe death,
The dreadful foul corruption with who knows
What future after it.
                            Well, I came back,
250   Back to my slough.[3] Who says I had my choice?
Could I stay there to die of some mad death?
And if I rambled out into the world
Sinless but penniless, what else were that
But slower death, slow pining shivering death
255   By misery and hunger? Choice! what choice
Of living well or ill? could I have that?
And who would give it me? I think indeed
If some kind hand, a woman's—I hate men—
Had stretched itself to help me to firm ground,
260   Taken a chance and risked my falling back,
I could have gone my way not falling back:
But, let her be all brave, all charitable,
How could she do it? Such a trifling boon°—   *favor*
A little work to live by, 'tis not much—
265   And I might have found will enough to last:
But where's the work? More seamstresses than shirts;
And defter hands at white work[4] than are mine
Drop starved at last: dressmakers, milliners,[5]
Too many too they say; and then their trades
270   Need skill, apprenticeship. And who so bold
As hire me for their humblest drudgery?
Not even for scullery slut;[6] not even, I think,
For governess although they'd get me cheap.
And after all it would be something hard,
275   With the marts° for decent women overfull,   *markets*
If I could elbow in and snatch a chance

---

[1]   *Refuge* Shelter.

[2]   *three per cents* British government stocks, which returned three per cent interest annually.

[3]   *slough* State of moral degradation.

[4]   *white work* White-thread embroidery on white cloth.

[5]   *milliners* Makers of women's hats.

[6]   *scullery slut* Maid who performs the most unpleasant kitchen tasks, such as dishwashing and floor cleaning.

And oust some good girl so, who then perforce
Must come and snatch her chance among our crowd.

Why, if the worthy men who think all's done
280   If we'll but come where we can hear them preach,
Could bring us all, or any half of us,
Into their fold, teach all us wandering sheep,
Or only half of us, to stand in rows
And baa them hymns and moral songs, good lack,[1]
285   What would they do with us? what could they do?
Just think! with were't but half of us on hand
To find work for ... or husbands. Would they try
To ship us to the colonies for wives?[2]

Well, well, I know the wise ones talk and talk:
290   "Here's cause, here's cure": "No, here it is, and here":
And find society to blame, or law,
The Church, the men, the women, too few schools,
Too many schools, too much, too little taught:
Somewhere or somehow someone is to blame:
295   But I say all the fault's with God Himself
Who puts too many women in the world.
We ought to die off reasonably and leave
As many as the men want, none to waste.
Here's cause; the woman's superfluity:
300   And for the cure, why, if it were the law,
Say, every year, in due percentages,
Balancing them with males as the times need,
To kill off female infants, 'twould make room;
And some of us would not have lost too much,
305   Losing life ere we know what it *can* mean.

The other day I saw a woman weep
Beside her dead child's bed: the little thing
Lay smiling, and the mother wailed half mad,
Shrieking to God to give it back again.
310   I could have laughed aloud: the little girl
Living had but her mother's life to live;

There she lay smiling, and her mother wept
To know her gone!

My mother would have wept.

Oh, mother, mother, did you ever dream,
315   You good grave simple mother, you pure soul
No evil could come nigh, did you once dream
In all your dying cares for your lone girl
Left to fight out her fortune helplessly
That there would be *this* danger?—for *your* girl,
320   Taught by you, lapped in a sweet ignorance,
Scarcely more wise of what things sin could be
Than some young child a summer six months old,
Where in the north the summer makes a day,
Of what is darkness ... darkness that will come
325   Tomorrow suddenly. Thank God at least
For this much of my life, that when you died,
That when you kissed me dying, not a thought
Of this made sorrow for you, that I too
Was pure of even fear.

Oh yes, I thought,
330   Still new in my insipid treadmill life,
(My father so late dead), and hopeful still,
There might be something pleasant somewhere in it,
Some sudden fairy come, no doubt, to turn
My pumpkin to a chariot, I thought then
335   That I might plod and plod and drum the sounds
Of useless facts into unwilling ears,
Tease children with dull questions half the day
Then con° dull answers in my room at night   memorize
Ready for next day's questions, mend quill pens
340   And cut my fingers, add up sums done wrong
And never get them right; teach, teach, and teach—
What I half knew, or not at all—teach, teach
For years, a lifetime—*I*!

And yet, who knows?
It might have been, for I was patient once,
345   And willing, and meant well; it might have been
Had I but still clung on in my first place—
A safe dull place, where mostly there were smiles

---

[1] *good lack* A polite exclamation.
[2] *ship ... wives* Reference to Sir Sidney Herbert's proposal to send half a million "surplus" women, such as those driven to prostitution by a lack of employment, to the colonies, where there was a shortage of women from whom to choose for settlers who wished to marry.

But never merry-makings; where all days
Jogged on sedately busy, with no haste;
350 Where all seemed measured out, but margins broad:
A dull home but a peaceful, where I felt
My pupils would be dear young sisters soon,
And felt their mother take me to her heart,
Motherly to all lonely harmless things.
355 But I must have a conscience, must blurt out
My great discovery of my ignorance!
And who required it of me? And who gained?
What did it matter for a more or less
The girls learnt in their schoolbooks, to forget
360 In their first season?[1] We did well together:
They loved me and I them: but I went off
To housemaid's pay, six crossgrained[2] brats to teach,
Wrangles and jangles, doubts, disgrace … then this;
And they had a perfection found for them,
365 Who has all ladies' learning in her head
Abridged and scheduled, speaks five languages,
Knows botany and conchology[3] and globes,
Draws, paints, plays, sings, embroiders, teaches all
On a patent method never known to fail:
370 And now they're finished and, I hear, poor things,
Are the worst dancers and worst dressers out.[4]
And where's their profit of those prison years
All gone to make them wise in lesson-books?
Who wants his wife to know weeds' Latin names?
375 Who ever chose a girl for saying dates?
Or asked if she had learned to trace a map?

Well, well, the silly rules this silly world
Makes about women! This is one of them.
Why must there be pretence of teaching them
380 What no one ever cares that they should know,
What, grown out of the schoolroom, they cast off

Like the schoolroom pinafore,[5] no better fit
For any use of real grown-up life,
For any use to her who seeks or waits
385 The husband and the home, for any use,
For any shallowest pretence of use,
To her who has them? Do I not know this,
I, like my betters, that a woman's life,
Her natural life, her good life, her one life,
390 Is in her husband, God on earth to her,
And what she knows and what she can and is
Is only good as it brings good to him?

Oh God, do I not know it? I the thing
Of shame and rottenness, the animal
395 That feeds men's lusts and preys on them, I, I,
Who should not dare to take the name of wife
On my polluted lips, who in the word
Hear but my own reviling, I know that.
I could have lived by that rule, how content:
400 My pleasure to make him some pleasure, pride
To be as he would have me, duty, care,
To fit all to his taste, rule my small sphere
To his intention; then to lean on him,
Be guided, tutored, loved—no not that word,
405 That *loved* which between men and women means
All selfishness, all cloying talk, all lust,
All vanity, all idiocy—not loved,
But cared for. I've been loved myself, I think,
Some once or twice since my poor mother died,
410 But *cared for*, never—that's a word for homes,
Kind homes, good homes, where simple children come
And ask their mother is this right or wrong,
Because they know she's perfect, cannot err;
Their father told them so, and he knows all,
415 Being so wise and good and wonderful,
Even enough to scold even her at times
And tell her everything she does not know.
Ah the sweet nursery logic!

                                        Fool! thrice fool!
Do I hanker after that too? Fancy me
420 Infallible nursery saint, live code of law!

---

[1] *first season* The London social season, when Parliament is in session and everyone of social importance is in the city.

[2] *crossgrained* Difficult to manage.

[3] *conchology* The study of sea-shells.

[4] *out* I.e., appearing in society. Young girls did not attend public social functions, so it was said that they "came out" when they became old enough to do so.

[5] *pinafore* Garment worn by little girls.

Me preaching! teaching innocence to be good!
A mother!

    Yet the baby thing that woke
And wailed an hour or two, and then was dead,
Was mine, and had he lived … why then my name
425 Would have been mother. But 'twas well he died:
I could have been no mother, I, lost then
Beyond his saving. Had he come before
And lived, come to me in the doubtful days
When shame and boldness had not grown one sense,
430 For his sake, with the courage come of him,
I might have struggled back.

    But how? But how?
His father would not then have let me go:
His time had not yet come to make an end
Of my "forever" with a hireling's fee
435 And civil light dismissal. None but him
To claim a bit of bread of if I went,
Child or no child: would he have given it me?
He! no; he had not done with me. No help,
No help, no help. Some ways can be trodden back,
440 But never our way, we who one wild day
Have given goodbye to what in our deep hearts
The lowest woman still holds best in life,
Good name—good name though given by the world
That mouths and garbles with its decent prate,[1]
445 And wraps it in respectable grave shams,
And patches conscience partly by the rule
Of what one's neighbour thinks, but something more
By what his eyes are sharp enough to see.
How I could scorn it with its Pharisees,[2]
450 If it could not scorn me: but yet, but yet—
Oh God, if I could look it in the face!

    Oh I am wild, am ill, I think, tonight:
Will no one come and laugh with me? No feast,
No merriment tonight. So long alone!
455 Will no one come?

    At least there's a new dress
To try, and grumble at—they never fit
To one's ideal. Yes, a new rich dress,
With lace like this too, that's a soothing balm
For any fretting woman, cannot fail;
460 I've heard men say it … and they know so well
What's in all women's hearts, especially
Women like me.

    No help! no help! no help!
How could it be? It was too late long since—
Even at the first too late. Whose blame is that?
465 There are some kindly people in the world,
But what can *they* do? If one hurls oneself
Into a quicksand, what can be the end,
But that one sinks and sinks? Cry out for help?
Ah yes, and, if it came, who is so strong
470 To strain from the firm ground and lift one out?
And how, so firmly clutching the stretched hand
As death's pursuing terror bids, even so,
How can one reach firm land, having to foot
The treacherous crumbling soil that slides and gives
475 And sucks one in again? Impossible path!
No, why waste struggles, I or anyone?
What is must be. What then? I where I am,
Sinking and sinking; let the wise pass by
And keep their wisdom for an apter use,
480 Let me sink merrily as I best may.

    Only, I think my brother—I forgot;
He stopped his brotherhood some years ago—
But if he had been just so much less good
As to remember mercy. Did he think
485 How once I was his sister, prizing him
As sisters do, content to learn for him
The lesson girls with brothers all must learn,
To do without?

    I have heard girls lament
That doing so without all things one would,
490 But I saw never aught to murmur at,
For men must be made ready for their work
And women all have more or less their chance

---

1 *prate* Lengthy and empty talk.

2 *Pharisees* I.e., hypocrites.

Of husbands to work for them, keep them safe
Like summer roses in soft greenhouse air
That never guess 'tis winter out of doors:
No, I saw never aught to murmur at,
Content with stinted fare and shabby clothes
And cloistered silent life to save expense,
Teaching myself out of my borrowed books,
While he for some one pastime (needful, true,
To keep him of his rank; 'twas not his fault)
Spent in a month what could have given me
My teachers for a year.

        'Twas no one's fault:
For could he be launched forth on the rude sea
Of this contentious world and left to find
Oars and the boatman's skill by some good chance?
'Twas no one's fault: yet still he might have thought
Of our so different youths and owned at least
'Tis pitiful when a mere nerveless girl
Untutored must put forth upon that sea,
Not in the woman's true place, the wife's place,
To trust a husband and be borne along,
But impotent blind pilot to herself.

        Merciless, merciless—like the prudent world
That will not have the flawed soul prank[1] itself
With a hoped second virtue, will not have
The woman fallen once lift up herself ...
Lest she should fall again. Oh how his taunts,
His loathing fierce reproaches, scarred and seared
Like branding iron hissing in a wound!
And it was true—*that* killed me: and I felt
A hideous hopeless shame burn out my heart,
And knew myself forever that he said,
That which I was—Oh it was true, true, true.

        No, not true then. I was not all that then.
Oh, I have drifted on before mad winds
And made ignoble shipwreck; not today
Could any breeze of heaven prosper me
Into the track again, nor any hand
Snatch me out of the whirlpool I have reached;

5
10
15
20
25
530

---

[1] *prank* Dress up, adorn.

But then?

        Nay, he judged very well: he knew
Repentance was too dear a luxury
For a beggar's buying, knew it earns no bread—
And knew me a too base and nerveless thing
To bear my first fault's sequel and just die.
And how could he have helped me? Held my hand,
Owned me for his, fronted the angry world
Clothed with my ignominy? Or maybe
Taken me to his home to damn him worse?
What did I look for? for what less would serve
That he could do, a man without a purse?
He meant me well, he sent me that five pounds,
Much to him then; and, if he bade me work
And never vex him more with news of me,
We both knew him too poor for pensioners.
I see he did his best; I could wish now
Sending it back I had professed some thanks.

        But there! I was too wretched to be meek:
It seemed to me as if he, everyone,
The whole great world, were guilty of my guilt,
Abettors and avengers: in my heart
I gibed° them back their gibings; I was wild.   *mocked*

        I see clear now and know one has one's life
In hand at first to spend or spare or give
Like any other coin; spend it, or give,
Or drop it in the mire, can the world see
You get your value for it, or bar off
The hurrying of its marts to grope it up
And give it back to you for better use?
And if you spend or give, that is your choice;
And if you let it slip, that's your choice too,
You should have held it firmer. Yours the blame,
And not another's, not the indifferent world's
Which goes on steadily, statistically,
And count by censuses not separate souls—
And if it somehow needs to its worst use
So many lives of women, useless else,
It buys us of ourselves; we could hold back,
Free all of us to starve, and some of us,

535
540
545
550
555
560
565

570 (Those who have done no ill, and are in luck)
To slave their lives out and have food and clothes
Until they grow unserviceably old.

Oh, I blame no one—scarcely even myself.
It was to be: the very good in me
575 Has always turned to hurt; all I thought right
At the hot moment, judged of afterwards,
Shows reckless.

Why, look at it, had I taken
The pay my dead child's father offered me
For having been its mother, I could then
580 Have kept life in me—many have to do it,
That swarm in the back alleys, on no more,
Cold sometimes, mostly hungry, but they live—
I could have gained a respite trying it,
And maybe found at last some humble work
585 To eke the pittance out. Not I, forsooth,
I must have spirit, must have womanly pride,
Must dash back his contemptuous wages, I
Who had not scorned to earn them, dash them back
The fiercer that he dared to count our boy
590 In my appraising: and yet now I think
I might have taken it for my dead boy's sake;
It would have been *his* gift.

But I went forth
With my fine scorn, and whither did it lead?
Money's the root of evil do they say?
595 Money is virtue, strength: money to me
Would then have been repentance: could I live
Upon my idiot's pride?

Well, it fell soon.
I had prayed Clement might believe me dead,
And yet I begged of him—That's like me too,
600 Beg of him and then send him back his alms![1]
What if he gave as to a whining wretch
That holds her hand and lies? I am less to him

Than such a one; her rags do him no wrong,
But I, I wrong him merely that I live,
605 Being his sister. Could I not at least
Have still let him forget me? But 'tis past:
And naturally he may hope I am long dead.

Good God! to think that we were what we were
One to the other ... and now!

He has done well;
610 Married a sort of heiress, I have heard,
A dapper little madam dimple cheeked
And dimple brained, who makes him a good wife—
No doubt she'd never own but just to him,
And in a whisper, she can even suspect
615 That we exist, we other women things:
What would she say if she could learn one day
She has a sister-in-law? So he and I
Must stand apart till doomsday.

But the jest,
To think how she would look! Her fright, poor thing!
620 The notion! I could laugh outright ... or else,
For I feel near it, roll on the ground and sob.

Well, after all, there's not much difference
Between the two sometimes.

Was that the bell?
Someone at last, thank goodness. There's a voice,
625 And that's a pleasure. Whose though? Ah, I know.
Why did she come alone, the cackling goose?
Why not have brought her sister? She tells more
And titters less. No matter; half a loaf
Is better than no bread.

Oh, is it you?
630 Most welcome, dear: one gets so moped alone.
—1870, 1893

---

[1] *alms* Money given as charity.

By the Looking-Glass

Alone at last in my room—
    How sick I grow of the glitter and din,
Of the lips that smile and the voices that prate
To a ballroom tune for the fashion's sake:
5   Light and laughters without, but what within?
Are these like me? Do the pleasure and state
Weary them under the seeming they make?
But I see all through my gloom.

For why should a light young heart
10 Not leap to a merry moving air,
Not laugh with the joy of the flying hour
And feed upon pleasure just for a while?
But the right of a woman is being fair,
And her heart must starve if she miss that
    dower,°   *endowment*
15 For how should she purchase the look and the smile?
And I have not had my part.

A girl, and so plain a face!
Once more, as I learn by heart every line
In the pitiless mirror, night by night,
20 Let me try to think it is not my own.
Come, stranger with features something like mine,
Let me place close by you the tell-tale light;
Can I find in you now some charm unknown,
Only one softening grace?

25 Alas! it is I, I, I,
Ungainly, common. The other night
I heard one say "Why, she is not so plain.
See, the mouth is shapely, the nose not ill."
If I could but believe his judgement right!
30 But I try to dupe my eyesight in vain,
For I, who have partly a painter's skill,
I cannot put knowledge by.

He had not fed, as I feed
On beauty, till beauty itself must seem
35 Me, my own, a part and essence of me,
My right and my being—Why! how am I plain?

I feel as if this were almost a dream
From which I should waken, as it might be,
And open my eyes on beauty again
40 And know it myself indeed.

Oh idle! oh folly! look,
There, looking back from the glass, is my fate,
A clumsy creature smelling of earth,
What fancy could lend her the angel's wings?
45 She looks like a boorish peasant's fit mate.
Why! what a mock at the pride of birth,
Fashioned by nature for menial things,
With her name in the red-bound book.[1]

Oh! to forget me a while,
50 Feeling myself but as one in the throng,
Losing myself in the joy of my youth!
Then surely some pleasure might lie in my reach.
But the sense of myself is ever strong,
And I read in all eyes the bitter truth,
55 And I fancy scorning in every speech
And mocking in every smile.

Ah! yes, it was so tonight,
And I moved so heavily through the dance,
And answered uncouthly like one ill taught,
60 And knew that ungentleness seemed on my brow,
While it was but pain at each meeting glance,
For I knew that all who looked at me thought
"How ugly she is! one sees it more now
With the other young faces so bright."

65 I might be more like the rest,
Like those that laugh with a girlish grace
And make bright nothings an eloquence;
I might seem gentler and softer souled;
But I needs must shape myself to my place,
70 Softness in me would seem clumsy pretence,
Would they not deem my laughters bold?
I hide in myself as is best.

---

[1] *red-bound book* *Burke's Peerage*, a book listing the nobility and their
genealogy, history, titles, etc.

Do I grow bitter sometimes?
They say it, ah me! and I fear it is true,
75 And I shrink from that curse of bitterness,
And I pray on my knees that it may not come;
But how should I envy—they say that I do—
All the love which others' young lives may bless?
Because *my* age will be lone in its home
80 Do I weep at the wedding chimes?

Ah no, for they judge me ill,
Judging me doubtless by that which I look,
Do I not joy for another's delight?
Do I not grieve for another's regret?
85 And I have been true where others forsook
And kind where others bore hatred and spite,
For there I could think myself welcome—and yet
My care is unpitied still.

Yes, who can think it such pain
90 Not to be fair "Such a trifling thing."
And "Goodness may be where beauty is not"
And "How weak to sorrow for outward show!"
Ah! if they knew what a poisonful sting
Has this sense of shame, how a woman's lot
95 Is darkened throughout! Oh yes I know
How weak—but I know in vain.

I hoped in vain, for I thought,
When first I grew to a woman's days,
Woman enough to feel what it means
100 To be a woman and not be fair,
That I need not sigh for the voice of praise
And the beauty's triumph in courtly scenes
Where she queens with her maiden-royal air,
Ah! and so worshipped and sought.

105 But I, oh my dreaming! deemed
With a woman's yearning and faith in love,
With a woman's faith in her lovingness,
That that joy might brighten on me, even me,
For which all the force of my nature strove,
110 Joy of daily smiles and voices that bless,

And one deeper other love it might be—
Hush, *that* was wrong to have dreamed.

I thank God, I have not loved,
Loved as one says it whose life has gone out
115 Into another's for evermore,
Loved as I know what love might be
Writhing but living through poison of doubt,
Drinking the gall of the sweetness before,
Drinking strange deep strength from the bitter lee[1]—
120 Love, love in a falsehood proved!

Loving him on to the end,
Through the weary weeping hours of the night,
Through the wearier laughing hours of the day;
Knowing him less than the love I gave,
125 But this one fond dream left my life for its light
To do him some service and pass away;
Not daring, for sin, to think of the grave
Lest it seemed the only friend.

Thank God that it was not so,
130 And I have my scatheless° maidenly pride,   unharmed
But it might have been—for did he not speak
With that slow sweet cadence that seemed made deep
By a meaning—Hush! he has chosen his bride.
Oh! happy smile on her lips and her cheek,
135 My darling! And I have no cause to weep,
I have not bowed me so low.

But would he have wooed in vain?
Would not my heart have leaped to his will,
If he had not changed?—How, *changed* do I say?
140 Was I not mocked with an idle thought,
Dreaming and dreaming so foolishly still?
By the sweet glad smile and the winning way
And the grace of beauty alone is love bought.
He woo me! Am I not plain?

145 But yet I was not alone
To fancy I might be something to him.

---

[1] *lee* Dregs.

They thought it, I know, though it seems so wild
Now, in this bitterer Now's hard light.
Vain that I was! could his sight grow dim?
50 How could he love me? But she, when she smiled
Once, the first once, by her beauty's right
Had made all his soul her own.

It is well that no busy tongue
Has vexed her heart with those bygone tales.
55 But I think he fears he did me some wrong,
I see him watch me at times, and his cheek
Crimsons a little, a little pales,
If his eye meets mine for a moment long.
But he need not fear, I am not so weak
60 Though I *am* a woman and young.

I had not grown to my love,
Though it might have been. And I give no blame:
Nothing was spoken to bind him to me,
Nothing had been that could make him think
65 My heart beat stronger and fast when he came.
And if he *had* loved me; was he not free,
When the fancy passed, to loose that vague link
That only such fancy wove?

No he has done no such ill
170 But that I can bear it, nor shame in my heart
To call him my brother and see her his,
The one little pearl that gleams through our gloom:
He has no dishonour to bar them apart.
I loving her so, am rested in this;
175 Else I would speak though I spoke her doom,
Though grief had the power to kill.

When she came a while ago,
My young fair sister bright with her bloom,
Back to a home which is little glad,
180 I thought "Here is one who should know no care,
A little wild bird flown into a room
From its far free woods; will she droop and grow sad?
But, here even, love smiles upon one so fair.
And I too might feel that glow."

185 But now she will fly away!
Ah me! and I love her so deep in my heart
And worship her beauty as he might do.
If I could but have kept her a little time!
Ah she will go! So the sunbeams depart
190 That brightened the winter's sky into blue,
And the dews of the chill dusk freeze into
    rime,°   *hoar-frost*
And cold cold mists hang grey.

I think she loved me till now—
Nay doubtless she loves me quietly yet,
195 But his lightest fancy is more, far more,
To her than all the love that I live.
But I cannot blame (as if love were a debt)
That, though I love, he is held far before;
And is it not well that a bride should give
200 All, all her heart with her vow?

But ah, if I smiled more sweet
And spoke more soft as one fairer could,
Had not love indeed been more surely mine?
Folly to say that a woman's grace
205 Is only strong o'er a man's light mood!
Even the hearts of the nearest incline
With a gentler thought to the lovely face,
And the winning eyes that entreat.

But I—yes flicker pale light,
210 Fade into darkness and hide it away,
The poor dull face that looks out from the glass,
Oh wearily wearily back to me!
Yes, I will sleep, for my wild thoughts stray
Weakly, selfishly—yes let them pass,
215 Let self and this sadness of self leave me free,
Lost in the peace of the night.
        —1866

The Happiest Girl in the World

A week ago; only a little week:
  It seems so much much longer, though that day
Is every morning still my yesterday;
As all my life 'twill be my yesterday,
For all my life is morrow to my love.   5
Oh fortunate morrow! Oh sweet happy love!

A week ago; and I am almost glad
To have him now gone for this little while,
That I may think of him and tell myself
What to be his means, now that I am his,   10
And know if mine is love enough for him,
And make myself believe it all is true.

A week ago; and it seems like a life,
And I have not yet learned to know myself:
I am so other than I was, so strange,   15
Grown younger and grown older all in one;
And I am not so sad and not so gay;
And I think nothing, only hear him think.

That morning, waking, I remembered him,
"Will he be here today? he often comes—   20
And is it for my sake or to kill time?"
And, wondering "Will he come?" I chose the dress
He seemed to like the best, and hoped for him;
And did not think I could quite love him yet.
And did I love him then with all my heart?   25
Or did I wait until he held my hands
And spoke "Say, shall it be?" and kissed my brow,
And I looked at him and he knew it all?

And did I love him from the day we met?
But I more gladly danced with someone else   30
Who waltzed more smoothly and was merrier:
And did I love him when he first came here?
But I more gladly talked with someone else
Whose words were readier and who sought me more.
When did I love him? How did it begin?   35

The small green spikes of snowdrops in the spring
Are there one morning ere you think of them;
Still we may tell what morning they pierced up:
June rosebuds stir and open stealthily,
And every new-blown rose is a surprise;   40
Still we can date the day when one unclosed:
But how can I tell when my love began?

Oh, was it like the young pale twilight star
That quietly breaks on the vacant sky,
Is sudden there and perfect while you watch,   45
And though you watch you have not seen it dawn,
The star that only waited and awoke?

But he knows when he loved me; for he says
The first time we had met he told a friend
"The sweetest dewy daisy of a girl,   50
But not the solid stuff to make a wife";
And afterwards, the first time he was here,
When I had slipped away into our field
To watch alone for sunset brightening on
And heard them calling me, he says he stood   55
And saw me come along the coppice walk
Beneath the green and sparkling arch of boughs,
And, while he watched the yellow lights that played
With the dim flickering shadows of the leaves
Over my yellow hair and soft pale dress,   60
Flitting across me as I flitted through,
He whispered inly, in so many words,
"I see my wife; this is my wife who comes,
And seems to bear the sunlight on with her":
And that was when he loved me, so he says.   65

Yet is he quite sure? was it only then?
And had he had no thought which I could feel?
For why was it I knew that he would watch,
And all the while thought in my silly heart,
As I advanced demurely, it was well   70
I had on the pale dress with sweeping folds
Which took the light and shadow tenderly,
And that the sunlights touched my hair and cheek,
Because he'd note it all and care for it?

85 Oh vain and idle poor girl's heart of mine,
Content with that coquettish mean content!
He, with his man's straight purpose, thinking "wife,"
And I but that 'twas pleasant to be fair
And that 'twas pleasant he should count me fair.
90 But oh to think he should be loving me
And I be no more moved out of myself!
The sunbeams told him, but they told me naught,
Except that maybe I was looking well.
And oh had I but known! Why did no bird,
95 Trilling its own sweet lovesong as I passed,
So musically marvellously glad,
Sing one for me too, sing me "It is he,"
Sing "Love him," and "You love him: it is he,"
That I might then have loved him when he loved,
100 That one dear moment might be date to both?

And must I not be glad he hid his thought
And did not tell me then, when it was soon
And I should have been startled and not known
How he is just the one man I can love,
105 And only with some pain lest he were pained,
And nothing doubting, should have answered "No."
How strange life is! I should have answered "No."
Oh can I ever be half glad enough
He is so wise and patient and could wait!

100 He waited as you wait the reddening fruit
Which helplessly is ripening on the tree,
And not because it tries or longs or wills,
Only because the sun will shine on it:
But he who waited was himself that sun.

105 Oh, was it worth the waiting? was it worth?
For I am half afraid love is not love,
This love which only makes me rest in him
And be so happy and so confident,
This love which makes me pray for longest days
110 That I may have them all to use for him,
This love which almost makes me yearn for pain
That I might have borne something for his sake,
This love which I call love, is less than love.
Where are the fires and fevers and the pangs?

115 Where is the anguish of too much delight,
And the delirious madness at a kiss,
The flushing and the paling at a look,
And passionate ecstasy of meeting hands?
Where is the eager weariness at time
120 That will not bate a single measured hour
To speed to us the far-off wedding-day?
I am so calm and wondering, like a child
Who, led by a firm hand it knows and trusts
Along a stranger country beautiful
125 With a bewildering beauty to new eyes
If they be wise to know what they behold,
Finds newness everywhere but no surprise,
And takes the beauty as an outward part
Of being led so kindly by the hand.
130 I am so cold: is mine but a child's heart,
And not a woman's fit for such a man?
Alas am I too cold, am I too dull,
Can I not love him as another could?
And oh, if love be fire, what love is mine
135 That is but like the pale subservient moon
Who only asks to be earth's minister?
And oh, if love be whirlwind, what is mine
That is but like a little even brook
Which has no aim but flowing to the sea,
140 And sings for happiness because it flows?

Ah well, I would that I could love him more
And not be only happy as I am;
I would that I could love him to his worth,
With that forgetting all myself in him,
145 That subtle pain of exquisite excess,
That momentary infinite sharp joy,
I know by books but cannot teach my heart:
And yet I think my love must needs be love,
Since he can read me through—oh happy strange,
150 My thoughts that were my secrets all for me
Grown instantly his open easy book!—
Since he can read me through and is content.

And yesterday, when they all went away,
Save little Amy with her daisy chains,
155 And left us in that shadow of tall ferns,

And the child, leaning on me, fell asleep,
And I, tired by the afternoon long walk,
Said "I could almost gladly sleep like her,"
Did he not answer, drawing down my head,
160 "Sleep, darling, let me see you rest on me,"
And when the child awaking wakened me,
Did he not say "Dear, you have made me glad,
For, seeing you so sleeping in your peace,
I feel that you do love me utterly;
165 No questionings, no regrettings, but at rest."

    Oh yes, my good true darling, you said well
"No questionings, no regrettings, but at rest":
What should I question, what should I regret,
Now I have you who are my hope and rest?
170 I am the feathery wind-wafted seed
That flickered idly half a merry morn,
Now thralled° into the rich life-giving earth   *bound*
To root and bud and waken into leaf
And make it such poor sweetness as I may;
175 The prisoned seed that never more shall float
The frolic playfellow of summer winds
And mimic the free changeful butterfly;
The prisoned seed that prisoned finds its life
And feels its pulses stir and grows and grows.
180 Oh love who gathered me into yourself,
Oh love, I am at rest in you, and live.

    And shall I for so many coming days
Be flower and sweetness to him? Oh pale flower,
Grow, grow, and blossom out and fill the air,
185 Feed on his richness, grow, grow, blossom out
And fill the air, and be enough for him.

    Oh crystal music of the air-borne lark,
So falling, nearer, nearer, from the sky,
Are you a message to me of dear hopes?
190 Oh trilling gladness flying down to earth,
Have you brought answer of sweet prophecy?
Have you brought answer to the thoughts in me?
Oh happy answer, and oh happy thoughts!
And which is the bird's carol, which my heart's?

195 My love, my love, my love! And I shall be
So much to him, so almost everything:
And I shall be the friend whom he will trust,
And I shall be the child whom he will teach,
And I shall be the servant he will praise,
200 And I shall be the mistress he will love,
And I shall be his wife. Oh days to come,
Will ye not pass like gentle rhythmic steps
That fall to sweetest music noiselessly?

    But I have known the lark's song half sound sad,
205 And I have seen the lake which rippled sun
Toss dimmed and purple in a sudden wind;
And let me laugh a moment at my heart
That thinks the summer-time must all be fair,
That thinks the good days always must be good:
210 Yes, let me laugh a moment—maybe weep.

    But no, but no, not laugh; for through my joy
I have been wise enough to know the while
Some tears and some long hours are in all lives,
In every promised land some thorn-plants grow,
215 Some tangling weeds as well as laden vines:
And no, not weep; for is not my land fair,
My land of promise flushed with fruit and bloom?
And who would weep for fear of scattered thorns?
And very thorns bear oftentimes sweet fruits.

220   Oh, the black storm that breaks across the lake
Ruffles the surface, leaves the deeps at rest—
Deep in our hearts there always will be rest;
Oh, summer storms fall sudden as they rose,
The peaceful lake forgets them while they die—
225 Our hearts will always have it summer-time.

    All rest, all summer-time. My love, my love,
I know it will be so; you are so good,
And I near you shall grow at last like you;
And you are tender, patient—oh I know
230 You will bear with me, help me, smile to me,
And let me make you happy easily;
And I, what happiness could I have more
Than that dear labour of a happy wife?

I would not have another. Is it wrong
35 And is it selfish that I cannot wish,
That I who yet so love the clasping hand
And innocent fond eyes of little ones,
I cannot wish that which I sometimes read
Is women's dearest wish hid in their love,
40 To press a baby creature to my breast?
Oh is it wrong? I would be all for him,
Not even children coming 'twixt us two
To call me from his service, to serve them;
And maybe they would steal too much of love,
45 For, since I cannot love him now enough,
What would my heart be halved? Or would it grow?
But he perhaps would love me something less,
Finding me not so always at his side.

       Together always, that was what he said;
250 Together always. Oh dear coming days!

Oh dear dear present days that pass too fast,
Although they bring such rainbow morrows on!
That pass so fast, and yet, I know not why,
Seem always to encompass so much time.
255 And I should fear I were too happy now,
And making this poor world too much my Heaven,
But that I feel God nearer and it seems
As if I had learned His love better too.

       So late already! The sun dropping down,
260 And under him the first long line of red—
My truant should be here again by now,
Is come maybe. I will not seek him, I;
He would be vain and think I cared too much;
I will wait here, and he shall seek for me,
265 And I will carelessly—Oh, his dear step—
He sees me, he is coming; my own love!
—1870

ALGERNON CHARLES SWINBURNE
<u>1837 – 1909</u>

Victorian poet and critic Algernon Swinburne was physically slight, but he had a powerful personality, and he left behind a vast literary output. Much of his writing, however, on topics such as incest, cannibalism, sadomasochism, and necrophilia, was too outrageous for "respectable" Victorian tastes. Although he was born into a distinguished family of British aristocracy, Swinburne's opinions on politics, religion, and sexuality were offensive enough to have earned him the nickname "Swineborn" in *Punch* magazine. Swinburne's poetry, however, was also metrically innovative, musical, and often erudite. Oscar Wilde claimed him as his literary master but said of Swinburne's writing, "Words seem to dominate him. Alliteration tyrannizes over him. Mere sound often becomes his lord. He is so eloquent that whatever he touches becomes unreal." This "diffuseness" was, according to T.S. Eliot, one of his "glories." Although few have disputed the musicality of Swinburne's poetry, some critics have accused him of being vague and soporific.

Algernon Swinburne was born in 1837 into a highly respectable aristocratic family. His father, Admiral Charles Henry Swinburne, was the son of a baronet, and his mother, Lady Jane, was the daughter of an earl. Raised a devout Anglo-Catholic, Swinburne read profusely and acquired an intimate knowledge of the Bible, as well as a proficiency in French and Italian. His early years at Eton, however, were troubled ones; as a result of disciplinary problems, he was removed from the school before he graduated. After private tutoring, he entered Balliol College at Oxford in 1856. During his first two years there, Swinburne excelled in the Classics and won a scholarship for French and Italian; his unruliness got the better of him again, and he was forced to leave Balliol without a degree. He nevertheless made many important friends at Oxford, including Benjamin Jowett (then master of Balliol) and the Pre-Raphaelites Edward Burne-Jones, William Morris, and Dante Gabriel Rossetti (with whom he lived in London after Rossetti's wife, Elizabeth Siddal, died).

In London during the 1860s, Swinburne gained notoriety for his wild, drunken revelries and experiments with flagellation, as much as for the publication of two important works, *Atalanta in Calydon* (1865) and *Poems and Ballads* (1866). The classical Greek tragic form of the verse-play *Atalanta* and its concentration on fate and divine intervention belied the long poem's modern revolt against religious institutions and its sympathy, instead, with the "holy spirit of man." While Victorians might have been expected to rail against Swinburne's chastisement of religious orthodoxy, the lyrical and mellifluous tragedy held many in its sway, and won accolades from reviewers. John Ruskin said that it was the "grandest thing ever done by a youth—though he is a Demoniac youth," and Tennyson wrote to Swinburne praising the metrical creativity of *Atalanta*.

Poems and Ballads, on the other hand, had the public (Ruskin included) up in arms. In such poems as "The Triumph of Time," "Dolores," "The Leper," "Hymn to Proserpine," and "Laus

Veneris," Swinburne explored themes of sexual perversion, paganism, and moral and spiritual decay. One reviewer said the author was an "unclean, fiery imp from the pit," while another, referring to Swinburne's association with the Aesthetes, called him the "libidinous laureate of a pack of satyrs." Amid this outcry, the publishing house withdrew the book from publication, angering Swinburne and prompting his eloquent riposte in *Notes on Poems and Reviews*. *Poems and Ballads* was re-released shortly afterward by another publisher.

Swinburne's notoriety continued into the late 1860s and 1870s, as he cultivated his image as a "scandalous poet," to use his own words. He wrote at a feverish rate—even though his alcoholism was by then prompting seizures and blackouts—and produced such works as *A Song of Italy* (1867), a defense of Italian liberation; *Ave Atque Vale* (1868), an elegy to Baudelaire; the brilliant essay *William Blake* (1868); and *Songs before Sunrise* (1871), which continued the theme of spiritual and political revolution. By the end of the 1870s, however, Swinburne was near death, his nerves destroyed by alcohol, and his body depleted from overwork. Luckily, in 1879, his friend Theodore Watts-Dunton took him to his house in Putney and helped nurse him back to health. There Swinburne lived in quiet solitude for the remaining 30 years of his life, writing and publishing prolifically, and finally succumbing to pneumonia in 1909.

In those final decades, Swinburne won the respect of many Victorians. Although the *Guardian* noted upon his death that his verse could be "careless, trivial, or inharmonious," the newspaper also acknowledged that "the greatest poet lately living is dead … and we cannot doubt that much of his poetry will live by virtue of its exquisite music."

⌘ ⌘ ⌘

The Triumph of Time

Before our lives divide forever,
  While time is with us and hands are free
(Time, swift to fasten and swift to sever
  Hand from hand, as we stand by the sea),
5 I will say no word that a man might say
Whose whole life's love goes down in a day;
For this could never have been; and never,
  Though the gods and the years relent, shall be.

Is it worth a tear, is it worth an hour
10   To think of things that are well outworn?
Of fruitless husk and fugitive flower,
  The dream foregone and the deed forborne?
Though joy be done with and grief be vain,
Time shall not sever us wholly in twain;°   *two*
15 Earth is not spoilt for a single shower;
  But the rain has ruined the ungrown corn.°   *grain*

It will grow not again, this fruit of my heart,
  Smitten with sunbeams, ruined with rain.
The singing seasons divide and depart,
20   Winter and summer depart in twain.
It will grow not again, it is ruined at root,
The bloodlike blossom, the dull red fruit;
Though the heart yet sickens, the lips yet smart,
  With sullen savour of poisonous pain.

25 I have given no man of my fruit to eat;
  I trod the grapes, I have drunken the wine.
Had you eaten and drunken and found it sweet,
  This wild new growth of the corn and vine,
This wine and bread without lees° or leaven,   *sediment*
30 We had grown as gods, as the gods in heaven,
Souls fair to look upon, goodly to greet,
  One splendid spirit, your soul and mine.

In the change of years, in the coil of things,
   In the clamour and rumour of life to be,
35 We, drinking love at the furthest springs,
   Covered with love as a covering tree,
We had grown as gods, as the gods above,
Filled from the heart to the lips with love,
Held fast in his hands, clothed warm with his wings,
40   O love, my love, had you loved but me!

We had stood as the sure stars stand, and moved
   As the moon moves, loving the world; and seen
Grief collapse as a thing disproved,
   Death consume as a thing unclean.
45 Twain halves of a perfect heart, made fast
Soul to soul while the years fell past;
Had you loved me once, as you have not loved;
   Had the chance been with us that has not been.

I have put my days and dreams out of mind,
50   Days that are over, dreams that are done.
Though we seek life through, we shall surely find
   There is none of them clear to us now, not one.
But clear are these things; the grass and the sand,
Where, sure as the eyes reach, ever at hand,
55 With lips wide open and face burnt blind,
   The strong sea-daisies feast on the sun.

The low downs lean to the sea; the stream,
   One loose thin pulseless tremulous vein,
Rapid and vivid and dumb° as a dream,   *silent*
60   Works downward, sick of the sun and the rain;
No wind is rough with the rank° rare flowers;   *lush*
The sweet sea, mother of loves and hours,
Shudders and shines as the grey winds gleam,
   Turning her smile to a fugitive pain.

65 Mother of loves that are swift to fade,
   Mother of mutable winds and hours.
A barren mother, a mother-maid,
   Cold and clean as her faint salt flowers.
I would we twain were even as she,
70 Lost in the night and the light of the sea,

Where faint sounds falter and wan beams wade,
   Break, and are broken, and shed into showers.

The loves and hours of the life of a man,
   They are swift and sad, being born of the sea,
75 Hours that rejoice and regret for a span,
   Born with a man's breath, mortal as he;
Loves that are lost ere they come to birth,
Weeds of the wave, without fruit upon earth.
I lose what I long for, save what I can,
80   My love, my love, and no love for me!

It is not much that a man can save
   On the sands of life, in the straits of time,
Who swims in sight of the great third wave
   That never a swimmer shall cross or climb.
85 Some waif washed up with the strays and spars[1]
That ebb-tide shows to the shore and the stars;
Weed from the water, grass from a grave,
   A broken blossom, a ruined rhyme.

There will no man do for your sake, I think,
90   What I would have done for the least word said.
I had wrung life dry for your lips to drink,
   Broken it up for your daily bread:
Body for body and blood for blood,
As the flow of the full sea risen to flood
95 That yearns and trembles before it sink,
   I had given, and lain down for you, glad and dead.

Yea, hope at highest and all her fruit,
   And time at fullest and all his dower,
I had given you surely, and life to boot,
100   Were we once made one for a single hour.
But now, you are twain, you are cloven apart,
Flesh of his flesh, but heart of my heart;
And deep in one is the bitter root,
   And sweet for one is the lifelong flower.

105 To have died if you cared I should die for you, clung
   To my life if you bade me, played my part

---

[1] *spars* Pieces of wood.

As it pleased you—these were the thoughts that stung,
    The dreams that smote with a keener dart
Than shafts of love or arrows of death;
110 These were but as fire is, dust, or breath,
Or poisonous foam on the tender tongue
    Of the little snakes that eat my heart.

I wish we were dead together today,
    Lost sight of, hidden away out of sight,
115 Clasped and clothed in the cloven clay,
    Out of the world's way, out of the light,
Out of the ages of worldly weather,
Forgotten of all men altogether,
As the world's first dead, taken wholly away,
120   Made one with death, filled full of the night.

How we should slumber, how we should sleep,
    Far in the dark with the dreams and the dews
And dreaming, grow to each other, and weep,
    Laugh low, live softly, murmur and muse;
125 Yea, and it may be, struck through by the dream,
Feel the dust quicken[1] and quiver, and seem
Alive as of old to the lips, and leap
    Spirit to spirit as lovers use.

Sick dreams and sad of a dull delight;
130   For what shall it profit when men are dead
To have dreamed, to have loved with the whole soul's
        might,
    To have looked for day when the day was fled?
Let come what will, there is one thing worth,
To have had fair love in the life upon earth:
135 To have held love safe till the day grew night,
    While skies had colour and lips were red.

Would I lose you now? would I take you then,
    If I lose you now that my heart has need?
And come what may after death to men,
140   What thing worth this will the dead years breed?
Lose life, lose all; but at least I know,
O sweet life's love, having loved you so,

Had I reached you on earth, I should lose not again,
    In death nor life, nor in dream or deed.

145 Yea, I know this well: were you once sealed mine,
    Mine in the blood's beat, mine in the breath,
Mixed into me as honey in wine,
    Not time, that sayeth and gainsayeth,°   *contradicts*
Nor all strong things had severed us then;
150 Not wrath of gods, nor wisdom of men,
Nor all things earthly, nor all divine,
    Nor joy nor sorrow, nor life nor death.

I had grown pure as the dawn and the dew,
    You had grown strong as the sun or the sea,
155 But none shall triumph a whole life through:
    For death is one, and the fates are three.
At the door of life, by the gate of breath,
There are worse things waiting for men than death;
Death could not sever my soul and you,
160   As these have severed your soul from me.

You have chosen and clung to the chance they sent you,
    Life sweet as perfume and pure as prayer.
But will it not one day in heaven repent you?[2]
    Will they solace you wholly, the days that were?
165 Will you lift up your eyes between sadness and bliss,
Meet mine, and see where the great love is,
And tremble and turn and be changed? Content you;
    The gate is strait;° I shall not be there.   *narrow*

But you, had you chosen, had you stretched hand,
170   Had you seen good such a thing were done,
I too might have stood with the souls that stand
    In the sun's sight, clothed with the light of the sun;
But who now on earth need care how I live?
Have the high gods anything left to give,
175 Save dust and laurels[3] and gold and sand?
    Which gifts are goodly; but I will none.

---

[1] *quicken* Come alive.

[2] *repent you* Cause you to repent.

[3] *laurels* Wreaths of laurel were traditionally awarded to recognize achievement, especially in poetry.

O all fair lovers about the world,
  There is none of you, none, that shall comfort me.
My thoughts are as dead things, wrecked and whirled
180 Round and round in a gulf of the sea;
And still, through the sound and the straining stream,
Through the coil and chafe, they gleam in a dream,
The bright fine lips so cruelly curled,
  And strange swift eyes where the soul sits free.

185 Free, without pity, withheld from woe,
  Ignorant; fair as the eyes are fair.
Would I have you change now, change at a blow,
  Startled and stricken, awake and aware?
Yea, if I could, would I have you see
190 My very love of you filling me,
And know my soul to the quick, as I know
  The likeness and look of your throat and hair?

I shall not change you. Nay, though I might,
  Would I change my sweet one love with a word?
195 I had rather your hair should change in a night,
  Clear now as the plume of a black bright bird;
Your face fail suddenly, cease, turn grey,
Die as a leaf that dies in a day.
I will keep my soul in a place out of sight,
200 Far off, where the pulse of it is not heard.

Far off it walks, in a bleak blown space,
  Full of the sound of the sorrow of years.
I have woven a veil for the weeping face,
  Whose lips have drunken the wine of tears;
205 I have found a way for the failing feet,
A place for slumber and sorrow to meet;
There is no rumour about the place,
  Nor light, nor any that sees or hears.

I have hidden my soul out of sight, and said
210 "Let none take pity upon thee, none
Comfort thy crying: for lo, thou art dead,
  Lie still now, safe out of sight of the sun.
Have I not built thee a grave, and wrought
Thy grave-clothes on thee of grievous thought

215 With soft spun verses and tears unshed,
  And sweet light visions of things undone?

"I have given thee garments and balm and myrrh,
  And gold, and beautiful burial things.
But thou, be at peace now, make no stir;
220 Is not thy grave as a royal king's?
Fret not thyself though the end were sore;
Sleep, be patient, vex me no more.
Sleep; what hast thou to do with her?
  The eyes that weep, with the mouth that sings?"

225 Where the dead red leaves of the years lie rotten,
  The cold old crimes and the deeds thrown by,
The misconceived and the misbegotten,
  I would find a sin to do ere I die,
Sure to dissolve and destroy me all through,
230 That would set you higher in heaven, serve you
And leave you happy, when clean forgotten,
  As a dead man out of mind, am I.

Your lithe hands draw me, your face burns through me,
  I am swift to follow you, keen to see;
235 But love lacks might to redeem or undo me;
  As I have been, I know I shall surely be;
"What should such fellows as I do?" Nay,
My part were worse if I chose to play;
For the worst is this after all; if they knew me,
240 Not a soul upon earth would pity me.

And I play not for pity of these; but you,
  If you saw with your soul what man am I,
You would praise me at least that my soul all through
  Clove° to you, loathing the lives that lie; *clung*
245 The souls and lips that are bought and sold,
The smiles of silver and kisses of gold,
The lapdog loves that whine as they chew,
  The little lovers that curse and cry.

There are fairer women, I hear; that may be;
250 But I, that I love you and find you fair,
Who are more than fair in my eyes if they be,
  Do the high gods know or the great gods care?

Though the swords in my heart for one were seven,
Would the iron hollow of doubtful heaven,
255 That knows not itself whether night-time or day be,
    Reverberate words and a foolish prayer?

I will go back to the great sweet mother,
    Mother and lover of men, the sea.
I will go down to her, I and none other,
260   Close with her, kiss her and mix her with me;
Cling to her, strive with her, hold her fast:
O fair white mother, in days long past
Born without sister, born without brother,
    Set free my soul as thy soul is free.

265 O fair green-girdled mother of mine,
    Sea, that art clothed with the sun and the rain,
Thy sweet hard kisses are strong like wine,
    Thy large embraces are keen like pain.
Save me and hide me with all thy waves,
270 Find me one grave of thy thousand graves,
Those pure cold populous graves of thine
    Wrought without hand in a world without stain.

I shall sleep, and move with the moving ships,
    Change as the winds change, veer in the tide;
275 My lips will feast on the foam of thy lips,
    I shall rise with thy rising, with thee subside;
Sleep, and not know if she be, if she were,
Filled full with life to the eyes and hair,
As a rose is fulfilled to the roseleaf tips
280   With splendid summer and perfume and pride.

This woven raiment° of nights and days,   *garment*
    Were it once cast off and unwound from me,
Naked and glad would I walk in thy ways,
    Alive and aware of thy ways and thee;
285 Clear of the whole world, hidden at home,
Clothed with the green and crowned with the foam,
A pulse of the life of thy straits and bays,
    A vein in the heart of the streams of the sea.

Fair mother, fed with the lives of men,
290   Thou art subtle and cruel of heart, men say.

Thou hast taken, and shalt not render again;
    Thou art full of thy dead, and cold as they.
But death is the worst that comes of thee;
Thou art fed with our dead, O mother, O sea,
295 But when hast thou fed on our hearts? or when,
    Having given us love, hast thou taken away?

O tender-hearted, O perfect lover,
    Thy lips are bitter, and sweet thine heart.
The hopes that hurt and the dreams that hover,
300   Shall they not vanish away and apart?
But thou, thou art sure, thou art older than earth;
Thou art strong for death and fruitful of birth;
Thy depths conceal and thy gulfs discover;
    From the first thou wert; in the end thou art.

305 And grief shall endure not forever, I know.
    As things that are not shall these things be;
We shall live through seasons of sun and of snow,
    And none be grievous as this to me.
We shall hear, as one in a trance that hears,
310 The sound of time, the rhyme of the years;
Wrecked hope and passionate pain will grow
    As tender things of a springtide sea.

Sea-fruit that swings in the waves that hiss,
    Drowned gold and purple and royal rings.
315 And all time past, was it all for this?
    Times unforgotten, and treasures of things?
Swift years of liking and sweet long laughter,
That wist° not well of the years thereafter   *know*
Till love woke, smitten at heart by a kiss,
320   With lips that trembled and trailing wings?

There lived a singer in France of old
    By the tideless dolorous midland sea.
In a land of sand and ruin and gold
    There shone one woman, and none but she.
325 And finding life for her love's sake fail,
Being fain to see her, he bade set sail,
Touched land, and saw her as life grew cold,
    And praised God, seeing; and so died he.

Died, praising God for his gift and grace:
330   For she bowed down to him weeping, and said
"Live"; and her tears were shed on his face
    Or° ever the life in his face was shed.   *before*
The sharp tears fell through her hair, and stung
Once, and her close lips touched him and clung
335 Once, and grew one with his lips for a space;
    And so drew back, and the man was dead.

O brother, the gods were good to you.
    Sleep, and be glad while the world endures.
Be well content as the years wear through;
340   Give thanks for life, and the loves and lures;
Give thanks for life, O brother, and death,
For the sweet last sound of her feet, her breath,
For gifts she gave you, gracious and few,
    Tears and kisses, that lady of yours.

345 Rest, and be glad of the gods; but I,
    How shall I praise them, or how take rest?
There is not room under all the sky
    For me that knows not of worst or best,
Dream or desire of the days before,
350 Sweet things or bitterness, any more.
Love will not come to me now though I die,
    As love came close to you, breast to breast.

I shall never be friends again with roses;
    I shall loathe sweet tunes, where a note grown strong
355 Relents and recoils, and climbs and closes,
    As a wave of the sea turned back by song.
There are sounds where the soul's delight takes fire,
    Face to face with its own desire;
A delight that rebels, a desire that reposes;
360   I shall hate sweet music my whole life long.

The pulse of war and passion of wonder,
    The heavens that murmur, the sounds that shine,
The stars that sing and the loves that thunder,
    The music burning at heart like wine,
365 An armed archangel whose hands raise up
All senses mixed in the spirit's cup
Till flesh and spirit are molten in sunder[1]—
    These things are over, and no more mine.

These were a part of the playing I heard
370   Once, ere my love and my heart were at strife:
Love that sings and hath wings as a bird,
    Balm of the wound and heft of the knife.
Fairer than earth is the sea, and sleep
Than overwatching of eyes that weep,
375 Now time has done with his one sweet word,
    The wine and leaven of lovely life.

I shall go my ways, tread out my measure,
    Fill the days of my daily breath
With fugitive things not good to treasure,
380   Do as the world doth, say as it saith;
But if we had loved each other—O sweet,
Had you felt, lying under the palms of your feet,
The heart of my heart, beating harder with pleasure
    To feel you tread it to dust and death—

385 Ah, had I not taken my life up and given
    All that life gives and the years let go,
The wine and honey, the balm and leaven,
    The dreams reared high and the hopes brought low?
Come life, come death, not a word be said;
390 Should I lose you living, and vex you dead?
I never shall tell you on earth; and in heaven,
    If I cry to you then, will you hear or know?
—1866

---

[1] *in sunder* Apart.

Itylus[1]

Swallow, my sister, O sister swallow,
   How can thine heart be full of the spring?
      A thousand summers are over and dead.
What hast thou found in the spring to follow?
5   What hast thou found in thine heart to sing?
      What wilt thou do when the summer is shed?

O swallow, sister, O fair swift swallow,
   Why wilt thou fly after spring to the south,
      The soft south whither thine heart is set?
10 Shall not the grief of the old time follow?
    Shall not the song thereof cleave[2] to thy mouth?
      Hast thou forgotten ere I forget?

Sister, my sister, O fleet sweet swallow,
   Thy way is long to the sun and the south;
15   But I, fulfilled of my heart's desire,
Shedding my song upon height, upon hollow,
   From tawny body and sweet small mouth
      Feed the heart of the night with fire.

I the nightingale all spring through,
20   O swallow, sister, O changing swallow,
      All spring through till the spring be done,
Clothed with the light of the night on the dew,
   Sing, while the hours and the wild birds follow,
      Take flight and follow and find the sun.

25 Sister, my sister, O soft light swallow,
   Though all things feast in the spring's guest chamber,
      How hast thou heart to be glad thereof yet?
For where thou fliest I shall not follow,
   Till life forget and death remember,
30   Till thou remember and I forget.

Swallow, my sister, O singing swallow,
   I know not how thou hast heart to sing.
      Hast thou the heart? is it all past over?
Thy lord the summer is good to follow,
35   And fair the feet of thy lover the spring:
      But what wilt thou say to the spring thy lover?

O swallow, sister, O fleeting swallow,
   My heart in me is a molten ember
      And over my head the waves have met.
40 But thou wouldst tarry or I would follow,
   Could I forget or thou remember,
      Couldst thou remember and I forget.

O sweet stray sister, O shifting swallow,
   The heart's division divideth us.
45   Thy heart is light as a leaf of a tree;
But mine goes forth among sea-gulfs hollow
   To the place of the slaying of Itylus,
      The feast of Daulis,[3] the Thracian sea.

O swallow, sister, O rapid swallow,
50   I pray thee sing not a little space.
      Are not the roofs and the lintels wet?
The woven web that was plain to follow,
   The small slain body, the flowerlike face,
      Can I remember if thou forget?

55 O sister, sister, thy first-begotten!
   The hands that cling and the feet that follow,
      The voice of the child's blood crying yet.
Who hath remembered me? who hath forgotten?
   Thou hast forgotten, O summer swallow,
60   But the world shall end when I forget.
—1866

---

[1] *Itylus* In Greek mythology, son of Tereus, the King of Thrace, and Procne. After Tereus raped Procne's sister Philomela and cut out her tongue to silence her, Procne murdered her son, cut up his flesh, and served him to Tereus as an act of vengeance. The gods then transformed Procne into a nightingale and Philomela into a swallow.

[2] *cleave* Adhere.

[3] *feast of Daulis* Feast at which Tereus unwittingly ate Itylus's flesh.

Hymn to Proserpine[1]

(After the Proclamation in Rome of the Christian Faith[2])

Vicisti, Galilæe[3]

I have lived long enough, having seen one thing, that
    love hath an end;
Goddess and maiden and queen, be near me now and
    befriend.
Thou art more than the day or the morrow, the
    seasons that laugh or that weep;
For these give joy and sorrow; but thou, Proserpina,
    sleep.
5 Sweet is the treading of wine, and sweet the feet of the
    dove;
But a goodlier gift is thine than foam of the grapes or
    love.
Yea, is not even Apollo,[4] with hair and harpstring of
    gold,
A bitter God to follow, a beautiful God to behold?
I am sick of singing: the bays[5] burn deep and chafe: I
    am fain
10 To rest a little from praise and grievous pleasure and
    pain.
For the Gods we know not of, who give us our daily
    breath,
We know they are cruel as love or life, and lovely as
    death.

O Gods dethroned and deceased, cast forth, wiped
    out in a day!
From your wrath is the world released, redeemed from
    your chains, men say.
15 New Gods are crowned in the city; their flowers have
    broken your rods;
They are merciful, clothed with pity, the young
    compassionate Gods.
But for me their new device is barren, the days are bare;
Things long past over suffice, and men forgotten that
    were.
Time and the Gods are at strife; ye dwell in the midst
    thereof,
20 Draining a little life from the barren breasts of love.
I say to you, cease, take rest; yea, I say to you all, be at
    peace,
Till the bitter milk of her breast and the barren bosom
    shall cease.
Wilt thou yet take all, Galilean? but these thou shalt
    not take,
The laurel, the palms and the pæan,[6] the breast of the
    nymphs in the brake;[7]
25 Breasts more soft than a dove's that tremble with
    tenderer breath;
And all the wings of the Loves,[8] and all the joy before
    death;
All the feet of the hours that sound as a single lyre,
Dropped and deep in the flowers, with strings that
    flicker like fire.
More than these wilt thou give, things fairer than all
    these things?
30 Nay, for a little we live, and life hath mutable wings.
A little while and we die; shall life not thrive as it may?
For no man under the sky lives twice, outliving his day.
And grief is a grievous thing, and a man hath enough
    of his tears:
Why should he labour, and bring fresh grief to
    blacken his years?

---

[1] *Proserpine* In Roman mythology, daughter of Jupiter and Ceres and wife of Pluto, King of the underworld, who stole her from her mother.

[2] *Proclamation ... Faith* Roman Emperor Constantine the Great legalized the Christian faith when he proclaimed the Edict of Milan in 313 CE.

[3] *Vicisti, Galilæe* Latin: "Thou hast conquered, Galilee," said to be the dying words in 363 of Julian the Apostate, half-brother of Constantine the Great. Julian eventually became emperor after the deaths of Constantine I and II; he was a pagan who opposed instituting Christianity as the state religion (as it was eventually proclaimed by Emperor Theodosius in 380).

[4] *Apollo* Greek sun god; also god of the arts.

[5] *bays* Wreaths of bay laurel were traditionally awarded to recognize achievement, especially in poetry.

[6] *palms* Symbol of victory; *pæan* Hymn of praise.

[7] *brake* Ferns.

[8] *Loves* Cupids or other gods representing sexual love.

35 Thou hast conquered, O pale Galilean; the world has
         grown grey from thy breath;
   We have drunken of things Lethean,[1] and fed on the
         fullness of death.
   Laurel is green for a season, and love is sweet for a day;
   But love grows bitter with treason, and laurel outlives
         not May.
   Sleep, shall we sleep after all? for the world is not
         sweet in the end;
40 For the old faiths loosen and fall, the new years ruin
         and rend.
   Fate is a sea without shore, and the soul is a rock that
         abides;
   But her ears are vexed with the roar and her face with
         the foam of the tides.
   O lips that the live blood faints in, the leavings of
         racks and rods!
   O ghastly glories of saints, dead limbs of gibbeted[2]
         Gods!
45 Though all men abase them before you in spirit, and
         all knees bend,
   I kneel not neither adore you, but standing, look to
         the end.
   All delicate days and pleasant, all spirits and sorrows
         are cast
   Far out with the foam of the present that sweeps to
         the surf of the past:
   Where beyond the extreme sea-wall, and between the
         remote sea-gates,
50 Waste water washes, and tall ships founder, and deep
         death waits:
   Where, mighty with deepening sides, clad about with
         the seas as with wings,
   And impelled of invisible tides, and fulfilled of
         unspeakable things,
   White-eyed and poisonous-finned, shark-toothed and
         serpentine-curled,

Rolls, under the whitening wind of the future, the
      wave of the world.
55 The depths stand naked in sunder[3] behind it, the
      storms flee away;
   In the hollow before it the thunder is taken and
      snared as a prey;
   In its sides is the north-wind bound; and its salt is of
      all men's tears;
   With light of ruin, and sound of changes, and pulse of
      years:
   With travail of day after day, and with trouble of hour
      upon hour;
60 And bitter as blood is the spray; and the crests are as
      fangs that devour:
   And its vapour and storm of its steam as the sighing of
      spirits to be;
   And its noise as the noise in a dream; and its depth as
      the roots of the sea:
   And the height of its heads as the height of the utmost
      stars of the air:
   And the ends of the earth at the might thereof
      tremble, and time is made bare.
65 Will ye bridle the deep sea with reins, will ye chasten
      the high sea with rods?
   Will ye take her to chain her with chains, who is older
      than all ye Gods?
   All ye as a wind shall go by, as a fire shall ye pass and
      be past;
   Ye are Gods, and behold, ye shall die, and the waves
      be upon you at last.
   In the darkness of time, in the deeps of the years, in
      the changes of things,
70 Ye shall sleep as a slain man sleeps, and the world shall
      forget you for kings.
   Though the feet of thine high priests tread where thy
      lords and our forefathers trod,
   Though these that were Gods are dead, and thou
      being dead art a God,

---

[1] *Lethean* Of the Greek mythological river Lethe in Hades (the underworld), the waters of which cause the dead to forget the past; also called the "River of Oblivion."

[2] *gibbeted* Hung on a gibbet, a device used to display the bodies of executed people.

---

[3] *in sunder* Apart.

Though before thee the throned Cytherean[1] be fallen,
and hidden her head,

Yet thy kingdom shall pass, Galilean, thy dead shall go
down to thee dead.

75   Of the maiden thy mother men sing as a goddess with
grace clad around;

Thou art throned where another was king; where
another was queen she is crowned.

Yea, once we had sight of another: but now she is
queen, say these.

Not as thine, not as thine was our mother, a blossom
of flowering seas,

Clothed round with the world's desire as with
raiment,° and fair as the foam,   *clothing*

80   And fleeter than kindled fire, and a goddess, and
mother of Rome.

For thine came pale and a maiden, and sister to
sorrow; but ours,

Her deep hair heavily laden with odour and colour of
flowers,

White rose of the rose-white water, a silver splendour,
a flame,

Bent down unto us that besought her, and earth grew
sweet with her name.

85   For thine came weeping, a slave among slaves, and
rejected; but she

Came flushed from the full-flushed wave, and
imperial, her foot on the sea.

And the wonderful waters knew her, the winds and
the viewless ways,

And the roses grew rosier, and bluer the sea-blue
stream of the bays.

Ye are fallen, our lords, by what token? we wist[2] that
ye should not fall.

90   Ye were all so fair that are broken; and one more fair
than ye all.

But I turn to her still, having seen she shall surely
abide in the end;

Goddess and maiden and queen, be near me now and
befriend.

O daughter of earth, of my mother, her crown and
blossom of birth,

I am also, I also, thy brother; I go as I came unto earth.

95   In the night where thine eyes are as moons are in
heaven, the night where thou art,

Where the silence is more than all tunes, where sleep
overflows from the heart,

Where the poppies[3] are sweet as the rose in our world,
and the red rose is white,

And the wind falls faint as it blows with the fume of
the flowers of the night.

And the murmur of spirits that sleep in the shadow of
Gods from afar

100   Grows dim in thine ears and deep as the deep dim
soul of a star,

In the sweet low light of thy face, under heavens
untrod by the sun,

Let my soul with their souls find place, and forget
what is done and undone.

Thou art more than the Gods who number the days
of our temporal breath;

For these give labour and slumber; but thou,
Proserpina, death.

105   Therefore now at thy feet I abide for a season in
silence. I know

I shall die as my fathers died, and sleep as they sleep;
even so.

For the glass of the years is brittle wherein we gaze for
a span;

A little soul for a little bears up this corpse which is
man.[4]

So long I endure, no longer; and laugh not again,
neither weep.

110   For there is no God found stronger than death; and
death is a sleep.

—1866

---

1   *throned Cytherean* Venus, Roman goddess of love and beauty
(Aphrodite in Greek mythology), who was born of the foam of the sea
and, according to some accounts, came ashore on the Greek island of
Cythera.

2   *wist* Know.

---

3   *poppies* Flowers representing sleep, sacred to Proserpine.

4   [Swinburne's note] ψυχάρτον εἶ βαστάζον νεκρόν.—Epictetus
[Greek: You are a little soul, carrying around a corpse.]

The Leper[1]

Nothing is better, I well think,
    Than love; the hidden well-water
Is not so delicate to drink:
    This was well seen of me and her.

5 I served her in a royal house;
    I served her wine and curious meat.
For will to kiss between her brows,
    I had no heart to sleep or eat.

Mere scorn God knows she had of me,
10   A poor scribe, nowise great or fair,
Who plucked his clerk's hood back to see
    Her curled-up lips and amorous hair.

I vex my head with thinking this.
    Yea, though God always hated me,
15 And hates me now that I can kiss
    Her eyes, plait° up her hair to see   *braid*

How she then wore it on the brows,
    Yet am I glad to have her dead
Here in this wretched wattled[2] house
20   Where I can kiss her eyes and head.

Nothing is better, I well know,
    Than love; no amber in cold sea
Or gathered berries under snow:
    That is well seen of her and me.

25 Three thoughts I make my pleasure of:
    First I take heart and think of this:
That knight's gold hair she chose to love,
    His mouth she had such will to kiss.

Then I remember that sundawn
30   I brought him by a privy[3] way
Out at her lattice, and thereon
    What gracious words she found to say.

(Cold rushes for such little feet—
    Both feet could lie into my hand.
35 A marvel was it of my sweet
    Her upright body could so stand.)

"Sweet friend, God give you thank and grace;
    Now am I clean and whole of shame,
Nor shall men burn me in the face
40   For my sweet fault that scandals them."

I tell you over word by word.
    She, sitting edgewise on her bed,
Holding her feet, said thus. The third,
    A sweeter thing than these, I said.

45 God, that makes time and ruins it
    And alters not, abiding God,
Changed with disease her body sweet,
    The body of love wherein she abode.

Love is more sweet and comelier
50   Than a dove's throat strained out to sing.
All they spat out and cursed at her
    And cast her forth for a base thing.

They cursed her, seeing how God had wrought
    This curse to plague her, a curse of his.
55 Fools were they surely, seeing not
    How sweeter than all sweet she is.

He that had held her by the hair,
    With kissing lips blinding her eyes,
Felt her bright bosom, strained and bare,
60   Sigh under him, with short mad cries

Out of her throat and sobbing mouth
    And body broken up with love,

---

[1] *The Leper* In an early version of this poem, Swinburne attached an endnote in an attempt to deceive the public into believing that it was based on a true story, *Grandes Chroniques de France*, 1505.

[2] *wattled* Built out of intertwining twigs and mud.

[3] *privy* Here, private, secluded.

With sweet hot tears his lips were loth°   *averse*
    Her own should taste the savour of,

65 Yea, he inside whose grasp all night
    Her fervent body leapt or lay,
Stained with sharp kisses red and white,
    Found her a plague to spurn away.

I hid her in this wattled house,
70   I served her water and poor bread.
For joy to kiss between her brows
    Time upon time I was nigh dead.

Bread failed; we got but well-water
    And gathered grass with dropping seed;
75 I had such joy of kissing her,
    I had small care to sleep or feed.

Sometimes when service made me glad
    The sharp tears leapt between my lids,
Falling on her, such joy I had
80   To do the service God forbids.

"I pray you let me be at peace,
    Get hence, make room for me to die."
She said that: her poor lip would cease,
    Put up to mine, and turn to cry.

85 I said, "Bethink yourself how love
    Fared in us twain, what either did;
Shall I unclothe my soul thereof?
    That I should do this, God forbid."

Yea, though God hateth us, he knows
90   That hardly in a little thing
Love faileth of the work it does
    Till it grow ripe for gathering.

Six months, and now my sweet is dead
    A trouble takes me; I know not
95 If all were done well, all well said,
    No word or tender deed forgot.

Too sweet, for the least part in her,
    To have shed life out by fragments; yet,
Could the close mouth catch breath and stir,
100   I might see something I forget.

Six months, and I sit still and hold
    In two cold palms her cold two feet.
Her hair, half grey half ruined gold,
    Thrills me and burns me in kissing it.

105 Love bites and stings me through, to see
    Her keen face made of sunken bones.
Her worn-off eyelids madden me,
    That were shot through with purple once.

She said, "Be good with me; I grow
110   So tired for shame's sake, I shall die
If you say nothing": even so.
    And she is dead now, and shame put by.

Yea, and the scorn she had of me
    In the old time, doubtless vexed her then.
115 I never should have kissed her. See
    What fools God's anger makes of men!

She might have loved me a little too,
    Had I been humbler for her sake.
But that new shame could make love new
120   She saw not—yet her shame did make.

I took too much upon my love,
    Having for such mean° service done   *lowly*
Her beauty and all the ways thereof,
    Her face and all the sweet thereon.

125 Yea, all this while I tended her,
    I know the old love held fast his part,
I know the old scorn waxed heavier,
    Mixed with sad wonder, in her heart.

It may be all my love went wrong—
130   A scribe's work writ awry and blurred,

Scrawled after the blind evensong[1]—
    Spoilt music with no perfect word.

But surely I would fain have done
    All things the best I could. Perchance
35 Because I failed, came short of one,
    She kept at heart that other man's.

I am grown blind with all these things:
    It may be now she hath in sight
Some better knowledge; still there clings
40   The old question. Will not God do right?
    —1866

A Forsaken Garden

In a coign° of the cliff between lowland and   *wedge*
    highland,
    At the sea-down's edge between windward and lee,[2]
Walled round with rocks as an inland island,
    The ghost of a garden fronts the sea.
5 A girdle of brushwood and thorn encloses
    The steep square slope of the blossomless bed
Where the weeds that grew green from the graves of
      its roses
    Now lie dead.

The fields fall southward, abrupt and broken,
10   To the low last edge of the long lone land.
If a step should sound or a word be spoken,
    Would a ghost not rise at the strange guest's hand?
So long have the grey bare walks lain guestless,
    Through branches and briars if a man make way,
15 He shall find no life but the sea-wind's, restless
    Night and day.

The dense hard passage is blind and stifled
    That crawls by a track none turn to climb

To the strait° waste place that the years have   *narrow*
    rifled
20   Of all but the thorns that are touched not of time.
The thorns he spares when the rose is taken;
    The rocks are left when he wastes the plain.
The wind that wanders, the weeds wind-shaken,
    These remain.

25 Not a flower to be pressed of the foot that falls not;
    As the heart of a dead man the seed-lots are dry;
From the thicket of thorns whence the nightingale
    calls not,
    Could she call, there were never a rose to reply.
Over the meadows that blossom and wither
30   Rings but the note of a sea-bird's song;
Only the sun and the rain come hither
    All year long.

The sun burns sere° and the rain dishevels   *dry*
    One gaunt bleak blossom of scentless breath.
35 Only the wind here hovers and revels
    In a round where life seems barren as death.
Here there was laughing of old, there was weeping,
    Haply, of lovers none ever will know,
Whose eyes went seaward a hundred sleeping
40   Years ago.

Heart handfast in heart as they stood, "Look thither,"
    Did he whisper? "look forth from the flowers to
      the sea;
For the foam-flowers endure when the rose-blossoms
    wither,
    And men that love lightly may die—but we?"
45 And the same wind sang and the same waves
    whitened,
    And or° ever the garden's last petals were shed, *before*
In the lips that had whispered, the eyes that had
    lightened,
    Love was dead.

Or they loved their life through, and then went whither?
50   And were one to the end—but what end who knows?
Love deep as the sea as a rose must wither,

---

1 *evensong* Evening prayers.

2 *sea-down* Dune; *lee* Sheltered from the wind.

As the rose-red seaweed that mocks the rose.
Shall the dead take thought for the dead to love them?
   What love was ever as deep as a grave?
55 They are loveless now as the grass above them
    Or the wave.

All are at one now, roses and lovers,
   Not known of the cliffs and the fields and the sea.
Not a breath of the time that has been hovers
60   In the air now soft with a summer to be.
Not a breath shall there sweeten the seasons hereafter
   Of the flowers or the lovers that laugh now or weep,
When as they that are free now of weeping and
    laughter
    We shall sleep.

65 Here death may deal not again forever;
   Here change may come not till all change end.
From the graves they have made they shall rise up
    never,
   Who have left nought living to ravage and rend.
Earth, stones, and thorns of the wild ground growing,
70   While the sun and the rain live, these shall be;
Till a last wind's breath upon all these blowing
    Roll the sea.

Till the slow sea rise and the sheer cliff crumble,
   Till terrace and meadow the deep gulfs drink,
75 Till the strength of the waves of the high tides humble
   The fields that lessen, the rocks that shrink,
Here now in his triumph where all things falter,
   Stretched out on the spoils that his own hand
    spread,
As a god self-slain on his own strange altar,
80   Death lies dead.
—1876

Anactoria[1]

τίνος αὐ τὺ πειθοῖ
μὰψ σαγηνεύσας φιλότατα ;[2]—SAPPHO

My life is bitter with thy love; thine eyes
  Blind me, thy tresses burn me, thy sharp sighs
Divide my flesh and spirit with soft sound,
And my blood strengthens, and my veins abound.
5 I pray thee sigh not, speak not, draw not breath;
Let life burn down, and dream it is not death.
I would the sea had hidden us, the fire
(Wilt thou fear that, and fear not my desire?)
Severed the bones that bleach, the flesh that cleaves,[3]
10 And let our sifted ashes drop like leaves.
I feel thy blood against my blood: my pain
Pains thee, and lips bruise lips, and vein stings vein.
Let fruit be crushed on fruit, let flower on flower,
Breast kindle breast, and either burn one hour.
15 Why wilt thou follow lesser loves? are thine
Too weak to bear these hands and lips of mine?
I charge thee for my life's sake, O too sweet
To crush love with thy cruel faultless feet,
I charge thee keep thy lips from hers or his,
20 Sweetest, till theirs be sweeter than my kiss:
Lest I too lure, a swallow for a dove,
Erotion or Erinna[4] to my love.
I would my love could kill thee; I am satiated
With seeing thee live, and fain would have thee dead.
25 I would earth had thy body as fruit to eat,
And no mouth but some serpent's found thee sweet.

---

[1] *Anactoria* One of the lovers of Sappho, a Greek lyric poet of the sixth century BCE. Swinburne once said: "Judging even from the mutilated fragments fallen within our reach from the broken altar of her sacrifice of song, I for one have always agreed with all Grecian tradition in thinking Sappho to be beyond all question and comparison the very greatest poet that ever lived. Aeschylus is the greatest poet who was also a prophet; Shakespeare is the best dramatist who was also a poet, but Sappho is simply nothing less—as she certainly is nothing more—than the greatest poet who ever was at all."

[2] τίνος... φιλότατα Greek: Whom shall I make to give thee room in her heart's love?

[3] *cleaves* Adheres.

[4] *Erotion* Greek man's name; *Erinna* Greek woman's name; Sappho had a student (who may have also been a lover) named Erinna.

I would find grievous ways to have thee slain,
Intense device, and superflux° of pain;   *excess*
Vex thee with amorous agonies, and shake
30   Life at thy lips, and leave it there to ache;
Strain out thy soul with pangs too soft to kill,
Intolerable interludes, and infinite ill;
Relapse and reluctation° of the breath,   *resistance*
Dumb[1] tunes and shuddering semitones of death.
35   I am weary of all thy words and soft strange ways,
Of all love's fiery nights and all his days,
And all the broken kisses salt as brine
That shuddering lips make moist with waterish wine,
And eyes the bluer for all those hidden hours
40   That pleasure fills with tears and feeds from flowers,
Fierce at the heart with fire that half comes through,
But all the flowerlike white stained round with blue;
The fervent underlid, and that above
Lifted with laughter or abashed with love;
45   Thine amorous girdle,[2] full of thee and fair,
And leavings of the lilies in thine hair.
Yea, all sweet words of thine and all thy ways,
And all the fruit of nights and flower of days,
And stinging lips wherein the hot sweet brine
50   That Love was born of burns and foams like wine,[3]
And eyes insatiable of amorous hours,
Fervent as fire and delicate as flowers,
Coloured like night at heart, but cloven° through   *split*
Like night with flame, dyed round like night with blue,
55   Clothed with deep eyelids under and above—
Yea, all thy beauty sickens me with love;
Thy girdle empty of thee and now not fair,
And ruinous lilies in thy languid hair.
Ah, take no thought for Love's sake; shall this be,
60   And she who loves thy lover not love thee?
Sweet soul, sweet mouth of all that laughs and lives,
Mine is she, very mine; and she forgives.
For I beheld in sleep the light that is
In her high place in Paphos,[4] heard the kiss

65   Of body and soul that mix with eager tears
And laughter stinging through the eyes and ears;
Saw Love, as burning flame from crown to feet,
Imperishable, upon her storied seat;
Clear eyelids lifted toward the north and south,
70   A mind of many colours, and a mouth
Of many tunes and kisses; and she bowed,
With all her subtle face laughing aloud,
Bowed down upon me, saying, "Who doth thee wrong,
Sappho?" but thou—thy body is the song,
75   Thy mouth the music; thou art more than I,
Though my voice die not till the whole world die;
Though men that hear it madden; though love weep,
Though nature change, though shame be charmed to
      sleep.
Ah, wilt thou slay me lest I kiss thee dead?
80   Yet the queen laughed from her sweet heart and said:
"Even she that flies shall follow for thy sake,
And she shall give thee gifts that would not take,
Shall kiss that would not kiss thee" (yea, kiss me)
"When thou wouldst not"—when I would not kiss thee!
85   Ah, more to me than all men as thou art,
Shall not my songs assuage her at the heart?
Ah, sweet to me as life seems sweet to death,
Why should her wrath fill thee with fearful breath?
Nay, sweet, for is she God alone? hath she
90   Made earth and all the centuries of the sea,
Taught the sun ways to travel, woven most fine
The moonbeams, shed the starbeams forth as wine,
Bound with her myrtles, beaten with her rods,
The young men and the maidens and the gods?
95   Have we not lips to love with, eyes for tears,
And summer and flower of women and of years?
Stars for the foot of morning, and for noon
Sunlight, and exaltation of the moon;
Waters that answer waters, fields that wear
100   Lilies, and languor of the Lesbian[5] air?
Beyond those flying feet of fluttered doves,
Are there not other gods for other loves?
Yea, though she scourge thee, sweetest, for my sake,

---

[1] *Dumb* Silent or inarticulate.

[2] *girdle* I.e., belt. Here, symbol of Aphrodite, the Greek goddess of love.

[3] *Love ... wine* Aphrodite was born out of the foam of the sea.

[4] *Paphos* Island on which, according to some accounts, Aphrodite came ashore after her birth.

---

[5] *Lesbian* Of the Greek island of Lesbos, where Sappho and Anactoria lived; the common usage of the term "lesbian" is derived from the name of the island and harks back to Sappho's love of women.

Blossom not thorns and flowers not blood should break.
105 Ah that my lips were tuneless lips, but pressed
To the bruised blossom of thy scourged white breast!
Ah that my mouth for Muses'[1] milk were fed
On the sweet blood thy sweet small wounds had bled!
That with my tongue I felt them, and could taste
110 The faint flakes from thy bosom to the waist!
That I could drink thy veins as wine, and eat
Thy breasts like honey! that from face to feet
Thy body were abolished and consumed,
And in my flesh thy very flesh entombed!
115 Ah, ah, thy beauty! like a beast it bites,
Stings like an adder, like an arrow smites.
Ah sweet, and sweet again, and seven times sweet
The paces and the pauses of thy feet!
Ah sweeter than all sleep or summer air
120 The fallen fillets° fragrant from thine hair!   hair ribbons
Yea, though their alien kisses do me wrong,
Sweeter thy lips than mine with all their song;
Thy shoulders whiter than a fleece of white,
And flower-sweet fingers, good to bruise or bite
125 As honeycomb of the inmost honey-cells,
With almond-shaped and roseleaf-coloured shells,
And blood like purple blossom at the tips
Quivering; and pain made perfect in thy lips
For my sake when I hurt thee; O that I
130 Durst crush thee out of life with love, and die,
Die of thy pain and my delight, and be
Mixed with thy blood and molten into thee!
Would I not plague thee dying overmuch?
Would I not hurt thee perfectly? not touch
135 Thy pores of sense with torture, and make bright,
Thine eyes with bloodlike tears and grievous light
Strike pang from pang as note is struck from note,
Catch the sob's middle music in thy throat,
Take thy limbs living, and new-mould with these
140 A lyre of many faultless agonies?
Feed thee with fever and famine and fine drouth,° drought
With perfect pangs convulse thy perfect mouth,
Make thy life shudder in thee and burn afresh,

And wring thy very spirit through the flesh?
145 Cruel? but love makes all that love him well
As wise as heaven and crueller than hell.
Me hath love made more bitter toward thee
Than death toward man; but were I made as he
Who hath made all things to break them one by one,
150 If my feet trod upon the stars and sun
And souls of men as his have always trod,
God knows I might be crueller than God.
For who shall change with prayers or thanksgivings
The mystery of the cruelty of things?
155 Or say what God above all gods and years
With offering and blood-sacrifice of tears,
With lamentation from strange lands, from graves
Where the snake pastures, from scarred mouth of slaves
From prison, and from plunging prows of ships
160 Through flamelike foam of the sea's closing lips—
With thwartings of strange signs, and wind-blown hair
Of comets, desolating the dim air,
When darkness is made fast with seals and bars,
And fierce reluctance of disastrous stars,
165 Eclipse, and sound of shaken hills, and wings
Darkening, and blind inexpiable[2] things—
With sorrow of labouring moons, and altering light
And travail of the planets of the night,[3]
And weeping of the weary Pleiads[4] seven,
170 Feeds the mute melancholy lust of heaven?
Is not his incense bitterness, his meat
Murder? his hidden face and iron feet
Hath not man known, and felt them on their way
Threaten and trample all things and every day?
175 Hath he not sent us hunger? who hath cursed
Spirit and flesh with longing? filled with thirst
Their lips who cried unto him? who bade exceed
The fervid will, fall short the feeble deed,
Bade sink the spirit and the flesh aspire,
180 Pain animate the dust of dead desire,
And life yield up her flower to violent fate?

---

[1] *Muses* Nine daughters of Zeus and Mnemosyne, each of whom presided over and provided inspiration for an aspect of learning or the arts.

[2] *inexpiable* Impossible to make amends for.

[3] *With sorrow … the night* Both "labour" and "travail" mean "eclipse," in addition to their usual sense of "work, suffering, or exertion."

[4] *Pleiads* Seven daughters of Atlas, who were changed into doves and later a constellation of stars after fleeing from Orion, the hunter.

Him would I reach, him smite, him desecrate,
Pierce the cold lips of God with human breath,
And mix his immortality with death.
185 Why hath he made us? what had all we done
That we should live and loathe the sterile sun,
And with the moon wax paler as she wanes,
And pulse by pulse feel time grow through our veins?
Thee too the years shall cover; thou shalt be
190 As the rose born of one same blood with thee,
As a song sung, as a word said, and fall
Flower-wise, and be not any more at all,
Nor any memory of thee anywhere;
For never Muse has bound above thine hair
195 The high Pierian[1] flower whose graft outgrows
All summer kinship of the mortal rose
And colour of deciduous days, nor shed
Reflex and flush of heaven about thine head,
Nor reddened brows made pale by floral grief
200 With splendid shadow from that lordlier leaf.
Yea, thou shalt be forgotten like spilt wine,
Except these kisses of my lips on thine
Brand them with immortality; but me—
Men shall not see bright fire nor hear the sea,
205 Nor mix their hearts with music, nor behold
Cast forth of heaven, with feet of awful gold
And plumeless wings that make the bright air blind,
Lightning, with thunder for a hound behind
Hunting through fields unfurrowed and unsown,
210 But in the light and laughter, in the moan
And music, and in grasp of lip and hand
And shudder of water that makes felt on land
The immeasurable tremor of all the sea,
Memories shall mix and metaphors of me.
215 Like me shall be the shuddering calm of night,
When all the winds of the world for pure delight
Close lips that quiver and fold up wings that ache;
When nightingales are louder for love's sake,
And leaves tremble like lute-strings or like fire;
220 Like me the one star swooning with desire
Even at the cold lips of the sleepless moon,
As I at thine; like me the waste white noon,

Burnt through with barren sunlight; and like me
The land-stream and the tide-stream in the sea.
225 I am sick with time as these with ebb and flow,
And by the yearning in my veins I know
The yearning sound of waters; and mine eyes
Burn as that beamless fire which fills the skies
With troubled stars and travailing things of flame;
230 And in my heart the grief consuming them
Labours, and in my veins the thirst of these,
And all the summer travail of the trees
And all the winter sickness; and the earth,
Filled full with deadly works of death and birth,
235 Sore spent with hungry lusts of birth and death,
Has pain like mine in her divided breath;
Her spring of leaves is barren, and her fruit
Ashes; her boughs are burdened, and her root
Fibrous and gnarled with poison; underneath
240 Serpents have gnawn it through with tortuous teeth
Made sharp upon the bones of all the dead,
And wild birds rend her branches overhead.
These, woven as raiment° for his word and   *clothing*
    thought,
These hath God made, and me as these, and wrought
245 Song, and hath lit it at my lips; and me
Earth shall not gather though she feed on thee.
As a shed tear shalt thou be shed; but I—
Lo, earth may labour, men live long and die,
Years change and stars, and the high God devise
250 New things, and old things wane before his eyes
Who wields and wrecks them, being more strong than
    they—
But, having made me, me he shall not slay.
Nor slay nor satiate, like those herds of his
Who laugh and live a little, and their kiss
255 Contents them, and their loves are swift and sweet,
And sure death grasps and gains them with slow feet,
Love they or hate they, strive or bow their knees—
And all these ends he hath his will of these.
Yea, but albeit he slay me, hating me—
260 Albeit he hide me in the deep dear sea
And cover me with cool wan foam, and ease
This soul of mine as any soul of these,
And give me water and great sweet waves, and make

---

[1] *Pierian* From Pieria, Greek district said to be the home of the
Muses.

The very sea's name lordlier for my sake,
265 The whole sea sweeter—albeit I die indeed
And hide myself and sleep and no man heed,
Of me the high God hath not all his will.
Blossom of branches, and on each high hill
Clear air and wind, and under in clamorous vales
270 Fierce noises of the fiery nightingales,
Buds burning in the sudden spring like fire,
The wan washed sand and the waves' vain desire,
Sails seen like blown white flowers at sea, and words
That bring tears swiftest, and long notes of birds
275 Violently singing till the whole world sings—
I Sappho shall be one with all these things,
With all high things forever; and my face
Seen once, my songs once heard in a strange place,
Cleave to men's lives, and waste the days thereof
280 With gladness and much sadness and long love.
Yea, they shall say, earth's womb has borne in vain
New things, and never this best thing again;
Borne days and men, borne fruits and wars and wine,
Seasons and songs, but no song more like mine.
285 And they shall know me as ye who have known me
        here,
Last year when I loved Atthis,[1] and this year
When I love thee; and they shall praise me, and say
"She hath all time as all we have our day,
Shall she not live and have her will"—even I?
290 Yea, though thou diest, I say I shall not die.
For these shall give me of their souls, shall give
Life, and the days and loves wherewith I live,
Shall quicken me with loving, fill with breath,
Save me and serve me, strive for me with death.
295 Alas, that neither moon nor snow nor dew
Nor all cold things can purge me wholly through,
Assuage me nor allay me nor appease,
Till supreme sleep shall bring me bloodless ease;
Till time wax faint in all his periods;
300 Till fate undo the bondage of the gods,
And lay, to slake and satiate me all through,

Lotus and Lethe[2] on my lips like dew,
And shed around and over and under me
Thick darkness and the insuperable° sea.   *unconquerable*
—1866

The Garden of Proserpine[3]

Here, where the world is quiet;
    Here, where all trouble seems
Dead winds' and spent waves' riot
    In doubtful dreams of dreams;
5   I watch the green field growing
    For reaping folk and sowing,
    For harvest-time and mowing,
        A sleepy world of streams.

I am tired of tears and laughter,
10   And men that laugh and weep;
Of what may come hereafter
    For men that sow to reap:
I am weary of days and hours,
Blown buds of barren flowers,
15 Desires and dreams and powers
        And everything but sleep.

Here life has death for neighbour,
    And far from eye or ear
Wan waves and wet winds labour,
20   Weak ships and spirits steer;
They drive adrift, and whither
They wot° not who make thither;   *know*

---

[1] *Atthis* The subject of a number of Sappho's poems.

[2] *Lotus* In Greek mythology, plant whose fruit produced a blissful state of forgetfulness when eaten; *Lethe* Greek mythological river in Hades, sometimes called "the waters of oblivion" as those who drank from it forgot the past.

[3] *Proserpine* Proserpina, or Persephone in Greek myth, is the daughter of Jupiter (Zeus) and Demeter (Ceres), goddess of the grain harvest. Proserpina was abducted by Pluto (Hades) and carried to the underworld, where she became queen of the dead. Ceres, enraged, refused to allow the grain to grow until a compromise was reached by which Proserpina would spend a third of the year in Pluto's house and two thirds of the year in the world above. See John Milton's description of her in *Paradise Lost* 4.269–72 (1667) as well as Dante Gabriel Rossetti's famous painting of her, *Proserpina Holding the Pomegranate* (1874).

But no such winds blow hither,
    And no such things grow here.

25   No growth of moor or coppice,[1]
    No heather-flower or vine,
But bloomless buds of poppies,
    Green grapes of Proserpine,
Pale beds of blowing rushes
30   Where no leaf blooms or blushes
Save this whereout she crushes
    For dead men deadly wine.

Pale, without name or number,
    In fruitless fields of corn,°   *grain*
35   They bow themselves and slumber
    All night till light is born;
And like a soul belated,
In hell and heaven unmated,
By cloud and mist abated
40   Comes out of darkness morn.

Though one were strong as seven,
    He too with death shall dwell,
Nor wake with wings in heaven,
    Nor weep for pains in hell;
45   Though one were fair as roses,
His beauty clouds and closes;
And well though love reposes,
    In the end it is not well.

Pale, beyond porch and portal,
50   Crowned with calm leaves, she stands
Who gathers all things mortal
    With cold immortal hands;
Her languid lips are sweeter
Than love's who fears to greet her
55   To men that mix and meet her
    From many times and lands.

She waits for each and other,
    She waits for all men born;
Forgets the earth her mother,

60   The life of fruits and corn;
And spring and seed and swallow
Take wing for her and follow
Where summer song rings hollow
    And flowers are put to scorn.

65   There go the loves that wither,
    The old loves with wearier wings;
And all dead years draw thither,
    And all disastrous things;
Dead dreams of days forsaken,
70   Blind buds that snows have shaken,
Wild leaves that winds have taken,
    Red strays of ruined springs.

We are not sure of sorrow,
    And joy was never sure;
75   To-day will die to-morrow;
    Time stoops to no man's lure;
And love, grown faint and fretful,
With lips but half regretful
Sighs, and with eyes forgetful
80   Weeps that no loves endure.

From too much love of living,
    From hope and fear set free,
We thank with brief thanksgiving
    Whatever gods may be
85   That no life lives for ever;
That dead men rise up never;
That even the weariest river
    Winds somewhere safe to sea.

Then star nor sun shall waken,
90   Nor any change of light:
Nor sound of waters shaken,
    Nor any sound or sight:
Nor wintry leaves nor vernal,°   *spring*
Nor days nor things diurnal;[2]
95   Only the sleep eternal
    In an eternal night.
    —1866

---

1 *coppice* Thicket or grove of small trees or shrubs.

2 *diurnal* Active in the daytime rather than at night.

WALTER PATER
_1839 – 1894_

K nown as the leader of the nineteenth-century Aesthetic Movement, the unassuming and reserved critic and theorist Walter Pater was somewhat surprised at the influence his writings commanded because of their advocacy of "art for art's sake." (The phrase _"l'art pour l'art"_ was first coined in 1818 by the French philosopher Victor Cousins, who in turn based his theory on Kantian notions of art and beauty.) In the famous conclusion to his collection of essays, _Studies in the History of the Renaissance_ (1873), Pater repeated in altered form words he had written in 1868 in his essay "Poems by William Morris" (1868):

> What we have to do is to be for ever curiously testing new opinions and courting new impressions, never acquiescing in a facile orthodoxy of Comte or Hegel, or of our own. ... Great passions may give us this quickened sense of life, ecstasy and sorrow of love, the various forms of enthusiastic activity, disinterested or otherwise, which come naturally to many of us. Only be sure it is passion—that it does yield you this fruit of a quickened, multiplied consciousness. Of such wisdom, the poetic passion, the desire of beauty, the love of art for its sake, has most. For art comes to you proposing frankly to give nothing but the highest quality to your moments as they pass, and simply for those moments' sake.

Without specifically advocating hedonism, Pater was reacting against the prevailing moral aesthetic (articulated compellingly by Carlyle, Ruskin, and Arnold) that charged the artist with ethical responsibilities. The response was in some quarters embarrassingly positive; so influential was this essay upon such "decadents" of the 1890s as Oscar Wilde that Pater withdrew the controversial conclusion from the book's second printing. He allowed it to be reprinted in subsequent editions, while making slight alterations "which," he claimed, "bring it closer to my original meaning."

The events of Walter Horatio Pater's early life did not give any indication of the effect his work would eventually have upon Victorian aesthetics. Born in London, Pater lost his father, Dr. Richard Glode Pater, at a young age, and moved with his siblings and mother, Maria Hill Pater, to Enfield. At the age of 13, the year before his mother died, Pater entered the King's School in Canterbury and five years later entered Queen's College, Oxford, where, to his disappointment, he graduated in 1862 with only second class honors. After tutoring for two years (Gerard Manley Hopkins was among his students), Pater became a fellow at Brasenose College. He remained a teacher at Oxford for most of his life. Soon after his appointment, Pater began publishing critical essays, beginning with "Coleridge's Writings," in which he spoke of abandoning his faith in the High Church for the "religion of art." Previously influenced by Ruskin's _Modern Painters_, Pater began to rethink his notions of beauty upon reading about the classical scholar Johann Winckelmann (1717–68), in whose life he saw a model for an ideal critic's dedication to the aesthetic. He set out these thoughts in his essay "Winckelmann," published in the _Westminster Review_ in 1867. This essay was a key moment not only in the development of Pater's thought but also in his career; the essay so impressed the editor of the *Fortnightly Review* that it initiated a decades-long relationship between Pater and the magazine.

In 1873, the essay on Winckelmann and essays on Botticelli, Michelangelo, Leonardo da Vinci, and others, were collected in *The Renaissance*. Pater's preface and conclusion attracted much attention, setting out as they did his Epicurean theories. The "Preface" defines the work of the aesthetic critic:

> The aesthetic critic ... regards all objects with which he has to do, all works of art, and the fairer forms of nature and human life, as powers or forces producing pleasurable sensations, each of a more or less peculiar or unique kind .... What is important ... is not that the critic should possess a correct abstract definition of beauty for the intellect, but a certain kind of temperament, the power of being deeply moved by the presence of beautiful objects. To him all periods, types, schools of taste, are in themselves equal.

For many, Pater's subjective vision of art, literature, and music—and indeed of one's responsibility to enjoy life—appeared self-indulgent and even amoral. The book, however, with its rich and eloquent prose style, established him as an important critic and placed him at the center of a school of aesthetes that included Wilde, Algernon Swinburne, Katharine Bradley, and Edith Cooper.

Possibly as a result of the controversy over *The Renaissance*, Pater was passed over for a proctorship at Oxford, and thereafter, although his lectures were popular, he was never considered for important positions at the university. He did, however, continue to publish articles and reviews, and worked on a novel, *Marius the Epicurean* (1885), which brought together his philosophies on art and religion, expanding in fictional form the ideas from the "Conclusion" to his first book. In 1887 he published *Imaginary Portraits*, a series of essays on intellectually and artistically rebellious people; in 1889 *Appreciations: With an Essay on Style*; and in 1893 a group of lectures, *Plato and Platonism*. His literary style was so meticulous and eloquent that decades after his death in 1894, Yeats reprinted Pater's description of the *Mona Lisa* in verse form as the opening piece in the *Oxford Book of Modern Verse* (1936). This style, along with his theories of aesthetics, influenced not only Yeats but many modernists, most notably Virginia Woolf and Ezra Pound.

Pater died suddenly of rheumatic fever, at Oxford, on 30 July 1894, at the age of 54. He is buried at Oxford's Holywell Cemetery.

⌘ ⌘ ⌘

from *The Renaissance: Studies in Art and Poetry*

PREFACE

Many attempts have been made by writers on art and poetry to define beauty in the abstract, to express it in the most general terms, to find a universal formula for it. The value of these attempts has most often been in the suggestive and penetrating things said by the way. Such discussions help us very little to enjoy what has been well done in art or poetry, to discriminate between what is more and what is less excellent in them, or to use words like beauty, excellence, art, poetry, with a more precise meaning than they would otherwise have. Beauty, like all other qualities presented to human experience, is relative; and the definition of it becomes unmeaning and useless in proportion to its abstractness. To define beauty, not in the most abstract, but in the most concrete terms possible, to find, not a universal formula for it, but the formula which expresses most adequately this or that special manifestation of it, is the aim of the true student of aesthetics.

"To see the object as in itself it really is,"[1] has been justly said to be the aim of all true criticism whatever; and in aesthetic criticism the first step towards seeing one's object as it really is, is to know one's own impression as it really is, to discriminate it, to realize it distinctly. The objects with which aesthetic criticism deals—music, poetry, artistic and accomplished forms of human life—are indeed receptacles of so many powers or forces; they possess, like the products of nature, so many virtues or qualities. What is this song or picture, this engaging personality presented in life or in a book, to *me*? What effect does it really produce on me? Does it give me pleasure? and if so, what sort or degree of pleasure?

How is my nature modified by its presence, and under its influence? The answers to these questions are the original facts with which the aesthetic critic has to do; and, as in the study of light, of morals, of number, one must realise such primary data for oneself, or not at all. And he who experiences these impressions strongly, and drives directly at the discrimination and analysis of them, has no need to trouble himself with the abstract question what beauty is in itself, or what its exact relation to truth or experience—metaphysical questions, as unprofitable as metaphysical questions elsewhere. He may pass them all by as being, answerable or not, of no interest to him.

The aesthetic critic, then, regards all the objects with which he has to do, all works of art, and the fairer forms of nature and human life, as powers or forces producing pleasurable sensations, each of a more or less peculiar and unique kind. This influence he feels, and wishes to explain, analyzing it, and reducing it to its elements. To him, the picture, the landscape, the engaging personality in life or in a book, *La Gioconda*, the hills of Carrara, Pico of Mirandola,[2] are valuable for their virtues, as we say, in speaking of a herb, a wine, a gem, for the property each has of affecting one with a special, a unique, impression of pleasure. Our education becomes complete in proportion as our susceptibility to these impressions increases in depth and variety. And the function of the aesthetic critic is to distinguish, analyze, and separate from its adjuncts, the virtue by which a picture, a landscape, a fair personality in life or in a book, produces this special impression of beauty or pleasure, to indicate what the source of that impression is, and under what conditions it is experienced. His end is reached when he has disengaged that virtue, and noted it, as a chemist notes some natural element, for himself and others; and the rule for those who would reach this end is stated with great exactness in the words of a recent critic of Sainte-Beuve: *De se borner à connaître de près les belles choses, et à s'en nourrir en exquis amateurs, en humanistes accomplis.*[3]

What is important, then, is not that the critic should possess a correct abstract definition of beauty for the intellect, but a certain kind of temperament, the power of being deeply moved by the presence of beautiful objects. He will remember always that beauty exists in many forms. To him all periods, types, schools of taste, are in themselves equal. In all ages there have been some excellent workmen, and some excellent work done. The question he asks is always: In whom did the stir, the genius, the sentiment of the period find itself? where was the receptacle of its refinement, its elevation, its taste? "The ages are all equal," says William Blake, "but genius is always above its age."[4]

Often it will require great nicety to disengage this virtue from the commoner elements with which it may be found in combination. Few artists, not Goethe or

---

Italian Neoplatonist philosopher (1463–94), the subject of chapter 2 of *The Renaissance*.

[3] *De se borner ... accomplis* Quotation by French literary critic Charles Augustin Saint-Beuve (1804–69): "To restrict themselves with knowing beautiful things thoroughly and to nourish themselves by these, as do perceptive amateurs and accomplished humanists."

[4] *The ages ... age* From Blake's annotations to *The Works of Sir Joshua Reynolds* (1798).

---

[1] *To see ... really is* From Matthew Arnold's *The Function of Criticism at the Present Time* (1865).

[2] *La Gioconda* The painting the *Mona Lisa* (1506) by Leonardo da Vinci, the subject of chapter 6 of Pater's *The Renaissance*; *Carrara* Region in Italy, center of the marble industry; *Pico of Mirandola*

Byron[1] even, work quite cleanly, casting off all *débris*, and leaving us only what the heat of their imagination has wholly fused and transformed. Take, for instance, the writings of Wordsworth.[2] The heat of his genius, entering into the substance of his work, has crystallised a part, but only a part, of it; and in that great mass of verse there is much which might well be forgotten. But scattered up and down it, sometimes fusing and transforming entire compositions, like the *Stanzas on Resolution and Independence*, and the *Ode on the Recollections of Childhood*,[3] sometimes, as if at random, depositing a fine crystal here or there, in a matter it does not wholly search through and transform, we trace the action of his unique, incommunicable faculty, that strange, mystical sense of a life in natural things, and of man's life as a part of nature, drawing strength and colour and character from local influences, from the hills and streams, and from natural sights and sounds. Well! that is the *virtue*, the active principle in Wordsworth's poetry; and then the function of the critic of Wordsworth is to follow up that active principle, to disengage it, to mark the degree in which it penetrates his verse.

The subjects of the following studies are taken from the history of the *Renaissance*, and touch what I think the chief points in that complex, many-sided movement. I have explained in the first of them what I understand by the word, giving it a much wider scope than was intended by those who originally used it to denote only that revival of classical antiquity in the fifteenth century which was but one of many results of a general excitement and enlightening of the human mind, of which the great aim and achievements of what, as Christian art, is often falsely opposed to the Renaissance, were another result. This outbreak of the human spirit may be traced far into the middle age itself, with its qualities already clearly pronounced, the care for physical beauty, the worship of the body, the breaking down of those limits which the religious system of the middle age imposed on the heart and the imagination. I have taken as an example of this movement, this earlier Renaissance within the middle age itself, and as an expression of its qualities, two little compositions in early French, not because they constitute the best possible expression of them, but because they help the unity of my series, inasmuch as the Renaissance ends also in France, in French poetry, in a phase of which the writings of Joachim du Bellay[4] are in many ways the most perfect illustration; the Renaissance thus putting forth in France an aftermath, a wonderful later growth, the products of which have to the full that subtle and delicate sweetness which belongs to a refined and comely decadence; just as its earliest phases have the freshness which belongs to all periods of growth in art, the charm of *ascêsis*,[5] of the austere and serious girding of the loins in youth.

But it is in Italy, in the fifteenth century, that the interest of the Renaissance mainly lies—in that solemn fifteenth century which can hardly be studied too much, not merely for its positive results in the things of the intellect and the imagination, its concrete works of art, its special and prominent personalities, with their profound aesthetic charm, but for its general spirit and character, for the ethical qualities of which it is a consummate type.

The various forms of intellectual activity which together make up the culture of an age, move for the most part from different starting points, and by unconnected roads. As products of the same generation they partake indeed of a common character, and unconsciously illustrate each other; but of the producers themselves, each group is solitary, gaining what advantage or disadvantage there may be in intellectual isolation. Art and poetry, philosophy and the religious life, and that other life of refined pleasure and action in the

---

[1] *Goethe* Johann Wolfgang von Goethe (1749–1832), German novelist, playwright, and natural philosopher; *Byron* George Gordon, Lord Byron (1788–1824), English Romantic poet.

[2] *Wordsworth* William Wordsworth (1770–1850), English Romantic poet.

[3] *Stanzas ... Childhood* Two poems by Wordsworth. The exact titles are "Resolution and Independence" (1807) and "Ode: Intimations of Immortality from Recollections of Early Childhood" (1803–06).

[4] *Joachim du Bellay* French poet (c. 1522–60) and subject of Chapter 8 of *The Renaissance*.

[5] *ascêsis* Asceticism; defined by Pater in his essay "Style" (1888) as "Self-restraint, a skillful economy of means."

open places of the world, are each of them confined to its own circle of ideas, and those who prosecute[1] either of them are generally little curious of the thoughts of others. There come, however, from time to time, eras of more favorable conditions, in which the thoughts of men draw nearer together than is their wont, and the many interests of the intellectual world combine in one complete type of general culture. The fifteenth century in Italy is one of these happier eras; and what is some-times said of the age of Pericles is true of that of Loren-zo:[2] it is an age productive in personalities, many-sided, centralised, complete. Here, artists and philosophers and those whom the action of the world has elevated and made keen, do not live in isolation, but breathe a common air, and catch light and heat from each other's thoughts. There is a spirit of general elevation and enlightenment in which all alike communicate. It is the unity of this spirit which gives unity to all the various products of the Renaissance; and it is to this intimate alliance with mind, this participation in the best thoughts which that age produced, that the art of Italy in the fifteenth century owes much of its grave dignity and influence.

I have added an essay on Winckelmann,[3] as not incongruous with the studies which precede it, because Winckelmann, coming in the eighteenth century, really belongs in spirit to an earlier age. By his enthusiasm for things of the intellect and the imagination for their own sake, by his Hellenism,[4] his lifelong struggle to attain to the Greek spirit, he is in sympathy with the humanists of an earlier century. He is the last fruit of the Renais-sance, and explains in a striking way its motive and tendencies.
—1873

---

[1] *prosecute*   Pursue.

[2] *Pericles*   Athenian political leader and great patron of the arts of the fifth century BCE; *Lorenzo*   Lorenzo de Medici, an Italian prince and art patron of the fifteenth century CE.

[3] *Winckelmann*   Johann Joachim Winckelmann (1717–68), German classical scholar and art historian, the subject of Chapter 9 of *The Renaissance*.

[4] *Hellenism*   Embrace of ancient Greek culture.

CONCLUSION[5]

Αέγει που Ἡράκλειτος ὅτι πάντα χωρεῖ καὶ οὐδέν μένει.[6]

To regard all things and principles of things as incon-stant modes or fashions has more and more become the tendency of modern thought. Let us begin with that which is without—our physical life. Fix upon it in one of its more exquisite intervals, the moment, for instance, of delicious recoil from the flood of water in summer heat. What is the whole physical life in that moment but a combination of natural elements to which science gives their names? But these elements, phosphorus and lime and delicate fibres, are present not in the human body alone; we detect them in places most remote from it. Our physical life is a perpetual motion of them—the passage of the blood, the wasting and repairing of the lenses of the eye, the modification of the tissues of the brain by every ray of light and sound—processes which science reduces to simpler and more elementary forces. Like the elements of which we are composed, the action of these forces extends beyond us; it rusts iron and ripens corn.[7] Far out on every side of us those elements are broadcast, driven by many forces; and birth and gesture and death and the springing of violets from the grave[8] are but a few out of ten thousand resultant combinations. That clear, perpetual outline of face and limb is but an image of ours, under which we group them—a design in a web, the actual threads of which

---

[5] [Pater's note]   This brief "Conclusion" was omitted in the second edition of this book, as I conceived it might possibly mislead some of those young men into whose hands it might fall. On the whole, I have thought it best to reprint it here, with some slight changes which bring it closer to my original meaning. I have dealt more fully in *Marius the Epicurean* with the thoughts suggested by it.

[6] *Αέγει ... μένει*   Greek (Pater's translation): "Heracleitus says, 'All things give way; nothing remains!'" From Plato's *Cratylus* (360 BCE). Heracleitus (c. 500 BCE), Greek philosopher.

[7] *corn*   Grain.

[8] *birth ... grave*   Cf. Shakespeare's *Hamlet* 5.1.238–40: "Lay her i' the earth: / And from her fair and unpolluted flesh / May violets spring!"

pass out beyond it. This at least of flame-like our life has, that it is but the concurrence, renewed from moment to moment, of forces parting sooner or later on their ways.

Or if we begin with the inward world of thought and feeling, the whirlpool is still more rapid, the flame more eager and devouring. There it is no longer the gradual darkening of the eye and fading of colour from the wall—the movement of the shoreside, where the water flows down indeed, though in apparent rest—but the race of the midstream, a drift of momentary acts of sight and passion and thought. At first sight experience seems to bury us under a flood of external objects, pressing upon us with a sharp and importunate reality, calling us out of ourselves in a thousand forms of action. But when reflexion begins to act upon those objects they are dissipated under its influence; the cohesive force seems suspended like a trick of magic; each object is loosed into a group of impressions—colour, odour, texture—in the mind of the observer. And if we continue to dwell in thought on this world, not of objects in the solidity with which language invests them, but of impressions unstable, flickering, inconsistent, which burn and are extinguished with our consciousness of them, it contracts still further; the whole scope of observation is dwarfed to the narrow chamber of the individual mind. Experience, already reduced to a swarm of impressions, is ringed round for each one of us by that thick wall of personality through which no real voice has ever pierced on its way to us, or from us to that which we can only conjecture to be without. Every one of those impressions is the impression of the individual in his isolation, each mind keeping as a solitary prisoner its own dream of a world. Analysis goes a step farther still, and assures us that those impressions of the individual mind to which, for each one of us, experience dwindles down, are in perpetual flight; that each of them is limited by time, and that as time is infinitely divisible, each of them is infinitely divisible also; all that is actual in it being a single moment, gone while we try to apprehend it, of which it may ever be more truly said that it has ceased to be than that it is. To such a tremulous wisp constantly reforming itself on the stream, to a single sharp impression, with a sense in it, a relic more or less fleeting, of such moments gone by, what is real in our life fines[1] itself down. It is with this movement, with the passage and dissolution of impressions, images, sensations, that analysis leaves off—that continual vanishing away, that strange, perpetual weaving and unweaving of ourselves.

Philosophiren, says Novalis, *ist dephlegmatisiren vivificiren*.[2] The service of philosophy, of speculative culture, towards the human spirit is to rouse, to startle it into sharp and eager observation. Every moment some form grows perfect in hand or face; some tone on the hills or the sea is choicer than the rest; some mood of passion or insight or intellectual excitement is irresistibly real and attractive for us—for that moment only. Not the fruit of experience, but experience itself, is the end. A counted number of pulses only is given to us of a variegated, dramatic life. How may we see in them all that is to be seen in them by the finest senses? How shall we pass most swiftly from point to point, and be present always at the focus where the greatest number of vital forces unite in their purest energy?

To burn always with this hard, gemlike flame, to maintain this ecstasy, is success in life. In a sense it might even be said that our failure is to form habits, for, after all, habit is relative to a stereotyped[3] world, and meantime it is only the roughness of the eye that makes any two persons, things, situations, seem alike. While all melts under our feet, we may well catch at any exquisite passion, or any contribution to knowledge that seems by a lifted horizon to set the spirit free for a moment, or any stirring of the senses, strange dyes, strange colours, and curious odours, or work of the artist's hands, or the face of one's friend. Not to discriminate every moment some passionate attitude in those about us, and in the brilliancy of their gifts some tragic dividing of forces on their ways, is, on this short day of frost and sun, to sleep before evening. With this sense of the splendour of our

---

[1] *fines* Refines.

[2] *Philosophiren ... vivificiren* German: To philosophize is to cast off apathy, to come alive. Novalis is the pseudonym of German poet Friedrich von Hardenberg (1772–1801).

[3] *stereotyped* Unchanging.

experience and of its awful[1] brevity, gathering all we are into one desperate effort to see and touch, we shall hardly have time to make theories about the things we see and touch. What we have to do is to be forever curiously testing new opinions and courting new impressions, never acquiescing in a facile orthodoxy of Comte, or of Hegel,[2] or of our own. Philosophical theories or ideas, as points of view, instruments of criticism, may help us to gather up what might otherwise pass unregarded by us. "Philosophy is the microscope of thought."[3] The theory or idea or system which requires of us the sacrifice of any part of this experience, in consideration of some interest into which we cannot enter, or some abstract theory we have not identified with ourselves, or what is only conventional, has no real claim upon us.

One of the most beautiful passages in the writings of Rousseau is that in the sixth book of the *Confessions*,[4] where he describes the awakening in him of the literary sense. An undefinable taint of death had always clung about him, and now in early manhood he believed himself smitten by mortal disease. He asked himself how he might make as much as possible of the interval that remained; and he was not biased by anything in his previous life when he decided that it must be by intellec-

tual excitement, which he found just then in the clear, fresh writings of Voltaire.[5] Well! we are all *condamnés*, as Victor Hugo says: we are all under sentence of death but with a sort of indefinite reprieve—*les hommes sont tous condamnés à mort avec des sursis indéfinis*:[6] we have an interval, and then our place knows us no more. Some spend this interval in listlessness, some in high passions, the wisest, at least among "the children of this world,"[7] in art and song. For our one chance lies in expanding that interval, in getting as many pulsations as possible into the given time. Great passions may give us this quickened[8] sense of life, ecstasy and sorrow of love, the various forms of enthusiastic activity, disinterested[9] or otherwise, which come naturally to many of us. Only be sure it is passion—that it does yield you this fruit of a quickened, multiplied consciousness. Of this wisdom, the poetic passion, the desire of beauty, the love of art for art's sake, has most, for art comes to you professing frankly to give nothing but the highest quality to your moments as they pass, and simply for those moments' sake.

—1868

---

[1] *awful* Awe-inspiring.

[2] *Comte* French philosopher Auguste Comte (1798–1857); *Hegel* German philosopher Georg Wilhelm Friedrich Hegel (1770–1831).

[3] *Philosophy ... thought* From Victor Hugo's *Les Miserables* (1862) 2.2.

[4] *Confessions* Autobiographical work by Jean-Jacques Rousseau (1712–78), Swiss writer and Enlightenment philosopher.

[5] *Voltaire* French writer and Enlightenment intellectual (1694–1778).

[6] *les hommes ... indéfinis* From Victor Hugo's *Le dernier jour d'un condamné* (1829).

[7] *the children of this world* From Luke 16.8: "The children of this world are in their generation wiser than the children of light."

[8] *quickened* Enlivened.

[9] *disinterested* Not self-interested.

Leonardo da Vinci, *The Last Supper*, 1498. "On the damp wall of the refectory, oozing with mineral salts, Leonardo painted the *Last Supper*. A hundred anecdotes were told about it, his retouchings and delays. They show him refusing to work except at the moment of invention, scornful of whoever thought that art was a work of mere industry and rule, often coming the whole length of Milan to give a single touch. He painted it, not in fresco, where all must be impromptu, but in oils, the new method which he had been one of the first to welcome, because it allowed of so many afterthoughts, so refined a working out of perfection. It turned out that on a plastered wall no process could have been less durable" (from *The Renaissance*).

Titian (previously attributed to Giorgione), *The Pastoral Concert*, 1508–09. "It is to the law or condition of music, as I said, that all art like this is really aspiring; and, in the school of Giorgione, the perfect moments of music itself, the making or hearing of music, song or its accompaniment, are themselves prominent as subjects. On that background of the silence of Venice, so impressive to the modern visitor, the world of Italian music was then forming. In choice of subject, as in all besides, the *Concert* of the Pitti Palace is typical of everything that Giorgione, himself an admirable musician, touched with his influence; and in sketch or finished picture, in various collections, we may follow it through many intricate variations—men fainting at music; music heard at the poolside while people fish, or mingled with the sound of the pitcher in the well, or heard across running water, or among the flocks; the tuning of instruments; people with intent faces, as if listening, like those described by Plato in an ingenious passage of the *Republic*, to detect the smallest interval of musical sound, the smallest undulation in the air, or feeling for music in thought on a stringless instrument, ear and finger refining themselves infinitely, in the appetite for sweet sound; a momentary touch of an instrument in the twilight, as one passes through some unfamiliar room, in a chance company" (from *The Renaissance*).

THOMAS HARDY
1840 – 1928

The work of Thomas Hardy—highly original and yet intimately connected with centuries-old traditions—is as important to the history of English poetry as it is to that of the novel in English, and as central to twentieth-century literature as it is to that of the Victorian era. Hardy was born in 1840 in Dorset, where much of his fiction was later set. A frail child, he did not attend the local school until the age of eight. However, his ill health fostered his love of reading. In his walks in the area, Hardy also came into contact with the local farmers and laborers, whose hardship and poverty deeply touched him. At the age of 15, he was apprenticed to a local architect, a career that would sustain him until he became established as a writer.

In 1862 Hardy moved to London to work with another architect. Always driven, he would rise at five in the morning to complete three or four hours of reading—in Homer, the Greek Testament, the Renaissance poets—before going to the office. On his return from work, he would often stay up reading and writing until midnight. It was during this time that he began writing poetry and short stories. Although he submitted many pieces to various magazines and the editors often wrote that he showed promise, his work was consistently rejected.

The hectic schedule that Hardy was following caused his health to deteriorate, and he was forced to return to the countryside in 1867 to recuperate. In Dorchester, he worked as an architect during the day and wrote in his spare time. It was in the course of his employment that he met his first wife, Emma Gifford. He had been sent to St. Juliot to draw plans for a church restoration, and Emma was the sister-in-law of the rector. The two struck up a close friendship, and Emma was very supportive of his writing. With Emma's encouragement, Hardy published his first novel, *Desperate Remedies* (1871). The novel, which has much in common with sensation fiction, a popular sub-genre of the 1860s, met with mixed reviews, but he continued to write. *Under the Greenwood Tree* (1872), his next novel, brought him popular acclaim.

In his early novels, Hardy began to include real places from the Dorset area, renamed Wessex— and was praised for his portrayal of the countryside and the people of the region. *A Pair of Blue Eyes* (1873) mirrored his own courtship with Emma, whom he married in 1874. That year also saw the publication of *Far from the Madding Crowd*, the first of what are now regarded as his classic novels. It depicts the life and loves of Bathsheba Everdene, and provides a convincing portrait of rural life. The novel also includes one of Hardy's "fallen women"; the case of Fanny Robin, who is seduced and eventually dies in a workhouse, shocked many readers. Despite this, the novel was very popular, and allowed him to give up his architectural work and concentrate solely on writing.

The Return of the Native, published in 1878, was also very successful. All of Hardy's novels were by now appearing in serialized form in monthly family magazines—a development which affected both the way that he wrote and the content of his fiction. Like most serialized writers, Hardy incorporated a steady flow of incidents in his novels; he was catering to an audience that needed to be encouraged to keep reading and buy the next issue. The "family" nature of the magazines often led his editors (one of whom was Leslie Stephen, the father of Virginia Woolf) to caution him to tone down the racier scenes and rewrite large sections. Because of the strict morality that dominated editorial policy, for example, Hardy could not state explicitly that some of his characters might have been involved in extra-marital activities.

Censure of Hardy's depiction of "immoral" subject matter reached its peak with the publication of his next two major novels, *Tess of the d'Urbervilles* (1891) and *Jude the Obscure* (1895). In the first of these, the aristocratic Alec d'Urberville forces himself upon Tess, who then bears his illegitimate child. Both the "seduction" itself and Tess's attempt to have the illegitimate child baptized shocked readers. Hardy rewrote many of the novel's explicit or controversial sections for serialization in *Longman's Magazine*, but when the novel was published as a complete volume, the controversial sections were restored.

Jude the Obscure depicts the thwarted life of Jude Fawley, a village mason who dreams of attending university but whose hopes are derailed by romantic entanglements—first with Arabella Dunn and later with Sue Bridehead—and by the deadening exclusions of class-conscious English society of the later nineteenth century. Hardy's marriage was on shaky ground at the time, and his wife Emma attempted to halt the publication of the novel. Publication went forward, but criticism of the book was swift and cruel. The Bishop of Wakefield, for one, said he had "bought one of Mr. Hardy's novels, but was so disgusted with its insolence and indecency" that he "threw it into the fire." Unfavorable and uncomprehending responses to *Jude* encouraged Hardy to give up fiction; this was the last novel he wrote.

Hardy's stories—of which he considered "The Son's Veto" to be his best—are, like his novels, frequently rooted in the details of traditional rural and small town life, although they often touch on highly contemporary issues. Also like his novels, they often take in the broad sweep of his characters' lives, which are typically subject to remorseless twists of fate; the gods may haunt his texts, but no God is there. Ongoing tensions between the city and the countryside, the educated and the uneducated, and the rich and the poor frequently contribute to the tragedy that lies at the heart of the life of a typical Hardy character, although these material factors frequently combine with a more philosophically grounded pessimism.

From the mid 1890s, Hardy concentrated on composing poetry, continuing in a different genre the portrayal of the Wessex region he had made famous in the novels. *Wessex Poems* appeared in 1898, *Satires of Circumstance* in 1914, and *Moments of Vision* in 1917. Hardy's poems form a body of work strongly rooted in the physical details of place—but even more than that, one strongly rooted in the past. Hardy often borrows from traditional poetic forms (such as the ballad), and he often employs archaic diction. In subject matter, too, the poems tend to be strongly rooted in the past—more often than not a very personal past, with love and the loss of love being recalled by the speaker; in very many of Hardy's poems an elegiac tone is pervasive.

Hardy's poetry is sometimes discussed as constituting a reaction to modernism; perhaps it would be more accurate to think of it standing as a strong counterweight to modernism. Certainly the simplicity and emotional resonance of his poetry have exerted a strong influence on the works of many subsequent poets (Philip Larkin perhaps most prominent among them). So too has Hardy's formal approach. His rhythms, his rhymes, and the way in which he varies quantity are all tightly controlled and finely modulated; the extraordinary degree of technical accomplishment in much of Hardy's poetry does not call attention to itself, and is perhaps all the more impressive for so often being unobtrusive.

Hardy's poetic reputation continues to rest on his lyrics and ballads—most of them tightly compact works. His most ambitious poetic work is much longer; *The Dynasts* is an extraordinary epic poem set in the Napoleonic Wars. It was published in three parts between 1903 and 1908.

The death of Emma in 1912, and Hardy's subsequent remorse for what had become of their relationship, resulted in some of his finest poetry and love poems, which appeared in *Satires of Circumstance* (1914). Hardy remarried in 1914; his second wife, Florence, is listed as the author of a two-volume biography that appeared in 1928 and 1930, but it has since been established that Hardy wrote the work himself. Hardy was awarded the Order of Merit in 1910 and the Gold Medal of the Royal Society of Literature in 1912. When he died in 1928, his ashes were interred in Poets' Corner at Westminster Abbey, but his heart was buried with Emma in Stinsford, in southern England.

⌘⌘⌘

The Son's Veto

I

To the eyes of a man viewing it from behind, the nut-brown hair was a wonder and a mystery. Under the black beaver hat, surmounted by its tuft of black feathers, the long locks, braided and twisted and coiled like the rushes of a basket, composed a rare, if somewhat barbaric, example of ingenious art. One could understand such weavings and coiling being wrought to last intact for a year, or even a calendar month; but that they should be all demolished regularly at bedtime, after a single day of permanence, seemed a reckless waste of successful fabrication.

And she had done it all herself, poor thing. She had no maid, and it was almost the only accomplishment she could boast of. Hence the unstinted pains.

She was a young invalid lady—not so very much of an invalid—sitting in a wheeled chair, which had been pulled up in the front part of a green enclosure, close to a band-stand, where a concert was going on, during a warm June afternoon. It had place in one of the minor parks or private gardens that are to be found in the suburbs of London, and was the effort of a local association to raise money for some charity. There were worlds within worlds in the great city, and though nobody outside the immediate district had ever heard of the charity, or the band, or the garden, the enclosure was filled with an interested audience sufficiently informed of all these.

As the strains proceeded many of the listeners observed the chaired lady, whose back hair, by reason of her prominent position, so challenged inspection. Her face was not easily discernible, but the aforesaid cunning tress-weavings, the white ear and poll,[1] and the curve of a cheek which was neither flaccid nor sallow, were signals that led to the expectation of good beauty in front. Such expectations are not infrequently disappointed as soon as the disclosure comes; and in the present case, when the lady, by a turn of the head, at length revealed herself, she was not so handsome as the people behind her had supposed, and even hoped—they did not know why.

For one thing (alas! the commonness of this complaint), she was less young than they had fancied her to be. Yet attractive her face unquestionably was, and not at all sickly. The revelation of its details came each time she turned to talk to a boy of twelve or thirteen who stood beside her, and the shape of whose hat and jacket implied that he belonged to a well-known public school.[2] The immediate by-standers could hear that he called her "Mother."

When the end of the programme was reached, and the audience withdrew, many chose to find their way out by passing at her elbow. Almost all turned their

---

1 *poll* Nape of the neck.

2 *public school* In England, private school.

heads to take a full and near look at the interesting woman, who remained stationary in the chair till the way should be clear enough for her to be wheeled out without obstruction. As if she expected their glances, and did not mind gratifying their curiosity, she met the eyes of several of her observers by lifting her own, showing these to be soft, brown, and affectionate orbs, a little plaintive in their regard.

She was conducted out of the garden, and passed along the pavement till she disappeared from view, the school-boy walking beside her. To inquiries made by some persons who watched her away, the answer came that she was the second wife of the incumbent of a neighbouring parish, and that she was lame. She was generally believed to be a woman with a story—an innocent one, but a story of some sort or other.

In conversing with her on their way home the boy who walked at her elbow said that he hoped his father had not missed them.

"He have been so comfortable these last few hours that I am sure he cannot have missed us," she replied.

"*Has,* dear mother—not *have!*" exclaimed the public-school boy, with an impatient fastidiousness that was almost harsh. "Surely you know that by this time!"

His mother hastily adopted the correction, and did not resent his making it, or retaliate, as she might well have done, by bidding him to wipe that crumby mouth of his, whose condition had been caused by surreptitious attempts to eat a piece of cake without taking it out of the pocket wherein it lay concealed. After this the pretty woman and the boy went onward in silence.

That question of grammar bore upon her history, and she fell into reverie, of a somewhat sad kind to all appearance. It might have been assumed that she was wondering if she had done wisely in shaping her life as she had shaped it, to bring out such a result as this.

In a remote nook in North Wessex, forty miles from London, near the thriving county-town of Aldbrickham, there stood a pretty village with its church and parsonage, which she knew well enough, but her son had never seen. It was her native village, Gaymead, and the first event bearing upon her present situation had occurred at that place when she was only a girl of nineteen.

How well she remembered it, that first act in her little tragi-comedy, the death of her reverend husband's first wife. It happened on a spring evening, and she who now and for many years had filled that first wife's place was then parlor-maid in the parson's house.

When everything had been done that could be done, and the death was announced, she had gone out in the dusk to visit her parents, who were living in the same village, to tell them the sad news. As she opened the white swing-gate and looked towards the trees which rose westward, shutting out the pale light of the evening sky, she discerned, without much surprise, the figure of a man standing in the hedge, though she roguishly exclaimed, as a matter of form, "Oh Sam, how you frightened me!"

He was a young gardener of her acquaintance. She told him the particulars of the late event, and they stood silent, these two young people, in that elevated, calmly philosophic mind which is engendered when a tragedy has happened close at hand, and has not happened to the philosophers themselves. But it had its bearings upon their relations.

"And will you stay on now at the Vicarage, just the same?" asked he.

She had hardly thought of that. "Oh yes—I suppose," she said. "Everything will be just as usual, I imagine."

He walked beside her towards her mother's. Presently his arm stole round her waist. She gently removed it; but he placed it there again, and she yielded the point. "You see, dear Sophy, you don't know that you'll stay on; you may want a home; and I shall be ready to offer one some day, though I may not be ready just yet."

"Why, Sam, how can you be so fast? I've never even said I liked 'ee; and it is all your own doing, coming after me."

"Still, it is nonsense to say I am not to have a try at you, like the rest." He stooped to kiss her a farewell, for they had reached her mother's door.

"No, Sam; you sha'nt!" she cried, putting her hand over his mouth. "You ought to be more serious on such a night as this." And she bade him adieu without allowing him to kiss her or to come indoors.

The vicar just left a widower was at this time a man about forty years of age, of good family, and childless.

He had led a secluded existence in this college living, partly because there were no resident landowners; and his loss now intensified his habit of withdrawal from outward observation. He was still less seen than heretofore, kept himself still less in time with the rhythm and racket of the movements called progress in the world without.[1] For many months after his wife's decease the economy[2] of his household remained as before; the cook, the house-maid, the parlor-maid, and the man out-of-doors performed their duties or left them undone, just as nature prompted them—the vicar knew not which. It was then represented to him that his servants seemed to have nothing to do in his small family of one. He was struck with the truth of this representation, and decided to cut down his establishment. But he was forestalled by Sophy, the parlor-maid, who said one evening that she wished to leave him.

"And why?" said the parson.

"Sam Hobson has asked me to marry him, sir."

"Well—do you want to marry?"

"Not much. But it would be a home for me. And we have heard that one of us will have to leave."

A day or two after she said: "I don't want to leave just yet, sir, if you don't wish it. Sam and I have quarreled."

He looked at her. He had hardly ever observed her before, though he had been frequently conscious of her soft presence in the room. What a kitten-like, flexuous,[3] tender creature she was! She was the only one of the servants with whom he came into immediate and continuous relation. What should he do if Sophy were gone?

Sophy did not go, but one of the others did, and things proceeded quietly again.

When Mr. Twycott, the vicar, was ill, Sophy brought up his meals to him, and she had no sooner left the room one day than he heard a noise on the stairs. She had slipped down with the tray, and so twisted her foot that she could not stand. The village surgeon was called in; the vicar got better, but Sophy was incapacitated for a long time; and she was informed that she must never again walk much or engage in any occupation which required her to stand long on her feet. As soon as she was comparatively well she spoke to him alone. Since she was forbidden to walk and bustle about, and, indeed could not do so, it became her duty to leave. She could very well work at something sitting down, and she had an aunt, a seamstress.

The parson had been very greatly moved by what she had suffered on his account, and he exclaimed, "No, Sophy; lame or not lame, I cannot let you go. You must never leave me again."

He came close to her, and, though she could never exactly tell how it happened, she became conscious of his lips upon her cheek. He then asked her to marry him. Sophy did not exactly love him, but she had a respect for him which almost amounted to veneration. Even if she had wished to get away from him she hardly dared refuse a personage so reverend and august in her eyes, and she assented forthwith to be his wife.

Thus it happened that one fine morning, when the doors of the church were naturally open for ventilation, and the singing birds fluttered in and alighted on the tie-beams of the rood,[4] there was a marriage-service at the communion rails which hardly a soul knew of. The parson and a neighbouring curate[5] had entered at one door, and Sophy at another, followed by two necessary persons, whereupon in a short time there emerged a newly-made husband and wife.

Mr. Twycott knew perfectly well that he had committed social suicide by this step, despite Sophy's spotless character, and he had taken his measures accordingly. An exchange of livings had been arranged with an acquaintance who was incumbent of a church in the south of London, and as soon as possible the couple

---

[1] *without* Outside.

[2] *economy* Management.

[3] *flexuous* Curvy.

[4] *rood* Cross.

[5] *curate* Member of the clergy, usually one who assists the clergy member in charge of a parish.

removed thither, abandoning their pretty country home with trees and shrubs and glebe[1] for a narrow, dusty house in a long, straight street, and their fine peal of bells for the wretchedest one-tongue clangor that ever tortured mortal ears. It was all on her account. They were, however, away from every one who had known her former position, and also under less observation from without than they would have had to put up with in any country parish.

Sophy the woman was as charming a partner as a man could possess, though Sophy the lady had her deficiencies. She showed a natural aptitude for little domestic refinements, so far as related to things and manners; but in what is called culture she was less intuitive. She had now been married more than fourteen years, and her husband had taken much trouble with her education; but she still held confused ideas on the use of "was" and "were," which did not beget a respect for her among the few acquaintances she made. Her great grief in this relation was that her only child, on whose education no expense had been or would be spared, was now old enough to perceive these deficiencies in his mother, and not only to see them but to feel irritated at their existence.

Thus she lived on in the city, and wasted hours in braiding her beautiful hair, till her once apple cheeks waned to pink of the very faintest. Her foot had never regained its natural strength after the accident, and she was mostly obliged to avoid walking altogether. Her husband had grown to like London for its freedom and its domestic privacy; but he was twenty years his Sophy's senior, and had latterly been seized with a serious illness. On this day, however, he had seemed to be well enough to justify her accompanying her son Randolph to the concert.

2

The next time we get a glimpse of her is when she appears in the mournful attire of a widow.

Mr. Twycott had never rallied, and now lay in a well-packed cemetery to the south of the great city, where, if all the dead it contained had stood erect and alive, not one would have known him or recognized his name. The boy had dutifully followed him to the grave, and was now again at school.

Throughout these changes Sophy had been treated like the child she was in nature though not in years. She was left with no control over anything that had been her husband's beyond her modest personal income. In his anxiety lest her inexperience should be overreached he had safeguarded with trustees all he possibly could. The completion of the boy's course at the public school, to be followed in due time by Oxford and ordination, had been all provisioned and arranged, and she really had nothing to occupy her in the world but to eat and drink, and make a business of indolence, and go on weaving and coiling the nut-brown hair, merely keeping a home open for the son whenever he came to her during vacations.

Foreseeing his probable decease long years before her, her husband in his lifetime had purchased for her use a semi-detached villa in the same long, straight road whereon the church and parsonage faced, which was to be hers as long as she chose to live in it. Here she now resided, looking out upon the fragment of lawn in front, and through the railings at the ever-flowing traffic; or, bending forward over the window-sill on the first floor, stretching her eyes far up and down the vista of sooty trees, hazy air, and drab house façades, along which echoed the noises common to a suburban main thoroughfare.

Somehow, her boy, with his aristocratic school-knowledge, his grammar, and his aversions, was losing those wide infantile sympathies, extending as far as to the sun and moon themselves, with which he, like other children, had been born, and which his mother, a child of nature herself, had loved in him; he was reducing their compass[2] to a population of a few thousand wealthy and titled people, the mere veneer of a thousand million or so of others who did not interest him at all. He drifted further and further away from her. Sophy's *milieu* being a suburb of minor tradesmen and under-clerks, and her almost only companions the two servants

---

[1] *glebe* Land granted to a member of the clergy.

[2] *compass* Here, social circle.

of her own house, it was not surprising that after her husband's death she soon lost the little artificial tastes she had acquired from him, and became—in her son's eyes—a mother whose mistakes and origin it was his painful lot as a gentleman to blush for. As yet he was far from being man enough—if he ever would be—to rate these sins of hers at their true infinitesimal value beside the yearning fondness that welled up and remained penned in her heart till it should be more fully accepted by him, or by some other person or thing. If he had lived at home with her he would have had all of it; but he seemed to require so very little in present circumstances, and it remained stored.

Her life became insupportably dreary; she could not take walks, and had no interest in going for drives, or, indeed, in traveling anywhere. Nearly two years passed without an event, and still she looked on that suburban road, thinking of the village in which she had been born, and whither she would have gone back—oh, how gladly!—even to work in the fields.

Taking no exercise, she often could not sleep, and would rise in the night or early morning and look out upon the then vacant thoroughfare, where the lamps stood like sentinels waiting for some procession to go by. An approximation to such a procession was indeed made every early morning about one o'clock, when the country vehicles passed up with loads of vegetables for Covent Garden market.[1] She often saw them creeping along at this silent and dusky hour—wagon after wagon, bearing green bastions of cabbages nodding to their fall, yet never falling; walls of baskets enclosing masses of beans and pease; pyramids of snow-white turnips, swaying howdahs[2] of mixed produce—creeping along behind aged night-horses, who seemed ever patiently wondering between their hollow coughs why they had always to work at that still hour when all other sentient creatures were privileged to rest. Wrapped in a cloak, it was soothing to watch and sympathize with them when depression and nervousness hindered sleep, and to see how the fresh green-stuff brightened to life as it came opposite the lamp, and how the sweating animals steamed and shone with their miles of travel.

They had an interest, almost a charm, for Sophy, these semi-rural people and vehicles moving in an urban atmosphere, leading a life quite distinct from that of the daytime toilers on the same road. One morning a man who accompanied a wagon-load of potatoes gazed rather hard at the house fronts as he passed, and with a curious emotion she thought his form was familiar to her. She looked out for him again. His being an old-fashioned conveyance with a yellow front, it was easily recognizable, and on the third night after she saw it a second time. The man alongside was, as she had fancied, Sam Hobson, formerly gardener at Gaymead, who would at one time have married her.

She had occasionally thought of him, and wondered if life in a cottage with him would not have been a happier lot than the life she had accepted. She had not thought of him passionately, but her now dismal situation lent an interest to his resurrection—a tender interest which it is impossible to exaggerate. She went back to bed, and began thinking. When did these market-gardeners, who traveled up to town so regularly at one or two in the morning, come back? She dimly recollected seeing their empty wagons, hardly noticeable among the ordinary day-traffic, passing down at some hour before noon.

It was only April, but that morning, after breakfast, she had the window opened, and sat looking out, the feeble sun shining full upon her. She affected to sew, but her eyes never left the street. Between ten and eleven the desired wagon, now unladen, reappeared on its return journey. But Sam was not looking round him then, and drove on in a reverie.

"Sam!" cried she.

---

[1] *Covent Garden market* Longstanding London market associated with the fruit and vegetable trade.

[2] *howdahs* Seats carried by elephants.

Turning with a start, his face lighted up. He called to him a little boy to hold the horse, alighted, and came and stood under her window.

Hobson came and stood under her window.[1]

"I can't come down easily, Sam, or I would!" she said. "Did you know I lived here?"

"Well, Mrs. Twycott, I knew you lived along here somewhere. I have often looked out for 'ee."

He briefly explained his own presence on the scene. He had long since given up his gardening in the village near Aldbrickham, and was now manager at a market-gardener's on the south side of London, it being part of his duty to go up to Covent Garden with wagon-loads of produce two or three times a week. In answer to her curious inquiry, he admitted that he had come to this particular district because he had seen in the Aldbrickham paper a year or two before the announcement of

the death in South London of the aforetime vicar of Gaymead, which had revived an interest in her dwelling-place that he could not extinguish, leading him to hover about the locality till his present post had been secured.

They spoke of their native village in dear old North Wessex, the spots in which they had played together as children. She tried to feel that she was a dignified personage now, that she must not be too confidential with Sam. But she could not keep it up, and the tears hanging in her eyes were indicated in her voice.

"You are not happy, Mrs. Twycott, I'm afraid," he said.

"Oh, of course not! I lost my husband only the year before last."

"Ah! I meant in another way. You'd like to be home again!"

"This is my home—for life. The house belongs to me. But I understand"—She let it out then.

"Yes, Sam. I long for home—*our* home! I *should* like to be there, and never leave it, and die there." But she remembered herself. "That's only a momentary feeling. I have a son, you know, a dear boy. He's at school now."

"Somewhere handy, I suppose? I see there's lots of 'em along this road."

"Oh no! Not in one of these wretched holes! At a public school—one of the most distinguished in England."

"Chok' it all! of course! I forgot, ma'am, that you've been a lady for so many years."

"No, I am not a lady," she said, sadly. "I never shall be. But he's a gentleman, and that—makes it—oh, how difficult for me!"

3

The acquaintance thus oddly reopened proceeded apace. She often looked out to get a few words with him by night or by day. Her sorrow was that she could not accompany her one old friend on foot a little way, and talk more freely than she could do while he paused before the house. One night, at the beginning of June, when she was again on the watch after an absence of some days from the window, he entered the gate and said, softly, "Now, wouldn't some air do you good? I've

---

[1] The illustrations that appear with this story accompanied "The Son's Veto" when it was first published in the *Illustrated London News*, 1 December 1891.

only half a load this morning. Why not ride up to Covent Garden with me? There's a nice seat on the cabbages, where I've spread a sack. You can be home again in a cab before anybody is up."

She refused at first, and then, trembling with excitement, hastily finished her dressing, and wrapped herself up in cloak and veil, afterwards sidling downstairs by the aid of the handrail, in a way she could adopt on an emergency. When she had opened the door she found Sam on the step, and he lifted her bodily on his strong arm across the little forecourt into his vehicle. Not a soul was visible or audible in the infinite length of the straight, flat highway, with its ever-waiting lamps converging to points in each direction. The air was fresh as country air at this hour, and the stars shone, except to the north-eastward, where there was a whitish light—the dawn. Sam carefully placed her in the seat and drove on.

They talked as they had talked in old days, Sam pulling himself up now and then, when he thought himself too familiar. More than once she said with misgiving that she wondered if she ought to have indulged in the freak.[1] "But I am so lonely in my house," she added, "and this makes me so happy!"

"You must come again, dear Mrs. Twycott. There is no time o' day for taking the air like this."

It grew lighter and lighter. The sparrows became busy in the streets, and the city waxed denser around them. When they approached the river it was day, and on the bridge they beheld the full blaze of morning sunlight in the direction of St. Paul's,[2] the river glistening towards it, and not a craft stirring.

Near Covent Garden he put her into a cab, and they parted, looking into each other's faces like the very old friends they were. She reached home without adventure, limped to the door, and let herself in with her latch-key unseen.

The air and Sam's presence had revived her; her cheeks were quite pink—almost beautiful. She had something to live for in addition to her son. A woman of pure instincts, she knew there had been nothing really wrong in the journey, but supposed it conventionally to be very wrong indeed.

Soon, however, she gave way to the temptation of going with him again, and on this occasion their conversation was distinctly tender, and Sam said he never should forget her, notwithstanding that she had served[3] him rather badly at one time. After much hesitation he told her of a plan it was in his power to carry out, and one he should like to take in hand, since he did not care for London work; it was to set up as a master gardener down at Aldbrickham, the county-town of their native place. He knew of an opening—a shop kept by aged people who wished to retire.

"And why don't you do it, then, Sam?" she asked, with a slight heart-sinking.

"Because I'm not sure if—you'd join me. I know you wouldn't—couldn't! Such a lady as ye've been so long, you couldn't be a wife to a man like me."

"I hardly suppose I could!" she assented, also frightened at the idea.

"If you could," he said, eagerly, "you'd on'y have to sit in the back parlor and look through the glass partition when I was away sometimes—just to keep an eye on things. The lameness wouldn't hinder that. I'd keep you as genteel as ever I could, dear Sophy—if I might think of it," he pleaded.

"Sam, I'll be frank," she said, putting her hand on his. "If it were only myself I would do it, and gladly, though everything I possess would be lost to me by marrying again."

"I don't mind that. It's more independent."

"That's good of you, dear, dear Sam. But there's something else. I have a son. I almost fancy when I am miserable sometimes that he is not really mine, but one I hold in trust for my late husband. He seems to belong so little to me personally, so entirely to his dead father. He is so much educated and I so little that I do not feel dignified enough to be his mother. Well, he would have to be told."

"Yes. Unquestionably." Sam saw her thought and her fear. "Still, you can do as you like, Sophy—Mrs.

---

[1] *freak* Whim.

[2] *St. Paul's* Cathedral in London.

[3] *served* Treated.

Twycott," he added. "It is not you who are the child, but he."

"Ah, you don't know! Sam, if I could, I would marry you, some day. But you must wait awhile, and let me think."

It was enough for him, and he was blithe at their parting. Not so she. To tell Randolph seemed impossible. She could wait till he had gone up to Oxford, when what she did would affect his life but little. But would he ever tolerate the idea? And if not, could she defy him?

She had not told him a word when the yearly cricket-match came on at Lord's[1] between the public schools, though Sam had already gone back to Aldbrickham. Mrs. Twycott felt stronger than usual. She went to the match with Randolph, and was able to leave her chair and walk about occasionally. The bright idea occurred to her that she could casually broach the subject while moving round among the spectators, when the boy's spirits were high with interest in the game, and he would weigh domestic matters as feathers in the scale beside the day's victory. They promenaded under the lurid July sun, this pair, so wide apart, yet so near, and Sophy saw the large proportion of boys like her own, in their broad white collars and dwarf hats, and all around the rows of great coaches under which was jumbled the débris of luxurious luncheons—bones, pie-crusts, champagne-bottles, glasses, plates, napkins, and the family silver; while on the coaches sat the proud fathers and mothers; but never a poor mother like her. If Randolph had not appertained to these, had not centred all his interests in them, had not cared exclusively for the class they belonged to, how happy would things have been! A great huzza at some small performance with the bat burst from the multitude of relatives, and Randolph jumped wildly into the air to see what had happened. Sophy fetched up the sentence that had been already shaped; but she could not get it out. The occasion was, perhaps, an inopportune one. The contrast between her story and the display of fashion to which Randolph had grown to regard himself as akin would be fatal. She awaited a better time.

It was on an evening when they were alone in their plain suburban residence, where life was not blue but brown, that she ultimately broke silence, qualifying her announcement of a probable second marriage by assuring him that it would not take place for a long time to come, when he would be living quite independently of her.

The boy thought the idea a very reasonable one, and asked if she had chosen anybody. She hesitated; and he seemed to have a misgiving. He hoped his step-father would be a gentleman, he said.

"Not what you call a gentleman," she answered, timidly. "He'll be much as I was before I knew your father"; and by degrees she acquainted him with the whole. The youth's face remained fixed for a moment; then he flushed, leaned on the table, and burst into passionate tears.

His mother went up to him, kissed all of his face that she could get at, and patted his back as if he were still the baby he once had been, crying herself the while. When he had somewhat recovered from his paroxysm he went hastily to his own room and fastened the door.

Parleyings[2] were attempted through the key-hole, outside which she waited and listened. It was long before he would reply, and when he did it was to say sternly at her from within: "I am ashamed of you! It will ruin me! A miserable boor! a churl! a clown![3] It will degrade me in the eyes of all the gentlemen of England!"

"Say no more—perhaps I am wrong! I will struggle against it!" she cried, miserably.

Before Randolph left her that summer a letter arrived from Sam to inform her that he had been unexpectedly fortunate in obtaining the shop. He was in possession; it was the largest in the town, combining fruit with vegetables, and he thought it would form a home worthy even of her some day. Might he not run up to town to see her?

She met him by stealth, and said he must still wait for her final answer. The autumn dragged on, and when

---

[1] *yearly cricket-match ... Lord's* Lord's cricket ground in London has been the site of an annual cricket match between two of the most prestigious public schools in England, Eton and Harrow, since 1805.

[2] *Parleyings* Negotiations.

[3] *boor* Unrefined person; *churl* Peasant or ill-mannered person; *clown* Rustic or unsophisticated person.

Randolph was home at Christmas for the holidays she broached the matter again. But the young gentleman was inexorable.

It was dropped for months; renewed again; abandoned under his repugnance; again attempted, and thus the gentle creature reasoned and pleaded till four or five long years had passed. Then the faithful Sam revived his suit with some peremptoriness. Sophy's son, now an undergraduate, was down from Oxford one Easter, when she again opened the subject. As soon as he was ordained, she argued, he would have a home of his own, wherein she, with her bad grammar and her ignorance, would be an encumbrance to him. Better obliterate her as much as possible.

He showed a more manly anger now, but would not agree. She on her side was more persistent, and he had doubts whether she could be trusted in his absence. But by indignation and contempt for her taste he completely maintained his ascendancy; and finally taking her before a little cross and shrine that he had erected in his bedroom for his private devotions, there bade her kneel, and swear that she would not wed Samuel Hobson without his consent. "I owe this to my father!" he said.

The poor woman swore, thinking he would soften as soon as he was ordained and in full swing of clerical work. But he did not. His education had by this time sufficiently ousted his humanity to keep him quite firm; though his mother might have led an idyllic life with her faithful fruiterer and green-grocer, and nobody have been anything the worse in the world.

Her lameness became more confirmed as time went on, and she seldom or never left the house in the long southern thoroughfare, where she seemed to be pining her heart away. "Why mayn't I say to Sam that I'll marry him? Why mayn't I?" she would murmur plaintively to herself when nobody was near.

Some four years after this date a middle-aged man was standing at the door of the largest fruiterer's shop in Aldbrickham. He was the proprietor, but to-day, instead of his usual business attire, he wore a neat suit of black; and his window was partly shuttered. From the railway station a funeral procession was seen approaching; it passed his door and went out of the town towards the

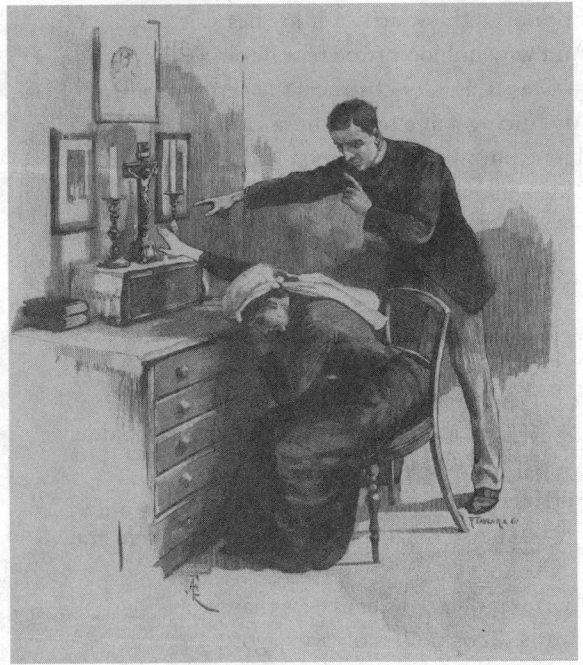

He made her swear before a little cross and shrine in his bed-room that she would not wed Samuel Hobson without his consent.

village of Gaymead. The man, whose eyes were wet, held his hat in his hand as the vehicles moved by; while from the mourning coach a young smooth-shaven priest in a high waistcoat looked black as a cloud at the shopkeeper standing there.

—DECEMBER 1891

Hap°   chance

If but some vengeful god would call to me
From up the sky, and laugh: "Thou suffering thing,
Know that thy sorrow is my ecstasy,
That thy love's loss is my hate's profiting!"

5   Then would I bear it, clench myself, and die,
Steeled by the sense of ire unmerited;
Half-eased in that a Powerfuller than I
Had willed and meted° me the tears I shed.   allotted

But not so. How arrives it joy lies slain,
10   And why unblooms the best hope ever sown?
      —Crass Casualty obstructs the sun and rain,
      And dicing Time for gladness casts a moan. . . .
      These purblind Doomsters[1] had as readily strown
      Blisses about my pilgrimage as pain.
      —1898 (WRITTEN 1866)

Neutral Tones

We stood by a pond that winter day,
      And the sun was white, as though chidden
         of God,
And a few leaves lay on the starving sod;
      —They had fallen from an ash, and were gray.

5   Your eyes on me were as eyes that rove
    Over tedious riddles of years ago;
    And some words played between us to and fro
       On which lost the more by our love.

The smile on your mouth was the deadest thing
10 Alive enough to have strength to die;
    And a grin of bitterness swept thereby
       Like an ominous bird a-wing . . .

Since then, keen° lessons that love deceives,   *sharp*
    And wrings with wrong, have shaped to me
15 Your face, and the God-curst sun, and a tree,
       And a pond edged with grayish leaves.
    —1898 (WRITTEN 1867)

In a Wood

Pale beech and pine-tree blue,
      Set in one clay,
Bough to bough cannot you
      Bide out your day?
5   When the rains skim and skip,
    Why mar sweet comradeship,

Blighting° with poison-drip   *infecting, spoiling*
      Neighbourly spray?

Heart-halt and spirit-lame,
10   City-opprest,
Unto this wood I came
      As to a nest;
Dreaming that sylvan° peace   *woodland*
Offered the harrowed ease—
15 Nature a soft release
      From men's unrest.

But, having entered in,
      Great growths and small
Show them to men akin—
20   Combatants all!
Sycamore shoulders oak,
Bines° the slim sapling yoke,   *climbing vines*
Ivy-spun halters° choke   *nooses*
      Elms stout and tall.

25 Touches from ash, O wych,°   *elm*
      Sting you like scorn!
You, too, brave hollies, twitch
      Sidelong from thorn.
Even the rank poplars bear
30 Illy[2] a rival's air,
Cankering[3] in black despair
      If overborne.[4]

Since, then, no grace I find
      Taught me of trees,
35 Turn I back to my kind,
      Worthy as these.
There at least smiles abound,
There discourse trills around,
There, now and then, are found
40   Life-loyalties.
    —1898

---

[1] *purblind Doomsters* Half-blind judges.

[2] *Illy* In an ill manner.

[3] *Cankering* Developing areas of diseased plant tissue.

[4] *overborne* I.e., overgrown.

The Darkling[1] Thrush

I leant upon a coppice gate[2]
    When Frost was spectre-grey,
And Winter's dregs made desolate
    The weakening eye of day.
5 The tangled bine[3]-stems scored the sky
    Like strings of broken lyres,
And all mankind that haunted nigh
    Had sought their household fires.

The land's sharp features seemed to be
10   The Century's corpse outleant,[4]
His crypt the cloudy canopy,
    The wind his death-lament.
The ancient pulse of germ and birth
    Was shrunken hard and dry,
15 And every spirit upon earth
    Seemed fervorless as I.

At once a voice arose among
    The bleak twigs overhead
In a full-hearted evensong
20   Of joy illimited;
An aged thrush, frail, gaunt, and small,
    In blast-beruffled plume,[5]
Had chosen thus to fling his soul
    Upon the growing gloom.

25 So little cause for carolings
    Of such ecstatic sound
Was written on terrestrial things
    Afar or nigh around,
That I could think there trembled through
30   His happy good-night air
Some blessed Hope, whereof he knew
    And I was unaware.
    —1901 (WRITTEN 31 DECEMBER 1900)

---

[1] *Darkling* Being in the dark; obscure.

[2] *coppice gate* Gate leading to a thicket or small forest.

[3] *bine* Hop, a climbing plant.

[4] *The Century's corpse outleant* I.e., as if the century were leaning out of its coffin.

[5] *plume* I.e., feathers.

The Ruined Maid

"O'Melia, my dear, this does everything crown![6]
    Who could have supposed I should meet you
        in Town?
And whence such fair garments, such prosperi-ty?"—
"O didn't you know I'd been ruined?" said she.

5 —"You left us in tatters, without shoes or socks,
Tired of digging potatoes, and spudding up docks;[7]
And now you've gay bracelets and bright feathers
    three!"—
"Yes: that's how we dress when we're ruined," said she.

—"At home in the barton° you said 'thee'   *barnyard*
    and 'thou,'
10 And 'thik oon,' and 'theäs oon,' and 't'other'; but now
Your talking quite fits 'ee for high compa-ny!"—
"Some polish is gained with one's ruin," said she.

—"Your hands were like paws then, your face blue
    and bleak
But now I'm bewitched by your delicate cheek,
15 And your little gloves fit as on any la-dy!"—
"We never do work when we're ruined," said she.

—"You used to call home-life a hag-ridden dream,
And you'd sigh, and you'd sock;[8] but at present you seem
To know not of megrims° or melancho-ly!"— *depression*
20 "True. One's pretty lively when ruined," said she.

—"I wish I had feathers, a fine sweeping gown,
And a delicate face, and could strut about Town!"—
"My dear—a raw country girl, such as you be,
Cannot quite expect that. You ain't ruined," said she.
    —1901 (WRITTEN 1866)

---

[6] *this does everything crown* This surpasses everything.

[7] *spudding up docks* Uprooting weeds.

[8] *sock* Mouth your displeasure.

A Broken Appointment

You did not come.
And marching Time drew on, and wore me numb.—
Yet less for loss of your dear presence there
Than that I thus found lacking in your make
5 That high compassion which can overbear
Reluctance for pure lovingkindness' sake
Grieved I, when, as the hope-hour stroked its sum,
     You did not come.

You love not me,
10 And love alone can lend you loyalty;
—I know and knew it. But, unto the store
Of human deeds divine in all but name,
Was it not worth a little hour or more
To add yet this: Once you, a woman, came
15 To soothe a time-torn man; even though it be
     You love not me?

—1902

A Trampwoman's Tragedy

I

From Wynyard's Gap[1] the livelong day,
     The livelong day,
We beat afoot the northward way
     We had travelled times before.
5 The sun-blaze burning on our backs,
Our shoulders sticking to our packs,
By fosseway,[2] fields, and turnpike tracks
     We skirted sad Sedge-Moor.[3]

2

Full twenty miles we jaunted on,
10   We jaunted on,
My fancy-man,[4] and jeering John,
     And Mother Lee, and I.
And, as the sun drew down to west,
We climbed the toilsome Poldon[5] crest,
15 And saw, of landskip° sights the best,   landscape
     The inn that stood thereby.

3

For months we padded side by side
     All side by side,
Through the Great Forest, Blackmoor[6] wide,
20   And where the Parret[7] ran.
We'd faced the gusts on Mendip[8] ridge,
Had crossed the Yeo[9] unhelped by bridge,
Been stung by every Marshwood midge,[10]
     I and my fancy-man.

4

25 Lone inns we loved, my man and I,
     My man and I;
King's-Stag, Windwhistle[11] high and dry,
     The "Horse" on Hintock Green,
The cozy house at Wynyard's Gap,

---

[1] *Wynyard's Gap*   Place between hills in Dorset county, in the southwest of England, where an inn is located. All the places mentioned in the poem are in Dorset or Somerset (the county immediately north of Dorset).

[2] *fosseway*   Ancient Roman road running from southwestern to central England.

[3] *Sedge-Moor*   Marshy area in Somerset; it was the site of the brutal defeat of the Duke of Monmouth, who attempted a rebellion against King James II in 1685.

[4] *fancy-man*   Here, common-law husband of a low woman.

[5] *Poldon*   Ridge of hills where an Ancient Roman road was located, immediately north of Sedgemoor.

[6] *Blackmoor*   Vale (wide valley) straddling northwest Dorset and south Somerset.

[7] *Parret*   River that runs south to north, beginning near Wynyard's Gap and flowing past the Polden Hills.

[8] *Mendip*   High ridge north of the Polden Hills.

[9] *Yeo*   River that flows through Dorset and Somerset, near Blackmore Vale.

[10] *Marshwood*   Marshy vale in west Dorset; *midge*   Biting, gnat-like fly, found in swarms near water.

[11] [Hardy's note]   The highness and dryness of Windwhistle Inn was impressed upon the writer two or three years ago, when, after climbing on a hot afternoon to the beautiful spot near which it stands and entering the inn for tea, he was informed by the landlady that none could be had, unless he would fetch water from a valley half a mile off, the house containing not a drop owing to its situation. However, a tantalizing row of full barrels behind her back testified to a wetness of a certain sort, which was not at that time desired.

30 The "Hut" renowned on Bredy's Knap,
And many another wayside tap[1]
        Where folk might sit unseen.

                    5
Now as we trudged——O deadly day,
        O deadly day!—
35 I teased my fancy-man in play
        And wanton idleness.
I walked alongside jeering John,
I laid his hand my waist upon;
I would not bend my glances on
40   My lover's dark distress.

                    6
Thus Poldon top at last we won,
        At last we won,
And gained the inn at sink of sun
        Far-famed as Marshal's Elm.[2]
45 Beneath us figured tor and lea,[3]
From Mendip to the western sea—
I doubt if any finer sight there be
        Within this royal realm.

                    7
Inside the settle° all arow—   *long bench*
50   Ay, all arow—
We sat, I next to John, to show
        That he had wooed and won.
And then he took me on his knee,
And swore it was his turn to be
55 My favoured man, and Mother Lee
        Passed to my former one.

                    8
Then in a voice I'd never heard,
        I'd never heard,
My only love to me: "One word,

60 My lady, if you please!
Whose is the child you are like to bear?
His? After all my months o' care?"
Gods knows 'twas not! But, O despair!
        I nodded—still to tease.

                    9
65 Then he sprung, and with his knife—
        And with his knife
He let out jeering Johnny's life;
        Yes; there, at sink of sun.
The slant ray through the window nigh
70 Gilded[4] John's blood and glazing eye,
Ere scarcely Mother Lee and I
        Knew that the deed was done.

                    10
The taverns tell the gloomy tale,
        The gloomy tale,
75 How that at Ivel-chester jail
        My man, my lover, swung;
Though stained till now by no misdeed
Save one horse ta'en° in time o' need;   *taken*
(Blue Jimmy stole right many a steed
80   Ere his last fling he flung).[5]

                    11
Thereaft I walked the world alone
        Alone, alone!
On his death-day I gave my groan
        And dropt his dead-born child.
85 'Twas nigh° the jail, beneath a tree,   *near*
None tending me; for Mother Lee

---

[1] *tap* Taproom, i.e., inn with a pub.

[2] [Hardy's note] Marshal's Elm, so picturesquely situated, is no longer an inn, though the house, or part of it, still remains. [Marshal's Elm is an inn near Polden Hills, at the site of the first skirmish of the English Civil War in 1642.]

[3] *tor* Exposed rock at the peak of a hill; *lea* Flat, fertile ground.

---

[4] *Gilded* I.e., painted gold.

[5] [Hardy's note] "Blue Jimmy" was a notorious horse-stealer of Wessex [Dorset and nearby counties] in those days, who appropriated more than a hundred horses before he was caught. He was hanged at the now demolished Ivel-chester or Ilchester jail above mentioned, that building formerly of so many sinister associations in the minds of the local peasantry. Its site is now an innocent-looking, green meadow. [Hardy's mention of "sinister associations" likely refers to the Duke of Monmouth's failed rebellion; hundreds of rebels were imprisoned in Ilchester jail, and some were executed.]

Had died at Glaston,[1] leaving me
    Unfriended on the wild.

12

And in the night as I lay weak,
90   As I lay weak,
The leaves a-falling on my cheek,
    The red moon low declined—
The ghost of him I'd die to kiss
Rose up and said: "O tell me this!
95 Was the child mine, or was it his?
    Speak, that I rest may find!"

13

O, doubt not but I told him then,
    I told him then,
That I had kept me from all men
100   Since we joined lips and swore.
Whereat he smiled, and thinned away
As the wind stirred to call up day....
—'Tis past! And I alone now stay
    Haunting the Western moor.
—1903

---

1 *Glaston* Glastonbury, near the Polden Hills.

IN CONTEXT

Hardy's Reflections on the Writing of Poetry

The Life of Thomas Hardy, published under the name of his second wife, Florence Hardy, was later discovered to have been written by Hardy himself. When this third-person autobiography discusses Hardy's poetic career in relation to his fiction writing, the author reveals his sensitivity to suggestions that he had taken up poetry only as a result of the reaction against his later novels:

> In the early weeks of this year [1899] the poems were reviewed in the customary periodicals— mostly in a friendly tone, even in a tone of respect, and with praise for many pieces in the volume; though by some critics not without umbrage at Hardy's having taken the liberty to adopt another vehicle of expression than prose fiction without consulting them....
>
> Almost all the fault-finding was, in fact, based on the one great antecedent conclusion that an author who has published prose first, and that largely, must necessarily express himself badly in verse, no reservation being added to except cases in which he may have published prose for temporary or compulsory reasons, or prose of a poetical kind, or have written verse first of all, or for a long time intermediately. ... In the present case, although it was shown that many of the verses had been written before their author dreamt of novels, the critics' view was very little affected that he had "at the eleventh hour," as they untruly put it, taken up a hitherto uncared-for art.

A few pages on, the account is again at pains to emphasize the purity of Hardy's motives in abandoning prose fiction and devoting himself to poetry:

> When one considers how he might have made himself a man of affluence by taking the current of popularity as it served, writing "best sellers," and ringing changes upon the novels he had already written, his bias towards poetry must have been instinctive and disinterested.

Hardy includes few reflections on the nature of his own poetry, but he does take issue with Wordsworth's famous strictures against poetic diction, asserting that Wordsworth "should have put the matter somewhat like this: in works of *passion and sentiment* (not 'imagination and sentiment') the language of verse is the language of prose. In works of *fancy* (or *imagination*), 'poetic diction' (of the real kind) is proper, and even necessary."

GERARD MANLEY HOPKINS
_1844 – 1889_

The Victorian priest and poet Gerard Manley Hopkins lived only 45 years, but his work spans three eras of literary history. A Romantic in his notions of the beauty and power of the natural world and of the imagination's importance, Hopkins shared some affinities with Keats and other poets of the Romantic period. He also shared affinities with the Victorian Pre-Raphaelites and, like them, was very influenced by the writings of John Ruskin. But because his poems and letters, in which he outlined his innovative poetic theories, were not published until 1918, some 30 years after his death, he is sometimes grouped with such Modernists as T.S. Eliot and Ezra Pound. Indeed these poets were influenced by Hopkins's experimental verse, with its unconventional syntax, dense alliteration, and "sprung rhythm" (the term Hopkins coined to describe his unique metric style).

Hopkins was born in Essex of affluent parents and showed promise as a scholar from an early age, but he was clearly also talented in music and the visual arts. His early schooling was at Highgate, where he studied under, and formed a lifelong friendship with, the Pre-Raphaelite poet R.W. Dixon. Hopkins went on to study classics at Oxford, where he became known as the "Star of Balliol [College]" and was educated by such luminaries as Benjamin Jowett and Walter Pater. While Pater's aestheticism was indeed an influence on Hopkins's artistic philosophies, no one at Oxford had a greater impact on him than did John Henry Newman. A convert to Roman Catholicism who later became a Cardinal, Newman was one of the leaders of the "Oxford Movement" of the 1830s and early 1840s, a Tractarian movement (so called because of the "Tracts for the Times" that Newman and others wrote) that called for the Church of England to recognize points of communion with the Roman Catholic Church.

Hopkins's conversion to Roman Catholicism in 1866 estranged him from his devout Anglican parents, who wrote "terrible" letters to try to dissuade him from his decision to become a Jesuit priest. He replied to his father's concerns by saying: "I am surprised you shd. say fancy and aesthetic tastes have led me to my present state of mind: these wd. be better satisfied in the Church of England, for bad taste is always meeting one in the accessories of Catholicism." Hopkins served the Catholic Church for the rest of his life, and for many of those years he renounced his own poetry, burning much of it in the belief that, with the exception of sermons, authorship was not becoming for a priest. It was obvious, however, that he did not cease thinking about the techniques of writing, as is attested by his journals and letters, many written to his Oxford friend the poet (later Poet Laureate) Robert Bridges.

After a famous shipwreck in 1875, Hopkins's superiors encouraged him to write of the fate of five Franciscan nuns, exiled from Germany by the Falk Laws, who had drowned in the disaster. In the long ode _The Wreck of the Deutschland_ he began experimenting with the rhythms he had been thinking about for so long. According to Hopkins, every object in the natural world has a unique and fluid identity, or "inscape," an essence that comprises its form and its meaning. Hopkins also coined the term "instress" to describe the way in which objects or people perceive "inscape." Instress is a powerful burst of energy that allows an observer to penetrate and experience the object's essence. Poetry, for Hopkins, is instress, and that which it seeks to penetrate is the divine.

In creating a poetic sound that would present the inscape of objects and of speech itself, Hopkins was inspired by the rhythms of Welsh nursery rhymes and Old English poetry. "Sprung rhythm" was the result, a syntactically disjunctive, highly alliterative, and densely rhyming style that reconfigured the nature of stresses and line length. The poems in this style that followed *Deutschland*—among them the famous "God's Grandeur"—often aimed to celebrate the spiritual and the divine.

Hopkins continued to write poetry, but his duties as a priest took priority. He served from 1877 to 1879 in various parishes in Sheffield, Oxford, and London, and then went on to fulfill demanding duties in the dreary slums of Manchester, Liverpool, and Glasgow. In 1881 he began teaching at Stonyhurst College in Lancashire, and in 1884 was appointed Professor of Greek and Latin at University College in Dublin. Hopkins disliked both his duties at this university and the city itself, which was still recovering from the Great Famine. Years of illness and depression followed, combined with doubts about his ability to give himself completely to God. During these years of angst, Hopkins composed what are now called his "terrible sonnets," among them "[Not, I'll not, carrion comfort]," and "[No worst, there is none]," their titles reflecting their themes of anguish and desolation.

Hopkins was not to live long in Ireland; he contracted typhoid fever and died in 1889 at the age of 45. Robert Bridges edited a volume of his poetry, *The Poems of Gerard Manley Hopkins*, and released it to the public thirty years after Hopkins's death, presumably waiting until the world was ready to hear the sound of the poet who acknowledged his "oddness" by saying, "The effect of studying masterpieces is to make me admire and do otherwise." Although his output was relatively small, the poet who "did otherwise" made an enormous impact on the literary world, and has influenced several generations of poets.

⌘ ⌘ ⌘

God's Grandeur

The world is charged with the grándeur of God.
   It will flame out, like shining from shook foil;[1]
   It gathers to a greatness, like the ooze of oil
Crushed.[2] Why do men then now not reck°   regard   10
   his rod?
5 Génerátions have trod, have trod, have trod;
   And all is seared with trade; bleared, smeared, with
      toil;

And wears man's smudge and shares man's smell:
      the soil
Is bare now, nor can foot feel, being shod.

Ánd, for° all this, náture is never spent;   *despite*
   There lives the dearest freshness deep down things;
And though the last lights off the black West went
   Oh, morning, at the brown brink eastward,
      springs—
Because the Holy Ghost óver the bent
   World broods with warm breast and with ah!
      bright wings.
—1918 (WRITTEN 1877)

---

[1] [Hopkins's note] I mean foil in its sense of leaf or tinsel. ... Shaken goldfoil gives off broad glares like sheet lightning and also, and this is true of nothing else, owing to its zigzag dints and creasings and network of small many cornered facets, a sort of fork lightning too.

[2] *oil / Crushed* I.e., as olive oil.

The Wreck of the Deutschland [1]

December 6. 7.1875

To the happy memory of five Franciscan nuns, exiles by
the Falck Laws,[2] drowned between midnight and
morning of December 7

PART THE FIRST

1

Thou mastering me
God! giver of breath and bread;
Wórld's stránd,° swáy of the séa;   shore
Lord of living and dead;
5 Thou hast bóund bónes and véins in me, fástened
    me flésh,
And áfter it álmost únmade, what with dréad,
    Thy doing: and dost thou touch me afresh?
Óver agáin I féel thy fínger and fínd thée.

2

I did say yes
10   O at líghtning and láshed ród;
Thou heardst me, truer than tongue, confess
    Thy terror, O Christ, O God;
Thou knówest the wálls, áltar and hour and níght:
The swoon of a heart that the sweep and the hurl
    of thee trod
15   Hárd dówn with a horror of height:
And the midriff astrain with leaning of, laced with fire
    of stress.

3

The frown of his face
Before me, the hurtle of hell
Behind, where, where was a, where was a
    place?—
20   I whirled out wings that spell

And fled with a fling of the heart to the heart of
    the Host.[3]—
My heart, but you were dovewinged, I can tell,
    Cárrier-wítted, I am bóld to bóast,
To flash from the flame to the flame then, tower from
    the grace to the grace.

4

25   I am sóft síft
In an hourglass—at the wall
Fast, but mined with a motion, a drift,
    And it crowds and it combs to the fall;
I stéady as a wáter in a wéll, to a póise, to a páne,
30   But roped with, always, all the way down from the
        tall
    Fells or flanks of the voel,[4] a vein
Of the góspel próffer, a préssure, a prínciple, Christ's
    gift.

5

I kiss my hand
To the stars, lovely-asunder
35   Starlight, wafting him out of it; and
        Glow, glory in thunder;
Kiss my hand to the dappled-with-damson[5] west:
Since, thóugh he is únder the wórld's spléndour
    and wónder,
    His mýstery múst be instréssed,[6] stressed;
40 For I greet him the days I meet him, and bless when I
    understand.

6

Not out of his bliss
Springs the stress felt
Nor first from heaven (and few know this)
    Swings the stroke dealt—

---

[1] *The Wreck of the Deutschland*   The *Deutschland*, a German ship, ran
aground on a shoal off the coast of England in December 1875. With
the lifeboats of the ship stripped away by the storm, five nuns drowned
in its hold. As they awaited death, their leader reportedly called out
"O Christ, come quickly!"

[2] *Falck Laws*   Anti-Catholic German legislation.

[3] *Host*   The consecrated bread of the Holy Eucharist, which represents the Body of Christ.

[4] *Fells* Pastures; *voel* Mountain.

[5] *damson* Dark purple.

[6] *instréssed*   The word, invented by Hopkins, means imbued with
that force which sustains the uniqueness of an object, or the essential
quality of a thing.

45 Stroke and a stress that stars and storms deliver,
   That guilt is hushed by, hearts are flushed by and
        melt—
        But it rídes tíme like ríding a ríver
   (And here the faithful waver, the faithless fable and
        miss).

                    7
                It dates from day
        Of his going in Galilee;[1]
50   Warm-laid grave of a womb-life grey;
        Manger, maiden's knee;
   The dense and the driven Passion, and frightful
        sweat:
   Thence the discharge of it, there its swelling to be,
        Though félt befóre, though in high flood
        yét—
55 What none would have known of it, only the heart,
        being hard at bay,

                    8
                Is out with it! Oh,
        We lash with the best or worst
   Word last! How a lush-kept plush-capped sloe[2]
        Will, mouthed to flesh-burst,
60 Gush!—flush the man, the being with it, sour or
        sweet
   Brim, in a flásh, fúll!—Híther then, lást or fírst,
        To hero of Calvary,[3] Christ's feet—
   Never ask if méaning it, wánting it, wárned of
        it—mén gó.

                    9
65   Be adored among men,
        God, three-numberèd form;[4]
   Wring thy rebel, dogged in den,

Man's malice, with wrecking and storm.
   Beyónd sáying swéet, past télling of tóngue,
70 Thou art lightning and love, I found it, a winter
        and warm;
   Father and fondler of heart thou hast wrung:
   Hast thy dark descending and most art merciful then.

                    10
                With an anvil-ding
        And with fire in him forge thy will
75   Or rather, rather then, stealing as Spring
        Through him, melt him but master him
        still:
   Whether át ónce, as ónce at a crásh Pául,
        Or as Áustin,[5] a língering-óut swéet skíll,
        Make mercy in all of us, out of us all
80 Mástery, bút be adóred, bút be adóred King.

                PART THE SECOND

                    11
        "Some find me a swórd; sóme
        The flánge° and the ráil; fláme,   rim
        Fang, or flood" goes Death on drum,
        And stórms búgle his fáme.
5 But wé dréam we are róoted in éarth—Dúst!
   Flesh falls within sight of us: we, though our
        flower the same,
        Wave with the meadow, forget that there must
   The sóur scýthe crínge, and the bléar sháre cóme.

                    12
        —On Saturday sailed from Bremen,[6]
10   American-outward-bound,
        Take settler and seamen, tell men with
        women,
        Two hundred souls in the round—

---

[1] *Galilee* Region in what is now the north of modern Israel, location of Nazareth, where Mary learned she would give birth to the son of god; Jesus later performed miracles there.

[2] *sloe* Fruit of the blackthorn.

[3] *Calvary* Site of Jesus' crucifixion.

[4] *God, three-numberèd form* According to the Christian doctrine of the Trinity, God is a single god who exists in three persons: father, son, and holy spirit.

---

[5] *Pául ... Áustin* St. Paul, whose conversion in an instant on the road to Damascus (Acts 9.1–19) was very different from the conversion over many years of St. Augustine (354–430 CE).

[6] *Bremen* Port city in north Germany.

O Father, not under thy feathers[1] nor ever as
    guessing
The goal was a shoal, of a fourth the doom to be
    drowned;
15   Yet *did* the dark side of the bay of thy blessing
Not vault them, the million of rounds of thy mercy
    not reeve[2] even them in?

13

     Into the snows she sweeps,
     Hurling the Haven behind,
    The Deutschland, on Sunday; and so the sky
     keeps,
20   For the infinite air is unkind,
    And the sea flint-flake, black-backed in the regular
     blow,
    Sitting Eastnortheast, in cursed quarter, the wind;
     Wiry and white-fiery and whírlwind-swivellèd
     snów
Spins to the widow-making unchilding unfathering
    deeps.

14

25   She drove in the dark to leeward,
     She struck—not a reef or a rock
    But the combs of a smother of sand: night
     drew her
     Dead to the Kentish Knock;[3]
    And she beat the bank down with her bows and
     the ride of her keel;
30   The breakers rolled on her beam[4] with ruinous
     shock;
     And, canvass and compass, the whorl and the
     wheel
Idle for ever to waft her or wind her with, these she
    endūred.

15

     Hope had grown grey hairs,
     Hope had mourning on,
35   Trénched with téars, cárved with cáres,
     Hope was twelve hours gone;
And frightful a nightfall folded rueful a day
Nor rescue, only rocket and lightship,[5] shone,
    And lives at last were washing away:
40 To the shrouds[6] they took,—they shook in the
    hurling and horrible airs.

16

     One stirred from the rigging to save
     The wild woman-kind below,
    With a rope's end round the man, handy and
     brave—
     He was pitched to his death at a blow,
45 For all his dreadnought° breast and braids   *fearless*
     of thew:°   *muscle*
    They could téll° him for hóurs, dándled the   *see*
     tó and the fró
     Through the cobbled foam-fleece. What could
     he do
With the burl of the fóuntains of aír, búck and the
    flóod of the wave?

17

     They fought with God's cold—
50   And they could not, and fell to the deck
    (Crushed them) or water (and drowned them)
     or rolled
     With the searomp over the wreck.
    Night roared, with the heartbreak hearing a
     heartbroke rabble,
    The woman's wailing, the crying of child
     without check°—   *restraint*
55   Till a líoness aróse bréasting the bábble,
A próphetess tówered in the túmult, a virginal tóngue
    tóld.

---

[1] *under thy feathers* Reference to Psalm 91.4: "He will cover you with His feathers, and under His wings you will find refuge."

[2] *reeve* Nautical term: to lace up with ropes.

[3] *Kentish Knock* Sandbank near the mouth of the Thames River.

[4] *beam* Widest point of a ship's hull.

---

[5] *lightship* Floating warning light.

[6] *shrouds* Ropes constituting part of a ship's standing rigging.

18

Ah, touched in your bower° of bone,   *dwelling*
Are you! turned, for an exquisite smart,
Have you! make words break from me here all
    alone,
60   Do you!—móther of béing in me, héart.
O unteachably after evil, but uttering truth,
Why, tears! is it? tears; such a melting, a
    madrigal° start!   *song*
Never-eldering revel and river of youth,
What can it be, this glee? the good you have there of
  your own?

19

65   Sister, a sister calling
A master, her master and mine!—
And the inboard seas run swirling and hawling;
The rash smart sloggering brine
Blinds her; but shé that wéather sees óne thing,
    óne;
70 Has óne fetch[1] ín her: she réars hersélf to divíne
Éars, and the cáll of the táll nún
To the mén in the tóps and the táckle rode óver the
  stórm's brawling.

20

She was first of a five and came
Of a coifèd sisterhood.[2]
75 (O Deutschland, double a desperate name!
O wórld wíde of its góod!
But Gertrude, lily, and Luther,[3] are two of a town,
Christ's líly, and béast of the wáste wóod:
From life's dáwn it is dráwn dówn,

80 Ábel is Cáin's brother[4] and bréasts they have súcked
  the sáme.)

21

Loathed for a love men knew in them,
Banned by land of their birth,
Rhíne[5] refúsed them, Thámes would rúin
    them;
Surf, snow, river and earth
85 Gnashed: but thou art above, thou Orion of light;
Thy unchancelling poising palms were weighing
    the worth,
Thou mártyr-máster: in thý síght
Storm flákes were scróll-leaved flówers, lily
  shówers—sweet héaven was astréw in them.

22

Five! the finding and sake
90   And cipher of suffering Christ.
Márk, the márk is of mán's máke
And the word of it Sacrificed,
But he scores it in scarlet himself on his own
  bespoken,
Before-time-taken, dearest prizèd and priced—
95   Stigma, signal, cinquefoil[6] token
For léttering of the lámb's fléece, rúddying of the
  róse-fláke.

23

Joy fall to thee, father Francis,
Drawn to the Life that died;
With the gnarls of the nails in thee, niche of
    the lance,[7] his
100   Lovescape crucified
And seal of his seraph-arrival![8] and these thy
    daughters
And five-livèd and leavèd favour and pride,

---

[1] *fetch* Solution.

[2] *coifèd sisterhood* Reference to the nuns' veils.

[3] *Gertrude … Luther* Hopkins contrasts St. Gertrude the Great (1256–1301), the first nun's namesake, with Martin Luther (1483–1546) the Protestant reformer, whose doctrinal descendants enacted the laws that exiled the nuns. St. Gertrude is thought to have been born in the town of Eiselben, the birthplace of Luther.

[4] *Ábel is Cáin's brother* See Genesis 4. Cain, the oldest son of Adam and Eve, killed his younger brother, Abel. As punishment, God exiled Cain into the wilderness and set a mark of sin upon him.

[5] *Rhíne* Major European river passing through Germany.

[6] *cinquefoil* Five-leaved plant.

[7] *lance* A spear was used to pierce Jesus' side during his crucifixion.

[8] *seraph-arrival* A seraph is a type of angel.

Are sísterly séaled in wíld wáters,
To bathe in his fall-gold mercies, to breathe in his all-
    fire glances.

24

105   Away in the loveable west,
            On a pastoral forehead of Wales,
        I was under a roof here, I was at rest,
            And they the prey of the gales;
        She to the black-about air, to the breaker, the
            thickly
110   Falling flakes, to the throng that catches and
            quails,
            Was calling "O Christ, Christ, come quickly":
        The cross to her she calls Christ to her, christens her
            wild-worst Best.

25

            The majesty! what did she mean?
            Breathe, arch and original Breath.
115   Is it lóve in her of the béing as her lóver had
            béen?
            Breathe, body of lovely Death.
        They were élse-mínded then, áltogéther, the mén
        Wóke thee with a *We are périshing* in the wéather
            of Gennésaréth.[1]
            Or ís it that she críed for the crówn thén,
120   The keener to come at the comfort for feeling the
            combating keen?

26

        For how to the heart's cheering
            The down-dugged ground-hugged grey
        Hovers off, the jay-blue heavens appearing
            Of pied° and peeled May!   *dappled*
125   Blue-beating and hoary-glow height; or night, still
            higher,
        With bélled fíre and the móth-soft Mílky Wáy.
        What bý your méasure is the héaven of desire,

The tréasure never éyesight gót, nor was éver guessed
    whát for the héaring?

27

            Nó, but it was nót thése.
130   The jáding and the jár of the cárt,°   *vessel*
        Time's tásking, it is fáthers that ásking for éase
            Of the sódden-with-its-sórrowing héart,
        Not danger, electrical-horror; then, further, it finds
        The appéaling of the Pássion is ténderer in práyer
            apárt:
135   Other, I gather, in measure her mind's
        Búrden, in wínd's búrly and béat of endrágonèd séas.

28

        But how shall I … Make me room there;
            Reach me a … Fancy, come faster—
        Strike you the sight of it? look at it loom there,
140   Thing that she … There then! the Master,
        Ipse,° the ónly one, Chríst, Kíng, Héad: *himself*
        He was to cure the extremity where he had cast
            her;
            Do, deal, lord it with living and dead;
        Let him ride, her pride, in his triumph, despatch and
            have done with his doom there.

29

145   Ah! thére was a héart right!
            There was single eye!
            Réad the unshápeable shóck níght
            And knew the who and the why;
        Wording it how but by him that present and past,
150   Heaven and earth are word of, worded by?—
            The Símon-Péter[2] of a sóul! to the blást
        Tárpéïan-fast,[3] but a blówn béacon of líght.

---

1   *Gennésaréth*   Sea of Galilee. In Matthew 8.23–27, Jesus and his disciples are caught in a boat during a storm on the Sea of Galilee. His disciples cry out in fear, and Jesus calms the storm.

2   *Símon-Péter*   St. Peter, one of Christ's apostles and a leader of the early Church. According to Christian tradition, he was crucified in Rome during a wave of religious persecutions.

3   *Tárpéïan-fast*   In the Roman Republic, convicted criminals were executed by being thrown off the Tarpeian Rock.

30

    Jésu, héart's líght,
    Jésu, máid's són,
55   Whát was the féast fóllowed the níght
    Thou hadst glóry of thís nún?—
Féast of the óne wóman withóut stáin.
For so conceivèd, so to conceive thee is done;
  But here was heart-throe, birth of a brain,
60 Wórd, that héard and képt thee and úttered thee
  óutríght.

31

    Well, shé has thée for the pain, for the
    Pátience; but píty of the rést of them!
  Heart, go and bleed at a bitterer vein for the
  Comfortless unconfessed of them—
165 No not uncomforted: lovely-felicitous Providence,
Finger of a ténder of, O of a féathery délicacy, the
  bréast of the
    Maiden could obey so, be a bell to, ring óf it, and
Stártle the poor shéep back! is the shópwrack then a
  hárvest, does témpest carry the gráin for thee?

32

    I admire thee, máster of the tídes,
170   Of the Yóre-flood,[1] of the yéar's fáll;
  The recúrb and the recóvery of the gúlf's sídes,
    The girth of it and the whárf of it and the
    wáll;
Stánching, quénching ócean of a mótionable mínd;
Gróund of béing and gránite of it: pást áll
175   Grásp Gód, thrónèd behínd
Déath, with a sóvereignty that héeds but hídes, bódes[2]
  but abídes;

33

    With a mércy that oútrides
    The all of water, an ark

For the lístener; for the língerer with a lóve
  glídes
180   Lówer than déath and the dárk;
A véin for the vísiting of the pást-prayer, pént in
  príson,
The-last-breath penitent spirits—the uttermost
  mark
    Our passion-plungèd giant risen,
The Christ of the Father compassionate, fetched in
  the storm of his strides.

34

185   Now burn, new born to the world,
    Double-naturèd name,
  The heaven-flúng, heart-fléshed, máiden-fúrled
    Míracle-in-Máry-of-fláme,
Mid-numberèd he in three of the thunder-throne!
190 Not a dóomsday dázzle in his cóming nor dárk as
  he cáme;
    Kind, but róyally recláiming his ówn;
A released shówer, let flásh to the shire, not a
  líghtning of fíre hard húrled.

35

    Dáme, at óur dóor
    Drówned, and among óur shóals,
195   Remémber us in the róads, the heaven-háven
    of the rewárd:
    Our kíng back, Oh, upon Énglish sóuls!
Let him éaster in us, be a dáyspring to the dímness
  of us, be a crímson-cresseted[3] east,
More bríghtening her, ráre-dear Britain, as his
  réign rólls,
    Príde, rose, prínce, hero of us, high-príest,
200 Oür héart's charity's héarth's fíre, oür thóughts'
  chivalry's thróng's Lórd.
—1918 (WRITTEN 1875–76)

---

[1] *Yóre-flood* Ancient flood (i.e., the biblical flood).

[2] *bódes* Preaches the Gospel; also, foretells.

[3] *cresseted* Lit by a cresset, a type of oil lamp.

The Windhover[1]
To Christ Our Lord

I caught this morning morning's minion, king-
   dom of daylight's dauphin,[2] dapple-dáwn-drawn
     Falcon, in his riding
  Of the rólling level úndernéath him steady air, and
     striding
High there, how he rung upon the rein of a
    wimpling° wing   *rippling*
5 In his écstasy! then off, off forth on swing,
  As a skate's heel sweeps smooth on a bow-bend:
     the hurl and gliding
Rebuffed the bíg wind. My heart in hiding
Stírred for a bird,—the achieve of, the mástery of the
    thing!

Brute beauty and valour and act, oh, air, pride, plűme,
    here
10   Buckle! AND the fire that breaks from thee then, a
    billion
Tímes told lovelier, more dangerous, O my
    chevalier!°   *knight*

   No wőnder of it: shéer plód makes plóugh down
    síllion°   *furrows*
Shíne, and blue-bleak embers, ah my dear,
  Fall, gáll themsélves, and gásh gőld-vermílion.
—1918 (WRITTEN 1877)

Pied[3] Beauty

Glóry be to God for dappled things—
  For skies of couple-colour as a brinded° cow; *spotted*
    For rose-moles all in stipple upon trout that
     swim;
Fresh-fírecoal chestnut-fálls;[4] fínches' wings;

---

5   Lándscape plotted and pieced—fold,°   *pasture*
    fallow, and plough;
   And áll trádes, their gear and tackle and
    trim.°   *equipment*

Áll things counter,° original, spáre,° stránge; *contrary / rare*
  Whatever is fickle, frecklèd (who knows how?)
    With swíft, slów; sweet, soũr; adázzle, dím;
10 He fathers-forth whose beauty is pást chánge:
          Práise hím.
—1918 (WRITTEN 1877)

Felix Randal

Félix Rándal the fárrier,[5] O is he déad then? my
  dúty all énded,
Who have watched his mould of man, big-bóned and
  hardy-handsome
Pining,[6] píning, till time when reason rámbled in it
  and some
Fatal four disorders, fléshed there, all contended?

5 Síckness bróke him. Impatient, he cursed at first, but
  mended
Being anointed[7] and all; though a heavenlier heart
  began some
Mónths éarlier, since I had our swéet repríeve and
  ránsom[8]
Téndered to him. Áh well, God rést him áll road
  éver[9] he offénded!

This séeing the síck endéars them tó us, us tóo it
  endéars.
10 My tongue had taught thee comfort, touch had
  quenched thy tears,

---

1 *Windhover* Another name for a kestrel, a small falcon that appears to hover in the wind.

2 *dauphin* Title of the eldest son of the King of France—the heir.

3 *Pied* Multicolored.

4 *Fresh ... fálls* Freshly fallen, brightly colored chestnuts.

5 *fárrier* One who shoes horses.

6 *Pining* Languishing; weakening.

7 *anointed* As in the sacrament of Extreme Unction, performed for the dying.

8 *had our swéet repríeve and ránsom* I.e., had received Holy Communion.

9 *áll road éver* However.

Thy tears that touched my heart, child, Félix, poor
  Felix Randal;

How far from then forethought of, all thy more
  boisterous years,
When thou at the random[1] grim fórge, pówerful
  amídst péers,
Didst fettle° for the great grey drayhorse[2] his   *prepare*
  bright and battering sandal!
—1918 (WRITTEN 1880)

Spring and Fall: To a Young Child

Márgarét, áre you gríeving
  Over Goldengrove unleaving?
Leáves, like the thíngs of mán, you
With your fresh thoughts care for, can you?
5 Ah! ás the héart grows ólder
  It will come to such sights colder
  By and by, nor spare a sigh
  Though worlds of wanwood leafmeal[3] lie;
  And yet you *will* weep and know why.
10 Now no matter, child, the name:
  Sórrow's spríngs áre the sáme.
  Nor mouth had, no nor mind, expressed
  What héart héard of, ghóst° guéssed: *spirit*
  It ís the blíght mán was bórn for,
15 It is Margaret you mourn for.
  —1918 (WRITTEN 1880)

[As kingfishers catch fire]

As kingfishers catch fire, dragonflies draw flame;
  As tumbled over rim in roundy wells
  Stones ring; like each tucked° string   *plucked*
    tells, each hung bell's
Bow swung finds tongue to fling out broad its name;

Each mortal thing does one thing and the same: 5
  Deals out that being indoors each one dwells;
  Selves—goes its self; *myself* it speaks and spells,
Crying *What I do is me: for that I came.*

I say more: the just man justices;
  Keeps grace: that keeps all his goings graces;   10
Ácts in God's eye what in God's eye he is—

  Chríst. For Christ plays in ten thousand places,
Lovely in limbs, and lovely in eyes not his
  To the Father through the features of men's faces.
—1918 (WRITTEN 1879–82)

[*No worst, there is none*]

No worst, there is none. Pitched past pitch of grief,
  More pangs will, schooled at forepangs, wilder
    wring.
Comforter, where, where is your comforting?
Mary, mother of us, where is your relief?
My cries heave, herds-long; huddle in a main, a chief— 5
Woe, world-sorrow; on an áge-old ánvil wínce and
    síng—
Then lull, then leave off. Fury had shrieked "No ling-
Ering! Let me be fell:° force[4] I must be brief."   *fierce*
O the mind, mind has mountains; cliffs of fall
Frightful, sheer, no-man-fathomed. Hold them cheap 10
May who ne'er hung there. Nor does long our small
Durance deal with that steep or deep. Here! creep,
Wretch, under a comfort serves in a whirlwind: all
Life death does end and each day dies with sleep.
—1918 (WRITTEN 1884–85)

[*I wake and feel the fell[5] of dark, not day*]

I wake and feel the fell of dark, not day
  What hours, O what black hours we have spent

---

1 *random* Roughly built.

2 *drayhorse* Powerful horse used for drawing a sled.

3 *wanwood leafmeal* Decaying wood and leaves.

4 *force* Perforce, or out of necessity.

5 *fell* Bitterness; also an animal hide, used as a covering.

This night! what sights you, heart, saw, ways you went!
And more must, in yet longer light's delay.

5   With witness I speak this. But where I say
Hours I mean years, mean life. And my lament
Is cries countless, cries like dead letters sent
To dearest him that lives alas! away.

I am gall, I am heartburn. God's most deep decree
10   Bitter would have me taste: my taste was me;
Bones built in me, flesh filled, blood brimmed the curse.

Selfyeast of spirit a dull dough sours. I see
The lost are like this, and their scourge to be
As I am mine, their sweating selves; but worse.
—1918 (WRITTEN C. 1885–86)

[*Not, I'll not, carrion*[1] *comfort*]

Not, I'll not, carrion comfort, Despair, not feast
on thee;
Not untwist—slack they may be—these last strands of
man
In me ór, most weary, cry *I can no more*. I can;
Can something, hope, wish day come, not choose not
to be.
5   But ah, but O thou terrible, why wouldst thou rude
on me[2]
Thy wring-world right foot rock? lay a lionlimb
against me? scan
With darksome devouring eyes my bruisèd bones? and
fan,
O in turns of tempest, me heaped there; me frantic to
avoïd thee and flee?

Why? That my chaff[3] might fly; my grain lie, sheer
and clear.
10   Nay in all that toil, that coil,° since (seems)   *tumult*
I kissed the rod,
Hand rather, my heart lo! lapped strength, stole joy,
would laugh, cheer.
Cheer whóm though? The hero whose héaven-
handling flúng me, fóot tród
Me? or mé that fóught him? O which one? is it éach
one? That níght, that yéar
Of now done darkness I wretch lay wrestling with (my
God!) my God.
—1918 (WRITTEN C. 1885–86)

That Nature Is a Heraclitean Fire[4] *and of the Comfort of the Resurrection*

Cloud-puffball, torn tufts, tossed pillows | flaunt
forth, then chevy° on an air—   *race*
Built thoroughfare: heaven-roysterers,[5] in gay-gangs |
they throng; they glitter in marches.
Down roughcast,[6] down dazzling whitewash, |
wherever an elm arches,
Shivelights[7] and shadowtackle[8] in long | lashes lace,
lance, and pair.
5   Delightfully the bright wind boisterous | ropes,
wrestles, beats earth bare
Of yestertempest's creases; in pool and rut peel
parches
Squandering ooze to squeezed | dough, crúst, dust;
stánches,° stárches   *dries up*

---

[1]   *carrion* Dead flesh.

[2]   *rude on me* Roughly against me.

[3]   *chaff* Outer covering that must be removed from grain before it is
eaten. See Matthew 3.12: "he will thoroughly purge his floor, and
gather his wheat into the garner; but he will burn up the chaff with
unquenchable fire."

[4]   *Heraclitean Fire* Heraclitus (c. 535–475 BCE), a Greek philosopher,
taught that everything is derived from fire, and therefore in a constant
state of change.

[5]   *roysterers* Noisy party-goers.

[6]   *roughcast* Wall plastering made of lime and gravel.

[7]   *Shivelights* Strips of light.

[8]   *shadowtackle* Shadows which resemble a ship's rigging.

Squadroned masks and manmarks | treadmire toil
    there
Fóotfretted in it. Million-fuelèd, | nature's bonfire
    burns on.
10   But quench her bonniest, dearest | to her, her
    clearest-selvèd spark
Mán, how fást his fíredint, | his mark on mind, is
    gone!
Bóth are in an ŭnfáthomable, áll is in an enórmous
    dárk
Drowned. O pity and indig | nation! Manshape, that
    shone
Sheer off, disseveral,° a star, death blots black   *separate*
    out; nor mark
15   Is any of him at all so stark
But vastness blurs and time | beats level. Enough! the
    Resurrection,
A héart's-clarion! Awáy grief s gásping, | joyless days,
    dejection.
            Across my foundering deck shone
A beacon, an eternal beam. | Flesh fade, and mortal
    trash
20   Fáll to the residuary worm; | world's wildfire, leave
    but ash:
            In a flash, at a trumpet crash,
I am all at once what Christ is, | since he was what I
    am, and
This Jack,° jóke, poor pótsherd,[1] | patch,[2]   *fellow*
    matchwood,° immortal diamond,   *kindling*
            Is immortal diamond.
—1918 (WRITTEN 1888)

[*Thou art indeed just, Lord*]

*Justus quidem tu es, Domine, si disputem tecum:
verumtamen justa loquar ad te: Quare via impiorum
prosperatur?[3] etc.*

Thou art indeed just, Lord, if I contend
    With thee; but, sir, so what I plead is just.
Whý do sínners' ways prosper? and why must
Dísappóintment all I endeavour end?
5   Wert thou my enemy, O thou my friend,
How wouldst thou worse, I wonder, than thou dost
Defeat, thwart me? Oh, the sots° and thralls   *drunkards*
    of lust
Do in spare hours more thrive than I that spend,
Sir, life upon thy cause. See, banks and brakes°   *thickets*
10   Now, leavèd how thick! lacèd they are again
With fretty chervil,[4] look, and fresh wind shakes
Them; birds build—but not I build; no, but strain,
Time's eunuch, and not breed one work that wakes.
Mine, O thou lord of life, send my roots rain.
—1918 (WRITTEN 1889)

---

[1] *pótsherd* Piece of broken pottery.

[2] *patch* Simpleton.

[3] *Justus … prosperatur* Latin: You are always righteous, O Lord,
when I bring a case before you. Yet I would speak with you about your
justice: why does the way of the wicked prosper? (Jeremiah 12.1).

[4] *fretty chervil* Interlaced leaves and stems of a garden herb.

IN CONTEXT

The Growth of "The Windhover"

Manuscript copies of Hopkins's poems open a remarkable window on his unique approach to poetic rhythm—and to poetic composition; "The Windhover" is a particularly interesting example.

The first page reproduced here (headed "Another version") is entirely in Hopkins's hand, and probably dates from 1877. The second dates from 1883; it is from an album of "fair copy" transcriptions of Hopkins's (often not very legible) manuscripts that was prepared by his friend and mentor, the poet Robert Bridges, and then corrected by Hopkins in 1884. According to Hopkins scholar Norman H. Mackenzie, the corrections and revisions here in Hopkins's handwriting include the addition of ": to Christ our Lord" to the title; the alteration of "o air" to "oh, air"; the replacement of the ampersand with the word "AND" in line 10; the addition of stress marks in lines 2, 3, 12, and 14; the addition of a "slur" between "the" and "hurl" in line 6, and the addition of seven "outrides" (as Hopkins termed the curved marks below the line).

Adding marks to indicate particularly strong stresses and adding "slurs" and "outrides" were among the many ways Hopkins endeavored to direct the reading of his poems according to the principles of what he termed "sprung rhythm" (see the Glossary in the online component of this volume for a definition). The meaning of the "slur" mark is fairly straightforward; it indicates where two syllables should be compressed together so as to be pronounced as one—much as in this case an apostrophe might be used to do (*th'hurl*). The "outride" denotes a much less familiar concept, and it may be best to quote Hopkins directly here. At one point he writes that "the outride under one or more syllables makes them extrametrical: a slight pause follows as if the voice were silently making its way back to the highroad of the verse." Elsewhere, he describes syllables so marked as "hangers or outriders," meaning "one, two or three slack syllables added to a foot and not counted in the nominal scanning. They are so called because they seem to hang below the line or ride forward or backward from it in another dimension than the line itself, according to a principle needless to explain here."

When entering corrections and revisions in 1884 Hopkins also added at lower right the date and place of the poem's original composition. The marginal notes, however, were evidently added by Bridges when he transcribed them; "= A", for example, indicates that the hyphen Bridges has added to line 6 is taken from an early manuscript of the poem (referred to as manuscript A).

The Windhover (Another version) - to Christ our Lord.

96

I caught this morning morning's minion, king-
dom of daylight's dauphin, dapple-dawn-drawn Fal-
con, in his riding   [and striding
Of the rolling level underneath him steady air,
High there
O how he rung upon the rein of a wimpling wing
In his ecstacy! then off, then off forth on swing,
As a skate's heel sweeps smooth on a bow-bend:
the hurl and gliding
Rebuffed the big wind. My heart in hiding
Stirred for a bird — for the mastery of the thing!
the achieve of

Brute beauty and valour and act, oh, air, pride, plume,
here   [then, a billion
Buckle! And the fire that breaks from thee
times told lovelier, more dangerous, O my
chevalier!

No wonder of it: sheer plod makes plough down
sillion
Shine, and blue-bleak embers, ah my dear,
Fall, gall themselves, and gash gold-vermilion.

(8)

The Windhover: to Christ our Lord

I caught this morning morning's minion, king-
dom of daylight's dauphin, dapple-dawn-drawn Falcon, in his riding
Of the rolling, level underneath him steady air, & striding
High there, how he rung upon the rein of a wimpling wing
In his ecstacy! then off, off forth on swing
As a skate's heel sweeps smooth on a bow-bend: the hurl & gliding
Rebuffed the big wind. My heart in hiding
Stirred for a bird, — the achieve of, the mastery of the thing!

Brute beauty & valour & act, oh, air, pride, plume, here
Buckle! AND the fire that breaks from thee then, a billion
Times told lovelier, more dangerous, o my chevalier!
No wonder of it: sheer plód makes plough down sillion
Shine, & blue-bleak embers, ah my dear,
Fall, gall themselves, & gash gold-vermilion.

St. Beuno's. May 30 1877

from *Journal* 1870–74

[*"Inscape" and "Instress"*]

[April 15] The white violets are broader and smell; the blue, scentless and finer made, have sharper whelking[1] and a more winged recoil in the leaves.

Take a *few* primroses in a glass and the instress[2] of—brilliancy, sort of starriness: I have not the right word—so simple a flower gives is remarkable. It is, I think, due to the strong swell given by the deeper yellow middle.

"The young lambs bound As to the tabour's sound."[3]

They toss and toss: it is as if it were the earth that flung them, not themselves. It is the pitch of graceful agility when we think that.

April 16—Sometimes they rest a little space on the hind legs and the fore-feet drop curling in on the breast, not so liquidly as we see it in the limbs of foals though.

Bright afternoon; clear distances; Pendle[4] dappled with tufted shadow; west wind; interesting clouding, flat and lying in the warp of the heaved but the pieces with rounded outline and dolphin-backs showing in places and all was at odds and at Z's, one piece with another. Later beautifully delicate crisping. Later rippling. …

April 21—We have had other such afternoons, one today—the sky a beautiful grained blue, silky lingering clouds in flat-bottomed loaves, others a little browner in ropes or in burly-shouldered ridges swanny and lustrous, more in the Zenith[5] stray packs of a sort of violet paleness. White-rose cloud formed fast, not in the same density—some caked and swimming in a wan whiteness, the rest soaked with the blue and like the leaf of a flower held against the light and diapered out[6] by the worm or veining of deeper blue between rosette and rosette. Later / moulding, which brought rain: in perspective it was vaulted in very regular ribs with fretting between: but these are not ribs; they are a "wracking" install[7] made of these two realities—the frets, which are scarves of rotten cloud bellying upwards and drooping at their ends and shaded darkest at the brow or tropic where they double to the eye, and the whiter field of sky showing between: the illusion looking down the "wagon" is complete. These swaths of fretted cloud move in rank, not in file.

April 22—But such a lovely damasking[8] in the sky as today I never felt before. The blue was charged with simple instress, the higher, zenith sky earnest and frowning, lower more light and sweet. High up again, breathing through woolly coats of cloud or on the quains[9] and branches of the flying pieces it was the true exchange of crimson, nearer the earth / against the sun / it was turquoise, and in the opposite south-western bay below the sun it was like clear oil but just as full of colour, shaken over with slanted flashing "travellers," all in flight, stepping one behind the other, their edges tossed with bright ravelling,[10] as if white napkins were thrown up in the sun but not quite at the same moment so that they were all in a scale down the air falling one after the other to the ground. …

[May 9] This day and May 11 the bluebells in the little wood between the College[11] and the highroad and in one of the Hurst Green[12] cloughs.[13] In the little wood

---

[1] *whelking* Ridges.

[2] *instress* Hopkins's own term, meaning the force or energy which sustains an inscape, which is the individual or essential quality of a thing.

[3] *The … sound* From William Wordsworth's *Ode: Intimations of Immortality*, lines 20–21; *tabour's* Drum's.

[4] *Pendle* Pendle Hill in Lancashire, England.

[5] *swanny* Swan-like; *Zenith* Point in the sky directly overhead.

[6] *diapered out* Patterned or variegated.

[7] *install* Here, installation.

[8] *damasking* Intricate pattern in the style of damask, a weaving technique.

[9] *quains* Angles (Hopkins's own term).

[10] *ravelling* Frayed edges.

[11] *College* Stonyhurst College, the seminary where Hopkins studied, in Lancashire, England.

[12] *Hurst Green* Village in Blackburn, Lancashire, England.

[13] *cloughs* Ravines.

/ opposite the light / they stood in blackish spreads or sheddings like the spots on a snake. The heads are then like thongs and solemn in grain and grape-colour. But in the clough / through the light / they came in falls of sky-colour washing the brows and slacks[1] of the ground with vein-blue, thickening at the double, vertical themselves and the young grass and brake fern combed vertical, but the brake struck the upright of all this with light winged transomes.[2] It was a lovely sight.—The bluebells in your hand baffle you with their inscape, made to every sense: if you draw your fingers through them they are lodged and struggle / with a shock of wet heads; the long stalks rub and click and flatten to a fan on one another like your fingers themselves would when you passed the palms hard across one another, making a brittle rub and jostle like the noise of a hurdle strained by leaning against; then there is the faint honey smell and in the mouth the sweet gum when you bite them. But this is easy, it is the eye they baffle. They give one a fancy of panpipes and of some wind instrument with stops—a trombone perhaps. The overhung necks—for growing they are little more than a staff with a simple crook but in water, where they stiffen, they take stronger turns, in the head like sheephooks[3] or, when more waved throughout, like the waves riding through a whip that is being smacked—what with these overhung necks and what with the crisped ruffled bells dropping mostly on one side and the gloss these have at their footstalks they have an air of the knights at chess. Then the knot or "knoop" of buds some shut, some just gaping, which makes the pencil of the whole spike, should be noticed: the inscape of the flower most finely carried out in the siding of the axes, each striking a greater and greater slant, is finished in these clustered buds, which for the most part are not straightened but rise to the end like a tongue and this and their tapering and a little flattening they have made them look like the heads of snakes.

[July 19, 1872] Stepped into a barn of ours, a great shadowy barn, where the hay had been stacked on either side, and looking at the great rudely[4] arched timber-frames—principals(?) and tie-beams, which make them look like bold big *As* with the cross-bar high up—I thought how sadly beauty of inscape was unknown and buried away from simple people and yet how near at hand it was if they had eyes to see it and it could be called out everywhere again. …

After the examinations we went for our holiday out to Douglas in the Isle of Man.[5] Aug. 3—At this time I had first begun to get hold of the copy of Scotus[6] on the Sentences in the Baddely library and was flush with a new stroke of enthusiasm. It may come to nothing or it may be a mercy from God. But just then when I took in any inscape of the sky or sea I thought of Scotus. …

Aug. 10—I was looking at high waves. The breakers always are parallel to the coast and shape themselves to it except where the curve is sharp however the wind blows. They are rolled out by the shallowing shore just as a piece of putty between the palms whatever its shape runs into a long roll. The slant ruck[7] or crease one sees in them shows the way of the wind. The regularity of the barrels surprised and charmed the eye; the edge behind the comb or crest was as smooth and bright as glass. It may be noticed to be green behind and silver white in front: the silver marks where the air begins, the pure white is foam, the green / solid water. Then looked at to the right or left they are scrolled over like mouldboards[8] or feathers or jibsails seen by the edge. It is pretty to see the hollow of the barrel disappearing as the white combs on each side run along the wave gaining ground till the two meet at a pitch and crush and overlap each other.

---

[1] *brows and slacks* Upward and downward slopes in terrain.

[2] *transomes* Crossbeams.

[3] *sheephooks* Shepherds' crooks.

[4] *rudely* Roughly.

[5] *Isle of Man* Self-governing island between England and Ireland.

[6] *Scotus* Duns Scotus (c. 1266–1308), Scottish-born theologian and philosopher. In his *Lectura*, he analyzes Thomas Lombard's *Sentences*.

[7] *ruck* Ridge.

[8] *mouldboards* Boards attached to plows, used to form furrows.

About all the turns of the scaping[1] from the break and flooding of wave to its run out again I have not yet satisfied myself. The shores are swimming and the eyes have before them a region of milky surf but it is hard for them to unpack the huddling and gnarls of the water and law out[2] the shapes and the sequence of the running: I catch however the looped or forked wisp made by every big pebble the backwater runs over—if it were clear and smooth there would be a network from their overlapping, such as can in fact be seen on smooth sand after the tide is out; then I saw it run browner, the foam dwindling and twitched into long chains of suds, while the strength of the backdraught shrugged the stones together and clocked them one against another. …

April 8 [1873]—The ashtree growing in the corner of the garden was felled. It was lopped first: I heard the sound and looking out and seeing it maimed there came at that moment a great pang and I wished to die and not to see the inscapes of the world destroyed any more. …

July 23—To Beaumont: it was the rector's day. It was a lovely day: shires-long of pearled cloud under cloud, with a grey stroke underneath marking each row; beautiful blushing yellow in the straw of the uncut rye fields, the wheat looking white and all the ears making a delicate and very true crisping along the top and with just enough air stirring for them to come and go gently; then there were fields reaping. All this I would have looked at again in returning but during dinner I talked too freely and unkindly and had to do penance going home. One field I saw from the balcony of the house behind an elmtree, which it threw up, like a square of pale goldleaf, as it might be, catching the light.
—(WRITTEN 1871–73)

from *Letter to Robert Bridges*
St. Giles's, Oxford.
25 February 1879

… No doubt my poetry errs on the side of oddness. I hope in time to have a more balanced and Miltonic[3] style. But as air,[4] melody, is what strikes me most of all in music and design in painting, so design, pattern or what I am in the habit of calling "inscape" is what I above all aim at in poetry. Now it is the virtue of design, pattern, or inscape to be distinctive and it is the virtue of distinctiveness to become queer. This vice I cannot have escaped. …
—(WRITTEN 1879)

Author's Preface[5]

The poems in this book are written some in Running Rhythm, the common rhythm in English use, some in Sprung Rhythm, and some in a mixture of the two. And those in the common rhythm are some counterpointed,[6] some not.

Common English rhythm, called Running Rhythm above, is measured by feet[7] of either two or three syllables and (putting aside the imperfect feet at the beginning and end of lines and also some unusual measures in which feet seem to be paired together and double or composite feet to arise) never more or less.

Every foot has one principal stress or accent, and this or the syllable it falls on may be called the Stress of the foot and the other part, the one or two unaccented syllables, the Slack. Feet (and the rhythms made out of them) in which the stress comes first are called Falling Feet and Falling Rhythms, feet and rhythm in which the slack comes first are called Rising Feet and Rhythms,

---

[1] *scaping* Hopkins's term for a reflection or impression of the individual quality of a thing or action.

[2] *law out* Determine the rules or organizing scheme of.

[3] *Miltonic* In the manner of John Milton (1608–74), English poet.

[4] *air* Tune.

[5] *Author's Preface* Prefatory to accompany Hopkins's manuscript poems.

[6] *counterpointed* Containing two types of rhythm in a line of verse.

[7] *feet* Metrical units.

and if the stress is between two slacks there will be Rocking Feet and Rhythms. These distinctions are real and true to nature; but for purposes of scanning it is a great convenience to follow the example of music and take the stress always first, as the accent or the chief accent always comes first in a musical bar. If this is done there will be in common English verse only two possible feet—the so-called accentual Trochee[1] and Dactyl,[2] and correspondingly only two possible uniform rhythms, the so-called Trochaic and Dactylic. But they may be mixed and then what the Greeks called a Logaoedic Rhythm[3] arises. These are the facts and according to these the scanning of ordinary regularly-written English verse is very simple indeed and to bring in other principles is here unnecessary.

But because verse written strictly in these feet and by these principles will become same and tame the poets have brought in licences and departures from rule to give variety, and especially when the natural rhythm is rising, as in the common ten-syllable or five-foot verse, rhymed or blank. These irregularities are chiefly Reversed Feet and Reversed or Counterpoint Rhythm, which two things are two steps or degrees of licence in the same kind. By a reversed foot I mean the putting the stress where, to judge by the rest of the measure, the slack should be and the slack where the stress, and this is done freely at the beginning of a line and, in the course of a line, after a pause; only scarcely ever in the second foot or place and never in the last, unless when the poet designs some extraordinary effect; for these places are characteristic and sensitive and cannot well be touched. But the reversal of the first foot and of some middle foot after a strong pause is a thing so natural that our poets have generally done it, from Chaucer[4] down, without remark and it commonly passes unnoticed and

cannot be said to amount to a formal change of rhythm, but rather is that irregularity which all natural growth and motion shows. If however the reversal is repeated in two feet running, especially so as to include the sensitive second foot, it must be due either to great want[5] of ear or else is a calculated effect, the super-inducing or *mounting* of a new rhythm upon the old; and since the new or mounted rhythm is actually heard and at the same time the mind naturally supplies the natural or standard foregoing rhythm, for we do not forget what the rhythm is that by rights we should be hearing, two rhythms are in some manner running at once and we have something answerable to counterpoint in music, which is two or more strains of tune going on together, and this is Counterpoint Rhythm. Of this kind of verse Milton is the great master and the choruses of *Samson Agonistes*[6] are written throughout in it—but with the disadvantage that he does not let the reader clearly know what the ground-rhythm is meant to be and so they have struck most readers as merely irregular. And in fact if you counterpoint throughout, since only one of the counter rhythms is actually heard, the other is really destroyed or cannot come to exist, and what is written is one rhythm only and probably Sprung Rhythm, of which I now speak.

Sprung Rhythm, as used in this book, is measured by feet of from one to four syllables, regularly, and for particular effects any number of weak or slack syllables may be used. It has one stress, which falls on the only syllable, if there is only one, or, if there are more, then scanning as above, on the first, and so gives rise to four sorts of feet, a monosyllable and the so-called accentual Trochee, Dactyl, and the First Paeon.[7] And there will be four corresponding natural rhythms; but nominally the feet are mixed and any one may follow any other. And hence Sprung Rhythm differs from Running Rhythm in having or being only one nominal rhythm, a mixed or "logaoedic" one, instead of three, but on the other hand in having twice the flexibility of foot, so that any two

---

[1] *Trochee* Metrical foot consisting of an accented syllable followed by an unaccented syllable.

[2] *Dactyl* Metrical foot consisting of an accented syllable followed by two unaccented syllables.

[3] *Logaoedic Rhythm* Rhythm in which dactyls are combined with trochees.

[4] *Chaucer* Geoffrey Chaucer (1343–1400), English poet best known for *The Canterbury Tales*.

[5] *want* Lack.

[6] *Samson Agonistes* Dramatic poem published by Milton in 1671.

[7] *Paeon* Metrical foot consisting of one stressed and three unstressed syllables.

stresses may either follow one another running or be divided by one, two, or three slack syllables. But strict Sprung Rhythm cannot be counterpointed. In Sprung Rhythm, as in logaoedic rhythm generally, the feet are assumed to be equally long or strong and their seeming inequality is made up by pause or stressing.

Remark also that it is natural in Sprung Rhythm for the lines to be *rove over*, that is for the scanning of each line immediately to take up that of the one before, so that if the first has one or more syllables at its end the other must have so many the less at its beginning; and in fact the scanning runs on without break from the beginning, say, of a stanza to the end and all the stanza is one long strain, though written in lines asunder.

Two licences are natural to Sprung Rhythm. The one is rests, as in music; but of this an example is scarcely to be found in this book, unless in the *Echos*, second line. The other is *hangers* or *outrides*, that is one, two, or three slack syllables added to a foot and not counting in the nominal scanning. They are so called because they seem to hang below the line or ride forward or backward from it in another dimension than the line itself, according to a principle needless to explain here. These outriding half feet or hangers are marked by a loop underneath them, and plenty of them will be found.

The other marks are easily understood, namely accents, where the reader might be in doubt which syllable should have the stress; slurs, that is loops *over* syllables, to tie them together into the time of one; little loops at the end of a line to show that the rhyme goes on to the first letter of the next line; what in music are called pauses ⌢, to show that the syllable should be dwelt on; and twirls ⌣, to mark reversed or counter-pointed rhythm.

Note on the nature and history of Sprung Rhythm —Sprung Rhythm is the most natural of things. For (1) it is the rhythm of common speech and of written prose, when rhythm is perceived in them. (2) It is the rhythm of all but the most monotonously regular music, so that in the words of choruses and refrains and in songs written closely to music it arises. (3) It is found in nursery rhymes, weather saws,[1] and so on; because, however these may have been once made in running rhythm, the terminations having dropped off by the change of language, the stresses come together and so the rhythm is sprung. (4) It arises in common verse when reversed or counterpointed, for the same reason.

But nevertheless in spite of all this and though Greek and Latin lyric verse, which is well known, and the old English verse seen in "Pierce Ploughman"[2] are in sprung rhythm, it has in fact ceased to be used since the Elizabethan age, Greene[3] being the last writer who can be said to have recognized it. For perhaps there was not, down to our days, a single, even short, poem in English in which sprung rhythm is employed—not for single effects or in fixed places—but as the governing principle of the scansion. I say this because the contrary has been asserted: if it is otherwise the poem should be cited. ...
—1883

---

[1] *saws* Sayings.

[2] *Pierce Ploughman* I.e., *Piers Plowman*, by William Langland (written c. 1360–99).

[3] *Greene* Robert Greene (1558–92).

"MICHAEL FIELD"
KATHARINE BRADLEY AND EDITH COOPER
1846 – 1914 and 1862 – 1913

In May 1884, a volume of two plays by an unknown author, Michael Field, was published to critical acclaim. One reviewer wrote in *The Spectator*: "We know nothing of the author, but we have found a wealth of surprises in the strength, the simplicity, and the terseness of the imaginative feeling. ... [The work] has the true poetic voice of fire in it. If this is the work of a young author, it is the work of the highest possible promise." The two authors who had taken the pen name "Michael Field," Katharine Bradley[1] and Edith Cooper had wished to receive the serious criticism accorded to male authors and also to conceal their relationship as lovers. The authors' identities did become widely known during their lifetimes, but "Michael" (Bradley) and "Field" (Cooper), as they called themselves, continued to collaborate on many books of plays and poetry, sometimes as "Michael Field," sometimes under other pseudonyms.

Bradley's father, a tobacco manufacturer, died in 1848, when she was two. Her mother educated her at home, and she later attended Newnham College, the new women's college at Cambridge. When her older sister, Emma, married James Cooper, the family stayed together with the married couple in Kenilworth, near Birmingham in central England. Bradley's mother died when Bradley was twenty-two, and not long afterward Emma also passed away. Bradley stayed on to help raise her sister's children, Amy and Edith Cooper; Edith was then six years old. Katharine and her niece Edith shared a love of literature and writing, evident from the time Edith was young, and the two later attended Bristol University together.

Bradley wrote one volume of poetry on her own in 1875 (*The New Minnesinger*, published under the pseudonym Arran Leigh), but thereafter published only in collaboration with Cooper. A stanza from their poem "It Was Deep April" describes their moment of decision: "The world was on us, pressing sore; / My love and I took hands and swore, / Against the world, to be / Poets and lovers evermore." The two eventually wrote some thirty plays and eleven volumes of poetry together in such a close collaboration that they later claimed in their journals that when they reviewed their work they could not distinguish who had written what. When their first collaborative work under the name "Michael Field" was published, the plays *Callirrhoë* and *Fair Rosamund*, they sent a copy to Robert Browning and revealed their true identities. Browning loved their work and became a close friend, but unfortunately he let slip to the public the authorship of the plays, a move that Bradley wrote back to tell him would "dwarf and enfeeble our work. ... We cannot be stifled in drawing room conventionalities."

But even though critical reception of their work cooled somewhat after their identities were exposed, Bradley and Cooper did not allow themselves to be stifled. They continued to live and travel together, and many of their poems address the subject of love between women. In its form and content their earlier work was influenced by figures associated with the aesthetic movement, such as

---

[1] Though Bradley's first name is spelled various ways, the spelling here is that she used when signing her own name.

Dante Gabriel Rossetti and Walter Pater, and by classical poets, especially Sappho (though Sappho's sexuality was a subject of speculation in the Victorian era, Bradley and Cooper were influential in claiming her as a lesbian foremother—as many other poets would do in the twentieth century). The figure and poetry of Sappho provides key inspiration for their 1889 volume *Long Ago*, which was called by the journal *The Academy* "one of the most exquisite lyrical productions of the latter half of the nineteenth century." In the last years of their lives, Bradley and Cooper converted to Catholicism, which replaced classicism as a driving influence in their work.

For nearly half a century, Bradley and Cooper together kept a diary that they called *Works and Days*, which incorporated critical discussions, letters to friends such as Pater and Browning, and descriptions of their travels and their daily lives. In these diaries, Bradley and Cooper also describe their abiding love for each other: "closer married" than the Brownings, they said, because they also shared an artistic partnership. The younger, Cooper, was the first to die, of cancer, in 1913; eight months later Bradley died of the same disease.

⌘ ⌘ ⌘

Maids, Not to You My Mind Doth Change

Maids, not to you my mind doth change;
Men I defy, allure, estrange,
Prostrate, make bond or free:
Soft as the stream beneath the plane
5   To you I sing my love's refrain;
Between us is no thought of pain,
Peril, satiety.

Soon doth a lover's patience tire,
But ye to manifold desire
10   Can yield response, ye know
When for long, museful days I pine,
The presage at my heart divine;
To you I never breathe a sign
Of inward want or woe.

15   When injuries my spirit bruise,
Allaying virtue ye infuse
With unobtrusive skill:
And if care frets ye come to me
As fresh as nymph from stream or tree,
20   And with your soft vitality
My weary bosom fill.
—1889

The Magdalen

Timoteo Viti[1]

This tender sylph[2] of a maid
Is the Magdalen—this figure lone:
Her attitude is swayed
By the very breath she breathes,
5   The prayer of her being that takes no voice.
Boulders, the grass enwreathes,
Arch over her as a cave
That of old an earthquake clave°   split open
And filled with stagnant gloom:
10   Yet a woman has strength to choose it for her room.

Her long, fair hair is allowed
To wander in its thick simpleness;
The graceful tresses crowd
Unequal, yet close enough
15   To have woven about her neck and breast
A wimple[3] of golden stuff.

---

[1] *The Magdalen Timoteo Viti*   Painting of the biblical Mary Magdalene by Renaissance painter Timoteo Viti (reproduced here as an illustration).

[2] *sylph*   Slight, graceful woman.

[3] *wimple*   Medieval headdress often worn by nuns.

Timoteo Viti, *St. Mary Magdalene*, 1521.

Though the rock behind is rude,°   *rough*
The sweetness of solitude
Is on her face, the soft
20 Withdrawal that in wildflowers we have loved so oft.

Her mantle is scarlet red
In folds of severe resplendency;
Her hair beneath is spread
Full length; from its lower flakes
25 Her feet come forth in their naked charm:
A wind discreetly shakes
The scarlet raiment,° the hair.   *dress*
Her small hands, a tranquil pair,

Are laid together; her book
30 And cup of ointment furnish scantily her nook.

She is happy the livelong day,
Yet her thoughts are often with the past;
Her sins are done away,
They can give her no annoy.
35 She is white—oh! infinitely clean
And her heart throbs with joy;
Besides, there is joy in heaven
That her sins are thus forgiven;
And she thinks till even-fall°   *dusk*
40 Of the grace, the strangeness, the wonder of it all.

She is shut from fellowship;
How she loved to mingle with her friends!
To give them eyes and lip;
She lived for their sake alone;
45 Not a braid of her hair, not a rose
Of her cheek was her own:
And she loved to minister
To any in want of her,
All service was so sweet:
50 Now she must stand all day on lithe, unsummoned feet.

Among the untrodden weeds
And moss she is glad to be remote;
She knows that when God needs
From the sinning world relief,
55 He will find her thus with the wild bees,
The doves and the plantain leaf,
Waiting in a perfect peace
For His kingdom's sure increase,
Waiting with a deeper glow
60 Of patience every day, because He tarrieth so.

By her side the box of nard[1]
Unbroken … God is a great way off;
She loves Him: it is hard
That she may not now even spread

---

[1] *nard* Ointment made from the aromatic plant of the same name.

65 The burial spice, who would gladly keep
    The tomb where He lay dead,
    As it were her rocky cave;
    And fold the linen and lave°   wash
    The napkin that once bound
70 His head; no place for her pure arts is longer found.

    And these are the things that hurt;
    For the rest she gives herself no pain:
    She wears no camel shirt,[1]
    She uses nor scourge, nor rod;
75 But bathes her fair body in the well
    And keeps it pure for God:
    The beauty, that He hath made
    So bright, she guards in the shade,
    For, as an angel's dress,
80 Spotless she must preserve her newborn loveliness.

    Day by day and week by week,
    She lives and muses and makes no sound;
    She has no words to speak
    The joy that her desert brings:
85 In her heart there is a song
    And yet no song she sings.
    Since the word *Rabboni*[2] came
    Straightway at the call of her name
    And the Master reproved,
90 It seems she has no choice—her lips have never moved.

    She stole away when the pale
    Light was trembling on the garden ground
    And others told the tale,
    Christ was risen; she roamed the wide,
95 Fearful countries of the wilderness
    And many a riverside,
    Till she found her destined grot,°   grotto
    South, in France, a woody spot,
    Where she is often glad,
100 Musing on those great days when she at first grew sad.
    —1892

---

[1] *camel shirt* I.e., hairshirt, worn to cause discomfort as an act of
penitence or asceticism. See Matthew 3.4.

[2] *Rabboni* Hebrew: Master, teacher.

Saint Sebastian[3]
Correggio[4]
The Dresden Gallery[5]

Bound by thy hands, but with respect unto thine
    eyes how free—
Fixed on Madonna,[6] seeing all that they were born to see!
    The Child thine upward face hath sighted,
        Still and delighted;
5   Oh, bliss when with mute rites two souls are plighted![7]

As the young aspen-leaves[8] rejoice, though to the stem
    held tight,
In the soft visit of the air, the current of the light,
    Thou hast the peril of a captive's chances,
        Thy spirit dances,
10 Caught in the play of Heaven's divine advances.

While cherubs straggle on the clouds of luminous,
    curled fire,
The Babe looks through them, far below, on thee with
    soft desire.
    Most clear of bond must they be reckoned—

---

[3] *Saint Sebastian* Early Christian saint and martyr, killed during the
Roman emperor Diocletian's campaign against Christians c. 288 CE,
he is typically represented as bound to a stake and pierced by arrows.
Many scholars have noted the homoerotic tenor of the iconography
surrounding Saint Sebastian, and his name and image were often
invoked, in the late nineteenth century, as a coded reference to same-
sex love.

[4] *Correggio* Antonio Allegri da Correggio (1489–1534), one of the
foremost painters of the Italian Renaissance, perhaps best known for
his *Madonna and Child with the Young Saint John*.

[5] *The Dresden Gallery* The Gemäldegalerie Alte Meister, or the Old
Masters Picture Gallery, is an important venue in Dresden, Germany,
and is renowned for its collection of notable Italian Renaissance
paintings.

[6] *Madonna* Mary, the mother of Jesus.

[7] *plighted* Bound by a vow.

[8] *aspen-leaves* The leaves of this poplar-type tree are prone to a
trembling movement. (In Eastern Orthodoxy, Judas is sometimes
believed to have hanged himself from an aspen tree following his
betrayal of Christ, causing the tree's leaves to forever quiver, though
the tree is not native to the Middle East.)

         No joy is second
15 To theirs whose eyes by other eyes are beckoned.

    Though arrows rain on breast and throat they have no
        power to hurt,
    While thy tenacious face they fail an instant to avert.
        Oh might my eyes, so without measure,
           Feed on their treasure,
20 The world with thong° and dart might   *leather whip*
        do its pleasure!
    —1892

La Gioconda[1]

Leonardo Da Vinci

Historic, sidelong, implicating eyes;
A smile of velvet's lustre on the cheek;
Calm lips the smile leads upward; hand that lies
Glowing and soft, the patience in its rest
Of cruelty that waits and doth not seek   5
For prey; a dusky forehead and a breast
Where twilight touches ripeness amorously:
Behind her, crystal rocks, a sea and skies
Of evanescent blue on cloud and creek;
Landscape that shines suppressive of its zest   10
For those vicissitudes by which men die.
—1892

A girl

A girl,
Her soul a deep-wave pearl
Dim, lucent° of all lovely mysteries;   *shining*
    A face flowered for heart's ease,
    A brow's grace soft as seas   5
    Seen through faint forest trees:
    A mouth, the lips apart,
Like aspen leaflets trembling in the breeze
From her tempestuous heart.
Such: and our souls so knit,   10
I leave a page half-writ—
    The work begun
Will be to heaven's conception done,
    If she come to it.
—1893

---

1   *La Gioconda*   Da Vinci's painting *The Mona Lisa* (c. 1503–19).

[It was deep April, and the morn]

It was deep April, and the morn
   Shakespeare was born;[1]
The world was on us, pressing sore;
My Love and I took hands and swore,
5   Against the world, to be
Poets and lovers evermore,
To laugh and dream on Lethe's[2] shore
To sing to Charon[3] in his boat,
Heartening the timid souls afloat;
10 Of judgment never to take heed,
But to those fast-locked souls to speed,
Who never from Apollo[4] fled,
Who spent no hour among the dead;
     Continually
15   With them to dwell,
Indifferent to heaven and hell.
—1893

Beloved

Mortal, if thou art beloved,
   Life's offences are removed;
All the fateful things that checked thee,
Hearten, hallow, and protect thee.
5 Grow'st thou mellow? What is age?
Tinct° on life's illumined page,   *color*
Where the purple letters[5] glow
Deeper, painted long ago.
What is sorrow? Comfort's prime,
10 Love's choice Indian summer[6] clime.

Sickness? Thou wilt pray it worse
For so blessed, balmy nurse.
And for death? When thou art dying
'Twill be Love beside thee lying.
15 Death is lonesome? Oh, how brave
Shows the foot-frequented grave!
Heaven itself is but the casket
For Love's treasure, ere he ask it,
Ere with burning heart he follow,
20 Piercing through corruption's hollow.
If thou art beloved, oh then
Fear no grief from mortal men!
—1893

[Sometimes I do despatch my heart]

Sometimes I do despatch my heart
   Among the graves to dwell apart:
On some the tablets are erased,
Some earthquake-tumbled, some defaced,
5 And some that have forgotten lain
A fall of tears makes green again;
And my brave heart can overtread
Her brood of hopes, her infant dead,
And pass with quickened footsteps by
10 The headstone of hoar° memory,   *aged*
     Till she hath found
     One swelling mound
With just her name writ and *beloved*;
From that she cannot be removed.
—1893

[She mingled me rue and roses]

She mingled me rue[7] and roses,
   And I found my bliss complete:
     The roses are gone,

---

[1] *morn … was born* It is traditional to celebrate Shakespeare's birthday on 23 April, St. George's Day.

[2] *Lethe* In Greek mythology, a river in Hades (the underworld), the waters of which cause the dead to forget the past.

[3] *Charon* Greek mythological ferryman of the underworld who transports the souls of the dead across the River Styx.

[4] *Apollo* Classical god associated with the sun, poetry, and prophecy.

[5] *purple letters* Perhaps an allusion to "purple prose," a literary term referring to ornate passages of writing.

[6] *Indian summer* Period of unseasonal warmth occurring in autumn.

[7] *rue* Garden rue, a shrub with yellow flowers and bitter, strongly scented leaves.

But the rue lives on,
5 The bitter that lived with the sweet.

Life will mingle you rue and roses;
The roses will fall at your feet:
But deep in the rue
That their leaves bestrew
10 The bitter will smell of the sweet.
—1893

[Our myrtle is in flower]

Our myrtle is in flower;
Behold Love's power!
The glorious stamens'[1] crowded force unfurled,
Cirque[2] beyond cirque
5 At breathing, bee-like, and harmonious work;
The rose-patched petals backward curled,
Falling away
To let fecundity have perfect play.

O flower, dear to the eyes
10 Of Aphrodite,[3] rise
As she at once to bare, audacious bliss;
And bid us near
Your prodigal,° delicious hemisphere,   extravagant
Where thousand kisses breed the kiss
15 That fills the room
With languor of an acid, dark perfume!
—1893

Cyclamens[4]

They are terribly white:
There is snow on the ground,
And a moon on the snow at night;
The sky is cut by the winter light;
5 Yet I, who have all these things in ken,[5]
Am struck to the heart by the chiselled white
Of this handful of cyclamen.
—1893

Unbosoming

The love that breeds
In my heart for thee!
As the iris[6] is full, brimful of seeds,
And all that it flowered for among the reeds
5 Is packed in a thousand vermilion°-beads   red
That push, and riot, and squeeze, and clip,
Till they burst the sides of the silver scrip,°   bag
And at last we see
What the bloom, with its tremulous, bowery[7] fold
10 Of zephyr[8]-petal at heart did hold:
So my breast is rent°   torn
With the burthen° and strain of its great content;   burden
For the summer of fragrance and sighs is dead,
The harvest-secret is burning red,
15 And I would give thee, after my kind,
The final issues of heart and mind.
—1893

---

[1] stamen In botany, the fertilizing (hence "male") portion of a plant.

[2] Cirque Round arena, typically designated for games.

[3] Aphrodite In classical mythology, the goddess of love and sexuality, renowned for her beauty.

---

[4] Cyclamens Type of perennial plant best known for its flowers, which have upswept petals and patterned leaves.

[5] ken Field of vision.

[6] iris Type of plant, prized for its vivid flowers.

[7] bowery Like a bower, that is, a place enclosed by trees, a leafy retreat.

[8] zephyr Mild breeze.

[When I grow old]

When I grow old,
    I would be bold
To ask of heaven this boon:°   *request*
Like the thin-circled and translucent moon,
5   That makes intrusion
        Unnoted on the morning sky,
        And with soft eye
Watches the thousand, grassy flowers unfold,
        I would be free,
10   Without confusion
        Of influence cold,
        To pause and see
The flush of youth in its felicity.
        —1893

To Christina Rossetti[1]

Lady, we would behold thee moving bright
    As Beatrice or Matilda[2] mid the trees,
Alas! thy moan was as a moan for ease
And passage through cool shadows to the night:
5 Fleeing from love, hadst thou not poet's right
To slip into the universe? The seas
Are fathomless to rivers drowned in these,
And sorrow is secure in leafy light.
Ah, had this secret touched thee, in a tomb
10 Thou hadst not buried thy enchanting self,
As happy Syrinx[3] murmuring with the wind,

Or Daphne,[4] thrilled through all her mystic bloom,
From safe recess as genius or as elf,
Thou hadst breathed joy in earth and in thy kind.
—1896

Nests in Elms

The rooks[5] are cawing up and down the trees!
    Among their nests they caw. O sound I treasure,
Ripe as old music is, the summer's measure,
Sleep at her gossip, sylvan[6] mysteries,
5 With prate and clamour to give zest of these—
In rune[7] I trace the ancient law of pleasure,
Of love, of all the busy-ness of leisure,
With dream on dream of never-thwarted ease.
O homely birds, whose cry is harbinger
10 Of nothing sad, who know not anything
Of sea-birds' loneliness, of Procne's[8] strife,
Rock round me when I die! So sweet it were
To die by open doors, with you on wing
Humming the deep security of life.
—1907

---

[1] *Christina Rossetti* English poet (1830–94) often associated with the Pre-Raphaelites.

[2] *Beatrice* From Dante's *Divine Comedy*, Book 3, *Paradise*: a woman who personifies love and acts as Dante's guide through Paradise; *Matilda* From Book 2, *Purgatory*: a beautiful virgin who meets Dante in the Garden of Eden and leads him to the river Lethe to wash away his sins.

[3] *Syrinx* In Greek mythology, the nymph Syrinx turned herself into a bed of reeds in order to escape Pan's advances.

[4] *Daphne* In Greek mythology, the nymph Daphne fled from the god Apollo's advances and was transformed into a laurel tree in her escape.

[5] *rooks* Crows known for their loud, grating voice.

[6] *sylvan* Associated with the woods. In classical mythology, a spirit of the woods.

[7] *rune* Poem or incantation, a spell. Also, the movement of the stars and other celestial bodies, or, more generally, rapid movement.

[8] *Procne* In classical mythology, Procne's husband Tereus raped her sister Philomela and cut out the girl's tongue so that she would not be able to tell what he had done to her. Philomela then wove a tapestry depicting the rape and sent it to Procne, who avenged her sister by killing Tereus's son and serving the body to her husband for dinner. When Tereus discovered he had eaten his child, he tried to kill the two sisters. The gods intervened and turned all three into birds. Tereus was transformed into a hawk or a hoopoe, Philomela into a nightingale, and Procne into a swallow.

The Mummy[1] Invokes His Soul

Down to me quickly, down! I am such dust,
  Baked, pressed together; let my flesh be fanned
With thy fresh breath; come from thy reedy land
Voiceful with birds; divert me, for I lust
5 To break, to crumble—prick with pores this crust!—
And fall apart, delicious, loosening sand.
Oh, joy, I feel thy breath, I feel thy hand
That searches for my heart, and trembles just
Where once it beat. How light thy touch, thy frame!
10 Surely thou perchest on the summer trees …
And the garden that we love? Soul, take thine ease,
I am content, so thou[2] enjoy the same
Sweet terraces and founts,° content, for thee,   fountains
To burn in this immense torpidity.
  —1908

Old Ivories

A window full of ancient things, and while,
  Lured by their solemn tints, I crossed the street,
A face was there that in its tranquil style,
Almost obscure, at once remote and sweet,
5 Moved me by pleasure of similitude—
For, flanked by golden ivories, that face,
Her face, looked forth in even and subdued
Deep power, while all the shining, all the grace
Came from the passing of Time over her,
10 Sorrow with Time; there was no age, no spring:
On those smooth brows no promise was astir,
No hope outlived: herself a perfect thing,

She stood by that time-burnished reliquary[3]
Simple as Aphrodite[4] by the sea.
  —1908

Ebbtide[5] at Sundown

How larger is remembrance than desire!
  How deeper than all longing is regret!
The tide is gone, the sands are rippled yet;
The sun is gone; the hills are lifted higher,
5 Crested with rose. Ah, why should we require
Sight of the sea, the sun? The sands are wet,
And in their glassy flaws huge record set
Of the ebbed stream, the little ball of fire.
Gone, they are gone! But, oh, so freshly gone,
10 So rich in vanishing we ask not where—
So close upon us is the bliss that shone,
And, oh, so thickly it impregns° the air!   impregnates
Closer in beating heart we could not be
To the sunk sun, the far, surrendered sea.
  —1908

Power in Silence

I

Though I sing high, and chaunt° above her,   chant
  Praising my girl,
It were not right
To reckon her the poorer lover;
5   She does not love me less
For her royal, jewelled speechlessness,
She is the sapphire, she the light,
The music in the pearl.

---

[1] *The Mummy* Fascination with mummies, and ancient Egypt more generally, was high during the Victorian era. Victorian travelers would sometimes purchase mummies on their travels, returning with their souvenirs and hosting "unwrapping" parties.

[2] *so thou* Provided you.

[3] *reliquary* Something that preserves memories of the past events or people.

[4] *Aphrodite* Greek goddess of love, beauty, and pleasure, said to have been born from sea foam.

[5] *Ebbtide* Outward flowing tide.

2

Not from pert° birds we learn the spring-tide   *lively*
10   From open sky.
    What speaks to us
Closer than far distances that hide
In woods, what is more dear
Than a cherry-bough, bees feeding near
15 In the soft, proffered blooms? Lo, I
    Am fed and honoured thus.

3

She has the star's own pulse; its throbbing
    Is a quick light.
She is a dove
20 My soul draws to its breast; her sobbing
    Is for the warm dark there!
In the heat of her wings I would not care
My close-housed bird should take her flight
    To magnify our love.
        —1913

Where the Blessed Feet Have Trod

Not alone in Palestine those blessed Feet have trod,
    For I catch their print,
I have seen their dint°   *impression*
On a plot of chalky ground,
5   Little villas dotted round;
On a sea-worn waste,
Where a priest, in haste,
Passeth with the Blessèd Sacrament[1] to one dying, frail,
Through the yarrow, past the tamarisk,[2] and the
        plaited snail:
10 Bright upon the grass I see
        Bleeding Feet of Calvary[3]—
And I worship, and I clasp them round!
On this bit of chalky, English ground,
Jesu, Thou art found: my God I hail,
15   My Lord, my God!
—1913

---

[1] *Blessèd Sacrament* In Catholicism, the consecrated host, believed to be Christ's body and blood.

[2] *yarrow* Type of plant with gray stems and flat flower-heads, sometimes used medicinally; *tamarisk* Evergreen shrub.

[3] *Calvary* Site of Jesus' crucifixion, also known as Golgotha.

T.N. MUKHARJI
1847 – 1919

Writer, civil servant, scientist, and curator Troilokyanath Mukhopadhyay (T.N. Mukharji) had a distinguished career in the Government of India at the height of the British Raj. As a curator for the Indian Museum in Calcutta and for several international exhibitions, he created exhibits and accompanying guidebooks that promoted Indian art and industry throughout the Western world. As a writer, he was prolific in both English and his native Bengali, pioneering the fantasy genre in Bengali literature through his novels and short stories. In Western literature, he is best remembered for *A Visit to Europe*, his penetrating account of his nine months spent traveling abroad as an official representative of the Indian government for the 1886 Colonial and Indian Exhibition in London.

Mukharji, the second of six children in a high-caste family, was born in 1847 in Rahuta, a rural village in what is now West Bengal. His early education took place at local village schools and later the Free Mission Institute, an English school for boys founded by the Scottish evangelist Alexander Duff in nearby Chinshurah. Unfortunately, a malaria outbreak in the region left Mukharji orphaned as a teenager and marked the end of his formal education, though he continued to self-educate throughout his life.

At eighteen Mukharji left Rahuta in search of work and initially found employment as a schoolteacher. Later, through a family connection, he secured a position as a police inspector in Cuttack, Orissa (modern-day Odisha). In the course of this work, Mukharji met and befriended Sir William Wilson Hunter, a Scottish-born member of the Indian Civil Service and compiler of various statistical and historical surveys of the Indian Empire. In 1870, Hunter helped Mukharji secure a job as a clerk at the Bengal Gazetteer Office in Calcutta (now Kolkata). From there he became the chief clerk and, later, assistant director of the Indian government's Agricultural Department before transferring to the Revenue Department in 1881. At the peak of his civil service career, he was the highest-ranking South Asian official in the British government in India.

While working for the Revenue Department, Mukharji was appointed the officer in charge of curating the Indian exhibits for various international colonial exhibitions—in Paris, Melbourne, Amsterdam, Calcutta, London, and Glasgow—throughout the 1870s and 1880s. He wrote detailed catalogues for several of these exhibitions, beginning with *A Descriptive Catalogue of Indian Produce Contributed to the Amsterdam Exhibition* (1883). This was followed by *A Rough List of Indian Art-ware* (1883), so successful that a second edition was released only three months after the first; *A Hand-book of Indian Products, Art-manufactures and Raw Materials* (1883); and *Art-Manufactures of India* (1888), commissioned by the Indian government for the Glasgow Exhibition.

Mukharji's position as curator gave him a powerful role in shaping perceptions of India on an international stage at the height of Britain's colonial presence in the country. He viewed these exhibits and their corresponding catalogues as a means to facilitate India's economic prosperity by showcasing the nation's artistry and artisanal skill, as well as its natural resources. As he writes in his preface to *A Hand-book of Indian Products, Art-manufactures and Raw Materials,*

> The object of this work is to interest European visitors at the Exhibition in the old Indian arts, which of late have attracted so much attention for the beauty of their design, the excellent selection and arrangement of colours, the minuteness of patterns and the high "finish" displayed in their execution, and to invite the attention of mercantile gentlemen to the innumerable raw materials which abound in every part of India, many of which are capable of being developed into articles of commerce.

Mukharji also had a concrete impact on the Indian economy through his achievements as a scientist and industrial innovator. He discovered new uses for several plants, including the manufacture of paper from the wild Indian creeper; he also encouraged the growth of the silk industry in Assam and popularized the farming of carrots as a means of mitigating famine.

Mukharji was appointed assistant curator of the Art and Economics exhibit at the Indian Museum in Calcutta in 1886, a post he held until his retirement in 1896. That same year, he was invited to serve as an official representative of the Government of India at the Colonial and Indian Exhibition in London and spent nine months traveling throughout the British Isles and the European Continent. When he returned to India, the magazine *Indian Nation* invited Mukharji to write an account of his experiences and impressions. These weekly installments were compiled into a single volume and published simultaneously in London and Calcutta as *A Visit to Europe* (1889). English-language readers continue to find much that is compelling in the perspective of a colonial subject incisively observing British society and comparing it with his own—while, at the same time, engagingly describing his experience as a visitor subjected to the curiosity of the British.

Having suffered from poor health for most of his life, Mukharji retired from civil service at 49 and relocated to the coastal town of Puri, Orissa, where he remained until his death in November 1919. Here, he enjoyed a successful career as a fiction writer in his native Bengali. His supernatural novella *Kankabati* was praised by such Bengali literary luminaries as Rabindranath Tagore; also especially well-received was his innovative *Damarucharita* (*Epic of Damarudhar*, 1910–17) a story cycle blending black comedy, realism, and social commentary with elements of myth, fantasy, and science fiction. Praised for his contributions as a satirist, and for an original approach to ghost fiction and fantasy that anticipates the development of magic realism, Mukharji made a significant mark on Indian literature. His work is still frequently read and studied in Bangladesh and West Bengal.

⌘ ⌘ ⌘

from *A Visit to Europe*

from CHAPTER 3
THE EXHIBITION AND ITS VISITORS

... Another place of considerable interest to the natives of England was the Indian Bazar where Hindu and Muhammadan artisans carried on their avocations, to witness which men, women and children flocked from all parts of the kingdom. A dense crowd always stood there, looking at our men as they wove the gold brocade, sang the patterns of the carpet and printed the calico[1] with the hand. They were as much astonished to

---

[1] *brocade* Fabric with a woven, raised pattern; *sang the patterns of the carpet* Refers to the practice of singing or chanting while weaving, possibly as a means of memorizing complex patterns; *calico* Woven cotton fabric often painted with floral patterns.

see the Indians produce works of art with the aid of rude apparatus they themselves had discarded long ago, as a Hindu would be to see a chimpanzee officiating as a priest in a funeral ceremony and reading out Sanskrit texts from a palm leaf book spread before him. We were very interesting beings no doubt, so were the Zulus before us, and so is the Sioux chief at the present time (1887). Human nature everywhere thirsts for novelty, and measures out its favours in proportion to the rarity and oddity of a thing. It was from the ladies that we received the largest amount of patronage. We were pierced through and through by stares from eyes of all colours—green, gray, blue and black—and every movement and act of ours, walking, sitting, eating, reading, received its full share of "O, I, never!" The number of wives we left behind at home was also a constant theme of speculation among them, and shrewd guesses were sometimes made on this point, 250 being a favourite number. You could tell any amount of stories on this subject without exciting the slightest suspicion. Once, one of our number told a pretty waitress—"I am awfully pleased with you, and I want to marry you. Will you accept the fortieth wifeship in my household which became vacant just before I left my country?" She asked—"How many wives have you altogether?" "Two hundred and fifty, the usual number," was the ready answer. "What became of your wife, number 40?" "I killed her, because one morning she could not cook my porridge well." The poor girl was horrified, and exclaimed—"O you monster, O you wretch!" Then she narrated the sad fate of a friend of hers. She was a sweet little child, when an African student studying in Edinburgh came and wooed her. They got married in England and fondly loved each other. Everything went well as long as the pair lived in England, but after a short time he took his fair wife to his desert home in Liberia. Not a single white man or woman could she see there, and she felt very lonely. But the sight of her mother-in-law, who dressed in feathers and skins came dancing into the house half-tipsy, was more than she could bear. She pined for a short time and died.

Of course, every nation in the world considers other nations as savages or at least much inferior to itself. It was so from the beginning and it will be so as long as human nature will retain its present character. We did not therefore wonder that the common people should take us for barbarians, awkward as we were in every respect. They have very strict notions of dress, manners and the general bearing of a man, any deviation from which is seriously noticed. Utmost indulgence was however shewn to us everywhere. Her Majesty was graciously pleased to lay aside the usual rules, and this favour was shewn us wherever we went. Gentlemen and ladies of high education and culture, however, honoured us as the representatives of the most ancient nation now existing on the face of the earth. They would frequently ask us home, get up private parties and arrange for all sorts of amusements. In other houses we grew more intimate and formed part of the family party. To these we were always welcome, and could go and come whenever we liked. We got some friends among them, and these gentlemen would often come and fetch us home if we absented ourselves for more than the ordinary length of time. I fondly remember the happy days I passed with them, and feel thankful for the kindness they showed me during my sojourn in their country.

In public matters non-official gentlemen were also very partial to us. "We want to hear the turbanned gentleman" was the wish often and often expressed. But we ceased not to be a prodigious wonder to strangers and to the common people. Would they discuss us so freely if they knew that we understood their language? It was very amusing to hear what they said about us. Often when fatigued with work, or when cares and anxieties cast a gloom upon our mind, we found such talks about us more refreshing than a glass of port wine. I wish I had the ability to do justice to the discussing power of these ladies and gentlemen exercised in their kind notice of us, for in that case I could produce one of the most interesting books ever published. Or if I had known that I would be required to write an account of my visit to Europe, I would have taken notes of at least some of the remarkable hits on truth unconsciously made by ignorant people from the country, which are applicable to all nations and which set one to philosophise on the material difference that exists between our own estimate of ourselves and the estimate which others form of us.

If we were interesting beings in the eyes of the Londoners, who had oftener opportunities of seeing their fellow subjects from the far East, how much more would we be so to the simple villagers who came by thousands to see the wonders of the Exhibition. Their conduct towards us was always kind and respectful. They liked to talk to us, and whenever convenient we tried to satisfy their curiosity. Men, women and children, whose relations are in India serving as soldiers or in any other capacity, would come through the crowd, all panting, to shake hands with us and ask about their friends. Many queer incidents happened in this way. "Do you know Jim—James Robinson you know of——— Regiment?" asked a fat elderly woman, who one day came bustling through the crowd and took me by storm, without any of those preliminary manoeuvres usually adopted to open a conversation with a stranger. I expressed my regret in not having the honour of Jim's acquaintance. The good old lady then explained to me that she was Jim's aunt, and gave me a long history of her nephew, and the circumstances which led to his enlistment as a soldier. If the truant nephew lost the golden opportunity of sending through us his dutiful message to his aunt, she on her part was not wanting in her affectionate remembrances of him. Among other things, most of which I did not understand, for she did not speak the English we ordinarily hear nor was her language quite coherent at the time, she begged me to carry to Jim the important intelligence that Mrs. Jones' fat pig obtained a prize at the Smithfield Agricultural Show. I showed my alacrity to carry the message right off to Jim in the wilds of Upper Burma by immediately taking leave of the lady, who joined her friends and explained to them that I was a bosom friend of her nephew.

Once, I was sitting in one of the swellish[1] restaurants at the Exhibition, glancing over a newspaper which I had no time to read in the morning. At a neighbouring table sat a respectable-looking family group evidently from the country, from which furtive glances were occasionally thrown in my direction. I thought I might do worse than having a little fun, if any could be made out of the notice that was being taken of me. I seemed to be suddenly aware that I was being looked at, which immediately scared away half a dozen eyes from my table. It took fully five minutes' deep undivided attention to my paper again to reassure and tempt out those eyes from the plates where they took refuge, and the glances from them, which at first flashed and flickered like lightning, became steadier the more my mind seemed to get absorbed in the subject I was reading. The closer inspection to which I submitted ended in my favour. Perhaps, no symptom being visible in my external appearance of the cannibalistic tendencies of my heart, or owing probably to the notion that I must have by that time got over my partiality for human flesh, or knowing at least that the place was safe enough against any treacherous spring which I might take into my head to make upon them, or owing to whatever other cause, the party gradually grew bolder, began to talk in whispers and actually tried to attract my attention towards them. The latter duty ultimately devolved upon the beauty of the party, a pretty girl of about seventeen. Of course it was not intended for my ears, but somehow I heard her say—"Oh, how I wish to speak to him?" Could I withstand such an appeal? I rose and approaching the little Curiosity asked—"Did you speak to me, young lady?" She blushed and hung down her head. Her papa came to the rescue. "My daughter, Sir, is delighted with the magnificent things brought from your country to this Exhibition. She saw some writing in your language on a few plates and shields, and is anxious to know its meaning. We did not know whom to ask, when we saw you. Will you take a seat here, and do me the honour to take a glass of something with me? What will it be? Sparkling moselle I find is good here; or shall it be champagne or anything stronger?" He said. The proferred glass was declined with thanks, but I took a chair and explained the meaning of some of the verses damascened on the

---

[1] *swellish* Stylish.

Koftgari ware.[1] The young lady soon got over her bashfulness, and talked with a vivacity which I did not expect from her. She was delighted with everything I said, expressed her astonishment at my knowledge of English, and complimented me for the performance of the band brought from *my country*, *viz.*, the West Indian band composed of Negroes and Mulattos, which compliment made me wince a little, but nevertheless I went on chattering for a quarter of an hour and furnishing her with sufficient means to annihilate her friend Minnie, Jane or Lizzy or whoever she might be, and to brag among her less fortunate relations for six months to come of her having actually seen and talked to a genuine "Blackie."

On another occasion in a poorer place called the Grill Room, where less elaborate food and cheaper refreshments were sold, a sailor came up to me and begged hard for the favour of my speaking to his wife. He said that he had returned from Australia the day before, and obtained a day's leave to bring his wife to the Exhibition. He wanted to please her and to satisfy her wishes as far as it lay in his power. The woman took into her head the fancy that she would not be happy nor would she enjoy the sights of the Exhibition unless I spoke to her. In utter vexation at the absurdity of the request I cried—"Nonsense, I can't speak to your wife?" But the man would take no denial, and his pleadings became more and more importunate as now and then he glanced at his petulant queen, who with downcast eyes gloomily sat at a distant table. Well, her ambassador succeeded in his mission, and I had to carry balm to the mind of the unhappy lady. She cheered up at once, and as a reward allowed her husband to have another glass of whisky. That settled him. With the assistance of his wife I had soon to pack him off to his home in a cab or otherwise he would have got into trouble.

How did the Anglo-Indians treat us? I am sure my countrymen would want to know that. They treated us as gentlemen would treat gentlemen. What kinder and warmer friend could any man hope to get than Sir George Birdwood?[2] A fellow-feeling existed between the Anglo-Indians and ourselves as if they were our countrymen in that strange land. Here inequality of official position separated us, there we were guests. Their sojourn in an oriental land would have been for nothing if they had not learned how honoured a guest is. Occasionally, however, we met with some queer characters who, specially if they had ladies with them, pompously displayed their acquaintance with the Hindi language, however slight it might be, and their power and superiority over us. That was as much as to tell the ladies—"Look, how great I am!" So far it was all right. And we did our best to look surprised at his unlimited command over the vernacular languages of India, and to look submissive before him to help him to be the Great Mogul[3] he wished to look in the eyes of the ladies. The ladies would smile and giggle, his face would be all animation with pleasure and pride, his urbanity would know no bounds, and at the end, ten to one, it would end in an invitation. Lord, what villains we thought we were! But it was all done in charity. At any rate here is a hint for one or two swindling Indians we met in London, whose business was rather slack. Once, but once only, I met with a little rudeness from an Anglo-Indian. I do not give the *exact words* he used, but I give his meaning and materialise his tone into words. He majestically stalked towards me and said—"Slave, show me ——'s office." "I am sorry I cannot obey your command just at this moment, Sir, as I am engaged, but if you go straight, turn to the right and then to the left, you will find yourself before that office," I replied. He got angry and said—"You must, Sir; who is your master?" "My master, Sir, is the Government of India. I cannot go with you for the reason that I am engaged

---

[1] *Koftgari ware* Metal ware that is damascened (inlaid with silver or gold designs) in an Indian style.

[2] *Sir George Birdwood* Anglo-Indian surgeon, museum curator, and writer (1832–1917). He was born in India to British parents and educated in England.

[3] *Great Mogul* I.e., emperor; the Mughal Empire, which included present-day India, existed from the mid-sixteenth to the mid-nineteenth centuries.

with this gentleman, who is the Reporter for ———." His rudeness did not annoy me more than his servility to the gentleman I named.

Outside the Exhibition we never experienced a single act of unkindness. We travelled alone in the East End, the West End and everywhere, and frequently got ourselves lost. Boys and girls would gather round, but they never molested us in any way. Beggars and bad women would no doubt be bolder with us than with the natives (of England), but they never gave us any trouble worth speaking of. No street Arab or London ruffian ever took advantage of our inexperience. On the other hand men who idly lounge about public houses in low quarters, were always ready to help us, and frequently showed us the way when we got lost. Places where even cockneys[1] would be afraid to go in the daytime we went to in search of adventures, but no adventure will happen to one who would keep clear of disreputable enticements. Once a villainous-looking Jew tried to cut a practical joke upon me. More than a dozen hands were at once raised in my protection, those hands belonged to English roughs, perfect strangers to me. At another time somebody called me a foreigner. "He is no foreigner!" cried several voices, "He is a British subject as you and I."

Speaking of British kindness, I may as well mention a little incident which happened to my friend, Mr. Gupte. He and Sir Edward Buck[2] one morning went to the Covent Garden Market, where fresh fruits brought from all parts of the world are sold in prodigious quantities. In this place in all seasons of the year the finest flower and the most delicious fruit which man can produce can always be procured. The busiest time in this market is six in the morning, especially on Tuesdays, Thursdays and Saturdays. Sir Edward asked my friend whether he had ever tasted raspberries. On his answering in the negative, Sir Edward tried to procure some, but it was then too late, all were sold and none could be had. A retail stall-keeper, however, bought some baskets earlier in the morning with which he was preparing to depart. Sir Edward asked him for one, but he would not sell. It was then explained to him, who it was wanted for, and without a word, he instantly handed over a basket. He would take no price. "He is the guest of my nation, Sir, and I make a present of it to him," said the patriotic fruit-seller. …

… Thus what I have said above about the kindness of the British people to strangers, and specially to the Indians, corroborates what has been often said on the same subject by other Indians who lived for a time in England. The British people take a pride in being kind to strangers who happen to be in their land, they consider it mean to be otherwise, and they feel it their duty to resent on their behalf any unmannerly conduct that may be shewn towards them by the rude and the rough who are to be found in all countries and among all nations. The manners of an Englishman, however, undergo some change when he is outside his own country, whether it be in France, Germany or Italy. Outside his own country, he is proud, somewhat disdainful, and not too anxious to conceal in his breast that opinion which every nation in the world entertains—that all other nations are inferior to itself. Not only with him, but as a rule with every man, this feeling of superiority is intensified when he finds himself amongst a people manifestly and vastly inferior to his own. He finds it impossible, for instance, to be on equal terms with a people whose low organization permitted their being reduced from time immemorial to the position of cattle, and who has been rescued from this position solely by his clemency. That portion of the human race which gave such a signal proof of its low organisation was always distinguished by the colour of its skin; and the universal decadence of *all* coloured races in the present cycle has in the eyes of the Europeans effaced all nicety of distinction among them, has divided the human race by one broad line into two main classes—the white and the coloured—and has established in their mind the idea of a more or less close consanguinity[3] between the Chinaman and the

---

1 *cockneys* Working-class people native to East London.

2 *Gupte … Buck* Both B.A. Gupte and Sir Edward Buck (an Anglo-Indian) were members of the delegation Mukharji was also a part of.

3 *consanguinity* Commonality of blood.

Hottentot and between Kálidása and Hiawatha.[1] The actual condition of things in a non-European country—acting on the mind of a European predisposed by traditions, tales and historical teachings, prepared by examples set by others before him, and narrowed by caste-rules already established around him—leaves no room for the full play of that broad sympathy which is a prominent feature in the character of an Englishman in his native home. He is therefore often judged by the non-European races among whom he lives under very unfavourable circumstances. A fish *out of* water is not exactly the fish *in* water. …

… My countrymen should think and ponder over the wonderful progress which Australia has made during the last thirty years. …

… If we could only bring a fraction of those sterling qualities to the aid of British administration in its struggles to subdue the wild forces of tropical nature, to utilise its blind unguided energy for the benefit of man, to wipe away all trace of savagery from the country, to cleanse the land of filth and dirt as old as the Himalayas, to stamp out preventable diseases which cut off vigorous manhood and shock civilised humanity, to make roads and railways, to impart the benefits of education to the ignorant masses, to show them the road to wealth and prosperity, to teach them to eat, dress and live like men, and generally to bring this interesting people within the pale of modern civilisation, then in a couple of generations India would wear altogether a different aspect. How many English lads, burning with enthusiasm to rush into this struggle, must allow their minds to revel in hopes of victory and glory on sleepless nights just before their departure for India! Vain hopes! They counted only on battle with inanimate nature and not with the intellectual darkness that has shrouded the country from time immemorial. To awake the sleeping

Himalaya and to make it walk bodily to Land's End[2] would be an easier task than to open the eyes of 250 millions of human beings, to invest them with the power to discriminate good from evil, to instill into their weak heart the courage to do what is good and to shun with loathing what is evil, to shake out from their system all dreaminess, indolence and apathy, and to infuse into it the life and vigour of a youthful nation. The disappointment of noble-hearted Englishmen may be great, but *our* disappointment and *our* impatience are acutely painful. They feel the same sympathy as a doctor feels for the sufferings of a child after his fruitless ministrations for its relief, but *we* feel the keen nervous longing of the mother for the power to wipe away with a brush of her hand the agonies of her beloved offspring. In my own humble way I have worked for the benefit of my nation for the last seventeen years, in new lines which I could never have dreamt of but for the example set before me by English friends and superior officers, and I speak with that authority which practical experience gives, when I say that the greatest difficulty one has to meet in this country is from the opposition of those forces of intellectual darkness I have just mentioned. The people of the country, the material with which and for which, you have to work are not fit or yet ready to receive and assimilate to any appreciable extent innovations, however profitable they may be. Their deep-rooted confidence in the existing state of things, their disbelief in the efficacy of change, their sentiment of human helplessness to contend with natural evils and to surmount difficulties, their short-sighted covetousness that prompts them to kill the goose that lays the golden egg, their habits of slovenliness, indolence and procrastination, their careless talk and reckless promises and assertions, all combine to make earnest work slow, exasperating and very often abortive. So we have now a treble[3] duty to perform; first, to conquer the natural shortcomings of our own character, to extirpate from

---

[1] *Hottentot* Derogatory (and formerly common) term for a member of the Khoekhoe people of southern Africa; *Kálidása* Classical Sanskrit poet and playwright (c. fourth–fifth century CE) considered to be one of the greatest Indian writers; *Hiawatha* Fifteenth-century Indigenous political figure known for his role in establishing the Haudenosaunee (also known as the Iroquois Confederacy).

[2] *Land's End* Kanyakumari, at the southernmost tip of continental India. The Himalayas mark the northernmost part of the Indian subcontinent.

[3] *treble* Triple.

our mind the deep-rooted effects of early teachings and to withstand the baneful influences of our everyday surroundings; second, to teach and help those elected to co-operate in the work to do the same; and third, to organise the work itself. Generations will pass away before the country will attain the state of a thorough working order, but nevertheless it behoves each individual to do however little he can to pioneer his nation in its march to that state, first by working in his own person, second by working on those with whom he comes in contact.

Vanity, undue reverence for the past, and reluctance to alter the present, seem at present to be serious obstacles in the way of our progress towards a new national life. Pressing needs of life are however too strong for such sentimentalities. Vain now we are no doubt, full of conceit, the result of imperfect knowledge. We hold that with our present acquirements we are capable of those deeds which make the English great; only opportunity is wanted, forgetting that if we were really worthy of those deeds opportunity could have been made, with the start that we have got and under the causes that are working around us. But we are not worthy. Our presumption is due to the fact that the conception we have formed in our mind of those deeds is superficial and vague. Nor have we rightly understood the necessity that led to their accomplishment in Europe, nor the circumstances which begot the power to perform them and favoured their being built one over the other. Neither have we yet formed a clear conception of the diverse and complex manifestations of human faculties which in the same regions have further differentiated man from the lower animals. In a transition like ours, conceit must have its course. It is the pride of ignorance, which can only be dispelled by the influx of additional light. Our past has long since gone, as it must; and its work is in ruins. We do not quite know what that work was, in all its details; nor do we pretend to make that the guide of our life. We fall back upon a vague surmise of it owing to vanity and ignorance, and bewilder our mind with a sublime mysticism borrowed from that unintelligible mass of gloomy ruins, among which historians weep, anti-

quarians grope, philologists feel for clues, and dyspeptic dreamers find solution of all doubts. It may deceive and lead astray the national mind, but only for a time; for hard facts are immediate, positive, solid and incontrovertible, and wants of life will not be put off or put down. This clamourous noise, therefore, about Vedas and Yogas,[1] esoteric and exoteric doctrines, denotes merely an expression of regret for the decay and disintegration of things existing. Such regret often dooms a nation to destruction; but happily we have been at the bottom of the wheel long ago; it is now turning round, forced by English education and English example, and we are rising. As a first step, we have acknowledged the superiority of western civilisation. We have accepted from that source a well-organised Government that has verified the wildest hyperbolical proverbs of old about peace, justice and safety of life and property, and we have gazed with wondering idiotic eyes at its railways, telegraphs, postal arrangements and steamships. We have humbly bowed before its mechanical contrivances that with gigantic powers spin and weave more ingeniously than he with hands, feet and brain who, fanned by the blossoming *Pipal* tree, wove under its shade of a wet summer evening the delicate muslin, which even aided by the early sun no eye could perceive as it peacefully lay on the grass wet with the dews of overnight, and hence the name *shabnam*.[2] Moreover, we have paid the highest tribute to western civilization by our willing bondage to nearly everything connected with it in the supply of the minutest necessaries of life, from nails, hinges and locks, knives, scissors and razors, needles, thread and sewing machines, to clothing, doctoring and educating materials. Above all, we owe to it that perception which is slowly taking a definite shape in our mind of the rights and duties of man.

Thus vanity and conservatism can only retard the nation's march; yet sometimes a moderate pace is

---

[1] *Vedas* The oldest sacred Hindu texts; *Yogas* Spiritual disciplines.

[2] *Pipal tree* Fig tree considered sacred in Hinduism; *muslin* Lightweight cotton fabric; *shabnam* Urdu word for "dew" that is applied to very fine muslin.

necessary to allow new ideas to take root. At any rate they do not establish the *unfitness* of a nation for a higher destiny. But other things or want of other things do. For instance up to this time we have not displayed much solidity of character, or discernment, or tact and power to give cohesiveness to loose floating ideas, and to discover and invent, wisely plan, arrange and organise ways and means and to work them out for our material good. Prophets innumerable we have had since the British came to this country, not to speak of former times, who added to content where discontent was wanted, and prophets of the most recent fashion too, who in search of light lead their countrymen to pursue the will-o'-the-wisp that dances fitfully among the pool of Indian ignorance, where the putrid mass of ages has been stirred up by a freshet[1] from the West. If we go on working for shadows and sentiments, as we have been hitherto doing, then I would despair of a bright future for India. My hope however, rests in the great intellectuality of the Indian races which will not allow their being killed off the face of the earth. This fact is sometimes forgotten by a certain section of Englishmen, and that forgetfulness is proving to be a strong, very strong incentive to bring out all the forces of the Indian mind, to bring about a common understanding among Indians of all creeds and nationalities. What a world of meaning, for instance, does that word NATIVE contain in it? Like one of those magic words of old it is performing wonders in all parts of the land wherever its true significance is understood. For Sir, we are all "natives." We were never "natives" before: we might have been *Gabars*[2] which signified a difference in religion, but did not carry with it any humiliation or disabilities; not even anything like those to which enlightened and liberal England subjected her "Papists"[3] only a short time ago. We are all "natives" now—We

poor Indians, the aborigines of Australia and the South Sea Islands, the Negroes, the Kaffirs,[4] the Hottentots and other races of Africa. The Egyptians have lately become "natives." The Chinese, the Japanese, the Persians and the Turks are not "natives." While I was in England, the English people came to see the "natives" at the Exhibition and often asked me where the "natives" were working, and English papers wrote about "natives." In England a French, German or Italian is a "foreigner," an Indian or an African is a "native." Colour has much to do with the making of a "native," but as Harris of "Uncle Tom's Cabin"[5] found to his cost, human beings of the "native" kind are not always distinguished by colour. Fair or dark, we in India are all "natives." The Kashmiri is a native, the Madrasi is a native; the Muhammadan is a native, the Hindu is a native; the Bráhman is a native, the Sudra[6] is a native; the prince is a native, the peasant is a native; I am native, thou art native, he is native. Sir, we are all natives. O Muhammad, Muhammad, thou the destroyer of all mockery in God-worship, thou, who established in the actual practices of life the fundamental principle of all religions—The Fatherhood of God and the Brother-hood of Man—thou, the great redeemer of coloured races, O Muhammad, well art thou rewarded by the gratitude of millions of souls who even to this day come flocking into thy fold in countries of Africa, where, if I am rightly informed, Christianity, with its sublime doctrine of "Do to others as you would be done by," but unhappily associated with brandy and gin, unheard-of diseases, rifles and bayonets, rapine[7] and spoliation, and other ordinary dealings with the "natives," cries in vain, as in a wilderness!

---

[1] *will-o'-the-wisp* In folk tradition, a mischievous spirit that appears as a fluttering light and draws a traveler away from the path; *freshet* Stream.

[2] *Gabars* Zoroastrians, members of a religious minority concentrated in India and Iran.

[3] *Papists* Derogatory term for Catholics.

[4] *Kaffirs* Derogatory term for Black South Africans.

[5] *Harris of "Uncle Tom's Cabin"* George Harris, a character in Harriet Beecher Stowe's 1852 antislavery novel *Uncle Tom's Cabin*. Harris, an enslaved man in the novel, is biracial and described as light-skinned.

[6] *Bráhman* Member of the highest-ranking Hindu caste, which traditionally consists of priests and teachers; *Sudra* Member of the lowest-ranking Hindu caste.

[7] *rapine* Robbery, plunder.

The word "Native," or rather all that it signifies, is having a miraculous effect in India. For, if we cannot cease to be "native" as we could cease to be *Gabar* or Hindu and become one of the imperial race in the Muhammadan times, we can now make "native" command respect. With a people who pay such high honours to Mammon,[1] wealth alone can do that. Every one of us cannot have Mammon in his house, and so cease to feel the humiliation of being a "native," but our people can be ardent votaries[2] of his heavenly counterpart and so practically become co-religionists of those that look down upon them. We have no Mammon in this country, but we have a lovely little goddess in heaven, benevolent and kind, who presides over wealth and prosperity and who occupies a foremost place among our three hundred and thirty millions of gods including their wives and children, and we have allowed her to usurp a day of the week, although it properly belongs to Jupiter, and we worship her many times in the year.[3] For all that we have lost her favour. Her affection must have to be won back, by worship according to western method. But remember it is not for us Bráhmans to do that. We care very little whether they call us "natives" or "niggers."[4] Our ambition should be always higher. It is to make the nation rich, whole humanity powerful, comfortable and happy. Our duty is to teach the people how to achieve these objects.

The real inequality between Europeans and "natives" rests not on the fact of the former filling a few high posts in this country, but the difference is in the race which the whole world is running ever and for ever. The great question will not be settled by the settlement of the minor and consequential question—who is to fill this post or that post? The great question is, who is better capable of reducing the devastating cyclones, the destroying floods of our mighty rivers, the hot blasts of the summer, the parching rays of the sun and other uncontrolled forces of our wild nature to the submission and service of man? These are for time to come. But now, answer me the question, who of us two is better able to disembowel the earth for her hidden treasures, to span mighty rivers, bore mountains, and bring to the service of man the various substances which lie in all parts of India? The answer is that the European is able to do these things and the native is not, and practically for that very reason he is "native." We have not yet the preliminary knowledge necessary for the attainment of such power. The European knows more of our mountains and rivers than we do; he knows more of the seas that girt our land on three sides; he knows more of the plants that grow around us, their names, their properties even to the size and shape of their leaves; he knows more of what is interred in the bosom of our earth; he knows more about the capabilities of our land; in everything he knows more than we do of our own country. Then he knows better how to use that knowledge for the benefit of man. We do not know these things, hence we are "natives." And necessarily the only way of getting over being a "native" is by our being equal to the European. I say again that our people have that high order of intellectuality which if rightly directed will enable them to equal if not to surpass the Europeans. No doubt like the power of the Niagra Falls in America various forces of nature are lying unused in this country, but those are insignificant when compared with the vast intellectual force of the most brilliant type that goes to waste in every part of India, in search of miserable clerkships, for want of proper guidance to better things. Our honour, our safety, and our salvation lie in the ardent pursuit after knowledge and wealth. …
—1889

[1] *Mammon* Personification of wealth and profit, regarded as a false god.

[2] *votaries* People bound by solemn oaths, usually to religious orders.

[3] *We have no … in the year* Odia Hindus, native to Odisha, celebrate Lakshmi, the Hindu goddess of wealth and prosperity, during the Mānabasā Gurubāra festival, which takes place every Thursday during Margasira, the ninth month of the Hindu calendar. Thursday is associated with the Roman god Jupiter in Western traditions, and with the planet Jupiter in Hindu astrology.

[4] *niggers* By the nineteenth century, this word had acquired the extremely derogatory connotations it carries today; it was, however, used freely by many white people.

ROBERT LOUIS STEVENSON
1850 – 1894

Due in part to his belief in romance rather than realism and in part to the success of *Treasure Island* and *Kidnapped*, Robert Louis Stevenson was once considered primarily a writer of adventure fiction for children. His large body of work has been re-evaluated in the past half century, however. His most famous work, the fantastic novella *Strange Case of Dr. Jekyll and Mr. Hyde*, has now taken a place among the canonical works of late Victorian literature. Stevenson's interest in the nature of good and evil lends this short novel a provocative moral complexity that has captivated the interest of a wide audience, with some readers viewing the book as a critique of Victorian double standards, others looking to the myth of the *doppelgänger*, or spiritual double, to explain the wicked Mr. Hyde, and still others adopting Freudian theories of the ego and the id to explain the two incarnations of Dr. Jekyll. Although he was long fascinated by the duality of the human psyche, in later years Stevenson turned to the concerns of his adopted country, Samoa, for subject matter, writing about the evils of imperialism and the damage done by foreign merchants. In all he wrote over 50 books in the course of his short life.

Stevenson's life was adventurous, but most of his travels were undertaken in search of respite from his ailments, which he wrote about in so much detail that he was once described as a "connoisseur of disease." He was an only child, born in Edinburgh in 1850 to Margaret Balfour, the daughter of a clergy member, and Thomas Stevenson, a well-known engineer for the Board of Northern Lighthouses. When he was young Stevenson contracted tuberculosis, and he remained frail ever after. He was put under the care of a nurse, who stimulated his interest in literature by reading to him everything from the Bible to serial adventure novels. Even as a child, he began spinning the raw material of these tales into stories of his own. In *Memories and Portraits* (1887), Stevenson said: "All through my boyhood and youth, I was known and pointed out for the pattern of an idler; and yet I was always busy on my own private end, which was to learn to write. I kept always two books in my pocket, one to read, one to write in. As I walked, my mind was busy fitting what I saw with appropriate words."

Stevenson continued writing in university, even though he was there initially to take an engineering degree and thereby continue the family tradition of his father and grandfather. He found himself uninterested in the profession, and switched to law, but after he had been called to the bar he decided to defy his father and pursue a career in writing. Stevenson began his legendary peregrinations soon after graduation; his first full-length published works, *An Inland Voyage* (1878) and *Travels with a Donkey in the Cévennes* (1879), record his travels through France. Both books found an enthusiastic audience. Two years later Stevenson published *Virginibus Puerisque*, a collection of essays previously published in *Macmillan's*, *Cornhill*, and *London* magazines. Many of these essays display the same gentle humor and wit that appears in the letters Stevenson wrote to his friends and family.

On one of his trips to France Stevenson met his future wife, Fanny Osbourne, an American who was then married, with two children. He followed her to California, where she obtained a divorce, and the two were married in 1880. It was for his stepson Lloyd's pleasure that Stevenson created *Treasure Island* (1883), the "boy's story" of a man who procures a secret map and sets out alongside Long John Silver in a quest for hidden treasure. *Kidnapped* (1886) and its sequel *Catriona* (1893) were equally successful. 1886 also saw the publication of Stevenson's most enduring work of fiction, *Strange Case of Dr. Jekyll and Mr. Hyde*, whose mystery concerns Dr. Jekyll's development of a drug that enables him to separate the good and bad parts of his nature. In these stories Stevenson saw himself as a romancer, eschewing the domestic realism that had defined the English novel as written by Dickens and George Eliot, with its complex focus on the home and the good woman who gives it moral definition. "This is a poison bad world for the romancer, this Anglo-Saxon world," he wrote; "I usually get out of it [the demand for morality in fiction] by not having any women in it at all." Later he would add: "Beware of realism; it is the devil."

Stevenson also enjoyed success as a poet and as a writer of short stories. His book of children's poetry, *A Child's Garden of Verses* (1885), was enormously popular. His first collection of short stories, *New Arabian Nights* (1882), includes "The Pavilion on the Links," which Arthur Conan Doyle called "the high-water mark of [Stevenson's] genius." *The Merry Men and Other Tales and Fables* was published in 1887, and *Island Nights' Entertainment* in 1893. The latter deals largely with the problems of imperialism in the South Sea islands; "The Beach of Falesà," for instance, concerns discord between colonial merchants and native islanders. Stevenson had come to live in Samoa after searching the South Seas for a more salubrious climate than that of his Scottish homeland.

Though he continued to express longing for Scotland in his final years, Stevenson also came to love Samoa profoundly. After his death from a cerebral hemorrhage in 1894, his many island friends carried his remains up Mt. Vaea to bury him as he had requested in his poem "Requiem," which also provided the epitaph engraved on his tombstone. Stevenson was in his prime at the time of his death, at work on *Weir of Hermiston* (1896)—a book that, although unfinished, is regarded by many as a masterpiece.

⌘ ⌘ ⌘

Requiem

U nder the wide and starry sky
   Dig the grave and let me lie.
Glad did I live and gladly die,
   And I laid me down with a will.

5 This be the verse you 'grave for me:
   Here he lies where he longed to be;
Home is the sailor, home from the sea,
   And the hunter home from the hill.[1]
—1879

---

[1] *Home … hill* These final two lines are engraved on Stevenson's tombstone.

from *A Child's Garden of Verses*

Whole Duty of Children

A child should always say what's true
   And speak when he is spoken to,
And behave mannerly at table;
At least as far as he is able.

Looking Forward

When I am grown to man's estate
I shall be very proud and great,
And tell the other girls and boys
Not to meddle with my toys.

The Land of Nod

From breakfast on through all the day
At home among my friends I stay,
But every night I go abroad
Afar into the land of Nod.

5   All by myself I have to go,
With none to tell me what to do—
All alone beside the streams
And up the mountain-sides of dreams.

The strangest things are there for me,
10 Both things to eat and things to see,
And many frightening sights abroad
Till morning in the land of Nod.

Try as I like to find the way,
I never can get back by day,
15 Nor can remember plain and clear
The curious music that I hear.

Good and Bad Children

Children, you are very little,
And your bones are very brittle;
If you would grow great and stately,
You must try to walk sedately.

5   You must still be bright and quiet,
And content with simple diet;
And remain, through all bewild'ring,
Innocent and honest children.

Happy hearts and happy faces,
10 Happy play in grassy places—
That was how, in ancient ages,
Children grew to kings and sages.

But the unkind and the unruly,
And the sort who eat unduly,
15 They must never hope for glory—
Theirs is quite a different story!

Cruel children, crying babies,
All grew up as geese and gabies,°   fools
Hated, as their age increases,
20 By their nephews and their nieces.

Foreign Children

Little Indian, Sioux or Crow,
Little frosty Eskimo,
Little Turk or Japanee,
Oh! don't you wish that you were me?

5   You have seen the scarlet trees
And the lions over seas;
You have eaten ostrich eggs,
And turned the turtles off their legs.

Such a life is very fine,
10 But it's not so nice as mine:
You must often, as you trod,
Have wearied *not* to be abroad.

You have curious things to eat,
I am fed on proper meat;
15 You must dwell beyond the foam,
But I am safe and live at home.
    Little Indian, Sioux or Crow,
    Little frosty Eskimo,
    Little Turk or Japanee,
20 Oh! don't you wish that you were me?
    —1885

Strange Case of Dr. Jekyll and Mr. Hyde

The concept of "Jekyll and Hyde" is now such a cultural commonplace that few twenty-first-century readers can experience the original story's twist ending the way a reader might have when it was first published in 1886. Though its shocking conclusion is too often already known to readers coming to the book for the first time, *Strange Case of Dr. Jekyll and Mr. Hyde* continues to fascinate general readers as well as critics, who have seen it variously as sensationalist escapism, a morally instructive fable, an early detective novel, and a Gothic examination of human psychology. Many have shared the view of critic Julia Wedgewood, who shortly after its publication described it as "a shilling story, which the reader devours in an hour, but to which [the reader] may return again and again, to study a profound allegory and admire a model of style."

At the time he conceived of *Jekyll and Hyde*, in the fall of 1885, Robert Louis Stevenson was in some personal difficulty. His typically poor health was particularly bad during this period, and he longed to become financially independent from his parents but frequently found himself requesting more support from them. He was in just such a state of financial distress when, as he would later claim, inspiration for a money-making story came to him in the form of a dream: "For two days I went about racking my brains for a plot of any sort; and on the second night I dreamed the scene at the window, and a scene afterwards split in two, in which Hyde, pursued for some crime, took the powder." After this moment of inspiration, *Jekyll and Hyde* was written in "white-hot haste": Stevenson composed the first draft in just three days. This draft, however, was just as quickly discarded when Fanny Stevenson argued that, by emphasizing sensationalism over moral substance, it had failed to fulfill its literary potential. It has been claimed that in this original draft Hyde was not an alternative personality but only an outer disguise, and some critics have speculated that the draft may have contained explicit sexual or violent content—but these conjectures cannot be confirmed because, after an intense disagreement, Stevenson is said to have burned the pages. He undertook his second draft with similarly punishing speed, and would later write that "*Jekyll* was conceived, written, re-written, re-rewritten, and printed inside ten weeks."

Released both as a cloth-bound volume and as a cheaply printed "shilling shocker," *Jekyll and Hyde* was an immediate hit and a major step in the establishment of Stevenson's writing career. Within half a year, it had sold 40,000 copies. Stevenson himself was somewhat uncomfortable with the book's mass success and its lowbrow elements, dismissing *Jekyll and Hyde* as "a fine bogey tale" and confiding in a letter to a friend that "[t]here must be something wrong in me, or I would not be popular." Although the book was favorably received by critics, who lauded Stevenson's style and originality, some of them also seemed hesitant to praise too highly a work with such broad appeal. In his 1894 criticism of the novella, Henry James would muse, "Is *Doctor Jekyll and Mr. Hyde* a work of high philosophic intention, or simply the most ingenious and irresponsible of fictions?"

The novella's popularity quickly prompted what would become the first of many theatrical adaptations of the *Jekyll and Hyde* story. Capitalizing on its most sensational elements, playwright Thomas Russell Sullivan and the prominent actor Richard Mansfield transformed Stevenson's narrative into an 1887 melodrama complete with a romance plot of which the original text contains no trace. After acclaimed performances in Boston and New York, the production was moved to London, where, despite initial success, the melodrama's run was closed down early. The infamous "Jack the Ripper" murders had begun, and Mansfield's convincing portrayal of Hyde reminded Londoners so strongly of the feared serial killer that Mansfield himself became a rumored suspect.

Though Jack the Ripper entered public consciousness after *Jekyll and Hyde* was published, it is perhaps not surprising that audiences drew a connection between them. Hyde's dwelling in Soho reflects anxieties that were made concrete in the figure of Jack the Ripper, but that pre-existed him—fears about the impoverished regions of London and the crime and vice they bred. Although it was immediately adjacent to the affluent Mayfair, Soho was a rough neighborhood, inhabited by poor families and associated with prostitution and other illicit activities. At the time *Jekyll and Hyde* was written, Victorian anxieties about such neighborhoods were particularly focused on sexual crimes; in the summer of 1885, Londoners were horrified to learn of the extent and violence of the city's underground child prostitution industry, disturbingly documented in an investigative newspaper report titled "The Maiden Tribute of Modern Babylon."

Consensual encounters between men were also a subject of public censure and discussion during this period; the Labouchère Amendment, passed in the same month as *Jekyll and Hyde*'s publication, expanded the range of sexual acts between men that could be punished by law. Many critics have drawn parallels between Jekyll's double life and that lived by participants in late-nineteenth-century middle-class gay subculture—a subculture with which Stevenson's own social circle overlapped (though it is not clear whether he himself was ever sexually attracted to men). It is worth noting, however, that Stevenson discouraged sexual interpretations of the novella, claiming that "people are so filled full of folly and inverted lust, that they can think of nothing but sexuality" and that "the beast Hyde ... is no more sensual than another, but ... is the essence of cruelty and malice, and selfishness and cowardice: and these are the diabolic in man."

Stevenson's evocation of "the beast Hyde" reflects another touchpoint for class anxieties in the last quarter of the nineteenth century: the pseudoscientific belief that criminality and moral degeneracy were caused by atavism—regression to an earlier point in biological evolution. This notion originated with the Italian criminologist Cesare Lombroso, who argued that in physiology as well as behavior criminals resembled the primates from which humans evolved. Cranial deformity, small brain size, and left-handedness were among the characteristics that, according to Lombroso, were associated with criminality. Though Lombroso's work was not published in English until the early twentieth century, he had many English popularizers, including some whom Stevenson knew personally.

Another contemporary theory regarding the physiology of disordered behavior was that of the double brain. According to this account, each half of a human brain was capable of independent functioning but possessed different dominant characteristics: the left brain was associated with reason, civilization, and masculinity, the right brain with emotion, instinct, and femininity. (These associations were informed by Victorian assumptions regarding race and gender; the left brain's influence was said to be strongest in healthy white men.) Misalignment of brain hemispheres was thought to cause all manner of criminal behaviors and mental illnesses, including multiple personalities. There is evidence to suggest that Stevenson—who had long been interested in the concept of the double—read medical case studies of dual personalities before composing his own "strange case."

Informed though it was by the ideological landscape of his own era, *Strange Case of Dr. Jekyll and Mr. Hyde* continues to hold a place in popular consciousness; it has never been out of print, and it has been adapted for the stage, film, and television hundreds of times. Although the novella's stature among scholars has never matched its tremendous mass appeal, *Jekyll and Hyde* has lent itself to an extraordinarily wide range of critical frameworks, from Freudian psychoanalysis to postmodern theories of language. Twenty-first-century readers continue to reinterpret the novella's suggestion that, as Stevenson's friend Andrew Lang put it, "every Jekyll among us is haunted by his own Hyde."

Strange Case of Dr. Jekyll and Mr. Hyde

STORY OF THE DOOR

Mr. Utterson the lawyer was a man of a rugged countenance, that was never lighted by a smile; cold, scanty, and embarrassed in discourse; backward in sentiment; lean, long, dusty, dreary, and yet somehow lovable. At friendly meetings, and when the wine was to his taste, something eminently human beaconed from his eye; something indeed which never found its way into his talk, but which spoke not only in these silent symbols of the after-dinner face, but more often and loudly in the acts of his life. He was austere with himself; drank gin when he was alone, to mortify a taste for vintages; and though he enjoyed the theatre, had not crossed the doors of one for twenty years. But he had an approved[1] tolerance for others; sometimes wondering, almost with envy, at the high pressure of spirits involved in their misdeeds; and in any extremity inclined to help rather than to reprove. "I incline to Cain's heresy,"[2] he used to say quaintly: "I let my brother go to the devil in his own way." In this character, it was frequently his fortune to be the last reputable acquaintance and the last good influence in the lives of down-going men. And to such as these, so long as they came about his chambers, he never marked a shade of change in his demeanour.

No doubt the feat was easy to Mr. Utterson; for he was undemonstrative at the best, and even his friendship seemed to be founded in a similar catholicity[3] of good nature. It is the mark of a modest man to accept his friendly circle readymade from the hands of opportunity; and that was the lawyer's way. His friends were those of his own blood or those whom he had known the longest; his affections, like ivy, were the growth of time, they implied no aptness in the object.

Hence, no doubt, the bond that united him to Mr. Richard Enfield, his distant kinsman, the well-known man about town. It was a nut to crack for many, what these two could see in each other, or what subject they could find in common. It was reported by those who encountered them in their Sunday walks, that they said nothing, looked singularly dull, and would hail with obvious relief the appearance of a friend. For all that, the two men put the greatest store by these excursions, counted them the chief jewel of each week, and not only set aside occasions of pleasure, but even resisted the calls of business, that they might enjoy them uninterrupted.

It chanced on one of these rambles that their way led them down a bystreet in a busy quarter of London. The street was small and what is called quiet, but it drove a thriving trade on the weekdays. The inhabitants were all doing well, it seemed, and all emulously hoping to do better still, and laying out the surplus of their gains in coquetry; so that the shop fronts stood along that thoroughfare with an air of invitation, like rows of smiling saleswomen. Even on Sunday, when it veiled its more florid charms and lay comparatively empty of passage, the street shone out in contrast to its dingy neighbourhood, like a fire in a forest; and with its freshly painted shutters, well-polished brasses, and general cleanliness and gaiety of note, instantly caught and pleased the eye of the passenger.

Two doors from one corner, on the left hand going east, the line was broken by the entry of a court; and just at that point, a certain sinister block of building thrust forward its gable on the street. It was two stories high; showed no window, nothing but a door on the lower story and a blind forehead of discoloured wall on the upper; and bore in every feature, the marks of prolonged and sordid negligence. The door, which was equipped with neither bell nor knocker, was blistered and distained.[4] Tramps slouched into the recess and struck matches on the panels; children kept shop upon the steps; the schoolboy had tried his knife on the mouldings; and for close on a generation, no one had appeared to drive away these random visitors or to repair their ravages.

---

[1] *approved* Proven.

[2] *Cain's heresy* Cain, the eldest son of Adam and Eve, murdered his younger brother, Abel, in an act of jealousy (see Genesis 4). His "heresy" refers to his denial of responsibility for his brother in Genesis 4.9.

[3] *catholicity* All-inclusiveness.

[4] *distained* Stained, discolored, or tarnished.

Mr. Enfield and the lawyer were on the other side of the bystreet; but when they came abreast of the entry, the former lifted up his cane and pointed.

"Did you ever remark that door?" he asked; and when his companion had replied in the affirmative, "It is connected in my mind," added he, "with a very odd story."

"Indeed?" said Mr. Utterson, with a slight change of voice, "and what was that?"

"Well, it was this way," returned Mr. Enfield: "I was coming home from some place at the end of the world, about three o'clock of a black winter morning, and my way lay through a part of town where there was literally nothing to be seen but lamps. Street after street, and all the folks asleep—street after street, all lighted up as if for a procession and all as empty as a church—till at last I got into that state of mind when a man listens and listens and begins to long for the sight of a policeman. All at once, I saw two figures: one a little man who was stumping along eastward at a good walk, and the other a girl of maybe eight or ten who was running as hard as she was able down a cross street. Well, sir, the two ran into one another naturally enough at the corner; and then came the horrible part of the thing; for the man trampled calmly over the child's body and left her screaming on the ground. It sounds nothing to hear, but it was hellish to see. It wasn't like a man; it was like some damned Juggernaut.[1] I gave a view halloa,[2] took to my heels, collared my gentleman, and brought him back to where there was already quite a group about the screaming child. He was perfectly cool and made no resistance, but gave me one look, so ugly that it brought out the sweat on me like running. The people who had turned out were the girl's own family; and pretty soon, the doctor, for whom she had been sent, put in his appearance. Well, the child was not much the worse, more frightened, according to the Sawbones;[3] and there you might have supposed would be an end to it. But there was one curious circumstance. I had taken a loathing to my gentleman at first sight. So had the child's family, which was only natural. But the doctor's case was what struck me. He was the usual cut-and-dry apothecary, of no particular age and colour, with a strong Edinburgh accent, and about as emotional as a bagpipe. Well, sir, he was like the rest of us; every time he looked at my prisoner, I saw that Sawbones turn sick and white with the desire to kill him. I knew what was in his mind, just as he knew what was in mine; and killing being out of the question, we did the next best. We told the man we could and would make such a scandal out of this, as should make his name stink from one end of London to the other. If he had any friends or any credit,[4] we undertook that he should lose them. And all the time, as we were pitching it in red hot, we were keeping the women off him as best we could, for they were as wild as harpies.[5] I never saw a circle of such hateful faces; and there was the man in the middle, with a kind of black, sneering coolness—frightened too, I could see that—but carrying it off, sir, really like Satan. 'If you choose to make capital out of this accident,' said he, 'I am naturally helpless. No gentleman but wishes to avoid a scene,' says he. 'Name your figure.' Well, we screwed him up to a hundred pounds for the child's family; he would have clearly liked to stick out; but there was something about the lot of us that meant mischief, and at last he struck.[6] The next thing was to get the money; and where do you think he carried us but to that place with the door?—whipped out a key, went in, and presently came back with the matter of ten pounds in gold and a cheque for the balance on Coutts's,[7] drawn payable to bearer and signed with a name that I can't mention, though it's one of the points of my story, but it was a name at least very well known and often printed. The figure was stiff; but the signature was good for more than that, if it was only genuine. I took the liberty of pointing out to my gentleman that

---

1. *Juggernaut*   Huge, powerful force that destroys whatever is in its path.

2. *view halloa*   Shout made by a hunter who sights a fox.

3. *Sawbones*   Slang: Doctor or surgeon.

4. *credit*   Good reputation.

5. *harpies*   Cruel, vengeful monsters of Greek and Roman mythology described as part woman and part bird.

6. *struck*   Surrendered.

7. *Coutts*   London bank that served only upper-class clients.

the whole business looked apocryphal,[1] and that a man does not, in real life, walk into a cellar door at four in the morning and come out of it with another man's cheque for close upon a hundred pounds. But he was quite easy and sneering. 'Set your mind at rest,' says he, 'I will stay with you till the banks open and cash the cheque myself.' So we all set off, the doctor, and the child's father, and our friend and myself, and passed the rest of the night in my chambers; and next day, when we had breakfasted, went in a body to the bank. I gave in the cheque myself, and said I had every reason to believe it was a forgery. Not a bit of it. The cheque was genuine."

"Tut-tut," said Mr. Utterson.

"I see you feel as I do," said Mr. Enfield. "Yes, it's a bad story. For my man was a fellow that nobody could have to do with, a really damnable man; and the person that drew the cheque is the very pink of the proprieties, celebrated too, and (what makes it worse) one of your fellows who do what they call good. Blackmail, I suppose; an honest man paying through the nose for some of the capers of his youth. Blackmail House is what I call that place with the door, in consequence. Though even that, you know, is far from explaining all," he added, and with the words fell into a vein of musing.

From this he was recalled by Mr. Utterson asking rather suddenly: "And you don't know if the drawer of the cheque lives there?"

"A likely place, isn't it?" returned Mr. Enfield. "But I happen to have noticed his address; he lives in some square or other."

"And you never asked about the—place with the door?" said Mr. Utterson.

"No, sir: I had a delicacy," was the reply. "I feel very strongly about putting questions; it partakes too much of the style of the day of judgment. You start a question, and it's like starting a stone. You sit quietly on the top of a hill; and away the stone goes, starting others; and presently some bland old bird (the last you would have thought of) is knocked on the head in his own back garden and the family have to change their name. No,

sir, I make it a rule of mine: the more it looks like Queer Street,[2] the less I ask."

"A very good rule, too," said the lawyer.

"But I have studied the place for myself," continued Mr. Enfield. "It seems scarcely a house. There is no other door, and nobody goes in or out of that one but, once in a great while, the gentleman of my adventure. There are three windows looking on the court on the first floor;[3] none below; the windows are always shut but they're clean. And then there is a chimney which is generally smoking; so somebody must live there. And yet it's not so sure; for the buildings are so packed together about that court, that it's hard to say where one ends and another begins."

The pair walked on again for a while in silence; and then, "Enfield," said Mr. Utterson, "that's a good rule of yours."

"Yes, I think it is," returned Enfield.

"But for all that," continued the lawyer, "there's one point I want to ask: I want to ask the name of that man who walked over the child."

"Well," said Mr. Enfield, "I can't see what harm it would do. It was a man of the name of Hyde."

"H'm," said Mr. Utterson. "What sort of a man is he to see?"

"He is not easy to describe. There is something wrong with his appearance; something displeasing, something downright detestable. I never saw a man I so disliked, and yet I scarce know why. He must be deformed somewhere; he gives a strong feeling of deformity, although I couldn't specify the point. He's an extraordinary looking man, and yet I really can name nothing out of the way. No, sir; I can make no hand of it; I can't describe him. And it's not want of memory; for I declare I can see him this moment."

Mr. Utterson again walked some way in silence and obviously under a weight of consideration. "You are sure he used a key?" he inquired at last.

---

[1] *apocryphal* Dubious.

[2] *Queer Street* Slang term referring to a personal predicament, usually of a financial nature.

[3] *first floor* I.e., the floor immediately above street level; in North American usage, it would be called the second floor.

"My dear sir …" began Enfield, surprised out of himself.

"Yes, I know," said Utterson; "I know it must seem strange. The fact is, if I do not ask you the name of the other party, it is because I know it already. You see, Richard, your tale has gone home. If you have been inexact in any point, you had better correct it."

"I think you might have warned me," returned the other with a touch of sullenness. "But I have been pedantically exact, as you call it. The fellow had a key; and what's more, he has it still. I saw him use it, not a week ago."

Mr. Utterson sighed deeply but said never a word; and the young man presently resumed. "Here is another lesson to say nothing," said he. "I am ashamed of my long tongue. Let us make a bargain never to refer to this again."

"With all my heart," said the lawyer. "I shake hands on that, Richard."

SEARCH FOR MR. HYDE

That evening Mr. Utterson came home to his bachelor house in sombre spirits and sat down to dinner without relish. It was his custom of a Sunday, when this meal was over, to sit close by the fire, a volume of some dry divinity on his reading desk, until the clock of the neighbouring church rang out the hour of twelve, when he would go soberly and gratefully to bed. On this night, however, as soon as the cloth was taken away, he took up a candle and went into his business room. There he opened his safe, took from the most private part of it a document endorsed on the envelope as Dr. Jekyll's Will, and sat down with a clouded brow to study its contents. The will was holograph,[1] for Mr. Utterson, though he took charge of it now that it was made, had refused to lend the least assistance in the making of it; it provided not only that, in case of the decease of Henry Jekyll, M.D., D.C.L., L.L.D., F.R.S.,[2]

etc., all his possessions were to pass into the hands of his "friend and benefactor Edward Hyde," but that in case of Dr. Jekyll's "disappearance or unexplained absence for any period exceeding three calendar months," the said Edward Hyde should step into the said Henry Jekyll's shoes without further delay and free from any burthen or obligation, beyond the payment of a few small sums to the members of the doctor's household. This document had long been the lawyer's eyesore. It offended him both as a lawyer and as a lover of the sane and customary sides of life, to whom the fanciful was the immodest. And hitherto it was his ignorance of Mr. Hyde that had swelled his indignation; now, by a sudden turn, it was his knowledge. It was already bad enough when the name was but a name of which he could learn no more. It was worse when it began to be clothed upon with detestable attributes; and out of the shifting, insubstantial mists that had so long baffled his eye, there leaped up the sudden, definite presentment[3] of a fiend.

"I thought it was madness," he said, as he replaced the obnoxious paper in the safe, "and now I begin to fear it is disgrace."

With that he blew out his candle, put on a greatcoat, and set forth in the direction of Cavendish Square,[4] that citadel of medicine, where his friend, the great Dr. Lanyon, had his house and received his crowding patients. "If any one knows, it will be Lanyon," he had thought.

The solemn butler knew and welcomed him; he was subjected to no stage of delay, but ushered direct from the door to the dining room where Dr. Lanyon sat alone over his wine. This was a hearty, healthy, dapper, red-faced gentleman, with a shock of hair prematurely white, and a boisterous and decided manner. At sight of Mr. Utterson, he sprang up from his chair and welcomed him with both hands. The geniality, as was the way of the man, was somewhat theatrical to the eye; but it reposed on genuine feeling. For these two were old friends, old mates both at school and college, both

---

[1] holograph   Written out by the person who has signed it.

[2] M.D.   Doctor of Medicine; D.C.L.   Doctor of Civil Law; L.L.D. Doctor of Laws; F.R.S.   Fellow of the Royal Society, a prestigious organization of scientists.

[3] presentment   Mental picture.

[4] Cavendish Square   Affluent neighborhood in London's West End; many prominent doctors had offices in the area.

thorough respecters of themselves and of each other, and, what does not always follow, men who thoroughly enjoyed each other's company.

After a little rambling talk, the lawyer led up to the subject which so disagreeably preoccupied his mind.

"I suppose, Lanyon," said he "you and I must be the two oldest friends that Henry Jekyll has?"

"I wish the friends were younger," chuckled Dr. Lanyon. "But I suppose we are. And what of that? I see little of him now."

"Indeed?" said Utterson. "I thought you had a bond of common interest."

"We had," was the reply. "But it is more than ten years since Henry Jekyll became too fanciful for me. He began to go wrong, wrong in mind; and though of course I continue to take an interest in him for old sake's sake, as they say, I see and I have seen devilish little of the man. Such unscientific balderdash," added the doctor, flushing suddenly purple, "would have estranged Damon and Pythias."[1]

This little spirit of temper was somewhat of a relief to Mr. Utterson. "They have only differed on some point of science," he thought; and being a man of no scientific passions (except in the matter of conveyancing[2]), he even added: "It is nothing worse than that!" He gave his friend a few seconds to recover his composure, and then approached the question he had come to put. "Did you ever come across a protégé of his—one Hyde?" he asked.

"Hyde?" repeated Lanyon. "No. Never heard of him. Since my time."

That was the amount of information that the lawyer carried back with him to the great, dark bed on which he tossed to and fro, until the small hours of the morning began to grow large. It was a night of little ease to his toiling mind, toiling in mere[3] darkness and

besieged by questions.

Six o'clock struck on the bells of the church that was so conveniently near to Mr. Utterson's dwelling, and still he was digging at the problem. Hitherto it had touched him on the intellectual side alone; but now his imagination also was engaged, or rather enslaved; and as he lay and tossed in the gross darkness of the night and the curtained room, Mr. Enfield's tale went by before his mind in a scroll of lighted pictures. He would be aware of the great field of lamps of a nocturnal city; then of the figure of a man walking swiftly; then of a child running from the doctor's; and then these met, and that human Juggernaut trod the child down and passed on regardless of her screams. Or else he would see a room in a rich house, where his friend lay asleep, dreaming and smiling at his dreams; and then the door of that room would be opened, the curtains of the bed plucked apart, the sleeper recalled, and lo! there would stand by his side a figure to whom power was given, and even at that dead hour, he must rise and do its bidding. The figure in these two phases haunted the lawyer all night; and if at any time he dozed over, it was but to see it glide more stealthily through sleeping houses, or move the more swiftly and still the more swiftly, even to dizziness, through wider labyrinths of lamp-lighted city, and at every street corner crush a child and leave her screaming. And still the figure had no face by which he might know it; even in his dreams, it had no face, or one that baffled him and melted before his eyes; and thus it was that there sprang up and grew apace in the lawyer's mind a singularly strong, almost an inordinate, curiosity to behold the features of the real Mr. Hyde. If he could but once set eyes on him, he thought the mystery would lighten and perhaps roll altogether away, as was the habit of mysterious things when well examined. He might see a reason for his friend's strange preference or bondage (call it which you please) and even for the startling clause of the will. At least it would be a face worth seeing: the face of a man who was without bowels of mercy: a face which had but to show itself to raise up, in the mind of the unimpressionable Enfield, a spirit of enduring hatred.

---

[1] *Damon and Pythias*   Loyal friends of Greek mythology. Damon was condemned to execution, and Pythias offered himself as collateral so Damon could leave to settle his affairs. Impressed when Damon returned as promised, the sovereign pardoned him.

[2] *conveyancing*   Use of legal documents to transfer property from one owner to another.

[3] *mere*   Undiluted.

From that time forward, Mr. Utterson began to haunt the door in the bystreet of shops. In the morning before office hours, at noon when business was plenty, and time scarce, at night under the face of the fogged city moon, by all lights and at all hours of solitude or concourse, the lawyer was to be found on his chosen post.

"If he be Mr. Hyde," he had thought, "I shall be Mr. Seek."

And at last his patience was rewarded. It was a fine dry night; frost in the air; the streets as clean as a ballroom floor; the lamps, unshaken by any wind, drawing a regular pattern of light and shadow. By ten o'clock, when the shops were closed, the bystreet was very solitary and, in spite of the low growl of London from all round, very silent. Small sounds carried far; domestic sounds out of the houses were clearly audible on either side of the roadway; and the rumour[1] of the approach of any passenger preceded him by a long time. Mr. Utterson had been some minutes at his post, when he was aware of an odd, light footstep drawing near. In the course of his nightly patrols, he had long grown accustomed to the quaint effect with which the footfalls of a single person, while he is still a great way off, suddenly spring out distinct from the vast hum and clatter of the city. Yet his attention had never before been so sharply and decisively arrested; and it was with a strong, superstitious prevision[2] of success that he withdrew into the entry of the court.

The steps drew swiftly nearer, and swelled out suddenly louder as they turned the end of the street. The lawyer, looking forth from the entry, could soon see what manner of man he had to deal with. He was small and very plainly dressed, and the look of him, even at that distance, went somehow strongly against the watcher's inclination. But he made straight for the door, crossing the roadway to save time; and as he came, he drew a key from his pocket like one approaching home.

Mr. Utterson stepped out and touched him on the shoulder as he passed. "Mr. Hyde, I think?"

Mr. Hyde shrank back with a hissing intake of the breath. But his fear was only momentary; and though he did not look the lawyer in the face, he answered coolly enough: "That is my name. What do you want?"

"I see you are going in," returned the lawyer. "I am an old friend of Dr. Jekyll's—Mr. Utterson of Gaunt Street—you must have heard my name; and meeting you so conveniently, I thought you might admit me."

"You will not find Dr. Jekyll; he is from home," replied Mr. Hyde, blowing in the key. And then suddenly, but still without looking up, "How did you know me?" he asked.

"On your side," said Mr. Utterson, "will you do me a favour?"

"With pleasure," replied the other. "What shall it be?"

"Will you let me see your face?" asked the lawyer.

Mr. Hyde appeared to hesitate, and then, as if upon some sudden reflection, fronted about with an air of defiance; and the pair stared at each other pretty fixedly for a few seconds. "Now I shall know you again," said Mr. Utterson. "It may be useful."

"Yes," returned Mr. Hyde, "it is as well we have met; and à propos,[3] you should have my address." And he gave a number of a street in Soho.[4]

"Good God!" thought Mr. Utterson, "can he, too, have been thinking of the will?" But he kept his feelings to himself and only grunted in acknowledgment of the address.

"And now," said the other, "how did you know me?"

"By description," was the reply.

"Whose description?"

"We have common friends," said Mr. Utterson.

"Common friends?" echoed Mr. Hyde, a little hoarsely. "Who are they?"

"Jekyll, for instance," said the lawyer.

"He never told you," cried Mr. Hyde, with a flush of anger. "I did not think you would have lied."

---

[1] *rumour* Noise.

[2] *prevision* Foreknowledge.

[3] *à propos* French: with respect to (this) purpose.

[4] *Soho* Central London district known for bohemians, criminals, and sex workers.

"Come," said Mr. Utterson, "that is not fitting language."

The other snarled aloud into a savage laugh; and the next moment, with extraordinary quickness, he had unlocked the door and disappeared into the house.

The lawyer stood awhile when Mr. Hyde had left him, the picture of disquietude. Then he began slowly to mount the street, pausing every step or two and putting his hand to his brow like a man in mental perplexity. The problem he was thus debating as he walked, was one of a class that is rarely solved. Mr. Hyde was pale and dwarfish, he gave an impression of deformity without any nameable malformation, he had a displeasing smile, he had borne himself to the lawyer with a sort of murderous mixture of timidity and boldness, and he spoke with a husky, whispering, and somewhat broken voice; all these were points against him, but not all of these together could explain the hitherto unknown disgust, loathing, and fear with which Mr. Utterson regarded him. "There must be something else," said the perplexed gentleman. "There *is* something more, if I could find a name for it. God bless me, the man seems hardly human! Something troglodytic,[1] shall we say? or can it be the old story of Dr. Fell?[2] or is it the mere radiance of a foul soul that thus transpires through, and transfigures, its clay continent? The last, I think; for, O my poor old Harry Jekyll, if ever I read Satan's signature upon a face, it is on that of your new friend."

Round the corner from the bystreet, there was a square of ancient, handsome houses, now for the most part decayed from their high estate and let in flats and chambers to all sorts and conditions of men: map engravers, architects, shady lawyers, and the agents of obscure enterprises. One house, however, second from the corner, was still occupied entire; and at the door of this, which wore a great air of wealth and comfort, though it was now plunged in darkness except for the fanlight, Mr. Utterson stopped and knocked. A well-dressed, elderly servant opened the door.

"Is Dr. Jekyll at home, Poole?" asked the lawyer.

"I will see, Mr. Utterson," said Poole, admitting the visitor, as he spoke, into a large, low-roofed, comfortable hall, paved with flags,[3] warmed (after the fashion of a country house) by a bright, open fire, and furnished with costly cabinets of oak. "Will you wait here by the fire, sir? or shall I give you a light in the dining room?"

"Here, thank you," said the lawyer, and he drew near and leaned on the tall fender.[4] This hall, in which he was now left alone, was a pet fancy of his friend the doctor's; and Utterson himself was wont to speak of it as the pleasantest room in London. But tonight there was a shudder in his blood; the face of Hyde sat heavy on his memory; he felt (what was rare with him) a nausea and distaste of life; and in the gloom of his spirits, he seemed to read a menace in the flickering of the firelight on the polished cabinets and the uneasy starting of the shadow on the roof. He was ashamed of his relief, when Poole presently returned to announce that Dr. Jekyll was gone out.

"I saw Mr. Hyde go in by the old dissecting room door, Poole," he said. "Is that right, when Dr. Jekyll is from home?"

"Quite right, Mr. Utterson, sir," replied the servant. "Mr. Hyde has a key."

"Your master seems to repose a great deal of trust in that young man, Poole," resumed the other musingly.

"Yes, sir, he do indeed," said Poole. "We have all orders to obey him."

"I do not think I ever met Mr. Hyde?" asked Utterson.

"O, dear no, sir. He never *dines* here," replied the butler. "Indeed we see very little of him on this side of the house; he mostly comes and goes by the laboratory."

"Well, good night, Poole."

"Goodnight, Mr. Utterson."

And the lawyer set out homeward with a very heavy heart. "Poor Harry Jekyll," he thought, "my mind misgives me he is in deep waters! He was wild when he was young; a long while ago to be sure; but in the law of

1 *troglodytic* Like a cave person.

2 *Dr. Fell* Character in a rhyme beginning "I do not like thee, Dr. Fell; / The reason why, I cannot tell."

3 *flags* Flagstones.

4 *fender* Guard placed around a fireplace.

God, there is no statute of limitations. Ay, it must be that; the ghost of some old sin, the cancer of some concealed disgrace: punishment coming, *pede claudo*,[1] years after memory has forgotten and self-love condoned the fault." And the lawyer, scared by the thought, brooded awhile on his own past, groping in all the corners of memory, lest by chance some Jack-in-the-Box of an old iniquity should leap to light there. His past was fairly blameless; few men could read the rolls of their life with less apprehension; yet he was humbled to the dust by the many ill things he had done, and raised up again into a sober and fearful gratitude by the many that he had come so near to doing, yet avoided. And then by a return on his former subject, he conceived a spark of hope. "This Master Hyde, if he were studied," thought he, "must have secrets of his own; black secrets, by the look of him; secrets compared to which poor Jekyll's worst would be like sunshine. Things cannot continue as they are. It turns me cold to think of this creature stealing like a thief to Harry's bedside; poor Harry, what a wakening! And the danger of it; for if this Hyde suspects the existence of the will, he may grow impatient to inherit. Ay, I must put my shoulder to the wheel—if Jekyll will but let me," he added, "if Jekyll will only let me." For once more he saw before his mind's eye, as clear as a transparency, the strange clauses of the will.

DR. JEKYLL WAS QUITE AT EASE

A fortnight later, by excellent good fortune, the doctor gave one of his pleasant dinners to some five or six old cronies, all intelligent, reputable men and all judges of good wine; and Mr. Utterson so contrived that he remained behind after the others had departed. This was no new arrangement, but a thing that had befallen many scores of times. Where Utterson was liked, he was liked well. Hosts loved to detain the dry lawyer, when the light-hearted and the loose-tongued had already their foot on the threshold; they liked to sit awhile in his unobtrusive company, practising for solitude, sobering their minds in the man's rich silence after the expense and strain of gaiety. To this rule, Dr. Jekyll was no exception; and as he now sat on the opposite side of the fire—a large, well-made, smooth-faced man of fifty, with something of a slyish cast perhaps, but every mark of capacity and kindness—you could see by his looks that he cherished for Mr. Utterson a sincere and warm affection.

"I have been wanting to speak to you, Jekyll," began the latter. "You know that will of yours?"

A close observer might have gathered that the topic was distasteful; but the doctor carried it off gaily. "My poor Utterson," said he, "you are unfortunate in such a client. I never saw a man so distressed as you were by my will; unless it were that hidebound[2] pedant, Lanyon, at what he called my scientific heresies. Oh, I know he's a good fellow—you needn't frown—an excellent fellow, and I always mean to see more of him; but a hidebound pedant for all that; an ignorant, blatant pedant. I was never more disappointed in any man than Lanyon."

"You know I never approved of it," pursued Utterson, ruthlessly disregarding the fresh topic.

"My will? Yes, certainly, I know that," said the doctor, a trifle sharply. "You have told me so."

"Well, I tell you so again," continued the lawyer. "I have been learning something of young Hyde."

The large handsome face of Dr. Jekyll grew pale to the very lips, and there came a blackness about his eyes. "I do not care to hear more," said he. "This is a matter I thought we had agreed to drop."

"What I heard was abominable," said Utterson.

"It can make no change. You do not understand my position," returned the doctor, with a certain incoherency of manner. "I am painfully situated, Utterson; my position is a very strange—a very strange one. It is one of those affairs that cannot be mended by talking."

"Jekyll," said Utterson, "you know me: I am a man to be trusted. Make a clean breast of this in confidence; and I make no doubt I can get you out of it."

1   *pede claudo*   Latin: lame-footed. The phrase appears in Horace's *Odes* 3.2: "Lame-footed punishment has rarely abandoned a wicked man with a head start."

2   *hidebound*   Wedded to convention.

"My good Utterson," said the doctor, "this is very good of you, this is downright good of you, and I cannot find words to thank you in. I believe you fully; I would trust you before any man alive, ay, before myself, if I could make the choice; but indeed it isn't what you fancy; it is not so bad as that; and just to put your good heart at rest, I will tell you one thing: the moment I choose, I can be rid of Mr. Hyde. I give you my hand upon that; and I thank you again and again; and I will just add one little word, Utterson, that I'm sure you'll take in good part: this is a private matter, and I beg of you to let it sleep."

Utterson reflected a little, looking in the fire.

"I have no doubt you are perfectly right," he said at last, getting to his feet.

"Well, but since we have touched upon this business, and for the last time I hope," continued the doctor, "there is one point I should like you to understand. I have really a very great interest in poor Hyde. I know you have seen him; he told me so; and I fear he was rude. But, I do sincerely take a great, a very great interest in that young man; and if I am taken away, Utterson, I wish you to promise me that you will bear with him and get his rights for him. I think you would, if you knew all; and it would be a weight off my mind if you would promise."

"I can't pretend that I shall ever like him," said the lawyer.

"I don't ask that," pleaded Jekyll, laying his hand upon the other's arm; "I only ask for justice; I only ask you to help him for my sake, when I am no longer here."

Utterson heaved an irrepressible sigh. "Well," said he, "I promise."

THE CAREW MURDER CASE

Nearly a year later, in the month of October, 18—, London was startled by a crime of singular ferocity and rendered all the more notable by the high position of the victim. The details were few and startling. A maidservant living alone in a house not far from the river, had gone upstairs to bed about eleven. Although a fog rolled over the city in the small hours, the early part of the night was cloudless, and the lane, which the maid's window overlooked, was brilliantly lit by the full moon. It seems she was romantically given, for she sat down upon her box, which stood immediately under the window, and fell into a dream of musing. Never (she used to say, with streaming tears, when she narrated that experience), never had she felt more at peace with all men or thought more kindly of the world. And as she so sat she became aware of an aged and beautiful gentleman with white hair, drawing near along the lane; and advancing to meet him, another and very small gentleman, to whom at first she paid less attention. When they had come within speech (which was just under the maid's eyes) the older man bowed and accosted the other with a very pretty manner of politeness. It did not seem as if the subject of his address were of great importance; indeed, from his pointing, it sometimes appeared as if he were only inquiring his way; but the moon shone on his face as he spoke, and the girl was pleased to watch it, it seemed to breathe such an innocent and old world kindness of disposition, yet with something high too, as of a well-founded self-content. Presently her eye wandered to the other, and she was surprised to recognise in him a certain Mr. Hyde, who had once visited her master and for whom she had conceived a dislike. He had in his hand a heavy cane, with which he was trifling; but he answered never a word, and seemed to listen with an ill-contained impatience. And then all of a sudden he broke out in a great flame of anger, stamping with his foot, brandishing the cane, and carrying on (as the maid described it) like a madman. The old gentleman took a step back, with the air of one very much surprised and a trifle hurt; and at that Mr. Hyde broke out of all bounds and clubbed him to the earth. And next moment, with apelike fury, he was trampling his victim under foot and hailing down a storm of blows, under which the bones were audibly shattered and the body jumped upon the roadway. At the horror of these sights and sounds, the maid fainted.

It was two o'clock when she came to herself and called for the police. The murderer was gone long ago; but there lay his victim in the middle of the lane, incredibly mangled. The stick with which the deed had been done, although it was of some rare and very tough and heavy wood, had broken in the middle under the stress of this insensate cruelty; and one splintered half had rolled in the neighbouring gutter—the other, without doubt, had been carried away by the murderer. A purse and a gold watch were found upon the victim: but no cards or papers, except a sealed and stamped envelope, which he had been probably carrying to the post, and which bore the name and address of Mr. Utterson.

This was brought to the lawyer the next morning, before he was out of bed; and he had no sooner seen it, and been told the circumstances, than he shot out a solemn lip. "I shall say nothing till I have seen the body," said he; "this may be very serious. Have the kindness to wait while I dress." And with the same grave countenance he hurried through his breakfast and drove to the police station, whither the body had been carried. As soon as he came into the cell, he nodded.

"Yes," said he, "I recognise him. I am sorry to say that this is Sir Danvers Carew."

"Good God, sir," exclaimed the officer, "is it possible?" And the next moment his eye lighted up with professional ambition. "This will make a deal of noise," he said. "And perhaps you can help us to the man." And he briefly narrated what the maid had seen, and showed the broken stick.

Mr. Utterson had already quailed at the name of Hyde; but when the stick was laid before him, he could doubt no longer; broken and battered as it was, he recognised it for one that he had himself presented many years before to Henry Jekyll.

"Is this Mr. Hyde a person of small stature?" he inquired.

"Particularly small and particularly wicked looking, is what the maid calls him," said the officer.

Mr. Utterson reflected; and then, raising his head, "If you will come with me in my cab," he said, "I think I can take you to his house."

It was by this time about nine in the morning, and the first fog of the season. A great chocolate-coloured pall lowered over heaven, but the wind was continually charging and routing these embattled vapours; so that as the cab crawled from street to street, Mr. Utterson beheld a marvellous number of degrees and hues of twilight; for here it would be dark like the back-end of evening; and there would be a glow of a rich, lurid brown, like the light of some strange conflagration; and here, for a moment, the fog would be quite broken up, and a haggard shaft of daylight would glance in between the swirling wreaths. The dismal quarter of Soho seen under these changing glimpses, with its muddy ways, and slatternly passengers, and its lamps, which had never been extinguished or had been kindled afresh to combat this mournful reinvasion of darkness, seemed, in the lawyer's eyes, like a district of some city in a nightmare. The thoughts of his mind, besides, were of the gloomiest dye; and when he glanced at the companion of his drive, he was conscious of some touch of that terror of the law and the law's officers, which may at times assail the most honest.

As the cab drew up before the address indicated, the fog lifted a little and showed him a dingy street, a gin palace, a low French eating house, a shop for the retail of penny numbers[1] and twopenny salads, many ragged children huddled in the doorways, and many women of different nationalities passing out, key in hand, to have a morning glass; and the next moment the fog settled down again upon that part, as brown as umber, and cut him off from his blackguardly surroundings. This was the home of Henry Jekyll's favourite; of a man who was heir to a quarter of a million sterling.

An ivory-faced and silvery-haired old woman opened the door. She had an evil face, smoothed by hypocrisy; but her manners were excellent. Yes, she said, this was Mr. Hyde's, but he was not at home; he had been in that night very late, but had gone away again in less than an hour; there was nothing strange in that; his habits were very irregular, and he was often absent; for instance, it was nearly two months since she had seen him till yesterday.

"Very well, then, we wish to see his rooms," said the lawyer; and when the woman began to declare it was

---

[1] *gin palace* Pub; *penny numbers* Serial publications offering sensational stories at low prices.

impossible, "I had better tell you who this person is," he added. "This is Inspector Newcomen of Scotland Yard."

A flash of odious joy appeared upon the woman's face. "Ah!" said she, "he is in trouble! What has he done?"

Mr. Utterson and the inspector exchanged glances. "He don't seem a very popular character," observed the latter. "And now, my good woman, just let me and this gentleman have a look about us."

In the whole extent of the house, which but for the old woman remained otherwise empty, Mr. Hyde had only used a couple of rooms; but these were furnished with luxury and good taste. A closet was filled with wine; the plate was of silver, the napery[1] elegant; a good picture hung upon the walls, a gift (as Utterson supposed) from Henry Jekyll, who was much of a connoisseur; and the carpets were of many plies and agreeable in colour. At this moment, however, the rooms bore every mark of having been recently and hurriedly ransacked; clothes lay about the floor, with their pockets inside out; lock-fast drawers stood open; and on the hearth there lay a pile of grey ashes, as though many papers had been burned. From these embers the inspector disinterred the butt end of a green chequebook, which had resisted the action of the fire; the other half of the stick was found behind the door; and as this clinched his suspicions, the officer declared himself delighted. A visit to the bank, where several thousand pounds were found to be lying to the murderer's credit, completed his gratification.

"You may depend upon it, sir," he told Mr. Utterson: "I have him in my hand. He must have lost his head, or he never would have left the stick or, above all, burned the chequebook. Why, money's life to the man. We have nothing to do but wait for him at the bank, and get out the handbills."[2]

This last, however, was not so easy of accomplishment; for Mr. Hyde had numbered few familiars— even the master of the servant maid had only seen him twice; his family could nowhere be traced; he had never been photographed; and the few who could describe him differed widely, as common observers will. Only on one point, were they agreed; and that was the haunting sense of unexpressed deformity with which the fugitive impressed his beholders.

INCIDENT OF THE LETTER

It was late in the afternoon, when Mr. Utterson found his way to Dr. Jekyll's door, where he was at once admitted by Poole, and carried down by the kitchen offices and across a yard which had once been a garden, to the building which was indifferently known as the laboratory or the dissecting rooms. The doctor had bought the house from the heirs of a celebrated surgeon; and his own tastes being rather chemical than anatomical, had changed the destination[3] of the block at the bottom of the garden. It was the first time that the lawyer had been received in that part of his friend's quarters; and he eyed the dingy, windowless structure with curiosity, and gazed round with a distasteful sense of strangeness as he crossed the theatre,[4] once crowded with eager students and now lying gaunt and silent, the tables laden with chemical apparatus, the floor strewn with crates and littered with packing straw, and the light falling dimly through the foggy cupola. At the further end, a flight of stairs mounted to a door covered with red baize; and through this, Mr. Utterson was at last received into the doctor's cabinet.[5] It was a large room, fitted round with glass presses, furnished, among other things, with a cheval glass[6] and a business table, and looking out upon the court by three dusty windows barred with iron. A fire burned in the grate; a lamp was set lighted on the chimney shelf, for even in the houses the fog began to lie thickly; and there, close up to the warmth, sat Dr. Jekyll, looking deadly sick. He did not

---

1 *napery*   Tablecloths, napkins, etc.

2 *handbills*   I.e., wanted posters.

3 *destination*   Designated purpose.

4 *theatre*   Lecture theater (here, one originally designed for medical demonstrations).

5 *baize*   Felt-like fabric often tacked onto doors to insulate against noise; *cabinet*   Private office.

6 *cheval glass*   Freestanding mirror that tilts from the middle so that the angle of the reflection can be adjusted.

rise to meet his visitor, but held out a cold hand and bade him welcome in a changed voice.

"And now," said Mr. Utterson, as soon as Poole had left them, "you have heard the news?"

The doctor shuddered. "They were crying it in the square,"[1] he said. "I heard them in my dining room."

"One word," said the lawyer. "Carew was my client, but so are you, and I want to know what I am doing. You have not been mad enough to hide this fellow?"

"Utterson, I swear to God," cried the doctor, "I swear to God I will never set eyes on him again. I bind my honour to you that I am done with him in this world. It is all at an end. And indeed he does not want my help; you do not know him as I do; he is safe, he is quite safe; mark my words, he will never more be heard of."

The lawyer listened gloomily; he did not like his friend's feverish manner. "You seem pretty sure of him," said he; "and for your sake, I hope you may be right. If it came to a trial, your name might appear."

"I am quite sure of him," replied Jekyll; "I have grounds for certainty that I cannot share with anyone. But there is one thing on which you may advise me. I have—I have received a letter; and I am at a loss whether I should show it to the police. I should like to leave it in your hands, Utterson; you would judge wisely, I am sure; I have so great a trust in you."

"You fear, I suppose, that it might lead to his detection?" asked the lawyer.

"No," said the other. "I cannot say that I care what becomes of Hyde; I am quite done with him. I was thinking of my own character, which this hateful business has rather exposed."

Utterson ruminated a while; he was surprised at his friend's selfishness, and yet relieved by it. "Well," said he, at last, "let me see the letter."

The letter was written in an odd, upright hand and signed "Edward Hyde": and it signified, briefly enough, that the writer's benefactor, Dr. Jekyll, whom he had long so unworthily repaid for a thousand generosities, need labour under no alarm for his safety, as he had

means of escape on which he placed a sure dependence. The lawyer liked this letter well enough; it put a better colour on the intimacy than he had looked for; and he blamed himself for some of his past suspicions.

"Have you the envelope?" he asked.

"I burned it," replied Jekyll, "before I thought what I was about. But it bore no postmark. The note was handed in."

"Shall I keep this and sleep upon it?" asked Utterson.

"I wish you to judge for me entirely," was the reply. "I have lost confidence in myself."

"Well, I shall consider," returned the lawyer. "And now one word more: it was Hyde who dictated the terms in your will about that disappearance?"

The doctor seemed seized with a qualm of faintness: he shut his mouth tight and nodded.

"I knew it," said Utterson. "He meant to murder you. You have had a fine escape."

"I have had what is far more to the purpose," returned the doctor solemnly: "I have had a lesson—O God, Utterson, what a lesson I have had!" And he covered his face for a moment with his hands.

On his way out, the lawyer stopped and had a word or two with Poole. "By the by," said he, "there was a letter handed in today: what was the messenger like?" But Poole was positive nothing had come except by post; "and only circulars[2] by that," he added.

This news sent off the visitor with his fears renewed. Plainly the letter had come by the laboratory door; possibly, indeed, it had been written in the cabinet; and if that were so, it must be differently judged, and handled with the more caution. The newsboys, as he went, were crying themselves hoarse along the footways: "Special edition. Shocking murder of an M.P."[3] That was the funeral oration of one friend and client; and he could not help a certain apprehension lest the good name of another should be sucked down in the eddy of the scandal. It was, at least, a ticklish decision that he had to make; and self-reliant as he was by habit, he began to cherish a longing for advice. It was not to be

---

[1] *They were ... square* Newspaper-sellers frequently shouted the headlines to entice buyers.

[2] *circulars* Advertisements produced for mass distribution by mail.

[3] *M.P.* Member of Parliament.

had directly; but perhaps, he thought, it might be fished for.

Presently after, he sat on one side of his own hearth, with Mr. Guest, his head clerk, upon the other, and midway between, at a nicely calculated distance from the fire, a bottle of a particular old wine that had long dwelt unsunned in the foundations of his house. The fog still slept on the wing above the drowned city, where the lamps glimmered like carbuncles;[1] and through the muffle and smother of these fallen clouds, the procession of the town's life was still rolling in through the great arteries with a sound as of a mighty wind. But the room was gay with firelight. In the bottle the acids were long ago resolved; the imperial[2] dye had softened with time, as the colour grows richer in stained windows; and the glow of hot autumn afternoons on hillside vineyards was ready to be set free and to disperse the fogs of London. Insensibly the lawyer melted. There was no man from whom he kept fewer secrets than Mr. Guest; and he was not always sure that he kept as many as he meant. Guest had often been on business to the doctor's; he knew Poole; he could scarce have failed to hear of Mr. Hyde's familiarity about the house; he might draw conclusions: was it not as well, then, that he should see a letter which put that mystery to rights? and above all since Guest, being a great student and critic of handwriting, would consider the step natural and obliging? The clerk, besides, was a man of counsel; he would scarce read so strange a document without dropping a remark; and by that remark Mr. Utterson might shape his future course.

"This is a sad business about Sir Danvers," he said.

"Yes, sir, indeed. It has elicited a great deal of public feeling," returned Guest. "The man, of course, was mad."

"I should like to hear your views on that," replied Utterson. "I have a document here in his handwriting; it is between ourselves, for I scarce know what to do about it; it is an ugly business at the best. But there it is; quite in your way: a murderer's autograph."

Guest's eyes brightened, and he sat down at once and studied it with passion. "No, sir," he said: "not mad; but it is an odd hand."

"And by all accounts a very odd writer," added the lawyer.

Just then the servant entered with a note.

"Is that from Dr. Jekyll, sir?" inquired the clerk. "I thought I knew the writing. Anything private, Mr. Utterson?"

"Only an invitation to dinner. Why? Do you want to see it?"

"One moment. I thank you, sir"; and the clerk laid the two sheets of paper alongside and sedulously compared their contents. "Thank you, sir," he said at last, returning both; "it's a very interesting autograph."

There was a pause, during which Mr. Utterson struggled with himself. "Why did you compare them, Guest?" he inquired suddenly.

"Well, sir," returned the clerk, "there's a rather singular resemblance; the two hands are in many points identical: only differently sloped."

"Rather quaint,"[3] said Utterson.

"It is, as you say, rather quaint," returned Guest.

"I wouldn't speak of this note, you know," said the master.

"No, sir," said the clerk. "I understand."

But no sooner was Mr. Utterson alone that night than he locked the note into his safe, where it reposed from that time forward. "What!" he thought. "Henry Jekyll forge for a murderer!" And his blood ran cold in his veins.

REMARKABLE INCIDENT OF DR. LANYON

Time ran on; thousands of pounds were offered in reward, for the death of Sir Danvers was resented as a public injury; but Mr. Hyde had disappeared out of the ken of the police as though he had never existed. Much of his past was unearthed, indeed, and all disreputable: tales came out of the man's cruelty, at once so callous and violent; of his vile life, of his strange associates, of the hatred that seemed to have surrounded his career;

---

[1] *carbuncles* Red gemstones, especially those cut round, without facets.

[2] *imperial* Deep, reddish purple.

[3] *quaint* Strange, illogical.

but of his present whereabouts, not a whisper. From the time he had left the house in Soho on the morning of the murder, he was simply blotted out; and gradually, as time drew on, Mr. Utterson began to recover from the hotness of his alarm, and to grow more at quiet with himself. The death of Sir Danvers was, to his way of thinking, more than paid for by the disappearance of Mr. Hyde. Now that that evil influence had been withdrawn, a new life began for Dr. Jekyll. He came out of his seclusion, renewed relations with his friends, became once more their familiar guest and entertainer; and whilst he had always been known for charities, he was now no less distinguished for religion. He was busy, he was much in the open air, he did good; his face seemed to open and brighten, as if with an inward consciousness of service; and for more than two months, the doctor was at peace.

On the 8th of January Utterson had dined at the doctor's with a small party; Lanyon had been there; and the face of the host had looked from one to the other as in the old days when the trio were inseparable friends. On the 12th, and again on the 14th, the door was shut against the lawyer. "The doctor was confined to the house," Poole said, "and saw no one." On the 15th, he tried again, and was again refused; and having now been used for the last two months to see his friend almost daily, he found this return of solitude to weigh upon his spirits. The fifth night he had in Guest to dine with him; and the sixth he betook himself to Dr. Lanyon's.

There at least he was not denied admittance; but when he came in, he was shocked at the change which had taken place in the doctor's appearance. He had his death warrant written legibly upon his face. The rosy man had grown pale; his flesh had fallen away; he was visibly balder and older; and yet it was not so much these tokens of a swift physical decay that arrested the lawyer's notice, as a look in the eye and quality of manner that seemed to testify to some deep-seated terror of the mind. It was unlikely that the doctor should fear death; and yet that was what Utterson was tempted to suspect. "Yes," he thought; "he is a doctor, he must know his own state and that his days are counted; and the knowledge is more than he can bear." And yet when

Utterson remarked on his ill looks, it was with an air of greatness that Lanyon declared himself a doomed man.

"I have had a shock," he said, "and I shall never recover. It is a question of weeks. Well, life has been pleasant; I liked it; yes, sir, I used to like it. I sometimes think if we knew all, we should be more glad to get away."

"Jekyll is ill, too," observed Utterson. "Have you seen him?"

But Lanyon's face changed, and he held up a trembling hand. "I wish to see or hear no more of Dr. Jekyll," he said in a loud, unsteady voice. "I am quite done with that person; and I beg that you will spare me any allusion to one whom I regard as dead."

"Tut-tut," said Mr. Utterson; and then after a considerable pause, "Can't I do anything?" he inquired. "We are three very old friends, Lanyon; we shall not live to make others."

"Nothing can be done," returned Lanyon; "ask himself."

"He will not see me," said the lawyer.

"I am not surprised at that," was the reply. "Some day, Utterson, after I am dead, you may perhaps come to learn the right and wrong of this. I cannot tell you. And in the meantime, if you can sit and talk with me of other things, for God's sake, stay and do so; but if you cannot keep clear of this accursed topic, then, in God's name, go, for I cannot bear it."

As soon as he got home, Utterson sat down and wrote to Jekyll, complaining of his exclusion from the house, and asking the cause of this unhappy break with Lanyon; and the next day brought him a long answer, often very pathetically worded, and sometimes darkly mysterious in drift. The quarrel with Lanyon was incurable. "I do not blame our old friend," Jekyll wrote, "but I share his view that we must never meet. I mean from henceforth to lead a life of extreme seclusion; you must not be surprised, nor must you doubt my friendship, if my door is often shut even to you. You must suffer me to go my own dark way. I have brought on myself a punishment and a danger that I cannot name. If I am the chief of sinners, I am the chief of sufferers also. I could not think that this earth contained a place for sufferings and terrors so unmanning; and you can do but one thing, Utterson, to lighten this destiny, and that is to respect my silence." Utterson was amazed; the dark influence of Hyde had been withdrawn, the doctor had returned to his old tasks and amities; a week ago, the prospect had smiled with every promise of a cheerful and an honoured age; and now in a moment, friendship, and peace of mind, and the whole tenor of his life were wrecked. So great and unprepared a change pointed to madness; but in view of Lanyon's manner and words, there must lie for it some deeper ground.

A week afterwards Dr. Lanyon took to his bed, and in something less than a fortnight he was dead. The night after the funeral, at which he had been sadly affected, Utterson locked the door of his business room, and sitting there by the light of a melancholy candle, drew out and set before him an envelope addressed by the hand and sealed with the seal of his dead friend. "PRIVATE: for the hands of G.J. Utterson ALONE and in case of his predecease *to be destroyed unread*," so it was emphatically superscribed; and the lawyer dreaded to behold the contents. "I have buried one friend today," he thought: "what if this should cost me another?" And then he condemned the fear as a disloyalty, and broke the seal. Within there was another enclosure, likewise sealed, and marked upon the cover as "not to be opened till the death or disappearance of Dr. Henry Jekyll." Utterson could not trust his eyes. Yes, it was disappearance; here again, as in the mad will which he had long ago restored to its author, here again were the idea of a disappearance and the name of Henry Jekyll bracketed. But in the will, that idea had sprung from the sinister suggestion of the man Hyde; it was set there with a purpose all too plain and horrible. Written by the hand of Lanyon, what should it mean? A great curiosity came on the trustee, to disregard the prohibition and dive at once to the bottom of these mysteries; but professional honour and faith to his dead friend were stringent obligations; and the packet slept in the inmost corner of his private safe.

It is one thing to mortify curiosity, another to conquer it; and it may be doubted if, from that day forth, Utterson desired the society of his surviving friend with the same eagerness. He thought of him kindly; but his thoughts were disquieted and fearful. He went to call indeed; but he was perhaps relieved to be denied admittance; perhaps, in his heart, he preferred to speak with Poole upon the doorstep and surrounded by the air and sounds of the open city, rather than to be admitted into that house of voluntary bondage, and to sit and speak with its inscrutable recluse. Poole had, indeed, no very pleasant news to communicate. The doctor, it appeared, now more than ever confined himself to the cabinet over the laboratory, where he would sometimes even sleep; he was out of spirits, he had grown very silent, he did not read; it seemed as if he had something on his mind. Utterson became so used to the unvarying character of these reports, that he fell off little by little in the frequency of his visits.

INCIDENT AT THE WINDOW

It chanced on Sunday, when Mr. Utterson was on his usual walk with Mr. Enfield, that their way lay once again through the bystreet; and that when they came in front of the door, both stopped to gaze on it.

"Well," said Enfield, "that story's at an end at least. We shall never see more of Mr. Hyde."

"I hope not," said Utterson. "Did I ever tell you that I once saw him, and shared your feeling of repulsion?"

"It was impossible to do the one without the other," returned Enfield. "And by the way, what an ass you must have thought me, not to know that this was a back way to Dr. Jekyll's! It was partly your own fault that I found it out, even when I did."

"So you found it out, did you?" said Utterson. "But if that be so, we may step into the court and take a look at the windows. To tell you the truth, I am uneasy about poor Jekyll; and even outside, I feel as if the presence of a friend might do him good."

The court was very cool and a little damp, and full of premature twilight, although the sky, high up overhead, was still bright with sunset. The middle one of the three windows was halfway open; and sitting close beside it, taking the air with an infinite sadness of mien,[1] like some disconsolate prisoner, Utterson saw Dr. Jekyll.

"What! Jekyll!" he cried. "I trust you are better."

"I am very low, Utterson," replied the doctor, drearily, "very low. It will not last long, thank God."

"You stay too much indoors," said the lawyer. "You should be out, whipping up the circulation like Mr. Enfield and me. (This is my cousin—Mr. Enfield—Dr. Jekyll.) Come, now; get your hat and take a quick turn with us."

"You are very good," sighed the other. "I should like to very much; but no, no, no, it is quite impossible; I dare not. But indeed, Utterson, I am very glad to see you; this is really a great pleasure; I would ask you and Mr. Enfield up, but the place is really not fit."

"Why then," said the lawyer, good-naturedly, "the best thing we can do is to stay down here and speak with you from where we are."

"That is just what I was about to venture to propose," returned the doctor with a smile. But the words were hardly uttered, before the smile was struck out of his face and succeeded by an expression of such abject terror and despair, as froze the very blood of the two gentlemen below. They saw it but for a glimpse, for the window was instantly thrust down; but that glimpse had been sufficient, and they turned and left the court without a word. In silence, too, they traversed the bystreet; and it was not until they had come into a neighbouring thoroughfare, where even upon a Sunday there were still some stirrings of life, that Mr. Utterson at last turned and looked at his companion. They were both pale; and there was an answering horror in their eyes.

"God forgive us, God forgive us," said Mr. Utterson.

But Mr. Enfield only nodded his head very seriously and walked on once more in silence.

THE LAST NIGHT

Mr. Utterson was sitting by his fireside one evening after dinner, when he was surprised to receive a visit from Poole.

"Bless me, Poole, what brings you here?" he cried; and then taking a second look at him, "What ails you?" he added; "is the doctor ill?"

"Mr. Utterson," said the man, "there is something wrong."

"Take a seat, and here is a glass of wine for you," said the lawyer. "Now, take your time, and tell me plainly what you want."

"You know the doctor's ways, sir," replied Poole, "and how he shuts himself up. Well, he's shut up again in the cabinet; and I don't like it, sir—I wish I may die if I like it. Mr. Utterson, sir, I'm afraid."

"Now, my good man," said the lawyer, "be explicit. What are you afraid of?"

"I've been afraid for about a week," returned Poole, doggedly disregarding the question, "and I can bear it no more."

The man's appearance amply bore out his words; his manner was altered for the worse; and except for the moment when he had first announced his terror, he had not once looked the lawyer in the face. Even now, he sat with the glass of wine untasted on his knee, and his eyes directed to a corner of the floor. "I can bear it no more," he repeated.

"Come," said the lawyer, "I see you have some good reason, Poole; I see there is something seriously amiss. Try to tell me what it is."

"I think there's been foul play," said Poole, hoarsely.

"Foul play!" cried the lawyer, a good deal frightened and rather inclined to be irritated in consequence. "What foul play? What does the man mean?"

"I daren't say, sir," was the answer; "but will you come along with me and see for yourself?"

Mr. Utterson's only answer was to rise and get his hat and great coat; but he observed with wonder the greatness of the relief that appeared upon the butler's face, and perhaps with no less, that the wine was still untasted when he set it down to follow.

It was a wild, cold, seasonable night of March, with a pale moon, lying on her back as though the wind had tilted her, and a flying wrack of the most diaphanous

---

1 *mien* Bearing, appearance.

and lawny[1] texture. The wind made talking difficult, and flecked the blood into the face. It seemed to have swept the streets unusually bare of passengers, besides; for Mr. Utterson thought he had never seen that part of London so deserted. He could have wished it otherwise; never in his life had he been conscious of so sharp a wish to see and touch his fellow creatures; for struggle as he might, there was borne in upon his mind a crushing anticipation of calamity. The square, when they got there, was all full of wind and dust, and the thin trees in the garden were lashing themselves along the railing. Poole, who had kept all the way a pace or two ahead, now pulled up in the middle of the pavement, and in spite of the biting weather, took off his hat and mopped his brow with a red pocket handkerchief. But for all the hurry of his coming, these were not the dews of exertion that he wiped away, but the moisture of some strangling anguish; for his face was white and his voice, when he spoke, harsh and broken.

"Well, sir," he said, "here we are, and God grant there be nothing wrong."

"Amen, Poole," said the lawyer.

Thereupon the servant knocked in a very guarded manner; the door was opened on the chain; and a voice asked from within, "Is that you, Poole?"

"It's all right," said Poole. "Open the door."

The hall, when they entered it, was brightly lighted up; the fire was built high; and about the hearth the whole of the servants, men and women, stood huddled together like a flock of sheep. At the sight of Mr. Utterson, the housemaid broke into hysterical whimpering; and the cook, crying out, "Bless God! it's Mr. Utterson," ran forward as if to take him in her arms.

"What, what? Are you all here?" said the lawyer peevishly. "Very irregular, very unseemly; your master would be far from pleased."

"They're all afraid," said Poole.

Blank silence followed, no one protesting; only the maid lifted up her voice and now wept loudly.

"Hold your tongue!" Poole said to her, with a ferocity of accent that testified to his own jangled nerves; and indeed, when the girl had so suddenly raised the note of her lamentation, they had all started and turned toward the inner door with faces of dreadful expectation. "And now," continued the butler, addressing the knife-boy, "reach me a candle, and we'll get this through hands[2] at once." And then he begged Mr. Utterson to follow him, and led the way to the back garden.

"Now, sir," said he, "you come as gently as you can. I want you to hear, and I don't want you to be heard. And see here, sir, if by any chance he was to ask you in, don't go."

Mr. Utterson's nerves, at this unlooked-for termination, gave a jerk that nearly threw him from his balance; but he recollected his courage and followed the butler into the laboratory building and through the surgical theatre, with its lumber[3] of crates and bottles, to the foot of the stair. Here Poole motioned him to stand on one side and listen; while he himself, setting down the candle and making a great and obvious call on his resolution, mounted the steps and knocked with a somewhat uncertain hand on the red baize of the cabinet door.

"Mr. Utterson, sir, asking to see you," he called; and even as he did so, once more violently signed to the lawyer to give ear.

A voice answered from within: "Tell him I cannot see any one," it said complainingly.

"Thank you, sir," said Poole, with a note of something like triumph in his voice; and taking up his candle, he led Mr. Utterson back across the yard and into the great kitchen, where the fire was out and the beetles were leaping on the floor.

"Sir," he said, looking Mr. Utterson in the eyes, "was that my master's voice?"

"It seems much changed," replied the lawyer, very pale, but giving look for look.

---

[1] *wrack* Body of high clouds moving quickly in the wind; *lawny* Like lawn, a sheer fabric made from linen or cotton.

[2] *knife-boy* Low servant who performs menial chores; *we'll get ... hands* A Scottish expression meaning "we'll fix this problem."

[3] *lumber* Household clutter.

"Changed? Well, yes, I think so," said the butler. "Have I been twenty years in this man's house, to be deceived about his voice? No, sir; master's made away with; he was made away with eight days ago, when we heard him cry out upon the name of God; and *who's* in there instead of him, and *why* it stays there, is a thing that cries to Heaven, Mr. Utterson!"

"This is a very strange tale, Poole; this is rather a wild tale, my man," said Mr. Utterson, biting his finger. "Suppose it were as you suppose, supposing Dr. Jekyll to have been—well, murdered, what could induce the murderer to stay? That won't hold water; it doesn't commend itself to reason."

"Well, Mr. Utterson, you are a hard man to satisfy, but I'll do it yet," said Poole. "All this last week (you must know) him, or it, or whatever it is that lives in that cabinet, has been crying night and day for some sort of medicine and cannot get it to his mind. It was sometimes his way—the master's, that is—to write his orders on a sheet of paper and throw it on the stair. We've had nothing else this week back; nothing but papers, and a closed door, and the very meals left there to be smuggled in when nobody was looking. Well, sir, every day, ay, and twice and thrice in the same day, there have been orders and complaints, and I have been sent flying to all the wholesale chemists in town. Every time I brought the stuff back, there would be another paper telling me to return it, because it was not pure, and another order to a different firm. This drug is wanted bitter bad, sir, whatever for."

"Have you any of these papers?" asked Mr. Utterson.

Poole felt in his pocket and handed out a crumpled note, which the lawyer, bending nearer to the candle, carefully examined. Its contents ran thus: "Dr. Jekyll presents his compliments to Messrs. Maw. He assures them that their last sample is impure and quite useless for his present purpose. In the year 18—, Dr. J. purchased a somewhat large quantity from Messrs. M. He now begs them to search with the most sedulous care, and should any of the same quality be left, to forward it to him at once. Expense is no consideration. The importance of this to Dr. J. can hardly be exaggerated." So far the letter had run composedly enough, but here with a sudden splutter of the pen, the writer's emotion had broken loose. "For God's sake," he had added, "find me some of the old."

"This is a strange note," said Mr. Utterson; and then sharply, "How do you come to have it open?"

"The man at Maw's was main angry, sir, and he threw it back to me like so much dirt," returned Poole.

"This is unquestionably the doctor's hand, do you know?" resumed the lawyer.

"I thought it looked like it," said the servant rather sulkily; and then, with another voice, "But what matters hand of write?" he said. "I've seen him!"

"Seen him?" repeated Mr. Utterson. "Well?"

"That's it!" said Poole. "It was this way. I came suddenly into the theatre from the garden. It seems he had slipped out to look for this drug or whatever it is; for the cabinet door was open, and there he was at the far end of the room digging among the crates. He looked up when I came in, gave a kind of cry, and whipped upstairs into the cabinet. It was but for one minute that I saw him, but the hair stood upon my head like quills. Sir, if that was my master, why had he a mask upon his face? If it was my master, why did he cry out like a rat, and run from me? I have served him long enough. And then …" The man paused and passed his hand over his face.

"These are all very strange circumstances," said Mr. Utterson, "but I think I begin to see daylight. Your master, Poole, is plainly seized with one of those maladies that both torture and deform the sufferer; hence, for aught I know, the alteration of his voice; hence the mask and the avoidance of his friends; hence his eagerness to find this drug, by means of which the poor soul retains some hope of ultimate recovery—God grant that he be not deceived! There is my explanation; it is sad enough, Poole, ay, and appalling to consider; but it is plain and natural, hangs well together, and delivers us from all exorbitant alarms."

"Sir," said the butler, turning to a sort of mottled pallor, "that thing was not my master, and there's the truth. My master"—here he looked round him and began to whisper—"is a tall, fine build of a man, and this was more of a dwarf." Utterson attempted to protest. "O, sir," cried Poole, "do you think I do not know my master after twenty years? Do you think I do not know where his head comes to in the cabinet door, where I saw him every morning of my life? No, sir, that thing in the mask was never Dr. Jekyll—God knows what it was, but it was never Dr. Jekyll; and it is the belief of my heart that there was murder done."

"Poole," replied the lawyer, "if you say that, it will become my duty to make certain. Much as I desire to spare your master's feelings, much as I am puzzled by this note which seems to prove him to be still alive, I shall consider it my duty to break in that door."

"Ah, Mr. Utterson, that's talking!" cried the butler.

"And now comes the second question," resumed Utterson: "Who is going to do it?"

"Why, you and me, sir," was the undaunted reply.

"That is very well said," returned the lawyer; "and whatever comes of it, I shall make it my business to see you are no loser."

"There is an axe in the theatre," continued Poole; "and you might take the kitchen poker for yourself."

The lawyer took that rude but weighty instrument into his hand, and balanced it. "Do you know, Poole," he said, looking up, "that you and I are about to place ourselves in a position of some peril?"

"You may say so, sir, indeed," returned the butler.

"It is well, then, that we should be frank," said the other. "We both think more than we have said; let us make a clean breast. This masked figure that you saw, did you recognise it?"

"Well, sir, it went so quick, and the creature was so doubled up, that I could hardly swear to that," was the answer. "But if you mean, was it Mr. Hyde?—why, yes, I think it was! You see, it was much of the same bigness; and it had the same quick, light way with it; and then who else could have got in by the laboratory door? You have not forgot, sir, that at the time of the murder he had still the key with him? But that's not all. I don't know, Mr. Utterson, if ever you met this Mr. Hyde?"

"Yes," said the lawyer, "I once spoke with him."

"Then you must know as well as the rest of us that there was something queer about that gentle-man—something that gave a man a turn—I don't know rightly how to say it, sir, beyond this: that you felt it in your marrow kind of cold and thin."

"I own I felt something of what you describe," said Mr. Utterson.

"Quite so, sir," returned Poole. "Well, when that masked thing like a monkey jumped from among the chemicals and whipped into the cabinet, it went down my spine like ice. Oh, I know it's not evidence, Mr. Utterson. I'm book learned enough for that; but a man has his feelings, and I give you my Bible word it was Mr. Hyde!"

"Ay, ay," said the lawyer. "My fears incline to the same point. Evil, I fear, founded—evil was sure to come—of that connection. Ay, truly, I believe you; I believe poor Harry is killed; and I believe his murderer (for what purpose, God alone can tell) is still lurking in his victim's room. Well, let our name be vengeance. Call Bradshaw."

The footman came at the summons, very white and nervous.

"Pull yourself together, Bradshaw," said the lawyer. "This suspense, I know, is telling upon all of you; but it is now our intention to make an end of it. Poole, here, and I are going to force our way into the cabinet. If all is well, my shoulders are broad enough to bear the blame. Meanwhile, lest anything should really be amiss, or any malefactor seek to escape by the back, you and the boy must go round the corner with a pair of good sticks and take your post at the laboratory door. We give you ten minutes to get to your stations."

As Bradshaw left, the lawyer looked at his watch. "And now, Poole, let us get to ours," he said; and taking the poker under his arm, led the way into the yard. The scud[1] had banked over the moon, and it was now quite dark. The wind, which only broke in puffs and draughts into that deep well of building, tossed the light of the candle to and fro about their steps, until they came into the shelter of the theatre, where they sat down silently to wait. London hummed solemnly all around; but nearer at hand, the stillness was only broken by the sounds of a footfall moving to and fro along the cabinet floor.

---

[1] *scud* Body of low, thin clouds moving quickly in the wind.

"So it will walk all day, sir," whispered Poole; "ay, and the better part of the night. Only when a new sample comes from the chemist, there's a bit of a break. Ah, it's an ill conscience that's such an enemy to rest! Ah, sir, there's blood foully shed in every step of it! But hark again, a little closer—put your heart in your ears, Mr. Utterson, and tell me, is that the doctor's foot?"

The steps fell lightly and oddly, with a certain swing, for all they went so slowly; it was different indeed from the heavy creaking tread of Henry Jekyll. Utterson sighed. "Is there never anything else?" he asked.

Poole nodded. "Once," he said. "Once I heard it weeping!"

"Weeping? how that?" said the lawyer, conscious of a sudden chill of horror.

"Weeping like a woman or a lost soul," said the butler. "I came away with that upon my heart, that I could have wept too."

But now the ten minutes drew to an end. Poole disinterred the axe from under a stack of packing straw; the candle was set upon the nearest table to light them to the attack; and they drew near with bated breath to where that patient foot was still going up and down, up and down, in the quiet of the night.

"Jekyll," cried Utterson, with a loud voice, "I demand to see you." He paused a moment, but there came no reply. "I give you fair warning, our suspicions are aroused, and I must and shall see you," he resumed; "if not by fair means, then by foul—if not of your consent, then by brute force!"

"Utterson," said the voice, "for God's sake, have mercy!"

"Ah, that's not Jekyll's voice—it's Hyde's!" cried Utterson. "Down with the door, Poole!"

Poole swung the axe over his shoulder; the blow shook the building, and the red baize door leaped against the lock and hinges. A dismal screech, as of mere animal terror, rang from the cabinet. Up went the axe again, and again the panels crashed and the frame bounded; four times the blow fell; but the wood was tough and the fittings were of excellent workmanship; and it was not until the fifth, that the lock burst in

sunder and the wreck of the door fell inwards on the carpet.

The besiegers, appalled by their own riot and the stillness that had succeeded, stood back a little and peered in. There lay the cabinet before their eyes in the quiet lamplight, a good fire glowing and chattering on the hearth, the kettle singing its thin strain, a drawer or two open, papers neatly set forth on the business table, and nearer the fire, the things laid out for tea: the quietest room, you would have said, and, but for the glazed presses full of chemicals, the most commonplace that night in London.

Right in the midst there lay the body of a man sorely contorted and still twitching. They drew near on tiptoe, turned it on its back and beheld the face of Edward Hyde. He was dressed in clothes far too large for him, clothes of the doctor's bigness; the cords of his face still moved with a semblance of life, but life was quite gone; and by the crushed phial in the hand and the strong smell of kernels[1] that hung upon the air, Utterson knew that he was looking on the body of a self-destroyer.

"We have come too late," he said sternly, "whether to save or punish. Hyde is gone to his account; and it only remains for us to find the body of your master."

The far greater proportion of the building was occupied by the theatre, which filled almost the whole ground story and was lighted from above, and by the cabinet, which formed an upper story at one end and looked upon the court. A corridor joined the theatre to the door on the bystreet; and with this the cabinet communicated separately by a second flight of stairs. There were besides a few dark closets and a spacious cellar. All these they now thoroughly examined. Each closet needed but a glance, for all were empty, and all, by the dust that fell from their doors, had stood long unopened. The cellar, indeed, was filled with crazy lumber, mostly dating from the times of the surgeon who was Jekyll's predecessor; but even as they opened the door they were advertised of the uselessness of further search, by the fall of a perfect mat of cobweb which had for years sealed up the entrance. Nowhere

---

[1] *kernels* Nuts or the insides of fruit pits; their smell here indicates the presence of cyanide.

was there any trace of Henry Jekyll, dead or alive.

Poole stamped on the flags of the corridor. "He must be buried here," he said, hearkening to the sound.

"Or he may have fled," said Utterson, and he turned to examine the door in the bystreet. It was locked; and lying nearby on the flags, they found the key, already stained with rust.

"This does not look like use," observed the lawyer.

"Use!" echoed Poole. "Do you not see, sir, it is broken? much as if a man had stamped on it."

"Ay," continued Utterson, "and the fractures, too, are rusty." The two men looked at each other with a scare. "This is beyond me, Poole," said the lawyer. "Let us go back to the cabinet."

They mounted the stair in silence, and still with an occasional awestruck glance at the dead body, proceeded more thoroughly to examine the contents of the cabinet. At one table, there were traces of chemical work, various measured heaps of some white salt being laid on glass saucers, as though for an experiment in which the unhappy man had been prevented.

"That is the same drug that I was always bringing him," said Poole; and even as he spoke, the kettle with a startling noise boiled over.

This brought them to the fireside, where the easy chair was drawn cosily up, and the tea things stood ready to the sitter's elbow, the very sugar in the cup. There were several books on a shelf; one lay beside the tea things open, and Utterson was amazed to find it a copy of a pious work, for which Jekyll had several times expressed a great esteem, annotated, in his own hand, with startling blasphemies.

Next, in the course of their review of the chamber, the searchers came to the cheval glass, into whose depths they looked with an involuntary horror. But it was so turned as to show them nothing but the rosy glow playing on the roof, the fire sparkling in a hundred repetitions along the glazed front of the presses, and their own pale and fearful countenances stooping to look in.

"This glass have seen some strange things, sir," whispered Poole.

"And surely none stranger than itself," echoed the lawyer in the same tones. "For what did Jekyll"—he caught himself up at the word with a start, and then conquering the weakness—"what could Jekyll want with it?" he said.

"You may say that!" said Poole.

Next they turned to the business table. On the desk among the neat array of papers, a large envelope was uppermost, and bore, in the doctor's hand, the name of Mr. Utterson. The lawyer unsealed it, and several enclosures fell to the floor. The first was a will, drawn in the same eccentric terms as the one which he had returned six months before, to serve as a testament in case of death and as a deed of gift in case of disappearance; but, in place of the name of Edward Hyde, the lawyer, with indescribable amazement, read the name of Gabriel John Utterson. He looked at Poole, and then back at the paper, and last of all at the dead malefactor stretched upon the carpet.

"My head goes round," he said. "He has been all these days in possession; he had no cause to like me; he must have raged to see himself displaced; and he has not destroyed this document."

He caught up the next paper; it was a brief note in the doctor's hand and dated at the top.

"O Poole!" the lawyer cried, "he was alive and here this day. He cannot have been disposed of in so short a space, he must be still alive, he must have fled! And then, why fled? and how? and in that case, can we venture to declare this suicide? Oh, we must be careful. I foresee that we may yet involve your master in some dire catastrophe."

"Why don't you read it, sir?" asked Poole.

"Because I fear," replied the lawyer solemnly. "God grant I have no cause for it!" And with that he brought the paper to his eyes and read as follows:

"My Dear Utterson,—When this shall fall into your hands, I shall have disappeared, under what circumstances I have not the penetration to foresee, but my instinct and all the circumstances of my nameless situation tell me that the end is sure and must be early. Go then, and first read the narrative which

Lanyon warned me he was to place in your hands; and if you care to hear more, turn to the confession of

"Your unworthy and unhappy friend,

"HENRY JEKYLL."

"There was a third enclosure?" asked Utterson.

"Here, sir," said Poole, and gave into his hands a considerable packet sealed in several places.

The lawyer put it in his pocket. "I would say nothing of this paper. If your master has fled or is dead, we may at least save his credit. It is now ten; I must go home and read these documents in quiet; but I shall be back before midnight, when we shall send for the police."

They went out, locking the door of the theatre behind them; and Utterson, once more leaving the servants gathered about the fire in the hall, trudged back to his office to read the two narratives in which this mystery was now to be explained.

DR. LANYON'S NARRATIVE

On the ninth of January, now four days ago, I received by the evening delivery a registered envelope, addressed in the hand of my colleague and old school companion, Henry Jekyll. I was a good deal surprised by this; for we were by no means in the habit of correspondence; I had seen the man, dined with him, indeed, the night before; and I could imagine nothing in our intercourse that should justify formality of registration. The contents increased my wonder; for this is how the letter ran:

"10th December,[1] 18—

"Dear Lanyon, You are one of my oldest friends; and although we may have differed at times on scientific questions, I cannot remember, at least on my side, any break in our affection. There was never a day when, if you had said to me, 'Jekyll, my life, my honour, my reason, depend upon you,' I would not have sacrificed my left hand to help you. Lanyon, my life, my honour, my reason, are all at your mercy; if you fail me tonight I am lost. You might suppose, after this preface, that I am going to

ask you for something dishonourable to grant. Judge for yourself.

"I want you to postpone all other engagements for tonight—ay, even if you were summoned to the bedside of an emperor; to take a cab, unless your carriage should be actually at the door; and with this letter in your hand for consultation, to drive straight to my house. Poole, my butler, has his orders; you will find him waiting your arrival with a locksmith. The door of my cabinet is then to be forced: and you are to go in alone; to open the glazed press[2] (letter E) on the left hand, breaking the lock if it be shut; and to draw out, *with all its contents as they stand*, the fourth drawer from the top or (which is the same thing) the third from the bottom. In my extreme distress of mind, I have a morbid fear of misdirecting you; but even if I am in error, you may know the right drawer by its contents: some powders, a phial and a paper book. This drawer I beg of you to carry back with you to Cavendish Square exactly as it stands.

"That is the first part of the service: now for the second. You should be back, if you set out at once on the receipt of this, long before midnight; but I will leave you that amount of margin, not only in the fear of one of those obstacles that can neither be prevented nor foreseen, but because an hour when your servants are in bed is to be preferred for what will then remain to do. At midnight, then, I have to ask you to be alone in your consulting room, to admit with your own hand into the house a man who will present himself in my name, and to place in his hands the drawer that you will have brought with you from my cabinet. Then you will have played your part and earned my gratitude completely. Five minutes afterwards, if you insist upon an explanation, you will have understood that these arrangements are of capital importance; and that by the neglect of one of them, fantastic as they must appear, you might have charged your conscience with my death or the shipwreck of my reason.

"Confident as I am that you will not trifle with this appeal, my heart sinks and my hand trembles at the bare thought of such a possibility. Think of me

---

[1] *10th December* The date of the letter is an error in Stevenson's original; for consistency it should be dated "9th January."

[2] *glazed press* Cupboard with glass in the doors.

at this hour, in a strange place, labouring under a blackness of distress that no fancy can exaggerate, and yet well aware that, if you will but punctually serve me, my troubles will roll away like a story that is told. Serve me, my dear Lanyon, and save

"Your friend,

"H.J.

"P.S.—I had already sealed this up when a fresh terror struck upon my soul. It is possible that the post office may fail me, and this letter not come into your hands until tomorrow morning. In that case, dear Lanyon, do my errand when it shall be most convenient for you in the course of the day; and once more expect my messenger at midnight. It may then already be too late; and if that night passes without event, you will know that you have seen the last of Henry Jekyll."

Upon the reading of this letter, I made sure[1] my colleague was insane; but till that was proved beyond the possibility of doubt, I felt bound to do as he requested. The less I understood of this farrago,[2] the less I was in a position to judge of its importance; and an appeal so worded could not be set aside without a grave responsibility. I rose accordingly from table, got into a hansom,[3] and drove straight to Jekyll's house. The butler was awaiting my arrival; he had received by the same post as mine a registered letter of instruction, and had sent at once for a locksmith and a carpenter. The tradesmen came while we were yet speaking; and we moved in a body to old Dr. Denman's surgical theatre, from which (as you are doubtless aware) Jekyll's private cabinet is most conveniently entered. The door was very strong, the lock excellent; the carpenter avowed he would have great trouble and have to do much damage, if force were to be used; and the locksmith was near despair. But this last was a handy fellow, and after two hours' work, the door stood open. The press marked E was unlocked; and I took out the drawer, had it filled up with straw and tied in a sheet, and returned with it to Cavendish Square.

---

[1] *made sure* I.e., was sure.

[2] *farrago* Mishmash, jumble.

[3] *hansom* Horse-drawn cab for hire.

Here I proceeded to examine its contents. The powders were neatly enough made up, but not with the nicety of the dispensing chemist; so that it was plain they were of Jekyll's private manufacture; and when I opened one of the wrappers I found what seemed to me a simple crystalline salt of a white colour. The phial, to which I next turned my attention, might have been about half-full of a blood-red liquor, which was highly pungent to the sense of smell and seemed to me to contain phosphorus and some volatile ether. At the other ingredients I could make no guess. The book was an ordinary version book[4] and contained little but a series of dates. These covered a period of many years, but I observed that the entries ceased nearly a year ago and quite abruptly. Here and there a brief remark was appended to a date, usually no more than a single word: "double" occurring perhaps six times in a total of several hundred entries; and once very early in the list and followed by several marks of exclamation, "total failure!!!" All this, though it whetted my curiosity, told me little that was definite. Here were a phial of some tincture, a paper of some salt, and the record of a series of experiments that had led (like too many of Jekyll's investigations) to no end of practical usefulness. How could the presence of these articles in my house affect either the honour, the sanity, or the life of my flighty colleague? If his messenger could go to one place, why could he not go to another? And even granting some impediment, why was this gentleman to be received by me in secret? The more I reflected the more convinced I grew that I was dealing with a case of cerebral disease; and though I dismissed my servants to bed, I loaded an old revolver, that I might be found in some posture of self-defence.

Twelve o'clock had scarce rung out over London, ere the knocker sounded very gently on the door. I went myself at the summons, and found a small man crouching against the pillars of the portico.

"Are you come from Dr. Jekyll?" I asked.

He told me "yes" by a constrained gesture; and when I had bidden him enter, he did not obey me without a

---

[4] *version book* Blank book often used by students for translation exercises.

searching backward glance into the darkness of the square. There was a policeman not far off, advancing with his bullseye[1] open; and at the sight, I thought my visitor started and made greater haste.

These particulars struck me, I confess, disagreeably; and as I followed him into the bright light of the consulting room, I kept my hand ready on my weapon. Here, at last, I had a chance of clearly seeing him. I had never set eyes on him before, so much was certain. He was small, as I have said; I was struck besides with the shocking expression of his face, with his remarkable combination of great muscular activity and great apparent debility of constitution, and—last but not least—with the odd, subjective disturbance caused by his neighbourhood. This bore some resemblance to incipient rigor,[2] and was accompanied by a marked sinking of the pulse. At the time, I set it down to some idiosyncratic, personal distaste, and merely wondered at the acuteness of the symptoms; but I have since had reason to believe the cause to lie much deeper in the nature of man, and to turn on some nobler hinge than the principle of hatred.

This person (who had thus, from the first moment of his entrance, struck in me what I can only describe as a disgustful curiosity) was dressed in a fashion that would have made an ordinary person laughable; his clothes, that is to say, although they were of rich and sober fabric, were enormously too large for him in every measurement—the trousers hanging on his legs and rolled up to keep them from the ground, the waist of the coat below his haunches, and the collar sprawling wide upon his shoulders. Strange to relate, this ludicrous accoutrement was far from moving me to laughter. Rather, as there was something abnormal and misbegotten in the very essence of the creature that now faced me—something seizing, surprising, and revolting—this fresh disparity seemed but to fit in with and to reinforce it; so that to my interest in the man's nature and character, there was added a curiosity as to his origin, his life, his fortune and status in the world.

These observations, though they have taken so great a space to be set down in, were yet the work of a few seconds. My visitor was, indeed, on fire with sombre excitement.

"Have you got it?" he cried. "Have you got it?" And so lively was his impatience that he even laid his hand upon my arm and sought to shake me.

I put him back, conscious at his touch of a certain icy pang along my blood. "Come, sir," said I. "You forget that I have not yet the pleasure of your acquaintance. Be seated, if you please." And I showed him an example, and sat down myself in my customary seat and with as fair an imitation of my ordinary manner to a patient, as the lateness of the hour, the nature of my preoccupations, and the horror I had of my visitor, would suffer me to muster.

"I beg your pardon, Dr. Lanyon," he replied civilly enough. "What you say is very well founded; and my impatience has shown its heels to my politeness. I come here at the instance of your colleague, Dr. Henry Jekyll, on a piece of business of some moment; and I understood …" He paused and put his hand to his throat, and I could see, in spite of his collected manner, that he was wrestling against the approaches of the hysteria—"I understood, a drawer …"

But here I took pity on my visitor's suspense, and some perhaps on my own growing curiosity.

"There it is, sir," said I, pointing to the drawer, where it lay on the floor behind a table and still covered with the sheet.

He sprang to it, and then paused, and laid his hand upon his heart: I could hear his teeth grate with the convulsive action of his jaws; and his face was so ghastly to see that I grew alarmed both for his life and reason.

"Compose yourself," said I.

He turned a dreadful smile to me, and as if with the decision of despair, plucked away the sheet. At sight of the contents, he uttered one loud sob of such immense relief that I sat petrified. And the next moment, in a voice that was already fairly well under control, "Have you a graduated glass?"[3] he asked.

---

[1] *bullseye* Lantern used to project a contained beam of bright light.
[2] *rigor* Shivering, goosebumps.

[3] *graduated glass* Glass container marked with gradations for measurement.

I rose from my place with something of an effort and gave him what he asked.

He thanked me with a smiling nod, measured out a few minims[1] of the red tincture and added one of the powders. The mixture, which was at first of a reddish hue, began, in proportion as the crystals melted, to brighten in colour, to effervesce audibly, and to throw off small fumes of vapour. Suddenly and at the same moment, the ebullition[2] ceased and the compound changed to a dark purple, which faded again more slowly to a watery green. My visitor, who had watched these metamorphoses with a keen eye, smiled, set down the glass upon the table, and then turned and looked upon me with an air of scrutiny.

"And now," said he, "to settle what remains. Will you be wise? will you be guided? will you suffer me to take this glass in my hand and to go forth from your house without further parley? or has the greed of curiosity too much command of you? Think before you answer, for it shall be done as you decide. As you decide, you shall be left as you were before, and neither richer nor wiser, unless the sense of service rendered to a man in mortal distress may be counted as a kind of riches of the soul. Or, if you shall so prefer to choose, a new province of knowledge and new avenues to fame and power shall be laid open to you, here, in this room, upon the instant; and your sight shall be blasted by a prodigy to stagger the unbelief of Satan."

"Sir," said I, affecting a coolness that I was far from truly possessing, "you speak enigmas, and you will perhaps not wonder that I hear you with no very strong impression of belief. But I have gone too far in the way of inexplicable services to pause before I see the end."

"It is well," replied my visitor. "Lanyon, you remember your vows: what follows is under the seal of our profession. And now, you who have so long been bound to the most narrow and material views, you who have denied the virtue of transcendental medicine, you who have derided your superiors—behold!"

He put the glass to his lips and drank at one gulp. A cry followed; he reeled, staggered, clutched at the table and held on, staring with injected[3] eyes, gasping with open mouth; and as I looked there came, I thought, a change—he seemed to swell—his face became suddenly black and the features seemed to melt and alter—and the next moment, I had sprung to my feet and leaped back against the wall, my arm raised to shield me from that prodigy, my mind submerged in terror.

"O God!" I screamed, and "O God!" again and again; for there before my eyes—pale and shaken, and half fainting, and groping before him with his hands, like a man restored from death—there stood Henry Jekyll!

What he told me in the next hour, I cannot bring my mind to set on paper. I saw what I saw, I heard what I heard, and my soul sickened at it; and yet now when that sight has faded from my eyes, I ask myself if I believe it, and I cannot answer. My life is shaken to its roots; sleep has left me; the deadliest terror sits by me at all hours of the day and night; I feel that my days are numbered, and that I must die; and yet I shall die incredulous. As for the moral turpitude that man unveiled to me, even with tears of penitence, I cannot, even in memory, dwell on it without a start of horror. I will say but one thing, Utterson, and that (if you can bring your mind to credit it) will be more than enough. The creature who crept into my house that night was, on Jekyll's own confession, known by the name of Hyde and hunted for in every corner of the land as the murderer of Carew.

HASTIE LANYON

HENRY JEKYLL'S FULL STATEMENT OF THE CASE

I was born in the year 18— to a large fortune, endowed besides with excellent parts,[4] inclined by nature to industry, fond of the respect of the wise and good among my fellow men, and thus, as might have been supposed, with every guarantee of an honourable and distinguished future. And indeed the worst of my faults

[1] *minims* Small amounts of liquid; a minim is approximately 0.002 ounces or 0.06 milliliters.

[2] *ebullition* Bubbling.

[3] *injected* Bloodshot or engorged.

[4] *parts* Talents or other positive personal attributes.

was a certain impatient gaiety[1] of disposition, such as has made the happiness of many, but such as I found it hard to reconcile with my imperious desire to carry my head high, and wear a more than commonly grave countenance before the public. Hence it came about that I concealed my pleasures; and that when I reached years of reflection, and began to look round me and take stock of my progress and position in the world, I stood already committed to a profound duplicity of life. Many a man would have even blazoned[2] such irregularities as I was guilty of; but from the high views that I had set before me, I regarded and hid them with an almost morbid sense of shame. It was thus rather the exacting nature of my aspirations than any particular degradation in my faults, that made me what I was, and, with even a deeper trench than in the majority of men, severed in me those provinces of good and ill which divide and compound man's dual nature. In this case, I was driven to reflect deeply and inveterately on that hard law of life, which lies at the root of religion and is one of the most plentiful springs of distress. Though so profound a double dealer, I was in no sense a hypocrite; both sides of me were in dead earnest; I was no more myself when I laid aside restraint and plunged in shame, than when I laboured, in the eye of day, at the furtherance of knowledge or the relief of sorrow and suffering. And it chanced that the direction of my scientific studies, which led wholly toward the mystic and the transcendental, reacted and shed a strong light on this consciousness of the perennial war among my members. With every day, and from both sides of my intelligence, the moral and the intellectual, I thus drew steadily nearer to that truth, by whose partial discovery I have been doomed to such a dreadful shipwreck: that man is not truly one, but truly two. I say two, because the state of my own knowledge does not pass beyond that point. Others will follow, others will outstrip me on the same lines; and I hazard the guess that man will be ultimately known for a mere polity of multifarious, incongruous,

and independent denizens. I, for my part, from the nature of my life, advanced infallibly in one direction and in one direction only. It was on the moral side, and in my own person, that I learned to recognise the thorough and primitive duality of man; I saw that, of the two natures that contended in the field of my consciousness, even if I could rightly be said to be either, it was only because I was radically both; and from an early date, even before the course of my scientific discoveries had begun to suggest the most naked possibility of such a miracle, I had learned to dwell with pleasure, as a beloved daydream, on the thought of the separation of these elements. If each, I told myself could but be housed in separate identities, life would be relieved of all that was unbearable; the unjust delivered from the aspirations might go his way, and remorse of his more upright twin; and the just could walk steadfastly and securely on his upward path, doing the good things in which he found his pleasure, and no longer exposed to disgrace and penitence by the hands of this extraneous evil. It was the curse of mankind that these incongruous faggots[3] were thus bound together that in the agonised womb of consciousness, these polar twins should be continuously struggling. How, then, were they dissociated?

I was so far in my reflections when, as I have said, a sidelight began to shine upon the subject from the laboratory table. I began to perceive more deeply than it has ever yet been stated, the trembling immateriality, the mist-like transience, of this seemingly so solid body in which we walk attired. Certain agents I found to have the power to shake and to pluck back that fleshly vestment, even as a wind might toss the curtains of a pavilion. For two good reasons, I will not enter deeply into this scientific branch of my confession. First, because I have been made to learn that the doom and burden of our life is bound forever on man's shoulders, and when the attempt is made to cast it off, it but returns upon us with more unfamiliar and more awful pressure. Second, because, as my narrative will make, alas! too evident, my discoveries were incomplete.

---

[1] *gaiety* In its most usual meaning during this period, "gay" meant "light-hearted"; it could also mean "licentious" but was not yet specifically related to sexual orientation.

[2] *blazoned* Publicly declared, i.e., bragged about.

[3] *faggots* Bundles, especially bundles of sticks used to make fires.

Enough, then, that I not only recognised my natural body for the mere aura and effulgence[1] of certain of the powers that made up my spirit, but managed to compound a drug by which these powers should be dethroned from their supremacy, and a second form and countenance substituted, none the less natural to me because they were the expression, and bore the stamp, of lower elements in my soul.

I hesitated long before I put this theory to the test of practice. I knew well that I risked death; for any drug that so potently controlled and shook the very fortress of identity, might by the least scruple[2] of an overdose or at the least inopportunity in the moment of exhibition, utterly blot out that immaterial tabernacle which I looked to it to change. But the temptation of a discovery so singular and profound, at last overcame the suggestions of alarm. I had long since prepared my tincture; I purchased at once, from a firm of wholesale chemists, a large quantity of a particular salt which I knew, from my experiments, to be the last ingredient required; and late one accursed night, I compounded the elements, watched them boil and smoke together in the glass, and when the ebullition had subsided, with a strong glow of courage, drank off the potion.

The most racking pangs succeeded: a grinding in the bones, deadly nausea, and a horror of the spirit that cannot be exceeded at the hour of birth or death. Then these agonies began swiftly to subside, and I came to myself as if out of a great sickness. There was something strange in my sensations, something indescribably new and, from its very novelty, incredibly sweet. I felt younger, lighter, happier in body; within I was conscious of a heady recklessness, a current of disordered sensual images running like a mill race[3] in my fancy, a solution of the bonds of obligation, an unknown but not an innocent freedom of the soul. I knew myself, at the first breath of this new life, to be more wicked, tenfold more wicked, sold a slave to my original evil; and the thought, in that moment, braced

and delighted me like wine. I stretched out my hands, exulting in the freshness of these sensations; and in the act, I was suddenly aware that I had lost in stature.

There was no mirror, at that date, in my room; that which stands beside me as I write, was brought there later on and for the very purpose of these transformations. The night, however, was far gone into the morning—the morning, black as it was, was nearly ripe for the conception of the day—the inmates of my house were locked in the most rigorous hours of slumber; and I determined, flushed as I was with hope and triumph, to venture in my new shape as far as to my bedroom. I crossed the yard, wherein the constellations looked down upon me, I could have thought, with wonder, the first creature of that sort that their unsleeping vigilance had yet disclosed to them; I stole through the corridors, a stranger in my own house; and coming to my room, I saw for the first time the appearance of Edward Hyde.

I must here speak by theory alone, saying not that which I know, but that which I suppose to be most probable. The evil side of my nature, to which I had now transferred the stamping efficacy, was less robust and less developed than the good which I had just deposed. Again, in the course of my life, which had been, after all, nine-tenths a life of effort, virtue, and control, it had been much less exercised and much less exhausted. And hence, as I think, it came about that Edward Hyde was so much smaller, slighter, and younger than Henry Jekyll. Even as good shone upon the countenance of the one, evil was written broadly and plainly on the face of the other. Evil besides (which I must still believe to be the lethal side of man) had left on that body an imprint of deformity and decay. And yet when I looked upon that ugly idol in the glass, I was conscious of no repugnance, rather of a leap of welcome. This, too, was myself. It seemed natural and human. In my eyes it bore a livelier image of the spirit, it seemed more express and single, than the imperfect and divided countenance I had been hitherto accustomed to call mine. And in so far I was doubtless right. I have observed that when I wore the semblance of Edward Hyde, none could come near to me at first without a visible misgiving of the flesh. This, as I take it, was

---

[1] *effulgence* Radiance.

[2] *scruple* Tiny quantity.

[3] *mill race* Fast-flowing water used to power a mill wheel.

because all human beings, as we meet them, are commingled out of good and evil: and Edward Hyde, alone in the ranks of mankind, was pure evil.

I lingered but a moment at the mirror: the second and conclusive experiment had yet to be attempted; it yet remained to be seen if I had lost my identity beyond redemption and must flee before daylight from a house that was no longer mine; and hurrying back to my cabinet, I once more prepared and drank the cup, once more suffered the pangs of dissolution, and came to myself once more with the character, the stature, and the face of Henry Jekyll.

That night I had come to the fatal crossroads. Had I approached my discovery in a more noble spirit, had I risked the experiment while under the empire of generous or pious aspirations, all must have been otherwise, and from these agonies of death and birth, I had come forth an angel instead of a fiend. The drug had no discriminating action; it was neither diabolical nor divine; it but shook the doors of the prison house of my disposition; and like the captives of Philippi,[1] that which stood within ran forth. At that time my virtue slumbered; my evil, kept awake by ambition, was alert and swift to seize the occasion; and the thing that was projected was Edward Hyde. Hence, although I had now two characters as well as two appearances, one was wholly evil, and the other was still the old Henry Jekyll, that incongruous compound of whose reformation and improvement I had already learned to despair. The movement was thus wholly toward the worse.

Even at that time, I had not yet conquered my aversion to the dryness of a life of study. I would still be merrily disposed at times; and as my pleasures were (to say the least) undignified, and I was not only well known and highly considered, but growing toward the elderly man, this incoherency of my life was daily growing more unwelcome. It was on this side that my new power tempted me until I fell in slavery. I had but to drink the cup, to doff at once the body of the noted professor, and to assume, like a thick cloak, that of Edward Hyde. I smiled at the notion; it seemed to me at the time to be humorous; and I made my preparations with the most studious care. I took and furnished that house in Soho, to which Hyde was tracked by the police; and engaged as housekeeper a creature whom I well knew to be silent and unscrupulous. On the other side, I announced to my servants that a Mr. Hyde (whom I described) was to have full liberty and power about my house in the square; and to parry mishaps, I even called and made myself a familiar object, in my second character. I next drew up that will to which you so much objected; so that if anything befell me in the person of Dr. Jekyll, I could enter on that of Edward Hyde without pecuniary loss. And thus fortified, as I supposed, on every side, I began to profit by the strange immunities of my position.

Men have before hired bravos[2] to transact their crimes, while their own person and reputation sat under shelter. I was the first that ever did so for his pleasures. I was the first that could thus plod in the public eye with a load of genial respectability, and in a moment, like a schoolboy, strip off these lendings[3] and spring headlong into the sea of liberty. But for me, in my impenetrable mantle, the safety was complete. Think of it—I did not even exist! Let me but escape into my laboratory door, give me but a second or two to mix and swallow the draught that I had always standing ready; and whatever he had done, Edward Hyde would pass away like the stain of breath upon a mirror; and there in his stead, quietly at home, trimming the midnight lamp in his study, a man who could afford to laugh at suspicion, would be Henry Jekyll.

The pleasures which I made haste to seek in my disguise were, as I have said, undignified; I would scarce use a harder term. But in the hands of Edward Hyde, they soon began to turn toward the monstrous. When I would come back from these excursions, I was often plunged into a kind of wonder at my vicarious

---

[1] *captives of Philippi* Cf. Acts 16.26, in which Paul and his followers were given an opportunity to escape from prison when an earthquake caused the doors of their prison to open. They chose to remain in their cells, but were freed as a result of their obedience.

[2] *bravos* Paid criminals, especially killers.

[3] *lendings* Borrowed clothes.

depravity. This familiar[1] that I called out of my own soul, and sent forth alone to do his good pleasure, was a being inherently malign and villainous; his every act and thought centred on self; drinking pleasure with bestial avidity from any degree of torture to another; relentless like a man of stone. Henry Jekyll stood at times aghast before the acts of Edward Hyde; but the situation was apart from ordinary laws, and insidiously relaxed the grasp of conscience. It was Hyde, after all, and Hyde alone, that was guilty. Jekyll was no worse; he woke again to his good qualities seemingly unimpaired; he would even make haste, where it was possible, to undo the evil done by Hyde. And thus his conscience slumbered.

Into the details of the infamy at which I thus connived (for even now I can scarce grant that I committed it) I have no design of entering; I mean but to point out the warnings and the successive steps with which my chastisement approached. I met with one accident which, as it brought on no consequence, I shall no more than mention. An act of cruelty to a child aroused against me the anger of a passerby, whom I recognised the other day in the person of your kinsman; the doctor and the child's family joined him; there were moments when I feared for my life; and at last, in order to pacify their too just resentment, Edward Hyde had to bring them to the door, and pay them in a cheque drawn in the name of Henry Jekyll. But this danger was easily eliminated from the future, by opening an account at another bank in the name of Edward Hyde himself; and when, by sloping my own hand backward, I had supplied my double with a signature, I thought I sat beyond the reach of fate.

Some two months before the murder of Sir Danvers, I had been out for one of my adventures, had returned at a late hour, and woke the next day in bed with somewhat odd sensations. It was in vain I looked about me; in vain I saw the decent furniture and tall proportions of my room in the square; in vain that I recognised the pattern of the bed curtains and the design of the mahogany frame; something still kept insisting that I was not where

I was, that I had not wakened where I seemed to be, but in the little room in Soho where I was accustomed to sleep in the body of Edward Hyde. I smiled to myself, and, in my psychological way began lazily to inquire into the elements of this illusion, occasionally, even as I did so, dropping back into a comfortable morning doze. I was still so engaged when, in one of my more wakeful moments, my eyes fell upon my hand. Now the hand of Henry Jekyll (as you have often remarked) was professional in shape and size: it was large, firm, white, and comely. But the hand which I now saw, clearly enough, in the yellow light of a mid-London morning, lying half shut on the bedclothes, was lean, corded, knuckly, of a dusky pallor and thickly shaded with a swart[2] growth of hair. It was the hand of Edward Hyde.

I must have stared upon it for near half a minute, sunk as I was in the mere stupidity of wonder, before terror woke up in my breast as sudden and startling as the crash of cymbals; and bounding from my bed, I rushed to the mirror. At the sight that met my eyes, my blood was changed into something exquisitely thin and icy. Yes, I had gone to bed Henry Jekyll, I had awakened Edward Hyde. How was this to be explained? I asked myself; and then, with another bound of terror—how was it to be remedied? It was well on in the morning; the servants were up; all my drugs were in the cabinet—a long journey down two pairs of stairs, through the back passage, across the open court and through the anatomical theatre, from where I was then standing horror-struck. It might indeed be possible to cover my face; but of what use was that, when I was unable to conceal the alteration in my stature? And then with an overpowering sweetness of relief, it came back upon my mind that the servants were already used to the coming and going of my second self. I had soon dressed, as well as I was able, in clothes of my own size: had soon passed through the house, where Bradshaw stared and drew back at seeing Mr. Hyde at such an hour and in such a strange array; and ten minutes later, Dr. Jekyll had returned to his own shape and was sitting down, with a darkened brow, to make a feint of breakfasting.

---

[1] *familiar* Spirit, often in animal form, that obeys and helps magic practitioners.

[2] *swart* Swarthy, i.e., dark.

Small indeed was my appetite. This inexplicable incident, this reversal of my previous experience, seemed, like the Babylonian finger on the wall, to be spelling out the letters of my judgment;[1] and I began to reflect more seriously than ever before on the issues and possibilities of my double existence. That part of me which I had the power of projecting, had lately been much exercised and nourished; it had seemed to me of late as though the body of Edward Hyde had grown in stature, as though (when I wore that form) I were conscious of a more generous tide of blood; and I began to spy a danger that, if this were much prolonged, the balance of my nature might be permanently overthrown, the power of voluntary change be forfeited, and the character of Edward Hyde become irrevocably mine. The power of the drug had not been always equally displayed. Once, very early in my career, it had totally failed me; since then I had been obliged on more than one occasion to double, and once, with infinite risk of death, to treble the amount; and these rare uncertainties had cast hitherto the sole shadow on my contentment. Now, however, and in the light of that morning's accident, I was led to remark that whereas, in the beginning, the difficulty had been to throw off the body of Jekyll, it had of late gradually but decidedly transferred itself to the other side. All things therefore seemed to point to this: that I was slowly losing hold of my original and better self, and becoming slowly incorporated with my second and worse.

Between these two, I now felt I had to choose. My two natures had memory in common, but all other faculties were most unequally shared between them. Jekyll (who was composite) now with the most sensitive apprehensions, now with a greedy gusto, projected and shared in the pleasures and adventures of Hyde; but Hyde was indifferent to Jekyll, or but remembered him as the mountain bandit remembers the cavern in which he conceals himself from pursuit. Jekyll had more than a father's interest; Hyde had more than a son's

indifference. To cast in my lot with Jekyll, was to die to those appetites which I had long secretly indulged and had of late begun to pamper. To cast it in with Hyde, was to die to a thousand interests and aspirations, and to become, at a blow and forever, despised and friendless. The bargain might appear unequal; but there was still another consideration in the scales; for while Jekyll would suffer smartingly in the fires of abstinence, Hyde would be not even conscious of all that he had lost. Strange as my circumstances were, the terms of this debate are as old and commonplace as man; much the same inducements and alarms cast the die for any tempted and trembling sinner; and it fell out with me, as it falls with so vast a majority of my fellows, that I chose the better part and was found wanting in the strength to keep to it.

Yes, I preferred the elderly and discontented doctor, surrounded by friends and cherishing honest hopes; and bade a resolute farewell to the liberty, the comparative youth, the light step, leaping impulses and secret pleasures, that I had enjoyed in the disguise of Hyde. I made this choice perhaps with some unconscious reservation, for I neither gave up the house in Soho, nor destroyed the clothes of Edward Hyde, which still lay ready in my cabinet. For two months, however, I was true to my determination; for two months I led a life of such severity as I had never before attained to, and enjoyed the compensations of an approving conscience. But time began at last to obliterate the freshness of my alarm; the praises of conscience began to grow into a thing of course; I began to be tortured with throes and longings, as of Hyde struggling after freedom; and at last, in an hour of moral weakness, I once again compounded and swallowed the transforming draught.

I do not suppose that, when a drunkard reasons with himself upon his vice, he is once out of five hundred times affected by the dangers that he runs through his brutish, physical insensibility; neither had I, long as I had considered my position, made enough allowance for the complete moral insensibility and insensate readiness to evil, which were the leading characters of Edward Hyde. Yet it was by these that I was punished. My devil had been long caged, he came out roaring. I was

---

[1] *the Babylonian ... judgment* Cf. Daniel 5, in which a message of judgment against Belshazzar, King of Babylon, was written on the wall by a disembodied finger. The writing foretold the king's assassination and the division of his kingdom, which happened that night.

conscious, even when I took the draught, of a more unbridled, a more furious propensity to ill. It must have been this, I suppose, that stirred in my soul that tempest of impatience with which I listened to the civilities of my unhappy victim; I declare, at least, before God, no man morally sane could have been guilty of that crime upon so pitiful a provocation; and that I struck in no more reasonable spirit than that in which a sick child may break a plaything. But I had voluntarily stripped myself of all those balancing instincts by which even the worst of us continues to walk with some degree of steadiness among temptations; and in my case, to be tempted, however slightly, was to fall.

Instantly the spirit of hell awoke in me and raged. With a transport of glee, I mauled the unresisting body, tasting delight from every blow; and it was not till weariness had begun to succeed, that I was suddenly, in the top fit of my delirium, struck through the heart by a cold thrill of terror. A mist dispersed; I saw my life to be forfeit; and fled from the scene of these excesses, at once glorying and trembling, my lust of evil gratified and stimulated, my love of life screwed to the topmost peg. I ran to the house in Soho, and (to make assurance doubly sure) destroyed my papers; thence I set out through the lamplit streets, in the same divided ecstasy of mind, gloating on my crime, light-headedly devising others in the future, and yet still hastening and still hearkening in my wake for the steps of the avenger. Hyde had a song upon his lips as he compounded the draught, and as he drank it, pledged[1] the dead man. The pangs of transformation had not done tearing him, before Henry Jekyll, with streaming tears of gratitude and remorse, had fallen upon his knees and lifted his clasped hands to God. The veil of self-indulgence was rent from head to foot.[2] I saw my life as a whole: I followed it up from the days of childhood, when I had walked with my father's hand, and through the self-denying toils of my professional life, to arrive again and again, with the same sense of unreality, at the damned

horrors of the evening. I could have screamed aloud; I sought with tears and prayers to smother down the crowd of hideous images and sounds with which my memory swarmed against me; and still, between the petitions, the ugly face of my iniquity stared into my soul. As the acuteness of this remorse began to die away, it was succeeded by a sense of joy. The problem of my conduct was solved. Hyde was thenceforth impossible; whether I would or not, I was now confined to the better part of my existence; and oh, how I rejoiced to think it! with what willing humility, I embraced anew the restrictions of natural life! with what sincere renunciation, I locked the door by which I had so often gone and come, and ground the key under my heel!

The next day, came the news that the murder had been overlooked,[3] that the guilt of Hyde was patent to the world, and that the victim was a man high in public estimation. It was not only a crime, it had been a tragic folly. I think I was glad to know it; I think I was glad to have my better impulses thus buttressed and guarded by the terrors of the scaffold. Jekyll was now my city of refuge; let but Hyde peep out an instant, and the hands of all men would be raised to take and slay him.

I resolved in my future conduct to redeem the past; and I can say with honesty that my resolve was fruitful of some good. You know yourself how earnestly in the last months of last year, I laboured to relieve suffering; you know that much was done for others, and that the days passed quietly, almost happily for myself. Nor can I truly say that I wearied of this beneficent and innocent life; I think instead that I daily enjoyed it more completely; but I was still cursed with my duality of purpose; and as the first edge of my penitence wore off, the lower side of me, so long indulged, so recently chained down, began to growl for licence. Not that I dreamed of resuscitating Hyde; the bare idea of that would startle me to frenzy: no, it was in my own person, that I was once more tempted to trifle with my conscience; and it was as an ordinary secret sinner, that I at last fell before the assaults of temptation.

---

[1] *pledged* Toasted.

[2] *The veil ... foot* Cf. Mark 15.38: "And the veil of the temple was rent in twain from the top to the bottom." This line immediately follows the death of Jesus; see also Matthew 27.51 and Luke 23.45.

[3] *overlooked* Witnessed from a higher viewpoint.

There comes an end to all things; the most capacious measure is filled at last; and this brief condescension to evil finally destroyed the balance of my soul. And yet I was not alarmed; the fall seemed natural, like a return to the old days before I had made discovery. It was a fine, clear, January day, wet underfoot where the frost had melted, but cloudless overhead; and the Regent's Park[1] was full of winter chirrupings and sweet with spring odours. I sat in the sun on a bench; the animal within me licking the chops of memory; the spiritual side a little drowsed, promising subsequent penitence, but not yet moved to begin. After all, I reflected, I was like my neighbours; and then I smiled, comparing myself with other men, comparing my active goodwill with the lazy cruelty of their neglect. And at the very moment of that vain-glorious thought, a qualm came over me, a horrid nausea and the most deadly shuddering. These passed away, and left me faint; and then as in its turn the faintness subsided, I began to be aware of a change in the temper of my thoughts, a greater boldness, a contempt of danger, a solution of the bonds of obligation. I looked down; my clothes hung formlessly on my shrunken limbs; the hand that lay on my knee was corded and hairy. I was once more Edward Hyde. A moment before I had been safe of all men's respect, wealthy, beloved—the cloth laying for me in the dining room at home; and now I was the common quarry of mankind, hunted, houseless, a known murderer, thrall to the gallows.

My reason wavered, but it did not fail me utterly. I have more than once observed that, in my second character, my faculties seemed sharpened to a point and my spirits more tensely elastic; thus it came about that, where Jekyll perhaps might have succumbed, Hyde rose to the importance of the moment. My drugs were in one of the presses of my cabinet; how was I to reach them? That was the problem that (crushing my temples in my hands) I set myself to solve. The laboratory door I had closed. If I sought to enter by the house, my own servants would consign me to the gallows. I saw I must employ another hand, and thought of Lanyon. How was he to be reached? how persuaded? Supposing that I

escaped capture in the streets, how was I to make my way into his presence? and how should I, an unknown and displeasing visitor, prevail on the famous physician to rifle the study of his colleague, Dr. Jekyll? Then I remembered that of my original character, one part remained to me: I could write my own hand; and once I had conceived that kindling spark, the way that I must follow became lighted up from end to end.

Thereupon, I arranged my clothes as best I could, and summoning a passing hansom, drove to an hotel in Portland Street,[2] the name of which I chanced to remember. At my appearance (which was indeed comical enough, however tragic a fate these garments covered) the driver could not conceal his mirth. I gnashed my teeth upon him with a gust of devilish fury; and the smile withered from his face—happily for him—yet more happily for myself, for in another instant I had certainly dragged him from his perch. At the inn, as I entered, I looked about me with so black a countenance as made the attendants tremble; not a look did they exchange in my presence; but obsequiously took my orders, led me to a private room, and brought me wherewithal to write. Hyde in danger of his life was a creature new to me; shaken with inordinate anger, strung to the pitch of murder, lusting to inflict pain. Yet the creature was astute; mastered his fury with a great effort of the will; composed his two important letters, one to Lanyon and one to Poole; and that he might receive actual evidence of their being posted, sent them out with directions that they should be registered.

Thenceforward, he sat all day over the fire in the private room, gnawing his nails; there he dined, sitting alone with his fears, the waiter visibly quailing before his eye; and thence, when the night was fully come, he set forth in the corner of a closed cab, and was driven to and fro about the streets of the city. He, I say—I cannot say, I. That child of Hell had nothing human; nothing lived in him but fear and hatred. And when at last, thinking the driver had begun to grow suspicious, he discharged the cab and ventured on foot, attired in his misfitting clothes, an object marked out for observation, into the midst of the nocturnal passengers, these two

[1] *Regent's Park*   Northwest London public park.

[2] *Portland Street*   Street on the edge of nineteenth-century Soho.

base passions raged within him like a tempest. He walked fast, hunted by his fears, chattering to himself, skulking through the less frequented thoroughfares, counting the minutes that still divided him from midnight. Once a woman spoke to him, offering, I think, a box of lights.[1] He smote her in the face, and she fled.

When I came to myself at Lanyon's, the horror of my old friend perhaps affected me somewhat: I do not know; it was at least but a drop in the sea to the abhorrence with which I looked back upon these hours. A change had come over me. It was no longer the fear of the gallows, it was the horror of being Hyde that racked me. I received Lanyon's condemnation partly in a dream; it was partly in a dream that I came home to my own house and got into bed. I slept after the prostration of the day, with a stringent and profound slumber which not even the nightmares that wrung me could avail to break. I awoke in the morning shaken, weakened, but refreshed. I still hated and feared the thought of the brute that slept within me, and I had not of course forgotten the appalling dangers of the day before; but I was once more at home, in my own house and close to my drugs; and gratitude for my escape shone so strong in my soul that it almost rivalled the brightness of hope.

I was stepping leisurely across the court after breakfast, drinking the chill of the air with pleasure, when I was seized again with those indescribable sensations that heralded the change; and I had but the time to gain the shelter of my cabinet, before I was once again raging and freezing with the passions of Hyde. It took on this occasion a double dose to recall me to myself; and alas! six hours after, as I sat looking sadly in the fire, the pangs returned, and the drug had to be re-administered. In short, from that day forth it seemed only by a great effort as of gymnastics, and only under the immediate stimulation of the drug, that I was able to wear the countenance of Jekyll. At all hours of the day and night, I would be taken with the premonitory shudder; above all, if I slept, or even dozed for a moment in my chair, it was always as Hyde that I awakened. Under the strain of this continually impending doom and by the sleeplessness to which I now condemned myself, ay, even beyond what I had thought possible to man, I became, in my own person, a creature eaten up and emptied by fever, languidly weak both in body and mind, and solely occupied by one thought: the horror of my other self. But when I slept, or when the virtue of the medicine wore off, I would leap almost without transition (for the pangs of transformation grew daily less marked) into the possession of a fancy brimming with images of terror, a soul boiling with causeless hatreds, and a body that seemed not strong enough to contain the raging energies of life. The powers of Hyde seemed to have grown with the sickliness of Jekyll. And certainly the hate that now divided them was equal on each side. With Jekyll, it was a thing of vital instinct. He had now seen the full deformity of that creature that shared with him some of the phenomena of consciousness, and was coheir with him to death: and beyond these links of community, which in themselves made the most poignant part of his distress, he thought of Hyde, for all his energy of life, as of something not only hellish but inorganic. This was the shocking thing; that the slime of the pit seemed to utter cries and voices; that the amorphous dust gesticulated and sinned; that what was dead, and had no shape, should usurp the offices of life. And this again, that that insurgent horror was knit to him closer than a wife, closer than an eye; lay caged in his flesh, where he heard it mutter and felt it struggle to be born; and at every hour of weakness, and in the confidence of slumber, prevailed against him, and deposed him out of life. The hatred of Hyde for Jekyll, was of a different order. His terror of the gallows drove him continually to commit temporary suicide, and return to his subordinate station of a part instead of a person; but he loathed the necessity, he loathed the despondency into which Jekyll was now fallen, and he resented the dislike with which he was himself regarded. Hence the apelike tricks that he would play me, scrawling in my own hand blasphemies on the pages of my books, burning the letters and destroying the portrait of my father; and

---

[1] *lights* Matches.

indeed, had it not been for his fear of death, he would long ago have ruined himself in order to involve me in the ruin. But his love of life is wonderful; I go further: I, who sicken and freeze at the mere thought of him, when I recall the abjection and passion of this attachment, and when I know how he fears my power to cut him off by suicide, I find it in my heart to pity him.

It is useless, and the time awfully fails me, to prolong this description; no one has ever suffered such torments, let that suffice; and yet even to these, habit brought— no, not alleviation—but a certain callousness of soul, a certain acquiescence of despair; and my punishment might have gone on for years, but for the last calamity which has now fallen, and which has finally severed me from my own face and nature. My provision of the salt, which had never been renewed since the date of the first experiment, began to run low. I sent out for a fresh supply, and mixed the draught; the ebullition followed, and the first change of colour, not the second; I drank it and it was without efficiency. You will learn from Poole how I have had London ransacked; it was in vain; and I am now persuaded that my first supply was impure, and that it was that unknown impurity which lent efficacy to the draught.

About a week has passed, and I am now finishing this statement under the influence of the last of the old powders. This, then, is the last time, short of a miracle, that Henry Jekyll can think his own thoughts or see his own face (now how sadly altered!) in the glass. Nor must I delay too long to bring my writing to an end; for if my narrative has hitherto escaped destruction, it has been by a combination of great prudence and great good luck. Should the throes of change take me in the act of writing it, Hyde will tear it in pieces; but if some time shall have elapsed after I have laid it by, his wonderful selfishness and circumscription[1] to the moment will probably save it once again from the action of his apelike spite. And indeed the doom that is closing on us both, has already changed and crushed him. Half an hour from now, when I shall again and for ever reindue[2] that hated personality, I know how I shall sit shuddering and weeping in my chair, or continue, with the most strained and fear-struck ecstasy of listening, to pace up and down this room (my last earthly refuge) and give ear to every sound of menace. Will Hyde die upon the scaffold? or will he find courage to release himself at the last moment? God knows; I am careless;[3] this is my true hour of death, and what is to follow concerns another than myself. Here then, as I lay down the pen and proceed to seal up my confession, I bring the life of that unhappy Henry Jekyll to an end.

—1886

---

[1] *circumscription* Restriction.

[2] *reindue* Dress (myself) again in.

[3] *I am careless* I do not care.

Oscar Wilde
1854 – 1900

For his epigrammatic genius, his challenges to bourgeois sensibilities, and his dazzling essays, dramas, and other writings, Oscar Wilde has been both reverenced and reviled for more than a century. Notorious for his flamboyance and wit before he had ever published a word, Wilde established himself in the literary world with his sole novel, *The Picture of Dorian Gray*, and even more with such sparkling social comedies as *An Ideal Husband* and *The Importance of Being Earnest*. He was a vocal advocate of aestheticism; Wilde saw in art the possibility for a life beyond the day-to-day monotony of ordinary existence. The "aesthetic movement," he writes, "produced certain colours, subtle in their loveliness and fascinating in their almost mystical tone. They were, and are, our reaction against the crude primaries of a doubtless more respectable but certainly less cultivated age."

Wilde began his life as Oscar Fingal O'Flahertie Wills Wilde. His parents, themselves no strangers to controversy, were Jane Francesca Elgee and Dr. William Wilde (later Lady and Sir Wilde). Both were accomplished writers. William, an ear and eye surgeon, wrote a book on medical and literary institutions in Austria and another about his voyage to North Africa and the Middle East. He achieved fame for his work on the Irish Census, for which he conducted a groundbreaking demographic study of the Great Famine, earning a knighthood in 1864. His reputation was somewhat tainted, however, by his womanizing; he fathered three children out of wedlock. Lady Wilde was also a prominent figure. Born Jane Frances Agnes Elgee, she adopted the more Italian-sounding "Francesca" to reinforce the family's claim that they were descended from Dante Alighieri (truth never stood in the way of a good Wilde family story). Lady Wilde took yet another name, "Speranza," when she published poems in *The Nation*, a weekly Dublin newspaper published by an anti-British revolutionary group called the Young Irelanders.

Wilde grew up in the colorful environment of his mother's famous salon, where she hosted leading Dublin artists and writers. Once when Wilde returned from college, he invited a friend to Lady Wilde's weekly "conversazione," saying, "I want to introduce you to my mother. We have founded a society for the suppression of virtue." Wilde was a brilliant student at Trinity College, graduating in 1874 with the Berkeley Gold Medal for Classics and receiving a scholarship to study at Oxford. Before long, he was celebrated at Oxford's Magdalen College for his wit, decadence, and ostentatious appearance. He was most influenced in his academic years by two rivals at Oxford, John Ruskin and Walter Pater. From Ruskin, perhaps the most influential art critic of the century, Wilde took counsel on what the older scholar believed to be the spiritual, ethical, and moral nature of art. From Pater, who was already infamous following the publication of his *Studies in the History of the Renaissance* (1873), Wilde picked up elements of aestheticism he would eventually transform into his own theories of art. Wilde would later describe Pater's *Renaissance* as "the holy writ of beauty."

After winning the Newdigate prize for poetry and graduating with first class honors, Wilde moved to London and began his career as a divisive public figure. He was known, for example, for a formal jacket, called his "cello coat," that he wore to the opening of the Grosvenor Gallery in 1877, and for being more generally a poster-boy of the emerging aesthetic movement. By the time he published a book of poems in 1881, he had already become the butt of many caricatures in *Punch* magazine; he had taken to modeling his look on the character of Bunthorne in Gilbert and Sullivan's satirical comic opera *Patience*. For the next few years Wilde delivered lectures in the United States and Great Britain about the aesthetic movement, for which he had ambitious plans: "I want to make this artistic movement the basis for a new civilization." In Boston he voiced some of the ideas about art and life for which he would become best known: "The supreme object of life is to live. Few people live. It is true life only to realize one's own perfection, to make one's every dream a reality. Even this is possible."

In 1884 Wilde married Constance Lloyd, with whom he would have two sons, Cyril and Vyvyan. From 1887 to 1889 he edited *Woman's World*, a popular magazine. Through the late 1880s, Wilde wrote reviews of many of his most famous contemporaries, including the painter James Whistler and the poets D.G. Rossetti, William Morris, and Algernon Swinburne. He was also at work on the volume *Intentions* (1891), which would ultimately constitute the most thorough account of his aesthetic philosophy, and would include his famous essays "The Decay of Lying" and "The Critic as Artist." The essays argue for the paramount importance of art in human life: "[Works of art] are ... the great archetypes of which things that have existence are but unfinished copies." Rather than artists copying from the world about them, writes Wilde, we as individuals interpret the world *through art*, through the "archetypes" presented to us by works of art. Hence "[t]here may have been fogs for centuries in London," but "no one saw them ... till Art had invented them." The early 1890s also saw the publication of Wilde's novel, *The Picture of Dorian Gray*, which both puts forward Wilde's aesthetic beliefs and suggests some of the dangers of a life given over to aesthetic consumption.

Wilde was clearly at his very best in the early 1890s. In addition to *Intentions*, *Dorian Gray*, and poems such as "Helas," Wilde penned a string of brilliant social comedies, including *Lady Windermere's Fan* (1892), *A Woman of No Importance* (1893), and *An Ideal Husband* (1895). His final comedy was his masterpiece of farce, *The Importance of Being Earnest*; it first played in 1895 to wildly enthusiastic crowds at the St. James Theatre in London. Success came to an end only through Wilde's ill-fated affair with a young aristocrat, Lord Alfred Douglas ("Bosie"). Douglas's father, the mentally unstable Marquess of Queensbury, was infuriated by the relationship, and in 1895 he publicly accused Wilde of sodomy. Convinced he had to defend his own and Douglas's honor, Wilde sued the Marquess for libel. After Wilde failed in his suit against Queensbury, the government used evidence from the trial to launch a criminal investigation against Wilde (sex between men was a crime during this period). Wilde was found guilty of "gross indecency" and sentenced to two years of imprisonment with hard labor.

Prison left Wilde financially and emotionally broken. The horrid conditions of late-Victorian prison life—including a poor diet, enforced silence, and physically taxing labor—were especially difficult to handle. From prison Wilde wrote a moving autobiographical letter to Bosie, later entitled *De Profundis*, that accuses the younger man of heartless and selfish behavior. (Bosie had treated Wilde poorly all along, and he abandoned Wilde during his imprisonment.) Even from his cell, however, Wilde wrote of seeing "new developments in Art and Life." Upon his release he composed "The Ballad of Reading Gaol " (1898), a heartfelt indictment of the prison system and capital punishment, as well as a meditation on the universal characteristics of human nature.

Wilde's last years were spent in Italy and France. He seems never to have recovered fully from his prison experience, and by late in 1900 he was quite ill. He died and was buried in Paris before the year ended; the immediate cause of his death has never been conclusively established. In 1995 a window in the Poets' Corner of Westminster Abbey was dedicated in his honor.

⌘ ⌘ ⌘

Helas![1]

To drift with every passion till my soul
  Is a stringed lute on which all winds can play,
Is it for this that I have given away
Mine ancient wisdom, and austere control?
5 Methinks my life is a twice-written scroll
Scrawled over on some boyish holiday
With idle songs for pipe and virelay,[2]
Which do but mar the secret of the whole.
Surely there was a time I might have trod
10 The sunlit heights, and from life's dissonance
Struck one clear chord to reach the ears of God:
Is that time dead? Lo! with a little rod
I did but touch the honey of romance—
And must I lose a soul's inheritance?[3]
—1881

Impression du Matin[4]

The Thames nocturne of blue and gold[5]
  Changed to a harmony in gray:
    A barge with ochre-coloured hay
Dropped from the wharf: and chill and cold

5 The yellow fog came creeping down
  The bridges, till the houses' walls
    Seemed changed to shadows and St. Paul's
Loomed like a bubble o'er the town.

Then suddenly arose the clang
10 Of waking life; the streets were stirred
    With country wagons: and a bird
Flew to the glistening roofs and sang.

---

[1] *Helas* Alas.

[2] *virelay* Short lyric poem.

[3] *with a … inheritance* Cf. 1 Samuel 14.43: "I did but taste a little honey with the end of the rod that was in mine hand, and, lo, I must die." Jonathan, son of King Saul, eats some honey from a honeycomb, unaware that his father has forbidden anyone in the land to eat before evening. For this, his father threatens to have him killed.

[4] *Impression du Matin* French: Impression of the morning.

[5] *gold* Cf. James McNeill Whistler's series of paintings, the "Nocturnes." Two of the most famous of these are *Nocturne in Blue and Gold: Old Battersea Bridge* and *Nocturne in Black and Gold: The Falling Rocket*, both of which were painted in the 1870s. These and other similar paintings were important precursors of the movement that came to be known as Impressionism; painters such as Claude Monet and Edgar Degas, like Whistler, strove to capture the transitory effects of light both on the landscape and on human figures. Much as Wilde was moved to write his own "impressions" in verse (this is one of several Wilde poems that include the word "impression" in their title), he did not respond positively to Whistler's radical experiments with impressions on canvas. His response to *Nocturne in Black and Gold: The Falling Rocket* on seeing it exhibited at the Grosvenor Gallery in 1877 was to call it "worth looking at for about as long as one looks at a real rocket, that is, for something less than a quarter of a minute." This judgment concurred with that of the famous art critic John Ruskin (who had been a teacher of Wilde's at Oxford). Ruskin criticized Whistler for "flinging a pot of paint in the public's face" with works such as *Nocturne in Black and Gold: The Falling Rocket*—an insult for which Whistler sued him in a famous trial. (Whistler won the case, but was awarded only one farthing in damages and had to pay the costs of the trial, which contributed to his eventual bankruptcy.)

But one pale woman all alone,
   The daylight kissing her wan hair,
15   Loitered beneath gas lamps' flare,
With lips of flame and heart of stone.
—1881

E Tenebris[1]

Come down, O Christ, and help me! Reach thy
   hand,
 For I am drowning in a stormier sea
   Than Simon on thy lake of Galilee:[2]
The wine of life is spilt upon the sand,
5 My heart is as some famine-murdered land
   Whence all good things have perished utterly,
   And well I know my soul in Hell must lie
If I this night before God's throne should stand.
"He sleeps perchance, or rideth to the chase,
10   Like Baal, when his prophets howled that name
   From morn to noon on Carmel's smitten height."[3]
Nay, peace, I shall behold, before the night,
   The feet of brass,[4] the robe more white than flame,
The wounded hands, the weary human face.
—1881

To Milton

Milton! I think thy spirit hath passed away
   From these white cliffs and high-embattled
     towers;
This gorgeous fiery-coloured world of ours

Seems fallen into ashes dull and grey,
5 And the age changed unto a mimic play
Wherein we waste our else too-crowded hours:
For all our pomp and pageantry and powers
We are but fit to delve the common clay,
Seeing this little isle on which we stand,
10 This England, this sea-lion of the sea,
By ignorant demagogues is held in fee,
Who love her not: Dear God! is this the land
Which bare a triple empire in her hand
When Cromwell spake the word "Democracy!"
—1881

from *"The Critic as Artist"*[5]

ERNEST.   … [S]urely, the higher you place the creative artist, the lower must the critic rank.

GILBERT.   Why so?

ERNEST.   Because the best that he can give us will be but an echo of rich music, a dim shadow of clear-outlined form. It may, indeed, be that life is chaos, as you tell me that it is; that its martyrdoms are mean and its heroisms ignoble; and that it is the function of Literature to create, from the rough material of actual existence, a new world that will be more marvellous, more enduring, and more true than the world that common eyes look upon, and through which common natures seek to realize their perfection. But surely, if this new world has been made by the spirit and touch of a great artist, it will be a thing so complete and perfect that there will be nothing left for the critic to do. I quite understand now, and indeed admit most readily, that it is far more difficult to talk about a thing than to do it. But it seems to me that this sound and sensible maxim, which is

---

[1] *E Tenebris* Latin: Out of the darkness.

[2] *Simon … Galilee* In Matthew 14.24–31, Simon Peter, one of the twelve apostles, nearly drowns in a storm at sea when Christ bids him to walk across the water to him. Christ reaches out his hand and saves him, saying "O thou of little faith, wherefore didst thou doubt?"

[3] *He sleeps … height* In 1 Kings 18.19–40, Elijah mocks the priests of Baal (who had called upon their God all day in vain) by saying, "either he is talking, or he is pursuing, or he is in a journey, or peradventure he sleepeth, and must be awaked." Here the speaker imagines a similar voice taunting him.

[4] *feet of brass* Revelation 1.13–16 describes a vision of the Son of man in which his feet are "like unto fine brass."

[5] *The Critic as Artist* In this dialogue, two men debate the merits of art criticism. Earlier, Ernest had questioned the usefulness of criticism, asking, "Why should the artist be troubled by the shrill clamour of criticism? Why should those who cannot create take it upon themselves to estimate the value of creative work?" In response, Gilbert argued that criticism is itself an art, that "there is no fine art without self-consciousness, and self-consciousness and the critical spirit are one," and, furthermore, that it is "very much more difficult to talk about a thing than to do it."

really extremely soothing to one's feelings, and should be adopted as its motto by every Academy of Literature all over the world, applies only to the relations that exist between Art and Life, and not to any relations that there may be between Art and Criticism.

GILBERT.   But, surely, Criticism is itself an art. And just as artistic creation implies the working of the critical faculty, and, indeed, without it cannot be said to exist at all, so Criticism is really creative in the highest sense of the word. Criticism is, in fact, both creative and independent.

ERNEST.   Independent?

GILBERT.   Yes; independent. Criticism is no more to be judged by any low standard of imitation or resemblance than is the work of poet or sculptor. The critic occupies the same relation to the work of art that he criticizes as the artist does to the visible world of form and colour, or the unseen world of passion and of thought. He does not even require for the perfection of his art the finest materials. Anything will serve his purpose. And just as out of the sordid and sentimental amours of the silly wife of a small country doctor in the squalid village of Yonville-l'Abbaye, near Rouen, Gustave Flaubert was able to create a classic and make a masterpiece of style,[1] so, from subjects of little or no importance, such as the pictures in this year's Royal Academy, or in any year's Royal Academy for that matter, Mr. Lewis Morris's poems, M. Ohnet's novels, or the plays of Mr. Henry Arthur Jones,[2] the true critic can, if it be his pleasure so to direct or waste his faculty of contemplation, produce work that will be flawless in beauty and instinct with intellectual subtlety. Why not? Dullness is always an irresistible temptation for brilliancy, and stupidity is the permanent *Bestia Trionfans*[3] that calls wisdom from its cave. To an artist so creative as the critic, what does

subject matter signify? No more and no less than it does to the novelist and the painter. Like them, he can find his motives everywhere. Treatment is the test. There is nothing that has not in it suggestion or challenge.

ERNEST.   But is Criticism really a creative art?

GILBERT.   Why should it not be? It works with materials, and puts them into a form that is at once new and delightful. What more can one say of poetry? Indeed, I would call criticism a creation within a creation. For just as the great artists, from Homer and Aeschylus down to Shakespeare and Keats,[4] did not go directly to life for their subject-matter, but sought for it in myth, and legend, and ancient tale, so the critic deals with materials that others have, as it were, purified for him, and to which imaginative form and colour have been already added. Nay, more, I would say that the highest Criticism, being the purest form of personal impression, is in its way more creative than creation, as it has least reference to any standard external to itself, and is, in fact, its own reason for existing, and, as the Greeks would put it, in itself, and to itself, an end. Certainly, it is never trammelled by any shackles of verisimilitude. No ignoble considerations of probability, that cowardly concession to the tedious repetitions of domestic or public life, affect it ever. One may appeal from fiction unto fact. But from the soul there is no appeal.

ERNEST.   From the soul?

GILBERT.   Yes, from the soul. That is what the highest criticism really is, the record of one's own soul. It is more fascinating than history, as it is concerned simply with oneself. It is more delightful than philosophy, as its subject is concrete and not abstract, real and not vague. It is the only civilized form of autobiography, as it deals not with the events, but with the thoughts of one's life; not with life's physical accidents of deed or circumstance, but with the spiritual moods and imaginative passions of the mind. I am always amused by the silly vanity of those writers and artists of our day

---

[1]   *masterpiece of style*   I.e., Flaubert's *Madame Bovary*.

[2]   *Mr. Lewis Morris*   Popular Anglo-Welsh poet;   *M. Ohnet* Georges Ohnet, nineteenth-century French novelist, many of whose works were successfully dramatized;   *Mr. Henry Arthur Jones*   Innovative playwright of the late nineteenth century.

[3]   *Bestia Trionfans*   Latin: Triumphant Beast. From the title of sixteenth-century philosopher Giordano Bruno's allegory *Spacio della Bestia Trionfante* (*Expulsion of the Triumphant Beast*).

[4]   *Homer*   Greek poet to whom the authorship of the *Iliad* and the *Odyssey* is attributed (?850 BCE);   *Aeschylus*   Ancient Greek playwright (c. 523–456 BCE);   *Shakespeare*   William Shakespeare, English poet and playwright (1564–1616);   *Keats*   John Keats, English poet (1795–1821).

who seem to imagine that the primary function of the critic is to chatter about their second-rate work. The best that one can say of most modern creative art is that it is just a little less vulgar than reality, and so the critic, with his fine sense of distinction and sure instinct of delicate refinement, will prefer to look into the silver mirror or through the woven veil, and will turn his eyes away from the chaos and clamour of actual existence, though the mirror be tarnished and the veil be torn. His sole aim is to chronicle his own impressions. It is for him that pictures are painted, books written, and marble hewn into form.

ERNEST.   I seem to have heard another theory of Criticism.

GILBERT.   Yes: it has been said by one whose gracious memory we all revere, and the music of whose pipe once lured Proserpina from her Sicilian fields, and made those white feet stir, and not in vain, the Cumnor cowslips, that the proper aim of Criticism is to see the object as in itself it really is.[1] But this is a very serious error, and takes no cognizance of Criticism's most perfect form, which is in its essence purely subjective, and seeks to reveal its own secret and not the secret of another. For the highest Criticism deals with art not as expressive but as impressive purely.

ERNEST.   But is that really so?

GILBERT.   Of course it is. Who cares whether Mr. Ruskin's views on Turner[2] are sound or not? What does it matter? That mighty and majestic prose of his, so fervid and so fiery-coloured in its noble eloquence, so rich in its elaborate symphonic music, so sure and certain, at its best, in subtle choice of word and epithet, is at least as great a work of art as any of those wonderful sunsets that bleach or rot on their corrupted canvases in England's Gallery;[3] greater indeed, one is apt to think at

times, not merely because its equal beauty is more enduring, but on account of the fuller variety of its appeal, soul speaking to soul in those long-cadenced lines, not through form and colour alone, though through these, indeed, completely and without loss, but with intellectual and emotional utterance, with lofty passion and with loftier thought, with imaginative insight, and with poetic aim; greater, I always think, even as Literature is the greater art.
—1890

from *"The Decay of Lying"*[4]

CYRIL.   … [I]n order to avoid making any error I want you to tell me briefly the doctrines of the new aesthetics.

VIVIAN.   Briefly, then, they are these. Art never expresses anything but itself. It has an independent life, just as Thought has, and develops purely on its own lines. It is not necessarily realistic in an age of realism, nor spiritual in an age of faith. So far from being the creation of its time, it is usually in direct opposition to it, and the only history that it preserves for us is the history of its own progress. Sometimes it returns upon its footsteps, and revives some antique form, as happened in the archaistic movement of late Greek Art, and in the Pre-Raphaelite movement of our own day. At other times it entirely anticipates its age, and produces in one century work that it takes another century to understand, to appreciate, and to enjoy. In no case does it reproduce its age. To pass from the art of a time to the time itself is the great mistake that all historians commit.

---

[1] *it has … really is*   Matthew Arnold, whose poem *Thyrsis* attempts to summon the goddess Proserpine from the pastoral landscape of Sicily to the Cumnor hills of England. Arnold discusses the aim of criticism in his essay *The Function of Criticism at the Present Time*.

[2] *Turner*   English landscape painter Joseph Mallord William Turner. Cf. John Ruskin's *Modern Painters*.

[3] *England's Gallery*   The Tate Gallery in London, upon which a major bequest of Turner's paintings was bestowed in 1856.

[4] *The Decay of Lying*   In this Platonic dialogue, Wilde sets out a new theory of aesthetics through the conversation of two characters, Vivian and Cyril (named after Wilde's two sons). Vivian, prompted by Cyril's questioning, has been reading from his essay in progress, called "The Decay of Lying," which explores and confirms Plato's claim in the *Republic* that art is falsehood, yet challenges his assertion that art is a mere imitation of life, and that the lies of art are morally repugnant. On the contrary, Vivian celebrates the lies of art, declaring, "if something cannot be done to check, or at least modify, our monstrous worship of facts, Art will become sterile and Beauty will pass from the land." At the heart of this work is a challenge to the Victorian adherence to realism and advocacy of faithful imitation of nature.

The second doctrine is this. All bad art comes from returning to Life and Nature and elevating them into ideals. Life and Nature may sometimes be used as part of Art's rough material, but before they are of any real service to art they must be translated into artistic conventions. The moment Art surrenders its imaginative medium it surrenders everything. As a method Realism is a complete failure, and the two things that every artist should avoid are modernity of form and modernity of subject matter. To us, who live in the nineteenth century, any century is a suitable subject for art except our own. The only beautiful things are the things that do not concern us. It is, to have the pleasure of quoting myself, exactly because Hecuba is nothing to us that her sorrows are so suitable a motive for a tragedy.[1] Besides, it is only the modern that ever becomes old-fashioned. M. Zola[2] sits down to give us a picture of the Second Empire. Who cares for the Second Empire now? It is out of date. Life goes faster than Realism, but Romanticism is always in front of Life.

The third doctrine is that Life imitates Art far more than Art imitates Life. This results not merely from Life's imitative instinct, but from the fact that the self-conscious aim of Life is to find expression, and that Art offers it certain beautiful forms through which it may realize that energy. It is a theory that has never been put forward before, but it is extremely fruitful, and throws an entirely new light upon the history of Art.

It follows, as a corollary from this, that external Nature also imitates Art. The only effects that she can show us are effects that we have already seen through poetry, or in paintings. This is the secret of Nature's charm, as well as the explanation of Nature's weakness.

The final revelation is that Lying, the telling of beautiful untrue things, is the proper aim of Art. But of this I think I have spoken at sufficient length. And now let us go out on the terrace, where "droops the milk-white peacock like a ghost,"[3] while the evening star "washes the dusk with silver."[4] At twilight nature becomes a wonderfully suggestive effect, and is not without loveliness, though perhaps its chief use is to illustrate quotations from the poets. Come! We have talked long enough.

—1889

Preface[5] to *The Picture of Dorian Gray*

The artist is the creator of beautiful things.

To reveal art and conceal the artist is art's aim.

The critic is he who can translate into another medium or a new material his impression of beautiful things.

The highest as the lowest form of criticism is a mode of autobiography.

Those who find ugly meanings in beautiful things are corrupt without being charming. This is a fault.

Those who find beautiful meanings in beautiful things are cultivated. For these there is hope.

They are the elect[6] to whom beautiful things mean only beauty.

There is no such thing as a moral or an immoral book. Books are well written, or badly written. That is all.

The nineteenth century dislike of Realism is the rage of Caliban[7] seeing his own face in a glass.

The nineteenth century dislike of Romanticism is the rage of Caliban not seeing his own face in a glass.

---

[1] *Hecuba ... tragedy* Hecuba, Queen of Troy when that city was conquered by the Greeks, saw her husband and her sons murdered. In Shakespeare's *Hamlet*, one of the players performing for Hamlet recites an emotional monologue on the terrible fate of Hecuba, prompting Hamlet to wonder, "What's Hecuba to him, or he to Hecuba, / That he should weep for her?" (2.2).

[2] *M. Zola* (Monsieur) Émile Zola, French novelist who played a significant role in the development of literary naturalism. His twenty-novel cycle *Les Rougon-Macquart* (1871–93) is set during the Second French Empire (1852–70).

[3] *droops ... ghost* From "The Princess" by Alfred, Lord Tennyson.

[4] *washes ... silver* From "To the Evening Star" by William Blake.

[5] *Preface* Published in 1891, the year after the novel's first appearance, this preface was a response to the charges of immorality leveled at the novel by numerous critics.

[6] *the elect* In some branches of Christianity, the "elect" are those chosen or preordained for salvation.

[7] *Caliban* The "monster" of Shakespeare's *The Tempest*, Caliban is a native of the island and has been enslaved by Prospero.

The moral life of man forms part of the subject matter of the artist, but the morality of art consists in the perfect use of an imperfect medium.

No artist desires to prove anything. Even things that are true can be proved.

No artist has ethical sympathies. An ethical sympathy in an artist is an unpardonable mannerism of style.

No artist is ever morbid. The artist can express everything.

Thought and language are to the artist instruments of an art.

Vice and virtue are to the artist materials for an art.

From the point of view of form, the type of all the arts is the art of the musician.

From the point of view of feeling, the actor's craft is the type.

All art is at once surface and symbol.

Those who go beneath the surface do so at their peril.

Those who read the symbol do so at their peril.

It is the spectator, and not life, that art really mirrors.

Diversity of opinion about a work of art shows that the work is new, complex, and vital.

When critics disagree the artist is in accord with himself.

We can forgive a man for making a useful thing as long as he does not admire it. The only excuse for making a useless thing is that one admires it intensely.

All art is quite useless.

—1891

The Importance of Being Earnest
A Trivial Comedy for Serious People

THE PERSONS IN THE PLAY

John Worthing, J.P.[1]
Algernon Moncrieff
Rev. Canon Chasuble, D.D.[2]
Merriman, *Butler*
Lane, *Manservant*
Lady Bracknell
Hon.[3] Gwendolen Fairfax
Cecily Cardew
Miss Prism, *Governess*

THE SCENES IN THE PLAY

ACT 1. Algernon Moncrieff's Flat in Half-Moon Street,[4] W.
ACT 2. The Garden at the Manor House, Woolton.[5]
ACT 3. Drawing-Room at the Manor House, Woolton.

TIME: The Present.

ACT 1

SCENE

(*Morning-room in Algernon's flat in Half-Moon Street. The room is luxuriously and artistically furnished. The sound of a piano is heard in the adjoining room.*)

(*Lane is arranging afternoon tea on the table, and after the music has ceased, Algernon enters.*)

ALGERNON.   Did you hear what I was playing, Lane?
LANE.   I didn't think it polite to listen, sir.
ALGERNON.   I'm sorry for that, for your sake. I don't play accurately—any one can play accurately—but I play with wonderful expression. As far as the piano is concerned, sentiment is my forte. I keep science for Life.
LANE.   Yes, sir.
ALGERNON.   And, speaking of the science of Life, have you got the cucumber sandwiches[6] cut for Lady Bracknell?

---

[1] *J.P.*   Justice of the Peace.

[2] *D.D.*   Doctor of Divinity.

[3] *Hon.*   I.e., The Honorable. The honorific in this case designates the daughter of a peer below the rank of Earl.

[4] *Half-Moon Street*   Street located in a fashionable area of London.

[5] *Woolton*   A fictional location.

[6] *cucumber sandwiches*   Small sandwiches of cucumber on thinly sliced bread, a staple of afternoon tea in polite English society.

LANE. Yes, sir. (*Hands them on a salver.*[1])

ALGERNON. (*Inspects them, takes two, and sits down on the sofa.*) Oh! … by the way, Lane, I see from your book that on Thursday night, when Lord Shoreman and Mr.
15 Worthing were dining with me, eight bottles of champagne are entered as having been consumed.

LANE. Yes, sir; eight bottles and a pint.

ALGERNON. Why is it that at a bachelor's establishment the servants invariably drink the champagne? I ask
20 merely for information.

LANE. I attribute it to the superior quality of the wine, sir. I have often observed that in married households the champagne is rarely of a first-rate brand.

ALGERNON. Good heavens! Is marriage so demoralising
25 as that?

LANE. I believe it is a very pleasant state, sir. I have had very little experience of it myself up to the present. I have only been married once. That was in consequence of a misunderstanding between myself and a young
30 person.

ALGERNON. (*Languidly.*) I don't know that I am much interested in your family life, Lane.

LANE. No, sir; it is not a very interesting subject. I never think of it myself.

35 ALGERNON. Very natural, I am sure. That will do, Lane, thank you.

LANE. Thank you, sir. (*Lane goes out.*)

ALGERNON. Lane's views on marriage seem somewhat lax. Really, if the lower orders don't set us a good
40 example, what on earth is the use of them? They seem, as a class, to have absolutely no sense of moral responsibility.

(*Enter Lane.*)

LANE. Mr. Ernest Worthing.

(*Enter Jack. Lane goes out.*)

ALGERNON. How are you, my dear Ernest? What brings
45 you up to town?

JACK. Oh, pleasure, pleasure! What else should bring one anywhere? Eating as usual, I see, Algy!

ALGERNON. (*Stiffly.*) I believe it is customary in good society to take some slight refreshment at five o'clock.
50 Where have you been since last Thursday?

JACK. (*Sitting down on the sofa.*) In the country.

ALGERNON. What on earth do you do there?

JACK. (*Pulling off his gloves.*) When one is in town[2] one amuses oneself. When one is in the country one amuses
55 other people. It is excessively boring.

ALGERNON. And who are the people you amuse?

JACK. (*Airily.*) Oh, neighbours, neighbours.

ALGERNON. Got nice neighbours in your part of Shropshire?

60 JACK. Perfectly horrid! Never speak to one of them.

ALGERNON. How immensely you must amuse them! (*Goes over and takes sandwich.*) By the way, Shropshire is your county, is it not?

JACK. Eh? Shropshire? Yes, of course. Hallo! Why all
65 these cups? Why cucumber sandwiches? Why such reckless extravagance in one so young? Who is coming to tea?

ALGERNON. Oh! merely Aunt Augusta and Gwendolen.

JACK. How perfectly delightful!

70 ALGERNON. Yes, that is all very well; but I am afraid Aunt Augusta won't quite approve of your being here.

JACK. May I ask why?

ALGERNON. My dear fellow, the way you flirt with Gwendolen is perfectly disgraceful. It is almost as bad as
75 the way Gwendolen flirts with you.

JACK. I am in love with Gwendolen. I have come up to town expressly to propose to her.

ALGERNON. I thought you had come up for pleasure? … I call that business.

80 JACK. How utterly unromantic you are!

ALGERNON. I really don't see anything romantic in proposing. It is very romantic to be in love. But there is nothing romantic about a definite proposal. Why, one may be accepted. One usually is, I believe. Then the
85 excitement is all over. The very essence of romance is uncertainty. If ever I get married, I'll certainly try to forget the fact.

---

1 *salver* Serving tray, typically silver.

2 *in town* In London.

JACK. I have no doubt about that, dear Algy. The Divorce Court was specially invented for people whose memories are so curiously constituted.

ALGERNON. Oh! there is no use speculating on that subject. Divorces are made in Heaven—(*Jack puts out his hand to take a sandwich. Algernon at once interferes.*) Please don't touch the cucumber sandwiches. They are ordered specially for Aunt Augusta. (*Takes one and eats it.*)

JACK. Well, you have been eating them all the time.

ALGERNON. That is quite a different matter. She is my aunt. (*Takes plate from below.*) Have some bread and butter. The bread and butter is for Gwendolen. Gwendolen is devoted to bread and butter.

JACK. (*Advancing to table and helping himself.*) And very good bread and butter it is too.

ALGERNON. Well, my dear fellow, you need not eat as if you were going to eat it all. You behave as if you were married to her already. You are not married to her already, and I don't think you ever will be.

JACK. Why on earth do you say that?

ALGERNON. Well, in the first place girls never marry the men they flirt with. Girls don't think it right.

JACK. Oh, that is nonsense!

ALGERNON. It isn't. It is a great truth. It accounts for the extraordinary number of bachelors that one sees all over the place. In the second place, I don't give my consent.

JACK. Your consent!

ALGERNON. My dear fellow, Gwendolen is my first cousin. And before I allow you to marry her, you will have to clear up the whole question of Cecily. (*Rings bell.*)

JACK. Cecily! What on earth do you mean? What do you mean, Algy, by Cecily! I don't know any one of the name of Cecily.

(*Enter Lane.*)

ALGERNON. Bring me that cigarette case Mr. Worthing left in the smoking-room the last time he dined here.

LANE. Yes, sir.

(*Lane goes out.*)

JACK. Do you mean to say you have had my cigarette case all this time? I wish to goodness you had let me know. I have been writing frantic letters to Scotland Yard about it. I was very nearly offering a large reward.

ALGERNON. Well, I wish you would offer one. I happen to be more than usually hard up.

JACK. There is no good offering a large reward now that the thing is found.

(*Enter Lane with the cigarette case on a salver. Algernon takes it at once. Lane goes out.*)

ALGERNON. I think that is rather mean of you, Ernest, I must say. (*Opens case and examines it.*) However, it makes no matter, for, now that I look at the inscription inside, I find that the thing isn't yours after all.

JACK. Of course it's mine. (*Moving to him.*) You have seen me with it a hundred times, and you have no right whatsoever to read what is written inside. It is a very ungentlemanly thing to read a private cigarette case.

ALGERNON. Oh! it is absurd to have a hard and fast rule about what one should read and what one shouldn't. More than half of modern culture depends on what one shouldn't read.

JACK. I am quite aware of the fact, and I don't propose to discuss modern culture. It isn't the sort of thing one should talk of in private. I simply want my cigarette case back.

ALGERNON. Yes; but this isn't your cigarette case. This cigarette case is a present from some one of the name of Cecily, and you said you didn't know any one of that name.

JACK. Well, if you want to know, Cecily happens to be my aunt.

ALGERNON. Your aunt!

JACK. Yes. Charming old lady she is, too. Lives at Tunbridge Wells.[1] Just give it back to me, Algy.

ALGERNON. (*Retreating to back of sofa.*) But why does she call herself little Cecily if she is your aunt and lives at Tunbridge Wells? (*Reading.*) "From little Cecily with her fondest love."

---

[1] *Tunbridge Wells* Town in western Kent, southeast of London, at one time a fashionable resort town.

JACK. (*Moving to sofa and kneeling upon it.*) My dear fellow, what on earth is there in that? Some aunts are tall, some aunts are not tall. That is a matter that surely an aunt may be allowed to decide for herself. You seem to think that every aunt should be exactly like your aunt! That is absurd! For Heaven's sake give me back my cigarette case. (*Follows Algernon round the room.*)

ALGERNON. Yes. But why does your aunt call you her uncle? "From little Cecily, with her fondest love to her dear Uncle Jack." There is no objection, I admit, to an aunt being a small aunt, but why an aunt, no matter what her size may be, should call her own nephew her uncle, I can't quite make out. Besides, your name isn't Jack at all; it is Ernest.

JACK. It isn't Ernest; it's Jack.

ALGERNON. You have always told me it was Ernest. I have introduced you to every one as Ernest. You answer to the name of Ernest. You look as if your name was Ernest. You are the most earnest-looking person I ever saw in my life. It is perfectly absurd your saying that your name isn't Ernest. It's on your cards. Here is one of them. (*Taking it from case.*) "Mr. Ernest Worthing, B. 4, The Albany."[1] I'll keep this as a proof that your name is Ernest if ever you attempt to deny it to me, or to Gwendolen, or to any one else. (*Puts the card in his pocket.*)

JACK. Well, my name is Ernest in town and Jack in the country, and the cigarette case was given to me in the country.

ALGERNON. Yes, but that does not account for the fact that your small Aunt Cecily, who lives at Tunbridge Wells, calls you her dear uncle. Come, old boy, you had much better have the thing out at once.

JACK. My dear Algy, you talk exactly as if you were a dentist. It is very vulgar to talk like a dentist when one isn't a dentist. It produces a false impression.

ALGERNON. Well, that is exactly what dentists always do. Now, go on! Tell me the whole thing. I may mention that I have always suspected you of being a confirmed and secret Bunburyist; and I am quite sure of it now.

JACK. Bunburyist? What on earth do you mean by a Bunburyist?

ALGERNON. I'll reveal to you the meaning of that incomparable expression as soon as you are kind enough to inform me why you are Ernest in town and Jack in the country.

JACK. Well, produce my cigarette case first.

ALGERNON. Here it is. (*Hands cigarette case.*) Now produce your explanation, and pray make it improbable. (*Sits on sofa.*)

JACK. My dear fellow, there is nothing improbable about my explanation at all. In fact it's perfectly ordinary. Old Mr. Thomas Cardew, who adopted me when I was a little boy, made me in his will guardian to his granddaughter, Miss Cecily Cardew. Cecily, who addresses me as her uncle from motives of respect that you could not possibly appreciate, lives at my place in the country under the charge of her admirable governess, Miss Prism.

ALGERNON. Where is that place in the country, by the way?

JACK. That is nothing to you, dear boy. You are not going to be invited … I may tell you candidly that the place is not in Shropshire.

ALGERNON. I suspected that, my dear fellow! I have Bunburyed all over Shropshire on two separate occasions. Now, go on. Why are you Ernest in town and Jack in the country?

JACK. My dear Algy, I don't know whether you will be able to understand my real motives. You are hardly serious enough. When one is placed in the position of guardian, one has to adopt a very high moral tone on all subjects. It's one's duty to do so. And as a high moral tone can hardly be said to conduce very much to either one's health or one's happiness, in order to get up to town I have always pretended to have a younger brother of the name of Ernest, who lives in the Albany, and gets into the most dreadful scrapes. That, my dear Algy, is the whole truth pure and simple.

ALGERNON. The truth is rarely pure and never simple. Modern life would be very tedious if it were either, and modern literature a complete impossibility!

JACK. That wouldn't be at all a bad thing.

---

1 *The Albany* Fashionable apartment block for London bachelors.

ALGERNON.   Literary criticism is not your forte, my dear fellow. Don't try it. You should leave that to people who haven't been at a University. They do it so well in the daily papers. What you really are is a Bunburyist. I was quite right in saying you were a Bunburyist. You are one of the most advanced Bunburyists I know.

JACK.   What on earth do you mean?

ALGERNON.   You have invented a very useful younger brother called Ernest, in order that you may be able to come up to town as often as you like. I have invented an invaluable permanent invalid called Bunbury, in order that I may be able to go down into the country whenever I choose. Bunbury is perfectly invaluable. If it wasn't for Bunbury's extraordinary bad health, for instance, I wouldn't be able to dine with you at Willis's to-night, for I have been really engaged to Aunt Augusta for more than a week.

JACK.   I haven't asked you to dine with me anywhere to-night.

ALGERNON.   I know. You are absurdly careless about sending out invitations. It is very foolish of you. Nothing annoys people so much as not receiving invitations.

JACK.   You had much better dine with your Aunt Augus-ta.

ALGERNON.   I haven't the smallest intention of doing anything of the kind. To begin with, I dined there on Monday, and once a week is quite enough to dine with one's own relations. In the second place, whenever I do dine there I am always treated as a member of the family, and sent down[1] with either no woman at all, or two. In the third place, I know perfectly well whom she will place me next to, to-night. She will place me next Mary Farquhar, who always flirts with her own husband across the dinner-table. That is not very pleasant. Indeed, it is not even decent ... and that sort of thing is enormously on the increase. The amount of women in London who flirt with their own husbands is perfectly scandalous. It looks so bad. It is simply washing one's clean linen in public. Besides, now that I know you to be a confirmed Bunburyist I naturally want to talk to you about Bunburying. I want to tell you the rules.

JACK.   I'm not a Bunburyist at all. If Gwendolen accepts me, I am going to kill my brother, indeed I think I'll kill him in any case. Cecily is a little too much interested in him. It is rather a bore. So I am going to get rid of Ernest. And I strongly advise you to do the same with Mr. ... with your invalid friend who has the absurd name.

ALGERNON.   Nothing will induce me to part with Bunbury, and if you ever get married, which seems to me extremely problematic, you will be very glad to know Bunbury. A man who marries without knowing Bunbury has a very tedious time of it.

JACK.   That is nonsense. If I marry a charming girl like Gwendolen, and she is the only girl I ever saw in my life that I would marry, I certainly won't want to know Bunbury.

ALGERNON.   Then your wife will. You don't seem to realise, that in married life three is company and two is none.

JACK.   (Sententiously.[2]) That, my dear young friend, is the theory that the corrupt French Drama has been propounding for the last fifty years.

ALGERNON.   Yes; and that the happy English home has proved in half the time.

JACK.   For heaven's sake, don't try to be cynical. It's perfectly easy to be cynical.

ALGERNON.   My dear fellow, it isn't easy to be anything nowadays. There's such a lot of beastly competition about. (The sound of an electric bell is heard.) Ah! that must be Aunt Augusta. Only relatives, or creditors, ever ring in that Wagnerian[3] manner. Now, if I get her out of the way for ten minutes, so that you can have an opportunity for proposing to Gwendolen, may I dine with you to-night at Willis's?

JACK.   I suppose so, if you want to.

ALGERNON.   Yes, but you must be serious about it. I hate people who are not serious about meals. It is so shallow of them.

---

[1] *sent down* I.e., sent from the drawing-room (typically upstairs) down to the dining-room (typically on a lower floor).

[2] *Sententiously* Pompously, as if imparting a moral lesson.

[3] *Wagnerian* Suggesting the music of German composer Richard Wagner (1813–83), known for dramatic, stirring compositions such as *Tannhäuser*, *Lohengrin*, and *Der Ring des Nibelungen*.

(*Enter Lane.*)

LANE. Lady Bracknell and Miss Fairfax.

(*Algernon goes forward to meet them. Enter Lady Bracknell and Gwendolen.*)

LADY BRACKNELL. Good afternoon, dear Algernon, I hope you are behaving very well.

330 ALGERNON. I'm feeling very well, Aunt Augusta.

LADY BRACKNELL. That's not quite the same thing. In fact the two things rarely go together. (*Sees Jack and bows to him with icy coldness.*)

ALGERNON. (*To Gwendolen.*) Dear me, you are smart!

335 GWENDOLEN. I am always smart! Am I not, Mr. Worthing?

JACK. You're quite perfect, Miss Fairfax.

GWENDOLEN. Oh! I hope I am not that. It would leave no room for developments, and I intend to develop in 340 many directions.

(*Gwendolen and Jack sit down together in the corner.*)

LADY BRACKNELL. I'm sorry if we are a little late, Algernon, but I was obliged to call on dear Lady Harbury. I hadn't been there since her poor husband's death. I never saw a woman so altered; she looks quite 345 twenty years younger. And now I'll have a cup of tea, and one of those nice cucumber sandwiches you promised me.

ALGERNON. Certainly, Aunt Augusta. (*Goes over to teatable.*)

350 LADY BRACKNELL. Won't you come and sit here, Gwendolen?

GWENDOLEN. Thanks, mamma, I'm quite comfortable where I am.

ALGERNON. (*Picking up empty plate in horror.*) Good 355 heavens! Lane! Why are there no cucumber sandwiches? I ordered them specially.

LANE. (*Gravely.*) There were no cucumbers in the market this morning, sir. I went down twice.

ALGERNON. No cucumbers!

360 LANE. No, sir. Not even for ready money.

ALGERNON. That will do, Lane, thank you.

LANE. Thank you, sir. (*Goes out.*)

ALGERNON. I am greatly distressed, Aunt Augusta, about there being no cucumbers, not even for ready 365 money.

LADY BRACKNELL. It really makes no matter, Algernon. I had some crumpets with Lady Harbury, who seems to me to be living entirely for pleasure now.

ALGERNON. I hear her hair has turned quite gold from 370 grief.

LADY BRACKNELL. It certainly has changed its colour. From what cause I, of course, cannot say. (*Algernon crosses and hands tea.*) Thank you. I've quite a treat for you to-night, Algernon. I am going to send you down 375 with Mary Farquhar. She is such a nice woman, and so attentive to her husband. It's delightful to watch them.

ALGERNON. I am afraid, Aunt Augusta, I shall have to give up the pleasure of dining with you to-night after all.

LADY BRACKNELL. (*Frowning.*) I hope not, Algernon. It 380 would put my table completely out. Your uncle would have to dine upstairs. Fortunately he is accustomed to that.

ALGERNON. It is a great bore, and, I need hardly say, a terrible disappointment to me, but the fact is I have just 385 had a telegram to say that my poor friend Bunbury is very ill again. (*Exchanges glances with Jack.*) They seem to think I should be with him.

LADY BRACKNELL. It is very strange. This Mr. Bunbury seems to suffer from curiously bad health.

390 ALGERNON. Yes; poor Bunbury is a dreadful invalid.

LADY BRACKNELL. Well, I must say, Algernon, that I think it is high time that Mr. Bunbury made up his mind whether he was going to live or to die. This shilly-shallying with the question is absurd. Nor do I in any 395 way approve of the modern sympathy with invalids. I consider it morbid. Illness of any kind is hardly a thing to be encouraged in others. Health is the primary duty of life. I am always telling that to your poor uncle, but he never seems to take much notice … as far as any 400 improvement in his ailment goes. I should be much obliged if you would ask Mr. Bunbury, from me, to be kind enough not to have a relapse on Saturday, for I rely on you to arrange my music for me. It is my last reception, and one wants something that will encourage conversation, particularly at the end of the season[1] when every one has practically said whatever they had to say, which, in most cases, was probably not much.

ALGERNON.   I'll speak to Bunbury, Aunt Augusta, if he is still conscious, and I think I can promise you he'll be all right by Saturday. Of course the music is a great difficulty. You see, if one plays good music, people don't listen, and if one plays bad music people don't talk. But I'll run over the programme I've drawn out, if you will kindly come into the next room for a moment.

LADY BRACKNELL.   Thank you, Algernon. It is very thoughtful of you. (*Rising, and following Algernon.*) I'm sure the programme will be delightful, after a few expurgations. French songs I cannot possibly allow. People always seem to think that they are improper, and either look shocked, which is vulgar, or laugh, which is worse. But German sounds a thoroughly respectable language, and indeed, I believe is so. Gwendolen, you will accompany me.

GWENDOLEN.   Certainly, mamma.

(*Lady Bracknell and Algernon go into the music-room, Gwendolen remains behind.*)

JACK.   Charming day it has been, Miss Fairfax.

GWENDOLEN.   Pray don't talk to me about the weather, Mr. Worthing. Whenever people talk to me about the weather, I always feel quite certain that they mean something else. And that makes me so nervous.

JACK.   I do mean something else.

GWENDOLEN.   I thought so. In fact, I am never wrong.

JACK.   And I would like to be allowed to take advantage of Lady Bracknell's temporary absence ...

GWENDOLEN.   I would certainly advise you to do so. Mamma has a way of coming back suddenly into a room that I have often had to speak to her about.

JACK.   (*Nervously.*) Miss Fairfax, ever since I met you I have admired you more than any girl ... I have ever met since ... I met you.

GWENDOLEN.   Yes, I am quite well aware of the fact. And I often wish that in public, at any rate, you had been more demonstrative. For me you have always had an irresistible fascination. Even before I met you I was far from indifferent to you. (*Jack looks at her in amazement.*) We live, as I hope you know, Mr. Worthing, in an age of ideals. The fact is constantly mentioned in the more expensive monthly magazines, and has reached the provincial[2] pulpits, I am told; and my ideal has always been to love some one of the name of Ernest. There is something in that name that inspires absolute confidence. The moment Algernon first mentioned to me that he had a friend called Ernest, I knew I was destined to love you.

JACK.   You really love me, Gwendolen?

GWENDOLEN.   Passionately!

JACK.   Darling! You don't know how happy you've made me.

GWENDOLEN.   My own Ernest!

JACK.   But you don't really mean to say that you couldn't love me if my name wasn't Ernest?

GWENDOLEN.   But your name is Ernest.

JACK.   Yes, I know it is. But supposing it was something else? Do you mean to say you couldn't love me then?

GWENDOLEN.   (*Glibly.*) Ah! that is clearly a metaphysical speculation, and like most metaphysical speculations has very little reference at all to the actual facts of real life, as we know them.

JACK.   Personally, darling, to speak quite candidly, I don't much care about the name of Ernest ... I don't think the name suits me at all.

GWENDOLEN.   It suits you perfectly. It is a divine name. It has a music of its own. It produces vibrations.

JACK.   Well, really, Gwendolen, I must say that I think there are lots of other much nicer names. I think Jack, for instance, a charming name.

GWENDOLEN.   Jack? ... No, there is very little music in the name Jack, if any at all, indeed. It does not thrill. It produces absolutely no vibrations ... I have known

---

1   *reception*   Evening party at which guests are formally received or welcomed by the hosts; *the season*   Traditionally, the period of the year when members of the upper classes left their country houses to spend time in London for social and political purposes.

2   *provincial*   "Province" does not indicate a formal British jurisdiction; "the provinces" is a colloquial term for all areas of the country that are some distance from London.

several Jacks, and they all, without exception, were more
than usually plain. Besides, Jack is a notorious
domesticity for John! And I pity any woman who is
married to a man called John. She would probably never
be allowed to know the entrancing pleasure of a single
moment's solitude. The only really safe name is Ernest.

JACK. Gwendolen, I must get christened at once—I
mean we must get married at once. There is no time to
be lost.

GWENDOLEN. Married, Mr. Worthing?

JACK. (*Astounded.*) Well … surely. You know that I love
you, and you led me to believe, Miss Fairfax, that you
were not absolutely indifferent to me.

GWENDOLEN. I adore you. But you haven't proposed to
me yet. Nothing has been said at all about marriage.
The subject has not even been touched on.

JACK. Well … may I propose to you now?

GWENDOLEN. I think it would be an admirable
opportunity. And to spare you any possible
disappointment, Mr. Worthing, I think it only fair to
tell you quite frankly before-hand that I am fully
determined to accept you.

JACK. Gwendolen!

GWENDOLEN. Yes, Mr. Worthing, what have you got to
say to me?

JACK. You know what I have got to say to you.

GWENDOLEN. Yes, but you don't say it.

JACK. Gwendolen, will you marry me? (*Goes on his
knees.*)

GWENDOLEN. Of course I will, darling. How long you
have been about it! I am afraid you have had very little
experience in how to propose.

JACK. My own one, I have never loved any one in the
world but you.

GWENDOLEN. Yes, but men often propose for practice.
I know my brother Gerald does. All my girl-friends tell
me so. What wonderfully blue eyes you have, Ernest!
They are quite, quite, blue. I hope you will always look
at me just like that, especially when there are other
people present. (*Enter Lady Bracknell.*)

LADY BRACKNELL. Mr. Worthing! Rise, sir, from this
semi-recumbent posture. It is most indecorous.

GWENDOLEN. Mamma! (*He tries to rise; she restrains
him.*) I must beg you to retire. This is no place for you.
Besides, Mr. Worthing has not quite finished yet.

LADY BRACKNELL. Finished what, may I ask?

GWENDOLEN. I am engaged to Mr. Worthing, mamma.

(*They rise together.*)

LADY BRACKNELL. Pardon me, you are not engaged to
any one. When you do become engaged to some one, I,
or your father, should his health permit him, will
inform you of the fact. An engagement should come on
a young girl as a surprise, pleasant or unpleasant, as the
case may be. It is hardly a matter that she could be
allowed to arrange for herself … And now I have a few
questions to put to you, Mr. Worthing. While I am
making these inquiries, you, Gwendolen, will wait for
me below in the carriage.

GWENDOLEN. (*Reproachfully.*) Mamma!

LADY BRACKNELL. In the carriage, Gwendolen!

(*Gwendolen goes to the door. She and Jack blow kisses to
each other behind Lady Bracknell's back. Lady Bracknell
looks vaguely about as if she could not understand what the
noise was. Finally turns round.*)

Gwendolen, the carriage!

GWENDOLEN. Yes, mamma. (*Goes out, looking back at
Jack.*)

LADY BRACKNELL. (*Sitting down.*) You can take a seat,
Mr. Worthing. (*Looks in her pocket for note-book and
pencil.*)

JACK. Thank you, Lady Bracknell, I prefer standing.

LADY BRACKNELL. (*Pencil and note-book in hand.*) I feel
bound to tell you that you are not down on my list of
eligible young men, although I have the same list as the
dear Duchess of Bolton has. We work together, in fact.
However, I am quite ready to enter your name, should
your answers be what a really affectionate mother
requires. Do you smoke?

JACK. Well, yes, I must admit I smoke.

LADY BRACKNELL. I am glad to hear it. A man should
always have an occupation of some kind. There are far
too many idle men in London as it is. How old are you?

JACK.   Twenty-nine.

LADY BRACKNELL.   A very good age to be married at. I have always been of opinion that a man who desires to get married should know either everything or nothing.
560 Which do you know?

JACK.   (*After some hesitation.*) I know nothing, Lady Bracknell.

LADY BRACKNELL.   I am pleased to hear it. I do not approve of anything that tampers with natural
565 ignorance. Ignorance is like a delicate exotic fruit; touch it and the bloom is gone. The whole theory of modern education is radically unsound. Fortunately in England, at any rate, education produces no effect whatsoever. If it did, it would prove a serious danger to the upper
570 classes, and probably lead to acts of violence in Grosvenor Square.[1] What is your income?

JACK.   Between seven and eight thousand a year.

LADY BRACKNELL.   (*Makes a note in her book.*) In land, or in investments?

575 JACK.   In investments, chiefly.

LADY BRACKNELL.   That is satisfactory. What between the duties[2] expected of one during one's lifetime, and the duties exacted from one after one's death, land has ceased to be either a profit or a pleasure. It gives one
580 position, and prevents one from keeping it up. That's all that can be said about land.

JACK.   I have a country house with some land, of course, attached to it, about fifteen hundred acres, I believe; but I don't depend on that for my real income. In fact, as far
585 as I can make out, the poachers are the only people who make anything out of it.

LADY BRACKNELL.   A country house! How many bedrooms? Well, that point can be cleared up afterwards. You have a town house, I hope? A girl with
590 a simple, unspoiled nature, like Gwendolen, could hardly be expected to reside in the country.

JACK.   Well, I own a house in Belgrave Square,[3] but it is let by the year to Lady Bloxham. Of course, I can get it

back whenever I like, at six months' notice.

595 LADY BRACKNELL.   Lady Bloxham? I don't know her.

JACK.   Oh, she goes about very little. She is a lady considerably advanced in years.

LADY BRACKNELL.   Ah, nowadays that is no guarantee of respectability of character. What number in Belgrave
600 Square?

JACK.   149.

LADY BRACKNELL.   (*Shaking her head.*) The unfashionable side. I thought there was something. However, that could easily be altered.

605 JACK.   Do you mean the fashion, or the side?

LADY BRACKNELL.   (*Sternly.*) Both, if necessary, I presume. What are your politics?

JACK.   Well, I am afraid I really have none. I am a Liberal Unionist.[4]

610 LADY BRACKNELL.   Oh, they count as Tories. They dine with us. Or come in the evening, at any rate. Now to minor matters. Are your parents living?

JACK.   I have lost both my parents.

LADY BRACKNELL.   To lose one parent, Mr. Worthing,
615 may be regarded as a misfortune; to lose both looks like carelessness. Who was your father? He was evidently a man of some wealth. Was he born in what the Radical papers call the purple of commerce,[5] or did he rise from the ranks of the aristocracy?

620 JACK.   I am afraid I really don't know. The fact is, Lady Bracknell, I said I had lost my parents. It would be nearer the truth to say that my parents seem to have lost me … I don't actually know who I am by birth. I was … well, I was found.

625 LADY BRACKNELL.   Found!

JACK.   The late Mr. Thomas Cardew, an old gentleman of a very charitable and kindly disposition, found me, and gave me the name of Worthing, because he happened to have a first-class ticket for Worthing in his

---

1 *Grosvenor Square*   Located in a fashionable part of central London.

2 *duties*   Taxes.

3 *Belgrave Square*   City square and garden in the affluent district of Belgravia in Central London, home at the time to several of the nobility.

4 *Liberal Unionist*   The Liberal Unionists, who in 1886 had broken away from the Liberal party in reaction to Prime Minister William Gladstone's support for Irish Home Rule, occupied the political center between the two large parties, the Liberals and the Conservatives.

5 *Was he born … the purple of commerce*   I.e., was he born into a wealthy merchant or trading family. (The color purple is traditionally associated with royalty.)

pocket at the time. Worthing is a place in Sussex. It is a seaside resort.

LADY BRACKNELL.   Where did the charitable gentleman who had a first-class ticket for this seaside resort find you?

JACK.   (*Gravely.*) In a hand-bag.

LADY BRACKNELL.   A hand-bag?

JACK.   (*Very seriously.*) Yes, Lady Bracknell. I was in a hand-bag—a somewhat large, black leather hand-bag, with handles to it—an ordinary hand-bag in fact.

LADY BRACKNELL.   In what locality did this Mr. James, or Thomas, Cardew come across this ordinary hand-bag?

JACK.   In the cloak-room at Victoria Station.[1] It was given to him in mistake for his own.

LADY BRACKNELL.   The cloak-room at Victoria Station?

JACK.   Yes. The Brighton line.

LADY BRACKNELL.   The line is immaterial. Mr. Worth-ing, I confess I feel somewhat bewildered by what you have just told me. To be born, or at any rate bred, in a hand-bag, whether it had handles or not, seems to me to display a contempt for the ordinary decencies of family life that reminds one of the worst excesses of the French Revolution. And I presume you know what that unfortunate movement led to? As for the particular locality in which the hand-bag was found, a cloak-room at a railway station might serve to conceal a social indiscretion—has probably, indeed, been used for that purpose before now—but it could hardly be regarded as an assured basis for a recognised position in good society.

JACK.   May I ask you then what you would advise me to do? I need hardly say I would do anything in the world to ensure Gwendolen's happiness.

LADY BRACKNELL.   I would strongly advise you, Mr. Worthing, to try and acquire some relations as soon as possible, and to make a definite effort to produce at any rate one parent, of either sex, before the season is quite over.

JACK.   Well, I don't see how I could possibly manage to do that. I can produce the hand-bag at any moment. It is in my dressing-room at home. I really think that

should satisfy you, Lady Bracknell.

LADY BRACKNELL.   Me, sir! What has it to do with me? You can hardly imagine that I and Lord Bracknell would dream of allowing our only daughter—a girl brought up with the utmost care—to marry into a cloak-room, and form an alliance with a parcel? Good morning, Mr. Worthing!

(*Lady Bracknell sweeps out in majestic indignation.*)

JACK.   Good morning! (*Algernon, from the other room, strikes up the Wedding March. Jack looks perfectly furious, and goes to the door.*) For goodness' sake don't play that ghastly tune, Algy. How idiotic you are!

(*The music stops and Algernon enters cheerily.*)

ALGERNON.   Didn't it go off all right, old boy? You don't mean to say Gwendolen refused you? I know it is a way she has. She is always refusing people. I think it is most ill-natured of her.

JACK.   Oh, Gwendolen is as right as a trivet.[2] As far as she is concerned, we are engaged. Her mother is perfectly unbearable. Never met such a Gorgon[3] ... I don't really know what a Gorgon is like, but I am quite sure that Lady Bracknell is one. In any case, she is a monster, without being a myth, which is rather unfair ... I beg your pardon, Algy, I suppose I shouldn't talk about your own aunt in that way before you.

ALGERNON.   My dear boy, I love hearing my relations abused. It is the only thing that makes me put up with them at all. Relations are simply a tedious pack of people, who haven't got the remotest knowledge of how to live, nor the smallest instinct about when to die.

JACK.   Oh, that is nonsense!

ALGERNON.   It isn't!

JACK.   Well, I won't argue about the matter. You always want to argue about things.

---

[1] *Victoria Station*   London railway station located in Belgravia.

[2] *as right as a trivet*   Proverbial expression indicating stability (a trivet is a three-footed stand or support).

[3] *Gorgon*   In Greek mythology the three Gorgons are sisters who have repulsive features (including snakes growing out of their heads instead of hair); anyone who looks at them turns into stone.

ALGERNON.   That is exactly what things were originally made for.

JACK.   Upon my word, if I thought that, I'd shoot myself … (*A pause.*) You don't think there is any chance of Gwendolen becoming like her mother in about a hundred and fifty years, do you, Algy?

ALGERNON.   All women become like their mothers. That is their tragedy. No man does. That's his.

JACK.   Is that clever?

ALGERNON.   It is perfectly phrased! and quite as true as any observation in civilized life should be.

JACK.   I am sick to death of cleverness. Everybody is clever nowadays. You can't go anywhere without meeting clever people. The thing has become an absolute public nuisance. I wish to goodness we had a few fools left.

ALGERNON.   We have.

JACK.   I should extremely like to meet them. What do they talk about?

ALGERNON.   The fools? Oh! about the clever people, of course.

JACK.   What fools!

ALGERNON.   By the way, did you tell Gwendolen the truth about your being Ernest in town, and Jack in the country?

JACK.   (*In a very patronising manner.*) My dear fellow, the truth isn't quite the sort of thing one tells to a nice, sweet, refined girl. What extraordinary ideas you have about the way to behave to a woman!

ALGERNON.   The only way to behave to a woman is to make love to her,[1] if she is pretty, and to some one else, if she is plain.

JACK.   Oh, that is nonsense.

ALGERNON.   What about your brother? What about the profligate Ernest?

JACK.   Oh, before the end of the week I shall have got rid of him. I'll say he died in Paris of apoplexy.[2] Lots of people die of apoplexy, quite suddenly, don't they?

ALGERNON.   Yes, but it's hereditary, my dear fellow. It's a sort of thing that runs in families. You had much better say a severe chill.

JACK.   You are sure a severe chill isn't hereditary, or anything of that kind?

ALGERNON.   Of course it isn't!

JACK.   Very well, then. My poor brother Ernest is carried off suddenly, in Paris, by a severe chill. That gets rid of him.

ALGERNON.   But I thought you said that … Miss Cardew was a little too much interested in your poor brother Ernest? Won't she feel his loss a good deal?

JACK.   Oh, that is all right. Cecily is not a silly romantic girl, I am glad to say. She has got a capital appetite, goes on long walks, and pays no attention at all to her lessons.

ALGERNON.   I would rather like to see Cecily.

JACK.   I will take very good care you never do. She is excessively pretty, and she is only just eighteen.

ALGERNON.   Have you told Gwendolen yet that you have an excessively pretty ward who is only just eighteen?

JACK.   Oh! one doesn't blurt these things out to people. Cecily and Gwendolen are perfectly certain to be extremely great friends. I'll bet you anything you like that half an hour after they have met, they will be calling each other sister.

ALGERNON.   Women only do that when they have called each other a lot of other things first. Now, my dear boy, if we want to get a good table at Willis's, we really must go and dress. Do you know it is nearly seven?

JACK.   (*Irritably.*) Oh! It always is nearly seven.

ALGERNON.   Well, I'm hungry.

JACK.   I never knew you when you weren't …

ALGERNON.   What shall we do after dinner? Go to a theatre?

JACK.   Oh no! I loathe listening.

ALGERNON.   Well, let us go to the Club?

JACK.   Oh, no! I hate talking.

ALGERNON.   Well, we might trot round to the Empire[3] at ten?

JACK.   Oh, no! I can't bear looking at things. It is so silly.

ALGERNON.   Well, what shall we do?

JACK.   Nothing!

---

1   *make love to her*   Flirt with her.

2   *apoplexy*   Stroke.

3   *the Empire*   Theater that often featured risqué variety shows.

ALGERNON. It is awfully hard work doing nothing. However, I don't mind hard work where there is no definite object of any kind.

(*Enter Lane.*)

LANE. Miss Fairfax.

(*Enter Gwendolen. Lane goes out.*)

ALGERNON. Gwendolen, upon my word!

GWENDOLEN. Algy, kindly turn your back. I have something very particular to say to Mr. Worthing.

ALGERNON. Really, Gwendolen, I don't think I can allow this at all.

GWENDOLEN. Algy, you always adopt a strictly immoral attitude towards life. You are not quite old enough to do that. (*Algernon retires to the fireplace.*)

JACK. My own darling!

GWENDOLEN. Ernest, we may never be married. From the expression on mamma's face I fear we never shall. Few parents nowadays pay any regard to what their children say to them. The old-fashioned respect for the young is fast dying out. Whatever influence I ever had over mamma, I lost at the age of three. But although she may prevent us from becoming man and wife, and I may marry some one else, and marry often, nothing that she can possibly do can alter my eternal devotion to you.

JACK. Dear Gwendolen!

GWENDOLEN. The story of your romantic origin, as related to me by mamma, with unpleasing comments, has naturally stirred the deeper fibres of my nature. Your Christian name has an irresistible fascination. The simplicity of your character makes you exquisitely incomprehensible to me. Your town address at the Albany I have. What is your address in the country?

JACK. The Manor House, Woolton, Hertfordshire.

(*Algernon, who has been carefully listening, smiles to himself, and writes the address on his shirt-cuff. Then picks up the Railway Guide.*)

GWENDOLEN. There is a good postal service, I suppose? It may be necessary to do something desperate. That of course will require serious consideration. I will communicate with you daily.

JACK. My own one!

GWENDOLEN. How long do you remain in town?

JACK. Till Monday.

GWENDOLEN. Good! Algy, you may turn round now.

ALGERNON. Thanks, I've turned round already.

GWENDOLEN. You may also ring the bell.

JACK. You will let me see you to your carriage, my own darling?

GWENDOLEN. Certainly.

JACK. (*To Lane, who now enters.*) I will see Miss Fairfax out.

LANE. Yes, sir. (*Jack and Gwendolen go off.*)

(*Lane presents several letters on a salver to Algernon. It is to be surmised that they are bills, as Algernon, after looking at the envelopes, tears them up.*)

ALGERNON. A glass of sherry, Lane.

LANE. Yes, sir.

ALGERNON. To-morrow, Lane, I'm going Bunburying.

LANE. Yes, sir.

ALGERNON. I shall probably not be back till Monday. You can put up my dress clothes, my smoking jacket, and all the Bunbury suits …

LANE. Yes, sir. (*Handing sherry.*)

ALGERNON. I hope to-morrow will be a fine day, Lane.

LANE. It never is, sir.

ALGERNON. Lane, you're a perfect pessimist.

LANE. I do my best to give satisfaction, sir.

(*Enter Jack. Lane goes off.*)

JACK. There's a sensible, intellectual girl! the only girl I ever cared for in my life. (*Algernon is laughing immoderately.*) What on earth are you so amused at?

ALGERNON. Oh, I'm a little anxious about poor Bunbury, that is all.

JACK. If you don't take care, your friend Bunbury will get you into a serious scrape some day.

ALGERNON. I love scrapes. They are the only things that are never serious.

JACK. Oh, that's nonsense, Algy. You never talk anything but nonsense.

855 ALGERNON. Nobody ever does.

(Jack looks indignantly at him, and leaves the room. Algernon lights a cigarette, reads his shirt-cuff, and smiles.)

ACT DROP

ACT 2

SCENE

(Garden at the Manor House. A flight of grey stone steps leads up to the house. The garden, an old-fashioned one, full of roses. Time of year, July. Basket chairs, and a table covered with books, are set under a large yew-tree. Miss Prism discovered[1] seated at the table. Cecily is at the back watering flowers.)

MISS PRISM. (*Calling.*) Cecily, Cecily! Surely such a utilitarian occupation as the watering of flowers is rather Moulton's duty than yours? Especially at a moment when intellectual pleasures await you. Your German

5 grammar is on the table. Pray open it at page fifteen. We will repeat yesterday's lesson.

CECILY. (*Coming over very slowly.*) But I don't like German. It isn't at all a becoming language. I know perfectly well that I look quite plain after my German

10 lesson.

MISS PRISM. Child, you know how anxious your guardian is that you should improve yourself in every way. He laid particular stress on your German, as he was leaving for town yesterday. Indeed, he always lays stress

15 on your German when he is leaving for town.

CECILY. Dear Uncle Jack is so very serious! Sometimes he is so serious that I think he cannot be quite well.

MISS PRISM. (*Drawing herself up.*) Your guardian enjoys the best of health, and his gravity of demeanour is

20 especially to be commended in one so comparatively

---

[1] *discovered* Revealed.

young as he is. I know no one who has a higher sense of duty and responsibility.

CECILY. I suppose that is why he often looks a little bored when we three are together.

25 MISS PRISM. Cecily! I am surprised at you. Mr. Worthing has many troubles in his life. Idle merriment and triviality would be out of place in his conversation. You must remember his constant anxiety about that unfortunate young man his brother.

30 CECILY. I wish Uncle Jack would allow that unfortunate young man, his brother, to come down here sometimes. We might have a good influence over him, Miss Prism. I am sure you certainly would. You know German, and geology, and things of that kind influence a man very

35 much. (*Cecily begins to write in her diary.*)

MISS PRISM. (*Shaking her head.*) I do not think that even I could produce any effect on a character that according to his own brother's admission is irretrievably weak and vacillating. Indeed I am not sure that I would desire to

40 reclaim him. I am not in favour of this modern mania for turning bad people into good people at a moment's notice. As a man sows so let him reap.[2] You must put away your diary, Cecily. I really don't see why you should keep a diary at all.

45 CECILY. I keep a diary in order to enter the wonderful secrets of my life. If I didn't write them down, I should probably forget all about them.

MISS PRISM. Memory, my dear Cecily, is the diary that we all carry about with us.

50 CECILY. Yes, but it usually chronicles the things that have never happened, and couldn't possibly have happened. I believe that Memory is responsible for nearly all the three-volume novels that Mudie sends us.[3]

MISS PRISM. Do not speak slightingly of the three-

55 volume novel, Cecily. I wrote one myself in earlier days.

CECILY. Did you really, Miss Prism? How wonderfully clever you are! I hope it did not end happily? I don't like novels that end happily. They depress me so much.

---

[2] *As a man sows so let him reap* Galatians 6.7: "whatsoever a man soweth, that shall he also reap."

[3] *nearly all ... Mudie sends us* Commercial lending libraries of the time, such as Mudie's, specialized in lending novels that were published in three volumes.

MISS PRISM.   The good ended happily, and the bad unhappily. That is what Fiction means.

CECILY.   I suppose so. But it seems very unfair. And was
your novel ever published?

MISS PRISM.   Alas! no. The manuscript unfortunately
was abandoned. (*Cecily starts.*) I use the word in the
sense of lost or mislaid. To your work, child, these
speculations are profitless.

CECILY.   (*Smiling.*) But I see dear Dr. Chasuble coming
up through the garden.

MISS PRISM.   (*Rising and advancing.*) Dr. Chasuble! This
is indeed a pleasure.

(*Enter Canon Chasuble.*)

CHASUBLE.   And how are we this morning? Miss Prism,
you are, I trust, well?

CECILY.   Miss Prism has just been complaining of a slight
headache. I think it would do her so much good to have
a short stroll with you in the Park, Dr. Chasuble.

MISS PRISM.   Cecily, I have not mentioned anything about
a headache.

CECILY.   No, dear Miss Prism, I know that, but I felt
instinctively that you had a headache. Indeed I was
thinking about that, and not about my German lesson,
when the Rector came in.

CHASUBLE.   I hope, Cecily, you are not inattentive.

CECILY.   Oh, I am afraid I am.

CHASUBLE.   That is strange. Were I fortunate enough to
be Miss Prism's pupil, I would hang upon her lips. (*Miss
Prism glares.*) I spoke metaphorically.—My metaphor
was drawn from bees. Ahem! Mr. Worthing, I suppose,
has not returned from town yet?

MISS PRISM.   We do not expect him till Monday
afternoon.

CHASUBLE.   Ah yes, he usually likes to spend his Sunday
in London. He is not one of those whose sole aim is
enjoyment, as, by all accounts, that unfortunate young
man his brother seems to be. But I must not disturb
Egeria and her pupil any longer.

MISS PRISM.   Egeria? My name is Lætitia, Doctor.

CHASUBLE.   (*Bowing.*) A classical allusion merely, drawn
from the Pagan authors.[1] I shall see you both no doubt
at Evensong?[2]

MISS PRISM.   I think, dear Doctor, I will have a stroll
with you. I find I have a headache after all, and a walk
might do it good.

CHASUBLE.   With pleasure, Miss Prism, with pleasure.
We might go as far as the schools and back.

MISS PRISM.   That would be delightful. Cecily, you will
read your Political Economy in my absence. The
chapter on the Fall of the Rupee you may omit. It is
somewhat too sensational. Even these metallic problems
have their melodramatic side.[3]

(*Goes down the garden with Dr. Chasuble.*)

CECILY.   (*Picks up books and throws them back on table.*)
Horrid Political Economy! Horrid Geography! Horrid,
horrid German!

(*Enter Merriman with a card on a salver.*)

MERRIMAN.   Mr. Ernest Worthing has just driven over
from the station. He has brought his luggage with him.

CECILY.   (*Takes the card and reads it.*) "Mr. Ernest
Worthing, B. 4, The Albany, W." Uncle Jack's brother!
Did you tell him Mr. Worthing was in town?

MERRIMAN.   Yes, Miss. He seemed very much
disappointed. I mentioned that you and Miss Prism
were in the garden. He said he was anxious to speak to
you privately for a moment.

CECILY.   Ask Mr. Ernest Worthing to come here. I
suppose you had better talk to the housekeeper about a
room for him.

MERRIMAN.   Yes, Miss.

---

[1]   *A classical allusion … Pagan authors*   In Roman mythology, the
nymph Egeria taught Numa, the second King of Rome, the lessons of
wisdom and law which he then used to found the institutions of
Rome.

[2]   *Evensong*   The evening service in the Anglican church (and various
other Christian denominations).

[3]   *The chapter … melodramatic side*   The rupee (India's currency)
declined dramatically in the early 1890s as a result of a variety of
disasters, including an outbreak of plague.

(*Merriman goes off.*)

CECILY. I have never met any really wicked person before. I feel rather frightened. I am so afraid he will look just like every one else. (*Enter Algernon, very gay and debonair.*) He does!

130 ALGERNON. (*Raising his hat.*) You are my little cousin Cecily, I'm sure.

CECILY. You are under some strange mistake. I am not little. In fact, I believe I am more than usually tall for my age. (*Algernon is rather taken aback.*) But I am your 135 cousin Cecily. You, I see from your card, are Uncle Jack's brother, my cousin Ernest, my wicked cousin Ernest.

ALGERNON. Oh! I am not really wicked at all, cousin Cecily. You mustn't think that I am wicked.

140 CECILY. If you are not, then you have certainly been deceiving us all in a very inexcusable manner. I hope you have not been leading a double life, pretending to be wicked and being really good all the time. That would be hypocrisy.

145 ALGERNON. (*Looks at her in amazement.*) Oh! Of course I have been rather reckless.

CECILY. I am glad to hear it.

ALGERNON. In fact, now you mention the subject, I have been very bad in my own small way.

150 CECILY. I don't think you should be so proud of that, though I am sure it must have been very pleasant.

ALGERNON. It is much pleasanter being here with you.

CECILY. I can't understand how you are here at all. Uncle Jack won't be back till Monday afternoon.

155 ALGERNON. That is a great disappointment. I am obliged to go up by the first train on Monday morning. I have a business appointment that I am anxious … to miss!

CECILY. Couldn't you miss it anywhere but in London?

160 ALGERNON. No: the appointment is in London.

CECILY. Well, I know, of course, how important it is not to keep a business engagement, if one wants to retain any sense of the beauty of life, but still I think you had better wait till Uncle Jack arrives. I know he wants to 165 speak to you about your emigrating.

ALGERNON. About my what?

CECILY. Your emigrating. He has gone up to buy your outfit.

ALGERNON. I certainly wouldn't let Jack buy my outfit. 170 He has no taste in neckties at all.

CECILY. I don't think you will require neckties. Uncle Jack is sending you to Australia.[1]

ALGERNON. Australia! I'd sooner die.

CECILY. Well, he said at dinner on Wednesday night, 175 that you would have to choose between this world, the next world, and Australia.

ALGERNON. Oh, well! The accounts I have received of Australia and the next world are not particularly encouraging. This world is good enough for me, cousin 180 Cecily.

CECILY. Yes, but are you good enough for it?

ALGERNON. I'm afraid I'm not that. That is why I want you to reform me. You might make that your mission, if you don't mind, cousin Cecily.

185 CECILY. I'm afraid I've no time, this afternoon.

ALGERNON. Well, would you mind my reforming myself this afternoon?

CECILY. It is rather Quixotic[2] of you. But I think you should try.

190 ALGERNON. I will. I feel better already.

CECILY. You are looking a little worse.

ALGERNON. That is because I am hungry.

CECILY. How thoughtless of me. I should have remembered that when one is going to lead an entirely 195 new life, one requires regular and wholesome meals. Won't you come in?

ALGERNON. Thank you. Might I have a buttonhole[3] first? I never have any appetite unless I have a buttonhole first.

200 CECILY. A Maréchal Niel?[4] (*Picks up scissors.*)

ALGERNON. No, I'd sooner have a pink rose.

CECILY. Why? (*Cuts a flower.*)

ALGERNON. Because you are like a pink rose, Cousin Cecily.

---

[1] *Australia* A former penal colony, at the time still considered to be largely composed of wilderness.

[2] *Quixotic* Unrealistic; so idealistic as to be foolish.

[3] *buttonhole* Boutonniere, flower for one's lapel.

[4] *Maréchal Niel* Variety of yellow rose.

205 CECILY. I don't think it can be right for you to talk to me like that. Miss Prism never says such things to me.

ALGERNON. Then Miss Prism is a short-sighted old lady. (*Cecily puts the rose in his buttonhole.*) You are the prettiest girl I ever saw.

210 CECILY. Miss Prism says that all good looks are a snare.

ALGERNON. They are a snare that every sensible man would like to be caught in.

CECILY. Oh, I don't think I would care to catch a sensible man. I shouldn't know what to talk to him
215 about.

(*They pass into the house. Miss Prism and Dr. Chasuble return.*)

MISS PRISM. You are too much alone, dear Dr. Chasuble. You should get married. A misanthrope I can understand—a womanthrope,[1] never!

CHASUBLE. (*With a scholar's shudder.*) Believe me, I do
220 not deserve so neologistic a phrase. The precept as well as the practice of the Primitive Church[2] was distinctly against matrimony.

MISS PRISM. (*Sententiously.*) That is obviously the reason why the Primitive Church has not lasted up to the
225 present day. And you do not seem to realize, dear Doctor, that by persistently remaining single, a man converts himself into a permanent public temptation. Men should be more careful; this very celibacy leads weaker vessels astray.

230 CHASUBLE. But is a man not equally attractive when married?

MISS PRISM. No married man is ever attractive except to his wife.

CHASUBLE. And often, I've been told, not even to her.

235 MISS PRISM. That depends on the intellectual sympathies of the woman. Maturity can always be depended on. Ripeness can be trusted. Young women are green. (*Dr. Chasuble starts.*) I spoke horticulturally. My metaphor was drawn from fruits. But where is Cecily?

---

1 *misanthrope ... womanthrope* The correct word for someone who hates women is a "misogynist"; a "misanthrope" is someone who hates all humanity.

2 *Primitive Church* Early Christian church.

240 CHASUBLE. Perhaps she followed us to the schools.

(*Enter Jack slowly from the back of the garden. He is dressed in the deepest mourning, with crepe hatband and black gloves.*)

MISS PRISM. Mr. Worthing!

CHASUBLE. Mr. Worthing?

MISS PRISM. This is indeed a surprise. We did not look for you till Monday afternoon.

245 JACK. (*Shakes Miss Prism's hand in a tragic manner.*) I have returned sooner than I expected. Dr. Chasuble, I hope you are well?

CHASUBLE. Dear Mr. Worthing, I trust this garb of woe does not betoken some terrible calamity?

250 JACK. My brother.

MISS PRISM. More shameful debts and extravagance?

CHASUBLE. Still leading his life of pleasure?

JACK. (*Shaking his head.*) Dead!

CHASUBLE. Your brother Ernest dead?

255 JACK. Quite dead.

MISS PRISM. What a lesson for him! I trust he will profit by it.

CHASUBLE. Mr. Worthing, I offer you my sincere condolence. You have at least the consolation of
260 knowing that you were always the most generous and forgiving of brothers.

JACK. Poor Ernest! He had many faults, but it is a sad, sad blow.

CHASUBLE. Very sad indeed. Were you with him at the
265 end?

JACK. No. He died abroad; in Paris, in fact. I had a telegram last night from the manager of the Grand Hotel.

CHASUBLE. Was the cause of death mentioned?

270 JACK. A severe chill, it seems.

MISS PRISM. As a man sows, so shall he reap.

CHASUBLE. (*Raising his hand.*) Charity, dear Miss Prism, charity! None of us are perfect. I myself am peculiarly susceptible to draughts. Will the interment take place
275 here?

JACK. No. He seems to have expressed a desire to be buried in Paris.

CHASUBLE.   In Paris! (*Shakes his head.*) I fear that hardly points to any very serious state of mind at the last. You would no doubt wish me to make some slight allusion to this tragic domestic affliction next Sunday. (*Jack presses his hand convulsively.*) My sermon on the meaning of the manna in the wilderness[1] can be adapted to almost any occasion, joyful, or, as in the present case, distressing. (*All sigh.*) I have preached it at harvest celebrations, christenings, confirmations,[2] on days of humiliation and festal days. The last time I delivered it was in the Cathedral, as a charity sermon on behalf of the Society for the Prevention of Discontent among the Upper Orders. The Bishop, who was present, was much struck by some of the analogies I drew.

JACK.   Ah! that reminds me, you mentioned christenings I think, Dr. Chasuble? I suppose you know how to christen all right? (*Dr. Chasuble looks astounded.*) I mean, of course, you are continually christening, aren't you?

MISS PRISM.   It is, I regret to say, one of the Rector's most constant duties in this parish. I have often spoken to the poorer classes on the subject. But they don't seem to know what thrift is.

CHASUBLE.   But is there any particular infant in whom you are interested, Mr. Worthing? Your brother was, I believe, unmarried, was he not?

JACK.   Oh yes.

MISS PRISM.   (*Bitterly.*) People who live entirely for pleasure usually are.

JACK.   But it is not for any child, dear Doctor. I am very fond of children. No! the fact is, I would like to be christened myself, this afternoon, if you have nothing better to do.

CHASUBLE.   But surely, Mr. Worthing, you have been christened already?

JACK.   I don't remember anything about it.

CHASUBLE.   But have you any grave doubts on the subject?

JACK.   I certainly intend to have. Of course I don't know if the thing would bother you in any way, or if you think I am a little too old now.

CHASUBLE.   Not at all. The sprinkling, and, indeed, the immersion of adults is a perfectly canonical[3] practice.

JACK.   Immersion!

CHASUBLE.   You need have no apprehensions. Sprinkling is all that is necessary, or indeed I think advisable. Our weather is so changeable. At what hour would you wish the ceremony performed?

JACK.   Oh, I might trot round about five if that would suit you.

CHASUBLE.   Perfectly, perfectly! In fact I have two similar ceremonies to perform at that time. A case of twins that occurred recently in one of the outlying cottages on your own estate. Poor Jenkins the carter,[4] a most hard-working man.

JACK.   Oh! I don't see much fun in being christened along with other babies. It would be childish. Would half-past five do?

CHASUBLE.   Admirably! Admirably! (*Takes out watch.*) And now, dear Mr. Worthing, I will not intrude any longer into a house of sorrow. I would merely beg you not to be too much bowed down by grief. What seem to us bitter trials are often blessings in disguise.

MISS PRISM.   This seems to me a blessing of an extremely obvious kind.

(*Enter Cecily from the house.*)

CECILY.   Uncle Jack! Oh, I am pleased to see you back. But what horrid clothes you have got on! Do go and change them.

MISS PRISM.   Cecily!

CHASUBLE.   My child! my child!

(*Cecily goes towards Jack; he kisses her brow in a melancholy manner.*)

---

[1]   *manna in the wilderness*   See Exodus 16.

[2]   *christenings, confirmations*   Whereas a christening formally admits a person to the Christian church through baptism (usually as an infant), in many Christian denominations a person's standing as a full member of the church must be confirmed at a later ceremony (typically as a young adult).

---

[3]   *canonical*   Accepted by the Church.

[4]   *carter*   Cart driver.

CECILY.   What is the matter, Uncle Jack? Do look happy! You look as if you had toothache, and I have got such a surprise for you. Who do you think is in the dining-room? Your brother!

350 JACK.   Who?

CECILY.   Your brother Ernest. He arrived about half an hour ago.

JACK.   What nonsense! I haven't got a brother.

355 CECILY.   Oh, don't say that. However badly he may have behaved to you in the past he is still your brother. You couldn't be so heartless as to disown him. I'll tell him to come out. And you will shake hands with him, won't you, Uncle Jack? (*Runs back into the house.*)

360 CHASUBLE.   These are very joyful tidings.

MISS PRISM.   After we had all been resigned to his loss, his sudden return seems to me peculiarly distressing.

JACK.   My brother is in the dining-room? I don't know what it all means. I think it is perfectly absurd.

(*Enter Algernon and Cecily hand in hand. They come slowly up to Jack.*)

365 JACK.   Good heavens! (*Motions Algernon away.*)

ALGERNON.   Brother John, I have come down from town to tell you that I am very sorry for all the trouble I have given you, and that I intend to lead a better life in the future. (*Jack glares at him and does not take his*

370 *hand.*)

CECILY.   Uncle Jack, you are not going to refuse your own brother's hand?

JACK.   Nothing will induce me to take his hand. I think his coming down here disgraceful. He knows perfectly

375 well why.

CECILY.   Uncle Jack, do be nice. There is some good in every one. Ernest has just been telling me about his poor invalid friend Mr. Bunbury whom he goes to visit so often. And surely there must be much good in one who

380 is kind to an invalid, and leaves the pleasures of London to sit by a bed of pain.

JACK.   Oh! he has been talking about Bunbury, has he?

CECILY.   Yes, he has told me all about poor Mr. Bunbury, and his terrible state of health.

385 JACK.   Bunbury! Well, I won't have him talk to you about Bunbury or about anything else. It is enough to drive one perfectly frantic.

ALGERNON.   Of course I admit that the faults were all on my side. But I must say that I think that Brother John's

390 coldness to me is peculiarly painful. I expected a more enthusiastic welcome, especially considering it is the first time I have come here.

CECILY.   Uncle Jack, if you don't shake hands with Ernest I will never forgive you.

395 JACK.   Never forgive me?

CECILY.   Never, never, never!

JACK.   Well, this is the last time I shall ever do it. (*Shakes hands with Algernon and glares.*)

CHASUBLE.   It's pleasant, is it not, to see so perfect a

400 reconciliation? I think we might leave the two brothers together.

MISS PRISM.   Cecily, you will come with us.

CECILY.   Certainly, Miss Prism. My little task of reconciliation is over.

405 CHASUBLE.   You have done a beautiful action to-day, dear child.

MISS PRISM.   We must not be premature in our judgments.

CECILY.   I feel very happy.

(*They all go off except Jack and Algernon.*)

410 JACK.   You young scoundrel, Algy, you must get out of this place as soon as possible. I don't allow any Bunburying here.

(*Enter Merriman.*)

MERRIMAN.   I have put Mr. Ernest's things in the room next to yours, sir. I suppose that is all right?

415 JACK.   What?

MERRIMAN.   Mr. Ernest's luggage, sir. I have unpacked it and put it in the room next to your own.

JACK.   His luggage?

MERRIMAN.   Yes, sir. Three portmanteaus,[1] a dressing-

420 case, two hat-boxes, and a large luncheon-basket.

---

[1] *portmanteaus* Suitcases.

ALGERNON. I am afraid I can't stay more than a week this time.

JACK. Merriman, order the dog-cart[1] at once. Mr. Ernest has been suddenly called back to town.

425 MERRIMAN. Yes, sir. (*Goes back into the house.*)

ALGERNON. What a fearful liar you are, Jack. I have not been called back to town at all.

JACK. Yes, you have.

ALGERNON. I haven't heard any one call me.

430 JACK. Your duty as a gentleman calls you back.

ALGERNON. My duty as a gentleman has never interfered with my pleasures in the smallest degree.

JACK. I can quite understand that.

ALGERNON. Well, Cecily is a darling.

435 JACK. You are not to talk of Miss Cardew like that. I don't like it.

ALGERNON. Well, I don't like your clothes. You look perfectly ridiculous in them. Why on earth don't you go up and change? It is perfectly childish to be in deep
440 mourning for a man who is actually staying for a whole week with you in your house as a guest. I call it grotesque.

JACK. You are certainly not staying with me for a whole week as a guest or anything else. You have got to leave
445 … by the four-five train.

ALGERNON. I certainly won't leave you so long as you are in mourning. It would be most unfriendly. If I were in mourning you would stay with me, I suppose. I should think it very unkind if you didn't.

450 JACK. Well, will you go if I change my clothes?

ALGERNON. Yes, if you are not too long. I never saw anybody take so long to dress, and with such little result.

JACK. Well, at any rate, that is better than being always
455 over-dressed as you are.

ALGERNON. If I am occasionally a little over-dressed, I make up for it by being always immensely over-educated.

JACK. Your vanity is ridiculous, your conduct an
460 outrage, and your presence in my garden utterly absurd.

---

[1] *dog-cart* Small horse-drawn carriage in which the occupants would sit back-to-back; a box for conveying hunting dogs was also typically part of the contraption.

However, you have got to catch the four-five, and I hope you will have a pleasant journey back to town. This Bunburying, as you call it, has not been a great success for you. (*Goes into the house.*)

465 ALGERNON. I think it has been a great success. I'm in love with Cecily, and that is everything.

(*Enter Cecily at the back of the garden. She picks up the can and begins to water the flowers.*)

But I must see her before I go, and make arrangements for another Bunbury. Ah, there she is.

CECILY. Oh, I merely came back to water the roses. I
470 thought you were with Uncle Jack.

ALGERNON. He's gone to order the dog-cart for me.

CECILY. Oh, is he going to take you for a nice drive?

ALGERNON. He's going to send me away.

CECILY. Then have we got to part?

475 ALGERNON. I am afraid so. It's a very painful parting.

CECILY. It is always painful to part from people whom one has known for a very brief space of time. The absence of old friends one can endure with equanimity. But even a momentary separation from anyone to whom
480 one has just been introduced is almost unbearable.

ALGERNON. Thank you.

(*Enter Merriman.*)

MERRIMAN. The dog-cart is at the door, sir.

(*Algernon looks appealingly at Cecily.*)

CECILY. It can wait, Merriman for … five minutes.

MERRIMAN. Yes, Miss.

(*Exit Merriman.*)

485 ALGERNON. I hope, Cecily, I shall not offend you if I state quite frankly and openly that you seem to me to be in every way the visible personification of absolute perfection.

CECILY. I think your frankness does you great credit,
490 Ernest. If you will allow me, I will copy your remarks

into my diary. (*Goes over to table and begins writing in diary.*)

ALGERNON. Do you really keep a diary? I'd give anything to look at it. May I?

495 CECILY. Oh no. (*Puts her hand over it.*) You see, it is simply a very young girl's record of her own thoughts and impressions, and consequently meant for publication. When it appears in volume form I hope you will order a copy. But pray, Ernest, don't stop. I

500 delight in taking down from dictation. I have reached "absolute perfection." You can go on. I am quite ready for more.

ALGERNON. (*Somewhat taken aback.*) Ahem! Ahem!

CECILY. Oh, don't cough, Ernest. When one is dictating

505 one should speak fluently and not cough. Besides, I don't know how to spell a cough. (*Writes as Algernon speaks.*)

ALGERNON. (*Speaking very rapidly.*) Cecily, ever since I first looked upon your wonderful and incomparable

510 beauty, I have dared to love you wildly, passionately, devotedly, hopelessly.

CECILY. I don't think that you should tell me that you love me wildly, passionately, devotedly, hopelessly. Hopelessly doesn't seem to make much sense, does it?

515 ALGERNON. Cecily!

(*Enter Merriman.*)

MERRIMAN. The dog-cart is waiting, sir.

ALGERNON. Tell it to come round next week, at the same hour.

MERRIMAN. (*Looks at Cecily, who makes no sign.*) Yes, sir.

(*Merriman retires.*)

520 CECILY. Uncle Jack would be very much annoyed if he knew you were staying on till next week, at the same hour.

ALGERNON. Oh, I don't care about Jack. I don't care for anybody in the whole world but you. I love you, Cecily.

525 You will marry me, won't you?

CECILY. You silly boy! Of course. Why, we have been engaged for the last three months.

ALGERNON. For the last three months?

CECILY. Yes, it will be exactly three months on

530 Thursday.

ALGERNON. But how did we become engaged?

CECILY. Well, ever since dear Uncle Jack first confessed to us that he had a younger brother who was very wicked and bad, you of course have formed the chief

535 topic of conversation between myself and Miss Prism. And of course a man who is much talked about is always very attractive. One feels there must be something in him, after all. I daresay it was foolish of me, but I fell in love with you, Ernest.

540 ALGERNON. Darling! And when was the engagement actually settled?

CECILY. On the 14th of February last. Worn out by your entire ignorance of my existence, I determined to end the matter one way or the other, and after a long

545 struggle with myself I accepted you under this dear old tree here. The next day I bought this little ring in your name, and this is the little bangle with the true lover's knot I promised you always to wear.

ALGERNON. Did I give you this? It's very pretty, isn't it?

550 CECILY. Yes, you've wonderfully good taste, Ernest. It's the excuse I've always given for your leading such a bad life. And this is the box in which I keep all your dear letters. (*Kneels at table, opens box, and produces letters tied up with blue ribbon.*)

555 ALGERNON. My letters! But, my own sweet Cecily, I have never written you any letters.

CECILY. You need hardly remind me of that, Ernest. I remember only too well that I was forced to write your letters for you. I wrote always three times a week, and

560 sometimes oftener.

ALGERNON. Oh, do let me read them, Cecily?

CECILY. Oh, I couldn't possibly. They would make you far too conceited. (*Replaces box.*) The three you wrote me after I had broken off the engagement are so

565 beautiful, and so badly spelled, that even now I can hardly read them without crying a little.

ALGERNON. But was our engagement ever broken off?

CECILY. Of course it was. On the 22nd of last March. You can see the entry if you like. (*Shows diary.*) "To-day

570 I broke off my engagement with Ernest. I feel it is better

to do so. The weather still continues charming."

ALGERNON. But why on earth did you break it off? What had I done? I had done nothing at all. Cecily, I am very much hurt indeed to hear you broke it off. Particularly when the weather was so charming.

CECILY. It would hardly have been a really serious engagement if it hadn't been broken off at least once. But I forgave you before the week was out.

ALGERNON. (*Crossing to her, and kneeling.*) What a perfect angel you are, Cecily.

CECILY. You dear romantic boy. (*He kisses her, she puts her fingers through his hair.*) I hope your hair curls naturally, does it?

ALGERNON. Yes, darling, with a little help from others.

CECILY. I am so glad.

ALGERNON. You'll never break off our engagement again, Cecily?

CECILY. I don't think I could break it off now that I have actually met you. Besides, of course, there is the question of your name.

ALGERNON. Yes, of course. (*Nervously.*)

CECILY. You must not laugh at me, darling, but it had always been a girlish dream of mine to love some one whose name was Ernest. (*Algernon rises, Cecily also.*) There is something in that name that seems to inspire absolute confidence. I pity any poor married woman whose husband is not called Ernest.

ALGERNON. But, my dear child, do you mean to say you could not love me if I had some other name?

CECILY. But what name?

ALGERNON. Oh, any name you like—Algernon—for instance …

CECILY. But I don't like the name of Algernon.

ALGERNON. Well, my own dear, sweet, loving little darling, I really can't see why you should object to the name of Algernon. It is not at all a bad name. In fact, it is rather an aristocratic name. Half of the chaps who get into the Bankruptcy Court are called Algernon. But seriously, Cecily … (*Moving to her.*) … if my name was Algy, couldn't you love me?

CECILY. (*Rising.*) I might respect you, Ernest, I might admire your character, but I fear that I should not be able to give you my undivided attention.

ALGERNON. Ahem! Cecily! (*Picking up hat.*) Your Rector here is, I suppose, thoroughly experienced in the practice of all the rites and ceremonials of the Church?

CECILY. Oh, yes. Dr. Chasuble is a most learned man. He has never written a single book, so you can imagine how much he knows.

ALGERNON. I must see him at once on a most important christening—I mean on most important business.

CECILY. Oh!

ALGERNON. I shan't be away more than half an hour.

CECILY. Considering that we have been engaged since February the 14th, and that I only met you to-day for the first time, I think it is rather hard that you should leave me for so long a period as half an hour. Couldn't you make it twenty minutes?

ALGERNON. I'll be back in no time.

(*Kisses her and rushes down the garden.*)

CECILY. What an impetuous boy he is! I like his hair so much. I must enter his proposal in my diary.

(*Enter Merriman.*)

MERRIMAN. A Miss Fairfax has just called to see Mr. Worthing. On very important business, Miss Fairfax states.

CECILY. Isn't Mr. Worthing in his library?

MERRIMAN. Mr. Worthing went over in the direction of the Rectory some time ago.

CECILY. Pray ask the lady to come out here; Mr. Worthing is sure to be back soon. And you can bring tea.

MERRIMAN. Yes, Miss. (*Goes out.*)

CECILY. Miss Fairfax! I suppose one of the many good elderly women who are associated with Uncle Jack in some of his philanthropic work in London. I don't quite like women who are interested in philanthropic work. I think it is so forward of them.

(*Enter Merriman.*)

MERRIMAN. Miss Fairfax.

(*Enter Gwendolen. Exit Merriman.*)

CECILY. (*Advancing to meet her.*) Pray let me introduce myself to you. My name is Cecily Cardew.

GWENDOLEN. Cecily Cardew? (*Moving to her and shaking hands.*) What a very sweet name! Something tells me that we are going to be great friends. I like you already more than I can say. My first impressions of people are never wrong.

CECILY. How nice of you to like me so much after we have known each other such a comparatively short time. Pray sit down.

GWENDOLEN. (*Still standing up.*) I may call you Cecily, may I not?

CECILY. With pleasure!

GWENDOLEN. And you will always call me Gwendolen, won't you?

CECILY. If you wish.

GWENDOLEN. Then that is all quite settled, is it not?

CECILY. I hope so. (*A pause. They both sit down together.*)

GWENDOLEN. Perhaps this might be a favourable opportunity for my mentioning who I am. My father is Lord Bracknell. You have never heard of Papa, I suppose?

CECILY. I don't think so.

GWENDOLEN. Outside the family circle, Papa, I am glad to say, is entirely unknown. I think that is quite as it should be. The home seems to me to be the proper sphere for the man. And certainly once a man begins to neglect his domestic duties he becomes painfully effeminate, does he not? And I don't like that. It makes men so very attractive. Cecily, Mamma, whose views on education are remarkably strict, has brought me up to be extremely short-sighted; it is part of her system; so do you mind my looking at you through my glasses?

CECILY. Oh! not at all, Gwendolen. I am very fond of being looked at.

GWENDOLEN. (*After examining Cecily carefully through a lorgnette.*) You are here on a short visit, I suppose.

CECILY. Oh no! I live here.

GWENDOLEN. (*Severely.*) Really? Your mother, no doubt, or some female relative of advanced years, resides here also?

CECILY. Oh no! I have no mother, nor, in fact, any relations.

GWENDOLEN. Indeed?

CECILY. My dear guardian, with the assistance of Miss Prism, has the arduous task of looking after me.

GWENDOLEN. Your guardian?

CECILY. Yes, I am Mr. Worthing's ward.

GWENDOLEN. Oh! It is strange he never mentioned to me that he had a ward. How secretive of him! He grows more interesting hourly. I am not sure, however, that the news inspires me with feelings of unmixed delight. (*Rising and going to her.*) I am very fond of you, Cecily; I have liked you ever since I met you! But I am bound to state that now that I know that you are Mr. Worthing's ward, I cannot help expressing a wish you were— well, just a little older than you seem to be—and not quite so very alluring in appearance. In fact, if I may speak candidly—

CECILY. Pray do! I think that whenever one has anything unpleasant to say, one should always be quite candid.

GWENDOLEN. Well, to speak with perfect candour, Cecily, I wish that you were fully forty-two, and more than usually plain for your age. Ernest has a strong upright nature. He is the very soul of truth and honour. Disloyalty would be as impossible to him as deception. But even men of the noblest possible moral character are extremely susceptible to the influence of the physical charms of others. Modern, no less than Ancient History, supplies us with many most painful examples of what I refer to. If it were not so, indeed, History would be quite unreadable.

CECILY. I beg your pardon, Gwendolen, did you say Ernest?

GWENDOLEN. Yes.

CECILY. Oh, but it is not Mr. Ernest Worthing who is my guardian. It is his brother—his elder brother.

GWENDOLEN. (*Sitting down again.*) Ernest never mentioned to me that he had a brother.

CECILY. I am sorry to say they have not been on good terms for a long time.

GWENDOLEN. Ah! that accounts for it. And now that I think of it I have never heard any man mention his brother. The subject seems distasteful to most men.

Cecily, you have lifted a load from my mind. I was growing almost anxious. It would have been terrible if any cloud had come across a friendship like ours, would it not? Of course you are quite, quite sure that it is not Mr. Ernest Worthing who is your guardian?

CECILY.   Quite sure. (*A pause.*) In fact, I am going to be his.

GWENDOLEN.   (*Inquiringly.*) I beg your pardon?

CECILY.   (*Rather shy and confidingly.*) Dearest Gwendolen, there is no reason why I should make a secret of it to you. Our little county newspaper is sure to chronicle the fact next week. Mr. Ernest Worthing and I are engaged to be married.

GWENDOLEN.   (*Quite politely, rising.*) My darling Cecily, I think there must be some slight error. Mr. Ernest Worthing is engaged to me. The announcement will appear in the *Morning Post* on Saturday at the latest.

CECILY.   (*Very politely, rising.*) I am afraid you must be under some misconception. Ernest proposed to me exactly ten minutes ago. (*Shows diary.*)

GWENDOLEN.   (*Examines diary through her lorgnettte carefully.*) It is certainly very curious, for he asked me to be his wife yesterday afternoon at 5:30. If you would care to verify the incident, pray do so. (*Produces diary of her own.*) I never travel without my diary. One should always have something sensational to read in the train. I am so sorry, dear Cecily, if it is any disappointment to you, but I am afraid I have the prior claim.

CECILY.   It would distress me more than I can tell you, dear Gwendolen, if it caused you any mental or physical anguish, but I feel bound to point out that since Ernest proposed to you he clearly has changed his mind.

GWENDOLEN.   (*Meditatively.*) If the poor fellow has been entrapped into any foolish promise I shall consider it my duty to rescue him at once, and with a firm hand.

CECILY.   (*Thoughtfully and sadly.*) Whatever unfortunate entanglement my dear boy may have got into, I will never reproach him with it after we are married.

GWENDOLEN.   Do you allude to me, Miss Cardew, as an entanglement? You are presumptuous. On an occasion of this kind it becomes more than a moral duty to speak one's mind. It becomes a pleasure.

CECILY.   Do you suggest, Miss Fairfax, that I entrapped Ernest into an engagement? How dare you? This is no time for wearing the shallow mask of manners. When I see a spade I call it a spade.

GWENDOLEN.   (*Satirically.*) I am glad to say that I have never seen a spade. It is obvious that our social spheres have been widely different.

(*Enter Merriman, followed by the footman. He carries a salver, table cloth, and plate stand. Cecily is about to retort. The presence of the servants exercises a restraining influence, under which both girls chafe.*)

MERRIMAN.   Shall I lay tea here as usual, Miss?

CECILY.   (*Sternly, in a calm voice.*) Yes, as usual.

(*Merriman begins to clear table and lay cloth. A long pause. Cecily and Gwendolen glare at each other.*)

GWENDOLEN.   Are there many interesting walks in the vicinity, Miss Cardew?

CECILY.   Oh! yes! a great many. From the top of one of the hills quite close one can see five counties.

GWENDOLEN.   Five counties! I don't think I should like that; I hate crowds.

CECILY.   (*Sweetly.*) I suppose that is why you live in town?

(*Gwendolen bites her lip, and beats her foot nervously with her parasol.*)

GWENDOLEN.   (*Looking round.*) Quite a well-kept garden this is, Miss Cardew.

CECILY.   So glad you like it, Miss Fairfax.

GWENDOLEN.   I had no idea there were any flowers in the country.

CECILY.   Oh, flowers are as common here, Miss Fairfax, as people are in London.

GWENDOLEN.   Personally I cannot understand how anybody manages to exist in the country, if anybody who is anybody does. The country always bores me to death.

CECILY. Ah! This is what the newspapers call agricultural depression,[1] is it not? I believe the aristocracy are suffering very much from it just at present. It is almost an epidemic amongst them, I have been told. May I offer you some tea, Miss Fairfax?

GWENDOLEN. (*With elaborate politeness.*) Thank you. (*Aside.*) Detestable girl! But I require tea!

CECILY. (*Sweetly.*) Sugar?

GWENDOLEN. (*Superciliously.*) No, thank you. Sugar is not fashionable any more. (*Cecily looks angrily at her, takes up the tongs and puts four lumps of sugar into the cup.*)

CECILY. (*Severely.*) Cake or bread and butter?

GWENDOLEN. (*In a bored manner.*) Bread and butter, please. Cake is rarely seen at the best houses nowadays.

CECILY. (*Cuts a very large slice of cake, and puts it on the tray.*) Hand that to Miss Fairfax.

(*Merriman does so, and goes out with footman. Gwendolen drinks the tea and makes a grimace. Puts down cup at once, reaches out her hand to the bread and butter, looks at it, and finds it is cake. Rises in indignation.*)

GWENDOLEN. You have filled my tea with lumps of sugar, and though I asked most distinctly for bread and butter, you have given me cake. I am known for the gentleness of my disposition, and the extraordinary sweetness of my nature, but I warn you, Miss Cardew, you may go too far.

CECILY. (*Rising.*) To save my poor, innocent, trusting boy from the machinations of any other girl there are no lengths to which I would not go.

GWENDOLEN. From the moment I saw you I distrusted you. I felt that you were false and deceitful. I am never deceived in such matters. My first impressions of people are invariably right.

CECILY. It seems to me, Miss Fairfax, that I am trespassing on your valuable time. No doubt you have many other calls of a similar character to make in the neighbourhood.

(*Enter Jack.*)

GWENDOLEN. (*Catching sight of him.*) Ernest! My own Ernest!

JACK. Gwendolen! Darling! (*Offers to kiss her.*)

GWENDOLEN. (*Draws back.*) A moment! May I ask if you are engaged to be married to this young lady? (*Points to Cecily.*)

JACK. (*Laughing.*) To dear little Cecily! Of course not! What could have put such an idea into your pretty little head?

GWENDOLEN. Thank you. You may! (*Offers her cheek.*)

CECILY. (*Very sweetly.*) I knew there must be some misunderstanding, Miss Fairfax. The gentleman whose arm is at present round your waist is my guardian, Mr. John Worthing.

GWENDOLEN. I beg your pardon?

CECILY. This is Uncle Jack.

GWENDOLEN. (*Receding.*) Jack! Oh!

(*Enter Algernon.*)

CECILY. Here is Ernest.

ALGERNON. (*Goes straight over to Cecily without noticing any one else.*) My own love! (*Offers to kiss her.*)

CECILY. (*Drawing back.*) A moment, Ernest! May I ask you—are you engaged to be married to this young lady?

ALGERNON. (*Looking round.*) To what young lady? Good heavens! Gwendolen!

CECILY. Yes! to good heavens, Gwendolen, I mean to Gwendolen.

ALGERNON. (*Laughing.*) Of course not! What could have put such an idea into your pretty little head?

CECILY. Thank you. (*Presenting her cheek to be kissed.*) You may.

(*Algernon kisses her.*)

GWENDOLEN. I felt there was some slight error, Miss Cardew. The gentleman who is now embracing you is my cousin, Mr. Algernon Moncrieff.

CECILY. (*Breaking away from Algernon.*) Algernon Moncrieff! Oh!

---

[1] *agricultural depression* The British economy in general was in depression from 1873 until the mid-1890s; the agricultural sector was depressed from 1875 until the mid-1890s.

(The two girls move towards each other and put their arms round each other's waists as if for protection.)

870 CECILY.   Are you called Algernon?

ALGERNON.   I cannot deny it.

CECILY.   Oh!

GWENDOLEN.   Is your name really John?

JACK.   *(Standing rather proudly.)* I could deny it if I liked.

875   I could deny anything if I liked. But my name certainly is John. It has been John for years.

CECILY.   *(To Gwendolen.)* A gross deception has been practised on both of us.

GWENDOLEN.   My poor wounded Cecily!

880 CECILY.   My sweet wronged Gwendolen!

GWENDOLEN.   *(Slowly and seriously.)* You will call me sister, will you not? *(They embrace. Jack and Algernon groan and walk up and down.)*

CECILY.   *(Rather brightly.)* There is just one question I

885   would like to be allowed to ask my guardian.

GWENDOLEN.   An admirable idea! Mr. Worthing, there is just one question I would like to be permitted to put to you. Where is your brother Ernest? We are both engaged to be married to your brother Ernest, so it is a

890   matter of some importance to us to know where your brother Ernest is at present.

JACK.   *(Slowly and hesitatingly.)* Gwendolen—Cecily—it is very painful for me to be forced to speak the truth. It is the first time in my life that I have ever been reduced

895   to such a painful position, and I am really quite inexperienced in doing anything of the kind. However, I will tell you quite frankly that I have no brother Ernest. I have no brother at all. I never had a brother in my life, and I certainly have not the smallest intention

900   of ever having one in the future.

CECILY.   *(Surprised.)* No brother at all?

JACK.   *(Cheerily.)* None!

GWENDOLEN.   *(Severely.)* Had you never a brother of any kind?

905 JACK.   *(Pleasantly.)* Never. Not even of any kind.

GWENDOLEN.   I am afraid it is quite clear, Cecily, that neither of us is engaged to be married to any one.

CECILY.   It is not a very pleasant position for a young girl suddenly to find herself in. Is it?

910 GWENDOLEN.   Let us go into the house. They will hardly venture to come after us there.

CECILY.   No, men are so cowardly, aren't they?

(They retire into the house with scornful looks.)

JACK.   This ghastly state of things is what you call Bunburying, I suppose?

915 ALGERNON.   Yes, and a perfectly wonderful Bunbury it is. The most wonderful Bunbury I have ever had in my life.

JACK.   Well, you've no right whatsoever to Bunbury here.

ALGERNON.   That is absurd. One has a right to Bunbury

920   anywhere one chooses. Every serious Bunburyist knows that.

JACK.   Serious Bunburyist! Good heavens!

ALGERNON.   Well, one must be serious about something, if one wants to have any amusement in life. I happen to

925   be serious about Bunburying. What on earth you are serious about I haven't got the remotest idea. About everything, I should fancy. You have such an absolutely trivial nature.

JACK.   Well, the only small satisfaction I have in the

930   whole of this wretched business is that your friend Bunbury is quite exploded. You won't be able to run down to the country quite so often as you used to do, dear Algy. And a very good thing too.

ALGERNON.   Your brother is a little off colour, isn't he,

935   dear Jack? You won't be able to disappear to London quite so frequently as your wicked custom was. And not a bad thing either.

JACK.   As for your conduct towards Miss Cardew, I must say that your taking in a sweet, simple, innocent girl like

940   that is quite inexcusable. To say nothing of the fact that she is my ward.

ALGERNON.   I can see no possible defence at all for your deceiving a brilliant, clever, thoroughly experienced young lady like Miss Fairfax. To say nothing of the fact

945   that she is my cousin.

JACK.   I wanted to be engaged to Gwendolen, that is all. I love her.

ALGERNON.   Well, I simply wanted to be engaged to Cecily. I adore her.

950 JACK. There is certainly no chance of your marrying Miss Cardew.

ALGERNON. I don't think there is much likelihood, Jack, of you and Miss Fairfax being united.

JACK. Well, that is no business of yours.

955 ALGERNON. If it was my business, I wouldn't talk about it. (*Begins to eat muffins.*) It is very vulgar to talk about one's business. Only people like stock-brokers do that, and then merely at dinner parties.

JACK. How can you sit there, calmly eating muffins when we are in this horrible trouble, I can't make out. You seem to me to be perfectly heartless.

960 ALGERNON. Well, I can't eat muffins in an agitated manner. The butter would probably get on my cuffs. One should always eat muffins quite calmly. It is the only way to eat them.

965 JACK. I say it's perfectly heartless your eating muffins at all, under the circumstances.

ALGERNON. When I am in trouble, eating is the only thing that consoles me. Indeed, when I am in really great trouble, as any one who knows me intimately will tell you, I refuse everything except food and drink. At the present moment I am eating muffins because I am unhappy. Besides, I am particularly fond of muffins. (*Rising.*)

975 JACK. (*Rising.*) Well, that is no reason why you should eat them all in that greedy way. (*Takes muffins from Algernon.*)

ALGERNON. (*Offering tea-cake.*) I wish you would have tea-cake instead. I don't like tea-cake.

980 JACK. Good heavens! I suppose a man may eat his own muffins in his own garden.

ALGERNON. But you have just said it was perfectly heartless to eat muffins.

JACK. I said it was perfectly heartless of you, under the circumstances. That is a very different thing.

985 ALGERNON. That may be. But the muffins are the same.

(*He seizes the muffin-dish from Jack.*)

JACK. Algy, I wish to goodness you would go.

ALGERNON. You can't possibly ask me to go without having some dinner. It's absurd. I never go without my dinner. No one ever does, except vegetarians and people like that. Besides I have just made arrangements with Dr. Chasuble to be christened at a quarter to six under the name of Ernest.

JACK. My dear fellow, the sooner you give up that nonsense the better. I made arrangements this morning with Dr. Chasuble to be christened myself at 5:30, and I naturally will take the name of Ernest. Gwendolen would wish it. We can't both be christened Ernest. It's absurd. Besides, I have a perfect right to be christened if I like. There is no evidence at all that I have ever been christened by anybody. I should think it extremely probable I never was, and so does Dr. Chasuble. It is entirely different in your case. You have been christened already.

1005 ALGERNON. Yes, but I have not been christened for years.

JACK. Yes, but you have been christened. That is the important thing.

ALGERNON. Quite so. So I know my constitution can stand it. If you are not quite sure about your ever having been christened, I must say I think it rather dangerous your venturing on it now. It might make you very unwell. You can hardly have forgotten that some one very closely connected with you was very nearly carried off this week in Paris by a severe chill.

JACK. Yes, but you said yourself that a severe chill was not hereditary.

ALGERNON. It usen't to be, I know—but I daresay it is now. Science is always making wonderful improvements in things.

JACK. (*Picking up the muffin-dish.*) Oh, that is nonsense; you are always talking nonsense.

ALGERNON. Jack, you are at the muffins again! I wish you wouldn't. There are only two left. (*Takes them.*) I told you I was particularly fond of muffins.

JACK. But I hate tea-cake.

ALGERNON. Why on earth then do you allow tea-cake to be served up for your guests? What ideas you have of hospitality!

1030 JACK. Algernon! I have already told you to go. I don't want you here. Why don't you go!

ALGERNON. I haven't quite finished my tea yet! and

there is still one muffin left. (*Jack groans, and sinks into a chair. Algernon still continues eating.*)

ACT DROP

ACT 3

SCENE

(*Morning-room at the Manor House. Gwendolen and Cecily are at the window, looking out into the garden.*)

GWENDOLEN. The fact that they did not follow us at once into the house, as any one else would have done, seems to me to show that they have some sense of shame left.

5   CECILY. They have been eating muffins. That looks like repentance.

GWENDOLEN. (*After a pause.*) They don't seem to notice us at all. Couldn't you cough?

CECILY. But I haven't got a cough.

10   GWENDOLEN. They're looking at us. What effrontery!

CECILY. They're approaching. That's very forward of them.

GWENDOLEN. Let us preserve a dignified silence.

CECILY. Certainly. It's the only thing to do now.

(*Enter Jack followed by Algernon. They whistle some dreadful popular air from a British Opera.*)

15   GWENDOLEN. This dignified silence seems to produce an unpleasant effect.

CECILY. A most distasteful one.

GWENDOLEN. But we will not be the first to speak.

CECILY. Certainly not.

20   GWENDOLEN. Mr. Worthing, I have something very particular to ask you. Much depends on your reply.

CECILY. Gwendolen, your common sense is invaluable. Mr. Moncrieff, kindly answer me the following question. Why did you pretend to be my guardian's

25   brother?

ALGERNON. In order that I might have an opportunity of meeting you.

CECILY. (*To Gwendolen.*) That certainly seems a satisfactory explanation, does it not?

30   GWENDOLEN. Yes, dear, if you can believe him.

CECILY. I don't. But that does not affect the wonderful beauty of his answer.

GWENDOLEN. True. In matters of grave importance, style, not sincerity is the vital thing. Mr. Worthing,

35   what explanation can you offer to me for pretending to have a brother? Was it in order that you might have an opportunity of coming up to town to see me as often as possible?

JACK. Can you doubt it, Miss Fairfax?

40   GWENDOLEN. I have the gravest doubts upon the subject. But I intend to crush them. This is not the moment for German scepticism.[1] (*Moving to Cecily.*) Their explanations appear to be quite satisfactory, especially Mr. Worthing's. That seems to me to have the

45   stamp of truth upon it.

CECILY. I am more than content with what Mr. Moncrieff said. His voice alone inspires one with absolute credulity.

GWENDOLEN. Then you think we should forgive them?

50   CECILY. Yes. I mean no.

GWENDOLEN. True! I had forgotten. There are principles at stake that one cannot surrender. Which of us should tell them? The task is not a pleasant one.

CECILY. Could we not both speak at the same time?

55   GWENDOLEN. An excellent idea! I nearly always speak at the same time as other people. Will you take the time from me?

CECILY. Certainly.

(*Gwendolen beats time with uplifted finger.*)

GWENDOLEN and CECILY. (*Speaking together.*) Your
60   Christian names are still an insuperable barrier. That is all!

JACK and ALGERNON. (*Speaking together.*) Our Christian names! Is that all? But we are going to be christened this afternoon.

---

1   *German scepticism* According to the school of philosophy deriving from Immanuel Kant, we do not always perceive the true state of things-in-themselves.

GWENDOLEN. (*To Jack.*) For my sake you are prepared
65   to do this terrible thing?

JACK. I am.

CECILY. (*To Algernon.*) To please me you are ready to
face this fearful ordeal?

ALGERNON. I am!

70 GWENDOLEN. How absurd to talk of the equality of the
sexes! Where questions of self-sacrifice are concerned,
men are infinitely beyond us.

JACK. We are. (*Clasps hands with Algernon.*)

CECILY. They have moments of physical courage of
75   which we women know absolutely nothing.

GWENDOLEN. (*To Jack.*) Darling!

ALGERNON. (*To Cecily.*) Darling! (*They fall into each
other's arms.*)

(*Enter Merriman. When he enters he coughs loudly, seeing
the situation.*)

MERRIMAN. Ahem! Ahem! Lady Bracknell!

80 JACK. Good heavens!

(*Enter Lady Bracknell. The couples separate in alarm. Exit
Merriman.*)

LADY BRACKNELL. Gwendolen! What does this mean?

GWENDOLEN. Merely that I am engaged to be married
to Mr. Worthing, Mamma.

LADY BRACKNELL. Come here. Sit down. Sit down
85   immediately. Hesitation of any kind is a sign of mental
decay in the young, of physical weakness in the old.
(*Turns to Jack.*) Apprised, sir, of my daughter's sudden
flight by her trusty maid, whose confidence[1] I purchased
by means of a small coin, I followed her at once by a
90   luggage train. Her unhappy father is, I am glad to say,
under the impression that she is attending a more than
usually lengthy lecture by the University Extension
Scheme[2] on the Influence of a permanent income on
Thought. I do not propose to undeceive him. Indeed I
95   have never undeceived him on any question. I would

---

[1] *confidence* Sharing of a secret.

[2] *University Extension Scheme* Attempt to broaden access to education by offering public lectures and part-time courses.

consider it wrong. But of course, you will clearly
understand that all communication between yourself and
my daughter must cease immediately from this moment.
On this point, as indeed on all points, I am firm.

100 JACK. I am engaged to be married to Gwendolen, Lady
Bracknell!

LADY BRACKNELL. You are nothing of the kind, sir. And
now, as regards Algernon!… Algernon!

ALGERNON. Yes, Aunt Augusta.

105 LADY BRACKNELL. May I ask if it is in this house that
your invalid friend Mr. Bunbury resides?

ALGERNON. (*Stammering.*) Oh! No! Bunbury doesn't
live here. Bunbury is somewhere else at present. In fact,
Bunbury is dead.

110 LADY BRACKNELL. Dead! When did Mr. Bunbury die?
His death must have been extremely sudden.

ALGERNON. (*Airily.*) Oh! I killed Bunbury this
afternoon. I mean poor Bunbury died this afternoon.

LADY BRACKNELL. What did he die of?

115 ALGERNON. Bunbury? Oh, he was quite exploded.

LADY BRACKNELL. Exploded! Was he the victim of a
revolutionary outrage? I was not aware that Mr. Bunbury was interested in social legislation. If so, he is well
punished for his morbidity.

120 ALGERNON. My dear Aunt Augusta, I mean he was
found out! The doctors found out that Bunbury could
not live, that is what I mean—so Bunbury died.

LADY BRACKNELL. He seems to have had great
confidence in the opinion of his physicians. I am glad,
125   however, that he made up his mind at the last to some
definite course of action, and acted under proper
medical advice. And now that we have finally got rid of
this Mr. Bunbury, may I ask, Mr. Worthing, who is that
young person whose hand my nephew Algernon is now
130   holding in what seems to me a peculiarly unnecessary
manner?

JACK. That lady is Miss Cecily Cardew, my ward.

(*Lady Bracknell bows coldly to Cecily.*)

ALGERNON. I am engaged to be married to Cecily, Aunt
Augusta.

135 LADY BRACKNELL. I beg your pardon?

CECILY.   Mr. Moncrieff and I are engaged to be married, Lady Bracknell.

LADY BRACKNELL.   (*With a shiver, crossing to the sofa and sitting down.*) I do not know whether there is anything peculiarly exciting in the air of this particular part of Hertfordshire, but the number of engagements that go on seems to me considerably above the proper average that statistics have laid down for our guidance. I think some preliminary inquiry on my part would not be out of place. Mr. Worthing, is Miss Cardew at all connected with any of the larger railway stations in London? I merely desire information. Until yesterday I had no idea that there were any families or persons whose origin was a Terminus.[1]

(*Jack looks perfectly furious, but restrains himself.*)

JACK.   (*In a clear, cold voice.*) Miss Cardew is the granddaughter of the late Mr. Thomas Cardew of 149 Belgrave Square, S.W.; Gervase Park, Dorking, Surrey; and the Sporran, Fifeshire, N.B.

LADY BRACKNELL.   That sounds not unsatisfactory. Three addresses always inspire confidence, even in tradesmen. But what proof have I of their authenticity?

JACK.   I have carefully preserved the Court Guides[2] of the period. They are open to your inspection, Lady Bracknell.

LADY BRACKNELL.   (*Grimly.*) I have known strange errors in that publication.

JACK.   Miss Cardew's family solicitors are Messrs. Markby, Markby, and Markby.

LADY BRACKNELL.   Markby, Markby, and Markby? A firm of the very highest position in their profession. Indeed I am told that one of the Mr. Markbys is occasionally to be seen at dinner parties. So far I am satisfied.

JACK.   (*Very irritably.*) How extremely kind of you, Lady Bracknell! I have also in my possession, you will be pleased to hear, certificates of Miss Cardew's birth, baptism, whooping cough, registration, vaccination, confirmation, and the measles; both the German and the English variety.

LADY BRACKNELL.   Ah! A life crowded with incident, I see; though perhaps somewhat too exciting for a young girl. I am not myself in favour of premature experiences. (*Rises, looks at her watch.*) Gwendolen! the time approaches for our departure. We have not a moment to lose. As a matter of form, Mr. Worthing, I had better ask you if Miss Cardew has any little fortune?

JACK.   Oh! about a hundred and thirty thousand pounds in the Funds.[3] That is all. Goodbye, Lady Bracknell. So pleased to have seen you.

LADY BRACKNELL.   (*Sitting down again.*) A moment, Mr. Worthing. A hundred and thirty thousand pounds! And in the Funds! Miss Cardew seems to me a most attractive young lady, now that I look at her. Few girls of the present day have any really solid qualities, any of the qualities that last, and improve with time. We live, I regret to say, in an age of surfaces. (*To Cecily.*) Come over here, dear. (*Cecily goes across.*) Pretty child! your dress is sadly simple, and your hair seems almost as Nature might have left it. But we can soon alter all that. A thoroughly experienced French maid produces a really marvellous result in a very brief space of time. I remember recommending one to young Lady Lancing, and after three months her own husband did not know her.

JACK.   And after six months nobody knew her.

LADY BRACKNELL.   (*Glares at Jack for a few moments. Then bends, with a practised smile, to Cecily.*) Kindly turn round, sweet child. (*Cecily turns completely round.*) No, the side view is what I want. (*Cecily presents her profile.*) Yes, quite as I expected. There are distinct social possibilities in your profile. The two weak points in our age are its want of principle and its want of profile. The chin a little higher, dear. Style largely depends on the way the chin is worn. They are worn very high, just at present. Algernon!

ALGERNON.   Yes, Aunt Augusta!

---

1   *Terminus*   Railway terminal.

2   *Court Guides*   Directory of names and addresses of those members of the nobility, gentry, and society who have been presented at court.

3   *the Funds*   Investments in government debt offering a reliable amount of interest.

LADY BRACKNELL.   There are distinct social possibilities in Miss Cardew's profile.

ALGERNON.   Cecily is the sweetest, dearest, prettiest girl in the whole world. And I don't care twopence about social possibilities.

LADY BRACKNELL.   Never speak disrespectfully of Society, Algernon. Only people who can't get into it do that. (*To Cecily.*) Dear child, of course you know that Algernon has nothing but his debts to depend upon. But I do not approve of mercenary marriages. When I married Lord Bracknell I had no fortune of any kind. But I never dreamed for a moment of allowing that to stand in my way. Well, I suppose I must give my consent.

ALGERNON.   Thank you, Aunt Augusta.

LADY BRACKNELL.   Cecily, you may kiss me!

CECILY.   (*Kisses her.*) Thank you, Lady Bracknell.

LADY BRACKNELL.   You may also address me as Aunt Augusta for the future.

CECILY.   Thank you, Aunt Augusta.

LADY BRACKNELL.   The marriage, I think, had better take place quite soon.

ALGERNON.   Thank you, Aunt Augusta.

CECILY.   Thank you, Aunt Augusta.

LADY BRACKNELL.   To speak frankly, I am not in favour of long engagements. They give people the opportunity of finding out each other's character before marriage, which I think is never advisable.

JACK.   I beg your pardon for interrupting you, Lady Bracknell, but this engagement is quite out of the question. I am Miss Cardew's guardian, and she cannot marry without my consent until she comes of age. That consent I absolutely decline to give.

LADY BRACKNELL.   Upon what grounds may I ask? Algernon is an extremely, I may almost say an ostentatiously, eligible young man. He has nothing, but he looks everything. What more can one desire?

JACK.   It pains me very much to have to speak frankly to you, Lady Bracknell, about your nephew, but the fact is that I do not approve at all of his moral character. I suspect him of being untruthful.

(*Algernon and Cecily look at him in indignant amazement.*)

LADY BRACKNELL.   Untruthful! My nephew Algernon? Impossible! He is an Oxonian.[1]

JACK.   I fear there can be no possible doubt about the matter. This afternoon during my temporary absence in London on an important question of romance, he obtained admission to my house by means of the false pretence of being my brother. Under an assumed name he drank, I've just been informed by my butler, an entire pint bottle of my Perrier-Jouet, Brut, '89; wine I was specially reserving for myself. Continuing his disgraceful deception, he succeeded in the course of the afternoon in alienating the affections of my only ward. He subsequently stayed to tea, and devoured every single muffin. And what makes his conduct all the more heartless is, that he was perfectly well aware from the first that I have no brother, that I never had a brother, and that I don't intend to have a brother, not even of any kind. I distinctly told him so myself yesterday afternoon.

LADY BRACKNELL.   Ahem! Mr. Worthing, after careful consideration I have decided entirely to overlook my nephew's conduct to you.

JACK.   That is very generous of you, Lady Bracknell. My own decision, however, is unalterable. I decline to give my consent.

LADY BRACKNELL.   (*To Cecily.*) Come here, sweet child. (*Cecily goes over.*) How old are you, dear?

CECILY.   Well, I am really only eighteen, but I always admit to twenty when I go to evening parties.

LADY BRACKNELL.   You are perfectly right in making some slight alteration. Indeed, no woman should ever be quite accurate about her age. It looks so calculating … (*In a meditative manner.*) Eighteen, but admitting to twenty at evening parties. Well, it will not be very long before you are of age and free from the restraints of tutelage. So I don't think your guardian's consent is, after all, a matter of any importance.

JACK.   Pray excuse me, Lady Bracknell, for interrupting you again, but it is only fair to tell you that according to the terms of her grandfather's will Miss Cardew does not come legally of age till she is thirty-five.

---

[1] *Oxonian*   One who has attended Oxford University.

LADY BRACKNELL.   That does not seem to me to be a grave objection. Thirty-five is a very attractive age. London society is full of women of the very highest birth who have, of their own free choice, remained thirty-five for years. Lady Dumbleton is an instance in point. To my own knowledge she has been thirty-five ever since she arrived at the age of forty, which was many years ago now. I see no reason why our dear Cecily should not be even still more attractive at the age you mention than she is at present. There will be a large accumulation of property.

CECILY.   Algy, could you wait for me till I was thirty-five?

ALGERNON.   Of course I could, Cecily. You know I could.

CECILY.   Yes, I felt it instinctively, but I couldn't wait all that time. I hate waiting even five minutes for anybody. It always makes me rather cross. I am not punctual myself, I know, but I do like punctuality in others, and waiting, even to be married, is quite out of the question.

ALGERNON.   Then what is to be done, Cecily?

CECILY.   I don't know, Mr. Moncrieff.

LADY BRACKNELL.   My dear Mr. Worthing, as Miss Cardew states positively that she cannot wait till she is thirty-five—a remark which I am bound to say seems to me to show a somewhat impatient nature—I would beg of you to reconsider your decision.

JACK.   But my dear Lady Bracknell, the matter is entirely in your own hands. The moment you consent to my marriage with Gwendolen, I will most gladly allow your nephew to form an alliance with my ward.

LADY BRACKNELL.   (*Rising and drawing herself up.*) You must be quite aware that what you propose is out of the question.

JACK.   Then a passionate celibacy is all that any of us can look forward to.

LADY BRACKNELL.   That is not the destiny I propose for Gwendolen. Algernon, of course, can choose for himself. (*Pulls out her watch.*) Come, dear, (*Gwendolen rises*) we have already missed five, if not six, trains. To miss any more might expose us to comment on the platform.

(*Enter Dr. Chasuble.*)

CHASUBLE.   Everything is quite ready for the christenings.

LADY BRACKNELL.   The christenings, sir! Is not that somewhat premature?

CHASUBLE.   (*Looking rather puzzled, and pointing to Jack and Algernon.*) Both these gentlemen have expressed a desire for immediate baptism.

LADY BRACKNELL.   At their age? The idea is grotesque and irreligious! Algernon, I forbid you to be baptized. I will not hear of such excesses. Lord Bracknell would be highly displeased if he learned that that was the way in which you wasted your time and money.

CHASUBLE.   Am I to understand then that there are to be no christenings at all this afternoon?

JACK.   I don't think that, as things are now, it would be of much practical value to either of us, Dr. Chasuble.

CHASUBLE.   I am grieved to hear such sentiments from you, Mr. Worthing. They savour of the heretical views of the Anabaptists,[1] views that I have completely refuted in four of my unpublished sermons. However, as your present mood seems to be one peculiarly secular, I will return to the church at once. Indeed, I have just been informed by the pew-opener[2] that for the last hour and a half, Miss Prism has been waiting for me in the vestry.

LADY BRACKNELL.   (*Starting.*) Miss Prism! Did I hear you mention a Miss Prism?

CHASUBLE.   Yes, Lady Bracknell. I am on my way to join her.

LADY BRACKNELL.   Pray allow me to detain you for a moment. This matter may prove to be one of vital importance to Lord Bracknell and myself. Is this Miss Prism a female of repellent aspect, remotely connected with education?

---

[1] *heretical views ... Anabaptists* Although Anabaptists, members of a Protestant sect that rejects Anglican doctrine, believe in baptism, they reject the Anglican custom of baptizing infants. Dr. Chasuble is suggesting that Jack is heretical in denying the value of baptism in the Anglican church.

[2] *pew-opener* One assigned to open the doors of pews for privileged churchgoers.

CHASUBLE. (*Somewhat indignantly.*) She is the most cultivated of ladies, and the very picture of respectability.

LADY BRACKNELL. It is obviously the same person. May I ask what position she holds in your household?

CHASUBLE. (*Severely.*) I am a celibate, madam.

JACK. (*Interposing.*) Miss Prism, Lady Bracknell, has been for the last three years Miss Cardew's esteemed governess and valued companion.

LADY BRACKNELL. In spite of what I hear of her, I must see her at once. Let her be sent for.

CHASUBLE. (*Looking off.*) She approaches; she is nigh.

(*Enter Miss Prism hurriedly.*)

MISS PRISM. I was told you expected me in the vestry, dear Canon. I have been waiting for you there for an hour and three-quarters.

(*Catches sight of Lady Bracknell, who has fixed her with a stony glare. Miss Prism grows pale and quails. She looks anxiously round as if desirous to escape.*)

LADY BRACKNELL. (*In a severe, judicial voice.*) Prism! (*Miss Prism bows her head in shame.*) Come here, Prism! (*Miss Prism approaches in a humble manner.*) Prism! Where is that baby? (*General consternation. The Canon starts back in horror. Algernon and Jack pretend to be anxious to shield Cecily and Gwendolen from hearing the details of a terrible public scandal.*) Twenty-eight years ago, Prism, you left Lord Bracknell's house, Number 104, Upper Grosvenor Street,[1] in charge of a perambulator that contained a baby of the male sex. You never returned. A few weeks later, through the elaborate investigations of the Metropolitan police, the perambulator was discovered at midnight, standing by itself in a remote corner of Bayswater.[2] It contained the manuscript of a three-volume novel of more than usually revolting sentimentality. (*Miss Prism starts in involuntary indignation.*) But the baby was not there!

---

[1] *Upper Grosvenor Street* Street in Mayfair, an affluent area in London's West End.

[2] *Bayswater* District of London.

(*Every one looks at Miss Prism.*) Prism! Where is that baby? (*A pause.*)

MISS PRISM. Lady Bracknell, I admit with shame that I do not know. I only wish I did. The plain facts of the case are these. On the morning of the day you mention, a day that is for ever branded on my memory, I prepared as usual to take the baby out in its perambulator. I had also with me a somewhat old, but capacious hand-bag in which I had intended to place the manuscript of a work of fiction that I had written during my few unoccupied hours. In a moment of mental abstraction, for which I never can forgive myself, I deposited the manuscript in the bassinette, and placed the baby in the hand-bag.

JACK. (*Who has been listening attentively.*) But where did you deposit the hand-bag?

MISS PRISM. Do not ask me, Mr. Worthing.

JACK. Miss Prism, this is a matter of no small importance to me. I insist on knowing where you deposited the hand-bag that contained that infant.

MISS PRISM. I left it in the cloak-room of one of the larger railway stations in London.

JACK. What railway station?

MISS PRISM. (*Quite crushed.*) Victoria. The Brighton line. (*Sinks into a chair.*)

JACK. I must retire to my room for a moment. Gwendolen, wait here for me.

GWENDOLEN. If you are not too long, I will wait here for you all my life.

(*Exit Jack in great excitement.*)

CHASUBLE. What do you think this means, Lady Bracknell?

LADY BRACKNELL. I dare not even suspect, Dr. Chasuble. I need hardly tell you that in families of high position strange coincidences are not supposed to occur. They are hardly considered the thing.

(*Noises heard overhead as if some one was throwing trunks about. Every one looks up.*)

CECILY. Uncle Jack seems strangely agitated.

CHASUBLE. Your guardian has a very emotional nature.

LADY BRACKNELL.   This noise is extremely unpleasant. It sounds as if he was having an argument. I dislike arguments of any kind. They are always vulgar, and often convincing.

CHASUBLE.   (*Looking up.*) It has stopped now. (*The noise is redoubled.*)

LADY BRACKNELL.   I wish he would arrive at some conclusion.

GWENDOLEN.   This suspense is terrible. I hope it will last.

(*Enter Jack with a hand-bag of black leather in his hand.*)

JACK.   (*Rushing over to Miss Prism.*) Is this the handbag, Miss Prism? Examine it carefully before you speak. The happiness of more than one life depends on your answer.

MISS PRISM.   (*Calmly.*) It seems to be mine. Yes, here is the injury it received through the upsetting of a Gower Street omnibus[1] in younger and happier days. Here is the stain on the lining caused by the explosion of a temperance beverage,[2] an incident that occurred at Leamington. And here, on the lock, are my initials. I had forgotten that in an extravagant mood I had had them placed there. The bag is undoubtedly mine. I am delighted to have it so unexpectedly restored to me. It has been a great inconvenience being without it all these years.

JACK.   (*In a pathetic voice.*) Miss Prism, more is restored to you than this hand-bag. I was the baby you placed in it.

MISS PRISM.   (*Amazed.*) You?

JACK.   (*Embracing her.*) Yes … mother!

MISS PRISM.   (*Recoiling in indignant astonishment.*) Mr. Worthing! I am unmarried!

JACK.   Unmarried! I do not deny that is a serious blow. But after all, who has the right to cast a stone[3] against one who has suffered? Cannot repentance wipe out an act of folly? Why should there be one law for men, and another for women? Mother, I forgive you. (*Tries to embrace her again.*)

MISS PRISM.   (*Still more indignant.*) Mr. Worthing, there is some error. (*Pointing to Lady Bracknell.*) There is the lady who can tell you who you really are.

JACK.   (*After a pause.*) Lady Bracknell, I hate to seem inquisitive, but would you kindly inform me who I am?

LADY BRACKNELL.   I am afraid that the news I have to give you will not altogether please you. You are the son of my poor sister, Mrs. Moncrieff, and consequently Algernon's elder brother.

JACK.   Algy's elder brother! Then I have a brother after all. I knew I had a brother! I always said I had a brother! Cecily,—how could you have ever doubted that I had a brother? (*Seizes hold of Algernon.*) Dr. Chasuble, my unfortunate brother. Miss Prism, my unfortunate brother. Gwendolen, my unfortunate brother. Algy, you young scoundrel, you will have to treat me with more respect in the future. You have never behaved to me like a brother in all your life.

ALGERNON.   Well, not till to-day, old boy, I admit. I did my best, however, though I was out of practice. (*Shakes hands.*)

GWENDOLEN.   (*To Jack.*) My own! But what own are you? What is your Christian name, now that you have become some one else?

JACK.   Good heavens! … I had quite forgotten that point. Your decision on the subject of my name is irrevocable, I suppose?

GWENDOLEN.   I never change, except in my affections.

CECILY.   What a noble nature you have, Gwendolen!

JACK.   Then the question had better be cleared up at once. Aunt Augusta, a moment. At the time when Miss Prism left me in the hand-bag, had I been christened already?

LADY BRACKNELL.   Every luxury that money could buy, including christening, had been lavished on you by your fond and doting parents.

JACK.   Then I was christened! That is settled. Now, what name was I given? Let me know the worst.

LADY BRACKNELL.   Being the eldest son you were naturally christened after your father.

---

[1]   *Gower Street omnibus*   Public horse-drawn bus on a route in central London.

[2]   *temperance beverage*   Non-alcoholic drink. (The temperance movement aimed to prohibit all alcoholic beverages.)

[3]   *who has … stone*   See John 8.7.

515 JACK. (*Irritably.*) Yes, but what was my father's Christian name?

LADY BRACKNELL. (*Meditatively.*) I cannot at the present moment recall what the General's Christian name was. But I have no doubt he had one. He was eccentric, I 520 admit. But only in later years. And that was the result of the Indian climate, and marriage, and indigestion, and other things of that kind.

JACK. Algy! Can't you recollect what our father's Christian name was?

525 ALGERNON. My dear boy, we were never even on speaking terms. He died before I was a year old.

JACK. His name would appear in the Army Lists[1] of the period, I suppose, Aunt Augusta?

LADY BRACKNELL. The General was essentially a man of 530 peace, except in his domestic life. But I have no doubt his name would appear in any military directory.

JACK. The Army Lists of the last forty years are here. These delightful records should have been my constant study. (*Rushes to bookcase and tears the books out.*) M. 535 Generals … Mallam, Maxbohm, Magley, what ghastly names they have—Markby, Migsby, Mobbs, Moncrieff! Lieutenant 1840, Captain, Lieutenant-Colonel, Colonel, General 1869, Christian names, Ernest John. (*Puts book very quietly down and speaks quite calmly.*) I 540 always told you, Gwendolen, my name was Ernest, didn't I? Well, it is Ernest after all. I mean it naturally is Ernest.

LADY BRACKNELL. Yes, I remember now that the General was called Ernest, I knew I had some particular 545 reason for disliking the name.

GWENDOLEN. Ernest! My own Ernest! I felt from the first that you could have no other name!

JACK. Gwendolen, it is a terrible thing for a man to find out suddenly that all his life he has been speaking 550 nothing but the truth. Can you forgive me?

GWENDOLEN. I can. For I feel that you are sure to change.

JACK. My own one!

CHASUBLE. (*To Miss Prism.*) Lætitia! (*Embraces her.*)

555 MISS PRISM. (*Enthusiastically.*) Frederick! At last!

ALGERNON. Cecily! (*Embraces her.*) At last!

JACK. Gwendolen! (*Embraces her.*) At last!

LADY BRACKNELL. My nephew, you seem to be displaying signs of triviality.

560 JACK. On the contrary, Aunt Augusta, I've now realized for the first time in my life the vital Importance of Being Earnest.

TABLEAU

—1895

---

1 *Army Lists* Directories of officers.

IN CONTEXT

Wilde and "The Public"

Interview with Oscar Wilde, *St. James Gazette* (January 1895)

I found Mr. Oscar Wilde (writes a Representative) making ready to depart on a short visit to Algiers,[1] and reading—of course, nothing so obvious as a time-table, but a French newspaper which contained an account of the first night of *The Ideal Husband*[2] and its author's appearance after the play.

"How well the French appreciate these brilliant willful moments in an artist's life," remarked Mr. Wilde, handing me the article as if he considered the interview already at an end.

"Does it give you any pleasure," I inquired, "to appear before the curtain after the production of your plays?"

"None whatsoever. No artist finds any interest in seeing the public. The public is very much interested in seeing an artist. Personally, I prefer the French custom, according to which the name of the dramatist is announced to the public by the oldest actor in the piece."

"Would you advocate," I asked, "this custom in England?"

"Certainly. The more the public is interested in artists, the less it is interested in art. The personality of the artist is not a thing the public should know anything about. It is too accidental." Then, after a pause—

"It might be more interesting if the name of the author were announced by the *youngest* actor present."

"It is only in deference, then, to the imperious mandate of the public that you have appeared before the curtain?"

"Yes; I have always been very good-natured about that. The public has always been so appreciative of my work I felt it would be a pity to spoil its evening."

"I notice some people have found fault with the character of your speeches."

"Yes, the old-fashioned idea was that the dramatist should appear and merely thank his kind friends for their patronage and presence. I am glad to say I have altered all that. The artist cannot be degraded into the servant of the public. While I have always recognized the cultured appreciation that actors and audience have shown for my work, I have equally recognized that humility is for the hypocrite, modesty for the incompetent. Assertion is at once the duty and privilege of the artist."

"To what do you attribute, Mr. Wilde, the fact that so few men of letters besides yourself have written plays for public presentation?"

"Primarily the existence of an irresponsible censorship. The fact that my *Salomé* cannot be performed is sufficient to show the folly of such an institution. If painters were obliged to show their pictures to clerks at Somerset House, those who think in form and colour would adopt some other mode of expression. If every novel had to be submitted to a police magistrate, those whose passion is fiction would seek some new mode of realization. No art ever survived censorship; no art ever will."

"And secondly?"

---

[1] *Algiers*   North African city on the Mediterranean coast, capital of modern-day Algeria.

[2] *The Ideal Husband*   I.e., Wilde's play *An Ideal Husband*. The play, which had opened on 3 January 1895, was currently enjoying a very successful run at the Haymarket Theatre.

"Secondly to the rumour persistently spread abroad by journalists for the last thirty years, that the duty of the dramatist was to please the public. The aim of art is no more to give pleasure than to give pain. The aim of art is to be art. As I said once before, the work of art is to dominate the spectator—the spectator is not to dominate art."

"You admit no exceptions?"

"Yes. Circuses where it seems the wishes of the public might be reasonably carried out."

"Do you think," I inquired, "that French dramatic criticism is superior to our own?"

"It would be unfair to confuse French dramatic criticism with English theatrical criticism. The French dramatic critic is always a man of culture and generally a man of letters. In France poets like Gautier[1] have been dramatic critics. In England they are drawn from a less distinguished class. They have neither the same capacities nor the same opportunities. They have all the moral qualities, but none of the artistic qualifications. For the criticism of such a complex mode of art as the drama the highest culture is necessary. No one can criticize drama who is not capable of receiving impressions from the other arts also."

"You admit they are sincere?"

"Yes; but their sincerity is little more than stereotyped[2] stupidity. The critic of the drama should be versatile as the actor. He should be able to change his mood at will and should catch the colour of the moment."

"At least they are honest?"

"Absolutely. I don't believe there is a single dramatic critic in London who would deliberately set himself to misrepresent the work of any dramatist—unless, of course, he personally disliked the dramatist, or had some play of his own he wished to produce at the same theatre, or had an old friend among the actors, or some natural reasons of that kind. I am speaking, however, of London dramatic critics. In the provinces both audience and critics are cultured. In London it is only the audience who are cultured."

"I fear you do not rate our dramatic critics very highly, Mr. Wilde; but, at all events, they are incorruptible?"

"In a market where there are no bidders."

"Still their memories stand them in good stead," I pleaded.

"The old talk of having seen Macready[;][3] that must be a very painful memory. The middle-aged boast that they can recall *Diplomacy*:[4] hardly a pleasant reminiscence."

"You deny them, then, even a creditable past?"

"They have no past and no future, and are incapable of realizing the colour of the moment that finds them at the play."

"What do you propose should be done?"

"They should be pensioned off, and only allowed to write on politics or theology or bimetallism,[5] or some subject easier than art."

"In fact," I said, carried away by Mr. Wilde's aphorisms, "they should be seen and not heard."

"The old should neither be seen nor heard," said Mr. Wilde with some emphasis.

---

[1] *Gautier*   Théophile Gautier (1811–72), French poet, novelist, and dramatist.

[2] *stereotyped*   I.e., repeated without variation.

[3] *Macready*   William Charles Macready (1793–1873), English actor and theater manager.

[4] *Diplomacy*   An English adaptation of the French play *Dora* (1878), by Victorien Sardou (1831–1908).

[5] *bimetallism*   Monetary standard in which currency value is fixed to two types of precious metals, typically gold and silver.

"You said the other day there were only two dramatic critics in London. May I ask—"

"They must have been greatly gratified by such an admission from me; but I am bound to say that since last week I have struck one of them from the list."

"Whom have you left in?"

"I think I had better not mention his name. It might make him too conceited. Conceit is the privilege of the creative."

"How would you define ideal dramatic criticism?"

"As far as my work is concerned[,] unqualified appreciation."

"And whom have you omitted?"

"Mr. William Archer, of the *World*."[1]

"What do you chiefly object to in his article?"

"I object to nothing in the article, but I grieve at everything in it. It is bad taste in him to write of me by my Christian name, and he need not have stolen his vulgarisms from the *National Observer* in its most impudent and impotent days."

"Mr. Archer asked whether[,] if it was agreeable to you to be hailed by your Christian name when the enthusiastic spectators called you before the curtain."

"To be so addressed by enthusiastic spectators is as great a compliment as to be written of by one's Christian name is, in a journalist, bad manners. Bad manners make a journalist."

"Do you think French actors, like French criticism, superior to our own?"

"The English actors act quite as well; but they act best between the lines. They lack the superb elocution of the French—so clear, so cadenced, and so musical. A long sustained speech seems to exhaust them. At the Théâtre Français we go to listen, to an English theatre we go to look. There are, of course, exceptions. Mr. George Alexander, Mr. Lewis Waller, Mr. Forbes Robertson, and others I might mention, have superb voices and know how to use them. I wish I could say the same of the critics; but in the case of the literary drama in England there is too much of what is technically known as 'business.'[2] Yet there is more than one of our English actors who is capable of producing a wonderful dramatic effect by aid of a monosyllable and two cigarettes."

For a moment Mr. Wilde was silent, and then added, "Perhaps, after all, that is acting."

"But are you satisfied with the interpreters of *The Ideal Husband*?"

"I am charmed with all of them. Perhaps they are a little too fascinating. The stage is the refuge of the too fascinating."

"Have you heard it said that all the characters in your play talk as you do?"

"Rumours of that kind have reached me from time to time," said Mr. Wilde, lighting a cigarette, "and I should fancy that some such criticism has been made. The fact is that it is only in the last few years that the dramatic critic has had the opportunity of seeing plays written by anyone who has a mastery of style. In the case of a dramatist, also an artist, it is impossible not to feel that the work of art, to be a work of art, must be dominated by the artist. Every play of Shakespeare is dominated by Shakespeare. Ibsen and Dumas[3] dominate their works. My works are dominated by myself."

"Have you ever been influenced by any of your predecessors?"

"It is enough for me to state definitely, and I hope once for all, that not a single dramatist in this century has ever in the smallest degree influenced me. Only two have interested me."

"And they are?"

---

[1] *Mr. William … World* For Archer's criticism of Wilde, see "*An Ideal Husband*," *The World*, 9 January 1895, 26–27.

[2] *business* On-stage action, as opposed to dialogue.

[3] *Ibsen* Norwegian playwright Henrik Ibsen (1828–1906); *Dumas* French author and playwright Alexandre Dumas (1824–95).

"Victor Hugo and Maeterlinck."[1]

"Other writers surely have influenced your other works?"

"Setting aside the prose and poetry of Greek and Latin authors, the only writers who have influenced me are Keats, Flaubert, and Walter Pater;[2] and before I came across them I had already gone more than halfway to meet them. Style must be in one's soul before one can recognize it in others."

"And do you consider *The Ideal Husband* the best of your plays?"

A charming smile crossed Mr. Wilde's face.

"Have you forgotten my classical expression—that only mediocrities improve? My three plays are to each other, as a wonderful young poet has beautifully said,

> as one white rose
> On one green stalk to another one.

They form a perfect cycle, and in their delicate sphere complete both life and art."

"Do you think that the critics will understand your new play,[3] which Mr. George Alexander has secured?"

"I hope not."

"I dare not ask, I suppose, if it will please the public?"

"When a play that is a work of art is produced on the stage, what is being tested is not the play, but the stage; when a play that is *not* a work of art is produced on the stage, what is being tested is not the play, but the public."

"What sort of play are we to expect?"

"It is exquisitely trivial, a delicate bubble of fancy, and it has its philosophy."

"Its philosophy!"

"That we should treat all the trivial things of life very seriously, and all the serious things of life with sincere and studied triviality."[4]

"You have no leanings towards realism?"

"None whatever. Realism is only a background; it cannot form an artistic motive for a play that is to be a work of art."

"Still I have heard you congratulated on your pictures of London society."

"If Robert Chiltern, the Ideal Husband, were a common clerk, the humanity of his tragedy would be none the less poignant. I have placed him in the higher ranks of life merely because that is the side of social life with which I am best acquainted. In a play dealing with actualities to write with ease one must write with knowledge."

"Then you see nothing suggestive of treatment in the tragedies of everyday existence?"

"If a journalist is run over by a four-wheeler in the Strand, an incident I regret to say I have never witnessed, it suggests nothing to me from a dramatic point of view. Perhaps I am wrong; but the artist must have his limitations."

"Well," I said, rising to go, "I have enjoyed myself immensely."

---

[1] *Victor Hugo* French novelist, poet, and playwright (1802–85); *Maeterlinck* Maurice Maeterlinck (1862–1949), Belgian poet and playwright who was awarded the Nobel Prize for Literature in 1911.

[2] *Keats* John Keats, English poet (1795–1821); *Flaubert* French novelist Gustave Flaubert (1821–80), celebrated author of *Madame Bovary* (1867); *Walter Pater* English critic and scholar; he had reviewed some of Wilde's works.

[3] *new play* *The Importance of Being Earnest*, which opened on 14 February 1895.

[4] *That we should … triviality* The full title of the play is *The Importance of Being Earnest: A Trivial Comedy for Serious People*.

"I was sure you would," said Mr. Wilde. "But tell me how you manage your interviews."

"Oh, Pitman," I said carelessly.

"Is that your name? It's not a very *nice* name."

Then I left.

In Context

The First Wilde Trial (1895)

The following is an excerpt from the transcripts of the cross examination of Wilde by Edward Carson, the attorney defending the Marquess of Queensberry in the libel action[1] Wilde had brought against him.

Portrait of Oscar Wilde at the time of his trial, by Henri de Toulouse-Lautrec.

from The Transcripts of the Trial

CARSON.　You stated that your age was thirty-nine. I think you are over forty. You were born on 16th October 1854?

WILDE.　I have no wish to pose as being young. I am thirty-nine or forty. You have my certificate and that settles the matter.

CARSON.　But being born in 1854 makes you more than forty?

WILDE.　Ah! Very well.

---

[1] *Marquess ... libel action*　The Marquess of Queensberry, offended at the close friendship Wilde had formed with his son, Lord Alfred Douglas, had left a card at Wilde's club addressed to "Oscar Wilde posing as a sodomnite [sic]." Wilde felt that he had little choice but to prosecute, or to become publicly known as a man who was unable to deny such a charge. It was this prosecution which eventually led to his imprisonment and the exile of Lord Alfred Douglas.

CARSON.   What age is Lord Alfred Douglas?

WILDE.   Lord Alfred Douglas is about twenty-four, and was between twenty and twenty-one years of age when I first knew him. Down to the time of the interview in Tite Street, Lord Queensberry was friendly. I did not receive a letter on 3rd April in which Lord Queensberry desired that my acquaintance with his son should cease. After the interview I had no doubt that such was Lord Queensberry's desire. Notwithstanding Lord Queensberry's protest, my intimacy with Lord Alfred Douglas has continued down to the present moment.

CARSON.   You have stayed with him at many places?

WILDE.   Yes.

CARSON.   At Oxford? Brighton on several occasions? Worthing?

WILDE.   Yes.

CARSON.   You never took rooms for him?

WILDE.   No.

CARSON.   Were you at other places with him?

WILDE.   Yes; at Cromer and at Torquay.[1]

CARSON.   And in various hotels in London?

WILDE.   Yes; at one in Albemarle Street, and in Dover Street, and at the Savoy.[2]

CARSON.   Did you ever take rooms yourself in addition to your house in Tite Street?

WILDE.   Yes; at 10 and 11 St. James's Place. I kept the rooms from the month of October 1893 to the end of March 1894. Lord Alfred Douglas has stayed in those chambers, which are not far from Piccadilly.[3] I have been abroad with him several times and even lately to Monte Carlo. With reference to the writings which have been mentioned, it was not at Brighton, in 20 King's Road, that I wrote my article for *The Chameleon*.[4] I observed that there were also contributions from Lord Alfred Douglas, but these were not written at Brighton. I have seen them. I thought them exceedingly beautiful poems. One was "In Praise of Shame" and the other "Two Loves."

CARSON.   These loves. They were two boys?

WILDE.   Yes.

CARSON.   One boy calls his love "true love," and the other boy calls his love "shame"?

WILDE.   Yes.

CARSON.   Did you think that made any improper suggestion?

WILDE.   No, none whatever.

CARSON.   You read "The Priest and the Acolyte"?

WILDE.   Yes.

CARSON.   You have no doubt whatever that that was an improper story?

WILDE.   From the literary point of view it was highly improper. It is impossible for a man of literature to judge it otherwise; by literature, meaning treatment, selection of subject, and the like. I thought the treatment rotten and the subject rotten.

CARSON.   You are of opinion, I believe, that there is no such thing as an immoral book?

---

[1]   *Cromer … Torquay*   English seaside resort towns.

[2]   *the Savoy*   Hotel in central London, associated with luxury and quality of service.

[3]   *Piccadilly*   Road and principal shopping district in central London.

[4]   *The Chameleon*   Oxford undergraduate magazine, of which there was only one issue, that of December 1894 to which Wilde refers. In this issue Wilde's "Phrases and Philosophies for the Use of the Young" appeared, as well as an anonymous story about sexuality between men (actually written not by Wilde but by the editor), called "The Priest and the Acolyte." Though Wilde was not the author, the mere fact that a piece signed by him appeared juxtaposed to this story proved damaging to his reputation.

WILDE.   Yes.

CARSON.   May I take it that you think "The Priest and the Acolyte" was not immoral?

WILDE.   It was worse; it was badly written.

CARSON.   Was not the story that of a priest who fell in love with a boy who served him at the altar, and was discovered by the rector in the priest's room, and a scandal arose?

WILDE.   I have read it only once, in last November, and nothing will induce me to read it again. I don't care for it. It doesn't interest me.

CARSON.   Do you think the story blasphemous?

WILDE.   I think it violated every artistic canon[1] of beauty.

CARSON.   That is not an answer?

WILDE.   It is the only one I can give.

CARSON.   I want to see the position you pose in?

WILDE.   I do not think you should say that.

CARSON.   I have said nothing out of the way. I wish to know whether you thought the story blasphemous?

WILDE.   The story filled me with disgust. The end was wrong.

CARSON.   Answer the question, sir. Did you or did you not consider the story blasphemous?

WILDE.   I thought it disgusting.

CARSON.   I am satisfied with that. You know that when the priest in the story administers poison to the boy, he uses the words of the sacrament[2] of the Church of England?

WILDE.   That I entirely forgot.

CARSON.   Do you consider that blasphemous?

WILDE.   I think it is horrible. "Blasphemous" is not a word of mine.

[*Carson then read the following passage from "The Priest and the Acolyte."*]:

> Just before the consecration the priest took a tiny phial from the pocket of his cassock,[3] blessed it, and poured the contents into the chalice.
>
> When the time came for him to receive from the chalice, he raised it to his lips, but did not taste of it.
>
> He administered the sacred wafer to the child, and then he took his hand; he turned towards him; but when he saw the light in the beautiful face he turned again to the crucifix with a low moan. For one instant his courage failed him; then he turned to the little fellow again, and held the chalice to his lips:
>
> "The Blood of our Lord Jesus Christ, which was shed for thee, preserve thy body and soul unto everlasting life."

CARSON.   Do you approve of those words?

WILDE.   I think them disgusting, perfect twaddle.

CARSON.   I think you will admit that anyone who would approve of such an article would pose as guilty of improper practices?

---

[1] *canon* Rule.

[2] *sacrament* Holy Communion, a Christian ceremony in which wine and bread are sanctified and consumed.

[3] *cassock* Garment worn by clergy.

WILDE.   I do not think so in the person of another contributor to the magazine. It would show very bad literary taste. I strongly objected to the whole story. I took no steps to express disapproval of *The Chameleon* because I think it would have been beneath my dignity as a man of letters to associate myself with an Oxford undergraduate's productions. I am aware that the magazine may have been circulated among the undergraduates of Oxford. I do not believe that any book or work of art ever had any effect whatever on morality.

CARSON.   Am I right in saying that you do not consider the effect in creating morality or immorality?

WILDE.   Certainly, I do not.

CARSON.   So far as your works are concerned, you pose as not being concerned about morality or immorality?

WILDE.   I do not know whether you use the word "pose" in any particular sense.

CARSON.   It is a favorite word of your own?

WILDE.   Is it? I have no pose in this matter. In writing a play or a book, I am concerned entirely with literature—that is, with art. I aim not at doing good or evil, but in trying to make a thing that will have some quality of beauty.

CARSON.   Listen, sir. Here is one of the "Phrases and Philosophies for the Use of the Young" which you contributed: "Wickedness is a myth invented by good people to account for the curious attractiveness of others." You think that true?

WILDE.   I rarely think that anything I write is true.

CARSON.   Did you say "rarely"?

WILDE.   I said "rarely." I might have said "never"—not true in the actual sense of the word.

CARSON.   "Religions die when they are proved to be true." Is that true?

WILDE.   Yes; I hold that. It is a suggestion towards a philosophy of the absorption of religions by science, but it is too big a question to go into now.

CARSON.   Do you think that was a safe axiom to put forward for the philosophy of the young?

WILDE.   Most stimulating.

CARSON.   "If one tells the truth, one is sure, sooner or later, to be found out"?

WILDE.   That is a pleasing paradox, but I do not set very high store on it as an axiom.

CARSON.   Is it good for the young?

WILDE.   Anything is good that stimulates thought in whatever age.

CARSON.   Whether moral or immoral?

WILDE.   There is no such thing as morality or immorality in thought. There is immoral emotion.

CARSON.   "Pleasure is the only thing one should live for"?

WILDE.   I think that the realization of oneself is the prime aim of life, and to realize oneself through pleasure is finer than to do so through pain. I am, on that point, entirely on the side of the ancients—the Greeks. It is a pagan idea.

CARSON.   "A truth ceases to be true when more than one person believes in it"?

WILDE.   Perfectly. That would be my metaphysical definition of truth; something so personal that the same truth could never be appreciated by two minds.

CARSON.   "The condition of perfection is idleness: the aim of perfection is youth"?

WILDE.   Oh, yes; I think so. Half of it is true. The life of contemplation is the highest life, and so recognized by the philosopher.

CARSON.   "There is something tragic about the enormous number of young men there are in England at the present moment who start life with perfect profiles, and end by adopting some useful profession"?

WILDE.   I should think that the young have enough sense of humour.

CARSON.   You think that is humourous?

WILDE.   I think it is an amusing paradox, an amusing play on words.

CARSON.   What would anyone say would be the effect of "Phrases and Philosophies" taken in connection with such an article as "The Priest and the Acolyte"?

WILDE.   Undoubtedly it was the idea that might be formed that made me object so strongly to the story. I saw at once that maxims that were perfectly nonsensical, paradoxical, or anything you like, might be read in conjunction with it.

CARSON.   After the criticisms that were passed on *Dorian Gray*, was it modified a good deal?

WILDE.   No. Additions were made. In one case it was pointed out to me—not in a newspaper or anything of that sort, but by the only critic of the century whose opinion I set high, Mr. Walter Pater—that a certain passage was liable to misconstruction, and I made an addition.

CARSON.   This is in your introduction to *Dorian Gray*: "There is no such thing as a moral or an immoral book. Books are well written, or badly written." That expresses your view?

WILDE.   My view on art, yes.

CARSON.   Then I take it that no matter how immoral a book may be, if it is well written, it is, in your opinion, a good book?

WILDE.   Yes, if it were well written so as to produce a sense of beauty, which is the highest sense of which a human being can be capable. If it were badly written, it would produce a sense of disgust.

CARSON.   Then a well-written book putting forward perverted moral views may be a good book?

WILDE.   No work of art ever puts forward views. Views belong to people who are not artists.

CARSON.   A perverted novel might be a good book?

WILDE.   I don't know what you mean by a "perverted" novel.

CARSON.   Then I will suggest *Dorian Gray* as open to the interpretation of being such a novel?

WILDE.   That could only be to brutes and illiterates. The views of Philistines[1] on art are incalculably stupid.

CARSON.   An illiterate person reading *Dorian Gray* might consider it such a novel?

WILDE.   The views of illiterates on art are unaccountable. I am concerned only with my view of art. I don't care twopence what other people think of it.

CARSON.   The majority of persons would come under your definition of Philistines and illiterates?

WILDE.   I have found wonderful exceptions.

CARSON.   Do you think that the majority of people live up to the position you are giving us?

WILDE.   I am afraid they are not cultivated enough.

CARSON.   Not cultivated enough to draw the distinction between a good book and a bad book?

WILDE.   Certainly not.

CARSON.   The affection and love of the artist of *Dorian Gray* might lead an ordinary individual to believe that it might have a certain tendency?

WILDE.   I have no knowledge of the views of ordinary individuals.

CARSON.   You did not prevent the ordinary individual from buying your book?

WILDE.   I have never discouraged him.

[*Carson then read a long passage from Chapter 1 of* The Picture of Dorian Gray *(from "The story is simply this . . ." to "I must see Dorian Gray").*]

---

[1]   *Philistines*   Here, people who are uninterested in or hostile to the arts.

CARSON.   Now I ask you, Mr. Wilde, do you consider that that description of the feeling of one man towards a youth just grown up was a proper or an improper feeling?

WILDE.   I think it is the most perfect description of what an artist would feel on meeting a beautiful personality that was in some way necessary to his art and life.

CARSON.   You think that is a feeling a young man should have towards another?

WILDE.   Yes, as an artist.

[*Carson then read a long passage from Chapter 9 of* The Picture of Dorian Gray *(from "Let us sit down, Dorian" to "You are made to be worshipped").*]

CARSON.   Do you mean to say that that passage describes the natural feeling of one man towards another?

WILDE.   It would be the influence produced by a beautiful personality.

CARSON.   A beautiful person?

WILDE.   I said a "beautiful personality." You can describe it as you like. Dorian Gray's was a most remarkable personality.

CARSON.   May I take it that you, as an artist, have never known the feeling described here?

WILDE.   I have never allowed any personality to dominate my art.

CARSON.   Then you have never known the feeling you described?

WILDE.   No. It is a work of fiction.

CARSON.   So far as you are concerned you have no experience as to its being a natural feeling?

WILDE.   I think it is perfectly natural for any artist to admire intensely and love a young man. It is an incident in the life of almost every artist.

CARSON.   But let us go over it phrase by phrase. "I quite admit that I adored you madly." What do you say to that? Have you ever adored a young man madly?

WILDE.   No, not madly; I prefer love—that is a higher form.

CARSON.   Never mind about that. Let us keep down to the level we are at now?

WILDE.   I have never given adoration to anybody except myself. (*Loud laughter.*)

CARSON.   I suppose you think that a very smart thing?

WILDE.   Not at all.

CARSON.   Then you have never had that feeling?

WILDE.   No. The whole idea was borrowed from Shakespeare, I regret to say—yes, from Shakespeare's sonnets.

CARSON.   I believe you have written an article to show that Shakespeare's sonnets were suggestive of unnatural vice?

WILDE.   On the contrary I have written an article to show that they are not.[1] I objected to such a perversion being put upon Shakespeare.

CARSON.   "I have adored you extravagantly"?

WILDE.   Do you mean financially?

CARSON.   Oh, yes, financially! Do you think we are talking about finance?

WILDE.   I don't know what you are talking about.

CARSON.   Don't you? Well, I hope I shall make myself very plain before I have done. "I was jealous of everyone to whom you spoke." Have you ever been jealous of a young man?

WILDE.   Never in my life.

---

[1]   *an article ... not*   Cf. "The Portrait of Mr. W.H." first published in *Blackwood's Edinburgh Magazine*, 146.885 (July 1889), and then again in a limited edition in 1921.

CARSON. "I wanted to have you all to myself." Did you ever have that feeling?

WILDE. No; I should consider it an intense nuisance, an intense bore.

CARSON. "I grew afraid that the world would know of my idolatry." Why should he grow afraid that the world should know of it?

WILDE. Because there are people in the world who cannot understand the intense devotion, affection, and admiration that an artist can feel for a wonderful and beautiful personality. These are the conditions under which we live. I regret them.

CARSON. These unfortunate people, that have not the high understanding that you have, might put it down to something wrong?

WILDE. Undoubtedly; to any point they chose. I am not concerned with the ignorance of others.

CARSON. In another passage Dorian Gray receives a book. Was the book to which you refer a moral book?

WILDE. Not well written, but it gave me an idea.

CARSON. Was not the book you have in mind of a certain tendency?

WILDE. I decline to be cross-examined upon the work of another artist. It is an impertinence and a vulgarity.

[*Wilde then stated the book Carson referred to was* A Rebours, *by J.K. Huysmans; and, following an appeal by Sir Edward Clarke, Wilde's attorney, the judge ruled against further reference to it. Carson then read a long passage from Chapter 12 of* The Picture of Dorian Gray *(from "... I think it right that you should know the most dreadful things are being said about you in London" to "Dorian, your reputation is infamous ... ").*]

CARSON. Does not this passage suggest a charge of unnatural vice?

WILDE. It describes Dorian Gray as a man of very corrupt influence, though there is no statement as to the nature of the influence. But as a matter of fact I do not think that one person influences another, nor do I think there is any bad influence in the world.

CARSON. A man never corrupts a youth?

WILDE. I think not.

CARSON. Nothing could corrupt him?

WILDE. If you are talking of separate ages.

CARSON. No, sir, I am talking common sense.

WILDE. I do not think one person influences another.

CARSON. You don't think that flattering a young man, making love[1] to him, in fact, would be likely to corrupt him?

WILDE. No.

CARSON. Where was Lord Alfred Douglas staying when you wrote that letter to him?

WILDE. At the Savoy; and I was at Babbacombe, near Torquay.

CARSON. It was a letter in answer to something he had sent you?

WILDE. Yes, a poem.

CARSON. Why should a man of your age address a boy nearly twenty years younger as "My own boy"?

WILDE. I was fond of him. I have always been fond of him.

CARSON. Do you adore him?

---

[1] *making love* Until the 1960s this expression was generally used to refer to the process of wooing or courtship, not to any physical act of lovemaking.

WILDE.   No, but I have always liked him. I think it is a beautiful letter. It is a poem. I was not writing an ordinary letter. You might as well cross-examine me as to whether *King Lear* or a sonnet of Shakespeare was proper.

CARSON.   Apart from art, Mr. Wilde?

WILDE.   I cannot answer apart from art.

CARSON.   Suppose a man who was not an artist had written this letter, would you say it was a proper letter?

WILDE.   A man who was not an artist could not have written that letter.

CARSON.   Why?

WILDE.   Because nobody but an artist could write it. He certainly could not write the language unless he were a man of letters.

CARSON.   I can suggest, for the sake of your reputation, that there is nothing very wonderful in this "red rose-leaf lips of yours"?

WILDE.   A great deal depends on the way it is read.

CARSON.   "Your slim gilt soul walks between passion and poetry." Is that a beautiful phrase?

WILDE.   Not as you read it, Mr. Carson. You read it very badly.

CARSON.   I do not profess to be an artist; and when I hear you give evidence, I am glad I am not—

SIR EDWARD CLARKE.   I don't think my friend should talk like that. (*To witness*) Pray, do not criticize my friend's reading again.

CARSON.   Is that not an exceptional letter?

WILDE.   It is unique, I should say.

CARSON.   Was that the ordinary way in which you carried on your correspondence?

WILDE.   No; but I have often written to Lord Alfred Douglas, though I never wrote to another young man in the same way.

CARSON.   Have you often written letters in the same style as this?

WILDE.   I don't repeat myself in style.

CARSON.   Here is another letter which I believe you also wrote to Lord Alfred Douglas. Will you read it?

WILDE.   No; I decline. I don't see why I should.

CARSON.   Then I will.

Savoy Hotel,
Victoria Embankment, London.
Dearest of all Boys,
Your letter was delightful, red and yellow wine to me; but I am sad and out of sorts. Bosie,[1] you must not make scenes with me. They kill me, they wreck the loveliness of life. I cannot see you, so Greek and gracious, distorted with passion. I cannot listen to your curved lips saying hideous things to me. I would sooner——than have you bitter, unjust, hating. ... I must see you soon. You are the divine thing I want, the thing of grace and beauty; but I don't know how to do it. Shall I come to Salisbury? My bill here is £49 for a week. I have also got a new sitting-room. ... Why are you not here, my dear, my wonderful boy? I fear I must leave—no money, no credit, and a heart of lead.
Your own Oscar. ...

---

[1] *Bosie* Lord Alfred Douglas's nickname.

Is that an ordinary letter?

WILDE.   Everything I write is extraordinary. I do not pose as being ordinary, great heavens! Ask me any question you like about it.

CARSON.   Is it the kind of letter a man writes to another?

WILDE.   It was a tender expression of my great admiration for Lord Alfred Douglas. It was not, like the other, a prose poem. ...

---

from *De Profundis*[1]

... Suffering is one very long moment. We cannot divide it by seasons. We can only record its moods, and chronicle their return. With us time itself does not progress. It revolves. It seems to circle round one centre of pain. The paralysing immobility of a life every circumstance of which is regulated after an unchangeable pattern, so that we eat and drink and lie down and pray, or kneel at least for prayer, according to the inflexible laws of an iron formula: this immobile quality, that makes each dreadful day in the very minutest detail like its brother, seems to communicate itself to those external forces the very essence of whose existence is ceaseless change. Of seed-time or harvest, of the reapers bending over the corn, or the grape gatherers threading through the vines, of the grass in the orchard made white with broken blossoms or strewn with fallen fruit: of these we know nothing and can know nothing.

For us there is only one season, the season of sorrow. The very sun and moon seem taken from us. Outside, the day may be blue and gold, but the light that creeps down through the thickly-muffled glass of the small iron-barred window beneath which one sits is grey and niggard. It is always twilight in one's cell, as it is always twilight in one's heart. And in the sphere of thought, no less than in the sphere of time, motion is no more. The thing that you personally have long ago forgotten, or can easily forget, is happening to me now, and will happen to me again tomorrow. Remember this, and you will be able to understand a little of why I am writing, and in this manner writing. ...

A week later, I am transferred here. Three more months go over and my mother dies. No one knew how deeply I loved and honoured her. Her death was terrible to me; but I, once a lord of language, have no words in which to express my anguish and my shame. She and my father had bequeathed me a name they had made noble and honoured, not merely in literature, art, archaeology, and science, but in the public history of my own country, in its evolution as a nation. I had disgraced that name eternally. I had made it a low by-word among low people. I had dragged it through the very mire. I had given it to brutes that they might make it brutal, and to fools that they might turn it into a synonym for folly. What I suffered then, and still suffer, is not for pen to write or paper to record. My wife, always kind and gentle to me, rather than that I should hear the news from indifferent lips, travelled, ill as she was, all the way from Genoa to England to break to me herself the tidings of so irreparable, so irremediable, a loss. Messages of sympathy reached me from all who had still affection for me. Even people who had not known me personally, hearing that a new sorrow had broken into my life, wrote to ask that some expression of their condolence should be conveyed to me. ...

Three months go over. The calendar of my daily conduct and labour that hangs on the outside of my cell

---

[1] *De Profundis* Latin: From the Depths. "De profundis" is the opening phrase and conventional title of the Latin translation of Psalm 130, which in English begins "Out of the depths have I cried unto thee, O Lord." The psalm addresses divine mercy and the possibility of redemption.

When it was first published in 1905, *De Profundis* appeared with much of its autobiographical content expurgated in an effort to avoid offending the family of Lord Alfred Douglas, to whom the essay was addressed. Further editions followed over the course of the twentieth century, each reintroducing more of the cut material; the text did not appear in its full and correct version until 1962. The selections reprinted here are drawn from the 1913 edition.

door, with my name and sentence written upon it, tells me that it is May. ...

... I have lain in prison for nearly two years. Out of my nature has come wild despair; an abandonment to grief that was piteous even to look at; terrible and impotent rage; bitterness and scorn; anguish that wept aloud; misery that could find no voice; sorrow that was dumb. I have passed through every possible mood of suffering. Better than Wordsworth himself I know what Wordsworth meant when he said—

> Suffering is permanent, obscure, and dark
> And has the nature of infinity.[1]

But while there were times when I rejoiced in the idea that my sufferings were to be endless, I could not bear them to be without meaning. Now I find hidden somewhere away in my nature something that tells me that nothing in the whole world is meaningless, and suffering least of all. That something hidden away in my nature, like a treasure in a field, is Humility.

It is the last thing left in me, and the best: the ultimate discovery at which I have arrived, the starting-point for a fresh development. It has come to me right out of myself, so I know that it has come at the proper time. It could not have come before, nor later. Had anyone told me of it, I would have rejected it. Had it been brought to me, I would have refused it. As I found it, I want to keep it. I must do so. It is the one thing that has in it the elements of life, of a new life, Vita Nuova[2] for me. Of all things it is the strangest. One cannot acquire it, except by surrendering everything that one has. It is only when one has lost all things, that one knows that one possesses it.

Now I have realised that it is in me, I see quite clearly what I ought to do; in fact, must do. And when I use such a phrase as that, I need not say that I am not alluding to any external sanction or command. I admit none. I am far more of an individualist than I ever was. Nothing seems to me of the smallest value except what one gets out of oneself. My nature is seeking a fresh mode of self-realisation. That is all I am concerned with. And the first thing that I have got to do is to free myself from any possible bitterness of feeling against the world. I am completely penniless, and absolutely homeless. Yet there are worse things in the world than that. I am quite candid when I say that rather than go out from this prison with bitterness in my heart against the world, I would gladly and readily beg my bread from door to door. If I got nothing from the house of the rich I would get something at the house of the poor. Those who have much are often greedy; those who have little always share. I would not a bit mind sleeping in the cool grass in summer, and when winter came on sheltering myself by the warm close-thatched rick,[3] or under the penthouse of a great barn, provided I had love in my heart. The external things of life seem to me now of no importance at all. You can see to what intensity of individualism I have arrived—or am arriving rather, for the journey is long, and "where I walk there are thorns."[4]

Of course I know that to ask alms on the highway is not to be my lot, and that if ever I lie in the cool grass at night-time it will be to write sonnets to the moon. When I go out of prison, R——[5] will be waiting for me on the other side of the big iron-studded gate, and he is the symbol, not merely of his own affection, but of the affection of many others besides. I believe I am to have enough to live on for about eighteen months at any rate, so that if I may not write beautiful books, I may at least read beautiful books; and what joy can be greater? After that, I hope to be able to recreate my creative faculty.

---

[1] *Suffering ... infinity* From William Wordsworth's play *The Borderers* (1842).

[2] *Vita Nuova* Italian: New Life. See *La Vita Nuova* (1294), an autobiographical work in which the poet Dante Alighieri reflects on his unrequited love for an idealized woman and the spiritual growth that results from his feelings for her.

[3] *rick* Haystack.

[4] *where I ... thorns* From Wilde's 1893 play *A Woman of No Importance*, Act 4: "For me the world is shrivelled to a palm's breadth, and where I walk there are thorns."

[5] *R——* Robbie Ross (1869–1918), a critic and journalist who was close with Wilde for many years and served as his literary executor after his death.

But were things different: had I not a friend left in the world; were there not a single house open to me in pity; had I to accept the wallet and ragged cloak of sheer penury: as long as I am free from all resentment, hardness and scorn, I would be able to face the life with much more calm and confidence than I would were my body in purple and fine linen, and the soul within me sick with hate.

And I really shall have no difficulty. When you really want love you will find it waiting for you.

I need not say that my task does not end there. It would be comparatively easy if it did. There is much more before me. I have hills far steeper to climb, valleys much darker to pass through. And I have to get it all out of myself. Neither religion, morality, nor reason can help me at all.

Morality does not help me. I am a born antinomian.[1] I am one of those who are made for exceptions, not for laws. But while I see that there is nothing wrong in what one does, I see that there is something wrong in what one becomes. It is well to have learned that.

Religion does not help me. The faith that others give to what is unseen, I give to what one can touch, and look at. My gods dwell in temples made with hands; and within the circle of actual experience is my creed made perfect and complete: too complete, it may be, for like many or all of those who have placed their heaven in this earth, I have found in it not merely the beauty of heaven, but the horror of hell also. When I think about religion at all, I feel as if I would like to found an order for those who cannot believe: the Confraternity of the Faithless, one might call it, where on an altar, on which no taper burned, a priest, in whose heart peace had no dwelling, might celebrate with unblessed bread and a chalice empty of wine. Everything to be true must become a religion. And agnosticism should have its ritual no less than faith. It has sown its martyrs, it should reap its saints, and praise God daily for having hidden Himself from man. But whether it be faith or agnosticism, it must be nothing external to me. Its

symbols must be of my own creating. Only that is spiritual which makes its own form. If I may not find its secret within myself, I shall never find it: if I have not got it already, it will never come to me.

Reason does not help me. It tells me that the laws under which I am convicted are wrong and unjust laws, and the system under which I have suffered a wrong and unjust system. But, somehow, I have got to make both of these things just and right to me. And exactly as in Art one is only concerned with what a particular thing is at a particular moment to oneself, so it is also in the ethical evolution of one's character. I have got to make everything that has happened to me good for me. The plank bed, the loathsome food, the hard ropes shredded into oakum[2] till one's finger-tips grow dull with pain, the menial offices with which each day begins and finishes, the harsh orders that routine seems to necessitate, the dreadful dress that makes sorrow grotesque to look at, the silence, the solitude, the shame—each and all of these things I have to transform into a spiritual experience. There is not a single degradation of the body which I must not try and make into a spiritualising of the soul.

I want to get to the point when I shall be able to say quite simply, and without affectation that the two great turning-points in my life were when my father sent me to Oxford, and when society sent me to prison. I will not say that prison is the best thing that could have happened to me: for that phrase would savour of too great bitterness towards myself. I would sooner say, or hear it said of me, that I was so typical a child of my age, that in my perversity, and for that perversity's sake, I turned the good things of my life to evil, and the evil things of my life to good.

What is said, however, by myself or by others, matters little. The important thing, the thing that lies before me, the thing that I have to do, if the brief remainder of my days is not to be maimed, marred, and incomplete, is to absorb into my nature all that has been

---

1   *antinomian*   Literally, a Christian who believes that those who have received divine grace are above the laws of morality.

2   *oakum*   Separated rope fibers, used to stop up gaps in ships or windows. The task of picking rope apart to produce oakum was often forced upon prisoners sentenced to hard labor; the work was very unpleasant and damaging to the hands.

done to me, to make it part of me, to accept it without complaint, fear, or reluctance. The supreme vice is shallowness. Whatever is realised is right.

When first I was put into prison some people advised me to try and forget who I was. It was ruinous advice. It is only by realising what I am that I have found comfort of any kind. Now I am advised by others to try on my release to forget that I have ever been in a prison at all. I know that would be equally fatal. It would mean that I would always be haunted by an intolerable sense of disgrace, and that those things that are meant for me as much as for anybody else—the beauty of the sun and moon, the pageant of the seasons, the music of daybreak and the silence of great nights, the rain falling through the leaves, or the dew creeping over the grass and making it silver—would all be tainted for me, and lose their healing power, and their power of communicating joy. To regret one's own experiences is to arrest one's own development. To deny one's own experiences is to put a lie into the lips of one's own life. It is no less than a denial of the soul. …

Many men on their release carry their prison about with them into the air, and hide it as a secret disgrace in their hearts, and at length, like poor poisoned things, creep into some hole and die. It is wretched that they should have to do so, and it is wrong, terribly wrong, of society that it should force them to do so. Society takes upon itself the right to inflict appalling punishment on the individual, but it also has the supreme vice of shallowness, and fails to realise what it has done. When the man's punishment is over, it leaves him to himself; that is to say, it abandons him at the very moment when its highest duty towards him begins. It is really ashamed of its own actions, and shuns those whom it has punished, as people shun a creditor whose debt they cannot pay, or one on whom they have inflicted an irreparable, an irremediable wrong. I can claim on my side that if I realise what I have suffered, society should realise what it has inflicted on me; and that there should be no bitterness or hate on either side. …

I now see that sorrow, being the supreme emotion of which man is capable, is at once the type and test of all great art. What the artist is always looking for is the mode of existence in which soul and body are one and indivisible: in which the outward is expressive of the inward: in which form reveals. Of such modes of existence there are not a few: youth and the arts preoccupied with youth may serve as a model for us at one moment: at another we may like to think that, in its subtlety and sensitiveness of impression, its suggestion of a spirit dwelling in external things and making its raiment[1] of earth and air, of mist and city alike, and in its morbid sympathy of its moods, and tones, and colours, modern landscape art is realising for us pictorially what was realised in such plastic[2] perfection by the Greeks. Music, in which all subject is absorbed in expression and cannot be separated from it, is a complex example, and a flower or a child a simple example, of what I mean; but sorrow is the ultimate type both in life and art.

Behind joy and laughter there may be a temperament, coarse, hard and callous. But behind sorrow there is always sorrow. Pain, unlike pleasure, wears no mask. Truth in art is not any correspondence between the essential idea and the accidental existence; it is not the resemblance of shape to shadow, or of the form mirrored in the crystal to the form itself; it is no echo coming from a hollow hill, any more than it is a silver well of water in the valley that shows the moon to the moon and Narcissus to Narcissus.[3] Truth in art is the unity of a thing with itself: the outward rendered expressive of the inward: the soul made incarnate: the body instinct with spirit. For this reason there is no truth comparable to sorrow. There are times when sorrow seems to me to be the only truth. Other things may be illusions of the eye or the appetite, made to

---

[1] *raiment* Clothing.

[2] *plastic* Sculptural.

[3] *it is no … Narcissus* In Greek mythology, Echo, who is cursed so that she can only repeat the last words spoken by others, falls in love with the beautiful Narcissus. When Narcissus rejects her, she pines for him until she fades away, leaving only her voice behind. Narcissus then falls in love with his own reflection in a pool of water, and pines for the reflection until he, too, dies as a result of his desire, turning into the narcissus flower.

blind the one and cloy the other, but out of sorrow have the worlds been built, and at the birth of a child or a star there is pain. ...

... I remember when I was at Oxford saying to one of my friends as we were strolling round Magdalen's[1] narrow bird-haunted walks one morning in the year before I took my degree, that I wanted to eat of the fruit of all the trees in the garden of the world, and that I was going out into the world with that passion in my soul. And so, indeed, I went out, and so I lived. My only mistake was that I confined myself so exclusively to the trees of what seemed to me the sun-lit side of the garden, and shunned the other side for its shadow and its gloom. Failure, disgrace, poverty, sorrow, despair, suffering, tears even, the broken words that come from lips in pain, remorse that makes one walk on thorns, conscience that condemns, self-abasement that punishes, the misery that puts ashes on its head, the anguish that chooses sack-cloth for its raiment and into its own drink puts gall[2]—all these were things of which I was afraid. And as I had determined to know nothing of them, I was forced to taste each of them in turn, to feed on them, to have for a season, indeed, no other food at all. I don't regret for a single moment having lived for pleasure. I did it to the full, as one should do everything that one does. There was no pleasure I did not experience. I threw the pearl of my soul into a cup of wine.[3] I went down the primrose path[4] to the sound of flutes. I

lived on honeycomb. But to have continued the same life would have been wrong because it would have been limiting. I had to pass on. The other half of the garden had its secrets for me also. Of course all this is foreshadowed and prefigured in my books. ...

I see a far more intimate and immediate connection between the true life of Christ and the true life of the artist; and I take a keen pleasure in the reflection that long before sorrow had made my days her own and bound me to her wheel I had written in The Soul of Man[5] that he who would lead a Christ-like life must be entirely and absolutely himself, and had taken as my types not merely the shepherd on the hillside and the prisoner in his cell, but also the painter to whom the world is a pageant and the poet for whom the world is a song. I remember saying once to André Gide,[6] as we sat together in some Paris café, that while meta-physics had but little real interest for me, and morality absolutely none, there was nothing that either Plato or Christ had said that could not be transferred immediately into the sphere of Art and there find its complete fulfilment.

Nor is it merely that we can discern in Christ that close union of personality with perfection which forms the real distinction between the classical and romantic movement in life, but the very basis of his nature was the same as that of the nature of the artist—an intense and flamelike imagination. He realised in the entire sphere of human relations that imaginative sympathy which in the sphere of Art is the sole secret of creation. He understood the leprosy of the leper, the darkness of the blind, the fierce misery of those who live for pleasure, the strange poverty of the rich. Someone wrote to me in trouble, "When you are not on your pedestal you

---

1 *Magdalen*   I.e., Magdalen College, a prominent constituent college at Oxford University.

2 *sack-cloth*   I.e., coarse animal-hair fabric that is worn by Christians and biblical figures as an expression of mourning or repentance; *gall* Bitter substance. In Matthew 27.34, as Jesus is being crucified, Roman soldiers give him vinegar (or, in some translations, wine) mixed with gall to drink, which he refuses.

3 *the pearl ... cup of wine*   According to Pliny the Elder in his *Natural History* (77 CE), Cleopatra, to prove to Mark Antony that she was the most extravagant of the two, dissolved a precious pearl in a cup of wine vinegar and drank it.

4 *primrose path*   In Shakespeare's *Hamlet*, Ophelia tells her brother Laertes not to give her advice on virtue that he won't follow himself: "Do not, as some ungracious pastors do, / Show me the steep and thorny way to heaven, / Whiles, like a puffed and reckless libertine, / Himself the primrose path of dalliance treads / And recks not his own rede [advice]" (1.3.48–52).

5 *The Soul of Man*   "The Soul of Man under Socialism" (1891), an essay in which Wilde argues in favor of socialism and interprets Jesus as an exemplar of individualism.

6 *André Gide*   French writer and intellectual (1869–1951).

are not interesting." How remote was the writer from what Matthew Arnold calls "the Secret of Jesus."[1] Either would have taught him that whatever happens to another happens to oneself, and if you want an inscription to read at dawn and at night-time, and for pleasure or for pain, write up on the walls of your house in letters for the sun to gild and the moon to silver, "Whatever happens to oneself happens to another."

Christ's place indeed is with the poets. His whole conception of Humanity sprang right out of the imagination and can only be realised by it. What God was to the pantheist, man was to Him. He was the first to conceive the divided races as a unity. Before his time there had been gods and men, and, feeling through the mysticism of sympathy that in himself each had been made incarnate, he calls himself the Son of the one or the Son of the other, according to his mood. More than any one else in history he wakes in us that temper of wonder to which romance always appeals. There is still something to me almost incredible in the idea of a young Galilean peasant imagining that he could bear on his own shoulders the burden of the entire world; all that had already been done and suffered, and all that was yet to be done and suffered: the sins of Nero, of Cesare Borgia, of Alexander VI, and of him who was Emperor of Rome and Priest of the Sun:[2] the sufferings of those whose names are legion and whose dwelling is among the tombs:[3] oppressed nationalities, factory children, thieves, people in prison, outcasts, those who are dumb under oppression and whose silence is heard only of God; and not merely imagining this but actually achieving it, so that at the present moment all who come in contact with his personality, even though they may neither bow to his altar nor kneel before his priest, in some way find that the ugliness of their sin is taken away and the beauty of their sorrow revealed to them.

I had said of Christ that he ranks with the poets. That is true. Shelley and Sophocles[4] are of his company. But his entire life also is the most wonderful of poems. For "pity and terror"[5] there is nothing in the entire cycle of Greek tragedy to touch it. …

It is tragic how few people ever "possess their souls" before they die. "Nothing is more rare in any man," says Emerson, "than an act of his own."[6] It is quite true. Most people are other people. Their thoughts are some one else's opinions, their lives a mimicry, their passions a quotation. Christ was not merely the supreme individualist, but he was the first individualist in history. People have tried to make him out an ordinary philanthropist, or ranked him as an altruist with the scientific and sentimental. But he was really neither one nor the other. Pity he has, of course, for the poor, for those who are shut up in prisons, for the lowly, for the wretched; but he has far more pity for the rich, for the hard hedonists, for those who waste their freedom in becoming slaves to things, for those who wear soft raiment and live in kings' houses.[7] Riches and pleasure seemed to him to be really greater tragedies than poverty or sorrow. And as for altruism, who knew better than he that it is vocation not volition that determines us, and that one cannot gather grapes of thorns or figs from thistles?[8]

---

[1] *what Matthew … of Jesus* In *Literature and Dogma* (1873), poet and critic Matthew Arnold describes "the secret of Jesus" as a statement Jesus makes in John 12.25: "He that loveth his life shall lose it, and he that hateth his life in this world shall keep it unto life eternal."

[2] *Nero* Roman emperor (r. 54–68 CE) traditionally associated with corruption and debauchery; *Cesare Borgia* Italian political and military strategist (1475–1507) rumored to have played a role in many assassinations; *Alexander VI* Pope (r. 1492–1503) who was criticized for his corruption, especially in advancing the careers of the children he had illicitly fathered with several mistresses. Cesare Borgia was one of his children; *him who … the Sun* Roman emperor Elagabalus (r. 218–22), known for numerous transgressions against Roman sexual morality.

[3] *those whose … the tombs* In Mark 5.2–13, Jesus exorcises "a man with an unclean spirit, who had his dwelling among the tombs." Jesus asks the unclean spirit its name and receives the answer "My name is Legion: for we are many." He frees the man from possession by sending the spirits into a herd of pigs.

[4] *Shelley* I.e., Percy Bysshe Shelley (1792–1822), English Romantic poet; *Sophocles* Ancient Greek writer of tragedies (c. 496–406 BCE).

[5] *pity and terror* In his *Poetics*, Aristotle identifies these as the key emotions incited by tragedy.

[6] *Nothing … his own* See American writer Ralph Waldo Emerson's essay "The Preacher" (1880).

[7] *those who … houses* See Matthew 11.8.

[8] *one cannot … thistles* See Luke 6.44: "For every tree is known by his own fruit. For of thorns men do not gather figs, nor of a bramble bush gather they grapes."

To live for others as a definite self-conscious aim was not his creed. It was not the basis of his creed. When he says, "Forgive your enemies,"[1] it is not for the sake of the enemy, but for one's own sake that he says so, and because love is more beautiful than hate. In his own entreaty to the young man, "Sell all that thou hast and give to the poor,"[2] it is not of the state of the poor that he is thinking but of the soul of the young man, the soul that wealth was marring. In his view of life he is one with the artist who knows that by the inevitable law of self-perfection, the poet must sing, and the sculptor think in bronze, and the painter make the world a mirror for his moods, as surely and as certainly as the hawthorn must blossom in spring, and the corn turn to gold at harvest-time, and the moon in her ordered wanderings change from shield to sickle, and from sickle to shield.

But while Christ did not say to men, "Live for others," he pointed out that there was no difference at all between the lives of others and one's own life. By this means he gave to man an extended, a Titan[3] personality. Since his coming the history of each separate individual is, or can be made, the history of the world. Of course, culture has intensified the personality of man. Art has made us myriad-minded.[4] ...

But it is when he deals with a sinner that Christ is most romantic, in the sense of most real. The world had always loved the saint as being the nearest possible approach to the perfection of God. Christ, through some divine instinct in him, seems to have always loved the sinner as being the nearest possible approach to the perfection of man. His primary desire was not to reform people, any more than his primary desire was to relieve suffering. To turn an interesting thief into a tedious honest man was not his aim. He would have thought little of the Prisoners' Aid Society[5] and other modern movements of the kind. The conversion of a publican into a Pharisee[6] would not have seemed to him a great achievement. But in a manner not yet understood of the world he regarded sin and suffering as being in themselves beautiful holy things and modes of perfection.

It seems a very dangerous idea. It is—all great ideas are dangerous. That it was Christ's creed admits of no doubt. That it is the true creed I don't doubt myself.

Of course the sinner must repent. But why? Simply because otherwise he would be unable to realise what he had done. The moment of repentance is the moment of initiation. More than that: it is the means by which one alters one's past. The Greeks thought that impossible. They often say in their Gnomic aphorisms, "Even the Gods cannot alter the past."[7] Christ showed that the commonest sinner could do it, that it was the one thing he could do. Christ, had he been asked, would have said—I feel quite certain about it—that the moment the prodigal son[8] fell on his knees and wept, he made his having wasted his substance with harlots, his swine-herding and hungering for the husks they ate, beautiful and holy moments in his life. It is difficult for most people to grasp the idea. I dare say one has to go to prison to understand it. If so, it may be worth while going to prison. ...

Everything about my tragedy has been hideous, mean, repellent, lacking in style; our very dress makes us

---

[1] *Forgive your enemies*   See Matthew 5.44.

[2] *Sell all ... the poor*   Jesus gives this advice to a wealthy ruler who asks how he can obtain eternal life; see Luke 18.18–25.

[3] *Titan*   I.e., very large and powerful. In Greek mythology, the Titans are ancient gods.

[4] *myriad-minded*   Possessing vast imagination; or, mentally encompassing countless individuals.

[5] *Prisoners' Aid Society*   Organization intended to support people recently released from prison and help them integrate with "respectable" society.

[6] *publican into a Pharisee*   In a parable in Luke 18.9–14, Jesus contrasts the prayers of a publican (a tax-collector) with those of an upstanding member of the Pharisees (a branch of Judaism). The parable praises the publican, who humbly requests God's mercy, and condemns the Pharisee, who exalts himself for his own good actions.

[7] *Gnomic aphorisms*   Concise poetic statements of wisdom; *Even the ... the past*   Statement attributed to the fifth-century BCE Greek poet Agathon in Aristotle's *Nicomachean Ethics* 6.2.

[8] *prodigal son*   See the parable of the prodigal son in Luke 15.11–32. When a man gives each of his sons their inheritance, one son squanders the wealth but returns, repentant, after he begins to suffer during a famine. The father forgives his son and holds a feast to celebrate his return.

grotesque. We are the zanies[1] of sorrow. We are clowns whose hearts are broken. We are specially designed to appeal to the sense of humour. On November 13th, 1895, I was brought down here from London. From two o'clock till half-past two on that day I had to stand on the centre platform of Clapham Junction in convict dress, and handcuffed, for the world to look at. I had been taken out of the hospital ward without a moment's notice being given to me. Of all possible objects I was the most grotesque. When people saw me they laughed. Each train as it came up swelled the audience. Nothing could exceed their amusement. That was, of course, before they knew who I was. As soon as they had been informed they laughed still more. For half an hour I stood there in the grey November rain surrounded by a jeering mob.

For a year after that was done to me I wept every day at the same hour and for the same space of time. That is not such a tragic thing as possibly it sounds to you. To those who are in prison tears are a part of every day's experience. A day in prison on which one does not weep is a day on which one's heart is hard, not a day on which one's heart is happy.

Well, now I am really beginning to feel more regret for the people who laughed than for myself. Of course when they saw me I was not on my pedestal, I was in the pillory.[2] But it is a very unimaginative nature that only cares for people on their pedestals. A pedestal may be a very unreal thing. A pillory is a terrific reality. They should have known also how to interpret sorrow better. I have said that behind sorrow there is always sorrow. It were wiser still to say that behind sorrow there is always a soul. And to mock at a soul in pain is a dreadful thing. In the strangely simple economy of the world people only get what they give, and to those who have not enough imagination to penetrate the mere outward of things, and feel pity, what pity can be given save that of scorn? ...

... Of course to one so modern as I am, "Enfant de mon siècle,"[3] merely to look at the world will be always lovely. I tremble with pleasure when I think that on the very day of my leaving prison both the laburnum and the lilac will be blooming in the gardens, and that I shall see the wind stir into restless beauty the swaying gold of the one, and make the other toss the pale purple of its plumes, so that all the air shall be Arabia[4] for me. Linnaeus fell on his knees and wept for joy when he saw for the first time the long heath of some English upland made yellow with the tawny aromatic brooms of the common furze;[5] and I know that for me, to whom flowers are part of desire, there are tears waiting in the petals of some rose. It has always been so with me from my boyhood. There is not a single colour hidden away in the chalice of a flower, or the curve of a shell, to which, by some subtle sympathy with the very soul of things, my nature does not answer. Like Gautier, I have always been one of those "pour qui le monde visible existe."[6]

Still, I am conscious now that behind all this beauty, satisfying though it may be, there is some spirit hidden of which the painted forms and shapes are but modes of manifestation, and it is with this spirit that I desire to become in harmony. I have grown tired of the articulate utterances of men and things. The Mystical in Art, the Mystical in Life, the Mystical in Nature this is what I am looking for. It is absolutely necessary for me to find it somewhere.

All trials are trials for one's life, just as all sentences are sentences of death; and three times have I been tried.[7] The first time I left the box to be arrested, the

[1] *zanies* Clowns who ridiculously imitate other performers.

[2] *pillory* Apparatus for criminal punishment consisting of a wooden framework through which a person's head and arms were placed. The individual would remain locked in this position while being exposed to public ridicule and harassment.

[3] *Enfant de mon siècle* French: Child of my century.

[4] *Arabia* I.e., Paradise.

[5] *Linnaeus ... furze* Legendary moment in the life of Carolus Linnaeus (1707–78), Swedish scientist who laid the foundations of modern taxonomy, beginning with the classification of plants.

[6] *pour qui ... existe* French: for whom the visible world exists. This statement is attributed to the French poet and critic Théophile Gautier (1811–72) in the Goncourt Journal, kept by the writers Edmond and Jules de Goncourt for most of the latter half of the eighteenth century.

[7] *three times ... tried* In the gospels of Mark, Luke, and Matthew, Christ is tested in the wilderness by Satan, who, over the course of forty days, tempts Christ three times.

second time to be led back to the house of detention, the third time to pass into a prison for two years. Society, as we have constituted it, will have no place for me, has none to offer; but Nature, whose sweet rains fall on unjust and just alike, will have clefts in the rocks where I may hide, and secret valleys in whose silence I may weep undisturbed. She will hang the night with stars so that I may walk abroad in the darkness without stumbling, and send the wind over my footprints so that none may track me to my hurt: she will cleanse me in great waters, and with bitter herbs make me whole.

—1905 (WRITTEN 1897)

OLIVE SCHREINER
1855 – 1920

Considered a feminist pioneer and an important early contributor to South African literature in English, Olive Schreiner introduced readers of her fiction to the culture and landscape of southern Africa, while her political and social writings influenced the course of international feminism and challenged racial and sexual inequalities.

Olive Emilie Albertina Schreiner (so named after three of her brothers who had died in childhood) was born on a South African mission station on the frontier of what was then Cape Colony. Her parents had come to southern Africa some twenty years earlier as part of the London Missionary Society. Their constant poverty, and her father's eventual expulsion from his missionary position, necessitated a nomadic childhood, with Schreiner and her siblings divided up and moving from one friend or relative's house to another. She received no formal education but read widely, including from the works of John Ruskin, Charles Dickens, Herbert Spenser, John Locke, and Thomas Carlyle.

After taking work as a governess for various Afrikaaner families at age fifteen, Schreiner gradually became more disillusioned with the set of religious and political beliefs she had inherited from her parents. She devoted her free time to studying and writing, and when she left Africa for England in 1881, she brought with her three nearly completed novels. *The Story of an African Farm* (1883) was the first to be published, under the pseudonym Ralph Iron. This semi-autobiographical novel draws upon Schreiner's experience of growing up on the South African karoo (desert plain). Its first part examines the political tensions on the South African frontier through the microcosm of the attempted colonization of a small farm, while the second half follows the lives of three children raised on the farm—Waldo, Lyndall, and Em. The original subject matter and "exotic" setting appealed instantly to Victorian readers, and the novel was an immediate and huge success—though when the third edition was released under Schreiner's own name, many readers suddenly found it to have "anti-feminine" and "un-Christian" aspects.

Schreiner thrived in London's literary and political environment; she formed close relationships with numerous other free thinkers and writers, including social reformer Havelock Ellis, writer on sexuality Edward Carpenter, and socialist activist Eleanor Marx. She joined the Men and Women's Club, an organization for the frank discussion of sexuality, gender, and the "Woman Question," and lent her voice to the suffragette movement.

Following Schreiner's return to her homeland in 1889 (prompted by her severe asthma, which the English climate seemed to aggravate), she focused her writing on South Africa's social and political issues in a series of articles for various journals—posthumously collected as *Thoughts on South Africa* (1923). Throughout her life Schreiner also worked on allegorical short stories, collected in *Dreams* (1890), *Dream Life and Real Life* (1893), and the posthumous *Stories, Dreams, and Allegories* (1923).

In 1894 she married a cattle farmer, Samuel Cron Cronwright, who shared many of her convictions and, at her request, took the name Cronwright-Schreiner after their marriage. The couple had one daughter, who died in infancy. Throughout this time Schreiner published numerous pamphlets on behalf of worker rights and against tyranny and inequality of all kinds. During the Boer War of 1899–1902, she wrote strongly in support of the Boers and against Britain's capitalist mining interests, while during World War I she spoke out strenuously for pacifism.

Schreiner's best-known work of non-fiction focuses on the constructed nature of Victorian gender roles and of ideals of female sexuality. Once regarded as "the Bible of the international feminist movement," *Women and Labour* (1911) examines the author's thoughts on the institution of marriage, educational opportunities for women, the necessity of female suffrage, and the nature of female sexuality. Schreiner argues for greater freedom of women in society, particularly in the workforce, and laments the economic dependence—or "parasitism," as she calls it—that women have been reduced to.

After struggling with poor health for many years, Schreiner died at home of heart failure in 1920. Two novels unfinished at her death, *From Man to Man* (1926) and *Undine* (1928), were published posthumously. Schreiner's childhood dream had been to work in medicine, and her will honored that memory and her lifelong values by establishing a medical scholarship for women at South African College in Cape Town (now the University of Cape Town).

Since her death, Schreiner's politics have come under scrutiny; critics have detailed some of the ways in which she perpetuated, even as she attempted to challenge, the dominant racist and colonialist stereotypes of her time, and have argued that she used African landscape and people—especially in her early work—as a backdrop for her explorations of the status and rights of white women. Schreiner was indeed influenced at the beginning of her career by such pioneers of social Darwinism as Herbert Spencer and Karl Pearson, and some of her writing reproduces aspects of their hierarchically biological and eugenicist thinking about race. Other scholars, however, have contended that Schreiner's understanding of race became more sophisticated over time and that her later work offers an insightful analysis of the role of British imperialism and international capitalism in fostering South Africa's racial divides. Although the role of race in Schreiner's work remains a subject of scholarly debate, the importance of her literary and intellectual contributions is widely recognized: as Virginia Woolf put it shortly after Schreiner's death, "She remains … too uncompromising a figure to be disposed of."

⌘ ⌘ ⌘

The Woman's Rose

I have an old, brown, carved box; the lid is broken and tied with a string. In it I keep little squares of paper, with hair inside, and a little picture which hung over my brother's bed when we were children, and other things as small. I have in it a rose. Other women also have such boxes where they keep such trifles, but no one has my rose.

When my eye is dim, and my heart grows faint, and my faith in woman flickers, and her present is an agony to me, and her future a despair, the scent of that dead rose, withered for twelve years, comes back to me. I know there will be spring; as surely as the birds know it when they see above the snow two tiny, quivering green leaves. Spring cannot fail us.

There were other flowers in the box once; a bunch of white acacia flowers, gathered by the strong hand of a man, as we passed down a village street on a sultry afternoon, when it had rained, and the drops fell on us from the leaves of the acacia trees. The flowers were damp; they made mildew marks on the paper I folded them in. After many years I threw them away. There is nothing of them left in the box now, but a faint, strong smell of dried acacia, that recalls that sultry summer afternoon; but the rose is in the box still.

It is many years ago now; I was a girl of fifteen, and I went to visit in a small upcountry town. It was young in those days, and two days' journey from the nearest village; the population consisted mainly of men. A few were married, and had their wives and children, but most were single. There was only one young girl there when I came. She was about seventeen, fair, and rather fully-fleshed; she had large dreamy blue eyes, and wavy light hair; full, rather heavy lips, until she smiled; then her face broke into dimples, and all her white teeth shone. The hotel-keeper may have had a daughter, and the farmer in the outskirts had two, but we never saw them. She reigned alone. All the men worshipped her. She was the only woman they had to think of. They talked of her on the "stoep,"[1] at the market, at the hotel; they watched for her at street corners; they hated the man she bowed to or walked with down the street. They brought flowers to the front door; they offered her their horses; they begged her to marry them when they dared. Partly, there was something noble and heroic in this devotion of men to the best woman they knew; partly there was something natural in it, that these men, shut off from the world, should pour at the feet of one woman the worship that otherwise would have been given to twenty; and partly there was something mean[2] in their envy of one another. If she had raised her little finger, I suppose, she might have married any one out of twenty of them.

Then I came. I do not think I was prettier; I do not think I was so pretty as she was. I was certainly not as handsome. But I was vital, and I was new, and she was old—they all forsook her and followed me. They worshipped me. It was to my door that the flowers came; it was I had twenty horses offered me when I

could only ride one; it was for me they waited at street corners; it was what I said and did that they talked of. Partly I liked it. I had lived alone all my life; no one ever had told me I was beautiful and a woman. I believed them. I did not know it was simply a fashion, which one man had set and the rest followed unreasoningly. I liked them to ask me to marry them, and to say, No. I despised them. The mother heart had not swelled in me yet; I did not know all men were my children, as the large woman knows when her heart is grown. I was too small to be tender. I liked my power. I was like a child with a new whip, which it goes about cracking everywhere, not caring against what. I could not wind it up and put it away. Men were curious creatures, who liked me, I could never tell why. Only one thing took from my pleasure; I could not bear that they had deserted her for me. I liked her great dreamy blue eyes, I liked her slow walk and drawl; when I saw her sitting among men, she seemed to me much too good to be among them; I would have given all their compliments if she would once have smiled at me as she smiled at them, with all her face breaking into radiance, with her dimples and flashing teeth. But I knew it never could be; I felt sure she hated me; that she wished I was dead; that she wished I had never come to the village. She did not know, when we went out riding, and a man who had always ridden beside her came to ride beside me, that I sent him away; that once when a man thought to win my favour by ridiculing her slow drawl before me, I turned on him so fiercely that he never dared come before me again. I knew she knew that at the hotel men had made a bet as to which was the prettier, she or I, and had asked each man who came in, and that the one who had staked on me won. I hated them for it, but I would not let her see that I cared about what she felt towards me.

She and I never spoke to each other.

If we met in the village street we bowed and passed on; when we shook hands we did so silently, and did not look at each other. But I thought she felt my presence in a room just as I felt hers.

At last the time for my going came. I was to leave the next day. Someone I knew gave a party in my honour, to which all the village was invited.

It was midwinter; there was nothing in the gardens but a few dahlias and chrysanthemums, and I suppose that for two hundred miles round there was not a rose to be bought for love or money. Only in the garden of a friend of mine, in a sunny corner between the oven and the brick wall, there was a rose tree growing which had on it one bud. It was white, and it had been promised to the fair-haired girl to wear at the party.

The evening came; when I arrived and went to the waiting-room, to take off my mantle, I found the girl there already. She was dressed in pure white, with her great white arms and shoulders showing, and her bright hair glittering in the candlelight, and the white rose fastened at her breast. She looked like a queen. I said "Good evening," and turned away quickly to the glass to arrange my old black scarf across my old black dress.

Then I felt a hand touch my hair.

"Stand still," she said.

I looked in the glass. She had taken the white rose from her breast, and was fastening it in my hair.

"How nice dark hair is; it sets off flowers so." She stepped back and looked at me. "It looks much better there!"

I turned round.

"You are so beautiful to me," I said.

"Y-e-s," she said, with her slow Colonial drawl; "I'm so glad."

We stood looking at each other.

Then they came in and swept us away to dance. All the evening we did not come near to each other. Only once, as she passed, she smiled at me.

The next morning I left the town.

I never saw her again.

Years afterwards I heard she had married and gone to America; it may or may not be so—but the rose—the rose is in the box still! When my faith in woman grows dim, and it seems that for want of love and magnanimity she can play no part in any future heaven; then the scent of that small withered thing comes back: spring cannot fail us.

—1893

TORU DUTT
1856 – 1877

Shortly after Toru Dutt's death, the French writer James Darmesteter described her as "a phenomenon without parallel": "a daughter of Bengal, so admirably and so strangely gifted, Hindu by race and tradition, an Englishwoman by education, a Frenchwoman at heart … who blended in herself three souls and three traditions, and died … in the full bloom of her talent and on the eve of the awakening of her genius." The work of poet, novelist, and translator Toru Dutt reflects her erudition in French, English, and Bangla; her complex, deeply referential poetry combines a vast and multicultural array of influences including John Milton, Elizabeth Barrett Browning, numerous French and English Romantic poets, and such ancient Indian classics as the *Ramayana* and *Mahabharata*. Dutt was remarkably prolific and accomplished despite a very short career: she died at the age of twenty-one.

Dutt was born in Kolkata, the capital of British India, into a highly privileged and literary family. The Dutts' conversion to Christianity in 1862, when Toru was six, left them alienated from the local Hindu community, a distance later thematized in her writing. Dutt and her sister, unlike most women of their caste, received a thorough literary education at home from their father—one conducted in English and French rather than their native Bangla, though they also received a less formalized education in Bengali traditions from their mother. Dutt was a precocious student who developed her love of literature early; as children, she and her siblings read Milton's *Paradise Lost*, for example, so often that they memorized significant portions of the book. In 1869, Dutt and her sister attended school in France, followed by a few years in England, where the family lived near Cambridge University and Dutt attended lectures held for women there. The family returned to India in 1873, and Dutt would spend the rest of her life in Kolkata and at Baugmaree, her family's estate outside the city.

Dutt's work and letters reflect a complex, changing relation to the place of her birth. "We all long to go to Europe again," she writes in 1874. "We hope, if we go, to settle in England and not return to India any more." Two years later, however, she notes that Baugmaree "is as good as England; in some respects, at least in my opinion, it is better," and declares that "India is my *patrie* [fatherland]." Her later letters also reflect a growing consciousness of colonial oppression, with references to "prejudiced Anglo-Indians" and commentary on their racist behavior. After her return to India, Dutt began to study Sanskrit in addition to the three languages she had already mastered.

Dutt's works include essays and poems she published regularly in the *Bengal Magazine* and the *Calcutta Review*, along with two novels printed posthumously: one in English and unfinished, entitled *Bianca, or the Young Spanish Maiden* (published 1878 in the *Bengal Magazine*), and the other in French, *Le journal de Mademoiselle d'Arvers* (published in Paris, 1879). Her first full-length collection of poems, *A Sheaf Gleaned in French Fields* (1876), featured translations into English from French authors such as Victor Hugo and Charles Baudelaire. The *Calcutta Quarterly Review* praised the book as "most interesting and pleasing ... pleasing by its intrinsic beauties, and interesting as showing the high degree of natural taste, improved by culture and refinement, that may be found amongst the daughters of the country." These are works distinctly removed from Dutt's Indian origins, engaging predominantly with English and French literary traditions.

Dutt wrote prolifically in the last years of her life, despite frequent illness; in 1877 she died as a result of the tuberculosis she had probably contracted during her travels to Europe. Her last book of poetry, published posthumously, was also her most important and innovative: *Ancient Ballads and Legends of Hindustan* (1882), a collection of adaptations to English verse of ancient Sanskrit legends. Dutt—already deeply familiar with many of these legends through oral traditions passed on to her by her mother—also studied some of the original Sanskrit and read numerous translations both by Indian scholars, including her uncle Hur Chunder Dutt, and by English and French Orientalist writers such as Clarisse Bader (with whom Dutt corresponded). The longer poems of *Ancient Ballads and Legends* foreground heroic Indian women whose stories originated before colonization and before the conservative turn that limited women's access to the public sphere in response to Britain's colonial presence. Savitri, for example, the subject of the first poem in the volume, fiercely stands up to Death to save her husband's life. *Ancient Ballads and Legends* concludes with a number of shorter, wholly original poems, many of which are more personal in tone. "Our Casuarina Tree," arguably Dutt's best-known poem, suggests a complex matrix of influences—including Milton's *Paradise Lost* and Wordsworth's "Yew Trees"—while also foregrounding the rich landscape of her family estate.

Dutt's final collection was largely well-received in the English press. The London *Athenaeum* noted, for example, that "as a linguistic feat" *Ancient Ballads and Legends* "is a thing unparalleled" if we consider "its author's age, origin, and circumstances." Nonetheless, the journal found Dutt's personal life more compelling than her poetry, which it dismissed as "naïve and ... conventional." English poet and critic Edmund Gosse's essay on Dutt's life, which was printed as an introduction to *Ancient Ballads and Legends*, was partly to blame for this romanticization of the author at the expense of her work. Though Gosse champions Dutt and attempts to cast her in positive terms, his essay fully orientalizes her, imagining Dutt as a "poetess ... chanting to herself those songs of her mother's race to which she always turned with tears of pleasure." Her poems, too, Gosse praises with racist condescension, describing them as a "fragile exotic blossom of song."

Dutt's views on India and its relationship to the British Empire evolved significantly over the course of her short life, and her poems are difficult to pigeonhole politically. Readers may discover in them anticolonial sentiment alongside affection for English and French culture; feminist celebrations of strong women but also traditional depictions of domestic life; aesthetic styles inspired by British and French poetry as well as innovative challenges to conventional forms. Dutt's work was largely overlooked in the decades following its initial publication, but it began in the late twentieth century to receive scholarly attention for its intricacy and lyrical artistry, as well as for its provocative, nuanced, and cosmopolitan navigation of multiple literary traditions from a colonized position within an oppressive British Empire.

⌘ ⌘ ⌘

À mon Père[1]

The flowers look loveliest in their native soil
   Amid their kindred branches; plucked, they fade,
And lose the colours Nature on them laid,
Though bound in garlands with assiduous toil.
5 Pleasant it was, afar from all turmoil,
   To wander through the valley, now in shade
And now in sunshine, where these blossoms made
A Paradise, and gather in my spoil.
But better than myself no man can know
10 How tarnished have become their tender hues
E'en in the gathering, and how dimmed their glow!
Wouldst thou again new life in them infuse,
Thou who hast seen them where they brightly blow?
Ask Memory. She shall help my stammering Muse.
   —1876

Sonnet.—Baugmaree[2]

A sea of foliage girds our garden round,
   But not a sea of dull unvaried green,
   Sharp contrasts of all colours here are seen;
The light-green graceful tamarinds[3] abound
5 Amid the mango clumps of green profound,
   And palms arise, like pillars gray, between;
   And o'er the quiet pools the seemuls[4] lean,
Red—red, and startling like a trumpet's sound
But nothing can be lovelier than the ranges
10 Of bamboos to the eastward, when the moon
Looks through their gaps, and the white
     lotus° changes   water-lily
   Into a cup of silver. One might swoon
     Drunken with beauty then, or gaze and gaze
     On a primeval Eden, in amaze.
—1882

Sonnet.—The Lotus[5]

Love came to Flora asking for a flower
   That would of flowers be undisputed queen,
   The lily and the rose, long, long had been
Rivals for that high honour.[6] Bards of power
5 Had sung their claims. "The rose can never tower
   Like the pale lily with her Juno[7] mien"°—   bearing
   "But is the lily lovelier?" Thus between
Flower-factions rang the strife in Psyche's bower.[8]
"Give me a flower delicious as the rose
10 And stately as the lily in her pride"—
"But of what colour?"—"Rose-red," Love first chose,
   Then prayed—"No, lily-white,—or, both provide";
   And Flora gave the lotus, "rose-red" dyed,
And "lily-white"—the queenliest flower that blows.
   —1882

---

[5] *Lotus* Also called the water-lily, a flower important in Hinduism and Buddhism and long associated with Indian culture. Lotus flowers are white at the base with pink tips.

[6] *Love came … high honour* See English poet William Cowper's "The Lily and the Rose" (1782), in which Flora, the Roman goddess of flowers, resolves a dispute between the lily and the rose over which should be considered queen of the flowers. The poem concludes with Flora praising the color of the rose and the bearing of the lily:

   Yours is, she said, the nobler hue,
     And yours the statelier mien,
   And, till a third surpasses you,
     Let each be deemed a queen.

   Thus, soothed and reconciled, each seeks
     The fairest British fair;
   The seat of empire is her cheeks,
     They reign united there.

[7] *Juno* Queen of the Roman gods. White lilies are also known as "Juno lilies."

[8] *Psyche* Beloved of Cupid, god of love and desire, in Roman mythology; *bower* Enclosed place in a forest or garden.

---

[1] *À mon Père* French: To my Father.

[2] *Baugmaree* Name of the Dutt family home outside Kolkata.

[3] *tamarinds* Trees commonly grown in India for their fruit.

[4] *seemuls* Also called red cotton trees for their numerous, bright red flowers.

Our Casuarina Tree[1]

Like a huge Python, winding round and round
The rugged trunk, indented deep with scars
   Up to its very summit near the stars,
A creeper climbs, in whose embraces bound
5   No other tree could live. But gallantly
The giant wears the scarf, and flowers are hung
In crimson clusters all the boughs among,
   Whereon all day are gathered bird and bee;
And oft at nights the garden overflows
10 With one sweet song that seems to have no close,
Sung darkling[2] from our tree, while men repose.

When first my casement° is wide open thrown   *window*
   At dawn, my eyes delighted on it rest;
   Sometimes, and most in winter, on its crest
15 A gray baboon sits statue-like alone
   Watching the sunrise; while on lower boughs
His puny offspring leap about and play;
   And far and near kokilas[3] hail the day;
   And to their pastures wend our sleepy cows;
20 And in the shadow, on the broad tank cast
By that hoar° tree, so beautiful and vast,   *ancient*
The water-lilies spring, like snow enmassed.

But not because of its magnificence
   Dear is the Casuarina to my soul:
   Beneath it we have played; though years may roll,
25 O sweet companions, loved with love intense,
   For your sakes, shall the tree be ever dear!
Blent with your images, it shall arise
In memory, till the hot tears blind mine eyes!
   What is that dirge-like murmur that I hear
30 Like the sea breaking on a shingle-beach?[4]

It is the tree's lament, an eerie speech,
That haply° to the unknown land may reach.   *by chance*

Unknown, yet well-known to the eye of faith!
35   Ah, I have heard that wail far, far away
   In distant lands, by many a sheltered bay,
When slumbered in his cave the water-wraith
   And the waves gently kissed the classic shore
Of France or Italy, beneath the moon,
40 When earth lay trancèd in a dreamless swoon:
   And every time the music rose—before
Mine inner vision rose a form sublime,
Thy form, O Tree, as in my happy prime
I saw thee, in my own loved native clime.

45 Therefore I fain would consecrate a lay[5]
   Unto thy honour, Tree, beloved of those
   Who now in blessed sleep, for aye,° repose,   *ever*
Dearer than life to me, alas! were they!
   Mayst thou be numbered when my days are done
50 With deathless trees—like those in Borrowdale,
Under whose awful branches lingered pale
   "Fear, trembling Hope, and Death, the skeleton,
And Time the shadow";[6] and though weak the verse
That would thy beauty fain, oh fain rehearse,
55 May Love defend thee from Oblivion's curse.
—1882

---

[1] *Casuarina Tree* Evergreen tree with long, needle-like branches.
[2] *darkling* In the dark.
[3] *kokilas* The kokila or koel is a type of cuckoo with a loud call.
[4] *shingle-beach* Pebbled beach.

---

[5] *lay* Song or poem.
[6] *Fear ... the shadow* See William Wordsworth, "Yew Trees" (1815), which considers an ancient, solitary tree that has witnessed English history pass by, and under whose branches "ghostly Shapes / May meet at noontide; Fear and trembling Hope, / Silence and Foresight: Death the Skeleton / And Time the Shadow;—there to celebrate, / As in a natural temple scattered o'er / With altars undisturbed of mossy stone, / United worship."

VERNON LEE
1856 – 1935

Vernon Lee was the author of some fifty books of fiction, philosophical and intellectual criticism, and art history. Her reputation now rests mainly on her stories of the fantastic and on her first novel, *Miss Brown* (1884), but Walter Pater once called her one of "the very few best critical writers of all time"; among her other admirers were Robert Browning, Edith Wharton, Henry James, and George Bernard Shaw, all of whom recognized her intellectual prowess.

Violet Paget (Vernon Lee was her pen name) was born in Boulogne, France, in 1856. Her father, Henry Ferguson Paget, was a British expatriate who had previously fought in the Polish army before fleeing to Paris during the 1848 Warsaw uprising. He worked as a tutor, eventually marrying the mother of one of his students, and soon afterward the couple had their own child, Violet. They moved frequently, living briefly in Germany, Switzerland, France, and Italy—where Lee would eventually settle—so the children received schooling in many different languages. In Nice, France, when she was ten, Lee forged a friendship with an American child, John Singer Sargent; the two prophesied correctly that he would become a famous painter and she a writer.

Lee's parents recognized that their daughter was intellectually gifted, and they encouraged her scholarship. Her first story was published in French when she was just fourteen. Within a few years she was publishing articles in English under the name Vernon Lee, which she would use publicly—and, increasingly, in private—for the rest of her life. At the age of twenty-four Lee published her first full-length book, *Studies of the Eighteenth Century in Italy* (1880), a scholarly monograph that received considerable acclaim. On her move from Florence to London after its publication, she joined a literary and intellectual circle that included Browning and Pater. Although initially very supportive of her writing, Pater cooled somewhat for a time after Lee published *Miss Brown* in 1884. The novel was viewed by many as a thinly veiled *roman à clef* in which Lee satirized the Pre-Raphaelites (such as Dante Gabriel Rossetti) and Aesthetes (such as Oscar Wilde)—both groups Pater was associated with.

Lee wrote prolifically during the following two decades. Chief among her publications was *Euphorion: Being Studies of the Antique and the Medieval in the Renaissance* (1884), a study of Italian art and culture that the American journal *The Nation* called "clever with the cleverness of precocious and presumptuous youth, lively and amusing even in its pretentiousness." She also wrote fiction, much of which was rooted in fairy tales and the supernatural as well as in history, and which was collected in volumes such as *Hauntings: Fantastic Stories* (1890) and *Pope Jacynth and Other Fantastic Tales* (1904). Her oft-discussed story "Prince Alberic and the Snake Lady" was published in 1896 in *The Yellow Book*, a short-lived but influential avant-garde journal closely associated with the Aesthetic and Decadent artistic movements. Her work also included a number of plays, including *Ariadne in Mantua* (1903), which Lee regarded as among her best works.

Much of Lee's aesthetic criticism was written in collaboration with the aesthetic theorist Clementina (Kit) Anstruther-Thomson, who was for many years also Lee's romantic partner. The two collaborated on *Beauty and Ugliness and Other Studies in Psychological Aesthetics* (1912), which Lee followed with *The Beautiful: An Introduction to Psychological Aesthetics* (1913). On her own Lee also published *The Handling of Words and Other Studies in Literary Psychology* (1923), an analytical study that anticipated a number of later twentieth-century trends in theory and art criticism.

Lee's interest in and knowledge of other cultures yielded seven volumes of travel essays, including *The Enchanted Woods, and Other Essays on the Genius of Place* (1905), a book she described as a "pilgrimage through the open and hidden ways where, without any noisy calling, the *Genus Loci* [spirit of the place]" met her. Her travel writing was much admired by the novelists Aldous Huxley and Edith Wharton, and by the critic Desmond MacCarthy, who would later declare that there was "no doubt [that] Vernon Lee will be read by posterity, for her work is a rare combination of intellectual curiosity and imaginative sensibility."

Despite MacCarthy's assessment, Lee's popularity and influence were waning by the time of her death in Florence in 1935. Over the years her fervently held opinions had alienated many fellow intellectuals, and her reputation had been harmed by works such as *The Ballet of the Nations: A Present-day Morality* (1915), a satirical play that was disparaged by many who objected to its anti-war position. While scholars today often see Lee's work as representing an important link between late-Victorian and early Modernist literature, this quality of not fitting neatly into the intellectual movements of either period proved a challenge to Lee's contemporary reception, particularly later in her career. In the year of her death, Lee complained to a friend that she felt like "an alien, having no ties, either of nation, blood, class or profession." The late twentieth century, however, saw a substantial revival of interest in Lee, which has continued into the twenty-first. Her fiction in particular is a subject of interest for its use of the fantastical as a means of exploring psychological and aesthetic ideas.

⌘⌘⌘

from *The Handling of Words*

CHAPTER 3: AESTHETICS OF THE NOVEL

There seems a general notion that wherever literature is cultivated for its own sake it must become a fine art like painting and music; and that the novel, more especially, since it gives pleasure, must give the special pleasure due to beauty; and, as a result, we call many things in a book beautiful, and imagine them to be analogous to a fine picture or a lovely song, which, honestly considered, are simply and utterly ugly.

It has taken me years to get rid of this prejudice, and cost me several pangs to admit to myself that it is otherwise. Yet it ought merely to prove the richness of human nature thus to find that the novel, for instance, has ample resources for fascinating our attention without the help of the very special quality called beauty. In the first place, *we like words*, and, above all, *we like a statement*; the forms made by logical thought are full of the special attractions of logic, and the material in which all that concerns our ego is expressed, is steeped, it would seem, in a sort of interesting egotistic solution. Certain it is that there must be a real pleasure in such things, since it is sufficient to overcome the effort of gathering up thoughts and interpreting words. Think of the quite unnecessary statement and argument in which mankind indulges, and the eager, often delighted manner in which people will talk and listen about anything, particularly about nothing at all. The attraction of all kinds of literature is primarily based upon this double pleasure: the pleasure of using words and the pleasure of realizing a statement or demonstration; neither of which pleasures are more aesthetic than are those of moving our limbs or of indiscriminately using our eyes. For this reason we often take up a book or newspaper, absolutely irrespective of its contents; and if a book, why not a novel? After this elementary attractiveness of the spoken or written word come the satisfactions (rather than definite pleasures) of expectation and fulfilment, of watching movement and of sympathetic participation therein; of emotional excitement (there is an undoubted pleasure, for instance, even in being annoyed and certainly in being angry); the immense and altogether superior satisfaction of leaving one's own concerns behind and freeing oneself from the routine of life by identification with other folk; a kind of play, masquerade, eminently a holiday satisfaction, to which is closely allied the agreeable sense of irresponsibility which seems to grow with the perception of the responsibility of the characters we are watching, a feeling, by the way, in no way connected with fiction as such, since we have it equally in reading the newspaper, histories, and memoirs; are we not always ready to treat other folks' affairs as mere inventions, being delighted to rid ourselves of the perpetual consequences and complications which prevent our life from being the mere amusing play of perception and volition which it might be? Add to this, in greater or lesser degree, the perception, which is pleasant, of skill and tact on the part of the author; sometimes (what to some critical natures is equally pleasing) the lack of skill and tact of the author. When we have summed up these various items of literary satisfaction, we can pass on to a new kind of factor of pleasure, which is immensely attractive to certain minds, and which is especially present in the novel—I mean the gaining (or thinking we gain) a knowledge of mankind and of life. For when we are young, particularly, we are troubled by a delusive longing for such knowledge, and hoodwinked by a false sense of capability whenever we think we have got it.

These are what I should call the non-aesthetic attractions of the novel, attractions frequently sufficient to compensate for the most rough-and-ready disregard for all our instincts of beauty and harmony. The aesthetic attractions are wholly different. The novelist can show us beautiful places, make us live in company with delightful personalities—from Stendhal's Duchess to Tolstoy's Natasha,[1] from *Robinson Crusoe* to Diana Warwick.[2] I do not mean merely *ethically laudable* persons (no one, I am sure, would care to live with Romola or Daniel Deronda[3]), but creatures whose vigorous, harmonious personalities, sometimes mainly physical, the author has felt as he would feel a melody or a sunset, and, in consequence, conveyed to us not by mere reproduction of their characteristics, but by the far more efficacious means of direct emotional contagion—his admiration, love, delight, inevitably kindling ours. Besides this, there is the specific aesthetic quality of literature. What it is, I do not, and I suppose nobody nowadays does, know: a charm due to the complex patterns into which (quite apart from sound) the parts of speech, verbs and nouns and adjectives, actives and passives, variously combined tenses, can be woven even like lines and colours, producing patterns of action and reaction in our mind, our nerve tracks—who knows? in our muscles and heartbeats and breathing, more mysterious, even, than those which we can dimly discern, darkly guess, are effects of visible and audible form. Insofar as any of these effects are produced by the novel, the novel participates in the nature of other aesthetic productions; I do not say of other works of art, for we are continually reverting to the old use of *art* as mere craft, and confusing with beauty what is mere logic, dexterity, technical knowledge, or tact.

But the novel can get along perfectly without any such aesthetic qualities, as I hope to have shown by my

---

[1] *Stendhal's Duchess* Reference to the title character in *The Duchess of Palliano*, by French novelist Stendhal (Marie-Henri Beyle, 1783–1842); *Natasha* Character in *War and Peace*, by Russian novelist Leo Tolstoy (1828–1910).

[2] *Robinson Crusoe* Novel by Daniel Defoe (1660–1731); *Diana Warwick* Main character of *Diana of the Crossways*, by George Meredith (1828–1909).

[3] *Romola or Daniel Deronda* Characters in the eponymous George Eliot novels.

enumerations of the many other factors of pleasure, or, at least, of interest, which the novelist has at disposal. And such non-aesthetic interest is sufficient, not merely for the readers who are more scientific, or more dramatic, or more practical, or more technically ingenious, than aesthetic, but sufficient even for aesthetic readers in their scientific, or dramatic, or practical, or technical moments and capacities; for even the most aesthetically sensitive persons must have other sides to their characters, else they would be dunces, criminals, paupers, bores, and general incapables. The difference between the people who are aesthetically sensitive and those who are not (and here we have the key to the varying power of reading novels like, let us say, Zola's[1] *Pot-Bouille*), is not merely that the aesthetic people ask for beauty as the scientific do for knowledge and the dramatic for human emotion, but that the aesthetic people suffer very acutely whenever the novel contains downright ugliness, suffer in a much more positive manner than the scientific or dramatic reader suffers from glaring absurdity or hopeless tameness of situation; for in the one case there is irritation or boredom, in the other something verging on physical disgust. So that, regarding the novel, the question becomes simply: which, in the individual case, happens to be the stronger, the satisfaction of the many non-aesthetic capacities for pleasure, or the displeasure inflicted on the aesthetic instinct by subject or treatment which do not in the least offend any other craving of human nature? It is a question, in fact, between the individual writer and the individual reader; and I doubt whether it can ever be made a question of right and wrong. Some persons *can* read *A Vau l'Eau*[2] without any misery and with much satisfaction, even getting up from their reading decidedly the richer in knowledge and

sympathy. Others are so harrowed that any possibilities of pleasure or profit are absolutely paralysed, and there is no sort of use in going on with the book. A third class can get through the novel in a middle condition of balanced, neutralized satisfaction and dissatisfaction, occasionally varied by a momentary predominance of pleasure or loathing.

I have ventured to say that in such questions there is no absolute right or wrong, and that a book like this (I have purposely chosen the most excessive instance) may increase the spiritual health of some readers and momentarily jeopardize that of others, all equally estimable persons. But what, I hear a class of readers (and that class is represented, as well as the others, in my own person), what is the use of being utterly depressed and sickened by a hundred and fifty pages of trivial hideousness? The sickening and the depression do no good, quite the contrary; and, as I said, where there is nothing else, the book had best be thrown into the fire. But the stimulation which the book can give to sympathetic understanding is a good, a very good thing, since we can never have enough of it in life. A novel like *A Vau l'Eau* can give the right kind of reader an increased insight into the commonest, but also the most powerful, needs and passions of mankind, and insofar it can tend to make his attitude and action in life more useful, or at least less mischievous. It can teach, moreover, pity for people who may, perhaps, be helped; teach also resolute idealism in our own persons by disclosing the very unideal sloughs above which our common human nature has so insecurely and so partially raised itself. But in the question of novels, as in all others, the most useful thing, perhaps, is to be at the same time very aesthetic and very capable of momentarily shelving our aestheticism, or rather of being able to see and understand dispassionately, while keeping the most passionate aversions and preferences.

—1906

[1] *Zola* Emile Zola (1840–1902), French novelist and author of *Pot-Bouille* (1882).

[2] *A Vau l'Eau* French: *With the Flow*; an 1882 novella by French author Joris-Karl Huysmans (1848–1907).

SIR ARTHUR CONAN DOYLE
1859 – 1930

British detective Sherlock Holmes is so renowned that his fame outstrips that of his creator, Sir Arthur Conan Doyle. Conan Doyle wrote many other sorts of fiction, as well as books on history, war, and supernatural subjects, and although some were very successful, they never roused the interest

generated by the man with the deerstalker cap, calabash pipe, and magnifying glass, who solved crimes using "elementary" deductions, abetted by the faithful Dr. Watson. When Conan Doyle grew bored with his creation and tried to kill off Holmes and his evil nemesis Professor Moriarty, his reading public wore arm bands to display their mourning, and publishers offered such enormous sums to have Holmes revived that Conan Doyle eventually succumbed to pressure and brought his character back to life.

Conan Doyle was born in Edinburgh, Scotland, in 1859. His father, Charles Altamont Doyle, was a civil servant with artistic aspirations, but alcoholism and epilepsy eventually caused him to be institutionalized. Conan Doyle's mother, Mary Foley Doyle, encouraged her son's voluminous appetite for books and his literary aspirations, even though unrelieved poverty made educating her ten children a financial struggle. When Conan Doyle came of age, he studied medicine at Edinburgh University—where he met Dr. Joseph Bell, the man who became the model for Sherlock Holmes—and earned his medical degree in 1881. During a subsequent medical stint in Southsea near Portsmouth, a dearth of patients left him ample time for writing. During this period he met his first wife, Louisa Hawkins, who would suffer from tuberculosis for much of their marriage, eventually dying of the disease.

Conan Doyle's first Sherlock Holmes adventure, *A Study in Scarlet*, was written in Southsea and published in the 1887 *Beeton Christmas Annual*. After he had published his second Holmes story, *The Sign of the Four*, in *Lippincott's Magazine* in 1890, *The Strand Magazine* began featuring "The Adventures of Sherlock Holmes." (The illustrations by Sidney Paget that accompany "The Adventure of the Speckled Band," below, are from its original publication in *The Strand* in 1892.) In an age of great scientific discovery, the public became captivated by Holmes's cool, rational, almost superhuman reasoning skills, but readers also responded to his all-too-human problems, such as his fear of emotional ties and his cocaine habit. Conan Doyle created other memorable characters in such books as *Micah Clarke* (1889) and *The Lost World* (1912), but none attained Holmes's cachet, much to Conan Doyle's chagrin. In 1891—the same year that his popular success enabled him to leave medicine and pursue writing full-time—he complained that the Sherlock Holmes adventures held back his writing career: "I'm thinking of slaying Holmes," he said in a letter to his mother, "he takes my mind from better things."

Whether or not these other "things" were better, Conan Doyle penned much fine work alongside his Sherlock Holmes adventures, including the historical novel *The White Company* (1891) and the science-fiction novella *The Poison Belt* (1913). He also adapted some of his Holmes stories, such as "The Adventure of the Speckled Band," for the stage. After serving in the Boer War in South Africa, he was knighted in recognition of two treatises he had written in support of the war. In the final decades of his life, and especially after the death of his son due to injuries sustained during World War I, Conan Doyle became immersed in spiritualism and the occult, writing and lecturing extensively on the subject.

After returning from an exhausting lecture tour in 1929, Conan Doyle suffered a heart attack. He never regained his health, and he died in 1930. He is buried in the rose garden at Windlesham, his home in Sussex, where he had lived with his second wife and children.

⌘ ⌘ ⌘

The Adventure of the Speckled Band

In glancing over my notes of the seventy odd cases in which I have during the last eight years studied the methods of my friend Sherlock Holmes, I find many tragic, some comic, a large number merely strange, but none commonplace; for, working as he did rather for the love of his art than for the acquirement of wealth, he refused to associate himself with any investigation which did not tend towards the unusual, and even the fantastic. Of all these varied cases, however, I cannot recall any which presented more singular features than that which was associated with the well-known Surrey family of the Roylotts of Stoke Moran. The events in question occurred in the early days of my association with Holmes, when we were sharing rooms as bachelors, in Baker Street. It is possible that I might have placed them upon record before, but a promise of secrecy was made at the time, from which I have only been freed during the last month by the untimely death of the lady to whom the pledge was given. It is perhaps as well that the facts should now come to light, for I have reasons to know there are widespread rumours as to the death of Dr. Grimesby Roylott which tend to make the matter even more terrible than the truth.

It was early in April, the year '83, that I woke one morning to find Sherlock Holmes standing, fully dressed, by the side of my bed. He was a late riser as a rule, and, as the clock on the mantelpiece showed me that it was only a quarter past seven, I blinked up at him in some surprise, and perhaps just a little resentment, for

I was myself regular in my habits.

"Very sorry to knock you up,[1] Watson," said he, "but it's the common lot this morning. Mrs. Hudson has been knocked up, she retorted upon me, and I on you."

"What is it, then? A fire?"

"No, a client. It seems that a young lady has arrived in a considerable state of excitement, who insists upon seeing me. She is waiting now in the sitting room. Now, when young ladies wander about the metropolis at this hour of the morning, and knock sleepy people up out of their beds, I presume that it is something very pressing which they have to communicate. Should it prove to be an interesting case, you would, I am sure, wish to follow it from the outset. I thought at any rate that I should call you, and give you the chance."

"My dear fellow, I would not miss it for anything."

I had no keener pleasure than in following Holmes in his professional investigations, and in admiring the rapid deductions, as swift as intuitions, and yet always founded on a logical basis, with which he unravelled the problems which were submitted to him. I rapidly threw on my clothes, and was ready in a few minutes to accompany my friend down to the sitting room. A lady dressed in black and heavily veiled, who had been sitting in the window, rose as we entered.

"Good morning, madam," said Holmes cheerily. "My name is Sherlock Holmes. This is my intimate friend and associate, Dr. Watson, before whom you can

---

[1] *knock you up* I.e., "wake you up with a knock at the door." (This usage remains current in some parts of Britain.)

speak as freely as before myself. Ha, I am glad to see that Mrs. Hudson has had the good sense to light the fire. Pray[1] draw up to it, and I shall order you a cup of hot coffee, for I observe that you are shivering."

"It is not cold which makes me shiver," said the woman in a low voice, changing her seat as requested.

"What then?"

"She raised her veil."

"It is fear, Mr. Holmes. It is terror." She raised her veil as she spoke, and we could see that she was indeed in a pitiable state of agitation, her face all drawn and grey, with restless, frightened eyes, like those of some hunted animal. Her features and figure were those of a woman of thirty, but her hair was shot with premature grey, and her expression was weary and haggard. Sherlock Holmes ran her over with one of his quick, all-comprehensive glances.[2]

"You must not fear," said he soothingly, bending forward and patting her forearm. "We shall soon set matters right, I have no doubt. You have come in by train this morning, I see."

"You know me, then?"

"No, but I observe the second half of a return ticket in the palm of your left glove. You must have started early, and yet you had a good drive in a dog-cart, along heavy roads, before you reached the station."

The lady gave a violent start, and stared in bewilderment at my companion.

"There is no mystery, my dear madam," said he, smiling. "The left arm of your jacket is spattered with mud in no less than seven places. The marks are perfectly fresh. There is no vehicle save a dog-cart which throws up mud in that way, and then only when you sit on the left-hand side of the driver."

"Whatever your reasons may be, you are perfectly correct," said she. "I started from home before six, reached Leatherhead at twenty past, and came in by the first train to Waterloo.[3] Sir, I can stand this strain no longer, I shall go mad if it continues. I have no one to turn to—none, save only one, who cares for me, and he, poor fellow, can be of little aid. I have heard of you, Mr. Holmes; I have heard of you from Mrs. Farintosh, whom you helped in the hour of her sore need. It was from her that I had your address. Oh, sir, do you not think you could help me too, and at least throw a little light through the dense darkness which surrounds me? At present it is out of my power to reward you for your services, but in a month or two I shall be married, with the control of my own income, and then at least you shall not find me ungrateful."

Holmes turned to his desk, and unlocking it, drew out a small casebook which he consulted.

"Farintosh," said he. "Ah, yes, I recall the case; it was concerned with an opal tiara. I think it was before your time, Watson. I can only say, madam, that I shall be happy to devote the same care to your case as I did to that of your friend. As to reward, my profession is its reward; but you are at liberty to defray whatever expenses I may be put to, at the time which suits you best. And now I beg that you will lay before us everything that may help us in forming an opinion upon the matter."

---

[1] *Pray* Please.

[2] *She raised her veil … glances* The illustration of this scene is by Sidney Paget; it accompanied the story's original publication in *The Strand Magazine* in 1892. Paget's eight other original illustrations are also included in these pages.

[3] *Waterloo* London railway station located south of the Thames River, in Lambeth.

"Alas!" replied our visitor. "The very horror of my situation lies in the fact that my fears are so vague, and my suspicions depend so entirely upon small points, which might seem trivial to another, that even he to whom of all others I have a right to look for help and advice looks upon all that I tell him about it as the fancies of a nervous woman. He does not say so, but I can read it from his soothing answers and averted eyes. But I have heard, Mr. Holmes, that you can see deeply into the manifold wickedness of the human heart. You may advise me how to walk amid the dangers which encompass me."

"I am all attention, madam."

"My name is Helen Stoner, and I am living with my stepfather, who is the last survivor of one of the oldest Saxon families in England, the Roylotts of Stoke Moran, on the western border of Surrey."[1]

Holmes nodded his head. "The name is familiar to me," said he.

"The family was at one time among the richest in England, and the estate extended over the borders into Berkshire in the north, and Hampshire in the west. In the last century, however, four successive heirs were of a dissolute and wasteful disposition, and the family ruin was eventually completed by a gambler, in the days of the Regency.[2] Nothing was left save a few acres of ground and the two-hundred-year-old house, which is itself crushed under a heavy mortgage. The last squire dragged out his existence there, living the horrible life of an aristocratic pauper; but his only son, my stepfather, seeing that he must adapt himself to the new conditions, obtained an advance from a relative, which enabled him to take a medical degree, and went out to Calcutta, where, by his professional skill and his force of character,

he established a large practice. In a fit of anger, however, caused by some robberies which had been perpetrated in the house, he beat his native butler to death, and narrowly escaped a capital sentence. As it was, he suffered a long term of imprisonment, and afterwards returned to England a morose and disappointed man.

"When Dr. Roylott was in India he married my mother, Mrs. Stoner, the young widow of Major-General Stoner, of the Bengal Artillery. My sister Julia and I were twins, and we were only two years old at the time of my mother's re-marriage. She had a considerable sum of money, not less than a thousand a year, and this she bequeathed to Dr. Roylott entirely whilst we resided with him, with a provision that a certain annual sum should be allowed to each of us in the event of our marriage. Shortly after our return to England my mother died—she was killed eight years ago in a railway accident near Crewe. Dr. Roylott then abandoned his attempts to establish himself in practice in London, and took us to live with him in the ancestral house at Stoke Moran. The money which my mother had left was enough for all our wants, and there seemed no obstacle to our happiness.

"But a terrible change came over our stepfather about this time. Instead of making friends and exchanging visits with our neighbours, who had at first been overjoyed to see a Roylott of Stoke Moran back in the old family seat, he shut himself up in his house, and seldom came out save to indulge in ferocious quarrels with whoever might cross his path. Violence of temper approaching to mania has been hereditary in the men of the family, and in my stepfather's case it had, I believe, been intensified by his long residence in the tropics. A series of disgraceful brawls took place, two of which ended in the police-court, until at last he became the terror of the village, and the folks would fly at his approach, for he is a man of immense strength, and absolutely uncontrollable in his anger.

---

[1] *Saxon* One of several Germanic peoples, collectively referred to as Anglo-Saxons, who occupied England in the wake of the fifth-century collapse of the Roman Empire; *Surrey* County near London.

[2] *the Regency* I.e., 1810–20, the period in which George, Prince of Wales, acted as regent for his father, George III, who was incapacitated by mental illness.

"He hurled the blacksmith over a parapet."

"Last week he hurled the local blacksmith over a parapet[1] into a stream and it was only by paying over all the money that I could gather together that I was able to avert another public exposure. He had no friends at all save the wandering gypsies,[2] and he would give these vagabonds leave to encamp upon the few acres of bramble-covered land which represent the family estate, and would accept in return the hospitality of their tents, wandering away with them sometimes for weeks on end. He has a passion also for Indian animals, which are sent over to him by a correspondent, and he has at this moment a cheetah and a baboon, which wander freely over his grounds, and are feared by the villagers almost as much as their master.

"You can imagine from what I say that my poor sister Julia and I had no great pleasure in our lives. No servant would stay with us, and for a long time we did all the work of the house. She was but thirty at the time of her death, and yet her hair had already begun to whiten, even as mine has."

"Your sister is dead, then?"

"She died just two years ago, and it is of her death that I wish to speak to you. You can understand that, living the life which I have described, we were little likely to see anyone of our own age and position. We had, however, an aunt, my mother's maiden sister, Miss Honoria Westphail, who lives near Harrow,[3] and we were occasionally allowed to pay short visits at this lady's house. Julia went there at Christmas two years ago, and met there a half-pay Major[4] of Marines, to whom she became engaged. My stepfather learned of the engagement when my sister returned, and offered no objection to the marriage; but within a fortnight[5] of the day which had been fixed for the wedding, the terrible event occurred which has deprived me of my only companion."

Sherlock Holmes had been leaning back in his chair with his eyes closed, and his head sunk in a cushion, but he half opened his lids now, and glanced across at his visitor.

"Pray be precise as to details," said he.

"It is easy for me to be so, for every event of that dreadful time is seared into my memory. The manor house is, as I have already said, very old, and only one wing is now inhabited. The bedrooms in this wing are on the ground floor, the sitting rooms being in the central block of the buildings. Of these bedrooms, the first is Dr. Roylott's, the second my sister's, and the third my own. There is no communication between them, but they all open out into the same corridor. Do I make myself plain?"

"Perfectly so."

"The windows of the three rooms open out upon the lawn. That fatal night Dr. Roylott had gone to his room early, though we knew that he had not retired to rest, for my sister was troubled by the smell of the strong Indian cigars which it was his custom to smoke. She left her room, therefore, and came into mine, where she sat for some time, chatting about her approaching wedding.

[1] *parapet* Stone embankment.

[2] *gypsies* Term referring to the Roma or Romani people, now considered pejorative.

[3] *Harrow* Town near London.

[4] *half-pay Major* When retired or not in service, officers were paid half their wages.

[5] *fortnight* Two weeks.

At eleven o'clock she rose to leave me, but she paused at the door and looked back. 'Tell me, Helen,' said she, 'have you ever heard anyone whistle in the dead of the night?'

"'Never,' said I.

"'I suppose that you could not possibly whistle yourself in your sleep?'

"'Certainly not. But why?'

"'Because during the last few nights I have always, about three in the morning, heard a low clear whistle. I am a light sleeper, and it has awakened me. I cannot tell where it came from—perhaps from the next room, perhaps from the lawn. I thought that I would just ask you whether you had heard it.'

"'No, I have not. It must be those wretched gypsies in the plantation.'

"'Very likely. And yet if it were on the lawn I wonder that you did not hear it also.'

"'Ah, but I sleep more heavily than you.'

"'Well, it is of no great consequence, at any rate,' she smiled back at me, closed my door, and a few moments later I heard her key turn in the lock."

"Indeed," said Holmes. "Was it your custom always to lock yourselves in at night?"

"Always."

"And why?"

"I think that I mentioned to you that the doctor kept a cheetah and a baboon. We had no feeling of security unless our doors were locked."

"Quite so. Pray proceed with your statement."

"I could not sleep that night. A vague feeling of impending misfortune impressed me. My sister and I, you will recollect, were twins, and you know how subtle are the links which bind two souls which are so closely allied. It was a wild night. The wind was howling outside, and the rain was beating and splashing against the windows. Suddenly, amidst all the hubbub of the gale, there burst forth the wild scream of a terrified woman. I knew that it was my sister's voice. I sprang from my bed, wrapped a shawl round me, and rushed into the corridor. As I opened my door I seemed to hear

a low whistle, such as my sister described, and a few moments later a clanging sound, as if a mass of metal had fallen. As I ran down the passage my sister's door was unlocked, and revolved slowly upon its hinges. I stared at it horror-stricken, not knowing what was about to issue from it. By the light of the corridor lamp I saw my sister appear at the opening, her face blanched with terror, her hands groping for help, her whole figure

"Her face blanched with terror."

swaying to and fro like that of a drunkard. I ran to her and threw my arms round her, but at that moment her knees seemed to give way and she fell to the ground. She writhed as one who is in terrible pain, and her limbs were dreadfully convulsed. At first I thought that she had not recognized me, but as I bent over her she suddenly shrieked out in a voice which I shall never forget, 'O, my God! Helen! It was the band! The speckled band!' There was something else which she would fain have said, and she stabbed with her finger into the air in the direction of the doctor's room, but a fresh convulsion seized her and choked her words. I rushed out, calling loudly for my stepfather, and I met him hastening from his room in his dressing gown.

When he reached my sister's side she was unconscious, and though he poured brandy down her throat, and sent for medical aid from the village, all efforts were in vain, for she slowly sank and died without having recovered her consciousness. Such was the dreadful end of my beloved sister."

"One moment," said Holmes; "are you sure about this whistle and metallic sound? Could you swear to it?"

"That was what the county coroner asked me at the inquiry. It was my strong impression that I heard it, and yet among the crash of the gale, and the creaking of an old house, I may possibly have been deceived."

"Was your sister dressed?"

"No, she was in her nightdress. In her right hand was found the charred stump of a match, and in her left a matchbox."

"Showing that she had struck a light and looked about her when the alarm took place. That is important. And what conclusions did the coroner come to?"

"He investigated the case with great care, for Dr. Roylott's conduct had long been notorious in the county, but he was unable to find any satisfactory cause of death. My evidence showed that the door had been fastened upon the inner side, and the windows were blocked by old-fashioned shutters with broad iron bars, which were secured every night. The walls were carefully sounded, and were shown to be quite solid all round, and the flooring was also thoroughly examined, with the same result. The chimney is wide, but is barred up by four large staples. It is certain, therefore, that my sister was quite alone when she met her end. Besides, there were no marks of any violence upon her."

"How about poison?"

"The doctors examined her for it, but without success."

"What do you think that this unfortunate lady died of, then?"

"It is my belief that she died of pure fear and nervous shock, though what it was which frightened her I cannot imagine."

"Were there gypsies in the plantation at the time?"

"Yes, there are nearly always some there."

"Ah, and what did you gather from this allusion to a band—a speckled band?"

"Sometimes I have thought that it was merely the wild talk of delirium, sometimes that it may have referred to some band of people, perhaps to these very gypsies in the plantation. I do not know whether the spotted handkerchiefs which so many of them wear over their heads might have suggested the strange adjective which she used."

Holmes shook his head like a man who is far from being satisfied.

"These are very deep waters," said he; "pray go on with your narrative."

"Two years have passed since then, and my life has been until lately lonelier than ever. A month ago, however, a dear friend, whom I have known for many years, has done me the honour to ask my hand in marriage. His name is Armitage—Percy Armitage—the second son of Mr. Armitage, of Crane Water, near Reading.[1] My stepfather has offered no opposition to the match, and we are to be married in the course of the spring. Two days ago some repairs were started in the west wing of the building, and my bedroom wall has been pierced, so that I have had to move into the chamber in which my sister died, and to sleep in the very bed in which she slept. Imagine, then, my thrill of terror when last night, as I lay awake, thinking over her terrible fate, I suddenly heard in the silence of the night the low whistle which had been the herald of her own death. I sprang up and lit the lamp, but nothing was to be seen in the room. I was too shaken to go to bed again, however, so I dressed, and as soon as it was daylight I slipped down, got a dog-cart at the Crown Inn, which is opposite, and drove to Leatherhead, from whence I have come on this morning, with the one object of seeing you and asking your advice."

"You have done wisely," said my friend. "But have you told me all?"

"Yes, all."

"Miss Stoner, you have not. You are screening your stepfather."

---

[1] *Reading* Town west of London.

"Why, what do you mean?"

For answer Holmes pushed back the frill of black lace which fringed the hand that lay upon our visitor's knee. Five little livid spots, the marks of four fingers and a thumb, were printed upon the white wrist.

"You have been cruelly used," said Holmes.

The lady coloured deeply, and covered over her injured wrist. "He is a hard man," she said, "and perhaps he hardly knows his own strength."

There was a long silence, during which Holmes leaned his chin upon his hands and stared into the crackling fire.

"This is very deep business," he said at last. "There are a thousand details which I should desire to know before I decide upon our course of action. Yet we have not a moment to lose. If we were to come to Stoke Moran today, would it be possible for us to see over these rooms without the knowledge of your stepfather?"

"As it happens, he spoke of coming into town today upon some most important business. It is probable that he will be away all day, and that there would be nothing to disturb you. We have a housekeeper now, but she is old and foolish, and I could easily get her out of the way."

"Excellent. You are not averse to this trip, Watson?"

"By no means."

"Then we shall both come. What are you going to do yourself?"

"I have one or two things which I would wish to do now that I am in town. But I shall return by the twelve o'clock train, so as to be there in time for your coming."

"And you may expect us early in the afternoon. I have myself some small business matters to attend to. Will you not wait and breakfast?"

"No, I must go. My heart is lightened already since I have confided my trouble to you. I shall look forward to seeing you again this afternoon." She dropped her thick black veil over her face, and glided from the room.

"And what do you think of it all, Watson?" asked Sherlock Holmes, leaning back in his chair.

"It seems to me to be a most dark and sinister business."

"Dark enough and sinister enough."

"Yet if the lady is correct in saying that the flooring and walls are sound, and that the door, window, and chimney are impassable, then her sister must have been undoubtedly alone when she met her mysterious end."

"What becomes, then, of these nocturnal whistles, and what of the very peculiar words of the dying woman?"

"I cannot think."

"When you combine the ideas of whistles at night, the presence of a band of gypsies who are on intimate terms with this old doctor, the fact that we have every reason to believe that the doctor has an interest in preventing his stepdaughter's marriage, the dying allusion to a band, and finally, the fact that Miss Helen Stoner heard a metallic clang, which might have been caused by one of those metal bars which secured the shutters falling back into their place, I think there is good ground to think that the mystery may be cleared along these lines."

"But what, then, did the gypsies do?"

"I cannot imagine."

"I see many objections to any such a theory."

"And so do I. It is precisely for that reason that we are going to Stoke Moran this day. I want to see whether the objections are fatal, or if they may be explained away. But what, in the name of the devil!"

The ejaculation[1] had been drawn from my companion by the fact that our door had been suddenly dashed open, and that a huge man framed himself in the aperture. His costume was a peculiar mixture of the professional and of the agricultural, having a black top hat, a long frock-coat, and a pair of high gaiters,[2] with a hunting-crop swinging in his hand. So tall was he that his hat actually brushed the crossbar of the doorway, and his breadth seemed to span it across from side to side. A large face, seared with a thousand wrinkles, burned yellow with the sun, and marked with every evil passion, was turned from one to the other of us, while his deep-set, bile-shot eyes, and the high thin fleshless nose, gave him somewhat the resemblance to a fierce old bird of prey.

---

[1]   *ejaculation*   Exclamation.

[2]   *gaiters*   Coverings of cloth or leather for the lower legs.

"Which of you is Holmes?"

"Which of you is Holmes?" asked this apparition.

"My name, sir, but you have the advantage of me," said my companion quietly.

"I am Dr. Grimesby Roylott, of Stoke Moran."

"Indeed, Doctor," said Holmes blandly. "Pray take a seat."

"I will do nothing of the kind. My stepdaughter has been here. I have traced her. What has she been saying to you?"

"It is a little cold for the time of the year," said Holmes.

"What has she been saying to you?" screamed the old man furiously.

"But I have heard that the crocuses promise well," continued my companion imperturbably.

"Ha! You put me off, do you?" said our new visitor, taking a step forward, and shaking his hunting crop. "I know you, you scoundrel! I have heard of you before. You are Holmes the meddler."

My friend smiled.

"Holmes the busybody!"

His smile broadened.

"Holmes the Scotland Yard jack-in-office."[1]

Holmes chuckled heartily. "Your conversation is most entertaining," said he. "When you go out close the door, for there is a decided draught."

"I will go when I have had my say. Don't you dare to meddle with my affairs. I know that Miss Stoner has been here—I traced her! I am a dangerous man to fall foul of! See here." He stepped swiftly forward, seized the poker, and bent it into a curve with his huge brown hands.

"See that you keep yourself out of my grip," he snarled, and hurling the twisted poker into the fireplace, he strode out of the room.

"He seems a very amiable person," said Holmes, laughing. "I am not quite so bulky, but if he had remained I might have shown him that my grip was not much more feeble than his own." As he spoke he picked up the steel poker, and with a sudden effort straightened it out again.

"Fancy his having the insolence to confound me with the official detective force! This incident gives zest to our investigation, however, and I only trust that our little friend will not suffer from her imprudence in allowing this brute to trace her. And now, Watson, we shall order breakfast, and afterwards I shall walk down to Doctors' Commons,[2] where I hope to get some data which may help us in this matter."

It was nearly one o'clock when Sherlock Holmes returned from his excursion. He held in his hand a sheet of blue paper, scrawled over with notes and figures.

"I have seen the will of the deceased wife," said he. "To determine its exact meaning I have been obliged to work out the present prices of the investments with which it is concerned. The total income, which at the time of the wife's death was little short of £1,100, is now through the fall in agricultural prices not more than £750. Each daughter can claim an income of £250, in case of marriage. It is evident, therefore, that if both girls had married this beauty would have had a mere pittance, while even one of them would cripple him to

---

[1] *jack-in-office* Insolent minor official.

[2] *Doctors' Commons* Buildings that housed the association of Doctors of Civil Law in London.

a serious extent. My morning's work has not been wasted, since it has proved that he has the very strongest motives for standing in the way of anything of the sort. And now, Watson, this is too serious for dawdling, especially as the old man is aware that we are interesting ourselves in his affairs, so if you are ready we shall call a cab and drive to Waterloo. I should be very much obliged if you would slip your revolver into your pocket. An Eley's No. 2[1] is an excellent argument with gentlemen who can twist steel pokers into knots. That and a toothbrush are, I think, all that we need."

At Waterloo we were fortunate in catching a train for Leatherhead, where we hired a trap[2] at the station inn, and drove for four or five miles through the lovely Surrey lanes. It was a perfect day, with a bright sun and a few fleecy clouds in the heavens. The trees and wayside hedges were just throwing out their first green shoots, and the air was full of the pleasant smell of the moist earth. To me at least there was a strange contrast between the sweet promise of the spring and this sinister quest upon which we were engaged. My companion sat in front of the trap, his arms folded, his hat pulled down over his eyes, and his chin sunk upon his breast, buried in the deepest thought.

Suddenly, however, he started, tapped me on the shoulder, and pointed over the meadows.

"Look there!" said he.

A heavily timbered park stretched up in a gentle slope, thickening into a grove at the highest point. From amidst the branches there jutted out the grey gables and high roof-tree[3] of a very old mansion.

"Stoke Moran?" said he.

"Yes, sir, that be the house of Dr. Grimesby Roylott," remarked the driver.

"There is some building going on there," said Holmes; "that is where we are going."

"There's the village," said the driver, pointing to a cluster of roofs some distance to the left; "but if you want to get to the house, you'll find it shorter to go over this stile,[4] and so by the footpath over the fields. There it is, where the lady is walking."

"And the lady, I fancy, is Miss Stoner," observed Holmes, shading his eyes. "Yes, I think we had better do as you suggest."

"We got off, paid our fare."

We got off, paid our fare, and the trap rattled back on its way to Leatherhead.

"I thought it as well," said Holmes, as we climbed the stile, "that this fellow should think we had come here as architects, or on some definite business. It may stop his gossip. Good afternoon, Miss Stoner. You see that we have been as good as our word."

Our client of the morning had hurried forward to meet us with a face which spoke her joy. "I have been waiting so eagerly for you," she cried, shaking hands with us warmly. "All has turned out splendidly. Dr. Roylott has gone to town, and it is unlikely that he will be back before evening."

"We have had the pleasure of making the doctor's acquaintance," said Holmes, and in a few words he sketched out what had occurred. Miss Stoner turned white to the lips as she listened.

"Good heavens!" she cried, "he has followed me, then."

---

[1] *Eley's No. 2* Conan Doyle is likely referring to a small but powerful pistol called a "Webley No. 2," which could be loaded with cartridges made by the ammunition manufacturer Eley.

[2] *trap* Small, two-wheeled carriage.

[3] *roof-tree* Ridge pole.

[4] *stile* Set of steps passing over a fence.

"So it appears."

"He is so cunning that I never know when I am safe from him. What will he say when he returns?"

"He must guard himself, for he may find that there is someone more cunning than himself upon his track. You must lock yourself from him tonight. If he is violent, we shall take you away to your aunt's at Harrow. Now, we must make the best use of our time, so kindly take us at once to the rooms which we are to examine."

The building was of grey, lichen-blotched stone, with a high central portion, and two curving wings, like the claws of a crab, thrown out on each side. In one of these wings the windows were broken and blocked with wooden boards, while the roof was partly caved in, a picture of ruin. The central portion was in little better repair, but the right-hand block was comparatively modern, and the blinds in the windows, with the blue smoke curling up from the chimneys, showed that this was where the family resided. Some scaffolding had been erected against the end wall, and the stonework had been broken into, but there were no signs of any workmen at the moment of our visit. Holmes walked slowly up and down the ill-trimmed lawn, and examined with deep attention the outsides of the windows.

"This, I take it, belongs to the room in which you used to sleep, the centre one to your sister's, and the one next to the main building to Dr. Roylott's chamber?"

"Exactly so. But I am now sleeping in the middle one."

"Pending the alterations, as I understand. By the way, there does not seem to be any very pressing need for repairs at that end wall."

"There were none. I believe that it was an excuse to move me from my room."

"Ah! that is suggestive. Now, on the other side of this narrow wing runs the corridor from which these three rooms open. There are windows in it, of course?"

"Yes, but very small ones. Too narrow for anyone to pass through."

"As you both locked your doors at night, your rooms were unapproachable from that side. Now, would you have the kindness to go into your room, and to bar your shutters."

Miss Stoner did so, and Holmes, after a careful examination through the open window, endeavoured in every way to force the shutter open, but without success. There was no slit through which a knife could be passed to raise the bar. Then with his lens[1] he tested the hinges, but they were of solid iron, built firmly into the massive masonry. "Hum!" said he, scratching his chin in some perplexity, "my theory certainly presents some difficulties. No one could pass these shutters if they were bolted. Well, we shall see if the inside throws any light upon the matter."

A small side door led into the white-washed corridor from which the three bedrooms opened. Holmes refused to examine the third chamber, so we passed at once to the second, that in which Miss Stoner was now sleeping, and in which her sister had met her fate. It was a homely[2] little room, with a low ceiling and a gaping fireplace, after the fashion of old country houses. A brown chest of drawers stood in one corner, a narrow white-counterpaned bed in another, and a dressing-table on the left-hand side of the window. These articles, with two small wicker-work chairs, made up all the furniture in the room, save for a square of Wilton carpet[3] in the centre. The boards round and the panelling of the walls were brown, worm-eaten oak, so old and discoloured that it may have dated from the original building of the house. Holmes drew one of the chairs into a corner and sat silent, while his eyes travelled round and round and up and down, taking in every detail of the apartment.

"Where does that bell communicate with?" he asked at last, pointing to a thick bell-rope which hung down beside the bed, the tassel actually lying upon the pillow.

"It goes to the housekeeper's room."

"It looks newer than the other things?"

"Yes, it was only put there a couple of years ago."

"Your sister asked for it, I suppose?"

"No, I never heard of her using it. We used always to get what we wanted for ourselves."

---

[1] *lens* Magnifying glass.

[2] *homely* Simple, unsophisticated.

[3] *Wilton carpet* Brand of carpet made in Wilton, England.

"Indeed, it seemed unnecessary to put so nice a bell-pull there. You will excuse me for a few minutes while I satisfy myself as to this floor." He threw himself down upon his face with his lens in his hand, and crawled swiftly backwards and forwards, examining minutely the cracks between the boards. Then he did the same with the woodwork with which the chamber was panelled. Finally he walked over to the bed and spent some time in staring at it, and in running his eye up and down the wall. Finally he took the bell-rope in his hand and gave it a brisk tug.

"Why, it's a dummy," said he.

"Won't it ring?"

"No, it is not even attached to a wire. This is very interesting. You can see now that it is fastened to a hook just above where the little opening of the ventilator is."

"How very absurd! I never noticed that before."

"Very strange!" muttered Holmes, pulling at the rope. "There are one or two very singular points about this room. For example, what a fool a builder must be to open a ventilator in another room, when, with the same trouble, he might have communicated with the outside air!"

"That is also quite modern," said the lady.

"Done about the same time as the bell-rope," remarked Holmes.

"Yes, there were several little changes carried out about that time."

"They seem to have been of a most interesting character—dummy bell-ropes, and ventilators which do not ventilate. With your permission, Miss Stoner, we shall now carry our researches into the inner apartment."

Dr. Grimesby Roylott's chamber was larger than that of his stepdaughter, but was as plainly furnished. A camp bed, a small wooden shelf full of books, mostly of a technical character, an armchair beside the bed, a plain wooden chair against the wall, a round table, and a large iron safe were the principal things which met the eye. Holmes walked slowly round and examined each and all of them with the keenest interest.

"What's in here?" he asked, tapping the safe.

"My stepfather's business papers."

"Oh! you have seen inside, then?"

"Only once, some years ago. I remember that it was full of papers."

"There isn't a cat in it, for example?"

"No. What a strange idea!"

"Well, look at this!" He took up a small saucer of milk which stood on the top of it.

"Well, look at this."

"No; we don't keep a cat. But there is a cheetah and a baboon."

"Ah, yes, of course! Well, a cheetah is just a big cat, and yet a saucer of milk does not go very far in satisfying its wants, I daresay. There is one point which I should wish to determine." He squatted down in front of the wooden chair, and examined the seat of it with the greatest attention.

"Thank you. That is quite settled," said he, rising and putting his lens in his pocket. "Hullo! Here is something interesting!"

The object which had caught his eye was a small dog lash hung on one corner of the bed. The lash, however, was curled upon itself, and tied so as to make a loop of whipcord.

"What do you make of that, Watson?"

"It's a common enough lash. But I don't know why it should be tied."

"That is not quite so common, is it? Ah, me! It's a wicked world, and when a clever man turns his brain to crime it is the worst of all. I think that I have seen enough now, Miss Stoner, and, with your permission, we shall walk out upon the lawn."

I had never seen my friend's face so grim, or his brow so dark, as it was when we turned from the scene of this investigation. We had walked several times up and down the lawn, neither Miss Stoner nor myself liking to break in upon his thoughts before he roused himself from his reverie. "It is very essential, Miss Stoner," said he, "that you should absolutely follow my advice in every respect."

"I shall most certainly do so."

"The matter is too serious for any hesitation. Your life may depend upon your compliance."

"I assure you that I am in your hands."

"In the first place, both my friend and I must spend the night in your room."

Both Miss Stoner and I gazed at him in astonishment.

"Yes, it must be so. Let me explain. I believe that that is the village inn over there?"

"Yes, that is the Crown."

"Very good. Your windows would be visible from there?"

"Certainly."

"You must confine yourself to your room, on pretence of a headache, when your stepfather comes back. Then when you hear him retire for the night, you must open the shutters of your window, undo the hasp, put your lamp there as a signal to us, and then withdraw with everything which are likely to want into the room which you used to occupy. I have no doubt that, in spite of the repairs, you could manage there for one night."

"Oh, yes, easily."

"The rest you will leave in our hands."

"But what will you do?"

"We shall spend the night in your room, and we shall investigate the cause of this noise which has disturbed you."

"I believe, Mr. Holmes, that you have already made up your mind," said Miss Stoner, laying her hand upon my companion's sleeve.

"Perhaps I have."

"Then for pity's sake tell me what was the cause of my sister's death."

"I should prefer to have clearer proofs before I speak."

"You can at least tell me whether my own thought is correct, and if she died from some sudden fright."

"No, I do not think so. I think that there was probably some more tangible cause. And now, Miss Stoner, we must leave you, for if Dr. Roylott returned and saw us, our journey would be in vain. Goodbye, and be brave, for if you will do what I have told you, you may rest assured that we shall soon drive away the dangers that threaten you."

"Good-bye, and be brave."

Sherlock Holmes and I had no difficulty in engaging a bedroom and sitting room at the Crown Inn. They were on the upper floor, and from our window we could command a view of the avenue gate, and of the inhabited wing of Stoke Moran Manor House. At dusk we saw Dr. Grimesby Roylott drive past, his huge form looming up beside the little figure of the lad who drove him. The boy had some slight difficulty in undoing the heavy iron gates, and we heard the hoarse roar of the doctor's voice, and saw the fury with which he shook his clenched fists at him. The trap drove on, and a few minutes later we saw a sudden light spring up among the trees as the lamp was lit in one of the sitting rooms.

"Do you know, Watson," said Holmes, as we sat together in the gathering darkness, "I have really some scruples as to taking you tonight. There is a distinct element of danger."

"Can I be of assistance?"

"Your presence might be invaluable."

"Then I shall certainly come."

"It is very kind of you."

"You speak of danger. You have evidently seen more in these rooms than was visible to me."

"No, but I fancy that I may have deduced a little more. I imagine that you saw all that I did."

"I saw nothing remarkable save the bell-rope, and what purpose that could answer I confess is more than I can imagine."

"You saw the ventilator, too?"

"Yes, but I do not think that it is such a very unusual thing to have a small opening between two rooms. It was so small that a rat could hardly pass through."

"I knew that we should find a ventilator before ever we came to Stoke Moran."

"My dear Holmes!"

"Oh, yes, I did. You remember in her statement she said that her sister could smell Dr. Roylott's cigar. Now, of course that suggests at once that there must be a communication between the two rooms. It could only be a small one, or it would have been remarked upon at the coroner's inquiry. I deduced a ventilator."

"But what harm can there be in that?"

"Well, there is at least a curious coincidence of dates. A ventilator is made, a cord is hung, and a lady who sleeps in the bed dies. Does not that strike you?"

"I cannot as yet see any connection."

"Did you observe anything very peculiar about that bed?"

"No."

"It was clamped to the floor. Did you ever see a bed fastened like that before?"

"I cannot say that I have."

"The lady could not move her bed. It must always be in the same relative position to the ventilator and to the rope—for so we may call it, since it was clearly never meant for a bell-pull."

"Holmes," I cried, "I seem to see dimly what you are hitting at. We are only just in time to prevent some subtle and horrible crime."

"Subtle enough and horrible enough. When a doctor does go wrong he is the first of criminals. He has nerve and he has knowledge. Palmer and Pritchard[1] were among the heads of their profession. This man strikes even deeper, but I think, Watson, that we shall be able to strike deeper still. But we shall have horrors enough before the night is over; for goodness' sake let us have a quiet pipe, and turn our minds for a few hours to something more cheerful."

About nine o'clock the light among the trees was extinguished, and all was dark in the direction of the Manor House. Two hours passed slowly away, and then, suddenly, just at the stroke of eleven, a single bright light shone out right in front of us.

"That is our signal," said Holmes, springing to his feet; "it comes from the middle window."

As we passed out he exchanged a few words with the landlord, explaining that we were going on a late visit to an acquaintance, and that it was possible that we might spend the night there. A moment later we were out on the dark road, a chill wind blowing in our faces, and one yellow light twinkling in front of us through the gloom to guide us on our sombre errand. There was little difficulty in entering the grounds, for unrepaired breaches gaped in the old park wall. Making our way among the trees, we reached the lawn, crossed it, and were about to enter through the window, when out from a clump of laurel bushes there darted what seemed to be a hideous and distorted child, who threw itself on

---

[1] *Palmer and Pritchard*   Both men were doctors who, in unrelated cases, were executed in the mid-1800s for murdering people using poison.

the grass with writhing limbs, and then ran swiftly across the lawn into the darkness.

"My God!" I whispered, "did you see it?"

Holmes was for the moment as startled as I. His hand closed like a vice upon my wrist in his agitation. Then he broke into a low laugh, and put his lips to my ear.

"It is a nice household," he murmured, "that is the baboon."

I had forgotten the strange pets which the doctor affected. There was a cheetah, too; perhaps we might find it upon our shoulders at any moment. I confess that I felt easier in my mind when, after following Holmes's example and slipping off my shoes, I found myself inside the bedroom. My companion noiselessly closed the shutters, moved the lamp on to the table, and cast his eyes round the room. All was as we had seen it in the daytime. Then creeping up to me and making a trumpet of his hand, he whispered into my ear again so gently that it was all that I could do to distinguish the words:

"The least sound would be fatal to our plans."

I nodded to show that I had heard.

"We must sit without a light. He would see it through the ventilator."

I nodded again.

"Do not go to sleep; your very life may depend upon it. Have your pistol ready in case we should need it. I will sit on the side of the bed, and you in that chair."

I took out my revolver and laid it on the corner of the table. Holmes had brought up a long thin cane, and this he placed upon the bed beside him. By it he laid the box of matches and the stump of a candle. Then he turned down the lamp and we were left in darkness.

How shall I ever forget that dreadful vigil? I could not hear a sound, not even the drawing of a breath, and yet I knew that my companion sat open-eyed, within a few feet of me, in the same state of nervous tension in which I was myself. The shutters cut off the least ray of light, and we waited in absolute darkness. From outside came the occasional cry of a night bird, and once at our very window a long drawn, cat-like whine, which told us that the cheetah was indeed at liberty. Far away we could hear the deep tones of the parish clock, which

boomed out every quarter of an hour. How long they seemed, those quarters! Twelve o'clock, and one, and two, and three, and still we sat waiting silently for whatever might befall.

Suddenly there was the momentary gleam of a light up in the direction of the ventilator, which vanished immediately, but was succeeded by a strong smell of burning oil and heated metal. Someone in the next room had lit a dark lantern.[1] I heard a gentle sound of movement, and then all was silent once more, though the smell grew stronger. For half an hour I sat with straining ears. Then suddenly another sound became audible—a very gentle, soothing sound, like that of a small jet of steam escaping continually from a kettle. The instant that we heard it, Holmes sprang from the bed, struck a match, and lashed furiously with his cane at the bell-pull.

"Holmes lashed furiously."

"You see it, Watson?" he yelled. "You see it?"

But I saw nothing. At the moment when Holmes struck the light I heard a low, clear whistle, but the sudden glare flashing into my weary eyes made it impossible for me to tell what it was at which my friend lashed so savagely. I could, however, see that his face was deadly pale, and filled with horror and loathing.

He had ceased to strike, and was gazing up at the ventilator, when suddenly there broke from the silence

---

[1] *dark lantern* Lantern with a slide so that its light can be hidden.

of the night the most horrible cry to which I have ever listened. It swelled up louder and louder, a hoarse yell of pain and fear and anger all mingled in the one dreadful shriek. They say that away down in the village, and even in the distant parsonage, that cry raised the sleepers from their beds. It struck cold to our hearts, and I stood gazing at Holmes, and he at me, until the last echoes of it had died away into the silence from which it rose.

"What can it mean?" I gasped.

"It means that it is all over," Holmes answered. "And perhaps, after all, it is for the best. Take your pistol, and we shall enter Dr. Roylott's room."

With a grave face he lit the lamp, and led the way down the corridor. Twice he struck at the chamber door without any reply from within. Then he turned the handle and entered, I at his heels, with the cocked pistol in my hand.

It was a singular sight which met our eyes. On the table stood a dark lantern with the shutter half open, throwing a brilliant beam of light upon the iron safe, the door of which was ajar. Beside this table, on the wooden chair, sat Dr. Grimesby Roylott, clad in a long grey dressing gown, his bare ankles protruding beneath, and his feet thrust into red heelless Turkish slippers. Across his lap lay the short stock with the long lash which we had noticed during the day. His chin was cocked upwards, and his eyes were fixed in a dreadful rigid stare at the corner of the ceiling. Round his brow he had a peculiar yellow band, with brownish speckles, which seemed to be bound tightly round his head. As we entered he made neither sound nor motion.

"The band! The speckled band!" whispered Holmes.

I took a step forward. In an instant his strange headgear began to move, and there reared itself from among his hair the squat diamond-shaped head and puffed neck of a loathsome serpent.

"It is a swamp adder!" cried Holmes—"the deadliest snake in India. He has died within ten seconds of being bitten. Violence does, in truth, recoil upon the violent, and the schemer falls into the pit which he digs for another. Let us thrust this creature back into its den, and we can then remove Miss Stoner to some place of shelter, and let the county police know what has happened."

"He made neither sound nor motion."

As he spoke he drew the dog whip swiftly from the dead man's lap, and throwing the noose round the reptile's neck, he drew it from its horrid perch, and, carrying it at arm's length, threw it into the iron safe, which he closed upon it.

Such are the true facts of the death of Dr. Grimesby Roylott, of Stoke Moran. It is not necessary that I should prolong a narrative which has already run to too great a length, by telling how we broke the sad news to the terrified girl, how we conveyed her by the morning train to the care of her good aunt at Harrow, of how the slow process of official inquiry came to the conclusion that the doctor met his fate while indiscreetly playing with a dangerous pet. The little which I had yet to learn of the case was told me by Sherlock Holmes as we travelled back next day.

"I had," said he, "come to an entirely erroneous conclusion, which shows, my dear Watson, how dangerous it always is to reason from insufficient data. The presence of the gypsies, and the use of the word 'band,' which was used by the poor girl, no doubt, to explain the appearance which she had caught a horrid glimpse of by the light of her match, were sufficient to put me upon an entirely wrong scent. I can only claim the merit that I instantly reconsidered my position when, however, it became clear to me that whatever danger threatened an occupant of the room could not come either from the window or the door. My attention was speedily drawn, as I have already remarked to you, to this ventilator, and to the bell-rope which hung down to the bed. The discovery that this was a dummy, and that the bed was clamped to the floor, instantly gave rise to the suspicion that the rope was there as a bridge for something passing through the hole, and coming to the bed. The idea of a snake instantly occurred to me, and when I coupled it with my knowledge that the doctor was furnished with a supply of creatures from India, I felt that I was probably on the right track. The idea of using a form of poison which could not possibly be discovered by any chemical test was just such a one as would occur to a clever and ruthless man who had had an Eastern training. The rapidity with which such a poison would take effect would also, from his point of view, be an advantage. It would be a sharp-eyed coroner indeed who could distinguish the two little dark punctures which would show where the poison fangs had done their work. Then I thought of the whistle. Of course, he must recall the snake before the morning light revealed it to the victim. He had trained it, probably by the use of the milk which we saw, to return to him when summoned. He would put it through the ventilator at the hour that he thought best, with the certainty that it would crawl down the rope, and land on the bed. It might or might not bite the occupant, perhaps she might escape every night for a week, but sooner or later she must fall a victim.

"I had come to these conclusions before ever I had entered his room. An inspection of his chair showed me that he had been in the habit of standing on it, which, of course, would be necessary in order that he should reach the ventilator. The sight of the safe, the saucer of milk, and the loop of whipcord were enough to finally dispel any doubts which may have remained. The metallic clang heard by Miss Stoner was obviously caused by her father hastily closing the door of his safe upon its terrible occupant. Having once made up my mind, you know the steps which I took in order to put the matter to the proof. I heard the creature hiss, as I have no doubt that you did also, and I instantly lit the light and attacked it."

"With the result of driving it through the ventilator."

"And also with the result of causing it to turn upon its master at the other side. Some of the blows of my cane came home, and roused its snakish temper, so that it flew upon the first person it saw. In this way I am no doubt indirectly responsible for Dr. Grimesby Roylott's death, and I cannot say that it is likely to weigh very heavily upon my conscience."

—1892

RABINDRANATH TAGORE
1861 – 1941

In 1931, Mohandas Gandhi wrote of Rabindranath Tagore, "In common with thousands of his countrymen I owe much to one who by his poetic genius and singular purity of life has raised India in the estimation of the world." Tagore's importance to the Indian subcontinent and its literature is indeed difficult to overstate. As a poet, Tagore wrote what became the national anthems for India and Bangladesh and inspired Sri Lanka's anthem, and he became for his native Bengal what Shakespeare is for England, earning himself the informal title of "Bard of Bengal." As a dramatist, novelist, and short-story writer, he helped give those genres their modern South Asian form. As an activist, he was an important voice for the Swadeshi movement, an early anticolonial campaign, as well as for international unity and understanding. He preached freedom from the British Raj while remaining skeptical of Indian nationalism, and he dedicated himself to revitalizing his nation and society so that they could avoid perpetuating what he saw as the nationalistic evils—militarism and imperialism, exploitative greed, intolerant chauvinism—from which India had itself suffered. By the end of his long life, he had produced approximately eighty volumes' worth of poetry, fiction, drama, and nonfictional prose (as well as nearly three thousand paintings); founded an international university, Visva-Bharati in Santiniketan, West Bengal; and become an international literary celebrity and the first non-European winner of the Nobel Prize in Literature.

Tagore was born in Kolkata (known at the time as Calcutta) in 1861. His family were wealthy Brahmins, members of the highest Hindu caste, who owed their riches and status to large landholdings, commercial and industrial investments, and service to the British East India Company. The family was also noted for its scholarly and artistic interests and involvement in the Bengali Renaissance, a movement that encouraged philosophical and literary invention in Bengali rather than in the traditional prestige languages of India, Sanskrit and Persian. By the time of Rabindranath's birth, the Tagore home had become a hub of creativity and intellectual activity that drew on and synthesized both Indian and European traditions and modes of thought. Rabindranath Tagore was accordingly immersed in the arts from a young age, writing poetry and plays that his large family—he was the fourteenth of fifteen children—performed by and for themselves. His creativity went hand-in-hand with a free-spiritedness that led him to reject all formal schooling (an attitude he was to preserve throughout his life). He continued this pattern of nonconformity when his father dispatched him to England in 1878 to train as a barrister: Tagore was more interested in reading Shakespeare than studying law, and he returned to India without a degree in 1880. By the time of his English sojourn, he had already completed his first major poetic works, one of which he playfully—but successfully—presented as a lost poem by an imaginary seventeenth-century poet. Once back in India, he launched himself fully into a literary career and quickly made his name as a writer in Bengal. He also started a family of his own, marrying Mrinalini Devi in 1883 when she was about ten years old; child marriage was a common traditional practice that Tagore criticized in his writings despite engaging in it himself. He and Mrinalini eventually had five children before her early death in 1902.

In 1890, Tagore took over the management of his family's estates, work which required him to spend long stretches of time in rural areas of what is now Bangladesh; he also assumed a leading role in the literary journal *Sadhana* ("Endeavour"), one of several Bengali literary magazines feeding a growing demand for short fiction. Inspired by what he witnessed of rural Bengali life, and compelled to provide a steady stream of content for *Sadhana*, he began an extraordinarily intense phase of short-story writing: Tagore wrote fifty-nine short stories during the 1890s, including nearly one per month from 1891 to 1895. His stories depicted the natural beauty and human life of the Bengali countryside with what Tagore insisted—in response to critics who accused him of "poeticizing" rural realities—was complete realism. As he put it many years later, "I used to rove down Bengal's rivers, and I observed the wonderful way of life of Bengal's villages. … I wrote from what I saw, what I felt in my heart—my direct experience." Tagore's short fiction blends attention to everyday rural life with spiritual and philosophical themes in an innovative style that balances complex and earthy elements. He did not invent the Bengali short story, but he played a leading role in establishing it as a serious literary form addressing contemporary concerns.

Tagore's literary representation of Bengal acquired a new urgency in 1905, when the Viceroy of India, Lord Curzon, divided the province in two as part of a "divide and rule" strategy meant to weaken the political power of Bengal's primarily Hindu upper and middle classes. Outraged, Bengalis responded with the Swadeshi movement, a campaign of anticolonial agitation that included the boycotting of British goods (the adjective *swadeshi* connotes national autonomy). Tagore supported the movement through works such as "Amar Sonar Bangla" ("My Golden Bengal," later made the Bangladeshi national anthem), which gave voice to a unified Bengali identity. After the partition was reversed in 1911, however, Tagore sounded a more ambivalent note in *Ghare Baire* (*The Home and the World*, 1916), a portrayal of the Swadeshi era that is his most famous novel. The novel embodies the tension between home and world, India and the West, tradition and modernity, in the opposition it stages between Nikhilesh, a rationalistic landowner who opposes violence, and Sandip, a Swadeshi radical willing to resort to incendiary and even unscrupulous methods. Despite the ambivalence on display in such works, Tagore remained an outspoken critic of British imperial rule throughout his life. In 1919, for example, a massacre of anticolonial protesters in Amritsar prompted him to renounce his British knighthood.

While Tagore's achievements in prose fiction are also celebrated, poetry was his primary vocation and the main basis for his fame. His voluminous poetic work encompasses an enormous array of forms, styles, and topics; it mingles Tagore's inheritance from Sanskrit and Bengali literature with influences from British poetry, especially the English Romantics, but also demonstrates a consistent spirit of restless innovation that Tagore shared with what would become the modernist literary movement. Building on the work done by his nineteenth-century predecessors to make Bengali a modern literary language, Tagore greatly diversified Bengali poetry's meters and verse forms, enriched its diction by drawing extensively on Sanskrit, and revitalized its style and content by turning for inspiration and models to the folk music of rural Bengal. Tagore's poetry also brought about his first major breakthrough in the West in 1912, when his translation into English of his 1910 collection *Gitanjali* (*Song Offerings*) set off a brief craze that culminated a year later in his receipt of the Nobel Prize for Literature. Tagore's close contemporary William Butler Yeats, who penned an introduction for the English version of *Gitanjali*, wrote that, while carrying around the manuscript of the poems, "I have often had to close it lest some stranger would see how much it moved me," adding that "[t]hese lyrics … display in their thought a world I have dreamed of all my life long." Building on these achievements, Tagore continued to refine his poetic voice for the rest of his life, producing ever more pared-down and vulnerable work right up to his death.

Tagore's later life combined ongoing writing with political, social, and cultural activism in India and abroad. In 1901, he founded a spiritual retreat and experimental school at Santiniketan, one of his family estates, which in 1918 he developed into an alternative university called Visva-Bharati (which could be translated as "India in the World"). The university, which still operates today, embodies Tagore's revolt against what he considered the oppressiveness of formal education: its classes are individualized, freewheeling, tailored to student interests, and typically conducted outdoors. In 1921, Tagore complemented the university with a nearby "Institute for Rural Reconstruction," which he hoped would form a basis for reforming and modernizing Indian agriculture and village life. To raise funds for these projects, he traveled and lectured all over the world: he visited five continents and befriended such luminaries as Jawaharlal Nehru, Albert Einstein, Ezra Pound, Margaret Noble, John Maynard Keynes, and Helen Keller, among many others. His advocacy of a universalist "Religion of Man" made him easy to parody as an impractical idealist, as he himself acknowledged, but his tireless denunciation of all forms of bigotry and prejudice provided an important counterpoint to the forces that, when he died in 1941, were on the march worldwide.

While he is today revered in South Asia, especially Bengal, Tagore garnered considerable controversy in his time. He argued strenuously with Gandhi (with whom he also shared a mutual admiration) about a range of topics, including the necessity of nationalism, the importance of science and rationality, and the nature of social and economic development. Tagore also condemned the embrace of violence by some nationalists associated with the Swadeshi movement, which led to at least one assassination plot against him. Tagore's critical reputation has varied, especially in the West, and the difficulty of adequately translating his writing from its original Bengali has kept him under-recognized outside of the subcontinent. The rise of postcolonial theory, however, has led to an increasing recognition of Tagore's significance to not just Indian but world literature. A letter written to Tagore in 1920 by the mother of Wilfred Owen, the promising English poet killed in the last days of World War I, poignantly illustrates Tagore's ability to speak across linguistic and cultural divides: "the day he said goodbye to me ... he, my poet son, said those wonderful words of yours—beginning at 'When I go from hence, let this be my parting word'—and when his pocket book came back to me—I found these words written in his dear writing—with your name beneath."

⌘ ⌘ ⌘

The Postmaster[1]

On commencing service the postmaster had to come to Ulapur.[2] It was a petty village. Hard by, there was an indigo[3] factory. The *Sahib*[4] of the factory had after a great deal of trouble got this post office established.

Our postmaster was a Calcutta cockney.[5] He was like a fish out of water in this village post office. His office was held in a gloomy thatched house; at no great distance there was a pond mantled with duckweed, and dense jungle covered the banks. The officers of the factory had hardly any leisure nor were they fit company for gentlemen.

Besides a Calcutta cockney never feels himself at home among strangers. In a strange place he either bears himself haughtily or fights shy of the people. For this reason, he could not freely mix with the people of the locality. Nor had he much work on his hands. Sometimes he would dabble in poetry. His poems would give vent to the sentiment that life may pass very happily by gazing on the trees and creepers trembling in the wind and on the clouds flitting on the sky, but God knows that if some genie of the "Arabian Nights"[6] could, in a single night, level those trees, root and branch, and make paved roads and could by means of rows of houses screen from his view the clouds on the sky, then this half-dead gentleman would regain a new life.

The postmaster's pay was very small. He had to cook his own meals, and a homeless orphan girl of the village did the household work for him and got her meals there. The name of the girl was Ratan. She was about twelve or thirteen years of age. There was little prospect of her marriage.

When in the evening volumes of smoke rose in curly streams from up the village cowsheds, the army of mosquitoes, having struck up their band among the jungles of the *Shaora* plants for a long time and having enjoyed the evening breeze, developed a keen appetite and got access to human habitations, when from every bush the cicalas[7] chirped afar, tipsy bands of *bauls*[8] with cymbals and drums would set up loud noisy songs, when sitting alone on the dark verandah of the thatched house the trembling of the trees would wake up even in the poet's heart—the postmaster would light a dim lamp in a corner of his room and would call "Ratan." Seated at the door Ratan would wait for this call, she would say "Why Sir, do you want me?"

Postmaster—What are you at?

Ratan—I shall have to light the oven presently—of the kitchen.

Postmaster—Never mind your kitchen, look to it after; do let me have a smoke of tobacco.

Very soon after Ratan entered with inflated cheeks blowing upon the *chillum*.[9] Taking over the *chillum* from her hand the postmaster abruptly asked, "Well Ratan, do you remember your mother?" That was a long story; she remembered certain things and other things had slipped from her memory. Her father loved her more than her mother did—she had a faint recollection of him. Her father returned in the evening after the day's labour and of such evenings one or two had been clearly outlined in her memory as a picture. While thus

---

[1] *The Postmaster* Translated by Debendra Nath Mitter, 1911.

[2] *Ulapur* Village in Bengal.

[3] *Hard by* Nearby; *indigo* Rare and expensive blue dye imported from India to Europe.

[4] *Sahib* British manager of the factory. "Sahib" is a term of polite address, originally Arabic but adopted by several Indian languages, that Indians often used for Europeans during India's colonial era.

[5] *Calcutta cockney* Term for a sheltered city-dweller from Calcutta (now Kolkata), unfamiliar with and uninterested in life beyond the city.

[6] *Arabian Nights* More properly known as *One Thousand and One Nights*; a classic Arabic text (possibly of Indian origin) known for its many supernatural and fantastical stories.

[7] *cicalas* Cicadas.

[8] [Translator's note] A class of musicians. [*Bauls* are itinerant Bengali musicians and religious mystics whose beliefs and practices draw from and combine both Hindu and Muslim traditions. Their music, which frequently celebrates celestial love, strongly influenced Tagore's poetry.]

[9] *chillum* Part of a hookah containing the tobacco.

chatting Ratan would sit down on the dust at the feet of the postmaster. She remembered a little brother—long ago in the wet season one day they had played at angling with the broken branch of a tree for a fishing-rod in a pond. And this fact would come to her mind more readily than even graver events. In such chitchat the night would far advance and for sheer laziness the postmaster would feel disinclined to cooking. Some stale hodgepodge there was remaining from the morning's cooking and Ratan would hastily light the oven and bake some *chapatis*[1] which served as their evening meal.

Sometimes the postmaster sitting in a corner of the large thatched house on a wooden stool of his office would talk of his own home—talk about his little brother, mother and elder sister—those for whom his heart ached in this strange place far away from home. Things which were always uppermost in his mind but which could not at all be broached to the *gomastas*[2] of the Indigo factory, he would relate without the least thought of any impropriety to an unlettered village girl. At last the situation reached such intimacy that the girl would mention the people of his home as "mother," "sister," "brother," as if she had known them all her life. She had even managed to sketch out their figures in imagination on the tiny tablet of her heart.

It was on a cloudless noon in the rainy season, a soft warm breeze was blowing pleasantly, the wet grass and trees were giving out a peculiar fragrance under the sun—it seemed as if the warm breath of the tired earth was wafting over the bodies of men and a certain obstinate bird was persistently pouring out her complaints at the bar of Nature in a plaintive monotonous tune. The postmaster had no work on his hands—the quivering of the smooth, shining, rain-washed shoots of the leaves and the scattered sunlit piles of white clouds of this fag-end[3] of the rainy season were really enjoyable sights. The postmaster looked on and thought, "would there were some one dear to his heart near to him

now—some human idol of love and affection bound up with his heart!" Gradually it struck him that the bird too was repeating the same tale over and over. And the murmuring of the trees in that solitary shady noon conveyed the same idea. None will believe it, none can know it, but in the head of a sub-postmaster drawing a small salary in a small village such feelings are awakened in a deep silent noon of a long holiday.

The postmaster, heaving a deep sigh, called "Ratan." Ratan was then sitting with her legs stretched out, eating green guavas. On hearing the voice of her master she immediately came running and asked in a panting voice "*Dada Babu* (elder brother), do you want me?" The postmaster said, "I shall give you short lessons in reading from day to day." And the whole noon he taught her the alphabet. Thus in a few days the compound letters were gone through.

It was the month of *Sravan*,[4] rain poured down in unceasing torrents. Ditches, marshes—tanks overflowed with water. The noise of the rain and the croaking of frogs were heard day and night. The village thorough-fares were almost stopped—the *hat* (market) could be reached only in boats.

One day the rain had set in heavily from the morning. The postmaster's pupil waited long at the door but missing the usual call she entered the room slowly with her books and papers and saw the postmaster lying upon his bed. Thinking that he was taking a short nap she was about to retire from the room noiselessly again, when suddenly she heard "*Ratan.*" She turned back quickly and asked, "*Dada Babu*, were you sleeping?" The postmaster in a plaintive voice said, "I don't feel well—just feel my brow."

In the heavy rains, lying ill and alone in a strange place, a man craves for some nursing. He remembers the sweet touch of hands, with shell bracelets on, on his fevered brow. He craves for the presence of the womanly tenderness of mother and sister at the sick bed. In this case, the sojourner's wishes did not remain unfulfilled. The girl Ratan was no longer a girl. She immediately

---

[1] *chapatis*   Type of unleavened flatbread, a staple of Indian cuisine.

[2] *gomastas*   Indian clerks or agents working for British businessmen or administrators.

[3] *fag-end*   Final remnant.

[4] *Sravan*   Fifth month in the Hindu calendar, roughly late July to late August.

took up the mother's *role*, called in the physician and fully gave him pills, sat up the whole night at his bed, cooked the sick man's diet and asked hundreds of times "well *Dada Babu*, do you feel a little better now?"

After a long time, the postmaster left his sick bed weak in body and determined that he would stay there no more and anyhow he must get himself transferred from that place. He immediately applied to the authorities in Calcutta for a transfer on the ground of the unhealthiness of the locality.

Being freed from nursing, Ratan occupied her own place outside the room. But she received no calls as before. Sometimes she peeped in and saw the postmaster sitting on the stool or lying on his bed very much absent-minded. When Ratan was waiting expectant for his bidding he was awaiting a reply to his application with an uneasy heart. The girl sitting behind the door went through her old lessons many times. She was afraid lest she should make a muddle of her compound letters when the sudden call for her lessons would come. At last after a week one evening the call came. With a full heart Ratan entered the room and asked, "*Dada Babu*, did you call me?" The postmaster said "Ratan, I am going away tomorrow."

Ratan—Where are you going, *Dada Babu*?

Postmaster—I am going home.

Ratan—When do you come back?

Postmaster—I shan't come back again.

Ratan did not ask any more questions. The postmaster told her of his own accord that he had applied for a transfer and his application had been rejected. He had therefore resigned his post and was proceeding home. For a long time neither spoke a word. The lamp burnt dimly and pitpat the rain fell on an earthen plate through a chink in the dilapidated thatched roof.

A little while after Ratan went away slowly to the kitchen to prepare the *chapatis*, but it was not done so quickly as on other days. Probably there arose many thoughts in her head. After the postmaster had finished his meal the girl suddenly asked him, "*Dada Babu*, will you take me home with you?" The postmaster laughed and said, "how can it be?" Why the matter was not possible he did not think it worth his while to explain to her.

The whole night asleep or awake the laughing voice of the postmaster['s] "how can it be?" rang in her ears.

Early in the morning the postmaster saw that the water for his bath was ready. According to his habit in Calcutta he used to bathe in drawn water. For some reason the girl could not ask the postmaster when he would start; and lest he would want his bath in the morning Ratan had drawn water from the river late in the night. Having finished his bath the postmaster called Ratan. She entered noiselessly and looked up silently to his face awaiting his orders. Her master said, "Ratan, I shall leave instructions to the man who comes to relieve me to take care of you as I have done, you need not be anxious because I am going away." There was no doubt that these words were the outcome of a kind and affectionate heart; but who can read the heart of a woman? Ratan had many a time quietly taken the rebukes of her master but could not bear these gentle words. With a surcharged heart she wept aloud and said, "No, no, you need not tell anyone for me. I shall not stay here."

The postmaster had never seen Ratan behave thus and so he was struck dumb with amazement.

The new postmaster came. Having made over his charge the late postmaster was about to start. At the time of departing, he called "Ratan" and said, "Ratan, I have never been able to give you anything; now while taking my leave, I give you something which will keep you at ease for a few days." Saying this, he took out all he had earned as his salary, retaining only the fare for his journey. Then Ratan fell on the dust at his feet and clinging to them said, "*Dada Babu*, I beg you humbly, you need not give me anything, none should be anxious for me," and saying this she ran away from that place.

Our late postmaster drawing a long breath took up his carpet bag in his hand, an umbrella on his shoulder, put his queer tin-trunk striped blue and white on the head of a coolie[1] and slowly strode on towards the boat.

When he got to the boat and the boat started—the overflowing and widening river of the rainy season

---

[1] *coolie* Indigenous manual laborer.

splashed on all sides and sparkled like the overflowing tears of the earth—he felt a smart pang in his heart—the pitiful picture of a simple village girl's face expressed a vast world-wide inexpressible heartache. Once he actually thought of coming back to take with him the forlorn orphan-girl—but the sails had caught the wind, the swollen current of the rainy season was flowing fast, the village had been left behind, and the burning-ghat[1] by the riverside came in view. In the sad heart of the voyager floating down the river the truth crept in—in this life there are innumerable such partings, innumerable deaths, what is the good of going back?

But Ratan's mind knew not the light of such truth. Flooded in tears she hovered round and round the post office. Perhaps a faint flicker of hope was in her heart—that *Dada Babu* might come back and this though held her as a bond, and she could not leave the place.

Oh! foolish human heart, delusion never breaks off, the dictates of reason come but too late, the strongest proofs are set aside and false hopes are clung to with the whole life and heart, till at last the nerves torn asunder, the blood of the heart sucked up—hope flies away, then one comes to one's senses and again the heart yearns for the snares of a second delusion.

—1891

A Shattered Dream[2]

When I went to Darjeeling[3] I found the weather misty and cloudy—the kind of weather in which a man does not care to go out of doors, and yet finds it still more unpleasant to stay inside the house. I finished my breakfast at the Hotel and went out, in thick boots and overcoat, for my usual walk.

It had been drizzling fitfully, and the mist that covered the hills gave them the appearance of a picture which the artist had been trying to rub out. As I walked on in solitude along the Calcutta Road, I felt that life needed some more definite background than this. The cloudland of mist seemed unfit for human habitation. My heart longed to cling hungrily to mother earth with every bodily sense and suck at her breast for sustenance.

At that moment I heard the muffled cry of a woman's voice near at hand—a thing not so rare in itself as to attract special attention. Indeed, at other times I should have paid no heed to it. But amid this endless mist it came to me like the sob of a smothered world.

When I got near to the spot I found a woman sitting on a rock by the roadside. She had a tangled mass of hair, coiled on her head, bronzed by the sun, and the cry which came from the depth of her heart was as if some long weariness of hope forlorn had suddenly given way in the midst of the utter loneliness of that cloud-covered mountainside.

I said to myself, "This is rather promising—here is a romance[4] in the making. To meet a woman ascetic weeping on a hill top in Darjeeling, is something out of the common."

It was not easy to make out to what religious order she belonged; so I asked her in Hindi who she was and what was the matter. At first she gave me no answer, but only looked at me through the mist and through her tears. I told her not to be afraid. She smiled and answered me in perfect Hindustani[5]—

---

[1] *burning-ghat* Area on the riverbank where dead bodies are cremated, according to Hindu custom, in a way that allows the ashes to be washed away by the river.

[2] *A Shattered Dream* Translated by C.F. Andrews, 1917.

[3] *Darjeeling* Town in northern Bengal, on the edge of the Himalayas. The temperate climate resulting from its elevation made it a popular resort during the summer months.

[4] *romance* Story dealing with unusual, exciting, imaginatively stimulating events.

[5] *Hindustani* In the nineteenth century, "Hindustani" referred to the South Asian language spoken by the elite classes, both Hindu and Muslim, of northern India. Because northern India had been under the control of Muslim rulers for many centuries, the language was heavily influenced by Arabic and Persian. Over the course of the nineteenth century, Hindus developed a version of the language that drew more on Sanskrit, an ancient Indian language considered sacred in Hinduism; this became modern Hindi. The narrator uses this more recent, Sanskritized form of the language, which he calls Hindi, to address the woman, but she responds in its older, more aristocratic and Persianized form, which the narrator calls Hindustani.

"I have done with fear long ago; neither have I any shame left. Yet there was a time, Babu-ji,[1] when I lived in my own zenana,[1] and even my brother would have to get leave before he entered. But now I have no purdah[2] left in the wide world."

I was slightly annoyed at being called "Babu-ji," because my dress and manners were completely European, and it nettled me not a little to be suspected by this ignorant woman of belonging to the "Babu" class.

For a moment, I thought I had better put an end to this romance at its very start, and, like a railway train of Sahibdom,[3] steam off with my nose in the air and rings of cigarette smoke floating behind me. But my curiosity got the upper hand. I assumed a stiff and superior air, and asked:

"Do you want my assistance?"

She looked in my face with a steady gaze and answered:

"I am the daughter of Ghulam Qadir Khan, the Nawab of Badraon."[4]

Where Badraon was and who in the world was its Nawab, and why in the name of all wonder his daughter should have become an ascetic, weeping and crying at the bend of the Calcutta Road—all this I could neither imagine nor believe. But I said to myself, that there was no need to be too critical; for the story was getting interesting. So, with all due solemnity, I made a deep salaam[5] and said:

"Pardon me, Bibi Sahiba,[6] I could not guess who you were."

The Bibi Sahiba was evidently pleased, and beckoned me to take a seat upon a rock near by, and said with a wave of her hand:

"Baithiye" (please sit down).

I discovered by her manner that she had the natural grace and power to command; and somehow I felt it was an unlooked for honour to be allowed to take a seat on that hard, damp, moss-covered rock by her side. When I left my hotel, in my overcoat, that morning I could never have imagined that I should be privileged to sit on a muddy stone by the daughter of Ghulam Qadir Khan of Badraon, whose name might be "Light of the Realm" or "Light of the Universe," etc.—and this at the bend of the Calcutta Road!

I asked her, "Bibi Sahiba, what has brought you to this condition?"

The Princess touched her forehead with her hand and said:

"How can I say who did it? Can you tell me who has banished this mountain behind the purdah of the clouds?"

I was in no mood just then to get involved in a philosophical discussion. So I accepted her word for it and said:

"Yes, it is true, Princess. Who can fathom the mystery of Fate? We are mere insects."

I would have argued out the point with her, at another time, but my ignorance of Hindustani stood in the way. Whatever little knowledge of Hindi[7] I had picked up from the servants could never have carried me through a discussion on fate and free will at the Darjeel-

---

[1]   *Babu-ji*   In Bengal, "Babu" was and is an honorific term of address for a Hindu man. By the late nineteenth century, however, it had also become a derogatory term, used by both Indians and British, for a Bengali man with a superficial English education. "Ji" is a common honorific suffix in northern India; *zenana*   Area of a home reserved for women.

[2]   *purdah*   I.e., means of observing purdah, the practice, widespread among Muslims and upper-class Hindus in the late nineteenth century, of keeping women secluded and concealing their physical forms from men. This typically involves the division of a home into separate spaces for men and women, and the wearing of face- and body-concealing garments by women outside of the home.

[3]   *Sahibdom*   I.e., the British or European world. *Sahib* was a term of polite address, somewhat equivalent to "sir," conventionally used by Indians for British people and other white Europeans during the period of British rule in India.

[4]   *Nawab of Badraon*   "Nawab" is a high-ranking aristocratic title originally used for the semi-autonomous local rulers of territories nominally within the Mughal Empire. Badraon is a village in what is now the Indian state of Uttar Pradesh.

[5]   *salaam*   Gesture of respect, made by bowing while touching the forehead with hand or fingers.

[6]   *Bibi Sahiba*   Somewhat archaic, formal way of addressing a married Muslim woman. "Bibi" was a polite term of address for a lady.

[7]   *little knowledge of Hindi*   The narrator comes from Bengal and thus speaks Bengali as a primary language.

ing roadside with the Princess of Badraon, or with any one else for the matter of that.

The Bibi Sahiba said: "the marvellous romance of my life has just come to its close on this very day. With your permission, I will tell you all about it."

I caught up her word quickly—"Permission? It would be a privilege to hear!"

Those who know me will understand that, in the language I used, I honoured Hindustani more in the breach than in the observance. On the other hand, when the Princess spoke to me, her words were like the morning breeze, upon the shimmering fields of golden corn. To her, an easy flow and graceful eloquence came naturally, while my answers were short and broken. This was her story—

"In my father's veins there flowed the imperial blood of Delhi. That is why it was so difficult to find me a suitable husband. There was some talk of my betrothal to the Nawab of Lucknow, but my father hesitated; and in the meanwhile there broke out the Mutiny of the sepoys against the Company Bahadur.[1] Hindustan was blackened by the cannon smoke."

Never in all my life before had I heard Hindustani spoken so perfectly by a woman's lips. I could understand that it was a language of princes, unfit for this mechanical age of modern commerce. Her voice had the magic in it to summon up before me, in the very heart of this English Hill Station, the sky-capped domes of Moghal palaces of white marble, the gaily caparisoned horses with their trailing tails, the elephants surmounted by howdahs richly dight,[2] the courtiers with their turbans of all different gorgeous colours, the curved scimitars fastened in magnificent sashes, the high-pointed gold-embroidered shoes, the leisurely flowing robes of silk and muslin and all the unbounded courtly ceremonial that went with them.

The Princess continued her story: "Our fort was on the banks of the Jumna, in charge of a Hindu Brahmin,[3] Keshav Lal—"

Upon this name, Keshav Lal, the woman seemed to pour out all at once the perfect music of her voice. My stick fell to the ground, I sat upright and tense.

"Keshav Lal," she went on, "was an orthodox Hindu. At early dawn I could see him every day, from the lattice of my zenana, as he stood breast high in the Jumna offering his libations of water to the sun. He would sit, in his dripping garments, on the marble steps of the river *ghat*[4] silently repeating his sacred verses, and he would then go home singing some religious chant in his clear and beautiful voice.

"I was a Musalman[5] girl, but I had never been given any opportunity of studying my own religion, nor did I practise any manner of worship. Our men, in those days, had become dissolute and irreligious, and the harems were mere pleasure resorts from which religion had been banished. But somehow I had a natural thirst for spiritual things, and when I witnessed this scene of devotion in the early light of dawn, at the lowly white steps leading down to the placid calm of the blue Jumna my new-awakened heart would overflow with an unutterable sweetness of devotion.

"I had a Hindu slave girl. Every morning she used to take the dust of Keshav Lal's feet.[6] This act used to give

---

[1] *the Mutiny*   In 1857, Indian sepoys—native soldiers in the service of the British East India Company—mutinied, and a general uprising spread across much of northern India. The uprising was violently crushed by British forces in the following year, and the British Crown then took direct control of the Indian colonies; *Company Bahadur* Indian name of the East India Company, literally meaning "honorable company."

[2] *English Hill Station*   Hill stations were high-altitude towns, like Darjeeling, built to allow the British to escape the summer heat of India's tropical regions; *Moghal* The Mughals were the Turkic-Mongol Muslim rulers of most of the Indian subcontinent from the sixteenth to the nineteenth centuries, though their power waned considerably after the East India Company took over much of India in

the eighteenth century. Mughal rulers built the Taj Mahal, among many other great works of architecture, and were renowned for their administrative and military organization and their sponsorship of literature and the arts; *howdahs* Railed and sometimes canopied seating areas attached to an elephant's back; *dight* Adorned.

[3] *Jumna* River in northern India, also known as the Yamuna; *in charge of* I.e., administered by; *Brahmin* Member of the Hindu priestly caste.

[4] *ghat* Wharf or series of steps along a river.

[5] *Musalman* I.e., Muslim.

[6] *take … feet* I.e., bow down at his feet.

me a kind of pleasure and it was also the cause of slight jealousy in my mind. On auspicious occasions this girl would feed the Brahmins and offer them gifts. I used to help her with money and once I asked her to invite Keshav Lal to her feast. But she drew herself up and said, that her Lord, Keshav Lal, would never receive food or gifts from anyone. And so because I could not express my reverence for Keshav Lal either directly or indirectly, my heart remained starved. One of my ancestors had taken by force a Brahmin girl into his harem, and I used to imagine that her blood was stirring in my own veins. They would give me a certain satisfaction and a sense of clan-kinship with Keshav Lal. I listened to all the wonderful stories of the Hindu gods and goddesses recited from the epics in all their details by this Hindu slave girl and would form in my mind an ideal world in which Hindu civilization reigned supreme. The images of the gods, the sounds of the temple bells and conches, the sacred shrines with their gilded spires, the smoke of the incense, the smell of the flower offerings and sandal-wood, the *yogis*[1] with their super-human powers, the sanctity of the Brahmins, the legends of the Hindu gods who had come down to earth as men—these things filled my imagination and created a vast and vaguely distant realm of fancy. My heart would fly about in it like a small bird in the dusk fluttering from room to room in a spacious old-world mansion.

"Then the great Mutiny broke out, and we felt the shock of it even in our tiny fort at Badraon. The time had come round for Hindu and Musalman to begin once more that unfinished game of dice for the throne of Hindustan, which they had played of old; and the pale-faced slayers of kine would have to be driven away from the land of the Aryans.[2]

"My father, Ghulam Qadir Khan, was a cautious man. He poured abuse on the English, but said at the same time, 'These men can do impossible things. The people of Hindustan are no match for them. I cannot afford to lose my little fort in pursuit of a vain ambition. I am not going to fight the Company Bahadur.'

"We all felt ashamed that my father could observe such caution at a time when the blood was running hot in the veins of every Hindu and Musalman in Hindustan. Even the Begum[3] mothers within the zenanas became restless. Then Keshav Lal, with all the force at his command, gave utterance—'Nawab Sahib, if thou dost not stand on our side then as long as the fight goes on I shall keep thee prisoner and guard the fort myself.'

"My father replied that there was no need to be anxious for he himself was ready to take the side of the mutineers. When Keshav Lal asked for money from the Treasury he gave him a small sum and said that he would give more as occasion arose.

"I took off all the ornaments which had decked me from head to foot and sent them secretly to Keshav Lal by my Hindu slave. When he accepted them it gave me a thrill in all those limbs of mine which had shed their decorations. He began to make preparations, cleaning the rust out of the old-fashioned guns and the long unused swords. Then all of a sudden one afternoon the Commissioner Sahib[4] entered the fort at the head of the red-coated white soldiers. My father Ghulam Qadir Khan had informed him in secret about Keshav Lal's plot. Yet so great was the Brahmin's influence that even then his tiny band of retainers were ready to fight with their useless guns and rusty swords. I felt my heart breaking for very shame though no tears came to my eyes. I went out of my zenana in secret disguised in the dress of my brother. Then the dust and smoke of the fight, the shouts of the soldiers, the boom of the guns ceased. The terrible peace of Death brooded over land

---

[1] *conches* Shells used as ceremonial trumpets in Hindu temples; *yogis* Practitioners of yoga, a group of physical, mental, and spiritual disciplines associated with Hinduism.

[2] *kine* Cattle. Hindus consider cows to be sacred; the fact that the British killed and ate cows, and used grease derived from cow-fat in the cartridges of the rifles they issued to Indian sepoys, contributed to the resentment of the British that sparked the 1857 uprising; *Aryans* In the Indian context, "Aryan" refers to the Indo-Iranian peoples of

ancient India, who used "Aryan" as a religious label for themselves and whose beliefs gave rise to Hindu religion in its modern form.

[3] *Begum* Aristocratic female title.

[4] *Commissioner Sahib* Local representative of the East India Company.

and sky. The sun had tinged red the blue waters of the Jumna and had gone down to his rest in blood; upon the evening sky appeared the moon which was nearly at the full. The battle field was covered with the fearful sights of death and pain. At any other time it would have been impossible for me to walk through such a scene but on that night I was like one walking in his sleep. My only object was to seek out Keshav Lal and everything else was blotted out from my consciousness.

"When it wore on to midnight I found Keshav Lal in a mango grove near the Jumna. He was lying on the ground with the dead body of his devoted servant, Deoki, near him. I was sure that either the servant, though fatally wounded, had carried his master, or the wounded master had carried his servant to this secure place. My veneration, which had been growing so long in secret, now could be restrained no longer. I flung myself down at the feet of Keshav Lal and wiped the dust of his feet with the tresses of my hair which I let down. I touched those death-cold feet of his with my forehead and my pent up tears broke out.

"Just then Keshav Lal slurred and a faint cry of pain broke from him. I started up. His eyes were closed, but I heard him call faintly for water. At once I went down to the Jumna and soaked my dress in the stream and squeezed it into his half-closed lips. I tore a piece of my cloth and bandaged the left eye which had received a sword cut together with a deep wound along the scalp. When I had squeezed out the water for him several times and sprinkled it on his face, he came back gradually to his senses. I asked him if he wanted any more. He stared at me and enquired who I was. I could no longer contain myself, but answered—

"'I am your devoted slave—the daughter of Nawab Ghulam Qadir Khan.'

"I had the hope in my mind that Keshav Lal would take with him in his dying moments my last confession. Nobody would deprive me of this final happiness. But the moment he heard my name he shouted out:

"'Daughter of a traitor! Infidel! At the very hour of my death you have desecrated my whole life.'[1] With these words he gave me a fierce blow on my right cheek. I felt giddy, and everything became dark to me.

"You must know that my age, when this happened, was only about sixteen. For the first time in my life I had come out from my zenana. The greedy and hot glare of the outside sky had not yet robbed my cheeks of their delicate rose flush. Yet at the very first step into the outer air, I got my salutation from the god of my world in this form!"

I was listening to this story of the ascetic like one lost in dreams. I did not even notice that the light had gone out from my cigarette. Whether my mind was occupied with the beauty of the language, or the music of her voice, or with the story itself, it is difficult to say, but I remained perfectly silent. When, however, she came to this point in her narrative, I could not keep still, but broke out saying:

"The beast!"

The daughter of the Nawab said:

"Who is the beast? Would a beast relinquish the draught of water brought to his lips at the time of his death agony?"

I corrected myself at once, and said:

"Oh, yes! It was divine!"

But the daughter of the Nawab answered:

"Divine! Do you mean to tell me that the Divine will refuse worship brought to him by a heart sincere?"

After this, I thought the best thing to do was to keep silence. The Nawab's daughter then went on with her story:

"At first, this was a great shock to me. It seemed as if the wreck of my broken world had come down upon my head. I had made my obeisance from a distance to that hard, cruel, imperturbable, warrior Brahmin, and said in my mind: 'You never accept service from the lowly, food from the alien, money from the rich, youth from the young, love from woman! You are aloof, alone, apart, distant—above all the defilement of the world of

[1] [Translator's note] I.e., by giving him water touched by a Musalman.

dust. I have not even the right to dedicate myself to you.'

"When he saw that I, the proud daughter of the Nawab, was making obeisance to him, with head touching the ground, I know not what thoughts passed through his mind! But his countenance showed no sign of wonder, or other emotion. He looked into my face for a moment, and then slowly raised himself and sat up.

"I was quick to extend my arms to help him, but he silently rejected me and with great pain dragged himself to the landing place of the Jumna. A ferry-boat was tied there, but neither passengers nor ferryman were present. Keshav Lal got into the boat, and untied the rope, and was drawn into the mid-stream and disappeared.

"For a moment, I felt a strong impulse to fling myself into the Jumna, like a flower untimely torn from its stem, offering all my love and youth and rejected worship towards that boat which carried off Keshav Lal. But I could not. The rising moon, the deep black line of the trees on the other side of the Jumna, the motionless stretch of the dark blue water of the river, the rampart of our fort glimmering above the distant mango grove, everything sang to me the silent music of death. Only that one frail boat, carried by the stream into the hopeless distance, still drew me on to the pathway of life, dragging me from the embrace of this beautiful Death in the peace of the moon-lit night.

"I went on, like one in a trance, along the back of the Jumna, across the thick sedge and sandy waste, now wading through shallow water, now climbing up steep banks, now threading my way through jungle thick with undergrowth"—

She stopped at this point and I did not disturb her silence. After a long interval she resumed her story:

"Events, after this, became confused. I do not know how to put them down one by one and make my story clear. I seemed to be walking through a wilderness, and I had no sense of the direction. It is difficult for me to recall to mind my wanderings through those trackless shades. I do not know how to begin and how to end, what to include and what to reject, and how to make the whole story so distinct as to appear perfectly natural

to you. But I have come to learn in these years of suffering that nothing is impossible, or absolutely difficult in this world. At first the obstacles might seem quite insurmountable for a girl brought up in the zenana of a Nawab, but that is merely imaginary. When you are once out among the crowd you find some path or other. That path may not be a Nawab's path; but all the same it is a path that leads men to their different fates, a path rugged and varied and endless in its winding course, a path full of joys and sorrows and obstructions—always a path.

"The story of my many wanderings along this pathway of the common race of men will not sound attractive, and even if it did I have not the energy to complete it. In brief, I went through all kinds of troubles, dangers, insults—and yet life had not become altogether intolerable. Like a rocket, the more I burned, the more I rushed upward, So long as I had this feeling of speed, I was unconscious of the burning pain; but when the fire of my supreme happiness and my supreme misery became extinct, I dropped spent and exhausted upon the dust of the earth. My voyage has been ended today, and my story has come to its conclusion."

She stopped.

But I shook my head and said to myself that this could not be a proper ending, and in my broken, imperfect Hindi I told her:

"Pardon me if I am discourteous, Princess, but I can assure you it would greatly relieve my mind, if you could make the ending just a little more clear."

The daughter of the Nawab smiled. I found that my broken Hindi had its effect. If I had carried on my conversation in the purest Hindustani, she would not have been able to overcome her reluctance; but this very imperfection of my language acted as a screen. She continued:

"I used to get news of Keshav Lal from time to time, but I never succeeded in meeting him. He joined Tantia Topi,[1] and would break like a sudden thunderstorm, now in the east, and now in the west; and then he

---

[1] *Tantia Topi* Tatya Tope (1814–59), a leader and general in the 1857 uprising.

would disappear just as suddenly. I took the dress of an ascetic and went to Benares, where I had my lesson in the Sanskrit scriptures from Sivananda Swami,[1] whom I call 'father.' News from every part of India would come to his feet, and while I learnt from him with all reverence my scriptures, I would listen with a terrible eagerness to the news of the fighting. The British Raj trampled out, from the whole of Hindustan, the smouldering embers of the rebellion.

"After that, I could get no further news of Keshav Lal. The figures which shone fitfully on the distant horizon in the red light of destruction suddenly lapsed into darkness.

"Then I left the shelter of my guru and went out seeking Keshav Lal from door to door. I went from one pilgrimage to another, but never met him. Those few who knew him, said he must have lost his life, either in the battlefield, or under the martial law which followed. But a small voice kept repeating in my heart that this could never happen. Keshav Lal could never die. That Brahmin—that scorching flame of fire—could not be extinct. That fire was still burning on some solitary altar difficult of approach, waiting for the final offering of my life and my soul.

"There are instances in the Hindu Scriptures of low caste people becoming Brahmins by the force of their ascetic practices, but whether a Musalman could also become a Brahmin has never been discussed. I know that I had to suffer long delay before I could be united with Keshav Lal, because I must become a Brahmin before that. And thirty years passed by in this manner.

"I became a Brahmin in my mind and habits of life. That stream of Brahmin blood, which I had inherited from some Brahmin grandmother, again became pure in my veins and throbbed in all my limbs. And when this was accomplished, I would mentally place myself, with

no touch of hesitation left, at the feet of that first Brahmin of my first youth—that one Brahmin of all my world. And I would feel round my head a halo of glory.

"I had often heard stories of Keshav Lal's bravery during the fighting of the Mutiny, but these would leave hardly any impression on my heart. The one picture that remained bright in my mind was that ferry boat, carrying Keshav Lal, floating down the calm, moonlit waters of the Jumna. Day and night I saw him sailing towards a great pathless mystery, with no companion, no servant—the Brahmin who needed nobody, who was complete master of himself.

"At last I got news of Keshav Lal—that he had fled across the border of Nepal to avoid punishment. I went to Nepal. After a long sojourn there, I learnt that he had left Nepal years ago, and no one knew where he had gone. Since that time, I have been travelling from hill to hill. This country is not the country of the Hindus. These Bhutias and Lepchas[2] are a heathen people. They have no proper regulations about their food. They have their own gods and modes of worship. And I was nervously careful to keep my purity of religious life avoiding all contamination. I knew that my boat had nearly reached its haven and that the last goal of my mortal life was not very far off.

"And then—how must I end? All ending is short. It takes only one sudden breath to make the lamp go out. Why then should I draw this out into a long tale? ... This very morning after thirty-eight years of separation I have met Keshav Lal—"

When she stopped at this point I became too eager to contain myself, and I said:

"How did you find him?"

The daughter of the Nawab replied:

"I saw old Keshav Lal picking out the grains from the ears of wheat in a courtyard of a Bhutia village, with his Bhutia wife at his side, and his Bhutia grandsons and granddaughters around him."

Here ended the story.

---

[1] *Benares* Also known as Varanasi; city on the banks of the Ganges River in northern India that is regarded as the holiest city in Hinduism; *Sanskrit scriptures* The primary sacred texts of Hinduism, including the Vedas, the Upanishads, and the Bhagavad Gita, are written in Sanskrit, an ancient Indian language; *Sivananda Swami* A swami is a Hindu religious teacher.

[2] *Bhutias and Lepchas* Indigenous peoples of the Himalayas in northeast India (as well as Nepal and Bhutan).

I thought I should say something—just a few words—to console her. I said:

"The man who had to spend thirty-eight years at a stretch with those aliens, hiding himself in fear of his life—how was it possible for him to keep his purity of religion?"

The daughter of the Nawab replied:

"Do not I understand all that? But what delusion was it, which I had been carrying all these years—the spell of this Brahmin who stole my heart when I was young? Could I even suspect that it was merely a matter of habit with him? I thought that it was Truth, Eternal Truth. Otherwise, how could I have taken, as an act of consecration from my guru, that blow upon my head—that intolerable insult, which this Brahmin dealt me in return for the offering of my body and mind and youth, trembling as I was with the fervour of devotion when I was only sixteen and had come for the first time in my life from the shelter of my father's house? Ah, Brahmin! You yourself have accepted another habit in place of your former habit. But how am I to get another life and youth in exchange for the life and youth I have lost?"

As she uttered this lament the woman stood up and said, "Namaskar, Babu-ji."—And then, in a moment, she corrected herself and said, "Salaam, Sahib."[1]

With this Muhammadan greeting she took her last farewell from the wreck of Brahmin ideals which were lying in the dusk. And before I could say another word she had vanished in the grey mist of the Himalayas.

I shut my eyes for a moment and saw all the incidents of her story pass again before my mind—that girl of sixteen, the Nawab's daughter, sitting at her lattice window, on her Persian carpet, watching the Brahmin as he performed his morning ablution at the Jumna: that sad woman in the dress of an ascetic at the evening ritual of the lighted lamps in some pilgrim shrine: that bent figure bowed down with the burden of a broken home on the Calcutta Road, Darjeeling. I felt in my mind the stir of the sad music born of the compact of two different strains of blood in the body of one woman, blended in a language beautiful in its perfect dignity of sound.

Then I opened my eyes. The mist had cleared away and the hillside was glistening with the morning light. The English memsahibs[2] were out in their rickshaws, and the English Sahibs were on horseback. Every now and then a Bengali clerk, with his head muffled up in his scarf, cast a glance of curiosity at me through its folds.

I got up from my seat. In the bare naked sunlight it was difficult to believe the woman's cloudy, misty story to be true. And it is my firm conviction, that it must have been my own imagination which mingled its cigarette fumes with the mist of the hills, and that the Brahmin warrior, the daughter of the Nawab and the fort by the Jumna are all vapour.

—1898

The Sunset of the Century[3]
(*Written in the Bengali on the last day of last century*)

The last sun of the century sets amidst the blood-red
    clouds of the West and the whirlwind of hatred.
The naked passion of self-love of Nations, in
        its drunken delirium of greed, is dancing to the
        clash of steel and the howling verses of vengeance.

The hungry self of the Nation shall burst in a violence
        of fury from its own shameless feeding.
For it has made the world its food,
And licking it, crunching it, and swallowing it in
        big morsels,
            It swells and swells

---

1. [Translator's note] Namaskar would be the greeting of a Hindu, Salaam the greeting of a Musalman. [The term "Sahib," when addressed to an Indian man, as opposed to a European, was the Muslim equivalent of "Babu."]

2. *memsahibs* "Memsahib" was the polite form of address for a British woman in India.

3. *The Sunset of the Century* Translated by the author, 1917.

Till in the midst of its unholy feast descends the sudden
  shaft of heaven piercing its heart of grossness.

The crimson glow of light on the horizon is not
  the light of thy dawn of peace, my Motherland.
It is the glimmer of the funeral pyre burning to ashes
  the vast flesh—the self-love of the Nation—dead
  under its own excess.
10 Thy morning waits behind the patient dark of the East,
    Meek and silent.

Keep watch, India.
Bring your offerings of worship for that sacred sunrise.
Let the first hymn of its welcome sound in your voice,
  and sing,
15 "Come, Peace, thou daughter of God's own great
    suffering.

Come with thy treasure of contentment, the sword
  of fortitude,
    And meekness crowning thy forehead."

Be not ashamed, my brothers, to stand before the proud
  and the powerful
    With your white robe of simpleness.
20 Let your crown be of humility, your freedom the
    freedom of the soul.
Build God's throne daily upon the ample bareness
  of your poverty
And know that what is huge is not great and pride
  is not everlasting.

—1899

TEKAHIONWAKE / E. PAULINE JOHNSON
1861 – 1913

E. Pauline Johnson, or Tekahionwake, was a Kanien'ke-há:ka (Mohawk) writer and performer who rose to literary prominence in the late nineteenth century, achieving fame in Canada, the United States, and England. Johnson's widely varied oeuvre ranged from nature poetry celebrating the Canadian landscape, retellings of traditional Indigenous stories, pieces on canoeing, cowboy and adventure tales, travel sketches, and love poems. Much of the discussion surrounding her career and legacy, however, has focused on her racial background and on her poetic engagement with Indigenous culture and politics. Johnson claimed Mohawk, English, and Canadian identity, and her work expresses patriotic attachment to Canada and the British Commonwealth, but it is also deeply critical of colonization and emphatic in its endorsement of Indigenous culture and values.

Johnson was born in 1861 to George Henry Martin Johnson, a Mohawk chief of the Six Nations of Grand River, and Emily Susanna Johnson (nee Howells), an English woman who had immigrated to America with her family as a child. George Johnson was an interpreter and liaison between the Mohawk nation and the Canadian government, and at one time was both a member of the Six Nations council and the official interpreter to the Crown. Pauline Johnson grew up in the family's grand house, called Chiefswood, on the Six Nations Reserve near Brantford, Ontario. The youngest of four children, she was raised in both British and Mohawk traditions, educated in Kanien'ke-há:ka culture by her father and grandfather, and in English culture by her mother. She was educated by governesses at home, at the reserve's day school, and at Brantford Central Collegiate. As a child, Johnson was a voracious reader; the influence of the sentimental writers popular during her youth is reflected in the scenes of nobility and pathos that recur in her poetry as well as her prose.

Johnson's father died prematurely in 1884, having been beaten several times by white rum runners whose exploitation of the Six Nations community he opposed. The loss necessitated the family's removal from Chiefswood to Brantford, and Johnson began writing to earn an income. In a letter to a friend in 1890, she wrote that she had undertaken her career with a "double motive": "one is to upset the Indian Extermination and noneducation theory—in fact to stand by my blood and my race. The other is that I am not a millionairess." Johnson began to publish her poetry in both Canadian and American periodicals, especially the prominent Toronto magazines *Saturday Night* and *The Week*, and by the end of the decade she had begun to publish stories and sketches as well. Her inclusion in W.D. Lighthall's influential anthology *Songs of the Great Dominion* (1889), which helped to shape late nineteenth-century notions of the canon of Canadian literature, went a long way toward building her reputation in Canada and overseas; London critic Thomas Watts-Dunton remarked in his 1889 review of the volume that Johnson was, "on account of her descent, the most interesting English poetess now living."

A turning point in Johnson's career was a brief appearance at a reading in Toronto in 1892, an event hosted by the Young Liberal Club of Toronto in celebration of Canadian literature. Johnson performed "A Cry from an Indian Wife" (1885) to rousing success, prompting the event's organizer, Frank Yeigh, to organize a recital tour of Ontario for her. Her career accelerated quickly, and she would spend the next decade and a half as a literary performer with a demanding schedule that would include multiple tours of the United States and England as well as Canada. Through her travels she formed connections with eminent figures such as Squamish Chief Joe Capilano (Sahp-luk) and his wife Mary Agnes Capilano (Líxwelut). Johnson also made the acquaintance of suffragist Nellie McClung and other figures of the "New Woman" movement, with whom she shared an interest in women's intellectual, financial, and other freedoms.

Johnson soon came to present her performances as "costume recitals" featuring a fringed buckskin dress she had created, inspired by multiple Indigenous cultures and in part modeled after a portrait of Minnehaha, a Dakota character in Henry Wadsworth Longfellow's influential poem *The Song of Hiawatha* (1855). Johnson continued to modify her costume throughout her career, accessorizing it with various artefacts such as wampum, a scalp, a bear-claw necklace, and a hunting knife. Often, she wore this costume while performing her "Indian" poems, and then recited her more conventional work wearing a Victorian evening gown. In an account of one Canadian performance, McClung recalls that

> Pauline's advertising had shown only the Indian girl in her beaded chamois costume and feather headdress, so when a beautiful young woman in white satin evening dress came out of the vestry door and walked to the platform, there was a gasp of surprise from the audience. Pauline smiled at us reassuringly, knowing what was in our minds.
> "I am going to be a white woman first," she said in her deep voice. "The Indian part will follow."

Johnson usually performed with a partner; her first, with whom she traveled from 1892 to 97, was Owen Smily, a musician, ventriloquist, and impersonator who performed his own set as well as acting opposite her in sketches based on her short fiction. Smily acted as manager for their shared tours—as did the humorist and recitalist Walter McRaye, who would replace Smily as her performing partner from 1901 to 1909. In these latter years, the influence of vaudeville became increasingly visible in Johnson's performance style: she performed many of her poems in character, skilfully imitating the dialect of the speaker, and comedy playlets and sketches became a significant part of her act with McRaye.

Johnson's first book, *The White Wampum* (1895), was published by the prestigious English publishing house Bodley Head. The volume consists mostly of poetry on nature, religion, and love written in a sentimental style common among Canadian poets of her era. It begins, however, with a number of poems centered on specifically Indigenous characters, and for many readers and critics Tekahionwake's indigeneity (or lack thereof) was a subject of particular interest. In a review of the book, settler ethnologist Horatio Hale commented that "The first inclination of the reader will be to look in her poems for some distinctive Indian traits, and to be disappointed if these are not strikingly apparent. Her compositions will be judged as those of a 'wild Indian girl,' and not as those of a well-bred and accomplished young Canadian lady with a dash of Indian blood, such as she really is." *The White Wampum* was published under the name Tekahionwake (Kanien'ke-há:ka: Double Wampum)—her grandfather's name, which she had adopted into her signature in the 1880s—though her English name also appeared on the inside cover. She would write and perform under both names from the mid-1890s onward, emphasizing one name or the other depending on the content of her work and its intended audience.

After the publication of her second poetry collection, *Canadian Born* (1903), Johnson focused increasingly on articles and short fiction, writing prolifically for periodicals such as *Mother's Magazine* and *Boys' World*. In 1909, as she was becoming increasingly ill with breast cancer, she retired in Vancouver, where she deepened her pre-existing friendship with Joe and Mary Agnes Capilano. She adapted to written prose many of the stories told to her by the Capilanos, some of which were later collected into *Legends of Vancouver* (1911). Johnson's friends collected some of her poems and stories in *Flint and Feather* (1912) to support her financially through her illness; after her death, they also saw to the publication of many of her prose pieces in the collections *The Moccasin Maker* (1913) and *The Shaganappi* (1913).

When Johnson died in 1913, she was mourned as a celebrity. Vancouver declared a half-holiday in her honor, and a monument to her was built in the city's Stanley Park, where her ashes are buried. In the mid-twentieth century, however, the male-dominated critical establishment dismissed Johnson, whose popular sentimental style did not conform to its modernist aesthetic—though white poets whom she influenced, such as Duncan Campbell Scott, continued to be celebrated. Even by her settler admirers, Johnson was often reduced to a "Mohawk Princess"—as she was described in the title of the first book-length study of her work, published in 1931. In the later twentieth century, as feminist and Indigenous criticism returned academic attention to Johnson, scholarship often focused on her complex navigation of her marginalized identity as a woman, a Mohawk, a Canadian of English heritage, and a participant in the formation of Canadian literature. For Indigenous writers—and especially Indigenous women writers—Johnson has long been recognized as an inspiration and an influence. As Kanien'ke-há:ka poet and essayist Beth Brant wrote in 1997, "Pauline Johnson began a movement that has proved unstoppable in its momentum—the movement of First Nations women to write down our stories of history, of revolution, of sorrow, of love."

⌘ ⌘ ⌘

A Cry from an Indian Wife

My forest brave, my Red-skin love, farewell;
We may not meet to-morrow; who can tell
What mighty ills befall our little band,
Or what you'll suffer from the white man's hand?
5 Here is your knife! I thought 'twas sheathed for aye.[1]
No roaming bison calls for it to-day;
No hide of prairie cattle will it maim;
The plains are bare, it seeks a nobler game:
'Twill drink the life-blood of a soldier host.
10 Go; rise and strike, no matter what the cost.

Yet stay. Revolt not at the Union Jack,[2]
Nor raise Thy hand against this stripling pack
Of white-faced warriors, marching West to quell
Our fallen tribe that rises to rebel.
15 They all are young and beautiful and good;
Curse to the war that drinks their harmless blood.
Curse to the fate that brought them from the East
To be our chiefs—to make our nation least
That breathes the air of this vast continent.
20 Still their new rule and council is well meant.
They but forget we Indians owned the land
From ocean unto ocean; that they stand

[1] *for aye* Forever.

[2] *Union Jack* British flag, which Canada continued to use until 1965.

Upon a soil that centuries agone
Was our sole kingdom and our right alone.
25 They never think how they would feel to-day,
If some great nation came from far away,
Wresting their country from their hapless braves,
Giving what they gave us—but wars and graves.
Then go and strike for liberty and life,
30 And bring back honour to your Indian wife.
Your wife? Ah, what of that, who cares for me?
Who pities my poor love and agony?
What white-robed priest prays for your safety here,
As prayer is said for every volunteer
35 That swells the ranks that Canada sends out?
Who prays for vict'ry for the Indian scout?
Who prays for our poor nation lying low?
None—therefore take your tomahawk and go.
My heart may break and burn into its core,
40 But I am strong to bid you go to war.
Yet stay, my heart is not the only one
That grieves the loss of husband and of son;
Think of the mothers o'er the inland seas;
Think of the pale-faced maiden on her knees;
45 One pleads her God to guard some sweet-faced child
That marches on toward the North-West wild.
The other prays to shield her love from harm,
To strengthen his young, proud uplifted arm.
Ah, how her white face quivers thus to think,
50 Your tomahawk his life's best blood will drink.
She never thinks of my wild aching breast,
Nor prays for your dark face and eagle crest
Endangered by a thousand rifle balls,
My heart the target if my warrior falls.
55 O! coward self I hesitate no more;
Go forth, and win the glories of the war.
Go forth, nor bend to greed of white men's hands,
By right, by birth we Indians own these lands,
Though starved, crushed, plundered, lies our
        nation low …
60 Perhaps the white man's God has willed it so.
—1885 (REVISED 1895)

The Song My Paddle Sings

West wind, blow from your prairie nest,
    Blow from the mountains, blow from the west
The sail is idle, the sailor too;
O! wind of the west, we wait for you.
5 Blow, blow!
I have wooed you so,
But never a favour you bestow.
You rock your cradle the hills between,
But scorn to notice my white lateen.°   *sail*

10 I stow the sail, unship the mast:
I wooed you long but my wooing's past;
My paddle will lull you into rest.
O! drowsy wind of the drowsy west,
Sleep, sleep,
15 By your mountain steep,
Or down where the prairie grasses sweep!
Now fold in slumber your laggard wings,
For soft is the song my paddle sings.

August is laughing across the sky,
20 Laughing while paddle, canoe and I,
Drift, drift,
Where the hills uplift
On either side of the current swift.

The river rolls in its rocky bed;
25 My paddle is plying its way ahead;
Dip, dip,
While the waters flip
In foam as over their breast we slip.

And oh, the river runs swifter now;
30 The eddies circle about my bow.
Swirl, swirl!
How the ripples curl
In many a dangerous pool awhirl!

And forward far the rapids roar,
35 Fretting their margin for evermore.
Dash, dash,

With a mighty crash,
They seethe, and boil, and bound, and splash.

Be strong, O paddle! be brave, canoe!
40 The reckless waves you must plunge into.
Reel, reel.
On your trembling keel,
But never a fear my craft will feel.

We've raced the rapid, we're far ahead!
45 The river slips through its silent bed.
Sway, sway,
As the bubbles spray
And fall in tinkling tunes away.

And up on the hills against the sky,
50 A fir tree rocking its lullaby,
Swings, swings,
Its emerald wings,
Swelling the song that my paddle sings.
—1892

Kicking-Horse River

It does not care for grandeur,
    And it does not care for state,
It flips its little fingers
    In the very face of fate;
5 And when its course is thwarted
    Its current set at bay,
It just kicks up its saucy heels
    And takes another way.

It laughs among the monarchs,
10   It giggles at the kings.
It dances in the gorges,
    While a comic song it sings;
It ripples into waterfalls,
    It tipples into spray,
15 And when they raise their eyebrows up
    It—takes another way.

It does not care a button
    For the granite or the rocks.
It never gets discouraged,
20   For it's never in a box.
When mountains contradict it,
    And canyons have their say,
It kicks a little higher,
    And takes another way.
—1894

The Cattle Thief

They were coming across the prairie, they were
    galloping hard and fast;
For the eyes of those desperate riders had sighted
    their man at last—
Sighted him off to Eastward, where the Cree
    encampment lay,
Where the cotton woods fringed the river, miles
    and miles away.
5 Mistake him? Never! Mistake him? the famous
    Eagle Chief!
That terror to all the settlers, that desperate
    Cattle Thief—
That monstrous, fearless Indian, who lorded it over
    the plain,
Who thieved and raided, and scouted, who rode like
    a hurricane!
But they've tracked him across the prairie; they've
    followed him hard and fast;
10 For those desperate English settlers have sighted
    their man at last.

Up they wheeled to the tepees, all their British
    blood aflame,
Bent on bullets and bloodshed, bent on bringing
    down their game;
But they searched in vain for the Cattle Thief:
    that lion had left his lair,
And they cursed like a troop of demons—for the
    women alone were there.

15   "The sneaking Indian coward," they hissed;
        "he hides while yet he can;
He'll come in the night for cattle, but he's scared
        to face a *man*."
"Never!" and up from the cotton woods rang
        the voice of Eagle Chief;
And right out into the open stepped, unarmed,
        the Cattle Thief.
Was that the game they had coveted? Scarce fifty
        years had rolled
20   Over that fleshless, hungry frame, starved to the
        bone and old;
Over that wrinkled, tawny skin, unfed by the
        warmth of blood.
Over those hungry, hollow eyes that glared for the
        sight of food.

He turned, like a hunted lion: "I know not fear,"
        said he;
And the words outleapt from his shrunken lips in
        the language of the Cree.
25   "I'll fight you, white-skins, one by one, till I kill
        you all," he said;
But the threat was scarcely uttered, ere a dozen
        balls of lead
Whizzed through the air about him like a shower
        of metal rain,
And the gaunt old Indian Cattle Thief dropped
        dead on the open plain.
And that band of cursing settlers gave one
        triumphant yell,
30   And rushed like a pack of demons on the body that '
        writhed and fell.
"Cut the fiend up into inches, throw his carcass on
        the plain;
Let the wolves eat the cursed Indian, he'd have
        treated us the same."
A dozen hands responded, a dozen knives gleamed
        high,
But the first stroke was arrested by a woman's strange,
        wild cry.
35   And out into the open, with a courage past belief,

She dashed, and spread her blanket o'er the corpse
        of the Cattle Thief;
And the words outleapt from her shrunken lips in
        the language of the Cree,
"If you mean to touch that body, you must cut your
        way through me."
And that band of cursing settlers dropped backward
        one by one,
40   For they knew that an Indian woman roused, was a
        woman to let alone.
And then she raved in a frenzy that they scarcely
        understood,
Raved of the wrongs she had suffered since her earliest
        babyhood:
"Stand back, stand back, you white-skins, touch that
        dead man to your shame;
You have stolen my father's spirit, but his body I
        only claim.
45   You have killed him, but you shall not dare to touch
        him now he's dead.
You have cursed, and called him a Cattle Thief,
        though you robbed him first of bread—
Robbed him and robbed my people—look there,
        at that shrunken face,
Starved with a hollow hunger, we owe to you and
        your race.
What have you left to us of land, what have you left
        of game,
50   What have you brought but evil, and curses since
        you came?
How have you paid us for our game? how paid us
        for our land?
By a *book*, to save our souls from the sins you brought
        in your other hand.
Go back with your new religion, we never have
        understood
Your robbing an Indian's *body*, and mocking his soul
        with *food*.
55   Go back with your new religion, and find—if find
        you can—
The *honest* man you have ever made from out a
        starving man.

You say your cattle are not ours, your meat is not
    our meat;
When *you* pay for the land you live in, *we'll* pay for
    the meat we eat.
Give back our land and our country, give back our
    herds of game;
Give back the furs and the forests that were ours
    before you came;
Give back the peace and the plenty. Then come with
    your new belief,
And blame, if you dare, the hunger that *drove* him to
    be a thief."
—1894

Ojistoh

I am Ojistoh, I am she, the wife
  Of him whose name breathes bravery and life
And courage to the tribe that calls him chief
I am Ojistoh, his white star, and he
5 Is land, and lake, and sky—and soul to me.

Ah! But they hated him, those Huron braves,
Him who had flung their warriors into graves,
He who had crushed them underneath his heel,
Whose arm was iron, and whose heart was steel
10 To all—save me, Ojistoh, chosen wife
Of my great Mohawk, white star of his life.

Ah! but they hated him, and councilled long
With subtle witchcraft how to work him wrong;
How to avenge their dead, and strike him where
15 His pride was highest, and his fame most fair.
Their hearts grew weak as women at his name:
They dared no war-path since my Mohawk came
With ashen bow, and flinten arrow-head
To pierce their craven bodies; but their dead
20 Must be avenged. Avenged? They dared not walk
In day and meet his deadly tomahawk;

They dared not face his fearless scalping knife;
So—Niyoh![1]—then they thought of me, his wife.

O! evil, evil face of them they sent
25 With evil Huron speech: "would I consent
To take of wealth? be queen of all their tribe?
Have wampum ermine?"[2] Back I flung the bribe
Into their teeth, and said, "While I have life
Know this—Ojistoh is the Mohawk's wife."

30 Wah! how we struggled! But their arms were strong.
They flung me on their pony's back, with thong
Round ankle, wrist, and shoulder. Then upleapt
The one I hated most: his eye he swept
Over my misery, and sneering said,
35 "Thus, fair Ojistoh, we avenge our dead."

And we two rode, rode as a sea wind-chased,
I, bound with buckskin to his hated waist,
He, sneering, laughing, jeering, while he lashed
The horse to foam, as on and on we dashed.
40 Plunging through creek and river, bush and trail,
On, on we galloped like a northern gale.
At last, his distant Huron fires aflame
We saw, and nearer, nearer still we came.

I, bound behind him in the captive's place,
45 Scarcely could see the outline of his face.
I smiled and laid my cheek against his back:
"Loose thou my hands," I said. "This pace let slack.
Forget we now that thou and I are foes.
I like thee well, and wish to clasp thee close;
50 I like the courage of thine eye and brow;
I like thee better than my Mohawk now."

He cut the cords; we ceased our maddened haste.
I wound my arms around his tawny waist;

---

1 [Tekahionwake's note]   God, in the Mohawk language.

2 *wampum* Valuable shell beads used by various Indigenous peoples
for many purposes, including record-keeping, trade, and decorative
arts; *ermine* I.e., white. The white winter coat of the ermine or
stoat, a species of weasel, is worn by Indigenous and European people;
in Europe, it can connote specific political status.

My hand crept up the buckskin of his belt;
55   His knife hilt in my burning hand I felt;
One hand caressed his cheek, the other drew
The weapon softly—"I love you, love you,"
I whispered, "I love you as my life."
And—buried in his back his scalping knife.

60   Ha! how I rode, rode as a sea wind-chased,
Back to my Mohawk and my home. I lashed
That horse to foam, as on and on I dashed.
Plunging through creek and river, bush and trail,
On, on I galloped like a northern gale.
65   And then my distant Mohawk's fires aflame
I saw, as nearer, nearer still I came,
My hands all wet, stained with a life's red dye,
But pure my soul, pure as those stars on high—
"My Mohawk's pure white star, Ojistoh, still am I."
—1895

from His Sister's Son[1]

For they killed the best that was in me
When they said I must not return
To my father's lodge, to my mother's arms
When my heart would burn—and burn!
5   For when dead is a daughter's womanhood
There is nothing left that is grand and good.
—RECORDED 1896

The Corn Husker

Hard by[2] the Indian lodges, where the bush
Breaks in a clearing, through ill-fashioned fields,
She comes to labour, when the first still hush
    Of autumn follows large and recent yields.

5   Age in her fingers, hunger in her face,
    Her shoulders stooped with weight of work and years,
But rich in tawny coloring of her race,
    She comes a-field to strip the purple ears.

And all her thoughts are with the days gone by,
10   Ere might's injustice banished from their lands
Her people, that to-day unheeded lie,
    Like the dead husks that rustle through her hands.
—1896

The Art of Alma-Tadema[3]

There is no song his colours cannot sing,
    For all his art breathes melody, and tunes
The fine, keen beauty that his brushes bring
    To murmuring marbles and to golden Junes.

5   The music of those marbles you can hear
    In every crevice, where the deep green stains
Have sunken when the grey days of the year
    Spilled leisurely their warm, incessant rains

That, lingering, forget to leave the ledge,
10   But drenched into the seams, amid the hush
Of ages, leaving but the silent pledge
    To waken to the wonder of his brush.

And at the Master's touch the marbles leap
    To life, the creamy onyx and the skins

---

[1]   *His Sister's Son*   Tekahionwake frequently performed this poem, but no complete version of the text survives; the fragment reprinted here was quoted in *The Fort Wayne Indiana Gazette* on 25 November 1896. The poem's subject is an Indigenous girl who is taken from her family and compelled to attend a residential school. Canada's residential school system was established in the 1880s and the last schools closed in the 1990s; the schools were intended to eliminate Indigenous cultures by forcing Indigenous children to assimilate to white Canadian religion and culture.

[2]   *Hard by*   Near.

[3]   *Alma-Tadema*   Sir Lawrence Alma-Tadema (1836–1912), a popular Dutch-born English painter best known for his lavish scenes set in ancient Rome.

15 Of copper-coloured leopards, and the deep,
      Cool basins where the whispering water wins

Reflections from the gold and glowing sun,
      And tints from warm, sweet human flesh, for fair
And subtly lithe and beautiful, leans one—
20   A goddess with a wealth of tawny hair.
      —1903

The Lost Lagoon

It is dusk on the Lost Lagoon,
And we two dreaming the dusk away,
Beneath the drift of a twilight grey—

     Beneath the drowse of an ending day
5   And the curve of a golden moon.

It is dark in the Lost Lagoon,
And gone are the depths of haunting blue,
The grouping gulls, and the old canoe,
The singing firs, and the dusk and—you,
10 And gone is the golden moon.

O! lure of the Lost Lagoon—
I dream tonight that my paddle blurs
The purple shade where the seaweed stirs—
I hear the call of the singing firs
15 In the hush of the golden moon.
      —1910

IN CONTEXT

Tekahionwake/Johnson and Print Culture

Reproduced below are the front cover and title page of the first edition of Johnson's first book, *The White Wampum*, followed by photographs of Johnson and posters from her international tours.

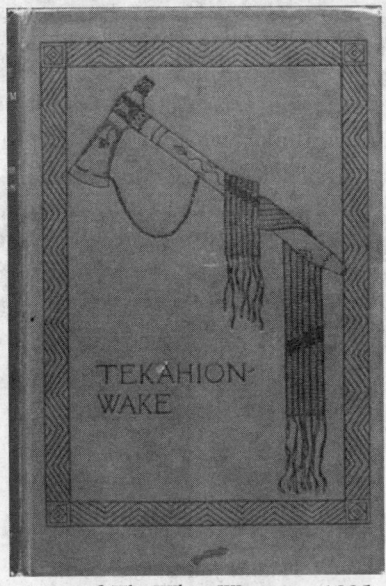

Cover of *The White Wampum*, 1895.

Title page of *The White Wampum*, 1895.

Pauline Johnson Performance Poster.

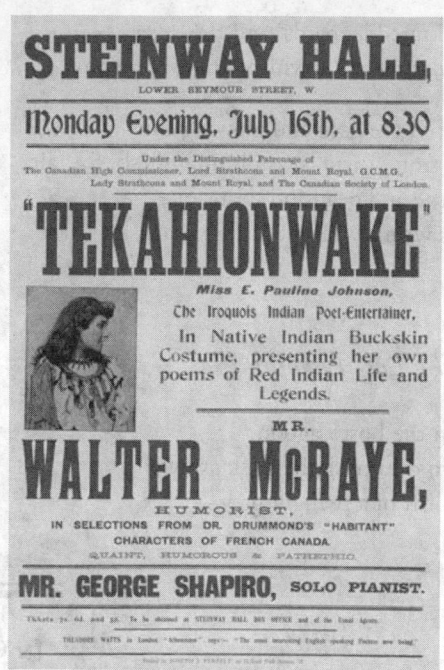

Poster advertising Johnson's London
performance at Steinway Hall, 1906.

Autographed portrait of
Pauline Johnson, undated.

Pauline Johnson, c. 1902.

AMY LEVY
1861 – 1889

As a novelist, short-fiction writer, essayist, and poet of the late Victorian era, Amy Levy is recognized for her work's emotional depth, its anticipation of Modernism through formal innovation and deployment of irony, its courageous "New Woman" politics of female independence, and its complex literary engagement with her own Anglo-Jewish culture. The extent of her contribution to English literature is especially striking given that she died before reaching 30. Her poetry, emotionally evocative as well as forthright in its feminist views, is also of interest to present-day critics for its evocation of eroticism between women. Her novels—one a "New Woman" novel, one an uncompromising examination of Anglo-Jewish society, and one a governess novel—have in common a realist engagement with feminist themes.

Levy, the daughter of Isabelle Levin and Lewis Levy, a stockbroker, grew up in a large, Anglo-Jewish, middle-class household in London. Intelligent and well educated, she began writing poetry at an early age, publishing her first work, "Ida Grey: A Story of Woman's Sacrifice," in a feminist journal at the age of thirteen. Contributions of poems, essays, and stories to many other journals followed, among them *The Cambridge Review*, *The Jewish Chronicle*, and the *Pall Mall Gazette*. In 1879 Levy became the first Jewish woman to attend Cambridge University, where she studied at Newnham College.

In 1881 Levy left the university without taking her exams, having published her first book of poetry, *Xantippe, and Other Verse*. The title poem is a defense of the wife of Socrates, who was much maligned for her outspokenness and intelligence. The volume, which quickly sold out, was followed by two more books of poems, many of the lyrics of which concentrated on melancholic and depressive themes; *A Minor Poet and Other Poems* appeared in 1884, and *A London Plane-Tree and Other Verse* was published posthumously in 1889. This last collection in particular offers an early example of the symbolist movement in English poetry, in some respects anticipating the development of poetic Modernism. Levy's first novel was *The Romance of a Shop* (1888), in which she writes of the determination of a family of orphaned sisters to support themselves by opening a photographic studio. The short novel vividly portrays the challenges facing independent, working, "new women" and the relatively uncharted territory they face when attempting to integrate the demands of self-employment and of romantic relationships.

In an 1886 article in *The Jewish Chronicle*, Levy criticized literary depictions of Jewish characters, saying that no one had as yet portrayed Jews with all their "surprising virtues and no less surprising vices." From this idea was born her most influential work, which was, ironically, criticized by *The Jewish Chronicle* and members of the Jewish community as anti-Semitic in its engagement with Jewish stereotypes. The novel *Reuben Sachs* (1888) proved to be very popular, notwithstanding its portrayal of, as one reviewer called it, "the less than refined aspects of Jewish society." Oscar Wilde praised the novel, saying, "Its directness, its uncompromising truths, its depth of feeling, and above all, its absence of any single superfluous word, make it, in some sort, a classic. Like all her best work it is sad, but the sadness is by no means morbid. The strong undertone of moral earnestness, never preached, gives a stability and force to the vivid portraiture, and prevents the satiric touches from degenerating into mere malice. Truly, the book is an achievement." Levy followed *Reuben Sachs* with a third novel, *Miss Meredith* (1889), a governess novel displaying the influence of Charlotte Brontë. This work is often dismissed as a blatant attempt to cater to a popular market, though some have seen an ironic sophistication in Levy's employment of genre clichés.

Levy moved in literary and artistic circles, counting among her friends Olive Schreiner (author of *The Story of an African Farm*), Beatrice Potter Webb (author and political activist), Eleanor Marx (daughter of Karl Marx and later a translator of Levy's poetry into German), and Vernon Lee (the *nom de plume* of author Violet Paget), for whom she was said to harbor a deep unrequited passion. She wrote a number of short essays, largely on literary matters (such as recent American fiction, and the poet James Thomson) or on Jewish issues, often seeking to explain to a gentile readership such topics as Jewish humor or contemporary middle-class Jewish women. Levy's writings often betray her self-conscious status as an outsider, and they reveal a fascination with others who felt themselves to be outsiders, whether by race or gender.

Levy suffered intense periods of depression that she called "the great-devil that lyeth ever in wait in the recesses of my heart." There is speculation that the press's negative reaction to *Reuben Sachs*, combined with health problems, contributed to her suicide at the age of 27. But the many difficulties experienced by a Jewish woman of her era attracted to other women and living an independent literary life may well also have been factors. Her marginal status certainly contributed to critical neglect of her work throughout much of the twentieth century, such that she was practically unknown when the 1993 publication of her *Complete Novels and Selected Writings* helped to rescue her work from obscurity. Her importance as a contributor to New Woman literature and to Anglo-Jewish literature, and as a forerunner of Modernism, has since come to be appreciated.

⌘ ⌘ ⌘

Xantippe[1] (*A Fragment*)

What, have I waked again? I never thought
　　To see the rosy dawn, or ev'n this grey,
Dull, solemn stillness, ere the dawn has come.
The lamp burns low; low burns the lamp of life:
5　The still morn stays expectant, and my soul,
All weighted with a passive wonderment,
Waiteth and watcheth, waiteth for the dawn.
Come hither, maids; too soundly have ye slept

That should have watched me; nay, I would not chide—
10　Oft have I chidden, yet I would not chide
In this last hour—now all should be at peace.
I have been dreaming in a troubled sleep
Of weary days I thought not to recall;
Of stormy days, whose storms are hushed long since;
15　Of gladsome days, of sunny days; alas!
In dreaming, all their sunshine seemed so sad,
As though the current of the dark To-Be
Had flowed, prophetic, through the happy hours.
And yet, full well, I know it was not thus;
20　I mind me sweetly of the summer days,
When, leaning from the lattice, I have caught
The fair, far glimpses of a shining sea:

---

[1] *Xantippe* Wife of Socrates, ancient Greek philosopher (469–399 BCE) who devoted his life to the study and teaching of ethics and moral behavior; Socrates was later sentenced to death for corrupting the youth and interfering with the religion of Athens. Xantippe was criticized for being headstrong.

And nearer, of tall ships which thronged the bay,
And stood out blackly from a tender sky
25 All flecked with sulphur, azure, and bright gold;
And in the still, clear air have heard the hum
Of distant voices; and methinks there rose
No darker fount° to mar or stain the joy   *fountain*
Which sprang ecstatic in my maiden breast
30 Than just those vague desires, those hopes and fears,
Those eager longings, strong, though undefined,
Whose very sadness makes them seem so sweet.
What cared I for the merry mockeries
Of other maidens sitting at the loom?
35 Or for sharp voices, bidding me return
To maiden labour? Were we not apart—
I and my high thoughts, and my golden dreams,
My soul which yearned for knowledge, for a tongue
That should proclaim the stately mysteries
40 Of this fair world, and of the holy gods?
Then followed days of sadness, as I grew
To learn my woman-mind had gone astray,
And I was sinning in those very thoughts—
For maidens, mark, such are not woman's thoughts—
45 (And yet, 'tis strange, the gods who fashion us
Have given us such promptings). …
                                        Fled the years,
Till seventeen had found me tall and strong,
And fairer, runs it, than Athenian maids
Are wont to seem; I had not learnt it well—
50 My lesson of dumb patience—and I stood
At Life's great threshold with a beating heart,
And soul resolved to conquer and attain. …
Once, walking 'thwart° the crowded marketplace,   *across*
With other maidens, bearing in the twigs,
55 White doves for Aphrodite's sacrifice,[1]
I saw him, all ungainly and uncouth,
Yet many gathered round to hear his words,
Tall youths and stranger-maidens—Sokrates—
I saw his face and marked it, half with awe,
60 Half with a quick repulsion at the shape. …
The richest gem lies hidden furthest down,

---

[1] *White doves … sacrifice* Aphrodite is the Greek goddess of love; white doves, Aphrodite's favorite birds, were sacrificed during her festival.

And is the dearer for the weary search;
We grasp the shining shells which strew the shore,
Yet swift we fling them from us; but the gem
65 We keep for aye° and cherish. So a soul,   *forever*
Found after weary searching in the flesh
Which half repelled our senses, is more dear,
For that same seeking, than the sunny mind
Which lavish Nature marks with thousand hints
70 Upon a brow of beauty. We are prone
To overweigh such subtle hints, then deem,
In after disappointment, we are fooled. …
And when, at length, my father told me all,
That I should wed me with great Sokrates,
75 I, foolish, wept to see at once cast down
The maiden image of a future love,
Where perfect body matched the perfect soul.
But slowly, softly did I cease to weep;
Slowly I 'gan to mark the magic flash
80 Leap to the eyes, to watch the sudden smile
Break round the mouth, and linger in the eyes;
To listen for the voice's lightest tone—
Great voice, whose cunning modulations seemed
like to the notes of some sweet instrument.
85 So did I reach and strain, until at last
I caught the soul athwart the grosser flesh.
Again of thee, sweet Hope, my spirit dreamed!
I, guided by his wisdom and his love,
Led by his words, and counselled by his care,
90 Should lift the shrouding veil from things which be,
And at the flowing fountain of his soul
Refresh my thirsting spirit. …
                                    And indeed,
In those long days which followed that strange day
When rites and song, and sacrifice and flow'rs,
95 Proclaimed that we were wedded, did I learn,
In sooth,° a-many lessons; bitter ones   *truth*
Which sorrow taught me, and not love inspired,
Which deeper knowledge of my kind impressed
With dark insistence on reluctant brain—
100 But that great wisdom, deeper, which dispels
Narrowed conclusions of a half-grown mind,
And sees athwart the littleness of life
Nature's divineness and her harmony,

Was never poor Xantippe's. ...

                     I would pause

105 And would recall no more, no more of life,
Than just the incomplete, imperfect dream
Of early summers, with their light and shade,
Their blossom-hopes, whose fruit was never ripe;
But something strong within me, some sad chord
110 Which loudly echoes to the later life,
Me to unfold the after-misery
Urges, with plaintive wailing in my heart.
Yet, maidens, mark; I would not that ye thought
I blame my lord departed, for he meant
115 No evil, so I take it, to his wife.
'Twas only that the high philosopher,
Pregnant with noble theories and great thoughts,
Deigned not to stoop to touch so slight a thing
As the fine fabric of a woman's brain—
120 So subtle as a passionate woman's soul.
I think, if he had stooped a little, and cared,
I might have risen nearer to his height,
And not lain shattered, neither fit for use
As goodly household vessel, nor for that
125 Far finer thing which I had hoped to be. ...
Death, holding high his retrospective lamp,
Shows me those first, far years of wedded life,
Ere I had learnt to grasp the barren shape
Of what the Fates[1] had destined for my life.
130 Then, as all youthful spirits are, was I
Wholly incredulous that Nature meant
So little, who had promised me so much.
At first I fought my fate with gentle words,
With high endeavours after greater things;
135 Striving to win the soul of Sokrates,
Like some slight bird, who sings her burning love
To human master, till at length she finds
Her tender language wholly misconceived,
And that same hand whose kind caress she sought,
140 With fingers flippant flings the careless corn.[2] ...
I do remember how, one summer's eve,
He, seated in an arbour's leafy shade,

Had bade me bring fresh wine-skins. ...

                     As I stood

Ling'ring upon the threshold, half concealed
145 By tender foliage, and my spirit light
With draughts of sunny weather, did I mark
An instant the gay group before mine eyes.
Deepest in shade, and facing where I stood,
Sat Plato,[3] with his calm face and low brows
150 Which met above the narrow Grecian eyes,
The pale, thin lips just parted to the smile,
Which dimpled that smooth olive of his cheek.
His head a little bent, sat Sokrates,
With one swart° finger raised admonishing,   *dark-skinned*
155 And on the air were borne his changing tones.
Low lounging at his feet, one fair arm thrown
Around his knee (the other, high in air
Brandished a brazen amphor,° which yet rained   *wine vessel*
Bright drops of ruby on the golden locks
160 And temples with their fillets of the vine),
Lay Alkibiades the beautiful.[4]
And thus, with solemn tone, spake Sokrates:
"This fair Aspasia, which our Perikles
Hath brought from realms afar, and set on high[5]
165 In our Athenian city, hath a mind,
I doubt not, of a strength beyond her race;
And makes employ of it, beyond the way
Of women nobly gifted: woman's frail—
Her body rarely stands the test of soul;
170 She grows intoxicate with knowledge; throws
The laws of custom, order, 'neath her feet,
Feasting at life's great banquet with wide throat."
Then sudden, stepping from my leafy screen,
Holding the swelling wine-skin o'er my head,
175 With breast that heaved, and eyes and cheeks aflame,
Lit by a fury and a thought, I spake:

---

[1] *Fates* Three Greek goddesses of destiny.

[2] *corn* Seed or grain.

---

[3] *Plato* Greek philosopher and student of Socrates (427–347 BCE).

[4] *Alkibiades the beautiful* The political leader Alcibiades (c. 450–404 BCE) was once a student of Socrates; his outstanding beauty was said to contrast with that of Socrates.

[5] *Aspasia ... set on high* Pericles, a political figure in ancient Athens, divorced his wife and married his lover, Aspasia, a woman of great education and intellect, who influenced the work of many philosophers, including Plato and Cicero.

"By all great powers around us! can it be
That we poor women are empirical?[1]
That gods who fashioned us did strive to make
180 Beings too fine, too subtly delicate,
With sense that thrilled response to ev'ry touch
Of nature's, and their task is not complete?
That they have sent their half-completed work
To bleed and quiver here upon the earth?
185 To bleed and quiver, and to weep and weep,
To beat its soul against the marble walls
Of men's cold hearts, and then at last to sin!"
I ceased, the first hot passion stayed and stemmed
And frighted by the silence: I could see,
190 Framed by the arbour foliage, which the sun
In setting softly gilded with rich gold,
Those upturned faces, and those placid limbs;
Saw Plato's narrow eyes and niggard° mouth,   *stingy*
Which half did smile and half did criticise,
195 One hand held up, the shapely fingers framed
To gesture of entreaty—"Hush, I pray,
Do not disturb her; let us hear the rest;
Follow her mood, for here's another phase
Of your black-browed Xantippe. ..."
                                                Then I saw
200 Young Alkibiades, with laughing lips
And half-shut eyes, contemptuous shrugging up
Soft, snowy shoulders, till he brought the gold
Of flowing ringlets round about his breasts.
But Sokrates, all slow and solemnly,
205 Raised, calm, his face to mine, and sudden spake:
"I thank thee for the wisdom which thy lips
Have thus let fall among us: prithee[2] tell
From what high source, from what philosophies
Didst cull the sapient° notion of thy words?"   *astute*
210 Then stood I straight and silent for a breath,
Dumb, crushed with all that weight of cold contempt;
But swiftly in my bosom there uprose
A sudden flame, a merciful fury sent
To save me; with both angry hands I flung
215 The skin upon the marble, where it lay

Spouting red rills° and fountains on the white;   *rivulets*
Then, all unheeding faces, voices, eyes,
I fled across the threshold, hair unbound—
White garment stained to redness—beating heart
220 Flooded with all the flowing tide of hopes
Which once had gushed out golden, now sent back
Swift to their sources, never more to rise. ...
I think I could have borne the weary life,
The narrow life within the narrow walls,
225 If he had loved me; but he kept his love
For this Athenian city and her sons;
And, haply, for some stranger-woman, bold
With freedom, thought, and glib philosophy. ...
Ah me! the long, long weeping through the nights,
230 The weary watching for the pale-eyed dawn
Which only brought fresh grieving: then I grew
Fiercer, and cursed from out my inmost heart
The Fates which marked me an Athenian maid.
Then faded that vain fury; hope died out;
235 A huge despair was stealing on my soul,
A sort of fierce acceptance of my fate,—
He wished a household vessel—well 'twas good,
For he should have it! He should have no more
The yearning treasure of a woman's love,
240 But just the baser treasure which he sought.
I called my maidens, ordered out the loom,
And spun unceasing from the morn till eve;
Watching all keenly over warp and woof,[3]
Weighing the white wool with a jealous hand.
245 I spun until, methinks, I spun away
The soul from out my body, the high thoughts
From out my spirit; till at last I grew
As ye have known me,—eye exact to mark
The texture of the spinning; ear all keen
250 For aimless talking when the moon is up,
And ye should be a-sleeping; tongue to cut
With quick incision, 'thwart the merry words
Of idle maidens. ...
                                        Only yesterday
My hands did cease from spinning; I have wrought
255 My dreary duties, patient till the last.

---

[1] *That we ... empirical* I.e., that we rely on experience rather than theory.

[2] *prithee* Please.

[3] *warp and woof* Cross threads in a weaving.

The gods reward me! Nay, I will not tell
The after years of sorrow; wretched strife
With grimmest foes—sad Want and Poverty;—
Nor yet the time of horror, when they bore
260 My husband from the threshold; nay, nor when
The subtle weed had wrought its deadly work.[1]
Alas! alas! I was not there to soothe
The last great moment; never any thought
Of her that loved him—save at least the charge,
265 All earthly, that her body should not starve. …
You weep, you weep; I would not that ye wept;
Such tears are idle; with the young, such grief
Soon grows to gratulation, as, "her love
Was withered by misfortune; mine shall grow
270 All nurtured by the loving," or, "her life
Was wrecked and shattered—mine shall smoothly sail."
Enough, enough. In vain, in vain, in vain!
The gods forgive me! Sorely have I sinned
In all my life. A fairer fate befall
275 You all that stand there. …

           Ha! the dawn has come;
I see a rosy glimmer—nay! it grows dark;
Why stand ye so in silence? throw it wide,
The casement,° quick; why tarry?—give me   *window*
   air—
O fling it wide, I say, and give me light!
—1881

Magdalen

All things I can endure, save one.
The bare, blank room where is no sun;
The parcelled hours; the pallet° hard;   *straw bed*
The dreary faces here within;
5 The outer women's cold regard;
The Pastor's iterated "sin"—
These things could I endure, and count
No overstrained, unjust amount;
No undue payment for such bliss—
10 Yea, all things bear, save only this:

That you, who knew what thing would be,
Have wrought this evil unto me.
It is so strange to think on still—
That you, that *you* should do me ill!
15 Not as one ignorant or blind,
But seeing clearly in your mind
How this must be which now has been,
Nothing aghast at what was seen.
Now that the tale is told and done,
20 It is so strange to think upon.

You were so tender with me, too!
One summer's night a cold blast blew,
Closer about my throat you drew
The half-slipped shawl of dusky blue.
25 And once my hand, on a summer's morn,
I stretched to pluck a rose; a thorn
Struck through the flesh and made it bleed
(A little drop of blood indeed!)
Pale grew your cheek; you stooped and bound
30 Your handkerchief about the wound;
Your voice came with a broken sound;
With the deep breath your breast was riven;
I wonder, did God laugh in Heaven?

How strange, that *you* should work my woe!
35 How strange! I wonder, do you know
How gladly, gladly I had died[2]
(And life was very sweet that tide)
To save you from the least, light ill?
How gladly I had borne your pain.
40 With one great pulse we seemed to thrill,—
Nay, but we thrilled with pulses twain.°   *two*

Even if one had told me this,
"A poison lurks within your kiss,
Gall[3] that shall turn to night his day":
45 Thereon I straight had turned away—
Ay, though my heart had cracked with pain—
And never kissed your lips again.

---

[1] *Nor … work* Socrates was condemned to die by suicide, which was accomplished by his drinking a cup of poison made from hemlock.

[2] *I had died* I would have died.

[3] *Gall* Bile; or bitter poison.

At night, or when the daylight nears,
I hear the other women weep;
50 My own heart's anguish lies too deep
For the soft rain and pain of tears.
I think my heart has turned to stone.
A dull, dead weight that hurts my breast;
Here, on my pallet-bed alone,
55 I keep apart from all the rest.
Wide-eyed I lie upon my bed,
I often cannot sleep all night;
The future and the past are dead,
There is no thought can bring delight.
60 All night I lie and think and think;
If my heart were not made of stone,
But flesh and blood, it needs must shrink
Before such thoughts. Was ever known
A woman with a heart of stone?

65 The doctor says that I shall die.
It may be so, yet what care I?
Endless reposing from the strife,
Death do I trust no more than life.
For one thing is like one arrayed,
70 And there is neither false nor true;
But in a hideous masquerade
All things dance on, the ages through.
And good is evil, evil good;
Nothing is known or understood
75 Save only Pain. I have no faith
In God or Devil, Life or Death.

The doctor says that I shall die.
You, that I knew in days gone by,
I fain would see your face once more,
80 Con° well its features o'er and o'er;   *study*
And touch your hand and feel your kiss,
Look in your eyes and tell you this:
That all is done, that I am free;
That you, through all eternity,
85 Have neither part nor lot in me.
—1884

To Lallie[1]
(*Outside the British Museum*)

Up those Museum steps you came,
   And straightway all my blood was flame,
      O Lallie, Lallie!

The world (I had been feeling low)
5 In one short moment's space did grow
      A happy valley.

There was a friend, my friend, with you;
A meagre dame, in peacock blue
      Apparelled quaintly:

10 This poet-heart went pit-a-pat;
I bowed and smiled and raised my hat;
      You nodded—faintly.

My heart was full as full could be;
You had not got a word for me,
15   Not one short greeting;

That nonchalant small nod you gave
(The tyrant's motion to the slave)
      Sole marked our meeting.

Is it so long? Do you forget
20 That first and last time that we met?
      The time was summer;

The trees were green; the sky was blue;
Our host presented me to you—
      A tardy comer.

25 You looked demure, but when you spoke
You made a little, funny joke,
      Yet half pathetic.

[1] *To Lallie* Critics suggest that Lallie may be British novelist and critic Vernon Lee, pseudonym for Violet Paget (1856–1935). See Terry Castle, *The Literature of Lesbianism*.

Your gown was grey, I recollect,
I think you patronized the sect
30   They call "aesthetic."[1]

I brought you strawberries and cream,
I plied you long about a stream
          With duckweed laden;

We solemnly discussed the—heat.
35 I found you shy and very sweet,
          A rosebud maiden.

Ah me, today! You passed inside
To where the marble gods abide:[2]
          Hermes, Apollo,

40 Sweet Aphrodite, Pan;[3] and where,
For aye° reclined, a headless fair   *ever*
          Beats all fairs hollow.

And I, I went upon my way,
Well—rather sadder, let us say;
45   The world looked flatter.

I had been sad enough before,
A little less, a little more,
          What *does* it matter?
—1884

A London Plane-Tree

Green is the plane-tree[4] in the square,
          The other trees are brown;

They droop and pine for country air;
          The plane-tree loves the town.

5 Here from my garret-pane, I mark
          The plane-tree bud and blow,°   *bloom*
Shed her recuperative bark,
          And spread her shade below.

Among her branches, in and out,
10   The city breezes play;
The dun fog wraps her round about;
          Above, the smoke curls grey.

Others the country take for choice,
          And hold the town in scorn;
15 But she has listened to the voice
          On city breezes borne.
—1889

London in July

What ails my senses thus to cheat?
          What is it ails the place,
That all the people in the street
          Should wear one woman's face?

5 The London trees are dusty-brown
          Beneath the summer sky;
My love, she dwells in London town,
          Nor leaves it in July.

O various and intricate maze,
10   Wide waste of square and street;
Where, missing through unnumbered days,
          We twain at last may meet!

And who cries out on crowd and mart?°   *market*
          What prates° of stream and sea?   *talk*
15 The summer in the city's heart—
          That is enough for me.
—1889

---

[1] *aesthetic* Late nineteenth-century artistic movement that valued art solely on its aesthetic qualities as opposed to valuing art for utilitarian or practical purposes.

[2] *inside ... abide* The British Museum holds a substantial collection of classical Greek marble statues, including pieces from the Acropolis.

[3] *Hermes* Ancient Greek messenger of the gods; *Apollo* Ancient Greek god of light, music, and poetry; *Aphrodite* Ancient Greek goddess of love and beauty; *Pan* Ancient Greek god of shepherds and flocks as well as rustic music.

[4] *plane-tree* London trees that are noteworthy for their ability to absorb pollution and then shed their bark.

"Ballade of an Omnibus"[1]

To see my love suffices me.
—Ballades in Blue China[2]

Some men to carriages aspire;
On some the costly hansoms° wait;   *two-wheeled carriage*
Some seek a fly,° on job or hire;   *one-horse stage-coach*
Some mount the trotting steed, elate.
5   I envy not the rich and great,
A wandering minstrel, poor and free,
I am contented with my fate—
An omnibus suffices me.

In winter days of rain and mire
10   I find within a corner strait;
The 'busmen know me and my lyre
From Brompton to the Bull-and-Gate.
When summer comes, I mount in state
The topmost summit, whence I see
15   Crœsus[3] look up, compassionate—
An omnibus suffices me.

I mark, untroubled by desire,
Lucullus'[4] phaeton° and its freight.   *four-wheeled carriage*
The scene whereof I cannot tire,
20   The human tale of love and hate,
The city pageant, early and late
Unfolds itself, rolls by, to be
A pleasure deep and delicate.
An omnibus suffices me.

25   Princess, your splendour you require,
I, my simplicity; agree

Neither to rate lower nor higher.
An omnibus suffices me.
—1889

London Poets
(In Memoriam)

They trod the streets and squares where now I tread,
With weary hearts, a little while ago;
When, thin and grey, the melancholy snow
Clung to the leafless branches overhead;
5   Or when the smoke-veiled sky grew stormy-red
In autumn; with a re-arisen woe
Wrestled, what time the passionate spring winds blow;
And paced scorched stones in summer:—they are dead.

The sorrow of their souls to them did seem
10   As real as mine to me, as permanent.
Today, it is the shadow of a dream,
The half-forgotten breath of breezes spent.
So shall another soothe his woe supreme—
"No more he comes, who this way came and went."
—1889

The Old House

In through the porch and up the silent stair;
Little is changed, I know so well the ways;
Here, the dead came to meet me; it was there
The dream was dreamed in unforgotten days.

5   But who is this that hurries on before,
A flitting shade the brooding shades among?
She turned—I saw her face—O God, it wore
The face I used to wear when I was young!

I thought my spirit and my heart were tamed
10   To deadness; dead the pangs that agonise.
The old grief springs to choke me. I am shamed
Before that little ghost with eager eyes.

---

[1] *Omnibus*   Horse-drawn public carriage traveling a fixed route with set stops.

[2] *To see ... Blue China*   Levy's epigraph is from Andrew Lang's poem "Ballade Amoureuse. After Froissart" in *Ballades in Blue China* (1880).

[3] *Crœsus*   Famously affluent king of Lydia (560–546 BCE), whose name came to signify anyone of great wealth.

[4] *Lucullus*   Roman general (110?–56? BCE) famous for luxurious banquets.

O turn away, let her not see, not know!
    How should she bear it, how should understand?
15 O hasten down the stairway, haste and go,
    And leave her dreaming in the silent land.
    —1889

The Last Judgment

With beating heart and lagging feet,
    Lord, I approach the Judgment-seat.
All bring hither the fruits of toil,
Measures of wheat and measures of oil;

5 Gold and jewels and precious wine;
No hands bare like these hands of mine.
The treasure I have nor° weighs nor gleams: *neither*
Lord, I can bring you only dreams.

In days of spring, when my blood ran high,
10 I lay in the grass and looked at the sky,
And dreamed that my love lay by my side—
My love was false, and then she died.

All the heat of the summer through,
I dreamed she lived, that her heart was true
15 Throughout the hours of the day I slept,
But woke in the night, at times, and wept.

The nights and days, they went and came,
I lay in shadow and dreamed of fame;
And heard men passing the lonely place,
20 Who marked me not and my hidden face.

My strength waxed faint, my hair grew grey;
Nothing but dreams by night and day.
Some men sicken, with wine and food;
I starved on dreams, and found them good.

        *   *   *

25 This is the tale I have to tell—
Show the fellow the way to hell.
    —1889

Cambridge in the Long[1]

Where drowsy sound of college-chimes
    Across the air is blown,
And drowsy fragrance of the limes,
    I lie and dream alone.

5 A dazzling radiance reigns o'er all—
    O'er gardens densely green,
O'er old grey bridges and the small,
    Slow flood which slides between.

This is the place; it is not strange,
10   But known of old and dear—
What went I forth to seek? The change
    Is mine; why am I here?

Alas, in vain I turned away,
    I fled the town in vain;
15 The strenuous life of yesterday
    Calleth me back again.

And was it peace I came to seek?
    Yet here, where memories throng,
Ev'n here, I know the past is weak,
20   I know the present strong.

This drowsy fragrance, silent heat,
    Suit not my present mind,
Whose eager thought goes out to meet
    The life it left behind.

25 Spirit with sky to change; such hope,
    An idle one we know;
Unship the oars, make loose the rope,
    Push off the boat and go. …

Ah, would what binds me could have been
30   Thus loosened at a touch!

---

[1] *the Long* Long vacation, the three summer months when universities and colleges are closed.

This pain of living is too keen,
  Of loving, is too much.
—1889

To Vernon Lee[1]

O Bellosguardo,[2] when the year was young,
  We wandered, seeking for the daffodil
And dark anemone, whose purples fill
The peasant's plot, between the corn-shoots[3] sprung.

5   Over the grey, low wall the olive flung
Her deeper greyness; far off, hill on hill
Sloped to the sky, which, pearly-pale and still,
Above the large and luminous landscape hung.

A snowy blackthorn flowered beyond my reach;
10 You broke a branch and gave it to me there;
I found for you a scarlet blossom rare.

Thereby ran on of Art and Life our speech;
And of the gifts the gods had given to each—
Hope unto you, and unto me Despair.
—1889

The End of the Day
To B.T.

Dead-tired, dog-tired, as the vivid day
Fails and slackens and fades away—
The sky that was so blue before
With sudden clouds is shrouded o'er.
5   Swiftly, stilly the mists uprise,
Till blurred and grey the landscape lies.

.   .   .   .   .   .

All day we have plied the oar; all day
Eager and keen have said our say
On life and death, on love and art,
10 On good or ill at Nature's heart.
Now, grown so tired, we scarce can lift
The lazy oars, but onward drift.
And the silence is only stirred
Here and there by a broken word.

.   .   .   .   .   .

15 O, sweeter far than strain and stress
Is the slow, creeping weariness.
And better far than thought I find
The drowsy blankness of the mind.
More than all joys of soul or sense
20 Is this divine indifference;
Where grief a shadow grows to be,
And peace a possibility.
—1889

---

[1] *Vernon Lee*   Pseudonym for British novelist and critic Violet Paget
(1856–1935), known for her work on aesthetics and her supernatural
fiction.

[2] *Bellosguardo*   Town in Italy, near Florence.

[3] *corn-shoots*   Young stalks of grain.

ARTHUR MORRISON
1863 – 1945

In the course of his long and varied literary career, Arthur Morrison wrote supernatural and detective fiction, novels, short stories, plays, journalism, and art scholarship. The common quality underlying this diverse output is aptly summarized in a review of one of Morrison's later books: "He does not flinch." Morrison's steadfastly honest mode of observation and description distinguishes, in particular, the work for which he is most famous: his literary portrayals of the lower-class London world in which he grew up. The unsparing realism of Morrison's East End fiction makes it a valuable portrait of this frequently misrepresented and misunderstood part of late nineteenth-century London by a writer with roots there.

Morrison was born in Poplar, a working-class East London district, in 1863. His father, who worked in the local dockyards, died in 1871, leaving his wife and three children to fend for themselves. In later life, Morrison had a complicated relationship with his East End origins, persistently seeking to downplay or conceal them even as he recurrently drew on them in his fiction. Because of his efforts to keep his personal history hidden, which extended to directing that all his private papers be destroyed after his death, little is known about his upbringing. By the 1880s, he was working as an office clerk for the People's Palace, a charitable institution meant to provide "technical education and rational recreation" for the East London poor. This job grew to include editing the institutional newsletter, the *Palace Journal*, which helped Morrison make the transition into full-time journalism and eventually into literature. His literary breakthrough occurred in 1891, when he published both *The Shadows Around Us*, a collection of supernatural tales, and "A Street," a sketch of a representative East End neighborhood. The latter work brought Morrison to the attention of W.E. Henley, an influential poet and editor whose other protégés included Rudyard Kipling and Joseph Conrad. Under Henley's patronage, Morrison began writing fictional snapshots of East End life, which were published in the *National Observer*, the journal Henley edited, and collected in 1894 as *Tales of Mean Streets*.

In their fine-grained focus on the experiences of factory girls, striking dockworkers, abused wives, unemployed scroungers, and other denizens of working-class London, the stories in *Tales of Mean Streets* reflect late-Victorian Britain's concern with the condition of the urban poor and the dangerous social consequences of their supposed degradation. That concern, however, frequently found expression in representations of the East End that were overly generalized, moralistic, paternalistic, or hyperbolic. Morrison's fiction sought to correct such impressions. His stories avoided editorializing and refrained from proposing solutions to the social ills to which they bore witness. They also conveyed the diversity of the East End, instead of offering an undifferentiated picture of it, and stressed the everyday nature of most of the struggle and suffering that went on there. The unsentimental objectivity of *Tales of Mean Streets* garnered controversy; critics especially took issue with the opening story, "Lizerunt," a matter-of-fact depiction of a young woman's brutalization by her violent, exploitative husband that ends with its protagonist being kicked out on the street to become a prostitute. Yet other readers detected, through the screen of what one reviewer called Morrison's "austerity of treatment," a "sympathetic comprehension of the pathos of poor life" that won the book esteem.

In the wake of *Tales of Mean Streets*' publication, Morrison was invited to research the Old Nichol, one of East London's most notorious slums, by a clergy member conducting missionary work in the area. Morrison spent eighteen months visiting the slum and interviewing its residents, which formed the basis for his first and best-known novel, *A Child of the Jago* (1896). The book transforms the Old Nichol into the fictional "Jago" and recounts the brief life there of Dicky Perrott, a boy who attempts to escape the slum but is—as Morrison put it of the character's real-life models—"fore-damned to a criminal or semi-criminal career" that ultimately destroys him. Like *Tales of Mean Streets*, *A Child of the Jago* shows hallmarks of naturalism, a variety of literary realism known for its direct portrayals of human suffering and its tendency toward deterministic depictions of people at the mercy of their heredity and environment. (Morrison himself, however, rejected the label of "realist," refusing "to be bound by any formula or prescription prepared by the cataloguers and the pigeon-holers of literature.") At the same time as it was being linked to contemporary trends in realism, the novel was also criticized for being unrealistic; one reviewer called its slum setting a "fairyland of horror." Morrison responded, in a preface to the novel's third edition, that he had merely fulfilled a writer's responsibility to depict life "as he sees it" and that each apparently outrageous incident was merely "the cold transcript of a simple fact, an ordinary, easygoing fact, a fact notorious in the neighbourhood, and capable of any amount of reasonable proof." Despite (or because of) disputes about its verisimilitude, *A Child of the Jago* became a bestseller, and by 1911 it had gone through six editions.

After *Tales of Mean Streets* and *A Child of the Jago*, Morrison continued his exploration of London's social geography in two other novels, *To London Town* (1899) and *The Hole in the Wall* (1902). He also wrote detective stories, another expression of the interest in the relationship between poverty and criminality he demonstrated in *A Child of the Jago*. Most of Morrison's detective fiction featured the respectable professional investigator Martin Hewitt, though Morrison also pushed the genre's boundaries by introducing the "criminal-detective" Horace Dorrington, a self-interested East End tough turned private investigator. Detective fiction proved to be a lucrative genre for Morrison, who published in *The Strand*—the periodical known for Arthur Conan Doyle's Sherlock Holmes stories—and was, after Conan Doyle, one of the most popular practitioners of the genre during its late nineteenth-century boom.

As he established himself as a successful writer, Morrison also became a connoisseur of Japanese art. When he began to collect Japanese prints in the mid-1890s, they were inexpensive enough to be accessible to a working writer such as Morrison, but by the early twentieth century they had attracted the interest of the English art world, and Morrison became considerably wealthy by selling portions of his collection to the British Museum. This second career enabled his retirement from fiction writing, and he cultivated his reputation as an expert on Japanese prints and paintings; his two-volume study *The Painters of Japan* (1910–11) became a standard reference work. In his later years, Morrison published little but remained a prominent member of London's intellectual elite. He became a member of the Royal Society of Literature in 1925, eventually serving on its governing council.

Partly because of this diminished output in the second half of his life, Morrison's significance for late-nineteenth century literary history went underappreciated for several decades after his death in 1945. A resurgence in scholarly interest in him began in the 1990s, and the importance of his treatment of urban poverty and the nature and aims of his realism are topics of robust ongoing study. But the extent of Morrison's impact, and the degree of his success in credibly conveying the experience of life in urban poverty, can be more immediately measured by the way his East End contemporaries responded to his depictions of their home. Almost as soon as *A Child of the Jago* was published, residents of the Old Nichol began to call their neighborhood by the fictional name Morrison had given to it, and "Jago" continues to serve as a signifier of local identity in East London today.

⌘ ⌘ ⌘

A Street

This street is in the East End.[1] There is no need to say in the East End of what. The East End is a vast city, as famous in its way as any the hand of man has made. But who knows the East End? It is down through Cornhill and out beyond Leadenhall Street and Aldgate Pump, one will say: a shocking place, where he once went with a curate; an evil plexus of slums that hide human creeping things; where filthy men and women live on penn'orths[2] of gin, where collars and clean shirts are decencies unknown, where every citizen wears a black eye, and none ever combs his hair. The East End is a place, says another, which is given over to the Unemployed. And the Unemployed is a race whose token is a clay pipe, and whose enemy is soap: now and again it migrates bodily to Hyde Park[3] with banners, and furnishes adjacent police courts with disorderly drunks. Still another knows the East End only as the place whence begging letters come; there are coal and

blanket funds[4] there, all perennially insolvent, and everybody always wants a day in the country. Many and misty are people's notions of the East End; and each is commonly but the distorted shadow of a minor feature. Foul slums there are in the East End, of course, as there are in the West; want and misery there are, as wherever a host is gathered together to fight for food. But they are not often spectacular in kind.

Of this street there are about one hundred and fifty yards—on the same pattern all. It is not pretty to look at. A dingy little brick house twenty feet high, with three square holes to carry the windows, and an oblong hole to carry the door, is not a pleasing object; and each side of this street is formed by two or three score[5] of such houses in a row, with one front wall in common. And the effect is as of stables.

Round the corner there are a baker's, a chandler's,[6] and a beer-shop. They are not included in the view from any of the rectangular holes; but they are well known to every denizen, and the chandler goes to church on Sunday and pays for his seat.[7] At the opposite end, turnings lead to streets less rigidly respectable: some

---

1 *the East End* Largely industrial and working-class area of London east of the City, London's historic core, and north of the River Thames. In the late nineteenth century, it bore a negative reputation for dire poverty and related social problems.

2 *Cornhill … Aldgate Pump* Cornhill and Leadenhall Street are streets in the City of London; Aldgate Pump is the landmark on the edge of the City that symbolically marks the start of the East End; *plexus* Complex, interconnected mass; *penn'orths* I.e., pennies' worth.

3 *Hyde Park* Park in the West End of London, the wealthier section of the city, that was frequently the site of political demonstrations.

4 *begging letters* Letters sent to rich people or organizations soliciting charity, very common in Victorian Britain; *coal and blanket funds* Charitable organizations intended to provide coal and blankets to the poor.

5 *two or three score* I.e., between forty and sixty.

6 *chandler* Seller of household goods.

7 *goes … his seat* Nineteenth-century Anglican churches frequently charged rent for church seats as a source of income. For small business owners and other members of the lower-middle class, renting such seats was a way of asserting social status.

where "Mangling[1] done here" stares from windows, and where doors are left carelessly open; others where squalid women sit on doorsteps, and girls go to factories in white aprons. Many such turnings, of as many grades of decency, are set between this and the nearest slum.

They are not a very noisy or obtrusive lot in this street. They do not go to Hyde Park with banners, and they seldom fight. It is just possible that one or two among them, at some point in a life of ups and downs, may have been indebted to a coal and blanket fund; but whosoever these may be, they would rather die than publish the disgrace, and it is probable that they very nearly did so ere submitting to it.

Some who inhabit this street are in the docks, some in the gasworks, some in one or other of the few ship-building yards that yet survive on the Thames. Two families in a house is the general rule, for there are six rooms behind each set of holes: this, unless "young men lodgers" are taken in, or there are grown sons paying for bed and board. As for the grown daughters, they marry as soon as may be. Domestic service is a social descent, and little under millinery and dressmaking is compatible with self-respect. The general servant may be caught young among the turnings at the end where mangling is done; and the factory girls live still further off, in places skirting slums.

Every morning at half-past five there is a curious demonstration. The street resounds with thunderous knockings, repeated upon door after door, and acknowledged ever by a muffled shout from within. These signals are the work of the night-watchman or the early policeman, or both, and they summon the sleepers to go forth to the docks, the gasworks, and the shipyards. To be awakened in this wise costs fourpence a week, and for this fourpence a fierce rivalry rages between night-watchmen and policemen. The night-watchman—a sort of by-blow of the ancient "Charley," and himself a fast vanishing quantity—is the real professional performer;

but he goes to the wall,[2] because a large connection must be worked if the pursuit is to pay at fourpence a knocker. Now, it is not easy to bang at two knockers three-quarters of a mile apart, and a hundred others lying between, all punctually at half-past five. Wherefore the policeman, to whom the fourpence is but a perquisite,[3] and who is content with a smaller round, is rapidly supplanting the night-watchman, whose cry of "Past nine o'clock," as he collects orders in the evening, is now seldom heard.

The knocking and the shouting pass, and there comes the noise of opening and shutting of doors, and a clattering away to the docks, the gasworks and the shipyards. Later more door-shutting is heard, and then the trotting of sorrow-laden little feet along the grim street to the grim Board School[4] three grim streets off. Then silence, save for a subdued sound of scrubbing here and there, and the puny squall of croupy[5] infants. After this, a new trotting of little feet to docks, gas-works, and shipyards with father's dinner in a basin and a red handkerchief, and so to the Board School again. More muffled scrubbing and more squalling, and perhaps a feeble attempt or two at decorating the blankness of a square hole here and there by pouring water into a grimy flower-pot full of dirt. Then comes the trot of little feet toward the oblong holes, heralding the slower tread of sooty artisans; a smell of bloater[6] up and down; nightfall; the fighting of boys in the street, perhaps of men at the corner near the beer-shop; sleep. And this is the record of a day in this street; and every day is hopelessly the same.

Every day, that is, but Sunday. On Sunday morning

---

[1] *Mangling*   Squeezing water from washed laundry by means of a mechanical press or "mangle," a widespread means of supplementing the income of poor households.

[2] *by-blow*   I.e., illegitimate child; *the ancient "Charley"*   Early nineteenth-century term for a person who performs a night watch; *goes to the wall*   Fails in business.

[3] *perquisite*   I.e., perk.

[4] *Board School*   State-run school of the kind established in Britain by the Elementary Education Act (1870). The act only created school boards for areas that did not have enough existing schools to serve all the children in the area; as a result, Board Schools tended to be concentrated in poorer districts.

[5] *croupy*   I.e., suffering from croup, a respiratory infection common in young children.

[6] *bloater*   Preserved herring.

a smell of cooking floats round the corner from the half-shut baker's, and the little feet trot down the street under steaming burdens of beef, potatoes, and batter pudding—the lucky little feet these, with Sunday boots on them, when father is in good work and has brought home all his money; not the poor little feet in worn shoes, carrying little bodies in the threadbare clothes of all the week, when father is out of work, or ill, or drunk, and the Sunday cooking may very easily be done at home—if any there be to do.

On Sunday morning one or two heads of families appear in wonderful black suits, with unnumbered creases and wrinklings at the seams. At their sides and about their heels trot the unresting little feet, and from under painful little velvet caps and straw hats stare solemn little faces towelled to a polish. Thus disposed and arrayed, they fare gravely through the grim little streets to a grim Little Bethel[1] where are gathered together others in like garb and attendance; and for two hours they endure the frantic menace of hell-fire.

Most of the men, however, lie in shirt and trousers on their beds and read the Sunday paper; while some are driven forth—for they hinder the housework—to loaf, and await the opening of the beer-shop round the corner. Thus goes Sunday in this street, and every Sunday is the same as every other Sunday, so that one monotony is broken with another. For the women, however, Sunday is much as other days, except that there is rather more work for them. The break in their round of the week is washing day.

No event in the outer world makes any impression in this street. Nations may rise, or may totter in ruin; but here the colorless day will work through its twenty-four hours just as it did yesterday, and just as it will tomorrow. Without there may be party strife, wars and rumors of wars,[2] public rejoicings; but the trotting of the little feet will be neither quickened nor stayed.

Those quaint little women, the girl-children of this street, who use a motherly management toward all girl-things younger than themselves, and toward all boys as old or older, with "Bless the child!" or "Drat the children!"—those quaint little women will still go marketing[3] with big baskets, and will regard the price of bacon as chief among human considerations. Nothing disturbs this street—nothing but a strike.

Nobody laughs here—life is too serious a thing; nobody sings. There was once a woman who sang—a young wife from the country. But she bore children, and her voice cracked. Then her man died, and she sang no more. They took away her home, and with her children about her skirts she left this street forever. The other women did not think much of her. She was "helpless."

One of the square holes in this street—one of the single, ground-floor holes—is found, on individual examination, to differ from the others. There has been an attempt to make it into a shop-window. Half a dozen candles, a few sickly sugar-sticks, certain shrivelled bloaters, some bootlaces, and a bundle or two of fire-wood compose a stock which at night is sometimes lighted by a little paraffin lamp in a tin sconce, and sometimes by a candle. A widow lives here—a gaunt, bony widow, with sunken, red eyes. She has other sources of income than the candles and the bootlaces: she washes and chars[4] all day, and she sews cheap shirts at night. Two "young men lodgers," moreover, sleep upstairs, and the children sleep in the back room; she herself is supposed not to sleep at all. The policeman does not knock here in the morning—the widow wakes the lodgers herself; and nobody in the street behind ever looks out of window before going to bed, no matter how late, without seeing a light in the widow's room where she plies her needle. She is a quiet woman, who speaks little with her neighbors, having other things to do: a woman of pronounced character, to whom it would be unadvisable—even dangerous—to offer coals or blankets. Hers was the strongest contempt for the helpless woman who sang: a contempt whose added

---

[1] *Little Bethel* Disparaging term for a church of a Protestant denomination other than the established Anglican Church.

[2] *Without* Outside; *wars and rumors of wars* See Matthew 24.6: "And ye shall hear of wars and rumours of wars: see that ye be not troubled: for all these things must come to pass, but the end is not yet."

---

[3] *marketing* Shopping.

[4] *chars* Does household cleaning work as an odd job.

bitterness might be traced to its source. For when the singing woman was marketing, from which door of the pawnshop had she twice met the widow coming forth?

This is not a dirty street, taken as a whole. The widow's house is one of the cleanest, and the widow's children match the house. The one house cleaner than the widow's is ruled by a despotic Scotchwoman, who drives every hawker off her whitened step, and rubs her door handle if a hand have rested on it. The Scotch-woman has made several attempts to accommodate "young men lodgers," but they have ended in shrill rows.[1]

There is no house without children in this street, and the number of them grows ever and ever greater. Nine-tenths of the doctor's visits are on this account alone, and his appearances are the chief matter of such conversation as the women make across the fences. One after another the little strangers come, to live through lives as flat and colorless as the day's life in this street. Existence dawns, and the doctor-watchman's door knock resounds along the row of rectangular holes. Then a muffled cry announces that a small new being has come to trudge and sweat its way in the appointed groove. Later, the trotting of little feet and the school; the midday play hour, when love peeps even into this street; after that more trotting of little feet—strange little feet, new little feet—and the scrubbing, and the squalling, and the barren flower-pot; the end of the sooty day's work; the last home-coming; nightfall; sleep. When love's light falls into some corner of the street, it falls at an early hour of this mean life, and is itself but a dusty ray. It falls early, because it is the sole bright thing which the street sees, and is watched for and counted on. Lads and lasses, awkwardly arm in arm, go pacing up and down this street, before the natural interest in marbles and doll's houses would have left them in a brighter place. They are "keeping company"; the manner of which proceeding is indigenous—is a custom native to the place. The young people first "walk out" in pairs. There is no exchange of promises, no troth-plight,[2] no engagement, no love-talk. They patrol the street side by side, usually in silence, sometimes with fatuous chatter. There are no dances, no tennis, no water-parties,[3] no picnics to bring them together: so they must walk out, or be unacquainted. If two of them grow dissatisfied with each other's company, nothing is easier than to separate and walk out with somebody else. When by these means each has found a fit mate (or thinks so), a ring is bought, and the odd association becomes a regular engagement; but this is not until the walking out has endured for many months. The two stages of courtship are spoken of indiscriminately as "keeping company," but a very careful distinction is drawn between them by the parties concerned. Never-theless, in the walking out period it would be almost as great a breach of faith for either to walk out with more than one, as it would be if the full engagement had been made. And love-making[4] in this street is a dreary thing, when one thinks of love-making in other places. It begins—and it ends—too soon.

Nobody from this street goes to the theatre. That would mean a long journey, and it would cost money which might buy bread and beer and boots. For those, too, who wear black Sunday suits it would be sinful. Nobody reads poetry or romance.[5] The very words are foreign. A Sunday paper in some few houses provides such reading as this street is disposed to achieve. Now and again a penny novel[6] has been found among the private treasures of a growing daughter, and has been wrathfully confiscated. For the air of this street is un-favorable to the ideal.

Yet there are aspirations. There has lately come into the street a young man lodger who belongs to a Mutual

[1] *rows* Arguments.

[2] *troth-plight* I.e., vow of mutual commitment to be married.

[3] *water-parties* Social events involving boating.

[4] *love-making* Professing or avowing love, especially in the context of courtship.

[5] *romance* Fiction dealing with exotic, exciting, or fantastic subject-matter.

[6] *penny novel* Cheap serialized novel.

Improvement Society.[1] Membership in this society is regarded as a sort of learned degree, and at its meetings debates are held and papers smugly read by lamentably self-satisfied young men lodgers, whose only preparation for debating and writing is a fathomless ignorance. For ignorance is the inevitable portion of dwellers here: seeing nothing, reading nothing, and considering nothing.

Where in the East End lies this street? Everywhere. The hundred and fifty yards is only a link in a long and a mightily tangled chain—is only a turn in a tortuous maze. This street of the square holes is hundreds of miles long. That it is planned in short lengths is true, but there is no other way in the world that can more properly be called a single street, because of its dismal lack of accent, its sordid uniformity, its utter remoteness from delight.

—1894

Without Visible Means[2]

All East London idled, or walked in a procession, or waylaid and bashed, or cried in an empty kitchen: for it was the autumn of the Great Strikes.[3] One army of men, having been prepared, was ordered to strike—and struck. Other smaller armies of men, with no preparation, were ordered to strike to express sympathy—and struck. Other armies still were ordered to strike because it was the fashion—and struck. Then many hands were discharged because the strikes in other trades left them no work. Many others came from other parts in regiments to work, but remained to loaf in gangs: taught by

the example of earlier regiments, which, the situation being explained (an expression devised to include mobbings and kickings and flingings into docks), had returned whence they came.[4] So that East London was very noisy and largely hungry; and the rest of the world looked on with intense interest, making earnest suggestions, and comprehending nothing. Lots of strikers, having no strike pay and finding little nourishment in processions, started off to walk to Manchester, Birmingham, Liverpool, or Newcastle,[5] where work might be got. Along the Great North Road[6] such men might be seen in silent companies of a dozen or twenty, now and again singly or in couples. At the tail of one such gang, which gathered in the Burdett Road and found its way into the Enfield Road by way of Victoria Park, Clapton, and Stamford Hill,[7] walked a little group of three: a voluble young man of thirty, a stolid workman rather older, and a pale, anxious little fellow, with a nasty spasmic cough and a canvas bag of tools.

The little crowd straggled over the footpath and the road, few of its members speaking, most of them keeping to their places and themselves. As yet there was nothing of the tramp in the aspect of these mechanics.[8] With their washed faces and well-mended clothes they might have been taken for a jury coming from a local inquest. As the streets got broken and detached, with patches of field between, they began to look about them. One young fellow in front (with no family to think of), who looked upon the enterprise as an amusing sort of tour, and had even brought an accordion, began to rebel against the general depression, and attempted a joke about going to the Alexandra Palace.[9] But in the rear, the

[1] *Mutual Improvement Society* Grassroots working-class organization in which the members educated one another and held political discussions and debates.

[2] *Without Visible Means* According to the Vagrancy Act (1824), "every person wandering abroad … not having any visible means of subsistence" was deemed a vagrant. Vagrancy was considered a crime punishable by imprisonment.

[3] *the autumn … Strikes* The dock workers of the Port of London went on strike on 14 August 1889. In the ensuing weeks, numerous sympathy strikes broke out among other groups of workers in London's East End. The strikes ended after most of the dock workers' demands were met, and they returned to work on 16 September.

[4] *Many others … whence they came* During the dock workers' strike, allegations spread that striking workers intimidated and occasionally assaulted strikebreakers.

[5] *Manchester … Newcastle* Industrial cities in northern England, all between 100 and 250 miles from London.

[6] *Great North Road* Main highway leading north from London.

[7] *Burdett Road … Stamford Hill* Locations in east and north London; in following this trajectory, the group has headed north out of the city.

[8] *mechanics* Members of the working class; industrial laborers.

[9] *Alexandra Palace* Public center for education, recreation, and the arts in north London, known as "the People's Palace."

little man with the canvas bag, putting his hand abstract-
edly into his pocket, suddenly stared and stopped. He
drew out the hand, and saw in it three shillings.

"S'elp me," he said, "the missis[1] is done that—
shoved it in unbeknown when I come away! An' she's
on'y got a bob[2] for 'erself an' the kids." He broke into a
sweat of uneasiness. "I'll 'ave to send it back at the next
post office, that's all."

"Send it back? not you!" Thus with deep scorn the
voluble young man at his side. "*She'll* be all right, you
lay your life. A woman allus[3] knows 'ow to look after
'erself. You'll bleed'n' soon want it, an' bad. You do as
I tell you, Joey: stick to it. That's right, Dave, ain't it?"

"Matter o' fancy," replied the stolid man. "My
missis cleared my pockets out 'fore I got away. Should-
n't wonder at bein' sent after for leavin' 'er chargeable[4]
if I don't soon send some more. Women's different."

The march continued, and grew dustier. The
cheerful pilgrim in front produced his accordion. At
Palmer's Green four went straight ahead to try for work
at the Enfield Arms Factory.[5] The others, knowing the
thing hopeless, turned off to the left for Potter's Bar.[6]

After a long silence, "Which'll be nearest, Dave,"
asked little Joey Clayton, "Newcastle or Middlesborough?"[7]

"Middlesborough," said Dave; "I done it afore."

"Trampin' ain't so rough on a man, is it, after all?"
asked Joey wistfully. "*You* done all right, didn't you?"

"Got through. All depends, though it's rough
enough. Matter o' luck. *I* 'ad the bad weather."

"If I don't get a good easy job where we're goin',"

remarked the voluble young man, "I'll 'ave a strike there
too."

"'Ave a strike there?" exclaimed Joey. "'Ow? Who'd
call 'em out?"

"Wy, *I* would. I think I'm equal to doin' it, ain't I?
An' when workin' men stand idle an' 'ungry in the
midst o' the wealth an' the lukshry an' the igstravagance
they've produced with the sweat of their brow, why,
then, feller-workmen, it's time to act. It's time to bring
the nigger-drivin'[8] bloated capitalists to their knees."

"'Ear, 'ear," applauded Joey Clayton; tamely, perhaps, for the words were not new. "Good on yer,
Newman!" Newman had a habit of practicing this sort
of thing in snatches whenever he saw the chance. He
had learnt the trick in a debating society; and Joey
Clayton was always an applausive audience. There was
a pause, the accordion started another tune, and
Newman tried a different passage of his harangue.

"In the shop they call me Skulky Newman. Why?
'Cos I skulk,[9] o' course" ("'Ear, 'ear," dreamily—from
Dave this time). "I ain't ashamed of it, my friends. I'm
a miker[10] out an' out, an' I 'ope I shall always remain a
miker. The less a worker does the more 'as to be
imployed, don't they? An' the more the toilers wrings
out o' the capitalists, don't they? Very well then, I mike,
an' I do it as a sacred dooty."

"You'll 'ave all the mikin' you want for a week or
two," said Dave Burge placidly. "Stow it."

At Potter's Bar the party halted and sat under a
hedge to eat hunks of bread and cheese (or hunks of
bread and nothing else) and to drink cold tea out of
cans. Skulky Newman, who had brought nothing, stood
in with his two friends. As they started anew and turned
into the Great North Road he said, stretching himself
and looking slyly at Joey Clayton, "If *I'd* got a bob or
two I'd stand you two blokes a pint apiece."

Joey looked troubled. "Well, as you ain't, I suppose
I ought to," he said uneasily, turning toward the little

---

[1] *S'elp me* So help me; *the missis* I.e., his wife.

[2] *bob* Shilling.

[3] *allus* Always.

[4] *chargeable* Dependent upon the parish for survival. Leaving one's
wife in this condition was a crime.

[5] *Palmer's Green* Village in Enfield, a suburban area on the northern
edge of London; *Enfield Arms Factory* I.e., the Royal Small Arms
Factory, where rifles for the British Army were manufactured.

[6] *Potter's Bar* Town on the Great North Road, thirteen miles north
of London.

[7] *Middlesborough* Middlesbrough, an industrial city 217 miles north
of London, slightly closer than Newcastle.

[8] *nigger-drivin'* The use of such highly pejorative racial terms was
common in Britain at the end of the nineteenth century; here,
Newman is comparing the industrial bourgeoisie to enslavers.

[9] *skulk* Avoid work.

[10] *miker* Someone who dodges work.

inn hard by. "Dave," he cried to Burge, who was walking on, "won't you 'ave a drink?" And, "Well, if you *are* goin' to do the toff,[1] I ain't proud," was the slow reply.

Afterward, Joey was inclined to stop at the post office to send away at least two shillings. But Newman wouldn't. He enlarged on the improvidence of putting out of reach that which might be required on an emergency, he repeated his axiom as to a woman's knack of keeping alive in spite of all things: and Joey determined not to send—for a day or so at any rate.

The road got looser and dustier; the symptoms of the tramp came out stronger and stronger on the gang. The accordion struck up from time to time, but ceased toward the end of the afternoon. The player wearied, and some of the older men, soon tired of walking, were worried by the noise. Joey Clayton, whose cough was aggravated by the dust, was especially tortured, after every fit, to hear the thing drawling and whooping the tune it had drawled and whooped a dozen times before; but he said nothing, scarce knowing what annoyed him.

At Hatfield Station[2] two of the foremost picked up a few coppers by helping with a heavy trap-load of luggage. Up Digswell Hill the party tailed out lengthily, and Newman, who had been letting off a set speech, was fain to save his wind. The night came, clear to see and sweet to smell. Between Welwyn and Codicote the company broke up to roost in such barns as they might possess: all but the master of the accordion, who had stayed at a little public-house at Welwyn, with the notion of earning a pot of beer and a stable-corner (or better) by a tune in the tap-room. Dave Burge lighted on a lone shed of thatched hurdles with loose hay in it, and Newman straightway curled in the snuggest corner on most of the hay. Dave Burge pulled some from under

him, and, having helped Joey Clayton to build a nest in the best place left, was soon snoring. But Joey lay awake all night, and sat up and coughed and turned restlessly, being unused to the circumstances and apprehensive of those months in jail which (it is well known) are rancorously dealt forth among all them that sleep in barns.

Luck provided a breakfast next morning at Codicote: for three bicyclists, going north, stood cold beef and bread round at The Anchor. The man with the accordion caught up. He had made his lodging and breakfast and eightpence: this had determined him to stay at Hitchin,[3] and work it for at least a day, and then to diverge into the towns and let the rest go their way. So beyond Hitchin there was no music.

Joey Clayton soon fell slow. Newman had his idea; and the three were left behind, and Joey staggered after his mates with difficulty. He lacked sleep, and he lacked stamina. Dave Burge took the canvas bag, and there were many rests: when Newman, expressing a resolve to stick by his fellow-man through thick and thin, hinted at drinks. Dave Burge made twopence at Henlow[4] level crossing by holding an unsteady horse while a train passed. Joey saw little of the rest of the day; the road was yellow and dazzling, his cough tore him, and things were red sometimes and sometimes blue. He walked without knowing it, now helped, now lurching on alone. The others of the party were far ahead and forgotten. There was talk of a windmill ahead, where there would be rest; and the three men camped in an old boathouse by the river just outside Biggleswade.[5] Joey, sleeping as he tottered, fell in a heap and lay without moving from sunset to broad morning.

---

1. *do the toff* Behave in a gentlemanly or upper-class manner.
2. *Hatfield Station* Hatfield, like Digswell, Welwyn, and Codicote (named in the following sentences), is a town on the Great North Road.
3. *Hitchin* Town 31 miles north of London.
4. *Henlow* Village 36 miles north of London.
5. *Biggleswade* Town on the River Ivel, about 40 miles from London, that was an important stage on the Great North Road.

When he woke Dave Burge was sitting at the door, but Newman was gone. Also, there was no sign of the canvas bag.

"No use lookin'," said Dave; "'e's done it."

"Eh?"

"Skulky's 'opped the twig[1] an' sneaked your tools. Gawd knows where 'e is by now."

"No—" the little man gasped, sitting up in a pale sweat. … "Not sneaked 'em … is 'e? … S'elp me, there's a set o' callipers[2] worth fifteen bob in that bag … 'e ain't gawn …?"

Dave Burge nodded inexorably.

"Best feel in your pockets," he said, "p'raps 'e's bin there."

He had. The little man broke down. "I was a-goin' to send 'ome that two bob—s'elp me, I was. … An' what can I do without my tools? If I'd got no job I could 'a pawned 'em—an' then I'd 'a sent 'ome the money—s'elp me I would. … O, it's crool!"

The walking, with the long sleep after it, had left him sore and stiff, and Dave had work to put him on the road again. He had forgotten yesterday afternoon, and asked, at first, for the others. They tramped in silence for a few miles: when Joey suddenly flung himself upon a tussock by the wayside.

"Why won't nobody let me live?" he snivelled. "*I'm* a 'armless bloke enough. I worked at Ritterson's, man and boy, very nigh twenty year. When they come an' ordered us out,[3] I come out with the others, peaceful enough; I didn't want to chuck it up, Gawd knows, but I come out promp' when they told me. And when I found another job on the Island, four big blokes set about me an' 'arf [4] killed me. *I* didn't know the place

was blocked.[5] And when two o' the blokes was took up, they said I'd get strike-pay[6] again if I didn't identify 'em; so I didn't. But they never give me no strike-pay—they laughed an' chucked me out. An' now I'm a-starvin' on the 'igh road. An' Skulky … blimey … *'e's* done me too!"

There were days wherein Joey learned to eat a swede[7] pulled from behind a wagon, and to feel thankful for an early turnip; might have learned, too, just what tramping means in many ways to a man unskilled both in begging and in theft, but was never equal to it. He coughed—and worse: holding to posts and gates, and often spitting blood. He had little to say, but trudged mechanically, taking note of nothing.

Once, as though aroused from a reverie, he asked, "Wasn't there some others?"

"Others?" said Dave, for a moment taken aback. "O, yes, there was some others. They're gone on ahead, y'know."

Joey tramped for half a mile in silence. Then he said, "Expect they're 'avin' a rough time too."

"Ah—very like," said Dave.

For a space Joey was silent, save for the cough. Then he went on: "Comes o' not bringing 'cordions with 'em. Every one ought to take a 'cordion what goes trampin'. I knew a man once that went trampin', an' 'e took a 'cordion. *He* done all right. It ain't so rough for them as plays on the 'cordion." And Dave Burge rubbed his cap about his head and stared; but answered nothing.

It was a bad day. Crusts were begged at cottages. Every rise and every turn, the eternal yellow road lay stretch on stretch before them, flouting their unrest. Joey, now unimpressionable,[8] endured more placidly than even Dave Burge. Late in the afternoon, "No," he said, "it ain't so rough for them as plays the 'cordion. They 'as the best of it…. S'elp me," he added suddenly,

---

[1] *'opped the twig* Departed suddenly.

[2] *callipers* Measuring tool used in mechanical engineering, metalworking, and woodworking.

[3] *When … out* I.e., when the union representing the workers at Joey's place of employment called a strike.

[4] *the Island* The Isle of Dogs, actually a peninsula in southeast London formed by a bend in the River Thames, site of the docks where the 1889 dock workers' strike began; *'arf* Half.

[5] *the place was blocked* I.e., striking workers were preventing anybody else from working there.

[6] *took up* Arrested; *strike-pay* Payment made to striking workers by their union in order to help support them and their families during the strike.

[7] *swede* Kind of turnip.

[8] *unimpressionable* Incapable of receiving impressions; numb.

"*we're* all 'cordions!" He sniggered thoughtfully, and then burst into a cough that left him panting. "We're nothin' but a bloomin' lot o' 'cordions ourselves," he went on, having got his breath, "an' they play any toon they like on us; an' that's 'ow they make their livin'. S'elp me, Dave, we're all 'cordions." And he laughed.

"Um—yus," the other man grunted. And he looked curiously at his mate; for he had never heard that sort of laugh before.

But Joey fondled the conceit,[1] and returned to it from time to time; now aloud, now to himself. "All 'cordions: playin' any toon as is ordered, blimy. … *Are* we 'cordions? *I* don't b'lieve we're as much as that … no, s'elp me. We're on'y the footlin'[2] little keys; shoved about to soot the toon. … Little tin keys, blimy … footlin' little keys. … I've bin played on plenty, *I* 'ave. …"

Dave Burge listened with alarm, and tried to talk of other things. But Joey rarely heard him. "I've bin played on plenty, *I* 'ave," he persisted. "I was played on once by a pal: an' my spring broke."

At nightfall there was more bad luck. They were driven from a likely barn by a leather-gaitered[3] man with a dog, and for some distance no dormitory could be found. Then it was a cut haystack, with a nest near the top and steps to reach it.

In the night Burge was wakened by a clammy hand upon his face. There was a thick mist.

"It's you, Dave, ain't it?" Clayton was saying. "Good Gawd, I thought I'd lawst you. What's all this 'ere—not the water is it?—not the dock? I'm soppin' wet."

Burge himself was wet to the skin. He made Joey lie down, and told him to sleep; but a coughing fit prevented that. "It was them 'cordions woke me," he explained when it was over.

So the night put on the shuddering gray of the foredawn. And the two tramps left their perch, and betook them, shivering and stamping, to the road.

That morning Joey had short fits of dizziness and faintness. "It's my spring broke," he would say after such an attack. "Bloomin' little tin key put out o' toon." And once he added, "I'm up to one toon, though, now: this 'ere bloomin' Dead March."[4]

Just at the outskirts of a town, where he stopped to cough over a gate, a stout old lady, walking out with a shaggy little dog, gave him a shilling. Dave Burge picked it up as it dropped from his incapable hand, and "Joey, 'ere's a bob," he said; "a lady give it you. You come an' git a drop o' beer."

They carried a twopenny loaf into the tap-room of a small tavern, and Dave had mild ale himself, but saw that Joey was served with stout with a penn'orth[5] of gin in it. Soon the gin and stout reached Joey's head, and drew it to the table. And he slept, leaving the rest of the shilling where it lay.

Dave arose, and stuffed the last of the twopenny loaf into his pocket. He took a piece of chalk from the bagatelle board in the corner, and wrote this on the table: "*dr. sir. for god sake take him to the work House.*"[6] Then he gathered up the coppers where they lay, and stepped quietly into the street.

—1894

---

[1] *conceit* Idea, metaphor.

[2] *footlin'* Insignificant.

[3] *leather-gaitered* I.e., wearing leather coverings over his shoes and lower legs.

[4] *Dead March* Piece of music played in a funeral procession.

[5] *penn'orth* Penny's worth.

[6] *bagatelle board* Table for playing bagatelle, a game resembling billiards; *dr.* Abbreviation: dear; *work House* Institution providing shelter and employment, often in the form of hard manual labor, to people unable to support themselves. Workhouses were designed to be as unpleasant as possible so as to discourage people from entering them.

RUDYARD KIPLING
1865 – 1936

The name "Rudyard Kipling" evokes images of the Raj in India, a time when Britannia ruled the waves and the sun never set on the British Empire. Indeed his life spanned most of the duration of British Colonial Office rule in India (1858–1947). Kipling, for many years considered England's unofficial poet laureate, was a strong proponent of imperialism; he believed it was Britain's duty to govern and civilize colonized lands. Though he was also capable of offering serious critiques of empire—and though he acknowledged that colonized people were "captives"—Kipling gave frequent voice to his belief that the British were in India to serve the native people. His famous 1899 poem, "The White Man's Burden," published in *McClure's Magazine*, aroused a storm of controversy, coming out at a time when many people were beginning to question the right of imperialist powers to subjugate other lands and peoples. Yet, for more than a half century Kipling's poems, short stories, and novels were wildly popular in India, Great Britain, and the United States, and in 1907 the Nobel Foundation honored him "in consideration of the power of observation, originality of imagination, virility of ideas and remarkable talent for narration which characterize the creations of this world-famous author." Thus Kipling became the first British writer to be awarded the Nobel Prize for Literature.

Kipling was named after Rudyard Lake in England, but he was born in Bombay (now Mumbai), India. Both his father, John Lockwood Kipling, professor of architectural sculpture at the University of Bombay, and his mother, Alice Macdonald, were children of Methodist ministers. Macdonald and her sisters were all associated with distinguished people—one sister married the neoclassical painter Sir Edward Poynter; another was the mother of Stanley Baldwin, who became Prime Minister of England in 1923; and another was the wife of the Pre-Raphaelite painter Sir Edward Burne-Jones. Kipling spent his first six years with his parents, learning the languages of his Indian friends and imbibing the cultural wealth of India. Of his school years, however, Kipling would say in his autobiography that his only happy moments were spent at the Burne-Jones home. Like many children of expatriates, he and his sister were sent to England for their education, where they spent five miserable years with severe, Calvinist foster parents in a home that Kipling would later call the House of Desolation. In 1878 he transferred to a boarding school in Devon (depicted in *Stalky and Co.*), which was also brutal at times, but where he acquired a schoolboy ethos—a sense of loyalty to and camaraderie with his peers—which later pervaded his work. It was at this school in Devon, too, where Kipling started to write in earnest.

Upon graduation, Kipling moved back to India, working first as a newspaper journalist for the *Civil and Military Gazette* in Lahore (now part of Pakistan) and then as an editor of *Pioneer* in Allahabad. Many of the poems and stories he wrote during that time were collected in *Departmental Ditties* (1886) and *Plain Tales from the Hills* (1888), in which Kipling wrote about the moral and psychological difficulties of integrating Indian and British cultures. The Indian Railway Library also published collections of Kipling's stories, notably *The Phantom Rickshaw and Other Eerie Tales* and *Wee Willie Winkie and Other Child Stories* (1888). The first of these collections included "The Man Who Would

Be King," which has remained one of Kipling's most popular stories. By the time he returned to England in 1889, Kipling was a well-established author in India and had become very popular in Britain as well. The British public loved his "tales of the exotic," which took them to worlds they could scarcely imagine and introduced them to cultures they would likely never experience first-hand.

Kipling published several collections of short stories and poems in the early 1890s; the volume *Barrack-Room Ballads and Other Verses* (1892), which included such well-known poems as "Mandalay" and "Gunga Din," went into more than 50 editions in the 30 years following. Two early novels, *The Light that Failed* (1891) and *The Naulahka* (1892), did not fare as well. Nevertheless, in this period Kipling acquired a reputation for using everyday language to express the thoughts of soldiers and other working Brits; his poems, for example, were often inspired by street ballads and music hall ditties.

In 1892 Kipling married an American, Caroline Balestier, and the couple settled in Vermont. Although Kipling was unhappy in the United States, he wrote some of his most esteemed works during his five-year stay there, including *The Jungle Book* (1894), *The Second Jungle Book* (1895), and *Captains Courageous* (1897).

The family eventually settled in Sussex, England, but Kipling continued to travel the world as a newspaper correspondent. He covered the Boer War in South Africa in 1899 and returned to the region annually thereafter, staying in a house given to him by Cecil Rhodes, the famous British imperialist and business magnate. Kipling's own imperialist political sentiments were disseminated widely at the turn of the century, most notably in the London *Times*, which published "Recessional," composed in honor of Queen Victoria's Diamond Jubilee, and "The White Man's Burden." The latter poem was soon afterward countered in the London magazine *Truth* with a poem by Henry Labouchère, which changed Kipling's opening refrain from "Take up the white man's burden," to "Pile on the brown man's burden." Amid the controversy that ensued, a letter to the editor was published that read, "There is something almost sickening in this 'imperial' talk of assuming and bearing burdens for the good of others. They are never assumed or held where they are not found to be of material advantage or ministering to honor or glory." Kipling himself suggested that his poem offered neither a noble call to arms nor a justification for colonization, but rather a warning of the costs involved on both sides of imperialist missions abroad.

Kipling's least controversial and best-loved novel appeared in 1901. *Kim* is a picaresque adventure tale of a British beggar boy, the orphaned son of an Irish soldier. Raised in Lahore by an opium-addicted, half-caste woman, Kim O'Hare comes to believe he is destined for greatness and eventually travels through India with a holy man in search of his glorious future. In 1907, the Nobel committee said that in *Kim* "there is an elevated diction as well as a tenderness and charm. … In sketching a personality he makes clear, almost in his first words, the peculiar traits of that person's character and temper. … [Kipling is] capable of reproducing with astounding accuracy the minutest detail from real life."

In the decades following his Nobel Prize, Kipling's literary output dwindled somewhat amid controversy over his politics and grief over the loss of two of his three children. Even former admirers, such as W.B. Yeats and T.S. Eliot, began to be critical of Kipling's unwavering allegiance to British imperialism. Nevertheless, the last half century has seen a resurgence of interest in his work.

Sir Ian Hamilton said that Kipling's death in January 1936 (two days before the death of Kipling's friend, King George V) placed "a full stop to the period when war was a romance and the expansion of our Empire a duty." When his ashes were interred in Poets' Corner of Westminster Abbey, Kipling's pallbearers included the then-prime minister of England, a field marshal, and the admiral of the fleet; the poem "Recessional" was sung as a hymn. Kipling's unfinished autobiography, *Something of Myself*, was published a year after his death.

⌘ ⌘ ⌘

Gunga Din

You may talk o' gin and beer
  When you're quartered safe out 'ere,
An' you're sent to penny-fights° an' Aldershot[1] it;   *skirmishes*
But when it comes to slaughter
5 You will do your work on water,
An' you'll lick the bloomin' boots of 'im that's got it.
Now in Injia's sunny clime,
Where I used to spend my time
A-servin' of 'Er Majesty the Queen,
10 Of all them blackfaced crew
The finest man I knew
Was our regimental bhisti,° Gunga Din.   *water carrier*
     He was "Din! Din! Din!
    You limpin' lump o' brick-dust, Gunga Din!
15   Hi! Slippy *hitherao*![2]
    Water, get it! *Panee lao*,[3]
    You squidgy-nosed old idol, Gunga Din."

The uniform 'e wore
Was nothin' much before,
20 An' rather less than 'arf o' that be'ind,
For a piece o' twisty rag
An' a goatskin water bag
Was all the field equipment 'e could find.
When the sweatin' troop train lay
25 In a sidin' through the day,
Where the 'eat would make your bloomin' eyebrows
    crawl,
We shouted "Harry By!"[4]
Till our throats were bricky-dry,
Then we wopped 'im 'cause 'e couldn't serve us all.
30   It was "Din! Din! Din!

You 'eathen, where the mischief 'ave you been?
    You put some *juldee*[5] in it
    Or I'll *marrow*[6] you this minute
  If you don't fill up my helmet, Gunga Din!"

35 'E would dot an' carry one[7]
Till the longest day was done;
An' 'e didn't seem to know the use o' fear.
If we charged or broke or cut,
You could bet your bloomin' nut,
40 'E'd be waitin' fifty paces right flank rear.
With 'is mussick° on 'is back,   *waterbag*
'E would skip with our attack,
An' watch us till the bugles made "Retire,"[8]
An' for all 'is dirty 'ide
45 'E was white, clear white, inside
When 'e went to tend the wounded under fire!
     It was "Din! Din! Din!"
  With the bullets kickin' dust spots on the green.
     When the cartridges ran out,
50   You could hear the front ranks shout,
  "Hi! ammunition mules an' Gunga Din!"

I shan't forgit the night
When I dropped be'ind the fight
With a bullet where my belt plate should 'a' been.
55 I was chokin' mad with thirst,
An' the man that spied me first
Was our good old grinnin', gruntin' Gunga Din.
'E lifted up my 'ead,
An' he plugged me where I bled,
60 An' 'e guv me 'arf-a-pint o' water green.
It was crawlin' and it stunk,
But of all the drinks I've drunk,

---

[1] *Aldershot* Town southwest of London, site of a military training center.

[2] *Slippy hitherao* I.e., *idhar ao*. Urdu: Come here!

[3] *Panee lao* Urdu: Bring water.

[4] *Harry By* I.e., *arré bhai!* Urdu: in this context, Hey, you!

[5] *juldee* I.e., *juldee karo*. Urdu: hurry!

[6] *marrow* I.e., *maro*. Urdu: hit.

[7] *dot an' carry one* From mathematics: calculate.

[8] *bugles … Retire* Bugles played the call indicating that troops should fall back.

I'm gratefullest to one from Gunga Din.
　　　It was "Din! Din! Din!
65　　　　'Ere's a beggar with a bullet through 'is spleen;
　　　　　'E's chawin' up the ground,
　　　　　An' 'e's kickin' all around:
　　　　For Gawd's sake git the water, Gunga Din!"

　　　'E carried me away
70　　To where a dooli° lay,　　　　　　　　　　stretcher
An' a bullet come an' drilled the beggar clean.
　　　'E put me safe inside,
　　　An' just before 'e died,
"I 'ope you liked your drink," sez Gunga Din.
75　So I'll meet 'im later on
At the place where 'e is gone—
Where it's always double drill and no canteen.
　　　'E'll be squattin' on the coals
　　　Givin' drink to poor damned souls,
80　An' I'll get a swig in hell from Gunga Din!
　　　　　Yes, Din! Din! Din!
　　　You Lazarushian[1]-leather Gunga Din!
　　　　　Though I've belted you and flayed you,
　　　　　By the livin' Gawd that made you,
85　　　You're a better man than I am, Gunga Din!
　　—1890

The Widow at Windsor [2]

'Ave you 'eard o' the Widow at Windsor
　　With a hairy gold crown on 'er 'ead?
She 'as ships on the foam—she 'as millions at 'ome,
　　An' she pays us poor beggars in red.[3]
5　　　　(Ow, poor beggars in red!)
There's 'er nick[4] on the cavalry 'orses,
　　There's 'er mark[5] on the medical stores—

An' 'er troopers° you'll find with a fair　　　troop-ships
　　wind be'ind
10　That takes us to various wars.
　　　　(Poor beggars!—barbarious wars!)
　　　Then 'ere's to the Widow at Windsor,
　　　　An 'ere's to the stores an' the guns,
　　　The men an' the 'orses what makes up the
　　　　forces
　　　　　O' Missis Victorier's sons.
15　　　(Poor beggars! Victorier's sons!)

Walk wide o' the Widow at Windsor,
　　For 'alf o' Creation she owns:
We 'ave bought 'er the same with the sword an' the flame,
　　An' we've salted it down with our bones.
20　　　(Poor beggars!—it's blue with our bones!)
Hands off o' the sons o' the Widow,
　　Hands off o' the goods in 'er shop,
For the kings must come down an' the emperors frown
　　When the Widow at Windsor says "Stop!"
25　　　(Poor beggars!—we're sent to say "Stop!")
　　　Then 'ere's to the lodge o' the Widow,
　　　　From the pole to the tropics it runs—
　　　To the lodge that we tile with the rank an' the file,
　　　　An' open in form with the guns.
30　　　(Poor beggars!—it's always they guns!)

We 'ave 'eard o' the Widow at Windsor,
　　It's safest to leave 'er alone:
For 'er sentries we stand by the sea an' the land
　　Wherever the bugles are blown.
35　　　(Poor beggars!—an' don't we get blown!)
Take 'old o' the Wings o' the Mornin',[6]
　　An' flop round the earth till you're dead;
But you won't get away from the tune that they play
　　To the bloomin' old rag over'ead.
40　　　(Poor beggars!—it's 'ot over'ead!)
　　　Then 'ere's to the sons o' the Widow,
　　　　Wherever, 'owever they roam.
　　　'Ere's all they desire, an' if they require

---

[1] *Lazarushian* Cf. Luke 16; the good Lazarus was a leper/beggar.

[2] *The Widow at Windsor* Queen Victoria, who, upon losing her husband in 1861, went into permanent mourning. (See the "In Context" section below for more information.)

[3] *red* Red coats of British soldiers.

[4] *'er nick* Mark distinguishing animals as belonging to the queen.

[5] *'er mark* "V.R.I.," the Queen's identification mark.

---

[6] *Wings o' the Mornin'* From Psalm 139.9–10: "If I take the wings of the morning, and dwell in the uttermost parts of the sea; / Even there shall thy hand lead me, and thy right hand shall hold me."

A speedy return to their 'ome.
(Poor beggars! they'll never see 'ome!)
45
—1890

Recessional[1]

God of our fathers, known of old,
Lord of our far-flung battle-line,
Beneath whose awful Hand we hold
    Dominion over palm and pine—
5   Lord God of Hosts, be with us yet,
Lest we forget[2]—lest we forget!

The tumult and the shouting dies;
    The captains and the kings depart:
Still stands Thine ancient sacrifice,
10   An humble and a contrite heart.[3]
Lord God of Hosts, be with us yet,
Lest we forget—lest we forget!

Far-called, our navies melt away;
    On dune and headland sinks the fire:
15 Lo, all our pomp of yesterday
    Is one with Nineveh and Tyre![4]
Judge of the nations, spare us yet,
Lest we forget—lest we forget!

If, drunk with sight of power, we loose
20   Wild tongues that have not Thee in awe,
Such boastings as the Gentiles use,
    Or lesser breeds without the law[5]—

Lord God of Hosts, be with us yet,
Lest we forget—lest we forget!

25 For heathen heart that puts her trust
    In reeking tube and iron shard,
All valiant dust that builds on dust,
    And guarding, calls not Thee to guard,
For frantic boast and foolish word—
30 Thy mercy on Thy people, Lord!
—1897

The White Man's Burden

THE UNITED STATES AND THE PHILIPPINE ISLANDS[6]

Take up the White Man's burden—
    Send forth the best ye breed—
Go bind your sons to exile
    To serve your captives' need;
5   To wait in heavy harness
    On fluttered folk and wild—
Your new-caught, sullen peoples,
    Half devil and half child.

Take up the White Man's burden—
10   In patience to abide,
To veil the threat of terror
    And check the show of pride;
By open speech and simple,
    An hundred times made plain.
15 To seek another's profit,
    And work another's gain.

Take up the White Man's burden—
    The savage wars of peace—
Fill full the mouth of Famine
    And bid the sickness cease;
20 And when your goal is nearest
    The end for others sought,

---

[1] *Recessional* Hymn written for Queen Victoria's sixtieth anniversary Jubilee.

[2] *Lest we forget* Cf. Deuteronomy 4.9: "[T]ake heed to thyself, and keep thy soul diligently, lest thou forget the things which thine eyes have seen, and lest they depart from thy heart all the days of thy life: but teach them thy sons, and thy sons' sons."

[3] *contrite heart* Cf. Psalms 51.17: "The sacrifices of God are a broken spirit: a broken and a contrite heart."

[4] *Nineveh and Tyre* Ruined cities that were once capitals of empires.

[5] *Gentiles ... law* Cf. Romans 2.14: "For when the Gentiles, which have not the law, do by nature the things contained in the law, these, having not the law, are a law unto themselves."

[6] *UNITED STATES AND THE PHILIPPINE ISLANDS* Response to the American takeover of the Philippines after the Spanish American War of 1898. (See the "In Context" section below for more information.)

Watch Sloth and heathen Folly
    Bring all your hope to nought.

25 Take up the White Man's burden—
    No tawdry rule of kings,
But toil of serf and sweeper—
    The tale of common things.
The ports ye shall not enter,
30   The roads ye shall not tread,
Go make them with your living,
    And mark them with your dead!

Take up the White Man's burden—
    And reap his old reward:
35 The blame of those ye better,
    The hate of those ye guard—
The cry of hosts ye humour
    (Ah, slowly!) toward the light:—
"Why brought ye us from bondage,
40   Our loved Egyptian night?"

Take up the White Man's burden—
    Ye dare not stoop to less—
Nor call too loud on Freedom
    To cloak your weariness;
45 By all ye cry or whisper,
    By all ye leave or do,
The silent, sullen peoples
    Shall weigh your gods and you.

Take up the White Man's burden—
50   Have done with childish days—
The lightly proffered laurel,[1]
    The easy, ungrudged praise.
Comes now, to search your manhood
    Through all the thankless years,
55 Cold-edged with dear-bought wisdom,
    The judgment of your peers!
—1899

---

[1] *laurel* Leaves of the bay laurel tree are a symbol of victory.

If[2]—

If you can keep your head when all about you
    Are losing theirs and blaming it on you,
If you can trust yourself when all men doubt you,
    But make allowance for their doubting too;
5 If you can wait and not be tired by waiting,
    Or being lied about, don't deal in lies,
Or being hated, don't give way to hating,
    And yet don't look too good, nor talk too wise:

If you can dream—and not make dreams your master;
10   If you can think—and not make thoughts your aim;
If you can meet with Triumph and Disaster
    And treat those two impostors just the same;
If you can bear to hear the truth you've spoken
    Twisted by knaves to make a trap for fools,
15 Or watch the things you gave your life to, broken,
    And stoop and build 'em up with worn out tools:

If you can make one heap of all your winnings
    And risk it on one turn of pitch-and-toss,[3]
And lose, and start again at your beginnings
20   And never breathe a word about your loss;
If you can force your heart and nerve and sinew
    To serve your turn long after they are gone,
And so hold on when there is nothing in you
    Except the Will which says to them: "Hold on!"

25 If you can talk with crowds and keep your virtue,
    Or walk with kings—nor lose the common touch,
If neither foes nor loving friends can hurt you,
    If all men count with you, but none too much;
If you can fill the unforgiving minute
30   With sixty seconds' worth of distance run,
Yours is the earth and everything that's in it,
    And—which is more—you'll be a man, my son!
—1910

---

[2] *If* It has been suggested that this poem may have been written in celebration of Dr. Leander Starr Jameson. Jameson launched the failed Jameson Raid of British troops against the Boers in South Africa in 1895, which ultimately led to the Boer War (1899–1902). Jameson went on to serve as Premier of the Cape Colony from 1904 to 1908.

[3] *pitch-and-toss* Coin tossing game.

The Story of Muhammad Din

"Who is the happy man? He that sees in his own house at home little children crowned with dust, leaping and falling and crying."

Munichandra, translated by Professor Peterson

The polo-ball was an old one, scarred, chipped, and dinted. It stood on the mantlepiece among the pipe-stems which Imam Din, *khitmatgar*,[1] was cleaning for me.

"Does the heaven-born want this ball?" said Imam Din deferentially.

The heaven-born set no particular store by it; but of what use was a polo-ball to a *khitmatgar*?

"By Your Honor's favor, I have a little son. He has seen this ball, and desires it to play with. I do not want it for myself."

No one would for an instant accuse portly old Imam Din of wanting to play with polo-balls. He carried out the battered thing into the verandah; and there followed a hurricane of joyful squeaks, a patter of small feet, and the *thud-thud-thud* of the ball rolling along the ground. Evidently the little son had been waiting outside the door to secure his treasure. But how had he managed to see that polo-ball?

Next day, coming back from office half an hour earlier than usual, I was aware of a small figure in the dining room—a tiny, plump figure in a ridiculously inadequate shirt which came, perhaps, halfway down the tubby stomach. It wandered round the room, thumb in mouth, crooning to itself as it took stock of the pictures. Undoubtedly this was the "little son."

He had no business in my room, of course; but was so deeply absorbed in his discoveries that he never noticed me in the doorway. I stepped into the room and startled him nearly into a fit. He sat down on the ground with a gasp. His eyes opened, and his mouth followed suit. I knew what was coming, and fled, followed by a long, dry howl which reached the servants' quarters far more quickly than any command of mine

had ever done. In ten seconds Imam Din was in the dining room. Then despairing sobs arose, and I returned to find Imam Din admonishing the small sinner who was using most of his shirt as a handkerchief.

"This boy," said Imam Din, judicially, "is a *bud-mash*,[2] a big *budmash*. He will, without doubt, go to the *jail-khana*[3] for his behavior." Renewed yells from the penitent, and an elaborate apology to myself from Imam Din.

"Tell the baby," said I, "that the *Sahib*[4] is not angry, and take him away." Imam Din conveyed my forgiveness to the offender, who had now gathered all his shirt round his neck, stringwise, and the yell subsided into a sob. The two set off for the door. "His name," said Imam Din, as though the name were part of the crime, "is Muhammad Din, and he is a *budmash*." Freed from present danger, Muhammad Din turned round, in his father's arms, and said gravely: "It is true that my name is Muhammad Din, *Tahib*,[5] but I am not a *budmash*. I am a *man*!"

From that day dated my acquaintance with Muhammad Din. Never again did he come into my dining room, but on the neutral ground of the compound, we greeted each other with much state, though our conversation was confined to "*Talaam, Tahib*"[6] from his side, and "*Salaam, Muhammad Din*" from mine. Daily on my return from office, the little white shirt, and the fat little body used to rise from the shade of the creeper-covered trellis where they had been hid; and daily I checked my horse here, that my salutation might not be slurred over or given unseemly.

Muhammad Din never had any companions. He used to trot about the compound, in and out of the castor-oil bushes, on mysterious errands of his own. One day I stumbled upon some of his handiwork far down the ground. He had half buried the polo-ball in dust,

---

[1] *khitmatgar* I.e., *khitmat-ghar*. Urdu: one who serves the household; houseboy.

[2] *budmash* Bad character; rascal.

[3] *jail-khana* Prison/jail.

[4] *Sahib* Title of respect (like "Sir"), used formerly by the natives of India in addressing Europeans.

[5] *Tahib* I.e., Sahib; Muhammad Din has a lisp.

[6] *Talaam, Tahib* Muhammad Din lisps out "Salaam, Sahib," "Peace be upon you, Sir"—an East Indian and Pakistani salutation.

RUDYARD KIPLING

and stuck six shrivelled old marigold flowers in a circle round it. Outside that circle again, was a rude[1] square, traced out in bits of red brick alternating with fragments of broken china; the whole bounded by a little bank of dust. The *bhisti*[2] from the well-curb[3] put in a plea for the small architect, saying that it was only the play of a baby and did not much disfigure my garden.

Heaven knows that I had no intention of touching the child's work then or later; but, that evening, a stroll through the garden brought me unawares full on it; so that I trampled, before I knew, marigold-heads, dust-bank, and fragments of broken soap-dish into confusion past all hope of mending. Next morning I came upon Muhammad Din crying softly to himself over the ruin I had wrought. Someone had cruelly told him that the *Sahib* was very angry with him for spoiling the garden, and had scattered his rubbish using bad language the while. Muhammad Din labored for an hour at effacing every trace of the dust-bank and pottery fragments, and it was with a tearful and apologetic face that he said, "*Talaam Tahib*," when I came home from the office. A hasty inquiry resulted in Imam Din informing Muhammad Din that by my singular favor he was permitted to disport himself as he pleased. Whereat the child took heart and fell to tracing the ground-plan of an edifice which was to eclipse the marigold-polo-ball creation.

For some months, the chubby little eccentricity revolved in his humble orbit among the castor-oil bushes and in the dust; always fashioning magnificent palaces from stale flowers thrown away by the bearer, smooth water-worn pebbles, bits of broken glass, and feathers pulled, I fancy, from my fowls—always alone and always crooning to himself.

A gayly-spotted seashell was dropped one day close to the last of his little buildings; and I looked that Muhammad Din should build something more than ordinarily splendid on the strength of it. Nor was I disappointed. He meditated for the better part of an hour, and his crooning rose to a jubilant song. Then he began tracing in dust. It would certainly be a wondrous palace, this one, for it was two yards long and a yard broad in ground-plan. But the palace was never completed.

Next day there was no Muhammad Din at the head of the carriage-drive, and no "*Talaam Tahib*" to welcome my return. I had grown accustomed to the greeting, and its omission troubled me. Next day, Imam Din told me that the child was suffering slightly from fever and needed quinine.[4] He got the medicine, and an English doctor.

"They have no stamina, these brats," said the doctor, as he left Imam Din's quarters.

A week later, though I would have given much to have avoided it, I met on the road to the Mussalman[5] burying-ground Imam Din, accompanied by one other friend, carrying in his arms, wrapped in a white cloth, all that was left of little Muhammad Din.

—1886

---

[1] *rude* Rough.

[2] *bhisti* Also spelled "bheestie"; servant who carries water from the well.

[3] *well-curb* Border around a well.

[4] *quinine* Medicine used to treat malaria.

[5] *Mussalman* Muslim.

IN CONTEXT

Victoria and Albert

Queen Victoria was widowed when Prince Albert died on 14 December 1861. His partnership with the Queen had been an extraordinarily successful one—as a professional partnership as well as in family life. For many years after his death the Queen was a recluse, so much so that the public began to lose patience with and sympathy for Victoria in her mourning. It was not until the early 1870s that the Queen began to re-emerge. As she did so she gradually regained public favor, and by the time Kipling's "The Widow at Windsor" was published in 1890 she was widely revered. Her 60th Anniversary Jubilee in 1897—for which Kipling composed "Recessional"—was a massive national celebration.

Franz Xaver Winterhalter, *The Royal Family in 1846.*

Queen Victoria and Prince Albert in the early
1850s. (Photograph by Roger Fenton.)

Queen Victoria in mourning, 1867.

Queen Victoria with John Brown, a servant who had been personal ghillie (the term applied to the attendant to a Highland Chief) to Prince Albert and who later served Queen Victoria; Brown is credited with helping to bring the Queen out from seclusion. (Photo by W & D Downy.)

The Queen with Princess Beatrice, Princess Victoria, and great-granddaughter Alice, c. 1885. (Photographer unknown.)

Queen Victoria in the Diamond Jubilee procession, 1897.

Victoria holding the future Edward VIII on the occasion
of his baptism; her son Edward (later Edward VII) and
grandson George (later George V) are in the background.

IN CONTEXT

The "White Man's Burden" in the Philippines

The Philippine Islands had long been a Spanish colony, but Spain's defeat in 1898 at the
hands of American Admiral George Dewey during the Spanish-American War was followed
by an agreement ceding the islands to the United States for $20 million. Local forces (under
Emilio Agninaldo) had been rebelling against the Spanish, and, expecting the American
victory to lead to liberation, declared a republic. The Americans, however, deciding that the
natives were not ready for independence, ruthlessly suppressed the insurrection of Agninaldo's
forces (which continued until 1905). Not until 1946 was the Republic of the Philippines
granted full independence. The American annexation of the islands in 1899 was widely
popular in the United States, but a significant minority loudly protested the expression of
American imperialism that was the occasion for Kipling's famous poem. Following are
excerpts from the platform adopted by one American organization at their founding meeting
in Chicago, 17 October 1899.

from Platform of the American Anti-Imperialist League (1899)

We hold that the policy known as imperialism is hostile to liberty and tends toward militarism, an evil from which it has been our glory to be free. We regret that it has become necessary in the land of Washington and Lincoln to reaffirm that all men, of whatever race or color, are entitled to life, liberty, and the pursuit of happiness. We maintain that governments derive their just powers from the consent of the governed. We insist that the subjugation of any people is "criminal aggression" and open disloyalty to the distinctive principles of our government.

We earnestly condemn the policy of the present national administration in the Philippines. It seeks to extinguish the spirit of 1776[1] in those islands. We deplore the sacrifice of our soldiers and sailors, whose bravery deserves admiration even in an unjust war. We denounce the slaughter of the Filipinos as a needless horror. We protest against the extension of American sovereignty by Spanish methods.

We demand the immediate cessation of the war against liberty, begun by Spain and continued by us. We urge that Congress be promptly convened to announce to the Filipinos our purpose to concede to them the independence for which they have so long fought and which of right is theirs.

The United States have always protested against the doctrine of international law which permits the subjugation of the weak by the strong. A self-governing state cannot accept sovereignty over an unwilling people. The United States cannot act upon the ancient heresy that might makes right.

Imperialists assume that with the destruction of self-government in the Philippines by American hands, all opposition here will cease. This is a grievous error. Much as we abhor the war of "criminal aggression" in the Philippines, greatly as we regret that the blood of the Filipinos is on American hands, we more deeply resent the betrayal of American institutions at home. The real firing line[2] is not in the suburbs of Manila. The foe is of our own household. The attempt of 1861 was to divide the country. That of 1899 is to destroy its fundamental principles and noblest ideals.

Whether the ruthless slaughter of the Filipinos shall end next month or next year is but an incident in a contest that must go on until the Declaration of Independence and the Constitution of the United States are rescued from the hands of their betrayers. Those who dispute about standards of value while the Republic is undermined will be listened to as little as those who would wrangle about the small economies of the household while the house is on fire. The training of a great people for a century, the aspiration for liberty of a vast immigration are forces that will hurl aside those who in the delirium of conquest seek to destroy the character of our institutions.

We deny that the obligation of all citizens to support their Government in times of grave national peril applies to the present situation. If an administration may with impunity ignore the issues upon which it was chosen, deliberately create a condition of war anywhere on the face of the globe, debauch the civil service for spoils to promote the adventure, organize a truth suppressing censorship and demand of all citizens a suspension of judgement and their unanimous support while it chooses to continue the fighting, representative government itself is imperiled.

We propose to contribute to the defeat of any person or party that stands for the forcible subjugation of any people. We shall oppose for reelection all who in the White House or in Congress betray American liberty in pursuit of un-American gains. We still hope that both of our great political parties will support and defend the Declaration of Independence in the closing campaign of the century.

We hold, with Abraham Lincoln, that "no man is good enough to govern another man without that other's consent. When the white man governs himself, that is self-government, but when he governs himself and also governs another man, that is more than self-government—that is

---

[1] *1776*   Year of the American Declaration of Independence, issued near the beginning of the American Revolution.

[2] *firing line*   Battle front.

despotism." "Our reliance is in the love of liberty which God has planted in us. Our defense is in the spirit which prizes liberty as the heritage of all men in all lands. Those who deny freedom to others deserve it not for themselves, and under a just God cannot long retain it."

We cordially invite the co-operation of all men and women who remain loyal to the Declaration of Independence and the Constitution of the United States.

BRITAIN, EMPIRE, AND A WIDER WORLD
CONTEXTS

In the Victorian era colonies in the British Empire were divided into two broad categories. In one category were crown colonies ruled by governments with no direct responsibility to the people they ruled, but only to the Colonial Office and the home country as a whole. The vast majority of the populace in such colonies did not share in the history, religion, or traditions of England or other European cultures, and were brown or black in color; in this category were the bulk of British possessions in Africa, Asia, and the Caribbean. In areas of the Empire where emigration from Britain and other European nations had created a majority or a substantial minority of a population sharing the cultural and racial makeup of "the old country," on the other hand, responsible government became the norm—though the Indigenous residents whose nations had been colonized were often denied voting rights (and many other fundamental rights as well). Under the terms of imperial arrangements in the latter category, administration was still overseen by British authority, but governments with a substantial degree of real power were elected by and responsible to the local settler populace, and were composed of local leaders rather than temporary appointees from abroad. Canada, the Australian colonies, and New Zealand were prominent in this second category.

India was in many ways a special case, with local hereditary rulers in some cases maintaining considerable authority under an umbrella of British rule over the subcontinent, and with this power structure complicated both by the existence of the India Office as a separate government department in Britain, and by the authority wielded (until 1858) by the East India Company. In the seventeenth century, the East India Company, the Hudson's Bay Company, and the Royal Africa Company were among the commercial entities given royal charters, empowering them not only to trade commercially in particular parts of the globe but also to exercise political authority over the local people. The empire continued to establish such charter companies into the late nineteenth century, even as the authority of earlier charter companies was transferred to government of a more conventional sort.

The nature of the Empire also changed in the course of the century, the last three decades of which saw a profound intensification of Britain's economic and ideological investment in imperialism. During this period—known as the "new imperialism"—Britain competed with other European powers to establish control of the territories Europeans saw as being ripe for imperial takeover. The largest arena of competition was the "scramble for Africa," where imperial domination was imposed with unprecedented speed; before 1870, European interest in Africa was focused mainly on coastal trade relationships, and by 1900 most of the continent had been divided among the empires of Europe.

Throughout the history of the British Empire various notions of "Empire" competed with one another. Perhaps the least complicated was the notion that Empire should be based purely on the commercial interests of the imperial power. It was this notion that was foremost in the minds of many commercial adventurers staking out an imperial claim—but also in the minds of many "little Englanders" in the nineteenth century who did not necessarily have any desire to abandon the Empire as a whole, but felt it would be expedient and appropriate to "cut loose" colonies that were perceived to represent a net drain on Britain's resources, financial and otherwise. For others, though, the Empire was a vital symbol of the nation's importance in the world—and of its "greatness" (a word in which power and morality came to be inextricably entangled). Finally, there were those whose notions of Empire were shaped by a hope and a confidence that Britain would improve the lot of its subject peoples—improve their economic conditions, certainly, but also bring to them literacy and an appropriate level of education, what were perceived to be the benefits of Christianity, and a broader set of cultural benefits, as well. It is easy to be cynical about this last set of ideas, and these "enlightened" notions of Empire were undoubtedly hypocritical, patronizing, and racist. That there was also frequently some kernel of altruism in the "enlightened imperialism" of the likes of William Gladstone or David Livingstone, however, is difficult to doubt, even as it must now be plain to all how horrifically misguided such impulses often were.

The pretense that British imperialism constituted a civilizing mission, however, is contradicted by the extremity of the horrors that were endured by the peoples they colonized. After a long struggle, outright slavery had been abolished in most British possessions in 1833, but in certain British colonies in the Caribbean, practices tantamount to slavery continued for decades thereafter—prompting incidents such as the uprising against British Governor Edward Eyre in Jamaica in 1865. Each colony had its own evils, such as the unspeakable atrocities meted out during the suppression of the Indian rebellion in 1857–58, and the brutal treatment accorded the Indigenous peoples of Australia, New Zealand, and Canada.

The feelings of cultural and racial superiority on which rationalizations of the subjugation of other peoples were founded took a variety of forms. The sort of anthropological theorizing that Adam Smith and other eighteenth-century thinkers had engaged in was one discourse that remained popular throughout the nineteenth century. According to this way of thinking, other peoples were not inherently inferior; they were simply at a less fully advanced stage of social and economic organization than were European peoples. An anthropological "stages of development" approach often led to an assumption by the British and other Europeans of a "childish" mentality among peoples elsewhere in the globe, but it also left room for the moral anthropology of Rousseau and others that ascribed to the "noble savage" the attribute of an innocence largely lost to "higher" stages of civilization. (It is this view with which Charles Dickens takes vehement issue in the essay from *Household Words* excerpted in this section.)

Although this approach was widely adopted throughout the Victorian era, pseudo-scientific claims of a biological sort were increasingly made. According to many making such claims, other peoples were not at a lower stage of development (from which they could, with assistance, be raised over the course of time to the level of Europeans); rather they were inherently, biologically inferior, and it would thus always be appropriate to treat them as creatures of a lower order.

One might assume that Victorian writers who deplored, for example, the brutality of conditions for workers in industry in England would also have deplored oppression and brutality overseas. However, this was simply not the case; imperialism and its racist justifications were an integral part of Victorian thought and culture. While John Stuart Mill and some others did indeed hold what could be considered relatively enlightened views on the subject of race and culture, many prominent Victorian writers—such as Charles Dickens, Thomas Carlyle, and John Ruskin—defended profoundly bigoted positions, bolstering the beliefs that have served to justify imperialism and other forms of large-scale racist violence in the Victorian era and beyond it.

⌘ ⌘ ⌘

Indigenous Negotiations

Woollarawarre Bennelong, Letter to Mr. Phillips, 29 August 1796

Born into the Wangal clan of the Eora people, Woollarawarre Bennelong (c. 1764–1813) was among the first Indigenous Australians to come into contact with British colonialists after their 1788 invasion of what is now called New South Wales, Australia. He learned English and traveled to England (1792–95), acting as an important cultural intermediary between his people and the British. Mr. and Mrs. Phillips, to whom the following letter is addressed, cared for him in London while he was ill.

The text below, including footnotes, has been transcribed from the earliest surviving version, a copy of the original letter Bennelong dictated to an unknown scribe; the manuscript (MS 4005) is held by the National Library of Australia.

Sidney Cove, New S. Wales, August 29 1796

Sir

I am very well. I hope you are very well. I live at the governor's. I have every day dinner there. I have not my wife: another black man took her away: we have had muzzy[1] doings: he speared me in the back, but I better now: his name is now[2] Carroway. All my friends alive & well. Not me go to England no more. I am at home now. I hope Sir you send me anything you please Sir. Hope all well in England. I hope Mrs. Phillips is very well. You nurse me Madam when I sick. You very good Madam: thank you Madam, & hope you remember me

Madam, not forget. I know you very well Madam. Madam I want stockings. Thank you Madam; send me two pair stockings. You very good Madam. Thank you Madam. Sir, you give my duty to Lord Sydney.[3] Thank you very good my lord. Very good: hope very well all family. Very well. Sir, send me you please some Handkerchiefs for Pocket. You please Sir send me some shoes: two pair you please Sir.

Bannelong

from Hannah Kilham, *The Claims of West Africa to Christian Instruction, through the Native Languages* (1830)

Hannah Kilham (1774–1832), an English-born convert to Methodism and Quakerism, was known for her work in West Africa as a missionary, translator, and educator. After Britain abolished the slave trade in 1807, Sierra Leone became home to many previously enslaved peoples from throughout the African continent who spoke a variety of distinct languages.

Kilham's text is excerpted from an 1830 pamphlet published in London.

The colony of Sierra Leone, interesting and important as it is, when regarded as a station inhabited by Africans from more than thirty different tribes, has not yet, it must be allowed, exhibited all those encouraging marks of advancement, either in civil or religious knowledge, which have been anxiously desired, and which indeed are still hoped for by many who look to this colony as a point from which, through the favor of divine goodness, may one day be extended the blessings of civilization and Christian instruction to many nations on the wide and almost unexplored continent of Africa.

This station having been formed and maintained on a principle of benevolent concern for the good of Africa,

[1] [Transcriber's note]   Meaning bad.

[2] [Transcriber's note]   They frequently change their names. [Indigenous Australians regularly use different names, or variations of one name, at different points in their lives, depending on age, status, and relationship of the speaker to the person named; names can also change or cease to be used on the deaths of the giver of a name, similarly named people, other community members, or the named person themselves.]

[3] *Lord Sydney*   Thomas Townshend, 1st Viscount Sydney (1733–1800), British politician and Cabinet member who originated the plan to settle convicts in what is now New South Wales; Sydney, Australia, was named after him. Bennelong met Sydney while in London.

and as a place of reception for the unhappy victims of cruelty and oppression, when rescued from the slave-ships, presents a very peculiar and a very powerful claim to our interest and regard[.] ...

And with regard to education, from what has been observed of African capacity, when intelligible means of instruction are given, it appears very evident, that were suitable measures adopted to prepare for them the elements of instruction, in a clear and simple form, these children would be far from being backward, either in applying to the acquisition of useful knowledge, or in imbibing what they are taught. But in the system hitherto pursued in the schools, of using English lessons only, for children, to whom English is quite a foreign language, (excepting that they have a very few words in occasional and colloquial use,) whilst the native languages, for conversation, are of course in general use among themselves, can it be expected that the lessons thus learned should prove any more than mere *sound* to the pupil? What would be the consequence, if we gave to an English child, at home, a Latin book to learn without any English translation, and just taught it to spell and read the Latin words? Would the child, by practicing in this way, acquire a knowledge of that language? Assuredly not: and it would be very unjust to complain of the want of capacity in the Africans in Sierra Leone, as the cause of their not having advanced more than they have, when that which has been offered to them as a medium of school instruction, must have been to them quite as unintelligible as a French, or Latin, or German book, without translation, would be to an English child.

... But, alas for poor Africa! how little has yet been done for that wide continent, with its thousands of peopled towns and villages: how little is yet known there of the great and important work of Scripture translations, or of the widely extended labors of the British and Foreign Bible Society, the rivers and streams of whose Christian bounty have so richly flowed, even far and near, in every other quarter of the habitable world. ...

It should never be forgotten, that translations are as indispensably requisite to the cause of Christian education in heathen lands, as schools are necessary to the effectual diffusion of the Holy Scriptures. We must be satisfied to commence with the earliest steps, and should surely feel great thankfulness for the favor of being permitted to take any step in a cause so precious as that of preparing, in the least degree, to open the way for our African brethren to a knowledge of those sacred records which direct to "Him of whom Moses and the prophets wrote."[1]

With an object in view so important, and so delightful to every feeling of Christian love, it is therefore proposed, that a few, to whom the advancement of truth and righteousness on the earth is precious, should, without further delay make arrangements for the introduction of a few native Africans into this country, selected from some of the most important tribes known in the colony of Sierra Leone, or other parts of West Africa ... and brought over with their own concurrence and desire, to be taught here the English language, and prepared to give assistance in translating from English into their own languages.

from Thomas Babington Macaulay, "Minute on Indian Education" (1835)

In this 1835 speech, Macaulay, then a member of the Council of India, argued that the sum set aside by the British Parliament for the education of Indian citizens should be used to teach the English language and the scientific and cultural advancements of Britain, rather than to promote the study of India's native cultures and languages. In the paragraphs immediately preceding this excerpt, Macaulay put forward the claim that the people of India should not be taught in any of their native

---

[1] *Him ... wrote* I.e., Jesus. See John 1.45: "Philip findeth Nathanael, and saith unto him, We have found him, of whom Moses in the law, and the prophets, did write, Jesus of Nazareth."

languages, as the various dialects are "poor and rude," and "contain neither literary nor scientific information." In addition, he asserted, the historical, philosophical, and literary achievements of works written in European languages far surpassed their Sanskrit, Arabic, and Persian equivalents.

...

How, then, stands the case? We have to educate a people who cannot at present be educated by means of their mother-tongue. We must teach them some foreign language. The claims of our own language it is hardly necessary to recapitulate. It stands preeminent even among the languages of the west. It abounds with works of imagination not inferior to the noblest which Greece has bequeathed to us; with models of every species of eloquence; with historical compositions, which, considered merely as narratives, have seldom been surpassed, and which, considered as vehicles of ethical and political instruction, have never been equalled; with just and lively representations of human life and human nature; with the most profound speculations on metaphysics, morals, government, jurisprudence,[1] and trade; with full and correct information respecting every experimental science which tends to preserve the health, to increase the comfort, or to expand the intellect of man. Whoever knows that language has ready access to all the vast intellectual wealth which all the wisest nations of the earth have created and hoarded in the course of ninety generations. It may safely be said that the literature now extant in that language is of far greater value than all the literature which three hundred years ago was extant in all the languages of the world together. Nor is this all. In India, English is the language spoken by the ruling class. It is spoken by the higher class of natives at the seats of government. It is likely to become the language of commerce throughout the seas of the East. It is the language of two great European communities which are rising, the one in the south of Africa, the other in Australasia; communities which are every year becoming more important, and more closely connected with our Indian Empire. Whether we look at the intrinsic value of our literature, or at the particular situation of this country, we shall see the strongest reason to think that, of all foreign tongues, the English tongue is that which would be the most useful to our native subjects.

The question now before us is simply whether, when it is in our power to teach this language, we shall teach languages in which, by universal confession, there are no books on any subject which deserve to be compared to our own; whether, when we can teach European science, we shall teach systems which, by universal confession, whenever they differ from those of Europe, differ for the worse; and whether, when we can patronize sound philosophy and true history, we shall countenance, at the public expense, medical doctrines which would disgrace an English farrier,[2] astronomy which would move laughter in girls at an English boarding-school, history abounding with kings thirty feet high, and reigns thirty thousand years long, and geography made up of seas of treacle[3] and seas of butter.

We are not without experience to guide us. History furnishes several analogous cases, and they all teach the same lesson. There are in modern times, to go no further, two memorable instances of a great impulse given to the mind of a whole society—of prejudices overthrown, of knowledge diffused, of taste purified, of arts and sciences planted in countries which had recently been ignorant and barbarous.

The first instance to which I refer is the great revival of letters among the western nations at the close of the fifteenth, and the beginning of the sixteenth, century. At that time almost everything that was worth reading was contained in the writings of the ancient Greeks and

---

[1] *jurisprudence* Law.

[2] *farrier* One who shoes or cares for horses.

[3] *treacle* Syrup produced by the process of refining sugar.

Romans. Had our ancestors acted as the Committee of Public Instruction has hitherto acted;[1] had they neglected the language of Cicero and Tacitus;[2] had they confined their attention to the old dialects of our own island; had they printed nothing, and taught nothing at the universities, but chronicles in Anglo-Saxon, and romances in Norman-French, would England have been what she now is? What the Greek and Latin were to the contemporaries of More and Ascham,[3] our tongue is to the people of India. The literature of England is now more valuable than that of classical antiquity. I doubt whether the Sanskrit literature be as valuable as that of our Saxon and Norman progenitors. In some departments—in history, for example—I am certain that it is much less so.

Another instance may be said to be still before our eyes. Within the last hundred and twenty years, a nation which had previously been in a state as barbarous as that in which our ancestors were before the crusades, has gradually emerged from the ignorance in which it was sunk, and has taken its place among civilized communities—I speak of Russia. There is now in that country a large educated class, abounding with persons fit to serve the state in the highest functions, and in no wise inferior to the most accomplished men who adorn the best circles of Paris and London. There is reason to hope that this vast empire, which in the time of our grandfathers was probably behind the Punjab,[4] may, in the time of our grandchildren, be pressing close on France and Britain in the career of improvement. And how was this change effected? Not by flattering national prejudices; not by feeding the mind of the young Muscovite[5] with old women's stories which his rude fathers had believed; not by filling his head with lying legends about St. Nicholas;[6] not by encouraging him to study the great question, whether the world was or was not created on the 13th of September; not by calling him "a learned native," when he has mastered all these points of knowledge: but by teaching him those foreign languages in which the greatest mass of information had been laid up, and thus putting all that information within his reach. The languages of Western Europe civilized Russia. I cannot doubt that they will do for the Hindu what they have done for the Tartar.[7] …

It is impossible for us, with our limited means, to attempt to educate the body of the people. We must at present do our best to form a class who may be interpreters between us and the millions whom we govern; a class of persons, Indian in blood and colour, but English in taste, in opinions, in morals, and in intellect. To that class we may leave it to refine the vernacular dialects of the country, to enrich those dialects with terms of science borrowed from the Western nomenclature, and to render them by degrees fit vehicles for conveying knowledge to the great mass of the population.

---

[1] *Committee … acted* The Committee of Public Instruction had hitherto used the allocated funds solely for promoting the study of Arabic, Persian, and Sanskrit literature and for encouraging those "learned natives" who studied the science, religions, and histories of their native cultures.

[2] *Cicero* Roman orator of the first century BCE; *Tacitus* First-century CE author of two works of Roman history, *Histories* and *Annals*.

[3] *More* Sir Thomas More (1478–1535), English lawyer and humanist scholar, author of *Utopia*; *Ascham* Roger Ascham (1515–68), Latin Secretary to Edward VI, Mary I, and Elizabeth I.

[4] *Punjab* Region in the northwest of British India, today divided between India and Pakistan.

[5] *Muscovite* Resident of Moscow.

[6] *St. Nicholas* Patron saint of sailors, revered in the Orthodox Christian tradition dominant in Russia.

[7] *Tartar* Here, Russian. The term originally referred to the nomadic Turkic and Mongol peoples of Central Asia and carried pejorative connotations of savagery and barbarism.

Felice Beato, an Italian-born British photographer, visited India early in 1858, at a time when much of the country was still engulfed in the uprising against British rule that had begun the year before. The photographs Beato took in India are some of the earliest extant photographs of battle scenes. This image depicts the aftermath of a massacre by British forces of over two thousand sepoys—native Indian troops who had joined the uprising—that took place in the Sikandar Bagh, a building in the fiercely fought-over city of Lucknow. The British war correspondent William Howard Russell visited the Sikandar Bagh on 12 March 1858, around the same time as Beato did, and wrote that "I walked as far as I could venture among the skeletons."

from Report of a Speech by William Charles Wentworth, Australian Legislative Council (1844)

In 1844 the Indigenous populace in Australia probably still outnumbered that of the whites. Official policy called for "amity and kindness" and forbade "any unnecessary interruption" of aboriginal existence, but, as the excerpt below suggests, attitudes towards native peoples that prevailed were often brutally harsh.

He could not see if the whites in this colony were to go out into the land and possess it, that the Government had much to do with them. No doubt there would be battles between the settlers and the border tribes; but they might be settled without the aid of the Government. The civilized people had come in and the savage must go back. They must go on progressing until their dominancy was established, and therefore he could think that no measure was wise or merciful to the blacks which clothed them with a degree of seeming protection, which their position would not allow them to maintain. ... It was not the policy of a wise Government to attempt the perpetuation of the aboriginal race of New South Wales. ... They must give way before the arms, aye! even the diseases of civilized nations—they must give way before they attain the power of those nations.

from Anonymous, "Australia," North British Review (1846)

This review article makes clear that Indigenous dispossession by settler colonial societies was understood even in the early nineteenth century, at least by some Britons, as grossly unjust and abhorrent.

One of the most revolting and disgraceful sophisms[1] by which private cupidity[1] has successfully deluded the British Government into measures for the interests of a few individuals, under the pretext of a principle of public law and right, sanctioned by reason and religion, is that the native uncivilized inhabitants of a country, the wild aborigines, are not the rightful owners of the land of their nativity, the land which they merely live upon, but do not cultivate; that the foreign colonists, who intrude into, settle on, and cultivate this land, become, *ipso facto*,[2] the legitimate owners, and may expel the aborigines who do not cultivate it, but merely live upon it by hunting, fishing, and gathering the roots, fruits, and spontaneous products of the soil; and may do so justly, by the law of God and man. The natives have no rights of property, according to this sophism, in the soil of their native land, because they do not plough, sow, and reap, and make it available for a civilized subsistence. ...

The earth is no doubt given to man for his support, and in a civilized, rather than in a savage state; but are we to conclude from this that we are to despoil, expel, or massacre our fellow-men who are in a savage state, instead of reclaiming, and enlightening, and civilizing them, if we can, and letting them alone if we cannot? The use and cultivation of that land are but relative terms. The savage who merely hunts over it, uses it for his subsistence as well as the farmer who ploughs and sows every foot of it. ... Civilization itself is but a relative term, and can confer no legitimate right on man in one state, to appropriate to themselves what is not their own, but the neglected property of men in another state. ... The principle and the practice of our colonization in Australia and New Zealand will be the indelible blot on British history in the nineteenth century.

---

[1] *sophisms* Fallacious arguments, often used to mislead or to advance an agenda; *cupidity* Desire for wealth.

[2] *ipso facto* Latin: by the fact itself; as a direct consequence.

Eliza M., "Account of Cape Town," *King William's Town Gazette* (1863)

The following account (brought to light by M.J. Daymond et al. and the *Women Writing Africa Project*[1]) is one of the most remarkable literary descriptions we have of the world of nineteenth-century British colonialism from the point of view of one of the colonized. King William's Town was a small town some 500 miles east of Cape Town, and Eliza M., as she was identified in the *King William's Town Gazette*, had attended school at St. Matthew's Mission in the area. As Daymond et al. suggest, such a piece as this would in all likelihood have "been written as a school exercise." It would have been published, they speculate, "partly because its naiveté was amusing to the whites, but also because it was proof of the civilizing policies of the missionaries. It was translated from Xhosa into English by an unknown translator." What may have seemed "amusing naiveté" to nineteenth-century settlers is more likely to strike the modern reader as a style of elemental freshness.

We left East London on the Sunday, while it was raining; the sea was fighting very much, and there were soldiers going to England and their wives. On the Tuesday we arrived at Algoa Bay, and boats came to fetch the people who were going there, and other people came in. The ship went off the same day. A great wind blew, and I thought myself that if it had been another ship, it would not have been able to go on, but in its going, it kept twisting about, it did not go straight, but it went well on the day of our arrival, for the wind was good. We arrived on the Friday. While I was in the ship, I forgot I was on the water, it was like a house inside, but outside it was not like a house. There is everything that is kept at home; there were fowls and sheep and pigs, and slaughtering every day. I kept looking at the thing which makes the ship go. There are two horses inside, made of iron, which make it go; and

when I looked inside, it was very frightful. There are many bed-rooms inside. The ship we were in is named the *Norman*, it is a steamer. It was unpleasant when nothing appeared, but when we left the Bay, we saw the mountains till we got to the Cape. One mountain is called the Lion's Head, and another is called Green Point, and I myself saw those mountains. That which is called the Lion's Head, is like a lion asleep. And another mountain above the town is that called Table Mountain; nevertheless it is not like a table, still that name is proper for it.

Before I came into the town, my heart said, "this place is not large," but when I entered it, I wondered, and was afraid. Oh, we slept that day. I have forgotten to relate something I saw the day I arrived. I saw black people, and I thought they were our kind, but they are not; they are Slams, called in English, Malays. Also, I was astonished at their large hats, pointed at the top, and large below. I saw some making baskets of reeds, and I wished I knew how to do it. On the Saturday evening, we went to a shop to buy butter and bread. At night lights were hung up throughout the whole town. I had thought we were going to walk in the darkness. I have not yet seen houses built with grass, like those we live in, they are high beautiful houses. The roads where people walk, are very fine. I have not yet seen a dirty, muddy place in the whole town. On the Sunday, bells sounded; there is one big one, and other small ones; we went to service in the great church.

Early on the Monday, wagons came about to sell things. Really people here get these things for nothing from their owners. A person can get men's trousers for three shillings each, yet in other places a person can never get them for that money. You can get three pairs of stockings for a shilling, a child's cap for a penny; you can get a width of a dress for threepence, if it is five widths, it is a shilling and threepence. There are little wagons, the man who drives the horses sits behind, the proprietor does nothing, he sits so.

Another thing. The shoes of the Malays astonished me. There is a heel, and yonder on before a piece of wood sticks out, and they put it between their toes, and so make a clattering like the Germans. As things are to be got for

---

[1] *Women Writing Africa Project*   M.J. Daymond et al., eds., *Women Writing Africa: The Southern Region* (New York: The Feminist Press, 2003), 98–104.

such little money, how cheap must they be in England!

On Friday I saw a man riding in a wagon, there was a barrel inside and a cross-bar, and the water came out there. I don't know how it came out. It watered the new road, which is being made. And on Tuesday I saw people working at slates, taking off their ends—it was a great heap; the people who were at work were four. On the day of our arrival, a house was burnt, the people escaped, but I don't know whether the goods escaped. There are carts which go every day, carrying earth to throw on the road which is being mended, drawn by one horse.

There is a house where there are all kinds of beasts, and there are figures of black people, as if they were alive; their blackness is very ugly; also the bones of a man when he is dead, and birds and elephants, and lions, and tigers and sea-shells. I was afraid of those people, and the skeleton. There is also an ape holding Indian Corn, and there are monkeys.

In the evening we went out again, we went to the houses of the Malays; we went to see their decorations, for they were rejoicing because their days of fasting were ended. They were very beautiful; they had made flowers of paper, you would never think they were made of paper. We went for the sole purpose of seeing these works. They made a great noise, singing as they walked; you would laugh to see the children dancing outside and clapping their hands.

There are also wagons there for the sale of fish. The proprietors sound a thing like a horn to announce that he who wishes to buy let him buy. There are others for collecting dust-heaps, they ring a bell. There are vehicles to convey two people, he who drives the horses, and he who sits inside. In some there are windows and lights lit at night: those windows are two.

There are not many trees in the town; in some places there are not many at all, but in one place it is like the bush; it is pleasant underneath the trees; there are stools to sit on when a person is tired. That path is very long; I saw two Newfoundland dogs. I did not know that I should ever come to see them when I heard them spoken of. They are dogs with large heads and great long ears; the hair is like sheep's wool, and they have

great claws; they are suited to assist people. It seemed as if they could swallow me without chewing; I was very much afraid, but one was not very big, it was about the size of the dogs of black people, when it barks, it says so with a great voice. Also, I saw sheep rather unlike others, in the tail here it was very large, the head was small, and the body was large and fat.

I have forgotten to mention something which I ought to have said before; when I came out of the ship and walked on land the earth seemed to move, and when I entered a house, it seemed to imitate the sailing of a ship, and when I lay down it seemed to move.

I saw an ox-wagon here, but I had not imagined that I should see a wagon.

We go to a very large beautiful Church; I don't forget the people who sing, the English; the prayers are said with thin voices as if it were singing; but the chief thing done is singing frequently, all the while there is continually singing, and then sitting. There is a Kafir[1] school here; I went one day, they were reading; they can read well; there are also carpenters &c.

There is another place besides that which I said is like the bush, and in that place there are trees and flowers, and two fountains; a thing is stuck in, and the water comes out above. I saw the date-tree when it is young; it is one leaf, yet when it is grown, it is a very large tree. In that place there are wild birds, doves are there, and those birds which the English call canaries, and a very beautiful bird, its tail is long, its bill is red.

Yesterday the soldiers had sports, the music-band played, and when they finished playing they fired. They were many, and they fired together. And as we were walking, they fired; I was very much startled and afraid. And to-day they are playing the music. It seems to-day it exceeds in sweetness, I mean its sound.

There came a person here who is a Kafir. I rejoiced very much when I heard that he too was one. He asked me what I had come to do here; I said "I am only travelling." He asked whether I was a prisoner, and I

---

[1] *Kafir*   During the colonial period, this word was used as a blanket term for all Black South Africans. It acquired openly derogatory connotations during the apartheid era in South Africa, and today its use there is considered unacceptable and is legally actionable.

said "No." He said he was very glad, he had thought I was a prisoner. I told him that I was going away again, and he said "May you go in peace, the Lord preserve you well till you arrive whence you came." I never saw a person like him of such kindness; he said he had come here to learn, he came from where I did; but I should not have known him to be a Kafir, and he did not know that I was one.

There are creatures which are eaten; they come from the sea, their name is called crawfish, they are frightful in appearance, yet their flesh is very fine and white.

The person of this house is a dyer of clothes, the white he makes red, and the red green, and the brown he makes black. I saw the wood with which they dye. Soap is cut in pieces, and put in water, and heated and boiled well, and continually stirred. This thing—dyeing clothes, is a great work. Water is even in the house; I don't know where it comes from, a person turns a thing, and fresh water comes out as if it were of a river.

There are also carts for selling meat, and for selling bread. I saw the fire-wagon, I did nothing but wonder. I did not know that it was such a big thing. It is long, with many wheels, they are not so large as those of an ox-wagon; people sit in places inside. The wheels run on metal; I say I could do nothing but wonder very much. I had not thought that it was such a great thing. And when it is about to proceed it says "Sh!" I don't know whether it is the boiling of the water; it hastens exceedingly, a person would be unable to notice it well, yet now some people say that this is a small one which I have seen. If it treads on anything, it must smash it, it is a very great thing. I shall never forget it. Where I saw it, the place was fenced on both sides, and I beheld it from the outside. I entered it another week after I had seen it; we went to Somerset West and slept one night. In the morning we returned by it: when I was inside, the earth seemed to move; it is pleasant to ride inside. I end now although this is not all the news about it. When I was in it, I saw a sugar plant; it is not a large plant, it is short with red flowers. I saw other trees at Somerset West which I had never seen before.

One day I saw people going to a burial, the carriages were black, but that people should wear black clothes is done also among the natives where a person has died; there were stuck up black feathers, and on the graves were placed stones with writing; the name of the person was written, and the years of his age, and the year in which he died.

I have seen to-day another thing which I did not know of, that thing which is said to be always done by white people in this month of May. They make themselves black people, they smear themselves with something black, with red patches on the cheeks; a thing is made with evergreens, and a man is put inside, and two people carry it, and another man carries a pan, and goes begging for money.

Another thing which I saw during the past month, was people going to the Governor's house—little chiefs, and chiefs of the soldiers, some had hats with red and white feathers, and silver coats, and gold swords, and the bishop went too. I heard it said that they were going to hear the things which were about to be spoken by people who had come from Graham's Town, King William's Town, Beaufort, and other places; it was said that these people were going to speak of the state of those towns and the doings of the people who live there. I do not say that those coats were really of gold, I say there was gold on some parts of them, on the arms and the back.

Also I have seen the fruit of the tree which the English call the chestnut; I did not see what the tree is like, the fruit is nice, the outside of it is hard; when you eat it it is sweet and edible like the potato, you can roast it or boil it. There is another fruit called Banana in English, it also is a nice fruit; it is not boiled or roasted, it is eaten like other fruits. There is a great white sweet potato, it is called Sweet Potato; those potatoes are very large, I had never seen them before, they are nearly all long: I do not know whether they are the potatoes named "Medicine" by the Fingoes.

I am puzzled to know how to begin to relate what was done yesterday, but I will try. Yesterday was said to be the wedding-day of the Great Son of Victoria,[1] but it

---

[1] *the wedding-day ... Victoria* Albert Edward (1841–1910), Queen Victoria's eldest son and the future King Edward VII, married Alexandra of Denmark in March 1863.

was not really the day of his marriage, for he has been married some time. The thing first done was arranging the children of the schools and I was there too. All walked in threes, going from one street to another. When we left the school-house we took up our station on an open piece of ground, other people climbed on the houses, and others looked on from below. On one house where we were standing there was the figure of a man like a king, a red cloth was put as if it were held by him, it is called in English a flag. Amongst all of us there were flags of different beautiful kinds; we stood there a great while, till we saw a multitude of soldiers and their officers and little chiefs and different sorts of people: one set wore clothes all alike, another had different clothes and ancient hats which were worn by the people of that time. All these now went in front, a very long line, then followed the ranks of another school, and we came after them. When we had finished going through many streets, we went to stand in another open spot of ground. All the time we were walking we were singing the song of Victoria. And there we saw the Governor and his wife; we all saluted. Although it seems that I have written a great deal I have not yet wondered at the things done at night, but let me finish those of the day. We were given food. We saw boats going along with people inside and boys wearing red clothes; there followed one with an old man, his hairs were long and white. There was a woman at his side wearing short clothes. Other boats followed with people in them, all the time they were appearing the drum and trumpets were sounded. I don't know how I shall make myself understood. I never saw such a beautiful thing; some of the men wore short dresses and short coats, and others wore short trousers like those of the French. All these things were red. When we had finished walking we went to stand in an open piece of ground, then we all went home. I do not know if any other things were done.

We went out again in the evening to see the fire-works. First we went into the gardens, where there were what I shall call candles; but nevertheless they are not called so in English. They were lights put inside little red and green glasses—When I was at a distance I thought they were little round things, all these were

hung up and fastened in the trees,—there were some large ones and there were others not put in glasses.

We walked and went to a great crowd of people, we could not tell what we should do to see that which we came to see. There we saw a tall man with a high hat, I did not understand how it was made, and another man wearing women's clothes continually playing with that tall man. All these things have their names in English, some were called *Punch & Judy*, *Spectre*, *Father of the Doomed Arm-chair*, or the *Maid, the Murderer and the Midnight Avenger*,[1] and many other plays besides these. We passed on from that woman and man and went to see white people smeared with soot, they went into a house made of a tent where there were stools, and two came out and spoke to the people saying, "Ladies and gentlemen, come in and see what we have got here inside." Some went in and others did not, afterwards they opened that the people might see; there were black people sitting on chairs and singing. So we left; at the entrance of the garden there was written in letters of fire, "GOD bless Albert and Alexandra." In another place there were other things of fire, that place is called in English the Parade, where there was a thing like a light-house, on all sides there were candles. Some people sent up fire from Table Mountain, others from Green Point, others sent up fire in the midst of the town, it went up and came down again.

Besides these things there was another thing done, an ox was baked whole, the legs were not removed, only the inside and the hoofs. Many tables were set under-neath the trees; that ox was intended for the poor people.

I am going to end now; I am very glad that I was brought here to see things which I never thought I should see.

There is another thing which has lately taken place, the birthday of Queen Victoria.[2] Two balloons were made, no one went in them, there were only lights. That sort is called fire-balloons. The first was sent up; it rose very high till it was like a star: I did not see it again

---

1 *Spectre … Avenger* Popular plays of the period.

2 *the birthday of Queen Victoria* 24 May.

where it went. The other reappeared, it did not rise high like the first, it burnt, and fire came down like two stars.

I saw where newspapers are printed; four people were at work. I do not know what I shall say to tell about it. There is a thing which folds the papers and another thing which continually receives them. It made us sleepy.

E.M.
Translator unknown

from Disasi Makulo, *The Life of Disasi Makulo*[1] (c. 1940, 1983)

> Born in the Congo, Disasi Makulo (c. 1871–1941) was enslaved as a child by Afro-Arab raiders, then purchased along with a number of other children by the explorer and colonizer Henry Stanley (1841–1904). Makulo came to be educated at a missionary school in Leopoldville (now Kinshasa), and as an adult he became a Christian missionary himself. Eventually he recounted his life story to his son, probably not long before his death in 1941; the resulting narrative was first published in Kinshasa in 1983. The excerpt presented here is from the first and longest chapter in the narrative. The translation, from the original French, is fairly literal; notably, it preserves the narrator's habit of shifting between past and present tenses.

from BIRTH AND CHILDHOOD OF DISASI MAKULO

My name is Makulo, Tolukato, Disasi, Samson, son of Asalo and Boheheli, from Bandio village, the Turumbu tribe in the Basoko Territory, Tshopo Province.[2]

I was born at the time when the white man had not yet arrived in our region. Back then, we did not know that there existed in the world human beings who had skin different from ours.

But alas! One day some people living along the river came to visit my parents. In their conversation, they said that they had seen something bizarre, perhaps a ghost, on the river. "We have seen," they said, "a huge mysterious canoe, which moves entirely on its own.[3] In this canoe there is a man all white, like an albino, and entirely clothed—one could not see anything except his head and his arms. He has some black men with him."

A long while after, some other rumors were heard; this time it was an army that had come from upriver. They were Arabs, called Batambatamba by the natives. After these slave traders had invaded Eastern Congo and reached Kisangani,[4] they then went down the river, equipped with their weapons, ravaging, burning villages, capturing and killing people mercilessly.

... Their grand chief Motipoli, or Tippo-Tip,[5] led this army, which was composed of true Arabs and people from the east of the country—people who had been first decimated and then forced to take up arms to fight their own compatriots. ...

The Batambatamba ... crossed the Aruwimi River and infiltrated the Turumbu region, ravaging, shooting, and capturing people. Those who had been the first to see them carrying their weapons ran to alert the rest of the population by crying: "We have seen people going back and forth: they carry a sort of hollow stick, when they hit it, a noise is heard—*PAM PAM!*—and then it sends out shots that wound and kill men. It's terrible!"

This news spread and sowed terror throughout the tribe. The village chiefs and the [people] gathered together in order to take measures to drive away these evildoers. Having learned that their camp was in Yalemba, a village situated by the river, they unanimously resolved to go and fight. The warriors gathered. After making their preparations, they went there during

---

1 *The Life of Disasi Makulo* Translated by Genevieve Kirk and Ian Johnston for Broadview Press, 2019.

2 *Tshopo Province* Region in the north-central part of what is today the Democratic Republic of Congo.

3 *a huge ... its own* On his 1875–77 expedition to the Congo, Stanley and his party traveled on *The Lady Alice*, a 40-foot boat powered by one sail.

4 *Kisangani* Town on the Congo River, today the capital of Tshopo Province; known as Stanleyville during the colonial era in the Congo.

5 *Tippo-Tip* Tippu Tip was the nickname of Hamad bin Muhammad bin Juma bin Rajab el Murjebi (1832–1905), an Afro-Arab merchant and explorer from Zanzibar who led many trading and enslaving expeditions into Central Africa, including the Congo.

the night. Having surrounded the camp, they began to cry, "Attack it!" Awakened by the noise and wanting to know what was happening, the Batambatamba were received by blows of spears. Many of them were wounded and one man was killed. No longer capable of resisting, they cleared out hurriedly[.] …

The natives, all joyful for their victory, returned to their villages singing and jumping for joy, believing it was the end. My father, Asalo, who was among the fighters, told my mother, Boheheli, as well as his brother Akambu, who had accompanied him: "Now the war is over, let's go back home because we must to go to Makoto to prepare the oil."[1]

My father, my mother, my little brother Kengo, and my two sisters set off for Makoto, while my uncle Akambu, my aunt Inangbelema, and their two children continued on for the village of Baonde. Upon their return, they stopped at Makoto, where we were, and spent the night. The next day, when they wanted to continue for Bandio, I asked my father and mother if I could go with my uncle, but my mother would not [agree]. Seeing this, I started screaming and crying insistently. My father then said, "Let him go."

All joyful, I went on my way laughing, believing I was on a happy journey: but this joy and laughter were only a farewell.

It was very hot that day. We arrived at a creek called Lohulu in between Makoto and Bandio; my uncle and I decided to take a bath. Aunt Inangbelema waited for us a certain distance from there. As we happily swam and splashed, the Batambatamba heard us and came and surrounded us. My aunt, to comfort her crying baby, was singing chants; none of us thought we could be in danger.

Suddenly, we heard a cry: "Help! Help! Brother Akambu, the warriors are assaulting me …"

Hastily leaving the bath, we saw my aunt already in the hands of the enemy. One of the assailants ripped the

baby from its mother's hands and went to drop it on the red ants. Terrified, none of us could approach. Uncle Akambu and my little cousin fled and hid themselves in the bushes. Me, I was standing a little ways away, waiting to see what they wanted to do to my aunt; unfortunately, one of these men saw me, ran, and managed to catch me. They also captured Uncle Akambu and my little cousin.

After our capture, those men brought us to our village of Bandio. Along the way, they continued to seize other people. Some people from our home followed behind us, and as they were moving along this path they heard the cries of a baby. As they approached, they saw the poor child had been attacked by ants. [They] took it and brought it to my parents' home in Makoto. It was these men who reported our capture to our parents.

My parents, upon learning this, came in haste to find us. While lamenting and crying, they begged these people to leave us alone, but our tears and our complaints did not affect them at all.

After four days, we left our village and were brought to the village of Yamokanda. That's where the one who was their chief, Montipoli or Tippo-Tip, was staying; it was to this place that we captives were bought. Many captives, whose parents had brought ivory, were released. My father also brought some ivory tips, but Tippo-Tip told him that it was not enough [to pay] for four people [to be released]. He released my Uncle Akambu, Aunt Inangbelema, and my cousin. As for me, he said to them, "Return home to search for two more ivory tips." I was left alone in the midst of the other captives who had not been ransomed.

The same day, after my parents' departure to search for ivory, Tippo-Tip orders his soldiers to cross to Camp Bandu. We leave Yamokanda amid cries, tears, and lamentations. The parents, in desperation, threw themselves on the ground, shouting heartbreaking cries. All the adults were tied up and put in chains; as for us, the children, we were treated kindly because, as our guard told us, they wanted to educate us and make us their fellow citizens.

---

[1] [Note from the original French publication]   Makoto means palm tree or place where one prepares palm oil. [The oil palm tree has a variety of uses in the traditional cultures of the Congo basin: oil for cooking is produced from its kernels, seeds and roots are used for food, and wine is produced from its sap.]

Soon we arrived at the bank of the Bokbili River, where we found several large canoes tied up, ready for us. One of these was reserved exclusively for us, the little ones. After all the other captives had embarked, we also took our place on ours. Very slowly the canoes drifted, and there we were, far from the banks of the river. All that could be heard during this gloomy journey was moans and sobs. We finally arrived at Bandu.

Upon disembarking, we were trembling more than ever, especially having seen in the camp a crowd of men and women who were in chains and were being subjected to hard labour. Our guard brought us inside a roughly built house—more like a shed, really—where there were other children, boys and girls both.

The following morning, after handing out food to us, our guard introduced us to a "*mwalimu*," or Islamic catechist, who had been charged with teaching us to read and write the Quran. The same day, while we were gathered together in class, another convoy coming from Yamokanda landed. Among the last captives [to disembark] was a man who knew my parents and who, speaking to me in our language, let me know that my father had come just after our departure with a few ivory tips [to exchange] for my release, and that he had returned in sadness. Having heard this, I started to cry.

Every day, some people were bringing ivory to buy back their children, while for us on the other bank that was no longer possible, because our parents did not have canoes and especially that they had for these people.[1]

Our slavemaster Tippo-Tip came to us from time to time, to ensure we were provided for as needed. He gave each of us a nickname. He nicknamed me DISASI, which means cartridge; one of my companions, Isalimba, had the name MAFUTA, which means oil.

If we the children were treated humanely, it was not the same with the adults. They were tortured, wounded, mutilated.

We stayed several months in Bandu, but without peace; while the Arabs continued their manhunt [for captives] during the day, the inhabitants of Bandu,

Barumbu, Bafamba, Basoko, and the surrounding villages found the night a favorable moment to take revenge. Almost every night, armed with their spears and armour, they entered the camp, and they sometimes succeeded in killing one or two of these evildoers. Because of these frequent attacks by the natives, the power and the number of the Arab soldiers gradually decreased, and it even became difficult to obtain food. Many of the captives had become thin; there were even some dead among them as a result of starvation.

Tippo-Tip, having had a premonition of defeat, saw fit to go back up the river to reorganize a new army.

For us, this voyage up the river was nothing more than a journey towards death, although they tried to persuade us that that they wanted to protect us so that we could become just like them.

Our convoy leaves Bandu; we are on our way, but to where? We do not know. …

A village appears in front of us. "*Yaombolé, Yaombolé*," cry our guards and the soldiers. We dock. The soldiers jump from the canoes, crying and shouting at the captives. Our master, Tippo-Tip, and some armed soldiers go first to the village to search for lodgings. Soon after, they return and order us all to head out. We are sent to the place indicated, and we the children are presented with a hut. …

One day,[2] something strange happened to us. While our "*mwalimu*" (teacher) was teaching us to read the Quran, we saw downstream on the river some kind of very large canoes; there were three of them coming in our direction. Everyone, the natives and ourselves, was seized with fear, believing that these were other aggressors, coming with the same goal of killing and massacring. Some of the residents fled in their canoes to take refuge in the islands; others went directly into the forest behind them. As for us, we stayed there frozen, our eyes fixed on these strange canoes. Soon all three are docking. Next we saw white and black men disembark; it was Stanley, accompanied by the other white men who had

---

[1] *especially … people* The meaning of the original French here ("et surtout qu'ils avaient pour de ces gens") is unclear.

[2] *One day* Though Makulo does not provide a date, this would in all probability have occurred during Stanley's second expedition to the Congo, beginning in 1879, during which Stanley began colonizing the area on behalf of the Belgian King Leopold II.

made the trip in order to set up a station at Kisangani (Stanleyville).

Stanley was no longer a stranger among the river people; the Lokelé called him "Bosongo," which means "Albino." This name had been given to him during his previous trips on the Congo River.

No sign of war having manifested itself, Tippo-Tip approached them. After he greeted them, they began to talk.

Our *mwalimu* led us near the riverbank. He let us know that these [craft] were not canoes like ours, but boats [of a different sort].

Stanley and his followers stayed in the same village for four days; then they continued on their way toward Kisangani.

After their departure, we also leave Yaombole to go back up the river. After two days we arrive at the village of Yangonde and we camp there.

A few days later, we see the three boats coming back down the river. Having seen us, they docked. Tippo-Tip went to meet Stanley. After a long discussion in an incomprehensible language, Tippo-Tip called our guard. That one came to round us up and he took us to where the two gentlemen were.

Soon after, we see the boat workers bring two rolls of fabric and a few bags of salt. Our *mwalimu*, while reluctant to separate from us, let us know that this white man wanted to buy us.

Stanley began to measure and cut the fabric; for each boy he had to cut one "doti" (4 metres), and for those who were bigger, two doti. We were, in number, twenty-three children, including three girls. The market ends, the two gentlemen shake hands, one of the workers takes us to the boat.

Soon, the three boats slowly move away from the bank, their pace accelerating more and more.

Something better starts to happen in these boats: the crew and us, we all enjoy a certain freedom. We shout, we laugh, we tell each other stories, no one has the rope around their neck, and we are never treated like animals as we had been when we were in the company of the Arabs.

The day after our departure from Yangonde, we arrive off the coast of our region (Yalemba). Surpris-ingly, we see that our boats do not stop, though we had believed when we were liberated that we would each be returned to our parents. I began to cry in our language: "*Ebiso hu été, ebiso hu été, toke boitike hu apa!* (Our home is over there; go leave me at my father's house!)" My companions and I, like the first day of our arrest, had sunk again into an extraordinary sadness.

To calm us down, Stanley approached. He leaned over the railing and began to advise us. [Realizing that we were not] comprehending what he was saying, one of his men translated into the Lingala language for us.

"My children," he said to us, "do not be alarmed. It is not to do you harm that I have bought you, but in order that you may regain true happiness and prosperity. You have all seen how the Arabs treat your parents, and even you little children. I cannot let you return to your parents' homes since I do not want you to become like them: savage people, cruel people, who do not know the Good Lord. Do not regret having lost your parents; I will get you other parents who will treat you well, teach you things. Later on, you will become like us."

Stanley brings out a roll of fabric; he cuts out some loincloths and distributes them to us. This offering makes us rejoice, and his goodness already gives us a sense of paternal love.

from Pixley Ka Isaka Seme, "The Regeneration of Africa" (1906)

Pixley Seme (1881–1951) was born in the Colony of Natal, now part of South Africa. He was an undergraduate at Columbia University in New York City, where in his senior year he was awarded the Curtis Medal for the speech excerpted here. He went on to study law at Oxford University. In 1912 he helped found the South African Native National Congress, which became the African National Congress, and he served as the organization's president from 1930 to 1937.

"The Regeneration of Africa" was delivered on 5 April 1906 and was published first in the *Columbia Monthly* and then the *Journal of the Royal African Society* (July 1906).

Ladies and Gentlemen:

I have chosen to speak to you on this occasion upon "The Regeneration of Africa." I am an African, and I set my pride in my race over against a hostile public opinion. Men have tried to compare races on the basis of some equality. In all the works of nature, equality, if by it we mean identity, is an impossible dream! Search the universe! You will find no two units alike. The scientists tell us there are no two cells, no two atoms, identical. Nature has bestowed upon each a peculiar individuality, an exclusive patent—from the great giants of the forest to the tenderest blade.[1] ... In all races, genius is like a spark, which, concealed in the bosom of a flint, bursts forth at the summoning stroke. It may arise anywhere and in any race.

I would ask you not to compare Africa to Europe or to any other continent. I make this request not from any fear that such comparison might bring humiliation upon Africa. The reason I have stated—a common standard is impossible! Come with me to the ancient capital of Egypt, Thebes, the city of one hundred gates. The grandeur of its venerable ruins and the gigantic proportions of its architecture reduce to insignificance the boasted monuments of other nations. The pyramids of Egypt are structures to which the world presents nothing comparable. The mighty monuments seem to look with disdain on every other work of human art and to vie with Nature herself. All the glory of Egypt belongs to Africa and her people. These monuments are the indestructible memorials of their great and original genius. It is not through Egypt alone that Africa claims such unrivalled historic achievements. I could have spoken of the pyramids of Ethiopia, which, though inferior in size to those of Egypt, far surpass them in architectural beauty; their sepulchres which evince the highest purity of taste, and of many prehistoric ruins in other parts of Africa. In such ruins Africa is like the golden sun, that, having sunk beneath the western horizon, still plays[2] upon the world which he sustained and enlightened in his career.

Justly the world now demands—

"Whither is fled the visionary gleam,
    Where is it now, the glory and the dream?"[3]

Oh, for that historian who, with the open pen of truth, will bring to Africa's claim the strength of written proof. He will tell of a race whose onward tide was often swelled with tears, but in whose heart bondage has not quenched the fire of former years. He will write that in these later days when Earth's noble ones are named, she has a roll of honor too, of whom she is not ashamed. The giant is awakening! From the four corners of the earth Africa's sons, who have been proved through fire and sword, are marching to the future's golden door bearing the records of deeds of valor done.

Mr. Calhoun,[4] I believe, was the most philosophical of all the slaveholders. He said once that if he could find a black man who could understand the Greek syntax, he would then consider their race human, and his attitude toward enslaving them would therefore change. What might have been the sensation kindled by the Greek syntax in the mind of the famous Southerner, I have so far been unable to discover; but oh, I envy the moment that was lost! and woe to the tongues that refused to tell the truth! If any such were among the now living, I could show him among black men of pure African blood those who could repeat the Koran from memory, skilled in Latin, Greek and Hebrew, Arabic and Chaldaic[5]—men great in wisdom and profound knowledge... There are many other Africans who have shown marks of genius and high character sufficient to redeem their race from the charges which I am now considering.

Ladies and gentlemen, *the day of great exploring expeditions in Africa is over!*

---

[1]   *blade* I.e., of grass.

[2]   *plays* Acts.

[3]   *Whither ... dream?* From William Wordsworth's "Ode: Intimations of Immortality" (1807).

[4]   *Mr. Calhoun* John C. Calhoun (1782–1850), American politician who devoted his long and varied career to promoting the interests of the Southern enslaving class to which he belonged.

[5]   *Chaldaic* I.e., Aramaic, an ancient Middle Eastern language in which several books of the Bible were originally written.

Man knows his home now in a sense never known before. Many great and holy men have evinced a passion for the day you are now witnessing—their prophetic vision shot through many unborn centuries to this very hour. "Men shall run to and fro," said Daniel, "and knowledge shall increase upon the earth."[1] Oh, how true! See the triumph of human genius today! Science has searched out the deep things of nature, surprised the secrets of the most distant stars, disentombed the memorials of everlasting hills, taught the lightning to speak, the vapors to toil and the winds to worship, spanned the sweeping rivers, tunneled the longest mountain range—made the world a vast whispering gallery, and has brought foreign nations into one civilized family. This all-powerful contact says even to the most backward race, you cannot remain where you are, you cannot fall back, you must advance! A great century has come upon us! No race possessing the inherent capacity to survive can resist and remain unaffected by this influence of contact and intercourse, the backward with the advanced. This influence constitutes the very essence of efficient progress and of civilization.

From these heights of the twentieth century I again ask you to cast your eyes south of the Desert of Sahara. If you could go with me to the oppressed Congos and ask, What does it mean, that now, for liberty, they fight like men and die like martyrs;[2] if you would go with me to Bechuanaland,[3] face their council of Headmen, and ask what motives caused them recently to decree so emphatically that alcoholic drinks shall not enter their country—visit their king, Khama,[4] ask for what cause he leaves the gold and ivory palace of his ancestors, its mountain strongholds and all its august ceremony, to wander daily from village to village through all his kingdom, without a guard or any decoration of his rank—a preacher of industry and education, and an apostle of the new order of things; if you would ask Menelik[5] what means this that Abyssinia is now looking across the ocean—oh, if you could read the letters that come to us from Zululand—you too would be convinced that the elevation of the African race is evidently a part of the new order of things that belong to this new and powerful period.

The African already recognizes his anomalous position and desires a change. The brighter day is rising upon Africa. Already I seem to see her chains dissolved, her desert plains red with harvest, her Abyssinia and her Zululand the seats of science and religion, reflecting the glory of the rising sun from the spires of their churches and universities. Her Congo and her Gambia whitened with commerce, her crowded cities sending forth the hum of business, and all her sons employed in advancing the victories of peace—greater and more abiding than the spoils of war.

Yes, the regeneration of Africa belongs to this new and powerful period! By this term, regeneration, I wish to be understood to mean the entrance into a new life, embracing the diverse phases of a higher, complex existence. The basic factor which assures their regeneration resides in the awakened race-consciousness. This gives them a clear perception of their elemental needs and of their undeveloped powers. It therefore must lead them to the attainment of that higher and advanced standard of life.

The African people, although not a strictly homogeneous race, possess a common, fundamental sentiment which is everywhere manifest, crystallizing itself into one common controlling idea. Conflicts and strife are rapidly disappearing before the fusing force of this enlightened perception of the true intertribal relation, which relation should subsist among a people with a common destiny. Agencies of a social, economic and religious advance tell of a new spirit which, acting as a leavening ferment, shall raise the anxious and aspiring mass to the level of their ancient glory. The ancestral greatness, the unimpaired genius, and the recuperative power of the race, its irrepressibility, which assures its

---

[1] *Men ... earth* See Daniel 12.4.

[2] *the oppressed ... martyrs* Under the colonial rule of King Leopold II of Belgium (1885–1908), the Congolese suffered extraordinary abuses.

[3] *Bechuanaland* Now the Republic of Botswana.

[4] *Khama* King Khama III of Bechuanaland (c. 1837–1923).

[5] *Menelik* King Menelik II of Ethiopia (1844–1913), formerly the Kingdom of Abyssinia.

permanence, constitute the African's greatest source of inspiration. He has refused to camp for ever on the borders of the industrial world; having learnt that knowledge is power, he is educating his children. You find them in Edinburgh, in Cambridge, and in the great schools of Germany. These return to their country like arrows, to drive darkness from the land. I hold that his industrial and educational initiative, and his untiring devotion to these activities, must be regarded as positive evidences of this process of his regeneration.

The regeneration of Africa means that a new and unique civilization is soon to be added to the world. The African is not a proletarian in the world of science and art. He has precious creations of his own, of ivory, of copper and of gold, fine plaited willow-ware[1] and weapons of superior workmanship. Civilization resembles an organic being in its development—it is born, it perishes, and it can propagate itself. More particularly it resembles a plant, it takes root in the teeming earth, and when the seeds fall in other soils, new varieties sprout up. The most essential departure of this new civilization is that it shall be thoroughly spiritual and humanistic—indeed a regeneration moral and eternal!

O Africa!
Like some great century-plant, that shall bloom
In ages hence, we watch thee; in our dream
See in thy swamps the Prospero[2] of our stream;
Thy doors unlocked, where knowledge in her tomb
Has lain innumerable years in gloom.
Then shalt thou, waking with that morning gleam,
Shine as thy sister lands with equal beam.

---

[1] *willow-ware* Popular blue and white, Chinese-inspired pattern on ceramic plates.

[2] *Prospero* Learned magician in William Shakespeare's *The Tempest* (1611).

Settler Colonial Perspectives

Thomas Pringle, "Afar in the Desert" (1824)

Born and raised in Scotland, Thomas Pringle spent six years in South Africa; much of his work, including the poem below, is inspired by his experiences there. "Afar in the Desert" was first published in Pringle's own literary journal in South Africa, but it was very well received abroad—Samuel Taylor Coleridge counted it "among the two or three most perfect lyric poems in our language." Pringle witnessed slavery in South Africa and became deeply opposed to the practice; after his return to the British Isles he devoted much of his time to campaigning for abolition as secretary to the Anti-Slavery Society.

Afar in the desert I love to ride,
  With the silent Bush-boy[3] alone by my side:
When the sorrows of life the soul o'ercast,
And, sick of the Present, I cling to the Past;
When the eye is suffused with regretful tears,   5
From the fond recollections of former years;
And shadows of things that have long since fled
Flit over the brain, like the ghosts of the dead:
Bright visions of glory—that vanished too soon;
Day-dreams—that departed ere manhood's noon;   10
Attachments—by fate or by falsehood reft;°   *taken away*
Companions of early days—lost or left;
And my Native Land—whose magical name
Thrills to the heart like electric flame;
The home of my childhood; the haunts of my prime;   15
All the passions and scenes of that rapturous time
When the feelings were young and the world was new,
Like the fresh bowers of Eden unfolding to view;
All—all now forsaken—forgotten—foregone!
And I—a lone exile remembered of none—   20
My high aims abandoned, my good acts undone,
Aweary of all that is under the sun,
With that sadness of heart which no stranger may scan,
I fly to the Desert afar from man!

---

[3] *Bush-boy* Term for a native person living in the wilderness.

25   Afar in the Desert I love to ride,
        With the silent Bush-boy alone by my side:
        When the wild turmoil of this wearisome life,
        With its scenes of oppression, corruption, and strife—
        The proud man's frown, and the base man's fear,
30   The scorner's laugh, and the sufferer's tear—
        And malice, and meanness, and falsehood, and folly,
        Dispose me to musing and dark melancholy;
        When my bosom is full, and my thoughts are high,
        And my soul is sick with the bondman's° sigh—   slave's
35   Oh! then there is freedom, and joy, and pride,
        Afar in the Desert alone to ride!
        There is rapture to vault on the champing steed,
        And to bound away with the eagle's speed,
        With the death-fraught firelock° in my hand—   musket
40   The only law of the Desert Land!

        Afar in the Desert I love to ride,
        With the silent Bush-boy alone by my side:
        Away—away from the dwellings of men,
        By the wild deer's haunt, by the buffalo's glen;
45   By valleys remote where the oribi[1] plays,
        Where the gnu,° the gazelle, and the   wildebeest
            hartèbeest[2] graze,
        And the kùdù and eland[3] unhunted recline
        By the skirts of grey forests o'erhung with wild-vine;
        Where the elephant browses at peace in his wood,
50   And the river-horse° gambols[4] unscared   hippopotamus
            in the flood,
        And the mighty rhinoceros wallows at will
        In the fen where the wild-ass is drinking his fill.

        Afar in the Desert I love to ride,
        With the silent Bush-boy alone by my side:

55   O'er the brown Karroo,[5] where the bleating cry
        Of the springbok's[6] fawn sounds plaintively;
        And the timorous quagga's[7] shrill whistling neigh
        Is heard by the fountain at twilight grey;
        Where the zebra wantonly tosses his mane,
60   With wild hoof scouring the desolate plain;
        And the fleet-footed ostrich over the waste
        Speeds like a horseman who travels in haste,
        Hying° away to the home of her rest,   hastening
        Where she and her mate have scooped their nest,
65   Far hid from the pitiless plunderer's view
        In the pathless depths of the parched Karroo.

        Afar in the Desert I love to ride,
        With the silent Bush-boy alone by my side:
        Away—away—in the Wilderness vast,
70   Where the White Man's foot hath never passed,
        And the quivered Coránna or Bechuán[8]
        Hath rarely crossed with his roving clan:
        A region of emptiness, howling and drear,
        Which Man hath abandoned from famine and fear;
75   Which the snake and the lizard inhabit alone,
        With the twilight bat from the yawning stone;
        Where grass, nor herb, nor shrub takes root,
        Save poisonous thorns that pierce the foot;
        And the bitter-melon, for food and drink,
80   Is the pilgrim's fare by the salt lake's brink:
        A region of drought, where no river glides,
        Nor rippling brook with osiered[9] sides;
        Where sedgy[10] pool, nor bubbling fount,
        Nor tree, nor cloud, nor misty mount,
85   Appears, to refresh the aching eye:
        But the barren earth, and the burning sky,
        And the black horizon, round and round,
        Spread—void of living sight or sound.

---

[1] *oribi*   Type of small brown antelope.

[2] *hartèbeest*   Another type of antelope, common to South Africa.

[3] *kùdù and eland*   Two other types of African antelope.

[4] *gambols*   Bounds playfully.

[5] *Karroo*   Semi-desert area in central South Africa.

[6] *springbok*   Type of antelope known for springing straight upward when startled.

[7] *quagga*   Type of zebra that was native to southern Africa; it is now extinct.

[8] *Coránna or Bechuán*   Two native tribes.

[9] *osiered*   Covered in osiers, or willow trees.

[10] *sedgy*   Filled with sedge—coarse grass or rushes.

And here, while the night-winds round me sigh,
90 And the stars burn bright in the midnight sky,
As I sit apart by the desert stone,
Like Elijah at Horeb's cave alone,[1]
"A still small voice" comes through the wild
(Like a Father consoling his fretful Child),
95 Which banishes bitterness, wrath, and fear,
Saying—MAN IS DISTANT, BUT GOD IS NEAR!

from William H. Smith, *Smith's Canadian Gazetteer* (1846)

Smith states in his preface that he was "induced to undertake the task" of writing his gazetteer by the "great ignorance" which he found to exist respecting the province of Canada West (now Ontario), "not only amongst persons in Great Britain, or newly arrived emigrants, but even amongst many of those who had been for years resident in the country." The *Gazetteer* included information on all towns and geographical areas in the province. The following excerpts are taken from the section of general reflections with which the work concludes.

It is most extraordinary, so long as Canada has been settled, that its great natural advantages should still be so little known; that so many persons who are either compelled by necessity to emigrate, or who do so from choice, should continue to pass it by and go on to the west of the United States, or otherwise emigrate to the more distant colonies of the Cape, New South Wales, or New Zealand and yet such is the case. …

In what respects will the advocates of emigration to the United States pretend to say that any portion of that country is superior to Canada. Is it in the climate? A tree may be judged of by its fruits, and very many of the native Canadians, in point of robust appearance and complexion, might be taken for English emigrants. Will any one venture to make the same assertion respecting a native of Ohio, Indiana, Illinois, or Missouri? And of what avail is it that the climate will grow cotton and tobacco, if the settler neither has the strength to cultivate them, nor a market in which to dispose of them, when grown? In the winter and spring of 1841–2, pork (a staple article of the State) was selling in Illinois, at from a dollar to a dollar and a half per 100 lbs.; and at that price it was almost impossible to obtain cash for it; wheat at a quarter dollar, and Indian corn from five to ten cents per bushel; butter, fifteen and sixteen pounds for a dollar; fowls, half a dollar per dozen; and other farming produce in proportion. At such prices farming could not be very profitable. A man certainly might live cheaply, and cram himself with bacon and corn bread till he brought on bilious fever;[2] but he could *make nothing* of what he raised. And a farmer having a fat ox, has even been known after killing it, to take from it the hide and tallow, and drag the carcass into the woods to be devoured by the wolves; finding from the small price the beef would fetch, that it was more profitable to do so than to sell the whole animal!

Is it from the nature of the government, that the States are so much more desirable as a place of residence—where the only law is mob law, and the bowie knife is the constant companion of the citizens, and is used even in the halls of legislature themselves? Or is New Zealand much to be preferred, where the settler in taking his morning ramble, to acquire an appetite for his breakfast, frequently receives a "settler" himself, and instead of returning to his morning's meal, is roasted for the breakfast of some native chief, and his interesting family. Canada, on the contrary, suffers under none of these disadvantages and annoyances. The government and constitution of the country are English; the laws English; the climate is fine and healthy; the Indians are tolerably civilized, none of them at any rate are cannibals, and few of them are even thieves; and bowie knives are not "the fashion." The settler, unless he has been guilty of the folly of planting himself down beyond the bounds of civilization and of roads, may always command a fair price and cash for whatever he can

---

1 *Like Elijah … cave alone* Reference to 1 Kings 19, which tells the story of Elijah, who journeyed for 40 days and nights to Horeb, the mount of God. After a great wind, an earthquake, and a fire, the Lord spoke to Elijah in "a still, small voice."

2 *bilious fever* Over-secretion of bile, causing indigestion.

raise—he need never be beyond the reach of medical attendance, churches, and schools—he can obtain as much land as he need wish to purchase, at a fair and moderate rate—he knows that whatever property he acquires is as secure as if he had it in England—his landed property, if he possesses any, is gradually increasing in value—and if he is only moderately careful and industrious, he need have no anxiety for the future—his sons, growing up in and with the country, and as they grow, acquiring a knowledge of the country and its customs, and the various modes of doing business in it, if steady, will have no difficulty in succeeding in any business they may select, or may be qualified for.

Much has been written on the subject of emigration, and many speculations entered into as to *who* are the proper persons to emigrate? The only answer that can be given to this question is—*those who are obliged to do so.* Let no person who is doing *well* at home, no matter what may be his profession or occupation, emigrate with the expectation of doing *better*,—let him not leave his home and travel over the world, in search of advantages which he may not find elsewhere. But those who are *not* doing well, who find it difficult to struggle against increasing competition, who fear the loss in business of what little property they possess, or who find it difficult with an increasing family to keep up appearances as they have been accustomed to do, and find it necessary to make a change—all these may safely emigrate, with a fair prospect of improving their condition. Persons of small, independent incomes may live cheaply in Canada, particularly in the country, and enjoy many comforts, and even luxuries, that were not within their reach at home. Retired military men do not generally make good settlers. They usually, when they leave the army, sell out, instead of retiring on half-pay; and when they emigrate they are apt to squander their property in purchasing land and in building, till at length they come to a stand for want of the means to proceed, frequently with their buildings half-finished, from being planned on too large a scale; although, if they had been asked in the commencement how they intended to *live* when the ready money was expended, they would have been unable to give an intelligible answer. If they succeed in getting some government office, the emoluments[1] of which are sufficient for their support, they will manage to get along very well; otherwise they will sink gradually lower and lower, and their children are apt to get into idle and dissipated habits. The idle and inactive life to which they have been accustomed while in the army, particularly during these "piping times of peace,"[2] totally incapacitates them for making good settlers in the backwoods. *A lounger, unless independent, has no business in Canada.* Naval officers, on the contrary, make settlers of a very different character. They have been accustomed, when on service, to a life of activity; and if they have been long on service, they have generally seen a great deal of the world—they have their half-pay to fall back on, which fortunately for them they cannot sell—and they generally make very excellent settlers. Lawyers are not wanted: Canada swarms with them; and they multiply in the province so fast, that the demand is not by any means equal to the supply. Medical men may find many openings in the country, where they will have no difficulty in making a tolerable living; but they will have to work hard for it, having frequently to ride fifteen, twenty-five, or even thirty miles to see a patient! And in the towns, the competition is as great as in England. …

from Agnes Macdonald, "By Car and Cowcatcher," *Murray's Magazine* (1887)

The essay from which the passages below are excerpted describes Macdonald's trip across Canada by train with her husband, Canadian Prime Minister Sir John A. Macdonald.

… The description of a cow-catcher is less easy. To begin with, it is misnamed, for it catches no cows at all.

---

[1] *emoluments* Salary, remuneration.

[2] *piping … peace* See William Shakespeare's *Richard III* 1.1.24: "Why, I, in this weak piping time of peace, / Have no delight to pass away the time."

Sometimes, I understand, it throws up on the buffer-beam whatever maimed or mangled animal it has struck, but in most cases it clears the line by shoving forward, or tossing aside, any removable obstruction. It is best described as a sort of barred iron beak, about six feet long, projecting close over the track in a V shape, and attached to the buffer-beam by very strong bolts. It is sometimes sheathed with thin iron plates in winter, and acts then as a small snow-plough.

Behold me now, enthroned on the candle-box, with a soft felt hat well over my eyes, and a linen carriage-cover tucked round me from waist to foot. Mr. E.[1] had seated himself on the other side of the headlight. He had succumbed to the inevitable, ceased further expostulation, disclaimed all responsibility, and, like the jewel of a Superintendent he was, had decided on sharing my peril! I turn to him, peeping round the headlight, with my best smile. "This is *lovely*," I triumphantly announce, seeing that a word of comfort is necessary, "*quite lovely*; I shall travel on this cowcatcher from summit to sea!"

Mr. Superintendent, in his turn, peeps round the headlight and surveys me with solemn and resigned surprise. "I—suppose—you—will," he says slowly, and I see that he is hoping, at any rate, that I shall live to do it!

With a mighty snort, a terribly big throb, and shrieking whistle, No. 374 moves slowly forward. The very small population of Laggan have all come out to see. They stand in the hot sunshine, and shade their eyes as the stately engine moves on. "It is an awful thing to do!" I hear a voice say, as the little group lean forward; and for a moment I feel a thrill that is very like fear; but it is gone at once, and I can think of nothing but the novelty, the excitement, and the fun of this mad ride in glorious sunshine and intoxicating air, with magnificent mountains before and around me, their lofty peaks smiling down on us, and never a frown on their grand faces!

The pace quickens gradually, surely, swiftly, and then we are rushing up to the summit. We soon stand on the "Great Divide"—5300 feet above sea-level—between the two great oceans. As we pass, Mr. E. by a gesture, points out a small river (called Bath Creek, I think) which, issuing from a lake on the narrow summit-level, winds near the track. I look, and lo! the water, flowing *eastward* towards the Atlantic side, turns in a moment as the Divide is passed, and pours *westward* down the Pacific slope!

Another moment and a strange silence has fallen round us. With steam shut off and brakes down, the 60-ton engine, by its own weight and impetus alone, glides into the pass of the Kicking Horse River, and begins a descent of 2800 feet in twelve miles. We rush onward through the vast valley stretching before us, bristling with lofty forests, dark and deep, that, clinging to the mountain side, are reared up into the sky. The river, widening, grows white with dashing foam, and rushes downwards with tremendous force. Sunlight flashes on glaciers, into gorges, and athwart[2] huge, towering masses of rock crowned with magnificent tree crests that rise all round us of every size and shape. Breathless—almost awe-stricken—but with a wild triumph in my heart, I look from farthest mountain peak, lifted high before me, to the shining pebbles at my feet! Warm wind rushes past; a thousand sunshine colours dance in the air. With a firm right hand grasping the iron stanchion, and my feet planted on the buffer-beam, there was not a yard of that descent in which I faltered for a moment. If I had, then assuredly in the wild valley of the Kicking Horse River, on the western slope of the Rocky Mountains, a life had gone out that day! I did not think of danger, or remember what a giddy post I had. I could only gaze at the glaciers that the mountains held so closely, 5000 feet above us, at the trace of snow avalanches which had left a space a hundred feet wide massed with torn and prostrate trees; on the shadows that played over the distant peaks; and on a hundred rainbows made by the foaming, dashing river, which swirls with tremendous rapidity down the gorge on its way to the Columbia in the valley below. ...

Halted at Palliser. The Chief and his friends walked up to the cow-catcher to make a morning call. I felt a little "superior" and was rather condescending. Some-

---

[1] *Mr. E.* John M. Egan, general superintendent of the western division of the Canadian Pacific Railroad at the time.

[2] *athwart* Run across in oblique direction.

what flushed with excitement, but still anxious to be polite, I asked "would the Chief step up and take a drive?" To the horror of the bystanders he carelessly consented, and in another moment had taken the place of Mr. E., the latter seating himself at our feet on the buffer-beam. There was a general consternation among our little group of friends and the few inhabitants of Palliser—the Chief rushing through the flats of the Columbia on a cow-catcher! and, worse still, possibly even among the wild Selkirk Mountains—those mountains of which scarcely three years before, in his charming book, "From Old Westminster to New," my friend Mr. Sandford Fleming[1] had said, "no one had been through the western slope of the Selkirks"! Every one is horrified. It is a comfort to the other occupant of the buffer to find some one else wilful, and as we steamed away towards Donald, at the eastern base of the Selkirks, I felt not so bad after all! …

Henry Lawson, "The Drover's[2] Wife" (1892)

Australian-born poet and prose writer Henry Lawson is best known for short stories like the one below, depicting the harshness of life in the Australian bush.

The two-roomed house is built of round timber, slabs, and stringy bark, and floored with split slabs. A big bark kitchen standing at one end is larger than the house itself, veranda included.

Bush all round—bush with no horizon, for the country is flat. No ranges in the distance. The bush consists of stunted, rotten native apple trees. No undergrowth. Nothing to relieve the eye save the darker green of a few she-oaks which are sighing above the narrow, almost waterless creek. Nineteen miles to the nearest sign of civilization—a shanty on the main road.

The drover, an ex-squatter,[3] is away with sheep. His wife and children are left here alone.

Four ragged, dried-up-looking children are playing about the house. Suddenly one of them yells: "Snake! Mother, here's a snake!"

The gaunt, sun-browned bushwoman dashes from the kitchen, snatches her baby from the ground, holds it on her left hip, and reaches for a stick.

"Where is it?"

"Here! Gone into the wood-heap!" yells the eldest boy—a sharp-faced urchin of eleven. "Stop there, mother! I'll have him. Stand back! I'll have the beggar!"

"Tommy, come here, or you'll be bit. Come here at once when I tell you, you little wretch!"

The youngster comes reluctantly, carrying a stick bigger than himself. Then he yells, triumphantly:

"There it goes—under the house!" and darts away with club uplifted. At the same time the big, black, yellow-eyed dog-of-all-breeds, who has shown the wildest interest in the proceedings, breaks his chain and rushes after that snake. He is a moment late, however, and his nose reaches the crack in the slabs just as the end of its tail disappears. Almost at the same moment the boy's club comes down and skins the aforesaid nose. Alligator takes small notice of this, and proceeds to undermine the building; but he is subdued after a struggle and chained up. They cannot afford to lose him.

The drover's wife makes the children stand together near the dog-house while she watches for the snake. She gets two small dishes of milk and sets them down near the wall to tempt it to come out; but an hour goes by and it does not show itself.

It is near sunset, and a thunderstorm is coming. The children must be brought inside. She will not take them into the house, for she knows the snake is there, and may at any moment come up through the cracks in the rough slab floor; so she carries several armfuls of firewood into the kitchen, and then takes the children there. The kitchen has no floor—or, rather, an earthen one—called a "ground floor" in this part of the bush. There is a large,

---

[1] *Sandford Fleming* Canadian engineer and inventor (1827–1915).

[2] *Drover* Person who drives livestock to market, often over great distances.

[3] *squatter* Someone who settles with livestock on government land. Initially, squatters struggled to establish themselves, but some eventually became wealthy as owners of large-scale grazing operations.

roughly made table in the centre of the place. She brings the children in, and makes them get on this table. They are two boys and two girls—mere babies. She gives them some supper, and then, before it gets dark, she goes into house, and snatches up some pillows and bedclothes—expecting to see or lay her hand on the snake any minute. She makes a bed on the kitchen table for the children, and sits down beside it to watch all night.

She has an eye on the corner, and a green sapling club laid in readiness on the dresser by her side, together with her sewing basket and a copy of the *Young Ladies' Journal*. She has brought the dog into the room.

Tommy turns in, under protest, but says he'll lie awake all night and smash that blinded snake.

His mother asks him how many times she has told him not to swear.

He has his club with him under the bedclothes, and Jacky protests:

"Mummy! Tommy's skinnin' me alive wif his club. Make him take it out."

Tommy: "Shet up you little—! D'yer want to be bit with the snake?"

Jacky shuts up.

"If yer bit," says Tommy, after a pause, "you'll swell up, an smell, an' turn red an' green an' blue all over till yer bust. Won't he mother?"

"Now then, don't frighten the child. Go to sleep," she says.

The two younger children go to sleep, and now and then Jacky complains of being "skeezed." More room is made for him. Presently Tommy says: "Mother! Listen to them (adjective) little 'possums. I'd like to screw their blanky necks."

And Jacky protests drowsily:

"But they don't hurt us, the little blanks!"

Mother: "There, I told you you'd teach Jacky to swear." But the remark makes her smile. Jacky goes to sleep.

Presently Tommy asks:

"Mother! Do you think they'll ever extricate the (adjective) kangaroo?"

"Lord! How am I to know, child? Go to sleep."

"Will you wake me if the snake comes out?"

"Yes. Go to sleep."

Near midnight. The children are all asleep and she sits there still, sewing and reading by turns. From time to time she glances round the floor and wall-plate, and whenever she hears a noise she reaches for the stick. The thunderstorm comes on, and the wind, rushing through the cracks in the slab wall, threatens to blow out her candle. She places it on a sheltered part of the dresser and fixes up a newspaper to protect it. At every flash of lightning, the cracks between the slabs gleam like polished silver. The thunder rolls, and the rain comes down in torrents.

Alligator lies at full length on the floor, with his eyes turned towards the partition. She knows by this that the snake is there. There are large cracks in that wall opening under the floor of the dwelling-house.

She is not a coward, but recent events have shaken her nerves. A little son of her brother-in-law was lately bitten by a snake, and died. Besides, she has not heard from her husband for six months, and is anxious about him.

He was a drover, and started squatting here when they were married. The drought of 18— ruined him. He had to sacrifice the remnant of his flock and go droving again. He intends to move his family into the nearest town when he comes back, and, in the meantime, his brother, who keeps a shanty on the main road, comes over about once a month with provisions. The wife has still a couple of cows, one horse, and a few sheep. The brother-in-law kills one of the sheep occasionally, gives her what she needs of it, and takes the rest in return for other provisions.

She is used to being left alone. She once lived like this for eighteen months. As a girl she built the usual castles in the air; but all her girlish hopes and aspirations have long been dead. She finds all the excitement and recreation she needs in the *Young Ladies' Journal*, and, Heaven help her! takes a pleasure in the fashion plates.

Her husband is an Australian, and so is she. He is careless, but a good enough husband. If he had the means he would take her to the city and keep her there like a princess. They are used to being apart, or at least she is. "No use fretting," she says. He may forget sometimes that he is married; but if he has a good cheque when he comes back he will give most of it to her. When he had money he took her to the city several times—hired a railway sleeping compartment, and put up at the best hotels. He also bought her a buggy, but they had to sacrifice that along with the rest.

The last two children were born in the bush—one while her husband was bringing a drunken doctor, by force, to attend to her. She was alone on this occasion, and very weak. She had been ill with a fever. She prayed to God to send her assistance. God sent Black Mary— the "whitest" gin[1] in all the land. Or, at least, God sent "King Jimmy" first, and he sent Black Mary. He put his black face round the door post, took in the situation at a glance, and said cheerfully: "All right, missus—I bring my old woman, she down alonga creek."

One of her children died while she was here alone. She rode nineteen miles for assistance, carrying the dead child.

It must be near one or two o'clock. The fire is burning low. Alligator lies with his head resting on his paws, and watches the wall. He is not a very beautiful dog to look at, and the light shows numerous old wounds where the hair will not grow. He is afraid of nothing on the face of the earth or under it. He will tackle a bullock[2] as readily as he will tackle a flea. He hates all other dogs—except kangaroo-dogs[3]—and has a marked dislike to friends or relations of the family. They seldom call, however. He sometimes makes friends with strangers. He hates snakes and has killed many, but he will be bitten some day and die; most snake-dogs end that way.

Now and then the bushwoman lays down her work and watches, and listens, and thinks. She thinks of things in her own life, for there is little else to think about.

The rain will make the grass grow, and this reminds her how she fought a bush-fire once while her husband was away. The grass was long, and very dry, and the fire threatened to burn her out. She put on an old pair of her husband's trousers and beat out the flames with a green bough, till great drops of sooty perspiration stood out on her forehead and ran in streaks down her blackened arms. The sight of his mother in trousers greatly amused Tommy, who worked like a little hero by her side, but the terrified baby howled lustily for his "mummy." The fire would have mastered her but for four excited bushmen who arrived in the nick of time. It was a mixed-up affair all round; when she went to take up the baby he screamed and struggled convulsively, thinking it was a "blackman"; and Alligator, trusting more to the child's sense than his own instinct, charged furiously, and (being old and slightly deaf) did not in his excitement at first recognize his mistress's voice, but continued to hang on to the moleskins[4] until choked off by Tommy with a saddle-strap. The dog's sorrow for his blunder, and his anxiety to let it be known that it was all a mistake, was as evident as his ragged tail and a twelve-inch grin could make it. It was a glorious time for the boys; a day to look back to, and talk about, and laugh over for many years.

She thinks how she fought a flood during her husband's absence. She stood for hours in the drenching downpour, and dug an overflow gutter to save the dam across the creek. But she could not save it. There are things that a bushwoman cannot do. Next morning the dam was broken, and her heart was nearly broken too, for she thought how her husband would feel when he came home and saw the result of years of labour swept away. She cried then.

She also fought the pleuropneumonia[5]—dosed and bled the few remaining cattle, and wept again when her two best cows died.

Again, she fought a mad bullock that besieged the house for a day. She made bullets and fired at him through cracks in the slabs with an old shotgun. He was dead in the morning. She skinned him and got seventeen-and-six[6] for the hide.

---

[1] *gin* Derogatory term used by white Australians to refer to an Aboriginal woman.

[2] *bullock* Young or castrated bull.

[3] *kangaroo-dogs* Large dogs used to hunt kangaroo.

[4] *moleskins* Trousers.

[5] *pleuropneumonia* Highly infectious disease afflicting cattle.

[6] *seventeen-and-six* Seventeen shillings and sixpence.

She also fights the crows and eagles that have designs on her chickens. Her plan of campaign is very original. The children cry "Crows, mother!" and she rushes out and aims a broomstick at the birds as though it were a gun, and says, "Bung!" The crows leave in a hurry; they are cunning, but a woman's cunning is greater.

Occasionally a bushman in the horrors,[1] or a villainous-looking sundowner,[2] comes and nearly scares the life out of her. She generally tells the suspicious-looking stranger that her husband and two sons are at work below the dam, or over at the yard, for he always cunningly inquires for the boss.

Only last week a gallows-faced swagman[3]—having satisfied himself that there were no men on the place—threw his swag down on the veranda, and demanded tucker.[4] She gave him something to eat; then he expressed his intention of staying for the night. It was sundown then. She got a batten[5] from the sofa, loosened the dog, and confronted the stranger, holding the batten in one hand and the dog's collar with the other. "Now you go!" she said. He looked at her and at the dog, said "All right, mum," in a cringing tone, and left. She was a determined-looking woman, and Alligator's yellow eyes glared unpleasantly—besides, the dog's chawing-up apparatus greatly resembled that of the reptile he was named after.

She has few pleasures to think of as she sits here alone by the fire, on guard against a snake. All days are much the same to her; but on Sunday afternoon she dresses herself, tidies the children, smartens up baby, and goes for a lonely walk along the bush-track, pushing an old perambulator[6] in front of her. She does this every Sunday. She takes as much care to make herself and the children look smart as she would if she were going to do the block in the city. There is nothing to see, however,

and not a soul to meet. You might walk for twenty miles along this track without being able to fix a point in your mind, unless you are a bushman. This is because of the everlasting, maddening sameness of the stunted trees—that monotony which makes a man long to break away and travel as far as trains can go, and sail as far as ships can sail—and further.

But this bushwoman is used to the loneliness of it. As a girl-wife she hated it, but now she would feel strange away from it.

She is glad when her husband returns, but she does not gush or make a fuss about it. She gets him something good to eat, and tidies up the children.

She seems contented with her lot. She loves her children, but has no time to show it. She seems harsh to them. Her surroundings are not favourable to the development of the "womanly" or sentimental side of nature.

It must be near morning now; but the clock is in the dwelling-house. Her candle is nearly done; she forgot that she was out of candles. Some more wood must be got to keep the fire up, and so she shuts the dog inside and hurries round to the wood-heap. The rain has cleared off. She seizes a stick, pulls it out, and—crash! The whole pile collapses.

Yesterday she bargained with a stray blackfellow[7] to bring her some wood, and while he was at work she went in search of a missing cow. She was absent an hour or so, and the native black made good use of his time. On her return she was so astonished to see a good heap of wood by the chimney, that she gave him an extra fig of tobacco, and praised him for not being lazy. He thanked her, and left with head erect and chest well out. He was the last of his tribe and a King; but he had built that wood-heap hollow.

She is hurt now, and tears spring to her eyes as she sits down again by the table. She takes up a handkerchief to wipe the tears away, but pokes her eyes with her bare fingers instead. The handkerchief is full of holes, and she finds that she has put her thumb through one, and her forefinger through another.

[1] *in the horrors* I.e., extremely drunk.
[2] *sundowner* Vagrant who arrives at sundown to avoid working in exchange for requested shelter.
[3] *swagman* Australian: man who travels the countryside in search of work.
[4] *tucker* Australian: food.
[5] *batten* I.e., board.
[6] *perambulator* Baby carriage.
[7] *blackfellow* Offensive Australian term for an Indigenous man.

This makes her laugh, to the surprise of the dog. She has a keen, very keen, sense of the ridiculous; and some time or other she will amuse bushmen with the story.

She has been amused before like that. One day she sat down "to have a good cry," as she said—and the old cat rubbed against her dress and "cried too." Then she had to laugh.

It must be near daylight. The room is very close and hot because of the fire. Alligator still watches the wall from time to time. Suddenly he becomes greatly interested; he draws himself a few inches nearer the partition, and a thrill runs though his body. The hair on the back of his neck begins to bristle, and the battle-light is in his yellow eyes. She knows what this means, and lays her hand on the stick. The lower end of one of the partition slabs has a large crack on both sides. An evil pair of small, bright, bead-like eyes glisten at one of these holes. The snake—a black one—comes slowly out, about a foot, and moves its head up and down. The dog lies still, and the woman sits as one fascinated. The snake comes out a foot further. She lifts her stick, and the reptile, as though suddenly aware of danger, sticks his head in through the crack on the other side of the slab, and hurries to get his tail round after him. Alligator springs, and his jaws come together with a snap. He misses, for his nose is large and the snake's body down in the angle formed by the slabs and the floor. He snaps again as the tail comes round. He has the snake now, and tugs it out eighteen inches. Thud, thud comes the woman's club on the ground. Alligator pulls again. Thud, thud. Alligator gives another pull and he has the snake out—a black brute, five feet long. The head rises to dart about, but the dog has the enemy close to the neck. He is a big, heavy dog, but quick as a terrier. He shakes the snake as though he felt the original curse in common with mankind. The eldest boy wakes up, seizes his stick, and tries to get out of bed, but his mother forces him back with a grip of iron. Thud, thud—the snake's back is broken in several places. Thud, thud—its head is crushed, and Alligator's nose skinned again.

She lifts the mangled reptile on the point of her stick, carries it to the fire, and throws it in; then piles on the wood, and watches the snake burn. The boy and dog watch, too. She lays her hand on the dog's head, and all the fierce, angry light dies out of his yellow eyes. The younger children are quieted, and presently go to sleep. The dirty-legged boy stands for a moment in his shirt, watching the fire. Presently he looks up at her, sees the tears in her eyes, and, throwing his arms around her neck, exclaims:

"Mother, I won't never go drovin'; blast me if I do!"

And she hugs him to her worn-out breast and kisses him; and they sit thus together while the sickly daylight breaks over the bush.

Debating Race

from Thomas Carlyle, "Occasional Discourse on the Negro Question," *Fraser's Magazine* (1849)

In the wake of the abolition of slavery in all British possessions in 1833, and of the ending of the preferential tariff on sugar in 1846, plantation owners in the British West Indies complained vociferously about their situation, arguing that they were placed in the unfair position of having to compete against sugar produced in countries such as Brazil where slavery was still permitted. Amongst the many in Britain who supported their arguments was Thomas Carlyle, who sets out his position in the essay excerpted below. Shortly thereafter, John Stuart Mill delivered a stinging reply, also excerpted below. In the 1860s the two also disagreed publicly over the Morant Bay rebellion, an uprising in Jamaica against the oppressive conditions under which Black Jamaicans were forced to work, which became a *cause célèbre* in England when the rebellion was suppressed, with extraordinary brutality, by Governor Edward John Eyre.

West Indian affairs, as we all know, and some of us know to our cost, are in a rather troublous condition this good while. In regard to West Indian affairs, however, Lord John Russell[1] is able to comfort us with one fact, indisputable where so many are dubious, that the negroes are all very happy and doing well. A fact very comfortable indeed. West Indian whites, it is admitted, are far enough from happy; West Indian colonies not unlike sinking wholly into ruin; at home, too, the British whites are rather badly off—several millions of them hanging on the verge of continual famine—and, in single towns, many thousands of them very sore put to it, at this time ... to live at all—these, again, are uncomfortable facts; and they are extremely extensive and important ones. But ... how pleasant to have always this fact to fall back upon; our beautiful black darlings are at last happy; with little labor except to the teeth, *which*, surely, in those excellent horse-jaws of theirs, will not fail!

Exeter Hall,[2] my philanthropic friends, has had its way in this matter. The twenty millions, a mere trifle, despatched with a single dash of the pen, are paid;[3] and, far over the sea, we have a few black persons rendered extremely "free" indeed. Sitting yonder, with their beautiful muzzles up to the ears in pumpkins, imbibing sweet pulps and juices; the grinder and incisor teeth ready for every new work, and the pumpkins cheap as grass in those rich climates; while the sugar crops rot round them, uncut, because labor cannot be hired. ... A state of matters lovely to contemplate, in these emancipated epochs of the human mind, which has earned us, not only the praises of Exeter Hall, and loud, long-eared hallelujahs of laudatory psalmody[4] from the friends of freedom everywhere, but lasting favor (it is hoped) from the heavenly powers themselves; which may, at least, justly appeal to the heavenly powers, and ask them,

if ever, in terrestrial procedure, they saw the match of it! Certainly, in the past history of the human species, it has no parallel; nor, one hopes, will it have in the future. ...

Truly, my philanthropic friends, Exeter Hall philanthropy is wonderful; and the social science ... which finds the secret of this universe in "supply and demand," and reduces the duty of human governors to that of letting men alone, is also wonderful. A dreary, desolate and, indeed, quite abject and distressing one; what we might call, by way of eminence, the *dismal science*.[5] These two, Exeter Hall philanthropy and the Dismal Science, led by any sacred cause of black emancipation, or the like, to fall in love and make a wedding of it—will give birth to progenies and prodigies: dark extensive moon-calves, unnameable abortions,[6] wide-coiled monstrosities, such as the world has not seen hitherto! ...

My philanthropic friends, can you discern no fixed headlands in this wide-weltering[7] deluge of benevolent twaddle and revolutionary grapeshot that has burst forth on us—no sure bearings at all? Fact and nature, it seems to me, say a few words to us, if, happily, we have still an ear for fact and nature. Let us listen a little, and try. And first, with regard to the West Indies, it may be laid down as a principle, which no eloquence in Exeter Hall, or Westminster Hall,[8] or elsewhere, can invalidate or hide, except for a short time only, that no black man, who will not work according to what ability the gods have given him for working, has the smallest right to eat pumpkin, or to any fraction of land that will grow pumpkin, however plentiful such land may be, but has an indisputable and perpetual *right* to be compelled, by the real proprietors of said land, to do competent work for his living. This is the everlasting duty of all men, black or white, who are born into this world. To do competent work, to labor honestly according to the

---

[1] *Lord John Russell* Russell (1792–1878) was British Prime Minister from 1846 to 1852 and from 1865 to 1866.

[2] *Exeter Hall* Exeter Hall, on the Strand, in London, was built in 1830 to serve as a meeting place for a variety of religious groups, benevolent associations, and other charitable institutions.

[3] *The twenty millions ... paid* When the British government abolished slavery in its possessions, it also paid £20 million in compensation to enslavers for the loss of their "property." This amounted to 5% of Britain's gross domestic product at the time, or nearly half of the British Treasury's annual income.

[4] *psalmody* Singing of psalms.

[5] *dismal science* This famous phrase describing the science now known as economics has often been cited as first used by Carlyle in his "Latter Day Pamphlet" (1850), rather than in the present essay.

[6] *moon-calves* Deformed creatures; *abortions* In this context, malformed or incompletely-gestated beings.

[7] *wide-weltering* State of turmoil, often used to describe the sea.

[8] *Westminster Hall* Location of British Parliament.

ability given them; for that, and for no other purpose, was each one of us sent into this world; and woe is to every man who by friend or by foe, is prevented from fulfilling this, the end of his being. ...

The idle black man in the West Indies had, not long since, the right, and will again, under better form, if it please Heaven, have the right (actually the first "right of man" for an indolent person) to be *compelled* to work as he was fit, and to *do* the Maker's will, who had constructed him with such and such prefigurements of capability. ...

And now observe, my friends, it was not Black Quashee,[1] or those he represents, that made those West India islands what they are, or can, by any hypothesis, be considered to have the right of growing pumpkins there. For countless ages, since they first mounted oozy on the back of earthquakes, from their dark bed in the ocean deeps, and reeking, saluted the tropical sun, and ever onward, till the European white man first saw them, some three short centuries ago, those islands had produced mere jungle, savagery, poison reptiles and swamp malaria till the white European first saw them, they were, as if not yet created; their noble elements of cinnamon—sugar, coffee, pepper, black and gray, lying all asleep, waiting the white Enchanter, who should say to them, awake! Till the end of human history, and the sounding of the trump of doom, they might have lain so, had Quashee, and the like of him, been the only artists in the game. Swamps, fever-jungles, man-eating caribs, rattle-snakes, and reeking waste and putrefaction: this had been the produce of them under the incompetent caribal[2] (what we call cannibal) possessors till that time; and Quashee knows, himself, whether ever he could have introduced an improvement. Him, had he, by a miraculous chance, been wafted thither, the caribals would have eaten, rolling him as a fat morsel under their tongue—for him, till the sounding of the trump of doom, the rattlesnakes and savageries would have held

on their way. It was not he, then—it was another than he! ... Quashee, if he will not help in bringing out the spices, will get himself made a slave again (which state will be a little less ugly than his present one), and with beneficent whip, since other methods avail not, will be compelled to work. ... The gods are long-suffering; but the law, from the beginning, was, He that will not work shall perish from the earth—and the patience of the gods has limits!

Before the West Indies could grow a pumpkin for any negro, how much European heroism had to spend itself in obscure battle; to sink, in mortal agony, before the jungles, the putrescences and waste savageries could become arable, and the devils be, in some measure, chained there! The West Indies grow pineapples, and sweet fruits, and spices; we hope they will, one day, grow beautiful, heroic human lives too, which is surely the ultimate object they were made for; beautiful souls and brave; sages, poets, what not—making the earth nobler round them, as their kindred from of old have been doing; ... heroic white men, worthy to be called old Saxons, browned with a mahogany tint in those new climates and conditions. But under the soil of Jamaica, before it could even produce spices, or any pumpkin, the bones of many thousand British men had to be laid. ...

Already one hears of black *Adscripti glebae*;[3] which seems a promising arrangement, one of the first to suggest itself in such a complicacy. It appears the Dutch blacks, in Java, are already a kind of *Adscripts*, after the manner of the old European serfs; bound by royal authority, to give so many days of work a year. Is not this something like a real approximation; the first step toward all manner of such? Wherever, in British territory, there exists a black man, and needful work to the just extent is not to be got out of him, such a law, in defect of better, should be brought to bear upon said black man! ...

---

[1] *Quashee* African first name, used by some eighteenth- and nineteenth-century writers to stand for all Black people.

[2] *caribal* Insulting combination of "Carib," Indigenous person of the West Indies, and "cannibal."

---

[3] *Adscripti glebae* Latin: Permanently tied to the land; serfs.

from John Stuart Mill, "The Negro Question,"
Fraser's Magazine (1850)

TO THE EDITOR OF *FRASER'S MAGAZINE*

Sir:

Your last month's number contains a speech against the "rights of Negroes," the doctrines and spirit of which ought not to pass without remonstrance. The author issues his opinions, or rather ordinances, under imposing auspices no less than those of the "immortal gods." "The Powers," "the Destinies," announce, through him, not only what *will* be, but what *shall* be done; what they "have decided upon, passed their eternal act of Parliament for." This is speaking "as one having authority"; but authority from whom? If by the quality of the message we may judge of those who sent it, not from any powers to whom just or good men acknowledge allegiance. This so-called "eternal act of Parliament" is no new law, but the old law of the strongest—a law against which the great teachers of mankind have in all ages protested—it is the law of force and cunning; the law that whoever is more powerful than an other, is "born lord" of that other, the other being born his "servant," who must be "compelled to work" for him by "beneficent whip," if "other methods avail not." I see nothing divine in this injunction. If "the gods" will this, it is the first duty of human beings to resist such gods. Omnipotent these "gods" are *not*, for powers which demand *human* tyranny and injustice cannot accomplish their purpose unless human beings cooperate. The history of human improvement is the record of a struggle by which inch after inch of ground has been wrung from these maleficent[1] powers, and more and more of human life rescued from the iniquitous[2] dominion of the law of might. Much, very much of this work still remains to do; but the progress made in it is the best and greatest achievement yet performed by mankind, and it was hardly to be expected at this period of the world that we should be enjoined, by way of a great reform in human affair, to begin *un*doing it.

---

[1] *maleficent* Harmful, evil.

[2] *iniquitous* Unjust, unrighteous.

... I must first set my anti-philanthropic opponent right on a matter of fact. He entirely misunderstands the great national revolt of the conscience of this country against slavery and the slave-trade if he supposes it to have been an affair of sentiment. It depended no more on humane feelings than any cause which so irresistibly appealed to them must necessarily do: Its first victories were gained while the lash yet ruled uncontested in the barrack-yard, and the rod in schools, and while men were still hanged by dozens for stealing to the value of forty shillings. It triumphed because it was the cause of justice; and, in the estimation of the great majority of its supporters, of religion. Its originators and leaders were persons of a stern sense of moral obligation, who, in the spirit of the religion of their time, seldom spoke much of benevolence and philanthropy, but often of duty, crime, and sin. For nearly two centuries had negroes, many thousands annually, been seized by force or treachery and carried off to the West Indies to be worked to death, literally to death; for it was the received maxim, the acknowledged dictate of good economy, to wear them out quickly and import more. In this fact every other possible cruelty, tyranny, and wanton oppression was by implication included. And the motive on the part of the slave-owners was the love of gold; or, to speak more truly, of vulgar and puerile[3] ostentation. I have yet to learn that anything more detestable than this has been done by human beings towards human beings in any part of the earth. ...

After fifty years of toil and sacrifice, the object was accomplished, and the negroes, freed from the despotism of their fellow-beings, were left to themselves, and to the chances which the arrangements of existing society provide for these who have no resource but their labour. These chances proved favorable to them, and, for the last ten years, they afford the unusual spectacle of a labouring class whose labour bears so high a price that they can exist in comfort on the wages of a comparatively small quantity of work. This, to the ex-slaveowners, is an inconvenience; but I have not yet heard that any of them has been reduced to beg his bread, or

---

[3] *puerile* Childish.

even to dig for it, as the negro, however scandalously he enjoys himself, still must. … If the [plantation owners] cannot continue to realize their large incomes without more labourers, let them find them, and bring them from where they can best be procured, only not by force. Not so, thinks your anti-philanthropic contributor. That negroes should exist, and enjoy existence, on so little work, is a scandal, in his eyes, worse than their former slavery. It must be put a stop to at any price. He does not "wish to see" them slaves again "if it can be avoided"; but "decidedly" they "will have to be servants," "servants to the whites," "compelled to labour," and "not to go idle another minute." "Black Quashee," "up to the ears in pumpkins," and "working about half an hour a day," is to him the abomination of abominations.

… To give it a rational meaning, it must first be known what he means by work. Does work mean everything which people *do*? No; or he would not reproach people with doing no work. Does it mean laborious exertion? No; for many a day spent in killing game, includes more muscular fatigue than a day's ploughing. Does it mean *useful* exertion? But your contributor always scoffs at the idea of utility. Does he mean that all persons ought to earn their living? But some earn their living by doing nothing, and some by doing mischief; and the negroes, whom he despises, still do earn by labour the "pumpkins" they consume and the finery they wear.

Work, I imagine, is not a good in itself. There is nothing laudable in work for work's sake. To work voluntarily for a worthy object is laudable; but what constitutes a worthy object? On this matter, the oracle of which your contributor is the prophet[1] has never yet been prevailed on to declare itself. He revolves in an eternal circle round the idea of work, as if turning up the earth, or driving a shuttle[2] or a quill, were ends in themselves, and the ends of human existence. Yet, even in the case of the most sublime service to humanity, it is not because it is work that it is worthy; the worth lies in the service itself, and in the will to render it—the noble

feelings of which it is the fruit; and if the nobleness of will is proved by other evidence than work, as for instance by danger or sacrifice, there is the same worthiness. While we talk only of work, and not of its object, we are far from the root of the matter; or, if it may be called the root, it is a root without flower or fruit.

In the present case, it seems, a noble object means "spices."—"The gods wish, besides pumpkins, that spices and valuable products be grown in their West Indies"—the "noble elements of cinnamon, sugar, coffee, pepper black and gray," "things far nobler than pumpkins." Why so? Is what supports life inferior in dignity to what merely gratifies the sense of taste? Is it the verdict of the "immortal gods" that pepper is noble, freedom (even freedom from the lash) contemptible? But spices lead "towards commerces, arts, polities, and social developments." Perhaps so; but of what sort? When they must be produced by slaves, the "polities and social developments" they lead to are such as the world, I hope, will not choose to be cursed with much longer.

The worth of work does not surely consist in its leading to other work, and so on to work upon work without end. On the contrary, the multiplication of work, for purposes not worth caring about, is one of the evils of our present condition. When justice and reason shall be the rule of human affairs, one of the first things to which we may expect them to be applied is the question, How many of the so-called luxuries, conveniences, refinements, and ornaments of life, are *worth* the labour which must be undergone as the condition of producing them? The beautifying of existence is as worthy and useful an object as the sustaining of it; but only a vitiated[3] taste can see any such result in those fopperies[4] of so-called civilization, which myriads of hands are now occupied and lives wasted in providing. In opposition to the "gospel of work," I would assert the gospel of leisure, and maintain that human beings *cannot* rise to the finer attributes of their nature compatibly with a life filled with labour. I do not include under the name labour such work, if work it be called, as is

---

[1] *prophet* With the publication of *Past and Present* in 1843, Carlyle began to be considered a visionary, even a prophetic voice, of social and cultural commentary in England.

[2] *shuttle* Instrument used in weaving.

[3] *vitiated* Corrupted.

[4] *fopperies* Here, useless consumer goods.

done by writers and afforders of "guidance," an occupation which, let alone the vanity of the thing, cannot be called by the same name with the real labour, the exhausting, stiffening, stupefying toil of many kinds of agricultural and manufacturing labourers. To reduce very greatly the quantity of work required to carry on existence is as needful as to distribute it more equally; and the progress of science, and the increasing ascendency of justice and good sense, tend to this result.

There is a portion of work rendered necessary by the fact of each person's existence: no one could exist unless work, to a certain amount, were done either by or for him. Of this each person is bound, in justice, to perform his share; and society has an incontestable right to declare to every one, that if he work not, at this work of necessity, neither shall he eat. Society has not enforced this right, having in so far postponed the rule of justice to other considerations. But there is an ever-growing demand that it be enforced, so soon as any endurable plan can be devised for the purpose. If this experiment is to be tried in the West Indies, let it be tried impartially; and let the whole produce belong to those who do the work which produces it. We would not have black labourers compelled to grow spices which they do not want, and white proprietors who do not work at all exchanging the spices for houses in Belgrave Square.[1] We would not withhold from the whites, any more than from the blacks, the "divine right" of being compelled to labour. Let them have exactly the same share in the produce that they have in the work. If they do not like this, let them remain as they are, so long as they are permitted, and make the best of supply and demand.

Your contributor's notions of justice and proprietary right are of another kind than these. According to him, the whole West Indies belong to the whites: the negroes have no claim there, to either land or food, but by their sufferance. "It was not Black Quashee, or those he represents, that made those West India islands what they are." I submit, that those who furnished the thews[2] and sinews really had something to do with the matter.

But the great ethical doctrine of the discourse, … than which a doctrine more damnable, I should think, never was propounded by a professed moral reformer, is, that one kind of human beings are born servants to another kind. "You will have to be servants," he tells the negroes, "to those that are born wiser than you, that are born lords of you—servants to the whites, if they are (as what mortal can doubt that they are?) born wiser than you." I do not hold him to the absurd letter of his dictum; it belongs to the mannerism in which he is enthralled like a child in swaddling clothes. By "born wiser," I will suppose him to mean, born more capable of wisdom: a proposition which, he says, no mortal can doubt, but which, I will make bold to say, that a full moiety[3] of all thinking persons, who have attended to the subject, either doubt or positively deny.

Among the things for which your contributor professes entire disrespect, is the analytical examination of human nature. It is by analytical examination that we have learned whatever we know of the laws of external nature; and if he had not disdained to apply the same mode of investigation to the laws of the formation of character, he would have escaped the vulgar error of imputing every difference which he finds among human beings to an original difference of nature. As well might it be said, that of two trees, sprung from the same stock one cannot be taller than another but from greater vigor in the original seedling. Is nothing to be attributed to soil, nothing to climate, nothing to difference of exposure—has no storm swept over the one and not the other, no lightning scathed it, no beast browsed on it, no insects preyed on it, no passing stranger stripped off its leaves or its bark? If the trees grew near together, may not the one which, by whatever accident, grew up first, have retarded the other's development by its shade? Human beings are subject to an infinitely greater variety of accidents and external influences than trees, and have infinitely more operation in impairing the growth of one another; since those who begin by being strongest, have almost always hitherto used their strength to keep the others weak. What the original differences are

---

[1] *Belgrave Square* Fashionable area of London.

[2] *thews* Muscles.

[3] *moiety* Half.

among human beings, I know no more than your contributor, and no less; it is one of the questions not yet satisfactorily answered in the natural history of the species. This, however, is well known—that spontaneous improvement, beyond a very low grade—improvement by internal development, without aid from other individuals or peoples—is one of the rarest phenomena in history; and whenever known to have occurred, was the result of an extraordinary combination of advantages; in addition doubtless to many accidents of which all trace is now lost. No argument against the capacity of negroes for improvement, could be drawn from their not being one of these rare exceptions. It is curious, withal, that the earliest known civilization was, we have the strongest reason to believe, a negro civilization. The original Egyptians are inferred, from the evidence of their sculptures, to have been a negro race: it was from negroes, therefore, that the Greeks learnt their first lessons in civilization; … but I again renounce all advantage from facts: [even if it *were* true that] whites [were] born ever so superior in intelligence to the blacks, and competent by nature to instruct and advise them, it would not be the less monstrous to assert that they had therefore a right either to subdue them by force, or circumvent them by superior skill; to throw upon them the toils and hardships of life, reserving for themselves, under the misapplied name of work, its agreeable excitements. …

Though we cannot extirpate[1] all pain, we can, if we are sufficiently determined upon it, abolish all tyranny; one of the greatest victories yet gained over that enemy is slave-emancipation and all Europe is struggling, with various success, towards further conquests over it. If, in the pursuit of this, we lose sight of any object equally important; if we forget that freedom is not the only thing necessary for human beings, let us be thankful to any one who points out what is wanting; but let us not consent to turn back. That this country should turn back, in the matter of negro slavery, I have not the smallest apprehension.

There is, however, another place where that tyranny still flourishes, but now for the first time finds itself seriously in danger. At this crisis of American slavery, when the decisive conflict between right and iniquity seems about to commence, your contributor steps in, and flings this missile, loaded with the weight of his reputation, into the abolitionist camp. The words of English writers of celebrity are words of power on the other side of the ocean; and the owners of human flesh, who probably thought they had not an honest man on their side between the Atlantic and the Vistula,[2] will welcome such an auxiliary. Circulated as his dissertation will probably be, by those whose interests profit by it, from one end of the American Union to the other, I hardly know of an act by which one person could have done so much mischief as this may possibly do; and I hold that by thus acting, he has made himself an instrument of what an able writer in the *Inquirer* justly calls "a true work of the devil."[3]

from Charles Dickens, "The Noble Savage,"[4] *Household Words* (1853)

Dickens wrote the essay presented below as a response to the popularity of various exhibitions of Indigenous peoples (some of which are described in the essay) in mid-nineteenth-century Britain. The essay was published in *Household Words*, a weekly magazine Dickens edited.

To come to the point at once, I beg to say that I have not the least belief in the Noble Savage. I consider him a prodigious nuisance, and an enormous superstition. His calling rum firewater, and me a pale face, wholly fail to reconcile me to him. I don't care what he

---

[1] *extirpate* To remove, literally pull out roots.

[2] *between the Atlantic and the Vistula* I.e., in Britain or in Continental Europe. (The Vistula is a river in Poland.)

[3] *writer … devil* From an article responding to Carlyle in *London Inquirer*: "It is a true work of the Devil, the fostering of a tyrannical prejudice."

[4] *Noble Savage* The notion of the "noble savage" is associated with the ideas of the French philosopher Jean-Jacques Rousseau (1712–78), who held that human beings are naturally innocent and good, but become corrupted by civilized society. According to this way of thinking, Indigenous peoples were seen as inherently nobler because they were closer to a "state of nature."

calls me. I call him a savage, and I call a savage a some-thing highly desirable to be civilised off the face of the earth. I think a mere gent (which I take to be the lowest form of civilisation) better than a howling, whistling, clucking, stamping, jumping, tearing savage. It is all one to me, whether he sticks a fish-bone through his visage, or bits of trees through the lobes of his ears, or bird's feathers in his head; whether he flattens his hair between two boards, or spreads his nose over the breadth of his face, or drags his lower lip down by great weights, or blackens his teeth, or knocks them out, or paints one cheek red and the other blue, or tattoos himself, or oils himself, or rubs his body with fat, or crimps it with knives. Yielding to whichsoever of these agreeable eccentricities, he is a savage cruel, false, thievish, mur-derous; addicted more or less to grease, entrails, and beastly customs; a wild animal with the questionable gift of boasting; a conceited, tiresome, bloodthirsty, monot-onous humbug.

Yet it is extraordinary to observe how some people will talk about him, as they talk about the good old times; how they will regret his disappearance, in the course of this world's development, from such and such lands where his absence is a blessed relief and an indis-pensable preparation for the sowing of the very first seeds of any influence that can exalt humanity; how, even with the evidence of himself before them, they will either be determined to believe, or will suffer themselves to be persuaded into believing, that he is something which their five senses tell them he is not.

There was Mr. Catlin,[1] some few years ago, with his Ojibbeway Indians. Mr. Catlin was an energetic, earnest man, who had lived among more tribes of Indians than I need reckon up here, and who had written a pictur-esque and glowing book about them. With his party of Indians squatting and spitting on the table before him, or dancing their miserable jigs after their own dreary manner, he called, in all good faith, upon his civilised audience to take notice of their symmetry and grace, their perfect limbs, and the exquisite expression of their

pantomime; and his civilised audience, in all good faith, complied and admired. Whereas, as mere animals, they were wretched creatures, very low in the scale and very poorly formed; and as men and women possessing any power of truthful dramatic expression by means of action, they were no better than the chorus at an Italian Opera in England—and would have been worse if such a thing were possible.

Mine are no new views of the noble savage. The greatest writers on natural history found him out long ago. Buffon[2] knew what he was, and showed why he is the sulky tyrant that he is to his women, and how it happens (Heaven be praised!) that his race is spare in numbers. For evidence of the quality of his moral nature, pass himself for a moment and refer to his "faithful dog." Has he ever improved a dog, or attached a dog, since his nobility first ran wild in woods, and was brought down (at a very long shot) by Pope?[3] Or does the animal that is the friend of man, always degenerate in his low society?

It is not the miserable nature of the noble savage that is the new thing; it is the whimpering over him with maudlin admiration, and the affecting to regret him, and the drawing of any comparison of advantage between the blemishes of civilisation and the tenor of his swinish life. There may have been a change now and then in those diseased absurdities, but there is none in him.

Think of the Bushmen.[4] Think of the two men and the two women who have been exhibited about England for some years. Are the majority of persons—who remem-ber the horrid little leader of that party in his festering bundle of hides, with his filth and his antipathy to water, and his straddled legs, and his odious eyes shaded by his

[1] *Mr. Catlin* George Catlin (1796–1872) pioneered the Wild West Show, which brought Indigenous peoples and cultures from the American West to the American east coast and to Europe.

[2] *Buffon* Georges-Louis Leclerc, Comte de Buffon (1707–88), French naturalist and mathematician.

[3] *Pope* Alexander Pope (1688–1744), British poet. Dickens refers to two passages in Pope's long didactic poem *An Essay on Man* (1733–34); in the first, Pope patronizingly describes "the poor Indian" and his belief that "this faithful Dog" will accompany him into the afterlife, while in the second, he condemns those who believe that virtuous actions will bring them material rewards after their death: "Go, like the Indian, in another life / Expect thy dog, thy bottle, and thy wife."

[4] *Bushmen* European name for peoples of the Kalahari desert.

brutal hand, and his cry of "Qu-u-u-u-aaa!" (Bosjesman[1] for something desperately insulting I have no doubt)—conscious of an affectionate yearning towards that noble savage, or is it idiosyncratic in me to abhor, detest, abominate, and abjure him? I have no reserve on this subject, and will frankly state that, setting aside that stage of the entertainment when he counterfeited the death of some creature he had shot, by laying his head on his hand and shaking his left leg—at which time I think it would have been justifiable homicide to slay him—I have never seen that group sleeping, smoking, and expectorating round their brazier, but I have sincerely desired that something might happen to the charcoal smouldering therein, which would cause the immediate suffocation of the whole of the noble strangers.

There is at present a party of Zulu Kaffirs[2] exhibiting at the St. George's Gallery, Hyde Park Corner, London. These noble savages are represented in a most agreeable manner; they are seen in an elegant theatre, fitted with appropriate scenery of great beauty, and they are described in a very sensible and unpretending lecture, delivered with a modesty which is quite a pattern to all similar exponents. Though extremely ugly, they are much better shaped than such of their predecessors as I have referred to; and they are rather picturesque to the eye, though far from odoriferous to the nose. What a visitor left to his own interpretings and imaginings might suppose these noblemen to be about, when they give vent to that pantomimic expression which is quite settled to be the natural gift of the noble savage, I cannot possibly conceive; for it is so much too luminous for my personal civilisation that it conveys no idea to my mind beyond a general stamping, ramping, and raving, remarkable (as everything in savage life is) for its dire uniformity. But let us—with the interpreter's assistance, of which I for one stand so much in need—see what the noble savage does in Zulu Kaffirland.

The noble savage sets a king to reign over him, to whom he submits his life and limbs without a murmur or question, and whose whole life is passed chin deep in a lake of blood; but who, after killing incessantly, is in his turn killed by his relations and friends, the moment a grey hair appears on his head. All the noble savage's wars with his fellow-savages (and he takes no pleasure in anything else) are wars of extermination—which is the best thing I know of him, and the most comfortable to my mind when I look at him. He has no moral feelings of any kind, sort, or description; and his "mission" may be summed up as simply diabolical.

The ceremonies with which he faintly diversifies his life are, of course, of a kindred nature. If he wants a wife he appears before the kennel of the gentleman whom he has selected for his father-in-law, attended by a party of male friends of a very strong flavour, who screech and whistle and stamp an offer of so many cows for the young lady's hand. The chosen father-in-law—also supported by a high-flavoured party of male friends—screeches, whistles, and yells (being seated on the ground, he can't stamp) that there never was such a daughter in the market as his daughter, and that he must have six more cows. The son-in-law and his select circle of backers screech, whistle, stamp, and yell in reply, that they will give three more cows. The father-in-law (an old deluder, overpaid at the beginning) accepts four, and rises to bind the bargain. The whole party, the young lady included, then falling into epileptic convulsions, and screeching, whistling, stamping, and yelling together—and nobody taking any notice of the young lady (whose charms are not to be thought of without a shudder)—the noble savage is considered married, and his friends make demoniacal leaps at him by way of congratulation.

When the noble savage finds himself a little unwell, and mentions the circumstance to his friends, it is immediately perceived that he is under the influence of witchcraft. A learned personage, called an Imyanger or Witch Doctor, is immediately sent for to Nooker the Umtargartie, or smell out the witch. The male inhabitants of the kraal[3] being seated on the ground, the learned doctor, got up like a grizzly bear, appears, and administers a dance of a most terrific nature, during the

---

[1] *Bosjesman* Language of the "Bushmen."

[2] *Kaffirs* Derogatory term for Africans.

[3] *kraal* A community of Indigenous people in southern or central Africa, typically dwelling in huts surrounded by a stockade.

exhibition of which remedy he incessantly gnashes his teeth, and howls:—"I am the original physician to Nooker the Umtargartie. Yow yow yow! No connexion with any other establishment. Till till till! All other Umtargarties are feigned Umtargarties, Boroo Boroo! but I perceive here a genuine and real Umtargartie, Hoosh Hoosh Hoosh! in whose blood I, the original Imyanger and Nookerer, Blizzerum Boo! will wash these bear's claws of mine. O yow yow yow!" All this time the learned physician is looking out among the attentive faces for some unfortunate man who owes him a cow, or who has given him any small offence, or against whom, without offence, he has conceived a spite. Him he never fails to Nooker as the Umtargartie, and he is instantly killed. In the absence of such an individual, the usual practice is to Nooker the quietest and most gentlemanly person in company. But the nookering is invariably followed on the spot by the butchering.

Some of the noble savages in whom Mr. Catlin was so strongly interested, and the diminution of whose numbers, by rum and smallpox, greatly affected him, had a custom not unlike this, though much more appalling and disgusting in its odious details.

The women being at work in the fields, hoeing the Indian corn, and the noble savage being asleep in the shade, the chief has sometimes the condescension to come forth, and lighten the labour by looking at it. On these occasions, he seats himself in his own savage chair, and is attended by his shield-bearer: who holds over his head a shield of cowhide—in shape like an immense mussel shell fearfully and wonderfully, after the manner of a theatrical supernumerary. But lest the great man should forget his greatness in the contemplation of the humble works of agriculture, there suddenly rushes in a poet, retained for the purpose, called a Praiser. This literary gentleman wears a leopard's head over his own, and a dress of tigers' tails; he has the appearance of having come express on his hind legs from the Zoological Gardens; and he incontinently strikes up the chief's praises, plunging and tearing all the while. There is a frantic wickedness in this brute's manner of worrying the air, and gnashing out, "O what a delightful chief he is! O what a delicious quantity of blood he sheds! O

how majestically he laps it up! O how charmingly cruel he is! O how he tears the flesh of his enemies and crunches the bones! O how like the tiger and the leopard and the wolf and the bear he is! O, row row row row, how fond I am of him!" which might tempt the Society of Friends[1] to charge at a hand-gallop into the Swartz-Kop location and exterminate the whole kraal.

When war is afoot among the noble savages—which is always—the chief holds a council to ascertain whether it is the opinion of his brothers and friends in general that the enemy shall be exterminated. On this occasion, after the performance of an Umsebeuza, or war song,— which is exactly like all the other songs, the chief makes a speech to his brothers and friends, arranged in single file. No particular order is observed during the delivery of this address, but every gentleman who finds himself excited by the subject, instead of crying "Hear, hear!" as is the custom with us, darts from the rank and tramples out the life, or crushes the skull, or mashes the face, or scoops out the eyes, or breaks the limbs, or performs a whirlwind of atrocities on the body, of an imaginary enemy. Several gentlemen becoming thus excited at once, and pounding away without the least regard to the orator, that illustrious person is rather in the position of an orator in an Irish House of Commons. But, several of these scenes of savage life bear a strong generic resemblance to an Irish election, and I think would be extremely well received and understood at Cork.[2]

In all these ceremonies the noble savage holds forth to the utmost possible extent about himself; from which (to turn him to some civilised account) we may learn, I think, that as egotism is one of the most offensive and contemptible littlenesses a civilised man can exhibit, so it is really incompatible with the interchange of ideas; inasmuch as if we all talked about ourselves we should soon have no listeners, and must be all yelling and screeching at once on our own separate accounts:

[1] *Society of Friends* Formal name of the Quakers, a Christian denomination known for its pacifism; many of its members were also prominent opponents of slavery.

[2] *Several gentlemen ... Cork* Dickens is displaying his prejudice against the Irish, who were frequently held, by many in England, to be "savages."

making society hideous. It is my opinion that if we retained in us anything of the noble savage, we could not get rid of it too soon. But the fact is clearly otherwise. Upon the wife and dowry question, substituting coin for cows, we have assuredly nothing of the Zulu Kaffir left. The endurance of despotism is one great distinguishing mark of a savage always. The improving world has quite got the better of that too. In like manner, Paris is a civilised city, and the Théâtre Français a highly civilised theatre; and we shall never hear, and never have heard in these later days (of course) of the Praiser THERE. No, no, civilised poets have better work to do. As to Nookering Umtargarties, there are no pretended Umtargarties in Europe, and no European powers to Nooker them; that would be mere spydom, subordination, small malice, superstition, and false pretence. And as to private Umtargarties, are we not in the year eighteen hundred and fifty-three, with spirits rapping at our doors?

To conclude as I began. My position is, that if we have anything to learn from the Noble Savage, it is what to avoid. His virtues are a fable; his happiness is a delusion; his nobility, nonsense.

We have no greater justification for being cruel to the miserable object, than for being cruel to a WILLIAM SHAKESPEARE or an ISAAC NEWTON; but he passes away before an immeasurably better and higher power than ever ran wild in any earthly woods, and the world will be all the better when his place knows him no more.

from J.J. Thomas, *Froudacity* (1889)

John Jacob Thomas (1841–89) was a Trinidadian schoolmaster, linguist, civil servant, and author. *Froudacity* is a pointed rejoinder to James Anthony Froude's racist defense of British colonialism, *The English in the West Indies* (1888).

from BOOK 3
THE NEGRO AS A WORKER

The laziness, the incurable idleness, of the Negro, was, both immediately before their emancipation in 1838, and for long years after that event, the cuckoo-cry[1] of their white detractors. It was laziness, pure and simple, which hindered the Negro from exhausting himself under a tropical sun, toiling at starvation wages to ensure for his quondam[2] master the means of being an idler himself, with the additional luxury of rolling in easily come-by wealth. Within the last twenty years, however, the history of the Black Man, both in the West Indies and, better still, in the United States of America, has been a succession of achievements which have converted the charge of laziness into a baseless and absurd calumny.[3] The repetition of the charge referred to is, in these waning days of the nineteenth century, a discredited anachronism, which, however, has no deterring features for Mr. Froude. As the running down of the Negro was his cue, he went in boldly for the game, with what result we shall presently see. … [O]ur author, speaking of the Negro garden-farms in Jamaica, says:

"The male proprietors were *lounging about* smoking. Their wives, as it was market-day, were tramping into Kingston with their baskets on their heads. We met them literally in thousands, all merry and light-hearted, their little ones with little baskets trudging at their side. Of the *lords of the creation* we saw, perhaps, one to each hundred of the women, and he would be riding on mule or donkey, pipe in mouth and *carrying nothing*. He would be generally *sulky* too, while the ladies, young and old, had a civil word for us, and curtsied under their loads. Decidedly if there is to be a black constitution I will give my vote to the women."

To the above direct imputation of indolence, heartlessness, and moroseness, Mr. Froude appends the following remarks on other moral characteristics of certain sable peasants at Mandeville, Jamaica, given on the authority of a police official, who, our author says, described them as—

"Good-humoured, but not universally honest. They stole cattle, and would not give evidence against each

---

[1] *cuckoo-cry* Insistently and monotonously repeated theme (after the monotonous mating call of the cuckoo bird); the term also carries connotations of foolishness.
[2] *quondam* Former.
[3] *calumny* Slander.

other. If brought into Court, they held a pebble in their mouth, being under the impression that when they were so provided, perjury did not count. *Their education was only skin-deep, and the schools which the Government provided had not touched their characters at all.*"

But how could the education so provided be otherwise than futile when the administration of its details is entirely in the hands of persons unsympathizing with and utterly despising the Negro? But of this more anon and elsewhere. We resume Mr. Froude's evidence respecting the black peasantry. Our author proceeds to admit, on the same subject, that his informant's duties (as a police official) "brought him in contact with the unfavourable specimens." He adds:

"I received a far pleasanter impression from a Moravian minister. … I was particularly glad to see this gentleman, for of the Moravians every one had spoken well to me. He was not the least enthusiastic about his poor black sheep, but he said that if they were not better than the average English labourer, he did not think them worse. They were called idle; *they would work well enough if they had fair wages and if the wages were paid regularly; but what could be expected when women servants had but three shillings a week and found themselves, when the men had but a shilling a day and the pay was kept in arrear in order that if they came late to work, or if they came irregularly, it may be kept back or cut down to what the employer [chose] to give? Under such conditions* ANY *man of* ANY *colour would prefer to work for himself if he had a garden, or would be idle if he had none.*"

Take, again, the following extract regarding the heroism of the emigrants to the Canal:[1]

"I walked forward" (on the steamer bound to Jamaica), "after we had done talking. We had five hundred of the poor creatures on their way to the Darien[2] pandemonium. The vessel was rolling with a heavy beam sea. I found the whole mass of them reduced to the condition of the pigs who used to occupy the fore decks on the Cork and Bristol packets. They were lying in a confused heap together, helpless, misera-

ble, without consciousness, apparently, save a sense in each that he was wretched. Unfortunate brothers-in-law! following the laws of political economy, and carrying their labour to the dearest market, where, before a year was out, half of them were to die. They *had souls*, too, *some* of them, and honest and kindly hearts."

It surely is refreshing to read the revelation of his first learning of the possession of a soul by a fellow-human being, thus artlessly described by one who is said to be an ex-parson. But piquancy[3] is Mr. Froude's strong point, whatever else he may be found wanting in.

Still, apart from Mr. Froude's direct testimony to the fact that from year to year, during a long series of years, there has been a continuous, scarcely ever interrupted emigration of Negroes to the Spanish mainland,[4] in search of work for a sufficing livelihood for themselves and their families—and that in the teeth of physical danger, pestilence, and death—there would be enough indirect exoneration of the Black Man from that indictment in the wail of Mr. Froude and his friends regarding the alarming absorption of the lands of Grenada and Trinidad by sable proprietors. Land cannot be bought without money, nor can money be possessed except through labour, and the fact that so many tens of thousand Blacks are now the happy owners of the soil whereon, in the days so bitterly regretted by our author, their forefathers' tears, nay, very hearts' blood, had been caused to flow, ought to silence for ever an accusation, which, were it even true, would be futile, and, being false, is worse than disgraceful, coming from the lips of the Eumolpids who would fain impose a not-to-be questioned yoke on us poor helots[5] of Ethiopia. It is said that lying is the vice of slaves; but the ethics of West Indian would-be mastership assert, on its behalf, that they alone should enjoy the privilege of resorting to misrepresentation to give colour, if not solidity, to their pretensions.

---

[1] *the Canal* Attempts to build a canal through the Isthmus of Panama had begun in 1881.

[2] *Darien* Province in Panama through which the canal was being built.

[3] *piquancy* Ability to excite, stimulate, or charm.

[4] *to the Spanish mainland* I.e., to Panama (on the mainland of Spanish America).

[5] *Eumolpids* Ancient Greek priests; *helots* Serfs; "helots" were originally members of the large population enslaved by the citizens of ancient Sparta.

The Great Exhibition of 1851

No single event is more expressive of the place Britain saw itself and its Empire occupying in the world than the Great Exhibition of the Industry of all Nations of 1851. It was intended as a celebration of the achievements of the entire world, but also of the special place that Britain saw itself occupying in the world—economic engine, most powerful nation, moral leader. The brainchild very largely of the Prince Consort, the event attracted exhibitors from throughout the Empire and from many other nations; more than 6,200,000 people visited what came to be regarded as the first world's fair. The exhibition hall—popularly known as the Crystal Palace—occupied over twenty-one acres in Hyde Park in central London over a six-month period (after which it was disassembled and rebuilt in a suburban location). The Exhibition was a success in every respect, not least of all financially; revenues helped to fund the construction of both the Albert Hall and the Victoria and Albert Museum.

Engraving by H. Bibby of a daguerreotype by John J.E. Mayall, *Great Exhibition, Main Avenue Looking East*, 1851.

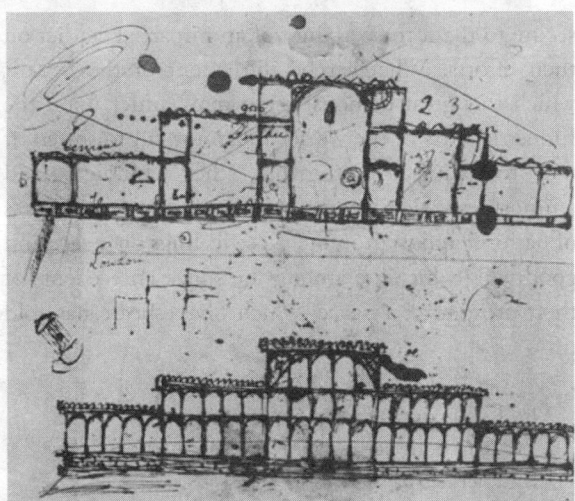

Joseph Paxton, first sketch for the Great Exhibition Building, 1850. From this initial sketch, drawn on blotting paper during a railway board meeting, Paxton developed the design of the Crystal Palace.

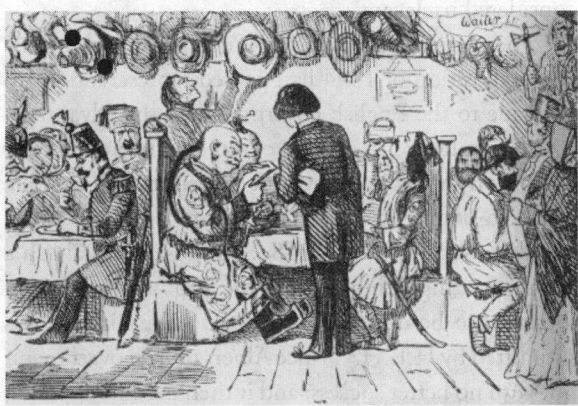

London Dining Rooms, 1851
Waiter (to Chinaman). "Very nice birds'-nest soup, Sir!—Yes, Sir!—Rat pie, Sir, just up—yes, Sir!—and a nice little dog to foller—yes, Sir!"

Cartoon from *Punch*, 1851. The Great Exhibition brought an unprecedented influx of foreign visitors to London—most from Europe, but some from much farther afield. The satirical magazine *Punch* was far from alone in engaging in casually racist ridicule of the cultural practices of foreigners. The original caption is reproduced above.

Prince Albert, Speech Delivered at the Lord Mayor's Banquet, London, 1849 (as reprinted in *The Illustrated London News*, 11 October 1849)

I conceive it to be the duty of every educated person closely to study and watch the time in which he lives; and as far as in him lies, to add his might of individual exertion to further the accomplishment of what he believes Providence to have ordained. Nobody, however, who has paid any attention to the features of our present era, will doubt for a moment that we are living at a period of most wonderful transition which tends rapidly to the accomplishment of that great end to which indeed, all history points—the realization of the unity of mankind. Not a unity which breaks down the limits and levels the peculiar characteristics of the different nations of the earth, but rather a unity, the result and product of those very national varieties and antagonistic qualities. The distances which separated the different nations and parts of the globe are gradually vanishing before the achievements of modern invention, and we can traverse them with incredible ease; the languages of all nations are known and their acquirements placed within the reach of everybody; thought is communicated with the rapidity and even by the power of lightning.

On the other hand, the great principle of the division of labour which may be called the moving power of civilization, is being extended to all branches of science, industry and art. Whilst formerly the greatest mental energies strove at universal knowledge, and that knowledge was confined to a few, now they are directed to specialities, and in these again, even to the minutest points; but the knowledge acquired becomes at once the property of the community at large. Whilst formerly discovery was wrapped in secrecy, the publicity of the present day causes, that no sooner is a discovery or invention made, than it is already improved upon and surpassed by competing efforts: the products of all quarters of the globe are placed at our disposal, and we have only to choose what is the cheapest and best for our purposes, and the powers of production are entrusted to the stimulus of competition and capital.

So man is approaching a more complete fulfillment of that great and sacred mission which he has to perform in this world. His reason being created after the image of God, he has to use it to discover the laws by which the Almighty governs His creation, and, by making these laws his standard of action, to conquer nature to his use—himself a divine instrument. Science discovers these laws of power, motion and transformation; industry applies them to raw matter which the earth yields us in abundance, but which becomes valuable only by knowledge; art teaches us the immutable laws of beauty and symmetry, and gives to our productions forms in accordance with them.

Gentlemen, the Exhibition of 1851 is to give us a true test and a living picture of the point of development at which the whole of mankind has arrived in this great task, and a new starting point from which all nations will be able to direct their further exertions.

from *The Art Journal Illustrated Catalogue of the Great Exhibition of the Industry of All Nations* (1851)

We commence this illustrated catalogue of the principal contents of the Great Exhibition with a brief but succinct History of the Building—and of the Project from its commencement up to the present time.

The experiment of an Exhibition of the Industry of all the civilised Nations of the World has been tried, and has succeeded beyond the most sanguine expectations of its projectors. It is, indeed, scarcely possible to instance any great enterprise of modern date which has so completely satisfied the anticipations which had been formed of its results. ... Other nations have devised means for the display and encouragement of their own arts and manufactures; but it has been reserved for England to provide an arena for the exhibition of the industrial triumphs of the whole world. She has offered an hospitable invitation to surrounding nations to bring the choicest products of their industry to her capital, and there to enter into an amicable competition with each other and with herself; and she has endeavoured to

secure to them the certainty of an impartial verdict on their efforts. Whatever be the extent of the benefit which this great demonstration may confer upon the Industrial Arts of the world, it cannot fail to soften, if not to eradicate altogether, the prejudices and animosities which have so long retarded the happiness of nations; and to promote those feelings of "peace and good will" which are among the surest antecedents of their prosperity; a peace, which Shakespeare has told us—

> Is of the nature of a conquest;
> For then both parties nobly are subdued,
> And neither party loses.[1]

It forms no part of our present object to enter, with any degree of minuteness, into the history of exhibitions of this class; but a brief glance at the origin and progress of such associations in France and England may not be considered irrelevant. ...

The great success which attended the French Industrial Exposition of 1844 had caused representations to be made to the English government of the advantages which would accrue to our commerce from a similar exhibition in this country; but the efforts which were made to obtain its cooperation appear to have been wholly unsuccessful. In 1848, a proposal to establish a self-supporting exhibition of the products of British industry, to be directed by a Royal Commission, was submitted by H.R.H.[2] Prince Albert to the government, but with no better success; and it then became apparent that no reliance whatever could be placed upon the active support of Her Majesty's ministers for any such plan. They had, in all probability, no objection to see the experiment tried, but were evidently unwilling to commit themselves to any responsibility in behalf of a scheme which seemed to be beset by so many difficulties. Meanwhile, the popular feeling in favour of such an undertaking was rapidly strengthening, and the success which has attended the experiment may, in a great measure, be referred to the freedom of action which this

---

[1] *Is ... loses* See Shakespeare's *Henry IV, Part 2* 4.1.340–42.

[2] *H.R.H.* His Royal Highness.

dissociation from the timid councils of the government secured for its projectors. It may be proper, in this place, to remark that, excepting in facilitating its correspondence with foreign nations; the provision of a site for the building; and the organisation of the police; no assistance has been either sought or obtained from the government for the present Exhibition; whilst, in every case in which it has been attended by expense, the cost has been defrayed out of the funds at the disposal of the Executive Committee. ...

H.R.H. Prince Albert ... on the termination of the Parliamentary session of 1849, took the subject under his immediate superintendence. But, indeed, for his indefatigable perseverance, his courageous defiance of all risks of failure, his remarkable sagacity in matters of business, and the influence which attached to his support, the whole project, notwithstanding the great exertions which had been made to secure its realisation, must have fallen to the ground. The maturely considered views of his Royal Highness, and the patriotic objects he proposed in making this great peace-offering to mankind, are admirably set forth in the speech delivered by him on the occasion of the banquet given by Mr. Alderman Farncomb, then Lord Mayor of London, to the municipal authorities of the United Kingdom in support of the project. "The Exhibition of 1851 would," he said, "afford a true test of the point of development at which the whole of mankind has arrived in this great task, and a new starting point from which all nations would be able to direct their further exertions." ...

On the 29th of June, 1849, at a meeting, at Buckingham Palace, of several of the gentlemen who afterwards became members of the Royal Commission, and Prince Albert, his Royal Highness communicated his plan for the formation of a great collection of works of Industry and Art in London, in 1851, for the purposes of exhibition, of competition, and of encouragement; when he proposed that these contributions should consist of four great divisions, namely: raw materials; machinery and mechanical inventions; manufactures; and sculpture and plastic[1] art generally. ...

Impressed with the truth of the proverb, *Ce n'est que le premier pas qui coûte*,[2] the council of the Society of Arts, after much fruitless negotiation with other parties, entered into an engagement with Messrs. Munday, the well-known contractors, by which those gentlemen undertook to deposit a prize fund of 20,000 *l.*; to erect a suitable building; to find offices; to advance the money requisite for all preliminary expenses; and to take the whole risk of loss; on the following conditions: The 20,000 *l.* prize fund, the cost of the building, and five percent on all advances, to be repaid out of the first receipts; the residue to be divided into three equal parts; one part to be paid over at once to the Society of Arts, in aid of future exhibitions; and out of the other two parts all other incidental costs, such as those of general management and preliminary expenses; the residue, if any, to be remuneration of the contractors for their outlay, trouble, and risk. ...

With a view to give Foreign nations as much time for preparation as possible, the Commissioners resolved, long before they had decided on the size and character of the building, to divide a certain large extent of space among foreign countries, amounting in the whole to 210,000 superficial feet, or rather more than the entire space which France had occupied for its two expositions of 1844 and 1849. Subsequently, the quantities of space allotted to foreign nations was increased; France obtaining 65,000 feet instead of 50,000. A definite amount of space proportioned to their presumed wants was also allotted to each of the British Colonies. ...

Every class appears, however, to have been satisfied with the final allocations, which were the best that could have been made under the circumstances.

When the time arrived for making definite arrangements for the erection of the building, the Commissioners had only 35,000 *l.* in hand; and, notwithstanding the guarantee to which they had themselves largely subscribed, they must have felt themselves committed to a very deep responsibility. Nothing daunted, however, an invitation was addressed, through the public prints,

---

[1] *plastic* Involving the manipulation or sculpting of physical materials.

[2] *Ce ... coûte* French: It is only the first step that costs.

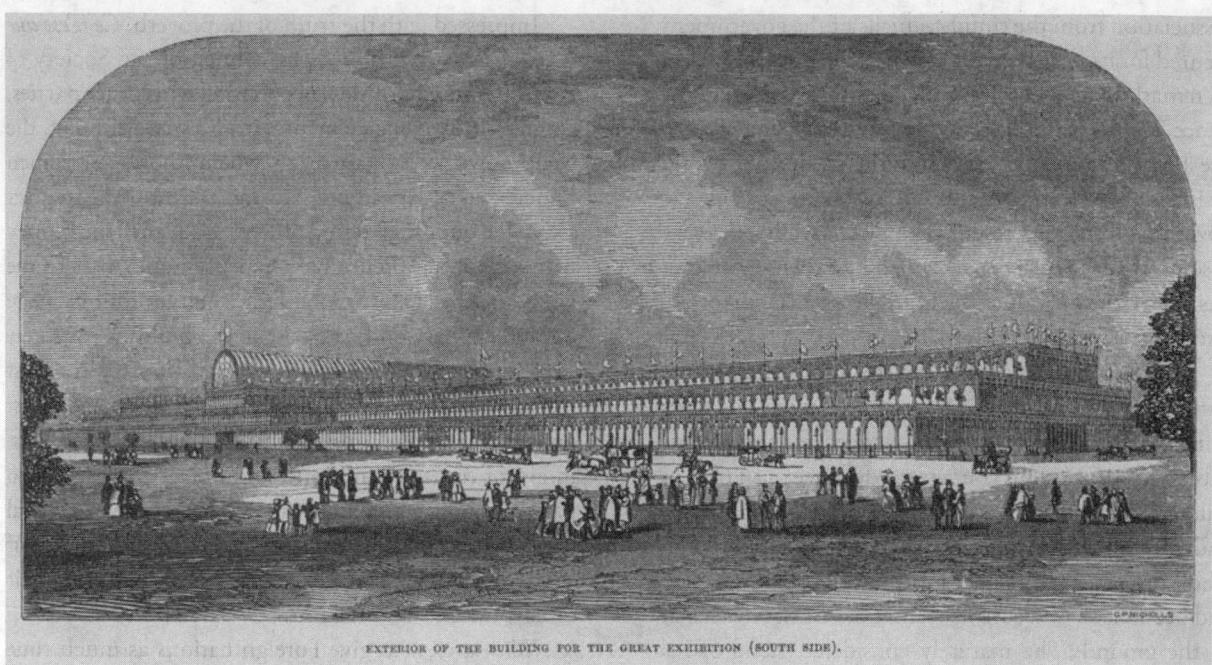

EXTERIOR OF THE BUILDING FOR THE GREAT EXHIBITION (SOUTH SIDE).

to architects of all nations, to furnish designs for an edifice, the roof of which was to cover 700,000 square feet; and the area of which, including the open spaces, was not to exceed 900,000 feet. Other conditions were enumerated which showed that the whole of the details had been carefully and judiciously considered. Although the time allowed for the preparation of the drawings was only a month, there were no fewer than two hundred and thirty-three competitors, many of whom sent in designs of a highly elaborate character. Of these, thirty-eight, or one-sixth of the whole, were from foreigners; 128 from London and its vicinity; and 51 from the provincial towns of England. ...

Among the contractors who had accepted the invitation of the Building Committee, was the firm of Fox & Henderson, who, availing themselves of the permission to alter and amend the plan of the Committee, contained in the latter part of the report, presented a tender for a building of an entirely different character from that which had been suggested by the Committee. This, we need scarcely add, was the plan which, with certain modifications and additions, was ultimately adopted; and for which, notwithstanding all that has

been said to the contrary, the public is wholly indebted to Mr. Paxton. ...

[A]nd if it be correct, as stated by Mr. Paxton at the dinner given to him at Derby, on the 6th of August, that his original sketch on a sheet of blotting paper indicates the principal features of the building as it now stands as much as the most finished drawings which have been made since, there can be no excuse for attempting to deprive him of any portion of the merit of the invention. But he appears to have done considerably more than merely furnish the idea. In nine days from that on which he had made the blotting paper sketch, he was in possession of nine plans, all, with a single exception, prepared by his own hand. And although his suggestion to Messrs. Fox & Henderson was offered so late as the 2nd June, 1850, his plan was engraved and published in the Illustrated News of the 6th July. ...

Tests had, as we have shown, been applied in the course of the work which had satisfied the scientific men who witnessed them that the iron girders would bear a strain upon them four times as great as they could ever be called upon to bear; but it was resolved to subject them to a still severer ordeal.

The first of these more elaborate experiments, which took place in the presence of Her Majesty, Prince Albert, and several scientific persons, was to ascertain the extent of oscillation that would be produced in the galleries by the regular motion of large bodies of persons. Three hundred workmen were accordingly deployed over the platform, and then crowded together as closely as possible. The load borne by the planks laid across the platform represented the degree of pressure that would be occasioned by the crowding of the bays of the galleries. The amount of deflection produced by this experiment was scarcely perceptible. The men next walked regularly and irregularly, and finally ran over the temporary floor, with little more effect. Even when packed in the closest order, and jumping simultaneously for several minutes, the play of the timbers and the wrought-iron work, was admirably developed, and the extreme deflection of any one girder did not exceed a quarter of an inch. As, however, the workmen were unable to keep military time in their step, the whole corps of Sappers and Miners employed on the ground, arranged in close order, marched several times over and around the bays without producing any other effect than is observable in a house in which dancing is going on. The crowning experiment suggested by Messrs. Maudslay & Field, the eminent civil engineers, rendered any further test wholly unnecessary. Seven frames, each capable of holding 36 cannon-balls, of 68 lbs. each, were constructed, and drawn with their contents over the floor. In this way a pressure on the flooring of seven and a half tons was obtained; the probable pressure from a crowd not exceeding 95 lb. The pressure of an ordinary crowd, however, at a public meeting or a theatre does not exceed 60 lbs. to the square foot. ...

The site of the Great Exhibition is the one originally proposed for it by H.R.H. Prince Albert. It consists of a rectangular piece of ground in Hyde Park, situated between the Queen's Drive and Rotten Row,[1] and contains about 26 acres, being 2300 feet in length by 500 feet in breadth. Its principal frontage extends from east to west. Several lofty trees which stretch across the

centre of its length have been allowed to remain, and it is to them we are indebted for the magnificent transept and semicircular roof, suggested after the first plans had received the approval of the Commissioners. The ground, although apparently level, has a fall from 1 to 250 inches from west to east. Among the most striking advantages of the spot were the facilities of access from all parts which it presented, and the ease with which it could be drained and supplied with gas and water; whilst the beauty of the neighbourhood can scarcely be exceeded within the same convenient distance from the metropolis. Indeed, however strong may have been the private objections urged against the adoption of this site, in the first instance, it is now universally admitted that a more desirable locality for the purpose to which it has been converted could not have been selected. ...

Two ... groups of trees, whose immolation was also interdicted, have rendered open courts necessary; but they are, nevertheless, included within the building. The entire area enclosed and roofed over comprises no fewer than 772,784 square feet, or about 19 acres; thus presenting an edifice about four times the size of St. Peter's, at Rome, and six times that of St. Paul's.[2] We have already described the principal entrance at the south front. Besides this, there is one at each end, and, at convenient intervals, no fewer than fifteen places of egress. ...

The first impression conveyed to the mind of a visitor, inexperienced in the science of architecture, on entering the building, is a sense of insecurity, arising from the apparent lightness of its supports as compared with the vastness of its dimensions. But this feeling is soon dissipated when he is informed how severely the strength of every separate part has been tested, and with what extreme care the connexion of all the supports with each other has been considered, so as to present the greatest possible combination of strength. ...

Among other striking examples of the ingenuity of the originators and constructors of the Crystal Palace is the ridge-and-furrow roof, by which the rain water is distributed into equal portions, and all ordinary chances

---

[1] *Queen's Drive and Rotten Row*   Carriage paths.

[2] *St. Peter's, at Rome*   St. Peter's Basilica, among the world's largest churches; *St. Paul's*   St. Paul's Cathedral in London, then the largest church in England.

of overflow averted; and the peculiar formation of the floor, which is a "trellised wooden pathway," with spaces between each board through which, on sweeping, "the dust at once disappears, and falls into the vacuity below." It may also be thoroughly washed without discomfort, for the water disappears as fast as the dust through the interstices; and the boards become fit for visitors almost immediately afterwards. ...

Such was the extraordinary eagerness of the public to be present at its inauguration, that upwards of 40,000 *l.* of season tickets were disposed of on the 29th of April; and but for the restriction that the holders of season tickets only should be admitted to this ceremony, the place would doubtless have overflowed with visitors. It is not our intention to enter into minute details of the circumstances which attended its inauguration; they were in every respect worthy of the occasion. It was opened by Her Majesty in person, accompanied by the Royal Family, and attended by the members of her cabinet, and by all the officers and ladies of her court. So soon as the music which hailed her entry had ceased, H.R.H. Prince Albert, as President of the Royal Commissioners, read a report of their proceedings since their appointment. This manifesto mentions that "for the suggestions of the principle of this structure, the Commissioners are indebted to Mr. Joseph Paxton, and expresses a hope that the undertaking, which has for its end the promotion of all branches of human industry, and the strengthening of the bonds of peace and friendship among all nations of the earth, may, under God's blessing, conduce to the welfare of Her Majesty's people, and be long remembered among the brightest incidents of her peaceful and happy reign."

To this address, Her Majesty returned a most gracious answer, and the Archbishop of Canterbury having invoked the blessing of the Almighty on the undertaking, the ceremony terminated with the performance of the Hallelujah chorus by the united choirs of the Chapel Royal, St. Paul's, Westminster Abbey, and St. George's Chapel, Windsor. The procession included all the persons who had been officially engaged in the work; the royal and foreign commissioners, Her Majesty's ministers, the whole of the lords and ladies of the court in waiting, and the foreign ambassadors. The vast but elegant proportions of the building, the richness and tastefulness of the costumes, and the large number (25,000) of well-dressed persons assembled on the occasion, rendered its inauguration one of the most imposing sights that had ever been witnessed in this country. But it is not in her regal capacity alone that Her Majesty has deigned to honour the Great Exhibition with her countenance. Day after day, accompanied by her children, and often at much personal inconvenience, has she flattered the various exhibitors by careful examinations of their productions; until it may fairly be presumed that there is scarcely one of her subjects who has more thoroughly inspected all that is worthy of attention within its walls than she has done. Whatever may have been the weather, or however crowded the interior, Her Majesty has devoted, almost daily, until the close of the session of parliament released her from attendance in London, several hours to visits to the Crystal Palace; inspecting each department in succession, and selecting from many of them such objects as gratified her taste, or were, for other reasons, considered to possess claims upon her attention.

On entering the building, for the first time, the eye is completely dazzled by the rich variety of hues which burst upon it on every side; and it is not until this partial bewilderment has subsided, that we are in a condition to appreciate as it deserves its real magnificence and the harmonious beauty of effect produced by the artistical arrangement of the glowing and varied hues which blaze along its grand and simple lines. After passing through the southern entrance, the whole extent of the transept,[1] interrupted only by the magnificent glass fountain of Messrs. Osler,[2] and the groups of sculpture and tropical plants and trees, that are intermixed throughout, flashes on the eye more like the

---

[1]   *transept* Transverse part of a building, i.e., part of it that crosses the main axis of the building at right angles. Originally, the transept was the portion of a Christian cathedral that intersected the nave, the main body of the cathedral.

[2]   *Messrs. Osler* Follett and Clarkson Osler, England's leading glass manufacturers.

fabled palace of Vathek,[1] than a structure reared in a few months by mortal hands. …

Forming the centre, or nearly so, of the entire building, and dividing alike the transept and the nave, rises the gigantic fountain of Messrs. Osler, the culminating point of view from every quarter of the building; whilst at the northern end the eye is relieved by the verdure of tropical plants and the lofty and overshadowing branches of forest trees.

On the right, looking from Messrs. Osler's glass fountain up the eastern division of the nave, towards the American organ and its enormous eagle, a combination of splendours bursts upon the sight of overpowering magnificence. …

The western division of the nave, devoted to the products of England and her Colonies, if less showy, on a superficial view, than its rival, has much of sterling merit to recommend it. Here, too, are interspersed statues, fountains, mirrors, organs, and other large ornamental objects.

Crossing the transept, and pursuing our course to the left, we enter the western division of the nave. We have here the Indian Court, Africa, Canada, the West Indies, the Cape of Good Hope, the Medieval Court, and the English Sculpture Court. … To these succeed Birmingham, the great British Furniture Court, Sheffield, and its hardware, the woollen and mixed fabrics, shawls, flax, and linens, and printing and dyeing. The long avenue leading from the Medieval Court to the end of the building is devoted to general hardware, brass and iron-work of all kinds, locks, grates, etc.; whilst behind it, and parallel with it, but occupying three times its breadth, is the department for agricultural machines and implements. At the back of this division is the long narrow gallery occupied by the mineral products of England. Passing the small compartment of glass which runs transversely under the great organ gallery, across the nave, we have the cotton fabric and carriage courts, leather, furs, and hair, minerals and mineral manufac-

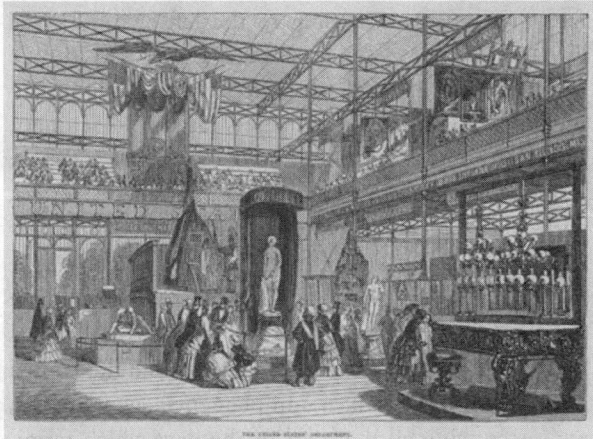

THE UNITED STATES' DEPARTMENT.

ENTRANCE TO THE TURKISH DEPARTMENT.

tures, and machinery; including cotton and woollen power-looms in motion. The next is the largest compartment in the building, comprising machinery in motion, flax, silk, and lace, rope-making lathes, tools, and mills; minerals and mineral manufactures, furniture, marine engines, ceilings, hydraulic presses, steam hammers, fire engines, etc. Then follow paper and stationery; Jersey, Ceylon, and Malta, with the Fine Arts Court behind them; railway and steam machinery in motion; building contrivances, printing, and French machinery, occupying the whole of the last compartments on both sides of the nave, as well as those which

---

[1] *palace of Vathek* In William Beckford's French novel *Vathek* (1782; first English translation 1786), the title character expands his already magnificent palace to incorporate five new wings, each for the satisfaction of one of the five senses.

face the transept. Crossing to the left of the Crystal Fountain, we have Persia, Greece, Egypt, and Turkey, Spain, Portugal, Madeira, and Italy, musical instruments, and chemicals; France, its tapestry, machinery, arms and instruments, occupying two large courts; Belgium her furniture, carpets, and machinery; Austria, with her gorgeous furniture courts, and machinery furniture; the Zollverein,[1] with its octagon room, the most tastefully-arranged compartment in the building; North of Germany and Hanse Towns;[2] Russia, with its malachite doors, vases, and ornaments; and the United States, with its agricultural implements, raw materials, etc., occupying all that part of the nave which terminates with its organ, if we except a small gallery on the north-east side, devoted to English paper-hangings. From this extremity of the building, and from the organ gallery more especially, the finest *coup d'œil*[3] of the nave and its adjoining galleries may be obtained. ...

Among the more striking objects in the southeastern gallery, in the British half of the nave, are the silks and shawls, abutting on the transept; lace and embroideries, jewellery, and clocks and watches; and behind them military arms and models, raw produce, substances used as food, and chemicals. Traversing the gallery for naval architecture, by the organ, we have philosophical instruments, civil engineering, architecture and building models, musical instruments, anatomical models, glass chandeliers, decorations, etc.; china and pottery above the left side of the northern part of the transept. On the opposite side, in the north-eastern gallery, are perfumery, toys, fishing materials, miscellaneous articles, wax flowers, stained glass, British, French, Austrian, Belgian, Prussian, Bavarian, and American products.

Clear passages under the galleries, of eight and ten feet broad, run the whole length of the building. Upon the extreme north and south sides, there are also longitudinal passages of similar width; the former interrupted by the offices of the commissioners and the entrances, and the latter by the refreshment rooms. With the exception of the offices, staircases, entrances, refreshment courts, and the various avenues and passages, including the transept, the whole of the ground-floor and galleries are available for exhibitors. As we have already shown, foreign countries, including the United States of America, occupy the east side of the transept above and below; whilst the United Kingdom, the East Indies, and the British Colonies are confined to the west side; with the exception of the United Kingdom, which extends into parts of the north and south galleries, on the east side of the transept. The productions of England and her Colonies occupy thirty separate sections. ...

In retiring from the contemplation of this magnificent edifice, the extraordinary expedition[4] with which it was constructed must be regarded as one of the marvels of the age.

Conservatives, Liberals, and Empire

The following excerpts from speeches by Liberal Prime Minister William Gladstone, Conservative Prime Minister Benjamin Disraeli, Secretary of State for the Colonies Joseph Chamberlain, and businessperson, mining magnate, politician, and colonizer Cecil Rhodes provide different perspectives on the attitudes taken by Britain's two main political parties towards issues of Empire in the second half of the nineteenth century.

from William Gladstone, "Our Colonies" (1855)

But an idea far more important and effective to a far greater extent has been the idea that the colonies ought to be maintained for the purpose of establishing an exclusive trade, the whole profit of which should be

---

[1] *Zollverein* Customs union of independent German states, founded in 1833, that formed one of the foundations of Germany's eventual unification in 1871.

[2] *Hanse Towns* I.e., the northern German cities of Lübeck, Hamburg, and Bremen, which in 1851 were the only remaining members of the once-powerful Hanseatic League, a trading alliance of city-states around the Baltic Sea.

[3] *coup d'œil* Here, line of sight.

[4] *expedition* Speed.

confined to the mother country, and should be enjoyed by the mother country. This was in fact the basis of the modern colonial system of Europe. I do not speak now of the political system, but it was the basis of the commercial laws of the countries which had colonies: that the industry of the colonists, instead of having a fair field and equal favour given to it, was attempted to be made entirely subservient to the interests and the profit of the mother country. It was placed in an unfair position. People were told in fact that they might go to the colonies, but that whatever they produced in the colonies must be sent to the British market—nay, that it must be sent in British vessels to the British market—nay, that whatever was produced must be sent to the British market in British vessels and in the state of raw produce, because if sent in other vessels, although it were sent better and cheaper, it would not be for the interest of the British shipowner, and if sent in a manufactured state it would not be for the interest of the British manufacturer. ...

Now, as I repudiate any and all of these reasons for desiring the possession of colonies, it is but fair that I should endeavour to state why I think colonies are desirable for a country circumstanced as England is. I have stated, that I do not think them desirable simply to puff up our reputation, apart from the basis and substance on which it rests. It is plain that they are not to be desired for revenue, because they do not yield it. It is plain that they are not to be desired for trading monopoly, because that we have entirely abandoned. It is plain they are not to be desired for patronage, properly so called, within their limits, because they will not allow us to exercise patronage, and I am bound to say, I do not think the public men of this country have any desire so to exercise it. With respect to territory, it is perfectly plain that mere extension of territory is not a legitimate object of ambition, unless you can show that you are qualified to make use of that territory for the purposes for which God gave the earth to man. Why then are colonies desirable? In my opinion, and I submit it to you with great respect, they are desirable both for the material and for the moral and social results which a wise system of colonisation is calculated to produce. As to the

first, the effect of colonisation undoubtedly is to increase the trade and employment of the mother country. Take the case of the emigrant going across the Atlantic. Why does he go across the Atlantic? Because he expects—and in general he is the best judge of his own interests—to get better wages across the Atlantic than he can get at home. If he goes across the Atlantic to get better wages, he leaves in the labour market at home fewer persons than before, and consequently raises the rate of wages at home by carrying himself away from the competition with his fellows. By going to the colony and supplying it with labour he likewise creates a demand for capital there, and by this means he creates a trade between the colony and the mother country. The capital and labour thus employed in the colony raise and export productions, for which commodities are wanted in return. ...

But I do not concede that the material benefit of colonies is the only consideration which we are able to plead. Their moral and social advantage is a very great one. If we are asked why, on these grounds, it is desirable that colonies should be founded and possessed, I answer by asking another question—Why is it desirable that your population at home should increase? Why is it that you rejoice, always presuming that the increase of population goes hand in hand with equally favourable or more favourable conditions of existence for the mass of the people—why is it that you rejoice in an increase of population at home? Because an increase of population is an increase of power, an increase of strength and stability to the state, and because it multiplies the number of people who, as we hope, are living under good laws, and belong to a country to which it is an honour and an advantage to belong. That is the great moral benefit that attends the foundation of British colonies. We think that our country is a country blessed with laws and a constitution that are eminently beneficial to mankind, and if so, what can be more to be desired than that we should have the means of reproducing in different portions of the globe something as like as may be to that country which we honour and revere? I think it is in a work by Mr. Roebuck that the expression is used, "that the object of colonisation is the creation of so many happy Englands." It is the reproduction of the image and likeness of England—the reproduction of a country in which liberty is reconciled with order, in which ancient institutions stand in harmony with popular freedom, and a full recognition of popular rights, and in which religion and law have found one of their most favoured homes. ...

from Benjamin Disraeli, "Conservative and Liberal Principles" (1872)

Gentlemen, there is another and second great object of the Tory party. If the first is to maintain the institutions of the country, the second is, in my opinion, to uphold the Empire of England. If you look to the history of this country since the advent of Liberalism—forty years ago—you will find that there has been no effort so continuous, so subtle, supported by so much energy, and carried on with so much ability and acumen, as the attempts of Liberalism to effect the disintegration of the Empire of England.

And, gentlemen, of all its efforts, this is the one which has been the nearest to success. Statesmen of the highest character, writers of the most distinguished ability, the most organised and efficient means, have been employed in this endeavour. It has been proved to all of us that we have lost money by our colonies. It has been shown with precise, with mathematical demonstration, that there never was a jewel in the Crown of England that was so truly costly as the possession of India. How often has it been suggested that we should at once emancipate ourselves from this incubus.[1] Well, that result was nearly accomplished. When those subtle views were adopted by the country under the plausible plea of granting self-government to the colonies, I confess that I myself thought that the tie was broken. Not that I for one object to self-government. I cannot conceive how our distant colonies can have their affairs administered except by self-government. But self-government, in my opinion, when it was conceded, ought to

---

[1] *incubus* Mythical demon said to rape sleeping women, and in so doing to drain their life force to sustain itself. Figuratively, an evil that drains vital energy.

have been conceded as part of a great policy of Imperial consolidation. It ought to have been accompanied by an Imperial tariff, by securities for the people of England for the enjoyment of the unappropriated lands which belonged to the Sovereign as their trustee, and by a military code which should have precisely defined the means and the responsibilities by which the colonies should be defended, and by which, if necessary, this country should call for aid from the colonies themselves. It ought, further, to have been accompanied by the institution of some representative council in the metropolis, which would have brought the colonies into constant and continuous relations with the Home Government. All this, however, was omitted because those who advised that policy—and I believe their convictions were sincere—looked upon the colonies of England, looked even upon our connection with India, as a burden upon this country, viewing everything in a financial aspect, and totally passing by those moral and political considerations which make nations great, and by the influence of which alone men are distinguished from animals.

Well, what has been the result of this attempt during the reign of Liberalism for the disintegration of the Empire? It has entirely failed. But how has it failed? Through the sympathy of the colonies with the Mother Country. They have decided that the Empire shall not be destroyed, and in my opinion no minister in this country will do his duty who neglects any opportunity of reconstructing as much as possible our Colonial Empire, and of responding to those distant sympathies which may become the source of incalculable strength and happiness to this land. ...

from Joseph Chamberlain, "The True Conception of Empire" (1897)

... It seems to me that there are three distinct stages in our Imperial history. We began to be, and we ultimately became a great Imperial power in the eighteenth century, but, during the greater part of that time, the colonies were regarded, not only by us, but by every European power that possessed them, as possessions valuable in proportion to the pecuniary advantage which they brought to the mother country, which, under that order of ideas, was not truly a mother at all, but appeared rather in the light of a grasping and absentee landlord desiring to take from his tenants the utmost rents he could exact. The colonies were valued and maintained because it was thought that they would be a source of profit—of direct profit—to the mother country.

That was the first stage, and when we were rudely awakened by the War of Independence in America from this dream that the colonies could be held for our profit alone, the second chapter was entered upon, and public opinion seems then to have drifted to the opposite extreme; and, because the colonies were no longer a source of revenue, it seems to have been believed and argued by many people that their separation from us was only a matter of time, and that the separation should be desired and encouraged lest haply[1] they might prove an encumbrance and a source of weakness. …

[W]e have now reached the third stage in our history, and the true conception of our empire.

What is that conception? As regards the self-governing colonies we no longer talk of them as dependencies. The sense of possession has given place to the sentiment of kinship. We think and speak of them as part of ourselves, as part of the British Empire, united to us, although they may be dispersed throughout the world, by ties of kinship, of religion, of history, and of language, and joined to us by the seas that formerly seemed to divide us.

But the British Empire is not confined to the self-governing colonies and the United Kingdom. It includes a much greater area, a much more numerous population in tropical climes, where no considerable European settlement is possible, and where the native population must always vastly outnumber the white inhabitants; and in these cases also the same change has come over the Imperial idea. Here also the sense of possession has given place to a different sentiment—the sense of obligation. We feel now that our rule over these territories can only be justified if we show that it adds to the happiness and prosperity of the people, and I maintain

that our rule does, and has, brought security and peace and comparative prosperity to countries that never knew these blessings before.

In carrying out this work of civilization we are fulfilling what I believe to be our national mission, and we are finding scope for the exercise of those faculties and qualities which have made of us a great and governing race. I do not say that our success has been perfect in every case, I do not say that all methods have been beyond reproach; but I do say that in almost every instance in which the rule of the Queen has been established and the great *Pax Britannica*[2] has been enforced, there has come with it the greater security to life and property, and a material improvement in the condition of the bulk of the population. No doubt, in the first instance, when these conquests have been made, there has been bloodshed, there has been loss of life among the native populations, loss of still more precious lives among those who have been sent out to bring these countries into some kind of disciplined order, but it must be remembered that that is the condition of the mission we have to fulfil. …

You cannot have omelettes without breaking eggs, you cannot destroy the practices of barbarism, of slavery, of superstition, which for centuries have desolated the interior of Africa, without the use of force; but if you will fairly contrast the gain to humanity with the price which we are bound to pay for it, I think you may well rejoice in the result of such expeditions as those which have been recently conducted[.] …

In regard to the self-governing colonies our task is much lighter. We have undertaken, it is true, to protect them with all the strength at our command against foreign aggression, although I hope that the need for our intervention may never arise. But there remains what then will be our chief duty—that is, to give effect to that sentiment of kinship to which I have referred and which I believe is deep in the heart of every Briton. We want to

---

[1] *haply* By chance.

[2] *Pax Britannica* Latin: "British peace," i.e., a peace imposed or made possible by Britain's imperial power. The phrase was coined in the late nineteenth century by analogy with the *Pax Romana*, the peace that the Roman Empire enforced throughout the territories under its rule.

promote a closer and a firmer union between all members of the great British race, and in this respect we have in recent years made great progress—so great that I think sometimes our friends are apt to be a little hasty, and to expect even a miracle to be accomplished. I would like to ask them to remember that time and patience are essential elements in the development of all great ideas. Let us, gentlemen, keep our ideal always before us. For my own part, I believe in the practical possibility of a federation of the British race, but I know that it will come, if it does come, not by pressure, not by anything in the nature of dictation from this country, but it will come as the realization of a universal desire, as the expression of the dearest wish of our colonial fellow-subjects themselves. ...

A transoceanic capital may arise across the seas, which will throw into shade the glories of London itself; but in the years that must intervene let it be our endeavor, let it be our task, to keep alight the torch of Imperial patriotism, to hold fast the affection and the confidence of our kinsmen across the seas, that so in every vicissitude of fortune the British Empire may present an unbroken front to all her foes, and may carry on even to distant ages the glorious traditions of the British flag.

from Cecil Rhodes, Speech Delivered in Cape Town, 18 July 1899

And, sir, my people have changed. I speak of the English people, with their marvellous common sense, coupled with their powers of imagination—all thoughts of a Little England are over. They are tumbling over each other, Liberals and Conservatives, to show which side are the greatest and most enthusiastic Imperialists. The people have changed, and so do all the parties, just like the Punch and Judy show[1] at a country fair. The people have found out that England is small, and her trade is large, and they have also found out that other people are taking their share of the world, and enforcing hostile tariffs. The people of England are

finding out that "trade follows the flag,"[2] and they have all become Imperialists. They are not going to part with any territory. And the bygone ideas of nebulous republics are over. The English people intend to retain every inch of land they have got, and perhaps, sir, they intend to secure a few more inches. ...

———

from David Livingstone, "Cambridge Lecture Number 1" (1858)

When I went to Africa about seventeen years ago I resolved to acquire an accurate knowledge of the native tongues; and as I continued, while there, to speak generally in the African languages, the result is that I am not now very fluent in my own; but if you will excuse my imperfections under that head, I will endeavour to give you as clear an idea of Africa as I can. ...

My object in going into the country south of the desert was to instruct the natives in a knowledge of Christianity, but many circumstances prevented my living amongst them more than seven years, amongst which were considerations arising out of the slave system carried on by the Dutch Boers. I resolved to go into the country beyond, and soon found that, for the purposes of commerce, it was necessary to have a path to the sea. I might have gone on instructing the natives in religion, but as civilization and Christianity must go on together, I was obliged to find a path to the sea, in order that I should not sink to the level of the natives. The chief was overjoyed at the suggestion, and furnished me with twenty-seven men, and canoes, and provisions, and presents for the tribes through whose country we had to pass. We might have taken a shorter path to the sea than that to the north, and then to the west, by which we went; but along the country by the shorter route, there is an insect called the tsetse, whose bite is fatal to horses, oxen, and dogs, but not to men or donkeys. You seem to think there is a connexion between the two. The habitat of that insect is along the shorter route to the sea. The bite of it is fatal to domestic animals, not

———

[1] *Punch and Judy show* Puppet show involving Mr. Punch and his wife Judy.

[2] *trade ... flag* Popular dictum of the period, meant to encourage colonization.

THE RHODES COLOSSUS
STRIDING FROM CAPE TOWN TO CAIRO.

Cecil Rhodes (1858–1902), nowadays best known for having endowed the Rhodes Scholarships for study at Oxford University, was the leading Briton in Southern Africa in the late nineteenth century—and a leading backer of the extension of British commercial and political interests in Africa as a whole. (The statue of the Colossus in the ancient city of Rhodes to which this cartoon alludes is said to have straddled the entrance to the harbor.)

immediately, but certainly in the course of two or three months; the animal grows leaner and leaner, and gradually dies of emaciation: a horse belonging to Gordon Cumming died of a bite five or six months after it was bitten.

On account of this insect, I resolved to go to the north, and then westwards to the Portuguese settlement of Loanda. Along the course of the river which we passed, game was so abundant that there was no difficulty in supplying the wants of my whole party: antelopes were so tame that they might be shot from the canoe. But beyond 14 degrees of south latitude the natives had guns, and had themselves destroyed the game, so that I and my party had to live on charity. The people, however, in that central region were friendly and hospitable: but they had nothing but vegetable productions: the most abundant was the cassava, which, however nice when made into tapioca pudding, resembles in its more primitive condition nothing so much as a mess of laundress's starch. There was a desire in the various villages through which we passed to have intercourse with us, and kindness and hospitality were shown us; but when we got near the Portuguese settlement of Angola the case was changed, and payment was demanded for every thing. But I had nothing to pay with. Now the people had been in the habit of trading with the slavers, and so they said I might give one of my men in payment for what I wanted. When I shewed them that I could not do this, they looked upon me as an interloper, and I was sometimes in danger of being murdered.

As we neared the coast, the name of England was recognized, and we got on with ease. Upon one occasion, when I was passing through the parts visited by slave-traders, a chief who wished to shew me some kindness offered me a slave-girl: upon explaining that I had a little girl of my own, whom I should not like my own chief to give to a black man, the chief thought I was displeased with the size of the girl, and sent me one a head taller. By this and other means I convinced my men of my opposition to the principle of slavery; and when we arrived at Loanda I took them on board a British vessel, where I took a pride in showing them that those countrymen of mine and those guns were there for the purpose of putting down the slave-trade. They were convinced from what they saw of the honesty of Englishmen's intentions; and the hearty reception they met with from the sailors made them say to me, "We see they are your countrymen, for they have hearts like you." On the journey, the men had always looked forward to reaching the coast: they had seen Manchester prints and other articles imported therefrom, and they could not believe they were made by mortal hands. On reaching the sea, they thought that they had come to the end of the world. They said, "We marched along with our father, thinking the world was a large plain without limit; but all at once the land said 'I am finished, there is no more of me'"; and they called themselves the true old men—the true ancients—having gone to the end of the world. On reaching Loanda, they commenced trading in firewood, and also engaged themselves at sixpence a day in unloading coals, brought by a steamer for the supply of the cruiser lying there to watch the slave-vessels. On their return, they told their people "we worked for a whole moon, carrying away the stones that burn." By the time they were ready to go back to their own country, each had secured a large bundle of goods. On the way back, however, fever detained them, and their goods were all gone, leaving them on their return home, as poor as when they started. ...

A prospect is now before us of opening Africa for commerce and the Gospel. Providence has been preparing the way, for even before I proceeded to the Central basin it had been conquered and rendered safe by a chief named Sebituane, and the language of the Bechuanas made the fashionable tongue, and that was one of the languages into which Mr. Moffat had translated the Scriptures. Sebituane also discovered Lake Ngami some time previous to my explorations in that part. In going back to that country my object is to open up traffic along the banks of the Zambesi, and also to preach the Gospel. The natives of Central Africa are very desirous of trading, but their only traffic is at present in slaves, of which the poorer people have an unmitigated horror; it is therefore most desirable to encourage the former principle, and thus open a way for the consumption of

David Livingstone, 1864. Photo by Thomas Annan.

free productions, and the introduction of Christianity and commerce. By encouraging the native propensity for trade, the advantages that might be derived in a commercial point of view are incalculable; nor should we lose sight of the inestimable blessings it is in our power to bestow upon the unenlightened African, by giving him the light of Christianity. Those two pioneers of civilization—Christianity and commerce—should ever be inseparable; and Englishmen should be warned by the fruits of neglecting that principle as exemplified in the result of the management of Indian affairs. By trading with Africa, also, we should at length be independent of slave labour, and thus discountenance practices so obnoxious to every Englishman.

Though the natives are not absolutely anxious to receive the Gospel, they are open to Christian influences. Among the Bechuanas the Gospel was well received. These people think it a crime to shed a tear, but I have seen some of them weep at the recollection of their sins when God had opened their hearts to Christianity and repentance. …

I beg to direct your attention to Africa; I know that in a few years I shall be cut off in that country, which is now open; do not let it be shut again! I go back to Africa to try to make an open path for commerce and Christianity; do you carry out the work which I have begun. I LEAVE IT WITH YOU!

WILLIAM BUTLER YEATS

1865 – 1939

It is widely acknowledged that in the twentieth century few poets contributed as much to the cultural, political, and social framework of Ireland, and to British literature in general, as William Butler Yeats. It is often forgotten, however, that by 1900 he was already an important poet—and an important influence on Irish culture.

William Butler Yeats was born in the Dublin suburb of Sandymount on 13 June 1865. His father, John Butler Yeats, had given up law to take up portrait painting, a decision that, though artistically and intellectually stimulating, led to many years of uprooted existence and strained finances for his family. When William was two, the family moved to London, yet much of his childhood was spent moving between schooling in London and retreats to the family home of his mother, Susan Pollexfen, in County Sligo, Ireland. In County Sligo, Yeats would find inspiration in the beauty of the countryside, the local folklore, and Irish tradition. In 1880, the family returned permanently to Ireland and settled in Howth, close to Dublin. In 1883, having completed high school, Yeats decided to become an artist and enrolled in the Metropolitan School of Art, but he soon left to pursue his true passion, poetry. His first published poems appeared in the *Dublin University Review* in 1885; three years later he wrote "The Lake Isle of Innisfree" (first published in 1890), which established his reputation as a poet of powerful emotions deeply rooted in Irish tradition and in the Irish landscape.

Also at an early age, influenced by his father's religious skepticism, Yeats developed a strong interest in occultism, folklore, and theosophism, a system of philosophical thought based on the direct and immediate experience of the divine. In 1885 he joined with friends to form the Dublin Hermetic Society, a group devoted to discussion of occult sciences and pseudo-sciences of the day. This group was predominantly influenced by a more famous mystical society, The Theosophical Society, founded in New York by Madame Helena Blavatsky. In 1887, Yeats met with Madame Blavatsky and later joined the Esoteric section of the London chapter of The Theosophical Society. In 1890, Yeats left the Society to join the Hermetic Order of the Golden Dawn, an occult society that drew upon astrology, tarot, kabbala, and Eastern mysticism for its teachings. Throughout his life and career, Yeats would turn to mythology and the occult as tools for developing his own vision of history and imagination. In much of his poetry, this vision is evident in an elaborate system of images and symbols that Yeats would continually investigate and refine.

In 1889 Yeats's first collection, *The Wanderings of Oisin and Other Poems*, was published. The collection was well received, but the attention of one reader in particular would be responsible for what Yeats would term "the troubling of my life." The beautiful actor and Irish nationalist Maud Gonne was introduced to Yeats by a mutual friend, John O'Leary, shortly after the collection was published. The meeting marked a fateful moment in the life of Yeats, as Gonne would become his obsession for the next quarter-century, and his poetry would resonate with his love and despair for her in poems such as "Adam's Curse" (1904), "No Second Troy" (1910), and "A Prayer for My

Daughter" (1921). She also helped to inspire him in two new cultural endeavors: the establishment of an Irish national theater and the development of a public voice for the Irish nationalist movement for independence.

Through the 1890s Yeats continued to gain literary prominence with further collections of poetry—among them *The Rose* (1893), and *Poems* (1895)—as well as anthologies, works of prose fiction, and studies of Irish folklore and fairy tales. The vivid lushness that characterizes much of Yeats's early poetry reaches a high point with poems such as "The Secret Rose" in the 1899 collection *The Wind Among the Reeds*.

In 1896 Yeats met Lady Augusta Gregory, a fellow writer and promoter of Irish literature, who invited him to stay in her country house at Coole Park. Through her influence, Yeats became involved in the founding of the Irish National Theatre in 1899. In writing for the theater, Yeats found a new voice for his interest in mythology, mysticism, and Irish nationalism. In 1904, the Irish National Theatre's permanent home, The Abbey Theatre, opened with Yeats's play *On Baile's Strand*. As the Abbey's director and dramatist, Yeats helped develop it into one of the world's leading theaters and, perhaps more importantly to him, into the center of the Irish literary renaissance.

The publication of *The Green Helmet and Other Poems* in 1910 marks Yeats's transition into the second phase of his poetic career. Where his early poems often offered romantic melancholy and idyllic meditations on pagan themes, the poetry of this second phase became more direct in its analysis of the events and attitudes of the period. As Yeats became embittered by the small-minded nationalism of The Abbey's middle-class audiences, and as he watched with horror the growing violence in the struggle for Irish independence, his poetry began to reflect his distrust of popular judgment and concern for the future of his country.

At the same time, Yeats continued to develop his complex system of symbolism and esoteric theories regarding the movement of history and human intellect. In 1917—having proposed several times to Maud Gonne and once to Gonne's daughter Iseult, both of whom refused him—Yeats married Georgie Hyde-Lees, whom he had met in 1911. On their honeymoon, Hyde-Lees delighted Yeats with her gift for automatic writing (believed by Yeats to be dictated by spirits), and for several years her writings inspired Yeats to refine his symbolic system, as described in his book *A Vision* (1925). Although Yeats's later poetry is by no means unintelligible without an understanding of *A Vision*, many of his poems refer directly to the patterns and imagery examined within its pages.

In 1922 Yeats was elected Senator of the Irish Free State; a year later, he was awarded the Nobel Prize for Literature, becoming the first Irish writer to receive the award. Yeats continued to produce major poetry well into his later years. As his health began to decline, his poetry took on a defiant tone, reflecting an awareness of his own mortality.

Following a long period of heart trouble, Yeats died on 28 January 1939; he was buried in Roquebrune, France, where he had been spending the winter. In 1948, his remains were reinterred, as he had wished, in Drumcliff, County Sligo. Also according to his wishes, his epitaph is taken from "Under Ben Bulben": "Cast a cold eye / On life, on death. / Horseman, pass by!"

A larger selection of Yeats's work appears in volume 6 of this anthology.

⌘ ⌘ ⌘

Ephemera[1]

"Your eyes that once were never weary of mine
   Are bowed in sorrow under
      pendulous° lids,   *heavy-hanging*
Because our love is waning."
   And then she:
5 "Although our love is waning, let us stand
By the lone border of the lake once more,
Together in that hour of gentleness
When the poor tired child, Passion, falls asleep:
How far away the stars seem, and how far
10 Is our first kiss, and ah, how old my heart!"

Pensive they paced along the faded leaves,
While slowly he whose hand held hers replied:
"Passion has often worn our wandering hearts."

The woods were round them, and the yellow leaves
15 Fell like faint meteors in the gloom, and once
A rabbit old and lame limped down the path;
Autumn was over him: and now they stood
On the lone border of the lake once more:
Turning, he saw that she had thrust dead leaves
20 Gathered in silence, dewy as her eyes,
In bosom and hair.
   "Ah, do not mourn," he said,
"That we are tired, for other loves await us:
Hate on and love through unrepining[2] hours;
25 Before us lies eternity; our souls
Are love, and a continual farewell."
—1887 (REVISED 1895)

The Lake Isle of Innisfree[3]

I will arise and go now, and go to Innisfree,
   And a small cabin build there, of clay and wattles[4]
     made;
Nine bean-rows will I have there, a hive for the honey
   bee,
And live alone in the bee-loud glade.

5 And I shall have some peace there, for peace comes
   dropping slow,
Dropping from the veils of the morning to where the
   cricket sings;
There midnight's all a glimmer, and noon a purple glow,
And evening full of the linnet's° wings.   *small songbird's*

I will arise and go now, for always night and day
10 I hear lake water lapping with low sounds by the shore;
While I stand on the roadway, or on the pavements grey,
I hear it in the deep heart's core.
    —1890

Into the Twilight[5]

Out-worn heart, in a time out-worn,
   Come clear of the nets of wrong and right;
Laugh heart again in the grey twilight,
Sigh, heart, again in the dew of the morn.

5 Your mother Eire° is always young,   *Ireland*
Dew ever shining and twilight gray;
Though hope fall from you and love decay,
Burning in fires of a slanderous tongue.

Come, heart, where hill is heaped upon hill:
10 For there the mystical brotherhood

---

[1] *Ephemera* Short-lived things, or things that are enjoyed only briefly.

[2] *unrepining* Contented, without brooding.

[3] *Lake Isle of Innisfree* A small island in Lough Gill, County Sligo; Innisfree (*Inis Fraoigh* in Gaelic) means "Heather Island."

[4] *wattles* Poles and reeds interwoven to create a thatched wall or roof.

[5] *Into the Twilight* Originally published under the title "The Celtic Twilight."

Of sun and moon and hollow and wood
And river and stream work out their will;

And God stands winding° His lonely horn, *blowing*
And time and the world are ever in flight;
15 And love is less kind than the gray twilight,
And hope is less dear than the dew of the morn.
—1893

The Secret Rose[1]

Far-off, most secret, and inviolate Rose,
Enfold me in my hour of hours; where those
Who sought thee in the Holy Sepulchre,[2]
Or in the wine vat, dwell beyond the stir
5 And tumult of defeated dreams; and deep
Among pale eyelids, heavy with the sleep
Men have named beauty. Thy great leaves enfold
The ancient beards, the helms of ruby and gold
Of the crowned Magi;[3] and the king whose eyes
10 Saw the Pierced Hands and Rood° of elder rise *cross*
In druid vapour and make the torches dim;
Till vain frenzy awoke and he died;[4] and him
Who met Fand walking among flaming dew
By a grey shore where the wind never blew,

15 And lost the world and Emer for a kiss;[5]
And him who drove the gods out of their liss,[6]
And till a hundred morns had flowered red,
Feasted, and wept the barrows° of his dead; *grave mounds*
And the proud dreaming king who flung the crown
20 And sorrow away, and calling bard and clown
Dwelt among wine-stained wanderers in deep woods:[7]
And him who sold tillage,° and house, *farmland*
  and goods,
And sought through lands and islands numberless years,
Until he found with laughter and with tears,
25 A woman, of so shining loveliness
That men threshed corn° at midnight by *grain*
  a tress,°   *lock of hair*
A little stolen tress.[8] I, too, await
The hour of thy great wind of love and hate.
When shall the stars be blown about the sky,
30 Like the sparks blown out of a smithy,° *blacksmith's forge*
  and die?
Surely thine hour has come, thy great wind blows,
Far-off, most secret, and inviolate Rose?
—1896

---

[1] *The Secret Rose* First published under the title "O'Sullivan Rua to the Secret Rose."

[2] *Holy Sepulchre* Cave in which Jesus Christ's body was placed before his resurrection.

[3] *Magi* Three wise men who came from the East to bring gifts to the baby Jesus.

[4] *the king ... he died* King Conchobar, who was said to have the same birth date and death date as Jesus Christ. Conchobar had an object embedded in his head, an injury from a past battle; when he was told of Christ's execution, he grew so angry that the object burst out of his skull and he died. Here, Yeats imagines Conchobar witnessing the crucifixion in a vision brought by Druids, priests of Celtic religion. Yeats identifies this and the poem's other references to Irish myth and folktale in an extensive note accompanying some editions of the poem.

[5] *and him ... a kiss* In Irish myth, the great hero Cúchulainn became a lover to the goddess Fand and accompanied her to the otherworld, leaving his wife Emer.

[6] *And him ... their liss* Caoilte, a hero of Irish legend. Seized by rage after almost all of his friends were killed in a battle, he drove the nearby gods out of their home; *liss* Circular fort common in iron-age Ireland.

[7] *And the proud ... deep woods* Legendary Irish king Fergus. According to Yeats, he fell so deeply in love with a woman that he was motivated to give up his throne to her son Conchobar, and he spent the rest of his days feasting and hunting in the forest.

[8] *And him who sold ... stolen tress* Reference to an Irish folktale in which a working man, while traveling on the road in the dark, discovers a box containing a brightly glowing lock of hair. He uses it as a lamp to work at night until the king learns of the hair and sends him to find the woman to whom it belongs.

He Remembers Forgotten Beauty[1]

When my arms wrap you round I press
   My heart upon the loveliness
That has long faded from the world;
The jewelled crowns that kings have hurled
5 In shadowy pools, when armies fled;
The love-tales wrought with silken thread
By dreaming ladies upon cloth
That has made fat the murderous moth;
The roses that of old time were
10 Woven by ladies in their hair,
The dew-cold lilies ladies bore
Through many a sacred corridor
Where such gray clouds of incense rose
That only the gods' eyes did not close:
15 For that pale breast and lingering hand
Come from a more dream-heavy land,
A more dream-heavy hour than this;
And when you sigh from kiss to kiss
I hear white Beauty sighing, too,
20 For hours when all must fade like dew
But flame on flame, deep under deep,
Throne over throne, where in half sleep
Their swords upon their iron knees
Brood her high lonely mysteries.
—1896

The Travail of Passion[2]

When the flaming lute-thronged angelic door is wide;
   When an immortal passion breathes in mortal
     clay;
Our hearts endure the scourge,° the plaited[3]   *whip*
   thorns, the way
Crowded with bitter faces, the wounds in palm and side,
5 The hyssop-heavy sponge,[4] the flowers by Kidron stream;[5]
We will bend down and loosen our hair over you,
That it may drop faint perfume, and be heavy with dew,
Lilies of death-pale hope, roses of passionate dream.
—1899

---

[1] *He Remembers … Beauty*   Originally published under the title "O'Sullivan Rua to Mary Lavell" (1896) and then, with small revisions, as "Michael Robartes Remembers Forgotten Beauty" (1899) before being reprinted under the present title (1906).

---

[2] *Travail*   Toil, struggle; *Passion*   Throughout this poem are allusions to the Passion of Christ, the sufferings of Jesus surrounding his crucifixion. Among other tortures, Christ was whipped, forced to wear a crown of thorns, made to carry his cross through a jeering crowd, nailed to the cross by his hands, and speared in the side.

[3] *plaited*   Braided (i.e., into a crown).

[4] *hyssop-heavy sponge*   In John 19.29 Christ, dying on the cross, is given a drink of vinegar on a sponge attached to a stick from a hyssop plant.

[5] *Kidron stream*   Small river that passes through the garden of Gethsemane, where Jesus spent the night in prayer before his arrest.

THE AESTHETIC MOVEMENT

From the Victorian *fin de siècle* to the early twentieth century, Aestheticism inspired poets, painters, playwrights, and innumerable others to reconsider the purpose of literature and art. Also known as "art for art's sake," the movement represented a break from the view that the arts must have a moral, social, or religious function. Aestheticism affirmed instead the autonomy of art and the belief that beauty and its appreciation are justifiable ends in themselves. Influenced in England by the writings of Walter Pater and a circle of young avant-garde writers at Oxford, leading Aesthetes such as Algernon Charles Swinburne and Oscar Wilde rejected the limits imposed on art by utilitarianism and conventional Victorian ethics and religion, and created in their place a body of literature determined to be uninhibited by the bourgeois standards of the day.

The term "aesthetics," derived from the Greek word for sense perception (*aesthesis*), was first used in 1750 by the German philosopher Alexander Baumgarten (1714–62) to describe "the science of sensitive knowing." All subsequent considerations of aesthetics maintain to some degree this concern with the "sensitive" origins of knowledge, and in particular the subjective experience by which individuals come to appreciate works of art. French philosopher Victor Cousin (1792–1867) later coined the phrase "*l'art pour l'art*," building on Kant's notion of disinterestedness in aesthetic judgment to proclaim that "the beautiful cannot be the way to what is useful, or to what is good, or to what is holy; it leads only to itself." In 1835, French author Théophile Gautier (1811–72) further developed the idea of "art for art's sake" in the preface to his novel *Mademoiselle de Maupin*: "nothing is truly beautiful except that which can serve for nothing; whatever is useful is ugly."

Aestheticism as defined by these writers emerged most powerfully in France through Charles Baudelaire's 1857 volume of poetry, *Les Fleurs du Mal* (*The Flowers of Evil*), which employed a language of symbolism to suggest "correspondences" among sounds, scents, and colors ("Les parfums, les couleurs et les sons se répondent"). On the other side of the English Channel a group of young artists who called themselves the "Pre-Raphaelite Brotherhood" advanced similar ideas through both poetry and painting. Originating in 1848 as a group of seven men including Dante Gabriel Rossetti, John Everett Millais, and others (Christina Rossetti and other women shared mutual influence with the group but were not formally admitted)—the Pre-Raphaelites set the stage for the Aesthetic Movement in England. With their attention to fine detail, symbolism, and brilliant use of color, the Pre-Raphaelites aimed to excite the senses of the spectator, to create a unique aesthetic experience through a combination of sense impressions.

British Aestheticism was effectively inaugurated as a movement in 1868 when Walter Pater published an unsigned essay on William Morris's poetry in the *Westminster Review*. Pater, who taught at Oxford, encouraged the constant pursuit of passionate experience, and especially the sort of passion that might come of reading literature or viewing works of art. When Pater republished his review of Morris as part of his 1873 *Studies in the History of the Renaissance*, it prompted a tidal wave of reaction, both for and against Aestheticism. "Great passions," Pater wrote, "may give us [a] quickened sense of life, ecstasy and sorrow of love, the various forms of enthusiastic activity." Pater valued above all "the poetic passion, the desire for beauty, the love of art for art's sake," precisely insofar as art might be separated from politics, ethics, and religion. The beauty of art, in other words, arises from its autonomy, from the moments of pleasure that arise "simply for those moments' sake."

For many writers associated with Aestheticism, however, the pursuit of "art for art's sake" did not mean an abdication of political views; for William Morris, for example, the valuation of human pleasure and creativity was inseparable from his socialist ideals. Wilde himself was a socialist, as was the author-activist Edward Carpenter, also known for his writing on same-sex love. Many of the most radical "New Woman" writers, such as Mona Caird, George Egerton, and Victoria Cross, were linked to the Aesthetic movement—though other "New Women," such as Sarah Grand, advocated a restrained sexual morality that was at odds with Aesthetic principles. In general, critics of Aestheticism saw its repudiation of political, ethical, and religious norms as a danger to British culture and society. A writer for *Blackwood's Edinburgh Magazine* worried in 1895 that a "wave of unrest" was passing over the world due in part to those authors who, following Pater's advice, sought "for new thrills and sensations." Critics took to characterizing this unrest as "decadence," a term that in many minds became synonymous with Aestheticism. In an 1893 *Harper's* magazine essay entitled "The Decadent Movement in Literature," Arthur Symons, once a pupil of Walter Pater and a self-proclaimed Aesthete, launched an attack on the Decadent Movement, calling it a "new and beautiful and interesting disease," epitomized by an "intense self-consciousness, a restless curiosity in research, an oversubtilizing refinement upon refinement, a spiritual and moral perversity." The German social theorist Max Nordau used many of the same terms to describe the Decadents—"diseased ... immoral ... anti-social"—but with the goal of illustrating the ways in which Aestheticism had led to what he called, in the title of his 1892 work, *Degeneration*, a deterioration of Western society and culture.

When Aestheticism wasn't being decried for its immorality, it was often the subject of parody. Gilbert and Sullivan's 1881 operetta *Patience* featured an Aesthetic poet, Bunthorne, whom Oscar Wilde himself took for a model (his career as the most prominent of Aesthetes was just getting under way), and the magazine *Punch* relentlessly parodied the Aesthetes, characterizing them as narcissistic, self-serving dandies. Authors such as Swinburne and Wilde ignored the derision of the critics and consciously dressed the part of dandies, donning clothes of flamboyant colors and wearing plumes, velvet jackets, and knee breeches. The movement became increasingly associated with sensuous beauty and the decorative arts, and for a time sales of blue china and peacock feathers, objects of the sort appreciated by the Aesthetes, soared, while the public clamored for books on decorating ideas. The movement also influenced architecture and design, inspiring the ornate and decorative motifs of the Art Nouveau movement as well as, paradoxically, the devotion to simplicity and handcrafted work of the Arts and Crafts Movement (exemplified by the works of the William Morris Company and the Scottish architect and designer Charles Rennie Mackintosh). In the arts, Aestheticism found expression in the paintings of Edward Burne-Jones and James McNeill Whistler and in the erotic illustrations of Aubrey Beardsley, many of which were published in *The Yellow Book*, a *fin de siècle* quarterly of the arts and literature that was a vehicle for Aesthetic works. It published many of the most prominent writers linked to the movement, including Vernon Lee, Max Beerbohm, Charlotte Mew, Lionel Johnson, and George Moore.

Although the Aesthetic Movement seemed to expire with the celebrated and humiliating trial of Oscar Wilde on charges of "gross indecency" with men, its after-effects were felt in the writing of such twentieth-century literary figures as William Butler Yeats and Henry James. More important, perhaps, Aestheticism helped break the Victorian loyalty to realism and moral aestheticism. Aestheticism's opposition to traditional forms, its concern with the self and individuality, and above all its principle of aesthetic autonomy, permanently altered the production and reception of art in Britain and elsewhere.

⌘ ⌘ ⌘

N.B. Because Aestheticism was not a formally defined movement, it can be difficult to determine which writers should be counted as Aesthetes, but the following authors appearing elsewhere in the anthology have, at least, significant links to Aestheticism: George Meredith, William Morris, Algernon Charles Swinburne, Walter Pater, Mathilde Blind, Michael Field (Katharine Bradley and Edith Cooper), Oscar Wilde, Vernon Lee, Amy Levy, and Charlotte Mew.

"MICHAEL FIELD"

KATHARINE BRADLEY (1848–1914) AND EDITH COOPER (1862–1913)

"Michael Field" was the pseudonym used by Katharine Bradley and her niece Edith Cooper, who together published eight volumes of poetry and numerous tragedies. The two women, who were also lovers, disguised their identity for fear that the truth would influence the reception of their work. A larger selection of their work appears under a separate author entry elsewhere in this volume; two poems whose themes relate strongly to those of the Aesthetes appear below.

From Baudelaire[1]

There shall be beds full of light odours blent,
Divans, great couches, deep, profound as tombs,
And, frown for us, in light magnificent,
Over the flower-stand there shall droop strange blooms.

5 Careful of their last flame declining,
As two vast torches our two hearts shall flare,
And our two spirits in their double shining
Reflect the double lights enchanted there.

One night—a night of mystic blue, of rose,
10 A look will pass supreme from me, from you,
Like a long sob, laden with long adieux.

---

[1] *Baudelaire* French poet and critic Charles Baudelaire (1821–67), whose volume of poetry *Les Fleurs du Mal* (1857) established a symbolic correspondence between sensory images of sound, scent, and color.

And, later on, an angel will unclose
The door, and, entering joyously, re-light
The tarnished mirrors and the flames blown to the night.
—1908

The Poet

Within his eyes are hung lamps of the sanctuary:
A wind, from whence none knows, can set in sway
And spill their light by fits; but yet their ray
Returns, deep-boled,[2] to its obscurity.

5 The world as from a dullard[3] turns annoyed
To stir the days with show or deeds or voices;
But if one spies him justly one rejoices,
With silence that the careful lips avoid.

He is a plan, a work of some strange passion
10 Life has conceived apart from Time's harsh drill,
A thing it hides and cherishes to fashion.

At odd bright moments to its secret will:
Holy and foolish, ever set apart,
He waits the leisure of his god's free heart.
—1908

JOHN DAVIDSON (1857–1909)

Poet, playwright, and novelist John Davidson spent his early life in Scotland before moving to London, where his work as a journalist provided him with a wealth of material for his poetry. Davidson remained marginal to the Aesthetic Movement, with which he had an ambivalent relationship. His poetry often relied upon deep philosophical enquiries into the nature of human existence and the pursuit of desire. He was unique among his contemporaries in

---

[2] *deep-boled* I.e., having deep apertures. A bole is a recess in the wall of a castle, etc., for admitting light.

[3] *dullard* Stupid or dull person.

his exploration of Nietzsche's poetic theories, and his deeply ironic tone, compelling urban images, and expressions of scientific materialism had an effect on many of the poets who followed him.

A Northern Suburb

Nature selects the longest way,
　　And winds about in tortuous grooves;
A thousand years the oaks decay;
　　The wrinkled glacier hardly moves.

5　But here the whetted fangs of change
　　Daily devour the old demesne°—　　　　　*district*
The busy farm, the quiet grange,°　　　　*country-house*
　　The wayside inn, the village green.

In gaudy yellow brick and red,
10　　With rooting pipes, like creepers rank,
The shoddy terraces o'erspread
　　Meadow, and garth,[1] and daisied bank.

With shelves for rooms the houses crowd,
　　Like draughty cupboards in a row—
15　Ice-chests when wintry winds are loud,
　　Ovens when summer breezes blow.

Roused by the fee'd° policeman's knock,　　　*hired*
　　And sad that day should come again,
Under the stars the workmen flock
20　　In haste to reach the workmen's train.

For here dwell those who must fulfil
　　Dull tasks in uncongenial spheres,
Who toil through dread of coming ill,
　　And not with hope of happier years—

25　The lowly folk who scarcely dare
　　Conceive themselves perhaps misplaced,

---

[1] *garth* Yard; garden.

Whose prize for unremitting care
　　Is only not to be disgraced.
—1897

CONSTANCE NADEN (1858–89)

Poet and philosopher Constance Naden was well educated in a range of sciences, including botany, chemistry, physics, and zoology. Her poetry demonstrates a particular interest in natural selection and evolutionary ethics, as well as a deep religious skepticism. Neither of the two volumes of poetry that Naden published in her lifetime received much notice, but those who reviewed her work praised it highly. One reviewer named her, Elizabeth Barrett Browning, and Christina Rossetti as the three finest female poets, while another described her second collection of poetry as displaying "both culture and courage—culture in its use of language, courage in its choice of subject matter." By 1887, Naden had stopped writing poetry, choosing to focus instead on her philosophical writing.

Illusions

Not in the heavens alone is Truth renowned;
　　Sad human hearts, that seem to love her less,
Even in mutiny her power confess:
We speak in fables, and are compassed round
5　With poesy, distilling song from sound,
Colour from light, and hope from happiness;
Subliming weakness, yearning, and distress,
To that high faith wherewith our life is crowned.

All fair deceits are prophets of the truth,
10　E'en as the desert mirage tells a tale
Of palms and wells, real, though far away:
The star-bright hopes that light the world's dim youth
Are not too brilliant, but too silvery pale,
To sparkle still, when dawns the golden day.
—1881

ERNEST DOWSON (1867–1900)

Dowson was a central figure of the Aesthetic Movement, and moved frequently in the London literary society of Lionel Johnson, Richard Le Gallienne, Oscar Wilde, Walter Pater, and Aubrey Beardsley, while contributing to most of the Aesthetic magazines of the time. Influenced by Charles Swinburne, classical Latin poets such as Horace, and the French symbolist Verlaine, Dowson also drew upon Roman Catholic liturgy in some poems. (He was received into the Church around 1891.) Throughout his work he demonstrates a technical mastery of the language and a lyrical, mellifluous style.

Nuns of the Perpetual Adoration

Calm, sad, secure; behind high convent walls,
　　These watch the sacred lamp, these watch and pray:
And it is one with them when evening falls,
　　And one with them the cold return of day.

5　These heed not time; their nights and days they make
　　Into a long, returning rosary,
Whereon their lives are threaded for Christ's sake;
　　Meekness and vigilance and chastity.

A vowed patrol, in silent companies,
10　Life-long they keep before the living Christ.
In the dim church, their prayers and penances
　　Are fragrant incense to the Sacrificed.

Outside, the world is wild and passionate;
　　Man's weary laughter and his sick despair
15　Entreat at their impenetrable gate:
　　They heed no voices in their dream of prayer.

They saw the glory of the world displayed;
　　They saw the bitter of it, and the sweet;
They knew the roses of the world should fade,
20　And be trod under by the hurrying feet.

Therefore they rather put away desire,
　　And crossed their hands and came to sanctuary;
And veiled their heads and put on coarse attire:
　　Because their comeliness was vanity.

25　And there they rest; they have serene insight
　　Of the illuminating dawn to be:
Mary's sweet Star[1] dispels for them the night,
　　The proper darkness of humanity.

Calm, sad, secure; with faces worn and mild:
30　Surely their choice of vigil is the best?
Yea! for our roses fade, the world is wild;
　　But there, beside the altar, there, is rest.
—1891

To One in Bedlam[2]

With delicate, mad hands, behind his sordid bars,
　　Surely he hath his posies, which they tear and
　　　twine;
Those scentless wisps of straw, that miserably line
His strait, caged universe, whereat the dull world stares,

5　Pedant and pitiful. O, how his rapt gaze wars
With their stupidity! Know they what dreams divine
Lift his long, laughing reveries like enchaunted wine,
And make his melancholy germane to the stars?

O lamentable brother! if those pity thee,
10　Am I not fain° of all thy lone eyes promise me;　　*glad*
Half a fool's kingdom, far from men who sow and reap,
All their days, vanity? Better than mortal flowers,
Thy moon-kissed roses seem: better than love or sleep,
The star-crowned solitude of thine oblivious hours.
—1892

---

[1] *Mary's sweet Star* I.e., Jesus; the star of Bethlehem, that announced his birth, is used here as a metaphor for Jesus.

[2] *Bedlam* I.e., London's Hospital of St. Mary of Bethlehem, a public asylum for the mentally ill. The term came to be used to refer to any asylum.

Spleen
For Arthur Symons[1]

I was not sorrowful, I could not weep,
And all my memories were put to sleep.

I watched the river grow more white and strange,
All day till evening I watched it change.

5 All day till evening I watched the rain
Beat wearily upon the window pane.

I was not sorrowful, but only tired
Of everything that ever I desired.

Her lips, her eyes, all day became to me
10 The shadow of a shadow utterly.

All day mine hunger for her heart became
Oblivion, until the evening came,

And left me sorrowful, inclined to weep,
With all my memories that could not sleep.
—1896

LIONEL JOHNSON (1867–1902)

Johnson, like his close friend Ernest Dowson, was central to the poetic movements of the 1890s. He was tutored at Oxford by Walter Pater and had close relationships with W.B. Yeats and Arthur Symons. His poems display a sensitivity to beauty, despite their often brooding tone, and frequently take literary themes as their topics. (Johnson was also a renowned scholar and critic.) His work also occasionally demonstrates religious anxiety—Johnson's Roman Catholic faith was a central part of his life, and he struggled to reconcile his religious beliefs with his same-sex desires. Johnson suffered from the effects of alcoholism throughout his adult life, and eventually died from complications of this disease.

Plato[2] in London
To Campbell Dodgson[3]

The pure flame of one taper° fall   candle
Over the old and comely page:
No harsher light disturb at all
This converse with a treasured sage.
5 Seemly, and fair, and of the best,
If Plato be our guest,
Should things befall.

Without,° a world of noise and cold: outside
Here, the soft burning of the fire.
10 And Plato walks, where heavens unfold,
About the home of his desire.
From his own city of high things,
He shows to us, and brings,
Truth of fine gold.

15 The hours pass; and the fire burns low;
The clear flame dwindles into death:
Shut then the book with care; and so,
Take leave of Plato, with hushed breath:
A little, by the falling gleams,
20 Tarry the gracious dreams;
And they too go.

Lean from the window to the air:
Hear London's voice upon the night!
Thou hast held converse with things rare:
25 Look now upon another sight!
The calm stars, in their living skies:
And then, these surging cries,
This restless glare!

---

1 *Spleen* Melancholy; ill-humor. (According to medieval physiology, the spleen was the source of these emotions.) *Arthur Symons* Literary scholar and editor (1865–1945) who established himself as a leading writer of the Aesthetic Movement. Some of Dowson's work was published in Symon's short-lived Aesthetic magazine *The Savoy* (1896).

2 *Plato* Greek philosopher (427?–347 BCE).

3 *Campbell Dodgson* Museum curator, art historian, and renowned scholar (1867–1948).

That starry music, starry fire,
30 High above all our noise and glare:
The image of our long desire,
The beauty, and the strength, are there.
And Plato's thought lives, true and clear,
    In as august a sphere:
35   Perchance, far higher.
—1889

The Dark Angel

Dark Angel, with thine aching lust
To rid the world of penitence:
Malicious Angel, who still dost
My soul such subtle violence!

5 Because of thee, no thought, no thing,
Abides for me undesecrate:
Dark Angel, ever on the wing,
Who never reachest me too late!

When music sounds, then changest thou
10 Its silvery to a sultry fire:
Nor will thine envious heart allow
Delight untortured by desire.

Through thee, the gracious Muses[1] turn
To Furies,[2] O mine Enemy!
15 And all the things of beauty burn
With flames of evil ecstasy.

Because of thee, the land of dreams
Becomes a gathering place of fears:
Until tormented slumber seems
20 One vehemence of useless tears.

When sunlight glows upon the flowers,
Or ripples down the dancing sea:
Thou, with thy troop of passionate powers,
Beleaguerest, bewilderest, me.

25 Within the breath of autumn woods,
Within the winter silences:
Thy venomous spirit stirs and broods,
O Master of impieties!

The ardour of red flame is thine,
30 And thine the steely soul of ice:
Thou poisonest the fair design
Of nature, with unfair device.

Apples of ashes, golden bright;
Waters of bitterness, how sweet!
35 O banquet of a foul delight,
Prepared by thee, dark Paraclete![3]

Thou art the whisper in the gloom,
The hinting tone, the haunting laugh:
Thou art the adorner of my tomb,
40 The minstrel of mine epitaph.

I fight thee, in the Holy Name!
Yet, what thou dost, is what God saith:
Tempter! should I escape thy flame,
Thou wilt have helped my soul from Death:

45 The second Death, that never dies,
That cannot die, when time is dead:
Live Death, wherein the lost soul cries,
Eternally uncomforted.

Dark Angel, with thine aching lust!
50 Of two defeats, of two despairs:
Less dread, a change to drifting dust,
Than thine eternity of cares.

---

[1] *Muses* In classical mythology, the nine daughters of Zeus and Mnemosyne, each of whom presided over and provided inspiration for an aspect of the arts and sciences.

[2] *Furies* Three winged deities of classical mythology who pursued and punished the doers of unavenged crimes, and who were terrifying in their appearance and behavior.

---

[3] *Paraclete* Comforter; advocate (a title usually given to the Holy Spirit).

Do what thou wilt, thou shalt not so,
Dark Angel! triumph over me:
55   *Lonely, unto the Lone I go*;
Divine, to the Divinity.
—1893, 1894

The Darkness
To the Rev. Fr. Dover, S.J.[1]

Master of spirits! hear me: King of souls!
I kneel before Thine altar, the long night,
Besieging Thee with penetrable prayers;
And all I ask, light from the Face of God.
5   Thy darkness Thou hast given me enough,
The dark clouds of Thine angry majesty:
Now give me light! I cannot always walk
Surely beneath the full and starless night.
Lighten me, fallen down, I know not where,
10   Save, to the shadows and the fear of death.
Thy Saints in light see light, and sing for joy:
Safe from the dark, safe from the dark and cold.
But from my dark comes only doubt of light:
Disloyalty, that trembles to despair.
15   Now bring me out of night, and with the sun
Clothe me, and crown me with Thy seven stars,[2]
Thy spirits in the hollow of Thine hand.
Thou from the still throne of Thy tabernacle[3]
Wilt come to me in glory, O Lord God!
20   Thou wilt, I doubt Thee not: I worship Thee
Before Thine holy altar, the long night.
Else have I nothing in the world, but death:
Thine hounding winds rush by me day and night,
Thy seas roar in mine ears: I have no rest,
25   No peace, but am afflicted constantly,
Driven from wilderness to wilderness.
And yet Thou hast a perfect house of light,
Above the four great winds, an house of peace:

Its beauty of the crystal and the dew,
30   Guard Angels and Archangels, in their hands
The blade of a sword shaken. Thither bring
Thy servant: when the black night falls on me,
With bitter voices tempting in the gloom,
Send out Thine armies, flaming ministers,
35   And shine upon the night: for what I would,
I cannot, save these help me. O Lord God!
Now, when my prayers upon Thine altar lie,
When Thy dark anger is too hard for me:
Through vision of Thyself, through flying fire,
40   Have mercy, and give light, and stablish me![4]
—1897, 1889

AUBREY BEARDSLEY (1872–98)

Few artists are as strongly associated with Aestheticism as Aubrey Beardsley, whose graceful and sumptuous black and white drawings made such an impact on British art that the 1890s, the height of his fame, were sometimes referred to as the "Beardsley period." His best-known work was entwined with the print culture of Aesthetic literature; he famously illustrated an 1894 publication of Oscar Wilde's play *Salomé*, and many of his works appeared in the pages and on the covers of *The Yellow Book* and its short-lived competitor, *The Savoy* (1896), of which Beardsley was also a co-founder. Beardsley's willingness to include erotic and macabre elements in his work was controversial; one critic remarked in 1894 that "There seems to be a peculiar tendency in Mr. Beardsley's mind to the representation of types without intellect and without morals. Some of the most dreadful faces in all art are to be found in the illustrations (full of exquisite ornamental invention) to Mr. Oscar Wilde's 'Salome.' ... There is distinctly a sort of corruption in Mr. Beardsley's art so far as its human element is concerned, but not at all in its artistic qualities, which show the perfection of discipline, of self-control, and of thoughtful deliberation at the very moment of invention."

---

[1] *S.J.* Member of the Society of Jesus; i.e., a Jesuit.

[2] *Thy seven stars* See Revelation 1.16, where Christ is described holding seven stars in his right hand.

[3] *tabernacle* Dwelling place (of God).

[4] *stablish me* Steady my faith.

Illustrations from *Salomé*, 1894.

Cover of *The Yellow Book*, Volume 1, 1894.

La Dame aux Camélias, from *The Yellow Book*,
Volume 4, 1894.

IN CONTEXT

French Influences and British Views on Aestheticism

The critical discussion of "art for art's sake" took hold in France decades before it did in England. The first two selections below reflect the mid-century French ideals that were later taken up by English Aesthetes; these are followed by popular and critical English responses to Aestheticism from the century's final decades.

Théophile Gautier, from Preface to *Mademoiselle de Maupin, A Romance of Love and Passion*[1] (1835)

Gautier was a French writer and critic who was claimed as a member by many of the artistic movements of the nineteenth century: Romanticism, Symbolism, Modernism, Decadence. His novel *Mademoiselle de Maupin* is based on the life of a French opera star who often dressed as a man and was known for her skills as a swordswoman. Gautier changed the story from the historical one (in which Maupin set fire to a convent, desperate with love for another woman) to a triangular love plot (in which a man and a woman both fall in love with Maupin, who is herself disguised as a man). The novel's dominant theme concerns the importance of purity in art and love; the author's preface, from which the following excerpt is taken, proved to be influential as an articulation of the value of "art for art's sake."

One of the greatest burlesques of the glorious epoch at which we have the good fortune to live, is unquestionably the rehabilitation of virtue undertaken by all the journals of every hue, red, green, or tricoloured.[2]

Virtue is assuredly very respectable, and we have no wish to fail in respect to her, God forbid! Good and worthy woman that she is! We think that her eyes are brilliant enough through their spectacles, that her leg is neatly gartered, that she takes her snuff in her gold box with all imaginable grace, that her little dog bows like a dancing-master. We think all this. We will even acknowledge that for her age, she is, in point of fact, not so much amiss, and that she carries her years as well as can be. She is a very agreeable grandmother—but she is a grandmother. It seems to me natural, especially at twenty years of age, to prefer some little immorality, very spruce and coquettish, and very good-natured, with her hair a little uncurled, her skirt short rather than long, an enticing foot and eye, her cheek lightly kindled, laughter on her lips, and her heart in her hand. The most monstrously virtuous journalists cannot be of a different opinion, and if they say the contrary, it is very probable that they do not think it. To think one thing and write another happens every day, especially in the case of virtuous people.

---

[1] *Preface to Mademoiselle de Maupin, A Romance of Love and Passion* Anonymously translated for the publisher Vizetelly and Co., 1887.

[2] *tricoloured* The "tricolor" is another word for the flag of Revolutionary France, which is still the French flag today. It is comprised of three bands of color: blue, white, and red.

I remember the jokes launched before the Revolution (that of July, I mean) against the unfortunate and virginal Viscount Sosthène de La Rochefoucauld,[1] who lengthened the skirts of the dancers at the Opera, and with his own patrician hands applied a modest plaster to the middle of all the statues. Viscount Sosthène de La Rochefoucauld has been far surpassed. Modesty has been greatly improved upon since that time, and we now indulge in refinements which he would not have dreamed of.

For my own part, not being accustomed to look at statues in certain places, I thought, like other people, that the vine leaf[2] carved by the chisels of the superintendent of the fine arts was the most ridiculous thing in the world. It appears that I was wrong, and that the vine leaf is among the most meritorious of institutions. …

I have been told, but I refused to believe it, so singular did it seem to me that people existed, who, standing before Michael Angelo's "Last Judgment," saw nothing in it but the episode of the licentious prelates, and veiled their faces, as they cried out against the abomination of the desolation![3] …

I confess that I am not virtuous enough for that. The impudent abigail Dorine[4] may safely display her plump breast before me. I shall certainly not take out my pocket-handkerchief to cover the bosom so that it cannot be seen. I shall look at her breast as at her face, and, if it is white and well-formed, I shall take pleasure in it[.] …

Say what they will, the age is an immoral one (if this word signifies anything, of which we have strong doubts), and we wish for no other proof than the quantity of immoral books it produces and the success that attends them. Books follow morals, and not morals books. … Someone has said somewhere that literature and the arts influence morals. Whoever he was, he was undoubtedly a great fool. It was like saying green peas make the spring grow, whereas green peas grow because it is spring, and cherries because it is summer. Trees bear fruits; it is certainly not the fruits that bear the trees, and this law is eternal and invariable in its variety; the centuries follow one another, and each bears its own fruit, which is not that of the preceding century; books are the fruits of morals.

By the side of the moral journalists, under this rain of homilies as under summer rain in some park, there has sprung up between the planks of the Saint-Simonian[5] stage a theory of little mushrooms, of a novel and somewhat curious species, whose natural history we are about to give.

---

[1] *Revolution* The French Revolution of 1830, or "July Revolution," overthrew the reinstated French Bourbon monarch, King Charles X, and installed another monarch, Louis Philippe; *La Rochefoucauld* Viscount Sosthène de La Rochefoucauld (1785–1864) was a Royalist politician and writer who was made Director of the Arts in 1824.

[2] *vine leaf* Used to cover the genitals on a sculpture.

[3] *Michel Angelo's … desolation* Michelangelo's fresco *The Last Judgment*, which covers the altar wall of the Sistine Chapel, shows the final judgment of humanity at the end of the world. The figures in the fresco are mostly nude, and this has long been a subject of controversy; some religious officials felt that nude portraiture was inappropriate to the holy setting, and another artist was hired to paint clothes on the figures after Michelangelo's death; *licentious prelates* Lustful priests; *the abomination of the desolation* See Matthew 24.15, where this phrase is used to describe the desecration of the Temple in Jerusalem.

[4] *abigail* Lady's maid; *Dorine* Wise lady's maid in Molière's comedy *Tartuffe* (1664). In Act 3, Scene 2, the hypocrite Tartuffe asks Dorine to cover her cleavage with a handkerchief, and she chastises him for being "so prone to lust" that the sight should tempt him.

[5] *Saint-Simonian* Saint-Simonianism is a nineteenth-century social movement based on the ideas of Henri de Rouvroy, Comte de Saint-Simon (1760–1825). Saint-Simon believed that scientific and technological improvements would create sweeping change that would do away with existing power and religious structures, creating a society based on equality and shared labor.

These are the utilitarian critics. Poor fellows! Their noses are too short to admit of their wearing spectacles, and yet they cannot see the length of their noses.[1]

If an author threw a volume of romance or poetry on their desk, these gentlemen would turn round carelessly in their easy chair, poise it on its hinder legs, and balancing themselves with a capable air, say loftily:

"What purpose does this book serve? How can it be applied for the moralisation and well-being of the poorest and most numerous class? What! not a word of the needs of society, nothing about civilisation and progress? How can a man, instead of making the great synthesis of humanity, and pursuing the regenerating and providential idea through the events of history, how can he write novels and poems which lead to nothing, and do not advance our generation on the path of the future? How can he busy himself with form, and style, and rhyme in the presence of such grave interests? What are style, and rhyme, and form to us? They are of no consequence (poor foxes! they are too sour). Society is suffering, it is a prey to great internal anguish[.] ... It is for the poet to seek the cause of this uneasiness and to cure it. He will find the means of doing so by sympathizing from his heart and soul with humanity (philanthropic poet! they would be something uncommon and charming). This poet we await, and on him we call with all our vows. When he appears, his will be the acclamations of the crowd, his the palm, his the crown, his the Prytaneum."[2]

Well and good! But as we wish our reader to remain awake until the end of this blissful preface, we shall not continue this very faithful imitation of the utilitarian style, which is, in its nature, tolerably soporific, and might, with advantage, take the place of laudanum and Academic[3] discourses.

No, fools, no, goitrous cretins that you are, a book does not make gelatine soup; a novel is not a pair of seamless boots; a sonnet, a syringe with a continuous jet; or a drama, a railway—all things which are essentially civilizing and adapted to advance humanity on its path of progress.

By the guts of all the popes past, present, and future, no, and two hundred thousand times no! ...

I know that there are some who prefer mills to churches, and bread for the body to that for the soul. To such I have nothing to say. They deserve to be economists in this world and also in the next.

Is there anything absolutely useful on this earth and in this life of ours? To begin with, it is not very useful that we are on the earth and alive. I defy the most learned of the band to tell us of what use we are, unless it be to not subscribe to the "Constitutionnel,"[4] nor any other species of journal whatsoever.

Next, the utility of our existence being admitted *a priori*, what are the things really useful for supporting it? Some soup and a piece of meat twice a day is all that is necessary to fill the stomach in the strict acceptation of the word. Man who finds a coffin six feet long by two wide more than sufficient after his death does not need much more room during his life. A hollow cube measuring seven or eight feet every way, with a hole to breathe through, a single cell in the hive, nothing more is wanted to lodge him and keep the rain off his back. A blanket properly rolled around his body will protect him as well and better against the cold than the most elegant and best cut dress coat[.] ...

---

[1] *cannot see ... noses*   Version of the old adage that one "cannot see past the end of one's nose," i.e., one cannot see beyond one's own immediate concerns.

[2] *palm ... crown*   Symbols of triumph and achievement; *Pyrtaneum*   Building in an ancient Greek city that housed the government; it was also where winners of the Olympic games were celebrated.

[3] *laudanum*   Drug containing opium; *Academic*   Related to the Academies, official organizations dedicated to intellectual and cultural pursuits.

[4] *Constitutionnel*   French journal that published from 1815 until 1914. It printed anti-church, pro-liberal writing and was suppressed many times by the authorities.

With this he will be able, literally, to subsist. It is truly said that it is possible to live on a shilling a day. But to prevent oneself from dying is not living; and I do not see in what respect a town organised after the utilitarian fashion would be more agreeable to dwell in than the cemetery of Père-la-Chaise.[1]

Nothing that is beautiful is indispensable to life. You might suppress flowers, and the world would not suffer materially; yet who would wish that there were no more flowers? I would rather give up potatoes than roses, and I think that there is none but an utilitarian in the world capable of pulling up a bed of tulips in order to plant cabbages therein.

What is the use of women's beauty? Provided that a woman be medically well formed, and in condition to bear children, she will always be good enough for economists.

What is the good of music? of painting? Who would be foolish enough to prefer Mozart to Monsieur Carrel,[2] and Michael Angelo to the inventor of white mustard?

There is nothing truly beautiful but that which can never be of any use whatsoever; everything useful is ugly, for it is the expression of some need, and man's needs are ignoble and disgusting like his own poor and infirm nature. The most useful place in a house is the water-closet.[3]

For my own part, may it please these gentlemen, I am one of those to whom superfluity is a necessity—and I like things and persons in an inverse ratio to the services that they render me. I prefer a Chinese vase, strewn with dragons and mandarins, and of no use to me whatever, to a certain utensil which is of service to me. ... I would most joyfully renounce my rights as a Frenchman and a citizen to see an authentic picture by Raphael, or a beautiful woman naked—Princess Borghese, for instance, when she posed for Canova, or Julia Grisi[4] entering her bath. ... Although I am no dilettante, I would rather have the noise of fiddles and tambourines than that of the bell of the President of the Chamber.[5] I would sell my breeches for a ring, and my bread for preserves. It appears to me that the most fitting occupation for a civilized man is to do nothing, or to smoke analytically his pipe or cigar. I also highly esteem those who play skittles[6] and those who make good verses. You see that the utilitarian principles are far from being mine, and that I shall never be a contributor to a virtuous journal, unless, of course, I become converted, which would be rather comical. ...

[E]njoyment appears to me to be the end of life and the only useful thing in the world. God has willed it so, He who has made women, perfumes, light, beautiful flowers, good wines, frisky horses, greyhound-bitches, and Angora cats; He who did not say to His angels, "Have virtue," but "Have love," and who has given us a mouth more sensitive than the rest of our skin to kiss women, eyes raised on high to see the light, a subtle power of smell to breathe the soul of flowers, sinewy thighs to press the sides of stallions, and to fly as quick as thought without railway or steam-boiler, delicate hands to stroke the long head of a greyhound, the velvety back of a cat, and the smooth shoulders of a creature of easy virtue, and who finally has granted to us alone the triple and glorious privilege of drinking when without thirst, of striking a light, and of making love at all seasons, a privilege which distinguishes us from brutes far more than the custom of reading papers and fabricating charters.

---

[1] *Père-la-Chaise* Large cemetery in Paris.

[2] *Monsieur Carrel* Armand Carrel (1800–36) was a French journalist whose political writing after the July Revolution in the *Le National*—a liberal pro-democracy journal—was hugely influential in Parisian politics.

[3] *water-closet* I.e., the bathroom.

[4] *Princess Borghese ... Canova* Italian sculptor Antonio Canova carved a life-size, semi-nude sculpture of Pauline Bonaparte, wife of Camillo Borghese, in Rome between 1805 and 1808; *Julia Grisi* Giulia Grisi (1811–69) was an Italian opera singer.

[5] *Chamber* Chamber of Deputies, the lower house of the French Parliament.

[6] *skittles* Lawn bowling game.

Good heavens! what a foolish thing is this pretended perfectibility of the human race which is continually being dinned into our ears! One would think, in truth, that man is a machine susceptible of improvements, and that some wheel-work in better gear or a counterpoise more suitably placed would make him work in a more convenient and easy fashion. When they succeed in giving man a double stomach so that he may ruminate like an ox, or eyes at the other side of his head that, like Janus,[1] he may see those who put out their tongues at him behind, and contemplate his *indignity* in a less inconvenient position than that of the Athenian Venus Callipyge,[2] when they plant wings upon his shoulder-blades that he may not be obliged to pay threepence for an omnibus, and create a new organ for him, well and good: the word *perfectibility* will then begin to have some meaning. …

Charles Baudelaire, "Correspondences"[3] (1857)

Arthur Symons wrote of French poet Charles Baudelaire's celebrated and controversial *Flowers of Evil* (1857) that "that book of his, in regard to my earliest verses, was at once a fascination and an influence, and … from that time onward his fascination has been like a spell to me." The following poem, from *Flowers of Evil*, articulates principles that were taken up by English Aesthetes.

In Nature's temple living pillars rise,
   And words are murmured none have understood,
And man must wander through a tangled wood
Of symbols watching him with friendly eyes.

5   As long-drawn echoes heard far-off and dim
Mingle to one deep sound and fade away;
Vast as the night and brilliant as the day,
Colour and sound and perfume speak to him.

Some perfumes are as fragrant as a child,
10   Sweet as the sound of hautboys,° meadow-green;   *oboes*
Others, corrupted, rich, exultant, wild,

Have all the expansion of things infinite:
As amber, incense, musk, and benzoin,[4]
Which sing the sense's and the soul's delight.

---

[1] *Janus*   Roman god of transitions and duality, usually depicted as a two-faced figure, with each face looking in opposite directions.

[2] *Venus Callipyge*   Ancient Roman statue of a woman whose head is turned to gaze at her own shapely buttocks.

[3] *Correspondences*   Translated by Frank Pearce Sturm, 1906.

[4] *benzoin*   Aromatic resin.

THE SIX-MARK TEA-POT.

Æsthetic Bridegroom. "It is quite consummate, is it not!"
Intense Bride. "It is, indeed! Oh, Algernon, let us live up to it!"

George Du Maurier, "The Six-Mark Tea-Pot," *Punch*, 1880. George Du Maurier's cartoons mocking the Aesthetic movement, published in the satirical magazine *Punch*, helped to popularize the stereotype of the Aesthete in the 1870s and 80s. This cartoon, lampooning the fashion for Japanese and Chinese porcelain, references a comment, supposedly made by Oscar Wilde, that he was finding it "harder and harder every day to live up to my blue and white china." Here, the "Æsthetic Bridegroom" declares that a teapot "is quite consummate, is it not?" His "Intense Bride" replies, "It is, indeed! Oh Algernon, let us live up to it!"

from Walter Hamilton, Introduction to *The Aesthetic Movement in England* (1882)

The first British critic to write a book explicitly addressing the English Aesthetic movement, Walter Hamilton includes in his discussion of the "Aesthetic school" Pre-Raphaelites such as Dante Gabriel and William Michael Rossetti, as well as writers now more definitively considered participants in the Aesthetic movement, such as Algernon Swinburne, William Morris, and Oscar Wilde. (All the key writers discussed in the book were men.) Hamilton's book also devotes considerable space to a defense of the movement against critical and satirical attacks, including the numerous cartoons mocking Aestheticism that appeared in *Punch* magazine.

... **W**hat then, is this school—what are its aims—and what has it achieved?

The term *Æsthetic* is derived from the Greek, *aisthesis*, signifying *perception*, or the science of the beautiful, especially in art, and the designation has long been applied by German writers to a branch of philosophical enquiry into the theory of the beautiful, or more accurately, into the philosophy of poetry and the fine arts. The term appears to have been invented, or adopted, by Baumgarten, a German philosopher, whose work entitled *Æsthetica* was published in 1750.

A great literary controversy has been going on in Germany for a century and a half, the chief topic in dispute being the question as to whether an object is actually beautiful in itself, or merely appears so to certain persons having faculties capable of appreciating it.

From this dispute came the origin of the school, and the *Æsthetes* are they who pride themselves upon having found out what is the really beautiful in nature and art, their faculties and tastes being educated up to the point necessary for the full appreciation of such qualities; whilst those who do not see the true and the beautiful—the outsiders in fact—are termed Philistines.[1]

Now up to a certain point, the theory that beauty is apparent only to some, is perfectly sound, for most persons will agree with Kant,[2] that there can be no strict mathematical definition, or science of beauty in nature, art, poetry or music, inasmuch as beauty is not altogether a property of objects or sounds, but is relative to the tastes and faculties brought to bear upon them.

Illustrations of the truth of this axiom will occur to every one; it is founded upon the old old truism, *tastes differ*. The Æsthetes recognise this truth to the fullest extent, but having first laid down certain general principles, they have endeavoured to elevate taste into a scientific system, the correlation of the arts being a main feature of the scheme; they even go so far as to decide what shall be considered beautiful, and those who do not accept their ruling are termed Philistines, and there is no hope for them.

Hence, the essence of the movement is the union of persons of cultivated tastes to define, and to decide upon, what is to be admired, and their followers must aspire to that standard in their works and lives. Vulgarity, however wealthy it may be, can never be admitted into this exclusive brotherhood, for riches without taste are of no avail, whilst taste without money, or with very little, can always effect much. So also those who prate most of Æsthetics are often those who have least of it to show in their houses, furniture, dress, or literary culture. …

from Arthur Symons, "The Decadent Movement in Literature," *Harper's New Monthly Magazine* (November 1893)

The English poet, critic, journalist, and translator Arthur Symons did a great deal to popularize in England the French developments in poetry and theory that influenced British Aesthetes. His essay on "The Decadent Movement in Literature," excerpted below, is among his most important critical pieces; it was later reworked to form the basis of his book *The Symbolist Movement in Literature* (1899).

The latest movement in European literature has been called by many names, none of them quite exact or comprehensive—Decadence, Symbolism, Impressionism, for instance. It is easy to dispute over words, and we shall find that Verlaine objects to being called a Decadent, Maeterlinck to being called a Symbolist, Huysmans[3] to being called an Impressionist. These terms, as it happens, have been adopted as the badge of little separate cliques, noisy, brainsick young people who haunt the brasseries of the Boulevard Saint-Michel,[4] and exhaust their ingenuities in theorizing over the works they cannot write. But, taken frankly as epithets which express their own meaning, both

---

[1] *Philistines* From the historical Philistines, enemies of the Israelites; the modern sense of the word denotes someone hostile or indifferent to culture and the arts.

[2] *Kant* German philosopher Immanuel Kant, whose ideas on aesthetics are most comprehensively treated in his book *Critique of Judgment* (1790).

[3] *Verlaine* Paul Verlaine (1844–96), French Symbolist poet; *Maeterlinck* Maurice Maeterlinck (1862–1949), Belgian Symbolist dramatist and poet; *Huysmans* Joris Karl Huysmans (1848–1907), a French novelist who worked in both the Naturalist and Decadent modes.

[4] *Boulevard Saint-Michel* Street in Paris's Latin Quarter.

Impressionism and Symbolism convey some notion of that new kind of literature which is perhaps more broadly characterized by the word Decadence. The most representative literature of the day—the writing which appeals to, which has done so much to form, the younger generation—is certainly not classic, nor has it any relation with that old antithesis of the Classic, the Romantic. After a fashion it is no doubt a decadence; it has all the qualities that mark the end of great periods, the qualities that we find in the Greek, the Latin, decadence: an intense self-consciousness, a restless curiosity in research, an over-subtilizing refinement upon refinement, a spiritual and moral perversity. If what we call the classic is indeed the supreme art—those qualities of perfect simplicity, perfect sanity, perfect proportion, the supreme qualities—then this representative literature of today, interesting, beautiful, novel as it is, is really a new and beautiful and interesting disease.

Healthy we cannot call it, and healthy it does not wish to be considered. The Goncourts, in their prefaces, in their *Journal*, are always insisting on their own malady, *la névrose*.[1] It is in their work, too, that Huysmans notes with delight "le style tacheté et faisandé"—high-flavoured and spotted with corruption—which he himself possesses in the highest degree. "Having desire without light, curiosity without wisdom, seeking God by strange ways, by ways traced by the hands of men; offering rash incense upon the high places to an unknown God, who is the God of Darkness"—that is how Ernest Hello,[2] in one of his apocalyptic moments, characterizes the nineteenth century. And this unreason of the soul—of which Hello himself is so curious a victim—this unstable equilibrium, which has overbalanced so many brilliant intelligences into one form or another of spiritual confusion, is but another form of the *maladie fin de siècle*.[3] For its very disease of form, this literature is certainly typical of a civilization grown over-luxurious, over-inquiring, too languid for the relief of action, too uncertain for any emphasis in opinion or in conduct. It reflects all the moods, all the manners, of a sophisticated society; its very artificiality is a way of being true to nature; simplicity, sanity, proportion—the classic qualities—how much do we possess them in our life, our surroundings, that we should look to find them in our literature—so evidently the literature of a decadence?

Taking the word Decadence, then, as most precisely expressing the general sense of the newest movement in literature, we find that the terms Impressionism and Symbolism define correctly enough the two main branches of that movement. Now Impressionist and Symbolist have more in common than either supposes; both are really working on the same hypothesis, applied in different directions. What both seek is not general truth merely, but *la vérité vraie*, the very essence of truth—the truth of appearances to the senses, of the visible world to the eyes that see it; and the truth of spiritual things to the spiritual vision. The Impressionist, in literature as in painting, would flash upon you in a new, sudden way so exact an image of what you have just seen, just as you have seen it, that you may say, as a young American sculptor, a pupil of Rodin, said to me on seeing for the first time a picture of Whistler's,[4] "Whistler seems to think this picture upon canvas—and there it is!" Or you may find,

---

[1]   *The Goncourts ... Journal*   Edmond Louis Antonine Huot de Goncourt (1822–96) and Jules Alfred Huot de Goncourt (1830–70) were brothers and writers; from 1850 until Jules's death in 1870, they collaborated on what is known as *The Goncourt Journal*, documenting life in the artistic and literary worlds of Paris. Edmond continued the *Journal* on his own until 1896. Pieces of the *Journal* were published in the nineteenth century, but the full 22 volumes were not published until the 1950s; *la névrose*   French: neurosis.

[2]   *Ernest Hello*   French essayist, best known for his *Renan, l'Allemagne et l'atheisme* (1861).

[3]   *maladie fin de siècle*   French: sickness of the end of the century. This phrase is a play on the phrase "mal de siècle," which was used by young people at the beginning of the nineteenth century to describe the listless melancholy that characterized the young at the time, and that came to be associated with the Romantic movement.

[4]   *Rodin*   Auguste Rodin (1840–1917), French sculptor; *Whistler*   James Abbott McNeill Whistler (1834–1903), an American-born painter and a major figure in the Aesthetic movement.

with Sainte-Beuve,[1] writing of Goncourt, the "soul of the landscape"—the soul of whatever corner of the visible world has to be realized. The Symbolist, in this new, sudden way, would flash upon you the "soul" of that which can be apprehended only by the soul—the finer sense of things unseen, the deeper meaning of things evident. And naturally, necessarily, this endeavor after a perfect truth to one's impression, to one's intuition—perhaps an impossible endeavor—has brought with it, in its revolt from ready-made impressions and conclusions, a revolt from the ready-made of language, from the bondage of traditional form, of a form become rigid. ...

---

[1] *Sainte-Beuve* Charles Augustin Sainte-Beuve (1804–69), French critic.

THE NEW WOMAN
CONTEXTS

The so-called "woman question" regarding women's status and role in society was a topic of consistent debate throughout the nineteenth century (as illustrated in this anthology's earlier Contexts section on "Women in Society")—a debate that inevitably spilled over into the related issues of sexuality, family structure, and the institution of marriage. As the century approached its close, the focus and terms of this debate shifted. In the 1870s and 80s, women seeking to alter their political and social status won a number of important victories: married women became legally allowed to retain full control of their own property, and reforms such as the establishment of women's colleges at Oxford and Cambridge improved women's educational and employment opportunities. By the 1890s, a new generation of women was coming of age that had been raised in the wake of these reforms, had benefited from them, and sought to build on them. At the same time, the literary and cultural avant-garde of the 1880s and 90s began to question and reject much conventional Victorian ideology. This countercultural critique—exemplified in literature and the arts by the Decadent and Aesthetic movements, and indelibly associated with the term *fin de siècle*—included a new embrace of sexual freedom and a reassessment of traditional gender roles.

This change in values was, of course, vehemently resisted—even by writers such as Grant Allen who were broadly sympathetic to some of the goals of social reformers. In some respects a radical thinker, Allen believed that the institution of marriage required extensive revision. In his "Plain Words on the Woman Question," however, he nonetheless attacks the abandonment of traditional gender roles as unnatural and harmful to society.

Despite such hostile responses, the new outlook persisted, and in the 1890s it was championed by an influential and controversial cohort of women writers. Prominent among these were Sarah Grand (the pen name of Frances Elizabeth Bellenden Clarke), Mona Caird, and George Egerton (the pen name of Mary Chavelita Dunne Bright), whose fiction and nonfiction levied a series of provocative criticisms of restrictive gender norms, the sexual double standard, and the institution of marriage. What would become the standard term for the kind of outspoken, emancipated woman exemplified by these writers was coined by Grand herself: "the new woman." This phrase first appeared in Grand's article "The New Aspect of the Woman Question" to name those of Grand's generation who had embraced the goals of political, educational, and economic equality with men. The importance of these goals is defended in Mona Caird's satirical response to the *Daily Telegraph*'s question "Does Marriage Hinder a Woman's Self-Development?" Caird's hypothetical reversal of men's and women's roles brings to light how arbitrary, and confining, definitions of "masculine" and "feminine" characteristics could be.

A distinct but complementary approach to the analysis of gender roles appears in George Egerton's short story "A Cross Line," which was published in her notorious—and phenomenally successful—1893 collection *Keynotes*. Like much of the rest of Egerton's fiction, this story depicts how marriage and domesticity stifle women's needs and desires—especially what Egerton characterizes as an anarchic urge for freedom, including sexual freedom, that she suggests is essentially "female." Another writer of the same generation, Julia M.A. Hawksley, echoes, in a different form, Egerton's implicit demand for more acknowledgment of women's sexuality, and for greater sexual frankness in general, in her article "A Young Woman's Right: Knowledge." Hawksley condemns the condition of ignorance about sexual matters in which young upper-class women (in particular) are kept and calls for more forthrightness about these matters—albeit mainly between mothers and their daughters.

Works such as these by the "new woman" writers immediately triggered intense debate. One of the most significant responses to Grand and her fellows was "The New Woman," a riposte to Grand's "New Aspect of the Woman Question" by "Ouida" (the pen name of the novelist Maria Louise Ramé). Ouida's fierce attack on Grand's article helped make the "New Woman" a stock cultural figure that could be deplored or ridiculed, as Ouida did, as well as celebrated. By the time Ouida's essay appeared, another front in the "New Woman" debate had already erupted in response to "The Revolt of the Daughters," a January 1894 article by Blanche Alethea Crackanthorpe that surveyed—not unsympathetically—the demands for greater freedom being made by many young women. This article garnered its own flurry of responses from some of the "daughters" in question in which they elaborated and defended the grounds for their "revolt"; Alys W. Pearsall Smith's essay "A Reply from the Daughters, II" is one of these.

These debates helped put the New Woman, and the broader questions and concerns that this figure distilled, at the forefront of the literary and cultural scene in the 1890s. Independent-minded women who challenged social conventions and insisted on pursuing their own desires and aspirations—for better or worse—took center stage in a range of literary works, including George Gissing's *The Odd Women* (1893), George Bernard Shaw's *Mrs. Warren's Profession* (1893), Sarah Grand's *The Heavenly Twins* (1894), Grant Allen's *The Woman Who Did* (1895), Thomas Hardy's *Jude the Obscure* (1895), and Bram Stoker's *Dracula* (1897). This last novel embodies a hostile view of the New Woman and what she stood for in the character of Lucy Westenra, whose transformation into a vampire is closely linked to her liberated sexuality and resistance to traditional marriage: at one point she asks, "Why can't they let a girl marry three men, or as many as want her, and save all this trouble?" Similarly unfavorable representations of the New Woman can also be found in the parodies of this figure that proliferated during the decade. *Punch* magazine particularly specialized in lampooning the New Woman, which it did in numerous cartoons as well as in comic poems such as "Donna Quixote," a satire of the New Woman's purportedly delusional crusade. *Cornhill Magazine's* "Character Note" on "The New Woman" is another work in the same vein. *Cornhill's* portrayal of the New Woman, like *Punch's* and Stoker's, reflects the hostility—and anxiety—that the New Woman prompted in many men. As H.E. Harvey's "The Voice of Woman" illustrates, however, other men welcomed the "new women" writers and sought to amplify their message.

That message was sounded in Britain's colonies, and resonated there, just as much as in Britain itself. At the same time as representatives of the New Woman were challenging restrictions and breaking down barriers in the "mother country," others were doing so in the Empire. Two of these were Cornelia Sorabji, from India, and Olive Schreiner, from South Africa. Sorabji's 1901 short story "Love and Death" reflects on the tension that educated professional women from the colonies—like herself—could experience between the values instilled by their British educations and those promoted by traditional religious and cultural institutions in their native lands. Olive Schreiner's *Woman and Labour* (1911) represents the culmination of its author's lifetime of feminist advocacy. This book, based on an older manuscript that was destroyed in the 1899–1902 Boer War, would go on to be hailed as the "bible" of the twentieth-century women's movement.

By the time *Woman and Labour* appeared, the New Woman had largely ceased to be a cultural touchstone. The stock caricature of the New Woman, with her latchkey and bicycle—a recently introduced mode of transportation that, together with the latchkey, symbolized the freedom and mobility that the new generation of women were claiming—quickly became a cliché. By 1896, as one of the illustrations reproduced below shows, the figure had been reduced to a costume idea for fancy-dress balls. Late in 1895, *Punch* was already proclaiming "THE END OF THE NEW WOMAN—The Crash has come at last." If the New Woman's career as a cultural archetype ended with the nineteenth century, however, the causes and demands underlying the archetype lived on, helping to give rise in the twentieth century to further seismic shifts in the ways gender and sexuality were conceived, institutionalized, and practiced.

The following authors and works appearing elsewhere in this anthology are also relevant to the figure of the New Woman: Thomas Hardy, "The Son's Veto"; Mathilde Blind; "Michael Field" (Katharine Bradley and Edith Cooper); Oscar Wilde, *The Importance of Being Earnest*; Olive Schreiner; Vernon Lee; Amy Levy; and Charlotte Mew.

⌘ ⌘ ⌘

from Grant Allen, "Plain Words on the Woman Question," *Fortnightly Review* (October 1889)

... Almost every woman must bear four or five children.[1] In doing so she must on the average use up the ten or twelve best years of her life: the ten or twelve years that immediately succeed her attainment of complete womanhood. ... Again, during these ten or twelve years of child-bearing at the very least, the women can't conveniently earn their own livelihood; they must be provided for by the labour of the men. ... It is true that in the very lowest state of savagery special provision is seldom made by the men for the women even during the periods of pregnancy, childbirth, and infancy of the offspring. The women must live (as among the Hottentots[2]) over the worst of these periods on their own stored-up stock of fat, like hibernating bears or desert camels. It is true also that among savage races generally the women have to work as hard as the men, though the men bear in most cases the larger share in providing actual food for the entire family. But in civilised communities—and the more so in proportion to their degree of civilisation—the men do most of the hardest work, and in particular take upon themselves the

duty of providing for the wives and children. The higher the type,[3] the longer are the wives and children provided for. Analogy would lead one to suppose (with Comte[4]) that in the highest communities the men would do all the work, and the women would be left entirely free to undertake the management and education of the children. ...

Seeing, then, that these necessities are laid by the very nature of our organization upon women, it would appear as though two duties were clearly imposed upon the women themselves, and upon all those men who sympathize in their welfare: First, to see that their training and education should fit them above everything else for this their main function in life; and, second, that in consideration of the special burden they have to bear in connection with reproduction, all the rest of life should be made as light and easy and free for them as possible. We ought frankly to recognise that most women must be wives and mothers: that most women should therefore be trained, physically, morally, socially, and mentally, in the way best fitting them to be wives and mothers; and that all such women have a right to the fullest and most generous support in carrying out their functions as wives and mothers.

---

[1] *Almost every ... five children* Earlier in the essay, Allen presents statistics to support his argument that women must maintain this average in order for the population to remain stable.

[2] *Hottentots* European term (now recognized as offensive) for the Khoikhoi people of southwestern Africa.

[3] *The higher the type* The more refined the society.

[4] *Comte* French philosopher Auguste Comte (1798–1857) wrote that in an ideal society women would be wholly isolated from political and material concerns in order to serve as parents and moral guardians.

And here it is that we seem to come in conflict for a moment with most of the modern Woman-Question agitators. …

For what is the ideal that most of these modern woman agitators set before them? Is it not clearly the ideal of an unsexed[1] woman? Are they not always talking to us as though it were not the fact that most women must be wives and mothers?… A woman ought to be ashamed to say she has no desire to become a wife and mother. Many such women there are no doubt—it is to be feared, with our existing training, far too many: but instead of boasting of their sexlessness as a matter of pride, they ought to keep it dark, and to be ashamed of it—as ashamed as a man in a like predicament would be of his impotence. They ought to feel they have fallen short of the healthy instincts of their kind, instead of posing as in some sense the cream of the universe, on the strength of what is really a functional aberration.

Unfortunately, however, just at the present moment, a considerable number of the ablest women have been misled into taking this unfeminine side, and becoming real "traitors to their sex" in so far as they endeavour to assimilate women to men[2] in everything, and to put upon their shoulders, as a glory and privilege, the burden of their own support. …

from Sarah Grand, "The New Aspect of the Woman Question," *North American Review* (March 1894)

… What [the new woman] perceived at the outset was the sudden and violent upheaval of the suffering sex in all parts of the world. Women were awakening from their long apathy, and, as they woke, like healthy hungry children unable to articulate, they began to whimper for they knew not what. They might have been easily satisfied at that time had not society, like an ill-conditioned and ignorant nurse,[3] instead of finding out what they lacked, shaken them and beaten them and stormed at them until what was once a little wail became convulsive shrieks and roused up the whole human household. Then man, disturbed by the uproar, came upstairs all anger and irritation, and, without waiting to learn what was the matter, added his own old theories to the din, but, finding they did not act rapidly, formed new ones, and made an intolerable nuisance of himself with his opinions and advice. He was in the state of one who cannot comprehend because he has no faculty to perceive the thing in question, and that is why he was so positive. The dimmest perception that you may be mistaken will save you from making an ass of yourself.

We must look upon man's mistakes, however, with some leniency, because we are not blameless in the matter ourselves. We have allowed him to arrange the whole social system and manage or mismanage it all these ages without ever seriously examining his work with a view to considering whether his abilities or motives were sufficiently good to qualify him for the task. We have listened without a smile to his preachments, about our place in life and all we are good for, on the text that "there is no understanding a woman." We have endured most poignant misery for his sins, and screened him when we should have exposed him and had him punished. We have allowed him to exact[4] all things of us, and have been content to accept the little he grudgingly gave us in return. We have meekly bowed our heads when he called us bad names instead of demanding proofs of the superiority which alone would give him a right to do so. We have listened much edified to man's sermons on the subject of virtue, and have acquiesced uncomplainingly in the convenient arrangement by which this quality has come to be altogether practised for him by us vicariously. We have seen him set up Christ as an example for all men to follow, which argues his belief in the possibility of doing so, and have

---

[1] *unsexed* Here, without the qualities traditionally associated with femininity.

[2] *assimilate women to men* Make women more like men.

[3] *nurse* Governess or nanny.

[4] *exact* Demand, extort.

not only allowed his weakness and hypocrisy in the matter to pass without comment, but, until lately, have not even seen the humor of his pretensions when contrasted with his practices, nor held him up to that wholesome ridicule which is a stimulating corrective. Man deprived us of all proper education, and then jeered at us because we had no knowledge. He narrowed our outlook on life so that our view of it should be all distorted, and then declared that our mistaken impression of it proved us to be senseless creatures. He cramped our minds so that there was no room for reason in them, and then made merry at our want of logic. Our divine intuition was not to be controlled by him, but he did his best to damage it by sneering at it as an inferior feminine method of arriving at conclusions; and finally, after having had his own way until he lost his head completely, he set himself up as a sort of god and required us to worship him, and to our eternal shame be it said, we did so. The truth has all along been in us, but we have cared more for man than for truth, and so the whole human race has suffered. We have failed of our effect by neglecting our duty here, and have deserved much of the obloquy[1] that was cast upon us. All that is over now, however, and while on the one hand man has shrunk to his true proportions in our estimation, we, on the other, have been expanding to our own; and now we come confidently forward to maintain, not that this or that was "intended," but that there are in ourselves, in both sexes, possibilities hitherto suppressed or abused, which, when properly developed, will supply to either what is lacking in the other.

The man of the future will be better, while the woman will be stronger and wiser. To bring this about is the whole aim and object of the present struggle, and with the discovery of the means lies the solution of the Woman Question. Man, having no conception of himself as imperfect from the woman's point of view, will find this difficult to understand, but we know his weakness, and will be patient with him, and help him with his lesson. It is the woman's place and pride and

pleasure to teach the child, and man morally is in his infancy. There have been times when there was a doubt as to whether he was to be raised or woman was to be lowered, but we have turned that corner at last; and now woman holds out a strong hand to the child-man, and insists, but with infinite tenderness and pity, upon helping him up. ...

from Mona Caird, "Does Marriage Hinder a Woman's Self-Development?" *Lady's Realm* (March 1899)

Perhaps it might throw some light on the question whether marriage interferes with a woman's self-development and career, if we were to ask ourselves honestly how a man would fare in the position, say, of his own wife.

We will take a mild case, so as to avoid all risk of exaggeration.

Our hero's wife is very kind to him. Many of his friends have far sadder tales to tell. Mrs. Brown is fond of her home and family. She pats the children on the head when they come down to dessert, and plies them with chocolate creams, much to the detriment of their health; but it amuses Mrs. Brown. Mr. Brown superintends the bilous[2] attacks, which the lady attributes to other causes. As she never finds fault with the children, and generally remonstrates with their father, in a good-natured way, when *he* does so, they are devoted to the indulgent parent, and are inclined to regard the other as second-rate. ...

John's faded cheeks, the hollow lines under the eyes, and hair out of curl, speak of the struggle for existence as it penetrates to the fireside. If Sophia but knew what it meant to keep going the multitudinous details and departments of a household! ...

If incessant vigilance, tact, firmness, foresight, initiative, courage and judgment—in short, all the qualities required for governing a kingdom, and more—

---

[1] *obloquy* Disgrace.

[2] *bilous* Angry, peevish.

have made things go smoothly, the wife takes it as a matter of course; if they go wrong, she naturally lays the blame on the husband. In the same way, if the children are a credit to their parents, that is only as it should be. But if they are naughty, and fretful, and stupid, and untidy, is it not clear that there must be some serious flaw in the system which could produce such results in the offspring of Mrs. Brown? What word in the English language is too severe to describe the man who neglects to watch with sufficient vigilance over his children's health and moral training, who fails to see that his little boys' sailor-suits and knickerbockers[1] are in good repair, that their bootlace ends do not fly out from their ankles at every step, that their hair is not like a hearth-brush, that they do not come down to dinner every day with dirty hands?

To every true man, the cares of fatherhood and home are sacred and all-sufficing. He realizes, as he looks around at his little ones, that they are his crown and recompense.

John often finds that *his* crown-and-recompense gives him a racking headache by war-whoops and stampedes of infinite variety, and there are moments when he wonders in dismay if he is really a true man! He has had the privilege of rearing and training five small crowns and recompenses, and he feels that he could face the future if further privilege, of this sort, were denied him. Not but that he is devoted to his family. Nobody who understands the sacrifices he has made for them could doubt that. Only, he feels that those parts of his nature which are said to distinguish the human from the animal kingdom are getting rather effaced.

He remembers the days before his marriage, when he was so bold, in his ignorant youth, as to cherish a passion for scientific research. He even went so far as to make a chemical laboratory of the family box-room, till attention was drawn to the circumstance by a series of terrific explosions, which shaved off his eyebrows,

blackened his scientific countenance,[2] and caused him to be turned out, neck and crop, with his crucibles, and a sermon on the duty that lay nearest him.... His own bent, however, has always been so painfully strong that he even yet tries to snatch spare moments for his researches; but the strain in so many directions has broken down his health. People always told him that a man's constitution was not fitted for severe brain-work. He supposes it is true. ...

John still hoped, after twenty years of experience, that presently, by some different arrangement, some better management on his part, he would achieve leisure and mental repose to do the work that his heart was in; but that time never came.

No doubt John was not infallible, and made mistakes in dealing with his various problems: do the best of us achieve consummate wisdom? No doubt, if he had followed the advice that we could all have supplied him with, in such large quantities, he might have done rather more than he did. But the question is: Did his marriage interfere with his self-development and career, and would many other Johns, in his circumstances, have succeeded much better?

from George Egerton, "A Cross Line" (1893)

... Summer is waning and the harvest is ripe for ingathering, and the voice of the reaping machine is loud in the land. She is stretched on her back on the short heather-mixed moss at the side of a bog stream. Rod and creel[3] are flung aside, and the wanton breeze, with the breath of coolness it has gathered in its passage over the murky dykes of black bog water, is playing with the tail fly, tossing it to and fro with a half threat to fasten it to a prickly spine of golden gorse. Bunches of bog-wool nod their fluffy heads, and through the myriad indefinite sounds comes the regular scrape of a

---

[1] *knickerbockers* Knee-length trousers.

[2] *box-room* Storage room; *countenance* Appearance, facial expression.

[3] *creel* Basket for holding fish.

strickle[1] on the scythe of a reaper in a neighbouring meadow. Overhead a flotilla of clouds is steering from the south in a north-easterly direction. Her eyes follow them. Old time galleons, she thinks, and with their wealth of snowy sail spread, riding breast to breast up a wide blue fjord after victory. The sails of the last are rose flushed, with a silver edge. Somehow she thinks of Cleopatra sailing down to meet Antony,[2] and a great longing fills her soul to sail off somewhere too—away from the daily need of dinner getting and the recurring Monday with its washing; life with its tame duties and virtuous monotony. She fancies herself in Arabia on the back of a swift steed. Flashing eyes set in dark faces surround her, and she can see the clouds of sand swirl, and feel the swing under her of his rushing stride. Her thoughts shape themselves into a wild song, a song to her steed of flowing mane and satin skin; an uncouth rhythmical jingle with a feverish beat; a song to the untamed spirit that dwells in her. Then she fancies she is on the stage of an ancient theatre out in the open air, with hundreds of faces upturned towards her. She is gauze-clad in a cobweb garment of wondrous tissue.[3] Her arms are clasped by jewelled snakes, and one with quivering diamond fangs coils round her hips. Her hair floats loosely, and her feet are sandal-clad, and the delicate breath of vines and the salt freshness of an incoming sea seems to fill her nostrils. She bounds forward and dances, bends her lissom waist, and curves her slender arms, and gives to the soul of each man what he craves, be it good or evil. And she can feel now, lying here in the shade of Irish hills with her head resting on her scarlet shawl and her eyes closed, the grand intoxicating power of swaying all these human souls to wonder and applause. She can see herself with parted lips and panting, rounded breasts, and a dancing devil in each glowing eye, sway voluptuously to the wild music that rises, now slow, now fast, now deliriously wild, seductive, intoxicating, with a human note of passion in its strain. She can feel the answering shiver of feeling that quivers up to her from the dense audience, spellbound by the motion of her glancing[4] feet, and she flies swifter and swifter, and lighter and lighter, till the very serpents seem alive with jewelled scintillations. One quivering, gleaming, daring bound, and she stands with outstretched arms and passion-filled eyes, poised on one slender foot, asking a supreme note to finish her dream of motion. And the men rise to a man and answer her, and cheer, cheer till the echoes shout from the surrounding hills and tumble wildly down the crags. The clouds have sailed away, leaving long feathery streaks in their wake. Her eyes have an inseeing[5] look, and she is tremulous with excitement. She can hear yet that last grand shout, and the strain of that old-time music that she has never heard in this life of hers, save as an inner accompaniment to the memory of hidden things, born with her, not of this time.

And her thoughts go to other women she has known, women good and bad, school friends, casual acquaintances, women workers—joyless machines for grinding daily corn,[6] unwilling maids grown old in the endeavour to get settled, patient wives who bear little ones to indifferent husbands until they wear out—a long array. She busies herself with questioning. Have they, too, this thirst for excitement, for change, this restless craving for sun and love and motion? Stray words, half confidences, glimpses through soul-chinks of suppressed fires, actual outbreaks, domestic catastrophes, how the ghosts dance in the cells of her memory! And she laughs, laughs softly to herself because the denseness of man, his chivalrous conservative devotion to the female idea he has created blinds him, perhaps happily, to the problems of her complex nature. Ay, she mutters musingly, the wisest of them can only say we are

---

[1] *strickle*   Tool for sharpening a scythe.

[2] *Cleopatra ... Antony*   The voyage, in 41 BCE, of the Egyptian queen Cleopatra to meet Mark Antony, the Roman politician and general with whom she had a love affair, is described in a famous passage in Shakespeare's play *Antony and Cleopatra* (1607). The play describes Cleopatra's ship as a gilded barge with purple sails.

[3] *tissue*   Rich, gauzy cloth.

---

[4] *glancing*   Rapidly moving.

[5] *inseeing*   Insightful.

[6] *corn*   Grain.

enigmas. Each one of them sets about solving the riddle of the *ewig weibliche*[1]—and well it is that the workings of our hearts are closed to them, that we are cunning enough or great enough to seem to be what they would have us, rather than be what we are. But few of them have had the insight to find out the key to our seeming contradictions. The why a refined, physically fragile woman will mate with a brute, a mere male animal with primitive passions—and love him—the why strength and beauty appeal more often than the more subtly fine qualities of mind or heart—the why women (and not the innocent ones) will condone sins that men find hard to forgive in their fellows. They have all overlooked the eternal wildness, the untamed primitive savage temperament that lurks in the mildest, best woman. Deep in through ages of convention this primeval trait burns, an untamed quantity that may be concealed but is never eradicated by culture—the keynote of woman's witchcraft and woman's strength. But it is there, sure enough, and each woman is conscious of it in her truth-telling hours of quiet self-scrutiny—and each woman in God's wide world will deny it, and each woman will help another to conceal it—for the woman who tells the truth and is not a liar about these things is untrue to her sex and abhorrent to man, for he has fashioned a model on imaginary lines, and he has said, "so I would have you," and every woman is an unconscious liar, for so man loves her. And when a Strindberg or a Nietzsche[2] arises and peers into the recesses of her nature and dissects her ruthlessly, the men shriek out louder than the women, because the truth is at all times unpalatable, and the gods they have set up are dear to them …

"Dreaming, or speering[3] into futurity? You have the look of a seer. I believe you are half a witch!"

And he drops his grey-clad figure on the turf. He has dropped his drawl long ago, in midsummer.

"Is not every woman that? Let us hope I'm, for my friends, a white one."

"A-ah! Have you many friends?"

"That is a query! If you mean many correspondents, many persons who send me Christmas cards, or remember my birthday, or figure in my address-book? No."

"Well, grant I don't mean that!"

"Well, perhaps, yes. Scattered over the world, if my death were belled out,[4] many women would give me a tear, and some a prayer. And many men would turn back a page in their memory and give me a kind thought, perhaps a regret, and go back to their work with a feeling of having lost something—that they never possessed. I am a creature of moments. Women have told me that I came into their lives just when they needed me. Men had no need to tell me, I felt it. People have needed me more than I them. I have given freely whatever they craved from me in the way of understanding or love. I have touched sore places they showed me and healed them, but they never got at me. I have been for myself, and helped myself, and borne the burden of my own mistakes. Some have chafed at my self-sufficiency and have called me fickle—not understanding that they gave me nothing, and that when I had served them, their moment was ended, and I was to pass on. I read people easily, I am written in black letter[5] to most—"

"To your husband!"

"He (quickly)—we will not speak of him; it is not loyal."

---

[1] *ewig weibliche* German: eternal feminine. The phrase, which refers to an unchanging essence supposedly shared by all women, comes from the end of the tragic play *Faust* (1832) by the German writer Johann Wolfgang von Goethe.

[2] *a Strindberg or a Nietzsche* The Swedish dramatist Johan August Strindberg (1849–1912) and the German philosopher Friedrich Nietzsche (1844–1900) were both major influences on the cultural and literary avant-garde in Europe at the end of the nineteenth century. Both wrote descriptions of women which have been construed as misogynistic, and Nietzsche in particular referred to women's supposed "inner wildness."

[3] *speering* Inquiring.

[4] *belled out* I.e., announced (deaths were traditionally announced by the ringing of church bells).

[5] *black letter* Form of script widely used throughout Western Europe from the twelfth to the seventeenth centuries. By the end of the nineteenth century, it had dropped out of use in most European countries, including Britain, and consequently was difficult for most people of the era to read.

"Do not I understand you a little?"

"You do not misunderstand me."

"That is something."

"It is much!"

"Is it? (searching her face). It is not one grain of sand in the desert that stretches between you and me, and you are as impenetrable as a sphinx at the end of it. This (passionately) is my moment, and what have you given me?"

"Perhaps less than other men I have known; but you want less. You are a little like me, you can stand alone. And yet (her voice is shaking), have I given you nothing?"

He laughs, and she winces—and they sit silent, and they both feel as if the earth between them is laid with infinitesimal electric threads vibrating with a common pain. Her eyes are filled with tears that burn but don't fall, and she can see his somehow through her closed lids, see their cool greyness troubled by sudden fire, and she rolls her handkerchief into a moist cambric[1] ball between her cold palms.

"You have given me something—something to carry away with me—an infernal want. You ought to be satisfied. I am infernally miserable."

"You (nearer) have the most tantalising mouth in the world when your lips tremble like that. I … What! can you cry? You?"

"Yes, even I can cry!"

"You dear woman! (pause) And I can't help you!"

"You can't help me. No man can. Don't think it is because you are you I cry, but because you probe a little nearer into the real me that I feel so."

"Was it necessary to say that? (reproachfully). Do you think I don't know it? I can't for the life of me think how you, with that free gipsy nature of yours, could bind yourself to a monotonous country life, with no excitement, no change. I wish I could offer you my yacht. Do you like the sea?"

"I love it, it answers one's moods."

"Well, let us play pretending, as the children say. Grant that I could, I would hang your cabin with your own colours; fill it with books, all those I have heard you say you care for; make it a nest as rare as the bird it would shelter. You would reign supreme; when your highness would deign to honour her servant I would come and humour your every whim. If you were glad, you could clap your hands and order music, and we would dance on the white deck, and we would skim through the sunshine of Southern seas on a spice-scented breeze. You make me poetical. And if you were angry you could vent your feelings on me, and I would give in and bow my head to your mood. And we would drop anchor and stroll through strange cities, go far inland and glean folklore out of the beaten track of everyday tourists. And at night when the harbour slept we would sail out through the moonlight over silver seas. You are smiling, you look so different when you smile; do you like my picture?"

"Some of it!"

"What not?"

"You!"

"Thank you."

"You asked me. Can't you understand where the spell lies? It is the freedom, the freshness, the vague danger, the unknown that has a witchery for me, ay, for every woman!"

"Are you incapable of affection, then?"

"Of course not, I share" (bitterly) "that crowning disability of my sex. But not willingly, I chafe under it. My God, if it were not for that, we women would master the world. I tell you men would be no match for us. At heart we care nothing for laws, nothing for systems. All your elaborately reasoned codes for controlling morals or man do not weigh a jot with us against an impulse, an instinct. We learn those things from you, you tamed, amenable animals; they are not natural to us. It is a wise disposition of providence that this untameableness of ours is corrected by our affections. We forge our own chains in a moment of softness, and then" (bitterly) "we may as well wear them with a good grace. Perhaps many of our seeming contradictions are only the outward evidences of inward chafing. Bah! the qualities that go to make a Napoleon—superstition, want of honour, disregard of opinion and the eternal

---

[1]   *cambric*   Fine white linen used for handkerchiefs.

I—are oftener to be found in a woman than a man. Lucky for the world perhaps that all these attributes weigh as nothing in the balance with the need to love if she be a good woman, to be loved if she is of a coarser fibre."

"I never met any one like you, you are a strange woman!"

"No, I am merely a truthful one. Women talk to me—why, I can't say—but always they come, strip their hearts and souls naked, and let me see the hidden folds of their natures. The greatest tragedies I have ever read are child's play to those I have seen acted in the inner life of outwardly commonplace women. A woman must beware of speaking the truth to a man; he loves her the less for it. It is the elusive spirit in her that he divines but cannot seize, that fascinates and keeps him."

There is a long silence, the sun is waning and the scythes are silent, and overhead the crows are circling, a croaking irregular army, homeward bound from a long day's pillage.

She has made no sign, yet so subtly is the air charged with her that he feels but a few moments remain to him. He goes over and kneels beside her and fixes his eyes on her odd dark face. They both tremble, yet neither speaks. His breath is coming quickly, and the bistre stains[1] about her eyes seem to have deepened, perhaps by contrast as she has paled.

"Look at me!"

She turns her head right round and gazes straight into his face. A few drops of sweat glisten on his forehead.

"You witch woman! What am I to do with myself? Is my moment ended?"

"I think so."

"Lord, what a mouth!"

"Don't, oh don't!"

"No, I won't. But do you mean it? Am I, who understand your every mood, your restless spirit, to vanish out of your life? You can't mean it. Listen; are you listening to me? I can't see your face; take down

your hands. Go back over every chance meeting you and I have had together since I met you first by the river, and judge them fairly. Today is Monday; Wednesday afternoon I shall pass your gate, and if—if my moment is ended, and you mean to send me away, to let me go with this weary aching …"

"A-ah!" she stretches out one brown hand appealingly, but he does not touch it.

"*Hang something white on the lilac bush!*"[2]

She gathers up creel and rod, and he takes her shawl, and, wrapping it round her, holds her a moment in it, and looks searchingly into her eyes, then stands back and raises his hat, and she glides away through the reedy grass. …

from Julia M.A. Hawksley, "A Young Woman's Right: Knowledge," *Westminster Review* (July 1894)

By this I do not mean scholarship. The battle of the higher education of women was long ago fought and won.[3] Every woman who is endowed with the necessary talents and tastes, and can command the needful time and money, may become, so far as study is concerned, almost what she will. Nor is the boon[4] the less because those who as yet avail themselves of their opportunities are an infinitesimal minority. But this is beside my subject.

The knowledge, a claim to which I urge on behalf of all maidenhood, is of a vastly different nature. It is a

---

[1] *bistre stains* I.e., areas of dark complexion (bistre is a brown pigment made from soot).

[2] *Hang … bush* Egerton's story ends with the following exchange, on the Wednesday afternoon, between the woman in this scene and her maid Lizzie:

   "Why, one nightgown will make a dozen little shirts …—and Lizzie!"

   "Yes, Ma'm!"

   "Just hang it out on the lilac bush; mind, the lilac bush!"

   "Yes, Ma'm."

   "Or Lizzie, wait—I'll do it myself!"

[3] *The battle … won* Women began to be permitted to take examinations and earn degrees from British universities in the late 1860s.

[4] *boon* Blessing.

knowledge which, no more than any other, comes by intuition or by inspiration. It is a knowledge the possession of which would mould differently many lives, change the destinies of sundry families and prevent the wreckage of much faith and hope. It is a knowledge the bestowal of which is at the option of each mother and is the right of every daughter. It is a knowledge which, from the nature of things, is most easily withheld from girls of the upper classes, since theirs are the lives most closely confined within the home radius and sheltered from outside influences. On them, therefore, falls the chief suffering. It is a knowledge the first glimmer of which caused Eve to make herself aprons of fig leaves,[1] but which does not dawn upon one and another of Eve's descendants until the apron is cast away, and the woman stands helpless and ashamed.

… Girls are today constantly married without any more idea of what matrimony implies than has been imparted by the prurient, whispered gossip of an impure-minded schoolfellow; and frequently—especially, as I have said, in the case of members of highborn families—without even that modicum of enlightenment. This condition of things, moreover, is regarded by many a satisfied matron as proving the perfection of watchful guardianship upon her own part and of sweet pliability upon that of her child.

And why?

Men, we are told, like to perform their own initiation. Men, it is constantly and truly said, prefer girls of innocent mind. In which latter statement, by the by, crops up the old, old confusion between innocence and ignorance. Men desire that their wives should realise nothing of the inner secrets and vast divergences of passing passion and of lasting love. This, too, in spite of, or, perhaps because of, the fact that they themselves almost invariably claim the privilege of ante-nuptial[2]

revelation, a revelation not only of theory, but also of practice. For what proportion of bridegrooms could declare that they present the same conditions of physical purity as they demand? And thus, as ever, are the women sacrificed for the men's gratification. Sacrificed in the most cruel, the most needless, the most irrevocable fashion of all. Because sacrificed in ignorance. …

A girl, four or five days before her marriage, went to her mother and implored to be told what that was which lay before her, to which her vows would commit her. She had heard much that to her seemed horrible to incredulity, repellent beyond words. She was half frantic with a vague dread, worse than any certainty. And she craved to know. But she was laughed at and refused. Why? A bride upon her husband's first approach believed him mad, and in her dread tried to reach a bell and summon help. Why? A man consulting a specialist upon a constitutional sexual ailment, mentioned his wife, who was also his confidante. The doctor deprecated any such confidence towards a wife, whose mind, he, considered, should be "like a sheet of white paper." Why?

Because men will to have it so, and mothers shrink from the task—truly a terrible task—involved. Perhaps they forget their own past suffering. Perhaps they are oblivious of the fact that every day women are becoming more sensitive, more highly strung, and therefore more and more capable of mental agony, more and more liable to the tortures of morbidity.[3] However that may be, certain it is that innumerable girls are still the victims, on the one hand, of ignorance, and, upon the other, of that natural inquisitiveness which causes them to seek from corrupt sources the intelligence which they crave. …

The matter remains with the mothers—mothers not merely in the carnal,[4] but also in the moral and spiritual sense—those elder women, in fact, in whose hands rest the education of the rising generation. The preservation of true innocence, that horribly maligned but most

---

[1] *It is … fig leaves* Genesis 3.7 relates that, after Adam and Eve ate the fruit of the tree of the knowledge of good and evil, "the eyes of them both were opened, and they knew that they were naked; and they sewed fig leaves together, and made themselves aprons."

[2] *ante-nuptial* Before marriage; in particular, before the consummation of marriage.

[3] *morbidity* Excessive, unhealthy anxiety or brooding.

[4] *carnal* Physical.

beautiful word; the dispelling of a blinding mist of misconception; the prevention of untold suffering; all hang upon their decision. Let them grant to their charges the right which those charges cannot claim. Otherwise will the young, rash creatures, in the first flush of unrecognised passion, determine, by a headlong rush into matrimony, the whole course of their lives; or, already in a measure demoralised[1] by a sense of secrecy and wrongdoing, seek enlightenment from unauthorised oracles. Let them give to their daughters a choice, a fair choice, lighted by understanding. Or let them themselves bear the reproach of soiled and strangled virtue, of discovery made too late. But the weight of sin and of pain they cannot assume. Such must for ever lie upon the persons and the souls of those whom they might have saved.

from Ouida, "The New Woman," *The North American Review* (May 1894)

It can scarcely be disputed, I think, that in the English language there are conspicuous at the present moment two words which designate two unmitigated bores: The Workingman and the Woman. The Workingman and the Woman, the New Woman, be it remembered, meet us at every page of literature written in the English tongue; and each is convinced that on its own especial W hangs the future of the world. Both he and she want to have their values artificially raised and rated, and a status given to them by favor in lieu of desert.[2] In an age in which persistent clamor is generally crowned by success they have both obtained considerable attention; is it offensive to say much more of it than either deserves? Your contributor avers that the Cow-Woman and the Scum-Woman,[3] man understands, but

that the New Woman is above him. The elegance of these appellatives[4] is not calculated to recommend them to readers of either sex; and as a specimen of style forces one to hint that the New Woman who, we are told, "has been sitting apart in silent contemplation all these years" might in all these years have studied better models of literary composition. We are farther on told "that the dimmest perception that you may be mistaken, will save you from making an ass of yourself." It appears that even this dimmest perception has never dawned upon the New Woman.

We are farther told that "thinking and thinking" in her solitary sphinx-like contemplation she solved the problem and prescribed the remedy (the remedy to a problem!); but what this remedy was we are not told, nor did the New Woman apparently disclose it to the rest of womankind, since she still hears them in "sudden and violent upheaval" like "children unable to articulate whimpering for they know not what." It is sad to reflect that they might have been "easily satisfied at that time" (at what time?), "but society stormed at them until what was a little wail became convulsive shrieks"; and we are not told why the New Woman who had "the remedy for the problem," did not immediately produce it. We are not told either in what country or at what epoch this startling upheaval of volcanic womanhood took place in which "man merely made himself a nuisance with his opinions and advice," but apparently did quell this wailing and gnashing of teeth since it would seem that he has managed still to remain more masterful than he ought to be. ...

Woman, whether new or old, has immense fields of culture untilled, immense areas of influence wholly neglected. She does almost nothing with the resources she possesses, because her whole energy is concentrated on desiring and demanding those she has not. She can write and print anything she chooses; and she scarcely ever takes the pains to acquire correct grammar or elegance of style before wasting ink and paper. She can

---

[1] *demoralised* Corrupted.

[2] *in lieu of desert* I.e., instead of deserving that higher status.

[3] *the Cow-Woman and the Scum-Woman* These terms, as well as the quoted passages in this paragraph and the following one, are references to Sarah Grand's essay "The New Aspect of the Woman Question," to which Ouida's essay is a direct response. "Cow-Woman" and "Scum-Woman" are Grand's terms for the functions of breeding and sexual

servicing, respectively, to which, Grand argues, men have reduced women.

[4] *appellatives* Descriptive names.

paint and model any subjects she chooses, but she imprisons herself in men's *atéliers*[1] to endeavor to steal their technique and their methods, and thus loses any originality she might possess. Her influence on children might be so great that through them she would practically rule the future of the world; but she delegates her influence to the vile school boards[2] if she be poor, and if she be rich to governesses and tutors; nor does she in ninety-nine cases out of a hundred ever attempt to educate or control herself into fitness for the personal exercise of such influence. Her precept and example in the treatment of the animal creation[3] might be of infinite use in mitigating the hideous tyranny of humanity over them, but she does little or nothing to this effect; she wears dead birds and the skins of dead creatures; she hunts the hare and shoots the pheasant, she drives and rides with more brutal recklessness than men; she watches with delight the struggles of the dying salmon, of the gralloched[4] deer; she keeps her horses standing in the snow and fog for hours with the muscles of their heads and necks tied up in the torture of the bearing rein; when asked to do anything for a stray dog, a lame horse, a poor man's donkey, she is very sorry, but she has so many claims on her already; she never attempts by orders to her household, to her *fournisseurs*,[5] to her dependents, to obtain some degree of mercy in the treatment of sentient creatures and in the methods of their slaughter.

The immense area which lies open to her in private life is almost entirely uncultivated, yet she wants to be admitted into public life. Public life is already overcrowded, verbose, incompetent, fussy, and foolish enough without the addition of her in her sealskin coat with the dead hummingbird on her hat. Woman in public life would exaggerate the failings of men, and would not have even their few excellencies. Their legislation would be, as that of men is too often, the offspring of panic and prejudice; and she would not put on the drag of common-sense as man frequently does in public assemblies. There would be little to hope from her humanity, nothing from her liberality; for when she is frightened she is more ferocious than he, and when she has power more merciless. ...

The "Scum-woman" and the "Cow-woman," to quote the elegant phraseology of your contributor, are both of them less of a menace to humankind than the New Woman with her fierce vanity, her undigested knowledge, her overweening estimate of her own value and her fatal want[6] of all sense of the ridiculous.

When scum comes to the surface it renders a great service to the substance which it leaves behind it; when the cow yields pure nourishment to the young and the suffering, her place is blessed in the realm of nature; but when the New Woman splutters blistering wrath on mankind she is merely odious and baneful.

The error of the New Woman (as of many an old one) lies in speaking of women as the victims of men, and entirely ignoring the frequency with which men are the victims of women. In nine cases out of ten the first to corrupt the youth is the woman. In nine cases out of ten also she becomes corrupt herself because she likes it.

It is all very well to say that prostitutes were at the beginning of their career victims of seduction; but it is not probable and it is not provable. Love of drink and of finery, and a dislike to work, are the more likely motives and origin. It never seems to occur to the accusers of man that women are just as vicious and as lazy as he is in nine cases out of ten, and need no invitation from him to become so. ...

The New Woman reminds me of an agriculturist who, discarding a fine farm of his own, and leaving it to nettles, stones, thistles, and wire-worms,[7] should spend

[1] *atéliers*   Artists' workshops or studios.

[2] *school boards*   Public bodies, created by the Elementary Education Act (1870), which established and administered elementary schools. The Elementary Education Act only created school boards for areas that did not have enough existing schools to serve all the children in the area; as a result, they tended to be concentrated in poorer districts.

[3] *the animal creation*   I.e., non-human animals.

[4] *gralloched*   Disemboweled.

[5] *fournisseurs*   Vendors or suppliers.

[6] *overweening*   Arrogant; *want*   Lack.

[7] *wire-worms*   Insects destructive to crops.

his whole time in demanding neighboring fields which are not his. The New Woman will not even look at the extent of the ground indisputably her own, which she leaves unweeded and untilled.

Not to speak of the entire guidance of childhood, which is certainly already chiefly in the hands of woman (and of which her use does not do her much honor), so long as she goes to see one of her own sex dancing in a lion's den, the lions being meanwhile terrorized by a male brute; so long as she wears dead birds as millinery[1] and dead seals as coats; so long as she goes to races, steeplechases, coursing and pigeon matches;[2] so long as she "walks with the guns";[3] so long as she goes to see an American lashing horses to death in idiotic contest with velocipedes;[4] so long as she courtesies before princes and emperors who reward the winners of distance rides; so long as she receives physiologists in her drawing-rooms, and trusts to them in her maladies; so long as she invades literature without culture and art without talent; so long as she orders her court-dress in a hurry; so long as she makes no attempt to interest herself in her servants, in her animals, in the poor slaves of her trades-people; so long as she shows herself as she does at present without scruple at every brutal and debasing spectacle which is considered fashionable; so long as she understands nothing of the beauty of meditation, of solitude, of Nature; so long as she is utterly incapable of keeping her sons out of the shambles of modern sport, and lifting her daughters above the pestilent miasma[5] of modern society—so long as she does not, cannot, or will not either do, or cause to do, any of these things, she has no possible title or capacity to demand the place or the privilege of man.

---

[1] *millinery* Women's hats.

[2] *steeplechases* Horse races in which the horses have to clear fences and other obstacles; *coursing* Hunting for sport with the aid of greyhounds who track the hunted animal by scent; *pigeon matches* Pigeon-shooting contests.

[3] *walks with the guns* I.e., goes on hunts.

[4] *velocipedes* Early bicycles.

[5] *shambles* Slaughterhouse; *miasma* Noxious atmosphere.

This depiction of "the New Woman" was published as a costume suggestion in *Fancy Dresses Described; Or, What to Wear at Fancy Balls*, by Ardern Holt (1896). The accompanying description of the figure reads: "She wears a cloth tailor-made gown, and her bicycle is portrayed in front of it, together with the *Sporting Times* and her golf club; she carries her betting-book and her latch-key at her side, her gun is slung across her shoulder, and her pretty Tam o'Shanter is surmounted by a bicycle lamp. She has gaiters to her patent leather shoes, and is armed at all points for conquest."

from Alys W. Pearsall Smith, "A Reply from the Daughters, II," *The Nineteenth Century* (March 1894)

Now that the mothers have been heard upon this subject, it seems only fair that the daughters should be heard also. If it is true that there is any widespread revolt of a race of beings so proverbially dutiful as daughters, it can only be because there is at bottom a sufficient reason and a crying need. And who so fitted to tell of this need and explain this reason as the daughters themselves? ...

Grown-up sons are started off in an independent career of their own, with the good wishes and kindly help of all their family and friends, and are afforded every facility for the development of any especial talents they may possess, or for the pursuit of any career they may choose. Grown-up daughters, on the other hand, often with equal and perhaps greater talents, and with at least as high purposes as their brothers, are condemned to a life of dependence at home, their energies limited to the social and domestic duties of the household, all their talents cramped and thwarted, and every impulse to do something for the world outside treated as unwomanly and revolutionary.

The suffering endured by many a young woman under these circumstances has never yet been told. Possessing no money in her own right, and obliged to beg, too often from an unwilling father, for all she gets, a girl of character, as she grows into maturity and lives on as a woman in her father's house, suffers from a sense of bitter humiliation that no one who has not experienced it can understand. Many young women under these circumstances would gladly engage in any honourable labour, however menial, that would enable them to be independent and to own themselves. But this, of course, "is not to be thought of for a moment." Could the parents of these daughters, who have never thought of them as independent beings, but only as appendages to themselves, created for the purpose of ministering to their pleasures, and waiting upon their fancies—could they for one single moment get a glimpse into the hearts of their quiet, uncomplaining daughters, they would be astonished and perhaps horrified. "What can our daughters want more than they have now?" they would ask. "They have a good home and every comfort, and the society of their parents' friends; perhaps a carriage to drive in and horses to ride. What more can they possibly desire?" To such parents I would reply: Your daughter wants herself. She belongs to you now, and can walk only in your paths, and enjoy your pleasures, and live your life. She wants to belong to herself. She has paths of her own she longs to walk in, and purposes of her

own she is eager to carry out. She is an independent being, created by God for the development of her own talents, and for the use of her own time. Her capacities were not given to her parents, but to herself; her life is not their possession, but her own; and to herself God looks for an account of it. Put yourselves in her place, and ask yourselves how you would like to have no independence, but be obliged to live always someone else's life, and carry out only someone else's purposes. You have had aims and purposes in your lives, and have been free, perhaps, to carry them out. Can you dare, as mere human beings like themselves, to lay hands upon the mature lives of your daughters and say, "It shall be as we please, not as they please"? If they yield to your demands it can only be at the expense of a grievous waste of energies and capabilities that were meant by God to accomplish, through their instrumentality, some personal and instrumental work for Him. But this is an aspect of the question that very few adequately realise. There is no sadder sight in the world than that of a wasted life. And when this waste is the result of carelessness or selfishness on the part of the strong towards the weak, it becomes no less a tragedy even although it is done under the name of parental love. Such tragedies are no fiction, but the very common occurrence of everyday life around us. How wanton is the waste continually going on in the lives of thousands of women, whose powers, by a long course of trivialities and mental starvation, deteriorate year after year, until they themselves and all their friends suffer incalculable loss. ...

A great deal is said about the duty and the beauty of "self-sacrifice," and as it is mostly said to the female part of creation, it is not to be wondered at that a conscientious girl feels herself to be a monster of selfishness if she ventures for a moment to assert her right to live her own life in her own way, should that way differ in the least from the ways of those around her. ...

But there is another aspect, apart from that which affects merely the home or the individual life, in which we must consider this question. No one of us can live to herself nor die to herself, nor even to her family. We are each a part of the society around us, of the nation to which we belong, of the world in which we live. And we must consider the claims that these have upon us, when we are trying to decide what our duty really is. Women must be taught to realise the solidarity of the human race, and to recognise the fact that we are all members one of another, and that if one member suffers all must necessarily suffer with it. No woman can permit her life to be dwarfed and thwarted without inflicting an injury not only upon herself and upon her family, but also upon the community in which she lives; and no woman can develop herself and make the most of all her powers without bestowing a positive benefit upon her friends and neighbours, and also upon the world.

Let every girl then claim her right to individual development, not merely for her own welfare and enjoyment or for that of her family, but chiefly that she may become a more perfect instrument to perform her allotted part in the world's work. It must be a matter of principle, not a matter of self-indulgence. She must be able to say not merely, "I want to do this or that," but "I believe I ought to do it." It is as fatal to a woman to live her life merely for her own enjoyment as it is for her to sacrifice her own life to other people's enjoyment. She must sacrifice herself, not *to* people, but *for* principles. She must ask herself frankly and honestly, "Have I any worthy purpose in my life? Am I doing the best with such powers as God has given me, or am I allowing them to be unused and wasted? Am I growing stronger and better with each year, or am I narrowing and deteriorating? Shall I be able rightly to fulfil my duties to the world in which I live if I allow myself to be frittered away in little nothings, and fail to strengthen and develop all my powers? Is it not my duty, even for the sake of others, to realise my best and highest self, and to make the most of all my capacities?"

If the community were only alive to its own high interests, it would hail with heartiest welcome the advent[1] of girls such as these, and all true lovers of humanity would reach out a hand to help them break through the trammels of prejudice or conventionality that have hitherto held them in check.

Hundreds of avenues are opening for the girls of today in which they can get the development and find the work they need. It ought, therefore, to be a matter of principle for every girl who has reached maturity to consider what is her own especial gift or capability; and, having discovered it, she ought to be as conscientious in trying to carry it out as she would be conscientious in carrying out any of the domestic duties which hitherto may have seemed to her to have been the only career allowed her.

The revolt of the daughter is not, if I understand it, a revolt against any merely surface conventionalities, that are after all of not much account one way or another, but it is a revolt against a bondage that enslaves her whole life. In the past she has belonged to other people, now she demands to belong to herself. In the past other people have decided her duties for her, now she asks that she may decide them for herself. She asks simply and only for freedom to make out of her own life the highest that can be made, and to develop her own individuality as seems to her the wisest and the best. She claims only the ordinary human rights of a human being, and humbly begs that no one will hinder her.

"Donna Quixote," *Punch* (April 1894)

The dreamy Don who to the goatherds told
Long-winded legends of the Age of Gold,[2]
Finds a fair rival in our later days;
The newest Chivalry brings the newest Craze.
Dear Donna QUIXOTE—and the sex is dear,
Even when querulous, or quaint, or queer—

_____

[1] *advent* Arrival.

_____

[2] *The dreamy … Gold* Don Quixote, the title character of the famous novel (1605, 1615) by Miguel Cervantes, is a foolish nobleman from the region of La Mancha in Spain who, after reading too many stories about chivalric knights, comes to believe he is such a knight himself and sets out to perform feats of chivalry. In one episode, he encounters a group of goatherds, to whom he narrates a story of the "Golden Age" of humanity, in which property did not exist, people lived in peace, and virgins could roam the countryside without fear. Don Quixote is also famous for attempting to fight battles with imaginary foes, such as windmills that he believes to be giants.

Dear Donna, like La Mancha's moonstruck knight,
Whose fancy shaped the foes he turned to fight,
Mere book-bred phantoms you for facts mistake;
10   Your *Wanderjahr*[1] will vanish when you—wake!

Yes, there you sit surrounded by wild hosts°   *multitudes*
Of warring wonders which indeed are "*Ghosts*":
"*Dolls-House*"[2] delirium sets your nerves a-thrill,
"DODO"[3] hysteria misdirects your will;
15   You yearn—indefinitely—to Advance!
You shake your lifted latch-key[4] like a lance!
And shout, "In spite of babies, bonnets, tea,
Creation's heir,[5] I must, I will be—Free!"

Morbid° conceptions born of books ferment   *unhealthy*
20   In brains a-burn with febrile° discontent!   *feverish*
So the dear Don, with dream-disordered head,
His fancy fired with all that he had read—
Enchantments, contests, challenges, and scars—
Found rustic Arragon[6] a world of wars,
25   Windmills fierce foes, and e'en domestic sheep
Destructive demons. Donna, could you keep
That trim-coiled "hair on"—pray forgive the slang!—
You do in *Dodo*!—let the fads go hang,
And "realise yourself" in natural sort,
30   For churls[7] and cynics you should make less sport.

These shapes are things of mirage and the mist,
Gendered° by genius with a mental twist;   *engendered*
By male hysteria, Amazonian sham,
And the smart world's great *Fin de Siècle* flam![8]
35   See Mrs. Cerberus[9] in your cloudy vision,
Keeping the portals of that Home Elysian[10]
Which cranks now call a Hades! Home, sweet home?
Nay, 'tis a jail to those who long to roam,
Unchaperoned, emancipate, and *free*
40   With the large Liberty of the Latch-key!
Materfamilias[11] and the chaperon grim,
Of watchful eye, firm mouth, and triple chin,
Are Mrs. GRUNDY'S[12] brace of stout supporters,
Three-headed guard of our Revolting Daughters![13]
45   You, Donna QUIXOTE, to this ward—or these—
Would but too gladly play the Hercules,[14]
Urged by the CAIRDS, and CRACKANTHORPES,
      and GRANDS![15]
These demon-weavers of domestic bands,
Who've snared the Daughter of the Day, and bound her,

---

[1] *Wanderjahr* German: Year of wandering.

[2] *Ghosts … Dolls-House* Plays (1881 and 1879, respectively) by the Norwegian dramatist Henrik Ibsen. Ibsen's plays, which frequently contain sympathetic portrayals of women's struggles in a male-dominated world, were considered to be a major influence on the thought of the "new woman." *A Doll's House* was especially controversial for its depiction of a married woman leaving her husband.

[3] *DODO* Controversial and bestselling 1893 novel by Edward Frederic Benson that depicts a young woman's adventures in high society.

[4] *latch-key* Latchkeys, symbolizing the ability to come and go freely that many women desired, were a stock accessory of the new woman in many representations of this figure.

[5] *Creation's heir* See Oliver Goldsmith's poem "The Traveller" (1764): "Creation's heir, the world, the world is mine!"

[6] *Arragon* I.e., Spain; the Kingdom of Aragon was one of two kingdoms that united to form the modern country of Spain.

[7] *churls* Low people.

[8] *smart* Fashionable; *Fin de Siècle* French term, meaning "end of the century," that was and is frequently used to describe the atmosphere of decadence thought to characterize the late nineteenth century; *flam* Falsehood.

[9] *Mrs. Cerberus* In classical mythology Cerberus, a dog with three heads, was the guardian of Hades, the underworld.

[10] *Elysian* Heavenly. Elysium, in classical mythology, was the dwelling place of the blessed after death.

[11] *Materfamilias* Female head of a household.

[12] *Mrs. GRUNDY* Character in the play *Speed the Plough* (1798), by the English playwright Thomas Morton, who represents conventional social disapproval, prudishness, and narrow-mindedness.

[13] *Revolting Daughters* Reference to a controversial January 1894 article, "The Revolt of the Daughters," by Blanche Alethea Crackanthorpe. The article, a discussion of the demands for greater freedom being made by many young women, garnered numerous responses, one of which is included in this Contexts section.

[14] *play the Hercules* In Greek myth, one of the labors of the hero Heracles was to capture Cerberus from Hades.

[15] *CAIRDS, and CRACKANTHORPES, and GRANDS* Mona Caird (1854–1932) and Sarah Grand (1854–1943) were, with Crackanthorpe, writers who made important contributions to the "New Woman" debate. Excerpts from works by both Caird and Grand appear elsewhere in this Contexts section.

50 As the bard sings, with dark Styx[1] nine times round her,
    Do not exist, dear Donna, save in dreams,
    Like QUIXOTE'S Caraculiambo![2] Gleams
    Of common sense and glorious hope illume
    (As dawn's first rosy streaks break night's black gloom)
55 The sex's future. The dull despot, man,
    Backed by the bondage of the social plan,
    Shall not for ever unrestricted sway.
    But Donna dear, not by the masher's° way,   *dandy's*
    Or MILL'S[3] or the sham Amazons, or CAIRD'S
60 Or HEDDA GABLER'S;[4] not through cranks ill-paired,
    Or franchise, or the female volunteers,
    EGERTON'S[5] fantasies or DODO'S jeers,
    Shall come the true emancipation. No!
    The Heavenly Twins, or *A Grey Eye or So*,
65 *The Yellow Aster*—or the *Yellow Book*,[6]
    Latch-keys or key-notes;[7] all the "thrills" that shook
    The Master-builder's minx,[8] or moved a soul
    Midway between a maniac and troll;

70 Music-hall freedom, laxity in love,
    Affinities that range all rites above;
    Soul-swell that outgrows marriage, as a plant
    Its pot-bound limitations—all the cants
    Of culture's cranks, and extra-ethic dolts,
    Whose fetish is the Gospel of Revolts—
75 Not these shall shed one single lustrous ray
    Of light divine upon the bitter way,
    Or help with human melody their songs
    Who'd "ride abroad redressing *woman's* wrongs."[9]

    Therefore, dear Donna QUIXOTE, be not stupid,
80 Fight not with Hymen, and war not with Cupid,[10]
    Run not amuck 'gainst Mother Nature's plan,
    Nor make a monster of your mate, poor Man,
    Or like La Mancha's cracked, though noble knight,
    You'll find blank failure in mistaken fight.

from "Character Note: The New Woman," *Cornhill Magazine* (October 1894)

> This parodic depiction of the New Woman is one of
> a series of satiric Character Notes published in
> *Cornhill* in the 1890s.

> *"L'esprit de la plupart des femmes sert plus a fortifier
> leur folie que leur raison."*[11]

She is young, of course. She looks older than she really is. And she calls herself a woman. Her mother is content to be called a lady, and is naturally of small account. Novissima's[12] chief characteristic is her unbounded self-satisfaction.

---

[1] *Styx*   According to classical mythology, all souls had to travel across the River Styx to reach Hades.

[2] *Caraculiambo*   Supposed giant who is one of Don Quixote's imaginary foes.

[3] *MILL*   The English philosopher John Stuart Mill (1806–73) was a noted advocate for women's rights who sought to extend the right to vote to women and compared women's condition in marriage to slavery.

[4] *HEDDA GABLER*   1890 play by Henrik Ibsen about a woman trapped in a loveless marriage; the play ends with her death by suicide.

[5] *EGERTON*   George Egerton was the pen name of Mary Chavelita Dunne Bright, an author of short stories—one of which is excerpted in this Contexts section—who was one of the most prominent and controversial of the "new woman" writers.

[6] *The Heavenly Twins*   1893 novel by Sarah Grand; *A Grey Eye or So* 1893 novel by Frank Frankfort Moore; *The Yellow Aster* 1894 novel by Kathleen Hunt Caffyn, writing under the pseudonym Iota; *Yellow Book* Controversial literary periodical, running from 1894–97, that was associated with avant-garde cultural movements, including Decadence and Aestheticism.

[7] *key-notes*   George Egerton's most popular and controversial work was titled *Keynotes* (1893).

[8] *Master-builder's minx*   In Henrik Ibsen's 1892 play *The Master Builder*, the life of the title character, a middle-aged architect, becomes entangled with a young woman whose pursuit of emotional and psychological thrills eventually causes his death.

[9] *ride … wrongs*   In "Guinevere" (1859), part of Alfred, Lord Tennyson's poetic collection *Idylls of the King*, the Knights of the Round Table swear an oath committing them "to ride abroad redressing human wrongs."

[10] *Hymen*   God of marriage in classical mythology; *Cupid* Roman god of love.

[11] *L'esprit … raison*   French: For the majority of women, the mind serves more to strengthen their madness rather than their reason.

[12] *Novissima*   Latin: Latest or very new; may also imply something extreme.

Gertrude. "MY DEAR JESSIE, WHAT ON EARTH IS THAT BICYCLE SUIT FOR?"
Jessie. "WHY, TO WEAR, OF COURSE."   *Gertrude.* "BUT YOU HAVEN'T GOT A BICYCLE!"
Jessie. "NO; BUT I'VE GOT A SEWING MACHINE!"

Gertrude. "My dear Jessie, what on earth is that Bicycle Suit for?" *Jessie.* "Why, to wear, of course." *Gertrude.* "But you haven't got a Bicycle!" *Jessie.* "No, but I've got a Sewing Machine!"

"The Bicycle Suit," a cartoon published in *Punch* in 1895. At the time, Jessie's style of clothing would have been considered acceptable for a woman to wear only when riding a bicycle—a recently introduced form of transportation stereotypically associated with the New Woman.

She is dark; and one feels that if she were fair she would be quite a different person. For fairness usually goes with an interest in children, and other gentle weaknesses of which Novissima is conspicuously innocent.

She dresses simply in close-fitting garments, technically known as tailor-made. She wears her elbows well away from her side. It has been hinted that this habit serves to diminish the apparent size of the waist. This may be so. Men do not always understand such things.

It certainly adds to a somewhat aggressive air of independence which finds its birth in the length of her stride. Novissima strides in (from the hip) where men and angels fear to tread.[1]

In the evening simplicity again marks her dress. Always close-fitting—always manly and wholly simple.

[1] *Novissima strides ... tread* The line "Fools rush in where angels fear to tread" was written by the English poet Alexander Pope in 1711 and quickly became proverbial.

Very little jewellery, and close-fitting hair. Which description is perhaps not technical. Her hands are steady and somewhat *en évidence*.[1] Her attitudes are strong and independent, indicative of a self-reliant spirit.

With mild young men she is apt to be crushing. She directs her conversation and her glance above their heads. She has a way of throwing scraps of talk to them in return for their mild platitudes—crumbs from a well-stored intellectual table.

"Pictures—no, I do not care about pictures," she says. "They are all so pretty nowadays."

She has a way of talking of noted men by their surnames *tout court*[2] indicative of a familiarity with them not enjoyed by her hearer. She has a certain number of celebrities whom she marks out for special distinction—obscurity being usually one of their merits. Prettiness is one of her pet aversions. Novissima is, by the way, not pretty herself. She is white. Pink girls call her sallow. She has a long face, with a discontented mouth, and a nose indicative of intelligence, and too large for feminine beauty as understood by men. Her equanimity, like her complexion, is unassailable. One cannot make her blush. It is the other way round.

In conversation she criticises men and books freely. The military man is the object of her deepest scorn. His intellect, she tells one, is terribly restricted. He never reads—Reads, that is, with a capital. For curates[3] she has a sneaking fondness—a feminine weakness too deeply engrained to be stamped out in one generation of advancement.

Literary men she tolerates. They have probably read some of the books selected out of the ruck[4] for her approval. But even to these she talks with an air suggestive of the fact that she could tell them a thing or two if she took the trouble. Which no doubt she could. …

---

[1] *en évidence*   French: conspicuous.

[2] *tout court*   French: without addition of title; i.e., familiarly, by surname alone.

[3] *curates*   Clergy members.

[4] *ruck*   Pile.

Albert Morrow, poster for the play *The New Woman* by Sydney Grundy, 1894.

from H.E. Harvey, "The Voice of Woman," *Westminster Review* (February 1896)

It is only during the last twenty years or so that the voice of woman has really been heard in literature. The women who distinguished themselves as writers before that time wrote under the influence of the social laws and literature which had been established by male feeling—because it was their interest to do so. Being entirely dependent on marriage as a profession, the woman of the past found it her interest to train herself in those qualities which made her attractive to men, humility being conspicuous among them. Even Charlotte Brontë,[5] one of the

---

[5] *Charlotte Brontë*   Novelist and poet best known for *Jane Eyre* (1847).

most original and independent of women writers, stoutly maintained the inferiority of women.

This necessity for meeting the demands of the marriage market has given to the sex an artificial character of subservience and servility which I suppose was pleasing to the men of the past, and is still to a large number; but I observe that for the most part the men of the present day are more ready to admire women of an independent turn of mind. The effects of this system showed themselves in many ways, notably in the writings of literary women, who always wrote from a masculine point of view, and preached subserviency to their own sex. … It showed itself in the special training which was formerly given to girls, who were taught chiefly showy accomplishments, which were likely to make them attractive to men, with merely a smattering of serious knowledge. Modesty, gentleness, and humility were much insisted on as suitable feminine qualifications.

It shows itself still in the readiness of women to blame one another, especially those among them who have fallen from the path of virtue, while they overlook the shortcomings of men.

It shows itself in the underhand arts practised by many women, more especially in the working classes, who do not scruple to deceive their husbands in order to carry on in private something which he has forbidden—the man, all the while, believing, in a blustering sort of way, that he is master in his own house. The woman does this in order to preserve the domestic peace, and have her own way at the same time.

The woman who is so indignant when anyone tries to prevent her husband beating her is another result of this teaching.

Man has always posed as the protector of the weaker sex; but, with the best intentions, is it possible that he can thoroughly understand the interests of a creature different from himself, without consulting her opinion? The law which denied property to married women[1] proved that he did not. Now, the woman of the present day has suddenly discovered[2] that she has opinions of her own respecting her welfare; and those men and women who deride the extravagance of some of the female writers of our times would do well, before they scoff, to consider calmly what these women have to say, and see if there is any cause for their complaints. Until now, men have had it all their own way in literature; and what they have written about women may be broadly divided under three heads—the first division being by far the largest.

1. Raptures written by men who are in love about the beauty and graces of women.

2. Complaints of married men about the trials of domestic life and the unreasonableness of women. (Good examples may be found in some of Lord Lytton's[3] novels.)

3. Ill-natured sneers at old maids or women who are supposed to wish to marry. (Such as those written by Dickens and Smollett.[4])

Of course, there are some notable exceptions to this rule, such as Solomon's description of the virtuous woman.[5]

Now, I do not for a moment suppose that the writings which I have mentioned show the average feeling of men towards women. The great majority of the men who are contented with their lot do not find it necessary to say so. We all know that the unfortunate have more to tell than the fortunate. The lover writes because he has not obtained what he desires. But I wish to point out that the women who were dissatisfied with their lot were obliged to make their complaints in private, to each other, because public feeling was such that if a wife did not agree with her husband she was blamed. The woman who complained of ceaseless child-

---

1 *The law … women* Before 1870, married women in Britain had no legal claim to their own property, which their husbands could dispose of as they pleased.

2 *discovered* Revealed.

3 *Lord Lytton* Edward Bulwer-Lytton, 1st Baron Lytton (1803–73), popular Victorian novelist.

4 *Smollett* Tobias Smollett (1721–71), Scottish novelist and poet who influenced Charles Dickens.

5 *Solomon's … woman* See Proverbs 31.10–31. The biblical Book of Proverbs was traditionally ascribed to the famously wise King Solomon.

bearing was told by husband and doctor that it was "the will of God" that she should spend her whole life in producing children. We see by the writings of Shakespeare how much meekness and subserviency was expected from a wife in his time. She must be ready to forgive any insult or backsliding on the part of her husband, being herself required to be blameless. No matter how badly he has treated her, she is ready to beg him, on her knees it may be, to receive her back again, because her honour and reputation depend on her being recognised as his wife. There is another, and still more degraded, modern type of heroine, who, I fancy, exists only in the imagination of male poets and novelists. This class of woman does not beg for her reputation; she is ready to sacrifice reputation, honour, happiness, life, everything that is hers, and a good deal that is not hers, for the sake of the man she loves, without receiving anything in return. ... But there is no place for self-respect in the manners and customs which owe their being to the marriage laws. Even at the present day, a woman whose husband has been unfaithful to her is allowed no redress. Dr. Johnson[1] distinctly stated that he would not receive back a daughter who left her husband on these grounds, because he considered that it would be her own fault that she had not succeeded in pleasing him!

The artificial distinction conferred by society on the married woman as compared with the unmarried, combined with the difficulty of qualifying themselves for other professions, is, of course, the great inducement to marriage with the majority of women, as very many women, who do not care for domestic life, would greatly prefer independence and liberty. But they marry because society expects it of them, and tempts them with the promise of its favours.

The unmarried woman who is deserted by her lover has, of course, always been a scapegoat in the eyes of society, and it is only since George Eliot took up her cause[2] that it has become the fashion to interest ourselves in her. ...

That such a woman, having become an outcast through the fault of a man, should be restored to her place in society by receiving the name of the villain who has injured her, is, I think, the most revolting of the principles which have been evolved from the marriage system. ...

But now those women who dare to make complaint of existing social institutions are told that they wish to overthrow morality and order, and introduce a state of chaos. The question is, Are we living just now in a state of morality and order? Are there no social laws that press unjustly on the hitherto silent part of the community? Now that so many complaints have been made, all these questions ought to be considered. As women have, on the whole, obediently conformed to the character which was required of them for six thousand years or so, I think that now that they have begun to announce publicly that they have opinions of their own, they are due, at the very least, a fair hearing.

Cornelia Sorabji, "Love and Death" (1901)

Cornelia Sorabji (1866–1954), the daughter of an Indian Parsi family that had converted to Christianity, pursued a distinguished legal career in which she won a succession of firsts, including first female graduate from Bombay University, first woman to study law at Oxford (1889–92), and first female legal advocate in India. After returning to India from Britain, she published *Love and Life Beyond the Purdah* (1901), a collection of short stories reflecting her commitment to women's rights—especially the rights of women kept in seclusion according to the South Asian practice of purdah. "Love and Death," the story reprinted below, appeared in this collection.

---

[1] *Dr. Johnson* Samuel Johnson (1709–84), English writer.

[2] *George Eliot took up her cause* The novel *Adam Bede* (1859), by the English novelist George Eliot (the pen name of Mary Anne Evans), is a sympathetic account of a young woman who is seduced and abandoned by her aristocratic lover.

Cornelia Sorabji.

"I tell you, Stewart, it's playing the very deuce[1] with a man's life to treat him as I've been treated."

"I thought that had been uncommonly well: by Fate certainly, in the way of fulfilled desires; and by your father, also undoubtedly, in the way of allowance. And what more can a man want?"

"Nothing—unless he's a married man."

"Ah! an indiscretion. You have my condolences, old chap: our follies always do vex us more than our sins, I know."

"Yes! and the offence is aggravated when you consider that it was someone else's folly. Listen, Stewart, and I'll tell you—I'm feeling communicative tonight, and this weed[2] draws nicely."

The two men stood on the forward deck of the P. & O. s.s. *Khartoum*, bound for India, and now in harbour off Brindisi,[3] awaiting the mails.

A bright moon looked down on the squalid town and the great expanse of sea, on the farther shore with its Turkish gardens and its tale of handsome brigands, and on the lithe Indian sailors, bending their supple bodies under the precious weight of the post-office consignments. One after another they crossed the bridge in well-trained rapidity. Pity the night was so brilliant! What thrill might not the darkness have lent to that scene of swift, noiseless activity!

Presently the foreigner spoke—"I was but seven years old," said he, "when my grandfather sent me to England, and, as you know, I have had no other home ever since. But there still linger with me Indian sights and sounds—music, and bright colours, and the scent of roses. I remember her, who must have been my mother, surrounded by chattering serving-women, who fed me with sweets, and flattered and spoilt me. But the memories all grow out of a noisy procession on a glaring day in midsummer. Dressed in garments of some startling hue, and smothered under the combined weight of heavy necklets and sickly odorous flowers, I rode gaily on a prancing nag, while the singers went before and the minstrels followed after. In the midst, however, was a single damsel, only—and she was not playing on a timbrel,[4] but drumming two small henna-dyed hands on the horse's neck, as she sat astride in front of me. … They tell me now that *that* meant my marriage! … It must, I think, have been almost immediately afterwards that I was packed away to the dear old dame's at Summerton, where we first met, you know, Stewart; for my memory comes to its *finis* about India

---

[1] *deuce* Devil.

[2] *weed* Cigar or cigarette.

---

[3] *P. & O. s.s.* I.e., a steamship of the Peninsular and Oriental line, a British shipping company that was one of the main carriers of passengers and mail between Britain and India; *Brindisi* Port in southern Italy that was on the P. & O. route to India via the Suez Canal.

[4] *timbrel* Tambourine.

when I have worried[1] the past so far. And not a word, it's odd, has my father said on the subject all this long while; but in his last letter he tells me placidly, that both a welcome *and a wife* await me, in the land of my birth! I tell you, Stewart, it is infamous! She has most likely been kept a semi-prisoner all her life, knowing certainly nothing of the world, either as God or man has made it, and probably also nothing of books, even in her vernacular. I daresay she can cook a palatable Indian dinner, and scour the cooking-pans—but, well! it has not been fair to me at all. Systems cannot alter in a day, you will say. Exactly so! But why alter them at all in this one-sided way? Why create a false position for a pair of innocent children—Oh yes! I know it's hard on her too. Everything is a huge mistake: new patches can never mean aught but worsened rents[2] to an old garment!"

"Poor old fellow!" said Stewart. "I never guessed such a complication. However, there'll be your work, you know, and perhaps she's not impossible, after all. You may even be able to educate her."

The conversation was not renewed through the voyage, and, on landing, the young Indian doctor and his friend found that stress of plague-work claimed their immediate presence. The welcome and the wife had alike to wait. "Incidental freedom," said the Indian grimly; but indeed there was scant time for reflection, whether congratulatory or self-compassionate. He was on search duty, and hunting the dread infection from street to street demanded the exercise of every nerve and faculty. Ah, the sadness of it all! The feeble subterfuges, the brave fight against the most patent[3] symptoms, the gasping attempt to propitiate the microbe—and finally, the sullen submission to Fate! The hearts of the two young doctors were heavy within them. Disease and

death were sufficiently appalling—but with superstition for ally!—

Only this morning they had passed a mad procession carrying the dead plague-infected rats on spikes, while broken-hearted mothers and anxious wives wailed a propitiatory serenade, ghastly in its pathos! "We can't hold out any longer," said the Indian one morning after breakfast. "Write to headquarters, Stewart, and beg for a lady-doctor and a nurse. They must spare them to us. The poor women whom we find in the bazaar have to submit to our ministrations. What alternative is there? But the better classes, as you see, choose death rather than be looked upon by a man; and indeed I must confess that I greatly dislike having to search their houses. Don't you yourself agree with me, that it is our inability to deal with this class of patient which fosters the microbe?"

"Yes," said Stewart, "I do, and I'll write this very moment. The fear of the microbe is the mother of virtue."

"I wish it were the mother of sanitation," growled the Indian. "That's the kind of offspring I'm seeking just now."

In a week came the answer. The request was only just in time. An Indian lady with European qualifications was temporarily at the disposal of the chief medical officer. He had meant to send her elsewhere, but, as this was so sacred and orthodox a town, and as she knew the vernacular of the district, Stewart might have her for six months. They might expect her and a nurse in a fortnight.[4]

"That's well done," said the Indian. "Now we'll get the thing under!"

She was tall and slender, intelligent and eager in face rather than pretty; and she carried herself with the ease and freedom of her race. Indeed her attraction lay in grace of movement, in fineness of proportion, and in a certain delicate sensitiveness, which could hardly escape even the least observant. For such work as fell to her she was pre-eminently suited—tactful, gentle, persuasive;

---

[1] *the dear ... Summerton* I.e., a dame school in England, where the speaker would have resided with and received his primary education from a local woman before, most likely, being enrolled in a boarding school for adolescent boys; *finis* Latin: end; *worried* "Chewed up," metaphorically—i.e., thought over comprehensively.

[2] *aught* Anything; *rents* Tears.

[3] *patent* Obvious.

---

[4] *fortnight* Two weeks.

and if she gave out so largely of her sympathising self to each sufferer, was that a fault? Her masculine colleagues thought that it was certainly so. "You'll break down," they said. "Besides, it's not professional!" And they devised common recreation to relieve the tension—golf, on the brown *maidan*[1] to westward, clear of the temples and the odours; and tennis in the garden of the civil engineer, whose wife and the wife of the padre were indeed the only other ladies in the station, and both were ready to do everything that was hospitable and kindly. Such patches of sunlight were those afternoons!

Suffering and death and all ugliness were forgotten in congenial and healthful companionship. The girl had evidently been responsive to all the best influences of her Western training, while losing nothing of her own charming individuality. The effect was that of brilliant colouring under the brush of a master-painter. Even the women loved her. What of the men? Well! as to one of them, you must have guessed. That which happened was hopelessly inevitable. Could it be avoided between two young people of similar tastes, doing the same work, bearing the same sad burden, seeing the best and most unselfish side of each other, day after day, amid scenes which excited the keenest of sympathies? That it was a surprise to both, made the remedy no easier. The ludicrous side of it all was the similarity of experience. The obstacle was double-barrelled. There was a baby-husband as there had been a baby-wife!

"I always thought it very nice of him to allow me an English education," she said; "and I have often built him up round that one kind fact. But I begged a year's freedom on coming to India—and now, how ever am I to face that inevitable introduction? 'Where is he?' Ah! that I cannot tell; but I expect you would find him in his native village, a pampered only son, too orthodox to cross the waters himself,[2] and managing the family property, in ignorant and comfortable self-satisfaction.

What I cannot understand is my own liberty! There must be some third person acting a reformed up-to-date Providence, I'm sure! Till lately I've been so curious about it all, but now curiosity is swallowed up in loathing!"

"Pity we can't marry those two!"[3] said the man.

It was the festival of the fire-god. "Though thou passest through the fire, thou shalt not be burned!"[4] Who would make good the promise of the deity and face the ordeal? Through long months of prayer and fasting, certain rapt fanatics, and of good women not a few, had been preparing themselves to answer that question. And here was the very day at last! Down the heights into the hollows came the crowds of pilgrims—intending victims and applauding gallery all huddled together—one chattering, rattling, rumbling, seething mass, like to some mountain torrent seeking the level, and, when found, glittering light-imprisoned under the brilliant rays of a lingering sun.

By their dress shall ye know them—many-hued, many-fashioned—and also by their equipages.[5] That long, low, wicker cart, likest to a racing-boat on lumbering wheels, has had other geographical genesis than that flat cradle-shaped construction of wooden poles and bambus.[6]

The great milk-white, soft-eyed bulls, easing tired necks with a graceful sweep of hoary[7] tongue, have not before known as neighbour the small, perky, wiry cattle, tossing impertinent heads to the jingle of aggressive bells, and bellowing staccato inquiries.

---

[1] *maidan* South Asian term for an urban park or other open space.

[2] *too orthodox ... himself* In Hindu religious culture, sea voyages are widely considered to be impurifying and to cause a loss of caste; consequently, crossing the sea was and remains taboo in some forms of Hinduism.

[3] *marry those two* I.e., have their spouses marry each other.

[4] *Though thou passest ... burned* Ordeal by fire as a proof of innocence or purity—a ritual known as *agni pariksha*—stems in Hindu culture from the *Ramayana*, the Hindu epic recounting the life and exploits of the hero Rama (considered to be one of the avatars, or incarnations, of the god Vishnu). In some versions of the epic, Rama's wife Sita undergoes a trial by fire after she is rescued from a demon who has abducted her, walking unscathed through flames and thereby proving her purity and fidelity to her husband.

[5] *equipages* Carriages.

[6] *bambus* I.e., bamboo.

[7] *hoary* Gray.

But the crowd has one manner of encamping. Under each cart is tied a primitive hammock, and into this are thrown the squalling babies, safely out of the way, while their parents water the beasts and cook the evening meal. Secure are they here from intrusion. Do not the mountains stand sentinel? And are not the very clouds frowning a watchful "*cave*"?[1] Yet it behoved them to do quickly that which they were purposing, for a wise Government approved not of the rash sacrifice of life; and even now some message of prohibition may be travelling from the camp of the nearest collector.[2]

"In the blackest watch of the night—the inrush!" said the priestly herald, beating a muffled drum among the *al fresco*[3] cooking-pots.

Gradually, like a long, stealthy shadow, silence creeps over the face of the valley, and out of the wordless darkness arises a great lurid fiery furnace. It shows the mass of onlookers, earnest, fanatic—ringing the sacred enclosure—a phalanx strong enough to withstand any band of venturesome intruders; and, at a sanctified distance, the knot of priests and white-robed devotees.

The head priest was speaking—"To the holy," said he, "this is no wanton sacrifice of life, but merely a hymn to the praise of the Deity—the rhythm of your bodies to the accompaniment of that angry roar. The *evil* do indeed take hurt, but is that not the just reward of their offences?"

"Let us go and see the festival," had said the doctor-girl to her friend. "My mother belonged to these hill-folk, and something stirs within me at thought of the great ordeal. I believe the instincts of the savage still survive. Do let us go, and I will—yes, I shall appear in the white garments of the devotee."

So they went, man and woman, in high spirits at the dubious adventure.

They arrived in time to hear the introductory address. The drums were growling now, and quaint pathetic incantations rose and fell on the midnight air. The first rush was just about to be made. One poor candidate has fainted. Carry her aside. Now!

They are through, unsinged, and a great shout of enthusiasm greets the semi-deities—canonization dearly bought!

But more stirring matters still are afoot. For now a group of young girls stand hand in hand, gladly responsive to the heavenly call, thrilling with the joy of martyrdom. But a moment, and the priest will give the signal for the fresh inrush!

"The gods will stay the plague," declares their messenger, "for the willing sacrifice of a band of virgins. Who will come, who will be the brides of death, to buy life for the millions? Who? Who? One short black moment for you, brave virgins. For others, years of glad happiness. See! the corn[4] is ready to harvest, but the hand which would gather it is stiff; the grain is garnered, but the arm which would grind it is withered; the meal is prepared, but they who would eat it are dead! dead *and defiled*! with no sacred rites to buy them the best eternity. ... Buy you it for them, O virgins! *You*! Buy life now, and life hereafter—a double gift—and your own the hand to bestow it. Virgin life-givers!" ...

In the silence one can almost hear life pulse! Then there is a sudden quick, convulsive sob—for, carried past all self-control, the doctor-girl has joined the band of vestal virgins.[5] The word is given, and there they are, the white-robed seven, treading the flames.

"O Agni![6] do not burn them altogether," chanted the priests. "Let the eye go to the sun, and the breath to the

---

[1] *cave* Latin: beware.

[2] *it behoved them* It was necessary for them; *collector* District magistrate—British colonial official in charge of the area. District magistrates in India are called "collectors" because one of their primary responsibilities is the collection of revenue.

[3] *al fresco* Open-air (from an Italian phrase meaning "in the fresh [air]").

[4] *corn* Grain.

[5] *vestal virgins* In ancient Rome, the vestal virgins were priestesses of Vesta, the goddess of the hearth, and tended the goddess's sacred flame.

[6] *Agni* Hindu god of fire.

wind! Go to sky or earth, as is right; or to the waters, if it is good to be there. But the immortal, the unborn part, warm it with thy heat and flame! Carry them in thy kindliest shape to the world of those who have done well!"

"*Peste*![1] Why sings he the death chant!" murmured the crowd. "It is ill luck!" And then—no one knew how it happened. … "The doctor-lady!" they shrieked.

"She was tainted with infidel observances!" said the didactic priest; "the gods were angry!"

"She was not quick enough," said her companions. "Hi! hi!" mourned the multitude. Her friend alone said not a word. And she, poor girl, lay terribly scarred in the accident ward of her own hospital.

The end was not long in coming. "The decision of the gods," she murmured, and so slept, her hand in his.

Postscriptum—It was a month later, and the doctor sat in his consulting room. His face wore the look of the man to whom life has proved a resented discipline. There were arrears[2] of correspondence clamouring for attention, and he settled wearily to the pile of multifarious envelopes.

Presently his eye flashed, and the sensitive mouth quivered, as he read a letter longer than the rest.

"Son," wrote, after much circumlocution, the father of whom he knew so little, "forgive the deception. It was part of your fate. The girl who worked in the hospital was your wife. We experimented for your good; but we were wrong. The gods resent experiments. In the path of orthodox monotony alone lieth safety. So perish all reform!"

But the man thought otherwise.

---

[1] *Peste* Curse or exclamation of anger.

[2] *arrears* I.e., a backlog.

from Olive Schreiner, *Woman and Labour* (1911)

from CHAPTER 5
SEX DIFFERENCES

If we examine the physical phenomenon of sex as it manifests itself in the human creature, we find, in the first stages of the individual's existence, no difference discernible, by any means we have at present at our command, between those germs which are ultimately to become male or female. Later, in the fetal life, at birth, and through infancy, though the organs of sex serve to distinguish the male from the female, there is in the general structure and working of the organism little or nothing to divide the sexes.

Even when puberty is reached, with its enormous development of sexual and reproductive activity modifying those parts of the organism with which it is concerned, and producing certain secondary sexual characteristics, there yet remains the major extent of the human body and of physical function little, or not at all, affected by sex modification. The eye, the ear, the sense of touch, the general organs of nutrition and respiration and volition are in the main identical, and often differ far more in persons of the same sex than in those of opposite sexes; and even on the dissecting-table the tissues of the male and female are often wholly indistinguishable.

It is when we consider the reproductive organs themselves and their forms of activity, and such parts of the organism modified directly in relation to them, that a real and important difference is found to exist, radical though absolutely complemental. It is exactly as we approach the reproductive functions that the male and female bodies differ; exactly as we recede from them that they become more and more similar, and even absolutely identical. Taking the eye, perhaps the most highly developed, complex organ in the body, and, if of an organ the term may be allowed, the most intellectual organ of sense, we find it remains the same in male and female in structure, in appearance, and in function throughout life; while the breast, closely connected with reproduction, though absolutely identical in both forms in infancy, assumes a widely different organisation when reproductive activity is actually concerned.

When we turn to the psychic phase of human life an exactly analogous phenomenon presents itself. The intelligence, emotions, and desires of the human infant at birth differ not at all perceptibly, as its sex may be male or female; and such psychic differences as appear to exist in later childhood are undoubtedly very largely the result of artificial training, forcing on the appearance of psychic sexual divergencies long before they would tend spontaneously to appear; as where sports and occupations are interdicted[1] to young children on the ground of their supposed sexual unfitness; as when an infant female is forcibly prevented from climbing or shouting, and the infant male from amusing himself with needle and thread or dolls. Even in the fully adult human, and in spite of differences of training, the psychic activities over a large extent of life appear to be absolutely identical. The male and female brains acquire languages, solve mathematical problems, and master scientific detail in a manner wholly indistinguishable; as illustrated by the fact that in modern universities the papers sent in by male and female candidates are as a rule absolutely identical in type. Placed in like external conditions, their tastes and emotions, over a vast part of the surface of life, are identical; and, in an immense number of those cases where psychic sex differences appear to exist, subject to rigid analysis they are found to be purely artificial creations, for, when other races or classes are studied, they are found non-existent as sexual characteristics; as when the female is supposed by ignorant persons in modern European societies to have an inherent love for bright colours and ornaments, not shared by the male; while experience of other societies and past social conditions prove that it is as often the male who has been even more desirous of attiring himself in bright raiment[2] and adorning himself with brilliant jewels; or as when, among certain tribes of savages, the use of tobacco is supposed to be a peculiarly

female prerogative, while, in some modern societies, it is supposed to have some relation to masculinity.[3]

But there remain certain psychic differences in attitude, on the part of male and female as such, which are inherent and not artificial: and, in the psychic human world, it is exactly as we approach the sphere of sexual and reproductive activity, with those emotions and instincts connected directly with sex and the reproduction of the race, that a difference does appear. ...

... [A]like in the sports, and joys, and sorrows of infancy; alike in the non-sexual labours of life; alike even in the possession of that initial instinct which draws sex to sex, and which, differing slightly in its forms of manifestation, is of corresponding intensity in both; the moment actual reproduction begins to take place, the man and the woman enter spheres of sensation, perception, emotion, desire, and knowledge which are not, and

---

[3] [Schreiner's note] The savage male of today when attired in his paint, feathers, cats' tails and necklaces is an immeasurably more ornamented and imposing figure than his female, even when fully attired for a dance in beads and bangles: the Oriental male has sometimes scarcely been able to walk under the weight of his ornaments; and the males of Europe a couple of centuries ago, with their powdered wigs, lace ruffles and cuffs, paste buckles, feathered cocked hats, and patches were quite as ridiculous in their excess of adornment as the complementary females of their own day, or the most parasitic females of this. ["Parasitism" is Schreiner's term for the condition of idle dependency to which, as she argues earlier in *Woman and Labour*, women are being reduced by modern technological and economic changes, which are causing women's "ancient fields of domestic labour" to "slip from (them)."] Both in the class and the individual, whether male or female, an intense love of dress and meretricious [superficial] external adornment is almost invariably the concomitant and outcome of parasitism. Were the parasite female class in our own societies today to pass away, French fashions with their easeless and grotesque variations (shaped not for use or beauty, but the attracting of attention) would die out. And the extent to which any woman today, not herself belonging to the parasite class and still labouring, attempts to follow afar off the fashions of the parasite, may be taken generally as an almost certain indication of the ease with which she would accept parasitism were its conditions offered her. The tendency of the cultured and intellectually labouring woman of today to adopt a more rational type of attire, less shaped to attract attention to the individual than to confer comfort and abstain from impeding activity, is often spoken of as an attempt on the part of woman slavishly to imitate man. What is really taking place is, that like causes are producing like effects on human creatures with common characteristics.

---

[1] *interdicted* Forbidden.
[2] *raiment* Clothing.

cannot be, absolutely identical. Between the man who, in an instant of light-hearted enjoyment, begets the infant (who may even beget it in a state of half-drunken unconsciousness, and may easily know nothing of its existence for months or years after it is born, or never at all; and who under no circumstances can have any direct sensational knowledge of its relation to himself) and the woman who bears it continuously for months within her body, and who gives birth to it in pain, and who, if it is to live, is compelled, or was in primitive times, to nourish it for months from the blood of her own being—between these, there exists of necessity, towards a limited but all-important body of human interests and phenomena, a certain distinct psychic attitude. At this one point, the two great halves of humanity stand confronting certain great elements in human existence, from angles that are not identical. From the moment the universal initial attraction of sex to sex becomes incarnate in the first concrete sexual act till the developed offspring attains maturity, no step in the reproductive journey, or in their relation to their offspring, has been quite identical for the man and the woman. And this divergence of experiences in human relations must react on their attitude towards that particular body of human concerns which directly is connected with the sexual reproduction of the race; and, it is exactly in these fields of human activity, where sex as sex is concerned, that woman as woman has a part to play · which she cannot resign into the hands of others.

It may be truly said that in the laboratory, the designing-room, the factory, the mart,[1] the mathematician's study, and in all fields of purely abstract or impersonal labour, while the entrance of woman would add to the net result of human labour in those fields, and though a grave injustice is done to the individual woman excluded from perhaps the only field she is fitted to excel in, that yet woman as woman has probably little or nothing to contribute in those fields that is radically distinct from that which man might supply; there would be a difference in quantity but probably

none in kind, in the work done for the race.

But in those spheres of social activity, dealing especially with certain relations between human creatures because of their diverse if complementary relation to the production of human life, the sexes as sexes have often each a part to play which the other cannot play for them; have each a knowledge gained from phases of human experience, which the other cannot supply; here woman as woman has something radically distinct to contribute to the sum-total of human knowledge, and her activity is of importance, not merely individually, but collectively, and as a class.

That demand, which today in all democratic self-governing countries is being made by women, to be accorded their share in the electoral, and ultimately in the legislative and executive duties of government, is based on two grounds: the wider, and more important, that they find nothing in the nature of their sex-function which exonerates them, as human beings, from their obligation to take part in the labours of guidance and government in their state: the narrower, but yet important ground, that, in as far as in one direction, *i.e.*, in the special form of their sex function takes, they do differ from the male, they, in so far, form a class and are bound to represent the interests of, and to give the state the benefit of, the insight of their class, in certain directions.

Those persons who imagine that the balance of great political parties in almost any society would be seriously changed by the admission of its women in public functions are undoubtedly wholly wrong. The fundamental division of humans into those inclined to hold by the past and defend whatever is, and those hopeful of the future and inclined to introduce change, would probably be found to exist in much the same proportion were the males or the females of any given society compared: and the males and females of each class will in the main share the faults, the virtues, and the prejudices of their class. The individuals may lose by being excluded on the ground of sex from a share of public labour, and by being robbed of a portion of their lawful individual weight in their own society; and the society as a whole may lose by having a smaller number to select

---

[1] *mart* Market.

its chosen labourers from; yet, undoubtedly, on the mass of social, political, and international questions, the conclusions arrived at by one sex would be exactly those arrived at by the other.

Were a body of humans elected to adjudicate upon Greek accents, or to pass a decision on the relative fineness of woollens and linens, the form of sex of the persons composing it would probably have no bearing on the result; there is no rational ground for supposing that, on a question of Greek accents or the thickness of cloths, equally instructed males and females would differ. Here sex plays no part. The experience and instructedness of the individuals would tell:[1] their sexual attributes would be indifferent.[2]

But there are points, comparatively small, even very small, in number, yet of vital importance to human life, in which sex does play a part.

It is not a matter of indifference whether the body called to adjudicate upon the questions, whether the temporary sale of the female body for sexual purposes shall or shall not be a form of traffic encouraged and recognised by the state; or whether one law shall exist for the licentious human female and another for the licentious human male; whether the claim of the female to the offspring she bears shall or shall not equal that of the male who begets it; whether an act of infidelity on the part of the male shall or shall not terminate the contract which binds his female companion to him, as completely as an act of infidelity on her part would terminate her claim on him; it is not a matter of indifference whether a body elected to adjudicate on such points as these consists of males solely, or females solely, or of both combined. As it consists of one, or the other,

or of both, so not only will the answers vary, but, in some cases, will they be completely diverse.[3] Here we come into that very narrow, but important, region, where sex as sex manifestly plays its part; where the male as male and the female as female have each their body of perceptions and experiences, which they do not hold in common; here one sex cannot adequately represent the other. It is here that each sexual part has something radically distinct to contribute to the wisdom of the race.

We, today, take all labour for our province! We seek to enter the non-sexual fields of intellectual or physical toil, because we are unable to see today, with regard to them, any dividing wall raised by sex which excludes us from them. We are yet equally determined to enter those in which sex difference does play its part, because it is here that woman, the bearer of the race, must stand side by side with man, the begetter; if a completed human wisdom, an insight that misses no aspect of human life, and an activity that is in harmony with the entire knowledge and the entire instinct of the entire human race, is to exist. It is here that the man cannot act for the woman nor the woman for the man; but both must interact. It is here that each sexual half of the race, so closely and indistinguishably blended elsewhere, has its own distinct contribution to make to the sum total of human knowledge and human wisdom. Neither is the woman without the man, nor the man without the woman, the completed human intelligence.

Therefore—*We claim, today, all labour for our province!* Those large fields in which it would appear sex plays no part, and equally those smaller in which it plays a part.

---

[1] *tell* Have an impact.
[2] *indifferent* Unimportant.
[3] *diverse* I.e., divergent.

CHARLOTTE MEW
1869 – 1928

Charlotte Mew, though she did not attain great fame, was beloved by her contemporaries in the literary world: Thomas Hardy, a close friend, called her "far and away the best living woman poet—who will be read when others are forgotten," while Virginia Woolf declared her to be "very good and interesting and unlike anyone else." Occupying a transitional space between Victorian and Modern literature, Charlotte Mew's oeuvre is distinctive for its formally complex, carefully structured verse and for its radical treatment of gender and sexuality. Mew's writing is also notable for its emotional intensity: many of her works evoke personal loss, unrequited love, and insanity, while others deal with isolation, loneliness, and sorrow.

Mew was born in London to Fred Mew, an architect, and Anna Maria Marden Kendall, who bore seven children but lost three in infancy. Two other siblings were eventually consigned to asylums for the mentally ill, and this experience left its pall over both Charlotte and her sister Anne, who vowed never to marry for fear of perpetuating the family history of schizophrenia. Though Mew's poems and stories are generally not autobiographical, their tone and subject matter is often informed by the suffering of her family, including many years spent in poverty.

Mew first came to the public's attention in 1894, when her short story "Passed" appeared in *The Yellow Book*, but it was with the publication of her poem "The Farmer's Bride" in a 1912 edition of *The Nation* that she truly arrived on London's literary scene. The poem is written from the point of view and in the dialect of a farmer, whose wife tries unsuccessfully to flee from him at the beginning of the marriage. Mew wrote in a letter after the publication of her first volume of poetry, *The Farmer's Bride* (1916), that she strove to present "not only the cry but the gesture and the accent … calling up witnesses to the real thing!" She became known as an eccentric personality with short hair who wore men's suits and smoked and swore—and who also wrote exquisite poems full of despair and pathos. The suffering in her poetry often mirrored the "real thing" of her life, with its unrequited love for Ella D'Arcy, an editor of *The Yellow Book*, and later for the novelist May Sinclair, who was said to have spurned Mew cruelly.

After her sister Anne—her only remaining family member and the one with whom she had lived her entire life—died of cancer in 1927, Mew fell into a deep depression and began suffering delusions. She checked herself into a nursing home, where she died by suicide less than a year later. Her friend Alida Monro edited a posthumous collection surveying Mew's poetic career, published in 1929 as *The Rambling Sailor*. Despite the acclaim of her peers—and of a few mid-century poets such as Marianne Moore—Mew's work was largely neglected until the late twentieth century, when it received a resurgence of critical interest.

⌘ ⌘ ⌘

The Farmer's Bride

*He asked life of thee, and thou gavest him a long life:
even forever and ever.*[1]

Three summers since I chose a maid,
  Too young maybe—but more's to do
At harvest-time than bide and woo.
  When us was wed she turned afraid
5 Of love and me and all things human;
Like the shut of a winter's day.
Her smile went out, and 'twasn't a woman—
  More like a little frightened fay.°   *fairy*
    One night, in the fall, she runned away.

10 "Out 'mong the sheep, her be," they said,
  Should properly have been abed;
  But sure enough she wasn't there
  Lying awake with her wide brown stare.
So over seven-acre field and up-along across the down
15   We chased her, flying like a hare
  Before our lanterns. To Church-Town
    All in a shiver and a scare
  We caught her, fetched her home at last
    And turned the key upon her, fast.

20 She does the work about the house
  As well as most, but like a mouse:
    Happy enough to chat and play

With birds and rabbits and such as they,
  So long as men-folk keep away.
25 "Not near, not near!" her eyes beseech
When one of us comes within reach.
  The women say that beasts in stall
  Look round like children at her call.
  I've hardly heard her speak at all.

30 Shy as a leveret,° swift as he,   *young hare*
Straight and slight as a young larch tree,
Sweet as the first wild violets, she,
To her wild self. But what to me?

The short days shorten and the oaks are brown,
35   The blue smoke rises to the low grey sky,
One leaf in the still air falls slowly down,
    A magpie's spotted feathers lie
On the black earth spread white with rime,°   *frost*
The berries redden up to Christmas-time.
40   What's Christmas-time without there be
    Some other in the house than we!

  She sleeps up in the attic there
  Alone, poor maid. 'Tis but a stair
Betwixt us. Oh! my God! the down,
45 The soft young down of her, the brown,
The brown of her—her eyes, her hair, her hair!
—1912

Madeleine[2] in Church

Here, in the darkness, where this plaster saint
  Stands nearer than God stands to our distress,
And one small candle shines, but not so faint
    As the far lights of everlastingness

---

1 *He asked … ever* From Psalms 21.4.

2 *Madeleine* "Madeleine" is an alternate spelling for Magdalene, and an allusion to the biblical Mary Magdalene.
Although nowhere in the Bible is Mary Magdalene named a prostitute, that has been a frequent historical speculation.
Hence "Magdalene" has become an epithet for a prostitute or for a woman whose sexual behavior is unconventional.

5 I'd rather kneel than over there, in open day
  Where Christ is hanging, rather pray
   To something more like my own clay,
    Not too divine;
   For, once, perhaps my little saint
10   Before he got his niche and crown,
  Had one short stroll about the town;
  It brings him closer, just that taint
   And anyone can wash the paint
  Off our poor faces, his and mine!

15 Is that why I see Monty now? equal to any saint, poor boy, as good as gold,
But still, with just the proper trace
Of earthliness on his shining wedding face;
And then gone suddenly blank and old
The hateful day of the divorce:
20 Stuart got his, hands down, of course
Crowing like twenty cocks and grinning like a horse:
But Monty took it hard. All said and done I liked him best—
He was the first, he stands out clearer than the rest.
    It seems too funny all we other rips°   *worthless people*
25   Should have immortal souls; Monty and Redge quite damnably
  Keep theirs afloat while we go down like scuttled° ships. *deliberately sunk*
    It's funny too, how easily we sink,
    One might put up a monument, I think
    To half the world and cut across it "Lost at Sea!"
30 I should drown Jim, poor little sparrow, if I netted him tonight—
    No, it's no use this penny light—
   Or my poor saint with his tin-pot crown—
   The trees of Calvary[1] are where they were,
    When we are sure that we can spare
35   The tallest, let us go and strike it down
  And leave the other two still standing there.
    I, too, would ask him to remember me
If there were any paradise beyond this earth that I could see.[2]

    Oh! quiet Christ who never knew
40   The poisonous fangs that bite us through
    And make us do the things we do,
    See how we suffer and fight and die,

---

[1] *trees of Calvary* I.e., crucifixes. Christ was crucified with two criminals at Calvary.

[2] *I, too … could see* See Luke 23.39–43.

How helpless and how low we lie,
God holds You, and You hang so high,
45   Though no one looking long at You,
Can think You do not suffer too,
But, up there, from your still, starlighted tree
What can You know, what can You really see
Of this dark ditch, the soul of me!

50   We are what we are: when I was half a child I could not sit
Watching black shadows on green lawns and red carnations burning in the sun,
Without paying so heavily for it
That joy and pain, like any mother and her unborn child were almost one.
I could hardly bear
55   The dreams upon the eyes of white geraniums in the dusk,
The thick, close voice of musk,
The jessamine° music on the thin night air,   *jasmine*
Or, sometimes, my own hands about me anywhere—
The sight of my own face (for it was lovely then) even the scent of my own hair,
60   Oh! there was nothing, nothing that did not sweep to the high seat
Of laughing gods, and then blow down and beat
My soul into the highway dust, as hoofs do the dropped roses of the street.
I think my body was my soul,
And when we are made thus
65   Who shall control
Our hands, our eyes, the wandering passion of our feet,
Who shall teach us
To thrust the world out of our heart; to say, till perhaps in death,
When the race is run,
70   And it is forced from us with our last breath
"Thy will be done"?[1]
If it is Your will that we should be content with the tame, bloodless things,
As pale as angels smirking by, with folded wings.
Oh! I know virtue, and the peace it brings!
75   The temperate, well-worn smile
The one man gives you, when you are evermore his own:
And afterwards the child's, for a little while,
With its unknowing and all-seeing eyes
So soon to change, and make you feel how quick
80   The clock goes round. If one had learned the trick—
(How does one though?) quite early on,

---

[1] *Thy will be done* The Lord's Prayer, from Matthew 6.10.

Of long green pastures under placid skies,
One might be walking now with patient truth.
What did we ever care for it, who have asked for youth,
85   When, oh! my God! this is going or has gone?

There is a portrait of my mother, at nineteen,
With the black spaniel, standing by the garden seat,
The dainty head held high against the painted green
And throwing out the youngest smile, shy, but half haughty and half sweet.
90   Her picture then: but simply Youth, or simply Spring
        To me today: a radiance on the wall,
        So exquisite, so heartbreaking a thing
      Beside the mask that I remember, shrunk and small,
        Sapless and lined like a dead leaf,
95 All that was left of oh! the loveliest face, by time and grief!

And in the glass, last night, I saw a ghost behind my chair—
Yet why remember it, when one can still go moderately gay—?
      Or could—with any one of the old crew,
        But oh! these boys! the solemn way
100   They take you, and the things they say—
      This "I have only as long as you"
When you remind them you are not precisely twenty-two—
      Although at heart perhaps—God! if it were
        Only the face, only the hair!
105   If Jim had written to me as he did today
      A year ago—and now it leaves me cold—
        I know what this means, old, old, *old!*
        Et avec ça—mais on a vécu, tout se paie.[1]

That is not always true: there was my mother—(well at least the dead are free!)
110   Yoked to the man that Father was; yoked to the woman I am, Monty too;
      The little portress at the convent school, stewing in hell so patiently;
The poor, fair boy who shot himself at Aix. And what of me—and what of me?
      But I, I paid for what I had, and they for nothing. No, one cannot see
      How it shall be made up to them in some serene eternity.
115 If there were fifty heavens God could not give us back the child who went or never came;
      Here, on our little patch of this great earth, the sun of any darkened day,
Not one of all the starry buds hung on the hawthorn trees of last year's May,
      No shadow from the sloping fields of yesterday;

---

[1] *Et avec ... paie* French: And with this—in living, everything has its cost.

For every hour they slant across the hedge a different way,
120   The shadows are never the same.

        "Find rest in Him"[1] One knows the parsons' tags—
Back to the fold, across the evening fields, like any flock of baaing sheep:
Yes, it may be, when He has shorn, led us to slaughter, torn the bleating soul in us to rags,
           For so He giveth His belovèd sleep.[2]
125   Oh! He will take us stripped and done,
           Driven into His heart. So we are won:
Then safe, safe are we? in the shelter of His everlasting wings—
I do not envy Him his victories. His arms are full of broken things.

          But I shall not be in them. Let Him take
130   The finer ones, the easier to break.
And they are not gone, yet, for me, the lights, the colours, the perfumes,
          Though now they speak rather in sumptuous rooms,
           In silks and in gemlike wines;
          Here, even, in this corner where my little candle shines
135   And overhead the lancet-window[3] glows
           With golds and crimsons you could almost drink
To know how jewels taste, just as I used to think
There was the scent in every red and yellow rose
           Of all the sunsets. But this place is grey,
140   And much too quiet. No one here,
           Why, this is awful, this is fear!
           Nothing to see, no face,
         Nothing to hear except your heart beating in space
           As if the world was ended. Dead at last!
145   Dead soul, dead body, tied together fast.
          These to go on with and alone, to the slow end:
       No one to sit with, really, or to speak to, friend to friend:
          Out of the long procession, black or white or red
Not one left now to say "Still I am here, then see you, dear, lay here your head."
150   Only the doll's house looking on the park
        Tonight, all nights, I know, when the man puts the lights out, very dark.
With, upstairs, in the blue and gold box of a room, just the maids' footsteps overhead,
Then utter silence and the empty world—the room—the bed—
          The corpse! No, not quite dead, while this cries out in me,

---

[1] *Find rest in Him*   From Matthew 11.29.

[2] *For so ... sleep*   From Psalms 127.2.

[3] *lancet-window*   Narrow, pointed window, a common feature of Gothic architecture.

155   But nearly: very soon to be
           A handful of forgotten dust—
       There must be someone. Christ! there must,
           Tell me there *will* be some one. Who?
       If there were no one else, could it be You?

160   How old was Mary out of whom You cast
       So many devils?[1] Was she young or perhaps for years
   She had sat staring, with dry eyes, at this and that man going past
       Till suddenly she saw You on the steps of Simon's house[2]
       And stood and looked at You through tears.[3]

165   I think she must have known by those
       The thing, for what it was that had come to her.
       For some of us there is a passion, I suppose
       So far from earthly cares and earthly fears
       That in its stillness you can hardly stir

170   Or in its nearness, lift your hand,
       So great that you have simply got to stand
       Looking at it through tears, through tears.
       Then straight from these there broke the kiss,
           I think You must have known by this

175   The thing for what it was, that had come to You:
           She did not love You like the rest,
       It was in her own way, but at the worst, the best,
           She gave You something altogether new.
           And through it all, from her, no word,

180   She scarcely saw You, scarcely heard:
       Surely You knew when she so touched You with her hair,
           Or by the wet cheek lying there,
   And while her perfume clung to You from head to feet all through the day
       That You can change the things for which we care,

185   But even You, unless You kill us, not the way.

       This, then was peace for her, but passion too.
       I wonder was it like a kiss that once I knew,
           The only one that I would care to take
   Into the grave with me, to which if there were afterwards, to wake.

---

1 *How old ... devils* See Luke 8.2 and Mark 16.9.

2 *Simon's house* I.e., Simon the Pharisee.

3 *Till suddenly ... tears* See Luke 7.37–50 for the biblical account of the story that follows, in which one unnamed woman "who was a sinner" washed Christ's feet with her tears, dried them with her hair, and anointed them with perfume.

190   Almost as happy as the carven dead
            In some dim chancel[1] lying head by head
        We slept with it, but face to face, the whole night through—
One breath, one throbbing quietness, as if the thing behind our lips was endless life,
      Lost, as I woke, to hear in the strange earthly dawn, his "Are you there?"

195   And lie still, listening to the wind outside, among the firs.

      So Mary chose the dream of Him for what was left to her of night and day,
It is the only truth: it is the dream in us that neither life nor death nor any other thing can
      away:
      But if she had not touched Him in the doorway of the dream could she have cared so much?
      She was a sinner, we are what we are: the spirit afterwards, but first, the touch.

200 And He has never shared with me my haunted house beneath the trees
Of Eden and Calvary, with its ghosts that have not any eyes for tears,
And the happier guests who would not see, or if they did, remember these,
           Though they lived there a thousand years.
        Outside, too gravely looking at me, He seems to stand,
205   And looking at Him, if my forgotten spirit came
           Unwillingly back, what could it claim
             Of those calm eyes, that quiet speech,
         Breaking like a slow tide upon the beach,
            The scarred, not quite human hand?—
210   Unwillingly back to the burden of old imaginings
          When it has learned so long not to think, not to be,
      Again, again it would speak as it has spoken to me of things
            That I shall not see!

      I cannot bear to look at this divinely bent and gracious head:
215   When I was small I never quite believed that He was dead:
          And at the Convent school I used to lie awake in bed
        Thinking about His hands.[2] It did not matter what they said,
He was alive to me, so hurt, so hurt! And most of all in Holy Week[3]
           When there was no one else to see
220   I used to think it would not hurt me too, so terribly,
           If He had ever seemed to notice me
           Or, if, for once, He would only speak.

—1916

---

[1] *chancel*   Area surrounding a church's altar.

[2] *His hands*   Christ's hands were nailed to the cross on which he was crucified.

[3] *Holy Week*   Week of the Christian calendar in which the events of Christ's passion, death, and resurrection are commemorated.

Sarojini Naidu
1879 – 1949

Called "the nightingale of India" by Mahatma Gandhi, Sarojini Naidu achieved international renown not only as a poet but also as a politician and activist who played a major role both in the nationalist struggle for Indian independence and in the fight to establish women's suffrage in the newly independent nation. Her strong political commitments are reflected in her poetry, which is passionately engaged with Indian cultural realties, and in the rhetorically powerful speeches she delivered on a national and global stage.

Born in the city of Hyderabad, the state capital of Telangana in contemporary India, on 13 February 1879, Sarojini Chattopadhyay was the eldest child of the well-known Bengali poet Barada Devi and of Aghorenath Chattopadhyay, the founder and principal of the Nizam's College in Hyderabad. Both her parents were members of Brahmo Samaj, an offshoot of Hinduism that rejected the caste system and held progressive views on gender relations and women's education. Naidu's father was a brilliant scientist who retained a lifelong fascination with the medieval science of alchemy. However, as an outspoken critic of the British government and a dedicated social reformer, he remained very connected to social realities of colonial India. Naidu grew up with seven talented siblings in a house filled with numerous pets, art, music, and a never-ending flow of eclectic guests including reformers, musicians, actors, writers, and scholars. That her first collection of poetry in English, *The Golden Threshold* (1905), was named after this house is a testament to the influence of her family and her home on her writing.

Naidu had a complicated relationship with the English language: as a nine-year-old, Naidu stubbornly refused to speak in English and was sent to her room by her father as punishment. When she came out of her room at the end of the day, she refused to communicate in any other language but English with her parents. Later in life, although proficient in Urdu, Telugu, Bengali, Hindi, and Persian, Naidu chose English as the medium for her speaking and writing.

A child prodigy, Naidu passed the Madras University matriculation examinations in her early teens, during which time she also wrote long poems and essays modeled after the British poets. As a young teenager she experienced bouts of serious illness and conducted a love affair with an older man of lower caste, Dr. Govindarajulu Naidu, against the wishes of her parents. At fifteen, Naidu traveled to England, where she continued her education at King's College, London, and then Girton College in Cambridge. While she returned to India after three years to marry Naidu, with whom she had continued an epistolary relationship, the years spent in England were important for the development of her original poetic voice and vision. In England, Naidu met Edmund Gosse, Arthur Symons, and W.B. Yeats, among other poets. Although Gosse and Symons' literary mentorship partly sprang from a place of Orientalist fascination for what Gosse described as "tropical and primitive" emotion and Symons called "Eastern magic" in her person and poetry, they spurred Naidu on to write poems more rooted in India. Following the advice of her mentors, Naidu reinvented herself as an artist specifically of India and destroyed the first volume of her poetry, written in imitation of British Romantic writers. After having four children in quick succession between the years of 1901 and 1904, Naidu was persuaded by Arthur Symons to publish her first book of poetry, *The Golden Threshold* (1905). This was followed by two other collections, *The Bird of Time: Songs of Life, Death and the Spring* (1912) and *The Broken Wing: Songs of Love, Death and Destiny, 1915–1916* (1917), which were well-received in the English press and brought her renown in India. In her poems, Naidu skillfully presented glimpses of everyday life, nature, and landscape drawn from the Deccan region in southern India as well as incorporating mythology and historical figures into her poetry. With each new volume, her work became increasingly patriotic, with several poems imploring a slumbering nation to awaken and usher in a future of secular harmony and freedom.

Through her friendship with Gopal Krishna Gokhale, a senior leader in the Indian National Congress, Naidu gradually became an active participant in political and social movements. Soon, she was a prominent figure in the Indian freedom movement: in powerful speeches delivered all across India, she addressed women's education, universal suffrage, communal harmony, labor rights, and India's need for self-governance. In fact, her status as a poet was somewhat eclipsed by her brilliance as an orator. Naidu was awarded the *Kaiser-e-Hind* medal by the British government in 1908 for her role in the relief efforts during the plague epidemic in India; she returned this award to protest the April 1919 Jallianwala Bagh massacre. In 1917, with the English writer and activist Annie Besant, Naidu co-founded the Women's India Association, an organization focused on women's rights.

In 1925 Naidu became the second woman to be elected president of the Indian National Congress, and she was instrumental in persuading the party to champion women's right to vote—and to follow through with their commitment to universal suffrage when India gained independence in 1947. Between 1930 and 1942, Naidu was sent to jail several times by the British colonial government because of her role in the *Satyagraha* (non-violent civil disobedience) protest against the exorbitant salt tax—especially as she emerged as one of the movement's prominent leaders after the imprisonment of Mahatma Gandhi. After independence, Naidu served as the first woman governor of Uttar Pradesh, a state in northern India, until her death in 1949.

In a 1913 letter to the well-known litterateur Rabindranath Tagore, Naidu describes herself as "a woman, a poet, and patriot." Indeed, both her poetry and oratory, working in tandem, articulate a vision for a self-governed, diverse, and egalitarian India.

⌘ ⌘ ⌘

Indian Weavers

Weavers, weaving at break of day,
   Why do you weave a garment so gay? ...
Blue as the wing of a halcyon[1] wild,
We weave the robes of a new-born child.

5 Weavers, weaving at fall of night,
   Why do you weave a garment so bright? ...
Like the plumes of a peacock, purple and green,
We weave the marriage-veils of a queen.

Weavers, weaving solemn and still,
10 What do you weave in the moonlight chill? ...
White as a feather and white as a cloud,
We weave a dead man's funeral shroud.
   —1905

---

[1] *halcyon* Kingfisher, a bird with bright blue wings.

Indian Dancers[1]

Eyes ravished with rapture, celestially panting,
    what passionate bosoms aflaming with fire
Drink deep of the hush of the hyacinth heavens that
    glimmer around them in fountains of light;
O wild and entrancing the strain of keen music that
    cleaveth the stars like a wail of desire,
And beautiful dancers with *houri*-like[2] faces bewitch
    the voluptuous watches of night.

5   The scents of red roses and sandalwood flutter and die
        in the maze of their gem-tangled hair,
And smiles are entwining like magical serpents the
        poppies of lips that are opiate-sweet;
Their glittering garments of purple are burning like
        tremulous dawns in the quivering air,
And exquisite, subtle and slow are the tinkle and tread
        of their rhythmical, slumber-soft feet.

Now silent, now singing and swaying and swinging,
        like blossoms that bend to the breezes or showers,
10 Now wantonly winding, they flash, now they falter,
        and lingering, languish in radiant choir;
Their jewel-girt arms and warm, wavering, lily-long
        fingers enchant through melodious hours,
Eyes ravished with rapture, celestially panting, what
        passionate bosoms aflaming with fire!
—1896 (REVISED 1905)

Nightfall in the City of Hyderabad[3]

See how the speckled sky burns like a pigeon's throat,
Jewelled with embers of opal and peridote.

See the white river that flashes and scintillates,
Curved like a tusk from the mouth of the city-gates.

5   Hark, from the minaret, how the *muezzin's*[4] call
Floats like a battle-flag over the city wall.

From trellised balconies, languid and luminous
Faces gleam, veiled in a splendour voluminous.

Leisurely elephants wind through the winding lanes,
10 Swinging their silver bells hung from their silver chains.

Round the high Char Minar[5] sound of gay cavalcades
Blend with the music of cymbals and serenades.

Over the city bridge Night comes majestical,
Borne like a queen to a sumptuous festival.
—1905

Street Cries

When dawn's first cymbals beat upon the sky,
    Rousing the world to labour's various cry,
To tend the flock, to bind the mellowing grain,
From ardent toil to forge a little gain,
5   And fasting men go forth on hurrying feet,
Buy bread, buy bread, rings down the eager street.

When the earth falters and the waters swoon
With the implacable radiance of noon,
And in dim shelters koils[6] hush their notes,
10 And the faint, thirsting blood in languid throats
Craves liquid succor from the cruel heat,
Buy fruit, buy fruit, steals down the panting street.

---

1   *Indian Dancers*   This poem was originally published under the title "Eastern Dancers."

2   *houri*   In Islam, beautiful women who await the faithful in Paradise.

3   *Hyderabad*   Largest city in and capital of the southern state of Telangana in contemporary India. At the time of the writing of the poem, Hyderabad was the princely state ruled by the Nizam Osman Ali Khan.

4   *muezzin*   Cleric who calls Muslims to pray from the minaret of a mosque.

5   *Char Minar*   Famous mosque and minaret located in the city of Hyderabad.

6   *koils*   The Asian Koel (a genus of cuckoo) is a small bird known for its melodious call; it is found in the Indian subcontinent, China, and Southeast Asia.

When twilight twinkling o'er the gay bazaars,
Unfurls a sudden canopy of stars,
15   When lutes are strung and fragrant torches lit
On white roof-terraces where lovers sit
Drinking together of life's poignant sweet,
Buy flowers, buy flowers, floats down the singing street.
—1905

To India

O young through all thy immemorial years!
  Rise, Mother, rise, regenerate from thy gloom,
And, like a bride high-mated with the spheres,
Beget new glories from thine ageless womb!

5   The nations that in fettered darkness weep
Crave thee to lead them where great mornings break ....
Mother, O Mother, wherefore dost thou sleep?
Arise and answer for thy children's sake!

Thy Future calls thee with a manifold sound
10   To crescent honours, splendours, victories vast;
Waken, O slumbering Mother and be crowned,
Who once wert empress of the sovereign Past.
—1905

Village-Song

Honey, child, honey, child, whither are you going?
  Would you cast your jewels all to the breezes
    blowing?
Would you leave the mother who on golden grain
  has fed you?
Would you grieve the lover who is riding forth to
  wed you?

5   Mother mine, to the wild forest I am going,
Where upon the *champa*[1] boughs the *champa* buds
  are blowing;
To the *köil*-haunted[2] river-isles where lotus lilies
  glisten,
The voices of the fairy folk are calling me: O listen!

Honey, child, honey, child, the world is full of pleasure,
10   Of bridal-songs and cradle-songs and sandal-scented
  leisure.
Your bridal robes are in the loom, silver and saffron
  glowing,
Your bridal cakes are on the hearth: O whither are
  you going?

The bridal-songs and cradle-songs have cadences of
  sorrow,
The laughter of the sun to-day, the wind of death
  to-morrow.
15   Far sweeter sound the forest-notes where
  forest-streams are falling;
O mother mine, I cannot stay, the fairy-folk are
  calling.
—1905

---

[1]   *champa*   Evergreen tree found in India and other southern Asian countries. The tree bears fragrant white flowers with long and thin petals.

[2]   *köil-haunted*   The Asian Koel (a genus of cuckoo) is a small bird known for its melodious call; it is found in the Indian subcontinent, China, and Southeast Asia.

ROKEYA SAKHAWAT HOSSAIN
1880 – 1932

The Bengali feminist Sarala Roy wrote of Rokeya Sakhawat Hossain, also known by her aristocratic honorific "Begum Rokeya," that her "very large heart … bled only for the improvement of the education of her own sex of the country." Through her writing and activism, Rokeya consistently advocated for women's education, liberation, and social and economic equality during the British rule in India. Her literary output—which comprises numerous essays, poems, short stories, and a novel in Bengali as well as a handful of works written in English—criticizes the social inequality of women in Bengali society, caused by its patriarchal practices and women's inequitable access to education, and outlines an alternative vision. She is celebrated today as a prominent figure in the early women's rights movement in South Asia and as the first and most notable Muslim female writer of the Bengali Renaissance, the late nineteenth- and early twentieth-century intellectual and artistic movement that established Bengal as a cultural and literary center of international significance. Shortly after her death in 1932, her fellow writer and countryman Kazi Abdul Wadud mused, "Among those living and dead, very few stand out as genuine Muslim writers[.] … Perhaps history will recognize Mrs. R.S. Hossain as the best among them. Mrs. R.S. Hossain occupies a lofty place not only among the Bengali Muslim writers but among all the female writers in the language."

Rokeya was born in 1880 in the village of Pairaband in what is now Bangladesh, then part of the province of Bengal in British India. She was the third of five children in an upper-class, conservative Muslim family. Her father, Jahiruddin Muhammad Abu Ali Haidar Saber, was the *zamindar*, or landlord, of the village. Rokeya's mother, Rahatunnessa Sabera Chaudhurani, was Saber's first wife. Rokeya and her sister Karimunnesa, a poet whose talent Rokeya felt was never properly recognized due to her sex, were taught to observe the strictest form of purdah (the cultural and religious practice of secluding and veiling women) beginning when they were as young as five years old. This restrictive upbringing shaped Rokeya's feminist views, and she frequently criticized the practice of extreme purdah in her writing.

While Rokeya herself received no formal education, her brothers were educated at St. Xavier's College in Kolkata (or Calcutta, as it was known at the time). Her eldest brother, Ibrahim, took pains to teach Rokeya both English and Bengali. Though Bengali was the common language of their homeland, the Saber family spoke Urdu at home, as Rokeya's father believed Bengali, a language of Hindu origin, to be inferior and a corrupting intrusion on their traditional Islamic cultural values. Rokeya's language lessons with her brother therefore took place in secret late at night, after their father had gone to bed. Bengali became Rokeya's language of choice for her writing, enabling her to reach the masses, and she dedicated her only novel, *Padmarag* (1924), to her brother.

The date of Rokeya's wedding is disputed but evidently took place in either 1896 or 1898, when she was sixteen or eighteen years old. She married an older widower, Khan Bahadur Syed Sakhawat Hossain, who had studied agriculture in England with government funding and was employed at the time in the Bengali civil service as deputy magistrate of Bhagalpur, a rural district in what is now the state of Bihar in India. The match was arranged by Rokeya's brother Ibrahim, who was acquainted with Hossain and knew him to hold progressive liberal views. These carried over into Rokeya and Hossain's marriage, as Hossain further supported Rokeya's study of languages and encouraged her to write. The couple had two daughters who both died in infancy. Hossain himself suffered from diabetes and passed away in 1909, leaving Rokeya widowed at twenty-nine years old.

Left a considerable sum of money after Hossain's death, Rokeya opened the first-ever school for Muslim girls in Bengal in the fall of 1909, naming it Sakhawat Memorial Girls' School in her husband's honor. However, Rokeya's stepdaughter and son-in-law from Hossain's first marriage disapproved of her choice to invest Hossain's legacy in female education. The resulting feud caused Rokeya to close the school the following year and relocate from Bhagalpur to Kolkata, where she reopened the school in 1911. Initially attended by just eight pupils, the school grew to over one hundred students within five years, and by 1930 it was serving all ten grades, funded both by private donations and government grants. It is still operating today. Rokeya later served as president of two women's rights organizations and founded a volunteer society that campaigned for women's educational and social advancement and provided aid and vocational training to women—particularly widows—living in the Kolkata slums.

As an advocate for the rights of Bengali Muslim women, Rokeya frequently used sardonic humor to make her points: in a speech as chair of the Bengal Women's Education Conference in 1926, for example, she reportedly remarked, "Although I am grateful to you for the respect that you have expressed towards me by inviting me to preside over the conference, I am forced to say that you have not made the right choice. I have been locked up in the socially oppressive iron casket of purdah for all my life. I have not been able to mix very well with people—as a matter of fact, I do not even know what is expected of a chairperson. I do not know if one is supposed to laugh, or to cry." This kind of wry humor characterized Rokeya's writing style as well. Her stories and essays—regarded as stylistically unembellished compared to the poeticism of her fellow Bengali Renaissance writers but incisively straightforward and compelling—often infused appeals to logic and reason with wit, satire, and allegory. Her literary career commenced with the publication of a short essay, "Pipasa," in the journal *Nabaprabha* in 1902. This was followed by more essays, poems, short stories, and novellas. She published two volumes of her collected works, entitled *Motichur*, in 1904 and 1922.

Though Rokeya wrote mostly in Bengali, her works also include a few works in English: two essays, "God Gives, Man Robs" (1927) and "Education Ideals for the Modern Indian Girl" (1931), and a short story, "Sultana's Dream" (1905), which Rokeya later translated into Bengali. "Sultana's Dream," originally published in the *Indian Ladies Magazine* and later in book form, is an early example of feminist science fiction and feminist utopian fiction. It envisions a place called "Ladyland," an idealistic, pacifistic, and technologically advanced society, complete with flying machines and solar power, made possible by the reversal of traditional gender roles and the advanced education of its female population. Sir Hugh McPherson, the divisional commissioner of Bhagalpur, was given a copy of the story by Rokeya's husband, his colleague, and commented that "[t]he ideas expressed in it are quite delightful and full of originality[.] … I wonder if she has foretold here the manner in which we may be able to move about in the air at some future time. Her suggestions on this point are most ingenious."

Rokeya continued to write, quite literally, until the day she died of heart failure on 9 December 1932. On her desk was an unfinished essay she had been working on late into the previous night: "Narir Adhikar," or "The Rights of Women." Her tomb is in Sodepur, near Kolkata, on the grounds of Panihati Balika Vidyalaya, a school for girls. The people of Bangladesh observe Begum Rokeya Day annually on the anniversary of her death.

⌘ ⌘ ⌘

Sultana's Dream

One evening I was lounging in an easy chair in my bedroom and thinking lazily of the condition of Indian womanhood. I am not sure whether I dozed off or not. But, as far as I remember, I was wide awake. I saw the moonlit sky sparkling with thousands of diamondlike stars, very distinctly.

All on a sudden a lady stood before me; how she came in, I do not know. I took her for my friend, Sister Sara.

"Good morning," said Sister Sara. I smiled inwardly as I knew it was not morning, but starry night. However, I replied to her, saying, "How do you do?"

"I am all right, thank you. Will you please come out and have a look at our garden?"

I looked again at the moon through the open window, and thought there was no harm in going out at that time. The menservants outside were fast asleep just then, and I could have a pleasant walk with Sister Sara.

I used to have my walks with Sister Sara when we were at Darjeeling.[1] Many a time did we walk hand in hand and talk lightheartedly in the botanical gardens there. I fancied Sister Sara had probably come to take me to some such garden, and I readily accepted her offer and went out with her.

When walking I found to my surprise that it was a fine morning. The town was fully awake and the streets alive with bustling crowds. I was feeling very shy, thinking I was walking in the street in broad daylight, but there was not a single man visible.

Some of the passersby made jokes at me. Though I could not understand their language, yet I felt sure they were joking. I asked my friend, "What do they say?"

"The women say that you look very mannish."

"Mannish?" said I. "What do they mean by that?"

"They mean that you are shy and timid like men."

"Shy and timid like men?" It was really a joke. I became very nervous when I found that my companion was not Sister Sara, but a stranger. Oh, what a fool had I been to mistake this lady for my dear old friend Sister Sara.

She felt my fingers tremble in her hand, as we were walking hand in hand.

"What is the matter, dear, dear?" she said affectionately.

"I feel somewhat awkward," I said, in a rather apologizing tone, "as being a purdahnishin[2] woman I am not accustomed to walking about unveiled."

"You need not be afraid of coming across a man here. This is Ladyland, free from sin and harm. Virtue herself reigns here."

By and by I was enjoying the scenery. Really it was very grand. I mistook a patch of green grass for a velvet cushion. Feeling as if I were walking on a soft carpet, I looked down and found the path covered with moss and flowers.

"How nice it is," said I.

---

[1] *Darjeeling* City in northern Bengal, on the edge of the Himalayas. The temperate climate resulting from its elevation made it a popular resort during the summer months for upper-class Bengalis as well as for the British.

[2] *purdahnishin* One who practices purdah, the custom of preventing women from being seen by men, either through the use of clothing that fully conceals women's bodies and faces or by keeping women in segregated and private spaces.

"Do you like it?" asked Sister Sara. (I continued calling her "Sister Sara," and she kept calling me by my name.)

"Yes, very much; but I do not like to tread on the tender and sweet flowers."

"Never mind, dear Sultana. Your treading will not harm them; they are street flowers."

"The whole place looks like a garden," said I admiringly. "You have arranged every plant so skillfully."

"Your Calcutta could become a nicer garden than this, if only your countrymen wanted to make it so."

"They would think it useless to give so much attention to horticulture, while they have so many other things to do."

"They could not find a better excuse," said she with a smile.

I became very curious to know where the men were. I met more than a hundred women while walking there, but not a single man.

"Where are the men?" I asked her.

"In their proper places, where they ought to be."

"Pray let me know what you mean by 'their proper places.'"

"Oh, I see my mistake, you cannot know our customs, as you were never here before. We shut our men indoors."

"Just as we are kept in the zenana?"[1]

"Exactly so."

"How funny." I burst into a laugh. Sister Sara laughed too.

"But, dear Sultana, how unfair it is to shut in the harmless women and let loose the men."

"Why? It is not safe for us to come out of the zenana, as we are naturally weak."

"Yes, it is not safe so long as there are men about the streets, nor is it so when a wild animal enters a marketplace."

"Of course not."

"Suppose some lunatics escape from the asylum and begin to do all sorts of mischief to men, horses, and

other creatures: in that case what will your countrymen do?"

"They will try to capture them and put them back into their asylum."

"Thank you! And you do not think it wise to keep sane people inside an asylum and let loose the insane?"

"Of course not!" said I, laughing lightly.

"As a matter of fact, in your country this very thing is done! Men, who do or at least are capable of doing no end of mischief, are let loose and the innocent women shut up in the zenana! How can you trust those untrained men out of doors?"

"We have no hand or voice in the management of our social affairs. In India man is lord and master. He has taken to himself all powers and privileges and shut up the women in the zenana."

"Why do you allow yourselves to be shut up?"

"Because it cannot be helped as they are stronger than women."

"A lion is stronger than a man, but it does not enable him to dominate the human race. You have neglected the duty you owe to yourselves, and you have lost your natural rights by shutting your eyes to your own interests."

"But my dear Sister Sara, if we do everything by ourselves, what will the men do then?"

"They should not do anything, excuse me; they are fit for nothing. Only catch them and put them into the zenana."

"But would it be very easy to catch and put them inside the four walls?" said I. "And even if this were done, would all their business—political and commercial—also go with them into the zenana?"

Sister Sara made no reply. She only smiled sweetly. Perhaps she thought it was useless to argue with one who was no better than a frog in a well.

By this time we reached Sister Sara's house. It was situated in a beautiful heart-shaped garden. It was a bungalow with a corrugated iron roof. It was cooler and nicer than any of our rich buildings. I cannot describe how neat and how nicely furnished and how tastefully decorated it was.

---

[1] *zenana* Sequestered area of a Muslim or Hindu home reserved for the women of the household, typically off-limits to men except for immediate family members.

We sat side by side. She brought out of the parlor a piece of embroidery work and began putting on a fresh design.

"Do you know knitting and needlework?"

"Yes: we have nothing else to do in our zenana."

"But we do not trust our zenana members with embroidery!" she said laughing, "as a man has not patience enough to pass thread through a needlehole even!"

"Have you done all this work yourself?" I asked her, pointing to the various pieces of embroidered teapoy[1] cloths.

"Yes."

"How can you find time to do all these? You have to do the office work as well? Have you not?"

"Yes. I do not stick to the laboratory all day long. I finish my work in two hours."

"In two hours! How do you manage? In our land the officers, magistrates, for instance, work seven hours daily."

"I have seen some of them doing their work. Do you think they work all the seven hours?"

"Certainly they do!"

"No, dear Sultana, they do not. They dawdle away their time in smoking. Some smoke two or three choroots[2] during the office time. They talk much about their work, but do little. Suppose one choroot takes half an hour to burn off, and a man smokes twelve choroots daily; then, you see, he wastes six hours every day in sheer smoking."

We talked on various subjects; and I learned that they were not subject to any kind of epidemic disease, nor did they suffer from mosquito bites as we do. I was very much astonished to hear that in Ladyland no one died in youth except by rare accident.

"Will you care to see our kitchen?" she asked me.

"With pleasure," said I, and we went to see it. Of course the men had been asked to clear off when I was going there. The kitchen was situated in a beautiful vegetable garden. Every creeper, every tomato plant, was

itself an ornament. I found no smoke, nor any chimney either in the kitchen—it was clean and bright; the windows were decorated with flower garlands. There was no sign of coal or fire.

"How do you cook?" I asked.

"With solar heat," she said, at the same time showing me the pipe, through which passed the concentrated sunlight and heat. And she cooked something then and there to show me the process.

"How did you manage to gather and store up the sun heat?" I asked her in amazement.

"Let me tell you a little of our past history, then. Thirty years ago, when our present Queen was thirteen years old, she inherited the throne. She was Queen in name only, the Prime Minister really ruling the country.

"Our good Queen liked science very much. She circulated an order that all the women in her country should be educated. Accordingly a number of girls' schools were founded and supported by the Government. Education was spread far and wide among women. And early marriage also was stopped. No woman was to be allowed to marry before she was twenty-one. I must tell you that, before this change, we had been kept in strict purdah."

"How the tables are turned," I interposed with a laugh.

"But the seclusion is the same," she said. "In a few years we had separate universities, where no men were admitted.

"In the capital, where our Queen lives, there are two universities. One of these invented a wonderful balloon, to which they attached a number of pipes. By means of this captive balloon, which they managed to keep afloat above the cloudland, they could draw as much water from the atmosphere as they pleased. As the water was incessantly being drawn by the university people, no cloud gathered and the ingenious Lady Principal stopped rain and storms thereby."

"Really! Now I understand why there is no mud here!" said I. But I could not understand how it was possible to accumulate water in the pipes. She explained to me how it was done; but I was unable to understand

---

[1]   *teapoy*   Ornamental three-legged table.

[2]   *choroots*   Cheroots; thin, open-ended cigars.

her, as my scientific knowledge was very limited. However, she went on:

"When the other university came to know of this, they became exceedingly jealous and tried to do something more extraordinary still. They invented an instrument by which they could collect as much sun heat as they wanted. And they kept the heat stored up to be distributed among others as required.

"While the women were engaged in scientific researches, the men of this country were busy increasing their military power. When they came to know that the female universities were able to draw water from the atmosphere and collect heat from the sun, they only laughed at the members of the universities and called the whole thing 'a sentimental nightmare'!"

"Your achievements are very wonderful indeed! But tell me how you managed to put the men of your country into the zenana. Did you entrap them first?"

"No."

"It is not likely that they would surrender their free and open air life of their own accord and confine themselves within the four walls of the zenana! They must have been overpowered."

"Yes, they have been!"

"By whom?—by some lady warriors, I suppose?"

"No, not by arms."

"Yes, it cannot be so. Men's arms are stronger than women's. Then?"

"By brain."

"Even their brains are bigger and heavier than women's. Are they not?"

"Yes, but what of that? An elephant also has got a bigger and heavier brain than a man has. Yet man can enchain elephants and employ them, according to his own wishes."

"Well said, but tell me, please, how it all actually happened. I am dying to know it!"

"Women's brains are somewhat quicker than men's. Ten years ago, when the military officers called our scientific discoveries 'a sentimental nightmare,' some of the young ladies wanted to say something in reply to those remarks. But both the Lady Principals restrained them and said they should reply not by word but by

deed, if ever they got the opportunity. And they had not long to wait for that opportunity."

"How marvelous!" I heartily clapped my hands.

"And now the proud gentlemen are dreaming sentimental dreams themselves.

"Soon afterward certain persons came from a neighboring country and took shelter in ours. They were in trouble, having committed some political offense. The King, who cared more for power than for good government, asked our kindhearted Queen to hand them over to his officers. She refused, as it was against her principle to turn out refugees. For this refusal the king declared war against our country.

"Our military officers sprang to their feet at once and marched out to meet the enemy.

"The enemy, however, was too strong for them. Our soldiers fought bravely, no doubt. But in spite of all their bravery the foreign army advanced step by step to invade our country.

"Nearly all the men had gone out to fight; even a boy of sixteen was not left home. Most of our warriors were killed, the rest driven back, and the enemy came within twenty-five miles of the capital.

"A meeting of a number of wise ladies was held at the Queen's palace to advise [as] to what should be done to save the land.

"Some proposed to fight like soldiers; others objected and said that women were not trained to fight with swords and guns, nor were they accustomed to fighting with any weapons. A third party regretfully remarked that they were hopelessly weak of body.

"If you cannot save your country for lack of physical strength, said the Queen, try to do so by brain power.

"There was a dead silence for a few minutes. Her Royal Highness said again, 'I must commit suicide if the land and my honor are lost.'

"Then the Lady Principal of the second university (who had collected sun heat), who had been silently thinking during the consultation, remarked that they were all but lost; and there was little hope left for them. There was, however, one plan [that] she would like to try, and this would be her first and last effort; if she failed in this, there would be nothing left but to commit suicide. All present solemnly vowed that they would never allow themselves to be enslaved, no matter what happened.

"The Queen thanked them heartily, and asked the Lady Principal to try her plan.

"The Lady Principal rose again and said, 'Before we go out the men must enter the zenanas. I make this prayer for the sake of purdah.' 'Yes, of course,' replied Her Royal Highness.

"On the following day the Queen called upon all men to retire into zenanas for the sake of honor and liberty.

"Wounded and tired as they were, they took that order rather for a boon! They bowed low and entered the zenanas without uttering a single word of protest. They were sure that there was no hope for this country at all.

"Then the Lady Principal with her two thousand students marched to the battlefield, and arriving there directed all the rays of the concentrated sun light and heat toward the enemy.

"The heat and light were too much for them to bear. They all ran away panic-stricken, not knowing in their bewilderment how to counteract that scorching heat. When they fled away leaving their guns and other ammunitions of war, they were burned down by means of the same sun heat.

"Since then no one has tried to invade our country any more."

"And since then your countrymen never tried to come out of the zenana?"

"Yes, they wanted to be free. Some of the Police Commissioners and District Magistrates sent word to the Queen to the effect that the Military Officers certainly deserved to be imprisoned for their failure; but they [had] never neglected their duty and therefore they should not be punished, and they prayed to be restored to their respective offices.

"Her Royal Highness sent them a circular letter, intimating to them that if their services should ever be needed they would be sent for, and that in the meanwhile they should remain where they were.

"Now that they are accustomed to the purdah system and have ceased to grumble at their seclusion, we call the system *mardana*[1] instead of zenana."

"But how do you manage," I asked Sister Sara, "to do without the police or magistrates in case of theft or murder?"

"Since the mardana system has been established, there has been no more crime or sin; therefore we do not require a policeman to find out a culprit, nor do we want a magistrate to try a criminal case."

"That is very good, indeed. I suppose if there was any dishonest person, you could very easily chastise her. As you gained a decisive victory without shedding a single drop of blood, you could drive off crime and criminals too without much difficulty!"

"Now, dear Sultana, will you sit here or come to my parlor?" she asked me.

"Your kitchen is not inferior to a queen's boudoir!" I replied with a pleasant smile, "but we must leave it now; for the gentlemen may be cursing me for keeping them away from their duties in the kitchen so long." We both laughed heartily.

"How my friends at home will be amused and amazed, when I go back and tell them that in the far-off Ladyland, ladies rule over the country and control all social matters, while gentlemen are kept in the mardanas to mind babies, to cook, and to do all sorts of domestic work; and that cooking is so easy a thing that it is simply a pleasure to cook!"

"Yes, tell them about all that you see here."

"Please let me know how you carry on land cultivation and how you plough the land and do other hard manual work."

"Our fields are tilled by means of electricity, which supplies motive power for other hard work as well, and we employ it for our aerial conveyances too. We have no railroad nor any paved streets here."

"Therefore neither street nor railway accidents occur here," said I. "Do not you ever suffer from want of rainwater?" I asked.

---

[1] *mardana* Area of a Muslim or Hindu house designated for men, off-limits to the women of the household.

"Never since the 'water balloon' has been set up. You see the big balloon and pipes attached thereto. By their aid we can draw as much rainwater as we require. Nor do we ever suffer from flood or thunderstorms. We are all very busy making nature yield as much as she can. We do not find time to quarrel with one another as we never sit idle. Our noble Queen is exceedingly fond of botany; it is her ambition to convert the whole country into one grand garden."

"The idea is excellent. What is your chief food?"

"Fruits."

"How do you keep your country cool in hot weather? We regard the rainfall in summer as a blessing from heaven."

"When the heat becomes unbearable, we sprinkle the ground with plentiful showers drawn from the artificial fountains. And in cold weather we keep our room warm with sun heat."

She showed me her bathroom, the roof of which was removable. She could enjoy a shower or bath whenever she liked, by simply removing the roof (which was like the lid of a box) and turning on the tap of the shower pipe.

"You are a lucky people!" ejaculated I. "You know no want. What is your religion, may I ask?"

"Our religion is based on Love and Truth. It is our religious duty to love one another and to be absolutely truthful. If any person lies, she or he is …"

"Punished with death?"

"No, not with death. We do not take pleasure in killing a creature of God—especially a human being. The liar is asked to leave this land for good and never to come to it again."

"Is an offender never forgiven?"

"Yes, if that person repents sincerely."

"Are you not allowed to see any man, except your own relations?"

"No one except sacred relations."

"Our circle of sacred relations is very limited, even first cousins are not sacred."

"But ours is very large; a distant cousin is as sacred as a brother."

"That is very good. I see Purity itself reigns over your land. I should like to see the good Queen, who is so sagacious and farsighted and who has made all these rules."

"All right," said Sister Sara.

Then she screwed a couple of seats onto a square piece of plank. To this plank she attached two smooth and well-polished balls. When I asked her what the balls were for, she said they were hydrogen balls and they were used to overcome the force of gravity. The balls were of different capacities, to be used according to the different weights desired to be overcome. She then fastened to the air-car two winglike blades, which, she said, were worked by electricity. After we were comfortably seated she touched a knob and the blades began to whirl, moving faster and faster every moment. At first we were raised to the height of about six or seven feet and then off we flew. And before I could realize that we had commenced moving, we reached the garden of the Queen.

My friend lowered the air-car by reversing the action of the machine, and when the car touched the ground the machine was stopped and we got out.

I had seen from the air-car the Queen walking on a garden path with her little daughter (who was four years old) and her maids of honor.

"Halloo! you here!" cried the Queen, addressing Sister Sara. I was introduced to Her Royal Highness and was received by her cordially without any ceremony.

I was very much delighted to make her acquaintance. In the course of the conversation I had with her, the Queen told me that she had no objection to permitting her subjects to trade with other countries. "But," she continued, "no trade was possible with countries where the women were kept in the zenanas and so unable to come and trade with us. Men, we find, are rather of lower morals and so we do not like dealing with them. We do not covet other people's land, we do not fight for a piece of diamond though it may be a thousandfold brighter than the Koh-i-Noor, nor do we grudge a ruler his Peacock Throne.[1] We dive deep into the ocean of knowledge and try to find out the precious gems that Nature has kept in store for us. We enjoy Nature's gifts as much as we can."

After taking leave of the Queen, I visited the famous universities, and was shown some of their factories, laboratories, and observatories.

After visiting the above places of interest, we got again into the air-car, but as soon as it began moving I somehow slipped down and the fall startled me out of my dream. And on opening my eyes, I found myself in my own bedroom still lounging in the easy chair!
—1905

---

[1] *Koh-i-Noor* Meaning "mountain of light" in Persian, a large and precious Indian diamond that belonged to the Mughal dynasty. The 1849 treaty that concluded the British conquest of Punjab in northwest India required the Maharajah of Punjab, who was then in possession of the Koh-i-Noor, to surrender it to Queen Victoria. It currently remains one of the British Crown Jewels, although the governments of various South Asian states, including India and Pakistan, have demanded its return; *Peacock Throne* Ornate, jewel-encrusted throne of the Mughal emperors of India, taken in a Persian invasion during the eighteenth century.

Maps

COUNTIES
OF BRITAIN
AND IRELAND

THE BRITISH ISLES IN
THE VICTORIAN ERA

GREATER LONDON
Finchley
Tottenham
Harrow
EPPING FOREST
Hampstead Heath
Wembley
Islington
Twyford Abbey
West Ham
London
Tower
Millenium Dome
Westminster
Fulham
Chelsea
Woolwich
Greenwich
Heathrow Airport
Richmond
Battersea
Deptford
Twickenham
Wandsworth
Dartford
Crystal Palace
Sydenham
Kingston
Wimbledon
Hampton Court
Merton
Bromley
Croydon

CENTRAL LONDON
1 Lambeth Palace
2 Westminster Bridge
3 Westminster Abbey
4 Whitehall
5 Tyburn
6 Covent Garden
7 The Temple
8 Blackfriar's Bridge
9 Swan Theatre
10 Bear Garden
11 Globe Theatre
12 London Bridge
13 St. Paul's Cathedral
14 Fortune Theatre
15 The Theatre
16 Bethlehem Hospital ("Bedlam")
17 The Tower
18 Tower Bridge
19 Waterloo Station
20 Houses of Parliament
21 Tate Gallery
22 Vauxhall Bridge
23 Victoria Station
24 Buckingham Palace
25 Royal Albert Hall
26 Kensington Palace
27 Paddington Station
28 Trafalgar Square
29 British Museum
30 Euston Station
31 St. Pancras Station
32 King's Cross Station
City Rd.
Edgeware Rd.
Gray's Inn Rd.
Aldersgate
Bishopsgate
Tottenham Court Rd.
Marylebone Rd.
Holborn
Cheapside
Drury Lane
Fleet St.
Oxford St.
Thames St.
Strand
Thames
Hyde Park
Piccadilly
Pall Mall
Green Park
St. James's Pk
Kensington Rd.
Chelsea Rd.
Lambeth
Chelsea
Vauxhall

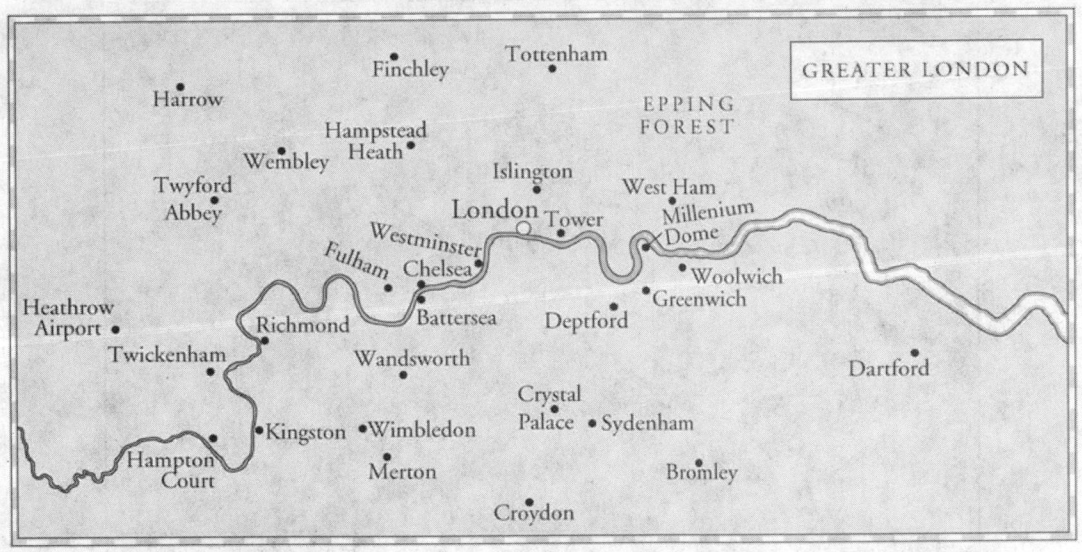

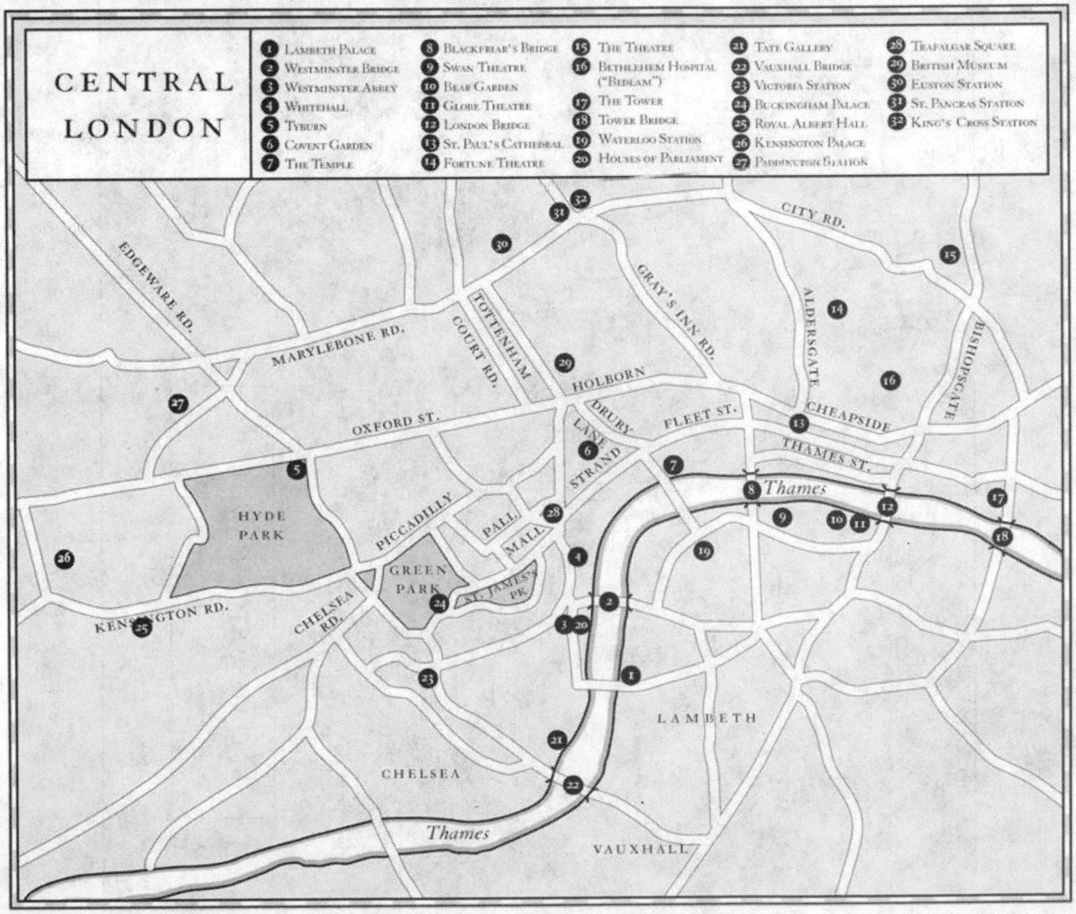

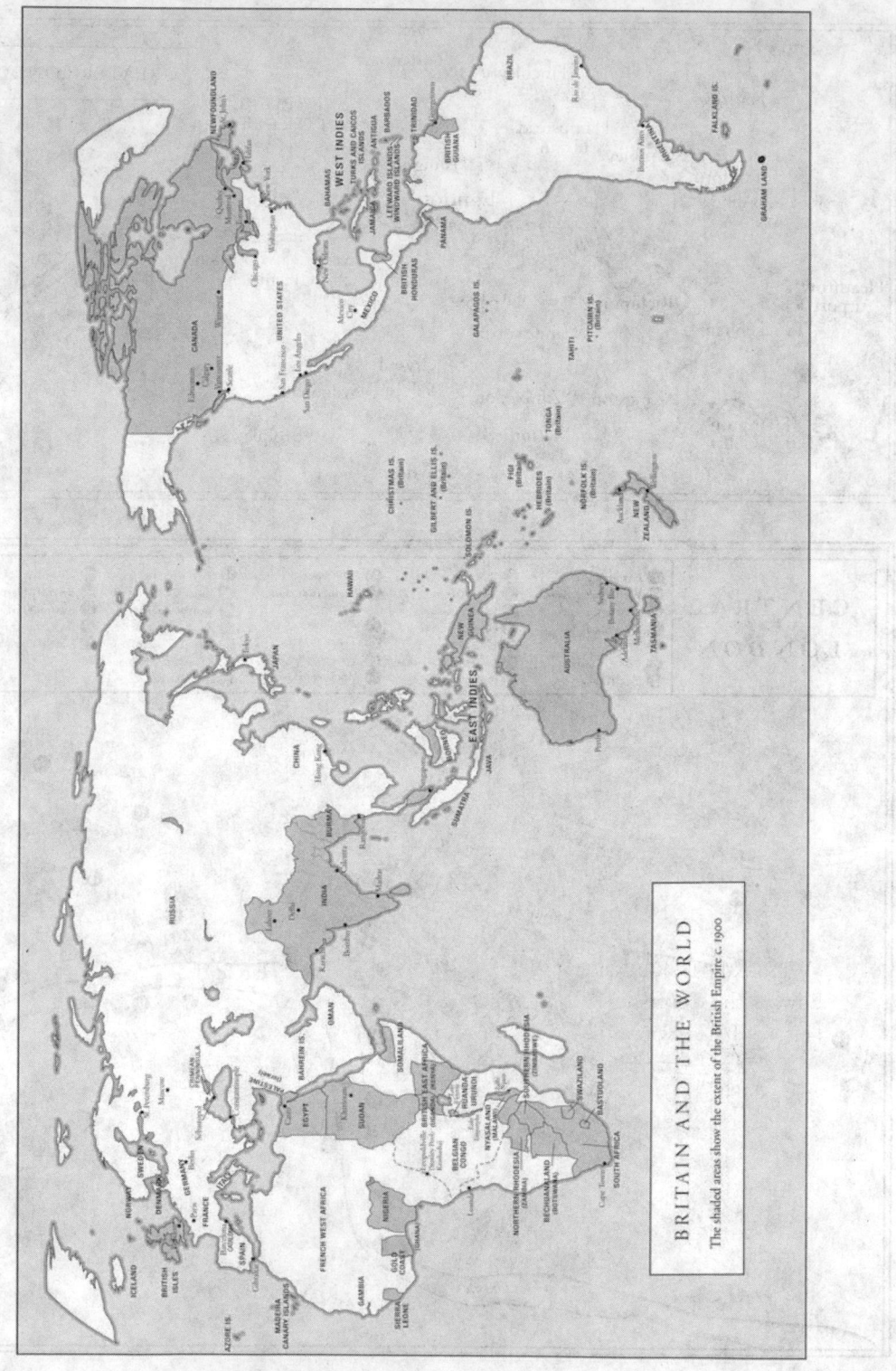

BRITAIN AND THE WORLD

The shaded areas show the extent of the British Empire c. 1900

MONARCHS AND PRIME MINISTERS

MONARCHS

HOUSE OF WESSEX

Egbert (Ecgberht)	829–39
Æthelwulf	839–58
Æthelbald	858–60
Æthelbert	860–66
Æthelred I	866–71
Alfred the Great	871–99
Edward the Elder	899–924
Athelstan	924–40
Edmund I	940–46
Edred (Eadred)	946–55
Edwy (Eadwig)	955–59
Edgar	959–75
Edward the Martyr	975–78
Æthelred II (the Unready)	978–1016
Edmund II (Ironside)	1016

DANISH LINE

Canute (Cnut)	1016–35
Harold I (Harefoot)	1035–40
Harthacnut	1040–42

Harold II

WESSEX LINE, RESTORED

Edward the Confessor	1042–66
Harold II (Godwinson)	1066

NORMAN LINE

William I (the Conqueror)	1066–87
William II (Rufus)	1087–1100
Henry I (Beauclerc)	1100–35
Stephen	1135–54
Matilda	1141

William I

MONARCHS

PLANTAGENET, ANGEVIN LINE

Henry II	1154–89
Richard I (Coeur de Lion)	1189–99
John (Lackland)	1199–1216
Henry III	1216–72
Edward I (Longshanks)	1272–1307
Edward II	1307–27
Edward III	1327–77
Richard II	1377–99

PLANTAGENET, LANCASTRIAN LINE

Henry IV	1399–1413
Henry V	1413–22
Henry VI	1422–61; 1470–71

Henry VIII

PLANTAGENET, YORKIST LINE

Edward IV	1461–70; 1471–83
Edward V	1483
Richard III	1483–85

HOUSE OF TUDOR

Henry VII	1485–1509
Henry VIII	1509–47
Edward VI	1547–53
Jane	1553
Mary I	1553–58
Elizabeth I	1558–1603

Mary I

HOUSE OF STUART

James I/VI	1603–25
Charles I	1625–49

(The Commonwealth)	1649–60
Oliver Cromwell	1649–58
Richard Cromwell	1658–59

MONARCHS		PRIME MINISTERS	
HOUSE OF STUART, RESTORED			
Charles II	1660–85		
James II	1685–89		
HOUSE OF ORANGE AND STUART			
William III and Mary II	1689–94		
William III	1694–1702		
HOUSE OF STUART			
Anne	1702–14		
HOUSE OF BRUNSWICK, HANOVER LINE			
George I	1714–27	Sir Robert Walpole (Whig)	1721–42
George II	1727–60	Earl of Wilmington (Whig)	1742–43
		Henry Pelham (Whig)	1743–54
		Duke of Newcastle (Whig)	1754–56
		Duke of Devonshire (Whig)	1756–57
George III	1760–1820	Duke of Newcastle (Whig)	1757–62
		Earl of Bute (Tory)	1762–63
		George Grenville (Whig)	1763–65
		Marquess of Rockingham (Whig)	1765–66
		William Pitt the Elder (Earl of Chatham) (Whig)	1766–68
		Duke of Grafton (Whig)	1768–70
		Frederick North (Lord North) (Tory)	1770–82
		Marquess of Rockingham (Whig)	1782
		Earl of Shelburne (Whig)	1782–83
		Duke of Portland (Whig)	1783
		William Pitt the Younger (Tory)	1783–1801
		Henry Addington (Tory)	1801–04
		William Pitt the Younger (Tory)	1804–06
		William Wyndham Grenville (Baron Grenville) (Whig)	1806–07

George III

George, Prince of Wales, Prince Regent

MONARCHS		PRIME MINISTERS	
		Duke of Portland (Tory)	1807–09
George, Prince of Wales, Prince Regent	1811–20	Spencer Perceval (Tory)	1809–12
		Earl of Liverpool (Tory)	1812–27
George IV	1820–30		
		George Canning (Tory)	1827
		Viscount Goderich (Tory)	1827–28
		Duke of Wellington (Tory)	1828–30
William IV	1830–37		
		Earl Grey (Whig)	1830–34
		Viscount Melbourne (Whig)	1834
		Duke of Wellington (Tory)	1834
		Sir Robert Peel (Tory)	1834–35
Victoria	1837–1901	Viscount Melbourne (Whig)	1835–41
		Sir Robert Peel (Tory)	1841–46
		Lord John Russell (later Earl) (Whig)	1846–52
		Earl of Derby (Con.)	1852
		Earl of Aberdeen (Tory/Peelite)	1852–55
		Viscount Palmerston (Lib.)	1855–58
		Earl of Derby (Con.)	1858–59
		Viscount Palmerston (Lib.)	1859–65
		Earl Russell (Lib.)	1865–66
		Earl of Derby (Con.)	1866–68
		Benjamin Disraeli (Con.)	1868
		William Gladstone (Lib.)	1868–74
		Benjamin Disraeli (Con.)	1874–80
		William Gladstone (Lib.)	1880–85
		Marquess of Salisbury (Con.)	1885–86
		William Gladstone (Lib.)	1886
		Marquess of Salisbury (Con.)	1886–92
		William Gladstone (Lib.)	1892–94
HOUSE OF SAXE-COBURG-GOTHA		Earl of Rosebery (Lib.)	1894–95
Edward VII	1901–10	Marquess of Salisbury (Con.)	1895–1902
		Arthur Balfour (Con.)	1902–05
		Sir Henry Campbell-Bannerman (Lib.)	1905–08
HOUSE OF WINDSOR			
George V	1910–36	Herbert Asquith (Lib.)	1908–16

Victoria

MONARCHS		PRIME MINISTERS	
		David Lloyd George (Lib.)	1916–22
		Bonar Law (Con.)	1922–23
		Stanley Baldwin (Con.)	1923–24
		Ramsay MacDonald (Labour)	1924
		Stanley Baldwin (Con.)	1924–29
		Ramsay MacDonald (Labour)	1929–35
Edward VIII	1936	Stanley Baldwin (Con.)	1935–37
George VI	1936–52	Neville Chamberlain (Con.)	1937–40
		Winston Churchill (Con.)	1940–45
		Clement Attlee (Labour)	1945–51
Elizabeth II	1952–	Sir Winston Churchill (Con.)	1951–55

Winston Churchill

Sir Anthony Eden (Con.)	1955–57
Harold Macmillan (Con.)	1957–63
Sir Alec Douglas-Home (Con.)	1963–64
Harold Wilson (Labour)	1964–70
Edward Heath (Con.)	1970–74
Harold Wilson (Labour)	1974–76
James Callaghan (Labour)	1976–79
Margaret Thatcher (Con.)	1979–90
John Major (Con.)	1990–97
Tony Blair (Labour)	1997–2007
Gordon Brown (Labour)	2007–10
David Cameron (Con.)	2010–16
Theresa May (Con.)	2016–19
Boris Johnson (Con.)	2019–

Permissions Acknowledgments

Illustration Credits

Cover: Painting by William Logsdail, reproduced by permission of Anne Evans. Page 525: Silvy, Camille. Portrait of James Pinson Labulo Davies; Sarah Forbes Bonetta (Sarah Davies). September 15, 1862. Copyright © National Portrait Gallery, London. Page 525: Silvy, Camille. Portrait of Sarah Forbes Bonetta (Sarah Davies). September 15, 1862. Copyright © National Portrait Gallery, London. Page 595: Male displaying the effects of onanism. Source: Wellcome Collection. Attribution 4.0 International (CC BY 4.0). Page 615: Image: How Long Have You Been. Courtesy of Mary Evans Library. Used under license. Page 759: Joanna Boyce Wells, "Fanny Eaton" (1861). Reproduced by permission of the Yale Center for British Art. Page 760: Study for the head of Morgan le Fay, drawing by Frederick Sandys, c. 1862. Copyright © Victoria and Albert Museum, London. Courtesy of Victoria and Albert Museum, London. Used by permission. Website: "Crossed Letter" of Susannah Moodie: c. 1850 by G.Staunton, Toronto, courtesy of Miss Kathleen McMussich.

Author Portraits

Page 104: Portrait of John Stuart Mill. National Portrait Gallery, London. Page 630: Portrait of John Ruskin. National Portrait Gallery, London. Page 642: Portrait of Matthew Arnold. National Portrait Gallery, London. Page 687: Portrait of George Meredith. National Portrait Gallery, London. Page 888: Portrait of Augusta Webster. National Portrait Gallery, London. Page 926: Portrait of Walter Pater. National Portrait Gallery, London. Page 935: Portrait of Thomas Hardy. National Portrait Gallery, London. Page 992: Portrait of Robert Louis Stevenson. National Portrait Gallery, London. Page 1097: Toru Dutt: Portrait by Rose McNeil. Page 1122: Rabindranath Tagore: Portrait by Rose McNeil. Page 1304: Rokeya Sakhawat Hossain: Portrait by Lisa Brawn. Website: Portrait of Thomas Babington Macaulay. National Portrait Gallery, London.

INDEX OF FIRST LINES

Index of Authors and Titles

From the Publisher

A name never says it all, but the word "Broadview" expresses a good deal of the philosophy behind our company. We are open to a broad range of academic approaches and political viewpoints. We pay attention to the broad impact book publishing and book printing has in the wider world; for some years now we have used 100% recycled paper for most of our books. Our publishing program is internationally oriented and broad-ranging. Our individual titles often appeal to a broad readership too; many are of interest as much to general readers as to academics and students.

Founded in 1985, Broadview remains a fully independent company owned by its shareholders—not an imprint or subsidiary of a larger multinational.

For the most accurate information on our books (including information on pricing, editions, and formats) please visit our website at www.broadviewpress.com. Our print books and ebooks are also available for sale on our site.

broadview press
www.broadviewpress.com

From the Publisher

A name never says it all, but the word "Broadview" expresses a good deal of the philosophy behind our company. We are open to a broad range of academic approaches and political viewpoints. We pay attention to the broad impact book publishing and book printing has in the wider world; for some years now we have used 100% recycled paper for most titles. Our publishing program is internationally oriented and broad-ranging. Our individual titles often appeal to a broad readership too; many are of interest as much to general readers as to academics and students.

Founded in 1985, Broadview remains a fully independent company owned by its shareholders—not an imprint or subsidiary of a larger multinational.

For the most accurate information on our books (including information on pricing, editions, and formats) please visit our website at www.broadviewpress.com. Our print books and ebooks are also available for sale on our site.

broadview press
www.broadviewpress.com